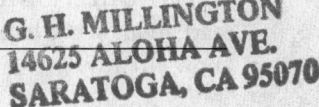

"THIS BOOK IS YOUR LIFE!... This fluent, likable, can't-put-it-down narrative history of America from the Bonus Army to Watergate is popular history in our special tradition... Reading Manchester, you run with the Bonus Army, lift up your chin like Roosevelt, put up the flag at Iwo Jima, and nervously dismiss MacArthur. You are against Communism *and* the Cold War. You participate!"

—Alfred Kazin, *The New York Times Book Review*

"UNQUESTIONABLY THE BEST BOOK PUBLISHED THIS YEAR."

—P. Albert Duhamel, *Boston Sunday Herald Advertiser*

"A WHOLE GENERATION OF READERS WILL RELIVE THEIR LIVES through this skilled mosaic of popular history...Manchester's book is a notable achievement."

—Paul Horgan

"WE ARE UNLIKELY TO SEE A FINER WORK OF ITS KIND IN MANY YEARS...A vibrant, teeming, colorful, populous story in which all of us played our parts."

—*John Barkham Reviews*

"BRILLIANT NARRATIVE HISTORY. Readers can dip into the book at any one of its 1302 pages and experience instant recognition and nostalgia."

—*Publishers Weekly*

"A STUNNING PERFORMANCE." —James MacGregor Burns

"WITH GREAT NARRATIVE SKILL, Manchester makes us want to read about what happens next, even when, maybe especially when, we know already." —John Brooks, *Chicago Tribune Book World*

"A REMARKABLE BOOK—and very good reading indeed...A most valuable, and readable, contribution to history." —Thomas K. Finletter

"A FASCINATING WORK OF HISTORY...Solidly researched, bold and imaginative in its conception, it is written with a fine sensitivity to the nuances of the American experience in the 40 years before, during, and after the second world war...For Americans who lived through those 40 fateful years, or through only a part of them, this book is invaluable." —William L. Shirer

"*THE GLORY AND THE DREAM* weighs five pounds on my bathroom scale, give or take a candy bar, which makes it a hard book to pick up. It is even harder to put down. With style and wit, William Manchester has written a history of the United States from 1932 to 1972 that crackles along like a well-paced novel." —Alfred Boas, *The Miami Herald*

"EXTRAORDINARILY VIVID HISTORY." —Cass Canfield

"A MAGNIFICENT BOOK...The kind of history that I really respect because it deals with humanity not with events." —Elia Kazan

---

"A REMARKABLE BOOK. It deserves quickly to become a bestseller... Every thoughtful American will benefit from reading *The Glory and the Dream.*" —Gardner Cowles

---

"THE ULTIMATE NOSTALGIA TRIP...Manchester organizes a huge mass of material with an eye for arresting detail." —Walter Clemons, *Newsweek*

"MAGNIFICENT NARRATIVE HISTORY OF THE LAST FORTY YEARS." —James Reston, *The New York Times*

"SPRAWLING, PROFLIGATE, BUSTING AT THE SEAMS with history's self-contradictions...*The Glory and the Dream,* depending on how one reads it, is Pop history, a nostalgia trip or the world's biggest trivia contest." —Melvin Maddocks, *Time*

"A REMARKABLE AND IMPRESSIVE PORTRAIT OF FOUR CRUCIAL DECADES OF THIS NATION." —Robert Kirsch, *Los Angeles Times*

BOOKS BY WILLIAM MANCHESTER

HISTORY

THE DEATH OF A PRESIDENT: *November 20–November 25, 1963*
*THE ARMS OF KRUPP: *1587–1968*
*THE GLORY AND THE DREAM: *A Narrative History of America, 1932–1972*
GOODBYE DARKNESS: *A Memoir of the Pacific War*

BIOGRAPHY

DISTURBER OF THE PEACE: *The Life of H. L. Mencken*
A ROCKEFELLER FAMILY PORTRAIT: *From John D. to Nelson*
PORTRAIT OF A PRESIDENT: *John F. Kennedy in Profile*
AMERICAN CAESAR: *Douglas MacArthur*
THE LAST LION: VISIONS OF GLORY, *Winston Spencer Churchill*
ONE BRIEF SHINING MOMENT: *Remembering Kennedy*

FICTION

THE CITY OF ANGER
SHADOW OF THE MONSOON
THE LONG GAINER

DIVERSION

BEARD THE LION

*Published by Bantam Books, Inc.

WILLIAM MANCHESTER

THE GLORY AND THE DREAM

A Narrative History of America

1932-1972

BANTAM BOOKS
NEW YORK · TORONTO · LONDON · SYDNEY · AUCKLAND

To
Laurie Manchester
and to
her future

Whither is fled the visionary gleam?
Where is it now, the glory and the
dream?
—Wordsworth

THE GLORY AND THE DREAM

A Bantam Book / published by arrangement with
Little, Brown and Company

PRINTING HISTORY

Little, Brown edition published November 1974

Literary Guild edition published December 1974

Bantam edition / September 1975
12 printings through March 1990

Portions of this book were first published in slightly altered form
in THE NEW YORK TIMES MAGAZINE *and* NEW YORK *magazine.*

Acknowledgments of permission to reprint excerpted material
appear on pages 1347–1349.

Library of Congress Cataloging-in-Publication Data
Manchester, William Raymond, 1922-
The glory and the dream: a narrative history of America,
1932-1972/William Manchester
p. cm.
Includes bibliographical references.
ISBN 0-553-34589-3
1. United States—History—1933-1945. 2. United States—
History—1945- I. Title.
E806.M34   1988   89-17671
973.9—dc20   CIP

Published simultaneously in the United States and Canada

Bantam Books are published by Bantam Books, a division of
Bantam Doubleday Dell Publishing Group, Inc. Its trademark,
consisting of the words "Bantam Books" and the portrayal of a
rooster, is Registered in U.S. Patent and Trademark Office and
in other countries. Marca Registrada. Bantam Books, 666 Fifth
Avenue, New York, New York 10103.

Contents

PROLOGUE: Rock Bottom   3

PART I
Rendezvous with Destiny
1932-1941

1   The Cruelest Year   31
    Depression Montage   70

2   Roosevelt!   71
    Portrait of an American: ELEANOR   91

3   Stirrings   94
    Mid-Thirties Montage   123

4   The Roosevelt Referendum   124
    Portrait of an American: STOCKBROKER RICHARD WHITNEY   145

5   The Conservative Phoenix   148
    Late Thirties Montage   172

6   A Shadow of Primitive Terror   173
    Portrait of an American: NORMAN THOMAS   206

7   Through the Night with a Light from Above   210
    Montage: The Last of Prewar America   237

8   America on the Brink   238

PART II
Sacrifice and Transformation
1941-1950

9   Counterattack   263
     Pacific Montage   288

10 The Home Front   289
     Home Front Montage   328

11 Lilacs in the Dooryard   329
     ETO Montage   363

12 A New World, Under a New Sun   364
     Portrait of an American: THE REDHEAD   388

13 The Fraying Flags of Triumph   392
     Postwar Montage   417

14 Life with Harry   418

15 A Little Touch of Harry in the Night   433
     Late Forties Montage   472

16 The Age of Suspicion   473
     Portrait of an American: EDWARD ROSCOE MURROW   513

17 Into the Abyss   517
     Early Fifties Montage   551

PART III
Sowing the Wind
1951-1960

18 A House Divided   555

19 Right Turn   599
     Montage: The Early Eisenhower Years   642

20 What Was Good for General Motors   643
     Portrait of an American: NORMA JEAN BAKER   688

21 Mr. Chairman, Mr. Chairman   692
     Montage: The Mid-Fifties   730

22 With All Deliberate Speed   731

23 The Pursuit of Happiness   772
     Montage: Eisenhower at Flood Tide   786

24 Beep Beep 787
    Portrait of an American: THE EDSEL 814

25 The Crusade Falters 818
    Late Fifties Montage 846

26 Tattoo for the General 847

PART IV
Reaping the Whirlwind
1961-1968

27 A New Generation of Americans 889
    Montage: The Early Sixties 924

28 Now the Trumpet Summoned Us Again 925
    Portrait of an American: PETER CARL GOLDMARK 972

29 Don't Let It Be Forgot 976
    Montage: JFK/LBJ 1009

30 The Long Arm 1010

31 A Dream of Greatness — and Disenchantment 1041
    Montage: The Johnson Years 1082

32 Up Against the Wall 1083
    Portrait of an American: KARL HESS III 1118

33 The Year Everything Went Wrong 1122
    Montage: The Late Sixties 1151

PART V
Nixon, After All
1969-1972

34 The Rise of the Silent Majority 1155
    Portrait of an American: BENJAMIN MCLANE SPOCK, M.D. 1187

35 Nattering Nabobs 1190
    Early Seventies Montage 1223

36 The Divided States of America 1224
    Portrait of an American: RALPH NADER 1255

37 Pride Goeth 1259

    EPILOGUE: Echoes 1298

Acknowledgments   1305

Chapter Notes   1306

Bibliography   1337

Copyright Acknowledgments   1347

Index   1350

THE GLORY AND THE DREAM

A Narrative History
of America

1932–1972

PROLOGUE

Rock Bottom

I N THE DESPERATE SUMMER of 1932, Washington, D.C., resembled the besieged capital of an obscure European state. Since May some twenty-five thousand penniless World War veterans had been encamped with their wives and children in District parks, dumps, abandoned warehouses, and empty stores. The men drilled, sang war songs, and once, led by a Medal of Honor winner and watched by a hundred thousand silent Washingtonians, they marched up Pennsylvania Avenue bearing American flags of faded cotton. Most of the time, however, they waited and brooded. The vets had come to ask their government for relief from the Great Depression, then approaching the end of its third year; specifically, they wanted immediate payment of the soldiers' "bonus" authorized by the Adjusted Compensation Act of 1924 but not due until 1945. If they could get cash now, the men would receive about $500 each. Headline writers had christened them "the Bonus Army," "the bonus marchers." They called themselves the Bonus Expeditionary Force.

BEF members had hoped in vain for congressional action. Now they appealed to President Hoover, begging him to receive a delegation of their leaders. Instead he sent word that he was too busy and then proceeded to isolate himself from the city. Presidential plans to visit the Senate were canceled; policemen patrolled the White House grounds day and night. For the first time since the Armistice, the Executive Mansion gates were chained shut. HOOVER LOCKS SELF IN WHITE HOUSE, read a New York Daily News headline. He went even further. Barricades were erected; traffic was shut down for a distance of one block on all sides of the Mansion. A one-armed veteran, bent upon picketing, tried to penetrate the screen of guards. He was soundly beaten and carried off to jail.

In retrospect this panoply appears to have been the overreaction of a frightened, frustrated administration. The bonus marchers were unarmed, had expelled radicals from their ranks, and — despite their evi-

dent hunger — weren't even panhandling openly. They seemed too weak
to be a menace. Drew Pearson, a thirty-four-year-old *Baltimore Sun*
reporter, described them as "ragged, weary, and apathetic," with "no
hope on their faces." Increasingly, the BEF vigil had become an exercise
in endurance. A health department inspector described the camps' sanitary
conditions as "extremely bad." Makeshift commissaries depended largely
upon charity. Truckloads of food arrived from friends in Des Moines and
Camden, New Jersey; a hundred loaves of bread were being shipped each
day from one sympathetic baker; a thousand pies came from another; the
Veterans of Foreign Wars sent $500, and the bonus marchers raised
another $2,500 by staging boxing bouts among themselves in Griffith
Stadium. It was all very haphazard. The administration was doing virtually nothing — Washington police had aroused Hoover's wrath by
feeding the District's uninvited guests bread, coffee, and stew at six cents
a day — and by mid-August brutal temperatures were approaching their
annual height, diminishing water reserves and multiplying misery.

In those years Washington was officially classified by the British Foreign
Office as a "sub-tropical climate." Diplomats loathed its wilting heat and
dense humidity; with the exception of a few downtown theaters which
advertised themselves as "refrigerated," there was no air-conditioning. In
summer the capital was a city of awnings, screened porches, ice wagons,
summer furniture and summer rugs, and in the words of an official guidebook it was also "a peculiarly interesting place for the study of insects."
Lacking shade or screens, the BEF was exposed to the full fury of the
season. When the vets' vanguard had entered the District, gardens were
flowering in their springtime glory. By July the blossoms of magnolia and
azalea were long gone, and the cherry trees were bare. Even the earth, it
seemed, was pitiless. The vets had taken on the appearance of desert
creatures; downtown merchants complained that "the sight of so many
down-at-the-heel men has a depressing effect on business." That, really,
was the true extent of their threat to the country.

But if the BEF danger was illusion, Washington's obscurity on the
international scene in that era, and its dependency upon Europe, were
more substantive. Among the sixty-five independent countries then in the
world, there was but one superpower: Great Britain. The Union Jack flew
serenely over one-fourth of the earth's arable surface — in Europe, Asia,
and Africa; North, Central, and South America; Australia, Oceania, and
the West Indies. The sun literally never sank upon it. Britain's Empire
commanded the allegiance of 485 million people, and if you wanted to
suggest stability you said "solid as the Rock of Gibraltar," or "safe as the
Bank of England," which with the pound sterling at $4.86 seemed the
ultimate in fiscal security. Air power was the dream of a few little-known
pilots and a cashiered American general named Mitchell; what counted
then was ships, and virtually no significant world waterway was free of

London's dominion. Gibraltar, Suez, the Gulf of Aden, the Strait of Singapore, and the Cape of Good Hope were controlled directly by the Admiralty. The Strait of Magellan was at the mercy of the British naval station in the Falkland Islands, and even the Panama Canal lay under the watchful eye of H.M.'s Caribbean squadron. As a consequence of all this, the United States was shielded by the Royal Navy as surely as any crown colony. Lloyd's of London offered 500-to-1 against any invasion of the U.S. And when *Fortune* assured its readers that the Atlantic and Pacific were "still a protection and will forever remain so, no matter how fast ships may sail or airplanes may fly," the magazine was assuming that the British fleet, which had ruled the waves throughout American history, would go right on ruling them.

Washington made the same assumption; the country lacked the status, the pretensions, and most of the apparatus of a great power. The capital was a slumbering village in summer, largely forgotten the rest of the year. In size it ranked fourteenth among American cities. Most big national problems were decided in New York, where the money was; when federal action was required, Manhattan's big corporation lawyers — men like Charles Evans Hughes, Henry L. Stimson, and Elihu Root — came down to guide their Republican protégés. President Coolidge had usually finished his official day by lunchtime. Hoover created a stir by becoming the first chief executive to have a telephone on his desk. He also employed five secretaries — no previous President had required more than one — and summoned them by an elaborate buzzer system.

Foggy Bottom, the site of the present State Department Building, was a Negro slum. The land now occupied by the Pentagon was an agricultural experimental station and thus typical of Washington's outskirts; "large areas close to the very heart of the nation's lawmaking," the *Saturday Evening Post* observed, "are still in farm hands." The government employed fewer than two thousand foreign service officers. It is an astonishing fact that the Secretaries of State, War, and Navy were all under one mansard roof, across the street from the White House in that ugly, smug mass of balusters, cupolas, and pillared porticoes known today as the Executive Office Building. Indeed, after a fire gutted the President's oval office in 1929, he and his staff had moved in with them and no one had felt crowded. There was little pomp. The East Wing of the White House, which would later house military attachés and social secretaries, hadn't been built. The Secret Service had not yet closed West Executive Avenue to the public; it was just another city street, and on a normal day you could park there within an easy stone's throw of the oval office. If you called on the Secretary of State, he sometimes met you at the door. Army Chief of Staff Douglas MacArthur, on the same floor of the Executive Office Building, was separated from his sole aide by a single slatted door. When the general wanted help he called "Major Eisenhower," and Ike came scurrying.

It was a *Fortune* writer, fortunately anonymous, who described the general as "shy and genuinely unsympathetic to publicity." That was nonsense. MacArthur, even then, spoke of himself in the third person, flourished a long cigarette holder as he talked, and had heightened his image by installing a fifteen-foot-high mahogany mirror behind him. As Eisenhower later recalled, when MacArthur felt slighted he was capable of expressing himself in "an explosive denunciation of politics, bad manners, bad judgment, broken promises, arrogance, unconstitutionality, insensitivity, and the way the world had gone to hell." He can hardly be blamed. Those were dog days for professional soldiers. Up through the rank of colonel, promotion was by seniority only, and by the early Thirties it took twenty-two years to climb from captain to major. There wasn't much to do except watch the calendar. Sheer boredom nearly drove Eisenhower to the point of resigning his commission, and it was in these years that he developed the habit of reading Street & Smith pulps: *Two-Gun Western, Western Story, Thrilling Western,* and *Cowboy Short Stories.* Across the Potomac at Fort Myer, George S. Patton Jr. — who had been a major since 1919 — could be observed playing polo Wednesdays and Saturdays at 4 P.M. Riding his own horses he had collected four hundred ribbons and two hundred cups; already known for his ivory-handled revolvers, he also pursued steeplechasing, fox hunting, skeet shooting, and flying. But Major Patton, unlike Major Eisenhower, was rich.

Perhaps nothing is more illustrative of American provincialism four decades ago than a brief glance at the military establishment; it requires no more. The U.S. had the sixteenth largest army in the world, putting it behind, among others, Czechoslovakia, Turkey, Spain, Romania, and Poland. When every $17.85-a-month private had suited up, there were 132,069 Americans in uniform. On paper they could have put up a stiff fight against Yugoslavia (138,934), but in reality they would have been torn to pieces, because most of MacArthur's men were committed to desk work, patrolling the Mexican border, and protecting U.S. possessions overseas. The chief of staff was left with 30,000 troops — fewer than the force King George sent to tame his rebellious American colonies in 1776.

Moreover, the quality of the Army was appalling. It cost roughly a quarter of one percent of today's military juggernaut, and looked it. *Fortune* called it the "worst equipped" of the world's armed forces; no one disputed the judgment. In a crisis MacArthur could have fielded 1,000 tanks, all obsolete; 1,509 aircraft, the fastest of which could fly 234 mph; and a single mechanized regiment, which had been organized at Fort Knox that spring, and which was led by cavalrymen on horses which wore mustard-gas-proof boots. The United States Army, one writer reported, "forever walks the wide land in the image of a gaping-mouthed private with an ill-fitting uniform carrying an obsolete rifle at an ungraceful angle."

MacArthur was the only four-star general in the country — and there were no three-star generals. As chief of staff he received $10,400 a year, a home at Fort Myer, and the exclusive use of the Army's only limousine. To his aide he seemed to occupy a distant pinnacle. Major Eisenhower's annual salary was $3,000. Because he doubled as the military's congressional lobbyist, he frequently went up to Capitol Hill. But his employer never loaned him the limousine. Nor was the major given taxi fare; in all of official Washington, there was no such thing as a petty cash fund. Instead, as he liked to recall in later life, Eisenhower would walk down the hall and fill out a form, in exchange for which he received two streetcar tokens. Then he would stand outside on Pennsylvania Avenue and wait for a Mt. Pleasant trolley car.

It wasn't a long wait. Washington was laced with trolley tracks; there were nearly seven hundred streetcars in service. Except in winter, when they were vulnerable to short-circuits, the cars were efficient, and traffic jams lay a generation away. If you drove to work (observing the 22 mph speed limit), you parked in front of your office. There was almost always room at the curb. There was also an extraordinary variety among the square-shouldered Packards, Studebakers, Grahams, Pierce Arrows, Terraplanes, and Stutzes, for the automobile business, by later corporate standards, was practically a cottage industry.

Men of all classes, including civil servants, worked Saturday mornings. In summer they wore a seasonal wardrobe: white linen, "Palm Beach," or cotton suits; straw boaters or Panama hats; shirts with "soft" collars; and light underwear, which was restricted to the warm months because central heating was recent and far from universal. The District's five daily papers were crowded with news of social unrest in 1932, but none of it was about Negroes. Although 26 percent of Washington was black (the highest ratio in any American city), Negroes accepted their appalling lot with remarkable unanimity. "Dark-skinned children of the South," a government guide explained, were confined to domestic service and "manual work." Department stores, movies, and government cafeterias were closed to them. Black workmen digging the foundations of the new Justice Department building on Pennsylvania Avenue either brought their lunches or went hungry; even if they wanted a glass of water they had to walk two miles out Seventh Street to find a restaurant which would serve them. The president of Howard University, the Negro college, was a white man. When President Hoover sent Gold Star mothers to France, black mothers were assigned to a second (and second-class) ship. And the most popular radio program in the country, *Amos 'n' Andy*, was a nightly racial slur, with its Negro parts played by two white men affecting minstrel show accents ("I'se regusted"; "Dat's de propolition").

Blacks occupied Foggy Bottom, southwest Washington, and all of Georgetown, which had not yet been discovered by lovers of the quaint, possibly because the rest of the city was so picturesque. The District was greener then; there were six shade trees for every inhabitant. The most exotic neighborhoods were Kalorama Heights and upper Massachusetts Avenue. As every Jew knew, the lovely mansions there were "restricted," but anti-Semitism was no more unfashionable than white racism; it didn't even trouble the diplomatic community, since there was no such nation as Israel. Embassy Row, now on Massachusetts Avenue, was then on Sixteenth Street, within walking distance of the White House, and the ambassadors wore striped pants and frock coats. They had to step carefully if they roamed the downtown area, for much of it was cobblestone. Supermarkets were still a California phenomenon; District food shopping was done in small groceries, in red-fronted outlets of the Great Atlantic & Pacific Tea Company, in open markets, or on pavements. Organ grinders and pushcart peddlers could be heard in the streets, together with the shouts of men wheeling grindstones and inviting housewives to bring them scissors and knives for sharpening. Downtown, flower and fruit stands provided vivid splashes of color on street corners. Oyster markets flourished down by the wharves. The Washington District Market was on Pennsylvania Avenue where the National Archives now stands. The Farmers Market was on K Street — a swarming spectacular celebrated for the cries of its fish hawkers and racks of dead rabbits. There was even a saddlery with a life-size wooden horse in front; there were still several thousand workhorses in the District in 1932. The K Street cobbles were dotted with their mementos, the scent of which, mingled with fragrances from the great markets and the corner stands, would soon vanish in deference to the great god macadam.

Even during the Depression Washington was visited by swarms of tourists, but they did not land at Washington National Airport, through which would pass in 1970 a total of 24,000 passengers a day. Those frantic acres then lay silent under the waters of the Potomac. Air travel was rare. The labor market being what it was, airlines could require that every stewardess be a registered nurse, but passenger planes, usually trimotor Fords, never flew at night or in bad weather. There were no coast-to-coast flights. The average airliner speed was 155 mph. By changing planes, one man crossed the country in eighteen hours; his picture was in all the papers. Although Washington had a field — Hoover Airport, on the Virginia side of what is now the Fourteenth Street Bridge (then called Highway Bridge) — it was used by only 250 passengers a day. The vast majority of travelers, eleven million of them each year, arrived at Union Station. The glorious reign of the steam engine was at the height of its Indian summer. There were 20,000 locomotives snuffling across the countryside (as compared to fewer than 300 in 1970), and the long, plaintive wail of the steam whistle stirred restless young men all over America. Fifteen-year-old John F. Kennedy heard it at the Choate School in Wallingford, Connecticut; Lyndon Johnson, then a teacher of public speaking, heard it in Houston; and in Whittier, California, a college student named Richard M. Nixon listened in the night, wondering what lay across the eastern horizon and what Washington, D.C., was like.

What did those who came see? To begin with, they looked at the train station. Union Station had become the first mass of masonry erected under the plan for a metropolis of classical buildings, and its imperial facade together with the Capitol dominated the city. The Capitol itself stood much as it does now, facing eastward, a tribute to one architect's belief in which direction the city would grow. Because the long expansion of presidential power had not begun, Congress was Washington's focal point, and tourists, like the BEF, made the Hill their first stop. For some it was also the last; the White House discouraged visitors, and there weren't many other attractions. There were the Lincoln Memorial and the Washington Monument, with its new elevator (though youngsters still felt challenged by the 898 steps up). The Botanical Gardens were open; so was the Folger Shakespeare Library. The Smithsonian Institution was popular in these months after the successful landing of Juan de la Cierva's Autogiro, a prototype of the helicopter, on the museum's lawn. If you liked drawbridges, there was the Arlington Memorial Bridge, which had been dedicated by President Hoover in January. Finally, there were a few — a very few — government office buildings: the Department of Agriculture on C Street, the old Interior Building on Eighteenth Street, the Civil Service Building on Seventh Street, and, bordering the Ellipse, the titanic Commerce Department Building, all of it under an eight-acre roof, erected in the 1920s by Secretary of Commerce Hoover as a shrine to American business.

What is most striking about 1932 Washington is the absence of so many landmarks which have since become familiar. There was no Jefferson Memorial, no Marine Corps Memorial, and no Supreme Court Building; the judges sat in the Capitol between the Senate and the House, almost directly under the Rotunda. The Tomb of the Unknown Soldier and the Washington Cathedral were under construction, the Shrine of the Immaculate Conception in the planning stage. Constitution Avenue, as we know it, did not exist. It was merely an extension of B Street. The long, clear mall could be found only in blueprints; the ground that summer was just another Washington park, thick with trees, crisscrossed by streets, and marred here and there by temporary World War buildings which had never been removed. Except for the Commerce Building, the Federal Triangle was unbuilt. Secretary Andrew Mellon and Senator Reed Smoot were especially interested, the *National Geographic* reported, in a four-billion-dollar program to line "the entire south side of Pennsylvania Avenue" with "monumental structures," and in September Hoover was scheduled to lay the cornerstone for a new Post Office Building. Meanwhile that great edifice and its neighbors — the Department of Labor, Interstate Commerce Commission, Department of Justice, National Archives, Federal Trade Commission, and National Gallery of Art — awaited the future. There were no FBI tours, no viewing of the Constitution and the Declaration of Independence. Until recently, most of the land had been in commercial use. Some of it still was, but here and there land had been broken, and some buildings to which the Treasury Department had taken title were scheduled for razing.

Of these, the most interesting were on a Pennsylvania Avenue tract now occupied by the National Gallery, the Federal Trade Commission, and the District tennis courts. There, on the morning of July 28, 1932, stood a row of ugly old red brick buildings which had once contained warehouses, a cheap hotel, automobile showrooms, a Chinese restaurant, and an undertaking parlor. Many of the walls had been knocked out, and the buildings would have been leveled weeks ago, but on the night of June 17 members of the Bonus Expeditionary Force had quietly occupied them. The District police superintendent, a retired brigadier named Pelham D. Glassford, was reluctant to deprive the veterans of shelter, especially since so many were accompanied by their wives and children. By midsummer, however, Glassford was under a cloud; Congress had rebuked him for allowing the vets to enter the city, and the White House let it be known that Hoover had reached the end of his patience. The President was determined to evict the ragged squatters even if he had to call out the Army — which, as things turned out, is exactly what he did.

That Pennsylvania Avenue camp was not BEF headquarters. The veterans' main force lay on the far side of the Anacostia River in southeast Washington, just across the Eleventh Street Bridge. But the Pennsylvania Avenue vets, living within three blocks of the Capitol, were the most conspicuous. To the administration they were an eyesore and a humiliation, and its determination to exorcise them reflected a general hardening throughout the land of the attitude of the well-fed toward the ill-fed. This was not true of those who moved among them. General Glassford liked them; so did General Billy Mitchell and Marine Corps General Smedley Butler, twice winner of the Medal of Honor. Drew Pearson wrote that the men "did not know what it was all about. They had no work, they were hungry, their families were hungry, they wanted to be paid. That was all they knew." Will Rogers said the BEF held "the record for being the best behaved" of any "hungry men assembled anywhere in the world."

But in the days before television newscasts it was possible to deny the obvious. Attorney General William D. Mitchell declared that the Bonus Army had been guilty of "begging and other acts." Vice President Charles Curtis had called out two companies of marines; bristling with fixed bayonets and steel helmets, they arrived on the faithful trolley cars, whereupon Glassford, pointing out that the Vice President of the United States lacks any authority over troops, ordered them back to barracks. Still, the appeal of force grew, here and elsewhere in the country. On March 7 three thousand hungry men and women had tried to demonstrate outside Henry Ford's plant in Dearborn, Michigan. The police had fired into their ranks, killing four and wounding a hundred others — who were then handcuffed to their hospital beds, charged with rioting. "Responsibility is not hard to fix," the *Detroit Free Press* thundered. "The inciters were William Z. Foster and the other Red agitators." Now other newspapers were egging on the President. The *Washington Evening Star* wondered editorially why no District policeman had "put into a healthy sock on the nose of a bonus marcher all the strength of healthy emotions," and the *New York Times* reported that the marchers were veterans who were "not content with their pensions, although seven or eight times those of other countries." Except for the disabled, there were no pensions at all, but sound men were beginning to make even more peculiar statements. One of Major Eisenhower's friends was Brigadier General George Moseley, whom Eisenhower later described as "a brilliant" and "dynamic" officer "always delving into new ideas." Among Moseley's new ideas that summer was a proposal to arrest the bonus marchers and others "of inferior blood," and then put them in concentration camps on "one of the sparsely inhabited islands of the Hawaiian group not suitable for growing sugar." There, he suggested, "they could stew in their own filth." He added darkly, "We would not worry about the delays in the process of law in the settlement of their individual cases."

Night and fog didn't worry the Pennsylvania Avenue vets; MacArthur had promised one of their leaders that if dispossession became necessary, he would permit them to retire with dignity, and as good soldiers they accepted the word of a four-star general. Reports had reached them that the Army might be on its way; they thought it a good rumor, thought that if men in khaki appeared they would fall into one another's arms. In their camp faded flags hung everywhere, and to them it was inconceivable that doughboys would attack the colors. Their greatest concern on that morning of Thursday, July 28, was the weather. By 9 A.M. they knew they were in for a day of extraordinary discomfort, and they talked wistfully of the new refrigerated theaters, whose current talkies featured Janet Gaynor and Charles Farrell in *The First Year,* William Powell and Kay Francis in *Jewel Robbery,* and Jackie Cooper and Chic Sale in *When a Feller Needs a Friend.* Compared to their present quarters, the thought of air-conditioning was an idyllic dream. Railroads had shipped them here free, to clear the yards; one bill of lading had read, "Livestock — Destination: Washington D.C. — 55 vets," and they had almost begun to think of themselves as livestock. The partially demolished buildings were largely reserved for women and young children, for whom straw mattresses had been provided by General Glassford. The men lay in what one reporter called a "conglomeration of tented huts made of tattered cloth fixed up on old boards with packing boxes serving as props." Here and there handmade signs read, "God Bless Our Home." They weren't meant to be witty. Men with their backgrounds didn't joke about God, home, or, if it came to that, about patriotism.

They were from the American yeomanry; if the term had been in use then, they would have been called members of the lower middle class. Five who would be in the direct line of any attack across Pennsylvania

Avenue were typical. Only one, J. A. Bingham of Harlan County, Kentucky, had been an officer in the American Expeditionary Force to France, and Bingham could hardly have been thought a member of the leisure class; his most recent employment had been as a strikebreaker, making life uncomfortable for Theodore Dreiser, Sherwood Anderson, John Dos Passos, and the crusade of Ivy League students who had come to Kentucky last March to protest violations of miners' civil rights. John Olson of Sacramento, and Charles P. Ruby, whose DSC had led to his selection as the first man to wish the President Happy New Year in 1931, had both been decorated for bravery in France. Eric Carlson of Oakland had been gassed and, as they said then, "shell-shocked." William Hrushka, whose life was to become a subject of considerable interest, had served as a private first class in the 41st Infantry. All were unemployed. Hrushka, a butcher, had been living in his brother-in-law's windowless basement flat on Chicago's southwest side.

Disaster wears many masks, and for these men, at 10 A.M. that oppressive morning, it was represented by two Treasury Department agents, who stood perspiring on the sidewalk and told them to leave. The veterans declined; the agents vanished. An hour passed and nothing happened except the relentless rise of the temperature. Then, shortly after eleven o'clock, General Glassford arrived on his blue motorcycle, drew up at Third and Pennsylvania, and announced that he had orders to clear the area. His men moved in, nightsticks at the ready.

It was a slow business, but there was little resistance at first, and by noon the first building was cleared. Meantime, however, word of what was happening had reached the main camp on Anacostia Flats. Belatedly, and rather desperately, the police tried to raise the Eleventh Street Bridge. It was too late; BEF reinforcements were on the way; arriving, they hurled brick fragments at the policemen there. Glassford himself was struck on the side of his face, and as he staggered backward he was horrified to see one of his own men, also dazed, pointing a pistol at him. The superintendent jumped behind a pillar. He heard a hoarse voice shout, "Let's get him!" Reappearing, Glassford saw a policeman who, in his words, had "gone wild-eyed" and was firing at a veteran. The vet — Hrushka — fell dead, a bullet in his heart. Other officers were also firing; in a moment three more vets fell, one — Carlson — mortally wounded. Glassford shouted, "Stop the shooting!" They did, but word of the incident was on its way to the White House. Attorney General Mitchell had already ordered the evacuation of all veterans from government property. Hoover learned of the shooting at lunch. After an interval, while everything was put into writing, the President told Secretary of War Patrick J. Hurley to use troops, and Hurley passed the word to the chief of staff.

Now came another, embarrassing lull. The chief wasn't in uniform. His aide didn't think he should be. "This is political, political," Eisenhower said again and again, arguing that it was highly inappropriate for a general to become involved in a street-corner brawl. The general disagreed. "MacArthur has decided to go into active command in the field," MacArthur declared. "There is incipient revolution in the air." So the soldiers, who were arriving from Fort Myer, milled around on the Ellipse, watched by Hoover from his oval office while an orderly dashed across the river to fetch the chief's tunic, service stripes, sharpshooter medal, and English whipcord breeches. The general also ordered Eisenhower into uniform. "We're going to break the back of the BEF," he said, and led his staff to the limousine. At Sixth and Pennsylvania (which later became the site of Washington's largest cut-rate liquor store) the car pulled over and began still another wait. "What's holding us up?" someone asked. "The tanks," MacArthur replied. He was going to use tanks. Everyone sat back and sweated — everyone, that is, except MacArthur. This is the first recorded instance of the general's remarkable inability to perspire. He remained cool, poised, and starched. It gave him an immense psychological advantage, and there were those who bitterly resented it.

Meanwhile the White House was issuing communiqués. President Hoover announced that the troops would "put an end to rioting and defiance of civil authority." A few minutes later the White House revealed that the men who had clashed with the police were "entirely of the Communist element." Reporters, finding MacArthur in his car, asked him what he was going to do. "Watch me," he replied. "Just watch me." Instead they were watching the astonishing display of force which was arriving, at last, down Pennsylvania Avenue. Troopers of the 3rd Cavalry, led by Major Patton, pranced along brandishing naked sabers. Behind the horses marched a machine gun detachment and men from the 12th Infantry, the 13th Engineers, and the 34th Infantry, the sun glinting on their bayonets. Behind these units rolled the six tanks, the caterpillar treads methodically chewing up the soft asphalt. It was now 4:45 P.M. The operation had become the worst-timed in MacArthur's career. Fifteen minutes earlier, the District's civil service workers had begun pouring into the streets, their day's work done; twenty thousand of them were massed on the sidewalks across from the bewildered, disorganized veterans. Someone was going to get hurt if the cavalry commander didn't watch out, and Major Patton was not celebrated for his solicitude toward civilians.

The veterans, assuming that this display was a dress parade for their benefit, applauded. The spectators clapped, too, though they were the first to be disillusioned. Abruptly Patton's troopers wheeled and charged into the crowd. "At first," wrote J. F. Essary, veteran Washington bureau chief of the *Baltimore Sun*, "it seemed that this attack upon the civilian observers was merely the act of a few of the armed horsemen. But later it appeared that it was a part of a concerted movement by the cavalry officers." Essary reported that the troopers charged "without the slightest warning" into "thousands of unoffending people"; that men and women were "ridden down indiscriminately"; and that one man who refused to move from the front of a telegraph office was beaten back into the doorway by two cavalrymen who flailed him with the flat side of their blades. Among those trampled was Senator Hiram Bingham of Connecticut — Panama hat, Palm Beach suit, and all.

"Clear out!" the mounted men yelled, and the spectators shouted back, "Shame! Shame!" The veterans, meanwhile, had hurriedly formed a solid line across the street. Their leaders were waving flags at rallying points, and it was these colors which became the troopers' second objective. Reforming in extended order, they bounded across Pennsylvania Avenue, converging on the faded standards. The vets were stunned, then furious. Some dared the soldiers to dismount and fight. "Jesus!" cried a graying man — "If we only had guns!"; and others demanded of cavalrymen, "Where were you in the Argonne, buddy?" By now all the bonus marchers were hooting and booing. One soldier in his late teens wrested a banner from the hands of a former AEF sergeant. "You crummy old bum!" the boy spat. A man near MacArthur called out, "The American flag means nothing to me after this." The general snapped, "Put that man under arrest if he opens his mouth again."

MacArthur's written instructions from the Secretary of War specified that "any women and children who may be in the affected area" must be "accorded every consideration and kindness." Given the chief of staff's plan, it is hard to see how such distinctions could have been drawn. In anticipation of this assignment, he had requisitioned three thousand gas grenades from the Aberdeen Proving Ground and Edgewood Arsenal, and gas could not discriminate between sexes and ages. The only participants with real protection would be the general's troops, who were now donning masks. Policemen tied handkerchiefs over their faces, storekeepers who had been warned slammed their doors and transoms, and those veterans who saw the masks spread the alarm, for they knew what was coming. But there wasn't time to do much. The infantry came running on the heels of the horsemen, pulling the blue tear gas bombs from their belts and throwing them ahead. Suddenly the air was sharply tainted; the spectators broke and fled. A sickly-sweet haze hung over Pennsylvania Avenue, and beneath it the BEF women, blinded and choking, stumbled from the occupied buildings clutching pots, pans, and children. "It was like a scene out of the 1918 no-man's land," reported the Associated Press. It wasn't quite. Washington was the capital of a nation at peace. The uneven struggle was being waged in the very shadow of Congress. Most of those present were noncombatants, and some were professionally neutral, though armed authority regarded newspapermen with suspicion. One reporter darted into a phone booth outside a filling station to call his office; a soldier tossed a bomb inside and drove him out.

Resistance vanished. Driven by sabers, bayonets, and a rising wind — which blew the vile gas southward — the stricken BEF retreated toward the Anacostia River. It was a clumsy withdrawal. The women were carrying infants and their husbands shabby suitcases, and the retirement was harried by the puffs of fresh gas bombs. Gallinger Hospital was beginning to fill up with casualties. The evening noises were frightening: ambulance sirens, fire engines, galloping horses, tramping soldiers, newsboys hawking extras, and the clanking of the tanks, whose role was, and would continue to be, quite vague; "so far as I can recall," Eisenhower wrote toward the end of his life, "they took no part whatever in the movements to evacuate the veterans," although there was plenty of time for them, because the retirement "proceeded slowly." Nevertheless, by 9 P.M. the refugees had crossed the Eleventh Street Bridge and joined the main BEF camp on the far shore. MacArthur's force had cleared out other camps on C Street, on Maryland and Maine Avenues, along the wharves, and near the Congressional Library. Stacking arms near a gas works at about eight o'clock, the troops messed at a field kitchen while their leader contemplated his next move.

To him the decision was obvious. His mission was the destruction of the BEF. There was no substitute for victory. His job wouldn't be complete until he had crossed the river, invaded the vets' sanctuary, and leveled their headquarters. General Glassford vehemently disagreed; he begged the chief of staff to abandon plans for a night attack, calling it "the height of stupidity." MacArthur was adamant, and the outranked police superintendent turned away. A direct order from the President of the United States was something else. Commander in Chief Hoover had his own ideas about how his army should be used, and they stopped at the water's edge. To make certain his instructions reached the general, he sent duplicate orders through General Moseley and Colonel Clement B. Wright, secretary of the General Staff. According to Eisenhower, the President "forbade any troops to cross the bridge into the largest encampment of the veterans, on open ground beyond the bridge." That was clear enough, and another general would have submitted instantly. Not MacArthur. He was choleric at this civilian meddling. He told the astonished Moseley that his plans had to go forward; he would not brook interference. To Eisenhower the chief of staff declared emphatically that he was "too busy and did not want either himself or his staff bothered by people coming down and pretending to bring orders." For the first but not the last time, the general decided to disobey a President.

Mounting heavy machine guns on the bridge to meet any counterattack, MacArthur led a column of infantry across, with Major Eisenhower at his side. They debouched on the other side in files of two — and marched into chaos. The Anacostia camp was a jumble of packing crates, fruit crates, chicken coops, burlap-and-tarpaper shacks, tents, lean-tos, wrecked touring cars, and dun-colored, tepee-like shelters. It didn't seem possible that anyone could have become attached to so preposterous an array of junk, but it was the only home the BEF families had. They were huddled here in the dark, praying for deliverance. What they got was another fusillade of tear gas bombs. Some fled screaming, some hid; one large group of about five hundred gathered on the edge of the camp and mocked the troops with the chant, "Yellow! Yellow! Yellow!" Veterans who had planted vegetable gardens pleaded with the infantrymen to spare their crops. The green rows were trampled anyhow. At 10:14, the Associated Press reported, soldiers put the torch to the hodgepodge of buildings. Flames leaped fifty feet in the air and spread to a nearby woods; six companies of firemen had to be summoned. From his White House window the President saw the glow in the eastern sky and demanded to know what had happened. To Eisenhower "the whole scene was pitiful. The veterans, whether or not they were mistaken in marching on Washington, were ragged, ill-fed, and felt themselves badly abused. To suddenly see the whole encampment going up in flames just added to the pity one had to feel for them."

The major's compassion wasn't universal. Seven-year-old Eugene King, a vet's son, tried to rescue his pet rabbit from the family tent. "Get out of here, you little son-of-a-bitch," said an infantryman, and before the boy could move, the soldier ran a bayonet through his leg. Again ambulances raced the two miles from Gallinger Hospital. There were over a hundred casualties. Two babies were dead of gas, and the angry editor of the BEF newspaper suggested the epitaph for one: "Here lies Bernard Myers, aged three months, gassed to death by order of President Hoover." That was unfair, but the veterans were bitter. They had seen soldiers pouring gasoline on their huts while well-to-do Washingtonians in yachts cruised close to look at the show. And at 11:15 P.M. they had watched Major George S. Patton Jr. lead his cavalrymen in a final destructive charge. Among the ragged bonus marchers routed by their sabers was Joseph T. Angelino, who, on September 26, 1918, had won the Distinguished Service Cross in the Argonne Forest for saving the life of a young officer named George S. Patton Jr.

Major Eisenhower advised his chief to avoid newspaper reporters; this operation had been more political than military, he continued to argue, and the politicians should do the talking. MacArthur shook his head. He enjoyed talking to the press. Furthermore, whether he liked it or not — it seems quite clear that he relished it — his decision to cross the Anacostia had put him squarely in the middle of presidential politics. At fifteen minutes past midnight he appeared before reporters with Secretary of War Hurley. From the outset his strategy was obvious: he disclaimed responsibility and praised Hoover for shouldering it. "Had the President not acted within twenty-four hours, he would have been faced with a very grave situation, which would have caused a real battle," the general said. "Had he waited another week, I believe the institutions of our government would have been severely threatened." Secretary Hurley added, "It was a great victory. Mac did a great job; he's the man of the hour." He paused thoughtfully and added, "But I must not make any heroes just now."

The real problem was the making of martyrs. Hounding men who fought for their country was not a political master stroke. Already sympathizers were offering the BEF farmland in Maryland and Virginia. Senators Hugo Black of Alabama, William Borah of Idaho, and Hiram Johnson of California were deeply shocked by the Army's behavior, and Representative Fiorello La Guardia of New York wired the President, "Soup is cheaper than tear gas bombs and bread is better than bullets in maintaining law and order in these times of Depression, unemployment, and hunger." General MacArthur dealt with this problem in an aside. The BEF were "insurrectionists," not ex-soldiers, he said. "If there was one man in ten in that group who is a veteran it would surprise me."

At the White House, which had announced that the President was staying up "until a late hour getting bulletins from the Bonus Army front," discrediting the BEF became the official line. Later Hoover would have private words of reproach for his insubordinate general, but now he declared that the bonus marchers were "not veterans," that they were "Communists and persons with criminal records." The percentage of nonveterans varied from spokesman to spokesman. MacArthur had put it at 90 percent. Hurley thought it was about 33 percent. Then Hoover wrote an American Legion post in Boston that it was his "impression" that "less than half of them ever served under the American flag." General Glassford protested that this was untrue, thereby assuring his early retirement in October. Some of the dirt was bound to stick. In an extraordinary charge to a Washington grand jury the day after the rioting, a member of the District Court said, "It is reported that the mob guilty of actual violence included few exservice men and was made up mainly of Communists and other disorderly elements. I hope you will find that it is so and that few men who have worn the nation's uniform engaged in this violent attack upon law and order."

Unfortunately for the Hoover administration's place in history, no one thought to check with the Veterans Administration. Before the BEF attacked law and order by becoming the targets of a gas attack, the VA had completed an exhaustive survey of its membership. According to the VA figures, 94 percent of the bonus marchers had Army or Navy records, 67 percent had served overseas, and 20 percent had been disabled. Glassford and the ragged men he had championed were vindicated. It cannot be said that it did them much good. Remarkably few newspapers reprinted the survey, and most of those that did ignored it on their editorial pages. The *New York Times* described the veterans as "ordinary trespassers" whose "insubordination" had "led to a violent outbreak, almost amounting to insurrection." The *Boston Herald* declared: "The people . . . have had enough of holdups by the undeserving." The *New York Herald Tribune* ventured that the BEF cause now found "not a shred of sympathy left anywhere." To the Cleveland *Plain Dealer,* "camping on the Capitol grounds" was "cheap heroics," and although *Time* was critical of the administration, *Fortune* concluded that MacArthur, by realizing that "bayonets and an overwhelming show of strength were the only means of preventing fatalities" (the fact that there *were* fatalities was overlooked) had earned the nation's gratitude for having "skillfully executed" a difficult task.

On the morning after the disorders, the general feeling in comfortable American homes was that the government had thwarted men bent upon violent revolution. There were exceptions. Noting that during the BEF's period of greatest frustration the chief executive had received a heavyweight wrestling champion, members of the Eta Upsilon Gamma sorority, and the winners of a high school essay contest, Walter Lippmann wrote, "Mr. Hoover does not shrink from holding conferences and issuing statements. How can he justify the fact that he never took the trouble to confer with the Bonus marchers?"

At the executive mansion in Albany, New York, the atmosphere was funereal. Eleanor Roosevelt read the papers with what she later called "a feeling of horror." Her husband seemed even more deeply affected. Professor Rexford Tugwell of Columbia, a house guest, was summoned to the master bedroom, where his host lay surrounded by clouds of newsprint. As Tugwell entered, Governor Roosevelt covered photographs of the rioting with his hands, as though in shame for his country. The governor recalled that in 1920 he had proposed Hoover as a presidential candidate. He apologized for that now. "There is nothing inside the man but jelly," Roosevelt said angrily. "Maybe there never was anything else. Why didn't Hoover offer the men coffee and sandwiches, instead of turning Pat Hurley and Doug MacArthur loose?" It was characteristic of Franklin Roosevelt that he saw the incident not in terms of principles or high policy, but as a human calamity. He might feel sorry for the President, he told Tugwell, if he weren't moved by a greater sorrow for the veterans and their families. "They're probably camping on the roads leading out of Washington," he said in anguish. "They must be in terrible shape."

They were in terrible shape, but they weren't bivouacked on those roads. The Democratic governors of Virginia and Maryland had seen to that. About two hundred veterans slipped into Arlington County before Sheriff Howard Fields blocked off the Potomac bridges; he told them that unless they left Virginia soil within twenty-four hours, Governor Pollard would call out the militia. Governor Ritchie's orders to the Maryland State Police were: "Make them go by the main highway toward Baltimore or don't let them enter Maryland." It was impossible to keep them out altogether, so motorcycle policemen met the exhausted bonus marchers at the District line and escorted them through sleeping Baltimore to the Pennsylvania line. In Pennsylvania a few found temporary sanctuary in Johnstown's Ideal Park. Most, however, were herded by the state police there to the Ohio line, where another uniformed escort waited. And so it went. Some, finding sympathy along the way, turned to begging. One railroad put together a special train to carry those bound for the plains states; Kansas City civic leaders raised $1,500 to keep it from stopping there, and the boxcars hurtled onward like Lenin's sealed car. There is no record of its eventual destination. All that is known is that by autumn most of the BEF had merged into the enormous transient population which roamed the land in 1932.

Roughly two million Americans — over a quarter-million of them between the ages of sixteen and twenty-one — were on the road that year. *Fortune* called them the Depression's "wandering population." In convoying the veterans from border to border, state policemen were following a ritual which had been established early in the Depression by county sheriffs. Every local government had more welfare cases than it could handle; impoverished strangers were charged with vagrancy and dumped across the nearest county line. A few cities, like East St. Louis, were famous for their compassionate Salvation Army stations. Most communities cultivated inhospitable reputations. California first set up forced labor camps and then posted guards on highways entering the state, to turn back the poor. In Atlanta shabby outsiders were sentenced to thirty days on the Fulton County chain gang. Eric Sevareid, who was one of the twenty-year-old wanderers in the early 1930s, later recalled that "cities were judged and rated on the basis of their citizens' generosity with handouts and the temperament of the railway 'deeks' who guard the freight yards. You did not, for example, attempt to travel through Cheyenne, Wyoming, if you had any alternative. You were apt to be chased from the yards there not only with clubs, which was fairly common, but with revolver shots, and it was a long walk to the next station."

Who were the vagabonds? There was a hard core of seasoned hoboes, whose "jungles" provided squalid havens for the others, but most Americans on the road were new to it. They were dispossessed sharecroppers, foreclosed farmers abandoning farmland parched by three summers of drought, ragged bands of youths who had graduated from school and could not find jobs — members of what was called the "locked-out" generation. Sevareid was a banker's son, and the percentage with middle-class backgrounds was very high. Mobility was in the American tradition; "'Scuse our dust," they had been fond of saying, and "You've got to be a go-getter if you want to get ahead," and "I'm on my way," and "Your Uncle Dudley's going places." Often an unemployed man would pile his family into the old car, head off in any direction optimistically looking for work, and wind up destitute and far from home.

"They are the people whom our post offices label 'address unknown,' and whom we call transients," Newton D. Baker wrote in the *New York Times* that year. "Every group in society is represented in their ranks, from the college graduate to the child who has never seen the inside of the schoolhouse. Expectant mothers, sick babies, young childless couples, grim-faced middle-aged dislodged from lifetime jobs — on they go, an index of insecurity in a country used to the unexpected. We think of nomads of the desert — now we have nomads of the Depression." It was true; in every city breadline there were sprinklings of chesterfields and homburgs, and magistrates never knew who would appear before them on vagrancy charges. One Brooklyn defendant, who pleaded guilty to sleeping in a vacant lot for forty-six days, was an alumnus of the University of Colorado and had served the governments of Panama, China, Chile, and Venezuela as a civil engineer. Another was one of the most famous chefs of the Twenties; he had been living in a condemned attic and tormenting himself reading his old menus.

The descent from the middle class was rapid and sickening. Among the unskilled laborers building a California reservoir were farmers, ministers, engineers, a school principal, and the former president of a Missouri bank. In Chicago two hundred women were sleeping nightly in Grant and Lincoln parks. They had no shelter, no blankets, no protection of any kind; when night fell they lay on the cold ground and shivered until dawn. In Babylon, New York, Long Island policemen found a registered nurse starving in a maple grove on a private estate where for two weeks she had slept in a bundle of old rags and papers. In Oskaloosa, Iowa, an unemployed teacher and her two children were preparing to spend their second winter in a tented hole in the ground. As Cabell Phillips of the *New York Times* observed, the man who knocked on your door at night "might be the same fellow who a few months or a year ago had cheerfully O.K.'d your loan at the bank or had written the editorials in your newspaper or had been the vice president of a leading real estate company."

Eminent writers were among the very poor in 1932, and some have left a record of what transient life was like. John Steinbeck washed his clothes with soap made from pork fat, wood ashes, and salt. He couldn't even afford postage on his manuscripts; his agent paid it, although none of them sold then. The prospect of illness, he later recalled, frightened the nomads most of all: "You had to have money to be sick then. Dentistry was out of the question, with the result that my teeth went badly to pieces." Steinbeck was in the country. City caravansaries were more foul. Thomas Wolfe regularly visited the public latrine in front of the New York City Hall, watching men quarrel over the possession of stools while foraging in their tattered overcoat pockets for crusts of bread or old bones with rancid shreds of meat still clinging to them. The nomads there, he wrote:

> . . . were just flotsam of the general ruin of the time — honest, decent, middle-aged men with faces seamed by toil and want, and young men, many of them boys in their teens, with thick, unkempt hair. These were the wanderers from town to town, the riders of freight trains, the thumbers of rides on highways, the uprooted, unwanted male population of America. They drifted across the land and gathered in the big cities when winter came, hungry, defeated, empty, hopeless, restless, driven by they knew not what, always on the move, looking everywhere for work, for the bare crumbs to support their miserable lives, and finding neither work nor crumbs. Here

in New York, to this obscene meeting place, these derelicts came, drawn into a common stew of rest and warmth and a little surcease from their desperation. . . . The sight was revolting, disgusting, enough to render a man forever speechless with very pity.

Years later Mrs. Lyndon Johnson would remember her husband's excited shout when he managed to get boys "out of boxcars and into jobs." That was the essence of the transients' problem. To workers in the U.S. Children's Bureau and the National Association of Travelers' Aid Societies it sometimes seemed that the youth of a nation was being destroyed on the rails. Paying Pullman passengers would find only one or two berths in a car occupied in 1932, but on the rods beneath them, and in the freight cars, humanity was dense. An average of seven hundred train hoppers a day passed through Kansas City. In twelve months, the Southern Pacific Railroad reported, its guards had thrown 683,000 people off freights. Riding the rods was dangerous. Testifying before a subcommittee of the Seventy-second Congress, R. S. Mitchell, chief special agent of the Missouri Pacific Railway, mentioned that he had taken "official notice" of 387,313 Depression nomads, of whom 335 had become casualties. He was asked for details.

> SENATOR COSTIGAN: Have you observed any ill effects on the health of people traveling under these conditions?
>
> MR. MITCHELL: The health conditions in the winter . . . is a very serious thing. It is a very serious thing for a tender individual not properly clothed, to ride outside in winter weather. I do not see how they can escape pneumonia.
>
> SENATOR COSTIGAN: There is considerable exposure?
>
> MR. MITCHELL: Yes, sir.

There were other kinds of exposure. Forty years ago the line between the sexes was sharply drawn, and girls, joining nomad caravans for the first time, frequently disguised themselves as boys. But they were soon unmasked; among other things, they lacked the strength and dash of boys who could hide in culverts at daybreak and raid passing produce trucks. To earn their keep, they offered themselves to fellow travelers. But the going rate for nomad prostitutes was only ten cents, and for a dime the girl was risking not only pregnancy — with the unlikelihood that a physician could be found nine months later — but also eventual venereal infection.

In the South there was an additional hazard. Both races were riding the freights. Intercourse between them was a crime, and a white girl under suspicion of working what was called "the black market" was strongly tempted to cry rape — with fatal consequences for her customer. In fact, this had happened the previous year on a slow gondola car between Chattanooga and Scottsboro, Alabama, giving rise to one of the great liberal causes of the decade. Nine illiterate Negro youths were sentenced to death on testimony from two white southern mill girls with police records, one of whom gave evidence in language so foul that reporters could not use any of it. The case went through countless appeals and two Supreme Court reversals of conviction until, twenty years later, the last of the Negro prisoners died of cancer. The Communist party made "the Scottsboro boys" known around the world, and their persecution provided incalculable fuel for black despair and, later, militancy.

But in 1932 you didn't have to be black to suffer on the road. Prison was often regarded as a godsend; as Agent Mitchell told Senator Costigan, when nomads were threatened with arrest, "they would laugh at the officers and say, 'That is what we want. That will give us a place to sleep and eat.'" To find out why they preferred jail fare, Thomas Minehan, a graduate student at the University of Minnesota, dressed in rags and joined a gang of young transients. Nourishment, he found, was acquired at breadlines, which might be in missions, churches, hospitals, Salvation Army flophouses, or municipal welfare stations. The lines should more accurately have been called soup kitchens: "the soup is invariably — I write from experience — thin, watery, lukewarm, tasteless, and served without even stale bread, and never with soda crackers. A portion equals about a small cupful." No second bowl was ever given, and eviction after the first or second day was inevitable.

Everywhere Minehan saw signs of malnutrition — prominent ribs, concave abdomens, arms and legs on which the skin was loose and baggy, hungry eyes, and nervous mannerisms. Newton D. Baker asked, "Can we afford to permit permanent injury to this generation of youth?" Baker was dismissed as a windy politician. Yet eight years later, when the children of the Depression were called to the draft, he was vindicated. National Physical Fitness Director John B. Kelly (father of Grace Kelly) found that 40 percent of the young men examined were unfit. Most rejections were for bad teeth. Other defects, in the order of prevalence, were poor eyesight, diseases of the heart and circulation, deformities of arms and legs, and mental disorders. To those were added the invisible scars inflicted in hobo jungles by thieves, drug addicts, and hardened inverts — men like the strapping homosexual who tried to seduce young Sevareid for a quarter.

Henry Ford said, "Why, it's the best education in the world for those boys, that traveling around! They get more experience in a few months than they would in years at school." If President Hoover believed otherwise, he never said so. Certainly nothing in his personal experience contradicted it. Because he couldn't bear to watch suffering, he never visited a breadline or a relief station, despite the pleas of William Allen White. He never turned his head when his limousine swept past apple salesmen on street corners. Not until that autumn did his train leave Washington to cross states he had never visited since taking his oath of office on March 4, 1929. It was then, staring out of his guarded car at night, that he saw the campfires of hundreds of thousands of his people, mostly boys and girls who, Gene Smith wrote, "were aimlessly traveling the highways by day and sleeping near them at night."

Hoover had considered economy in the White House kitchen, then decided that would be bad for the country's morale. Each evening he entered the dining room wearing black tie — he was the last President who unfailingly dressed for dinner — and addressed himself to seven complete courses. The reporter who had coined the 1928 Republican campaign slogan ("A chicken in every pot and two cars in every garage") was broke and pleading for loans to support his three children, but the chief executive believed that America would despair if its first family lost faith in the return of prosperity.

Usually some of the courses were out of season; so were the cut flowers on the table. A custom-built humidor held long thick cigars handmade in Havana to the President's specifications; he smoked twenty a day. As the Hoovers ate, a remarkable number of men stood around and watched. The butler and footmen — all had to be the same height — stood at attention, absolutely silent, forbidden to move unbidden. In the doorways were duty officers from the company of marines who stood by wearing dress blues, to provide ceremonial trappings, and there were buglers in Ruritanian uniforms whose glittering trumpets announced the President's arrival and departure from the nightly feast, even when the only other diner was his wife Lou. Hoover was proud of Lou. She spoke five languages fluently, was president of the Girl Scouts of America, and set what was conceded to be the finest table in White House history. Sometimes she wondered whether the President really appreciated the food. He wolfed it down with such incredible speed.

By the fourth year of his administration, Herbert Clark Hoover had become a national riddle. A sardonic Texan had written a bonus marcher, "Of course, you won't have to worry about chow, being so close to the world's greatest food administrator." Yet that is precisely what Hoover had been; his feat in rescuing starving Belgium is still one of the brightest chapters in the long history of American humanitarianism. Maxim Gorki had written him, "You have saved from death 3,500,000 children, 5,500,000 adults." Finland added a verb to its language; to "hoover" meant to help.

Now it was all turned round. As the nation's anger deepened and darkened, stories were spread that he had made a fortune in Belgium, that dogs instinctively disliked him, that he was the mastermind behind the kidnapping and murder of Charles Lindbergh's son in March 1932. Junky shantytowns of tin, cardboard and burlap were Hoovervilles — Manhattan had two big ones, below Riverside Drive and near the obelisk in Central Park. The unemployed (an adjective which had become a noun in these years) carried sacks of frayed belongings called "Hoover bags." In North Carolina the rural poor sawed the fronts off broken-down flivvers, attached scrawny mules, and called the result "Hoovercarts." (The government tried to change the name to "Depression chariots," but no one bought it.) "Hoover blankets" were old newspapers which park bench tenants wrapped around themselves for warmth. "Hoover flags" were empty pockets turned inside out. "Hoover hogs" were the jackrabbits hungry farmers caught for food. Vaudeville comedians called out, "What? You say business is better? You mean Hoover died?" or reported that Hoover asked Secretary of the Treasury Mellon for a nickel to telephone a friend and was told, "Here's a dime, phone both of them."

There was a fine irony in Hoover's plight, for by the standards of the Twenties he had been considered a liberal politician. President Coolidge had scorned his brisk Secretary of Commerce as "the miracle worker" and "the wonder boy." Republican conservatives had not been grateful to Hoover for regulating radio and making airwaves public property. His great dream, on the day of his inauguration, had been to become a mighty social engineer, manipulating industrial forces for the common good. That was not quite what the Grand Old Party stood for; when the first few paragraphs of his inaugural address reached the *Chicago Tribune*, Colonel McCormick had wired his Washington bureau, "This man Hoover won't do." Hoover had been sharply critical of Coolidge-Mellon easy money. He had predicted an economic downturn because of it, and one of his first acts as President had been to persuade the Federal Reserve Board to tighten credit in the hope that the blow might be softened.

When time came to sail near the wind, however, it developed that he wasn't so heretical after all. By manipulation he had meant that the government should act as a supervisor and coordinator. Its function was to bring about "a condition of affairs favorable to the beneficial development of private enterprise," he explained, and he added that the only "moral" way out of the Depression was self-help: the people should find inspiration in the devotion of "great manufacturers, our railways, utilities, business houses and public officials." Since by 1932 the people in large numbers had become convinced that the great manufacturers and their colleagues were a bunch of crooks, a credibility gap appeared and widened.

The President professed to ignore it. He was an apostle of what John Kenneth Galbraith later called the conventional wisdom. He believed the gold standard to be sacred — even though eighteen nations, led by Great Britain, had abandoned it. He was convinced that a balanced budget was "indispensable," an "absolute necessity," "the most essential factor to economic recovery," "the first necessity of the nation," and "the foundation of all public and private financial stability" — all this despite the fact that in 1932 he was running the federal budget four billion dollars into the red. When he became convinced at last that the government must do something, he created the Reconstruction Finance Corporation to prop up sagging banks, and agreed to spend twenty-five million dollars on feed for farm animals on the condition that a bill authorizing $120,000 for hungry people be tabled.

This sounds absurd today, but in those days sound men accepted it as the revealed word. "Federal feeding would set a dangerous precedent," argued the *Schenectady Star;* it would be too dangerously like the dole, which paralyzed British labor. "If this country ever votes a dole," said Silas Strawn, president of the United States Chamber of Commerce, "we've hit the toboggan as a nation." Everyone knew how England's moral fiber had been sapped; the *American Magazine* reported that pubs were crowded with topers on the dole. Henry Ford declared that unemployment insurance would only guarantee increased unemployment, and his logic was accepted as flawless The enlightened editors of *Fortune* explained that business should reject the very concept of social responsibility, on the ground that the introduction of any noneconomic factor would destroy the benign workings of a free market. Even Walter Lippmann, while taking the position that action was necessary, insisted that money be raised by state legislatures, not Congress.

It was a business country, Calvin Coolidge had said, and it wanted a business government. Coolidge went further. "The man who builds a factory," he wrote, "builds a temple," and "the man who works there worships there." During the Republican Twenties business had become much more than the accumulation of cash; it had come to be the guiding light in schools, press, even in churches. True believers continued reading Bruce Barton's best seller about Jesus Christ, *The Man Nobody Knows,* in which Barton claimed, among other things, that if Jesus were alive he would be an account executive in an advertising agency — a startling thought for those who had been taught that the Saviour had been a member of the building trades.

The harder times became, the greater Hoover's faith in business became. He reduced individual and corporate income taxes, thereby narrowing the government's tax base at a time when it desperately needed every source of revenue. To preside over the Reconstruction Finance Corporation he appointed Chicago banker Charles G. Dawes, who then loaned ninety million dollars to his own bank. As the impasse continued, the President turned to Mellon for counsel, and that social Darwinist replied, "Liquidate labor, liquidate stocks, liquidate the farmers, liquidate real estate." It almost seemed, as Galbraith later wrote, that everyone called upon for advice "was impelled by the conventional wisdom to offer proposals designed to make things worse."

Years later Richard Nixon came to believe that "Hoover had the misfortune to hold office at the wrong time." Certainly Hoover was trying desperately to find solutions. He worked eighteen hours a day, proclaimed a statesmanlike moratorium on war debts, and even cut his own salary. And he was hopeful. In the end, he felt, what he called "rugged individualism" would win.

Over and over the President explained that help for the poor must come from private charities and local or state governments. To be sure, no state had had a department of public welfare until Franklin Roosevelt opened New York's, but others would have to follow the governor's example.

Meanwhile, the President said firmly, there would be no irresponsible experiments performed simply to "do something." The United States, he wrote a public works advocate on May 20, 1932, couldn't "squander itself into prosperity." When the Democratic Congress passed a two-billion-dollar relief bill, he vetoed it and issued a scathing message calling the measure "an unexampled raid on the public treasury." He added, "Our nation was not founded on the pork barrel, and it has not become great by political log-rolling!"

At about this time men in power began to discover "outside agitators." It was always strangers, never "the deserving poor," who whipped mobs into a frenzy of irrational behavior. Hoover's contempt for mobs had been set down ten years earlier. In a little book entitled *American Individualism* he had written, "Above all, beware the crowd! The crowd only feels; it has no mind of its own which can plan. The crowd is credulous, it destroys, it consumes, it hates, and it dreams — but it never builds." Conceivably, he concluded, this "destructive criticism" could lead to revolution. Destructive critics were blamed for the hunger march on Ford's Dearborn plant, for the bonus riot, and especially for the unrest in Harlan County, Kentucky. Rugged individualists in both parties regarded the college students who had gone into Kentucky as fair game. They were beaten, jailed, and denounced by the county attorney as a "godless, self-appointed, nondescript, iconoclastic minority of grandiloquent egotists."

Riffling through Hoover's papers, one sometimes has the strange feeling that the President looked upon the Depression as a public relations problem — that he believed the nightmare would go away if only the image of American business could be polished up and set in the right light. Faith was an end in itself; "lack of business confidence" was a cardinal sin. Hoover's first reaction to the slump which followed the Crash had been to treat it as a psychological phenomenon. He himself had chosen the word "Depression" because it sounded less frightening than "panic" or "crisis." In December 1929 he declared that "conditions are fundamentally sound." Three months later he said the worst would be over in sixty days; at the end of May he predicted that the economy would be back to normal in the autumn; in June the market broke sharply, yet he told a delegation which called to plead for a public works project, "Gentlemen, you have come sixty days too late. The Depression is over."

Already his forecasts were being flung back at him by critics, but in his December 2, 1930, message to Congress — a lame duck Republican Congress; the Democrats had just swept the off-year elections — he said that "the fundamental strength of the economy is unimpaired." At about the same time the International Apple Shippers Association, faced with a surplus of apples, decided to sell them on credit to jobless men for resale at a nickel each. Overnight there were shivering apple sellers everywhere. Asked about them, Hoover replied, "Many people have left their jobs for the more profitable one of selling apples." Reporters were caustic, and the

President was stung. By now he was beginning to show signs of the most ominous trait of embattled Presidents; as his secretary Theodore Joslin was to note in his memoirs, Hoover was beginning to regard some criticism "as unpatriotic." Nevertheless he persevered, pondering new ways of waging psychological warfare. "What this country needs," he told Christopher Morley, "is a great poem." To Rudy Vallee he said in the spring of 1932, "If you can sing a song that would make people forget the Depression, I'll give you a medal." Vallee didn't get the medal. Instead he sang:

> They used to tell me I was building a dream
> And so I followed the mob.
> When there was earth to plough or guns to bear
> I was always there right on the job.
>
> Once I built a railroad, made it run
> Made it race against time.
> Once I built a railroad, now it's done.
> Brother, can you spare a dime?

But not everyone let Hoover down. A presidential commission reported that the country's number one problem was "law and order," which in those days meant prohibition gangsters. Hoover endorsed the report, and a spokesman for the National Association of Manufacturers endorsed the President's endorsement, observing that "Many of the bad effects of the so-called Depression are based on calamity howling." Catching the presidential mood, industrialists put up a brave front. One source of embarrassment to the administration was the stretch of Pennsylvania Railroad track between Washington and New York. It was lined with thousands of billboards. Half were blank, which raised awkward questions in the minds of passengers until admirers of the President began renting them to spread the slogan WASN'T THE DEPRESSION TERRIBLE? Agreeing that it had been, but that it was past, the International Association of Lions Clubs celebrated Business Confidence Week.

"Leaping lizards!" cried Little Orphan Annie, the President's favorite comic strip character. "Who said business is bad?" Not Nicholas Murray Butler, president of Columbia University; Dr. Butler assured Columbia men that "Courage will end the slump." Not the president of U.S. Steel; he said the "peak" of the Depression had passed. Not Owen D. Young, board chairman of General Electric; he announced that the "dead center of the Depression" had come and gone. Not Secretary of Commerce Thomas Lamont; he reported that "The banks of this country generally are in a strong position." And certainly not the *New York Times*, which had argued as early as New Year's Day 1931 that conditions were so dreadful that they had to better — that people would have to start spending all that money they must have saved and begin to replace their "worn-out private belongings."

There were, indeed, few alarmist voices in the press. Youngstown's mayor was chastised by its newspaper for "borrowing trouble"; the Depression would be over, the editor maintained, before relief would be needed. On July 28, 1932 — the day World War veterans and their wives and children were being driven through the streets of Washington like animals — the lead story of the International News Service began: "That the sun of a new prosperity is beginning to rise above the clouds of economic distress was indicated by developments in many parts of the country"; and that same week these headlines appeared on American newsstands:

BUSINESS PULSE
BEATING FASTER

FACTORIES REOPENING ALL OVER COUNTRY

BOOM AWAKENS
TEXTILE PLANTS
IN NEW ENGLAND

CAPACITY PRODUCTION REPORTED IN SOME
CITIES, IDLE EMPLOYEES FIND JOBS

REVIVAL IN TRADE
GAINS MOMENTUM
THROUGHOUT EAST

ROAD IS CLEAR
TO PROSPERITY
CAPITAL FEELS

MARK SULLIVAN NOTES A CALM CONFIDENCE;
OBSTACLES TO RECOVERY ARE GONE

SHOWING BEST
IN WEEKS FOR
RESERVE BANKS

TRADE UPTURN
WITHIN 90 DAYS
NOW EXPECTED

BRIGHT SPOTS
GROW ON U.S.
BUSINESS MAP

CURTIS SEES BETTER TIMES

Nowhere in any of these newspapers was there mention of the remarkable fact that in the United States of America, the richest country in the world, more than 15 million men were looking for jobs that did not exist.

I

——

RENDEZVOUS WITH DESTINY

1932-1941

ONE

The Cruelest Year

THAT AUGUST a writer for the *Saturday Evening Post* asked John Maynard Keynes, the great British economist, whether there had ever been anything like the Depression before. "Yes," he replied. "It was called the Dark Ages, and it lasted four hundred years." This was calamity howling on a cosmic scale, but on at least one point the resemblance seems valid. In each case the people were victims of forces they could not understand.

Some vaguely blamed "conditions," Hoover's euphemism. Others confused the Depression with the stock market Crash of 1929 — "We haven't been to the city since the Depression," they would say, or "I used to, but that was before the Depression." A remarkable number of sufferers stoically accepted the implicit charge of malingering made by President John E. Edgerton of the National Association of Manufacturers: "Many of those who are most boisterous now in clamor for work have either struck on the jobs they had or don't want to work at all, and are utilizing the occasion to swell the communistic chorus." An explanation lies in the strength of the Protestant ethic forty years ago in America. Although millions were trapped in a great tragedy for which there could plainly be no individual responsibility, social workers repeatedly observed that the jobless were suffering from feelings of guilt. "I haven't had a steady job in more than two years," a man facing eviction told a *New York Daily News* reporter in February 1932. "Sometimes I feel like a murderer. What's wrong with me, that I can't protect my children?"

Such men had been raised to believe that if you worked diligently, you would succeed. Now failure was dragging down the diligent and the shiftless alike. Men were demoralized, and "a demoralized people," as Walter Lippmann wrote then, "is one in which the individual has become isolated. He trusts nobody and nothing, not even himself." Seventeen years later, in *The Lonely Crowd*, Riesman explained the plight of the inner-directed man caught in such a crisis: "If repeated failures destroy his hope of future accomplishment, then it is likely that his internal strengths can no longer hold the fort against the external evidence. Overwhelmed with guilt, he will despise himself for his failures and inadequacies." Newspapers of that period are crowded with accounts of men who took their own lives rather than go on relief. Emile Durkheim had created a special category, "altruistic suicides," for men who killed themselves rather than become a burden to the community.

The real blame lay in the false underpinnings of the Coolidge-Hoover "New Era" prosperity. Seen in perspective, the Depression appears to have been the last convulsion of the industrial revolution, creating a hiatus before the technological revolution. In the aftermath of the World War, the techniques of mass production combined to increase the efficiency per man-hour by over 40 percent. This enormous output of goods clearly required a corresponding increase of consumer buying power — that is, higher wages. But the worker's income in the 1920s didn't rise with his productivity. In the golden year of 1929, Brookings economists calculated that to supply the barest necessities a family would need an income of $2,000 a year — more than 60 percent of American families were earning. In short, the ability to buy did not keep abreast of the volume of goods being turned out. It was part of the foolishness of the time to argue that the surge in production was no problem, that "a good salesman can sell anything." In practice this meant that while the rich (and many who weren't rich) were speculating in stocks, zealous salesmen were encouraging a kind of mass speculation. Customers of limited means were being persuaded to take products anyhow, the exchange being accomplished by an overextension of credit.

The stock market, honeycombed with credit in the form of brokers' loans, crashed of its own weight, calling to account the millions of little deals consummated by commercial travelers who had sold anything and everything to people lacking the means to pay for it. Thus ended the New Era prosperity. The panic followed, and the country couldn't cope with it. The last extended economic crisis had been in 1893; since then America had become so industrialized that a massive return to the farm was impossible. There was a certain rough justice in Herbert Hoover's ascent to the Presidency on the eve of the catastrophe, for as Secretary of Commerce he had been fascinated with productivity and indifferent to the dangerous lack of buying power. Long after he left the White House, he realized what had happened and wrote: "A margin of some thousands . . . got too much of the productive pie for the services they performed. . . . Another margin of some 20 percent got too little."

Between the Crash and 1932, the cruelest year of the Depression, the economy's downward spiral was accelerated by measures which, according to all accepted canons, ought to have brought recovery, and which in practice did the opposite. To protect investments, prices had to be maintained.

Sales ebbed, so costs were cut by laying off men. The unemployed could not buy the goods of other industries. Therefore sales dropped further, leading to more layoffs and a general shrinkage of purchasing power, until farmers were pauperized by the poverty of industrial workers, who in turn were pauperized by the poverty of farmers. "Neither has the money to buy the product of the other," an Oklahoma witness testified before a congressional subcommittee, explaining the vicious circle. "Hence we have overproduction and underconsumption at the same time and in the same country."

In June 1932, Ivy League seniors joined 21,974 other alumni hunting for jobs. By then New York department stores were requiring bachelor degrees for all elevator operators, and that was the best many of them could do, but twenty-year-old Sylvia Field Porter, Hunter '32, was an exception. She switched her major from English to economics because of what she later called "an overwhelming curiosity to know why everything was crashing around me and why people were losing their jobs" and talked her way into an investment counsel firm. At the same time she began a systematic study of the financial world, with the thought that one day she might write a column about it.* She then discovered that she was in the middle of a crisis without historical precedent.

Ever since the fiasco of England's South Sea Company in 1720, the phrase "South Sea bubble" had been used to describe a doomed business venture. The bubble had certainly burst; South Sea stock had plunged to 13.5 percent of its highest quotation. Yet it subsequently rallied, and the firm continued to do business for eighty years. By the time of Miss Porter's commencement, however, United States Steel and General Motors had dropped to 8 percent of their pre-Crash prices. Overall, stocks listed on the Big Board were worth 11 percent of their 1929 value. Investors had lost 74 billion dollars, three times the cost of the World War. More than 5,000 American banks had failed — in Iowa City, just across the county line from Hoover's native West Branch, all five banks were shut — and 86,000 businesses had closed their doors. The country's Gross National Product had fallen from 104 billion dollars to 41 billion (in 1973 it would be 2,177 billion). In 1932, 273,000 families were evicted from their homes, and the average weekly wage of those who had jobs was $16.21.

Some enterprises flourished. The contraceptive business was netting a quarter-billion dollars a year, a fact which the youth of that day conveniently forgot after they had become parents. Over half the population was going to the movies once a week (admission was a quarter for adults, a dime for children), and each year saw an increase in the number of cigarette smokers, none of them aware that the habit might be harmful. Kelvinator refrigerators and Atwater Kent radios were moving briskly. Miniature golf courses and circulation libraries were booming. Alfred C.

*Sylvia Porter began writing for the *New York Post* in 1935.

Fuller was doing very nicely with his corps of door-to-door brush sales-men; in the grim month of August 1932 his sales leaped from $15,000 to $50,000 and grew thereafter at the rate of a million dollars a year. A prodigy named J. Paul Getty was quietly picking up cheap petroleum wells; that February he gained control of 520,000 of the Pacific Oil Cor-poration's one million shares. Here and there a venture was lucky. In Quincy, Massachusetts, the owner of a curious restaurant with a bright orange roof and pseudo Colonial architecture was almost bankrupt when a stock company opened across the street. Its first play was Eugene O'Neill's nine-act *Strange Interlude*. Every evening there was an 8:30 intermission for supper, and the restaurateur, Howard Johnson, survived.

But these were exceptions. U.S. Steel, the key to heavy industry, was operating at 19.1 percent of capacity. The American Locomotive Company didn't need much steel. During the 1920s it had sold an average of 600 locomotives a year; in 1932 it sold one. Nor was the automotive industry the big steel customer it had been. Month by month its fine names were vanishing: the Stutz Motor Company, the Auburn, the Cord, the Edward Peerless, the Pierce Arrow, the Duesenberg, the Franklin, the Durant, the Locomobile. One rash man decided to challenge Ford with another low-priced car. He called it the Rockne, lost 21 million dollars, and killed him-self. In January an inventive bacteriologist named Arthur G. Sherman had become the sensation of the Detroit Auto Show by exhibiting the first crude, hand-carpentered, wooden trailer. In 1932 he sold just eighty of them. Air transport nose-dived. Airliners then had twelve seats, of which, the Department of Commerce reported, an average of seven were flying empty. And with the exception of the new talkies, most entertainers were foundering. In four years the jazz musician Eddie Condon landed four recording sessions; the phonograph recording industry had dwindled from 50 million dollars a year to a quarter-million. Sally Rand was making a precarious living with her celebrated fans; to a reporter who asked why she did it, she replied, "I never made any money till I took off my pants."

Because poverty was considered shameful, people tried to conceal desti-tution from neighbors, often with considerable success. One could never be sure about the family across the street. The smartly dressed young lawyer who always left home at the same time each morning may have been off to sell cheap neckties, magazines, vacuum cleaners, pressure cookers, or Two-in-One shoe polish door-to-door in a remote neighbor-hood. He may have changed his clothes and gone to another part of the city to beg. Or he may have been one of the millions who looked for work day after day, year after year, watching his children grow thinner and fighting despair in the night. There were certain skills developed by men who spent their days in the streets. You learned to pay for a nickel cup of coffee, to ask for another cup of hot water free, and, by mixing the hot water with the ketchup on the counter, to make a kind of tomato soup. In winter you stuffed newspapers under your shirt to ward off the cold; if you knew you would be standing for hours outside an employment office, you wrapped burlap bags around your legs and tied them in place. Shoes were a special problem. Pasteboard could be used for inner soles, and some favored cotton in the heels to absorb the pounding of the concrete. But if a shoe was really gone, nothing worked. The pavement destroyed the cardboard and then the patch of sock next to it, snow leaked in and accumulated around your toes, and shoe nails stabbed your heels until you learned to walk with a peculiar gait.

It was remarkable how ingenious an impoverished, thrift-minded family could be. Men resharpened and reused old razor blades, rolled their own cigarettes or smoked Wings (ten cents a pack), and used twenty-five-watt light bulbs to save electricity. Children returned pop bottles for two cents or stood in line for day-old bread at the bakery. Women cut sheets lengthwise and resewed them to equalize wear, retailored their clothes for their daughters, and kept up a brave front with the wife next door — who may have being doing the same thing on the same meager budget. Families sorted Christmas cards so they could be sent to different friends next year. Sometimes a man would disappear for weeks. All the neighborhood knew was that he had gone on a "business trip." It was a considerate husband who withheld the details of such trips from his wife, for they were often more terrible than anything she could imagine.

He was, of course, looking for work. The legends of job hunting had become folklore by 1932, and some of the unbelievable stories were true. Men *did* wait all night outside Detroit employment offices so they would be first in line next morning. An Arkansas man *did* walk nine hundred miles looking for work. People *did* buy jobs. In Manhattan a Sixth Avenue employment agency *did* have five thousand applicants for three hundred jobs. It is a matter of record that a labor subcommittee of the 72nd Congress heard testimony about men setting forest fires in the state of Washington so they would be hired to put them out. *Business Week* verified the fact that a great many people who no longer loved America either left it or attempted to. Throughout the early Thirties the country's emigration exceeded its immigration. Amtorg, the Russian trading agency in New York, was getting 350 applications a day from Americans who wanted to settle in Russia. On one memorable occasion Amtorg advertised for six thousand skilled workers and a hundred thousand showed up, including plumbers, painters, mechanics, cooks, engineers, carpenters, electricians, salesmen, printers, chemists, shoemakers, librarians, teachers, dentists, a cleaner and dyer, an aviator, and an undertaker.

New York drew countless job seekers from surrounding states, though the city had a million jobless men of its own. A few strangers joined Manhattan's seven thousand nickel shoeshine "boys" or found furtive roles in the bootleg coal racket — 10 percent of the city's coal was being sneaked in by unemployed Pennsylvania miners — but most outsiders wound up on one of New York's eighty-two breadlines. If a man had a dime he could sleep in a flophouse reeking of sweat and Lysol. If he was broke he salvaged some newspapers and headed for Central Park, or the steps of a subway entrance, or the municipal incinerator. The incinerator's warmth drew hundreds of men on winter nights, even though they had to sleep on great dunes of garbage.

Returning from such an expedition in or under an empty freight car, a husband would review family assets with his wife and estimate how long they could keep going. Wedding rings would be sold, furniture pawned, life insurance borrowed upon, money begged from relatives. Often the next step was an attempt at a home business, with its implicit confession to the neighborhood that the pretense of solvency had been a hoax. The yard might be converted to a Tom Thumb miniature golf course. The husband might open a "parlor grocery." The wife might offer other wives a wash, set, and manicure for a dollar. In Massachusetts, idle textile workers erected looms in their living rooms; in Connecticut, households strung safety pins on wires, toiling long hours and earning a total of five dollars a week for an entire family.

These last-ditch efforts rarely succeeded; there were so few potential customers with money. Finally hope was abandoned. The father went to the city hall, declared himself penniless, and became a statistic. Because those figures were poorly kept, the precise extent of poverty is unknown. Somewhere between 15 million and 17 million men were unemployed, with most of them representing a family in want. *Fortune*, in September 1932, estimated that 34 million men, women, and children were without any income whatever. That was nearly 28 percent of the population, and like all other studies it omitted America's 11 million farm families, who were suffering in a rural gethsemane of their own.

During the Nixon Presidency, when America's farm population had shrunk to 5.2 percent of the population, it was hard to realize that only forty years earlier 25.1 percent had been living, or trying to live, on the land. They had not shared in New Era prosperity; the Crash merely worsened a situation which had already become a national scandal. By 1932 U.S. farmers had come to remind one reporter of Mongolian peasants seen in the rotogravure sections of Sunday newspapers, and the shadow of imminent famine fell across the plains. Agricultural prices hadn't been so low since the reign of Queen Elizabeth. Farmers were getting less than twenty-five cents for a bushel of wheat, seven cents for a bushel of corn, a dime for a bushel of oats, a nickel for a pound of cotton or wool. Sugar was bringing three cents a pound, hogs and beef two and a half cents a pound, and apples — provided they were flawless — forty cents for a box of two hundred.

Translated into the bitter sweat of rural life, this meant that a wagon of oats wouldn't buy a pair of four-dollar Thom McAn shoes. A wagon of wheat would just do it, but with mortgage interest running at $3.60 an acre, plus another $1.90 in taxes, the wheat farmer was losing $1.50 on every acre he reaped. In cotton fields the strongest and most agile man would toil from "can see" to "can't see" — fourteen hours of daylight — and receive sixty cents for the 300 pounds he had picked. It was cheaper to burn corn than sell it and buy coal. With meat bringing such ruinous prices, a man would spend $1.10 to ship a sheep to market, where it would return him less than $1.00. In Montana a rancher bought bullets on credit, spent two hours slaughtering a herd of livestock, and left it rotting in a canyon. It wasn't worth its feed. Turning away, he muttered to a reporter, "One way to beat the Depression, huh?"

As farm prices caved in, tens of thousands of mortgage foreclosure notices went up on gateposts and county courthouses. It has been estimated that one-fourth of the state of Mississippi was auctioned off. William Allen White, the Republican country editor who had pleaded with Hoover to come and see what was happening to the Middle West, wrote, "Every farmer, whether his farm is under mortgage or not, knows that with farm products priced as they are today, sooner or later he must go down." When the farmer did fail, unable even to pay the small costs of binder twine, tool repair, and seed, the bank would take title as absentee landlord, and he would rent from it the land his family had owned for generations. Meantime, while ranchers fed mutton to buzzards and warmed their hands over corn fires, millions in the cities could not afford the low prices which were destroying farmers (butter at 39 cents a pound, prime rib roast at 21 cents, two dozen eggs for 41 cents) because so many were idle and those who had jobs were often earning what could only be called starvation wages.

There was no one to protect them. The President disapproved of wage cuts and said so, but he was equally opposed to wage-hour legislation, so that when U.S. Steel made its second big wage slash in the spring of 1932, the workers were helpless. The labor movement was almost extinct; AFL membership had dwindled from 4.1 million in 1920 to 2.2 million, about 6 percent of the work force. There were strikes of desperation in 1932. All were lost. Miners were paid $10.88 a month, were at the mercy of check-weight men, and were required to buy groceries at inflated prices in the company store; when they rebelled the protest was bloodily suppressed by armed strikebreakers backed by the National Guard. The United Mine Workers were too weak to offer the victims anything but sympathy.

In such New England mill towns as Lynn and Lowell, where only one worker in three was employed, men were treated like serfs; one of them left Manchester, New Hampshire, to apply for a job in New Haven, was arrested, brought before a judge on a charge of vagrancy, and ordered back to his Manchester mill. The immense pool of job seekers tempted employers to slash their wage bills again and again. Department stores paid clerks as little as five dollars a week. An investigation in Chicago disclosed that the majority of working girls were getting less then twenty-five cents an hour; for a fourth of them, it was less than a dime. In 1932 hourly rates had shrunk to ten cents in lumbering, seven-and-a-half cents in general contracting, six cents in brick and tile manufacturing, and five cents in sawmills. Before the Depression, Massachusetts textile mills rarely required skilled operators to be responsible for more than twenty looms eight hours a day. Then the mills introduced speedups and stretch-outs, and Louis Adamic saw teen-aged girls running thirty wide looms from before dawn until after sunset.

In the sweatshops of Brooklyn fifteen-year-olds were paid $2.78 a week. Women received as little as $2.39 for a fifty-hour week. In the summer of 1932 the Connecticut Commissioner of Labor reported that there were over a hundred shops in the state paying as little as sixty cents for a fifty-five-hour week. New York City was the worst sweat spot in that state, and its garment industry, employing fifty thousand women, was the most sweated trade. "Unscrupulous employers," *Time* reported, had "battered wages down to the Chinese coolie level." Hat makers crocheted hats for forty cents a dozen; in a week a worker could make two dozen. Apron girls were paid two-and-a-half cents an apron; they earned twenty cents a day. A slipper liner received twenty-one cents for lining seventy-two pairs; if she completed one slipper every forty-five seconds, she took home $1.05 after a nine-hour day. Girl cleaners in a pants factory were paid a half-cent for each garment they threaded and sponged. It was a five-minute operation; their income was six cents an hour. Honest employers could not survive that kind of competition. Welfare rolls grew longer and longer, the President continued to withhold federal help, and as the fourth Depression winter loomed the relief structure began to disintegrate.

When a senator declared the workers simply could not survive on one or two days' wages a week, President J. E. Edgerton of the National Association of Manufacturers said, "Why, I've never thought of paying men on the basis of what they need. I pay for efficiency. Personally, I attend to all those other things, social welfare stuff, in my church work." Doubtless he thought he did. As *Fortune* explained it, the theory was that now, as in the past, private charity and semipublic welfare groups could care for the old, the sick, and the indigent.

It wasn't working. The Depression, while multiplying the demands upon charities, had dried up their sources of contributions. By 1932, private help had dwindled to 6 percent of the money spent upon the needy, leaving some thirty million people to public welfare. Unfortunately, local governments couldn't handle the burden. State and city budgets had been in the red since 1930. About nine-tenths of municipal income came from taxation on real estate, which in terms of the Depression dollar was ludicrously overappraised. Landlords were liable to taxation if they held title to buildings; their inability to realize income from their houses was legally irrelevant, even when their tenants were on municipal relief, which never paid rentals. The landlords tried desperately to get their money. At first, in exasperation, they turned penniless occupants out. In New York there was hardly a block without a daily dispossession, and in Philadelphia so many families were put on the street that little girls invented a doll game called Eviction.

But empty tenements solved nothing; they merely contributed to the unpopularity of men of property while leaving tax bills unpaid. Eventually, as Professor Sumner H. Slichter of the Harvard Business School explained to the Senate Committee on Manufactures, there was "a more or less national moratorium on rents, insofar as the unemployed are concerned." Delinquent tax ratios hovered between 20 and 30 percent in metropolitan areas, and the cities, lacking this revenue, cut services. Roads were unpaved, sidewalks crumbled, streets blocked by winter snow were left unplowed. Chicago, deprived of two years' receipts by a taxpayers' strike, borrowed from the banks — and agonized over its unemployed population of 600,000.

Given the bankruptcy of public treasuries, and the widespread feeling that the poor were somehow responsible for their fate, it was inevitable that admittance to relief rolls would be made extremely difficult. Before applications were even considered, homes and possessions had to be sold, insurance canceled, credit exhausted, and evidence produced that all known relatives were broke. Even then, in many cities no assistance was granted to unmarried people or people without young children. Every possible stigma was attached to aid. In September 1932 Lewiston, Maine, voted to bar all welfare recipients from the polls, a goal already achieved by property requirements in the constitutions of ten states from Massachusetts to Oregon. West Virginia hospitals refused to admit patients unless payment for services was guaranteed; a referring physician suggested to one surgeon that he delay operating upon a child until the parents promised to pay $1,000. Two doctors in Royce City, Texas, put the following advertisement in the local paper:

> TO WHOM IT MAY CONCERN: If you are expecting the stork to visit your home this year and he has to come by way of Royce City, he will have to bring a checkbook to pay his bill before delivery.

In some communities taxpayer associations tried to prevent welfare children from attending schools, and families receiving public assistance were known to have been excluded from churches.

Even those who surmounted all barriers found that the approval of a welfare application was exceptional. In mill towns, mining communities, and on sharecropper farms, *Fortune* reported, "relief is merely a name." In the cities only 25 percent of qualified families were getting some form of help. The mayor of Toledo said in 1932: "I have seen thousands of these defeated, discouraged, hopeless men and women, cringing and fawning as they come to ask for public aid. It is a spectacle of national degradation."

Admittance to the rolls did not end the defeat, discouragement, and hopelessness. In Philadelphia a family of four was given $5.50 a week, which hardly encouraged the debauchery predicted by those who objected to the dole, and Philadelphia was munificent compared to New York ($2.39), Mississippi ($1.50) and Detroit ($0.60). At the most, assistance covered only food and fuel. Since welfare families had often been inadequately clothed before the Crash, their rags three winters later sometimes defied description. It was not uncommon to see the head of a family dressed like a vaudeville tramp, wearing a buttonless suit coat out at one elbow, a pair of trousers out at the knee and in the seat, an old summer cap that had hung for years in some furnace room, worn tennis shoes covered by patched rubbers, a pair of mismatched canvas gloves; the whole covered by a filthy old sheepskin.

Frequently public employees were almost indistinguishable from public wards, since money for both came from the same sources. As a rule community elders found a way to provide their policemen with decent uniforms, for it was a time of anxiety about public safety. This concern did not cover schoolteachers, who more than any other group were victims of local governments' inadequate tax base. At the beginning of the Depression they had been assessed part of their pay to finance soup kitchens. With the school population increasing by over two hundred thousand each year, further economies were inevitable. Desks were set up in corridors, in coal-heated portables, in tin shacks; courses in art and music were stricken from the curriculum; the same textbooks were handed down semester after semester, until they had become dog-eared, dirty, with pages defaced or missing. Classrooms became more and more crowded. Finally, the money to pay the teachers began to disappear.

By 1932, a third of a million children were out of school because of lack of funds. Teachers in Mississippi, northern Minnesota, Idaho, South Dakota, and Alabama managed to eat only by "boarding around" at the homes of parents. In Dayton, Ohio, schools were open only three days a week; in Arkansas over three hundred schools were closed ten months or more. In Kansas, twenty-five-cent wheat meant rural teachers were being paid $35 a month for an eight-month year — $280 a year. In Iowa they were receiving $40 a month, half the income Washington had said was necessary for industrial workers to exist. Akron owed its teachers $300,000, Youngstown $500,000, Detroit $800,000, and Chicago's debts to its teachers were more than 20 million dollars.

The story of the Chicago schools was a great Depression epic. Rather than see 500,000 children remain on the streets, the teachers hitchhiked to work, endured "payless paydays" — by 1932 they had received checks in only five of the last thirteen months — and accepted city scrip to be redeemed after the Depression, even though Chicago bankers would not accept it. Somehow the city found money to invest in its forthcoming World's Fair of 1933, when Sally Rand would gross $6,000 a week, but it turned a deaf ear to the Board of Education. A thousand teachers were dismissed outright. Those who remained taught on at immense personal sacrifice. Collectively the 1,400 teachers lost 759 homes. They borrowed $1,128,000 on their insurance policies and another $232,000 from loan sharks at annual interest rates of 42 percent, and although hungry themselves, they fed 11,000 pupils out of their thin pocketbooks.

Teachers, welfare workers, and policemen saw hardship at close range. Nobody called cops pigs in the early 1930s. Even when they were used to break strikes, it was widely acknowledged that they were as exploited as the workers.* In New York, men on the beat had been distributing food in the most stricken neighborhoods since 1930. The money came from city employees, including themselves, who contributed 1 percent of their salaries; as Caroline Bird pointed out, this was "the first public confession of official responsibility for plain poverty, and it came, not from the top, but from the lowest civil servants, who worked down where the poor people were."

Once more the teachers bore witness to the worst, for the most heartbreaking Depression martyrs were in the classrooms. In October of that terrible year, a month before the presidential election, the New York City Health Department reported that over 20 percent of the pupils in the public schools were suffering from malnutrition. In the mining counties of Ohio, West Virginia, Illinois, Kentucky, and Pennsylvania, the secretary of the American Friends Service Committee told a congressional committee, the ratio was sometimes over 90 percent, with deprived children afflicted by "drowsiness, lethargy, and sleepiness," and "mental retardation." A teacher suggested that one little girl go home and eat something; the child replied, "I can't. This is my sister's day to eat." A little boy exhibited his pet rabbit to a visitor and the boy's older sister whispered, "He thinks we aren't going to eat it, but we are." Lillian Wald, a social worker, asked in anguish, "Have you ever seen the uncontrolled trembling of parents who have starved themselves for weeks so that their children might not go hungry?" A bitter father said, "A worker's got no right to have kids any more," and a Massachusetts priest said, "One family I know has lived on lentils, nothing but lentils, all this year. They can't afford to buy bread. What is going to happen to our children?"

"Nobody is actually starving," President Hoover told reporters. "The hoboes, for example, are better fed than they have ever been. One hobo in New York got ten meals in one day." In September 1932 *Fortune* flatly called the President a liar and suggested that "twenty-five millions in want" might be a fairer description of the nation's economic health. Cases of starvation were being chronicled by *Fortune*, the *San Francisco Chronicle*, the *Atlantic*, the *New York Times*, and in congressional testimony. The New York City Welfare Council reported 29 victims of starvation and 110,

---

*The day after the bloody suppression of hungry marchers at the Ford plant on March 7, Detroit's police commissioner laid off 162 policemen.

mostly children, dead of malnutrition. Hoover simply hadn't seen the suffering, though he was not to be spared after his departure from the White House; on a fishing trip in the Rocky Mountains he was led by a native to a hut where one child had succumbed and seven others were dying of hunger.

Millions stayed alive by living like animals. In the Pennsylvania countryside they were eating wild weed-roots and dandelions; in Kentucky they chewed violet tops, wild onions, forget-me-nots, wild lettuce, and weeds which heretofore had been left to grazing cattle. City mothers hung around docks, waiting for spoiled produce to be discarded and then fighting homeless dogs for possession of it. After the vegetables had been loaded on trucks they would run alongside, ready to snatch up anything that fell off. A cook in a midwestern hotel put a pail of leftovers in the alley outside the kitchen; immediately a dozen men loomed out of the darkness to fight over it. In Long Beach, California, a sixty-six-year-old physician named Francis Everett Townsend glanced out his window while shaving and saw, among a group of refuse barrels, "three haggard very old women," as he later called them, "stooped with great age, bending over the barrels, clawing into the contents." Whole families were seen plunging into refuse dumps, gnawing at bones and watermelon rinds; a Chicago widow always removed her glasses so she wouldn't see the maggots. At night in New York Thomas Wolfe observed "the homeless men who prowled in the vicinity of restaurants, lifting the lids of garbage cans and searching around inside for morsels of rotten food." He saw them "everywhere, and noticed how their numbers increased during the hard and desperate days of 1932."

It was considered benevolent by well-to-do Americans that year to give your garbage to fellow countrymen who were famished. The Elks of Mount Kisco, New York, and the eating clubs of Princeton University instructed their servants to see that their leftovers reached the needy. The *Brooklyn Eagle* proposed a central depot where edible swill could be sent by charitable citizens and where the poor might apply for portions of it. In Oklahoma City John B. Nichlos, a gas company executive, worked out a plan under which restaurants, civic clubs, and hotel chefs would pack swill in "sanitary containers of five (5) gallons each," to be "labeled 'MEAT, BEANS, POTATOES, BREAD AND OTHER ITEMS.'" The Salvation Army would pick up the cans, the contents of which would then be distributed to jobless men who would first chop wood donated by — of all people — the farmers. "We expect a little trouble now and then from those who are not worthy of the support of the citizens," the gas man wrote Secretary of the Army Hurley, "but we must contend with such cases in order to take care of those who are worthy." Hurley thought it a marvelous idea, and urged the administration to adopt it. It was vetoed by the director of Hoover's Emergency Committee for Employment on the ground that the gesture might be misunderstood.

It never seems to have occurred to Nichlos, the *Eagle,* the Princetonians and the Elks that more dramatic solutions might lie ahead. But already there were those who pondered the contrast between the well-fed rich and the starving multitude, and who thought they saw the dark shadow of things to come. Thomas Wolfe would talk to the tragic men in New York's public toilets until he could not stand their anguish any more. Then he would mount the steps to the pavement twenty feet above and gaze out upon "the giant hackles of Manhattan shining coldly in the cruel brightness of the winter night. The Woolworth Building was not fifty yards away, and a little farther down were the silvery spires and needles of Wall Street, great fortresses of stone and steel that housed enormous banks. The blind injustice of this . . . seemed the most brutal part of the whole experience, for there . . . in the cold moonlight, only a few blocks away from this abyss of human wretchedness and misery, blazed the pinnacles of power where a large section of the entire world's wealth was locked in mighty vaults."

In adversity Americans have always looked for scapegoats, and by early 1932 other hunters, like Wolfe, were closing in on lower Manhattan. The prey there was fat and vulnerable. In the Twenties American financiers and industrialists had become national folk heroes. In vain had William Z. Ripley of Harvard warned President Coolidge that "prestidigitation, double-shuffling, honeyfugling, hornswoggling and skulduggery" were threatening the economy; Coolidge refused to be daunted by prophets of gloom and doom. For nine years, as Arthur Schlesinger Jr. later wrote, the government had treated business as though it had "discovered the philosopher's stone which would transmute the uncertainties of the capitalist system into permanent prosperity." Mellon had become known as "the greatest Secretary of the Treasury since Alexander Hamilton," and *Nation's Business* had reported that the American businessman was "the most influential person in the nation." But now, three years after the Crash, children were singing:

> *Mellon pulled the whistle,*
> *Hoover rang the bell,*
> *Wall Street gave the signal,*
> *And the country went to hell.*

The high priests of finance weren't listening. Their world remained insular, arrogant, and out of touch. In the *Literary Digest* they read of the Depression's blessings: "People are growing more courteous in business, and often more reasonable at home, thoughtless women especially. Unappreciative wives who were indifferent to their husbands and neglected their homes have become tame and cautious." A Republican candidate for governor of New Jersey had good news for the voters: "There is something about too much prosperity that ruins the moral fiber of the people." A member of the Du Pont family was reported to have rejected a suggestion that he sponsor a Sunday afternoon program on the ground that "at three o'clock on Sunday afternoons everybody is playing polo," and J. P. Morgan observed that if "you destroy the leisure class, you destroy civilization. By the leisure class, I mean the families who employ one servant — twenty-five or thirty million families." He seemed startled when told that census figures showed there were fewer than two million servants in the entire country. The people were not surprised by his misinformation; by then, Walter Lippmann wrote, industrial and financial leaders had fallen "from one of the highest positions of influence and power that they have ever occupied in our history to one of the lowest."

In 1932, 65 percent of American industry belonged to 600 corporations; 1 percent of the population owned 59 percent of the wealth. One man, Samuel Insull of Chicago, held 85 directorships, 65 board chairmanships, and 11 company presidencies. His utilities empire was a conglomerate of 150 companies, with 50,000 employees serving 3,250,000 customers. On New Year's Day its securities were valued at over three billion dollars, and unemployed men warming themselves over scrap wood fires on the lower level of Wacker Drive looked up at the Insull offices far above and wondered aloud to reporters why the old man couldn't help them.

He couldn't because he had problems of his own. His pyramid of holding companies was collapsing, and thousands of Chicagoans — including a great many schoolteachers — were about to learn in horror that their Insull stock had dropped to 4 percent of its 1931 value. Insull scurried about trying to salvage something, protected day and night by thirty-six bodyguards, but in April his two investment trusts went into receivership. By June he had fled to Europe, sixty million dollars in debt; a Cook County grand jury indicted him. In Paris he craftily scheduled a press conference, sneaked out the back door to board a midnight express for Rome, and flew on to Athens. His lawyers had told him he would be safe there, because there were no extradition treaties between Greece and the United States. It was true then, but by early November the diplomats had signed one. Disguised as a woman, the fugitive chartered a boat for Turkey. The Turks turned him over to American authorities; he was brought back, tried — and found not guilty, because holding companies were not subject to regulation. "A holding company," Will Rogers said dryly, "is a thing where you hand an accomplice the goods while the policeman searches you."

Rogers also said, "There's a lot of things these old boys have done that are within the law, but it's so near the edge you couldn't slip a razor blade between their acts and a prosecution." Looking for evidence, the Democratic Congress was turning over stones up and down Wall Street, and some remarkable specimens were crawling out. Banker Albert H. Wiggin had sold the stock of his own bank (the Chase) short and then lied about it. Because of the depressed economy, Charles E. Mitchell of the National City Bank had broken an agreement to merge with the Corn Exchange Bank; at the same time he was tormenting his own clerks and tellers by demanding that they keep up their installment payments on National City stock bought at pre-Crash prices ($200 a share, now down to $40) — and loaning $2,400,000 of the stockholders' money to bank officers, with neither collateral nor interest, for market speculation. Mitchell had avoided federal income tax by selling securities to a member of his family at a loss and later buying them back. Through similar loopholes J. P. Morgan had paid no income tax in 1929, 1930, or 1931. Colonel Robert R. McCormick of the *Chicago Tribune*, sent the government a token $1,500 a year while writing long editorials urging his subscribers to pay their taxes in full.

As Secretary of the Treasury, Andrew Mellon had also hounded people who were reluctant to meet their tax obligations — and had similarly applied a different standard to himself. The country was astonished to learn that at Mellon's request his commissioner of internal revenue had prepared a memorandum for him describing twelve ways to evade federal taxes. A Treasury Department tax expert had then been assigned to work on Mellon's personal returns. Five of the commissioner's suggestions had been followed, including the recording of fictitious gifts and losses to reduce tax liability. These disclosures aroused Representative Wright Patman of Texas, who on January 25, 1932, asked the House to impeach Secretary Mellon "for high crimes and misdemeanors," but there were those who still regarded Mellon with reverence. To them the publication of these singular facts was a form of *lèse majesté;* one admirer, Mellon's lawyer, sharply rebuked a *New York Times* reporter for "providing ammunition for radicals."

Like the Insull machinations, tax dodges were legal. But despite the tax legislation of the time, some men had crossed into criminal territory. Ivar Kreuger, "the Swedish Match King," was a Grand Officer of the French Legion of Honor, an adviser to President Hoover on European aspects of the Depression, and a man of such probity that in 1928, when the Boston firm of Lee, Higginson prepared to issue millions on Kreuger securities, its officers had agreed with the Match King that an audit of his books was unnecessary. On March 12, 1932, he bought a large pistol, locked the door of his luxury apartment in Paris, and killed himself. After all the moving eulogies had been delivered, it turned out that the king had been a common thief, guilty of swindling, fraud, and forging Italian government bonds. Among other things he had stolen over three hundred million dollars from trusting investors.

Every week brought fresh shocks. Joseph Wright Harriman, a banker (or "bankster," as *Time* had it) and a cousin of Averell Harriman, left his failing bank and took refuge in a Manhattan nursing home. As the law closed in, he escaped to a Long Island inn, registering under an alias. The Nassau County police found him anyhow. Harriman tried to drive a butcher's knife between his ribs, failed at that, too, and served two years in prison for falsifying his bank's books and misapplying its funds. Saul Singer, executive vice president of the Bank of the United States — the largest American bank ever to fail — went to the penitentiary on the same charges, and later Howard Hopson, president of the Associated Gas and Electric Company and responsible to 188,576 investors, was captured in

Washington after a wild taxicab chase and found guilty on seventeen counts of mail fraud. "Confidence in the erstwhile leadership of this country is gone," George Sokolsky wrote. Representative Fiorello La Guardia said of a stock manipulation case, "Sordid as these facts may seem, I believe the same sort of story could be told regarding every stock in which there was a pool," and Joseph P. Kennedy, himself a market tycoon, concluded, "The belief that those in control of the corporate life of America were motivated by honesty and ideals of honorable conduct" had been "completely shattered."

Viewed in this light, the conduct of Hoover's Reconstruction Finance Corporation can only be called a major political blunder. In 1932 the congressional leadership finally pushed through an act authorizing the RFC to advance the states 300 million dollars for unemployment relief. By the end of the year only 30 million had actually reached the states, one-third of the amount Dawes had loaned to his Central Republic Bank and Trust Company of Chicago. It was perhaps symbolic that when the President telephoned former Senator Atlee Pomerene of Ohio to appoint him Dawes's successor, Pomerene had exactly ninety-eight cents in his pocket, and that on his way to be sworn in, a dozen panhandlers approached him. As public policy the RFC was broke. Millions were calling it "a breadline for big business," which was exactly what it had become.

But such phrases, like the demand for Mellon's head, provoked violent reactions from men like General MacArthur, who believed that the national security was endangered. The well-to-do were becoming genuinely afraid of the hungry, and that fear does much to explain a sudden attack upon one Democratic leader by a former friend in the spring of 1932. Alfred E. Smith, born in an East Side tenement, had become a checker in the Fulton Fish Market at the age of fifteen and had risen through Tammany's ranks to become governor of New York. In 1928, during Al Smith's unsuccessful campaign against Hoover, Franklin D. Roosevelt had been elected to succeed him in Albany. "After I left Albany," Smith said later, "after living in a mansion for six years, I couldn't see First Avenue very well, so I went over to Fifth Avenue. I signed a lease for $10,000 a year." Smith had been riding around Manhattan in a chauffeured limousine since the Crash, a director of banks and insurance companies, a crony of tycoons, the president of the Empire State Building. He had found a new level, a higher level, and he liked it.

Then, on Thursday, April 7, 1932, the nation heard a new voice over a nationwide hookup — the warm, vibrant, confident voice of Franklin Roosevelt. The governor denounced the Hoover administration for relieving the big banks and corporations. He mocked "shallow thinkers" who knew no way to help the farmer. "These unhappy times," he said, "call for the building of plans that put their faith once more in the forgotten man at the bottom of the economic pyramid."

Smith exploded at a Jefferson Day dinner. Flushed and hoarse, he said,

"This country is sick and tired of listening to political campaign orators who tell us what is the matter with us," and that "this is no time for demagogues. I will take off my coat and vest and fight to the end any man who persists in any demagogic appeal to the masses of the working people of this country to destroy themselves by setting class against class and rich against poor!"

In retrospect Smith's outburst appears extraordinary both in its virulence and in the mildness of the sentiment which had triggered it. The governor had, after all, merely suggested that something be done for the starving poor.

The Roosevelt for President campaign was then being waged from an inconspicuous office at 331 Madison Avenue in New York City, and it was not going well. Since his smashing gubernatorial victory FDR had been the Democratic front runner, but as the convention approached he was losing ground rapidly. His most devoted subordinate was sixty-one-year-old Louis McHenry Howe, an uncomely little ex-newspaperman who liked to answer the telephone by saying, "This is the medieval gnome speaking." Many out-of-state politicians were repelled by him. But then, there wasn't much about the Roosevelt candidacy that critics found attractive. On the right, Bernard Baruch called the governor "wish-washy," Boss Frank Hague of Jersey City said he had "no chance of winning in November," and the Scripps-Howard newspapers, coming out for Al Smith, said, "In Franklin Roosevelt we have another Hoover."

He was the only leader in either party who had suggested progressive solutions for the national dilemma, yet the liberal abuse of him was even harsher. Heywood Broun, Elmer Davis, and Walter Lippmann scorned him. The *New Republic* dismissed him as "not a man of great intellectual force or supreme moral stamina." In an open letter to Roosevelt on May 11, editor Oswald Garrison Villard of the *Nation* wrote: "You have deeply stabbed the faith that is within Americans that an emergency brings a leader, that our institutions are to survive." Riffling through preconvention issues of the *Nation* one finds such anti-Roosevelt comments as ". . . there is small hope for better things in his candidacy" . . . "his candidacy arouses so little real enthusiasm" . . . "no evidence whatever that people are turning to him as a leader" . . . "weakness and readiness to compromise" . . . "To put into the Presidency at this hour another weak man in the place of Herbert Hoover would be all the more disastrous because of the mistaken idea that Franklin D. Roosevelt is really a liberal," and, picking up the Scripps-Howard refrain, "A Hoover, perhaps, by any other name is still a Hoover."

To win the Democratic nomination under the convention rules of 1932, a candidate needed two-thirds of the votes. Smith quickly became the leader of the coalition opposing FDR; both men entered the Massachusetts primary late in April, and Smith gave Roosevelt a beating, capturing all of the state's thirty-six convention votes. The popular margin was three to one. The following month red-baiting John Nance Garner, Speaker of the House and Hearst's candidate, carried the California primary by 60,000 votes, with FDR second and Smith a strong third. There was only one way Roosevelt could win the convention now, and that was by dealing with the bosses. Late in June the Democrats gathered in Chicago — where two weeks earlier the Republicans had renominated Hoover, after a delegate who wanted to nominate Coolidge had been muscled from the hall by Chicago policemen — and Howe began spinning his web from suite 1502 in the Congress Hotel. "What's your price?" he asked former Governor Harry Byrd of Virginia. Byrd said he wanted to be a U.S. Senator. "Is that your price?" the medieval gnome demanded. Byrd said that was it. Virginia already had two Democratic senators, but Howe said, "Very well. We'll put either Glass or Swanson in Franklin's cabinet." Politicians in those days were very direct.

Down at the podium of the Chicago Stadium John E. Mack was about to deliver a lackluster speech putting Roosevelt's name in nomination. Already the party had adopted an appalling platform promising a 25 percent reduction in federal spending, a balanced budget, loyalty to the gold standard, laissez-faire economics, and, its saving grace, repeal of Prohibition. The Roosevelt supporters didn't even have a theme song. Smith had preempted "The Sidewalks of New York." Since the governor's home town of Hyde Park didn't have sidewalks anyhow, Howe had decided to use "Anchors Aweigh" as a tribute to his man's naval service. While the judge approached the podium, Howe's secretary burst in on him and said "Anchors Aweigh" wouldn't do at all; it was being used in a radio commercial for a cigarette company. Instead she suggested a song written the year of the Crash for the MGM film *Chasing Rainbows*. She skipped up and down the bedroom of suite 1502, humming and snapping her fingers. Wearily agreeing, Howe picked up the phone and said, "Tell them to play 'Happy Days Are Here Again,'" thus giving a generation of Democrats its anthem. The judge finished, the demonstration began, and from the cheap pipe organ came:

> *Happy days are here again!*
> *The skies above are clear again!*
> *Let's all sing a song of cheer again —*
> *Happy days — are — here — a-gain!*

Although rousing, it wasn't enough; after three ballots the convention was still deadlocked. Some Roosevelt delegates were wavering. Under the unit rule the switch of a single vote in the Mississippi caucus would mean the loss of the entire state. The Roosevelt floor managers, led by a Long Island politician named Jim Farley, promised Garner the Vice Presidency. William Randolph Hearst was afraid that disintegration of FDR strength would bring in a League of Nations advocate, and on his advice Garner accepted the deal. From Washington, Garner phoned Sam Rayburn, his man on the floor. California switched — and the galleries, packed with Smith men, erupted in rage. Smith's delegates refused to make the party's choice unanimous; instead they ran around tearing up Roosevelt posters. Will Rogers said, "Ah! They was Democrats today. They fought, they fit, they split and adjourned in a dandy wave of dissension. That's the old Democratic spirit." Others were less kind. Heywood Broun jeered that Roosevelt was the "corkscrew candidate of a convoluting convention." H. L. Mencken wrote in the *Baltimore Sun* that the Democrats had picked their weakest candidate. The *San Francisco Chronicle* concurred, and so, during his daily medicine-ball workout with friends next morning, did President Hoover. They nodded; one assured him that the country was still conservative. Another said it was inconceivable that voters would elect a hopeless cripple. Already that whispering campaign had begun.

Roosevelt flew to Chicago in a trimotor Ford, writing his acceptance speech on the two-stop, turbulent, nine-hour flight from Albany. No one had ever accepted a presidential nomination with such alacrity, but this nominee believed that the Depression called for all sorts of unprecedented action; standing before the convention, his leg braces locked in place, he said he hoped the Democratic party would make it its business to break "absurd traditions." He cried, "I pledge you, I pledge myself, to a New Deal for the American people." Some delegates thought the phrase a brilliant combination of Theodore Roosevelt's Square Deal and Woodrow Wilson's New Freedom. Reporters, however, were discovering that FDR was a great borrower. "The forgotten man" had come from a speech delivered by William Graham Sumner in 1883, and Stuart Chase had just published a book entitled *A New Deal*. Roosevelt didn't much care about the genesis of a word, an idea, or a program. His statecraft was summed up in a speech at Oglethorpe University, when he said, "The country needs and, unless I mistake its temper, the country demands bold, persistent experimentation. . . . Above all, try something." He had already begun recruiting college professors to generate suggestions. James Kieran of the *New York Times* called them "the brains trust"; then everyone else, Roosevelt included, borrowed *that* and shortened it to "brain trust."

If one definition of genius is an infinite capacity to make use of everyone and everything, the Democratic nominee certainly qualified. He reminded John Gunther of "a kind of universal joint, or rather a switchboard, a transformer," through which the energy and intelligence of other people flowed. Within a year he would become obscured by the mists of legend, but as a candidate he was still seen as mortal — a big, broad-shouldered man of fifty whose paralyzed legs were partially offset by his long arms and huge, hairy, freckled hands. His hair was gray and thin, and he had a small paunch, deep blue eyes set close together over permanent brown shadows, and two long wrinkles that formed parenthetical curves around his mouth. Undoubtedly his breeding as a country gentleman, guided by the old-fashioned morality of Groton headmaster Endicott Peabody, contributed immeasurably to his inner strength; he was perhaps the only politician in the country who thought of economics as a *moral* problem. Rooseveltian confidence was striking — someone said "he must have been psychoanalyzed by God" — and so was his memory. He remembered Italian streets and buildings he hadn't seen since his youth. Once in wartime a ship sank off Scotland; either it had been torpedoed or it had struck a rock. FDR said it was probably the rock, and then proceeded to reel off the height of the tide at that season on that coast and the extent to which that particular rock would be submerged. One of his favorite performances (and he was always a showman) was to ask a visitor to draw a line in any direction across an outline map of the United States; he would then name, in order, every county the line crossed. He was an apostle of progress; as soon as he saw the Sahara he wanted to irrigate it. Now in a world bereft of progressive action he was already a world figure. In Brussels *Demain* was investigating his horoscope. Among other things, the astrologers found excessive idealism, zeal for too rapid reformation, and "great good judgment." After 1941 he would be in danger of accidents.

He was telling the country that "to accomplish anything worthwhile . . . there must be a compromise between the ideal and the practical." That wasn't at all what the ideologues wanted to hear. Roosevelt, Harold Laski sneered, was "a pill to cure an earthquake." Lippmann called him too soft, too eager to please and be all things to all men. The country yearned for a Messiah, Ernest K. Lindley reported, and Mr. Roosevelt did not "look or sound like a Messiah." John Dewey felt the argument that Governor Roosevelt was the lesser of two evils was "suicidal." Organized labor, such as it was, refused to endorse any candidate.

Disenchantment with the two major parties ran high. Will Rogers concluded, "The way most people feel, they would like to vote against all of them if it was possible." In Kansas, Republican gubernatorial candidate Alfred M. Landon was threatened by a third-party adventurer named Dr. John "Goat Glands" Brinkley; in California, District Attorney Earl Warren of Alameda County, running for reelection, was threatened by a half-dozen crank candidates. In FDR's own party he had the dubious honor of receiving support from Huey Long, the pasha of Louisiana, who packed a gun and who, in Roosevelt's private opinion, was one of the two most dangerous men in the country. (The other was General MacArthur.)

Lippmann saw "no issue of fundamental principle" between Roosevelt and Hoover, and defections on the left were particularly heavy. "If I vote at all," said Lewis Mumford, "it will be for the Communists. It is Communism which desires to save civilization." Professor Paul H. Douglas of the University of Chicago, later to become a brilliant ornament of the Democratic party, declared then that its destruction would be "one of the best things that could happen in our political life." John Chamberlain wrote in September that progressivism "must mean either Norman Thomas or William Z. Foster, ineffectual though one or both may be." Thomas supporters included Stephen Vincent Benét, Reinhold Niebuhr, Stuart Chase, Elmer Davis, Morris Ernst, and the editors of both the *New Republic* and the *Nation*. Villard continued his litany of the left; of Roosevelt he wrote: "He has spoken of the 'forgotten man,' but nowhere is there a real, passionate, ringing exposition of just what it is that the forgotten man has been deprived of or what should be done for him. ... we can see in him no leader, and no evidence anywhere that he can rise to the needs of this extraordinary hour."

This was overstated, but when TRB wrote in the *New Republic* of "the pussyfooting policy of Roosevelt's campaign," and *Time* said the governor "emerged from the campaign fog as a vigorous well-intentioned gentleman of good birth and breeding" who "lacked crusading convictions," they were reading the record correctly. The candidate delivered only one really radical speech, to the Commonwealth Club of San Francisco on September 23. It was not repeated. His own convictions at this time were largely conservative; he believed in the gold standard, a balanced budget, and unregulated business competition. Moreover, he had to hold his party together. For every Huey Long on the left there were ten men like Al Smith, who said, "We should stop talking about the Forgotten Man and about class distinctions" and Garner, who sent word to Roosevelt that if he went too far with "wild-eyed ideas" they would have "the shit kicked out of us." FDR didn't go too far. His speeches were laced with ambiguities and contradictions. Many passages seem to reflect a shallow optimism, and one address, delivered in Pittsburgh, was a dreadful blunder. Among the new members of his brain trust was General Hugh S. "Ironpants" Johnson, a friend of Baruch's who had been Douglas MacArthur's classmate at West Point and had later shared a tent with George Patton on the Mexican border. As a child he had chanted, "Everybody's a rink-stink but Hughie Johnson and he's all right." That was still his attitude; to him the other brain-trusters were rink-stinks, and during their absence from the campaign train he persuaded the Democratic standard-bearer to embrace the platform plank calling for a 25 percent slash in the federal budget. FDR would hear about that four years later.

But his audiences were less interested in his stand on tariffs and the power business than in taking the measure of the man, and what they saw was a magnificent leader — his leonine head thrown back, his eye flashing, his cigarette holder tilted at the sky, his navy boat cloak falling gracefully from his great shoulders. He was the image of zest, warmth, and dignity; he was always smiling; he always called people "my friends." If his speeches were inadequate as statements of public policy, politically they were brilliant. Editors read, "The only real capital of the nation is its natural resources and its human beings," and they groaned. Voters felt the governor's obvious sincerity and were moved. To them his messages were lucid, specific, and illumined by homely metaphors. He cared about people. They could feel that. And the campaign was as much of an education for him as for them. Heading westward across the plains, he realized for the first time just how desperate the country's economic situation had become. "I have looked into the faces of thousands of Americans," he told a friend. ". . . They have the frightened look of lost children."

Meanwhile, back at the White House, Herbert Hoover had come alive. Roosevelt's speeches hadn't done it. The *Literary Digest* poll predicting a Roosevelt victory may have helped; so may the gambling odds, which were running seven to one against the President. The real shock, however, came from Maine. Maine still voted in September then, and when the ballots were counted it turned out that the state had elected a Democratic governor and two Democratic Congressmen — the first such slippage from the GOP since the Civil War. Hoover had carried forty states in 1928; he was bewildered. He told his secretary that this meant "we have got to fight to the limit." Earlier he had said that in four months of campaigning Roosevelt would lose the confidence of business, which in some mysterious way would, he thought, decide the election. Such firms as the Ford Motor Company had in fact notified their employees that "To prevent times from getting worse and to help them get better, President Hoover must be elected." But apparently workers weren't listening to their employers. Futhermore, there had been several startling desertions from Republican ranks, notably Senators Borah of Idaho and Hiram Johnson of California.

So Hoover put on his high-button shoes and celluloid collar and went to the people. He was lucky to come back alive. He deliberately chose the low road; to a member of his cabinet he confided that there was "hatred" for him in the country, and that the only way to win was to incite "a fear of what Roosevelt will do." In Des Moines he said of his tariff, "The grass will grow in the streets of a hundred cities, a thousand towns; the weeds will overrun the fields of millions of farms if that protection is taken away." They jeered and paraded Hoovercarts bearing signs that read, WE'LL GET THERE REGARDLESS OF HOOVER, AND THIS AIN'T NO BULL. In Indianapolis he told listeners that Roosevelt was peddling "nonsense . . . misstatements . . . prattle . . . untruths . . . defamation . . . ignorance . . . calumnies," and they hissed. In Cleveland he promised that no "deserving" citizen would starve, and they hooted. In St. Paul, referring to the rout of the bonus marchers, he said, "Thank God we still have a government in Washington that still knows how to deal with a mob," and the crowd replied with one vast snarl. Detroit was the worst. The city was carrying a quarter-million people on its relief rolls. At the station he was greeted with boos and catcalls. Mounted police, swinging batons, scattered the throng, but all along his limousine route tens of thousands more shouted "Hang Hoover!" and shook their fists. Signs read, DOWN WITH HOOVER, SLAYER OF VETERANS!; BILLIONS FOR BANKERS, BULLETS FOR VETS. Afterward a Secret Serviceman told a reporter, "I've been traveling with Presidents since Teddy Roosevelt's time, and never before have I seen one actually booed, with men running out into the streets to thumb their noses at him. It's not a pretty sight." Chief Agent Sterling looked at Hoover and saw a man stricken. The President could hardly talk. By now people were throwing eggs and tomatoes at his train as it moved across the stricken land. He didn't know what else to do, so he phoned Calvin Coolidge.

Coolidge said his throat was bothering him and, what's more, "I find it terribly hard to know what to say." His difficulty was understandable. In Northampton, Massachusetts, his own bank was collapsing. Finally he agreed to speak in Madison Square Garden. Republicans thought the magic of his name would pack the Garden. Instead fewer than a third of the seats were filled, and frantic ushers ran outside begging passersby to come hear the country's only living ex-President. Inside, the party faithful gave him a two-minute ovation which he throttled by holding out his watch, showing that the cheers had wasted $340 of radio time. "That's Cal!" somone shouted. But it wasn't the Cal of old, nor was this the kind of audience he had known. He said, "The Republican party believes in encouraging business in order that the benefits from such business may minister to the welfare of the ordinary run of people." He waited for applause. There was silence. He began another sentence, "When I was in Washington —" and they roared with laughter. Baffled, he shook his head. No one had ever laughed at a Coolidge speech before. He stumbled through the text and went home declaring himself "burned-out"; in fifteen weeks he would be dead.

Now the party in power was really desperate. The Secretary of Agriculture maligned the New York governor as "a common garden variety of liar"; the Secretary of the Navy predicted, "If Roosevelt is elected, the homes and lives of a hundred million Americans might be in danger." Hoover cried, "My countrymen! The fundamental issue that will fix the national direction for one hundred years to come is whether we shall go in fidelity to American traditions or whether we shall turn to innovations." His shoulders sagged, the crow's-feet about his eyes deepened, the lines around his mouth grew harder. In his final radio plea to the electorate he premonished against "false gods arrayed in the rainbow colors of promises," and William Allen White noted "how infinitely tired" his voice was and "how hollow and how sad in disillusion" his words had become.

The contrast with Governor Roosevelt could not have been greater. "You may not have universally agreed with me, but you have universally been kind to me," FDR said to his radio audience; ". . . Out of this unity that I have seen we may build the strongest strand to lift ourselves out of this Depression." He was magnanimous and sure of himself, and no presidential challenger ever had better reason. Sitting in Democratic headquarters in New York on election night at the Hotel Biltmore, his Phi Beta Kappa key gleaming on his dark blue vest, he listened to reports of the growing avalanche until, at 12:17 A.M., Hoover conceded. The President-elect had carried 42 of the 48 states — all but Connecticut, Maine, Vermont, New Hampshire, Delaware, and Pennsylvania — and had won 472 electoral votes; the "President-reject," as *Time* cruelly called him, had but 59. It was the greatest victory in a two-party presidential race since Lincoln beat McClellan 212 to 21, though there were those who noted that the popular vote for Norman Thomas had jumped from 267,240 to 728,860. Louis Howe broke out a twenty-year-old bottle of sherry. Three babies born that night at Brooklyn's Beth-El Hospital were named Franklin Delano Mayblum, Franklin Delano Finkelstein, and Franklin Delano Ragin.

Franklin Delano Roosevelt retired to his town house at 49 East Sixty-fifth Street, where his mother embraced him and said elatedly, "This is the greatest moment of my life." Her son, however, seemed to have lost some of his campaign assurance. Upstairs his twenty-five-year-old son lifted him into bed, leaned over, and kissed him goodnight. Looking up, the President-elect said, "You know, Jimmy, all my life I have been afraid of only one thing — fire. Tonight I think I'm afraid of something else." The young man asked, "Afraid of what, Pa?" and his father replied, "I'm just afraid that I may not have the strength to do this job."

Next morning, propped in bed, he was heartened by the nation's editorial comment. Even the *Chicago Tribune* said that his "personality and his ideas pleased the people. They were impressed by his good will and good faith." Those qualities were there, but they could not be traded upon. He had not won the Presidency without a shrewd eye for hidden motives, and he needed it that morning. Hoover's congratulatory telegram had arrived; it must be answered. At first he wrote on the back of it that he was prepared "to cooperate with you" in the months ahead. Then he paused and struck that out. In its place he scrawled that he was "ready to further in every way the common purpose to help our country." In 1932 Presidents were not inaugurated until March 4. A four-month interregnum lay ahead. He had a hunch that Hoover would try to tie him to the discredited policies of the outgoing administration, and he was right.

On December 5 the lame-duck 72nd Congress limped back to Capitol Hill, and those of its members who were under the impression that the rout of the BEF had frightened jobless families away from Washington were in for a shock. Over 2,500 men, women, and children greeted them at the Capitol steps, chanting, "Feed the hungry, tax the rich! Feed the hungry, tax the rich!" The District's new police commissioner had orders not to humor such wraiths, and he followed them scrupulously. Policemen with gas guns and riot guns defended the Hill, then rounded up the throng and herded it down New Jersey Avenue to Camp Meigs, a wartime cantonment on New York Avenue. The commissioner told the press he had concentrated his wards in a "detention camp." Their guards ridiculed them and denied them water, food, medical attention or even the right to dig toilets; a Wisconsin congressman reported to his constituents that he had seen policemen deliberately provoking people. After huddling on the frozen ground for forty-eight hours, the prisoners were released. Leaving, they sang the newly learned words:

> *Arise, ye prisoners of starvation*
> *Arise, ye wretched of the earth*
> *For justice thunders condemnation*
> *A better world's in birth. . . .*

Throughout the early Thirties, and especially in the months bracketing the last session of the 72nd Congress, the sound of famished men on the march was heard from coast to coast. In New York thirty-five thousand men and women packed Union Square to hear Communist party orators. Crowds in Oklahoma City, Minneapolis, and St. Paul broke into groceries and meat markets to rifle shelves. Feelings of desperation were still internalized in most men (the suicide rate tripled that winter) but more and more mobs were beginning to coalesce. In Lincoln, Nebraska, four thousand men occupied the statehouse, another five thousand took over Seattle's ten-story County-City Building, and five thousand Chicago teachers, tormented beyond endurance, stormed the city's banks. The strains of "L'Internationale" were becoming increasingly familiar to the jobless; a forty-two-year-old radical named Louis Budenz led the Ohio Unemployed League mass march on the Columbus statehouse. His slogan was: "We must take control of the government and establish a workers' and farmers' republic."

The sense of institutions, authority, and private property — the intuitive discipline which Daniel Patrick Moynihan would later call "the glue that holds societies together" — was showing signs of disintegration. The tax strikes and the bootleg mining of company coal seams were ominous; so was the frequency with which empty lots were being gardened without their owners' consent, and the scattered, aimless rioting in Detroit, where relief had simply stopped. Some communities quit. Key West, Florida, was going into bankruptcy; there was no money to pay the sanitation department, and whole streets were filling up with rubbish and garbage. Here and there the starving were muttering violence. The mayor of a Massachusetts town, watching two thousand idle men milling around his city hall, wrote that "a spark might change them into a mob." Governor O. Max Gardner of North Carolina warned of the danger of "violent social and political revolution." Mayor Anton Cermak of Chicago, faced with the state's reluctance to appropriate funds for the city's six hundred thousand out-of-work men, told the legislature, "Call out the troops before you close the relief stations."

The well-fed were edgy. Company men in employment offices became curt, bank tellers nervous, elected officials quicker to call the police, policemen faster with the nightstick. Henry Ford had always been a pacifist. Now he carried a gun. In Richmond, Virginia, a delegation from the local Unemployed Council called on Mayor J. Fulmer Bright a few days after Thanksgiving; the mayor told his police chief, "Take these men by the scruff of the neck and the seat of the pants and throw them out." Jittery company guards killed four miners in Pennsylvania's Fayette County. New York ordered the apple sellers off its sidewalks, and John P. O'Brien, the new occupant of Gracie Mansion, promised his city, "You're going to have a mayor with a chin and fight in him. I'll preserve the metropolis from the Red Army." Plainclothesmen swinging truncheons waded into a Union Square rally; the *New York Times* reported "screams of women and cries of men with bloody heads and faces." Oklahoma City police used tear gas to break up meetings. Seattle police evicted the squatters from its County-City Building with fire hoses. Chicago law enforcement officers clubbed the unpaid teachers with billies, two of them holding one middle-aged woman while a third smashed her face.

Testifying before a Senate committee about the "sporadic uprisings in a number of our industrial cities," an AFL spokesman said that "the great bulk of those people know nothing about Communism. They wanted bread." To the propertied classes, the distinction was irrelevant. As Robert Sherwood wrote, the way ahead seemed to be clouded by "black doubt, punctured by brief flashes of ominous light, whose revelations are not comforting." If the government could not keep order, each man must look to his own. Businessmen in a number of cities formed committees to cope with nameless terrors should railroad and telephone lines be cut and surrounding highways blocked. Candles and canned goods were stockpiled; a Hollywood director carried with him a wardrobe of old clothes so that he could "disappear into the crowd" on a moment's notice. In New York, hotels discovered that wealthy guests who usually leased suites for the winter were holing up in their country homes. Some had mounted machine guns on their roofs.

They weren't paranoid. The evidence strongly suggests that had Roosevelt in fact been another Hoover, the United States would have followed seven Latin American countries whose governments had been overthrown by Depression victims. Charles M. Schwab was one of many tycoons who believed revolution was just around the corner. The dean of the Harvard Business School said, "Capitalism is on trial and on the issue of this trial may depend the whole future of Western civilization." Articles debating the imminence of revolt appeared in the *Yale Review, Scribner's, Harper's,* the *American Mercury,* and the *Atlantic.* Norman Thomas later said of the period "between the popular election and the inauguration" that "never before or since have I heard so much open and bitter cynicism about democracy and the American system."

There was a great deal of disagreement about which form of government the United States should adopt. Most intellectuals had turned leftward. Socialism to them was the middle of the road; John Dos Passos scornfully compared it to drinking near beer. Those who openly espoused Communism included Dos Passos, Sherwood Anderson, Erskine Caldwell, Malcolm Cowley, Lincoln Steffens, Granville Hicks, Clifton Fadiman, Upton Sinclair, and Edmund Wilson, who urged taking "Communism away from the Communists," and subsequently added that Russia was "the moral top of the world where the light really never goes out." William Allen White called the Soviet Union "the most interesting place on the planet." *New Russia's Primer* was a Book-of-the-Month Club choice; it compared American chaos with Russian order. "Those rascals in Russia," said Will Rogers, ". . . have got mighty good ideas. . . . Just think of everybody in a country going to work." Elmer Davis said the profit system was dead. Even Scott Fitzgerald was reading Marx and writing, "To bring on the revolution, it may be necessary to work inside the Communist Party." Stuart Chase asked in *A New Deal*, "Why should Russians have all the fun of remaking a world?" More than one man in office flirted with the left. Governor Theodore G. Bilbo of Mississippi confessed, "I'm getting a little pink myself," and Governor Floyd B. Olson of Minnesota, more forthright, told a Washingtonian to go back "and tell 'em Olson is taking recruits for the Minnesota National Guard, and he isn't taking anybody who doesn't carry a Red Card." To be sure he wasn't misunderstood he added, "Minnesota is a left-wing state."

But the greater danger lay at the other end of the political spectrum. Intellectuals lacked power, and Bilbo and Olson were political eccentrics. The money, the influence, and Secretary of War Hurley were on the right. As early as 1931 the administration had resisted attempts to reduce troop levels because the cut would "lessen our means of maintaining domestic peace and order," and that September the American Legion had passed a resolution asserting that the economic crisis could not be "promptly and efficiently met by existing political methods." The "American Facist [*sic*] Association and Order of Black Shirts" had been founded in Atlanta, and although its name was unpopular — asked if fascism would come to America, Huey Long said, "Sure, but here it will be called anti-fascism" — the Black Shirts had been joined by Silver Shirts, White Shirts, Khaki Shirts, the Minute Men, and the American Nationalists. A secret clique of reserve army officers was reported ready to act if the new President proved ineffective. General Smedley D. Butler testified that a New York bond salesman had attempted to recruit him for the right with an offer of $18,000 in cash. Nicholas Murray Butler told his students that totalitarian regimes brought forth "men of far greater intelligence, far stronger character, and far more courage than the system of elections," and if anyone represented the American establishment then it was Dr. Butler, with his Nobel Prize, his thirty-four honorary degrees, and his thirty-year tenure as president of Columbia University.

Who else was prepared to sacrifice constitutional government for this vision of expanded intelligence, character, and virility? Apart from the president of Columbia and General Butler's bond salesman, few came out for totalitarianism as such, but plenty advocated the principle. Governor Landon of Kansas declared, "Even the iron hand of a national dictator is in preference to a paralytic stroke." Congressman Hamilton Fish Jr. of New York said in 1932, "If we don't give it [dictatorship] under the existing system, the people will change the system." In February 1933 he wrote the President-elect that he and his fellow Republicans were ready to "give you any power you may need." Al Smith thought the Constitution ought to be wrapped up and laid "on the shelf" until the crisis was over. *Vanity Fair*, whose associate editors included Clare Boothe Brokaw (later Luce), demanded, "Appoint a dictator!" Walter Lippmann wanted to give the President full power at the expense of Congress; "the danger," he said, "is not that we shall lose our liberties, but that we shall not be able to act with the necessary speed and comprehensiveness," and Republican Senator David A. Reed said outright, "If this country ever needed a Mussolini, it needs one now."

In a *New Yorker* cartoon a girl at a Greenwich Village party told a limp young man, "Oh, it's all very simple. Our little group simply seizes the powerhouses and the radio station." That was where the danger lay, most people thought; in the cities. Secretary Hurley was believed to be concentrating the few troops he had near metropolitan areas, but rebellious populations have a way of outfoxing authority, and the opening revolt came where it was least expected. Farmers had always been considered the most conservative of Americans, yet it was in Republican Iowa — Hoover's home state — that sunburned men of native stock first reached for their pitchforks and shotguns. They were finally taking up arms against a system which paid them two cents a quart for milk that distributors sold for eight cents in Sioux City.

Under the leadership of Milo Reno, a sixty-four-year-old former president of the Iowa Farmers Union, they blocked all ten highways leading into the city. Spiked telegraph poles and logs were laid across the roads. Only milk for hospitals was allowed to pass. Other trucks were stopped and the milk cans emptied into ditches or taken into town and distributed free. Sympathetic telephone operators warned the insurgent farmers of approaching convoys an hour in advance; sheriffs were disarmed and their pistols and badges thrown into cornfields. Route 20 became known as Bunker Hill 20. Peering at Mary Heaton Vorse of *Harper's* from under the brim of a ten-cent straw hat, an old man said, "They say blockading the highway's illegal. I says, 'Seems to me there was a tea party in Boston that was illegal too.'"

The movement spread until Des Moines, Council Bluffs, and Omaha were isolated. In Wisconsin, embattled farmers invaded a dairy three times in one day, dumped 34,000 pounds of milk on the ground, and poured gasoline in the vats. A congressional subcommittee heard Oscar Ameringer of Oklahoma City describe a conversation with a rancher whom he had known to be conservative. The man had said, "We've got to have a revolution here like they had in Russia." Ameringer had asked him how he proposed to do it, and the man had replied, "We will have four hundred machine guns . . . batteries of artillery, tractors and munitions and rifles and everything else needed to supply a pretty good army. . . . If there are enough fellows with guts in this country to do like us, we will march eastward and we will cut the East off. We will cut the East off from the West. We have got the granaries; we have the hogs, the cattle, the corn, and the East has nothing but mortgages on our places. We will show them what we can do." Ameringer told the House Labor Committee, "I have heard much of this talk from serious-minded prosperous men of other days."

Will Rogers said, "Paul Revere just woke up Concord. These birds woke up America." And on Route 20 the Iowans sang:

> Let's call a farmers' holiday
> A holiday let's hold;
> We'll eat our wheat and ham and eggs
> And let them eat their gold.

The Sioux City siege was lifted shortly after a mysterious shotgun attack on the camp of some Milo Reno followers near the town of Cherokee, forty-eight miles east of the city. He quit, and farmers surrounding the other invested cities quit with him. But Reno said, "You can no more stop this movement than you could stop the revolution. I mean the revolution of 1776." Both in their violence and their uprising they were being faithful to American tradition. And they went unpunished. At Council Bluffs sixty had been arrested, but when a thousand of their fellow insurgents marched on the jail, they were hastily released. Deciding that direct action paid, the farmers now decided to do something about mortgage foreclosures.

On the outskirts of a Kansas village police found the murdered body of a lawyer who had just foreclosed on a five-hundred-acre farm. In Cheyenne County, Nebraska, the leaders of two hundred thousand debt-ridden farmers announced that if they didn't get help from the legislature they would converge on the statehouse and raze it, brick by brick. Throughout Hoover's last winter as President there were foreclosure riots in Iowa at Storm Lake, at Primghar, in Van Buren County, and at Le Mars. The Le Mars incident was particularly ugly. Black-shirted vigilantes invaded the courtroom of Judge Charles C. Bradley, dragged him from the bench, blindfolded him, and drove him to a lonely crossroads. Their leader demanded, "Will you swear you won't sign no more mortgage foreclosures?" The judge said no. Again and again the demand was repeated, and the answer was the same. He was slapped, kicked, and knocked to the ground. A rope was tied around his neck; the other end was thrown over a roadside sign. A greasy hubcap was clapped down on his head — "That's his crown," one of the men shouted. The judge never did give his word, but though he was stripped and beaten, he declined to press prosecution afterward.

When papers had been signed, hundreds of farmers would appear at the auction shouting, "No sale!" Prospective bidders would be shoved aside; then neighbors would buy the land for a few dollars and return it to its original owner. At one sheriff's sale a horse brought five cents, a Holstein bull five cents, three hogs another nickel, two calves four cents, and so on, until the entire property had changed hands for $1.18. It was deeded back to the householder for ninety-nine years. Lawyers representing insurance companies in the East were kidnapped and threatened with the noose until the home office relented and agreed to a mortgage moratorium. By the end of January 1933, John A. Simpson, president of the National Farmers Union, told the Senate Committee on Agriculture, "The biggest and finest crop of revolutions you ever saw is sprouting all over this country right now." Edward A. O'Neal III, president of the American Farm Bureau Federation, added, "Unless something is done for the American farmer we'll have revolution in the countryside in less than twelve months."

Here and there that troubled winter were sensitive boys now reaching the age of awareness who would, a generation later, become American leaders. Although their reactions to the world around them varied, none would ever forget the Great Depression. American history in their lifetimes would be a succession of crises, but for them this first crisis was formative.

A glance at some names is useful. In 1932 Robert F. Kennedy became seven years old; Frank Church and James Baldwin were eight; Mark Hatfield and Norman Mailer nine; John Lindsay, Nicholas Katzenbach, and Floyd McKissick ten; Whitney Young and John Glenn eleven; James Farmer, Stewart Udall, and Charles Percy twelve; Edward Brooke, George Wallace, McGeorge Bundy, and Russell Long thirteen; Billy Graham, Orville Freeman, and Arthur M. Schlesinger Jr. fourteen; John F. Kennedy, Robert Taft Jr., John Connally, and Lawrence F. O'Brien fifteen; Arthur Miller, Robert McNamara, Eugene McCarthy, and John Tower sixteen; David Rockefeller, Peter Dominick, Herman Wouk, Saul Bellow, Walter Heller and Theodore H. White seventeen; William Westmoreland, Tennessee Williams, Jonas Salk, and Stewart Alsop eighteen; and Gerald Ford and Richard M. Nixon nineteen.

Nixon had entered his junior year at Whittier College that autumn, majoring in history and running the fresh vegetable counter at Nixon's Market, the family store; each morning before dawn he drove to the Los Angeles Public Market to haggle with produce growers over prices. The family had enough to eat, which put Nixon in the great silent majority of eighty million Americans who were neither starving nor on relief. His collegiate status set him apart, however; fewer than one youth in eight between eighteen and twenty-two was in college, and only half had gone to high school. For millions, formal education was still confined to the one-teacher elementary school, of which there were 143,391 in the country.

If it were possible to be transported back in time to the typical middle-class neighborhood of that year, it would probably be in a city; suburban areas had begun to form, but only 18 percent of the population lived there. It was still feasible for a man and his family to live decently within walking distance of his office. Arriving on a street in the neighborhood, a visitor from the 1970s would first notice superficial differences — stop signs were yellow, mailboxes green; milk bottles thick and heavy — and then the seedy appearance of the houses. Few had been painted since 1929; often those which had been under construction had been left unfinished. On Detroit's East Jefferson Street, for example, the Elks suspended work on an eleven-story building, and its naked beams stood silhouetted against the sky for thirty-four years.

Appliances, gadgets, and creature comforts of the 1970s were rare. There were no power mowers, home air-conditioning units, automatic dishwashers, clothes driers, electric blankets, clock-radios, thermopane windows, nylons, drip-dry clothes, frozen foods, automatic coffee makers, cordless shavers, filter cigarettes, electric toothbrushes, vinyl floors, ballpoint pens, electric typewriters, modern Dictaphones, Xerox machines, Styrofoam, hi-fi stereo sets, Scotch tape, home freezers, cassette recorders, color or Polaroid film, Fiberglas fishing rods, garbage disposal units, tape recorders, snow blowers, electric knives, home hair driers, electric can openers, or Muzak, and although Gilbert Seldes was predicting in *Harper's* that soon "we shall probably have the simple and comparatively inexpensive mechanisms, now being perfected, which will throw on a small screen set up beside the home radio set a moving picture projected from a central broadcasting station," there was no television, not even plain black-and-white. Somehow the middle class survived the Depression — the entire decade of the Thirties — with none of these. O Pioneers!

Most American homes were heated by hand-stoked hot air furnaces, which had to be tended twice daily. The country needed nearly 400 million tons of coal to get through a winter, and it was brought to a house by a grimy man who would back his truck to a cellar window and empty the coal down a chute into a bin near the furnace. "Refrigerator" didn't mean an *electric* refrigerator; it was an icebox, kept filled by an iceman who knew how many pounds a housewife wanted because she notified him by placing in her kitchen window a card with the figure 100, 75, 50, or 25 turned up. It was an affluent husband who bought his wife a toaster that would scorch both sides of a piece of bread simultaneously ("Our SUPREME toaster!" cried the Sears, Roebuck catalogue that year), for in most homes bread was singed in a gas oven or a coal or wood-burning "kitchen range." The stove might also be used to heat heavy sadirons for pressing clothing that had come back from the laundry rough-dried, or, in a home without hot water, for heating bucketfuls before a bath.

Phonographs had to be wound by hand; they might be called Victrolas or Gramophones, but never record players. A housewife began her heavy cleaning by donning a dustcap, and as a rule her only mechanical help was a carpet sweeper; in December 1932, in all the houses served by the Alabama Power Company, there were exactly 185 vacuum cleaners. Most farms depended upon kerosene lamps for illumination. Electricity was available to one American farmer in every ten — in Mississippi the ratio was one in a hundred — and 90 percent of all rural families were without either bathtubs or showers. Seventy-five percent lacked indoor plumbing. Half carried their water from wells or brooks and did their laundry — and washed their children — outdoors. (For that matter, millions of urban housewives also had only a washboard to cope with the family laundry, which was usually hung out on Mondays.) Insects were always a summer problem. There was no DDT. Both on farms and in cities the only preventives were spray guns ("Quick, Henry, the Flit!") and flypaper. A mother who wanted fruit juice for her children had to work at it. She bought Sunkist oranges and laboriously squeezed them, one by one, on an aluminum juice extractor.

Before a girl learned how to handle bobby pins — at about the same age that boys were acquiring their first long pants — her mother had explained the difference between a lady and a woman. Being a lady had certain advantages. Men opened doors for her, stood up to give her a seat on buses and streetcars, and removed their hats when she entered elevators; butchers cut her meat to order, grocers took orders over the telephone and delivered to her door, and when she had a baby she was expected to stay in bed ten days (at a total cost, including the doctor's fee, of $25). On the other hand, she was expected to defer to her husband; at the altar she had sworn "to love, honor, and *obey* him." Her activities in public were circumscribed by convention. A middle-class lady could neither smoke on the street nor appear with hair curlers. In her purse she carried cosmetics in a small disc called a compact, but this, too, could be produced only in private or a ladies' room. She never swore or told dirty jokes. (Sometimes she wondered what a lesbian was. But whom could she ask?) Advertising copywriters saw to it that she had enough worries anyway: halitosis, B.O., undie odor, office hips, paralyzed pores, pink toothbrush, ashtray breath, colon collapse, pendulosis, and athlete's foot. Her skirts came to mid-calf. (Any woman whose hem did not cover the knee was assumed to be a prostitute.) A lady would no more leave the house without her cloche than her husband would without his snap-brim felt hat. She might squirt Ipana (for the smile-of-beauty) on her Dr. West toothbrush, and even use Tangee lipstick, but fingernail paint and hair dye were highly dubious. Hairdressers didn't know how to use dye. Respectable women didn't even talk about it; a clever young NYU chemistry major, who sold his homemade Clairol dye from door to door, discovered that to make ends meet he had to talk about hair "coloring."

As a mother, the middle-class wife often had to double as a nurse. Illnesses were long and painful then. Even a visit to the dentist meant an hour of agony; Procaine, a primitive form of Novocaine, was widely used, but it had to be mixed at the chair and was accompanied by disagreeable side effects. Thousands of patients still had to take the big burring drill straight, and since fast drills hadn't been invented, not much could be accomplished in one visit. In many hospitals, anesthesiologists were limited to chloroform; ether would soon succeed it, though the improvement was questionable. There were no sulfa drugs and no antibiotics. Meningitis killed 95 percent of its victims; pneumonia was often fatal. Even viral infections (called "the grippe" then) were a serious business. Though hospitals were comparatively inexpensive, practically no one had hospital insurance — the American Medical Association didn't approve Blue Cross until 1933 — so most patients remained at home, which meant with mother. She seldom had the help of medication. Ethical drugs were largely limited to a few barbiturates, notably phenobarbital. So remote was the drug nightmare of the next generation that 3,512 drug firms failed between 1932 and 1934, leaving liabilities of over 59 million dollars.

If motherhood was more difficult, it was also a greater challenge. Parents had a tremendous influence upon their children. The teen-age subculture did not exist; indeed "teenage," as defined by Merriam-Webster, meant "brushwood used for fences and hedges." Young people were called youngsters, and youngsters were loyal to their homes. Since the brooding omnipresence of the peer group had not yet arrived, children rarely felt any conflict between their friends and their families. No youngster would dream of discussing parental conflicts with other youngsters. If a middle-class family was going to take a drive in the country on Sunday afternoon, as it usually was, children quit the baseball or hopscotch game and hopped in the back seat. The Depression increased all family activities; a study of over a hundred white-collar and professional families in Pittsburgh discovered that a majority had increased family recreation — ping-pong, jigsaw puzzles, checkers, parlor games, bridge, and most of all listening to the radio.

As often as not, the radio was the most prominent piece of furniture in the living room. Whether an Atwater Kent, Philco, Silvertone, or Majestic set, it was likely to be a rococo console in high Grand Rapids style. Network programs were scheduled with the family in mind. Mother's serials came during the day; news, comedians, and variety programs in the evening. Between the two was sandwiched the children's hour, part of which might be listed in the local newspaper as:

5:15	WTIC	1040	Tom Mix
	WEAF	660	Story Man
5:30	WTIC	1040	Jack Armstrong
	WJZ	760	Singing Lady
5:45	WJZ	760	Little Orphan Annie
6:00	WOR	710	Uncle Don

In the winter of 1932–33 a young middle-class boy wore, almost as a uniform, a sheepskin-lined tan cloth coat, a knitted hat, corduroy knickers, and high-cut lace-up boots with a small pocket on the side of one of them for a jackknife. (In summertime he wore short pants and Keds.) If he was lucky, he owned a Ranger 28-inch-wheel bike with a coaster brake and cushion tires, the tires protected by Neverleak and the whole locked, when not in use, by a $1.50 slip-shackle padlock. The times being what they were, he was very much aware of money and what it bought. A nickel would bring a three-flavored cake of brick ice cream, a Horton's Dixie Cup, a candy bar, a loaf of bread, a local telephone call, a cup of coffee, or a copy of the *Saturday Evening Post, Collier's*, or *Liberty*. For a penny you could get candy, a pencil, a postcard, a pad of paper, a glass marble, or your best friend's thoughts.

If you had an allowance (a Sunday nickel, say) or had earned some money shoveling snow or mowing lawns at a quarter apiece, the quickest place to spend it was at the corner drugstore, drinking a Coke at one of the marble-topped, wire-legged tables, though in Youngstown, Ohio, children bought ice-cream-on-a-stick from a confectioner who drove slowly through the suburbs in a white truck, ringing a bell, and who called himself the Good Humor man. A boy who accumulated as much as fifty cents could get the latest in the Tom Swift series. As David Riesman has pointed out, the heroes of boys' literature were "ambitious. They had goals. And the reader identified with them and tried to emulate them. . . . The virtue which brought victory was frequently an ability to control the self, for instance, to be brave." Significantly, the most widely read book in middle-class homes was Charles Lindbergh's *We*.

Inner-direction (or, as Paul Elmer More then called it, "the inner check") provided children with a built-in need to achieve, though the Depression discouraged them from reaching for anything beyond their grasp. In 1931 the *Literary Digest* had conducted a survey of vocation preference among children. Boys of eight wanted to be cowboys, aviators, or army officers when they grew up; girls wanted to be movie stars. At eighteen the boys were looking forward to being lawyers, electrical engineers, or architects; eighteen-year-old girls were taking stenographic and secretarial training. Adolescence was a sobering experience. But then, it wasn't supposed to be much fun. "Childhood is so short and the balance of life so long," Dorothy Dix explained. "At best, a mother can satin-pad the world for her children for a few years. Then they are bound to face realities, and it is a bitter price they must pay for her folly in turning them into weaklings, instead of strong men and women, and making them unable to cope with the difficulties that they are inevitably destined to encounter."

One of the first lessons a child learned — because it would be a future asset when he applied for a job — was the importance of personal appearance. "Sit up *straight!*" he was told, and "Here's fifteen cents, go get a haircut." He might prefer a Flexible Flyer sled or a Simplex typewriter, but what he got first was an $8.95 blue serge suit comprising a coat, vest, and knickers, and a pair of black $2.98 Gold Bond shoes. He wore them Sundays and on the first day of each semester, when every mother examined her son like a first sergeant going over his men before a white-glove inspection. (Somehow he always forgot his white handkerchief.) She wanted his new teachers to have a nice impression. It is not recorded that any child ever asked why.

To school he also brought a Masterpiece tablet, bearing on its cover a blurry reproduction of a great painting; in it he laboriously copied assignments with a big, circular Palmer Penmanship script. Seats in the classroom were frequently arranged alphabetically. The walls of at least one room would be decorated with the ruins of Pompeii or a bust of Caesar, etchings and statues which, as Riesman noted, would "signify the irrelevance of the school to the emotional needs of the child." Some of his lessons make interesting reading today. Young Lyndon Johnson had read in his geography book:

> French Indo-China resembles Siam both in climate and the character of people. Its forest-covered hills yield valuable teak and ironwood, and in its valleys are extensive fields of rice and millet. Silk, cotton, tea and spices are other products and there are also extensive coal beds.

A civics textbook explained:

> The child who has not learned obedience is handicapped for life. If he does not obey at home, he is not likely to observe the laws of the state, even though he helps elect the men who make them. Boys and girls who study our Government will quickly discover that obedience to authority is as necessary in a government by the people as in a monarchy.

And this paragraph appeared in Professor Thomas Marshall's widely used *American History*, published by Macmillan in 1930:

> *The slaves.* Although he was in a state of slavery, the Negro of plantation days was usually happy. He was fond of the company of others and liked to sing, dance, crack jokes, and laugh; he admired bright colors and was proud to wear a red or yellow bandana. He wanted to be praised, and he was loyal to a kind master or overseer. He was never in a hurry, and was always ready to let things go until the morrow. Most of the planters learned that not the whip, but loyalty, based upon pride, kindness, and rewards, brought the best returns.

Nor did unreality stop there. In schools of the Thirties — including, for several years, Washington, D.C. — teachers were forbidden to so much as mention the Soviet Union. On maps the area occupied by Russia was left blank, like the many "unexplored" tracts in Africa. School days usually opened with both the pledge of allegiance to the flag and a Protestant prayer, in which Jewish and Catholic children were expected to share. God was very much alive in 1932, and he was something of a prig. There is a great deal of social comment in *Time*'s prissy review of Earl Carroll's *Vanities* that October. Like Erskine Caldwell, Carroll sorely tested the Luce tolerance: "Mr. Carroll's shows have long held the record for borderline humor. In Comedian Milton Berle is to be found the acme of hysterical vulgarity. While one part of the audience blushes and the other part guffaws, Comedian Berle proceeds to imitate a person of uncertain gender, quip about the show girls' fundaments, shout depraved announcements into a loudspeaker. He seems to get a great deal of fun out of it." What especially entertained Berle — and infuriated *Time* — was that some of the chorines appeared with their brassieres clearly visible.

Mae West appeared that year with George Raft in *Night After Night,* and there were gasps in middle-class America when, in reply to a friend's remark, "Goodness, what beautiful diamonds," Mae replied, "Goodness has nothing to do with it, dearie." Will H. Hays, then czar of all the rushes, also overlooked an exchange in Busby Berkeley's first musical, *Forty-Second Street;* one chorus girl said, "I'm afraid I gotta run," the second said, "First door on your left," and the first said, "In my stocking." Such outrageous lewdness didn't get by often. For adolescents, sex was the most forbidden of all subjects. Like the myths about bogeymen and truant officers and the lists of New Year's resolutions which were faithfully made out each January 1 and broken within a week, the treatment of sex information virtually assured massive guilt feelings. Every growing boy knew masturbation led to brain damage and, in time, to the growth of hair on the palms of his hands.

Girls similarly worried over who had the reputation for being the "hottest" or "dirtiest" girl in school. Their difficulties were increased by the fact that the world of adolescence was largely male chauvinist. Girls were rarely invited to go bike riding, swap steelies or gum cards, discuss the Cleveland National Air Races, or play mumblety-peg, king-of-the-mountain, capture-the-flag, or (unless they were sisters or tomboys) ringolevio. A boy and girl might hold a strained conversation about the relative merits of the Ipana Troubadors, the Cliquot Club Eskimos, and the A & P Gypsies, but girls were largely spectators who emitted squeals during the great annual festival of July 4, when the anniversary of independence was celebrated by firing Bangsite cannon, hurling torpedos at the sidewalk, and blowing up tin cans with two-inchers and cherry bombs.

Middle-class parents who could afford it — and at eight dollars a week the cost was not prohibitive — sent their children away for at least part of the summer, if only because of the annual polio terror. When an epidemic of infantile paralysis struck, people stayed home from movies and meetings; some wouldn't even appear outdoors without gauze masks. Thus many a middle-class city child learned to swim at a Scout or YMCA camp, came to love the scent of honeysuckle and the flight of fireflies and June bugs around a campfire, and was told the sound of katydids in August meant frost in six weeks.

Sometimes the whole family would strap suitcases on the running boards of the new Chevrolet ($445, F.O.B. Detroit) and go "touring." Touring was an adventure, with real hazards. The spare tire mounted on the back of a roadster or a sedan was frequently needed, and with the tires of that era a blowup was a real explosion. Automobiles were uncomfortable. Meals in "roadhouses" were of uncertain quality. Overnight rest was difficult; rooms were hard to find. According to the American Automobile Association, the average American on tour spent a week getting to where he was going and a week coming back, which seems like a lot of touring until you realize that on the roads of that day he could average only 234 miles a day. Route 1 went right through the center of Washington, Philadelphia, New York and Boston; you had to use ferries at the Delaware River and the Hudson (the George Washington Bridge was still under construction); and in Maine, Depression winters had left the roads high-crowned and weak-shouldered. Speed traps were everywhere. There were no interstate highways. The only way you could drive coast to coast from the east was to take route 30 (the Lincoln Highway) into the center of Chicago, where you picked up route 66. Both were two-lane roads, both had stretches of unpaved dirt, and 66 traversed the Rockies with ungraded hairpin curves.

If all this sounds a trifle primitive, it must be added that, as Caroline Bird has pointed out, certain aspects of American society then could be quite pleasant. To be sure, you needed money, but not a great deal; an income of $5,000 or $6,000, or even less, brought comforts unknown today. The middle-class world was much quieter. There were no sonic booms, high-impact rock drills, air compressors, chain saw, hi-fi sets, tape recorders, playback units or 125-decibel rock groups, and very few riveters. It was more private. The FBI had fewer than three million fingerprints, and the digital society of social security numbers, zip codes, direct distance dialing, and credit card memory banks was unknown. Getting into college was relatively easy. Only thirty-five thousand applicants took college boards in 1932. If you preferred to fly the scheduling was primitive, but passengers received first-class service — the labor market being what it was, airlines could require extra effort from their R.N. stewardesses.

You never needed reservations at hotels, fine restaurants, hairdressing emporia, or hospitals. Nobody worried about pollution; factory chimneys were cold. Tutors, barbers, dressmakers, music teachers, and even physicians came to your house. If you worked in an office, secretaries arrived on time in the morning. They didn't disappear for coffee breaks, didn't make personal telephone calls from the office, and didn't object to working overtime. "The best guarantee of efficiency is a long line at the factory gate," was the way Samuel Insull put it (he would), but John Kenneth Galbraith stated the principle less cruelly. The more retrograde an economy becomes, he said, the more service improves.

Apart from amenities, the most cheerful feature of life then, as seen from the 1970s, lay abroad. Not only was America untroubled by foreign crises; as far as the vast majority of Americans were concerned, there were no foreign affairs at all. The Japanese were behaving badly in China, but who had time for that? In the German presidential elections eighty-four-year-old Paul von Hindenburg defeated forty-three-year-old Adolf Hitler. Americans were bored by both. In London the Prince of Wales made a date with a Mrs. Wallis Simpson, who had just been presented at court, but of course nothing could come of it because she already had a husband. Saigon was so remote that Hollywood used it as the background for *Red Dust,* an escapist film starring Clark Gable. The Middle East was quieter than the Middle West; as *Time* reported on April 4, the Jewish population of Palestine was "a minority (16.9 percent) without political power, save for the advisory powers conferred on the Jewish Agency by the mandate allotted to Great Britain ten years ago."

Although the decade was two years old, many figures who would later be identified with the 1930s were still relatively obscure. The name of Winston Churchill appeared in print as the author of *Amid These Storms,* an anti-Communist tract. (Other authors of 1932 were William Faulkner, Christopher Morley, Aldous Huxley, John Dos Passos, Robinson Jeffers, T. S. Stribling, Hendrik Willem van Loon, James M. Barrie, and Charles Nordhoff and James Norman Hall.) The men whose birthdays were matters of public note — e.g., George Bernard Shaw, Rudyard Kipling, George M. Cohan, and John Galsworthy — belong in memory to an earlier age. This was particularly true in the world of entertainment. The five top box office stars were Marie Dressler, Janet Gaynor, Joan Crawford, Charles Farrell, and Greta Garbo. Irene Dunne had just made her film debut; so had Claudette Colbert (with Maurice Chevalier). Ginger Rogers was simply another tap dancer in Busby Berkeley's chorus line. Nelson Eddy and Fred Astaire wouldn't arrive in Hollywood for another year. Four-year-old Shirley Temple was appearing on the nation's standard (eighteen feet high, twenty-four feet wide) screens in a series of one-reel shorts called *Baby Burlesks.* Benny Goodman was rooming with Tommy Dorsey, working in New York pit bands and playing clarinet cadenzas on radio for the Hoffman Ginger Ale Hour. In Beaumont, Texas, sixteen-year-old Harry Haag James approached a traveling band leader named Lawrence Welk and asked, "You don't happen to be looking for a trumpet player, do you?" The leader asked for a demonstration, James blasted away, and Welk shook his head. He said, "You play too loud for my band, son."

In retrospect, America seems to have been singularly blind to the future. When Professor Auguste Piccard penetrated the stratosphere in a balloon and wrote in his log, "We have attained an altitude of 54,120 ft. All human records broken!" there was no way of knowing that time would make the entry seem quaint. People were impressed by Dr. William Beebe's bathysphere and its brief dive to 2,200 feet off Bermuda; they wouldn't have believed that aquanauts a generation later would live at that depth for a month. It was in the naval maneuvers of 1932 that an American aircraft carrier, slipping past picket destroyers northeast of Oahu, attacked Pearl Harbor in a dawn "raid" and "sank" the warships anchored there. Nobody noticed the watchful Japanese in Honolulu, or knew that Tokyo was filing a long memorandum on the paper victory.

Most striking of all, newspaper readers were unaware that at Cambridge University Sir James Chadwick had discovered the neutron, the key to atomic fission. Its significance was unappreciated. According to physics doctrine at the time, only projectiles with fantastic penetrating power could split the nucleus of an atom. The very notion of such a split was highly theoretical, and certainly it couldn't be achieved by the neutron, which carried no electrical charge whatever. Lord Rutherford told a meeting that people who foresaw large-scale release of atomic energy were "talking moonshine." Albert Einstein, then en route to asylum at Cal Tech, agreed that the idea was "fantastic." The only practical use for uranium worth mentioning was to paint luminous figures on clock dials. Here it served as a substitute for radium, abandoned in the spring of 1932 when the owners of a New Jersey clock factory discovered that their dial painters were dying. Imbibed radium, they were shocked to learn, accumulated in the bones and led to certain death. The clockmakers turned in relief to uranium. It was so safe, so benign; no one could possibly associate it with death or even illness.

Depression Montage

FATHER OF TEN DROWNS SELF
Jumps from Bridge, Starts to Swim
Gives Up, Out of Work Two Years

REPEAL THE EIGHTEENTH AMENDMENT

COPS TRAIL LINDY BABY
KIDNAP CAR TO NEWARK

THE BEARDED LADY
TRIED A JAR
SHE'S NOW
A FAMOUS
MOVIE STAR —
BURMA SHAVE!

RIN TIN TIN DEAD AT 14

WHOLE INDUSTRIAL REGIONS IDLE

Work-is-what-I-want-and-not-charity-Who-will-help-me-get-a-job-7-years-in-Detroit-No-money-sent-away-furnish-best-of-references-Phone Randolph 8381: Room #59

WARNER BAXTER & BEBE DANIELS
in
FORTY-SECOND STREET
with
Guy Kibbee, Ruby Keeler, Dick Powell,
Una Merkel, George E. Stone,
Ned Sparks & Al Jenkins

A Scout is trustworthy loyal helpful friendly courteous kind obedient cheerful thrifty brave clean and reverent.

INTERNATIONAL CORRESPONDENCE SCHOOLS

DIRIGIBLE AKRON CRASHES IN LIGHTNING STORM AT SEA

BABE DIDRIKSON STARS IN Xth OLYMPIAD IN L.A.

ANNOUNCER: Olly-olly-in-free!

Wheaties, breakfast of champions, bring you the thrilling adventures of Jack Armstrong, the aaaaaaaaaallAmurrican boy. Jack Armstrong is climbing up the dangerous mountain trail to the cave of the glacier. High above him the towering peaks of the Andes press their eternal snows against the South American sky. And far below lies the valley with its hotel, "Winter Sports." Jack and his friends are seeking Hungster, whom enemy agent Lucano captured and brought to the cave of the glacier. Right now Uncle Jim leads the way . . .

I can't give you anything but love, baby
That's the only thing I've plenty of, baby

Tastyeast is tempting
To your appetite
Creamy, wholesome candy
Try a luscious bite.

DENTIST, WIFE, TAKE LIVES
RATHER THAN GO ON RELIEF

— Now the Miracle of Vitaphone —
Brings Broadway to Walla Walla!

Gee, I'd like to see you looking swell, baby
Wearing bracelets Woolworth's doesn't sell, baby
But until that day you know darned well, baby
I can't give you anything but love.

We understand that Mr. Gandhi has stated as part of his creed that civil disobedience is an effective substitute for violence or armed rebellion. In the opinion of this newspaper experience has proven time and time again that in India civil disobedience cannot be carried on without violence. Of course it would be another matter altogether in this country.

TWO

Roosevelt!

Shortly after the presidential election a band of Communists had arrived unheralded at 49 East Sixty-fifth Street. The President-elect received them, but when one said, "We want you to tell President Hoover that the federal government must —" Roosevelt broke in sharply. "I can't tell the President to do anything," he said. "I'm simply a private citizen as far as the federal government is concerned." He meant it. Until he had the power to act, he would not intervene. Meantime he went fishing on Vincent Astor's yacht, picked an unimpressive cabinet, and appeared to agree with everyone who saw him. Huey Long, battling the conservative influence of Arkansas's Senator Joseph Robinson, said of the President-elect, "When I talk to him he says, 'Fine! Fine! Fine!' But Joe Robinson goes to see him the next day and again he says, 'Fine! Fine! Fine!' Maybe he says 'Fine!' to everybody." So rapid had the processes of social disintegration become (even Eleanor Roosevelt wondered whether anyone could "do anything to save America now") that FDR's genial, vague, not-my-problem attitude seemed irresponsible. People thought that he ought to do *something* — and no one felt this more keenly than the outgoing President.

In November the President telegraphed the President-elect, suggesting that they confer. Roosevelt called at the White House on the way to Georgia, but although the meeting lasted the better part of an afternoon, it settled nothing. Word had reached Roosevelt that a member of the Hoover cabinet had said, "We now have the fellow in a hole that he is not going to be able to get out of." The hole had yet to be dug that FDR could not get out of; hour after hour he parried invitations to board the administration's sinking ship. After his visit he felt strengthened in his conviction not to commit himself, the wisdom of which grew upon him as he read the newspapers in Warm Springs. Hoover had sent the Hill his farewell State of the Union message, a recital of all his shibboleths. More taxes were needed. Europe should pay its war debts. "We have built a system of individualism. The background of our American system is that we should allow free play of social and economic forces." The country must have "confidence in the future."

America's patience was running out. So was its cash. On St. Valentine's Day 1933 — Hoover was singing his swan song at ten o'clock that evening before the Republican National Committee — the nation's banking system began its final collapse. That afternoon Governor William A. Comstock of Michigan had received an urgent telephone request to join a conference of bankers in downtown Detroit, and he had been there ever since. Detroit's Union Guardian Trust Company was in straits. If it failed it would probably take every other bank in the city with it, and the financiers were asking Comstock to declare a banking moratorium throughout Michigan. At midnight he agreed, drove to the state capitol at Lansing, and issued a proclamation closing the state's 550 banks for eight days. He called it a holiday.

In Washington, Hoover scribbled a letter to FDR; he was so distraught that he misspelled his successor's name on the envelope. The President-elect was becoming accustomed to jolts (the week before, an unemployed bricklayer had shot at him and fatally wounded Mayor Cermak of Chicago), and this communication was among the more outrageous. He read it carefully and then called it "cheeky." It was certainly that. Hoover said flatly that the country was afraid of what the new administration might do. In the name of patriotism (and of "confidence") he demanded that Roosevelt publicly promise not to change government programs. The outgoing President was fully aware of what he was asking; to Senator David A. Reed of Pennsylvania he wrote, "I realize that if these declarations are made by the President-elect, he will have ratified the whole major program of the Republican administration; that is, it means the abandonment of 90 percent of the so-called new deal." He had already told friends he thought FDR an amiable lightweight. Now he was treating him as a fool. When the declarations were not forthcoming, he changed his mind again; to Henry Stimson he said that Roosevelt was "a madman."

The President-elect would certainly have been of doubtful sanity had he associated himself with Hoover's policy, for by then it was clear that under that policy the entire country was going stone broke.

Michigan's plight had been especially aggravated by plunging real estate values, but the problem was nationwide. Since the Crash more than 5,500 banks had failed, and the public, understandably, was nervous. It responded by hoarding. Gold was vanishing from vaults at the rate of 20 million dollars a day, and depositors who couldn't get metal were taking paper, so that the Treasury was called upon to expand its currency at the very time the gold upon which it was based was disappearing.

Bank panics are always suicidal. In this crisis, however, the situation had been complicated by the three years of deflation. Even the soundest institutions held mortgages and securities which had fallen to a fraction of their former value. America's 18,569 banks had about six billion dollars in cash to meet 41 billion in deposits, and bankers forced to liquidate mortgages and securities to raise cash would suffer heavy losses.

Now that Michigan's banks had fallen, the daily outflow of gold from the rest of the country's banks abruptly jumped to 37 million; currency withdrawals to 122 million. Banks everywhere were swarming with breathless depositors taking out cash — in the Bronx a young mother rented her baby, at twenty-five cents a trip, to women who used it to claim preference at the head of withdrawal lines. During the week of February 20, while both houses of Congress were whooping through Prohibition repeal, the Baltimore Trust Company paid out 13 million dollars, nearly half of it on Friday. Late Friday night Governor Albert C. Ritchie declared a holiday for Maryland's two hundred banks. The second state had gone under.

Rallying to the standard of confidence, responsible men made painfully self-conscious efforts to keep their heads. The *Detroit News* commented, "It is an experience we shall have to look back upon, and no doubt grin over," and the *Baltimore Sun* said cheerily, "Life . . . will be filled with pleasant and unpleasant things as it was before. And it will have the additional advantage that everybody will have something to talk about." The president of the Baltimore Association of Commerce saw no reason why business should not continue as usual; the Bureau of Internal Revenue issued a stern reminder that income taxes were due in two weeks.

Nothing from Hyde Park dispelled the illusion of unreality. Roosevelt, as Robert Sherwood put it, knew that he had the advantage of "a good act to follow." Already a master of timing, he realized that the poorer Hoover's exit, the better his own entrance would be. If his refusal to cross bridges before he reached them was irresponsible — it is hard to see what he could have done — it was also in keeping with an old tradition in American politics. As Charles A. Beard pointed out, until Lincoln's hand was forced he "never adopted the system of unconditional emancipation. He understood it, but did not commit himself to it." All the same, there was an almost pixie quality about FDR's selection for Secretary of the Treasury — a puckish little railway equipment manufacturer who wore a gray toupee, loved puns, collected five-dollar gold pieces, and spent his leisure time composing on a guitar. A week later, when the new administration took office, the country was to know William H. Woodin as hard-driving and ingenious, but on the eve of office he was celebrated only as the composer of a song for children:

> *Let us be like bluebirds,*
> *Happy all day long,*
> *Forgetting all our troubles*
> *In a sunny song.*

In Indianapolis and Akron that Sunday, February 26, banks announced that withdrawals would be limited to 5 percent of balances. During the night institutions in a dozen other Ohio cities fell into line, and on Monday — as flames gutted the German Reichstag and Japanese troops marched into a Manchurian blizzard — the number grew to one hundred. Across the river from Cincinnati, five Covington, Kentucky, banks adopted similar restrictions. Monday evening Governor Gifford Pinchot of Pennsylvania signed a bill permitting individual institutions to close at will, and Thomas W. Lamont sent word to Hyde Park that in the view of J. P. Morgan, "the emergency could not be greater."

It could be, and soon was. By Wednesday, March 1, frantic governors had declared bank holidays in seventeen states. Pinchot acted so hurriedly he had to watch the inaugural five days later with 95 cents in his pocket. Governor Oscar K. Allen of Louisiana, on the other hand, withdrew his expense money for Washington and then entrained, leaving behind his dictated proclamation closing all banks. It was on Wednesday that the President-elect — who, Arthur Krock reported in the *New York Times*, was being asked by responsible men to seize power *now* — drove to his East Sixty-fifth Street town house and went into conference with Woodin. They did not emerge until Thursday afternoon, when, preceded by the screaming sirens of twenty motorcycles, they raced down Fifth Avenue and turned west toward the Hudson River ferry. During the morning a light snow had sifted over the city. New Yorkers stood silently in it, staring at the cavalcade. Outside Radio City Music Hall a cardboard King Kong, erected to dramatize his first Manhattan run, leered toothily. In the river the French Line steamer *Paris* lay quietly at berth, her cargo space reserved — though no one in the President-elect's party knew it yet — for nine million dollars in fleeing gold. On the other side of the ferry a special B & O train was waiting, and that afternoon, talking now with Woodin of banks, now with Farley of religion, Franklin Roosevelt thundered southward through a cold fog, toward Washington.

It was sleeting when they reached Union Station. In the presidential suite of the Mayflower Hotel a sheaf of telegrams awaited Roosevelt: banks were closed, or closing, in twenty-one states and the District of Columbia, and Federal Reserve figures showed the week's gold loss to be 226 million dollars. There wasn't enough money in the Treasury to meet the federal payroll, not to mention the 700 million dollars in short-term certificates which would fall due March 15. The President-elect had scarcely unpacked when Woodin drew him aside. Secretary of the Treasury Ogden Mills and Eugene Meyer of the Federal Reserve Board had telephoned to suggest a national proclamation closing all banks. President Hoover felt less drastic action would do. FDR's opinion was solicited. He shook his head; he still refused to advise anyone. Fair skies had been forecast for Saturday's inauguration, but now the barometer was falling.

The last page of the *New York Times* of Friday, March 3, carried an advertisement showing "John Doe" and "Jane Doe" acclaiming the "Good Work" of the Bowery Savings Bank. Presumably its purpose was to reassure depositors. It failed. By noon long lines of New Yorkers had formed opposite Grand Central Station and were filing into the world's largest private savings bank, demanding cash. At 3 P.M. the Bowery closed its doors with a huge crowd still unpaid. At the same hour Governor Henry Horner of Illinois sat in the Federal Reserve Bank of Chicago plucking nervously at his moustache, reading figures which showed that Chicago banks had paid out 350 million dollars in two weeks. After seventeen days in the hinterland, the storm was hammering at the nation's two financial strongholds.

That morning Miss Catherine Shea, a messenger for the Treasury Department, had brought Herbert Hoover his last $500 pay check. He received it with a semblance of cheer; reports reaching him before noon suggested that the panic might be lessening. After lunch it was clear that this was only an illusion. Minnesota and Kansas were gone, North Carolina and Virginia were going. Hoover, too exhausted and too embittered for the traditional inauguration eve dinner with the President-elect, formally received the Roosevelt family for tea at 4 P.M. By his lights, he had every right to be angry. In his words, the country was "on the verge of financial panic and chaos" — and all because this fellow from New York lacked confidence. At tea he reviewed his figures and asked Roosevelt to join him in bipartisan action. Once more FDR said he would wait; tomorrow he would be President. Preparing to go, he adjusted his leg braces. "Mr. President," he said, "I know it is customary to do so, but you don't have to return our call if you don't want to."

Hoover strode across the room and loomed above him menacingly. In his most cutting voice he said, "Mr. Roosevelt, when you have been in Washington as long as I have, you will learn that the President of the United States calls on nobody!" He turned his back to leave the room.

Jimmy Roosevelt glanced at his father; he had never seen him so angry. Before FDR could speak, Eleanor Roosevelt jumped up and said quickly, "It's been very pleasant, but we must go now."

In fact a complete break between the two men was impossible. Illinois and New York were on the brink; their governors, Horner and Herbert Lehman, had given up all hope of attending the inauguration. Back at the Mayflower, Roosevelt kept in touch with Hoover by telephone until 1 A.M., when he suggested that they both get some sleep. They did, and as they slept their advisers huddled at the Treasury Building and decided everything for them. Before them lay the latest bleak Federal Reserve report. During the last two days 500 million dollars had been drained from the nation's banking system. They were convinced that the New York bankers did not understand the enormity of the disaster and must be protected. Mills and Woodin agreed that Lehman must be persuaded to close the New York banks and that Horner must also declare a moratorium for Illinois. Horner proclaimed his holiday at 2 A.M.; Lehman's decision came at 4:20 A.M. Hoover was told at 6 A.M. "We are at the end of our string," he said. "There is nothing more we can do."

The financial heart of the country had stopped beating. Banking in every state was wholly or partly suspended. Flags flew in Wall Street honoring the inauguration, but the Stock Exchange was officially closed, and so, for the first time in eighty-five years, was the Chicago Board of Trade. On Manhattan's Fifth Avenue, Norman Vincent Peale was writing a sermon for delivery the following morning demanding that bankers and corporation heads get down on their knees before God and confess their sins. In Kansas, Governor Landon was calling industrialists "racketeers." Arthur Krock compared the atmosphere in Washington to "that which might be found in a beleaguered capital in wartime." The sky was the color of slate. Over a hundred thousand people blackened the forty acres of park and pavement in front of the Capitol's east facade, awaiting the inaugural. General MacArthur was in command of the inauguration parade, and he anticipated trouble. (It says something about the departing administration that Walter F. Brown, the outgoing Postmaster General, had requisitioned a new limousine for the occasion because he could not sit erect in the old one while wearing his tall silk hat.) Army machine guns had been mounted at strategic points. In many ways the occasion had the marks of an impromptu affair. John Nance Garner wore a borrowed muffler against the chill wind. Woodin, unable to reach his seat, perched on a railing with a cameraman.

The Capitol clocks struck twelve noon. Franklin Delano Roosevelt had at last become the thirty-second President of the United States.

Hatless and coatless, he threw back his great shoulders and repeated the oath after Chief Justice Charles Evans Hughes. The new President's hand lay on the three-hundred-year-old Roosevelt family Bible, open at the thirteenth chapter of Paul's First Epistle to the Corinthians:

Though I speak with the tongues of men and of angels, and have not charity, I am become as sounding brass, or a tinkling cymbal.

And though I have the gift of prophecy and understand all mysteries, and all knowledge; and though I have faith, so that I could remove mountains, and have not charity, I am nothing.

He turned to the podium. Ignoring applause, he drew from his pocket a longhand manuscript which he had written in his Hyde Park study the Sunday before. No phrase was borrowed; it was pure Roosevelt:

"Let me first assert my firm belief that the only thing we have to fear is fear itself — nameless, unreasoning, unjustified terror which paralyzes needed efforts to convert retreat into advance."

The radio networks carried his ringing voice out across the suffering land, over the sweatshops and flophouses, the Hoovervilles and hobo jungles, the rocky soil tilled by tenant farmers, the ragged men shivering in the iron cold outside factory gates.

"I shall ask the Congress for the one remaining instrument to meet the crisis — broad Executive power to wage a war against the emergency, as great as the power that would be given me if we were in fact invaded by a foreign foe."

Herbert Hoover slumped and stared at his feet, but in the three-decker tenements with radios the hungry children looked up; in county court-houses the embattled farmers looked up; housewives patching threadbare clothes looked up; there was a kind of magic in the air; and in Santa Monica Will Rogers pecked out on his typewriter: "If he burned down the Capitol, we would cheer and say, 'Well, we at least got a fire started somehow.'"

"The people of the United States have not failed. In their need they have registered a mandate that they want direct, vigorous action. They have asked for discipline and direction under leadership. They have made me the present instrument of their wishes. In the spirit of the gift I take it."

In Walt Whitman's phrase, the new President had made a "tremendous entrance"; Roosevelt's face was "so grim," wrote Arthur Krock, "as to seem unfamiliar to those who have long known him." Henry L. Stimson confided to his diary, "I was thoroughly scared." The new First Lady thought the inaugural "very, very solemn and a little terrifying" because "when Frank-lin got to that part of his speech when it might become necessary for him to assume powers ordinarily granted to a President in wartime, he re-ceived his biggest demonstration." Edmund Wilson, in Washington to cover the ceremonies for the *New Republic,* scorned "the old unctuousness, the old pulpit vagueness." At the same time he wrote, "The thing that emerges most clearly is the warning of a dictatorship." The intellectuals still didn't understand FDR; some of them never would. Indeed, the man was mys-terious even to those closest to him. It is a remarkable fact that he had not told his own wife of his decision to run for the Presidency; she had learned it from Louis Howe. Perhaps she came closest to the mood of thoughtful people in those first hours of his first administration when she said, "One has the feeling of going it blindly, because we're in a tremen-dous stream, and none of us know where we're going to land." Yet the peo-ple, on the whole, did not share her uncertainty. To them the speech had been a triumph; that weekend 450,000 wrote Roosevelt to tell him so.

Eleanor went to the inaugural ball while her husband stayed in the Executive Mansion to work with Howe. Sunday morning after breakfast the President had himself wheeled down newly installed ramps and into the empty oval office. Alone, he contemplated the room. The desk was empty. Hoover had taken everything movable except the flag and the great seal. There was no pad, no pencil, no telephone, not even a buzzer to summon help. Slowly it came to him that he could do nothing by himself here. He gave a great shout, and his secretary and an aide came running. The incident was notable because it was the last time he would feel utterly helpless as President. By that evening he was ready to act. His cigarette holder atilt, he invoked the World War's half forgotten Trading with the Enemy Act to declare a four-day holiday for all banks. The 73rd Congress was being called into special session Thursday, when emergency legislation would be ready. Meantime the country would have to manage without moneychangers.

It was a challenge to American ingenuity, and it was met by improvised combinations of scrip, credit, barter, stamps, streetcar tokens, Canadian dollars, and Mexican pesos. The Dow Chemical Company was coining magnesium into "Dow-metal Money," with an arbitrary value of twenty cents. A Wisconsin wrestler signed a contract to perform for a can of tomatoes and a peck of potatoes; an Ashtabula, Ohio, newspaper offered free ads in exchange for produce. A New York state senator arrived in Albany with twelve dozen eggs and a side of pork to see him through the week. The most spectacular transactions were conducted by the *New York Daily News,* which was sponsoring the semifinals of the Golden Gloves tournament in Madison Square Garden. The seat price was fifty cents, but any article worth that amount was accepted as admission provided the five-cent amusement tax was paid. An appraiser was engaged who during the evening inspected frankfurters, mattresses, hats, shoes, overcoats, fish, noodles, nightgowns, steaks, spark plugs, box cameras, jigsaw puzzles, sweaters, canned goods, sacks of potatoes, golf knickers, mechanics' tools, foot balm, copies of the New Testament, and what girls of that day called step-ins.

Nearly everyone assumed the holiday would end with the formal adoption of scrip — local currencies, managed by states, cities, and individual firms. Atlanta, Richmond, Mattituck, and Knoxville, of all places, were already on the stuff; before the week of March 6 was out Nashville would have a million dollars of it in circulation and Philadelphia eight million. In Nutley, New Jersey, a paper company which had been working three days a week went on three shifts, turning out six tons of scrip for Wisconsin and Tennessee. To Secretary of the Treasury Woodin, however, the thought of state and municipal currencies and company certificates floating around the country was appalling, and at breakfast on Tuesday, March 7, he told Ray Moley that he had decided scrip wasn't needed. "We can issue currency against the sound assets of the banks," he said. "It won't frighten people. It won't look like stage money. It'll be money that looks like money." There was nothing to lose. After all, he said publicly, "We're on the bottom. We're not going any lower."

Working around the clock in his Carlton Hotel suite with Senator Carter Glass, Woodin met Thursday's legislative deadline. As congressmen filed into the special session the finished bill was handed to the clerk — "My name's Bill, and I'm finished, too," Woodin muttered — and was read aloud. Few representatives heard it above the hubbub. They had no copies of their own; there had been no time to print them. Even the copy given to the clerk bore last-minute changes scribbled in pencil. In thirty-eight minutes they whooped it through while Mrs. Roosevelt sat knitting in the gallery like a benign Madame Defarge, counting votes. Then they crowded into the Senate chamber to hear Glass explain just what it was they had done.

The little Virginian backed it, though he acknowledged there were parts which shocked him. It was, in fact, a shocking measure, ratifying all acts "heretofore *or hereinafter* taken" by the President and the Secretary of the Treasury. It provided prison terms for hoarders, appointed "conservators" (receivers) for weak banks, and authorized the issue of two billion dollars in new currency based on bank assets. At 8:36 P.M. a rumpled Roosevelt signed it in the White House, surrounded by unpacked books and pictures from Hyde Park. That evening the Bureau of Engraving and Printing recruited 375 new workers. The official printing presses of the United States were going into action.

All that night and the next the lights of the Bureau twinkled across the tidal basin. There was no time to engrave new dies, so plates bearing the imprint "Series of 1929" were used. There wasn't even an opportunity to acquire facsimile signatures from each of the twelve Federal Reserve banks; signatures were taken from government files and sent by messenger to the American Type Foundry in Jersey City, where logotypes were cut. Early Saturday morning planes began taking off from Washington bearing bales of cash. The first were received in the New York Federal Reserve bank shortly before noon. Transfer to member banks began immediately.

The real trick was prying open the rigid fists of hoarders, who in one week had taken 15 percent of the nation's currency out of circulation. Even a bewitched Congress couldn't make the penal clauses apply to hoarding that had already taken place. Instead, the government turned to the spur of publicity. On Wednesday, March 8, the Federal Reserve Board announced that its banks would prepare lists of persons who had withdrawn gold since February 1 and who failed to bring it back by the following Monday. Newspapers had scarcely appeared with this announcement before bank switchboards were jammed. Callers were told only that if they had gold and wanted to return it, the banks would open for them and newspapermen would be kept out of the lobbies. In the next few hours thousands of mattresses were torn open, cans dug up, hidden boxes brought forth. Banks everywhere reported long queues, reminiscent of the preceding week's panic but comprised this time of men and women carrying Gladstones and briefcases. Encouraged, the board extended its order on Friday, asking for reports covering withdrawals of the past two years. The widened hunt brought bigger game; by Saturday night the Federal Reserve banks had recovered 300 million dollars in gold and gold certificates — enough to support 750 million dollars in additional circulation. And even before the planes flew out from Hoover Airport with new bank notes, Woodin had permitted individual savings banks to release ten dollars to each depositor. Business began to stir. Within a week 13,500 — 75 percent

— of the country's banks were back in business, and gongs were heard again in stock exchanges. In New York, where stocks jumped 15 percent, the Dow Jones ticker clicked off the message "Happy Days Are Here Again."

They weren't really. But the panic had ended without currency chaos or nationalization of the banks. Undoubtedly the medicine had been strong; the inflationary movement, once started, would prove irresistible in the long run. Yet Roosevelt had had very few options. A friend told him that if he succeeded he would go down in history as the greatest American President and that if he failed he would be known as the worst. FDR replied, "If I fail I shall be the last one." But he had no intention of failing. His Hundred Days had begun.

In the eye of the Hundred Days hurricane — from March 9, when the Emergency Banking Act was cheered into law, to the passage of the National Industrial Recovery Act (NIRA) on June 16 — the new Chief Executive was continually revealing fresh reservoirs of imagination and energy. Before Congress adjourned in exhaustion he would have delivered ten major speeches, given birth to a new foreign policy, presided over press conferences and cabinet meetings twice a week, taken the country off the gold standard, sent fifteen messages to the Capitol, and shepherded through its chambers thirteen major pieces of legislation, including insurance for all bank deposits, refinancing of home mortgages, Wall Street reforms, authorization for nearly four billion dollars in federal relief, legalization of beer, and laws creating the Civilian Conservation Corps (CCC), the Agricultural Adjustment Administration (AAA), and Tennessee Valley Authority (TVA). "Occasionally," he remarked at one point, "I think I am a bit shell-shocked."

It was all improvised. "Take a method and try it," he told his New Dealers. "If it fails, try another. But above all, try something." He interpreted his landslide victory as a mandate for change, almost any change, as long as it was quick. At first he had planned to put through Woodin's save-the-banks law, send Congress home, and work with the powers of the Presidency. Such a step would have been supported by the national consensus. The hour demanded "dictatorial authority," the conservative *Boston Evening Transcript* editorialized. "This is unprecedented in its implications, but such is the desperate temper of the people that it is welcome." Senator Burton K. Wheeler said congressmen would "jump through a hoop" for the new President, and their constituents, said Charles Michelson, were ready to believe FDR could "see in the dark." Later, John Gunther was to suggest that the President could easily have become a dictator: "We are apt to forget nowadays the immense, unprecedented, overwhelming authority conferred on FDR by an enthusiastically willing Congress during the first hundred days of his first administration. The Reichstag did not give Hitler much more."

Roosevelt preferred to work within the Constitution. He said he wanted to become a "preaching President," like his cousin Theodore Roosevelt, and the tremendous volume of White House mail suggested to him that his legislative revolution — for it amounted to that — might well be accompanied by a campaign to educate the people about the New Deal goals. He had no U.S. Information Agency, no Voice of America. He didn't need one; with him as teacher, the country became one vast classroom.

The first lesson came on his fifth day in power, when he assembled the White House correspondents around his desk. It was the first of what would become an unequaled number of press conferences (998), and it was an instant success. Will Rogers commented that Roosevelt could take a complicated subject like banking and explain it so that everyone could understand it, even the bankers; subsequently Charles A. Beard, no Roosevelt admirer, wrote that FDR discussed "more fundamental problems of American life and society than all the other Presidents combined." At the end the correspondents burst into applause. In one stroke the President had shifted the news capital of the country from New York to Washington. The United Press tripled its Washington staff; 25 percent of all Associated Press news was coming from the capital. Metropolitan newspapers sent men to cover the White House, and smaller papers began running syndicated Washington columnists, who were joined, in time, by the President's own wife.

On Sunday, March 12, Roosevelt preached his second lesson directly to the people. Microphones of the National, Columbia, and Mutual broadcasting systems were installed on the ground floor of the Executive Mansion in front of the fireplace in the Diplomatic Reception Room. The President said he wanted to catch the spirit of a man in his own home talking informally to his neighbors in their living rooms. In that case, said Harry C. Butcher, manager of the CBS Washington office, the talk might be called a "fireside chat," and so it was christened. His cigarette burning down in its long ivory holder, FDR spoke to the nation about the bank moratorium: "My friends, I want to tell you what has been done in the last few days, why it was done, and what the next steps are going to be. First of all, let me state the simple fact that when you deposit money in a bank the bank does not put the money into a safe-deposit vault. It invests your money in many different forms of credit — bonds, mortgages. In other words, the bank puts your money to work to keep the wheels turning around. . . ."

Somehow he did it without condescension, translating the complexities of an industrial economy into phrases and metaphors almost anyone could comprehend. His language was plain and functional — and so was the decor he was introducing into the White House. The elegant trappings of the previous administration were being chucked out. There were no footmen, no buglers, no trooping of the colors, no changing of the guard, and above all, no seven-course meals. Roosevelt's cuisine was perhaps the least distinguished in official Washington. He couldn't become a gourmet; he hadn't the time. Guests who spent any amount of time in the mansion compared the monotonous fare to that of a boardinghouse. One woman was served the same dessert three evenings in a row: a single slice of pineapple with two cherries and a walnut lying in a pool of watery whipped cream. Even so, she was getting something of a treat; the President's lunches — hash with one poached egg — cost nineteen cents.

In a sense all this was deceptive. He didn't need the accouterments of power because he had the real thing. In Arthur M. Schlesinger Jr.'s felicitous phrase, FDR was a "natural President." Few men in history have dominated their times as he did. He ran his administration as a one-man show, and loved to exercise authority. "Wouldn't you be President if you could?" he jovially asked one visitor. "Wouldn't anybody?" After meeting him, Dr. Carl Gustav Jung said, "Make no mistake, he is a force — a man of superior but impenetrable mind, but perfectly ruthless, a highly versatile mind which you cannot foresee." W. M. Kiplinger had never known any President "as omnipotent as this Roosevelt." Ed Flynn observed that FDR's aides and cabinet members were little more than messenger boys, that "he really made his own decisions." Arthur Krock reported that he was "the boss, the dynamo, the works." At no time, wrote Henry Morgenthau, was Roosevelt "anything else but a ruler." Morgenthau liked to argue with FDR. FDR enjoyed it, too — up to a point. Then the big freckled fist would bang down on the desk, then he would stop saying "I think" and start saying "The *President* thinks." The argument was over, and there was no doubt about who had won it.

The President opened a typical fourteen-hour day by breakfasting in bed while skimming through diplomatic cables and clouds of newspaper. The bedroom walls were decorated with pictures of ships, the mantel with family photographs and Victorian bric-a-brac. During the Hundred Days favored advisers would come in for bedside conferences, but usually he had this time to himself. Sometime after nine o'clock he would shave and then dress with the help of his valet, Irvin McDuffie, who would push him to his office in the small, armless presidential wheelchair. The day's appointments would begin at ten o'clock. If Congress was in session he would spend a full quarter of his time on the telephone. He always used first names. In the first week of his administration, before Washington had become accustomed to Secretary of Labor Frances Perkins's brown tricorne hat or she to Washington, one of her assistants picked up a phone and heard a voice say, "This is Frank. May I talk to Miss Perkins?" The assistant relayed the message. The secretary said, "Frank? I don't know any Frank. Ask him whom he's with." Questioned, the caller chuckled and said, "With the United States. This is the President."

He would accept calls at almost any time, even in the middle of a cabinet meeting. His availability was astonishing; about one hundred people could get through to him without first stating their business to a secretary.* It

---

*By contrast Robert S. McNamara, the most available high official thirty years later, could be so reached by only twenty-five people.

was hard to remember he was crippled; his sources of information seemed unlimited. In cabinet meetings he would quote people from all over the country, including Mrs. Roosevelt — "My Missus," he would remark, "says there's typhoid fever in that district." One of his first orders as President was that people in distress who telephoned the White House for help should never be shut off; someone in the administration must be found to talk to them. This brought him the most remarkable correspondence in presidential history. One note ran:

> Dear Mr. President:
>   This is just to tell you that everything is all right now. The man you sent found our house all right, and we went down to the bank with him and the mortgage can go on for a while longer. You remember I wrote you about losing the furniture too. Well, your man got it back for us. I never heard of a President like you.

Nor had anyone else. His daily mail was running between 5,000 and 8,000 letters, ten times Hoover's. One congressman compared him to Jesus Christ, and in a poll among New York schoolchildren God ran a poor second to FDR. Americans really felt that they *were* his friends. Forty-one popular songs were written about him. And when he locked his braces and appeared in public, people literally reached out to touch the hem of his cape. In New York, the cast for *Strike Me Pink* responded to curtain calls by singing, to the tune of "Wintergreen for President," Roosevelt is President!" — and never failed to bring the crowd to its feet in a roaring ovation. Anne O'Hare McCormick observed in the *New York Times* that "no President in so short a time has inspired so much hope." Even Pierre Du Pont and William Randolph Hearst were delighted; a tycoon told John T. Flynn that he considered Roosevelt the greatest leader since Jesus Christ, and he just hoped God would forgive him his vote for Hoover. Walter Lippmann, revising his earlier estimate, wrote, "In one week, the nation, which had lost confidence in everything and everybody, has regained confidence in the government and in itself."

Roosevelt's magnetism lured swarms of bright young men from campuses and offices. Suddenly the most flourishing business in the capital was the boardinghouse industry; the huge old brownstone mansions lining G Street, R Street, New Hampshire Avenue, and Twenty-first Street were converted to housing for New Deal bachelors. Traditionalists in the capital were appalled; Arthur M. Schlesinger Jr. later talked to one who said, "A plague of young lawyers settled on Washington. . . . They floated airily into offices, took desks, asked for papers and found no end of things to be busy about. I never found out why they came, what they did or why they left."

Some never left, or left to come back in other roles. Among those rallying to the New Deal banner were Dean Acheson, Undersecretary of the Treasury; J. W. Fulbright, a young lawyer in the Department of Justice; Hubert H. Humphrey, who quit studying pharmacy to become a relief administrator; and Henry Fowler, a TVA lawyer. One of the most efficient new-comers was Lyndon B. Johnson, administrative assistant to Congressman Richard Kleberg of Texas. Johnson contrived to step briefly into the public eye by persuading the White House that the first farmer to plow under a part of his cotton crop as part of the AAA war on agricultural surpluses should be one of Kleberg's constituents.

Minor deities in the New Deal constellation were Sam Rosenman, Rexford Tugwell, Adolf Berle, "Ironpants" Johnson; Harold Ickes, who secretly liked his public nickname, "the old curmudgeon" (and was unaware that Roosevelt privately called him "Donald Duck"), and Ray Moley, the lordly occupant of a Washington hotel suite and the brightest of the lot, of whom more obscure men sang:

> *Moley! Moley! Moley!*
> *Lord God Almighty!*

Morale was particularly high in the Department of Agriculture. The new general counsel there, Jerome N. Frank, had recruited a dazzling group of young attorneys: Thurmond Arnold, Abe Fortas, Adlai Stevenson, Nathaniel Weyl, John Abt, Nathan Witt, Lee Pressman, and Pressman's Harvard Law School classmate Alger Hiss. Admirers in other departments agreed that one day fame would come to most of them, especially Hiss.

Hiss, Pressman, Witt, Abt, and Weyl were members of a Communist party cell which met secretly in a Connecticut Avenue music studio. They were studying the new administration, and they were confused, which is not surprising; Moley was then regarded as a passionate liberal, while Secretary of Agriculture Henry A. Wallace was vehemently opposed to the diplomatic recognition of Russia. Communism set class against class, he argued, sounding like Al Smith. Most puzzling of all was the President. On inauguration day Roosevelt was empirical but still conservative, and his early measures strengthened his right-of-center support. It is curious to note that his first measure, once he had rescued the banks, was a bill cutting veterans' pensions and government salaries, including those of congressmen.

His Civilian Conservation Corps (CCC), which put slum youths to work on conservation projects, was also popular with conservatives. A Communist spokesman called it "forced labor" and William Green of the AFL said it smacked "of fascism, of Hitlerism, of a form of Sovietism." But the CCC was Roosevelt's pet project, and thanks to Army help it was an instant success. Organized by MacArthur, it brought to the President's attention a colonel named George C. Marshall, who made his reputation by his efficient administration of seventeen CCC camps in the South. (Major Eisenhower ran into trouble in Pennsylvania by appointing Republicans to all key posts; it hadn't occurred to him to consider their politics.) Eventually over two and a half million boys wore the forest-green CCC uniform, planting two hundred million trees in a shelterbelt conceived by FDR and stretching from Texas to Canada.

The President's departure from the gold standard on April 19 was less popular with the right, for reasons which now seem rooted in superstition. For centuries Europeans and Americans had clung to gold in the belief that it was the hallmark of Western culture; during the Victorian age gold had become identified with great powers, silver with backward countries. Some Republicans called devaluation a "rubber dollar program," Al Smith said that he was "for gold dollars as against baloney dollars," and Roosevelt's own budget director said the executive action meant "the end of Western civilization." However, an 88.5-cent dollar — by summer it had leveled off at 83 cents — meant America could once more compete in world markets with European nations which had already turned to inflation. If Main Street didn't understand this, Wall Street did. Charles G. Dawes applauded; so did the Republican leadership. Russell Leffingwell, a Morgan partner, wrote Roosevelt, "Your action in going off gold saved the country from complete collapse," and J. P. Morgan himself stifled criticism by declaring in a rare public statement that "I welcome the reported action of the President. . . . It seems to be clear that the way out of the Depression is to combat and overcome the deflationary forces."

Any move welcomed at 23 Wall Street could scarcely be called revolutionary or even liberal. Roosevelt's turn to the left didn't come until late March, when he asked Congress for the Agricultural Adjustment Act and the Federal Emergency Relief Act, and he signed both on May 12, the sixty-fifth of the Hundred Days. Triple-A was a direct response to the Iowa insurrectionists; it raised prices by creating scarcity. The idea of paying a farmer *not* to farm was a flagrant violation of the conventional wisdom. Henry Wallace spoke for millions when he said, "I hope we shall never have to resort to it again. To destroy a standing crop goes against the soundest instincts of human nature." Four months later he had to authorize the slaughter of six million little pigs. He hated to do it, and blamed Coolidge-Hoover policies for making it necessary. (FDR casually suggested birth control for hogs.)

Federal relief was more controversial in the long run, but as Harry Hopkins tartly observed at a congressional hearing, "People don't eat in the long run, Senator, they eat every day." Lanky, tousled, sardonic Hopkins, whose relationship with the President was to outlast the New Deal, had been fighting the Depression as a New York social worker. He had entered the administration underneath a staircase. He couldn't reach the President, so he buttonholed Frances Perkins at a crowded New York function, led her to a nook under the stairs — in the hubbub it was the only place he could make himself heard — and explained the urgent need for national relief. Miss Perkins recommended him to FDR, and FDR recommended his program to Congress. Republicans were shocked. Representative Robert Luce of Massachusetts called it "socialism"; Representative Carroll L. Beedy of Maine cried, "God save the people of the United States!"

But their God had failed; it was Roosevelt's turn, and on May 22 he brought Hopkins to Washington. Under changing leadership (Hopkins, Ickes, and back to Hopkins) and various titles — Civil Works Administration (CWA), Works Progress Administration (WPA), Public Works Administration (PWA) — federal relief was to continue until 1942. "I'm here to see that people don't starve," Hopkins said bluntly. Fiorello La Guardia said, "I can go down to the market here and buy a parrot for two dollars, and in one day I can teach it to say, 'Dole, dole, dole.' But that parrot would never understand an economic problem." Opponents of relief were unimpressed, and the words they used were far less polite than dole. Sweatshop owners in the North and southern planters were furious because their sources of cheap labor were depleted. To upper-middle-class critics, the symbol of the reliefer would forever be a man leaning on a shovel or a rake, and their greatest triumph was the distortion of an obscure word. Testifying before a New York aldermanic inquiry, a handicraft teacher named Robert Marshall explained that he taught unemployed men how to make boondoggles — a word coined in 1925 by an upstate scoutmaster to describe such useful pioneer handiwork as weaving belts from rope. Presently newspaper editorials all over the country were ridiculing "boondoggling," and they were so successful that millions of subscribers believed (and still believe) that make-work was all Hopkins and Ickes achieved.

In point of fact, both administrators despised idleness. Hopkins in particular felt that relief without jobs would destroy individual pride. He liked to hear women say, "We're not on relief any more. My husband works for the government." And for the most part it *was* work, and hard work at that. CWA, WPA, and PWA funds went into over thirty thousand New Deal projects, paying teachers and building waterworks, post offices, bridges, jails, airports, sewers, culverts, public swimming pools, athletic fields, playgrounds, power plants, and railroad stations. During Hopkins's years in Washington he was responsible for 10 percent of all new roads in America, 35 percent of all new hospitals, 65 percent of new city halls, courthouses, and health facilities, and 70 percent of new schools. Denver was given a water supply system; Ohio's Muskingum Valley a flood control system; Brownsville, Texas, a port; and Key West roads and bridges connecting it with the Florida mainland.

Investing in projects beyond the scope of private enterprise, the WPA, with its forerunners and derivatives, transformed America. It built the Lincoln Tunnel, connecting New York and New Jersey under the Hudson, and the Triborough Bridge, linking Manhattan and Long Island. It electrified the Pennsylvania Railroad. It underwrote the first diesel engines. The District of Columbia owes its zoo, its mall, and the Federal Trade Commission its building to the WPA. Without WPA workers California would lack the Camarillo Mental Hospital, Kentucky the Fort Knox gold depository, San Francisco its fairgrounds, Dallas its Dealey Plaza, St. Louis its floral conservatory, the Columbia River its Bonneville Dam, and the Colorado its Boulder Dam. Nearly two hundred WPA men lost their lives building Boulder Dam, which the Republicans liked so much that when they regained control of Congress in 1946 they renamed it Hoover Dam. And all the relief projects combined cost less than twenty billion dollars — one-fourth of the Pentagon's annual budget in the first Nixon administration.

The *Army and Navy Register* later reported that in these years, "when the regular appropriations for the armed services were so meager, it was the WPA worker who saved many army posts and naval stations from literal obsolescence." Without WPA undertakings the wartime and post-war expansion of American business would have been impossible, and without TVA, another inspiration of the Hundred Days, the two atomic bombs which ended World War II could never have been constructed — a mixed blessing, to be sure, but one which must be set against the dead certainty that the Soviet Union would have mastered the challenges of nuclear weapon production by the mid-1950s anyhow. Of course, that was not TVA's primary goal. It began with a series of Tennessee River dams, providing and selling electrical power to the people that lived in the valley. In the end it saved three million acres from erosion, multiplied the average income in the valley tenfold, and repaid its original investment in federal taxes. TVA had long been the dream of Senator George Norris; it came true because Franklin Roosevelt, while still unpacking in the White House, sent Norris a note saying that "as soon as this rush of emergency legislation is over" he hoped Norris would come and talk to him about "the Tennessee Basin development." Under such a President, people began to feel that anything was possible.

Some things were impossible. Banks could be saved, farmers rescued, the hungry fed, and the mighty Tennessee tamed, but the United States was an industrial nation, and no law could solve industry's problems. Roosevelt tried. The National Recovery Administration (NRA) was the New Deal's greatest effort. It cannot be dismissed as a total failure. The NRA lifted men's hearts, and it is arguable that by strengthening organized labor it contributed enormously to eventual recovery. If it did not fulfill Roosevelt's hopes for it — and clearly it did not — it did give the country a kind of temporary wartime unity. The NRA was like a spectacularly successful football rally followed by a lost game, or, as General Hugh Johnson predicted at the outset in a splendid mix of metaphors, "It will be red fire at first and dead cats afterwards. This is just like mounting the guillotine on the infinitesimal gamble that the ax won't work."

Johnson, the most colorful of the New Dealers, was chosen to administer the NRA. Possibly his everybody's-a-rink-stink-but-Hughie attitude injured its chances. He denounced people who obstructed him as men "in whose veins there must flow something more than a trace of rodent blood," or "perfumed guys from the State Department," or "merchants of bunk, guff, and hooey," and he hurt Herbert Hoover's feelings by comparing offices in the Commerce Building to pay toilets in Union Station. But NRA's problems were visible when the idea first surfaced in FDR's second fireside chat, on May 7. The President said he wanted "a partnership in planning" between business and government, with the government having the right to "prevent, with the assistance of the overwhelming majority in that industry, unfair practices and to enforce this agreement by the authority of government."

His purpose, which every decent businessman could endorse, was the elimination of cutthroat competition and the sweating of women and children. But the industry-by-industry codes inevitably meant the end of trust-busting and the return of price-fixing. Labor was jittery, so Donald R. Richberg, counsel for the Railway Brotherhoods, persuaded Johnson to write NRA's historic section 7(a), legitimizing collective bargaining and thus providing impetus to the labor movement of the 1930s. Big business saw it coming. In Senate hearings the National Association of Manufacturers and the Chamber of Commerce protested bitterly. Roosevelt summoned disputants and advocates of the bill to a White House conference, which lasted until they reached an agreement on wording. They emerged with 7(a) intact, but it was an inauspicious beginning. The industrialists and their legislative spokesmen had gone along only because some of them believed in abolishing all free enterprise. As Ralph Flanders, then president of the Jones & Lamson Machine Company, put it, they were "thoroughly sold on the idea that recovery and prosperity depended on the restraint of competition."

Ironpants Johnson was such a superb showman that these prickly issues were undiscovered through most of 1933. Henry Wallace had told him about thunderbirds, and the general drew a blue eagle based on the old Indian ideogram. Under it he lettered the legend *We Do Our Part*. To the press he growled, "May God have mercy on the man or group of men who attempt to trifle with this bird." Firms which complied with his codes were entitled to display blue eagles. Consumers affixed eagle decals on their windshields, *Time* printed the symbol on its covers each week. Four girls had it tattooed on their backs. In a San Francisco baseball park eight thousand children stood in formation to form a gigantic NRA eagle, and Busby Berkeley, not to be outdone, rewrote the finale of *Footlight Parade* so that Ruby Keeler, Dick Powell, Joan Blondell, and every extra in Hollywood formed (1) the American flag, (2) the profile of FDR, and (3) Johnson's eagle. It was dazzling, it was exhilarating, and with the general racing around the country getting his codes signed, it looked real.

Much of it was. By midsummer some nine million workers were under NRA work and wage codes signed by one million employers. But most of these were small businessmen. Of the ten largest industries — textiles, coal, petroleum, steel, automobiles, lumber, garments, wholesale trade, retail trade and construction — only textiles had signed up, and that had taken six weeks of furious campaigning. There were mutinous sounds in New Deal ranks; "Hugh," said Hopkins, "your codes stink." Indifferent to the blue thunderbird, coal mine guards were shooting miners, and Henry Ford refused to do his part. Johnson traded in his Lincoln for a Cadillac. The President ordered government departments and bureaus to do business only with NRA firms. A newspaperman asked Johnson what would happen to objectors who wouldn't go along with the codes. Wiping beer suds from his lips, he snapped, "They'll get a sock right on the nose."

Then the general changed his strategy. He launched a nationwide campaign to pledge all employers to a twelve-dollar, forty-hour week; formal codification would come later. The President made it the subject of his third fireside chat, on July 24, 1933: "In war, in the gloom of night attack, soldiers wear a bright badge on their shoulders to be sure that comrades do not fire on comrades. On that principle, those who cooperate in this program must know each other at a glance." The implication was plain — do your part or lie low. The NRA now took on an evangelical air. Mayor James Michael Curley assembled a hundred thousand children on Boston Common and led them in the pledge: "I promise as a good American citizen to do my part for the NRA. I will buy only where the Blue Eagle flies. I will ask my family to buy in September and buy American-made goods. I will help President Roosevelt bring back good times."

Every community with any civic pride held an NRA parade, with floats and bands playing "Happy Days Are Here Again." New York's eclipsed all the rest. For ten hours two million New Yorkers watched a quarter-million marchers. Symphony conductor Walter Damrosch led the radio workers, Charles Winninger the actors, Al Jolson the motion picture employees. There were a thousand barbers; ten thousand bankers, brokers, and stock exchange clerks; and twenty thousand garment workers. At the reviewing stand, fifty carrier pigeons were released, carrying good wishes to FDR. Night fell, the Fifth Avenue lights went on, and still the delegations came tramping out of Washington Square — grocers, jewelers, pawnbrokers, butchers, firemen, policemen, librarians, druggists, book publishers, and bartenders. But you didn't have to be in New York to feel the enthusiasm. In Tulsa, Hugh Johnson's seventy-seven-year-old mother led the parade, warning, "People had better obey the NRA, because my son will enforce it like lightning, and you can never tell where lightning will strike." Everywhere, wrote Heywood Broun, marchers felt hope and confidence: "When a line forms and your shoulder touches that of a fellow and a comrade, solidarity is about to be born." Suddenly General Johnson was flooded with draft codes, two million of them. Every major industry endorsed the NRA except automobiles and coal; then the car makers joined (Ford remained an exception) and, finally, coal. In the general enthusiasm, even Herbert Hoover signed an NRA pledge.

Then came the reaction. Hoover changed his mind and decided that the

NRA was totalitarian. Businessmen denounced it as "creeping socialism" and union leaders as "business fascism." William Randolph Hearst charged that NRA stood for No Recovery Allowed. A writer for *Harper's Magazine* toured four states and found that firms displaying blue eagles were guilty of monstrous NRA violations. Of the more than 700 codes, 568 had price-fixing clauses, which is presumably what Hopkins had had in mind. Walter Lippmann wrote of the NRA that "The excessive centralization and the dictatorial spirit are producing a revulsion of feeling against bureaucratic control of American economic life."

What had happened? Earlier in the year columnists and industrialists had been begging the President to become a dictator. The difference now was that he had turned the country around; he was paying the price of success. During his first four months in the White House, the Federal Reserve Board's adjusted index for industrial production had risen from 59 to 100. Brokers spoke of "the Roosevelt market." Men who would have been too weak or too frightened to oppose Johnson in March were now dealing from strength. "We have had our revolution," said *Collier's*, "and we like it." "Up go the prices of stocks and bonds, adding millions of value," cheered the *Literary Digest*. "Up go the prices of wheat, corn and other commodities, putting millions into the pockets of Depression-harried farmers." The *Digest* didn't mention the AAA, which was directly responsible for farm price rises, but the *New York Times* declared that Roosevelt had turned an unprecedented crisis into a personal triumph: "That was because he seemed to the American people to be riding the whirlwind and directing the storm. The country was ready and even anxious to accept any leadership. From President Roosevelt it got a rapid succession of courageous speeches and achievements which inclined millions of his fellow citizens to acclaim him as the heaven-sent man of the hour." Roosevelt, said Ray Moley, had saved capitalism.

The institution of the Presidency had been transformed. When Roosevelt rode up Capitol Hill bystanders clapped loudly; and Secret Service agent Richard Jervis, who had guarded Hoover for four years, said, "It sounds good to hear that again." In August the President jauntily greeted a press conference with the announcement, "I have some rather grand news for you." A year earlier it would have been incredible: a government 500-million-dollar issue of 3.25 percent bonds — the first long-term Treasury issue since September 1931 — had been oversubscribed *six times*. Despite Hearst, there could have been no more decisive proof of business confidence in the New Deal. For the first time since 1929 businessmen were discounting the future. And why not? Nothing, it seemed, could blunt Roosevelt's attack on the Depression. The Congress was his, and Thomas Reed Powell, professor of constitutional law at Harvard, declared that "In my judgment, there are sufficient doctrines of constitutional law to enable the Supreme Court to sustain any exercises of legislative or executive power that its practical judgment would move it to do." If Professor Powell didn't know, who did? The answer was Chief Justice Charles Evans Hughes. Unfortunately, no one had thought to ask him.

Portrait of an American

ELEANOR

HER FATHER was T.R.'s brother, her mother a famous beauty, and she was born Anna Eleanor Roosevelt in 1884. So sad, everyone said. Such an *ugly* child.

When visitors called she would hide and suck her fingers till her mother called, "Come in, Granny," explaining to the guest, "She's such a funny child, so old-fashioned that we call her Granny." And the little girl would want to sink through the floor.

Her mother died of diphtheria when she was eight, her father died of alcoholism when she was nine. She was sent to live with her maternal grandmother, a strict disciplinarian. Until she was fifteen she had no friends her own age.

At eighteen she was presented to Society. Society shuddered. The girl was nearly six feet tall. Her voice was loud and scratchy. Her front teeth protruded. She wouldn't use cosmetics. She giggled at odd times. Sometimes she burst into tears for no apparent reason. Her mind was going, the family said, and when Cousin Franklin proposed to her, his mother Sara fought the marriage for three years.

At the wedding, on March 17, 1905, Teddy gave the bride away. She had inherited his fantastic energy. Not proper in a woman, everyone clucked, and they disapproved of the way she spent it. Someone asked whether housekeeping bothered her. She said, "I rarely devote more than fifteen minutes a day to it." Instead she worked among the poor. And while she was out of the house in 1913, her young husband fell in love with her part-time social secretary, Lucy Mercer.

Lucy married a rich old man named Rutherfurd in 1920 and next year polio crippled Franklin. Sara wanted him to give up public life, to retire to Hyde Park as a cripple, but the doctor told Eleanor that he should return to politics; she could serve as his eyes and ears. The two women struggled. Eleanor joined the Women's Trade Union League, worked till she dropped for the Democratic party, and told Franklin that he must be governor. Sara's benevolent dictatorship grew weaker. She wrote her brother, "Eleanor is in the lead."

He was elected governor, then President.

And at the inaugural he arranged for a front-row seat and a private limousine for lovely Lucy Mercer Rutherfurd.

After the inauguration Eleanor visited the second encampment of the bonus marchers. She sang songs with them, and afterward they said, "Hoover sent the army, but Roosevelt sent his wife."

The President could seldom tour the country, so his First Lady covered forty thousand miles every year, delivering lectures and visiting slums, nursery schools, playgrounds, sharecroppers. Franklin always questioned her closely when she returned; he jocularly gave her the Secret Service code name Rover.

"For gosh sakes," said one goggle-eyed miner to another in a *New Yorker* cartoon, "here comes Mrs. Roosevelt!"

While she was away, Lucy called on the President.

In Washington, Eleanor held a press conference once a week for women reporters in the Treaty Room on the second floor of the White House. Her column, *My Day*, appeared in 135 newspapers. She wrote a question-and-answer page for each issue of the *Woman's Home Companion*. As a radio personality she was second only to Franklin. Her twice-a-week broadcasts were sponsored by Sweetheart toilet soap, Simmons mattresses, Johns-Manville building materials, Selby shoes, and Pond's cold cream; she gave all the money to the American Friends Service Committee. Once she kept two White House receptions going at once, moving back and forth between the connecting door.

The President would meet Lucy on roads beyond Georgetown and Arlington. Once his Washington to Hyde Park train detoured to a little-used siding at Allamuchy, New Jersey, so he could visit her at her estate.

Eleanor by now knew that she could have neither romance nor a close relationship with Franklin.

"Back of tranquillity lies always conquered unhappiness," was her favorite quotation.

To her admirers she was mother, wife, politician, stateswoman, journalist, and First Lady — all at once, and often all at the same time. She broke more precedents than her husband, had a greater passion for the underdog, and was always a little farther to the left. Once at Hyde Park she debated with Winston Churchill the best way to keep peace in the postwar world. By an Anglo-American alliance, said he; by improving living standards throughout the world, said she.

Her critics, led by Westbrook Pegler, called her a busybody, a do-gooder, a bleeding heart. Cartoonists drew savage caricatures of her. Anti-Eleanor jokes were cruel: "Eleanor can bite an apple through a picket fence." In London, Ambassador Joseph P. Kennedy said she was the greatest cross he bore — "She's always sending me a note to have some little Susie Glotz to tea at the embassy."

Once she wondered whether her outspokenness might be a liability to

Franklin. (At the time she was defending the right of Americans to be Communists.) He chuckled and said, "Lady, it's a free country."

She was at a meeting of Washington clubwomen when word came that he had died in Warm Springs.

In the White House she learned that Lucy had been with him at the end. She wept briefly; then, as always, she steadied herself.

Wounded by her mother, her father, her mother-in-law, and her husband, she now embraced all humanity. She continued her column, wrote fifteen books, reformed Tammany Hall, and represented the United States at the United Nations. Year after year in the Truman and Eisenhower administrations, American women voted her the woman they most admired. Gallup reported she was the most popular woman in any part of the world.

Aged seventy-four, she wrote, "We must regain a vision of ourselves as leaders of the world. We must join in an effort to use all knowledge for the good of all human beings. When we do that, we shall have nothing to fear."

Four years later she was dead. "Her glow," said Adlai Stevenson, had "warmed the world." The U.N. stood in silence in her honor. The three Presidents who had succeeded her husband bowed their heads as her coffin joined his in the Hyde Park garden. Over both stood a stone with an inscription she had chosen: "The only thing we have to fear is fear itself."

Lucy was absent. She had died in a New York City hospital fourteen years earlier.

THREE

Stirrings

I<small>N</small> M<small>AY</small> 1934 the first comics magazine, *Famous Funnies*, appeared on American newsstands. Its readers did not include J. Edgar Hoover, director of the Federal Bureau of Investigation. The nation's top cop enjoyed comics — his favorites were Dick Tracy and Secret Agent X–9 — but he had little time for them that spring. Hoover had his hands full getting ready to move the Justice Department into its new building on Pennsylvania Avenue, carrying out a presidential order to keep an eye on Fascist organizations, studying the new crime control acts just passed by Congress, and absorbing into his FBI agents from the now defunct Prohibition Bureau. The director wanted all the help he could get. "The criminal in America is on the march," he had told the public, and the public could only agree. It had hoped that prohibition repeal would wipe the dark stain of violence from the American national character. Instead, the bootleggers turned to holding up banks. The reputation of bankers being what it was, the thieves were widely regarded as Robin Hoods; an Indianapolis admirer of the FBIs Public Enemy Number One wrote, "Dillinger does not rob poor people. He robs those who became rich by robbing poor people. I am for Johnnie."

Johnnie's record of ten shootings, four bank stickups, and three jailbreaks ended when he lost a confrontation with the fastest guns in the FBI, led by Melvin Purvis. The lesson should have been obvious, but as a national commission was to find thirty-five years later — amid what could hardly be called a serene era — public tolerance of violence during the 1930s was the highest in American history. Dillinger was more dangerous dead than alive. He became a kind of folk hero, and people who had never even seen a pistol spoke casually of the rod, the roscoe, the equalizer, or the heat. Farmers had demonstrated that direct action worked; now all sorts of people were advocating it, including the governor of California, who congratulated a lynch mob for doing "a good job." Chester Gould, Dick

Tracy's creator and therefore presumably a man after J. Edgar Hoover's heart, said, "Big gangsters were running wild but going to court and getting off scot-free. I thought: why not have a guy who doesn't take the gangsters to court but shoots 'em?" If it came to that, why not shoot anybody big who angered you? An alarming number of letters threatened Eleanor Roosevelt; on the advice of the Secret Service, she never left White House grounds without a roscoe of her own in her purse.

It was symbolic that Dillinger had been equalized while leaving a theater featuring a gangster movie. Hollywood was churning out fifty such films each year, many of them casting crime in a romantic light. Opinions about the director's other gifts have varied, but no one ever doubted his genius for public relations. In 1934 the bureau's files were opened for the producers of *G-Men,* a new kind of movie with the part of an FBI man played by an appealing young actor named James Cagney. Then the director turned to radio. Melvin Purvis was dispatched to appear on the Fleischmann Yeast Hour. This was a near disaster; Purvis horrified Hoover and inflamed ulcers at the J. Walter Thompson advertising agency by belching into the microphone. On the other hand, a program called *Gangbusters* proved to be immensely popular. Dick Tracy himself could be heard during the children's hour; millions of children sent in Quaker Oats box tops for detective badges. But the country's flesh-and-blood super-sleuth was still Hoover himself. He was constantly running around the country, drawing up public enemy lists, and pursuing such outlaws as "Pretty Boy" Floyd, "Baby Face" Nelson, "Ma" Barker, "Machine Gun" Kelly, and — last and least in those days — Bonnie Parker and Clyde Barrow.

The most distinguished guest to call at 1600 Pennsylvania Avenue that May was John Maynard Keynes. Bearing a letter of introduction from Felix Frankfurter, the economist came to recommend deficit spending: "Nothing else counts in comparison with this." Afterward Roosevelt wrote that he and Keynes had had "a grand talk." In fact it had been rather chilly. The Keynesian manner was reserved, even arrogant, and FDR still had difficulty accepting the idea that a country could spend its way to prosperity. Still, he permitted Tugwell to introduce Keynes to key figures in his administration. Despite New Deal pyrotechnics, more than eighteen million Americans were reliefers. Some states — for example, Arkansas, Mississippi, and South Carolina — received 90 percent of their relief money from the federal government. Beyond doubt Roosevelt had saved the country from anarchy, but the Depression continued to be intractable, and Keynes's contention that complete recovery could be achieved only by annual deficits of 300 million dollars would be remembered in the capital long after he had left.

These were hard days for the New Deal. The NRA was collapsing under its own weight. In despair, General Johnson turned to the bottle and his secretary; he justified her salary to the press by saying she was "more than a stenographer," and when they printed that, he protested, "Boys, you're hitting below the belt" — an unhappy metaphor. The business community had begun to turn against Roosevelt two months earlier when he proposed legislation to regulate the stock market. George M. Humphrey, Sewell Avery, and Tom Girdler had led the fight against a Securities and Exchange Commission. A Republican congressman charged that it was part of a plot to "Russianize everything worthwhile." President Richard Whitney said of his New York Stock Exchange that it was "a perfect institution"; it was after Whitney's testimony that Will Rogers drawled, "Those Wall Street boys are putting up an awful fight to keep the government from putting a cop on their corner." They lost the fight, and their disappointment turned to fury when FDR appointed Joseph P. Kennedy, a notorious speculator, to head the commission. The President had acted on Moley's advice; since Kennedy knew all the loopholes, Moley argued, he could plug them. Wall Street was unappeased. When Whitney took Kennedy on a formal tour of the exchange floor, he surrounded him with bodyguards; otherwise, he explained coldly, the brokers might attack the new SEC chairman. Some tycoons were calling Kennedy "a traitor to his class." They weren't saying that about FDR yet, but that time was approaching, for the President had coupled insult to injury by firing Dean Acheson because he refused to sign the devaluation order. Already Acheson was toying with the idea of becoming a charter member of the nascent Liberty League.

A much greater storm lay over the horizon. Over a thousand cases involving New Deal legislation were in litigation. Individual judges could issue injunctions against federal laws in 1934, and as Attorney General Homer Cummings had warned Roosevelt, only 28 percent of the federal judiciary was Democratic. Eventually all cases would reach the Supreme Court, but that was small comfort. The high court judges were on the average seventy-eight years old and conservative. Eventually almost every strong President had come into conflict with the Court. Roosevelt was the strongest since Lincoln, and the battle, if it came, could be shattering.

One cabinet member, at least, had good news for the country. Secretary of State Cordell Hull pored over cables from Berlin and announced that "Mistreatment of Jews in Germany may be considered virtually terminated."

In a Pennsylvania Avenue cafeteria that same spring, Alger Hiss met Whittaker Chambers for the first time, though not under that name. The introductions were made by J. Peters, a Soviet agent, and Harold Ware of the American Communist party. They merely told Hiss that this was "Carl," to whom he would be answerable in party matters. The cafeteria was just a few doors away from the *Washington Post*, yet even if the city desk had known of the meeting, it seems highly unlikely that an account of it would have been published. Communists were not yet regarded as horrid. John W. McCormack of Massachusetts, chairman of the eight-week-old House Un-American Activities Committee, was preoccupied with the American right. It would be three years before J. Edgar Hoover would receive presidential instructions to put Communist organizations under surveillance, and even then the sole concern was espionage.

The United States had extended formal recognition to the Soviet Union the previous Thanksgiving. Russia's new ambassador had just been the guest of honor at a Waldorf-Astoria banquet; among the younger guests was an ex-president of the National Student Federation, Edward R. Murrow, who angrily wrote his future wife about America's economic system, which "damns some of us before we are born." (Murrow was indignant about the price of the banquet tickets, an unheard-of six dollars a plate.) In May 1934 the Popular Front was only six months away. Earl Browder would soon stand under banners proclaiming *Communism is Twentieth-Century Americanism*. Westbrook Pegler would call him "more Kansan than Landon," and Browder became the author of an unemployment insurance bill introduced by Congressman Lundeen of Minnesota. Before the decade was out he would achieve the acme of acceptability, an invitation to share a Cleveland platform with Robert A. Taft, who wanted all the votes from the left he could get.

On May 14, 1934, a Missouri relief administrator named Harry S. Truman filed for the Democratic statewide primary. He wrote a note to himself early that morning:

> It is 4 a.m. I am about to make the most momentous announcement of my life. I have come to the place where all men strive to be at my age . . . now I am a candidate for the United States Senate. If the Almighty God decides that I go there I am going to pray as King Solomon did, for wisdom to do the job.

The event went unnoticed in Washington. The only man in high office even to have met Truman was Harry Hopkins, and their acquaintance was confined to a single conference, in Hopkins's Pullman drawing room between Chicago and Kansas City the previous October. Had the New Dealers known more, they would have been unimpressed. The candidate wasn't even solvent; since the failure of his haberdashery he had been saddled with an unsatisfied judgment of $8,944.

The capital *was* intrigued by the formation of La Follette's Wisconsin Progressive party and Upton Sinclair's stunning primary triumph in California; Sinclair had received more votes than all eight of his Democratic opponents combined. But most of Washington was taking a political breather. The spectacles of the past year had exhausted them, and on the eve of the off-year elections they talked of other things. Hervey Allen's 1,224-page *Anthony Adverse* was leading all best-seller lists, though it was being challenged by James Joyce's *Ulysses*, which had just been cleared by a Manhattan judge. Ernest Hemingway had caught a record 468-pound Marlin without harness, Max Baer had outpunched Max Schmeling, Glenn Cunningham had run a 4:06.7 mile; Sir Malcolm Campbell had driven his *Blue Bird* 272.1 mph — faster than airliners. St. Louis was afflicted by sleeping sickness, New England elms by the Dutch elm disease. Movie-goers marveled at the eclipsing of Dolores Del Rio and Gene Raymond, the stars of *Flying Down to Rio*, by two "feature players," Fred Astaire and Ginger Rogers. The brightest comedian on adult radio was Jack Benny. During the past two years he had failed to catch the public ear with three sponsors, Canada Dry, Chevrolet, and General Tires. Now he was finally making it for Jell-O. Children preferred *The Lone Ranger*, who with his horse Silver had been thundering past microphones since New Year's Day.

In short, there was time for trivia. The despair of 1932 had fled. There was a feeling that almost anything could happen. In Canada, on May 28, Mr. and Mrs. Oliva Dionne had become the parents of quintuplets. Last fall the Washington Senators had actually been in the World Series. It might happen again sometime.* Most Washingtonians were enjoying the dry, pleasant spring and the flowering cherry blossoms, though Henry Wallace wished to God the country would get some rain.

Among the most unpleasant aspects of the mid-1930s, once the fear of chaos had subsided, was the weather. At one time or another the Mississippi, Ohio, Potomac, Tennessee, Delaware, Connecticut, Missouri, Susquehanna, Columbia, Allegheny, and Merrimack rivers — streams drain-ing virtually every major basin in America — rose over their banks and roared through the streets of cities. One flood, that of the Ohio River in 1937, was the worst in the nation's history; it destroyed the homes of a half-million people. Flood and windstorms in these years took 3,678 lives. Winters were uncommonly bitter, and in a single summer, 1936, while one of her inhabitants was trying to win the Presidency, Kansas recorded almost sixty days of 100 degree heat, but in the early Roosevelt years the most urgent problem was a combination of drought and high gales, bring-ing what were known as "black blizzards." That was Henry Wallace's nightmare. Before his Triple-A and CCC conservation could alter the country's agriculture, the topsoil of the Middle West was blowing away.

For years conservationists had warned that ecological catastrophe hov-ered over the Great Plains. The so-called short-grass country west of the hundredth meridian was favored by fewer than twenty inches of rain a year. Early explorers had labeled the frontier beyond the Missouri "the great American desert," and then it was relatively stable, hammered flat by millions of bison and untilled by the Indians. Then the settlers arrived with their John Deere plows. Before the Depression they were blessed by extraordinarily heavy rains, but as they pushed their luck by overgrazing

*It never did.

and overplowing, the ineludible drew nearer. Even in the 1920s a hundred counties in Colorado, Kansas, New Mexico, Texas, and Oklahoma had been called the "dust bowl." Now in 1934 the National Resources Board estimated that 35 million acres of arable land had been completely destroyed, the soil of another 125 million acres had been nearly or entirely removed, and another 100 million acres were doomed. Abruptly the bowl grew to 756 counties in nineteen states. Like Ireland and the Ukraine in the nineteenth century, the Plains were threatened with famine.

The first of the great storms had blustered out of the sky on Armistice Day 1933, in the ninth month of the new administration. In South Dakota the farms began blowing away that morning. By noon the sky was darker than night. Men were literally vomiting dirt, and when the sun reappeared, fields had been replaced by sand, while roads, trees, sheds, fences, and machinery had disappeared beneath great hanging dunes of soil. By then the wind was headed for Texas. A towering pall darkened Chicago, and was visible as far east as Albany.

That was only the beginning. The drought continued through 1934 and 1935, accompanied by fantastic windstorms howling down from such remote Dakota towns as Chugwater, Niobe, Wounded Knee, and Spotted Horse. "In 1934," wrote Tugwell, then Undersecretary of Agriculture, "rainfall had been so short that severe damage had been done." Actually that year's farm calamity could be traced back to the previous winter; light snows had left the land too hard to absorb what rain there was. The earth could be seen through the thin grass, and the wheat was so thin that Tugwell compared it to the stubble on an old man's chin. In the same month that Keynes visited Roosevelt and Truman filed for the Missouri primary, the first storms of 1934 struck the Texas Panhandle. Whole counties were transformed into shifting Saharas. Wives packed every windowsill, door frame, and keyhole with oiled cloth and gummed paper, yet the fine silt found its way in and lay in beachlike ripples on their floors.

A Texas schoolboy described the storms as "rolling black smoke." In Oklahoma Nathan Asch found that even food tasted gritty. He wrote that the dust "blew into the eyes, underneath the collar; undressing, there were specks of dust inside the buttonholes; in the morning it had gathered like fine snow along the window ledge; it penetrated even more; it seeped along the wiring of the house; and along the edges of the door . . . there was a rusty brown stain." For three weeks Oklahoma streetlights were on day and night. People wore dust masks, and to compound misery, the temperature seemed stuck at 108 degrees.

Lorena Hickok, on a field trip for Hopkins, reported from Huron, South Dakota:

> We started out about 8:30 in the morning intending to drive into the northern part of the county to see some farmers. We had gone less than ten miles when we had to turn back. It kept getting worse. You couldn't see a

foot ahead of the car. It was truly a terrifying experience. Like driving in a fog, only worse because of the wind that seemed as if it would blow the car right off the road. It was as though we were picked up in a vast, impenetrable black cloud which was hurling us right off the earth.

"Speaking nationally," Tugwell wrote, "that drought had been an ironic blessing — it had helped reduce embarrassing surpluses of wheat — but for the individuals and families involved it was disastrous." In fact, the Department of Agriculture inadvertently increased the human disaster; under the AAA acreage reduction programs, wealthy farmers were discovering that they needed less help. Their tenants, turned out, took to the road in rattletrap 1925 Dodges, 1927 La Salles, and 1923 Model Ts, looking for a greener land. They were joined by small farmers whose "For Sale" signs marked the start of the dust-bowlers' migrations. Drought had destroyed the wheatlands of Eric Sevareid's father and broken his bank; he moved on. In Hall County, Texas, the population abruptly dropped from 40,000 to less than 1,000. Most picturesque of all were Oklahoma's ragtag "Okies," to be immortalized five years later in John Steinbeck's *The Grapes of Wrath*. In the interim Steinbeck would conduct a dog census in California's Monterey County — one of the few idiotic Hopkins projects — and he was destined to see the migrants because California was their destination. It beckoned as a land of milk and honey: "I like to think how nice it's gonna be, maybe, in California," Ma Joad said. "Never cold. An' fruit ever' place, and people just bein' in the nicest places, little white houses in among the orange trees." In reality it would bring the Joads the drudgery and want which were the fruit pickers' lot. Simultaneously, the Okies' pilgrimage would help ruin the promising gubernatorial campaign of Upton Sinclair.

Those people in little white houses among the orange trees were appalled by the advancing army of dust-blown, indigent farmers who, as Arthur M. Schlesinger Jr. wrote, seemed to represent "the threat of social revolution by a rabble of crazed bankrupts and paupers — a horrid upheaval from below, led by a Peter the Hermit, which could only end in driving all wealth and respectability from the State." It was Louis B. Mayer, the motion picture tycoon, who cast Sinclair in the role of Peter the Hermit, thus sowing a seed in media manipulation which would bear weird fruit a generation later.

Sinclair was vulnerable. In a state celebrated for its eccentrics, the fifty-four-year-old author had emerged as one of the oddest. His candidacy had been launched in a pamphlet entitled *I, Governor of California, and How I Ended Poverty: A True Story of the Future*. He proposed to set up a statewide net of socialist communes toiling under the symbol of a wide-winged honeybee and the slogan "I Produce, I Defend." Roosevelt liked Sinclair, and the writer's program was endorsed by Theodore Dreiser, Archibald MacLeish, Dorothy Canfield Fisher, Stuart Chase, Morris Ernst, Clarence Darrow, and, curiously, Father Charles E. Coughlin of Royal Oak, Michigan. But Norman Thomas said it was "economically and politically absurd." Sister Aimee Semple McPherson, the shopworn Los Angeles evangelist, called Sinclair "a red devil." The California Boy Scouts were mobilized against the accused, who was then repudiated by the regular Democratic organization.

The Republican candidate, Frank Merriam, came out for the Townsend Plan — $200 a month for everyone over sixty — which had been launched in Long Beach on January 1, 1934, and presently legions of white-haired Californians were marching for the GOP, singing:

> Onward, Townsend soldiers,
> Marching as to war,
> With the Townsend banner
> Going on before.

Sinclair's slogan, "End Poverty in California" (EPIC), was twisted to mean "Empty Promises in California." The three big Los Angeles newspapers, *Time* noted, "simply quit reporting news of EPIC and its sponsor." Metro-Goldwyn-Mayer taxed its employees to underwrite the anti-Sinclair campaign, and though some stars revolted (Cagney and Jean Harlow among others), most not only went along but permitted their talents to be exploited in fake newsreels. Mayer, the state Republican chairman, had hired the big advertising firm of Lord & Thomas and put MGM studios at its disposal. Gangs of extras dressed as hoodlums and hookers tumbled off freight trains while MGM cameras ground and commentators explained that their audiences were witnessing actual Okie invasions. One elderly bit actress, dressed as a kindly grandmother, declared that she could never vote for Sinclair because he believed in free love, while elderly male actors appeared with fake beards and stage accents shouting aggressively that they were supporting the author ("Vell, his system vorked vell in Russia, vy can't it vork here?"). In October FDR thought Sinclair would win, but nothing could withstand the MGM offensive. California went Republican by a quarter-million votes, and the defeated writer returned to his typewriter to hammer out a new book, *I, Candidate for Governor: And How I Got Licked.**

Not everyone on the left was licked. In the state of Washington radicals rallying under an almost identical banner ("End Poverty in Washington") elected a senator, half the legislature, and, as prosecutor of King County, young Warren Magnuson. The La Follettes were triumphant in Wisconsin, winning the senatorial and gubernatorial races and taking seven of the ten congressional seats. Strapping Floyd B. Olson sat in the Minnesota statehouse, growling at interviewers, "You bet your life I'm a radical. You

---

*Among the interested California observers of the campaign were Jerry Voorhis, a Sinclair supporter who was later elected to Congress, and the man who would later unseat Voorhis, Richard M. Nixon, Whittier '34.

might say I'm radical as hell!" And the incomparable Fiorello La Guardia was now mayor of New York City.

"Too often, life in New York is merely a squalid succession of days," La Guardia said, "whereas in fact it can be a great, living, thrilling adventure." Under the swashbuckling five-foot-two-inch mayor, it became an adventure in light opera. He wore a black sombrero, shouted his commands in an incongruously shrill voice, and carried out his duties with piratical dash. One minute after he was sworn in he ordered the arrest of Lucky Luciano, the eminent hood. He used the city's building, fire, and health departments to help striking waiters. When laundry owners begged him to be neutral in a dispute over their sweatshop wages, he blandly picked up his telephone and ordered his water commissioner to show the city's impartiality by turning off the water in all laundries. (The owners settled immediately.) He ruled Manhattan like a laird, leading police raids in person, showing up without notice to preside over night court sessions, reading comic strips over the radio to children, and hanging on the back of a racing fire engine, an outsize helmet on his head. La Guardia's hymn was "Who's Afraid of the Big Bad Wolf?" His flair for the dramatic, even the preposterous, sometimes camouflaged his advocacy of socialism, yet none who worked with him ever doubted his views or his effectiveness.

The elected radicals allied themselves with the New Deal; the doctrinaire left kept its distance. Contemplating Marxism and FDR's experimentation, the *New Republic* stated flatly, "There is no middle course." When Tugwell boasted of the administration's aversion to "blind doctrine," James Wechsler, then the Marxist editor of Columbia's student daily, wrote that doctrine was precisely what the New Deal needed, and I. F. Stone and Max Lerner enthusiastically agreed. More than thirty years before Herbert Marcuse roused the New Left with his call for "selective tolerance," Lincoln Steffens said, "Get the notion of liberty out of your heads. . . . We want liberty for us, but not for Hitler and Mussolini." The *New Masses* used even more Marcusian language: "We would deny democratic rights to Fascists, to lynchers, to all those who wish to use them as a means of winning mass support for reaction."

Tom Wolfe, who was three years old at the time, would one day write a brilliant article for the *New York Magazine* about "radical chic." Wolfe had Leonard Bernstein and the Black Panthers in mind, but the concept was equally valid in the mid-Thirties. Hede Massing, a Soviet agent, was startled and amused when one of her earnest socialite protégés in the State Department sang "The International" to her in Russian from the steps of the Lincoln Memorial. As Budd Schulberg was to note in *The Disenchanted*, face styles had even changed among intellectuals since the Twenties; F. Scott Fitzgerald's "sleek, shiny, Arrow Collar perfection, finely etched, sharp-featured, a pretty-boy face drawn with the symmetry of second-rate art, pear-shaped, with a straight nose, cleft chin, dark hair parted smartly down the middle, combed back and plastered down with Vaseline or

Sta-comb," had been replaced by the heavy bone structure, unruly hair, and Slavic features of the proletarian image. Indeed, wrote Frederick Lewis Allen, if you listened carefully at certain cocktail parties "you might have heard a literary critic who had been gently nurtured in the politest of environments referring to *himself* as a proletarian, so belligerently did he identify himself with the masses." At dinner parties in New York's elegant upper Eighties the most recent caller at the Communist party's headquarters at 35 East Twelfth Street would be the cynosure of all artistic eyes, and if in his cups he could always find comradely voices to join him in the rousing refrain:

> *To make it Soviet*
> *One more S in the USA*
> *Oh, we'll live to see it yet.*
> *When the land belongs to the farmers*
> *And the factories to the working men —*
> *The USA when we take control*
> *Will be USSA then.*

The threat from the left was absurd, if colorful; the rightist threat was inchoate, if greater in potential. As the 1934 off-year elections approached, the most persistent criticisms of the New Deal came from businessmen. During the Hundred Days, most of them had approved of Joseph Medill Patterson's moratorium on harassment of the administration; in his *New York Daily News* he had promised, "Whatever President Roosevelt does or doesn't do, we're going to be for him. We're going to withhold hostile criticism for one year at least." Now over a year had passed, and on reflection they decided they didn't much like FDR's paraphrase, in his inaugural, of Matthew 21:12 — "The moneychangers have fled from their high seats in the temple of our civilization." The first to speak out had been Al Smith. In a December 1933 editorial in his *New Outlook* Smith scorned the New Deal's proliferation of acronyms: "It looks as if one of the absent-minded professors had played anagrams with the alphabet soup." He had added, "Some of my readers may ask why others have not pointed out the dangers in the CWA program. The answer is very simple. No sane official who has hung up an empty stocking over the municipal fireplace is going to shoot Santa Claus just before a hard Christmas."

"The hell they won't," Hopkins said dryly. "Santa Claus really needs a bullet-proof vest." Roosevelt himself wrote to one of his ambassadors, "The inevitable sniping has commenced, led by what you and I would refer to as the Mellon-Mills influence in banking and certain controlled industries." Congress approved increased relief spending in 1934, but the SEC battle thickened the ranks of snipers. On June 8 the President was sufficiently concerned to postpone his request for social security and its payroll tax until the following winter. It didn't matter; no truce was possible now; two months later the American Liberty League convened in

Miami and declared formal war. "All the big guns have started shooting," Roosevelt wrote William C. Bullitt in Moscow. "Their organization has been labeled the I CAN'T TAKE IT CLUB."

Sometimes he asked them to take a lot. Jesse Jones of his revitalized RFC castigated a meeting of financiers in Chicago, telling them that they were failures on their own terms, reminding them that half the audience represented institutions that had failed, and demanding that they "Be smart for once" and "take government into partnership with you." Perhaps the point of no return in Roosevelt's break with Wall Street was reached on October 24, 1934, when four thousand members of the American Bankers Association met in the DAR's Constitution Hall to hear FDR himself. Jackson E. Reynolds, president of the First National Bank of New York, delivered an introduction which can only be described as obsequious. He told the President that the financial community was in a "chastened and understanding mood" and actually thanked him for everything the New Deal had done to "rescue and rehabilitate our shattered banking structure." Roosevelt's reply was one of his more unfortunate lapses into Endicott Peabodyism, asking for an alliance of all economic forces in the nation, including business, banking, labor, capital, and government. "What an all-America team that would be!" he exulted — as though Ironpants Johnson had not just led precisely such a team to a dismal string of defeats. The applause was polite, though the bankers felt Reynolds's surrender had gone too far. Then, back in their hotels, they learned that they had been sold out. The White House had insisted upon censoring Reynolds's speech in advance, deleting such wry asides as his recollection of the days when he had been a Columbia law professor and Franklin Roosevelt his less than perfect student. Neither for the first nor the last time, FDR had been too clever for his own good.

Business baiting of the President mounted in the last days of the 1934 election campaign, but the great middle class was largely unaware of it. In a masterly fireside chat he said, "I am not for a return to that definition of liberty under which for so many years a free people were being gradually regimented into the service of the privileged few." At the same time he praised "the driving power of individual initiative and the incentive of fair private profit." Republicans were rediscovering that it was impossible to come to grips with such an opponent, and a note of ugliness began to creep into some of their speeches; in Wisconsin a Republican nominee bitterly referred to Roosevelt as "a man who can't stand on his own two feet without crutches." FDR, knowing that such tactics could boomerang, thought Democrats would do well at the polls, though even he was surprised by the results. On the morning of November 7 the country awoke to find that the party in power had actually increased its congressional margins to 229 seats in the House and 44 in the Senate; the Republicans were left with only seven governorships. Among the thirteen freshman senators, all Democrats, was Harry S. Truman of Missouri.

In his preelection fireside chat Roosevelt had questioned the price-fixing aspects of the NRA. Johnson then resigned — he assembled his employees in the Commerce Department auditorium and tearfully quoted, in Italian, the dying words of Madame Butterfly before she committed hara-kiri — and was replaced by Averell Harriman. The departure of old Ironpants made little difference. The NRA was due to expire in June 1935 anyway, and before it could die with dignity the Supreme Court declared it unconstitutional. Implications of that decision were ominous only insofar as they affected other New Deal legislative achievements. The execution of the blue eagle — which left as its only legacy trade-in allowances for buyers of new cars — was in many ways a relief. By then it had been superseded by the acts of the Second Hundred (actually a hundred and seventy-seven) Days of 1935.

Planning for those days was begun by Roosevelt and Hopkins in the wake of the election returns, which could only be interpreted as a mandate. The general goals of the new laws were to be a more sensible use of national resources, security against unemployment and old age, and slum clearance and better housing. The chief beneficiaries would be labor and the small farmer. Roosevelt sketched its broad outlines in his State of the Union message to the new, heavily Democratic Congress on January 4, 1935. Then he and his aides began drafting the bills. They were not the same aides who had dazzled the capital two years earlier. Moley, Tugwell, Acheson, Richberg, Berle, Douglas, and Johnson were gone or going. The new New Deal required different talents, which the President found in, among others, Felix Frankfurter, James M. Landis, Marriner S. Eccles, Tom Corcoran, and Ben Cohen. Cohen and Corcoran lived together in what soon became famous as "the little red house on R Street." They reminded *Fortune* of "those minor state counselors in Shakesperian comedies who serve the Duke, make astute comments, and are always perturbed at developments."

There was plenty of perturbation, but it lay elsewhere, notably in the Washington offices of the Liberty League and other conservative strongholds. The Holding Company Act provided a good example of how far big business would now go in fighting Roosevelt. It applied to public utilities and included a five-year "death sentence" clause which provided that any holding company not able to prove its usefulness to its community within that time would be dissolved. Opposition appeared on several different levels. On the most dignified plane there was Wendell L. Willkie, then a utilities attorney, with a counterplan for state regulation. Several notches down was the utilities lobby, which, the Scripps-Howard Washington bureau reported, employed more agents than there were senators and congressmen. Finally, at the very bottom, were the forgers of fake messages from voters. This extraordinary campaign almost killed the bill. It cost the utilities nearly two million dollars; they sent out 250,000 telegrams and five million letters demanding rejection of the death sentence. Senator

Truman alone received 30,000 such appeals. He burned them and remained loyal to Roosevelt. The House at first rejected the death sentence, however, and changed its mind only after a congressional committee headed by Hugo Black proved that the mail response was a fraud.

Social security was the most emotional issue that session. Republicans protested that if the administration bill were passed, children would no longer support their parents, the payroll tax would discourage workmen so much that they would quit their jobs, and that, taken all in all, the measure would remove the "romance of life." Throughout the rest of his life Roosevelt was especially proud of his battle for social security, and in retrospect it seems the greatest of his legislative achievements. But it was a battle hard won. Every conceivable argument was raised against it, including militant interruption of hearings; Frances Perkins was testifying in its behalf before a congressional committee when a woman leaped up and shouted that the bill had been copied, word for word, from "page eighteen of the Communist Manifesto, which I have right here in my hand, Mr. Chairman."

Coolidge-Hoover prosperity had identified the Republican party with big business, and as 1935 advanced into spring and then summer, antagonism toward FDR welded the two together. Utility lobbyists were so successful in their whispering campaign charging the President with insanity that by July the Washington press corps was being badgered by hometown offices inquiring whether Roosevelt had in fact lost his mind. The handful of Republicans in the Capitol took turns excoriating the New Deal's plan to "sovietize America." When Roosevelt proposed to raise income taxes in the higher brackets and introduce an inheritance tax, Hearst branded the program "essentially Communism," a "bastard" measure attributable to "a composite personality which might be labeled "Stalin Delano Roosevelt."

The Senate struck out the inheritance tax and reduced assessments in the top brackets, but FDR got most of what he wanted that session. Among the fruits of the Second Hundred Days were the Soil Conservation Act, a National Resources Board; a strengthened Federal Reserve Board; the Rural Electrification Act, which eventually brought electricity to a million farm families; the Guffey-Snyder Coal Act, which superseded the NRA in the mining industry; the Wagner-Connery Act, replacing section 7(a) and establishing a National Labor Relations Board; and the National Youth Administration, providing employment for youths from relief families and part-time jobs for needy students. Lyndon B. Johnson, who had just moved his young wife Lady Bird into a two-room apartment with a rollaway bed at 1910 Kalorama Road N.W., was appointed NYA administrator for the state of Texas, where he would soon meet and hire, at 17 cents an hour, a sharecropper's son named John B. Connally Jr. (The North Carolina administrator was more openhanded with Richard Nixon, who had moved from Whittier to Duke Law School; Nixon's NYA job paid 35 cents an hour.)

"Boys, this is our hour," a grinning Hopkins had told his staff after the off-year triumph. "We've got to get everything we want — a works program, social security, wages and hours, everything now or never. Get your minds to work on developing a complete ticket to provide security for all the folks of this country up and down and across the board." Despite charges that Hopkins used relief money to buy votes — Republicans insisted he had said, "We will tax, tax, spend, spend, and elect, elect" — he went to great lengths to keep the WPA above politics. Nevertheless, those who had been saved from want could hardly fail to be grateful, and it was in these early months of 1935 that Roosevelt turned the Democrats into the country's majority party by forging his grand coalition of labor, the South, women, ethnic minorities, city bosses, and Negroes.

Viewed from the 1970s, FDR's appeal to blacks may seem baffling. They were evicted from farms under the AAA crop reduction policies, and subject to new forms of discrimination by southern Democrats administering New Deal programs in Dixie. At its inception in June 1934, the Federal Housing Administration introduced restrictive clauses into its housing contracts. At the Warm Springs railroad depot there were separate toilets, waiting rooms, and even baggage rooms for "colored." New Dealers were lukewarm about anti-lynching bills; in 1934 Louis Howe buried one in his files with the note: "Not favored at this time — may create hostility to other crime bills."

Roosevelt benefited largely from comparison with Hoover, whom Walter White of the NAACP had called "the man in the lily-White House." (During his four years in the Executive Mansion Hoover had declined to speak to the two Negro porters there.) The Republicans continually promised to protect the Negro's economic status, which, as Jonathan Daniels observed, "was exactly what he wanted to escape." Championing of black causes by Eleanor Roosevelt, Frances Perkins, and Harold Ickes helped; Ickes desegregated the Interior Building cafeteria and brought Robert Weaver into the administration. Negroes were accepted by the CCC and WPA, social security was color-blind, Howard University received a three-million-dollar government grant, relief projects built schools for blacks, and three hundred thousand Negro adults learned to read under a New Deal emergency education program. It was all tokenism, perhaps, but blacks hadn't been able to get even tokens in the past.

The formation of every presidential cult is met by its opposite, and so it is with coalitions. By the end of the Second Hundred Days the first anti-Roosevelt bloc had emerged. It was a loose alliance of the Liberty League, Townsendites, William Dudley Pelley's anti-Semitic Silver Shirts, the Hearst press, admirers of red-baiting Elizabeth Dilling, Huey Long's Share Our Wealth movement; the Reverend Gerald L. K. Smith, Long's chief lieutenant; and Father Charles E. Coughlin's National Union for Social Justice, formed on November 11, 1934. The Liberty League supplied much of the money. Followers were recruited from the lower middle class — often from the same neighborhoods which were to support Senator Joseph R.

McCarthy in the early 1950s, Governor George Wallace in the late 1960s, and Spiro Agnew in the early 1970s.

During the Second Hundred Days the anti-Rooseveltians scored twice — both times in the name of isolationism, then at the height of its appeal. Defying the President's reluctance to have his hands tied in foreign affairs, they lobbied through the Neutrality Act of 1935, which required him to prohibit arms traffic with nations at war and to forbid American citizens to travel on belligerent vessels, except at their own risk. The measure was immediately applied to the Ethiopian War. In the second instance, they turned back an FDR appeal to Congress asking American adherence to the World Court. On the Senate floor Long enlisted the support of Hiram Johnson and Borah; in the nationwide mail campaign Will Rogers joined Hearst and Father Coughlin. The Radio Priest claimed rejection of the Court as a personal victory, and since his audience at the time was esti- mated at 45 million listeners, his claim was undisputed.

The building of Father Coughlin's empire had been a brilliant one-man accomplishment in media manipulation, exploiting aspects of the national character which were then but little understood: American innocence, the nation's yearning for simple solutions, its joiner complex, and the carnival instinct for collecting shiny junk. Had the priest been born a generation later, he would have made a superb host on a television talk show or a Madison Avenue account executive, for he was a born salesman. He could have merchandised almost anything. He chose to peddle hate.

Now in his forty-fifth year, he was a big, sleek, well-groomed, bespec- tacled Canadian with a voice like an organ. Detroit had first heard that marvelous voice in 1926, when the Ku Klux Klan — toward which he would later display a peculiar tolerance — burned down his church in Royal Oak, a Detroit suburb. The shocked director of the local radio station WJR suggested that he deliver a series of sermons over the air asking contributions for a new church. By the end of 1930 Coughlin had organized the Golden Hour of the Little Flower, broadcast over seventeen CBS stations, plus occasional local cut-ins, from 6 to 7 P.M. CST Sundays. Members of his vast unseen audience could not only hear the radio priest's florid metaphors and rolling tirades; they could also acquire a Sacred Relic by sending him money. In return they received a tiny chrome-plated cross stamped "Radio League of the Little Flower," and with it this letter:

My dear Friend:

   With this letter it is my privilege to send you a souvenir crucifix. As I announced over the air, it has touched a relic of the True Cross. . . .

Devotedly yours in Christ,
CHAS. E. COUGHLIN

P.S. If some friend wants a crucifix, let me know.

C.E.C.

Three months after he joined CBS, he was getting an average of 80,000 letters a week enclosing more than $20,000. Eventually, after especially popular broadcasts, the number of envelopes would pass a million and require 150 clerks to sort out the bills and stock the change. In 1934 he was getting more mail than anybody in the country, including President Roosevelt. His church had been rebuilt long ago (with nonunion labor). The marble and granite tower of its seven-story Shrine could be seen all over Royal Oak; at night dazzling spotlights played across a gigantic bas-relief figure of Christ spread across it. Beneath the Saviour was carved the single word, "Charity." On the stones of the church were various inscriptions, some from the Scriptures and some just good service club slogans. *Time* claimed that "Charity Crucifixion Tower reminds many Detroiters of a silo" and christened its architect "Silo Charlie." In riposte Coughlin cried that the news magazine "is not forgiven for indirectly insulting the crucified Christ whose monument is described by *Time* as a 'silo.' By inference, are we Catholics and Protestants who receive our spiritual food and drink from the Victim of the cross — are we cattle, content to fill ourselves with silage? By printing such classical billingsgate *Time* has stubbed its toes against eternity."

From the side of Charity Crucifixion Tower, Christ's agonized expression looked out upon a bizarre scene — a gasoline station beneath a gigantic sign reading "Shrine Super-Service," a "Shrine Inn," and a Little Flower hot dog stand. Inside the church itself other vendors spread their wares: picture postcards of Silo Charlie, crucifixes "personally blessed" by him, Bibles, anti-Semitic pamphlets, copies of the Brooklyn *Tablet*, and, after 1934, stacks of the Father's *Social Justice* magazine. (At the height of its popularity, *Social Justice* was on sale in two thousand American churches.) Tourists were asked to make as little noise as possible — not, as one might suppose, because they were in a place of worship, but because at the very top of the tower, accessible only by a circular staircase, the radio priest sat chain-smoking, stroking his Great Dane, and composing his weekly sermon. The enormity of this task was well-known to the visitors. After CBS dropped him because he had become controversial, the priest organized his own network of over sixty stations, supported by contributions from the faithful. His flock had become the largest in the history of Christianity. *Fortune* called him "just about the biggest thing that ever happened to radio"; he outdrew *Amos 'n' Andy*, *Dr. Fu Manchu*, and Ed Wynn. So great was his weekly harvest of currency that he had become the country's principal speculator in silver, which he described on his Sunday programs as "the Gentile metal." Like a Pope, he granted audiences; occasionally he would graciously consent to receive the President's personal emissary, Joseph P. Kennedy, who was frantically trying to find some common ground between them.

It was impossible. No such ground existed. Father Coughlin had supported FDR in the beginning; his war cry in 1932 had been "Roosevelt or ruin," and as late as April 1934 he assured a rally in New York's Hippodrome Theater, "I will never change my philosophy that the New Deal is Christ's deal." It was a rash promise. For one thing, he now had 500,000 ounces of silver, and the President wasn't being very cooperative with the silver bloc. The radio priest was mortified when the Secretary of the Treasury gave the press a list of silver speculators, headed by Coughlin's private secretary. He could have survived that — after all, Woodin's successor at the Treasury was Henry Morgenthau, who as a Jew could be depicted as a born enemy of the Gentile metal — but in his need to create new sensations or lose his audience, the radio priest was being driven to excesses which, in the long run, could only lead to hostility toward a President who had preempted the political center.

The hostility grew as Coughlin's power grew. His National Union for Social Justice claimed a signed-up membership of 7,500,000, the most militant of whom took to the streets in what *Social Justice* called "platoons" of twenty-five each, looking for Jews. The preferred method for creating an incident was to offer copies of the magazine for sale to passersby who were known to be or just looked Semitic, and jump them when they declined; it was employed several times in front of Nedick's orange juice stand on Times Square, where Irish policemen were admirers of the radio priest. Meanwhile he was opening fire on Roosevelt's new allies in the labor movement. He denounced the American Federation of Labor, recommending that the government, following the example of Italy and Germany, settle industrial disputes by decree. What he wanted, Raymond Gram Swing pointed out, was "a fascist solution of the labor problem."

Supported by Bishop Michael Gallagher of Detroit, Coughlin insisted that he also had the backing of Pius XI. It was true that the Pontiff had said "every minister of the holy religion must throw himself, heart and mind, into the conflict for social justice," but the *Osservatore Romano*, speaking for the Holy Father, took pains to point out that he hadn't meant the kind of Social Justice advocated by the priest of Royal Oak, and William Cardinal O'Connell of Boston accused Coughlin of disseminating "demagogic stuff to the poor." By this time the radio priest was beginning to display the arrogance of power; he informed his ecclesiastical betters that his magazine was a private venture and therefore none of their business. Anyone who crossed him now was going to have his knuckles rapped. La Guardia was awarded the Shrine's "ill will" prize for criticizing Adolf Hitler and thus "breeding international bad feeling." Liberals were called Communists. Organized labor, the flock was told, was being masterminded in Moscow. The faithful must "think Christian, act Christian, buy Christian" and beware of world Jewry: "Call this inflammatory if you will. It is inflammatory. But rest assured we will fight and we will win."

Early in 1935 Coughlin published the totalitarian program of his National Union for Social Justice. Point One set the tone: he demanded "Liberty of conscience and education," but no freedom of speech, which would have meant the end of his Radio League — unless he was running the country, which presumably was what he had in mind. At the same time he broke with Roosevelt. The New Deal became the "Jew Deal." The President was "a liar," an "anti-God"; in a Cincinnati speech Coughlin advocated the elimination of FDR by "the use of bullets." This was too much for Westbrook Pegler, a Catholic layman and admirer of European strong men; in his column he wrote that federal investigators of subversion should have treated Coughlin just as they were treating Earl Browder, instead of tiptoeing "around him for fear he would cry up a holy war."

It wasn't too much for Mrs. Dilling, whose list of powerful Communists included Senator Borah, Chiang Kai-shek, Eleanor Roosevelt, H. L. Mencken, and Mahatma Gandhi. It didn't offend James True, inventor of the "kike-killer" (Pat. No. 2,026,077), a short rounded club made in two sizes (one for ladies). It didn't offend Joe McWilliams, the soapbox Führer, or Lawrence Dennis, the intellectual of the radical right. Most interesting of all, no reproaches were found in the Hearst press. "Whenever you hear a prominent American called a 'Fascist,'" Hearst declared, "you can usually make up your mind that the man is simply a LOYAL CITIZEN WHO STANDS UP FOR AMERICANISM." Beginning in November 1934, Hearst sent reporters disguised as students into college classrooms, to trap teachers in unconventional comments. Nobody wanted to change the American economic system, he said, except for "a few incurable malcontents, a few sapheaded college boys, and a few unbalanced college professors."

Considering the tens of millions who were reading and listening to incendiary remarks, it is not surprising that some of them reacted violently. Between June 1934 and June 1935 the American Civil Liberties Union noted "a greater variety and number of serious violations of civil liberties" than in any year since the World War, and the ACLU records were incomplete, owing to the suspension of all constitutional guarantees in the state of Louisiana.

If Father Coughlin was the propaganda minister of Depression extremism, Senator Huey Pierce Long Jr. was universally acknowledged as its leader. The radio priest had the audience, but he preached nihilism. Dr. Townsend, who had become their ally, could count ten million followers, but he didn't know how to get things done. Huey Long, the consummate politician, had everything: constituents, a program, and an intuitive sense of when and how to seize power. He was the only antagonist who genuinely frightened Franklin Roosevelt.

The legend of Huey Long has been set down in two memorable novels, by John Dos Passos in *Number One* and Robert Penn Warren in *All the King's Men*. The truth is at least as compelling. Huey was born in a log cabin, in the bitter poverty of Winn Parish, and he was distinguishable from other wool-hats only by his genius. He began by selling a shortening called Cottolene to the gallused men and calicoed women who would trust him to the grave and beyond. In eight months he completed the Tulane University three-year law course and, by special dispensation from the Louisiana Supreme Court, became a lawyer at the age of twenty-one, an achievement that no Tulane student, before or since, has ever matched. Later he displayed his virtuosity before the United States Supreme Court, establishing the constitutionality of a school book law which had been rejected in the lower courts. He presented his argument without legal assistance, without a lawbook, with only a one-page brief; and he won the admiration of Chief Justice William Howard Taft.

Huey could never have been elected governor without back-room deals with Standard Oil lawyers. He took it the way he could get it. But Huey, unlike the corrupt politicians of New Orleans, saw what had to be done. Louisiana was held in thrall by out-of-state corporations. There were only thirty miles of paved roads in the entire state, hospitals were virtually closed to the poor, the major rivers were unspanned by bridges, there was no schooling for half the children. As Secretary of Commerce, Herbert Hoover came to visit Louisiana. It amused him. He even smirked at the state's treasured Evangeline myth. Very little was known about her, he said; even her name was questionable; she might have been called Gwendoline. It was an unforgivable thrust, and in the autumn of 1928 Huey, now thirty-five and a candidate for governor, parried it for the wide-eyed rednecks and Cajuns. Standing on a cotton bale beneath flickering torches at Martinville, he delivered one of the most moving perorations in American politics:

"And it was here that Evangeline waited for her lover Gabriel who never came. This oak is an immortal spot, made so by Longfellow's poem. But Evangeline is not the only one who has waited here in disappointment. Where are the schools that you have waited for your children to have that have never come? Where are the roads and highways that you spent your money to build, that are no nearer now than ever before? Where are the institutions to care for the sick and disabled? Evangeline wept bitter tears in her disappointment. But they lasted through only one lifetime. Your tears in this country, around this oak, have lasted for generations. Give me the chance to dry the tears of those who still weep here."

Elected, he broke the power of the corporations. Louisiana's poll taxes were abolished, new taxes were levied on business, a debt moratorium was declared, the poor were exempted from the general property tax, textbooks were free, children rode in school buses. In three years he gave the state 2,500 miles of paved roads, 6,000 miles of gravel roads. Twelve bridges went up. Property assessments were reduced 20 percent, and at his new night schools 175,000 illiterate adults were taught to read and write. He was the only southern governor to treat blacks as equals; when the head of the Ku Klux Klan threatened to come into the state and campaign against him, Huey told reporters, "Quote me as saying that that Imperial bastard will never set foot in Louisiana, and that when I call him a son of a bitch I am not using profanity, but am referring to the circumstances of his birth."

He had been elected on the slogan "Every man a king, but no man wears a crown." One man did. Huey did. He called himself Kingfish after the head of Amos 'n' Andy's lodge, the Mystic Knights of the Sea, and "by the spring of 1935," Hodding Carter wrote, "Huey Long owned Louisiana." Newspaper critics like Carter went armed day and night. Some were beaten, kidnapped, and jailed. When his secretary's husband threatened to sue him for alienation of affections on the eve of his election to the Senate, Huey had him put in an airplane and flown through the skies all over the state until votes were in; then he was brought down. Every state judge was in his pocket, including the entire state supreme court. All policemen, state and municipal, reported directly to him. He alone held power over the schoolteachers, tax collectors, the state government, the banks, and the governor. Finally his legislature outlawed democracy. Huey, not voters, would decide who had been elected to what. When New Orleans rumbled with discontent, he called out the militia and entered the city at the head of his troops, like Caesar. He said he had tried to reason with his opponents: "That didn't work and now I'm a dynamiter. I dynamite 'em out of my path."

Early in 1935, after his legislature had shouted through forty-four bills in twenty-two minutes, one of the few honest men left in it rose to say, "I am not gifted with second sight. Nor did I see a spot of blood on the moon last night. But I can see blood on the polished floor of this capitol. For if you ride this thing through, you will travel with the white horse of death." He was hooted down. If any blood was spilled, it wouldn't be Huey's; he was surrounded by bodyguards carrying revolvers and submachine guns. And soon, his henchmen prophesied, he would be protected by the U.S. Secret Service, because it was clear to them — and to many of his enemies — that Huey's next address would be 1600 Pennsylvania Avenue in Washington.

Already he was a national figure, second only to FDR. He was the most widely discussed politician in the country. Clearly he was preparing to move beyond the borders of Louisiana. He was deeply involved in Texas politics, and he was planning to purge Joe Robinson of Arkansas, Senate majority leader, and Pat Harrison of Mississippi, chairman of the Senate finance committee. His outrageous clowning was the subject of editorials and cartoons in every metropolitan newspaper. At a Long Island party he drank too much, sauntered into the men's room, and ordered a tall young man standing at the urinal to "Step aside for the Kingfish of Louisiana." When the youth wouldn't, Huey, unconventional as always, attempted to direct the trajectory of his stream between the other's legs. He missed, and left the party with a black eye. That was low comedy, but there was little laughter in a Senate cloakroom when he told his colleagues, "Men, it will not be long until there will be a mob assembling here to hang Senators from the rafters of the Senate. I have to determine whether I will stay and be hung with you, or go out and lead the mob."

The President wrote his ambassador to Italy that Americans "are going through a bad case of Huey Long and Father Coughlin influenza — the whole country is aching in every body." That included Roosevelt. Like the radio priest, Huey had supported Roosevelt in 1932. (Unlike Coughlin, the Kingfish could rightly claim that FDR couldn't have been nominated without him.) Now he was angry at the entire New Deal. His income tax returns were being questioned, Farley was withholding federal patronage from him, and WPA projects in Louisiana had been suspended because of irregularities in local administration. The Kingfish's chief grievance, however, was that he wasn't President, and he felt he ought to be. He wrote a book, *My First Days in the White House*. (Roosevelt, he wrote, would be his Secretary of the Navy.) Asked if there would be a Long-for-President movement in 1936, he snapped, "Sure to be. And I think we will sweep the country." One of the few men on Capitol Hill to stare Huey down was Harry S. Truman. The obscure Missourian was carrying out one of the traditional chores of freshman senators, presiding over the Senate, when Long delivered one of his more venomous speeches. Afterward the Kingfish asked him what he thought of it. Truman answered sharply, "I had to listen to you because I was in the chair and couldn't walk out." But as the New Deal approached its second anniversary there were fewer and fewer Trumans. Huey was openly ridiculing the President on the Senate floor as "a liar and a faker," and it is a measure of Roosevelt's desperation that he was driven to solicit support from Theodore Bilbo of Mississippi, the most noisome racist in the South. Bilbo scorched "that madman Huey Long," but all he achieved was to attract a tornado of angry mail from his own constituents.

On February 5, 1935, the Louisiana peril cropped up in a discussion of federal appointments. The proceedings of the National Emergency Council recorded this exchange:

THE PRESIDENT: Don't put anybody in and don't keep anybody that is working for Huey Long or his crowd! That is a hundred percent!

VICE-PRESIDENT GARNER: That goes for everybody!

THE PRESIDENT: Everybody and every agency. Anybody working for Huey Long is not working for it.

SECRETARY OF STATE HULL: It can't be corrected too soon.

THE PRESIDENT: You will get a definite ruling any time you want it.

It made little difference. As Hodding Carter later noted, "On our side we had only the federal patronage. In a vote-getting sense, this consisted mainly of WPA work orders which were distributed by the thousands to the anti-Long organizations. They didn't help much. The poor jobless devils took the work orders readily enough, but they didn't vote WPA. Few among us could have won even an honestly conducted election."

On March 5, the second anniversary of Roosevelt's inaugural, the administration formally conceded that the country had something to fear besides fear itself. Speaking at a Waldorf-Astoria banquet, Ironpants Johnson, now the WPA administrator for New York, attacked the right-wing alliance "between the great Louisiana demagogue and this political padre." The Kingfish and the radio priest replied over the networks. Johnson returned to the attack — "If you put quotations from Hitler and Father Coughlin in parallel columns, you can't tell them apart, including anti-Semitism" — and the New Deal's heavy artillery joined him. Harold Ickes permitted himself to be quoted as saying, "The trouble with Senator Long is that he is suffering from halitosis of the intellect. That's presuming Emperor Long has an intellect."

Huey's intellect was greater than the old curmudgeon's; he seized equal time to lay his Share Our Wealth program before a nationwide radio audience. Fortunes would be limited to five million dollars. No one's annual income could be greater than $1,800,000 or less than $2,000. Provisions would be made for old-age pensions, bonuses for veterans, and cheap food through AAA surpluses. Children would receive a free education from kindergarten through college. Every family would be entitled to a $6,000 homestead grant and a radio, an automobile, and a washing machine. In their one foray outside Louisiana, members of Huey's Share Our Wealth clubs (there were no dues) had elected Mrs. Hattie W. Caraway to fill out her dead husband's Arkansas Senate seat. Now Huey's catchy ditty could be heard in slums all over the country:

> *Every man a king, every man a king,*
> *For you can be a millionaire*
> *But there's something belongs to others.*
> *There's enough for all people to share.*
> *When it's sunny June and December too*
> *Or in the wintertime or spring*
> *There'll be peace without end*
> *Every neighbor a friend*
> *With every man a king.*

To Forrest Davis, author of *Huey Long: A Candid Biography,* the Kingfish confided that he intended to outlaw the Democratic and Republican parties and serve four terms "as the dictator of this country." Throughout that spring and summer his popularity snowballed to frightening size. Turner Catledge of the *New York Times* felt that the administration had blundered in striking back at him; its replies had "probably transformed Huey Long from a clown into a real political menace." The Democratic National Committee conducted a secret poll showing that Huey, running for the Presidency on a third-party ticket, might take four million votes away from Roosevelt and capture enough key states to throw the 1936 election into the House. Jim Farley, the country's most skillful political fortuneteller, told Ickes in September that the Kingfish's vote would exceed six million. Already Huey and his allies were a visible influence in the Second New Deal; social security had acquired much of its momentum from the Townsend Plan, which Long backed, and the raising of taxes in the upper brackets and the Holding Company Act owed much to Huey's charge that FDR was a prisoner of the rich and the utilities. Huey knew it. In July he charged that Roosevelt was "copying my share-the-wealth speeches that I was writing when I was fourteen years old. So he's just now getting as smart as I was when I was in knee breeches."

Late in August, when Congress adjourned, the Kingfish was still skipping up and down Senate aisles, mocking "Prince Franklin," "Lord Corn" Wallace, "Sitting Bull" Johnson, and Ickes, "the Chicago Chinch Bug." Yet Huey, like his lonely scold in Baton Rouge, was visited by premonitions. A month earlier he accused his enemies of plotting his assassination with "one man, one gun, and one bullet" and a presidential pardon for the assassin. Now he said that in the next session he expected Congress to obey his orders, "provided I am back here — I may not be back here. This may be my swan song, for all I know."

It was. On September 8 he was in the Baton Rouge statehouse, cracking the whip over his legislature. Meanwhile one man with one gun was hiding behind a marble pillar in the capitol, ready to fire the one bullet. His name was Carl Austin Weiss; he was an idealistic young physician whose father-in-law, a district judge, had crossed foils with the Kingfish. Huey had retaliated by gerrymandering the judge out of his district and circulating rumors about his ancestry. At 9:20 P.M. Huey strutted across the capitol rotunda. Dr. Weiss stepped out and shot him in the stomach. In the next instant the Kingfish's bodyguards riddled the doctor's body with sixty-one bullets, but their chief was fatally wounded. "I wonder why he shot me?" he asked before he lapsed into a coma. Others wondered, too, and their speculation grew during the two days the body lay in state, dressed in white tie and tails. Floral tributes covered three acres; some 250,000 came to watch their leader's burial on the capitol's front lawn. "He was the Stradivarius, whose notes rose in competition with jealous drums, envious tomtoms," the Reverend Gerald L. K. Smith cried in his eulogy. "His was the unfinished symphony." Afterward Smith blamed the crime on the news media and Bilbo. Bilbo answered by describing Smith as "a contemptible, dirty, vicious, pusillanimous, with-malice-aforethought, damnable, self-made liar." Still, the speculation continued. In the bayous, Louisiana's poor, who owed the Kingfish everything, sang:

> Oh they say he was a crook
> But he gave us free school book
> Tell me why is it that they kill Huey Long?
>
> Now he's dead and in his grave
> But we riding on his pave'
> Tell me why is it that they kill Huey Long?

Over thirty years later Smith told students at the University of Illinois, "It cannot be proved that President Roosevelt ordered the assassination of Huey Long, but it can be proved that those who discussed his assassination were positively of the opinion that it would please the President." The President's first reaction to the murder — he was lunching with Father Coughlin and Joseph P. Kennedy at the time — was one of horror. No humane man could find pleasure in such a violent death. In the long run, however, the disappearance of the Kingfish from the national scene certainly brought FDR relief from a serpentine threat. Huey Long was one of the very few men of whom it can be said that, had he lived, American history would have been dramatically different.

Roosevelt knew he must face a third-party challenge from the right anyhow. Smith, Coughlin, and Townsend were determined to see Huey's symphony finished. Nine months after the funeral the radio priest announced to his vast audience — his hookup had grown to thirty-five stations — that a new party, the Union Party, had been formed. Its convention was held in Cleveland, where Coughlin ripped off his clerical collar, linked arms with Smith and Townsend, and brought admirers to their feet in a standing ovation. If they had come for a show, they got one. His oration was one long slander of the President. Every slur was greeted by waves of frantic applause, and the speech reached its climax in the most dramatic of all rabble-rousing techniques; Coughlin's great voice wavered and he staggered away from the lectern, collapsing into the arms of his guards as thousands screamed. That had never happened to him on radio. But he was more than a radio personality now, more than a priest; and it had been years since he had delivered anything remotely resembling a sermon.

In the spring of 1935 the President's closest advisers concluded that he was slipping in his role as a public educator. When they told him so, he replied, "People tire of seeing the same name day after day in the important headlines of the papers, and the same voice night after night over the radio. . . . Individual psychology cannot, because of human weakness, be attuned for long periods of time to constant repetition of the highest note in the scale."

Here the public wisdom may be deeper than it seems. There is more to history than politics. In the trivia of one decade the life style of another may lie, awaiting nothing but competent management and a change in the economy. This is not true of all minutiae; one searches in vain for any note of significance in the chain-letter craze that swept the country in May 1935. On the other hand, the excitement in Enrico Fermi's quaint little Roman laboratory appears in retrospect to be a study in understatement; it is clear from the humorous account by Fermi's wife Laura that by systematically bombarding all the elements with neutrons, Fermi and his students, though they didn't know it at the time, had just become the first physicists to split the uranium atom — establishing nothing less than a chain reaction.

Between the trifles and the stupefying are curious developments, some of them far more memorable than any congressional battle that year, which made 1935 a kind of technological watershed. Tiring of Father Coughlin and spinning the radio dial, for example, Sunday listeners might pick up twenty-year-old Orson Welles, playing The Shadow, alias Lamont Cranston:

MARGOT: Oh, Lamont, look! When that waiter started for the kitchen, the door opened without his touching it!

SHADOW (*casually*): Yes. Works by photoelectric ray.

MARGOT: Oh, what's that?

SHADOW: Look at each side of the door, Margot. See those chromium fixtures sticking out of the floor? Lights hidden at the top of them? There's a beam of light between those two bulbs. When anybody approaches the door, his body breaks that ray. Whenever the beam is broken the door opens without touching it.

MARGOT: How clever!

It *was* clever in 1935, and it was also the crude beginning of the electronics industry, which would eventually eliminate not only doormen but elevator operators, bowling alley pinboys, letter sorters, billing clerks, matchers of textile hues, counters of passing objects, guards at prison gates, insurance actuaries, accountants, magazine distributors, and a thousand other skilled and unskilled occupations. Automation, in a word, had begun.

So had the communications revolution, the displacement of privacy and the written word by Marshall McLuhan's global village. In June 1935 George Gallup conducted his first poll, for the advertising firm of Young & Rubicam. "Public relations" offices were opened by John Hill, Earl Newsom, and Carl Byoir. In 1935 *Becky Sharp*, starring Miriam Hopkins, began appearing in downtown theaters. Though many screens were not equipped to handle the process, it was the first feature-length Technicolor motion picture. To color film should be added certain allied developments. Nobel Laureate Guglielmo Marconi had discovered the microwaves which would first be used in World War II radar and, later, in television broadcasting. The Associated Press introduced its wirephoto service in 1935, to be followed by *Life* in 1936 and *Look* in 1937; the country was becoming accustomed to the concept of image. Combine all these with two other 1935 innovations — the first night baseball game, in Cincinnati, and the invention of the beer can — and the future middle-aged recreation of boys then in their teens begins to assume a familiar form.

Arthur Sherman's trailer industry had turned the corner during 1933's Hundred Days and was rapidly becoming America's fastest-growing business; within a year two thousand trailers and house cars would convene in

Sarasota, Florida. American youth was still expected to be mechanically minded then, and the hottest thing in *Mechanics Illustrated* was the General Motors independent front-wheel suspension, as described by G.M. President Alfred P. Sloan Jr.: "The simplest way to explain it is to say that we have put knees on our automobiles. Each front wheel will be attached individually to the chassis by its own soft spring. When it encounters a bump or a hole, it will rise or fall independently, as your leg is lifted or straightened by its knee without affecting your other leg or the equilibrium of your body. The result will be that the wheel, not the passenger, will get the jar." Knee action! But not even Alfred Sloan (or Arthur Sherman) foresaw the growth in American mobility and the interstate highway net.

In 1935 the sound of the Thirties — swing music — was heard for the first time. Benny Goodman, a forty-dollar-a-week clarinetist the year before, was trying to improve his situation by leading his own band. He wasn't having much luck; on the evening of August 21 the band was about to wind up an engagement at the Palomar Ballroom in Los Angeles, and no one had offered to pick up its option. The musicians were as bored by the saccharine, bland fox-trot music as the dancers. Goodman decided to go down in style to the swinging rhythm his sidemen preferred in after-hour sessions, using a Fletcher Henderson arrangement (Henderson, a Negro, was unacceptable to white ballroom managers). Suddenly the audience was aware of vibrant brasses, strong drums, singing saxophones smashing away at full speed, and wild improvisations as hot soloists, including Benny, rose in turn under the spotlight to embroider the theme. The result was electrifying; the room came to life, and in the eyes of the entertainment business the twenty-five-year-old Goodman overnight became king — King of Swing.

Not everyone was enthusiastic; a psychologist told the *New York Times* that swing was "dangerously hypnotic" because it was "cunningly devised to a faster tempo . . . than the human pulse" and would tend to "break down conventions." Yet it was characteristic of the decade that there was some form of swing for every age group. Goodman, Artie Shaw, Glenn Miller, and Tommy Dorsey — who was about to make his own memorable debut with "Marie" in Nixon's Grand Theater in Philadelphia — were idols of the tulle-and-white-buck Palomar, Roseland, Savoy, Hollywood Palladium, Glen Island Casino dancing youth. But there was also swing for children (Spike Jones), sweet swing for the middle-aged (Kay Kyser), sticky swing for the geriatric set (Guy Lombardo, Wayne King, Vincent Lopez), and even intellectual swing at Carnegie Hall, where one could hear subtle, intricate patterns for the most sophisticated ear. Through the reborn phonograph industry, every form of swing was available on 35-cent Bluebird and Decca or 50-cent Columbia records. The diversity, or, as some would have it, the balkanization of taste lay thirty years in the future.

This ecumenicalism was true of all lively arts. The concept of X, R, and

GP films would have been inconceivable. Everything had to be GP, because 85 million Americans went to the movies once a week, a large part of them as families; the average family annual movie budget was $25, astonishing in the light of Depression admittance prices. There were 17,000 theaters in the country, more than there were banks, twice as many as there were hotels and three times as many as department stores. Each theater owner showed between a hundred and four hundred films a year. He didn't have time to screen them all. Fortunately for him (and unfortunately for cinema art) the Hays Office, later the Breen Office, did it for him. The Catholic League of Decency, which began its vigil in 1934, saw to it that Hollywood avoided long kisses, adultery, nude babies, or married couples sleeping in anything except twin beds. Language on the silver screen was, as they said then, Rinso White; when Dennis King sang "to *Hell* with Burgundy," a thrill ran through audiences, as though a naked woman had run among them. Even titles went through the washing machine. *Infidelity* mysteriously became *Fidelity*, and *Good Girls Go to Paris Too* was transmogrified into *Good Girls Go to Paris*. In part this censorship is attributable to the values of the time. As Mae West said later, "We weren't even allowed to wiggle when we sang." Mae's films were picketed after her reply to Cary Grant's "Darling, you need a rest — let me take you away somewhere" slipped past Breen. (Stroking her coiffure and running her tongue over her teeth, she answered, "Would you call that a rest?") *Life* had to go to court for the right to distribute its issue on "Birth of a Baby," and *Time*'s thin-lipped comment on Erskine Caldwell's *God's Little Acre* was that it "underlines a recent tendency of U.S. publishers: to go as near the limits of censorship as possible."

In equal part, censorship reflected the needs of a depressed population seeking not realism but an escape into celluloid. Hollywood, John Dos Passos wrote, offered a "great bargain sale of five and ten cent lusts and dreams." Even in the Depression a dime didn't buy much lust, if only because blue movies, then as now, appealed to a selected audience. Everyone dreams, on the other hand, so escapism reached the largest possible audience. Americans of all ages and persuasions could enjoy *Mutiny on the Bounty, Little Miss Marker, Captain January,* Busby Berkeley, and the thrillers of Alfred Hitchcock, which began appearing in the United States in 1935.

Moviegoing in this period attained its own ambiance, only part of which was seen on the Magnascope screen or heard over the Fox sound-track-on-film which replaced Vitaphone recordings. Everything that came out of the projector became part of the aura. The double feature was important; so was the Saturday serial and selected short subjects — a Terrytoon cartoon, say, with a Pathé newsreel, a Thelma Todd–Patsy Kelly comedy, and a Fitzgerald Traveltalk (". . . and so we say *Auf Wiedersehen* to picturesque, peace-loving Germany"). There were also bank nights, dish nights, bingo, Fleer's Dubble Bubble Gum, Assorted Charm wrappers, sluglike Tootsie

Rolls, a carpet of cold popcorn underfoot, and a great deal of amorous foreplay in the back rows. Most important was the dreaming in the darkness inspired by The Face, The Look, or The Body on screen. The movie mystique began to dissolve with the advent of television, but while it lasted, its power was immense; Gore Vidal was probably right when he put into Myra Breckinridge's mouth his own conviction that the movies of 1931 to 1945 were the most formative influence upon those who came of age in that "post-Gutenberg and pre-Apocalypse" era.

Or rather, he was *half* right. The other great familial activity in the Thirties was listening to radio. Like the cinema, it was tightly controlled; seven hundred of the country's nine hundred stations were organized into four networks, NBC-Red, NBC-Blue, CBS, and Mutual. Radio, too, was more innocuous than television today. Television hosts are permitted a certain amount of room for maneuver, but the announcer for a child's program in the Thirties who, thinking he was off the air, muttered, "I guess that'll hold the little bastards for a while," was all through. The entire family was concerned with what the shiny wagon-wheel microphones of the time picked up. Symbolically, perhaps, one of the most durable programs was NBC-Red's *One Man's Family,* a Norman Rockwell myth heard in 28 million homes on Wednesdays at 8 P.M. The announcer always began by declaring that the play was "dedicated to the Mothers and Fathers of the Younger Generation and to their Bewildering Offspring."

For millions, twisting the dial was a kind of tribal ritual. It was a rare household that could not identify Kate Smith with "When the Moon Comes Over the Mountain," Ruth Etting with "Shine On, Harvest Moon," Amos 'n' Andy with "The Perfect Song," Rudy Vallee with "My Time Is Your Time," Morton Downey with "Carolina Moon," and Ray Noble with "The Very Thought of You." MUrray Hill 8-9933 was the best-known telephone number in the country; you called it to register your opinion of performers on the *Major Bowes Amateur Hour.* The national audience couldn't imagine Christmas without Lionel Barrymore's presentation of *A Christmas Carol.* It is improbable that many Americans lost sleep over the question "Can this girl from a mining town in the West find happiness as the wife of a wealthy and titled Englishman?" but if they thought it foolish, they kept it to themselves. Because every scene had to be staged in the imagination, and because imagination is more colorful than any twenty-one-inch screen, the best of radio can never be matched by television. Charlie McCarthy, Edgar Bergen's whittled imp, was so real that Louis B. Mayer, the king of Sweden, and Winston Churchill extended their hands upon being introduced to him.

The ultimate significance of radio's appeal is that through it the first steps were taken toward a manipulated consumer society. Advertising's pioneer then was George Washington Hill, president of the American Tobacco Company. Thanks to Hill, American became the first firm to buy testimonials (including one from Madame Schumann Heink, the opera singer, who didn't even smoke). The concept of product identification began with the comedians "Jones and Hare, the Interwoven Pair"; when you laughed at them, you were supposed to think about socks. *Gangbusters* meant Cue, the liquid dentifrice; Bergen and McCarthy, Chase & Sanborn coffee; *Your Hit Parade*, with its obnoxious tobacco auctioneer's chant, reminded you of Lucky Strikes. The chant was Hill's idea; explaining its usefulness, he once spat on a polished board of directors' table. The act was disgusting, he said, wiping up the bubbly spittle with his silk handkerchief, but for that very reason you would never forget it. "LS/MFT" was another Hillism. Announcers repeated, "Lucky Strike means fine tobacco. Yes, Lucky Strike means fine tobacco," until listeners thought they would lose their minds, and a grateful nation should not have forgotten the local news commentator who was handed a flash in mid-program on September 13, 1946, and said to the mike, "Ladies and gentlemen, George Washington Hill died today. Yes, George Washington Hill died today."

At the time, "Not a cough in a carload" (Old Golds), "Ask the man who owns one" (Packard), "First he whispers, then he shouts!" (Big Ben), "Banish tattletale gray" (Fels Naptha soap), and "Reach for a Lucky instead of a sweet" were regarded as nothing more than minor irritants. The idea that the mass-production-consumption society was, in George E. Mowry's words, tying together "big business and the masses in a symbiotic relationship so close that the health of one was the health of the other" had not yet emerged. Few would have understood it, anyhow. Had they been told that a later college generation would deprecate consumer orientation and scorn society's preoccupation with security, they would have been baffled. Mechanical servants were just becoming available in large numbers. A surfeit of labor-saving gadgets was unimaginable. Security, moreover, was the impossible dream of the Depression. Nobody could have enough of it, and the viability of President Roosevelt's limited concept of social security — the act of 1935 covered only wage earners, not their families — was to be displayed in the presidential election of 1936, which loomed ever larger in the American consciousness and which, everyone agreed, would be a referendum on the New Deal.

Mid-Thirties Montage

Hello, Mr. and Mrs. America and all the ships at sea! Flash!

Oh, you push the first valve down
And the music goes round and round
Whoa, ho ho, ho ho ho
And it comes out here!

Barbasol! Barbasol!
The brushless shaving cream supreme!
Leaves your face so smooth and clean!

John Barrymore, Lionel Barrymore, Marie Dressler
Jean Harlow, Wallace Beery, Lee Tracy, Billie
Burke, Edmund Lowe, Jean Hersholt and
Madge Evans

in

DINNER AT EIGHT
Mon. Tues. Wed.

FOX-POLI
Continuous Performances

Margaret Mitchell's "Gone With the Wind" (Macmillan, $3) is an outstanding novel of Civil War and Reconstruction in Georgia. It is, in all probability, the biggest book of the year: 1,087 pages ... Scarlett O'Hara is growing up on the family plantation, a magnificent place. In April, 1861, she and her sisters wear hooped skirts, their scores of Negro slaves are lovable and happy....

WILL ROGERS, WILEY POST KILLED IN PLANE CRASH

And now — The Romance of Helen Trent! The Romance of Helen Trent: the real-life drama of Helen Trent, who, when life mocks her, breaks her hopes, dashes her against the rocks of despair, fights back bravely, successfully, to prove what so many women long to prove in their own lives — that because a women is 35 — or more — romance in life need not be over — that romance can begin at 35!

ADVANCE TO GO (COLLECT $200)

EDWARD VIII RENOUNCES BRITISH CROWN

CANDID CAMERA SALES UP FIVEFOLD

Here in Lakehurst it's starting to rain again, the rain had slackened up a bit. The back motors of the Hindenburg are just holding it, just enough to keep it from — It's bursting into flames! Get that shot! Get that shot! It's cra-crashing, crashing, terrible, oh, my, get out of the way please, it's burning, bursting into flames, and is falling on the mooring paths and all the people agree this is one of the terrible, worst tragedies in the world! Oh, flames four or five hundred feet into the sky, it's a terrific crash ladies and gentlemen, the smoke and the flames now and the crashing to the ground, not quite to the mooring, oh the humanity, and I told you, I can't even talk, mass of smoking wreckage, I can, I can hardly breathe, ohh, ohhh, ohhhh

FIBBER: *Gosh darn it, I'll fix it myself. Where's my hammer? Oh, it's in the closet.*

MOLLY *(in alarm): Don't open that door, McGee! I'm putting all my eggs in one basket I'm betting everything I've got on you*

NRA

LINDBERGH RANSOM RECEIVER SEIZED, $13,759 FOUND AT HIS EAST BRONX HOME

Knock, knock.
Who's there?
Eskimo, Christian, and Italian.
Eskimo, Christian, and Italian who?
Eskimo Christian and Italian no lies.

Me Tarzan, you Jane

The trumpets blow so low, so um-pah-pah
While everybody's shouting "Hotchacha!"

FOUR

The Roosevelt Referendum

BEFORE REPEAL* Benito Mussolini had declared, "I can sum up the United States in two words: Prohibition and Lindbergh!" That was totalitarian dogma; America was a land of gangsters and kidnappers. Then he was asked his opinion of American foreign policy. He replied, "America has no policy." This time Il Duce came painfully close to the truth. There was no mention of events abroad in Roosevelt's first inaugural address. He silenced all official advocacy of American participation in the League of Nations, and in his first appearance on the world scene he torpedoed the International Monetary and Economic Conference of 1933, an attempt to knit together the gold bloc nations. Alone among economists, John Maynard Keynes was delighted; Keynes preferred managed currencies to the gold standard, and he pronounced Roosevelt "magnificently right." But the President had not been swayed by Keynesian theory. He was deliberately sacrificing international good will to domestic priorities, putting the American house in order before turning to threats overseas.

All this was to change five years later, after Hitler showed his fist at Munich. Yet the danger to peace became evident much earlier. Before Roosevelt's second presidential campaign, Mussolini had seized Ethiopia; Spain had burst into flame; Germany had rearmed, occupied the Rhineland, and, Hull's soporifics to the contrary, made life wretched for Jews, 80,000 of whom had arrived in the United States by 1935. In Tokyo militant young officers drove Hirohito's government toward expansionism and imperialism; when a Japanese soldier slipped across the Marco Polo Bridge to patronize a Chinese brothel, his officers accused the Chinese of kidnapping him and then attacked Peking and Tientsin. Amelia Earhart, America's most celebrated aviatrix, is believed to have caught a glimpse of Japanese fortifications in the mandated Marianas. She was almost certainly forced down and murdered. Her fate was unknown at the time, but repeated provoca-

*Of the Eighteenth Amendment. Repeal meant virtually nothing else in the early 1930s.

tions by the Japanese, all of them front-page news, seemed designed to determine whether or not America was chickenhearted.

America was. State Department spokesmen protested and talked vaguely of "moral embargoes." Roosevelt and Hull expressed confidence in something mysteriously called "world opinion" — as though there were such a thing, and as though dictators could be intimidated by it. Congress passed new neutrality acts and resolutions, which the President reluctantly signed. He hesitated largely because he disliked any curb on presidential power; there was then little difference between the administration's conduct of foreign affairs and opinion on Capitol Hill. The New Deal had no designs on other countries. In signing a neutrality pact with twenty-one Latin American countries, Hull made it quite clear that America wanted nothing so much as to be left alone, and one of the few Hoover decisions endorsed by FDR was a refusal to join Great Britain in a condemnation of Japanese aggression in Manchuria.

In the Depression most of this was sensible; the home front demanded every resource the government could summon. But there was no sense in the Johnson Debt Default Act of 1934, barring loans to countries which had failed to repay their World War debts, or the Pittman Neutrality Resolution of 1935, which notified the world that under no circumstances would the United States help victims of aggression. Such measures merely encouraged dictators and tied the President's hands. Yet the fact that he said so, together with his support of the World Court, angered the high priests of isolationism. "Believing that he is under moral obligation to help decide the agelong quarrels of Europe and Asia," Charles A. Beard wrote, "President Roosevelt has resisted every effort of Congress and the country to impose limits on his powers of intervention abroad. In case of a major war in Europe or Asia, there is ground for believing that he will speedily get the United States into the fray. But with what outcome? That Americans will be euchred at the peace conference, whether they lose or win the war, is fairly certain."

In reality, speedy intervention would have been impossible. The country's military establishment continued to shrink during Roosevelt's first term, until America had fewer soldiers than Henry Ford had auto workers. The Army's real enemy, as Eisenhower later noted, was "money, or its lack." In 1934, when the President visited Oahu, the commanding officer decided to stage an exercise in his honor. The spectacle turned into a travesty; half the trucks and seven of the twelve World War tanks broke down in front of the startled commander in chief. The following year *Fortune* reported that although the M-1 Garand rifle had been adopted by the infantry, there weren't enough of them to equip a single regiment. "At the present rate of purchase," the magazine calculated, "it will take about thirty years to equip just the Regular Army with the new Garand, by which time it might well be obsolete." The title of the article was "Who's in the Army Now?" Among those in uniform, it reported, were a forty-seven-year-old first lieutenant and a sixty-five-year-old sergeant. The average captain was forty-three.

A great many Americans believed that *nobody* should be in the Army. Scholars generally held that the country had been tricked into the World War by wicked Europeans, and for once the people — 71 percent of them, Gallup found — agreed with the professors. The Depression had started in Europe, they believed; Europeans didn't pay their debts. From *Three Soldiers* and *A Farewell to Arms* to *What Price Glory?* intellectuals had argued that peace was worth almost any price. Had the story of Amelia Earhart's death been known, it wouldn't have been accepted; Allied propaganda about Belgians had immunized Americans to atrocity stories. Richard H. Rovere was but one of millions of schoolchildren who would later recall an idealistic civics teacher fond of saying, "We have a War Department. Wouldn't it be a splendid thing, boys and girls, if we had a Peace Department, too?" In 1934 the Convention of Episcopal Bishops resolved that "The Christian Church . . . refuses to respond to that form of cheap patriotism that has as its slogan, 'In time of peace prepare for war.'" Their congregations approved. (So did Adolf Hitler. "Those who support the pacifist ideal," he observed, "inevitably support efforts to conquer the world to its fullest.") Scarcely anyone in America was paying attention to Germany's new Führer; even the Veterans of Foreign Wars were campaigning for 25 million signatures to convince Congress that more neutrality legislation was needed. Among those who needed no persuasion was Senator Gerald P. Nye of North Dakota. Nye was chairman of the Senate Munitions Investigating Subcommittee — his chief assistant legal counsel was Alger Hiss — and he achieved the ultimate in scapegoatism by uniting villainous Wall Street financiers with foreign warmongers. "We didn't win a thing we set out for in the last war," he cried from podiums across the land. "We merely succeeded, with tremendous loss of life, to make secure the loans of private bankers to the Allies."

Among college students wealthy enough to defy tradition, militant pacifism was something of a cult. Their poorer classmates, although usually silent, agreed with them. In a national poll, 39 percent of undergraduates said they would not participate in any war, and another 33 percent said they would do so only if the United States were invaded. At Columbia and Berkeley, strongholds of pacifism, only 8 percent were willing to fight under any circumstances. In 1935 over 150,000 students demonstrated in a nationwide Student Strike for Peace, despite attempts to intimidate them at Harvard, Johns Hopkins, and CCNY. Subsequently a half-million undergraduates signed a pledge that if Congress declared war they would refuse to serve. Their concept of what they called "the system" was not far removed from "the establishment" their children would later learn to loathe. They were opposed to compulsory ROTC, violations of academic freedom and student rights, and Fascist activities; they wanted reform of college administrations. Radicals were members of the Student League for Industrial Democracy (SLID), a forerunner of the Students for a Democratic

Society. Their bible was SLID's *Blueprint for Action: A Handbook for Student Revolutionists*. Among the more memorable undergraduate pests were James Wechsler of Columbia, Eric Sevareid of the University of Minnesota, and Clark Kerr, Swarthmore '32.

The character of "the movement" (it was called that, too) varied from one campus to another. At Minnesota "We didn't like the leaders we observed in political life, and we didn't like the university authorities, who we thought were merely serving the system and not the cause of truth," Sevareid recalled. "Of all the instruments designed to uphold the existing order, I think we most hated the military establishment. . . . We began to detest the very word 'patriotism,' which we considered to be debased, to be a synonym for chauvinism." ROTC was the target of the demonstrations in which Sevareid participated, and on his campus they abolished it.

Princetonians treated the military as a sick joke, advertising themselves as members of a new VFW — Veterans of Future Wars. Vassar played hostess to a national convention of the supermilitant American Student Union. When the president of the College of the City of New York received a delegation of Italian Fascist students, his own undergraduates hissed; he called them "guttersnipes," and next day CCNY blossomed with lapel buttons reading, "I am a guttersnipe." The president broke up one meeting of militants by swatting them with his umbrella. Such retaliation was rare, but not unknown. A less primitive reaction occurred at the University of Pittsburgh, which invited General MacArthur to speak at commencement. The leaders of a protest demonstration were arrested and fined. A higher court reversed the conviction, but the following week matriculating Pitt students were required to swear allegiance to the U.S. Constitution, the Pennsylvania laws, and the university regulations. The university business manager explained to the press, "We want right-minded students here."

The vast majority of undergraduates were, if not right-minded, at least well-behaved. Then, as now, the militants were a tiny minority — 1 percent at CCNY; three-tenths of 1 percent nationally. By demonstrating, marching for the rights of labor, raising money for the Scottsboro Boys, and picketing Hearst newsreels they created a lot of noise, as later in the decade a quite different group made front pages by swallowing goldfish. Generalizing from a small sample is a peculiarly American failing. In 1970 a national advertiser taunted middle-aged Americans by running a photograph of a 1930s marathon dance and asking pawkily, "Now What Were You Saying About Today's Youth?" He was under the impression that marathon dance contestants had been exhibitionists. Quite the contrary; they were submitting themselves to an appalling torture in hope of winning a little desperately needed cash.

As members of the locked-out generation, most college students of the 1930s were preoccupied with acquiring marketable skills. The Depression hit their age group hardest; in January 1935 there were still several million youths between the ages of sixteen and twenty-four who were on relief, and a college president told his seniors that the 150,000 students being awarded degrees that June were emerging into a society which did not want them. *Fortune* polled twenty-five universities and concluded that undergraduates wanted a haven in a "job that is guaranteed to be safe and permanent." Wryly they chanted:

> *I sing in praise of college,*
> *Of M.A.s and Ph.D.s*
> *But in pursuit of knowledge*
> *We are starving by degrees.*

It was a poor joke. With tuition out of reach for 80 percent of American parents, a diploma often represented a four-year fight for survival. It was not unknown for undergraduates to work forty hours a week when school was in session and eighty-four hours a week during vacations. A study at Duquesne University found students employed as filling station attendants, undertakers' helpers, railroad firemen, steel mill laborers, and tombstone cutters; one Duquesne boy held 27 odd jobs on campus and in adjacent Pittsburgh. At the University of Michigan, Arthur Miller washed dishes for board and earned $15 a month from the NYA by feeding a building full of mice. He lived on that. At Minnesota, Hubert Humphrey couldn't afford textbooks, so he used those in the university library.

Working one's way through college has never been easy, and considering the rigors of a depressed economy it is something of a marvel that anyone made it. For ambitious youth, the challenges of the Depression continued right down to Pearl Harbor. That was not true of the rest of middle-class America, however. By the third year of the Roosevelt administration the country had drawn back from the abyss, and Jonathan Mitchell could write in the *New Republic*, "It feels good to have money again. . . . Happy days are here again. Of course, things aren't so good. . . . A man can be fired, and next morning there are ten men in line waiting for his job. But the unemployed have been around a long time. No one can expect us to sit home and be sympathetic indefinitely." There was even enough change around to provide allowances for adolescent children. Not much, to be sure; not enough to support a Woodstock Nation; but sufficient to finance a few fads and some bizarre badges of juvenile distinction.

The music came first. The great thing was to see a big band in person, but you could often hear good live music on college campuses — from the University of North Carolina's student band, led by Hal Kemp, or from Les Brown's Blue Devils of Duke. In obscure halls and bars were unknown entertainers whose time would one day come: Alvino Rey, who played (an omen) an electric guitar, the first amplified instrument most Americans had ever heard, or young Frankie Sinatra. Between 1933 and 1937 Sinatra was one of the worst-paid entertainers in the country. He entered amateur contests, filled in on local radio stations, and sang at lodge meetings for carfare, seventy cents. The great Sinatra constituency was still too young to support him in the manner to which he would become accustomed, still distracted by Big Little Books, Shirley Temple hairdos, G-Man underwear, Yale-bred Flash Gordon, bike foxtails, and scooters fashioned from orange crates and roller skates.

Meanwhile their older brothers and sisters were evolving the first youthful life style since the jazzy Twenties. It had its own language (such as "keen," "gas," "copacetic"), its arcane humor ("Confucius say," "Knock, knock"), its virility symbols (jalopies), and its special uniforms. Both sexes wore rubber-soled brown-and-white saddle shoes, beer jackets autographed by their friends, and reversible raincoats, preferably dirty. Girls' daytime wear also prescribed twin-sweater sets (cashmere or angora cardigans for the affluent), mid-calf plaid dirndl skirts, ankle socks (later to be known as bobby sox), and babushkas. Sport coats and slacks were essential for boys; saddle shoes could be replaced by heavy brogues shod with V cleats of steel, so that the wearer could click as he walked; and it was rather a good thing to have an argyle sweater knitted by a heavy steady. At formal dances — one a year in high school, at least four a year in colleges — all this changed. Under a gym ceiling transformed by crepe paper, girls glided across the waxed floor in long swirling tulle gowns, an orchid or gardenia corsage pinned on the left shoulder strap, with boys wearing rented tuxedos or dark suits and white bucks.

If the dancers limited themselves to fox-trot shuffles or the sedate Carioca, it could all be incredibly dull, but if the band was swinging the steps became much more athletic. By the mid-Thirties the jitterbug was known all over the country. The legitimate descendant of the Charleston, the Lindy Hop, and a dance called the Texas Tommy — which went all the way back to the Darktown Follies of 1913 — jitterbugging became as diversified as events in a track meet, which it sometimes resembled. There was the Charleston Swing, Truckin', Peckin', the Shag, the Suzy-Q, the Circle Swing, the Praise Allah, and Kickin' the Mule, in which boys and girls leapfrogged one another. Because of its suggestiveness, and because spirited girls sometimes revealed their pants, jitterbugging was unpopular among chaperones; as late as 1942 it was banned at all Duke dances.

The continuing repression of sex may be seen as a reflection of apprehension that all customs might vanish in what was, by any standard, a turbulent decade. Pregnancy was treated as a disgrace, often even among married women; maternity clothes were advertised as designed to "keep your secret." Everything about sex was secretive. The closest thing to a girlie magazine was The Stocking Parade, which published photographs of fully clothed young women whose skirts were hoisted five or six inches above the knee. Pornographers were midgets in those days. A puritanical society held them in check for the same reason that it recoiled from the jitterbugging coeds — or, to turn to another face of the prism, with the same motivation as the radio station manager who cut Tommy Dorsey off the air for swinging "Loch Lomond." The manager felt that too many traditions were being challenged as it was. Conventions honored for generations were vanishing. Most conspicuously, the nation's workmen, too weak to protest in Hoover's last months, were now on the march. The thunder of their boots frightened white-collar, middle-class America, but Labor's time had come. The unions were organizing, there was fighting on the barricades, blood was being spilled on the streets outside the mines and mills, and the worst was yet to come.

In many ways John Llewellyn Lewis was a preposterous figure. A barrel-chested, beetle-browed, six-foot three-inch goliath of a man, he relaxed by reading Shakespeare, the Bible, the *Iliad*, the *Odyssey*, Oswald Spengler, and the *Panchatantra*, an Oriental book of fables. The son of a blacklisted Welsh miner, he had become president of the United Mine Workers at the age of forty, but under his leadership the UMW had dwindled to half its pre-Lewis size; in 1930 a miners' group said of him, "He killed more than the leaders of our union. He killed its very soul." During the 1930s he was to become loved and despised as the symbol of militant unionism. Yet he had entered the decade as a Hoover Republican, an apostle of free enterprise, and the sworn enemy of progressive union policies.

In private John L. Lewis was a brilliant and engaging conversationalist, the grand strategist and champion of oppressed working men. To the public he seemed to be a peculiar combination of evangelist, thespian, and hamfatter. He said incredible things. Of his own propensity for self-aggrandizement he observed, "He who tooteth not his own horn, the same shall not be tooted." At the opening of a labor convention he said, "Heed this cry from Macedonia that comes from the hearts of men! Methinks that upon this decision of this convention may rest the future of the American Federation of Labor." Of his opponent William Green, president of the AFL, he cried, "Alas, poor Green! I knew him well. He wishes to join in fluttering procrastination, the while intoning, 'O tempora, O mores!'" And after he had split organized labor in half he crowed, "They smote me hip and thigh, and right merrily did I return their blows."

Few laughed; liberals saw him as a man of vision, while to his critics he was evil incarnate. In certain circles he had a capacity for arousing hatred matched only by President Roosevelt. Once former Secretary of War Patrick J. Hurley, appearing at a hearing as a coal owners' attorney, boasted that while a young man he had belonged to the UMW. Lewis gathered his million muscles, rose, and said sonorously, "It is a matter of pride to a member of the United Mine Workers to see a man of that organization go out into the highways and byways of national politics and make a name for himself that is recognized throughout the country." He paused heavily. "But it is a matter of sorrow and regret to see a man betray the union of his youth" — he paused again — "for thirty lousy pieces of silver." Hurley flew at him and had to be restrained. Lewis said carelessly, "Strike out 'thirty pieces of silver.' Let it stand 'betray the union of his youth.' "

That was pure ham. It was also courageous. When the President's Commission on Violence reported in 1969 that the United States "has had the bloodiest and most violent labor history of any industrial nation in the world," it alluded specifically to the 1930s. Organizers of industrial unions were being murdered. Governors were calling out the National Guard to suppress unruly workers. In Georgia, Eugene Talmadge built a concentration camp for pickets. Mine owners in Duquesne, Pennsylvania, a typical coal town, invested $17,000 in munitions during one year, bombed miners' homes, and burned crosses on hillsides. In Johnstown, Pennsylvania, the mayor of a company town told reporters that "A world without policemen" — he made it clear that he meant company policemen — "would be like a world without music." His district attorney added, "Give me two hundred good, tough armed men and I'll clean up them sons-of-bitches on the picket line." When unrest spread among women in the textile sweatshops, the trade journal *Fibre and Fabric* declared editorially, "A few hundred funerals will have a quieting influence."

The wonder is that the unions survived the onslaughts against them. When Roosevelt entered the White House they had been very weak. Lewis's UMW membership had fallen to less than 100,000 members. The American Federation of Labor as a whole had dropped to 6 percent of the work force; it was losing seven thousand dues-paying members each week, and was so servile to management that in 1932 it had opposed unemployment insurance. Aggressive industrialists were convinced that in confronting organizers they were battling the devil himself. They didn't mean to lose. As the La Follette Civil Liberties Committee was to discover in December 1934, over 2,500 American employers employed strikebreaking companies, the largest of which were Pearl Bergoff Services and the Pinkerton National Detective Agency. Bergoff was a multimillion-dollar heavy; the Pinkertons, favored by Detroit's automobile industry, earned nearly two million dollars between 1933 and 1936. Each of them maintained a small standing army which was ready to move into struck jobs carrying machine pistols, gas guns, and clubs. Both also infiltrated workmen's ranks as undercover agents. When a senator asked Herman L. Weckler, vice president of the Chrysler Corporation, why he hired spies, he replied, "We must do it to obtain the information we need in dealing with our employees." Thousands of men were literally working at gunpoint; the Pittsburgh Coal Company, for example, kept machine guns trained on employees in its coal pits. A congressional committee asked why. Chairman Richard B. Mellon answered, "You cannot run the mines without them."

Under these circumstances, the eagerness of workers to organize was really a measure of their desperation. The frightened miners, the sweated garment workers in Manhattan, the dime-an-hour laborers at Briggs Manufacturing in Detroit, and the nickel-an-hour clerks in Detroit knew that nothing else worked. State laws had been tried. In Pennsylvania employers systematically checked off 33 cents a week from the pay of each child to indemnify themselves for $100 fines imposed upon them for working the children ninety hours a week. The average steelworker's clothes caught fire at least once each week. Rather than invest in safety devices, the Pittsburgh mills lost over 20,000 workers a year maimed by industrial accidents. Girls working in five-and-ten-cent stores at five-and-ten wages read of the various aristocratic marriages contracted in Europe by Babs Hutton, the Woolworth heiress, and sang bitterly:

> *Barbara Hutton has the dough, parlez-vous*
> *Where she gets it sure we know, parlez-vous*
> *We slave at Woolworth's five and dime*
> *The pay we get is sure a crime*
> *Hinkey-dinkey parlez-vous.*

Potbellied Bill Green — "Sitting Bill," Lewis called him — had been indirectly responsible for the National Recovery Act's section 7(a). He had been among those nervous labor men who had complained to Hugh Johnson that NRA's industrywide agreements might be used to throttle unions, so the impulsive cavalryman had scribbled in the collective bargaining guarantee. But Green didn't see the possibilities in the clause. It was, in fact, quite vague; employers were not obliged to recognize unions, they could deal with company unions if they wished, and the method by which workers might choose their bargainers was not spelled out. Lewis, however, realized that details could wait. What was important was 7(a)'s propaganda value. It was a declaration of intention by the federal government. He compared it with Lincoln's emancipation of slaves and sent his brawny lieutenants into the coal fields with sound trucks and leaflets: "The President wants you to unionize. It is unpatriotic to refuse to unionize. Here is your union. Never mind about the dues now. Just join up!"

The alacrity with which the miners responded startled even Lewis. The NRA, which was supposed to revive business, was stimulating industrial unions instead. Within three weeks after FDR's signing of the act, 135,000 former UMW workers had taken up their cards again; by early 1934 Lewis had nearly 400,000 men on its books. Then Sidney Hillman and David Dubinsky brought the sound trucks and leaflets into New York. In less than a year their International Ladies Garment Workers Union had tripled its membership, to 200,000; by the end of the decade it would stand at over 400,000.

Franklin Roosevelt missed few political cues, but he was slow picking up this one. Nothing in the President's background had prepared him for a role as confederate of organized labor. He regarded himself as a succorer, a Good Samaritan to exploited workmen, which was not the same thing as a trade union ally. While he wanted higher wages, shorter hours, and better safety precautions, he was not at all sure that Lewis's way was the best, or even the right, way to do it. If labor became a powerful new economic force, the President might be unable to stand aloof, as he wished, from industrial conflict. Therefore in these first years he hesitated. "Labor's public enemy number one is Franklin D. Roosevelt!" Heywood Broun cried at a mass meeting. That was absurd. Nevertheless, the President did believe that Frances Perkins and Francis Biddle were too prolabor, and the only labor advocate on the Hill whom FDR admired was Senator Robert Wagner of New York. Wagner, pressing for fresh labor legislation, was slowly bringing the President around. Unfortunately the situation was too volatile. There was no time for persuasion.

As Lewis signed up more and more workmen — watched uneasily by Green, who kept warning, "Now John, take it easy" — the inevitability of crippling strikes drew nearer. Industry was preparing to man the barricades, and sometimes even preparing the barricades. The domestic market for munitions had never been so great. During eight weeks in the summer of 1933, policemen in the tiny Kentucky town of Lynch bought 41 rifles, 21 revolvers, 500 cartridges, and a supply of tear gas canisters. When federal marshals pointed out that instigators of violence might face federal charges, the company towns hotly replied that they were private property; Washington had no power over them. In Muncie, Indiana, the research team of Robert and Helen Lynd found that General Motors was subsidizing an expanded police force to jail suspected organizers. The A & P shut down its Cleveland stores for several days and docked its bewildered employees for the lost time — just to show them what they might expect if they joined a union. When Lewis opened the labor wars of the Thirties by taking out 70,000 Pennsylvania miners in 1934, and the strike spread across the Allegheny valley, the mayor of Duquesne talked as though the strikers were Indians he intended to head off at the pass: "We're going to meet 'em at the bridge and break their goddam heads."

In all, there were 1,856 strikes in 1934, most of them for union recognition. It was a time of martyrdom; terrorism colored that year of labor history like one vast bloodstain. Outside the Frick mines hired guns shot union miners emerging from the shafts. In the company town of Kohler, Wisconsin, strikebreakers opened fire on an AFL picket line, killing two men and wounding thirty-five. At Toledo's Electric Auto-Lite Company, where the newly organized United Auto Workers were trying to bargain with an intransigent management, National Guardsmen shot twenty-seven workmen. Striking longshoremen were murdered in San Francisco, striking teamsters in Minneapolis, and striking textile workers — fifteen of them — in New England and the South. In Minneapolis two special deputies were also killed, one a businessman. Eric Sevareid covered that strike for the *Minneapolis Star*. He watched, horrified, as vengeful policemen delivered a fusillade of shotgun fire into an unarmed, unwarned crowd, shooting sixty-seven people, two of them fatally. "Suddenly I knew," he wrote afterward; "I understood deep in my bones and blood what Fascism was." John L. Lewis said, "Labor, like Israel, has many sorrows. Its women weep their fallen and lament for the future of the race."

Labor's sorrows were deeper, and the laments greater, because so many seemed to have died in vain. Local unions won recognition in Toledo, San Francisco, and Minneapolis, but in the big industries — steel, textiles, automobiles, rubber — anti-union employers were triumphant. When Congress established a National Labor Relations Board, the National Association of Manufacturers pressed its members to ignore it, and in a test case one firm did; what happened was that the company's right to fly the blue eagle was withdrawn. The administration was still vacillating. Late in February 1935 a federal district court found NRA section 7(a) unconstitutional. Immediately Senator Wagner and Congressman William P. Connery Jr. of Massachusetts introduced legislation creating a National Labor Relations Board, establishing the right of workers to bargain collectively with management through unions chosen in federally supervised elections, and defining unfair labor practices. Roosevelt signed it on July 5, won over by Wagner's argument that the Depression could not end until workmen's wages were high enough to make them consumers of the goods they produced. Businessmen were unswayed. The Liberty League circulated a statement signed by fifty-eight eminent members of the bar declaring that the Wagner Act was just as unconstitutional as 7(a). Clearly the labor movement still had far to go. Employer resistance remained high; thirty-two more strikers and strike sympathizers were killed in 1935, and National Guardsmen were called out in South Dakota, Illinois, Nebraska, Kentucky, Georgia, and Ohio. Progress was still measured in inches, with miles of assembly lines unorganized, underpaid, and sweated.

For all anyone could tell, Bill Green had never read the Wagner Act. But John L. Lewis had. He had studied it while it was in committee, and realized that under its canopy of government protection a new House of Labor could be built. The defects in the old house were obvious. The American Federation of Labor was a loose alliance of jealous little barons, mostly descended from early immigrants to America. Except for miners and textile workers, its members were divided into craft unions: boiler-makers, carpenters, machinists, upholsterers, punch machine operators, painters, etc. Ohio rubber workers, attempting to organize themselves, were visited by an AFL representative who quickly separated them out into nineteen locals because that many skills were required to make rubber. To Green the United Auto Workers was a temporary abomination; in time its members would be sundered into a hundred craft chapters.

It was at the October 1935 AFL convention in Atlantic City that Lewis voiced his cry from Macedonia. It was a call for industrial unionism, in which mass production workers would be bound together by the nature of their products. Steelworkers would have one union, for example; the building trades another. It was, he argued, the only way big business could be successfully struck. The cry went unheeded. The convention voted him down. In the parliamentary maneuvering which followed, Big Bill Hutcheson, the rajah of the carpenters, called Lewis a "bastard." It was a mistake; in full view of Green and the thousands of delegates, Lewis slugged his tormentor so hard that the carpenter, streaming blood, had to be carried off the stage. Lewis adjusted his clothes, lit a cigar and sauntered out of the hall and, as it developed, out of the AFL. He wrote a one-line resignation to Green and told the press, "The American Federation of Labor is standing still, with its face toward the dead past." Then he announced the formation of a rival union complex, the Committee for Industrial Organization (CIO), later reorganized as the Congress of Industrial Organizations.

Belting Hutcheson had been a bit crude, perhaps, but it made Lewis more of a hero than ever to the millions of unskilled and semiskilled workers awaiting deliverance from economic servitude. There was a kind of fire in the strapping tragedian's eye now, and it lit up a whole movement. CIO meetings became singing meetings. The men joined in the ballad of Joe Hill, who died at the hands of the goons. To the tune of "The Battle Hymn of the Republic" they sang:

It is we who plowed the prairies, built the cities where they trade,
Dug the mines and built the workshops, endless miles of railroad laid;
Now we stand outcast and starving mid the wonders we have made
But the union makes us strong!

Solidarity forever!
Solidarity forever!
Solidarity forever!
For the union makes us strong!

If the CIO represented the non-Communist left in 1936, a great many New Dealers were coming to believe that the non-Fascist right was located not far from the new temple of the United States Supreme Court, which opened for the fall session of 1935. Facing the Capitol across Second Street N.E., it bore the inscription, sculptured in its marble facade, "Equal Justice Under Law." From the White House — and from much of the rest of America, including the dust bowl and John L. Lewis's bastion in the coal-laced hills — it appeared that the "nine old men," as Drew Pearson and Robert S. Allen called them, were committed to strange notions of justice. To be sure, interpretation was the very purpose of the Court. "We are under a Constitution," Chief Justice Charles Evans Hughes had said nearly thirty years earlier, "but the Constitution is what the judges say it is." The difficulty, according to *Time*, was that "the pure white flame of Liberalism has burned out, in Hughes, to a sultry ash of conservatism." In this the Chief Justice typified both the bench and the bar of his time. Franklin Roosevelt's legislative program was the closest thing to a revolution the country had seen since the War of Independence. The lower courts, which had been sitting in judgment upon it, represented the old order. Most of the federal district judges had made their reputations under Republican leadership or in corporate law. They were stockholders, trustees, members of exclusive clubs; men of industrial power were their friends, and like them they looked upon the New Deal upheaval as an atrocity. By the end of FDR's first thousand days in the Presidency, over a hundred of them had issued some 1,600 injunctions against federal laws. In addition, blue-chip attorneys were writing what amounted to private rulings discrediting unwelcome laws. The Liberty League's refutation of the Wagner Act was typical of the technique. The National Association of Manufacturers distributed it among its members, encouraging defiance of legislation passed by Congress and signed by the President on the ground that it was illegal.

The eminence of Supreme Court justices should have freed them from any sense of alliance with the past, and in fact the Court was more divided than many had realized. Seated at the Court bench in their black robes they looked monolithic, but in chambers they split three ways. Willis Van Devanter, James C. McReynolds, George Sutherland, and Pierce Butler were more zealous in their homage to Adam Smith than Herbert Hoover had ever been; they believed it was downright criminal to interfere with the fundamental "laws" of laissez-faire economics. Hughes and Owen J. Roberts were right of center and usually voted that way, but because they held their convictions less deeply they were regarded as swing men. Only Benjamin N. Cardozo, Harlan Fiske Stone, and Louis D. Brandeis belonged wholly to the twentieth century.

The conflict between Roosevelt and the Court had begun in the early spring of 1935, when the President, learning that 389 fresh challenges of new legislation were on federal dockets and realizing that he could not postpone the issue of constitutionality much longer, approved an immediate appeal to the Supreme Court of a district judge's ruling that the NRA was unconstitutional. Choosing the NRA was unfortunate; all nine justices agreed that it was invalid (though their reasons varied), and May 27, thereafter known to New Dealers as Black Monday, Hughes read the majority decision. What made it so black was not the rejection of the NRA, which had become excess baggage, but the extraordinary vehemence of Hughes's opinion. He all but branded Roosevelt an outlaw, and he took the unprecedented step of warning the President and Congress not to base broad federal statutes on their constitutional right to regulate interstate commerce.

FDR was the last man in the country to be intimidated by a conservative fiat *de haut en bas*. He was pretty good at taking stands himself, and on Wednesday he called a press conference to do just that. While Eleanor sat beside him, knitting as furiously as she had during the First Hundred Days, he called Monday's ruling "more important than any decision probably since the Dred Scott case." He reviewed Hughes's opinion that business is essentially local and thus lying within the jurisdiction of the states — that even though it might have an impact on the country as a whole, intervention by the federal government was illegal. By rejecting the concept that the forty-eight states were members of one interdependent community, the Chief Justice seemed to be suggesting that no matter how great a national economic crisis might be, Washington could do nothing about it. This, said the President, was a "horse and buggy definition of interstate commerce." He, too, was issuing a warning.

Attorney General Cummings believed that prospects of a reconciliation were gloomy. "I tell you, Mr. President, they mean to destroy us," he said vehemently, adding, "We will have to find a way to get rid of the present membership of the Supreme Court." For a while Roosevelt was more optimistic. As late as December 1935 he wrote the chief U.S. delegate at a London naval conference, "Things are going well in spite of Supreme Court majority opinion and Hearst and an 85 percent newspaper opposition." The new year changed his mind. On January 6, 1936, by a 6 to 3 vote, the Court declared the AAA unconstitutional. Agriculture, Roberts argued for the majority, was not a national activity. The attempt to picture it as one was an invasion of states' rights, raising the specter of "a central government exercising uncontrolled police power in every state of the union." Near Ames, Iowa, farmers hanged in effigy the six justices who had joined in this staggering interpretation. The tories, undaunted, proceeded to strike down the Securities and Exchange Act (6 to 3); Sutherland compared the investigation of Wall Street to the "intolerable abuses of the Star Chamber." Next to fall was the Guffey-Snyder Coal Act (5 to 4), on the ground that mining was purely local, even though the coal might be shipped all over the country. Then the Municipal Bankruptcy Act was thrown out (5 to 4), on arguments so tenuous that the entire New Deal, including social security and the Wagner Act, seemed doomed. All the voided law had done was to permit state-federal cooperation in the readjustment of public debts, the initiative lying with the states. To the conservative justices, apparently, any federal participation in local problems was forbidden.

In the first 140 years of its history, the Court had invalidated only sixty laws. Now, in little more than one year, the Hughes Court had nullified eleven Roosevelt measures. Its last victory of the session came on the eve of the national conventions, and it was the most shocking. Having already dismissed federal wages and hours legislation, it proceeded, in Morehead v. Tipaldo, to consider a New York state law on minimum wages for women. The vote was against it, 5 to 4. Butler, for the majority, wrote that "The right to make contracts about one's affairs is a part of the liberty protected by the due process clause," and "In making contracts of employment, generally speaking, the parties have equal rights to obtain from each other the best terms they can by private bargaining." In other words, he held sacred the right of a fifteen-year-old girl in one of Manhattan's sweatshops to reach an agreement with a textile millionaire under which she would be allowed to earn $2.39 a week. Neither Washington nor the states could interfere. *Nobody* had the right to put a floor under wages or a ceiling over hours.

There was merrymaking that night in the stately mansions overlooking the mill towns of New England and North Carolina, but conservatives in public life were dismayed. Here, clearly, was too much of a good thing. Herbert Hoover said, "Something should be done to give back to the states the powers they thought they already had." Sixty newspapers called for a congressional amendment; Governor Landon agreed with them. The Republican platform that year offered a nebulous promise to do something to protect women and children, without saying how, and the Democrats called for a "clarifying amendment." Only the President was silent. He was weighing courses of action, but first he must be reelected, and as he told Ray Moley, "There's one issue in this campaign. It's myself, and people must be either for me or against me." He expected them to be for him. He also anticipated more 5 to 4 or 6 to 3 decisions, and in a sense he would welcome them. As Ickes noted, he could use them "as a background for an appeal to the people over the heads of the Court."

In 1936 the United States lacked the political sophistication which would later transform national elections. There were no computer consoles then, no studies of key precincts, and only the barest beginnings of scientific polling. Returns were a mystery until election day evening; meantime partisans could speculate and assemble supporting data. Afterward, of course, everything was clear (political scientists have always had superb hindsight) but few had predicted a Roosevelt landslide that year, and a great many had written him off as a one-term President.

Their arguments were not all tortured. Here was a President who had promised to balance the budget four years earlier, and was instead running an annual deficit of six or seven billions. Seven million Americans were still looking for work; the programs designed to rescue them were turning out to be unconstitutional and hence useless. For most of the past eighty years the party now in power had been a minority party. The election of one of its members to the Presidency was interpreted by many as a freak of circumstance, and support for this one was being diminished by the defection of such distinguished Democrats as Newton D. Baker, Dean Acheson, and John J. Raskob; former Democratic presidential candidates Al Smith and John W. Davis; and Democratic governors Joseph B. Ely of Massachusetts, Albert Ritchie of Maryland, and Eugene D. Talmadge of Georgia. The vast majority of the big newspapers were anti-Roosevelt. Hearst wrote front-page editorials denouncing the "Raw Deal." Switchboard operators at the *Chicago Tribune* answered calls by saying, "Good morning. Do you know you have only [number] days left to save your country?" *Tribune* headlines (ROOSEVELT AREA IN WISCONSIN IS HOTBED OF VICE) and stories ("Governor Alfred M. Landon tonight brought his great crusade for the preservation of the American form of government into Los

Angeles") strongly implied that its subscribers might be turned away from the President.

Walter Lippmann was against Roosevelt; so was Dorothy Thompson. Mark Sullivan, another distinguished political writer, had forecast an FDR defeat as early as 1935, and that same year Charles A. Beard had written that "Roosevelt's spell of leadership is definitely broken." Bankers and brokers, whose contributions had accounted for 25 percent of FDR's war chest in 1932, were giving only 4 percent of this one. Indeed, the Democrats' perennial shortage of money, which was to continue into the 1970s, began in 1936. The Republicans were to spend $9,000,000 on Landon; Roosevelt's candidacy attracted little more than half that.

There was irony here. Republicans could afford to splurge because the economy had turned round since the last campaign. In 1933 Roosevelt's role had been that of a receiver in bankruptcy, and the intervening years had been far more prosperous than anyone had then thought possible. Unemployment was less than half of that in 1932. The Federal Reserve Board's Adjusted Index of Industrial Production had climbed from 58 to 101 in 1935 and would reach 121 in 1936. (It had been 125 in 1929.) Insurance assets had increased by three billion since inauguration day. The banks had been rescued. The national income and company profits had risen by over 50 percent; the Dow Jones industrial average by 80 percent. For the first time since the Crash, Wall Street was nervous about inflation — the sure sign of a bull market — and investors who had papered the walls of one room in the Union League Club with worthless securities four years ago were steaming them off and cashing them in. Nevertheless, a huge electric sign attached to the front of the club read, LANDON AND KNOX 1936. LOVE OF COUNTRY LEADS.

Earlier in the year the Republican nomination had been worth more. FDR's popularity, according to the few yardsticks then available, had touched bottom; a Gallup report had given the opposition an even chance to unseat him. As late as July the Democratic National Committee was writing off New York and Illinois and clinging to only the faintest hope in Minnesota, Indiana, and Ohio. By then, however, the President had assumed personal command of the campaign. In February he told Secretary Wallace, "Henry, through July, August, September, October and up to the fifth of November, I want cotton to sell at twelve cents. I do not care how you do it. That is your problem. It can't go below twelve cents. Is that clear?" Like paving roads during a campaign, that was traditional politics. What was new was his coalition theory. He believed that the Democratic coalition would smash Republican strongholds and establish his party as the majority party — provided the Democrats were blessed with that greatest of political assets, luck.

They were so blessed. The first piece of luck came on January 25, 1936, when two thousand men in full dress and women wearing ermine assembled in Washington's Mayflower Hotel for a Liberty League banquet to launch its campaign against Roosevelt's reelection. It was perhaps the most ostentatious meeting in the history of American politics; the *New York Times* said that it represented, "either through principals or attorneys, a large portion of the capitalistic wealth of the country." The chief speaker was Al Smith, now busy fighting legislation which would prohibit child labor. He arrived wearing a high silk hat and delivered a hysteroid, anti-New Deal polemic ("The New Deal smells of the stench of Communistic Russia") which thrilled everyone with an annual income of $100,000. Pierre S. Du Pont called it "perfect." John Nance Garner agreed. The Democrats didn't have to spend a cent or deliver a speech, the Vice President said; their return to power had been assured by tycoons who had completely misjudged the American temper.

On June 11 the Republicans nominated Alfred M. Landon, thereafter to be known as Alf, in Cleveland. He was a good governor, and his platform was to the left of the one Roosevelt had run on in 1932. Unfortunately for Landon's chances, his essential liberalism was obscured by the men around him. Republican chairman Henry P. Fletcher defined the campaign issue as "constitutional government." Henry Ford said he hadn't voted in twenty years, but he would this time because "Landon is like Coolidge." Landon was christened "the Kansas Coolidge"; his symbol was to be the Kansas sunflower, of which FDR dryly noted that it was yellow, had a black heart, was useful only as parrot food, and always died before November.

For Landon there was the further embarrassment of Herbert Hoover. The thirty-first President arrived in Cleveland with an uninstructed California delegation — chaired by Earl Warren — and quietly let it be known that he could be prevailed upon once more to honor the ticket with his name. Republicans weren't that unbalanced, at least not in June, but they did greet him with a fifteen-minute ovation. Roosevelt's acronyms had almost exhausted the alphabet, he said slyly, "but of course the new Russian alphabet has thirty-four letters." For the next four months he bombarded Landon with advice. The Kansas Coolidge escaped his blandishments, if not the stigma of his endorsement, and Hoover was reduced to listening to Roosevelt's speeches over the radio and booing the loudspeaker whenever the President paused for breath.

On adjournment the GOP delegates had sung, to the tune of "Oh, Susanna":

> *The alphabet we'll always have but one thing sure is true,*
> *With Landon in, the New Deal's out and that means PDQ.*
> *Alf Landon's learned a thing or two, he knows the right solution,*
> *And in the White House he will stay within the Constitution.*
>
> *Oh, Alf Landon!*
> *He's the man for me!*
> *'Cause he comes from prairie Kansas*
> *His country for to free!*

Somehow one feels that Pierre Du Pont could have afforded something better. Certainly the gentle governor had deserved a more dignified scenario. For a few days political reporters thought they had witnessed the year's record in convention slapstick, and then Father Coughlin and his colleagues preempted the lunatic fringe, presenting for the voters' consideration their new Union Party. The Union candidate for President was Congressman William Lemke of North Dakota, a strange individual with a pocked face, a glass eye, and a shrill voice; to the radio priest's dismay he insisted upon wearing a gray cloth cap and an outsize suit. Coughlin baptized him "Liberty Bill," and Gerald L. K. Smith drew up plans to guard the November polls with a hundred thousand Townsendite youths. The radio priest promised to quit the air forever if he didn't deliver nine million votes for the Union ticket. That seemed extravagant, but in June both major parties were taking Lemke seriously. Unlike the song "Oh, Alf Landon!" the sobriquet "Liberty Bill" was catching on. Father Coughlin rather liked the alliterative resemblance to "Liberty Bell." Then, too late, he remembered something: the Liberty Bell was cracked.

The following week the Democrats descended upon Philadelphia, gleefully driving McCormick reapers up and down the streets to remind everyone of Hoover's prediction that grass would grow there if Roosevelt moved into the White House. They were euphoric; except for the shadows cast by the Hughes Court, they had just about everything they had wanted four years earlier. Even the soldiers' bonus had passed that spring; Roosevelt's veto had been halfhearted and easily overridden. Being Democrats, they had to have at least one fight; Senator "Cotton Ed" Smith of South Carolina walked out when a Negro minister delivered a convention prayer. But even that fitted the coalition plan. In that year the black vote was still to be had for a prayer.

Roosevelt had passed the word; he was going to run against the Liberty League, not Landon. Accordingly, Alben Barkley's keynote address brought the convention to its feet with his scorn for Wall Street's anguish over the AAA: "My friends, their bitter tears are not shed for the little pigs. Their real grief comes from the fact of the slaughter of the fat hogs of Republican plunder which they had fed on the substance of the American people." That was powerful political medicine, but the President himself was going to excoriate big business in his acceptance speech as the "enemy within the gates."

His address was delivered at Franklin Field on June 27 before over a hundred thousand, who according to Marquis Childs "cheered wildly at each pause, as though the roar out of the warm, sticky night came from a single throat." It was not a flawless performance. The President was awaiting his introduction, and Robert Trout was describing the scene to his CBS radio audience, when, to Trout's horror, "the braces of his legs gave way and he fell. The pages of his manuscript were scattered. They were picked up by willing hands. He put the pages together as best he could in the few minutes before he was introduced. The manuscript was damp, crumpled, and spattered with mud." Afterward Roosevelt said, "It was the most frightful five minutes of my life," and, in a phrase which would have lost him the black vote in the 1970s, "I was the damnedest, maddest white man at that moment you ever saw."

Once under way he was magnificent. That was the night he said, "Better the occasional faults of a government that lives in a spirit of charity than the consistent omissions of a government frozen in the ice of its own indifference," and the prophetic, "There is a mysterious cycle in human events. To some generations much is given. Of other generations much is expected. This generation has a rendezvous with destiny." Afterward the vast crowd joined him in two choruses of "Auld Lang Syne" and then stood to give him a long, mighty ovation as he circled the stadium track in an open car, beaming up at them and waving his battered campaign fedora.

He planned to remain detached until five weeks before the election, when, his sense of timing told him, the electorate would be ready for him. In the meantime he would do his job and hope his rivals made mistakes. They obliged him. Before the end of the summer the Union Party was dissolving in its own excesses. Gerald L. K. Smith permitted himself to be quoted as saying of the electorate, "I'll teach 'em to hate." Father Coughlin declared, "I take the road of Fascism." Coughlin was beginning to fear Smith, who said, "The blood memory of Huey Long is still hot in my eyes," and, astonishingly, "Dr. Townsend and I stood under the historic arch at Valley Forge and vowed to take over the government." Presently Dr. Townsend was in no position to take over anything; he was in a District of Columbia jail cell, sentenced for contempt after he had refused to testify at a congressional hearing. Roosevelt pardoned him, and then Smith was jailed for disturbing the peace and using obscene language in New Orleans.*

Had Governor Landon been a more forceful man, he might have salvaged something, if only his dignity. Unhappily he came across to the public as a colorless, bespectacled little man with a flat, raspy voice. He read his speeches badly, and they were bad speeches; opening his first campaign trip in Pennsylvania, he declared for the ages: "Wherever I have gone in this country, I have found Americans." Moreover, like all men who ran against FDR, he became increasingly maddened by the elusiveness of his opponent. He told amazed Baltimoreans that if the President remained in power, he would erect a guillotine and decapitate his critics. He tacitly accepted endorsement by Fritz Kuhn's German-American Alliance (later Bund), let the Republican National Committee identify FDR as the candidate of the Jews, and insinuated that the President was a Communist.

It was in this campaign, the first to schedule nationwide broadcasts, that

---

*At this point the political evangelist disappears from this narrative. In the late 1960s the Reverend Mr. Smith was discovered in Los Angeles, where he described himself as "for all practical purposes, the senior adviser and liaison contact for something over 1,700 right-wing organizations."

the concept of selling a presidential candidate was introduced. The GOP had set aside over a million dollars for radio, and Robert Choate of the *Boston Herald* wrote Landon that he felt "the handling of Republican publicity should be on the same basis as the handling of any other article that wants to be merchandised to the public." On the networks, issues were shelved; the people were to be manipulated, not convinced. Front-page Hearst editorials charged that the Democratic campaign was being masterminded by Moscow; the GOP national chairman, John D. M. Hamilton, cried that Roosevelt's hands were stained with the blood of murdered Spanish priests; and such firms as Johnson & Johnson and Ingersoll Rand stuffed workmen's pay envelopes with caveats that they would be fired if Landon didn't win.

Beginning in October, other employers put in slips implying that social security contributions would come only from workers' pay: "Effective January 1937 we are compelled by a Roosevelt 'New Deal' law to make a 1 percent deduction from your wages and turn it over to the government. . . . You might get your money back, but only if Congress decides to make the appropriation. . . . Decide before November 3 — election day — whether or not you wish to take these chances." This was part of the Republican game plan. Landon's strategists actually expected a ground-swell of hostility against retirement pay for sixty-five-year-old workmen. On radio spots, actors hired by the Republican National Committee revealed in shocked tones that each man would be given a number — as though there were any other way to keep track of social security accounts — and perpetrated the hoax that people would be fingerprinted. On October 20 mammoth signs in factories put readers on notice: "You're sentenced to a weekly tax reduction for all your working life. You'll have to serve the sentence unless you help reverse it November 3." Finally, Hamilton went on the air to disclose that every man and woman who worked for wages would be required to wear around his neck a steel dog tag ("like the one I'm now holding") stamped with his social security number.

Until then Roosevelt had been campaigning in low key; his speeches, Marquis Childs wrote, were "more like the friendly sermons of a bishop come to make his quadrennial call." But when the Republicans mounted their attack on social security, his proudest achievement, it lit a bonfire in him.

On the evening of October 31, 1936, before a capacity crowd in Madison Square Garden, the flame blazed high in one of his greatest fighting speeches. He identified his enemies: "business and financial monopoly, speculation, reckless banking . . . organized money." The audience, on its feet throughout, waving cowbells and horns, howled its approval. In an edged voice he said, "Never before in all our history have these forces been so united against one candidate as they stand today. They are unanimous in their hate for me — and I welcome their hatred." The *New York Times* compared the applause to "roars which rose and fell like the sound of waves pounding in the surf." The President said, "I should like to have it said of my first administration that in it the forces of selfishness and of lust for power met their match." Now his voice rose: "I should like to have it said —" He had to pause, the ovation had begun; then, as the din abated slightly: "I should like to have it said of my second administration that *in it these forces met their master.*" Like a mighty storm, the cheering rose and continued long after his departure.

A few blocks from the Garden, nine-year-old Daniel Patrick Moynihan chanted, "Roosevelt's in the White House, waiting to be elected, Landon's in the garbage, waiting to be collected." The Republican candidate wouldn't have agreed. He and Chairman Hamilton were confident. The *Literary Digest,* basing its straw vote on telephone listings and automobile registrations, predicted a large Republican victory — 32 states with 370 electoral votes against 16 states with 161 votes for the President. A Harvard professor of statistics foresaw an electoral vote of 241 for Landon, 99 for Roosevelt, and 91 uncertain. Congressman Connery, cosponsor of the Wagner Act, had written Farley that "it looks like 60-40 in favor of Landon." In September Arthur Krock had told readers of the *New York Times* that "the Republican party will poll a far larger popular and electoral vote than in 1932. . . . Roosevelt's big majorities are over." Later he called this a "conservative" estimate. The President himself thought in June that he would win in the electoral college 340 to 191; at the end of the campaign he revised this, giving himself 360 to 171. Farley told reporters that Roosevelt would carry every state but Maine and Vermont. Most political writers agreed with Frederick Lewis Allen: "Whoever believes a campaign manager's prophecies?"

On the night of November 3 they discovered that a great many people who lacked telephones and automobiles knew the way to the nearest voting booth. Roosevelt had won the greatest victory in the history of American politics. His plurality was eleven million votes, which meant that since the 1932 election over five million Republicans had turned Democratic. Farley had been absolutely right; Landon had won only Maine and Vermont. The electoral vote was 523 to 8. Even Joseph Schechter of Brooklyn, the plaintiff in the Supreme Court case which doomed the NRA, had voted for Roosevelt. So had the other fifteen members of his family. So, for that matter, had Huey Long's father. Lemke had fewer than a million votes, and Father Coughlin announced that he was quitting radio. Later he changed his mind, but his influential days were over. The *Literary Digest,* similarly ill-starred, sold out to *Time.*

FDR, it seemed, could have almost any legislation he wanted, for more than 75 percent of both houses of Congress were now Democratic. The Republicans were reduced to tiny minorities — 17 senators and 103 representatives. There was grave doubt that the GOP could survive. And Europe was more than ever aware of the new world statesman. Winston Churchill and the French Chamber of Deputies congratulated the President. "Henceforth," wrote *Paris-Soir*, "democracy has its chief!" The chief himself was indulging in one of his favorite recreations, enjoying the cut and thrust of fencing with the White House press corps. "I knew I should have gone to Maine and Vermont," he said quizzically, "but Jim wouldn't let me." He showed reporters his election eve electoral college guess. One of them asked why he had given himself only 360 votes. His eyes danced. He said, "Oh, just my well-known conservative tendencies."

Portrait of an American

STOCKBROKER RICHARD WHITNEY

HE WAS KNOWN as the patrician's patrician, the White Knight, the hero of Wall Street. With his background he could afford to cut Franklin Roosevelt, which he did whenever possible.

He was descended from a family which landed at Salem in 1630; he had been captain of the Groton baseball team, had rowed varsity for Harvard, and made the Porcellian Club.

When he married, his father-in-law was an ex-president of the Union League Club. When he took a mistress, she was a rich, redheaded, fox-hunting widow from Wilmington. When he opened his own brokerage firm in 1916, he became J. P. Morgan's man on the floor — his brother George was a Morgan partner.

Richard Whitney was a big, strapping man, proud of his membership in the ruling class; he owned an elegant house at 115 East Seventy-third Street in Manhattan and a 495-acre New Jersey estate, where he stabled his eighteen thoroughbred horses, raised champion Ayrshire cattle, and reigned as Master of Fox Hounds for the Essex Hunt. His two daughters made magnificent debuts. His wife was an organizer of the Butlers' Ball. The Whitneys contributed to all the proper charities. They were Society.

On Black Thursday, October 24, 1929, at 1:30 P.M., the first big day of the Crash, Richard Whitney kept his head while all about him were losing theirs. As the representative of a bankers' pool, he waded through the chaos on the floor, reached Post No. 2 and offered to buy 10,000 of U.S. Steel at $205. Although his quieting of the panic was only temporary, it made him a national figure.

Post No. 2 was permanently retired and placed on display in the lobby of Richard Whitney & Company.

For five years he was president of the New York Stock Exchange.

In Philadelphia he delivered a widely quoted speech before the Chamber of Commerce on "Business Honesty."

On Capitol Hill he was called "the most arrogant, supercilious witness in the history of congressional hearings." Jovially he agreed.

But the White Knight had problems with, of all things, money. The presidency of the stock exchange was unaccompanied by salary — it was considered honor enough in itself — and M.F.H. Whitney had expensive tastes. Between giving balls, serving on boards, supporting Republican candidates, breeding horses and cattle, chasing foxes, and fornicating with the well-born Mrs. Margery Pyle Montgomery in Delaware, he couldn't make both ends meet.

When Repeal came, he enviously watched Joseph P. Kennedy multiply his already considerable fortune by winning the right to import Haig & Haig and Gordon's gin. Kennedy was an upstart and a New Dealer. Whitney was sure he could do better. The coming drink, he believed, was applejack, and during Prohibition distilleries near his country estate had turned out a highly profitable brand called Jersey Lightning. Whitney took over, organized the Distilled Liquors Corporation, and issued 148,750 shares of stock on the Curb Exchange. The price shot up to over $45 a share and Whitney was elated; Distilled Liquors was going to drive Joe Kennedy's Somerset Importers up against the wall.

Suddenly — almost overnight — it was Richard Whitney who was at the wall. Nobody was buying Jersey Lightning. To recoup, he bought 106,000 gallons of Canadian rye, paying for it with Distilled Liquors stock and warrants. The rye didn't move either. Distilled Liquors dropped to $13 a share, and the Canadians demanded more collateral.

He mortgaged his estate for $300,000 and desperately plunged into get-rich-quick schemes: a patented air-pressure bearing, a process for spraying metal to repair rust. They were even more unpopular than Jersey Lightning, and after borrowing from everyone in sight he began to steal.

As one of the most trusted men in New York, with Morgan power behind him and a gilt-edged office address of his own at 15 Broad Street, he was in a position to steal quite a lot. His first theft was $150,200 in bonds belonging to the New York Yacht Club, which had been put in his care for safekeeping. This was criminal embezzlement, but no one knew of it; indeed, New York University conferred upon him the honorary degree of Doctor of Commercial Science ("Your career in the world of finance has now become of nationwide significance"). And of course he intended to pay everything, once Distilled Liquors stock went up.

It went down. Trying to peg it at $9 a share, he borrowed from everyone he knew — and all his friends were millionaires. It wasn't enough, so he filched bonds belonging to Harvard, St. Paul's School, and his wife's and then his sister-in-law's trust funds. In a stroke of luck, he was named a trustee of the Stock Exchange Gratuity Fund, set up for the widows and families of deceased brokers. He rifled it for $667,000.

Then, at a routine meeting of the Gratuity Fund trustees — which Whitney was too busy to attend — a clerk blurted out that over a half-million dollars was missing, that Whitney had taken it and hadn't put any back. At the same time William O. Douglas, representing federal regulation, threatened to audit the books of all brokers. The exchange decided to beat him to it. Accountants looked at the books of Richard Whitney & Company and recoiled.

By now Jersey Lightning was a national joke. Whitney had bought up every share of Distilled Liquors to come on the market, 139,400 of them, now down to $3.50 a share. Over the past four months he had borrowed $27,361,500, five million of it with no collateral, and a million taken in outright theft.

J. P. Morgan, Thomas W. Lamont, and George Whitney were told but kept quiet. They considered it the gentlemanly thing to do.

Confronted by Charles R. Gay, Whitney's successor as president of the stock exchange, the tarnished White Knight asked that the charges be dropped. "After all, I'm Richard Whitney," he said. "I mean the stock exchange to millions of people."

It was a point. All the haters of Wall Street would gloat. The New Dealers would celebrate. That grinning traitor-to-his-class in the White House would be triumphant.

Gay thought it over. Then he rang the exchange gong, announced that Richard Whitney & Company had been suspended for insolvency, and pressed charges.

New York County District Attorney Thomas E. Dewey drew up the indictment.

At the St. Elizabeth Street police station, awed Bowery derelicts stood aside while he was booked for grand larceny. The lieutenant at the desk said, "Mr. Whitney, I'm sorry to see you in all this trouble, and I wish you luck." The prisoner thanked him icily.

Whitney was released on bail, but at the trial he was sentenced to five to ten years in Sing Sing. His butler bowed double when he left his town house to serve time. A crowd of five thousand gathered at the train station to see him off, and all that day limousines drew up at his town house, delivering flowers to Mrs. Whitney. She remained true to him.

Harvard announced with regret his resignation from the Board of Overseers' Visiting Committee to the Department of Economics.

At Sing Sing other convicts took off their caps when he approached them, and in prison yard baseball games they always let him get a hit. People respected an important man in those days.

But when Post No. 2 was auctioned off for five dollars, William O. Douglas just laughed.

FIVE

The Conservative Phoenix

T O PUT THE AFTERMATH of the New Deal's great referendum in perspective: the year 1937 lay midway between FDR's entry into the White House and Pearl Harbor — at dead center, that is, of the prewar Rooseveltian experience. The inconveniences and economies of the Depression had been institutionalized; 98 percent of American families now lived on less than $5,000 a year. Excluding reliefers, the average was $1,348. Typically, that income supported a mother, a father, and one or two children who lived in a four-or-five-room apartment or a six-room house. The house was almost always rented; after the great shakedown of 1929–33, few white middle-class Americans owned their own homes. Taxes, on the other hand, were inconsequential. Most people paid no income tax, and the top earners of 1937 — Louis B. Mayer of MGM, $1,161,753; Major Edward Bowes, $427,817; and Thomas J. Watson of IBM, $419,398; and George Washington Hill, $380,976 — spent or kept most of what they made.

Between May or June of 1937 and April of 1938, Alger Hiss's Woodstock typewriter was clattering most of the time on Thirtieth Street N.W., though in August he, his wife, and Whittaker Chambers took a break and drove to New Hampshire to see *She Stoops to Conquer*. Richard M. Nixon was then being investigated by the FBI. He wasn't suspected of anything. He wanted to be an agent, had taken the bureau's examination, and, as he wrote his law school dean, "They have been investigating my character since that time." The FBI rejected him. For others of his generation, however, 1937 was the year of making it. Joe Louis knocked out James Braddock and became heavyweight champion of the world. A Colorado halfback named Byron "Whizzer" White became an all-American. Ann Sheridan, who had something called oomph, replaced Jean Harlow, who had just died, as Hollywood's sex bomb. Mary Martin was about to make her Broadway debut singing "My Heart Belongs to Daddy," supported by a chorus which included Gene Kelly and Van Johnson. It was, in short, a marvelous year for entertainers, and America's sweetheart was twenty-five-year-old Ginger Rogers. Housewives envious of her narrow waist shopped tirelessly in girdle departments, to the immense satisfaction of rubber planters in what was then called the Dutch East Indies.

Du Pont chemists had developed a synthetic rubber called Duprene, but its significance would be overlooked until the Japanese seized the Indies plantations five years later. Although all sorts of exciting discoveries were being made in laboratories — the sulfanilamides, insulin shock treatment for schizophrenics, and a polyamide fiber made from coal, air, and water named Nylon — the country was largely unaware of them. Business was wary of new products. In searching for prosperity it clung instead to its 1920s faith in salesmanship, and 1937 was preeminently the year of the hard sell. George Washington Hill was still the trail blazer. To compete with him, full-page advertisements announced that "By speeding up the flow of digestive fluids and increasing alkalinity, Camels give digestion a helping hand"; a midget bellboy called Johnny Roventini made America's ears ring with his howling, "Call for Philip Morris"; and Old Golds were tested for British thermal units in something called an oxygen bomb calorimeter.

But pioneer manipulators could be found in almost all industries. It is perhaps symbolic that John D. Rockefeller — the symbol of traditional capitalism, who had defiantly listed himself as "capitalist" in Who's Who in America — died in 1937. Replacing him were management executives, with their newfound manipulation techniques and their reliance on A. C. Nielsen's "Advertising Effectiveness" reports. Listerine reduced germs "up to 86.7 percent." Women got the Monday Blues while worrying about Flour Face, Dated Skin, and Housework Hands. Men were fired because of Five O'Clock Shadow, owed their inability to get a date to the fact that they were Ninety-Eight-Pound Weaklings, and became social bankrupts because they lacked Talon zipper flies. (Most trousers were still equipped with buttons. In mixed company one man would tell another that a button was unfastened by saying cryptically, "It's one o'clock." That watchword held no terrors for the Talon man, but the other poor slobs would have to feel around furtively to make sure they were Gap-Free.)

Increased leisure, with all its implications for family life, was becoming widespread in 1937. By introducing part-time employment in the bad years, industry had assured the five-day work week. In recreation, radio and the movies held their supremacy — that year audiences first saw Snow White and the Seven Dwarfs, and heard Nelson Eddy and Jeannette MacDonald bellowing at one another in Maytime — but with more free time there were also more choices: amateur photography, stamp collecting, Chinese checkers, bingo, golf, bicycling, skiing, bowling, and the softball craze. The National Football League was in the fourth year of its east-west championship play-offs, though professional football's great moments awaited television.

Taking the oath of office for the second time on January 20, 1937, Franklin Roosevelt saw "one-third of a nation ill-housed, ill-clad, ill-nourished." Social protest continued to be the overriding theme among intellectuals, and would be until the world crisis preempted their attention. But the well-housed, well-clothed, well-fed two-thirds was less given to vicarious suffering. For the first time since the Crash, youth was speaking in tongues. Girls spoke of boys as smooth; a boy called a girl neat, though he knew she might give him the shaft. The ultimate accolades were "in the groove" and "terrific." Among the terrific hit songs of 1937 were several whose lyrics were as obscure as the most esoteric rock: "The Dipsy Doodle," "Tutti Frutti," "Three Little Fishies," and "Flat Foot Floogee with the Floy Floy." It was that kind of year.

It was a strange year in Washington, too. The President's extraordinary victory, combined with his political skill and an overwhelmingly Democratic Congress, should have given him an even freer hand than in the First Hundred Days. It didn't. Indeed, very little went his way. At times he appeared to have lost control, both of the country and, even more dismaying, of the party which owed him so much. Part of the difficulty could be traced to errors of presidential judgment, though his miscalculations were not so obvious at the time. Certainly he was entitled to interpret his lopsided victory over Landon as approval of Rooseveltian leadership, and the most powerful force thwarting that leadership — and the will of the people — was the Supreme Court.

His "horse and buggy" press conference hadn't been well received, and for over a year after that he had said nothing on the record about the Court. Even then, his objection to the ruling that no one could regulate wages and hours was no stronger than Hoover's; he merely observed that that opinion created a "no-man's-land" into which neither Congress nor the legislatures could trespass. Meanwhile, however, he was scheming. The Court's challenge had been on his mind even before it had arisen; during the 1932 campaign he remarked that at the time of the Crash Republicans had been in charge of all branches of the federal government — the White House, the Capitol, "and, I might add for good measure, the Supreme Court as well." Thus he viewed the issue as partisan. He may have been right, but the American people, including the men on the Hill, believed the Court and the Constitution were above politics. That strategic blunder was compounded by a tactical error. The struggle brought out what John Gunther called Roosevelt's "worst quality," a "deviousness," a "lack of candor" that "verged on deceit." He gave the impression of sneaking up on the Nine Old Men; as John Randolph said of Martin Van Buren, he "rowed to his object with muffled oars."

Those oars first became audible, for those with highly sensitive ears, on that rainy January day when he took the oath of office for the second time. Afterward he told friends that when the Chief Justice "came to the words 'Support the Constitution of the United States,' I felt like saying, 'Yes, but it's the Constitution as I understand it — flexible enough to meet any new problem of democracy. . . .'" Actually he had said something very like that in the speech that followed, and Hughes had heard him. The American people were determined to go forward, the President declared, and they "will insist that every agency of popular government use effective instruments to carry out their will." One New Dealer who was watching Hughes's face noted, "There was no doubt that the Chief Justice understood."

Two weeks later the President and the Chief Justice came face to face again. This year the Court had agreed to attend the annual judiciary dinner, and everyone present left with the impression that both men had been in high good humor. The reason for the jurist's jollity is unknown. FDR, on the other hand, was enjoying a private joke, soon to become public. Digging back in Justice Department records, Attorney General Cummings had found a proposal to invigorate the federal judiciary by appointing a new judge for every judge who had reached the age of seventy and had failed to retire. The document was dated 1913, and its author had been Attorney General James C. McReynolds — now the most vehement of the Court's Four Horsemen. If the principle were applied to the Hughes Court, Cummings pointed out, the President could name enough liberal justices to reverse the reactionary tide of 6–3 and 5–4 decisions. Hence the origins of what was to become famous (and infamous) as the "Court pack."

"That's the one, Homer!" Roosevelt had cried. He had then flown off to a conference in Rio de Janeiro, leaving his attorney general to draft the legislation. Cummings thought the plan sound, though at the judiciary reception he was uneasy, whispering to a colleague, "I feel too much like a conspirator." Roosevelt felt conspirational, too. That was why he was enjoying himself. The occasion appealed to his love of irony and secret deals. On February 4, 1937, Roosevelt and Cummings unveiled the bill, S.1392, to the assembled cabinet and Democratic congressional leaders. Ickes was delighted, but he didn't have to carry the ball on the Hill. The congressional leadership, which did, said little. Riding back down Pennsylvania Avenue, Representative Hatton Sumners of Texas, chairman of the House Judiciary Committee, abruptly said to the others, "Boys, here's where I cash in." No one knew it at the time, but Vice President Garner had reached the same decision.

Predictably, the Liberty League came back to life and joined the fight against Court reform. Arrayed with it were the U.S. Chamber of Commerce, the National Association of Manufacturers, the Daughters of the American Revolution, and something called the Constitutional Government Committee, led by Frank Gannett, a right-wing newspaper publisher. All this had been predictable. But there was also a spontaneous surge of protest on the community level, from American Legion posts, Kiwanians, and women's clubs. Most dismaying of all, the independent Senate liberals — Borah, Hiram Johnson, and Burton K. Wheeler — came down hard on the Court's side. Roosevelt took off his gloves; in a fireside chat he accused the justices of usurping power and vetoing a reform program which had just been endorsed by the electorate. At a $100-a-plate Democratic dinner at the Mayflower he appealed to party loyalty and demanded passage of S.1392. Wheeler struck back, crying that "a liberal cause was never won by stacking a deck of cards, by stuffing a ballot box, or by packing a court," and Senator Edward R. Burke, in the unkindest cut of all, told a New York rally that constitutional government faced "a rendezvous with death."

Meanwhile the Supreme Court, for the first time in its history, was preparing to emerge from its cloister. The Chief Justice had been telling friends lightly, "If they want me to preside over a convention, I can do it." Inwardly he was splenetic, however, and when the President argued that an overaged, undermanned Court was unable to deal with a logjam of appeals, Hughes decided to challenge him. According to Burton K. Wheeler's recollection, Hughes telephoned him and invited him to his home. As the Senator entered, the Chief Justice said solemnly, "The baby is born," and handed him a letter. Rapidly scanning it, Wheeler saw that it was everything he had hoped for. The Court was abreast of its calendar, it declared; no one was overburdened, and even if the President's charge were true, the adding of justices would slow, not hasten, the administration of its business. Furthermore, the Court had closed ranks; Brandeis and Van Devanter had endorsed the letter. As the senator left, Hughes said, "I hope you'll see that this gets wide publicity." Wheeler did; next morning he read it to the Senate Judiciary Committee, and, as he recalled long afterward, "You could have heard a pin drop in the caucus room."

That crippled Court reform. Even more interesting, the tory justices discovered liberal sympathies hitherto concealed. On March 29 — which was immediately christened White Monday by New Dealers — the Court reversed itself on minimum wages for women and children. Next the Wagner Act was upheld, and then, to the immense relief of the administration, social security. When Van Devanter announced his decision to retire, S.1392 seemed pointless; with the President's appointment of Hugo Black to succeed him, the New Deal had a clear majority on the bench. But Roosevelt had committed his prestige to the bill. He refused to withdraw. Instead he turned patronage screws harder and harder, and drove Joe Robinson, his Senate majority leader, mercilessly. The result was catastrophe. On July 14 Robinson fell dead of a heart attack, the *Congressional Record* gripped in his hand.

Now the insurrection spread among regular Democrats. Alben Barkley of Kentucky, Roosevelt's choice to succeed Robinson, won by just a single vote, 38 to 37, over Pat Harrison of Mississippi, and the Vice President plotted S.1392's defeat on Robinson's funeral train, defiantly telling the President, "You are beat. You haven't got the votes." Garner was right, though his insurrection meant that he would never again run on a Roosevelt ticket. Meeting in executive session, the Judiciary Committee reported the bill unfavorably. Next the full Senate voted it down, 70 to 20, and while still in a mutinous mood it overrode the President's veto of a farm loan act. For the first time in over five years, FDR had sustained a major legislative defeat in the Senate. In the bedlam which followed, most of his other big measures — wages-and-hours legislation, executive reorganization, a comprehensive farm program, and the creation of small regional TVAs — were lost for that session. Challenging the White House, which would have been inconceivable for any Democrat in 1936, was now acceptable.

The long-term effects of the failure of his Court reform plan are difficult to assess. The President had won his immediate objective. Interpretation of the interstate commerce clause had been immensely broadened, and because the nine old men really were old, death and retirement would shortly permit Roosevelt to choose a Chief Justice and his eight associate justices. The price was extremely high, however, and was correctly gauged by young Congressman Lyndon Johnson, who took his seat that year. FDR's miscalculation, Johnson reasoned, was responsible for the formation of the Southern Democratic and Republican coalition — a cross which would be borne by all subsequent Democratic Presidents, including Johnson himself.

On February 4, 1937, the day before he sent his Supreme Court plan to Congress, the President had put through a person-to-person call to John L. Lewis in Detroit. Like millions of middle-class Americans, Roosevelt had been exasperated by reports that General Motors workers were sitting down on the job, tying up plants and costing GM a million dollars a day. Every twentieth-century President, including Roosevelt, had endorsed collective bargaining, but no President could approve of trespass. Moreover, Roosevelt told Lewis, strikes threatened the rising prosperity, of which the administration was so proud. In March 1934 he had successfully used that argument with the AFL, which was then organizing the auto workers. The AFL had obligingly canceled a strike date, provoking 75,000 men into turning in or tearing up their cards. Now the rank and file were at it again. The President sympathized with them, but the timing was inconvenient. Lewis could hardly have agreed more. For him the workmen's rebellion was a personal humiliation. Having organized the coal mines, his CIO was devoting its energy and money to the steel industry. He wasn't prepared for a new confrontation elsewhere, and had mustered all his rich eloquence to persuade auto workers that for the time being their assembly lines must be kept moving.

It wasn't enough. Labor's leaders had misjudged the temper of their followers. Even Sidney Hillman, the radical Lithuanian, had not sensed the significance of the Court's 9-0 vote against the NRA. He had been downcast by Brandeis's vote. The justice had once devoted himself to closing sweatshops, Hillman protested; now he had "cleared the way for their reopening." What the junking of the NRA had really done was to open the way for revolt. The men had taken all they could. They were literally prepared to die rather than take more, and before the uproar was over some of them would do just that. It was not a popular strike. General Motors was well regarded by the general public. Its cars were popular, and somehow it had acquired the reputation of being a benevolent employer. That was unjustified. GM paid its twenty top executives an average of $200,000 a year; its workmen scarcely $1,000. Its spy system was one of the most vicious in the country. Complainers were dismissed on trumped-up charges, and foremen controlling the tempo of the assembly lines — the great moving belts carrying frames to which men would fasten and tighten bolts, rims, fenders, engine blocks, doors, and axles, hour after relentless hour — were merciless. "So I'm a Red?" a malcontent told a reporter. "I suppose it makes me a Red because I don't like making time so hard on these goddamned machines. When I get home I'm so tired I can't sleep with my wife." Another said, "It takes your guts out, that line. The speedup, that's the trouble."

Late in 1936 the United Auto Workers had written William S. Knudsen, GM's executive vice president, requesting a conference on the general subject of collective bargaining. Knudsen replied that the UAW should seek adjustment of grievances with local plant managers — as though GM policy weren't determined at the top. UAW leaders were debating their next step when the men decided it for them. The origins of the sit-down were European. Two years earlier, groups of Welsh and Hungarian miners had refused to come to the top until their wages were raised. It was in America, however, that the all-night sit-down, the affirmation that the worker has a vested interest in his job, became famous. It began on December 28, 1936, when workmen in Cleveland's Fisher Body Plant No. 1 spontaneously sat down and ignored the steel skeletons on the belt. Quick as fever the movement spread to Fisher Body Plant No. 2 in Flint, Michigan, and then to Pontiac, Atlanta, Kansas City, and Detroit itself, until 484,711 men employed by sixty plants in fourteen states were involved. To some it seemed almost miraculous. In Akron, for example, the men struck Firestone Plant No. 1 at 2 A.M. January 29. A puzzled foreman watched as a tire builder at the end of the belt moved three paces to the master safety switch. At this signal, with the perfect synchronized rhythm mass production had taught them, all the other tire builders stepped back. The switch was pulled, and a great hush fell over the plant. Into this silence a man cried, "We done it! We stopped the belt! By God, we done it!" The worker beside him burst into tears.

Some small firms capitulated to the early sit-ins, but the bigger plants, notably those of General Motors, didn't budge. Machine guns were being brought into Flint. In Dearborn, Harry Bennett, the former Navy boxer who had won the affection of Henry Ford, was recruiting a private army of three thousand, and blackjacks were stockpiled in the union camp. Inside each factory a cadre of tough young workers converted shops into fortresses. Armed with clubs and brake parts, they took turns guarding barricaded gates while those off duty played cards or made beds on the floor beside incomplete car chassis. Company property was carefully protected, but company men weren't allowed inside. When Fisher Body executives turned off the heat, the men roller-skated, sang, and danced. Periodically UAW men ran food in past the police.

To the management mentality of 1937, the sit-down was the ultimate outrage. Private property was held to be as sacred as human life, perhaps more so. White-collar executives had always suspected that the union leaders were Communists. Now they knew it. If subversives could prevent an owner from using his shop by draping their bodies across its doors, erecting flesh and blood blockades to keep him out, General Motors might as well turn the country back to the Indians. Their lawyers counseled patience. Obviously this tactic was unlawful. Why not turn it over to the forces of law and order? General Motors did, and instantly acquired an injunction ordering evacuation of the plants. Front offices were elated. But the moral force of the injunction collapsed when reporters discovered that the judge was a major GM stockholder.

Enter John L. Lewis. By now he had realized that if he didn't lead the auto workers he would lose them; therefore he went on the air to declare, "The CIO stands squarely behind these sit-downs." Father Coughlin called Lewis "a Communist stooge." Hermann Schwinn, Nazi leader on the West Coast, and General Nicholas Rodríguez, head of the Mexican Gold Shirts, offered their services to GM management. The NAM erected antilabor billboards all over the country. William Green, speaking for the AFL, denounced the strikers, and in the President's oval office Roosevelt, Garner, and Secretary Perkins debated the wisdom of issuing a statement.

Garner left the meeting under the impression that Roosevelt would take a stand. He didn't, and his silence meant that the man under the gun was Governor Frank Murphy of Michigan. GM lawyers had appealed to another judge, not a stockholder, and this time the evacuation order threatened the strikers with prison sentences and a fine of fifteen million dollars if they didn't quit the shops by 3 P.M. on February 3. By this time the workers were vowing that they were ready to die on their barricades. GM had selected the battleground: its Chevrolet plant in Flint. Murphy had called out the National Guard, and the plant was surrounded by soldiers, the Flint police force, and strikebreakers armed with pokers, clubs, and crowbars. Milling around in between were UAW sympathizers from Detroit, Akron, and Toledo. Over the mail gate hung a strikers' placard: THEY SHALL NOT PASS.

Murphy was ready to send Guard bayonets against the workers. Then, at the last moment, he called John L. Lewis and uneasily asked him what he would do. "You want my answer, sir?" roared Lewis. "I shall personally enter General Motors Chevrolet Plant Number Four. I shall order the men to disregard your order, to stand fast. I shall walk up to the largest window in the plant, open it, divest myself of my outer raiment, remove my shirt and bare my bosom. Then, when you order your troops to fire, mine will be the first breast that those bullets will strike. And as my body falls from the window to the ground, you will listen to the voice of your grandfather as he whispers in your ear, 'Frank, are you sure you are doing the right thing?'"

Murphy hesitated; his grandfather had been hanged after an Irish uprising. And the threat of blood was no Lewisian metaphor. Already it had begun to flow in Flint. During night skirmishes fourteen strikers had been wounded. The police had retreated, and the strikers were derisively describing the "Battle of the Running Bulls" to newspapers, a taunt which was almost certain to trigger police brutality. Wearily the governor tore up his orders. Then he forbade General Motors to impede delivery of food to the sit-downers. Embittered conservatives afterward claimed that Murphy had broken GM's morale. He had helped. So had Lewis. So, by remaining silent, had the President. The crushing blow, however, had been the UAW's technique. Under it the union had immobilized General Motors while making only token demonstrations at Chrysler, Ford, Nash and Packard. In theory — Liberty League theory — the others should have stood with GM in antilabor solidarity. In practice they had been carving up the GM market for their own cars. On February 7 GM directors had to cut its dividend in half. This cost Pierre Du Pont an estimated $2,500,000. From Wilmington came word that principles were all right, in their place, but management should not lose its head, not to mention Du Pont cash. At that General Motors capitulated. After forty-four days of crisis, Knudsen agreed to a conference. When the sit-downers heard about it they square-danced wildly in the frozen yards outside the plants.

Chrysler fell in line, and by summer every firm except Ford — who held out until 1941 — had signed a contract recognizing the UAW, seniority, grievance committees, surveys of speedup evils, the forty-hour week, and time and a half for overtime. It was nothing less than total victory. For a while perching on the job, any job, was the rage. New Jersey barbers sat in a nonunion shop, chefs in Washington's Willard Hotel sat on cold stoves, striking seamen sat in deck chairs, Woolworth clerks sat on their counters, striking waitresses persuaded their friends to occupy all seats and then order coffee, Chicago wet nurses sat until they were paid a higher rate per ounce, and a New York motion picture projection operator stopped the show to tell the infuriated audience that he was underpaid.

Now John L. Lewis's CIO had eclipsed the AFL. Industrial labor had put a very large foot in Detroit's very large door. The fact that Lewis had contributed a quarter-million dollars to Roosevelt's reelection campaign came to light, and a chill fell over the Union League Club. The *New York Sun* warned of THE CALLOUS SELFISHNESS OF JOHN L. LEWIS. The man's agents seemed to be everywhere. He learned that the Vice President had opposed him and thundered, "All labor asks is twenty-five lousy cents an hour. The genesis of the campaign against labor is a labor-baiting, poker-playing, whiskey-drinking, evil old man whose name is Garner. Garner's knife is searching for the quivering, pulsating heart of labor. I am against him officially, individually and personally, concretely and in the abstract." It was suggested that the CIO "explore" the possibility of a reunion with the AFL. Lewis snorted, "Explore the mind of Bill Green? I give you my word there is nothing there."

Everyone in industry knew his next target was U.S. Steel. He admitted it. "If we can organize here," he said, "the rest will follow. If the crouching lion can be routed, it's a safe bet that the hyenas in the adjacent bush may be scattered along the plain." The prospect of a conflict between the CIO and Big Steel was appalling. Huge as General Motors was, it was dwarfed by U.S. Steel, or "the Corporation," as it was more simply known to its officers. In 1934, despite the Depression, the Corporation earned $35,218,359. Its by-products alone — from ammonia to cement — came to more than a quarter-million tons a year. It owned mills and mines from Canada to Brazil, a fleet of ships rivaling the U.S. Navy, and thousands of miles of railroad track. It was the largest thing in American industry. Yet the average steelworker, working in constant danger, earned $369 a year and had to support six people with it. If anyone in America was ready for revolution, he was. By comparison, the auto worker was affluent, and now, with the heavily publicized settlements in Detroit, the steelworker knew it. It was noted that when *Modern Times* was shown in Pittsburgh, blue-collar audiences did not laugh at Charlie Chaplin's parody of a workman's five-minute break, in which his hands continued to mime the machine at first and then slowed down just long enough to allow him to grab a glass of water. The pantomime was too close to their real routines, the lockstep lives they meant to change.

But how? The right to organize, it seemed, could only be bought with blood. And then came a surprise. There would be more bloodshed in 1937, but none of it at Big Steel. On the lazy Saturday of January 9, when the GM sit-downs were entering the third week, Lewis had been in Washington, lunching at the Hotel Mayflower with Senator Guffey. There was a stirring around the maître d'hôtel's post and in walked bespectacled Myron Charles Taylor, the patrician chairman of U.S. Steel's board of directors and chief executive of the Corporation. Taylor bowed to the two men; then, after escorting Mrs. Taylor to another table, he strolled across the room to chat with Guffey and Lewis. The senator left, and the president of the CIO joined the Taylors for a pleasant twenty-minute talk. It was one of the more sensational moments in the history of the Mayflower, but no reporter was there to record it, and the lobby was empty next day when

Lewis, at Taylor's invitation, arrived at the industrialist's hotel suite for another conversation.

At first they discussed Gothic tapestries, medieval manuscripts, and Elizabethan drama. Taylor, finding his guest captivating, suggested the two of them begin conferring at his New York home, in secret, to resolve differences between Big Steel management and the CIO Steel Workers Organizing Committee (SWOC). Lewis brought more than charm to these meetings. He had figures showing that SWOC had signed up enough U.S. Steel workers to cripple it just as orders were piling up. For fifty years the Corporation had fought its own employees with guns and strikebreakers; surely, he suggested, it was time for a truce, formal talks, and a contract. Taylor reflected awhile and consented. Eight weeks later he initialed a pact agreeing to an eight-hour five-dollar day and a forty-hour week for steel-workers, and to paid vacations and seniority rights. Then they called in the press. When an organizer stumbled into Philip Murray's SWOC office and said he had just heard on the radio that U.S. Steel had been meeting with the CIO, Murray told him he was crazy and threw him out. Taylor's subordinates were equally shocked, though when the contract was signed March 7 Benjamin Fairless, president of U.S. Steel, came over to Murray and told him that he was the son of a miner. "Call me Ben," he asked. Murray answered, "Yes, Mr. Fairless."

Lewis had reached the peak of his glory. In the afterglow of the GM and Big Steel triumphs, firm after firm came round until the CIO had 30,000 contracts and three million members. Organized labor had become a significant American constituency, with partisans far beyond working-class wards. Thirty New York clergymen qualified for AFL admission as Ministers Union of America, Local 1; college students began singing labor's new anthems, and altered meanings of liberal (pro-union) and conservative (anti-union) came into general use. The CIO had won two famous victories. However, the routing of the crouching lion did not mean the scattering of the hyenas, by which Lewis had meant Little Steel — Republic, National, Inland, Bethlehem, and Youngstown Sheet and Tube. None of them would speak to CIO organizers. Tom M. Girdler of Republic, the tycoon who became the leader of Little Steel's intransigents, said he would quit his $130,000-a-year presidency and go back to hoeing potatoes before he would meet workers' demands.

On May 26 Lewis took the men out — 70,000 workers in 27 plants. Little Steel company police, and hired guns wearing local police uniforms but paid by management, expanded by 7,000 men. A Senate investigation subsequently reported, "Over $4,000,000 was expended directly attributable to the strike. A total of $141,000 worth of industrial munitions was assembled for use." Strikebreakers inside the mills were fed by parcel post and parachute drops, and local newspapers cooperated in back-to-work campaigns. Girdler paid strikers who played informer $25 a week while accusing union leaders of "interference in a man's private affairs." He added, "An ominous fact was repeated in the sketchy facts we had about some of these fellows: they were Communists." He refused to permit "intimidation" of "loyal workers" by "outside agitators." And he pledged: "I won't have a contract, verbal or written, with an irresponsible, racketeering, violent, communistic body like the CIO, and until they pass a law making me, I am not going to do it." The fact that the Wagner Act was such a law, and that it had been signed by the President and upheld a few days earlier by the Supreme Court, was unmentioned.

Violence came on Memorial Day, outside Republic Steel's South Chicago plant. Several thousand strikers and their families had gathered on a stretch of flat, sparsely inhabited prairie east of the factory. They were planning a protest parade. From the beginning of the strike, the police had interfered with token picketing; this time, however, Mayor Edward Kelly had announced that a peaceful demonstration would be permitted. It was hot and humid. Vendors with refrigerated pushcarts bearing nickel-a-cake brick ice cream were mobbed. On a signal the marchers formed ranks quickly, displaying their hand-lettered signs: REPUBLIC STEEL VIOLATES LABOR DISPUTES ACT, REPUBLIC STEEL SHALL SIGN A UNION CONTRACT, and WIN WITH THE CIO. Two men carrying American flags led the procession. Reporters and photographers swarmed around, and there was a camera crew from Paramount News. Like a long crocodile, the marchers crossed the fields singing "Solidarity Forever."

Just ahead, between them and the mill, the singers saw a line of five hundred heavily armed Chicago policemen. They hadn't expected this. It was, in fact, in direct contravention of the mayor's orders. The cops were there, it later developed, because an "anonymous source" had informed them that the pickets planned to march into the mill and seize it — that defenseless families, in other words, would try to overpower the professional strikebreakers manning Browning 30-caliber heavy machine guns at the gate. Anyhow, the bluecoats believed it, or said they did. To the approaching pickets a police captain shouted, "You dirty sons of bitches, this is as far as you go."

The parade slowed, but doggedly it edged toward the factory. There was no further warning. About 250 yards from the mill a wedge of bluecoats attacked a band of workers' wives, nightsticks thrusting into breasts. Other cops were aiming gas guns or yanking revolvers free. The men with flags shouted, "Stand fast! Stand fast! We got our rights! We got our legal rights to picket!" But police shouted back, "You got no legal rights!" and "You Red bastards, you got no rights!" In that instant the provocations later cited by Chicago police spokesmen took place; a few empty soda pop bottles were thrown, and workers called out taunts. At that, police grenades began to fly, a pall of nauseous tear gas settled over the procession, children screamed in terror, and the line buckled and broke. Then the murdering began.

At first the shots were scattered. As the general flight began, however, the bluecoats fired volleys. Some policemen pursued individuals. A woman tripped and fell; four cops held her down, smashing in her face with the butts of their pistols. Pickets lay on the grass or crawled about aimlessly on all fours, vomiting blood, and officers stood over them and fired into their backs. It was all there on the Paramount newsreels. Ten were dead, over ninety were wounded. The reporters called it the Memorial Day Massacre, but Tom Girdler said, "There can be no pity for a mob. As that artistic brawler, Benvenuto Cellini said, 'Blows are not dealt by measure.' Some of the mob were clubbed after they had started to run from the wrath they had aroused. Some women were knocked down. The policemen were there performing a hazardous and harsh duty. What were women doing there?"

The Paramount newsreel was suppressed on the fatuous ground that movie audiences — though conditioned by years of gangster films — might be incited to riot. The *St. Louis Post-Dispatch* exposed the suppression, but the *Chicago Tribune* described members of the unarmed procession as "lusting for blood." Both the McCormick and the Hearst press branded the CIO (and, by implication, the wives and children of CIO men) as communistic. No one was ever prosecuted, though eight more workers were killed, one of them a crippled veteran who was selling tickets to a CIO dance, before the strike was over. It ended when the men returned to work without a contract. Girdler's tactics had been too much for them.

They were not, however, too much for Robert M. La Follette Jr. The Wisconsin senator launched one of the most exhaustive and memorable investigations of the decade. His committee found that:

> . . . provocation for the police assault did not go beyond abusing language and the throwing of isolated missiles from the rear ranks of the marchers. . . . From all the evidence we think it plain that the force employed by the police was far in excess of that which the occasion required. Its use must be ascribed either to gross inefficiency in the performance of the police duty, or a deliberate attempt to intimidate the strikers.

Photographs had been enlarged and distributed, testimony from participants and witnesses published, and the story unfolded bit by bit for a public which, until then, had assumed that all strikers were suspect. When the casualty list first appeared, President Roosevelt had probably spoken for the middle class when he quoted Shakespeare: "A plague on both your houses." Lewis had replied, "It ill behooves one who has supped at labor's table and who has been sheltered in labor's house to curse with equal fervor and fine impartiality both labor and its adversaries when they become locked in deadly embrace." Roosevelt explained that he meant the extremists on both sides. It was not often that the President felt it necessary to explain anything, and when it developed that all the extremists in South Chicago that day had been antiunion, he moved to labor's side. Public opinion moved with him, and the National Labor Relations Board brought

Girdler to his knees. Thus the Little Steel strike was won after all, with union shops in all its plants except Bethlehem Steel.

The killings and beatings of CIO men continued throughout the year, and when all incidents had been reported to Secretary Perkins, she remarked that 1937 had been the most savage in the history of twentieth-century labor. It was in fact the high-water mark of the decade's spectacular picket line confrontations. Of the 4,720 strikes in 1937, the Department of Labor estimated that 82 percent had ended in settlements favorable to unions. By the year's end, nearly eight million workers were carrying union cards. "For the past four and one-half years," *Fortune* observed late in 1937, "the United States has been in the throes of a major labor upheaval which can fairly be described as one of the greatest mass movements in our history."

In 1941, when Ford and Bethlehem Steel were swept up in the tidal wave, there would be ten million union men; late in the 1940s the figure reached fifteen million. Lewis fell into public disfavor during the war, when he seemed to be blackmailing the President by threatening to withhold coal from war industries. The CIO, embarrassed to find that there really were some Communists in its ranks (Lee Pressman was for a time the CIO general counsel) was obliged to purge itself of them. Nevertheless, the original goal had been reached and was never again in jeopardy; American workmen had gained security and dignity, and with a new surge of prosperity they themselves would move to suburbs and join the expanding middle class.

Hardly anyone noticed when, on February 27, 1939, the U.S. Supreme Court declared the sit-down strikes illegal. The circumstances at the time had seemed to render that point irrelevant. If labor had sometimes stepped outside the law in its great struggle, liberals could argue, then surely it had been provoked. Any suggestion that the sit-downs had been a form of collective violence was denied or shrugged off; any mention of other incidents in which labor was at least as guilty as management — such as the bloody strike against the Aluminum Company of America in Alcoa, Tennessee, or of jurisdictional disputes between AFL and CIO pickets — brought hostile stares.

But a people cannot escape its past so easily. Certain precedents had been established, and would be remembered. Nor were those precedents to be altered by the fact that union men had been acting in concert with American history. They were, but that would merely strengthen the resolve of the rebels of the future. Violence had brought the United States independence, freed the slaves, and first conquered the West and then tamed it. Now it had raised working men up from the industrial cellar. Labor might forget that and turn conservative, but for liberals to deny other oppressed groups the right to revolt would prove impossible. Thus were the seeds of later anguish planted in innocence, even in idealism.

By late summer of 1937 the President felt he had to get out of Washington for what he called a "look-see" trip. In September his air-conditioned ten-car train nosed out of Union Station and rolled westward, pausing at selected stations long enough for him to deliver his simple little discourses from the back platform, remind constituents of what the administration had done ("How do you like your new high school?"), and enjoy the warmth of their affection. At Boise he told his audience that he felt like Antaeus: "I regain strength just by meeting the American people." Their enthusiasm seemed even greater than in the last campaign, and reporters, noting it, saw something else. Invitations to the presidential car were following an interesting pattern. Senators Burke of Nebraska, Wheeler of Montana, and O'Mahoney of Wyoming — Democrats who had fought FDR's Supreme Court bill — were being deliberately overlooked. At Casper, Wyoming, the President told the crowd that voters didn't have much use for politicians who gave lip service to ideals and then did nothing to put their ideals to work.

This was correctly interpreted as a threat to mutinous Democrats, though he didn't follow it up immediately. As usual, Roosevelt's mind was exploring several channels at once. He was pondering new legislation, looking toward the coming off-year elections, sifting the alternatives in foreign policy, watching the strikes, and brooding over his budget, which he had promised to balance in his first campaign. Until now that had been impossible, but he still wanted to do it if he could. This looked like the year. In its first months *Time* had reported: "Last week, with Depression lapsing into memory, the portents of Boom drummed excitingly throughout the land," and now, in report after report, Morgenthau was noting a small but accumulating surplus in the Treasury. To be sure Leon Henderson, the WPA economist, was worrying about rising prices; he had written a troubled memorandum expressing fear of a business collapse. Roosevelt had seen it, but he didn't want to renege again on the commitment to balance. During the Court fight he had assured Garner, "I have said fifty times that the budget will be balanced for the fiscal year 1938. If you want me to say it again, I will say it either once or fifty times more."

The prescription was as wrong for Roosevelt as it had been for Hoover. Stocks slumped. The President was tempted to say that conditions were "fundamentally sound" — he really believed that they were — but then, remembering his predecessor, he held his tongue. It made no difference. On October 19, "Black Tuesday," wave after wave of selling orders hit the market, the tape was twenty-five minutes behind the trading, and the backup of new selling orders indicated that bottom had not yet been touched. The following winter brought painful memories of 1929–30.

The New York Stock Exchange blamed the Securities and Exchange Commission, the SEC blamed the exchange, businessmen blamed a loss of confidence in the administration, New Dealers muttered darkly of a "capital strike." Certainly the year's real strikes, affecting 1,950,000 workers, had scarred the economy. In any event, the recession, as it was called, deepened the gloom in what was already a dark year for the President and the country. The skid downward was actually steeper than in the first months after the Crash. By the spring of 1938 five million people who had found jobs since 1933 were out of work again, and nearly 14 percent of the population was on relief.

It was hard for the President to abandon hope in a balanced budget, but Roosevelt was not Hoover; the spectacle of millions in want moved him more than Manchester economics ever could. And this was not 1930. A growing number of Democrats, including Henderson and the President's son James, had become Keynesian advocates. FDR hadn't read Keynes — he rarely opened a book when he could pick up the same information in conversation — and he was unimpressed by a long letter from England dated February 1, 1938 ("You received me so kindly when I visited you some three years ago that I make bold to send you some bird's-eye impressions"), in which Keynes recommended massive deficit spending. It couldn't be massive. In politics some goals, no matter how enchanting to the academy, are unattainable. Still, limited deficits had already passed Roosevelt's supreme test: they worked. In 1934 and 1935 they had fueled better times, increasing the money supply and pushing indices up. With his advisers recommending a Keynesian solution, and with the recession deepening as 1938 grew older, the President capitulated. On April 2, lunching on the train between Warm Springs and Washington, he told Harry Hopkins and Andrew Williams, director of NYA, that he was going to quit trying to balance the budget. Twelve days later, in a fireside chat, he explained to the country that he planned to ask Congress for three billion dollars to increase public works, relief, flood control, and housing. In June the stock market came to life, and in eight months the Dow index spurted from 99 to 158. Happier days, if not happy days, lay ahead.

His critics were unimpressed. Long ago the most vociferous of them had turned aside from any serious inquiry into current affairs and abandoned themselves to orgies of presidential vilification. When he floated one of his little valentines for them the week after the April fireside chat — he attacked big business's control over "other people's money, other people's labor, other people's lives" — they salivated as predictably as a Pavlovian kennel. Keynes thought that very naughty of Roosevelt. In that February 1 letter he had attempted to advise the President on the management mentality. Businessmen were not snarling beasts, he wrote. It was best to treat them as "domestic animals by nature, even though they have been badly brought up and not trained as you would wish."

This was one Keynesian recommendation that Roosevelt didn't even acknowledge. Let the Englishman stick to his last; FDR was the reigning expert on public opinion, and he wasn't going to dangle olive branches before his sworn enemies. Anyway, by then it was too late to reconcile the quarrels between the President and the American business community. Too much had been said, too many slights inflicted, too many ritualistic needles rammed into waxen images, too many stakes driven into imaginary hearts.

Willard M. Kiplinger, whose weekly newsletter circulated in business offices, later dated the reaction against the administration among the well-to-do from March 1, 1934. By that September *Time* had noted that "Private fulminations and carpings against the New Deal have become almost a routine of the business day," but the President himself was still too popular for open attacks upon him, let alone his family.

A stronger reaction was inevitable once the propertied classes had convalesced from their terror of early 1933 and discovered that by "recovery" FDR did not mean a return to New Era prosperity. He wanted changes, and those changes would benefit not the rich, to whose schools he had gone and in whose circles he had moved, but the oppressed. Talk of the Forgotten Man, businessmen agreed among themselves, merely fomented unrest. Anti-New Deal columns began appearing under the bylines of David Lawrence in *U.S. News*, Mark Sullivan in the *New York Herald Tribune*, and Frank R. Kent in the *Baltimore Sun*. The *Saturday Evening Post* was a particular haven for mourners of the past. One of its editorial writers declared indignantly, "We might just as well say the world failed as that American business leadership failed." The *Post* published a spirited defense of child labor, insisting that "the surest prescription for starting an American boy toward understanding success is to let him go to work before he is fully grown," and when Carter Glass said of New Dealers, "Why, Thomas Jefferson wouldn't even speak to these people," it was clear that opposition to Roosevelt was along class lines, not party lines.

The 1936 election returns indicated that excoriation of Roosevelt was counterproductive. It did not disappear, though. Instead it turned more virulent and went underground: to Westchester County and Orange County, Grosse Pointe and Miami Beach, Brookline and Longmeadow; Greenwich, Shaker Heights, Scottsdale, Kenilworth, and Winnetka; Wall Street, State Street, Chestnut Street, and La Salle Street. In lighter forms it could be amusing. There were the stories of the psychiatrist who went to heaven and was immediately sent to God "because He has delusions of grandeur; He thinks He's Franklin D. Roosevelt," and "Why is a WPA worker like King Solomon? Because he takes his pick and goes to bed." When FDR saw the celebrated Peter Arno cartoon of the overdressed rich on their way "to hiss Roosevelt" at the Trans-Lux Theater, he scribbled "Grand!" across it.

But there was nothing grand about the anti-Roosevelt sewage being circulated in upper-class and upper-middle-class clubs and homes in the late 1930s. Of course, they told one another knowingly, everyone in Washington knew That Fellow had caught gonorrhea from "El-ea-nor." (A

Negro had infected her.) Franklin D. was dying of VD, and that was the reason El-ea-nor was gallivanting around the country; after he was dead she was going to turn the country over to the Russians. Then she was going to Moscow and learn unspeakable sexual practices, taught only in the Kremlin. "Jimmee" Roosevelt would probably stay; his protection racket, selling "insurance" to honest businessmen, was battening.

"One is apt to forget nowadays," John Gunther wrote in 1950, "the furtive vindictiveness of the whispering campaign against Roosevelt, the sheer defamatory wickedness of the calumny that descended on him. . . . One forgets the atmosphere of the 'better' country clubs in the late 1930s, the ghoulish talk at the bankers' lunches, the burble of poisonous gossip at fashionable dinners." There were the Army officers who, even in uniform, refused to toast the President of the United States. There were the old men in mahogany-walled city clubs repeating the incantation, "Just another Stalin — only worse," or "We might just as well be living in Russia right now." There was even the Boston bookstore which informed Bennett Cerf, the President's publisher, that it would sell FDR's collected speeches "only if bound in that man's skin."

And over and over there were the clichés: That Man, That Fellow, trying to destroy the American way of life, you can't spend your way out of a Depression, our children's children will be paying, half the people on relief are foreigners anyhow, cut the relief rolls and enlarge the police and let trouble come, John L. Lewis has a key to the back door of the White House, That Man's smile has been grafted on his face by plastic surgeons, he has never earned a nickel in his life and just lives off his mother's income, and he's only a Jew anyway, descended from Dutch sheenies who changed their names, nothing but a New York kike. (An elaborate genealogy was worked out for this last, going back to a fictitious Colonel van Rosenfeld.)

In two striking magazine articles ("They Hate Roosevelt," *Harper's,* May 1936, and "They Still Hate Roosevelt," *New Republic,* September 14, 1938) Marquis W. Childs analyzed the haters. His first study cited "a phenomenon which social historians of the future will very likely record with perplexity if not with astonishment: the fanatical hatred of the President which today obsesses thousands of men and women of the American upper class. No other word than hatred will do," he went on. "It is a passion, a fury, that is wholly unreasoning." Childs suggested that "It permeates, in greater or less degree, the whole upper stratum of American society. It has become with them an *idée fixe.*"

What especially baffled him was that the majority of those who railed against the President had to a large extent "had their incomes restored and their bank balances replenished since the low point of March 1933." The value of some stocks had doubled, tripled, or quadrupled — "and indeed has multiplied some of them by ten." Corporate dividends were up over 40 percent. Thus far the incomes of the wealthy had not been heavily taxed.

(A man who made $16,000 a year was taxed $1,000.) Much of the burden in Roosevelt's tax programs had been passed along to the mass of consumers through processing or excise taxes.

Nevertheless the rich — Childs called them "the 2 percent" — regarded the administration of Washington as though it were an alien government. Indeed, in repeating the "Rosenfeld" myth they were quoting a Goebbels tract word for word. Some of them said outright that they would prefer Hitler to Roosevelt. While this was nonsense, it does suggest the depth of their feeling. Atwater Kent retired in June 1936 because he refused to do business while Roosevelt was President; a Du Pont vice president was honestly indignant when his servants left him because they could get more money from the WPA; a Bethlehem Steel executive had a heart attack when FDR was quoted — accurately for once — as saying of Bethlehem's president, "Go tell Eugene Grace he'll never make a million dollars a year again!" As Childs discovered, the fury of the rich was passed along to the middle-class white-collar workers who still believed in them, who had retained their faith in the shibboleths of the 1920s. Reviling Roosevelt became a status symbol among men who, unlike their "betters" (as the 2 percent were still called), were unthreatened by the labor unions and the transfer of power from financiers and big businessmen to Washington.

The President's reaction to this was puzzling. In Madison Square Garden he had said that he welcomed their hatred, but he was not the kind of man to relish widespread detestation of anyone, let alone himself and his family. Childs wrote, "He doesn't seem to mind." There is some evidence that he did. Raymond Moley has left an account of how Roosevelt, planning a conciliatory address on the role of American industry, would listen to New Dealers repeat the stories going the rounds of Forsyte homes until his face stiffened and it became clear that the speech would be "more like a thistle than an olive branch." The President told Norman Thomas that he was saving capitalism and resented the criticism of the capitalists. At one of his press conferences he quietly handed around, with minimal comment, a "confidential backgrounder" from a national news service to subscribing editors hinting at proof that FDR had syphilis.

As long as he lived, the 2 percent and their admirers would be ready to spring on his most innocuous move. When in 1939 he proposed that Thanksgiving be celebrated a week early to extend the Christmas shopping season — a boon to small businesses — the country split wide open; twenty-five governors agreed, twenty-three revolted (including the governor of Maine, who ate a symbolic can of sardines), and the issue had to be solved by a joint resolution of Congress. Even in death there were those who reviled him. One of them was Harold Gray, creator of *Little Orphan Annie*. Shortly before the President was stricken in 1945, Daddy Warbucks, unable to stand the thought of another term under Roosevelt, threw himself to his death. After the President's funeral, Gray brought Daddy back on the ground that "since the climate is different around here recently," it would be possible for a man of property and decency to breathe freely again.

Daddy Warbucks and the man behind him belonged to what Teddy Roosevelt once called the lunatic fringe. Pearl Harbor thinned the ranks of the haters, who had reached their crest during the late 1930s. In the opinion of Frederick Lewis Allen, their rage "flared higher and higher during 1934 and 1935 and continued at a high temperature until about 1938, when it appeared to weaken somewhat, if only through exhaustion." Meantime they had enjoyed FDR's 1937 reverses as much as if they were reading Defoe's *Journal of the Plague Year*, and though they were disappointed by the swiftness with which his 1938 recession faded, they were to feast joyously on a Roosevelt defeat once again in the fall.

Clearly the New Deal was on its last legs. The two Hundred Days periods had just about exhausted the administration's legislative creativity; the few presidential measures which hadn't passed contravened the growing conservatism in the country. Reforming zeal was nearly dead on the Hill. Only a man with Roosevelt's extraordinary gift for leadership could have held his huge, amorphous coalition together in November 1936. Next time only a war would keep it intact. The South was its weak link, and the conservative bloc fused in the Court reform fight was developing stronger ties each month.

Congressman Martin Dies of Texas, chairman of the House Un-American Activities Committee, explained that it would be incorrect to identify the bloc as southern, because it had "the support of nearly all small-town and rural congressmen." Its enemies, he continued, were "the men from the big cities which . . . are politically controlled by foreigners and transplanted Negroes," whose "representatives have introduced insidious influences into the New Deal."

The influences had been there all along; it was the congressmen who had changed. As one embittered New Dealer put it, "The farmers have forgotten that they were just as hungry and desperate as the people in city slums before the President bailed both out." It was true, but irrelevant. The anti-urbanism which Dies expressed was a powerful new force in the country, and in its hostility to the ways and ideas of city slickers, it was essentially conservative. Opinion polls in 1938 reported that while the President retained his popularity, his methods and his power were being questioned. Furthermore, the quality of his support had changed. According to a *Fortune* survey, about 62 percent of the voters were still for him, but those who felt he was essential — as against those who believed merely that the good in his administration outweighed the bad — had dropped from 34.9 to 17.7 percent. There had been little faith in pollsters since the *Literary Digest* debacle, but the coming off-year campaigns would confirm the trend, and congressmen who read their mail could sense it.

The last New Deal reform measure was the Fair Labor Standards Act, introduced early in 1937. It had a dreadful time. It provided for a forty-cent hourly minimum, a maximum work week of forty hours, with time and a half for overtime and no labor for children under sixteen. Employers were to be given eight years to meet the standards, starting with twenty-five cents an hour. In retrospect it does not seem Draconian. All the same, it was first forgotten in the battle over the Court plan, and then pigeonholed by southerners from low-wage states. FDR called Congress back into special session after his "look-see" trip convinced him that the country was behind him. The wages-and-hours law came up in the House and was trounced. It came up again, and lost again. Finally, in late June of 1938, it was sent to the White House for Roosevelt's signature.

By then he had decided he must do something about the Hill. Good Democrats up for reelection must win; the others should leave Washington. In the spring he had written a "Dear Alben" letter to Barkley, who faced a popular primary candidate in Kentucky's Governor A. B. "Happy" Chandler. Alben's opponent, Roosevelt wrote, was "a dangerous person . . . of the Huey Long type, but with less ability." Next he invited John L. Lewis to the White House and persuaded him to put his men and his money behind Barkley. Finally — or it should have been final — FDR announced that he would personally stump Kentucky to campaign for Alben. Unhappily local WPA administrators, eager to please the chief, also showed favoritism toward Barkley, and this blunder was documented in the Scripps-Howard press. It was an ugly overture.*

The entire country learned firsthand of the President's determination to intervene in local primaries through a fireside chat late in June 1938. Democrats in the 75th Congress, he reminded the electorate, had been elected by running on an "uncompromisingly liberal" platform. Citing the year-long battle over wages and hours, he said, "Never before have we had so many Copperheads." Copperhead was not a flattering term; it meant people in northern states who sympathized with the South during the Civil War. He explained liberal principles and then said that "as head of the Democratic party" he felt that he had "every right to speak in those few instances where there may be a clear issue between candidates for a Democratic nomination involving these principles, or involving a clear misuse of my own name."

That was all. Yet newspaper editorial writers, who had popularized the phrase "Court pack" so successfully that most readers did not know it had been introduced as a measure for Court reform, promptly christened this new venture a "purge" — thus inviting dark comparisons with the bloody events in Moscow a year earlier. To read some papers one would have thought that the President intended to bound back and forth across the land with a sickle, lopping off the heads of inoffensive men who had been audacious enough to disagree courteously with him once in a while.

And yet — one wonders precisely what FDR *did* have in mind. Jim

---

*It led directly to the Hatch Act (1939), forbidding political participation by federal employees below the policy-making level.

Farley, who knew when to leave a ship, fled to Alaska, groaning, "It's a bust." By any gauge of conventional politics, it was. Here was the leader of a national party — generally regarded as the most skillful politician ever to occupy the White House — deliberately inviting reverses. In off-year campaigns local personalities are usually far more important than national policy. Issues also tend to be local, and in 1938 there was a bewildering array of them: corruption in Pennsylvania, a state pension plan in California, the sit-downs in Michigan, a Rhode Island race track scandal, bribery in Massachusetts, bossism in New Jersey, strikes everywhere, and, in Connecticut, an uproar over a revolutionary proposal to build a four-lane, fifteen-million-dollar landscaped highway through the townships of Greenwich, Stamford, New Canaan, Norwalk, Westport, Fairfield, and Trumbull. As James MacGregor Burns has noted, "Putting out campaign brush fires all over the country was no way to leave the President in a commanding position."

But to Roosevelt this was no ordinary campaign. Ever since the Court fight he had been planning a realignment of the parties. Most conservatives were Republicans; let that party be their home. He saw the Democratic party as the instrument of liberalism. As the first national hero of peace, he was ready to spend his popularity in a gigantic political reform, and the first stage of his crusade was encouraging. His appeal to the people was undiminished. Everywhere crowds were unprecedented. In Marietta, Ohio, an elderly woman knelt to pat the dust where he had stepped; in Idaho, where the railroad tracks ran beside a quiet lake, a man had erected two American flags on a tiny homemade pier, and as the presidential car passed he stood at attention between them, his hand raised in a military salute.

FDR gave Happy Chandler the back of his hand. Chandler was so thick-skinned, and so determined to seize a piece of the President's coattails, that he had to be all but kicked and dragged from the platform. It was done, and Roosevelt leveled him with such magnificent scorn that Kentuckians could have no doubt about the presidential choice. In Texas the hallowed hands fell on the brows of Congressmen Lyndon B. Johnson and Maury Maverick; Senator Tom Connally, who had voted against the Court plan, was almost incoherent with rage when he heard Roosevelt announce — and from the train's rear platform at that — the appointment to the federal bench of a Texan the senator loathed. In Oklahoma, Colorado, Nevada, and California blessings were bestowed more discreetly, and one marked man, Senator Pat McCarran of Nevada, demonstrated that he was a better athlete than Chandler by actually fighting his way to FDR's side. On the whole the President's surgical job had been well done, however, and boarding the warship *Houston* the commander in chief wore a triumphant glow. In the big races, including Kentucky, his men had won. McCarran had barely slipped in, and in lesser contests little presidential prestige had been committed.

Now he was prepared to commit a lot. In Barnesville, Georgia, he cast the evil eye on Senator Walter George while George sat on the same plat-form. When FDR finished reading him out of the party, the senator said, "Mr. President, I regret that you have taken this occasion to question my democracy and to attack my public record. I want you to know that I accept the challenge." "Let's always be friends," FDR replied fatuously. The rest of the Georgia politicians present were jittery; they were trying to think how on earth they could survive such a feud. Traveling north, Roosevelt hexed "Cotton Ed" Smith of South Carolina and Millard Tydings of Mary-land. In early September he spent two days speaking against Tydings, a man who, he charged, wanted to campaign "with the Roosevelt prestige and the money of his conservative Republican friends both on his side." His New York scourge was Congressman John J. O'Connor, who, although he was the brother of the President's former law partner, had used his position as chairman of the House Rules Committee to bottle up New Deal legislation.

Then the people voted. The result, for FDR, was calamity and humilia-tion — the only election in which it can be said that the President was crushed. Of the ten principals marked for the political void, only O'Connor fell, brought down by an attractive candidate backed by La Guardia, Hopkins, Corcoran, and boss Edward J. Flynn. All the rest, including Tydings, George, and the medieval Smith, coasted in on landslides or sweeps. The southern Democratic party, with an identity all its own, was a mighty force now. Of it, President Kennedy was to observe ruefully in 1962, "Some Democrats have voted with Republicans for twenty-five years, really since 1938 . . . so that we have a very difficult time, on a controversial piece of legislation, securing a working majority."

In November surviving Democrats collided with rejuvenated Republi-cans. Conservatives beat George Earle in Pennsylvania, Philip La Follette in Wisconsin, and Frank Murphy in Michigan.* Among the new Republi-can faces were Robert A. Taft and John Bricker of Ohio, Leverett Saltonstall of Massachusetts, and Thomas E. Dewey, who ran Governor Lehman of New York such a close race that he was already being spoken of as a presi-dential possibility in 1940. Although Democrats retained control of both congressional houses, liberal strength in the House had been cut in half (Lyndon Johnson made it, but Maverick didn't). Overall, the GOP, which only two years earlier had seemed to be on its way to joining the extinct Whigs, had picked up a dozen governorships, eighty-two House seats, and eight new Senate seats. Republican incumbents had not lost a single race.

At his first post-election press conference the President was asked, "Will you not encounter coalition opposition?" FDR replied that he didn't think so. The reporter said, "I do!" and his colleagues laughed. Cryptically the President commented, "The trees are too close to the forest."

And so they were. The challenges to freedom's leaders no longer lay within the United States; they were on the other side of the world's two

*But labor took care of its own. Murphy was appointed to the Supreme Court.

greatest oceans, in Germany and Japan. As early as Christmas 1935 Roosevelt had written Baruch, "I still worry about world affairs more than domestic problems which include the election." Now, two elections later, his worries had multiplied. The country was still overwhelmingly isolationist; alerting it to the distant threats was a challenging task, so vast that it beggared description. But this much seemed certain: coalition politics on Capitol Hill would be irrelevant for some time. Even the hard-core Roosevelt haters would swing in line if the nation faced an outside enemy. Childs had conceded that; in 1936 he had written, "A major war would serve, of course, as it did for Wilson, to dissolve the fury," and, in 1938, "One thing, and one thing alone, could bring about a shift in the attitude of the hating class, and that, of course, is a war. . . . It is no accident that those who rail most violently against the Roosevelt domestic policies speak with grudging approval of the President's foreign policy."

What made this phenomenon remarkable was that his critics were endorsing something which did not exist. At this time he still had no foreign policy. He needed one; he knew that. He had begun looking for it during his first administration, and the search, still unfulfilled, had been pressed in earnest since a December day, nearly eleven months before the 1938 off-year election, when the United States gunboat *Panay*, lying at anchor on the Yangtze River above Nanking, had been deliberately bombed and sunk by aircraft from the Empire of Japan.

Late Thirties Montage

KARPIS CAPTURED IN NEW ORLEANS BY HOOVER

There's a small hotel
By a wishing well
I wish that we were there
Together

Miss Otis regrets she's unable to lunch today, madam.

Feed it to me Gene

MAN: *They found Lefty!*
AGATE: *Where?*
MAN: *Behind the carbarns with a bullet in his head!*
AGATE: (crying): *Hear it, boys hear it? Hell, listen to me! Coast to coast! HELLO, AMERICA! HELLO. WE'RE STORMBIRDS OF THE WORKING CLASS. WORKERS OF THE WORLD . . . OUR BONES AND BLOOD! And when we die they'll know what we did to make a new world! Christ, cut us in little pieces. We'll die for what is right! Put fruit trees where our ashes are!*

Bei mir bist du schön
Please let me explain,
Bei mir bist du schön
Means that you're grand

"Isn't this Los Angeles?" inquired Flier Corrigan. "Los Angeles! This is Dublin!" he was told. Flying a $900 plane which authorities had described as "not airworthy," traveling without official permission, passport, visa, parachute, or radio, he made the trip on $62.26 for gas and oil and has been dubbed "Wrongway" Corrigan.

Spank the skin

Rush, says the boss, work like a hoss;
I'll take the profits and you take the loss,
I've got the brains, I've got the dough,
The Lord Himself decreed it so

Mamma's little baby
loves a union shop

NAZIS SEIZE AUSTRIA AFTER HITLER ULTIMATUM GERMAN TROOPS ENTER, INVITED BY VIENNA

Who's afraid of the big bad wolf!
The big bad wolf! The big bad wolf!

Any evening, any day
If you come down Lambeth way
You'll find us all
Doin' the Lambeth Walk — oy!

FORD BRINGS OUT MERCURY, FIRST NEW CAR SINCE CRASH

HUMPHREY BOGART
and
LESLIE HOWARD
in
THE PETRIFIED FOREST

A fine romance!
With no kiss-es!
A fine romance!
My friend, this is!

BRENDA FRAZIER CATCHES COLD ON DEBUT EVE

SIX

A Shadow of Primitive Terror

LIKE ANOTHER BRIGHT SUNDAY four years later, December 12, 1937, was a day of rest for the ships of the U.S. Navy. The officers and men of the U.S.S. *Panay* felt they deserved it. Although the 450-ton, shoal-draft gunboat had been designed merely to protect American shipping and American citizens from irresponsible guerrilla bands roaming the shores of the Yangtze, her crew had worked around the clock for the past two nights. Nanking was about to fall to the Japanese army. Chiang Kai-shek's foreign office advised Americans in the city to leave. All that Saturday the gunboat had been taking aboard staff from the U.S. embassy, foreign correspondents, photographers, and American businessmen. Fully loaded, and with shellfire uncomfortably close, the *Panay* weighed anchor. Pursued by Japanese artillery, she sailed twenty-seven miles upstream and anchored in quieter waters beside three Standard Oil tankers. Afterward, American isolationists charged that the *Panay* was "convoying" the tankers and deserved her fate. But this was ridiculous. By treaty the Yangtze was an international waterway. It was spangled with the flags of all trading nations. Nobody was convoying anybody.

Indeed, the *Panay*'s commanding officer, Lieutenant Commander J. J. Hughes, had special reason to be tranquil. Twelve days earlier the American ambassador in Tokyo had informed the Japanese government of the gunboat's position and its probable mission. Hughes was flying the Stars and Stripes prominently. Japanese officers storming Nanking knew precisely where he was — which, as it turned out, was unfortunate for him, his ship, and Standard Oil's vessels. At 1:30 P.M. two flights of Mitsubishi warplanes with the rising sun on their wings dive-bombed and strafed the gunboat and the tankers until they all sank. Then, as lifeboats carried the survivors shoreward, they, too, were machine-gunned. Two American bluejackets and one civilian were killed; eleven sailors were gravely wounded.

Ambassador Joseph C. Grew, remembering the *Maine*, expected the United States to declare war.

Nothing of the sort happened. In Washington Tokyo's explanations and apologies were eagerly accepted. The State Department agreed that the attack had been a "mistake." It wasn't. A court of inquiry in Shanghai later brought out incontrovertible evidence that the sinking was ordered by responsible Japanese officers. The likeliest explanation was that it had been a test of American nerve. If so, the attackers had reason to be pleased. In Tokyo Grew was told that the Open Door policy was no longer applicable in China — although if the Chinese door was really shut, the biggest intruder was the Imperial Japanese Army. This inherent contradiction didn't trouble the aggressors. They knew now that America was a paper tiger. Gallup had polled voters with an opinion about the *Panay* incident and found that 70 percent favored complete withdrawal of U.S citizens from the Far East, including clergymen and medical missions. "Apparently no American except Mr. Grew," Samuel Eliot Morison wrote acidly, "remembered the *Maine*."

Those who did might have pointed out that the *Maine* had blown up ninety-two miles from the continental United States; the *Panay* had sunk seven thousand miles away. In the 1930s distances meant more than in the Seventies. A courier couldn't take off on the next international flight. There weren't any. It would be another eighteen months before Pan American would inaugurate the first regular transatlantic passenger service. Even coast-to-coast flights still took a day and a night, and the China Clipper, flying mail only, flew from San Francisco to Manila in 59 hours 48 minutes.* Most Americans who went abroad (they were few) sailed on ocean liners. A superb steamer took New Yorkers to Rome in ten days; Californians could reach Tokyo in fifteen days if the captain was deft and the weather right. Only when this enormity of prewar oceans is borne in mind does the isolationism of the Depression become comprehensible.

But there were other factors. To pacifists a repetition of the last war's insensate horrors was unthinkable. America's European allies of 1918 were despised as people who welshed on their debts. England was a special demon; only along the eastern seaboard and in the South could anglophiles be found in great number. Inevitably antagonism toward the Old World found political expression. As Richard H. Rovere and Arthur M. Schlesinger Jr. have pointed out, "Among oceans, the Pacific has always been the favorite of American isolationists: this is true for the simple reason that the Pacific is not the Atlantic. . . . Isolationism is opposed to the introduction of 'European ideas' in American politics; it has never had to oppose the introduction of 'Asian ideas' because scarcely anyone has tried to introduce them. Among the more virulent isolationists, indeed, one detects almost a

---

*Of course, in the summer of 1938 Howard Hughes *did* encircle the world in less than four days, but he was a daredevil. A lot of people thought he did it for the publicity.

hatred of Europe." And, one might add, an even deeper hatred of those rich, overeducated Easterners who still doted on Europe.

In 1937 these feelings were compounded by ignorance. The Depression had obscured foreign affairs by turning the country inward. Americans simply hadn't had time for the troubles of others. At each deepening of the international crisis, their attention had been diverted by developments at home. The following parallels are suggestive:

Hitler becomes dictator	March 1933	Roosevelt becomes President
Germany rearms	March 1935	Second Hundred Days
Italy invades Ethiopia	October 1935	Assassination of Huey Long
Germany reoccupies Rhineland	March 1936	Supreme Court challenge to New Deal reaches peak
Formation of Rome-Berlin Axis	October 1936	Reelection campaign
Sino-Japanese War begins	July 1937	Labor strife
Austrian Anschluss	March 1938	Recession

The men who went down with the *Panay* were not forgotten, but the time to speak for them had not arrived, as the President had discovered two months before the incident. On the way back from his "look-see" trip he had stopped in Chicago to dedicate the Outer Link Bridge, a PWA project. He stayed overnight in the home of George William, Cardinal Mundelein, the first prelate to speak against totalitarianism. (It was Mundelein who had called Hitler "an Austrian paperhanger, and a poor one at that.") Next day, in his dedication speech, Roosevelt floated a trial balloon: "The epidemic of world lawlessness is spreading. When an epidemic of physical disease starts to spread, the community approves and joins in a quarantine of the patients in order to protect the health of the community against the spread of the disease." Peace-loving nations, he said, must act in concert with other nations of the world community. The colorful homily was typical of him. It caught the country's attention, as he had hoped, but the howls of protest were deafening. Editorials and his personal mail charged him with warmongering. Quarantine aggressors? It sounded like Woodrow Wilson. A typical wire to the White House read, IF YOU "HATE" WAR DO NOT TRY TO INCITE IT BY SUCH APPEALS. He had touched one of the country's most sensitive nerves. Overnight he was driven to the defensive. Later he confided to a friend, "It is a terrible thing to look over your shoulder when you are trying to lead and to find no one there."

Some of his constituents were there. Cardinal Mundelein was; so were Rabbi Stephen S. Wise of New York and Henry L. Stimson, who had been Hoover's Secretary of State. After the quarantine proposal was shot down, Stimson wrote, "Mr. Roosevelt seemed to conclude that the country was not ready for strong political medicine." Certainly the President was warier. Although the League of Nations condemned Japanese aggression, the

State Department blandly joined Japanese diplomats in a conference on the situation in the Far East, which could hardly be construed as an act of quarantine. Ickes thought the President had "the appearance of a man who had more or less given up."

It was deceptive. The quality of FDR's leadership was complex, and consistency was not his strong suit. He was no Winston Churchill, a lone voice in the darkness. He had to remain in the cockpit of action, and therein lay his genius: he rarely let the distance between himself and the American consensus grow too wide. But he never retracted the quarantine speech. On the contrary, he quietly hewed to the same line. On December 21 he said American isolation from the twentieth century was impossible — he wouldn't want peace at any price — and in Kingston, Ontario, he promised that the United States would not "stand idly by" if Canada were attacked.

Every now and then he reaffirmed his hatred of war, or even claimed credit for neutrality legislation which he detested. He was the first President since Wilson to assert American presence in world affairs, and he was making his historic pivot when isolationist enthusiasm stood at flood tide. Any presidential move abroad, in any direction, provoked outcries. Liberal senators of both parties — Wheeler, Hiram Johnson, Pittman, Borah — were united in their stand for Fortress America. To Borah diplomacy was "power politics." *Time*, then staunchly isolationist, expressed anxiety over "Roosevelt's bent for international power politics," admired Borah, and for a time carried all foreign news under the standing head "Power Politics." Americans who had fought Franco in Spain lost their passports. American firms continued to provide half of Japan's oil and scrap iron needs — without which the war with China would have been impossible — and the National Council for the Prevention of War even tried to ban newsreels of the sinking *Panay* because they had "the unquestioned effect of arousing the American temper."

These were the months when the Dies committee discovered that the New Deal was Communistic while ignoring Father Coughlin, who gave a Nazi salute at a rally in the Bronx and shouted, "When we get through with the Jews in America, they'll think the treatment they received in Germany was nothing." Dies seemed to be blind to the activities of the Coughlin "Crusaders," the Citizen's Protective League, the Christian Front, American Patriots, Inc., and the German-American Bund. Right-wing organizations were trying to intimidate Congress, and sometimes they succeeded; the House rejected Roosevelt's request for funds to defend Guam because Tokyo might interpret it as a provocative gesture. At the final vote, 205 to 168, Congressman-adman Bruce Barton merrily cried out, "Guam, Guam with the wind!" Guam was gone, all right; the Japanese were to seize it the week after Pearl Harbor, and its recapture in August 1944 would cost the Marine Corps nearly eight thousand casualties.

Late in April 1937, when Congress extended the Neutrality Act, the *New York Times* observed editorially, "The passage of this misnamed neutrality bill may mark the high tide of isolationist sentiment in this country." The *Times* was too optimistic. The crest came nine months later, in a piece of legislative inanity introduced by Representative Louis Ludlow of Indiana. The Ludlow resolution stated that the authority of Congress to declare war could not become effective until confirmed by a majority vote in a nationwide referendum. President Roosevelt wrote Speaker William B. Bankhead that such an amendment would make the conduct of foreign affairs impossible. Nevertheless, a national poll reported that 73 percent of the people favored the idea, and only a second poll, showing support had dropped to 68 percent, sent the resolution back to the committee. At that, the House vote was 209 for the Ludlow resolution and 188 against it. A two-thirds majority being required, the country was saved from a situation in which, as Roosevelt had told Bankhead, other nations could have mistreated the United States with impunity.

"Democracy is sand driven by the wind," Mussolini said that year. At times it certainly looked that way. Shackled by neutrality legislation, the State Department watched helplessly while a Japanese general seized Kwangsi province, reached the border of Indochina, and shook hands with a French officer in Lang Son — Lang Son, the mountain pass through which munitions would pour into Vietnam for the next third of a century. Isolationists, always hypersensitive, sometimes seemed paranoid. The President's simplest moves were misinterpreted. When the king and queen of England decided to visit America (to heal the scars of what was known in polite society as "*l'affaire Simpson*"), Congressman Hamilton Fish predicted that America would revert to its status as a British colony, Congressman George Holden Tinkham of Boston said that "a sinister secret diplomacy is now directing American foreign policy," and Senator Borah suggested that the President wait until there was a lull in the conversation and then ask casually when it would be convenient for Their Majesties to repay the $21,385,000,000 borrowed from Americans in 1914–18.

It is important to remember the character of this opposition. Because of it, and because the President knew America to be in jeopardy, he was caught in a historic dilemma. In the coming months he would be driven to set new precedents — extensions of executive authority which would later be abused by other chief executives who forgot that the power to declare war is vested in Congress. Yet had Roosevelt acted otherwise he would have been false to his oath, in Samuel Eliot Morison's opinion, and would have deserved impeachment. Unlike critics on the Hill, Roosevelt and Hull had access to European diplomatic cables. In 1938 they saw the Czechoslovakian crisis coming, saw through Hitler, and saw little fiber or imagination in the British and French governments. The fear of another war had infected Whitehall and the Quai d'Orsay. Certainly Roosevelt's Washington was not without its defeatists; in the last fiscal year the Army's plans for new equipment had been limited to 1,870 more Garand rifles. Perhaps the generals were only being realistic; they would have had a difficult time getting much more on the Hill. But Roosevelt saw an alternative. The most resolute hard-core isolationist, believing only in Fortress America, conceded the need for a strong Navy. Therefore the President rode down Pennsylvania Avenue on January 28, 1938, and asked for a billion-dollar "two-ocean" Navy.

He got it, in the Vinson Naval Act. At the same time he sent Hopkins to the Pacific Coast for a survey; he wanted to know how quickly aircraft factories could convert to the production of warplanes. As Hopkins later noted, the President felt certain that war was coming to America "and he believed that air power would win it." His statement in 1938 that the United States needed 8,000 planes distressed almost everyone, including generals and admirals. An exception was Air Corps General Arnold. Briefing the commander in chief, Arnold had estimated that Germany then had 8,000 bombers and fighters. America had 1,650 pilots, a few hundred obsolete planes, and thirteen B-17s on order, to be delivered at the end of 1938. The general added pointedly that the lead time for modern weapons was very long. Roosevelt gave him the green light for expansion. Without that sanction, Arnold declared after the war, the sky over Normandy could not have been cleared of the Luftwaffe in 1944, and D-Day could not have been scheduled for June 6.

Lacking a military establishment in those years of the locust, Roosevelt was left with the power of persuasion, which had never been conspicuously successful in increasing the comity of nations. Still, he could try. His attempts to replace aggression with international understanding had failed in Spain and China. Undaunted, he wrote Prime Minister Neville Chamberlain proposing a great conference at which treaties would be altered without resorting to force and all nations assured access to raw materials. Chamberlain declined. He had his own plan. Roosevelt's conference, he replied, would merely undermine Great Britain's new policy to grant "a measure of appeasement" to the dictators.

He didn't say how large the measure would be, but the world was about to find out. In the spring of 1938 the German Führer screamed that Germans living in the Sudetenland — mountainous, heavily fortified Czech territory along the German frontier — were being mistreated. Goebbels further accused Prague of harboring Soviet warplanes and permitting the Russians to build airdromes on Czechoslovakian soil. Despite Czech protests, these accusations were repeated, and at the height of the Nazi campaign of denunciation, former President Thomas Masaryk died. Prague police suppressed Sudeten demonstrations during the funeral, Sudeten deputies boycotted the Czech parliament, and Hitler rattled his saber. Suddenly Europe was in the middle of a desperate crisis — and the American public, thanks to radio, had a ringside seat.

There had been few precedents for the transatlantic radio coverage of contemporary history. NBC and CBS had sent home shortwave summaries of the London Naval Conference of 1930; six BBC announcers had described the coronation of George VI; early in 1938 London and Chicago had exchanged signals; and that same year Americans heard their first coast-to-coast broadcast, between Al Goodman's orchestra in New York and W. C. Fields in Hollywood. Regularly scheduled commentators such as Lowell Thomas and rapid-fire Floyd Gibbons (he delivered a fantastic 217 words a minute) took their material right off the wire service tickers. CBS didn't even have a regular Washington correspondent; when one was needed, Senator Lewis B. Schwellenbach filled in. There had been nothing approaching serious radio coverage of a big European story until the Nazis lunged into Austria six months before the Czech crisis. With all Europe in an uproar, Paul White, a CBS executive in New York, called William L. Shirer in London and asked for a half-hour Paris-Rome-Berlin-Vienna-London "roundup." He asked, "Can you do it?"

There was every reason to say no. Ed Murrow was six hundred miles away in Vienna, and with the German armies marching, vital lines could be cut at any time. Shirer and Murrow would have to recruit inexperienced commentators in five great capitals, hire engineers, lease transmitters, and coordinate a live broadcast down to the second. Furthermore, there was almost no time. New York wanted the roundup that evening — and the day was a Sunday; offices were closed, technicians were on holiday, and responsibility for communications was in the hands of caretakers who had no authority and could scarcely understand sophisticated radio jargon in their own language, let alone in English. Technically the challenge was almost insurmountable. The very idea was madness. Shirer said they would try.

He got through to Murrow, who was watching gangs of Seyss-Inquart thugs racing between the chestnut trees and shouting, *"Ein Volk, Ein Reich, Ein Führer!"* Bit by bit the two young Americans put a skeletal framework together: Frank Gervasi of INS in Rome, Edgar Ansel Mowrer of the *Chicago Daily News* in Paris, a newspaper friend of Shirer's in Berlin, and a lady M.P. who agreed to leave her weekend in the country and speak from a BBC studio. All transmitting problems were solved except Rome's — the Italians couldn't figure out a way to "landline" Gervasi's voice across the Swiss border to a big transmitter in Geneva. They *could* put him through to London via radiophone, however, so he read his account from a booth, and Shirer reread it to New York. Such were the humble beginnings of the world news "roundup," with all its implications for the future and American public opinion.

In July 1914 Karl von Wiegand of the United Press had cabled 138 words on Austria-Hungary's ultimatum to Serbia which set off World War I, and he had been reprimanded for wasting money. Now, despite the strength of isolationism, Americans wanted to know what was happening overseas. There was a lull in late spring; the Czechs stood firm and Hitler backed down, agreeing to negotiations. His absorption of Austria, however, had altered the strategic complexion of central Europe; the expanded Reich now threatened Czechoslovakia from three sides. Prague continued to be refractory, and thus an embarrassment to England and France, who were committed to the Czechs by treaty and were beginning to wish they weren't. But the talks dragged on all summer. Apparently nothing was going to happen.

Then came the German chancellor's September 12 address to the annual Nazi rally in Nuremberg. As *Variety* explained, America's two big networks were handling the event differently. NBC would carry the speech live, but had adopted a policy of "playing down the current agitation and tension in Europe." CBS decided it was history and built it up. On that Monday morning CBS announcers reminded listeners that "the entire civilized world is anxiously awaiting the speech of Adolf Hitler, whose single word may plunge all of Europe into another world war." At 2:15 P.M. an announcer cut into the net to say, "We interrupt the program of Enoch Light in order to bring our listeners the world-awaited talk on Germany's foreign policy to be delivered by Adolf Hitler to the Nazi Congress at Nuremberg. . . . We take you now to Nuremberg, Germany." The address, relayed by a shortwave station in Berlin, came through clearly. Next day *Variety* was to comment: "A dynamic, spellbinding speaker, the broadcast was most impressive when he worked up the thousands of Nazis in attendance to frenzied cheers, 'Heil Hitlers' and 'Sieg Heils' ('Hail Victory')."

Kurt Heiman of CBS's New York staff translated passages of the address as it ran along, with some help from Kurt von Forstmeyer in Nuremberg. *Variety* complained that NBC's man "appeared to be soft-pedaling" and that he refrained from editorial comment. CBS's commentary came from an obscure, sixty-year-old Harvard graduate of German descent named Hans von Kaltenborn. At 3:36 P.M., after Hitler had finished speaking, Kaltenborn came on with a thorough analysis: "Adolf Hitler has spoken and the world has listened. . . . There was in it, and through it all, a very definite declaration that Germany would no longer tolerate the oppression, as he called it, of the Sudeten Germans in Czechoslovakia, and that Czechoslovakia would have to reach a settlement with the Sudeten Germans or the Germans would see to it that a settlement was reached." Kaltenborn didn't miss a detail, noting all such new information as Hitler's revelation that 280,000 Germans were working around the clock on the Siegfried Line.

American newspapers, which had not yet come to terms with radio journalism, published special editions when a big story broke. These were hurriedly printed and newsboys were sent into the streets calling, "Extra! Extra! Read all about it!" Suddenly they were on every corner shouting about mobilization in Germany, Italy, Czechoslovakia, France, and England. Great troop movements were under way. Fleets were at sea. Aircraft had been sent to camouflage fields. Smudged newsprint photographs showed Chamberlain, always carrying an umbrella, scooting back and forth between Godesberg, Berchtesgaden, and London. English children carrying tiny gas masks were being taken into the country, Frenchmen were digging trenches in public parks, and Europe was expected to burst into flame at any moment.

Millions of Americans, hearing Hitler for the first time over shortwave, were shaken by the depth of his hatred; on his lips the Teutonic language sounded cruel, dripping with venom. Those fluent in German — Franklin Roosevelt was one — could take it straight. The rest depended upon translators, and especially on CBS's chief analyst, who, *Variety* reported, was drawing "the greatest and most profoundly interested listening audience in radio history, next to the English king's abdication address." It was an exhausting ordeal for a man of Kaltenborn's age. During eighteen days starting that Monday he delivered eighty-five extemporaneous broadcasts from Studio Nine on the seventeenth floor of the CBS Building in New York, dozing on a deskside cot whenever the tension eased. On the nineteenth day he emerged, rumpled, haggard, and with a slight alteration in his name which had been made earlier because of the public animosity toward Germany. He was now plain H. V. Kaltenborn, and at that moment he was one of the most famous men in the United States.

At 7:30 that Monday evening, when the Czechoslovakian countdown began, Robert Trout had taken over the CBS network:

TROUT: Tonight, as nations of the world digest the long-anticipated talk of Chancellor Adolf Hitler at Nuremberg, we will hear in rapid succession from London, Berlin, Prague, and Paris. . . . The four speakers are to be: Edward R. Murrow, chief of Columbia's European staff, speaking from London; Melvin Whiteleather of the Associated Press, speaking from Berlin; William L. Shirer, Columbia's Central European representative, speaking from Prague; and John T. Whitaker, of the Chicago *Daily News* Syndicate, speaking from Paris. Mr. Murrow will speak to you from London, England. . . .

MURROW: There is little optimism in London tonight. . . .

It sounded very professional. Only a veteran journalist could have sensed how thin CBS coverage was. Despite their elaborate titles, thirty-year-old Murrow and thirty-four-year-old Shirer were still the sole CBS analysts on the program — were, for that matter, the network's only two men in Europe. They had been scurrying around the continent talking to one another from phone booths. It was a zany, patchwork quilt they were putting together, a kind of Rube Goldberg approach to broadcasting, and one explanation for its success — which was enormous — was European ignorance of what was going on. Finding out took a while; when Eric Sevareid arrived in the Netherlands a few months later as a CBS reinforcement, the Dutch were bewildered when they learned that he intended to send back news of the day. All previous broadcasts from Holland to America had been about tulips and windmills. To Europeans broadcasting was entertainment — as indeed it had been for most Americans.

To the astonishment of conservatives in the news media, radio coverage of European turmoil not only held its own, it became increasingly efficient. Kaltenborn, installed in Studio Nine with his sandwiches and black coffee, was fed streams of accurate information from the jerry-built Murrow-Shirer structure across the ocean. Because censorship was gagging native journalists there, while American speech remained free, people in the United States knew more about the September crisis than European listeners. The BBC wouldn't even allow Winston Churchill to speak; there was suspicion (well founded) that he might try to sabotage the peace. One British magazine editor suggested that readers who really wanted to know what was going on in the Czechoslovakian crisis ought to tune to shortwave broadcasts from the United States.

Murrow was rapidly becoming almost as famous as Kaltenborn. He made thirty-five broadcasts himself that September and set up another 116 from eighteen European cities. As the European chief he was Studio Nine's link with the continent; when communications became difficult or fadeouts frequent, the fascinated country would hear Kaltenborn say in a querulous hush, "Calling Ed Murrow! Calling Ed Murrow!" In the first days of the crisis this sort of thing was infrequent. European staffs had improved enormously since spring; one Czech switchboard girl was keeping track of a hundred placed calls. The weather was so clear that two-way conversations were possible. It was actually possible to hold "round table" discussions with correspondents overseas. The listening audience, holding "crisis maps" which the networks mailed on request, could listen to Murrow or Shirer talking to Kaltenborn or Trout, and follow reported movements of troops toward the Maginot Line, say, or in Silesia. It was almost like Monopoly, if you didn't think about it too much.

Then, on September 15, the fourth day, something went wrong. With armies in place, diplomatic confrontations reported hourly, and Hitler and Chamberlain eyeball to eyeball — no one then knew how quickly the prime minister's eyes would become shifty — the weather went bad. Shortwave transmissions, unlike those over ordinary frequencies, are highly vulnerable to atmospheric conditions. Day after day CBS frequencies remained inaudible; Kaltenborn called Murrow in vain, and was left to rely on cabled news. Suddenly, to the horror of CBS, NBC men in Europe began coming through loud and clear. The other network had found a fantastic solution, relaying shortwave over a Capetown to Buenos Aires to New York circuit. Broadcasts originating from Europe were traveling three times the distance on this circuit, but the delay was only a few seconds. And they were clear. CBS caught on, though direct broadcasts were still preferred.

The weather over the Atlantic was still unspeakable (what *was* going on out there?) when events in Prague reached a climax. The Czechs, as punishment for standing firm, were being treated shabbily by their two great allies. At 2:15 A.M. on September 21, the British and French ministers to Czechoslovakia routed President Eduard Benes out of bed and bluntly told him that their governments intended to break their covenants. In spite of their pledged word, they would not march; either the Czechs would capitulate to the Nazi dictator or they would be left to fight alone. All through the day Benes, staggering from fatigue, consulted with his cabinet, party leaders, and generals. At about five o'clock that afternoon of September 21 his government submitted. A Czech communiqué explained to the world: "We had no choice, because we were left alone." Benes said, "We have been basely betrayed."

At 5 P.M. it was still only 11 A.M. in New York and New England. Radio engineers were still complaining of the weather at sea, and merchant sailors were muttering about the strange copper-colored sky at last evening's sunset, but no one else worried about it. The forecast in that morning's paper wouldn't have panicked anyone. It read: "Rain and cooler."

It actually said just that.

In 1938 the United States Weather Bureau was but a shadow of its future self. It lacked the superb instruments of the next generation: radar-scopes, jet-propelled aerial surveillance, and weather-reporting satellites equipped with television cameras. Its chief devices then were the sixteenth-century thermometer, the seventeenth-century mercurial barometer, and the medieval weathervane. The greatest need was oceanographic information. Outposts on land could exchange reports with one another, but the seas were mysterious. Meteorologists relied entirely upon voluntary observations from merchant ships and aircraft. In the Depression the government wasn't going to let weathermen fly around in expensive planes of their own, observing conditions there. So the metereologists wondered, or guessed. They had long known that one of their guesses might be tragically wrong, and now the law of probability was closing in.

Yet it would be wrong to limn them as helpless scapegoats. Not to put too fine a point on it, the Weather Bureau was a slack outfit. *Some* new skills were known, to others if not to them. Estimating the approach of a big storm by studying wind velocity and barometric readings, a proficiency required of all licensed navigators, baffled many veteran forecasters. And when one remembers their great need for data, it is an astonishing fact that key meteorologists did not even attempt to phone one another that day until the blow had already fallen, carrying the telephone lines with it. Ironically, the *New York Times* ran an editorial praising the bureau on September 21. The humdrum forecast was published on the lower left corner of page 27. Nowhere was there any suggestion that the most destructive hurricane in American history — and the first to hit Long Island and New England since September 23, 1815 — was on its way.

It is possible to trace the progress of the storm with some confidence.

Atlantic hurricanes, known to seamen as tropical cyclones, begin as small disturbances in the doldrums, west of the Sahara Desert and east of the Cape Verde Islands, a calm area between the trade winds that blow from the northeast and southeast. The first stage of a tropical cyclone occurs when a column of hot moist air starts to rise. Cooler air moves in below it, the cycle accelerates, and the eastward rotation of the earth sends it spiraling off counterclockwise toward the western hemisphere. The longer the cyclone is over the water, the more powerful it becomes. This one was first sighted at 9:30 P.M. on September 16 by the captain of a Brazilian freighter, the S.S. *Alegrete*. It was 350 miles northeast of Puerto Rico, and the captain radioed that he could find nothing good to say about it.

The closest U.S. weather station was in Jacksonville, Florida. It was also the one most experienced in judging hurricanes. But the storm lay in the area most dreaded by American meteorologists — the triangle of sea between Long Island, Bermuda, and Georgia. Weather there was notoriously unstable, yet they had no idea what was happening. They kept listening for signals from afflicted ships. None came; if any merchantmen were there, they were either lacking in public spirit or already in Davy Jones's locker. Despite its ignorance, Jacksonville made the right moves. Warnings went out on Sunday, September 18, and Monday, September 19. Floridians, accustomed to this sort of thing, bought candles and boarded up windows. Many from New England, anxious to miss the winds, took the train home. At that point trains were moving faster than the cyclonic winds. They weren't going to miss anything after all.

Monday night the hurricane turned away from Miami. Jacksonville dutifully reported that the storm was "moving rapidly north" and only possibly "east of north." The eye was then estimated to be 275 miles south of Cape Hatteras; that is, just off North Carolina. At Hatteras it automatically passed from Jacksonville's jurisdiction to Washington's, and here an incompetence bordering on the criminal began to creep into forecasts. To grasp what was happening one should bear in mind that a fully developed hurricane, blowing 75 mph, is as powerful as 500 Nagasaki-type atomic bombs and contains more electricity than the entire United States uses in six months. That is an *ordinary* hurricane. *This* cyclone was churning around at over 200 mph. How far over is a matter of speculation, but on Wednesday the Harvard University observatory at Blue Hill, ninety miles from the vortex, was measuring a steady 121 mph, with 186 mph gusts, and New York City, far west of the storm center, noted 120 mph on top of the Empire State Building. Washington didn't know that, but it had a report from the skipper of the Cunard White Star liner *Carinthia*. His barometer measured its pressure at 27.85, one of the lowest barometric readings ever taken off the Atlantic coast. Nevertheless, the Washington station, staffed by the most seasoned meteorologists in the country, dropped the word "hurricane" from its forecast. As late as 2 P.M. September 21, when the storm had torn up Atlantic City's boardwalk and was transporting entire houses across Long Island Sound, Washington reported that the "tropical storm" was rapidly blowing out to sea.

New York and Boston went along with the Washington brass. Every meteorologist knew there was a lot of commotion just offshore, but it had been 123 years since a tropical cyclone had turned inward, and they just couldn't believe it would happen now. As it passed along the Carolinas, Virginia, Delaware, and New Jersey, the forecasters, snug inland, watched their barometers dip and rise again as the eye moved on. They sighed; *that* was over. Yet their instruments were warning them that it was far from over. Since 8:30 A.M. the hurricane's isobars — lines of equal barometric pressure — had been lengthening into ovals, all pointing north. Nevertheless, the forecasters kept talking about "shifting gales," as though this were a good day to fly heavy kites. Their folly was compounded by a cruel coincidence. The hurricane was coming when the moon was nearest the earth, and the sun and moon, pulling together in phase, caused tides a foot higher than usual. And the storm wave was going to hit precisely at high tide.

The weathermen hadn't thought of that; implicit in their logs was the assumption that once Miami was saved, it was all over. What they had failed to see (apart from their own instruments) was that just when the storm seemed about to swing northeastward at Cape Hatteras, its path had been blocked by an unusually broad high-pressure plateau covering almost the entire North Atlantic. Caught between that and another high pressure area just inland, the cyclone was unable to spread out and dissipate its power. On the contrary, the winds doubled and redoubled in force.

Long Island and New England had been lashed by rain for four straight days and nights. The air there was unnaturally warm and muggy. Ears felt queer, because atmospheric pressure was decreasing. In Vermont people noticed the smell of the seashore in the air. Hurricanes love nothing so much as warmth and dampness, and this one lurched toward the broad moist carpet six hundred miles long. Moreover, at the instant it crossed the shore, another dreadful principle would come to bear upon it. Usually hurricanes weaken over land, but the soggy ground, extending all the way to Canada, meant the storm would continue to blow as hard as though it had been in the Caribbean — picking up speed from the sticky air until the eye was moving at 60 mph, as fast as a tornado, fast enough to reach Montreal that same night.

The 1 P.M. news broadcast from New York brought the first sign that some forecasters were belatedly coming to terms with reality. The announcer said the storm had changed course and would "probably hit Long Island." That was something, more warning than New England was going to get, but it was too late for effective precautions. Besides, the vast majority of people missed the broadcast, and the Coast Guard had not been alerted. The richest seaboard in the world, from Cape May to Maine, was completely unprotected. Among the striking stories which later came to light was the experience of a Long Islander who had bought a barometer a few days earlier in a New York store. It arrived in the morning post September 21, and to his annoyance the needle pointed below 29, where the dial read "Hurricanes and Tornadoes." He shook it and banged it against a wall; the needle wouldn't budge. Indignant, he repacked it, drove to the post office, and mailed it back. While he was gone, his house blew away.

It happened that quickly. One moment the barometer read 27.95 inches. A moment later the winds struck, and people on the south shore saw what one of them described as "a thick and high bank of fog rolling in fast from the ocean." He added, "When it came closer we saw that it wasn't fog. It was water." With gusts already bellowing and the wind raving at every door jamb, the great wall of brine struck the beach between Babylon and Patchogue at 2:30 P.M. So mighty was the power of that first storm wave that its impact registered on a seismograph in Sitka, Alaska, while the spray, carried northward at well over a hundred miles an hour, whitened windows in Montpelier, Vermont. As the torrential forty-foot wave approached, some Long Islanders jumped into cars and raced inland. No one knows precisely how many lost that race for their lives, but the winners later estimated that they had to keep the speedometer over 50 mph all the way. Manicured lawns a mile inland at Quogue were under breakers two feet high, and a cottage near there floated away with ten people on its roof.

J. P. Morgan's multimillion-dollar estate at Glen Cove was blown to flinders. Thirty-room mansions at Westhampton were swept away, and owners couldn't rebuild because the land had gone with them. Seventeen people were huddled chest-deep in brine on the second floor of one of these châteaux; then the walls collapsed. The 190-foot Mackay radio tower, out toward Montauk Point, was gone. The Bridgehampton freight station had been moved to the wrong side of the tracks. Pullman cars weighing sixty-seven tons were rocking. Fishing craft were split apart, fishermen's shacks were sailing into Connecticut. The entire coastline had been altered, and obviously this was only a beginning; thirteen million people lay in the storm's path, which could now be projected through New Haven, Hartford, Springfield, Northampton, Vermont, and Montreal. Had the hurricane come three weeks earlier, six thousand dead could have been expected. Even as it was, Long Island Sound, beaten into one solid mass of foam, was hurling corpses at the wreckage of what had been comfortable cottages only that morning.

At 3:40 P.M., when the forward edge of the doughnut-shaped storm was uprooting Yale's famous old elms, the eye of the storm reached Long Island. The survivors assumed that they had been saved. The sun came out, the sky was blue, zephyrs whispered in the wreckage. Then the distant roaring drew near again, and they knew they were in for it again. Actually, the worst was to come; the mightiest force in a hurricane lies in the swifter, titanic winds behind the eye. The most remarkable accounts of this phase will never be told, for the participants were dead before evening. We know that the second storm wave destroyed the Westhampton section of the outer barrier beach, blew the dunes away, leveled most of the houses left standing, flooded the Maidstone Club golf course, and swamped the Montauk Highway and the Long Island Rail Road tracks at Napeague Beach, temporarily cutting Long Island in two. At the height of it, one couple actually swam across Moriches Bay with two dogs and a Coast-guardsman. Arriving, the drenched woman dismayed bystanders by an-nouncing that Long Island was sinking. That part of it nearly did. Of 179 Westhampton houses, 153 had completely vanished, and most of the others were too battered ever to be inhabited again. In and around them were twenty-nine corpses.

In effect, Long Island was serving as a breakwater for the seventy-mile stretch of Connecticut shore across the sound, including New Haven and Bridgeport (which were having other problems). The exposed Connecticut and Rhode Island shores east of Montauk Point were being belted by even stronger seas, and the city struck hardest was Providence, at the mouth of Narragansett Bay. One huge wave, a hundred feet high, swept up the bay, crushed the docks into kindling, and broke near City Hall, drowning pedes-trians outside. The sea pulled people from automobiles, sometimes from behind the wheel, thereby saving their lives. When it subsided, downtown Providence was under thirteen feet of water. Policemen in motorboats patrolled the Mall and Exchange Place. The headlights of thousands of automobiles shone under water, and short-circuited car horns blew steadily, like a traffic jam in a nightmare.

Meanwhile, the hurricane had been thundering through Connecticut and Massachusetts. There was a grayness around everything that afternoon, as though the storm were veiling its atrocities. Wesleyan University's hundred-year-old stone chapel steeple had been blown down. New London was burning. In Hartford and Springfield men were toiling with sandbags, holding back the Connecticut River, already at flood. Among the waiting mobs of refugees — no one had time for them now — was Katharine Hep-burn; she had waded to safety from her parents' summer cottage an hour before it was carried away.

By nine o'clock that evening Dartmouth College, in New Hampshire, was as embattled as Yale had been at 4 P.M., with the wind building and the rain slanting vertically, but by the next morning the sky, as the Weather Bureau cheerfully reported, was clear. Conditions were hardly normal, though. The New Haven Railroad estimated that 1,200 trees and 700 tele-phone poles lay across its tracks. The Shore Line of the New York, New Haven and Hartford was trying to find a missing train and wondering what to do with a 300-foot steamship that lay across its tracks in New London. American Airlines was searching for an empty plane that had blown away from Logan Field in Boston. Not one Connecticut highway was open. The *Hartford Courant* described September 21 as the "most calamitous day" in the history of the state. "As near as the crippled communications can indicate," the editorial said, "no community of any size escaped damage. New Haven is still dark and battered. The heart of New London is in smoking ruins."

The Red Cross reported 700 people killed and 1,754 injured, and that 63,000 had lost their homes. President Roosevelt sent Hopkins north with 100,000 men from the Army, the Coast Guard, and the WPA. Before long they had the current running again, but much that had been lost in the storm could never be brought back. New England mourned its trees; 16,000 were down in Springfield alone, and someone calculated that the hurricane had toppled enough wood to build 200,000 houses. The season's apple crop was a total loss. Maimed shore cottages that had lost their beaches were being auctioned off for pittances. And because only 5 percent of the losses had been insured, many factories which had been in trouble since the Crash went out of business.

For a while an imaginative beggar roamed Boston Common wearing a placard which read, "For 25¢ I will listen to your story of the hurricane." One of the best tales was about the American flag on New York's Whitehall Building. It had been torn to shreds. Inside, a few feet away, was the regional office of the U.S. Weather Bureau.

Long Islanders and New Englanders traveling to other parts of the country that fall were startled by the number of well-informed men and women who knew nothing of the hurricane. In part this reflected the magnitude of the disaster. For the first twenty-four hours the New York Times hadn't been able to get any reliable news at all. Even the Boston Globe's editors, who could see overturned freighters in their own harbor, didn't publish an interview with a survivor until Friday, two days after the big wind. That same morning the Times, piecing together scattered reports, realized that the country had suffered a greater disaster than the Chicago fire, the San Francisco earthquake, or any Mississippi flood. Then the paper ran eight-column headlines about the hurricane. Surprisingly, few readers read them or retained what they read; within a week they had forgotten it, and the story has been one of the forgotten fragments of American history.

The big reason for this mnemonic failure was that the country's attention was still riveted on Czechoslovakia. The crisis in Europe had become the first of those mass communications phenomena which might be called the shared simultaneous experience. Unlike those which followed — the Army-McCarthy hearings of 1954, for example, or the Kennedy funeral of 1963 — Czech developments were not televised. Yet the impact was immense. Listeners became helpless spectators following events which they knew might alter their own lives. After the Munich Pact was signed on September 29, CBS hailed the arrival of radio "not merely as a disseminator of the news, but as a social power."

This was true, but it was not all good. Over radio, fear had fed on fear; everyone had wanted a happy ending, and when eventually it did end, the best possible construction was put upon the agreement. Chamberlain was the hero of the hour, as much in America as in Britain. It took a while for people to realize that he was a weak old man who had sold out a resolute and embattled ally for a worthless Hitler promise. Churchill knew it, and said, "Britain and France had to choose between war and dishonor. They chose dishonor. They will have war." Roosevelt knew it; to his ambassador in Portugal he wrote, "The dictator threat from Europe is a good deal closer to the United States." Murrow and Shirer knew it. Meeting in Paris, they agreed that war was likely after next year's harvest. And H. V. Kaltenborn knew it; even before Chamberlain's visit to Berchtesgaden he said, "My own feeling is that it will be little more than a truce. There is grave doubt as to whether or not the visit will bring peace."

The people were beginning to understand. A *Fortune* survey showed that only 11.6 percent of the American people thought the Munich agreement commendable, and 76.2 percent believed that the United States would participate in a general European war. The percentage held in every part of the country. "This is news," the editors commented. "Eighteen months ago only about 22 percent of the population thought that we would be drawn into a foreign war in the next two or three years. Now more than three times that many believed that we actually would have been embroiled in the war that was so narrowly averted. . . . Thus has been shattered our sense of secure alliance upon the sentiment: 'Thank God for two wide oceans!'"

In short, the Czech crisis had awakened America from a long slumber, and the country was anxious, biting its nails, drumming its fingers. Bombs, invasions, war — all that had been unthinkable as recently as last summer — were suddenly very real. Radio had transformed the country into one vast theater crowded with skittish spectators, and four weeks after the Munich Pact a brilliant twenty-three-year-old producer shouted, "Fire!"

The journalistic hoax has a long, picaresque, and not entirely dishonorable history. Edgar Allan Poe became famous on the strength of his "Unparalleled Adventure of One Hans Pfall"; H. L. Mencken's spurious account of how the first bathtub was invented became a national joke and found its way into some encyclopedias. The most successful of all, Richard Adams Locke's Moon Hoax of 1835, told wide-eyed readers of the *New York Sun* that one "Sir John Herschel," using "an immense telescope based on an entirely new principle," had identified bat-man inhabitants of the moon. Poe, Mencken, and Locke were quickly forgiven, for newspapers, being what Marshall McLuhan calls a "cool medium," are not likely to incite a riot. The mass media are "hot," and radio has never been hotter than the night before Halloween in 1938.

The recipient of that heat was then the most versatile and successful young man on Broadway. Actor-director, producer, at the age of twenty Orson Welles had been radio's "Lamont Cranston" (*The Shadow*). He had dressed Julius Caesar in a business suit, put on a Negro *Macbeth* with Haiti as the background — and made money with both. When his WPA production of *The Cradle Will Rock* was ordered canceled on opening night by Washington — on political grounds — Welles defied the government. He and his theatrical company led the customers through the streets to an empty theater. The play became an enormous success, and CBS invited the prodigy of show business to broadcast a one-hour drama from the network's Studio One each Sunday evening at 8 P.M. There were no sponsors; the program was what was called "sustaining." CBS wasn't making much of a gesture. It couldn't sell the time, because its NBC competitor, the Chase and Sanborn Hour, was the most popular program of the week. Don Ameche was the master of ceremonies there, Dorothy Lamour the singer, and high comedy was provided by ventriloquist Edgar Bergen and his redheaded dummy Charlie McCarthy. Carved by a Chicago bartender for $35, and based on a Bergen sketch of a Chicago newsboy, Charlie had been No. 1 for eighteen months. His witty, insolent personality dominated Sunday prime time.

When it came to a choice between great theater and listening to Bergen talk to himself, most Americans preferred Bergen. Both the Crossley and Hooper radio censuses conducted the week before that Halloween gave the Chase and Sanborn Hour 34.7 percent of the total possible audience and Welles's Mercury Theater 3.6 percent. (There was a hidden factor here, withheld from advertisers because it would damage their morale; we shall encounter it presently. Still, the figures doubtless held up on an average Sunday.) Of the 32 million families then living in the United States, about 27.5 million owned radios. Thus when CBS played the opening strains of the Tchaikovsky Piano Concerto in B Flat Minor — the Mercury's opening theme each week — Welles could assume that about a million people were tuned to him. On October 30 that figure would grow.

Roosevelt had sent a personal message to Hitler on September 26 asking him to stop issuing ultimatums and proposing instead a conference of "nations directly interested in the present controversy" as an alternative to the battlefield. He suggested it be held immediately in some "neutral spot in Europe." It never came off — other conferences were being arranged — but on that same day Orson Welles had an inspiration. Why not dramatize H. G. Wells's *War of the Worlds?* His agent thought the idea silly, and Howard Koch, his writer, believed it was impossible. The young producer insisted. Being a strong personality, he won, and Koch went off to translate Wells into Welles. On Tuesday, October 25, five days before the show, he phoned John Houseman, the Mercury's editor. He was throwing in the towel, he said; science fantasy couldn't be turned into radio drama. The Mercury's secretary agreed. "You can't do it!" she cried. "Those old Martians are just a lot of nonsense! We're going to make fools of ourselves! Absolute fools!" Houseman thought of substituting *Lorna Doone,* but Orson wouldn't discuss it, so writing the Wells script became a team effort. By Thursday they had a show — a dull show, everyone agreed.

Then someone — later no one remembered who — made a suggestion. Wouldn't it be a good idea to make the whole thing a simulated news broadcast? As realistic as possible? Even a voice like Roosevelt's? It was all possible, including the voice; Kenneth Delmar, whom Fred Allen would later make famous as Senator Claghorn, could summon commanding tones. The actor who would play Carl Phillips, the first network "announcer," dug into the CBS record library and listened, over and over, to the semihysterical radio commentator's description of the *Hindenburg* exploding at Lakehurst. Welles himself would appear as a Princeton scientist. They were to open with a weather report, dance music, and then the special bulletins. The cast thought Welles dragged this part much too long. He shook his head; that, he explained, was what gave it authenticity.

It certainly did. The public had become accustomed to sudden interruptions during the Czech crisis; each had provided a significant development later confirmed in the newspapers. Radio, indeed, had become the accepted vehicle for important announcements. And there were other circumstances which would increase authenticity. Since the 1936 election, *Fortune* had found, people had more faith in commentators than in newspapers. Indeed, for many the line between reality (news) and fantasy (drama) had become hopelessly blurred. In one of the more penetrating postmortems of the performance, *Variety* doubted that "any explanation would have prevented some people taking the whole thing in deadly earnest," because "evidence of the seriousness with which many listeners take radio dramas is the concerned letters numerous dialers write in about the characters and happenings in the daily serial shows."

It was, furthermore, an era in which people still respected authority, and Kenneth Delmar would be identified as "the Secretary of the Interior." For audiences in New York and New Jersey, real streets were to be named: the Pulaski Skyway, South Street, route 23. Added to all these, a Princeton University study later found, were intellectual and emotional immaturity, Depression insecurity ("Things have happened so thick and fast since my grandfather's day that we can't hope to know what might happen now," one respondent said afterward) and, outweighing everything else, the "recent war scare in Europe."

Welles seems to have had some apprehension. The script opened and closed with explanations that this was only a play, and four CBS station breaks were to interrupt the actors and say the same thing. All that was fine, given their assumption that listeners would join them at eight o'clock and stay till the end. But the assumption was unsound. Here the rating surveys' little secret assumed tremendous significance. Their discovery, which would have discouraged sponsors, was that when a commercial or an unpopular entertainer came on, people reached over and twisted their radio dials. Everyone enjoyed Edgar Bergen and Charlie McCarthy, but they were only part of a variety show.

The Mercury's relatively small but faithful audience heard the Tchaikovsky theme, the introduction, an authentic weather report, and "We now take you to the Meridian Room in the Hotel Park Plaza in downtown New York, where you will be entertained by the music of Ramón Raquello and his orchestra." Periodic bulletins traced the progress of Carl Phillips and Professor Pierson to the New Jersey town of Grovers Mill. There were sirens and crowd noises in the background. At that moment, 8:12 P.M., Charlie McCarthy finished his first skit and a soothing voice began to recommend the rich flavor of Chase and Sanborn coffee.

Nearly six million people spun dials to CBS. This is what they heard:

ANNOUNCER: . . . I'll move the microphone nearer. Here. (*Pause*) Now we're not more than twenty-five feet away. Can you hear it now? Oh, Professor Pierson!

PIERSON: Yes, Mr. Phillips?

ANNOUNCER: Can you tell us the meaning of that scraping noise inside the thing?

PIERSON: Possibly the unequal cooling of its surface.

ANNOUNCER: Do you still think it's a meteor, Professor?

PIERSON: I don't know what to think. The metal casing is definitely extra-terrestrial . . . not found on this earth. Friction with the earth's atmosphere usually tears holes in a meteorite. The thing is smooth and, as you can see, of cylindrical shape.

PHILLIPS: Just a minute! Something's happening! Ladies and gentlemen, this is terrific. The end of the thing is beginning to flake off! The top is beginning to rotate like a screw! The thing must be metal!

Excited crowd voices were heard; then back to the microphone.

ANNOUNCER: Ladies and gentlemen, this is the most terrifying thing I have ever witnessed! . . . Wait a minute! Someone's *crawling out of the hollow top*. Someone or . . . something. I can see peering out of that black hole two luminous discs . . . are they eyes? It might be a face. It might be . . .

(*Shout of awe from the crowd*)

ANNOUNCER (*sobbing and retching*): Good heavens, something's wriggling out of the shadow like a gray snake. Now it's another one, and another! They look like tentacles to me. There, I can see the thing's body. It's large as a bear and it glistens like wet leather. But that face. It . . . it's indescribable. I can hardly force myself to keep looking at it. The eyes are black and gleam like a serpent. The mouth is V-shaped with saliva dripping from its rimless lips that seem to quiver and pulsate. . . .

The announcer temporarily loses control. Silence. A few bars of "Clair de Lune." A second announcer, cool and professional, says, "We are bringing you an eyewitness account of what's happening on the Wilmuth farm, Grovers Mill, New Jersey." A few more bars of Debussy, then the cool announcer again: "We now return you to Carl Phillips at Grovers Mill." Policemen, it develops, are advancing on the thing, but the Martians turn a sheet of flame upon them. Screams are heard, and unearthly shrieks. A barn blows up; then the mike goes dead. In comes the second announcer, saying quietly, "Ladies and gentlemen, due to circumstances beyond our control, we are unable to continue the broadcast from Grovers Mill. Evidently there's some difficulty with our field transmission. However, we will return you to that point at the earliest opportunity." Now the action escalates. The state police have been burned to cinders. "Brigadier General Montgomery Smith, commander of the State Militia in Trenton," makes an official statement, in behalf of the governor of New Jersey, placing the counties of Mercer and Middlesex, as far west as Princeton and east to Jamesburg (all real places), under martial law. New space-ships are landing, and Pierson, who has made a miraculous escape, says the invaders are armed with something which "for want of a better term, I shall refer to . . . as a heat-ray."

Now the second announcer is upset:

> ANNOUNCER: Ladies and gentlemen, I have a grave announcement to make. Incredible as it may seem, both the observations of science and the evidence of our eyes lead to the inescapable conclusion that those strange beings who landed in the Jersey farmlands tonight are the vanguard of an invading army from the planet Mars.

In shocked tones he reveals that Martians have annihilated the New Jersey National Guard. Martial law is declared throughout New Jersey and eastern Pennsylvania. The President has declared a national emergency. The Secretary of the Interior, sounding like FDR and even using his phrases, begs the country to do its duty and pray God for help. The Army Air Corps is wiped out. An operator comes cn jerkily:

> OPERATOR: This is Newark, New Jersey. . . . This is Newark, New Jersey! . . . Warning! Poisonous black smoke pouring in from Jersey marshes. Reaches South Street. Gas masks useless. Urge population to move into open spaces . . . automobiles use routes 7, 23, 24. . . . Avoid congested areas. Smoke now spreading over Raymond Boulevard. . . .

In the last sequence before the middle break, Ray Collins, the only surviving announcer, is standing on a New York rooftop. Bells are ringing in the background warning New Yorkers that it's time to evacuate the city; the Martians are coming. "Hutchinson River Parkway is still kept open for motor traffic. Avoid bridges to Long Island . . . hopelessly jammed." Voices in the background are singing a hymn; you can just hear them as Collins, his voice choking, reads a bulletin announcing that "Martian cylinders are falling all over the country. One outside Buffalo, one in Chicago, St. Louis. . . ."

Toward the end of Collins's speech (8:32 P.M.) Davidson Taylor, a CBS program supervisor, was asked to leave the Studio One control panel; an urgent phone call awaited him. He left and returned, his face a white knot. Already 60 percent of local stations had broken into the broadcast to reassure listeners that all this was make-believe, and New York policemen were surrounding the CBS Building. None of the performers or technicians would be allowed to leave after the show; some urgent questions needed answering. When Taylor came back to the control booth, Collins was describing the Martians, tall as skyscrapers, astride the Pulaski Skyway, preparing to wade through the Hudson River. It was seconds before the break, so Taylor decided to let Collins end, which he did in a voice ravaged by gas:

> COLLINS: . . . Now they're lifting their metal hands. This is the end now. Smoke comes out . . . black smoke, drifting over the city. People in the streets see it now. They're running toward the East River . . . thousands of them, dropping like rats. Now the smoke's spreading faster. It's reached Times Square. People are trying to run away from it, but it's no use. They're falling like flies. Now the smoke's crossing Sixth Avenue . . . Fifth Avenue . . . 100 yards away . . . it's 50 feet . . .
>
> OPERATOR FOUR: 2X2L calling CQ . . . 2X2L calling CQ . . . 2X2L calling CQ . . . New York. Isn't there anyone on the air? Isn't there anyone . . . 2X2L . . .

Now came the break; now a regular CBS announcer told them that they were listening to a CBS presentation of Orson Welles and his Mercury Theater. The second half of the program followed. It was sensitively written, with no hysterics, but that didn't matter any more. Before the break hundreds of thousands of screaming Americans had taken to the streets, governors were begging their constituents to believe that martial law had *not* been declared, and the churches were jammed with weeping families asking for absolution of their sins before the Martians came to *their* town. Altogether, the Princeton study discovered, approximately 1,700,000 believed the program to be a news broadcast, and about 1,200,000 were sufficiently distressed to do something about it. "For a few horrible hours," the study concluded, "people from Maine to California thought that hideous monsters armed with death rays were destroying all armed resistance sent against them; that there was simply no escape from disaster; that the end of the world was near."

In every state, telephone operators were overwhelmed. Local stations reported a 500 percent increase in incoming calls. In New York CBS and police switchboards were jammed. Riverside Drive became impassable; it was packed with mobs of sobbing people. Conditions were worst in northern New Jersey, where the first Things had been "discovered." Weeping families clung to one another, terrified men ran blindly across fields, and drivers raced about in all directions, all hoping to escape asphyxiation and flaming death. Train terminals and bus stations were filled with wild-eyed people demanding tickets to anywhere; one New York woman phoning the Dixie Bus Terminal for information gasped, "Hurry, please, the world is coming to an end and I have a lot to do."

When Dorothy Thompson wrote, "Nothing about the broadcast was in the least credible," there was a tendency among those who had not heard the program to dismiss the stricken mobs as ignorant. It was untrue. Miss Thompson to the contrary, *War of the Worlds* was a magnificent technical achievement; even today a transcription of it is chilling. And while there was some correlation between fear, education, and economic status — the most vulnerable were listeners who had not completed grammar school and had been on relief for more than three years — the well-to-do could not be let off so easily. Princeton found that 28 percent of the college graduates who were tuned to the program, and 35 percent of those with high incomes, believed they were hearing straight news. On a southern university campus, sorority girls wept in each other's arms and took turns telephoning their parents for a last goodbye, and an Ivy League senior, driving back from a Vassar check-in, was convinced when he flipped on the car radio that "Princeton was wiped out and gas was spreading over New Jersey and fire."

In Studio One, Welles signed off jovially: "Goodbye everybody, and remember, please, for the next day or two the terrible lesson you learned tonight . . . and if your doorbell rings and nobody's there, that was no Martian! It's Halloween." The red light went out; the Mercury Theater was off the air. But it was Studio One's doorbell that was ringing, and somebody was out there — not Martians but New York's finest, determined to teach Orson Welles a lesson he would never forget. Before opening the door, Welles and Houseman answered a shrill telephone in the control room. As Houseman later remembered it, the call came from "the mayor of some Midwestern city, one of the big ones. He is screaming for Welles. Choking with fury, he reports mobs in the streets of his city, women and children huddled in the churches, violence and looting. If, as he now learns, the whole thing is nothing but a crummy joke — then he, personally, is coming up to New York to punch the author of it on the nose!"

They hung up, the door burst open, the studio was suddenly crowded with dark blue uniforms, and what Houseman called "the nightmare" began — interrogations hinting darkly at countless suicides, traffic deaths, and a "fatal stampede in a Jersey hall." At the moment the police could think of no law that had been broken, so the two men were released to a more terrible fate: the press. It seemed to Houseman that the press was being vindictive because radio had eclipsed newspaper coverage of the Czech crisis. Reporters countered that the broadcast was a big story, which it certainly was. Next morning scare headlines read:

RADIO WAR TERRORIZES U.S.

PANIC GRIPS NATION
AS RADIO ANNOUNCES
"MARS ATTACKS WORLD"

TIDAL WAVE OF TERRORISM SWEEPS NATION

PHONE CALLS SWAMP POLICE
AT BROADCAST OF FANTASY

"The show came off," Houseman said wryly. There was no doubt about that. For two days it drove Hitler off front pages, while CBS put to rest the fears of those still distressed by following its hourly time signal ("9 P.M. B-u-l-o-v-a, Bulova Watch Time") with an explanation that "the entire story and all of its incidents were fictitious." The Federal Communications Commission issued a statement describing the program as "regrettable" and proposing a new radio code. For a while there was talk of criminal action, but it died away. By then Orson Welles had rocketed to national fame, and his Mercury Theater, no longer CBS's poor relation, had acquired a lavish sponsor in Campbell Soups. Eventually Welles was invited to a White House function. The President took him off to one side and said, "You know, Orson, you and I are the two best actors in America." He seemed serious, but Welles wasn't sure how to take it, so he merely bowed.

The *War of the Worlds* broadcast revealed, as clearly as any mass convulsion can, that American nerves were being stretched ever tauter. In a popular phrase of the time, the country was "all balled up." *Fortune* noted a mood of fatalism among people. It did not, however, report despair. Though men might feel that they had little control over their individual futures, there was a kind of momentum to the decade, a feeling that America had touched bottom at the start of it and was moving inexorably toward some grand historic climax. Radio was part of it; the European tempo mounted month by month, and ignoring its crises was impossible. There was also the immense vitality of the time; looking back on it Frank Brookhouser wrote, "It was, granted, a grim and heartbreaking period in many ways. But the people triumphed over the loss and the disappointment and the suffering and the heartache. And never was the nation's heartbeat so loud and clear." Finally, Roosevelt discouraged any sense of mindlessness. He believed in generational destiny, and as long as he was the conductor, beaming and flourishing his baton, it was almost impossible to doubt that eventually it would all make sense.

Sometimes, when the fire is low and the bourbon just right, the images and lost notes may drift down from the past, evoking memories for those who were then alive of what 1939 was like for a quite ordinary American in that year. If his morning newspaper was the *Chicago Tribune*, he was relieved to learn that Colonel Robert R. McCormick had just abandoned his crusade for simplified spelling ("agast," "staf," "lether," "jaz," "fantom"). The *Tribune* was elated by the new congressional coalition against a Roosevelt spending bill ("Mutiny on the bounty!") but wrathful about a Court of Appeals ruling that schoolchildren needn't salute the flag. *Tribune* editors expressed dismay that New York children thought habeas corpus was a kind of disease, approval of Senator Taft's maiden speech on governmental economy, sadness over Lou Gehrig's farewell to baseball, awe over the twenty-three-stitch gash Joe Louis inflicted on Two-Ton Tony Galento, resentment of those enemies of tradition who had changed the Boston Braves to the Boston Bees, and pleasure that the new Pope, Pius XII, had appointed conservative Francis Joseph Spellman an archbishop. Colonel McCormick would have given a great deal to know that an apostate Communist named Whittaker Chambers was visiting Adolf Berle at Berle's Washington home on Woodley Road and telling him of subversion in the government — which Berle then disregarded. It remained a secret — then. But the colonel's time would come.

J. Edgar Hoover was wrapped in combat with, of all people, District Attorney Thomas E. Dewey. Dewey thought the FBI wiretappings were invasions of privacy, and one high police official in Manhattan accused Hoover of being a "publicity hound," a "David Belasco in the squad car." Fighting back, the FBI director issued a blast: "Communists at a meeting yesterday in New York have instructed two of their best writers to portray me as a Broadway glamour-boy." At the American Legion's national convention he said, "Intellectual license and debauchery is un-American. In righteous indignation it is time to drive the debauchers of America out in the open." Dewey announced for the Presidency, which may not have been what Hoover had in mind.

The fastest-selling record was Hildegarde's "Deep Purple." Frankie Sinatra was still plugging along at $25 a week, but one night in a hotel Harry James's wife turned up the volume on her radio and said, "Honey, listen to this boy sing." Harry drove to Englewood, New Jersey, found Sinatra in a roadhouse called the Rustic Cabin, and signed him up. Their first record, "All or Nothing at All," sold only eight thousand copies, but the Sinatras were eating regularly now. The Lone Ranger was being heard three times a week by twenty million people over 140 stations . . . Bette Davis, Spencer Tracy, and Frank Capra won Oscars . . . Alfred Hitchcock was making a lady vanish . . . Bobby Breen had to retire at the age of twelve because his voice was changing.

Otherwise — or moneywise, as they were already saying in the motion picture industry — Hollywood was at the crest of its supercolossal glory. Shirley Temple was only ten. At box offices the top three were Mickey Rooney, Tyrone Power, and Spencer Tracy. Every movie was marvelous, amazing, spellbinding, sensational, and the reigning genies were entitled to leave their imprints in the wet cement slabs of Grauman's Chinese Theatre on Hollywood Boulevard. On the prewar silver screen, stars demonstrated incredible, magnificent deeds. Judy Garland persuaded a humbug Frank Morgan to confer courage upon cowardly Bert Lahr. Laurence Olivier, David Niven, and Merle Oberon recklessly pursued one another across the foggy moors ("Heathcliff! Heathcliff!") of *Wuthering*

Heights. Gene Autry sang of the West. Watching Robert Donat as *Mr. Chips,* you knew the Empire would last forever. Clark Gable was something of a cutup. He took his shirt off right in front of Claudette Colbert,* and to the consternation of cotton mill owners he turned out to be topless; textile stocks dropped 8¼ in one week. Gable got that raffish "damn" into GWTW, though when the world premiere was held in Atlanta, the president of the United Daughters of the Confederacy was reported to have succumbed to the vapors. Even worse, Gable led a mutiny against Charles Laughton, who had kept calling him "Mr. Christian."

George Arliss was a man of such dignity, such sang froid, that he became typecast as a historical figure, and a school superintendent expressed anxiety that a whole generation of schoolchildren might grow up believing that all great men of the past looked like George Arliss. He outmaneuvered Gladstone, outwitted D'Artagnan and the Three Musketeers, and outspent the rest of the Rothschild brothers. Arliss left audiences feeling euphoric; the French Revolution always left them sobbing. In *Marie Antoinette* Norma Shearer rode bravely to the guillotine in a tumbril. Ronald Colman rolled right behind her in *A Tale of Two Cities,* and as he laid his handsome neck under the blade you knew then, before his head even dropped into the basket, that it was a far, far better thing that he did than he had ever done; it was a far, far better rest that he went to than he had ever known.

Both Europe and America had suffered through one of the coldest winters on record. There were a million dead in Spain. Heinrich Himmler banned *Time* from Germany, to the delight of Henry Luce, and Hitler posed before the $396 Volkswagen he had helped to design. (Later the price would go up, but the little auto would look the same.) There were *two* world's fairs in America in 1939, and if you could swing it, an excursion train would take you to both at a cut rate. Not many took advantage of the bargain. For most fairgoers one was enough, and that one was usually New York's. San Francisco's Golden Gate Exposition was designed with taste; its aeronautic display took your breath away, and its color floodlighting revealed a genuine flair. But the Golden Gate Exposition had no gimmicks, no camp, no corn, no sideshows — and, most important, no Grover Whalen.

At fifty-three Grover Aloysius Whalen, who had never been seen in

---

*One of the more entertaining aspects of showbiz was its ethnic deodorization. A generation later this practice would be challenged, but in the 1930s the lively arts were — apparently — wholly Anglo-Saxon. Though debatable, the custom endures. Thus we have or have had Doris Day (her real name, Doris Kapplehoff), Judy Garland (Frances Gumm), Claudette Colbert (Claudette Chauchoin), Karl Malden (Malden Sekulovich), Laurence Harvey (Larry Skikne), Tony Curtis (Bernie Schwartz), Tab Hunter (Arthur Gelien), Mitzi Gaynor (Mitzi Gerber), Ethel Merman (Ethel Zimmerman), Vic Damone (Vito Farinola), Judy Holliday (Judy Tuvim), Rita Hayworth (Margarita Carmen Cansino), Jane Wyman (Sarah Fulks), Kirk Douglas (Issur Danielovitch), Danny Kaye (David Kaminsky), and Jack Benny (Benjamin Kubelsky).

public without a gardenia in his lapel, was New York's official "greeter." Visiting dignitaries who were not met by Whalen and presented with a key to the city felt insulted, and rightly so; it was like breaking diplomatic relations. The New York fair — he called it "The World of Tomorrow" — was conceived as his masterpiece. He intended to greet all guests by offering them anything they could possibly want, from great art to skin shows, from a robot called Elektro that could talk and smoke a cigarette to the Lord's Prayer in three hundred languages. "It was the paradox of all paradoxes," Sidney M. Shalett wrote of the fair in *Harper's* the year it closed. "It was good, it was bad; it was the acme of all crazy vulgarity, it was the pinnacle of all inspiration." Meyer Berger of the *New York Times* called it "Mad Meadow." But there was a method in its madness, and in retrospect that motive seems more significant than its lapses of taste, even more important than the snub from Nazi Germany, the only major power that stayed away. In a word, the fair was a triumph of technology, the force that would do so much to shape postwar American society.

The hit of the fair was GM's Futurama, which drew 28,000 paying customers a day, each of whom sat on a conveyor belt armchair for fifteen minutes, listening to a recorded explanation while he observed Norman Bel Geddes's notion of what the American landscape would be like in 1960. Bel Geddes's prescience was less than twenty-twenty. He predicted tall, tanned, vigorous people spending most of their time having fun. (There was no mention of black people; blacks, apparently, would have ceased to exist.) Possessions would bore Americans in his 1960, so there weren't many in the Futurama. The countryside was crisscrossed by fat highways. Cars were air-conditioned and cost $200. Most of the land was forested. The luckiest Americans dwelt in one-factory villages producing a single industrial item and growing their own food.

Inventors and engineers would use a little atomic energy, but their chief source of power would be liquid air. Tremendous telescopes permitted men to see the moon a hundred times more clearly. Cancer would be cured; the average life span was seventy-five years. Houses were light and disposable; when you tired of one you just threw it away. (Where you threw it was unmentioned.) Most people had high school educations. Every village had an airport, with elevators taking aircraft to and from underground hangars. Office buildings and apartment condominiums were 1,500 feet high and were bordered by fourteen-lane turnpikes.

John Brooks has pointed out Bel Geddes's most conspicuous Futurama flaw. He had no grasp whatever of the urban problems which would produce the crisis of America's next generation. Cities were to be divided by the superhighways, and neighborhoods were to be zoned residential, commercial, or industrial. The dreamland was built to bring more automobiles into cities faster, yet there was no provision for parking. That was Bel Geddes's most accurate forecast. It is precisely what has happened — to our despair. As Brooks observes of the Futurama, "many of its prophecies of Heaven have become facts; the only trouble is that now that they are here they look more like the lineaments of Hell."

Among the foreign visitors to arrive at Mad Meadow's gate in mid-June of 1939 was an Englishman with an awkward stutter and the name George the Sixth, by the Grace of God, of Great Britain and Northern Ireland and of his other Realms and Territories, King; Emperor of India; Head of the Commonwealth; Defender of the Faith. He was accompanied by his queen, the former Elizabeth Angela Marguerite Bowes-Lyon, and a host of protocol officers, secretaries, and aides. It was probably the biggest moment in the greeter's life. His smile benevolent above a flowing white stock, he gave them his blue-ribbon personal tour and then saw them off to Hyde Park.

FDR was very much the squire that day. He drove his royal guests around the county in his custom-built Ford with manual brakes and served them hot dogs and — at the request of the Defender of the Faith — Ruppert's beer. In Washington, 600,000 people lined the parade route, John Nance Garner cackled "Here come the British!" and Kate Smith, again by royal request, sang "When the Moon Comes Over the Mountain." It was all very low-key, but its political significance was prodigious. Three months earlier Hitler had seized the rump Czech state. War was now imminent, and the President was letting the world know that he could do more than send pious messages to the Wilhelmstrasse. America had been a slumbering giant, he said, but now she was awakening; the aggressors had better watch out. The Führer displayed his customary charm by describing the President as a "pettifogging Jew" and adding that "the completely negroid appearance of his wife" showed that she was "half-caste."

Hitler had an adoring Reichstag; Roosevelt faced a coalition Congress, and for the White House the difference was painful. The President asked the Führer for assurance that weak nations would not be attacked; William L. Shirer noted how "the paunchy deputies rocked with raucous laughter" when their leader solemnly promised not to invade the United States. Senator Nye, speaking for the isolationist bloc, said Roosevelt had "asked for it." The strong wind FDR had sowed in the off-year primaries reaped a whirlwind in the Senate Foreign Relations Committee; after the shock of Munich the committee had been expected to recommend repeal of the neutrality laws, but the vote was 12-11 against it, and the majority included Walter George and Guy Gillette, two of the senators Roosevelt had tried to retire.

Second only to the President among public figures, Charles A. Lindbergh could command the largest radio audience. "We must not be misguided by this foreign propaganda that our frontiers lie in Europe," he said. "What more could we ask than the Atlantic Ocean on the east, the Pacific on the west? An ocean is a formidable barrier, even for modern aircraft." Later he would put his case more strongly. Senator Arthur H. Vandenberg swore never to send American boys to war under any circumstances. Earl Browder, speaking at the summer Institute of Politics at the University of Virginia, was asked whether Stalin might form an alliance with Hitler; as Browder later recalled, "I replied that I could easier imagine myself being elected president of the U.S. Chamber of Commerce." Fritz Kuhn was convicted of forgery and theft; his German-American Bund called him Roosevelt's first political prisoner. Hitler issued his first demand for Danzig on August 20, and when Berlin and Moscow jointly announced their nonaggression pact on August 21 the Poles were doomed. Yet military analysts kept talking about Poland's bad roads and "General Mud," as though World War II might be called off because of bad weather.

America's yearning for simplism prevented any rational debate over foreign policy and the threat to national security. Chamberlain hadn't understood why British lives depended upon Czech fortifications in the Sudetenland, and U.S. public opinion couldn't see beyond the fastness of its seascapes. But Roosevelt and Hull realized that the British Empire was no longer the world's great stabilizing force; Munich had exposed its flabby muscle. H.M.'s fleet remained intact, but if France fell and the English were cornered on their island, the center of geopolitical gravity would inevitably move westward. Hitler had declared that his ultimate goal was "*die ganze Welt*" (the whole world), and already German agents were active in Argentina. Roosevelt believed that he could buy peace for his generation, but he knew the price; the next generation of Americans would have to fight alone, against overwhelming odds. Lincoln had said that you could do anything with public opinion, and nothing without it. What was the public's opinion now? Dr. Gallup reported that 65 percent of his pollees favored boycotting Germany, 57 percent wanted neutrality legislation revised, 51 percent expected war in Europe in 1939, 58 percent believed the United States would be drawn into it, 90 percent said they would fight if America were invaded, and 10 percent said they would fight if America were not invaded.

Anything approaching a declaration of war, then, would be an invitation to insurrection. The President had to cut his cloth to fit the public mood. That boxed him in. But he could make two important moves now: keep the congressional leadership informed and strengthen the armed forces, which were, that summer, weaker than Poland's. The President did not know — or could not prove — that Hitler had decided in May to destroy Poland and then move on England and France. His intelligence services were quite good, however; a mountain of data could admit of but one conclusion: that the Wehrmacht was preparing to rupture the borders of the Reich.

In the last week of July the President invited the leaders of Capitol Hill to his second-floor oval study. With Hull at his elbow, he reviewed the evidence of Hitler's intentions, estimated that the Allies had only a fifty-fifty chance of surviving, and asked for neutrality revision. Hitler had acknowledged to Roosevelt that the one American force which impressed him was "the vastness of your nation and the immense wealth of your nation." Why not intimidate him with it? Under the neutrality law's present working, the United States was required to withhold sales of arms to aggressors and victims alike. Revision now might deter the Nazi dictator and so save the peace. To his guests the President said, "I've fired my last shot. I think I ought to have another round in my belt."

He was really talking to one man, Borah, who could carry the Senate if he would. He wouldn't. "There's not going to be any war this year," he said. "All this hysteria is manufactured and artificial."

In despair Hull said, "I wish the senator would come down to my office and read the cables."

Borah said impassively, "I have sources of information in Europe that I regard as more reliable than those of the State Department." He explained what he meant: foreign newspapers.

With Hull near tears, Garner polled the room on embargo repeal. To the President he said, "Well, Captain, we may as well face the facts. You haven't got the votes, and that's all there is to it."

Roosevelt remarked quietly to the leadership that the responsibility was theirs and bade them good evening.

There remained for him the state of national defense. For the first time in five years the U.S. Navy was maneuvering in the Atlantic — the excuse was a ceremonial visit to Mad Meadow — but that was about all that could be said for American naval might; the most memorable naval event of 1939 was the inexplicable sinking of the submarine *Squalus* off Portsmouth in 240 feet of water. The House had authorized $499,857,936 for the Army, including $50,000,000 to increase the Air Corps from 5,500 to 6,000 planes. "Bluff and jitterism," snorted Borah, and this time he was right. None of the aircraft belonged in the same sky with the British Spitfire, the French Nieuport, or the German ME-109. Even the new P-40s which were beginning to appear on American bases carried only machine guns synchronized to fire through the propellers — as in 1918 — and these planes had just reached the experimental stage.

In May the President had once more demonstrated his skill in picking men by choosing as his new chief of staff Brigadier General George C. Marshall (who was to be sworn in the same day that Germany invaded Poland). Marshall had 227,000 soldiers but equipment for only 75,000: Garand and Springfield rifles, twenty-year-old machine guns, and a few French 75s brought home after the Armistice in 1918. In August Lieutenant General Hugh Drum assembled his First Army for maneuvers and reported with a straight face that he was short of combat strength by 246,000 men, 3,063 machine guns, 348 howitzers, and 180 field guns. In European terms, *Time* wrote, "the U.S. Army looked like a few nice boys with BB guns." Dean Acheson quoted the old chestnut about America's lack of military preparedness: "God looks after children, drunkards, and the United States." J. P. Morgan capsulated the country's myopia when, upon sailing for Scotland to shoot grouse, he said, "If they start war, my shooting will be interrupted."

They started it at 5:20 A.M. Polish time, September 1, when a German warplane bombed Puck, a fishing village and air base on the northwest coast of the Gulf of Danzig. At 5:45 A.M. the German ship *Schleswig-Holstein* fired the opening shell, a direct hit on a Polish ammunition dump at Westerplatte. Then the first Wehrmacht infantry attack went in through a gentle rain, under gray skies. Four hours later, at 2:30 A.M. Washington time, the telephone beside the President's bed rang. It was his ambassador in Paris. "This is Bill Bullitt, Mr. President."

"Yes, Bill."

"Tony Biddle has just got through from Warsaw, Mr. President. Several German divisions are deep in Polish territory, and fighting is heavy. Tony said there were reports of bombers over the city. Then he was cut off. . . ."

"Well, Bill, it's come at last. God help us all."

In the beginning the war went swiftly. The German General Staff had calculated that it needed a month to conquer Poland. After eleven days essentially all was over but the screaming in Himmler's new concentration camps. In its September 25 issue *Time* introduced its readers to a new word: "This was no war of occupation, but a war of quick penetration and obliteration — *Blitzkrieg*, lightning war." Every thirty seconds Americans tuned to shortwave could hear eleven stirring notes — the opening of a Chopin polonaise — a sign that although the rest of the country had been overrun, Radio Warsaw was still free. Then, at 4 A.M. on September 17, the Russians burst into Poland through the back door. Radio Warsaw fell silent. When next heard from it burst into a triumphant "Deutschland über Alles."

Kenneth Crawford rhetorically inquired for the *Nation,* "Is the Roosevelt Administration neutral? Certainly not. Is there any chance for the United States to stay out of another world war? Practically none." That was not the line the White House was taking, however. "This nation will remain a neutral nation," Roosevelt announced in a fireside chat on September 3, "but I cannot ask that every American remain neutral in thought as well." At the President's first wartime press conference, Phelps Adams of the *New York Sun* asked, "Can we stay out of it?" After a pause FDR answered slowly, "I not only sincerely hope so, but I believe we can, and every effort will be made by this administration to do so." Shoring up Latin America, he suggested that the Inter-American Conference warn warships to avoid naval action in the western hemisphere south of Canada, and in a declaration from Panama it did so. At a second press conference he was asked how far U.S. territorial waters extended toward Europe. He said evasively, "As far as U.S. interests require them to go." The reporter inquired, "Does that reach the Rhine, Mr. President?" The President laughed. He was, he explained "talking only about salt water."

He was thinking about it, too. The only place Americans might encounter Germans in force was on the high seas. Already a U-boat had sunk the S.S. *Athenia*, and in England furious U.S. survivors had been interviewed by Ambassador Kennedy's twenty-two-year-old son Jack. Young Kennedy's words to them — "We are still neutral and the Neutrality Act still holds" — had satisfied few. That viewpoint didn't satisfy Roosevelt, either. Now that war had begun, his policy was changing. Neutrality, in his rather unusual definition, was now defined as meaning no American soldiers shooting at German soldiers. It did not preclude helping the Allies exploit their command of the sea. He therefore closed U.S. waters to "belligerent submarines" (subs, of course, were Nazi vessels) and called Congress into special session, asking that foreign powers be permitted to buy American munitions on a "cash-and-carry" basis. In her column Mrs. Roosevelt had concluded that "much as we may dislike to do it, it may be necessary to use the forces of this world in the hope of keeping civilization going until spiritual forces gain sufficient strength everywhere to make an acceptance of disarmament possible." That is what her husband really meant by neutrality.

But it wasn't what Lindbergh meant, or Borah, or Vandenberg, or Wheeler, or even — at first — a majority of newspaper editors. Thus cash-and-carry became America's first wartime issue. It marked the emergence of a new Lindbergh. In a radio speech on September 15 he said, "This is not a question of banding together to defend the white race against foreign invasion"; this was "a quarrel arising from the errors of the last war." His wife Anne had just finished a book, *The Wave of the Future*, which seemed to argue that a worldwide Nazi victory was inevitable. But Anne's mother was working on a William Allen White committee supporting cash-and-carry. It was a time of divided families, divided loyalties, and hard words. Harold Ickes asked publicly, "How can any American accept a decoration at the hand of a brutal dictator who, with that same hand, is robbing and torturing thousands of fellow human beings? Perhaps Henry Ford and Colonel Charles A. Lindbergh" — both decorated by Hitler in 1938 — "will be willing to answer."

The German chargé d'affaires protested Ickes's remarks, Sumner Welles coldly rejected the protest, and suddenly the issue wasn't just neutrality revision; it had become one of patriotism. Roosevelt proclaimed an unprecedented "limited national emergency." Lawyers and scholars asked one another what a limited national emergency was. It wasn't anything; it was just FDR's way of showing the flag. The only people in the country who tried to honor the vague proclamation were the managers of movie theaters, where "The Star-Spangled Banner" was played at the end of each evening's performance (a practice which was to continue for nearly six years). In the sharp exchange with the isolationist bloc, the President won. The captain had the votes now. Both houses passed the cash-and-carry amendment, and arriving British merchantmen began picking up harbor pilots on November 3.

In the subsequent legislative lull, Americans noticed something, or, to be more precise, the absence of something. Wasn't there supposed to be a war in Europe? There was, but the only bellicose sounds came from London's music halls, where Cockney harpies were breaking up audiences with a dreadful ballad called "We'll Hang Our Washing on the Siegfried Line." There was some action at sea, where the British held the initiative. On the Western front, however, Hitler was playing a waiting game, letting French morale drop ever lower. On the Maginot Line the cooped-up French Army squatted and grew flabby — "the strongest army in the world," as a British general would put it, "facing no more than twenty-six divisions, sitting still and sheltering behind steel and concrete." German civilians were calling it Sitzkrieg, "sit-down war." "This so-called war," said Senator Vandenberg, "is nothing but about twenty-five people and propaganda." Senator Borah called it the "phony war," and the epithet stuck.

Thus the 1930s, which had begun with a cry for bread, ended with a yawn. There was no Battle of the Marne this time, nor even a sizable border skirmish. It was a period in American history when international challenges were about to replace domestic problems, but it was marked in little ways. Granville Hicks resigned from the Communist party because of the Hitler-Stalin pact; hardly anyone noticed. Tyrone Power and his wife Annabella flew home from Lisbon. Rhodes Scholars were recalled — Byron White entered Yale Law School — and then they all felt rather foolish; they had run away from nothing but a silent confrontation. In the first days of the war grocers were selling sugar in hundred-pound sacks, canned goods by the case, flour in fifty-pound bags. Presently the squirrelers too felt silly; there were no food shortages.

For a while there *was* a shortage of pins with colored heads for armchair strategists, and Rand McNally & Company was briefly sold out of large-scale European maps. New York's Transportation Board announced that subways would make excellent bomb shelters. A Standard Oil subsidiary at Bayonne, New Jersey, replaced German natives on its tanker crews with American-born seamen, and a rug manufacturer changed the name of his most popular line, Dictator Carpets, to Liberty Carpets. But when boredom set in, the early, impulsive gestures were regretted. By Christmas, European maps were a glut on the seasonal market. Elmo Roper found that 67.4 percent of the people wanted no part of the war. And by New Year's Day 1940, the country was much more interested in whether a scrappy, lightweight Tennessee team could dance its way around Southern California's musclemen in the Rose Bowl. (They couldn't; USC won, 14-0.) Jukeboxes were announcing that "Annie Doesn't Live Here Any More," and Bonnie Baker's Lolita lisp was describing the assets of her steady with "Oh,

Johnny!" At the University of Illinois a member of the Pi Kappa Phi house wrapped five baby white mice in lettuce and swallowed the lot. People were lining up under marquees to see Bette Davis in *Dark Victory* and James Stewart in *Mr. Smith Goes to Washington.* President Roosevelt sent a final conciliatory message to Hitler and was informed that the Führer was asleep. He did not, however, sleep long.

Portrait of an American

———

NORMAN THOMAS

HE WAS THE AMERICAN ISAIAH,
     the nation's conscience,
     the voice of the mute,
     the advocate of the dispossessed,
     the patrician rebel,
     the prophet who spoke out when others fled into silence.

He ran for the Presidency six times and never came close to a single electoral vote. Yet he refused to yield his idealism to despair, declined to quit the system, and in the end he found he had won as much as the winners — and without the loss of integrity.

Norman Thomas was an evangelist. It was in his blood, in the bone of his bone. His father and both his grandfathers had been Presbyterian ministers, and as a boy in Ohio, delivering copies of the Marion *Star,* owned by Warren G. Harding, he practiced intonation alone until he had developed the spellbinding delivery of a Bryan, a Debs, a Theodore Roosevelt.

He had the style. What he needed now was something to say. A trip around the world after leaving Princeton — he was class valedictorian — persuaded him that colonialism was evil. Back in New York, he became a social worker in Manhattan's blighted Spring Street neighborhood. The misery and want there tore at him, he looked for answers, and found some from Walter Rauschenbusch at the Union Theological Seminary. Later he said: "Life and work in a wretchedly poor district in New York City drove me steadily toward Socialism, and the coming of the war completed the process. In it there was a large element of ethical compulsion."

That war came in 1917. He campaigned against it, was stoned, and founded with Roger N. Baldwin the American Civil Liberties Bureau, later League. In 1918 he wrote Gene Debs:

    I am sending you an application for membership in the Socialist party. I
  am doing this because I think these are the days when radicals ought to

stand up and be counted. I believe in the necessity of establishing a cooperative commonwealth and the abolition of our present unjust economic
institutions and class distinctions based thereon.

He was moved by:

. . . grotesque inequalities, conspicuous waste, gross exploitation and unnecessary poverty all around me.

Debs died in 1926; Thomas became the party's new leader. He was now
forty-two, six-foot-two, 185 pounds, with merry blue eyes — a gentle moralist, a good-humored Puritan. His health was oddly affected by the human
condition. If the world was peaceful and prosperous, he glowed with
vitality; if world conditions deteriorated, so did he. But he never let illnesses stop him.

In 1932 he knew he could not be elected, and warned his young followers to prepare for defeat. But, "Vote your hopes and not your fears,"
he told them, and, "Don't vote for what you won't want and get it."

The planks in his presidential platform were public works, unemployment insurance, minimum wage laws, low-cost housing, slum clearance, the
five-day week, abolition of child labor, health insurance for the aged, anti-
Communism, civil liberties, civil rights for Negroes, and old age pensions.
Nearly every one of these proposals was then considered radical.

The program was approved by 728,860 voters and by the man from New
York who won the election.

In 1936 Thomas's vote dwindled to 187,342, and he knew why: ". . . the
Socialists watched with some eagerness as Democrats adopted policies they
had long recommended in such fields as tariffs and trade barriers, labor
legislation, social legislation, social security, and . . . farm policy, such as
the Resettlement Administration."

He would join almost any picket line, mount any stump, whatever the
danger. In March 1935, in a Mississippi county called Birdsong, he spoke
out for black sharecroppers, and a drunken mob of whites dragged him
from the platform, beat him bloody, and threw him across the county line.
One said, "We don't need no goddam Yankee bastard to tell us what to do
with our niggers."

Three years later he went into Jersey City to speak against Mayor Frank
("I am the law") Hague. Hague forbade the rally and warned Thomas to
stay away. Thomas came. Hague's police slugged him, drove him across the
Hudson, and ordered him never to enter Jersey again. He returned to it an
hour later. The cops mauled him again and again threw him, hemorrhaging,
on a Manhattan sidewalk. This time he went to a federal court. A judge
issued an injunction against the mayor and his heavies, and Thomas, ban-
daged but upright, denounced "Hagueism" to an enormous throng in Jersey
City's Journal Square.

Communists hated him. He visited Moscow during the purge trials and
later declared:

For the believer in the dignity of the individual, there is only one standard by which to judge a given society and that is the degree to which it approaches the ideal of a fellowship of free men. Unless one can believe in the practicability of some sort of anarchy, or find evidence there exists a superior and recognizable governing caste to which men should by nature cheerfully submit, there is no approach to a good society save by democracy. The alternative is tyranny.

Leon Trotsky hooted, "Norman Thomas called himself a Socialist as the result of a misunderstanding." But Thomas was firm: one must work within the system. He believed the New Deal should have nationalized the steel industry, but he became convinced that Roosevelt's election had brought "the salvation of America . . . the welfare state and almost a revolution."

In World War II he battled against the internment of Japanese-Americans and Roosevelt's demand for unconditional surrender. He believed "the lowest circle of hell" would be a Nazi victory, but thought a call for a statement of democratic peace terms would be more reasonable.

Almost alone in 1945 he condemned America's use of atomic bombs: "We shall pay for this in a horrible hatred of millions of people which goes deeper and farther than we think."

His last campaign was in 1948; he entered only because he saw how the Communist party was manipulating Henry Wallace. The day after the election an eminent New York Democrat said, "The wrong man lost." "Dewey?" asked a friend. "No," said the Democrat, "Thomas."

In later years he spoke not as a candidate, but as the evangelist he had always been. In 1960 he anticipated the ecological crisis and the need for disarmament. He was convinced that ultimate disaster lay in military aid to other nations, and he believed in the wisdom of the Marshall Plan.

Along the way he wrote twenty books. His energy was unbelievable. In his eighties, crippled by arthritis, this old man deformed by sickness crisscrossed the country by auto or in trains — sleeping in upper berths to save money — speaking out against the Vietnam war. And college students, who had sworn to distrust everyone else of his generation, crowded halls to hear his indictment of the war. But he never counseled them to violence:

"The secret of a good life is to have the right loyalties and to hold them in the right scale of values. The value of dissent and dissenters is to make us reappraise those values with supreme concern for truth. Rebellion per se is not a virtue. If it were, we should have some heroes on very low levels."

A reporter once asked him what he considered to be his achievements over the years. He replied in part:

"I suppose it is an achievement to live to my years and feel that one has kept the faith, or tried to . . . to be able to sleep at night with reasonable satisfaction . . . to have had a part . . . in some of the things that have been accomplished in the field of civil liberties, in the field of better race relations, and the rest of it. It is something of an achievement, I think, to keep the idea of socialism before a rather indifferent or even hostile American public."

When he died in his sleep in December 1968, President Johnson, Vice President Humphrey, Governor Nelson Rockefeller, United Nations ambassador Arthur Goldberg, and New York Mayor John Lindsay issued shining tributes to him. Everyone agreed he had kept the faith.

They omitted the end of Norman Thomas's answer to the reporter's question: "That's the kind of achievement that I have to my credit. As the world counts achievement, I have not got much."

Not much. Only a beam of immortality.

SEVEN

Through the Night
With a Light from Above

I N HITLER'S THIRD REICH the science of fundamental physics did not
exist. There was Jewish physics, which was against the law, and
German physics, the responsibility for which was vested in the Ministerium
für Wissenschaft, Erziehung und Volksbildung (Ministry of Science, Education and National Culture) at No. 69 Unter den Linden. Actually a Jewish
woman was, until March 1938, one of the ministry's brightest stars. Working with Otto Hahn and Fritz Strassmann, Lise Meitner had been bombarding uranium with neutrons in the laboratories of Berlin's Kaiser
Wilhelm Institut, and logging unbelievable results. Dr. Meitner was an
exception to anti-Semitic legislation because she wasn't a German. She was
Viennese.

After the Anschluss all Austrians were transformed into citizens of the
Reich, however, and as a non-Aryan, Lise Meitner found herself locked out
of her own laboratory. The shadow of the concentration camp lay across
her path. Her eminent colleagues went to the Führer himself. Race had
nothing to do with science, they argued. Physics was either true or false,
and because Germany had been guided by truth, the fatherland led the
world in Nobel laureates — three times as many as the Americans. Hitler
angrily dismissed them as "white Jews." A warrant for Lise Meitner's arrest
was issued. She slipped over the Dutch border disguised as a tourist and
made her way to the small Swedish seaside town of Kungälv, near Göte-
borg. Two great physicists, Niels Bohr in Copenhagen and Hahn, now in
Stockholm, were hospitable and kind, but to her it seemed that her career
was over, her life in ruins.

In point of fact all of them, and their colleagues in the United States,
stood on the threshold of science's Elizabethan Age. Astonishing discoveries
were being made simultaneously in a half-dozen countries. Enrico Fermi
had won a Nobel Prize for his work with neutrons. Hahn, Strassmann,
Bohr, Chadwick at Cambridge, and the Joliot-Curies in Paris were at the

frontier of investigation and driving hard. Over thirty years earlier Albert Einstein measured atomic energy in the abstract from his theory of relativity. Einstein observed that a body in motion has a greater mass than a body at rest, the difference being defined by the velocity of light. Now real neutrons were splitting real nuclei, new elements were being discovered, three isotopes (types) of uranium were under investigation, and formulae had been committed to paper which, under conceivable circumstances, might translate Einstein's theory into a stupendous reality. The nuclear physicists didn't expect the world to understand. They could hardly credit their own work. When Hahn posted a report on his atom splitting to *Naturwissenschaften* on December 22, 1938, he felt that somehow he must be wrong: "After the manuscript had been mailed, the whole thing once more seemed so improbable to me that I wished I could get the document back out of the mailbox." But when Bohr read it, he struck himself on the forehead and cried, "How could we have overlooked that so long?"

They were fascinated, awestricken, frightened, and at odds with one another over what it all meant. Einstein told William L. Laurence of the *New York Times* that fission could not produce an explosion. Bohr, arguing with a colleague, ticked off ten persuasive reasons why such a device could never be built, and Hahn said of it, "That would surely be contrary to God's will!" But across the Atlantic there was disagreement. On February 2, 1939, Leo Szilard wrote Joliot-Curie from America:

> When Hahn's paper reached this country about a fortnight ago, a few of us at once got interested in the question whether neutrons are liberated in the disintegration of uranium. Obviously, if more than one neutron were liberated, a sort of chain reaction would be possible. In certain circumstances this might then lead to the construction of bombs which would be extremely dangerous in general and particularly in the hands of certain governments.

He did not identify "certain governments." Everyone knew; it was on all their minds: with such bombs, Hitler could rule or destroy the world.

Haunted by this specter, the giants of European physics joined Lise Meitner in a general migration. Leaving Fascist Italy to receive his prize in Stockholm, Fermi canceled his return ticket in Sweden and headed for New York and the laboratories of Columbia University. Young Edward Teller went to George Washington University. Victor F. Weisskopf joined the Rochester faculty, and Bohr was packing to join Einstein in Princeton. He suggested that Lise Meitner and her nephew Dr. O. R. Frisch remain in Copenhagen long enough to conduct a confirming experiment. On January 16, 1939, Bohr reached New York. Awaiting him was a cable from Meitner and Frisch. The experiment had been affirmative — staggeringly so; the atom they split had freed 200 million volts of electricity. If uranium could be harnessed, theoretically it would be twenty million times as powerful as TNT.

Had the man on the street grasped this, he would have been as astonished by the source as by the fact. Popular notions of the scientist were of wildly impractical eccentrics — Dr. Frankensteins, giggling madly as they juggled retorts and vials and threw enormous switches. It is worth noting that when General Leslie R. Groves later recruited a staff to work with the nuclear scientists, he said: "Your job won't be easy. At great expense we have gathered here the largest collection of crackpots ever seen." The scientists were aware of their reputation and were indifferent toward it. There was about prewar nuclear physicists an informality, a casual air which would vanish in a terrible cloud six years later. In 1939 the very word "physicist" was uncommon; many Americans couldn't even pronounce it. Universities paid men with Ph.D.s in science $1,500 to $1,800 a year. They accepted because they had little choice. Industry didn't want them. In one year, 1937, there were only four research openings for them in the whole country, and the mite set aside for government research was largely confined to the Department of Agriculture.

In return, science was left alone. Genuinely international, scientists had no secrets from one another. Even in the Soviet Union, A. I. Brodsky could publish an article on the separation of uranium isotopes in 1939, and two of his colleagues carried out fission experiments in a shaft of the Moscow subway. (The Kremlin then ordered the work discontinued on the ground that it had no practical value.) Even when the concept of security crept in, scientific investigators didn't worry about it. They could talk shop with confidence that no layman could understand them. Indeed, only a handful of their own colleagues knew of fission in its new context. Before leaving Denmark, Bohr had been well aware that the Wehrmacht might invade his little country, and he was concerned about his precious hoard of heavy water — water in which the hydrogen has an atomic mass of two, invaluable for slowing down neutrons. But how many Nazis had heard of it? Very few, so he solved his problem by pouring it into a large beer bottle and putting it in his refrigerator, where it sat through five years of alien rule.

It was in America, perhaps, that dedication to academic freedom was greatest, and it was here that the first moves on the atomic chessboard were made in full view of an incurious public. The Meitner-Frisch cable had been sent in clear. The idea of coding information would have been considered absurd. Similarly, the experiment was reconfirmed by the simple expedient of reserving a Columbia laboratory for the night of January 25, calling in Fermi as an adviser, staging the uranium test, setting up an oscilloscope to measure energy, and pushing a button. The needle registered precisely 200 million volts; duplication was that exact. To discuss interpretations, everyone moved into lecture room 301 of Columbia's Pupin Physics Laboratory at Broadway and 119th Street. The door wasn't even closed, let alone locked. Anyone could have walked in from the pavement and learned of the latest developments in nuclear science — provided, of course, he could understand the jargon and the graphs, charts, formulae, and chalk scribbles on the blackboard.

Even a Washington conference was free in 1939. Fermi and Bohr were among those attending the spring meeting of the American Physical Society there, and Bohr went to the lectern to report on their work. He stated flatly that a projectile armed with a tiny fragment of U-235 under bombardment from slow neutrons could blow up most of the District of Columbia. As he lectured, delegates slipped in and out of the hall, placing long-distance calls to their campuses, and one young American, Robert Oppenheimer, was scrawling furiously away on a yellow pad, roughly calculating what the critical mass would be. There was a *New York Times* reporter at that meeting, but either he or his editors failed to grasp the full weight of what had happened. The *Times* did carry a brief account on the achievement of uranium fission. The next morning Dr. Luiz W. Alvarez was getting a haircut at the University of California when the story caught his eye. He leaped right out of the barber's chair, swirled the sheet around him like a toga, and dashed into the Radiation Laboratory to spread the news.

Aside from the moral issue — which was being raised even then — a thousand questions needed answering. Ahead lay the discovery that uranium was not only rare; 99.6 percent of it was U-238, too stable for fission. U-235 had to be separated from the masses of U-238 and refined until the metal had reached a degree of purity unknown in America. Any bomb would have to be designed, a task which in the event would be entrusted to a German refugee named Klaus Fuchs with interesting political opinions. Most important, the move from theoretical physics to an actual device would be so expensive that private sponsorship would be inadequate. Thousands of millions of dollars would be needed, and only one man in the country commanded resources that great. Probably they would have gone to Roosevelt in any event. Moral checks were not strong yet, and scientific curiosity was. But debate became pointless, because a single argument swept all before it. The scientists were now absolutely convinced that Hitler was building his own bombs — was, on the evidence, far ahead of them.

The Nazis knew about nuclear fission, of course; Hahn had told them in his *Naturwissenschaften* article. Early in 1939 two German physicists called at No. 69 Unter den Linden and suggested the possibility of constructing a "uranium machine." In April the Reich's six most distinguished atomic scientists met twice in Berlin; they agreed to join in such an undertaking and keep quiet about it. Then Dr. S. Flügge, an anti-Nazi physicist, learned the details. Nobody had sworn Flügge to secrecy, and he thought the world's scientific community ought to know what was going on. He published an extensive report on uranium chain reaction for the July 1939 number of *Naturwissenschaften* and then gave a simplified version to an interviewer from the *Deutsche Allgemeine Zeitung*, a conservative newspaper Goebbels hadn't yet suppressed. The inevitable copies found their way out through Zurich, slipping past the censors because the material was as incomprehensible to ordinary Nazis as it was to ordinary Americans. But the scientists in America didn't know the where or the why. They thought Flügge was showing them only the tip of the iceberg, and if the tip was that large, the world was in trouble. Then, that summer of 1939, came the most alarming development of all. Suddenly, without explanation, the Germans forbade the export of uranium ore from Czechoslovakia and ordered a blackout of all news about uranium. Since the known uses of uranium were confined to pottery and the painting of luminous dials on clocks, there could be only one interpretation of the embargo. The gentlemen at No. 69 Unter den Linden must be on their way. And in truth, they were. Being Germans, they had naturally tricked out their project with lines of authority, word of which also drifted through Zurich. It was Operation U, directed by appointed members of the Uranium Verein (Uranium Society) and responsible to the Heereswaffenamt (Army Weapons Department) in Berlin.

Roosevelt must be warned. But how? Most of the nuclear physicists in the United States who knew about fission were newly arrived expatriates. They had no friends in power; some were still learning the language. Szilard and Teller went to Washington and were met with blank stares. Even Fermi, with his Nobel Prize, was received coldly. The Army and Navy needed all their energies to acquire conventional weapons; they had no time for Buck Rogers games. The State Department saw no reason for urgency. According to their files, uranium was a rare and rather useless metal which was found, among other places, in Czechoslovakia and Belgium. Europe was in the last days of peace, armies were mobilizing, the crisis was desperate, and foreign service officers had no time for disheveled men who talked like organ grinders about splitting atoms.

But there was one tousled scientist, the sloppiest of them all, who could not be ignored. Albert Einstein was so famous that when he decided to wear his hair long he added a phrase to the American idiom. By July, after bureaucratic Washington's last turndown of Fermi, Einstein left Princeton for his summer holiday on Long Island. When Szilard and Eugene Wigner sent word that they must see him, however, he consented. Their plans were vague. They doubted that even Einstein could get through to the President; it seemed more practical to warn Brussels through Einstein's friendship with the Belgian queen mother. First, of course, they had to find Einstein on Long Island, and that turned into quite an expedition. On the hottest day of the year they set out for an address which had been given to them over the telephone. It had sounded like "Patchogue" but was really Peconic. Even after reaching Peconic they were bewildered. Szilard was arguing that they ought to quit, that they ought to go home and think it over, when a small boy volunteered to lead them to Einstein's house.

The great man shuffled out in slippers and led them to his study. According to Szilard, "the possibility of a chain reaction in uranium had not occurred" to Einstein. "But almost as soon as I began to tell him about it he realized what the consequences might be and immediately signified his readiness to help us and if necessary 'stick his neck out,' as the saying goes." They proposed the Belgian solution — which might have altered the outcome of the whole war, since Hitler would be in Brussels by spring — with Einstein writing the queen. Unsure of the protocol, they decided after leaving him that a copy should go to the State Department; the original would be held for two weeks, to give the State Department a chance to protest. But during the following week, as they discussed the mission with friends, the question of another approach was raised. Gustav Stolper, former editor of *Der deutsche Volksvirt* (*The German Economist*), was acquainted with Alexander Sachs, a financier and adviser to President Roosevelt. Why not go straight to the White House? Sachs thought the idea excellent, and on August 2 Szilard returned to Long Island with Teller. Einstein dictated a letter to the President in German; Teller translated it. Hitler's embargo on Czech uranium was cited, and the work in Berlin. The key passage explained the possible implications of a nuclear chain reaction: ". . . extremely powerful bombs of a new type may thus be constructed. A single bomb of this type, carried by boat and exploded in a port, might very well destroy the whole port, together with some of the surrounding territory."

Sachs handed the letter to Roosevelt on October 11, and to make certain that it wasn't lost in a shuffle of other papers, he read it to him aloud. That was a mistake. The letter was too long. Roosevelt became bored and said at the end that he thought government intervention might be premature at this stage. Sachs begged for another meeting, at breakfast the following day, and the President nodded. The financier couldn't sleep that night. Repeatedly he left his room at the Carlton Hotel and walked the two blocks to Lafayette Park, directly across Pennsylvania Avenue from the White House. He was trying to think of a way to dramatize the issue. The way he chose at breakfast was to remind FDR that Robert Fulton had taken his steamship invention to Napoleon, who had dismissed it as impractical, thus losing the vessel which might have permitted an invasion of England and victory. The President thought a moment, then produced a bottle of Napoleon brandy and two glasses.

Filling them and lifting his to Sachs, he said, "Alex, what you are after is to see that the Nazis don't blow us up."

"Precisely."

Roosevelt summoned his military aide, General Edwin "Pa" Watson, and handed him Einstein's letter, together with supporting documents Sachs had brought. The President said, "Pa, this requires action!"

So began the secret war, or S-1, as it was known to a few selected Americans — a very few, not even including the Vice President. Like the other war, this one had its triumphs and heroes, not all of them in laboratories. Seven months after Roosevelt and Sachs toasted their new understanding, France's nuclear physicists carried out a daring plan to thwart the Nazi scientists at No. 69 Unter den Linden. The Germans knew that the French owned virtually all the heavy water in Europe — 185 kilograms in twelve sealed aluminum containers, bought in March 1940 from a Norwegian firm, Norsk Hydro. Led by Frédéric Joliot-Curie, and with enemy troops all around them, the French scientists concealed their cache in the death cell of the Riom prison. Although the Nazis knew it was nearby and were looking for it, the French smuggled it out of Bordeaux aboard a British collier while Joliot-Curie duped his German interrogators into believing the heavy water was on another ship.

Senator Borah died in January 1940, and his phony war died three months later when the Wehrmacht invaded Denmark and Norway, but the seismic shock of 1940 was Hitler's campaign in the west. It was like a seven-week Halloween broadcast by Orson Welles. Daily, hourly, the armchair strategists moved their colored pins while commentators described panzer thrusts far behind the Allied lines, the slaughter of refugees by Stuka dive bombers, and endless lines of blond Aryan youths who hurtled into the Lowlands and France shouting, "Heil Hitler!" Apart from the relentless advance of the field-gray columns, it was hard to tell exactly what was happening. Europe was obscured by a haze of conflicting reports. In this mist men like Joliot-Curie and Pierre Laval forged their separate destinies, while other figures, new leaders, tried to rally the demoralized Allied troops. Premier Paul Reynaud replaced Premier Edouard Daladier, Generalissimo Maxime Weygand succeeded Generalissimo Maurice Gamelin, and in London Chamberlain stepped down for Churchill, whose magnificent prose began to roll across the Atlantic.

Every American now knew what blitzkriegs were, and this was the greatest of them all. The German offensive opened on May 10. Four days later Holland surrendered. On the sixteenth day Belgium quit, and over the following weekend the British Army conducted its desperate, heroic evacuation from the beaches of Dunkerque. That left the French Army. It had been accounted the best in the world, but now in this seventh and last week of the Nazi *coup de main*, shortwave sets in Washington were picking up an impassioned but vain plea for Roosevelt to intervene, delivered by Reynaud himself.

On June 22 France capitulated. Paris was German, and a new fascistic government was established in the resort city of Vichy under Marshal Henri Philippe Pétain and Laval.* One of its first acts was to try *in absentia* a French tank general who had flown to England, sentencing him to death. Scornful of the men of Vichy, Charles de Gaulle sat in a Chelsea flat writing his first broadcasts to the people with whom he felt a mystical union, and whose destiny he would share. Like Reynaud, he was counting on the United States. So was Churchill, though he was too adroit a politician to beg. Instead he made grand references to the time when "the New

---

*As the ministers, deputies, and civil servants left Paris for Vichy, the two American films playing at the Champs Elysées were *Going Places,* and *You Can't Take It with You.*

World, with all its power and might," would step forth "to the rescue and the liberation of the Old."

Now came the Battle of Britain, the RAF struggling with the Luftwaffe for mastery of the skies over England. The city of Coventry was destroyed and thousands of Londoners were slain in the streets as a lesson to British stubbornness. The lesson did not take. The people huddled in bomb shelters and subway tubes — in one of them, four-year-old Julie Andrews was learning to sing — while their prime minister told Hitler that England would rather die than submit: ". . . we shall not flag or fail. We shall go on to the end. We shall fight in France, we shall fight on the seas and oceans, we shall fight with growing confidence and growing strength in the air, we shall defend our island, whatever the cost may be, we shall fight on the beaches, we shall fight on the landing grounds, we shall fight in the fields and in the streets, we shall fight in the hills; we shall never surrender."

Now the mass media began to show their real power. In retrospect the Martian broadcast appeared to have been a kind of shakedown cruise, to steady the nerves of the high-strung. But this war was real, it was happening in Europe as listeners heard about it, and there was no way to avoid emotional alliances. Not many Americans favored the Nazis. The Germans were displaying a genius for bad public relations. They not only committed atrocities; they advertised them. They had been shooting hostages from the outset, and there was hardly an ethnic group in the United States whom they had not alienated. And there was worse to come. Nazi offenses against Italy, their present ally, lay in the future; so did conquest of Greece, with that unforgettable moment when a Wehrmacht officer ordered a Greek soldier to lower the blue-and-white colors of Greece from the Acropolis. The soldier did it. Then he wrapped the flag around him and stepped off the edge of the Acropolis parapet, falling silently to his death three hundred feet below.

You didn't have to be an American of Greek descent to be moved by that, and those who were praying for England in 1940 weren't all anglophiles. Just before the French collapse, Edna St. Vincent Millay had written in the *New York Times:*

> *Oh, build, assemble, transport, give,*
> *That England, France and we may live*
> *Lest we be left to fight alone.*

Now night had fallen over France, and about all that England had left that summer were RAF courage, Churchill's voice, and the legacy of Shakespeare: *This England never did, nor ever shall/ Lie at the proud feet of a conquerer.* But since Shakespeare's language was also America's, it could rouse some Americans to extraordinary pitches of emotion. In the late summer of 1940 the American writer Alice Duer Miller published from England a slim volume of verse — that least popular of art forms. It was entitled *The White Cliffs,* and in three months it went through eleven printings. There were people who could recite long passages from it, including the closing quatrain, which so eloquently expressed the anglophilia of the author — and millions of her readers:

> *I am American bred,*
> *I have seen much to hate here — much to forgive,*
> *But in a world where England is finished and dead,*
> *I do not wish to live.*

The destiny of Britain had become a national obsession for the multitudes of interventionists; now, for the first time, many realized how much they owed England, and how closely they were bound to England's fate. Radio addicts — and there were those who hardly ventured more than a few feet from a loudspeaker that summer — could hear the tramp of jackboots as German soldiers marched into the Channel ports, could hear the troops singing "Wir Fahren Gegen England" (We're Sailing Against England). It sounded hopeless. There was no way of knowing then that the Spitfires and Hurricanes were winning their dogfights over the Channel. On one September night a Luftwaffe air fleet of 1,500 planes dropped 4,400,000 pounds of high explosives on London. It was the city's greatest catastrophe since the Great Fire of 1666. The priceless windows of St. Mary le Bow were lost; the House of Lords was hit by one bomb; Buckingham Palace by five. In her tube little Julie Andrews joined the other children in chanting:

> *Now come the incendiaries to light you to bed,*
> *Bring out the sandbags and kill them all dead.*

Over 32,000 British children had been evacuated to the United States. In the way of things that year, the children had to have a song. The fall of France had inspired "The Last Time I Saw Paris," the Battle of Britain "A Nightingale Sang in Berkeley Square," and so, in honor of America's young guests, Tin Pan Alley turned out a haunting tune for the lyrics:

> *My sister and I recall the day*
> *We left our friends and we sailed away*
> *And we think of the ones who had to stay —*
> *But we don't talk about that.*

This went on until men were willing to leave perfectly good drinks in bars not to hear the voices not talking about that. But there really was no escape. Kate Smith seemed to be singing "God Bless America" everywhere. The movies needed a longer lead time; it would be many months before the premiere of *Mrs. Miniver,* with Walter Pidgeon sailing out in his little boat to do his bit in picking up the Tommies at Dunkerque, but already Edward G. Robinson was the FBI man in *Confessions of a Nazi Spy,* listening to such hissed threats as, "I vill get efen mit you for zis zometime, Mister G-Mann!" It made you squirm but was ineluctable; every great moment in history has its sleazy exploiters and souvenir salesmen. This propaganda campaign turned out some classic films — including *Casablanca,* which some regard as the greatest movie of all time — and one immortal stratagem, which was so successful that it has been used by political movements ever since.

It was invented by a Belgian refugee named Victor de Laveleye. Like Charles de Gaulle, de Laveleye made daily shortwave broadcasts to his countrymen telling them to keep stiff upper lips. One evening late in 1940 he suggested that they chalk the letter V (for *victoire*) in public places to show their confidence in an ultimate Allied triumph and create a nuisance for the Nazis. It became the most popular symbol since the introduction of the crucifix. V was an astonishingly versatile letter. In Serbian it stood for *vitestvo* (heroism), in Czech *vitzstvi* (victory), and in Dutch *vrijheid* (freedom). The BBC began introducing its programs beamed to the continent with the first four notes of Beethoven's Fifth Symphony, three dots and a dash — the Morse code symbol for V. In the occupied countries the did-dit-dit-dah was used to knock on doors, blow train whistles, honk car horns, and fetch waiters. People waved to one another with two stretched fingers of the hand. In restaurants, cutlery was arranged in Vs. Stopped clocks were set at five minutes past eleven, and crayoned Vs were everywhere, even in the private toilets of German officers. Goebbels tried to steal the thunder by insisting the symbols all represented *Viktoria,* complete triumph for Hitler, but no one, not even Germans, believed him. Then the craze leaped the Atlantic. Rhinestone V brooches were on sale in department stores, and at Tiffany's you could get a quite good one, set in diamonds, for $5,000.

"Don't think you will win the war by making silly noises in restaurants," jeered one of Quisling's Norwegian henchmen. He was right, of course. Hitler's empire was now larger than Napoleon's, and his power was as absolute. On land he was strong enough to launch offensives in four directions simultaneously; at sea his three hundred U-boats were strangling Britain's lifelines. Only the consecration of embattled Britain stood between him and absolute mastery of Europe — unless the United States intervened.

In the United States nearly everyone was now either an isolationist or an interventionist, and while there were degrees to both, all interventionists believed that *something* ought to be done. In the dazed aftermath of the French armistice, their gestures, like their V brooches, were rather ineffectual. In Jeannette, Pennsylvania, a gun club practiced marksmanship so they would be ready to pick off descending Nazi parachutists. A coffee shop in Kirkland, Washington, changed "hamburger" on its menu to "liberty steak." The American Legion, hot for war, booed from its platform Senator Bennett Champ Clark and Congressman Fish, who had come to state the case for isolationism. There was a lot of nonsense about America's "going soft," as though the country's youth had lain around eating banana splits during the Depression; even Ed Murrow wrote his parents, "The price for soft living must be paid, and we may soon be paying that price." For all interventionists the arch villain was Charles A. Lindbergh. Charlotte, North Carolina, changed the name of Lindbergh Drive to Avon Terrace, the *New York Times* said he was "a blind young man," liberal columnists referred to him as "Herr von Lindbergh," and President Roosevelt mildly insulted him (he called him "a Copperhead") — whereupon Lindbergh angrily resigned his reserve commission as an Air Corps colonel.

A surprising number of people believed Lindy was a traitor. It seems fair to suggest that they felt betrayed because they had adored him when he flew the Atlantic alone, and now his feet had turned to clay. In the beginning, at least, he was one of the less abrasive isolationists. "Let us not delude ourselves," he said in the first month of the war. "If we enter the quarrels of Europe during war, we must stay in them in peace as well," and "This war is the climax of all political failure." As Nazi spearheads were knifing through France in May 1940, he said, "We are in danger of war today not because European people have attempted to interfere in America, but because we American people have attempted to interfere with the internal affairs of Europe. Our danger in America is an internal danger. We need not fear a foreign invasion unless American people bring it on through their own quarreling and meddling with affairs abroad." He saw interventionists as men seizing "every opportunity to push us closer to the edge."

That was above the belt; some interventionists could accept the charge and even exult in it. But Lindbergh was being driven to excesses by some of his supporters, who unlike him were pro-German, and by his briery relationship with the press. He was neither the first nor the last public figure to become persuaded that the news media hated him. On several counts one must sympathize with him; their behavior during the kidnapping and death of his child had been shocking. All the same, he was fighting a war of words — at a New York rally he addressed himself to "that silent majority of Americans who have no newspaper, or newsreel, or radio station at their command," but who believed in isolation — and he was beginning to choose the wrong words. In Des Moines, with Senator Nye beside him, he all but destroyed the America First movement. He actually warned American Jews to shut up — or else. Because of Jewish "ownership and influence in our motion pictures, our press, our radio and our government," he said, if war came "they will be blamed for it." In a stroke he lost all Jewish support and, among others, Thomas E. Dewey, who called the speech "inexcusable."

But then, all isolationist rhetoric had become scorching. The favorite adjective of the season was "tantamount"; every Roosevelt order was "tantamount to a declaration of war." Key Pittman, chairman of the Senate Foreign Relations Committee, proposed that the British give up their home islands and retreat to Canada; that, he thought, would satisfy Hitler. Pittman was even agreeable to letting the Nazis control the Atlantic. Senator Ernest Lundeen of Minnesota recommended American seizure of all British and French possessions in the western hemisphere. Senator Vandenberg thought cash-and-carry was "like the first drink of whiskey." Joseph P. Kennedy, back from London, said talk that Britain was fighting for democracy was "bunk." Ironpants Johnson accused his old chief in the White House of "a reckless shooting craps with destiny." John Foster Dulles, who would be contributing to America First groups as late as November 1941, said, "Only hysteria entertains the idea that Germany, Italy, or Japan contemplates war upon us." Burton K. Wheeler told the Senate that Roosevelt's "new triple-A plan" was "to plow under every fourth American boy." ("Dastardly," said the President, and Wheeler took it back.) Perhaps the most interesting remark in the Senate came from Robert A. Taft. He noted White House displeasure over a growing Japanese presence in Vietnam. Taft said no American mother was ready to have her son die "for some place with an unpronounceable name in Indochina."

KEEP THE U.S. OUT OF WAR! read a telegram to the President signed by a thousand Dartmouth students. Having been schooled by isolationist and pacifist teachers since they were children, it was not surprising that undergraduates found it impossible to shift gears on such short notice. Here they split with their faculties. College teachers saw the issues much as Roosevelt did — they were, if anything, impatient with him for not going faster. A few idealistic students crossed into Canada and enlisted; Charles G. "Chuck" Bolte, whose interventionist editorials in the Dartmouth newspaper had offended his classmates, joined the British Army and lost a leg at El Alamein. But most students wanted only to be left alone, as British ambassador Lord Lothian discovered when he spoke at Yale's commencement in June 1940. The most extreme isolationists saw Hitler satisfied with conquest of the United Kingdom, while the British fleet cheerfully steamed westward to put itself at the disposal of Washington. Lothian tried to confront his audience with reality. Isolation, he declared, was completely impossible. The world would force itself on America as it had on Britain. American wealth and strength would become a magnet to other powers; it would be an irresistible challenge to Hitler or anyone who dreamed of international power. The Yale faculty was enthusiastic. Most of the seniors sat on their hands.

Roosevelt's thoughts were along Lothian's lines, and he carried the analogy with Britain a step farther. The keystone in the arch of Whitehall's foreign policy had always been the principle that no one nation must ever control the continent. That was why Marlborough and Wellington had crossed the Channel, why the Kaiser's crushing of Belgium had been intolerable in 1914, why England was at war now. In the long cycles of history, Roosevelt believed, the United States must take the same position in the Atlantic community.

The President's quandary was intensified by the fact that 1940 was an election year, and no President had served more than two terms. Running for a third term wasn't unconstitutional, but the two-term Presidency was a powerful tradition. He hadn't planned to flout it. He had expected to retire in January 1941, but he didn't see how he could now. The country might elect an isolationist President, and that would be a disaster whose limits were beyond imagining. Just helping Britain and at the same time winning the election was going to be quite a trick. To carry it off, he felt — and Hull agreed with him — they would have to drop their policy of being frank with the American people.

A certain deviousness had marked administration conduct from the first days of the war. One of the new top-secret Douglas A-20 bombers had crashed in a test flight, and the Associated Press reported that among the men injured was a M. Chmedelin of the French Air Ministry. The Senate Military Affairs Committee had hit the roof. Again, on FDR's instructions, the State Department had reached an agreement with the British under which freedom of the seas would be restricted by H.M.'s vessels. Any German goods — made there or destined for there — could be seized at sea, and this policy applied even if a ship was sailing between two neutral countries. The neutrals protested, but Whitehall said that was hard cheese; there was a war on. And after Dunkerque the British Army was not only soaking wet but, worse, disarmed; therefore Roosevelt sent the whole surplus store of new American arms by fast freighters to England.

America at this time was still not even a third-rate military power. The basic machine tool industry had almost vanished since the Crash. The biggest forges in the country could hold only bathtubs and auto frames; howitzers were being turned out on machines made for streetcar axles. On the day the Wehrmacht invaded Holland, Hull told the President he should go before Congress and ask for 50,000 planes a year. Roosevelt gasped, but he did it, and since even the isolationists believed in the Fortress America concept, they voted him the money. "Unbelievable!" Hermann Göring said, but eventually the United States would be turning out 60,000 planes a year.

The President repeatedly spoke out as an enemy of the Axis — when Italy declared war on France, then in her extremity, he said, "On this tenth day of June, 1940, the hand that held the dagger has struck it into the back of its neighbor" — and in the middle of the presidential campaign he gave the British fifty overage U.S. destroyers in exchange for ninety-nine-year leases on British naval and air bases in the western hemisphere. The swap wasn't even legal, and it made the United States a nonbelligerent ally of Britain. But General Pershing and George Fielding Eliot spoke up for it. *Time* agreed with the President that it was the most important event in American defense since the Louisiana Purchase, and an isolationist senator said, "Listen, you can't attack a deal like that. . . . Roosevelt outsmarted all of us when he tied up the two deals."

Two days after the destroyer swap papers were signed, the largest, richest, and most influential antiwar organization was founded by a Yale law student, R. Douglas Stuart Jr., a son of the first vice president of Quaker Oats. This was the Committee to Defend America First. Its argument was that the country should prepare to fight for the United States, not Britain — thus sacrificing a valuable ally, though America Firsters never put it that way — and its leader became General Robert A. Wood, chairman of the Sears, Roebuck board of directors.

In less than six months they had 60,000 members. Every isolationist on Capitol Hill was enrolled. Novelist Kathleen Norris became the movement's chief propagandist, Charles Lindbergh its most popular speaker, and Wood, Henry Ford, Robert Young, Sterling Morton, Edward Ryerson Jr., and Lessing Rosenwald its financial sponsors. America First's war chest seemed inexhaustible. At one point it ran full-page advertisements attacking Roosevelt's foreign policy in sixty newspapers and then repeated the ad in another seventy-nine. Joseph P. Kennedy, Alice Longworth, and John Foster Dulles made it respectable. Rally after rally was held in Madison Square Garden and in Chicago, where the audience, to Lindbergh's embarrassment, repeatedly booed Churchill's name.

William Allen White countered by forming the Committee to Defend America by Aiding the Allies, which formed its own chapters across the country — its greatest support, significantly, came from the eastern seaboard — and which gathered signatures, mailed pamphlets, and distributed handbills taking the other side. The White committee's spokesmen included John J. McCloy; writer Elizabeth Cutter Morrow, Lindbergh's mother-in-law; and the intellectual community, led by Robert Sherwood. The committee was strongly backed by most big newspapers, except the *Chicago Tribune* and the *Washington Times-Herald*.

The depth of feeling became apparent in the debate over the country's first peacetime draft, perhaps the most controversial issue ever raised by a President campaigning for reelection. Not even George Washington had ever persuaded a Congress at peace to approve conscription. In 1940 only Canada, Cuba, and a few South American countries shared with the United States the lack of compulsory military training. Millions of Americans wanted it to continue that way; to them a draft represented the Europe they had fled. But General Marshall needed the men, and if the nation was to have an effective defense, he needed them at once. Roosevelt first raised the issue in his June 10 speech; he pledged that America would have "the equipment and training equal to the task of every emergency defense." The operative word was "training," and legislation to translate it into action went into the House hopper as the Selective Training and Service Bill.

John L. Lewis testified that conscription smacked of "dictatorship and fascism." Norman Thomas, Oswald Garrison Villard, and the Reverend Harry Emerson Fosdick said it was immoral — one clergyman predicted it would reduce American youth to "syphilis and slavery" — and Bill Green of the AFL, whose testimony was less than lucid, seemed to be arguing that the draft would be acceptable to him only when an invading army stood on American soil. To the embarrassment of Eleanor Roosevelt, the American Youth Congress, one of her pet projects, vowed that its members would refuse induction. More than a score of Union Theological Seminary students announced they would refuse to register despite the fact that they would be automatically deferred. The Mohawk Indians argued with more persuasive eloquence that they wouldn't fight because they had never been treated as U.S. citizens.

The peace lobby was luckless. The bill came out of the committee in September, when pictures of Nazi bombers and burning London were on every front page. On June 1 Gallup had reported the public feeling on conscription was running fifty-fifty. After the fall of France conscription had been favored by 67 percent, and now 71 percent were for it. Congress approved a one-year draft requiring registration of all men between twenty-one and thirty-five. Overnight New York's J. R. Wood & Sons, one of the country's largest manufacturers of wedding rings, reported a 250 percent increase in business; America was being swept by a wave of beat-the-draft marriages, on the theory that married men would receive permanent deferments. Little did they know their antagonist. As director of the draft Roosevelt appointed an Army officer who had been studying conscription plans since 1926 and knew all the loopholes. His name was Lewis B. Hershey.

Senator Wheeler had been muttering that rather than submit to such slave labor legislation American youth would rise in revolution. They did nothing of the sort. On October 16 over sixteen million men registered. There were no incidents; spirits seemed high. The Secretary of War drew the first numbers on October 29, and presently thousands of mailmen were carrying form letters which began:

> Greeting:
> Having submitted yourself to a local board composed of your neighbors for the purpose of determining your availability for training and service in the land or naval forces of the United States, you are hereby notified that you have been selected . . .

Living in new pine barracks, the draftees or selectees — it was considered impolite to call them "soldiers" — were soon maneuvering with wooden rifles and cardboard boxes marked "tank." After a while that became dull. It wasn't as though the United States were at war. Furthermore, they were dealing with the American peacetime military establishment, always an awkward and uninspiring institution. As the months passed, bored draftees took to studying the calendar. By summertime chalked inscriptions in the camps read OHIO — over the hill in October. Over the hill, in Army cant, means being absent without leave, and when the conscription law expired in October, they would be free. By then it was impossible to release them. War was very near. Yet the House vote on extending the draft eighteen months was 203 to 202 — a margin of one vote, an indication of the thinness of the ice on which Roosevelt was skating.

Hitler would have preferred another American President, and after the war it was discovered that the German government had, in fact, spent a lot of money on the 1940 election, most of it in vain. The man with the bag was one Hans Thomsen, an attaché in the German embassy. Thomsen repeatedly placed full-page advertisements in the *New York Times* backing isolationists in both parties, and in his report to the Wilhelmstrasse he took credit for a plank in the Republican platform stressing "Americanism, preparedness, and peace." He added slyly: "Nothing has leaked out about the assistance we rendered in this."

It was a doubtful claim; the Democrats had a similar plank, pledging that American troops would not be sent overseas "except in case of attack." The key to the campaign was the Republican candidate, and friends of Britain could hardly have picked a better man. Racketbuster Thomas E. Dewey of New York had won all the primaries, and Taft had set up headquarters with the confident phone number ME-1940, but this was one convention in which the politicians lost control. The delegates desperately wanted a winner; they were angered by Roosevelt's deft appointment, on the eve of the convention, of Republicans Henry Stimson and Frank Knox as Secretaries of War and Navy. The galleries kept chanting "We want Willkie! We want Willkie!" until on the sixth ballot the convention gave them Wendell L. Willkie.

Willkie was a better man than his campaign. He was plagued by small disasters. His larynx wasn't strong enough for leather-lunged oratory. After two days of speeches in September, his voice literally disappeared. In Rock Island County, Illinois, he croaked gamely, "The spirit is — *squawk* — but the voice is — *squawk.*" The rest of it was weird, like a silent movie; the lips moved, but no sound issued from them. Specialists told him to shut up, that was the only cure, but it is one thing no presidential candidate can do. Despite ointments and gargling, his voice cracked and scratched and never did return to normal until after the election.

Some party regulars rejected him on the ground that until recently he had been a registered Democrat. Willkie asked Senator James E. Watson for support, and the old man snorted, "If a whore repented and wanted to join the church, I'd personally welcome her and lead her up the aisle to a pew, but by the Eternal, I'd not ask her to lead the choir the first night." Blue-collar toughs booed him, and an egg hit his wife. More seriously, he was weakened by some of the gut-fighters in his own party who had learned nothing in 1936. A Philadelphia lawyer was quoted as saying that Roosevelt's support was confined to "paupers, those who earn less than $1,200 a year and aren't worth that, and the Roosevelt family." The Republican National Committee's antiwar radio spots were so rough they created sympathy for the President: "When your boy is dying on some battlefield in Europe . . . and he's crying out, 'Mother! Mother! — don't blame Franklin D. Roosevelt because he sent your boy to war — blame YOURSELF because YOU sent Franklin D. Roosevelt back to the White House!"

Willkie was blameless in this. The war was the one issue which might have been turned against the President, but Willkie was too good a man, and too gallant an American, to stoop to use it. He encouraged Roosevelt to send arms to England, supported a peacetime draft and the destroyer deal, and though he faulted the President for bypassing Congress in the swap, the criticism was fair. He didn't deserve the charge of the Old Guard that he was a "me-too" candidate. He could hardly have taken any other stand when the national security was threatened. Above all, he should never have been subjected to the accusation from Henry Wallace, FDR's new vice-presidential candidate, that Willkie was the Nazis' choice.

During all this, the President went smilingly about his business, giving no indication that he had ever heard of a man named Wendell Willkie. His renomination was masterminded by Harry Hopkins, sitting in a tan-walled bedroom in Chicago's Blackstone Hotel with a direct line to the White House in the bathroom. The names of Farley, Garner, and Tydings were placed in nomination — a sign that since their last quadrennial meeting the Democrats had become a divided party. But the convention was plainly rigged. Chicago's Mayor Edward J. Kelly had hooked a microphone in the basement of the Chicago Stadium to the public address system. At the key moment a Chicago official triggered the demonstration by shouting "We want Roosevelt!" into the mike. Republicans thought it significant that the official was Chicago's Superintendent of Sewers.

The only really controversial moment in Roosevelt's campaign came in Boston five days before the election. Local politicians kept urging him to repeat his promise that American boys would not have to fight abroad. He was weary of this, he told them; he had done it so many times. But he finally consented to say: "And while I am talking to you mothers and fathers, I give you one more assurance. I have said this before, but I shall say it again and again and again: Your boys are not going to be sent into any foreign wars."

Sam Rosenman protested; that wasn't the language of the platform. The President should add the proviso "except in case of attack." Roosevelt shook his head. It was too obvious, he replied: "Of course we'll fight if we're attacked. If somebody attacks us, then it isn't a foreign war, is it? Or do they want me to guarantee that our troops will be sent into battle only in the event of another Civil War?" John Gunther afterward suggested that this was "disingenuous." Robert Sherwood, who had argued for the passage, said afterward that he burned inwardly whenever he thought of those words "again — and again — and again," and other Roosevelt admirers still cringe whenever those lines are repeated. Until this year Roosevelt had always leveled with the American people. That was one of the reasons he was about to be returned to the White House.

The morning after the election John L. Lewis found a huge sign draped across the facade of his United Mine Workers Building: RESIGNATION ACCEPTED. The popular vote was the closest of FDR's career — 27 million to 22 million — but the indisputable fact was that he still was, as Willkie had called him: "the Champ." Two days after the election the Champ returned to Union Station and rode triumphantly down Pennsylvania Avenue to the White House, beaming and doffing his old fedora as the 200,000 people lining the curbs cheered. The Roosevelt lovers were still legion. Their opposites were around, too. It is entertaining to find that the election results were buried on page six of that day's *Wall Street Journal*.

In the interval between the conventions and the campaign, Roosevelt visited the 94,000 officers and men of the First Army. He sent word that he wanted no gun salutes, no brass band, no reviewing of troops, and no saluting — the Army, being the Army, gave him all of them — but he did want to see what their equipment was like. There still wasn't much to see. The commanding general told him, "We are using broomsticks for machine guns and rain pipes for mortars." The President laughed and said everyone seemed to be in the same boat.

Not quite everybody; not the British. Roosevelt had not only sent them everything he could lay his hands on after Dunkerque; he was now assigning current production of P-40 fighter planes to Britain. It was a sensible decision; the stronger the British became, the longer America would have to get ready. Explaining its wisdom to the American public would probably have been impossible, however, and as he entered his third term, with events escalating at home and abroad, the secrecy surrounding his moves increased. Except when he needed money from Congress, he tended to act independently, sending personal emissaries like Harry Hopkins to London instead of following regular diplomatic channels. Not until the congressional investigation of Pearl Harbor in 1946 did Congress know that the British military staffs flew to Washington for secret conversations with the Combined Chiefs from January 29 to March 27, 1941. Although the two countries were not yet allies, they were, in T. R. Fehrenbach's phrase, "associated powers" with a common goal.

Clare Boothe Luce, who thought the President should be tougher with Hitler, accused him of waging a "soft war." Every leader has his symbolic gesture, she said: Churchill's fingered V, Hitler's stiff arm, Mussolini's strut. When she was asked about Roosevelt, she moistened her finger and held it up to test the wind. It was clever, it was true, and it was absolutely necessary. The President had to know how Americans felt. Divided countries do not win great wars. He could be a step ahead of the people, perhaps even two steps. But if he ever lost them he would fail them and his oath of office. "To serve the public faithfully and at the same time please it entirely," Benjamin Franklin wrote, "is impossible."

The polling business was among the booming new industries. Some of the pollsters' findings were predictable. New York City was more interventionist in spirit than the rest of the country. Yet Texas was more belligerent toward Hitler; anglophilia was rare in Texas, but nationalism was intense. The only section of the country with genuine war fever was Dixie. (No America First rally was ever held in Georgia.) White Anglo-Saxon Protestant southerners were six times as ready to fight Nazis as their countrymen — perhaps, as Dean Acheson has suggested, because so many southern heroes are soldiers. Taking the country as a whole, 62 percent of America had approved the destroyer swap. Ethnic groups whose homelands had been overrun were passionately hostile to Germans, with the exception of Scandinavians. The upper classes tended to be interventionist; by the early summer of 1940 better than two-thirds of America's business and intellectual leadership favored increased shipments to Britain, and almost half the men and women listed in *Who's Who in America* wanted Congress to declare war at once. By then virtually everyone in the nation (93.6 percent) favored building up the armed forces.

But many of the straw votes defied understanding. In the fall of 1939, 40 percent of all Americans believed the United States would be drawn into the European war. After the fall of France, when the danger was much greater, only 7.7 percent believed it. Late in 1940 60 percent believed Britain was fighting for American interests, but only 13 percent approved American participation. And by 1941 a *Fortune* survey reported that 67 percent of the American people were ready to follow President Roosevelt into a war that 70 percent did not want. "The fact is," Lincoln had said in 1862, "that the people have not yet made up their minds that we are at war."

The *New York Times* concluded in late 1940 that the country was suffering from "a form of schizophrenia." But one set of figures was consistent and indicated a trend. To the Gallup question "Do you think the United States should keep out of war or do everything possible to help England, even at the risk of getting into war ourselves?" the response was:

	STAY OUT	HELP ENGLAND
May 1940	64	36
November	50	50
December	40	60

The President was under immense pressure from extremists at both ends of the spectrum; it came from congressional leaders, aides, cabinet members; even from his wife. In retrospect, his policy seems clearer than it did then. He was giving Britain everything he could lay his hands on. He was mobilizing American industry and arming the country to the teeth. And by drifting ever closer to Hitler's periscopes in the Atlantic, he was hoping for an incident which would weld the entire nation into a single aggressive instrument. He gave little thought to the Pacific, nor, so far as is known, was he shown one poll which in some respects was the most interesting of all. On the West Coast Americans weren't much interested in Germany, but they were ready to take on the Japanese any time.

It was the first aspect of his policy which was weakest in late 1940. The United Kingdom was taking terrible punishment, British arms had been defeated on all fronts, and the pound was disappearing. Roosevelt was brooding about all this while basking in the Caribbean sun aboard the cruiser *Tuscaloosa,* recovering from his third presidential campaign and a subsequent sinus attack, when a seaplane arrived alongside to deliver a personal letter from Winston Churchill — "perhaps the most important letter of his [Churchill's] life," James MacGregor Burns has called it. England was running out of supplies and money to buy more; the exchequer was down to its last two billion dollars. The United States was the greatest industrial nation on earth. Indeed, two days after this last election Hitler himself had declared publicly, "As far as American production figures are concerned, they cannot even be formulated in astronomical figures. In this field, therefore, I do not want to be a competitor."* But this, Churchill felt, was the very ground upon which Hitler should be *required* to compete. Was there some way that the President, working within the American Constitution, could prevent the British from being "stripped to the bone"?

Hopkins was aboard the *Tuscaloosa* when the letter arrived. He saw no immediate sign that Roosevelt had been impressed by it. It took a while for Hopkins to realize that the President was thinking hard — "refueling," Hopkins put it, "the way he so often does when he seems to be resting and carefree." According to Churchill's memoirs, Hopkins later told him that the President read and reread the letter as he sat alone in his deck chair. For two days he appeared to be undecided; he was deep in thought, reflecting silently. Knowing his moods, Hopkins asked no questions. "Then," according to Hopkins, "one evening, he suddenly came out with it — the whole program. . . . there wasn't much doubt that he'd find a way to do it." The program, the answer to Churchill's dilemma and the weapon Hitler could not match, was to be fortuitously numbered House Bill 1776 and known around the world as lend-lease.

Roosevelt returned to Washington December 16. Next morning he called a press conference, and after saying, "I don't think there is any particular news, except possibly one thing," he proceeded to give them one of the biggest stories in American history, explaining the lend-lease concept for forty-five minutes. "Suppose my neighbor's house catches fire, and I have a length of garden hose," he began. "If he can take my garden hose and connect it up with his hydrant, I may help him put out the fire. Now what do I do? I don't say to him before that operation, 'Neighbor, my garden hose cost me fifteen dollars; you have to pay me fifteen dollars for it.' What is the transaction that goes on? I don't want fifteen dollars — I want

*In 1940 the slowly wakening United States forged 66,993,000 tons of steel while the German Reich, running full tilt, produced only 28,000,000.

my garden hose back after the fire is over. All right. If it goes through the fire all right, intact, without damage to it, he gives it back to me and thanks me very much for the use of it." If the hose were destroyed, the neighbor replaced it "in kind."

As reasoning, the parable was both brilliant and specious. He proposed to loan the British, not hoses, but tanks, warplanes, and ships. How could they be returned "in kind" after the war? Moreover, to accept his own metaphor, the hose was the smallest part of lend-lease. With it he would also be signing over to his "neighbor" the hydrant and a great deal of expensive plumbing. Finally, the President alone would decide what to lend, when to lend it, and to whom. H.R. 1776, entitled "A Bill to Further Promote the Defense of the United States, and for Other Purposes," would give him powers no other President had ever requested. It provided for aid to "any country whose defense the President deems vital to the defense of the United States."

As a precedent, the measure would reach far into the future, eventually penetrating the jungles of Southeast Asia, but at the time the debate over it was seen merely as an epic struggle between isolationists and interventionists. The President described the proposal to the country on December 29 — the night of one of London's worst fire-bombings — in a fireside chat. The intent of the program, he said, was confined to lending, leasing, and selling war goods. He named the enemy — the Berlin-Rome-Tokyo Tripartite Axis — and he renewed his pledge to keep out of war. "We must," he said, "be the great arsenal of democracy." It was an exceptionally effective speech; letters and telegrams to the President supported him a hundred to one. The polls reported that 71 percent of the people agreed with him, and 54 percent wanted lend-lease to start now.

It couldn't start now, because the isolationists on Capitol Hill realized that this was their Little Bighorn. Hamilton Fish cried that 1776 would leave Congress "with no more authority than the German Reichstag." Ironpants Johnson testified that lend-lease meant "humanitarian lollipopping all over the world." Senator Nye alone spoke for twelve hours; Clark of Missouri called it a "war bill." But their power to intimidate was gone. Alexis de Tocqueville had observed that "Time, events, or the unaided individual action of the mind will sometimes undermine or destroy an opinion, without any outward sign of the change," and this is what had happened to isolationism. The pendulum of history had swung away from it. Its loyalists were little people in the way. A group called the Mother's Crusade Against Bill 1776 staged a sit-down strike before the office door of Senator Carter Glass of Virginia. Glass called the FBI and then told the press: "It would be pertinent to inquire whether they are mothers. For the sake of the race, I devoutly hope not."

Roosevelt's floor managers had signed up the Republican moderates, every one of them. When Homer Bone of Washington asked the question which had cornered interventionists in the past — "What is worse than war?" — Warren Austin of Vermont replied, "I say that a world enslaved to Hitler is worse than war, and worse than death." The galleries cheered. Bone disappeared into a cloakroom. On February 11, 1941, Willkie testified for lend-lease, assuring its passage. He said, "It is the history of democracy that under such dire circumstances, extraordinary powers must be granted to the elected executive." The bill became law in March, and FDR asked Congress to give him nine billion dollars for starters — which raised the money going to arms at home and abroad to twenty-six billion. American flags flew all over London. Hitler said that despite lend-lease, "England will fall." In Italy Mussolini's press said ominously, "Roosevelt's gesture may cause some unpleasant surprises to England and the United States in the Pacific." But who listened to the Duce any more?

Now developments began to gather momentum. Heavy industry, retooling for war production, hired three million new workers. Red, white, and blue banners over assembly lines warned, TIME IS SHORT. Government regulatory agencies were established, and Washington saw the first influx of top-notch managerial talent since the President and big business had crossed swords. Civilians began to encounter shortages; Harold Ickes had turned 150 tankers over to the British, cutting America's tanker fleet by 40 percent and creating the East Coast's first gasoline famine.

In February Mussolini had ordered United States consulates in Palermo and Naples closed. Roosevelt retaliated by shutting down Italian consulates in Detroit and New York; then he declared an "unlimited national emergency," freezing German and Italian assets in the United States. Axis ships, and ships from countries which had been overrun by Axis troops, including Vichy France's *Normandie*, were seized "to prevent their sabotage." The Army Air Corps announced that it would train eight thousand fledgling RAF pilots. Roosevelt transferred ten Coast Guard cutters — old rumrunner chasers, relics of Prohibition — to the British and, in sublime defiance of *de facto* hostilities, he opened up the Red Sea to American freighters by declaring Egypt neutral and therefore not in a war zone. On April 9 the United States and Greenland signed a treaty under which Washington, in exchange for the right to establish U.S. weather stations and other bases there, pledged itself to defend Greenland from invasion. A terse announcement said German weathermen already on the island had been "cleaned out." The defense of Greenland, the President declared, was essential to the security of the western hemisphere.

But how far did the western hemisphere extend? That was what Senator Taft kept asking, and responses from the White House were nebulous. The hottest issue that spring, at both ends of Pennsylvania Avenue, was convoying. Gallup first reported that the public attitude was almost entirely negative. A private poll of the Senate disclosed that forty-five senators would approve of U.S. warships escorting freighters halfway across the Atlantic. But forty were against even that, and appalling figures from the

British Admiralty left no doubt that the U-boats were winning the Battle of the Atlantic. If the President wanted his lend-lease supplies to reach England he would have to be very clever out on the deep, and far more daring than the Tafts of the Senate would approve.

In February and March, German raiders and submarines operating in what they called "wolf packs" sank or captured twenty-two ships (115,000 tons). The opening of American shipyards to damaged British ships helped, but not enough; the Atlantic was fast becoming a German sea. The President announced that the United States "safety belt" — reporters called it "the chastity belt" — now reached a thousand miles into the Atlantic. At the same time he disclosed that American warships were "cooperating" with the British fleet. He cabled Churchill on April 11: "The United States will extend its 'security zone' to about west longitude 26 degrees." He requested the prime minister to see to it that the Admiralty notify American naval units in "great secrecy" of its convoy dates, plans and destinations, "so that our patrol units can seek out any ships or planes of aggressor nations operating west of the new line." As Fehrenbach has pointed out, "It was under this policy, and these conditions — unannounced military orders — that America entered the North Atlantic war."

In June popular support for U.S. convoys was up to 52 percent, with 75 percent approving if it appeared that British would lose the war without convoys. But Roosevelt remained elusive. Knox and Stimson were publicly arguing for convoying; the President told reporters he was against it, and against Americans being sent overseas. That was duplicity, as we now know. Walter Lippmann saw the credibility gap and wrote a bitter column accusing FDR of treating the American people "cleverly, indirectly, even condescendingly and nervously." It was Roosevelt who had to lead a united country, however, and he knew unity would be strengthened if the flag were attacked on the high seas, which, under his policy, was inevitable.

The first incident occurred on April 10. There wasn't much to it. The U.S.S. *Niblack*, a destroyer picking up survivors from a torpedoed Dutch freighter, made sound contact with a U-boat and drove it away with depth charges. Not even Roosevelt could make much out of that. Still, with the British continuing to lose 400,000 tons of shipping every month, he felt he had to make *some* move. As he told the press, "It would be suicide to wait until they are in our front yard." Therefore he extended the western hemisphere some more. Now, apparently, it would almost reach the North Sea. The spark plug behind the new move was the Chief of Naval Operations, who on June 17 sent Hopkins a memorandum proposing that the 1st Brigade, U.S. Marine Corps, relieve the British troops in Iceland and ready themselves for "operations." Back came the memo, initialed: OK FDR.

On July 7 the marines landed at Reykjavik, Iceland's capital, backed by a presidential statement noting that the Icelandic government had invited the troops and that Roosevelt agreed to prevent the use of Iceland "for use as a naval or air base against the Western Hemisphere." That was absurd. As the bomber flew, Reykjavik was 3,900 miles from New York but only 2,800 miles from Berlin. Iceland was being "protected" from other powers. Confronted with a variation of the very stratagem they used so often and so effectively, the Nazis were indignant. The German Navy wanted to turn loose its U-boats against American shipping, but Hitler, sensing that Roosevelt was looking for just that sort of trouble, refused to be baited. He ordered Admiral Erich Raeder to take every possible precautionary step to see that no American vessel was attacked. Of course, he added, he understood the possibility of an honest U-boat error. So did Roosevelt. The American presence in Iceland put U.S. troops and ships squarely into the Battle of the Atlantic. "If ever there was a point when Roosevelt knowingly crossed some threshold between aiding Britain in order to stay out of war and aiding Britain by joining in the war," Burns wrote, "July 1941 was probably the time."

It was also a time when the Führer had to exercise self-control. Two weeks earlier, on Sunday, June 22, he had taken the boldest gamble of all, invading the Soviet Union on a two-thousand mile front from the Arctic to the Ukraine. If there was one thing he didn't need right now, it was another enemy. In any event, he suspected that this new invasion would not be entirely unpopular in the United States. It wasn't. *Time* probably expressed the average American's lack of commitment when it commented, "Like two vast prehistoric monsters lifting themselves out of the swamp, half-blind and savage, the two great totalitarian powers of the world now tore at each other's throats." Senator Harry Truman — in a remark Stalin would never forgive — said he hoped "the Nazis will kill lots of Russians and vice versa." Washington's generals and admirals thought Russia a lost cause and recommended that no supplies be sent there. Roosevelt and Hopkins disagreed. On October 1 a billion-dollar lend-lease protocol was signed with Soviet diplomats, and Russian freighters began making the long, dangerous Murmansk run.

Hopkins and Averell Harriman, lend-lease coordinator, were working with their staffs in seventeen hastily cleared rooms of the Federal Reserve Building. Mobilization was changing the face of Washington. Both the Pentagon and the new State Department Building were finished that autumn. Temporary buildings were rising on the Mall — though the "temporaries" of World War I were still in use. Here and there a name suggestive of the future appeared. Aboard the U.S.S. *Augusta* a young Knox assistant briefly conferred with the President over a labor problem; the ship log noted the call by "Adelai" Stevenson. In the Louisiana Army maneuvers Robert Sherrod told Eric Sevareid, "Be sure you see Colonel Eisenhower — he makes more sense than the rest of them." Eisenhower himself was amused to see his photograph accompanied by the caption *Lt. Col. D. D. Ersenbeing*. ("At least the initials were right," he said wryly.)

Hopkins was now the second most powerful man in the country. He occupied a suite of rooms on the southeast corner of the White House second floor, right in the family's private living quarters. Because Churchill admired him and respected him — he called him "Lord Root of the Matter" — he was trusted in London, too. Late in July 1941, sitting with his host in the garden behind 10 Downing Street, he remarked that the President would like to meet Churchill "in some lonely bay or another." The prime minister was delighted. He very much wanted to see his chief ally in the flesh, and the trip would also provide first-rate propaganda. They chose one of the most desolate places in the world, Placentia Bay in southeast Newfoundland. On August 9 the *Augusta* and its escort steamed into position beside the British battleship *Prince of Wales* and its escorts; between them they formed a fleet large enough to fight a major naval engagement, which was perhaps the idea. All meetings were held aboard the *Augusta* except on Sunday, when Roosevelt crossed a short gangplank to attend a religious service. After the British and American crews had sung "Oh God, Our Help in Ages Past," Churchill told the President, "I'm not a religious man, but I thank God that such a man as you is the head of your government at a time like this." For over three days the two leaders conferred with their staffs, were photographed together, and drew up a joint statement of principles called the Atlantic Charter.

After they had returned to London and Washington, the photographs were released to the press and the charter was issued in the form of a communiqué. It endorsed the rights of free peoples to choose their own leaders, regain lands wrested from them by force, trade freely with one another, have access to raw materials on equal terms, improve the lot of backward countries, disarm aggressors, and enjoy freedom of the seas, freedom from want, and freedom from fear. Largely based on FDR's most recent State of the Union address — he had also included freedom of speech and of worship — the Atlantic Charter was endorsed by fifteen anti-Axis nations, including (ironically) the Soviet Union, in September. The curious thing is that the charter, in the tactile sense at least, did not exist. A reporter asked FDR about it. The President replied, "There isn't any copy . . . so far as I know. I haven't got one. The British haven't got one. The nearest thing you will get is the [message of the] radio operator on the *Augusta* or *Prince of Wales*. . . . There was no formal document."

There was an understanding, though, and it wasn't confined to strategies of peace. Back in the White House, the President announced that the convoy question was settled; he had settled it by executive order. American warships would convoy merchant vessels west of Iceland. U.S. ships were to darken their lights at sea and be ready for combat, and although the freighters being convoyed were presumed to be American, the operation plan for the Navy stipulated that "shipping of any nationality" could attach itself to the convoys.

The next incident was likely to involve an exchange of fire, and it did.

On September 4, in the waters off Iceland, the commander of the German sub U-652, finding himself under bombardment by depth charges and noting that a destroyer was cruising in the water overhead, drew the obvious conclusion: those were Englishmen in that ship, trying to make him *kaputt*. He was in error. The depth charges were coming from a British plane; the destroyer, the *Greer*, was American. When its captain saw two torpedoes churning toward him, he took evasive action and fired his own depth charges in self-defense. Neither the sub nor the *Greer* was damaged, but the fact of the matter was that Germans had fired the first shot. Roosevelt called it "piracy" and changed his naval orders from "search and patrol" to "search and destroy" — in other words, to shoot on sight. The Nazis and the United States were now in an undeclared naval war, and two out of every three Americans told the pollsters that they approved.

On October 15 a sub wolf pack attacked a British convoy about four hundred miles south of Iceland. The convoy commander radioed for help, and steaming to the rescue came five American warships, led by the U.S.S. *Kearny*, a crack destroyer, barely a year old. She took a torpedo in the side, and though she didn't sink, Americans read their first casualty list of World War II: two men wounded and eleven missing, presumed dead. The President declared that this was no random encounter; the Nazis were carrying out a long-range plan to drive American shipping off the seas. History had recorded which side fired the first shot, he said, "We Americans have cleared our decks and taken our battle stations. We stand ready in the defense of our nation."

Two weeks later another destroyer, the *Reuben James*, also on escort duty in Icelandic waters, came within torpedo range of a U-boat commander. This time the American ship went down; with her went over a hundred U.S. bluejackets. The sinking created a sensation in the U.S. press. Woody Guthrie wrote a ballad about it:

> *What were their names, tell me, what were their names?*
> *Did you have a friend on the good* Reuben James?

There was real war fever now, all over the country, but the isolationists on the Hill were unimpressed. The President argued that under present circumstances, some clauses in neutrality legislation were obsolete. One of them forbade American merchant ships to carry any weapon larger than a captain's pistol or a harpooner's gun. It should be repealed, he said, and replaced by a measure arming the freighters and permitting them to carry cargoes to belligerent ports. The intensity of the battle in Congress was almost on the lend-lease level, and the administration margin much thinner: 13 votes in the Senate and 18 in the House. Barring dramatic developments, no declaration of war would get past this Congress. Roosevelt wasn't at all sure he even wanted such a declaration. Under the Tripartite Pact of September 27, 1940, all-out war between the United States and any one of the signing powers — Germany, Italy, and Japan — meant war declarations against the U.S. from the other two. Roosevelt didn't believe the United States was strong enough to take on Japan, too.

The more he and his advisers thought about it, the more dismayed they became. For seventeen months FDR had been more or less making up policy as he went along, improvising affronts to Hitler which would have brought Teutonic wrath down upon anyone else's head. But the Führer never lost his temper; he merely knew how to use it. Twice Admiral Raeder had begged him to strike back. The flow of supplies into Britain worried the admiral. He goaded his leader by drawing up a list of twenty bellicose actions by the American Navy. Unperturbed, Hitler counseled patience; once Russia was defeated he would deal "severely" with Roosevelt. After the President's shoot-on-sight order Raeder pleaded again; either let him attack U.S. warships, he asked, or withdraw all U-boats from the Atlantic. Hitler shook his head. Soon "the great decision in the Russian campaign" would have been reached. Then the wolf packs could be turned loose on the American Navy.

The President had hoped that by putting the United States on a collision course with Germany, events would take over and lead to outright hostilities. But Hitler was still the master manipulator of events, and he kept turning his cheek. On the other side of the world the Japanese, who had been similarly provoked, had given every sign that they, too, would refuse to be drawn. They were here in Washington now, negotiating. As the talks dragged on, the Axis powers drew ever closer to world conquest. Roosevelt felt impotent. "He had no more tricks left," Sherwood said afterward. "The bag from which he had pulled so many rabbits was empty." Sherwood, sharing the gloom in Washington, thought he might run up to New York before Christmas and see what was new in the theater.

Late in November the producing firm of José Ferrer and Ruth Wilk announced the imminent arrival on Broadway of *The Admiral Had a Wife,* a new comedy by Lowell Barrington. Those who had seen out of town tryouts described it as a light piece, the haps and mishaps of an ambitious Navy wife in Hawaii and her attempts to win promotion for her husband by using an uncle in Washington. In its exposure of service nepotism it was also called "a good-natured spoof on the Navy." It was scheduled to open at the Playhouse on Wednesday, December 10, 1941.

Montage: The Last of Prewar America

MAN WITH PICKAX ASSASSINATES TROTSKY IN MEXICO

ANNOUNCER: *The Lone Ranger!* (Bugle) *Heigh-ho Silver!* (Salvo of pistol shots) *A fiery horse with the speed of light; a cloud of dust and a hearty "Heigh-ho Silver!" The Lone Ranger! With his faithful Indian companion Tonto, the daring and resourceful masked rider of the plains led the fight for law and order in the early western United States! Nowhere in the pages of history can one find a greater champion of justice! Return with us now to thrilling days of yesteryear, when out of the past come the thundering hoofbeats of the great horse Silver! THE LONE RANGER RIDES AGAIN!*

LONE RANGER: *Come, Silver! Let's go, big fella! Heigh-ho Silver! Away!*

And now — "Gangbusters!" The only national program to bring you authentic police histories! Gangbusters, America's crusade against crime!

A man without a woman
Is like a ship without a sail

WONDER DRUG SCIENTISTS FIND "BLOOD PLASMA"

HITLER BEGINS WAR ON RUSSIA, WITH ARMIES ON MARCH FROM ARCTIC TO THE BLACK SEA

Thanks for the memory
Of sentimental verse, nothing in my purse
And chuckles when the preacher said
"For better or for worse."
How lovely it was!

What's cookin', good-lookin'?

FDR BUDGET HITS 8.8 BILLION

CLAGHORN: Claghorn's the name, Senator Claghorn. I'm from the South.
ALLEN: Yes, I know. You're from the South . . .
CLAGHORN: When I'm in New York I never go near the Yankee Stadium.
ALLEN: Now wait a minute . . .
CLAGHORN: I won't even go to see the Giants unless a southpaw is pitchin'.
ALLEN: Well, look, now . . .
CLAGHORN: And I refuse to watch the Dodgers unless Dixie Walker's playin'.
ALLEN: Now wait a minute . . .
CLAGHORN: Stop interruptin', where's your manners?
ALLEN: Manners! I have . . .
CLAGHORN: Stop interruptin'. You might learn something.
ALLEN: Listen, if I ever learn . . .
CLAGHORN: Your tongue's waggin' like a blind dog in a meat market.

Last week in Wilmington, Del., Du Pont's sheeny, much-publicized hosiery went on sale, sold quickly when salesgirls claimed that one pair of them would outwear four of silk, that they would dry in ten minutes when washed

DRIVES FROM CHI TO INDIANAPOLIS IN SIX HOURS

And strictly entre nous
Darling, how are you
And how are all the little dreams
That never did come true? . . .
And thank you so much

POPE'S AIR RAID SHELTER IN VATICAN NEARLY READY

BEARS, LED BY LUCKMAN, WHIP REDSKINS 73-0

$2 complete with 20 blades Schick injector razor

EIGHT

America on the Brink

THE AMERICA Kate Smith kept asking God to bless in the blitzkrieg spring of 1940 had changed mightily since the pit of the Depression, but it was still a very different country from the superpower of the early 1970s. The war boom wouldn't bring real prosperity until the nation went to war. The morning after Roosevelt's third inaugural, in 1941, *PM* — Marshall Field's seven-month-old adless New York newspaper — covered its front page with a picture of ragged, jobless men. There were still such tableaux to be seen in the United States. Nearly nine million men were unemployed, nearly three million were on WPA rolls, and 30 percent of all Negroes were on relief. And this was more than eleven years after the Crash. Millions in their late teens or early twenties had no memories of a healthy economy. Their fathers had come to manhood in World War I, but before World War II could touch the sons they had been tempered and toughened by a struggle for sheer survival.

Since the country needed a lot of soldiers in a hurry, Roosevelt convened a National Nutrition Conference in the spring of 1941 to find out why Army doctors were turning back nearly half of the men called up by Selective Service. They discovered what any welfare caseworker could have told them; the largest single cause was malnutrition during the previous decade. According to the 1940 census, over half of the nation's children were in families with an annual income of less than $1,500 a year. A quarter of the population still lived on farms; the typical farmer made $1,000. As late as the autumn of 1939, Toledo schools were closed two months because of lack of funds. In Manhattan, the unskilled workers who were using the ruins of bombed-out Bristol, England, to build a foundation for the East River Drive were being paid $832 a year.

Even then, visiting Europeans were scornful of American materialism, but young Europeans today would not have thought prewar America cosseted. Though rural electrification was making steady progress, three farms out of every four were still lit by kerosene lamps. Taking the country as a whole, there was one telephone for every seven Americans, one car for every five. One-fourth of all homes lacked running water, one-third were without flush toilets. The average American had left school after the eighth grade. In Washington, lobbyists for the American Medical Association had just defeated Senator Wagner's health insurance plan, and the biggest killer of children between the ages of five and fifteen was rheumatic heart disease.

The country's population was 132,000,000. Demographers agreed that it wouldn't get much larger. Only 17 percent of married women were working — although the number of women working had crept up, almost unnoticed, by a half-million during the 1930s. Doing housework, wives listened to soap operas, the most popular of which was *Vic and Sade,* and to the new singing commercials. One ditty, "Chiquita Banana" was being sung 2,700 times a week.

The Gross National Product was 90 billion dollars a year; the Dow Jones industrial average drifted back and forth over the 150 mark. America's economy, in short, was still depressed. Sylvia Porter, who then constituted the entire financial staff of the *New York Post,* has provided a vivid picture of what deflation was like then. Renters of bachelor apartments paid $25 a month. Hot dogs were a nickel. Prewar movie admission was twenty cents, most magazines were a dime, a dinner was forty-five cents, the average wristwatch repair ten cents, a fifth of scotch $1.25, and the typical bet with a friend five cents.

Business continued to blame its problems on government interference, labor unions, federal spending, lazy workers, and Roosevelt's refusal to accept Hoover's policy of permitting a "healthy readjustment" of wages and prices. Caroline Bird has offered another solution; the businessmen of the 1930s, she thinks, were not really very good businessmen. They thought prosperity depended upon Wall Street financiers and the so-called basic industries — steel, for example. The real key, which eluded them, was the consumer and the inexpensive goods and services he required. "Demand for shoes, drugs, foods, soap, cigarettes, clothes and gas for the jalopy grew directly with the population," Miss Bird points out. "Buses, trucks, gas, electricity, stores, laundries, beauty parlors stayed in business." In the last months of the prewar era, *Fortune* reported in amazement that one industry which had boomed since the Crash was the manufacture of disposable goods: paper napkins, cups and plates; bottles which could not be returned; and sanitary napkins. Men spent more on condoms than haircuts.

To some degree, products seem to have been withheld because entrepreneurs vaguely felt that they wouldn't be good for people. A woman was supposed to wash dishes; it wasn't right to let her throw them away. Drive-in services were wrong because they made everything too easy. For these and other reasons, among them simple failures of imagination, men of property refused to invest in supermarkets, postage meters, air-conditioning, ski resorts, neon lights, transistors, plywood, and motels. Except for the rich, consumer credit was almost unknown. Most people paid small bills with cash; banks discouraged checking accounts by requiring large minimum balances. The suggestion that a bank should give wigs to depositors, or finance "go now, pay later" vacations, would have been attended by as much shock as if the community's leading citizen had committed a public nuisance in the lobby.

Many of the discoveries which were to alter the postwar landscape had been made before Pearl Harbor. Not only radar but even television was receiving finishing touches from engineers. NBC had beamed an experimental telecast from Grover Whalen's Mad Meadow on April 30, 1939, and receivers on Manhattan had picked it up, though the picture on those early DuMont sets was tiny. Professor Chester L. Dawes of Harvard didn't think television would ever achieve popularity, because "it must take place in a semidarkened room, and it demands continuous attention." Fluorescent lighting was coming in, too, and just as nylon and dacron foretold a revolution in fabrics, so were plastics about to replace steel, aluminum, zinc, and nickel in everything from steering wheels to fountain pens (and, later, ballpoint pens). In the spring of 1940 Igor Sikorsky made his first ascent at the Bridgeport, Connecticut, airport in what one reporter described as "a strange, spindle-shanked machine." A news magazine speculated that Sikorsky's helicopters might be useful on a battlefield.

The American automobile had not yet become what one social critic would call an "insolent chariot," but it was on its way. Oldsmobile advertised a $57 extra called its "hydraulic clutch," which in time would dispense with the need for shifting gears, and the Lincoln Zephyr convertible actually had a magic button the mere touching of which would raise or lower the top. Conservative Detroit shrugged at such gimmicks, just as the publishing business, in those last months of peace, scorned the plans of Pocket Books, Inc. Its first paperback volume, James Hilton's *Lost Horizon*, was on sale at selected drugstores. It cost a quarter.

Advance information on the fate of any of these developments would have made a man's fortune. But sometimes it is just as well that we cannot hold the mirror up to the future. As Hitler blazed his way back and forth across Europe, Washington was completing plans to extend the withholding tax principle from social security to federal income taxes, and a brief story on page 20 of the September 2, 1939, *New York Times* reported that a researcher named A. H. Roffo, addressing the International Cancer Congress, described how he had produced cancer in mice by painting them with tobacco tars.

If you were visiting a distant community in the autumn of 1941, you would almost certainly have traveled by train. The new crack diesels were at the peak of their efficiency and popularity. There were always plenty of redcaps at the station. Roadbeds were maintained so that sleepers in Pullmans — in lower berths, at least — could really rest. The porter shined your shoes, carried your bags, and tugged gently at the green curtain when it was time to wake up. If you gave him a half-dollar as you left he said, "Thank *you*, sir," and meant it. Meals on the train were a pleasure. The tables were covered by immaculate linen, the menu offered a genuine choice, and everyone was courteous.

Your reasons for not flying may have been poor food, inaccessible airports, or fear. To be sure, service and schedules were improving, and now Pan American's Yankee Clipper could take you from Long Island to Lisbon in twenty-six and a half hours, but most people weren't in that much of a hurry. You might drive, though it would be an ordeal. The Merritt Parkway and the Pennsylvania Turnpike had just opened; the rest of the roads were still two-lane and three-lane highways, and every town along the way had its speed traps, fines from which paid the local constable's salary. Tourist cabins were little known and rather disreputable; the campaign against them was being led by J. Edgar Hoover. Writing in the *American Magazine,* Hoover called the precursors of motels "a new home of disease, bribery, corruption, crookedness, rape, white slavery, thievery, and murder." What's more, he warned, husbands and wives might occupy mattresses previously sullied by people who had engaged in "illicit relations."

As the train passed through settled areas, you would see no signs advertising discount houses or roadside food franchises. Like the superhighways that would carry customers to them, they lay over a far horizon. People didn't need cars as much then. They could go to work, shop, or reach schools via public transportation. The number of local bus lines which have been discontinued since then is beyond calculation, but we know something about streetcars. In 1940 there were 19,600 miles of electric railway track in the United States. By the late 1960s the figure had dwindled to 2,049 — most of them no longer used.

Near the train station stood at least one Victorian hotel with a mansard roof, alert bellboys, and clean beds for a dollar a night. The bellboy always had liquor available; the town hooker hired herself out for three dollars or, if you were a soldier, two. The hotel dining room would be quiet and inexpensive, though if you wanted something livelier, you might look around for a diner, with its inevitable jukebox and local gossip. Some of the slang might baffle youth in the 1970s. A party was a bash. People didn't split; they scrammed. A Casanova was a wolf. If you wanted a wolf to scram, you told him to get lost, drop dead, or just to dry up and blow away. If a girl approved of him, she would call him nobby, cute, nifty, or snazzy. Alone with him, she might find that he was a sap, but if he was pretty sharp, a smooch could end in her going all the way.

The hotel, the diner, movies, and the hooker were diversions for the traveling salesmen. If you were visiting friends or relatives, they met you at the depot, and if you were male and from a well-to-do family, like as not you would be wearing a double-breasted glen plaid suit. Their home might be in what later would be called "the inner city." But for every Beacon Hill there was a Brookline, a suburb, and here one must come to a full stop. The suburb and suburban life of Greenwich or Winnetka were very different from the Levittowns and Park Forests of the 1970s. Prewar suburbia was rich, exclusive, prep school- and college-educated, and an immense status symbol — an extension not of the shopping center but of the country club. It was inhabited by John P. Marquand characters, by the people John O'Hara envied and James Gould Cozzens knew: the Republican white Protestant upper middle class. Joseph P. Kennedy had to battle as only a Kennedy could to establish his enclave in Hyannisport, and if a Catholic could barely make it, a Jew didn't have a chance. Neighborhoods for him, like his summer camps and winter cruises, would advertise "dietary rules strictly enforced." If his son went to college, bigotry would be translated into separate fraternities.

Unless you objected to this insularity, life in a prewar suburb could be very pleasant. The old houses were roomy and the new mansions elegant. Ten to twenty thousand dollars bought a lot of house in the Depression; the preferred styles were Tudor or Colonial, though here and there spectacular structures of modern design were rising. Handy-andies mowed the grass and cut the wood. Fathers golfed, mothers gardened, and the young "set" or "crowd" danced Saturday evenings at the club. Nobody complained about the rat race. Gray flannel was an acceptable cloth, and anyone who misbehaved might be expelled from the club. Summer evenings a family sat in the yard; the lawn furniture included a rocking couch called a glider, restful for the elderly (but absolutely impossible for young sex). No date would have been caught wearing blue jeans, a fabric spun for cowboys and manual laborers. Despite juvenile fads, youth wanted what age had achieved: dignity and respectability. Nothing then visible could stop them. Even if war came, everyone assumed that boys with this background would be officers. Inasmuch as the armed forces were making the same assumption, the perpetuation of a privileged caste in uniform, with all its implications, was inevitable.

The future for young American blacks was quite different. Jim Crow was practically a member of the military establishment. In 1940 there were two Negro officers in the Army and none in the Navy. Black soldiers were usually assembled in the "port" battalions that loaded and unloaded ships; only three regiments accepted Negro recruits. Black sailors were confined to the mess; if they were lucky they could wear short white jackets, wait upon officers, and bow deeply when spoken to. Early in 1942 Eisenhower rounded up reports on what was called "the colored troop problem" (no one suggested that it was anyone else's problem). He found it virtually intractable, but he took a step forward by removing racial incidents from the war correspondents' censorship list. Some correspondents argued with him; they were afraid "troublemakers" at home would exaggerate their stories. The general refused and asked them, in effect, why America was fighting this war.

They had no answer, but if one had been from South Carolina, he could have pointed out that the legislature there had passed a resolution declaring that American troops were "fighting for white supremacy." Bigotry openly stalked the countryside in those last weeks of peace. It was bad enough for the Jews, who were barred from prestigious law firms, admitted to medical schools on a quota basis, and excluded from employment by the phrase "Christian only"; none of his peers censured Mississippi Congressman John Rankin when he stood in the well of the House and described a newspaperman as "a little kike." But anti-Semitism never achieved the depths of anti-Negro racism. Senator Theodore G. "The Man" Bilbo, Rankin's fellow Mississippian, enlivened official proceedings from time to time with such Bilboisms as "We people of the South must draw the color line tighter and tighter," "The white man is the custodian of the gospel of Jesus Christ," and "We will tell our nigger-loving Yankee friends to go straight to hell."

It was outside a Mississippi fence that a sign read, "Easter egg hunt. White children 9:30 A.M. — colored children 3:30 P.M." But white racism flourished north of the Mason and Dixon line, too. Congress refused to go on record against lynching. The *Baltimore Sun*, which regarded itself as an enlightened newspaper, reported as a scandal the fact that in a federal work relief camp "colored women live in screened-in cabins." In the celebrated Rhinelander divorce suit, the husband claimed that he hadn't known that his wife was part Negro, and Alice Rhinelander had to strip to the waist to prove he must have known it. Amos 'n' Andy's devoted fans included J. Edgar Hoover, who reported to President Roosevelt that "a good proportion of unrest as regards race relationships results from Communist activities." Chicago's great Negro newspaper the *Defender* warned its southern readers to shed their illusions; they weren't wanted in the North.

But remaining in the South meant more than suffering indignities from such thugs as T. Eugene "Bull" Connor, who even then was Birmingham's head of public safety. Staying home meant trying to live on $634 a year in southern cities, or $566 a year in the rural South. That could be doubled in New York or Detroit, and so the migration of a million blacks began, northward to a living wage, but north to ghettos, too. In exchange for food, clothing, and a better education, they paid a terrible price in social disintegration and mass frustration. It was in these years, in northern slums, that many of the militant blacks of the 1960s were born.

Their early heroes were black musicians, and great black athletes like Jesse Owens and Joe Louis. Sportswriters were acclaiming Louis as the greatest prizefighter in history — he had just defended his title successfully for the ninth time — and he was aware of his social role. "I want to fight honest," he said, "so that the next colored boy can get the same break I got.

If I cut the fool, I'll let them down." Among his adoring audience was Malcolm X, who wrote in his autobiography that "Every Negro boy old enough to walk wanted to be the next Brown Bomber."

Some of the greatest music ever heard in America was recorded in these years, and the treatment black musicians received from white Americans was a national disgrace. Benny Goodman broke the color line by adding Teddy Wilson to his band, but even then hotel managers refused to let Wilson play with the band on dance floors. In New York, the magnificent Duke Ellington band was allowed to play at Loew's State Theater on Broadway but was barred from the Paramount and the Strand. Road trips were worse. Finding a place to eat and a bed were daily humiliations. On one of Goodman's southern swings two policemen were hustling Lionel Hampton to jail when their chief appeared; he turned out to be a jazz fan and Hampton was saved. Billie Holiday had to enter and leave hotels by the back door, and in Detroit, where a theater manager thought she looked too light-skinned to appear with blacks, she had to apply dark makeup. Once she made a southern tour with Artie Shaw's band. Of it she said, "It got to the point where I hardly ever ate, slept, or went to the bathroom without having a major NAACP-type production."

Now and then they got a little of their own back. Pearl Bailey recalls a confrontation in one of Chicago's Chinese restaurants. A Chinese waiter came over and, she remembers, "started with a language I couldn't understand, but . . . kept ending with 'Me no serve.' That did it. I told him in a slow, Oriental drawl, 'You think I came to America to pick cotton. I was told you came to do laundry. So, brother, serve.' And you know what? He did." Lena Horne made a magnificent gesture of defiance in one of the first prisoner of war camps. The camp commander had filled the front rows with German soldiers. Their black guards had been seated in back. Lena slowly stepped down from the stage, walked down the aisle, and with her back turned to the Germans, sang to her own people.

President Roosevelt was inclined to postpone a civil rights program until after the war, but now and then his hand was forced. Black leaders, watching federal money pouring into defense plants, saw Negro job applicants being turned away. In the spring of 1941 A. Philip Randolph, head of the Brotherhood of Sleeping Car Porters, told the President that the government was, in effect, subsidizing discrimination, and if it didn't stop he was going to lead a massive protest march on Washington. The President hesitated. Randolph mobilized his men and set the date: July 4. Roosevelt, dismayed at the prospect of a spectacle which would damage the illusion of national unity, yielded on June 25 and issued Executive Order 8802, establishing a Committee on Fair Employment Practices. Employers and unions were required "to provide for the full and equitable participation of all workers in defense industries, without discrimination because of race, creed, color, or national origin." The policing power was weak, and Negro leaders, who had wanted an order with real teeth, felt defeated. Nevertheless the moment was historic; the great movement which eventually emerged from it would challenge all subsequent American Presidents.

Within the administration, Eleanor Roosevelt and Harold Ickes were those most sensitive to the injustices inflicted upon American blacks, and they joined to give prewar America's civil rights record one shining moment of glory. Marian Anderson was widely regarded as the finest singer in the world; "a voice like yours," Toscanini had told her, "comes but once in a century." But she was also Negro, and when a peppy, redheaded newspaperwoman named Mary Johnson heard of plans for an Anderson concert in Constitution Hall, she played a hunch. Constitution Hall, Miss Johnson knew, belonged to the Daughters of the American Revolution. Calling upon the DAR president, Mrs. Henry M. Robert Jr., she asked her where the Daughters' position was in all this. Right in the driver's seat, Mrs. Robert snapped, and the plans could stop right where they were. Neither Marian Anderson nor any other Negro artist would ever be heard in Constitution Hall.

The next move was made by Walter White of the NAACP. He suggested that one way to draw attention to DAR prejudice would be for Miss Anderson to sing in an open-air, free concert in Washington. She consented, and the universal feeling in the NAACP was that the Lincoln Memorial would be appropriate. That was where Ickes came in; the concert could not be staged without permission from the Secretary of the Interior. Told of the DAR's stand, he phoned the White House. The President was just about to leave for Warm Springs. Ickes asked him to wait until he could get over there. When Roosevelt heard the details, he ordered Ickes to stage the greatest outdoor concert possible.

Eleanor Roosevelt resigned from the DAR, and at White's suggestion she and Ickes recruited a blue-ribbon sponsoring committee of cabinet members, Supreme Court justices, senators, congressmen, and other distinguished men and women. What the president of the Daughters had done was to provide the concert with a massive surge of publicity, literally beyond price. A few prospective sponsors weaseled out with the excuse that their positions prohibited them from participation in controversial issues, but the overwhelming majority came, including the diplomatic corps. The audience was seventy-five thousand. From the opening bars of "America" to the last notes of "Nobody Knows the Trouble I've Seen," they sat spellbound. Then there was a convulsive rush toward the singer which for a moment or two threatened to become a stampede. Among those thrusting their hands toward Miss Anderson, White noticed, was a slender black child dressed in Easter finery. Her cheeks were wet with tears, and despite her youth, her fingers bore the marks of manual labor. White said afterward, "If Marian Anderson could do it, the girl's eyes seemed to say, then I can, too."

Such an event briefly attracted the attention of millions, but it would be misleading to suggest that on the eve of Pearl Harbor Americans were preoccupied with great issues or, indeed, with any issues. Most of them were absorbed in personal problems, trivia, shoptalk. Even in Detroit, where engineers were studying the vulnerability of Italy's light Fiat tank, the most popular topic of conversation was sales. This was turning into Detroit's best year. Dealers had sold five million cars, and executives were tingling with pleasure — to the horror of British officers who had come over for consultations. British shock deepened when Henry Ford first threatened to close his factories rather than accept defense contracts and then stipulated that under no circumstances would he make planes for Canada. Pratt and Whitney, in Hartford, was having trouble producing engines for pursuit planes, as fighter aircraft were then called. Glenn L. Martin had signed a $131,000,000 contract for a thousand B-26s, but at last report only twenty were on the assembly line.

In Hollywood, Louella Parsons and Hedda Hopper exulted over Dorothy Lamour's generosity; the actress had just donated the sarong she wore in *Her Jungle Love* to the Los Angeles Museum of History, Science and Art, which, being in Los Angeles, had accepted it. Elsewhere in the same city the body of F. Scott Fitzgerald had been laid out in a cheap funeral parlor; Dorothy Parker stood over it for a long moment and then said quietly, "The poor son of a bitch." It was a season for mourning authors: within six months of one another came the deaths of Fitzgerald, James Joyce, Sherwood Anderson, and Virginia Woolf.

In 1941 the *Boston Evening Transcript* expired after one hundred and eleven years of continuous publication. That was an omen: the long, slow attrition of American newspapers was gathering momentum; within the next two decades one in every four morning dailies would go. Harvard, alma mater of *Transcript* editors, lamented its passing. The university wanted straight news, now of all times, for like all campuses in periods of great change, it was seething with ideas. In 1941 W. H. Auden published his poem "The Age of Anxiety," William Barrett brought out *What Is Existentialism?*, Henry Luce appalled nonchauvinists with *The American Century*, and the *Kenyon Review* carried John Peale Bishop's optimistic appraisal of "The Arts." Bishop saw the crisis of the West as a great cultural opportunity for America; he welcomed Europe's refugee intellectuals and artists, and he thought they would stay. "The future of the arts is in America," he wrote, "for only here can the intelligence pursue its inquiries without hindrance from the state and publish its discoveries unmolested by authority."

As subscribers pored over Bishop's hopeful essay, a former chicken farmer named Joseph R. McCarthy, who had put himself through law school by working as a gasoline station attendant, a dishwasher, a pie baker, and a pick-and-shovel man on a road construction gang, was presiding as circuit judge, an elective office, in Wisconsin's District 10. Spiro T.

Agnew was a claims adjuster for the Lumbermen's Mutual Casualty Company in Baltimore. Whittaker Chambers, now a fat, sad-looking man who wore baggy blue suits, was the third-string book reviewer for *Time*. Alger Hiss, still living at 3210 P Street, in Washington, was a rising man in the State Department. It is startling to reflect that if the Xerox duplicating machine had been invented by the mid-Thirties, Hiss wouldn't have needed to copy documents on his Woodstock typewriter, Chambers couldn't have proved his case, and it is highly doubtful that Richard Nixon, Chambers's champion, would have ever reached a national audience and the White House.

Sportswriters had a dull time in 1941. There was Seabiscuit, of course. Bob Feller threw a no-hitter, and Joe DiMaggio hit safely in fifty-six consecutive games. But Lou Gehrig died in June, the University of Chicago quit intercollegiate football, and the war canceled all Davis Cup, Wightman Cup, and Wimbledon matches. The Olympics were out, too; they were to have been held in Helsinki. The editors of sports pages covered professional football but not with much enthusiasm; it hadn't yet caught on. Its fans included Ensign John F. Kennedy, who had a ticket to the Washington Redskins home game on December 7, 1941.

It had been a fine, golden autumn, a lovely farewell to those who would lose their youth, and some of them their lives, before the leaves turned again in a peacetime fall. The girls, who would be women before the troopships came home, would never again be so willowy. It is startling to learn that the average American girl was five feet five inches tall (less than now) and weighed 120 pounds (more than now). Perhaps nostalgia blurs hindsight, though changes in fashion doubtless play a part. The prevailing hair style in the fall of 1941 was a shoulder-length pageboy or curled bob. Tossing their hair behind them, they crossed campuses like young goddesses, and as Frederick Lewis Allen said, "every girl appeared good-looking from behind."

College girls wore knee socks, came to dances in strapless organdy dresses, and if they were Smithies their daily uniform included a sweater, or sweater set, and a single strand of pearls. (Vassar girls preferred three strands.) Their shoes were broad and low. Girls not living on campuses wore snoods around their hair, or bare-midriff dresses, but any public nudity would have been an anomaly; it would have destroyed the charm. Boys were less appealing. Their lapels were too broad, and their pants were so wide at the cuff that in old photographs they are almost embarrassing. White shirts (two dollars apiece in department stores in 1941) were standard. With their steadies in mind, early shoppers after Thanksgiving were inclined to take the copywriter's advice and say "Merry Christmas with fragrant whimsies from Coty."

"God Bless America" was number three on the Lucky Strike Hit Parade, and older people choked up whenever Hildegarde sang "The White Cliffs of Dover," but the swing generation remained loyal to its own. In five years they had increased the sales of phonograph records a hundredfold. They argued over who was the best canary — Martha Tilton, Helen O'Connell, and Marion Hutton were much favored — and whenever possible they went to hear live jive. New York's West Fifty-second Street was known as the Street of Swing: at spots like the Famous Door, the Onyx Club, and Kelly's Stables you could, within a single evening, hear Count Basie, Bunny Berigan, and Bud Freeman. T. Dorsey was playing at the Terrace Room of the New Yorker Hotel, Goodman in the Manhattan Room of the Pennsylvania Hotel. And if you really wanted to swing out and shine, you and your date headed for such gymnasiums as the Roseland Dance Hall on Broadway, with its mirrored walls, its ceiling studded with electric stars, and its sharp hostesses.

Those who suspect that there was more than a little hanky-panky amid all this innocence are quite right. Sex went with swing, was even a part of it. The girl whose 1-A date kept playing "Please Give Me Something to Remember You By" knew exactly which something he wanted. The Lynds found that seven of every ten interviewees admitted having premarital sexual relations. While the figure was doubtless lower in the college population, the percentage of "technical virgins" was certainly high. Marriage was out of the question for most. Until long after the war, middle-class Americans regarded early marriage as a lower-class phenomenon, so campus pregnancies were avoided by recourse to what Dr. Kinsey would later call substitute "outlets."

Predictably, the older generation expressed displeasure at the customs of the young. Professor William H. Kilpatrick, formerly of Columbia Teachers College, deplored the breakup of "old authoritarian morals," which was pretty nervy, considering the job he had been doing to traditional values in the classroom. The Pope appealed to Catholic girls urging them to abandon their "immodest fashions," which made little sense, because most of the time everything was covered except the shins, hands, and face. Maybe he meant bathing suits. The New York Times did, and protested against the "almost naked people on beaches."

In Alhambra, a Los Angeles suburb, high school girls moving into a new building discovered that they would have to undress and shower in a common shower room. Sixteen-year-old Joan Aveline Lawrence refused. She would rather flunk gym than have other girls see her in all her nakedness, and her father, an engineer, backed her modesty 100 percent. Joan filed suit for an injunction on the grounds that requiring her to show her birthday suit was immoral, violated a California statute about disrobing in public, and encroached upon her constitutional right to life, liberty, and the pursuit of happiness. It was a popular stand, even within her peer group; 275 of Joan's classmates signed a petition demanding private showers.

The judge was on a spot. He leaned on Solomon: since the school had already been built, the girls had to choose between having their parts examined and going dirty. No injunction was issued. The New York judiciary was of sterner stuff, however, and perhaps nothing is more illustrative of prewar Grundyism and the permissiveness of the 1970s than the case of the third Earl Russell — Bertrand Arthur William Russell. Everybody in academia knew Bertrand Russell was a caution, with unusual ideas above love and marriage. Nevertheless, he was at the height of his mathematical and philosophic powers, he wrote the clearest prose on either side of the Atlantic, and he had taught at Berkeley and the University of Chicago. The College of the City of New York rejoiced when he agreed to become a CCNY professor and chairman of its philosophy department. New York reporters, descending upon him, described the philosopher as an elderly man with very blue eyes, an outsize nose, and a receding chin. One wrote: "The British upper classes believe that he is mad."

The Right Reverend William T. Manning, Episcopal Bishop of New York and himself a Briton, thought his lordship was just a dirty old man, and in a letter to newspaper editors he said so. Quoting Russell's books ("Outside human desires there is no moral standard. . . . In the absence of children, sexual relations are a purely private matter which does not concern either the state or the neighbors") the bishop demanded to know whether this was the sort of man to hold up before youth as an example. CCNY's acting president answered, "Mr. Russell has been invited to teach courses in mathematics and logic and not to discourse on his personal ethical and moral views."

Round one to his lordship. But by now indignation was spreading in all the places one might expect it to spread: the Hearst papers, the Ancient Order of Hibernians, the Catholic Daughters of America, the Lutheran Society, the Baptist Ministers Conference, and the American Legion. All of them passed resolutions, wrote to newspapers, held rallies, and staged protest marches. The city's Board of Higher Education went into executive session. It voted to stand by the philosopher. He had won round two.

Today that would have been the end of it — assuming that any modern bishop would launch such a crusade, which seems improbable. In the early 1940s, however, parents would go to great lengths to save their children from wickedness. Mrs. Jean Kay, the wife of a Brooklyn dentist, was such a mother. Suppose, she reflected, that her little daughter grew up, went to CCNY, and fell into the clutches of this fiend? Mrs. Kay consulted Joseph Goldstein, an attorney, who filed a taxpayer's suit in her behalf. They appeared before New York Supreme Court Judge John E. McGeehan with four of Lord Russell's books, which Goldstein described as "lecherous, salacious, libidinous, lustful, venereous, erotomaniac, aphrodisiac, atheistic, irreverent, untruthful, bereft of moral fiber," and "narrow-minded."

Judge McGeehan was a Tammany appointee. He knew a good issue when he saw one. In press clippings he found rumors that Russell had run an English nudist colony, tolerated homosexuality, and enjoyed obscene limericks. Then he dashed off a sizzling seventeen-page decision. McGeehan said that in making this appointment the Board of Higher Education had, in effect, established a "Chair of Indecency" at CCNY. Academic freedom, he ruled, could not permit a teacher to teach that sexual intercourse between students was proper. Besides, Lord Russell was an alien. The judge revoked CCNY's appointment and cast the offender into outer darkness, which, in his case, was a full professorship at Harvard — and Harvard couldn't have been happier about it.

Bertrand Russell had at first been stunned. When a reporter told him the judge's verdict, he gasped. "It strikes me between the eyes," he said. "I don't know what to think or say. I want it understood that I am not as interested in sex as Bishop Manning." He authorized the American Civil Liberties Union to act in his behalf. After a while he began to brood. Three years later he returned to England to become one of the most caustic and bitter critics of the United States.

In the spring of 1940 Pat Ryan and Dick Nixon became engaged, and after a June wedding they rented an apartment over a Whittier garage. On the weekend of December 6–7, 1941, he was thinking of applying for a government job. Twelve miles northwest of Whittier, Norma Jean Baker, a fifteen-year-old, sexually precocious girl, was spending less time in her tenth-grade classes than in movie theaters. Dean Acheson left a California Street mortuary in Washington, where he had bowed his head over the body of Justice Louis Brandeis. On the morning of December 7 he had visitors on his Maryland farm; Archibald MacLeish and his wife had driven out to help clear fallen timber in the woods and share a picnic lunch. President Roosevelt was in his oval study, wearing an old pullover sweater and going through his stamp collection. Hamilton Fish was celebrating his fifty-third birthday. Senator Harry S. Truman was writing letters, trying to get more defense contracts for small Missouri businessmen. Richard Whitney, who had been paroled four months earlier, was resting at the home of a friend. At Fort Sam Houston in Texas, Brigadier General Dwight D. Eisenhower, exhausted by his staff work during the recent maneuvers, was taking a nap. Donald Nelson, one of the able executives who had come to the capital to help mobilize the economy, was enjoying a Sunday luncheon at the Maryland farm of Harold Ickes and redheaded young Mrs. Ickes. Senator Nye was enroute to an isolationist rally in Pittsburgh. Myron Taylor had just praised the peace efforts of the Pope and the President at a communion breakfast of the Notre Dame Club of New York. Three days earlier the *Chicago Tribune*, attempting to prove Roosevelt a warmonger, had published top-secret plans — the hypothetical kind that all war offices prepare, to meet any emergency — showing an invasion of Germany by five million Americans in 1943, and at weekend parties Justice Department lawyers were seriously debating the wisdom of charging Colonel McCormick with treason. Norman Mailer was playing scrub football on a Harvard lot. Edward R. Murrow was shaving with particular care; he was to be the President's dinner guest that evening. Seventy-year-old Cordell Hull was on his way to the old State, War and Navy Building, beside the White House. He had just scheduled a meeting with two Japanese diplomats at their urgent, inexplicable request.

Two of the best sellers that weekend were *Reveille in Washington* by Margaret Leach and *The Sun Is My Undoing* by Marguerite Steen.

The Sunday papers advertised Matson Line cruises to Hawaii.

The rising sun, Japan's ensign, appeared over Pearl Harbor on the wings of hostile aircraft that morning, and bombing with devastating precision, the enemy proceeded to cripple the U.S. battle fleet, damage the base, and kill 2,403 Americans.

The attack can never be adequately explained, because it was an irrational response to a miscalculated provocation — or, more accurately, a series of provocations. The first step in the long minuet which ended that disastrous Sunday had been taken nearly two years earlier, when Congress, at the urging of Senator Vandenberg, ended the U.S.-Japanese trade agreements of 1911. Hull then informed Tokyo that future trade between the two nations would be on a day-to-day basis. At the time Walter Lippmann had strongly condemned the move as a step toward war. It put the United States, Lippmann wrote, "in the position of challenging a great power." It did more. It opened the way to a chain of diplomatic moves which made the Japanese jittery, cost them face, and deprived them of vital imports, including, toward the end, the lifeblood of their armed forces — oil.

All that is clear now. It was not so obvious at the time. The administration was too busy following developments on the Atlantic to give the Pacific more than an occasional glance. To the President, the issue in Asia was a moral one. The Japanese were aggressors; they should go home. But he regarded Hitler as the prime disturber of the international peace and dreaded a two-front war. He was always ready to negotiate, and as late as December 6 he sent a message to Emperor Hirohito urging Japanese withdrawal from Indochina. Had it arrived in time, the course of events would almost certainly have been altered. Grew, his ambassador in Tokyo, wanted a softer line from Washington. But Hull and his senior advisers at State were hard-liners, and they could be steely because Congress, including most of the isolationist bloc — even Senator Wheeler — was vehemently anti-Japanese.

The fall of France, Holland, and Belgium had wholly altered the strategic picture in Asia. Their colonies there were now almost defenseless, and Washington felt avuncular. Hull warned Tokyo on September 4, 1940, to leave Vietnam alone. Later in the month the President proclaimed an embargo on scrap iron and steel to all nations outside the western hemisphere, Great Britain excepted. The following day the Japanese, goaded by what they called this "unfriendly act," signed the Tripartite Pact with Germany and Italy.

The point of no return was reached in the summer of 1941. On July 24 Japanese troops formally occupied Indochina, including Vietnam. Two days later President Roosevelt froze all Japanese credits in the United States, which meant no more oil from America. Great Britain took the same action. This was serious but not desperate; Japan's chief source of petroleum was the Netherlands East Indies, which sold her 1,800,000 tons a year. Then came the real shock. The Dutch colonial governor in Djakarta froze Japanese assets there — and immediately suspended its current oil contract with Tokyo. For Prince Fumimaro Konoye, Hirohito's premier, this was a real crisis. Virtually every drum of gas and oil fueling the army's tanks and planes had to be imported. Worse, the navy, which until now had counseled patience, joined the army in calling for war. Civilian petroleum was rationed immediately; when Ambassador Kichisaburo Nomura arrived in Washington in September he sadly told the press, "All over Tokyo are no taxicab."

His country could hold out for a few weeks; no more. Until Christmas they could count on a trickle of petroleum from private sources, Anglo-American companies with storage tanks on neutral soil. But every day counted now. Konoye submitted his government's demands to Grew: if the United States would stop arming Chiang-kai Shek, stop building new fortifications in the Pacific, and help the emperor's search for raw materials and markets, Konoye promised not to use Indochina as a base, to withdraw from China after the incident there had been "settled," and to "guarantee" the neutrality of the Philippines. Grew warned Washington that there were worse men around the throne than Konoye; humble him, and one of them would replace him. Unimpressed, Hull sent back an ultimatum: Japan must withdraw all troops from China and Indochina, denounce the Tripartite Pact, and sign a nonaggression pact with neighboring countries.

Hull seemed to feel that the United States could treat the Japanese in any way it chose. As far as politics was concerned, he could. If such an ultimatum had been sent to Berlin, there would have been America First rallies all over the country and impeachment proceedings on the Hill. But Grew had been right; Konoye stepped down on October 16 and was succeeded by General Hideki Tojo, the fiercest hawk in the Orient.

The embargoed Japanese now believed that they had no choice. They had to go to war, unless they left China, which was unthinkable. They began sharpening samurai swords. American intelligence, in possession of the Japanese code, could follow almost every development. On November 22 a message from Tokyo to Nomura and Saburo Kurusu, who were still negotiating in Washington, warned that in a week "things are automatically going to happen." On November 27 the Signal Corps transcribed a conversation between Kurusu in Washington and Isoroku Yamamoto in

Tokyo. They were using a voice code in which "Miss Umeko" referred to Hull and "Miss Kimiko" meant President Roosevelt. The term "matrimonial question" meant the negotiations in Washington. Yamamoto asked, "How did the matrimonial question go today?" Kurusu replied, "There wasn't much that was different from what Miss Umeko said yesterday." Then he asked, "Does it seem as if a child will be born?" Yamamoto answered in a very definite tone, "Yes, the birth of the child seems imminent. It seems as if it will be a strong, healthy boy." Finally, on November 29, a conversation was monitored in which an embassy functionary asked, "Tell me what zero hour is. Otherwise I can't carry on diplomacy." The voice from Tokyo said softly, "Well, then, I will tell you. Zero hour is December 8" — that is, December 7 — "at Pearl Harbor."

Washington now knew that the negotiations were a meaningless minuet, a stall for time; that an attack was coming, and when it would come. The objective of the assault was unknown, so commanders in Hawaii and the Philippines received this message:

> THIS DISPATCH IS TO BE CONSIDERED A WAR WARNING. NEGOTIATIONS WITH JAPAN LOOKING TOWARD STABILIZATION OF CONDITIONS IN THE PACIFIC HAVE CEASED. AN AGGRESSIVE MOVE BY JAPAN IS EXPECTED WITHIN THE NEXT FEW DAYS. EXECUTE AN APPROPRIATE DEFENSIVE DEPLOYMENT PREPARATORY TO CARRYING OUT THE TASKS ASSIGNED IN WPL-46.

WPL-46 was the war plan. On December 6 General Walter Short, the Army commander in Hawaii, was handed another message, from Army intelligence:

> JAPANESE NEGOTIATIONS HAVE COME TO PRACTICAL STALEMATE. HOSTILITIES MAY ENSUE. SUBVERSIVE ACTIVITIES MAY BE EXPECTED.

Short concluded that this was a reference to Japanese civilians on Oahu. Therefore he ordered all aircraft lined up in the middle of their fields, wing tip to wing tip — where they could be instantly destroyed by hostile warplanes. He and Admiral Husband E. Kimmel, the naval commander in the Pacific, decided not to execute the war plan. Put on constant alert, they felt, the men would become exhausted. In fact, officers and men were given their customary Saturday evening liberty. No special guards were mounted on the United States Pacific Fleet — 94 ships, including eight battleships and nine cruisers — the only force-in-being which could prevent further Japanese invasions.

All this is baffling. Short and Kimmel later testified that neither had considered an attack on Pearl Harbor a possibility. Yet it is difficult to think of many moves in military history which had been predicted more often. Confronting one another across the Pacific, each nation had long pondered the strategy of a surprise raid on the base. The U.S. naval maneuvers around Pearl in 1932 have been noted. Japan's interest in them arose from the fact that beginning in 1931, every member of each graduating class in Japan's naval academy had been required to answer one question: "How would you execute a surprise assault on Pearl Harbor?" In January 1941 Ambassador Grew alerted Washington to the possibilities of a sneak raid on Pearl. (In his diary he wrote, "There is a lot of talk around town to the effect that the Japanese, in case of a break with the United States, are planning to go all out in a surprise mass attack on Pearl Harbor. I rather guess the boys in Hawaii are not precisely asleep.") The Peruvian ambassador in Tokyo heard the same talk, and obligingly sent it to Washington via Grew. The American military establishment was not perturbed. Men in striped pants! Peruvians! What would they know about war?

But other Americans had seen the future clearly. In July 1941 Richmond Kelly Turner, then chief of the Navy War Plans Division, had named Hawaii as the "probable" target of any Japanese offensive, and he also predicted that the attack would be made by aircraft. Navy Secretary Knox had written Stimson, "Hostilities would be initiated by a surprise attack on Pearl Harbor." There were warning flags everywhere. An intercepted Tokyo message on December 3, four days before the raid, had inquired whether there were "any observation balloons above Pearl Harbor," and on December 5 FBI agents in Honolulu had told the high command at Pearl that the Japanese consulate there was burning its confidential papers. Admiral Kimmel himself — his memory to the contrary — had warned his staff that "Declaration of war might be preceded by a surprise attack on Pearl Harbor."

What happened? Four years later, with the war won and Congress investigating the catastrophe over which Kimmel and Short had presided, the question was still unanswered. That the commanding officers had failed was evident enough, but why? Part of the answer may lie in the fact that Americans, for complex reasons that included racial chauvinism, had never taken the Japanese people seriously. They were such funny little men, with their thick spectacles, buck teeth, and bowlegs. Everyone knew America might go to war with them, but no one believed it. It was both inevitable and out of the question. On August 11 *Time* reported that "the Navy is fairly well off with its . . . own defenses"; on November 24 it declared that official Washington felt the chances "were nine-to-ten that Japan and the U.S. would go to war"; and in its December 8 issue, which was on the presses when the base on Oahu was going up in flames, *Time* reflected the general confidence: "From Rangoon to Honolulu, every man was at battle stations."

Every *Japanese* was at battle stations, and troop formations were poised to strike at Manila, Hong Kong, Malaya. Months of planning and rehearsal had gone into this coordinated effort. Secrecy had been perfect; no word of the offensive, not even a rumor, had reached foreign agents. And yet, in the end, the Japs bungled it. They had outfoxed themselves. The crux of their diplomatic maneuver had been to declare war on the United States and *then* bomb Pearl Harbor, before the dazed Americans could respond. In the 1970s, after a quarter-century of undeclared hostilities, this may seem too fine a point, but in 1941 most great powers did not make war until the declaration had been made. To do otherwise was considered treacherous.

The schedule drawn up in Tokyo required the two Japanese envoys in Washington to telephone Hull at 10:20 A.M. on December 7 and ask for a 1 P.M. appointment. Tokyo was cabling a fourteen-point message to its Washington embassy, the last part of which contained a carefully worded end of diplomatic relations — in effect a war declaration. Twenty minutes after Hull had the document, the carrier-borne warplanes would swarm over Pearl Harbor. At 10:20 A.M. Nomura obediently arranged the appointment — and then made a dreadful discovery. Yesterday, when he left his embassy, his decoders had been working on the long document. Now, to his horror, he learned that the decoders had quit work early Saturday and would need two or three hours to finish. It was nearly 11 A.M. They were fighting the clock, and they couldn't beat it.

At 12:32 P.M. Eastern Standard Time (7:02 A.M. in Hawaii) a radar operator on Oahu reported the imminent arrival of a large force of aircraft. His superior officer told him to forget it, that the blips were probably U.S. planes coming from the mainland. At 1:20 P.M. Washington time the attack on Pearl Harbor began. At 1:48 P.M. the Navy's traffic chief was called to the Washington-Honolulu circuit by an alert to stand by for an urgent message from the Honolulu operator. At 1:50 it came in:

> NPM 1516
> Z $\emptyset$F₂ 183$\emptyset$ $\emptyset$F3 $\emptyset$F4 $\emptyset$₂F$\emptyset$ O
>
> FROM: CINCPAC
>
> ACTION: CINCLANT CINCAF OPNAV
>
> AIR RAID ON PEARL HARBOR THIS IS NOT A DRILL

Nomura and Kurusu reached the old State, War and Navy Building at 2:05 P.M., and they were a sorry sight. For three hours they had been struggling with codes and hunting and pecking on typewriters. The message was marred by typographical errors, but they hadn't had time for another draft. As they entered the building, Hull's phone rang. It was the President. He quickly gave his Secretary of State the few scraps of information which had come in, confirming what they already knew from Signal Corps decoding. Meet Nomura and Kurusu, Roosevelt ordered Hull; don't mention Pearl Harbor, and then icily bow them out.

The Japanese envoys were ushered into his office at 2:21 P.M. Nomura held out the translation and said apologetically, "I was instructed to hand this reply to you at 1:00 P.M."

His voice trembling with anger, Hull said, "Why should it be handed to me at 1 P.M.?"

"I do not know why," said Nomura.[*]

Glancing at the translation, Hull said bitterly, "I must say that in all my conversations with you during the last nine months I have never uttered one word of untruth. . . . In all my fifty years of public service I have never seen a document that was more crowded with infamous falsehoods and distortions — infamous falsehoods and distortions on a scale so huge that I never imagined until today that any government on this planet was capable of uttering them."

Nomura moved to speak; Hull dismissed him with a curt nod toward the door.

Moments later Associated Press tickers chimed in the country's newsrooms:

FLASH

WASHINGTON — WHITE HOUSE SAYS JAPS ATTACK PEARL HARBOR

222PES

Curiously, only one network interrupted a program for the start of the war. Len Sterling, staff announcer for the Mutual Broadcasting System, broke into a professional football game between the Dodgers and the Giants at the Polo Grounds. NBC and CBS continued with a Sammy Kaye serenade and a program of studio music; both networks had scheduled news broadcasts at 2:30, and they decided to let their listeners wait until then. Meanwhile, more was coming in:

BULLETIN

WASHINGTON, DEC. 7 (AP) PRESIDENT ROOSEVELT SAID IN A STATE-MENT TODAY THAT THE JAPANESE HAD ATTACKED PEARL HARBOR, HAWAII, FROM THE AIR.

THE ATTACK OF THE JAPANESE ALSO WAS MADE ON ALL NAVAL AND MILITARY "ACTIVITIES" ON THE ISLAND OF OAHU.

THE PRESIDENT'S BRIEF STATEMENT WAS READ TO REPORTERS BY STEPHEN EARLY, PRESIDENTIAL SECRETARY. NO FURTHER DETAILS WERE GIVEN IMMEDIATELY.

AT THE TIME OF THE WHITE HOUSE ANNOUNCEMENT, THE JAPANESE AMBASSADORS KICHISABURO NOMURA AND SABURO KURUSU, WERE AT THE STATE DEPARTMENT.

FLASH

WASHINGTON — SECOND AIR ATTACK REPORTED ON ARMY AND NAVY BASES IN MANILA.

[*]How much the Japanese ambassadors knew has never been established. It is thought that they — like Hull — had known everything except the target.

The second flash was a rumor; the Philippines were to have a day's grace
— though when the Jap Zeros did arrive, they found that MacArthur, like
Short, had huddled his planes together, and in the middle of Clark Field
they were gutted just as easily. The radio networks, having canceled all
scheduled programs, were now putting everything they could get on the
air, including some canards.

Millions of Americans first learned of the attack when they turned on
their radios to hear the CBS broadcast of the New York Philharmonic
concert at 3 P.M., and one of them was Rear Admiral Chester Nimitz. He
was waiting for his set to warm up; at the announcer's first phrase
("Japanese attack on Pearl Harbor today"), Nimitz was up and away — to
replace, it subsequently developed, Pearl's unfortunate Admiral Kimmel.
Simultaneously a telephone rang at Fort Sam Houston, arousing Brigadier
General Eisenhower. His wife heard him say, "Yes? When? I'll be right
down," and then he was running for the door, dressing as he went and
calling over his shoulder to her that he was on his way to headquarters and
didn't know when he would be back.

Inevitably, some reactions were odd. Len Sterling, who had interrupted
WHN's account of the football game at the Polo Grounds, was being
hounded by calls from infuriated fans who wanted to know what was
happening on the field. The same was true in Phoenix, where people were
phoning the *Arizona Republic* to say irritably, "Have you got any score on
the game between the Chicago Bears and the Cardinals? Aren't you
getting anything besides that war stuff?" In Denver a KFEL religious program was canceled; a caller wanted to know whether the station considered
war news more important than the gospel. A girl in Palm Springs said,
"Everybody knew it was going to happen, so why spoil a perfectly good
Sunday afternoon worrying about it?" In New Jersey an elderly man
cackled, "Ha! You got me on that Martian stunt; I had a hunch you'd try it
again." A reporter asked Senator Nye his reaction. The senator, who
perhaps could hear the bell of political oblivion tolling in the distance,
growled, "Sounds terribly fishy to me."

But Senator Wheeler caught the national mood: "The only thing to do
now is to lick hell out of them." So divided had the country been before
this Sunday that President Roosevelt, at a White House lunch the week
before, said he doubted he could get a declaration of war out of Congress
if the Japs invaded the Philippines. Now the country was united as it had
never been. The sneak attack, the presence of two Japanese ambassadors in
Washington pretending to negotiate peace, and an old distrust of what
some still called the Yellow Peril combined to transform the war into a
crusade against treacherous Orientals.

"No!" the President had gasped when the Secretary of the Navy telephoned him the news. Like Knox, Roosevelt had thought that the first
blow would fall on the Philippines. No American officer, including General

Marshall, had expected a carrier strike on Hawaii now, because Hirohito's crack divisions were in Indochina, ready to jump off for Malaya, Singapore, and the oil fields of the Netherlands East Indies. Pearl Harbor wasn't anywhere near this corridor of advance. Pearl was a logical target in war games, but in the context of the December 1941 strategic picture it seemed almost irrelevant. Now they saw the bitter truth. The enemy had decided to win in a stroke by sinking the Navy. Except for the American aircraft carriers, which had been at sea, Tokyo had made a good job of it. All eight battleships had been knocked out, with the three cruisers and many destroyers. The United States no longer had a Pacific Fleet.

After calling Hull, the President of the United States did nothing for eighteen minutes. He may have been praying, or planning, or merely adjusting to the new situation. He sat perfectly still. Then he looked up and personally dictated the first news bulletin. He was composed, and so, to a remarkable degree, was the capital. There were exceptions; some zealous superpatriot chopped down one of the Japanese cherry trees around the tidal basin, Civil Defense Director Fiorello La Guardia was racing around in a sirening police cruiser yelling "Calm! Calm! Calm" — and announcing over the radio, "We are not out of the danger zone by any means" — while a crowd gathered across the street from the Japanese embassy watching the smoke of burning diplomatic papers rise from the chimney and looking, as one woman said, like "a lynch mob I once saw in Valdosta, Georgia."

There was no necktie party at the embassy, La Guardia collected himself, the rest of the cherry trees remained intact, and the President was working swiftly and efficiently. He called in the cabinet, talked to Churchill on the transatlantic phone, briefed the congressional leadership, ordered guards around defense plants, advised Hull to keep South American governments informed, and reviewed the Army's troop dispositions with Marshall. Ed Murrow, who had heard the news while golfing on the Burning Tree course, had assumed their dinner engagement would be canceled, but Mrs. Roosevelt called Janet Murrow and said, "We all have to eat. Come anyway."

They ate, though the President's chair was empty. The Executive Mansion's lovely oval study had abruptly become the commander in chief's general headquarters. While Sumner Welles stood by, Roosevelt dictated tomorrow's war message, and from time to time, when a door was opened, his resonant voice could be heard in the hall: "Yesterday comma December seventh comma nineteen forty-one dash a date which will live in infamy dash the United States of America was suddenly and deliberately attacked by naval and air forces of the Empire of Japan period. Paragraph The United States was at peace with that nation and comma at the solicitation of Japan comma was still in conversation with that government and its Emperor looking toward the maintenance of peace. . . ."

Murrow thought he ought to go, but several times the First Lady left the table, and she always returned with a message from the President: he wanted Murrow to stay. At 11 P.M. Janet went home. It was a half-hour after midnight when Roosevelt, obviously exhausted, invited the commentator to share a tray of sandwiches and beer. He took Murrow into his confidence, described the damage at Pearl, and told him that every member of the administration responsible for defense — himself, Knox, Stimson — was incredulous. They just couldn't understand how a major military base could have been so vulnerable, could have suffered such losses. He was still stunned, still angry.

"Our planes were destroyed *on the ground!*" he said again and again, pounding his fist on the table. "On the *ground!*"

Across Pennsylvania Avenue, in Lafayette Park, anonymous Washingtonians stood in a dense mass that evening. Some were singing "God Bless America," but most of them stared up at the White House in silence. There wasn't much to see. The Executive Mansion was dark; the great light over the north portico was unlit for the first time in memory. Already Henrietta Nesbitt, the mansion's housekeeper, was taking measurements for blackout curtains. West Executive Avenue had been closed to traffic; it passed too near the President's office. In the White House basement engineers were chalking off the entry for a tunnel which would pass beneath East Executive Avenue and enter the old vaults under the Treasury Building — the safest shelter in Washington if the capital should be bombed.

Secretary Morgenthau had ordered the White House guard doubled. On the roof of the old State, War and Navy Building, over the room where Hull had confronted the wretched Japanese envoys, soldiers worked in the dark siting antiaircraft guns, and the fifth floor of the old structure was being transformed into a barracks for the troops who would man the guns. At the time none of these precautions seemed extravagant.

Downstairs Marshall was leaving. A presidential adviser asked him about conflicting rumors from Hawaii. Every war has its rumors, the general said, and sometimes it was impossible for anyone to distinguish between myth and reality. He explained: "We're now in the fog of battle."

In Chicago a newsstand was mobbed by people trying to buy *Tribune* extras. In passing, a stocky woman said to a stranger, "What's this?" He replied, "We're at war, lady, for crying out loud." She said, "Well, what do you know. Who with?" The anecdote enjoyed a brief vogue during the next few days, and was usually worth a chuckle. Actually the question was highly relevant. The President was committed to an Atlantic first strategy. When Churchill phoned him that afternoon and asked "Mr. President, what's this about Japan?" Roosevelt replied that yes, it was true: "They have attacked us at Pearl Harbor. We are all in the same boat now." But were they? The nation's shock and anger were directed at the Japanese. The outrage at Pearl couldn't be blamed on Nazis. Emotional as the Congress was, it would probably balk at involvement in a two-front war. Even if it went along with war declarations against the European Axis, the country would be divided again, and morale, now so high, would dive.

Luckily for the Allied cause, Adolf Hitler was no longer entirely rational. He had begun to crack under the strain of the Russian campaign. Increasingly he was given to uncontrollable rages and decisions guided by intuition — by what he called his "artistic" side. On December 8 he left his Wolfsschanze headquarters in East Prussia and hurried back to Berlin by train; the Japanese were invoking the Tripartite Pact. Hitler could have ignored Tokyo. It wouldn't be the first solemn pledge he had made and then broken, and the nature of the Pearl attack could have been called an extenuating circumstance; the text of the treaty bound Germany and Italy to assist Japan only in case of an attack on Japan itself. If the Führer turned his back on Tokyo he could scarcely have been punished. Japan and Germany were on opposite sides of the globe, with the Soviet Union between them.

So his advisers argued. With the exception of Ribbentrop, who vacillated, the men around Hitler begged him not to add the United States to his long list of anti-Nazi belligerents while he chose this, of all times, to recall a verbal commitment he had made to Hirohito's foreign minister: "If Japan should go to war with the United States, Germany, for her part, would immediately take the necessary steps at once." He argued, "if we don't stand on the side of Japan, the pact is politically dead." The Nazi leadership was unconvinced. The debate raged day and night between December 8 and December 11 — an anxious time in Tokyo — and then Hitler conceded that his true motive was vengeance. Frustrated by the endless steppes of Russia, he had been seething more and more over the behavior of American destroyers in the Atlantic. In short, Roosevelt's accelerating provocations had driven the Führer to the end of his tether after all. According to the Nuremberg documents, Hitler said that the "chief reason" for opening formal hostilities "is that the United States is already shooting against our ships. They have been a forceful factor in this war and through their actions have already created a situation of war." Thereupon he proclaimed a state of war against America. Mussolini followed suit — by now he was entirely the Führer's creature — and suddenly Roosevelt's problem was solved. Congress had no choice; it reciprocated later that same Thursday. Dean Acheson, who thought Hitler was acting with "colossal folly," later wrote, "At last our enemies, with unparalleled stupidity, resolved our dilemmas, clarified our doubts and uncertainties, and united our people for the long, hard course that the national interest required."

II

SACRIFICE
AND
TRANS-
FORMATION
1941-1950

NINE

Counterattack

T HE JAP," as MacArthur called the enemy — nearly everyone else called Japanese "Nips," short for "Dai Nippon," the Japanese word for their homeland — may have been the most underrated infantry weapon in history. On parade he resembled a poorly wrapped parcel of brown paper — soiled, crumpled, and threatening to come apart. His leggings were sloppy, his blouse bulged, his trousers were baggy, and his bandy legs were ridiculously short. The image was deceptive, but illusions die hard; even after the ax fell at Pearl, Admiral William F. Halsey Jr. predicted Japan would be crushed by 1943, and at home jukeboxes rasped, "Goodbye, Mama, I'm off to Yokohama," and "I'm gonna slap a dirty little Jap." Any barhop could tell you: America had been winning battles since 1775, and had never lost a war.

But the *Japanese* hadn't lost a war since 1598. The men in the badly wrapped brown uniforms were anything but inept in combat. As sharpshooters they were accurate up to a thousand yards. Each carried 400 rounds of ammunition (twice as many as an American infantryman) and five days' rations of fish and rice. They were absolutely fearless; since childhood they had been taught that there could be no greater glory than dying for the emperor. Moreover, the hardware backing them up was awesome. At Pearl they had sunk America's battlewagons, and presently Washington was learning that Nips' ships were faster, their guns bigger, their torpedoes better, and their air power matchless in number and quality. Over Hawaii they had flown four warplanes, the Kawasaki, the Mitsubishi Zero, the Nakajima B5N1, and the Mitsubishi G4M1, each of them superior to anything comparable the United States could put in the sky then.

Secretary Stimson warned the country in the fourth week of the war: "We'll defeat the Japanese in the end, but we shouldn't look at the war with them through rose-colored glasses. There have been reports that the

Japanese . . . are badly trained troops, ill equipped. The cold truth is that the Japanese are veterans and they are well equipped. The Japanese soldier is short, wiry and tough. He is well disciplined." By then the fiction that any red-blooded American could lick ten Orientals had yielded, in Washington at least, to a shocked realization that the capital had entered its grimmest period since the Civil War. U.S. military intelligence — it was called intelligence — had ruled out an air strike at Pearl because, among other things, the enemy was known to be massing troops in Saigon, and everyone knew that Tojo couldn't mount more than one offensive at once.

Everyone was wrong. By New Year's Day the troops of Dai Nippon had not only thrust southward from Saigon; they had also made landings on Guam, Hong Kong, Borneo, Wake, and the Philippines. Tojo was out-blitzing Hitler. He was carving out an enormous salient — a tenth of the globe — into the direct route between the West Coast and Tokyo, and he was receiving invaluable assistance from Admiral Raeder's unleashed U-boats. Shipping had been short from the outset. Raeder was determined to break the Anglo-American alliance, making the supply of overseas garrisons impossible by sinking every vessel flying the Stars and Stripes or Union Jack. In early 1942 it looked as though he would succeed. Merchantmen were being torpedoed almost nightly within view of Americans living on the East Coast. Within a few hours of each other that January, Nazi submarines dispatched the 6,768-ton British tanker *Coimbra* and the freighter *Norness* off Long Island and the U.S. merchantman *Allan Jackson* and tanker *Malay* off North Carolina. That year U-boats blew up 1,160 ships, better than three a day, including the destroyer *Jacob Jones*, which, when it went down off Cape May, New Jersey, became the first American warship to be torpedoed in her own coastal waters.

It was in these desperate months, with defeat following defeat, that the Axis powers seemed invincible. The Nazis were taking Stalingrad and re-forming for their final leap on Moscow. Rommel was approaching Cairo — British diplomats there were burning their papers — and it seemed only a question of time before the Germans would be at the gates of India, where they would greet their Nipponese allies sweeping in from the east. Like Hitler, Tojo seemed unstoppable. General Joseph Stilwell limped out of Burma muttering, "We got a hell of a beating. We got run out of Burma and it is as humiliating as hell." In Washington there were strategists who thought it might take ten years to beat Japan. The two protective oceans appeared to have shrunk; not only were American seamen being killed within sight of the eastern seaboard, but the Pacific Coast heard gunfire, too. A Jap submarine shelled the Oregon coast at Fort Stevens. Militarily the attack was only of nuisance value but as a psychological thrust it was brilliant. The President decided to calm the nation. He scheduled a fire-side chat and asked the newspapers to publish world maps so listeners could follow him. But the Japanese had access to American radio, and while Roosevelt was quietly assuring the public that there was no reason for defeatism, another Jap U-boat launched a small plane that dropped incendiary bombs on the southern Oregon coast.

Apart from Pearl, the first movement in the concert of offensives Tojo had prepared for December 7 was Malaya. A few foreign service officers in Washington, proud of their ability to read the Oriental mind, had hazarded a guess that the Japanese might trespass in Thailand. In a way they were right — as right, say, as forecasters who had predicted that New England might get a little rain that memorable September day three years earlier. Having taken advantage of Vichy weakness to convert Indochina into a staging area, General Tomoyuki Yamashita had entered into secret negotiations with the Thai government. As a consequence, the Thais surrendered to him after four hours of sham fighting on December 7. Now he was ready for his first big show: Malaya.

Surging through Thailand, three bristling columns invaded the peninsula under an umbrella of planes from Vietnam, driving the British back and back. The Japs didn't really need so large a force, but they hoped to divert the RAF and lure the British Navy into a trap. It worked. Admiral Sir Tom Phillips went for the bait with the pride of H.M.'s Navy — the *Prince of Wales,* Britain's finest battleship, and the heavy battle cruiser *Repulse.* His one carrier ran aground, depriving him of his eyes, and on the third day of the war Mitsubishi torepdo bombers sank the only two Allied capital ships then off Hawaii. Nothing could save Malaya now. The enemy advance accelerated — wild stories were circulated of Jap "monkey men" who swung from tree to tree, like Tarzan (in fact they were using bicycles), and Winston Churchill learned to his horror that the great guns of Singapore pointed only at sea and couldn't be turned.

Those were Hirohito's crack troops. While they had lunged southward, Lieutenant General Masaharu Homma had been landing regular divisions on Luzon since December 10, the day Tom Phillips drowned and unfortified Guam fell into the Jap bag. In less than three weeks Homma was ashore at nine points. MacArthur declared Manila an open city (it was immediately bombed) and American soldiers and Filipino scouts were retreating into Bataan peninsula. Roosevelt wanted to save MacArthur. He knew how difficult the general could be, but respected his military judgment. He ordered him to Australia, and in the darkness of a February night MacArthur boarded a PT boat with his wife, his son, and the son's governess. The men left behind sang bitterly:

> We're the battling bastards of Bataan:
> No momma, no poppa, no Uncle Sam,
> No aunts, no uncles, no nephews, no nieces
> No rifles, no guns or artillery pieces
> And nobody gives a damn.

Their complaint about the lack of weapons was painfully close to the truth. The defense was disintegrating; the only U.S. regiment on the peninsula, the 31st Infantry, was down to 636 men, so they withdrew into the tadpole-shaped island fortress of Corregidor, supported by ten obsolete planes and a few PT boats. The ranking naval officer, Admiral Tom Hart, had left the day after Christmas flying his four-star flag from the biggest warship he had, the submarine *Shark*. For a while the men in Corregidor's underground chambers hung around the Signal Corps radio, but then they quit; the news broadcasts were too depressing. Hong Kong had fallen, its nurses raped in the streets by Jap soldiers. Wake was gone too, after a valiant two-week stand by five hundred marines under Major James Devereux, who beat off an attempted landing and then waited, in vain, for relief. By New Year's Day, when Admiral Hart surfaced off Java and joined Field Marshal Wavell's Allied command, Nips in defeated Singapore were taking dead aim on Java and Sumatra. Wavell studied his war map and flew off to India, leaving the Indies, as the angry Dutch said, to their fate.

It was a terrible fate. Led by a Dutch admiral whose orders had to be translated to Allied captains, seventeen Allied warships without air power sailed out to stop the invasion of Java. They were hopelessly outmatched. The largest among them were two cruisers, and looming over the horizon were the pagoda-like forecastles of seventy-four Jap ships, including four battlewagons and five carriers. In the seven-hour Battle of the Java Sea half the Dutchman's ships went down with him; Jap planes proceeded to polish off most of the rest. The last two surviving vessels, the American *Houston* and the Australian *Perth*, tried to escape through Sunda Strait. The enemy had closed it, and in the night of March 1 they went down fighting, the *Houston* encircled by enemy steel, all her guns blazing defiantly and a bluejacket bugler standing on the sloping fantail sounding Abandon Ship.

It was difficult for people at home to understand what was happening in the Pacific. Pearl Harbor, like the Alamo and the *Maine,* is better remembered than the war that followed. One reason is that except for the West Coast, America was preoccupied with Hitler. Another is geography. Men on Iwo Jima got V-mail from relatives who thought they were still fighting in the "South Pacific." Names from the European theater were a familiar echo from school days, but who had heard of Yap? Where was Ioribaiwa? And what was the difference between New Britain, New Caledonia, New Guinea, New Ireland, and the New Hebrides?

American teachers, unfortunately, hadn't gone into that. They couldn't be blamed. Until the air age, islands like Wake, Midway, and Iwo had been almost worthless, and as late as 1941 entire archipelagoes were of interest only to Standard Oil or Lever Brothers. The U.S. Navy started the war with obsolete eighteenth-century charts; sea battles were actually broken off because no one knew where the bottom was. The Marine Corps had to survey King Solomon's Isles as they went along. Their first engagement there was fought on the wrong river — they thought it was the Tenaru, and discovered afterward it was the Ilu.

Most of what the public did know about the Pacific had been invented by B movie scriptwriters. The South Seas were pictured as exotic isles where lazy winds whispered in palm fronds, and Sadie Thompson diddled with missionaries, and native girls dove for pearls in fitted sarongs, like Dorothy Lamour. It was an appealing myth, and there was a flicker of truth in it. The girls looked more like Lister bags than Lamour, but most veterans of the Greater East Asia War, as the enemy called it, can recollect scenes of great natural beauty — the white orchids and screaming cockatoos in Guadalcanal's dense rain forests, for example, or the smoking volcano in Bougainville's Empress Augusta Bay, or Saipan's lovely flame trees.

But American men hadn't come as tourists. They were fighting a savage war, and the more breathtaking the jungle looked, the more ferocious the combat turned out to be. Some islands were literally uninhabitable — Army engineers sent to survey the Santa Cruz group for airstrips were wiped out by cerebral malaria — and the battles were fought under fantastic conditions. Guadalcanal was rocked by an earthquake. Volcanic steam hissed through the rocks of Iwo. On Bougainville, bulldozers vanished in the spongy, bottomless swamps, and at the height of the fighting on Peleliu the temperature was 115 degrees in the shade. Sometimes the weather was worse than the enemy. At Cape Gloucester sixteen inches of rain fell in one day. The great sea battle of Leyte Gulf was halted by a double monsoon, and a month later a typhoon sank three American destroyers.

Like any war, this one had its special sights and sounds, to be remembered in later years as a kind of blurred kaleidoscope or a random selection of old film clips, enough to jog quiescent memories later, and sometimes even to stir the dark recesses of the mind where the terror of those days still lurked. There were the Quonseted troops on sandy outposts ringed by the brasslike sea — castaways on cartoon islands, vindicating Justice Holmes's definition of war as an "organized bore." There was scratchy monotony on the ship PA systems, the smell of sweat, the sickening heft of an empty canteen. Temporary airstrips were paved with slabs of perforated metal like pieces from a gigantic Erector set. There were the blossoms of artillery crumps in the banyan jungles, the meatballs on Zero wings flashing under the equatorial sun, the way phosphorescent organisms in the water would light up when a zigzagging prow taking evasive action creamed through them, and the image of carrier pilots scrambling across a flattop deck, helmets flapping and chart boards clutched under their arms.

To former marines and GIs, however, the most poignant memory is likely to be of that almost unbearable tension in the small hours of Z-day or A-day or L-day of a new operation, when they stumbled down from their hard transport bunks, toyed with a 3 A.M. breakfast, watched the warships sock the shore with their fourteen-inch salvos and then crawled down in the swinging cargo nets to rocking Higgins boats, those unbelievably small landing craft, with their packs tugging hard on their already aching backs. Peering nervously toward the purply land mass ahead, they would highball in toward Red Beach One, say, or Green Beach Two, hoping there would be no reefs this time to hold them in Jap machine gunners' sights, wondering what the terrain would be like, and knowing it would be another miserable blast furnace — torture for the foot soldier, yet touched, as all the islands were, with a wild, unearthly splendor.

Lurid settings produced bizarre casualties. Twenty-five marines were killed during the Battle of Cape Gloucester by huge falling trees. Shipwrecked sailors were eaten by sharks. Japanese swimming ashore after the Battle of the Bismarck Sea were carved up by New Guinea headhunters, and others, on Guadalcanal, were eaten by their own comrades. The jungle was cruel to defeated soldiers, who, as America's growing sea power cut off lines of escape, were usually Nips. If they were surrounded, only cannibalism and ferns were left to them, and they had to share the bush with snakes and crocodiles. Even when they had an escape route the odds were against survival. Just one man in five was able to bear arms after Admiral Mori's retreat across New Guinea's Huon Peninsula, and during General Horii's disastrous flight across the Owen Stanley Mountains, the general actually drowned.

Japanese surrenders were proscribed until the Son of Heaven ordered it, and even after Hirohito had done so, diehards sulked in caves until well into the 1950s and even afterward. Japs considered it disgraceful to be taken alive. Some carried suicide pistols with a single bullet in the magazine. When defeat loomed in the middle years of the war, officers would round everybody up for a traditional *banzai* (hurrah) suicide charge. Men without rifles were issued clubs, men unable to walk were given hand grenades or land mines and told to blow themselves up. No one was exempt. The Saipan commander was too senile to kill himself, so an aide shot him, and it was on Saipan that five-year-old Japanese children formed circles and tossed grenades back and forth until they exploded.

Hara-kiri had always been highly regarded in Japan, but to the samurai warlords last-ditch resistance also made military sense. Having captured more of Oceania than they needed in half the time they had allowed, they were maneuvering for a negotiated peace. "We are prepared to lose ten million men in our war with America," General Homma had warned in 1939. "We will build a barricade across the Pacific with our bodies," said a crudely lettered sign over the Jap dead on Peleliu. Their propaganda never mentioned anything except total victory over the Yankees, though in their inner councils they were more realistic. If the U.S. regained the initiative, the admirals and generals planned a war of attrition. The closer Americans came to their homeland, the more determined the Japanese would become.

Tokyo would mobilize suicide boats, human torpedoes, and great clouds of kamikaze planes. Faced with landings on Japan itself, the national slogan would be: "One hundred million people die proudly!" They knew Mac-Arthur expected fifty thousand U.S. casualties the first day of an invasion of Japan, followed by a campaign which might last years. The American people, they reasoned, would not pay such a sacrifice for unconditional surrender. Therefore they prepared posters to be put up in Tokyo toward the end: "The sooner they [the Americans] come, the better."

What made Pacific combat so ferocious, and turned it into a conflict in which few prisoners were taken, was that Japs thought it shameful for their enemies to surrender, too. Their captives were not treated gently. Corregidor's survivors were led on a "death march" after their capitulation — that is, the weak and the wounded were literally marched to death. Nips beheaded marine raiders captured on Makin Island, and at Milne Bay they left behind bayoneted Australian prisoners whose penises had been lopped off and the foreskins sewn to their lips. Above hung a taunting sign: "It took them a long time to die."

Such behavior brought swift retaliation; not since the French and Indian War had American troops been so brutal. Women and children were excluded; there were none of the atrocities against civilians which were to stain the Army's honor a quarter-century later in Vietnam. But in combat there were no truces, no chivalric gestures. The U.S. Navy waged unrestricted submarine warfare. Nips in the Admiralty Islands who preferred starvation to surrender were left in the bush and used for target practice. It was a hard war. Generals and flag officers could be as bloodthirsty as riflemen. Lieutenant General Lesley J. McNair told his troops, "We must hate with every fiber of our being. We must lust for battle; our object in life must be to kill." Admiral William F. Halsey ordered the erection of a huge billboard on a Tulagi hillside, visible to passing ships:

KILL JAPS. KILL JAPS.
KILL MORE JAPS.

You will help to kill the yellow
bastards if you do your job well.

In the same mood, MacArthur told General Robert L. Eichelberger that if he didn't take Buna he needn't come back alive, and in 1943, when spies reported where Japan's great Admiral Yamamoto was, American commanders deliberately sought him out with P-38 fighter planes and killed him.

Yamamoto was a genius, an Oriental Nelson. He had masterminded the multipronged naval offensive which had seized 300,000 square miles of Oceania in six months. Had he known that the U.S. Signal Corps had broken his Purple Code, the war would have taken a very different turn. As it was, he came so close to annihilating American power that he became a perennial Pentagon argument for staggering defense budgets long after he was dead.

After his total victory in the Battle of the Java Sea, the rising sun was blinding. Singapore had capitulated on February 17 ("All I want from you," Lieutenant General Yamashita told Britain's Lieutenant General A. E. Percival, "is *yes* or *no*"), and fourteen of her huge Vickers naval guns were moved to an atoll in the Gilbert Islands exotically named Tarawa. Burma followed swiftly. By the second week in March 1941 the Nips were on the Road to Mandalay, which they took on May Day, sealing off China.

Singapore had been a big name; its loss was shocking. Less familiar, but more vital, was Rabaul, an Australian outpost in New Britain captured by the enemy in January. He moved in 100,000 troops, paved five airfields, and built Rabaul into an impregnable fortress, the key to a chain of outposts in New Ireland, the Solomons, and New Guinea. Jap pilots were now within range of Australia; after heavy air raids, Darwin, on the north coast, had to be abandoned. In New Zealand every man under sixty-five was called up, and the country's pursuit planes were readied for combat — all nine of them. The prime minister of Australia warned his people to expect invasion hourly. In Washington Ernest J. King, the new Admiral of the Fleet or COMINCH (the abbreviation had been hastily changed from CINCUS), was arguing against the abandonment of both dominions. "The Pacific situation is now very grave," Roosevelt cabled Churchill, and Tokyo Rose jeered, "Where are the United States Marines hiding?"

Apart from the southern Solomon Islands, Port Moresby (the tail of bird-shaped New Guinea) and dying Corregidor, the Japanese controlled the entire Pacific west of Midway and north of the Coral Sea. They had expected 20 percent casualties in their blitz, and they had been scarcely touched — one of their fleets had sunk five Allied battleships, a carrier, two cruisers, and seven destroyers without receiving a scratch. MacArthur spoke brave words in Australia; King ordered Admiral Nimitz, who had been hastily sent out in mufti as the Pacific's new commander, to hold the Midway-Samoa-Fijis-Brisbane line "at all costs." Yet this seemed like whistling in the dark. After the Java Sea disaster America was fielding scratch teams. U.S. forces in the Pacific were beset by every conceivable calamity, including subversion. U.S. headquarters at French Nouméa were infested with Vichyite colonials, who sent the enemy bulletins on U.S. ship and troop movements.

At home, American morale was being braced with cheerful lies: that an Air Corps flier named Colin Kelly had sunk the battleship *Haruna* (he didn't); that a naval brush in Macassar Strait, off Borneo, was a great victory for the U.S. (it wasn't); and that the marines on Wake had radioed "Send us more Japs" (they certainly hadn't). Tojo and Yamamoto, undeceived, confidently reviewed the Japanese war plan of 1938. Guadalcanal and nearby Tulagi in the Solomons were next on the timetable, and were easily taken May 3. On May 6 Corregidor surrendered. The Philippine tragedy was now complete. In Australia MacArthur wrote, "Corregidor needs no comment from me. But through the bloody haze of its last reverberating shot I shall always seem to see the vision of its grim, gaunt and ghostly men, still unafraid."

The following day a Japanese amphibious force steamed into the Coral Sea, east of Australia, intent upon capturing Port Moresby. They were heartened by the conquest of the Philippines and flushed with what Admiral Hara, the carrier commander, later called a "victory disease." The battle which followed was the first carrier versus carrier action in history, and it was a curious engagement. The Americans were desperate. To save Australia they had to save Moresby, and two of the five surviving U.S. flattops had been sent to block the way. For the enemy, this was a sideshow. Yamamoto was saving his strength for the great Battle of Midway. Even so, Japanese airmen inflicted heavy losses in the Coral Sea; among others they sank the *Lexington* and crippled the *Yorktown*. U.S. Navy fliers picked off seven ships, including a light carrier — "Scratch one flattop," the pilot radioed. A draw, at best. Yet Moresby and Australia had been reprieved. The pagoda forecastles turned back. And at Pearl 1,400 mechanics, working around the clock, took less than two weeks to repair the *Yorktown* in time for Midway.

Now came the first great crisis in the Pacific war. The Allies were running out of islands. Japanese troops had seized the islands of Attu and Kiska in the Aleutians, and Roosevelt, like the Australians, had to contemplate the incredible possibility of an invasion of his own homeland. Hirohito's navy had never been more confident. It had three times as many warships as the decimated U.S. fleet. May 27, 1942, was the thirty-seventh anniversary of Japan's great victory over the Russian Navy, in which Yamamoto had fought as a junior officer, and he chose that day to make his historic move on Midway. Steaming seaward, his force was led by a screen of sixty-five destroyers. Then came twenty-two heavy cruisers and eleven battleships, headed by the admiral's flagship, the superdreadnought *Yamato*. Twenty-one submarines ringed this armada, four fast fleet carriers kept seven hundred planes overhead, and eighty transports bulged with troops. Bulling through the water, the men gaily sang war songs, and the Jap marines, who were to land in the first wave, were issued beer. "It looks, at this moment," Roosevelt told MacArthur on June 2, "as if the Japanese fleet is heading toward the Aleutian Islands or Midway and Hawaii, with a remote possibility it may attack Southern California or Seattle by air."

That was precisely what Yamamoto wanted — confusion over where the blow would fall. He had sent a second task force (Japan at this point had more ships than the admiral knew what to do with) in a feint toward Alaska, hoping to humbug the Americans into splitting their forces. Here the admiral overreached himself. He wasn't as invincible as he thought. "Magic," the Signal Corps cover name for the broken Purple Code, was deciphering his messages almost as fast as he was sending them and passing them along to Admiral Nimitz, who was organizing Midway's defense. Every foot of the island was crammed with troops; every warship that could be spared was at sea: seven heavy cruisers, a light cruiser, seventeen destroyers, twelve submarines, and the carriers, *Hornet, Enterprise,* and the patched-up *Yorktown.*

In the beginning the battle went badly for the Americans. The first Jap air strike, a hundred seagoing bombers, softened up Midway for the invasion, and the U.S. pursuit planes were pitifully inadequate. Nimitz had two new advantages, however. Not only was Magic telling him where the enemy was; Yamamoto hadn't the foggiest notion where the U.S. fleet was. And then the Jap carrier commander committed a grave tactical error. He cleared his decks to recover his planes from the Midway strike — leaving himself almost defenseless when U.S. aircraft arrived overhead first.

American torpedo bombers went in first that morning of June 4, 1942 — and they were massacred by flak. Of forty-one, only six survived, and none scored a hit. The pilots of those obsolete planes sacrificed themselves as surely as any kamikaze, and they died believing it was in vain. In fact they had provided the thin edge of victory. The Jap carriers, frantically wagging their fantails to dodge torpedoes, hadn't been able to get any planes off, and the few Zeros that were in the air were down low, intercepting the martyred American pilots. At that decisive moment Lieutenant Commander Clarence McClusky's two squadrons of Dauntless bombers from the *Enterprise* arrived high overhead and swooped down in 70-degree dives. They blew three carriers apart, then jumped another that afternoon and sent her down, too. Since four carriers were all Yamamoto had brought with him, he had to retire; he had lost his umbrella. He sat slumped on his bridge, listlessly sipping rice broth.

Eight weeks later the U.S. Marines whom Tokyo Rose had twitted were in the Fijis, rehearsing the first American offensive of World War II. It was to be a shoestring operation, first to last. With every modern weapon headed for Europe, the 1st Marine Division was armed with 1903 bolt-action Springfield rifles. Their leggings dated from 1918; their Browning machine guns and their mortars had been cosmolined since the Argonne.

The only first-class part of the push was the quality of the troops. The Marine Corps was an elite force, and these were its picked regiments. On August 7, 1942, they waded ashore at Guadalcanal and immediately wished they hadn't. The 'Canal, as it was known evermore, had been accurately described by a former British colonial resident as a "bloody, stinking hole." Taking it would have been difficult any time, and in the summer of 1942 it presented a special difficulty. In capturing Java, the Japanese had acquired the Allies' source of quinine, the only known cure for malaria. In the 1930s German chemists had discovered a substitute called atabrine, and American firms were working feverishly to synthesize it. But not much was available yet. The order was: no man could leave the line unless his temperature rose to 102 degrees. Even so, two thousand were hospitalized by October.

On the first day the marines had been lucky. The landing had been unopposed; a handful of Nips fled into the jungle, leaving a 3,600-foot airstrip they had been building. But the second night was disastrous. Yamamoto still had lots of ships and skilled seamen, and after dark he sent a Rabaul task force down the Slot, the channel between the Solomon Islands. The volcanic cone of Savo Island obscured its approach, and the Battle of Savo Island, as that night's engagement was to be called, was one of the most crushing defeats in the history of the U.S. Navy or, for that matter, any navy. Four precious cruisers were sunk; a thousand bluejackets drowned. Next morning the remaining American warships withdrew southward, and the transports, only partially unloaded, followed. As the marine general put it, his troops had been left "bare-arse." They had to go on half rations at once and defend themselves with only a four-day supply of ammunition. Meantime transports of what the marines called the Tokyo Express began landing Jap soldiers from Rabaul on the far shore of the 'Canal — nine hundred a night, forty-five hundred one night.

Supplied via their crude airstrip, the marines hung on in their muddy foxholes, shelled by enemy artillery, attacked by mass formations of charging Jap troops, swept by tropical rains, and weakened not only by malaria but by dysentery and fungus infections ("jungle rot") as well. Then, slowly, the world began to grasp the significance of the struggle for Guadalcanal. Now they were there, withdrawing them was unthinkable. By mid-October MacArthur was warning Roosevelt, "If we are defeated in the Solomons . . . the entire Southwest Pacific will be in gravest danger." Roosevelt wrote Churchill that he was praying that the men could hold their beachhead. Both sides were making the 'Canal a test of strength. In Tokyo Emperor Hirohito announced that Guadalcanal was "a decisive battle." Like Stalingrad and El Alamein, which were reaching their peaks at the same time, the jungle island became a powerful magnet, attracting forces far out of proportion to its strategic importance because each side had decided to commit all, in confidence that it could win all.

MacArthur's plea for Guadalcanal reinforcements contained a sharp barb, as MacArthur communiqués often did. He asked that America's "entire resources" be diverted to the Southwest Pacific. This would have meant stopping all shipments to Britain and Russia and diverting every U.S. troopship bound for Europe to Australia. In his opinion the Japanese threat was that great. But the President was bound to see things differently. Unlike theater commanders, he had to take a global view of the war. That meant risks, and the greater risk would lie in throwing everything at the Japanese. What would he gain if he succeeded there, only to turn and find he had to face Hitler alone? Needing the Anglo-Russian alliance, he was committed to the Atlantic first strategy. Nazi Germany could not be defeated until the Wehrmacht had been destroyed. The Russians were appealing for a second front, and he and Churchill would have to provide it, or something like it, very soon. He knew the peril in the Solomons; he even intervened to send Guadalcanal reinforcements. Beyond that, the embattled Americans and Australians down under would have to manage.

It is improbable that MacArthur could even have imagined what had happened to Washington. Outwardly the capital looked like a city at peace: the cars were shiny, they became entangled in traffic jams, there was plenty of food in the stores, there were almost as many parties as ever. In high places, however, men were driving themselves furiously, trying to deal with high-priority crises. Winston Churchill's visit and his speech before a joint session of Congress had been a matter of very high priority. Even more pressing was the continuing Battle of the Atlantic. The first step had been to turn off a lot of light switches; the glare of cities like Miami, whose six miles of neon shone far out to sea, had been silhouetting merchantmen for U-boat captains. Starting in May 1942 dimouts (or "Byrne-outs," after Economic Mobilizer Jimmy Byrnes) had deprived the subs of that advantage, although another year passed before improved radar, air surveillance, and new destroyer tactics turned back the U-boat challenge.

Building a twelve-million-man Army was expensive, and Roosevelt was sending Congress a $108,903,047,923 military budget, then the greatest in world history. The production challenge was tremendous. Boeing was responsible for the B-17 Flying Fortress (and later for the B-29 Superfortress). Consolidated was making B-24 Liberators, North American P-51 Mustangs, Vought F4U Corsairs. The names of Hughes, Kaiser, and Frazer were becoming familiar. Factories with good records were awarded Army-Navy E (for Excellent) pennants to fly over their shops, and the largest shop of all would soon be Ford's Willow Run. On Pearl Harbor Sunday a lazy creek had meandered over untilled land there, where now stood the biggest room in the world, with a half-mile assembly line. In it Ford expected to turn out a thirty-ton Consolidated bomber every hour. They would be coming off the line so fast that he wouldn't even try to store them; they would be taxied to an adjacent airfield, make their test flights there, and then fly off to combat.

The Willow Run contracts, like everything else, wound up on some Washington desk. In mid-June 1942 Nazi submarines landed six English-speaking spies on Long Island and the Florida shore. Two turned themselves in; the others were captured and their dynamite caches seized. Someone in Washington had to arrange the trial and, later, the execution of the defiant six. Yale wanted to protect its ivy walls with sandbags; somebody in Washington approved it. Sometimes the orders, decisions, and colloquies were ludicrous. In early summer members of the Women's Army Corps (WACs) began to don their new uniforms, designed by Lord & Taylor. *Women's Wear Daily* exulted: "Adoption of girdles and brassieres as part of the women's Army wardrobe will add to the prestige of the corset and brassiere industry." Then the Brooklyn *Tablet* started an arble-garble by revealing that the WAC concept was subversive, cunningly designed "to break down the traditional American and Christain opposition to removing woman from the home and to degrade her by bringing back the pagan female goddess of de-sexed, lustful sterility." Even the liberal Catholic *Commonweal* opposed the recruiting of women. Girls joined up anyhow. Everyone wanted to serve, including dog lovers. The Army gamely organized a K-9 Corps of useful pets and gave it the nickname "Wags." Arthur Roland, dog editor of the *New York Sun*, even wrote a K-9 marching song:

> *From the kennels of the country,*
> *From the homes and firesides too,*
> *We have joined the canine army,*
> *Our nation's work to do.*

America, Philip Wylie observed at about this time, bestows its affection in peculiar ways; it was, for example, the only World War II army which formed an entire division on a parade ground to spell out MOM. But trivia helped mask the significant and the top secret, some of which needed all the camouflage they could get. In Oak Ridge, Tennessee, eighteen miles northwest of Knoxville, workers were clearing a hillside and putting down footings for a series of buildings. No one there had the slightest notion of what it was all about. Asked what he was making, a worker replied, "A dollar thirty-five an hour." Two thousand miles westward, in the lazy New Mexico town of Santa Fe, tourists, many with foreign accents, were strolling up to a house at 109 East Palace Street and then being ferried thirty-five miles away to a camp they knew only as Site Y which the world would later come to know as Los Alamos.

Huge industrial complexes were rising in the Pacific northwest, and employees who asked the boss what they were doing were told they were turning out "the front part of horses, to be shipped to Washington," or "wheels for miscarriages." The boss himself didn't know. The secret was confined to a few scientists, a major general, and a handful of civilians personally chosen by President Roosevelt. The two billion dollars being spent was hidden in various categories of the federal budget, and when Senator Harry Truman came nosing around to be sure the taxpayers' money wasn't being misspent, the White House warned him off.

The scientists believed they were working against time. British intelligence reported that Berlin had ordered Norway's Norsk Hydro plant to produce 3,000 pounds of heavy water, and then increased the order to 10,000 pounds. Czech uranium was moving steadily into the Reich. On the night of October 15, 1942, a party of commandos parachuted into Norway and destroyed part of the Hydro works. That provided a respite, but no one doubted that the Nazis would rebuild it.

In this instance Senator Truman's time had been wasted. In most cases it was well spent. Roosevelt's introduction of rationing and controls brought expected howls from civilians, and Bumbledom being what it was, some howling was justified. That spring saw the creation of what may have been the longest and least successful acronym attempt in history, the PWPGSJSISIACWPB (Pipe, Wire Product and Galvanized Steel Jobbers Subcommittee of the Iron and Steel Industry Advisory Committee of the War Production Board). There was also something called the Biscuit, Cracker and Pretzel Subcommittee of the Baking Industry of the Division of Industry Operation, War Production Board, and in the first week of December the Office of Price Administration (OPA) decreed that "Bona fide Santa Clauses shall be construed to be such persons as wearing a red robe, white whiskers, and other well-recognized accouterments befitting their station of life, and provided that they have a kindly and jovial disposition and use their high office of juvenile trust to spread the Christmas spirit they shall be exempt from the wage-freezing Executive Order of October 3."

This was the Washington Richard Nixon first knew. As a Quaker he wasn't at all sure he should fight, so after Pearl Harbor he took Pat east and joined the OPA at $61 a week. Nixon had left college a liberal, but, as he later recalled, he became "more conservative" after watching the men administering rationing. Although he was making $90 a week by August, his feelings about how "political appointees at the top feathered their nests with all kinds of overlapping and empire building" led him, one is told, to resign, overcome his Quaker scruples, and join the Navy. Since he had become subject to the draft, the point is irrelevant. As an attorney he was entitled to a commission as lieutenant (j.g.), and he was sent to the South Pacific, where another Navy lieutenant (j.g.) named John F. Kennedy commanded a PT boat. Unlike Kennedy, Nixon spent most of his time in the backwash of the war with an air transport organization (SCAT), playing marathon poker and becoming so adept at scrounging delicacies and even bourbon from visiting ships that his billet became known as Nixon's Hamburger Stand. One day he was on Bougainville when a plane carrying Harold Stassen, then a member of Halsey's staff, touched down. Nixon knew Stassen was a political comer, a man whose presidential chances were ranked high, and he managed to be at the bottom of the ramp in time to greet the visitor. He was greatly impressed by Stassen's firm handshake, though when he mentioned the meeting to him after the war, Stassen couldn't remember it.

In his suite on the second floor of the White House, always within hailing distance of the chief, Harry Hopkins was briefing another future President on the coming strategy in the European Theater of Operations, known henceforth to the swing generation as the ETO. Eisenhower was still a relatively obscure figure. He had made his Army reputation in the Louisiana maneuvers of 1941. Roosevelt, reading reports of it and consulting General Marshall, had decided this was precisely the sort of man to wage that most difficult of conflicts, the coalition war.

Everyone in high office knew that Lieutenant General Eisenhower was a comer, but few resented it. He was the typical American's concept of what the typical man should be, a Norman Rockwell general taken right off a cover of the *Saturday Evening Post*. He was canny, openhanded, brisk, candid, and modest; he enjoyed dialect jokes and singing "Abdul Abulbul Amir" to the thirty-eighth verse. Born in Texas, he had grown up in a small town in Kansas, the American heartland. Most men liked him, and he liked most of them. He must be one of the few Republicans of consequence to have put in a kind word for Hopkins: "He had a grasp of the broad factors in military problems that was almost phenomenal and he was selflessly devoted to the purpose of expediting victory. He never spared himself, even during those periods when his health was so bad that his doctors ordered him to bed."

It was June 1942, and high time the President named an ETO commander. Roosevelt had rashly promised Molotov that Stalin could expect a second front "this year." American troops had sent a token body of troops to Ireland after Pearl Harbor — inspiring one of Tin Pan Alley's more unfortunate wartime ballads — "Johnny Doughboy Found a Rose in Ireland" — and now GIs were crossing to Britain itself. They were being thrust into odd corners, and the British had begun to complain that the trouble with Yanks was that they were "overpaid, oversexed, and over here." Clearly a sense of direction was needed. With Eisenhower installed in Mayfair's Grovesnor Square, renamed "Eisenhowerplatz," the Yanks and Tommies were ready to move.

But where? The Americans wanted a cross-Channel stroke from England; the British preferred what Churchill called "the soft underbelly of Europe." They weren't strong enough to take on either, so they compromised on French North Africa. Timed to match a Montgomery offensive from Egypt, it could knock the Germans out of Africa. The code name for the operation was Torch.

It began, bizarrely, with an American attack not upon Germany, her sworn enemy, but on France, her oldest ally. The invaders lay in eight hundred ships off the coast of Algeria and Morocco on the night of Saturday, November 7, 1942, exactly eleven months after Pearl Harbor. Hiding so large a force was impossible; Berlin and Rome knew of it, tried to guess the convoy's destination, and decided it would be either Malta or Egypt. When the landing craft began putting infantry on French African soil at 3 A.M., Europe was dumbfounded, no one more than Marshal Pétain. The trespass of ninety thousand Yankees offended him deeply. FDR's shortwave broadcast to the people of French Africa (*"Mes amis . . . We have come to help you repulse the invaders . . . Vive la France éternelle!"*) distressed him so deeply that he wrote the President, "It is with stupor and sadness that I learned tonight of the aggression of your troops. You have taken such a cruel initiative."

The American commander in chief was naturally in a very different mood. He was spending the weekend with Hopkins and a few other friends at Shangri-La, his Catoctin Mountain hideaway sixty miles north of Washington. It was still Saturday evening there when the invasion began. The President's phone rang. Grace Tully answered it. It was Stimson. Roosevelt's hand trembled as he lifted the receiver. He listened a moment and then said, "Thank God, thank God. Congratulations. Casualties are comparatively light — much below your predictions. Thank God." He replaced the receiver and turned to his friends. "We have landed in North Africa," he said. "We are striking back."

Eisenhower had directed the landings from a command post deep in the damp tunnels of Gibraltar. On November 23 he transferred his headquarters to the white, hilly city of Algiers; his presence ashore was essential, even if only to boost morale. Americans were beginning to learn how the Wehrmacht had won its reputation. Although caught off balance by Torch, the Germans had moved swiftly and effectively. Before the unblooded American troops could advance, Axis troops had occupied Tunisia and fortified it with men and arms from Sicily. While the GIs trudged through the winter rains and the mud, Stuka dive bombers and Krupp 88 artillery pieces pounded them, their tanks, and the Allied air cover. Then, in February 1943, counterattacking Germans hurled the Americans back through Kasserine Pass.

At the time, the pass seemed an Allied disaster. It turned out to be disastrous for the Axis. Patton replaced the corps commander there, recaptured the pass, and teamed up with Montgomery, who had arrived after chasing Rommel's Afrika Korps all the way from El Alamein. The Germans in Africa were doomed; Rommel flew off to tell Mussolini and Hitler that his men must be evacuated. To survive, the Korps needed at least 140,000 tons of supplies every month, and the Allied navies' command of the Mediterranean was reducing the German trickle from 29,000 to 23,000 to 2,000 tons. Mussolini and Hitler told Rommel he was a Cassandra. Look at Kasserine Pass, they said triumphantly; that was what happened when Aryan troops met mongrelized Americans. To Rommel's horror, they were shipping men *into* the beachhead. Thus, when the Allies snapped their trap shut in early May, they bagged nearly a quarter-million POWs. This, combined with battlefield losses, meant the Axis had lost 349,206 in French Africa. The Americans, in their first campaign, had sustained just 18,500 casualties.

Patton wasn't there at the finish; Eisenhower had sent him off to plan the invasion of Sicily. Here, again, Montgomery and Patton were to work in tandem under Eisenhower. The troops for Husky, the operation's cipher, included a French corps. Despite Anglo-American snubs, Charles de Gaulle had been working behind the lines, dominating the freed French by political maneuvering and sheer force of will, and inspiring them to enlist. Of the Gaullist troops Mark Clark would later say, "A more gallant fighting organization never existed," but all Allied troops looked fearsome now. Europe had turned a psychological corner. The Germans had lost Stalingrad — and another 330,000 men there — and now that they had been thrown out of Africa, the Wehrmacht no longer looked invincible. By this summer of 1943 it was the Allies who terrified their enemies, particularly such half-hearted Axis partners as the Italians and Sicilians.

Sicily was a political battle, fought to knock Italy out of the war, and on those terms it was successful. It was also a military victory; the Allies conquered a barren, mountainous island defended by 255,000 troops, and did the job in little more than a month. In Rome, King Victor Emmanuel bluntly told the dazed Mussolini that he was no longer head of the government: "The soldiers don't want to fight any more. At this moment you are probably the most hated man in Italy." Mussolini was arrested, and a new government under Marshal Pietro Badoglio began furtive peace talks with Eisenhower's representatives. The upshot was that Badoglio agreed to announce the Italian capitulation over the radio on September 8. That same night, the Allies would be landing troops at Salerno, in the Italian shin. The code name was Avalanche. Its purpose was to capture the startled Germans and clear the entire Italian peninsula of Axis troops.

How they thought they could bring it off is inexplicable. Keeping so big a secret was impossible; talky Italians had given the whole thing away to the Gestapo and Nazi intelligence. Badoglio surrendered unconditionally on September 8, as promised, but by then elite German divisions had poured into Italy and disarmed their former ally. Mark Clark's Fifth Army was pinned down at Salerno, and the GIs, who had been told of Italy's surrender and expected an easy time of it, were angry and confused. Now enemy tank and artillery fire confined them to a beachhead less than five miles deep. Every night loudspeakers, commanded by a bilingual German who evidently admired Hollywood Westerns, roared at the hemmed-in infantry, "O.K., you guys. Come in and give yourself up. We got you covered." This sort of thing went on for four months. In Berlin "Lord Haw-Haw," the renegade Englishman who broadcast propaganda for Goebbels, was predicting "another Dunkerque."

This was the beginning of the Italian tragedy, of useless battles, needless suffering, and endless siege warfare. On the east coast of Italy, Montgomery's Eighth Army had moved swiftly, joining the 1st British Airborne Division — which had taken the naval base of Taranto — and then racing on to the Adriatic port of Bari. The British accelerated their advance to take the pressure off the American infantry. American airmen bombed the hills overlooking Salerno. The beachhead was jammed with artillery until, on September 5, the Germans at last began to withdraw slowly toward Naples.

Company commanders knew what was wrong with the Italian war, even if generals didn't. The Fifth Army was fighting geography. It took them three weeks and nearly 12,000 casualties to reach Naples. The spine of the country was traversed by the Apennines. Since this mountain chain was the source of Italy's rivers, infantry had to cross an endless succession of valleys, beyond each of which would rise a ridge held by entrenched Germans. The most famous crest was Monte Cassino, the site of a fourteen-hundred-year-old monastery and the western anchor of Kesselring's Gustav Line. Dug in along the heights around the monastery, the enemy decimated American infantrymen with mortars and *nebelwerfers* — "screaming meemies," GIs called them — while U.S. tanks were destroyed by 88s. The Allies believed the monastery was being used as an observation point and bombed it to rubble. Nothing had been solved. Enemy fire was as accurate and pitiless as ever.

To compound the foot soldiers' misery, Eisenhower, recalled to England for planning the cross-Channel invasion of France, took with him his best generals: Patton, Montgomery, and Omar Bradley. In Italy icy winds and heavy snow lashed the jagged ridges. The mud was waist-deep in the daytime and frozen solid at night. Bill Mauldin thought there was something almost supernatural about the muck: "I'm sure Europe never got this muddy during peacetime. I'm equally sure that no mud in the world is so deep or sticky or wet as European mud. It doesn't even have an honest color like ordinary mud." Day after day the war of attrition went on; dead bodies were wrapped in bloody bed sacks or ponchos and stacked like cordwood, bound together by Signal Corps wire. Scavenging dogs ate the throats of the dead. Frostbite and trench foot were epidemic. Sentries shivered at their posts. It was one of the worst Italian winters in memory.

After V-E Day and V-J Day the Army informed American newspapers and magazines that they should stop calling infantrymen GIs, on the ground that GI meant General Issue and was therefore "dehumanizing, demeaning, and disrespectful." In the spirit of victory, editors and publishers quickly submitted. It seemed absurd at the time, but in the long run it turned out to be a good thing, for just as "doughboys" meant the foot soldiers of 1918, and "grunts" those of Vietnam, the GI belongs almost exclusively to World War II. He is the symbol of the swing generation's youth, or the erosion of it: the fresh-faced adolescent who left home in ill-fitting khaki and returned much quieter at twenty-three with dull, resigned eyes and a way of tensing up when the old Third Avenue El or anything else approached overhead with a whir, a whoosh, a whiz, a whistle, or a sound like rapidly ripped canvas.

The sad part is that hardly anyone remembers GIs as they were. Actors pretending to be in the armed forces of those days appear in television situation comedies on TV so often that children are seduced into believing that the war was all thrills and high good humor. Every dogface in the ETO assumed that if he grew old enough to father children at home, one of them would ask one day, "Daddy, what did you do in the big war?" He never imagined that the question would be rhetorical, to be followed by the child's observation that doubtless it was great to have been one of Hogan's Heroes or in McHale's Navy or — cruelest of all — "What fun it must have been to fight with Patton!" There are other dogface images around, but they are just as irrelevant. The harpies of the DAR, the VFW and the Legionnaires see the doggie as a clean-shaven, well-barbered, selfless hero, and college students of the 1970s wonder whether once upon a time it was really possible to wear the country's uniform with pride, shoulder a rifle, and righteously shoot to kill.

There was such a time, and these were its men. By the winter of 1943–44 the ETO foot soldier had become a veteran of war, a skilled foot soldier who would have been valued by Alexander the Great or Napoleon Bonaparte. He was more subdued than they were (or than we have been told they were; combat makes a man suspicious of all warrior legends), and if he had rank he didn't wear it on the line; up front the Krauts, as everyone called them, enjoyed sniping at leaders. GIs didn't shave or get their hair cut while in combat, not because they wanted to become flower children but because they lacked razors, shaving cream, mirrors, hot water, and time.

After two weeks of Italy's driving rain, lying in a muddy foxhole while the enemy tried to hit him with bombs, tanks, grenades, bullets, flame-throwers, booby traps, and HE (high explosive) and phosphorescent shells, a man looked like a tramp. His behavior was often uncivilized. He moved his bowels in full view of his peers, many of whom took a critical interest in his performance. He was foul-mouthed, and especially insulting to men who hadn't been up front ("rear echelon bastards"). The dogface had been wet so long that his combat jacket was disintegrating, and sometimes he smelled vile. Most of all he was tired. Some men took years to recover from that weariness. Some never did.

When it was all over, and the generals had finished decorating and congratulating each other — that sounds cynical, but the GI would have put it that way; you can never understand the dogface until you have grasped the extent of his cynicism — a civilian employee of the Quartermaster Corps did a little historical research and disclosed that the average American infantryman in World War II had carried 84.3 pounds each day. That made him the most heavily laden foot soldier in the history of warfare. The figure startled some people, including, inexcusably, generals. It didn't surprise the former GI. He knew he had been a beast of burden. Moving into the line, he had worn or carried his uniform, his steel chamberpot helmet and helmet liner, an M-1 rifle, a knife, his canteen, an entrenching tool (a combination pick and shovel), his bayonet, his first-aid pouch, a web belt with cartridge magazines in each pocket, two bandoliers of extra ammo, hand grenades hung by their handles from his belt and the suspender harness supporting his pack, and the contents of the pack: a poncho, Primacord fuses, mess kit, cigarettes, a Zippo lighter, writing paper, letters from home, and various rations — C, K, or canned ham and eggs from H. J. Heinz Co., winners of the Army-Navy E pennant. In addition, the GI had to carry part of the outfit's communal weapons: a Browning automatic rifle or its tripod, or Browning light or heavy machine gun or its tripod, or a 60- or 81-millimeter mortar or its base.

These were essentials. He was supposed to carry a gas mask, too, but he had discarded that before he left North Africa; he couldn't bear another ounce on his back. The Army wished he could shoulder more, not because it was sadistic but because he needed more. He ought to have had a blanket at night. He should have had a shelter half, so he and the man beside him could ward off the rain at night. Most of all he needed extra socks. Without a change of socks, GIs accumulated wet mud around their feet and, eventually, trench foot. The pain became excruciating, and when they crawled to the battalion aid station (nobody with trench foot has ever walked), and the medics cut off their shoes, their feet swelled to the size of footballs. Sometimes they had to be amputated. That happened with frostbite, too. Late in the war privileged divisions were issued "shoe packs," which helped keep feet dry, but there was no real substitute for the warmth of socks.

To the strange mud-caked creatures who fought battles, however, the greatest source of anxiety was German artillery. "That artillery did things to you," said a corporal quoted in Yank, the GI weekly. "We'd been told not to duck when we heard the screaming of shells; it would be too late. But we ducked anyway. Even the almost silent pop of the mortars was frightening. We got to know exactly where they would land." Of all the Nazi big guns, the most feared was the Krupp 88. Sometimes it almost seemed that it could shoot around corners. At the time, doggies believed that nothing could be as bad as their "incoming mail" (German shells), but the men with iron crosses on the other side of the hill wouldn't have agreed. By 1944 American "outgoing mail" included radar-guided rockets, proximity-fused shells, and a flamethrower fuel invented by Harvard chemists in partnership with Standard Oil technicians, a wicked brew of soap powder and gasoline called napalm.

In a revealing moment President Roosevelt lamented that no one had thought of a fitting title for the war (he rather liked "The Tyrants' War") and that there were no stirring songs like "Tipperary" and "Over There." It tipped his hand because that was the kind of thoughts commanders in chief and five-star generals had. GIs would have hooted. To them giving the war a number was fine; if calling them GIs dehumanized them, and numbering wars deglorified them, they approved; it was justice. Walter Johnson has pointed out that despite the title of Eisenhower's Crusade in Europe, the ETO war lacked a crusading spirit. Disillusion with World War I had discredited in advance any slogans or parades, and "the Depression had left its mark, as those unsure of their future in hard times now had war added to their doubts about the future. An adolescent thirst for glory was replaced by a grim determination to defeat the enemy. The justness of the cause was not doubted, but the nation fought with a dead-pan face."

Significantly, the two most famous GI cartoon characters in the ETO were anything but comic. War can be preposterous at times, and when the ETO was ridiculous, Willie and Joe noted it with a wry, throwaway wit. But most of the time they were melancholy. Their creator, writing at the time, explained: "We don't have to be indoctrinated or told there is a war on. We know there is a war on because we see it. We don't like it a darned bit, but you don't see many soldiers quitting, so fancy propaganda would be a little superfluous."

And yet, ironically, they were perhaps the best-prepared generation ever to go to war willingly — willingly only because they knew the job had to be done. And that was how they looked at it: it was a job. A dirty, nauseating job, but what else could you do if you were a young, ruddy, well-nourished male with the right reflexes? To be sure, there were those who refused to go. Robert Lowell was a conscientious objector. In his imagination he could see the mutilated victims of air bombings, and he wanted no part of that. But few had his vision, and most of those who did were unwilling to turn the world over to Hitler.

Most of the swing generation, including those who loathed violence, approved of Dr. Henry Sloane Coffin, president of the Union Theological Seminary and uncle of a future Yale chaplain, when he warned that the seminary would not become "a haven for draft dodgers." Doubtless he would have taken another position on the Vietnam War, for the two con-flicts are very different. To a shocking degree the American casualties in Vietnam were to be children of the poor; until 1972 college students were exempt and knew loopholes in the draft law by the time they graduated. In World War II everybody who was fit went. Lieutenant Colonel Henry Cabot Lodge Jr. commanded tanks in the African desert. William Fife Knowland was a major in France. Hank Greenberg, the great Detroit slugger, was a shavetail. Jimmy Stewart and Clark Gable were Air Corps officers, Walter Winchell and John Ford naval officers. John Huston be-came a major, Darryl Zanuck and Frank Capra lieutenant colonels. Jackie Coogan was a glider pilot. Paul Douglas, aged forty, enlisted in the Marine Corps as a private, and other volunteers included Joe DiMaggio, Red Skelton, Robert Montgomery, Douglas Fairbanks Jr., Henry Fonda, Louis Hayward, Tyrone Power and David Niven.

In January 1942 Joe Louis knocked out Buddy Baer in exactly two min-utes and fifty-six seconds, then turned his purse over to the New York Auxiliary of the Navy Relief Society and went into the Army — this despite the appalling fact that throughout World War II the Red Cross kept "white blood" and "Negro blood" in segregated containers. Joe might have hesitated if the color line had been drawn in combat, with the rich and the privileged in safe zones. But they weren't. Among those cited for bravery in the naval battle off Casablanca was Lieutenant Franklin D.

Roosevelt Jr., a gunnery officer on a destroyer. Major Glenn Miller went down with his plane, and the men killed in action included Lieutenant Wells Lewis, son of Sinclair Lewis; Lieutenant Peter G. Lehman, son of New York's Herbert Lehman; Marine Sergeant Peter B. Saltonstall, son of the Massachusetts senator; Joseph P. Kennedy Jr., son of the ambassador; and eighteen-year-old Stephen P. Hopkins, Harry Hopkins's youngest boy.

The guys up front read about all this in the *Stars and Stripes, Yank,* or the "pony editions" (small and adless) of *Time* and the *New Yorker.* They were proud of America's democratic Army, just as they were proud of their engineers, who could erect Bailey bridges overnight, and the Seabees, who leveled the mountains of Ascension Island and built a mile-long airstrip there after the British engineers had said it couldn't be done. But they rarely bragged about their country, even among themselves. They got through what they had to go through by adopting a tough, sardonic facade. They griped about rear echelon pleasures that never reached the front — movies, Bob Hope shows, Red Cross girls — though if a gripe turned into a whine they came down on the whiner: "See the chaplain," they would taunt, or "Tough shit," or "Hell, you found a *home* in the Army."

Subjects that could be used for communal grousing were greeted with relish. The K-9 Corps was fair game. So were members of the women's services, who, they told one another, were all sleeping with officers — "Hey! You hear what happened to Halsey? He got sucked under a bridge by a Wave!" (Marines, lacking an acronym, called women marines BAMs — broad-assed marines; the girls struck back by calling them HAMs — hairy-assed marines.) But the greatest source for the mass gripe and the best guffaws was probably advertising from home. That was their one complaint about pony editions. They *wanted* to see the ads, and wrote home asking for them, and they could hardly wait to see what Madison Avenue would do next.

What Madison Avenue was doing, if you believed every word, was winning the war. THE GREAT GIFT TO THE MOTHERS OF MEN! one classic began. The gift, the first two paragraphs of the copy explained, was sulfa drugs, but the advertiser, you learned in the third paragraph, was the air-conditioning company which kept comfortable the scientists who discovered sulfa. Challenged by this creative stroke, a competitor claimed an assist for the torpedoing of a Jap freighter — "air-conditioning made possible the hit itself" because the periscope used by the American sub had been ground and polished in an air-conditioned workshop.

FERTILIZER CAN WIN THE WAR! another plug began, and the guys agreed that if that was true, Madison Avenue was doing the job. A maker of ball bearings assured the home front that GIs would have "a safe highway home" because the soldier's bearings "still ride with him." Sugar was a Nazi-killer. Castor beans had left the medicine chest for Anzio. Lucky Strike green had gone to war. Gillette razor blade steel was going into bayonets. Alarm clocks kept generals on time. The guys read that "cotton cloth can help win an air fight," that "back of every attack is wire rope," that heavy equipment was "playing its part in the clearing away of the rubble of destruction and in the building of a better world," that a manufacturer of metal fasteners — a soldier was shown lying in a hammock — had made certain that "*his* cradle won't drop, because it's furnished with clamps 30 percent stronger than specified." As a rule, the fruitier the prose, the more soldiers enjoyed it, though some pitches were adjudged to be foul. One New York cemetery deliberately timed its commercials to be broadcast after bulletins about heavy fighting overseas; after the guys had heard about it the commercials were hastily withdrawn. In another unbelievable campaign, parents were warned that they should have the right brand of spectacles so they could recognize their returning sons. Again, a blizzard of angry V-mail arrived on the advertiser's desk. And when a copywriter for an aircraft company asked in print, "Who's afraid of the big Focke-Wulf?" the fliers at an Air Corps base wrote, "*We* are," followed it with the signatures of every airman there, including the commanding officer, and mailed it to the sponsoring firm.

The most famous ad of the war was "The Kid in Upper 4," a description of a young soldier lying awake in a Pullman berth remembering "the taste of hamburgers and pop . . . the feel of driving a roadster . . . a dog named Shucks, or Spot, or Barnacle Bill." It continued: "There's a lump in his throat, and maybe a tear fills his eye. It doesn't matter, Kid. Nobody will see . . . it's too dark. . . ." GIs thought that was a lot of fertilizer, too, but at least it was in a good cause (making room for traveling soldiers), like the appeals to buy war bonds, avoid the black market, collect scrap iron, and, if readers learned about troop movements, to "Keep it under your Stetson." The doggies passed over them in silence. What really doubled them up were the flagrant attempts to exploit the war for private gain — the assertion that war production would be increased if everyone chewed a few more sticks of Wrigley's every day, for example, or advertising Munsingwear's foundation garments with a picture of a WAC saying, "Don't tell me bulges are patriotic!" or Sergeant's flea powder advertisement showing "Old Sarge" reporting, "Sighted flea — killed same."

One such plug, "Angel in Muddy Boots," was in a class by itself. A nurse was shown leaning over a wounded GI. The huckster read the soldier's mind: "I remember you . . . you are the girl with flying feet who led the way to laughter . . . you are all the girls I ever liked who brightened a fellow's life. . . . You didn't always wear muddy boots. Once you raced over summer lawns, in bright, skylarking shoes. . . ." This sent the adman to dreaming: "Yes, she grew up. . . . Her muddy boots are an example of that. The men and women — skilled craftsmen all . . . that first gave her the delight of casual shoes in color, turned their hand to meeting the need for a sturdy boot that would carry a nurse through mud and rain. . . . When the war came, these same bootmakers . . . created the Nurses' Arctic, the

Soldiers' Arctic, the Jungle Boot, the War Pilots' Boot, the deck-gripping Sea Boot, the Arctic Mukluk. . . . Someday there will be girls again who . . . fly over sun-flecked lawns with the lilt of summer in their hearts and rainbows on their feet." Only the copywriter didn't want them to wear the rainbows. "Playshoes would be back," he promised, "and everyone should remember the brand name. . . ." Somehow one has forgotten it.

What made the Angel in Muddy Boots particularly tasteless was that it was trading on something very precious to infantrymen: their secret dream of love and postwar peace. The dreams of different soldiers were remarkably alike. Loping through fields sown with Teller mines, their legs swinging in the awkward gait of the eternal foot soldier, they had come to resemble one another. Willie and Joe might have been twins; Willie had the big nose and Joe the little one, but sometimes even their creator confused them, and in their propinquity, in their shared agony, they had formed a common vision of paradise. It had nothing to do with headlines, salients, or pincer movements; that was the generals' war. The other war, as John Steinbeck explained it, was "the war of homesick, weary, funny, violent, common men who wash their socks in their helmets, complain about the food, whistle at Arab girls, or at any girls for that matter, and lug themselves through as dirty a business as the world has ever seen and do it with humor and dignity and courage." That was Bill Mauldin's war, it was Ernie Pyle's war, and Sad Sack's war, it was the war of men who cherished their Betty Grable and Rita Hayworth pinups in *Yank*, the war which was completely misunderstood by Postmaster General Frank Walker, who banned *Esquire* from the mails because he thought the magazine appealed to GI prurience.

It appealed to their yearning for tenderness and passion, for beauty and warmth, for real girls to replace the pinups; for a home that was not in the Army. Betty Friedan, then fresh from Smith, later recalled that "women as well as men sought the comforting reality of home and children. . . . We were all vulnerable, homesick, lonely, frightened." Fannie Hurst wrote that American girls "are retrogressing into . . . that thing known as The Home." In Europe GIs moodily listened to the strains of "Lili Marlene," the greatest song of the war, broadcast from behind German lines but universal in its appeal —

> *Vor der Kaserne, vor dem grossen Tor,*
> *Steht 'ne Laterne und steht sie noch davor.*
> *Dort wollen wir uns mal wiederseh'n,*
> *Bei der Laterne wollen wir steh'n*
> *Wie einst, Lilli Marlene*
> *Wie einst, Lilli Marlene.*

— while at home girls, standing on tiptoe for the postwar world, heard:

> *I'll walk alone*

Because, to tell you the truth, I'll be lonely
I don't mind being lonely
When my heart tells me you
Are lonely too

Or:

I'll be with you in apple blossom time
I'll be with you to change your name to mine
Some day in May
I'll come and say
"Happy the bride that the sun shines on today."

Possibly because there was so much correspondence between the front and home, the girls and the men in the ETO and the Pacific not only longed for the same future; they often agreed about its most minute details. The house would have a white picket fence. It would be within walking distance of a school. The girl would have a chest of silverware, the ex-GI a den. They would garden together. He would probably commute to work, because they lived in a quiet suburb. Naturally they would have children who would be adorable as babies, cute as grade school pupils, and striking as they entered their teens. After high school they would attend the best colleges and universities in the country, where their parents would be very, very proud of them.

Pacific Montage

always the rain and the mud, torrid heat and teeming insect life, the stink of rotten jungle and rotting dead; malaria burning the body and fungus infection eating away

Now hear this! Now hear this!
Sweepers, man your brooms!
A clean sweep-down, fore and aft!

Oh, Captain Colin Kelly
Put a bomb in her belly
And sent the ship *Haruna*
To the bottom of the sea

Corregidor here   Corregidor here   0200 5 May 42   They are not here yet   We are waiting for God only knows what   How about a chocolate soda   Lots of heavy fighting going on   We may have to give up by noon   We don't know yet   They are throwing men and shells at us and I feel sick at my stomach   They bring in the wounded every minute   We will be waiting for you guys to help   The jig is up   Everyone is bawling like a baby   They are piling dead and wounded in our tunnel   I know now how a mouse feels   Caught in a trap waiting for guys to come along and finish it up   Got a treat   Canned pineapple   My name is Irving Strobing   Get this to my mother Mrs. Minnie Strobing 605 Barbey Street Brooklyn New Yo

In the film version the charm is heightened by the innocence and utter lack of guile on the part of twelve-year-old Elizabeth Taylor, making her screen debut

Mammoth new Pentagon Building in Washington, D.C. Souwespac will be glad to know the fabulous new building has eight cafeterias and two big chow halls serving 40,000 meals a day

Bell-bottomed trousers, coat of navy blue,
He'll climb the riggin' like his daddy used to do!

WCTU OBJECTS TO NATIVES GIVING GI'S WINE

Oh, we sent for MacArthur to come to Tarawa, but General MacArthur said no.
He gave as the reason, it wasn't the season, besides there was no USO.

Mairzy doats and dozy doats and liddle lamzy divey
A kiddley divey too, wouldn't you?

Dear John,
This is the hardest letter I've ever had to write. But I've been thinking it over and I now see that it wasn't wise for us to be married. I don't want to hurt you but

I'll be seeing you
In all the old familiar places
That this heart of mine embraces
All night long

ITALY QUITS!
One Down, Two to Go!

Say a prayer for your pal
On Guadalcanal
He needs God's help it's true

My mama done tol' me . . . .
A woman's a two-face
A worrisome thing who'll leave ya t' sing
The blues in the night

AMBASSADOR KENNEDY'S SON DECORATED FOR "EXTREME HEROIC CONDUCT"

Pardon me, boy. Is this the Chattanooga Choo-choo?
Track twenty-nine. And I can give you a shine.
Can you afford to board the Chattanooga Choo-choo?
I've got my fare — and just a trifle to spare

As we go marching
And the band begins to p-l-a-y
You can hear the people shouting,
"The raggedy-ass Marines are on parade!"

KILROY WAS HERE

TEN

The Home Front

DURING MARCH 1942, according to an anecdote then sweeping the country, a woman on a bus was reported to have said loudly, "Well, my husband has a better job than he ever had and he's making more money, so I hope the war lasts a long time." At that, another woman rose and slapped her face, blurting out, "That's for my boy who was killed at Pearl Harbor. And this" — a second slap — "is for my boy on Bataan."

The story has an air of apocrypha (what mother had sons on Oahu *and* Luzon?), but its widespread acceptance suggests that it told wartime America something about itself. For tens of millions the war boom was in fact a bonanza, a Depression dream come true, and they felt guilty about it. Not so guilty that they declined the money, to be sure — that would have been asking too much of human nature and wouldn't have helped combat troops a bit — but contrite enough to make them join scrap drives, buy war bonds, serve in Civil Defense units, and once in a while buy a lonely soldier a drink.

Every great war is accompanied by social revolution, and the very dimensions of this war were bound to alter America greatly. Few realized that then. The *New York Daily News* really believed that GIs were fighting "to get back to the ball game and the full tank of gas," and GIs themselves sometimes thought they were in there battling for Mom and apple pie. But history does not let those who make it get off that easily. No country could have survived America's convulsive transformation of 1941–45 without altering its essence and its view of itself. The home front was in reality a battleground of ideas, customs, economic theory, foreign policy, and relationships between the sexes and social classes. Rosie the Riveter, like Kilroy, was everywhere, and she would never be the same again.

The most obvious source of change was the immense transfusion of cash into what had been an austere economy. In 1942 Washington was pumping three hundred million dollars a day into U.S. wallets and purses. After the windup in 1945 the total cost of the war was reckoned at 245 billion dollars — more than the merged annual budgets of the United States from 1789 to 1940, which included the financing of five wars. In 1939 the Gross National Product, the total value of the goods and services produced by the American people, had been 91 billion dollars. In 1945 it was 215 billion, a jump without precedent in the history of the world. The stubborn tumor of jobless men — there had been eight million as late as 1940 — had disappeared. The number of working Americans had grown from 45 million to 66 million, over five million of them women. Paul Bunyan was back. The country's old, pre-Crash confidence in itself had returned. Corporate profits in 1943 exceeded those of 1929.

Joseph Paul Goebbels cried, "The Americans are so helpless that they must fall back again and again upon boasting about their matériel. Their loud mouths produce a thousand airplanes and tanks almost daily, but when they need them they haven't got them and are therefore taking one beating after another!" This was mindless, even antic, but there was something disconcerting about a country which could field an Army of twelve million men, fight two awesome empires at the same time, build a Navy larger than the combined fleets of its enemies and its allies — and still record a 20 percent increase in civilian spending over 1939. The phenomenon troubled some commentators. "We live in the light, in relative comfort and complete security," said Edward R. Murrow. "We are the only nation in this war which has raised its standard of living since the war began. We are not tired, as all Europe is tired." Eric Sevareid, observing that most people at home were better off because of the war, warned that "if hardships do things to the mind, so do comforts."

Time trumpeted that America was "getting suddenly rich — everywhere, all at once," but not many Americans were accumulating fortunes. It was true that big, efficient corporations were crowding many small businesses off the stage. However, tax returns testify that the real beneficiary of the war boom was the small family which had saved little or nothing during the Depression. It was all unplanned, but part of the explanation lay deep in the American national character. D. W. Brogan, the Tocqueville of the twentieth century, explained to his fellow Europeans that their new ally took a different view of the conflict: "To the Americans war is a business, not an art; they are not interested in moral victories, but in victory. . . . the United States is a great, a very great corporation whose stockholders expect (with all their history to justify the expectation) that it will be in the black."

Even farmers flourished in the boom, and for a significant reason. At first, wary of the surpluses which had been their undoing in the past, they had held back. By the fall of 1942 their leaders had convinced them that they must become the breadbasket of the world, and when they returned to their fields their crops were 25 percent more bountiful than ever before. Therein lies the significance: during the Depression inventors, chemists, engineers, and horticulturalists had developed new fertilizers, high-yielding seeds, insecticides, and new machinery. Technology had emerged to alter the face of the land. It was the same elsewhere. Forced by the war to work together, scientists, military officers, economists, corporate executives, and public officials were pooling their talents and finding immediate solutions not only to wartime problems but to the challenges of the postwar world. Inventions which had been gathering dust throughout the 1930s were helping win the war. Young men with a managerial bent, like Robert S. McNamara, assistant professor of business administration at Harvard, saw no reason why radar, prefabricated housing, frozen foods, diesel power, and catalytic cracking of crude oil should not contribute to an abundant life in years of peace. The war boom had created the nucleus of a mass market; it seemed clear that a greater mass market would lie beyond victory. "Certainly there took place during the war a cross-fertilization of thinking that was stimulating to all concerned," Frederick Lewis Allen wrote. "All in all, during the war American technology underwent a hothouse growth."

Thirty years later, when the production miracle had long since been taken for granted, its long-range implications began to emerge. World War II gave tremendous impetus to egalitarianism. Traditional criteria vanished; wealth, social class, age, race, sex, and family identity no longer commanded instinctive deference. What James MacGregor Burns has called the war's "equality of bodies" destroyed the tradition that men were entitled to respect because of "background." Sing Sing would no longer treat men like Richard Whitney as honored guests. Even position based upon achievement would mean little. The scientists and engineers who had helped unlock America's productive capacities, making the new world of technology possible, would soon be dismissed as "eggheads."

All this was not the work of World War II. The social revolution had been gathering momentum for more than a half-century. World War I, Prohibition, the Depression, and, later, the cold war and the impotence of all leaders in the shadow of nuclear warheads, helped discredit all symbols of authority, from the flag to the cross, from Presidents in the White House to each father in his home. Nevertheless, the years between Pearl Harbor and V-J Day were decisive, partly because national mobilization blurred the lines between the classes by putting everyone shoulder to shoulder. Even more important, the war led to the transfer of economic power to the disfranchised. Before the boom America had been a country in which people sought products. With the postwar arrival of the consumer society, products would seek people, and the origin of lower-class affluence would lie in the accumulated pay envelopes of the early 1940s. At the time, big spending was considered unpatriotic, and scarcities and anti-inflation controls discouraged buying sprees anyhow. Still, bankrolls were thickening, and economists worried. By the summer of 1943 the Treasury Department estimated that Americans on the home front had saved some seventy billion dollars in cash, checking accounts, and redeemable war bonds. Randolph Paul, the department's general counsel, called it "liquid dynamite," which, considering what it would eventually do to the character and quality of American life, hardly seems an overstatement.

Until victory had been assured, such considerations yielded to expediency. It would have been presumptuous, and even dangerous, to brood over the challenges of peace until the Axis had been defeated. In 1942 the administration did propose a study of postwar issues by the National Resources Planning Board, but Congress killed that by abolishing the board. At times the President himself seemed to have difficulty focusing on domestic issues. To a correspondent who lingered after his December 28, 1943, press conference he confessed that he was weary of the phrase "New Deal." Ten years earlier, he said, "Dr. New Deal," an internist, had treated the country for an acute internal illness. After recovery, however, the patient had suffered "a very bad accident" on December 7, 1941. Dr. New Deal, knowing nothing about curing such afflictions, had referred his patient to "an orthopedic surgeon, Dr. Win-the-War."

Editorial writers rejoiced. Wrote *Time:* "DEATH REVEALED: The New Deal, 10, after long illness; of malnutrition and desuetude. Child of the 1932 election campaign, the New Deal had four healthy years, began to suffer from spots before the eyes in 1937, and never fully recovered from the shock of war. Last week its father, Franklin Roosevelt, pronounced it dead." But had he? Reform by any other name was still appealing to FDR, and he was preparing two major pieces of legislation for the Hill: the GI Bill of Rights, providing educational and other rights for veterans of the war, and a proposal that men in uniform be permitted to vote.

He had to move warily with Congress these days. The years when he was received there as a constitutional monarch were past. The conservative coalition had picked up strength in the new 78th Congress. Yet it is notable that isolationism had become a dead issue. Senator Arthur Vandenberg was in the middle of his long, historic swing toward advocacy of a world community. Only Hiram Johnson of California, dying with his cause, continued to argue that America should "go it alone." In the autumn of 1943 Johnson delivered the last major isolationist speech. Then, on the question "Should the Senate resolve its willingness to join in establishing international authority to preserve peace?" the vote was 85 yes, 5 no, 6 absent. The House had already passed a similar resolution—introduced by young Representative J. William Fulbright of Arkansas — 360 to 29. The way was then clear for the Dumbarton Oaks Conference in Washington, which drew up a preliminary draft for American participation in the U.N. The Senate ratified it, 89 to 2, and in Bretton Woods, New Hampshire, diplomats hammered out agreements providing for an international bank and a world fund for stabilizing currencies and rebuilding war-torn countries. It seemed that Wendell Willkie had chosen precisely the right title for his 1943 book: *One World*.

Meanwhile the great assembly lines were moving round the clock, preparing the armies of Russia, Britain, the Commonwealth, the Free French, and America's own servicemen for the decisive assaults of 1944. Typewriter factories were making machine guns; auto plants, bombers. In Connecticut Igor Sikorsky had opened the world's first helicopter assembly line. Another Connecticut plant, in Stratford, was making more than 6,000 Corsair fighter planes. Chrysler was turning 25,507 tanks over to the Army.

Because of the complexity of sophisticated machines, there was no way to predict what next week's civilian shortage might be. Only a professional hoarder, with a large staff and unlimited funds, could even have attempted to stay a jump ahead of the quirky market. Sugar, butter, alcohol, meat, cigarettes — scarcities of these made sense; they were needed for the troops or war industry. But why was it that in the very week that cigarettes came back, every store was out of book matches? How did it happen that tire-rationed motorists, deciding to ride bicycles, hurried downtown to find that bicycle rationing had begun only yesterday? And why on earth did the war effort absorb hair curlers, wigs, kitchen utensils, lawn mowers, paper, girdles, tea, diapers, bronze caskets, electric toasters, waffle irons, egg-beaters, tin soldiers, electric trains, asparagus tongs, beer mugs, spittoons, birdcages, cameras, cocktail shakers, corn poppers, exotic leather goods, and lobster forks? The invariable answer to every plaintive question was the snarl, "Don't you know there's a war on?" Well, yes, one knew, but still . . .

It still didn't make much sense, a fact well known to Jimmy Byrnes, who ran his Office of War Mobilization in the cramped East Wing of the White House, which was still being built. (Byrnes's news ticker was in the men's room.) In many cases the makers of the missing oddments were now producing cams and cogs for the war machine, of course; like civilian pleasure boats, waffle irons and lobster forks weren't going to be manufactured for the duration. But that was no excuse for not unloading backlogs of stock. The only real answer was that a nationwide mobilization of this size was bound to be marred by kinks and foibles. You couldn't expect to issue sugar ration cards to an estimated 122,604,000 Americans — 91 percent of the population — without something going awry. There were blunders, some of them incredible. The Philadelphia ration office had to close down temporarily because it had neglected to ration fuel for itself. Everyone plagued by the housing shortage had heard the story of the Los Angeles murder. A local reporter named Chick Felton arrived at the scene, verified that the corpse was dead, and headed for the victim's address at a run. "Can I rent his apartment?" he panted. The landlady shook her head and said, "I already rented it to that police sergeant over there."

Apart from black marketeers, or strategically placed civilians — like the Detroiters who slipped across the Canadian border and stripped bare the shelves of prosperous Windsor — most home-front civilians had to resign themselves to involuntary asceticism, and did so cheerfully. It did, after all, take some gall to gripe while standing beneath a war bond poster showing a dying GI and the legend: "He gives his life — you only loan your money." Naturally some wants were easier to bear than others. Except for the inhabitants of skid rows, few Americans felt frantic about the War Production Board's whiskey drought, which lasted from the autumn of 1942 to the summer of 1944. (Incorrigible drinkers put up with unappealing substitutes like Olde Spud, bearing spirits distilled from waste potatoes and skins, just as incorrigible smokers puffed desperately away at such obscure cigarette brands as Fleetwoods.)

Transportation was another matter. On February 1, 1942, when the last auto assembly line was converted to war production, Detroit had 500,000 precious new cars in stock. The OPA took title to all of them, stored them in government warehouses, and doled them out to applicants with airtight priorities, such as country physicians. By July 1944 only 30,000 autos were left — a three-day peacetime supply for the country's car salesmen, even in the shabby 1930s — and the monthly OPA quota was arbitrarily cut by 22 percent.

If you already had a car, you had to face the gasoline shortage. An ordinary citizen without a defense job received a black "A" stamp on his windshield entitling him to three gallons a week. This was death for racetracks and roadhouses; they had to fold. Trolley cars were popular in cities. When distances were short, walking seemed a sensible solution, but even this posed special problems; civilians were rationed two pairs of shoes a year, and J. Edgar Hoover reported that shoes were third on hijackers' lists, behind liquor and rayon. In the last year of the war remarkable varieties of vehicles were to be seen in America: horses and buggies, resurrected bicycles built for two, elegant Baker Electrics, and puffing Stanley Steamers, the most recent of them made in 1925, when the Stanley company went out of business.

People were fed up with red tape and bureaucratic arrogance; here young Richard Nixon had correctly diagnosed a national mood. Men didn't mind wearing pants without cuffs or coats without lapels, women didn't object to painting "bottled" stockings on their legs and drawing seams down them with mascara pencils, children became accustomed to little butter, less beef, and no bacon; but the tokens and ration stamps in those little OPA books remained a mystery to millions, including the grocers, who almost lost their minds when meats, fats, and cheeses were added to the point system. What made this particularly insufferable was that everyone had heard, from a friend of a friend, of how well captured Nazis were eating in their plush POW camps.

Now and then the government felt it must resort to stern measures. Roosevelt seized the railroads and put their executives in colonels' uniforms; it was the only way he could get the engineers back in their cabs. Sewell Avery, the board chairman of Montgomery Ward, was carried from his office by soldiers because he refused to obey a directive from the War Labor Board. (The boff that week was, "Know what's going to be on the cover of Montgomery Ward's new catalogue? 'We take orders from everybody.' ") And War Manpower Commissioner Paul McNutt did "freeze" in their jobs 600,000 Detroit craftsmen, 110,000 merchant seamen, and 1,500,000 aircraft workers on the West Coast.

In 1942, the war's darkest year, the Axis destroyed 1,664 ships — over 7,790,000 tons. Admiral Dönitz had calculated — and he was dead right — that if his wolf packs could average 700,000 sunken tons a month, Britain would starve. Elated by his successes, he wanted to send every U-boat he had to the American seaboard. It would have changed the whole complexion of the war, with unfathomable (and chilling) consequences, but Hitler restrained his admiral. He had just had one of his attacks of intuition. Norway, he said emphatically, would be "the zone of destiny." Norway? Dönitz was incredulous. He spread out a chart. Only a dozen German submarines were lying off the American shore, and in a few weeks they had sunk nearly a half-million tons of shipping, 57 percent of it in tankers. Hitler rolled his eyes toward Scandinavia. "Norway," he repeated, and there the sub reserves went, right where the Allied admirals wanted them.

The Allies were unaware of the maneuver then, of course. The Atlantic threat was far from over; the Germans were building new U-boats every week, and the figures for sunken tonnage continued to rise. The British were grim. The Americans told them to take heart. If there was no other way to win the Battle of the Atlantic, they would simply have to outbuild the U-boats. It was at this moment that Henry J. Kaiser, an aggressive, sixty-year-old industrialist, entered American history. Kaiser had played key roles in the building of Boulder Dam, Grand Coulee Dam, Bonneville Dam, Grand Shasta Dam, and the Oakland–San Francisco Bay Bridge. In March 1942 he had just acquired shipyards in California and Oregon, and there he was introducing revolutionary techniques of prefabrication and assembly which would lead to the mass production of shipping without loss of quality.

From the outset Kaiser's industrial triumphs became legend. Beginning with an initial keel-to-delivery time of over two hundred days, he cut the average work time on a Liberty ship to forty days, and that September, in the tenth month of the war, he established a world record by launching the 10,000-ton Liberty ship *John Fitch* just twenty-four days after laying the keel. By then he had a hundred ships in the Atlantic. And that was only the beginning. In 1944 he was launching a new escort aircraft carrier every week — and he and his fellow shipbuilders were turning out entire cargo ships in seventeen days. During the first 212 days of 1945 they completed 247 of these, better than one a day, but long before then Kaiser had cast an eye elsewhere. If he could make Liberty ships, he argued in Washington, why couldn't he build cargo planes, too? Immediately he was surrounded by government designers and engineers telling him his plans were impossible. But mastering the impossible had been the story of his life, and this time he acquired a partner, Howard Hughes, who had done almost every-thing Kaiser had done and established a few flying records besides. In late 1942 they struck a bargain: each would invest 50 percent of the capital and harvest 50 percent of the profits.

Kaiser and Hughes were charismatic; they became celebrities. Yet they are best remembered as representatives of their time. The production miracle was accomplished by thousands of hard-driving executives and millions of workers, some skilled veterans and some young women fresh from the kitchen or the bargain counter. American resources and Ameri-can freedom had united them in a joint effort that Nipponese emperor wor-ship, Mussolini's rhetoric, and Albert Speer's productive genius could not match. To a generation which has grown up under the sound of supersonic booms, some miracles doubtless seem unimpressive. Aerospace designers of the 1970s, for example, are inclined to regard the B-17 Flying Fortress as merely quaint, like a World War I Spad or a De Havilland Tiger Moth. But in the early 1940s the B-17 was a technical triumph, just right for its time. If the passage of a quarter-century has rendered obsolete the weapons which came off World War II assembly lines, it cannot touch the exploits of those who toiled there, competing with equally determined workers in Krupp, Fiat, and Mitsubishi factories and overwhelming them.

To put U.S. military production in perspective, it may be useful to note that on May 10, 1940, when the Wehrmacht burst through the Lowlands and the Ardennes, its historic blitzkrieg was supported by 3,034 aircraft, 2,580 tanks, 10,000 artillery pieces, and 4,000 trucks. In the five years fol-lowing the French collapse, America turned out:

Warplanes	296,429
Tanks (including self-propelled guns)	102,351
Artillery pieces	372,431
Trucks	2,455,964
Warships	87,620
Cargo ships	5,425
Aircraft bombs (tons)	5,822,000
Small arms	20,086,061
Small arms ammunition (rounds)	44,000,000,000

At Teheran, late in 1943, Marshal Stalin proposed a toast: "To American production, without which this war would have been lost." Twelve years earlier, the U.S. government had doled out streetcar tokens to its command-ing general's chief (and sole) aide, Major Eisenhower. In 1938 General George C. Marshall had testified that American armed forces were too weak to repel an invasion of the country. In August 1941 Hitler told Mus-solini that the United States was a soft country "whose conceptions of life are inspired by the most grasping commercialism." He should have read the papers of his World War I predecessor. After the Armistice in 1918 Paul von Hindenburg had summed up American war production in one sentence: *They understood war.*

They did not understand Japanese-Americans, though, and their treatment of California's Issei and Nisei constituted what can only be set down as a national disgrace. Those who like to stamp labels on public figures should find it instructive, for the racist repression did not come from the right, where according to liberal dogma it always lurks; it was advocated and administered by men celebrated for their freedom from bigotry — Earl Warren, Walter Lippmann, Henry L. Stimson, Abe Fortas, Milton Eisenhower, Hugo Black, and John J. McCloy. One man in the cabinet pleaded for compassion: Attorney General Francis Biddle — and he was supported by J. Edgar Hoover. One senator took the floor to protest — and he was Republican Robert A. Taft. The persecution of 125,000 immigrants, the majority of them naturalized citizens (all would have been except for discriminatory immigration laws), and many with sons in the Army, was a violation of their rights, a shirking of the government's responsibilities, and an abrogation of the very principles for which — if the Roosevelt-Churchill Atlantic Charter meant anything — the country was fighting.

The air strike at Pearl Harbor started the harassment, and the long string of Japanese victories in 1942 stirred a blind yearning for vengeance among American Caucasians — so runs the justification. It might be more persuasive had the judges at Nuremberg not ruled that the fever of war is not an extenuating circumstance. If Germans punished civilians on a racial pretext, so did Americans. To be sure, Japanese-Americans were not tortured, gassed, cremated, or used in sadistic medical experiments. Nevertheless, American authorities took steps down the dark road toward atrocities. Their contemporaries did not judge them; history must.

Why intolerance should have been particularly intense on the West Coast is something of a mystery. In Hawaii, which had a much higher proportion of Oriental aliens, the Army moved quickly and sensibly; leaders of the Japanese cooperated closely with G2 and the FBI, and a few suspects were questioned. There were no charges, or even rumors, of discrimination. But in California, where only 1 percent of the population were Issei (first-generation Japanese-Americans) or Nisei (children of Issei), the trouble began the morning after Pearl Harbor. Governor Culbert L. Olson and Attorney General Earl Warren, working with sheriffs and district attorneys, set a ghastly example. Issei-Nisei were dismissed from civil service jobs; their licenses to practice law and medicine were revoked; in some communities they were forbidden to do business of any sort, and those who made their living as commercial fishermen were barred from their boats. Attorney General Warren, using the same sort of convoluted reasoning which would later be turned against him when he became Chief Justice, said that the absence of any domestic sabotage by Japanese showed just how devious their plotting was. "Opinion among law enforcement officers in this state," he further informed Washington, "is that there is more potential danger among the group of Japanese who were born in this country than from the alien Japanese."

Launched thus by men in public office, and whipped up by the press, the hate campaign against the Yellow Peril became progressively more ugly. On January 29, 1942, a syndicated West Coast columnist wrote, "Why treat the Japs well here? They take the parking positions. They get ahead of you in the stamp line at the post office. They have their share of seats on bus and streetcar lines. Let 'em be pinched, hurt, hungry, and dead up against it. Personally I hate the Japanese, and that goes for all of them." He advocated expulsion to the interior of Americans with Japanese ancestry — all of them, including infants and the infirm — and added: "I don't mean a nice part of the interior, either. Herd 'em up, pack 'em off, and give 'em the inside room in the badlands." Westbrook Pegler declared that every Japanese in California should be under guard "and to hell with *habeas corpus* until the danger is over," and columnists Damon Runyon and Henry McLemore concurred.

The sheep followed the shepherds. Insurance companies canceled Issei-Nisei policies. Milkmen refused to deliver their milk. Grocers wouldn't sell them food. Warren had frozen their funds, and banks declined to honor their checks. Throughout early 1942 white Californians became increasingly fearful and suspicious. The state suggested to the Japanese-Americans that they might prefer to move inland, and it is a sign of their plight that eight thousand took the hint during the next three weeks.

That didn't solve the problem; it merely moved part of it. The germ of racism was spreading. The Nevada Bar Association resolved, "We feel that if Japs are dangerous in Berkeley, California, they are likewise dangerous in the State of Nevada," and Governor Chase Clark of Idaho told the press that "Japs live like rats, breed like rats, and act like rats." Governor Homer M. Adkins of Arkansas followed by announcing, "Our people are not familiar with the customs or peculiarities of the Japanese, and I doubt the wisdom of placing any in Arkansas." Governor Payne Ratner ordered his state police to forbid their cars on state highways, explaining, "Japs are not wanted and not welcome in Kansas."

Life became terrifying for the eight thousand on the run. They found signs in barbershop windows reading JAPS SHAVED. NOT RESPONSIBLE FOR ACCIDENTS, or in restaurant windows, THIS MANAGEMENT POISONS BOTH RATS AND JAPS. Gas stations refused them gas. They couldn't get water, or even the use of public toilets. Five Nisei reached New Jersey and were hired by a farmer; a vigilante committee put the farmer's barn to the torch and threatened to kill his youngest child. In Denver, where a Nisei girl found a job, she tried to attend church. The minister himself blocked the way. He asked, "Wouldn't you feel more at home in your own church?" Lieutenant General John L. De Witt, commanding general of the Western Defense Command and an old Philippine hand, thought that letting Japanese-Americans roam the countryside was folly anyhow. "A Jap's a Jap!" he said. "It makes no difference whether he's an American or not."

California was pressing for federal action. Roosevelt, weary of the issue and preoccupied with theaters of war, told Stimson and McCloy, then Assistant Secretary of War, to handle it; he asked only that they be as reasonable and humane as possible. Stimson was busy with his own maps and pins, so the initiative passed to McCloy, who became the administration's prime mover for resettlement, *con brio.* On instructions from General De Witt, Major Karl R. Bendetsen, head of the War Department Aliens Division, had already drawn up an evacuation plan. He was in San Francisco putting the final touches on it when McCloy telephoned him on February 8 to say, "We have carte blanche to do what we want as far as the President is concerned." De Witt, who had already endorsed the Bendetsen draft, promptly mailed it to Washington.

Six days later Attorney General Biddle urged caution, advising FDR that "the Army has not yet advised me of its conclusions in the matter." But at this point he was crossing foils with Stimson, the strong man of the cabinet, who felt that he must support McCloy and De Witt. As Biddle recalled twenty years later, "If Stimson had insisted, had stood firm, as he apparently suspected that this wholesale evacuation was needless, the President would have followed his advice. And if . . . I had urged the Secretary to resist the pressure of his subordinates, the result might have been different. But I was new to the Cabinet, and disinclined to insist on my view to an elder statesman."

Something else happened that Saturday; Walter Lippmann weighed in with what Biddle's staff later called the decisive opinion. "It is a fact that the Japanese have been reconnoitering the Pacific Coast for a considerable period of time, testing and feeling out the American defenses," Lippmann wrote in his column of February 14. He understood Washington's reluctance to adopt "a policy of mass evacuation and mass internment," but "The Pacific Coast is officially a combat zone: some part of it may at any moment be a battlefield. Nobody's constitutional rights include the right to reside and do business on a battlefield." General De Witt could hardly have put it more forcefully. The offices of Undersecretary of the Interior Fortas and Director Milton Eisenhower of the War Relocation Authority were alerted for supporting roles, and on February 19 the President signed Executive Order 9066 authorizing the War Department to establish "military areas" and to exclude from them "any or all persons."

It was not Roosevelt's finest hour. With a stroke of his pen he had consigned to De Witt's mercies an innocent and bewildered people who, like most first- and second-generation immigrants, were more loyal to their new country than old settlers. The middle-aged Issei had been producing more than half California's fruits and vegetables before Pearl Harbor; by traditional American standards they had made good. The Nisei were in their teens or early twenties. Nativeborn, conditioned in California's public schools, they talked, dressed, behaved, and danced like their Caucasian peers.

Under Executive Order 9066, as interpreted by De Witt, voluntary migration ended on March 27. People of Japanese descent were given forty-eight hours to dispose of their homes, businesses, and furniture; during their period of resettlement they would be permitted to carry only personal belongings, in hand luggage. All razors and liquor would be confiscated. Investments and bank accounts were forfeited. Denied the right to appeal, or even protest, the Issei thus lost seventy million dollars in farm acreage and equipment, thirty-five million in fruits and vegetables, nearly a half-billion in annual income, and savings, stocks and bonds beyond reckoning.

Beginning at dawn on Monday, March 30, copies of General De Witt's Civilian Exclusion Order No. 20 affecting persons "of Japanese Ancestry" were nailed to doors, like quarantine notices. It was a brisk Army operation; toddlers too young to speak were issued tags, like luggage, and presently truck convoys drew up. From the sidewalks soldiers shouted, "Out, Japs!" — an order chillingly like the "'Raus, Juden, 'Raus!" which Anne Frank was hearing from German soldiers on Dutch pavements. The trucks took the internees to fifteen assembly areas, among them a Yakima, Washington, brewery, Pasadena's Rose Bowl, and racetracks in Santa Anita and Tanforan. The tracks were the worst; there families were housed in horse stalls.

These areas, as reports from Milton Eisenhower and Fortas make clear, were only temporary quarters. The prisoners (for that is what they now were) received identity cards and periodic inspections of their belongings and their persons. Although no one told them, they were awaiting the construction of eleven huge "relocation centers." Because state governors felt as they did, all the centers were to be on federal land — the most desolate such land in the country.

The President never visited these bleak garrisons, but he once referred to them as "concentration camps." That is precisely what they were. The average family of six or seven members was allowed an "apartment" measuring twenty by twenty-five feet. None had a stove or running water. Each block of barracks shared a community laundry, mess hall, latrines, and open shower stalls, where women had to bathe in full view of the sentries. Modesty was one characteristic both Issei and Nisei women had in common with their ancestors, but when they raised the point, their guards told them to forget it; weren't they Americans now?

They were to spend three years on dreary tracts east of the Sierra Nevadas, in California's desolate Owens Valley, and at Tule Lake, in northern California's remote Siskiyou County. Surrounded by barbed wire, with powerful searchlights in watchtowers sweeping their windows each night, they struggled to recapture something of the life they had known before Pearl Harbor, teaching the children, holding church services, and attending what eventually turned out to be 2,120 marriages, 5,981 christenings, and 1,862 funerals.

Their cause should have been the cause of everyone who believed in freedom; the American Civil Liberties Union would call it "the worst single wholesale violation of civil rights of American citizens in our history." But that was not a popular view at the time. If the federal government intended to wait upon public opinion in California, the barracks might as well have been made permanent. Racists there had no intention of putting up with free Japs, despite what others said, and the Supreme Court could go hang.

But even the Supreme Court was tepid in its support of liberty. On Monday, December 18, 1944, the Court handed down findings which would have been inconceivable in peacetime. Justice Douglas dodged the issue of constitutionality; Justice Black, in what is now remembered by students of the law as a bad decision, wrote that California had been threatened with invasion, the authority of the military was paramount, and the Japanese hadn't been excluded because of racial prejudice anyhow. (Roberts, Murphy, and Jackson dissented.) In two cases the Court offered divided advice. It upheld the mass evacuation as a proper exercise of the power to wage war and ruled that there was no justification for continuing to detain American citizens whose loyalty was unquestioned. The Army began moving Japanese-Americans back to the coast on December 19 — and was confronted by fifty-seven separate acts of violence by anti-Japanese vigilantes. To crown this tragicomedy, the Hearst press raged over reports of a prisoner riot at Camp Tule, citing it as evidence that the interned families were "disloyal."

There had been no riot at Tule. At no time during the detentions were there any disturbances in the camps. The staggering irony is that the patriotism of the Japanese-Americans had been almost wholly unaffected by their mistreatment. With incredible stoicism they had accepted a double standard under which — to cite one instance — a white intern was paid $500 for a schedule of examinations and minor operations while an experienced Issei physician beside him, completing identical tasks, received $19. Others had planted trees, carried out experiments in developing artificial rubber, and painted Army recruiting posters, knowing that they would be paid nothing. To the confusion of their guards, they assembled each morning to raise the Stars and Stripes and salute it while their Boy Scout drum and bugle corps (every camp had one) played the national anthem. At Camp Topaz 3,250 adults were enrolled in camp courses; the two most popular were the English language and American history. Saturday evenings they sang "America the Beautiful," and after January 28, 1943, the men of military age did a lot more than sing.

On that Thursday Stimson announced that the Army would accept Nisei volunteers. Immediately more than 1,200 signed up, and before the war's end 17,600 Japanese had joined the Army, taking the recruit's oath of allegiance while still behind barbed wire. In Italy they served with great distinction in the 100th Infantry and the 442nd Infantry. No Nisei ever deserted. During the Italian campaign the 442nd alone suffered the loss of three times its original strength while winning 3,000 Purple Hearts with

500 oak leaf clusters, 810 Bronze Stars, 342 Silver Stars, 47 Distinguished Service Crosses, and 17 Legion of Merit awards. In Europe these units were a legend. Bill Mauldin wrote that "to my knowledge and the knowledge of numerous others who had the opportunity of watching a lot of different outfits overseas, no combat unit in the Army could exceed them in loyalty, hard work, courage, and sacrifice. Hardly a man of them hadn't been decorated at least twice, and their casualty rates were appalling."

Those who fought beside the Nisei knew what drove them. They were trusting that when word of their war records reached California, attitudes toward their families would improve, and that the Issei's prewar possessions would be returned to them. It was a vain hope. Japanese-American homes, farms, and businesses had been taken over by white Californians, most of whom, with Hearst's aggressive support, kept their loot. The Nisei themselves, returning in uniform, were rejected by barbershops and restaurants. After the *San Francisco Examiner* had run the headline SOLDIERS OF NIP ANCESTRY ALLOWED TO ROAM ON COAST, a Nisei who had lost a leg in the ETO was publicly beaten. That was too much even for bigots, and overt outrages subsided.

To imply that everyone in the state was a xenophobe would be to compound injustice. But a great many people sat on their hands and looked the other way. The War Department became concerned about Nisei incidents; white officers who had served with them were sent on West Coast lecture tours to describe their gallantry to farmers and businessmen. One first lieutenant was asked by a lanky farmer, "How many of them Japs in your company got killed?" The lieutenant replied, "All but two of the men who started in my platoon were killed by the end of the war." The farmer said, "Too goddam bad they didn't get the last two." People stared at the ceiling, at the floor, at their laps. No one said a word.

Pressing demands of the Western Defense Command kept Lieutenant General John L. De Witt at his desk throughout the war, far from the excitement and challenge of combat. His fidelity did not go unnoticed, however. The Army awarded him the Distinguished Service Medal with two oak leaf clusters, the Navy honored him with its Distinguished Service Medal, France made him an officer in its Legion of Honor, and Mexico decorated him with its Order of the Aztec Eagle. In 1947 he retired with full honors, whereupon, in a remarkable display of Occidental inscrutability, he became an ardent member of the Japan-America Society.

Three weeks after Pearl Harbor, Secretary of Agriculture Claude R. Wickard casually offered Americans a tip. Farmers were going to be busy feeding the Army, he said, so civilians who liked fresh vegetables might like to plant home gardens — he called them victory gardens. Millions of urbanites who didn't know a harrow from a spade and thought a rake was what Errol Flynn was put down peas, carrots, spinach, tomatoes, radishes, beets, lettuce, and cabbages in every open place they could find — backyards, parking lots emptied by gas rationing, playgrounds, Chicago's Arlington Racetrack, the Portland (Oregon) zoo, Ellis Island, and Alcatraz. Guided by advice from the Department of Agriculture and seed firms, victory garden farmers surprised and delighted the country. By 1943 a third of America's fresh vegetables were coming from twenty million victory gardens.

The U.S. wasn't that fond of greens, but it was something to do. In wartime the nation had become one huge transient station inhabited by people saying goodbye, people on the move, or people just waiting, if only for an end to the Kleenex and hairpin shortages. Middle-aged men painted their World War I helmets white and joined Civil Defense, testing sirens, filling boxes with sand and pails with water, practicing first aid and standing watches night after night, scanning the skies for a glimpse of an Axis plane. In government drives women and small children collected scrap rubber, wastepaper, aluminum, tin cans, and toothpaste tubes. Housewives salvaged cooking grease and rolled Red Cross bandages — two and a half billion of them, from Pearl Harbor to V-J Day. A Seattle shoemaker gave six tons of rubber heels. "Cotton Ed" Smith contributed the rubber mat that supported his favorite spittoon. In Boston, Beacon Hill held a black-tie scrap rally, donations to which included an eighty-year-old Gatling gun, a buggy, and Governor Leverett Saltonstall's rowing machine.

Hollywood helped kill time during the long wait. It was primarily addressing itself to GIs; during the war 982 movies were filmed and 34,232 prints sent overseas. The pictures were also available to civilians, and theaters were jammed nightly. These were the years of *H. M. Pulham, Esq.* (Robert Young), *The Man Who Came to Dinner* (Monty Woolley), *Woman of the Year* (Katharine Hepburn, Spencer Tracy), *My Gal Sal* (Victor Mature), *This Above All* (Tyrone Power, Joan Fontaine), *The Song of Bernadette* (Jennifer Jones), *Going My Way* (Bing Crosby, Barry Fitzgerald), *Double Indemnity* (Fred MacMurray, Barbara Stanwyck, Edward G. Robinson), *The Outlaw* (Jane Russell), *For Whom the Bell Tolls* (Gary Cooper and Ingrid Bergman), *Saratoga Trunk* (Cooper and Bergman again), *The Lost Weekend* (Ray Milland), *Casablanca* (all the immortals), Hitchcock's *Shadow of a Doubt*, and *Bambi*. As usual, show business had some bad moments, including one when press agents joyfully announced that Lassie had given birth to a litter of puppies — whereupon a veterinarian revealed that Lassie was male. Still, the level of screen quality remained high, an exceptional achievement when it is remembered that many reviewers were testing not only excellence but patriotism as well. Dorothy Thompson faulted *Lifeboat* because she thought Hitchcock made the Nazi more competent than his fellow passengers, and Bosley Crowther of the *New York Times* agreed that it was "a strangely undemocratic film, excusable on no basis, even in our enlightened society." Hitchcock protested that he had been producing a thriller, not a message; his demurrer was filed in wastebaskets. Even so professional and detached a critic as the *New Yorker's* Wolcott Gibbs wrote that John Steinbeck's *The Moon Is Down* evinced "a curious tenderness toward the Germans." Audiences were more tolerant; they had come for other reasons. More than ever, with so many people so far from home and family, movies offered brief asylum and tranquillity.

In these years the mass media were also a bond between those who were separated, continents apart, for years. The media gave the lonely something in common when they had little else. Some of it was cloying; "White Christmas," America's first hit tune of the war, was a bleat of self-pity, and "I'll Be Home for Christmas" was even worse. Some was just obnoxious. There were times — as when Jimmy Savo and the rest of the country were singing, "You gets no bread with ONE meatball" — which were almost unbearable for people with sensitive eardrums. "Makes No Difference Now" and "You Are My Sunshine" fell in the same category, and it is a depressing fact that throughout the war Nelson Eddy was the highest-paid singer in the United States. But Broadway promised a brighter tomorrow. *Bloomer Girl, I Remember Mama, The Voice of the Turtle,* and *Harvey* were entering their lusty youth. In the summer of 1942 two men down on their luck, Richard Rodgers and Oscar Hammerstein II, had begun experimenting with a dog-eared script called *Green Grow the Lilacs.* As a play, it had closed in 1931 after only sixty-four performances. "The RH factor," as *Life* later called it, transformed the turkey into *Oklahoma!* It opened at the St. James on March 31, 1943, and before it closed in 1948 it had played 2,248 performances — then a record for musicals. Meanwhile a twenty-six-year-old musician named Leonard Bernstein had composed *On the Town,* another rollicking musical. For the first time in fifteen years ticket scavengers were lurking in Broadway alleys.

Americans on the home front were reading more. Crossley and Hooper raters reported that radio was still the country's prime source of entertainment, with *Fibber McGee and Molly* and *Town Meeting of the Air* leading the pack, but the biggest audiences gathered at news time. In radio, as in bookstores and libraries, the great swing from fiction to nonfiction had begun. The Pentagon was the world's biggest publisher; in 1945 alone it distributed over sixty million copies of its armed services editions, covering every conceivable topic, and while their double-column format was irritating, they were read hungrily and often sent home. New titles were: Marion Hargrove *See Here, Private Hargrove,* Major Alexander de Seversky *Victory Through Air Power,* Ilka Chase *Past Imperfect,* Elliot Paul *The Last Time I Saw Paris,* William L. White *They Were Expendable,* Richard Tregaskis *Guadalcanal Diary,* John Hersey *A Bell for Adano,* Willkie *One World,* and Ernie Pyle *Here Is Your War* and *Brave Men.* Two clues to a major postwar issue, Richard Wright's *Black Boy* and Lillian Smith's *Strange Fruit,* were hardly noticed by social scientists, though they sold well.

The biggest sellers were magazines. Every popular periodical in the United States increased its sales during the war; in 1944 advertisers invested a hundred million dollars more in them than in 1942. Here again, as Eric Hopkins observed at the time, "Their percentage of nonfiction has . . . been steadily rising; for one thing, facts since 1939 have been outrunning fantasy." (They would continue to do so; by the 1970s serious fiction would be nearly obsolescent.) Magazines for women were of special interest. To countless numbers of their subscribers the war was a four-year bore. Of the 16 million volunteers and draftees who wore a uniform between 1941 and 1945, only a quarter-million were female. At any given time the size of the military establishment was 12 million males — the fittest 12 million — withdrawn from a population of 131 million. So great an imbalance inevitably meant masses of frustrated women.

On blind dates with servicemen, girls had about them an air of enterprise if not of aggression; they weren't wholly jesting when they called their cosmetics "war paint." Older women were more subtle. Lacking counsel from the high priests of Paris, Manhattan's couturiers copied military uniforms — a giveaway to where feminine thoughts were. One popular evening gown was adorned with a huge swooping Air Corps wing of gold lamé, beginning at one hip and curving upward across the bosom to the opposite shoulder. Eisenhower jackets were models for evening wraps or blouses with drawstring waists. Imitations of British commando berets made very dashing hats for daytime wear, and girls who had no intention of joining the Women's Army Corps wore copies of WAC hats decked out with sequins. Even the cloth shortages were exploited; the "Dido," a sort of outsize romper suit, became a playsuit by day and pajamas at night.

Putting horns on overseas GIs was just about the most unpopular thing a soldier's wife could do, and she wasn't often tempted anyhow; as a popular song of the day put it, "They're Either Too Young or Too Old." Doomed to purdah, married women in large numbers took to wearing slacks. The home front wasn't much of a life for them. The younger wives were prey to secret misgivings. Many weddings had been held just before the troop transports left, and the lonely brides wondered whether lasting marriages could be built upon impulse. The tough ones turned to booze; by 1943 the ratio of male to female alcoholics had jumped from 1-to-5 to 1-to-2. Others buried themselves in Emily Post or Dorothy Dix, or lived vicariously with Oona O'Neill, who, to the disgust of her playwriting father, had been named debutante of the year by the Stork Club. Once again, however, the multitude turned to magazines — in particular to three of them created during the war with a feminine mystique in mind: Street & Smith's *Mademoiselle*, Condé Nast's *Glamour*, and Walter Annenberg's *Seventeen*.

Here another wartime phenomenon appears: the emerging adolescent. The end of the Depression had restored interest in nubility. At the same time, high school students whose mothers were working for Lockheed or Boeing came home to a key beneath the doormat, and with so much cash around they either received allowances or earned money themselves. Lester Markel, editor of the *New York Times Magazine*, began trying to work the word "teen-ager" into articles, but the country wasn't quite ready for it yet. High school boys, intent upon military service, seemed more grim than carefree. The girls were gayer and more spirited, and because they all wore short socks they were called bobby-soxers.

The fashions of the swing generation were dead or dying; saddle shoes had been replaced by flat-soled loafers, cardigan sweater sets by Sloppy Joe sweaters, and convertible raincoats by the steady's parka, worn with — another omen — blue jeans. For a while jeans were accompanied by a vogue for men's white shirts (with the shirttails always flapping loose); after V-J Day fathers and older brothers would return to find the closets empty. Beer jackets were still around, but scarcely recognizable to aging jitterbugs; bobby-soxers had decorated them with the divisional insignia of boyfriends, real or imagined, in the service. Another rage was the wearing of rings of black jet symbolizing absent GI friends, and bobby-soxers congregating after school for a bull session (not yet a rap), if asked what they were doing, would reply, "Just messing around."

Yo-Yos, slumber parties, mismatched shoes and socks, striped football stockings — their capacity for fads was no more tasteless or greater than that of middle-class youth of the 1930s. But there was a difference. The country had changed. Older Americans were more inclined to watch them, listen to them, and indulge them. On some issues the generations were united. One was organized labor. They were against it. Looking at labor's wartime record, one wonders why. General Brehon Somervell, the Army's chief of supply, told a Senate committee, "Make no mistake about it, no one has suffered from a lack of supplies. The boys at the front have had everything that could possibly be moved to the front." But the United Mine Workers' ill-timed demands for overtime and extra pay seemed almost designed to wreck labor's reputation, and James C. Petrillo, czar of the musicians' union, was just as inept. Petrillo was a special bogey for bobby-soxers. He demanded royalties for bands and orchestras whose records were played over radio stations, and for twenty-seven months he kept most popular music from the public. Youth seemed to feel that a strike was directed at it, though the real victims were the big swing bands. Between Petrillo's ban, rationing, the cost of road trips, and changes in public taste — bobby-soxers preferred sentimental ballads — the great bands broke up, and the swing era that the GIs had loved quietly died.

Parents beamed. They had favored ballads all along. They were proud of their children's participation in the rubber and paper drives and delighted by much in the new youth culture. In 1944 the country's top song hit was a novelty song for bobby-soxers, "Swinging on a Star." With almost no male college students, there were hardly any college athletes (an exception was West Point, which built its great point-a-minute team around Doc Blanchard and Junior Davis). Attention was thus diverted to high school teams, and revisions of rules made basketball for the first time an exciting spectator sport. Dads and sons could go together, just as moms and daughters could pore over the same features in *Glamour*. Youth is always excited by innovation, and in the summer of 1944 adolescents were among the first to adopt the invention of a Hungarian refugee in Argentina, a pen which used a ball bearing instead of a point. It was imported under the brand name Stratopen, but users simply called them ball-point pens. Approving adults began buying them, too. On everything from politics to writing instruments, it seemed, the generations on the home front were at peace.

Then a huge gap yawned. The guilty party was a frail, pallid, bow-tied, hundred-and-thirty-five-pound crooner with jug-handle ears and a starved look. He was Francis Albert Sinatra, last seen in this narrative tagging along behind the Harry James band. To his worshippers he looked vulnerable, innocent, and in his teens. Actually he wasn't any of them. Born in a cold-water Hoboken tenement, the son of a Sicilian bantamweight prizefighter, he was a tough, profane loner who believed his patent-leather lungs would carry him to stardom; of any rival he would snarl, "I can sing that son of a bitch off the stage any day of the week." Far from being in high school, he was in his mid-twenties. His explanation for the illusion was, "I'm twenty-five. I look maybe nineteen. Most kids feel I'm one of them — the pal next door, say. So maybe they feel they know me. And that's the way I want it to be. What the hell, they're nice kids."

Sinatra wasn't healthy enough for the Army — he had an occupational handicap, a punctured eardrum — so he overcompensated with fierce drive. His real appetite was for fame. Swing sidemen were often adept at sabotaging crooners, but when Buddy Rich taunted Sinatra by playing little drum riffs during tender moments in his songs, Rich wound up with a mouse and a fat lip. Frankie's obsession with success meant that he couldn't remain in any bandleader's shadow very long. After six months with James he switched to Tommy Dorsey. He attracted some attention with his versions of "Fools Rush In," "Night and Day," and "White Christmas"; then he bought out his Dorsey contract and hired a press agent. He was ready to make it alone. On the night of December 30, 1942, he was singing with all he had on the stage of New York's Paramount Theater when something happened in the audience. A girl in the twelfth row who hadn't eaten lunch fainted — or "swooned." Another girl, startled, stood up and screamed. No one knows exactly what happened in the next few seconds, but Sinatra continued to sing — nobody was going to scream *him* down — and by the time he had finished the theater was a charivari, with every girl in the theater on her feet, shrieking.

The screeching spread like the plague. He became known as the Voice. Wherever the Voice appeared, pandemonium followed. His weekly mail rose to five thousand letters, and two thousand Frankie fan clubs were organized across the country. Autograph hunters chased him through drugstores, restaurants, department stores, and his home. They climbed his roof to peer into his bedroom. If he walked in mud, they dug up the earth and dried it to preserve his footprints. They weren't all kids and they weren't all nice. Twice he was almost strangled by hoydens tugging for possession of his bow tie. They tried to tear his clothes off, with considerable success, and one harpy in her forties cornered him in the Waldorf, ripped open her blouse, and insisted that he autograph her brassiere. By 1944 his reappearance at the Paramount for a three-week engagement was greeted by thirty thousand wailing adolescents; controlling them required 421 riot policemen, twenty policewomen, and over twenty squad cars.

In less time than the GIs needed to capture Sicily, the Voice — alias Frank Swoonatra, alias the King of Swoon — was rich. He had signed contracts guaranteeing him a weekly appearance on the Lucky Strike Hit Parade, an annual RKO movie, and unprecedented royalties from Columbia Records. His annual income was over a million dollars. Despite wartime controls, he seemed to be spending most of it. In Hollywood he built a pink house with every known convenience and some that had previously been unknown; to spare himself the trouble of rising to close the drapes on one wall he installed a gadget which cost $7,000. His tailored clothes were gaudy and enormous in every dimension, from the floppy bow ties and high-waisted slacks to the bulging padded shoulders. His friends, and by now he had accumulated a lot of them, gathered around him like barons doting on a king. They felt privileged just to be in his company, but he made them happy in other ways; among his idiosyncrasies was handing out 150-dollar gold cigarette lighters as casually as Major Bowes distributed Mars Bars. His feminine confidantes were changing, too. Before the war he had married his childhood sweetheart, Nancy Barbate, and early in his celebrity he answered all matrimonial questions with "Nobody comes before my wife Nancy. That goes for now and all time." Then he stopped answering the questions. Ahead lay Ava Gardner and, much later, Mia Farrow.

Frankie's talent, or lack of it, had become a burning issue, like General Patton's slapping of a soldier. "Sinatra's voice," *Time* said, "has become a national feature comparable to Yosemite Valley," but *Life*, *Time*'s sister publication, thought that the "swooner-crooner" made "every song sound like every other song" because he knew only one rhythm: *large alla marcia funebre*. The *New York Herald Tribune* quoted a congressman as saying, "The Lone Ranger and Frank Sinatra are the prime instigators of juvenile delinquency in America." Elsa Maxwell accused the Voice of "musical illiteracy" and suggested his fans be given "Sinatraceptives." Even his old boss Harry James conceded that Frankie's new wardrobe made him look "like a wet rag." Someone told Bing Crosby that "A voice like Sinatra's comes only once in a lifetime." Bing replied, "Sure, but why does it have to be in *my* lifetime?"

Parents were angry and confused. The hero of the hour was supposed to be a strapping, steel-helmeted GI in full battle array, leaping through surf to storm an enemy shore. Frankie, in the idiom of the time, looked as though he had been strained through a condom. Adolescent refugees from

Europe thought him a noisome freak. A fugitive from a German concentration camp, herself seventeen, inquired, "Is there no way to make those kids come to their senses? The time they are wasting outside the Paramount Theater could be used for other purposes — for instance, to help win this war." Her American peers went right on shrieking, and speculation over the source of his magic grew. "As a visible object of female adulation," *Newsweek* observed, "Sinatra is baffling."

Psychiatrists and psychologists denied being baffled. They recalled the medieval dance craze and spoke of "mammary hyperesthesia," a "maternal urge to feed the hungry," "mass frustrated love," and "mass hypnosis." Some of Frankie's flip critics said the same thing more pointedly: "It's as if he had musk glands instead of vocal cords," and, "Let's face it — Sinatra's just about the only male left around." The last seems the likeliest. Girls might sing of boys absent in the New Guinea bush — "He's 1-A in the Army and he's A-1 in my heart" — but a male in hand was worth two of them. Besides, it wasn't like dating a 4-F. That would have been treacherous. This was merely a bobby-soxer rite.

If older civilians didn't understand that, the GIs he was replacing did. It is not too much to say that by the end of the war Sinatra had become the most hated man in the Army, Navy, Air Corps, and Marine Corps. Like the bobby-soxers, Frankiephobes in uniform saw in the Voice a symbol; to them he stood for all available civilians. Frankie made just one USO tour in Italy, and that was after V-E Day, when the Axis guns had been spiked. Then he flew off sneering that the USO was strictly for cheap hacks. The *Stars and Stripes* commented that "Mice make women faint, too," and Marlene Dietrich, who had performed near the front, observed that, after all, "you could hardly expect the European Theater to be like the Paramount."

Exactly five weeks before Frankie's first hungry girl fainted in that twelfth row, John J. McCloy ordered the acquisition of the Los Alamos Ranch School for Boys, where Robert Oppenheimer had been educated as a child, for a special war project. Oppenheimer had recommended Los Alamos because it was isolated, and the other Allied scientists agreed that they must have privacy if they were to stand any chance of building a bomb before the Nazis — a possibility most of them felt was exceedingly remote at the time. By now, late in 1942, the Americans and their refugee colleagues were desperate. They had made little progress on the bomb, despite Roosevelt's commitment. Allen Dulles was reporting from Switzerland that large consignments of uranium and heavy water were entering the Reich every week. Germany's atomic physicists were the finest in the world. Moreover, the scientists in America suspected that their own project had been compromised. That autumn two German agents had been picked up in the wild hills near Oak Ridge, Tennessee. How they got there, and what became of them, are questions Washington still prefers to leave unanswered. But coupled with other evidence, it added one more touch of authenticity to the nightmare the physicists then thought they saw in the future: Hitler with an arsenal of atomic weapons and the Allies with nothing.

Of this much they were now certain: such a bomb was practical. The hypothesis had been sound from the outset, but there had been a hitch in its application. In theory, a chain reaction should have developed when neutrons were introduced into a U-235 pile. The neutrons would split the U-235 atoms, each of which would liberate from one to three neutrons — which, in turn, would split more atoms, and so on, until the critical mass was reached. Obviously they couldn't permit that mass to form in a laboratory; that was why they used graphite, to slow neutrons down while they observed the process. In practice, they found, some neutrons went astray and some were "cannibalized" by the pile. A chain reaction was possible only if successive "generations" of neutrons became larger and larger. This was christened the K factor, otherwise known as "the great god K." It was reached under the following conditions. If 100 neutrons which had caused fission in 100 U-235 atoms gave birth to a generation of new neutrons, 105 of which were left to cause fission, the ratio would be 105 to 100, and the K factor would have a value of 1.05. The third generation would be 105 multiplied by 1.05, and so on, until the mass was formed. As William L. Laurence put it, "When the K factor is greater than one, the pile will be chain-reacting, as the birth rate will be greater than the death rate." Conversely, if 100 neutrons produced only 99, the K factor, 0.99, would be inadequate. By purifying the graphite in early experiments, the best they could get in those early months was a birth rate of .87 per 100. Their greatest problem lay in the impurity of the uranium. Dr. Arthur H. Compton called the Westinghouse director of research and — at a time when the world's total hoard of pure uranium metal did not exceed a few grams — asked him, "How soon can Westinghouse supply three tons of pure uranium?" He heard a gagging sound at the other end of the line, but the firm's response was an illustration of American industry's versatility in World War II. Uranium fabrication was stepped up from eight ounces a day to over five hundred pounds, and by November 1942 Westinghouse had delivered the three tons.

The delivery address could hardly have aroused less interest. On Ellis Avenue in Chicago, between Fifty-sixth and Fifty-seventh streets, the ivied Gothic walls of University of Chicago buildings parted to reveal a recess and, within, a door. Beyond that door was a large squash court which had been unused since the outbreak of war. The court lay directly beneath the west stands of Stagg Field, and scarcely anyone had come this way since the university had abandoned intercollegiate football. It was there, that November, that a pile of unprecedented size was being assembled with materials of unique purity. Two carbon companies, working with the National Bureau of Standards, had turned out a graphite highly resistant to neutrons. Other bureau scientists had joined Professor Frank H. Spedding of Iowa State College in further improving the Westinghouse uranium; in the new method the metal was transformed into lumps called "Spedding's eggs." Lastly, engineers were prepared to create a vacuum in the pile — by enclosing it in an enormous square balloon and pumping the air out — to prevent neutron absorption by nitrogen. Dr. Compton predicted that the new mass would yield a K factor "somewhere between 1.04 and 1.05"; others believed it might reach 1.07.

So great a prospect of success raised new questions. Atoms had been split before, but no one in history had ever created a viable chain reaction, and it was impossible to gauge the efficiency of decelerating techniques. The great god K might defy their checks and restraints, might break loose and take all Chicago, or even Illinois, with it. To reduce the risk, seven strips of cadmium and three rods of boron steel — cadmium and boron being gluttonous consumers of neutrons — were passed completely through the pile; sliding them in and out was expected to give the Frankensteins control over the monster they were creating. No one could be sure that would be successful, however, so two young physicists volunteered to form what was called the "suicide squad." The two would stand on scaffolding overlooking the pile with buckets of cadmium solution in their hands. If all other controls failed and the apparatus started to go, they would hurl the liquid at it.

Layer after layer was added, and the speed of neutron counters grew with the pile, until, during the bitterly cold night of December 1–2, 1942, the twelfth layer was in place. The contrivance now weighed 12,400 pounds, and the rapid clicking of the counters was unmistakable. "We knew then," W. H. Zinn later told William L. Laurence, "that if we pulled out the control rods, the thing would pop." At 3:30 the following afternoon, with Fermi present and the suicide squad in position overhead, all the controls except one cadmium strip were removed; then that was partly withdrawn. The counter clicking was so intense that it reminded one of the witnesses of a burring drill. The K factor mounted to 0.98, 0.99, 1.00 — and then 1.01, 1.02, 1.03, 1.04, 1.05, 1.06, 1.07, 1.08, 1.09, and 1.10. They had done it: each successive generation of neutrons would now exceed the last. Pure science had gone as far as it could. The chain was now self-perpetuating; transforming it into a deliverable bomb had become a technological problem.

On that same December 2, the technological issue was being discussed only three blocks away, in room 209 of the university's Eckhert Hall. Neither group was aware of the other's presence in the city. Security was very tight; Roosevelt wanted it that way. The President's attitude toward the Manhattan Project was ambivalent, and, like so many of FDR's traits, a reflection of the American national character. Instinctively he trusted people, enjoyed sharing knowledge, and wanted the United States to contribute toward the world's store of learning. But while he spoke of brotherhood — and meant it — he also liked secrets. As James MacGregor Burns has noted, "If Roosevelt was both realist and idealist, both fixer and preacher, both a prince and a soldier, the reason lay not only in his own mind and background, but also in his society and its traditions. Americans have long had both moralistic and realistic traditions."

In Chicago the President was being realistic; the squash court and Eckhert Hall might as well have been separated by a continent. Nevertheless, they were part of the same design, destined to merge in a B-29 bomb bay thirty-one months later. General Groves had called them here to review the Chicago Metallurgical Project. They were America's technological elite — captains of heavy industry, professors from Cal Tech and MIT — and the general was asking them to take a lot on faith. They were being asked to produce material they had never seen for a purpose unknown to them. Their only assurances were that the project was vital to the war effort and that Washington would pay the bills.

They agreed, and beginning that month, contracts were signed with clauses which must surely rank among the vaguest in industrial law. Groves pledged four hundred million dollars for a down payment; the ultimate cost would exceed two billion. Beyond that the contractors knew very little, and the few who had to be told certain secrets were forbidden to mention them even to their wives. They couldn't talk to the scientists because the scientists had, in effect, been removed from society; all their families knew of them was an address: U.S. Army, Post Office Box 1663.

The secrecy seemed excessive to the physicists working at Los Alamos. Certainly some aspects of it seem to have been absurd. The man most closely watched was J. Robert Oppenheimer, and the man watching him was one Boris Pash, an overweight former football coach at Hollywood High School whom the Army's G2 had transmogrified into a specialist in "Communist infiltration." Pash fixed his professional eye on Oppenheimer when he heard that the scientist had contributed generously to liberal causes before the war and had twice been on the verge of marrying Dr. Jean Tatlock, a San Francisco psychiatrist who was also a Communist. In 1943 Oppenheimer picked Jean up at her Telegraph Hill home and took her to the Top of the Mark for a drink. He told her that he would be unable to see her again for months, perhaps years, and that because his work was classified he couldn't tell her what it was or where he would be doing it. Then he disappeared. Seven months later, despairing of ever seeing him again, she committed suicide. Pash, meantime, had shadowed them in San Francisco and had completely misinterpreted their meeting; he thought Oppenheimer had been slipping secrets to a fellow Commie. Telling his superiors that he was on to Oppenheimer's little game, he demanded that the physicist be fired. Groves replied that this was impossible: "Irrespective of the information you have concerning Mr. Oppenheimer, he is absolutely essential to the project."

All this might be dismissed as low comedy were it not for the uncomfortable fact that real Communist spies, following instructions from Moscow, were casting a highly professional espionage net around Los Alamos. The control was a certain Anatoli A. Yakovlev, who operated out of New York's Soviet consulate. Yakovlev worked through Harry Gold, a Philadelphian and a former industrial spy. Another thread in Yakovlev's web led from Julius and Ethel Rosenberg in New York to David Greenglass, Ethel's brother, who as a privileged Army enlisted man at Los Alamos had access to almost every blueprint, sketch, or valuable document and was bright enough to know which would be most valuable to Russians interested in building a bomb of their own. Greenglass wasn't Yakovlev's prize, though. The real treasure was Klaus Emil Fuchs. Fuchs, like Oppenheimer, Compton, and Fermi, was a highly gifted atomic physicist — a member of the Los Alamos inner circle. A native German, he had fled to England when the Nazis started rounding up their enemies. His hatred of Hitler and his loyalty to the Allied war effort were never questioned, and as a naturalized subject of the United Kingdom he had been granted top clearance. Nobody had asked why the Nazis had been after a theoretical physicist; such questions weren't raised then. Only after the war, when the Soviet apparatus came apart, would Fuchs's friends learn that he was a whole-souled Communist.

Usually Harry Gold let other carriers pick up data from Greenglass, but he often met Fuchs, and on one trip he saw both of them. His call on David Greenglass and David's pregnant young wife Ruth has been memorialized by the top of a raspberry Jell-O box, just as the Hiss-Chambers case would be remembered for a pumpkin. Julius Rosenberg had torn the Jell-O top in half and given one piece to his brother-in-law, David. When a man bearing the other half appeared, Julius had said, David should tell the man everything he knew, in the interest of "sharing information for scientific purposes." Gold was therefore welcomed to the Greenglass flat upstairs at 209 North High Street, Albuquerque, when he said, "Julius sent me," and produced his half of the box top. David dutifully produced a sheaf of paper upon which he had set down the best information he could get. It was very good: working in the smallest of the top-secret technical shops at Los Alamos, he had copied several schematic drawings of flat-type lens mold experiments for detonating an atomic bomb. This device bore little relationship to lenses as laymen know them. It was a mix of high explosives which would focus detonation waves as a glass lens focuses light waves, thus triggering the bomb. In Russian hands it would permit Soviet scientists to skip an expensive and time-consuming experimental stage. When David Greenglass put those sketches in Harry Gold's hands, he was making history. He was also opening his wife's eyes. Until that moment he had persuaded Ruth that in some obscure way they really were sharing information for the good of all mankind. But when Gold handed David an envelope bearing $500 in cash, her illusions vanished. After their visitor had left she cried, "Now I see how it is: you turn over the information and you get paid. Why, it's just — it's just like C.O.D.!" The weakest link in the Los Alamos to Moscow chain had just been formed.

Gold had brought no money for Klaus Fuchs. He had offered him $1,500 last time, and Fuchs had politely declined it. He wasn't a man to be bought; he was betraying the bomb project on principle. In Santa Fe Fuchs picked Gold up on Alameda Street, as arranged, and took him on a country ride in his battered Chevrolet coupe. When they parted, Gold was carrying a thick packet of typed notes on the application of theoretical fission to the building of a bomb. It was highly technical, way over Gold's head, but Moscow was elated. The information from both sources, Yakovlev was instructed to tell Gold, was "particularly excellent and very valuable." Six years later a production chief of the Atomic Energy Commission was shown duplicates of the Greenglass sketches. He said, "Why, they show the atomic bomb, substantially as perfected!"

How much this apparatus helped the Soviet Union when it was supplemented by data from Morton Sobell and Alan Nunn May, two other spies, is a matter of conjecture, even among scientists. It was all a question of time. The Russians had the theoretical knowledge and the technologists; sooner or later they would have found the great god K. Greenglass may, in fact, have given them nothing at all. There was really only one way to build the bomb. Edward Teller described its most intimate mechanism — two hemispheres brought into contact until the mass reaches the critical point and detonates — in an early Los Alamos seminar. Beyond that lay a farrago of details: the amount of U-235 needed, the size of the two halves, the speed with which they must collide, the scattering angle, the range of the neutrons to be projected by the chain reaction, and so on. It seemed endless. It was certainly dangerous. Dr. O. R. Frisch, Lise Meitner's nephew and the supervisor of this task, nearly lost his life in one experiment, and two other physicists were in fact killed.

Luckily for those working near Harry Dagnian, the first of them, he was holding only a small amount of fissionable material when he accidentally set off a chain reaction. It lasted only a fraction of a second and he was instantly hospitalized, but his right hand had been saturated with radiation. Within an hour he had lost his sense of touch. Gamma rays had penetrated his skin; his viscera were deteriorating. He became delirious, his hair fell out, the white corpuscles in his blood increased, and he died in agony. After that the tensions in Frisch's labs increased perceptibly. Indeed, the entire settlement was on edge, especially when a carefree young Canadian named Louis Slotin was looking for "the crit." Slotin was literally playing with cosmic fire — he called it "twisting the dragon's tail" — and if he had been guilty of a really big blunder, no one would have survived to tell of it. Los Alamos would have been annihilated, Hiroshima and Nagasaki spared, and history greatly altered.

Slotin was an adventurer and a follower of causes. He had fought with the Loyalists in Spain and with the RAF during the Battle of Britain.

Grounded for nearsightedness, he had drifted into the Manhattan Project because he had the right scientific training. Under Frisch he found his métier, though many of his associates ardently wished he were back in a Spitfire. He would tinker away with two live hemispheres, using screwdrivers to slide them toward one another on a rod while he watched, engrossed. It was like Russian roulette. Sooner or later the law of probability would claim its own and he would neglect to separate the halves in time. It happened. One day a screwdriver slipped. The hemispheres came too close to one another; the lab was filled with a blinding blue glare. He tore the halves apart, breaking the chain and saving the community. He knew that in the process he had forfeited his own life. On the way to the hospital with a friend who had been working near him, he said, "You'll come through all right. But I haven't the faintest chance myself." After nine days of suffering he died. The man assigned to study the incident and ascertain what, if anything, could be learned from it, was Klaus Fuchs.

Most other physicists grumbled about security arrangements — Niels Bohr never became accustomed to his code name "Nicholas Butler" and kept forgetting it — but Fuchs, who knew the real joke, said little. Or rather, Fuchs knew *half* the joke. The Germans remained an enigma. Hitler kept talking about secret weapons, and early in 1944 he unleashed three of them: jet aircraft, snorkel submarines, and his V-1s, the first buzz bombs. None of the intelligence coming from the Reich undercut the original hypothesis of the scientific community in America. Either Hitler had a bomb, they reasoned, or he was about to get one. He might have an arsenal of them deployed as his last line of defense. The man was capable of anything. Today it is impossible to re-create the terror, hatred, and awe that the German Führer roused; yet without a semblance of it, the motivation of the atomic scientists in the New Mexico desert remains obscure.

The issue was discussed on the highest levels in Washington and London (though not in Moscow; Roosevelt and Churchill rightly suspected that Stalin would not share the discoveries of Soviet laboratories). In the autumn of 1943 a special intelligence unit, to be landed in Normandy on D-Day, was formed under the code name Alsos, the Greek word for Groves. Its members, though dressed as soldiers, would wear on their battle dress a recognition badge bearing the alpha sign in white and a jagged line of red forked lightning. Their mission was to collect data about the extent of the Reich's atomic research. Such documents would be translated and appraised on the spot by the team's senior scientist, Dr. Samuel A. Goudsmit of Holland, a distinguished experimental physicist whose hobby was the study of new developments in criminal investigation.

On Thursday, January 7, 1943, the President of the United States delivered his tenth annual State of the Union address to a joint session of Congress — "The Axis powers knew that they must win the war in 1942 or eventually lose everything," he said; "I do not need to tell you that our enemies did not win the war in 1942" — and late Saturday evening, when the capital was quiet, a small cavalcade of limousines glided away from the south portico of the White House, turned right on Fifteenth Street, and parked at a little-known train siding near the Bureau of Engraving and Printing. The President's train was waiting. Following him into the "Ferdinand Magellan," his private car, were Harry Hopkins, Dr. Ross T. McIntire, and a glittering staff of generals and flag officers. In Miami a Pan American Clipper waited to fly the presidential party across the Atlantic, to Casablanca and Winston Churchill.

This was to be a year of Allied summit meetings. After Casablanca — where he sized up Eisenhower and announced his controversial demand for "unconditional surrender" from the enemy coalition — the commander in chief would confer in Quebec (Churchill again), Washington (Churchill and joint military staffs), Cairo (Churchill and Chiang Kai-shek), Hawaii (Nimitz and MacArthur), Teheran (Churchill and Stalin), and then back to Cairo (Churchill once more). During that year the torch of leadership passed from the British Prime Minister to the American President, and both men knew it. The shift had nothing to do with personalities. America was putting more men and matériel into the conflict, and American generals, notably Eisenhower, would be commanding combined forces in the great battles ahead.

Roosevelt's performance as commander in chief was not without critics; nothing in his life was. Stalin believed FDR's insistence on unconditional surrender would merely prolong the war by uniting the German people, and most historians agree with him. In the Pacific the President may have given MacArthur too strong a hand in what was essentially a war for sea power and was to be won by Admiral Nimitz. But no one doubted that Roosevelt, from 1943 on, was the commander of Allied armies and navies. As early as November 1942 William D. Hassett, a special assistant to Roosevelt, observed in his diary, "The President becomes more and more the central figure in the global war, the source of initiative and authority in action, and, of course, of responsibility." Louis Johnson cabled from New Delhi, "The magic name over here is Roosevelt," and most professional soldiers admired his leadership. Eisenhower wrote, "With some of Mr. Roosevelt's political acts I could never possibly agree. But I knew him solely in his capacity as leader in a nation at war — and in that capacity he seemed to me to fulfill all that could possibly be expected of him." Stimson said that "the Army never had a finer commander in chief," and Major George Fielding Eliot wrote that FDR's grasp of total and global strategy made him "one of the greatest war presidents." American casualties were proportionately lighter than those of any other World War II power, yet on Navy Day 1944 the President could say that during the past year Americans in uniform had participated in twenty-seven landings on enemy beachheads and "every one of those twenty-seven D-days has been a triumphant success."

He certainly didn't look like a military genius. In his flannel shirt, old hat, and carelessly knotted bow tie — his invariable costume when visiting troops — he looked more like a hearty grandfather casually dressed for a weekend of trout fishing. But then, the troops he commanded were casual, too. The United States was not a European country; it was a different kind of nation, and no one represented it better than the American in the White House. David Lilienthal might write that FDR had "the handsomest fighting face in the world," and General Eisenhower might be dazzled by the President's gift for terrain, for grasping and remembering all the features of a countryside; to GIs and bluejackets, however, his greatest gift was his warmth, his concern, his appearance on the world scene as a shirt-sleeved President in a shirt-sleeved America. "As no other man in his time," Jonathan Daniels wrote, "he could speak to the American confidence always underlying American fears. And because he believed in the dignity of the American, he was never afraid to ask or expect America's courage." Nothing is more illustrative of the Roosevelt touch, of his sensitivity to the needs of people, than his visit to a military hospital in Hawaii. He had come to talk to generals and admirals, to plan the great offensives which would bring Japan to its knees. But before he left, he asked to be wheeled through the ward for combat victims whose arms and legs had been amputated. He smiled and waved; he said nothing; his presence said everything. Here was a man who had lost the use of both legs. He knew their bitterness; he had shared it. Yet he had overcome it to become President, and there was no reason for them to despair of their prewar dreams.

Roosevelt was tired now, and he looked it. The White House press corps was convinced he didn't want to run for President again in 1944, and he himself wrote Robert Hannegan, chairman of the Democratic National Committee, "All that is within me cries out to go back to my home on the Hudson River." But there were pressures to stay in office, too. Like any President, he was thinking of history's judgment. He had plans for postwar America; he was as committed to the United Nations as Wilson had been to the League of Nations. And then there were the letters: "Please President Roosevelt don't let us down now in this world of sorrow and trouble," one man wrote. "If we ever needed you it's now. I believe within my heart God put you here in this world to be our guiding star." There were petitions, one signed by over six thousand steelworkers: "We know you are weary — yet we cannot afford to permit you to step down." And from the Third Reich came the voice of Douglas Chandler, a former Hearst man who had turned traitor to broadcast from Berlin under the name Paul Revere: "Get that man out of the house that was once white!"

Roosevelt was politician enough to be swayed, if ever so slightly, by such voices. He eyed Wendell Willkie wistfully. Both men saw things alike, and each secretly admired the other. The President called Sam Rosenman to his office and asked him to serve as an emissary to Willkie. "We ought to have two parties — one liberal and the other conservative," FDR said. "As it is now, each party is split by dissenters." He thought the parties should be realigned after the election, and asked Rosenman to sound out Willkie. "You tell the President that I'm ready to devote almost full time to this," Willkie told Rosenman. In 1940 they might have worked something out — though it is hard to see how — but this was four years later. Willkie had just been discredited in the Wisconsin Republican primary, running be-hind Dewey, MacArthur, and Stassen. He too was tired; he was angry at the Republican Old Guard, and disillusioned with the political process. He was also sick; on October 8 he died after three heart attacks.

The passing of the Republicans' most impressive presidential candidate since Hughes in 1916 brought out a vindictive streak in the GOP anti-Willkie Old Guard. "One-worlder" became their pet sneer. Spokesmen for the extreme right, silenced since Pearl Harbor, reappeared in 1944 — Lawrence Dennis; Mrs. Elizabeth Dilling; and Joseph E. McWilliams, who alluded to FDR as the "Jew King." Congressman Fish's secretary was convicted of perjury for testifying that certain congressmen hadn't used their franking privileges to mail Nazi propaganda as late as November 1941. Newspapers like the *Chicago Tribune*, the *New York Daily News*, Eleanor ("Cissy") Patterson's *Washington Times-Herald,* and the Hearst chain refused to keep military secrets — one *Tribune* correspondent actually gave away American knowledge of the Purple Code, but the Japanese missed his story — and the President thought the Justice Department should crack down on them. The government did have a strong sedition case, but Attorney General Biddle didn't think jailing conservative pub-lishers in an election year would sit well with the electorate, so he side-tracked Roosevelt. Still, the issue was very much on the President's mind. Isolationists remained entrenched in the press and on Capitol Hill, and after victory they might drum up enough support in the country to sabotage American foreign policy. That threat appears to have been decisive. A week before the Democratic National Convention met the President wrote Hannegan:

> If the people command me to continue in this office and in this war I have as little right to withdraw as a soldier has to leave his post in the line.
>
> For myself I do not want to run. By next spring, I shall have been Pres-ident and Commander in Chief of the Armed Forces for twelve years. . . .
>
> Reluctantly, but as a good soldier, I repeat that I will accept and serve in this office, if I am so ordered by the Commander in Chief of us all — the sovereign people of the United States.

On July 20, while the convention was nominating him in Chicago, Roosevelt was perched on a towering California cliff, watching hinge-prowed Higgins boats land ten thousand marines in an amphibious re-hearsal. As he saw it, he was doing his job while the politicians went through their routine. But the quadrennial meeting of the Democrats has never been routine. United on Roosevelt's candidacy, united on the platform, they were in turmoil over the Vice Presidency. Either the President had overlooked the matter or couldn't make up his mind; the evidence suggests indecision. He thought Henry Wallace had done a poor job, neglecting his duties and needlessly bruising the congressional leadership, but he refused to disown him. Wallace believed he would stay on the ticket, and with reason; Roosevelt had written of him, in a letter to the convention chairman, "I like him and I respect him and he is my personal friend. For these reasons I personally would vote for his renomination if I were a delegate to the convention."

Yet William O. Douglas and Alben Barkley were just as sure that FDR preferred them, and Jimmy Byrnes thought he already had the President's endorsement. Harry Truman was equally certain that Byrnes had the inside track, and had agreed to nominate him. But with Roosevelt indifferent, the National Committee had been looking for the man who would hurt the President least. They decided upon Truman. He was a loyal Democrat, had gone down the line for administration bills on the Hill, came from a midwestern border state, and had led his committee investigating the war effort — a difficult task — with tact and skill. The President didn't know him, scarcely knew his name. When Hannegan raised it, FDR murmured, "Yes . . . yes . . . I put him in charge of that war investigating committee, didn't I?" Roosevelt had not had anything to do with it, of course, but Hannegan's reasoning made political sense. Roosevelt agreed; it would be Truman.

"My God!" the Missouri senator said when told. He was flabbergasted. Truman hadn't even considered running. Convinced only when he heard FDR's voice over the phone — characteristically he asked friends, "Why the hell didn't he tell me in the first place?" — he went off to square things with Byrnes. Even so, the convention took two ballots to nominate him. Then Roosevelt accepted the nomination in a radio address from the Marine Corps San Diego base while Americans were asking one another who Truman was. "The second Missouri compromise," the New York Times called him. "A triumph of the bosses," wrote James A. Hagerty. His opposite number, Republican vice presidential candidate John Bricker, said "Truman — that's his name, isn't it?" He scratched his head and murmured, "I never can remember that name." In its July 31 issue Time patronizingly referred to Roosevelt's running mate as "the gray little junior Senator from Missouri."

Thomas E. Dewey, who led the Republican ticket, was a man of wisdom and courage, and there is every reason to believe he would have made an able President. But the Democratic challenge was too great. Prosperity had returned, the people still identified the GOP with Hoover, the armed forces were chalking up victories every day, and FDR was by now the most experienced politician in U.S. history. "There is nothing I love so much as a good fight," he had once told the Times, and time had increased his enjoyment of it. His idea of fighting was to shadowbox with Old Guard

Republicans and ignore his opponent. These tactics had crushed Hoover, Landon, and Willkie; and in a celebrated speech he displayed a new and even deadlier weapon — derision. Singling out a congressional trio celebrated for obstructionist tactics — Joe Martin, Bruce Barton, and Hamilton Fish — he defended his achievements and said everyone approved except "Martin . . . Barton . . . and Fish." By the third time he used the phrase his audience had caught its cadence and was chanting with him, "Martin . . . Barton . . . and Fish." It was funny, and it was powerful political medicine. Even more effectively, he seized upon a GOP whispering campaign that he had left his Scottie behind on the Aleutian Islands and dispatched a destroyer to bring the dog back. In a voice edged with sarcasm he told the Teamsters Union — and the country, by radio — that "These Republican leaders have not been content with attacks on me, or my wife, or my sons. No, not content with that, they now include my little dog Fala. . . . I think I have a right to resent, to object to libelous statements about my dog."

Dewey was burning. The President's sardonic tone had reached him, and from then on, as someone remarked, the campaign was between "Roosevelt's dog and Dewey's goat." It seemed that each Roosevelt campaign became rougher than the last, as though presidential politics were powered by some invisible but malevolent engine. This one turned increasingly bitter. One GOP target was Sidney Hillman, whose CIO Political Action Committee (PAC) was organizing to bring out the working-class vote for FDR. The story went round that when Truman's name was suggested for the Democratic ticket, Roosevelt had said, "Clear it with Sidney." CLEAR IT WITH SIDNEY, read billboards across the country. SIDNEY HILLMAN AND EARL BROWDER'S COMMUNISTS HAVE REGISTERED. HAVE YOU? In the last weeks of the campaign Dewey returned again and again to the issue of Communism. Within a decade such charges would make politicians tremble, but in 1944, with Russia a welcome ally against Hitler, their value was doubtful.

Fortune favored the Republicans when Lewis B. Hershey, still director of the draft and now a major general, remarked in public that enlisted men could be kept in the Army as cheaply as discharging them and creating an agency to take care of them. General Hershey's name will reappear in this volume; his gaucheries were to enliven the administrations of other Presidents. In this instance, however, Roosevelt stopped him cold. Stimson was ordered to gag him and clarify the government's plans for rapid demobilization. But a general with foot-in-mouth disease wasn't to put Dewey in the White House anyhow. Neither were attacks on Fala or Sidney Hillman. Dewey needed an issue. Roosevelt was murdering him.

Speaking from his car on Chicago's Soldier Field, with a hundred thousand people in the amphitheater and another hundred thousand standing outside, the President said this was the strangest campaign in his career. The Republicans were calling the Democratic party incompetent and praising the legislation it had passed. They were saying that "Quarrelsome, tired old men" had built the greatest Army and Navy in the history of the world, that none of this would be changed, and "therefore it is time for a change. They also say in effect," said FDR, " 'Those inefficient and worn-out crackpots have really begun to lay the foundations of a lasting world peace. If you elect us, we will not change any of that, either. But,' they whisper, 'we'll do it in such a way that we won't lose the support even of Gerald Nye or Gerald Smith — we won't lose the support of any isolationist campaign contributor. Why, we will be able to satisfy even the *Chicago Tribune!*' "

His adversaries had one sound issue: Roosevelt's health. Had this been debated responsibly, with all medical evidence before the electorate, the outcome might have been different. But this was impossible. No one really knew the true state of the President's health, including the President and his physicians, and there was no way to raise the question in public without inviting charges of bad taste. The rabidly anti-Roosevelt press damned the torpedoes and went full speed ahead anyway. "Let's not be squeamish . . ." began a front-page editorial in the *New York Sun* that October. "It is convention, not the Constitution, which forbids open comment on the possibility that a President may be succeeded by his Vice President. Six Presidents have died in office." The *New York Daily News* mentioned in each edition, as a matter of policy, that Franklin D. Roosevelt was sixty-two years old and Thomas E. Dewey forty-two. *Time* said: "Franklin Roosevelt at sixty-two is an old man."

The White House reply came from Dr. McIntire, and he bears heavy responsibility for it. Like most presidential physicians, he bore a military rank — vice admiral — and was a qualified ophthalmologist (eye doctor) and otolaryngologist (ear, nose and throat doctor). He was a wizard at clearing Roosevelt's sinuses. To the press Dr. McIntire announced that his patient was:

> . . . eight or nine pounds under his best weight. Frankly, I wish he'd put on a few pounds. He hasn't been in the pool since before going to Quebec. But he's going to start in the pool again now. He is a powerful swimmer and that gives him a good workout. The buoyancy of the water enables him to walk and he gets exercise there that he can't get any other way. Nothing wrong organically with him at all. He's perfectly O.K. He does a terrific day's work. But he stands up under it amazingly. The stories that he is in bad health are understandable enough around election time, but they are not true.

The doctor thought that should satisfy anyone. It didn't suit Roosevelt. Perhaps because of his paralysis, the President was hypersensitive to rumors about his physical capacities, and he resolved to prove the doctor right by submitting himself to a physical ordeal. The first opportunity arose in New York. He was to lead a four-hour, fifty-mile motorcade from Ebbets Field in Brooklyn through Queens to the Bronx, then to Harlem and mid-Manhattan and down Broadway to the Battery. It was raining that day — a hard, steady, drenching, cold autumn rain which saturated clothes and inflicted misery on everyone not sheltered. The cavalcade was madness. Yet FDR refused to consider ending or even shortening it. Twice he paused for rubdowns and a quick change of clothes, at a Coast Guard motor pool in Brooklyn and in his wife's Washington Square apartment. The rest of the time he stood — smiling, waving his fedora, utterly wretched.

Eleanor, in the Secret Service follow-up car, felt desperate. She had a roof, and she thought that at the very least Franklin should order the canvas top raised over his presidential Packard. La Guardia and Wagner, occupying the jump seats in front of Roosevelt and soaked to the skin, were also worried about him. The downpour grew heavier and heavier, silvering his boat cloak. The President's hair — thinner and whiter than in the last campaign — was plastered down. He could see little through his pince-nez. But hundreds of thousands of Americans were shivering under umbrellas and sodden newspapers for a glimpse of the country's most famous smile, and he was determined to give it to them if he had to grit his teeth all the way. Six days later he repeated the performance in Philadelphia, riding around for hours in the open car, wrapped in sheets of freezing rain. After it the press corps, including reporters from Rooseveltphobic papers, wrote that he appeared to be the very image of vitality.

On November 7 he appeared as usual at the Hyde Park village polling place with Eleanor, told officials his occupation was "tree grower," was solemnly identified as voter number 251, and was introduced for the first time to a polling machine. He failed to master it. After some muttering and bouncing about, his matchless voice came through the curtain: "The goddamned thing won't work." Advice was offered through the curtain, and with it he overcame what was to be his only difficulty of the day. Even before the ballots from absentee servicemen had been counted (they were heavily pro-Roosevelt) he had won 54 percent of the vote. In the electoral college his margin over Dewey was 432 to 99. His coattails had brought Fulbright of Arkansas and McMahon of Connecticut to the Senate; Helen Gahagan Douglas and Adam Clayton Powell would be in the new House; Ham Fish and Gerald Nye had been defeated; and despite John L. Lewis's endorsement of Dewey in mining precincts, the Democratic ticket had swept them. Roosevelt was elated. Repeatedly during the campaign he had told voters that the election was also a referendum on United States participation in the United Nations, and now the ghost that had haunted Woodrow Wilson to his grave had been forever laid.

In triumph the President was also vindictive. Dewey's red-baiting, he had said, deserved "unvarnished contempt." Now, wheeling himself toward his New York bedroom after the Republican's 3 A.M. concession, he told Hassett, "I still think he's a son of a bitch." He never said that in public, of course. By all outward signs, the country had survived a wartime election with no scars.

And yet . . .

If the Fala speech had got Dewey's goat, the implications that Roosevelt was physically unfit had not only touched Roosevelt to the quick; the hurt lingered afterward. In public appearances he now made a point of being brisk and hearty. Returning to Washington like a victorious Caesar, he found the capital engulfed in rain. It was eerie; this was happening to him every time he moved from one city to another. Ten years ago farmers had cheered the downpours that had accompanied his visits, and his staff had called it Roosevelt luck. Now it was unlucky, and could become dangerous to a man his age. The President calmed their fears — and then ordered the Packard top down. In Union Plaza thirty thousand soggy people awaited him. Flanked by Truman and Wallace, he made a joke about the weather. Then the limousine drove slowly down Pennsylvania Avenue past three hundred thousand cheering Washingtonians. FDR (and Truman and Wallace) were deluged. Nevertheless, when they reached the White House Roosevelt was radiant, even euphoric. He had never seemed so robust.

And yet, and yet . . .

Among those close to him Franklin Roosevelt's well-being had been a matter of concern for some time. That October *Time* had reported that sinus trouble was "Franklin Roosevelt's most nagging health problem." The situation was graver than that. His entire cardiovascular system — a branch of medicine in which Dr. McIntire had no special training — was afflicted. As early as 1937 systolic hypertension had been diagnosed in the President, and four years later diastolic hypertension, much more serious, had joined it. McIntire remained cheerful; although his patient was exercising less and worrying more, he remained jovial. But Roosevelt was not as healthy as his physician led the public to believe. Early in 1943 he had been afflicted by two serious illnesses, influenza and an unexplained fever which he blamed on his North African trip, and after returning from Teheran he caught flu again. He complained of evening headaches. By mid-morning, after a good night's rest, he would be exhausted. Sometimes he fell asleep in the middle of a conversation, and once he dropped off while signing his name; the pen just dribbled off the paper. Frightened, his daughter Anna and his secretary Grace Tully confided in Dr. McIntire. He said he shared their anxiety and wanted a hospital checkup, but he seemed intimidated at the very thought of confronting his imperious patient with anything so drastic. Finally Anna spoke to her mother. Eleanor simply told the President that he was going to be bundled off to Bethesda Naval Hospital for an examination, and on March 27, 1944, he meekly went. This time he would be observed not by a single physician, but by a whole battery of specialists.

Among them was a Lieutenant Commander Howard G. Bruenn, a consultant in cardiology and chief of Bethesda's electrocardiograph department. Bruenn was shocked at Roosevelt's condition. The President was worn out, feverish, and suffering from bronchitis. Worse: his heart was enlarged, the vessels around it were swollen, and his blood pressure was alarming. Dr. Bruenn reported hypertension, hypertensive heart disease, and cardiac failure. His colleagues agreed. They recommended rest, and the President, a good patient, went off to lie in the sun at Hobcaw, Bernard Baruch's South Carolina plantation. He cut his predinner drinking to one and a half cocktails (with no nightcap later) and his smoking from twenty or thirty Camels a day to five or six. He wrote Hopkins that he was having a splendid vacation sleeping twelve hours a night, basking in the sun, controlling his temper, and letting "the rest of the world go hang." Lucy Rutherfurd was a frequent visitor.

He was an incurious patient and never asked about the small green pills he was taking. They were digitalis. Commander Bruenn or any of the other Bethesda physicians could have explained his condition to him, but no one in medical school had told them how to inform a President of the United States that he is gravely ill. Besides, they lacked rank, which in wartime was important. All the charts and diagrams were turned over to Admiral McIntire. The Bethesda staff assumed McIntire would tell Roosevelt. There is no evidence that he ever did, and the President's working hours after leaving South Carolina certainly weren't those of an invalid. He traveled fifty thousand miles that year, leading two wars and campaigning for reelection. At the same time he had to supervise the home front and dispose of all the trivia Americans dump on their President's desk. In 1944 his domestic agenda included the seizure of Montgomery Ward in Chicago, drafting the GI Bill of Rights, persuading Alben Barkley to withdraw his resignation as Senate floor leader, approving plans for a Missouri authority patterned after TVA, talking Secretary Stimson out of retiring, submitting the biggest budget in the history of the world, stumping New York in a mayoralty election, studying a proposed moratorium for insurance companies, endorsing a program of postwar scientific research, carrying out secret negotiations with both labor and management in the secret atomic fission plants, and reviewing the court-martial sentence for a young marine who had shot a wounded calf. It was up to him to decide whether Marshall or Eisenhower would lead the invasion of Europe, which was fair enough; what was grossly unfair was that only the President could convince the Navy that it should share the Pentagon with the Army — the admirals wanted their *own* Pentagon — and he alone could decide whether or not to call off the Army-Navy game. "One man simply could not do it all," Stimson said afterward, "and Franklin Roosevelt killed himself trying."

Visitors to the White House were remarking to one another how "wasted" the President's face looked. In July James Roosevelt had his first augury of what lay ahead. They were in the "Ferdinand Magellan" just before the Marine Corps maneuvers off the California coast. Suddenly Roosevelt's face was drained of color. Writhing, with his eyes closed, he gasped, "Jimmy, I don't know if I can make it — I have horrible pains." His son wanted to cancel the appearance, but Roosevelt, recovering after several minutes, overruled him. There is no way of knowing what the attack was since it wasn't reported to Dr. Bruenn. The next incident, however, occurred in public. Leaving his son in California, he met a speaking engagement in Bremerton, Washington. The Secret Service had suggested that he address the civilian audience from the deck of a moored destroyer, with its guns as a background. The President liked the idea. Everything was in place, and he was in the first paragraph of his address, when he was stricken. Although no one knew it, he was in the grip of an agonizing angina pectoris attack. For fifteen minutes shooting waves of pain crossed and recrossed his chest, lacing his rib cage and both shoulders with excruciating pangs. The wonder is that he could keep his feet at all — his braces were insecure on the slanting deck — let alone deliver a speech.

But only he knew of the pain; Bruenn, standing directly behind him, didn't suspect anything wrong and couldn't find evidence of it until much later. The President's dismayed audience was aware only of the worst speech they had ever heard. His delivery was slurred, uninspired, and at times inaudible. The content rambled wildly, making little sense. He didn't even sound like Roosevelt. Sam Rosenman, listening to a radio, wrung his hands. Rumors that the President was dying were everywhere now, supported by a cruel news photograph showing him with a slack, gaping mouth, a skeletal face, and poached eyes. Mike Reilly of the Secret Service told FDR that some reporters insisted the President had been in a hospital, not South Carolina. Roosevelt said tightly, "Mike, those newspapermen are a bunch of goddamned ghouls."

His response was both understandable and unreasonable. Sometimes it becomes the duty of the press to keep a deathwatch, and this was one of them. Out of their long affection for him they had been writing little about his appearance; the photographer who had taken the ghastly picture of him was ostracized by his colleagues. Members of the President's official family and old acquaintances were far more outspoken. Years of accumulated strain seemed to be taking their toll all at once; within a single week, an observer wrote, the President appeared to have passed "from the prime of life to old age." Frances Perkins was immune to gossip about him (and herself), and she had dismissed all the stories about his decline. But at a cabinet meeting the day before his fourth inaugural, she was stunned. His eyes were glazed and looked as though they had been blackened, his complexion was gray, his face gaunt, and his clothes a size too large for him. His hands trembled. His lips were blue. He had to prop up his head with a hand. "We were all shocked by the President's appearance," Dean Acheson wrote in his memoirs. "Thin, gaunt, with sunken and darkly circled eyes, only the jaunty cigarette holder and his lighthearted brushing aside of difficulties recalled the FDR of former days." John Gunther, seeing him the next day, wrote, "I was terrified when I saw his face. I felt certain that he was going to die. All the light had gone out underneath the skin. It was like a parchment shade on a bulb that had been dimmed. I could not get over the ravaged expression on his face. It was gray, gaunt, and sagging, and the muscles controlling the lips seemed to have lost part of their function." At times, Gunther wrote, his exhaustion was so great that "he could not answer simple questions and talked what was close to nonsense."

Two weeks later, at the Yalta Conference in the Crimea, Anthony Eden thought the President hazy and confused on their first evening together; Lord Moran, Churchill's physician, took one look at the President and decided that he was a dying man. Their impressions, coupled with those formed in Washington, later contributed to the theory that FDR, "the sick man of Yalta," was outfoxed by the Russians at Yalta, and that in letting him run for a fourth term his family and friends had betrayed not only him but also his country. Yalta, in a Republican phrase of the 1950s, had been "a sellout."

There are certain difficulties here. The first is the assumption that anyone could have talked Roosevelt out of running. Eleanor had tried very hard in 1940; he had been unmoved. The second problem was that his ailment was maddeningly inconsistent. One day Dr. Bruenn's indices would warn that the President's condition was about to enter a critical phase; the next day his vitality would be superb. Bruenn found little correlation between his findings and the condition of his patient. Clearly his campaigning in the rain fatigued him; after it he lost color and appetite. Yet his blood pressure had dropped (to 210/112), his lungs were clear, and his heart showed every sign of being in excellent shape. Leaving the destroyer deck in Seattle, he had told Bruenn of his pain. Blood counts and electrocardiograph tracings were made within an hour; both were normal.

His ability to rally when needed was astonishing. Allen Drury, then a UP reporter, watched the President being wheeled in for the annual White House correspondents' dinner and thought how scrawny-necked, elderly, and senescent he seemed; yet before the President left he acknowledged the reporters' cheers "with the old, familiar gesture, so that the last we saw of Franklin Roosevelt was the head going up with a toss, the smile breaking out, the hand uplifted and waving in the old, familiar way." On September 25, 1944, he spoke to union leaders and party professionals in Washington's new Hotel Statler. Rosenman and the President's daughter arrived early, both tense; FDR's condition earlier in the day had been shocking. Anna whispered to Rosenman, "Do you think Pa will put it over? . . . If the delivery isn't just right, it'll be an awful flop." The audience was also nervous. They had all heard the rumors, seen the news photograph from California, and heard the dreadful destroyer speech. Roosevelt spoke sitting down, and his first words sounded odd, "as though," Burns wrote, "the President were mouthing them." He then recovered and delivered a fine fighting speech, as crisp and resonant as his first inaugural.

At Yalta his American staff — Harriman, Byrnes, Admiral William D. Leahy, Edward R. Stettinius — believed he was representing the United States effectively and with skill. In the early sessions he had a nocturnal cough, but Bruenn found his lungs clear and his heart and blood pressure unchanged. On February 8 (after a row with Stalin over Poland) Roosevelt's blood pressure bothered the doctor, who altered his regimen and his schedule for two days. By then the trouble had disappeared. At the same time Eden had changed his mind. His first impression had to be wrong, he felt. In spite of his poor color and loss of weight FDR was, in Eden's opinion, negotiating with rare good judgment. Not only was he keeping abreast of Churchill's agenda; he was finding time to carry on a conference-within-a-conference with Stalin over Soviet-American roles in Asia.

Unquestionably the Crimean conference hastened the President's death. The same was true of his 1944 campaign against a hard-hitting Republican challenger and his role as an energetic, participating commander in chief. Yalta will be recalled because the President sacrificed much of himself there. He sacrificed little else. *

Home Front Montage

They're Either Too Young Or Too Old

They're eith-er too gray — or too old, — They're eith-er too young — or too old,

REFRAIN 1. They're eith-er too young — or too

I dood it.

December 27, 1944

Dear Mrs. Witkowski,

As one who shares your great sorrow, let me introduce myself. I am George C. Fowler of Memphis, and it was my privilege to be your son's company commander for nineteen months. I am told that you will have received a War Department telegram by the time this reaches you, but I want you to know how bravely and gallantly John fought to the end. Every man in Fox Company regarded him as a pal, a real soldier in every way

Don't fence me in.

I left my heart
at the Stage Door Canteen
I left it there with
a girl named Eileen

WPB Directive No. 1 to OPA
All RED and BLUE stamps in War Ration Book 4 are WORTH 10 POINTS EACH. RED and BLUE tokens are WORTH 1 POINT EACH. RED and BLUE TOKENS are used to make CHANGE for RED and BLUE STAMPS only when purchase is made. IMPORTANT! POINT VALUES of BROWN and GREEN STAMPS are NOT CHANGED.

When The Lights Go On Again
(All Over The World)

Chorus

WHEN THE LIGHTS GO ON A-GAIN   All O-ver The World _____   And the

To Save Electricity
NIGHT BASEBALL RULED OUT

A
MILEAGE RATION

MOST ADMIRED BY U.S. TEENERS

Men	Women
Franklin D. Roosevelt	Florence Nightingale
Abraham Lincoln	Clara Barton
Douglas MacArthur	Sister Elizabeth Kenny
Joe DiMaggio	Louisa May Alcott
Babe Ruth	Doris Day
Roy Rogers	Vera-Ellen

Roll out the barrel!
We'll have a barrel of fun!
Roll out the barrel!
We've got the blues on the run!

And when I die, please bury me
'Neath a ton of sugar, by a rubber tree
Lay me to rest in an auto machine
And water my grave with gasoline.

LOUIS "LEPKE" BUCHALTER OF "MURDER, INC." ELECTROCUTED AT SING SING

JUNK MAKES FIGHTING WEAPONS
One old radiator will provide scrap steel needed for

KISSIMMEE, Fla. Nov. 14 (AP) -- Cartoonist Frank King, creator of Gasoline Alley, divulged today that Skeezix Wallett will not be killed in the war. King, who appeared exhausted, said that since the rumor that Skeezix would die in combat began circulating, he has been inundated with thousands of letters

Play it, Sam.

He's 1-A In The Army And He's A-1 In My Heart

Refrain

He's   1 - A   in the   ar - my   and he's   A - 1   in my heart.   He's

ELEVEN

Lilacs in the Dooryard

THE GI INVADERS OF ITALY, when last glimpsed in this account, had been wallowing in the cold brown porridge below Monte Cassino hoping for warmer weather and a breakthrough. That had been in 1943. The new year brought no change. The Germans still held two-thirds of Italy, including Rome. On January 22, 1944, the Allies tried to outflank the enemy's line with an amphibious landing in his rear at Anzio, but the American general commanding the end run was incompetent. Instead of exploiting his surprise he waited cautiously on the beach while Field Marshal Kesselring hemmed him in. Anzio turned into a bloody trap. The Allies couldn't break off contact and they couldn't advance. For over four months they huddled on the beachhead, taking casualties and improving nothing except perhaps German marksmanship. "They lived like men in prehistoric times," one reporter wrote, "and a club would have become them more than a machine gun. How they survived the dreadful winter was beyond us."

Spring arrived, washing out the Bailey bridges and turning iron-hard road ruts into mire again; and still the senseless siege went on. Both Allied armies, the Fifth (American) and Eighth (British), were bleeding to death in head-on assaults up the leg of Italy, on the west and east of its shinbone, the Apennines. At most they could hope to tie down Wehrmacht divisions that might be manning Hitler's Atlantic Wall — soon to be tested by the cross-Channel lunge — and wear down German strength by attrition. But attrition grinds both ways. Worse, it is more costly for attackers than defenders. Allied casualties rose and morale dropped. Friction between Allies, always a danger sign, was growing. Next to Mussolini, now under house arrest by non-Fascist Italians, Lieutenant General Mark Clark was the most unpopular man in the Italian peninsula. His attempt to blame the bombing of Monte Cassino on General Bernard Freyberg, the New Zealand

hero, was, to put the best face on it, an ungracious attempt to evade responsibility for what seemed at the time to be a necessary act of war.

Anzio *had* to be relieved. The Allied high command saw but one solution: a big push toward Rome. On June 4, 1944, at 7:30 P.M., elements of
the U.S. Fifth Army, with Clark in the vanguard, marched up the Piazza
Venezia, the heart of the Eternal City. The conqueror was greeted by
flowers, cheers, kisses, and more chianti than he could carry. It was a
moment any soldier might savor, but Clark didn't know when to stop. Next
morning he called for a meeting of his corps commanders, and when they
arrived they discovered they were to be used as foils in a press conference.
Clark was striking martial poses at the request of photographers. His subordinate generals, American and Allied, reddened with embarrassment.
Even some war correspondents colored. Clark didn't notice their uneasi-
ness. In fact, he decided to say a few words. "This," he began, "is a great
day for the Fifth Army."

The press stared. For the *Fifth Army!* How about the Eighth Army, the
angry British correspondents muttered to one another? The Eighth, that
had come all the way from Cairo fighting every step of the way? And what
of the Poles, and all the others? But beyond that, Eric Sevareid wondered,
wasn't every victory over Hitler a victory for Europe's enslaved civilians,
for the Jews on the beltlines of Nazi slaughter, for people all over the
world who had sacrificed so much and were still suffering in the mincing
machine of war? Not to Mark Clark, it wasn't. He saw to it that photographers and correspondents were given everything they needed, and cleared
cable traffic to make sure everything would be on editors' desks next morning. It arrived. But unhappily for Clark, the next day was June 6, 1944—
D-Day in Normandy.

Due north of Portsmouth dockyard, in a thicket of hazel trees near South-
wick House, one of the stately homes of England, stood a shabby trailer
whose unusual furnishings included a red telephone for scrambled conversations with Washington and a green phone, a direct line to No. 10 Downing Street. In it, sometime during that blustery week preceding the greatest
amphibious assault in history, Dwight Eisenhower, now wearing four stars,
scribbled two messages. The first, now long famous ("You are about to embark upon the Great Crusade"), would congratulate his troops if they
established a foothold on Normandy's shores. The other would be handed
to the press if Dunkerque was repeated:

> Our landings in the Cherbourg-Havre area have failed to gain a satisfac-
> tory foothold and I have withdrawn the troops. My decision to attack at this
> time and place was based upon the best information available. The troops,
> the air, and the Navy did all that bravery and devotion to duty could do. If
> any blame or fault attaches to the attempt it is mine alone.

Long after they happen, historic events take on an air of inevitability.

In thinking of D-Day, we assume that the Germans in France never had a chance — that with Eisenhower's huge armies and unlimited supplies, protected by Anglo-American armadas in the Channel and the air overhead, his crusade was as good as won. Even men who knew better at the time fall under the spell of myth: Montgomery later wrote that "the battle was fought exactly as planned before the invasion." It wasn't.

Much has been made of the rough weather, and how it hampered landing operations. It was really a blessing. Because the weather was poor, key German officers were absent from their headquarters when the blow fell — Rommel, the most gifted of Hitler's field marshals, had taken the day off to celebrate his wife's birthday with her in Ulm. Ten highly mobile panzer divisions were available to throw the invaders back into the Channel. On D-Day only one of them saw combat. Even so, it broke the British line at Caen and drove through to the beach. That force was too small, but if only three of the ten panzer divisions had been thrown into Normandy, wrote B. H. Liddell Hart, the eminent military strategist, "the Allied footholds could have been dislodged before they were joined up and consolidated."

Had Rommel not been so faithful a husband he would have remained in France, and the Allies might have been liquidated. To be sure, the field marshal would first have been obliged to phone Hitler. But the Führer was already convinced that a cross-Channel thrust must be stopped at the waterline; that, he believed, would prevent the reelection of Roosevelt, who, "with luck," would "finish up somewhere in jail." Curiously, Hitler's intuition had told him from the first that the landings would come in Normandy. Then he listened to his advisers and changed his mind. Calais, he said: their main force will land near Calais; Normandy is just a feint. This was the best possible piece of luck for Eisenhower. His troops had enough on their hands as it was. For the past year the Germans had been mining coastal waters, driving great antitank tripods of steel rails into the ground, erecting six-foot-thick concrete pillboxes, fortifying cement tunnels, and weaving military obstacles into natural defenses, using their vast stock of slave labor for the work. From the first, the British were on timetable on their beaches (Juno and Sword), but the American beaches (Omaha and Utah) were taken at great cost. Then the soldiers moved inland and encountered Normandy's hedgerows, ideal for stubborn defenders.

On the other side of the Atlantic a hundred million Americans hovered near radios, awaiting the latest word from France. Franklin Roosevelt was one of them. The President had followed every detail of the massive preparations. He knew how the landing ships built on Lake Michigan had been floated down the Illinois and Mississippi rivers, to sail eastward and then be packed beam to beam with GIs in British ports. Daily reports had briefed him on the construction of fleets of LSTs (Landing Ship, Tank) in California, and the trial runs of the tanks, bulldozers, and trucks they would carry. He had kept abreast of Ike's postponement of D-Day and the nerve-racking, inconclusive predictions of Army meteorologists. He had been told how the general paced the crunching cinder path outside his trailer, rubbing lucky coins from the invasions of North Africa and Sicily. And he had heard from SHAEF how the general had said in a strangled voice, "I'm quite positive we must give the order. . . . I don't like it, but there it is. . . ." Then, slamming his right fist into his left palm: "O.K. We'll go."

With those words, the great bound into Hitler's Europe began. Ed Murrow, a man not given to fantasy, stood beneath the roaring bombers headed for France, and thought he heard the strains of "The Battle Hymn of the Republic." The commander in chief, not that close, could only pray, and that is what he did. Over the weekend, at the Charlottesville home of "Pa" Watson, his military aide, he had reread the Book of Common Prayer, looking for D-Day invocations. On the evening of that Tuesday, June 6, he went on the radio to lead the nation in asking benediction for "our sons, the pride of our nation . . . lead them straight and true," he beseeched, "give strength to their arms, stoutness to their hearts, steadfastness in their faith. They will need Thy blessings. Their road will be long and hard. For the enemy is strong. He may hurl back our forces. Success may not come with rushing speed. But we shall return again and again." Then he asked guidance for those, like himself, who must watch from home: "Give us faith in Thee; faith in our sons; faith in each other; faith in our united crusade. . . ."

Meanwhile the issue was being decided amid the hedges and poppies of Normandy. After eleven days of fighting, Bradley announced his first casualties: 3,283 dead and 12,600 wounded. He had little to show for it, and London had a fresh reason for demanding results; on June 14 Dr. Wernher von Braun had begun the massacre of British civilians with his V-1 rockets, launched from Nazi sites in France and Belgium.* The Allies needed a victory, the generals needed a major port, and everyone wanted an end to the Battle of the Bridgehead. Cherbourg didn't fall until Tuesday, and the Germans had done everything they could think of to spoil the spoils. Breakwaters were smashed, cranes destroyed, piers sown with mines and boobytraps. It would be August before Army engineers could clean up the mess. For the present the expedition had to rely on Mulberry, the artificial harbor they had brought with them and sunk off Arromanches.

Nevertheless, the buildup continued. On July 4 Eisenhower reported to Washington that the millionth man had been landed in France, and 566,648 tons of supplies and 171,532 vehicles were ashore. Furthermore, the Battle of the Bridgehead was turning out to be a disguised blessing. The very ferocity of the fighting had drawn the bulk of Germany's western forces into the Cotentin Peninsula. Panzer divisions were thrown in piecemeal to plug holes in the German line and were methodically chewed up — thus

*In 1955 Dr. von Braun became a naturalized citizen of the United States. He has been among the leaders in the aerospace program. Fifteen American colleges and universities have conferred honorary degrees upon him.

depriving the Nazis of future mobility when they would need it most, behind the peninsula, in the open country of France's heartland. At the same time, Hitler's order not to retreat an inch shackled his field commanders and made tactical retreats impossible. Caen fell to the British on July 9, and Saint Lô — the road junction linking Normandy with Brittany — to U.S. troops on July 25. Now Patton was in the cockpit, driving hard. On July 25 he broke out in a powerful armored thrust toward Avranches and into Brittany, and by August 10 he had overrun Brittany and cut it off. Lord Beaverbrook's London *Express* said, "Americans have proved themselves to be a race of great fighters, in the very front rank of men at arms."

On Friday, August 25, General Leclerc's Free French jeeps entered the suburbs, and on Saturday de Gaulle made his triumphant march while across the Atlantic Lily Pons, wearing her USO uniform, sang "The Marseillaise" in Manhattan's Rockefeller Plaza. It was an electric moment, although observers in Paris found the aftermath of the city's liberation to be more complex than they had expected. The Gaullists and their comrades in the underground French Forces of the Interior had a blacklist of seven hundred thousand collaborators, and French girls who had slept with Germans were forced to submit while their heads were shorn and then shaved. But many collaborators escaped humiliation or bought their way to freedom. Paris disturbed some Americans. It didn't look at all like an enslaved capital. Compared to London, it was prospering. Ed Murrow was surprised by the number of well-dressed women on the streets. Not only had the French textile industry flourished throughout the war; the French had developed the first practical television transmitters and sets. All the famous couturiers were in business — Molyneux, Lanvin, Schiaparelli — and their French customers were wearing full skirts and mutton-legged sleeves, which had long been out of the question for American and British women limited by clothes rationing. Discussing the liberation with an American reporter, one Parisian designer sighed and spread his hands in a Gallic gesture. "What shall I do with all this nonsense going on?" he asked. "All my best customers are in concentration camps, because of course they were working for Vichy."

London was still in greater danger than Paris. On September 8 the British capital's lights were turned up after 1,843 dark nights, and for the first time in memory, eight-year-old Julie Andrews saw a lighted city. It didn't stay lit long. That same night von Braun began hurling his V-2 missiles at Britain — Englishmen called them "Bob Hopes" ("Bob down and hope for the best") — and a return to blackouts seemed sensible. For a few weeks the troops in France and the civilians in England had persuaded one another that the war was all but over. The broken Wehrmacht seemed finished; even Hitler, one thought, must realize that he had lost the war. On September 12 GIs crossed the border and entered Germany near Eupen and Trier and probed the outer defenses of the Siegfried Line; western Germany had been invaded. In rapid succession that autumn the Canadians cleared the Scheldt estuary, the U.S. First Army took Aachen and penetrated the Siegfried Line itself in the process, Patton's U.S. Third Army captured Metz and Strasbourg, and other American troops reached the Roer River. That was on December 3. Less than two weeks later, Hitler caught the Allies with a major counterattack. Crack troops flung themselves at the Americans with Field Marshal Gerd von Rundstedt's battle cry ringing in their ears: "Your great hour has struck. Strong attacking Armies are advancing today against the Anglo-Americans. I do not need to say more to you. You all feel it. Everything is at stake. You bear the holy duty to achieve the superhuman for our Fatherland and Führer!"

This was the overture to the Battle of the Bulge. The havoc wrought by English-speaking Germans in GI uniforms; the 101st Airborne's gallant stand at Bastogne; the German ultimatum and Brigadier General Mc-Auliffe's reply of "Nuts!"; Patton's classic maneuver in wheeling to relieve Bastogne, with his lead tank commanded by a thirty-year-old lieutenant colonel in the 4th Armored named Creighton Abrams — all this belongs to American military lore. It was the GIs' finest hour in the ETO. Asked what had turned the tide, Montgomery replied, "The good fighting qualities of the American soldier. I take my hat off to such men. I salute the brave fighting men of America — I never want to fight alongside better soldiers. I have tried to feel that I am also an American soldier myself."

The Bulge was Hitler's last mad gamble, and was followed by disintegration. The Russians opened their final offensive in January 1945. Beginning in early February the Allies cleared Holland, took the Saar, captured an unblown bridge at Remagen, and then threw nine more bridges across the Rhine than the Germans had at the beginning of the war, enveloped the Ruhr, captured 325,000 prisoners there, and then seized Mannheim and Frankfurt-am-Main. The end was approaching; everyone in Europe could sense it. Though London was to remain blacked out for another month, Paris became France's city of light once more in the first week of April. Berlin, Hamburg, Dresden, Essen, Düsseldorf, Nuremberg, and Frankfurt had been bombed to rubble; Hitler's fifty-sixth birthday was two weeks away, but there were no plans to celebrate it.

At noon on April 11, 1945, the U.S. Ninth Army reached the Elbe. In Warm Springs at 6 A.M. on April 12, President Roosevelt lay asleep in his corner bedroom. He had retired expecting to read of new developments in the morning, but the mail had been delayed. Instead of his usual newspapers — the *New York Times, New York Herald Tribune, Baltimore Sun,* and *Washington Post* — he would be limited to the *Atlanta Constitution.* Its headlines were:

9TH 57 MILES FROM BERLIN
50-MILE GAIN IN DAY
SETS STAGE FOR EARLY
U.S.-RUSS JUNCTURE

And, from the Pacific:

MARINES GAIN ON OKINAWA; FIGHTING HEAVY

150 SUPERFORTS HAMMER TOKYO IN TWO-HOUR DAYLIGHT RAID

Here in Georgia it was unseasonably warm for early April; the dogwood and wild violets were out, and a neighbor was planning an outdoor barbecue for FDR, with a chair under an old oak tree, where he could enjoy a breathtaking view of the valley. Since the mail had also held up his daily bale of paperwork, there was nothing for the President to do except sit for his portrait. Two years ago Lucy Rutherfurd had commissioned a painter to paint a watercolor of him; now he himself had asked the same artist to do another, as a gift from him to Lucy's daughter.

With the President down here, Bill Hassett and Dr. Bruenn breathed more easily, though they were beginning to despair of recovery. They had heard the gasps in the crowd at Warm Springs station on March 30 when he had been carried from his train to the platform; he had sagged in his wheelchair as he was pushed toward his car, his head bobbing out of control. He had rallied long enough to drive the car here, but they had learned to distrust these brief upturns. In the evening, after the President had retired, they had faced each other in anguish. Hassett had said that Roosevelt was just drifting toward death. His dashing, flamboyant signatures had faded out; they didn't even look like good forgeries. He was the President of the United States and he couldn't write his own name. Bruenn had given his professional opinion: Roosevelt's case was hopeless unless he could be protected from pressure. Hassett said that was out of the question; no President could be so isolated. The two men had been at the point of tears. Hassett confided to his diary:

> Shocked at his appearance — worn, weary, exhausted. He seemed all right when I saw him in the morning. He is steadily losing weight — told me he has lost twenty-five pounds — no strength, no appetite, tires easily — all too apparent whenever you see him after midday. Again observed this to Dr. Bruenn. He admits cause for alarm.

This morning, however, they agreed that his color was much better. The news was good; that helped. And the absence of mail was a godsend. Once more, as so often in these last few weeks, they persuaded one another — against all evidence — that he might, just might, make it.

Among the papers awaiting action on the President's Washington desk were an urgent note from Albert Einstein and an attached memorandum from Leo Szilard, both begging him to order an immediate suspension of all work on an atom bomb. The world situation had changed, they explained; much which they had taken for granted was either untrue or no longer relevant. Any brief military advantage the United States might gain with nuclear weapons would be offset by political and psychological losses and damage to American prestige. The United States, Einstein argued, might even touch off a worldwide atom armaments race.

Obviously something had happened — or not happened — in Hitler's Reich. The blunt truth was that the Nazis had no atomic weapons. This seemed so beyond comprehension that Allied scientists at first suspected an attempt to humbug them. Samuel A. Goudsmit, the senior member of the Alsos intelligence team which landed in Normandy, believed (and continued to believe in the 1970s) that Carl von Weizsäcker, and Nobel laureates Max von Laue and Werner Heisenberg, the three most brilliant German physicists, could have built bombs between them with support from the state. They asked German scientists: what about it?

In those days Germans were blaming Hitler for everything, but in this instance their account was plausible. The Führer's anti-Semitism had driven their most promising colleagues out of the country, the Nazi bureaucracy was indifferent toward long-term research, technical equipment was unavailable, and — a typical example of inept rivalry within the Nazi hierarchy — uncoordinated atomic research was being carried out by the Ministry of Education, the War Office, and even the Post Office Department. The turning point for the Germans had come on June 6, 1942, just as the American scientists were approaching their breakthrough. That Saturday Heisenberg briefed Albert Speer, Hitler's Minister of Supply, on progress in the Reich's uranium research. There was definite proof, he said, that Germany had the technical knowledge to build a uranium pile and acquire atomic energy from it, and theoretically an explosive for atom bombs could be produced from such a source. The next step would be to investigate technical problems — the critical size, for example, and the possibility of a chain reaction. At that point he and von Weizsäcker were talking about a pile not only as a weapon in itself but as a prime mover in weapon production. Speer gave them tentative approval. The work would continue, but on a smaller scale, and their target should be a pile usable as a generation of power. Speer was only echoing Hitler. The Führer, certain of imminent triumph, had just ordered the termination of all new weapon projects except those which would be ready for use in the field within six weeks.

According to Speer — he was convicted at Nuremberg and served twenty years as a war criminal — Hitler had sometimes mentioned to him the possibility of an atomic bomb. Speaking with the Führer on May 6, 1942, Speer raised the question of an all-out program to make one. He suggested that Göring be placed at the head of the Reich Research Council to emphasize its importance, and this was done.

On June 23, 1942, Speer reported to Hitler. The Führer was still interested, but he had no grasp of theoretical physics, and the project was shunted aside. German physicists were now talking to Speer of a three- or four-year project for bomb production. Instead, he recalls, "I authorized the development of an energy-producing uranium motor for propelling machinery. The Navy was interested in that for its submarines." Speer leaves no doubt that had he dreamed of the Manhattan Project, he would have moved heaven and earth to catch up with the Americans. He continued to make periodic inquiries, but now Hitler was discouraging him. The Führer's old party cronies were ridiculing America's reputation for efficiency, and he had taken to describing all physics as Jewish physics (*jüdische Physik*). But if the German dictator had given his own scientists the blank check Roosevelt had given their colleagues in the United States, the maps of Europe and even of the western hemisphere might have been sharply changed.

None of this was known outside the Reich until November 23, 1944, when Patton took Strasbourg. The Alsos detachment headed straight for the university and its new laboratories. Sam Goudsmit was looking for Weizsäcker, Strasbourg professor of theoretical physics, but his quarry had flown three weeks ago, and while Goudsmit debated the propriety of questioning other Strasbourg physicists, the German scientists solved his problem by refusing to have commerce with the enemy.

Strasbourg looked like a debacle until the Alsos team stumbled upon Weizsäcker's private papers. Translating them by candlelight, with GIs playing cards in the same room and the rumble of artillery from the right bank of the Rhine distinctly audible, Goudsmit and his assistant looked for this clue, that hint, for scholarly citations and casual references, until they leaped up with such triumphant cries that the edgy GIs reached for their M-1s and grenades. The scientists had just turned up a thick batch of closely typed pages — the full record of the Reich's U project and the Uranium Verein. There were a few pieces missing, of course, and no entries had been made during the past three months, but this, by all evidence, was the most complete file in Europe on Nazi uranium research.

Until that night Allied scientists had assumed that German physicists led them by a wide margin. To Goudsmit, squinting at Weizsäcker's manuscript in the flickering light, it was clear that the Nazis were two years behind the men at Los Alamos. The Reich lacked plants for the manufacture of PU-239 (Plutonium) and U-235. Apparently they didn't even have any uranium burners worth mentioning. When he cabled Washington reporting his findings, he was reminded that Weizsäcker's papers might be a hoax. He replied that the internal evidence was genuine; this was serious work. The Army suggested that other Germans, elsewhere in the Reich, might be manufacturing atom bombs. Goudsmit replied tartly, "A paperhanger may perhaps imagine that he has turned into a military genius overnight, and a traveler in champagne may be able to disguise himself as a diplomat. But laymen of that sort could never have acquired sufficient scientific knowledge to construct an atom bomb."

Nevertheless, the hunt had to continue. Heisenberg had been an enthusiastic advocate of nuclear weapons; it was conceivable that he and other equally ardent scientists had been at work in secret laboratories, defying official indifference to the possibilities in fissionable materials. In fact, something very like that had happened. During the winter of 1943–44, working through air raids, Heisenberg and his staff had built a small reactor in the Dahlem Institute with three tons of uranium and heavy water. To elude the bombers they had then transferred their laboratory to a tall warehouse, owned by a Stuttgart brewery, in the foothills of the Swabian Alps. Moving out beer vats, they had papered the inside of the warehouse with silver foil, equipped it with a powerful electric plant, and built workshops in the wing of a textile mill.

Once Hitler's Festung Europa began to break up, even this refuge wasn't inaccessible enough for them. Like the Allies, Heisenberg and his colleagues were harried by worries about security, and they moved again, to a great cave hollowed out of rock near Tübingen. It was in this cavern, in February 1945, that the construction of a large pile — roughly comparable to the one Allied scientists had built on the abandoned squash court under Stagg Field — began in earnest. By spring there was an atomic burner comprising heavy water, cubes of uranium, and a graphite jacket. The Germans were moving swiftly toward the accumulation of a critical mass. Shipments of uranium cubes arrived daily from the Thuringian Forest, where a second uranium burner had been built by Dr. Karl Diebner. The gap between Oppenheimer and Heisenberg was still wide, but it was rapidly closing. To the intense annoyance of Goudsmit, who believed in the preservation of all experimental data, the U.S. Army colonel who served as nomimal commander of Alsos sent a small unit of Rangers to the grotto with orders to destroy the German apparatus. Sending troops had been a good idea, though. Members of Heisenberg's staff were thwarted in a hasty attempt to smuggle the uranium cubes out under a hay load on an oxcart, and other cubes which had been filched by Hechingen peasants — the peasants didn't know what they were, but had guessed that they were valuable and might be sold to the French — were recovered. Presently all Nazi physicists were in Allied custody, including the elusive Heisenberg. Goudsmit was ecstatic. To a regular Army major who had been detached to serve as a liaison officer with the Alsos group he said, "Isn't it wonderful that the Germans have no atom bomb? Now we don't have to use ours." The major looked surprised. He replied, "Of course you understand, Sam, that if we have such a weapon we are going to use it."

From that moment, the officers and scientists who had worked on the Manhattan Project were divided into those who meant to use the bomb if it turned out to be practical, and those who were shocked at the thought. The split wasn't always between soldiers and civilians — Edward Teller was a hard-liner from the beginning — but the first ban-the-bomb advocates were nuclear physicists. Even before the myth of a Nazi bomb had been dispelled, some of them had become convinced that the United States should share its discoveries with the world's scientific community. At their urging Niels Bohr had called on the President at 4 P.M., August 26, 1944, to discuss that very issue. Bohr was an unwise choice. He was garrulous; he took a half-hour to come to the point, and the President's time was precious. In any event, Roosevelt disagreed with Bohr and bade him good day. Bohr then tried Churchill. After listening to his guest for thirty minutes the prime minister turned to Lord Cherwell, who had introduced him, and inquired testily, "What is he really talking about — politics or physics?"

He was talking about both. Many — perhaps a majority — of the scientists believed that in building the bomb they had acquired a moral obligation to all mankind. To confront a Hitler in possession of atomic bombs was one thing, but the Japanese in 1945 were not that advanced in theoretical physics or technology. They were unable to build such weapons themselves, and so, the argument went, using one against them was unthinkable. To introduce such a question raised politics and physics to a level of scientific statesmanship. There were no precedents for it, and wartime was not the best time to think it through, especially when the enemy in the Pacific had opened the war with an unprovoked, devastating air attack. Alexander Sachs was a better emissary than Bohr. He was a close friend of the President, and five years earlier he had persuaded him to launch this two-billion-dollar search. Sachs shared Bohr's convictions, and in December 1944 he called at the White House. It is known that he had a long talk with the President, but that is about all that is known. After FDR's death Sachs said that Roosevelt had agreed that if any test succeeded a second rehearsal should be held, attended by Allied and neutral scientists; that a detailed report on the weapon's implications should be circulated among Allied and neutral scientists; that the enemy should agree to evacuate a given area; and that after a demonstration of the weapon's power the enemy should be given an ultimatum to surrender or be annihilated.

Sachs's minute, submitted to Secretary of War Robert P. Patterson a year later, is an extraordinary document. Roosevelt had signed nothing. The conversation had been unwitnessed. The President had not mentioned it to Stimson, then the Secretary of War and FDR's liaison with X, as Stimson always called the Manhattan Project. Obviously a man of Sachs's integrity would not invent such a tale. But the President had a genius for telling people what they wanted to hear and then hedging it — by hypothetical statements, say, or by skillful use of the subjunctive — so that he stopped just short of commitment. In this case he may have been undecided. That would have been like him; he rarely made up his mind until he had to. The Sachs minute seems less convincing than Stimson's entry in his diary on March 15, 1945. That was the last time FDR and his war secretary talked of X. Stimson wrote: "I went over with him the two schools of thought that exist in respect to the future control after the war of this project, in case it is useful, one of them being the secret close-in attempted control of the project by those who control it now, and the other being international control based upon freedom of science. I told him that those things must be settled before the project is used and that he must be ready with a statement to come out to the people on it just as soon as that is done. He agreed to that."

Like Stalingrad, which had been raging at the same time, the issue at Guadalcanal had remained in doubt for six months — from mid-August 1942 to early February 1943. The valor of the outnumbered marines captured the public imagination, but the decisive struggle was between the two navies. In six separate engagements — "fire-away Flanagans," as nineteenth-century seamen would have called them — the admirals battled for command of the sea. Losses on both sides were shocking. Each lost an even dozen warships. To sailors the waters between the 'Canal, Tulagi, and Savo Island were "Iron-bottom Sound"; to marines, "Sleepless Lagoon." If reckoned by tonnage lost, the naval struggle would be called a draw. It wasn't, because at the end of it the marines still held Guadalcanal and its airstrip, and the Japanese troops were being evacuated, leaving behind twenty-five thousand of their dead. They still felt invincible. On New Georgia they reinforced their Munda base, a whistle-stop for Zeros and Zekes flying down the Slot to bomb the marines. But a corner had been turned. For the first time in the war the Jap had gone over to the defensive.

Nor was that all. Guadalcanal was one of two successful Pacific campaigns, waged at the same time and to the same end: the defense of Australia. The other was in MacArthur's theater, New Guinea. The Coral Sea battle hadn't discouraged the enemy there. In July 1942 he had seized a string of villages along the north shore of Papua, the New Guinea tail, and he was planning to envelop Port Moresby, on the south shore, in a land-and-sea pincer. Coast watchers — British colonial officials hiding in the jungle with radios — warned Americans that the sea assault was headed for Milne Bay, at the tip of the peninsula tail. U.S. warships arrived first and beat off that threat. The Japanese land drive took off from a village called Buna. It was only a hundred miles from there to Moresby as the crow flies, but the Nips had to cross the awesome 13,000-foot Owen Stanley Range on foot. Twenty miles from Moresby the Australians held them and, with the U.S. 32nd Division, began a counteroffensive.

This ordeal, costlier in lives than Guadalcanal, ended when the enemy was pushed all the way back across the mountains and General Eichelberger entered Buna on January 2, 1943. The Australians captured nearby Sanananda two weeks later, but the Japanese collected reinforcements and tried to land a counterattacking force with eight transports. On March 3, skip-bombing B-25s caught the convoy in the Bismarck Sea and sank all eight, together with their four escorts. In the grisly aftermath seven thousand Japanese were drowned or, if they reached land, beheaded by island natives, according to a local custom. Tokyo solemnly announced that Moresby had no military significance.

Rabaul did. The enemy wanted to keep Rabaul; had to, in fact, to hold the South Pacific. Rabaul itself was too strong to be assaulted, so the Americans neutralized it. GIs and marines began by moving into New Georgia in the summer of 1943 and pouncing at Munda. They had to attack through thickets and over flooded rivers, against pillboxed Nips in steel vests. Still, the airstrip fell in August, and American troops had a leg up the Slot. Vaulting to Vella Lavella and Kolombangara, they mopped up the central Solomons, and on November 1 the 3rd Marine Division steamed into Bougainville's Empress Augusta Bay and landed under a three-day-old moon. This was a big step, as steps were measured that year in the Pacific. If Seabees and Army engineers could somehow build a large airfield in this green slime, U.S. fliers would be within fighter range of Rabaul.

The enemy thought it unlikely. He buffeted the invaders by air and sea but held back his best troops, thinking the Americans would use the bay to stage a push elsewhere. On Christmas Day U.S. engineers finished their big strip, Piva Uncle, above the forks of the Piva River. The American* and 37th divisions ringed it with a perimeter of steel, and when the Japanese finally came howling down on it with their elite 6th Division they were stopped cold. By then Rabaul was just about surrounded. Emirau and the Green Islands had been occupied; the 112th Cavalry was in Arawe; the 1st Marine Division had taken Cape Gloucester in New Britain; and troopers of the 5th Cavalry, General Robert E. Lee's old outfit, and the 7th Cavalry, General Custer's, were ashore in the Admiralty Islands. Massive U.S. sorties from Piva Uncle were making Rabaul unlivable. The Japanese had no choice; they had to write Rabaul off. They evacuated what they called their "consolation units" — Korean whores — and left the garrison to suffer as U.S. bombers, unescorted and unchallenged, flew in daily and unloaded overhead.

Meanwhile, the character of the war was changing. It had to change; so far Americans had been only nibbling at the outer edges of the expanded Japanese Empire. They had spent nine months moving 250 miles in the central Solomons, and Tokyo was still five thousand miles away. But new equipment was arriving from home. Makeshift World War I weapons — which had been sent here because of ETO priorities — were now being replaced by rockets, amphibious tractors, boats with wheels — DUKWs ("ducks") — and flamethrowers that could lick around corners. The Navy had more of everything: fifty carriers led by the fast *Independence* class, converted from cruiser hulls. If Nimitz could somehow get closer to Japan, his submarines, which had already sunk a million tons of enemy supplies, could destroy the Japanese merchant marine, and since Japan, like England, was surrounded by water, this would have the same impact as

---

*So named because it was formed on New Caledonia. Twenty-five years later its junior officers would include one William Calley Jr.

in the Battle of the Atlantic. With closer bases Tokyo could also be reached by air; the first B-29 Superfortresses, with a range of 1,500 nautical miles, would soon be on their way. The solution to all this was to open up a new theater of war, the Central Pacific, and on November 20, 1943, the 2nd Marine Division did that. It wasn't supposed to be easy. Everyone knew the Gilbert Islands bristled with Japanese defenders. But no one anticipated a Tarawa.

Tarawa was the battle America almost lost. The enemy commander had boasted that Betio, the key island in the atoll, couldn't be taken by a million men in a hundred years. "Corregidor," said Samuel Eliot Morison, "was an open town by comparison." The marines going in had other problems: the naval bombardment had been too light, the tides betrayed them, they missed H-hour, and at the end of the first day their beachhead was exactly twenty feet wide. Officers stood waist-deep in the water, directing the battle by radio and praying against a counterattack. Only the breakdown of Japanese communications prevented one. The next day the marines drove through and split the defenses, but the attackers had lost three thousand men. The following month Kwajalein and Eniwetok, in the Marshall Islands, were taken more cheaply. Nevertheless, from the very first, battles in the Central Pacific were short and terrible — the 4th Marine Division, blooded on Kwajalein, was in action only sixty-one days during the entire war, yet it suffered 75 percent casualties.

There were several reasons for this sudden lengthening of casualty lists. On Guadalcanal the enemy had been taken by surprise. He would never be caught unprepared again. Furthermore, in storming the Marshalls and the Marianas, U.S. troops were attacking islands which had been mandated to Japan after World War I; the Japanese had been digging in for nearly a quarter-century. The greatest reason for greater bloodshed in the Pacific, however, was a dramatic change in Jap tactics. The Oriental masters of amphibious offense had gone over to an iron defense. Dai Honei, Imperial headquarters, radioed reminders to every outpost that they must prepare a last-man resistance. One of them did more than that. On Biak, an island near the tail of the New Guinea bird, the enemy had ten thousand men. Their commander, Colonel Naoyuki Kuzume, decided that while dying on the beach was all very fine, dying inland would be better; by skillful use of caves and cliffs, his men could prolong the slaughter of what one Japanese diary keeper contemptuously called "these blue-eyed Americans."

Kuzume had made the most murderous discovery of the island war. Tokyo might never had heard of it had Biak not lain directly in the path of MacArthur's drive on the Philippines. Having mopped up the bird's tail, the general was skipping up its back in the spring of 1944, using a new U.S. tactic, "leapfrogging." Americans had stumbled upon this course while retaking Attu and Kiska, the Alaskan isles with which Yamamoto had tried to mislead Nimitz during the Battle of Midway. Lacking strength to attack both, operations officers bypassed Kiska — and discovered, after

Attu had been retaken, that the Japanese had quietly evacuated it. Mac-Arthur caught on. Late in April he leaped into Hollandia, and a month later the 41st Division hit Biak. Until now the cost of the offensive had been relatively light, but Kuzume's cliff-and-cave defenders exacted a terrible toll; before the island was secured casualty lists were approaching Tarawa's.

They might have been worse. The Japanese Navy, in hiding for a year, was preparing to emerge and reinforce the garrison. The ships were already at sea when, in mid-June, word reached Admiral Jisaburo Ozawa that Nimitz's Central Pacific drive was about to pounce on the Marianas' key islands — Saipan, Tinian, and Guam. This was the greater threat, and prows were turned that way. The resulting Battle of the Philippine Sea was another of those long-distance aircraft duels that disappointed old line-of-battle salts. It was, nonetheless, a stunning American victory. Hellcats knocked out the enemy's land-based air power on Guam and, in eight hours of continuous fighting in the sky, beat off four massive attacks on the U.S. fleet. It was the most spectacular carrier battle of the war; by the end of the following day Ozawa's air arm had been reduced from 430 operational warplanes to 35. After this Great Marianas Turkey Shoot, as Navy pilots called it, Ozawa withdrew — and Japanese soldiers on Saipan were cut off.

The Nips swore that they would make the Americans pay the highest possible price for Saipan. There were twice as many defenders as intelligence had predicted, and U.S. casualties dismayed Washington. After three thousand Japs had staged the war's biggest *banzai* attack, driving GIs into the surf, surviving soldiers and marines wiped out the rest of the enemy or waited while the suicides saved them the trouble. Two weeks later other marines were fanning out across Guam's reefs. Guam was only half as expensive as Saipan, partly because the *banzai* was less effective. U.S. casualties on Tinian, where the Japanese hadn't thought a north shore landing possible, were even lighter. Even so, the Marianas Islands had cost twenty-five thousand Americans killed or wounded. Yet they were priceless. They gave the B-29s their first base within flying range of the Japanese home islands. Marine Lieutenant General Holland M. "Howlin' Mad" Smith, the commanding officer in the U.S. struggle for Saipan, called it the decisive battle of the Pacific war. Tokyo agreed; the German naval attaché there had reported to Berlin that the island was "understood to be a matter of life or death." The Tojo cabinet fell, and for the first time Americans saw a way to victory in the Pacific, and were heartened.

At the outset MacArthur had opposed the marines' invasion of Guadalcanal, and these thrusts in the Central Pacific so far from his own theater in the Southwest Pacific, suited him even less. "Island hopping," as he now called it scornfully, seemed to him a waste of time — though it was indistinguishable from his own "leapfrogging." By the summer of 1944 he was beside himself. Admiral King was suggesting that U.S. forces bypass the Philippines. America had to keep faith with the Filipinos, MacArthur insisted; it was a matter of honor. A matter of sentiment, King replied, and both appealed to Roosevelt.

The President, whose political advisers wanted him in Chicago at the Democratic national convention, went to Hawaii instead. He had to settle the military issue. On July 26, as the battle for Guam raged, the presidential aircraft touched down at Hickam Field. Nimitz and MacArthur, up from Australia, stated their cases. In a private session MacArthur actually threatened Roosevelt with political reprisals if his strategic plan was set aside; should the general's promise to return to the Philippines be unredeemed, he said, "I dare say that the American people would be so aroused that they would register most complete resentment against you at the polls this fall." This was insolent and probably untrue, but FDR had seen it coming and had made his choice before leaving the White House. He answered, "We will not bypass the Philippines. Carry on your existing plans. And may God protect you."

The Combined Chiefs of Staff weren't satisfied. In Washington they argued for two months before agreeing that MacArthur should return to the Philippines. In the meantime Halsey had made a startling suggestion. The Philippine timetable called for early landings on Peleliu, Yap, and Mindanao. Air strikes convinced Halsey that the enemy's air force was a broken lance. He proposed skipping the preliminaries and charging right into Leyte. His motion was carried, though the Peleliu operation, too far advanced to be canceled, went ahead as scheduled. The consequences were tragic. Biak had become a magic word in Tokyo. Kuzume's lesson had been passed on to the commanding officer on Peleliu, who had made his men moles. Burrowed in natural limestone caves linked by underground tunnels and protected by layers of coral sand and concrete, they cut the 1st Marine Division to pieces, giving all American regiments a bitter taste of what was to come.

By the time the jagged ridges north of Peleliu airfield had been cleared, four American divisions were swarming over the beach at Leyte Gulf. Less than an hour after the main landings on October 20, 1944, the 382nd Infantry had the Stars and Stripes up; four days later General Walter Krueger's Sixth Army command post was ashore and Yamashita's Thirty-fifth Japanese Army was marching against it. Krueger seemed stuck in the mud, and in Leyte Gulf the stage had been set for the greatest naval battle of all time.

Yamamoto was dead, but the Japanese Navy still cherished his dream of a decisive action at sea, preferably while U.S. ships were busy covering a landing. Now, if ever, was the time for it. Four separate Japanese task forces sailed against Halsey's main fleet, which was protecting the Leyte operation, and Admiral Thomas Kinkaid's weaker group of old battleships and small carriers. The enemy admirals knew they couldn't match America's new power — the U.S. had 218 warships, the Japanese had 64 — so they hatched a brilliant plan. Leyte Gulf could be reached through two straits, San Bernardino to the north and Surigao to the south. Their center force, led by Admiral Takeo Kurita, was to head for San Bernardino while two southern forces entered Surigao. At the same time the fourth force, Ozawa's, was to lure Halsey away to the north. Kinkaid would then be helpless. *Banzai.*

The southern prongs had no luck. Admiral Jesse Oldendorf had Surigao Strait corked. Torpedoes and gunfire exterminated the first Jap column; the second turned back after firing at radar pictures which later turned out to be islands. In the beginning Kurita's luck seemed bad, too. On the way to San Bernardino, American submarines destroyed two of his heavy cruisers, and his largest battleship was sunk by U.S. aircraft. Actually these losses were a stroke of fortune for Kurita. Halsey, learning of them, thought him finished, and when Ozawa's decoy was sighted Halsey took off after the bait — leaving San Bernardino Strait unguarded. In the darkness of October 24 Kurita slipped through. The following morning he sprang on Kinkaid's exposed carriers in the first moments of daylight.

The carriers' only protection was their screen — destroyers (DDs) and destroyer escorts (DEs), vulnerable vessels ordinarily used for antisubmarine work and manned mostly by married draftees. The destroyers counterattacked Kurita's battleships, and then their gallant little escorts, who hadn't even been taught to form a line of battle, steamed toward the huge Japanese guns. Kurita's goliaths milled around in confusion as the DEs, some already sinking, made dense smoke. The U.S. carriers sent up everything that could fly, and Kurita, with the mightiest Japanese fleet since Midway, turned tail. The rout was complete, for Halsey was thorough in his error; he chewed up Ozawa's bait, and in the final Leyte Gulf reckoning the enemy lost three battleships, four carriers, and twenty other warships. The emperor's sea power was finished.

On Leyte the Sixth and Eighth Armies were now pulling a drawstring around the enemy bag. Yamashita, in Manila, privately wrote off the island at Christmas, though it wasn't freed until the following St. Patrick's Day. By then Yamashita could have done nothing about it anyway. GIs had hit the island of Mindoro on December 12; three weeks later four divisions made an almost unopposed landing at Luzon's Lingayen Gulf. Bypassing the northern defenses of the Yamashita Line, they jumped Bataan, then Corregidor, and finally, in early March, Manila.

On Bataan and Corregidor, as an Army officer wryly remarked at the time, the United States was "right back where we started." B-29s had begun to scar the Japanese homeland, but it was still a remote fortress. Bringing it closer was the task of the other American pincer — the Central Pacific thrust that had driven from Tarawa through the Marshalls to Saipan. Its next target was the volcanic pile of Iwo Jima, "on the ladder of the Bonins," as Admiral King put it. Saipan was within B-29 range of the Japanese capital, but only just. Superfort bomb loads were limited to two tons; those damaged in raids couldn't get back. But if the Americans held

Iwo, they would be 660 miles from Japan. The B-29s could carry seven tons of bombs and Tokyo would miss warnings of coming raids now radioed to the capital by Japs on Iwo.

The enemy thought a lot of Iwo's eight square miles. The Navy's seventy-four days of preinvasion bombardment scarcely jarred the defenders, because they had no barracks aboveground. Most of their caves were shielded by at least thirty-five feet of overhead cover. Nearly every Jap weapon could reach the beaches. The first two hours ashore were comparatively tranquil. Then the beachhead was blanketed with mortar fire. Despite this, Mount Suribachi and Motoyama Airfield No. 1 were taken in the early days of the battle, which, in the first year of the war, would have been it. Everyone waited for the Nips to form a *banzai* charge and come in to be slaughtered. They didn't. Enemy soldiers had been thoroughly trained in Biak tactics. They stuck to their pillboxes and ravines, and when the end came in March the grim abacus showed 19,000 marine casualties.

The abacus was grimmer for the enemy. The Japanese equivalent of "It never rains but it pours" is "When crying, stung by bee in the face." Stinging Superforts were swarming low over his homeland, beginning the methodical destruction of eighty Jap cities, killing one hundred thousand people in a single day in the great Tokyo raid of March 9, 1945. Halsey's carriers had broken into the South China Sea, cutting the enemy's oil and rice lines. Hirohito's merchant navy was a skeleton; soon the American submarine score would be over a thousand ships. Shantytowns were rising in Yokohama and Osaka. Jap civilians were racked by tuberculosis and malaria. There was no food for their ration cards. Menacing reports from Japanese commanders in Manchuria reported that Russian troops were mobilizing on their frontier. When crying, stung by bee in the face.

Yet the Japanese morale showed no signs of cracking. Old men and women were being armed with bamboo spears. "Come and get us," Tokyo Rose dared. To oblige, the Americans needed one more invasion base: Okinawa. General Mitsuri Ushijima, Okinawa's commanding officer, had guessed in March that he would be receiving hostile visitors near Yontan Airfield on April 1. He was right. And he had a surprise for them. April 1 was Easter Sunday, but it still looked like April Fools' Day to the GIs and marines wading ashore. There didn't seem to be any enemy soldiers around. No one then guessed that it would take nearly three months to conquer the island, or that Okinawa would be the bloodiest battle of the Pacific war. Actually Ushijima had a hundred thousand soldiers concentrated in the southern third of the island. By April 12 it was clear that this would be another Iwo. Okinawa's burial vaults had been converted to pillboxes; caves masked heavy artillery that could be rolled in and out on railroad tracks. Ushijima expected to win, too. The Japanese strategy was to wait until all American troops were ashore, knock out the U.S. fleet with suicidal kamikaze bombers, and slaughter marines and GIs at leisure.

In Warm Springs, Georgia, where President Roosevelt had dressed and settled in his leather armchair, the global situation was more promising. Chatting with Lucy Rutherfurd and two visiting cousins, Miss Margaret Suckley and Miss Laura Delano, the President was all smiles and optimism. Strategically, American arms were victorious on all fronts. Germany had been cut in half. Apart from a few obstinate pockets the Wehrmacht was disintegrating, surrendering by the tens of thousands. Japan would be more difficult, of course. Iwo Jima had fallen, in time Okinawa would, too; there could be no doubt about the eventual outcome. Yet as of this April 12, the war against the Axis had cost the lives of 196,669 Americans; total U.S. casualties were 899,669 Americans — 6,481 of them in the past week. There could be no glossing that over. After so great a sacrifice, he had told those around him, world peace would be absolutely secure.

Shortly before noon Bill Hassett appeared, dragging a leather pouch from Washington. The mail had arrived. Hassett suggested that the President postpone his paper work until after lunch, but FDR said he would do it right now. Hassett put before him a State Department paper requiring his approval. Roosevelt brightened. "A typical State Department letter," he cheerily told the ladies. "It says nothing at all." He worked through the rest of the papers, affixing his weakened signature to a batch of postmaster appointments, routine correspondence, and Legion of Merit awards to eminent Allied statesmen. The White House still regarded ballpoint pens as a passing fad. Fountain pen ink could easily be smeared, blemishing a document, so as the President worked, Hassett laid out the signed papers on a divan, empty chairs, and the rug. When he came to Senate Bill 298, extending the Commodity Credit Corporation, he winked at Lucy Rutherfurd and said, "Here's where I made a law." Just then there was a sound in the outer hall. Madame Elizabeth Shoumatoff, the portrait painter, had arrived. She glanced in, puzzled by the sheets of paper everywhere. "Oh, come right ahead," Roosevelt called. "Bill is waiting for his laundry to dry."

Hassett went about it quickly, and with averted eyes. He did not approve of Madame Shoumatoff. She distracted the President too much, he thought, with her measurements of his nose and requests to turn this way or that, and she even dictated his apparel; this morning, for example, he was wearing a Harvard tie and a vest, neither of which he liked. To Hassett all this was "unnecessary hounding of a sick man." He didn't even think she was much of an artist, but Lucy liked her, and so did FDR. As Hassett left, handing Roosevelt a batch of State Department reports, Madame erected her easel and slipped his boat cloak over his shoulders. Instantly he became engrossed in the state documents.

Because the papers were diplomatic, and because FDR had been troubled all week by Russian duplicity (less than two hours ago he had cabled Churchill, "We must be firm"), it is not too fanciful to suggest that in the last moments of his life the President may have been reflecting upon the Yalta Conference in the Crimea, two months earlier. He had gone there because his military advisers had told him that it was necessary. General MacArthur, General Albert Wedemeyer, and the Joint Chiefs had spoken with one voice: they wanted the Soviet Union to declare war on Japan, and they believed it worth almost any price. At that time — six months before atomic weapons were to alter permanently the nature of war and geopolitics — none of those who knew of the Manhattan Project thought it worth mentioning. "The bomb will never go off," wrote Admiral Leahy, Roosevelt's chief of staff, "and I speak as an expert in explosives."

At Yalta, Roosevelt and Churchill got more from Stalin than they had expected. In the past they had found the Soviet dictator a hard bargainer. He liked to sit impassively behind the impenetrable screen of the Slavic language — his stock of English phrases was confined to "So what?" "You said it," "The toilet is over there!" and "What the hell goes on here?" — and in his present position he could afford to gloat. For nearly three years he had been the weakest of the three, begging the Anglo-Americans to open a second front in Europe and unable to offer them anything in exchange. Now they had to come to him. Nevertheless he was mellow. He secretly agreed to enter the anti-Japanese coalition. In return the Soviet Union would be given certain privileges in Manchuria (notably a half-interest in the eastern end of the Trans-Siberian Railway), the Kurile Islands, half of Sakhalin (another island north of Japan), an occupation zone in Korea, a U.N. veto for major powers, and, in another secret agreement which would later cause domestic difficulties in the United States, U.N. seats for the Ukraine and Belorussia. The Anglo-Americans further agreed to recognize the autonomy of Outer Mongolia.

Poland's borders were to be redrawn, adding lands that had been German. Stalin solemnly joined his allies in guaranteeing all eastern European countries, including Poland, the right to choose their leaders and governments in free elections. Long afterward the American President and the British prime minister were assailed as naive; how, it was asked, could they have trusted pledges from so implacable an enemy of democracy? The fact is that they had very little choice. They were at war with Japan; Russia wasn't; the Red Army could do as it pleased, promises or no promises. At the time it appeared the Russian dictator, flushed from the European victory, was in a generous mood. The greatest beneficiary of the conference seemed to be Chiang Kai-shek. Stalin signed a treaty with Chiang recognizing him as the ruler of all China and promising to persuade Mao Tse-tung's Chinese to cooperate with him.

Pat Hurley and Henry Luce praised the Yalta agreements; so did the American and British press. Averell Harriman and George Kennan, both veteran Kremlinologists, were skeptical. But that was not a popular view in early 1945. Winston Churchill had urged Eisenhower to "shake hands with the Russians as far east of the Elbe as possible." Ike disagreed. He countermanded an order which would have sent Patton into Prague and withdrew his GIs west of the Elbe, permitting the Russians to free Czechoslovakia, eastern Germany, and Berlin. After visiting Moscow Eisenhower declared: "Nothing guides Russian policy so much as desire for friendship with the United States."

In Warm Springs Roosevelt stirred and glanced at his watch. It was 1 P.M. To Madame Shoumatoff he said, "We've got just fifteen minutes more."

She wasn't doing much now. He had become so engrossed in his papers that she hadn't dared ask him to resume his pose. She was occupying her time filling in colors.

Lizzie McDuffie, an elderly black servant, paused at the door and glanced into the living room. She saw Lucy Rutherfurd facing the President. He had just said something witty; she was smiling. "That is the last picture I have in my mind of Mr. Roosevelt," she said afterward. "The last I remember he was looking into the smiling face of a beautiful woman."

FDR slipped a cigarette into his holder and lit it. He had now fallen so far from his pose that the painter despaired of regaining his attention. Watching, she saw him raise his left hand to his temple and press it. He appeared to be squeezing his forehead. The hand fell, the fingers twitched; it was as though he were fumbling for something. Miss Suckley put down her crocheting and stepped over, asking, "Did you drop something?" He pressed his left hand behind his neck, closed his eyes, and said softly — so softly only she heard him — "I have a terrific headache." His arm fell. His head drooped to the left. His chest slumped. It was 1:15 P.M.

Daisy Suckley phoned for Dr. Bruenn and asked Madame Shoumatoff to find the nearest Secret Service agent. The painter did, and then headed toward her car. Flying after her was Lucy Rutherfurd; Eleanor Roosevelt must never know of her presence here. Of course he would recover. As the word spread through the household, everyone felt that way. The thought of an America without Franklin Roosevelt in the White House was insupportable; the young men fighting overseas could hardly remember a time when he had not been President. This was a passing thing. The doctors would fix it, everyone assured everyone else, and all were convinced of it except the doctors.

On orders from Dr. McIntire, Dr. Bruenn had become virtually a member of the presidential staff; he was always just around the corner. At 9:30, just before the President's breakfast, Bruenn had examined his patient. There had been nothing wrong with Roosevelt's heart. His blood pressure was high — 180 systolic over 110 to 120 diastolic — but not alarming. It had been running at those levels for some time now. He hadn't been tense. In conversations with the doctor during the past week he had commented bitterly on Stalin's behavior since Yalta, but he hadn't mentioned that this morning. Now Bruenn, racing into the cottage, saw Roosevelt sagging against, and held up by, the arms of his chair. FDR's cousins sat petrified on the couch.

Momentarily the President stopped breathing. Then his breath became harsh. His tongue was blocking his throat. His neck was rigid, his systolic blood pressure over 300, and his left eye was dilating wildly. What had happened was that an artery in Roosevelt's brain had developed a tiny puncture, probably because it was old, fragile, and easily ruptured. Blood from this perforation had seeped into cavities around the brain, and the brain, sensitive to the slightest change, was sending frantic distress signals. The victim's eyes were distorted; he suffered from vertigo; his breathing became more audible; he sounded as though he were snoring. To a physician those signals had but one meaning. The patient was suffering from a massive cerebral hemorrhage. At this point Bruenn could not gauge the severity of the stroke, but he could provide emergency relief. Swiftly scissoring away Roosevelt's clothes, he injected doses of papaverine and amyl nitrite into the President's arm, re-dressed him in striped blue pajamas, and, with the help of a male servant and a Navy physiotherapist who had arrived to give FDR his daily rubdown, gently carried him to his maple bed. The only sound those outside the room could hear were the great gasping, anguished snores.

Bruenn called McIntire in Washington, who endorsed Bruenn's diagnosis and the treatment. Physicians today would hesitate to administer amyl nitrite, which depresses blood pressure and decreases the vital flow of blood to the brain, but the President was beyond help anyway. He had now been unconscious for fifty minutes. Bruenn reported intense narrowing of the blood vessels (vasoconstriction) and partial paralysis. McIntire phoned an eminent Atlanta specialist, Dr. James E. Paullin, and begged him to reach Warm Springs as quickly as possible. Speeding down back roads and shortcuts and expecting, as he later put it, "to be picked up any moment," Paullin made Warm Springs in less than an hour and a half. As he explained in his report to McIntire, "The President was *in extremis* when I reached him. He was in a cold sweat, ash gray and breathing with difficulty. Numerous rhonchi in the chest. . . . Within five minutes of my entrance into the room, all evidence of life passed away. The time was 3:35 o'clock."

Until that moment Fala had been sitting quietly in the bedroom. Now he seemed to sense the change. Abruptly the dog leaped from his corner, brushed the screen door open, and raced, frantically yelping, to the top of the nearest hill. There he stopped barking and stood immobile, as though on vigil.

Inside the bedroom, the first mourner was Grace Tully: "Without a word or glance toward the others present, I walked into the bedroom, leaned over and kissed the President lightly on the forehead." Good taste and form required that the First Lady and the Vice President, the new President, be informed before the press learned what had happened. Hassett and Bruenn asked McIntire to put them through to Steve Early, the President's press secretary. Stifling his own grief, Early told them to say nothing until he could reach Eleanor Roosevelt.

The President's widow was at that moment preparing to speak at the annual tea of the Sulgrave Club at 1801 Massachusetts Avenue N.W. in Washington. Shortly after 3 P.M., when the President had been unconscious for forty-five minutes, Laura Delano called from Warm Springs and guardedly told her that the President had "fainted." A few minutes later McIntire phoned the First Lady. He saw no reason for panic, he said, but he had requisitioned a Navy plane to carry her and him to Georgia. She inquired: should she cancel her speech? Not at all, he said; it might lead to rumors. On that advice she spoke on the United Nations. Afterward Evalyn Tyner, a pianist, began to play selections. Again Mrs. Roosevelt was called to the phone; this time it was Steve Early, "very much upset," in her words, asking her "to come home at once." She had a sinking feeling "that something dreadful had happened. Nevertheless the amenities had to be observed, so I went back to the party." She listened to Miss Tyner complete a piece and then excused herself, saying, "Now I'm called back to the White House and I want to excuse myself for leaving before this delightful concert is finished."

Outside, a presidential limousine awaited her. She "got into the car and sat with clenched hands all the way to the White House. In my heart I knew what had happened, but one does not actually formulate these terrible thoughts until they are spoken." Back in the sitting room on the second floor of the Executive Mansion, she sent for Early. Afterward he quoted her to the press as saying, "I am more sorry for the people of this country and of the world than I am for ourselves." It would have been appropriate, but the truth is that she never said it. The thought was Early's. What Eleanor really did tell him was that she wanted to see Harry Truman at once.

Framed dramatically against a background of red Levanto marble pilasters and heavy blue velvet embellished with a gold embroidered border, the sixty-year-old thirty-fourth Vice President was ostensibly presiding over the United States Senate. In reality he was scrawling:

Dear Mama & Mary: I am trying to write you a letter today from the desk of the President of the Senate while a windy Senator . . . is making a speech on a subject with which he is in no way familiar. The Jr. Sen. from Arizona made a speech on the subject, and knew what he was talking about. . . .

He hoped they were having nice weather, said it was "raining and misty" in Washington, and told them he would be flying to Providence Sunday morning. He added:

Turn on your radio tomorrow night at 9:30 your time, and you'll hear Harry make a Jefferson Day address to the nation. I think I'll be on all the networks, so it ought not to be hard to get me. I will be followed by the President, whom I'll introduce.

Hope you are both well and stay that way.

Love to you both.

Write when you can.

Senator Alexander Wiley surrendered the floor, Alben Barkley moved for a recess until the following day, and at 4:56, his official day over, the Vice President — ignorant of the fact that he had been America's thirty-third President for over an hour — dropped in on Speaker Sam Rayburn for a drink. He was there, sipping bourbon and water, when the White House switchboard located him. Early told him, "Please come right over and come in through the main Pennsylvania Avenue entrance." Puzzled, Truman thought Roosevelt had returned from Warm Springs early and wanted a word with him on some minor matter. Upstairs, one glance at Eleanor Roosevelt's face told him this was nothing slight. She put her hand on his shoulder gently and said quietly, "Harry, the President is dead." Dazed, he asked if there was anything he could do for her. She said, "Is there anything *we* can do for *you?* You are the one in trouble now."

Seventeen minutes later, at 5:47 P.M., the White House switchboard alerted the Associated Press, the United Press, and the International News Service* to an imminent conference call. Newspapermen for the three wire services were plugged in. They heard: "This is Steve Early. I have a flash for you. The President died suddenly this afternoon at . . ."

That was enough for Hearst's INS; it was first on the wire with:

FLASH

WASHN — FDR DEAD

INS WASHN 4/12/547 PPH36.

UP followed thirty seconds later with:

FLASH. WASHINGTON. PRESIDENT ROOSEVELT DIED THIS AFTERNOON.

Two minutes later, at 5:49 P.M., AP sent:

FLASH — WASHINGTON — PRESIDENT ROOSEVELT DIED SUDDENLY THIS AFTERNOON AT WARM SPRINGS, GA.

At the United Press Washington Bureau a rewrite man was taking down Early's dictation in reportorial shorthand:

at Warm Springs, Ga. deth resulted from cerebal hemorrhage — V-P Truman has been notified. Called to W hse & informed By Mrs. R. Secy of State has been advised. Cab meeting has been called. 4 boys in service have been sent message by their mother which sed — (no quote) that the president slipped away this afternoon. he did his job to the end as he wud want you to do. Bless you and all our love. Mrs. R. signed the message "mother."†

*The last two later merged and became United Press International (UPI).

†The actual text: DARLINGS: PA SLEPT AWAY THIS AFTERNOON. HE DID HIS JOB TO THE END AS HE WOULD WANT YOU TO DO. BLESS YOU. ALL OUR LOVE. MOTHER.

Mrs. R, Adm. McIntyre & Steve Early will leave WA by air t aft for warm Springs. We expect (Steve talking) to leave Warm S tmro a.m. by train for Wa. funeral services will be held Sat. aft. east room of W hse. Interment will be at Hyde Park Sunday aft. Detailed No detailed aranns or exact times have been decided on as yet.

for details hv get from man at Warm Springs.

In the office of radio station WRC at New York Avenue and Fourteenth Street N.W., the deskman was twenty-four-year-old David Brinkley He heard the INS machine ring four bells, ripped off the flash, and took it to his boss. On radio this was the children's hour; NBC was broadcasting the juvenile serial *Front Page Farrell,* CBS *Wilderness Road,* ABC *Captain Midnight,* and Mutual *Tom Mix.* By 5:49, however, commentators were beginning to come through on every network and local station. Radio commercials had been canceled for the next four days; there was nothing else to talk about. A Bronx housewife was asked if she had heard the radio bulletins. "For what do I need a radio?" she cried. "It's on everybody's face." People told strangers, who phoned their friends, who put through long distance calls to relatives. The flashes were broadcast in London and Moscow, even in Tokyo and Berlin, before most people in Warm Springs knew what had happened. In Germany, where darkness had fallen, Eisenhower was conferring with Patton and Bradley. They had retired for the night when Patton, realizing that he had forgotten to wind his watch, turned his radio to get the right time. He heard a BBC commentator, his voice breaking with emotion, say, "We regret to announce that the President of the United States has died." Patton woke Bradley, and together they roused Ike. At almost the same time, on a highway near Macon, Georgia, Lucy Rutherfurd asked Madame Shoumatoff if she might turn on the car radio. The painter nodded. They heard soft music, then the break: "We interrupt this program to bring you a special bulletin. . . ." Lucy gasped and covered her face with her hands.

In telegraphing her sons that their father had done his job to the end as he would "want you to do," Eleanor Roosevelt had meant just that. The Victorian sense of duty was strong in her. In leaving the Sulgrave Club she had been careful not to interrupt the proceedings or embarrass anyone. She believed in propriety, and her sons understood her. In the waters off Okinawa, Lieutenant John Roosevelt, USNR, was standing watch on the flag bridge of the carrier *Hornet* when he received a voice contact from the destroyer *Ulvert L. Moore,* under the command of Lieutenant Commander Franklin D. Roosevelt, USNR. In enemy waters identification was impossible but unnecessary; Groton-Harvard accents were rare. "Are you making it home, old man?" inquired the voice from the destroyer. "No," said the man on the *Hornet*'s bridge. "Are you?" Young FDR Jr. said, "Nope. Let's clean it up out here first. So long, old man — over." John Roosevelt: "So long — out."

Americans were incredulous, shocked, and above all, afraid. He had been leading them so long. Who would lead now? Cabell Phillips of the *New York Times* recalls that when the implications of what had happened sank in, the White House press corps was aghast: " 'Good God,' we said, 'Truman will be President!' " But at the moment it was unnecessary, and indeed impossible, to think of Truman. The long shadow of Roosevelt's passing lay dark across the land. Only then, Eleanor later conceded, did she realize how direct FDR's dialogue with the American people had been. Anne O'Hare McCormick wrote in the *New York Times* that he had "occupied a role so fused with his own personality after twelve years that people in other countries spoke of him simply as 'The President,' as if he were President of the World. He did not stoop and he did not climb. He was one of those completely poised persons who felt no need to play up or play down to anybody. In his death this is the element of his greatness that comes out most clearly."

Some responses were surprising. His voice trembling with unexpected emotion, Robert A. Taft said, "He dies a hero of the war, for he literally worked himself to death in the service of the American people." The author of the *New York Times* obituary editorial appeared to be almost overwhelmed with grief: "Men will thank God on their knees a hundred years from now that Franklin Roosevelt was in the White House when a powerful and ruthless barbarism threatened to overrun the civilization of the Western World." For the first time since Abraham Lincoln's death in 1865, the New York Philharmonic canceled a Carnegie Hall concert. In London, Churchill was told while entering his study at No. 10 Downing Street. He said he "felt as if I had been struck a physical blow." Buckingham Palace's Court Circular broke precedent by reporting the death of a head of state who was not a member of the royal family. Black-bordered Moscow flags flew at half-mast, and a *Times* correspondent cabled that people there said over and over, "We have lost a friend."

In Washington vast crowds gathered around the White House while Dean Acheson looked down on them from his window next door in the Executive Office Building. "There was nothing to see," he would write in his memoirs, "and I am sure they did not expect to see anything. They merely stood in a lost sort of way." In Berlin, where Russian artillery shells were falling outside the Führerbunker, Goebbels babbled, "My Führer! I congratulate you! Roosevelt is dead! It is written in the stars that the second half of April will be the turning point for us. This is Friday 13 April. It *is* the turning point!" Hitler was impressed. Radio Tokyo, on the other hand, amazed the world by quoting Premier Admiral Kantaro Suzuki as saying, "I must admit that Roosevelt's leadership has been very effective and has been responsible for the Americans' advantageous position today. For that reason I can easily understand the great loss his passing means to the American people and my profound sympathy goes to them." An announcer added, "We now introduce a few minutes of special music in honor of the passing of the great man."

Obscure mourners offered special eulogies. In San Diego, Petros Proto-papadakis petitioned a court to change his name to Petros FDR Proto-papadakis. The alarm system of the New York Fire Department sounded "four fives" to all fire stations — the signal that a fireman had died on duty. A little boy in Chicago picked a bouquet in his backyard and sent it with a note, saying he was sorry he couldn't come to the funeral. Other boys at Groton were told just before supper that the President, a member of the class of 1900, had just died. Leaving their meal untouched, they followed the headmaster into the chapel for prayer. In the village of Hyde Park, the bells of St. James Episcopal Church were tolling for its senior warden. And the *New York Post,* in a gesture which would have moved the President, simply headed its daily casualty list:

> Washington, Apr. 16 — Following are the latest casualties in the military services, including the next of kin.
>
> ARMY-NAVY DEAD
>
> ROOSEVELT, Franklin D., Commander-in-Chief, wife, Mrs. Anna Eleanor Roosevelt, the White House.

A *Yank* editor wrote, "We made cracks about Roosevelt and told Roosevelt jokes. . . . But he was still Roosevelt, the man we had grown up under. . . . He was the Commander-in-Chief, not only of the Armed Forces, but of our generation." An elderly black Georgian said, "He made a way for folks when there wasn't no way." Again and again, strangers told John Gunther, "I never met him, but I feel as if I had lost my best friend." Gunther himself could not, at first, comprehend the tragedy: "He was gone, and it seemed impossible to believe it. FDR's belief in the basic goodness of man, his work to better the lot of humble people everywhere, his idealism and resourcefulness, his faith in human decency, his unrivaled capacity to stir great masses and bring out the best of them — to realize that all this was now a matter of memory was hard to absorb." On Capitol Hill Congressman Lyndon B. Johnson said brokenly, "He was just like a daddy to me always. He was the one person I ever knew, anywhere, who was never afraid. God, God — how he could take it for us all!"

There were a great many Americans, of course, who did not think of him as a war hero, did not feel that they had lost their best friend, and certainly had not regarded him as a daddy. Often their feelings were mixed. One who had fought him bitterly said sadly, "Now we are on our own." Some were delighted to be on their own. In a Park Avenue hotel elevator, when news of the first flash was being whispered about, the wife of a prominent Wall Street lawyer nervously clutched a glove. She couldn't wait to get to a radio. Suddenly, directly behind her, a man said aloud, "So he's finally dead. Isn't it about time?" The woman turned and lashed her glove across the man's cheek.

Of all the eulogies, one by Samuel Grafton may have come closest to the feelings of those who would always think of Franklin D. Roosevelt as *the* President: "One remembers him as a kind of smiling bus driver, with that cigarette holder pointed upward, listening to the uproar from behind as he took the sharp turns. They used to tell him that he had not loaded his vehicle right for all eternity. But he knew he had stacked it well enough to round the next corner, and he knew when the yells were false and when they were real, and he loved the passengers. He is dead now, and the bus is stalled, far from the gates of heaven, while the riders hold each other in deadlock over how to make the next curve."

At 4701 Connecticut Avenue, in a second-floor five-room apartment, twenty-year-old Margaret Truman was dressing for a dinner date when the telephone rang. She remembered afterward that her father's voice sounded "tight and funny," but she, with her mind on the exciting evening ahead, said gaily, "Hi, Dad."

"Let me speak to your mother."

"Are you coming home for dinner?"

"Let me speak to your mother."

"I only asked a civil question!"

"Margaret, will you let me speak to your mother?"

Hurt, her eyes damp, the girl returned to her makeup table. Seconds later she glanced up and saw her mother standing in the doorway looking at her — or, as it seemed to Margaret, *through* her.

"Mother, what's the matter? What is it?"

Bess Truman answered slowly, "President Roosevelt is dead."

"Dead!"

Bess was phoning a friend when the doorbell rang. Margaret answered it. A strange woman was standing on the threshold.

"Miss Truman?"

"Yes?"

"I'm from the Associated Press. I would like a —"

Horrified, Margaret realized that she had come to the door in her slip. She slammed the door, and at that instant she comprehended that her days of privacy were over. Looking down from a window, she saw a crowd gathering — newspapermen, photographers, friends, curious onlookers, and, as the apartment manager was discovering, a crowd of applicants for a large, conveniently located $120 a month rent-controlled apartment which was about to be vacated.

The widowed First Lady was circling over Fort Benning's landing strip waiting for her plane to land, and in Atlanta Bill Hassett was buying a coffin at the undertaking firm of H. M. Patterson & Co. Hassett wanted a solid mahogany casket with copper lining, but there were none; all copper was going into the war effort. He then specified that the coffin must be six feet four inches long; Franklin Roosevelt had been a big man. Even that seemed unattainable. The undertaker *did* have a long mahogany casket, but he had promised it to a New Jersey funeral home. They haggled and bargained until Hassett, a shrewd Vermonter backed by the prestige of the Presidency, got the best coffin in the house. It arrived in Warm Springs at 10:45, accompanied by two hearses. Forty minutes later Eleanor Roosevelt, Dr. McIntire, and Steve Early drew up.

Mrs. Roosevelt had long talks with Grace Tully and each of her cousins. Who told her about Lucy Rutherfurd is not known; nevertheless she learned of it then, at the worst possible time. She shook visibly, then composed herself and went into the bedroom. Five minutes later she emerged, grave and solemn but dry-eyed. The time had come to plan the funeral, map its route, choose the service, name the clergymen, select the hymns, and decide who, under protocol, would be entitled to occupy the two hundred seats in the East Room of the White House, where the rites would be held. There were no precedents. Warren G. Harding had been the last chief executive to die in office, and the State Department had just discovered that Harding's funeral files were missing. Everything would have to be improvised, with the President's widow as chief improviser.*

A stout bier of thick Georgia pine was installed in the last car of the presidential train and draped with dark green Marine Corps blankets. In the coffin, the lower part of the President's body was covered by his boat cloak. Mrs. Roosevelt nodded her approval, and a flag was draped over the casket. They had worked through the night, in bright starlight, the air around them thick with the fragrance of honeysuckle. It was 9:25 on the morning of Friday the 13th before the procession moved down the red clay road to the train depot, led by the casket on its caisson and Fort Benning musicians beating muffled drums. Helmeted paratroopers lined both sides of the winding road. Many were white-faced, some faces were tear-stained, and one soldier wobbled as the caisson passed and then collapsed and rolled into a ditch. Graham Jackson, a black accordionist and the President's favorite musician, played "Going Home." Military pallbearers carried the coffin into the waiting car, and then, taking advantage of the one-degree grade, the engineer let the train glide silently away. This was to be the four-hundredth and final trip of Roosevelt's special train. The last two cars had been reversed. Mrs. Roosevelt rode in the "Ferdinand Magellan," now next to the last. Behind it, in the car FDR had used as an office, lay the coffin on its crude catafalque. Servicemen stood at attention on either side. Elsewhere on the train most blinds were drawn; here they remained up, and the lights over the flag-draped casket were to be left on all night, to permit outsiders to view it.

No one attempted to estimate the number of anonymous mourners camping by the tracks waiting for a glimpse of that casket. In Atlanta they

---

*One copy of the Roosevelt funeral plans was deposited in the archives of the State Department, and was used by Jacqueline Bouvier Kennedy for President Kennedy's funeral arrangements eighteen years afterward, in late November 1963.

weren't allowed near it; as the train slowly chugged down the station's track 9 it passed through an aisle of white-gloved soldiers holding bayoneted rifles at present arms. Nevertheless, the faithful had come; traffic was at a standstill for blocks around, and men and women could be seen on the roofs of garages, warehouses, factories, and tenements, peering down from vast distances while private planes circled overhead. Beyond Atlanta that afternoon silent crowds stood at every grade crossing, and as they were approaching Gainesville, Merriman Smith, in the press car, cried "Look!" and pointed. In the middle of a cotton field a group of black sharecropper women wearing bandannas were kneeling and holding out clasped hands.

At Greenville, South Carolina, the train paused to refuel, change crews, and acquire another American flag, this one fastened across the front of the locomotive by the new engineer. For at least five blocks on either side of the track, packed masses stood wide-eyed. Then a Boy Scout troop started singing "Onward, Christian Soldiers." It was "ragged at first," Merriman Smith later recalled, "but then it spread and swelled. Soon eight or ten thousand voices were singing like an organ." Heading north in the gathering darkness, Eleanor Roosevelt "lay in my berth all night with the window shade up, looking out at the countryside he had loved and watching the faces of the people at stations, and even at the crossroads, who had come to pay their last tribute all through the night. . . . I was truly surprised by the people along the way; not only at the stops but at every crossing. I didn't expect that because I hadn't thought a thing about it." She had always like Millard Lampell's poem about Lincoln's death, and now, peering into the night, with Fala at her feet, one quatrain kept running through her mind:

> A lonesome train on a lonesome track
> Seven coaches painted black
> A slow train, a quiet train,
> Carrying Lincoln home again. . . .

At 6:20 A.M. on Saturday the train passed through Charlottesville, Virginia. Dawn promised a lovely spring day; over the forests dogwood spread like a pink mist, and everywhere azaleas and lilacs were in full bloom. Less than four hours later President Truman met the train and the funeral procession began, down Delaware Avenue and turning west on Constitution. Franklin Roosevelt had come this way many times, beaming and waving his campaign fedora to the cheering thousands. They were here again today, more of them than ever, but the stillness was unnatural, broken only when twenty-four Air Corps Liberators passed overhead.

The capital had never seen such panoply before. Helmeted soldiers lined the sidewalks. A squadron of policemen on gleaming motorcycles paced the slow procession. The Navy and Marine bands played Chopin's "Funeral March," "Onward, Christian Soldiers," and the "Dead March" from *Saul*. A battalion of midshipmen marched. There were tanks, troop carriers, infantry in trucks, detachments of WACs, WAVEs, SPARs (the Coast Guard women), the Liberators overhead again — and then the little black-draped caisson bearing the casket suddenly appeared, led by six white horses and a seventh outrider: eyes hooded, stirrups reversed, sword and boots turned upside down and hanging from the stirrups: the mark of a fallen warrior since the days of Genghis Khan. Arthur Godfrey was describing the event to the nation over live radio; when he saw the caisson his voice broke and he sobbed. "It was so sudden," Bernard Asbell wrote. "It came so quietly. It seemed so peculiarly small. Just a big-wheeled wagon, dragged slowly, bearing the flag-covered oblong box. It was not a huge thing at all, as somehow everyone expected it to be. It was small, as though it might be any man's."

A right turn into Fifteenth Street, a left on Pennsylvania past weeping women — "Oh, he's gone. He's gone forever. I loved him so. He's never coming back"; "Oh Lord, he's gone, forever and forever and forever" — then through the White House northwest gate and up to the north portico. The Navy Band began to play "The Star-Spangled Banner," and a spry figure edged away and hurried toward the presidential office — Harry Truman, already on the job. Scarcely anyone noticed him. All eyes were on the doorway as the honor guard carried the coffin inside to the East Room, followed by the President's widow.

That Saturday afternoon was probably the quietest of the war. Across the country department stores were draped in black. The Ringling Brothers Barnum & Bailey circus had canceled its matinee. Movie theaters — seven hundred in New York alone — were closed. Newspapers had finished their runs early, for they were carrying no advertisements this day. Even grocery stores were locked up from two o'clock to five, and at four o'clock, when services began in the East Room, America simply stopped. AP, UP, and INS teletypes slowly tapped out: s i l e n c e . Buses and automobiles pulled over to curbstones. Trolley cars were motionless. Airplanes in the sky just circled overhead; those that had landed parked on their runways and did not approach terminals. Radios went dead. There was no phone service, not even a dial tone. In New York's subway tunnels, 505 trains halted where they were, and everywhere you saw men taking off their hats and women sinking to their knees. In that long moment the United States was as still as the two hundred worshippers gathered in the East Room of the Executive Mansion.

The walls in the room were almost obscured by ten-foot banks of lilies, whose cloying scent was overpowering. The congregation forgot to rise when President Truman entered, but almost no one noticed the lapse, not even Truman, and in every other respect the service went well. Roosevelt's empty wheelchair stood apart from the improvised altar, a mute reminder of the handicap he had overcome. At the widow's request the guests sang the Navy Hymn ("Eternal Father, strong to save . . .") and heard FDR's favorite passage from his own speeches, "The only thing we have to fear is fear itself," quoted by Episcopal Bishop Angus Dun in his eulogy. The

benediction was said at 4:23 P.M. Mrs. Roosevelt left first, and it was upstairs, in the private apartment of the First Family, that she exchanged bitter words with Anna. Her daughter had served as official hostess when the
First Lady was out of town, and when the President had asked Anna
whether she felt dinner invitations to "an old friend" — Lucy Rutherfurd —
would be proper, Anna had hesitated, knowing the implications, and then as-
sented. Eleanor felt doubly betrayed. Then she rallied. Drying her tears, she
descended to the East Room for a last goodbye. An officer opened the coffin
for her. She laid a bouquet within, and the coffin was then sealed forever.

At Union Station two trains awaited passengers to Hyde Park: the first
for the Roosevelts, the Trumans, the Supreme Court, the cabinet and close
friends, the second for congressmen, diplomats, and the press. At 9:30 P.M.
the funeral cortege retraced its morning route, past the stiffly erect soldiers
and the hushed public mourners on the pavements. Men in public life
being what they are, politics was under discussion the moment the train
left Washington. In the "Ferdinand Magellan," Harry Truman was talking
earnestly to Jimmy Byrnes and sizing him up as a future Secretary of
State, because Byrnes had been at Yalta and had an exact knowledge of
the agreements reached there. Harold Ickes was the loudest man in his car,
ridiculing Truman and bickering with his own wife. Henry Wallace sat
alone, dour and glum. Morgenthau had seen FDR in Warm Springs on
Wednesday evening, and he said that although the President's hand had
trembled a trifle more than usual when he poured drinks, he had been as
alert and well-informed as ever. Harry Hopkins was telling everyone who
would listen that the new President's name had definitely not been "picked
out of a hat" five months ago, that Roosevelt had been watching Truman's
performance for some time and had put him on the ticket because he had
led his committee well, was popular, and enjoyed prestige in the Senate,
where the peace treaties would be sent for ratification.

In the Bronx they paused again. When they left the Mott Haven yards
the second train was leading the President's, and word of the switch was
swiftly telegraphed up the Hudson shore to sorrowing New Yorkers waiting there. At daybreak a writer for the *New Yorker*'s "Talk of the Town"
drew up at the depot in Garrison, New York, a village directly across the
river from West Point. He asked the railroad crossing watchman when the
President's car would pass. "Be here between seven-thirty and eight," the
man said. "First there'll be the train with the congressmen and then, maybe
a quarter of an hour later, the President will go through." A crowd had
begun to gather. Among the spectators was a man with a shivering little
boy. "You've got to remember everything you see today," the father said.
"It's awfully cold," said his son.

Presently two or three dozen cars arrived, from Model A Fords to 1942
Cadillacs. The occupants seemed more excited than stricken, and it struck
the writer that maybe this was proper, that "Franklin Roosevelt would have

preferred to have left his world with more of a bang than a whimper." As they waited, they gossiped. ("I couldn't tell old Mrs. Beldon on Friday. The shock would have been too much for her." "I wish to God he'd managed to hang on until Germany was licked." "I wish the people would all stand in one place on the platform. It would make a bigger tribute.") A party of bearded brothers from Glenclyffe Monastery appeared in brown cassocks and sandals; they stood in a line, almost with military precision. A nervous woman said, "It will be just terrible if I don't see him." A man assured her, "They'll slow up when they see us."

They did. The first train passed, and then the second locomotive crawled past the station, trailing a plume of white smoke. Men took off their hats, as they had eighty years ago when Lincoln's casket passed here. First a Garrison youth in a red-and-blue-striped mackinaw gave a shout, and then for an instant they all had a clear view of the flag-covered coffin with its military guard of honor.

"I saw him!" a little girl cried. "I saw him real plain!"

"You couldn't have seen him," her embarrassed mother said. "He was sleeping under the American flag." But the child repeated, "I saw him."

The crowd dissolved slowly, as though uncertain what to do next. As the father and his shivering son left, the boy said, "I saw everything." The man said, "That's good. Now make sure you remember it."

Cold Spring, Poughkeepsie, Chelsea, Bacon, Stoneco, New Hamburg — names which would have been increasingly familiar to FDR — passed in succession, and at 8:40 A.M. that Sunday morning the locomotive veered off to a private Hyde Park siding on the edge of the Roosevelt estate. The moment it stopped, a cannon roared. Fifteen seconds later it roared again, and then again and again until the twenty-one-gun salute had been delivered. The West Point Band led the caisson and horses up the steep, wriggling, unpaved road that James Roosevelt had cleared in 1870, a wide trail that James's son Franklin had always called "the river road." Along this shore the boy had learned to swim, to row a boat, and, on the sunlit uplands, to ride a horse. Now one horse scrambled up the bank with an empty saddle and reversed harness.

The family estate was at the top of the hill. There, behind a ten-foot hedge in the rose garden, the fresh grave had been dug. The plan was for the brief ceremony here; every relative, dignitary, friend, and neighbor was escorted to his place. As the cadet escort presented arms, six servicemen bore the casket into the rose garden. Eleanor Roosevelt walked behind it. A crucifix appeared through a trellis green with woven leaves; the Hyde Park Episcopal vicar led the prayers in a ceremony which, Margaret Truman wrote in her diary that evening, "was simple and very impressive."

Raising his hand as the pallbearers slowly lowered the coffin into the ground, the rector ended:

> *Now the laborer's task is o'er;*
> *Now the battle day is past;*
> *Now upon the farther shore*
> *Lands the voyager at last.*
> *Father, in Thy gracious keeping*
> *Leave we now Thy servant sleeping.*

A lone plane circled overhead. Advancing with precision, a squad of cadets fired three rounds in the air, terrifying Fala. The little dog yelped, rolled over, and cringed. He was still trembling, looking frightened and lost, when the bugler blew taps.

Eleanor Roosevelt left slowly. In New York, wearing on her black dress the pearl fleur-de-lis Franklin had given her as a wedding present, she dismissed a gathering of reporters with four words. "The story," she said quietly, "is over."

ETO Montage

I've got sixpence, jolly, jolly sixpence
I've got sixpence to last me all my life
I've got tuppence to spend
And tuppence to lend
And tuppence to send home to my wife
Poor wife

*I'm dreaming of a white Christmas
Just like the ones I used to know*

PATTON SLAPS GI FUROR AT HOME

She Copies Nearly Everything with COPYFLEX

"Just gimme a coupla aspirin. I already got a Purple Heart."

O.K., you guys. Reveille. Drop your cocks and grab your socks.

I'm a sa-a-ad sack!

Out of Wartime Needs Has Come Startling Progress in Dry Batteries

"You'll get over it, Joe. Oncet I wuz gonna write a book exposin' the army after the war myself."*

*Unattributed quotations in this montage are captions from Bill Mauldin cartoons and appear in his *Up Front* (Holt, New York, 1945).

"Oh, I likes officers. They make me want to live till the war's over."

VICTORY and a BURBERRY

Radio Warsaw, this is Radio Warsaw. We lack food and medical supplies. Warsaw is lying in ruins. The Germans are murdering the wounded in the hospitals. They are driving women and children before their tanks as screens. Our sons are dying. Hear us, Holy Father, Vicar of Christ.

To many a truly discriminating man, not the least of the fruits of Victory will be the privilege of buying a Burberry topcoat . . .

cornball

and then Hope said, "Were the soldiers at the last camp happy to see me! They actually got down on their knees! What a spectacle! What a tribute! What a crap game!"

"This is Fragrant Flower Advance. Gimme yer goddam number."

While on pass you will be observed by civilians who will judge the United States Army by your appearance and conduct as an individual. Failure on your part to conform to regulations with respect to wearing your uniform and to live up to the highest traditions of the service will result in unfavorable criticism of the Army, your organization, and yourself.

I have read and understand the above statement and am familiar with the provisions of paragraphs 1 to 59 of the Soldier's Handbook.

Situation Normal All Fucked-Up

*I wouldn't give a bean
To be a fancy-pantsied Marine
I'd rather be a dog-faced soldier boy.*

Man Going on Leave

So what? I'm free, white, and twenty-one.

"Th' hell this ain't th' most important hole in th' world, I'm in it."

"This damn tree leaks."

PARIS LIBERATED!

Picasso Well, Busy In Rue Saint Augustin Studio

"Th' krauts ain't followin' ya so good on 'Lili Marlene' tonight, Joe. Ya think maybe somethin' happened to their tenor?"

flaking out

It's almost over and I'm almost home and I'm scared that maybe just a lucky shot will get me. And I don't want to die now, not when it's almost over. I just don't want to die now. Do you know what I mean?

shackup-job

"Beautiful view. Is there one for the enlisted men?"

I'm just a dog-faced soldier with a rifle on my shoulder
And I eat a kraut for breakfast every day
So feed me ammunition — keep me in the Third Division
Your dog-faced soldier boy's oh-kaaay!

"Ever notice the funny sound these zippers make, Willie!"

TWELVE

A New World, Under a New Sun

A T 6:30 ON THE WARM MORNING of April 13, 1945 — the Friday that
My Day's author submitted no column — Harry Truman stirred
on his pillow at 1701 Connecticut Avenue N.W., roused by the dreamy
feeling that some extraordinary urgency was awakening him. Then it hit
him: *he was President of the United States.* He bounded out of bed in one
motion and dove for his clothes as though ready for instant action, because,
as he later wrote in his memoirs, watching Roosevelt had convinced him
that "being a President is like riding a tiger. A man has to keep on riding
or be swallowed. . . . I never felt that I could let up for a single moment."

Truman was a hard rider, an up-with-the-sun Missouri farm boy with
the mulish strength of the Middle Border, an incisive mind, and a deeper
understanding of world history than most Presidents, including Franklin
Roosevelt. Little of this was visible at the time. With "almost complete
unanimity," *Time* wrote, his friends "agreed last week that he 'would not
be a great President.'" Speaker Sam Rayburn saw Truman as a man "right
on all the big things, wrong on most of the little ones." Nothing big
surfaced in the first hours of his Presidency, and the country was inclined
to take the word of the *Kansas City Star*'s Roy Roberts for it that "Harry
Truman is no man to rock the boat." To Roberts and other conservatives
the new President was a good-natured but poor politician, a dapper ex-
haberdasher who delivered tepid speeches with singsong rhetoric and a
flatter Midwest accent than Alf Landon's. He would sit out Franklin
Roosevelt's fourth term, they told one another, and then return to obscurity.

That was how they typecast the new President, and that, in the beginning, was how he looked. Washington believed that he had landed on the
1944 ticket as a compromise candidate. Roosevelt never denied it. If
memoirs are to be believed, he scarcely mentioned Truman to anyone
after their joint victory. The consequence was that Truman came into
office as the worst-prepared President in history.

All transitions have their awkward moments, and no one could be expected to match Roosevelt's flamboyance, but his successor somehow gave the impression of a country cousin who had just arrived in Washington for a quick tour and was stunned by the thought of his own insignificance. As Truman himself recalled it, Secret Service agents arrived at his apartment that first morning and led him down the back stairs, yet despite their presence he kept forgetting that he was the chief executive. A newspaperman addressed him as "Mr. President," and he winced; "I wish you didn't have to call me that," he said. In his first public statement after his hurried oath taking at the White House he had said, "It will be my effort to carry on as I believe the President would have done." To him, as to most of his constituents, the man who had died in Warm Springs remained "the President."

Arriving on the sidewalk that first Friday morning, he hailed an AP correspondent: "Hey, Tony, if you're going down to the White House, you may as well hop in with me." The Secret Service agents looked pained, and their displeasure turned to alarm when, downtown, he insisted upon walking to his bank. They were unaccustomed to a President who walked anywhere. News that the new chief executive was a pedestrian swept adjacent blocks, creating the greatest traffic jam in memory, and Truman ruefully conceded that his bodyguards were right — Presidents couldn't go to banks; it had to be the other way round. He enjoyed the deference, but whenever his new duties were mentioned, he paled. "Boys, if newspapermen pray," he told the White House press corps, "pray for me now."

In perspective his behavior seems natural. The death of the great leader had unnerved everyone; yesterday Truman had been sworn in — after a frantic search for a Bible — by a confused Chief Justice who thought the new President's middle name was Shippe, when in fact the S stood for nothing. Afterward Truman had impulsively kissed the Bible. At that time he knew no more about prosecution of the war than the average reader of the *Washington Post* — which, in fact, had been his principal source of information. Roosevelt had told him nothing. Truman had never been in the White House war room. It is astonishing to reflect that during his first day in office he had never heard of an atomic bomb, while Joseph Stalin knew almost everything about the Manhattan Project. Stimson had tried to take the new President aside for a quick briefing, but there wasn't time then. On the second day, as Truman tells it, "Jimmy Byrnes came to see me, and even he told me few details, though with great solemnity he said that we were perfecting an explosive great enough to destroy the whole world." Truman, from Missouri, just stared. Nearly two weeks were to pass before he would be properly briefed on the developments at Los Alamos, and then Admiral Leahy, speaking once more as an explosions expert, would snort that the project was a complete waste of taxpayers' money, "the biggest fool thing we have ever done."

Washington sophisticates were diverted by anecdotes of Truman's artlessness, though the stories lacked the malice of anti-Roosevelt lore and were sometimes funny. After attending a concert, the new President was invited backstage to meet the virtuoso. Vice President Truman had been photographed playing an upright piano with Lauren Bacall, looking very leggy, perched on top of it, and the virtuoso murmured politely, "I understand that you, too, play the piano, Mr. President." The President replied modestly, "Oh, no, not like you, maestro." The true significance of such stories is that President Truman could laugh at them, too. Ridicule couldn't touch him. He knew what he was, a rare trait in Washington, and was proud of his lack of ostentation, an even rarer one.

To be sure, he *did* lack grace, tact, brilliance, charisma. But millions who had been daunted by FDR's remote grandeur were delighted by HST's earthiness and unpretentiousness. Roosevelt hadn't told his own wife that he was going to run against Hoover, but after taking the oath Truman phoned his ninety-one-year-old mother in Grandview, Missouri. After that first flash from Warm Springs, the family home in Grandview had been under siege by reporters and photographers who phoned, rang the doorbell, and peered in windows. The elder Mrs. Truman ignored them. She did come to the phone for her son. "Mama, I'm terribly busy," he said. He assured her everything would be all right, but said, "You probably won't hear from me for some time." Reaching home, laden with documents, he followed Bess and Margaret to the apartment of a hospitable family next door. In his words: "They had a turkey and then gave us something to eat. I had not had anything to eat since noon. Went to bed, went to sleep, and did not worry any more that day." The Trumans wouldn't have dreamed of troubling the White House kitchen, or sending out to a restaurant. As in most Depression families, caution with money had become ingrained in their lives. In his faithful weekly letter to Missouri he described how he had learned of FDR's death with humility — "When I arrived at the Pennsylvania [*sic*] entrance to the most famous house in America, a couple of ushers met me" — and told of problems with the Connecticut Avenue apartment: "Our furniture is still there and will be for some time. . . . But I've paid the rent for this month and will pay for another month if they don't get the old White House redecorated by that time." He ended:

> I have had a most strenuous time for the last six days. I was sworn in at 7:09 p.m. Eastern War Time Apr. 12 and it is now 9 p.m. April 18th. Six days President of the United States! It is hardly believable. This day has been a dinger, too. I'm about to go to bed, but I thought I had better write you a note. Soon as we get settled in the White House you'll both be here to visit us. Lots of love from your very much worried son and bro.
>
> HARRY

Awaiting Eleanor Roosevelt's departure, the new First Family was living out of suitcases in Blair House, diagonally across Pennsylvania Avenue from the Executive Mansion. In her diary, Margaret was breathless: "It is perfectly beautiful. All old and priceless. Visiting dignitaries stay here. Dad is the first President to do so." But then, she was always euphoric these days — "Mother, Dad and I went to the Walter Reed chapel today," reads her entry for April 22. "Then we called on General Pershing! Such *excitement!*" The pejoratives "campy" and "square" were unknown in 1945, but "corny" was, and jaded Washingtonians applied it to Margaret and her natty father, who wore double-breasted gray suits with two-toned wingtip shoes, and opened his first coast-to-coast address by forgetting Sam Rayburn, so that the Speaker had to interrupt him with a hoarse, "Wait, Harry, until I introduce you." "To err," Washington said wittily, "is Truman." Very little was known about Bess Truman until a reporter found a county employee in Independence, Missouri, who had grown up with her. "She was a great girl," Henry P. Chiles said enthusiastically. "She was the first girl I ever knew who could whistle through her teeth."

Harry Truman was usually indifferent to criticism. Slurs on his wife and daughter were another matter. The most celebrated incident followed Margaret's debut as a professional singer in Constitution Hall. Paul Hume, the *Washington Post* music critic, wrote that the President's daughter "cannot sing very well," was "flat a good deal of the time," and "communicates almost nothing of the music she presents." Minutes after that day's copy of the *Post* reached the White House this holograph was dispatched to Hume:

> I have just seen your lousy review of Margaret's concert. . . . It seems to me that you are a frustrated old man. . . . Some day I hope to meet you. When that happens you'll need a new nose, a lot of beefsteak for black eyes, and perhaps a supporter below.
>
> H.S.T.

Margaret was humiliated. She told the press, "I am absolutely positive that my father wouldn't use language like that," and then ran upstairs in tears. HST humbly acknowledged that "Sometimes the frailties of the human get the better of me" (Hume opened his next recital review with "If I may venture to express an opinion"), and the episode was written off by everyone except those Republicans, Congressman Richard M. Nixon among them, who said they thought Presidents should conduct themselves with greater dignity.

To Truman's critics he was a joke, and a poor one at that. Roosevelt had at least behaved like a chief of state. He could never have forgotten himself long enough to excoriate a music critic or, as in another ill-tempered Truman missive, say that the Marine Corps had "a propaganda machine that is almost equal to Stalin's." Outside Washington, HST behaved like a Legionnaire at a national convention. In Florida he wore a white cap, crazy-colored Hawaiian shirts, and carried an outsize cane. En route to Fulton, Missouri, with Winston Churchill, he donned an engineer's cap and gaily drove the locomotive. In Kansas City he hopped into Frank Spina's barbershop and reminded Frank, "None of that fancy stuff. I don't want anything that smells." The press recorded it all, including his farewell kiss to his mother before boarding the *Sacred Cow* and her last words: "You be good, but be game, too."

In the days and weeks after FDR had been lowered into the earth at Hyde Park, no one expected much of the new President, and only a handful slowly reached the conclusion that by any standards HST was both good and game. In the White House war room, Marshall and Leahy found that they never had to tell him anything twice. Troop units, names of warships, battle plans, enemy dispositions, logistics data — he retained it all and cited it in his own concise appraisals. Before his first week had ended, he had tackled the prickly Palestine problem, was preparing for the first U.N. conference in San Francisco, had shaken up Washington's bureaucracy, and made three cabinet changes. He almost countermanded Eisenhower and sent GIs into Berlin and Prague; it was one of the few times in his life he didn't play a hunch, and the postwar history of Europe would have been far different if he had. In Moscow, Ambassador Averell Harriman, knowing almost nothing of his new boss, had boarded an embassy plane and flown across Asia, Europe, and the Atlantic — a record at the time — to be sure Truman wasn't beguiled by Stalin's deceit. On Monday, April 23, Harriman was admitted to the oval office and met the new President:

> I had talked to Mr. Truman for only a few minutes when I began to realize that this man had a real grasp of the situation. What a surprise and relief this was! He had read all the cables and reports that had passed between me and the State Department, going back for months. He knew the facts and the sequence of events, and he had a keen understanding of what they meant.

Roosevelt had tried to charm the Russians. Truman was blunt. When V. M. Molotov entered the oval office with Andrei Gromyko, the President said briskly that the United States and the United Kingdom had observed every Yalta covenant, but that honoring vows wasn't a one-way street. Molotov replied that the Soviet Union had been equally faithful to its word. Not in Poland, it hadn't, Truman shot back, and he wanted Molotov to know here and now that as long as Red puppets sat in eastern Europe, Poland would not be admitted to the U.N. Moreover, he hoped that sentiment would be conveyed to Stalin in exactly those words. Molotov answered indignantly, "I have never been talked to in my life like this." Truman said dryly, "Carry out your agreements and you won't get talked to like this." Afterward Harriman, who had lurked in the background, recalled, "He got quite rough with Molotov, so much so, in fact, that I was becoming a little concerned. But I must say I was quite proud of the new President."

Back from Hyde Park, Truman had invited Byrnes to join the new cabinet as Secretary of State, and Byrnes, in the President's words, "almost jumped down my throat taking me up on it." Dean Acheson, the new Undersecretary of State, wrote his son on April 30, "The new President has done an excellent job." By chance, he went on, he and Truman had spoken at length just two days before Roosevelt's death, and Acheson had "for the first time got a definite impression of him. He is straightforward, decisive, simple, entirely honest. . . . I think he will learn fast and will inspire confidence. It seems to me a blessing that he is the President and not Henry Wallace."

Marshall, Leahy, Harriman, and Acheson were among the early converts. Others took longer, and some had to be all but struck on the head with a blunt instrument, a skill at which HST was proficient. He had decided to appoint an old Missouri friend, John W. Snyder, as Federal Loan Administrator, and he called in Jesse Jones, the former head of the agency, to tell him the news. Jones was startled. He had expected to be consulted. He asked, "Did the President make the appointment before he died?"

"No," replied Truman. "He made it just now."

In late April the *Geneva Tribune* ran a headline: EVENTS SEEM TO BE SUCCEEDING ONE ANOTHER WITH GREAT RAPIDITY. They certainly were. The Führer's death was announced May 1, and that evening Julie Andrews saw London alight after dark for the second time. Berlin fell May 2. Later in the day the Germans in Italy surrendered. Two days later Wehrmacht commanders capitulated in Holland, Denmark, and northwest Germany. Then, on May 7, General Alfred Jodl and his staff signed unconditional surrender documents at Reims while Field Marshal Wilhelm Keitel was going through the same painful ceremonies under the eye of Soviet Marshal Georgi Zhukov in Berlin. It was a half-hour before midnight. For the first time in modern history the entire armed forces of a nation, officers and enlisted men alike, on land, at sea, and in the air, had become prisoners of war. During the following week all commanders in all armies moved troops, had orders cut, and synchronized watches for a common cease-fire, and suddenly it was V-E Day — May 8, 1945, Harry Truman's sixty-first birthday. The President was on the air at 9 A.M. (Churchill in London and Stalin in Moscow were giving their people the news at the same instant). His first words were, "The Allied Armies, through sacrifice and devotion and with God's help . . ." Hardly anyone remembered what he said after that. They were in the streets, in Times Square, hurling bales of ticker tape out Wall Street windows, dancing in the Chicago Loop, on Boston Common, at Hollywood and Vine, around Indianapolis's war monument and on Washington's Mall, on campuses and in war plants, wherever there was room to dance and sometimes where there was none: department store windows, telephone booths, elevators. Men wanted to kiss, women wanted to be kissed, and for one long moment they felt entitled to forget that other, more complicated war with an empire larger than Germany's and even more determined to fight on until every member of its race was extinct — taking with them the largest possible number of Japan's enemies. V-E Day hadn't dampened Tokyo's morale. The emperor was still divine; sacrificing your life in his name continued to be a guarantee of immortality. To all peace feelers Tokyo made the same reply; capitulation was and always would be out of the question.

History had been moving at breakneck speed since the relief of Bastogne on December 26, and since the momentum was to continue through September, survivors of that time are understandably hazy about the sequence of events. Many had no time for news anyhow. Fighting men were still in replacement centers, canteens, hospitals, cockpits, or on warships. They were mourning their dead, convalescing from military surgery, rereading mail from home, collecting autographs for short snorters, fighting boredom. At home their wives and mothers welcomed home crippled GIs or pored anxiously over casualty lists. In these circumstances, commentators often spoke to deaf audiences, piles of newspapers were thrown out unread, and months merged into a bewildering kaleidoscope.

Earthshaking events had passed in a blur. The United Nations Charter had been signed in San Francisco. Winston Churchill, in American eyes the very embodiment of indomitable Britain, was swept out of office in a Labour party landslide. MacArthur reconquered the Philippine archipelago. Fantastic drugs (drug was a benign word then) were emerging from war laboratories. For the first time in eleven years Fiorello La Guardia was no longer mayor of New York, and the familiar old Bond sign was coming down in Times Square. Americans scarcely had time to comprehend the pilotless V-2 buzz bombs when they were confronted by reports of the slaughter of six million Jews in Nazi killing centers, of Japan's kamikaze ("divine wind") pilots, who loaded their warplanes and then dove into U.S. ships, and finally — this time at American hands — of the annihilation of two Japanese cities, the first of them the size of Denver and the second larger than Newark.

V-E Day had aroused hope west of Hawaii, but little elation. The ETO had been somebody else's war; in the islands its chief significance lay in the promise of early reinforcement from Europe. Pacific veterans recited doggerel: "Home alive in '45," "Back in the sticks in '46," "Back to heaven in '47," "Golden Gate in '48." Barring a million-dollar wound (serious enough to make a soldier unfit for combat but fit for anything else), the men facing Japan were reconciled to the hard fact that expectations of returning home in '45, '46, or even in '47 were unrealistic. Most of them would have settled for '48; the chances of falling with an unlucky, mortal wound were growing with each battle. In Washington the Joint Chiefs agreed. The capture of Iwo Jima, less than eight square miles of volcanic ash, had cost 25,849 marines, a third of the landing force. Okinawa's price had been 49,151; kamikazes diving from the skies over Okinawa had sunk 34 U.S. warships and damaged another 368. If the Japanese could draw that much blood in the outer islands of their defense perimeter, how formidable would they be on the 142,007 square miles of their five home islands, where they would be joined — as they had been on Saipan — by every member of the civilian population old enough to carry a hand grenade?*

The Joint Chiefs had made an educated guess, based on the Yalta guarantee that Anglo-American forces would receive full support from the Red Army. Assuming a November 1 landing on Kyushu and a midwinter invasion of Honshu, the number of battle deaths, it was anticipated, would eclipse all other U.S. casualty lists, ETO and Pacific, combined. In the February 1947 *Harper's,* Stimson wrote: "I was informed that such operations might be expected to cost over a million casualties to American forces alone." (Total U.S. Pacific losses in World War II in breaching Japan's outer perimeter of defense were 170,596.) General MacArthur was less optimistic. So far, he pointed out, GIs and marines had been fighting isolated island garrisons, cut off from reinforcements. The vast mass of the Imperial Japanese Army, between five and six million troops with thousands of tons of ammunition stowed in underground caves, had never been defeated in battle. They were being brought home from China to defend the sacred soil of Dai Nippon, and were digging in. Unless the Japanese islands were to be blockaded and the people left to starve — the least humane of all solutions — that force must be met and defeated. MacArthur predicted the greatest bloodletting in history. He expected to take 50,000 casualties just in establishing that November 1 beachhead. Before an assault on Honshu could be contemplated, Allied navies must devise some way of protecting themselves against the 5,350 kamikazes known to be waiting in underground hangars, prepared to take that many vessels down with them. Finally, MacArthur warned Washington, all contact with an organized enemy might disappear. The Japs might fade into the mountains to fight as guerrillas. If they made that choice in Japan he predicted a ten-year war with no ceiling on Allied losses.

It was with this prospect that President Truman prepared for the coming conference in the Brandenburg city of Potsdam, seventeen miles southwest of Berlin. He *had* to have the Red Army. When Patton declared to a British audience that the U.K. and the U.S. must weld bonds of postwar friendship "because undoubtedly it is our destiny to rule the world," Stimson quickly told the press that the general spoke only for himself. U.S. newspaper editorials urged Patton to confine his public remarks to "For-

*Japan comprises four main islands, Kyushu, Honshu, Shikoku, and Hokkaido. Tokyo is in southeastern Honshu. In 1945 the population of these four was 72,598,077. When Radio Tokyo spoke of "one hundred million" Japanese, they were including such settled colonies as Saipan, mandated to the emperor by the Treaty of Versailles.

ward, men," "Fix bayonets," and "Open fire." Had Russia not been America's ally, General Marshall told the press, twice as many GIs would have been needed in the ETO, and General Eisenhower flew to the Kremlin to further cement bonds between Moscow and Washington. The marshals admired him, the commissars liked him, and Joseph Stalin beamed on his distinguished guest. The Soviet dictator presented Ike with a photograph of himself and saw to it that the American general was invested with the Order of Suvorov and Order of Victory. The second of these was a magnificent ornament.' With the possible exception of a gold sword trimmed with pearls from Queen Wilhelmina of Holland, it was the most expensive award Eisenhower ever received. Star-shaped and platinum, the medal was three inches in diameter and was set with ninety-one matched sixteen-carat diamonds. It is a historic irony that the holder of this decoration would later preside over an America in which men who had been favored in any way by the Soviet Union would lose their jobs, be browbeaten by congressional committees, and hounded in the streets by their neighbors. But in 1945 all that lay in the future. This was an era of good feeling between the world's two new superpowers. In pleasing Stalin, Eisenhower served his country well, and if two columns of cosmic fire had not intervened that summer, his service might have been even greater.

Stalin was a busy man then, entertaining the Allied supreme commander at the Kremlin, taking the new President's measure in Potsdam, and studying intelligence reports on the untried American super weapon known to the British as "tube alloys," to Stimson as X, to the Joint Chiefs as S-1, to a select few at Oak Ridge as S-Y, and among an even smaller number of scientists in the Los Alamos Tech Area — where the thing existed — as "the gadget."

The crowning achievement of scientific wisdom, the most expensive piece of hardware ever built, it had been designed to become the most efficient instrument of mass murder in history — if, of course, it worked; no one could be sure in advance. Meanwhile military security, unaware of the Fuchs-Gold-Rosenberg-Greenglass leaks, was keeping a tight lid not only on details, but also on the gadget's very existence. Early that spring seventy-five picked fliers had been ordered to Wendover Field in Utah, where they formed the 509th Composite Group of the 313th Wing of the 21st Bombing Command of the 20th Air Force. None of them knew the 509th's mission. All were volunteers, but when they asked just what it was they had volunteered for, they were told that they belonged to an organization which was "going to do something different."

They already knew that. Their flight maneuvers were highly unusual. One B-29 would simulate a high-level raid alone while two others watched for unusual weather, especially electrical storms. The lone raider would carry no blockbusters, the huge high-explosive demolition bombs dropped by normal B-29s. Instead it would be loaded with a large, oddly shaped missile armed with ordinary explosives. In point of fact, the missile was a precise reproduction of the shell of the Los Alamos device, constructed from blueprints while the first bomb was being perfected. The 509th didn't know what to make of it, and remained ignorant when sent overseas to Tinian, within easy bombing range of Japan. Here maneuvers were resumed while Dr. Philip Morrison, a young nuclear physicist, supervised the building of an advance laboratory on the island. The fliers weren't introduced to Morrison; for all they knew, he might have been the planner of a new PX. To add to their frustration, they were receiving warnings against hazards which, to their knowledge, didn't exist. Apparently someone in Washington thought they were all in danger of going blind; they were instructed to wear welders' goggles when airborne and never to look in the direction of a target after the bombardier had emptied the bomb bay.

Each evening at dusk other B-29s took off for Japan, and Dr. Morrison later told a Senate Committee: "We came often to sit on top of the coral ridge and watch the combat strike of the 313th Wing in real awe. Most of the planes would return the next morning, standing in a long single line, like beads on a chain, from just overhead to the horizon. You could see ten or twelve planes at a time, spaced a couple of miles apart. As fast as the next plane would land, another would appear at the edge of the sky. There were always the same number of planes in sight. The empty field would fill up, and in an hour or two all the planes would have come in."

To Morrison it was a majestic sight; to the 509th Composite Group it was a daily humiliation. They were all crack airmen, and leisure was eroding their morale. Tokyo Rose had greeted their unit by name when it arrived on Tinian; maybe *she* knew. Worst of all were the taunts from other fliers in the 313th who nightly dodged flak over the Empire, as B-29 crews called Japan. Some never came back, some returned wounded, while all the 509th did was cruise over tracts of the Empire so barren and strategically useless that the airmen never encountered antiaircraft fire. Now and then they would be told to drop a bomb — one lonely little bomb. It was demeaning, it was bewildering, and to compound their indignity a bombardier from another group mocked them in verse:

> Into the air the secret rose,
> Where they're going, nobody knows.
> Tomorrow they'll return again,
> But we'll never know where they've been.
> Don't ask us about results or such,
> Unless you want to get in Dutch.
> But take it from one who knows the score,
> The 509th is winning the war.

Tokyo Rose, with her omnipresent sources, picked up the satire. Take it from one who knew the score, she jeered, the 509th was winning the war.

Late in May the pariahs of Tinian were joined by a towering civilian named Luis W. Alvarez. Although no one on the island knew it or would have believed it, Alvarez had risked his life more often than any of them; working in remote canyons far from the mesa where the living quarters and Tech Area of Los Alamos stood, he had perfected the complex release mechanism of the gadget. He called it a "gun-type" contrivance — that is, a bomb in which one hemisphere of U-235 would be shot as a bullet into the second U-235 hemisphere. The Alvarez device, now accurate to one millionth of a second, completed technology's answer to the challenge posed a year and a half earlier under the empty stands of Alonzo Stagg stadium in Chicago.

This is what the bomb looked like in the spring of 1945, and these were its secrets:

Black, whale-shaped, and exquisitely machined, it was 28 inches in diameter and ten feet long. The entire assembly weighed 9,000 pounds; most of it was ballast. Its uranium core weighed only 22 pounds. (If 100 percent efficiency had been achieved, only 2.2 pounds would have been required, but in those primitive days even 10 percent effectiveness was an impressive achievement.) Not only were the 22 pounds, or 10 kilograms, separated to make a premature buildup of the critical mass impossible; it was also important that they be unequal. The "bullet" part was perhaps five pounds, the "target" about seventeen. Obviously the shield dividing the two was crucial. The prime requisite of this shield, or envelope, was that it deflect the fast neutrons which would split U-235 atoms. If the shield failed, the 509th wouldn't win anything, because it would be blown into oblivion — together with its hecklers and the entire island of Tinian. In the Chicago pile purified graphite had served the neutron-resistant function. But building a bomb was far more difficult than a pile. When Germany's nuclear physicists first heard that America had exploded a nuclear weapon, Goudsmit reported, they "believed that what we had dropped on Hiroshima was a complete uranium pile." Because graphite was impractical in a portable missile, the Allied scientists in New Mexico had spent months searching for some other neutron-resistant substance to serve as what was called in the Los Alamos Tech Area the "tamper." The tamper had to be a metal of high density. Gold was a possibility, and at one point Oppenheimer had seriously considered asking for some. An alloy proved to be just as useful, and so twin wombs were woven around the two U-235 eggs, with layer after layer of shrapnel outside, until the completed device would occupy most of the space in a B-29 bomb bay. Contrary to widespread belief later, the bomb was not to be parachuted to its target. B-29s flew high enough and fast enough to permit pilots and crews to escape, so the missile was to be dropped free. It would never reach the ground, however. To achieve maximum effect, the Alvarez mechanism would trigger the explosion in the air above the target area, or, as the target was called in Los Alamos jargon, "Zero." The actual fuse was the lens David Greenglass had sketched for Harry Gold on papers now in Moscow. At that fantastic micromoment when it was touched off by remote control, the neutrons would build up so rapidly that the explosion would take place in one-tenth of a millionth of a second.

Whatever his private misgivings, General Groves had to assume that the gadget wouldn't misfire. He was a soldier and a committed man; after the expenditure of two billion dollars which had been hidden from Congress in countless appropriation bills, he had no intention of writing the project off on any grounds. As early as December 30, 1944, when Bastogne was still on half-rations and flags of the rising sun flapped confidently over Iwo Jima and Okinawa, Groves had written General Marshall that he felt "reasonably certain" a gun-type bomb would be operational at some point during the coming year. At that time Groves thought preliminary testing would be unnecessary. He estimated that the first bomb would be ready about August 1, 1945, the second by January 1, 1946, and the third at some later date, as yet undetermined.

On April 24 President Truman received his first complete briefing on the Manhattan Project from Stimson and Groves in the oval office. The President received them standing, and then, after he had heard it all, he abruptly sat down. The scenario had been changed somewhat, Stimson told him. A test would be held in the uninhabited desert near Los Alamos around the middle of July. If it succeeded, Stimson said, the test device would yield the equivalent of 500 tons of TNT, while the first "operational" bomb would be twice as powerful, yielding the equivalent of 1,000 tons. If anything were needed to show how little these men understood the evil jinni waiting to be born, these figures should suffice, for the test would reveal that the real force locked in that first missile would exceed 20,000 TNT tons. Even so, Truman was wary of it. His first decision on the bomb, reached toward the end of that April 24 briefing, was to order a search for other choices. The hunt would be conducted by two teams, an interim committee of soldiers and civilians and a scientific panel. On May 31 and June 1 the two met together — and discovered that each group while working independently had reached the same conclusions.

Moral implications were not ignored. The interim committee (whose members included Stimson, General Marshall, James F. Byrnes, Vannevar Bush, Karl T. Compton, and President James Bryant Conant of Harvard) was sensitive to the fact that atomic energy could not be "considered simply in terms of military weapons" but must also be viewed "in terms of a new relationship to the universe." At the same time, the investigators were aware that every industrialized nation had its community of atomic physicists; nuclear arms were on the way, whatever the United States decided. Both the interim committee and the scientific committee (Oppenheimer, Fermi, E. O. Lawrence, and Arthur H. Compton) had studied the likeliest alternatives to operational use — a detailed advance warning or a demonstration in some uninhabited area. Both were rejected as infeasible. The nature of atomic explosions was still unfamiliar. Even the forthcoming Los Alamos test, if successful, would not guarantee that a missile would detonate when dropped from a B-29. The desert test would be static. It would tell the technicians nothing about the problem of exploding a bomb at a predetermined height by a complex, untried mechanism. Operational failure was a very real possibility, and if the Americans warned the Japanese and then dropped a dud, enemy morale would stiffen, intensifying last-ditch resistance. Finally, the Americans had no bombs to waste. Apart from the static apparatus to be exploded in the desert, there were just two, bearing the names "The Thin Man" and "The Fat Man."

On June 1, therefore, the President's advisers recommended that the bomb "should be used against Japan as soon as possible," that it be directed at a dual target — a military installation near other buildings more susceptible to damage — and that it should be dropped "without prior warning." The four scientists submitted a unanimous opinion: "We can promise no technical demonstration likely to bring an end to the war; we see no acceptable alternative to direct military use." In a subsequent memorandum to the President, Stimson wrote: "Once started in actual invasion" — preparations for which would have begun instantly if Truman vetoed use of the bomb — "We shall in my opinion have to go through with an even more bitter finish fight than in Germany. I think that the attempt . . . will tend to produce a fusion of race solidarity and antipathy which has no analogy in the case of Germany." Writing a year later in the *Atlantic*, Karl Compton said of the bomb, "I believe that no man could have failed to use it and afterwards looked his countrymen in the face." Compton was not blind to the horror of Hiroshima's 80,000 dead. He did suggest, however, that critics should remember the fire storms of Dresden and Hamburg and the two B-29 incendiary raids over Tokyo, one of which killed 125,000 Japanese and the other nearly 100,000. If morality was to be judged by statistics, he implied, the men who decided to use nuclear weapons against Japan were far from being the war's greatest war criminals.

On Friday, July 13, exactly three months after Franklin Roosevelt's death in Warm Springs, the U-235 hemispheres, the tamper, and the detonator for the test device left Los Alamos from the Tech Area's "back door," a secret road leading to Site S, a stretch of semidesert fifty miles from Alamogordo, New Mexico. The nearest village was called Obscuro — Spanish for "dark" — and natives knew the site itself as Jornada del Muerto — "Death Tract." The coincidence evoked no gallows humor from the nuclear physicists. They knew they were taking a giant step into the unknown. The warnings to the 509th about lightning had not been fanciful. It was the one imponderable in equations. A stray bolt from an electrical storm could atomize all of them, and since the outer limits of a chain reaction were unknown, conceivably the entire planet might be destroyed.

The weight of scientific opinion was against it, but no one could be sure. They drove past Obscuro in the dark, and no one said much.

In the middle of the Jornada del Muerto a 100-foot frame of iron scaffolding had been built against the facade of an old farmhouse. The bomb core would be fitted inside the house, but only at the last moment. The fear of lightning had increased. July was a bad month for thunderstorms in this barren wasteland, and a few days earlier, after a conventional bomb had been strung up here during a rehearsal, a bolt of forked light had struck and exploded it. The scaffolding and farmhouse were absolute Zero. Dr. Robert F. Bacher, head of the Los Alamos Bomb Physics Division, was inside putting the real thing together when, at about dusk, he had a bad moment. Every component had been machine-tooled to the finest measurement, and one of them got stuck in another. He waited, tried again, waited again, tried once more, and in it went, perfecting the mesh.

Oppenheimer and the rest of the scientific command waited, watches in hand, in a bunker ten miles to the southwest, while two B-29s cruising overhead radioed weather conditions. The Oppenheimer bunker, S-10, was the control center and general headquarters. Three other forts of reinforced concrete had been built at other points of the compass, each 10,000 yards from Zero. Preliminary plans had called for a 4 A.M. shot, but the weather was playing hob with the schedule; every time the skies cleared, the B-29s reported new flashes on the horizon. The shot was postponed until 5:30 A.M. That held; the storms vanished. At 5:29:15 on July 16 — forty-five seconds before the dawn of the Atomic Age — a University of California physicist flipped a switch activating a master transmitter, which set off second- and third-generation transmitters as each prearranged cumulation of electrons moved into position at exactly the right microsecond.

5:29:50.

A voice rang out, "Zero minus ten seconds!" It was the first countdown. Wordlessly lips formed in the new ritual — 5:29:51, 5:29:52, 5:29:53, 5:29:54, 5:29:55, 5:29:56, 5:29:57, 5:29:58, 5:29:59 —

At 5:30 everything happened at once. Human beings cannot distinguish between millionths of a second, so no one saw the first flash of atomic fire. They did see its dazzling reflection on far hills. All of them went into mild shock — Oppenheimer was clinging to an upright in his bunker — and thirty seconds later they were jarred again as a wind of hurricane force, followed by a deafening roar, swept the desert. Meanwhile the rising emanation in the sky over Zero stunned and silenced its creators. It was, wrote William L. Laurence:

> . . . a sunrise such as the world had never seen, a great green supersun climbing in a fraction of a second to a height of more than eight thousand feet, rising ever higher until it touched the clouds, lighting up earth and sky all around with a dazzling luminosity. Up it went, a great ball of fire about a mile in diameter, changing colors as it kept shooting upward, from deep purple to orange, expanding, growing bigger, rising as it expanded, an ele-

mental force freed from its bonds after being chained for billions of years. For a fleeting instant the color was unearthly green, such as one sees only in the corona of the sun during a total eclipse. It was as though the earth had opened and the skies had split. One felt as though one were present at the moment of creation when God said: "Let there be light."

Up and up it went, a giant column whose internal pressures found relief in a supramundane mushroom, then up, then another mushroom, finally disappearing into the night sky at an altitude of 41,000 feet, higher than Mount Everest. Oppenheimer was reminded of two passages from the Bhagavad-Gita: "If the radiance of a thousand suns were to burst into the sky, that would be the splendor of the Mighty One" and "I am become Death, the shatterer of worlds." Others groped for words. "Good God!" a senior officer croaked. "I believe those long-haired boys have lost control!" One jubilant physicist shouted, "The sun can't hold a candle to it!" It was literally true: at 5:30 the temperature at Zero had been one hundred million degrees Fahrenheit, three times the temperature in the interior of the sun and ten thousand times the heat on its surface. Sleeping Americans in New Mexico and western Texas had been wakened by the mysterious flash and then frightened as the storm wind blew angrily against their windowpanes.

At Zero nothing could be seen. Fermi, advancing toward it in a Sherman tank lined with lead, gathered earth samples with a mechanical scoop for laboratory examination, but a thorough study had to be postponed; the radiation was too great. When the scientists could enter safely, they found that all life, plant and animal, including rattlesnakes, cacti and desert grass, had been destroyed within a mile of Zero. An antelope herd which the B-29s had spotted miles from the blast had vanished, and the skin of cattle in other parts of New Mexico had developed gray spots. A thirty-two-ton steel tower eight hundred yards from Zero was now a snarled wreck. Around Zero itself sand had been hammered into the desert like a white-hot saucer eight hundred yards in diameter. It wasn't even sand any more. The heat had turned it into a jade-green substance unknown to man but resembling a heavy, unbreakable plastic. The farmhouse and the scaffolding were gone, just gone. They had been transformed into gas and blown away.

General Groves, the first to regain his composure, said to his deputy, "The war's over. One or two of those things and Japan will be finished." The scientists standing around them said little, but one of them crossed his fingers, since "One or two" was all they had. The code name for the Los Alamos test had been Trinity, an allusion to the three gadgets-in-being. If Tokyo guessed the truth (and one of the emperor's warlords was later to suspect it) America's position would be difficult. The better part of a year would pass before any other missile could be readied. Two blasts now, however, just might bring instant peace.

Only one man could make the next decision. Preparation for the test had been in final stages when President Truman sailed for Potsdam. As he later noted in his memoirs, he had been "anxiously awaiting word on the results" because "no one was certain of the outcome of this full-scale atomic explosion." On the morning of July 16 two messages in improvised code reached Potsdam by courier plane. The first was from General Groves to the presidential party: "Operated on this morning. Diagnosis not yet complete but results seem satisfactory and already exceed expectations." The second was addressed to Churchill on the personal stationery of the Secretary of War. Stimson had written, "Babies satisfactorily born." The prime minister muttered, "This is the Second Coming, in wrath." According to Truman's recollection, he "casually mentioned" to Marshal Stalin that the United States had developed "a new weapon of unusual destructive force." The Russian, who might have filled him in on a few details, evinced little interest. He merely replied that he was glad to hear it and hoped the Americans would make "good use of it against the Japanese."

On his desk top in the oval office Truman had put a small sign: "The buck stops here." This buck was now his; he could pass it to no one. His *ad hoc* committee of advisers had just cabled its final conclusion: WE CAN PROPOSE NO TECHNICAL DEMONSTRATION LIKELY TO BRING AN END TO THE WAR. WE CAN SEE NO ACCEPTABLE ALTERNATIVE TO DIRECT MILITARY USE. As Truman saw it, he had no options. His military advisers were already urging him to let them press forward with what he called "the existing plans for the invasion of the Japanese home islands."

On July 24, eight days later, the President tentatively approved atomic strikes: "The 509th Composite Group, 20th Air Force, will deliver its first special bomb as soon as weather will permit visual bombing after about 3 August 1945, on one of the targets: Hiroshima, Kokura, Niigata and Nagasaki. . . ." In print it looked cold-blooded to Truman. Stimson agreed. As early as June 19 the Secretary of War had written in his diary that a "last-chance warning" must be given to Tokyo. On the President's initiative, he, Churchill and Chiang Kai-shek broadcast to the Japanese what subsequently became known as the Potsdam Declaration. Its first seven points gave detailed assurances of humane treatment, no recriminations, a Japanese "new order of peace, security and justice," freedom of speech, religion, and thought; new industry, "participation in world trade relations," and a limited occupation of strategic points in the home islands — an occupation which would swiftly end once stability had been achieved. The eighth and last point called upon Tokyo to proclaim unconditional surrender of all its armed forces. The alternative, the declaration warned, was "prompt and utter destruction."

In Tokyo the broadcast aroused mixed feelings. There were those who read in it a promise to let the Japanese determine their own form of government after American troops were withdrawn, and they were right; that was precisely what Truman was trying to tell them. But the samurai influence was too strong. Foreign Minister Shigenori Togo favored a waiting game, arguing that no answer at all would be preferable to the flat rejection which the military men in the cabinet could force. Then the premier, Admiral Baron K. Suzuki, blundered. During a July 28 press conference he called the Potsdam Declaration a rehash of old proposals, beneath Japanese contempt. Byrnes told correspondents that this was "disheartening." Truman, hoping against hope that the enemy would reconsider, delayed giving the green light to Tinian until August 2, when he was back on the U.S.S. *Augusta* and sailing home. Then the orders were coded and radioed more than halfway round the world. The point of no return had been passed.

The Thin Man had been flown to Tinian in three Superforts, and on the afternoon of Sunday, August 5, it hung, partially assembled, in the bomb bay of the B-29 *Enola Gay*, flagship of Colonel Paul W. Tibbetts, Jr., commanding officer of the 509th Composite Group, who had named the plane for his mother long ago. In less than twenty-four hours, he was told, he and his plane would enter history. By now his men had guessed that their days of ennui were over. Jeeps raced back and forth, bearing brass. Brigadier General T. F. Farrell, Groves's deputy, had just arrived from Los Alamos and was explaining the gadget to Captain William S. Parsons, a naval ordnance expert who would ride to the Empire tomorrow aboard the *Enola Gay*. The more Parsons heard, the more he frowned. Since reaching the island he had seen several B-29s crack up in taking off. If that happened to a Superfort with an assembled bomb aboard it would become the most spectacular accident of all time. Farrell said they would just have to pray that there would be no crash. "Well," Parsons persisted, "if I made the final assembly of the bomb after we left the island, that couldn't happen." Farrell asked, "Have you ever assembled a bomb like this before?" Parsons said no, but he had all day to learn. His decision meant he would be the only man on the *Enola Gay* who knew all the gadget's secrets. Through a fluke he might wind up in enemy hands. As insurance against that, he borrowed a pistol from a young intelligence officer.

That evening the 509th was ordered to meet in its assembly hall, and there, for the first time, Colonel Tibbetts told them their purpose: "We are going on a mission to drop a bomb different from any you have ever seen or heard about. The bomb contains a destructive force of twenty thousand tons of TNT."

He paused, awaiting questions. There were none. The fliers looked stricken.

An extraordinary weapon, he went on, called for extraordinary tactics. That was why their maneuvers had been so peculiar. In a few hours, at 1:45 A.M., three Superforts would take off for the Empire. They would relay weather reports over targets and alternate targets. At 2:45 the second three B-29s would take off. He would be driving the *Enola Gay,* the strike plane, and his two escorts would rendezvous with him over Iwo Jima fifteen minutes after dawn. Then they would go in together. There was a final briefing at midnight, reviewing reports from Los Alamos and explaining why a naval ordnance captain would be aboard the lead bomber. Then the men lay sleepless, most of them wondering whether Captain Parsons could really put the bomb together in the air, Parsons wondering more than any of them.

It was almost a milk run. Dodging large cumulus clouds south of the Bonins, they sailed under starlight until dawn, picked up their escorts at the Iwo tryst, and then soared northwest in the big left-hand turn toward Japan. Apart from a high thin cirrus, the overarching sky was cloudless, cerulean — and free of enemy aircraft. The crew had become restless; there was little conversation and no banter.

Something of their mood is preserved in a Dear-Mom-and-Dad letter written during the flight by Captain Robert A. Lewis, Tibbetts's copilot. "At 4:30," he wrote on the plane, "we saw signs of a late moon in the east. I think everyone will feel relieved when we have left our bomb with the Japs and get half way home. Or, better still, all the way home." The first sign of daybreak came at five o'clock. Nearly an hour later Lewis wrote, "It looks at this time (5:51) that we will have clear sailing for a long spell. Tom Ferebee" — the bombardier — "has been very quiet and methinks he is mentally back in the midwest part of the old U.S.A." A minute later: "It is 5:52 and we are only a few miles from Iwo Jima. We are beginning to climb to a new altitude, at which we will remain until we are about one hour away from the Empire."

Over Honshu Parsons silently set about arming the device. Copilot Lewis's handwriting became jagged and cramped: ". . . Captain Parsons has put the final touches on his assembly job. We are now loaded. The bomb is alive. It is a funny feeling knowing it is right in back of you. Knock wood." Then: "We have set the automatic. We have reached proper altitude. . . . Not long now, folks. . . ."

They had a clear, straight, four-mile run over the target. Ferebee's eye was concentrated on the sight's cross hairs. At 9:15 he pressed his toggle, releasing the single missile. It descended in less than sixty seconds — timepieces below, some of them wristwatches later found on severed arms, confirmed the time — and as it fell its delicately adjusted cams and mechanisms moved faultlessly toward ignition. Captain Lewis had just written his parents: "There will be a short intermission while we bomb our target." Then he scrawled wildly: *My God!*

Through their welder's goggles they first saw a tiny point of purplish-red fire, which within a millisecond expanded to a purple fireball a half-mile wide. The whole monstrous seething mass of red and purple fire rose, accompanied by vast gray smoke rings encircling the column of flames until, at ten thousand feet, the seething mass roiled outward to form the first mushroom. The base of the column was now three miles; it was sucking what was left of the city toward Zero and cremating everything combustible. At 50,000 feet the cloud's second mushroom appeared. Taking evasive action from time to time, the *Enola Gay* and its two escorting Superforts snapped photographs and fled. Even after they had put 270 miles between them and Hiroshima they could still see the mushroom cloud entering the stratosphere and flashing every color in the spectrum.

At 9:20 Tibbetts had radioed Tinian: "Mission successful." Successful hardly seemed the right word, but no word was right. Suddenly Tibbetts realized that the 509th fliers would be kings of Tinian. Nobody back at field would mock them any more, and in America millions would believe they had won, or soon would win, the war. But something had been lost too. Hiroshima, a thriving city of 344,000 people at 9:14 A.M., had by 9:16 A.M. lost 60,175 in dead and missing. Four square miles of civilization had been vaporized. In Washington President Truman was soon announcing, "Sixteen hours ago an American airplane dropped one bomb on Hiroshima. . . . It is a harnessing of the basic power of the universe. The force from which the sun draws its power has been loosed against those who brought war to the Far East." That was correct, but when he added that America had "spent two billion dollars on the biggest scientific gamble in history — and won," it was wrong. To speak of such slaughter as a winning bet was tasteless. In savage irony, imprisoned Hermann Göring put it better. "A mighty accomplishment," he said. "I don't want anything to do with it."

Much indelicacy and outright vulgarity of those first days of the Atomic Age can be set down to incomprehension. The concept was too big, it couldn't be grasped at once. It was one thing to say that under the Einstein formula a single gram of matter, four-tenths the weight of a dime, would lift a million-ton load to the crest of a mountain six miles high, or that a breath of air could fuel a powerful airplane, flying day and night, for a year. Accepting the facts was something else. Burlesque queens who advertised themselves as "anatomic bombs," and Sam Goldwyn's unfortunate quip, "That A-bomb, that's dynamite!" betrayed as much ignorance of nuclear fission as the farmer in Newport, Arkansas, who wrote the nonexistent "Atomic Bomb Co." at Oak Ridge, "I have some stumps in my field that I should like to blow out. Have you any atomic bombs the right size for the job? If you have, let me know by return mail, and let me know how much they cost. I think I should like them better than dynamite." Thousands who laughed at the Arkansas rube knew as little about a chain reaction as he did, and many more couldn't, or wouldn't, credit it. William L. Laurence of the *New York Times*, preparing to accompany the second atomic bomb to Nagasaki, eyed the Fat Man with wonder. He thought it "so exquisitely shaped that any sculptor would have been proud to have created it," and although he had witnessed the Alamogordo desert test he asked himself, "Could it be that this innocent-looking object, so beautifully designed, so safe to handle, would in much less time than it takes to wink an eye annihilate an entire city and its population?" It could, it had, and on August 9 it did it again, destroying 35,000 lives in the second target city. Even then there were doubters. On Tinian Lieutenant General Carl Spaatz, commander of the Pacific Strategic Air Command, examined the dimensions of the case in which the U-235 destined for Nagasaki had been brought from New Mexico. "Of course," he said to Dr. Charles P. Baker of Cornell, "the atoms in the material carried in here served as a fuse that set off the atoms of the air over Nagasaki." "Oh no, General!" said Baker. "The explosion came entirely from the material in this case." General Spaatz stared at him. "Young man," he said, "you may believe it. I don't."

Returning from Nagasaki, the second crew of atomic bombers learned that Russia was invading Manchuria. B-29s were ranging over the Japanese homeland, sowing the air with millions of pamphlets:

TO THE JAPANESE PEOPLE
America asks that you take immediate heed of what we say on this leaflet.
We are in possession of the most destructive force ever devised by man . . .

The message warned, "We have just begun to use this weapon against your homeland"; advised readers to cease resistance before they were all exterminated; and urged them to "petition the Emperor to end the war." It made Occidental sense but bewildered Orientals. Hirohito was a god, not a politician. Gods are not swayed by appeals and referendums. Besides, propaganda was unnecessary now. Confronted by declarations of war from every other major power on earth, the Japanese government was past the point of reason. Various emotional tides were tugging it in different directions. The great struggle was between those who wanted to live and those who wanted to die, and only much later did American scholars discover how close to fulfillment the national death wish had come.

Hirohito, like Hitler, had an air-raid shelter in the ground beneath his palace, and it was there, amid scenes of passion and acrimony, that many of the most crucial meetings were held in that second week of August. In the beginning the government had very little information about the pulverization of Hiroshima. Throughout August 6 Tokyo had been unable to establish routine communications with the city, and no one knew why. At dawn next day Lieutenant General T. Kawabe, deputy chief of the army general staff, received a single-sentence report that made no sense to him: "The whole city of Hiroshima was destroyed instantly by a single bomb." Subsequent details sounded to Kawabe like ravings. Later accounts to the contrary, Hiroshima had not been without military significance; the Japanese Second Army had been quartered there. At 9:15 August 6 the entire army had been doing calisthenics on a huge parade ground. The Thin Man had exploded almost directly overhead, wiping it out. That was one of the messages which reached Kawabe. It was as though the Pentagon had been informed that the United States Marine Corps had been annihilated in less than a second while turning somersaults.

Although unable to build nuclear weapons themselves, the Japanese did have one nuclear physicist of international distinction, Yoshio Nishina. Nishina was summoned before the Japanese general staff at nine o'clock that morning and provided with a summary of the situation in Hiroshima. While out of touch with his colleagues abroad since Pearl Harbor, he had been worried about the possibility of a nuclear weapon and had even written out rough estimates of the damage such a weapon could do. It corresponded with everything he was told now, and he said so. This offered the generals little solace, and they dismissed him. Later, a reporter from Domei, the official Nippon news agency, called at Nishina's laboratory. The Americans were circulating stories that they had atomic bombs, said the newspaperman; it was impossible, wasn't it? The scientist turned away. He was almost certain now. The government then flew him over the desolate city, and as Nishina later told American officers who questioned him, "As I surveyed the damage from the air, I decided at a glance that nothing but an atomic bomb could have created such devastation."

On Thursday, August 9, word of Stalin's declaration of war against Japan reached Tokyo just before sunrise, proverbially the darkest hour of the day, but at 11:01 A.M. an even darker word reached the Supreme Council for the Direction of the War, then in session: a second nuclear device had just exploded over Nagasaki. The SCDW promptly moved in a body to the Imperial Palace, from which Hirohito had just sent a covert message to Premier Suzuki urging immediate acceptance of the Potsdam Declaration. The emperor, his premier, and their civilian advisers were in unanimous agreement, and in any other part of the world that would have guaranteed instant capitulation. Not here; the country was going down in flaming ruin, but Japanese custom required that great care be taken to save face, Hirohito's above all. That could be accomplished if the armed forces joined everyone else. The emperor could then vanish into his palace and behave as though the war had been none of his doing.

There was an obstacle, however. The armed forces weren't going along. In the palace they rose one by one, holding their jeweled samurai swords stiffly, and stated their terms. War Minister General S. Anami, General Y. Umezu, army chief of staff; and Admiral S. Toyoda, navy chief of staff, insisted that Washington accept three conditions: Japanese officers were to disarm their own troops, war criminals would be tried in Japanese courts, and enemy occupation must be limited in advance. In a less savage conflict these stipulations might have been acceptable, but from the outset this had been a war without quarter, and the Americans were in no mood to bargain. Foreign Minister Togo said as much. Japan was defeated, he reminded them; immediate peace was mandatory. Anami, Umezu, and Toyoda looked grim and folded their arms. It was a stalemate.

Next a cabinet meeting raged for over seven hours, interrupted only by shocking dispatches from Hiroshima, Nagasaki, and the Manchurian front. At 9:30 on the evening of that August 9, Suzuki and Togo called upon the emperor to report that both the SCDW and the cabinet were deadlocked. They suggested that the SCDW meet as an Imperial Conference in the air-raid shelter with the emperor in the background. Hirohito agreed, and the session began at 11:30 P.M. Hour after hour the wrangling went on, with the two generals and the admiral holding the civilians in check. They were asked for their solution, and their response reveals how well MacArthur had read the enemy's mind. Thus far, they stubbornly insisted, the war had been confined to indecisive skirmishes. Now was the time for Japan's finest hour — to "lure" the Americans ashore and then "annihilate" them, as the original kamikaze "divine wind" had wiped out Kublai Khan in 1281. It sounded very much like Goebbels's words of encouragement to Hitler when Roosevelt died. Reminded that this had been their strategy in defense of Iwo and Okinawa, they answered sullenly that whatever happened, "national honor" required "one last battle on Japanese soil." Suzuki finally appealed to the emperor for an "Imperial Decision." This was unprecedented; the Son of Heaven traditionally limited himself to hovering around, blessing them by his presence. Nevertheless, Hirohito replied at once. He rose, said their only choice was to end the war immediately, and left the room. As the council broke up Suzuki declared that "His Majesty's decision should be the decision of this conference as well."

The military, it appeared, had been defeated. But nobody dies harder than a warlord. Outwardly, the finer points of protocol were carefully observed. The cabinet went into session as the council broke up — it was now 3 A.M., Friday, August 10 — and unanimously approved identical messages to Washington, London, Moscow and Chungking accepting Truman's Potsdam Declaration with the understanding that the emperor would remain sovereign. The cables went out at 7 A.M. The momentous news was kept from the Japanese public — still under the impression that Nippon was winning the war — for fear of a coup. The fear was justified. That same morning General Anami, the highest-ranking officer in the Empire, summoned all Tokyo officers down to the rank of lieutenant colonel and told them what had happened. Here, if anywhere, the seeds of incipient revolt would find rich earth. Many did take root; by evening growing restlessness was reported at the War Ministry and in the fleet. All the conspirators needed now was time, and in Washington the Americans were unwittingly giving it to them. Truman, Byrnes, Stimson, Forrestal, and Leahy were pondering the possibility of political repercussions when the American people knew that Hirohito would remain on his throne. Once more the buck stopped with Truman. He decided to let the Japanese keep their emperor, and so advised Suzuki via Switzerland. That was on Saturday, August 11. Now, maddeningly, Hirohito seemed to stall. For the next three days Radio Tokyo was silent, a silence so ominous that the President contemplated a resumption of mass bombing. At one point over a thousand B-29s were actually winging toward the Empire before he changed his mind and countermanded the order.

Insofar as it is possible to interpret Hirohito's thoughts, the emperor seems to have been determined to bring the militant Anami, Umezu, and Toyoda into line. For three days and three nights the struggle of wills went on in the palace air-raid shelter. At least one of those present, General Anami, knew officers elsewhere in the capital were plotting to seize power, though he stopped short of permitting them to use his name. Shortly after noon on Tuesday, August 14, in Tokyo — still August 13 in Washington — Hirohito invoked his imperial powers. He taped a broadcast to his subjects, who had never before been allowed even to hear his voice, telling them to bow their heads to the coming conqueror and ending, "We charge you, Our loyal subjects, to carry out faithfully Our will." The tape was to be played over Radio Tokyo at noon next day, after the United States had agreed to the formalities of capitulation.

Truman learned that Japan had quit at ten minutes before four on that Tuesday afternoon. At 7 P.M. he announced it to the country and declared a two-day holiday of jubilation.

Yet the danger in Tokyo remained. During the night of August 14–15 — after the emperor had made his decision but before the people had been told — firebrands were still planning to overthrow the government. They approached the general commanding Hirohito's Imperial Guards Division demanding that he order his troops to disobey the imminent order to surrender. When he refused, they murdered him. Two of his subordinates joined the insurgents and prepared forgeries of imperial orders that would permit them to isolate the emperor and impound the tape of his surrender message. At 8 A.M. the fake orders were ready, and clever counterfeits of Hirohito's seal were being affixed to them, when another Guards general arrived and put them under arrest.

Throughout Wednesday morning Radio Tokyo alerted the nation to the "most important broadcast" coming at noon. These were violent hours in the capital. Hotheads tried to assassinate Suzuki and two members of his cabinet. General Anami, in despair at the loss of national honor, committed hara-kiri. Four of the leading conspirators followed his example. Inexplicably, to the western mind, the general who had suppressed their coup at eight o'clock that morning also knelt and buried a hara-kiri knife in his abdomen. More fittingly, Admiral Takijishi, father of the Kamikaze Corps, followed his example.

Americans were amazed by the docility with which the Japanese accepted defeat. It was a closer shave than they knew. Generals were reconciled to ceremonial suicide, but among younger officers the plotting and counterplotting continued right down to August 28, when the U.S.S. *Mis-*

souri sailed into Tokyo Bay to accept the Japanese surrender while armed bluejackets and the 4th Marines landed at Yokosuka. Last-ditch insurgents had sworn to massacre the landing party, and kamikaze bombers were taxiing into position at the Atsugi airfield, their cockpits occupied by airmen who had sworn upon the honor of their ancestors that they would dive-bomb the *Missouri* and sink her. As she went down, fighter pilots, who were also warming up, intended to strafe the bay until all on the *Missouri*, including Admiral Nimitz and General MacArthur, were dead. Had they succeeded, the vengeance of the American people, confronted with what they would certainly have regarded as a final example of treachery, is terrible to contemplate. Yet it almost happened. In the last frantic hours before the surrender Hirohito was sending members of his family to every stronghold demanding assurances that the imperial promise would be kept. His younger brother, Prince Takamatsu, reached the Atsugi strip just in time to coax the fire-eaters into grounding their planes. It was touch and go right up to the end. To those who later asked whether the bombing of Hiroshima and Nagasaki had been necessary, Samuel Eliot Morison replied that in the light of all the facts, "the atomic bomb was the keystone of a very fragile arch."

The surrender ceremonies abroad the *Missouri* on September 2 marked the official end of World War II. For the first time since September 1, 1939, the *New York Times* observed, no war communiqué had been issued anywhere in the world, and a London headline read, THIS IS THE FIRST UN-CENSORED DAILY EXPRESS IN EXACTLY SIX YEARS. But people do not find peace when governments do. For civilian soldiers the war would be over only when they were on their way home. The Army had worked out a sensible demobilization plan in 1944, and ten days before V-E Day it had begun returning the bravest and weariest GIs to the United States.

The plan became famous as "the point system." Each month in the Army counted a point; each month overseas another one. Presence in a battle was worth five points, and combat wounds and decorations for valor brought five each. Thus a soldier who had been drafted forty months earlier, had been overseas thirty-two months, had come under fire in six separate engagements and had been wounded twice, was on his way home with 112 points. So was every other GI who had at least 85 points, or any WAC with 44. Special provisions were made for fathers, WACs married to men being discharged, and other WACs who had been found PWOP (pregnant without permission).

The system was as fair as any could be, and it enraged sailors and marines, whose services had no arrangements at all. By summer the Navy Department got around to announcing its plans for point counting. The minimum was so high that few qualified, and six marines who wrote their congressmen in protest were put in the brig. Meanwhile Stimson was making more friends by lowering soldiers' minimum counts. By July 1945 enough red tape had passed through enough hands to launch a great transatlantic passenger movement. On one day seven transports docked in New York with 31,445 GIs. The *Queen Elizabeth* brought one division; the *Queen Mary* another. In one 72-hour period the Army Transport Service flew in 125,370 veterans from the European and Mediterranean theaters. By summer over a half-million men were home, even though the federal budget continued to anticipate a long war against Japan.

The Bomb changed that. Before it, fresh divisions were being dispatched to the Pacific on attack transports while high-point veterans waited in Brest or Le Havre for one of the *Queens* or an empty C-54. Now vessels bound for the international date line were rerouted. One of them was the transport *General Henry Taylor,* sailing under Captain Leonard B. Jaudon. A few days after the V-J celebrations the transport passed through the Panama Canal, east to west, and headed for the Hawaiian Islands. Abruptly the fo'c'sle bullhorn blared, "Now hear this! This is the captain. Watch the shadow of this ship" — he paused — "as it turns toward New York." The three thousand men from the ETO cheered. Now they believed it. The war was really over. And they were going home — although home, in 1945, was very different from home as they remembered it. The world had changed, America had changed, and so, though they were unaware of it, had the men on the *General Henry Taylor.*

Portrait of an American

THE REDHEAD

APPROPRIATELY, WALTER REUTHER was born on Labor Day eve, 1907. Walter's grandfather Jacob, a Social Democrat, had emigrated from a German farm in 1892 to flee Prussianism. Jacob's son Valentine became an American Socialist and a fiery leader of the Brewery Workers Union. Valentine, in turn, raised his boys to admire Eugene Debs, Big Bill Haywood, and social justice, and when redheaded Walter and his brother Victor arrived in Detroit from Wheeling, West Virginia, they were already on a collision course with the overlords of the automobile industry.

Working in the factories by day, they finished high school by night and enrolled at Wayne University, where they led a successful student protest against ROTC. In 1932, when Norman Thomas was running for President, Walter made a speech for him and was fired by Ford, whereupon the two brothers pooled their savings and bought steerage tickets for Europe. They defied Nazis in Germany, worked in a Russian plant for two years, crossed Asia on the Trans-Siberian Railway, worked their way across the Pacific in the crew of the *President Hoover* — and arrived back in Detroit just in time for the sit-down strikes.

Walter led one of the first of them. He had been elected president of Local 174 of the United Automobile Workers (UAW-CIO). Borrowing three hundred dollars, he hired a sound truck, rented an office, and waited by the telephone while Victor got a job working a punch press for 36.5 cents an hour at the Kelsey-Hayes factory. At Victor's urging the brake assembly line sat down. A bewildered personnel man begged him to get the men back on the job. "Only Walter Reuther can do that," said Victor, and the man, innocent of the future, asked, "Who's Walter Reuther?" Summoned by phone, Walter mounted a packing case and exhorted the men to join Local 174. The anxious personnel man said, "You're supposed to get them back to work, not organize them," and Walter, his eyes sparkling, replied, "How can I get them back to work if they aren't organized?"

In the end an agreement was signed establishing a 75-cent minimum. In six months the local's membership jumped from 78 to 2,400. Suddenly the redhead was everywhere, signing up auto workers all over town and directing strike strategy. He became a marked man. On May 26, 1947, company goons armed with rubber hoses and blackjacks attacked him while he was distributing UAW leaflets on an overpass outside Ford's Rouge plant in Dearborn, beating him and another union organizer to a pulp. A year later Ford gunmen invaded the Reuthers' La Salle Boulevard apartment and threatened his life.

The only result was to increase the redhead's popularity among Detroit's workmen. He became director of the UAW's General Motors department in 1939 and president of the union in 1946. Two years later, on a cool April evening, he was in his kitchen talking to his wife May when a hired killer standing a few feet away fired both barrels of a ten-gauge shotgun loaded with "00" buckshot. Walter collapsed on the floor, his right arm almost gone and his condition critical. While he was still in the hospital an assassin shot out Victor's right eye and dynamiters tried to blow up UAW headquarters.

The thugs were never caught, but they weren't necessarily hirelings of management. Walter made plenty of other enemies. He drove Communists out of the union and numbers operators out of the shops, and his campaigns against every form of racial segregation in UAW social life alienated bigots. His name attracted lightning like a Franklin rod. To Jimmy Hoffa he was a prig; to John L. Lewis "a pseudo-intellectual nitwit"; to Henry Wallace "the greatest single obstacle" to his Progressive Party. At the same time, his leadership in the ADA, the NAACP, and the United World Federalists had won him many liberal admirers. After he became president of the CIO in 1952, British Labour intellectuals regarded him as the most exciting man in

America. Reuther votaries included Chester Bowles, Jawaharlal Nehru, and Eleanor Roosevelt, who thought he might even be qualified for the White House.

While other labor leaders tended to become voluptuaries, Walter was recognized as a true ascetic — a man who shrank from pleasures, sometimes from normal conviviality, and always from ostentation. After his narrow brushes with death he recognized the need for bodyguards, but when the union had Packard build an elegant $12,000 armored car to convoy him around, he protested, "I can't be seen in a limousine." And he wasn't. If he went downtown to the movies, he dismayed his lookouts by insisting that he disembark in an alley, violating the most elementary security precautions. Finally, when the wheels locked in Canada and the car smashed another auto, he sprang out and snapped, "That does it. I'm not going another inch in that." He finished the trip by bus and never entered the limousine again.

Providing the Reuthers with a safe house proved more successful. An isolated, easily defensible one-room summer cottage was found in the country. Walter, being Walter, began wondering how he could improve it. His doctors told him that constant exercise of his injured hand was necessary if he wanted to avoid having a claw hand. For four years he worked at making the cottage livable. He started surrounding it with other rooms, attaching a kitchen here, a bedroom and study there, adding a second story, screening in a porch. He even built the furniture, including an elaborate hi-fi set. At the end his hand was well and his home was complete. Of the original building only the hand-hewn beams in the living room and the rainspouts (which were on the inside) could be seen.

His energy became legendary. So did the creative ferment of his mind. In ideas he found the exhilaration others got from cronies, liquor, or tobacco, none of which appealed to him. He could talk endlessly, on anything; Murray Kempton called him the only man he knew who could reminisce about the future. "Ask Walter the time," said Spencer McCulloch of the *St. Louis Post-Dispatch*, "and he tells you how to make a watch." Sometimes in the torrent wildly confused metaphors would tumble out. Once Walter charged that Hoffa, Dave Beck, and Joe McCarthy were "in bed together, hand in glove," and another time he described a company negotiator as "a man with a calculating machine for a heart, pumping ice water."

The negotiator was not amused. In bargaining sessions the redhead's verbosity was a powerful weapon. The union negotiated with Ford, General Motors, and Chrysler simultaneously, in different parts of town. This was part of Walter's "one-at-a-time" stratagem. It was based on the belief that competition among auto's big three was stronger than their distrust of the UAW. Separate one from the group, he argued; none wanted to be strike-bound while the other two seized its share of the market. The whipsaw worked — the tip-off that Walter had picked his prey came when he stowed his briefcase and toothbrush under one table — and one reason for its success was his multiloquence. Flexing his powerful jaw muscles hour after hour, he suggested this, suggested that, expatiated, rebutted, lost his temper, was contrite, turned accusing, and expostulated in a dry monotone until the others were numb.

Sometimes they were numb with fury. The Hoffas and Becks of labor held that it was the union's job to win money and management's to decide whether the stockholders or the public paid the bill. Walter disagreed. He contended that another nickel in the pay envelope wouldn't help a worker if the corporation charged more for its cars, stoking the fires of inflation and raising the cost of living, and he asked the big three to pay higher wages without raising their prices. In corporate boardrooms this was seen as an outright attempt to usurp the traditional prerogatives of the boss. To make matters worse he demanded to look at the companies' books so he could prove his claims were sound. (This came out of the Reuther euphonium as "democracy in the economic sphere.") He didn't get it, but he altered the concept of labor-management relations all the same.

For while his rivals in the union were mocking him as an "egghead" pursuing "pie in the sky," and management spokesmen scorned his "Alice-in-Wonderland things," the redhead from Wheeling was successfully demonstrating that there was more to the job than what Detroit workmen call Cadillac money. After his guaranteed annual wage, after the escalator clauses — after the blue-collar proletariat had been lifted into the middle class — Walter turned his Solidarity House staff loose on broader matters: slum clearance, recreation for the elderly, UAW radio programs, a union newspaper, interracial bowling leagues. And the working stiffs followed their leader. Often puzzled, sometimes even resentful, they nevertheless moved toward what his father had called the brotherhood of man.

On May 9, 1970, Walter and May Reuther were killed in the crash of a chartered plane near Pellston, Michigan. Walter's coffin was draped in the UAW banner, a white gear wheel on a blue background. Mrs. Martin Luther King delivered the eulogy. At the end the mourners sang that most moving of union ballads:

> From San Diego up to Maine
> In every mine and mill
> Where working men defend their rights,
> It's there you'll find Joe Hill.

And one redhead.

THIRTEEN

The Fraying Flags of Triumph

INDIAN SUMMER, 1945.

Up before 6 A.M. for his daily predawn raid on a well-stocked White House refrigerator — installed for his convenience near the presidential bedroom — Harry Truman showers, shaves, and dresses with haberdasher nattiness in a white shirt, bow tie, and double-breasted suit. He is alone; the presidential tradition of retaining a valet educes from him a scornful snort. Riffling through the morning papers, he dashes off several memos to his staff while sitting erect at his desk in the stiff, no-nonsense, Palmer penmanship posture he learned as a schoolboy. At seven o'clock sharp he is out of the mansion, hitting the pavement on his prebreakfast constitutional. Accompanied by Secret Service bodyguards and a few panting reporters, he steps off at his brisk, 120-paces-a-minute clip — cutting across Lafayette Square, up Connecticut Avenue to K Street, east to Fifteenth Street, south to New York Avenue, and then down past the Treasury Building and the future office of John W. Snyder, Truman's choice for Secretary of the Treasury after Fred Vinson is elevated to the Supreme Court. His advisers are telling the President that Snyder is too conservative to become a cabinet member in a Democratic administration. Truman shakes his head and reminds them that Snyder, like his military aide General Harry Vaughan, is an old friend. The new President believes in relying on old friends, in trusting them.

The First Family's breakfast is served at eight o'clock: fruit, toast, bacon, milk, coffee, and a little conversational pepper from the head of the household, who tells Bess and Margaret that he wishes Jimmy Byrnes would stop treating him like a freshman senator, that Henry Wallace were less gullible about the Russians, that MacArthur would stop acting like ceremonial viceroy in Tokyo, and that the damned admirals, especially the s.o.b. Radford, would suppress the Navy's mutiny against the administration's plan to unify the armed forces.

Among the issues not discussed by the President are militant students, Black Power, Women's Lib, presidential income tax returns, airplane hijacking, wife swapping, heroin epidemics, heart transplants, SDS trashing, spacecraft modules, racial integration, domestic riots, hard-core pornography, economic game plans, the bombing of office buildings, the CIA, the Middle East, Red China, Indochina, Krebiozen, law and order, the sound barrier, foul-mouthed college girls, ungovernable cities, the Symbionese Liberation Army, the Pill, ecology and charisma — two words then found only in *Saturday Review* puzzles — and the John Birch Society.

The mutilated body of twenty-seven-year-old Captain John Birch, Mercer '39, lay that morning in a fresh grave on a wooded hillside overlooking the Chinese town of Suchow. A Baptist fundamentalist and a brave OSS officer, Birch had met a fate which struck many who had known him as almost predestined. Before it, Major Gustav Krause, his commanding officer, had written in his diary: "Birch is a good officer, but I'm afraid is too brash and may run into trouble." On August 25, 1945, the zealous captain had encountered a Chinese Communist patrol and quarreled violently with its leader, whose men then fell upon him. "In the confusing situation," Krause later said, "my instructions were to act with diplomacy. Birch made the Communist lieutenant lose face before his own men. Militarily, John Birch brought about his own death."

By that autumn Betty Goldstein, *summa cum laude* Smith '42 — in college she demanded that her first name be spelled Bettye and was so independent that she stamped on a boy's foot if he tried to open a door for her — had become disillusioned with her Berkeley psychology fellowship. Returning to the East Coast she married a summer stock producer named Carl Friedan. He entered the advertising business, acquired a lovely mansion overlooking the Hudson, staffed it with servants, and came to share with his wife a joint pride in their three handsome children. To neighbors' eyes it would seem that as suburban wives and mothers go, Betty — no longer Bettye — was thriving. In her spare time Betty Friedan began to write short stories about feminine heroines for women's magazines.

Allen Ginsberg had begun working his way through Columbia as a spot-welder in the Brooklyn Navy Yard. He was studying to be a market research consultant. He rarely swore, and he shaved every day.

In the new State Department Building on Virginia Avenue, Alger Hiss, director of the Office of Special Political Affairs, was moving into a larger office. He had just completed his tenure as secretary general of the United Nations Conference in San Francisco and was now principal adviser to the United States delegation to the U.N. General Assembly.

While winning an E certificate as a war worker, Norma Jean Baker had also been photographed for *Yank*. The picture had caught the eye of the Blue Book Model Agency, and by V-J Day Norma Jean was taking the agency's modeling course. Her husband was still overseas; he knew nothing about it. She earned the modeling course's hundred-dollar fee by keeping her war job, calling in sick, and doing a ten-day stint as a hostess.

Joe McCarthy, late of the Marine Corps, was reelected circuit judge in 1945. He immediately began laying plans to stump his state the following year under the slogan "Wisconsin Needs a Tail Gunner in the Senate," telling voters of the hell he had gone through in the Pacific. In reality McCarthy's war had been chairborne. As intelligence officer for Scout Bombing Squadron 235, he had sat at a desk interviewing fliers who had returned from missions. His only wartime injury, a broken leg, was incurred when he fell down a ladder during a party on a seaplane tender. Home now, he was telling crowds of harrowing nights in trenches and dugouts writing letters to the families of boys who had been slain in battle under his leadership, vowing that he would keep faith with the fallen martyrs by cleaning up the political mess at home — the mess that had made "my boys" feel "sick at heart." Sometimes he limped on the leg he broke. Sometimes he forgot and limped on the other leg.

In Boston a skinny, twenty-eight-year-old former naval lieutenant returned home after covering the U.N. opening in San Francisco and the British elections in London as an INS reporter. Newspaper work had an uncertain future, he lacked a graduate degree for college teaching, and the thought of becoming a businessman was unappealing. So John F. Kennedy decided to file for congressman in the Eleventh Massachusetts District, his chief qualifications being his father's money and boyhood memories of his grandfather as mayor of Boston. Meanwhile he established a legal address by renting apartment 36 at 122 Bowdoin Street, just around the corner from the gold-domed capitol. An astonishing number of well-bred young women found their way there.

Republicans in California's Twelfth Congressional District were desperately in need of a presentable candidate to run against incumbent Jerry Voorhis, a liberal protégé of Upton Sinclair's. In the late spring of 1945 a committee of GOP "citizen fact-finders" had advertised in the newspapers for a qualified candidate. None had replied. Then the president of Whittier College mentioned one of his alumni, Richard M. Nixon. After a talk with Nixon's parents, two members of the Republican fact-finders reported that the young man was still in uniform, negotiating naval contracts in Baltimore while awaiting release from the service. A third committeeman, a banker named Herman Perry, then put through a historic long-distance call to Maryland. Perry was uneasy; further inquiries had revealed that Nixon, though a lawyer, hadn't voted until he was twenty-five years old. Even his party affiliation was a mystery. Over the phone he said sure, he'd be glad to run. Perry asked, "Are you a Republican?" There was a pause. Then Nixon replied, "I guess so. I voted for Dewey last time." That would be good enough, Perry said, and he asked Nixon to fly west as soon as possible. At last the citizen fact-finders had a candidate, though his skills needed some honing. His own instinct, as first revealed, was to appear in dress blues outside factory gates where former enlisted men would be leaving work, look them squarely in the eye, hold out his hand, and say sternly, "I am Lieutenant Commander Richard M. Nixon."

In Washington another former lieutenant commander, Lyndon B. Johnson, was once more representing Texas's Tenth Congressional District. Congressman Johnson deplored speedy demobilization in the wake of peace. "We must keep strong!" he cried from the well of the House. "We must have military strength to fulfill our moral obligations to the world. Our supreme duty today is to underwrite the future. We must have a strong police force to protect us from criminals, an Army and Navy strong enough to carry out our pledge to help the United Nations police the world."

A fourth naval officer, Lieutenant Commander Benjamin M. Spock, a former instructor in pediatrics at the Cornell Medical College and now a naval physician, was putting the final touches on his first book, *The Common Sense Book of Baby and Child Care.*

In distant Hanoi, French colonial soldiers had returned on the heels of the withdrawing Japanese army. Ho Chi Minh, a native politician with a mixed background but most recently known as a Chiang Kai-shek protégé, had applied week after week for official recognition of his popular Viet Minh (Viet Nam Independence League), but Admiral Thierry D'Argenlieu, General de Gaulle's representative, had refused to see him. Still independent and still a peaceful advocate, Ho carried his cause to Paris. If thwarted there, he resolved, he would order his followers to blow up the Hanoi reservoir and wage guerrilla warfare from the hills.

A few blocks from Ho's room in Paris, thirty-seven-year-old Major William F. Knowland, presiding over an Army historical section, was notified that he had just become the youngest member of the United States Senate. Governor Earl Warren of California had chosen him to succeed the late Hiram Johnson, confident that he was the most qualified man available. Among Knowland's merits were his youth, his military service, six years in the state legislature, a fine record as a charity-drive organizer, a wife and three children, and his father, Joseph Russell Knowland, a millionaire and the chief contributor to Warren's political war chests.

In May 1945 a strong-minded widow named Marguerite Oswald had remarried, but by fall it had become clear that the marriage was a mistake. The bride insisted upon taking her five-year-old son Lee with them wherever they went, and Marguerite's husband and child found themselves competing for her attention. To Lee, who seemed fond of his new step-father, the parental quarrels were baffling. He was becoming moody and withdrawn.

The press that autumn was unfamiliar with the public personalities of Jane Alpert, Mark Rudd, Stokely Carmichael, Angela Davis, Diana Oughton, Bernadine Dohrn, H. Rap Brown, Kathy Boudin, the Soledad Brothers, Bill Ayres, Huey Newton, Jerry Rubin, Linda Fitzgerald, William L. Calley Jr., Tom Hayden, Cathlyn Wilkerson, and Patricia Campbell Hearst, because none of them had any.

Descending from the presidential apartment in a small elevator shortly before nine o'clock each morning, the thirty-third President of the United States strode smartly to his oval office in the West Wing of the White House and plunged into work. His zest was genuine and his manner direct. Roosevelt had enjoyed intrigue and sleight of hand; Truman liked clear-cut decisions, the harder the better. To prevent misunderstandings, all of them were put into writing. He never regretted one, never lost sleep over consequences, never glanced over his shoulder. Procrastination was a sin to him, and he despised it. His customary air was that of an alert shopkeeper, all business, and in fact visitors on his daily appointment schedule, from Anthony Eden to advocates of National Poultry Week, were always referred to by the President as "the customers." Each was welcomed with a manly two-pump handshake and escorted to the presidential desk, where, in those first months of peace, Truman liked to call attention to the tiny plow which had replaced his model gun on V-J Day. "It's the little things that count," he would say sententiously. "I like the feeling of having the new little fellow there."

His optimistic air disquieted informed callers, who wondered among themselves when he would face the inevitable reappearance of the De-pression. "A war boom?" Frederick Lewis Allen had written in *Since Yesterday* (1940). "No gain thus made could be lasting." In *Harper's* Bernard De Voto warned his readers to be prepared for the return of all of it: labor-baiting, Father Coughlin, and hand-to-hand fighting on the barricades as "the waves of reaction" gathered strength "in the years immediately ahead of the United States." Leo Cherne peered into the future and saw a "cold breeze" sweeping through America. Hungry veterans would roam the streets in packs, he predicted; "Occasionally you will see them in strikes and riots . . . The newly set up employment offices, particularly at first, will grind slowly . . . an occasional soldier will be found on a street corner selling a Welcome Home sign. Others will start house-to-house canvassing in their uniforms." Some economists foresaw another 1932, with 15 million jobless men. Political scientists spoke of revolution, and from his deathbed H. G. Wells concluded in 1945 that since faith in scientific progress had plummeted, man, already "at the end of his tether," was doomed to rapid extinction.

The harder they looked, the more convinced employers were that there was no way to turn industry's juggernaut of superproductivity toward peaceful pursuits without stumbling into disaster. Preoccupied as they were by the Crash and all that had followed, they overlooked one massive difference between Herbert Hoover's America and Harry Truman's. In 1932 people couldn't enter stores, because they were broke. If hard times had taught them nothing else, the importance of saving had been drilled into them. Since Pearl Harbor average weekly earnings in the United States had almost doubled, rising from $24.20 to $44.39 for the 48-hour week — soon to be the 40-hour week, with no loss in pay, after Truman set the example with federal employees. Partly because the Depression had made them frugal and partly because there had been so little on store shelves, the American people had spent the four war years accumulating Liberty Bonds and queuing up at bank deposit windows. There were 85 million bondholders alone. With the shooting over, the public had socked away 136.4 billions in savings institutions and liquid securities. It was burning a hole in their pockets, and the administration's real quandary — one which could never be solved to everyone's satisfaction — was how to prevent a national buying spree in the black market.

Thus the nightmare of factory gates being stormed by jobless GIs was the last bitter legacy of the shabby 1930s. Those terrible years were dead at last; 52-20 unemployment compensation was evidence of it, and so was the GI Bill. Finding jobs for all discharged soldiers would take time, but meanwhile they could learn trades, start small businesses of their own, or move to college campuses. And jobs weren't all that tight anyhow. Women war workers were quitting beltlines by the million to go home and have babies.

A *New York Daily News* headline read:

PRICES SOAR, BUYERS SORE,
STEERS JUMP OVER THE MOON

In Kansas City the President of the United States strutted through downtown streets at the head of an American Legion parade. From a curb Eddie Jacobson, his old partner in haberdashery, called, "Harry, what about inflation?"

"I've got my eye on it," Truman called back.

He needed a quick eye. The economy was shifting daily as it hurtled ahead, trying to catch up with black marketeers peddling five-dollar nylons, fifteen-dollar shirts, and twenty-dollar recapped tires. The war had receded into history and the convulsions of readjustment were at their height. Affluence lay in the certain future, but reaching it was an agonizing struggle. When Vinson had prophesied "the pleasant predicament of having to learn to live 50 percent better," he had failed to mention that first the people must face shortages, riots, labor strikes, and the skyrocketing prices of postwar inflation.

Yet controls were exasperating. By the war's end the Office of Price Administration had become a government-within-a-government, with 73,000 full-time employees, 200,000 volunteers, and an office in every community down to the town level. It was an intolerable tyranny, a mockery of freedom, and all that could be said for it was that there was no alternative. Somehow it had managed to hold price rises to 30 percent over their 1939 levels. Not to put too fine a point on it, in 1946 the economy was virtually glued together by the gum on the back of red and green stamps. Even so, it was near chaos. There were a thousand ways to circumvent OPA regulations, and sharpers found them all. You could tip the head waiter twenty dollars and a choice roast would appear. You might barter an automobile for an apartment, say, or a car battery for scotch whisky. The scotch might have been acquired by also agreeing to buy a case of wine or beer. That ruse was called the "tie-in" sale, and its possibilities were unlimited. In Oklahoma City, for example, a car dealer would sell you an automobile if you also bought his dog for $400; afterward the dog would find his way back. Other dealers offered new cars if you would trade your old one in for a two-dollar bill, and in Cincinnati an imaginative customer greeted an auto salesman by saying: "I'll bet you seven hundred dollars I can hold my breath for three minutes." In addition there were endless "bonuses" — a $150 bonus for the landlady who would rent an $80-a-month cold-water flat, or three dollars to the butcher who found a thick steak in his refrigerator.

It was impractical to wipe out the black market with stiff fines and heavy prison sentences, and infeasible, now that the war was won, to retain bipartisan support for controls. The Republicans were feeling truculent once more. In August 1945 they reluctantly decided not to challenge Truman's "hold-the-line" executive order, which envisaged a gradual reduction of wage and price controls, but in September party lines were drawn tight on this issue for the first time since Pearl Harbor. Calling Congress back into special session, the President demanded broad domestic powers. He wanted rationing to continue — some controls were due to expire automatically six months after the war's end — and in addition he asked for congressional approval of a social and economic program whose most notable measures were a 65¢-an-hour minimum wage, nationalization of the housing industry, expansion of natural resources development, federal control of all unemployment compensation, and a fair employment practices bill with teeth. Republican congressmen gagged. Minority leader Joe Martin accused the

President of "out-dealing the New Deal," and Charlie Halleck said, "This is the kick-off. This begins the campaign of 1946."

On January 14, 1946, Congress reassembled to hear Truman's first State of the Union message. The heart of it was a request for another year of OPA, with controls being relinquished, commodity by commodity, as the supply and demand of each reached their natural level. But he had telegraphed his punch in September, and now he confronted a formidable alliance: the National Association of Manufacturers, the U.S. Chamber of Commerce, and the Republican leadership. They had prepared intricate charts and graphs to persuade committees that free enterprise was doomed unless Congress struck "the shackles from American business." Outside the Senate's marbled caucus room, corporation public relations men fought for a sellers' market by marshaling parades of clerks, junior executives, ministers, physicians, Legionnaires, Rotarians, and newspaper boys, all of whom testified to the virtues of John Stuart Mill and the wickedness of Karl Marx, who, they insisted, was their true adversary. There was even a sad troupe of bankrupt businessmen, who told of their former prosperity in a free market and how mischievous OPA officials had ruined them.

Lobbying was intense on both sides. OPA's Chester Bowles fielded his own team of expert witnesses, Truman's congressional liaison men swarmed through the Capitol buttonholing congressmen, and the unions, consumer groups, and women's clubs paraded in the plaza outside, holding pro-OPA signs aloft. On April 19 they staged what the following morning's *New York Times* called "the climax" of the consumers' "crusade." Over a thousand housewives, representing every state, marched up the Hill demanding a twelve-month extension of controls without crippling amendments. According to the *Times*, the demonstration

> . . . served to emphasize that the fight over OPA, in and out of Congress, has reached proportions of bitterness, stridency, and obfuscation which have not been matched in years. . . . The NAM has spearheaded the fight over OPA with the . . . enthusiastic assistance of associations representing the meat industry, retail trade, real estate and others. . . . As the battle has grown each side has become progressively more voluble, they have started to call each other names, and a few blows have been struck below the belt.

Congress's reflex reaction to so savage a struggle was to compromise, and as Bowles had pointed out, wage and price controls were all or nothing. OPA's death rattle followed. So did inflation. Within a month food prices had doubled, angry consumers formed The Militant Marketers to picket stores, livestock men kept cattle in the stockyards until beef would bring over a dollar a pound, and the overall cost of living rose 33 percent and then 75 percent. In August worried congressmen reconvened to pass new controls, dropping Taft's amendment, but it was too late. OPA had lost its grip on the economy. There was no way to turn the spiral back upon itself, and in October Truman bowed to the irresistible force; the lifting of all controls began. Two years later, when the electorate's memory of OPA had mellowed, he would remind voters that he had been battling for price regulation while Republicans had fought on the NAM's side. By then he would be moving in stride with events. At the time, however, the first Taft-Truman confrontation could only be called a draw at most. Presidential popularity dipped in the polls.

Luckily Truman seldom worried about polls. In general he was suited by temperament for the hard choice. This was true even when his decisions hurt those who had supported his political fortunes, which, in the unsettled years after the war, it often did. Taking on the NAM and the U.S. Chamber of Commerce was relatively easy for a Democratic chief executive. Disciplining organized labor was something else. Not only was labor essential to the coalition Franklin Roosevelt had forged; its leaders had been among those who had urged Truman's vice-presidential candidacy upon FDR in 1944. Without labor he would have remained a senator, and another man, either Jimmy Byrnes or Henry Wallace, would be in the White House. Nevertheless, nagging management about prices was pointless unless the administration was ready to take an equally strong stand on wages. And there was no point in that if the workers were always on strike, which at times in 1946 they seemed to be. During that first full year after the war, nearly five million men struck at one time or another and 107,476,000 man-days of work were lost to strikes. Coming when they did, these disruptions deepened middle-class antagonism toward labor. Young couples awaiting their first car were infuriated by photographs of an idle automotive worker. They were applying a double standard, judging the unions more harshly than employers, but that had always been the posture of the middle class. Even Truman, so representative of the American center, was more respectful of white collars than blue.

Blue-collar contributions to the 1941–45 production miracle deserved more recognition than they were getting. Army-Navy E pennants had been earned because employees, sharing their employers' vision of peace and triumph, had sweated themselves for long hours on the line, agreed to speed-ups, volunteered for swing shifts, and put their money in war bonds. In the week after the Japanese attack on Hawaii, President Roosevelt had asked the unions for no-strike pledges, to be honored until the fighting was over. Every labor leader had agreed, and with the exception of two coal miners' strikes and a threatened walkout by railroad workers — all in 1943 — the pledges were kept. Even when the few wildcat strikes were counted, less than .0006 of 1 percent of total production time had been lost. By V-J Day, however, the pressure of accumulated grievances was intolerable.

The first sign of trouble came in September 1945; Ford was held up by a rash of spontaneous suppliers' strikes. Then, as the GM walkout was followed in 1946 by wave after wave of strikes from Montauk Point to Malibu Beach, paralyzing the oil, lumber, textile, and electrical industries, newspapers began talking about the workers' "revolt" and labor's "rebellion." It was hard to believe that so widespread an upheaval wasn't planned, that it was a spontaneous backfire to the end of wartime austerity. This much was certain: the cumulative effect of the disruptions was threatening reconversion. If strikes against the public interest loomed, the President might feel it his duty to take a longer step than the appointment of impotent commissions. That is precisely what happened, and in the process Truman reached the low point of his Presidency.

His anger was understandable. No sooner had the GM strike been settled than 750,000 steelworkers banked their fires and hit the bricks. After eighty days they returned, but before the country could take a deep breath the 400,000 soft coal miners in twenty-one states left their pits. On April 18, with the miners still out, the railroads' two key brotherhoods announced that they would withdraw all their men in thirty days. The nation's transportation grid would stop functioning. The leaders of the two unions had long been allies of the Democratic party, and when Truman called them to the White House three days before the strike deadline and offered generous arbitration awards, he expected them to accept. Instead they shook their heads stubbornly.

"If you think I'm going to sit here and let you tie up this whole country," he said, "you're crazy as hell."

"We've got to go through with it, Mr. President," one of them replied. "Our men are demanding it."

Truman rose. "All right," he said. "I'm going to give you the gun. You've got just forty-eight hours — until Friday at this time — to reach a settlement. If you don't, I'm going to take over the railroads in the name of the government."

The forty-eight hours passed, the deadlock remained unbroken, and so, on that Friday, May 17, 1946, he signed an executive order seizing the railroads. He was now the brotherhoods' new employer. In that role he gave them another five days of reprieve. Nothing happened. The best he could get in exchange for his leniency was a curt note from them ending: "Your offer is unacceptable." By now it was Friday of the following week. The effect of the soft coal strike was beginning to reach the cities; to conserve the little they had, some were already cutting electricity during certain hours. A railroad strike at this juncture would have the effect of a national strike. He couldn't allow it. At issue was less what he would do than how he did it. The method he chose was deplorable.

Summoning his cabinet, he informed it that he would appear before a joint session of Congress Saturday and ask for authority to draft all railroad men, regardless of age or situation, into the Army. His attorney general said, "Unconstitutional." The President snapped, "We'll draft 'em first and think about the law later." He told his press secretary, Charles G. Ross, to clear all networks for a coast-to-coast fireside chat that same evening, and he handed him a dozen-page holograph on ruled tablet paper.

"Here's what I'm going to say," he said tautly. "Get it typed up. I'm going to take the hide right off those sons of bitches."

Back in his own office, Ross couldn't believe what he was reading. It was probably the most splenetic outburst ever set down in the White House. It was also inaccurate, slanderous, and, toward the end, a dangerous incitement. He planned to tell the country that while America's young men had "faced bullets, bombs and disease to win the victory," the leaders of the coal and railroad unions had as much as fired "bullets in the backs of our soldiers" by holding "a gun at the head of the government." They were all liars, he said, and he singled out John L. Lewis and "Mr. Murray and his communist friends" for intimidating "a weak-kneed Congress." Next came the extraordinary statement:

> Every single one of the strikers and their demigog [sic] leaders have been living in luxury, working when they pleased and drawing from four to forty times the pay of a fighting soldier.

The coda read:

> Let's give the country back to the people. Let's put transportation and production back to work, *hang a few traitors,* and make our own country safe for democracy.* Come on, boys, let's do the job!

It might as well have ended, "Right on!" Here was a President who proposed to demand power for the people and save democracy by stringing up labor leaders. The expletives uttered in the elegant Grosse Pointe mansions of automobile executives in darkest 1937 had scarcely been worse. Ross didn't think Truman really wanted to encourage necktie parties, certainly not that explicitly, and Clark Clifford concurred. Together they persuaded the President to accept a different draft. Even so, it was scathing. "The crisis at Pearl Harbor was the result of action by a foreign enemy," he began. "The crisis tonight is caused by a group of men within our own country who place their private interests above the welfare of the nation." He announced that he was calling Congress in session Sunday afternoon at four o'clock. If the engineers and trainmen weren't on the job then, he would turn them over to General Hershey.

It was a strange way to run railroads, his advisers privately thought, but their chief was going through with it. Sunday afternoon arrived with no capitulation from the brotherhoods. Their leaders were locked in a Statler Hotel room at Sixteenth and K streets, slowly giving ground to a jawboning administration negotiator, when the President rode down Pennsylvania Avenue, entered the House chamber through the Speaker's office, and mounted the podium to ask for authority permitting him, as commander in chief, "to draft into the Armed Forces of the United States all workers who are on strike against their own government." In Rayburn's office Clark Clifford kept vigil over the telephone. Five minutes after

*Author's italics.

Truman had begun his speech, it rang. The negotiator said, "It's signed!" Clifford scribbled frantically on a scrap of paper, "Mr. President, agreement signed, strike over," and sent it to the lectern. Truman glanced at it. He looked up from his text, and smiled at the packed chamber. He said, "Gentlemen, the strike has been settled."

They gave him an ovation, and when he went on anyhow to ask for the legislation permitting him to draft future strikers jeopardizing the public welfare, the House whooped it through on the spot. Still, this was far from his finest hour. At a stroke he had alienated the labor movement, the American Civil Liberties Union, the liberal community, and every thoughtful conservative who had read the constitution the President had sworn to uphold. In the Senate Robert A. Taft, no champion of the unions, used his influence to table the bill; the proposal, he declared, "offends not only the constitution, but every basic principle for which the American Republic was established. Strikes cannot be prohibited without interfering with the basic freedom essential to our form of government." The embittered president of the railroad trainmen announced that every penny in his brotherhood's 47-million-dollar treasury would be spent defeating Truman in 1948. In New York the CIO stigmatized the President as the country's "number one strikebreaker," and from his aerie in the hills of West Virginia, John L. Lewis cried, "You can't mine coal with bayonets."

Maybe not, but the aroused vigilante in the White House was going to try. Lewis was courting disaster. Truman could survive the strikebreaker brand; he would later win labor back with his vetos of the anti-union Case and Taft-Hartley bills. What he could not tolerate was the mine leader's arrogance and growing irresponsibility. The President came close to the truth when he said Lewis had "called two strikes in wartime to satisfy his ego." He had marched his 400,000 men in and out of the mines with no thought for the GIs overseas, and they knew it; in 1943 an editorial in the Middle Eastern edition of *Stars and Stripes* had ended, "Speaking for the American soldier — John L. Lewis, damn your coal-black soul." The Democratic party owed the old thespian nothing. He hadn't supported the ticket for ten years. The way was clear, therefore, for a confrontation between two bristling leaders. The very nature of the strike invited federal intervention. The American economy was still based on coal. It provided 62 percent of the country's electricity and 55 percent of its industrial power. Putting the railroad men back to work would have been useless if the miners didn't go too; nineteen out of every twenty locomotives in the United States burned coal.

Truman was so determined to stare down Lewis that he hadn't waited until the brotherhoods were tamed. Five days before they yielded at the Statler he had signed an executive order taking over the mines. Lewis's strike was then in its sixth week, and at first it appeared that this effort to intimidate him would be as ill-starred as all the others. "Truman doubts the legality of our demands?" he bellowed at a newspaperman. "What does Truman know about the legality of anything?" The President knew enough to be cagier this time. Putting his Secretary of the Interior in management's seat, he approved a compromise giving the United Mine Workers most of their demands. (The employers, who would have to pay, raged helplessly; in this struggle, reason was as irrelevant as constitutionality.) Then the President waited for the UMW chief to make his next move. Lewis's swaggering and blustering were sure signs that he was looking for an opening. When he found none, he created one. Raising a trivial point over vacation pay, he repudiated the contract in October and declared that he was reopening negotiations on all its clauses. He wanted "portal-to-portal" pay for his men (payment for travel time from the mine gate to the pithead). Truman told the Interior Department to stand fast while he, like Lewis, found a pretext for action. To their consternation, his New Deal lawyers discovered that there was nothing except the despised anti-union court injunction, which had been outlawed in the Norris–La Guardia and Wagner acts.

Truman wasn't disconcerted. He decreed that the law covered *private* employers, not the government. It was a novel interpretation, but now that the duel was in the open neither man could retire without loss of face. Even as the court papers were being served on Lewis in his UMW headquarters at Fifteenth and I streets, his lieutenants were passing the watchword in the mines: "No contract, no work." While he holed up in his Alexandria mansion, the mines were shut down one by one. In ten days cities were again cutting back electric power, industrial plants were shutting down, and locomotives and empty coal cars were being stranded on sidings. By then the struggle was approaching its climax. UMW lawyers had exhausted their repertoire of stratagems. On Thursday, November 21, Federal District Judge T. Alan Goldsborough cited Lewis for contempt of court, and on Tuesday, November 26, Goldsborough ruled that "The defendants, John L. Lewis and the United Mine Workers of America, have beyond a reasonable doubt committed and continue to commit a civil and criminal contempt of this Court." The fine was $3,510,000.

Lewis sat down, flabbergasted. It was the heaviest fine in labor history, and he saw himself facing a limited number of options. He couldn't choose jail, as Debs and Gompers had, because the government had dropped the charge of criminal contempt. He could include the judge among his enemies, and he seemed to be pondering that when he croaked, "Sir, I have already been adjudged in contempt of your court —" but he broke off there. His lawyers were dragging him back to his seat. A judge who would hand down multimillion-dollar fines was dangerous. Appeal was inevitable, but that would only delay the decision. Meanwhile the defendant had become entangled in court orders, writs, citations, briefs, and restraining orders. He had lost sight of his adversary. Where was Harry Truman?

The President had wisely withheld comment from the moment Lewis had knocked his own chip off his own shoulder. Yet a presidential triumph was far from a certainty. The initiative was still with Lewis, and there was only one sure way to wrench it from him. His power base must be eliminated or threatened. If both men remained mute while his lawyers threw up a new screen of legal motions, the national crisis would pass from the inconceivable to the unendurable. The miners might dislike Lewis, and some of them hated him, but they were convinced, almost to a man, that they needed his protection. The pits and tunnels would remain vacant until the men were told to return by him or by an equally persuasive voice. Perhaps the President's voice was strong enough. Harry Truman decided to try. That Saturday morning, the fifth anniversary of Pearl Harbor, Charlie Ross told the press that the President would broadcast a direct appeal to the miners in the evening, asking them to save their country by ignoring their chief and going back to work at once.

It was a breathtaking gamble, with presidential prestige at hazard, but it succeeded. Lewis had been stared down. At four o'clock he called a press conference at Fifteenth and I. Declaring that the Supreme Court deliberations "should be free from public pressure superinduced by the hysteria of an economic crisis," he said, "all mines in all districts will resume production of coal immediately. . . . Each member is directed to return to work immediately under the wages and conditions of employment on or before November, 1946." With those lines he tottered off the stage and into oblivion. He would never again hold the country in ransom, and his defeat, in becoming Truman's victory, made the President feel like a President, possibly for the first time. "I can tell you, there was a big difference in the Old Man from then on," Clark Clifford later told Cabell Phillips of the *New York Times.* "He was his own boss at last." Another presidential aide put it more succinctly. "When Harry walked back to the mansion," he said, "you could hear his balls clank."

Emil Mazey, Walter Reuther's right-hand man, was not available to the automobile workers' union that winter. He didn't even know what was happening in Detroit. As a draftee and leader of demobilization riots in Manila, Sergeant Mazey was deprived of mail and visitors and kept under constant watch. The surveillance didn't stop the rioting. Demonstrations intensified and spread to Tokyo, Guam, China, Calcutta, Hawaii, London, and Vienna; to Le Havre, Paris, and Frankfort. By spring the disturbances had weakened U.S. military morale, damaged American prestige abroad, and dealt the Army a heavy blow.

Morale was already at its lowest since Pearl Harbor. That was why soldiers were so susceptible to skillful agitators. On V-J Day demobilization points had been frozen; service after that date won no credits toward an early discharge. Some inequities were unavoidable under the point system anyway, and the unexpectedly early end of the Pacific war increased them. Instead of transporting high-point outfits home in the summer of 1945, the

Army had found it convenient to discharge low-point troops who had never seen a ship. The most abrasive issue, however, had nothing to do with mustering out. It was a universal grievance of enlisted men who felt that they were being systematically mistreated by their superiors.

Military precedence lay athwart the thrust of egalitarianism, twentieth-century America's most powerful social force. Under the best of circumstances enlisted men were anti-authoritarian, and with the coming of peace and the return to barracks life, gaps between the haves and have-nots had widened. Hanson W. Baldwin, military editor of the *New York Times* and no enemy of privilege, concluded afterward that there had been "solid grounds for real discontent." Generals, he noted, were literally feasting on caviar and champagne while the troops were fed C rations. Junior officers laid claim to the plushest quarters, the prettiest Red Cross girls, the most comfortable seats at the finest movies. The best buildings were reserved for their clubs, where GI bartenders served them choice liquors until their GI chauffeurs put them to bed. Some commanding officers retained unneeded men merely to defer relinquishment of their own temporary wartime ranks, and the accumulation of legitimate complaints was heightened by inexcusable ignorance and insensitivity at the highest levels, notably on the part of Secretary of War Robert P. Patterson.

Nevertheless there was something disgraceful about the Army's near-mutiny of 1946. Since the previous September officers had been discharging nearly a million men a month while cutting a soldier's point requirement to 50 and then to 38. The Navy suffered fewer embarrassing episodes despite greater grievances, and the Marine Corps avoided demonstrations by simply issuing an order forbidding them. The Army riots would have been less shameful if the rioters had been the combat veterans who had won the war, but they weren't. By Christmas of 1945 most of Bill Mauldin's Willies and Joes were home and out of uniform.

The first man to cast doubt on the Army's demobilization policy was, of all people, General MacArthur. On September 17, 1945, without consulting anyone in Washington, he called a press conference to announce that the occupation force in Japan would be cut from 400,000 to 200,000 within six months. Questioned by reporters, President Truman said feebly that though he hadn't been told, he was glad the general didn't need as many troops as he had thought. Dean Acheson commented that the size of MacArthur's force would be determined by policy makers, not the general, and instantly ran afoul of MacArthur's champions in Congress. (Had the administration been able to see into the future, Acheson later wrote, "we might have recognized this skirmish as the beginning of a struggle leading to relief of General MacArthur from his command on April 11, 1951.") If a five-star general could cut his garrison in half, restless soldiers reasoned, generals with fewer stars could, too.

The exact opposite happened. On January 6, 1946, the *Daily Pacifican*, a soldier's newspaper, reported that Army demobilization schedules had been

cut from 800,000 men a month to 300,000 because of the difficulty in obtaining replacements. The replacement shortage, the *Pacifican* charged in a
front-page appeal to President Truman, was of the Army's own making;
General Hershey had cut his monthly draft quota from 88,000 to 21,000.
Maintenance of large contingents in Manila was particularly vexing. As the
Pacifican saw it, the only legitimate use of citizen soldiers in peacetime was
to occupy conquered countries, and Filipinos weren't enemies: they were to
become independent on July 1. Combat training for GIs, which had been
resumed to take their minds off worries, had increased them; rumor had it
that they would be used to hunt down Communist guerrillas in the Philippines or on the Chinese mainland. To cap it all, Secretary Patterson told an
interviewer on Guam that he was "surprised" to hear of the V-J Day five-
month-old point freeze.

With Mazey were hundreds of other CIO workers who had been blooded
on Detroit picket lines in the late 1930s. In a matter of hours they had
mimeographed leaflets, distributed them, and formed a cavalcade of fifteen
trucks and jeeps. Honking horns and flourishing such signs as WHEN DO WE
GO HOME? and WE DON'T LIKE THIS DEAL, they paused at each camp to pick
up volunteers. Altogether there were perhaps 150 of them in that first procession. After hearing a few speeches and passing the hat for a protest ad
in the *New York Times*, they broke up, their fire apparently spent. But the
incident had attracted the attention of the press, which served as a megaphone for grievances. Almost overnight, posts on Luzon were transformed
into rebellious communes. The crowd that began to form the following
evening in front of Manila city hall grew to 2,500, and its mood was ugly.
This time the hat was returned to the speakers with a surplus, and supple-
mentary cables were sent to Drew Pearson and Walter Winchell. The word
was passed all over the island — write your congressman. With time on
their hands and nothing better to do, 18,000 soldiers did it. Lieutenant
General W. D. Styer, commander of the armed forces in the Western
Pacific, then committed a major strategic error. The best way to calm the
mob, he concluded, was to let it hear the soothing sound of his voice over a
public address system in Manila's huge Rizal Stadium. All he achieved was
a tenfold increase in the crowd's size. The *Times* put the story on page one:
20,000 MANILA GI's BOO GENERAL; URGE CONGRESS TO SPEED SAILINGS.

A chain reaction had begun. As radio broadcasts and newspapers described the behavior of Styer's men, sympathetic demonstrations were
staged on bases around the world. In Calcutta instigators demanded the
liquidation of the China-Burma-India war theater. Secretary Patterson tried
to explain the situation to occupation troops in Yokohama and was heckled.
In Tokyo men paraded under signs reading, SERVICE, YEA, BUT SERFDOM
NEVER and JAPS GO HOME, WHY NOT US? Calling "Eleanor! Eleanor! Eleanor!"
thousands of London-based soldiers gathered beneath Mrs. Roosevelt's window in Claridge's Hotel and asked her to find out why transport room was
found for GI brides and not them. (She appeared briefly, smiled, and told

them she would try to find out.) The Paris reaction began early one afternoon when soldiers tacked up crudely lettered red-crayoned signs on the bulletin boards of both the Columbia and Rainbow Corner Red Cross Clubs: BACK UP YOUR MANILA BUDDIES. MEETING TONITE 8:30 ARC DE TRIOMPHE. At the Place d'Etoile polite gendarmes explained that because the arch was a French shrine, the rally must be held elsewhere. One group headed for the Trocadéro, across the Seine from the Eiffel Tower, yelling "Scabs!" at soldiers who refused to join them. The other column marched four abreast down the Champs Elysées to the Place de la Concorde, brandishing magnesium flares and chanting: "We wanna go home! We wanna go home! We wanna go home! We wanna go home. . . ."

The most offensive of the Wanna-Go-Home riots, as they were thereafter known, was in Germany. The Paris demonstrators at least knew how to keep step. In Frankfort four thousand GIs turned into a mindless, howling rabble. Agitators shinnied up lampposts and waved the horde on toward the I. G. Farben Building with flashlights. Turned back there by the points of MP bayonets, the protesters shouted derisively that General Joseph T. McNarney was too cowardly to confront them. McNarney was in Berlin at the time. On his return he became one of the few commanding officers to call ringleaders in and talk to them plainly. Eisenhower had referred all inquiries to his theater commanders, vaguely telling the press that he was in favor of sending home any soldiers "for whom there is no military need," and Wedemeyer all but apologized to China-Burma-India men for red tape that delayed their discharges. McNarney explained American commitments in Europe. Then he said, "We will get you home as quickly as we possibly can, but if your congressman gets the impression from his mailbag that what the public wants is 'to get the boys home and to hell with international commitments,' then you'll go home regardless of what happens to . . . chores in Europe that the nation accepted."

The general was sarcastic. In reality he had hit upon the key to the worldwide campaign. Already Capitol Hill was being swamped with complaints bearing APO return addresses. And that was only the beginning. In the second wave, parents, wives, and sweethearts joined the din with what Undersecretary of War Kenneth C. Royall called "that philosophy of 'me and my son John' that's flooding our congressmen with a deluge of criticism of demobilization." One senator received over two hundred pairs of baby bootees with "I miss my daddy" notes. The campaign was a test of congressional courage, and Congress flunked. "Every father, every mother, every child want their loved one to be with them at home," Robert F. Rich of Pennsylvania said. He added: "Remember, there is no place like home." John Rankin introduced a measure which would release every soldier who had been in uniform eighteen months, had dependents, or wanted to go to school — in other words, every draftee. Representative Mike Mansfield of Montana told reporters that he saw "no reason why the men overseas cannot be sent home and discharged as quickly as possible." Senators Tom

Connally (Democrat) and Arthur Vandenberg (Republican) issued a bipartisan statement pledging support of the rebels, and a Senate subcommittee flew to the Philippines to take testimony from Sergeant Mazey and other instigators.

The *New York Times,* horrified, expressed dismay at the impact of the "breakdown of Army discipline" on foreign spectators. It pointed out that the demonstrators "are not yet civilians; they are still soldiers. What they have done," the editorial said bluntly, "is indefensible, and they must be made to understand this." In the *Times* view, Congress was guilty of abetting "a bring-the-boys-home campaign which disregards our international responsibilities and encourages such exhibitions as those in Manila and Le Havre."

From the administration's standpoint, the timing of the disturbances could scarcely have been worse. President Truman was trying to rally congressional approval for his plan to integrate all three armed forces into a single Department of Defense. Senior officers were touchy enough as it was. The brass already distrusted the White House. If the administration let them down in this new matter, the entire reorganization plan might be jeopardized. Therefore the President announced that after reviewing Army and Navy procedures he was "convinced that the services are carrying out demobilization with commendable efficiency and with justice to all concerned." All he achieved was a switch in congressional targets, from the War and Navy departments to himself.

Like Roosevelt before him, Truman had strongly endorsed universal military training. Now hope for it evaporated overnight. Instead there was grave doubt that the military establishment could maintain a skeletal force abroad. Armed strength was already down 80 percent. What had been the mightiest air force in the world had dwindled from 2,385,000 men to 165,000. The Navy was discharging 245,000 sailors each month; Nimitz warned that not a single squadron was fit for combat. With the draft due to expire on May 15, the Joint Chiefs were contemplating a withdrawal of all occupation troops from Korea. Already five million trained soldiers were back in mufti. Generals were contemplating grim arithmetic. At the very least they needed 350,000 troops in Germany, 375,000 in the Pacific, and between 725,000 (Eisenhower's estimate) and 1,375,000 (Truman's) elsewhere. But only 400,000 soldiers were volunteers. With reenlistments declining, General Eisenhower told congressional leaders, there was very real danger that the United States would "run out of Army."

The general met the leadership in an unused room in the rear of the Congressional Library. Open testimony was out of the question. The political fires were too high. He had approached the Hill by side streets, uncomfortably aware that GIs chanting "We like Ike!" in new disturbances were endorsing his hazy comment as an endorsement of their insurgency. He told the congressmen that he had to have 1,550,000 men, and he quoted the Eighth Army chief of staff in Japan: "If any Japanese decided the time was ripe for revolt they would certainly pick a time when they believed there was dissatisfaction in the American Army. It appears that subversive forces are deliberately at work, for obscure reasons, to undermine the morale of our Army." Eisenhower added that in his opinion it might become necessary to let U.S. influence in Europe "go by default" to "some other country."

The other country was unnamed. In those months after the Japanese surrender it was unfashionable to speak of any nation as a potential enemy, but only one adversary was strong enough to challenge the United States. At the end of the war there had been ten million men in the Red Army, and ten million were still there. Russian soldiers stationed outside the Soviet Union staged no Wanna-Go-Home riots. Stalin could move at will through eastern Europe. Because Congress listened to its constituents instead of Eisenhower and Truman, by the summer of 1946 American military power had dwindled to two and a half divisions, largely replacements, with a combat efficiency at about 50 percent of the Army's wartime peak. After Churchill had called attention to the Iron Curtain running from Stettin in the Baltic to Trieste in the Adriatic, a large block of public opinion turned savagely on Truman. The ex-soldiers who had demonstrated, and the wives who had sent congressmen bootees, blamed the President, the State Department, intellectuals, and fellow travelers for the situation abroad. So far as is known, none of them looked in a mirror.

Sir William Hayter once compared negotiations with the Kremlin to a confrontation with an old-fashioned slot machine: you rarely got what you wanted, but you usually got something; you could "sometimes expedite the process by shaking the machine," but it was "useless to talk to it." Roosevelt had talked to it at Yalta, and he had hardly told Congress about Soviet promises before the Russians were openly flouting them. Stalin thought it magnanimous of him to treat with the western allies at all. Britain had provided time for the victory over Hitler, he said, and the United States contributed supplies, but Russia, with six million battle deaths, had "paid in blood." From Moscow Truman looked like a weakling and the United States like a disintegrating nation; Soviet economists had assured their leader that America was about to collapse into depression and chaos. Therefore Stalin demanded control of the Dardanelles, a slice of Turkish territory, a fixed share of Middle East oil, Caspian territory to shield his Baku oil fields, a Titoist Trieste, an Austrian Carinthia, a role in the occupation of Japan, and a physical presence in the Ruhr.

Truman's tongue-lashing of Molotov on April 23, 1945, had been the first intimation that the new President wasn't going to yield on any of them. The Russian, shaken, extended a formal invitation to Potsdam. As originally conceived, the conference there was to have implemented the decisions made at Yalta. Truman had misgivings about going, but there were many reasons he should, "the most urgent to my mind," as he wrote, being "to get from Stalin a personal reaffirmation of Russia's entry into the war against Japan, a matter our military chiefs were most anxious to clinch." The only part he really looked forward to was the ocean voyage aboard the U.S.S. *Augusta*. It was his first trip abroad since World War I, and his gossipy letters to Dear Mamma and Mary convey a delightful picture of Harry, wearing a sport shirt and white sailor hat, running all over the ship to inspect every corner of it, finding a distant cousin in the crew, and snubbing the officers to eat with the enlisted men. After that: Potsdam. The meeting was instructive but depressing. He now knew beyond doubt that "Force is the only thing the Russians understand" and the Russians were "planning world conquest." Afterward he was "glad to be on my way home."

Potsdam left the future of the former Axis satellites unchanged; that is, papered over with ambiguities and occupied by Russians. The conference had been as pointless as Truman had thought it would be. He was so disheartened during it that at one moment — one of those fascinating moments which tempt the historian to speculate — he offered General Eisenhower the White House. The two of them were touring bombed Berlin, looking at rubble, when the President suddenly turned and said, "General, there is nothing you may want that I won't try to help you get. That definitely and specifically includes the Presidency in 1948." Eisenhower didn't know what to do, so he decided to treat the offer as a splendid joke. "Mr. President, I don't know who your opponent will be," he said, "but it will not be I."

As the months passed, Russian manners deteriorated. American scientists led by Oppenheimer toiled to perfect a sensible plan for the control of atomic armaments; when they had finished, Andrei Gromyko curtly rejected it out of hand. The behavior of the many Soviet front groups was, if possible, worse. Undersecretary of State Dean Acheson left a desk groaning with work to address the National Council of Soviet-American Friendship in Madison Square Garden. He expressed the hope that nations could reconcile their differences short of the point when "a knock on the door at night strikes terror into men and women." For this he was driven from the hall with boos and catcalls. "I have often wondered," he said, "who convinced the foreign offices of Communist countries that bad manners were a basic requirement for the conduct of international relations. Marx or Engels? Whoever did so, it was a great pity."[*]

The only member of the administration who retained his illusions about the Soviet Union was Secretary of Commerce Wallace. A visionary and a dreamer, Henry Wallace had long been suspicious of U.S. chauvinists; when Henry Luce hailed the coming century as the "American Century," Wallace had retorted that the postwar years "can and must be the century of the common man." Now, sitting in cabinet meetings and watching Harry

*Acheson's presence in Madison Square Garden was later cited by his critics as evidence of sympathy for Communism.

Truman with hooded eyes, Secretary Wallace reached the conclusion that the President was an out-and-out warmonger. Something must be done about him, he decided. The people must be warned. He would warn them.

In retrospect, Wallace's defiant challenge of American foreign policy is less surprising than the fact that he had remained a member of the government that long. With Byrnes at State and Wallace at Commerce, there were two members of Truman's cabinet who thought they should be sitting in his chair. If Truman had possessed the charm of Franklin Roosevelt, he might have overridden the differences between personalities. Utterly lacking in wiles, he was fated instead to cross one New Dealer after another. Byrnes had run afoul of him early. Leaving a Moscow conference, he had cabled the White House that he expected to broadcast a complete report to the people with a fireside chat as soon as he returned. Truman had reminded him that it was his first duty to report to the President, who would then make the chat, if any. Soon afterward Truman became embroiled with Harold Ickes in a struggle over patronage. On February 12, 1946, Ickes submitted his resignation, suggesting that it become effective March 31. Truman tartly made it February 15; Ickes then publicly charged him with collecting "a nondescript band of political Lilliputians" in the White House, and reporters observed that seldom had Washington seen such a sharp exchange between a cabinet member and his President.

It was repeated before the year was out. On March 5 Churchill, as a token of esteem for Truman, delivered his Iron Curtain speech on the campus of little Westminster College in Fulton, Missouri. His criticism of Soviet foreign policy was not well received; he was, as so often before, ahead of his time. The angriest sounds in Washington came from the Secretary of Commerce. Wallace resolved to put all Russophobes in their place when the moment came. It came in September, when Byrnes was in Paris for a crucial meeting of foreign ministers. On September 10 Wallace brought the President the final draft of a speech he meant to deliver before a U.S.-Soviet friendship rally. Truman didn't have time to read it; he thumbed through the manuscript while Wallace gave him the gist of it — he would, he said, take a more critical view of the Russians than he had in the past. Preoccupied, the President nodded casually and said he hoped the address would boost the prospects of liberal and left-wing congressional candidates and the Democratic state ticket in New York. In the lobby outside, reporters asked Wallace what he and the President had discussed. He suggested they listen to his speech.

Wallace kept his word in one respect. He rapped the Kremlin's knuckles. He rapped Whitehall's just as hard, however, and then delivered a powerful blow to the Truman-Byrnes foreign policy. Washington had no business interfering with the Russian presence in eastern Europe, he said; that was Stalin's sphere of influence. Next he argued that the administration should distribute atomic bomb plans to all governments, regardless of political persuasion. After that, he wanted the United States to disarm — whatever the other countries were doing. He felt that the mere thought of collective security treaties with Britain and western Europe countries was, on the face of it, wicked. "To make Britain the key to our foreign policy would, in my judgment, be the height of folly," he said. "Make no mistake about it: the British imperialist policy in the Near East alone, combined with Russian retaliation, would lead the United States straight to war." Then came these two sentences, written in since he had left 1600 Pennsylvania Avenue: "I am neither anti-British nor pro-British; neither anti-Russian nor pro-Russian. And just two days ago, when President Truman read these words, he said they represented the policy of his administration."

Reporters who had read advance copies massed at a 4 P.M. presidential press conference, three hours before the speech was to be delivered. Truman was asked whether he had approved the Secretary of Commerce's address, and he nodded. Did it accurately reflect administration policy? He replied that it did. Then, under the impression that Wallace would endorse established policy, he attended a stag party at Clark Clifford's house. He was there when lightning struck. The first rumble of thunder came at 6 P.M. At that time one of the advance copies reached the State Department desk of Will Clayton, who was Acting Secretary in Byrnes's absence. Calling Charlie Ross on the White House direct line, Clayton protested that "This will cut the ground right out from under Jimmy at Paris." He wanted a presidential repudiation, but Ross said it was too late; Truman had already approved Wallace's remarks. Next morning's newspapers heralded the "about-face" of American policy in end-of-the-world type. In Paris Senator Vandenberg told a newspaperman, "I can cooperate with only one Secretary of State at a time." Byrnes learned of the catastrophe from a British correspondent. After stewing for four days he cabled the President: "If it is not possible for you for any reason to keep Mr. Wallace, a member of your Cabinet, from speaking on foreign affairs . . . I must ask you to accept my resignation immediately."

Dean Acheson felt that "President Truman was naive. This is not a serious indictment. In the first place he was still learning the awesome responsibilities of the President of the United States. It did not occur to him that Henry Wallace, a responsible and experienced high officer of government, should not make a speech he had carefully prepared." If Truman had said that, he would have been understood. Instead he attempted to stamp out the fire with what *Time* called "a clumsy lie." He called a press conference to "clarify" what he called "a natural misunderstanding." He hadn't endorsed the speech at all, he explained; he had merely wished to defend Wallace's right to speak out. Above all, he had not approved the speech as "a statement of the foreign policy of this country." In the edgy question and answer period that followed, Truman was reminded that Wallace had in fact told his audience that his own refusal to choose between London and Moscow had been commended by the President as "the policy of this administration." This disastrous exchange followed:

THE PRESIDENT: That is correct.

Q: My question is, does that apply just to that paragraph, or to the whole speech?

THE PRESIDENT: I approved the whole speech. . . .

Q: Mr. President, do you regard Wallace's speech a departure from Byrnes' policy —

THE PRESIDENT: I do not.

Q: — toward Russia?

THE PRESIDENT: They are exactly in line.

James Reston wrote scathingly in next morning's *Times,* "Mr. Truman seems to be the only person in the capital who thinks that Mr. Wallace's proposals are 'in line' with Mr. Truman's or Mr. Byrnes'." While mollifying the British, the President had nettled the reporters. To make a bad situation worse, Wallace refused to climb down. Calling his own press conference on the White House lawn, he declared: "I stand on my New York speech. Feeling as I do that most Americans are concerned about and willing to work for peace . . . I shall within the near future speak on this subject again."

That was too much. Confronted by the Secretary of State's ultimatum and the Secretary of Commerce's intransigence, Truman decided to dismiss Wallace. First he wrote him a longhand note laced with every profanity and blasphemy he could summon. Then he dispatched it to the Department of Commerce by hand. Wallace, stunned, telephoned Ross and said he thought the letter was not only unfit for publication; in his opinion it was too raw even to be filed in the National Archives as a presidential paper. After Wallace had read it over the phone, Ross agreed. The former secretary, as he had just become, sent it back to the White House, where Ross promptly burned it. That evening the President, purged of bitterness, wrote:

Dear Mama and Mary:

Well, I had to fire Henry today, and of course I hated to do it. . . . If Henry had stayed Sec. of Agri. in 1940 as he should have, there'd never have been all this controversy, and I would not be here, and wouldn't that be nice? . . . Henry is the most peculiar fellow I ever came in contact with. I spent two hours and a half with him Wednesday afternoon arguing with him to make no more speeches on foreign policy — or to agree to the policy for which I am responsible — but he wouldn't. . . . Well, now he's out and the crackpots are having conniption fits. I'm glad they are. It convinces me I'm right. . . .

He had been wrong, of course; he had handled things badly. Coming on top of the strikes, shortages, rising prices, the black market, and the general frustrations of reconversion, the Wallace incident contributed heavily to the erosion of Truman popularity. On the eve of his voyage to Potsdam in

July 1945, Gallup had reported that 87 percent of the American people had approved of the way he was doing his job — an extraordinary vote of confidence in light of the fact that FDR's wartime high, just after Pearl Harbor, had been 84 percent. Then came a shift. "Washington has begun to turn against him," John Chamberlain wrote in the November 26, 1945, issue of *Life*. While Chamberlain's wish may have fathered that thought, a turning point was clearly reached sometime in 1946.

It was evident in little ways. On the right came a roar from the President of the NAM: "The President lets the public freeze while his guts quiver." On the left the liberal columnist Samuel Grafton called Truman "an object for pity." Even mainstream Democrats told one another, "You just sort of forget about Harry until he makes another mistake." Ickes called upon him to unite the country by announcing that he would not be a candidate in 1948. Truman's first eighteen months had been so inept, said Democratic freshman Congressman J. W. Fulbright of Arkansas, that in the national interest the President ought to step aside for a Republican successor. In California, Nixon was drawing heavy applause with such bromides as "I promise to preserve our sacred heritage in the name of my buddies and your loved ones, who died that these might endure." The people were restless, fed up with the Ins and receptive to the blandishments of the Outs, whose two-word slogan, provided by the Harry M. Frost advertising agency in Boston and written large on billboards from coast to coast was, "Had enough?"

The people said yes. For the first time in eighteen years the Republicans captured both houses of Congress — the 80th Congress, as Truman would later memorialize it, the most ultra-conservative since the Fighting 69th of the 1920s. Richard Nixon and Joe McCarthy were swept into office. The *Los Angeles Times* saw Stassen's star rising, and Nixon's with it: "Mr. Nixon is a friend of Governor Stassen, and his political philosophy is along the lines advocated by Stassen." *Life* jubilantly hailed the victory as a "significant shift in the government's center of gravity." Congress, which for years had been a "rubber stamp and whipping boy for the White House" would now, *Life* predicted, determine the direction of public life. A conference of Republican leaders proposed a slash of ten billion dollars from the budget, lower taxes, "abandonment of the philosophy of government interference with business and labor," and repeal of all social and welfare legislation passed since 1932, including social security and the Wagner Act. Senator Styles Bridges of New Hampshire crowed that "The United States is now a Republican country."

It wasn't. The returns of any political contest reflect, at most, the persuasion of those people who voted. As Theodore H. White has pointed out, mid-century America was always Republican until 5 P.M. on election day, when working men and women, on their way home, decided whether or not to stop at the polls. If they did, and only if they did, the country would go Democratic. In 1946 they didn't. A low vote — 34 million — meant that

Democrats in large numbers, discontented with the times and missing White House leadership, had stayed away. But Republicans misinterpreted the returns. They thought the people were disillusioned with the New Deal and wanted a swift return to the simplistic, pre-Crash, golden 1920s. That being true, they reasoned, they need only bait Truman during the next two years. Then the mansion at 1600 Pennsylvania would be returned to them.

Postwar Montage

A Walk in the Sun

Brief Encounter

JOLSON SINGS AGAIN!

Mammy, Mammy,
I'd walk a million miles
for one of your smiles,
My Mam-a-a-ammy!

B'WAY BIZ DROPS 50 PERCENT AS WORLD SERIES TELECAST

Introducing: POLAROID!

Moppin' up soda pop rickeys
To our hearts' delight
Dancin' to swingeroo quickies
Juke box Saturday night

*The girl that I marry
Will have to be
As soft and as pink
As a nursery*

Give me five minutes more
Only five minutes more
Let me stay, let me stay
In your arms

AMERICANS ATE 714 MILLION GALLONS OF ICE CREAM IN 1946

LYNCH 6 IN SOUTH IN '46

Senator Theodore Bilbo (D., Miss.) called on "every red-blooded white man to use any means to keep the niggers away from the polls."

FTC REVEALS: *BOTH TONI* TWINS WENT TO HAIRDRESSER

MORON'S ECSTASY $1.00

8 FLAVORS OF ICE CREAM, APPROXIMATELY A QUART

8 FRUIT AND NUT TOPPINGS, WHICH INCLUDE: BANANAS — 2 HALVES MELBA PEACH — RASPBERRIES — MIXED NUTS — MARASCHINO CHERRIES — TUTTI-FRUTTI — PINEAPPLE — WHIPPED CREAM

NOTICE: THE MANAGEMENT ASSUMES NO RESPONSIBILITY OF ANY KIND, SHAPE, OR MANNER. Any person moron enough to finish a Moron's Ecstasy is eligible for membership in the Royal Order of Morons.

SINATRA PAYS OUT $9,000 FOR SLUGGING NY DAILY MIRROR MAN IN HOLLYWOOD

LUCKY STRIKE MEANS FINE TOBACCO!

NEW SURVEY SHOWS NUREMBERG TRIALS BORE U.S. PUBLIC

BEST SELLERS: Fiction

Try and Stop Me by Bennett Cerf
Black Boy by Richard Wright
The Egg and I by Betty MacDonald
Top Secret by Ralph Ingersoll
Pleasant Valley by Louis Bromfield

MUZAK

BEST SELLERS: Fiction

Arch of Triumph by Erich Maria Remarque
Brideshead Revisited by Evelyn Waugh
The Snake Pit by Mary Jane Ward
The Foxes of Harrow by Frank Yerby
Cass Timberlane by Sinclair Lewis

The word canasta means basket in Spanish and most likely was suggested by the tray placed on the table to hold the stock and discards — according to Hoyle

FORTUNE POLL SHOWS 8.8 PERCENT OF U.S. STRONGLY ANTI-SEMITIC

THE ICEMAN COMETH

STRAPLESS, WIRED BRA KEY TO BARE-SHOULDERED LOOK

For Men of Discernment . . . LORD CALVERT

Best actress of 1947: Loretta Young in *The Farmer's Daughter*

Gentlemen's Agreement   Crossfire   Miracle on 34th Street

Monsieur Verdoux   Great Expectations

That's just Elmer's tune

BIKINI BANG NO. 2 ROCKS RUSS

FOURTEEN

Life with Harry

I N WARTIME the streams of history merge. Each of the republic's constituencies sees the struggle as a whole because everyone shares it and even participates in it, if only vicariously. Afterward the currents divide again. Insularity returns. The week remembered at the State Department for a reciprocal trade agreement recalls a merger in Wall Street, a fire sale on Main Street, a beauty contest in Pine Bluff, the installation of an Oriental rug for a young matron, and the World Series to fifty million baseball fans.

For President watchers, the four years, ten months, and ten days between V-J Day and Korea were one long succession of crises. In Washington the kitchen was always hot, and Harry Truman was always in it. Once he slipped away to visit Mexico, whose president showed him an erupting volcano. Harry said, "That's nothing compared to what I have back home." But of course there was more to the era than that. Truman saw events in a special light. He was the President, and men in high places have always been preoccupied with national destiny.

The hiatus between the two wars was certainly a time of tremendous flux. But it *was* peaceful. The guns were mute, the bombers grounded, the warships at anchor, the marines off doing pushups. It was a lacuna, a breathing space for the children of the Depression who had come of age overseas, and in this gentle nexus the college graduates of the swing generation — those likeliest to emerge as America's leaders in the 1960s and 1970s — returned to the arms of their girls, now young women. "Do you know what you are?" Elspeth Rostow would ask her husband early one morning in 1961 during the Bay of Pigs crisis. "You are all the junior officers of the Second World War, come to responsibility."

Later, in the Johnson years, a Washington wit described the capital as "a city inhabited by powerful men and the women they married when they were young." That was unkind, and in its implication that postwar weddings had been casual detours from the highway of ambition it was also inaccurate. To the young veterans and their brides the late 1940s were exquisite years of easy laughter and lovers' vows, whose promises lingered like the fragrance of incense burning in little golden vessels on the altars of the heart. To be young and uncrippled was to be unbelievably lucky; to marry was to give of oneself, an exchange of gifts that multiplied in joy. It was a kind of fragile kaleidoscopic montage, held together by youthful passion, of a million disjointed sounds, colors, scents, tastes and snatches of quite ordinary Tin Pan Alley music; of an advertisement half glimpsed over a stranger's upturned collar on a Fifth Avenue double-decker bus; of the oleomargarine that came white in plastic bags with a yellow dye pill and had to be squeezed; of Kem-tone that came in a powder that you mixed; of knowing what it was like to lie in bed together chain-smoking in that last decade before they took the fun out of cigarettes.

And it was playing charades with other young couples. And Alec Guinness's punting scene in *Kind Hearts and Coronets*. And that six-month wait for the first postwar Ford or Chevy, and shopping for the first crackly wash-and-wear shirts, and joking about the mad money she still kept pinned in her dirndl skirt; the shared jubilance of that cafeteria luncheon after you picked her up at the doctor's office and she said yes, it was true; the wonder at the supple touch of her breasts in that first pregnancy, and, all in the same mélange, the weekends of reading *The Death of a Salesman* to her in bed and choking up, of reading *1984* and sweating bullets, of watching Mary Martin wash her hair, hating Captain Queeg, and listening to Edith Piaf and Paul Robeson on the old Magnavox covering the place where the Kem-tone had run out; of Sunday afternoons spent taking instant pictures of each other when the first black-and-white Polaroids came out in 1948, and playing Columbia's first ten- and twelve-inch 33⅓ LP Microgroove records in the summer of that same year and RCA Victor's 45 rpm the following January and then feeling the sudden hunger for the old 78s, and playing *them*, and afterward haunting Nick's and Eddie Condon's after hours in the Village and walking the dead pavements of Fifty-second Street where Petrillo had killed swing and made way for bop, the tungsten-edged "progressive" jazz of Charlie Parker and Dizzy Gillespie. Outside Jimmy Ryan's darkened bar you bowed your head.

It was a time of emerging social distinctions, of an awareness of taste, when the men you didn't know wore clocks on their socks, called money "moola," yelled "Hubba! Hubba!" at passing girls, bowled Mondays, sent singing telegrams to each other at 3 A.M., tied tiny bells to the bedsprings of newly married couples and listened outside, did imitations of Franklin Roosevelt saying, "I hate wah, Eleanor hates wah," wore Robert Hall suits Sundays, tied foxtails to radio antennas, suspended baby boots from their rear-view mirrors, devoted Saturday mornings to ritualistic car washes, said "Long time no see" when they met, married wives who went to market with curlers in their hair and were always chewing gum, took their families to movies like *Four Jills in a Jeep* and *Sands of Iwo Jima,* but boycotted *Monsieur Verdoux* because *Parade* had exposed Charlie Chaplin as a Red.

Youngsters were now teen-agers (the word, which had come into general use, joined the language as "teen age" in the January 7, 1945, issue of the *New York Times Magazine*) and they were increasingly visible. Some inner-directed households kept them in their place. In her memoirs, *Souvenir* (1956), Margaret Truman wrote that she "was still called 'the little Truman girl' — a designation for which I had the usual teen-age distaste." Beyond the White House, however, Youth Power was reshaping social behavior, usually, older Americans grumbled, with excessive noise or bad taste. The younger ones were enthusiastic riders of scooters made from orange crates and roller-skate wheels.

With the number of popular songs up tenfold over the 1930s, there were now a half-million jukeboxes in the country, earning their owners 250 million dollars a year, all of it in nickels. The tunes were unmemorable, the words forgettable, but the jukeboxes were loved for themselves. They became so cherished an icon for the young that in 1947 the seniors of a Hudson Valley high school — Scarborough's — presented one to the school as a class gift while beaming parents and teachers looked on.

It was during the Truman years that America irrevocably joined the community of nations. The phrase "United Nations" had come to FDR in the middle of one night during the bleak Christmas of 1941, when Churchill was his White House guest. In its January 10, 1942, issue, *Time* reported that "a new phrase, the United Nations," had "slipped into the world's vocabulary. The year before, a *Fortune* survey had found that barely 13 percent of the electorate wanted to see America in any international organization. By March 1944, 68 percent did. A cross-section of college students that same year endorsed the proposal to send a U.S. delegation to a permanent U.N., fifty to one. Sumner Welles favored the idea and had written an eloquent plea for world government, *The Time for Decision.* It was the August 1944 selection of the Book-of-the-Month Club and sold almost a half-million copies. On the motion of Arkansas's Congressman Fulbright, the House of Representatives resolved 360 to 20 to support "the creation of appropriate international machinery with power adequate to establish and maintain a just and lasting peace among the nations of the world, and . . . participation by the United States therein." In the Senate the measure also had bipartisan support.

Philadelphia, Atlantic City, Chicago, San Francisco, and the Black Hills of South Dakota were competing vigorously with New York for the honor of providing the United Nations with a tax-free enclave. One small Connecticut city — Greenwich — had testily voted *not* to receive the new world organization, but that was put down to anti-Willkie, anti–*One World* spite. These were the months in which Senator Arthur Vandenberg was brooding in his Wardman Park* apartment, making his historic pivot toward faith in the viability of international interdependence. Crouched in a London air raid shelter as German robot bombs rocked the ground overhead, he had asked his escort, "How can there be immunity or isolation when man can devise weapons like that?" Vandenberg broke the power of his party's go-it-alone faction when he told a hushed Senate, "I have always been frankly one of those who believed in our own self-reliance. I still believe that we can never again — regardless of collaborations — allow our national defense to deteriorate to anything like a point of impotence. But I do not believe that any nation hereafter can immunize itself by its own exclusive action. . . . I want maximum American cooperation. . . . I want a new dignity and a new authority for international law. I think self-interest requires it."

Senators from both parties gave Vandenberg a rising ovation. The press hailed him for delivering a speech "of unquestioned greatness," "the most important address to come from the Senate in the last eighty years," "a courageous pledge to meet all aggression with force," "a promise that there will be no more Munichs," and "a shot heard round the world." In the excitement Washington turned a deaf ear toward a shot fired on the other side of the world. Returning from Paris in a barely controlled rage, Ho Chi Minh declared the independence of Vietnam, proclaimed himself president, and took to the hills. The State Department's Far Eastern desk issued no special directives to its men on the spot. After all, the rebels were only natives. Their insurgency was nothing a few companies of U.S. Marines couldn't break up, if it came to that. But, of course, it wouldn't. Vietnam was a French colony: the French Foreign Legion was on hand ready to suppress any serious uprising.

There was an elusive semantic problem here, and some grasp of it is important to an understanding of postwar weltpolitik. A quarter-century ago "the world," "the free world," and even "the United Nations," were not global concepts. As late as 1947, when Secretary of State George C. Marshall delivered his celebrated speech at Harvard launching the plan which would bear his name, it was clear from the text of the address that Marshall's "world" was confined to North America, western Europe, and their allies and dependencies. There was no "Third World" then, or anything like it. It is startling to note that the United Nations declaration of New Year's Day 1942 had been signed by just twenty-six countries: the United States, the United Kingdom, the USSR, and Nationalist China; five British dominions; eight European states, all of them then Nazi thralls; and nine South American republics. A united nation, in short, was one pledged to Hitler's defeat. In 1945 there were only four independent African countries: Egypt, where British influence was still paramount; Liberia, a peculiar kind of puppet of the United States; Ethiopia, which had just been freed from Italian Fascists;

*Now the Sheraton-Park. It still stands at the corner of Connecticut Avenue and Woodley Road N.W. and is still a rookery for eminent legislators.

and South Africa, then as now ruled by a white oligarchy. On V-J Day U.N. membership had risen to 51 by the addition of liberated European states, the Scandinavian countries, and scattered small countries, but it was still largely a gentleman's club where one might clap his hands and call "Boy!" or assert independence by saying "I'm free, white, and twenty-one" without offending other members, including those whose skin happened to be black. The neighborhood, in other words, hadn't started to go.

At postwar dinner parties in Manhattan's opulent lower East Seventies, one of the smartest neighborhoods on that glittering island, the usual opening moves were to call for a drink — "Seabreezes," gin and citrus, were in vogue — while making it quite clear that (A) you never watched television and (B) you thought Christian Dior had taken leave of his senses. In the first instance you may or may not have been on the level, but in the second you were dead wrong. Christian Dior was at least as sane as you were. An obscure, middle-aged Parisian designer at the war's end, he had shrewdly guessed that women in the United States were still servile to fashions decreed in Paris and were ready to celebrate the end of Washington's hated Government Regulation L-85, which had limited them to two inches of hem, one patch pocket per blouse, no coat cuffs, no belts wider than two inches, no attached hoods or shawls, and no skirt more than 72 inches around. In the five years since Paris had fallen, a great many American girls had become accustomed to unpocketed and ruffleless blouses, spartan suits, and short skirts, the last of which had also brought enjoyment to men. But Dior said no. In late 1945, the orphic couturier sketched abundant skirts barely twelve inches from the floor, with unpadded shoulders but stuffed brassieres (or "falsies," as they were known), and shoes and hats that made men gasp. What Dior had going for him was that if women adopted his styles they would have to invest in entire new wardrobes. That brought the three-billion-dollar garment industry and the women's magazines down on his side with a thump. The ecstasy of *Harper's Bazaar* and *Vogue* and *Glamour* was unbounded. "Your bosoms, your shoulders and hips are round," one writer sang out. "Your waist is tiny, your skirt's bulk suggests fragile feminine legs. You are *you!*" Down with the barren, the harsh, and the sterile, they trumpeted on their slick pages, and up with Dior's full, luxurious, abundant (and expensive) New Look.

The New Look: that became fashion's war cry of '46. For American husbands, apart from their dismay over Dior's hidden leg, there was the prospect of bills running anywhere from $17.95 for a taffeta afternoon dress in Arkansas to $450 for a Paris original. In the case of their wives the stakes were more complicated. Most of them didn't like the costs, either. To many the V-plunge necklines, curving waists, sloping shoulders, midi-lengths, and the frothy organdy blouses erupting from peg-top skirts were downright ugly. But there was more to it than that. The promotional drive was an insult to their intelligence. The very prose in the slicks was crackers: "In this issue," *Vogue* giggled, "the merits of the cautious discard." What did that mean? It wasn't even a sentence. If women bought these absurd new outfits they would be conceding that they were dupes, the weaker sex, dithering little fools who couldn't be trusted with the family budget and were a menace on the roads.

The difficulty was that women lacked options, because society was still tightly sheathed in taboos — or, if you like, self-discipline. Their mothers had taught them to be modest and gentle in all ways, so they glowed in their wrath and did what, within the context of the time, could be done. In Kentucky 676 working women signed an anti–New Look manifesto. The loudest complaints were over skirt lengths, because girls were accustomed to showing more leg, and this was one alteration Singer couldn't make; it was impossible to let a short skirt down. "LBK" ("Little Below the Knee") clubs sprang up in several cities; 1,300 Dallas LBK members marched through the shopping district with hems just below their kneecaps and LBK placards demanding freedom from French tyrants. In Paris Dior cried, "My God, what have I done?" — as though he didn't know.

The crisis came in 1946–47. It had to be resolved quickly; millions of yards of full-flowered chiffon and lace were piling up in the garment warehouses of Manhattan awaiting decisions from Little Rock, Denver, and Seattle. Customers were under pressure, too. Every time one girl passed another on a sidewalk, each was frantically deliberating which way to go. Some found brief refuge in what might have been called the third world of postwar fashion: new looks that weren't the New Look. Austere Britain, for example, was still rationing materials. Heels could be no higher than two inches, and clever Portobello Road modistes had designed "wedgies" with solid insteps that were cheap and looked smart. America's own dressmakers had revived the bare midriff and introduced the strapless wired brassiere in 1946. As Easter approached — it came on April 6 in 1947 — the strugglers seemed locked neck-and-neck. And then feminine resistance suddenly vanished. Pushovers and dunces they might be, but no middle-class woman with cash or credit was willing to look like a frump that Sunday. Parading up the aisles, they clearly demonstrated to the rest of the country — that is, to their groaning husbands — that in matters of haut monde, a phrase which was not French by accident, they still danced to the music of a foreign piper.

In the aftermath of the struggle, the women guests not only struck their colors, they managed to forget that they had ever raised them. Women went about wearing, among other things, espadrilles, clogs, backless linen boots, spike-heeled "naked sandals," and fezzes garnished with veils, feathers, and even birdcages. The excesses of the shoemakers followed a certain logic; limited in the length of leg they could show, women with trim ones were trying to attract attention with odd footwear, varicolored nylons, and multiple ankle straps. But the hats made no sense whatever. Neither did impractical matching gloves nor the bizarre handbags. If they were making any social statement at all, it was an assertion of feminine intuition and a woman's right to be wrong, trivial, and fickle.

Over Seabreezes or Martinis at the typical Manhattan dinner party the general discussion of the gathering guests might touch upon Larry Mac-Phail's coup in picking up the Yankees for three million dollars; Nicholas Murray Butler's retirement from Columbia University; the Pope's creation of four new American cardinals; and, on a gloomier note, a report from the University of Denver's National Opinion Research Center: 36 percent of Americans expected the country to be at war again within twenty-five years and another 23 percent within fifty years. Only 20 percent thought World War II was the last global struggle. And the poll had been conducted late in 1945, before the public knew how shaky relations with Stalin had become.

Buffet dinners were not acceptable in the lower East Seventies during these years, nor was dress optional. Wearing black tie and evening gowns, the guests found their places at a linened table, the guest of honor at the host's right, and all flanked by members of the opposite sex to whom they were not married. You were expected to divide your conversational time between them until, with the the last wineglass empty and the candles burning low, the sexes took leave of one another. The men gathered around their host for brandy and Havana cigars, while the women went upstairs to do whatever women did on such occasions. It seems likely that at least part of the time they discussed prevalent topics of special interest. Yale pediatrician Arnold Gesell's *The First Five Years of Life* was still selling briskly and usually sparked interest in powder rooms. (*The Robe* and *Peace of Mind* were better sellers, but to mention them in this company would have been social suicide.) There was a current rage for matched purses and hats, adhesive black silk "beauty patches" for the face, and new dress fabrics featuring huge portraits of the wearer. Women were very much aware of the technological revolution, and like their sisters out on the farm they were grateful for it. Synthetic fabrics were changing their lives in Manhattan as well as in Iowa. Servants had almost vanished, but so had many of the reasons for hiring them. Electric clothes dryers had appeared in appliance stores less than a year after V-J Day, and during each year in the late 1940s women were buying 225,000 automatic dishwashers and 750,000 garbage disposal units. Frozen orange juice had come in 1947. Of course, some of the new devices were absurd. A young Chicago industrial designer named Jean Otis Reinecke was taking out a patent on an electric guitar which could be tuned up to such a pitch that it challenged the endurance of the human eardrum. Well, people said, it was a free country, and everybody knew it took all kinds, but some people were the absolute limit.

Advertising was about to enter a kind of Golden Age. A Navy veteran's best-selling roman à clef (Frederic Wakeman's *The Hucksters,* 1946) was making Madison Avenue a household word. Yet the very heralds of advertising's prosperity — the mass circulation magazines — would later become the communications industry's most prodigious failures. During the war periodical publishers had been as busy as foremen at Willow Run. Between Pearl Harbor and V-J Day each of them had gained, on the average, a quarter-million subscribers. Before the war they had sold at most a few thousand copies abroad; now that America was the acknowledged leader of the West, their readers included hundreds of thousands of Europeans. In one two-year period alone they increased their advertising income by a hundred million dollars. Even in the full flush of this prosperity, however, there were warnings of trouble ahead. Surveys by advertisers, John Fischer reported in *Harper's,* had disclosed that literate Americans were turning more and more to periodicals aiming at specific clienteles — *Yachting, Holiday, The New Yorker.* As for the mass audience, it was restless. Diverting it was no longer enough; it wanted to be captivated, enthralled, carried away. The days of the newsstand giants would be numbered, once the public discovered TV.

Television made stimulating conversation in the early Truman years, but it didn't make much else, certainly not money. The early DuMont sets were tiny, expensive, and limited in number, and there usually wasn't much to see. Two sports telecasts hinted at its great potential: TV's coverage of the Louis-Conn fight on June 19, 1946, and of the 1947 World Series. In each case the spectator who stayed home by his set saw more than men who had paid fifty dollars for a ringside or Yankee Stadium seat. But advertising sponsors were waiting before committing themselves. There were still far too few sets in living rooms to justify big budgets for the tube — only 172,000 of them as late as January 1, 1948, with fewer than twenty television stations. So radio remained smug. Hollywood didn't. The movie moguls came hat in hand to the great Madison Avenue advertising agencies, where brisk account executives mounted a nationwide offensive, suggesting to readers of hoardings and subway and trolley ads, "Why Not Go to a Movie Tonight?" and reassuring them that "Movies Are Better Than Ever." It wasn't true, and it didn't work; as word spread that nearly a quarter-million television sets a month were going into American homes, it couldn't. But that didn't seem to matter. The admen and their half-brothers the P.R. men were the alchemists and sorcerers of postwar society, the wizards whose florid wartime institutional advertising had softened up the market for the new fabrics and appliances, the new canned beer, and cigarettes double-wrapped in cellophane. When they cleared their throats at a Manhattan party, in Detroit's auto styling suites, or among oilmen and lobbyists, others fell silent. The image makers were known to have special insight. Attention must be paid. Everyone understood that polling skills and manipulative techniques were the experimental stage, like Newton watching the apple fall or Fleming finding the penicillin mold in his laboratory, but give it time, give it time; its possibilities knew no horizon, and some visionaries, remembering the rout of Upton Sinclair's EPIC in 1934, thought that one day its refined techniques might even be used in a presidential campaign.

Determining the communications industry's precise role in the boom was impossible, but media influence had clearly grown during the war, and it wasn't confined to the marketplace. Already ads and magazine articles were trying to form internalized profiles of what an individual was, or ought to be. Thus GIs had been bombarded with the puerile assurances that they were fighting for blueberry pie, while the girl next door — or the young bride left in the trailer camp at the point of embarkation — was wondering how much Joe had changed and what he was like now. She had his letters, of course, but censorship was crude and most soldiers were inarticulate about the things that really mattered. So she stopped at the newsstand or corner drugstore and turned to articles whose authors were only too eager to help her understand her faraway loved one, now about to return.

They told her that a "readjustment" problem lay ahead, and that she had better be ready to solve it. "Has Your Husband Come Home to the Right Woman?" the *Ladies' Home Journal* asked. Psychiatrists, sociologists, and writers explained over and over that Joe couldn't be the same. *Good Housekeeping* counseled patience: "After two or three weeks he should be finished with talking, with oppressive remembering. If he still goes over the same stories, reveals the same emotions, you had best consult a psychiatrist." To *House Beautiful* the solution was obvious. "Home must be the greatest rehabilitation center of them all!" it trumpeted, displaying the living room decor for a shell-shocked general. There were even primers on taking the bends out of WACs and WAVEs. Surprise her, her parents were urged, by redecorating her bedroom: "GI Jane will retool with ruffles." Irresponsible newspapers dwelt on the threat of deranged ex-servicemen at large. CRAZED VET RUNS AMOK, ran one headline.

Through Bill Mauldin and others, rumors of this sort of thing had reached the troops overseas. Anger flared when they heard embroidered versions of home front advice or outright lies; in 1944 the story made the rounds that Eleanor Roosevelt had recommended that combat divisions be quarantined in a Panama detention camp before their homecomings, to be taught how to behave among civilized people, and that even after discharge they should be required to wear conspicuous armbands warning decent girls that a potential rapist was in the vicinity. They weren't that way at all, the guys on the line said indignantly. It wasn't true that they were preoccupied with sex.

But they were.

After the Battle of El Alamein a Reuters correspondent reportedly asked an Eighth Army Tommy, "What's the first thing you're going to do after the war?"

"Hump my wife," was the soldier's instant reply.

"And the second thing?"

"Take off these goddamned hobnail boots."

It was much the same in all armies, and has been true of troops since the beginning of military history. Once the Betty Grable pinups came down and skirts were hoisted in bedrooms and parks, talk of readjustment disappeared; "the veteran question," noted William L. O'Neill, "never materialized. . . . Of all the surprising developments in the postwar years, the easy accommodation of this mass of men was perhaps the most astonishing."

In the 1940s, love American style was marked by three distinct features. The first was the speed with which wartime marriage contracts had been drawn, the second the frequency with which they were dissolved after the gunfire died down, and the third the swiftness with which nurseries became overpopulated. Before Hiroshima quick weddings were chic. The communications industry encouraged them; in a memorable film, *The Clock*, Robert Walker went to the altar with a girl exactly twenty-four hours after he had encountered her in Pennsylvania Station, despite the fact that they came from different backgrounds, didn't know each other's families, and had nothing in common except physical attraction. On some military bases near cities teeming with girls, nuptials were encouraged by the construction of special chapels. The press made much of celebrity weddings: Artie Shaw to Ava Gardner, Oona O'Neill to Charlie Chaplin, Judy Garland (after divorcing David Rose) to Vincente Minnelli, Gloria Vanderbilt (twenty-one) to Leopold Antoni Stokowski (fifty-eight), and, after starring in twenty-four Westerns together without exchanging a kiss, Roy Rogers to Dale Evans. Then the boys came home, and romances began to disintegrate. One of the chief reasons was limned in *The Best Years of Our Lives*, a movie about middle-class homecomings. Dana Andrews played a young flier who had married on impulse just before sailing. During his absence his bride, a shallow blonde, dreamed of him as he had been then, silver wings, smashed-down pilot's cap, and all. Mustered out, he couldn't wait to get back in civvies, and when she took one look at him in them she was as good as on the train to Reno, which in 1946 granted eleven thousand divorces, still an all-time high.

In those years, these matters — among them the engaging case of Loveless v. Loveless — attracted the interest of the young veterans' wives, who might have been found attending any one of several thousand kaffeeklatsches in, among other communities, Los Angeles. They were all a winning lot; unless they had suffered from prolonged malnutrition in the Depression, they showed no outward sign of those desperate years. (When they smiled the effect may have been different. Orthodontists and braces had been a luxury when they were young. Some would be wearing dentures before they were thirty.) According to a study of fifteen thousand girls completed in 1945 by New York's American Museum of American History, the average young American woman that year had longer legs, fractionally heavier hips, and a slightly thicker waist than her grandmother in 1890, but was slimmer-hipped and less voluptuous than Aphrodite of Cyrene. On her wedding day she stood about 5 feet 3½ inches (slightly taller if she had been born in California) and measured 33.9–26.4–37.4. By the time she had become eligible for L.A.'s morning kaffeeklatsches, motherhood had scored a few local gains in the battle of inches, but she continued to be trim, pert, and celebrated by European journalists of the time for her readiness to laugh at almost anything, including, self-deprecatingly, herself and her friends — "We're such a bunch of cows here," she would say, "just a yard of cackling hens." Her hair was brown, her eyes blue, and "dear," the most popular term of endearment in her parents' generation, had been succeeded by "honey." Unless she was a college graduate or a member of the League of Women Voters, her interest in public affairs was nil. She took pride in belonging to "the uncommitted generation." She and her husband seldom scanned a newspaper. All she expected of him was that he hold a steady job, and as a child of the Depression himself, that was what he expected of himself. The name of the game was security.

Except for patios and their tiny subtropical gardens, these young women could have been found anywhere in the country. They were in California because it was growing faster than any other state, was especially attractive to veterans ready to settle down, and had become known as the birthplace of postwar America's life-style. In these years the number of American supermarkets was tripling and would soon pass the twenty-thousand mark, but San Francisco's Crystal Palace Market, their prototype, had opened in 1922. Before Pearl Harbor, California had pioneered in the development of drive-in theaters, restaurants, banks, churches, and machines which would wash and wax a car with the driver in it; after it they popularized backyard barbecue pits and kidney-shaped swimming pools. California engineers laid out the first eight-lane superhighways, designed the first cloverleaf interchanges, and developed the exact-change toll booth. The first guest to arrive at a dinner party in a sport shirt was a Californian; so was the first wearer of an electric blue tuxedo jacket. On their beaches California women pioneered bathing suit seminudity and then nudity, and elsewhere they introduced the nation to street slacks, illuminated shrubbery, split-level living, and the custom of women smoking in public. In a word, they were imaginative; in another, casual. The coffee, unsurprisingly, was instant.

Typically, kaffeeklatsch conversation was about their children. They had become the beaming creators of a population explosion which was wholly unexpected. The government had unwittingly encouraged mushrooming births. "Instead of dating many girls until college and profession were achieved," Betty Friedan has noted, the veteran "could marry on the GI bill." Demographers hadn't expected the new couples to lie in bed and just neck, but they had thought they would exercise some restraint, like their older brothers and sisters in the 1930s. Parental moods had changed, however. "The veterans and their wives grabbed for the good things as if there were no tomorrow," Caroline Bird wrote. "They wanted everything at once

— house, car, washing machine, children. . . . They had babies without worrying about how much it would cost to straighten their teeth or send them to college." It was easy to do, and lots of fun; if the figures Dr. Alfred Kinsey of Indiana University published in the third year after the war are set beside census data of the late 1940s, a few simple calculations reveal that America's 55,311,617 married men were reaching 136,666,060 sexual climaxes a week, or one emission every .0048 seconds. During those years a wife was being impregnated once every seven seconds, and the U.S. Bureau of the Census was blushing.

For the bureau this was a debacle. Every pre–Pearl Harbor population estimate went out the window. The war years had not been barren. "Goodbye babies" were being born throughout it, with the annual birth rate just below three million. But in 1946, the year after the troop transports began unloading, a half-million more infants were born than the year before. And that wasn't the end, or anything like it. The next year's crop passed 1946's record-breaker by over 400,000. By the mid-Sixties there would be between 20 and 30 million more Americans than long-range planners had counted on, with the greatest expansion in the teen-age population: the student generation which was destined to make so much news. Even in the Johnson-Goldwater election of 1964, before the bulk of the war babies reached their majority, fewer than one voter in four had been a Depression adult. It was then, in Johnson's second term, that certain generational differences began to emerge. Thus the conceptions of the Truman years would begin to exert a conspicuous influence upon society just as the parents were settling into middle age, and alter it in ways which would not always arouse their enthusiasm.

It was in these years that Dr. Spock's manual of baby care became the greatest best seller since best seller lists began in 1895. Spock devoted a section to what he called "permissiveness." He wrote: "It's basic human nature to tend to bring up your children about as you were brought up." Nevertheless, they should bear in mind that "Doctors who used to conscientiously warn young parents against spoiling are now encouraging them to meet their baby's needs, not only for food, but for comforting and loving." The Age of Spock had begun.

At the outset it was in many ways a marvelous age. One of Bill Mauldin's cartoons in *Back Home*, his sequel to *Up Front*, shows a father clutching groceries and wheeling a stroller while a uniformed sergeant heckles: "How's it feel to be a free man, Willie?" Veterans without number thought it felt great. Women's magazines began to note a phenomenon: the new fathers were volunteering to mix the baby's formula, take the 2 A.M. feeding, and even cope with the diaper service. (Disposable diapers wouldn't be available for another fifteen years.) As new gadgets and conveniences came on the market, parental chores became easier. (There were no electric knives, but electric knife sharpeners took the butchery out of carving; no central vacuuming systems, but vacuum cleaners became lighter and more efficient.) And if a couple wanted to dine out and take in a movie, older girls in the neighborhood were glad to sit for a price. (A quarter an hour was considered generous.) Emerging households, in fine, had been freed of their worst drudgery and most backbreaking tasks. The only difficulty was finding a home.

The postwar housing shortage was a direct consequence of the baby boom and the rapid Wanna-Go-Home demobilization. With the Army discharging nearly a million men a month by December 1945, and the Navy another quarter-million, there was almost no place to put them. America needed at least five million homes, and it needed them now. Clearly it wasn't going to get them from the housing industry. Once wartime controls were removed, labor and materials went into industrial construction; between V-J Day and Christmas ground had been broken for only 37,000 houses. President Truman asked Congress for price ceilings on housing and authority to channel half the country's building materials into low-cost ($10,000 or less) houses. The powerful housing lobby blocked him. The Senate did approve turning 75,000 temporary wartime buildings over to veterans and their families; government dormitories were remodeled for another 11,000 married GIs, and with winter blowing colder every day, 14,000 families were crowded into empty Army barracks. It was a dent, no more. Over a million families were doubling up. In arctic Minneapolis a husband, wife, and their little war baby spent seven nights in their car. In Atlanta two thousand people answered an ad for one apartment. Atlanta's distressed city fathers bought a hundred trailers for veterans' families. Trailer camps were springing up around every community of any size, especially those with campuses. The University of Missouri conducted a house-to-house canvass, reserving every foot of available space for children of Missouri parents, and then wrote out-of-state applicants that despite their qualifications, there was no room. North Dakota veterans converted grain bins into housing, and Benny Goodman and his band played for a Cleveland benefit at which citizens pledged rooms for rent. There wasn't anywhere near enough of this, though. Landlords were famous for their cold shoulders. Mauldin was bitter — his wrath continued to be a guide to the temper of his generation — and he expressed his anger in a savage drawing showing a GI and his wife and daughter confronting a fat, arrogant landlady. A sign by the door reads: "ROOMS/No Children or Dogs." The landlady is saying, "You soldiers just don't seem to understand our problems."

At the height of the crisis, every encampment of married GIs had its repertoire of gruesome stories. Their most striking advocate was an improbable U.S. Senator named Glen Taylor, a cowboy singer sent to the capital by the people of Idaho on the strength of his skill with a banjo. Standing on the Capitol steps with his wife and children, he wailed:

Oh, give me a home near the Capitol dome,

With a yard where little children can play;
Just one room or two, any old thing will do,
Oh, we cain't find a pla-ace to stay.

The country desperately needed a ten-year program to erect 1,500,000 homes a year, and for a while it looked as though the only answer would be tents. The housing industry's lobby had enough muscle to block a huge government effort, but the industry was too expensive and too slow, with its brick-by-brick methods, to do the job itself. Somehow the vacuum had to be filled, and by early 1949 it had become evident that assembly-line prefab developers — the peacetime equivalent of those who had wrought wartime production miracles — were going to do the job. The Henry J. Kaiser of housing was to be the emerging firm of Levitt & Sons. In shaping postwar society, William J. Levitt's purchase of a 1,500-acre potato field in Long Island's Nassau County ranks with DuMont's seven-inch TV screen and Howard Aiken's construction of the first U.S. computer at Harvard. The origins of suburbia as it is today can be traced to the staking out of that field, and those who scorn Levitt's first Levittown cannot know how grateful its first inhabitants were. Levitt made no announcement and bought no advertising. Word of mouth was enough; when he opened his modest sales office on the cold, blustery morning of March 7, 1949, over a thousand couples were waiting. Some of them had been there four days and nights living on coffee and doughnuts. When the doors opened it was like the Oklahoma Land Rush of 1889, with the Young Marrieds, as they were now beginning to be called, rushing around, resolved to be among the first to buy the basic four-room house for $6,990 or, with closing fees, landscaping, and kitchen appliances included, well under $10,000.

Levitt built homes as Kaiser had ships, on beltlines — 17,500 houses in that first eruption, each like the other. On signal his bulldozers moved across the landscape in echelon, pivoting at red flags. Street pavers followed, then electricians with light poles and men bearing stamped street signs. Next, house lots were marked off. Convoys of trucks moved over the hardened pavements, tossing out prefabricated sidings at 8 A.M., toilets at 9:30, sinks and tubs at ten, sheetrock at 10:45, flooring at eleven. And so it went. Levitt's carpenters used only power tools; there wasn't a handsaw in town. Paint came from spray guns, and at first in just one two-toned "color scheme." Calculating that two thousand families could swim in a pool occupying the same amount of space as a tennis court, Levitt decreed eight pools and no courts. Everything was uniform. On Mondays wash was hung in 17,500 backyards; under no circumstances could it flap on Sundays. Picket fences were prohibited. Lawns had to be cut regularly. It was all in the deed. Even pleasant innovations conformed to Levitt's game plans. Trees were introduced at the rate of one every 28 feet (2.5 for each house), and the distance from trunk to trunk was precise to the inch. Curbstones curved gently, but always at the same angle. Families struggling to assert their identity were limited to interior decorating and the pitch of the door chime. (It had to be a chime, though; buzzers and bell-pulls were out.) Architects and sociologists were aghast. To them this was the entrepreneur as a totalitarian. Yet the Levittowners didn't mind. To ex-GIs who remembered military regimentation, and their wives from Quonset huts and trailer camps, the hearths were no less warm for having been built according to standard specifications.

Bill Levitt became an instant legend, a checkout counter Paul Bunyan unscarred by the outraged aesthetes. As his imitators sprang up across the country he assembled his men, crossed the Pennsylvania state line, and targeted on eight square miles on the Delaware River which until then had been used to grow spinach. Levitt's draftsmen had plans for 1,100 streets accompanied by schools, churches, baseball diamonds, a town hall, factory sidings, parking lots, offices for doctors and dentists, a reservoir, a shopping center, a railroad station, newspaper presses, garden clubs — enough, in short, to support a densely populated city of 70,000, the tenth largest in Pennsylvania. Levitt called Levittown II "the most perfectly planned community in America," and when he spoke of it his voice grew husky. "Sure, there's a thrill in meeting a demand with a product no one else could meet," he said. "But I'm not here just to build and sell houses. To be perfectly frank, I'm looking for a little glory, too. It's only human. I want to build a town to be proud of." After a pause he added, "You have to have nerve. You have to think big."

Curiously, his own home was everything a Levittown house wasn't — a lovely old Bucks County farmhouse with thick stone walls, hand-hewn rafters, stout beams, expansive rooms, and a stunning view of thick, uninhabited woods. He liked it, he admitted. But, he quickly added, most Americans, especially women, would not. "It isn't fair," he told a visitor, "to ask the public to pay for things they don't need and can't afford." Pointing at the old building's ornate moldings and other dust catchers, he said, "Imagine asking a modern housewife to clean this place. Imagine sticking your own wife way off in the country like this. People like people." They'd better, his tone suggested. They weren't going to get much choice.

FIFTEEN

A Little Touch of Harry in the Night

I T IS POSSIBLE to fix the time and place when the flag of world leadership began to pass from the dying British Empire to the United States. Late in the morning of Friday, February 21, 1947, Lord Inverchapel, the British ambassador in Washington, telephoned the State Department to request an emergency appointment with General George C. Marshall, who had just replaced Byrnes as Secretary of State. His lordship explained that he had been instructed to deliver "a blue piece of paper" — diplomatic cant for a formal and important message — from Whitehall. Dean Acheson replied that Marshall was away, speaking at the Princeton bicentennial. Could the matter wait until Monday?

Actually it couldn't, Inverchapel replied. He would ask his First Secretary, H. M. Sichell, to make the delivery now. Here a bit of stage business intruded. As Undersecretary, Acheson couldn't receive a First Secretary without violating protocol. Someone of lower rank was needed; therefore he designated as his representative Loy Henderson, director of the Office of Far Eastern and African Affairs. Thus it happened that two low-level diplomats, meeting in a dismal office in the Executive Office Building late that afternoon, took the first step in transferring world power westward.

Sichell had in fact brought two documents, both of them, as Acheson later recalled, "shockers." Acheson knew Greece was troubled. The Communists were reported ready to take over the country, there were rumors of British troop withdrawals, and Henderson had submitted a memorandum entitled "Crisis and Imminent Possibility of Collapse," urging massive aid to a coalition government as Greece's only hope of salvation. But nothing heretofore had signified the extent of Hellenic despair. If the Greeks didn't receive a first installment of over two hundred million dollars in the immediate future, he now read, they would succumb to a new barbaric invasion from Russia. Turkey was also in straits — that was the second piece of blue paper. The Turks were somewhat stronger, but lacking aid they, too, would be overwhelmed. Britain couldn't give either country anything more. The English were exhausted and depleted by their six-year struggle with Nazi Germany. Indeed, they, too, were in urgent need of fresh dollar transfusions; presently Lord Inverchapel would be approaching the Americans again, this time holding out his own silk hat.

Apprised of all this, Truman was startled. He had no idea the situation was that bad. To be sure, Churchill had warned that Europe had become "a rubble heap, a charnel house, a breeding ground of pestilence and hate," but that had been largely discounted as a peal of Churchillian thunder. The press had either ignored the extent of Europe's agony or underplayed it; *Time*, ever fortunate in its search for the epigrammatic bystander, had quoted the anonymous widow of a Czech partisan as saying, "We don't need much, but we need it quickly." That had made sense in Washington, where the premise had been that after a short period of turmoil and adjustment the continent, like the United States, would rebuild its peacetime economy. The week after V-J Day the President had reviewed Allied appeals for extensions of lend-lease and turned them down. Forty billion lend-lease dollars, he had said, was enough. The program must be liquidated as soon as possible; he was dead set against America's playing the role of a global Santa Claus after September 1945.

De Gaulle had protested, so had Chiang Kai-shek, and Churchill had cried: "I cannot believe that this is the last word of the United States. I cannot believe that so great a nation would proceed in such a rough and harsh manner." It didn't. One loaning device was merely discarded to be replaced by others, notably the United Nations Relief and Rehabilitation Administration (UNRRA). Yet despite the loans, credits, and outright gifts of eleven billion dollars, deprivation and want continued to stalk the Low Countries, France, Italy, Western Germany and the Balkans. In each of the two postwar autumns methodical Berliners had dug thousands of graves before the ground froze to accommodate neighbors whom they knew would never see another spring; UNRRA's gifts to Greece had barely sufficed to replace the rusted pipes and pumps of Athens's ruined water system. From the Aegean to the North Sea, Nazi tyranny had been succeeded not by freedom, but by hunger and disorder. Looted by the Germans, pounded by bombs, and gutted by resistance fighters, the blackened factories stood cold and mute. There were no raw materials for them anyway, and even if raw materials had magically appeared, the shattered railroad grid could not have brought them to the plants. Political leadership seemed about to pass to the Soviet Union, if only because there was no viable alternative.

The State Department, upon learning of the need for a massive rescue operation, had at first counted on Britain and her far-flung empire to provide it. In July 1946 Truman had signed a bill authorizing a fifty-year loan of $3,750,000,000 to His Majesty's government, and that, he had thought, should liquidate American obligations to Europe. But now the money was gone, with little to show for it. Some 17,000 homes, a quarter of London, still lay in ruins; the erection of 10,000 Nissen huts as emergency shelters had met the housing needs of only a fraction of the supplicants. While American women argued about the New Look, their English sisters were limited each year to one dress, four ounces of knitting wool, two yards of material, one-third of a petticoat, one-fourth of a suit, and one-fifth of a nightgown. Victory had brought America's great ally survival, but not much else.

Even that was menaced by the terrible winter which began in January 1947. Throughout that month and the next, temperatures remained below zero while blizzards piled layer upon layer of record-breaking snow accumulations. It paralyzed England. Agricultural production dropped below nineteenth-century levels. Industry shut down. Electricity was limited to a few hours each morning, unemployment rose to over six million, and rations were tighter than in wartime. On that bitter Friday when Sichell rode to Pennsylvania Avenue with the two blue pieces of paper, one for Greece and one for Turkey, Whitehall predicted "even worse things to come in the year ahead." The *Times* of London called the forecast "the most disturbing statement ever made by a British government." Any doubts about the magnitude of Europe's plight vanished when Herbert Hoover returned from touring twenty-four countries at the President's request to report that their populations — and especially their children, the flotsam of war — were on the verge of starvation and could be saved only by American largess on an unprecedented scale.

Hoover's fellow Republicans in Congress weren't so sure. There was much talk about Uncle Sam being played for a sucker, of pouring money down a rathole or into a global WPA, of the American dream ending in bankruptcy. Europeans, in turn, were stung by such callous appraisals.

Anti-Americanism had spread. An Army chaplain noted that in continental eyes U.S. soldiers were pathetic young men who had no idea why they had fought or what victory meant, and who were interested in finding only three things: women to sleep with, brandy to steal, and the next boat home. "There he stands in his bulging clothes," the Reverend Renwick C. Kennedy wrote of the typical U.S. occupation soldier, "fat, overfed, lonely, a bit wistful, seeing little, understanding less — the Conqueror, with a chocolate bar in one pocket and a package of cigarettes in the other. . . . The chocolate bar and the cigarettes are about all that he, the Conqueror, has to give the conquered."

The transmittal of this mood to Capitol Hill raised congressional hackles, and for the first time since the 1930s legislators began muttering about Europe's failure to repay its debts. But there was more to the Greco-Turk issue. Communists were a genuine threat there. Since the British could no longer disperse them with a whiff of grapeshot, Washington had to face a hard choice. An enslaved Europe under the hammer and sickle seemed unthinkable. The Soviet Union would double its steel capacity, shipbuilding facilities, skilled labor, electrical and chemical output, scientific and technical knowledge, and industrial plant. That way, and only that way, Russia could match American power. "I believe that if we lose Western Europe," Admiral Forrest Sherman testified before a congressional committee, ". . . we would have an increasingly difficult time in holding our own. Whereas if we lost all of the Asiatic mainland, we could still survive and build up and possibly get it back again."

That was logical, although in 1947 it was less than compelling. The Russians were still remembered as a brave ally. Disillusion had just begun to sink in, and thus far its effect had been confined to depressed morale; savage as World War II had been, the conflict between good and evil had been plain, and the prospect of more strife on new issues was disheartening. In 1946 Herbert Bayard Swope had introduced the phrase "cold war" in a Bernard Baruch speech. Baruch had thought it too strong then and struck it out. On April 13, 1947, after another year of Soviet crudity, Baruch did use it in Columbia, South Carolina, but even then it was limited to what was called "the war of ideas," and as late as May 1950 — just before Korea — Paul Hoffman could argue that "The cold war is a good war. It is the only war where the question of destruction doesn't enter into it at all."

Even in 1947, however, it was clear that General Markos and his 20,000 Communist (EAM) guerrillas could not be driven from Greek hills by better ideas. The legitimate government needed what the State Department's Policy Planning Staff called "massive nonideological aid" — in a word, guns. Guns were better than butter in attracting congressional votes from anti-Communist Republicans. Truman and his advisers were determined to send both. Yet their experience in piecemeal commitments had been discouraging. Europe required reconstruction, not relief. America needed a genuine foreign policy. Casting about for a philosophy to fit its deeds, the administration found one in a current issue of the prestigious quarterly *Foreign Affairs*. The article was titled "The Sources of Soviet Conduct"; its author was identified only as "X."

"X" was George F. Kennan, then a brilliant if obscure student of the Russian mind. He had first written his treatise in America's Moscow embassy, where he had served as counselor. He had been motivated by a careful study of Stalin's hard-line 1946 speech to a gigantic rally of Communist party functionaries, in which the dictator denounced coexistence with democracies and pledged himself to a world revolution of the proletariat. In Kennan's view Soviet leaders were frightened Marxist evangelists who had been unbalanced by a quarter-century of western distrust. Communism was their pseudoreligion, the opiate for their insecurity. Seen as theology rather than politics, it emerged in Kennan's analysis as one of the world's great faiths, complete with dogma, rituals, and historic mission. It was as indestructible as, say, Mohammedanism, and like Islam it would take hold wherever weakened societies had made men yearn for change. Once embraced it could never be wholly eliminated. It could, however, be *contained* — limited to the frontiers of nations already under its spell.

In the context of the 1940s, containment was realistic. It made excellent sense to Harry Truman; as the largest and richest of the free nations, he declared, America must meet her obligations to "the free world." The President became so staunch an advocate of Kennan's views that they became known as "the Truman Doctrine." On his order they were incorporated in Policy Paper Number 68 of the National Security Council, and in Dean Acheson's opinion, NSC-68 became "one of the great doctrines in our history." In fact, even before Kennan's article became America's cold war strategy, Acheson, in the President's presence, outlined its principles to a meeting with the congressional leadership. At stake was the future of Turkey and Greece; "never," he wrote later, "have I spoken under such a pressing sense that the issue was up to me alone." When he had finished, there was a long pause. Then Arthur Vandenberg turned to Truman and said, "Mr. President, if you will say that to the Congress and the country, I will support you, and I believe that most of its members will do the same."

He did, and they did. On March 12 Truman asked a joint session to appropriate 400 million dollars — 250 million for Greece and 120 million for Turkey. Then he, Marshall, Acheson and Vandenberg hit the sawdust trail to preach the gospel of containment before every influential group in the country, until, on May 22, the President signed the Greco-Turk aid bill into law in his temporary office in Kansas City's Muehlebach Hotel.

At the time, the Truman Doctrine looked like a master stroke. Its loudest critics then were right-wing mastodons who wanted to "roll" the Communists "back" to their prewar frontiers. Yet there were other dissenters whose questions, raised mildly at the time, remained unanswered a quarter-century later. Senator Taft, pointing out that the two governments were to receive American arms, suggested that Capitol Hill should be exceedingly careful about delegating its war-making powers to any chief executive, whatever the issue. General Albert C. Wedemeyer thought containment was an invitation to military folly, because the Russians could bleed America white by provoking aggression on the boundaries of its satellites, where the conflict would be "their third team opposing our first team." Most haunting of all, Walter Lippmann adopted Wedemeyer's arguments and added others of his own in a brilliant riposte to Kennan's reasoning.

Lippmann's slim volume was called *The Cold War: A Study in U.S. Foreign Policy* (1947). In it he was polite — Kennan was called "Mr. X" throughout — and devastating. Quoting the article in *Foreign Affairs,* he noted Kennan's view that it demanded "unalterable counterforce" to the Communists "at every point where they show signs of encroaching." If the Soviet Union were an island like Japan, he wrote, it could be blockaded by American air and sea power. Unfortunately, it was a land power, and as such it could only be contained by trench warfare or the endless hemorrhages of guerrilla warfare. "The Eurasian continent is a big place," he wryly commented, "and the military power of the United States has certain limitations." Already, in Greece, partisans had carried the struggle to the hills, where sophisticated weapons were useless ar⁷ infantry skills were everything. Under containment, Lippmann continu. 1, the outcome would depend upon draftees or satellite troops. Despair lay either way. America must "disown our puppets, which would be tantamount to appeasement and defeat and the loss of face," or must support them at an incalculable cost "on an unintended, unforeseen and perhaps undesirable issue." Repeatedly Lippmann returned to Asia and its traps for containment-minded diplomats. To accept a challenge there would permit the Communists to choose the battlefield, the weapons, and even the nationality of the Red battalions. "I find it hard," he concluded, "to understand how Mr. X could have recommended such a strategic monstrosity."

In eighteen months Greece was pacified, Turkey was invulnerable, and George Kennan was a hero. Washingtonians reminded one another that Lippmann wasn't infallible: after all, he had misjudged Roosevelt. But this time his instincts were right. While the triumph of the center in Greece would have been unlikely without American assistance, it would have been inconceivable if Tito hadn't quarreled with the Cominform and closed the border between Yugoslavia and Greece, depriving General Markos of his sanctuary. Superficial resemblances between Greece and Korea later strengthened advocates of containment and limited war without solving this problem of asylum, thereby contributing to Vietnam. It is worth noting that professional soldiers as far apart in other ways as MacArthur and Bradley agreed that the kind of conflict Lippmann had foreseen would be a strategic nightmare.

That was one side of the containment coin. The brighter side was the Marshall Plan, which grew out of the Truman Doctrine and became its great sequel. If the Greek and Turkish debt to Kennan's vision is less than had been supposed, western Europe's obligation is beyond price. Eventually the Marshall Plan — formally known as the European Recovery Program (ERP) — became as noncontroversial as social security.

If ERP began with any one man, it was Undersecretary of State Will Clayton. Flying home from a six-week canvass of Europe, Clayton put it on paper as the only alternative to war in the coming decade. In every country he had visited, subversive campaigns were destroying national integrity and independence. "Feeding on hunger, economic misery, and frustration," he wrote, "these attacks have already been successful in some of the liberated countries." He proposed that the President and the State Department shock the American people into action. After his plane from Zurich reached Washington, Clayton handed his memorandum to Acheson, who took it to the President. Acheson reminded Truman that the President had asked him to speak for him at a small southern function on May 8.

If shock was the right prescription, perhaps he should strike a few sparks there.

Truman concurred, and so it happened that the ERP concept was first presented to an American audience on the campus of the Delta State Teachers College in remote Cleveland, Mississippi. Abroad, Acheson told his listeners, the margins of survival were so narrow that the cruel winter just passed had threatened the people of northern Europe with extinction. He said: "It is one of the principal aims of foreign policy today to use our economic and financial resources to widen these margins. It is necessary if we are to preserve our own freedoms and our own democratic institutions. It is necessary for our national security. And it is our duty and privilege as human beings."

That, in sum, was the Marshall Plan. It wasn't Marshall's yet, however. The Mississippians liked it, and the *New York Times,* forewarned, put it on page one with an analysis by James Reston, but the wire services were indifferent; economic stories were considered almost as dull as public addresses by long-winded bureaucrats. The press would listen to General Marshall, though, and so a second trial balloon was readied, to be launched by him. It is a measure of the speed with which the European economy was deteriorating that delivery of his speech was moved up from the Amherst College commencement on June 16 to Harvard's on June 5, while Dean Acheson was drumming up support among reporters. Acheson was particularly active with British correspondents. To Leonard Miall of the British Broadcasting System, Malcolm Muggeridge of the *Daily Telegraph,* and René MacColl of the *Daily Express* he said, "Don't waste time writing about it. As soon as you get your hands on a copy telephone the whole thing to London. And one of you must ask your editor to see that Ernie Bevin gets a full copy of the text at once. It will not matter what hour of the night it is; wake Ernie up and put a copy in his hand."

General Marshall spoke for fifteen minutes in Harvard Yard. He first described the torn "fabric of the European economy." The remedy lay in "breaking the vicious circle and restoring the confidence of the European people in the economic future of their own countries and of Europe as a whole." Aid must be continued. He was now thinking in terms of seventeen billion dollars. But UNRRA's random spending must be replaced by a program in which there was "some agreement among the countries of Europe as to the requirements of the situation and the part those countries themselves will take to give proper effect to whatever action might be undertaken by this government." America had made its move. Now it was Europe's turn.

Thanks to Muggeridge, that next move was made almost at once. In England the small hours of the following day had arrived, yet a boy from the *Daily Telegraph* bicycled to the home of sleeping Foreign Minister Ernest Bevin with a carbon of Muggeridge's story, dictated over a transatlantic phone, as Acheson had suggested. Almost at once Bevin and

France's Georges Bidault called an all-European conference in Paris, after which applications for economic aid reached Washington from Britain, France, Italy, Greece, Turkey, Belgium, Holland, Denmark, Norway, Austria, Ireland, Iceland, Portugal, Sweden, Switzerland, Luxembourg, and, later, West Germany. After six weeks of debate and the rejection of a Taft amendment which would have slashed a billion dollars from the program, Congress passed it and then voted 597 million dollars to tide over the "Marshall gap" — the months that would pass before long-term aid could take hold.

On April 14, 1948, eleven days after President Truman had signed ERP into law, the appropriately named freighter *John H. Quick* left Galveston harbor with nine thousand long tons of wheat for Bordeaux. It was the first in a six-vessel fleet carrying emergency food cargoes for France. All told, the Marshall Plan was to give Europe 12.5 billion dollars, less than Marshall had thought necessary. In addition, there were such tangential programs as the Displaced Persons Plan, under which 339,000 DPs became American citizens. It was a proud page in history. The Russians were furious, of course. They announced the imminence of something called "the Molotov Plan," which was never heard from again. Henry Wallace, now sidestepping rapidly to the left, called ERP "the Martial Plan." In the lower house of Congress seventy-five representatives had fought it, and in the upper house freshman Senator Joseph R. McCarthy had demanded that for every dollar spent the United States should receive the equivalent of a dollar in strategic materials or foreign bases.

McCarthy notwithstanding, European leaders were both moved and exultant. This was especially true in Britain. Churchill hailed ERP as "the most unsordid act in history." The London *Economist* described it as "the most straight-forward, generous thing that any country has ever done for others." Thirty months later, when England was back on its feet, the *Manchester Guardian* said, "Ordinary thanks are inadequate. Here is one of the most brilliant successes in the history of international relations," and Hugh Gaitskell, then chancellor of the exchequer, added: "We are not an emotional people . . . and not very articulate, but these characteristics should not . . . hide the real and profound sense of gratitude toward the American people."

Across the Channel from England, the continent was transformed. Malnutrition vanished, people could dress warmly in winter, raw materials moved swiftly, pulled by new diesel locomotives on new railroad tracks; the Saar and the Ruhr sprang to life, and factories were busier than they had been before the war. In 1951 the Marshall Plan would lead directly to Jean Monnet's Coal and Steel Community. Six years after that the Coal and Steel Community would lead to the Treaty of Rome and the European Economic Community, or Common Market, which in turn would grow in power until it could compete with the United States and the Soviet Union as an equal. But in the late 1940s America glittered on a solitary peak. No other nation could even come close to it. It could only lose its lead by some extraordinary misfortune, such as a President or Presidents who would squander its wealth and youth on a distant, Orwellian war. At that time the possibility was too remote to be raised. Not to worry, as the English say, was the American mood. The United States was, and would continue to be, rich, chivalrous, peaceful, and Number One.

Number Two was becoming more and more difficult. Mutilated and ravaged by the full force of the Nazi war machine, unable or unwilling to understand why their western allies had delayed the second front until 1944, the Russians were hypersensitive to any sign of life in prostrate Germany. This national apprehension, fortified by the paranoia of Joseph Stalin, had become a wretched cross borne by western soldiers and statesmen. It grew heavier as signs of European health — and, as a concomitant, German vigor — began to return. In 1948 it peaked. During those spring weeks when Congress was winding up its Marshall Plan debate, Soviet conduct became increasingly aggressive. In February Stalin had seized Czechoslovakia, and on June 24 he imposed a blockade on Berlin.

The immediate issue was currency control. To thwart German recovery, the Russians had been flooding the western zone with paper money printed with plates that had been in use since the beginning of the occupation. To suppress this inflation, the western authorities issued new money, and at the same time they signed the Brussels Defense Pact and agreed upon a constitution for awakening West Germany. Russians fought these reforms step by step. They walked out of conferences. They issued their own currency. They stopped rail traffic between Berlin and West Germany for two days, stopped traffic on a highway bridge for "repairs," and then, by ordering a full blockade, invited a complete rupture.

The western allies decided against retaliation. If possible, Truman wanted to avoid face-to-face confrontations. The only glimmer of hope was in the sky. Air traffic was moving in and out of West Berlin's two airports, Tempelhof in the American sector and Gatow in the British. No blockade could be built in the air. Soviet aircraft might challenge western planes, but the responsibility for an incident could easily be evaded with no loss of prestige on either side.

Still, an airlift of these dimensions brought perils of its own. West Berlin was home to two and a half million people, more than Los Angeles, Philadelphia, Detroit, or Cleveland. No one had ever tried to supply a community that large, or anything like it, by air. Just keeping Berliners alive would require 4,000 tons a day — the takeoff or landing of one C-47 every three minutes and 36 seconds around the clock. Furthermore, every eastward plane would have to be overloaded, ten tons to the flight. That was enough for bare essentials. It was a possibility, a mathematical possibility, though it would mean danger for the fliers and hardship for Berlin. Enough coal could be brought in to keep the lights on, but there would be no fuel for warmth. To function normally, the city needed 8,000 tons a day, a takeoff or landing every minute and 48 seconds. It couldn't be done — yet.

The Germans promised a disciplined civilian response. The U.S. Air Force and the RAF worked out a carefully planned, split-second operation. To train new pilots, a duplicate of Berlin's air corridor approach paths and navigational aids was built in Montana. They learned to fly four-engine transports blindfolded with the new GCA (Ground Control Approach) radar. Crews had to go up with very little sleep. Maintenance men, hosing out fuselages black with coal dust, developed ugly skin diseases. And the schedule didn't always work. Twenty-eight Americans lost their lives in the Berlin airlift of 1948–49.

The fliers called it "Operation Vittles." In the beginning it didn't begin to bring enough victuals. During June and July 1948 the airlift averaged just 1,147 tons a day, and it looked as though the siege would succeed. The first break came on June 30, when squadrons of C-54s began arriving from Panama, Hawaii, and Alaska. These were larger ships; they could carry heavier loads and permit longer periods between landings and takeoffs. General Lucius Clay flew back to Washington to request more of them and was given 160. As winter approached the airlift began to hit 4,000 daily tons with consistency. West Berlin would survive and might do better, depending upon the young American, British and, now, French fliers.

They needed more room to land in Berlin, and now they were getting it. Two new airstrips were built at Tempelhof and a third on the British field. What they really needed was a third airdrome. In September the French offered a site at Tegel, in their occupational zone. They doubted that it would prove useful. The number of laborers needed would probably be prohibitive. Furthermore, they lacked rock crushers and other heavy equipment. The western allies were about to receive a useful lesson in what German tenacity could do when harnessed to American ingenuity. Over 20,000 Berliners, of both sexes and all ages, volunteered to work three shifts a day. Meanwhile C-54s began landing the necessary equipment. At the first planning session, Clay dryly recalls in his memoirs, his engineers advised him that the new airport would be ready in March, whereupon "I found it necessary to tell them that it would be completed in December." They met his timetable with the help of a little audacity on the part of General Jean Ganeval, the French commander. Getting into the spirit of the project, he removed a radio transmitting tower that obstructed the new runway. The tower was in the Soviet zone. He asked the Russians to remove it, and when they refused he marched in with a demolition team and blew it up.

That third field in the French sector put Operation Vittles over the top. In December the airlift's daily average reached 4,500 tons; in January and February, 5,500 tons. It was clear now that Berlin would make it and then some; coal rations could be doled out for homes and some industry. Clay's

C-54 fleet had grown to 224. By early spring the airlift was landing 8,050 tons a day, and one day it put down 13,000 tons. Besieged Berlin was fast becoming one of the most affluent cities in Europe, with warehouses crammed, just in case the Russians didn't know they were beaten.

They knew. On May 12 the barricades came down. The airlift was now history. The impossible had been achieved. Counting the first weeks of a partial "little blockade" in early 1948, the siege had lasted fifteen months, and in it Americans and their allies had logged 277,264 flights, hauling 2,343,315 tons of food, fuel, medicine, and clothing — nearly one ton for every citizen of Berlin. Its feats had become legend, and the miracles wrought by its pilots did much to balance the loutish behavior of immature U.S. soldiers on leave. "America has saved the world," Churchill said grandly. Not the world, surely; but certainly a vital part of central Europe. If the airlift was not typically American, it was America at its best, living up to the Seabee–Air Force boast, "The difficult we do immediately; the impossible takes a little longer," and carrying it off with grace and generosity.

The country was generous and so were the men who drove its planes. American pride was divided almost equally between Operation Vittles and Operation Little Vittles, the inspiration of a first lieutenant named Carl S. Halverson. On his way in and out of Tempelhof, Halverson parachuted bags of candy to Berlin children watching below. The idea caught on; soon all the fliers were doing it. In December 1948 they mounted Operation Santa Claus. Day and night thousands of tiny parachutes floated down bearing gifts from the unseen "amis" soaring overhead to Berliners too young to understand the blockade. Every toy, every doll, every piece of candy was bought by the crews with their own money.

In this as in all ways, the continent was becoming curious about the American national character, with its faith in solutions, its technological know-how, its pragmatism, its interest in things rather than ideas, and, less fortunately, its philistinism. General MacArthur spoke for legions of his countrymen when he condescendingly told a visitor, "It is fascinating to go back and read Plato's vision of Utopia and see how far we have progressed . . . What a remarkable vision — what intellectual flashes — those old fellows had, living under their backward conditions!" To the MacArthurs of America, and they probably constituted a majority, good plumbing and get-up-and-go outweighed the exquisite winding of Socratic reasoning.

Europeans could often identify Americans in civilian clothes before they opened their mouths. In part this was attributable to table manners, tailoring, informality, and the 35-mm cameras that seemed to dangle from every American's shoulder. There was also something about the way they carried themselves. "Conquerors?" Eric Sevareid had said of the GIs. "They had no sense of conquering a country; they were just after the Germans and had to walk over this particular piece of the earth's surface to get at them." Even before the war, when living in Munich, Sevareid had noticed that whenever he or his countrymen went for a stroll, Germans turned to watch. He had concluded, "Nobody on earth walks as easily as the American. His body is neither rigid like an Englishman's nor compact and crowded like a Frenchman's, and his head turns very easily upon his neck." Some called it insolence, others called it self-confidence; conceivably it was indefinable, but it was real. Someone else said, "The British walk the earth as if they owned it; the Americans walk the earth as if they don't give a damn who owned it."

In the past, Hollywood had given Europeans a distorted view of Americans, like figures in a carnival fun house mirror. Now their impressions were based upon the homesick soldier, or, more and more, the American traveling abroad. It wasn't much of an improvement. Tourists from other countries represented its privileged classes; well-educated, well-read, and frequently multilingual. Because of the extraordinary standard of living in the United States citizens from all levels were crossing the ocean, often with loud wives and louder children in tow. It spoke well of their country that second-generation Americans could return to the lands of their fathers, but it played hob with the national reputation.

It was U.S. popular culture on this level — somewhere below what Orwell called "the lower-upper-middle class" — which gave rise to continental concern over the Americanization of the world. Arriving in large numbers from the Atlantic seaboard, a small army of tourists, technicians, exchange scholars, diplomats, journalists, USIS librarians, Red Cross girls, ECA administrators, Point Four agronomists, Stage Door Canteen hostesses, and American businessmen — five thousand of them in Paris alone — were carving out beachheads at customs offices and deploying inland in swelling numbers. Meanwhile the Fulbright and Smith-Mundt programs would soon bring forty thousand foreign students each year to study in America. Europeans asked one another what were these people bringing to Europe? And what were Pierre and Gretchen learning across the water?

To the disgust of French traditionalists, a beloved guillotine had been replaced in 1945 by a shiny new U.S. electric chair. It was somehow symbolic. (Americans agreed, though for other reasons.) In public places once brightened by colorful native dancers at Christmas, Europeans were captives of what had become the most widely heard voice in the history of man — Bing Crosby crooning "White Christmas" (1,700,000 records sold by V-J Day), "Silent Night" (1,500,000 records) or "Don't Fence Me In" (1,250,000). Peasants who for generations had been proud of their vital role in European society now learned that their countrymen were being fed by "The American Middle West — Breadbasket of the World," and palates once soothed by the finest wines from the choicest grapes were being washed by a cheap brown fluid called Coca-Cola — the notorious "Coke," now in the late 1940s selling 50 million bottles a day, enough to float a light cruiser. Frenchmen struck back. The continent had hardly recovered from the airlift when the National Assembly in Paris voted 366 to 202 "to prohibit the import, manufacture and sale of Coca-Cola in France, Algeria, and the French colonial empire."

Resentment of what had come to be called "Americanization" was as widespread as the unpopularity of John Bull in the long century of British domination, and as inevitable. In Europe's view, the colossus from across the sea was smothering its pride with a new economic imperialism even more demeaning than the old. One didn't need to be a Marxist to sympathize. What were the Oxford don's feelings when he read in the *Times* that the British Marketing Council was sending fifty executives each year to the Harvard Business School, with the Crown footing the bill? Or a Roman who learned that once more the lira was being devalued because of a "technical readjustment" on the New York Stock Exchange? Or the independent little Belgian service station owner upon discovering that Esso sold more gas on the continent than in the United States? Or any European when told that to the U.S. Department of Commerce Lausanne was known only as the capital of Union Carbide Overseas, Zurich as the home of the Corn Products Company abroad, and Paris, Brussels, and London, respectively, as the European headquarters of IBM, the Celanese Corporation, and Standard Oil of New Jersey?

Yet apart from the heavy-handed campaigns of these commercial Caesars, it did appear that the country's best men and best efforts were often badly abused. It seemed hard that the embassies of a country which had given over a hundred billion dollars in foreign aid should have to weigh the advantages of installing shatterproof window glass because they were so frequently the target of hostile demonstrations. The gifts had been taken quickly enough, and within a month, sometimes less, those who received them had publicly displayed their contempt for the dollar. It was in these Truman years that Louis Kronenberger, an American intellectual with a following in Europe, and certainly no chauvinist, wrote in exasperation:

> Americans have every right to be proud of a pioneer heritage that, first conquering and subduing the land, has gone on harnessing and commandeering the air waves. Americans have a right to exalt a national ideal and a native *modus operandi* that, beginning with maximum hardship, has ended in maximum comfort. Why shouldn't we be proud of how openhanded and hospitable we are, how alive and alert, of how the American way has conferred unimaginable opportunity on the poor and the elsewhere rejected?

Others struck back at European critics; *Time,* in a memorable issue, called France a prostitute. (Another riotous scene in the National Assembly.) Doubtless cutting all foreign aid from the budget would have enhanced presidential popularity, but it was never seriously considered. Even Senator Taft knew a return to isolationism was impossible, and conceded that an American President could no longer concern himself solely with domestic pressures. In an age of thermonuclear weapons, on a globe shrunk to a fraction of its prewar size, understanding the hopes and aspirations of other countries had become a matter of national security. It was precisely in this area that Harry Truman defied all the form sheets drawn up in the early weeks of his Presidency. Lacking brilliance in statecraft, he compensated for it with courage and native shrewdness. "When the Truman government found its feet," Dean Acheson later wrote, "its policies showed a sweep, a breadth of conception and boldness both new in this country's history and obviously centrally planned and directed." And at the time, quoting Shakespeare's *Henry V*, Acheson said that America's allies had been reassured, and her enemies discomfited, by the realization that in the darkest hour of any international crisis, the President would be a formidable adversary, providing "a little touch of Harry in the night."

Throughout the spring before the Berlin airlift, Republicans were watching the calendar with a mounting sense of pleasure. Sixteen years had passed since Franklin Delano Roosevelt had first cast them into outer darkness. They continued to despise everything about That Man, and in a sense thousands of them were still running against him, but his sorcery, they believed, had died with him; nevermore would the Grand Old Party be daunted by that wicked grin, that maniacal laughter, that tilted cigarette holder and flashing pince-nez.

In his place stood a humbler politician, who looked very much like a man of straw. HST could hardly have resembled FDR less. Truman's height was average, he wore ordinary spectacles, and his flat, high-pitched voice carried no echo of the cultivated, prep-school accent which had identified his predecessor as a patrician. Since it was assumed that Roosevelt alone had infused his programs with dynamic appeal, the obvious corollary was that all of them could be repealed, like the Eighteenth Amendment, after the American people had spoken in the next quadrennial referendum. That would come on November 2. They could hardly wait.

It was going to be so easy. "Truman is a gone goose," said Congresswoman Clare Boothe Luce, the lovely blonde lawmaker from Connecticut, and although Democrats flinched, no one contradicted her. Since the Republican sweep of the off-year elections in November 1946, every public opinion poll, every survey of political experts had spoken with one voice: if Harry Truman ran for the Presidency, he would be doomed. Gallup reported that between October 1947 and March 1948 the percentage of Americans who thought the President was doing a good job had dropped sharply — to 36 percent — and that if he ran then he would lose to Dewey, Stassen, MacArthur, or Vandenberg.

"If Truman is nominated," Joseph and Stewart Alsop told their readers, "he will be forced to wage the loneliest campaign in recent history." Even he had misgivings. His approach to Eisenhower at Potsdam was repeated in the autumn of 1947; he asked Secretary of the Army Kenneth C. Royall to tell the general that if Ike would run for President on the Democratic ticket, Truman would be proud to be his running mate. Eisenhower asked Royall to convey his heartfelt gratitude to the President, but with it his regrets. Possibly he thought that with Truman as his vice presidential nominee he would lose.

In the middle of November 1947 presidential Special Counsel Clark Clifford handed his chief a thirty-five-page reelection scenario. In it Clifford pointed out that Truman had achieved far more than most people realized. He had been good to the farmer. He was the man who had faced down John L. Lewis. Jews were happy because he was an enthusiastic Zionist, blacks because he had ordered the commissioning of Negro officers. He had unified the armed forces and vetoed antilabor bills, and it was the Republican reactionaries on Capitol Hill — Taft, Wherry, Millikin, Bridges, Joe Martin and Charlie Halleck — who had turned back his proposals for a massive housing program and a social security base for medical care for the elderly. Clifford wanted the President to run as an underdog, and against the Eightieth Congress.

Truman's overtures to Eisenhower are unmentioned in his memoirs; he gives the impression that he never considered standing aside. In reality, he appears to have been hesitant as late as March 1, 1948, when he told a Key West press conference that he had been "so darned busy with foreign affairs and other situations that have developed that I haven't had any time to think about any presidential campaign." During the following week the CIO took a firm stand against Henry Wallace's third party candidacy. Apparently that persuaded him that he could make it. On March 9 he called in Chairman J. Howard McGrath of the Democratic National Committee and said, "Well, Howard, if you think so, let's do it." McGrath was puzzled (he hadn't asked the President to run, only to make up his mind), but in the lobby outside he gamely faced the White House press and announced: "The President has authorized me to say that if nominated by the Democratic National Committee, he will accept and run." Truman's stetson was in the ring.

Immediately most of the party's leaders demanded that he withdraw it. Ed Flynn, boss of the Bronx and a former Democratic national chairman, refused to appear on the same platform with the President in New York; a husky presidential aide literally had to drag him from his car. Senator Olin Johnson of South Carolina publicly snubbed Truman. Fulbright of Arkansas proposed that he resign so that a Republican could take over at once and restore national confidence. A six-man delegation of southern governors led by Strom Thurmond, alienated by the administration efforts at racial integration, prepared to secede from the party and back a southern candidate — thus guaranteeing a *four*-party race, two of them formed from Democratic splinters. In Manhattan McGrath had to cancel a meeting of wealthy Democratic contributors — only three men would come — and when he mentioned Truman's name at a Los Angeles rally he was drowned out by boos. The hecklers were led by James Roosevelt and other apostles of the New Deal. They were in good company. Among those vowing to dump Truman were James's brother Elliott, Leon Henderson, Claude Pepper of Florida, Chester Bowles, Walter Reuther, Wilson Wyatt, and young Mayor Hubert Humphrey of Minneapolis. Boss Jake Arvey of Illinois announced that he would no longer support Truman, and the ADA hierarchy came up with what *Time* called "an extraordinary idea." It was breathtaking. Why hadn't it been discovered before? They would draft General Eisenhower!

There is a strain of high comedy in the Democrats-for-Eisenhower movement of 1948. Unaware that he had twice turned down such a proposal from the President, or that he regarded himself as a conservative Republican — even Truman didn't know that — the prospect of Ike as the leader of their party swept up all the dumpers cited above, plus Frank Hague of Jersey City, John Bailey of Connecticut, Happy Chandler of Kentucky, Richard Russell of Georgia, Mayor Edward J. Kelly of Chicago, and Senators Lister Hill and John Sparkman of Alabama. The final antic touch — it was also an unforgivable insolence — was a telegram to the White House from Hugh Mitchell, Democratic leader in the state of Washington, asking the President to serve as chairman of the Draft Eisenhower Committee.

So appealing was the Ike-or-die movement that as long as there was a glimmer of hope that the general might change his mind, it was quite clear that Truman couldn't be nominated by his own party. On the eve of the conventions Eisenhower slammed the door shut by announcing that "I would refuse to accept the nomination under any conditions, terms, or premises." With that, the party rank and file abandoned hope. A pall fell over Democratic delegates. Convinced that they would lose in November, and trying to cut their losses wherever possible, they asked the Republicans, who would be the first to convene in Philadelphia's Convention Hall, to leave their flags and bunting in place. *Noblesse oblige;* the GOP charitably agreed. Democratic gratitude was almost pathetic. They were already saving for a head start in 1952. Maybe Eisenhower would be willing to lead them then.

Meantime, Truman's staff was busily refurbishing what Clifford called his "portrait." ("Image" still hadn't come into general use.) The President was disdainful of the public relations approach — he called it "gimmickry" — but the idea of attacking the Republican Congress aroused his militant instincts. The first tactic in the grand strategy was to hit the Hill every Monday with a popular proposal that Taft and his colleagues were sure to table. In swift succession Truman proposed a St. Lawrence Seaway, broader civil rights legislation, federal housing, aid to China, extension of wartime controls, highway construction, and extension of the Reciprocal Trade Act — all destined to become issues in November.

If the polls are to be believed, Truman's prospects looked dimmest in April. It was then that the greatest inspiration of the campaign struck his staff, and it was perhaps indicative of the general confusion there that afterward none of three men — Clifford, George M. Elsey, and Charles S. Murphy — could remember whose idea it had been. All of them knew that the President had never learned to read a speech. He hung his head over the manuscript, had no sense of pace or emphasis, and usually killed his applause. In extemporaneous remarks, on the other hand, he was lively and effective. The question therefore arose, why not talk him into delivering an off-the-cuff speech before a sizable audience? He liked the idea, and on April 17, after reading a prepared text before the American Society of Newspaper Editors, he improvised for a half-hour on American-Soviet relations. The difference was startling and heartening; the editors cheered him at the end and remarked to one another on how well he had spoken. Four more extemporaneous addresses followed, climaxing in a political chalk-talk before a thousand young Democrats at the Mayflower Hotel on May 14. At the end of it he brought them all to their feet with: "I want to say to you that for the next four years there will be a Democrat in the White House — and you're looking at him!" Next morning's *New York Times* called it a "fighting" speech, delivered "in the new Truman manner." Satisfied that he had found the right campaign style, he and his staff now proposed to submit it to a coast-to-coast trial run.

Here they encountered a financial obstacle. It looked immovable. The party war chest was almost empty. Poverty was destined to haunt the Democrats throughout the campaign; few men of means had any confidence in the candidate's chances. Even in April suggestions for cutting costs were valued, and after the Mayflower dinner the staff came up with a big idea. Why shouldn't Truman dip into his $30,000-a-year presidential travel allowance to make a nationwide railroad journey to educate the people about his achievements at home and abroad, and, while he was at it, to say a few choice words about his problems with Congress?

This was the politics of desperation, a sign of how long the odds looked to Truman. To be sure, Presidents seeking reelection had frequently advertised themselves by finding it necessary to ride around dedicating monuments or opening bridges. Such jaunts were considered a legitimate use of taxpayers' money, justifiable because their purposes were ostensibly nonpartisan. This junket was something else. From the first, Truman served notice that he intended to spend every minute strafing the Republican Congress, and that, as Chairman Carroll Reece of the Republican National Committee observed, made it as "nonpolitical as the Pendergast machine." Doubtless Reece would have made more of the issue if Truman's cause hadn't seemed so hopeless, and if the tour itself, seen from a distance, hadn't looked like a debacle.

At 11:05 P.M. on June 3, over two weeks before the adjournment of Congress for the conventions, the sixteen-car "Presidential Special" glided out of Washington's Union Station and headed westward; although Truman usually flew from city to city, people then expected Presidents and presidential candidates to travel by rail. The last car in the caravan was the luxurious, armor-plated "Ferdinand Magellan," built by the Association of American Railroads for FDR. Walnut-paneled, in continuous radio contact with Washington, its most conspicuous feature was an outsize platform in the rear, protected by a striped canopy and equipped with a public address system. Unlikely as it seemed at the time, that platform was to become the stage for a campaign drama as stirring, in its way, as anything in the history of presidential politics.

Often it seemed likelier to be remembered for its small disasters. Democrats under the impression that he had in fact agreed to draft Eisenhower turned out with homemade signs reading: IKE FOR PRESIDENT! HARRY FOR VP! One state chairman — William Ritchie of Nebraska — tried to board the "Ferdinand Magellan" and was ejected; he angrily told reporters, "I'm convinced that he cannot be elected. He has muffed the ball badly. He seems to prefer his so-called buddies to the persons who have done the work and put up the money for the party." Elsewhere one of these so-called buddies, a 1918 veteran who had been asked to make speaking arrangements, thought it was to be a reunion of the 35th Division. Others were turned away, with the consequence that the President spoke to fewer than a thousand people in an auditorium with a capacity for ten thousand. Photographers had a marvelous time standing high in the rear and taking shots that showed him addressing acres of empty seats. Literally nobody, the pictures implied, was interested in what the President had to say, though *Time* commended his "growing entertainment value."

At least twice he appeared on the train platform in pajamas and a bathrobe. "I understand it was announced that I would speak here," he told one gaping crowd. "I'm sorry that I had gone to bed, but I thought you would like to see what I look like, even if I didn't have on any clothes." In Barstow, California, a girl eyed his blue dressing gown and asked him if he had a cold. He shook his head. She persisted, "You sound like it." He twinkled and said, "That's because I ride around in the wind with my mouth open." It was the truth. In Eugene, Oregon, after his usual introduction of Bess ("my boss") and Margaret ("who bosses my boss"), he launched into an off-the-cuff discussion of Potsdam and, forgetting that reporters were present, said, "I like old Joe! He's a decent fellow. But Joe is a prisoner of the Politburo. He can't do what he wants to." Back East Mrs. Luce gave him both barrels. She was glad the Democrats had got round to admitting it, she said poisonously: "Good old Joe! Of course they like him. Didn't they give him all Eastern Europe, Manchuria, the Kuriles, North China, coalitions in Poland, Yugoslavia, and Czechoslovakia?"

From Washington, Halleck told reporters that Truman would be remembered as America's worst President, and Congressman Cliff Clevenger of Ohio said he was a "Missouri jackass." Then Taft slipped. It was a little thing. Speaking before the Union League Club in Philadelphia, he deplored Truman's "blackguarding Congress at whistle-stops all over the country." He had coined a word, and from the Republican viewpoint it was an unfortunate one. Democratic headquarters telegraphed the mayors of all the little towns and cities through which Truman's train had passed. They were indignant at the slur, and he happily distributed their replies to the press. In Los Angeles, where an enormous throng awaited the President, he grinned and cried, "This is the biggest whistle-stop!"

On June 18 he returned to Washington. He had been away two weeks, had covered 9,504 miles, and had delivered seventy-three speeches in sixteen states. For the most part he had followed Clifford's suggestion that he be "controversial as hell," and toward the end he had felt an intangible meshing of the crowd's mood and his own. After a new Congress was chosen in November, he had said in Illinois, "Maybe we'll get one that will work in the interests of the people and not the interests of men who have all the money." A murmur of agreement had risen from the upturned faces. In Bremerton, Washington, the strong voice of a lumberjack had rung out: "Pour it on, Harry!" and he had shot back, "I'm going to — I'm going to!" In Spokane a man said, "What about throwing eggs at Taft?" Truman replied, "I wouldn't throw *fresh* eggs at Taft!" "You've got the worst Congress you've ever had!" he had cried, and, "If you send another Republican Congress to Washington, you're a bigger bunch of suckers than I think you are!" The crowds had roared approval: "Pour it on!" and "Give 'em hell, Harry!" And he had flung back savagely, "That's what I'm doing! That's what I'm doing!"

Taft was right, of course. It was demeaning, it was in ghastly taste, its precedents had ugly implications for future campaigns, and it was unfair to Republicans like Vandenberg, without whom there would be no Truman Doctrine in the Balkans, no Marshall Plan, no Berlin airlift. But as the spectacle of one man fighting against all odds it was stirring. The White House correspondents thought so. Now and then, they told their wives back in the capital, the President had almost made them forget that he didn't have a chance.

In Philadelphia the city fathers had spent $650,000 sprucing up for the Republican, Democratic, and Progressive conventions, in that order; the "Dixiecrats," so named by a copyreader on the Charlotte, North Carolina, *News,* would convene on the hallowed ground of the old Confederacy. An eastern city was preferable because the Atlantic seaboard was the farthest reach of the coaxial cable bringing live transmission; the speakers knew that while Edward R. Murrow and the other famous commentators stubbornly clung to radio, the podium in Philadelphia's Convention Hall could be seen on some 400,000 little TV screens in the East. In those days that was something.

In 1948 newspapermen paid as much as $12 for a room and bath and muttered about inflation; in 1948 they assumed that a hotel's menial tasks would all be done cheaply by Negroes. Truman had been trying to do something about the plight of colored people, but the Republican platform committee, after weighing a civil rights plank, discarded it without qualms. The issue hadn't yet caught the imagination of the intellectual community; they were still half persuaded by the plea for more time in William Faulkner's 1948 novel *Intruder in the Dust*. Southern filibusters continued to kill every measure prohibiting poll taxes, and southern blacks, like their fathers before them, lived in terror of the rope; there had been a lynching in 1947, there would be two more in this convention year.

The big names in the Republican party were Thomas E. Dewey, Harold Stassen ("Man the oars and ride the crest,/Harold Stassen, he's the best"), General Douglas MacArthur, Halleck, Vandenberg, Taft ("To do the job, name our Bob," and "To steer our craft, let's have Taft"), Earl Warren, and Joseph W. Martin Jr. Joe McCarthy of Wisconsin and Richard Nixon were present, but were very small potatoes; McCarthy had been a Stassen delegate in the Wisconsin primary, and Nixon, also for Stassen, was up in the galleries — too insignificant to be seated in the California delegation. Their big issue was there, however. Voters in the Oregon primary had found Stassen's advocacy of a measure to outlaw Communists absurd, but the convention keynoter was declaring, "We shall ferret out and drive out every Red and pink on Federal payrolls."

Dewey was the Republican front runner, though he had taken a few nasty falls since announcing his candidacy on January 15 — or, rather, telling young Jim Hagerty to make the announcement *for* him. He was always leaving such vulgar details to other men, explaining that he preferred to concentrate on issues. Actually he spent a lot of time worrying about his appearance. With his toothbrush moustache and his stiff manner, he reminded people of a Keystone cop, or the man on the wedding cake. During the primaries photographers had persuaded him to wear a ten-gallon hat and an Indian headdress which had been worn by Queen Marie of Romania on her visit to the United States in the 1920s. He never forgave himself; in the pictures he looked preposterous. Of his tepid manner, wicked gossips said — unjustly — "You have to know Tom Dewey well to dislike him."

It was a cruel mischance that had made Stassen Dewey's principal challenger that spring. Dewey's height was five feet eight inches, Stassen was six feet three inches, and when they posed together in primary lulls, the effect was that of a man and his son. By convention time Dewey had acquired elevator shoes. Still, the damage was done. It was particularly annoying because Stassen hadn't been expected to do as well as he had in the primaries. In Wisconsin, it had been thought, MacArthur's slate would carry all before it. The general's partisans were well financed, and the state had been flooded with instant biographies: *MacArthur: Hero of Destiny*, *MacArthur: Fighter for Freedom*, and *MacArthur the Magnificent*. On

March 29 a *New York Times* headline guessed, MACARTHUR VICTORY DUE IN WISCONSIN. The next day delegates representing the general won only eight convention votes. Senator McGrath told reporters, "This leads me to the conclusion that to insure the election of the Democratic ticket in November we need only have the commentators united in predicting defeat." They had chuckled politely; national chairmen have their little jokes.

Despite Dewey's convention eve come-from-behind triumph in Oregon, he could hardly be called the choice of the party's rank and file. Gallup now reported that the country's registered Republicans preferred the Minnesota giant, 37 percent to Dewey's 24 percent. Figures like that deserved more study than Dewey gave them. The summer before, every other Republican voter had wanted the dapper New Yorker. Such an erosion of strength ought to have alarmed him, especially since the Democrats, under Roosevelt, had become the country's majority party. After his nomination he should have come on slugging. Instead his acceptance speech lulled the delegates to sleep: "The unity we seek is more than material. It is more than a matter of things and measures. It is most of all spiritual. Our problems are not outside ourselves, our problems are within ourselves."

After photographers had taken pictures of him and Earl Warren, his vice-presidential candidate, Dewey went home to rest. He would not leave Albany until September 19, six weeks before the election, which, as the *New York Times* noted, would make his campaign "the shortest undertaken in recent years by the presidential candidate of the major party out of power." He seemed to regard it almost as a formality. And the rest of the Republican leadership agreed. Several powerful Republicans, knowing that they would be members of the new administration, had traveled home from Philadelphia via Washington, stealing a march on their colleagues by picking up good houses at bargain prices.

"The Democrats act as though they have accepted an invitation to a funeral," the Associated Press observed on July 12, as delegates of the party in power trudged into Convention Hall through the soggy sauna of a Philadelphia heat wave. The bunting, gay three weeks ago, was stained and flyblown. KEEP AMERICA HUMAN WITH TRUMAN, said a high banner. Hardly anyone looked up at it. Truman "Victory Kits" were distributed, each with a notebook, pencil, and whistle — "For the Democratic graveyard," someone said. On the marquee of the Bellevue-Stratford a huge mechanical donkey flashed electric blue eyes at passersby, but that was just about the extent of the gaiety. Democratic delegates had a grim, hammered look. There were a few feeble signs of animation in rebel delegations which had recovered from the collapse of the Draft Eisenhower movement and were now reaching frantically, groping for any straw before they went down for the third time. Nineteen state chairmen held an election eve caucus. They approached Justice Douglas. He declined and they gave up. Then Truman phoned Douglas and asked him to run for the Vice-Presidency. He said he wouldn't do that, either. For a while it looked as though the President might have to run alone. At last Alben Barkley, faithful old Alben, said he'd be glad to run the race.

In his humiliation Truman was spared nothing. He knew that a majority of the delegates didn't want him, that if he freed them now they would give him a standing ovation — and quickly choose someone else. It seemed inevitable that Henry Wallace would poll several million votes — enough, at any rate, to cost him New York. Now the Solid South was about to break up. Young (thirty-seven) Mayor Humphrey of Minneapolis, and Paul Douglas and Adlai Stevenson, the party's senatorial and gubernatorial candidates in Illinois, were leading the fight for a strong civil rights plank. Truman would have preferred to avoid heroics on this point. But North and South were groping for one another's throats; the Dixiecrats lost the key roll call 651½ to 582½. "We bid you goodbye!" cried Alabama's Handy Ellis, leading the way to the door.

It was Wednesday evening, July 14, when the Confederates left. The President almost ran into them when he arrived. His special train had left Union Station just as the evening session had been gaveled to order in Convention Hall. Seated in the "Ferdinand Magellan" between Clark Clifford and Sam Rosenman, Truman read through the notes for the speech. He was under the impression that he would go straight to the podium upon arriving. He didn't; he couldn't; the nominating speeches were just getting under way. He would have to wait four hours sweltering offstage. It is somehow appropriate that at that low point — the lowest point in his career — he was led to a small bleak room under the platform with a little balcony overlooking a littered alley. It was near the railroad tracks; he could hear the locomotives thundering by, feel them in the tremors of his straight chair. Talking now with Barkley, now with Homer Cummings, he squinted out at the grime and trash, mopping his forehead, rewriting the outline of his talk, glancing at the outline, brooding alone, and waiting.

At 12:42 A.M. on Thursday the President was finally nominated, 947½ votes to 362 for Georgia's Richard Russell and half a vote for Paul McNutt, former governor of Indiana. Despite the hour, the weariness, and clinging heat, Cabell Phillips wrote, the demonstration for Truman had "developed a sudden spontaneity; the whoops and rebel yells sounded real; delegates who had listlessly kept their seats while others paraded up and down the aisles picked up their banners and noisemakers and joined the aimless snake dance. Reporters standing on their benches in the press bank looked at one another in disbelief and said, 'This looks like it is for real.'"

Barkley was nominated by acclamation — underscoring the convention's failure to thus honor its presidential candidate — and at 1:45 A.M. he and Truman mounted the dais to the strains of "Hail to the Chief." At any other convention it would have been a sublime moment: the two leaders raising one another's arms high, the glaring lights, the tempo of the organ, the men standing on the collapsible chairs, and the excited women crying into handkerchiefs. There was all that, to be sure, but there was something else, too — a note of burlesque that seemed in keeping with the rest of it. Chairman Rayburn had just begun his introduction of Barkley when a stout, overdressed woman interrupted him. All evening a floral Liberty Bell had stood by the podium awaiting the emergence of the President. Now she presented it to him, or tried to; there was a sudden swishing under it — she just had time to stammer "doves of peace" — and abruptly flock after flock of white pigeons emerged from beneath the floral display and sailed back and forth and back and forth over the assembled delegates bearing their own tributes. Anyone familiar with pigeons, as the planners of this bit of stage business clearly were not, knew what came next. "Watch your clothes!" farmers in the crowd shouted. It was too late. People had been muttering it all through the long session, and here was the real thing, ruining their shirts and dresses. Luckily for the party's public image, or portrait, the press in 1948 considered such matters too indelicate for readers of family newspapers. Sam Rayburn saved the moment at the rostrum. He captured a passing bird and hurled it high overhead. The delegates cheered, and to their surprise and pleasure discovered that in that moment of slapstick their tensions had fled. They were relaxing, chuckling as they put away their pocket handkerchiefs and telling one another that whatever Harry had in store for them, it couldn't be fouler than that.

It was another, greater surprise. After Barkley's brief remarks, "the weary crowd," Irwin Ross tells us, "steeled itself for a dose of presidential oratory." Instead, the President spoke from the outline of his address, jotted down while waiting in the cheerless window over the alley near the coughing locomotives. Using his extemporaneous new style, he delivered a lashing, vibrant, give-'em-hell speech, and in Ross's words, "his strident, high-pitched tones electrified the audience." Stabbing the air with quick, awkward gestures, he cried, "Senator Barkley and I will win this election and make the Republicans like it — don't you forget it!" He shouted: "If the voters don't do their duty by the Democratic party, they are the most ungrateful people in the world!"

He then turned to the Republicans, reviewing the list of programs he had proposed, and the Hill had rejected, for medical care, housing, price controls, aid to education. They had killed such measures, he said — and then, in an unparalleled display of cynicism and hypocrisy, they had approved a presidential platform calling for all of them. Very well. He would test their sincerity.

He delivered his haymaker: "On the twenty-sixth day of July, which out in Missouri we call 'Turnip Day,' I am going to call that Congress back in session, and I am going to ask them to pass some of these laws they say they are for in their platform. Now, my friends, if there is any reality behind that Republican platform, we ought to get some action from a short session of the Eightieth Congress. They can do this job in fifteen days if they want to do it, and they will still have time to go out and run for office."

This, the *New York Times* reported, "set the convention on fire." The weather, the hour, the bitter internal strife and the impending defeat in November were for the moment forgotten. Truman waited till the din abated a bit, and then he drove it all home: "They are going to try to dodge this responsibility," he called, "but what that 'worst' Eightieth Congress does in this special session will be the test of whether they mean what they say!"

They were on their feet, giving him a standing ovation. He was hewing to the plan, keeping himself "controversial as hell," and the reaction outside Convention Hall confirmed it. Editorial writers were all but speechless; using federal funds for a campaign swing was bad enough, but calling a special congressional session to score partisan points was almost grounds for impeachment. Vandenberg told a reporter, "This sounds like a last hysterical gasp from an expiring administration." Congressman Hugh D. Scott Jr. of Pennsylvania deplored "the act of a desperate man who is willing to destroy the unity and dignity of his country and his government for partisan advantage after he himself has lost the confidence of the people"; and Walter George of Georgia, in a splendid Catherine wheel of mixed metaphors, cried, "The South is not only over a barrel — it is pilloried! We are in the stocks!"

Yet here and there men gave Truman grudging admiration. "There was no doubt that he had lifted the delegates out of their doldrums," said *Time*. "He had roused admiration for his political courage."

July was dominated by the two splinter parties and what everyone was calling "the Turnip session." Dixiecrat morale was high. The southern strategy was to throw the election into the House of Representatives. They believed they would win as many votes as Truman, and on July 14 they met in Birmingham. In one day they zipped through the entire convention ritual. Their nominees were Strom Thurmond for President and Governor Fielding L. Wright of Mississippi for Vice President. Here and there were omens that Dixie's thin white line might break. Russell and Harry Byrd of Virginia stayed away from Birmingham, not out of love for equal rights but because they thought their seniority on the Hill might be in jeopardy. Still, the Dixiecrat loss was a blow to the Democrats, particularly to Clifford, whose campaign scenario had assumed the continuing solidarity of the Democratic South.

Ten days later Wallace's Progressive Citizens of America (PCA) arrived in Philadelphia to form the Progressive Party of America (PPA). On December 29, when their leader had launched the movement by announcing his candidacy, the PCA future had looked very bright. "We have assembled a Gideon's army," he had said then. Progressives hadn't expected to win the Presidency in 1948, but they believed it might be theirs in 1952. The average delegate was about thirty years old, some twenty years younger than those at major party conventions. American campuses were heavily represented — more Ivy than Big Ten — and so were unions whose leaders had moved into deep left field. Boys with crew cuts, then part of the student life-style, wore open-necked sport shirts; girls were in bobby socks and dirndls; Negroes were heavily represented; there were many guitars and much singing of folk songs in the manner of Pete Seeger and vice-presidential candidate Glen Taylor. Everyone seemed to be having a lot of fun. To the casual eye Progressivism appeared to be flourishing.

In reality it was racked by internal strains. Rexford Guy Tugwell was the only New Deal recruit Wallace had managed to enlist, and he was in constant conflict with Lee Pressman, the Communist CIO general counsel who would later be ousted by Walter Reuther. One does not lightly affix Communist labels, particularly to public figures in the first postwar decade, and there was much confusion at the time among voters, who were under the impression that the Progressives were merely providing a liberal alternative to Truman. The confusion was deliberate, fomented by Communist party (CP) members who could hardly believe their luck in capturing a former Vice President of the United States. PCA was the mirror image of the Americans for Democratic Action (ADA), which had been formed in January 1947 to combat it. Three years after the 1948 election Michael Quill, who had broken with the CP, described its role in the Progressive movement to a CIO committee taking testimony about it. Quill was president of the Transport Workers Union and no red-baiter. In the autumn of 1947, he said, when his own sympathies were with the CP, Eugene Dennis, general secretary of the Communist party, told him and other labor leaders that the party hierarchy had "decided to form a third party led by Henry Wallace" and that Wallace "would come out in the next few weeks and announce his candidacy."

Wallace seems to have embarked on this extraordinary adventure wearing blinders. Late in the campaign, as he later told friends, he realized that he was being used, that nearly everyone around him was an avowed Communist. He must have been among the last to find out. The *New Republic* had tried to warn him; the *Nation* tried; so did *PM*. The *New York Post* had begged Wallace to join ADA, in vain. His candidacy had been supported by only two newspapers in the country, the *Daily Worker* and Pennsylvania's *York Gazette and Daily*. Reporters invited him to repudiate Red support, as FDR had in the 1930s. He refused.

The consequence was shattering publicity. Despite the vigor and enthusiasm of 3,200 attractive PPA delegates in Philadelphia — more than at either of the major party conventions — Wallace's Communist aides undid him at every turn. Potentially, his acceptance speech in Philadelphia's Shibe Park had the makings of one of the most memorable events in American politics. With tickets selling for $2.60 to 65¢ — the proletariat in the bleachers — more than thirty thousand wildly cheering admirers attested to his continuing popularity. Given a reasonably fair press, which he might easily have had, he could have won over the Walter Reuthers and Jimmy Roosevelts, who needed very little persuading that July. He had only to disassociate himself from the Lee Pressmans. He declined; he wouldn't "repudiate any support that comes to me on the basis of interest in peace." A *Time* reporter called his attention to the resemblance between the PPA's platform and the CP's. "I'd say that they have a good platform," Wallace said of the Communists. He added gratuitously, "I would say that the Communists are the closest things to the early Christian martyrs."

With that, the wave of the Wallace movement broke. He would go on to the end doggedly, undeterred by hecklers who could see little resemblance between Communists and early Christian martyrs, his hand out, his brow damp, the familiar Wallace lick of hair in his eye. Invading the South, he was pelted with eggs, tomatoes, and firecrackers in three North Carolina towns. To the press, Truman regretted 'this "violation of the American concept of fair play." With that exception, the President ignored the PPA threat, trusting that it would shrink as Wallace's novelty appeal wore off. It did. With each passing week of the campaign, the Progressive effort lost momentum. Tugwell quietly withdrew his support, the left-leaning United Electrical Workers refused to endorse Wallace, and Progressive congressional candidates withdrew from local races. In the spring political analysts had conceded Wallace 3,500,000 votes at the least, approaching Robert La Follette's 1924 high of 4,800,000 for a third-party race. Gallup had given him 7 percent of the total vote then. By the third week in October, Gallup's forecast was down to 4 percent, and on November 2 the actual Wallace turnout would be less than that — 1,157,172 votes. Democratic defections to the PPA undoubtedly cost Truman New York, but a careful reading of the returns strongly suggests that for every vote he lost to Wallace elsewhere, he picked up two or three sympathetic votes from the independent center.

Thurmond's popular vote was to be 1,169,021. His concentration in the old Confederacy did bring him 39 electoral votes (Alabama, Louisiana, Mississippi, South Carolina, and one Tennessee elector), but it can be argued that this was worse than nothing. The discovery that the party could win without the Solid South freed Democrats from the need to compromise with it; in attempting to thwart advocates of civil rights for Negroes, Thurmond had hastened their victories.

On July 26 Truman appeared before a hostile joint session on the Hill to present what he called his "shopping list" of needed legislation. During the thirty-minute speech he was interrupted only six times by applause, all of it from Democrats. The Republican members sat on their hands. Dewey, wary as always, refusing to "get in the gutter with Truman," as he called it, evaded reporters' questions about the Turnip session. He turned the whole thing over to Herbert Brownell and disappeared into his Albany study. Brownell was uneasy. He suggested to Taft that the party's congressional leadership might give the green light to a few noncontroversial bills, thereby crippling Truman's charge that it was obstructive. Why not amend the Displaced Persons Act, eliminating discriminatory clauses against Jews and some Catholics? Everyone agreed that the revision was needed, he argued, and Republican initiative now would cut the big Democratic pluralities in eastern metropolitan areas. Taft shook his head. It was a matter of principle, he said. In calling this session, the President had abused his powers. The shopping list must be ignored. Brownell having failed, Taft's GOP colleagues on the Hill tried to reason with him. Vandenberg said, "Bob, I think we ought to do something. We ought to do whatever we can to show that we are trying to use the two weeks as best we can. Then we have a better case to take before the public." According to Hugh Scott, who was there, "Bob Taft would have none of it. 'No,' he said, 'we're not going to give that fellow anything.' Anyone familiar with Bob Taft's method of ending a conversation will know that was the end of it."

Truman was delighted. In his message he had asked for legislation to control inflation, expand civil rights, increase minimum wages, extend social security coverage, and support housing programs — most of which had been vaguely endorsed in Dewey's platform. In agreeing to the hazy wording in Philadelphia, the Republican congressional leadership had never dreamed that they would be held accountable for it before the election. Taft's principle was sound, but there was also something to be said for keeping promises to the public. By sulking, the GOP seemed to be confirming the President's judgment of it.

On August 12 the White House issued a detailed report contrasting presidential proposals with inactivity on the Hill. At that day's press conference Truman deplored the "do-nothing" session and its "do-nothing Congress." Every name he had called it had been justified, he said; it had proved itself to be the "worst" Congress in history.

Before leaving, one Washington correspondent, pursuing a different story, reminded the President that it was nearly two weeks now since a plain, stocky woman in her mid-thirties named Elizabeth Bentley had begun testifying before the Senate Committee on Expenditures in the Executive Departments. Since then she and a House Committee on Un-American Activities witness, Time editor Whittaker Chambers, had charged that a number of government employees had spied for the Soviet Union. The accused included Alger Hiss, William T. Remington, and Lauchlin Currie. Did the President wish to say something about these espionage hearings?

"They are simply a red herring," Truman snapped. His thoughts still on the Eightieth Congress, he said: "They are using this as a red herring, as an excuse to keep from doing what they ought to do. Yes, you can quote me."

At 3:40 P.M. on Sunday, September 5, the engineer in the cab of the

"Truman Special" blew his steam whistle twice and left Union Station in pursuit of six million enfranchised spectators. A Democratic campaign, financed from party coffers, was finally in business. There would be two major transcontinental tours of ten days each, a tour of the northeastern United States, and shorter trips into the states around the District of Columbia. In this first thrust the President would ride 32,000 miles and deliver over 250 speeches, then a record in campaigning. From each rural dawn to the day's last whistle-stop eighteen hours later, with the wide-eyed citizens of a small town gathered around the back of the "Ferdinand Magellan," holding torches high to see the scrappy little fellow on the platform, Truman was unfailingly full of fight — and always quotable.

Following the script of June's dress rehearsal, he was good-humored most of the time, admiring the local band, introducing Bess and Margaret, and ending his informal little talks with a plea to "Go to the polls on the second of November and cast your ballot for the Democratic ticket — and then I can stay in the White House for four more years," or "Do the right thing that will keep me from suffering a housing shortage on January 20, 1949." At the end of each stop the engineer would give a warning toot, and the medicine show would be on its way.

In the cities, crowds grew larger: 50,000 in Indianapolis; 50,000 in Denver; 250,000 in Boston; 250,000 in Detroit. "Nobody stomps, shouts, or whistles for Truman," Richard H. Rovere wrote in the October 9, 1948, New Yorker. "Everybody claps. I should say that the decibel count would be about the same as it would be for a missionary who had just delivered a mildly encouraging report on the inroads being made against heathenism in Northern Rhodesia. This does not necessarily mean that the people who come out to hear him intend to vote against him — though my personal feeling is that most of them intend to do exactly that."

Much that Truman said was absurd or irresponsible, and some of it mischievous. Harried and forlorn, supported by only 15 percent of the nation's newspapers, told on every side that he was wasting his time and everyone else's, he was capable of delivering demagogic lines. "The Republicans," he said, "have begun to nail the American consumer to the wall with spikes of greed." He called them "gluttons of privilege," called Dewey a "fascist" and compared him to Hitler, and to over 80,000 listeners at the National Plowing Contest in Dexter, Iowa, he charged that "This Republican Congress has already stuck a pitchfork in the farmer's back."

September became October, the days grew shorter, the nights deepened, cider appeared in the supermarkets, children scooped out pumpkins for jack-o'-lanterns, geese honked on their way southward at the first frost, bobwhites and barn swallows fled after them, squirrels hoarded white oak acorns, and still the Truman train crossed and recrossed the great fields of hayshocks, brown now but in trim straight rows, the locomotive meandering gracefully through the forests where maple tops were turning gold and staghorn sumac scarlet, where the long lonely whistle called those who could hear it to listen to the spry man introduce his wife and daughter, state his case, make his jokes, and then wave his hand and depart.

The low point for that train, according to Clifford, came toward the middle of October. As they paused in a small Midwest town, a member of the staff jumped off and bought the October 11 issue of *Newsweek*. The big black type read: FIFTY POLITICAL EXPERTS UNANIMOUSLY PREDICT A DEWEY VICTORY. "Unanimously," someone said hollowly, and there was a long silence. One of them trudged back and showed it to Truman. He blinked, grinned, and said lightly, "Oh, those damned fellows; they're always wrong anyway. Forget it, boys, and let's get on with the job." At that point, Clifford believes, neither Bess nor Margaret believed that the President had a chance. He himself did, however, and afterward he could prove it. On the afternoon of October 13, while riding from Duluth to St. Paul, he wrote out his state-by-state analysis of the coming vote on the back of a mimeographed copy of his Duluth speech and handed it to George Elsey, who sealed it and put it away until the day after the election. It then developed that Truman had predicted 340 electoral votes for himself, 108 for Dewey, 42 for Thurmond, with 37 marked "doubtful." It wasn't on the nose, and it omitted four electoral votes, but a great many men whose job was forecasting elections would have given almost anything to have written it.

Meanwhile the man who was following Harry around continued his triumphant tour of the nation. Superbly organized, rigorously on schedule, always met by liaison men, with facilities for distributing advance speech texts to the ninety-eight reporters aboard and a high-fidelity public address system which could carry the candidate's deep baritone tones from the rear platform to the press's bar car, Thomas E. Dewey's "Victory Special" provided the very latest thing in media equipment, designed to carry, spread, and disseminate whatever he wished to say.

He wished to say nothing. "Governor Dewey," Leo Egan reported in the *New York Times* late in September, "is acting like a man who has already been elected and is merely marking time, waiting to take office. In his speeches and in his manner there is an attitude that the election will . . . confirm a decision already made. . . . Governor Dewey is deliberately avoiding any sharp controversy with the Democratic incumbent."

Once in a while, in the Middle West and again in California, the two campaign trains would be only a day or two apart. Truman always noted the fact and reeled off a list of prickly questions for his opponent. Dewey declined the bait. He preferred to dwell upon the "incredible beauty" of the Rocky Mountains, the "soft, rolling, wooded country" through which he had been passing, the "teeming cities" and "fertile plains" — in sum, "the sheer majesty" of the United States.

Truman discussed housing, minimum wages, medical care for the elderly, crops. Dewey took his stand in behalf of water: "By adequate soil conservation," he said resonantly in Denver, "we can do much to preserve our own future. We must also use the water we have wisely and well. We need the water from our rivers for power as well as agriculture. . . . The mighty rivers of the west should be developed with a view to the widest possible use for conservation, power, navigation, flood control, reclamation, and irrigation."

In Des Moines, two days after Truman's "pitchfork in the back" speech, with the country waiting for the Republican standard-bearer's reply, Dewey said, "On January 20 we will enter into a new era. We propose to install in Washington an administration which has faith in the American people, a warm understanding of their needs, and the competence to meet them. We will rediscover the essential unity of our people and the spiritual strength that makes our country great. We will begin to move forward again shoulder to shoulder toward an even greater America and a better life for every American, in a nation working effectively for the peace of the world."

So thin was the meat in Dewey's formal addresses that resourceful newspapermen began looking for some anecdote, some light feature to relieve the gray paragraphs. On October 12, at Beaucoup, Illinois, the train abruptly moved backward, toward the crowd. It halted again after a few feet, and there were no casualties, but the governor was upset and angry. Depending upon which version you heard, he said either, "That's the first idiot I've ever had for an engineer" or "That's the first lunatic I've had for an engineer. He probably ought to be shot at sunrise but I guess we can let him off because no one was hurt." Possibly because it was one of the rare times that he had said anything real, the remark was passed on and on until it became an anti-Dewey slogan in union halls and railroad roundhouses all over the country.

Other Republicans were on the warpath. Hugh Scott, now national chairman, had seized upon the Bentley-Chambers testimony, judging it as an issue with too many implications to be dismissed as a "red herring." Dewey made one tame reference to it and then soared off toward his most elegant generalities: "We have sometimes failed in our faith and often fallen short of it. But in our hearts we believe and know that every man has some of the Divine in him, that every individual is of priceless importance." To be fair, it must be set down that in the closing weeks of the campaign Dewey began to doubt his strategy. His crowds were dwindling and Truman's, the newspapers told him, were growing. His strategy board — Brownell, Scott, Elliott Bell and Russell Sprague — had decided to aim the final thrust at the industrial northwest; midwestern farmers were Republican by birth and would take care of themselves. Stung by Truman's hooks and jabs, he wanted to strike back, and in four communities he let loose. Truman's message vetoing the Taft-Hartley Law, for example, he said was "the wrongest, most incompetent, most inaccurate document ever put out of the White House in a hundred and sixty years." The crowds enjoyed it, and so did he, but his advisers were alarmed. Hagerty polled the newsmen and reported that all of them believed a slugfest would be a mistake, that it would be a confession of weakness. To be sure Dewey was getting the best counsel, Brownell set up a series of conference calls around the nation tying the candidate into round robin conversations with ninety of the ninety-six Republican state committeemen and committeewomen. All save one urged the governor to press forward on the high road and let Truman totter down the low road into oblivion. The exception, Harry Darby of Kansas, warned that the farm belt was in a mutinous mood. He was dismissed as a Cassandra, and Dewey resumed his crusade for unity, cleanliness, better water, and faith.

Down to the wire, the Truman train was bombarded with bills from managers of service industries terrified of being left unpaid. But after the disheartening *Newsweek* issue spirits began to lift a little. In bull sessions late on the train the younger staff members argued back and forth about the President's chances, though whenever they grew optimistic one of them would remind the others that every poll in the country contradicted them. In the last days Clifford thought there was something in the air, that Truman was picking up strength; when he rose to speak at the traditional Friday night before election rally in the Brooklyn Academy of Music, some of whose backers had been leaders of the "Dump Truman" movement before Philadelphia, the crowd gave him a twelve-minute standing ovation. Clifford reflected that if only the campaign could last two weeks more, they might have a chance.

In Chicago Adlai Stevenson and Paul Douglas stood side by side in an open car on their way to a Truman rally at the stadium. The silent crowds were four or five deep on the sidewalk. Fifteen years ago these had been the forgotten men and women at the bottom of the economic pyramid, the starving teachers and threadbare workers Insull had betrayed and Roosevelt had saved. Stevenson marveled at the size of the turnout. All Chicago seemed to be there, yet there was almost no cheering, hardly any sound at all. Douglas said, "They've come out today to see the death of the dream that they cherish."

In Baltimore, editor in chief Hamilton Owens of the *Sun* stopped by a young reporter's desk. "I've finished my editorial congratulating the new President," he said. "It's in type and on the stone." He paused and added with a twinkle, "If Truman won, I'd have to write another one, wouldn't I?" The little sally delighted him; he strode off chuckling.

Subscribers to *Life* that last weekend in October saw on page 37 of the new issue, dated November 1, a full-page photograph of Governor and Mrs. Dewey over the caption: THE NEXT PRESIDENT TRAVELS BY FERRY BOAT OVER THE BROAD WATERS OF SAN FRANCISCO BAY. Accompanying it was an eight-page windup on the campaign, in which the editors concluded that the U.S. was "about to ditch Truman and take Dewey" for reasons that involved "the brain as well as the emotions." The cover of Willard Kiplinger's weekly *Changing Times* for November 1 carried a 72-point type head announcing disclosures inside on WHAT DEWEY WILL DO. On Sunday, October 31, the *New York Times* reported the results of a month-long survey during which its sizable national staff had studied voter sentiment in every state. Its conclusion: Dewey would carry 29 states with 345 electoral votes (266 needed to win); Truman 11 states with 105 electoral votes; Thurmond 4 states with 38 electoral votes; in doubt, 43 electoral votes. The survey also found that the Republicans would retain control of both houses of Congress. To make sure it was right, the *Times* polled the forty-seven shrewdest journalists covering Dewey. In a secret ballot, they unanimously agreed that the governor would win handily.

In an editorial which would appear on November 3, the morning after the election, the *Detroit Free Press* would call upon Secretary of State Marshall to resign and urge Truman to appoint John Foster Dulles, Dewey's adviser on foreign affairs, in his place. "That," its editors argued, "would restore confidence in our foreign policy abroad and at home." (That same Truman Doctrine was pacifying Greece, the Marshall Plan was in full swing, and the Berlin airlift had entered its fifth month.) "True," the *Free Press* conceded, "that is asking a great deal of Mr. Truman. Yet these are times which, with all our unity and patriotism, will ask a great deal more of millions of other Americans." The editors generously described America's "lame duck" President as "a game little fellow, who never sought the Presidency and was lost in it, but who went down fighting with all he had." *Free Press* readers were assured that Harry Truman would still make a living: "There's first the prospect of a $25,000 pension as a former President. Then there are all the radio contracts and the magazine articles and books which he can look forward to and which will net him a handsome income — close, they say, to a million. The path for him doesn't lead from the White House to the poorhouse."

Not everyone in the fourth estate wrote about the crushed President with such benevolence; one syndicated columnist wondered "how long Dewey is going to let Truman interfere with the running of this country." Like the *Free Press*, some writers had to complete their Wednesday columns on Monday for setting on Tuesday, while the voters made their choice. Thus Drew Pearson would astonish his millions of readers the day after the returns had been counted by disclosing, in his opening paragraph, "I surveyed the close-knit group around Tom Dewey, who will take over in the White House 86 days from now." He then triumphantly named the new President's entire cabinet. That same Wednesday Joseph and Stewart Alsop revealed that "The first post-election question is how the government can get through the next ten weeks. . . . Events will not wait patiently until Thomas E. Dewey officially replaces Harry S. Truman. Particularly in the fields of foreign and defense policy, somebody somewhere in Washington must have authority to give answers that will still be valid after

January 20." The Alsops proposed that Dewey's cabinet nominees for the State and Defense posts immediately move in as "special assistants," guiding their lame-duck predecessors until Dewey's inaugural.

How did this happen? How could so many seasoned observers have climbed out so far on so shaky a limb? The answer is that they didn't think of it as a limb, let alone a shaky one. They had been telling one another that Truman's cause was hopeless for so long, and reading each other's analyses of why Dewey would easily defeat him, that they believed no other outcome was possible. Truman's campaign claim that "Everybody's against me but the people" had this seed of truth: unlike the pundits, he and the voters thought of the election as a contest, not a coronation. To those who had devoted their careers to the study of electoral trends, all the signposts pointed one way. When the party out of power captured control of Congress, as the Democrats had in 1930, it was virtually certain to win the Presidency two years later, as FDR had then. Besides, the Republicans were long overdue. Roosevelt's four straight victories could be attributed only to his charming personality, the Alsops and Pearsons told one another, and if there was one thing Truman lacked, it was charm. The Republican ticket had the money, the overwhelming support of the press — newspapermen naturally thought that this counted heavily — and, most important of all, the blessing of the public opinion polls.

It was twelve years since the *Literary Digest* fiasco. In the aftermath of the Democratic landslide of 1936, embittered Republicans had sworn that they would never again trust a straw vote. Afterward, however, they learned that George Gallup and Elmo Roper, then lesser known than the *Digest*'s pollsters, had spurned its direct mail for statistical samplings, which had forecast a big Roosevelt triumph. Since then these pollsters had been vindicated in every election. Metropolitan newspapers subscribed to their services — the *New York Times* was thought quaint for spending so much money on its own survey — and any pundit who contradicted them would have been considered a fool. Thus the beginning of the cycle: polls foresaw a Republican sweep, and columnists and editorial writers took it for gospel. It is even possible that men and women who planned to vote Democratic misled the pollsters because they wanted to keep up with the Joneses. Error was feeding upon error, and this chain was strengthened by poll takers who had become smug and, in at least one instance, arrogant.

Elmo Roper was arrogant. In a column dated September 9, nearly eight weeks before the election, he announced that he had surveyed the electorate for the last time. "Thomas E. Dewey," he wrote, "is almost as good as elected. . . . That being so, I can think of nothing duller or more intellectually barren than acting like a sports announcer who feels he must pretend he is witnessing a neck-and-neck race." Like so many professional election watchers, Roper believed in what some had come to call Farley's Law. After his sensational prediction in 1936, Farley had said that in his opinion, voters made up their minds during conventions; the campaigns, he implied, were ineffective carnivals. In laying his reputation on the line that first week in September, Roper was using figures gathered by his staff in August. Ironically, he did take another poll in the last week of the election showing a slight shift to Truman; it still gave Dewey a heavy lead, however, so he decided not to hedge his bet.

All three of the national polls — Roper, Gallup, and Crossley — erred in failing to ask interviewees whether they actually intended to vote and in excluding from their samples most voters with grade school educations, who were likely to be Truman partisans. The pollsters' greatest blunder, however, was their indifference to the last-minute impact of Truman's great effort. Roper had closed his books before the Truman Special could pull out of Union Station. Crossley's last report (predicting 49.9 percent for Dewey and 44.8 for Truman, the rest going to Thurmond and Wallace) was a reflection of mixed state samplings taken in mid-August, mid-September, and mid-October. Gallup, the most industrious of the three, should have sensed what was happening in the country. His September 24 report foresaw 46.5 percent of the vote for Dewey to 38 percent for Truman. His last column, appearing in Sunday papers two days before the election, showed Truman gaining sharply — to 44 percent — and the interviews on which it was based had been conducted two weeks earlier. Clifford was right. The national mood was shifting daily, almost hourly.

In the memories of Americans now over forty, four events stand apart: Pearl Harbor, the death of Roosevelt, the election of 1948, and the assassination of John Kennedy. A man may have forgotten what happened on his twenty-first birthday, or a woman how she lost her virginity, but each can recall where he was when he heard about these four. They became milestones in the lives of people; even as their parents had said, "We met after the Armistice," or "We moved just before the Crash," so the swing generation came to date incidents in their private lives from the moment news reached them of the shots in Dallas, the attack on Hawaii, the stroke in Warm Springs, and the Truman miracle.

Everyone expected an early night. In the ballroom of New York's Roosevelt Hotel, Jim Hagerty told reporters, "We may be out of the trenches by midnight"; Governor Dewey, after voting in an East Fifty-first Street school ("Good luck, Mr. President!" a clerk called from an office window overhead), predicted that Truman's telegram of concession would arrive while he and Mrs. Dewey were dining at the home of his good friend Roger Straus at 6 East Ninety-third Street. In Washington the Statler Hotel, Republican by tradition as the Mayflower is Democratic, had redecorated its ballroom and set aside a corsage for each Republican lady, to be presented to her as she arrived. The Mayflower, on the other hand, was quiet as a stone. The Democratic National Committee was so sure of defeat that it hadn't bothered to reserve the hotel's ballroom. Putting the money aside for '52, the committeemen retired to their office suite, took the phone off the hook, broke out a couple of bottles of whiskey, and settled in for a wake. None of them had brought a radio; this was one evening when they could do without the news. (In the 1960s or 1970s one of them might have brought a transistor in his pocket, but in 1948 "portable" radios were comparatively heavy and bulky, and had to be plugged into wall outlets.) This was going to be one night when the committeemen would be far behind the swiftly developing political picture. Cabell Phillips of the *New York Times* was also out of touch. Back in Manhattan after Truman's campaign, he had boosted his spirits by buying a $47.50 topcoat — a real investment in those days — and a ticket to Lynn Fontanne and Alfred Lunt's latest play. As the first scattered returns came in from New Hampshire, Phillips entered the theater's Forty-seventh Street door and sat through two acts, unaware of the greater drama outside.

Those early figures from New Hampshire surprised Dewey; though he was leading, his margin was less than in 1944, less than any Republican candidate would expect from so staunch a party stronghold. Hurrying back to his hotel suite, he sat by a radio with his family and a few intimate friends, listening, reading wire service returns as they were brought to him, and jotting figures on a scratch pad.

Out in Missouri, President Truman had eluded the press several hours earlier with the help of Secret Service agents Henry Nicholson and Jim Rowley.[*] At 4:30 P.M. they had driven to Excelsior Springs, a resort thirty miles northeast from Independence, and checked into the Elms Hotel. The President took a Turkish bath and retired to his room at 6:30 with a ham sandwich and a glass of milk. He turned on the bedside radio. An announcer reported that he had taken an early lead of a few thousand votes. He went to bed and fell asleep almost instantly.

At 7:45 P.M. a Chicago *Tribune* editor faced an agonizing decision. The paper's bulldog edition was going to press, to reach the streets in time for the late theater crowd. The editor had to compose a headline. He couldn't just report that a national election had been held; they knew *that;* he needed a piece of hard news. Truman was now leading, but those first returns from New England were meaningless unless you knew where they came from. The Republican ticket might sweep Connecticut, for example, but if Hartford reported before the rest of the state, as it usually did, the figures would suggest a Democratic victory. Even the commentator in Connecticut couldn't tell you where the figures were from. He didn't know himself. In the race to be first on the air, he read scrawled notes the moment they were handed to him.

So the editor in the Tribune Building had to write his headline before he

---

[*]Who would be chief of the Secret Service on November 22, 1963.

knew what was happening. He fell back on the one certainty in this election and blocked out the banner head: DEWEY DEFEATS TRUMAN.

By now the running totals made no sense. Truman had taken an early lead, as expected; Democratic strength lay in the cities, whose returns came in first because so many of them had voting machines and superior communications facilities. Correcting for this bias, Dewey seemed to be taking New York and New Jersey (but only because of a heavy Wallace vote in each). He was winning throughout the industrial East, with the exception of Massachusetts and Rhode Island. This reassured him; traditionally it was Democratic ground. Furthermore, Thurmond was depriving Truman of Mississippi, Louisiana, Alabama, and South Carolina. However, the Dewey margins were incredibly thin. Some counties that were GOP bastions were going Republican by a handful of votes. And Truman, outpolling Roosevelt in some places, was holding the popular vote lead in key cities.

The real shocks came from the other side of the Appalachian Range. The Democratic ticket had seized a strong lead in Wisconsin, Iowa, and Colorado, all three Republican fiefs; and as early reports came in from the eleven western states, only Oregon seemed to be going to Dewey.

At 10:30 in New York the curtain came down on the Lunts' second act. Cabell Phillips was thirsty. He had remained seated during the first intermission, but he decided to spend this one in a nearby bar. As he ordered scotch he became aware of a voice coming from the bar's radio, reciting the names of states, the number of wards and precincts, and a jumble of bewildering figures. Phillips had paid the bartender, and the first swallow of whisky was halfway down his throat when the clear voice of a commentator said, "Truman's lead now looks almost unassailable. If he can hold his lead in Ohio . . ."

Phillips gagged. Coughing scotch, he ran out the door and headed for Times Square. Midway in his sprint he remembered his new topcoat, paused, decided to forget it, and raced on.

Every fifteen or twenty minutes Dr. George Gallup was interviewed by a network announcer asking for his interpretation of the running tabulation. Gallup explained that the present Democratic plurality would be wiped out by the farm vote. By eleven o'clock the farm vote began to come in, and it was Democratic. Out on the plains they had remembered which party had given them parity and grain storage.

At 11 P.M. Herbert Brownell entered the Roosevelt Hotel ballroom and claimed a Dewey victory. Party workers cheered, but before they could ask details he hurried upstairs again. It seemed that Hagerty had overestimated the size of the landslide; they weren't going to be out of the trenches at midnight after all.

At midnight Harry Truman woke up. It took him a moment to adjust to the unfamiliar hotel room. Then he turned the radio on again. The voice was that of H. V. Kaltenborn, explaining that although Truman was 1,200,000 votes ahead in the count he was "still undoubtedly beaten." The President turned him off and went back to sleep.

In the Washington headquarters of the Democratic National Committee a latecomer who had passed a radio brought word that the President wasn't being overwhelmed after all; in some states he was even leading, though of course "the farmers haven't been heard from yet." One of the staff suggested they send out for a radio. They shrugged, then nodded. Might as well have a few laughs before it was all over.

"Meanwhile," Richard H. Rovere wrote, "the solid Statler walls were crumbling. Republican matrons were eating their corsages, Republican gentlemen were wilting their collars with nervous perspiration."

Shortly after midnight the party mood in the Roosevelt ballroom began to be replaced by anxiety and then consternation. Only now, at this late hour, had they been assured that Dewey had carried his home state — and by a mere 60,000 votes at that; if Wallace hadn't been on the ballot, Truman would have trounced him here.

It now appeared that the outcome hung on Ohio, Illinois, and California. Unbelievable as it was, any one of them could give Truman a winning combination. He would take a slight lead in one, then Dewey would pass him; all three were seesawing. At 1:45 A.M. Brownell, for reasons known only to him, returned to the ballroom and issued a second victory statement. He roused a few faint cheers. The others just stared at him.

At 4 A.M. Agent Rowley awoke the President and suggested he switch the radio on again. His lead was now a stunning two million votes, though H. V. Kaltenborn — whose voice Truman would gleefully mimic for friends to the end of his life — said he couldn't see how the President could be elected.

Dressing, the President told the agents to drive him back to the Muehlebach Hotel in Kansas City, because "It looks as if we're in for another four years." They arrived there at 6 A.M. Wan reporters wondered where he had been and how he managed to look as though he had had some sleep.

At 4:30 A.M., as the President's car pulled away from the Elms Hotel in Excelsior Springs, Hagerty had assembled the reporters at the Roosevelt and told them he had just been conferring with Dewey. He said: "We're in there fighting. The returns are still coming in, but it looks as if we won't know definitely until morning." Thirty-five minutes later he was back again. "We are not making any predictions or claims," he said.

Sometime after dawn, still unable to grasp that he was being beaten, the exhausted governor went to bed, and as he dozed the last hope slipped away from his haggard aides. Truman took Ohio at 9:30 A.M. — by 7,000 votes — putting him over the top with 270 electoral votes. An hour later, when Dewey awoke, he learned that he had also lost Illinois and California. At 11:14 A.M. he conceded. President Truman had not only won the race; he had forged a smashing victory in the electoral college — 304* to 189, with 38 going to the Dixiecrat ticket. Moreover, he had carried Congress in with him. In the 80th Congress the Republicans had controlled the Senate 51 to 45, and the House 246 to 188. Now the Democrats held the whip hand in the Senate, 54 to 42 (a gain of 9 seats), and the House, 263 to 171 (a gain of 75). Paul Douglas, Hubert Humphrey, Lyndon Johnson, and Estes Kefauver were Senators-elect; G. Mennen Williams was governor of Michigan, Chester Bowles governor of Connecticut, and Adlai Stevenson governor of Illinois.

Taft was fit to be tied. "I don't care how the thing is explained," he said. "It defies all common sense to send that roughneck ward politician back to the White House." Elsewhere the character of Truman's achievement overrode rancor. "You just have to take off your hat to a beaten man who refuses to stay licked!" said the arch-conservative New York *Sun.* "Mr. Truman won because this is still a land which loves a scrapper, in which intestinal fortitude is still respected." The triumph was more than a personal victory, though. Two days after the election Walter Lippmann wrote, "Mr. Truman's own victory, the Democratic majorities in both houses of Congress, the Democratic victories in so many states, attest the enormous vitality of the Democratic party as Roosevelt led it and developed it from 1932 to 1944 . . . the party that Roosevelt formed has survived his death and is without question the dominant force in American politics."

In newsrooms and editorial chambers men avoided one another's eyes the morning after the election. The fourth estate and its sources were the laughingstock of the country and knew it. The Alsop brothers wrote: "There is only one question on which professional politicians, polltakers, political reporters and other wiseacres and prognosticators can any longer speak with much authority. This is how they want their crow cooked." When the President and his Vice-President-elect returned to Washington (Truman holding aloft the *Chicago Tribune's* "Dewey Defeats Truman" headline) they were greeted by 750,000 cheerers and a huge sign across the front of the Washington Post Building: "Mr. President, we are ready to eat crow whenever you are ready to serve it." In a letter to his own paper, Reston of the *Times* wrote that "we were too isolated with other reporters; and we, too, were far too impressed by the tidy statistics of the poll." *Time* said the press had "delegated its journalist's job to the polls." Several angry publishers canceled their subscriptions to the polls. The pollsters themselves were prostrate. Gallup said simply, "I don't know what happened." One

*One Truman elector in Tennessee later defected to Thurmond.

New York Times reporter thought to call Wilfred J. Funk, the last editor of the *Literary Digest*, and ask for his comment. "I don't want to seem malicious," Funk replied, "but I can't help but get a good chuckle out of this."

Afterward the Survey Research Center of the University of Michigan conducted a poll on the polls, while Gallup and Roper scrupulously investigated themselves. The results of the studies are startlingly alike. The Michigan group found that of the 24,105,000 Truman voters, 14 percent, or 3,374,800, decided to vote for him in the last fortnight of the campaign. Gallup and Roper, taking a different approach, learned that one voter in every seven (6,927,000) made up his mind in the last two weeks of the election. Of these, 75 percent (5,195,000) picked Truman; 25 percent (1,732,000) chose Dewey, a difference of 3,463,000. Inasmuch as Truman's plurality over Dewey on November 2 had been 2,135,000, the inference is inescapable. Using either the Michigan figures or Gallup-Roper's, one finds that some 3,300,000 fence-sitters determined the outcome of the race in its closing days — when Dewey's instincts were urging him to adopt Truman's hell-for-leather style and slug it out with him, and when he didn't because all the experts told him he shouldn't.

Late Forties Montage

GALLAGHER: Some fuggin mornings like this I wish I'd catch a bullet.

WILSON: Only goddam trouble with that is you can't pick the spot.

STANLEY: You know if you could, the Army wouldn't be keeping me long.

GALLAGHER: Aaah, there ain't a goddam place you can get a million-dollar wound that it don't hurt.

Now is the hour
For me to say good-bye
Soon I'll be sailing
Far across the sea
While I'm away
Oh, please remember me

PYRAMID CRAZE SWEEPS U.S.

Paisan   **The Search**   **Treasure of Sierra Madre**   **Snake Pit**

Best actor of 1949: Broderick Crawford in **All the King's Men**

Battleground   **Sands of Iwo Jima**   **The Bicycle Thief**   **Quartet**

Home of the Brave   **Letter to Three Wives**

We've a date in '48
Watch us roll up the vote in every state . . .
For the U.S.A. and the G.O.P.
On the great day of victory

So in love
with you
am I

Dear Seventeen:

I think you should have more articles on dates and shyness and put in some more about movie stars, too. Stories like those on atomic energy are very boring.

Nobody dast blame this man. You don't understand: Willy was a salesman. And for a salesman, there is no rock bottom to the life. He don't put a bolt to a nut, he don't tell you the law or give you medicine. He's a man way out there in the blue, riding on a smile and a shoeshine. And when they start not smiling back — that's an earthquake. And then you get yourself a couple of spots on your hat, and you're finished. Nobody dast blame this man. A salesman is got to dream, boy. It comes with the territory.

BEST SELLERS: Fiction
Came a Cavalier by Frances Parkinson Keyes
Raintree County by Ross Lockridge, Jr.
Parris Mitchell of King's Row by Henry and Katherine Bellamann
The Naked and the Dead by Norman Mailer
The Young Lions by Irwin Shaw

GM'S 1949 INCOME TAX PUT AT $444,377,889

BEST SELLERS: Nonfiction
The Gathering Storm by Winston Churchill
Crusade in Europe by Dwight D. Eisenhower
Peace of Mind by Joshua L. Liebman
Cheaper by the Dozen by Frank B. Gilbreth and Ernestine G. Carey
The Seven Storey Mountain by Thomas Merton

Now the reason this club hasn't made a deal is why should we? When you got players good enough to win a pennant on the road and a World Series on the road which is where they win the majority of their games and against a treemendous club like this one which you know is a great ball club because why have they played us more games in the World Series than anybody, then why would you want to change? . . . And whenever I make a deal I get swindled.

BIRTH RATE ZOOMS

Highbrow, lowbrow, upper middlebrow, and lower middlebrow . . . gradually they are finding their own levels and confining themselves more and more to the company of their own kind. You will not find a highbrow willingly attending a Simon & Schuster cocktail party any more than you will find an upper middlebrow at a Rotary Club luncheon or an Elks' picnic.

INDIA FREE

Goodnight, sweetheart
Though I'm not beside you
Goodnight, sweetheart
Still my love will guide you
Dreams enfold you
In each one I hold you
Goodnight, sweetheart
Goodnight

I'm just wild about Harry
And Harry's wild about me.
The fates decreed it, we concede it,
Harry made history

. . . Friendly Henry Wallace is O.K.
He'll end Jim Crow
Warmongers will all know
That with Henry peace will have its day

Kiss Me Kate

RED-BLOODED AMERICANS!
Fight progressive education, mental health, fluoridation, vivisectionists, Freudianism, planned parenthood!

SIXTEEN

The Age of Suspicion

BEFORE CHECKING OUT of the Muehlebach and returning to Washington, President Truman was advised that he could not enter the White House. No coup; it just wasn't safe. The most famous home in America was in imminent danger of collapse. Its householder wasn't altogether surprised. According to the National Archives, "President Truman became concerned because of a noticeable vibration in the floors in his study." There had been more to it than that. The great chandeliers in the East Room had been tinkling when there was no breeze, and when the President held his physician's stethoscope against the walls, he could hear them creaking.

He had appointed a commission to look into the matter — just in time, as it turned out. In the last week of the campaign horrified engineers had discovered that blackened beams, burned by the British in 1814 and never replaced, were about to give way; frescoed ceilings weighing seventy pounds to the square foot were sagging six inches. While the First Family had been walking out one door en route to Independence, frantic construction men had rushed in another with props and scaffolding. The reconstruction would cost $5,400,000. It might have been cheaper to erect a new building, but tearing down the White House was unthinkable. The next tenant would have air-conditioning, fireproofing, and multiple outlets for television cables. Meanwhile the Trumans would pig it in Blair House, diagonally across the street at 1648 Pennsylvania Avenue.

The Fair Deal was christened in Blair House. During the first three years of his Presidency Truman had regarded himself as the executor of FDR's political will. But a third of the nation was no longer in want. The altered economy called for a new liberalism, "focused," as Cabell Phillips put it, "on the creation and equitable distribution of abundance, which now loomed as an attainable reality." Even before the miracle at the polls, a group of key Truman aides had conceived a program during a series of

Monday evening seminars in the Wardman Park apartment of Oscar Ewing, director of the Federal Security Agency, whose advocacy of a national medical plan would soon make him the bugbear of the American Medical Association.* In embryonic form their list of proposals had first appeared on the Hill in the President's Turnip session proposals. Fully developed now, it included new measures for civil rights, housing, unemployment benefits, agricultural aid, and inflation control; a 3.2-billion-dollar tax cut for poor wage earners, federal aid to schools, and Taft-Hartley repeal. Together with Ewing's Medicare, they would later form the nucleus of Kennedy's New Frontier and Johnson's Great Society.

After a week of postelection convalescence at Key West, Truman put his back into his forthcoming State of the Union message. In time it would indeed alter history, but of the innovations which emerged from those last weeks in 1948, the one that would be most closely identified with Truman's name was to appear not in the January 5 State of the Union address, but at his inauguration two weeks later. As Clark Clifford recollects, "We were having a real problem during late December putting the inaugural speech together. Our man had won a smashing and surprising victory at the polls, and he and all of us felt that when he stood up to take the oath of office on January 20, he should have something big and new and challenging to present to the country." The message to Congress dwelt upon domestic issues; the inaugural would look abroad. The difficulty was that the great links of Truman's foreign policy had already been forged in Greece, Turkey, Berlin, and the European Recovery Plan. Then Clifford remembered "a State Department memorandum that had crossed my desk a few weeks or a few months earlier. A technical assistance program had been tried on a very modest scale in Latin America, and this memo raised the question — not very hopefully as I recall — whether it might not be adapted to the Far East as a sort of substitute for the ERP." Clifford suggested it to the President, who said after a moment's reflection, "This looks good. We'll use it. We can work out the operating details later." Truman had already decided to tell the inauguration crowd that in dealing with other nations the United States would be sustained by faith in the United Nations, the Marshall Plan, and a new North Atlantic alliance. In addition to these three points he now had another, technical aid to backward countries. In the final draft it appeared as:

> Fourth. We must embark on a bold new program for making the benefits of our scientific advances and industrial progress available for the improvement and growth of underdeveloped areas. . . .

Point Four stirred the world. Endorsed by the U.N.'s Economic and Social Council on March 4, 1949, it roused the hope that American technical skills might revolutionize primitive agricultural techniques, raise the stan-

* In addition to Ewing the planners were Clifford, Charles S. Murphy, C. Girard Davidson, David A. Morse, and Leon Keyserling.

dard of living in Asia and Africa, and tame their rivers with new TVAs. "While there is some criticism of the President for having shot first and questioned later," James Reston wrote from Washington, "there is general approval of his colonial development program here." The *Christian Science Monitor* reported that "President Truman's dedication of United States technological resources to improve the lot of the globe's less fortunate people has kindled the imagination of thinking people throughout Britain and Western Europe." Predictably, there were rumbles of dissent on Capitol Hill from "the primitives," as Dean Acheson called them. Senator Kenneth Wherry and Joe Martin groaned, Senator Jenner of Indiana said the whole thing had been invented by Earl Browder, and Senator Taft wanted to know where the money was coming from.

Taft knew. It had to come from Congress. But many Democratic candidates who had ridden in on the President's coattails were turning out to be ungrateful; once again the Republican and southern Democratic coalition was bucking the administration. The chairmen of eighteen powerful Senate committees were from the South, and the President pro tempore of the Senate, the Speaker of the House, and the two party whips were all coalition members. Point Four, with a humble allotment of 45 million dollars, did not reach Truman's desk until June 5, 1950. Even then it was hedged with multiple restrictions which, as Cabell Phillips wrote, largely vitiated "the great propaganda value it had when President Truman first proposed it."

In the aftermath of his election, problems abroad bore upon Truman with special urgency. General Marshall was in Walter Reed Hospital having a kidney removed; he would continue as Secretary of State until the inaugural but step down then. Truman gave hard thought to the choice of a successor. He couldn't pick a crony, a faceless bureaucrat, or a free-spending campaign contributor like Louis Johnson, who would succeed James Forrestal as Secretary of Defense in March. Marshall's successor must be esteemed in friendly chancelleries, respected in Moscow, and known on the Hill.

Three weeks after the election he sent for Dean Acheson, who had retired to the private practice of law. As Acheson remembers it, he passed the Executive Mansion, of which only the outside wall had been left standing "for sentimental reasons," and was escorted to the President's "minute office" in Blair House. The President asked him to sit down, then grinned.

"You had better be sitting down when you hear what I have to say to you," he began. Without pausing he continued, "I want you to come back and be Secretary of State. Will you?"

Acheson recalls that he was "utterly speechless." The President suggested that he talk it over with his wife. Mrs. Acheson being agreeable, her husband accepted. He would take oath on January 21 and become the fifty-second and, with the possible exception of Seward, the most controversial of U.S. Secretaries of State.

As one crew of workmen rebuilt the White House, others were encircling the country's inner cities with America's new suburbs — the Hillendales, Gardenvilles, Northwoods, Parkvilles, Stoneleighs, Baynesvilles, Drumcastles, Anneslies, Wiltondales, Dunbartons, and Cedarcrofts. Levittown had become an American institution, with thousands of imitators, and outside Chicago a group of businessmen broke ground for another pilot development, Park Forest. Recognizing the housing needs of veteran families with small nest eggs but stable jobs, Park Forest's founders first erected rental "garden apartments" around a central shopping plaza. Then, as their tenants' savings accumulated, they added split-level ranch houses financed by themselves. The end result was a constantly recycling population of 30,000 whose predictable wants were supplied by stores in the shopping center — owned, again, by the businessmen. The inhabitants knew they were being exploited and loved it, and the envious hardhats who built Park Forest could hardly wait to reach the new suburbia themselves.

Baltimore spawned no fewer than sixteen developments, and it is worth noting that the president of the PTA in one of them, Loch Raven Village, was a 10th Armored veteran named Spiro T. Agnew. Agnew was in many ways representative of homeowners in the packaged communities. Although he had held a commission he was a zealous egalitarian ("Call me Ted"). He was active in the VFW and Kiwanis. As a licensed though not practicing lawyer, he was naturally interested in public office, but his style was the new politics. Thomas D'Alesandro Jr., Baltimore's incumbent mayor, advertised his background by remaining in his Little Italy home; Agnew, also a product of a downtown ethnic neighborhood, was doing his best to forget it. He attended the Episcopalian church. His favorite musician was Lawrence Welk. His leisure interests were all midcult: watching the Baltimore Colts on television, listening to Mantovani, and reading the sort of prose the *Reader's Digest* liked to condense. He was a lover of order and an almost compulsive conformist. Saturday mornings he happily joined other Loch Raven men in washing and waxing their '48 Fleetline Chevies, '49 Buick Specials, and Oldsmobile 88s. Mondays he donned his double-breasted — later three-button — suit, set his snap-brim squarely on his head, and arrived in his Schreiber Food Stores office at 8:45 on the dot. Anyone who came in after nine o'clock heard about it. Agnew, the manager, believed firmly in punctuality, a stitch in time, and plenty of elbow grease.

Had they met, he would have aroused the professional interest of William H. Whyte Jr., a former Marine Corps officer only a year older than Agnew. As a staff writer for *Fortune*, Whyte had begun to type the Agnews as Organization Men. They might call their work a treadmill or a rat race, but they belonged to the firm — or whatever lay at the other end of their occupational umbilical cord, since junior executives were only one of the many species found in the developments. They included the young physician completing his residency in internal medicine and destined for group practice, the dental intern, the FBI agent, the salaried young attorney working for a prestigious law partnership, the promising young major attending staff school, the physicist in corporate shop, the Ph.D. in a pharmaceutical laboratory, the apprentice engineer at Pratt & Whitney; even the vicar who would wind up a member of the church hierarchy. Most were well aware of the bond that joined them; as some frequently put it, they were "all in the same boat." They had few doubts about the boat's destination. Within a quarter-century, when their turn came, they and others like them would set the national tone, becoming what *Time* would later call the "command generation." Then they would have their hands full. For the present, they enjoyed their families while they could, met their peers at mixers, and enjoyed the communal sports of the development: canasta, ping-pong, Chinese checkers — and, in that presidential election year when their man lost, hushed conversations about an Indiana University research investigation which was becoming known to the whole world as the Kinsey Report.

In a Peter Arno cartoon of the time, a shocked woman looked up from the report (*Sexual Behavior in the Human Male*, 804 pages, $6.50, over 275,000 copies sold in 1948) and asked her husband, "Is there a *Mrs.* Kinsey?" There was, and there were also three Kinsey children, all conceived before he embarked upon his major work. Not that he had been idle before; his passion for taxonomy could be traced back to his school days in South Orange, New Jersey, when he submitted an account of the behavior of birds in the rain to a nature journal, which accepted it. Then, and thereafter, he was a stickler for explicit detail. Until he became interested in certain extracurricular activities of his Indiana students, his fellow zoologists thought he would be remembered for his prodigious study of the gall wasp, a harmless species found in eastern Central America. Kinsey traveled 80,000 miles collecting examples, and he measured, catalogued, and preserved 3,500,000 of them, to demonstrate their individual variations. Peering through his microscope, he recorded twenty-eight different measurements of each specimen. *PM* called it "a landmark in the history of entomology." As a scientist he had naturally played no favorites; every gall wasp was just as good as the next one to him; he rendered no judgment on their behavior. It was an attitude which would subsequently prove even more useful to him. It would also amaze the country.

Until the late 1930s the career of Alfred C. Kinsey had varied scarcely a jot from those of thousands of his colleagues: Harvard, graduate study, years of junior faculty teaching, tenure, and all those gall wasps. In Bloomington he had become a familiar campus figure, tall, heavyset, with sandy hair and a preoccupied manner. His students admired his patience and forbearance. He had all the right professorial hobbies: gardening, hiking, pottery, classical music. No scandal had touched him or even come within whispering distance of him. He was, in short, just the sort of educator a cautious dean would choose to teach a course on marriage problems. Certainly Indiana's dean never suspected that he would *create* problems — and, to boot, make the university a mecca for collectors of erotica.

Before he could reach even a tentative view of matrimonial difficulties, Kinsey reasoned, he must steep himself in facts about biological transactions between *Homo sapiens* mates. He went to the university library and received the jolt of his life. There were no facts worth mentioning, in Indiana or elsewhere. The staggering truth was that men and women knew more about gall wasps than each other. Human beings were even uninformed about the erotic behavior of members of their own sex, and therefore had no way of knowing whether or not they were normal. To a disciple of truth, this was unacceptable. He was seized with a determination to right the wrong which would glow within him until the end of his life, sustaining him through long periods of exhausting research. It was at about this time that Mrs. Kinsey said, "I hardly see him at night since he took up sex."

His friends saw him, though not informally. While on the job he no longer thought of them as friends. As an objective investigator he regarded them as just so many specimens, to be measured and catalogued in all their variations. Working with them, he developed his basic two-and-a-half-hour, 300-to-500-question interview. It covered the whole sexual spectrum — masturbation, nocturnal emissions, lewd fantasies, petting, intercourse before and after marriage, adultery, inversion, frequency of ejaculations, oral sex, anal sex, relations with animals, exotic pleasures. Whether his friendships survived this test is unknown, but in Bloomington and elsewhere word got around that he was turning over rocks no one had come near before. Nothing was beyond his scope. Babies, measured in the nursery with special instruments, were found to experience orgasms at the age of four or five months. Elderly spinsters confided that restrictive clothing brought them to climax. One preadolescent child had 26 orgasms in 24 hours; a scholarly and skilled attorney had averaged over 30 ejaculations a week for over 30 years.

Bankers, tramps, criminals, writers, diplomats, poets, pimps, editors, cowboys, teachers, cab drivers, literary agents, hospital orderlies, idle patricians — the responses of all of them were transcribed in code, filed, and later fed into IBM computers. As the completed interviews mounted into the thousands, Kinsey acquired a staff; university funding was supplemented by grants from the National Research Council and the Rockefeller Foundation. By the time the first volume on the human male reached the manuscript stage, Kinsey and his three chief interviewers had devoted forty manyears to the compilation of over 12,000 case histories. Now they were breaking down data on the human female. The first volume was scheduled to reach book counters in January 1948.

Americans since grown jaded by literature on mate swapping and the St. Louis laboratories of Masters and Johnson — where nurses and doctors' wives volunteered, in the name of science, for intercourse with total strangers — may find it hard to recapture the innocence of sex before Kinsey. Youths in their early teens held sotto voce discussions with other youths, spreading ignorance. Adults talked of it only to their spouses, and here too the blind were leading the blind. Kinsey interviewed thousands of married couples who said they had never experienced intercourse; gynecological examinations of the women confirmed them. One Kinsey investigator found 1,000 wives who were virgins and had no idea why their marriages had been childless. (Their husbands were equally perplexed.) For millions like them, the facts of life were mysteries as obscure as the interior of unexplored Brazil.

Apart from the dubious studies of Havelock Ellis — over a third of Ellis's patients reported that they had been seduced in their parents' homes by servants of the opposite sex, which suggests the narrowness of his social base — educated Americans lacked qualified guides. The rest of the population had no guides at all. Marriage manuals going back to Ovid's, in the first century of the Christian epoch, were flawed by error. In the absence of knowledge, superstition flourished. Boys believed that masturbation was a practice of degenerates; girls were told that "deep" or "French" kissing led to pregnancy and venereal disease. Because the sex drive is stronger than fear, onanism and mutual exploration by boys and girls continued — to be followed by paroxysms of remorse. What is perhaps hardest to grasp is the conviction of powerful social institutions that they had a sacred obligation to propagate these private terrors. Both church and secular leaders believed that only children scared stiff could be counted on to approach the altar as virgins. (How they would conquer their irrational fright in bed that first night was unmentioned and, like the rest of it, unmentionable.) Except for hurried and inept father/son, mother/daughter sessions, mature society went along with the incubi and the bogeys. The general feeling was rather like that of lodge brothers toward an initiate. They had been hazed; so must their offspring.

All this was predicated upon the assumption that the system worked — that boys who had been properly reared "saved themselves" for well-bred girls who had remained "pure" — hence white for brides — and that after marriage and until death they remained faithful to one another. Male homosexuals, usually called fairies or perverts, were considered indistinguishable from the criminally insane. Even among sophisticates such practices as pederasty, fellatio, cunnilingus, and sodomy with barnyard quadrupeds were presumed to exist only in fantasy and locker room jokes.

Then Kinsey told Americans this about themselves:

Eighty-five percent of all married men had engaged in sexual intercourse before marriage.

The average groom had experienced 1,500 orgasms before his wedding day.

Fifty percent of American husbands had committed adultery.

Fifty percent of American females "were nonvirgins, if single, or had been nonvirgins before marriage."

Two out of every three single women had engaged in premarital sex of some kind.

Ninety-five percent of all males were sexually active before their fifteenth birthday, and maximum activity occurred at sixteen or seventeen.

The average unmarried male had three or four orgasms a week.

One girl in every six had experienced orgasm before adolescence, and one in four by the age of fifteen.

By the age of forty, more than one wife in every four (26 percent, or over seven million) had committed adultery at least once. (In view of the tendency to conceal infidelity, Kinsey believed that the actual figures were much higher.) Adultery tended to increase as a marriage lengthened.

One male in every three, and one female in every seven, had some adolescent homosexual experience.

Ten percent of the male population was "more or less exclusively homosexual" for at least three years between the ages of sixteen and fifty-five.

Four percent (2,600,000) of American men were "exclusively homosexual throughout their lives, after the onset of adolescence."

Women who weren't virgins on their wedding day were twice as likely to commit adultery.

One in every six American farm boys had copulated with farm animals.

Nearly 70 percent of men had had relations with prostitutes by the age of thirty-five.

Among the thousands of interviewees were 2,094 single women who reported a total of 460,000 acts of sexual intercourse; 476 of them had become pregnant. To Kinsey's surprise, four out of five of the unmarried mothers expressed no regret.

Among American females, three out of every four nonvirgins did not regret their sexual experiences. The least regretful were those who had been the most promiscuous, the most regretful those who had had the least sex activity. Asked why they remained chaste, 22 percent of the virgins "frankly conceded lack of opportunity."

Nobody was neutral about the Kinsey Report. Sacks of mail descended upon the professor's office on the second floor of Bloomington's old Zoology Building. Kinsey became one of the first instant celebrities. His face, or something resembling it, appeared on the cover of *Time,* and to his horror strangers sought him out to reveal closely guarded secrets of their estral lives — secret to them, but to him repetitive accounts of acts practiced by millions. Late in the 1940s a teen-age sex club craze swept the country; girls were admitted to membership after coupling with a boy in the presence of the group and promising to engage in sexual congress at least once a week thereafter. When the wave reached Indiana, a reporter asked Kinsey to comment. In his matter-of-fact way — it was this, as much as anything, which offended those who held sex to be sacred — the zoologist pointed out that according to his studies there were 450,000 acts of fornication in Indiana every week. "And that," he said, "is why I don't get excited when the newspapers report three or four teen-agers having such experiences." On December 31, 1948, the *New York Times* reported that fake telephone calls from spurious Kinsey interviewers were harassing respectable matrons. After a year of Kinsey statistics people were beginning to wonder just what respectability was, and the issue was further clouded when the *Times* switchboard was jammed by female New Yorkers eager to be put in touch with *real* interviewers.

There was something peculiarly American about both the Kinsey project and its reception. "No other people has been so curious about itself," Clyde Kluckhohn observed, "nor so willing to subject itself to scientific analysis, nor so avid to read even the most sneering and superficial criticisms of outsiders. . . . More than anything else, the Kinsey studies testify to the continued vitality of a childlike trust in knowledge, particularly scientific knowledge, as an instrument for individual and social improvement." Within a generation it appeared that the country had come to regard the statistics as a challenge; if the new thing was to have bigger and better orgasms, the U.S. intended to be first. In 1970 the two best-selling titles on U.S. nonfiction lists told readers how to make themselves more sensual by extrapolating from Kinsey data. Indeed, by the late 1960s and early 1970s the children of Americans who had felt guilty about strong sex drives were becoming anxious if they weren't lusty enough. "America had no sooner got rid of being ashamed about sex," wrote Louis Kronenberger, "than it grew ashamed about the lack of it." In the Nixon years advocates of a vigorous new feminism waged a running battle with their critics over whether careers for women masculinized them or increased their sexual gratification. Both sides accepted Kinsey's figures as valid and, more significantly, both agreed that satisfied desire was important to the individual and even to society.

There, as elsewhere, the Truman and Nixon eras seem more than a generation apart. In 1972 the concept of chaperones, say, or the sight of men tipping their hats to approaching young women would seem as anachronistic as microskirts or four-letter words on the screen of your neighborhood theater would have been in 1948. It is singular to recall that when Norman Mailer published *The Naked and the Dead* that year, he could convey soldiers' profanity only by coining a new verb, to fug (fugging, fugger, motherfugger, etc.). In 1949 Joseph W. Gannon, the arbiter of what the *New York Times* saw fit to print in its advertising columns, revised, bowdlerized, or rejected 1,456 submissions, mostly because he considered them prurient. Gannon had a genius for the right word. He always cut it out. An ad publicizing lingerie as "naughty but nice" was altered to read "Paris-inspired — but so nice." A night club ad featuring "50 of the hottest girls this side of hell" emerged from Gannon's laundromat as "50 of the most alluring maidens this side of paradise." Curves were painted out of models in girdle displays, giving them an eerie, unisex appearance and raising the question of why they needed foundation garments at all, and the *Times* airbrushes dressed photographs of Sally Rand from clavicle to femur.

Those were desperate days for Sally. Bumping and grinding in Milwaukee, she was arrested for the nth time by a policewoman, Geraldine Sampson. Officer Sampson testified that the defendant had been appearing in a carnival sideshow without panties — "nude as could be." Indignantly Sally protested that she was stone broke; she didn't *have* any pants. Lacking a civil liberties lawyer to rescue her, she was convicted and shown to a cell. The cops took everything she had, including her woman's right to conceal her age. "I'm sorry, I just don't tell that," she demurred, but the bulls wangled it out of her anyhow, and then it was in all the papers. She was forty-six, a prophet before her time. On the West Coast a younger exhibitionist, who in 1946 had changed her name from Norma Jean Baker to Marilyn Monroe, was fired by Columbia Pictures in September 1948 after playing her first part. (Studio comments included "Can't act," "Voice like a tight squeak," "Utterly unsure of herself," and "Unable even to take refuge in her own insignificance.") But Norma Jean at liberty under the new name of Marilyn Monroe could make both ends meet by posing naked for girlie photographs, the most provocative of which was reproduced in vivid color on the tip of a best-selling condom.* That door was closed to Sally; in the world of commercial sex she was over the geriatric hill. Kinsey characteristically saw no difference between Sally and Marilyn, however. To him they were just two more digits to be fed into Bloomington's computers.

"All the standards are harum-scarum," Mark Sullivan complained after reading the Kinsey Report. "Children running the homes or the President of the United States barnstorming up and down the country — it's all the same dissolution of traditional, dependable ways." A Harvard graduate of '00, Sullivan didn't accept the New Deal, let alone Truman's Fair Deal. For men like him the postwar years were especially rough; it was a time of sharp breaks with the past and of accelerating change, that cruel solvent of custom.

The White House wasn't all that was falling down. The reputation of Brink's, banker to banks, was set back when a mob wearing Halloween masks heisted it for a million dollars in Boston. In a Jersey election, Frank Hague's once mighty machine was stripped of its gears by a reform slate. The medical profession was embarrassed when a New Hampshire physician was charged with the "mercy killing" of a doomed and suffering patient. (He was acquitted.) White supremacists were begining to suspect that the road ahead would be bumpy for them. When the limousine bearing Governor Strom Thurmond approached the reviewing stand in Truman's inaugural parade, the President found it necessary to turn his back and speak to someone behind him. Washington hotels trying to hang on to Jim Crow during the inauguration were bluntly told to integrate or face condemnation by the District's Commissioner of Housing. They integrated. In Okla-

*It was not advertised in the *New York Times*.

homa a court order — the first of thousands to come — directed the state university to admit a Negro woman student, and the Nobel Prize was awarded to an American diplomat named Ralph Bunche for negotiating an Arab-Israeli truce. When rednecks and wool-hats heard Bunche was black, they reached for their bottle of Hadacol.

Around the cracker barrels of northern New England, their Yankee counterparts grumbled about progress and its value, or lack of it. New York was building the largest airport in the world at Idlewild. Who for? California's Mount Palomar was completing the world's biggest telescope. To look at the moon? Everybody knew there was no future in that. The prevailing winds of style were setting weathervanes spinning. In Europe the guns had hardly cooled and already the Germans were exporting their first snub-nosed little Volkswagens, selling in the United States for $1,280. American women were reading *Flair,* a magazine with holes in it, and buying Tide, the first detergent, which began appearing on shelves in 1948. A lot of old-timers around a lot of country store barrels would have approved of anything that could scrub a youth named Eden Ahbez. Ahbez was the first hippie — or prehippie, if you like — and he surfaced in 1948: a shy, gentle vegetarian with shoulder-length hair and a full beard. He encapsulated his philosophy in a song, "Nature Boy." Nat King Cole made it the hit of the year:

> *There was a boy, a very strange, enchanted boy . . .*
> *A little sad and shy of eye.*
> *But very wise was he . . . This he said to me:*
> *"The greatest thing you'll ever learn*
> *Is just to love and be loved in return."*

In 1948 Allen Ginsberg was expelled by Columbia University for scribbling obscene anti-Semitic phrases on his dormitory window. The proud National Football League surprised everyone in the world of sport by deciding to merge with the All-America Football Conference. Frankie Sinatra suffered a massive throat hemorrhage; bobby-soxers drifted away to Perry Como and Frankie Laine. In *Down Beat* Stan Kenton nosed out Woody Herman as the country's number one jazz band, though some critics were beginning to wonder whether musical improvisation, like the swing generation itself, wasn't déjà vu; after touring Greenwich Village, Mary McCarthy gave the back of her tongue to "middle-aged jazz musicians in double-breasted suits trumpeting in a whisky transfiguration for middle-aged jazz aficionados, also in double-breasted suits."

Looking back over the first half of the twentieth century, Bruce Bliven was struck by "the alteration in the moral climate from one of overwhelming optimism to one which comes pretty close to despair." He noted that "during the first forty years of the century" there had been "a steady drift away from a sense of identification with the faiths for which the churches stood." Bliven was looking in the wrong places. God, or someone like Him, had leaped over the altar rail and hit the sawdust trail. In 1949 His presence was identified in the vicinity of a mammoth tent erected in Los Angeles by a thirty-year-old North Carolina evangelist named William Franklin Graham — "Billy" to the chosen. That year Billy Graham drew over 300,000 Californians to his canvas shrine and converted 6,000 of them, including a crooner, a cowboy, a racketeer, and a professional athlete.

On July 4, 1946, the Philippines had become a sovereign nation. The British raj had then withdrawn from India and Burma, and in 1949 the Dutch reluctantly granted independence to Indonesia. Colonialism, another prewar institution, was withering away. The United States approved of the demise; in the light of its own origins, it could hardly have done otherwise. But older Americans who found comfort in the familiar were losing one more well-worn bench mark, and they felt uneasy. Apart from the tension crackling between Blair House and the Kremlin — which was unsettling enough — lesser stories on foreign affairs were puzzling or disturbing. Most stories about Nazi crimes had become boring. Closer to home, a cabal of Puerto Rican fanatics tried to assassinate the President in Blair House. The plot failed in spite of Harry Truman, who kept running around trying to get a better view of what was going on. Then the country relaxed; men remembered that with the incomparable Secret Service in charge, no one could kill a President.

Most Americans learned of such events from radio. The number of people who had seen a television screen was still smaller than those who had heard about it, though some popular radio programs, such as *Major Bowes Amateur Hour* and *Town Meeting of the Air*, had gone over to the tube. TV certainly needed them. Its seven-inch peepholes had been succeeded by twelve-inch and even fourteen-inch screens, and there was less of what was called "snow" in the pictures, but what the audiences were looking at was hardly worth watching. First there were the wrestlers, notably Gorgeous George, whose appearance in the ring was usually preceded by that of his valet, a small man wearing a tailcoat and bearing on a silver tray a monogrammed "GG" towel, a prayer rug, and various spray guns and atomizers, to spare his employer the stench of his competitor's sweat. At the outset there was always a bit of contrived suspense over which outfit George would wear. ("He's going to be in chartreuse tonight, folks! Correction, it'll be cherry red!") GG had 88 satin costumes and a weakness for ermine jockstraps. Describing a Georgeous George entrance for *Sport* in 1949, Hannibal Coons wrote:

> Knotted loosely at his throat is a scarf of salmon-colored silk. His hair, a mass of golden ringlets, looks as though he has just spent four hours in a beauty parlor. George makes the grand entrance, sneering at the peons. Slowly and calmly he removes his Georgie pins — gold-plated and sequined bobby pins — and casts them to the crowd. And shakes his hair like a lordly spaniel.

After the wrestlers came the lady wrestlers. They were worse, if that is possible — great hulking earth bitches with breasts like half-loaded gunnysacks and pubic hair dangling down their thighs. They always seemed to have cut themselves shaving. One of their pet tricks was to pin the referee beneath them until he shrieked for mercy; their fans loved that. After the network producers had more than even they could stomach, the girls were sent back to wherever they had come from, and the gaps between baseball games and prizefights were filled with Leo Selzer's Roller Derby. The Derby was almost indescribable. Shapely hoydens were outfitted in hockey uniforms, crash helmets and roller skates and sent spinning around an old marathon dance ring, crashing into one another, clawing at each other, swearing, bleeding, crying, and, yes, pinioning the ref beneath and belting him with their steel rollers. It was thought to be merry. Families gathered round their sets couldn't get enough of it. One of the skaters, Gerry Murray, had almost as many followers as Gorgeous George. Sportswriters were too squeamish to approve either of them. In 1949, when GG was at his peak and earning $70,000 a year, Red Smith raged in the *New York Herald Tribune*: "Groucho Marx is prettier, Sonny Tufts a more gifted actor, Connie Mack a better rassler, and the Princeton Triangle Club has far better female impersonators." After watching Gerry and her fellow gamines mix it up, John Lardner wrote, "The Roller Derby is a sport. Defenestration is also a sport, for those who like it."

Along the Atlantic seaboard television viewers, or "gawks," as Mencken called them, were fewest per thousand inhabitants in the District of Columbia, probably because there was so much else going on there. Washington society had by now acquired a style appropriate to the seat of a great power. Georgetown was being restored; Cleveland Park had a new elegance. Chefs from benighted Europe were establishing their reputations in the huge embassies on or just off Massachusetts Avenue. In the Virginia and Maryland suburbs of Alexandria, Arlington, Bethesda, and Chevy Chase, Friday cocktail parties were the chief adult sport. Republicans were rarely seen. In the grander affairs liberal Democrats set the tone, as they had for sixteen years.

Aside from shoptalk, cocktail and dinner party conversations in Greater Washington didn't vary much from those on the outer rims of other American metropolitan areas. In Pawling or Chestnut Hill more of the guests would know the finer points of expense account living; more would be aware that the Dow had broken through the 225 barrier and that General Motors would pay $444,377,889 in taxes this year. Here on Washington's Macomb Street, say, or Kalorama Circle, men would have a more detailed knowledge of the status of bills in committee, and women would be likelier to rhapsodize about the marvelous job young Telford Taylor was doing in Nuremberg. But until the end of the decade had all but arrived, the enthusiasms of other well-to-do communities in the 1940s were shared by educated Washingtonians. Everyone was amused, for example, by Russell

Lynes's clever stratification of Americans into highbrows, lowbrows and middlebrows in the February 1949 *Harper's* — the beginning of a whimsical parlor game that sociologists would later take up with high seriousness. Adventure stirred in the blood of male Martini drinkers marveling over the exploit of a Norwegian anthropologist who had crossed the Pacific in 101 days on a raft. Women, wearing the same mid-calf skirts to be seen in Sutton Place or Dallas's Highland Park, might tick off the latest list of eligible bachelors, with multimillionaire Congressman John F. Kennedy near the top. (Jacqueline Bouvier was a temporary expatriate; she had dropped out of Vassar the year before to study at the Sorbonne.)

The cinema continued to be the most widely discussed form of entertainment. In its Indian summer the silver screen was showing some of its finest films: Joseph L. Mankiewicz's *All About Eve* (Bette Davis, George Sanders, Anne Baxter); Harry Cohn's *Born Yesterday* (Judy Holliday, Broderick Crawford); Carol Reed's *The Third Man* (Orson Welles, Joseph Cotten, Trevor Howard); *Twelve O'Clock High* (Gregory Peck); *Sunset Boulevard* (Gloria Swanson); *Father of the Bride* (Spencer Tracy, Elizabeth Taylor); MGM's $3,200,000 musical *Annie Get Your Gun* (Betty Hutton), and Roberto Rossellini's *Stromboli*, which would be picketed by Catholic groups because Ingrid Bergman, Rossellini's star, had proudly borne his illegitimate son.

To put coming events in greater perspective: *South Pacific* was just beginning its four-year run (1,694 performances) in those last months of the 1940s. In New Haven, Ethel Merman was learning to bellow *Call Me Madam*. T. S. Eliot's *The Cocktail Party*, Carson McCullers's *The Member of the Wedding*, and William Inge's *Come Back, Little Sheba* were running well. The best musical play of the year was Gian-Carlo Menotti's *The Consul*. Critics were panning Ernest Hemingway's *Across the River and Into the Trees* — one wag called it "Across the Ribs and Between the Knees." Hemingway himself was about to become the victim of a vicious Lillian Ross profile in the *New Yorker*. In London, George Orwell lay desperately ill. His reputation had finally been established the year before with *1984*; now admirers were discovering his earlier achievements: *Down and Out in Paris and London*, *Burmese Days*, and *Coming Up for Air*. Orwell, supremely a figure of the 1940s, would breathe his last in the first month of the new decade.

It is of some interest that two memorable hits then in rehearsal were about witches — Christopher Fry's *The Lady's Not for Burning* and John Van Druten's *Bell, Book and Candle* — for the United States was about to enter upon the greatest witch-hunt in its history. And ironies were not confined to Broadway. It was in 1949 that Tin Pan Alley churned out a catchy tune called "I'd Like to Getcha on a Slow Boat to China." No sooner had it displaced Huddie Ledbetter's "Goodnight, Irene" on *Your Hit Parade* than the blow fell. Owing to certain events on the mainland of Asia, the country learned, no Americans were going to China for a long time. Not

to put too fine a point on it, the United States had suffered the worst diplomatic defeat in its two centuries. Like the rest of the capital, Washington
hostesses had known that the debacle was imminent. Not even they could
have guessed the savagery of the coming recriminations, but there was a
distinctly brittle quality to social functions in that first full year of Truman's second administration. Something big was coming, it was in the air;
there was no place for men to hide; soon the pall of the great suspicion
would fall across the city.

On April 4, 1949, the day the NATO alliance was signed in the new
State Department auditorium under the approving eye of Dean Acheson,
a Communist general named Chu Teh began massing a million of Mao
Tse-tung's seasoned troops on the north bank of the Yangtze, the last
natural barrier between Mao and the few southern provinces still loyal to
Chiang Kai-shek's Nationalist Chinese, or Kuomintang (KMT). Chu Teh's
veterans stormed across the Yangtze on April 24, meeting only token resistance; Chiang had withdrawn 300,000 of his most reliable soldiers to
form a rear-guard perimeter around Shanghai. In the first week of May
Chu Teh was hammering at the gates of Shanghai, and Chiang fled across
the Formosa Strait to Taiwan, taking as many Nationalist Chinese as he
could. By now China was as good as lost to him. A few formalities remained: on June 26 KMT gunboats began blockading the ports of mainland China; Mao proclaimed Red China's sovereignty on September 21 —
the same day as West Germany's proclamation of sovereignty — and on
December 8 Chiang announced the formation of his new government in
Taipei. The world now had two Chinas. Sun Yat-sen's fifty-year-old vision
of a democratic China was dead, and Franklin Roosevelt's expectation that
Chiang would provide the non-Communist world's eastern anchor had died
with it.

The American response was slow. Troops had been fighting in China
under one flag or another since September of 1931. U.S. newspapers had
carried regular accounts of Chinese Communist offenses and the progressive disintegration of Chiang's KMT since V-J Day. But China was so vast,
its geography so unfamiliar, and the movements of its unmechanized
armies so slow, that Americans had lost interest in the distant battles. They
knew of Chiang, of course, and from time to time newspapers had carried
photographs of Mao, sleek and guileful, stripped to the waist for summer
marches and always chain-smoking or chewing melon seeds. But the conflict had been too complicated and too far away for the general reader. If
developments became important, he had reasoned, his government would
tell him about them.

It did. With the collapse of the Kuomintang, Acheson decided to lay the
whole story before the people. On August 5, 1949, the State Department
issued a 1,054-page White Paper conceding that the world's largest nation
had fallen into Communist hands, announcing the cessation of aid to Na-

tionalist China, and setting forth the chain of events which had led to this tragic end. Three American generals — Stilwell, Hurley, and Marshall — had tried in vain to persuade Chiang to break the power of his KMT warlords and rid the Nationalist Army of corruption and defeatism. Over two billion dollars of U.S. aid had come to Chiang since V-J Day. Virtually all of it had been a waste of powder and shot; 75 percent of the American arms shipped to the KMT had wound up in Mao's hands. In his introduction to the White Paper, Acheson bluntly called Chiang's regime incompetent, corrupt, and insensitive to the needs of its people. He added:

> The unfortunate but inescapable fact is that the ominous result of the civil war in China was beyond the control of the government of the United States. Nothing that this country did or could have done within the reasonable limits of its capabilities could have changed that result. . . . It was the product of internal Chinese forces, forces which this country tried to influence but could not.

To knowledgeable Washingtonians this was apparent, even superfluous. But the U.S. public was bewildered. All this talk of KMT inefficiency was a switch. The China it knew — Pearl Buck's peasants, rejoicing in the good earth — had been dependable, democratic, warm, and above all pro-American. Throughout the great war the United Nations Big Four had been Churchill, Roosevelt, Stalin, and Chiang. Stalin's later treachery had been deplorable but unsurprising. But Chiang Kai-shek! Acheson's strategy to contain Red aggression seemed to have burst wide open. His own White Paper admitted that Mao's regime might "lend itself to the aims of Soviet Russian imperialism." Everything American diplomats had achieved in Europe — the Truman Doctrine, the Marshall Plan, NATO — momentarily seemed annulled by this disaster in Asia.

Nor was that all. In late August, while editorial writers were still digesting the White Paper and the last daring Chinese Nationalists were sailing in junks from mainland ports to Taiwan, a B-29 flying laboratory returned from an Asian flight with dismaying photographs. The B-29's mission had been to gather stress routine. Its pictures were expected to interest only low-level technicians. When developed, however, they revealed clear traces of radioactive material. There could be but one explanation: an atomic explosion somewhere in Russia. This was a massive jolt; Americans had been told that the Soviet Union could not develop a nuclear weapon before the late 1950s, if ever. Told the news, President Truman shook his head again and again, asking, "Are you sure? Are you *sure?*" Then, convinced, he said heavily, "This means we have no time left."

He waited three weeks before telling the public. On September 23 he authorized the release of a terse statement: "We have evidence an atomic explosion occurred in the USSR." When they were handed copies of it, White House correspondents raced to their phones. After they had gone, the President lay low, anticipating an angry public reaction. His cabinet also made itself scarce, with one notable exception. Acheson was beginning to suspect that Secretary of Defense Louis Johnson was afflicted by mental illness, and Johnson's behavior that Friday seemed probative. He made himself available to the press, discussed troop dispositions, and said lightly of the Russian bomb, "Now, let's keep calm about this. Don't overplay the story." Most responsible editors, worried about the possibility of mass hysteria, were already trying to understate the announcement, but there was no way to soften the blow. In Chicago physicist Harold C. Urey told reporters he felt "flattened." He said: "There is only one thing worse than one nation having the atomic bomb — that's two nations having it."

Now the administration began to pay for the President's campaign excesses the year before. Then the Republicans had nominated a gentleman who had been beaten by a slugger. Studying campaign stories from small newspapers through whose towns Truman had passed, they had discovered after November 2 how savage he had really been. They were going to flay this administration any way they could, and the Asian crisis and the loss of America's nuclear monopoly were gut issues. Increasingly one heard from the Republican side of the Senate floor that the administration had "lost" China — that the responsibility for Chiang's defeat lay in Washington, among traitors who had cunningly worked with other Communists abroad to bring Mao to power. It was all a Red conspiracy, the litany ran, and it all began when Roosevelt went to Yalta.

For hard-core anti-Communist vigilantes, the conspiracy went back even farther. The issue of Communists in the government predated the war and had a faithful constituency; the House Committee on Un-American Activities had been consistently high in Gallup polls since its inception. To be sure, there was considerable disagreement over what a Communist was. To some it meant Soviet spies, to others it signified dues-paying members of the Communist Party of America, and to countless implacable adversaries of Franklin Roosevelt and everything he represented, Communism was a vague term embracing all advocates of social change.

No one quarreled over the first definition. Russian espionage would clearly constitute a threat to national security. On that point Americans were united, and any fuzzing of the definition served only to fragment that unity. Yet hazier interpretations of Communism had become the meat upon which ultraconservatives fed.* To them, anyone who had altered the world they had known in their youth was suspect. If they could pin a Red label on one New Dealer and make it stick, they felt, they would discredit everything left of center in one stroke.

The rise of the loyalty issue began in the last months of the war. Like almost everything else the Committee on Un-American Activities tackled, the case of *Amerasia*, a reputable scholarly journal, turned into a hopeless

---

*In postwar America the terms "ultraconservatism" and "the right" have become as irrelevant to traditional conservatism as the New Left is to prewar liberalism and radicalism. All are in revolt against the world as it is. Any attempt to rechristen them here would merely compound the confusion. Therefore here, as elsewhere, the author has reluctantly adopted the usage of the time.

muddle. Early in 1945 a research analyst for the Office of Strategic Services (OSS), while riffling through the January 26 issue of the magazine, discovered that one article contained information from a restricted OSS report, some of it quoted verbatim. There was nothing sinister in that. Like so many governmental agencies, the OSS routinely stamped "Confidential" on virtually every document, including, in this case, an innocuous briefing which the State Department had earlier made available to American foreign correspondents in China. Despite this, a heavy-handed OSS officer raided *Amerasia*'s office and found other "confidential" information: reports on rice yields in selected provinces, water tables, livestock populations. The Justice Department's prosecution fell apart when a grand jury refused to indict anyone. But the *Amerasia* case would never be forgotten by those who had pressed it. The charge of treason had been raised, and the fact that the topic of the classified data had been China would later seem portentous.

The "do-nothing" 80th Congress had hurt the Democrats more than anyone realized at the time. After capturing control of the Hill, the Republican leadership had projected no fewer than thirty-five major loyalty investigations. Uneasy over the *Amerasia* uproar, Truman named a commission in late 1946 to study possible threats to internal security, and on March 21, 1947, acting upon its recommendation, he issued Executive Order 9835 establishing a Federal Employee Loyalty Program. Nevertheless the din continued. Reluctantly, and ill-advisedly, the State Department permitted a team of congressional investigators, led by a Republican and an anti-Communist vigilante with the engaging name of Robert E. Lee, to examine its loyalty files. Lee left carrying information on 108 past, present, and prospective State Department employees. The files were completely unscreened. They included allegations, unconfirmed statements, malicious gossip, and data which had later been proved to be false. Some sources weren't even identified. Other material reflected the biases of Lee's team; the American Civil Liberties Union was listed as a Communist front, and a labor leader was identified as a Communist on the strength of a charge from a manufacturer whose plant he had struck. After a long lull another congressional team asked State to bring the Lee list up to date. The department replied that of the original 108, only 57 were still employed. With that, the list and its accompanying folders went back on a shelf to collect dust. But the figure 57 would be heard again.

Early in 1948 yet another House committee demanded the federal record of Dr. Edward U. Condon, the director of the National Bureau of Standards. Learning that Condon had become the victim of a whispering campaign, Truman declared that he was fed up with Republican fishing expeditions. On March 13 he directed all government offices to keep personnel files in strictest confidence; any congressional requests or subpoenas for them were to be rejected. The President's position had become intolerable — isolated passages in the files, wrenched from context, were implicating the administration as a helpless accomplice in slander — but his directive solved nothing. Freed from the hazard that official records might contradict them, the vigilantes merely stepped up their recklessness; Nixon of California, for example, flatly stated that Democrats were responsible for "the unimpeded growth of the Communist conspiracy in the United States." The Democratic leadership heatedly denied it, though some of their backbenchers chimed in with the opposition. On February 21 Congressman John F. Kennedy of Massachusetts said that at Yalta a "sick" Roosevelt, on the advice of General Marshall and other chiefs of staff, "gave" the Kuriles and other strategic places to the USSR. The administration had tried to force Chiang into a coalition with Mao, he said. President Truman had even treated Madame Chiang with "indifference," if not "contempt." The State Department had squandered America's wartime gains by listening to such advisers as Owen Lattimore of Johns Hopkins University. "This," Kennedy concluded, "is the tragic story of China, whose freedom we once fought to preserve. What our young men saved, our diplomats and our President have frittered away."

The fact that Kennedy briefly found common cause with the vigilantes has long been forgotten, possibly because of his later career. Others in the China debate had become more inflammatory. As early as October 1947 William C. Bullitt, ex-ambassador to France and a zealous vigilante, had published a "Report on China" in Life charging that Washington bureaucrats were shackling Chiang by withholding arms from him. The Luce publications were vehement on the issue; Henry Luce had been born in China's Shantung province, the son of a missionary, and he had become a key figure in what was beginning to be called the "China Lobby" — men whose commitment to the Kuomintang was so great that it seemed to preclude all else, including their allegiance to the United States. The September 6, 1948, issue of Life declared that Yalta had been the "high tide" of appeasement. After that the level of rhetoric descended rapidly. Republicans began referring to their congressional adversaries as members of "the party of treason" — a slur that Rayburn attributed to Nixon, and never forgave. Mundt of South Dakota demanded that the President "ferret out" those on the federal payroll "whose Soviet leanings have contributed so greatly to the deplorable mess of our foreign policy."* Congressman Harold Velde of Illinois announced that Soviet spies were "infesting the entire country," like gypsy moths; Congressman Robert Rich of Pennsylvania charged that Dean Acheson was on Joseph Stalin's payroll. To Jenner of Indiana, every American whose advice to Chiang Kai-shek had failed to stanch the Red tide was, almost by definition, a criminal. Jenner called General Marshall "a front man for traitors," a "living lie" who had joined

---

*The Communist issue was acquiring an idiom all its own. "Enemies of the Free World" were to be "ferreted out" despite "commiecrats" who "coddled" security risks and were "soft" on "fellow travelers." As Robert Griffith of the University of Georgia has pointed out, long before the rise of McCarthy, Congressman Eugene Cox of Georgia — among others — had begun a speech on subversion with the solemn declaration, "I hold in my hand . . ."

hands "with this criminal crowd of traitors and Communist appeasers who, under the continuing influence of Mr. Truman and Mr. Acheson, are still selling America down the river."

Each excess seemed to surpass the last. Democrats on the Hill thought the opposition touched bottom in December 1949, when Republicans in both houses of Congress overwhelmingly resolved that the Secretary of State had lost the confidence of the country, could not regain it, and should be fired by the President. Eventually this singular resolution reached the desk of Harry Truman, who promptly ripped it in half. But that wasn't the bottom. They hadn't even begun to see the bottom.

The liberal community regarded Republican vigilantes as stage heavies. Certainly some of them were behaving as though they had not only been cast as villains but were enjoying every minute of it. On a typical afternoon spectators might enter the Senate visitors' gallery to hear the administration denounced as one of "egg-sucking phony liberals" whose "pitiful squealing" would "hold sacrosanct those Communists and queers" who had "sold China into atheistic slavery." The ripest phrases were reserved for those "prancing mimics of the Moscow party line in the State Department" who were "spewing the Kremlin's malignant smear" while "the Red Dean" (Acheson) "whined" and "whimpered" and "cringed" as he "slobbered over the shoes of his Muscovite masters." There were times when correspondents wondered whether anti-American polemics in the Soviet Politburo could possibly be as scathing as those heard under the Capitol dome.

Occasionally the voice of reason was heard on the Hill, most memorably when a Joint Congressional Committee was pondering the nomination of David E. Lilienthal, a distinguished public servant, for the chairmanship of the Atomic Energy Commission. Senator Kenneth D. McKellar of Tennessee, a Democratic vigilante, insisted that Lilienthal had harbored Communists in the TVA. Did he, McKellar asked Lilienthal, carry in his head a blueprint for Soviet revolution? The witness replied in part:

> This I *do* carry in my head, Senator. . . . One of the tenets of democracy . . . is a . . . repugnance to anyone who would steal from a human being that which is most precious to him — his good name — either by imputing things to him by innuendo or by insinuation. And it is especially an unhappy circumstance that occasionally that is done in the name of democracy. This, I think, can tear our country apart and destroy it if we carry it further. . . . This I deeply believe.

Such moments were rare, and apart from heartening men of good will, they achieved almost nothing. The Lilienthals of America erred in assuming that fear of internal subversion could be resolved by evidence and reason. It couldn't; otherwise there would have been no crisis in the first place. The anti-Communist terror was pathological. It would have to run its course before the delirium could end. In the meantime it would be a savage force in the hands of men who had fathomed how to use it. Senator Taft understood it. He knew precisely what he and his fellow Republicans were doing, and he knew why. After a vigilante exercise in verbal overkill ("The greatest Kremlin asset in our history has been the pro-Communist group in the State Department who promoted at every opportunity the Communist cause in China") Taft cut close to the bone when he told reporters: "The only way to get rid of Communists in the State Department is to change the head of government." In other words, he was warming up for 1952, when the people would have an opportunity to choose a new President, hopefully Robert A. Taft. Tom Coleman, the Republican boss in Wisconsin and a Taft supporter, was more explicit. "It all comes down to this," he said. "Are we going to try to win an election or aren't we?"

But Democrats liked to win, too. Harry Truman was well aware that the stain of suspicion was spreading. Moreover, other issues were at stake for him. The Republicans were hunting witches, but the NKVD had been running real agents from Moscow, and the country's chief executive was responsible for its internal security. Truman's first inkling that the NKVD was at large in North America had come shortly after that evening in September 1945 when a Russian cipher clerk named Igor Gouzenko, stationed in the Soviet embassy at Ottawa on the staff of the military attaché, snatched up an armful of incriminating documents — all he could carry — and staggered out into the night and political asylum. The Canadians established a commission to investigate the Gouzenko papers. It uncovered a widespread apparatus of English and Canadian citizens whose trail ultimately led to two British physicists with Most Secret clearance: Dr. Alan Nunn May and Dr. Klaus Fuchs. The net comprised dedicated Communists and participants in a scheme, which had been largely successful, to pry loose atomic and other defense secrets Washington had shared with its Canadian allies.

At first the President appears to have been slow in grasping the implications of the Ottawa ring. The following February J. Edgar Hoover sent Truman confessions from Communist agents Elizabeth Bentley, a former employee in the Italian Library of Information in New York, and Whittaker Chambers. The Bentley and Chambers cases hardly qualified as FBI exploits. It was now seven years since Chambers had first tried to find someone in the government who would take him seriously, and when Miss Bentley first tried to turn herself in at the FBI's New Haven office, she had been ignored; agents believed her only after seeing a Soviet operative slip her two thousand dollars in a sidewalk stakeout. She and Chambers were strangers to one another, but they had this in common: their statements were sufficiently fantastic to raise questions about their sanity. Miss Bentley, a middle-aged Vassar graduate, declared that for five years she had served as a Soviet courier, picking up highly classified documents in Washington and turning them over to her Russian contact in New York. Among thirty-odd former government employees she accused of treachery were Lauchlin

Currie, who had served as special assistant to President Roosevelt from 1939 to 1945, headed two missions to China, and now headed a Park Avenue import-export firm; Harry Dexter White, a former Assistant Secretary of the Treasury and the current executive director of the International Monetary Fund; and William W. Remington, a handsome young Dartmouth graduate who had become a rising star in the Department of Commerce. Chambers identified nine of the brighter lights in the Roosevelt administration as Communist party members, notably Alger Hiss, who was about to leave the State Department to become president of the Carnegie Endowment for International Peace.

Like others who had heard them out, Truman was skeptical. The Canadian ring had shaken him, however, and in that autumn's off-year election several GOP congressional candidates had used fallout from the *Amerasia* case to raise doubts about the administration. In response, on December 4 Attorney General Tom C. Clark made public a list of ninety organizations which in the opinion of the Justice Department were Communist fronts. Throughout the following year the list was repeatedly expanded — on one day, May 27, 1948, thirty-two additions were made. Suspicion fell upon everyone who had ever belonged to, say, the Anti-Fascist Refugee Committee, even though its original purpose had been confined to contributing food and medicine to America's Russian ally. Civil servants who had thus "followed the party line" were dismissed. In the vernacular of the time, they had been found to be "bad security risks."

At the time, the Truman administration's most spectacular contribution to vigilantism seemed to be its invocation of the Smith Act of 1940 to try eleven leaders of the Communist Party of America. The real terror seldom reached newsprint, however, because it was so ordinary, like being jobless in 1932. Apart from its other outrages, Executive Order 9835 encouraged Americans to snoop on colleagues, friends, neighbors, and even relatives. Furthermore, the loyalty program was an administrative monstrosity. On May 22, 1947, the FBI began stalking "disloyal and subversive persons" by conducting a "name check" of the two million people on federal payrolls, from mailmen to cabinet members. In addition, the bureau was answerable for disloyalty among the five hundred thousand annual applicants for government jobs. "Derogatory information" about an individual brought a "full field investigation" into his past, sometimes all the way back to childhood, with agents interrogating those who remembered him, or thought they remembered him, about his habits, associates, and convictions. Accumulated data were weighed by a regional loyalty board which could either dismiss charges or hold a hearing and reach a verdict. Adverse decisions could be appealed to a National Loyalty Review Board in Washington, whose rulings were final.

On what grounds could a good and faithful letter carrier, say, be fired? Pink slips went to those who had committed treason, engaged in espionage, advocated violent overthrow of the government (already forbidden by the

Hatch Act), disclosed official confidences, or belonged to an association which the attorney general defined as subversive. Proof that a man had engaged in any of these activities need not be absolute; "reasonable grounds for belief" of subversion was enough. The ground rules for hearings were Kafkaesque. Charges were to be stated "specifically and completely" only if, in the judgment of the employing department, "security considerations permit." If not, the accused wasn't even told how or where he was said to have slipped. He might have learned of it if he had been granted the time-honored right to confront his accuser, but this, too, was denied him. FBI policy held that identification of informants would hamper future investigations, thus jeopardizing national security. Similarly, the attorney general's list of proscribed organizations, which had been drawn up by the FBI, was above challenge. The groups on it were not allowed to argue their innocence. If a civil servant had held membership in one of them — or, in many cases, if he merely *knew* someone who belonged — he was given notice. Guilt was, quite literally, by association.

Those victims who were privileged to know why they were being fired received a form which began, "The evidence indicates that," and continued with such accusations as these, taken from files of the time:

> Since 1943 you have been a close associate of ———, an individual who, evidence in our files indicates, has displayed an active, sympathetic interest in the principles and policies of the Communist Party.

> Your name appeared in an article in the 4 April 1946 edition of the *York Gazette and Daily* as a sponsor of a Philadelphia, Pa. mass meeting . . . sponsored by the National Committee to Win the Peace. The National Committee to Win the Peace has been cited by the Attorney General as Communist.

> During your period of employment by Williams College, in Williamstown, Mass., you made statements to the effect that you believed "the House Committee on Un-American Activities hearings in Washington, D.C. are a greater threat to civil liberties than the Communist Party because they infringe upon free speech. . . ."

> Your name appeared among the signers of an open letter . . . of the National Federation for Constitutional Liberties dated 28 December 1941 and urging speedier shipments of arms to the Union of Soviet Socialist Republics. The National Federation for Constitutional Liberties has been cited by the Attorney General as Communist.

The form would conclude with a formal notice of dismissal: "The foregoing information indicates that you have been and are a member, close affiliate, or sympathetic associate of the Communist Party." The luckless ex-employee had been cashiered by a court which "could proceed on mere rumor" — Webster's definition of a star chamber. The mere opening of the full field investigation was often enough to humiliate a man and shame his family. Guilty in the eyes of many until innocence had been proven, he became suspect the day his loyalty check began. Neighbors questioned by security officers cut him on the street, ignored invitations from his wife, and forbade their children to play with his. His sons might be barred from the Cub Scouts. He couldn't even call upon civil service friends without putting them, too, in the shadow of the ax. In the end he had to fall back upon his savings, if any, and his family.

In June of 1949 former Attorney General Clark, now a member of the Supreme Court, remarked that "never before" had the morale of federal officials been so high, "thanks to the Loyalty Order." It is hard to imagine what had made him think so. Nearly every other lawyer in the country knew that the program had made a sham of due process. Tom Paine's proud boast that the New World had become "the asylum for the persecuted lovers of civil and religious liberty from every part of Europe" mocked his memory. The most popular book in Washington was Bert Andrews's *Washington Witch Hunt,* a recital, by the respected chief of the *Herald Tribune's* Washington Bureau, of the loyalty program's more flagrant injustices. John Lord O'Brian, writing in the *Harvard Law Review* of April 1948, had pointed out that the effect of an assertion of guilt by association was "analogous to that of a criminal conviction — loss of occupation, lasting disgrace, and a continued impairment of . . . ability to earn a livelihood." Already the program had cost twelve million dollars, and among the more diverting cases awaiting appeal was that of a man who had been dismissed for deserting the Army during World War I, when he was nine years old.

Those who trusted the National Loyalty Review Board to set things straight were grasping at a frail reed. In President Truman's memoirs he identifies Seth Richardson, the board's chairman, as "a prominent conservative Republican" who "worked in close contact with the Department of Justice." Doubtless the Richardson appointment was good politics — he had been a protégé of Harding and Coolidge — but it led to wretched equity. In his late sixties, the appeals chairman was best known in the capital as counsel for the American Medical Association and the Pullman Corporation. He was an American Legionnaire, an Elk, and a member of the Metropolitan, Burning Tree, and Chevy Chase clubs — exactly the sort of establishmentarian who defined loyalty negatively, as something which was not un-American, and who confused patriotism with orthodoxy.

Sometimes a single incident may illumine an entire era. The appeal of Dorothy Bailey sheds considerable light on this one. A graduate of Bryn Mawr and the University of Minnesota, Miss Bailey was forty-one in the spring of 1948. She had worked at the United States Employment Service for fourteen years and was regarded as an exemplary employee; her only public activity was in the United Public Workers of America, an organization not cited by the attorney general. Miss Bailey was president of her UPWA local, which may have inspired jealous gossip, though she had no known enemies. On the strength of unsupported charges that she was, or had been, a Communist and had "associated with known Communist Party members," she had been haled before the District of Columbia's regional loyalty board. The prosecution presented no evidence. No witnesses testified against her. She categorically denied the reports, presented several character witnesses — and was sacked anyway.

During Miss Bailey's appearance before Seth Richardson's review board, Paul Porter, her attorney, suggested that she may have been prey for hidden spite. The chairman answered that "five or six of the reports came from informants certified to us by the Federal Bureau of Investigation as experienced and entirely reliable." Pressed by Porter, Richardson refused to identify the sources. He then added that he couldn't if he wished to, because "I haven't the slightest knowledge as to who they are or how active they have been in anything." One of Richardson's fellow board members noted a damning phrase in the dossier, and this exchange followed:

BOARD MEMBER: Then another one says it first came to the informant's attention about 1936, at which time [you were] a known member of the so-called "closed group" of the Communist Party operating in the District of Columbia.

MISS BAILEY: First of all, I didn't know, or don't know, that there is a "closed group." The terminology is unfamiliar to me. I can say under oath and with the strongest conviction that I was not then and have never been a member of the Communist Party.

BOARD MEMBER: Here is another that says you were a member of the Communist Party, and he bases his statement on his knowledge of your association with known Communists for the past seven or eight years. That is part of the evidence that was submitted to us.

MR. PORTER: It is part of the allegations. I don't think that can be considered evidence.

CHAIRMAN RICHARDSON: It is evidence.

MR. PORTER: We renew our request, although we recognize the futility of it, that some identification of this malicious gossip be given this respondent or her counsel.

CHAIRMAN RICHARDSON: Of course, that doesn't help us a bit. If this testimony is true, it is neither gossip or [sic] malicious. We are under the difficulty of not being able to disclose this.

MR. PORTER: Is it under oath?

CHAIRMAN RICHARDSON: I don't think so.

BOARD MEMBER: It is a person of known responsibility who had proffered information concerning Communist activity in the District of Columbia.

MISS BAILEY: You see, that point in it worries me, because if I am convicted here that will make this person who has made these charges considered a reliable witness; and they are not, because the charges are not true, and whatever is said here should not add to their reliability.

Her appeal was denied. Reminded that the board's procedures were in flagrant contempt of constitutional guarantees, Richardson took refuge in the meaningless cliché that government service is "a privilege, not a right."

He then glanced at his agenda, pored over the next batch of unsigned accusations, and began conferring with his colleagues. That was justice under the vigilantes.

Seldom in the long history of bureaucracy has there been such a waste of time and paper. Even in Richardson's kangaroo court, with every conceivable card stacked against the pleader, such a conviction as Miss Bailey's was rare. During the loyalty program's five years the FBI screened over 3,000,000 Americans and conducted 10,000 full field investigations. Preliminary indictments were filed against 9,077, of whom 2,961 were arraigned before regional boards and 378 were given notice. Asked to sum up his findings for a congressional committee, Richardson said: "Not one single case or evidence directing toward a case of espionage has been disclosed in the record. Not one single syllable of evidence has been found by the FBI indicating that a particular case involves a question of espionage."

"A specter is haunting Europe," Marx and Engels had written in 1848 — "the specter of Communism." Now in the centennial of their Communist Manifesto the shadow of the same apparition had fallen across the United States. It seldom made sense. Richardson, for example, had been boasting to the congressmen: no spies had been found; therefore the searchers must have driven them out. This inverted logic was not confined to federal employees. Irène Curie, arriving in New York for a scientific meeting, was interned overnight on Ellis Island; anonymous telephone calls had warned that she might be an enemy agent. After the publication in *Liberty* magazine of "Reds in Our Atomic Bomb Plants," an article by J. Parnell Thomas insinuating that all scientists were security risks, the government for a time found it almost impossible to recruit young nuclear physicists.* Physicians subscribing to the *American Review of Soviet Medicine,* a professional journal issued by the American-Soviet Medical Society, asked that issues be mailed to them in plain paper wrappers.

Firms active in defense work were jittery — one spent $3,000,000 on new safes and strongboxes for classified documents entrusted to it — and colleges and universities were torn by a double allegiance, to the flag and to academic freedom. Legislature after legislature was requiring loyalty oaths from teachers, 11,000 of them at the University of California alone; UCLA fired 157 professors who balked. On the local level teacher oaths were administered by school board chairmen, PTA presidents, and police chiefs. In many communities Legion or VFW officers also studied classroom texts for subversive material.

If any occupation had to endure more than the teaching profession, it was show business. In New York three aggressive ex-FBI agents, egged on by vigilantes in the American Federation of Radio Artists, published *Counter-*

---

*J. Parnell Thomas was chairman of the House Committee on Un-American Activities when the article appeared. He was convicted of fraud on December 3, 1949, fined $10,000, and sent to prison.

Attack, a pamphlet listing 151 actors, directors, and writers whose names had appeared in the files of various congressional committees. *Counter-Attack* was circulated among communications executives, who were urged to fire anyone in it and to check it before hiring new people. Next the three issued *Red Channels,* a thicker directory of entertainers and announcers whose friends or "affiliations" were dubious. The industry trembled — *Counter-Attack* had described CBS as "the most satisfying network for the Communists" — and vice presidents kept copies of *Red Channels* in their bottom desk drawers. On Madison Avenue and throughout Hollywood it was rechristened "the blacklist."

Blacklisting was to be a feature of the entertainment industry for over a decade. It was a blunt instrument of blackmail, used to cow administrators whose livelihood depended upon public opinion. Time has blurred many sharp contours of the Age of Suspicion, but no brief can be held for those company heads who permitted themselves to be intimidated. Often they knew that a star had been blacklisted by a jealous competitor, and at the other end of the wage scale they summarily dismissed stagehands and deodorant demonstrators on preposterous charges that they were "disloyal" or "security risks." If one executive had stiffened his backbone the counter-attackers' house of cards might have collapsed. None did.

The experience of Jean Muir was typical. One day she was the leading actress in *The Aldrich Family,* NBC's most popular radio serial. The next day her name was added to *Red Channels.* By afternoon the network had torn up her contract and put her on the street. NBC's explanation to the press set a new low in what had already become a low era, and established a precedent its competitors soon followed. Of course Miss Muir wasn't a Communist, the network spokesman said blandly. She was loyal to her country and always had been. Unfortunately, she had become controversial. Controversy alarmed sponsors, stirred up the public, and hurt the product. In short, she had been fired because someone had lied about her. From then on, "controversial" was almost a synonym for "disloyal" — and just as likely to ruin a career. Eventually most people stopped trying to justify the blacklist. If questions were raised about its iniquities, there always seemed to be someone around who would shake his head and say maddeningly, "Where there's smoke, there's fire."

The worst of it was that he was right, there *was* a flame beneath all that smog. Not that Dorothy Bailey and Jean Muir had anything to do with it. They were martyrs, sacrificed to ignorance and fear as surely as any Salem "witch" in 1692. But it was a chilling fact that real agents had made off with real secrets. Once Stalin had the Bomb, few gave peace more than an even chance — Lloyd's of London didn't — and the swiftness with which Russian scientists built their first nuclear weapon owed almost everything to the ingenious espionage web Soviet Vice Consul Anatoli A. Yakovlev had spun between New York and Los Alamos during the war.

Yakovlev's apparatus would never have been discovered without the defection of Gouzenko in Ottawa. Even so, it took four years and the combined efforts of the Canadian Mounties, Scotland Yard, and the FBI to unravel the snarl. Fuchs was the key to it. His confession to a Yard inspector in Harwell and London led to Harry Gold in New York. Gold broke down when FBI agents found a New Mexico map in his apartment showing the routes he followed in his rendezvous with Fuchs and Greenglass. When Julius Rosenberg read of Gold's arrest in the *New York Herald Tribune* he took the paper to Ruth Greenglass. She and David would have to leave the country, he said; David could implicate all of them, including Ethel Rosenberg, his own sister. Ruth said, "We can't go anywhere. We have a ten-day-old infant." Rosenberg said, "Your baby won't die. Babies are born on the ocean and in trains every day. My doctor says that if you take enough canned milk and boil the water the baby will be all right."

Julius gave the Greenglasses a thousand dollars and mapped out a complex journey from Mexico City to Sweden to Czechoslovakia to Moscow. Local Communists would meet them and guide them on each leg of the trip, he said. They had passport photos taken and then hesitated again. Ruth was ill. Julius, climbing walls, gave them four thousand dollars more, but they told him they were going to stay and face punishment. Eleven days later the FBI picked David up. He then had to choose between his wife and his sister. He chose Ruth. Early one summer evening while the Rosenbergs were listening to *The Lone Ranger* the FBI knock came. Only Julius was taken then; Ethel was left to care for their two sons. Then she had to make other arrangements. She too was jailed. They had betrayed the country in wartime, and Sing Sing and electrocution lay ahead for both of them.

That was real treason, not the paranoid fantasies of superpatriots demanding loyalty oaths of kindergarten teachers and movie extras. Beyond doubt the Rosenberg-Greenglass-Gold-Fuchs-Nunn-May ring was one of the most successful in the history of international espionage. In Moscow it disgorged charts, formulae, and hundreds of pages of closely written data describing in detail everything from Oak Ridge's gaseous diffusion process for separating U-235 and U-238 to blueprints of the missile itself. The Russians could scarcely have learned more about nuclear weapons had they been full partners in the undertaking. At the cost of two billion dollars America had assembled the best scientific minds in western Europe and the United States, mobilized American industry, and united the two in a three-and-a-half-year search that culminated in success at Alamogordo and terror over Japan. By then the Soviet director of intelligence had a full account of the making of the bomb and even an eyewitness account, from Fuchs, of that first blast in the New Mexico desert. The information was beyond price. USSR physicists could not have duplicated it then. They grasped the theoretical physics involved, but in the late 1940s Russia simply did not have adequate industrial resources for so huge a venture.

Treachery permitted them to close the nuclear gap. The Anglo-American traitors had hastened the onset of the Cold War by at least eighteen months.

So enormous were their crimes, and so leaky the British and American counterespionage nets through which they slipped, that public opinion might well have demanded new governments at 10 Downing Street and 1600 Pennsylvania Avenue. Nothing of the sort happened. As far as the electorate was concerned, the whole thing might have been an act of God. The security failures were lamented, of course, but in neither country was there any sustained search for scapegoats in the laboratories. The man in the street lacked sufficient scientific sophistication to appreciate what had happened. Gaseous diffusion processes would have made poor campaign issues. Furthermore, none of the guilty persons could be identified with any party except the Communist party. What the Republicans needed was a ring of full-fledged New Dealers, or at least one of them, who had turned U.S. secrets over to the USSR.

It is a central fact of mid-century American politics that they found what they wanted. Not the real thing, perhaps, but close enough to it to divide the country and make heads roll. If their Communists-in-government had not betrayed atom bomb plans, it was only because they didn't know any. All were cut from the same cloth as the spies in the labs — intelligent, sensitive and idealistic men who had been born shortly after the turn of the century and retained grim memories of the First World War. They had witnessed the collapse of the economy after the Crash, the unchecked aggression which had followed in Spain, Ethiopia, China, and central Europe, and the shame of Munich. Despairing of the western democracies, they had embraced Communism as the faith that would remake the world. Like religious fanatics they would do anything for the cause. Most of them were denied the golden opportunity of the physicists, but everyone could do something. Those in the administration could filch state secrets. If in the sub-cabinet, one might recommend Soviet solutions, such as the plowing under of Germany's Ruhr. Even ordinary people could serve as couriers. Harry Gold was a courier. Whittaker Chambers was another.

This is very complicated, and even today it cuts across beliefs so deeply held that confessions and overwhelming evidence are denied; Dean Acheson went to his grave believing Harry Dexter White innocent and the Hiss affair a "mystery." To comprehend the enormity of what began happening in the summer of 1948, one may imagine a large household whose children insist that they are pursued by a bogeyman. Others in the family repeatedly assure them that there is no such thing as a bogeyman. The house is searched over and over. Nothing is found, and although the children persist in their preposterous stories, everyone else in the home ignores them. Then one evening when the family is gathered together one child notices that a closet door is ajar. He flings it open — and out steps a real bogeyman, ten feet tall and all teeth. Igor Gouzenko in Canada had been such a child. Three years afterward American defectors began giving other evidence in Washington. The difference was that their door didn't open on a closet. It led to the master bedroom.

Early in the Age of Suspicion liberals and intellectuals tried to drown the Red bogey in laughter. For ten years the House Committee on Un-American Activities had been trying to discredit Roosevelt reforms by frightening the country. It seemed inconceivable that anything of conse-quence could turn up now. When Elizabeth Bentley began testifying before a subcommittee of the Senate Committee on Expenditures in the Executive Department, the *New Yorker* turned the pitiless wit of A. J. Liebling on her. "Behind Schrafft's saccharine facade," he wrote, "Miss Bentley had handed Al* the secret formula for making synthetic rubber out of garbage, which has not yet been discovered, or a redundant tip on the approximate date of D Day, which the Allied Chiefs of Staff had communicated to their Russian colleagues as soon as it was decided upon. I forget where she passed on the information that she had received from a man who, she testified, told her he got it from Lauchlin Currie, former administrative assistant to President Roosevelt, on a subject that Currie has since sworn he knew nothing about — the breaking of a Russian code."

There was no end to the fun Liebling had with Miss Bentley that August. To him she was "the Nutmeg Mata Hari," and after the *New York World-Telegram* stopped calling her a "Red Spy Queen" and began re-ferring to her as "striking" and "a blonde" (she was neither) the *New Yorker's* press critic gaily rechristened her "the Red blonde Spy Queen." Then his comments became sharper. A joke was a joke, but this woman was damaging the reputations of decent men. The hearings, he wrote, "were reminiscent of a group of retarded children playing deteckative." Liebling thought that "An editor who couldn't smell an odor of burning synthetic rubber about Miss Bentley's inside-policy data has an extremely insensitive nose for news." To have suggested the suppression of testimony would have been entirely out of character for him, a violation of his most deeply held convictions; still, when South Dakota's bumbling Karl Mundt said, "Evidence is clouding up, but it isn't clear enough yet," Liebling remarked, "I feel that the press has been slighting the low-comedy aspects of the hearings."

As the summer wore on, they became less amusing. In sworn testimony Miss Bentley and Whittaker Chambers accused thirty-seven former govern-ment employees of participation in Soviet espionage. Of these, seventeen refused under oath to say whether they were Communists or spies. The names of those who took the Fifth Amendment are faintly evocative today, like a scratchy old Paul Robeson recording of "The Peat-Bog Soldiers" or "The Four Insurgent Generals." None of them had been known to

*Her lover and chief contact. His real name was Jacob Golos. Before his death in 1944 Golos was a link in the chain whose other links included Harry Gold and Klaus Fuchs.

the public before 1948, but all had been close to the seats of power and decision. Six others were not called to testify. Of those remaining, Harold Ware had died in 1935; Lee Pressman and John Abt admitted they were Communists but denied espionage; Laurence Duggan, a fourteen-year veteran of the State Department, either jumped or fell to his death from a sixteenth-floor Manhattan window after two witnesses had identified him as a Communist; former Assistant Secretary of State Harry Dexter White, against whom the evidence was formidable, died of a heart attack; and the other twelve swore that the charges against them were false. Two of these were then accused of perjury. The first, William Remington, was found guilty and later murdered in prison. The other was Alger Hiss.

His biographical sketch in the 1948–1949 edition of *Who's Who in America* read:

HISS, Alger, lawyer, B. Baltimore, Md. Nov. 11, 1904; s. Charles Alger and Mary L. (Hughes) H.; A.B., Johns Hopkins, 1926; LL.B., Harvard, 1929; m. Priscilla Fansler Hobson, Dec. 11, 1929; children — Timothy Hobson (stepson), Anthony. Mem. bars of Mass., N.Y. and U.S. Supreme Court; sec. and law clerk to Supreme Court Justice, 1929–30; asst. to gen. counsel and asst. gen. counsel, Agrl. Adjustment Administrn., Washington, D.C. 1933–35; legal asst., special Senate com. investigating munitions industry, 1934–35; special atty. U.S. Dept. Justice, 1935–36 . . . pres. Carnegie Endowment for Internat. Peace since Feb. 1, 1947; exec. sec. Dumbarton Oaks Conf., 1944; accompanied Pres. Roosevelt to Crimea Conf., Feb. 1945; sec. gen. United Nations Conf. on Internat. Organization, San Francisco, 1945; principal advisor, U.S. Del. to U.N. Gen. Assembly, Jan.–Feb. 1946. Mem. Phi Beta Kappa, Alpha Delta Phi. Club: Metropolitan (Washington). Home: 3210 P Street N.W., Washington 7, D.C. Office: 522 Fifth Avenue, New York 18, N.Y.

It would have been difficult to find a more attractive Rooseveltian figure. In the word of the man who became his prosecutor, he was "a prototype." Lean, tanned, elegantly tailored, he was every inch the patrician-as-idealist — the public servant who was also a member of a law firm with the name Choate in it, the reform Democrat who was listed in the Washington *Social Register*. At Johns Hopkins he had been a debater, a track star, and the "best hand-shaker" in his class. His reputation was flawless: Governor Adlai Stevenson of Illinois was prepared to testify to that; so were two U.S. Supreme Court justices, a former solicitor general of the United States, John W. Davis (a former presidential candidate) and John Foster Dulles. Hiss's presence was imposing. His well-modulated voice carried just the right trace of a Harvard accent. He smiled easily and broadly, like FDR at his most charming, and moved with a casual grace suggestive of Baltimore Cotillions or Gibson Island tennis matches, at both of which he was a familiar figure. Attending his own trials, he would seem less the defendant than a distinguished spectator. To call such a man a Communist was as unthinkable as calling him a liar.

Whittaker Chambers, who accused him of being both, was by his own admission a scoundrel and a blackguard. Before breaking with the party to join *Time* he had perjured himself a thousand times over. As a boy he had formed a suicide pact with his brother Dick; Dick had killed himself but Whittaker had backed out. Aged seventeen, he had set up housekeeping in a New Orleans flophouse with a prostitute named One-Eyed Annie. Later he brought another female tramp to live with him in his mother's Long Island home — she let him do it, he said, "because she had lost one son and did not want to lose another." He had been expelled from Columbia for writing a sacrilegious play. He had been a thief. Confronted with an oath he had taken upon going to work for the WPA, he readily conceded, in his phlegmatic way, that he had broken it in every particular. Now in 1948 he was a fat, rumpled, middle-aged, sad-looking man with a sickly complexion and heavily lidded eyes.

Yet it was Chambers who saw one aspect of the issue between the two men most clearly: "No feature of the Hiss case is more obvious, or more troubling as history," he wrote afterward, "than the jagged fissure, which it did not so much open as reveal, between the plain men and women of the nation, and those who affected to act, think and speak for them. It was not invariably, but in general, the 'best people' who were for Alger Hiss and who were prepared to go to almost any length to protect and defend him." That was certainly part of it. The other part was that to partisans on both sides Alger Hiss quickly became a symbol. Liberal Democrats saw him as representative of the New Deal achievements now under attack. To conservative Republicans he stood for the hated eastern elite. The liberals made the first commitment in the case. Hiss's innocence was so obvious to them that they staked everything on it and invited the opposition to do the same. Conservatives were slower on the field. In the beginning Chambers seemed an unlikely champion for them. But Congressman Richard M. Nixon showed them the way, and long before the true import of the Chambers-Hiss uproar was known — that is, before the charge of treason had been lodged — both sides had closed ranks and raised their banners. Thereafter the role of reason steadily diminished; the case incited blind, violent emotions in every quarter. It was the tragedy of the liberals that they were wrong. It was the triumph of Richard Nixon and his party that Chambers was not only right; he could prove it.

He didn't look right at first. Hiss played his part superbly. Others had taken refuge in the Fifth Amendment or in transparent evasions. Not he. On August 4, 1948, upon learning that Chambers had identified him as a Communist the day before in testimony before the House Committee on Un-American Activities, he telegraphed the committee from New York demanding that he be given the right to deny the charge under oath. Next day he faced the committee, the very picture of righteous indignation. He answered every question and denied each of Chambers's specifications. At the end Chairman Mundt thanked Hiss for his "very cooperative attitude" and "forthright statements." John Rankin walked round to shake Hiss's hand. Everyone was smiling except Nixon, who hadn't taken his eyes off Hiss's face. Before the month was out the young California congressman would appear to have had second sight. In fact he was blessed by an excellent source. The FBI had begun checking Hiss. An agent named Ed Hummer was phoning the results of each day's investigation to a priest named John Cronin, and Father Cronin was relaying it to Nixon. Still, there was little to go on in that first week in August, and Nixon deserves full marks for persistence and perspicacity. He said he wanted to see Chambers and Hiss face to face.

The rest of the committee decided to hear Chambers again; they thought Hiss might be the victim of mistaken identity. It was during this second session, which was closed to the public (and to Hiss), that the accuser began to reveal his encyclopedic knowledge of Hiss, Hiss's wife, and the Hiss household. The couple called one another "Hilly" and "Pross," he remembered. They had been devoted to their cocker spaniel. Their Volta Place house had been furnished with Hitchcock chairs stenciled in gilt, a gold mirror with an eagle on top, walls papered halfway with a mulberry pattern and the lower half paneled. Chambers knew much more about them than that, but for the moment he said just enough to establish his bona fides — little details about children, servants, food, books, furniture, and hobbies. One of Hiss's hobbies was bird-watching. Chambers told of how excited Hiss had become upon seeing a prothonotary warbler on the Potomac. By chance one of the congressmen, John McDowell, was himself an amateur ornithologist, and when Hiss was recalled before the committee McDowell asked him whether he had ever seen a prothonotary warbler. Hiss's eyes lit up. He replied brightly, "I have, right here on the Potomac. Do you know that place?" A moment later he said, "They come back and nest in those swamps. Beautiful head, a gorgeous bird." It had been a small feat. It impressed the committee more than he knew.

Clearly Chambers's knowledge of the Hisses was the sort that comes from only the closest friendship. Nixon therefore got his confrontation, on August 25, in suite 400 of the Commodore Hotel in New York. It was a critical point in the case. Hiss, rattled by Nixon's questioning and Chambers's evident knowledge of him, identified his accuser as one George Crosley, a free-lance writer and deadbeat he had met in the 1930s. Now Nixon began to close in. Hiss was asked to produce three people who would also testify that they knew Chambers as Crosley. Visibly upset, he replied, "I will if it is possible. Why is that a question to ask me? I will see what is possible. This occurred in 1935. The only people that I can think of who would have known him as George Crosley with certainty would have been the people who were associated with me in the Nye [munitions investiga-

tion] committee." After another sharp Nixon-Hiss exchange this colloquy
followed, between the two principals, Congressmen Nixon and McDowell,
and Louis Russell, a committee investigator:

MR. McDOWELL: Then your identification of George Crosley is complete?

MR. HISS: Yes, as far as I am concerned, on his own testimony.

MR. McDOWELL: Mr. Chambers, is this the man, Alger Hiss, who was also
a member of the Communist Party at whose home you stayed?

MR. NIXON: According to your testimony.

MR. McDOWELL: You make identification positive?

MR. CHAMBERS: Positive identification.
   (*At this point Mr. Hiss arose and walked in the direction of Mr. Chambers.*)

MR. HISS: May I say for the record at this point, that I would like to invite
Mr. Whittaker Chambers to make those same statements out of the presence of this committee without their being privileged for suit for libel. I
challenge you to do it, and I hope you will do it damned quickly. I am
not going to touch him (*addressing Mr. Russell*). You are touching me.

MR. RUSSELL: Please sit down, Mr. Hiss.

MR. HISS: I will sit down when the chairman asks me, Mr. Russell, when the
chairman asks me to sit down —

MR. RUSSELL: I want no disturbance.

MR. HISS: I don't —

MR. McDOWELL: Sit down, please.

MR. HISS: You know who started this.

MR. McDOWELL: We will suspend testimony here for a minute or two, until
I return.

But it was too late. Hiss had blundered. Until this moment his gamble
had made sense. He was right, 1935 *had* been a long time ago. It was his
word against Chambers's, and given the differences between their reputations there could be small doubt about the outcome. Having been a
Communist wasn't a crime anyhow, and the statute of limitations had
expired on the felony of stealing government secrets. The committee had
just about given up hope of making any case out of the Bentley-Chambers
testimony. By daring Chambers to shed the privilege of congressional
immunity, however, and by promising to sue for libel, Hiss had created a
new situation. Now Chambers would be forced to produce his evidence.
The whole wretched business would be moved into a court of law, which
would determine which of them was lying. The loser would be found
guilty of perjury and imprisoned.

Eight days later there was another Hiss-Chambers confrontation in
Washington, for the public, under lights. Here Hiss's assurance had plainly
ebbed. He had brought his lawyer, and he prefaced his answers with such
circumlocutions as, "To the best of my recollection." Even when asked

whether he came to the hearing in response to a subpoena he replied, "To the extent that my coming here quite voluntarily after having received the subpoena is in response to it — I would accept that statement." Chambers had told the congressmen that Hiss had given him a 1929 Model A Ford, to be used as the Communist party saw fit. This was something that could be checked in motor vehicle records. Hiss responded weakly; it had been an old car, just deteriorating on the street, of "practically no financial value," so he had let Crosley have it. Or thought he had: "I gave Crosley, to the best of my recollection," he began, whereupon Nixon broke in to say, "Well, now, just a minute on that point, I don't want to interrupt you on that 'to the best of my recollection,' but you certainly can testify 'Yes' or 'No' as to whether you gave Crosley a car. How many cars have you given away in your life, Mr. Hiss?" The laughter was unfriendly, and when Hiss clung to the periphrasis, insisting that it was only his "best recollection" that he had given Crosley the car, "as I was able to give him the use of my apartment," the laughter gave way to a heavy silence. Every member of the committee had the same thought: you do not turn your home and your automobile over to someone known to you only as a deadbeat. The three names Hiss had given them were useless. One man had died, a second couldn't be found, and the third had no memory of anyone named Crosley.

Two nights later Chambers appeared on *Meet the Press,* then a radio program, to accept Hiss's challenge. Hiss "was a Communist and may be one now," he said. The country waited for Hiss to take him to court. And waited. And waited. Finally, on September 27, Hiss sued for defamation in Baltimore. Before anything else could happen the national election intervened. This would have been a good time for Hiss to quit, and as things turned out, it was his last chance to do so. The Republicans were stunned by Truman's victory. They had lost control of the House of Representatives and with it control of the House Committee on Un-American Activities. In addition, two Republicans on the committee had been defeated for reelection. But events were about to move far beyond the scope of congressmen. On Wednesday, November 17, Chambers was scheduled to appear at a pretrial hearing in Baltimore as a defendant. Then he would have to show Hiss's lawyers his proof, if he had any, of an earlier association with the plaintiff. Thus cornered, he proceeded to establish beyond any reasonable doubt a fact that stunned the country: ten years earlier Alger Hiss, his wife Priscilla, and Whittaker Chambers had been members of a Soviet espionage apparatus passing state secrets to the Russians.

Between May or June of 1937 and April 1938, when Chambers broke with the party, Alger Hiss had given him every classified document, cable, report, and dispatch he could lay his hands on. They had been transmitted in three forms. Some had been originals which Chambers had microfilmed and then returned to Hiss. Hiss had summarized others in his own handwriting. Priscilla Hiss had copied the rest at home on her Woodstock typewriter; her husband had then slipped them back into State Department files. He hadn't been the only one doing this. Henry Julian Wadleigh, director of State's trade agreements section and another descendant of fine old American stock, had been another Chambers source. Wadleigh now admitted it. The statute of limitations protected him. But Hiss had denied it. He had gone too far. He had perjured himself, and now he was trapped.

Before dropping out of sight in 1938 Chambers had put three strips of microfilm and 84 papers — 43 documents copied on Priscilla's typewriter and 41 memoranda in Alger's hand — in a large brown paper envelope. He had taken the envelope to Nathan Levine, a Brooklyn attorney and his wife's nephew, and had asked him to put it in a safe place. Now, ten years later, on November 14, 1948, he came to Levine and asked him for it. Covered with grime, it lay in a dumbwaiter shaft; Levine had to stand on his bathtub to fetch it. Chambers dusted it off in the kitchen and took the typewritten copies and longhand memoranda to the pretrial hearing in Baltimore. Their appearance there must have been shattering for Hiss, but he kept his head; he directed his attorneys to put the documents before the Justice Department at once. It was a clever move. If the Truman administration announced that the material was secret, Chambers just might be prevented from talking about it. There was another danger for Chambers: producing the documents had revealed him as a receiver of classified material. Nixon's staff was at its wits' end, afraid the wrong man might be arrested. But Hiss wasn't the only clever one. Chambers hadn't brought everything to the pretrial hearing. He had hidden the microfilm in a hollowed-out pumpkin on his Maryland farm. On the night of December 2, when House investigators asked him if he had anything else, he led them there. The House Committee on Un-American Activities ordered that a twenty-four-hour watch be mounted over the pumpkin's contents, and two days later the newspapers had the story.

Democrats howled. The "pumpkin papers" seemed to be the last absurd act in the Chambers melodrama. The nature of the papers which had been released to the press made the twenty-four-hour watch seem ridiculous. As A. J. Liebling wrote in the New Yorker, they constituted "a mixed bag of trivia." None of it had been of much significance in 1938, let alone 1948. One paper had reported that the Japanese were trying to buy manganese from a Costa Rican island which had no manganese. Another solemnly noted that Hitler and Mussolini were exchanging staff officers. A third had been written at a time when the whole world knew the Nazi seizure of Austria was imminent. It recorded an opinion of the American consul general in Vienna: "it seems possible Hitler is seeking a foreign political triumph at the expense of Austria."

That was good for a chuckle, but it was the last laugh liberal Democrats were going to have from this business. As other papers were declassified it became evident that some of them had been enormously helpful in Moscow, and others were being withheld from newspapermen because the State Department had ruled that they were too secret, even in 1948, to be published without risking the national security. Moreover, the content of the documents was really beside the point. Had they been confined to weather reports or traffic accidents, their appearance in the hands of a former Communist courier would still have been shocking, and an occasion for a broad federal inquiry, because all of them had been transmitted in Code D, the department's most secret cipher. That meant the code had been broken and American diplomacy compromised on a very high level; agents of another government had been able to eavesdrop at will, picking up information on exchanges with foreign secretaries of friendly powers, names of confidential informers, troop transfers, presidential directives — the lot. And indeed, when former Undersecretary of State Sumner Welles examined enlargements of the pumpkin papers he declared that their acquisition by another government in 1938, and especially the loss of Code D, had been "most perilous to the interests of the United States."

Now the administration had no choice. In his press conferences President Truman continued to maintain that talk of spies had been nothing more than a campaign red herring, but already his Justice Department was moving to preempt ground hitherto held by the House Committee on Un-American Activities. In New York the government recalled a grand jury and showed it some of the enlargements. Subpoenas were issued for Hiss, Chambers, and Mrs. Hiss. On December 15 Hiss was indicted on two counts of perjury. His first trial began on May 31, 1949, and ended on July 8 with the jury hung, eight for conviction and four not. There was a great deal of unpleasantness about the judge. He had been solicitous of the Hiss cause throughout, overruling the prosecution, sustaining the defense, and excluding witnesses who, had they been permitted to testify, would have clarified several points that baffled the jury. Those who had expected a guilty verdict were chagrined.

It was at this point that Richard Nixon first came to the attention of the country's liberal constituency and offended it deeply. Democrats had followed the trial numbly, hoping that the mountain of circumstantial evidence would somehow be explained away. The deadlock disappointed them, too. It was a blow to learn that eight jurors had believed Chambers, and they were in no mood to be jarred by a contentious young Republican congressman. He did go far. It was doubtless true that "the Truman administration," as he charged, was "extremely anxious that nothing bad happen to Mr. Hiss," and even fair to add that the court's "prejudice against the prosecution" had been "obvious and apparent." But it was unwise to demand an investigation of the judge, and unwiser still to raise the hackles of those who believed in simple justice by saying that "the average American wants all technicalities waived in this case." A trial without technicalities is a lynching bee. A. J. Liebling, stuck with Hiss and not much liking it, observed that apparently "it is un-American not to convict anybody Congressman Nixon doesn't like," and, in another thrust, that Nixon was "in the plight of a young bank teller who has bet his life savings on a horse that looks like faltering."

Chambers wasn't faltering. He was surer of himself when the second trial opened November 17 under an impartial judge and with a new attorney, less histrionic than the first, representing Hiss. Another consideration was working against the defense. Great political trials must be seen in the context of their times, and throughout 1949 and January 1950, when the second trial ended, the temperature of the cold war was dropping steadily. During every day of both trials Chiang Kai-shek was giving ground to the Chinese Communists until, on the day the second verdict came in, he had lost all of it. In eastern Europe the Red Army was suppressing one democratic government after another. NATO was coalescing to protect western Europe from it. Between the two trials Russia exploded its first atomic bomb. At home the attorney general's list of subversive organizations grew by the month. Accusations of spying were losing their novelty, and with it their incredibility. The FBI had arrested Judith Coplon on charges of espionage. The Smith Act defendants were being tried in the same building as Hiss; during quiet moments in his trial you could hear Communists demonstrating outside in Foley Square. In August 1948, when Chambers and Hiss had faced one another for the first time in a decade in that Commodore Hotel room, it had been possible to argue that Henry Wallace might be right. Seventeen months later, when Hiss's second jury retired to deliberate, opinion against Russia and its American admirers had hardened. The jurors found Hiss guilty on both counts.

That does not mean that Alger Hiss was a victim of world politics, except in the sense that it was world politics which had got him in trouble in the first place. Reading through transcripts of the two trials, one can only wonder that four people had voted to acquit him at the end of the first one, despite the biased judge. The documents alone should have been enough to condemn him. He admitted that the handwriting in the memoranda was his. He said that it had been his practice to summarize long documents for his chief, Francis B. Sayre. Sayre denied it, his secretary denied it; nobody in the State Department had heard of such a custom. In the trials Hiss was asked how Chambers had acquired these digests. He didn't know; he supposed someone had gone through his wastebaskets in the 1930s and saved them. Then, the relentless prosecutor asked, why had they been folded and not crumpled? Hiss agreed that it was a mystery.

U.S.A. v. Alger Hiss was a puzzle fashioned with such pieces: the Woodstock typewriter, the prothonotary warbler, the Hitchcock chairs stenciled in gilt, the Volta Place walls papered with a mulberry pattern, "Hilly" and "Pross," the handwritten notes — and the $400 "loan." The loan was in some ways the most convincing fragment of all. In the autumn of 1937

Chambers had needed a new automobile. After his trade-in he was short $400. He went to the Hisses and they gave it to him.

Here the records were very precise. On November 17, 1937, Mrs. Hiss had withdrawn $400 from their savings account. Four days later Chambers bought his auto. The bankbook and the car dealer's bill of sale were submitted as evidence. Mrs. Hiss testified that she had taken the money out to furnish their new home. She had no receipts, and the withdrawal had just about wiped out their savings. It left them a balance of $14.69 — so little that Hiss had to borrow $300 from the bank to meet the monthly installments on his own car. In the depressed 1930s families didn't make such a sacrifice for a slight acquaintance who was known to be a poor credit risk. As for Mrs. Hiss's story, the prosecutor asked the jury, "Is that the way you do it when you have a checking account and a charge account, and you're not moved in? Do you take the $400 out in one lump? Do you go out and buy items for the house to be delivered later and pay for them in cash?" Two lady jurors smiled. Of course they didn't. Neither had Priscilla Hiss.

On that blustery Saturday in January 1950 when the jury reached its verdict, Congressman Nixon was flooded with congratulatory messages, including one from Herbert Hoover: "The conviction of Alger Hiss was due to your patience and persistence alone. At last the stream of treason that existed in our government has been exposed in a fashion that all may believe." Hoover had rarely displayed warmth, but the elation in those lines is unmistakable. It is easy to imagine his feelings that weekend. He had taken the measure of that New Deal crowd from the very beginning and now at last, at last, the country could see how right he had been.

At the other end of the emotional spectrum stood Dean Acheson. The Secretary of State had known Hiss since the younger man's graduation from Harvard Law School. In his United Nations liaison work Hiss had worked under Acheson's supervision, and when Acheson had resigned as Undersecretary of State in 1947, briefly to resume his private practice, his closest associates had presented him with a thermos carafe for ice water on a silver tray. Their names, inscribed around it, included Chip Bohlen, Loy Henderson, Dean Rusk, and Alger Hiss. On the Wednesday after the conviction, the same day that Hiss was sentenced to five years in the Lewisburg Federal Penitentiary, Acheson held a press conference. Homer Bigart of the *New York Herald Tribune* asked the inevitable question: "Mr. Secretary, do you have any comment on the Alger Hiss case?" The response is remembered where other aspects of the trials have faded: "I should like to make it clear to you that whatever the outcome of any appeal which Mr. Hiss or his lawyers may take in this case, I do not intend to turn my back on Alger Hiss." Everyone must act according to his principles, he explained, and there could be no doubt about his: "I think they were stated for us a very long time ago. They were stated on the Mount of Olives, and if you are interested in seeing them you will find them in the 25th Chapter of the Gospel according to St. Matthew beginning with verse 34."*

That night Acheson wrote his daughter Mary:†

> . . . today I had my press conference. Alger's case has been on my mind incessantly. As I have written you, here is stark tragedy — whatever the reasonable probable facts are. I knew I would be asked about it and the answer was a hard one — not in the ordinary sense of do I run or do I stand. That presented no problem. But to say what one really meant — forgetting the yelping pack at one's heels — saying no more and no less than one truly believed. This was not easy.

The pack at his heels included Nixon, who told reporters he thought the secretary's comment "disgusting," and Congressman Walter Judd of Minnesota, who said Truman ought to turn his back on Acheson. The Hill was not interested in the Mount of Olives that month. It wanted scalps. Here it was less than five years after the war and the world had begun to disintegrate. China was gone, Stalin had the bomb, the State Department had been harboring spies — and there was worse to come. Six days after Acheson's press conference the President announced that work had begun on the deadly hydrogen bomb. Albert Einstein chilled the country by appearing on television to warn that "radioactive poisoning of the atmosphere and, hence, annihilation of any life on earth has been brought within the range of possibilities. . . . General annihilation beckons," and four days after *that* Scotland Yard arrested Fuchs for betraying America's atom bomb to the Russians. "How much more are we going to take?" Homer Capehart cried in the Senate. "Fuchs and Acheson and Hiss and hydrogen bombs threatening outside and New Dealism eating away the vitals of the nation. In the name of heaven, is this the best America can do?"

On January 7 the junior senator from Wisconsin dined at Washington's Colony Restaurant on Connecticut Avenue, halfway between the White House and Dupont Circle, with a Catholic priest, a professor of political science, and a Washington lawyer. He was, he told them, in desperate need of advice.

The past year had brought nothing but bad news to Joseph R. McCarthy. He had angered prestigious senators in both parties, and he had problems at home. Among other things, Wisconsin's State Board of Bar Commissioners had nearly disbarred him in 1949 over a breach of ethics: he had run for the Senate while holding judicial office. The commissioners had let

---

*"Naked, and ye clothed me: I was sick, and ye visited me: I was in prison, and ye came unto me. . . . Inasmuch as ye have done it unto one of the least of these my brethren, ye have done it unto me."

†Wife of William P. Bundy, who in the 1960s became one of the chief architects of the government's Vietnam policies.

McCarthy off with a warning. As he himself paraphrased the ruling, "It was illegal — Joe was naughty — but we don't think he'll do it again."

They didn't know their man. In a crisis he would do anything, and he had reached such a turning point now. In Washington he had attracted public attention chiefly by his defense of some Nazi war criminals. A poll of Washington correspondents had chosen him America's worst senator. In two years, he reminded his dinner guests at the Colony, he would be up for reelection.

He needed a campaign issue. Did they have any ideas?

Portrait of an American

EDWARD ROSCOE MURROW

SOMETIMES, when the wind is right and the London night plays tricks with the memory, one can almost hear the flak, the Luftwaffe armada droning overhead, and the din below. With a little imagination you can see the searchlights springing up. It is then, in fancy, that you can picture the lone figure of a gallant young American defying annihilation to tell his countrymen, through the static and the sputter of shortwave, what he felt they must know:

> *This — is London.* . . .
>
> I'm standing on a rooftop looking out over London. . . . I think probably in a minute we shall have the sound of guns in the immediate vicinity. The lights are swinging over in this general direction now. You'll hear two explosions. There they are! . . . I should think in a few minutes there may be a bit of shrapnel around here. Coming in, moving a little closer all the while.
>
> The plane's still very high. Earlier this evening we could hear occasional — again, those were explosions overhead. Earlier this evening we heard a number of bombs go sliding and slithering across, to fall several blocks away. Just overhead now the burst of the antiaircraft fire. Still the nearby guns are not working. The searchlights now are feeling almost directly overhead. Now you'll hear two bursts a little nearer in a moment. There they are! That hard stony sound.

He was on top of the BBC building, a major German target, a place so dangerous that Winston Churchill's personal intervention was required before broadcasts from it could be permitted. Night after night Murrow went up there and elsewhere to describe the havoc around St. Paul's, the Abbey, Trafalgar Square. Buildings collapsed around him, his CBS office was destroyed three times, yet his measured, authoritative tones continued to bring the war ever closer to American homes. His effectiveness owed much to understatement. There were never any heroics in his newscasts. At the end he would simply sign off with the current London phrase: "So long — and good luck."

Though few realized it — particularly during his later duel with Joe McCarthy — Murrow was essentially a conservative. He believed in patriotism, personal honor, and the values of western civilization. At Washington State College, where he worked his way through in the traditional manner of ambitious poor boys, he was the cadet colonel of the ROTC unit. He had chosen Washington State because it offered the country's first collegiate course in radio broadcasting; in his steady, level-headed way he already knew what he wanted to be. He liked to describe himself as an accurate, objective old-time newsman ("I try to be a reporter; a commentator is a kind of oracle, and I am never so sure I'm right"), but in practice he was closer to an old-time missionary. In a revealing letter to his parents from London he wrote: "I remember you once wanted me to be a preacher, but I had no faith, except in myself. But now I am preaching from a powerful pulpit. Often I am wrong but I am trying to talk as I would have talked were I a preacher. One need not wear a reversed collar to be honest."

He had joined CBS in 1935 after five years with student and educational organizations, and in 1937, at the age of twenty-nine, he sailed for England to take over the CBS European bureau. It wasn't much of a job then. Most of his work was boring: scheduling speeches, concerts, cultural broadcasts. He was traveling to Poland in 1938 to set up a CBS School of the Air program when Hitler entered Austria. Chartering a plane, he reached Vienna in time to describe the arrival of the Nazi troops. Then he hired William L. Shirer, built a staff, and went on to cover Munich, the fall of Czechoslovakia, the London blitz, and the major European battles of World War II.

In 1945 CBS made him a vice president, but he quit after two years; he didn't understand budgets and couldn't bring himself to fire anybody. He returned to the air with a nightly 7:45 newscast which opened with the letters N-E-W-S in Morse code. London having made him, he retained the well-remembered phrases of those years in altered form, beginning each broadcast with "This — is the news," and signing off, "Goodnight — and good luck." In 1948 he and Fred W. Friendly produced their first *I Can Hear It Now* album, preserving voices which had made history in their time, and soon Murrow's annual year-end news roundups with CBS correspondents became as much a part of the Christmas holidays as Lionel Barrymore playing Scrooge.

He was reluctant to leave radio for television, but the switch was inevitable; he had become the country's most celebrated newscaster, and as *Cue* noted, he was "handsome enough to play a movie war correspondent." Millions who had never seen him had read of his "Doomsday look," or read Ernie Pyle's description of Murrow at his mike during the war: gesticulating, nodding, perspiring, glancing at the clock — and fumbling, always, for another cigarette. Beginning in 1951, with the debut of *See It Now* on CBS-TV, Americans could see Murrow at work on their living room screens. Because he was now at the height of his powers and insisted on complete independence from the network, they also saw some of the greatest broadcasts in the history of mass communications.

On December 28, 1952, Murrow took his cameras into the Korean front line to show the country what Christmas was like in foxholes. Nothing was too difficult, or too controversial, for *See It Now* and a companion program, *CBS Reports*. He interviewed Truman on MacArthur, MacArthur on Truman, and Khrushchev in the Kremlin. He investigated the cases of Harry Dexter White, Annie Lee Moss, J. Robert Oppenheimer, Irving Peress, and Lieutenant Milo Radulovich. *See It Now* was the first television program to discuss the relationship between cigarettes and lung cancer — a subject which Murrow, more than any other commentator, would have preferred not to think about. Most memorably, on the evening of March 9, 1954, *See It Now* tackled Senator McCarthy when he was his most powerful and exposed him as a fraud.

He said at the end: "This is no time for men who oppose Senator McCarthy's methods to keep silent. We can deny our heritage and our history, but we cannot escape responsibility for the result. There is no way for a citizen of a republic to abdicate his responsibilities."

It would be difficult to exaggerate the courage Murrow displayed on this program, or the malice it aroused. Merely by saying at the end of it, "I want to associate myself with every word just spoken by Ed Murrow," Don Hollenbeck, the network's regular 11 P.M. newscaster, touched off a Hearst crusade against himself which ended in his suicide. CBS — which was administering loyalty oaths to its own employees and hiring ex-FBI agents to investigate them — was appalled. (Murrow, now a director of the network, described the reaction of his colleagues at their next meeting as, "Good show. Sorry you did it.") McCarthy himself said scornfully that he hadn't seen it: "I never listen to the extreme left-wing, bleeding heart elements of radio and TV." He wouldn't deign to reply on the air, so CBS gave the time to Vice President Nixon, who spent it begging McCarthy to follow the Republican party line.

If Murrow's zeal as a cold-warrior was not fully appreciated then, it was only because it was shared by virtually everyone in the country, in public life and out. Like his countrymen he was an ardent advocate of NATO, the Truman Doctrine in Greece and Turkey, more spending on U.S. armaments, a stronger U.S. military presence in Europe, and the right of a President to send American troops abroad without congressional approval. He backed the Korean War — "We have drawn a line," he said approvingly, "not across the peninsula but across the world" — and he predicted that "some form of intervention" in Vietnam "may prove inescapable."

But he also shared the liberal vision of Wilsonian self-determination. After Pearl Harbor he had said that the State Department had "misjudged the nature of this war. It is a worldwide revolution, as well as a war." That in itself was enough to recommend him to John Kennedy when the new President was looking for a United States Information Agency (USIA) director in 1960.

Murrow accepted, partly because he reciprocated Kennedy's admiration but also because he was discouraged by what was happening to mass communications in the United States. With situation comedies, quiz shows, and mindless Westerns, television was grossing a billion dollars a year. Murrow spoke out bitterly against TV's "decadence, escapism, and insulation from the realities of the world in which we live," but the titans of the industry weren't listening. Already CBS had killed *See It Now* as a weekly program and replaced it with occasional specials. Admen called the new broadcasts *See It Now and Then*.

His last years were sad. Uncomfortable as a bureaucrat, he saw USIA's reputation for integrity fall, a casualty of the Johnson administration's decision to use the agency for the dissemination of propaganda about the Vietnam War. One of the grimmest of his Doomsday predictions was coming true; demonstrations were being staged for TV, and cameramen, by their very presence, were encouraging urban rioting. The networks were becoming increasingly shameless in their pursuit of the advertising dollar. "Station breaks" were lengthened from 32 to 42 seconds, to cram in more commercials. *CBS Reports*, the last of Murrow's great news programs, was replaced by a show about a talking horse. On the day he died in the spring of 1965, CBS announced his death — and followed the bulletin with a cigarette commercial.

His ashes were scattered over his farm in Pawling, New York. But that wasn't the end of Ed Murrow. Buried six feet below the farm's soil lay a new television cable. As long as it lies there, as long as the social function of communications retains its great potential, the spirit of the man will live

That — was Murrow.

SEVENTEEN

Into the Abyss

ILL HEALTH had forced Mary Acheson Bundy to leave her small son with her parents and enter a sanatorium in Saranac, New York. There, in that month of the Hiss verdict, she received a letter from her father noting that soon:

> . . . in a public speech I shall do my best to carry some sense of the problem in the Far East, the limitation of our power, the direction of our purpose. So much that is foolish, disloyal, and generally contemptible has been going on that it is good that we are — as I hope — free to go ahead on a clear and sensible course.

It was, in Acheson's words, "a supercharged moment to be speaking on Asian matters." The Chiang Kai-shek tragedy was now complete. He had been the generalissimo of a vast and superbly equipped army on V-J Day, and he had staggered from one setback to another until his forces melted away and he himself was a refugee on an island off the Chinese coast. Chiang's ineptness had been evident to nearly everyone who had been watching the disintegration of his strength. Even Colonel Robert R. McCormick of the *Chicago Tribune* had told the Associated Press, "The Chiang Kai-shek government cannot put down an insurrection which is falsely called a Communist insurrection." The colonel would soon change his mind, recognizing in the loss of China the most effective political issue since Roosevelt had wrested control of the White House from Hoover.

As Acheson posted the letter to his daughter, the Red Chinese regime was in its fourth month. Mao Tse-tung was in Moscow negotiating a Sino-Soviet friendship treaty with Joseph Stalin. Having just exploded his first atomic bomb, the Russian dictator had become a very useful friend to have. The American people knew that, and they were in no mood for gradations in guilt. Republicans on the attack encouraged the confusion in which Chiang, Fuchs, Hiss, Mao, the Rosenbergs, Yalta, and Acheson were all being wrapped up in one scarlet bundle. Senator Taft was being widely quoted as charging in the Senate that the State Department had "been guided by a left-wing group who obviously have wanted to get rid of Chiang and were willing at least to turn China over to the Communists for that purpose."

That was politics. Military strategy was something else. In 1947 the Joint Chiefs of Staff had unanimously agreed that South Korea was not worth fighting for, and on March 1, 1949, General MacArthur had told a *New York Times* correspondent in Tokyo:

> Our defensive dispositions against Asiatic aggression used to be based on the west coast of the American continent. The Pacific was looked upon as the avenue of possible enemy approach. Now the Pacific has become an Anglo-Saxon lake, and our line of defense runs through the chain of islands fringing the coast of Asia. It starts from the Philippines and continues through the Ryukyu Archipelago, which starts in its main bastion, Okinawa. Then it bends back through Japan and the Aleutian Island chain to Alaska.[*]

A glance at that bend on a map shows that strategically, at least, Mac-Arthur felt that he could live with hostile forces controlling Formosa or the Korean peninsula. But the general was a better politician than the Secretary of State. By the end of 1949 he was beginning to realize that American public opinion, shocked by the red star rising over mainland China, would interpret any further expansion by Communist arms as a stinging U.S. defeat. Acheson, for his part, remained resigned to a Maoist Taiwan. On December 18, 1949, he advised U.S. Asian missions that the importance of Formosa should be minimized since "its fall is widely anticipated." Two weeks later MacArthur leaked his copy of that memorandum to the press. In the general uproar Taft and Herbert Hoover demanded a naval defense of Formosa, but Truman vetoed it, and it was against this background that Acheson delivered the speech, first mentioned in the letter to his daughter, before the National Press Club on January 12, 1950.

Clearly it was no time for a Secretary of State to speak extemporaneously. His staff had therefore given him a thick folder of marked-up drafts. "But in the end," he writes in his memoirs, without further explanation, "I put the drafts aside and made the speech from a page or two of notes." For his audience he retraced the same defensive perimeter MacArthur had drawn ten months earlier, before the fall of China had altered the political picture in Washington: from the Aleutians to Japan, to the Ryukyus, to the Philippines. "So far as the military security of other areas in the Pacific is concerned," he added — and here he obviously had Formosa and South

---

[*]The general said substantially the same thing to G. Ward Price, the British journalist, that same month and to William R. Mathews of the *Arizona Daily Star* later in the year.

Korea in mind — "it must be clear that no person can guarantee these areas against military attack. Should such an attack occur," he declared, "the initial resistance" must come from "the people attacked." If they proved to be resolute fighters, he vaguely concluded, they were entitled to an appeal under the charter of the United Nations.

To the end of his life Acheson would bitterly deny that he had given the green light for aggression in South Korea by excluding it from the defensive perimeter. But when he told the Press Club that the United States was waiting "for the dust to settle" in China and added that America's line of resistance ran "along the Aleutians to Japan and then goes to the Ryukyus," the Communists could only conclude, as they did, that the United States was leaving people northwest of the Korea Strait to fend for themselves.

It was not like Acheson to misinterpret American policy, and in fact he had not done so. Like MacArthur the previous March, he had ruled out U.S. participation in an Asian land war. American intentions change, however. Hitler had failed to appreciate that, and as a consequence he had been destroyed. Now Stalin was repeating the error. The Soviet leader was dictating North Korean war plans (at this point Mao wasn't even advised of them) and he took Acheson at his word. The day after the secretary's Press Club speech Jacob Malik, the Russian representative at the United Nations, walked out on the Security Council because it had refused to reject the Chinese Nationalists and welcome emissaries from the new mainland regime. Stalin was putting the Americans on notice. From his point of view, the timing was perfect. The United States was drafting a Japanese peace treaty without consulting Moscow. Since V-J Day the Russians had been hoping that Washington would give them a free hand in Korea. In George Kennan's opinion, "When they saw it wasn't going to work out that way, they concluded: 'If this is all we are going to get out of a Japanese settlement, we had better get our hands on Korea fast before the Americans let the Japanese back in there.' "

Meanwhile Truman's global strategy had begun to pivot. In April the President, presiding over a meeting of the National Security Council, abandoned defense perimeters and moved toward a new strategy under which the country could meet any threat to non-Communist governments. It was at that session that the council adopted NSC 68, the paper which, among other things, determined that 20 percent of the country's future income would be set aside for military use. Wise or not, the decision should never have been kept secret. Stalin, unaware of it, assumed that South Korea was as ripe for plucking as Czechoslovakia had been in 1938. Later, congressional critics taxed Acheson for calling poor signals, though they were in no position to throw stones. A week after the secretary's Press Club speech the economy-minded lower house defeated 193 to 192 a small appropriation which would have provided five hundred U.S. Army officers to supervise the equipping of South Korean troops. That night Acheson wrote Mary:

> This has been a tough day, not so much by way of work, but by way of troubles. We took a defeat in the House on Korea, which seems to me to have been our own fault. One should not lose by one vote. We were complaisant and inactive. We have now a long road back.

The first intersection on that road lay dead ahead.

In January 1950 Joseph R. McCarthy was forty-one years old, and in more ways than one he was a man on the skids. Elected four years earlier in the Republican sweep of 1946, he was in a fair way to becoming a disgrace to the United States Senate — a cheap politician who had sunk to taking $10,000 from the Lustron Corporation, a manufacturer of prefabricated housing, and an unsecured $20,000 from the Washington lobbyist for Pepsi-Cola. He had spent it recklessly in speculation in soybean futures and long phone conversations with bookies. A few men on the Hill know that McCarthy's battered tan briefcase always carried a bottle of whiskey. He was in fact a borderline alcoholic, boastful among friends of his ability to "belt a fifth" every day. But at the rate he was going, he had six, maybe seven years left.

He was a rogue, and he looked the part. His eyes were shifty. When he laughed, he snickered. His voice was a high-pitched taunt. On the Senate floor he could be quickly identified by his heavy beard. He was in fact a prime specimen of what has been called the Black Irish: the thickset, bullshouldered, beetle-browed type found on Boston's Pier Eight and in the tenements of South Chicago. He lacked the genius of Huey Long and the faith in himself. What he had going for him was a phenomenal ability to lie and an intuitive grasp of the American communications industry. That and ruthlessness. If he had a creed it was nihilism, a belief in nothing, or next to nothing. He enjoyed reading his name in the newspapers, and he wanted to remain a senator.

Sometime after the Colony dinner, which had not been particularly helpful to him, McCarthy telephoned the Republican National Committee to say that he would be available on the Lincoln's birthday weekend, five weeks hence, for speeches about Communists in the government. If the committee staff was elated, they concealed it. Certainly they weren't surprised. This, after all, was the party line. Richard Nixon, the anti-Communist hero of the hour, was warning that the Hiss case was just "a small part of the shocking story of Communist espionage in the United States." Nixon was much in demand, but to the best of the Republican National Committee's knowledge, McCarthy knew nothing about Communism. The only Lincoln Day booking the staff could find for him was a spot before the Ohio County Women's Club in Wheeling, West Virgina, followed by dates in Salt Lake City and Reno. En route to Wheeling, the dutiful airline hostess, observing a U.S. Senator on her passenger list, said, "Good afternoon, Senator McCarthy." He looked startled. "Why, good afternoon," he said. "I'm glad somebody recognizes me."

Before enplaning he had done a little — a very little — homework. It would be too much to call it research. For the most part his "rough draft," as he later described it to reporters, was a scissors-and-paste job made up of passages from other Republican addresses, only slightly altered. According to the *Wheeling Intelligencer*, he had hacked out a paragraph from a speech Nixon had delivered in the House of Representatives on January 26:

NIXON IN CONGRESS	MCCARTHY IN WHEELING
The great lesson which should be learned from the Hiss case is that we are not just dealing with espionage agents who get 30 pieces of silver to obtain the blueprint of a new weapon . . . but this is a far more sinister type of activity, because it permits the enemy to guide and shape our policy.	One thing to remember in discussing the Communists is that we are not dealing with spies who get 30 pieces of silver to steal the blueprint of a new weapon. We are dealing with a far more sinister type of activity because it permits the enemy to guide and shape our policy.

So far as is known, his own investigation of subversion was limited to a single telephone call. He phoned Willard Edwards of the *Chicago Tribune* Washington staff and told him he needed help for his speech. From Edwards he learned of two inquiries, both brief and largely forgotten, into the loyalty of State Department workers. The first could be found in files of the *Congressional Record*. On July 26, 1946, James F. Byrnes, then Secretary of State, had written Congressman Adolph J. Sabath of Illinois explaining that during a preliminary screening of some 3,000 employees who had been transferred to the State Department from wartime agencies, the screeners had recommended against the permanent employment of 284. Of these, 79 had been discharged. By subtracting 79 from 284, McCarthy acquired the magical figure of 205 — 205 people whose dismissal had been suggested but who had still been on the rolls at the time of Byrnes's letter.* The senator's other source was known to anti-Communist vigilantes as "the Lee list." Robert E. Lee was the investigator for a House appropriations subcommittee who had been permitted to examine 108 State Department personnel files in connection with the *Amerasia* case. In 1948 the department had sent the committee a statistical summary reporting that of the 108, those still in departmental employ numbered 57 — the "Heinz Varieties figure," as Richard H. Rovere would soon call it in the *New Yorker*.

*The implication is that by the time of McCarthy's Wheeling speech the figure may have become out of date. It was. In the August 1950 *Harper's* Alfred Friendly reported that as of February 1950 just 65 of the 205 were still in the State Department's employ. Of course Friendly had made more than one phone call. That kind of digging was beyond McCarthy's comprehension.

Thus Senator McCarthy had two numbers, 205 and 57. But that was *all* he had. To grasp the dimensions of his fraud, one must remember that at this point he had no dossiers, no raw data, and no specifications, however vague. He knew of the two outdated lists, but he had neither. If pressed, he was incapable of producing a single name, and was embarking on a speaking tour which would take him to West Virginia, to Utah after a change of planes in Colorado, and then to Reno, Nevada. On the other hand, it is highly unlikely that he anticipated a challenge. He expected to deliver a few time-honored homilies before small audiences of Republican women and return to find that Wisconsin papers had carried accounts of his trip, reminding Republican functionaries and contributors back home of his existence. Of course, he would make two or three wild charges, but they would be no wilder than those of other GOP speakers that weekend. Later he realized that he had stumbled upon a brilliant demagogic technique. Others deplored treachery. McCarthy would speak of *traitors*.

Wheeling's radio station WWVA recorded his remarks there and put them on the air that night. Unfortunately for history, the tape was erased immediately after the broadcast. All that survives, beyond the recollections of others present, are the notes of a *Wheeling Intelligencer* reporter named Frank Desmond. According to Desmond, the famous passage was:

> While I cannot take the time to name all the men in the State Department who have been named as members of the Communist Party and members of a spy ring, I have here in my hand a list of 205 that were known to the Secretary of State as being members of the Communist Party and are still working and shaping the policy of the State Department.

He may have been holding a laundry list, a shopping list, or an old Christmas card list. Whatever it was, it cannot have been important, because afterward he threw it away. Back in Washington the following week, with half the capital demanding that he prove his charges, he would try desperately — without success — to find out exactly what he had said. He even tried appealing to ham radio operators in the area who might have made a recording of the speech. He found none.

Desmond's story appeared in the *Intelligencer* and was reprinted inside the *Chicago Tribune* and on the front page of the *Denver Post*. Three days were to pass before the *New York Times* published the senator's charges. The Associated Press put two paragraphs of Desmond's account on its B wire, however, and someone in the State Department read them, for when the senator changed planes in Denver a newspaperman told him the department wanted the names of those accused so that investigations could begin at once. McCarthy said he had been misquoted; he had spoken not of 205 Communists but of 205 "bad security risks." The reporter asked if he might see the list. Of course, said the senator. Then he said he had left it in his baggage on the plane. The *Denver Post* has preserved a photograph showing McCarthy peering forlornly into his battered briefcase, searching for the fugitive list.

Late in the afternoon of February 20 a three-bell quorum call sounded in the Senate, and Joe McCarthy strode out on the floor carrying the tan briefcase, now bulging. The Democrats had demanded evidence, and twice since his return to the capital he had assured newspapermen that if he couldn't come up with it, he would resign. Now he was going to give the Senate one of the wildest evening sessions in its history. He had more than figures this time, though not much more. Lee had provided him with photostated copies of the 108 two-year-old dossiers prepared from State Department files for the House appropriations subcommittee. Of their subjects, only 40 still worked for the department. All had been subjected to a full field FBI investigation and cleared. Nevertheless, McCarthy stacked 81 obsolete dossiers on his desk and those of nearby senators and grandly announced that he had penetrated "Truman's iron curtain of secrecy."

The next few minutes were awful. Shuffling the first folders, he said that he would identify them by number only. That in itself was suspicious — after all, anything said on the floor was privileged — but what followed was shocking. Spectators realized that McCarthy was looking at these dossiers *for the first time.* He had to pause before each, riffling through papers to see what it contained. Another man would have been embarrassed beyond endurance. Not McCarthy. He stood there almost six hours, carrying the absurd farce forward, shrugging heavily when the files baffled him but never yielding the floor.

Some of his cases had nothing to do with the State Department. Numbers 21 through 26 worked for the Voice of America. Number 12 had once been employed by the Department of Commerce; McCarthy blandly conceded that he had no idea "where he is today. I frankly do not know." Number 62 was "not important insofar as Communistic activities are concerned." Of number 40 he said, "I do not have much information on this except that there is nothing in the files to disprove his Communist connections." Number 72 had the senator stumped. It was significant, he lamely said, "in that it is the direct opposite of the cases I have been reading. . . . I do not confuse this man as being a Communist. This individual was very highly recommended by several witnesses as a high type of man, a democratic American who . . . opposed Communism." (In addition, 72 had never worked for the State Department.) Astounded, Richard Rovere asked, "Could anything but sheer lunacy lead a man discussing 81 Communists to say that one of the Communists was an important example because he was not a Communist?"

But McCarthy plodded on doggedly. Number 9 was the same as number 77. Numbers 15, 27, 37, and 59 did not exist — they were just empty folders. Numbers 13 and 78 had only applied for jobs. Number 14, who was "primarily a morals case," appeared in the dossier of number 41. Number 52 was of note only because he worked for number 16 — "who," McCarthy said, with the tone of a man finding gold at last, was "one of the most dangerous espionage agents in the Department."

He wasn't, of course. There wasn't a spy in the lot. But by inserting a phrase in a file here, deleting another there, and embellishing the whole performance with spurious investigative paraphernalia, he created an impression of subversion among those who read their newspapers by studying the comics first, the sports page next, and then glancing carelessly through the headlines. Sometimes McCarthy's alterations of truth in that February 20 performance were small. Three people "with Russian names" became "three Russians." Words like "reportedly" and "allegedly" vanished; "may have been" and "may be" were replaced by "was" and "is"; "considerable derogatory information" was translated into "conclusive evidence of Communist activity." Other changes were startling. Notations of FBI clearance were omitted or turned into FBI findings of guilt. If a "good American" had been turned away by State Department recruiting agents it was because they hired only Communists; the fact that the applicant may have been nearly seventy years old was unmentioned. The Republicans were aghast. Kenneth Wherry, the party's floor leader, did wha: he could for McCarthy with parliamentary motions, but avoided iden:ification with him. Taft, who hardly knew McCarthy, told reporters afterward, "It was a perfectly reckless performance."

By the following morning the obsolescence of the folders was known and revealed on front pages. Jubilant Senate Democrats caucused and instructed their majority leader, Scott Lucas of Illinois, to call for "a full and complete" inquiry into "whether persons who are disloyal to the United States are or have been employed by the Department of State." Since the other Republicans were keeping their distance from McCarthy, and since he had insisted that he would welcome an investigation, Lucas's Senate Resolution 231 passed unanimously. Wherry did try to refer it to the Appropriations Committee, whose right-wing chairman, Kenneth McKellar of Tennessee, would have seen to it that liberal Democrats were given the least possible aid and comfort. That move failed on a straight party vote, and the matter went to Foreign Relations. There Tom Connally of Texas appointed a tough committee chaired by Millard E. Tydings, the aggressive patrician who had dominated Maryland politics for a quarter-century. Even before the naming of his fellow members (Brien McMahon of Connecticut and Theodore Francis Green of Rhode Island, Democrats; Henry Cabot Lodge of Massachusetts and Bourke B. Hickenlooper of Iowa, Republicans), McCarthy was calling it a kangaroo court. Tydings promised "neither a witch hunt, nor a whitewash." In private, however, he spoke patronizingly of Wisconsin's junior senator as "that boy." He had no way of knowing that this would be the first of five senatorial attempts to investigate McCarthy's charges, none of which would find anyone at the bottom of it all except McCarthy himself.

Of course, he had *some* help. Nobody, not even Joe McCarthy, could build that big a bonfire all alone. No congressional endeavor can get very far without lobbyists of some sort, and the fact that McCarthy had phoned a *Chicago Tribune* correspondent before flying to Wheeling is an indication that he knew where help lay. The role of investigator Lee is another sign. From the moment McCarthy's star began to rise over West Virginia, these men and their allies mounted a massive rescue operation, amassing names and data which would be available to him whenever he needed help. They hadn't chosen him, but he had chosen their issue. No alliance formed to influence legislation lands a U.S. Senator every day; when one does, the last thing it wants is to see him discredited.

This was the pressure group known as the China Lobby. For the most part it consisted of men employed by right-wing newspaper publishers: Willard Edwards and Walter Trohan of Colonel McCormick's *Tribune*; George Waters of the McCormick-owned *Washington Times-Herald*; Fulton Lewis Jr., whose broadcasts were heard over McCormick's Mutual radio network; Lawrence Kerley of William Randolph Hearst's *New York Journal-American*; Hearst reporters Howard Rushmore, Ken Hunter, and Ray Richards; and two Hearst columnists, George Sokolsky and J. B. Matthews. Matthews owned a copy of "Appendix Nine," the vigilante equivalent of anti-Semitism's Protocols of the Elders of Zion. Put together in 1944 by investigators for the House Committee on Un-American Activities, Appendix Nine comprised seven volumes containing 22,000 names gathered indiscriminately from letterheads and programs of organizations whose patriotism had been challenged, from informers, and from ultraconservative pamphlets published in the 1930s. Even the House Committee on Un-American Activities had thought it outrageous. The full membership had called it back and suppressed it, but Matthews had kept a pirated copy. Armed with it, McCarthy could talk endlessly, and anything missing from it could usually be acquired from Alfred Kohlberg, founder of the China Policy Association and chief patron of the China Lobby. For thirty years Kohlberg had profitably imported Oriental textiles from the mainland; with the collapse of Chiang Kai-shek he had been cut off, and now he funneled contributions from his considerable fortune into such publications as *Counter-Attack*, the *Freeman*, and Isaac Don Levine's *Plain Talk*.

These forces had been wandering around Washington looking for a leader. Now they were McCarthy's, and for the most part they served him well. His adversaries were formidable: the Democratic leadership on the Hill, President Truman (who said of him off the record that "the son of a bitch ought to be impeached"), and virtually every journalist to the left of McCormick and Hearst. In that first onrush of McCarthy, Joseph and Stewart Alsop were particularly effective, ridiculing the M.I.5 theatrics in

McCarthy's office — how during phone conversations he would strike the mouthpiece with a pencil "to jar the needle of any listening device," and how toward the end of a telephone conversation obviously staged for the benefit of his interviewers, he gripped the receiver and muttered: "Yeah, yeah, I can listen, but I can't talk. Get me? You really got the goods on the guy? Yeah? Well, I tell you. Just mention this sort of casual to Number One, and get his reaction. Okay? Okay, I'll contact you later."

Walter Lippmann reported the impact of the senator's pyrotechnics on the Secretary of State: "No American official who has represented this government abroad in great affairs, not even Wilson in 1918, has ever been so gravely injured at home." Many old liberal publications such as the *Baltimore Sun* were strangely reticent in McCarthy's first year, but the *Washington Post* fought him every inch of the way; so did the *New York Times* and the *St. Louis Post-Dispatch*; and *Time* climbed on his back and stayed there. Probably the greatest stroke on either side of the battle was the work of Herbert Block ("Herblock"), the *Post's* cartoonist. Block created an eponym by crudely lettering "McCarthyism" on a barrel of mud shakily supported by ten mud-bespattered buckets.

Yet the senator and his gamy henchmen always seemed to be gaining. Lippmann's stately prose was a pale thing beside McCarthy's description of the country's majority party: "The Democratic label is now the property of men and women who have . . . bent to the whispered pleas from the lips of traitors . . . men and women who wear the political label stitched with the idiocy of a Truman, rotted by the deceit of an Acheson, corrupted by the red slime of a [Harry Dexter] White." Even Herblock's contribution was turned around when Fulton Lewis told his listeners, "To many Americans, McCarthyism is Americanism," and the senator, addressing a Wisconsin audience, said, "McCarthyism is Americanism with its sleeves rolled."*

None of his sloganeering and billingsgate would have mattered much had it not been for one painful fact: McCarthy had kindled a fire in America's grass roots. Even as his facade was torn asunder, as his fellow senators took his accusations apart one by one and exposed his lies two by two, till he sat exposed (and grinning) before them, his support grew and stiffened across the land. The evidence was unmistakable. Gallup consistently found that 50 percent of the public had a "favorable opinion" of the senator and thought he was helping the country; only 29 percent disapproved of him and 21 percent had no opinion at all. Reporters who accompanied McCarthy on post-Wheeling campaign trips were shocked by the tributes to him, and those on the Hill who discounted their stories were confronted by the most convincing attestation of all: the pyramids of rumpled dollar bills and change which arrived in McCarthy's mail each morning.

McCarthy invested the money in soybean futures while his fellow Repub-

---

* "Communism is twentieth-century Americanism" — Earl Browder, 1936 (see page 97).

licans began having second and then third thoughts. Wherry began throwing an arm around Joe's husky shoulders. William E. Jenner asked to be photographed with him. Homer Ferguson exchanged subversive lists with him. Owen Brewster and Karl E. Mundt offered the services of their staffs. Hickenlooper, sitting on the Tydings committee, began coming down hard on the side of his embattled colleague from Wisconsin. Over in the House, a District of Columbia subcommittee took testimony on one of McCarthy's most preposterous claims, "links between homosexuality and Communism," notably a Soviet plot to ensnare "women employees of the State Department by enticing them into a life of lesbianism." Finally the last GOP pillar fell. The possibility of unearthing another bona-fide Democratic traitor who would do to the administration's China policy what Hiss had done to the New Deal was too much for Robert A. Taft, and that monument of integrity announced that "the pro-Communist policies of the State Department fully justify Joe McCarthy in his demand for an investigation." He then said to McCarthy, "If one case doesn't work, try another." As though Joe needed to be told.

On March 21 the conjurer's bag of tricks was empty, or so it appeared. Then McCarthy concocted the greatest prank of all. He told the Tydings committee that he was about to name the "top Russian espionage agent" in the United States. The committee assembled for an emergency session. There McCarthy blandly admitted that he had nothing new. "There's nothing mysterious about this one," he said. "This has all been put in the record already, plus some exhibits." And so it had. Owen Lattimore, a professor at Johns Hopkins and specialist in Asian studies — he was at that moment in the interior of Afghanistan — was neither a Communist nor an employee of the State Department. He had advised the government in Far Eastern matters, and the cold realism of his reports on Chiang Kai-shek had aroused the wrath of the China lobbyists, particularly Kohlberg. Everything there was to know about the man was known on the Hill. All the same, McCarthy informed the incredulous Tydings that Lattimore was "definitely an espionage agent," that his file was "explosive." He added: "If you crack this case, it will be the biggest espionage case in the history of this country." The following morning he laid all this before the press, withholding only Lattimore's name. He said, "I am willing to stand or fall on this one. If I am wrong on this, I think the subcommittee would be justified in not taking my other cases too seriously." The man whose name was in his pocket, he said, was that of the superspy who had been "Alger Hiss's boss in the espionage ring in the State Department."

That was on a Tuesday. By the end of the week Lattimore was being mentioned with increasing frequency in the Senate press gallery, and on Sunday, March 26, Drew Pearson broke the story. McCarthy, meantime, was going into one of his disappearing acts, vanishing only to return with an entirely different charge. Summoned from Afghanistan, Lattimore had sent word that he really wasn't the top Russian espionage agent in the United States, and he was flying back to clear up any misunderstandings on that score. But McCarthy had begun to say that he, too, had been misunderstood. "I fear in the case of Lattimore," he said on the Senate floor the following Thursday, "I have perhaps placed too much stress on the question of whether or not he has been an espionage agent." What he had really meant to say was that the professor was "the chief architect of our Far Eastern policy." The man was a "policy risk," McCarthy said, and then he said, "I believe you can ask almost any schoolchild who the architect of our Far Eastern policy is, and he will say, 'Owen Lattimore.'" The press gallery, where men were still trying to get information about the obscure professor, rocked with laughter.

Lattimore testified before the committee under klieg lights on April 6. The crowd in the marble-columned Senate caucus room, the largest since Wendell Willkie's appearance there to endorse lend-lease nine years earlier, heard the witness deny every allegation. He produced personal letters from Chiang Kai-shek and Madame Chiang expressing profound gratitude for his services. Tydings then revealed that four members of the committee had studied his loyalty file and found no evidence of subversion in it. Lattimore received an ovation and departed. Four days later McCarthy produced Louis Budenz, a former managing editor of the *Daily Worker,* who swore that in 1944 his superiors in the party had told him "to consider Owen Lattimore as a Communist."

The right-wing senators crowed. There, they said triumphantly; Joe had proved it; Budenz had been Lattimore's Whittaker Chambers. Two conservative newspapermen were briefly gulled. William S. White reported that Budenz had been "officially informed" that Lattimore was a traitor, and Arthur Krock observed that "many fair-minded persons" were changing their minds about McCarthy. They didn't keep them changed long. Abe Fortas and Paul Porter, Lattimore's lawyers, led Budenz through a devastating cross-examination. Yes, he conceded, in four years of FBI interviews he had told everything he knew about the Communist party. No, he had never mentioned Owen Lattimore. Yes, in 1947 he had advised a State Department security officer that Lattimore was not a Communist. Yes, in early 1949 he had written an article for *Collier's* magazine denying that Lattimore was a Communist. Yes, it was true that Owen Lattimore's name had appeared in none of Budenz's books about American Communists. How did he reconcile all this with his present testimony? He replied weakly that "in another book which I am writing Mr. Lattimore is very prominent." He stepped down and was succeeded by two other ex-Communists, Bella V. Dodd and Freda Utley. Miss Dodd ridiculed the notion that Lattimore was a Communist. Miss Utley was hazier, but she was certain he hadn't been a spy — and when it came to that, even Budenz found the allegation of espionage startling. McCarthy was unrepentant. He set his sights on another old China hand who, he averred, had written "a book which sets forth his pro-Communist answer to the problems of Asia as clearly as Hitler's *Mein Kampf* set forth his solutions for the problems of Europe." Questioned after reporters had left, he admitted that he hadn't read the book. In fact, he didn't even know the title. He promised to look it up. Once more he had been confuted; once more his name was in all the headlines.

Tydings's confidence was ebbing. He was being outfoxed and out-bludgeoned, and he was too skillful a politician not to sense it. While he was shaping the report — which would be read only by Americans already aware of McCarthy's infamy — public support for McCarthy continued to grow. Even as Republican Margaret Chase Smith of Maine promulgated her anti-McCarthy "Declaration of Conscience," signed by her and five other liberal Republican senators, Majority Leader Lucas, counting noses, discovered that just twelve Senate Democrats had spoken out against McCarthy. Tydings had won all the battles of reason and decency, but McCarthy had never tried to be reasonable or decent; he was a political charlatan, and his brand of quackery was sweeping the spring primaries. While the committee which had investigated him debated whether to use this adjective or that adverb, Willis Smith was ousting North Carolina Senator Frank P. Graham with a McCarthyite campaign; Congressman George A. Smathers was defeating Florida's liberal Senator Claude Pepper with a second McCarthyite campaign; and the senatorial candidacy of California's Helen Gahagan Douglas was being smeared by Manchester Boddy in a third McCarthyite primary — with Richard Nixon preparing yet a fourth McCarthyite campaign which would defeat her in the general election.

Thus the report was discredited before it had been written. In the end it ran pretty much as expected, accusing McCarthy of perpetrating "a fraud and a hoax" and engaging in deliberate, willful falsehoods. Knowing what it would be like, McCarthy had already branded it "a disgrace to the Senate" and "a green light to the Red fifth column in the United States." Taft had called the proceedings a "farce," a "whitewash," and an insult to "a fighting Irish Marine." Owen Brewster of Maine echoed him, Wherry assailed Acheson, and Republican National Chairman Guy Gabrielson maintained that the GOP was uncovering "spies, emissaries, agents and members of the Communist party" who "infest the government of the United States."

By summer optimists thought they saw signs that McCarthy had run his course. The wire services were reducing his news conferences to an inch or two of type, and most papers weren't printing that. Events in the struggle with Reds abroad had overwhelmed his sideshow; when he took the floor to brandish an "FBI report" exposing "three Communist agents" in the State Department, J. Edgar Hoover's repudiation of the performance surprised no one. For the moment, at least, McCarthyism seemed to be finished.

It was an illusion. Against all logic, Americans by the tens of millions had come to regard Wisconsin's junior senator as the symbol of anti-Communism, and as long as Communism remained an issue, he would be a hero to them. His arrogance continued to grow. Reminded that he had not replied to the committee's indictment, he said, "I don't answer charges, I make them." A reporter asked, "Wasn't that a classified document you were reading?" The senator snapped, "It *was*. I declassified it." At a cocktail party a girl inquired, "Senator McCarthy, when did you discover Communism?" Leering, he shot back: "Two and a half months ago."

While the government of the United States was engrossed in the question of how many Communists, if any, had worked in the State Department (205? 57? 108? 40? 66? 25? 1? 0?), the government of North Korea was deploying nine superbly equipped divisions to invade the almost defenseless Republic of Korea. Led by 20,000 Korean Communists who had been blooded in the great Russo-German battles of World War II, including Stalingrad, the 120,000-man North Korea Peoples Army (NKPA) was an elite force by any military standard. Supporting its troops were 122-mm howitzers, 76-mm divisional howitzers, 76-mm self-propelled guns, 120-mm mortars, the whole family of Soviet antiaircraft guns, and every imaginable infantry weapon from antitank rifles to burp guns. Sharpening the tip of the assault spear were 150 T-34 Soviet tanks — the steel giants that had shattered Krupp's Tigerpanzers in the Kursk salient — and clouds of Yak and Stormovik fighter planes. In the expert opinion of Colonel Robert D. Heinl Jr., USMC, the NKPA "was, among the Armed Forces of the Far East, probably better trained and equipped for its intended work than any other Army but Russia's."

Against it South Korean President Syngman Rhee could field little more than a constabulary. Ironically, the Pentagon had deliberately weakened Rhee's 65,000-man Army of the Republic of Korea (ROK). Each of the two Koreas had repeatedly announced its intention to invade the other and unite the peninsula in blood, but although the NKPA had regularly crossed the 38th Parallel with patrols — some of them as large as 1,500 men — Washington's main worry was seventy-five-year-old Rhee. To thwart his aggressive instincts, his ROK units were armed with ancient Japanese model 99 Mausers, short-range M-3 105-mm howitzers, obsolete 2.36-inch bazookas, no mortars larger than 81 mm, no recoilless rifles, no tanks, no offensive artillery, and no warplanes. The administration in Washington was the chief culprit in this negligence, but Capitol Hill was an accessory. Truman had earmarked sixty million dollars for South Korea in his 1950–51 budget, and Congress had cut it out. American hope for South Korean defense was vested in a U.S. Military Advisory Group. It was a frail hope; in Seoul, Rhee's capital, the advisory officers were training ROK troops as MPs. Beyond that, the Americans provided only bombast. As late as June 13, 1950, the administration's William C. Foster testified before a congressional committee that "the rigorous training program [in South Korea] has built up a well-disciplined Army of 100,000 soldiers, one that is prepared to meet any challenge by the North Korean forces and one that has cleaned out the guerrilla bands in South Korea in one area after another"; and in a *Time* interview on the very eve of hostilities, homeward-bound Brigadier General William L. Roberts, the group's CO, called his protégés "the best damn Army outside the United States."

It wasn't true, and it wasn't saying much. The greatest shock awaiting the American people was the feeble state of their own military establishment. Its decline had begun with the Wanna-Go-Home riots, which had turned postwar demobilization into a rout; the United States had "fought the war like a football game," said General Albert C. Wedemeyer, "after which the winner leaves the field and celebrates." Then the unification controversy had torn service morale asunder. Secretary of Defense Louis Johnson announced his intention to "trim the fat out of the Armed Forces" and slashed away a lot of muscle by cutting their budgets from 30 billion dollars to 14.2 billions. The Pentagon abandoned defensive radar screens and protective devices to counter the new Russian submarines. By 1950 Russia had as many combat airplanes as the United States, four times as many troops, and thirty tank divisions to America's one. Only one U.S. infantry division approached top combat efficiency; altogether the Army had just 592,000 men in uniform, less than half its strength on Pearl Harbor Sunday. Lastly, the four divisions of U.S. occupation troops in Japan had been allowed to deteriorate until, in the later words of General William F. Dean, they had become a flabby force accustomed to "Japanese girl-friends, plenty of beer, and servants to shine their boots."

Their commanders could not plead ignorance of enemy intentions. Korea had an unhappy history of partitions reaching back to 108 B.C., and since V-J Day the 38th Parallel had become increasingly troubled. Apart from the patrolling back and forth and the saber-rattling of Rhee and Kim Il Sung, Rhee's counterpart in the North Korean capital of Pyongyang, the Central Intelligence Agency had alerted Washington to the probability of coming violence. CIA reports describing the immense NKPA buildup along the frontier warned that it could be justified only by plans for a large-scale offensive. If no one else read CIA briefs, the Secretary of State did; in testifying before congressional committees he had read several intelligence cables into the record, including one dated March 10, 1950, predicting that the "PA [NKPA] will attack South Korea in June 1950." To be sure, thirty months earlier the Joint Chiefs had told the White House that "from the standpoint of military security" the United States had "little strategic interest" in Korea. It hadn't had it then, perhaps, but any President who refused to confront fresh Communist aggression now would risk impeachment. Afterward the administration pointed out that Korea had been but one of many danger spots. Berlin had been threatening to erupt, the French had faced disaster in Indochina, and Romanian and Bulgarian troops were massing on Yugoslavia's frontiers. Administration defenders argued that it couldn't be on its toes everywhere. Precisely. That was the trouble with containment.

Entering the last weekend in June 1950, the United States stirred feebly in the hundred-degree temperatures of that summer's first heat wave. Those who could do it left their little television screens for air-conditioned theaters. Children were watching Robert Newton as Long John Silver in Walt Disney's *Treasure Island*. Joyce Cary's *The Horse's Mouth* offered literate escape in hammocks. On Morningside Heights Dwight Eisenhower, president of Columbia University, holed up with *The Maverick Queen*, Zane Grey's fifty-first novel, published posthumously. Dean Acheson spent the afternoon gardening on Harewood Farm, his Maryland home, and read himself to sleep after dinner. Outside, stealthy shadows flicked back and forth; since the rise of McCarthy the secretary's hate mail had become so great that he needed bodyguards around the clock.

Secretary of Defense Louis Johnson and Omar Bradley, chairman of the Joint Chiefs of Staff, were somewhere over the Pacific, flying home from Tokyo. President Truman was also airborne early that afternoon; at 2 P.M. Saturday his aircraft *Independence* darted down through a bank of storm clouds and entered its glide pattern above the Kansas City municipal airfield. Two hours before, the President had dedicated Baltimore's new Friendship International Airport ("to the cause of peace in the world"); now he expected to spend the rest of the weekend going over some family business with his brother Vivian and enjoying the company of old friends. White House correspondents had been told that the lid was on; no presidential activities were expected before Monday.

As usual, the higher echelons of the government were celebrating the President's absence from Washington by relaxing. Dean Rusk, the Assistant Secretary of State for Asian Affairs, was uncoiling at the home of Joseph Alsop. W. Bradley Connors, the department's public affairs officer for the Far East, was playing with his children in his Washington apartment. The last place any of them might have expected new developments was the United Nations; the U.N. had been deadlocked since January, when Jacob Malik of the USSR had begun boycotting the Security Council. The U.S. Representative on the Council was Warren Austin. He was pruning his apple orchard in Vermont. His deputy, Ernest Gross, was also away from the office, supervising a teen-age party in his Manhasset home on Long Island. Trygve Lie, secretary general of the United Nations, was loafing in nearby Forest Hills.

It was early afternoon in New York, noon in the Middle West, and 4 A.M. on the faraway 38th Parallel when, as MacArthur later put it, "North Korea struck like a cobra."

The summer monsoon had just begun there. Heavy rains were falling on the green rice paddies and the barren brown and gray mountain slopes when the North Korean artillery — forty miles of big guns, standing side by side — opened fire. The shelling was sporadic at first, as smaller batteries awaited flare signals from the 122-mm NKPA howitzers, but presently all artillery pieces were erupting flame, sheet after sheet of it, while officers studied the crumps to the south and corrected their ranges. Overhead, Yaks and Stormoviks winged through the warm moist air toward Seoul, less than fifty miles away. Like the Chinese, the North Koreans still used the bugle to herald charges, and with its first notes infantrymen lunged across the border toward their first objectives. Despite the rain and inevitable confusion in the darkness, NKPA General Chai Ung Jun put 90,000 men into South Korea without any traffic jams. Junks and sampans were landing amphibious troops ashore behind ROK lines to the south. Awakening to the din, South Koreans fumbled for their clothes. In a few hours they would be on the roads, hurrying away from the roar over the horizon. Some would be refugees for the rest of their lives.

Six hours later, at 8 P.M. Eastern Daylight Saving Time, Bradley Connors became the first U.S. official in Washington to hear the news. Donald Gonzales of the United Press phoned to tell him that the UP correspondent in Korea was cabling fragmentary bulletins reporting heavy North Korean attacks all along the 38th Parallel. Did State know anything about it? Not to the best of his knowledge, Connors replied, but he would find out for certain right away. Hanging up, he tried to place a call to the U.S. embassy in Seoul. It was impossible, the operator told him; Sunday morning had arrived there, and all overseas circuits were closed. Connors hurried to the C Street entrance of the New State Department Building, but before an emergency circuit could be put together the department's communication center received a cable from John J. Muccio, the American ambassador in Seoul. Stamped in at 9:26 P.M., it read:

> North Korean forces invaded Republic of Korea at several places this morning. . . . It would appear from the nature of the attack and the manner in which it was launched that it cons
titutes an all-out offensive against the Republic of Korea.

Dean Rusk and John Hickerson, the department's assistant secretary for United Nations affairs, were quickly summoned, and at 10 P.M. Hickerson awoke Dean Acheson. Hickerson proposed a special meeting of the U.N. Security Council in the morning to call for a cease-fire. Since Warren Austin was in Vermont, he added, Ernest Gross should take the initiative in New York. Acheson agreed, instructed him to summon the Security Council through Trygve Lie, and picked up the white telephone that tied him in to the White House switchboard.

In Independence the Trumans had finished their evening meal. In the library of their home on North Delaware Street, the householder had begun to yawn; it was nearly his bedtime. Nevertheless, after Acheson's opening words — "Mr. President, I have very serious news. The North Koreans have invaded South Korea" — he said he would fly back at once. Better get a good night's sleep, Acheson advised him. Apart from putting the U.N. wheels in motion, nothing could be done now; they had to wait for more information. He would call again in the morning. The President asked if he could do anything now, and Acheson said yes, as a matter of fact, he could; Louis Johnson had imposed absurd restrictions on communications between the State and Defense departments. He would like to deal directly with Secretary of the Army Frank Pace. Done, said Truman; he hung up, and the secretary began gathering in his hands the reins of American initiative. As he saw it, the chief theater of action now, even more important than the battlefield, was at Lake Success, New York.

"My God, Jack," said Trygve Lie when Hickerson called him, "this is war against the United Nations!" And so it was. The two Koreas were wards of the U.N. The United States merely represented it in the south. At Potsdam the Big Three had agreed that the peninsula's future would be determined in supervised elections; then the Russians had changed their minds and refused to allow U.N. commissioners above the 38th Parallel. At Acheson's direction, his staff drafted a Security Council resolution determining that the "armed attack on the Republic of Korea by forces from North Korea" constituted "a breach of the peace" and should be terminated at once in a cease-fire. Since the Soviet boycott of the council continued to be in effect, the measure passed 9 to 0.

Sunday morning the news from Muccio was all bad. A strong NKPA tank column was driving toward Seoul and Kimpo airport, apparently advancing at will; "South Korean arms," Acheson concluded, were "clearly outclassed." At 12:35 P.M. he phoned Independence and asked the President to return. Before boarding his aircraft Truman had a few words for reporters: "Don't make it alarmist. It could be a dangerous situation, but I hope it isn't. I can't answer any questions until I get all the facts." Back at 1628 Pennsylvania Avenue, he ordered an immediate conference of all his diplomatic and military advisers around Blair House's large mahogany dining table. There he made three decisions: MacArthur would be told to use all the planes and ships necessary for the evacuation of American civilians from Korea, going above the 38th Parallel if necessary; the general was to provide the ROK troops with ammunition; and the U.S. Seventh Fleet would patrol Formosa Strait, against the possibility that the Korean thrust was a feint masking a leap to Taiwan. Had Mao pursued Chiang there a year earlier, the Americans would have stood aside. Now domestic politics made U.S. neutrality impossible.

Monday, the fifth anniversary of the United Nations, was a dark day, "a day," said Acheson "of steadily worsening reports from Korea." Ignoring the U.N. appeal for a cease-fire, NKPA troops were enveloping Rhee's Seoul in a six-pronged drive. Already Rhee's government was moving south. The roads were solid with terrified people. ROK soldiers were still running; a desperate stand at Chunchon had disintegrated with the arrival of the first T-34 tank. Dr. John Myun Chang, the Korean ambassador to the U.S., called at the White House. Spinning the big globe in his office and putting his hand on Korea, the President said, "This is the Greece of the Far East. If we are tough enough now, there won't have to be any next step." Unconsoled, Dr. Chang left in tears. At 9 P.M. Truman convened another emergency session in Blair House. The "war cabinet," as he now called it, heard Chip Bohlen and George Kennan say that Russia's absence from the Security Council offered a great opportunity for the United States; they needn't worry about a Russian veto. With this in mind, the President approved a new Council resolution calling upon all U.N. members to lend a hand in throwing the North Koreans back. Obviously the most help would be expected from the Americans, and Truman was prepared to provide it. With the approval of his advisers, he directed naval and Air Force units in MacArthur's command to give direct tactical support to ROK defenders south of the 38th Parallel. At Acheson's urging, he also increased support of French troops fighting in Indochina.

Seoul fell Wednesday, and the ROK defenders retreated to the Han River. In Long Island's Stockholm Restaurant that noon, three unlikely diplomats — Trygve Lie, Jacob Malik, and Ernest Gross — met to keep a long-standing luncheon date. Naturally they talked about the war; there was nothing else to talk about. Malik held that Sunday's Security Council resolution was "illegal" because no Russian delegate had been present and Red China had not been admitted. While Gross waited tensely, Lie met his responsibilities as a scrupulous Secretary General. Forget about Sunday, he advised Malik; come to this afternoon's Council meeting and hear the new American resolution. "Won't you join us?" he asked. "The interests of your country would seem to me to call for your presence." But the Russian shook his head. He said vehemently, "No, I will not go there." Outside, Gross mopped his brow. He said to Lie, "Think what would have happened if he had accepted your invitation." What would have happened would have been a Soviet veto of the new U.S. move and then, in all probability, American intervention in Korea unsupported by the U.N. — in short, an earlier Vietnam.

Tuesday evening Americans with TV sets watched their first U.N. session, oddly interspersed between commercials and the performances of two children's puppets named Foodini and Pinhead. Malik's seat remained vacant, and the strong U.S. resolution carried. For the first time in history, an international organization had decided to resist aggression with force. That was how editorial writers put it the following morning, for Truman's decision to provide the ROK troops with naval support and air cover was enormously popular. When it was announced on the Hill, Congress rose in a standing ovation. The White House press received it with broad smiles. As titular head of the Republican party, Governor Dewey enthusiastically supported U.S. intervention. Even the *Chicago Tribune* congratulated the President, noting that approval of his stand was unanimous.

It wasn't quite. One man stood against the tide. All day Tuesday, while the Senate debated the new course of foreign policy, Robert Taft had sat apart, his head resting in his hand, thoughtful and silent. Now on Wednesday he took the floor. He charged that the administration had "invited" the NKPA attack by declaring that Korea lay beyond the American defensive perimeter. No wonder the North Koreans felt they could strike south with impunity, he said; "If the United States was not prepared to use its troops and give military assistance to Nationalist China against Chinese Communists, why should it use its troops to defend Nationalist Korea against Korean Communists?" Make no mistake, Taft said; he approved using U.S. might to throw the invaders back across the 38th Parallel, and if the administration had brought the issue before the Senate, he would have voted for it. But it hadn't. Instead it had "usurped the power of Congress," creating dangerous precedents for the future. The Constitution extended the right to declare war to Congress alone, and the President's action "unquestionably has brought about a de facto war." Taft concluded: "So far as I can see, and so far I have studied the matter, I would say there is no authority to use Armed Forces in support of the United Nations in the absence of some previous action by Congress dealing with the subject."

He sat down. The right-wing Republican senators gave him token applause, and, when the moment arose, expressed other views. On the question of whether the President "arrogates to himself the power to declare war," said William Knowland of California, "I believe that in the very important steps the President of the United States has taken to uphold . . . the United Nations and the free peoples of the world, he should have the overwhelming support of all Americans regardless of their party affiliation." The rest of the Taft bloc broke into loud, sustained applause. What with the prospect of a ROK stand on the Han, a Chiang Kai-shek offer of 33,000 Kuomintang veterans to fight the North Korean aggressors, and news that all British warships in the Pacific had been placed under the command of the U.S. Navy, the country was in no mood to weigh fine points of constitutional law. Yet Harry Truman agreed with Taft. He wanted a congressional resolution of support. Acheson argued against it. In his opinion Taft's speech, though "basically honest," was "bitterly partisan and ungracious." He insisted that the President "should not ask for a resolution of approval, but rest on his constitutional authority as Commander in Chief of the Armed Forces."

Among historical ironies, few are sharper than this: Dean Acheson, excoriated during his years of power as a tool of international Communism, was so implacable in his hostility toward it that he believed the President could commit America's armed might to an anti-Communist conflict without consulting anyone, acting on the strength of his position as commander in chief. Acheson never changed his mind. During the missile crisis of 1962, he wanted President Kennedy to invade Cuba. In his last years he became one of the most zealous of Vietnam hawks, wearing a red, white, and blue armband and lecturing Washington high school students on the need to stand up to the Reds. By then, of course, presidential authority to intervene in foreign wars had become much greater — largely because of precedents established, at Acheson's urging, in June 1950.

Between communiqués from Washington, Lake Success, Tokyo, and Seoul, the public was thoroughly muddled, and in a presidential press conference Thursday afternoon, the first since the outbreak of hostilities, Truman was urged to clarify matters:

Q. Mr. President, everyone is asking in this country, are we or are we not at war?
A. We are not at war.
Q. Mr. President, could you elaborate on that statement, "We are not at war," and could we use that in quotes?
A. Yes, I will allow you to use that in quotes. The Republic of Korea was set up with United Nations help. It was unlawfully attacked by a bunch of bandits who are neighbors, in North Korea. The United Nations held a meeting and asked the members to go to the relief of the Korean Republic, and the members of the United Nations are going to the relief of the Korean Republic to suppress a bandit raid on the Republic of Korea. That is all there is to it.
Q. Would it be correct to call it a police action under the United Nations?
A. Yes, that is exactly what it amounts to.

It amounted to more than one hundred thousand American casualties over the next three years, and the Republicans, who after their initial enthusiasm found less and less to like in the war, never let Harry Truman forget that he had once thought of it as a "police action." Homely phrases work only if the policies they epitomize work; had lend-lease failed, FDR's comparison of it with "a length of garden hose" would be less charitably remembered. The difference, unappreciated in June 1950, was that Roosevelt's goal had been total victory. The purpose in Korea was not unconditional surrender; it was a cease-fire, an end to aggression, a negative aim.

Thursday morning's communiqué from Tokyo reported that of South Korea's 65,000 defenders, nearly half had been killed, wounded, or taken prisoner. Plainly this mounting sacrifice could not go on much longer. Equally obvious, tactical support from U.S. naval and air units would not be enough to turn the war around. Hourly, now, the momentum of events was tugging Truman toward a stronger commitment. From the Dai Ichi Building in Tokyo came news that MacArthur had flown into Korea for a firsthand look at the struggle. Disregarding his Air Force weathermen, who had grounded all other aircraft at Haneda Airfield, the seventy-year-old general had boarded his old C-54, the *Bataan,* and told his pilot, "We go." Upon landing — Syngman Rhee met him at the airstrip — MacArthur said, "Let's go to the front and look at the troops. The only way to judge a war is to see the troops in action." He then drove northward under shellfire and reached the Han just in time to see the last, hopeless attempt to hold the bridges. For twenty minutes the general stood on a little mound just off the road watching the demoralized retreat, the screaming refugees, and the continual bombardment from the north. As a member of his staff noted, he had "encountered all the dreadful backwash of a defeated and dispersed Army." Back at his Japanese headquarters, he cabled the Pentagon: "The only assurance for holding the present line and the ability to regain later the lost ground is through the introduction of United States ground combat forces into the Korean battle area."

There it was. They had known all week that it was coming, and now it came chattering from a Pentagon telecom machine at 3 A.M. Friday, while most of the capital lay asleep. General J. Lawton Collins, in Mac-Arthur's old role as the Army's chief of staff, answered that before taking such a momentous step the President would doubtless want to consult his advisers. Couldn't the war wait a few hours? Absolutely not, MacArthur replied. Every minute was crucial now. If the Republic of Korea was to be saved, America troops must be sent into the breach at once.

General Collins phoned Secretary of the Army Frank C. Pace Jr., and Pace called Blair House. It was just before 5 A.M. in Washington, but Truman was already up and shaved. Taking the call at his bedside table, he hesitated briefly and then authorized the commitment of one regiment to combat. He would assemble the members of his war cabinet at once, he said, to propose an expansion of this expeditionary force. Their approval was unanimous. Orders were cut that morning, and at 1:22 P.M. that June 30, the seventh day of the crisis, the calling up of reserve units was under way. The United States was at war all the way — with warships, warplanes, tanks, artillery, and ground troops — and Congress hadn't even been asked for an opinion.

Six weeks of agony followed. Americans assumed that the moment the U.S. 24th and 25th divisions left Japan and arrived in Korea, the fighting would take on a new cast. If the North Koreans didn't panic and flee, it was thought, they would at least lose their momentum. In fact, the U.S. divisions began crumbling as quickly as their new ROK allies. Out of condition and outnumbered by as much as twenty to one, the first detachments to arrive were for the most part green troops; fewer than 20 percent of them had seen action in World War II. Their only antitank weapons were ten-year-old bazookas, hopelessly ineffective against the mighty Soviet T-34s. Isolated and cut off from one another, in the first weeks many surrendered, including the major general commanding the 24th, before learning that the North Koreans took few prisoners. More often the NKPA tied the hands of captives behind their backs and bayoneted them. U.S. infantrymen then became afflicted by "bugout fever" — a yearning to return to their soft billets in Japan. MacArthur did what he could, skillfully maneuvering

U.S. and ROK battalions so as to delay the enemy as much as possible while building a defensive perimeter around the Pusan bridgehead, but defeatism crept into the high command.

Osan, Yongdok, Hadong, Chindong'mi, the Nakton Bulge — the strange names appeared in headlines as a succession of front-page maps depicted the Pusan perimeter, smaller each morning. Ferocious NKPA attacks threw the 24th Division out of Taejon on July 20 and then began hammering the 25th at Taegu, the main U.S. supply base and communications hub. In the tough phrase of the hour, war correspondents wrote that MacArthur might "run out of real estate," and be driven into the sea. Then, on August 6, the long retreat ended. Infantrymen of the 27th Regiment and their ROK allies dug in their heels and stopped the Red tide at the walls of Taegu. Late in August the North Koreans staged one last massive attack in an attempt to capture Pusan, but by now the defenders had tanks and heavy artillery. The lines held on a 120-mile arc from the Sea of Japan on the east to the Korea Strait on the south. There, as summer waned, the line of opposing trenches grew stronger every week. It was a stalemate, and commentators wondered how it could become anything else. The mood of the men on the line was fatalistic. Their favorite expression was, "That's the way the ball bounces," and they sang:

> The Dhow, the Gizee, and Rhee
> What do they want from me?

But Douglas MacArthur was too gifted a strategist to be bottled up by an unimaginative siege, and the military force now arriving from an aroused America was too great to be contained within so narrow an enclave. At home selected National Guard units were being called up. Recruiting drives had been intensified and draft quotas increased to put 600,000 men in uniform as soon as possible. To be sure, the replacements were often neither enthusiastic nor cheerful. No one called them gung ho; Kilroy wasn't there; and a Corporal Stephen Zeg of Chicago doubtless spoke for thousands of others in Pusan when he told a reporter, "I'll fight for my country, but I'll be damned if I see why I'm fighting to save this hellhole." Yet there were few organized protests against the war and fewer demonstrations in the States. The new infantrymen were the younger brothers of the men who had fought in World War II. Patriotism was still strong, and that early rout of American infantry by North Koreans had stung the country's pride.

Each day the stockpiles of men and steel behind the Pusan front grew larger. The 1st Cavalry Division arrived from Japan and the 2nd Infantry from home; then came 2,000 Tommies from the 27th British Brigade in Hong Kong and French, Turkish, Australian, Dutch, and Philippine troops — the van of supporting units from fifteen other U.N. members.

While the North Koreans worried about their long supply lines, their heavy casualties, and the inferior quality of teen-age replacements who were being drafted in the north at bayonet point, MacArthur was preparing the most brilliant stroke of his career. Against all advice, he proposed to divide his force, holding part of it here and staging an intricate amphibious attack with the other part, landing at the port of Inchon, twenty-four miles west of Seoul and one hundred and fifty miles from the present NKPA rear.

Two days before D-day, ten warships swept the harbor of mines and bombarded shore batteries. At 6:30 A.M. on September 15, the appointed day, as the first pink streaks of dawn broke in the east, the commanding admiral broke out the traditional amphibious signal "Land the landing force" — whereupon waves of small boats darted for the shore bearing the 1st Marine Division, which had sailed secretly from San Francisco two weeks earlier. It took the marines exactly forty minutes to seize Wolmi Island, the key to Inchon's defense. Racing down a thousand-foot causeway, they then headed for Seoul while MacArthur announced to the world: "The Navy and Marines have never shone more brightly." By October 1 the North Korean army was all but destroyed. Half its men were in prisoner of war pens; the rest were divided into small detachments that moved furtively at night, trying to reach home. U.N. troops held everything in the peninsula south of the 38th Parallel. MacArthur appealed to the NKPA to lay down its arms, and at Lake Success a resolution backed by eight nations asked the U.N. General Assembly to "take all appropriate measures to ensure a stable situation in the whole of Korea" — thus approving a crossing into North Korea. But the Joint Chiefs were again urging caution upon MacArthur, and ominous rumbles were heard in Peking. U.S. intelligence reported that Chinese divisions were massing in Manchuria, just across the Yalu River from North Korea. President Truman decided that it was time he and General MacArthur had a little talk.

It was long overdue. As early as June, John Foster Dulles, the chief Republican foreign affairs adviser, had called on Truman to recommend that the general be "hauled back to the United States." Dulles had just returned from Tokyo. At the outbreak of the war, he said indignantly, MacArthur's headquarters had been caught unprepared. No one in the Dai Ichi Building would rouse the general — "they were afraid to disturb him" — so Dulles had to do it himself.

Late in July the general's dabbling in affairs which were none of his concern had prompted a second glance from the White House. At a time when diplomatic maneuvering in the U.N. required that Chiang Kai-shek be kept under wraps, MacArthur had flown to Formosa to call on the generalissimo and tell reporters that the U.S. ships patrolling Formosa Strait were "leashing" Chiang and should be withdrawn. The President, disturbed, had dispatched Averell Harriman to the Dai Ichi Building for a consultation with MacArthur. Harriman had returned gloomy. He felt that the general hadn't understood him, that he seemed to have "a strange idea that we should back anybody who will fight communism."

The next Truman knew, AP, UP, and INS were carrying the text of a special message MacArthur had sent to the annual convention of the Veterans of Foreign Wars. In it the general had proposed nothing less than a new foreign policy in the Pacific, with American arms holding a defensive line from Vladivostok to Singapore. Obviously this would commit the United States to an alliance with Chiang. The general thought that a sound idea. Those who believed such a move might provoke the Chinese Communists were appeasers, he said, guilty of offering a "fallacious and threadbare argument," while what was needed was "aggressive, resolute and dynamic leadership." The President, furious, demanded that the statement be withdrawn. MacArthur obeyed, but that accomplished nothing; it was already in the papers. Now, with the threat of a wider war, the White House arranged a face-to-face conference between the President and his most colorful general on lonely Wake Island.

They met on October 15 in an ugly cinder block outpost of the Civil Aeronautics Authority. In the crucial session, both men assumed that they were alone, but a zealous diplomat — Philip Jessup — had stationed a secretary with a shorthand pad in the shadow of the door, which was ajar. Though MacArthur later challenged the accuracy of her stenographic transcript, there is no other reason to doubt it. If it is correct, MacArthur apologized handsomely for his message to the VFW. He also predicted that the war would be over by Thanksgiving. Then the Japanese peace treaty could be signed with or without Soviet cooperation, he said, and Korea could be reconstructed for as little as a half-billion dollars. Truman asked about the chance of either Russian or Chinese intervention in the war. The general replied that it was:

> Very little. Had they interfered in the first or second months it would have been decisive. We are no longer fearful of their intervention. We no longer stand hat in hand. The Chinese have 300,000 men in Manchuria. Of these probably not more than 100,000 to 125,000 are distributed along the Yalu River. Only 50,000 to 60,000 could be gotten across the Yalu River. They have no air force. Now that we have bases for our Air Force in Korea, if the Chinese tried to get down to Pyongyang, there would be the greatest slaughter.

There certainly would, though it would not be the kind of slaughter MacArthur had in mind. His intelligence was defective. Mao had assembled 850,000 soldiers in Manchuria. Already 120,000 men, the vanguard of his veteran Fourth Field Army, were south of the Yalu. They had been slipping over every night, bringing their armor and heavy guns with them and hiding before daybreak in the rugged hills of North Korea. The discovery of this momentous ruse was subsequently used to discredit MacArthur. That was unjust. He was not blameless in his autumn conduct of the war — his failure to issue winter clothing to his men against the possibility of a wider conflict is inexplicable — but his major oversights and aberrances, including his insubordination, came later. At Wake he was a loyal commander, telling his commander in chief what he believed to be the truth. In the six weeks which followed, his behavior was flawless. No blueprints for a new foreign policy issued from the Dai Ichi Building, and although technically he needed no authorization to cross the 38th Parallel in force, he waited until the U.N. General Assembly, recalling that the essential objective of his expedition was "the establishment of a unified, independent, and democratic Korea," directed him to move north.

He now led a splendid army built around seven U.S. divisions, the most recent of which was the magnificent old Third. By their side marched six seasoned ROK divisions and contingents from England, Australia, New Zealand, Thailand, and Turkey. Pyongyang fell on October 20. There, in the enemy capital, six years to the day after he had waded ashore at Leyte, MacArthur struck an antic pose and called out, "Any celebrities here to meet me? Where's Kim Buck Too?"

The general was convinced that his foes had lost heart. In this he was tragically mistaken — so wrong, in fact, that from this point forward there were two wars, one in Korea and the other in MacArthur's mind. The real battlefield was a bleak tract of towering heights and plunging chasms, a region so dismal that until now it had been largely uninhabited. There were no reliable maps of it. Here and there faint trails in the dirt hinted at earlier visitors, but they led nowhere. Passes between the windswept precipices were unexplored, and the spines of the mountain ranges ran north to south, so that any force moving northward on a broad front would have to be split into detachments inaccessible to one another in an emergency. It would be hard to imagine terrain better suited to guerrilla warfare. Tanks were useless in it, heavy artillery had to be left behind, and its deep gorges and canyons provided superb concealment for ambushers or troops hiding from aerial observation. So adaptable was it to the enemy's purpose that by October he had successfully tucked away in it 250,000 well-disciplined, sturdy-legged peasant riflemen who awaited only the signal to charge, sounded by their buglers and cymbal-swinging bandsmen, before throwing themselves on the flanks of the unsuspecting United Nations armies. Behind the ambushers, in the vastness of Manchuria, another 600,000 blue-uniformed Chinese soldiers stood ready to reinforce them. It was one of the greatest natural traps in the history of warfare.

MacArthur was euphoric. To his quartermasters in Japan he sent word to prepare billets for the Eighth U.N. Army, his left wing. He informed Omar Bradley that he expected to have the U.S. 2nd Division ready for reassignment to Europe in January, and he promised the country that he would "have the boys home by Christmas." It was all over but the mopping up, he told correspondents. On October 24 he advised the Joint Chiefs that he had drawn up his forces on a line between Pyongyang and Wonsan, a seaport forty-five miles to the east. Then he announced — actually *announced* — his battle plan. It was to be a giant pincer, with the Eighth Army driving north from Pyongyang while the rest of his troops, designated X Corps, moved out from Wonsan. The Eighth Army would be the western claw of the pincer, X Corps the eastern claw, and the high ground between them would be lightly held by ROK units. To the astonishment of officers who fought by the book, the general blandly notified them that he had decided to violate a basic military axiom. He had deliberately split his command between two ground commanders, giving the left wing to Lieutenant General Walton H. Walker and the right to his Dai Ichi GHQ. Intoxicated by his successs at Inchon, he seemed to be increasing the difficulties already inherent in the terrain by assuring that neither hand would know what the other was doing.

In the last week of October a dozen U.N. spearheads began this northward sweep, striking out toward the Chongchon River on the left and the Changjin Reservoir on the right. Almost at once they ran into trouble. Major General Charles A. Willoughby, MacArthur's G2, had told them that the NKPA was completely demoralized, but a sharp North Korean counterattack isolated the 7th ROK Division and cut it up. Then, on October 26, an Eighth Army patrol picked up a Chinese soldier fully ninety miles south of where he should have been. Eyebrows went up as far back as 1600 Pennsylvania Avenue; presidential approval of MacArthur's drive had been based on his virtual guarantee that there would be, indeed could be, no effective Chinese intervention. The U.N. general replied that there was nothing to worry about, that Peking, like Moscow, made a practice of sending idealistic "volunteers" to fight under other Communistic flags, and had in fact advertised its intention to do it in Korea.

Four days later sixteen soldiers from no known NKPA unit were taken north of Hamhung, in northeastern Korea. Interrogated by a Nisei officer who had grown up in Honolulu's Chinatown, they too were found to be Chinese. The following day a whole regiment of MacArthur's presumed volunteers was reported near the Changjin and Pujon reservoirs; prisoners from it said that they had crossed the Yalu on an ammunition train two weeks earlier. On November 1 a group of Soviet MIG-15 jets challenged U.S. fighters, briefly scrimmaged with them, and then returned to the Chinese side of the Yalu. By this time Chinese foot soldiers had been identified on every divisional front. On November 2 the 1st Cavalry sent back word that while reconnoitering the north bank of the Chongchon one of its battalions had been decimated by machine gun fire and screaming soldiers in blue Mao jackets. "We don't know whether they represent the Chinese government," the report said, but the battle had been "a massacre, Indian-style, like the one that hit Custer at Little Big Horn."

Inevitably, American officers were becoming preoccupied with the yellow peril. They were fighting in forbidden country, with long and vulnerable supply lines, and they weren't equipped for an extensive campaign. They knew little about China, but what they had heard was disturbing: its new regime regarded America as its natural enemy, and it held life cheap. The prospect of a confrontation with endless waves of charging Orientals was frightening. On November 3 the 24th Infantry actually disregarded an instruction from MacArthur. Informed that "the order of the day is full speed ahead to the Yalu River," the 24th turned about-face and retreated fourteen miles. Before anyone in GHQ could deal with this insubordination, the situation reports for November 4 had come in. The 1st Marine Division had identified three Chinese divisions in its sector; the 1st Cavalry had found five.

Reaction in the Dai Ichi Building was mixed. At first MacArthur told the Pentagon that while Chinese Communist intervention was "a distinct possibility," he did not have "sufficient evidence at hand to warrant immediate acceptance." After sleeping on it, he decided that the presence of eight hostile divisions was pretty good evidence. He advised the Joint Chiefs that his left wing had eluded "a possible trap . . . surreptitiously laid" and that there had not been "any possibility of a great military reverse." Still, he was upset. Having destroyed the North Koreans, the U.N. force had found that "a new, fresh army now faces us, backed up by a possibility of large alien reserves and adequate supply within easy reach to the enemy but beyond the limits of our present sphere of military action." These newcomers were operating from a "privileged sanctuary" across the Yalu. "Whether and to what extent these reserves will be moved forward to reinforce units now committed remains to be seen and is a matter of the gravest significance," he said. Already he was "in hostile contact with Chinese military units deployed for action against the forces of the Unified Command," and the Chinese were capable of massing in such numbers as "to threaten the ultimate destruction of my command."

Until this point the Joint Chiefs had interdicted bombing within five miles of the Yalu. MacArthur now asked for authority to destroy the Yalu bridges. He was still unconvinced that the Chinese intended to come in all the way, but as a lifelong student of the Asian mind, he said, he knew that "it is the pattern of the Oriental psychology to respect and follow aggressive, resolute, and dynamic leadership." Taking out those bridges would be aggressive, resolute and dynamic, and it would also serve the purpose of discouraging replacements. Permission to bomb was granted. The Joint Chiefs were disturbed, too. They didn't like the deployment of his forces, and they were beginning to wonder about Willoughby. Still, MacArthur was the senior soldier in the U.S. Army ("Senior," said one junior officer, "to everyone but God"). He was also seven thousand miles away, the commander on the spot, and to overrule him would break a standing U.S. military policy going back to 1864. They were unwilling to give him a blank check, however. He was reminded that "extreme care must be taken to avoid violation of Manchurian territory and airspace." His pilots must avoid targets inside Manchuria and, above all, the Yalu dam and power installations.

As the teletypes in the Dai Ichi Building rattled off these instructions, the Korean front fell silent. Patrols couldn't flush a single Chinese soldier. Apparently they had all vanished. General Willoughby was sure of it, had known it all along, and was in a mood to crow. As an old China hand he had spotted Peking's bluff. It had been called, and now the war was over. In Korea the ground commanders weren't so sure. The Chinese could have broken off action because they had had enough, as MacArthur and Willoughby now believed, or conversely because they were regrouping for a full-fledged attack. Altogether, they agreed, it was a mystery.

The fact that they were mystified is itself mysterious. For over two months Chou En-lai, foreign minister of the Central People's Government, had been trying every way he could think of to tell these Occidental intruders to go home. On August 25, when MacArthur was still boxed in at Pusan, Chou had notified the U.N. that Washington's support of Chiang Kai-shek's right to remain on Formosa was in itself a "criminal act" of "armed aggression," and he had pledged himself to "liberate from the tentacles of the United States aggressors" all Oriental territories which didn't belong to them. Asia for the Asians, Chou was saying, and while Korea wasn't his either, his argument was no weaker than, and in many ways resembled, the Monroe Doctrine.

Since the Americans hadn't heard him the first time, Chou had tried again after Inchon. China, he had warned, would not "supinely tolerate their North Korean neighbors being savagely invaded by imperialists." Then, on October 3, he had summoned Sirdar K. M. Panikkar, the Indian ambassador to Peking. Chou solemnly informed him that the Chinese People's Republic would ally itself with North Korea and enter the war against the United Nations if U.N. troops crossed the 38th Parallel south to north. This message was transmitted to the State Department through New Delhi, Moscow, and Stockholm. It was published in all the great newspapers in the world, and just in case Washington had overlooked it, Chou repeated it over Peking's official government radio station a week later. MacArthur and Willoughby dismissed it as "diplomatic blackmail." They were wrong, though the administration could hardly reproach them for that. Remarking that Panikkar had in the past "played the game of the Chinese Communists fairly regularly," Truman concluded that Chou's message was probably "a bald attempt to blackmail the United Nations by threats of intervention in Korea."

In all probability, MacArthur was no more responsible for the approaching catastrophe than Eisenhower for the Battle of the Bulge — the analogy is Truman's — but his handling of the events leading up to it was another matter. Afterward he would say of himself that "no more subordinate soldier ever wore the uniform," yet on at least one sensitive issue he had treated Joint Chiefs' directive with something less than respect. In their view, the deployment of Caucasian troops near Korea's northern frontiers was needlessly provocative. On September 27 they had informed him that "as a matter of policy, no non-Korean ground forces will be used in the northeast provinces bordering the Soviet Union or in the area along the Manchurian border." He not only ignored this order; on October 24 told his lieutenants in the field to "use any and all ground forces at their commands, as necessary, in order to capture all of North Korea." To the Chiefs he sent word that the Chinese despised weakness, while a show of strength "would effectively appeal to the reason in the Chinese mind."

MacArthur's racial chauvinism — for that is what it was — led him into a snare of his own making. By Thanksgiving nearly three weeks had passed since the last sign of Chinese activity at the front, and he concluded that his militance had scared them off. The CIA warned him that "at a minimum" Red China would increase its presence in Korea, try to tie up U.N. forces in battles of attrition, and "maintain the semblance of a North Korean state in being." Ignoring this, MacArthur went over to the attack for the second time that month, and again he provided the press with a preview of his strategy.

This, he told the correspondents, would be a "general offensive" to "win the war." He repeated his October promise to the men, directing Major General John B. Coulter to tell the troops that "They will eat Christmas dinner at home." The drive would open early on the morning of November 24, and he would fly over from Tokyo for the occasion. It was inconceivable that this final drive might fail. In a special communiqué to the U.N. he reported that the Air Force had "completely interdicted the rear areas." His left wing, he said, would advance against "failing resistance," while his right wing, "gallantly supported by naval air and surface action," continued to exploit its "commanding position." The juncture of the two "should for all practical purposes end the war." A reporter asked him if he knew how many Chinese soldiers were in Korea. "About thirty thousand regulars," the general fired back, "and thirty thousand volunteers." Losses would be "extraordinarily light."

In Washington the President was bemused. Earlier in the month the general had sounded an alarm in his messages that had seemed, in Truman's opinion, to portend impending disaster. Now, apparently, the grave danger did not exist, since the same commander was announcing victory even before the first men started marching. Indeed, the troops were celebrating it in advance; the day before the offensive was Thanksgiving, and American ingenuity saw to it that every man received a hot turkey dinner with buttered squash, Waldorf salad, cranberry sauce, mince pie, and after-dinner mints.

That was on Thursday. On Friday the attack went in, and on Sunday the Chinese struck with thirty-three divisions — 300,000 men.

At 6:15 A.M. General Bradley phoned the White House. "A terrible message has come from General MacArthur," he told the President. "The Chinese have come in with both feet."

They had ruptured the entire U.N. front. The center, held by ROK divisions, simply caved in, and in those central mountain ranges the ROK II Corps disintegrated. Turks, British units, and the 1st Cavalry rushed up to replace them. They were driven back thirty miles to Tokchon, lost Tokchon, and took off for the south in two-and-a-half-ton trucks, firing back at their tormentors as they fled. The Turks chose to make a stand. They ran out of bullets, went after the enemy with scimitars, and were wiped out. The 24th Division was driven back across the Chongchon River. Altogether the Chinese had slashed off forty miles of front. Pausing on the hilly ground between the Eighth Army on their right and X Corps on their left, they then swung east and west to envelop them. General Walker had to choose between retreat and annihilation. He sensibly withdrew. X Corps received the same order, but there the outcome was different.

Despite appalling casualties, Walker's command had remained intact. To be sure, every night seemed worse than the last. Heralded by the bugles and cymbals — and sometimes police whistles — masses of screaming Chinese would swoop down under flares. There was no end to them. In MacArthur's phrase, the enemy had a "bottomless well" of manpower. Still, Walker eventually stopped running and was able to re-form down by the 38th Parallel. X Corps, on the other hand, came apart. There the key force was the 1st Marine Division. As usual, the marines had been out in front of every other U.N. unit — about forty miles ahead. They had been way up on the Chosin Reservoir when the first bugles blew, and being alert, they decided that this would be a good time to wheel around, come down behind the Chinese assaulting the Eighth Army, and pounce on their rear. But the enemy had anticipated them. The next thing MacArthur knew, the marines had been cut off and surrounded. They were forty miles away from the nearest help, at Hungnam.

Their breakout was one of the great stories of the Korean War. "Retreat, hell!" the Marine general snapped at a war correspondent. "We're only attacking in a different direction." And Colonel Lewis B. "Chesty" Puller told his regiment, "The enemy is in front of us, behind us, to the left of us, and to the right of us. They won't escape *this* time." Joined by men from the 3rd and 8th divisions and the ROK Capital Division, they formed a column and hacked their way through walls of Chinese, moving ever eastward over a corkscrew trail of icy dirt for fourteen days of sub-zero cold, blizzards, and thousand-foot chasms. At one point they seemed utterly lost, confronted by an impassable gorge; then the pilots of the Combat Cargo Command arrived overhead with a huge suspension bridge dangling from their flying boxcars and parked it in the canyon. Once the column had to bury 117 marines in one frozen grave. Another time it took 2,651 casualties in four days of fighting and, lacking a hospital, had to carry every one of them. At last it reached the port of Hungnam and was evacuated.

The valor of individuals and units could not obscure the central fact: MacArthur's men had been dealt a stunning defeat, "the worst," *Time* said, "the United States has ever suffered." Correspondent Homer Bigart declared that "Unsound deployment of United Nations forces and a momentous blunder by General MacArthur helped insure the success of the enemy's strategy." An editorial in the *New York Herald Tribune*, a Republican paper, described the rout as a "colossal military blunder" which had demonstrated that MacArthur "can no longer be accepted as the final authority on military matters."

MacArthur took a different view. Although he was deeply depressed — "near panic," Acheson thought, reading his telecom messages — he couldn't see that he could be held responsible. On the fourth day of the Chinese blitz his communiqué recognized that "We face an entirely new war," and he seemed to be attributing it to bad faith in Peking. The enemy drive, he declared, had "shattered the high hopes we had entertained that the intervention of the Chinese was only of a token nature on a volunteer and individual basis as publicly announced."

At the end of the first week in December, while the Eighth Army was still in disarray and the 1st Marine Division was pinned in around the Chosin Reservoir, he told the Joint Chiefs that his men were reaching the end of their strength. He could see no alternative to "steady attrition leading to final destruction" unless the terms of the U.N. commitment were changed. The new situation, he said, "calls for political decisions and strategic plans in implementation thereof adequate fully to meet the realities involved." Translated from MacArthurese, this meant that he wanted the one thing no one in Washington or Lake Success could give him — freedom to invade Manchuria. To Acheson, in Washington, the communiqués from Tokyo "depicted MacArthur in a blue funk, sorry for himself, complaining of the restrictions against expanding the war, and sending to press and Pentagon what Lovett called 'posterity papers.'" No doubt. The general never forgot that he would be a figure in history. In the Dai Ichi Building, however, his request for authority to cross the Yalu made sense. There was no other way to win the war.

Unfortunately, winning it was out of the question. The nature of hostilities had changed since 1945. Hiroshima and Nagasaki had changed it. In a world with weapons capable of inflicting megadeaths, war was no longer the last argument of kings and presidents; if it spread and became global, it would mean the end of the human race. To be sure, MacArthur's enemies in Korea had no U-235 bombs, but their ally in Moscow did, and that in itself was enough to put a checkrein on him. There were other reasons, equally persuasive. The other fifteen members of the United Nations with men in his command wanted no part of a wider war. And even if the United States was prepared to discard the mantle of U.N. approval and go it alone, the logic of its global strategy argued against further Asian entanglement. A Manchurian campaign would have brought a sharp increase of anti-Americanism among nations in the emerging Third World and a virtual halt to American aid in the rebuilding of Europe.

If MacArthur couldn't win without crossing the Yalu — and clearly he now could not — new dilemmas arose. A United Nations defeat was unthinkable. At the same time, the two great adversaries could not, in the present circumstances, walk away. The mad solution, then, was war with neither triumph nor subjugation — a long, bloody stalemate which would end only when the exhausted participants agreed to a truce. That, in effect, is what ultimately happened, and in light of the later experience in Vietnam it seems bearable. At the time it was infuriating, especially to MacArthur, a proud officer steeped in nineteenth-century concepts of honor, who with every fiber of his being believed, as he would soon tell his countrymen, that "In war there is no substitute for victory."

Christmas was unreal that December. If you belonged to the swing generation and weren't a "two-time loser" — a World War II veteran trapped by reserve status into fighting the new war, too — your children were just becoming old enough to give the season a special charm and poignancy. The threat of the mushroom cloud hung over them, too. The number one tune on the hit parade was a lugubrious ballad called "The Tennessee Waltz." While you shopped for gifts among the agitated but strangely silent crowds and wondered whether there would even be a Christmas in 1951, loudspeakers moaned:

> I was waltzing with my darlin' to the Tennessee Waltz
> When an old friend I happened to see
> I introduced him to my loved one, and while they were waltzing,
> My friend stole my sweetheart from me. . . .

The headlines in kiosks were odd, even grotesque. While Chinese soldiers and young Americans were killing one another on the far side of the Pacific, a Chinese Communist delegation arrived in Lake Success to state their case. Between the U.N. sessions, one read, General Hu Hsiu-chuan and his thirteen aides bought Mixmasters and nylons for their wives and books on atomic bombs, presumably for themselves. A Montana draft board refused to allow the induction of any more boys until MacArthur was given nuclear weapons and the right to use them. Word reached Washington that a Soviet diplomat had assured Peking that Russia would enter the war if Manchuria were bombed. In a subsequent press conference the President hinted that atomic bombs might be used in Korea, and that MacArthur might be the man to decide when. That brought Prime Minister Clement Attlee over on the next plane from London. Truman told him to forget it, he hadn't said anything like that, it was all a rhubarb. Nevertheless, Attlee returned home looking grim. He had learned something else. Both Truman and Acheson had confided that the Korean situation looked hopeless. The President had just instructed MacArthur: "We consider that the preservation of your forces is now the primary consideration. Consolidation of forces into beachheads is concurred in."

Administration figures in the White House, the Pentagon, and the New State Building were quietly frantic. The President presided over a council of war every morning, as soon as that day's communiqués were in. Telecom circuits to the Dai Ichi Building were in use twenty-four hours a day. The National Security Council was in almost constant session. And all of it appeared to be in vain. Truman covered memorandum pages with his random thoughts. On one surviving page from that Christmas he scrawled: ". . . conference after conference on the jittery situation facing the country. Attlee, Formosa, Communist China, Chiang Kai-shek, Japan, Germany, France, India, etc. I have worked for peace for five years and six months and it looks like World War III is near."

It was the worst year's end since the Bulge in 1944. The Communists recrossed the 38th Parallel the day after Christmas. Three days later the Joints Chiefs told MacArthur that while "a successful resistance [to aggression] would be of great importance to our national interest," it wasn't worth "serious losses." If he was forced back to the Kum River, they told him, they would order him "to commence a withdrawal to Japan." Replying on December 30, he called upon the administration to "recognize the state of war imposed by the Chinese authorities." It was his recommendation to follow this up by "dropping from 30 to 50 atomic bombs on air bases and other sensitive points" in Manchuria, and landing an amphibious force of 500,000 Chinese Nationalist troops from Formosa, supported by two divisions of U.S. Marines, at either end of the border between Korea and China. He added that further Communist incursions into Korea should be precluded "by laying down, after the defeat of the Chinese," a belt of radioactive cobalt all along the Yalu.*

That same Saturday South Koreans abandoned Seoul for the second time since spring. Temperatures along the Parallel fell below zero and stayed there. The Communists attacked every night. MacArthur's lines bent and began to buckle, and on New Year's Eve, at the very hour of "Auld Lang Syne," the greatest onslaught of all came billowing down through the dense snow and sailed into the U.N. lines.

---

*This from two mutually supporting interviews granted by the general during his retirement and withheld until his death.

Early Fifties Montage

CONGRESS REPEALS OLEO TAX

Best actress of 1950: Judy Holliday in **Born Yesterday**

Best supporting actor of 1950: George Sanders in **All About Eve**

Sunset Boulevard   **The Asphalt Jungle**   **Twelve O'Clock High**

Tight Little Island   **The Third Man**

BATTLESHIP MISSOURI RUNS AGROUND

FRANKIE SEEN SWOONING INTO OBSCURITY

It doesn't quite jell with me, T.J. When you glim the over-all picture You savvy that there are certain rock-bottom Slants which have got to be considered Before the final wrap-up if you're going to Housebreak it for the top brass — If it's going to grab them where they live

Queeg looked up in horror. A vast dark bulk was bearing down on the Caine. Queeg opened and closed his mouth three times without uttering a sound, then he choked out, "All engines back full — bah — bah— belay that —All stop."

The bag of groceries that cost a city housewife $5 in 1935-1939 now costs her $9.83, the Bureau of Labor Statistics reported today

SMOKEY

Only you can prevent forest fires.

When the sun in the morning creeps over the hill
And kisses the roses round my windowsill
Then my heart fills with laughter when I hear the trill
Of the birds in the treetops on Mocking Bird Hill

WOMEN'S SKIRTS RISE TO MID-CALF

What'll you have? PABST!

Chinese checkers — an ingenious new marble game

an odd-looking, snub-nosed little car drew some mildly curious stares. Few of the onlookers realized that it was a postwar model of the Volkswagen, the car which Hitler once promised to put in every German garage. With an air-cooled rear engine, and a luggage compartment under the hood, it was the first of 600 which Germany is shipping to the U.S. to sell at $1,280 to $1,977.

To at least one observer, it seemed that the men who sadly watched the humiliation of Joe Louis last week in Yankee Stadium were really feeling sorry for themselves. So many, in the uncomfortable long span of Louis's greatness, had themselves picked up fortyish weight and lost twentyish confidence.

I keep picturing all these little kids playing some game in this big field of rye and all. Thousands of little kids, and nobody's around — nobody big, I mean — except me. And I'm standing on the edge of some crazy cliff. What I have to do, I have to catch everybody if they start to go over the cliff . . . I'd just be the catcher in the rye and all. I know it's crazy but that's the only thing I'd really like to be. I know it's crazy.

BEST SELLERS: Fiction

The Cardinal by Henry Morton Robinson
From Here to Eternity by James Jones
Melville Goodwin, U.S.A. by John P. Marquand
Dinner at Antoine's by Frances Parkinson Keyes
A Rage to Live by John O'Hara

Best actor of 1951: Humphrey Bogart in **The African Queen**

Best actress of 1951: Vivien Leigh in **A Streetcar Named Desire**

An American in Paris   **The Red Badge of Courage**   **Detective Story**

The Lavender Hill Mob   **Strangers on a Train**   **Quo Vadis**   **The River**

BEST SELLERS: Nonfiction

Betty Crocker's Picture Cook Book
Look Younger, Live Longer by Gaylord Hauser
A King's Story by the Duke of Windsor
The Greatest Story Ever Told by Fulton Oursler
The Far Side of Paradise by Arthur Mizener

HEARST DEAD AT 88

*Irene, goodnight, Irene, goodnight,
Goodnight, Irene, goodnight, Irene,
I'll kiss you in my dreams*

III

SOWING
THE WIND
1951-1960

EIGHTEEN

A House Divided

Seoul fell again on January 4, 1951. Once more the Communists achieved a major breakthrough, cutting off the U.S. 2nd Division at Wonju in the center of the Korean peninsula and rupturing the entire U.N. front. Lieutenant General Matthew B. Ridgway, MacArthur's new Eighth Army commander, had 200,000 men — half of them Koreans — to match the enemy's 400,000. In Washington Acheson was depressed by "the stench of spiritless defeat."

The U.N. lines held. Ridgway plugged the Wonju gap, throwing in his reserves, exploiting his superiority in the air, and adroitly moving in troops from his flanks. By the middle of January the fury of the enemy's New Year's Eve drive had been spent, and in the last week of the month the U.N. went over to the counteroffensive. The end of February found the Eighth Army back in the outskirts of Seoul. Ridgway recaptured the city on the night of March 14–15, and two weeks later the two great armies again squatted opposite one another on the 38th Parallel, almost exactly where they had been three months earlier — or, for that matter, nine months earlier, at the outbreak of the war.

A generation still flushed by the mighty triumphs of World War II and dazzled more recently by the miracle at Inchon could not accept the stalemate gracefully. To many Americans, the language of containment — the advocacy of limited objectives as an alternative to unlimited warfare — sounded sour and heretical. A *Life* editorial rejected "the pap" and the "pernicious fallacy" of " 'coexistence' with Soviet communism." China lobbyists scorned administration reluctance to invade Manchuria as "appeasement," and ultraconservative Republicans found Dean Acheson's calls for restraint just short of treason.

Prewar isolationism was now passing through an extraordinary transformation. In December, as thirty-three divisions of Chinese began pouring through the sieve of MacArthur's defenses, two isolationists had publicly washed their hands of the Korean expedition. Speaking in Charlottesville, Virginia, on December 12, Joseph P. Kennedy had called upon his country-men to "mind our own business and interfere only when someone threatens . . . our homes." Herbert Hoover had then joined Kennedy on December 17. American arms, he reasoned, could never triumph in a global conflict with Communist armies, but U.S. air and sea power *could* dominate the oceans and defend North and South America. He recommended that they resign themselves to that, meantime feeding "the hungry of the world" and — Hoover's perennial solution to national crises — balancing the budget.

Alert isolationologists noted something new, however. Hoover's go-it-alone hypothesis wasn't as lonely as it at first seemed and was not, indeed, confined to the western hemisphere. He wanted to hold the Atlantic and Pacific "with one frontier on Britain and the other on Japan, Formosa, and the Philippines." On the Senate floor Robert A. Taft, Hoover's successor as leader of the Republican right, made the same concession. Taft accepted the need to protect "the island democracies" if they were attacked and if a successful defense was possible. The Hoover-Taft doctrine, variously called the principle of Fortress America or Continentalism, was being set forth by New Year's Day as a viable alternative to NATO. The argument over which was best came to dominate all other news from Capitol Hill. Newspaper-men called it the Great Debate.

The immediate issue before the country was an appropriation for four U.S. divisions which Truman had pledged to NATO. On January 5, 1951, Taft told the Senate, "The commitment of a land army to Europe is a pro-gram never approved by Congress into which we should not drift." Three days later Senator Wherry introduced Senate Resolution 8, opposing the assignment of U.S. ground forces to Europe pending the adoption of con-gressional policy, and on February 15 a majority of House Republicans signed a manifesto endorsing Hoover's Continentalism. Taft's adversaries were determined to depict him as an obstructionist, but what they failed to understand, and he neglected to clarify, was the prop behind his whole position: the fact that the Constitution assigned war-making powers to Capitol Hill, not the White House. He did not mean to hobble the executive branch. On January 15 he declared that he was "quite prepared to sit down with the President . . . or anyone on the majority side, and try to work out a program which could command the unanimous and consistent support of the people of the United States." But Truman now had no intention of shar-ing the growing powers of the modern Presidency, accumulated through precedents dating back to Roosevelt's Hundred Days.

From the perspective of the 1970s, one of the most remarkable aspects of the debate was the tacit agreement on both sides to accept certain postu-lates which, twenty years later, were far from being accepted as eternal truths. "The free world" was a phrase favored by administration rhetoricians as well as those on the Hill, and by unanimous consent it included Chiang's Formosa, Rhee's South Korea, Bao Dai's Vietnam, Salazar's Portugal,

Farouk's Egypt, Franco's Spain, Batista's Cuba, Perón's Argentina, French Algeria, the military dictatorship ruling Haiti, and all European colonies in Africa and Asia. Continentalists and internationalists alike assumed that any application of U.S. military power would be benign, and that no matter who won the debate, the American people would accept the result without demonstrations, protests, or even discussion. All debaters took it for granted that Communism was monolithic — that a central intelligence guided all Red activities, from Shanghai to the Elbe, so that any move, anywhere, by any Marxist, was presumed to have been made after calculating its effect on all of the free world. So closely held was this extraordinary belief that afterward President Truman would write in his memoirs:

> We were seeing a pattern in Indo-China and Tibet timed to coincide with the attack in Korea as a challenge to the Western world. It was a challenge by the Communists alone, aimed at intensifying the smoldering anti-foreign feeling among most Asian peoples. Our British allies and many statesmen of Europe saw in the Chinese moves a ruse to bring to a halt American aid in the rebuilding of Europe.

The debate arose over substantive disagreements between Hoover-Taft Republicans and Truman-Acheson Democrats, but it was far from being a party issue. Joseph Kennedy was still a Democrat; so were Senators George and Douglas, both of whom held that a President could not send soldiers abroad without congressional approval. Republican Senators Lodge and Knowland, on the other hand, believed that since the Senate had already approved of NATO in principle, Truman could provide the troops to implement it. Thomas E. Dewey, Earl Warren, Harold Stassen, and John Foster Dulles also threw their weight behind NATO, and in the end it was testimony by a future Republican President which determined the outcome of the debate.

The witness was Eisenhower. General Marshall had spoken eloquently of the need for what was being called "collective security," but Marshall had been identified with Roosevelt-Truman policies too long to be considered above the battle. This was not true of Eisenhower, who had left Columbia to become supreme commander of the western European defense force only the week before Christmas. There was, he told Congress, no acceptable alternative to "the rearmament and defense of western Europe." He reported that the will to resist Stalin was strong among Europeans, recommended that the United States assume leadership of the North Atlantic alliance, and urged a larger U.S. military presence in Europe, with no congressional strings attached to future increases.

Taft protested that this would make the matter "more hazy and indefinite and uncertain in outline," but the debate was over, and he had lost it. As James Reston observed in the *New York Times*, Eisenhower had what Acheson lacked, "political support in the country." Moreover, he had "Republican support, a commodity that has been in short supply at the State Department ever since Senator McCarthy, Republican of Wisconsin, invaded West Virginia last spring." Wherry's resolution was withdrawn, and on April 4 Congress accepted a substitute measure approving the dispatch of the four divisions to Europe. The President was admonished not to send more without "further congressional approval," but there was nothing to stop his doing it.

It had been a hard winter for Republicans. Out of office for eighteen years, and unaware of the political strength gathering behind General Eisenhower, they looked toward more bleak seasons ahead. McCarthy was now the most famous figure in the party. In November he had gone into Maryland to purge Millard Tydings. It had been a disgraceful campaign. Tydings had been opposed by John Marshall Butler, a Republican nonentity. Backing Butler, McCarthy and the *Washington Times-Herald* pooled their talents to produce a one-issue tabloid called *From the Record*. It appeared on every Maryland doorstep the night before the election. In it was every shabby lie McCarthy had used against the Democratic senator, the whole topped off by a fake photograph doctored to make it appear that Tydings was shaking hands with Earl Browder. Tydings lost by 40,000 votes. He had been considered invincible. If he could be eliminated, no one was safe. Looking around at his senatorial colleagues on the morning after the election, a senior Democrat asked, "For whom does the bell toll?" He answered dryly, "It tolls for thee."

The following month an incident at Washington's Sulgrave Club offered a sign of how far Lincoln's party had fallen. Leaving a dinner there on the eve of Drew Pearson's fifty-third birthday, Senator Nixon found a drunken Senator McCarthy in the men's room, beating up Pearson. "This one's for you, Dick," McCarthy jeered, belting the columnist in the face. He added, "I'm going to prove a theory. If you knee a man in the balls hard enough, blood'll come out of his eyeballs." Nixon stepped in and said, "Let a Quaker stop this fight." He took McCarthy's arm. "Come on, Joe," he said, "it's time for you to go home." McCarthy said, "No, not till he goes first. I'm not going to turn my back on that son of a bitch." After Pearson had gone, McCarthy confessed to Nixon that he couldn't remember where he had left his car. For a half-hour the two of them searched the area, the California senator reading license plates while the Wisconsin senator lurched after him in the dark. Nixon found it and McCarthy roared off. It would have been better for Joe to sleep it off before driving, just as it would have been better for party morale if some other Republican had won the allegiance of millions, but the party had little choice; it had run out of idols some time ago.

Then came spring, and all that changed. On April 11 Harry Truman presented them with a martyred hero. He fired Douglas MacArthur, turned the Great Debate into a greater debate, and touched off the country's greatest emotional convulsion between V-J Day and Dallas twelve years later.

Unlike Eisenhower, MacArthur was not widely admired by fighting men. But generals are not measured by popularity. On any rating of performance,

MacArthur eclipses other U.S. military leaders of his generation, and he may have been the most brilliant commander in the country's history. In 1918 he was named commander of the Rainbow Division in France, thereby becoming, at thirty-eight, the youngest general in the Army. Coming out of retirement to lead U.S. land troops against the Japanese, and then ruling postwar Japan as a kind of presidential viceroy, Douglas MacArthur had, by 1951, become a deity for many Americans. In forty-eight years as an officer, he had learned and practiced every soldierly virtue, with one exception: he made a poor second in command.

We shall never know what was in his mind that terrible winter after the Chinese came into the war. This much seems certain: he had lost his fighting spirit. According to Major General Chester V. Clifton, then aide to General Bradley and later military aide to Presidents Kennedy and Johnson, the Joint Chiefs of Staff decided as early as January that the general would have to be recalled on military, not political grounds: "What really counted was that MacArthur had lost confidence in himself and was beginning to lose the confidence of his field officers and troops. . . . And when he committed the final error of insubordination to the Commander-in-Chief — and there's absolutely no question about that — they had no trouble at all deciding what had to be done." Most Washingtonians doubted that the President had the nerve to tell him off, however. The *Washington Post* headline on the morning of April 11 read: MACARTHUR RECALL RULED OUT BY PRESIDENT, HILL HEARS; REPRIMAND IS STILL SEEN POSSIBLE.

By then the entire country knew of the dispute between the two men. The spirit of Wake had been long forgotten. As early as December the general had begun sniping at the President in the press, sending sharply worded letters to *U.S. News and World Report* and the president of the United Press. "I should have fired MacArthur then and there," Truman later said. Instead he had the Joint Chiefs tell the general that "no speech, press release, or public statement" on policy was to be released without prior clearance in Washington. After Christmas the President wrote MacArthur, praising his talents while gently reminding him that it was a presidential responsibility to "act with great prudence as far as extending the area of hostilities is concerned." To make certain that MacArthur understood the directive, two of the Chiefs — Collins and Hoyt S. Vandenberg — flew to Tokyo on Janauary 12, delivered the letter to him in the Dai Ichi Building, and told him they were prepared to provide any additional clarification he might require. He said he needed none. During the next two months he was inaccessible to reporters. Then, in Dean Acheson's words, he perpetrated "a major act of sabotage of a Government operation . . . sabotage of an operation of which he had been informed, and insubordination of the grossest sort to his commander in chief."

The President had felt it was time for a cease-fire and peace negotiations. On March 20 he drafted a statement saying so, and copies were sent to each of the U.N. allies for comment. The Joint Chiefs dispatched the text to

Tokyo in confidence, whereupon, to their amazement and horror, MacArthur called in the press and announced that he was prepared to negotiate with the enemy on his own terms. This torpedoed the Truman plan while achieving nothing. The general offered Peking annihilation, and as Walter Lippmann dryly noted, "Regimes do not negotiate about their survival." The Red Chinese merely reaffirmed their faith in victory. The peace offensive had failed before it could get started, leaving the President in a thin-lipped rage. He later wrote, "MacArthur left me no choice. I could no longer tolerate his insubordination." Then, before he could act, he was confronted by the last straw: a letter from the general to Congressman Joe Martin.

Martin, the Republican leader in the House, was one of several men on the Hill who had been treating MacArthur as a friendly foreign prince. Another of them, Republican Senator Homer Ferguson of Michigan, actually proposed that a congressional committee go to Tokyo so they could learn, from the general's own lips, what the goals of American policy should be and how to reach them. Since Martin was known to be one of Truman's more ferocious critics, MacArthur must have known that the only result of a letter to him would be mischief. On April 5 Martin rose in the House, declaring, "I owe it to the American people to tell the information I have from a great and reliable source." The information was a full-fledged assault on the administration by the general and a demand for the deploying of Nationalist Chinese troops on the Korean front. Later that day word came from London that MacArthur had made the same statements, for publication, in an interview with Lieutenant General H. G. Martin of the British Army. That evening Acheson received word that the President wanted to confer with him and General Marshall the next morning, immediately after the cabinet meeting. "I was," Acheson said in his memoirs, "in little doubt what the subject of our discussion would be."

The next day was April 7, a Friday. None of those close to him now doubted what Truman's response to MacArthur's latest insubordinations should be, but Acheson suggested that he wait until after the weekend for an opinion from the Joint Chiefs. On Monday Marshall reported that the Chiefs unanimously recommended that MacArthur be stripped of all his commands and replaced by Lieutenant General Matthew B. Ridgway, and that he and Bradley concurred in the recommendation. The next step was notifying MacArthur, and it cannot be said that this was handled well. Learning that the *Chicago Tribune* had the story, Truman snapped, "He's not going to be allowed to quit on me. He's going to be fired!" He ordered Bradley to push the thing through as quickly as possible. From the Pentagon Bradley sent word to Secretary of the Army Frank Pace, who was in Korea, advising him of the change of command and telling him to fly to Japan at once to inform MacArthur. Unfortunately for those who wished to soften the blow to the general's pride, Pace was cut off by a power failure, trapped in a tent during a hailstorm. Meanwhile the White House press secretary announced the news to a hastily called 1 A.M. press conference, releasing the text of the message which, Truman mistakenly thought, had just been delivered in Tokyo:

To General MacArthur from the President.

I deeply regret that it becomes my duty as President and Commander-in-Chief of the United States military forces to replace you as Supreme Commander, Allied Powers; Commander-in-Chief, United Nations Command; Commander-in-Chief, Far East; and Commanding General, U.S. Army, Far East.

You will turn over your commands, effective at once, to Lieutenant General Matthew B. Ridgway. You are authorized to have issued such orders as are necessary to complete desired travel to such place as you select.

My reasons for your replacement will be made public concurrently with the delivery to you of the foregoing message.

But it wasn't concurrent; the hailstorm fixed that. As Pace waited for it to abate, reporters at the White House hastily copied the presidential statement — "With deep regret I have concluded that General of the Army Douglas MacArthur is unable to give his wholehearted support to the policies of the United States and of the United Nations . . ." — and sent it flashing around the world. In Tokyo, where the time was 3 P.M., an aide who happened to be listening to a news broadcast told Mrs. MacArthur and then the general, who was lunching with Senator Warren Magnuson of Washington.

MAC IS SACKED, the London *Evening Standard* announced, and Murray Schumach of the *New York Times* cabled from Seoul, "The widespread feeling among officers of field rank is that the relationship between General Headquarters in Tokyo and the Eighth Army in Korea will become more pleasant." But that was not the reaction in the United States. There a large part of the public, frustrated by the war no one could win, registered its displeasure with Harry Truman in every way short of actual violence. Flags were flown upside down or at half-mast from Eastham, Massachusetts, to Oakland, California. In San Gabriel, California, and Worcester, Massachusetts, Truman was burned in effigy; Ponca City, Oklahoma, burned an effigy of Acheson. Petitions were circulated. Clergymen fulminated in their pulpits. New anti-Truman jokes were heard: "This wouldn't have happened if Truman were alive," and "I'm going to have a Truman beer — just like any other beer except that it hasn't got a head." The *Los Angeles Herald-Examiner* suggested that the President was befuddled by drugs, and the *Daily Oklahoman* called the dismissal "a crime carried out in the dead of night," overlooking the fact that the dead of night in Oklahoma was broad daylight in Tokyo.

The Los Angeles City Council adjourned "in sorrowful contemplation of the political assassination" of MacArthur. The California, Florida, and Michigan legislatures passed resolutions censuring Truman. In Charlestown, Maryland, a woman was told she couldn't send a telegram to the White House calling the President a moron; she and the clerk rummaged through a *Roget's Thesaurus* until they found the acceptable "witling." Other Western Union offices were more permissive. Among the wires from constituents inserted in the *Congressional Record* by proud representatives on the Hill were IMPEACH THE IMBECILE; WE WISH TO PROTEST THE LATEST OUTRAGE ON THE PART OF THE PIG IN THE WHITE HOUSE; IMPEACH THE JUDAS IN THE WHITE HOUSE WHO SOLD US DOWN THE RIVER TO THE LEFT WINGERS AND THE UN; SUGGEST YOU LOOK FOR ANOTHER HISS IN BLAIR HOUSE; WHEN AN EX-NATIONAL GUARD CAPTAIN FIRES A FIVE-STAR GENERAL IMPEACHMENT OF THE NATIONAL GUARD CAPTAIN IS IN ORDER; IMPEACH THE B WHO CALLS HIMSELF PRESIDENT; IMPEACH THE LITTLE WARD POLITICIAN STUPIDITY FROM KANSAS CITY; and IMPEACH THE RED HERRING FROM THE PRESIDENTIAL CHAIR.

The White House mail room was swamped. The President's press office ruefully acknowledged that in the first 27,363 letters and telegrams counted, critics of the dismissal outnumbered those who supported it twenty to one. George Gallup found that 69 percent of the voters backed MacArthur, and only 29 percent Truman. Truman was booed at Griffith Stadium — the first public booing of a President since Hoover in 1932. Senator Jenner said, "This country today is in the hands of a secret coterie which is directed by agents of the Soviet Union." Senator McCarthy told a Milwaukee meeting that the President was "a son of a bitch" surrounded by henchmen drunk on "bourbon and benedictine," and Congressman Martin, in whose office the first GOP caucus was held the morning after the dismissal, told reporters that "the question of impeachments was discussed," implying that not just Truman but his entire administration might be tried.

After that caucus Martin invited MacArthur to address a joint session of Congress. The general accepted immediately; for an orator of his gifts, this was the chance of a lifetime. He was accepting his ouster philosophically, even serenely. "I have just left him," Major General Courtney Whitney told the press. "He received the word of the President's dismissal from command magnificently. He never turned a hair. His soldierly qualities were never more pronounced. This has been his finest hour." On April 17 the *Bataan* put down at the San Francisco airport and he set foot on his native soil for the first time since his first retirement from the Army fourteen years earlier. As he appeared at the head of the gangway, his gold-encrusted hat and his dramatic trench coat bathed in spotlights, the elated crowd surged toward him. Two hours were required for his motorcade to crawl through fourteen miles of cheering people to the St. Francis Hotel, where the city's police force linked arms to save him, his wife, and thirteen-year-old Arthur MacArthur II from being trampled to death. Next day one hundred thousand Californians hurrahed again when he stood on the steps of San Francisco's City Hall and declared, "The only politics I have is contained in a single phrase known well by all of you — God Bless America!"

At Washington National Airport MacArthur was greeted by a seventeen-gun salute and the Joint Chiefs, who presented him with a silver tea service. There was an awkward moment then. He was cordial to the Chiefs, unaware of their role in his martyrdom, but frosty toward the President's representative, an old National Guard crony of Truman's. Harry Vaughan slipped away muttering, and the way was clear for the hero's triumphant ride through three hundred thousand rooting Washingtonians. The hour's most memorable moment came at 12:30 P.M., April 19, when the listening country heard the radio networks pick up the House doorkeeper's announcement: "Mr. Speaker, General of the Army Douglas MacArthur."

The general strode to the rostrum and stood erect and impassive as the senators and congressmen cheered until they were hoarse. "I address you," he said at last, "with neither rancor or bitterness in the fading twilight of life, with but one purpose in mind: To serve my country." They went wild again. And again. And again. Altogether his thirty-four-minute address was interrupted by thirty ovations. Of those who argued that America could not fight a two-front war he said, "I can think of no greater expression of defeatism. If a potential enemy can divide his strength on two fronts, it is for us to counter his effort. You cannot appease or otherwise surrender to Communism in Asia without simultaneously undermining our efforts to halt its advance in Europe." His voice dropped a register: "Why, my soldiers asked of me, surrender military advantages to an enemy in the field?" After a pause he almost whispered, "I could not answer."

In tears, he said at the end: "I am closing out my fifty-two years of military service. When I joined the Army, even before the turn of the century, it was the fulfillment of all my boyish hopes and dreams. Since I took the oath at West Point, the hopes and dreams have all vanished. But I still remember the refrain of one of the most popular barracks ballads of that day, which proclaimed most proudly that old soldiers never die, they just fade away. And like the old soldier of that ballad, I now close my military career and just fade away, an old soldier who tried to do his duty as God gave him the right to see that duty. Good-bye."

Sperry Rand had announced that MacArthur had joined its board of directors, but obviously he was not going to fade away there or elsewhere. His peroration had struck so deep a chord in the hearts of his admirers that some of them thought of him as divine. "We heard God speak here today," cried Representative Dewey Short of Missouri, "God in the flesh, the voice of God." Herbert Hoover, another President whom the general had crossed, now spoke of him as "a reincarnation of St. Paul into a great General of the Army who came out of the East." One senator said, "It's disloyal not to agree with General MacArthur," and six thousand Daughters of the American Revolution, whom he addressed later in the afternoon, agreed. It was the DAR's Sixtieth Continental Congress in Constitution Hall. The ladies had voted to remove their hats so they wouldn't obscure one another's view of the general. He didn't disappoint them. "In this hour of crisis, all patriots look to you," he said, and "I have long sought personally to pay you the tribute that is in my heart."

Reading her minutes the next day, the DAR recording secretary general, Mrs. Warren Shattuck Currier, observed that the general's speech was "probably the most important event" in the history of the hall. Instantly Mrs. Thomas B. Throckmorton was on her feet. She moved, and the convention agreed with one voice, to strike the word "probably." By then MacArthur was in New York, the center of a historic demonstration. Over 2,859 tons of litter were being dumped on him, four times the previous record (for Eisenhower). Police put the number of spectators at 7,500,000, which was absurd, but it was certainly the largest crowd Manhattan had ever seen. Forty thousand longshoremen walked off their jobs to be there. Schools were closed. People crossed themselves as the general's limousine passed. Women sobbed into handkerchiefs. Eighteen victims of hysteria were hospitalized. Enterprising notion vendors with MacArthur buttons, pennants, and corncob pipes from the 1948 MacArthur-for-President campaign were sold out, and the only other business in business was Tin Pan Alley, whose tune-smiths were turning out five recordings of:

> Old soldiers never die, never die, never die,
> Old soldiers never die,
> They just fade away.*

"The country," said Senator James Duff of Pennsylvania, "is on a great emotional binge." Florists were offering a Douglas MacArthur tea rose ("needing no coddling or favor") and MacArthur orchids, cacti, gladioli, geraniums, peonies, and irises. At the Waldorf Astoria, where the Mac-Arthurs checked into a $130-a-day suite, the switchboard began receiving three thousand calls a day from people who wanted to speak to the general. There he paid his respects to Hoover and was himself visited by Cardinal Spellman and a parade of powerful Republicans: Senator Taft, Senator Styles Bridges, Colonel McCormick, Henry Luce, and William Randolph Hearst. It was evident that politics was very much on the general's mind. In a series of speeches before state legislatures, beginning in Massachusetts, he attacked Truman's "appeasement on the battlefield" and his "timidity" in domestic and foreign policy. The President let these criticisms pass until MacArthur, speaking to an American Legion convention, claimed that his March offer to negotiate with the enemy had wrecked a "secret plan" by U.S. leaders to abandon Formosa to the Chinese Communists and give Peking a U.N. seat in exchange for peace in Korea. Truman said that was a lie, and that the general knew it. But by then the emotional binge was over. MacArthur was in politics up to his pipe and braided cap, and everybody knew it now, for he had been chosen to deliver the keynote address at the 1952 Republican National Convention.

*A British army ballad, it was based on an American gospel hymn, "Kind Words Can Never Die."

Ten days after MacArthur's dismissal public opinion polls noted the first signs of a decline in his popularity. Simultaneously, another Communist offensive burst upon the U.N. line in Korea. It came as no surprise to Ridgway. Observing the ominous buildup behind the enemy's earthworks, he had ordered a salient thrust forward into the middle of them. The salient fell to the Chinese in the first phase of their new push, and over the next two weeks, as one ROK unit after another broke and ran, the Eighth Army once more reeled backward across the 38th Parallel. But the Reds again failed to break through. After a month they paused, exhausted, whereupon General James A. Van Fleet reversed the momentum of battle with a skillful counterattack. No sooner had he straightened the line than the Chinese bent it southward. Ridgway bent it right back. By the end of May 1951, he had cleared South Korea of Communist troops, and the jagged front stretched across the waist of the Korean peninsula, from the Sea of Japan on the east to the Yellow Sea on the west. The western anchor for both armies lay near the obscure village of Panmunjom.

The fighting was grim, colorless, and depressing. To enliven it, Ridgway's staff gave geographical features homely American names — "the Kansas-Wyoming Line," "the Utah Line," "Porkchop Hill," "the Punch Bowl" — a practice which would ultimately lead to Vietnam's grotesque "Operation Cedar Rapids" and "Operation Attleboro." Gone were World War II's crisp code words: Torch, Husky, Overlord, Anvil, Dragoon, Iceberg. If the horrors of war could not be liquidated, it seemed, military public relations men would wrap them in euphemisms until they had been thoroughly Americanized. Like the ubiquitous comic books and the turkey dinners served in foxholes on Thanksgiving, battlefield nomenclature would remind the men of home.

People at home stopped following news about the war. Suspecting that literally no one was reading about it any more, the editors of an Oregon newspaper ran one war story two days in a row — the same text, same byline, same head, and even the same position, halfway down column two on page one. Their hunch was confirmed; not a single subscriber noticed the repetition. In the Nebraska town of Hastings, Eric Goldman reported, an Army corporal named William Jensen, who had been shot in the thigh during the first Chinese attack, limped downtown, stared at the prosperous stores on Second Street, and said, "Man, I never saw anything like it. This town is just one big boom."

It was; all America was. Although at war abroad, the country had been neither invaded nor attacked, and nothing cherished was in peril. Unlike Kipling's nineteenth-century Tommy Atkins, who also fought in distant lands, the American soldier did not even have the feeling that he was contributing to the glory of empire. He was fighting battles whose sole objective was peace in another land, participating in a police action whose felons were not going to be punished, and it wasn't good enough. In James A. Michener's later view, "starting with the Korean War in 1950 our nation developed a seductive and immoral doctrine which I questioned at the time and about which I have become increasingly dubious. The mistaken doctrine was this: that we could wage with our left hand a war in which a few men chosen at random sacrificed their lives, while with our right hand we maintained an undisturbed economy in which the fortunate stay-at-homes could frolic and make a lot of money."

Seen in this light, the acclaim for MacArthur appears to have been an escape valve for a thwarted people. In addition it may have goaded administration peace efforts, which badly needed the energies of dedicated men. Arranging an armistice was a delicate business. Officially, the United States government had not even conceded the existence of North Korea and Communist China. The Chinese continued to insist that all its troops along the 38th Parallel were volunteers and therefore not subject to its discipline. Russia disclaimed any responsibility for the conflict. The State Department was wary of discussing peripheral issues — Formosa, Indochina, and diplomatic recognition of Peking and Pyongyang. The very fact that negotiations were under consideration would increase casualties as field commanders sparred to improve their positions. Lastly, there was no reliable go-between for peace feelers. Discretion was essential. Experience had demonstrated the impossibility of keeping a secret at the United Nations. Neutral nations, notably India, were also leaky; indeed, Krishna Menon, India's ambassador to the U.N., was an Americophobe who seemed bent upon terms which would humiliate the United States.

George Kennan found a way out. On leave from the State Department, he called Jacob Malik from Princeton and suggested they meet for unofficial conversations in Russian. These began on May 31 at Malik's Long Island summer home. After an awkward beginning they settled into a series of talkathons, interrupted only when Malik felt the need to "consider matters"; that is, to check with Moscow. Eventually he suggested initiatives between commanders in the field, and these were taken, although early results were discouraging. The Chinese remained suspicious. Ridgway, more tactful and less haughty than his predecessor, did persuade them to sit down in the ancient city of Kaesong, between the lines, on July 10, but quarrels about the agenda followed. In early autumn the talks were moved to Panmunjom. While they were better than nothing, communications kept breaking down. Korean hostilities dragged on through a second year of battle and into a third. American enthusiasm for the war, in Acheson's tart phrase, had "reached an irreducible minimum."

By now cold war temperatures had sunk to arctic levels. Tension between the Communist and free worlds dominated world affairs. It was a kind of pollution which was found everywhere: in novels, plays, movies, magazine articles; in newspaper serials (Herbert Philbrick's *I Led Three Lives,* the account of an FBI informer who had been a Communist party member for nine years, ran in more than five hundred papers throughout the 1950s);

and on radio and television. The Cincinnati Reds changed their name for a time. Social studies teachers either came down hard on the evils of "Communist slavery" or risked dismissal. The highest lecture fees went to anti-Communist zealots and the biggest Americanism awards to contestants whose reasons for loathing Communists and fellow travelers, or pinkos, were most persuasive.

Even Miss America aspirants had to state their opinions of Karl Marx, and the most popular writer of the new decade was a former Brooklyn lifeguard whose hymns to sex and anti-Communist sadism had, by the end of 1951, sold over thirteen million copies. Wiry, with a crew cut, loudly contemptuous of "longhairs," thirty-three-year-old Mickey Spillane had published his first Mike Hammer novel, *I, the Jury,* in 1947. As he grew more prolific, turning out *My Gun Is Quick, Vengeance Is Mine, One Lonely Night,* and *The Big Kill,* he was recognized as the latest expression of the vigilante streak of violence in the American national character. Mike Hammer was more than just another tough private eye. He brought his creator $50,000 a book by killing for justice and democracy. A typical scene in *One Lonely Night,* which appeared in 1951 and sold three million copies, ended with the gloat:

> "I killed more people tonight than I have fingers on my hands. I shot them in cold blood and enjoyed every minute of it. . . . They were Commies, Lee. They were Red sons-of-bitches who should have died long ago. . . . They never thought that there were people like me in this country. They figured us all to be soft as horse manure and just as stupid."

The nebulous figures behind Mike were variously described as "a new McCarthy," "another McCarthy," or a nameless reformer who had the courage to expose Commies in government, thereby winning the hatred of disloyal Ivy League graduates. To be consistent, Mike ought to have been a Jacobin hunting aristocrats, but much of the time Spillane wasn't coherent. Some of his passages were so dense that even the non sequitur was buried. In *The Girl Hunters,* while mourning for a McCarthy type named Leo Knapp, Mike reflects that "Reds just aren't the kind who can stand a big push. Like it or not, they are still a lousy bunch of peasants who killed to control but who can be knocked into line by the likes of us. They're shouting slobs who'll run like hell when class shows and they know this inside their feeble little heads." Class shows elsewhere when the author, pondering the gulf between Mike and Communist peasants, muses:

> Damn their stinking hides anyway. Damn them and their philosophies! Death and destruction were the only thing the Kremlin crowd was capable of. They knew the value of violence and death and used it over and over in a wild scheme to smash everything flat but their own kind.

Then, presumably to distinguish between these apostles of death and destruction, whose currency is violence and death, and the clean, decent, American way, Mike tells a female captive what will happen if she tries to kill him with a shotgun whose barrels have been plugged with heavy clay.

> "The barrel would unpeel like a tangerine and you'd get that whole charge right down your lovely throat and if you ever want to give a police medical examiner a job to gag a maggot, that's the way to do it. They'd have to go in and scrape your brains up with a silent butler and pick pieces of your skull out of the woodwork with needle-nosed pliers."

She vomits, and he continues:

> "The worst of all is the neck because the head is gone and the neck spurts blood for a little bit while the heart doesn't know its vital nerve center is gone — and do you know how high the blood can spurt? No? Then let me tell you."

After throwing up again she says, "Man, are you mean." He wasn't as mean as comic books of the time, however. As a sop to reformers and child psychologists they ran pious credos. "This magazine is dedicated to the prevention of crime and subversion," appeared on the cover of one 1951 issue. "We hope that within its pages the youth of America will learn to know crime and treason for what they really are: sad, black, dead-end roads of fools and tears." But its pages taught American youth a lot more than that. Graphic drawings showed Negro corpses strung up by their wrists, boys driving white-hot pokers between thighs of disloyal girls, and girls, not to be outdone, stabbing Communist criminals in the eyes with icepicks ("P-put that down!!! NO! AG, AG, AG, UGG . . .").

These were recurring themes, together with rape, murder, stamping on children's faces, and drinking the blood of the opposite sex ("As she bites into his neck he feels a burning poisonous venom seeping through his veins paralizing [sic] his every muscle . . . He realizes the answer to it all!"). Phantom Lady's specialty was tying up victims and whipping them to death. How to hurt people was another common motif. Anatomical diagrams showed everything from "Eyes — finger jab or thumb gouge" to "Arch heel stamp," while the accompanying text explained, "There are certain spots in the body more sensitive than the rest. . . . The charts made for the use of government agents in training show just where those spots are and what to use against them." Some of the tableaux offered Mike Hammerism to the illiterate, as in the illustrations accompanying this message:

> So NOW you KNOW, fiends. Now you know WHY there is a ball game being played in the moonlight at midnight in the deserted Central City ball park. Look CLOSELY. SEE this STRANGE BASEBALL GAME! See the long strings of pulpy intestines that mark the base lines. See the two lungs and the liver that indicate the bases . . . the heart that is home plate. See Doc White bend and whisk the heart with the mangy scalp, yelling . . . "PLAY BALL . . . Batter up!" See the batter come to the plate swinging the legs, the arms, then throwing all but one away and standing in the box waiting for the pitcher to hurl the head in to him. See the catcher with the torso strapped

on as a chest-protector, the infielders with their hand-mits [*sic*], the stomach-rosin bag, and all the other pieces of equipment that was once Central City's star pitcher, Herbie Satten.

Seasoned readers of the comics were not surprised to learn that villainous old Doc White, who had carved Herbie up, was an enemy agent. In that episode evil had won. More often Reds were depicted dangling from lynch ropes, pistol-whipped, buried alive, fed to sharks, or dangling from the bumpers of loyal Americans' jalopies — "These travel roads are tough on tires!" "But ya gotta admit, there's nothing like 'em for erasing faces!" "Yeah, even Stalin couldn't identify this meat!" The lesson was plain. Because organized society was helpless against the free world's enemies, the only hope lay with brutal men who weren't afraid to take the law into their own hands, men who were undeniably uncouth but obviously necessary. This was what people meant when they said, "I don't approve of McCarthy's methods, but he's got the right idea."

The right idea was to thumb your nose at authority, kick over the traces, take Commies down behind the gas works and break their necks. Ordinary men believed it because, like MacArthur, they were fed up with national policy. It was at loggerheads with everything they had learned as children, inimical to their traditions. Korea's war without victory was but one example. America, they had been taught, avoided entangling alliances. Now they were expected to forget all that. U.S. troops were the backbone of a NATO force which would comprise fifty divisions and 4,000 warplanes by the end of 1952. To support military bases around the globe, an unprecedented proportion of the national income was being poured into military hardware. In Washington the federal bureaucracy grew larger each month. Nor was that all; having suffered through its own Depression just a few years earlier, the United States now seemed to be doling out its new wealth to poor countries all over the world. The bill for all this was being passed along to U.S. taxpayers, who grew increasingly resentful.

Where could they turn? Their only seasoned allies were in the thinning ranks of prewar isolationism. The old America Firsters shared their dismay over America's new directions. "It's almost unbelievable in its grant of unlimited power to the Chief Executive," Vandenberg had written to his wife when he read the first Military Assistance Program. ". . . It would virtually make him the number one war lord of the earth." Taft had voted against it because it carried "an obligation to assist in arming, at our expense, the nations of Western Europe. With that obligation, I believe it will promote war in the world rather than peace"; and Senator Forrest Donnell of Missouri had condemned the concept of collective security as a "moral commitment" that would draw the United States into other peoples' wars.

Twenty years later those words would sound prophetic, but they did not seem so then. The right appeared to be the province of the discredited fossils who had applauded Munich. It occurred to almost no one in public life that the whole structure of international politics had become obsolescent on August 6, 1945, that the dropping of the first atomic bomb then had been a revolutionary act, and that all the panoply of diplomatic relations and military alliances — indeed, the very concept of the nation state — might now be as quaint and irrelevant as a senseless little barrack tune running through the mind of a seventy-year-old general. Armies and navies were useful only if threats to use them were believable. If a course of action has become incredible, all the assumptions based on it have lost their justification. In the atomic age, military solutions were still possible in disputes between little countries, or between little and big countries. Between great countries they meant nothing. One British military analyst saw this. Sir John Slessor said, "We have at last arrived at the point when war — in the sense of total world war as we have known it in our generation — has abolished itself as a practical instrument of policy." The flight of the *Enola Gay* over Hiroshima and of her sister ship over Nagasaki had demonstrated that warfare between superpowers would be a thousandfold more ghastly than the bloodiest Spillane fiction or the most revolting comic, and nothing since then had scattered this awful cloud. On the contrary, bombs had been growing much bigger.

After Japan's surrender, Los Alamos had gone into a temporary eclipse. Its celebrities left for college campuses, and key technicians moved to Albuquerque, where a new factory was about to begin assembly line production of nuclear weapons. Laboratories in the old Tech Area were stripped of equipment. Road repair was discontinued. Buildings decayed. After an inspection David Lilienthal reported to Washington that "We found a great many health hazards and fire hazards that were very damaging to morale." Nothing seemed likely to prevent the decay of Los Alamos into a ghost town — and then in the early 1950s something did. Overnight streets were paved. A hospital went up, then schools, and then a library. Stores, a theater, and a community center were built around a central mall; ground was broken for a stadium; athletes were recruited for a sports club called the "Los Alamos Atomic Bombers."

These signs of prosperity in the death business owed much to the dark, bushy-browed Hungarian named Edward Teller. His enthusiasm for ever greater explosions overcame moral qualms in the scientific community, the Pentagon, and the federal government. It is not too much to call him, as he was called, "the chief architect of the hydrogen bomb."

The H-bomb is the ultimate in deathmanship, a missile which may be anywhere from twenty-five to a thousand times more destructive than the weapons dropped in 1945. The energy for the A-bomb comes from fission, the splitting of uranium atoms; the H-bomb's power comes from fusion, the uniting of hydrogen atoms — the very process by which the sun gives light. Fusion can occur only at very high temperatures; therefore H-bombs are called thermonuclear weapons. Their theoretical possibilities had long been known, but after the horrors of Hiroshima conversations about them among atomic physicists were awed and guarded. The hypothetical new bomb was called the "Super." From time to time cryptic references to it appeared in the *Bulletin of the Atomic Scientists*, but the editors never defined it. In their opinion, the less the world knew about the Super, the better.

Teller disagreed. At Berkeley in the summer of 1942 he had been one of seven physicists who had mulled over the feasibility of man-made fusion, and he never forgot what he later called the thrilling "spirit of spontaneous expression, adventure and surprise." To his disappointment, the consideration of thermonuclear possibilities was discontinued in 1943. Since the temperatures required were so high that only a fission bomb could produce them, the fission riddle had to be solved first, anyhow, and once that happened, it was thought, they ought to stop. At about this time Teller began speaking of the mythic Super as "my baby." His colleagues were glad to leave it to him.

After V-J Day he said he would stay on at Los Alamos if he could start thermonuclear experiments. When the response was negative, he accepted an appointment at the University of Chicago's Institute for Nuclear Studies. The following year he returned for a conference on the Super, where he argued that the bigger bomb could be perfected in two years. He was in a minority. The leader of anti-Super physicists was Albert Einstein. Einstein thought it wrong even to consider construction of an H-bomb. Teller couldn't see why. The Hiroshima bomb, he pointed out, had been built because Nazi scientists were thought to be on the track of it. Now Soviet physicists were believed to be working on a thermonuclear device. Was Stalin any safer or saner than Hitler?

The turning point for the development of a new U.S. nuclear arsenal was the announcement, on September 23, 1949, that the Russians had exploded an atomic bomb. From this point on, the rise of the fusion bomb owed much to a series of stimuli which served to break down objections to it. First there was the discovery that Leningrad physicists had been investigating the possibility of fusing light nuclei as early as 1932. That convinced Alvarez and Ernest O. Lawrence; they came down hard on Teller's side, and the three of them became known in the scientific community as "the Supermen." The Supermen's chief adversaries were Einstein, Oppenheimer, and President James B. Conant of Harvard, the three biggest names in American science. All other things being equal, the opposition should have won easily, and in the beginning it did. On October 25, 1949, the Atomic Energy Commission met in Washington to weigh arguments in favor of a weapon which, if dropped on a major city, would instantly kill somewhere between 80 and 90 percent of the inhabitants. They rejected it. Apart from moral objections, the H-bomb project was thought to be so expensive and complex that it would slow down the mass production of A-bombs in Albuquerque, and even if it proved feasible, the only Russian targets large enough to justify its use were Moscow and Leningrad, both of which could be annihilated with fissionable materials.

That was a triumph for common sense, but it was only the beginning of the struggle. The Supermen had picked up an ally in Rear Admiral Lewis A. Strauss, USNR, one of AEC's five directors (the other four were then opposed), and they were gaining other converts in Secretary of Defense Louis Johnson, the Joint Chiefs, the Joint Congressional Committee on Atomic Energy, and Paul Nitze, director of the State Department's Policy Planning Staff. The prestige of the United States, the Supermen insisted, owed much to the dominance of American technology; if the Russians built the first fusion bomb, the U.S. would lose face. On January 13, 1950, Omar Bradley decided to approve the Super on the ground that as chairman of the JCS he could endorse no move which might lead to any Russian advantage, however temporary, in the accelerating arms race. Hiss had been convicted that month, setting the stage of McCarthyism, and four days after Bradley made his commitment word of the second stimulus favoring the H-bomb partisans came from London; Fuchs had been charged with treason. It was impossible to say with any certainty how much Fuchs had known, but he had sat in the highest councils of Anglo-American science, and official Washington was in a mood to overreact. Meeting in the Executive Office Building on January 31, a three-man *ad hoc* special committee — Secretaries Acheson and Johnson, AEC chairman Lilienthal — again pondered the advisability of a thermonuclear crash program. Lilienthal was outvoted. That afternoon President Truman announced that he had directed the AEC to develop "the 'hydrogen' or super bomb."

The consciences of many scientists were outraged. Speaking for them Oppenheimer said, "In some crude sense, which no vulgarity, no humor, no overstatement can quite extinguish, the physicists have known sin and this is a knowledge they cannot lose." The cover of the *Bulletin of Atomic Scientists* in each issue had carried a clock registering eight minutes to twelve; now it was moved up to three minutes before twelve. Under the leadership of Hans Bethe of Cornell, twelve U.S. senior physicists issued a statement deploring Truman's decision. They declared: "We believe that no nation has the right to use such a bomb, no matter how righteous its cause. The bomb is no longer a weapon of war but a means of extermination of whole populations. Its use would be a betrayal of all standards of morality and of Christian civilization itself." Their sincerity was beyond question, but Bethe's indignation proved evanescent. In less than five months the resolution of the protesters was tested by the outbreak of the Korean War and the challenge of the new project to their scientific curiosity. The first was his undoing; he decided that patriotism required him to drop his objections to the H-bomb and plunge into the search for its early perfection — which he did with such vigor that his contribution to it became a major factor in its success. Curiosity was the greater goal for most, however. In June of 1951, on the first anniversary of North Korea's rupture of the 38th

Parallel, Teller spoke before several distinguished associates at the Institute for Advanced Study at Princeton. Gordon Gray, the new chairman of the AEC, made notes of the discussion. They read in part:

> Out of the meeting came something which Edward Teller brought into the meeting with his own head, which was an entirely new way of approaching a thermonuclear weapon. . . . Calculations were made, Dr. Bethe, Dr. Teller, Dr. Fermi participating the most in this. Oppy [*sic*] very actively as well. . . . everyone around that table without exception, and this included Dr. Oppenheimer, was enthusiastic now that you had something foreseeable.

That same week Gray committed the AEC to the financing of America's first H-bomb plant. Thirteen years were to pass before the savage parody of Teller in the film *Dr. Strangelove*. By then the monsters of which he had dreamed at Berkeley would lie in underground silos, available at the touch of a button.

The first riddle to be solved was a math problem, or a series of them. Equations for the A-bomb had been complicated enough; the new ones went right off the blackboard. Each step in the completed device required a staggering number of precise calculations to gauge its impact on millions of tiny parts in the bomb, and since the steps succeeded one another in tiny fractions of a second — for all practical purposes they were instantaneous — the human mind could not cope with them. Nor were the calculating machines of 1951 much help. Despite its 500 miles of wire and 3,000,000 electrical connections, the instrument IBM had built for Harvard was nowhere near fast enough. Improved models were coming along, but the best of them, the new ENIAC, could recall only twenty-seven words. They were maddeningly temperamental. Storms put them out of commission. Tubes went out. Circuits went wrong. Repair crews couldn't find the trouble. Technicians would sit up night after night with a sick computer, spending months on one problem while other specialists in their design teams awaited an answer. Los Alamos added a day to the work week and round-the-clock shifts for computer crews. The Tech Area still marked time until one of the scientists, John von Neumann, decided to tackle the bottleneck. Neumann reflected the ambivalence of the Supermen; he called their goal "the hell weapon" and drove himself mercilessly in the search for it. In the 1930s he had acquired an international reputation in mathematics. His hobby was the construction of robots and mechanical toys, and now his most enduring contribution to the Superhunt became a kind of Supertoy. It could retain and remember 40,000 bits of "software" — computerspeak for data — and complete three months of equations in a day; he called it a "Mathematical Analyzer, Numerical Integrator and Computer." Only after the device was patented, and its name irretrievably registered with the AEC, did his colleagues realize that the acronym for it was MANIAC.

With maniacal help, then, the Supermen completed a sixty-five-ton

H-bomb in the last year of the Truman Presidency. In that era of the Kansas-Wyoming Line and the Punch Bowl, it is perhaps unsurprising that they christened it "Mike." Mike was towed to Eniwetok atoll in the Marshalls and housed in a shed on the tiny island of Elugelab with various ion chambers, high-speed cameras, beta ray spectrographs, containers of uranium and heavy hydrogen, and other nuclear paraphernalia. There the ritual worked out seven years earlier on the semidesert near Alamogordo, New Mexico, was repeated. On the night of October 31–November 1, 1952, all ships withdrew forty miles while a team of volunteers made last-minute preparations. After they, too, had left, the countdown began on the boats over public address systems. At dawn the counters reached zero and Mike was immediately transformed into the first man-made star. Dumbfounded sailors saw a ball of fire rise five miles into the sky followed by a gigantic cauliflower-shaped cloud, all mauve and blue and gray-green, that rose twenty-five miles into the stratosphere while beneath it Elugelab burned, broke in two, and sank.

Divers found a mile-long, 175-foot-deep canyon in the ocean floor. The scientific observers calculated that the bomb's four-mile-wide fireball would have vaporized all of downtown Spokane or San Francisco, most of St. Louis or Pittsburgh, or everything in Manhattan from Central Park to Washington Square. Navy security was slack; descriptive letters were passed by censors. They were chilling; one witness wrote that "It would take at least ten suns" to equal the light of the explosion. Some of the letters found their way into local newspapers, and presently the whole world knew of the test and its awesome results. Nine months later Georgi Malenkov triumphantly announced in Moscow that "the United States no longer has a monopoly of the hydrogen bomb." Radioactive traces found in the skies over Asia by B-29 flying laboratories confirmed him. The British had meanwhile exploded their first atomic device, distinguished by a macabre Z-shaped cloud. The nuclear club was growing. The nightmare envisioned by Einstein, Oppenheimer, and Conant had come true, and the imbalance of terror had begun. "General annihilation," Einstein told reporters, "beckons."

Absolute weapons, it now developed, were to be provided with absolute transportation. In the early 1950s automation had not yet eliminated the human factor from bombing. Responsibility for America's nuclear arsenal was vested in the Strategic Air Command, which employed 270,000 men in a ceaseless B-29 shuffle around the globe, making certain that even if the United States ceased to exist, posthumous vengeance would be wreaked. SAC can hardly be called attractive. Each of its pilots was riding with more explosives than all the Allied air raids in World War II. Its generals put up billboards proclaiming PEACE IS OUR PROFESSION. They called sonic booms "the sound of freedom," and their annual maneuvers, in which who-hit-what-target was recorded in railroad boxcars stuffed with radar, were "the World Series of Bombing." Still, the generals and their pilots were people. As such, they were about to become obsolete.

Their replacements were to come from, of all places, the smoking ruins of the Third Reich's laboratories. Alone among World War II's belligerents, the Germans had foreseen the martial possibilities of rocket propulsion. The scientists who had hatched the V-1 and V-2 weapons were now the men of the hour, and SAC strategists were beating paths to their doors. With the thrust of rocket engines, a nuclear explosive could cross the Atlantic or the North Pole in less than a half-hour. SAC had considered rockets before and rejected them as too inaccurate. Their margin of error could not be honed below two-tenths of one percent. At a range of 5,000 miles this meant a deviation of ten miles, too much for an A-bomb. But it wasn't too much for an H-bomb. The sinking of Elugelab had cast matters in a new and brutal light. In the chilling words of *Fortune,* "Because of the quantum jump in the destructive power of the thermonuclear warhead, not to mention the still greater area of lethal fallout, delivery within eight or ten miles of the center of the target became militarily acceptable."

The admittance of the sinister word "fallout" into the language, and the expansion it implied in a bomb's circle of death, signaled a change in the whole concept of war. Another significant new term was "overdestroying." With the refinement of the H-bomb into a "fission-fusion-fusion" or FFF bomb — to the A-bomb trigger, and the fusion of the fuel, it added fusion of the bomb casing — the area of lethal fallout could be increased to 300 square miles.

It was at this point that people started digging. World War II's civil defense program had been something of a joke; the oceans had been too wide for Axis bombers to constitute a real menace, and the air-raid wardens in their flat white tin hats had been a little shamefaced about the whole thing. Now their long vigils made some sense. Reactivated, they supervised drills in schools. Elsewhere there was a brisk trade in amulets and quackery. Medicasters advertised lead-foil brassieres, lead girdles, aluminum pajamas, and drawstring bags to be pulled over the head in time of danger. One crank hawked a "U-235 Atomic Shock Cure" until the U.S. Public Health Service found its active ingredients to be bicarbonate of soda, table salt, and water. Another advocated shaving all pets so their hair wouldn't become radioactive. The SPCA protested, and nothing came of it.

Still, there was something unreal about *all* civil defense campaigns. The most determined, with the greatest potential for enterprising entrepreneurs, was the shelter program. In an attempt to encourage excavations, a construction company in Los Angeles staged a ground-breaking ceremony for one of the first family shelters in January 1951. A Mrs. Ruth Colhoun, a mother of three, ceremoniously turned over the first spadeful for television cameramen. She had contracted to pay $1,995 for an underground refuge with brightly painted concrete walls, shamrock green plastic carpeting, storage space concealed by clever sliding doors, and a lightweight Geiger counter. "I do a lot of canning and bottling in the summer," she cheerfully told the television audience, "and it will make a good storehouse." As an afterthought she added, "It will make a wonderful place for the children to play in, too."

For $3,000 you could have the "Mark I Kidde Kokoon." That included a three-way portable radio, air blower, wind-up clock, first aid kit, Sterno stove, radiation charts, protective apparel suits, chemical toilet, gasoline-driven generator, pick-and-shovel combination ("for digging out after blast"), and everything else needed for a family of five to spend three to five days underground.

For most people the sticking point was the problem of what to do on D-day about improvident neighbors who had neglected to build refuges of their own. After retreating to your own dugout you would have no room for them. It would be necessary to lock them out, and you might have to use force. Some kits began including pistols with this in mind, but the public wasn't prepared to be *that* realistic. In time the backyard cavities became curiosities. Some were converted to barbecue pits. Others were used to stow garden tools, snow tires, and children's bikes.

After a while stories of the horrors which would accompany a nuclear holocaust became familiar to Pentagon strategists, and they moved almost effortlessly from the consideration of megatons to megadeaths — each megadeath being the killing of one million persons, with ten or fifteen possible in a single day. The threat of a thermonuclear holocaust which could envelop the world in flame remained very real for some thoughtful people outside the military establishment, but they felt impotent. Cold-warriors had become deaf to warnings of doomsday, men in public life seemed paralyzed by McCarthyism, and intellectuals who had been in the grip of one international crisis or another since Munich could not summon the wit or strength to break the hold of this one.

Meanwhile, the passage of time had brought a new generation of Americans to maturity. Surely, sensitive men thought, the air-raid drills in public schools, with their apocalyptic implications, must have aroused the children. Their elders looked hopefully toward them and suffered a cruel disappointment.

In the twilight months of the Truman administration, college teachers gradually became aware of a slow, creeping rot in the country's intellectual life, which, it turned out, was the younger generation. It is curious to recall that in those years students were chastised for their apathy, but they were, and with justice; never had American youth been so withdrawn, cautious, unimaginative, indifferent, unadventurous — and silent.

The silent generation was a phenomenon of the 1950s, as characteristic of it as tailfins and white bucks. A vast hush had settled over the universities. Liberalism had become tired and dull. There seemed to be no indignant young men on campuses, no burning causes, and no militancy, except among a reactionary handful on the far right. Protest was confined to a few "beats," who like their peers were in full retreat from idealism and contention. For the majority, acts of social significance were replaced by the panty raid or something called "stuffing," in which the largest possible number of undergraduates would squash themselves into some small space — forty of them in a Volkswagen, say, or a dozen in an outdoor phone booth. At Fresno State in California, students lowered a booth into the deep end of the college swimming pool; seven volunteers then held their breaths long enough to cram themselves in it.

A few zealous sociologists tried to find significance in this — arguing that the stuffers were dramatizing interdependence — but the students themselves had no illusions. It was all meaningless, and they knew it; after the fun was over they could be found waiting in queues for interviews with recruiters from the nation's largest corporations. They waited so patiently for everything that visitors to campuses began commenting on their docility. Cartoonists depicted students as empty Brooks Brothers suits. Robert Frost said he was troubled by their "lack of decisiveness." A CCNY alumna returned for a social function and left shocked; the coeds could talk only of their future homes in suburbia, the very sort of trivial chatter which CCNY girls of other years had scorned as being typical of expensive women's colleges. Debaters from Oxford, touring American campuses, were startled to find free enterprise regarded not merely as an economic system, but as a way of life. "What is there to crusade about?" a bespectacled Princeton junior asked Professor Otto Butz. At Harvard David Riesman wrote of undergraduate complaints: "When I ask such students what they have done about these things, they are surprised at the very thought they could do anything. They think I am joking when I suggest that, if things came to the worst, they could picket!"

"Few young people," Murray Ross wrote in 1950, "share deeply in the life of a group dedicated, and actively devoted, to the highest goals of mankind." To find out what did stir youth, Life that year asked it for its heroes and heroines. Back like a straight arrow came the answers: Lincoln, Franklin Roosevelt, Joe DiMaggio, MacArthur, Babe Ruth, and Roy Rogers; Clara Barton, Vera-Ellen, Florence Nightingale, Doris Day, and Sister Elizabeth Kenny. Parental opinions could scarcely have been much different. Indeed, one of the most remarkable features of the new decade was the degree to which young Americans adopted the values of the older generation. The "dedication of bourgeois America to personal security," wrote William O'Neill of the University of Wisconsin, had produced "a generation with strongly middle-aged values." In the past it had been a safe assumption that a young man's politics would crystallize on the left and then move slowly to the right as he grew older. No more; college youth in the 1950s started in dead center and stayed there.

Of course, a majority in any student generation is silent; it is the articulate minority which win it its label. Not many undergraduates in the 1920s wore raccoon coats and only a few drove Stutz Bearcats; a handful in the 1930s joined the Young Communist League or struck for peace. But in the

1950s it was hard to find *any* who were articulate, *any* who could be called leaders. Typically, varsity football teams elected cocaptains, or revolving captains, and Phi Beta Kappa keys were quietly pocketed. Undergraduates seemed to spurn the very concept of leadership, preferring someone they called "the well-rounded man," who under close scrutiny resembled a faceless blob. Of this apotheosis William H. Whyte Jr. wrote in *The Organization Man* that it was "obtrusive in no particular, excessive in no zeal." Believing that leadership came from the group, that progress lay in something called problem-solving meetings, the well-rounded campus men had no use for drive and imagination. Above all, they distrusted individualism. The individual sought prestige and achievement at the expense of others. He was abrasive; he rocked the boat; he threatened the corporate One, and they wanted no part of him.

In their mystique the deadliest sin was to be controversial. The silent generation shunned commitments of any sort, and it was above all politically illiterate. Its members could not be disillusioned because they had no illusions. They kept their mouths shut, avoided serious discussions, and eschewed reformers as "bleeding hearts." In the conflict between independence and the system, they came down hard on the side of the system. They sought not fame, but the approval of others. Eager to collaborate in group actions, they deliberately suppressed traits which might set them apart. It was in these years that wealthy students began to cultivate shabby appearances, wearing denim to discourage any suggestion that they were different from others. Riesman was approached by a varsity swimmer who said, "I get sore at the guys I'm competing against. Something's wrong with me. I wish I could be like ———, who really cooperates with the other fellows. He doesn't care so much about winning." Whyte observed that students no longer dreamed of going into business for themselves. They wanted to work for someone else, and the bigger the firm, the more they trusted it. They were not much interested in becoming salesmen, however, or in rising to be key executives. Salesmen were contenders; executives sometimes had to be tough. Seniors more frequently told company recruiters that they wanted to be in personnel, because they liked people, or in public relations, where, Whyte dryly noted, they could "be nice to everybody on company time."

Protest was clearly alien to such an outlook. For professors, hostility to McCarthyism was the great passion of the time, but students weren't much interested. The senator won few recruits on campuses, but he didn't stir up much resentment, either; most undergraduates found the issue boring. This indifference was noticeable in all fields — including theology, journalism, and law — although it is significant that the occupational preferences of students had sharply changed. The great thing now was business administration. Between 1940 and 1950 the primacy of the humanities had declined, until fewer than three undergraduates in ten were majoring in a fundamental discipline. Vocational training had the allegiance of the young, and business was the most popular vocation because it offered the highest return on their investment of choice. At the end of the 1940s business majors had accounted for 19.4 percent of all college students in the United States. By 1955 they had come to constitute the largest undergraduate group.

If they had a paradigm, he was Tom Rath, Sloan Wilson's *Man in the Gray Flannel Suit*. At the beginning of the novel, Wilson's hero has a wife named Betsy, three children, a six-room house in Westport, a 1939 Ford, $10,000 in GI life insurance, and a $7,000-a-year job at a charitable foundation, where his duties are negligible. Life is pleasant, but rather austere; he needs a new car, the kitchen linoleum is starting to go, etc. Then Tom gets what looks like a break. He is offered a public relations job paying $9,000. He takes it and finds there is a hitch. In his new career he is expected to work. No more three-hour lunches, no long coffee breaks, being nice on company time; he has to produce now, and sometimes he has to stay at his desk after five o'clock or even come in on Saturdays, cutting into his time with Betsy and the kids. That incenses him. He tells the boss where to get off. Tom doesn't mind getting rich, but if in exchange he has to curtail his roles as husband, father, and all-around good fellow, he wants no part of it. This is the climax of the story, and the denouement is extraordinary. The boss backs down.

> "Of course," Hopkins said kindly, getting up and pouring himself another drink. "There are plenty of good positions where it's not necessary to put in an unusual amount of work. Now it's just a matter of finding the right spot for you."

The silent generation really believed that. Beneath its ersatz camaraderie lay an essential innocence, a Hans Christian Andersen belief that clock watchers, for some supernatural reason, would be rewarded with what was variously called "the good life," the "good, sensible life," and "the right, full life." Hopkins says defensively, "*Somebody* has to do the work," and Tom replies sympathetically, "I know." Somebody, but not him. No driven neurotic he:

> "I don't want to give up the time. I'm trying to be honest about this. I want the money. Nobody likes money better than I do. But I'm just the kind of guy who can't work evenings and weekends and all the rest of it forever. I guess there's even more to it than that. I'm not the kind of person who can get all wrapped up in a job — I can't get myself convinced that my work is the most important thing in the world."

Convinced that all great discoveries had been made, all great dreams realized, and all great fortunes amassed, the Toms of the 1950s were content to tinker with techniques and technicalities from nine to five, five days a week, while devoting the bulk of their energies to nonvocational interests — the church, civic activities, "getting to know" the kids, golf, Little Leagues, leading a rewarding life with Betsy and laying pipe with her. All this was to be theirs once they had signed up with the right recruiters before commencement, entered their names in the rat race, and roistered away down the superhighways of consumption. It was significant, as one social critic pointed out, that college students no longer spoke of "playing the game." Instead they "knew the score." They were aware that the score would change from time to time, but when that happened, they felt sure, somebody would tell them what to do.

There was no longer much talk of selling out. It was unnecessary. They were in bondage from the outset, as committed to the American way as any medieval youth off for the monastery. To them the world that awaited them after commencement was neither cold nor cruel, and certainly not hostile. Writing in *Daedalus,* the journal of the American Academy of the Arts and Sciences, one academician reported, "A dominant characteristic of students in the current generation is that they are gloriously contented both in regard to their present day-to-day activity and their outlook for the future. Few of them are worried — about their health, their prospective careers, their family relations, the state of national or international society or the likelihood of their enjoying secure and happy lives." Graduating seniors were prepared to embrace — and if need be, to defend — the status quo; they would obey the law, pay taxes, fulfill their military obligations, and vote, though thereafter politics would be none of their concern. They would conform to the dictates of society in their dress, speech, worship, choice of friends, length of hair, and above all, in their thought. In exchange they would receive all the rights and privileges of the good life; *viz.,* economic security.

That was the deal, and it shocked their teachers. Having survived the challenges of poverty and fascism, it seemed, the national legacy was to be betrayed by puerile hobbledehoys who preferred mink-handled beer can openers and fourteen-karat gold charge plates to ideals, and who accepted General Eisenhower's definition of an intellectual: "a man who takes more words than is necessary to say more than he knows."

In New York's Temple Rodeph Sholom, Rabbi Lewis I. Newman blamed panty expeditions on McCarthyism. By making "serious discussion and dissent on major issues dangerous," he argued, the Wisconsin senator had made it necessary for students to "find an expression for their bottled-up energies in foolish and unseemly 'raids' upon dormitories." This was stretching things; yet there was a seed of truth in it. If thoughtful discussion was not downright risky, it was certainly being discouraged on almost every level of organized society. A jet propulsion engineer was arrested, apparently on no other ground than that he had been a friend of the Rosenbergs. Owen Lattimore was indicted on seven counts of perjury before a congressional investigating committee.* The State Department banned travel in Communist countries. The dismissal of American employees at the U.N. as "security risks" had begun, and passage of the McCarran-Walter Immigration Act all but guaranteed the public humiliation of European scholars arriving to lecture on American campuses.

Now that McCarthy was at his height, nearly every week brought news of some fresh outrage against free thought, and pensive students could hardly avoid the conclusion that conformists were rewarded and heretics punished. Washington was the great battleground for the senator and his foes, but colorful skirmishes were being fought in almost every community of any size. San Antonio, Texas, for example, was going through agonies over a proposal that the public library brand books whose authors had been called Communists or were suspected of Communist sympathies with a red stamp. The advocates were led by Myrtle Glasscock Hance, a local housewife. Mrs. Hance, the *New York Times* reported, "has never made any pretense to literary attainments or wide acquaintance with books." But that didn't mean that she didn't have a pretty good idea of the hanky-pank inside. She produced a list of suspected authors and said she wanted something done about their books. She didn't demand that the books be actually burned. The stamp would satisfy her, provided it was bright red and "large enough to be seen immediately." Affixed to the inside front cover, it would specify the writer's Communist affiliations and sympathies, together with the number of his "citations." "The reader," Mrs. Hance said, "will then realize that in many instances he is reading Communist propaganda." San Antonio's mayor, whose own wife was a member of the Minute Women, thought Mrs. Hance's suggestion an excellent one. Then it developed that there was more to it than met the eye. Watchers were to take note of people who consulted the branded books. Their names were then to be turned over to the FBI or, alternately, published in the *San Antonio News*. That aroused the city's powerful Maverick family, civil libertarians to the man. Before the clamor ended in the triumph of the antibranders, households had been divided and friendships torn asunder.

In Indiana another housewife, Mrs. Thomas J. White, a member of the Indiana State Textbook Commission, offered a novel interpretation of Anglo-Saxon folklore. She declared: "There is a Communist directive in education now to stress the story of Robin Hood. They want to stress it because he robbed the rich and gave to the poor. That's the Communist line. It's just a smearing of law and order." The Republican governor declined to take a stand, for Robin Hood or against him. In England William Cox, sheriff of Nottingham, told a reporter that in his opinion Hood (1160–?) had not been a Communist, but Wilbur Young, Indiana's superintendent of education, called a press conference to announce that he was rereading the tales of Robin Hood just the same. Nothing was

---

*Lattimore was indicted twice, in 1952 and 1954. The last of the charges was dismissed in 1955.

above suspicion in the early 1950s, and in some quarters to be suspect was tantamount to guilt. As though blacklisting was not enough, Samuel French, the country's leading publisher of drama, announced a playwriting contest in which it reserved "the right to declare ineligible any author who is, or becomes publicly involved, in a scholastic, literary, political, or moral controversy."

With FBI agents openly conducting security checks on campuses and trustee demands for loyalty oaths, it would have been surprising if undergraduates had not held their tongues. Almost everyone else did. Paul G. Hoffman, chairman of the board at Studebaker-Packard and a liberal Republican, was an exception. His views on freedom would scarcely have seemed daring in any other era, but holding any opinion strongly was unusual then. After he had spoken at a large southwestern university a student asked, "Do you think there ought to be any study of Communism in a school such as this?" Hoffman answered, "Yes, I think we ought to teach what Communism is, so that the new and most important generation of Americans can know exactly why it is such a menace to our way of life." The student said, "I think so, too, but it's dangerous to say that around here now." In fact it wasn't entirely safe for Hoffman to say it. He was being watched, and when he sought to speak in Indianapolis again under the auspices of the American Civil Liberties Union, the American Legion saw to it that he was denied the use of the city's War Memorial. His topic this time was to have been free enterprise.

Vigilante persecution, horror of the new thermonuclear weapons, and parental tales of the Depression were all formative forces in the making of the silent generation. It was not without defenders. Writing in the *New York Times Magazine*, Princeton's Otto Butz held that its elders misjudged it. His own students, he wrote, were merely prudent. He thought it wrong to condemn them for their lack of political militance: "The future, indeed, may show that they are precisely the kind of realistic idealists which this country, in both its domestic and international life, has long been badly in need of." It was faint praise, found no echo, and has not been justified by the passage of time. A more eminent educator, Philip E. Jacob of the University of Pennsylvania, held that the values of the silent generation represented a departure from American tradition. Although students spoke well of sincerity, honesty, and loyalty, he wrote, their own standards were "generally low in regard to academic honesty, systematic cheating being a common practice rather than the exception at many major institutions." Their hedonism and anti-intellectualism seemed to him to represent an abandonment of their Puritan heritage, and he suggested that "Perhaps these students are the forerunners of a major cultural and ethical revolution," the unconscious ushers of an essentially secular (though nominally religious), self-oriented (though group-forming) society."

If others saw the specter of revolution in the wings, they were keeping it to themselves. But Dr. Jacob had sketched an outline, and in time others would flesh it out. It is fascinating to speculate on how they felt about the voluntary gags worn then, for although they were too young to assess it, the mystique of the silent generation must have had an impact upon them in some dark place of the mind back beyond memory and below the level of speech. In the high summer of 1951, when the decade was just getting under way, Mark Rudd was a three-year-old in Maplewood, New Jersey; Mario Savio was eight and Kathy Boudin seven in Manhattan; Huey Newton ten in Oakland, California; Linda Sue Evans eight in Fort Dodge, Iowa; Cathlyn Platt Wilkerson six in New York; and Diana Oughton nine in Dwight, Illinois.

Early in the 1960s, when the silent generation had passed into history, a group of undergraduates at Wesleyan University, feeling a pang of nostalgia between periods in a basketball game, spontaneously burst into lyrics all had retained in their collective memory. They sang:

> *Winky Dink and you,*
> *Winky Dink and you,*
> *Always have a lot of fun*
> *To-geth-er!*

Then:

> *It's Howdy Doody time,*
> *It's Howdy Doody time,*
> *Bob Smith and Howdy too*
> *Say Howdy-Do to you!**

And then:

> *Mickey Mouse! Mickey Mouse!*
> *Forever let us raise our banners high!*
>
> *M - I - C*
> *— See you real soon!*
> *K - E - Y*
> *— Why? Because we like you!*
>
> *M - O - U - S - E!*

The chanting students shared bonds which had been unknown to their parents. They were members of the first television generation, reared in a time when public relations men had begun speaking of "images" and psychologists of "roles" — when "the public" in advertising jargon was being superseded by "the mass audience." In the 1930s the radio children's hour had been forty-five minutes. At other idle times its young admirers had either listened to adult programs or, if they were small and belonged to the great middle class, to parents reading fragments from a juvenile

*© Children's Songs, Inc. 1948.

literature unchanged since their own childhoods: Mother Goose, Grimms' fairy tales, *A Child's Garden of Verses*, *Treasure Island*, *Peter Pan*, *Little Women*, *The Wizard of Oz*. All that began to recede in the late Truman years. Unless enshrined by Disney (Pinocchio, Sleeping Beauty) or a popular entertainer (Peter Pan, Oz), tales once told at mothers' knees were to become progressively less familiar, until allusions to them were lost upon all but a select few from homes where children who read and were read to were not thought peculiar.

Winky, Howdy, Mickey, *Lucky Pup*, and *Life with Snarky Parker* were among the less objectionable survivors in the new medium. The general level was much lower. Really clever programs were given short shrift by sponsors. *Magic Cottage* and *Mr. I. Magination*, preferred by parents in a *TV Guide* survey, were swiftly cut down by the A. C. Nielsen and C. E. Hooper ratings. *Kukla, Fran, and Ollie*, Burr Tillstrom's charming puppet show, lasted longer, but eventually it, too, was trodden under by the prophets of violence: *Captain Video*, *Sky King*, *Space Cadet*, *Captain Midnight*, and *Superman*, whose young fans continued to cherish illusions of his indestructibility even after George Reeves, the actor who played him, drove his Jaguar into a stone wall in California, cut his forehead, and fainted at the sight of his own blood.

Roughly one-third of the new programs for children were devoted to crime and violence. The number of American firms manufacturing toy guns jumped from ten to nearly three hundred, and two-fisted, gunslinging William Boyd, who had been foresighted enough to buy up rights to his discarded celluloid horse operas, built one of television's first fortunes, grossing forty million dollars by 1950 in the sale of Hopalong Cassidy clothing alone. Hopalong's six-gun casualties contributed to the general television toll, which by 1954 actually exceeded the death rate in Korea. Some murders on the screen were quite horrible. Jack Gould of the *New York Times* campaigned against close-ups of young girls being strangled, but the predominant view in the network hierarchy was that TV was no gorier than, say, "Jack the Giant Killer," and that ferocity on the tube might even be doing some good by helping little watchers work out their aggression in fantasy. Anyway, violent programs were popular; kids wanted them. Therefore decisions to increase the homicidal level were reached in the sixty square blocks around Madison Avenue known as "the industry." It happened to be a short ride from the apartment where an eleven-year-old truant named Lee Harvey Oswald was watching all the TV mayhem he could get.

Almost everything about the new medium was debatable except its significance. Clearly that was immense. The Age of Television was dawning more rapidly than the Age of Radio. At the peak of radio's expansion, Americans had bought about 165,000 receivers a month. During every month of 1948 and 1949, more than 200,000 TV sets were sold, and that was only the beginning. On January 1, 1950, there were three million television owners in the United States. In that swing year — the year of McCarthy and Korea — another seven million sets were installed in American homes. Radio still dominated the airwaves, broadcasting to forty million receivers, but that was only because the majority hadn't yet bowed to salesmanship ("Is *your* little girl left out . . . ?") and social pressure. In metropolitan communities those forces were often augmented by newspaper campaigns. Misjudging the appeal of radio, newspapers had allowed station franchises to go to others, leaving them in the cold. This time they were in at the start. Baltimore provided an excellent illustration of how effective skillful merchandising, backed by journalistic indoctrination, can be. In the spring of 1949 Hooper's figures showed that 82 percent of the city's inhabitants listened to radio, while only 18 percent watched television. Then the *Baltimore Sun, Evening Sun,* and *Sunday Sun* began urging subscribers to enjoy programs on WMAR-TV, which was owned by them. As a consequence, in May 1950 the city became the first in which television's evening audience (50.2 percent) was larger than radio's.

It was not as satisfied, though. Once the novelty had worn off, WMAR-TV's delivery was found to be snowy and its programming so shabby at times as to constitute almost a new form of air pollution. "What happens to old, broken-down wrestlers?" Baltimoreans asked one another on street corners, and the answer was, "Nothing. They're still wrestling." *Time* declared, "Television became a major industry and cultural force in 1950," but during the first part of the year its performance level remained poor. Bright spots were appearing here and there: *Duffy's Tavern,* Jack Webb's *Dragnet,* and an elfin Amazon from West Virginia named Dagmar. Still, even the best of it was mostly second-bill vaudeville, and in fact the man of the hour, acclaimed as "Mr. Television," was Milton Berle, a mugging, vaudevillian joke stealer. Most of the big entertainers were veteran radio personalities. Two years earlier the Goldbergs had moved to the screen ("Enter, whoever"; "If it's nobody, I'll call back"), but for most the pendulum had not yet swung. Those who wanted the news from Ed Murrow or the latest ballad from Bing Crosby had to listen, not see, and Arthur Godfrey continued to keep in touch with his forty-million flock by radio, caressing them with what Fred Allen called Godfrey's "barefoot voice."

Part of TV's problems were technical. Cameramen were still feeling their way, installers put antennas up wrong, the first mass-produced sets kept breaking down, and repairmen were incompetent. Chicago's Hallicrafters Company didn't develop the first rectangular picture tube until January 1950. That permitted use of the whole tube face and saved 50 percent in cabinet space. The great obstacle to national television remained: curvature of the earth's surface. AM radio waves bend; FM and television beams do not. In those pioneer years TV receivers over the horizon could not pick up a station's picture, so program directors were limited to local talent. During the 1948 Republican National Convention engineers had tinkered with something called Stratovision, putting an antenna in a B-29 and sending it up to circle 25,000 feet above Pittsburgh. It was a good stunt — signals flickered on screens within a 250-mile radius — but something more substantial was required. The solution lay in coaxial cable and microwave relays. Within another three years a significant grid of cable was in the ground and working. Its first coast-to-coast television broadcast was President Truman's address at the Japanese Peace Treaty Conference in San Francisco on September 4, 1951, beamed to forty million viewers by 94 stations. With that, the networks began signing up local channels and the massive shift from radio to television began.

On the eve of it, *Radio Daily* announced its awards for 1950, and in them the standoff between the two giants then was evident:

RADIO	TELEVISION
Man of the Year: Jack Benny	*Man of the Year:* Sid Caesar
Woman of the Year: Eve Arden	*Woman of the Year:* Faye Emerson
Drama Show: Lux Radio Theater	*Drama Show:* Studio One
Comedy Show: Jack Benny	*Comedy Show:* Milton Berle

Over the next five years, dealer sales averaged five million TV sets a year, and they continued high until 88 percent of American families — forty million homes — had tubes, with 13 percent owning two or more and some with as many as six. For every farmer watching the screen in 1949, there were 27 ten years later. As early as 1950 one study had found that some junior high school students were spending an average of nearly thirty hours a week in front of tubes. Surveys were predicting, accurately, that the average American youth on the day of his high school graduation would have spent 11,000 hours in classrooms and 15,000 hours watching television, and a Westinghouse study later discovered that Americans were spending more man-hours in front of the screen than in working for pay.

Those who weren't watching — and in the 1950s few self-respecting intellectuals would admit to owning a set — were fascinated by those who were. Norman Cousins reported to his appalled readers that "the standardized television formula for an evening's entertainment is a poisoning, a variety show, a wrestling show"; Max Lerner held that TV was "the poor man's luxury because it is his psychological necessity"; and judges held that it was indeed a necessity, not subject to seizure by creditors. In 1954 the TV dinner appeared, obviating the need for people to tear themselves away from the screen to bolt supper, and that same year the water commissioner of Toledo made a remarkable discovery. Baffled by why water consumption surged upward during certain three-minute periods, he conducted a discreet little survey and found that all over Toledo, during television commercials, viewers were simultaneously dashing into bathrooms, voiding, and flushing their toilets in unison.

By then the average American family was watching TV between four and five hours a day; Louis Kronenberger commented that television was returning people to the home, whence the auto had lured them, but destroying the home in the process:

> Where Mother and Father, Jane and John on their treks and travels exchanged pleasantries and ideas, they sit now for hours, side by side, often shoulder to shoulder, scarcely exchanging a glance. Or if they do address one another, they do so crossly, campaigning for this program or that.

What were their choices? Some early network presentations were quite good. In 1950 the March of Time's *Crusade in Europe*, telecast by ABC, became the first documentary to win a Peabody Award. Murrow's *See It Now* began the following year, and the year after that Alistair Cooke started bringing an hour and a half of *Omnibus* into living rooms on Sunday afternoons, courtesy of the Ford Foundation. On other channels Jimmy Durante was funny, if broad; Victor Borge, the happy Dane, was charming, if *manqué*; Bishop Fulton J. Sheen, literate, if glib; NBC's televised operas outstanding by any standard. Sunday evenings NBC's *Philco-Goodyear Playhouse* and CBS's *Studio One* introduced live dramas by fine new playwrights, beginning with Paddy Chayefsky's *Marty*. Among commentators, CBS's Murrow was still supreme, but viewers could also switch to ABC's John Charles Daly or NBC's John Cameron ("Now hopscotch in the world for headlines") Swayze. David Brinkley was also at NBC, and in 1955 Chet Huntley joined him to form the famous newscasting team which would move to the top when Murrow retired.

Had these programs been typical, the quality of American life might have risen. Instead it sank. Those interested enough to monitor television fare and perceptive enough to judge it waged bitter disputes over who was responsible for its tasteless sludge. No one was, really; there simply wasn't enough talent to fill all those empty hours, and the very size of the waiting audience meant that concepts comprehensible to the majority had to be banal. Families were really amused by:

> OZZIE: Er . . . uh . . . oh, dear . . . have you . . . seen the . . . the paper?
> HARRIET: Gee, dear, Ricky may have seen it.
> OZZIE: Uh . . . oh . . . well, gee . . . I . . .
> RICKY (*bursting in*): Hi, Pop. I gave the paper to Dave to give to Thorny. (*Leaves*)
> OZZIE: Oh, well . . . gee, dear, I . . . I wanted to read the . . . the paper.

Young viewers — and not only the young — caught their breaths at:

> BOYD: Lucky, round up a posse. Bart Slime's kidnapped the judge's daughter.
> GABBY HAYES: Wh-h-h-y, them dirty, no good — c'mon, Hoppy, let's go git them varmints.

And four million housewives hunched over their irons and ovens were actually moved when 203 stations broadcasted:

HELEN: Oh, Paul! The operation was a success!

PAUL: You mean that little guy will live to play shortstop again?

HELEN: Yes! Oh, I prayed for this so hard last night!

PAUL (*gently*): And your prayer was answered.

HELEN (*after a long pause*): Yes, Paul — my prayer — was answered.

Space Cadet was just as trite as *Hopalong Cassidy, My Favorite Husband* as inane as *Ozzie and Harriet* and *As the World Turns* or *The Edge of Night* as florid as *Helen Trent*. On TV the pot competed with the kettle. The real Sunday evening contest was not between *Studio One* and *Philco-Goodyear;* it was the 8 P.M. duel between CBS's Ed Sullivan and NBC's Steve Allen, and Sullivan won it going away by signing up the most expensive guest star of the time, young Elvis Presley, a former Memphis truck driver whose most memorable line was, "*Goan . . . git . . . luhhv.*" For the privilege of presenting Presley on three Sullivan shows, CBS paid $50,000, which would have bought a lot of serious drama or documentary film.

TV morality made no more sense than Hollywood's. Presley's pelvis and Faye Emerson's plunging necklines were acceptable, but the chairman of the Federal Communications Commission called Godfrey's double-entendres "livery stable humor," and when Noel Coward retained the hells and damns in *Blithe Spirit* for CBS's Ford Star Jubilee, *Time* commented, "Viewers last week were treated to the raciest — and most profane — language that has ever been heard on TV." Groucho Marx was also in and out of trouble with network watchdogs, while the antics of Jerry ("I'm a bean bag") Lester, offensive to some, were passed over in silence. In part censorship seemed to be a matter of whose ox was being gored. Almost any vulgarity was tolerated on the giveaway shows. Yet when anti-Communist blacklisters formed an organization called AWARE, Inc., and smeared John Henry Faulk, a wit in the Will Rogers tradition, CBS quickly let him go. Faulk had to sue to be reinstated. After six years in the courts he won, but no action was taken against the vigilantes, among them Clayton (Bud) Collyer of *Break the Bank*.

Trendex ratings that February offer some insight into American mass taste in the 1950s. The top ten programs were *Ed Sullivan, The $64,000 Question, Perry Como, I Love Lucy, December Bride, Talent Scouts, You Bet Your Life, Red Skelton, What's My Line?,* and *Walt Disney*. On the whole they were bland and slick, and the dominant theme was slapstick, which may say something about television as a new medium, the national character, or the times. Allen Tate thought the tragedy of the 1950s lay in the mass media's destruction of ways to communicate through love. Louis Kronenberger believed it significant that with the advent of TV's square eye, all walls guarding privacy were crumbling. We had, he said, become a nation of peeping Toms.

But all words spoken in the United States were not for microphones, and millions of words were not being spoken at all. They were in print, in Braille, on tape, on newsprint, in phonographs, on celluloid, on plastic, on canvas, and even in architecture. Communications was having its revolution, as economics did in the 1930s and sex would in the 1960s. Never had there been so much information to transmit, or so many ways to transmit it. The volume was breathtaking. Beginning in 1950 the paperback industry alone sold over a quarter-billion books each year in drugstores and newsstands for twenty-five cents, thirty-five cents, and (for giants then) fifty cents. Already the industry had 81,000 titles in print, including seventeen editions of Jane Austen's *Pride and Prejudice.* "There is," D. W. Brogan argued, "abundant evidence that popular taste in the United States is improving." A random glance at paperback sales in January 1952 shows 400,000 for Ruth Benedict's *Patterns of Culture,* 1,250,000 for *The Naked and the Dead,* 750,000 for *Nineteen Eighty-four,* 500,000 for *A Streetcar Named Desire,* and — for a translation of the Odyssey with an abstract cover design — 350,000. The broad rivers coming down from Canada were choked with logs waiting to sacrifice their pulp at mills so that America might be educated as well as entertained, inspired as well as amused, aroused as well as inflamed, and their thousands of square miles of paper went to *U.S. News* and the *New York Times, Commentary* and *Playboy, Holiday* and Grove Press, the *Encyclopaedia Britannica* and *Peyton Place, Mad* and the *American Scholar,* the books of Harold Robbins and John Crowe Ransom, and the works of Norman Cousins, Max Lerner, Allen Tate, and Louis Kronenberger.

Across America five thousand motion picture theater marquees had been darkened in the great box office recession which had accompanied the rise of television. Ernie Kovacs and *Queen for a Day* had stolen hearts once pledged to Clark Gable and Ginger Rogers. The tarnish of time clouded the stars' names embedded in Hollywood Boulevard's sidewalks. Bitter signs there read, "Buy Christmas Seals and Stamp Out TV," and studios would have had to close down without revenue from abroad, which now, for the first time, was providing 50 percent of the movie industry's gross. President Eric Johnston of the Motion Picture Association of America said, "We will simply have to face the fact that we are in for a leveling off in the future because of the public's driving habits and television." In vast tracts of countryside films had become a summer business; since V-J Day the number of drive-in theaters had grown from 351 to 7,000. Meanwhile the gaudy old movie palaces on Main Street, the Paramounts and Capitals and Bijous and Foxes and Hippodromes — once the pride of the only big business to flourish throughout the Depression — went into eclipse.

Nationwide weekly attendance figures showed that about forty-five million people had stopped going to the pictures. Things perked up briefly with the Cinerama vogue and then dropped off again. Owners shut off their balconies. They let help go and took over the popcorn concessions themselves. After a while they took to showing films only on weekends, and finally many of them closed down altogether. Some became bowling alleys, supermarkets, banks, apartment houses, or even churches; in Manhattan, ironically, they were converted to television studios. In metropolitan neighborhoods and little cities, where they were abandoned to dust and mice, they turned into fire hazards and eyesores. Because the old exit doors were easily forced, some became trysting places for tramps and lovers. Beneath screens on which Paul Muni had defended Alfred Dreyfus and Gary Cooper had submitted to torture rather than divulge the cavalry's location, empty whiskey bottles accumulated, and where Charles Boyer had begged Hedy Lamarr to run away from the Casbah with him, and Jennifer Jones as Bernadette had been visited by the Virgin Mary, aisles became cluttered with cigarette butts, sanitary napkins, and used contraceptives.

Movies were still a social force. On certain occasions they brought the community together again, as for a reunion. Mike Todd's *Around the World in Eighty Days* did it with its 29 stars, 68,894 extras, and 7,959 animals, including four ostriches, six skunks, fifteen elephants, seventeen bulls, 512 monkeys, 800 horses, 950 donkeys, 2,448 bison, 3,800 sheep, and a scared cow. There were others: *Strangers on a Train, Moby Dick, Twelve O'Clock High, The Third Man, The Man with the Golden Arm, Guys and Dolls, The Desperate Hours,* and *The Bridge on the River Kwai.* Of the new stars, Judy Holliday, Kirk Douglas, Marilyn Monroe, William Holden, and Shirley MacLaine were at least as good as those in prewar constellations.

The chief problem was that the box office dollar was now much smaller, but there were other factors. Foreign films had become increasingly popular. Before the war most moviegoers had never seen a European picture; the few to come over were mostly British, tedious, and dull. J. Arthur Rank changed that. Alec Guinness, Jack Hawkins, and Michael Redgrave became as familiar to American audiences as American actors. The Italians sent Anna Magnani and Gina Lollobrigida, the Austrians Maria and Maximilian Schell, the French Brigitte Bardot and Yves Montand, the Japanese Toshiro Mifune, and the Swedes whole troupes whose performances suggested that Paris really wasn't the sexiest place in the world. In the late 1940s Hollywood pressure had kept these actors off neighborhood screens; to see them one had to seek out what were called "art theaters" in large cities.

Then, in February 1950, a federal court in New York dissolved corporate articles binding producers and distributors of films to local exhibitors. Exhibitors no longer showed what they were sent, sight unseen. They bought features one by one, and they could buy from anyone. All America was an open market for enterprising Europeans. The ruling had broad ramifications. Hollywood had been built on the assurance that every picture would have its chance with the public. To get Shirley Temple or Robert Taylor, exhibitors had had to buy a quota of B movies and experimental films. The result had been the double feature and "selected short subjects"; the unknown was shown with the known, and if it caught on, a star was born. No more. Improvisation was too risky after 1950. Exhibitors were free to turn down the obscure picture, making it a dead loss. As a result, the moguls on the Coast began sinking everything into superspectacles which, if they failed, entailed losses in the millions.

Altogether, it was to be a wretched decade for Hollywood. Month by month the film industry's once massive role in the national economy declined. Grimly refusing to open their treasure of old movies to the television networks, and as yet unable to interest them in using movie lots for TV production, the moguls watched the film capital deline until it had become all but a ghost town.

The film makers were caught in a wrenching transition. The nation's mores still proscribed the showing of sexual acts, or even nudity; of the harmless *Baby Doll, Time* said that it was "just about the dirtiest American-made motion picture that has ever been legally exhibited." Producers continued to be attuned to generalized entertainment. The notion that a film might appeal to one group in society was yet to come. Its first success was to be *Rock Around the Clock* (1954), and even then American youth was largely indifferent to it. The movie's breakthrough — and the emergence of rock 'n' roll as a worldwide phenomenon — came first in Britain, where upheavals dating from World War II had first created an autonomous teen-age class. After the film had triggered rioting by three thousand Teddy boys that September, councils in a dozen English towns met in special session to discuss banning it, and police cordons were thrown around theaters where it was still being shown. The Teds' hair was of special interest. At a time when adolescent males in the United States remained faithful to the crew cut, the Teds wore theirs long, combing it in the back in a style which can be traced to wartime Los Angeles. It was called — not in mixed company, of course — the DA, or Duck's Ass. The Teds did not let it hang loose on their shoulders, to be sure; that would come later.

Before the transition, motion pictures had served as a social unifier. Appealing as they did to all ages and slighting no class — except blacks, who remained unnoticed even by themselves — films had strengthened familial ties and reminded moviegoers of values they shared. Wartime films warmed the melting pot by showing WASPs, ethnics, and minority Americans working together. In addition, Hollywood served as a social mentor. Consciously and unconsciously, fans modeled their behavior after that of the stars. By ruling that couples in films must not be shown sleeping in double beds, for example, the Hays Office, later the Breen Office, had altered styles in the entire bedding industry, and by excluding even the mildest profanity it helped keep the language, as was then said, clean. Moreover, to an extent unappreciated at the time, the generalized pretransition movies provided the country with a common lore. Even in the 1970s middle-aged strangers could relate to one another and find a meeting ground by references to *The Philadelphia Story, Mutiny on the Bounty,* or any other of a hundred films remembered and cherished, over thirty years later, by virtually an entire generation. Their children lacked that; no motion picture of the early Nixon years knitted itself into the American experience.

Of course, none of this had anything to do with art. Judged by that yardstick, the best movies of the 1960s and 1970s outshone almost everything before them. By then the transition was complete and it was possible to explore emotions and relationships which had been freed from the old taboos. Films had attained maturity; high seriousness on the screen had become possible; brilliant directors were using celluloid in ways undreamed of before. Still, something had been lost. Pictures had become divisive. Small children went to weekend matinees, teen-agers to movies made for them by stars their own age, and adults to films rated for them alone. Hollywood's old unifying force was gone.

The signposts, too, were different, and the possibilities for misunderstanding greatly increased. One misleading word was "nonconformity." In the 1950s some teen-agers began warning parents that they had decided to stop conforming to the rest of society. But within their subculture, conformity was absolute — "How," Irving Howe asked pointedly, "can a bobby-soxer admit to not enjoying Vaughn Monroe?" — and some examples of it were unconsciously entertaining: "Join the beat generation!" cried an ad in an early issue of *Playboy*. "Buy a beat generation tieclasp! A beat generation sweatshirt! A beat generation ring!" That subcult was swiftly forming in the early 1950s. Money had become more plentiful for it in the prosperity accompanying the Korean War, and in 1955 it acquired its first martyr with the flaming death of James Dean, who had just starred in *Rebel Without a Cause.**

The social sciences were rising in prestige. There was an immense curiosity about all the media — what they were doing, their influence, their meaning, their potential. David Riesman at Harvard and Reuel Denney in Chicago were investigating their role in the shaping and socialization of people, instilling in them a sense of what it meant to be an American man or woman, boy or girl, mature or old. At the University of Toronto Marshall

---

*Dean is as important in American legend as Jean Harlow and Marilyn Monroe. Nearly twenty years afterward, he would still be receiving fan mail. Excluding microfilm, the New York Public Library finds it impossible to keep Dean material. His worshippers steal it. The Lincoln Center Library for the Performing Arts has just one book about him. It is in French, and all the pictures in it have been cut out.

McLuhan was defining "the visual, linear, older generation" and "the aural, tactile, and suffusing younger generation," and in Baltimore H. L. Mencken had completed his documentation of the growth of a national speech, "standard American," and the accompanying decline in regional speech.*

In these same years the publicity business grew from a cloud no larger than a handout to the vastness of Marlboro Country. In 1948, when the Public Relations Society of America was founded, there were about a hundred PR firms in the country, many of them operating out of hole-in-the-wall offices, and fewer than fifty PR departments in industry. The number of public relations companies in Manhattan alone swiftly expanded to a thousand, and it was a rare business — or an impoverished governmental bureau — without its complement of mimeograph machines and amiable men eager to plant plugs and puffs. Very soon ranking PR advisers rose to the vice-presidential level in industry and, in Washington, became members of the subcabinet. With their arrival, images often came to supersede truth. They wrote commencement speeches for heads of corporations, cajoled newspapermen with free rides on company planes, subsidized the new call girl business, and, with Robert Montgomery's coaching of Eisenhower, made PR skills indispensable to political campaigns.

Meantime advertising had begun to move in subtler patterns. During the 1940s it had continued with straightforward appeals to vanity, sentiment, ambition, greed, and fear — Listerine's "Always a Bridesmaid, Never a Bride," "I was a 98-lb. Weakling," "Your Best Friends Won't Tell You," and "They Laughed When I Sat Down at the Piano." Hyperbole had made superlatives so ordinary that R. H. Macy & Co. ran a six-column ad in the *New York Times* to taunt the rest of the industry with a glossary of "Unfamiliar Words & Phrases — As Used by Advertising Writers to Describe Female Apparel and Appurtenances." Included in it were "*gossamer*: the nearest thing to nothing — and better in black"; "*lush*: anything softer than stone"; "*glamorous*: anything plus a sequin"; and "*fabulous*: we haven't seen anything like it for an hour." By the time the 1950s were well under way, Madison Avenue's hacks had been shouldered aside by brighter account executives. The bark of the television auctioneer and the specter of B.O. had been replaced by "Cloud Nine, Calling Earth," "Bendix Starter Drive Puts 20 Million Women in the Driver's Seat," "A Bacardi Daiquiri Has Less Calories Than a Glass of Skim Milk," and "Steel Is As Big As All Outdoors!" Motivational advertising research had arrived in all its Day-Glo splendor. For a while there was even scary talk of something called subliminal advertising — slogans flashed on TV screens so rapidly that they eluded the conscious eye and embedded themselves in the subconscious, whence, presumably, they would emerge at the crucial shopping moment.

*One of the last, charming manifestations of which came ten years later, just after Lyndon Johnson moved into the White House, when a woman in Houston remarked, "Isn't it nice to have a President without an accent?"

Beginning with the postwar vogue of Frederic Wakeman's *The Hucksters*, sophisticated Americans had been giving Madison Avenue and its works the sort of spellbound attention once invoked by Emile Coué and Howard Scott. By the end of the Truman era almost everyone in Winnetka or Bel Air could describe the difference between the hard sell and the soft sell; the significance of Roper, Nielsen, and Hooper; and what it meant to say, "Let's run this one up the flagpole," or "Put this on the train and see if it gets off at Westport."

The most beloved creatures of the soft sell were probably the Piel Brothers, though serious students of modern advertising honor above all others the name of Henry Morgan. An eccentric figure during the last of radio's great days, Morgan was capable of doing almost anything on the air. Once he auctioned off his entire staff for $83. He frequently interviewed himself, and on the assumption that Hollywood's Coming Attractions were more exciting than the features they were hawking, he would devote a full half hour to running off their sound tracks. Advertising a breakfast cereal — "Snap! Crackle! Pop!" — Morgan would put on earmuffs to muffle the deafening racket. One infuriated sponsor after another fired Morgan. Eventually he wound up in a dull, unimaginative hard-selling job, a talented casualty in the endless war for the consumer dollar.

Advertisers were spending ten billion dollars a year — 2.2 percent of the Gross National Product — to manipulate the public, creating ever larger wants for ever more ingenious products. By stimulating the economy, the theory went, commercials were striking blows for the American way. Thus the glib adman came to occupy roughly the same place in the firmament which, in Coolidge's New Era, had been reserved for the financier. Nearly everyone believed in them; even Joseph Stalin bought two thousand transmitters to jam Free World electronic spiels before they could corrupt his people. Sports fans accepted without protest TV's fake rest periods, fake injuries, and "two-minute warnings" in the last period of football games, knowing that all of them were merely excuses for commercials. The Billy Graham Crusade invested in a special survey on the habits of subway straphangers to ascertain the best strategic location for Crusade ads; God, too, believed in motivational research.

Less than a quarter-century had passed since the Roaring Twenties collapsed in 1929, and the country was off on another binge in another bull market. The Fat Fifties, some were calling it. The New York Stock Exchange reported that one out of every nine Americans owned stocks, but most of the rest seemed to be debtors; Eric Goldman wrote that department stores were advertising plans under which customers could spend the rest of their lives owing a specified balance — $500, for instance — and for a fee "debt counselors" would give you a living allowance in exchange for your pay envelope, which they would then distribute among your creditors.

Automobiles were growing wider, longer, and lower. Each autumn's new models were hooked up with more junk, more chrome, and bigger tailfins.

The dashboard on Cadillac's $13,074 Eldorado Brougham included lipstick, a Kleenex box, and four tumblers finished in gold. Outside Detroit the market offered those who had everything solid gold toothpicks, whiskey-flavored toothpaste, and His and Her submarines. The *Wall Street Journal* discovered a thriving mail-order business which offered life-size plastic replicas of famous models equipped with real hair, real fingernails, and real toenails; bachelors bought them and took them to bed, and some had invested thousands of dollars in wardrobes for them. Living women, meanwhile, were emerging from hairdressers with coiffures tinted Champagne Beige, Autumn Apricot, Fire Silver, Golden Cinnamon, Apple Green, Peacock Blue, and Sparkling Sherry. On weekends their husbands were exploring the possibilities of new radar-equipped fishing rods which sent out an electric impulse, found fish, and reported their bearings. At parties businessmen were showing curious friends little rectangles of plastic issued by the Diners Club. Ahead, for middle-class America, lay the wonders of credit card living.

All these were part of the tenor of the time. Throughout the decade tastelessness and vulgarity shrieked out from billboards and TV screens — wherever the peddler opened his pack and hawked his wares. If there was one moment which summed up the rest, it came on CBS-TV at the climax of *Judgment at Nuremberg,* a brilliant piece of theater produced by the network's *Playhouse 90.* The theme was the injustice of justice in Nazi Germany. Claude Rains, the American judge, confronted Paul Lukas, a German jurist. "How in the name of God," Rains asked, "can you ask me to understand the extermination of men, women, and children in — ?" His lips moved soundlessly. The missing phrase was "gas ovens." It had been cut at the insistence of *Playhouse 90*'s sponsor, the American Gas Association.

It was the age of Lawrence Welk and of Suzy Parker, of Lavrenti P. Beria and of Albert Schweitzer, of the Superbomb and the Salk vaccine, of Orwellian despair and Reutherian hope. In the Kremlin sat a victor of World War II with a stubborn jaw and little sense of the comic; in the White House sat a victor of World War II with an equally stubborn jaw and just as small a sense of the comic. To the inhabitants of each country it was clearer than crystal that the rulers of the other must be humbled soon, probably by armed might. Both believed that the state of their own internal affairs had, in general, been fixed forever, and would be little changed by the passage of time. Neither trusted their own intellectuals, each worried about its children. Washington smiled on technology; so did Moscow. Fundamentalist preachers of state-approved faith were enjoying a vogue in the U.S.A. and in the USSR also.

Dr. Herman N. Sander, forty-one, of Candia, New Hampshire, was acquitted of first-degree murder in Manchester; he had been charged with the "mercy killing" of Mrs. Abbie Borroto, fifty-nine, an incurable cancer patient, by injecting air in her veins. The year of Our Lord one thousand nine hundred and fifty-one was succeeded by the year one thousand nine hundred and fifty-two. In Akron a convention of sheriffs deplored the lack of law and order. Officials of the 1950 census reported that the new population center of the United States was just outside Olney, Illinois. Puerto Rico became the first commonwealth of the United States, and William Randolph Hearst, dead at eighty-eight, was mourned in a requiem service at the Orphans of the Storm Shelter for Homeless Pets in Chicago.

Greek-born shipping tycoon Aristotle Socrates Onassis, forty-eight, was indicted on charges of conspiring to defraud the United States while buying surplus ships. Dore Schary told the Harvard Club of Los Angeles, "America is a happy-ending nation." Tornadoes in Arkansas, Tennessee, Missouri, Mississippi, Kentucky, and Alabama killed 236. Deploring the country's lackluster youth, a social critic in New York declared, "I am old-fashioned enough to think that the young should break ground, heave rocks, smash idols, even create a perceptible amount of damage." He concluded that if undergraduates "don't revolt in the name of sense, they ought to do it in the name of style."

Uranium mining began at Beaver Lodge Lake in Saskatchewan, Canada, reportedly the largest deposit of the metal in North America. Visiting Lincoln's tomb in Illinois, President Sukarno of newly independent Indonesia was heard saying to himself over and over again, "I love Americans!" Newark Airport was closed following three fatal crashes in two months, but Britain's De Havilland Comet flew the 6,724 miles from London to Johannesburg in less than 24 hours, opening the world's first jetliner passenger service. Secretary of State Dean Acheson, remaining faithful to propeller-driven aircraft, crossed the Atlantic in fourteen hours aboard the *Sacred Cow* and called it "a magnificent aircraft." Acting on CIA reports that Russians planned to spike the cocktails of American diplomats with the compound lysergic acid diethylamide, which was said to cause strange behavior, Dr. Louis Lasagna administered the drug to several Boston volunteers in 1952 and confirmed accounts of its remarkable properties. The more unstable an individual's personality, he found, the greater his sensitivity to LSD. Captured in Brooklyn after a clothing salesman spotted him, Willie Sutton was asked why he robbed banks. He said, "Because that's where the money is."

In Cairo a junta of army officers led by General Mohammed Naguib and Colonel Gamal Abdel Nasser deposed King Farouk and proclaimed Egypt a republic. The Dionne quintuplets, living near Callander, Ontario, turned sixteen. Connie Mack turned ninety-two. In the Soviet zone of Austria copies of Dwight D. Eisenhower's *Crusade in Europe* were confiscated as "fascist literature." A House subcommittee headed by Representative Ezekiel Gathings of Arkansas opened an investigation of obscene literature and was inundated with letters and packages containing pornography. Fleet Admiral Chester Nimitz confessed to Tex McCrary and Jinx Falkenburg that aboard boats "I always get seasick."

In a Maryland referendum voters approved by a four-to-one margin the state's controversial new Ober Anti-Subversive Act, whose provisions included periodic investigations of Communist activity. Actor John Barrymore Jr., twenty-two, was arrested in Las Vegas for driving recklessly while whooping it up on his second wedding anniversary. General Fulgencio Batista ousted the government of Carlos Piros in Havana and seized control of Cuba. The California Supreme Court voided the University of California's loyalty oath but upheld the state loyalty oath. The U.S. Supreme Court approved New York's released time program in schools but threw out the state's ban of the motion picture *The Miracle,* thereby extending to films for the first time constitutional guarantees of free speech and a free press.

Joe Adonis was sentenced to prison for conspiring to violate New Jersey's gambling laws. The Missouri, Mississippi, and Red rivers rose over their banks, leaving three dead, 100,000 homeless, and damage estimated at $300,000,000. A House committee investigating the Katyn forest massacre of 10,000 Polish army officers in World War II declared that the Soviet NKVD was responsible. The junta which had ruled Bolivia was overthrown during riots in which two hundred were killed, and the Argentine government seized the independent newspaper *La Prensa.* The South African Supreme Court invalided a law putting colored voters on separate lists, but Prime Minister Daniel F. Malan declared the Supreme Court itself illegal. In Paris Arthur Koestler finished the manuscript of *The Age of Longing,* got drunk and then, "conditioned by my past experiences with policemen," as he later said, punched a gendarme. An Indiana parole board paroled David C. Stephenson, onetime Grand Dragon of the state's Ku Klux Klan and a sadistic murderer of the 1920s. The Dow Jones industrial average moved in the range between 206 and 236. Since Pearl Harbor, the Census Bureau reported, the number of air conditioners in the U.S. had tripled.

Five atomic explosions set off near Las Vegas, Nevada, included a small-scale bomb detonated in mid-air and the first atomic bomb maneuvers, in which five thousand troops took part. The U.S. Supreme Court upheld the convictions of eleven Communist leaders tried in 1949 for intent to overthrow the government, and the Massachusetts legislature banned the Communist party from the ballot. President Truman signed legislation extending the draft on June 19, 1951. The U.S. closed the Hungarian consulate in New York and banned American travel in Hungary.

The White House announced on October 3, 1951, that a second atomic explosion had taken place in the Soviet Union. A third was reported on October 22. West Germany swept Chancellor Konrad Adenauer into office and ratified the European Defense Community Pact. In Prague, Rudolf Slansky and nine other purged Communists were hanged for espionage and treason. Tariff concessions by the United States to the Soviet Union and Red China were suspended. Radio Free Europe opened a transmitter in Munich to broadcast anti-Communist propaganda to Czechoslovakia, while the Russians restricted travel by foreign diplomats to within twenty-five miles of Moscow and, in New York, forced U.N. Secretary General Trygve Lie to step aside for Dag Hammarskjöld of Sweden.

All these things, and a thousand like them, passed as the falling calendar pages accumulated in the early 1950s. The snows yielded to greenery, summers passed in their heavily handsome way, leaves turned and snow returned as the seasons moved in sequence; the decade settled in; the Cold War deepened; politics grew uglier at the approach of another national election; and among the swing generation, now entering its thirties as the parents of learning children, a nagging feeling grew that the nation was in trouble.

NINETEEN

Right Turn

SOMETHING WAS IN A DECLINE, that was certain; if not the country's well-being, then its morals, its pride, its self-respect. Since the beginning of the Korean War cartoonists in Communist countries had been depicting Uncle Sam as an evil, leering old man, and accumulating headlines suggested that they might have a case. In both public life and private, a dismaying number of Americans in key positions were turning out to be thieves or worse. Their crimes seemed particularly outrageous when the criminals were in the federal government. The miscreants were called "influence peddlers" and "five-percenters" responsible for "the mess in Washington," and the issue grew into a severe handicap to Democratic hopes of extending the party's twenty-year hegemony for four more years.

That was precisely what Republicans meant it to be. Every shady implication was pushed to the very threshold of the White House until, by the spring of 1952, it was possible to infer that in one way or another the administration was responsible for most of the corruption in the country. No responsible Republican suggested that Harry Truman's hand had been in any till, of course, and as it happened, the first eminent crook of the 1950s — and TV's first superstar — had never been on the public payroll. He had contributed to Democratic war chests, however, and had become a figure in New York politics, and that was enough to attract the attention of an ambitious Tennessee senator investigating nationwide crime.

Frank Costello, alias Francisco Castaglia, alias Frank Severio, was a man of the period, an organization man of organized crime. He had been arrested only once, long ago, for assault and robbery. Thereafter he let others carry the guns. Moving up the rungs of his trade, he had become in turn a small-time henchman, bootlegger, slot machine operator, owner of gambling houses, and ultimately a friend and sponsor of New York politicians. By then he was trying to cover his tracks. He invested in real estate and oil wells and assured reporters that whatever he had been in the past, he was now a legitimate businessman. But he wasn't. He had been Lucky Luciano's chief lieutenant, and when Lucky was deported, Costello became his legatee, the biggest racketeer. His underworld connections crisscrossed the country. Carmine De Sapio of Tammany was Costello's creature. So, some said, was New York's Mayor William O'Dwyer.

Had Estes Kefauver's senatorial road show toured the country in the late 1940s or the mid-1950s, it would have attracted minimal attention — in the first period because not enough television stations had been established, and in the second because network programs had come to fill the hours of daytime TV. But the committee opened its hearings in May 1950. Lacking anything better to put on the air, local television directors in outlying cities covered the proceedings as a public service, and when the investigators pitched their tents in New York's Foley Square Courthouse on March 12, 1951, cameramen for WPIX-TV were prepared to do the same thing. Here the situation was somewhat different. The incidence of set ownership in New York was extremely high; the mass audience was already assembled. And here in the capital of the communications industry the facilities for relaying transmissions elsewhere had already been developed.

Costello's lawyer tried to circumvent the tube. He asked that the cameras be turned away from his client, explaining that "Mr. Costello doesn't care to submit himself as a spectacle." The senators agreed, but one of the technicians craftily suggested that they concentrate on Costello's hands. The result was superb theater: tense dialogue accompanied by clenched hands, fingers drumming the table top, gestures with papers and water glasses, nervous hands ripping sheets of paper to shreds. Yes, Costello conceded, he kept "a little cash" at home in a "little strongbox." No, he couldn't remember how much. Senator Charles Tobey threatened a search of his mansion, and the gangman suddenly recalled that he had $50,000 there. How had he acquired it? He muttered that he had generous friends. One friend, a fellow golfer who administered Roosevelt Raceway, had admitted that he paid Costello $15,000 a year for four years to see to it that the New York State Harness Racing Commission did not revoke the track's license because of bookie operations there. Rudolph Halley, the committee counsel, asked Costello if that was true. Not at all, said Costello, making fists; there had been some sort of misunderstanding, and he had "spread the propaganda around" that his friend was "a nice fellow" who didn't deserve mean treatment.

Costello's hands began to sweat. He had taken about all he could. Was this, he asked aggrievedly, any way to treat a hardworking businessman? His throat was sore. The television lights bothered him. He wanted to go home. Kefauver bluntly told him to continue answering questions, but Costello shook his head. Then:

KEFAUVER: You refuse to testify further? . . .

COSTELLO: Mr. Senator, I want to think of my health first. When I testify, I want to testify truthfully, and my mind don't function.

KEFAUVER: Your mind seems to be functioning pretty well.

COSTELLO: With all due respect to the senators . . . I have a lot of respect for them, I am not going to answer another question. . . . I am going to walk out.

He then did, thereby winning an eighteen-month stretch in Lewisburg Federal Penitentiary for contempt. His departure was witnessed by thirty million televiewers. According to Videodex figures, nearly 70 percent of New York's sets were tuned to the Kefauver hearings, giving it twice as large an audience as the previous autumn's World Series.

After eight days in Foley Square, the Kefauver committee returned to Washington. Its chairman was now a candidate for the Presidency, and thirty million households had been left with the distinct impression that something was rotten in U.S. cities. Ed Murrow said that "the television performance has been fascinating, the audience fantastic — perhaps because the midgets in the box have been real," and the advertising firm of Young & Rubicam, summing up the general impression, placed ads in New York newspapers to deplore sin and ask: "*Is there anything we can do about it?*"

One thing that could be done was to teach children the difference between right and wrong. Presumably that had already been accomplished, but while the Kefauver committee was still in session newspapers were documenting charges of corruption in the last place to be suspected, among college youth. For several winters the City College of New York had fielded one of the best basketball teams in the country. It now developed that three of its five starters had been taking money — as much as $1,500 each — to throw games in Madison Square Garden. And no sooner had they been indicted than similar confessions were signed by basketball players at New York University, Toledo University, Bradley University, and the University of Kentucky.

The Fagin of the Garden, one Salvatore T. Sollazo, went to prison for eight years; the others received lesser terms. Sollazo was a convenient scapegoat, and given an exciting sports season that fall, the stain on collegiate copybooks would have been quickly forgotten. Unfortunately another scandal emerged that August. West Point announced that ninety cadets had been expelled for cheating on examinations.

Shaving basketball points and cribbing in exams were symptomatic. The country was going through one of its periodic romps with vice — the first since the 1920s — and as always in such scarlet eras people were more tolerant of sin than they would admit. Grasping what was happening required a lot of reading between the lines. A spade was rarely called a spade; newspaper accounts of dissolution were larded with euphemisms. Typically, prostitutes were described as "call girls" or "party girls"; sometimes they were also "fun girls." In bed with a man they invariably "partied."

("After partying with this John, what did you do?" "I went into the bathroom for a towel.") The cumulative effect was to make the oldest profession sound glamorous.

In their furs and jewels, the whores of the 1950s practiced a harlotry far removed from the dime-a-hump "wild girls" who had ridden the rails in the early 1930s or the six-bit "victory girls" of World War II. Call girls never haunted pavements or bus terminals; they lounged around between silk sheets and made appointments by phone, like doctors. Many were beauty contest winners and/or college graduates. Some had majored in economics, and in court they almost seemed to regard themselves as generous contributors to the Gross National Product. In point of fact, the services they provided did play a certain role in business. Firms provided girls for out-of-town buyers as a matter of course, with the burgeoning public relations departments acting as procurers. Accounting stratagems saw to it that the fees were deductible. Only girls known for their discretion were recruited for this sort of work, but the payoffs were big, as much as five hundred dollars a trick. One wry madam marked her dossier for them "VIP" — for "Very Important Pieces."

In a way it made sense. Amateur entanglements were risky for star entertainers and executive vice presidents. The girl picked up under a streetlamp or at a big cocktail party came without references. She might be diseased, or a spy for a competitor, or the wife of a man with blackmail on his mind. She could show up a month later at the office or even at home, determined to parlay a casual encounter into a permanent liaison. Putting everything on a business basis removed those possibilities. It did the job and left no aftertaste. The bigger a man's name, the greater was the likelihood that he would be in the market for professional lust; the bit actors who played the star's ranch hands could prowl for lonesome waitresses, but the star himself needed a pro. And this was true of distinguished men in any occupation requiring a great deal of travel, including politicians of national distinction. The voters didn't know that then. Not that they had any illusions about men in high office. Far from it. They merely thought public figures were too busy stealing the country blind.

Major General Harry H. Vaughan was a big, genial Missourian with a vague resemblance to Hermann Göring and a natural talent for draw poker. He was not conspicuously talented otherwise, or even particularly shrewd. As military aide to Harry S. Truman he might have been expected to know that he would often be on display, yet he continued to be the sloppiest general officer ever in uniform. He simply couldn't remember to put on a blouse or cinch up his necktie on historic occasions, and was always making deals. Nothing shady, to be sure; just borderline things. In his first speech after Truman's ascension to the Presidency in 1945, for instance, he had told the Women's Auxiliary of the Alexandria Westminster Presbyterian Church about the terrible black market prices in occupied Germany, and as an example he revealed that he had sold his own fifty-five-dollar American watch to a Russian officer for five hundred dollars.

In the White House, Vaughan became celebrated for his gregariousness and his affability. His social energy seemed inexhaustible. He was always ready to grace a cocktail party or a dinner party. Making new friends there, he would be ready, in the morning, to grease the machinery of government with a letter or a well-placed phone call. In almost any other line of endeavor this would have been unexceptionable. In his it was dangerous business.

The general's undoing was a sleazy ex-colonel in the Quartermaster Corps named James V. Hunt. There were others of Hunt's stripe around, but he was typical of them and, for that matter, representative of the influence peddlers of the time. For a fee — in Truman's Washington it was 5 percent of profits — the man with influence who "knew the ropes" and had "pull" saw to it that a difficult deal went through. At Hunt's request, Vaughan put outrageous pressure on regulatory agencies, procurement officers at the Pentagon, the State Department's passport office, and the Department of Agriculture. In occupied Europe a businessman with a to-whom-it-may-concern letter from the White House bought up essential oils for a perfume manufacturer. Federal trade regulations were bent for one Hunt client, surplus property disposal procedures for a second, public housing schedules for a third. In the readjustment to a peacetime economy scarce structural steel went to a California racetrack, scarce commercial sugar to a soft drink manufacturer. Vaughan let himself be the channel for campaign contributions from the beneficiaries. Worst of all, he accepted from one of them a personal gift which would become famous. It was a $520 Deepfreeze.

Three other Missouri cronies of the President were Donald Dawson, E. Merle Young, and William M. Boyle Jr. Their turf was the Reconstruction Finance Corporation. The RFC, established by Herbert Hoover to shore up firms facing ruin, had financed defense industries in the early 1940s and eased the pangs of adjustment after the war. Lately there hadn't been much need for it, but suddenly business over there began humming. A senatorial subcommittee under J. William Fulbright of Arkansas went to take a look and stumbled into a cesspool. Government appropriations were being used to plunge in all sorts of speculative ventures, including gambling hotels in Las Vegas and Miami. Some records were missing. Others showed out-and-out favoritism. After being turned down three times in its application for $565,000 in RFC funds, the American Lithfold Company had paid an $8,000 retainer to Boyle, who among other things was vice chairman of the Democratic National Committee. The loan was then approved. Dawson, a special assistant to the President, had repeatedly made inquiries on behalf of politically well-connected persons seeking loans from the RFC. Young was an RFC loan examiner. For ten years he had been supplementing his salary with "retainers" from firms whose loans he put through. After getting one for $150,000, a company showed its gratitude by sending Mrs. Young a present. It was a $9,540 mink coat.

That gift was disastrous. If there was one thing most American housewives wanted more than anything else, and never expected to get, it was a coat of mink. And here was a woman who had been given one because her husband had been defrauding the government. Fueled by Republicans — who overlooked the fact that their own national chairman had intervened to get a big RFC loan for the Carthage Hydrocol Company, of which he was president — rumors grew until there were those who thought everybody in the administration had a Deepfreeze in the basement and a mink on his wife's back. The wife of Senator Blair Moody wore on her new fur coat a receipt showing that it was mink-dyed muskrat, $381.25 with taxes. Harold W. Reed of the Mink Ranchers' Association found it necessary to issue a statement saying that all women with mink coats weren't married to crooks, that many were in fact "highly respectable people of discriminating taste."

Harry Truman said Fulbright's RFC investigation was "asinine." It wasn't, and Fulbright proved it wasn't. Under klieg lights and amplifying equipment in the Senate Caucus Room, he paraded before the press evidence that Dawson, while sitting at the President's right hand, had been closely associated with men who had been lining their pockets at the expense of the public. One memorable exhibit was the office diary of Walter Dunham, director of the RFC. In it were carefully logged scores of phone calls from people putting in the fix for disreputable and discredited speculators who had found the door to politicians of easy virtue. Washington had seen nothing like it since Teapot Dome, but Truman continued to wear blinders. Young was indicted by a grand jury for perjury; the White House had no comment. Boyle was allowed to resign "for reasons of health" after the President had staunchly defended him for three months. Dawson, like Vaughan, continued to sit on presidential councils and make final decisions on personnel matters. It was literally wicked.

And there was more to come. As then organized, the Bureau of Internal Revenue was a standing invitation to malefaction. Its sixty-four regional offices were each headed by a collector of internal revenue. They, their deputy collectors, and the hierarchy in Washington were all political appointees. The jobs went to Democrats who had done the best job of shepherding voters to the polls in the last national election. Secretary of the Treasury Snyder, an honest Missourian, had felt scandal coming for some time and had been trying to nail down hearsay about bribery. He had gone so far as to demand the resignation of James P. Finnegan, the St. Louis collector, but Finnegan's ties to Truman were strong, and he hung on.

Now all that changed. With circumstantial evidence from a congressional committee, Finnegan was indicted by a grand jury; he quit then, and was later convicted of failing to report $103,000 on his own tax returns. Next Snyder suspended collector James G. Smyth of San Francisco and eight members of his staff; indictments for conspiracy to defraud the government followed. Dennis Delaney, the Boston collector, resigned and was indicted for accepting bribes. Collector Joseph Marcelle of Brooklyn was found to have omitted $32,000 in taxable income from his returns; he and Mordecai Miller, a sidekick, were sacked for refusing to identify the sources of their outside income for the committee. George J. Schoenman, the Commissioner of Internal Revenue and a former White House aide, handed in his resignation, pleading ill health. Altogether, nine Democrats were on their way to prison, including Matthew H. Connelly, who had been President Truman's appointments secretary.

The sheer weight of evidence finally provoked Truman into reacting. Dismissing T. Lamar Caudle, chief of the Justice Department's tax division, the President sent Congress plans for reorganization of the RFC and the Bureau of Internal Revenue.* In the future the bureau would be known as the Internal Revenue Service; its personnel would all be under the civil service. But that was no longer enough to appease administration critics. The next presidential election was now less than a year away. The "mess in Washington" had become a vigorous campaign issue. Something had to be done to steal the Republican thunder, and therefore he announced the establishment of a presidential commission to investigate charges of corruption in the federal government.

Republicans wondered aloud whether there was a Democrat upright enough to head the commission. That was no joke to Truman. He first appointed Thomas F. Murphy, the prosecutor of Alger Hiss and now a federal district court judge. After accepting, Murphy changed his mind at the last minute without giving a reason — a stinging blow to presidential prestige. Next Truman announced that the housecleaning would be conducted by his Attorney General, J. Howard McGrath. The critics said that would be worse than nothing. The scandals had touched his department, too, and as a former chairman of the Democratic National Committee, McGrath had brought the very men now being indicted into the government. The GOP cried whitewash; so did the ADA; so did the House Judiciary Committee, which voted its own investigation of McGrath and Justice.

The farce now approached its climax. The desperate President named Newbold Morris, a liberal New York Republican lawyer, as chief commissioner. In rapid succession Morris appeared on *Meet the Press* to divulge unsupported suspicions of the Justice Department, rejected McGrath's offer of office space and had quarters opened in a downtown Washington office building instead, asked Congress for subpoena power and was turned down, and finally was subpoenaed himself — as a witness before a Senate committee which wanted to question him about the role of his own law firm in the illegal sale of surplus oil tankers to a foreign government. Morris then offended everyone in the government by mailing long questionnaires

*President Kennedy pardoned Connelly in 1962; President Johnson pardoned Caudle in 1965.

to all U.S. employees, including cabinet members, instructing them to list their net worth and their sources of income. When McGrath's questionnaire arrived, he blew up. Under the mistaken impression that Morris was answerable to him, he sent him a five-word memorandum: "Your employment is hereby terminated." Truman learned about it from an AP teletype. Then *he* blew up — and dismissed McGrath.

In those last months before the political conventions of 1952, Truman's grip seemed less and less firm. His handling of the steel strike that year was a parody of his resourceful disciplining of John L. Lewis six years earlier. When the steel companies refused to abide by a Wage Mediation Board award of March 20, offering higher wages to workers without any rise in steel prices, Truman directed Secretary of Commerce Charles Sawyer to seize the mills and run them as government property. He thought his emergency powers allowed him to do that, and he believed the Supreme Court would agree. It didn't; on June 2 it ruled that the seizure was illegal. The United Steel Workers then struck anyway, and to get the union's 600,000 men back on the job with a 16-cent increase, the President had to accept a $5.20 per ton rise in the cost of steel — the very thing he had been trying to avert.

Accompanying this stumbling performance in the White House was a dismaying rise in Republican irresponsibility. Too long out of power, losing faith in an electorate which had rejected it in five straight presidential elections, the minority party was determined to discredit the Democrats at all costs. Exposing the pilferers hiding under Truman's umbrella was its prerogative and even its duty. Hammering away at administrative incompetence was an additional service to the country; that is how the democratic system is supposed to work. But the GOP's extraordinarily savage attacks on Dean Acheson and General George C. Marshall were another matter. Neither had any connection with crooks like Caudle and Finnegan. As America's spokesmen abroad they represented the entire country. They deserved, at the very least, an acknowledgment that they were decent men in pursuit of honorable objectives.

Acheson was a patrician, with a distant, even arrogant manner toward his adversaries. General Marshall was altogether different. He was a military hero, like Eisenhower, identified with neither party. His service as presidential envoy to China had been as nonpartisan as Eisenhower's invasion of Europe. In the cabinet he had avoided all political winds. His only controversial position had been taken in the uproar which followed the dismissal of MacArthur. He had argued eloquently then for the concept of limited war. Doubtless that had angered MacArthur's admirers on the Hill, but the same position had been warmly defended by Omar Bradley and the Joint Chiefs. Besides, Republican antagonism toward Marshall had been marked before MacArthur's recall. In September 1950 twenty Republican senators had gone on record against his appointment as Secretary of

Defense. Congressman Dewey Short of Missouri had called him "a cat's-paw and a pawn" for Truman; Joe Martin had characterized him as "an appeaser" responsible for Mao's takeover of China.* What had aroused them? Why were they stalking a distinguished officer who had been called the "greatest living American"?

The answer lay right there: Marshall was above the battle, a national symbol, and in the ruthless struggle for power any man who was above criticism was a threat to them. If he was not with them now, he might be ranged against them one day. That being so, they needed to spike his guns now, discrediting him so thoroughly that any future opinion from him would be discounted in advance. The last stage of the job went to McCarthy. In midafternoon on June 14, 1951, he began his longest and most famous Senate speech, charging Marshall with "a conspiracy so immense and an infamy so black as to dwarf any previous such venture in the history of man."

Liberal Republicans were trying to establish an intelligent, responsible opposition to the Truman administration. Margaret Chase Smith had declared that she did not want to see her party ride to victory on "the Four Horsemen of Calumny — Fear, Ignorance, Bigotry and Smear." Emmet John Hughes shunned the phrase "mess in Washington" as "petty, self-righteous, and extravagant." Hughes also thought it dangerous to challenge the patriotism of Democrats, but by early 1952 such advice had been rejected by the party's dominant Old Guard. Throughout that year Republican polemicists even persisted in calling the opposition "the Democrat party," insisting that it was grammatically correct, when in fact it was meant as a slight.

Speeches from the Republican right divided all Democrats into five categories: the criminals, the traitors, the cowards, the incompetents who always blundered into war, and the effete, who lacked sufficient vigor to invade China and conquer it. Differing politicians are usually tolerant of one another, but the consequence of this sort of oratorical thrust was to drive a deep schism between the parties.

The GOP line was popular. Most Americans had come to disapprove of Truman's Presidency, and no amount of whistle-stopping could have restored him to their good graces now. According to recurring Gallup samplings, his first-term low in public support had come in 1946, when just 32 percent of his constituents had been for him. Throughout 1950 the figure had varied between 37 and 46 percent. Thereafter — during his last two years in office — approval of him never rose above 32 percent. At times it dipped to 23 percent, which meant that fewer than one American in four stood behind him. He had never displayed the charm and magnetism of personal leadership. At best he had seemed to be a plucky fellow who had

---

*On the eve of World War II Martin had led the successful fights which rejected legislation to fortify Guam and Wake. Arming them, he had said then, might provoke Japanese warlords.

overcome his lack of talent by sheer determination. He saw himself that way. At his three hundredth press conference in April 1952 he told reporters: "I have tried my best to give the nation everything I have in me. There are a great many people — I suppose a million in this country — who could have done the job better than I did it. But I had the job and I had to do it. I always quote an epitaph which is in the cemetery at Tombstone, Arizona. It says: 'Here lies Jack Williams. He done his damnedest.'"

Nevertheless, to a Democrat of his convictions the prospect of a Republican administration was something to be regarded with horror. Who besides Truman could head the Democratic ticket? Estes Kefauver's name was heard everywhere. He had entered his name in all the primaries; his following was immense. Truman was unimpressed. A machine politician and proud of it, the President had no use for reformers who blackened the names of fellow Democrats. Yet most of the other possible candidates carried one handicap or another. Alben Barkley was seventy-two, too old. Russell of Georgia was anathema to the liberal wing. Harriman had never run for office. In the autumn of 1951 Truman thought he had found the best of all possible successors. Inviting Chief Justice Fred M. Vinson to the presidential retreat on Key West, he proposed that he step down from the bench and became the standard-bearer. Vinson hemmed and hawed, argued that the Supreme Court should not be a stepping-stone to the White House, and finally agreed to talk it over with his wife. She liked the idea even less; the chief judge, Truman regretfully noted in his papers, "firmly declined." With that, the President turned to Illinois. In the election of November 1948 the head of the state ticket there had forged a remarkable personal triumph, winning by the historic margin of 572,067 votes. Truman's own margin in Illinois had been 33,612. Alone, he doubtless would have lost the state. To David Lloyd, one of his presidential assistants, he said that he wanted to be notified of the next Washington visit of Governor Adlai E. Stevenson.

In that same month a Republican governor, Sherman Adams of New Hampshire, became chairman of the state's Eisenhower for President committee. At once he encountered a problem. To enter a name in New Hampshire's approaching presidential primary, he was required by law to offer evidence that his candidate was a member of the Republican party. Adams sent an inquiry to Eisenhower's county seat in Kansas. Back came this reply from County Clerk C. F. Moore:

> Mr. Eisenhower has never voted in this county as far as I know, the Primary laws were first put into operation in the year 1928 and he has never voted since then, I have been county clerk since January 14th, 1927, Dwight has never been in the city as far as I know of until after war No. 2 at least he has never voted or I would have known it as the party filiation books are still here ever since the primary or branding law was passed in the spring

of 1927 and never went into effect until the Primary Election of 1928.

Dwights father was a republican and always voted the republican ticket up until his death, however that has nothing to do with the son as many differ from their fathers of which I am sorry to see, the multitude beleives in going into debt and see how much they can spend, it has become a habit & will sink this nation into bankrupsy.

I don't think he has any politics.

Not only had Eisenhower no politics; he had no religion, no conspicuous guiding principles, and few known views on most of the great issues of his time. For the second time in four years he was being offered the most powerful office in the world, yet the men making the proposal had no idea what he would do with it if he got it. To be sure, as president of Columbia University he had made such conservative remarks as "If all that Americans want is security, they can go to prison." At the same time, he had used his prestige to rally public opinion behind the Roosevelt-Truman foreign policy, and his accomplishments, including his present post as commander of NATO in Europe, had been achieved while representing Democratic administrations. All his fellow countrymen could be sure of was that he was a man of strength, decency, and tolerance; that he had won the respect of European statesmen; and that he displayed many of the ordinary characteristics which a democratic people like to find in their leaders — a fondness for dialect jokes, for example, and a bent for informal dress best expressed in the Eisenhower jacket.

He turned out to be a Republican, though the question remained unsettled for several agonizing weeks. Returning from France on January 6, 1952, Senator Henry Cabot Lodge Jr. of Massachusetts told reporters that the general would accept the Republican nomination if it were offered, and that he would not disown this statement by Lodge. He came close to it, though. In Paris next day he refused to identify his party affiliation for reporters; he merely said that the senator had given "an accurate account of the general tenor of my political convictions and of my Republican voting record." He dodged the question of accepting a draft. Persons working in his behalf, he warned, did so at his displeasure. While there could be "no question of the right of American citizens to organize in pursuit of their common convictions," their convictions in this case were not shared by the man they were meant to honor. He added: "Under no circumstances will I ask for relief from this assignment in order to seek nomination to political office, and I shall not participate in the preconvention activities of others who have an intention with respect to me."

Apparently the door was closed. In the next breath, however, he reopened it a crack. If he had no choice he would, of course, answer a call to "duty that would transcend my present responsibility." That was enough for Adams and Lodge, and they were off running for him. Among those now convinced that Eisenhower would be the Republican choice — and that he would soon forget his pledge to remain in Paris — was Harry S. Truman.

On January 20 Governor Stevenson spoke before the annual banquet of the Urban League in New York. He arrived in Washington at four o'clock the following afternoon for a conference on mine inspection and found that the Metropolitan Club had no room for him. A room had been reserved for him at the Roger Smith Hotel. Checking in, he was handed a message from Blair House; the President wanted to see him that very evening. At 11:15 P.M. Stevenson was back in his hotel room, feeling dazed. Calling a friend, he said, "This is Adlai, and I've just had the most incredible experience. Would you mind terribly coming down to the hotel for a little talk?" The friend found him in his shirtsleeves. Stevenson said, "I've just come from Blair House, and the President wants me to save the world from Dwight Eisenhower."

In Truman's memoirs he wrote that he had told the governor:

> . . . that I would not run for President again and that it was my opinion that he was best-fitted for the place. . . . I told him what I thought the Presidency is, how it has grown into the most powerful and greatest office in the history of the world. I asked him to take it and told him that if he would agree he could be nominated. . . . But he said: No! He apparently was flabbergasted.

Stevenson had reminded Truman that he was an announced candidate for gubernatorial reelection, and "One does not treat the highest office within the gift of the people of Illinois as a consolation prize." He had obligations toward his two younger sons, who had been virtually abandoned by their socialite mother; blinding publicity could warp their lives. In addition, he doubted that he was ready for the Presidency. After another term in Springfield he might be equipped for it, but not now. Stevenson did not, of course, suggest that this would be a difficult year for the Democratic nominee, but it must have crossed his mind; unlike Truman, he knew how much the administration had been hurt by the recent scandals.

Ironically, Eisenhower briefly thought — while watching a telecast of the Democratic convention the following summer — that had he known that the other party would nominate a man of Stevenson's caliber, he would have stayed in Paris. Like millions of others, in America and around the world, Dwight Eisenhower had been touched by the magic of Adlai Stevenson. Physically the governor was unprepossessing: short, bald, broad of beam. Yet he came close to political genius. His integrity and devotion to public service were sensed at once; his intellect and wit deighted admirers in both parties. No twentieth-century politician, including Franklin Roosevelt and John Kennedy, won so loyal a following among liberal intellectuals. When he spoke, he evoked a lyrical sense of America's past and what she might be in the future. Stevenson dreamed Lincoln's dream; vast audiences sat hushed as he swept them up in it; for the young and the idealists in his party he became a kind of religion that year. Like Wendell Willkie twelve years earlier, he made his countrymen better just for pausing to reflect upon what he represented, and eight years later the lamp he had held so high for so long would show the way upward to another, younger Democratic nominee.

Truman refused to accept his withdrawal. Shortly after the President had breakfasted with Senator Paul Douglas of Illinois the next morning, January 22, the news of Stevenson's call at Blair House was on front pages across the country. The dismayed governor found himself accompanied by swarms of reporters. His name appeared in speculative accounts by all syndicated columnists, and he was featured in a *Time* cover story which said, "Whatever the truth behind the rumors, this much is evident: in a cold season for the Democrats, Adlai Stevenson is politically hot, and Harry Truman feels the need of a little warmth." Asked by the press whether he would accept a draft, Stevenson grappled with his conscience. How, he asked those close to him, could anyone in good health and already in public life refuse the greatest honor and greatest responsibility in American politics? His reply to reporters was as negative as he could make it; "No one," he said, could be "drafted by a modern convention against his oft-expressed wish." In fact it had not happened in seventy-two years. In January Stevenson thought a repetition of that inconceivable.

Six weeks later he wasn't so sure. On March 4 he and the President met again — at his request, according to Truman in his memoirs; at Truman's, according to Stevenson's papers. To avoid encouragement of the rising presidential boom, the governor flew to Washington under the name of an aide, William McCormick Blair Jr. During a refueling stop at Louisville, Barry Bingham, publisher of the *Louisville Courier-Journal* and an old friend, urged him to let the people "judge for themselves on the basis of the public record." Laughing, Stevenson said, "Well, you certainly haven't been much help to me!" At Blair House he reaffirmed to Truman that re-election in Illinois was the full measure of his ambition. But the President wasn't much help, either. "I felt," he later wrote, "that in Stevenson I had found the man to whom I could safely turn over the responsibilities of party leadership. . . . I felt certain that he would see it as his duty to seek the nomination."

On March 29, 1952, the governor was one of 5,300 Democrats gathered in Washington's National Guard Armory for the party's annual Jefferson-Jackson Day Dinner. Other guests included the Achesons, and on the way there Alice Acheson asked her husband whether he thought the President might disclose his political plans during his after-dinner remarks. Out of the question, the Secretary of State said briskly; this was too early for him to announce that he would run again, and if he had decided not to, he wouldn't reveal it before this audience, so many of whom would be disappointed. As it happened, Alice Acheson was the first person outside the

Truman family to learn what was coming. She was seated beside the President, and as the time for speeches approached he showed her the last page of his. On it he had written in his own hand his decision not to seek another term. "You, Bess, and I," he said, "are the only ones here who know that." Distressed, she wanted to bring her husband over to argue with him, but he shook his head. "A little later," Acheson wrote, "we were stunned by the announcement. The party was quite unprepared to find a new leader and the material from which to choose seemed thin."

That was a Saturday evening. On Sunday Stevenson appeared on *Meet the Press*, now a television program, before a large number of studio spectators. The most heavily freighted question centered on his deposition in the Hiss case. The key testimony had been brief:

Q: Have you known other persons who have known Mr. Alger Hiss?

A: Yes.

Q: From the speech of those persons, can you state what the reputation of Alger Hiss is for integrity, loyalty, and veracity?

A: Yes.

Q: Specify whether his reputation for integrity is good or bad?

A: Good.

Q: Specify whether his reputation for loyalty is good or bad?

A: Good.

Q: Specify whether his reputation for veracity is good or bad?

A: Good.

In the cross-interrogation in behalf of the government, the following testimony had been taken:

Q: Were you ever a guest in the home of defendant Alger Hiss at any time in 1935, to and including 1938?

A: No, I have never been a guest in Mr. Hiss's home.

Q: Did you, prior to 1948, hear that the defendant Alger Hiss during the years 1937 and 1938 removed confidential and secret documents from the State Department and made such documents available to persons not authorized to see or receive them?

A: No.

Q: Did you, prior to 1948, hear reports that the defendant Alger Hiss was a Communist?

A: No.

After two years of McCarthyism, however, bland material like this was being transformed into political poison. Richard Nixon, California's new senator, was saying that Stevenson had "testified as a character witness for Alger Hiss" and "in defense of Alger Hiss."* Everett Dirksen, the Repub-

---

*At the time of Nixon's first speech on this subject, the governor had been virtually unknown outside Illinois, and in the version which went into the *Congressional Record* his name was misspelled "Stephenson."

lican senatorial candidate in Illinois, was taking the same line ("What would Dirksen have said?" asked Stevenson. "Would he have told a lie?") and the *Chicago Tribune* had argued editorially that the governor should have avoided testifying because by giving evidence he had "arrayed himself willingly beside Alger Hiss."

Now on *Meet the Press* Stevenson said: "I am a lawyer, and I think it is the duty of all citizens and particularly of lawyers — it is the most fundamental responsibility of lawyers — to give testimony in a court of law, honestly and willingly. And I think it will be a very unhappy day for Anglo-Saxon justice when a man in public life is too timid to state what he knows or has heard about a defendant in a criminal case for fear that a defendant would be ultimately convicted. That is the ultimate timidity."

In response to other questions he said once more, "I must run for governor. I want to run for governor. I seek no other office. I have no other ambition." Lawrence Spivak asked, "Governor, doesn't this large studio audience give you any indication of how some people in the country feel about that?" Stevenson smiled. "It's very flattering indeed," he said, "and I suppose flattery hurts no one — that is, if he doesn't inhale."

What he had avoided saying was that among the members of the Carnegie Endowment's board of trustees, which had voted in favor of making Alger Hiss president of the foundation and against accepting his resignation during his trials, was Dwight D. Eisenhower.

On March 11 Eisenhower had won the New Hampshire primary, 44,497 to Taft's 35,820; eight days later Stassen won the Minnesota primary with 128,605 votes, but Ike was right behind him with 106,946 write-ins. From Paris came word that his showing in these two races had persuaded the general to "reexamine" his "political position." In short, he was packing.

Kefauver was winning Democratic delegates, humiliating the President in state after state, but the Republican primaries, after that first burst of enthusiasm for Eisenhower, were not a runaway for anyone. Taft beat the general in Nebraska, beat Warren in Wisconsin, and trounced Stassen in Illinois by over 700,000 votes; write-ins for Eisenhower put him third. On April 15 the general took New Jersey away from Taft. He won in Pennsylvania, and Governor Dewey's support guaranteed him the lion's share of New York's delegates. He picked up 20 delegates in Kansas, but only one in Kentucky, which gave the other 19 to Taft. Indiana went to Taft. On June 3, in the last two primaries, Warren won in California and Taft beat Ike in South Dakota. Nationally, Taft's lieutenants counted 588 convention votes — with 604 needed for the nomination.

Early in April Eisenhower had announced that his "surprising development as a political figure" was interfering with his military duties; he asked to be relieved, and the White House granted the request at once, naming General Matthew Ridgway as his successor in Paris. Ike's campaign opened on June 2 in his home town of Abilene, Kansas, where twenty thousand stood in a driving rain to hear him speak in the local ball park. As he saw it, the most pressing issue before the country was "liberty versus socialism." He wanted the Senate to have a stronger role in determining foreign policy, and he called for lower taxes, an improved Taft-Hartley law, "a decent armistice" in Korea, abolition of needless federal agencies, continuing membership in NATO, and the "rooting out" of "subversive elements." He was against controls to fight inflation and against "socialized medicine," and he thought protection of civil rights should be left to the states.

There didn't seem to be much there that Taft could quarrel with. On June 19, in an "Answer to Abilene," he criticized the general for misunderstanding Taft-Hartley, lacking an agricultural policy, failure to name "the persons responsible for the loss of China," and refusal to condemn the administration's handling of the Korean War. That was quibbling, and everybody who could read a newspaper knew it. Someone pointed out that the only real issue upon which it was easy to differentiate between the two candidates was General MacArthur. Taft had promised to give MacArthur a government job. Eisenhower promised to listen to anything MacArthur had to say.

On July 7, when the Republican National Convention opened in Chicago's International Amphitheater, hard by the stockyards, those present included Betty Furness, a thirty-six-year-old former actress who had contracted to appear on television commercials with the message, "You can be sure if it's Westinghouse." Before Betty had finished opening and closing refrigerator doors she would entrance seventy million viewers, including one GOP delegate who would try to put her name in nomination.

The three major networks had shipped thirty tons of equipment and over a thousand workers to the amphitheater, but the Taft forces who controlled the convention had made few concessions to the new medium. Apart from agreeing to the installation of a TelePrompTer, or "idiot board," at the lectern, they had spurned requests from the TV networks. Later in the week, as word spread among those in the hall that they were on television, repeated motions would be made to "poll the delegation," so that everybody could be sure he was seen by the folks back home. Viewers found it maddening. In the beginning, however, there was none of this, and when Delegate Cecil B. De Mille told reporters that this was the greatest show on earth, he meant the proceedings, not their transmission on television, which he as a movie mogul had sworn to stamp out.

Since conservatives had written the scenario, events bore an unmistakable rightist tinge. The keynote address was delivered by Douglas MacArthur. It was a great chance for a dark horse, but to the disappointment of his supporters he bungled it. Ike in mufti retained his appeal; MacArthur was merely another retired executive with a hairpiece. Whenever he mentioned God, which was often, his voice had a disconcerting way of rising a register and breaking, and he had developed a peculiar way of jumping up and down for emphasis. Toward the end of MacArthur's speech the delegates were babbling so much among themselves that the general could scarcely be heard. This time he did fade away. After speaking he returned to the Waldorf in New York to await the decision of the convention. For three days the *Bataan* stood on the tarmac at La Guardia Field, its motor warm and its tanks full, ready to fly him back if the party should turn to him. On Friday the plane went back to its hangar.

The most popular speech was Joe McCarthy's. Here Taft's program committee had correctly judged the temper of the audience. When Chairman Walter Hallanan said he would give the delegates "Wisconsin's fighting Marine," a man who had suffered much for his dedication to "exposing the traitors in our government," and the band struck up "The Marines' Hymn," a wild demonstration swept up half the men in the hall. Placards advertised his victims: "Hiss," "Acheson," "Lattimore." Joe grinned satanically. After a tribute to MacArthur ("the greatest American that was ever born") he launched into his text on a note of high drama: "We are at war tonight." Solemnly he recited statistics of the conflict — the number of square miles which the "Commie-loving" Democrats had handed over to the beasts in the Kremlin, the millions of souls they had plunged into torment, the perfidy of the "slimy traitors" who slithered even now in "the Red Dean's State Department." He said he had documents to prove all this. Huge graphs and charts were wheeled to the lectern. The data were meaningless, the scales unreadable, but that didn't matter; Joe explained it all while waving a pointer like a cattle prod.

That was the real keynote, and subsequent performances adjusted to Joe's level. Apart from the Westinghouse commercials and the attractive wives and daughters of candidates — most memorably "Honeybear" Warren and her sisters — the fare was grim. Young Senator Richard Nixon cried that "the American people have had enough of the whining, whimpering, groveling attitude of our diplomatic representatives, who talk of America's weaknesses and of America's fears, rather than of America's strengths and of America's courage." The platform was hewn from the same lumber. In writing the foreign policy plank, John Foster Dulles excoriated every aspect of the Democratic record abroad, from Roosevelt's failure to defend the Baltic republics in 1939 to Korea. A reporter reminded him that at the time of the Baltic seizure Dulles himself, an America Firster, was urging FDR to stay out of the "senseless, cyclical struggle" to maintain national sovereignties, and that as recently as last May 19 Dulles had written in *Life* that Truman's decision to defend South Korea had been "courageous, righteous, and in the national interest." How could he say otherwise now? He replied that if he were speaking as an individual, he couldn't. As a platform writer, however, he was merely setting forth the Republican case against the Democrats. It was, he agreed, a nice point.

Combative as the words at the podium were, the struggle for the nomination was fiercer. Its ferocity is suggested by an appeal from David S.

Ingalls, Taft's cousin and campaign manager. Circulated among delegates that week, it began:

SINK DEWEY!!

TOM DEWEY IS THE MOST COLD-BLOODED, RUTHLESS, SELFISH POLITICAL BOSS IN THE UNITED STATES TODAY. He stops at nothing to enforce his will. His promises are worthless. He is the greatest menace that the Republican Party has. Twice he has led us down the road to defeat, and now he is trying the same trick again hidden behind the front of another man.

But how could Dewey do it? Taft seemed to have the nomination sewed up before the first gavel had fallen. On Sunday, July 6, when party functionaries were still arriving, the senator had walked briskly into a press meeting in the basement of Chicago's Conrad Hilton Hotel carrying a large, neat bundle of telegrams — 530 of them — from delegates who had banded together in their determination to stick with him to the end. By Monday morning Taft had 607 such assurances — three more than needed. Both the temporary and the permanent chairman were pledged to him. He had a majority in the Platform Committee, the Credentials Committee, and the National Committee. His aides had even picked the music to be played and the singers who would sing it. There was, it seemed, no way he could be turned back.

The Eisenhower forces' only hope lay in challenging accredited delegates. Ever since the Civil War the Republican faith had been defended in southern states by skeletal organizations of loyal party workers. They had but two tasks: to serve as postmasters when a Republican President was in the White House, and to vote in the quadrennial conventions. As regulars, they were now backing Taft to a man.

Eisenhower men questioned their right to sit on the convention floor. The first contest arose in Texas, and it was typical. Only five voters had attended the Republican party's 1950 Fort Worth caucus, so Henry Zweifel, the national committeeman for Texas, had decided to hold the May 3, 1952, caucus in his own home. To his dismay his garden had been trampled by a hundred strangers wearing Ike buttons. On the ground that Democrats without standing in the Republican party had no right to choose the Republican nominee, Zweifel had ordered them out of the yard. Three weeks later, at the state convention in Mineral Wells, regular Republicans had chosen the delegates they would send to Chicago: 30 Taft men, 4 for Eisenhower, and 4 for MacArthur. The Eisenhower people had convened in a separate hall, picking 33 Ike delegates and 5 for Taft. Thus there were two slates of Texans at the national convention.

The party officials who would choose between them were, of course, Taft men. But Eisenhower spokesmen were denouncing what they called "the Texas Steal" and demanding that Taft himself denounce such tactics. The senator replied with some heat that he had never stolen anything in his life. GOP slates in the South had been chosen according to procedures which had been followed for eighty-four years, he said, and only those with larceny in their own hearts were saying otherwise. He was right. The issue was bogus. The Eisenhower delegations from the South were no more representative than the Taft southerners, and the Taftites were at least lifelong Republicans. Unfortunately for the senator, he was not the idol of a grateful nation. Shielded by Ike's five-star mantle, his floor managers had expanded operations; they were now challenging the slates from Georgia and Louisiana, too. Even more important, they had coaxed their leader into the ring.

Eisenhower had been against going to Chicago. He thought it unseemly. Instead, he would spend the week with his wife's family in Denver. On July 1 he and Mamie had celebrated their thirty-sixth wedding anniversary at the Dowds' eight-room gray brick house at 750 Lafayette Street, the closest thing to a home he had known in a tumbleweed marriage that had been spent on military posts. In an evening discussion his supporters now persuaded him that he must move on to Chicago. The next morning he told reporters that he was ready "to roar clear across the country for clean decent operations." He would fight "to keep our party clean and fit to lead the nation." The battle being waged in the Credentials Committee was a "straight-out issue of right and wrong." He deplored "smoke-filled rooms," "star chamber methods," and "chicanery," and he was "shocked" at the National Committee's decision temporarily seating pro-Taft delegations from the South. He demanded "fair play."

Fair play: that became the rallying cry of his followers. Lodge said Taftite southerners must be banished as "stains on the integrity of our party." There was a good deal of this sort of talk, some of it in the form of out-and-out charges that Taft was a thief, and the impact of it on the conservatives was galvanic. During two decades in the political Sahara they had learned much about bitterness, but their anger in the amphitheater transcended everything they had felt toward the Democrats. This convention wanted to nominate Taft. New Englanders excepted, if its members had felt free to follow their convictions they would have chosen him by acclamation and campaigned for him around the clock. Even the New York delegation eyed him longingly; only Dewey's whip kept it in line. One by one the men whose telegrams the senator had held were drifting toward Eisenhower's floor managers, doing it sneakily and hating themselves for it. Emotionally the high point of the week was reached Wednesday evening, at the climax of the debate over the Georgia slate, when Dirksen, his hair carefully mussed, mounted the podium in Taft's behalf, pointed at the New York standard, and intoned, "Reexamine your hearts before you take this action. We followed you before and you took us down the path to defeat." Crooking his finger at Dewey, he cried, "And don't take us down that road again!"

They roared their approval — and then reached for Ike buttons. It was the polls that did it. Loving Taft as they did, they loved victory more, and they believed that the general, unlike the senator, would lead them to 1600 Pennsylvania Avenue. A majority were looking for an honorable way into the Eisenhower camp. Unwittingly the Taft forces gave them one. By banning cameras and reporters from the credentials hearings, they created the impression that they were trying to steamroller their men through. "Fair play" had acquired a convincing ring. The issue was joined when an Eisenhower leader, Governor Arthur B. Langlie of Washington, put a motion before the convention asking that the contested delegates from Georgia, Texas, and Louisiana remain unseated until their qualifications had been approved by a majority of all the delegates. At that the senator's strategists skidded again. Ohio congressman Clarence J. Brown, a Taft manager, offered an amendment to the Langlie resolution which would have given Ike's people just about everything they wanted while keeping control of the proceedings in Taftite hands. Brown seemed to be conceding that play in fact had been less than fair. It gave his amendment the semblance of a deal — which is precisely what the Eisenhower floor managers called it. The roll call which followed determined the outcome of the entire convention. Brown's amendment was defeated, 658 to 548. By that margin control of the Republican party had passed into the hands of Dwight Eisenhower. His nomination followed, a few minutes before noon on Friday, the fifth day of the GOP marathon, when at the end of the first ballot the count stood: Eisenhower 595, Taft 500, Warren 81, Stassen 20, MacArthur 10. Senator Edward J. Thye waved the Minnesota standard and yelled above the roar, "Minnesota wishes to change its vote to Eisenhower!" Senators Bricker, for Taft, and Knowland, for Warren, then moved that the choice be made unanimous. Ike had it.

He had watched it on television in his suite at the Blackstone Hotel, standing with his four brothers and nervously fingering two good luck charms, a Salvation Army coin and a Boy Scout souvenir. As Minnesota switched, Herbert Brownell rushed up and embraced him. The general's eyes filled. Too moved to speak, he sought out Mamie for a private moment. Then he picked up a phone and asked to speak to Taft. It was precisely the right thing to do, and he, the presumed amateur in politics, was the one who had thought of it. He asked the senator if he could pay his respects. Fighting crowds all the way, he made his way to Taft's lair in the Conrad Hilton. Both men were exhausted, stunned, and dazed. Photographers begged them to smile. They complied, though Taft was clearly in agony. He was going through this for the sake of the party, and his devotion to it had never made a greater demand. Though his eyes were bleak with pain, he managed to keep on grinning. He said huskily, "I want to congratulate General Eisenhower. I shall do everything possible in the campaign to secure his election and to cooperate with him in his administration."

Eisenhower expressed surprise when Brownell told him that it was customary for presidential candidates to name their running mates. This would be the nominee's first decision as Republican standard-bearer, and it was characteristic of him that he turned instinctively toward a procedure of the Army's staff system. He wanted "a man who had a special talent and an ability to ferret out any kind of subversive influence," but he would withhold his decision until Brownell could get "the collective wisdom of the leaders of the party."

It was too soon to invite conservatives to the conference; those summoned were all Ike men. They gathered in a room, which quickly became smoke-filled, in the Conrad Hilton. According to Paul Hoffman, the first name discussed was Taft. It was knocked down; they wanted a younger man, preferably a westerner. Dewey waited until all but one of the other possibilities had been considered and rejected. "Then," he said later, "I named Nixon as the logical nominee." The senator met all qualifications. He was thirty-nine, popular with conservatives, a hard campaigner, and had never been accused of being a security risk. After a brief discussion everyone agreed to the recommendation. Brownell phoned Eisenhower and asked the operator to find Nixon. The senator had loaned his car to Earl Behrens of the *San Francisco Chronicle* and had then gone off, no one knew where, with Murray Chotiner. He was one of the last men at the convention to learn he had been picked. By the time he could call his sister-in-law in Whittier, she knew it; it had been on television, too.

In one sense the freshman senator was a natural choice for the second spot on a presidential ticket: he was everything his leader was not. An extrovert and a genius at compromise, Eisenhower was a natural master of social situations. Shy, taciturn, and introverted, Nixon was a perfectionist. He couldn't stand cocktail parties. Humorless but earnest, a loner, proud of being the fastest dresser in the capital — eight minutes for formal clothes, two and a half for regular wear — he always carried in his inside pocket a list of things to do. Ike let others carry lists; that was what they were for. He was a backslapper; Nixon was a brooder. In economics and political ethics the general was a fundamentalist. The senator was a relativist, an opportunist, and a fatalist. The older man's strength lay in his appeal for independent voters, while Gallup traced the popularity of the younger man to registered Republicans, most of them his senior.

Of course, there was more to Richard Nixon than that. Twenty years later, after everything in his life had been subjected to minute analysis, aspects of his life would intrigue his countrymen. Somewhere in his impoverished Yorba Linda childhood lay the secret of the immense drive which brought him fame in Chicago only five years after a Washington newspaper story had featured him as the "Greenest Congressman in Town." Nixon's eye for detail had been Alger Hiss's nemesis, and in a way his own behavior was a pattern of odd little details. His sales executive manner, his indifference to what most men would call matters of principle, his extraordinary way of wolfing down lunches of cottage cheese and ketchup, his loathing of psychiatrists, the need always to wear a vest — hundreds of such Nixonian traits, each insignificant in itself, formed a fascinating mosaic. At the time of his elevation to the GOP's national ticket, however, he was still a one-dimensional politician, important only to the extent that he added or subtracted to Eisenhower's appeal. It seemed reasonable to believe that he would add something. As the man who had brought Hiss to justice Nixon commanded respect. It was not enough to say, as Democrats did, that he was a clean-shaven McCarthy, and that he had won his Senate seat by crucifying his opponent, Helen Gahagan Douglas. Mrs. Douglas had been crucified, all right, but the worst spikes had been driven into her by fellow Democrats. It was a conservative Democrat who had first called her the Communist candidate, making her primary triumph a pyrrhic victory and assuring her defeat before the Republicans had chosen their nominee.

Republicans were eager to give Nixon tangible evidence of their confidence in him. To those who asked how they could do it, Chotiner and Bernard Brennan replied that the best proof was cash. A vigorous campaigner needed a reservoir of it. The apparatus to receive it was already set up. Two years earlier Nixon and his staff had established a pipeline for contributions. Money was conveyed to what had become, in essence, an $18,000 contingency fund maintained for him by friends and admirers.

During the week between the departure of the Republicans and the arrival of the Democrats, Chicago was as serene as a hurricane's eye. Conventions are the lifeblood of hotels, and the Loop's hostelers had booked several small ones for the hiatus. The corridors where Ike had prevailed and Adlai would soon charm were momentarily swarming with safe driving instructors, life insurance salesmen, and the Ralston Purina sales force. It was a curious fact that memories of Taft seemed more viable than those of the general who had beaten him. For days after the Ohio senator had departed for his father's old summer place in Murray Bay, Quebec, his ghost haunted the scenes of his last great struggle to follow the elder Taft into the White House.

In that midsummer of 1952 it was by no means certain that the vanquished Taft conservatives would remain loyal to the Grand Old Party. Colonel McCormick's *Chicago Tribune* was describing Eisenhower as the candidate of Wall Street, Europe, Harry Truman, and Tom Dewey. Asked by a *Sun-Times* reporter what he thought of Republican chances in November, Colonel McCormick said, "Zero." A bitter *Tribune* editorial described the governor of New York as "the most unpopular figure in the Republican party today," and a reader in Racine, Wisconsin, wrote in that although he had been voting Republican since 1916, "I will not vote for Eisenhewey. Phewey on Eisenhewey!" Clearly the GOP house was badly divided.

Obviously much hinged on the outcome of what was already being called the second Betty Furness Show. Democratic hopes had been broaching and yawing since April 16, when Governor Stevenson had to all intents and purposes taken himself out of the race. En route to a fund-raising dinner at the Waldorf — where his presence, he felt, might be misconstrued — he had issued a firm statement saying that in view of his decision to run for reelection in Illinois, "I could not accept the nomination for any other office this summer." That, it appeared, had been that. Stevenson, the *New York Times* had observed, "seems effectively to have closed the door to his nomination."

Had any other state been chosen for the convention, he might have kept it closed, but as governor he would have to welcome the delegates. Those who knew how well he spoke believed the convention would be smitten by him, and his admirers set up a national Stevenson for President Committee headquarters on the fifteenth floor of the Conrad Hilton. Unlike the outposts of other candidates, this one had no contact, direct or indirect, with its man. The governor continued to do everything in his power to shut it down. At his request, friends reluctantly promised not to put his name in nomination, and on Sunday, July 20, the day before proceedings opened, he made an extraordinary appeal to a closed caucus of the Illinois delegation begging it not to join in a draft. Reporters outside, lying on the floor and putting their ears to a crack beneath a sliding partition, heard him say of the Presidency that "I do not dream myself fit for the job — temperamentally, mentally, or physically. And I ask therefore that you all abide by my wishes not to nominate me, nor to vote for me if I should be nominated."

No successful candidate in history had gone that far, but next day two events conspired against him. The first was a breakfast bid by Alben Barkley for the support of sixteen labor union leaders. Lacking a Stevenson commitment, the Vice President had a fair claim on Truman's support, and had the leaders backed him, Truman wrote in his memoirs, Barkley would have become the party's choice. They didn't, thereby taking him out of the race. The second event was, as predicted, the governor's stirring salute to the convention. He said: "Here, my friends, on the prairies of Illinois and of the Middle West we can see a long way in all directions. . . . Here there are no barriers . . . to ideas and to aspirations. We want none; we want no shackles on the mind or the spirit, no rigid patterns of thought, and no iron conformity. We want only the faith and the conviction that triumph in free and fair contest."

He reviewed the years since Franklin Roosevelt's first nomination to the Presidency in Chicago twenty years before, and spoke movingly of the proud achievements since. Then his eyes sparkled mischievously. "But our Republican friends," he continued, "have said it was all a miserable failure. For almost a week pompous phrases marched over this landscape in search of an idea, and the only idea they found was that the two great decades of progress" were "the misbegotten spawn of bungling, of corruption, of socialism, of mismanagement, of waste and of worse. They captured, they tied and they dragged that ragged idea into this hall and they furiously beat it to death for a solid week." Indeed: "After listening to this everlasting procession of epithets about our misdeeds I was even surprised the next morning when the mail was delivered on time. . . . But we Democrats were by no means the only victims here. First they slaughtered each other, and then they went after us. And the same vocabulary was good for both exercises, which was a great convenience. Perhaps the proximity of the stockyards accounts for the carnage."

It was at that point that Eisenhower, watching in a Colorado fishing lodge, had misgivings. Simultaneously, the Democratic delegates took heart. "In one day," Anne O'Hare McCormick wrote in next morning's *New York Times*, "all the confused and unchanneled currents seemed to converge upon the shrinking figure of Governor Adlai Stevenson as the one and only, the almost automatic choice of the convention. Nothing but action by the President could alter the picture, and the general feeling here is that even that would now be too late."

Late Thursday afternoon Governor Henry F. Schricker of Indiana took the lectern and said: "Ninety-two years ago, the nation called from the prairies of Illinois the greatest of Illinois citizens, Abraham Lincoln. Lincoln, too, was reluctant. But there are times when a man is not permitted to say no. I place before you the man we cannot permit to say no, Adlai E. Stevenson of Illinois."

Fifteen minutes earlier, as Schricker made his way to the podium, Stevenson had bowed to the inevitable. In a call to the White House he had asked whether the President would be embarrassed if Stevenson allowed his name to be put in nomination. Truman said, "I have been trying since January to get you to say that. Why should it embarrass me?"

The balloting proceeded while Stevenson, sitting in a second-floor bedroom at 1416 North Astor Street, the home of William McCormick Blair Jr.'s father, wrote out his acceptance speech in longhand on a yellow ruled tablet. Kefauver led on the first two ballots. After the third Stevenson was two and a half votes short of a majority. Utah then switched its twelve votes, and early in the morning of Saturday, July 26, the reluctant governor became the Democratic choice of 1952.

The first moments of his candidacy were inauspicious. Over and over the organ bleated out the campaign song "Don't Let Them Take It Away," a crude appeal to mass cupidity, and the nominee was then introduced to the delegates by Harry Truman. Four years earlier, the President had ridden an underdog role to victory. Since then his political stock had depreciated, however, and Stevenson's smile seemed wan when the President cried, "You have nominated a winner, and I am going to take off my coat and do everything I can to help him win." To seventy million television watchers the scene was a reminder of Truman's least attractive side, his fondness for Pendergast politics. The new man accordingly looked like a Pendergast protégé, and moments later the governor dealt his own chances a blow. In a rare lapse of taste, he told them: "I have asked the merciful Father, the Father of us all, to let this cup pass from me. But from such dread responsibility one does not shrink in fear, in self-interest or in false humility. So, 'If this cup may not pass from me, except I drink it, Thy will be done.' "

To the devout, repeating Christ's prayer at Gethsemane was sacrilege. Ike switched off his television set, saying to his fishing companions, "After hearing that, fellows, I think he's a bigger faker than all the rest of them."

He missed a remarkable speech. When memories of the conventions had faded, Stevenson said, there would remain: "the stark reality of responsibility in an hour of history haunted with those gaunt, grim specters of strife, dissension and materialism at home, and ruthless, inscrutable, and hostile power abroad. The ordeal of the twentieth century — the bloodiest, most turbulent era of the Christian age — is far from over. Sacrifice, patience, understanding, and implacable purpose may be our lot for years to come. Let's face it — let's talk sense to the American people. Let's tell them the truth, that there are no gains without pains, that we are now on the eve of great decisions — not easy decisions, like resistance when you're attacked, but a long, patient, costly struggle which alone can assure triumph over the great enemies of man — war, poverty, and tyranny — and the assaults upon human dignity which are the most grievous consequences of each. . . .

"Better we lose the election than mislead the people," Stevenson said; "and better we lose the election than misgovern the people."

After posing on the rostrum with John Sparkman of Alabama, his vice-presidential nominee, Stevenson took the train to Springfield. There he resolved to disassociate himself from Truman and fashion his own identity. His headquarters would be here, not in Washington or even in New York. National Chairman Frank McKinney, a Truman man, would be replaced by Stephen A. Mitchell, a Chicago lawyer and Stevenson friend.

In declaring his political independence, he went so far as to tell an Oregon reporter that one of his major goals, if elected, would be to clean up "the mess in Washington." Referring to this in his memoirs, Truman dryly noted, "How Stevenson hoped he could persuade the American voters to maintain the Democratic party in power while seeming to disown powerful elements of it, I do not know."

In fact, political legacies meant little to either candidate. Eisenhower and Stevenson were each too strong and too genuine to be called anyone's foil. For all that, on the eve of their great match they were very different. As John Mason Brown pointed out, the center of Ike's celebrated smile was his mouth, while Stevenson's was in his eyes. The general's waves to crowds were sweeping, with his arms straight out, and while speaking he would frequently say, "I am told," or "someone told me." The governor would say instead, "It strikes me," or "I am reminded by." He gestured tentatively, keeping his elbows at his sides. He worried about the country's smug materialism, its "spiritual unemployment." Eisenhower would have been embarrassed by such phrases. Even "status quo" bothered him; if he had to say it in a speech, he would follow it with an apologetic, " 'Course, I'm not supposed to be the educated candidate." And material prosperity did not alarm him; he saw it as a blessing, and as an American he was proud of it.

He was not a born speaker like his adversary. He needed time to find the natural rhythm of his campaign — so much time, in fact, that along the way some of his aides despaired of his ever getting it. Winding up his fishing trip, he said, "The great problem of America today is to take that straight and narrow road down the middle." It wasn't an arresting phrase to begin with, and when he used it the next day, and then the day after that, there was talk among the correspondents of crossing the 38th platitude. He was drawing large crowds, Richard H. Rovere reported on September 6, but "those that show up to lend an ear when he pleads for their assistance in unhorsing the Democrats are often rather thin."

During that first month almost the only bright note for the Republicans was their newspaper support. Just 201 daily papers were backing Stevenson, and their daily circulation was 4.4 million readers. Eisenhower, by contrast, was supported by 993 dailies with 40.1 million subscribers. But even here the news columns tended to undermine the pro-Ike editorials just by carrying quotations from the Democratic candidate. The governor's sense of timing was superb. Picking up Ike's concession that he would retain some Democratic programs, the governor remarked that he would be proud to stand on much of his party's record "if only . . . the general would move over and make room for me." The Republicans had lacked fresh ideas since the turn of the century, he charged, and "As to their platform, well, nobody can stand on a bushel of eels." Ending a 6,500-mile tour of the West on September 12, he learned that Taft had brought a conservative manifesto to the general's New York home, and that after a two-hour conference Eisenhower had agreed to it in every particular. Stevenson called it "the Surrender of Morningside Heights." He said, "Taft lost the nomination but won the nominee," and when an anguished Ike protested that the Presidency was no laughing matter, the governor jabbed him again: "My opponent is worried about my funnybone, but I'm worried about his backbone."

Television critic John Crosby wrote in the *New York Herald Tribune* that "To both the Republicans and the Democrats it's now fairly clear that Governor Adlai E. Stevenson is a television personality the like of which has not been seen ever before. The man is setting a pace that will not only be almost impossible for succeeding candidates to follow but one that will be pretty hard for Stevenson himself to maintain." To discouraged Republicans the race looked like 1948 all over again, with the other man lengthening his lead. After six weeks of it, the pro-Eisenhower Scripps-Howard chain ran a desperate editorial on the front page of all nineteen of its papers. "Ike," it said, was "running like a dry creek" because he was not "coming out swinging." He had said that he didn't know whether General Marshall had made mistakes. "If Ike doesn't know," the editorial continued, "he had better find out. For that's one of the big issues of this campaign. Ask any mother, father, or wife of a soldier now in Korea." It concluded, "We still cling to the hope that . . . he will hit hard. If he doesn't, he might as well concede defeat."

That was one of the turning points in the election. It led to a general decline in the level of the campaign, which was deplorable, but it also stiffened Eisenhower's resolve and made him a more militant competitor, which, from the Republican standpoint, was a good switch. At about the same time, Stevenson's wit began to generate a backlash. Louis Kronenberger has suggested that in an important context Americans "tend to fear and fight off humor." Some voters began saying that the general was right, that the struggle for the White House wasn't funny. Another September surprise was the realization that the Democratic candidate's intellect might not be an unqualified asset, that there were voters who would distrust it. A broad streak of anti-intellectualism had always been part of the American national character, and the fall of Hiss and the rise of McCarthy had been accompanied by a marked rise in the political use of anti-intellectual pejoratives — "longhairs," "do-gooders," "highbrows," "double-domes," "bleeding hearts." Now the 1952 campaign gave birth to another, a kind of watchword for Philistinism whose popularity was destined to remain high for the next five years.

Its coiner was John Alsop, the younger brother of two columnists, an insurance executive who was chairman of Connecticut's Republican speakers' bureau. In mid-September, when Stewart Alsop called to ask him how things stood, John said fine; it looked like a big GOP year in New England. He in turn asked how everything looked elsewhere. Stewart observed that while most intellectual celebrities had championed Eisenhower against Taft, many of them were now rooting for Stevenson. John thought a minute. As he later explained, he reflected that "while Stevenson was appealing and appealed strongly to people's minds, Eisenhower, as a man and as a figure, was appealing far more strongly to far more people's emotions." As his brother awaited his comment, John's mind's eye pictured the countenance of a typical intellectual in politics — a smooth, faceless, haughty, and very oval head. "Sure," he said, "all the eggheads are for Stevenson, but how many eggheads are there?"

Stewart put it in his column. Neither Alsop thought of the word as disparaging, but they quickly lost control of it. It answered a need and became a coast-to-coast sneer overnight. Louis Bromfield, an anti-intellectual intellectual, was one who seized upon it. Not knowing its origin, he wrote that "It seems to have arisen spontaneously from the people themselves." To him it stood for "a person of intellectual pretensions, often a professor or the protégé of a professor," who was "superficial in approach to any problem," and who was in addition "feminine," "supercilious," "surfeited with conceit," a "doctrinaire supporter of middle-European socialism," a "self-conscious prig" and, yes, "a bleeding heart." If Stevenson were elected, Bromfield prophesied, "the eggheads will come back into power and off again we will go on the scenic railway of muddled economics, Socialism, Communism, crookedness and psychopathic instability."

Suddenly the campaign became a pitched battle. Descending from the high plane established by the principals, partisans of both parties let fly wild charges, innuendos, absurd hyperbole — all the excesses that offend decency but stigmatize important elections all the same. Afterward there was some bewilderment over who had said what, understandable in the heat of the conflict and the confusion, in some quarters, over who was running. Harry Truman acted as though he was, and Henry Luce appeared to agree with him. Whistle-stopping all the way to the Pacific Northwest and back through the Middle West, the President spent two weeks questioning both Eisenhower's acumen and his character. Anthony Leviero of the *New York Times* said Truman had engaged the general in "an epic political conflict," and Arthur Krock described the tour as "a protracted assault on the personal integrity of General Eisenhower that is without parallel for a man in Mr. Truman's position." You could read all about it in *Time* and *Life*. You could not, however, find much there about the Democratic candidate for President. One issue of *Life* was devoted to pictures of the President and the general — there were none at all of Governor Stevenson.

Ike himself wasn't responsible for that. By and large his campaigning was as irreproachable as Stevenson's, and it is hard to fault his speeches. Doubtless he later wished that he could reword some of them. (On September 3 he said in Little Rock: "Thank goodness for a Supreme Court.") Others were naive, most memorably his egg lecture, in which he would hold aloft an egg and express outrage that a hundred different taxes might be levied on this little product of nature, to which the government had, he would say, made no contribution whatsoever. (As Taft had pointed out, the general didn't know much about agricultural policy.) Yet this was hardly demagogy, or even flamboyance. Emmet John Hughes was running a vigilant blue pencil over Ike's major speeches before they were delivered, crossing out such words as "crusade" in domestic affairs and "liberation" in foreign policy. Most of what was left was honest Eisenhower wrath. He may not always have had his facts quite right, but like his audiences he knew something had gone wrong for America, and it had put his dander up.

The crowds were with him now. The chant "We like Ike" was less a political call to arms than a hymn of praise. As John Alsop had noted, Stevenson sought to persuade men, but Eisenhower wanted to move them. And he was succeeding. The public, wrote James Reston, "likes his angry little outbursts against corruption, and his essays on America." Afterward Marquis Childs wrote that Ike had represented "strength, triumph, unswerving confidence. Millions were happy to take him on faith, on his face, on his smile, on the image of American manhood, on the happy virtue of his family life."

This was on a far higher level than Karl Mundt's formula for a Republican victory: K_1C_3 (Korea, Crime, Communism, Corruption). There were a lot of Mundts in the GOP, and by becoming the Republican nominee Ike had inherited them. He would have pleased their critics if he had repudiated them outright, but that wasn't his way. (It is fair to add that it wasn't FDR's way with Frank Hague or Stevenson's with Pat McCarran.) We know how the general felt about the Republican ultraconservatives. When Jenner tried to embrace him on a public platform in Indianapolis, Eisenhower recoiled. "I felt dirty," he told Hughes afterward, "from the touch of the man." In Green Bay, Wisconsin, on October 3, he refused to pose for photographers with Joe McCarthy, telling an audience that "The differences between me and Senator McCarthy are well known to him and to me, and we have discussed them."

McCarthy stalked off, furious, though the incident was soon forgotten in the candidate's failure to break openly with the senator later that day in Milwaukee. Feeling belligerent when the Milwaukee speech was being planned, Ike had said to Hughes, "Listen, couldn't we make this an occasion for me to pay a personal tribute to Marshall — right in McCarthy's backyard?" It was so decided, and a Marshall encomium was included in the advance copies of the speech distributed to the press. Then Governor Walter J. Kohler Jr. boarded the train in Peoria. He convinced Adams and General Wilton B. "Jerry" Persons, Eisenhower's military aide, that the tribute might split Republican strength in the state. When they approached Ike, he said, "Are you trying to suggest that I take out that paragraph on Marshall?" Adams said, "That's right, General." Ike said, "Well, take it out. I covered that subject thoroughly in Colorado a few weeks ago."

He hadn't, though. Praising his old superior in Colorado wasn't the same as going after Tailgunner Joe in Wisconsin. As he himself had been the first to see, Milwaukee would have been a superb place to strike a blow for decency. He had forfeited it, and the press had let the country know why. That was not the first time the general had taken a bold stand and changed his mind. He had said he would remain in Paris and then asked to be relieved, had said he would not go to Chicago and then did. It was to become a disconcerting habit of his political years, giving his adversaries the impression that he was weak and giving his staff apoplectic moments, but it did not mean that he was afraid of McCarthy — he would later prove that he was not — or that he himself was any readier to campaign in the gutter.

Some Democrats said he was. That was probably inevitable. Any election with McCarthy in it was going to be the occasion for squalor. McCarthy himself was seeing to that. There is no way of determining his impact on the November outcome. While he was picking up votes from people who believed him or thought Eisenhower in the White House could handle him better than Stevenson, others, affronted by his tactics, were being driven into the Democratic camp. Election results were inconclusive. Four Democratic senators against whom he campaigned, Tydings among them, went down in defeat. At the same time, however, his own showing at the polls was unimpressive. Eisenhower carried Wisconsin 979,744 to 622,175. McCarthy won 870,444 to 731,402, which was not only smaller than the general's plurality; it made him low man on the winning state ticket.

Still, he was a force. His most striking performance was his televised attempt to pin a Communist tag on Stevenson. "Alger," he began, smirking as he corrected himself, "— I mean Adlai." No one else plumbed the political depths so thoroughly as McCarthy, but plenty of others were knee — or hip — deep. Either it was impossible to be elected without suggesting that Democrats were treasonous, or Republicans thought it impossible. Even in Green Bay, where Eisenhower had drawn the line between himself and Joe, he had felt obliged to add: "I want to make one thing very clear. The purposes that he and I have of ridding this government of the incompetents, the dishonest, and above all the subversives and the disloyal are one and the same. Our differences, therefore, have nothing to do with the end result we are seeking. The differences apply to method."

His running mate was more direct. Nixon repeatedly charged that a Democratic victory in November would mean "more Alger Hisses, more atomic spies, more crises." He was still flagellating Hiss, now in stir, and in a major address, televised nationally from New York on October 13, he once more took up the trial deposition which had been given then by the Democratic candidate. After declaring that the Russians had acquired hundreds of secret documents "from Hiss and other members of the ring" which meant "that the lives of American boys were endangered and probably lost because of the activities of a spy ring," he added: "Mr. Stevenson was a character witness, or should I say a witness for the reputation, and the good reputation, of Alger Hiss. He testified that the reputation of Alger Hiss for veracity, and for loyalty was good. . . . This testimony . . . was given after all these facts, this confrontation in which Hiss had to look into Chambers' mouth to identify him, after these papers came out of the pumpkin, after all of those facts were known . . . it was voluntary on Mr. Stevenson's part."

Democratic speakers were now charging that while Eisenhower was taking a high road to November, his running mate was on a low one. It was working out that way, though not because anyone had planned it. That was the kind of men they were. Ike was cautious and, for a general, remarkably unaggressive. That was part of his appeal. He was no readier to climb into a ring with Stevenson than with McCarthy. Nixon was by contrast a lunger, a street fighter with a long shiv and a jugular instinct. If he wounded good men that autumn, it is fair to add that there were Democrats with knives, too.

"Secret Nixon Fund!" cried the page one headline in the *New York Post*. A two-line banner on page two read:

SECRET RICH MEN'S TRUST FUND KEEPS NIXON IN STYLE FAR BEYOND HIS SALARY
By Leo Katcher

Los Angeles — The existence of a "millionaire's club" devoted exclusively to the financial comfort of Senator Nixon, GOP vice presidential candidate, was revealed today. . . .

Katcher, a Hollywood movie writer, had managed to get most of the facts wrong, including the amount of money in the fund and the legality of it. The special bank account was well within both the letter and the spirit of the law. Men in public life seldom have enough money to meet their obligations. Some men put their wives on the payroll, or accepted extravagant legal fees, or spoke at $100-a-plate dinners. Stevenson had established a fund to backstop men who had left high-salaried jobs to serve Illinois. Other businessmen contributed to it, and as Stevenson said, there was "no question of improper influence, because there was no connection between the contributors and the beneficiaries."

There wasn't any in the Nixon fund, either. Contributions, none of which could exceed $500 in one year, were sent to Dana C. Smith, a Pasadena lawyer who acted as trustee and manager of the fund. Over a two-year period, 76 contributors had given an average of $240 each; the $18,235 had paid for recordings of speeches, travel vouchers, postage, and Christmas cards sent to former campaign workers. All of it had been accounted for. None had gone to Nixon or his wife. In addition, it had never been "secret." The account and Smith's administration of it had been a matter of public knowledge from its inception. In a way, Nixon was being hoist by his own petard. In his anti-Communist evangelism he had become a master of irrelevant minutiae. What had been in Chambers's mouth, or in the pumpkin, had nothing to do with Hiss's reputation. Indeed, the more spotless a spy's reputation, the more damaging the case against him, since he has been exploiting the trust of others. This was what had made Hiss's treachery so shocking. In that sense, by testifying to the faith men had had in him, Stevenson's deposition had made the verdict more damning. But Nixon had made it look the other way round. His syllogism had been: Hiss was a spy; Stevenson had known him; therefore Stevenson was under a cloud. The syllogism slandering him was: Some politicians take bribes; Nixon had taken money; Nixon was thus corrupt. The impact of the *Post* accusation was increased by the sanctimoniousness of his own campaign. His first reaction to the *Post* was in character. The Nixon train was about to pull out of Sacramento when a heckler yelled, "Tell 'em about the $16,000!" "Hold the train!" he shouted. "Hold the train!" It stopped, and he gave the crowd not the reasonable facts, but a muddled version of them. "You folks know the work I did investigating Communists for the United States," he said. "Ever since I have done that work, the Communists, the left-wingers, have been fighting me with every smear that they have been able to. Even when I received the nomination for the Vice Presidency, I want you folks to know — and I'm going to reveal it today for the first time — I was warned that if I continued to attack the Communists and crooks in this government they would try to smear me. . . ."

The country was not so easily diverted. The CIO was charging that Nixon had been bought by capital-gains Republicans who "knew a good investment when they saw one." California's franchise tax board had announced that it would investigate the fund. The Democratic National Committee was mailing a reminder to newspaper editors of criminal law provisions on "bribery and graft . . . by members of Congress," and Chairman Mitchell was wondering when Eisenhower would "cast away" his running mate. Mitchell's speculations were of no consequence to Nixon; Stevenson refused to make a judgment until all the facts were in. Eisenhower's opinion was another matter, though. If the standard-bearer thought a case could be made against his vice-presidential candidate, the result would be havoc. The general hadn't said he believed that, but he hadn't called it absurd, either, and as the long hours passed the silence aboard Ike's train, the Look Ahead, Neighbor Special, grew deafening.

Ike was getting conflicting advice. Taft approved of the fund. Hoover was issuing a statement to the effect that "If everyone in the city of Washington possessed the high level of courage, probity, and patriotism of Senator Nixon, this would be a far better nation." Chairman Arthur Summerfield made a few calculations on what the party's printing bill would be if Ike switched running mates and said it was out of the question.

The general himself was undecided. He had Brownell summon Senator Knowland from Hawaii as a possible replacement for Nixon, and Paul Hoffman was instructed to supervise a thorough investigation of the fund. On Hoffman's orders, fifty lawyers and accountants began a round-the-clock audit of it. They found it aboveboard in every respect. By now the reporters on Ike's train were begging him for a comment. For the record he said he had faith in Nixon's honesty and felt sure that the senator would vindicate him by putting "all the facts before the people, fairly and squarely." That wasn't quite what the vice-presidential candidate had been expecting. It sounded as though he would have to prove his innocence. The general had just that in mind. When he joined the reporters covering his tour for a glass of beer and was asked, "Do you consider the Nixon thing a closed incident?" he frowned and replied, "By no means." He really didn't know Nixon very well, he said — he had only met him a couple of times — and he wanted evidence of the senator's probity — facts, figures, names, dates. "What was the use," he asked rhetorically, "of campaigning against this business of what has been going on in Washington if we ourselves aren't as clean as a hound's tooth?"

The general's comment reached Nixon in Portland, Oregon. According to Earl Mazo of the *Herald Tribune,* if the ballot had been cast there that night "Eisenhower would not have gotten a single vote from the Nixon staff." With the embattled vice-presidential candidate were Chotiner and William P. Rogers.* "We had calls from everybody, all offering advice," Rogers said later. "There were only a few of us that day who were reasonably sure it would work out all right."

At about this time pressure began to build for a radio-television report to the people. Dewey suggested to Nixon that he make it as soon as possible. Nixon agreed, but he thought he was entitled to a word with Eisenhower first. The call went through to the Look Ahead, Neighbor Special. After pleasantries, the senator described Dewey's proposal. "I'm at your disposal," he said. Then he said, "I want you to know that if you reach a conclusion either now or any time later that I should get off the ticket, you can be sure that I will immediately respect your judgment and do so." Ike said he didn't think that decision ought to be up to him, and Nixon bridled. He was being pilloried for nothing; he was offering to sacrifice himself for the cause; certainly the standard-bearer could do *something*. In earthy language he told the five-star general either to make a decision or get off the seat of power.

Two hours later Nixon received word that the Republican National Committee and Senatorial Congressional Campaign Committee had pledged $75,000 for a half-hour nationwide explanation of the fund. Batten, Barton, Durstine, and Osborn, the party's advertising agency, had put together a hookup of 64 NBC television stations, 194 CBS radio stations, and the 560-station Mutual Radio Network. They asked how soon the senator could be ready — there was a choice spot open the following night, right after *I Love Lucy.* Impossible, said Nixon; he had to return to California and marshal his thoughts. He could make it the night after that, however, and so it was decided that he would go on the air then, immediately after Milton Berle. Reserving a seat on the next United Airlines flight to Los Angeles, the senator made arrangements to go into seclusion there at the Ambassador Hotel.

En route, he pulled a sheaf of United's souvenir postcards from the seat in front of him and made sketchy notes:

*Who served as Nixon's Secretary of State from 1969 to 1973.

Checkers . . .
Pat's cloth coat —
Lincoln ref. to common people (?)

He later explained that he had thought of Checkers, the Nixon family dog, because FDR had used Fala so cleverly in the 1944 campaign. In Eugene, Oregon, a placard had read "No mink coats for Nixon," and sure enough, he thought, his wife didn't have one. The Lincoln reference was more complex. Mitchell had said, "If a fellow can't afford to be a senator, he shouldn't seek the office." It was a stupid remark. If it meant anything, it was that only wealthy men should go to Washington. Hadn't Lincoln said something about God loving the common people because he made so many of them?* At the Ambassador Hotel, after acknowledging the airport crowd — it was disappointingly small — Nixon put through a call to Paul Smith, his old Whittier history professor, asking him to pin down the quotation.

Meanwhile, something extraordinary had happened to the campaign. It was stalled. The public had forgotten about the presidential candidates. All eyes were on the GOP candidate for Vice President. TV programs were being interrupted for rumors that he had suffered a nervous breakdown and interrupted again to reveal that he was in good health, and speculation over what he was going to say was building. Even Eisenhower was becoming curious about it. At his direction Adams called Chotiner and asked what it would be. Chotiner said he didn't have the foggiest idea.

"Oh, come now, Murray, you must know," Adams said. "He has a script, doesn't he?" Chotiner said he didn't, and Adams asked, "What about the press?"

"We've set up television sets in the hotel for them," Chotiner replied, "and we have shorthand reporters to take it down, page by page."

"Look," said Adams, "we have to know what is going to be said."

"Sherm," Chotiner said, "if you want to know what's going to be said, you do what I'm going to do. You sit in front of the television and listen."

It was true. Nixon had a general idea of his theme, but there was no text, and he hadn't decided how to end it. Dewey had suggested that he ask voters to write to the Republican National Committee. It seemed to be a good idea, but what should they write? He didn't know. The pressure, he knew, was growing hourly, and press comment continued to be hostile to him. The Los Angeles *Daily News* was reporting that "Anything short of an enthusiastic burst of public support . . . will be interpreted in favor of what Eisenhower and his staff have already decided — that corruption cannot remain a campaign issue as long as one of their candidates is tainted with the slightest suspicion. Thus, Nixon will probably be asked to resign." Eisenhower and his staff had decided no such thing, though the general

*In fact Lincoln had said "common-looking people."

was certainly preoccupied with the issue. It seemed crucial. "There is one thing I believe," the general said to Adams; "if Nixon has to go, we cannot win." That evening Ike was interested only in a seat in front of a television set. The manager of the Cleveland Public Auditorium, where he was scheduled to speak afterward, led him up three flights of stairs to one. Mamie and William Robinson, publisher of the anti-fund *Herald Tribune*, sat with him; Summerfield and Jim Hagerty stood against the wall.

Nixon, meantime, was preparing to leave the Ambassador Hotel for NBC's El Capitan Theater in Hollywood. The cameramen, the electricians, and the men in the control room had been rehearsing there all day; everyone was ready except the star, who still hadn't decided how to wind up his talk. He was talking to Chotiner and Rogers, debating the best way for the audience to express its opinion of him — by writing to him, to Eisenhower, or to the National Committee — when the phone rang. The operator said it was long distance; a Mr. Chapman was calling. "Mr. Chapman" was Dewey's code name. Chotiner was told that the senator was unavailable, but the governor was adamant. Nixon reluctantly picked up the receiver.

Dewey said to him, "There has just been a meeting of all of Eisenhower's top advisers. They've asked me to tell you that in their opinion at the conclusion of the broadcast you should submit your resignation to Eisenhower. As you know, I haven't shared this point of view, but it's my responsibility to pass this recommendation to you."

Nixon was too shocked to speak. Dewey jiggled the receiver. He said, "Hello? Can you hear me?"

Nixon asked, "What does Eisenhower want me to do?" Dewey didn't know; he hadn't spoken directly to the general. Nixon said, "It's kind of late to pass on this kind of recommendation to me now."

"What shall I tell them you're going to do?" Dewey persisted.

Nixon exploded, "Just tell them that I haven't the slightest idea what I'm going to do, and if they want to find out they'd better listen to the broadcast! And tell them I know something about politics, too!"

It was 6 P.M. in Los Angeles, 9 P.M. in the East — a half-hour till broadcast time. After shaving, showering, and dressing, Nixon found he was too wrought up from Dewey's call to memorize his notes; he would have to go on holding them. At the theater the program director led him and Pat in and asked him what movements he would be making. Nixon said, "I don't have the slightest idea. Just keep the camera on me." With three minutes to go, he thought wildly of backing out. To Pat he said, "I just don't think I can go through with this one." She said of course he could, and it was too late to do anything else; already the camera was showing his calling card. It switched to him. He said: "My fellow Americans, I come before you tonight as a candidate for the Vice-Presidency and as a man whose honesty and integrity has been questioned."

He described the purpose of the fund and how it worked. The money had been used solely for campaign expenses, he said. Since he had never even seen it, none of it had been taxable or even reportable under federal law. He continued: "There are some that will say, 'Well, maybe you were able, Senator, to fake this thing. How can we believe what you say — after all, is there a possibility that maybe you got some sums in cash? Is there a possibility that you might have feathered your own nest?' And so now what I am going to do — and incidentally, this is unprecedented in the history of American politics — I am going at this time to give to this television and radio audience a complete financial history, everything I have earned, everything I have spent, everything I own."

Going back to his youth, he led up to the present and said he now owned:

> A 1950 Oldsmobile.
> A 3,000 equity in his California house, where his parents were living.
> A $20,000 equity in his Washington house.
> $4,000 in life insurance, plus a GI term policy.
> No stocks, no bonds, nothing else.

He owed:

> $10,000 on the California house.
> $20,000 on the Washington house.
> $ 4,500 to the Riggs National Bank in Washington.
> $ 3,500 to his parents.
> $ 500 on his life insurance.

"Well, that's about it," he said. "That's what we have and that's what we owe. It isn't very much, but Pat and I have the satisfaction that every dime that we have got is honestly ours."

By then he had doubtless won his audience. After running against FDR's forgotten man in five straight presidential elections, the Republicans had finally nominated a man with whom millions could identify. Nixon was carefully presenting himself as an ordinary man. Although he had been around "when the bombs were falling" during the war and was probably entitled to a star or two, he claimed no heroics. The key to the speech, however, was the detailed discussion of finances. This was, after all, a talk about money, and in laying every penny he had, or had had, on the line, he was telling a tale familiar to his listeners — the two-year-old car, the mortgages, the inadequate life insurance. Here, clearly, was a man who knew what it was to worry about getting the kids' teeth straightened, or replacing the furnace, or making the next payment on the very set now tuned to him. Of course, he said adroitly, it was fine that a man like Governor Stevenson, "who inherited a fortune from his father," could run for President. But it was equally fine that "a man of modest means" could also make the race, because they would all remember what Lincoln had said about the common man. . . .

Overeager Democrats had slandered him, panicky Republicans had talked of jettisoning him, and now he had exonerated himself. But Nixon, with his immense drive, was unwilling to settle for that. This was an opportunity to leave an indelible impression on the national memory — to do what Bryan had done with the cross of gold and Coolidge with the Boston police strike — and he meant to exploit it every way he could.

He told the audience: "I should say this — that Pat doesn't have a mink coat. But she does have a respectable Republican cloth coat. And I always tell her that she would look good in anything.

"One other thing I should probably tell you, because if I don't they'll be saying this about me, too. We did get something, a gift, after the nomination. A man down in Texas heard Pat on the radio mention the fact that our two youngsters would like to have a dog and, believe it or not, the day before we left on this campaign trip we got a message from Union Station in Baltimore, saying they had a package for us. We went down to get it. You know what it was?

"It was a little cocker spaniel dog in a crate that he had sent all the way from Texas — black and white, spotted, and our little girl Tricia, the six-year-old, named it Checkers. And you know, the kids, like all kids, love that dog, and I just want to say this, right now, that regardless of what they say about it, we're going to keep it."

It wasn't easy to appear on a nationwide hookup and "bare your life, as I have done," he said; he was doing it because his country was in danger, and the only man who could save it was Dwight Eisenhower. ("You say, why do I think it is in danger? And I say, look at the record. Seven years of the Truman-Acheson administration, and what's happened? Six hundred million people lost to the Communists.") He was approaching the peak. The clock told him that he was also running slow.

"I know that you wonder whether or not I am going to stay on the Republican ticket or resign. Let me say this: I don't believe that I ought to quit, because I am not a quitter. And, incidentally, Pat is not a quitter. After all, her name was Patricia Ryan and she was born on Saint Patrick's Day — and you know the Irish never quit."*

But the decision, he went on, was not his to make. He had decided — at this moment, while talking — to turn the whole thing over to the Republican National Committee "through this television broadcast." And he was going to ask his listeners to help the Committee decide: "Write and wire the Republican National Committee whether you think I should stay on or whether I should get off. And whatever their decision is, I will abide by it."

A director slipped into the studio and signaled vigorously that his time was almost up. Nixon didn't appear to see him. His eyes glassy, he kept talking to the camera: ". . . just let me say this last word. Regardless of what happens, I am going to continue this fight. I am going to campaign

*Actually she was born on March 16, 1912, the day before Saint Patrick's Day, and christened Thelma Catherine Ryan. Her father gave her the nickname Pat. Her mother was a native of Germany.

up and down America until we drive the crooks and those that defend them out of Washington. And remember, folks, Eisenhower is a great man. Folks, he is a great man, and a vote for Eisenhower is a vote for what is good for America —"

It was over. In Cleveland Eisenhower turned to Summerfield. He said, "Well, Arthur, you certainly got your seventy-five thousand dollars' worth."

In the El Capitan Theater Nixon was saying to the director, "I'm terribly sorry I ran over. I loused it up, and I'm sorry." Thanking the technicians, he gathered up his notes, stacked them neatly — and then, in a spasm of rage, flung them to the floor. Chotiner came in beaming and tried to congratulate him, but Nixon was inconsolable. "No, it was a flop," he said. "I couldn't get off in time." In the dressing room he wheeled away from his friends and burst into tears.

Later he was to have another memory of this moment. In his book, *Six Crises,* he would recall that the tears had been in the eyes of cameramen who had been moved by his eloquence. The makeup man, in his recollection, growled, "That ought to fix them. There has never been a broadcast like it before," while well-wishers jammed the studio switchboard and "everyone at the station agreed that the broadcast had been successful beyond expectations."

That came later. In the immediate aftermath of the speech he was haunted by the realization that the red camera light had blinked off just as he had been about to begin his most important sentence, giving his audience the address of the Republican National Committee. His faulty timing meant they didn't have it. Lacking it, he reasoned, they would be unable to respond, and the committee would receive no messages at all. As he approached his car outside, a huge Irish setter bounded up, wagging its tail. He said gloomily to Pat, "Well, we made a hit in the dog world, anyhow."

At the Ambassador Hotel he discovered that the impact of the broadcast had, in fact, been immense. The lobby cheered as he entered. He took a call there from Darryl Zanuck, who told him it had been "the most tremendous performance I've ever seen." Within the hour word arrived that people were appearing at Western Union offices all over the country. Bit by bit his staff began putting together the story of the nationwide reaction. According to Nielsen figures, half of the TV receivers in the country had been tuned to the broadcast. Counting radio, the audience had been 60,000,000. Of these, roughly 1,000,000 called, wired, or wrote. The mails brought $60,000 in small contributions, almost enough to pay for the broadcast. It was a remarkable personal triumph, and although he was at first unaware of its scale, by the end of the evening he knew that he had received messages of praise from virtually every outstanding member of the Republican party, with one exception. There had been nothing from Dwight Eisenhower.

This imagined slight — Ike had wired his congratulations, but the telegram had been lost in the avalanche of incoming messages — was to leave permanent scars on the relationship between Nixon and the general's advisers. The first word from Cleveland to reach the Ambassador Hotel was that the half-hour presentation hadn't been enough for Eisenhower; he wanted a face-to-face confrontation. That was partly true. Eisenhower did feel that the half-hour had been inadequate. For the sake of appearances he felt that the two of them ought to have a private word together the following evening, in Wheeling, before putting the fund behind them. However, he had expected that Nixon would receive the suggestion in the context of his admiration for the television performance. Coming this way, after the days of excruciating tension, it was a cruel disappointment, and Nixon blew up. "What more can he possibly want of me?" he shouted, and calling in Rose Mary Woods, his secretary, he dictated a telegram to Summerfield resigning as vice-presidential candidate pending the selection of a successor. Chotiner destroyed it before it could be sent, and Nixon himself had second thoughts, but both of them decided it was best to ignore the invitation to Wheeling. Instead, Nixon would pick up his own campaign train in Missoula, Montana. An insubordinate wire went to Ike: "Will be in Washington Sunday and will be delighted to confer with you at your convenience any time thereafter."

While that message was on its way, a call came in from Summerfield. He asked Chotiner, "Well, Murray, how are things out there?"

Chotiner replied, "Not so good."

"What in hell do you mean, 'Not so good'?"

"Dick just sent a telegram of resignation to the general."

"What! My God, Murray, you tore it up, didn't you?"

"Yes, I tore it up, but I'm not so sure how long it's going to stay torn."

"Well, Dick is flying to Wheeling to see the general, isn't he?"

"No, we're flying tonight to Missoula."

"What? My God, Murray, you've got to persuade him to come to Wheeling."

"Arthur, we trust you. If you can give us your personal assurance direct from the general that Dick will stay on the ticket with the general's blessing, I think I can persuade him. I know I can't otherwise."

Before Summerfield could call back the Nixon party was off for Montana, but a phone call from Bert Andrews in Cleveland reached Nixon at the airport. Andrews reminded him that he could hardly expect Eisenhower, a five-star general and the leader of the party, to fly to him. It was time to forget the fund. The press critics had turned around. The *Herald Tribune* was saying, "The air is cleared."* The Republican National Com-

---

*There were dissenters. Walter Lippmann said the response had been "with all the magnification of modern electronics, simply mob law," and to *Variety* the telecast had been "a slick production . . . parlaying all the schmaltz and human interest of the 'Just Plain Bill' – 'Our Gal Sunday' genre of weepers."

mittee had been polled and had voted to keep the ticket intact, 107 to 31. To underscore this, in Montana word at last reached Nixon from Ike: "Your presentation was magnificent. . . . My personal decision is to be based on personal conclusions. I would most appreciate it if you can fly to see me at once. Tomorrow I will be at Wheeling, W. Va. Whatever personal affection and admiration I had for you — and they are very great — are undiminished."

After a few token appearances in Missoula and a two-hour nap, Nixon flew to West Virginia. On the field in Wheeling he was still on the plane, helping Pat into her Republican cloth coat, when a solitary figure detached itself from the crowd below and darted up the ramp. It was Eisenhower. Surprised, Nixon blurted out, "What are you doing here, General? You didn't have to come up here to meet us." Putting his arm around his running mate's shoulders, Ike said, "Why not? You're my boy." As they posed for pictures in the terminal, Nixon's eyes began to fill.

He had lots of sympathizers now. Well-wishers had sent Checkers a vast assortment of dog collars, hand-woven dog blankets, a kennel, and a year's supply of dog food. The little spaniel had become the most famous pet in the country. Even those who had deplored the speech used it as a standard for measuring Nixon's later performances. "This mawkish ooze ill became a man who might become the President of the United States," said the Montgomery, Alabama, *Advertiser*; then, finding something in him to praise, the *Advertiser*'s editorial writer added a phrase to the language: "We have found ourselves dissolving our previous conception . . . the New Nixon rejoices us."

The first of Eisenhower's two most important campaign speeches was delivered on the evening of October 16 at the Alfred E. Smith Memorial Foundation dinner in Detroit; its statesmanlike approach to foreign policy won an endorsement of his candidacy from the *New York Times*, which had been leaning toward Stevenson. In the second speech, on October 24 in Detroit, the general promised that if elected, "I shall go to Korea." Truman called the pledge a stunt, and Stevenson delighted his followers by saying, "If elected, I shall go to the White House," but Eisenhower had struck a deep chord. The war continued to be America's most vexing issue; surely, people felt, progress would follow a visit to the front by the nation's greatest military hero. "For all practical purposes," Jack Bell of the Associated Press later wrote, "the contest ended that night."

But the wild swirls of accusations and countercharges continued right down to the wire. Outrageous stories were circulated over that first November weekend: Stevenson was a homosexual, Mamie was an alcoholic, "Adlai" was a Jewish name, Ike was dead but his aides wouldn't admit it. The campaign had been the ugliest since the Roosevelt-Landon donnybrook of 1936. That Sunday, November 2, an automobile with a Stevenson bumper sticker was forced off the Pennsylvania Turnpike and its driver beaten senseless. In Joplin, Missouri, one Raymond Nixon, no relation to the senator, received three threatening phone calls, and the New Orleans Police Department reported eleven brawls, all of them over politics. Sherman and Rachel Adams spent election day in New York. That evening Sinclair Weeks asked where they had been. At the Bronx Zoo, they said, watching the wild animals.

"Quite a change from a political campaign," he said.

"No," said Rachel, "not much."

In Libertyville, Illinois, on election day Stevenson visited a school which was also a polling place. "I would like to ask all of you children to indicate, by holding up your hands, how many of you would like to be governor of Illinois, the way I am," he said. Nearly every hand went up. "Well, that is almost unanimous," he said. "Now I would like to ask all the governors if they would like to be one of you kids." He raised his own hand. He was in good spirits, and confident. His staff formed a betting pool, each man contributing five dollars to it and writing his guess of the electoral vote on a slip of paper. His own slip predicted he would win 381 electoral votes, a landslide. The others were less optimistic, though none thought he would be defeated.

The front-page headline in the *New York Times* the previous morning had been: ELECTION OUTCOME HIGHLY UNCERTAIN, SURVEY INDICATES. "Neither Gen. Dwight D. Eisenhower, Republican, nor Gov. Adlai E. Stevenson, Democrat, can be regarded as now certain of election," the story began, summing up the last of seven exhaustive surveys conducted by *Times* reporters. Those burned four years earlier were making cautious forecasts. The public opinion polls warily noted unusually high numbers of undecided voters and suggested that this floating vote would be divided rather evenly between the two candidates. Nearly all of it went to Eisenhower. What the pollsters had overlooked, or ignored, was that the vast majority of this central group were new registrants. When previously indifferent voters register they usually augur a protest vote, and so it was this time. In the first great swing since 1932, the country went Republican.

Eisenhower won, 33,936,234 to 27,314,992. Republican editorial writers interpreted the victory as an endorsement for free enterprise, predicting that at the stroke of noon on inaugural day an efficient businessman's administration would turn the Pendergast politicians out. The *Chicago Tribune*, examining returns from the new suburbs, chortled that fresh air had done wonders for the judgment of those who had moved out from urban wards. It had certainly changed their politics. Coming from neighborhoods which had given lopsided majorities to Roosevelt and Truman, the young couples in the new developments had been converted to Ike's cause. The winning ticket had carried Levittown, Long Island, by 66 percent and Park Forest, Illinois, by 69.4 percent.

Adlai Stevenson could hardly be called discredited. He had polled more votes than any losing presidential candidate in the country's history —

more, indeed, than any *winning* candidate except FDR in 1936 and Ike this time. Though Eisenhower wound up with 442 of the 531 electoral votes, his triumph was less impressive than those of the last three Republican Presidents. His plurality was below 11 percent. Theirs had been 28 percent (Harding), 30 percent (Coolidge), and 18 percent (Hoover). Moreover, despite his margin of six million votes, he had just barely managed to pull in a Republican Congress. The GOP majority in the new House was ten votes; in the Senate, merely one.

Nevertheless, 1952, like 1932, was a pivotal election. The Democrats remained the larger party, with a 5 to 3 ratio in registered voters, but registration meant less; the number of staunch Democrats — "knee-jerk liberals," Republicans were calling them — had diminished. It had become fashionable to say that you voted "for the man, not the party," as though those who had cast their ballots for FDR had done anything else. Independent registrations had now increased to more than 20 percent of the electorate. On Capitol Hill control was securely anchored in the Republican-Southern Democratic coalition first formed to fight Roosevelt's court reform bill fifteen years earlier. Its skepticism toward legislative innovation suited the country's new mood, which was conservative, content, and above all wary of nonconformity.

Adlai Stevenson spent election day evening in his basement office in Springfield, working on state business and listening to returns on a small portable radio. He had written out two statements, an acknowledgment of victory and a concession of defeat, and when Blair came in at nine o'clock he asked blandly, "Well, Bill, which is it to be — 'A' or 'B'?" Blair replied, "I'm afraid it's 'B,' Governor." "O.K.," said Stevenson.

He reached the Leland Hotel lobby at 1:43. Smiling cheerfully at downcast volunteers, he stepped to a battery of microphones and said, "General Eisenhower has been a great leader in war. He has been a vigorous and valiant opponent in the campaign. These qualities will now be dedicated to leading us all through the next four years. . . ." After reading his telegram of concession, he looked out across the crowd. It was the end of an age, and they all felt it. Democrats of the swing generation had grown up under administrations of their own party. Now, with the age of reform over, they could not see the way ahead. Neither could he, but as their leader he wanted to say another word. After a pause he said: "Someone asked me, as I came down the street, how I felt, and I was reminded of a story that a fellow townsman of ours used to tell — Abraham Lincoln. He said he felt like a little boy who had stubbed his toe in the dark. He said that he was too old to cry, but it hurt too much to laugh."

He left, and millions discovered that tonight, at least, they were not too old for tears. In that broken moment of time they felt the first pangs of the barren loneliness Republicans had known for two decades — the frustrations of men accustomed to power but relegated to impotence.

Democrats slept late in the White House and at the Leland that Wednesday, November 5. Not so General Eisenhower; up early, he flew to Augusta. The day was still crisp and golden when the President-elect teed up for the first hole. The first ball he hit soared nearly 250 yards straight down the fairway. Two well-built young men congratulated him on his powerful drive, and he introduced them to the rest of his party as members of the Secret Service.

EAST BERLINERS RISE, BATTLE RUSSIAN TANKS

BARDAHL does it again!

BEST SELLERS: Fiction

The Silver Chalice by Thomas B. Costain
Lord Vanity by Samuel Shellabarger
East of Eden by John Steinbeck
The Old Man and the Sea by Ernest Hemingway
Too Late the Phalarope by Alan Paton

How much is that doggie in the window
The one with the waggly tail
How much is that doggie in the window
I do hope that doggie's for sale

I like Ike
I'll shout it over a mike
Or a phone,
Or from the highest steeple
I like Ike
And Ike is easy to like
Stands alone, the choice
Of we the people

STATE DEPT. BANS TRAVEL TO RUSSIA

CAIRO JUNTA SEIZES HELM

"OMNIBUS" SEEN LURING HIGHBROWS TO TELEVISION

He was an old man who had fished alone in a skiff in the Gulf Stream and he had gone eighty-four days now without taking a fish.

GAMMA GLOBULIN CUTS POLIO FEAR

GEORGE VI DIES — LIZ IS QUEEN

Best actor of 1953: William Holden in *Stalag 17*
Best supporting actress of 1953: Donna Reed in *From Here to Eternity*

Lila   Moulin Rouge   Shane   Roman Holiday

BEST SELLERS: Nonfiction

The Holy Bible Revised Standard Edition
Witness by Whittaker Chambers
Anne Frank: The Diary of a Young Girl
The Power of Positive Thinking by Norman Vincent Peale
A Man Called Peter by Catherine Marshall

"I like Ike, too," said Governor Stevenson.

MAU MAU LEADERS SENTENCED: KENYATTA GIVEN SEVEN YEARS

PUERTO RICO BECOMES 1st U.S. COMMONWEALTH

IKE CHRISTENS ATOMS-FOR-PEACE PROGRAM "OPERATION WHEATIES"

ARREST WILLIE SUTTON IN BROOKLYN

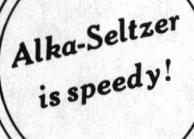

LINK CIGARETTES TO LUNG CANCER, HEART DISEASE

Best actor of 1952: Gary Cooper in *High Noon*
Best actress of 1952: Shirley Booth in *Come Back, Little Sheba*

The Member of the Wedding   The Man in the White Suit   Singing' in the Rain

Viva Zapata!   Limelight

TWENTY

What Was Good for General Motors

Late that autumn, while Washington awaited instructions from the first President-elect since FDR, the rest of the country turned, so to speak, from the bomb shelter to the barbecue pit, moving in rhythm to the tempos of the time. In the early 1950s that was easy. Rock 'n' roll lay in the future. Record stores had not yet been overwhelmed by teenagers. Their typical customer was in his early twenties. His favorite songs were about love, not lust, and they were rendered tenderly by such mellow vocalists as Mario Lanza, Julie London, and Tony Bennett. Harry Belafonte, a U.S. Navy veteran, was earning $750,000 a year in the early 1950s — his album *Calypso* became the first LP to sell a million copies — and straight-arrow customers were buying 100,000 Mitch Miller albums every month. Miller was not only a performer; he was also the director of the Columbia Records popular music division, which meant that he profited twice from each sale. Yet it was all so relaxed that the public forgot that it was big business. On his Saturday evening television show Perry Como, one of Miller's fellow entrepreneurs, said he wouldn't mind going back to cutting hair for a living, and nobody in the studio audience laughed.

After seventeen years *Your Lucky Strike Hit Parade* was still going strong Saturday evenings on NBC, advertising a product still thought to be harmless. The number one hit in 1952 was Johnnie Ray's "Cry." It would be replaced in 1953 by Percy Faith's "Where Is Your Heart." Other melodies oozing from jukeboxes were "April in Portugal," "On Top of Old Smoky," Vera Lynn's "Auf Wiederseh'n, Sweetheart," Rosemary Clooney's "Come on-a My House," and Tex Ritter's "High Noon." "High Noon" was the first big movie "theme." It was from the Gary Cooper picture of the same name. The tune was billed as "an original folk song by Dimitri Tiomkin," and it was so catchy that General Eisenhower couldn't get it out of his mind; he went around whistling it for months. In none of the lively arts was there anything startling or jumpy, anything that rocked the boat. This was a seedtime, a breathing spell, a space to stretch and regroup. Sensible Democrats knew it: "I agree that it is a time for catching our breath," said Adlai Stevenson; "I agree that moderation is the spirit of the times"; and Dean Acheson advised friends to "Do what nature requires, that is to have a fallow period."

In the hiatus between the Truman and Eisenhower administrations a Pueblo, Colorado, businessman and amateur named Morey Bernstein was preparing to make psychic history by mesmerizing an attractive thirty-three-year-old woman named Virginia Tighe. Until Bernstein fixed her with his eye she had been an ordinary Colorado housewife. Under his spell she spoke with a soft brogue, danced a jig, and identified herself as an Irishwoman named Bridey Murphy. Careful inquiries in Ireland disclosed that there had been such a person; she had been born in Cork in 1758 and was buried there. It then developed that Virginia, while speaking as Bridey, possessed an encyclopedic knowledge of early nineteenth-century Cork — its people, its places, and its customs. After a newspaper series about her appeared in the *Denver Post*, Virginia became a nationwide sensation. Bernstein's book about her, *The Search for Bridey Murphy*, went through eight printings; 30,000 long-playing records of her voice, speaking as Bridey, were sold at $5.95.

Psychiatrists, though stumped, suggested that Virginia could have woven together fragments of memory that lay in her subconscious. Sure enough, the *Chicago American* found that a Mrs. Anthony Corkell, née Murphy, had lived just across the street during Virginia's impressionable childhood. Mrs. Corkell had come from Cork. At the child's urging, she had repeatedly described her early life in Ireland and stories about it she had heard from her mother.

Receipts for motion picture theaters continued to be low. The storm that greeted Brigitte Bardot's performance in *And God Created Woman* says much about the 1950s. "There lies Brigitte," *Time* gasped, "stretched from end to end of the Cinemascope screen, bottoms up and bare as a censor's eyeball." The bowdlerizers did their duty. France's most famous piece of baggage could be seen only in the art theaters of very large cities, and not always there; Providence, Fort Worth, Memphis, and Philadelphia banned her outright. For a while, in the month of the Eisenhower landslide, movie exhibitors thought they might have something new in the deepies. Deepies were being hailed by their developers as the sequel to talkies. They were in 3-D photography; you put on a pair of glasses with cardboard rims, and you were on a roller coaster run amok, hurtling downward at 150 mph, or watching a spear sail right out of the screen headed for your throat. The first feature-length deepie, *Bwana Devil*, opened in Los Angeles on November 26, 1952. In one week it earned $95,000, and a Paramount executive, scoffing at the suggestion that the need to wear spectacles would ultimately mean poor box office, said, "They'll wear toilet seats around their necks if you give them what they want to see!"

Then the novelty wore off, and sure enough, the deepies were as dead as Vitaphone.

The Ike-Stevenson campaign had been accompanied by two other fads: flying saucers and painting by the numbers. The first sighting of an airborne saucer is believed to have occurred in 1947, when a pilot in the state of Washington reported nine unidentified flying objects (UFOs) resembling shallow dishes and moving at about 1,200 mph in the skies above Yakima Indian Reservation. By the time of Ike's election the baffled Air Force was investigating fifty UFO reports a month; at the end of the decade $500,000 would have been spent on them, and the mystery would be as great as ever.

There was nothing unfathomable about enumerated art. It was a kind of crib for the inartistic, allowing them to pass themselves off as painters without creating anything. In a decade remarkable for its high incidence of sham, it served as a cultural weathercock. The idea of providing color-coded canvases is attributed to the Palmer Paint Company of Detroit. Customers bought an intricate outline of a still life, say, or a portrait — Milton Berle was a favorite. With it came as many as fifty oils or watercolors, each numbered. Matching numbers were stamped on the canvas, or paper. If sepia was 14, you covered every 14 area with it, and so on. Using the Palmer method, you could reproduce Leonardo da Vinci's *The Last Supper* for $11.50 plus tax, with a "beautiful antique gold frame" thrown in. The frame was plastic.

At 5:30 in the starlit morning of Saturday, November 29, 1952, two men in heavy overcoats, their collars turned up against the cold, emerged from 60 Morningside Drive in Manhattan and entered a black limousine waiting at the curb. One of them was Secret Service agent Edward Green; the other was the President-elect of the United States. At that hour there was no traffic in the city. The car moved swiftly down the deserted streets toward the East River, crossed the Triborough Bridge, and swung across Long Island to a back road paralleling Mitchel Field. There two Constellations were waiting, the fastest aircraft in that pre-jet age. One was for the general, who hurriedly mounted the ramp, buffeted by a sharp, chill wind.

The other plane would carry Ike's staff. All over metropolitan New York, Secret Service automobiles had been coming and going through the small hours of that Saturday morning, their movements synchronized with those of the President-elect's limousine. Extraordinary measures had been taken to make certain that no outsider's curiosity was aroused. Eminent men awaiting transport had left home and dawdled at unfamiliar street corner rendezvous; Defense Secretary-designate Charles E. Wilson, the president of General Motors, had awaited his driver by hanging around Grand Central Station pretending to be a stranded passenger. Press Secretary Jim Hagerty had prepared a simulated Eisenhower agenda crowded with fake appointments. These would be released to the press, which would be told that the general was working busily at home. Reporters conscientiously standing watch at 60 Morningside Drive would see a steady procession of distinguished statesmen arriving and departing, for Hagerty had left nothing to chance. It was thought unlikely that Communists would make an attempt on Eisenhower's life, but with international tension as taut as it was, nobody was taking any chances.

The two planes landed outside Seoul Tuesday at 8 P.M. Generals Mark Clark and James A. Van Fleet met them. Their former commanding officer and next commander in chief spent three days in Korea, studying situation maps, listening to artillery fire, and visiting infantrymen. The American people first learned of the journey on Saturday, December 6. In a statement released by Hagerty they were warned that their next President had "no panaceas, no solutions," but assured that "much can be done and much will be done" to back the embattled U.N. forces along the 38th Parallel. Ike, meantime, was bound for Honolulu aboard the U.S. Navy cruiser *Helena* with his advisers. Caustic Democrats assumed that his only reason for flying the Pacific had been to fulfill his campaign pledge. It is true that he had achieved little in his seventy-two hours there, but there was more to the trip than that. Word that he had gone to the front was a sorely needed boost to U.S. morale, and the sight of the ice-rimmed foxholes had reminded him, as nothing else could, of the desperate need for a truce. Finally, there was the cruise on the *Helena*. During it he received and pondered advice from Douglas MacArthur, met and chose the next chairman of the Joint Chiefs, Admiral Arthur W. Radford, and became better acquainted with the man he had designated Secretary of State, John Foster Dulles. Since each of these last three believed that America's adversaries understood nothing but naked force, the trip was a fateful one.

The general had never before met the admiral, who came on board at Iwo Jima in his role as Commander in Chief, Pacific. Omar Bradley's second term as JCS chairman would expire in August, and Eisenhower had come to the conclusion that Bradley's successor must be a man who believed, as Charles E. Wilson did, that Asia would be the pivot of the cold war in the 1950s. Radford more than met that test; he was so ardent a champion of the Pacific theater that he wouldn't even hear of closing down Sand Point Naval Station in Seattle. He also agreed with their choice of a new strategic concept. Ike believed that huge defense budgets played into Stalin's hands; if the new administration tried to meet every Communist threat around the globe, he argued, it would spend the country into oblivion. More sensible, in his view, was a policy of discouraging aggression by building up a large stockpile of nuclear weapons. If the Soviet Union knew that a hopeless confrontation could end in bombs being unloaded on the Kremlin, the chances for world peace would be greater, or so the theory went. Dulles liked it. Later he would call it "massive retaliation."

It was dangerous, of course, and the subsequent debate over it became one of the great political issues of the 1950s. Some Democrats blamed it on George Humphrey, who would be Ike's Secretary of the Treasury. Humphrey was a passionate advocate of balanced budgets, and the Pentagon was the biggest spender of federal money. But Humphrey was only one of many converts to massive retaliation. Another was MacArthur. While aboard the *Helena* Eisenhower read that his old chief had told an NAM convention that he had "a clear and definite solution to the Korean conflict," involving "no increased danger of provoking universal conflict." He refused to disclose it publicly, but said he would give it to the President-elect. Most of the notables on the *Helena* no longer took MacArthur seriously. Ike disagreed. He wired the Waldorf that he looked forward to a meeting where "I may obtain the full benefit of your thinking and experience." MacArthur replied that he was pleased, "especially so because, despite my intimate personal and professional concern therewith, this is the first time that the slightest official interest in my counsel has been evidenced since my return."

On December 9 Hagerty released the exchange to the press. Harry Truman read it next morning while returning to Washington from his mother-in-law's funeral, and he all but went through the roof. If General MacArthur knew of a sensible way to end the fighting, he said, it was his duty to lay it before the President of the United States. At a press conference the following day he said he doubted that MacArthur had a workable plan. While still seething, he fired a salvo at the *Helena*. Ike's pledge to visit Korea, he said, had been an irresponsible piece of campaign demagogy. Everybody was angry now. MacArthur's thoughts were scarcely worth the price — calling at the Waldorf when he reached New York, Ike learned that his idea was to threaten Peking with extermination — and all hope was now gone for a smooth transition between incoming and outgoing administrations.

Prospects for it had never been great. Before flying to Seoul Eisenhower and his aides had called at the White House in an attempt to mesh the two foreign policies. Truman had introduced Acheson, who had reviewed world trouble spots. He dwelt at length on Vietnam, where the big question, he said, was whether the French had the will to carry on the fight against the Communists.

Ike wanted a good start, but he had his own way of preparing for it. His concept of leadership reflected his faith in experts and the delegation of authority. Sherman Adams was to be his chief of staff, with the title "the Assistant to the President." Beneath Adams would be the cabinet. Selecting it was the President-elect's first crucial task. Most Presidents have found the cabinet too unwieldy to be of much use as a deliberative body; they have preferred to work with the White House staff, leaving the secretaries to administer the departments. Eisenhower intended to treat his cabinet as a national council, laying all important matters before it; so instead of working in tandem with Truman and Acheson in the weeks before his inauguration, he would put his designated secretaries through two rehearsals at the Commodore Hotel in New York on January 12 and 13.

His appointees reflected his admiration for the American business community. Ike wanted his stewardship to be remembered as a business administration, and said so frequently. In his opinion, businessmen were abler than military men, and both more competent than politicians. To him, politicians were men of very small caliber. At the pinnacle of his value scale were the great captains of industry. His designated cabinet was so heavily weighted with them that Stevenson called it "the Big Deal," and TRB, writing in the *New Republic*, said it comprised "eight millionaires and a plumber." The plumber was Martin P. Durkin, a union leader. He was chosen to lead the Labor Department.

Humphrey at the Treasury, Wilson in the Pentagon, Attorney General Brownell, Postmaster General Summerfield, Secretary of Agriculture Ezra Taft Benson, Douglas McKay at Interior, Secretary of Commerce Sinclair Weeks, Oveta Culp Hobby, who would become the first Secretary of Health, Education and Welfare when the department was created April 11 — the change from the Democratic appointees was breathtaking. Three of the newcomers would be General Motors men: Wilson and Summerfield and McKay, who were Chevrolet dealers. (During one stormy session of the new cabinet, Jerry Persons passed a note to Emmet John Hughes: "From now on, I'm buying nothing but Plymouths.") Since GM accounted for 7.8 percent of all Pentagon business, Wilson had to sell his stock in it. Then Ike insisted that all his nominees do the same.

Like Eisenhower himself, his designated secretaries were farther to the right on some issues than Republican politicians — Taft confided to friends that he had misgivings over the number of industrialists high in the government — and their rhetoric was more conservative still. In the coming months the country would be provided with some striking examples of it. The most voluble member of the new administration was Wilson, nicknamed "Engine Charlie" (the president of General Electric was named Charles E. Wilson, too). Engine Charlie sometimes claimed that he was misquoted, and he was sometimes right. He never said, "What's good for General Motors is good for the country." What he said, in testifying before a Senate committee weighing his confirmation, was, "What was good for our country was good for General Motors, and vice versa" — a very different remark, one that was turned round by liberal reporters unsympathetic to the new regime. Wilson was capable of gaffes of his own, however. In dismissing complaints of excessive Pentagon spending he said, "I didn't come down here to run a grocery store."

Hughes has left a memorable description of Eisenhower's slow burn whenever he learned of a feisty Wilson remark; first came an "audible grinding of teeth," then a "strained tightening of the mouth," and lastly a "slow, pained rolling of the bright blue eyes heavenward." Engine Charlie's colleagues were sometimes stricken by foot-in-mouth attacks, too. George Humphrey said of Ernest Hemingway's 1952 novel, *The Old Man and the Sea*, "Why should anyone be interested in some old man who was a failure and never amounted to anything, anyway?" Weeks admitted that he didn't really believe in government regulation of trade, his job under Ike. Benson liked to talk about the "spiritual side" of farm prices. Confronted by a proposal to provide the country's children with free Salk vaccine, Mrs. Hobby denounced it as "socialized medicine" by "the back door." Another member of the administration, Howard Pyle, who as a deputy assistant to the President was privy to cabinet confidences, permitted himself to be quoted as saying that "the right to suffer is one of the joys of a free economy."

Seen in retrospect, the incoming cabinet was more impressive than any of those remarks would indicate. As a group it was characterized by dedication, industry, sobriety, and patriotism. Week after week the secretaries punctually took their places at their long coffin-shaped table in the West Wing of the White House, sitting erect on their high-backed black leather chairs, solemnly fingering the little white notebooks before them and nodding gravely whenever the chief executive spoke. Luckily they were not easily daunted, for their new burdens were immense. None of them, not even Wilson, had been asked to cope with anything anywhere near as large as the U.S. government of January 1953. The last time a Republican had occupied the White House there had been 630,000 civilian employees on the federal payroll. Now there were 2,561,000, a fourfold increase, and the budget, having risen from $3,863,000,000 to $85,400,000,000, was more than twenty times as large.

In some ways the most interesting figure in the new administration was the youngest and most partisan Republican at the cabinet table. Hughes saw Vice President Nixon as "crisp and practical and logical: never proposing major objectives, but quick and shrewd in suggesting or refining methods — rather like an effective trial lawyer, I kept thinking, with an oddly slack interest in the law." Like the others, Nixon sometimes made Ike wince. In discussing early Eisenhower decisions on television he said, "Incidentally, in mentioning Secretary Dulles, isn't it wonderful, finally, to have a Secretary of State who isn't taken in by the Communists, who stands up to them?" When Earl Warren was appointed to replace Fred Vinson, the Vice President incensed Ike by calling Warren "a great Republican Chief Justice,"* and he was photographed smiling over the rim of a wineglass at the Dominican Republic's Rafael Trujillo Molina while proposing "A toast to this great country and its illustrious ruler."

Those preinaugural cabinet meetings in the Commodore foreshadowed much that would follow in the Eisenhower years. From the very beginning they were devout. Each meeting opened with a silent prayer or a few

---

*Afterward he said he had meant to insert a comma between "Republican" and "Chief." Ike was unpropitiated.

prayerful words from Benson, who was one of the Council of Twelve Apostles of the Mormon Church. If Eisenhower forgot it, Dulles would clear his throat and murmur a reminder, and Ike would blurt out, "Oh my gosh! And I really need all the help we can get up there this morning. Ezra, please . . ." There was also a tremendous amount of talk. At that time the chief topic was the coming ceremony in Washington. Despite Democratic grumbling Ike had decided to replace the traditional toppers with homburgs — an illustration of his preference for the informal, one reason for his popularity in the new suburbs. He also read to the group the remarks he would make after taking the oath and, when they applauded, modestly protested that he had presented it "more for your blue pencils than your applause." Wilson said, "You flew the flag! It was wonderful!" Engine Charlie, it quickly developed, relished having the first word on any subject. When the President-elect spoke of one of his most cherished beliefs — the need for free trade with all nations, including the Communists — Wilson snapped, "Well, I'm a little old-fashioned. I don't like selling fire-arms to the Indians." That secretly pleased the anti-Communist vigilantes, but he could shock them, too; in a discussion of the possibilities for a cease-fire in Korea he asked, "Is there any possibility for a package deal? Maybe we could recognize Red China and get the Far East issues settled."

Eisenhower's preparations having gone well in New York, he left there on Sunday, January 18, 1953, and rode to Washington with his family on the Pennsylvania Railroad's Business Car No. 90, the same one he had used on his return from Europe in 1945. The capital's quadrennial upheaval had already begun. Every hotel room was occupied. The *New York Times* reported that hairdressers were offering a "Mamie bang" for $2 a coiffure if the customer wanted her own hair curled and anywhere up to $17.50 for "store hair." The President-elect was too busy to notice such trivia. His train had left Manhattan an hour late because he had been revising his inaugural address at the Commodore, and he and his staff continued to hone it Monday in the Statler's twelfth-floor presidential suite, three blocks from the White House. Unfortunately, too many advisers had a hand in it. As delivered Tuesday noon, it was prosy and tedious. The prayer preceding it, on the other hand, was entirely his own, and it gave that day its one really unforgettable moment. It reminded the country of the new President's most prized attribute, that of a unifier and healer. During the parade down Pennsylvania Avenue that followed, a button vendor checked his stock and made an interesting discovery. Two of his novelty pins read "I like every-body" and "I hate everybody." His supply of the first was exhausted; that of the second was almost untouched. To a bystander he remarked, "Most people like everybody today. We're not moving the 'hate' ones, except to kids."

Democrats had little reason to feel cheerful, though. Still smarting from Truman's brickbats, Ike had declined the outgoing President's invitation to share his last White House breakfast. Dulles had already twice called on

Acheson, who rather wished he hadn't. Though both men were cold war hard-liners, they agreed on little else. Acheson suspected — correctly, it later developed — that his successor would bow to McCarthy pressure and dismiss John Carter Vincent, an able foreign service officer who had drawn the senator's fire.

McCarthy became a Republican problem at the stroke of noon on January 20. The GOP had been dishing out criticism for twenty years — the tenure of only one Republican senator reached back to the last Republican President — and now they would be taking it. Departing Democrats felt a surge of relief. Riding from 1600 Pennsylvania Avenue to Acheson's Georgetown home, Margaret Truman turned to her father and said jubilantly, "Hi, *Mister* Truman!" He looked astonished for an instant; then he laughed. There had been no advance word of his plans, yet the pavement outside Acheson's P Street home was crowded with five hundred well-wishers, and at Union Station five thousand had gathered to see the last departure of the "Ferdinand Magellan" for Independence. From the platform Truman told them that he would never forget this gesture "if I live to be a hundred"; chopping air in a parody of his awkward campaign gesture, he added with mock stridency, "And that's just what I expect to do!" The engineer gave a warning toot, the train lurched forward. A lone voice sang the first few bars of "Auld Lang Syne"; then, as the crowd joined in a thundering chorus, Truman receded into history.

The Executive Mansion, early Wednesday, January 21, 1953:

Although visits to two inaugural balls kept him up until nearly 2 A.M., the new President rises as usual at 7:30 and breakfasts alone in his bedroom with his customary half-grapefruit and coffee. Washington is a city of late risers, but West Point taught Ike that an early start is a virtue, and he still believes it; despite anguished protests he will schedule his weekly breakfast meetings with the National Security Council and the legislative leadership at 8 A.M., and his daily calendar will start no later than 8:30. Now, slipping into a dark brown suit and knotting a figured tie, he descends to the first floor and strides vigorously to the oval office in the West Wing, where Sherman Adams, also a lifelong early bird, awaits him. Squatting on a table behind the President's red leather desk chair is an ornate green marble clock-barometer, bought during the Grant administration for $400. Ike sets it. He is a methodical man; he will do it every morning.

His first appointment, at 8:02 A.M., is with Brownell. They discuss a few procedural matters; the cabinet will be sworn in at 5:30 P.M. in the East Room, and Wilson won't be able to make it because he is still selling his $2,500,000 of GM stock. (Republican Wayne Morse of Oregon will take the Senate floor today to urge that Wilson's name be withdrawn. Morse will be a liberal thorn in the administration's side throughout the decade, and eventually he will switch to the other party.) Brownell leaves for the Justice Department and is succeeded by Mr. and Mrs. James Bradshaw

Mintener of Minneapolis. Mintener is general counsel for Pillsbury Mills. This is a social visit. Last spring he organized the Eisenhower write-in campaign in the Minnesota primary, and this is his reward.

The morning fills up with routine presidential business. Twenty-nine horsemen wearing red jackets and white caps swarm in; they are members of the Palomino Mounted Patrol of Colorado, which rode in yesterday's parade, and each gets an Eisenhower handshake. They are followed by the Junior Police Band of Denver, shepherded by Police Chief Herbert E. Forsyth. The mail room sends up good news: yesterday's events have inspired 1,500 congratulatory telegrams. Two Republican governors arrive for a fried chicken lunch. It is afternoon before Ike, preparing for a conference over his first State of the Union address, discovers that he doesn't have a key to his desk.

The key is provided by Adams, who also deals with most of the paperwork which, under Ike's predecessors, had been handled by the chief executive. With Persons and Hagerty, Adams is one of the three aides closest to the President. Except for Dulles, who can talk to Eisenhower at any time, everyone in the administration must approach the President through the former New Hampshire governor. On most matters his scrawled "OK, SA" is as good as a presidential signature. On a typical day he will handle 250 calls. Adams runs a trim ship; White House workers are warned against gossip sessions, smoking in corridors, putting their feet on desks, or other "eccentric habits" in "deportment."

While his executive officer toils, the commander ponders larger issues and keeps himself fit. At sixty-two the thirty-fourth President of the United States is a bald, handsome, energetic, ruddy, square-shouldered man standing five feet ten inches tall and weighing 178 pounds, just six pounds over his cadet weight forty years earlier. He holds his head high, his jaw set, and his strong mouth taut. In anger he will sock his right fist into his left palm and squeeze it; in repose his expression is stern, and if he chooses to be aloof his manner can be arctic. His most striking feature, however, is his famous grin.

Hoover kept fit with a medicine ball, FDR swam, Truman walked; Ike golfs. Outside, by the White House rose garden, the United States Golf Association is installing a putting green for him, and in good weather he will make iron shots across the Mansion's south grounds. On wet days he can swing clubs in his high-ceilinged bedroom. Directly across the hall from it he will soon convert a spare bedroom into a studio. The new First Lady gave him his first oils for Christmas after the war, and painting has become a serious hobby for him. At present he is working on portraits of his chief advisers. Democratic critics will tell how Adams, trying to handle a half-dozen crises at once, received a call from his chief asking, "Are your eyes blue?" They will remind the country that no President since Coolidge has relaxed more. An Eisenhower agenda, they will gibe, is a list of steps he will refrain from taking, and TRB will write in the *New Republic*: "The public loves Ike. The less he does the more they love him. That, probably, is the secret. Here is a man who doesn't rock the boat."*

Like most men in public life, Eisenhower dislikes wearing spectacles. Ann Whitman, his secretary, copies manuscripts of his speeches on a special machine with outsize type. Rather than carry his bifocals in his pocket, he leaves a dozen pairs lying around the Mansion; when thoughtful he will pick one up and chew at the earpiece. Paperback westerns are still his favorite light reading. His favorite author is Luke Short, though he has also read the first two books of Bruce Catton's Civil War trilogy, *Mr. Lincoln's Army* and *Glory Road,* and soon he will tackle the third, *A Stillness at Appomattox.* At his direction the collected works of Jefferson and Lincoln have been put on his office shelves. He will dip into them when he has time. One passage from Lincoln — Volume II, 1848–1858 — describes his own approach to the Presidency. He likes to quote it:

> The legitimate object of government, is to do for a community of people, whatever they need to have done, but can not do at all, or can not, so well do, for themselves — in their separate, and individual capacities.
> In all that the people can individually do as well for themselves, government ought not to interfere.

Beginning at 10:30 A.M. next Wednesday, he will meet White House correspondents regularly in the Indian Treaty Room of the Executive Office Building next door. In those sessions he will often seem unaware of major events. To the embarrassment of his aides, he will admit it is true: "You're telling me something about my own administration I never heard of," he will say. He will dismay them with awkward straggling sentences that wander over the landscape in defiance of all grammatical and syntactic rules. Clever reporters will write an Eisenhower version of the Gettysburg address:

> I haven't checked these figures, but 87 years ago, I think it was, a number of individuals organized a governmental set-up here in this country, I believe it covered certain Eastern areas, with this idea they were following up based on a sort of national independence arrangement and the program that every individual is just as good as every other individual. . . .

It is true that the only newspaper he usually reads is the Republican *Herald Tribune.* It is not true that his press conference manner is wholly inept (when Adams worries about a delicate subject before a press conference Ike will say with a wicked grin, "I'll just confuse 'em!") or that he spends most of his evenings watching television. His only regular TV program is the *Fred Waring Show,* Sunday evenings from nine to nine-thirty. He will attend the movies shown in the White House basement theater but rarely. His idea of pleasant diversion is a dinner with eight or

*Some of the moves Ike did not make are worth noting. He did not invade Manchuria, send American troops to Indochina, wage preventive war, replace containment with a policy of "liberation," or end American participation in NATO — all measures that were urged on him by powerful advocates in his own party and administration.

ten congenial men in the solarium on the White House roof, with himself broiling steaks on a portable charcoal grill. Those invited to such an evening receive a note on monogrammed "DDE" stationery, usually addressed to them by their first names:

> I wonder if it would be convenient for you to come to an informal stag dinner on the evening of Tuesday, May twenty-eighth. I hope to gather together a small group, and I should like very much for you to attend if it is possible for you to do so. . . . Because of the informality of the occasion, I suggest that we meet at the White House about seven-fifteen, have a reasonably early dinner, and devote the evening to a general chat . . . I shall probably wear a dinner jacket, but a business suit will be entirely appropriate.
>
> With warm regard,
>
> Sincerely,
> DE

Who will be invited? Not politicians; in his opinion his responsibilities require him to see too much of them as it is. Not his administrators; once he has found a competent manager for a department or a bureau he assumes that he has done his duty and promptly forgets him and it. If Ike wants the evening to end in a bridge game, he taps one of his favorite partners — General Alfred M. Gruenther of NATO; William E. Robinson, president of Coca-Cola; or Clifford Roberts, an investment banker. For general conversation the President casts a wider net, but the guest list is drawn from the same group. A *U.S. News & World Report* survey of "presidential playtime companions" finds only one man associated even remotely with public life, an ex-governor of Colorado. Among the others are two cattlemen, two oilmen, two distillers, two golf champions, two realtors, and three bank presidents. Businessmen prevail — executives from hotel, soft drink, publishing, insurance, home appliance, and tire enterprises — and those not in industry are established conservatives: Herbert Hoover, Douglas MacArthur, Francis Cardinal Spellman, Bernard Baruch.

What will they discuss? If this is to be their first visit, some time must be spent admiring mementos presented to the general by grateful Allied governments. There is no way to avoid them; Ike has filled the presidential apartment's white oval study with cases displaying the awards and called it his "trophy room."* But in an hour the banter may run from rock gardens to modern architecture, Pat and Mike jokes, French cooking, good bourbon, Turkish baths, automobile styling, vegetable farming, Jewish humor, and poker. As a conversationalist, he prefers the specific to the general; mention McCarthy's flouting of constitutional rights and his attention wanders, but describe a victim of witch hunts and he is with you all the way, provided, that is, you are not bitter. The venomous and mean-spirited are unwelcome

---

*To allay confusion: there are two oval rooms in the White House. The oval *office* is in the West Wing. The oval *study*, on the second floor of the Mansion, is in the First Family's living quarters.

here. Ike is generous, and expects his friends to be the same. Only gentlemen are admitted to these rooms. The rest must deal with Sherman Adams.

Robert A. Taft's political skills had never been more masterful, or his energy so inexhaustible. He was swarming all over the Hill, organizing the 83rd Congress, outwitting his adversaries, rewarding his allies, deciding who should have which office — doing everything, in short, but painting the Capitol dome, and some days he seemed capable of that. Taft made himself majority leader and put all key committee chairmanships in the hands of his ultraconservative friends: Eugene Millikin, Styles Bridges, William Langer, Hugh Butler, Homer Ferguson, and William Knowland. The Ike-before-Chicago senators — Carlson of Kansas, Ives of New York, Duff of Pennsylvania — found themselves consigned to unpopular, insignificant duties. In cutting up the senatorial pie Taft made but one slip. He thought he had outmaneuvered Joe McCarthy into the Government Operations Committee. There, it was expected, he would spend his time poring over figures from the General Services Administration. Taft said, "We've got McCarthy where he can't do any harm."

The first gavel had hardly fallen before Joe began looking for trouble. He found it in the list of administration nominees up for senatorial confirmation. At first glance the names seemed flawless, but McCarthy could find sin anywhere. James B. Conant was Ike's choice for high commissioner in Germany. The senator declared that as president of Harvard Conant held opinions "contrary to the prevailing philosophy of the American people." Eisenhower wanted General Walter Bedell Smith as Undersecretary of State. Smith was a formidable figure; he had been Eisenhower's chief of staff in World War II, and since then he had served as director of the CIA and as U.S. ambassador to the Soviet Union. Joe countered that Smith had testified at a pretrial hearing in a libel suit against McCarthy, and was known to have defended diplomat John Paton Davies despite charges made against him by McCarthy and Pat McCarran. The Senate wasn't ready to defy a popular President on such dubious grounds. Conant and Smith were approved. But McCarthy had staked his claim. The White House had been put on notice; he meant to be reckoned with.

The serious reckoning was over the appointment of Charles E. Bohlen to the Moscow embassy. Bohlen was important to Eisenhower and Dulles. He was the State Department's authority on the Soviet Union. In that role he had served as FDR's interpreter at Yalta, and anyone associated with that hated name was anathema to the Republican Right. In hearings before the Foreign Relations Committee Bohlen steadfastly refused to condemn the Yalta Conference. He even defended it against its senatorial critics as having been in the best interests of the United States at that time. With that, the gauntlet was down. Power was at stake; somebody had to lose.

The ultraconservatives subjected the Bohlen nomination to a rising stream of abuse. Bridges told the Senate that the Moscow appointment should go to "a deserving Republican." On March 20 McCarran charged that R. W. Scott McLeod, a McCarthy man who had been appointed the State Department's security chief, had been "unable to clear" Bohlen on the basis of "information received by the FBI"; McLeod had been "summarily overridden" by Dulles. The secretary immediately denied it. Later in the day McCarthy called Dulles a liar and demanded that he testify under oath. He said he knew what was in Bohlen's file, and that calling him a security risk was "putting it too weak." By now McLeod was distraught. Trapped between warring giants, he sought refuge in the White House. It was all a grotesque mistake, he told Adams and Persons. He had merely called Dulles's attention to certain "derogatory material" in Bohlen's FBI file. McLeod offered to resign, but Adams told him that if he did, the already unpleasant situation would only seem worse.

Dulles assured the Foreign Relations Committee that FBI investigators had "no doubt" of Bohlen's loyalty, but to the Senate ultraconservatives even a conservative Secretary of State was suspect. The only solution was for Taft and Sparkman of Alabama, who had been Stevenson's running mate, to form a two-man commission and study the FBI's Bohlen file together. On March 25 Taft reported their findings to the Senate:

> There was no suggestion anywhere by anyone reflecting on the loyalty of Mr. Bohlen in any way or any association by him with Communism or support of Communism or even tolerance of Communism . . . There was not any suggestion that would in my opinion create even a *prima facie* case or a *prima facie* charge of any ill doing on the part of Mr. Bohlen.

Nevertheless, McCarthy still wanted Bohlen's scalp. Eisenhower told White House correspondents that the diplomat's name would remain before the Senate. America's best interests would be served by the appointment, and that, said the President, was that. Responsible Republicans were left with little choice. Taft's personal opinion of Bohlen was low, but as majority leader he could hardly lead a revolt against Ike, especially since the evidence all ran the other way. With his great strength in the Senate he put the nomination through, 74 votes to 13.

At a glance McCarthy seemed to have sustained a defeat. Actually it was the other way round. The issue had divided Taft's forces; he didn't want to see another like it, and he sent Ike the price of his support: "No more Bohlens!" The President's aides had come to the same conclusion on their own. Meanwhile, the Wisconsin senator planned fresh outrages. In all Washington, it seemed, there was not one Republican prepared to defy Joseph R. McCarthy.

Forming battle lines against him, the new administration was weakened by several unwise campaign promises. The party platform adopted in Chicago had been a hodgepodge reflecting two decades of broken hopes, myths nursed in defeat, and promissory notes for heavy Republican contributors. One of them pledged Eisenhower to return rich submerged coastal lands to the states. The President redeemed it in full, despite a Wayne Morse filibuster, but his prestige suffered; he had entered politics as a crusader, and the quarrel over tidelands oil was no crusade. At George Humphrey's urging he met another campaign commitment on February 6, ordering an immediate end to wage controls and removing from controls a vast range of consumer goods, including meat, furniture, clothing, meals in restaurants, and almost all articles sold in retail stores. Then Humphrey also demanded tighter federal credit and a deep cut in defense appropriations. Here, too, Ike acceded, disappointing consumer advocates and paving the way, it later developed, for recession in late 1953 and the first half of 1954.

Republican myths were wildest in foreign affairs. Taiwan was the subject of one. In sending ships and planes to Korea on June 27, 1950, Truman had also declared:

> The occupation of Formosa by Communist forces would be a direct threat to the security of the Pacific area and to the United States forces pursuing their lawful and necessary functions. Accordingly, I have ordered the Seventh Fleet to prevent any attack on Formosa. As a corollary of this action, I am calling upon the Chinese government on Formosa to cease all air and sea operations against the mainland. The Seventh Fleet will see that this is done.

Acheson had called this "neutralizing" Formosa. The Republican ultra-conservatives disapproved of it. In their view measures to neutralize Chiang Kai-shek were neither sensible nor loyal to the United States. Against all evidence, they were convinced that Chiang could easily defeat Mao Tse-tung's armies now, and that keeping him bottled up on the island was part of a sinister conspiracy. As a demonstration of their faith in Kuomintang arms, McCarthy, Knowland, and Bridges attended a formal dinner in the Chinese embassy and joined in the shouted Nationalist pledge, "Back to the mainland!" They stood up to do it, and the Chinese ambassador applauded vigorously.

They had vowed to "unleash Chiang Kai-shek." Eisenhower never used the phrase, but it was in the platform, and at his order the Joint Chiefs cabled the Seventh Fleet:

2 FEB 53

OPERATIONAL IMMEDIATE
TO: CINCPAC PEARL HARBOR TH
INFO: CINCFE TOKYO JAPAN

THAT PORTION UR CURRENT DIRECTIVE WHICH REQUIRES YOU INSURE THAT FORMOSA AND PESCADORES WILL NOT RPT NOT BE USED AS BASES OPNS AGAINST CHI MAINLAND BY CHI NATS IS RESCINDED.

But how could Chiang reconquer the mainland? Lacking ships, how could he even reach it? Still, Eisenhower went along with the fantasy. In drafting his State of the Union message he wrote that as a consequence of Truman's order, "the United States Navy was required to serve as a defensive arm of Communist China." Lewis Carroll could not have turned things round more. Furthermore, talk of reopening China's civil war was provocative; when word of it leaked through the press Anthony Eden warned the President that it might have "very unfortunate political repercussions without compensating military advantages." Disturbed, Ike decided on the way to Capitol Hill to end the passage on a peaceful note: "Permit me to make it crystal clear this order implies no aggressive intent on our part." What really became crystal clear was that Chiang, having been unleashed, possessed no teeth. Unhampered by Seventh Fleet patrols, Communist Chinese made a few exploratory amphibious moves and found that the Nationalists lacked strength to dominate or even make a showing in Formosa Strait. As the months passed Chiang came to miss American warships more and more, and on the first anniversary of Eisenhower's order to the Joint Chiefs the *New York Times* reported the results: eleven coastal islands had been lost to the Communists. The administration had by no means heard the last of Formosa. Because of possible political ramifications in the United States, or just to ward off Democratic horse laughs, the Seventh Fleet was recalled. The term for that was "releashing Chiang."

The Chicago platform had further vowed to "repudiate all commitments contained in secret understandings such as those of Yalta which aid Communist enslavements." In writing that plank Dulles, like the rest of his party's leaders, had believed some things about the American State Department which simply were not true. They were convinced that the Communist empire had been built by Communists and Democrats at Teheran, Yalta, and Potsdam. They had resolved to set this wrong right. In his first speech as Secretary of State Dulles advised eastern Europe that it could "count on us," and he wrote this passage in the President's State of the Union address: "I shall ask the Congress at a later date to join in an appropriate resolution making clear that this government recognizes no kind of commitment contained in secret understandings of the past which permit . . . enslavement." The reference to Yalta, Potsdam, and Teheran was clear. When Eisenhower read it, the Republicans leaped to their feet cheering. The secret agreements did exist, then, they told one another; they had known it all along. Dulles at the time was still sure he would find the incriminating documents in some obscure vault at the State Department. But they weren't there. They weren't anywhere. They didn't exist. As the truth emerged, both the President and his Secretary of State began to revise their expectations. But the Republican mastodons of the Senate were already preparing a Yalta resolution. As worded by them, it would renounce all wartime agreements. If it went through, Eisenhower realized, the position of Americans in Berlin and Vienna would be extremely awkward.

The upshot was the first serious rift between the White House and the

GOP leadership on the Hill. At his February 16 weekly meeting with the Republican legislative leaders Ike presented a waffled draft prepared by him and Dulles. It was virtually meaningless; the United States would express regret over the plight of eastern Europeans and assure them that "all peaceful means" would be used to help them. Taft bridled. That wasn't at all what he had in mind. Ike pointed out that stronger wording would, among other things, offend congressional Democrats, who would look upon it as an insult to the memory of FDR. But Taft had precisely that in mind. At the next weekly meeting between the President and the legislative leadership, on February 23, Ike and the majority leader squared off again. Taft would settle for nothing less than an outright repudiation of all agreements between Roosevelt and the Russians.

At this point an outside force intruded upon the intraparty row. It was Lyndon Johnson of Texas, the Senate's new minority leader. Johnson advised the White House that Democrats were just as unhappy about the situation in eastern Europe as Republicans, and would be glad to join them in lamenting it. However, they had no intention of pleading guilty to something neither they nor their Presidents had done. Emmet Hughes and Assistant Secretary of State Thruston Morton sympathized, and the administration resolution went to the Hill without teeth. Bitter ultras there trotted out all their old clichés about the "betrayals" of Roosevelt and Truman. Taft joined other members of the Foreign Relations Committee in adding an amendment asserting that the measure "does not constitute any determination by Congress as to the validity or invalidity of any provisions" of agreements between the United States and the Soviet Union. The Senate Democratic Policy Committee took this as a reflection upon Roosevelt. They rejected the amendment, and the issue was deadlocked.

Thus a central political fact of the 1950s emerged in the fifth week of the Eisenhower Presidency: Ike's foreign policy would be backed by Democratic senators and opposed by diehards in his own party. The President, resolved to forget the past, was baffled by the ultras' determination to hold an eternal inquest into the iniquities of Yalta. For their part, they came to believe that all their misgivings at Chicago had been justified. They saw Ike as the puppet of men like Dewey and Lodge, about whose patriotism they had grave doubts. They weren't quite sure where Dulles stood (neither, at times, was Eisenhower), and they were vigilant for any State Department attempt to succor what Knowland called "the Trojan horse of containment."

In 1953 Lyndon Johnson and his Democrats saved administration measures no fewer than fifty-eight times. The "enslaved peoples" resolution was not among them, however. The question would continue to bedevil Washington until 1955, when Dulles authorized the publication of all Yalta papers and chagrined Senate ultras found no campaign ammunition in them. All this had almost come to a head two years earlier. The administration draft of the resolution had again headed the agenda for the March 9,

1953, meeting between Eisenhower and the congressional leadership, but before they could meet, fate intervened and tabled it. Stalin would be giving no more orders to anyone. On March 4 he had been mortally stricken in Moscow.

The President was dining with Mrs. Eisenhower when the bulletin came in from Moscow Radio: "The heart of the inspired continuer of Lenin's will, the wise leader and teacher of the Communist Party and Soviet people — Joseph Vissarionovich Stalin — has stopped beating." The President sent formal condolences to Moscow. To the cabinet he remarked acidly the following morning, "Ever since 1946, I know all the so-called experts have been yapping about what would happen when Stalin dies and what we, as a nation, should do about it. Well, he's dead. And you can turn the files of our government inside out — in vain — looking for any plans laid. We have no plan. We are not even sure what difference his death makes."

Alone in his office with Emmet Hughes, he paced the oval room in a wide arc. Hughes's notes of that hour offer an exceptional glimpse of Ike in action. He said:

> Look, I am tired — and I think everyone is tired — of just plain indictments of the Soviet regime. I think it would be wrong — in fact, asinine — for me to get up before the world now to make another one of those indictments. Instead, just one thing matters: what have we got to offer the world? What are we ready to do, to improve the chances of peace? . . .
>
> Here is what I would like to say.
>
> The jet plane that roars over your head costs three-quarters of a million dollars. That is more money than a man earning ten thousand dollars a year is going to make in his lifetime. What world can afford this sort of thing for long? We are in an armaments race. Where will it lead us? At worse, to atomic warfare. At best, to robbing every people and nation on earth of the fruits of their own toil.

But there could be "another road before us," he said, "the road of disarmament." If taken it would give everyone "bread, butter, clothes, homes, hospitals, schools." How could it be reached?

> Let us talk straight: no double talk, no sophisticated political formulas, no slick propaganda devices. Let us spell it out, whatever we really offer . . . withdrawal of troops here or there by both sides . . . United Nations-supervised free elections in another place . . . free and uncensored air-time for us to talk to the Russian people and for their leaders to talk to us . . . and concretely all that we would hope to do for the economic well-being of other countries.
>
> What do we say about the Soviet government? I'd like to get up and say: I am not going to make an indictment of them. The past speaks for itself. I am interested in the future. Both their government and ours now have new men in them. The slate is clean. Now let us begin talking to each other. And let us say what we've got to say so that every person on earth can under-

stand it. Here is what we propose. If you — the Soviet Union — can improve on it, we want to hear it.

This is what I want to say. And if we don't really have anything to offer, I'm not going to make a speech about it.

Sherman Adams believed that "The Chance for Peace," Ike's April 16 speech to the American Society of Newspaper Editors, was the greatest in his career. Writing in the *New Yorker,* Richard H. Rovere called it "an immense triumph," one which "firmly established his leadership in America and re-established American leadership in the world." The *New York Times* found it "magnificent and deeply moving," and even the opposition *New York Post* agreed that it was "America's voice at its best." Long afterward in the 1960s, Hughes would chiefly remember the struggle to bring it off. Dulles fought it through every draft. Once Hughes asked him whether he thought American interests would be served by any armistice in Korea. Dulles shook his head. He said, "We'd be sorry. I don't think we can get much out of a Korean settlement until we have shown — before all Asia — our clear superiority by giving the Chinese one hell of a licking." Hughes passed this along to Eisenhower, who snapped, "If Mr. Dulles and his sophisticated advisers really mean that they cannot talk peace seriously, then I am in the wrong pew." Later he said, "Sometimes Foster is just too worried about being accused of sounding like Truman and Acheson." It was a difficult speech all the way; even delivering it was agony. That day Eisenhower was suffering from a vicious stomach upset. He could hardly hold up his head and nearly collapsed at the end.

Unlike hundreds of other such addresses in the 1950s, this one launched an effective peace offensive. The Chinese were tired of fighting, too. Dulles's rigid diplomacy had given Asia the impression that the new administration was immovable; that the Americans, as an Indian newspaper put it, were "hunting peace with a gun." Now their President said they weren't. A new spirit quickened at Panmunjom. More than peaceful intentions were needed to cut the knot there, of course; the negotiators were held fast in a vise of accumulated fears, hatreds and recriminations which had reached a climax in Peking's accusations that the Americans had resorted to bacteriological warfare.* Stalin's death undoubtedly contributed to a solution by removing the hardest of all the hard-liners. Dulles subsequently became convinced that Peking was cowed by blunt warnings, relayed by Nehru, that the United States was planning to issue tactical nuclear weapons to U.N. field commanders. Threats that the war would soon spread to Manchuria were certainly made; Eisenhower later told Adams about them. However, Adams

---

*This propaganda campaign enjoyed an astonishing success in neutral nations, despite the fact that American appeals for an investigation by the International Red Cross, accepted by the Red Cross, were rejected by Peking. At the time Chinese motives were obscure. Later it was learned that their leaders used the occasion to rid China of billions of insects and rats — for centuries the source of devastating Chinese epidemics — by telling the population that they had been put there by an unscrupulous enemy.

doubted Dulles's dramatic assertion that the United States went "to the brink of total war" three times — in the Korean truce crisis of 1953, the Indochinese crisis of 1954, and the grave situation which arose from Mao's threat to invade Formosa in late 1954 and early 1955. Adams wrote: "Whether the Dulles policy was actually put to three crucial tests, as the Secretary believed it was, is a matter that is open to question. I doubt that Eisenhower was as close to the brink of war in any of these three crises as Dulles made him out to be."

In any event, Ike's appeal to reason was at the very least one clear note in an orchestration of events which roused the men on the other side and brought them back to the bargaining table. In the first sessions of the new beginning, progress was slow. The bottleneck was the fate of 132,000 North Korean soldiers in U.S. hands. The U.S. was determined to give them the right to decide whether or not they would go home. In 1945 the Allies had delivered Russian POW's, freed from the Germans, to Soviet commanders; many had then been sent to Siberia, and in some cases executed, for having allowed themselves to be captured. On May 7, 1952, Truman had declared: "We will not buy an armistice by turning over human beings for slaughter or slavery." Eisenhower was equally determined. More and more it became evident that the destiny of the POW's would determine the outcome of the talks.

The negotiations, resumed eleven days after the President's peace speech, dragged all through May. Holding the U.N. coalition together was becoming increasingly difficult. Some leaders of the European left thought there might be something to Mao's bacteriological warfare charges. At the other end of the political spectrum, ultraconservatives were urging the U.S. to ignore its timid allies and answer MacArthur's call for total victory. Ike declined. "If you go it alone in one place," he told them, "you have to go it alone everywhere." The most chauvinistic hawk in the U.S. camp was Syngman Rhee. The seventy-eight-year-old South Korean President refused to consider any agreement which would leave Korea divided. Rather than accept as a border the 38th Parallel or the front line, he was prepared to face certain annihilation by driving toward the Yalu without the U.N. Later Adams observed: "The endless efforts to appeal to Rhee's sense of reason and to make him understand that the United States could not hazard a possible world war for a unified Korea left Eisenhower and Dulles limp and baffled." The dispute with Rhee, he added, was "more nerve-racking and frustrating than the haggling with the Communists."

The old man almost sabotaged the peace. On June 4 the Chinese and North Koreans consented to an arrangement under which prisoners who declared before a neutral Repatriation Commission that they did not wish to go home would, after a 120-day waiting period, be freed and demobilized. On June 8 a protocol was initiated, and everything seemed set when, on June 18 at two o'clock in the morning in Washington, Dulles was awakened by a call from a State Department watch officer. On Rhee's orders guards had opened stockyard gates and released 25,000 anti-Communist North Koreans. The operation had been painstakingly prepared; South Korean police had provided the refugees with food, shelter, and civilian clothing. Dulles called the President — the only time Eisenhower was awakened during his eight years in the White House. Ike was shocked. As expected, the Communists that morning accused the U.N. of "deliberately conniving" with Rhee and demanded that the POW's be recaptured "immediately" — an impossibility. They broke off negotiations on June 20 and launched a major offensive.

Dulles was undiscouraged. Convinced that the enemy would be receptive to new overtures, he told Ike that if the other side was as anxious for a cease-fire as he thought, "They will overlook Rhee's impetuosity and will be content to sign an agreement, provided they are given proper assurances." Peking confirmed him, through New Delhi. That left the assurances, which required further pressure on the intractable Rhee. Ike cabled the South Korean president that he had put the U.N. command in "an impossible situation." He sent Walter S. Robertson, Assistant Secretary of State for Far Eastern Affairs, to talk to him. Robertson sat down with Rhee in Seoul and listened hour after hour, and then day after day, while the angry old man poured out his pent-up feelings. After Rhee had run out of steam Robertson explained the U.S. dilemma. After two weeks Rhee gave in.

The armistice terms, announced two weeks before the signing ceremony, satisfied no one. After 37 months of bloodshed and 2,000,000 dead, 80 percent of them civilians and 33,629 of them Americans, Korea would be returned to its *status quo ante*. Rhee had gained 2,350 square miles as against Kim Il Sung's 850, but in all other respects the settlement was a draw. No principles had been vindicated. The U.N. had not even succeeded in putting through a reliable inspection system to prevent Kim from launching another attack. The end had come as a result of negotiations begun by President Truman, yet his terms for a truce had been harsher; as Paul Douglas pointed out, Truman "would have been flayed from one end of Washington to the other if he had accepted the present agreement."

When a photographer asked Eisenhower how he felt, he said simply, "The war is over, and I hope my son is coming home soon." The White House had no other comment on the coming truce. In official Washington only the Secretary of State spoke of it with satisfaction: "For the first time in history, an international organization has stood against an aggressor . . . All free nations, large or small, are safer today because the ideal of collective security has been implemented."

This was also the interpretation of the liberal community. Liberals then were faithful to the Roosevelt-Truman concept of world government and were determined to put the best possible face on its first effort to keep the peace. Richard H. Rovere summed up their conviction that Korea had been a blazing success:

In Korea, the United States proved that its word was as good as its bond — and even better, since no bond had been given. History will cite Korea as the proving ground of collective security, up to this time no more than a plausible theory. It will cite it as the turning point of the world struggle against Communism.

Conservatives were not so easily hoodwinked. Walter Lippmann wrote in the *Herald Tribune,* "What has really happened is that both sides and all concerned have been held within a condition of mutual deterrent." The Old Guard was another matter. As Hanson W. Baldwin explained in the *New York Times,* ultraconservatives had taken it as an article of faith that Korea was "the right war in the right place at the right time if we wished to stop the spread of Asiatic Communism." They had not forgotten that the GOP platform had charged that under Truman the war had been waged by men "without will to victory" who "by their hampering orders" had "produced stalemates and ignominious bartering with our enemies." Now Korea, like Germany, was to be cut in twain. "Truman's war," as they saw it, was to become "Eisenhower's appeasement."

Jenner of Indiana and Malone of Nevada saw the approaching cease-fire as a Chinese victory. On the Senate floor Malone asked: "Does the distinguished Senator remember any change in State Department policy . . . by Mr. Dulles since he has taken office?" And Jenner responded: "I have noticed no change."

Knowland of California was asked in a broadcast interview, "Is this a truce with honor that we are about to get?" He replied, "I don't believe so," and predicted that under its terms, "Inevitably we will lose the balance of Asia." In Korea General Mark Clark said, "I cannot find it in me to exult in this hour," and General James A. Van Fleet, to whom U.N. copies of the convention would be brought for safekeeping after the ceremonies, turned away from correspondents who asked his opinion of it. "I don't know," he said tightly. "The answer must come from higher authority." The makings of an Old Guard revolt were present. All that was necessary was a signal form Robert A. Taft.

None came. The Senator from Ohio had been passing through a conversion much like that of Arthur Vandenberg seven years earlier. A gadfly and obstructionist under Roosevelt and Truman, Taft was now becoming a tower of administration strength. The crisis had come on April 30, 1953, in the Cabinet Room. Eisenhower had summoned the legislative leadership to break bad news; contrary to expectations, he would be unable to balance his first budget. Originally drawn up by Truman, it had anticipated a 9.9 billion-dollar deficit. Ike could cut that to 5.5 billion, he said, but he could slice no more without jeopardizing national security. Supportive presentations followed from Secretary Humphrey; Joseph M. Dodge, director of the budget, and Undersecretary of Defense Robert M. Keyes. The gist of them was that the cost of changing the country's static defense posture to a fluid stance, while anticipating an attack against the United States at any time, would be too expensive to permit further reductions.

Taft exploded. He lost control of himself, hammering the cabinet table with his fist and shouting in his hard, metallic voice that this Republican administration was turning out to be no different than those of the Democrats. The Pentagon was as greedy as ever. The budget would exceed 30 percent of the national income, and that was too much. Unless the government raised taxes — which at this point was inconceivable — the deficit would be outrageous. He yelled, "The one primary thing we promised the American people was reduction of expenditures! With a program like this, we'll never elect a Republican Congress in 1954! You're taking us down the same road Truman traveled! It's a repudiation of everything we promised in the campaign!" Addressing Taft at last, and speaking deliberately, Eisenhower began, "There are certain essential elements in the global strategy of the United States. They are not difficult to grasp. . . ." A concise review of cold war strategy followed.

It was a critical moment. Had Taft stalked out of the meeting, denounced the President's budget to the press, and set up a shadow cabinet on the Hill to battle the administration's foreign policy, Eisenhower's legislative program would have collapsed. Old Guard sentiment was hostile to Ike anyhow; one word from the powerful majority leader would have been enough But Taft stayed. In possession of himself once more, he merely expressed the hope for substantial reductions in next year's budget — hopes which Eisenhower assured him were justified.

The storm had passed. Taft from that moment forward was the President's most important champion. Privately he gagged on the terms of the Korean cease-fire, but he suppressed his feelings; in speaking to the press he was more cautious than the Knowlands, Jenners, and Malones. To be sure, he could be as blunt as ever. (He once said, "It isn't honest to be tactful.") He conceded that he found the prospect of a divided Korea "extremely distasteful" because it left "a condition likely to bring war at any moment" and gave the Chinese freedom to attack Vietnam. But he refused to sow discontent or counsel despair.

At about this time reporters began to notice the change in him. For six months the majority leader had served his party's President with distinction. His one goal since the inaugural, they wrote, had been to make this Republican administration a success. It had been a lonely struggle. Other senators on the Right were puzzled by his sense of loyalty, and to Democrats he was, as he always had been, an implacable adversary. Moreover, though none of them knew it yet, he was carrying another new burden. Over the past several weeks he had become increasingly aware that he was in ill heath.

It mystified him. Before launching his campaign for the GOP presidential nomination the year before, he had submitted to a thorough physical checkup. Doctors assured him that he had never been fitter. In the first three months of the 83rd Congress he had been a legislative whirlwind. Then, in mid-April while golfing with Eisenhower in Augusta, he suffered a sharp, excruciating hip pain. During the next week he couldn't sleep. Massive doses of aspirin were ineffective; so was a rest at White Sulphur Springs, Montana, in May. On June 12 he checked into New York Hospital for a battery of tests. He used the name "Howard Roberts."

Physicians there prescribed deep X-rays and cortisone, put him on crutches, told him to keep his weight off his hipbone, and insisted that he relinquish the routine chores which went with being majority leader. On June 10 he delegated day-to-day decisions to Knowland. The appointment was to be considered temporary; Taft would continue to handle policy matters and attend White House meetings insofar as his treatments would permit. Before the next congressional session he expected to be back on the floor, heartier than ever. Minority Leader Lyndon Johnson was the last man to see him on the Hill. Taft waved at him and called twice, "I'll be back in January! I'll be back in January!"

There was something heroic about Robert Taft that June. Though in almost unbelievable pain, he dragged himself to Washington garden parties with his wife Martha, herself a cripple and almost wholly dependent upon him, rather than reveal his condition to her. Like many formidable men in public life he had always removed his stern mask when crossing his own threshold. Martha knew him as a devoted husband, and to their four sons he was "Gop," a delightful companion on camping trips who loved to play hearts, chew nickel candy, and entertain them hours on end with his encyclopedic memory of Gilbert and Sullivan.

He reentered New York Hospital in early July. His condition then was reported to be "good." The doctors expected him to be back at his desk by the end of the year and able to vote in close contests before then. He was to be discharged July 23. Then they suddenly announced that he needed more therapy. Signs of leukemia had appeared in blood tests. His return to Washington was postponed indefinitely.

Progress at Panmunjom continued to be smooth. The Chinese had just erected a new pagoda there, and on a freshly lacquered table eighteen copies of the armistice agreement were executed at 10:01 A.M. July 27 (8:01 P.M. July 26 in Washington). The signers were General William K. Harrison for the U.N., tieless and without decorations, and North Korea's General Nam Il, sagging in a baggy tunic weighed down with medals. No words were spoken, no hands shaken, and on Rhee's order no South Korean participated.

President Eisenhower was on television within the hour. He said, "With special feelings of sorrow and with special gratitude, we think of those who were called to lay down their lives in that far-off land to prove once again that only courage and sacrifice can keep freedom alive on the earth." He warned that the United States had "won an armistice on a single battlefield, not peace in the world," and said he hoped it would convince people of the wisdom of negotiating differences instead of resorting to "futile battle."

It was a time to review American foreign policy and strengthen the legislative role in it, but the man who would have recognized it as such, and explained it to American conservatives, lay stricken at New York Hospital that Sunday evening. At 10:30 P.M. Thursday Taft went into a coma. Thirteen hours later he was dead.

His departure at that juncture was a catastrophe. William S. White wrote in next morning's *New York Times*, "The death of Senator Robert A. Taft of Ohio has shaken the Republican party as it has not been shaken in half a lifetime. It has removed the one real bridge between the East and Midwest in the Eisenhower administration. The loss to the administration . . . is beyond calculation."

It was in fact a national tragedy. The only American statesman who really understood the role of congressional prerogative and the danger of an omnipotent Presidency — the one man who could have foreseen the end of the long road running from Pusan to My Lai — was mourned on the Hill by politicians who by their very expressions of grief revealed how little they had understood him. The eulogy was delivered by John Bricker, Ohio's junior senator. After thirty-five thousand mourners had passed through the Capitol rotunda, where the coffin lay on the black catafalque which had been used for Taft's father and Lincoln before him, the muffled brasses of the Marine Band struck up "America the Beautiful." Bricker said: "Senator Taft never hesitated to recommend the coercion of the law. . . . During life our departed leader created to himself an everlasting memorial. His services to his government, and through government to his fellow man, go on."

That was the best Bricker could do: Taft acclaimed as a law and order man. It was an ominous sign for Eisenhower. In the months ahead the snowy-haired Ohioan would distress the administration by his advocacy of a constitutional amendment which would have sharply limited the scope of treaties to which the U.S. could be a party and the President's authority to negotiate executive agreements. After Vietnam the measure would take on a somewhat different look, but at the time Ike believed it unwise. To Knowland he wrote:

> Adoption of the Bricker Amendment . . . by the Senate would be notice to our friends as well as our enemies abroad that our country intends to withdraw from its leadership in world affairs. The inevitable reaction would be of major proportions. It would impair our hopes and plans for peace and for the successful achievement of the important international matters now under discussion.

Knowland didn't see it that way. He rarely saw things Ike's way. Over the next five years he would make the President's weekly meetings with the legislative leadership a torment from which Ike would emerge livid, exhausted, and at times almost incoherent. Ironically, Eisenhower himself was responsible for Knowland's succession to the role as majority leader. Once Taft was dead, custom dictated that the President, as head of the majority party, select the new Senate leader. But here Eisenhower's concept of his office, so very different from FDR's and Truman's, disserved him. He firmly maintained that the Executive Department was but one of the government's three equal branches, and that presidential attempts to manipulate the men on the Hill were in contempt of the Founding Fathers. This was what he meant when he called himself a "constitutional President." Because of his respect for Congress, he stood aside in the days after Taft's death. On the day of the obsequies he pointedly told the cabinet, "I want to say with all the emphasis at my command that this administration has absolutely no personal choice for new majority leader. We are not going to get into their business."

They, however, were determined to get into his. During their long struggles against programs of the last five administrations the ultras had become skillful legislative guerrillas adept at penetrating executive agencies and making the lives of civil servants unlivable. Their chief weapon was the congressional investigation. Ike had assumed that inquiries on the Hill would be held in abeyance during his first year in the White House. In his opinion, he told the cabinet, Americans had been living too long on too high a level of tension; the endless hearings under klieg lights were unnecessary now; his administration should be allowed a period of grace to clean house. Only if it failed would Congress be justified in stepping in.

Brownell wryly observed that the 83rd was already in with both feet. These were ten separate investigations of the State Department alone; State men scarcely had time to read their mail. Ike replied that the administration must cooperate with the Hill: probably they were just checking up on Truman's people anyway. In fact they were turning over every stone in sight, including many which weren't in the government and some which had always been regarded as out of bounds for politicians. McCarthy was in pursuit of the Voice of America. Jenner's Internal Security subcommittee was looking for Communists in high schools, and the House Committee on Un-American Activities, now piloted by Republican Harold R. Velde of Illinois, was preparing to invade places of worship. On a radio program Velde explained that the committee had just about finished sweeping out subversives in show business. Now it was ready for a searching investigation of Christianity. The hunt, he said, would focus on "individual members of the cloth, including some who seem to have devoted more time to politics than . . . to the ministry."

To the end of Ike's life he never wavered in his belief that "our long-term good requires that leadership on the Hill be exercised through the party organization there," but there were times when even a constitutional President must rap knuckles. "Are you in favor of the federal government, through the Congress of the United States, investigating Communism in the churches?" Eisenhower was asked at his next press conference. No, he said; houses of God were the last places to look for disloyalty; he could see no possible good in questioning their patriotism. Maybe in this instance the investigators should be investigated, he said — hard words from a chief executive who believed in leaving the legislators alone.

But Republicans were running Congress, and Republicans of a very special breed at that. At times their ultraconservatism went beyond reaction. Judgment Day was approaching for Joe McCarthy; the Senate had begun to form ranks against him. Soon every member of the chamber would be asked to choose between him and Eisenhower, and the men of the right would be revealed as enemies of the President. With the single exception of Leverett Saltonstall of Massachusetts, every senior Republican Senate leader — Knowland, Dirksen, Styles Bridges, and Eugene Millikin — would vote for the demagogue.

George Sokolsky, McCarthy's muezzin, charged that under Eisenhower the Republican party "has gone so modern that it is indistinguishable from the New Deal," and Colonel McCormick had tried to read Ike out of the party in the *Washington Times-Herald* the morning after his inaugural. Most publicists were on the President's side, however. Seven months after Taft's funeral the *Times-Herald* was absorbed by the *Washington Post,* a very different kind of newspaper, which observed sharply that "Senator Knowland does not seem able to separate administration objectives from his own pet phobias." *Business Week* commented that "it is only natural for people to ask themselves whether Republicans are equal to the responsibilities of power," and Roscoe Drummond wrote in the *New York Herald Tribune* of a new sort of "mess in Washington."

> What is to be the consequence, what is to be the political harvest of this heedless divisiveness, this feuding, this name-calling, this miasmic preoccupation with bitter negative controversy within the Republican Administration? . . . The effect of this new kind of "mess" is to exhibit the Republican Government as quarrelsome, unproductive and legislatively nearly impotent."

There were days then when capital correspondents wondered in print whether the federal government was becoming an exercise in self-parody. Here was William Knowland, the helmsman of the Senate, pounding away at the President on the urgent need to institute a full naval blockade of the Chinese coast and vetoing Paul Nitze, Wilson's choice to be his Assistant Secretary of Defense for Foreign Affairs, on the ground that as a member of the State Department Nitze had been one of "Acheson's architects of disaster." Here was Everett McKinley Dirksen triumphantly tacking a rider on an appropriations bill to provide that should Peking be admitted to the United Nations, all U.S. contributions to the U.N. should be terminated instantly. Five drafts of the rider passed the Senate, five times the President took up his pen, five times he put the pen down saying he couldn't live with this and still conduct foreign affairs. The impasse was broken by Styles Bridges's resolution asserting it to be the "sense of

Congress" that Red China should forever be barred from U.N. member-ship. It passed both houses unanimously — the unanimity in the Senate being recorded approvingly by Vice President Richard M. Nixon. The height of these follies was reached when Hubert Humphrey drew up a bill making membership in the Communist party a felony. This had to be changed — it would have destroyed the McCarran Act, which required Communists to register, by making registration self-incriminating and thus evadable under the Fifth Amendment — but CP membership was never-theless outlawed. Attorney General Brownell was horrified. The bill was still unconstitutional on at least six counts, and it canceled out several existing anti-Communist laws. Nevertheless, no one on Capitol Hill in the early 1950s was prepared to explain a no vote to his constituents. Hum-phrey's absurdity passed the Senate 79-0 and the House 265-2.

Apart from the coming struggle with McCarthy, that first year of the Eisenhower Presidency was his worst in Washington. Foster Dulles, prompted by Scott McLeod, was sacking seasoned foreign service officers on the flimsiest of pretexts. State's passport office, now headed by Frances G. Knight — like McLeod a McCarthy appointee — was looking into the loyalty of Edward R. Murrow. Murrow's unpopularity in ultra circles arose from his October 20, 1953, *See It Now* CBS-TV program broadcast, in which Murrow described the plight of a University of Michigan senior named Milo Radulovich. After eight years of active duty in the Air Force Reserve, Radulovich had suddenly been classified as a security risk. He was accused of violating Air Force Regulation 36-52 by close association with "Communists or Communist sympathizers." Stripped of his lieu-tenant's rank, he was dismissed from the service, making him, in the politi-cal climate of the time, virtually unemployable. His case had been heard by a board of three colonels. The Air Force had produced no witnesses, specified no charges, had refused to identify the lieutenant's accuser, and had kept the evidence it said it had in an envelope which had remained sealed during the hearing. Murrow found out what was in it. The persons with whom Radulovich had been in close association were his father and his sister. Their questionable activity was reading a Serbian-language news-paper. The newspaper was published in Yugoslavia. Yugoslavia had broken with Moscow five years earlier, but the Air Force was taking no chances; it wanted no officers whose relatives read a journal using a foreign lan-guage which might be spoken by people who had once admired the late Joseph Stalin.

Five weeks after the Radulovich broadcast Secretary of the Air Force Harold E. Talbott appeared on *See It Now* to announce that he had decided, on second thought, that Lieutenant Radulovich's commission would be returned on the ground that he wasn't a threat to the nation's safety after all. It was a humiliating experience for Talbott, and it wasn't his last; in the summer of 1955 he was accused of shady dealings with firms holding Air Force contracts, and resigned under a cloud. In 1953 the administration felt protective toward him, however, and blamed Murrow. The credibility of the press was becoming a major problem. There were other Murrows, because there were other Radulovichs.

Abraham Chasanow, a civil servant who had worked in the Navy Hydrographic Office for twenty-three years, always to the satisfaction of his superiors, was one of them. Chasanow was suspended without pay on July 29, 1953. The personnel director informed him that he had been called a security risk. Two months later a naval board examined the evidence, found it worthless, and unanimously recommended that he be reinstated. Months passed; nothing happened. By now Chasanow, having exhausted his savings, was living on loans from his wife's relatives. On April 7, 1954, despite the lack of proof, Assistant Secretary of the Navy James H. Smith Jr. ordered Chasanow's dismissal. The messenger who laid this news before the public — together with the background details — was Anthony Lewis of the *Washington Daily News*. His stories about the case won a Pulitzer Prize, vindication for Chasanow, and further alienation of Republican conservatives and the press.

The trouble, said the reporters, was that in loyalty cases the administration's right hand sometimes didn't know what the left hand was doing, or, if it did, didn't care. They cited the unseemly row over the patriotism of Wolf I. Ladejinsky. The Ladejinsky incident was especially ridiculous because of his demonstrable patriotism. A militant anti-Communist and an expert on land reform, his work under MacArthur in Japan was regarded as a textbook example of how to outwit agrarian Communists. Ladejinsky's politics had in fact been commended by Scott McLeod. All the same, Ezra Taft Benson didn't want him in the Department of Agriculture. Benson discharged him as a security risk — whereupon Stassen cleared him, hired him with the President's approval, and sent him off to match wits with agrarian Communists in Asia.

For Ike, the pursuit of Communists was what he called, in a favorite expression, "a can of worms." The difficulties here, as elsewhere, went back to his campaign for the Presidency. The Republicans had said that the Democrats weren't doing enough about spies, yet it was hard to devise a harsher internal security program than the one Truman had established in 1947. Eisenhower tried it, on April 27, 1953, with his Executive Order 10450. Under it the mere suspicion of treachery brought termination of employment. So did suspicion of a great many other deviations from the accepted norm — drunkenness, drug addiction, participation in unusual sexual practices, conviction of a felony, mental illness, membership in a nudist colony, unsanitary habits, a reputation for lying — anything, in fact, deemed "inconsistent with the national security."

The regulation certainly thinned employee rolls. On October 23 the White House announced that in 10450's first four months 1,456 persons had left federal service, only five of whom had been hired since Eisenhower took office. To give further evidence of progress in the struggle against world

Communism the White House issued a statement pointing to the conviction of 41 U.S. Communist party leaders under the Smith Act, verdicts against two other party members for spying and one for treason, the banishment of 84 alien subversives from American soil, and the addition of 62 new organizations to the attorney general's already bloated list of subversive organizations. In his second State of the Union message Eisenhower announced a new score. The number of "security risks" dismissed from government service, he said, had risen to 2,200. Later Nixon, declaring that "thousands of Communists, fellow travelers, and security risks have been thrown out" of government jobs, reported that 6,926 had been dropped from the payroll.

There, said delighted Republicans; it was true after all; the government had been infested with reds and pinks, and Ike had found them and booted them out. But the Democrats weren't having any of that. They went through civil service records and found that of the workers on the first list, only 863 had been discharged. The rest had resigned or retired; they would have left anyhow. As for Nixon's figures, only 1,743 of those dropped had been accused of disloyalty — and 41.2 percent of them had been hired by the Eisenhower administration. Stevenson guyed the Republican loyalty program as a "numbers game." So, in private, did the President. Dulles complained to the cabinet that he found himself wasting whole evenings reading files sent to him because someone in a worker's family — or even in his neighborhood — was reported to be a pacifist, a member of the United World Federalists, or an advocate of fluoridation.

The unkindest cut of all for 10450 came in a broadside from Harry P. Cain. Cain was a former Republican senator from Washington; defeated in the 1952 election, he had been appointed to the Subversive Activities Control Board as a favor to his old sidekicks on the Hill. Since they had included Jenner, McCarthy, and Dirksen, and since his own outlook had been ultraconservative, no one had dreamed that he might become a civil libertarian. Yet he did. In an emotional speech he flayed the White House for having "swung too far on the side of injustice." The President called Cain an ingrate; Adams reminded him that he belonged to a team and should not let the side down.

But the team had not yet learned to play together. McCarthy was raising hob with the Mutual Security Administration. Secretary of the Interior McKay had drummed out the distinguished director of the Fish and Wildlife Service and replaced him with a public relations flack. Secretary of Commerce Weeks continued to play politics with the National Bureau of Standards, a sanctuary that Harry Vaughan and Donald Dawson had not dared enter, and Dr. Clarence E. Manion, a former Notre Dame law school dean and extreme right-winger who had been appointed chairman of the President's Commission on Intergovernmental Relations, threw the White House into a turmoil by endorsing the Bricker amendment.*

---

*As a result, Adams forced him to resign.

The Bricker amendment had conservative chic. Some of its most ardent supporters didn't know what was in it; they had put their names and their money behind it because in certain boardrooms and clubrooms it was the thing to do, just as backing the Liberty League had been stylish in those same places in 1936. It *must* be right, they felt; why else would those lobbying for it include the Daughters of the American Revolution, the American Medical Association, the Committee for Constitutional Government, the *Chicago Tribune,* and the Vigilant Women for the Bricker Amendment — "a volunteer organization of housewives and mothers of boys overseas" — which had brought to the Hill petitions signed by over a half-million Americans?

Similarly, those opposing it must be wrong; why else would *they* include the League of Women Voters, the Americans for Democratic Action, the *New York Times,* the *Washington Post,* the American Bar Association's Section on International and Comparative Law, the Association of the Bar of the City of New York, the American Association for the United Nations, and Eleanor Roosevelt?

Capital correspondents called the Bricker sortie "our greatest debate about the constitutional ordering of our foreign relations since 1788." It probably was. Had it not been obscured by the even graver struggle between Joseph R. McCarthy and the United States government, it would have been remembered as the greatest ultraconservative travail of the decade. When introduced in the Senate on January 7, 1953, the amendment had sixty-four senatorial cosponsors — the two-thirds of the Senate needed for a constitutional amendment. Dulles's plea that it was "dangerous to our peace and security" was ignored; after six months of begging Senate Republicans not to mortify their own President, Nixon had to tell the cabinet, "Well, there's just no doubt there's a lot of public support for this amendment."

Offering amendments to the U.S. Constitution had become an ultraconservative fashion of the early 1950s. Herblock depicted it as a kind of Scrabble. No fewer than 107 such proposals had been introduced in the 83rd Congress and referred to committees, among them one which would have interpreted treason not only as advocacy of the overthrow of the government but also of "weakening" it, "whether or not by force or violence." Others would have put the soil of any foreign country off limits to draftees unless Congress had declared war against it; prohibited the spending of taxpayers' money on welfare; limited new states to one senator; enjoined the federal government from meddling in any state's right to regulate the "health, morals, education, marriage, and good order" of its inhabitants; and affirmed that "this nation devoutly recognizes the authority and law of Jesus Christ, Saviour and Ruler of Nations through Whom are bestowed the blessings of Almighty God."

Six of the measures had reached the Senate floor, where each of them had been approved by majority vote, and four had received the two-thirds majority needed to send a proposed amendment on to the House of Representatives. From there, provided it was supported by two-thirds of those voting, it would go on to the state legislatures. This was senatorial irresponsibility. The prevailing sophistry was expressed by Dirksen: "If the legislatures say 'No,' that will be all right with the junior senator from Illinois; if they say 'Yes,' it will also be all right with me." Knowland took the same line. What, he asked, were the opponents of the Bricker amendment afraid of? Didn't they trust the people's judgment? The answer, of course, was that the founding fathers never meant Congress to be a transom through which schemes to alter the Constitution were to be passed, and that the state legislatures, lopsided with representatives of special interests and vulnerable to special pleaders, were no tribunes of the people. That reply was seldom made. Freshman Senator John Kennedy of Massachusetts argued that "reluctance to amend the Constitution is one of our most valuable safeguards and bulwarks of stability," but his colleagues were not listening to him yet.

Yalta was what the Bricker amendment was all about. The ghost refused to be exorcised. By now every informed citizen should have known what had happened in the Crimea during the first half of February 1945, but hallucinations of "secret agreements" continued to haunt Washington, kept alive by such bogeymen as William Jenner, who revealed in hushed tones that anti-Bricker forces were being masterminded by a "secret revolutionary corps" that included Owen Lattimore, Henry Wallace, Alger Hiss (who was in prison), and Harry Hopkins and Harry Dexter White (both of whom had died in the 1940s). Manion was not the only administration figure infected by the Bricker fever. In a January 29, 1954, cabinet meeting, after having listened to discussions of the amendment for over a year, Charlie Wilson volunteered that he shared the feelings of its backers that treaties should not be able to deprive people of their rights, and that conventions like Yalta and Potsdam ought to be outlawed. The President patiently explained once again that the Bricker amendment could not have prevented Yalta and Potsdam, because they had been political accords, not treaties or executive agreements.

Back in his office Ike raged, "I'm so sick of this I could scream! The whole damn thing is senseless and plain damaging to the prestige of the United States. We talk about the French not being able to govern themselves — and we sit here wrestling with a Bricker Amendment." He had been going to the mat with it ever since his pre-inaugural cabinet rehearsals in the Commodore Hotel. At that time the idea had appealed to him. He had been caught up in the indignation at stories of FDR and Stalin carving up the world (somehow Churchill's presence was always forgotten), and he believed — as Bricker said he did — that resentment of the treaty-making process might be turned against the United Nations. The amendment sounded plausible; the United States would be insured against the possibility that an inept chief executive and a slumbering Senate might usurp the constitutional rights of the people and the individual states.

Then Dulles studied it. The more he thought about it, the more alarmed he became. Bricker's real hostility seemed to be toward *all* treaties and executive agreements. One of his remedies was to transfer the power to make them from the White House to the Hill. As Dulles saw it, this would mean that other governments would doubt the sanctity of treaties with the United States; what one Congress could do, another Congress could undo.°
Eisenhower began to change his mind about the proposal. His complete conversion to the anti-Bricker camp was the byproduct of a tangential dispute over the so-called Status of Forces agreements. Under them, foreign governments were given legal jurisdiction in cases of offenses committed by American servicemen who were not acting in the line of duty. (The classic example was that of a U.S. soldier in Japan who fired an empty mortar shell at a group of women and killed one of them.) Ultraconservatives felt strongly that the armed forces should have complete jurisdiction over all American troops overseas. As it happened, Eisenhower knew more about Status of Forces treaties than anyone else in Washington, because as commander of NATO he had drafted some of them, negotiated them, and then kept watch over those administering them. He tried to explain their theory and practice to Knowland, but the majority leader flared up. Pounding the table he roared, "A young man drafted in peacetime, sent overseas against his will, assigned to a duty — by God, I don't think he ought to be turned over for trial! He's wearing the uniform of our country. I wouldn't want *my* son treated that way!"

Bricker felt the same way. His real motives were unmasked in an emotional attack on two State Department men. They opposed his amendment, but that was not why he went after them; they had testified for the NATO Status of Forces agreement, and he chastised them on that. It was a tactical error. The President was listening. Ike had already set the best constitutional lawyers he could find to work on the amendment. To his dismay they now reported that under it the United States could not have entered NATO. It specified that unless the Constitution assigned a specific matter to Congress, the Senate was powerless to act upon it. Such a treaty could become law under Bricker only if it was approved by legislation in each of the states. This, said Eisenhower, would permit state legislatures to renounce American treaties.† The President and his Secretary of State would, Ike said, be faced with the "impossible task of representing forty-eight governments."

The Bricker showdown came on February 26, 1954, at the end of a stunning sequence of parliamentary maneuvers. Bricker was defeated in the Status of Forces fight. To save his face, Ike proposed a mild procedural measure; when treaties came up votes would have to be recorded; they

---

°Other advocates of a strong Presidency trotted this out. But by the same reasoning, administrations could repudiate treaties made by their predecessors.
†Bricker denied this interpretation.

could not be shouted through. Bricker rejected the gesture. On February 25 his amendment fell short of the two-thirds vote; 50 senators were for it and 42 opposed.

Here, in the last desperate hour of the struggle, was a tragic incident. Chairman Walter George of the Senate Foreign Relations Committee drafted an amendment similar to Bricker's. It deserved serious attention. Not all Bricker supporters were irresponsible. One of them was Frank E. Holman, a former president of the American Bar Association. The ABA Committee on Peace and Law Through the United Nations had been behind Bricker, too, and so had some constitutional scholars. That did not make it good legislation, but it did suggest that amid all the clamor there were a few voices worth listening to. Since FDR's arrival in Washington the powers of the Presidency *had* grown to dismaying size. A chief executive with Eisenhower's scruples would not abuse them, but as subsequent events were to demonstrate, later inhabitants of the White House were not so circumspect. Furthermore, George was not just offering a restylized, Simonized Bricker amendment. His language was carefully drawn. It was more temperate than Bricker's, and he had omitted Bricker's notorious "which" clause, proscribing congressional action in matters beyond its delegated powers. That had been the sticking point for Ike, the provision that would have required that certain treaties be approved by the states. Without it, the heart of the administration's case against Bricker was gone. George's measure was farsighted in many ways, but because it, too, would have restricted presidential freedom in foreign policy, the White House decided to resist it.*

By the late 1960s and early 1970s senators who remembered the George amendment were having long second thoughts about it, and in the general mutiny against presidential behavior in Vietnam some of them could hear the voice of Knowland, by then long since defeated at the polls and retired to private life in California.† Knowland had endorsed the George proposal because, he said, he could not ignore "a dangerous tendency toward executive encroachment on legislative powers." Had Taft stood in Knowland's place that day he might have clothed the debate in dignity, but as it was all hope for rational contemplation was lost in the fog of emotion. A senator was either an Eisenhower man or he wasn't; that was all there was to it, and so Bricker dragged George down with him. Even so, the administration just squeaked through. There were 60 yeas and 31 nays on the George amendment — a margin of one vote, since it required a two-thirds margin. Had that thirty-first senator been ill, or in the men's room, and had affirma-

---

*The key clause in the George proposal provided that any provision of a treaty or other international agreement that conflicted with the Constitution — e.g., one which did not recognize that the war-making power is vested in Congress — should not be effective. In addition, international nontreaty agreements could not be effective as internal law except by act of Congress.

†He committed suicide in February 1974.

tive action followed in the House and the legislatures, the history of American foreign policy over the next two decades would have been very different; to cite but one example, the notorious Tonkin Gulf resolution, authorizing U.S. intervention in Vietnam on a grand scale, would have been rejected as unconstitutional.

John Foster Dulles celebrated his sixty-sixth birthday the very day Bricker's amendment was defeated. He was an elder statesman and looked it. Everything about him emanated distinction: his leonine head and craggy face; his membership in the Metropolitan, Piping Rock, Down Town, and Century clubs; his chairmanships of the Carnegie Foundation and the Federal Council of Churches Commission on a Just and Lasting Peace; his Phi Beta Kappa key; and his degrees from Princeton, the Sorbonne, and George Washington Law School.

The most important fact in Dulles's life was his membership in the Presbyterian church. He regarded his religiosity as a great strength. In fact it was an encumbrance. In him anti-Communism was an extension of Presbyterianism — just as Communism itself, in George Kennan's view, was a gospel in the minds of Soviet leaders — and as a result his diplomacy, like theirs, was rigid and dogmatic. Eisenhower believed in compromise and conciliation, but the man he had chosen to conduct his foreign policy deeply distrusted both. Dulles skillfully sabotaged Stassen's disarmament plans on the ground that America's NATO partners would look upon them as a sign of slackening U.S. resolve. To him flexibility was worse than frailty; it was downright immoral. Dissent from his hard doctrines carried with it the stigma of sin. On one of his first trips abroad in 1953 he presented President Mohammed Naguib of Egypt, as a present from President Eisenhower, a nickel-plated automatic pistol. It was a reminder to statesmen in all uncommitted nations that militant vigilance against designing Communists was the price of American friendship. To neutral leaders like India's Nehru the world was not that simple. Nehru was trying to stake out a position between the two great rival blocs. He believed it important to be anti-colonialist as well as anti-Communist. Dulles saw neutralism as wicked; he virtuously shipped arms to Pakistan and lost India's friendship.

Despite Dulles's rhetoric, the only pro-Soviet government to be unseated in the 1950s was in Guatemala, a little country in America's back yard. Even that success was questionable; it sowed the seeds of later defeats in Latin America. The most disturbing aspect of Dulles evangelism, however, was its deliberate appeal to the populations of eastern Europe — his promises of a "rollback" of Russian tryanny there. In a cabinet meeting on July 17, 1953, he reported with immense satisfaction that Georges Bidault of France and Britain's Marquess of Salisbury had joined him three days earlier in an expression of concern over "true liberty" for East Europeans. This, he said, was "the first time to my knowledge that London and Paris have been willing to embrace this principle."

In his notes on that meeting Hughes wrote furiously, "Does he really believe that *words* are going to free anyone, any people?" But what Dulles believed was less important than the credulity of his listeners from Stettin to Trieste. There his failure to explain that America's determination to hasten their liberation must be confined to "every peaceful means" — a qualification Eisenhower was always careful to include — was to have tragic consequences. East German cities erupted in strikes, arson, and rioting. After Soviet tanks had suppressed an uprising by thirty thousand East Berliners, Ike emphasized to the press that the United States planned no physical intervention in eastern Europe, but by late November Dulles was inciting unrest in Lithuania, Latvia, and Estonia by declaring that the United States would not recognize Russia's incorporation of them and thereby "confirm their captivity."

To the relief of those who preferred diplomacy in a lower key, Dulles was frequently absent from the capital. In effect he was traveling round offering alliances as insurance policies against aggression, knitting the non-Communist world together with the steel thread of American military might. To NATO were added a rejuvenated Organization of American States (OAS), the Southeast Asia Treaty Organization (SEATO), and, in the Middle East, the Baghdad Pact, later to become the Central Treaty Organization (CENTO), which the United States did not join but backed heavily. Year by year new clauses were added to the covenants encircling the Communist countries, until America was committed by eight security treaties to the defense of forty-two nations. "Dulles," Walter Lippmann wrote in the *New York Herald Tribune*, "has shown himself to be not a prudent and calculating diplomat but a gambler who is more lavish than any other secretary of state has ever dreamed of being with promissory notes engaging the blood, the treasure, and the honor of this country."

Although none of the notes was called in Dulles's lifetime, there was considerable anxiety among those who would be called to account if they were. A parade of alarmed witnesses marched into congressional committee rooms to protest that while the administration was expanding U.S. military obligations, it was reducing the country's strength. For a general, Eisenhower was showing scant regard for the Pentagon. In one maneuver he cut five billion dollars from an Air Force budget, thereby estranging General Hoyt Vandenberg; another directive, issued while Formosa was approaching one of its periodic boiling points, reduced the size of the armed services from 3,200,000 men to 2,850,000. Only a President who had worn five stars could have accomplished that. He rejected all the strategic arguments that were raised as inapplicable in the nuclear age. "If you want to be coldly logical about it," he said at one White House meeting called to discuss further reductions in Army force levels, "the money being spent for ground forces could be used to better advantage on new highways to facilitate the evacuation of large cities in case of an enemy attack."

The President knew what he wanted, and George Humphrey, who had become the strong man of the cabinet, was behind him. Their goal was relief for the taxpayer, and they believed that this was the right way to go about getting it. "The New Look, with its planning predicated on nuclear retaliation," Sherman Adams wrote, obviously "led to an order from Eisenhower to reduce the number of army ground troops." Ike was commander in chief; the responsibility was his. To dispel any further confusion he instructed the Pentagon to assume that the United States would fight any future war with nuclear weapons. Democrats on the Hill complained that America was being lulled into a false sense of security, that the President's motives were political. They were, partly. One of the tinnier administration promises was "a bigger bang for a buck." Strategic monism also appealed to searchers for simplistic solutions. Clearly the United States planned no wars of conquest. Therefore, they said, the Department of Defense should be concerned, literally, with just defense. They only wanted America left alone, and the threat of massive retaliation was designed to guarantee that it would be.

Of course, their doctrine did no such thing, and with the Secretary of State marching to a different drum there was no way it could. It is amazing that so few observers spotted the discrepancies between the largesse of the administration's foreign policy and the relative parsimony of its military policy. Retaliation might have been an effective deterrent between the two world wars, when Presidents were sedulously avoiding entanglements abroad, but America was no longer that kind of country. The Pax Britannica had been replaced by a Pax Americana; where the British had once sent gunboats the United States now sent John Foster Dulles and his ballpoint pen. Superpowers need a wide range of deterrents to keep the peace, and it was precisely here that phrasemongering about a bigger bang for a buck — as though global politics were an old-fashioned Fourth of July celebration — became so irrelevant.

Young Henry Kissinger saw it. After taking his Ph.D. in 1954 and becoming a junior member of Harvard's government department, Kissinger wrote *Nuclear Weapons and Foreign Policy,* a closely reasoned examination of America's world posture. Massive retaliation, he concluded, was a fallacy: with the government's capacities for fighting a limited war sharply reduced, and with nothing left but the bomb, national survival became a stake in every diplomatic disagreement that verged on the use of force. Dean Acheson also saw the inconsistency. In a magazine article he examined administration claims that massive retaliation gave the United States "initiative" and rejected them as absurd; retaliation, he pointed out, is a response to somebody else's initiative. Richard Rovere saw the anomaly vividly; in a "Letter from Washington" dated April 8, 1954, he predicted that "if the worst happens in Indochina, where atomic bombs would be about as useless as crossbows, the ground forces will have to be restored to their former strength — and then some."

Washington and Indochina are exactly twelve hours apart — midnight in one is noon in the other — and so evening darkness had already enveloped the Maison de France, French army headquarters in Hanoi, when, at 10:30 on the morning of February 10, 1954, President Eisenhower entered the Indian Treaty Room for his regular Wednesday press conference. He was asked about the critical military situation half a world away. He said, "No one could be more bitterly opposed to ever getting the United States involved in a hot war in that region than I am. Consequently, every move that I authorize is calculated, so far as humans can do it, to make certain that that does not happen."

"Mr. President," the next reporter asked, "should your remarks be construed as meaning that you are determined not to become involved or, perhaps, more deeply involved in the war in Indochina regardless of how that war may go?"

Eisenhower replied that he could not forecast the future. However, he added: "I say that I cannot conceive of a greater tragedy for America than to get heavily involved now in an all-out war in any of those regions, particularly with large units."

Compared to what would come later, the American presence in Indochina at that time was slight. It dated from the previous administration. Until the late 1940s the three states of Indochina — Vietnam, Cambodia, and Laos — had been French colonies. On December 30, 1949, their status had changed somewhat; Paris had recognized them as "independent states" within "the French Union." That was mostly show, a token gesture of anticolonialism designed to counter Russia's support of Ho Chi Minh's insurgent Viet Minh. On February 7, 1950, Washington and London had recognized the three states, Acheson stressing America's "fundamental policy of giving support to the peaceful and democratic evolution of dependent peoples toward self-government and independence." He had hoped that recognition from some Asian nations would follow, but they hung back, repelled by France's puppet ruler of Vietnam, Prince Bao Dai, an absentee chief of state who preferred to lie in the Riviera sun. Undeterred by the widespread contempt for Bao Dai, Acheson had doggedly continued to risk American prestige in Indochina. Later he would ruefully recall that one State Department colleague, John Ohly, had warned him that the U.S. was moving into a position in which "our responsibilities tend to supplant rather than complement those of the French." America could become a scapegoat for the French and be sucked into direct intervention, said Ohly, noting that "These situations have a way of snowballing." In his memoirs Acheson commented: "I decided . . . that having put our hand to the plow, we would not look back."

By the time of Eisenhower's inaugural the United States was paying a third of French costs, shipping arms to Indochina, and providing two hundred U.S. Air Force technicians. Ike continued the aid, but it was no longer enough. The Vietnam crisis deepened. On the morning of that February press conference it had come to center around one battle, a classic engagement which would alter world history and affect the United States more profoundly than Shiloh or the Argonne. For seven years now, the French army had been kept off balance by Ho Chi Minh's brilliant generalissimo, General Vo Nguyen Giap. Baffled by Giap's guerrilla tactics, so unfamiliar to officers trained at Saint-Cyr-l'École, the French had vowed to lure the Viet Minh into a pitched battle. On November 20, 1953, they had dropped 15,000 parachute troops on a strategic point almost two hundred miles west of Hanoi. The position covered lines of communications linking China, Tonkin, and Laos. This was Thai country, and the name of the place was a combination of three Thai words: *dien* (big), *bien* (frontier) and *phu* (administrative center). Dienbienphu: a big administrative center on the frontier. No name could have been more ordinary.

Geographically, that part of Southeast Asia is mostly chaos: cliffs, jagged peaks, unfathomable jungle, impenetrable canyons, impassable rivers. Here and there, however, the face of the land is dimpled by relatively smooth hollows, the larger of which may be cleared and used for airstrips. Dienbienphu was such a basin. Shaped like a long oak leaf in which brooks represent the ribs of the leaf and a central stream the median line, it was eleven miles long and three miles wide. Hills darkened by forests surrounded Dienbienphu. The French paratroopers built an airfield and then a series of *porc-épics* (porcupines) — strongholds to protect the field and harass the enemy. Military strategists since the time of Machiavelli have urged commanders to seize high ground, pointing out that should one side become entrenched on it, it can crush the other side with its artillery. The French, however, failed to seize the crests overlooking Dienbienphu. Holding them against guerrillas would have been difficult, and the high command in Hanoi decided that it was unnecessary. In the Maison de France war correspondents were told that French artillery was superior to anything Giap could mount, and besides, the Viet Minh couldn't possibly drag cannon through the mountains studding the countryside all around.

The Maison de France was wrong. Since November, 90,000 Vietnamese peasants had been hauling batteries of 105-mm field guns across the savage land to Dienbienphu. By January the greater part of Giap's artillery was in position overlooking the plain of gray and yellow clay below, and on February 10 in Washington, as Eisenhower was answering questions about Indochina in the Indian Treaty Room, Viet Minh soldiers of the 57th Regiment, resting from their backbreaking toil, were looking down the moonlit slopes to the blockhouses shielding twelve sleeping French battalions. Later the guerrillas' commanding officer, Captain Hien, would tell how the flickering torches around the airstrip that night had reminded him of the flames of the little sticks of firewood traditionally left on the thresholds of huts in his village to honor the dead.

Giap opened the siege of Dienbienphu with a dawn bombardment on March 13. A smoke screen which the French laid down to hide the airfield was unsuccessful, and pilots began to call the shallow basin *"un pot de chambre."* Three days earlier, at another Wednesday press conference, a correspondent had reminded the President of an observation by Senator John Stennis of Mississippi. Stennis had warned that the presence of the Air Force technicians already in Vietnam might be enough to bring the United States into the war. Not so, said Ike; there would be no U.S. intervention in Indochina unless Congress exercised its constitutional right to declare war.

Historians may wonder why the question of American involvement was even being discussed. The United Nations had no commitments in Indochina, and until the recent past the United States had had nothing to do with it; the only President who had expressed a genuine interest in the place was Franklin Roosevelt, and he had wanted to see it freed from French colonial rule. Eisenhower had refused to widen one Asian war against Communists only a year before. He had pointed out that even an air strike at Dienbienphu would be hazardous; it might pit U.S. airmen against the Chinese air force. Chances of a decisive blow were slight anyhow. French military strength in Indochina was much smaller than the U.N. force in Korea.

With the exception of Eisenhower, however, most administration leaders did not see it that way. In their view, the United States, as the strongest power in the free world, was the leader of a global struggle against world Communism. Since the Korean armistice Indochina had been the scene of the only active conflict in it. If the Communists were victorious on one front, interventionists reasoned, the security of all fronts would be endangered. That was also the reasoning of the intellectual community; writing in *Daedalus*, Walt W. Rostow, professor of economic history at the Massachusetts Institute of Technology, argued:

> The balance of power in Eurasia could be lost to the United States by the movement of Soviet or Chinese ground forces. And, equally, it could be lost if, in hope or despair, men and women in the decisive regions of Eurasia should turn to Communism. . . . the survival of the United States . . . would be in jeopardy if we were to become a democratic island in a totalitarian sea.

The consensus was that as long as American troops had been engaged in Korea, sending the French money, guns, and advice had been enough. Now more was needed, the argument went; failure to provide it would endanger the free world.

Eisenhower had authorized larger payments to the French the previous September — $385,000,000 before the end of 1954. At that time Dulles had defined America's goal in Indochina as success for the Navarre Plan, named for the French commander there. This, Dulles had explained, would defeat "the organized body of Communist aggression by the end of the 1955 fighting season," leaving only mopping-up operations, "which could in 1956 be met for the most part" by Vietnamese troops. The Navarre Plan failed, but as late as January 4, 1954, when the President reviewed his forthcoming State of the Union message with the congressional leadership, no consideration had been given to the possibility of shipping U.S. troops to Indochina. Ike planned to ask congressional approval of continued military aid to France. A Republican senator asked whether this meant sending American boys to Vietnam. "No," the startled President replied. He said, "I can write in 'material assistance,'" and he did.

By the end of the third week in March the situation in Indochina had deteriorated. Dulles's faith in the French continued to be strong — on March 23 he predicted that they would win — but the Pentagon was not so sure. The news from Dienbienphu was bleak. Giap's guns on the rim of the basin had rendered the airfield virtually inoperable. Attempts to parachute supplies to the twelve surrounded battalions from C-54s were only partly successful. If the drops were made from 6,000 to 8,000 feet, half the material landed in the Viet lines, and at 4,000 feet Viet antiaircraft batteries hit most of the planes. On all sides enemy trenches nibbled toward the French strongpoints, splitting up here and there to allow the installation of automatic weapons. Diplomatic channels brought Washington an appeal from Paris for an American air strike to take the pressure off the isolated garrison, and on March 22 General Paul Ely, the French chief of staff, flew over to ask for it.

Ridgway was vehemently opposed. Once the use of American air power was approved, he said, dispatching infantry would only be a matter of time. He knew something of the terrain: rice paddies, jungle, an impossible road net, wretched communications. Even the harbors were poor. U.S. intervention would be a "tragic adventure." He sent this opinion to Eisenhower, he later wrote in *Soldier,* his memoirs, explaining that "to a man of his military experience its implications were immediately clear." But Radford, also a man of military experience, thought sending U.S. bombers was a good idea. And any doubts over where the Secretary of State stood were removed in a speech he delivered before the Overseas Press Club on Monday, March 29. Its tone says as much about cold war rhetoric as its text:

> Under the conditions of today, the imposition on Southeast Asia of the political system of Communist Russia and its Chinese Communist ally, by whatever means, would be a grave threat to the whole free community. The United States feels that the possibility should not be passively accepted, but should be met by united action. This might have serious risks, but these risks are far less than would face us a few years from now if we dare not be resolute today.

On Saturday Dulles conferred with the congressional leaders of both parties at the State Department to explain the need for collective defense of the French position — expeditions from Britain, Australia, and New Zealand, as well as the United States. He felt confident that he could frighten the Chinese Communists into forsaking Ho Chi Minh. That failing, he said, the Viet Minh must be wiped out. No compromise was possible, even in theory. One observer was left with the impression that the Secretary of State had "grave doubts whether the United States could survive the establishment of Communist power in Indochina."

Sunday evening Dulles joined Eisenhower and Radford in the President's oval study. The immediate issue before them was whether intervention was justified, and if so on what terms. In Paris Bidault was pressing Ambassador Dillon hard. It was a measure of French despair that they were asking for atomic bombs. Two aircraft carriers with nuclear weapons aboard were cruising in the Gulf of Tonkin with the Seventh Fleet, but virtually no one in Washington seriously considered using them.* In fact, Eisenhower forbade any air strike. He was willing to consider Dulles's "united action" — an allied effort — under certain circumstances. The French must agree to see the war through. They must grant complete independence to Vietnam, Cambodia, and Laos. Both the French and the Indochinese states must ask the allies — the U.S. and Britain — to come in. Lastly, the decisive step must be taken by Congress, which had the power to declare war, rather than by the President, who did not. Dulles was to do what he could within that context, and after an exploratory exchange of cables between Eisenhower and Churchill (whose reservations were later to become even greater than Ike's), the Secretary of State took off to see whether he could put an alliance together in London and Paris.

Three days later the President added a metaphor to the language. Although reluctant to make any U.S. commitment in Vietnam, he remained a firm believer in cold war catechisms. He had read and approved Dulles's Overseas Press Club speech before its delivery. Much more than French prestige was at stake in Indochina, he told the correspondents at that week's press conference. A Communist triumph there would enlarge the Red empire and deprive the United States of vital raw materials. It could mean the loss to the free world of all Southeast Asia, followed by threats to the U.S. defense perimeter in the Pacific: Australia, New Zealand, the Philippines, Formosa, and Japan. He said: "You have a row of dominoes set up, and you knock over the first one, and what will happen to the last one is the certainty that it will go over very quickly. So you have a beginning of a disintegration that would have the most profound influences."

Dulles, back from Europe, felt the chances for swift intervention were bright. Whitehall and the Quai d'Orsay had seemed receptive to suggestions for united action. If there was any moment during the crisis in which substantial allied aid for the beleaguered Maison de France was a possibility, this was it. Churchill had not yet thrown his great weight against the idea. To get it, the French were ready to give up almost anything except the Arc de Triomphe (where noisy demonstrators were protesting the

*The French had a different impression. See Jules Roy *La Bataille de Dien Bien Phu*, Paris 1963, 270 ff.

course of the war). Eisenhower seemed immovable, but he might have changed his mind; if he didn't, Congress could act.

It was precisely at this point in the drama that Richard Nixon moved to stage center. His motives were obscure then, and he has never clarified them. At the time he appeared to be the fiercest hawk in Washington, but there is a large body of opinion in the capital which held then, and holds now, that the Vice President was merely floating a trial balloon for the administration. The occasion for its launching was the annual convention of the American Society of Newspaper Editors in Washington on Friday, April 16. His remarks were supposedly made off the record, but they were too sensational to remain there. What should the United States do, he was asked, if the French withdrew their troops and abandoned Vietnam? Should U.S. soldiers take their place? Nixon answered that they should. The plight of the free world was desperate, he said; any further retreat in Asia was unthinkable. He prayed that the French would dig in and win. "But under the circumstances, if in order to avoid further Communist expansion in Asia and particularly in Indochina — if in order to avoid it we must take the risk now by putting American boys in, I believe that the Executive Branch has to take the politically unpopular position of facing up to it and doing it, and I personally would support such a decision."

Reaction was immediate. Some members of the administration may have been ready for a new war, but the newspapers weren't; editorials called on Ike to repudiate his Vice President. Congress wasn't ready; Nixon was accused of irresponsible chauvinism. Abroad, garbled reports of imminent U.S. troop movements triggered nervous reactions which shattered all possibilities of an allied expeditionary force. London decided to see what could be accomplished at a nineteen-nation conference on Asia due to open in Geneva later in the month. On Monday Dulles returned from Augusta, where Eisenhower was golfing, to tell the press that American intervention in Vietnam was "unlikely."

Late in April the French made their third and last appeal for help. Dulles and Radford were in Paris on NATO business. Bidault begged the secretary for an American air strike. Otherwise, he said, Dienbienphu would fall. Dulles said he would sleep on it, but he was just being polite. Eisenhower had told him once more that only an act of Congress could put American servicemen in Indochina. Besides, Dulles could read the Paris newspapers. All hope for the beleaguered French garrison had been abandoned.

By now the agony of Dienbienphu had captured the imagination of the world: editors were playing the most fragmentary dispatches from Vietnam on their front pages. The French code name for the operation, one learned, was Vautour (Vulture). Page one maps depicted the strongpoints within the surrounded fortress — little hills named Anne-Marie, Gabrielle, Dominique, Isabelle, Huguette, Françoise, Claudine, Béatrice, and the twin hillocks of Eliane One and Eliane Four — "the Lollobrigidas." Christian de Castries, the senior French officer, had been promoted from colonel to brigadier on the theory that a hero ought to be a general. Geneviève de Galard-Terraube, a French nurse, had refused to board the last plane back to Hanoi; she became "the Angel of Dienbienphu." Several stories told how de Castries, discovering that his part of the post was doomed, had called down artillery fire upon himself.

Many accounts of the siege were apocryphal. De Castries sent no orders to his artillery because he had no artillery left. The Beau Geste stories being featured in American newspapers had no connection with actual conditions in the entrenched camp. War correspondents were not to blame, for the French high command was also uninformed. By Easter Sunday, April 18, when beribboned officers from the Maison de France sang their annual hallelujahs in Hanoi Cathedral, they no longer knew much about their Vautour. Observation planes arriving overhead to see what was happening to the post were either destroyed by Giap's flak or driven away. The whole of the airstrip was being raked by Viet machine guns. A final attempt by C-54s to parachute supplies — together with de Castries's brigadier's stars, brandy to celebrate his promotion, and boxes of Croix de Guerre and Légion d'Honneur awards — failed completely. Recoilless guns on blockhouses, now in Viet hands, picked off Frenchmen pursuing the parachutes, and next morning the Viet Minh radio triumphantly announced the capture of everything dropped, including the brandy.

The men of Dienbienphu were now wretched beyond imagining. Half of them had already fallen. Alternately baked by the pitiless tropical sun and wrapped in sheets of rain, they lay burrowed under mounds of excrement and decaying corpses. Futile counterattacks on the lost emplacements left them in despair. Giap's barrages of 105s never slackened. Zagging Viet trenches continued to inch toward the French, bringing enemy infantry closer. For a while hopeful rumors had predicted a relief column from Hanoi, then an American air armada. The reports were believed by the men, by their officers, and even by de Castries, who found it hard to accept the fact that Navarre had sent him here to die. Now in April he knew: Hanoi ordered him to destroy all arms and supplies before they could fall into enemy hands. His men, he was told, were to be rallied for a last stand by the knowledge that they were holding up a Viet battle corps and defending the honor of France.

On May 7, the fifty-sixth day of siege, the tricolor over Dienbienphu was replaced by a white flag and then by the Viet Minh colors, red with a star of gold. The honor of France would never be the same again. In Geneva the multination conference on Asia had already begun. There was still talk of a U.S. expeditionary force. "No decision has been made to send American troops to Indochina," said Ed Murrow in a broadcast on the conference, "but neither has a decision been made not to send troops under any circumstances. And the second statement may prove to be more important than the first. If it comes down to the bare choice of losing Indochina to the Communists or saving it, some form of intervention may prove inescapable."

Then Dulles informed the conferring powers that although Indochina was important, it was not essential to the salvation of Southeast Asia from Communist domination. That cleared the way for a compromise. Vietnam was to be temporarily divided at the 17th Parallel, with the understanding that free elections in both halves of the country would reunite it on July 20, 1956. It was the best of a bad bargain, wrote Robert J. Donovan of the *New York Herald Tribune;* the domino had been kept "from going all the way over with a crash."

Meanwhile the Secretary of State's attempts to put together an Asian alliance continued, spurred by Eisenhower's declaration that "the free world" knew that "aggression in Korea and Southeast Asia" were "threats to the whole free community to be met only through united action." In September Dulles's mission ended successfully in Manila, where delegates from Australia, Britain, France, New Zealand, Pakistan, Thailand, the Philippines, and the United States pledged a joint defense against aggression. Article Four of their pact, creating the Southeast Asia Treaty Organization, committed them to act together if any one of them was attacked; provision was made to counter not only external threats but also internal subversion. A separate protocol extended the treaty's protection to Vietnam, Cambodia, and Laos.

American diplomacy seemed to be riding high. Few thought it important that the Geneva agreement had not been signed by representatives from either South Vietnam or the United States — Dulles's official role at the conference had been that of an observer — and that neither, therefore, was bound by the pledge to hold elections in Vietnam two years hence. Thus was set a historic trap. Failure to hold elections would lead to a renewal of hostilities. The difference would be that this time the Viet insurgency would be branded "aggression" — and thus a direct challenge to every member of the alliance forged in Manila. John Ohly's "snowballing" had begun.

In October the Secretary of State, speaking with great deliberation, told the cabinet: "The United States has never been so respected nor had such good relations as now."

In a private conversation afterward he said of Vietnam: "We have a clean base there, without the taint of colonialism. Dienbienphu was a blessing in disguise."

Portrait of an American

NORMA JEAN BAKER

SHE WAS THE BASTARD DAUGHTER of a paranoid schizophrenic — Gladys Pearl Baker, a film cutter for MGM, Paramount, and Columbia studios who was in and out of asylums all her life. Madness also claimed both Gladys's parents and her brother, who killed himself. She named her unwanted baby after Norma Talmadge, a silent star of that year: 1926. Years later, when the infant was grown, the casting director at Twentieth Century–Fox rechristened her Marilyn Monroe. Once, before she became famous, Marilyn tried to telephone the man who had fathered her. A secretary said, "He doesn't want to see you. He suggests you see his lawyer in Los Angeles if you have some complaint."

She hung up without replying, but if ever a girl emerging from childhood had reason to complain, she did. At one time or another she had lived with twelve sets of foster parents. Their standards varied wildly. In one home she was given empty whiskey bottles as toys; two others were ruled by religious fanatics. In one of them she was taught to sing "Jesus Loves Me" in time of trial, punished with a razor strop for thinking impure thoughts, and, when she undressed with a little boy to compare the differences in their bodies, called a slut. She loved a dog; a neighbor killed it. On a visit, her grandmother tried to smother her with a pillow. She spent twenty-one months in an orphanage, and when she became sixteen she married an older man she didn't love to escape her wretched situation as a ward of the state. Already she was a stammerer, a chronic insomniac — and a girl with a desperate, insatiable yearning to be wanted.

Her first husband taught her sexual ecstasy on a Murphy bed. She gloried in it and would pursue it for the rest of her life, but it wasn't enough; she craved the adoration of millions. As a child she had spent Saturday afternoons in Grauman's Egyptian Theatre, watching Bette Davis in *Jezebel* and Norma Shearer in *Marie Antoinette* and wishing she were up there on the screen. Outside, she would try to fit her feet into the concrete prints of Clara Bow, Janet Gaynor, and Gloria Swanson. After *Yank* ran a picture of her in an article on women in war work, she was given a screen test. In it she entered a room, sat down, and lit a cigarette. The first man to see the rushes said: "I got a cold chill. This girl had something I hadn't seen since silent pictures. This is the first girl who looked like one of those lush stars of the silent era. Every frame of the test radiated sex."

Billy Wilder, who later directed her in *Some Like It Hot,* called it "flesh impact," and said the only other stars who had it were Clara Bow, Jean Harlow, and Rita Hayworth. Audiences first saw it in a Marx Brothers comedy, *Love Happy.* Playing a bit part, Marilyn came swaying into the office of a private detective played by Groucho and said anxiously, "Some men are following me." Suddenly everyone was tremendously interested in her problem. After *The Asphalt Jungle* and *All About Eve* had made her a celebrity, that provocative walk was heavily insured by Lloyd's of London.

She was worth it. Her twenty-three films between 1950 and 1961 grossed 200 million dollars. Only Brigitte Bardot of France approached her in popularity. Each week on an average Marilyn received five thousand letters, a score of them proposals of marriage. In Turkey a distraught admirer slashed his wrists when she didn't accept him. *Pravda* and the Vatican's *L'Osservatore Romano* agreed that she symbolized a sinful society. Nunnally Johnson called her "a phenomenon of nature, like Niagara Falls and the Grand Canyon." To *Life* she was "a busty Bernhardt," and her voluptuous dimensions — 37.5-23-36 — were familiar to millions of men who didn't know those of their own wives. At various times her immense appeal was attributed to her breathless voice, her incandescence, her ash-blonde hair, her moist-lipped open mouth, her dreamy blue eyes, and that tremulous gait.

It was more elusive than that — and more earthy. Marilyn's need to be desired was so great that she could make love to a camera. Because of this, her lust aroused lust in audiences, sometimes even among women. There was nothing subtle about it. She was no tease. She was prepared, and even eager, to give what she offered. By the time she was fourteen the fathers of her friends had pawed her, and one summer an off-duty policeman had cut through a screen door to get at her. She never pretended to be shocked, or even resentful.

She became the mistress of a theatrical agent. He lost weight; his physician told him he had a weak heart and must avoid strenuous exercise; but Marilyn's demands increased until he collapsed while with her in Palm Springs and died. Once, when she was married to Joe DiMaggio and he was away, she slipped on moccasins and prowled the foggy streets of San Francisco looking for a companion. Costarring with Yves Montand in *Let's Make Love* while she was Mrs. Arthur Miller, she seduced Montand on the set — and Miller knew it.

She exulted in her carnality. As a rising star she posed naked for a calendar. She didn't need the fifty dollars; she just liked the idea. ("You mean you didn't have anything on?" a scandalized woman reporter asked. "Oh yes," said Marilyn, "I had the radio on.") Acquiring from the photographer transparencies which showed her pubic hair, she gave them to DiMaggio as a wedding present. "Slugger," as she called him, was rather prim about sex, and she offended him deeply by straddling a New York sidewalk grating, during the filming of *The Seven-Year Itch*, until a gathering of cheering fans saw a blast of air toss her skirt above her hips. To her it had been one of the most exciting moments of her life.

In the last days of her life she was poring over *Playboy* prints of her taken in the nude. It was her ambition to have these pictures appear simultaneously on the covers of girlie magazines all over the world. She anticipated the coming of X-rated movies and yearned for it. When John Huston cut a shot of her exposed breasts from *The Misfits*, she was crushed. "Let's get the people away from the television sets," she said. "I love to do things the censors won't pass. After all, what are we all here for, just to stand and let it pass us by? Gradually they'll let down the censorship — sadly, probably not in my lifetime."

She became as big a star as Chaplin and Garbo, she gave a command performance for the Queen of England — and yet a feeling of achievement eluded her. Her three marriages ended disastrously; she suffered two miscarriages and couldn't have a child. Hollywood kept casting her in dumb blonde roles. She fled eastward and studied serious acting with the Strasbergs, but after two years she returned to California, still searching for the unattainable.

The release of *Some Like It Hot* in January 1959 was a personal triumph for her, but under the glitter there was a dark side the public had not yet seen. She was drinking heavily and had become addicted to barbiturates. Never prompt, she had become so unpunctual that she had alienated her fellow actors; Jack Lemmon and Tony Curtis, playing a pair of merry transvestites, had had to stand around all day waiting for her to appear. Attempts to wake her would begin at 6:30 A.M. with vats of black coffee and masseurs. Her snoring body would be rolled back and forth as attendants made her up horizontally. Sometimes shooting wouldn't begin until 4 P.M.; sometimes it would be postponed until the next morning, when the ritual would begin again.

She wouldn't learn her lines. In one scene she was supposed to say, "It's me, Sugar" at a certain moment. That required forty-seven takes. She seemed to be wholly indifferent to the inconvenience and the expense, which would add as much as a million dollars to the production costs of a movie. Once an assistant director knocked on the door of her dressing room and told her that the other actors were waiting. Marilyn replied, "Go fuck yourself."

Finally Fox fired her for being absent for all but five days during seven weeks of shooting *Something's Got to Give*. It was the summer of 1962, she was thirty-six years old, and she seemed to have lost her zest for life. To a *Life* reporter she said: "It might be kind of a relief to be finished. It's sort of like, I don't know what kind of a yard dash you're running, but then you're at the finish line, and you sort of sigh — you've made it! But you never have — you have to start all over again."

Her last affair was with a Washingtonian, a lawyer and a public man. She was afraid of destroying his political career, afraid that she was pregnant by him — and, finally, furious at him because he wanted her to join him for an evening with some friends and two prostitutes. She put a stack of Sinatra records on a spindle, swallowed all the Nembutals in her medicine cabinet, and sank into a lethal coma.

Her corpse, Coroner's Case No. 81128, lay unclaimed at the Los Angeles County Morgue until Joe DiMaggio arrived to arrange the funeral. Marilyn had given no thought to the disposal of her coffin, but it would be incorrect to say that she had not anticipated her last act. She had, and she had left exact instructions for it. As she had requested, her makeup was by Allan Snyder, her costume by Margie Plecher, and her hair style by Agnes Flanagan.

TWENTY-ONE

Mr. Chairman, Mr. Chairman

LATER THE SPECTER of Dienbienphu would loom ever larger in the American consciousness, but at the time it was something that was happening to somebody else. Its downfall wasn't the only major event of 1954, or even one of the top stories. That was a newsy year in the United States. In January the world's first atomic submarine, *Nautilus,* was launched in Groton, Connecticut. Six weeks later in Detroit six leaders of the Communist Party in Michigan were found guilty of conspiring to overthrow the U.S. government. Confronted by indisputable evidence of an approaching recession, the President decided in his March 12 cabinet meeting to call it a "rolling readjustment."

The Easter 1954 issue of *McCall's* introduced "togetherness," a concept which quickly became so popular that it took on overtones of a social crusade and became almost a national purpose of the 1950s. The Air Force Academy was created on April 1; its first class was sworn in at Lowry Air Force Base, Denver, Colorado. Rejecting a lower British bid, Secretary of Defense Charles E. Wilson awarded contracts for construction of the Chief Joseph Dam in the state of Washington to an American firm, and both houses of Congress approved the St. Lawrence Seaway.

Julius and Ethel Rosenberg had been executed after a demonstration outside the White House in which picketers protesting the sentence were accosted by noisy young demonstrators bearing placards which read TWO FRIED ROSENBERGERS COMING RIGHT UP. Admiral Robert B. Carney, Chief of Naval Operations, contributed to cold war tensions by telling reporters that he and his staff expected a Chinese Communist attack on the offshore islands of Quemoy and Matsu within a month. "They have information I do not have," said the President. Nevertheless, he warned that any assault on Formosa "will have to run over the Seventh Fleet." The cabinet was elated at its July 23 meeting to learn that economic indicators would soon turn upward, ending the rolling readjustment. August's Hurricane Carol blew down the steeple of Boston's historic Old North Church. Other hurricanes named Edna and Hazel followed in September.

Eisenhower and Churchill conferred in Bermuda on world peace. The Atomic Energy Commission on October 5 approved a contract under which a West Memphis power plant would be built for the TVA by a southern utility group headed by Edgar H. Dixon and Eugene A. Yates. President Eisenhower described his administration's political philosophy as "dynamic conservatism," then as "progressive, dynamic conservatism," then as "progressive moderation," then as "moderate progressivism," and then as "positive progressivism." On December 21, 1954, Dr. Samuel H. Sheppard, a Cleveland osteopath, was convicted of murdering his wife Marilyn on July 4. Sir Edmund Hillary, conquerer of Mount Everest, was thrilling lecture audiences in the Middle West, and nationwide circulation was given to the first authoritative reports linking cigarette smoking and heart disease.

Playboy was selling for fifty cents, competing on newsstands with such other publications of the decade as *Flair* (fifty cents), *Confidential*, "Uncensored and Off the Record" (a quarter), *Mad* (a dime), and, at fifteen cents, the most successful periodical of the 1950s, *TV Guide*, which by the end of the decade would be running fifty-three regional editions for seven million subscribers.

America's drug culture lay far in the future, but the roots of its idiom could be heard at bebop sessions where one heard the esoteric jazz of such maestros as Miles Davis and Thelonious Monk. They called money bread and girls chicks. To understand was to flip; something which in the past had been fabulous was now crazy. Superlatives of crazy were cool, groovy, the end, and far out (later to become out of sight). To be appreciative was to be hip, and someone who was so hip that he had passed into an ecstatic trance would soon be called a hippy.

Better known then, and a source of amusement in intellectual circles throughout the decade, was advertising cant. As society became more aware of advertisers, and as they became more clever, their instant clichés briefly became part of the language. In 1954 the reigning platitude was the suffix "wise," meaning "with regard to," "in respect of," or "in the manner of." Battered by overuse, it became an all-purpose word. Instead of saying "This year's cars are all chrome," you said, "Stylewise, this year's cars are all chrome." Moneywise, a tycoon was rich. Sequencewise, a loser was last. Agewise, a girl was young; clotheswise, she might be chic; and personalitywise, she would be attractive. Boozewise, you might have a big night. Headwise, you would feel terrible in the morning, but jobwise, you would make it to the office.

On the other side of the island from Madison Avenue lay Tin Pan Alley, and there sovereignty still rested in the clammy hands of the balladeers. The biggest hit of 1954 was Kitty Kallen's "Little Things Mean a Lot." Runners-up included Perry Como's "Wanted," Frank Sinatra's "Young at Heart," and the Crew Cuts' (only classical musicians wore their hair long then)

"Sh-Boom." Archie Bleyer's "Hernando's Hideaway" was another memorable ditty that year. The Four Aces' "Three Coins in the Fountain" was from the motion picture of the same name, a Cinemascope production in De Luxe Color starring Dorothy McGuire, Clifton Webb, and Jean Peters. Waterfront corruption in New York was a running story throughout 1954 — on April 15 Albert Anastasia was deprived of his citizenship — and the Academy of Motion Picture Arts and Sciences awarded its Oscar for the best picture of the year to *On the Waterfront*. Other honored films were *The Caine Mutiny, The Country Girl, Seven Brides for Seven Brothers, Sabrina, Executive Suite, Dial M for Murder, Rear Window*, and Disney's *20,000 Leagues Under the Sea*. Movies still weren't making much money, but for the time being the big talent was staying in Hollywood.

Variety listed as 1954's most popular television programs *I Love Lucy, Dragnet*, and the mixed bags of Groucho Marx and Ed Sullivan. The only really bright hour of TV comedy, Sid Caesar and Imogene Coca's Saturday evening *Your Show of Shows*, folded in 1954 after 160 performances; the network blamed lack of audience interest. Above all, 1954 was the year of the quiz show: *I've Got a Secret, Stop the Music, Place the Face, Name That Tune*, and *What's My Line*. The big money quiz programs, *Twenty-one* and *The $64,000 Question*, were in the wings. TV spectaculars — long, lavish, one-performance extravaganzas — were more interesting. *Amahl and the Night Visitors*, a Christmas Eve opera written for television by Gian-Carlo Menotti in 1951, had been acclaimed everywhere. As it happened, 1954's chief spectacular, *Satins and Spurs*, was so terrible that its star, Betty Hutton, retired from show business. Next year promised to be much better, though. Contracts were out for Mary Martin's superb *Peter Pan*, to be telecast March 7, 1955.

Obviously television was having an immense impact on American mores, but defining the nature of the impact was difficult. Some thought the networks were too wide-open, too permissive. TV fare was more violent than radio, and franker about sex. Plunging necklines, an exciting development of the early 1950s, left little doubt that female performers were mammary and proud of it. When Desi Arnaz impregnated his wife and costar, Lucille Ball, the producers of *I Love Lucy* took it as an opportunity; each week's episode offered late bulletins on Lucy's condition, and Desi was even depicted suffering from sympathetic morning sickness.

In reality TV was merely noting a trend here, one whose implications would not emerge until another decade. The medium itself would never be a pace-setter. Like the life-styles of the 1950s of which it was so faithful a mimic, it was bland, innocuous, noncontroversial. Its most familiar themes were charming but irrelevant to real issues: the bromides Loretta Young read at the end of each program, Dave Garroway's "Peace," and the "Ho-Ho Song" to which Red Buttons danced offstage.

Commercial? Absolutely: the profit motive was as sacred as togetherness. Sneering at it was almost prima facie evidence of subversion. Everybody was selling something, and Americans approved; the diversity of their marketplace was the marvel of the world. A confidential survey made for the Republican National Committee by Batten, Barton, Durstine, and Osborn reported that foreign policy was the number one issue for American voters, with Communist infiltration in the U.S. second, but it was untrue. The agency was telling its clients what they wanted to hear. Prosperity was what Americans wanted, and they had it, were getting fat with it, and enjoyed reading the scales. It was a bull market that was going to get bullier. Detroit was counting on Chevrolet's Dinah Shore to be especially alluring in 1955. The automotive industry's confident — and justifiable — expectation was that nearly eight million cars would be sold, nearly a million more than in any previous year.

In February 1954 over 7,500 Republicans descended on Washington to eat fried chicken box lunches in the Ellipse and observe Lincoln Day by singing "God Bless America." The President came out for a few brief remarks. At the moment he wasn't toying with "moderate progressivism" or any of that; he used the simple term "conservative," paused, then added firmly: "And don't be afraid to use that word." They cheered. Middle-class Republicans were feeling their oats. They were proud to be conservative, prosperous, conformist, and vigilant defenders of the American way of life, and they wanted no truck with crackpots, Reds, heretics, Bohemians, radicals, nuts, Bolsheviks, loonies, pinkos, fellow travelers, galoots, geezers, or screwballs. Eggheads were subjects of particular scorn. No wild-eyed college professors were going to be allowed to gum up the works. On April 13, 1954, James Reston reported in the *New York Times* that the Atomic Energy Commission, at the direction of President Eisenhower, had withdrawn the security clearance of Dr. J. Robert Oppenheimer pending an investigation of charges that he had, among other things, "worked tirelessly from January 21, onward, to retard the United States H-bomb program."

The accusation had been lodged five months earlier by William L. Borden, former executive secretary of the Joint Congressional Committee on Atomic Energy and senior assistant to Senator Brien McMahon. Borden had written J. Edgar Hoover on November 7, 1953, that "more probably than not J. Robert Oppenheimer is an agent of the Soviet Union." A bill of particulars followed, including charges that prior to April 1942 "He was contributing substantial monthly sums to the Communist Party," that "His wife and younger brother were Communists," and that "He had no close friends except Communists."

Borden's motives are obscure. He had nothing new. The government had long known that Oppenheimer had been a freewheeling left-of-center ideologue in the 1930s. It hadn't affected his work. Lately he hadn't had much to do with Washington anyhow. At one time he had been a member of no fewer than thirty-five government committees, but in July 1952 he had resigned as chairman of the AEC General Advisory Commission, and since the beginning of the Eisenhower administration he had been devoting most of his energies to the Institute for Advanced Study in Princeton, of which he was the director. As a government consultant he retained his top-secret Q clearance, but he never used it. At the time of Borden's accusations Oppenheimer wasn't even in the country. He had been chosen to deliver the BBC's prestigious Reith Lecture for 1953, and while he was in Britain Oxford decided to award him his sixth honorary degree. It was a question of who was more honored by the occasion, Oppenheimer or Oxford. By this time America's most eminent scientist had been elected to every learned society in Europe. Prizes, awards, and foreign decorations had been showered upon him. At home he had been chosen for everything from the American Academy of Arts and Sciences to the *Popular Mechanics* Hall of Fame.

Now Borden said he was a Russian spy. What is far more likely is that he was a victim of scientific politics. A savage dispute was raging between nuclear physicists belonging to two schools of thought named for America's two great nuclear laboratories, Los Alamos and Livermore. The Los Alamos group, comprising Oppenheimer's colleagues and protégés, held that nuclear missiles should be only one of many kinds of weapons in the American arsenal. This was called "finite containment." The Livermore, or Teller, group believed that the nation's security depended upon the unlimited development of nuclear striking power. That was "infinite containment." Most scientists took the finite view, but an administration that advocated "massive retaliation" was plainly thinking in infinite terms. The Livermore men were in power, and this, in fact, was one reason Oppenheimer had withdrawn to Princeton. But that wasn't enough for his adversaries. The debate had turned some men of science into fanatics — which is not really surprising, since the issue could determine the future of the human race — and certain admirers of Edward Teller were determined to discredit Oppenheimer. Almost certainly they were behind Borden.

Borden, however, merely wrote a letter. Washington desks were covered with such letters then. There was no reason why an official should pay attention to a new smear, unless, of course, he thought there was something in it. That was true in this instance. J. Edgar Hoover had been suspicious of J. Robert Oppenheimer for a long time. In 1947 Hoover had done all he could to tag Oppenheimer as a security risk. The *Herald Tribune* reported that the FBI file on Oppenheimer was four feet six inches high. Borden could hardly have sent his letter to a more receptive addressee, and the chances are that he knew it.

Hoover spent the next three weeks preparing an inch-thick digest of the Oppenheimer file. On November 30 he sent it to the White House. Copies went to Lewis A. Strauss at the Atomic Energy Commission and Charlie Wilson at the Pentagon. After reading his, Wilson phoned the President; he wanted Oppenheimer barred from all military installations at once. Eisenhower called it "very disturbing" (which of course it was, however you felt about Oppenheimer) and called an emergency meeting to weigh the charges. Had the scientist ever been confronted with them? he asked. Told he hadn't, Ike ordered a hearing. Meantime, he said, he wanted a "blank wall" put between Oppenheimer and all government secrets. It was an arresting phrase, and although only Wilson, Strauss, Brownell, and Robert Cutler of the National Security Council had been present, word of the decision reached the Washington gossips and, through them, the Capitol Hill home of Senator Joseph R. McCarthy.

Upon returning from England Oppenheimer found a message to call Admiral Strauss. Strauss urged him to come to the capital at once; the matter was pressing and couldn't be discussed over the telephone. On the afternoon of December 21 the scientist entered the AEC's gleaming marble building on Constitution Avenue, and in room 236, the admiral's large, paneled office, he found Strauss in conference with Major General Kenneth D. Nichols, the commission's general manager. They asked him to join them at a conference table. There, after an exchange of pleasantries and news of mutual friends, Strauss told Oppenheimer, as gracefully as you can tell a man such a thing, that he was suspected of treason. Eisenhower's directive was explained to him, and then the possibility of a graceful exit was discussed. Oppenheimer refused to take it.

On Christmas Eve a special indignity was visited upon him. Security men from the AEC arrived in Princeton to confiscate all classified material in his possession. The hearing was then scheduled for April. Reston knew of it. He intended to publish nothing until a decision had been reached, but since McCarthy was planning to announce it in the Senate to claim that he had forced the administration's hand, Reston went ahead. The news was sensational, and the determination to avoid further sensationalism gave the subsequent hearing a furtive air. The sessions, closed to the press and public, were held in temporary building T-3, a shabby relic of OPA's wartime bureaucracy. To hoodwink any reporters who might learn of the location, Oppenheimer used a back door. The trial — for that is what it amounted to — was held in T-3's room 2022, a 24- by 12-foot office which had been converted to its temporary purpose by an arrangement of tables, chairs, and a seedy old leather couch. Oppenheimer used the couch; afterward a participant would recall that the scientist "leaned back lazily, sometimes as though his thoughts were elsewhere, on the sofa which had been turned into a dock for the occasion."

A bench had been set up at the opposite end of the room. There sat Oppenheimer's judges: Gordon Gray; Thomas A. Morgan, a retired industrialist; and Ward V. Evans, emeritus professor of chemistry at Northwestern. The AEC was represented by Robert Robb, counsel to its Personnel Security Board. Robb contributed to the inquisitional aura by adopting the abrasive manner of a prosecuting attorney. His attitude toward Oppenheimer was one of contempt. A stranger entering room 2022 would never have guessed that the man under interrogation had been director of the laboratory that had perfected the atomic bomb. Robb used all the time-worn trial tricks, including keeping the sunlight in the defendant's eyes by putting his own back to a window. The 992-page transcript of the hearings bristles with his disdain.

Periodically Oppenheimer's disembodied voice would be heard over a portable public address system — recordings of wartime G-2 telephone taps which had been made without his consent or even knowledge. It was humiliating; at times it was almost unbelievable. When André Malraux read the record of the proceedings he expressed astonishment that Oppenheimer, who after all was a free man, had remained to hear Robb's studied insults. Malraux said, "He ought to have stood up and shouted, 'Gentlemen, I am the atomic bomb.'" But Oppenheimer was too diffident, too introverted for that, and he had suffered much brooding over the destruction of Hiroshima; he felt, as he told a friend, that "We did the devil's work."

After taking testimony from forty witnesses, the tribunal retired to write its opinion. The allegation that Oppenheimer had been an enemy agent was rejected: "We have given particular attention to the question of his loyalty and we have come to the clear conclusion, which should be reassuring to the people of this country, that he is a loyal citizen." Indeed, the panel observed, "It must be said that Dr. Oppenheimer seems to have had a high degree of discretion reflecting an unusual ability to keep to himself vital secrets." Evans, the only scientist on the tribunal, wanted to restore Oppenheimer's security clearance, but Gray and Morgan wouldn't go that far. They didn't like some of Oppenheimer's friends. It was their opinion that his "associations have reflected a serious disregard for the requirements of the security system." Then there was his troubling lack of enthusiasm for the superbomb:

> We find his conduct in the hydrogen bomb program sufficiently disturbing as to raise a doubt as to whether his future participation, if characterized by the same attitudes in a government program relating to the national defense, would be clearly consistent with the best interests of security.

Oppenheimer appealed the two-to-one decision to the AEC, which upheld it in a four-to-one vote. Commissioner Henry D. Smyth urged the others to see that Oppenheimer's "loyalty and trustworthiness emerge clearly," that in the light of his distinguished attainments "his services could be of great value to the country in the future," and that "the security system has . . . neither the responsibility nor the right to dictate every detail of a man's life." But it was precisely there that the others parted company with him; a man of great achievements might be forgiven much, and the commissioners were less rigid than the Gray board in passing judgment on Oppenheimer's mixed feelings about thermonuclear weapons, but failure to repudiate friends and relatives with unorthodox political persuasions could not be overlooked.

Ironically, the effect of purging Oppenheimer was the exact opposite of what his enemies had intended. In martyrdom he acquired new stature. Teller, on the other hand, became something of an outcast. The plotters had expected him to become the new wise man of nuclear physics. Instead he was ostracized. The only established scientist who had spoken against Oppenheimer, he was looked upon as an FBI informer, a turncoat who had betrayed both a fellow scientist and science itself. At scientific meetings he was snubbed by the others; when he protested they walked away. Eventually he came to be tolerated, but he was never really trusted again; in panel discussions and conversations his fellow physicists were formal and guarded. He appealed to Enrico Fermi, now near death, and the great Italian scientist supported him in an article in the magazine *Science,* but to Teller's critics this was just one more breach of ethics. They put him down as a publicity seeker and continued to ignore him. In the world of science his Dr. Strangelove image had already formed.

Meantime the human condition which would be symbolized by Strangelove had been brought into focus by a chance wind in the western Pacific Ocean, giving Americans a brief but terrible glimpse of what they were doing to themselves and to the world. On March 1, when Robb was preparing his case against Oppenheimer, the AEC had exploded its second hydrogen bomb on Bikini atoll, just east of Eniwetok. Outstripping all expectations, it ripped open the coral reef with a force of some 18 million to 22 million tons of TNT — the equivalent of 900 to 1,000 Hiroshima bombs. Then the wind picked up the fallout. Meteorologists had predicted a stiff breeze to the north. Instead, it blew southward until, 120 miles from Bikini and far from the danger zone marked by the bomb testers, it dropped clouds of radioactive dust on a Japanese trawler grimly misnamed the *Lucky Dragon No. 5.* The startled Japanese fishermen at first thought themselves to be in the world's first tropical snowstorm. By the time they reached their home port of Yaizu, the ghastly truth had begun to emerge. All twenty-three of them were sick and had to be hospitalized. Subsequently one, the wireless operator, died. Meanwhile sensitive devices had picked up traces of radioactivity from rainfall in Japan, Australia, the United States, Europe, and even in the oil in airliners which had been flying over India.

This brought new term to the vocabulary of death: strontium 90, or radiostrontium, a heavy radioactive isotope of strontium with a half-life of 25 years. That was what had been in the lethal blizzard which had struck the *Lucky Dragon No. 5.* Deposited in the bones, like calcium, and combined with radioactive iodine, which had been discovered in the thyroid glands of the fishermen, strontium 90 was a cause of cancer. It was further believed to threaten posterity, though its impact there could not be measured for several generations. Admiral Strauss called the scientists who warned of these dangers, "appeasers" and "alarmists." He dispatched his own teams of technicians around the world, and their findings appeared to justify his name for the project, "Operation Sunshine." Other investigators were gloomy. A. H. Sturtevant, emeritus professor of biology at Cal Tech, said that "the bombs already exploded will ultimately result in the production of numerous defective individuals." Curt Stern, professor of genetics at

Berkeley, said, "By now everyone in the world harbors in his body small amounts of radioactivity from past H-bomb tests," and physicist Ralph Lapp, a consultant for the Bikini tests and head of the Office of Naval Research nuclear branch, predicted that at some time in the 1970s the buildup of radioactive material in the stratosphere would exceed the maximum permissible amount and begin to affect the health of everyone on earth.

At the distance of twenty years this issue may seem to transcend all others of that spring — the uproar over the Bricker amendment, the crisis in Indochina, the fall of Oppenheimer — but at the time it, like them, was overshadowed by a question so absurd, so petty, so devoid of significance or even seriousness as to cast grave doubts upon the ability of democratic institutions to survive the challenges of the second half of the twentieth century. Incredible as it seems now, for thirty-five days the nation was engrossed in a dispute which began as a quarrel over who had granted a routine promotion, from captain to major, to a left-wing Army dentist named Irving Peress.

"Who promoted Peress?" Senator McCarthy demanded over and over. He never found out, and the truth is that he wasn't much interested. Peress merely gave him an excuse to wade into the Army. Actually the dentist's majority had come to him not because any of his superiors approved it, but because he was entitled to it under automatic provisions of the Doctor Draft Law, a measure meant to correlate military pay with civilian earnings — and one which McCarthy had approved. Peress had entered the Army in October 1952. He received his bronze oak leaves a year later. Next it developed that he had belonged to the American Labor Party, then tantamount to being a Communist. In testifying before McCarthy's subcommittee at Camp Kilmer, New Jersey, on January 30, 1954, he invoked the Fifth Amendment. The Office of the Adjutant General had already instructed the First Army to discharge him, and three days later it did, but that wasn't good enough for the junior senator from Wisconsin. McCarthy thought the Army should have court-martialed Peress. He took its failure to do so as proof that Communists had infiltrated the Department of the Army, a situation which he meant to remedy by his investigative powers.

McCarthyologists reasoned that there must be more to it than that, and in fact there was much more. To be sure, as a nihilist Joe McCarthy was opposed to the Army for no better reason than that it represented established authority. His first appearance as a Washington mischief-maker, predating his discovery of Communism, had pitted him against the Army. During the Battle of the Bulge seventy-three SS troopers had murdered 150 captured American GIs at Malmedy. After the war they had been sentenced to death, and in 1949 Joe had taken up the SS cause. The furor had brought the senator the sort of headlines he craved (MCCARTHY HITS BRUTALITY; MCCARTHY HINTS AT MYSTERY WITNESS; MCCARTHY CHARGES WHITEWASH).

The Germans' lives had been spared, and nothing that had happened since then suggested that he would be reluctant to take on the Pentagon again. Yet he bore it no grudge. There was no conflict between his interests and the Army's. In early 1954 he had stronger motives for attacking other institutions. The decision to attack the Army was not really his; it was made for him by two remarkable young men, two members of McCarthy's staff who might be called the Leopold and Loeb of the 1950s. Their names were Roy M. Cohn and G. David Schine.

Cohn typified young political militants of his generation, just as Mario Savio and Mark Rudd would later typify theirs. Short, dark, insensitive, and haughty, he also possessed a photographic memory. His drooping eyelids and his curiously sensual mouth gave him a sullen, vulpine expression. Like McCarthy, he loved a quarrel for its own sake. The fact that Cohn always kept his dark hair combed was just about the only sign that he came from a good family. His father — a Democrat — was a judge in the appellate division of the New York Supreme Court. Roy's mother worshipped him. Once in his childhood, when he was invited on an excursion to be supervised by the father of one of his friends, the father had a phone call from Mrs. Cohn. She said, "You're in for a great treat. Roy's going with you. He's such a smart boy and knows so much about so many things. I'm sure you'll get a lot of pleasure out of him and probably learn a lot from him, too."

Certainly he was precocious. At twenty he was graduated from Columbia Law School; he had to loiter around Manhattan waiting to turn twenty-one before he could be admitted to the bar. On that day he was sworn in as an Assistant U.S. Attorney. He became a specialist in what was called subversive activities, working on, among other cases, the Remington and Rosenberg trials. At twenty-three he was an inside source for Walter Winchell and George Sokolsky, and while he was scratching their backs, they scratched his with flattering references which gave him a start on his next goal: appointment as special assistant to U.S. Attorney General James McGranery. He reached it in September 1952. Cohn's first day in Washington was a portent: he was sworn in McGranery's private office, although no new oath was necessary; he held a press conference to announce his duties but forgot to reveal his title, held a second press conference to correct the oversight, demanded a private cable address and a private telephone line to his former boss in New York, and was turned down both times but somehow managed to have three other junior lawyers evicted from the office they shared so that it could become his private office. In December he prepared the indictment which charged Owen Lattimore with perjury. That case collapsed, but by then Cohn didn't care; on January 14, 1953, he had resigned from the Justice Department to become chief counsel for Senator Joseph R. McCarthy's Permanent Investigations Subcommittee.

Schine was the sleeker of the two, a fair, languid youth with the face and physique of a fledgling Greek god. Born to wealth, he was a graduate of

Andover and Harvard, '49. In Cambridge he had been conspicuous for his valet and his big black convertible with a two-way phone-radio. The Harvard *Crimson* took note of his way of arriving at parties:

> This consisted of phoning from his car and saying, "This is G. David Schine. I'm now driving through Copley Square. Could you direct me a little further," and then later, "This is G. David Schine. I'm now at Kenmore Square. Could you give me more directions please."

Like Cohn, he became interested in Communism. In school he wrote a paper about it which he afterward published as a six-page pamphlet, *Definition of Communism*. After Schine became famous *Time* called it "remarkably succinct." The *New Yorker,* more critical, reported that "It puts the Russian Revolution, the founding of the Communist Party, and the start of the First Five Year Plan in years when these things did not happen. It gives Lenin the wrong first name. It confuses Stalin with Trotsky. It confuses Marx with Lenin. It confuses Alexander Kerensky with Prince Lvov. It confuses fifteenth-century Utopianism with twentieth-century Marxism." By then copies of it had become extremely rare, but when it first appeared, *Definition of Communism* could be found beside the Gideon Bible in every Schine hotel — the Roney Plaza in Miami Beach, the Ten Eyck in Albany, the Ambassador in Los Angeles, the Ritz Carlton in Atlantic City, and the Boca Raton in Boca Raton. One guest who read it with pleasure was a certain Rabbi Benjamin Schultz, the director of something called the American Jewish League Against Communism. Rabbi Schultz sought Schine out and introduced him to George Sokolsky. Through Sokolsky, Schine met Cohn, and through Cohn he met McCarthy.

Putting a multimillionaire on the subcommittee payroll would have been ridiculous. Besides, Schine didn't have any qualifications, as the word is understood on Capitol Hill. Early in 1953 Cohn persuaded McCarthy to appoint his new friend chief consultant on psychological warfare. There was no such position. Cohn made it up. Schine was delighted to serve without pay. In New York the two young men set up temporary headquarters in the Waldorf Towers, where Schine had a permanent suite, and there they planned an ingenious investigation of the Voice of America. Voice employees were quietly urged to put the finger on fellow workers with odd ideas or habits — it was these informants McCarthy had in mind when he talked of his "Loyal American Underground" — and after televised hearings under klieg lights there was general agreement in the press that the Senator's exuberant protégé had demoralized the Voice program. Cohn and Schine were still only twenty-six. There was no limit to how far they might go.

They flew to Europe, surfacing in Paris on Easter Sunday, April 4. Eighteen days of madness followed: in-and-out trips to European capitals during which they strutted and posed for the press and exercised, to the greatest possible degree, their rights and prerogatives as representatives of the U.S. Congress. And wherever they went they were trailed by a gleeful corps of correspondents who chanted:

> *Positively, Mr. Cohn!*
> *Absolutely, Mr. Schine!*

Or sang:

> *Oh, the Cohn Schines east!*
> *The Cohn Schines west!*
> *McCarthy knows*
> *Where the Cohn Schines best!*

By late 1953 McCarthy's hostility toward the White House was apparent to all around him. Two days before Thanksgiving he made it public. In a November 16 broadcast Harry Truman had referred scathingly to "McCarthyism." Joe had demanded equal time to reply. Like the administration, the networks were trying desperately to appease him, and the request was granted. But after the first few minutes the senator turned his wrath from Truman to Eisenhower. At a press conference the week before Ike had said he didn't know what McCarthyism meant. He would soon find out, Joe said ominously. Ike had also expressed confidence in his ability to rid the government of security risks; in next year's congressional elections, he said, the issue would be a dead one. Far from it, the senator told his radio and television audience. The "raw, harsh, unpleasant fact" was that "Communism is an issue and will be an issue in 1954."

Of course, he said patronizingly, the Republican administration was doing "infinitely" better than the Democrats in this respect. But there were "a few cases where our batting average is zero — we struck out." As always he got down to cases: names, dates, figures, dossiers — the wrong ones, though his listeners couldn't tell that. Joe said that was shameful, it was disgraceful, it made McCarthy sick way down deep inside. But there was worse. Despite admonitions from him, Eisenhower, like Truman before him, persisted in adhering to mutual aid treaties with Britain while the British insulted the memory of American boys who had fallen in Korea by trading with Peking. McCarthy's voice rose nasally:

"Are we going to continue to send perfumed notes? . . . it is time that we, the Republican Party, liquidate this blood-stained blunder . . . we promised the American people something different. Let us deliver — not next year or next month — let us deliver now. . . . We can do this by merely saying to our allies and alleged allies, "If you continue to ship to Red China . . . you will not get one cent of American money."

Eisenhower was furious. C. D. Jackson and Paul Hoffman urged him to repudiate McCarthy as a Republican at the next presidential press conference. Hagerty agreed; so did Bryce Harlow and four other presidential assistants. But Nixon said the real victim in such a showdown would be the Republican party. It was decided that Dulles should answer McCarthy at his own press conference on December 1 with a statement that Eisenhower would approve word by word. McCarthy, the secretary said, had attacked "the very heart of U.S. foreign policy." That policy was to treat other nations as sovereign, not to pick their trade partners or "make them our satellites." As a real anti-Communist hard-liner — unlike McCarthy — Dulles observed that the United States must alway be prepared "to retaliate with a devastating blow against the vitals of Russia," and that it retained the capacity to do this "only because we share the well-located bases of other friendly countries."

McCarthy was now on favorite turf. He liked nothing better than a slugging match with a Secretary of State, and he hadn't had one for nearly a year. Besides, this was an exceptionally good time to do mischief. Eisenhower was about to confer with Churchill in Bermuda. An emotional televised appeal to the American people on the eve of the conference could go a long way toward sabotaging it and embarrassing the President. And that was in fact Joe's next move. On the evening of December 3, as Ike was leaving for the meeting, McCarthy took the air to cry out against Englishmen who fattened their bankrolls by dealing with the murderers of U.S. soldiers. He implored "every American who feels as I do about this blood trade with a mortal enemy to write or wire the President . . . so he can be properly guided." Five days later the White House acknowledged that over fifty thousand messages had been received. No one in Washington had been deceived by the moonshine about guidance. This was a straight-out contest between the two men, and the presidential spokesman who reported the mail count did not pretend otherwise. McCarthy won among letter writers, he announced, while Eisenhower held the edge among those who had sent telegrams. Since the White House receives comparatively few wires, this was an artful way of saying that the senator had overwhelmed the President.

It was at this point that it became fashionable in Washington to describe McCarthy as the second most powerful man in the country. Certainly any demagogue who could trigger that sort of response had become formidable. There were other indications that McCarthyism was approching a new crest. In the next month, January 1954, Gallup reported that public approval of the senator had risen sixteen percentage points in the past six months. Fewer than three Americans in every ten disapproved of him. It is improbable that one in ten knew what a mountebank he was, so dexterous had he become in his manipulation of the press, but if the reactions of the man on the street can be put down to ignorance — and they probably can — those of the U.S. Senate cannot. Nowhere else was his wickedness so well known, yet in February, when the time came to vote on a $214,000 appropriation for his permanent subcommittee, the membership of the Senate was reduced to quivering jelly. Exactly one senator, Fulbright of Arkansas, had the courage to vote against it. Among those who did not find it possible to join Fulbright were Kennedy of Massachusetts, Johnson of Texas, Humphrey of Minnesota, Kefauver of Tennessee, Mansfield of Montana, Magnuson of Washington, Russell of Georgia, Long of Louisiana, Williams of Delaware, Kuchel of California, Douglas of Illinois, Lehman of New York, and Margaret Chase Smith of Maine. All were resolute, their characters were strong, they were enormously popular with their constituents. But they had never before encountered a prodigy like Joseph R. McCarthy.

Who believed him? Where was his strength? Who were the hard-core McCarthyites? They were Legionnaires, Minute Women, Texas millionaires, and people who felt threatened by fluoridation of public reservoirs and campaigns for mental health. They belonged to organizations like the DAR, the Sons of I Shall Return, We the Mothers Mobilize, the Nationalist Action League, and the Alert Council for America. They were anti-egg-heads like Louis Bromfield, John Chamberlain, Max Eastman, James Burnham, and William F. Buckley Jr. ("McCarthyism," Buckley wrote, ". . . is a movement around which men of good will and stern morality can close ranks.") They were fugitives from lost battles against Roosevelt legislation, the alliance with western Europe, the United Nations, the communications revolution, anti-anti-Semitism, the egalitarian passion, racial equality, the great internal migration of the 1940s, and social upheavals which were destroying the lines between the classes and the sexes, and widening those between the generations. At McCarthy rallies they sang reedily, "Nobody Loves Joe but the People," and politicians were convinced that dark masses of troubled voters stood behind them. It was believed on Capitol Hill, in the winter of 1953–54, that eight men in the Senate owed their presence there to McCarthy support.

As the second year of the Eisenhower administration began, the junior senator from Wisconsin stood on an awesome pinnacle, and Roy M. Cohn was right up there with him. G. David Schine was missing. He had been drafted. His absence was thought unimportant in Washington. Schine wasn't bright, like Cohn. In fact, McCarthy had secretly found him a pain in the neck. He hadn't mentioned this to Cohn, because McCarthy needed Cohn. What he was just discovering was that Cohn needed someone, too. Cohn needed Schine.

Schine's greeting from the Army had arrived in July. Apparently the blow was unexpected; he seems to have forgotten that he had even registered. Until then he and Cohn had been busy having a lively time — adjoining rooms in the Statler from Monday to Friday, merry weekends in Manhattan, and the anticipatory pleasure of planning antic forays into stodgy bureaucratic agencies. Joe, a lazy demagogue, had left the running of the subcommittee to them. They had felt, and had seemed to be, invulnerable. If no one in the capital dared strike back at them, who would? The answer was Schine's Gloversville draft board. There was irony here. The good citizens of Gloversville were too far from the power structure to know of Schine's mighty friends. They were also safe from a political fix:

the one thing Washington feared more than McCarthy was a selective service scandal.

Cohn's first thought was that his friend should be commissioned immediately. It was impossible; the Army, Navy, and Air Force in turn rejected Schine as unqualified. Cohn then summoned to his office Brigadier General Miles Reber, the Army's chief of liaison on the Hill. Later Joseph N. Welch, special Army counsel, was to question Reber about that.

WELCH: Were you actually aware of Mr. Cohn's position as counsel for this committee?

REBER: I was, Mr. Welch.

WELCH: Did that position . . . increase or diminish the interest with which you pursued the problem?

REBER: . . . I feel that it increased the interest.

WELCH: Disregarding the word "improper" influences or pressure, do you recall any instance comparable to this in which you were put under greater pressure?

REBER: . . . I recall no instance in which I was put under greater pressure.

The Pentagon hadn't taken this lightly. Indeed, to outsiders the most remarkable aspect of the Schine case was not the pressure from Cohn, but the favoritism which the military establishment had voluntarily displayed over a rich young McCarthy protégé who was, after all, only one of nearly a half-million Americans to be drafted that year. Schine's situation had been studied by the Secretary of Defense, the Secretary of the Army, two Army chiefs of staff, a vice chief of staff, the adjutant general of the Army, the commanding general of the Transportation Corps, the Air Force major general directing legislative liaison, and the judge advocate of the Navy.

At the direction of Secretary of the Army Robert T. Stevens, a New York textile manufacturer whose role in the affair would soon grow, two full colonels and a lieutenant colonel were ordered to reconsider the possibility that Schine might be officer material. Meanwhile the young applicant himself had begun to take an interest in the matter. The first time General Reber interviewed him, Schine was ready to raise his right hand and be sworn in as an officer right there. He was put out when Reber explained that there was more to it than that. As the general later testified, "he apparently felt that the business of filling out forms and going through with the processing was an unnecessary routine step."

On November 3, 1953, Schine went into uniform, and after fifteen days of temporary duty in New York ("to complete committee work") he was assigned to Company K, Fort Dix, New Jersey, for four weeks of basic training. Thanks largely to Cohn's persistence, the case remained open. Indeed, it grew even more interesting. The Army cannot be said to have been inflexible. Unlike other recruits, Schine was given a pass almost every weekend. His limousine was allowed inside the camp to pick him up and bring him back. He was released from drill for no fewer than 250 long-distance telephone calls. One rainy day, when everybody else was on the rifle range, Company K's commander found Private Schine goldbricking. Schine threw a comradely arm over the captain's shoulder and explained that he had been studying logistics "to remake the military along modern lines" — an excuse which actually was accepted. Schine's unusual ideas about how he might serve his country might, in fact, have been taken more seriously had not McCarthy, in his own talks with the Pentagon, let it be known that he did not share Cohn's unqualified enthusiasm for Schine. In a monitored call to Stevens the senator asked the secretary, as a "personal favor," not to assign "Dave . . . back on my committee." He said that Schine was "a good boy but there is nothing indispensable about him . . . it is one of the few things I have seen Roy completely unreasonable about."

John G. Adams, counselor for the Department of the Army, was now receiving the brunt of Cohn's anger. In his phone conversations with Schine, at the camp, Cohn would learn of little ways in which his friend's life might be made easier. He would then call Adams at any hour. Once he phoned Amherst College, where Adams was speaking, in an effort to have Schine relieved from KP duty the following day. If his suggestions were rejected, he became cross. During a heated discussion in New York he ordered Adams out of his car in the middle of three lanes of traffic, at Park Avenue and Forty-sixth Street, and on January 14, 1954, when Adams told him that Schine, like 90 percent of all inductees, would probably draw overseas duty, Cohn said this would "wreck the Army" and cause Stevens to be "through as Secretary of the Army."

By now the bizarre situation was being whispered about. In mid-December Drew Pearson ran an account of the Schine story. The following week the *Baltimore Sun* carried a long piece about it, and a *New York Post* article appeared in January. At the same time, McCarthy's view of the Army was darkening. Goaded by Cohn, wrathful over the discharge of Peress, and spurred, perhaps, by his need for daily victories, he erupted at a subcommittee hearing in New York on February 18. The unlucky witness at the time was Brigadier General Ralph W. Zwicker, a hero of the Bulge and the commanding officer of Camp Kilmer in New Jersey. McCarthy told Zwicker that he was "not fit to wear that uniform," that he should "be removed from any command," and that he did not have "the brains of a five-year-old child." When word of this reached the Pentagon, Stevens, under pressure from Ridgway, told the press that McCarthy would not be given the names of officers answerable for the discharge of Peress. Stevens deplored the "humiliating treatment" and "abuse" of Zwicker. He ordered the general not to appear before the subcommittee again, and said that he would testify instead. The secretary promptly received a phone call from McCarthy. "Just go ahead and try it, Robert," the senator said menacingly. "I am going to kick the brains out of anyone who protects Communists! . . . You just go ahead . . . I will guarantee you that you will live to regret it."

This was followed on February 24 by what became celebrated as "the chicken luncheon" in Dirksen's Senate office, an attempt by senior Republicans to close the widening breach between McCarthy and the Army. Stevens found himself facing McCarthy, Dirksen, Karl Mundt and Charles Potter; Nixon was in an adjoining office. The secretary, as one reporter put it, was like a goldfish in a tankful of barracuda. Believing himself safe in the hands of these genial, sympathetic fellow Republicans, Stevens lowered his guard. All he wanted, he said, was to live and let live. Sure, he would be glad to put his name on a statement to that effect. He then did. The next thing he knew, the doors opened to admit a crowd of newspapermen. Mundt waded into them, distributing copies of the "memorandum of understanding," which was what Stevens, disarmed by the senatorial bonhomie all around him, had just signed. Now in anguish he found that in neglecting to read the fine print he had capitulated to virtually all McCarthy's demands. Among other things, the memorandum stipulated:

> There is complete agreement that the Secretary . . . will give the committee the names of everyone involved in the promotion and honorable discharge of Peress and that such individuals will be available to appear before the committee. If the committee decides to call General Zwicker . . . General Zwicker will be available.

In the Pentagon next morning officers greeted one another by waving handkerchiefs. "Private Schine," said one of them, "is the only man left in the Army with any morale." The *Times* of London commented that "Senator McCarthy achieved today what General Burgoyne and General Cornwallis never achieved — the surrender of the American Army." Herblock depicted Eisenhower whipping a white feather from a scabbard and saying to McCarthy, "Have a care, sir!" Palmer Hoyt of the *Denver Post* telegraphed Sherman Adams: FROM HERE IT LOOKS AS THOUGH STEVENS' COMPLETE CAVE-IN HAS SPATTERED MORE MUD ON THE U.S. ARMY UNIFORM THAN HAVE ALL OUR ENEMIES IN ALL OUR WARS. A story going the rounds in Washington went, "Stevens didn't mean to surrender to the senators. He just thought they wanted to look at his sword," and McCarthy, brutal in triumph, told a reporter that Stevens could not have yielded "more abjectly if he had got down on his knees."

For the next two weeks matters drifted. Republicans were huddling all over the capital. National Chairman Leonard W. Hall, having called McCarthy a "great asset" less than a month earlier, now criticized his conduct with Stevens. The President praised Zwicker at his March 3 press conference and said his administration would not stand having any official "submit to any kind of personal humiliation when testifying before congressional committees or elsewhere." Extraordinary efforts continued to be made in the hope of accommodating Joe. All that was required of him at this point was that he show the same spirit of compromise. He wouldn't do it. Instead he taunted the Pentagon, calling Peress the "sacred cow of certain Army brass" and saying that his investigation of the case had established "beyond any possibility of a doubt" that "certain individuals in the Army have been promoting, covering up, and honorably discharging known Communists."

"Just damn tommyrot," Defense Secretary Wilson replied. McCarthy was ridiculed in the Senate for the first time, by Ralph E. Flanders of Vermont: "He dons his warpaint. He goes into his war dance. He emits his warhoops. He goes forth to battle and proudly returns with the scalp of a pink Army dentist. We may assume that this represents the depth and seriousness of the Communist penetration in the country at this time." Senator John Sherman Cooper of Kentucky congratulated Flanders, and the President wrote to him: "I was very much interested in reading the comments you made in the Senate today. I think America needs to hear from more Republican voices like yours." Attacking McCarthy still took courage, but it had begun, and the Army took heart. The senator's impact on the military had been fearful, Hanson Baldwin wrote in the *New York Times:* "Its morale is depressed; discipline and efficiency leave much to be desired." Now it was ready to go over to the counteroffensive, and the weapon it chose was the Schine affair. A strong case could be made that McCarthy and Cohn had been punishing the Army for allowing Cohn's friend to be drafted; it was probably true, and in any event it was the weakest spot in Joe's armor. On March 11 the Army leaked (through a Democrat) a chronology of the Schine case, including Cohn's threat to "wreck the Army."

Next day McCarthy countercharged that the Army had attempted to "blackmail" him into calling off his "exposure of Communists" by holding Schine as a "hostage." Plainly a full-dress congressional investigation was needed to hear both sides. The White House hoped it would be made by the Senate Armed Services Committee — McCarthy influence was relatively weak there — but the chairman, Leverett Saltonstall of Massachusetts, was up for reelection in November and wanted no part of it. A mazurka of parliamentary moves followed. The Democrats tried to have it assigned to the full Senate Committee on Government Operations; their own senators there, with Margaret Chase Smith, would outnumber McCarthy's men. The Republicans wouldn't stand for that, however, and the only solution acceptable to all parties was foolish: the conduct of McCarthy and Cohn was to be investigated by their own subcommittee. McCarthy agreed to step down as chairman; Mundt, one of his most ardent admirers, would preside. Cohn was similarly unqualified to serve as chief counsel. The task of finding a successor for him seemed insurmountable; what was needed was an able attorney who had not expressed an opinion about McCarthy. Dirksen came up with Ray Jenkins, a Knoxville, Tennessee, trial lawyer. Procedural questions followed. Dirksen protested against public hearings, but Lyndon Johnson successfully demanded televised sessions, and McCarthy won the right of cross-examination — one he had adamantly denied to witnesses when he sat in the chair.

The hearings opened in the floodlit Corinthian splendor of the Senate

Caucus Room shortly after 10:30 on the morning of April 22, 1954. Everything seemed to be in order. Jenkins was at the microphone. The gavel was in Mundt's hand. McCarthy sat far to his left, at the very end of the coffin-shaped table. Nine months earlier Democratic members of the committee had begun boycotting its meetings in protest against McCarthy's tactics, but now they were back with their minority counsel, twenty-eight-year-old Robert F. Kennedy, then known chiefly for his hostility to Cohn. Mundt exchanged banalities with John McClellan of Arkansas, the ranking Democrat;* then he rapped for order. Mundt said, "Our counsel, Mr. Jenkins, will call the first witness." Jenkins opened his mouth — it was enormous — but before he could speak there was an interruption. The record reads:

McCARTHY: A point of order, Mr. Chairman; may I raise a point of order?

According to H. M. Robert's *Rules of Order,* a chairman may be interrupted on a point of order, provided that the question is one of propriety under the rules. McCarthy had something else in mind. His resonant voice rose.

McCARTHY: I have heard from people in the military all the way from generals with the most upstanding [*sic*] combat records down to privates recently inducted and they indicate they are very resentful of the fact that a few Pentagon politicians attempting to disrupt our investigations are naming themselves the Department of the Army. . . . The Department of the Army is not doing this. It is three civilians in the Army and they should be so named.

An impartial chairman would have gaveled McCarthy into silence the moment it became clear that, far from raising a procedural matter, he was making a speech. Mundt let him make it. Placidly he agreed to a preposterous McCarthy proposal: that judgment be witheld on whether the Secretary of the Army represented the Army. With that as an opening, McCarthy interrupted to make the same speech again. "Mr. Chairman, Mr. Chairman," he sang out in that tight whine. Mundt looked down the table and nodded, and Joe made his point again:

McCARTHY: I maintain it is a disgrace and a reflection upon every one of the million outstanding men in the Army to let a few civilians who are trying, trying to hold up an investigation of Communists labelling themselves as the Department of the Army.

McClellan quietly pointed out that the 46 countercharges against the Army had been signed for the subcommittee by "Joe McCarthy, Chairman," but Mundt ruled in favor of the Wisconsin senator. A pattern was forming. Joe would dominate the hearings as surely as though he were in the chair. Between his "points of order" and his cross-examinations, he would say everything he wanted to say. Mundt was his man, and so, it developed, was

---

*McClellan followed details of the privileges which had been extended to Private Schine with great interest. He had lost two of his three sons in World War II.

Ray Jenkins. Chosen for his supposed impartiality, the subcommittee's special counsel openly encouraged McCarthy's excesses, swearing him in and asking him to explain "just what the set-up of the Communists is." To the dismay of those who had been through this so many times before, Joe produced maps mounted on easels and a pointer. At the end of his lecture he said, "There are many people who think that we can live side by side with Communists." Eagerly Jenkins said, "What do you say about that, sir?" The answer consumed most of that afternoon. Even so, Jenkins was not done with encouraging Joe:

> JENKINS: Senator McCarthy. . . . it is about closing time. . . . Now, while you have an audience of perhaps twenty or thirty million Americans . . . I want you to tell . . . what each individual American man, woman and child can do . . . to do their bit to liquidate the Communist party.

McCarthy's critics were in despair. The senator seemed invincible. Nothing, not even the U.S. Army, was a match for him. By the force of his personality he was turning each session into a McCarthy melodrama, with doctored photographs, phony FBI reports, memoranda lifted from Pentagon files by the Loyal American Underground, and savage little McCarthy homilies, such as the bit of advice he attributed to one of his childhood mentors, someone called Indian Charlie, to the effect that "if one was ever approached by another person in a not completely friendly fashion, one should start kicking at the other person as fast as possible below the belt until the other person was rendered helpless." The moment any testimony unfavorable to him began to get interesting he would rumble into the record with one of his vibrant calls for "A point of order," or "Mr. Chairman, Mr. Chairman," and then he would be off with a digression about how "sick and tired" he was of "sitting down here" and hearing all these "packs of lies." So one-sided were the hearings becoming that the Caucus Room audience, which had come to see a fight, cheered Senator Stuart Symington just for having the courage to talk back to Joe: "You said something about being afraid. I want you to know from the bottom of my heart that I'm not afraid of anything about you or anything you've got to say any time, any place, anywhere."

No one else around the table seemed prepared to go farther than that, and of all of them the man who appeared least likely to bell the McCarthy tiger was the Army's special counsel. Tall, portly, and birdlike, Joseph N. Welch was sixty-three, a lifelong Republican and a senior partner in the eminently respectable Boston firm of Hale and Dorr. He had undertaken this assignment for no fee. And that, said reporters, must have been why he had been chosen. Hour after hour he sat quietly with an elbow on the table, his chin in the palm of his hand or his fingers tracing the furrows on his forehead. He might have been another spectator. He let McCarthy browbeat his client, Stevens, without an objection. The few remarks he did make were almost comic in their grave courtesy. With his green bow ties, his fussy manner, and his high-pitched voice, Welch seemed more like a Dickensian solicitor than a successful American trial lawyer.

Rarely had the capital seen a man whose appearance was more deceptive. He knew the impression he conveyed and was content; at times, he had found, it was useful to be underestimated. Life on Beacon Hill and Boston Common had not prepared him for the McCarthy demimonde of bluster, intimidation and transparent lies, so Welch cocked his head and listened. His hands deep in his pockets, his toes pointed outward, he could be seen during recesses lurking on the fringes of groups, taking everything in. And when he spoke up at the hearings, as in time he did, the contrast between him and McCarthy could not have been greater. As Michael Straight put it in his *Trial by Television,* "McCarthy never forgot the vast audience. Welch seemed not to remember it. McCarthy spoke with contempt for the mob. Welch seemed to be conversing respectfully with one individual, and so he gained the audience's devotion to the end."

Bit by bit those watching Welch for this first time sensed the steel in him. He and McCarthy were the real duelists here, and their first significant encounter came on the ninth day of the hearings, when Welch cross-examined the senator over a confidential FBI letter which had found its way into McCarthy's hands. Along the way it had been retyped, an important point because under the law the retyping of a classified document amounted to publication. Joe crouched over the microphone, tense and swarthy. Under the klieg lights a roll of flesh beneath his dark eyebrows gave his upper eyelids a slanted, demonic expression. Welch let him wait awhile. The Bostonian lolled almost puckishly on an elbow, finger crooked on the purplish veins of his cheek, his brow wrinkled as though he were looking for the first time at something which was quite incredible. Now he was ready.

WELCH: Senator McCarthy, when you took the stand you knew of course that you were going to be asked about this letter, did you not?

McCARTHY: I assumed that would be the subject.

WELCH: And you, of course, understood that you were going to be asked the source from which you got it.

McCARTHY: . . . I won't answer that. . . .

WELCH: Have you some private reservation when you take the oath that you will tell the whole truth that lets you be the judge of what you will testify to?

McCARTHY: The answer is that there is no reservation about telling the whole truth.

WELCH: Thank you, sir. Then tell us who delivered the document to you!

McCARTHY: The answer is no. You will not get the information.

Jenkins came to the senator's rescue with the amazing opinion that McCarthy's position was justified because he was a "law enforcing officer . . . ferreting out crime," and the committee members turned to other matters.

Only gradually did they and their audience realize what Welch had done. He had exposed McCarthy as an outlaw. In acknowledging his possession of the purloined letter the senator had violated a federal statute, and by refusing to answer Welch's questions he had put himself in contempt of Congress. There was something else. His defiance of the Boston attorney had been somehow familiar. Comparing impressions at the end of that session they realized why. For four years the country had watched McCarthy bully witnesses who refused to respond to his own interrogations. He had held these people up to public scorn as "Fifth Amendment Communists," reducing the Bill of Rights to an epithet. Now he was behaving in the same way.

Demagogues are conspicuously vulnerable to ridicule, but masters of derision are rare. Since the emergence of Cohn and Schine there had been speculation over whether their relationship was an unusual one, but no one could think of the right way to touch upon this very delicate subject. Welch found a way to do it. He had been honing the rapier of his wit since the hearings began, waiting to thrust it under McCarthy's bludgeon. The opportunity arose in an exchange over a cropped photograph. Cohn had given Jenkins, in proof of an obscure point, what appeared to be a picture, taken at McGuire Air Force Base, of Stevens beaming at Schine. Then the original turned up. In it Stevens was smiling at someone else, who had been cropped out to produce the fake. There was a thoughtful silence in the Caucus Room. Cohn strenuously denied knowing that this picture had been cropped. He said he didn't even know where it had come from. Welch innocently asked the witness at the time, another member of McCarthy's staff, "Do you think it came from a pixie?"

There was a rumbling at the end of the table. The bludgeon was being raised. McCarthy asked, "Will the counsel for my benefit define — I think he might be an expert on that — what a pixie is?"

Welch's rapier flashed: "Yes, I should say, Mr. Senator, that a pixie is a close relative of a fairy."

The chuckles were suppressed, but the giant had been wounded. From that moment forward McCarthy reserved his most venomous tones for Welch and searched for a way of retribution. On June 9, in the eighth week of testimony, he thought he had it. Cohn was in the chair at the time. Welch was asking him about the subcommittee's hunt for subversives among Army Signal Corps employees at Fort Monmouth in New Jersey.

> WELCH: Mr. Cohn, if I told you now that we had a bad situation at Monmouth, you'd want to cure it by sundown if you could, wouldn't you?
>
> COHN: Yes, sir.
>
> WELCH: May I add my small voice, sir, and say whatever you know about a subversive or a Communist or a spy, please hurry! Will you remember these words?

McCarthy's voice rose, tense and vibrant.

McCARTHY: Mr. Chairman, in view of that question —

MUNDT: Do you have a point of order?

McCARTHY: Not exactly, Mr. Chairman, but in view of Mr. Welch's request that the information be given once we know of anyone who might be performing any work for the Communist Party, I think we should tell him that he has in his law firm a young man named Fisher . . . who has been for a number of years a member of an organization which was named, oh years and years ago, as the legal bulwark of the Communist Party. . . .

Welch looked stricken. A hush had fallen over the table. Smiling, licking his lips, his words freighted with sarcasm, McCarthy went on:

McCARTHY: . . . Knowing that, Mr. Welch, I just felt that I had a duty to respond to your urgent request. . . . I have hesitated about bringing that up. But I have been rather bored with your phony requests to Mr. Cohn here that he personally get every Communist out of government before sundown. Therefore we will give you the information about the young man in your own organization. . . .

And he did, while Welch, obviously desolate, sat with his head in his hands, staring at the table before him. By now it was clear that something had gone wrong. Cohn, still at the microphone, was staring at the senator and shaking his head in silent entreaty. If anything, he seemed more distressed than Welch. But McCarthy went on to the end, shredding the reputation of someone whose very existence had not been a matter of public knowledge until now.

McCARTHY: . . . Whether you knew he was a member of that Communist organization or not I don't know. I assume you did not, Mr. Welch, because I get the impression that while you are quite an actor, you play for a laugh, I don't think you have any conception of the danger of the Communist Party. I don't think you would ever knowingly aid the Communist cause. I think you are unknowingly aiding it when you try to burlesque this hearing in which we are trying to bring out the facts, howeve.·.

He snickered. In that silence it was eerie. The room awaited Welch's reply. It was long in coming; once while McCarthy was still speaking the Bostonian's lips had formed the mute word "stop," but now he seemed to be groping for words. To Mundt he said, leaning forward, "Mr. Chairman, under these circumstances I must have something approaching a personal privilege." Mundt said quickly, "You may have it, sir. It will not be taken out of your time." He, too, was upset. Everyone at the table appeared to be affected, with the exception of McCarthy, who was talking loudly to one of his aides. Welch had to begin three times before he could attract the senator's attention. "I can listen with one ear," McCarthy said to him. "This time," said the Bostonian, "I want you to listen with both." McCarthy ordered the aide to bring a clipping showing that Frederick G. Fisher had belonged to the Lawyers Guild, the proscribed organization. "I think," said the senator, "that should be in the record."

WELCH: You won't need anything in the record when I have finished telling you this. Until this moment, Senator, I think I never really gauged your cruelty or your recklessness. Fred Fisher is a young man who went to the Harvard Law School and came into my firm and is starting what looks to be a brilliant career with us.

He then told the television audience what insiders at the hearings already knew. Welch's one misgiving about coming to Washington had been the possibility that because of him, someone at Hale and Dorr might be slandered. In talking to the two young assistants he had planned to bring to the capital with him he learned that one of them — Fred Fisher — had briefly belonged to the Lawyers Guild after leaving law school.* On learning more about it, he had resigned. Welch had left Fisher in Boston, and McCarthy and Cohn, who knew of him, had agreed not to mention his name. In 1954 few worse things could happen to a man than being identified over national television as a subversive. That was what McCarthy, to pay off a score, had done to Fisher. Welch now told the full story. At the end of it he turned back to the senator.

WELCH: . . . Little did I dream you could be so reckless and so cruel as to do an injury to that lad. It is true he is still with Hale and Dorr. It is true that he will continue to be with Hale and Dorr. It is, I regret to say, equally true that I fear he shall always bear a scar needlessly inflicted by you. If it were in my power to forgive you for your reckless cruelty I would do so. I like to think that I am a gentle man, but your forgiveness will have to come from someone other than me.

McCarthy afterward told a friend that as Welch spoke he could feel knots in his stomach. It wasn't contrition. He was probably incapable of that. What he grasped was that he had stumbled badly, that Welch had outwitted him again. Trying desperately to regain his footing, he growled that Welch had no right to mention cruelty because he had "been baiting Mr. Cohn here for hours."

WELCH: Senator, may we not drop this? We know he belonged to the Lawyers Guild, and Mr. Cohn nods his head at me.

Cohn, in evident agony, was indeed nodding at Welch. He was also biting his lips and trembling visibly.† He had crushed too many witnesses himself not to see what Welch was doing to McCarthy. To Cohn Welch said: "I did you, I think, no personal injury, Mr. Cohn."

---

*The other was James D. St. Clair, who became counsel to President Nixon during the House of Representatives impeachment inquiry twenty years later.

†Writing in the February, 1968, *Esquire,* Cohn revealed that McCarthy had consented not to bring up Fisher if Welch promised not to explore Cohn's lack of a military record. Welch had kept his word. Thus Cohn had reason to be concerned over his leader's violation of the agreement.

COHN: No, sir.

WELCH: I meant to do you no personal injury and if I did I beg your pardon.

Again Cohn nodded. Again McCarthy tried to shape a reply, and again Welch turned him away.

WELCH: . . . Let us not assassinate this lad further, Senator. You have done enough. Have you no sense of decency, sir, at long last? Have you no sense of decency?

The senator stared into his lap, looked up, and tried one more time. He tried to ask Welch if it was not true that Fisher had been his assistant. This time the Bostonian silenced him with superb disdain.

WELCH: Mr. McCarthy, I will not discuss this with you further. You have sat within six feet of me and could have asked me about Fred Fisher. You have brought it out. If there is a God in heaven it will do neither you nor your cause any good. I will not discuss it further. I will not ask Mr. Cohn any more questions. You, Mr. Chairman, may, if you will, call the next witness.

But there would be no more testimony that day. The audience was struggling to its feet, cheering Welch. Even Mundt was with them. He put down his gavel, and six policemen, who had been told at the opening of each session to eject anyone who applauded, stood impassive. Mc-Carthy's face was grim; he was breathing hard. Welch moved toward the door, and a woman there touched his arm and then began to cry. As he stepped into the hall the press corps surged after him. Suddenly everyone broke for the door. It was as though someone had yelled, "Fire!" They couldn't wait to get out, and presently McCarthy, who had not left his chair, was left with the guards and the television technicians. He looked around, stretching his neck, trying to catch someone's eye. At first no one would look at him, then one man did. The senator turned his palms up and spread his hands. He asked, "What did I do?"

After thirty-six days of testimony the Army-McCarthy hearings ended on June 17. The subcommittee then studied the 7,400 printed pages of testimony and issued a report blaming both sides. At first the extent of the damage done to McCarthy was unknown. He had been exposed before and had recovered quickly each time. His physical stamina was unimpaired, he retained the loyalty of eight to ten key senators, his influence with the Republican legislative leadership continued to be great, and with his customary vigor he announced new investigations of Communists in the Army, the defense industry, and the CIA.

All died stillborn. New voices were being heard in the land on the subject of McCarthy, and old voices spoke in different tones. From Nebraska, Republican leader Jim Schramm wrote Sherman Adams that every member of the Republican State Central Committee felt that GOP candidates had been hurt by the "public spectacle" of the hearings. In

Colorado Palmer Hoyt said, "It is now time for the Republican party to repudiate Joe McCarthy before he drags them down to defeat," and in Ohio conservative Republican congressman George Bender, campaigning for Taft's Senate seat, declared that "McCarthyism has become a synonym for witch-hunting, star-chamber methods, and the denial of those civil liberties which have distinguished our country in its historic growth." Cohn, it was generally agreed, had been discredited. With every subcommittee member except McCarthy against him, he resigned July 19. ("A great victory for the Communists," Joe said bitterly.) Since the first open rupture between the senator and the Army, at the beginning of the year, poll takers had been observing a vast change in the public's view of McCarthy. By late August some 22 percent of the adult population had revised their opinion of him downward. Over 24 million Americans now looked upon him with disfavor.

Ralph Flanders didn't wait until all the evidence was in. Two days after McCarthy's disastrous attack on Fisher, the Vermont Republican introduced a resolution calling on the Senate to strip its junior member from Wisconsin of his chairmanships. McCarthy said, "I think they should get a net and take him to a good quiet place." The measure was given little chance then. Knowland denounced it next day at a hurriedly called press conference, and southern Democrats let it be known that they were wary of a precedent which might threaten the seniority system. Debate opened on Friday, June 30. That evening Flanders, shifting tactics, substituted a simple motion of censure: "Resolved, That the conduct of the Senator from Wisconsin, Mr. McCarthy, is contrary to senatorial traditions, and tends to bring the Senate into disrepute, and such conduct is hereby condemned." Knowland proposed that it be referred to a select committee of three Republicans and three Democrats. That seemed safe. The members, chosen by Knowland and Lyndon Johnson, were all conservatives. Their chairman was Utah Republican Arthur V. Watkins. The McCarthy men felt they had won.

They misjudged Watkins. Determined to avoid another carnival, the chairman banned television from the new hearings and laid down strict ground rules. Even smoking was forbidden. Either Joe or his attorney would be allowed to cross-examine witnesses, but not both. Since McCarthy was a poor courtroom lawyer, this meant that he had to yield the center of the stage. At the first session he tested Watkins with cries of "Mr. Chairman, Mr. Chairman." The chairman's gavel came down like an executioner's ax. He said crisply, "The Senator is out of order. . . . We are not going to be interrupted by those diversions and sidelines. We are going straight down the line." McCarthy bolted into the corridor, where the television crews were waiting, and spluttered into a microphone, "I think this is the most unheard of thing I ever heard of." Unimpressed, the select committee reported out the Flanders resolution with the recommendation that McCarthy be censured, and the full Senate agreed 67 to 22 — this in a chamber which had produced exactly one anti-McCarthy vote, Fulbright's, the previous January.

Vice President Nixon, exercising his prerogative as presiding officer of the Senate to alter the title of a measure, struck out the word "censure," changing it to "Resolution relating to the conduct of the Senator from Wisconsin, Mr. McCarthy." He was trying to help Joe, and McCarthy's admirers sought semantic solace in that. McCarthy himself was undeceived. "Well," he told reporters, "it wasn't exactly a vote of confidence." He said, "I'm glad to have this circus ended so I can get back to the real work of digging out Communism, crime, and corruption." In the White House Eisenhower greeted his cabinet with a slow grin. "Have you heard the latest?" he asked. "McCarthyism is McCarthywasm."

So it was. Missing the stimulus of Cohn, Joe became listless, flabby, and easily depressed. His devoted followers had formed a Committee of Ten Million Americans Mobilizing for Justice, with a retired rear admiral as "chief of staff," to protest the censure; they delivered to the Capitol, in an armored truck, a petition bearing 1,000,816 signatures. In New York thirteen thousand attended a "Who Promoted Peress?" rally. Its sponsors included Governor Bracken Lee of Utah, Alvin M. Owsley of the American Legion, Mrs. Grace Brosseau of the D.A.R., a former governor of New Jersey, and a former ambassador to Russia. A high school band played "On, Wisconsin." A rock singer intoned that he would "shake, rattle, and roll" for their leader, and Cohn told the crowd that "Joe McCarthy and I would rather have American people of this type than all the politicians in the world." But Joe himself wasn't there. He had hurt his arm shaking hands with a voter. In what some saw as a symbolic act, the other man had inadvertently shoved Joe's elbow through a glass table top. The senator went into Bethesda Naval Hospital and emerged with a sling.

McCarthy's successor as chief Republican campaigner was Richard Nixon. The Democrats said they couldn't see much difference. Nixon charged that their party was "bending to the Red wind." When Adlai Stevenson observed that the American economy appeared to be in the doldrums, Nixon accused him of "spreading pro-Communist propaganda." If the Democrats endorsed by Stevenson were elected, he said, "the security risks which have been fired by the Eisenhower administration will all be hired back," and he urged patriotic Democrats to "put their party in their pocket and vote for an Eisenhower Congress" because "we recognize the Communist menace and this administration is determined to crush that menace." The Communist party, he warned, was battling "desperately and openly" against Republicans because "the candidates running on the Democratic ticket are, almost without exception, members of the Democratic party's left-wing clique which has been so blind to the Communist conspiracy and has tolerated it in the United States."

"By golly," said Eisenhower, "sometimes you sure get tired of all this clackety-clack." Nixon was weary of it, too; "I'm tired, bone tired, my heart's not in it," he told a friend. Barnstorming the country seemed particularly fatiguing this time, but the President's decision not to campaign actively left Nixon as the party's highest-ranking politician, and he believed that much was at stake. "The election of a Democratic Eighty-fourth Congress in November," he told the Ohio Republican state convention in Columbus, "will mean the beginning of the end of the Republican party. It is that simple." To stave it off he delivered 204 speeches, held over a hundred press conferences, flew 26,000 miles, and visited 95 cities in 31 states, By the end of it he had become the country's second most controversial figure. "McCarthyism in a white collar," said Stevenson of his tactics. Walter Lippmann went further. He described the Vice President as a "ruthless partisan" who "does not have within his conscience those scruples which the country has a right to expect in the President of the United States."

It was characteristic of the 1950s that even Eisenhower's adversaries were anxious to believe the best of him, and he was not held responsible for Nixon's speeches. How he could have avoided knowing about them was unexplained. The *Herald Tribune,* whose most loyal subscriber he was, played them on its front page. Somehow it was felt, as James Reston wrote, that the President would never imply that the Democrats had winked at treason, "but things are done in his name he knows not of." To be sure, Nixon's style was not Eisenhower's style. Ike wanted to be regarded, he said, as "President of all the people," and invective wasn't his forte anyway. Nevertheless, he wanted the candidates of his party to win, believed Nixon was helping them, and cheered him accordingly.

Both men had hoped that Republicans could stow campaign rhetoric and run on the administration's record. "The time, the right time to start winning the 1954 elections is *now,*" Nixon had told the cabinet in April 1953. Eisenhower believed that his 1954 legislative accomplishments were worth boasting about. It had been a good session, despite the sideshow in the Senate Caucus Room. He had signed into law bills extending the federal housing program and reciprocal trade agreements, liberalizing the Atomic Energy Act, broadening unemployment insurance and social security, simplifying customs procedures, establishing a new farm program, authorizing two billion dollars for federal highways, and providing more than a billion dollars in tax relief. He calculated that his "batting average" had been .830 and was delighted. The *Congressional Quarterly,* figuring differently, put it at .646; even so, he had done well, and Democratic predictions that a Republican administration would bring back the Depression — as irresponsible, in their way, as Nixon's Red issue — had been exposed as myth.

But the twenty-year trend toward Democratic voter registrations had given the party out of power the same advantage that the Republicans once had. All other things being equal, the man in the middle tended to favor the Democrats. Eisenhower and Nixon were also fighting history; the party in power has nearly always lost strength in off-year elections. Furthermore, postwar prosperity had paused to catch its breath. There were no breadlines in 1954, but farm prices had taken a downward lurch, and the recession had given some employers the jitters.

In view of the hurdles ahead, party councils had decided that a Republican hatchet man was needed. The Vice President had been chosen because he handled hatchets well, because using this one would endear him to the rank and file of his party, and because, as Eisenhower pointed out, it would add to his fame. Nixon was game — "Every campaign has to have someone out front slugging," he said — but he was also unenthusiastic. It wasn't pleasant to return to Whittier as commencement speaker, which he did in the spring of 1954, to find that two reception lines had been set up, one for students who didn't want to shake his hand. His wife liked strife even less than he did, and in mid-February, after a long talk, they had discussed the possibility of his retirement from public life when his present term ended in 1956. According to Murray Chotiner, Nixon weighed the relative merits of opening his own law practice and joining an established firm while flying back to Washington on election eve. As the plane entered its glide pattern he handed Chotiner seven pages of notes. "Here's my last campaign speech," he said. "You may want it as a souvenir, I'm through with politics."

The results of the election were perplexing. The Democrats did regain control of Congress, whereupon Nixon had to admit that the survival of Republicanism hadn't been at stake after all. McCarthy called it "a bad defeat" and held the administration responsible for waging "jungle warfare among those of us who were trying to expose and root out Communists." But it wasn't bad at all. The Republican edge in the 83rd Congress had been so slight that realists had conceded its loss in advance. After the dust had cleared the Democrats had recaptured twenty House seats — they had expected fifty — and in the Senate they had won just two. "The administration," the *Washington Post and Times Herald* concluded two days later, "has experienced neither victory nor overwhelming defeat at the polls."

Nixon interpreted the returns for the cabinet that same day. What they showed, he said, was "really a dead heat." He thought he knew a way to improve performance. The key to future campaigns, he said, was a good public relations program. The American people had to be "sold." The party with the best image would win elections; the secret to control of 1600 Pennsylvania Avenue would lie not on Main Street or Wall Street, but on Madison Avenue. Parties would invest in catchy jingles, not pretentious campaign songs. How a candidate looked on the television screen would be as important as what he had to say. It would all be one big package, Nixon told them, and he offered to show them the gist of it. Reaching into his pocket he drew out a mechanical toy drummer, wound it up, and sent it clattering down the polished table past the astonished President and his secretaries. The Vice President said, "Just keep beating that goddamned drum."

The most memorable singing commercial of that year, as evocative of the Army-McCarthy hearings as Joe's sonorous "Mr. Chairman, Mr. Chairman," went:

> *When the values go up, up, up,*
> *And the prices go down, down, down,*
> *Robert Hall this season*
> *Will show you the reason,*
> *Low overhead, low overhead!**

Robert Hall, clothier, was a precursor of the discount houses which had begun to rise, like vast gymnasiums, on the outskirts of metropolitan areas and in suburban shopping centers. The first of them, E. J. Korvette, had opened its doors in 1948. It had been an instant success. In the past, discounting had been largely confined to shabby little factory annexes, difficult to find and seldom clean. Labels had been removed from wares; the wholesaler didn't want the retailer to know that he was competing with him. Now an entirely new approach to merchandising was emerging. Businessmen had begun to grasp the implications of America's automotive economy. In the 1930s and 1940s, when the greater part of customers had arrived on buses and streetcars, downtown streets lined with retail stores had made sense. But now public transportation had begun to atrophy. The typical urban shopper of the 1950s came in a car and had no place to put it. Downtown parking had become almost impossible. Millions of meters were being installed, but the results were disappointing; as often as not a Main Street merchant, blind to his own interests, would allow his clerks to occupy the spaces in front of his store and feed the meters every hour while potential customers cruised up and down.

Shopping centers were the obvious solution. Planners provided them with ample parking facilities, great tracts paved with macadam. Nationwide firms began erecting discount wonderlands: Korvette's, Topp's, Bradlee's, Grant's, King's, etc. By selling directly to the consumer there, manufacturers avoided the retailers' overheads. Those Main Street merchants who could afford suburban annexes built them. The rest joined a long, slow decline into what sociologists began to call "inner-city blight."

Meantime the discount marts were acquiring problems of their own. Shoplifting grew to epidemic proportions, encouraged by the discounters' practice of substituting checkout counters for aisle clerks. After hours, shopping center parking areas were often inhabited by restless teen-agers. Mobile like their parents, they needed a place to rendezvous. Unfortu-

*Copyright 1946, 1954, 1963, and 1972 by Robert Hall Clothes, Inc. Reprinted by permission.

nately, police discovered, the paved expanses became staging areas for gang fights and drag racing.

Fueled by affluence, the teen subculture continued to develop its separate identity in the 1950s, with its own customs, status symbols, stigmata, rites, and fads — the ducktail haircuts and sleeves rolled up to a prescribed length for boys, and, for girls, poodle cuts and pop-it necklaces that could be changed from chokers to waist-length. Long hair and peculiar modes of dress lay a decade away, but the new language which would go with them was already developing. Like the bop musicians they admired, teenagers frequently used the term cool, though for them the emphasis was different; it meant pretty much what keen, neat, swell, snazzy, or smooth had meant twenty years earlier. "Like" had become an all-purpose pause-word and modifier.

Scram had been replaced by blast-off, and a drip was now a drag. The draggiest were variously described as spastics, turkeys, nerds, yo-yos, or — the most popular of all pejoratives — square. A teen-ager would say, "She's a —," switching to mimicry and drawing a square in the air with his index finger. It was considered tactful, if the square was present, to refer to her obscurely as an "L7" (because the letter and the numeral could form a crude square). The ultimate in squares was the cube. Wits would say that he was so square he could block his own hat. That might elicit a grudging laugh, but as a rule joking with teen-agers of that period was a risky business; they would often riposte with a withering "Hardee-harhar."

Every adolescent familiar with the facts of life, as they were still called, knew that a drive-in movie was a passion pit. Admittance to these arenas of foreplay was restricted, of course, to those with automobiles (wheels), but almost every boy in the great middle class either had wheels or knew someone who could get them; the Allstate Insurance Company found that nationally 75 percent of all high school juniors had driver's licenses and nearly 60 percent had access to the family car for "social purposes." The auto was so fundamental a part of the subculture that teen-age argot was often almost indistinguishable from hot-rod slang (also called jive), though subtle distinctions could be detected. To a pure hot-rodder, drag, for instance, had nothing to do with social acceptability; it was a race, from a standing start, between motor vehicles powered by souped-up engines. The hot-rod itself was also known as a hack, a stormer, a bomb, a screamer, or a draggin' wagon. Substantial alterations, a sure way to acquire greater prestige within the peer group, were chopping (lowering the roof) and raking (lowering the front end). Tires were skins; whitewalls, snowballs. Driving around for the sheer joy of the trip was bombing or spooking.

That was for lovers of speed, which did not then mean amphetamines. The vast majority of adolescents were much more interested in exploring sexual diplomacy. Unless he had been grounded — enjoined from the use of the family car — a young male who had taken his date to the passion pit would attempt to make out (the equivalent of the long-gone pitching woo) under cover of darkness. The eternal scourge of seducers and the most common of all female complaints was still known almost universally as the curse, or the monthly, though girls' boarding schools in New England clung to the more proper, and more engaging, "off the sports list." This could be frustrating for the fledgling roué, unless the date was a blind one and had been revealed to him, during a moment under a strong light, as a dog, or a beast. Of course, the girl also had discriminatory rights. If she reached the conclusion that her escort was a drag, she might incinerate him with "DDT" (drop dead twice). That was the ultimate insult. His position would then be extremely uncomfortable, or, to use his word for it, hairy.

Teen-agers and their younger brothers and sisters were emerging as a major target group for national advertisers. They not only had their fashions; increasingly they had a voice in what their parents bought. David Riesman observed: "One must listen to quite young children discussing television models, automobile styling, or the merits of various streamliners to see how gifted they are as consumers . . . their influence in family councils must not be underestimated." Eugene Gilbert, who was then establishing a consulting firm to advise businessmen on marketing policies for young customers, told his clients:

> An advertiser who touches a responsive chord in youth can generally count on the parent to finally succumb to purchasing the product. . . . It is not to be denied that a parent subjected to requests from the youngster who thinks he is in dire need of an item, witnessed on television, may find it easier to "give in" rather than dispute rationally with a highly emotionalized child.

A survey found that 94 percent of the mothers interviewed said that their children had asked them to buy goods they had seen on television. Testers of small children discovered that they could recognize the word "detergent" before they could even read. Exposed to TV while still in their playpens and then put in front of the tube to keep them quiet, they looked upon the world of goods with a sophisticated awareness new to their generation. *American Girl*, the magazine of the Girl Scouts, noted that their subscribers "use their first lipstick, wear their first nylons and first bra sooner than girls ten years ago." Brassiere styles for twelve-year-olds were named Allowance, Freshman, Little Angel and Littlest Angel — "the bra that expands as a girl develops." Bernice Fitz-Gibbon, merchandising consultant for *Seventeen* magazine, told advertisers attending a "fashion clinic" that "Your fashion department is the wooing chamber. Get the teen-age fly to come into your parlor and little by little the web will be spun. Then when the girl marries you haven't lost a customer. You've gained a goldmine." Miss Fitz-Gibbon advised her audience to lure "the teen tycoons, not in the sweet by-and-by, but in the much sweeter now-and-now." She described young girls as "women of means."

Often they were women of very substantial means. *Teen Times,* the magazine of the Future Homemakers of America, put weekly spending by seventh-graders at 30 cents to $8.50 and by high school seniors at $1.65 to $19.50, but in some cases it was much more. In a pictorial essay *Life* described the expenditures of a suburban seventeen-year-old girl who was given $4,000 each year. Among her budget items were $1,300 for bedroom decorations, $1,500 for clothes (including seven bathing suits), and $500 for entertainment, not counting "a jaunt to Hawaii for having survived high school." *Life* noted that "more and more teen-agers will be moving into Suzie's bracket." It ended on what was meant to be a cheerful note: "Her parents' constant indulgence has not spoiled Suzie. She takes for granted all the luxuries that surround her because she has had them all her life."

National statistics on this emerging leisure class of youth were awesome. As the flood of war and postwar babies approached puberty the new market expanded until there were between eighteen and twenty million of the new consumers in the country. Their annual purchases rose to 10 billion dollars, then to 25 billion. Gilbert reported that girls between fourteen and seventeen were spending 773 million dollars on "back to school" outfits alone. In one year of the 1950s, *Teen Times* found, the average American adolescent spent $555 "for goods and services, not including the necessities normally supplied by their families."

Entire industries retooled to accommodate the young. The phonograph record business offered them two lines, "singles" (45 rpm) for subteens and "albums" (33⅓ rpm) for the teen-age market. Together they bought 43 percent of all records sold in the United States. Adolescent purchases accounted for 53 percent of movie admissions, 44 percent of camera sales, 39 percent of new radios bought, and 9 percent of new automobile sales. Each year the fifteen-to-nineteen group was spending 20 million dollars on lipstick, 25 million on deodorants, and 9 million on home permanents. The total spent annually on toiletries by teen-agers of both sexes was almost a third of a billion dollars.

Some parents raised in the austere 1930s were becoming accustomed to such phenomena as a twelve-year-old daughter's weekly trip to the hairdresser, or a fourteen-year-old son engrossed in a brochure on retirement insurance written for his age bracket. In certain places the younger generation had its own credit accounts, with such enticing names as the 14 to 21 Club, the Campus Deb Account, and the Starlet Charge Account. They might order merchandise over Princess phones in their own rooms, or exchange Going Steady rings ($12.95, "nothing down, payments of 50 cents a week") with boyfriends or girlfriends. In California one firm built a

$2,500,000 teen-age shopping center, with six stores, a milk bar, a swimming pool, an ice-skating rink, and a bank.

On the evening of December 15, 1954, Walt Disney touched off a children's craze that showed the whole country how very young consumers could be successfully wooed. *Disneyland* was then the high point of Wednesday TV for 40 million viewers, most of them youngsters and their parents, and that week's program was the first in a series on Davy Crockett. As played by twenty-nine-year-old Fess Parker, a hitherto unknown actor, Davy was a hero of irresistible charm. Mesmerized by his folksiness, tiny America was easy prey for hawkers of Crockett pseudomemorabilia. By the following spring every playground and supermarket seemed to be populated by five-year-olds wearing coonskin caps. The price of coonskins jumped to $8 a pound. Before the boom ended the following summer 100 million dollars' worth of coons had been marketed, not to mention Davy Crockett sweat shirts, sleds, blankets, snowsuits, toothbrushes, school lunch boxes, swing sets, playhouses, sandboxes, stools, toy guns, and bicycles. An entrepreneur overstocked with 200,000 pup tents stenciled "Davy Crockett" on them and sold them all in two days. Some adults were pushed past endurance; a department store buyer said, "The next person who says Davy Crockett to me gets a Davy Crockett flintlock over his head," and it was a rare mother who didn't want to stop her ears after the thousandth rendering of Fess Parker's "Ballad of Davy Crockett," which sold four million copies during his six-month hegemony:

> *Born on a mountain top in Tennessee,*
> *Greenest state in the Land of the Free,*
> *Raised in the woods so's he knew ev'ry tree,*
> *Kilt him a b'ar when he was only three.*
>
> *Davy, Davy Crockett,*
> *King of the wild frontier!*

Fred M. Hechinger of the *New York Herald Tribune* feared that a "passion for possession" might be putting a spiritual blight on youth. In that regard two forms of entertainment introduced in 1954 were troubling. The new music of Bill Haley and the Comets, billed as "the first R 'n' R Pop Smash," gave rise to fears that the children of the new prosperity, like those of the Twenties, might be seduced into a mindless hedonism. To this Stanley Kramer's *The Wild One* added a prophecy of savage violence. Marlon Brando played the title character, Johnny, the apelike "president" of a scruffy motorcycle club whose members wore skin-tight jeans and black leather jackets with a skull and crossbones painted on the back. In the film Brando's gang rides into a quiet town on a lazy Saturday afternoon and, for want of anything else to do, takes the place apart. Obviously the movie was an indictment, but of what? Youth? Permissiveness? Disrespect for law and order? Most critics wrote that Kramer was showing a seamy

side of postwar opulence, of crass acquisitiveness run amuck. Some, repelled by the movie's brutality — in that gentler time it *was* rough — suggested that such censure might be carried too far.

One small group of youthful Bohemians thought that no indictment of
materialism could be strong enough. To them affluence was an outrage.
They had grappled with it and lost. Now they conceded that they were
beaten, or, more succinctly, beat. The beat generation first surfaced in the
early 1950s amid the peeling billboards and crumbling stucco of Los
Angeles's seedy Venice West. Nurtured in dimly lit coffeehouses there, the
movement then leaped 350 miles north and found a Mecca at 261 Columbus Avenue in San Francisco, soon to be famous throughout the movement
as the City Lights Bookshop. The store's colorful co-owner was Lawrence
Ferlinghetti, a bearded native of Paris who had served in the Navy, worked
at *Time* as a mail boy, and taken degrees at Columbia and the Sorbonne.
In 1953 he and Peter D. Martin founded their emporium as the first all-
paperback bookstore in the United States. Ferlinghetti took the name from
the Chaplin film. Expanding, he established City Lights Books, a publishing
house. The first poet on its list was himself. The title of one of Ferlinghetti's
poems, "Tentative Description of a Dinner to Promote the Impeachment
of President Eisenhower," gives some idea of how far he was from the
typical merchant of the 1950s.

The City Lights Bookshop served as an address for certain authors who
had no fixed address of their own. They were unusual, even in their profession. Gregory Corso had been captured in 1946 for trying to seize New
York City by carrying out a series of elaborate robberies with his friends;
when arrested, Corso was attempting to coordinate the attempt with a
walkie-talkie. After three years in prison he educated himself in Harvard's
Widener Library and wrote such poems as "Marriage," in which he advised
a young man planning an evening with his fiancée:

> ... *Don't take her to movies but to cemeteries*
> *tell all about werewolf bathtubs and forked clarinets*
> *then desire her and kiss her and all the preliminaries*
> *and she going just so far and I understanding why*
> *not getting angry saying You must feel! It's beautiful to feel!* ...

The ages of beat writers put them in the swing generation, though they
had now opted out of it. As social prophets they advocated spontaneous
expression, travel, Oriental mysticism, singing folk ballads, playing the
guitar, the blues, sex in all its forms, and their version of the American
dream. Some of them became celebrities. The most famous was a husky
French-Canadian who had played football at Columbia, served as a merchant seaman during World War II, and taught at the New School for
Social Research in the late 1940s. Born Jean-Louis Kerouac, he changed
his first name to Jack for his first book, *The Town and the City*, in 1950.

Kerouac rebuked commentators who called him and other new renaissance authors negative. He insisted that they were in fact passionately affirmative. On television Ben Hecht asked him why he didn't write more about "what's wrong with this country." Kerouac wrote afterward:

> . . . all he wanted me to do was speak out my mind AGAINST people, he sneeringly brought up Dulles, Eisenhower, the Pope, all kinds of people like that . . . No, I want to speak FOR things, for the crucifix I speak out, for the Star of Israel I speak out . . . for sweet Mohammed I speak out, for Lao-tse and Chuang-tse I speak out, for D. T. Suzuki I speak out . . . why should I attack what I love out of life. This is Beat. Live your lives out? Naw, LOVE your lives out. When they come and stone you at least you won't have a glass house, just your glassy flesh.

His *On the Road* was written in three weeks. Truman Capote said of it, "It isn't writing at all — it's typing." Yet it told people something they wanted to hear; they bought 500,000 copies. *On the Road*'s wenching episodes were dull, the visions of the characters were puerile, and for all their expeditions back and forth across the country they never seemed to get anywhere or find anything, not even themselves. But perhaps that was the point. At least Kerouac's people were looking; they refused to be encapsulated by things they owned. The Beats were honest men offended by the sterile myths of their decade. Allen Ginsberg, a more powerful writer than Kerouac, was devastating on the cold war:

> *America you don't really want to go to war.*
> *America it's them bad Russians.*
> *Them Russians them Russians and them Chinamen.*
>   *And them Russians.*
> *The Russia wants to eat us alive. The Russia's pow-*
>   *er mad. She wants to take our cars from out our*
>   *garages.*
> *Her wants to grab Chicago. Her needs a Red Reader's*
>   *Digest. Her wants our auto plants in Siberia. Him big*
>   *bureaucracy running our fillingstations.*
> *That no good. Ugh. Him make Indians learn read. Him*
>   *need big black niggers. Hah. Her make us all work*
>   *sixteen hours a day. Help.*
> *America this is quite serious.*
> *America this is the impression I get from looking in the*
>   *television set.*
> *America is this correct?*
> *I'd better get right down to the job.*
> *It's true I don't want to join the Army or turn lathes in*
>   *precision parts factories, I'm nearsighted and psy-*
>   *chopathic anyway.*
> *America I'm putting my queer shoulder to the wheel.*

Ginsberg wasn't really demented, but a year of psychotherapy had changed his life. That was in 1954 and early 1955. It ended his career as a fledgling market research consultant. Coming off the couch he turned out "Howl" in a nonstop frenzy. San Francisco policemen confiscated it as obscene, but a judge found "redeeming social importance" in the long poem, and Ginsberg joined Kerouac, Corso, Ferlinghetti, and other stars in the beat firmament.

No sooner had they arrived than prim admirers tried to sanitize them. Entranced English teachers averted their eyes from Ginsberg's homosexuality and Kerouac's amorality. Beat, they said, was short for "beatitude"; these poets were blessed. The beats were understandably nettled. Whatever the intrinsic value of their work, and it is probably slight, they did succeed in their social purpose of raising doubts about thoughtless conformity. Denying them would have turned them into literary eunuchs. But there was little chance of the attempt succeeding; the continuing uproar over them assured that.

Twenty years later the only odd aspect of their movement would be that it had been so controversial. It was never revolutionary. Its poets were yea-sayers and minstrels, not challengers of the social order. They broke no windows, planted no bombs, profaned no faiths, and were no threat to the establishment — a word which, in its later sense, did not then exist in the American language. Kenneth Rexroth, at fifty their senior citizen, did declaim sardonically, "I write poetry to seduce women and overthrow the capitalist system." In reality, however, Rexroth was married, the father of two children, the proud holder of several literary awards, and, as a former popcorn salesman, something of an entrepreneur. So, in fact, was Kerouac; in *The Subterraneans* he ingenuously describes the hero's disappointment and frustration when he learns that another beat writer has received a larger publisher's advance than his own. Elsewhere Kerouac said, "We love everything — Billy Graham, the Big Ten, Rock and Roll, Zen, apple pie, Eisenhower — we dig it all." They didn't, of course, and he didn't expect to be taken seriously, but the beats were incapable of militance. The thought of them marching on the Pentagon or stoning National Guardsmen is ludicrous. They would have been startled by anyone who called policemen pigs, and the closest any of them came to a demonstration was Ginsberg wearing a sandwich board that said SMOKE POT.

But that was enough to affront convention then. Smoking marijuana was believed to be wicked beyond imagining. In addition, beats were known to use foul language, sometimes in public. It was an intolerant time. Exotic life-styles were suspect. The mere fact that members of the movement said they were different put them beyond the pale. "Beatnik" was coined as a term of opprobrium. Male beatniks wore khaki trousers, sandals, and beards. (Their hair, however, was short.) The movement's females could be distinguished by their tousled hair and black leotards. Though they scorned lipstick, they put so much make-up around their eyes that they were sometimes called "raccoons." Beatniks were said to live in what they called "pads," surrounded by unwholesome books and records. They didn't pick up after themselves. The beds were unmade — did not, in fact, have proper bedclothes. Reportedly they slept naked on bare mattresses and did disgraceful things in the dark, even when they weren't married. Some had actually advocated bearing children out of wedlock.

Eisenhower's America was horrified. Fathers told daughters that they could not date beatniks. Ronald Reagan told jokes about football players in sandals. Slick magazine writers described beatnik debauchery. Commuters exchanged stories about beatnik orgies. Hollywood cranked out morality tales with beatnik villains. Even Helen Trent acquired a beatnik character. In Middletown, Connecticut, teen-agers in a convertible tried to run down a bearded man on a bicycle because they thought that such a defier of conventions must be beat. And at the bottom of all this commotion was nothing more sinister than a few romantic poets who recoiled from the prevailing life-style. They were individualists, and in that sense their claim to be the real Americans was valid. They asked only to secede from the majority, and they expounded nothing more than the eternal bohemia, as in this passage from *On the Road*:

> . . . they danced down the street like dingledodies, and I shambled after as I've been doing all my life after people who interest me, because the only people for me are the mad ones, the ones who are mad to live, mad to talk, mad to be saved, desirous of everything at the same time, the ones who never yawn or say a commonplace thing, but burn, burn, burn like fabulous yellow roman candles exploding like spiders across the stars and in the middle you see the blue centerlight pop and everybody goes "Awww!"

That was what passed for nonconformity then. The alarm next time would be triggered by the real thing.

Montage: The Mid-Fifties

DAISY: You the policeman?

JOE: Yes ma'am (Shows ID) My name's Friday. . . .
    This is Frank Smith.

FRANK: Hello.

not a recession, said the White House, but a "rolling readjustment"

Best actress of 1955: Anna Magnani in The Rose Tattoo

And here is the best part
You have a head start
If you are among
The very young
At heart

The Man With the Golden Arm   Bad Day at Black Rock   East of Eden
    Mister Roberts   Diabolique   The Desperate Hours

She's the sweetest little rosebud that Texas ever knew
Her eyes are bright as diamonds, they sparkle like the dew
You may talk about your Clementine and sing of Rosalee
But the yellow rose of Texas is the only girl for me

"Sincerity," said Vice President Nixon, "is the quality that comes through on television."

AFL, CIO TO MERGE

Better dead than Red

See the U.S.A.
in your
Chevrolet

According to Nancy Mitford, "England" is U and "Britain" non-U, and "dentures" is non-U for false teeth.

"A Classic"
— Brooks Atkinson
New York Times

KURT WEILL'S

THE THREE-PENNY OPERA

MARTY (in a low, intense voice): *You don't like her. My mother don't like her. She's a dog, and I'm a fat, ugly little man. All I know is I had a good time last night. I'm gonna have a good time tonight. If we have enough good times together, I'm going down on my knees and beg that girl to marry me.*

English adaptation of book and lyrics by
MARC BLITZSTEIN

Original text by
BERT BRECHT

McCALL'S
The magazine of Togetherness

When it seems that everything is lost
I will smile and never count the cost
If you love me, really love me,
Let it happen, darlin', I won't care

EINSTEIN DEAD

THEATRE DE LYS
121 Christopher Street
WAtkins 4-8782

BEST SELLERS: Nonfiction
Gift from the Sea by Anne Morrow Lindbergh
Life Is Worth Living by Fulton J. Sheen
MacArthur 1941-1951 by Major General Charles A.
    Willoughby and John Chamberlain
Call to Greatness by Adlai E. Stevenson
The Scrolls from the Dead Sea by Edmund Wilson

Best actor of 1954: Marlon Brando in
On the Waterfront

Best actress of 1954: Grace Kelly in
The Country Girl

BEST SELLERS: Fiction
Not As a Stranger by Morton Thompson
Marjorie Morningstar by Herman Wouk
Andersonville by Mackinlay Kantor
The Man in the Gray Flannel Suit by Sloan Wilson
Something of Value by Robert Ruark

"In the opinion of the Joint Chiefs, MacArthur's strategy would involve us in the wrong war, at the wrong place, at the wrong time and with the wrong enemy."

Seven Brides for Seven Brothers   Three Coins in the Fountain
Twenty Thousand Leagues Under the Sea   Dial M for Murder
    Executive Suite   Rear Window   Mr. Hulot's Holiday

two doctors working together, Gregory Pincus of the Worcester Foundation for Experimental Biology and John Rock of the Reproductive Study Center in Brookline, Mass., have discovered a drug which, when taken as a pill by a woman, interrupts the process of ovulation.

Hey there you with the stars in your eyes
Love never made a fool of you
You used to be too wise

Better Red than dead

Mama   Make Room for Daddy   Our Miss Brooks   Mr. Peepers

Burns and Allen Show   December Bride   Leave It To Beaver

Father Knows Best   The Phil Silvers Show   Ozzie and Harriet

Dobie Gillis   The Honeymooners   *Goodnight, Mrs. Calabash*

TWENTY-TWO

With All Deliberate Speed

THE AVERAGE AMERICAN MALE in 1954 stood five feet nine inches tall and weighed 158 pounds, according to Dr. George Gallup's Institute of Public Opinion, a diligent collector of such Americana. The average female was five feet four and weighed 132. Husbands thought the knack of running a smooth, orderly household was more important in a wife than anything else, and most of them — 55 percent — felt that American women were spoiled.

In announcing these and other results of an elaborate study of American life, the institute observed that "Throughout history, races and nations have sometimes been remembered for their small human quirks rather than for their great deeds and battles. Here," it said, "are some of the small things that 'homo Americanus' may be famous for in 1,000 years' time." In fact they have become of interest after only twenty years' time, and although some are frivolous, it is interesting, and sometimes even significant, to know the little details of everyday life — what people thought of themselves and others, what they worried about, and how they lived. Already some of the findings of this survey seem quaint.

No audible voices protested the traditional distinctions between the sexes. Wives believed that men drank too much and that one of the chief faults of husbands was "just not paying enough attention," but nothing was said about chauvinism. The typical woman said she preferred marriage to a career. She wanted the word "obey" taken out of the wedding ceremony — it is rather astonishing that it was still there — but in other ways she accepted the double standard. For example, 61 percent of all women agreed that a wife should never open her husband's mail, even if a letter arrived in a scented envelope addressed in feminine handwriting, and when asked, "Should a wife's adultery be more condemned than a husband's?" an overwhelming majority of women — four out of every five — replied, "Yes, of course it should."

Most people listed money as their greatest worry; only 21 percent checked "the threat of world war, keeping the peace." Confidence in the United States and pride of country ran high. Generosity was voted the most conspicuous American characteristic, followed by friendliness, understanding, piety, love of freedom, and progressivism. The American faults listed were petty: shallowness, egotism, extravagance, preoccupation with money, and selfishness.

There were still enough farmers for them to be treated as a separate category. They were the first to rise in the morning; 69 percent of them were out of bed before 6 A.M. The typical American, on the other hand, got up at 6:30 A.M. weekdays and 8 A.M. Sundays. (Women, surprisingly, rose a bit later than men.) The average bedtime was 10 P.M. weekdays and 11 P.M. Saturdays. The typical breakfast was served at 7 A.M., the typical lunch at noon, and the typical supper or dinner at 6 P.M. The postwar custom of a fifteen-minute coffee break was catching on, but less than half of the population enjoyed it; to the question, "At your place of work are employees given time off for coffee, refreshments, or rest?" 51 percent checked "No." Farmers suffered more from the well-named common cold than any other group. The peak month for colds was February, when 15 percent of the adult population, or 15 million people, had them. The low point was July, but even then 5 percent, or five million, were coughing and sneezing and generally miserable.

Even without a war or scandal to divide the country, living was a strain. Every other adult complained of trouble getting to sleep. It was a greater problem for women than men, worse for the unmarried than the married, greatest for the divorced and the widowed. The main cause given was "nervous tension." Sedatives had not achieved wide acceptance; most insomniacs just tossed and turned. Among other complaints, one American in three said his feet hurt, one in five had trouble hearing, two in seven were worried about being overweight, and two out of three wore glasses, half of them all the time.

By gourmet standards their eating habits were dull. If allowed to order anything for dinner, regardless of cost, they said they would choose fruit cup, vegetable soup, steak and french fried potatoes, peas, rolls and butter, apple pie à la mode, and coffee. Three million Americans were vegetarians. Nearly six in ten drank wine, beer or liquor, but they didn't drink much; fewer than one in five had something every day. Their favorite sport was bowling. A startling eight million bowled at least once a week, and there were three occasional bowlers for every golfer or ping-pong player, the second and third most popular recreations. Only 52 percent of all adults knew how to swim, a reflection of the fact that opportunities for swimming were fewer then, for vacations were shorter and less frequent. Over 15 million, or 15 percent of all adults, had not been more than 250 miles from home — the equivalent, then, of one day's ride in an automobile. After Sunday dinner half of all families with cars took an afternoon pleasure ride, but they didn't go far. One American in four had not seen either the Atlantic Ocean or the Pacific.

Nine out of ten adults had been on a train, and four in ten had spent at least one night on a Pullman sleeper. Trips by air, though rising in frequency, were still preferred by a minority. Cars were used for short trips, but traffic was lighter than it has since become. One reason was that there were about 50 million fewer people living in the country. Farmers excluded, the average worker lived two miles from his job, and he could get there in about eighteen minutes. One man in three went home for lunch. Less than one-third of all families said grace at meals, but 95 percent said they believed that prayer helped "in one way or another," 94 percent believed in God, and 68 percent in life after death; 69 percent were in favor of adding the phrase "under God" to the pledge of allegiance, which was done on June 14, 1954. The highest proportion of Bible readers was in the South, the lowest in New England and the Middle Atlantic states. America's two favorite mottoes were "Do unto others as you would have them do unto you," and "Live and let live."

In winter the average family with a house kept it heated at 70 degrees in the daytime and 60 degrees at night. The smallest amount of money a family of four needed to get along in an average U.S. community was $60 a week. (In 1937 it had been $30 a week.) The impression fostered by movies and television was that twin beds had become increasingly popular, but only one couple in eight had them; the rest still slept in double beds. Men preferred showers to bathtubs. Women favored tubs, three to one. The average family had a pet, with dogs outnumbering cats two to one. Most Americans said they liked and trusted their neighbors. Prudence with money, instilled during the Depression, was habitual. If suddenly given $10,000, the average American said, he would buy a home. The next largest group would pay off debts, put the money in a bank, or invest in securities. Only a few said they would take life easy, travel, or go on a spending spree. A twenty-three-year-old Chicago stenographer replied that she would get married right away. Another working girl answered that she would move to California, "where there are plenty of men."

On the whole, America remained a nation of optimists. In spite of grousing about high taxes and high prices — though even then they were considered high — a clear majority said they believed they were better off than their parents had been. The average American wanted to live to be a hundred, and more men than women wanted it, though women, with their longer life expectancy, had a greater chance of reaching it. Asked to single out the age he would most like to live over again, the typical adult chose twenty-one. Nearly half of all those polled had a pet superstition. The superstitions named most often were knocking on wood, avoiding black cats when walking, and throwing spilled salt over the shoulder. Women were more superstitious than men.

Most people thought the ideal family had three youngsters. Mothers felt that the first child should not arrive until the second year of marriage. Parental opinions of 1954's young people were high; they were regarded as more sensible and level-headed than the parents had been at that age. But the children were more critical: only one in five had no complaints about his father or mother. Nearly all adult Americans felt that a child ought to have an allowance, even though fewer than three out of ten parents had had one when young. While disturbed about juvenile delinquency, which had been rising since World War II and was already a source of anxiety, most adults took the position that parents, not youngsters, were chiefly to blame for it. Typical parents of that time thought a girl should not begin dating until she was sixteen.

Mixed marriages, a term which then meant marriages between Christians of different religious faiths, were a subject of lively discussion. Slightly more than half the people — 54 percent — approved of them, but only one American in four believed they had much chance of turning out successfully. Marriages between Gentiles and Jews were statistically insignificant. Unions between whites and Negroes, as blacks were then called, were unknown to the great middle class. Their possibility wasn't even discussed.

Negroes still did not exist as people for mainstream America. In popular entertainment they were more like pets. Stepin Fetchit, Hattie McDaniel, Butterfly McQueen, and Eddie Anderson — these were good for the nudge and the guffaw but they weren't looked upon as human beings. If Hollywood wanted to portray human feelings in a man with a black face, it put burnt cork on the face of somebody like Al Jolson. Black America was unnoticed by white America. "I am an invisible man," cried the hero of Ralph Ellison's 1953 novel. ". . . I am invisible, understand, simply because other people refuse to see me. I can hear you say, 'What a horrible, irresponsible bastard!' And you're right. . . . But to whom can I be responsible, when you refuse to see me?"

Now, after three centuries of black submission and black servitude, "the long habit of deception and evasion," as Ellison once called it, was about to end. The Supreme Court of the United States had pondered the matter and concluded that Negroes were real people after all, and that as such they must become visible to their white compatriots and treated as equals everywhere, beginning in the public schools.

By the U.S. Supreme Court clock it was 12:52 P.M., May 17, 1954. A concealed hand parted the red velour draperies at the front of the Court's magnificent chamber, and nine men robed in black, stepping past the gleaming Ionic columns, seated themselves in the leather chairs at the long mahogany bench. Editors all over the world were awaiting what was already being called the greatest moment in the Court's history since the Dred Scott decision of 1857. Associate Justice Robert Jackson, who was convalescing from a heart attack, had left his hospital bed that morning so that the full Court, including its three southerners, would be present for the occasion. In a departure from custom, newsmen had not been given advance copies of the decision. They had no inkling of which way it would go. The new Chief Justice had been on the bench only six months. At the time of his appointment lawyers had been appalled by his total lack of judicial experience, and few in Washington had been willing to predict how he would stand in this case of Brown v. Board of Education of Topeka. Earl Warren was no racist, but he had the reputation of being a staunch believer in states' rights.

Wire service reporters who cover Court sessions scribble bulletins in longhand at the press table, just below the bench, and send them on their way in pneumatic tubes. At 12:57 the Associated Press A wire came alive:

> Chief Justice Warren today began reading the Supreme Court's decision in the public school segregation cases. The Court's ruling could not be determined immediately.

Delivery of an opinion by the Chief Justice meant that he sided with the majority. This was Warren's first important ruling, and for a while all that spectators could be sure of was that he was taking an unconscionable amount of time to say what the decision was. Instead of delivering a brisk text he was meandering, stopping to cite such psychologists and sociologists as Kenneth Clark and Gunnar Myrdal on the mental development of Negro children. At 1:12 the exasperated AP correspondent dispatched a second bulletin. Warren was clearly opposed to segregation on principle, he said, but "the Chief Justice had not read far enough in the court's opinion for newsmen to say that segregation was being struck down as unconstitutional."

The decision's constitutional pivot was the Fourteenth Amendment: "Nor shall any state deny to any person the equal protection of the laws . . . ," but there was no judicial precedent for this application of it. The Supreme Court had never ruled on the issue of school segregation. In 1896 it had laid down a "separate but equal" doctrine in a case involving segregation of train passengers. Since then it had found against segregated housing and railroad transportation and ordered Negro students admitted to graduate schools of six southern and border state universities. Now at 1:20 P.M. Warren came to the climax of the ruling:

> To separate [Negro children] from others of similar age and qualifications solely because of their race generates a feeling of inferiority as to their status in the community that may affect their hearts and minds in a way never to be undone . . . We conclude that in the field of public education the doctrine of "separate but equal" has no place. Separate educational facilities are inherently unequal.

Segregation in schools, then, was unconstitutional: against the law. And the decision was unanimous, a special triumph for the National Association for the Advancement of Colored People and its scholarly counsel, Thurgood Marshall, himself a graduate of Jim Crow schools. Acknowledging that compliance would take time, the Court said it would withhold further instructions until its fall term. Meanwhile all sides were asked to prepare arguments on when segregation should be abolished and who — a special master or the federal district courts — should establish and enforce the terms under which it would end.

In the white South there was gloom. No greater blow to its social structure could be imagined. In seventeen states and the District of Columbia public school segregation was required by law, and four other states permitted it. Altogether, schools with a total population of twelve million children were affected. The first reactions of the authorities responsible for them varied according to their geographical location. In Kansas and Oklahoma, border states, officials were calm; they predicted that the change would be made with little commotion, if any. In Austin Governor Allan Shivers said Texas would submit, though he warned that full compliance might "take years." After studying the full opinion, Virginia's Governor Thomas Stanley told the press: "I shall call together . . . representatives of both state and local governments to consider the matter and work toward a plan which will be acceptable to our citizens and in keeping with the edict of the court."

The Deep South was more hostile. South Carolina's Governor James F. Byrnes, now seventy-five, said he was "shocked." He could scarcely claim to be surprised. In the hope of intimidating the Court, South Carolina had amended its constitution to allow for abandonment of the public school system. The question now was whether it would carry out its threat. Georgia had taken the same step, and its leaders were fiercer. Senator Richard Russell argued that racial matters were in the jurisdiction of the legislative, not the judicial, branch of government, and he accused the Warren Court, as some were already calling it, of "a flagrant abuse of judicial power." Governor Herman Talmadge delivered a diatribe: "The United States Supreme Court . . . has blatantly ignored all law and precedent . . . and lowered itself to the level of common politics . . . The people of Georgia believe in, adhere to, and will fight for their right under the U.S. and Georgia constitutions to manage their own affairs." They would, he said, "map a program to insure continued and permanent segregation of the races."

By autumn there was a lot of that sort of rhetoric as local candidates in southern elections fell to quarreling over who would be the greater defender of white supremacy. The Court, wary of civil disorder, set no rigid schedule for compliance. At the same time the justices let it be known that having laid down the law, they meant to see that it was enforced. Federal courts and local school districts were directed to evaluate their situations and study administrative problems. Then they were to take steps toward a "prompt and reasonable start" in carrying out the decision with "all deliberate speed" as soon as was "practicable."

President Eisenhower was troubled by all this. He knew there was a certain inevitability in it — that the end of European colonialism in Africa and Asia was bound to be matched in the United States by rising protests against discrimination, and that Americans were increasingly aware that the country's position of world leadership was being jeopardized by racism at home. Still, his innate conservatism distrusted sudden change. Privately he called the Warren appointment "the biggest damfool mistake I ever made." While believing in eventual integration, he argued that "if you try to go too far too fast . . . you are making a mistake." Nixon disagreed. He said that he felt strongly that "civil rights is primarily a moral rather than a legal question." But Ike remained reticent on this very delicate issue. To one of his advisers he said emphatically: "I am convinced that the Supreme Court decision set back progress in the South at least fifteen years. . . . It's all very well to talk about school integration — if you remember you may also be talking about social *dis*integration. Feelings are deep on this, especially where children are concerned. . . . We can't demand perfection in these moral questions. All we can do is keep working toward a goal and keep it high. And the fellow who tries to tell me that you can do these things by force is just plain nuts."

Still, as an old soldier he knew that orders must be obeyed. The Court had interpreted the Constitution; the chief executive had to carry out its instructions. At his direction all District of Columbia schools were integrated at once. He ended segregation on all Navy bases where it was still practiced — Truman had abolished it on Army posts — and overnight, literally over one night, the COLORED and WHITE signs over drinking fountains and rest room doors disappeared from naval installations. Lois Lippman, a Boston Negro, became the first black member of the White House secretarial staff; a few months later another Negro, E. Frederic Morrow, was appointed an administrative assistant to the President. Hagerty saw to it that all these facts reached the press; no one would say that Eisenhower wasn't practicing what he expected of others.

Over the next several months Oklahoma, Texas, Kentucky, West Virginia, Maryland, Tennessee, Arkansas, and Delaware reported partial integration in 350 school districts. Elsewhere the picture was less encouraging. Legislatures in Virginia and the Deep South passed complex measures designed to lead to long, involved court battles and circumvent the Supreme Court's ruling. Their governors were speaking stubbornly of "state sovereignty," "nullification," and the "interposition" of state authority to balk enforcement of federal laws — antebellum expressions which had not been heard since the death of John C. Calhoun. Encouraged by the warlike stance of their leaders, southerners on the lower rungs of the social ladder were reviving the Ku Klux Klan and organizing White Citizens' Councils to resist integration. Tempers were short throughout the white South.

But there could be no turning back now. Blacks had tempers, too. Over a century earlier de Tocqueville had predicted that once Negroes "join the ranks of free men, they will be indignant at being deprived of almost all the rights of citizens; and being unable to become the equals of the whites, they will not be slow to show themselves their enemies." That was the alternative to substantial integration. The Court had stirred hope in Negro hearts, and it is hope, not despair, that is the fuel of social action. J. Edgar Hoover reported to the White House that the sale of small arms had increased all over the South. In some communities it was up by as much as 400 percent. The most volatile rhetoric was coming from whites, but it was also notable that throughout the winter of 1954–55 the Black Muslims, with their gospel of inverted racism and retaliatory violence, were expanding rapidly.

Americans found, to their consternation, that they were rapidly moving into an era of racial incidents. Given the deeply held convictions at either end of the spectrum, such episodes were unavoidable. Militant whites vowed to defend the racial status quo, which the NAACP and the new Negro organizations springing up around it were bound to challenge. As often as not the officials in the middle simply came apart. With Thurgood Marshall as her adviser a twenty-six-year-old black woman, Autherine Lucy, announced her intention to enroll at the University of Alabama. The university trustees were distraught. After three days of unruly crowds at Tuscaloosa, during which her car was stoned and pelted with rocks, Miss Lucy reached the registrar's office, only to be handed this telegram from the trustees: FOR YOUR SAFETY AND THE SAFETY OF THE STUDENTS AND FACULTY MEMBERS OF THE UNIVERSITY, YOU ARE HEREBY SUSPENDED FROM CLASSES UNTIL FURTHER NOTICE. Marshall led her to a court, which lifted the suspension. The trustees then met that night, accused Miss Lucy of making "false, defamatory, impertinent, and scandalous charges" against the university authorities — and ordered her permanent expulsion.

Frustration ran high on both sides in such episodes. With the power of the federal courts behind her, Autherine Lucy was bound to win in the end, and the trustees knew it. Only a bullet could stop her — a haunting possibility. Not only were guns and gunmen all around; it was possible, and indeed in some cases probable, that such a killer would go free. The same Constitution which required desegregation entitled a defendant to trial before a jury of his peers. His peers, in large areas of the South, were likely to acquit him. This happened. The first such incident occurred in Greenwood, Mississippi, in August 1955. Emmett Till, a fourteen-year-old black youth from Chicago, was visiting relatives there. Rumor spread that he had insulted a white woman, and three white men dragged him from his relatives' home and drowned him. Witnesses identified two of the three killers to federal agents, but an all-white jury acquitted them. The two — they were half-brothers — were then charged with kidnapping by a U.S. attorney, but a grand jury refused to indict them, and the FBI, which had painstakingly assembled irrefutable evidence, reluctantly closed its file.

By the first anniversary of the Supreme Court decision, racism lay like an ugly blight across much of the South. Rabble-rousers stirred up mobs which frightened, and sometimes attacked, blacks insisting on their constitutional rights. The cruelest incidents were in the grade schools, where children, most of them too small to understand the savage struggle being waged over them, were subjected to intimidation and outright terror. The return to school each September is a familiar American ritual. Mothers dress youngsters in new clothes, brush their hair, give them pencil cases, and send them off to their new classrooms. It is at precisely this time that boards of education introduce whatever changes in regulations there are to be — such as desegregation. Beginning the year after the Supreme Court decision and extending to the end of the 1950s, American front pages each fall carried accounts of ghastly demonstrations in front of bewildered pupils. Sometimes there was violence.

Two representative incidents erupted almost simultaneously in one week of 1956. In Clinton, Tennessee, mob hysteria was whipped up by John Kasper, a racist zealot from Washington, D.C. (He saw no irony in his charge that desegregation was the work of "outside agitators.") Until Kasper arrived, Clinton had been a quiet backwater town of four thousand people, where twelve black students were preparing to enroll in the local high school. Goaded by him, a thousand Clinton citizens disrupted the school, blocked traffic, battered the cars of Negroes who happened to be passing through, and then threw themselves on the eight-man Clinton police force shouting, "Let's get the nigger lovers! Let's get their guns and kill them!" After a night of fear 100 state troopers, 633 National Guardsmen, and seven M-41 tanks put down what looked like an incipient revolution. That was a lot of law enforcement for one township, but the country was learning how vulnerable to hotheads schools were. Mansfield, Texas, with a population of 1,450, was even smaller than Clinton. There a federal district court had ordered the integration of three blacks with three hundred white high school students. On registration day four hundred men barged into the school waving placards that read DEAD COONS ARE THE BEST COONS and $2 A DOZEN FOR NIGGER EARS. The three Negro students quickly withdrew. A fourteen-year-old white girl told a reporter: "If God wanted us to go to school together He wouldn't have made them black and us white."

It was easy for Americans outside the South to be scornful of it, but it wasn't necessarily fair. The fact that racist vigilantes could disrupt the peace did not make them a majority. In the aftermath of the Clinton disorders the town looked like a stronghold of bigotry. Kasper, arrested on charges of instigating a riot, was freed. In a current election campaign the White Citizens' Council there nominated its own candidate for mayor. Bumper stickers urging his election seemed to be everywhere. In the school students wearing Confederate flags sewn on their sweaters stoned black boys, shouted "Nigger bitches" and "Dirty nigger whores" at black girls, and poured ink over the blacks' books. On the morning of election day a white minister attempting to escort the Negro children past a mob outside the school was badly beaten; so were two people who tried to come to his assistance. The principal expelled a thirteen-year-old white boy for assaulting a black girl and then, after he himself had been threatened, announced that the school was being closed "because of lawlessness and disorder." At that point, just as Clinton seemed lost to decency, the tide shifted. On orders from Attorney General Brownell, the FBI arrested sixteen of the mob's ringleaders. Fifty white high school students, led by the seventeen-year-old football captain, asked people to comply "with the federal court order to provide an education for all the citizens of Anderson County who desire it." Then came a surprise, even to those who thought they knew the town well. The polls closed, the votes were counted — and every segregationist candidate for local office was defeated by a margin of nearly three to one.

That year a new phrase was on the lips of public speakers: "the winds of change." The expression came out of Morocco, where French troops transferred from Vietnam were fighting another losing battle against anticolonialists, but it also seemed applicable to the United States. The Warren Court in particular appeared to be a storm center for winds of change. In time its reinterpretations of the Constitution would bar prayer from classrooms, expand defendants' rights to counsel (notably in Miranda v. Arizona), extend freedom of speech and freedom of the press to moviemakers, strike the bonds of censorship from pornographers, and lay down guidelines for legislative apportionment in the states.

Diehard conservatives dug in. IMPEACH EARL WARREN billboards went up all over the South. The Chief Justice had become the most controversial figure in the government since Franklin Roosevelt; all turmoil and racial tensions were laid at his door. Yet the Supreme Court was but one of many federal institutions which were acting to alter the system. Congress was fashioning the first of what would eventually be five civil rights acts. The Civil Service Commission was speeding up the advancement of black workers, and federal regulatory agencies were taking a sudden interest in charges of discrimination. One of them, the Interstate Commerce Commission, was weighing a proposal to forbid the interstate segregation of travelers on trains, buses, and in waiting rooms when a black seamstress in Montgomery, Alabama, anticipated it.

Her name was Rosa Parks, she was forty-two years old, and on Thursday, December 1, 1955, she was very tired. She found a seat on a Montgomery bus, but when the bus filled up the driver told her to stand so a white man could sit there. It was an old southern custom for Negroes to surrender their seats to whites. It was also against the law for anyone to disobey a bus driver's instructions. Mrs. Parks thought about it for a moment and then said she wouldn't move. At that moment, Eldridge Cleaver later wrote, "somewhere in the universe a gear in the machinery had shifted."

Arrested at the next stop, she was charged with a misdemeanor, found guilty, and fined ten dollars. That made Mrs. Parks's friends angry, and she was a popular woman; within forty-eight hours mimeographed pamphlets being distributed in Negro neighborhoods called for a one-day boycott of all city transportation. The boycott was so spectacular a success that leaders of Montgomery's black community started asking one another larger questions. The city's 25,000 blacks accounted for 75 percent of the bus company's patronage. Suppose they extended the boycott and set terms for an end to it? Eventually the management would either yield or go bankrupt.

That was how it started. The company was told that it would have no more black passengers until Negroes were seated on a first come first served basis and allowed to keep their seats. In addition the Negro leaders demanded that drivers be ordered to treat blacks courteously and that black drivers be hired for buses in Negro districts. The management replied that white drivers would be polite, but that was all. So the passenger strike continued. It was 95 percent effective, and as the weeks passed with no compromise on either side, the determination of the blacks simply increased. The rest of Alabama began to watch Montgomery; then the rest of the country; and then the world. The segregationists were led by W. A. Gayle, Montgomery's mayor. Gayle and his fellow members of the city commission ceremoniously joined the local White Citizens' Council. Then he declared that the city would never capitulate to the boycotters. He said, "We have pussyfooted around long enough and it has come time to be frank. There seems to be a belief on the part of the Negroes that they have the white people hemmed in a corner and they are not going to give an inch until they can force the white people of the community to submit to their demands."

Gayle's chief adversary, the leader of the blacks, was Martin Luther King, an unknown twenty-six-year-old clergyman. King had come to Montgomery the year before to become pastor of the Dexter Avenue Baptist Church. The white South paid grudging respect to black clergymen, but King was one of the new Negroes, and he lay outside the southern white experience. He was a Ph.D., a product of Harvard, and a genuine scholar. In his sermons he dwelt less on the river Jordan than on the wisdom of Socrates, Aristotle, Shakespeare, Galileo, and Toynbee. Writing in his small white Montgomery bungalow to the soft accompaniment of classical music, he had fused Christianity, Hegelianism, and Gandhiism into a philosophy teaching strength through struggle and harmony out of pain. Gandhi's satyagraha — passive resistance and noncooperation as a way of opposing mistreatment — had become King's "soul force." He showed his congregation films of the Indian mahatma and said of the boycott:

> This is not a tension between the Negroes and whites. This is only a conflict between justice and injustice. We are not just trying to improve Negro

Montgomery. We are trying to improve the whole of Montgomery. If we are arrested every day; if we are exploited every day; if we are triumphed over every day; let nobody pull you so low as to hate them.

He taught the Dexter Avenue church's worshippers the meaning of "victory over your enemies through love," and he inspired them with rousing old Baptist hymns and camp-meeting tunes, sometimes with new words:

> *Deep in my heart,*
> *I do believe*
> *We shall overcome*
> *One day.*

Hard-core segregationists were derisive. One described King as "just another rabble-rouser the Communistic N-double-A-C-P is sending down here to stir up our decent Nigras." Not all whites felt that way. Mayor Gayle was discovering that families accustomed to Negro help were giving rides to their cooks and handymen or paying their taxi fares. He protested that the domestics "are fighting to destroy our social fabric just as much as the Negro radicals who are leading them," and he said, "The Negroes are laughing at white people behind their backs. They think it's very funny that whites who are opposed to the Negro boycott will act as chauffeur to Negroes who are boycotting the buses."

After three months of deadlock the city attorney produced a 1921 state antilabor law enjoining restraint of trade. Under it a grand jury indicted King and 114 other black leaders. "In this state," the indictment read, "we are committed to segregation by custom and law; we intend to maintain it." The defendants were fingerprinted and freed on $300 bond each. Late in March King became the first of them to come to trial on the charge of conspiring "without a just cause or legal excuse" to hinder a company in its conduct of business. Black witnesses testified that they certainly did have just cause. One told how a bus driver had shut the door on her blind husband's leg and then stepped on the accelerator. A second described a Negro being forced from a bus at pistol point because he did not have correct change. A third said his pregnant wife had been compelled to surrender her seat to a white woman, and a fourth said a driver had called her an "ugly black ape."

King, who had waived a jury trial, pointed out that the boycott had begun spontaneously and that he had become its spokesman only after it was in full swing. The judge nevertheless found him guilty; he was ordered to pay $1,000 in fines and court costs and released on bond pending appeal. If the verdict was meant to intimidate Montgomery's Negroes, its effect was the exact opposite. They promptly held a rally on the lawn outside the courthouse. One black shouted, "We ain't going to ride the buses now for sure." A middle-aged woman pushed through the crowd to tell King,

"My heart and my pocketbook are at your disposal." A mass prayer meeting was scheduled for that evening. One man called to the others, "Are you going to be there?" They called back, "Yes!" He asked, "Are you going to ride the buses?" and they roared, "No!"

And they didn't. Spring passed, summer passed, and still the spirit of the blacks showed no signs of flagging. The mayor confided to friends that he had never dreamed that Negroes could be this determined. The bus company sank into debt. Drivers drifted into other jobs or left the city. The Negroes showed every sign of being able to survive without them. Some had become accustomed to walking to work, some had bicycles, and for the others King had organized a vast car pool with two hundred automobiles. The mayor announced that this was illegal. In the twelfth month of the customer strike King and the other black leaders were arrested for running a business enterprise without a franchise. They were on trial in state circuit court when electrifying news arrived. The Supreme Court, which had already overturned the "separate but equal" doctrine for recreational facilities as well as in schools, had now killed it in public transportation. Discrimination on buses was now a violation of federal law. Martin Luther King was free. He was in addition a world celebrity. The unprecedented boycott had dealt Alabama segregation a devastating blow. American Negroes everywhere had found new hope, and the young black preacher had been catapulted into the first rank of the struggle for civil rights.

King did not gloat. He advised his flock to act with dignity and without pride. He said, "We have been going to the back of the bus for so long that there is danger that we will instinctively go straight back there again and perpetuate segregation." At the same time, he continued, "I would be terribly disappointed if any of you go back to the buses bragging, 'We, the Negroes, won a victory over the white people.' If you do, our struggle will be lost all over the South. Go back with humility and meekness."

He would have been less than human if he hadn't ridden a bus himself when the boycott ended, 381 days after Rosa Parks had started it. The driver said to him, "Is this the Reverend?" The clergyman said, "That's right. How much?" It was fifteen cents — up a nickel from the year before — and putting the coins in the slot he took a front seat. He said afterward, "It was a great ride." Most Montgomery whites were relieved to have it all over, and some were in good humor. A bank teller wryly told a reporter, "They'll find that all they've won in their year of praying and boycotting is the same lousy service I've been getting every day." On one bus a white man said to nobody in particular, "I see this isn't going to be a white Christmas." A nearby black smiled. "Yes sir," he said. "That's right."

Long after an event has passed, its place in the scheme of things becomes clear, but at the time it often seems insignificant. Doubtless the driver who told Mrs. Parks to stand merely thought he was dealing with one uppity Nigra; had he known that his own grandchildren would one day study the incident in school, he might have been more circumspect. Presidents are more conscious of history than bus drivers, but they, too, may be blind to the consequences of their decisions. Dwight Eisenhower was above all a man of peace. That and his respect for congressional prerogatives had caused him to stop other members of his administration from making unwise commitments on Indochina. Yet in the same year that Rosa Parks altered destiny, Ike took the country a step down the long road toward madness in Vietnam.

It was not the first such step. Any assessment of the growth in presidential war-making powers should note the precedents set by Franklin Roosevelt in 1941 and 1942. Before then, congressional authority in this area was intact. It was shakier afterward; FDR, with his brilliant display of political legerdemain, had used executive agreements to create a situation in which the Axis powers were virtually compelled to attack the United States. Then came Korea. Cabell Phillips, Harry Truman's biographer, observes that "His decision to intervene in Korea . . . came close to preempting the right to declare war . . . all Presidents are now armed with the Truman precedent to strike swiftly on their own, wherever and with whatever force is necessary, when they believe the national interest demands it."

The last steps in the erosion of congressional authority, and the accompanying executive ascendancy, were to be taken by Lyndon Johnson and Richard Nixon against the backdrop of Southeast Asia, but each link in the chain of precedent deserves notice. The Formosa resolution of 1955 was one of them. It was a special consequence of the cold war, but its implications for the future were broad and grave.

Dean Acheson had wanted to wait "until the dust has settled" in China before formulating a new policy there. By 1955 it was as settled as it would ever be, yet the eastern edge of the picture remained murky. The Communists controlled the mainland and the Nationalists Formosa, but the status of Formosa Strait, which separated them, was unresolved. Here and there the 115-mile-wide sound was sprinkled with tiny, barren islands whose only real significance, in 1955, was as a bone of contention between the Peoples Republic of China, on the one hand, and Chiang and his American allies on the other.

The islands varied in size and proximity to larger land masses. One group of sixty-four islets, the Pescadores, was thirty miles from Formosa and was considered a part of it; the White House let it be known that any attack on the Pescadores would be interpreted as preliminary to an invasion of Formosa and as such would be resisted by the Seventh Fleet. Congressional approval was not needed for a defense of the Pescadores because they had been captured from Japan in World War II; under international law the United States was entitled to protect them. The situation on the far side of the strait was different. The islands there were Quemoy, Matsu, and the Tachen group, each of which was more than a hundred miles from

Formosa and within five to ten miles of the mainland. As Adlai Stevenson pointed out, they lay "almost as close to the coast of China as Staten Island does to New York," had "always belonged to China," and were properties to which neither the U.S. nor the Nationalists on Formosa had any legal claim. Walter Lippmann underscored the implications of this: ". . . were we to intervene in the offshore islands, we would be acting on Chinese territory in a Chinese civil war."

Nothing would have given John Foster Dulles greater satisfaction. He was ready to fight for the offshore islands any time, and he complained to Sherman Adams about the inability of the British and other U.S. allies to understand "the tremendous shock that a retreat from Quemoy and Matsu would be to the free people of East Asia." That was how Dulles saw the world. He conjured up visions of mass meetings in places like Sumatra and Tibet, with millions of stern peasants gathered under banners reading FREE PEOPLE OF EAST ASIA UNITE and SUPPORT COLLECTIVE SECURITY. The Chinese Communists knew of Dulles's intractability and liked to twit him. While he was in Manila signing the Southeast Asia Treaty Organization protocols in September 1954 they had bombarded Quemoy, and the following January 18 they occupied the islet of Yikiang in the Tachens. Since Yikiang was so microscopic that it wasn't even shown on State Department maps, and since the Tachens were two hundred miles north of Formosa, the threat to Chiang's Nationalists was obscure. Nevertheless, the Joint Chiefs went into emergency session. A majority was hawkish. Admiral Radford, Admiral Carney, and General Nathan F. Twining felt that it was time to take a stand against the Communists and bring about a showdown once and for all.

General Ridgway was the lone dissenter. He advised the President that "Such an action would be almost impossible to limit. It would bring us into direct conflict with the Red Chinese. It could spread to full and all-out war, employing all the terrible weapons at our command." Even if China were conquered, Ridgway went on, the situation would still be highly unsatisfactory; the United States would have created "by military means a great vacuum. Then we would have to go in there with hundreds of thousands of men to fill that vacuum — which would bring us face to face with Russia along a seven-thousand-mile frontier."

With Ridgway the only dove, the Joint Chiefs voted to move against the Reds. Dulles agreed; so did Senator Knowland. But Eisenhower concluded that Ridgway was right. Once again he refused to be drawn into a war on the Asian mainland. The war fever abated. Nevertheless, Dulles did succeed in persuading Ike that face was involved. After the seizure of Yikiang the Peking radio had declared that the thrust showed a "determined will to fight for the liberation of Taiwan." If under these circumstances America did nothing, Dulles warned, Asians would conclude that the U.S. was a paper tiger. The President agreed to do something. He would ask Congress for a resolution.

His message of January 24 was unprecedented in American history. Ike was asking Congress for something more and something less than a declaration of war. He wanted it to let him decide when and where America would fight. He said:

> The situation has become sufficiently critical to impel me, without awaiting action by the United Nations, to ask the Congress to participate now, by specific resolution, in measures designed to improve the prospects for peace. These measures would contemplate the use of the armed forces of the United States, if necessary, to assure the security of Formosa and the Pescadores.

The President then suggested that whether or not a Chinese attack off the offshore islands invited retaliation depended upon the character of the assault. If they just wanted Quemoy and Matsu he might let them have it. If they had a leap toward Formosa in mind, he might not. He wanted Congress to let him read the Communist mind and take whatever action he thought appropriate.

For a measure which was meant to remove doubts, this one bewildered a lot of people. Liberal Democrats contended that Ike already had authority to take the steps he had in mind. As champions of Roosevelt-Truman foreign policy, they were believers in a strong Presidency. His constitutional power as commander in chief, they insisted, permitted him to deploy American military might any way he wished. Some of the arguments spun that winter make curious reading today. Vietnam was destined to become the graveyard of many U.S. policies, none more so than this one. As in the struggle over the Bricker amendment, conservatives wanted to keep the prerogative of making great decisions abroad on Capitol Hill, while liberals insisted that it belonged in the White House. The absolutist nature of the liberal position was most clearly stated by Richard H. Rovere. On March 19, 1955, he wrote that:

> . . . the President's power to defend Formosa does not rest on the hastily composed resolution that Congress passed in January. As President of the United States he has the right to take whatever action he deems necessary in any area he judges to be related to the defense of this country, regardless of whether it is related to the defense of Formosa or anything else.

Eisenhower himself was uncertain over whether he was giving Congress something or taking it away. Before sending the message to the Capitol he made one change. It had read, "The authority I request may be in part already inherent in the authority of the Commander-in-Chief." He crossed this out and wrote in its place, "Authority for some of the actions which might be required would be inherent in the authority of the Commander-in-Chief." Congress was no surer of itself than he was. The most common interpretation there was that the administration was looking for a way to get off the hook on the offshore islands.

Hubert Humphrey tried in vain to tack on an amendment which would have restricted the grant of power to Formosa and the Pescadores. Others in Congress were worried that the United States might be trapped into a war over some obscure place that had nothing to do with American security. Senator Ralph E. Flanders went further. "We have had intimations from the highest quarters," he said, "that it would be militarily advisable to prevent the massing of troops and equipment gathered for the purpose of making an assault on the islands. Put in plain English, this is preventive war. And it is seriously proposed as a possible action pursuant to the purposes of this resolution."

Opposition receded when Senator George threw his great weight behind the bill, saying, "I hope no Democrat will be heard to say that because the President of the United States came to Congress he is thereby subject to criticism." The resolution passed the Senate 85 to 3 and the House 410 to 3. Eisenhower signed it on January 29. That happened to be George's seventy-seventh birthday, and a great fuss was made over the senator when he arrived for the ceremony. Yet in less than a month the Seventh Fleet seemed to show how pointless the whole debate had been by evacuating fourteen thousand Chinese Nationalist troops from the Tachens. So much for the Formosa resolution, Washington said, assuming that it would now become a meaningless scrap of paper. But one man saw it differently. Adlai Stevenson observed that the President had asked for, and had received from Congress, a "blank check." That is precisely what it was. One day Eisenhower or another occupant of his office could present it for payment without consulting Congress further. The delicate balance of constitutional powers had shifted again; another restraint on the chief executive had been removed.

Eisenhower's greatest foreign policy coup, which came six months later, was a public relations triumph. To achieve it he had to all but run over John Foster Dulles. For ten years the Republican Old Guard had resolutely opposed any meeting with the Soviet leaders. Winston Churchill had been proposing a top-level meeting for some time — he called it a "summit" — but for American conservatives the mere suggestion that an American President might clink cocktail glasses with the Russians was like a Pavlovian bell. It set them to protesting against another Yalta or Potsdam, to them synonyms for sellout. Dulles agreed; as an anti-Communist fundamentalist he recoiled from any bargaining with men as steeped in sin as the Soviets.

He couldn't come right out and say that, because the President had repeatedly declared that he would meet anyone, anywhere, in the name of peace. Therefore Dulles tried to establish impossible prerequisites for such a meeting. Before it could be seriously considered, he said, Moscow must show by its deeds that the Soviet Union belonged to the comity of nations and would cooperate in settling differences. When pressed for an example of such a deed, he would reply with vague generalities. He gave the impression that he might be impressed by a withdrawal of all Russian troops from eastern Europe, say, or free elections throughout Russia under U.N.

supervision. Sometimes he implied that he would expect handsome apologies from them, too, for their transgressions in the past.

To mollify him and the Republican ultras, Eisenhower called in key senators and congressmen and promised them that he would not be party to "another Yalta." He assured them that no commitments would be made without their approval. Dulles, who was there, said he wouldn't put it past the Russians to make some grandstand play in the name of world peace. He would be on the lookout for it, he said grimly.

Eisenhower had said nothing when Dulles spoke scornfully of dramatic peace proposals. Inwardly, however, he must have been troubled. He himself had that very thing in mind. Nothing definite had been decided, but the draft of a fresh approach to disarmament lay on his desk. In March the President had appointed Nelson Rockefeller chairman of a panel of experts in arms control and psychological warfare. He had given Rockefeller office space at the Marine Corps base at Quantico and asked him to come up with new recommendations which might be produced at a summit meeting. Dulles heard about the task force, but he didn't know its mission. All the same, he was suspicious. To Sherman Adams he said of Rockefeller, "He seems to be building up a big staff. He's got them down at Quantico, and nobody knows what they're doing."

They were studying European opinion surveys. People in the NATO nations, they learned, were weary of the alliance, unenthusiastic about the American bases on the continent, and in favor of banning nuclear weapons. That was disturbing. Lacking Russia's huge standing army, America needed the bombs and the bases as a deterrent. Some way must be found to keep them and still convince Europeans that the U.S. was seeking peace. The Quantico group's answer was a proposal for aerial inspection — in a felicitous phrase, "Open Skies." The idea was not new. Aerial inspection had been suggested as early as 1946 in a Bernard Baruch plan for the international control of atomic energy, and later it had appeared in the report of a U.N. disarmament commission and an Acheson plan for "international disclosure and verification" of all armed forces and weapons. Until now, though, it had been overlooked. Eisenhower thought it both appealing and practical. He hadn't made up his mind over whether to present it at the summit, but on the way to the *Columbine*, his plane, he stuffed it in his briefcase.

The *Columbine*'s destination was Geneva. There he unpacked in the fifteen-room Château Creux de Genthod, which the wife of a Swiss perfume tycoon had placed at his disposal. Meantime Plane No. 001 of the Ilyushin fleet landed and discharged down its ramp Stalin's two successors, Nikita Khrushchev and Nikolai Bulganin, the first looking like a labor union boss and the second bearing an uncanny resemblance to Colonel Sanders, the fried chicken magnate of the early 1970s. Later that afternoon, Anthony Eden and French Premier Edgar Faure arrived to complete the roster of participants in the Big Four talks, or, in the neat Swiss phrase, the

Conférence à Quatre. Already the Spirit of Geneva, the newsmen's name for it, was casting a magic spell, attracting crowds of tourists and some celebrities. Pastor Martin Niemöller was there to hold a press conference, and an American clergyman, Billy Graham, was presiding over a revival in the Parc des Eaux-Vives.

In the Palais des Nations Dulles looked disconsolate. Ike, by contrast, was in fine form. At first he tried to match Dulles's stony expression, agreeing with the secretary that it would be unwise to raise false hopes that might be quickly dashed if the meetings were unfruitful. But Eisenhower was too genial, too optimistic, too bursting with good spirits to stay gloomy. He allowed himself to tell the press that "a new dawn may be coming," and in chairing the opening session on Monday, July 18, he spent the first quarter-hour greeting Marshal Zhukov.

The Russians, for their part, seemed more relaxed than at any time since the war. Khrushchev assured his listeners that "neither side wants war," and back home *Pravda* and *Izvestia* were telling the Russian people the same thing — a major shift in the party line, which until now had held that the rest of the world was implacably against them. Khrushchev, Bulganin, and Zhukov rode around Geneva in open cars and took long walks without bodyguards, something of an embarrassment to the Americans, because Eisenhower's every move was screened by Secret Service details and monitored by men in helicopters overhead.

Nevertheless, it was Ike who dominated the Conférence à Quatre. His smile, his candor, and his obvious concern for all mankind captivated the Europeans. *Le Monde* of Paris, usually anti-American, observed that "Eisenhower, whose personality has long been misunderstood, has emerged as the type of leader humanity needs today." Addressing himself to the Soviets, he said earnestly: "The American people want to be friends with the Soviet people. There are no natural differences between our peoples or our nations. There are no territorial or commercial rivalries. Historically, our two countries have always been at peace." He then proposed freer communications between East and West, disarmament, and a united, democratic Germany.

Despite their better manners, the Russians were still Russians when the chips were down. They had a few favorable words to say about peaceful coexistence, but in exchange for it they wanted nothing less than the dissolution of NATO. They dusted off and presented a plan which all those present had heard before: America, Russia, and China would each limit itself to 1,500,000 soldiers; Britain and France would have 650,000 each; and all nuclear weapons would be banned. When they laid that on the table the talks bogged down. After a two-hour huddle of the Americans in the château, Stassen went off to draw up a general disarmament proposal while the President himself drafted an Open Skies presentation. He continued to be undecided about submitting it; he wanted to hear what Bulganin had to say in the morning. Bulganin said nothing new. Not much was expected from Ike, either; this was the fourth day of the conference, and the others assumed that he had already spoken his mind. His first words were familiar: the United States was "prepared to enter into a sound and reliable agreement making possible the reduction of armaments." Then he paused, squared his shoulders against the high windows looking out over Lake Geneva, took off his glasses, and laid them down. He said:

> I should address myself for a moment principally to the delegates from the Soviet Union, because our two great countries admittedly possess new and terrible weapons in quantities which do give rise in other parts of the world, or reciprocally, to the fears and dangers of surprise attack.
>
> I propose, therefore, that we take a practical step, that we begin an arrangement, very quickly, as between ourselves — immediately. These steps would include:
>
> To give each other a complete blueprint of our military establishments, from beginning to end, from one end of our countries to the other; lay out the establishments and provide the blueprints to each other.
>
> Next, to provide within our countries facilities for aerial photography to the other country — we to provide the facilities within our country, ample facilities for aerial reconnaissance, where you can make all the pictures you choose and take them to your own country to study; you to provide exactly the same facilities for us and we to make these examinations, and by this step to convince the world that we are providing as between ourselves against the possibility of great surprise attack, thus lessening danger and relaxing tension.
>
> Likewise we will make more easily attainable a comprehensive and effective system of inspection and disarmament, because what I propose, I assure you, would be but a beginning. . . .
>
> The United States is ready to proceed in the study and testing of a reliable system of inspections and reporting, and when that system is proved, then to reduce armaments with all others to the extent that the system will provide assured results.
>
> The successful working out of such a system would do much to develop the mutual confidence which will open wide the avenues of progress for all our peoples.

During the translation a blinding flash of lightning filled the room, thunder rolled across the lake, and all the electricity in the Palais des Nations went dead. Ike chuckled. He said, "I didn't mean to turn the lights off." They flickered on again, revealing a dumbfounded Russian delegation. The Soviet Union was still in the grip of Stalinist paranoia. Diplomats in Moscow were shadowed, foreign correspondents were limited in their movements, the telephones of foreigners were tapped, and any Soviet citizen seen in conversation with them was closely questioned. The idea of providing the Americans with detailed maps of their military bases and then allowing U.S. photographers to fly over and take all the pictures they liked was stupefying. Khrushchev and his fellow delegates didn't know what to say. They just stared.

The Europeans were overjoyed. They hailed the proposal as a diplomatic masterstroke. Premier Faure said, "I wish the people of the world could have been in this conference room to hear the voice of a man speaking from great military experience. Had this been possible, they would believe that something had changed in the world in the handling of this question of disarmament. I am sure that this conference has scored its first victory over skepticism." Next morning newspaper editorials all over western Europe echoed Faure. Opening the skies was something everyone could understand. It was simple and direct, and only a President whose country had nothing to hide could have proposed it.

In practice it was impossible, as out of the question for Americans as for Russians. Ike's military advisers knew that. They had read the fine print he had skipped in his extemporaneous delivery — Open Skies was described there as a suggestion to "instruct our representatives in the Subcommittee on Disarmament in discharge of their mandate from the United States to give priority effort to the study of inspection and reporting" — and they had concluded that he was talking about a distant goal, something that could become practical only after a great many other agreements had been reached and tested. The Pentagon was not paranoid, but it did have a great many hoops through which anyone must jump before he could look at classified material. A government that withheld data from J. Robert Oppenheimer wasn't going to turn it over to the NKVD. This was still the McCarthy era. The senator might be discredited, and the country might be willing to forgive the promoters of Peress, but that was a far cry from filling the sky over Los Alamos with MIGs.*

At the end of the conference Bulganin drew the President aside and said, "Don't worry — this will come out all right." Ike left Geneva convinced that the Soviet leaders, especially Zhukov, were persuaded that he had been sincere. In the following months they treated Open Skies gingerly, mindful, perhaps, of the enthusiasm which had greeted it elsewhere. As late as March 1, 1956, Eisenhower was writing Bulganin to propose the merger of Open Skies and another plan, for the peaceful use of atomic energy. By then, however, Bulganin was being shouldered aside by Khrushchev, who wasn't interested in conciliatory gestures. He preferred to deliver speeches about "wars of national liberation." The Spirit of Geneva was dead. There had been no detente. The conference had achieved nothing that lasted, and is now remembered only for the warmth of Ike's grin and the density of the ice which it didn't melt.

Mercifully, disillusionment was slow to emerge. As the President flew home, Geneva was being acclaimed as a thundering success. Gallup reported that 84 percent of the American people could not think of a single

---

*Assuming, that is, that the Russian photographers would have been in Russian planes. They could have been carried in American transports while the American photographers flew over the Soviet Union in Russian planes. Eisenhower hadn't made that clear, and no one asked him. Perhaps even elated Europeans knew in their hearts that Open Skies was too redolent of BBD&O.

thing in the Eisenhower administration that deserved criticism. The *Columbine* brought the President home in the early hours of Sunday, July 24. It was still dark, the Washington National Airport was drenched in rain. Nevertheless, people were there to cheer him as he descended the ramp, and others lined the roads to the White House. It was a peak in his Presidency, one of the great moments of the 1950s. He had left determined to lessen world tensions, he was returning in apparent triumph, and now he looked forward to a long golfing vacation in Denver.

On September 23, 1955, President Eisenhower awoke early on Byers Peak Ranch outside Denver, where he was the guest of Aksel Nielsen, a Colorado banker, and cooked his own breakfast: beef bacon, pork sausage, fried mush, and flapjacks. He stopped off at the stucco administration building at Lowry Air Force Base, spent two intensive hours working with aides, and then drove to the Cherry Hills Country Club for eighteen holes of golf. He shot 84, which was better than it seemed because twice his game had been interrupted by urgent phone calls, one of them from Dulles about the Soviet responses to Open Skies.

The President lunched on hamburger and raw onions, then golfed another nine holes. On the eighth hole he paused, frowning, and rubbed his chest. To the club pro he said, "Maybe I can't take those onions any more. They seem to be backing up on me. I seem to have a little heartburn." The rest of his afternoon was spent in the basement of his mother-in-law's Lafayette Street home painting; he was copying a photograph of an Argentine woman in the July 11 issue of *Life*. Then George and Mary Allen arrived for dinner. Over roast lamb, potatoes, and vegetables Ike mentioned being troubled by the onions earlier, but then he appeared to forget it. At 10 P.M. he retired to his second-floor bedroom. Mamie's bedroom was directly across the hall.

She awoke at 2:30 A.M. and heard him tossing about. Crossing the corridor, she found him asleep but restless. "What's the matter, Ike?" she asked. "Are you having a nightmare or something?" No, he mumbled; he was fine; she left. But he wasn't fine. And he couldn't get back to sleep. Suddenly an agonizing pain gripped his chest. He rose and crossed the hall to her. He couldn't speak; he rubbed his chest to show where it hurt. Remembering the onions, she gave him milk of magnesia. She was troubled. This was something new; he had never complained of a pain there before. Picking up the phone, she called Major General Howard McC. Snyder, the President's personal physician, at Lowry's bachelor officers' quarters four miles away. She told him what was happening and said, "You'd better come over."

Snyder didn't need to be told. Those symptoms would alarm any doctor. Flinging his clothes over his pajamas, he told his driver, "Seven-fifty Lafayette Street, and step on it." They raced through red lights all the way; at 3:12 the doctor was at the President's bedside. Ike was flushed, sweating, and in extreme discomfort. His pulse was rapid and his blood pressure was high. Listening to his chest with a stethoscope, Snyder reached a diagnosis within minutes. The President had been stricken by a coronary thrombosis. His heart had been damaged; how much, Snyder could not tell. He administered amyl nitrate, papaverine hydrochloride to dilate Ike's arteries, and morphine for shock. Then he gave him a shot of heparin to prevent clotting. At 3:45 he administered a second injection of morphine. Ike fell into a deep sleep. His crisis was passing, but Snyder decided that for the time being he would tell no one of it, not even Mrs. Eisenhower. There was nothing they could do, and the commotion of an alarmed household would only decrease the President's chances.

For nearly four hours the doctor sat alone by the bed. A little before 7 A.M., when others in the gray brick house began to waken, he sent for Ann Whitman. The President was indisposed, he told the secretary; it was a digestive upset. At 10:30 this word was given to the press and flashed around the world. By then, however, Snyder knew he couldn't withhold the truth much longer. He quietly informed Mrs. Eisenhower of it and called the chief of cardiology at Fitzsimons General Hospital, just outside Denver, asking him to bring an electrocardiograph. Ike awoke at 11:45. He was conscious but feeble. The tracing of the electrocardiograph, when spread out on Mrs. Doud's dining room table, confirmed the diagnosis, and Snyder told Ike what had happened. He said, "We would like to take you to Fitzsimons." Then he said that an ambulance would not be necessary. The President nodded and asked him to inform the Secret Service. Assisted down the stairs and into a limousine waiting in the driveway, Ike was driven nine miles to the hospital. There a wheelchair took him to a special suite and an oxygen tent.

At 2:30 P.M. a press aide at Lowry told the White House correspondents there: "The President has just had a mild anterior — let's cut out the word 'anterior' — the President has just had a mild coronary thrombosis. He has just been taken to Fitzsimons General Hospital. He was taken to the hospital in his own car and walked from the house to the car."

His last words were drowned by pandemonium.

In Washington, where it was 4:30 P.M., Jim Hagerty had returned from vacation that morning. Informed by phone of the heart attack shortly before the announcement to the press in Denver, he immediately put through a call to Vice President Nixon's white brick home in Washington's fashionable Spring Valley neighborhood. The Nixons had just returned from a wedding, and the Vice President was reading the *Washington Evening Star*'s brief account of Eisenhower's digestive upset. Hagerty asked him, "Dick, are you sitting down?" Nixon said he wasn't, and then the President's press secretary, speaking very slowly, told him what happened. He said, "The press will be told about it in a half-hour or so." Nixon said, "My God!"

Hanging up, the Vice President walked into his living room in a daze and sat down. According to his later recollection, he said nothing for at least five minutes. After the shock had worn off he phoned William Rogers, then deputy attorney general, and asked him to come at once. By the time Rogers's taxi drew up, the news had been broken in Denver. Nixon's phone was ringing constantly. Outside, a crowd was gathering: neighbors, reporters, photographers. Determined to say nothing to newspapermen, Nixon remained inside as long as he could. By the time he had finished dinner, however, the din outside had become alarming, and he decided to hide out in Rogers's Bethesda home. It was like a movie escape. Rogers called his wife and told her to come and park a block away keeping the motor running. Then, while nine-year-old Tricia Nixon distracted the crowd on the lawn, the two men darted out a side door, raced down an alley, and jumped into the car.

In Prestwick, Scotland, the weather was cold and drizzly as Sherman Adams, the assistant to the President, checked into headquarters of the U.S. base there with Colonel Andrew J. Goodpaster. Adams had just completed a four-week tour of U.S. installations in Europe; he was meeting General Gruenther for a return flight to Washington that night. Before they could exchange a word the commanding officer of the base darted up and told them that he had just learned the President had been hospitalized in Denver with a heart attack. No details were available. Fleetingly Adams wondered whether Denver's elevation of five thousand feet would be good for a mending heart. Then it occurred to him that if Eisenhower had to be ill, this was a good time for it. Congress was in recess, Ike had no pending obligations as head of state, presidential duties were at a minimum, and planning for the coming year's program, then in its early stages, would not require the President's attention for some time.

Wall Street did not know that. The stock market, which is a kind of fun-house mirror exaggerating ups and downs in the American mood, opened nervously Monday morning as the plane bearing Adams approached the U.S. coast. Then stocks dove. The Dow Jones average plummeted to 444.56; losses were estimated at twelve billion dollars; it was the Street's worst day since the Crash.

The extent of Ike's illness was the only topic of conversation at 1600 Pennsylvania Avenue that noon when Adams arrived in time to lunch with Nixon, Rogers, and Jerry Persons. Halfway through the meal a call came from Denver. Dr. Paul Dudley White, the eminent Boston heart specialist, had completed his first examination of the President and was surprisingly optimistic. Ike's condition was satisfactory, he said, and his morale was good. He would be able to meet a light schedule in two weeks if all went well, and could probably return as a full-time President within a few months. Indeed, Dr. White said, barring the unforeseen, Eisenhower ought to be able to run for reelection. The stock market, delighted with this prognosis, surged back on Tuesday, and administration leaders lunched again, this time in the office of Secretary Humphrey in the Treasury Building, to consider ways of carrying on in the chief's absence.

All that week Washington buzzed with rumors of mistrust and misunderstandings on the highest levels of the government, and all of them were false. Eisenhower's much maligned staff system worked smoothly while he himself lay on a hospital bed 1,551 miles away. On Thursday the cabinet met with Nixon presiding. He read the morning bulletin from Denver — the President had had an excellent night, his first one out of the oxygen tent — and after a review of the diplomatic fronts by Dulles, Brownell led a discussion on the delegation of powers. As things worked out in the days ahead, Nixon signed some papers "in behalf of" the President while Adams really ran the office. Once a week during the rest of Eisenhower's convalescence Adams flew to Denver to report on meetings of the cabinet and the National Security Council. Only urgent problems were brought to the President's bedside. There were few of those; the one topic of substance was the coming State of the Union message, and that wasn't due until January.

In Adams's opinion, "the real key figure in the government" that autumn was Paul Dudley White. By the end of September Dr. White had become the most famous physician in the country. His candid medical briefings reassured the press and the country, and with his encouragement — sometimes, in fact, at his insistence — presidential aides overcame their reluctance to burden the hospitalized chief executive. "Look," White said to Hagerty, "he's not so much of an invalid as he is the President of the United States lying in there. He wants to do his job." On October 14 Ike told Adams he felt fine. "Funny thing," he said. "If the doctors didn't tell me differently, I would think this heart attack belonged to some other guy."

That was his sixty-fifth birthday, and sacks of congratulatory mail were piled high in the hospital auditorium. Over and over the President told visitors how moved he was by them; to Mamie he said, "It really does something for you to know that people all over the world are praying for you." The White House correspondents gave him his gayest moment of the day. Their gift was a suit of fire-engine red pajamas with five tiny gold stars embroidered on each collar tab and "Much Better, Thanks" embroidered over the breast pocket. To complete the gaudy costume, Merriman Smith of the United Press and Laurence H. Burd of the *Chicago Tribune* had contributed a 39-cent black cowboy tie tricked out with silver sequins. Ike was delighted. He told Dr. White these were the most marvelous pajamas he had ever owned. The doctor encouraged him to wear them as often as possible. They were more important than they seemed, White privately told the presidential staff; one of the worst aspects of a heart attack was the depression that accompanied recovery.

For a time it seemed that Ike might be spared that. Discharged from Fitzsimons after a fluoroscopic examination, he returned to Washington on

November 11 for a long White House weekend, and on November 14 he drove to his Gettysburg farm with Mrs. Eisenhower. Seven thousand Pennsylvanians greeted him there, waving placards saying GLAD YOU'RE HOME, IKE and WELCOME HOME, IKE AND MAMIE. On November 22 he presided over a cabinet meeting, his first since the attack, at Camp David. All of those present noticed that he had lost weight, but his spirits appeared to be fine. He had seen an editorial expressing surprise that the cabinet could work well without him, he said. In fact, he said with a smile, there were hints that it had worked better. Adams noted: "He was quick, decisive, and keen. I could see that the Cabinet liked what they saw. Some of them were openly astonished by the President's fast recovery and all of them were agreeably surprised."

Then, back in Gettysburg, gloom struck. December was dark, cold, and wet; the putting green at the farm was brown and soggy. Cooped up indoors, he faced, as Hagerty put it, "the sheer, God-awful boredom of not being President." For five terrible weeks he stalked around the farmhouse using a golf club as a cane, suffering in that special hell known only to victims of severe depression. In the two months since his coronary neither he nor anyone close to him had seriously supposed that he might run for another term. Now he began to have second thoughts. Paul Dudley White saw no reason why he shouldn't stay in the White House. It was, the President told those around, something to think about.

Newspapermen raised the question on January 8, 1956, at a Key West press conference. Ike had flown down for a few days of work and exercise. After a thirty-minute stroll he faced the reporters and was asked about his political future. He replied: "All the considerations that apply to such things are complicated. Naturally I will want to confer with my most trusted advisers." He noted that the Presidency was probably the most tiring job in the world but that "it also has, as I have said before, its inspirations." Afterward newsmen asked one another what that had meant. By a margin of nearly five to one they concluded that Ike would retire at the end of this term.

The minority wasn't so sure; they were picking up persistent rumors that the President was scheduling a meeting to weigh that very question. It was true, and the meeting was held that same week. Puckishly Ike called it for the evening of Friday, January 13, and made out place cards for exactly thirteen men. Mrs. Eisenhower joined them for dinner in the Mansion's state dining room and retired when they withdrew into the second-floor Trophy Room. Sitting with his back to the fireplace, Ike explained that he wanted each of them to speak out frankly on the question of whether he should try for another term and why. There was, of course, little doubt about which way the wind would blow. As Adams dryly observed afterward, "I don't imagine that the President expected to get a cross-fire of pro-and-con arguments from a group like that one. . . . If Eisenhower was looking for cogent reasons for leaving his office, he would have hardly sought them from his own appointees."

Adams, Humphrey, Dulles, Hagerty, Summerfield, Lodge, Persons, Len Hall, Brownell, Howard Pyle, Tom Stephens — one by one they told him how indispensable he was. Then Milton Eisenhower, who didn't want his brother to run again, summed up the arguments on both sides. The President made no decision then. He appeared to be undecided as late as February 13. That morning he reminded a cabinet meeting that he had wanted to put into his inaugural address his intention of remaining in office for only one term. He had been dissuaded, he said, and now he regretted it. Adams, however, was already proceeding on the assumption that they would be in the White House for another four years. While the President had been in Key West his chief assistant had called in government carpenters to shorten the office of the presidential appointments secretary, thereby creating a small room adjacent to the office large enough for a cot and a lounging chair — a retreat where Ike could rest before lunch, as Paul Dudley White had recommended. Adams counted on continuing strong support from the doctor for a second term, and he wasn't disappointed; on February 14, in his last medical briefing, White was able to remove the last traces of doubt about his patient's stamina. X-rays of his heart now and before the attack were almost identical, showing that there had been no enlargement of it since he had resumed normal activity in January. If the President ran again, White said, he would vote for him.

The following day the President flew to Secretary Humphrey's Georgia plantation and tested his strength golfing and hunting. He felt fine, and that convinced him: he was going to run. At 4 P.M. Tuesday he told Adams, Nixon, Persons, and Hall, and at 10:37 A.M. on Wednesday, February 29, he announced the news to the press in the Indian Treaty Room. If asked to make the race again, he said, "My answer will be positive, that is, affirmative."

The radio networks broadcast their first bulletin at 10:52, and in the next moment a House Armed Services subcommittee was given a startling glimpse of the postwar revolution in communications. A witness there was reciting a long list of statistics. Congressmen were dozing, reporters doodling. Only Chairman F. Edward Hebert of Louisiana was bright-eyed. Suddenly he whacked his gavel and cried, "Gentlemen, the President has just announced his candidacy for reelection!" After the excitement had died down a colleague from Illinois asked Hebert how he had known. The telephone hadn't rung, no notes had been passed, no one had entered the room. Shamefacedly, Hebert confessed; instead of listening to the witness he had been tuned into one of the tiny new transistor radios, tucked inside the pocket of his coat and hooked up with an earphone that looked like a hearing aid.

In a telecast that evening from the oval office Ike told an audience estimated at 65 million: "I wanted to come into your homes this evening because I felt the need of talking to you directly about a decision I made today after weeks of the most careful and devoutly prayerful consideration. . . . I have decided that if the Republican party chooses to nominate me I shall accept the nomination. Therefore, if the people of this country should elect me I shall continue to serve them in the office I now hold. I have concluded that I should permit the American people to have the opportunity to register their decision in this matter."

Beforehand, he had been chatting with television adviser Robert Montgomery when a network assistant asked him about an inch-high plaque on his desk bearing the Latin motto *Suaviter in Modo, Fortiter in Re,* and the translation "Gently in Manner, Strongly in Deed." The President chuckled and said, "Maybe I'd better hide that; it proves I'm an egghead."

The country's ranking egghead was also in a witty mood. Asked about the President's decision, Adlai Stevenson said, "The real reason Eisenhower is running again is that he can't afford to retire to his farm at Gettysburg while Benson is Secretary of Agriculture."

In the high summer of 1956 the corn stood tall from Mount Rushmore to the panhandle. America seemed to have returned, momentarily at least, to the frivolous 1920s, to wonderful trivia, hot music, placid politics, glamorous athletes, and automobile worship. General Motors president Harlow Curtice was *Time*'s Man of the Year. The compact Rambler was Detroit's current success; Republicans were wondering whether George Romney of American Motors might make a future President.

President Eisenhower's contribution to the American landscape, the interstate highway system, was just getting under way; ultimately it would provide 41,000 miles of new roads — high-speed, limited access, nonstop travel arteries. It was going to be the biggest public works project in the nation's history; the cost was expected to run somewhere between 33 and 41 billion dollars. (It came to 76 billions.) Landlocked cities in the Middle West would be opened to new commerce. The driving time between Chicago and Indianapolis alone would be cut from six hours to three. Roadside services would become a billion-dollar industry, and people and goods would move quickly and safely across the country on well-engineered ribbons of concrete.

It was appropriate that in 1956 Oregon miler Jim Bailey was clocked at 3:58.6, the first under-four-minute mile run in the United States. Americans were not only moving toward new horizons; they could hardly wait to get there. The Gross National Product was 400 billion dollars' worth of goods and services that year, and inflation was still negligible, though a warning of what lay ahead came when, after a quarter-century of unchanged postal rates, first-class mail went from three cents to four and airmail from six cents to seven.

Businessmen pointed with pride to the increase in productivity, and sermons and editorials viewed with alarm the frantic pace of American life. Popular misconceptions to the contrary, however, America did not lead the world in suicides. According to the World Health Organization, the U.S. suicide rate was 10.8 per 100,000 (16.1 for men and 4.3 for women), which put it far down the list, below Denmark (24.1), Austria, Switzerland, Japan, Sweden, West Germany, Finland, France, and England and Wales. Of course, psychiatric help was now more available for Americans, and beginning in 1956 jittery executives could find peace with meprobamate, an exceptionally effective tranquilizer better known by its trade name, Miltown. *Time* called Miltown "Don't-Give-a-Damn Pills." Their first big markets were Madison Avenue and Hollywood. In Hollywood, a drugstore at Sunset and Gower pasted a huge red sign across its display window: "Yes, we have Miltown!" Milton Berle said, "I'm thinking of changing my name to Miltown Berle." It was a poor year for humor.

Popular athletes of the 1940s were entering the cruel twilight of their trade: Joe DiMaggio was in his forties, and now that Floyd Patterson was heavyweight champion, Joe Louis, overweight and slow, was stumbling into the oblivion of professional wrestling. Jackson Pollock died and Liberace arrived, accompanied by his ubiquitous mother. Grace Metalious and Françoise Sagan also emerged, edifying nobody, and so did a new minstrel of youth whose voice seemed to be everywhere, singing, "Hi luh-luh-luh-luv yew-hew," or

> *Awopbopaloobop! alopbamboom!*
> *Tutti Frutti! Aw rutti!*
> *Tutti Frutti! Aw rutti!*

Elvis Aaron Presley made his movie debut that fall in *Love Me Tender*. He sang four songs in a secondary role, and his curious amalgam of rock 'n' roll, bluegrass, and boogie dominated the show. All year he toured the South and West, fighting off hysterical teen-agers in pedal pushers and boosting his first LP album — it went straight to the top of *Billboard*'s weekly ratings — and such singles as "Don't Be Cruel" and "Heartbreak Hotel," each of which sold over a million copies.

Presley shocked the parents of young girls. Drape-suited and tight-panted, his petulant eyes glassy and his pouting lips hanging open, he would grip the microphone, crouch, and then buck his hips against his dangling guitar. Television producers refused to show him below the waist. They called him lewd, and they were right; that was the secret of his appeal. Teen-aged girls carved his name on their forearms with pen knives while older women bestowed gifts upon him and tried to lure him away. In Amarillo a reporter asked him if he was contemplating marriage. He replied, "Why buy a cow when you can get the milk through the fence?"

Offstage Presley could be refreshingly straightforward. Unlike Liberace, Presley had no musical pretensions. He recalled that he had been given a guitar when he was twelve. "I beat on it for a year or two," he said. "Never did learn much about it." Tired of driving trucks, he had taken the guitar to a recording studio. "It sounded like somebody beatin' on a bucket lid," he said, "but the engineer at this studio had a recording company called Sun, and he told me I had an unusual voice, and he might call me up sometime." When Presley records started to sell, he acquired a manager who said, "He may not sound like a hillbilly, but he gets the same response."

The pervasive vulgarity of Elvis the Pelvis was part of his appeal. He liked to spend hours at amusement parks riding dodgem cars, wore $10,000 gold lamé suits, and bought a fleet of Cadillacs painted in pastels. Obsessed with his hair — it was turning prematurely gray — and guarded by a rat-pack of muscular young men who doubled as companions, he settled down in a garish estate ringed with sentry boxes. When he wanted to go night-clubbing word would be phoned ahead, so that precautions could be taken. Like royalty, he carried no cash. Then, like G. David Schine, he was drafted. In Germany, where he was stationed, he received much attention from the local press, in which he was identified as a symbol of American culture.

Presley in the flesh wasn't much different from the comic opera roles he played on the screen. In this he was supremely a man of the time. There was little room in the ambiance of 1956 for genuine tragedy. Sober events were ignored or externalized. It is significant that on July 20, 1956, one of the most important dates in American history, headline writers were en-thralled by the fact that Eisenhower had at last balanced a budget. None noted that on that day, according to the Geneva agreement of 1954, free elections were to be held in Vietnam. The failure to hold them would produce the Viet Cong, civil war, and American intervention; but com-mentators had no time for its implications then.

The catastrophes that did attract attention were explicit, obvious; the kind that tabloids feed on. It was a time of sensations. Victor Riesel, a New York labor columnist, was blinded by a man who threw acid in his face. Dr. Jesús de Galíndez disappeared outside a Manhattan subway station; presumably he was kidnapped by henchmen of Rafael Trujillo, the dictator of the Dominican Republic, and murdered. On Parris Island, South Caro-lina, a Marine Corps drill instructor led 74 recruits into a treacherous tidal stream; six of them drowned. In Boston the FBI solved a $2,775,000 Brink's robbery, and the great Hungarian uprising was encouraged by Radio Free Europe in an act of criminal irresponsibility.

In June of 1956 Phyllis Brown, an editor at the Research Institute of America, entertained Wisconsin bankers at their annual convention with a charming little talk on the innate frailties of her sex. Never tell a woman she is being illogical, she said: "The average woman starts off on the premise that the way she feels about something is itself a most compelling argu-ment." Miss Brown further recommended that they praise women more than men and remember that women always take things personally.

Time reprinted this Aunt Tom's remarks with a manly good humor. In another issue *Time*'s editors put a woman of intellectual pretensions in her place by reporting that "Like many of her sisters in what she bitterly refers to as the Second Sex, France's Simone de Beauvoir would rather talk than eat." Women's magazines, edited by men, treated their subscribers with similar condescension. A *Ladies' Home Journal* editor explained to a writer, "If we get an article about a woman who does anything adventurous, out of the way, something by herself, you know, we figure she must be terribly aggressive, neurotic." At the peak of feminine achievement the *Journal* introduced to its readers a Texas housewife who had her face made up an hour after breakfast and could say, "By 8:30 A.M., when my youngest goes to school, my whole house is clean and neat and I am dressed for the day, I am free to play bridge, attend club meetings, or stay home and read, listen to Beethoven, and just plain loaf."

There were signs, for those who could read them, that not all of her sisters were satisfied with bridge or club meetings. In 1956 *McCall's* published an innocent little piece called "The Mother Who Ran Away" and was dumbfounded to find that it drew more readers than anything they had ever carried. Later *Redbook* ran an article on "Why Young Mothers Feel Trapped." Young mothers who felt that way were encouraged to write in — and more than twenty-four thousand of them did. But the notion that a woman should aspire to become something other than a fetching housewife was too heretical to take hold. The altar remained the only acceptable destination for single girls, and those who managed to reach it with a prize groom in tow became celebrities. Memorable brides of 1956 included Mrs. E. Clifton Daniel Jr., née Margaret Truman, and the former Odile Rodin, who became the fifth wife of Porfirio Rubirosa. (Her predecessors were Danielle Darrieux, Doris Duke, Barbara Hutton, and the daughter of Rafael Trujillo.) The ultimate prize, however, was won that year by a pretty actress from Philadelphia who, after being wooed by dress designer Oleg Cassini and actor Jean-Paul Aumont, hooked the most eligible bachelor in Europe: Prince Rainier III of Monaco. How Grace Kelly did it was a secret to be pondered by the wives of America as they loaded their automatic washing machines and scoured the blades of their husbands' electric carving knives. All her father would say was: "Grace met him when she was on the French Riviera. She went there to make a picture called *To Catch a Thief* — and look what she came back with."

The father, a Philadelphia contractor and politician who had been national sculling champion and therefore something of a catch himself, recalled that when the prince first called at the Kelly mansion, "I was under the impression he was going to stay just a couple of hours. But he stayed and stayed and stayed." Kelly was wary. ("I don't generally approve of these oddballs she goes out with.") Then Rainier asked for Grace's hand. This being too important a matter for her, she was sent off while the menfolk conferred. In a speech which might be memorized by every American tycoon whose daughter is being courted by a sovereign, Kelly warned Rainier to beware the occupational weaknesses of his class: "I told the prince that royalty didn't mean a thing to us. I told him that I certainly hoped he wouldn't run around the way some princes do, and I told him that if he did, he'd lose a mighty fine girl." Mrs. Kelly sold her as-told-to memoirs to Hearst (*My Daughter Grace Kelly, Her Life and Romances*). The *Chicago Tribune,* in an allusion to Monaco's Monte Carlo, complained, "She's too well-bred a girl to marry the silent partner in a gambling parlor." Aristotle Onassis, who virtually owned Monte Carlo and would continue to pay no French taxes if Grace presented her husband with an heir, cried, "I am mad with joy," and gave the Monaco Red Cross a million francs.

The Kelly-Rainier wedding was an MGM press agent's dream, one reason being that the MGM publicity department had a hand in it. On April 12 the American Export liner *Constitution* hovered off the French coast and set Grace on the deck of the Prince's white yacht *Deo Juvante II.* Accompanying her were 80 wedding guests, 24 columnists, four trunks, 20 hatboxes, 36 other pieces of luggage, and the bride's black French poodle, Oliver. Overhead, an aircraft from Onassis's private squadron bombarded the yacht with red and white carnations. From the shore came a din: klaxons, sirens, rockets, and cannon firing 21-gun salutes. The dock was literally black with newspapermen — 1,500 of them from all over the world, more than had covered the Geneva summit the year before. Ashore and with Grace beside him in his green Chrysler Imperial, Rainier discovered that his way was temporarily blocked by fifty photographers. Everyone seemed to be in Monaco except the ones the couple most wanted: Europe's more famous crowned heads. Elizabeth II had declined to come, and other members of European royalty had followed her example. England was represented in Monaco by a minor diplomat and Randolph Churchill, who yelled in a moment of pique, "I didn't come here to meet vulgar people like the Kellys."

If Elizabeth was wary of being exploited by the world press, others with famous names didn't mind at all. President Eisenhower was represented at the wedding by Conrad Hilton, the hotel magnate. The Aga Khan was there with his begum. Somerset Maugham led Monte Carlo's literary contingent, and former King Farouk of Egypt, now obese and besotted, distressed the wedding marshals by waddling up the central staircase of St. Nicholas Cathedral, supposedly reserved for the bridal party. He was whisked aside and the principals arrived. Grace said *"Je veux,"* thereby becoming twice a princess, four times a duchess, nine times a baroness, eight times a countess, four times a marchioness, and once a viscountess. Her wedding gifts included a quarter-million dollars in diamonds alone. Pickpockets at the festivities made off with $150,000, but to Onassis, who kept picking up tabs, it was all worth it. In August Rainier disclosed that his wife was pregnant. Monaco celebrated the announcement with fireworks, trumpets, bonfires, and dancing in the street and the *New York Daily Mirror* used a line it had been saving almost a year: MONACO WEATHER FORECAST: A LITTLE RAINIER IN FEBRUARY.

In the four years since Farouk had fled Cairo, taking his priceless collection of pornography with him, Egypt had become the stronghold of a military clique. Lieutenant Colonel Gamal Abdel Nasser emerged in June 1956 as the leader of the junta. John Foster Dulles believed he had Nasser's number, and he decided to teach him a lesson. The upshot was a minor war and, ironically, a tremendous boost for President Eisenhower in his campaign for reelection.

As a neutral in the cold war, Nasser was naturally anathema to Dulles. The United States had been trying to coax Egypt into the western camp. With that in view, Washington had told Cairo the previous winter that it would loan the Egyptians 56 million dollars for their three-mile Aswan High Dam on the Nile. But Nasser was ungrateful. He recognized Red China, tried to break up the Baghdad Pact, announced plans to visit Moscow, and traded 200 million dollars' worth of cotton for Czechoslovakian guns. Thereupon Dulles, on July 19, publicly canceled the American loan. Foreign service officers on the State Department's Middle Eastern desk had warned that Nasser might seize the Suez Canal in retaliation. He did. He cried, "I look at Americans and say: may you choke to death on your fury!" He said, "We shall build the high dam as we desire. The annual income of the Suez Canal is 100 million dollars. Why not take it ourselves?" Then: "We shall rely on our own strength, our own muscle, our own funds. And it will be run by Egyptians! Egyptians! Egyptians!"

The full weight of this blow fell not upon the United States, but on Britain and France. At the urging of anticolonialists in Washington, the British had withdrawn the last of their troops from Suez in June. Now Nasser had cut Anglo-French industry off from its chief source of petroleum. Of the 1.5 million barrels of oil that passed through the canal each day, 1.2 million went to western Europe. Suez provided two-thirds of the fuel the continent needed for heat and production, and the other third came overland through pipes that could easily be sabotaged by the Arabs. Therefore this was a real crisis for London and Paris. It would have taxed the gifts of a Disraeli, and the householder at 10 Downing Street was no Disraeli. He was Sir Anthony Eden, once Churchill's great foreign secretary and now worn to a shadow. The office of prime minister was simply too much for him. Struggling along with less than five hours sleep a night, he became addicted to amphetamines. Years later medical scientists discovered that amphetamines could rob a sensible man of his good judgment, and that was what happened to Eden in 1956.

Blaming Dulles for their plight, Eden and Guy Mollet, the French premier, turned their backs on Washington. They decided to tackle the problem in their own way — or, to be precise, in the way advocated by David Ben-Gurion. To the Israeli premier, this seemed a perfect time to settle accounts with the hated Egyptians. Russia was preoccupied by a developing crisis in Hungary, the United States was in the middle of a national election, and the British and the French, furious at Nasser, were spoiling for a fight. Ben-Gurion reminded them that under certain circumstances an Anglo-French expeditionary force could act in the Middle East under a cloak of legitimacy. The Tripartite Declaration of 1950 provided that Britain and France could reoccupy the Suez Canal if war erupted between Israel and Egypt. Ben-Gurion said he would be delighted to provide that excuse, and Eden and Mollet endorsed the plan.

In the last week of October the CIA received troubling reports. Israel was mobilizing. More than 100,000 Israeli troops were poised along their border with Egypt, and Israeli tanks were in position for a lunge westward. Whitehall and the Quai d'Orsay had lapsed into a studied silence. To Washington the very correctness of their behavior was puzzling. They were like men building up an alibi. It was hard to believe that they could be plotting with Jerusalem, though. Eisenhower, who was in Walter Reed for a physical checkup on Sunday, October 28, rejected the idea. Drafting notes to Ben-Gurion between trips up and down hospital corridors for tests, Ike said wryly, "Israel and barium make quite a combination."

The Israelis struck the next day. At 3 P.M. Washington time teletypes chattered out the first bulletin: Israeli forces were crossing into Egyptian territory. Eden and Mollet now had their justification. They went through the motions of sending ultimatums to Jerusalem and Cairo demanding that both sides lay down their arms. In the House of Commons Eden said, "We have asked the Egyptian government to agree that Anglo-French forces should move temporarily into key positions." If the request was ignored, he said, British and French troops would intervene in Suez "in whatever strength may be necessary."

Eisenhower had left the hospital to campaign in the South. Now he rushed back to Washington. At 7 P.M. that Monday, as dusk began to gather in the capital, his limousine entered the southwest gate of the White House grounds. After conferring with Adams, Radford, Persons, and the Dulles brothers, he authorized a statement from Hagerty: "At the meeting the President recalled that the United States, under this and prior administrations, had pledged itself to assist the victim of any aggression in the Middle East. We shall honor our pledge."

On Wednesday British bombers based in Cyprus attacked Egyptian airfields. Ike said, "I just don't know what got into those people. It's the damnedest business I ever saw supposedly intelligent people get themselves into." But: "We cannot subscribe to one law for the weak, another for those allied with us." In a Wednesday telecast he told the American people just that. The British and the French, who held Dulles responsible for the whole mess, were furious. Eden let it be known that he would reject any U.N. cease-fire proposal. On Saturday Dulles, exhausted and distraught, collapsed; an ulcer had penetrated his abdominal wall; he was taken to

Walter Reed for two and a half hours of surgery. The world seemed very near war that weekend. On Sunday the White House learned that British and French troops were boarding transports at Cyprus for an invasion of Suez. Early Monday British paratroopers began landing on the north end of the canal. That evening Bulganin warned Eden, Mollet, and Ben-Gurion that unless they withdrew immediately they would become targets for Red missiles loaded with nuclear warheads. At the same time Bulganin proposed to Eisenhower that the United States and the Soviet Union form an alliance to stop the invasion. Ike was indignant. To an aide he said, "Those British — they're still my right arm!" He told Bulganin that Russo-American intervention was "unthinkable" and accused the Soviet premier of trying to divert attention from Hungary, where the Red Army "at this very moment is brutally repressing the human rights of the Hungarian people."

This was more than cold war rhetoric. Ike was right: the Russians were also guilty of atrocities that week. Afterward the Communists would remember Suez while the West remembered Hungary; in fact the two were equally ugly. On Wednesday, the day of the first RAF raids on the canal zone, anti-Soviet rioters in Budapest had made Imre Nagy premier of Hungary. By Saturday the entire country had risen. Nagy denounced the Warsaw Pact, which made Hungary a Soviet satellite. Russian troops withdrew from Budapest and then regrouped to crush the revolt. The streets were carpeted with the bodies of Budapest's martyrs, Joseph Cardinal Mindszenty took refuge in the besieged American embassy, and the Hungarian delegation to the United Nations begged the U.N. to intervene. Lodge introduced a measure which would do that. The Russians vetoed it. Eisenhower spent twenty million dollars in Mutual Security funds on food and medicine for Hungary. He ordered that 21,500 Hungarian refugees be admitted to the United States and told his staff to see to it that the administration found homes and jobs for them, and he sent protests to Bulganin. The Soviet premier coldly replied that Russia and Hungary would settle their differences without outside help.

On the morning of Tuesday, November 6, 1956, French infantry seized the east side of the canal, Russian troops captured Nagy, the U.N. General Assembly condemned Soviet aggression, and 61,616,938 Americans went to the polls. War was on everyone's mind, and the country's most famous general was on the ballot. The conclusion that the voters put the two together is inescapable. Perhaps they were right to do so. Certainly Ike retained his poise throughout that terrible week. Adams was with the President in his oval office when Eden phoned. Eisenhower said heartily, "Well, Anthony, how *are* you?"

It was a question, Adams dryly observed, which, "it seemed to me at the time, would have required a long and involved answer."

Afterward there is a certain inevitability to political landslides, and this one was no exception. Eisenhower would have been reelected if Nasser had kept his hands off Suez and Hungary had remained servile. No Democratic candidate could have driven him from office, and to those who enjoy hindsight it may seem surprising that a man as intelligent as Adlai Stevenson didn't realize that. Gallup figures showed that the President retained the confidence of better than seven out of every ten Americans. In his first term he had accomplished much that had seemed unattainable four years earlier. The Korean War had been ended, and without a depression. McCarthy had been routed. The Bricker amendment was a dead issue. Knowland stood isolated in the Senate. The Republican party was now committed to the United Nations, and except for Styles Bridges no Republican with a safe seat was advocating the invasion of China or a preventive war against Russia. Futhermore, Ike's management of domestic problems suggested that he was a wiser politician than he appeared to be. His federal highway program was outspending the WPA. Inflation had been checked. Labor was getting a larger share of the national income. Social security had been extended. The administration had built a sound antitrust program, and its soil bank, by appeasing farmers, had robbed the Democrats of a major issue.

The President had still other assets, less tangible but very real, which could be redeemed at the polls. His personality was gilt-edged political capital. Joseph Alsop wrote that "Eisenhower's greatest single contribution has been bringing us back to a sense of the true American style — setting the style, in fact, by his own example and in the most trying circumstances," and Richard H. Rovere concluded that "when Eisenhower has spoken for the nation, he has . . . in general appeared before the world as a not unworthy successor to those few American presidents whom the world has known and respected."

This account is, of course, incomplete. If those had been the only issues, the Democrats would not have battled so hard for the nomination. To them the administration seemed highly pregnable. The GOP was more than ever the party of big business. The schism between liberal Republicans and the Old Guard continued to be unsightly. Dulles's performance abroad had been less than brilliant, as the mess in the Middle East demonstrated. Apart from these, there were three overriding major points at issue: the President's health, Vice President Nixon, and the eloquence and charm of the Democratic nominee.

Hopes for Dwight Eisenhower's longevity were at best precarious. If reelected he would be seventy before he left office. Only a year ago he had suffered a massive heart attack, and he himself had observed that the Presidency was the most demanding job in the world. Moreover, there was worry about more than his heart. Less than ten weeks before the national conventions he was stricken with another ailment, taken from the White House in an ambulance, and subjected to a two-hour ordeal on the operating table.

At first the Denver scenario seemed to be repeating iself. In the small hours of June 9 Dr. Snyder was awakened in his Connecticut Avenue apartment by an anxious Mamie Eisenhower. The President was tossing and turning. He complained of stomach pains. What should she do? Milk of magnesia was ineffective, and Snyder hurried to the Executive Mansion. After breakfast Hagerty issued a brief statement: "The President has an upset stomach and headache. Dr. Snyder has been with him since early this morning. There is nothing wrong with his heart." But that was far from reassuring. The Denver crisis had also begun with a "digestive upset." A second statement was more specific: "The President has had an attack of ileitis (inflammation of the lower portion of the small intestine)." As a "precaution" he was entering Walter Reed Hospital.

It was a wretched day for Hagerty. He kept telling reporters that ileitis wasn't serious while appearances indicated that it was. The ambulance left the Mansion behind a screen of motorcycles with screaming sirens. Paul Dudley White appeared. ("They wanted me on hand in case anything needed to be done," he said.) Another specialist was stopped by state policemen in South Carolina and hurried aboard a jet trainer for a supersonic trip to Walter Reed, where a dozen surgeons were examining the lower part of the President's digestive system. Surgery was necessary — without it the condition could lead to gangrene of the bowel — but Hagerty had been right, there was nothing to worry about. Afterward Dr. Leonard D. Heeton, the leading surgeon, was asked whether he thought Ike should decline to run for reelection. He said, "I certainly do not." Of the President's life expectancy Snyder said, "We think it improves it." The physicians estimated that he would be back on the job in four to six weeks, and headlines across the country read OKAY FOR IKE TO RUN SAY DOCTORS.

Kenneth S. Davis, Stevenson's biographer, believed afterward that the frailty of Eisenhower's health, "far from being a hazard to his reelection, was probably a political asset. Having passed through the valley of the shadow of death, he was now a greater hero, more beloved of the populace than before." Davis thinks this was due to Ike's personal qualities, "to the perfection with which he expressed the dominant mood of the country and to the warm affection he personally inspired." Democrats were aware of Eisenhower's appeal and treated him gingerly.

Nixon was another matter. The leaders of the party out of power had noted with grim pleasure that he had reconsidered and decided to run again. They took it as an article of faith that the rest of the country despised the Vice President as much as they did, and they went for him with sandbags. Stevenson called the Vice President "shifty," "rash," "inexperienced," and a "man of many masks," and in Minneapolis on November 5 he told listeners that Nixon "has put away his switch-blade and now assumes the aspect of an Eagle Scout." The Vice President, he reminded them, had recently declared in their city that there would be no war in the Middle East. Like many other Democrats, Stevenson honestly thought that a Nixon succession to the Presidency would be a catastrophe.

Nixon could ignore the opposition, and he did. The critics in his own party were more serious. Ironically, the GOP leader of the "Dump Nixon movement," as it was called, was Harold Stassen, Nixon's first political idol. Not without reason, Stassen believed that the President wouldn't be heartbroken if the movement succeeded. To an adviser Ike expressed doubts about Nixon's stature and then said: "Well, the fact is, of course, I've watched Dick a long time, and he just hasn't grown. So I just haven't honestly been able to believe that he is presidential timber."

At that point the party's rank and file took a hand. Republican voters, always strong for Nixon, let their wishes be known; in the New Hampshire and Oregon primaries 52,202 of them wrote his name in under Ike's. That impressed Nixon, if not Stassen. On April 26 the Vice President asked for an appointment with the President and told him he would be happy to make the race again. Eisenhower rang for Hagerty, who came in to find the two running mates of 1952 grinning at each other. According to Hagerty's recollection, the President said, "Jim, Dick just told me he would be happy to be on the ticket, and he has made up his mind that he would like to run again with me." Adams and Persons came in, and after they had the news Ike said to Hagerty, "What do you think we ought to do on the announcement?" The press secretary suggested that Nixon make it to White House correspondents right now. Eisenhower nodded and said, "Jim, you go with him, and after he finishes his announcement, you say I was delighted to hear this news from the Vice President."

That was the end of serious attempts to dump Nixon in 1956, and for all practical purposes it was the end of Harold Stassen's political career. His arguments had convinced only one delegate, an eccentric Nebraskan named Terry Carpenter who had been identified with the Coughlin-Townsend fringe in the 1930s. In the roll call of states Carpenter expressed his displeasure with Nixon by casting one vice-presidential vote for a mythical "Joe Smith," thereby providing the San Francisco convention with its most memorable moments.

Four years earlier Governor Stevenson had won the admiration of the commentators by his dignity and grace in defeat. This was his second time round, and it was too much to expect that he could repeat that sparkling performance. He didn't. He dulled the memory of it. Musing over the tactics which had won in 1952, the Democratic standard-bearer succumbed to the fatal charms of the media manipulators. He allowed himself to be drawn into discussions of the relative merits of the "old" Stevenson and the "new" Stevenson, as if there were two of him running around, and there was a lot of mindless chatter in his entourage about the "blurring" of his "image."

"The campaign of 1956 was curious and special," a veteran Democrat later told Emmet John Hughes. "It was nearly a classic of its kind. For it's almost impossible to recall anything you people did wrong — and nearly as hard to remember anything we did right." The worst thing was Truman's emergence from retirement. Trying to secure the nomination for Governor Averell Harriman of New York, he drew Stevenson into a wasting intraparty fight for political survival, and when he found he couldn't rule the convention he seemed bent upon ruining Stevenson's hopes. In his anger the former President gave the Republicans ammunition beyond their wildest hopes. He called Stevenson a "conservative" who followed the "counsel of hesitation" and lacked "the kind of fighting spirit we need to win."

Stevenson had other handicaps. He should have been dueling with Eisenhower, not Truman and Nixon. But the President had taken a lofty stance above the battle. Like President Roosevelt, he wouldn't let his opponent come to grips with him. When not preoccupied with the deepening crises abroad, he ran serenely on the GOP's bland campaign slogan, "Peace, Progress, Prosperity." Nixon, meantime, had discovered what would later become one of his most familiar political stratagems. Confronted by alternatives, he would choose the popular one while insisting that it was really the harder of the two. It would be "easy," he said, for him to endorse an end to hydrogen bomb testing, as Stevenson was urging. Then, his voice vibrating, the Vice President announced that his conscience compelled him to defy public opinion and call for continuing tests. Actually it was Stevenson who was taking the hard road; few votes were lost that year by demanding bigger and better bombs. Nixon was having it both ways, pleasing the majority while winning marks for audacity.

The professionals in Stevenson's camp warned that the testing issue would alienate large blocs of Democrats, especially in ethnic and bluecollar neighborhoods. He knew it, and his decision to plunge ahead anyway, insisting that what he had to say needed saying, was an example of true political courage. In such moments the gallant candidate of 1952 could still be seen. He hadn't lacked heart then and didn't now. His difficulties were with shrewdness and native cunning — small virtues, perhaps, but essential in a political leader.

To laymen, Eisenhower's testing argument — that improved bombs must be built so that the U.S. could "negotiate" from a "position of strength rather than weakness," that "the only way to win World War III is to prevent it" — sounded persuasive. While time would later vindicate Stevenson, elections are not won by such moral victories. The cold war was still a formidable reality in 1956. Stevenson misjudged its impact, and not only on the question of testing. In the middle of one address he declared that it was time to take a "new look" at American defenses and to consider "ending the draft." So many voices were raised in protest that he was thrown on the defensive, never a good stance for the challenger.

As November approached, Stevenson's campaign became wobbly. He was tired, he was careless, and in his election eve telecast he was guilty of bad taste. Repugnant as the matter was, he said, "I must say bluntly that every piece of scientific evidence we have, every lesson of history and experience, indicates that a Republican victory tomorrow would mean that Richard M. Nixon would probably be President of the country within the next four years." It was true. Saying it in a nationwide broadcast was another matter. It jarred Stevenson's followers, and it was an unhappy note upon which to end a brave battle against odds.

The dimensions of the second Eisenhower avalanche were awesome. He won 457 electoral votes to Stevenson's 72, amassing a triumphant margin of nearly ten million votes. For the first time in a quarter of a century, Negroes were voting Republican. The President had won two-thirds of the nonunion labor vote and 45 percent of the votes of union members. He had swept all the new suburbs. His plurality was 16 percent, just two points behind Hoover's in 1928.

This time Eisenhower celebrated in the presidential suite of Washington's Sheraton Park. By 9 P.M. what little suspense there had been was over. Sherman Adams was sitting on the floor staring rapturously at a small TV tube. Jerry Persons called out in his Alabama accent: "I want all of you to know that the cradle of the Confederacy — Montgomery, Alabama — has just voted for a Republican for the first time in its history!" Ike led the cheering. To Emmet Hughes he said, "There's Michigan and Minnesota still to see. You remember the story of Nelson — dying, he looked around and asked, 'Are there any of them still left?' I guess that's me. When I get in a battle, I just want to win the whole thing . . . six or seven states we can't help. But I don't want to lose any more. Don't want any of them 'left' — like Nelson. That's the way I feel."

All in all it had been a tedious election. Yet there had been one exciting moment at the Democratic convention. Declining to select his running mate, Stevenson had announced that the delegates would make the choice, and in the ensuing turmoil the watching nation had been given a glimpse of the future.

The scramble was between Estes Kefauver, Albert Gore, Robert Wagner, John F. Kennedy, and — the only man who had come to Chicago as an avowed vice-presidential candidate — Hubert Humphrey. Kefauver won, but Kennedy, in nearly beating him, had made a greater impression on the watching audience. The nomination had seemed to be in his grasp after Senator Lyndon Johnson came out for him, shouting tremulously, "Texas proudly casts its vote for the fighting sailor who wears the scars of battle," but at that moment Missouri switched from Gore to Kefauver. Next day the *New York Herald Tribune*'s convention story began, "The famous Kennedy luck ran out today." Actually, losing the vice-presidential nomination was the luckiest thing that had ever happened to Kennedy. He had appeared on the rostrum to make a short, charming speech of concession, and his winning manner had created an instant Kennedy constituency. The country was now aware of him. As James MacGregor Burns noted, "Kennedy's near-victory and sudden loss, the impression he gave of a clean-cut boy who had done his best and who was accepting defeat with a smile — all this struck at people's hearts in living rooms across the nation."

That was half of it. The other half was that since he hadn't made the ticket, its subsequent defeat couldn't be blamed on him or, more especially, on his Catholicism, which had been regarded as a crushing political handicap since Hoover's rout of Al Smith in 1928. Shortly after the election Kennedy was told that he would easily win the vice-presidential nomination in 1960. "I'm not running for Vice President any more," he said crisply. "I'm now running for President."

TWENTY-THREE

The Pursuit of Happiness

T HE EISENHOWER SIESTA, as it may be called, extended from the Korean armistice in 1953 to the autumn of 1957, when Americans who had assumed that their technical supremacy would never be challenged were dismayed to learn that rocketeers in the Soviet Union had stolen a long march on them. After that, the country's self-confidence was never the same. Ahead lay a frantic hundred-billion-dollar scramble to reassert the U.S. technological lead by exploring the stars while, year by year, disheartening developments on earth were causing a new and different erosion of American pride. To those who had cherished it, the 1953–57 breather would come to be remembered as an uncomplicated, golden time, mourned as lost childhoods are mourned and remembered, in nostalgia, as cloudless.

If it was never that splendid, neither was it as flatulent as its intellectuals made it out to be. In their view these were dreary, complacent years of an all-out, pedal-to-the-floor materialistic binge in which mass society bred alienation, conformity, facelessness, and moral emptiness; a frivolous boredom and a joyless vulgarity; a time of rootlessness, when small-town hotels were being replaced by 41,000 motels, at the more pretentious of which you could, for a quarter, lie on a bed and have your erogenous zones jiggled. The disillusioned saw America as a country in which religion had been reduced to Dial-a-Prayer, *Modern Screen*'s series on "How the Stars Found Faith," and prepackaged sixty-second solutions for every spiritual problem. In this judgment the mid-1950s were entirely lacking in merit, with status being represented by the key to the executive washroom, virility by the Mennen After-Shave Club, democracy by a vote for Miss Rheingold, decor by the knotty pine rumpus room, and economics by You Auto Buy Now.

There *were* a lot of gadgets. Technological change had never held a greater fascination for Americans. Men talked wonderingly of transistors, those slivers of germanium or silicon no bigger than a shoelace tip which, when not running tiny radios like Congressman Hebert's, were powering hearing aids so small that they could fit in the frames of spectacles and lightening the load of fighter planes by 1,500 pounds. But all the gadgetry wasn't necessarily bad. Only an ascetic crank could despise the Simmons Company for promoting king- and queen-sized Beautyrest mattresses. If it was absurd to find strips of paper across motel toilet seats reading "This seat has been sterilized for your protection," the fact remained that too much cleanliness was preferable to too little. And after Los Alamos and all that it was rather engaging to find that American technologists were now making life more comfortable.

There was nothing inherently wrong with the innovations, though their sheer number was sometimes bewildering: central vacuuming, vinyl floor-ing, push-button phones, stereo FM sets, washer-dryers, automatic trans-missions, drive-in shopping malls, air-conditioned buses, electric blankets, electric floor polishers, electric pencil sharpeners, electric can openers, and electric floor waxers, to name only the most conspicuous. One by one they appeared, were assimilated into the general experience, and became a part of the average middle-class American's routine. And little by little the more practical innovations altered everyday existence. At one time or another in the mid-1950s millions of men and women of the swing generation realized that in countless little ways life had become easier, more tolerable, more convenient, more interesting — in a word, more livable. At about the same time they remembered the Depression. With a sense of awe they realized: *It's gone.*

And so it had. Evidence of a surge to abundance was everywhere. The boom arose from many springs; natural resources, global politics after World War II, demography, the altered economy of Western Europe, and Americans' love of work. The United States was producing half of the world's goods. Since the war the Gross National Product had doubled. (By the early 1970s it would double again.) U.S. investment abroad had in-creased from twelve billion dollars to eighty billions. The budget of one firm, General Motors, had grown to the size of Poland's.

The consequence of all this was a standard of living beyond the compre-hension of the rest of the world. Nearly 60 per cent of all American families were reporting wages in the middle-class brackets. Just since the late 1940s the median family income had risen from $3,083 to $5,657; even when cor-rected for inflation this meant a rise of 48 percent. America, in Adolf A. Berle's phrase, was in the throes of "galloping capitalism." The proletariat was being transformed. Assembly line workers with working wives were driving expensive new automobiles and buying stocks. *Fortune* in May 1954 suggested that it was "time to change the stereotype of the American middle-class consumer. He is not, and has not been for some years, a small landlord or drugstore proprietor. If any stereotype at all is meaningful, it might be the machinist in Detroit."

No sooner had the Depression survivor comprehended the new prosperity than he became obsolescent. Economic prosperity had been the impossible dream of his youth. His fiscal instincts were timid, defensive; if he could get a hundred dollars together, he squirreled it away. But thrift had suddenly become old-fashioned. Americans who had come of age since World War II, who had no memory of the lean years, were spending every cent they could lay their hands on together with other income they wouldn't earn for a long time to come. "Big spender" became a term of approbation. The spenders were living on credit and buying on margin like the speculators of 1929, except that they were acquiring consumer goods, not securities. Life for them was life on the installment plan. Between 1952 and 1956 consumer debt in the United States increased from 27.4 billion dollars to 42.5 billions, or 55 percent. Installment credit grew 63 percent and that for automobiles almost 100 percent. Though these were boom years, disposable income for individuals increased by merely 21 percent. The new Americans were in hock to the future, and they were plainly enjoying it. They spoke with easy confidence of "debt consolidation" and revolving credit plans. A new profession, debt counseling, sprang up to advise them on ways of handling their credit.

Even the big earners among the new suburbanites saved little. In both Long Island's Levittown and Illinois's Park Forest, the average bank deposit was about $300. Accustomed to tax withholding and packaged mortgages, the young couples were indifferent to rates of interest. Installment buyers asked of a new purchase only the size of the monthly payments. They actually seemed to find security in the entrapment of bank loans, in the obligations of coupon books with specified payments and debts. And the banks were delighted to oblige them. "Instead of merchandising the idea of saving," William H. Whyte Jr. observed, they were providing "the apparatus of it."

Grasshoppers, their scandalized parents called them. Older brothers and sisters were also shocked. Over and over one heard couples in their thirties say of those in their twenties, "When we were that age we wouldn't have dreamed of going into debt." But in the past Americans had lacked the protection of such institutions as hospital insurance and expanded social security. There were fewer reasons for nest eggs now. In a short-term emergency the new people could always float another loan. That clearly violated the precepts of rugged individualism — what Max Weber called the Protestant ethic — but it was individualism, the young hedonists in the developments pointedly replied, which had led to the Depression. In ads one noted a decline in the very vocabulary of the Protestant ethic: such verbs as "compel," "force," "climb," and "control" had become unfashionable. Spending was not only more fun, the young argued; it was more sensible. Some thought it more patriotic, too. One radio station recorded a five-voice choir singing a jingle which ended, "Buy, buy something that you need today" and played it seventy times a day.

Even if you didn't need what you bought, you were still fueling the boom. Any tendency to go the other way was considered alarming. One New York newspaper reported that a "rise in thrift" was "disturbing the administration." Madison Avenue quoted Samuel Butler — "All progress is based upon a universal desire on the part of every organism to live beyond its income" — and a researcher for the J. Walter Thompson agency came up with an indulgent quotation from, of all people, Benjamin Franklin: "Is not the hope of being one day able to purchase and enjoy luxuries a great spur to labor and industry? . . . May not luxury therefore produce more than it consumes, if, without such a spur, people would be, as they are naturally enough inclined to be, lazy and indolent?" (In the ad citing this reflection the agency said that it "appears to be a mature afterthought, qualifying his earlier and more familiar writings on the importance of thrift.")

John Kenneth Galbraith maintained that talk of customer sovereignty had become nonsense. Demand was managed; consent was engineered; the public was being subjected to organized bamboozlement. This was consumership, as essential to an understanding of the evolving new economy as Dullesship was to an understanding of American policy abroad. In the packaged suburbs it was called the "good life." It meant the gratification of acquisitive desires — the split-level home, two cars in the two-car garage, a boat, a place at the beach, more new possessions as old ones wore out or became unfashionable (which was often, thanks to the wizards of planned obsolescence), and, somewhere in the nebulous future, college educations for the children, who would then begin to repeat the process. But the prosperity psychology was not confined to the suburbanites. It was meant to include everyone in the growing middle class. It had to be; mass production assumed mass consumption. Farther down the status ladder, Americans whose lower incomes would not permit a move to the Park Forests, Park Merceds, and Drexelbrooks (that is, an income below $4,800 to $5,200) participated by buying other wares, notably those hawked in television commercials: beers, dentifrices, pain-killers, rinses, cake mixes, laxatives, detergents, razor blades, skin conditioners, cigarettes, and — the big purchase for most families — new cars. In the relentless propaganda for goods in general, viewers were ceaselessly urged to be on the lookout for advertised brands, to get them, to incur debt with approved finance companies if that was necessary, and to participate in the huckstered vision of the good life or risk the loss of everything they prized, including their own sense of identity.

The concepts of consumer exploitation and manipulation were not new to the mid-1950s, but widespread awareness of them was. Motivational research, with all it implied, was becoming highly sophisticated. Its seductive presence was felt in virtually every walk of life. The candor of advertising's chief legerdemainists was sometimes breathtaking. They gloried in building empires on the smell of soap, the texture of its suds, the whiteness of textiles. At their wish, they boasted — and they had polls and sales figures to confirm them — buyers from Oregon to Cape Cod switched to Marlboros, discarded their undershorts for jockey shorts by Fruit of the Loom, or made pilgrimages to the loan companies so their wives and daughters could answer affirmatively the famous question which, Philip Wylie had said, was inherent in all ads beamed at American women: "Madam, are you a good lay?"

Of the creative pitchmen A. C. Spectorsky said:

> These people, God save us all, set the styles, mold the fashions, and populate the dreams of the rest of the country. What they do will be done, a few weeks or months later, by their counterparts in Lake Forest and Santa Barbara and on the Main Line. What they decree, via such esoteric channels as the "People Are Talking About . . ." feature in *Vogue*, will all too often be picked up and actually talked about, in Beverly Hills, Grosse Pointe, and Sewickley. What they tell us to buy, by God, we buy.

Spectorsky was fascinated by these transactions. Others were more judgmental. The deliberate encouragement of irrational behavior and impulse buying constituted an invasion of privacy, they said; people were being victimized. The creation of wants was a form of enslavement, and the critics believed that they could detect symptoms of profound disturbance beneath the prosperous surface of Eisenhower America. The figures on alcoholism and addiction to the new tranquilizers were alarming. By 1957 drug sales had increased sevenfold since the end of the war. There was much more shoplifting. In one Illinois community the average shoplifter was not, as might be expected, a figure of destitution or even want. She was, the chief of police said, a housewife married to a junior executive making $8,000 a year; she was a churchgoer, active in the PTA, a member of a bridge club, and a consumer with about $50 a week to spend.

Galbraith was troubled by society's double standard: "Anything which increases production from given sources is good and implicitly important; anything which inhibits or reduces output is, *pro tanto*, wrong." The prophets of self-indulgence and accumulation applauded private goods but recoiled from public services — education, public health, crusades against urban blight. According to that reasoning, Galbraith contended, it was "unquestionably more rewarding, in purely pecuniary terms, to be a speculator or a prostitute than a teacher, preacher or policeman." The younger generation was being "prevulgarized," Louis Kronenberger wrote, "as materials are said to be preshrunk." Edmund Wilson wrote: "Production, consumption and profit have come to play the role that religion played in our grandfather's generation." Such things, he said, could not even be discussed, since "they have taken the place of the Book of Genesis and the divinity of Jesus Christ." To some observers the admen seemed to be stockbrokers in neuroses. Walter Lippmann scorned them as "new barbarians," and Galbraith, in a striking passage, indicted consumerism and at the same time provided later writers with a bench mark against which to measure the very different society of the late 1960s and early 1970s:

> These are the days in which even the mildly critical individual is likely to seem like a lion in contrast with the general mood. These are the days when men of all social disciplines and all political faiths seek the comfortable and the accepted; when the man of controversy is looked upon as a disturbing influence; when originality is taken to be a mark of instability; and when, in minor modification of the scriptural parable, the bland lead the bland.

An understanding of the social revolt that came fifteen years later is impossible without some grasp of the 1950s life-style which arose from the new prosperity. Here, as elsewhere, the character of the time is most easily discerned in the new suburbs. They were not representative of all America (hardly anyone ever died there, for example, and there were almost no unmarried adults) but they did represent what America was becoming. It was there that junior executives unwound after each day, there that their wives honored what Betty Friedan would call the "feminine mystique" — and there that future hippies and straights roamed the community playgrounds.

The vast internal migration of the early 1940s had continued, in a somewhat lower key, in the postwar period. Throughout the 1950s over a million farmers were leaving their farms each year — 17 million altogether for the postwar era by the 1960s. At the same time the centers of the cities, once so splendid, were being deserted — to become ghettos of the poor and bastions of the rich. The rest fled and camped outside. Even in so settled a prewar suburb as Stratford, Connecticut, commutation tickets had doubled and then tripled, and in the new cities the figures comprised virtually the entire male population. Every weekday morning now hundreds of thousands of white-collar workers rode or drove into Manhattan; every evening they returned home. At the end of the 1950s the population of the island south of City Hall was over a million by day — and about two thousand at night. During the decade more than a million New Yorkers left the city to live in the postwar communities ringing it. The suburbs, John Brooks wrote, were "draining downtown of its nighttime population, except for night watchmen and derelicts; it was becoming a part-time city, tidally swamped . . . when the cars and commuter trains arrived and abandoned again at nightfall when the wave sucked back — left pretty much to the thieves, policemen, and rats."

It was the same in all American metropolises. Of the thirteen million new homes which were built in settled areas in the ten years before 1958, about eleven million — 85 percent — were outside the inner cities. Refugees from both the farms and the central cities were converging on townships which hadn't even existed on V-J Day. The loss of metropolitan vigor was especially significant. In the past it had served as a magnet for the young and ambitious. Now it was flowing into the rising communities on the perimeters of the cities, to the curving superblocks, garden duplexes, and red brick labyrinths and manicured lawns of suburbia. There stood the dormitories of the new people, the swing generation and its younger cousins. In these developments the new life-style flourished.*

Its most conspicuous quality was a tremendous emphasis on social skills. Rural and small-town America had been strongholds of what David Riesman called "inner-directed" men and women. The source of their direction — he compared it to a gyroscope — was planted early in life by parents and never wavered afterward. The classic example of inner direction was the Englishman who dressed for dinner in the jungle. In the suburbs an entirely different type was gaining ascendancy: the "other-directed Americans." Their impetus came from an insatiable need to be liked. Riesman likened this to radar picking up impulses. The response was an adjustment to what the group wanted. In the Hillendales and Gardenvilles the accolade was to be called "well-adjusted."

These characteristics were not new to the postwar United States. Seymour Martin Lipset argues persuasively that Americans, with their lack of an autocracy and their emphasis on egalitarianism, have always been other-directed, and Alexis de Tocqueville found supportive evidence more than a hundred years ago. Though Americans took great pride in talking about their individualism, he noted, their special genius — and the source of their greatest potential weakness — lay in their ways of cooperation with each other. If America ever lost that drive, he predicted, it would be through strengthening social virtues at the expense of all others, creating a dictatorship of the majority. "In times of equality," he wrote, "no matter what political laws men devise for themselves, it is safe to foresee that trust in common opinion will become a sort of religion, with the majority as its prophet." The danger in this was that the individual might be "overwhelmed by the sense of his insignificance and weakness."

This is precisely what such critics as William Whyte thought they saw emerging in the suburbs of the 1950s. The great stress on behavior acceptable to the team was inhibiting to the individual, they believed; it was thwarting natural leaders and creating a new breed of yes-men. In some ways that was inevitable. Small business was going under everywhere. Americans increasingly were employed by bureaucracies, both private and public. In 1956 the country passed a milestone as important, in its way, as the closing of the frontier in 1890: the number of blue-collar workers (people producing things) was surpassed by that of white-collar workers (in middle-class, service occupations). Increasingly the representative wage earner became the pencil pusher working for a large, impersonal entity. In the newly developed areas it sometimes seemed that everyone was employed by a vast floating cooperative. The swing generation had become a

---

*The word "development" has since come to mean a publicly financed housing project. Here it is used in its earlier sense, as a tract of developed land.

generation of technicians, of interchangeable parts. It members knew it — and for the most part they liked it.

To be sure, they often spoke of life as a treadmill, but their despair was a mock despair; if they felt imprisoned, their prison was the most comfortable in history, as they would have been the first to point out. Paternalism had become benevolent. The most modest example was RCA's issuance of company neckties. Other corporations went farther. Richfield Oil erected model homes and IBM built country clubs; Reynolds Tobacco engaged company chaplains and Eastman Kodak and Du Pont employed staff psychiatrists. To junior executives who spent their weekdays in such corporate wombs, a carryover of organizational principles in the home neighborhood was only natural.

"It seemed to me," John Steinbeck wrote of the newly organized, "that they looked at me for a place to insert a coin." That was unfair. There was nothing inherently wrong in Park Merced's employment of uniformed attendants to cut the grass, or in Drexelbrook's annual Christmas decoration contest for its 1,223 garden apartments, in which the rivalry between garden courts became so imaginative that a hundred thousand Philadelphians drove out every year to see it. Life in the developments was in many ways an improvement over the life its dwellers had known as children in the 1930s, and not just because everyone was now prosperous. Even as modern business kept all ways of advancement open in order that any junior executive might graduate one day to Westchester, Bull Valley, or Bloomfield Hills, so were the new suburbs free, unstructured, and genuinely hospitable to anyone from any background except blacks, whose time had not yet come. Families moving in found that their new neighbors were eager to help them unpack, take care of their children, and feed them until they had settled down. Even William Whyte conceded that the young suburbanites had achieved "a pretty high quotient of kindliness and fundamental decency."

They owned their own homes, and that was important; it satisfied an old American yearning. Their sense of community was rooted in the American past, too; the pioneers had also been generous and hospitable. The new people were relaxed and informal, almost to a fault. Sport shirts and denim pedal pushers replaced collars and hose. Mother wouldn't have dreamed of going downtown without dressing; now her daughter went with her hair in curlers, and if anyone thought the kerchief over it suggestive of the babushkas worn by the peasant women of eastern Europe, she didn't care. Her concern was the attitude of the other girls in her neighborhood. They did the same thing and would have been disappointed in her if she had done anything else.

Children in the developments exchanged toys and clothes almost as though they were community property, which they almost were. If little Bobby had outgrown his playsuit, it went to little Billy across the way. It wasn't unusual for a mother to recognize a familiar garment on a strange child long afterward; since she had given it away it had passed through several households. Bikes and scooters were also exchanged. Front doors were unlocked; neighbors felt free to enter without knocking. Doors inside were disappearing. So were the massive overstuffed chairs of the Thirties, the heavy rugs and the inside walls; the formal dining room mother had dusted every day and used only for big meals had been replaced by a single living-dining-kitchen area, and the suburbanites saw little reason to mourn its loss, even when guests came. The sitdown dinner had been succeeded by casserole dinners, served buffet style. Sometimes they were awkward, but no one seemed to mind. This way a hostess could enjoy her own party.

The host usually mixed the drinks beforehand, which in 75 percent of the dwellings were martinis. If there was an uprising in the nursery he hurried off to suppress it. Suburban fathers took a livelier interest in their children; home had become a place for companionship and recreation. Nearly two-thirds of all American husbands were helping with housework by 1954, and in the developments the percentage was higher. In addition, and to a degree which often amazed their own parents, the young fathers there were pitching in to help with the dishes, the cooking, and the diapering of the babies. Russell Lynes complained that the young wives were beginning to treat their husbands as part-time servants or as the latest new appliance, but to the new men there was nothing emasculating about stopping at the supermarket for extra groceries on the way home from work, or filling in at the laundromat, or pushing the stroller around the block. They believed it was good for them and good for their families. Spock was the grandfather clock by which the new fathers set their watches, and he approved, and that made it right.

Suburban mothers, in the togetherness vanguard, seemed very young and often were. During the 1950s the age at which U.S. women married dropped from twenty-two to twenty and into the teens. High school marriages became an accepted phenomenon. Children began going steady in junior high school. Girls began thinking about their weddings then or even earlier; a *New York Times* advertisement for a child's dress said, "She Too Can Join the Man-Trap Set."

Being a successful man-trap entailed being desirable — a good lay, in Wylie's phrase; ideally, a great lay. To achieve this happy state females of all ages invested in wardrobes, cosmetics, and exotic perfumes whose makers claimed that they incited rape. Since 1939 the average woman had shrunk three or four sizes. Instead of shopping for a dress her size, she now found one she liked and then dieted to fit it. Metrecal made its appearance and found an eager mass market. So did a new Clairol slogan: "If I have only one life, let me live it as a blonde." Some social scientists and aging suffragettes worried about women's reckless haste to abandon their hard-won independence, but their voices were muffled. *Life* applauded the mass movement of girls into the home, and in a cover story on the suburban wife *Time* reported that wives were "having too good a time . . . to believe that they should be unhappy." The truth, Carl N. Degler wrote, was that "American society in general, which includes women, shuns like a disease any feminist ideology."

By the late 1950s the U.S. birth rate was approaching India's. The number of U.S. mothers who had given birth to three or more children had doubled in twenty years. The increase was most spectacular among college women; they were abandoning careers to bear four, five, and six or more children. The percentage of females in the American college population (35 percent) was lower than that in any European country and smaller than the prewar figure on U.S. campuses (40 percent). Nearly two-thirds of matriculating girls dropped out before graduation, while more than half the men stayed. Many coeds left the classroom to take menial jobs, supporting their partners, who remained on campus; this was called the degree of "Ph.T." (Putting Husband Through). Other women quit because they had *not* acquired spouses. Deans' offices found that coeds were leaving at the end of the first year or two because they had found the pickings slim and wanted to try their luck elsewhere.

To ambitious junior executives hanging their hats in Levittown and casting covetous eyes on Westchester, the right spouse was as important as a hearty chuckle and a sincere necktie. Corporations set up training programs to show company wives what they should and should not do, and *Fortune* found in interviews that the wives, especially the young ones, approved of the idea. They felt that women should become gregarious if they were shy, and, if they were smarter than men, learn to hold their tongues. Several movies of the time dramatized their situation, among them *Executive Suite* and *Woman's World*. The theme in each was a corporation's search for the right man to fill a big job and how a wise mate could help her man by wearing the right dress, hiring the right interior decorator, choosing the right friends, and serving the boss his favorite menu when he came to dinner.

The very anonymity of the big corporation served to sap confidence and independence in men and women dependent on it. So did their own lack of roots. In the front office, where employees were so many pins on a map, personnel chiefs seemed to move them about with reckless abandon. Each relocation meant farewells to friends and the search for new ones elsewhere. The *Wall Street Journal* reported that a Montgomery Ward executive and his family had been moved twenty-eight times in twenty-six years of marriage. Growing mobility was a fact of suburban life. According to Atlas Van Lines, the average corporate manager now moved fourteen times in his lifetime, once every two and a half years. For him the ability to adjust to new circumstances was important to a degree beyond the comprehension of men who live their lives in one place. Though the premium on socialization in the developments sometimes became excessive, the alternative — a family dependent upon its own emotional resources — was considered worse.

Suburbia was superbly equipped to meet the needs of newcomers. Its inhabitants had little reason to feel lonely. The American compulsion to join every association on sight found its ultimate expression there. Meetings were scheduled by one organization or another at every hour from breakfast to late in the evening. Partners were always available for bridge, canasta, poker and bowling. Camera, bird-watching, gun, embroidering, archery, and ping-pong clubs flourished; so did PTAs, the League of Women Voters, the ADA, the Minute Women and, beginning in 1958, the John Birch Society.

Many Americans who would later rise in public life began to acquire their political expertise in suburbia's constant shuffle of adjustment. Here they were likelier to be Republican than in their old neighborhoods. Socially ambitious couples arriving from the inner cities switched their party affiliations — much as they abandoned other lower-class ways. Their parents had contributed to the Democratic party's huge great urban majorities. They didn't. Now that they had made it, they wanted to pull the ladder up behind them. In Europe the postwar expansion of labor unions was leading to the formation of a large, militant, class-conscious force. Not here; although eighteen million industrialized U.S. workers were now unionized, their craving for middle-class status, and the frequency with which it was being satisfied, created instead a large new middle group. Uneasy in their new roles, distrustful of liberalism, and deeply hostile toward further social reforms, they constituted a neoconservative force which would become increasingly significant as the old Roosevelt coalition faltered.

The most common indictment of suburbia's life-style was that it was oppressive. Its passion for informality was so intense that preference for privacy was treated almost as a sign of malaise. Picture windows became windows for looking in. Couples who wanted to lock out the neighbors occasionally were expected to provide an explanation afterward. The group felt it had a right to know everything — "Did you have your period yesterday?" or "Who was that woman you were talking to at Stop and Shop?" or "Your Roger was looking daggers when he left for the office this morning. What's his problem?"

The term "polite society" fell into disuse because society wasn't polite any more. The increasing use of first names was extraordinary. Once it had been limited to family and friends. Then it was extended to colleagues at work and the neighborhood. At office parties and neighborhood cocktail parties finding out who you were talking to became increasingly difficult. Last names were used only in introductions; afterward everyone was Al, Debby, Chuck, or Beth. Eventually the circle of first-namers widened to include virtually everyone who knew who you were: doctors, tradesmen, the children of others, etc. The suburbanite who arrived home to find her bathroom being used by a strange boy might be greeted, "Hi, Doris." In suburbia this was looked upon as just friendliness. Any objection to it would be regarded as snobbish and resented.

One option closed to the suburbanite was scolding someone else's child — in the idiom of earlier generations, "correcting" him. Any correction had to come from his own parents, and there wasn't much of it. Children were special people in the new communities. Whether or not they benefited from their status was a question which would later be debated nationally. Certainly they weren't neglected. Permissiveness took time and patience, and the parents in the developments were among the most permissive in the country. Children made other demands on their time. A mother was expected to plan her youngster's activities and then chauffeur him to them. At times this required the energy and ingenuity of a Grossinger's social director, for suburbia's children were busy all the time. Sociologists were struck by the remarkable degree to which their lives were organized for them. After school and on Saturdays, hurrying station wagons crisscrossed suburbia, carrying their charges to dancing lessons, Little League practice, tennis lessons, sailing lessons, play groups, parties, piano lessons, Cub Scouts, dramatic school — schedules which returned them home just in time for dinner and evenings in front of the television set. So occupied were they, Henry A. Murray protested in *Daedalus*, that their chances of growing into individuals were being curtailed sharply, if not crushed altogether; "parents make their babies play with other babies," he wrote, "as soon as they can toddle." The swing generation wasn't much interested in individuality. Though older executives still paid lip service to it, their juniors were more anxious to raise children who, as they put it, could "get along with other people." They admired that quality in one another, sought to develop it in themselves, and saw it becoming the key to success in the next generation.

The upshot was that millions of pupils approached the age of awareness equipped with marvelous radar but no gyroscopes. They were well instructed about society's need for morale but hadn't been told what it produced; they knew a great deal about achieving popularity but very little about achieving anything else. "Give me a boy for the first seven years and he will be a Catholic for life," a prelate had said. The apostles of adjustment had more than seven years, and it is doubtful that even the church could have done a more thorough job than they did. First mothers instilled in children the necessity for wooing their peers. Next came practice workouts in sandboxes and on swing sets. Activities followed: Brownies, Little Leagues, etc. The propaganda for good fellowship was relentless. Sunday schools in the modern churches taught that God was really just a pal; that religion was fun, like the movie nuns who played softball and rode around in helicopters. Any fledgling Luther who felt inclined to cultivate his own identity was exhorted not to by the mass media, while the last layers of goodguymanship polish were zealously applied in the new suburban schools.

The character and quality of classroom instruction in America varied from one community to another. In some, McGuffey readers and rote memorization were still prevalent. One-teacher public elementary schools were on the way out, however; their number dropped from 143,391 in 1932 to 59,652 in 1950, and at the end of the Eisenhower era they would be down to 20,213. The leaders in the profession, honored at teachers' conventions and teachers colleges and extolled by the National Education Association, were advocates of what was called progressive education. It wasn't really progressive. It had been that, in its beginnings as a movement, when it was dedicated to freeing the imaginative child from lockstep classroom discipline and encouraging him to develop his own individuality. Then, as educators became more enthusiastic about developing social skills, teachers replaced the old stress on intellectual attainments with the even greater constraints involved in turning a child into what Gesell profiles suggested he should be.

Pupils in these schools were not told what they must learn. They were asked to choose their own electives. To avoid fixed standards of performance ("straitjackets," they were called), grades were often limited to "satisfactory" and "unsatisfactory." Courses in "family living" replaced algebra, geometry, grammar, and foreign languages. At times the attitude of the new educators toward the traditional academic disciplines bordered on outright hostility. Eric Baber, superintendent of the Park Forest, Illinois, high school, which in 1954 was chosen one of the five winners in the "All America Schools" contest of the National Municipal League, deplored the stubbornness with which college admissions offices clung to entrance requirements. "The so-called 'bright student,'" he said, "is often one of the dumbest or least apt when he gets away from his textbooks and memory work. This is evidenced by the fact that many $20,000-to-$100,000 jobs in business, sales, sports, radio . . . are held by persons with I.Q.s of less than ninety."

Alert to signs of what was denigrated as "maladjustment," teachers in schools participated in their pupils' choices of friends, their games at recess, their very fantasies. Instead of visiting national monuments, classes visited dairies or grocery stores. Learning to become consumers, they gathered information that, they were told, would be useful to them in later life. In such "doing" sessions, supervisors explained at PTA meetings, pupils were participating in actual situations. Abjuring what was called "elitism," they were concentrating not on what changes might be made in life, but how to make them "without upsetting human relationships." "Ours is an age of group action," Dr. Baber told a teachers' workship, stressing the need to emphasize the extroverted side of their pupils' nature. So the children were taught, and so they learned to be "well-rounded" — people who understood that the goals of the individual and the goals of society were identical. If uncertain about a problem, they polled one another.

Some parents objected. They wanted to bring back Latin, chemistry, integral calculus — courses that colleges and universities also wanted. Smiling principals shook their heads and replied, "We teach the child, not the subject." They believed that in preparing pupils for participation in the consumer world they were taking a practical, realistic, hardheaded approach which would be vindicated by the future.

On October 4, 1957, Tass, the Soviet news agency, had an interesting item for the American public. "The first artificial earth satellite has now been created," it announced. "This first satellite was successfully launched in the USSR . . . Artificial earth satellites will pave the way for space travel and it seems that the present generation will witness how the freed and conscious labor of the people of the new socialist society turns even the most daring of man's dreams into reality."

To grasp the full impact of this announcement, it must be remembered that in 1957 the United States was still regarded as the home of scientific innovation. It was a running joke of the postwar years that from time to time Moscow would announce that this or that Russian — usually some Ivan or Ilya no one had ever heard of — was responsible for a discovery which everyone outside the Soviet Union knew had been made in the United States. Americans had grown up believing they held a virtual monopoly on technological ingenuity. Now the proud were fallen. In addition they were mortified. Nikita Khrushchev was crowing, "People of the whole world are pointing to the satellite. They are saying that the U.S. has been beaten." And so they were. Tass called the space vehicle a *sputnik;* literally a "traveling companion" or, more appropriately, a "fellow traveler." It instantly won the attention of the world. To the United States it came as a shock on the order of the Crash.

Montage: Eisenhower At Flood Tide

Best actor of 1956: Yul Brynner in **The King and I** · Best actress of 1956: Ingrid Bergman in **Anastasia**

Stevenson, Stevenson
If you vote for Stevenson
He will be, easily,
President next year
Help him win, get him in
Now the fight's begun
Gotta be, gotta be, gotta be
Believe in Stevenson!

Dear <u>Modern Screen</u>:

I think you had a hand in the reconciliation of the Dean Martins. You wrote on "open letter" in <u>Modern Screen</u> telling Dean and Jeanne how silly they were to stay apart when they really love one another. I read your words, and I bet they did, too.

And after this fling Maria, New York
Who could blame Mr. Bing
If he shipped Madam Callas to Dallas?

Shortly after 8 o'clock on Sunday night, Staff Sergeant Matthew C. McKeon limped into the barracks of Platoon 71 at the U.S. Marine Corps Recruit Depot, Parris Island, S.C.... The 74 boots of Platoon 71 followed him toward the salt tidal marshes of Parris Island, where death was waiting.

ALTHEA GIBSON WINS WIMBLEDON TROPHY

La Strada

SCOTT paper has WET STRENGTH

A white sport coat and a pink carnation
I'm all dressed up for the dance
A white sport coat and a pink carnation
I'm all alone in romance

The wedding day burst fair and warm; Margaret Truman walked out of the 91-year-old house a last time on the arm of her ever-punctual, this time solemn father. "She looks beautiful, Mr. Truman," called a voice from the crowd. "Thank you, thank you very much," said the father of the bride. "I think so, too."

Around the World in 80 Days

YOUTHFUL INSURGENTS ATTACK BATISTA'S PALACE: 46 DIE

BEST SELLERS: Fiction
Don't Go Near the Water by William Brinkley
By Love Possessed by James Gould Cozzens
The Last Hurrah by Edwin O'Connor
Auntie Mame by Patrick Dennis
Peyton Place by Grace Metalious

U.S. INTERSTATE HIGHWAY SYSTEM TO BE LAUNCHED

The Catered Affair

PLEASE INFORM EUROPE AND THE AUSTRIAN GOVERNMENT . . . THEY OPENED FIRE ON EVERYBODY . . . A FEW HUNDRED TANKS ATTACKED BUDAPEST . . . THERE IS HEAVY FIGHTING . . . I STAY OPEN AND CONTINUE W.TH THE NEWS . . . WE SHALL INFORM THE WORLD ABOUT EVERYTHING. LONG LIVE HUNGARY AND EUROPE. THE RUSSIANS ARE USING PHOSPHORUS BULLETS. ANY NEWS ABOUT HELP? QUICKLY, QUICKLY, WE HAVE NO TIME TO LOSE. NO TIME TO LOSE. I AM RUNNING OVER TO THE WINDOW IN THE NEXT ROOM TO SHOOT BUT I WILL BE BACK. WE WILL HOLD OUT TILL THE LAST DROP OF BLOOD. GOOD-BYE FRIENDS. GOOD-BYE FRIENDS. GOD SAVE OUR SOULS. THE RUSSIANS ARE TOO NEAR. The Edsel performs fine, rides well, and handles good.

WEST SIDE STORY

Book by Arthur Laurents
Music by Leonard Bernstein
Lyrics by Stephen Sondheim

◆

WINTER GARDEN

Try **Zest** — the soapless soap

BEST SELLERS: Nonfiction
Arthritis and Common Sense by Dan Dale Alexander
Kids Say the Darndest Things by Art Linkletter
The Search for Bridey Murphy by Morey Bernstein
Profiles in Courage by John F. Kennedy
Too Much, Too Soon by Diana Barrymore and Gerold Frank

Just walking in the rain gettin' soaking wet
Torturing my heart by trying to forget
Just walking in the rain so alone and blue
All because my heart still remembers you

Standing on the corner watching all the girls go by
Standing on the corner watching all the girls go by
Brother you don't know a nicer occupation
Matter of fact neither do I
Than standing on the corner watching all the girls
watching all the girls watching all the girls
go by

Make me feel real loose
Like a long-necked goose
Oh, baby, that's what I like

You ain't nothin'
but a hound dawg

My baby
rocks me
with a
steady roll

Bus Stop

By ABIGAIL VAN BUREN

DEAR ABBY

The funniest questions, and the wittiest and wisest answers, from the famous "Dear Abby" column

Where there's life — there's BUD

TWENTY-FOUR

Beep Beep

THE FIRST WORD that a Russian sphere the size of a beachball was circling the earth once every 96.2 minutes, traveling at a speed of 18,000 mph and emitting beeping sounds as it did so, had reached Washington, quite by chance, during a cocktail party in the Soviet embassy at 1125 Sixteenth Street. Scientists from twenty-two countries were observing 1957–58 as an International Geophysical Year, or IGY as they called it — a general sharing of data — and Russian diplomats were entertaining fifty IGY luminaries that historic Friday evening when one of the guests, Walter Sullivan of the *New York Times*, was called away for an urgent telephone call. At the phone he learned of the Tass announcement. He hurried back and whispered to an American scientist, Dr. Lloyd Berkner, who rapped on the hors d'oeuvre table until the hubbub quieted. "I wish to make an announcement," he said. "I am informed by the *New York Times* that a satellite is in orbit at an elevation of 900 kilometers.* I wish to congratulate our Soviet colleagues on their achievement."

The room burst into applause. Eminent scientists are indifferent to national loyalties, and the Americans there were particularly generous. Dr. Joseph Kaplan, chairman of the U.S. IGY program, called the Russian achievement "tremendous" and added, "If they can launch one that heavy, they can put up much heavier ones." The White House, however, was momentarily speechless. The advent of the first sputnik astounded U.S. intelligence even though the Soviets had made no great secret of their satellite plans. At an IGY planning conference in Barcelona Russian delegates had spoken openly and confidently of their plans to launch a space vehicle. As early as November 1954, Defense Secretary Wilson had been asked whether he was concerned over the possibility that the USSR might win the satellite race. He had snorted, "I wouldn't care if they did."

That continued to be the Republican line now that Sputnik was an

*Approximately 559 miles.

accomplished fact. Administration spokesmen seemed to suggest that the press was making molehills out of molehills. Hagerty issued a statement describing the satellite as a matter "of great scientific interest" but adding that "we never thought of our program as one which was in a race with the Soviet's." Wilson, now in retirement, called the Russian feat "a nice technical trick." Rear Admiral Rawson Bennett, chief of the Office of Naval Research, wondered why there was so much fuss over a "hunk of iron almost anybody could launch." White House adviser Clarence Randall described the space vehicle as "a silly bauble" — thereby infuriating the President — and Sherman Adams said disparagingly that the government wasn't interested in "an outer-space basketball game." (In his memoirs Adams regretted this. "I was only trying to reflect the President's desire for calm poise," he wrote, "but I had to admit on reflection that my observation seemed to be an overemphasis of the de-emphasis.")

Others in Washington were in no mood to dismiss Sputnik so lightly. Trevor Gardner, who as former Assistant Secretary of the Air Force had tried to mediate interservice quarrels over who should run the American space program, said bitterly, "We have presently at least nine ballistic missile programs, all competing for roughly the same kind of facilities, the same kind of brains, the same kind of engines and the same public attention." Electronics and airframe experts recalled Wilson's casual attitude toward space research. "The basic reason we're behind the Russians," a major defense contractor said, "is that we haven't gone all out." One of the President's closest aides said he felt an urge to "strangle" Budget Director Percival Brundage. Knowland privately warned Ike that the worldwide impact of the Soviet accomplishment had all but nullified the value of America's Mutual Security program, and some publicists were actually suggesting a negotiated peace with the Russians "before it is too late."

The Democrats, predictably, were indignant. Senator Henry Jackson of Washington wanted the President to proclaim "a week of shame and danger." Missouri's Symington demanded a special session of Congress. Fulbright of Arkansas said, "The real challenge we face involves the very roots of our society. It involves our educational system, the source of our knowledge and cultural values. And here the Administration's program for a renaissance of learning is disturbingly small-minded." Majority Leader Johnson saw cosmic implications in the Russian success. "The Roman empire controlled the world because it could build roads," he said. "Later — when men moved to the sea — the British Empire was dominant because it had ships. Now the Communists have established a foothold in outer space. It is not very reassuring to be told that next year we will put a 'better' satellite into the air. Perhaps," he concluded sarcastically, "it will even have chrome trim — and automatic windshield wipers."

This was more than partisan oratory. Periodically Americans feel a need to agonize over why the country has gone soft. The last time it had happened had been in the spring of 1940, when France was falling and the older generation thought American youth too engrossed in swing to hear the Nazi jackboots. Now, as then, the press was aroused. "It is downright terrifying with [Sputnik] staring down at us," the Portland *Oregonian* said, and *Time* said that "the U.S. takes deep pride in its technical skills and technological prowess, in its ability to get things done — first. Now, despite all the rational explanations, there was a sudden, sharp national disappointment that Americans had been outshone by the Red moon." John Kenneth Galbraith had been awaiting publication of *The Affluent Society*. Neither he nor his publishers had expected much of a sale. "Then, in the autumn of 1957," he wrote in an introduction to the second edition, "the Soviets sent up the first Sputnik. No action was ever so admirably timed. Had I been younger and less formed in my political views, I would have been carried away by my gratitude and found a final resting place beneath the Kremlin Wall. I knew my book was home."

Americans were learning humility — and humiliation. They had become an international laughingstock. At a scientific conference in Barcelona Leonid I. Sedov, Russia's chief space scientist, taunted a U.S. colleague: "You Americans have a better standard of living than we have. But the American loves his car, his refrigerator, his house. He does not, as we Russians do, love his country." Anti-Americans were derisive. RUSSIANS RIP AMERICAN FACE, read a headline in Bangkok's *Sathiraphab,* and a Beirut professor said dryly of his students, "You would have thought they launched it themselves." The editors of London's *Economist* saw the Russians scoring a brilliant psychological triumph in the Afro-Asian world. French journalists saw the catch, the price the Soviet masses had paid. Thierry Maulnier wrote in *Le Figaro*, "The Russian people can . . . see in the sky a brilliant star which carries above the world the light of Soviet power, thanks to millions of pots and shoes lacking," and *Combat* commented: "We ourselves would like it if the Russians would put some of their pride into the evolution of a better world — an end to the world of concentration camps." But in all Europe only the London *Express*, faithful to Britain's old ally, predicted that somehow the United States would muddle through: "The result will be a new drive to catch up and pass the Russians in the sphere of space exploration. Never doubt for a moment that America will be successful."

Americans themselves had plenty of doubts, and the more they knew about the implications of the Soviet achievement the more apprehensive they became. In those first days virtually all the details about the man-made star came from Tass and *Pravda;* the Smithsonian Institution was building an astrophysical observatory in Cambridge to track precisely this sort of phenomenon, but it was unfinished and unable even to correlate visual observations being phoned to it by widely scattered moonwatchers. The Russians disclosed that their first sputnik was a polished steel ball twenty-two inches in diameter, weighing 184.3 pounds and equipped with four radio antennas. Its orbit was higher than U.S. scientists had thought possible. Because of that height it would avoid the atmosphere and could keep circling the earth for years. Sputnik's weight was also stunning; the directors of America's Vanguard Project, still in the theoretical stage, had been hoping to send a 21.5-pound Navy Viking research projectile to a maximum of 300 miles. That would have required 27,000 pounds of rocket thrust. The Russian catapult had used 200,000 pounds — an incredible figure, clearly indicative of a new source of power.

As new data came in and were digested by MIT computers, American appreciation of Soviet technical virtuosity soared. The orbit was stunning. It was elliptical, of course, carrying the sputnik from an apogee 583 miles above the earth to a perigee 143 miles down, but since both of these distances were added to the radius of the earth (3,960 miles) the ellipse was almost a circle, showing that the Russians had precise control as well as power. Moreover, the launch had been daring. The simplest way to orbit the satellite would have been to aim it eastward from the equator, taking advantage of the earth's rotation to give the object about 1,000 mph of free speed — in effect, a tailwind. Vanguard's planners had expected to do this; according to their calculations the Viking rocket, rising due east from Florida, would have had a 914 mph boost. But Vanguard rocketeers working under lights those first nights were astounded to learn that the Russian course was 65 degrees the other way. That indicated that they had power to burn. It had another significance. Vanguard's course would have kept it south of Europe and most of Russia. Sputnik's journey took it over most of the inhabited earth, meaning most of the world's peoples could see it, as well as hear it and read about it — a propaganda coup in itself.

Americans would be among the last to have a clear view of it, owing, perhaps, to a sly bit of Muscovite humor. The launch had been timed so that during its first weeks the satellite would pass over the United States during the day, when it would be invisible against the glare of the sun, or at night, when the shadow of the earth would hide it. The curious — and there were tens of thousands of them — had to peer up at daybreak and twilight, when the object could be briefly glimpsed against the gray sky. That would change. The orbit was shifting around the earth at four degrees a day, Dr. Joseph A. Hynek of the Smithsonian observatory explained; on about October 20 the sputnik would come into view overhead for those with binoculars or small telescopes. But Americans, impatient as always, wanted to know everything now. They had been huddling over their radios and television sets since that Friday night when an NBC commentator had told them, "Listen now for the sound which forevermore separates the old from the new." Then they had heard it for the first time, alternating between 20 and 40 megacycles — an eerie A-flat beeping from outer space.

It was generally assumed in those early days that the object was sending back signals in cipher, and CIA cryptographers worked in shifts to break the code. A man who could enlighten them happened to be right there in Washington; he was General Anatoly Arkadievich Blagonravov, chief of the three-man delegation Moscow had sent to the IGY conference. There was no code, the general said. The designers had put the beeps in to track the sputnik and reassure themselves that the satellite was still out there. There was nothing in the steel ball except the transmitter and the batteries. The power of the signal was one watt — just about enough for a conversation between hams in Australia and the United States. In about three weeks the batteries would be exhausted, Blagonravov said, and the beeping would stop. A likely story, Americans snorted. Who could trust a Russian general? There was something fishy about those signals. "Many believe that the whole story has not been told," *Time* noted darkly. The CIA had better get to the bottom of it, the man on the street muttered, or the U.S. taxpayer would know the reason why.

Sputnik I dealt the coup de grace to Ford's fading Edsel, which had been introduced to the public the month before, and which was now widely regarded as a discredited symbol of the tinny baubles Americans must thrust aside. There were other scapegoats. The administration was one. It was M. Robert Bendiner who suggested that until now the Republican idea of a scientist had been a man who tore and compared cigarettes on television. Public education was another conspicuous target and did, in fact, have much to answer for. American parents were angered to learn that while their children were being taught "life adjustment," Russian education had been acquiring a reputation for being tough and competitive, ruthlessly winnowing out mediocrities beginning in the fourth grade and awarding to outstanding students the laurels which, in the United States, were reserved for athletes and baton-twirling, tail-twitching cheerleaders.

Parental wrath would grow with the publication of John Gunther's *Inside Russia Today*, then in galleys. Gunther reported that "In the schools which prepare for college, the Soviet child must absorb in ten years what an American child gets in twelve — perhaps more." Russian pupils, he said, went to school six hours a day, six days a week, attending classes 213 days a year as against 180 in the United States, and in the last two years of schooling four hours of homework were assigned each day. Gunther continued:

> . . . the main emphasis is on science and technology, for both boys and girls, and herein lies the greatest challenge to our system. In addition to ten solid years of mathematics, every child must take four years of chemistry, five of physics, six of biology. By contrast, only about half of American high schools have *any* physics, and only 64 percent have *any* chemistry. An American authority told me that the average Soviet boy or girl graduating from the tenth grade (our twelfth) has a better scientific education — particularly in mathematics — than most American college graduates!

Emphasis on science came early in Soviet schools; pupils began studying optics and quantum theory in grade school. By the mid-1950s the USSR was graduating twice as many scientists and engineers as the United States, and in a sixty-four-page report the National Science Foundation estimated that 14 percent of all Soviet scientists were allowed to pursue basic research — that is, inquiries which may or may not have practical significance. Such work often seems pointless at the time, but it is the restless search for answers by the laboratory man with insatiable curiosity which makes possible the technological miracles of the next generation. Thomas Edison could not have developed the incandescent lamp without Henry Cavendish and Michael Faraday; the atomic bomb became a reality because in 1905 Albert Einstein had published an obscure volume setting forth the proposition, then wholly inapplicable, that energy is encompassed in every bit of matter; and the H-bomb was created by men who had been studying the stars. Charles E. Wilson thought basic research ridiculous. As Secretary of Defense he had once mocked it as finding out "what makes grass green and fried potatoes brown," a remark scientists now remembered and quoted bitterly. The number of Americans in long-range studies was fractional, and the funds allotted to them — about 450 million dollars a year — represented only one-tenth of one percent of the national income.

Now scientists were beginning to speak up. Norbert Wiener had something to say about science and society. Wiener blamed the tight lid government had clamped on research, beginning with radar and the Manhattan Project. The consequence, he said, was that the individual scientist was often not only unaware of the vast problem he was dealing with, but even worse, that his scientific inquisitiveness was frequently discouraged. Physicists pointed out that the Soviets had an 8.3-billion electron-volt particle accelerator (atom smasher), better than America's best, the University of California's betatron, and UCLA's Joseph Kaplan, the U.S. IGY chairman, said, "In oceanography, meteorology, and upper-atmosphere physics, the indications are that they are certainly as good as we are."

Edward Teller also spoke up. Though still a pariah among most of his fellow physicists, Teller remained a brilliant and prescient scholar. His Pentagon friends pointed out that in last April's issue of *Air Force* magazine, six months before the first beep, he had gloomily written: "Ten years ago there was no question where the best scientists in the world could be found — here in the U.S. . . . Ten years from now the best scientists in the world will be found in Russia." In the Soviet Union, he had pointed out, science was almost a religion; its ablest men were singled out and treated as a privileged class while their underpaid American colleagues lacked status in their society and could offer few incentives to bright protégés. His appeal for respect for the dignity of scientific inquiry was well taken. The number of cartoons about mad scientists dropped sharply. There were also fewer jokes about them. And it was extraordinary how quickly the word egghead dropped out of the language.

For some time Walter Lippmann had been urging his countrymen to consecrate themselves to a national purpose. Few had grasped what he had in mind, but now they knew: the national purpose was to rescue education and, with it, America's next generation. Suddenly Rudolf Flesch's *Why Johnny Can't Read — and What You Can Do About It,* which had come out in 1955 without making much of a dent, was on everyone's best-seller list. Hardly anyone had a good word for schools as they were except people like Dr. Ruth Strang of Teachers College, Columbia, and she and TC were in disgrace. Social critics' heaviest guns trained on just such educators, or, as they were derisively christened, "educationists." Chancellor Lawrence A. Klimpton of the University of Chicago explained how the Strangs and the William Heard Kilpatricks had distorted and misrepresented the ideas of John Dewey. Dewey had held that thinking begins in an interest, or a concern. But this had been twisted into an insistence that teachers must amuse, or entertain, pupils.

Herbert Hoover said that the Communists "are turning out twice or possibly three times as many" scientists "as the U.S." He scorned the "too prevalent high-school system of allowing a thirteen- or fourteen-year-old kid to choose most of his studies." That same week another distinguished engineer from whom more would be heard on this score observed in Detroit that one root of the trouble lay in the "misconception of the worth" of the American high school. "We have always overvalued it," said Rear Admiral Hyman G. Rickover, the man responsible for America's atomic submarines. "It comes out," he continued, "that we have many more children in high school and in college than [Europeans] have in secondary schools and universities, and this makes us proud. But all these comparisons are meaningless because the European secondary school graduate has learned more than most of our college graduates. As to the high school diploma," he added heavily, "the less said about it the better."

Even resolute Republicans were uneasy. Clare Boothe Luce, in other ways a steadfast defender of the status quo during the Eisenhower years, found complacency on this issue impossible. She called the sputnik's beep an "outer-space raspberry to a decade of American pretensions that the American way of life is a gilt-edge guarantee of our national superiority." Her husband was also troubled by heretical thoughts. "Turning to Washington for reassurance," *Time* said nervously, "the U.S. saw administrative confusion, sensed a crisis in leadership and demanded action." The stock market tobogganed dizzily downward that week, and with Russia's man-made moon flashing across the skies all America seemed depressed. A contagion of black humor cropped up — proposals to change Project Vanguard's name to Project Rearguard and a story about a Washington reporter who called the U.S. Space Agency, asked how the program was going, and was asked by the girl on the phone, "Sir, are you calling *for* information or *with* information?"

Sputnik I's beeps died away in the last week of October, as General Blagonravov had predicted. It was still there and could be tracked, but at

794 | SOWING THE WIND: 1951–1960

least you couldn't hear it any more. Then, just as Americans had begun to catch their breath, Sputnik II went up on November 3. In some ways it was a more breathtaking achievement than its predecessor. The new satellite weighed 1,120.29 pounds — making it six times as heavy as Sputnik I — and its orbit carried it 1,056 miles away from the earth. "The unfathomed natural processes going on in the cosmos," Moscow radio proclaimed, "will now become more understandable to man." It was true; American scientists were envious. A space vehicle that large would house a maze of instruments radioing back data on cosmic rays, solar radiation above the atmosphere, atmospheric temperature and composition, the danger of meteors, the earth's gravitation, its magnetic field, its electric charge, and the cloud patterns of its weather. The Russians had another surprise. There was a little dog of the *laika* breed aboard, strapped with contrivances which would provide other information about the ability of fauna to survive in space.

It was another luckless day for administration image makers. Ideally news of the event should have found the leaders of the government at their desks furiously striving to catch up. As it happened, Eisenhower was just returning from a West Point class of '15 reunion and homecoming football game, while a Big Ten game had taken Charlie Wilson's successor, the new Secretary of Defense, Neil McElroy, to Columbus.

The United States was in an uproar. The presence of the dog in Sputnik II clearly meant that eventually the Russians intended to put a man on the moon. Most people in the U.S. were determined to beat them there, and they were becoming impatient with the composure of their President. *Time* said: "The storm showed promise of being the most serious that Dwight Eisenhower had ever faced." A headline in the *Pittsburgh Press* begged: SHOOT THE MOON, IKE.

Ike wasn't going to do it. He refused to be stampeded. Unlike the three Presidents who followed him in the White House, he had grave doubts about the wisdom of investing the national resources in space exploration. He was General Eisenhower now, pondering what he saw as a military threat. He knew he was falling in public esteem. To Gallup's question, "Do you approve of the way Eisenhower is handling his job as President?" only 57 percent now answered affirmatively. Previously the figure had rarely dropped below 71 percent. The present decline was greatest in the South, where it had dropped from 72 percent the previous January to an all-time low of 36 percent.* No President enjoys an erosion of popularity, and Ike valued public esteem more than most. But on matters of national security he was the expert, and he had regarded rocketry from the first as a military matter. He suspected his opinion was shared in the Kremlin, and from mid-October on he was certain of it, largely thanks to a remarkable interview with Nikita Khrushchev by James Reston of the *New York Times*.

*Much of the loss here was attributable to the Little Rock crisis. See pages 799–810.

The first secretary of the Soviet Communist party was in an expansive mood. Elated by the triumphs of his scientists, he boasted that the space satellites were only the beginning of Russia's rocket wonders. "When we announced the successful launching of an Intercontinental Ballistic Missile," he gloated, "some American statesmen did not believe us. Now that we have successfully launched an earth satellite, only technically ignorant people can doubt this. The U.S. does not have an intercontinental ballistic missile; otherwise it would also have easily launched an earth satellite of its own." The West, he said, might as well scrap its B-52s and abandon its airfields: "If you study our latest proposals you will no longer find any mention of control posts at airfields* . . . It is useless to create control posts to watch obsolete airplanes." In another interview that same week with two visiting British M.P.s he said even more vividly: "Bombers are obsolete. You might as well throw them on the fire. You cannot send human flesh and blood to fight things like that." A few days later the Russians announced that they had successfully tested a new hydrogen warhead for a guided missile. To General Eisenhower there could be but one interpretation of all this. The skeptics of Russian advances in rocketry had been wrong. Khrushchev had to be believed now. Manned bombers might not yet be obsolete, but they were becoming obsolete. The Soviet Union had in fact developed the dreaded ICBM. The touch of one button in Moscow and Washington would vanish.

The danger then confronting the United States is evident in retrospect:

June 5, 1957   An Army Jupiter travels over 1,500 miles from Cape Canaveral, the first successful flight of an intermediate range weapon (IRBM) for the United States.

August 26, 1957   The USSR reports that it has successfully tested a multi-stage ICBM.

November 28, 1958   An American Atlas completes a 6,325-mile flight from Cape Canaveral to Ascension Island, the first full-range flight for a U.S. ICBM.

Thus Soviet rocketry held a clear lead for fifteen perilous months. The U.S., to be sure, was hardly defenseless. Despite Khrushchev's jeers at bombers, at every hour of the day and night the vigilant Strategic Air Command had fleets of B-52 jets in the air in a state of readiness with nuclear warheads on board, and the Jupiter IRBMs, poised on NATO bases ringing the Soviet Union, were a powerful deterrent to Russian aggression. Nevertheless, the fact remained that America had fallen behind in the vital ICBM race and would remain there for well over a year.

In the seclusion of the presidential mansion, Ike was very different these days from the cool-headed, almost tranquil chief executive who exasperated the White House press corps. "Although Eisenhower maintained an official air of serenity," Sherman Adams later wrote, "he was privately as concerned

*Control posts: radar installations.

as everybody else in the country by the jump ahead that the Russians had made in scientific enterprise." Even before the ascent of Sputnik II he had ordered McElroy, sworn in only the day before, to undertake an immediate, urgent review of the country's missile program, and when Emmet John Hughes suggested to him that popular concern could be an advantage, winning support for new programs, the President quickly replied, "Oh, absolutely. Anything that will get us out of this complacency — and make this next Congress realize how serious things are — that's all to the good."

His problem was more complicated than that. If he had revealed the real stakes in this contest with the Russians, Congress and the people would not only have lost their complacency, they might very well have lost their perspective, or even their minds. The previous spring the President had asked H. Rowan Gaither Jr., then chairman of the board of the Ford Foundation, to evaluate the nation's state of defense readiness with the cooperation and guidance of the National Security Council. The results were submitted in November, just after Sputnik II went into orbit. They were so shocking that the President decided to suppress them. The Gaither Report endorsed a proposal for a nationwide nuclear bomb shelter program. The shelter plan was financially impossible, Ike concluded, and he saw no point in publication of a text which would merely terrify the people without offering any hope of a solution.

He believed a solution could be found, however. The answer was to draw ahead, or at least abreast, of the Soviet missile achievements. As he saw it, that was the task before the country, not exploits in outer space. It was as great a challenge as any President had ever faced, and because of it he had no difficulty in keeping his eyes off the stars, though not many in the country, or even in his own administration, could resist the fascination of space travel. Knowland couldn't; Ike had to tell him curtly that he had no intention of being "pushed into an all-out effort in every one of these glamour performances without any idea of their eventual cost." The President's determination to keep all rocket programs in the Defense Department, at least for the present, was also challenged, by Vice President Nixon and President James R. Killian of MIT, whom Ike appointed special assistant to the President for science and technology on November 7. Eisenhower said to both that the mechanics of launching space rockets and long-range missiles were virtually the same; a costly duplication of effort made no sense to him. Killian was doubtful, and Nixon, supporting Killian, argued that America's image abroad would be more favorable if the peaceful aspects of space exploration were handled by an agency without ties to the country's military establishment. The President, less concerned with image than with survival, replied that he would rather have "one good Redstone nuclear-armed missile than a rocket that could hit the moon." He added pungently, "We have no enemies on the moon."

His wisdom is apparent to a generation accustomed to nuclear weapons housed in hardened silos, Polaris submarines, and fail-safe mechanisms —

all the horrid realities of the future from which Ike flinched but which he nevertheless faced. ICBMs, which the Russians had, and the inferior IRBMs, which America had, had not yet found their way into the language. Even the sophisticated had not come to terms with the implications of joining H-bomb warheads to unmanned missiles capable of traversing oceans and continents at speeds even greater than Sputnik I's 18,000 mph. All that was beyond the mind of the average American in 1957. A paragraph in the October 28 *Time* gives some idea of the innocence of the well-informed then. It was headed "What About Armed Satellites?" and it might have been written by Jules Verne:

> Many imaginative military planners have dreamed of satellite fortresses armed with nuclear missiles to shoot at the earth below. All space vehicles must be lightly built to conserve weight. They would therefore be vulnerable, and since they are forced to move on predictable orbits, they should not be too hard to shoot down. One suggested method of dealing with a hostile satellite is to shoot a modest rocket into its orbit, but moving in the opposite direction. The warhead would burst and fill the orbit with millions of small particles. Any one of these, hitting the satellite with twice its orbital speed (36,000 mph) would have the effect of a meteor, punching a hole and sending a blast of flame and shock into its interior.

That was in 1957, with a Soviet projectile in orbit and fresh information about the phenomenon accumulating hourly. Another five months would pass before *Time* reported: "A word coming more and more into Pentagon usage is 'overkill' — a blunt but descriptive term implying a power to destroy a military target many times more than necessary." By then the country was learning fast. But when Eisenhower had taken office the very theory of guided missiles had been almost as remote as the atomic bomb concept when Einstein's famous letter reached FDR's desk in October 1939. During the eight years after V-J Day government spending on long-range ballistic missile projects had averaged less than a million dollars a year. In 1954 American physicists advised Washington that they now believed they could design a hydrogen warhead small enough to be carried in the nose of a missile. The administration then gave the green light to ballistic missile development. But the United States was already behind — the Russians had decided to push on with missile research without knowing whether one would ever be capable of carrying a warhead — and the lag grew greater after a fateful recommendation of the U.S. IGY committee.

In 1954 Wernher von Braun, the Nazi V-2 scientist who was to become a naturalized U.S. citizen the following year, had persuaded the Army and the Navy to share in a joint venture under his leadership. Von Braun planned to soup up the Army's tested Redstone missile with booster rockets and send a tiny (five-pound) satellite into orbit. The endeavor was christened Project Orbiter. It was coming along nicely until October of that year, when an International Geophysical Year panel meeting in Rome proposed earth satellite launchings during the IGY — from July 1957 to December 1958. The Americans on the panel agreed. They recommended that the United States undertake a satellite project as part of the country's IGY contribution. The White House consented. At the same time certain administration policy makers insisted that any appearance of using an IGY undertaking for military purposes must be avoided. Their reasoning was the same as that set forth three years later by Killian and Nixon; neutral governments might misunderstand and become offended. It made sense to the National Security Council, which thereupon separated satellite research from military ballistic work. This decision, ending von Braun's Project Orbiter, was reached in mid-1955, when, as it happened, up in Dearborn the Ford Motor Company was deciding to produce the star-crossed Edsel.

After Sputnik I went up, I. M. Levitt, director of Philadelphia's Fels Planetarium, called the separation of the rocketeers and the missilemen an "astonishing piece of stupidity." Army projectile engineers echoed him. In 1955 progress on their Jupiter IRBM had been sufficiently advanced for it to launch a satellite; in September 1956 a modified Jupiter-C reached a height of 650 miles, higher than Sputnik I's orbit, and sailed on for a distance of 3,500 miles. There was no appeal from the National Security Council, however. Orbiter's rocket men were transferred to Project Vanguard, its successor. Vanguard was then assigned to the Navy on the ground that the Navy's Vikings and Aerobees represented greater advances in high-altitude missile research than similar enterprises in the other services. There Vanguard had languished. As a first step under the new management, Director John P. Hagen, the Canadian astronomer now at the helm, announced his intention of launching a 20-pound satellite — one-eighth the weight of Sputnik I — late in 1954. But then there were snags, delays, postponements. Hagen issued a revised schedule, under which the first 21½-pound satellite would go up in the spring of 1958, provided the 27,000-pound thrust of its Viking launcher worked perfectly. Hagen and his colleagues were still working on this when Soviet scientists began hurtling Red moons across the skies.

In Eisenhower's mind the distinction between scientific inquiry and military necessity continued to be sharply defined, and he drew it in his first press conference after the launching of Sputnik I. Vanguard was a scholarly undertaking, he said, "merely an engagement on our part to put up a vehicle of this kind." It was all very well in its way; if the ambitions for it were realized, mankind's knowledge would be enriched with information about "temperatures, radiation, ionization, pressures." But it had nothing to do with any race to the moon, and he didn't know where that idea had started, and he wished someone would tell him.

The launching of the sputnik, Ike said, was something else again. It meant Soviet possession "of a very powerful thrust in their rocketry, and that is important." Unfortunately the figures he had received up to now were militarily meaningless: "I don't know anything about their accuracy, and until you know something about their accuracy, you know nothing at all about their usefulness in warfare." He acknowledged that he was deeply concerned: "I wish we were farther ahead and knew more as to accuracy and to the erosion and to the heat-resistant qualities of metals, and all the other things we have to know about. I wish we knew more about it at this moment."

It was Russian weaponry, he explained, that was the source of his anxiety. The administration had spent $110 million on its satellite project and would spend more. All the same, missile research and development would continue to have priority over it. Almost disdainfully he said: "So far as the satellite itself is concerned, that does not raise my apprehensions, not one iota."

Over at the Vanguard offices, Dr. Hagen and his staff appeared to be equally tranquil. They acknowledged some obstacles, some disappointments, but that was always the way of things on the drawing boards and in the labs. Nodding and puffing thoughtfully on his pipe, the soft-spoken Hagen conceded that his launching vehicle was still undergoing tests, but neither he nor his colleagues admitted to any sense of failure. They had promised to put a satellite in orbit before IGY's end, and that was over a year away. Time, they gently reminded journalists, has little meaning in basic research.

> *fau-bus* (faw-bus), v.i.; FAUBUSED, FAUBUSING. 1. To commit an error of enormous magnitude through malice and ignorance. 2. To make a serious error, to commit a fault through stupidity or mental confusion. Syn. Blunder, err, bollix.

Thus Jack Mabley of the *Chicago Daily News* proposed, in October 1957, that the name of Arkansas Governor Orval Faubus be added to the language. The suggestion never caught on, partly because Faubus's period of notoriety, though great, was brief, and also because under it all he was really quite colorless. If Faubus had not existed it would not have been necessary to invent him. All over the South white politicians were campaigning against the Supreme Court's three-year-old decision striking down the concept of separate but equal education. In Alabama alone four gubernatorial candidates were pledging unyielding opposition to school integration, one of them vowing he would go to jail for segregation and another going one better by swearing that he would die for it. The difference between them and Faubus was that he was already in office and therefore able to attract and hold national attention by official action. In that tumultuous fall he moved in counterpoint with the momentous developments at Cape Canaveral and in outer space, his parochialism juxtaposed against their promises of glory.

There was never any doubt about Faubus's motives. In Arkansas he faced an uphill fight for reelection. The state had a strong tradition against a third-term governor, and his popularity was waning; he had offended liberal constituents by approving rate increases for utilities and railroads and disillusioned others by raising taxes. His strategy was to build a new base in red-neck, racist eastern Arkansas. On August 20, 1957, he made his first move, calling on Deputy Attorney General William Rogers in Washington to ask what the government would do to prevent violence when Little Rock schools opened in September. This was the first time anyone had intimated that violence might come to Little Rock. All the signs indicated that integration would proceed smoothly. On the initiative of Mayor Woodrow W. Mann the city had worked out a model seven-year integration program, carefully picking black pupils likely to do well. Startled by Faubus's question, Rogers replied that local disorders were usually handled by local police.

To be certain that federal officials were still abreast of developments there, the deputy attorney general sent the head of the Justice Department's civil rights division to Little Rock. The official, himself a native of Arkansas, explained to Faubus how federal injunctions could pinion conspirators. He asked the governor why he expected trouble. Faubus's answer was evasive; his evidence, he said, was "too vague and indefinite to be of any use to a law-enforcement agency." Back in Washington, the official reported that he believed the governor intended to play racial politics with schoolchildren.

Faubus's next step confirmed him. On August 29 the governor asked a state court to block the city's integration schedule on the ground that it would lead to bloodshed. The local judge gave him his injunction and was promptly overruled by U.S. District Judge Ronald Davies. The board of education proceeded with its integration arrangements. They were modest enough; nine black pupils were to be enrolled with the two thousand whites in Little Rock's Central High School. There were still no signs of unrest, but to be safe Mayor Mann and his 175-man police force worked out tactics for controlling possible demonstrations.

It was a waste of time. The governor had no intention of consulting the mayor. His plan was rather to call out the National Guard and order it to stop the nine Negro children from registering. Getting wind of this on September 1, Arkansas's most famous citizen, Winthrop Rockefeller, hurried to the statehouse and for two hours begged Faubus not to do it. The governor refused. He said, "I'm sorry, but I'm already committed. I'm going to run for a third term, and if I don't do this, Jim Johnson and Bruce Bennett" — racists who would oppose him in the primary — "will tear me to shreds." At 9 P.M. on September 2, the evening before schools would reopen, National Guardsmen carrying M-1s with fixed bayonets set up a perimeter defense around Central High while their leader, a major general in the Air National Guard, set up his command post in the principal's office. An hour later Faubus appeared on Little Rock's KTHV-TV and announced that he had called out the militia "to maintain or restore the peace and good order of this community." The city, he said, was on the brink of riot: "the evidence of discord, anger, and resentment has come to me from so many sources as to become a deluge!"

Little Rock was astonished. The mayor said, "There was no indication whatever. We had no reason to believe there would be violence." The governor had said that the city's stores were running out of knives (sold "mostly to Negro youths"), but an FBI check of 100 stores revealed that the sale of knives and guns was below normal. The only weapons in sight were those of the National Guard. There had been every reason to believe that the capital of the state would follow the pattern of three other Arkansas communities — Fort Smith, Ozark, and Van Buren — which were quietly integrating that same day. Now the nine black youngsters, arriving at Central High in a group, were turned away by National Guardsmen who said, "Governor Faubus has placed this school off limits to Negroes." One fifteen-year-old black girl tested the perimeter. The Guardsmen raised their rifles against her, and as she retreated a spectator called out, "Go home, you burr head"; then the white-haired wife of a teacher shielded the child and led her to a bus stop. That was the extent of Faubus's "violence," and Judge Davies denied a new petition for further delay of integration.

At the judge's request, fifty FBI agents had roamed Little Rock, looking once more for signs of racial tension. Their 500-page report disclosed not a shred of evidence to support the claim that the peace was threatened. Accordingly, Davies summoned the governor to appear in court September 20 and show cause why he should not be enjoined from interfering with the school board's program. Faubus had retired to the salmon-pink gubernatorial mansion and ringed it with Guardsmen, but a U.S. marshal easily penetrated this screen and handed him the summons on the executive lawn. For the first time the governor looked worried. He wired President Eisenhower, complaining that he was being investigated by federal agents, that his telephone was being tapped, and that he had learned of a scheme to take him "into custody, by force." He asked for a presidential assurance of "understanding and cooperation." Eisenhower replied, "The only assurance I can give you is that the federal constitution will be upheld by me by every legal means at my command."

Representative Brooks Hays, Little Rock's congressman, thought Eisenhower and Faubus ought to sit down together and talk things over. It was arranged; on September 14, the eleventh day of the crisis, they met at the summer White House in Newport, Rhode Island. Sherman Adams's impression of Faubus was that "he would not be unreasonable or difficult to deal with," and Eisenhower thought Faubus seemed confused about the course he should take. Both were wrong. The governor continued to stonewall, and the situation was unchanged six days later when Judge Davies called from his bench, "Civil case no. 3113 on a Motion for preliminary injunction." He was handling the hearing like any other, but it was historic. The governor of a state was being brought to justice in a federal court.

Faubus himself was not there. Ever since calling out the National Guard he had dodged questions about his evidence of violence by promising to produce it in open court, but the evidence wasn't there, either. In place of it were three Arkansas lawyers representing him. They filed motions asking first that Davies disqualify himself because of personal bias, and second that charges against the governor be dismissed here because they should be heard by a three-judge court. Davies quietly overruled them. Speaking from notes, their chief counsel then said, "The position of the respondent, Governor Faubus, and his military officers must be firm, unequivocal, unalterable: that the governor of the state of Arkansas cannot and will not concede that the United States in this court or anywhere else can question his discretion and judgment."

The attorney asked if he and his colleagues might be excused from the hearings, the judge nodded, and they walked out. The governor's defense had rested without summoning a witness. His argument was that federal courts had no jurisdiction over him in Arkansas. That issue had been raised in 1861 and presumably settled in 1865.

The U.S. attorney had planned to call nearly two hundred witnesses. Now eight were enough. They included the mayor, the police chief, and the superintendent of schools. All testified to the city's racial peace. Summing up the evidence afterward, the judge said it showed that the school board's integration program had been "thwarted by the governor of Arkansas by the use of National Guard troops," adding, "It is equally demonstrable from the testimony here today that there would have been no violence in carrying out the plan of integration." He thereupon issued orders that Faubus and the National Guard were to stop their interference. Asked to comment, Faubus scrawled a statement for reporters. He noted that his attorneys had not been present, omitting the fact that they had left on his instructions. He declared: "Now comes the crucifixion. There will be no cross-examination, no evidence presented for the other [his own] side. So now, by the use of carefully selected witnesses, the Justice Department's case can be continued. The results are a foregone conclusion." That night he issued a milder statement, attacking Davies's "unwarranted action" but saying that he would comply with the court order until its "certain reversal on appeal." The militia was withdrawn from Central High, and as the troops marched away Faubus and his wife Alta left Little Rock for a Southern Governors' Conference in Sea Island, Georgia. On the way they stopped to see a Georgia-Texas football game in Atlanta. Afterward a fellow governor told the press, "He's really lapping up the glory. There were 33,000 people at the game, and every time they cheered a play, Faubus got up and bowed."

That evening he was the cynosure of all eyes in the Silver Room of

Sea Island's Cloister Hotel, signing autographs, drinking bourbon and Seven-Up, and dancing. His partners included Mrs. James Karam, who was accompanying the governor's party. Her husband had been unable to make the trip. "Jimmy the Flash" Karam, as he was known in Little Rock, was one of the governor's closest friends. A former football player and professional strikebreaker, Karam was now head of the Arkansas State Athletic Commission. As such he had intimate knowledge of the world of locker rooms, sparring partners, and bullyboys. That was what was keeping him home. He had a special assignment from the governor, and it began at daybreak the following morning. While the Faubuses and his wife lay asleep in Sea Island recovering from the festivities in the Silver Room, Karam was deploying a force of husky young men outside Central High, whispering here, nodding there, and ducking in and out of a filling station phone booth.

At 6 A.M. seventy Little Rock policemen arrived swinging nightsticks and erected sawhorse barricades around the school. Three weeks earlier that would have been enough to keep the peace, but now the crisis had been building too long; Faubus's prediction of trouble was about to become self-fulfilling, especially with Karam there to rally faint hearts. Afterward the mayor blamed what happened on "professional agitators" and an assistant police chief said that "half the troublemakers were from out of town." Civic pride kept them from pointing out that many of the leaders were figures in Little Rock sports and therefore friends of the policemen. Some cops, sympathetic with them, were defensive about being here. "Do you think I like this?" one of them told spectators. "I'm just trying to do my job."

At 8:45 the Central High class bell sounded. In the next instant a yell went up: "Here come the niggers!" These blacks weren't schoolchildren. They were four Negro newspapermen who had arrived together. Retreating, they were pursued by about twenty bullyboys, who cut them off and began systematically beating them. One cop climbed on a car to get a better look. Others moved in to stop the mayhem, and as they did Jimmy Karam cried angrily, "The niggers started it!" A powerfully built youth hurried up to him and said, "Get me five or six boys and get them over there where the nigger kids came in last time." Karam rounded up five of the biggest and led them there. He was too late; while the mob had been watching the attack on the black reporters, the nine Negro children had arrived in two cars and walked into the school. Once there, they seemed safe. Most of the white students looked at them curiously. Some made friendly overtures. None appeared to be hostile.

Nevertheless, the position of the newcomers was untenable. The scene outside was rapidly deteriorating. Radio and television descriptions of the melee had attracted toughs from surrounding towns. The throng doubled and redoubled, until nearly a thousand men were milling around, spoiling for a fight. The ineffectual police response to the assault on the Negro newsmen had taught them that hooliganism would go unpunished. Looking for new targets, they settled on white journalists. Three *Life* men were mauled. Every reporter without a southern accent was in danger. So were the policemen and the state troopers who had answered their appeals for help. In the turmoil the sawhorse barricades were demolished. Surging toward Central High, the crowd was at its very doors when, at 11:50 A.M., Mayor Mann capitulated and ordered the black children withdrawn from the school. The toughs dispersed, chortling. Jimmy Karam darted into the filling station booth and put through a call. Shortly afterward Governor Faubus called a press conference in Sea Island. "The trouble in Little Rock," he said, "vindicates my good judgment."

President Eisenhower was in Washington that morning, speaking before the International Monetary Fund. All that week he had been depressed by the growing crisis in Arkansas. He told Sherman Adams that he was well aware that the Warren Court's resolution of Brown v. Board of Education was "cutting into established customs and traditions in such communities as Little Rock," and "You cannot change the hearts of people by law." Later in the week he would tell four moderate southern governors, "I have never said what I thought about the Supreme Court decision — I have never told a soul." He added, "But how I feel about it is immaterial. The fact is that it is the law, and as the President of the United States I have the responsibility of seeing to it that it is enforced." He had been about to leave the Monetary Fund meeting after speaking when he received an urgent call from Brownell. The attorney general gave him a terse account of the disorders outside Central High. The President then approved a tough statement:

> The federal law and orders of a United States District Court . . . cannot be flouted with immunity by any individual or any mob of extremists. I will use the full power of the United States including whatever force may be necessary to prevent any obstruction of the law and to carry out the orders of the Federal Court.

He was hoping to shake some sense into Faubus. But it was too late. He had barely returned to Newport when a second call from Brownell came in over the maximum-security telephone in his personal quarters. Reports from U.S. marshals in Arkansas disclosed that law enforcement had broken down on both the state and local levels. A mob had ruled at Central High. Moreover, Little Rock was asking Washington to intervene; School Superintendent Virgil Blossom had just called the Justice Department and said, "Mayor Mann wants to know who to call to get federal help." He had been put through to Brownell, who, after hanging up, had drafted a proclamation setting forth the traditional authority and responsibility of the President, reaching back to 1795, to use troops to enforce the federal law. If approved by Eisenhower, it would open the way to sending in the Army. Ike listened to it over the phone. He said, "I want you to send up that proclamation. It looks like I will have to sign it, but I want to read it."

He studied it that evening on the sun porch of his living quarters and went to bed leaving it unsigned. The prospect appalled him, he told Adams; using U.S. soldiers against U.S. citizens would never be "a wise thing to do in this country." But events in Little Rock had acquired a momentum of their own. It is doubtful that even Orval Faubus and Jimmy Karam could have controlled them now. Only strict obedience of the court order would keep the Army out, and a crowd which has successfully defied policemen obeys nobody. Walking to his Newport office just before eight o'clock the following morning, Ike squinted at the horizon and said, "There's a cold wind blowing up." It was an omen. In less than an hour Brownell was on the line again with bad news from Central High. The mob was even bigger today; pushing and shoving, it jeered cops who tried to break it up. The nine Negro students had stayed home. In the opinion of the U.S. marshals, only their absence had saved the school from an invasion. This time Mayor Mann had sent Washington a telegram formally requesting presidential intervention. Eisenhower hung up and signed the proclamation, and that evening he went on national television to explain: "The very basis of our individual rights and freedoms rests upon the certainty that the President and the executive branch of government will support and insure the carrying out of the decisions of the federal courts, even, when necessary, with all the means at the President's command. Unless the President did so, anarchy would result."

That morning, responding to the proclamation, Secretary of Defense Wilson had placed the Arkansas National Guard in federal service, beyond the reach of Governor Faubus, and General Maxwell Taylor, the Army chief of staff, had assigned the 327th Battle Group of the 101st Airborne Division to bring peace to Central High. Eight C-130 and C-123 transport planes had carried the paratroopers from Fort Campbell, in Kentucky, to Arkansas. As Eisenhower spoke to the nation the first trucks drew up in front of the school. For the first time since Reconstruction days southern intransigence on the issue of race had brought Army rule.

The difference between these troops and the militia was striking. Both wore the same uniform, but the resemblance ended there. The National Guard was made up of weekend soldiers, easygoing, casual in dress, and slow to obey. The 101st Airborne was a crack outfit, professional in all ways. While salty officers carrying swagger sticks barked commands, disciplined men spilled out of the trucks and formed ranks on the school grounds. Jeeps were parked just so, in a line. Immaculate tents, each the same distance from the others, rose in a field beyond Central High's tennis courts. Field telephone wires were strung from oaks in the school yard, and before dawn walkie-talkies crackled with the code names of communications men: "Hello, Defiance, this is Crossroads Six. Come in, Roadblock Alpha."*

Roadblock Alpha was the scene of the day's most dramatic incident. The barrier had been thrown up in an intersection a block east of Central High. There, in the first olive moments of Tuesday morning, ringleaders began organizing their men. A lanky, lantern-jawed major watched them from beside a sound truck. His voice rasped over the loudspeaker: "Please return to your homes or it will be necessary to disperse you." They didn't budge. "Nigger lover," one of them muttered, and another called, "Russian!" A man in a baggy brown suit shouted to the others, "They're just bluffing. If you don't want to move, you don't have to."

The major ripped out a command. Twelve paratroopers with fixed bayonets formed a line and braced their rifle butts against their hips in the on-guard position for riot control; it brought each bayonet on a line with the crowd's throats. Again the major snapped an order, and the soldiers moved forward. The mob retreated. The man in the brown suit held his ground until the last moment; then he broke and ran. He didn't run far, however. The Army had won the first skirmish, but the showdown was yet to come. The black children hadn't even reached the school.

That moment arrived in a crisp, swiftly executed maneuver. Central High's 8:45 bell rang. Simultaneously the barricade at Park Avenue and Sixteenth Street opened to admit a lead jeep, an Army station wagon, and a rear guard jeep. They braked together in front of the school, and the Negro children emerged from the station wagon as three platoons of paratroopers ran up on the double with rifles at port arms and formed a semicircle, shielding the children with a hedge of bayonets. A fourth platoon, lining up on either side of the black students, escorted them up the steps. The crowd watched in stunned silence. Then a woman cried brokenly, "Oh my God! The niggers are inside!" Others shouted, "They're in! They're in!" Another woman screamed and tore at her hair. The crowd shifted, tilting forward.

At Roadblock Alpha the throng had thickened. Again the major said harshly, "Let's clear this area right now. This is the living end! I'll tell you, we're not going to do it on a slow walk this time." Nothing happened, and he ordered the paratroopers to resume their advance. As they came on, the crowd recoiled, hopping, to the front lawn and then to the veranda of a private home, all the time yelling that this was private property, that the troopers had no right to come after them on it. The soldiers didn't miss a step. Up on the porch they came, and then across it as the mob scrambled backward from the bayonets.

Those who hesitated were being methodically pushed off the piazza

---

*The officer responsible for this impressive display, the 101st's commander, was Major General Edwin Walker. Later he was retired for circulating John Birch Society material among his men; later still, he was on the wrong side in a racial incident and was arrested. He retired in Dallas, where he flew the American flag upside down. In Little Rock his conduct was above reproach.

when one of them struck back. He was C. E. Blake, a Missouri-Pacific switchman who had been among the most active agitators during the past two days. Blake seized a soldier's rifle barrel and dragged him down. As they sprawled together another paratrooper reversed his M-1 and clouted the switchman's head with the steel butt. Blood streaming from his scalp, he crawled away on all fours shouting at photographers, "Who knows the name of that lowlife son of a bitch who hit me?" Without a glance in his direction the troopers continued to move out while a stony-eyed sergeant called, "Keep those bayonets high — right at the base of the neck."

Back from Sea Island, Orval Faubus joked with the press ("I feel like MacArthur. I've been relieved of my job") and asked the networks for equal time to answer President Eisenhower. ABC-TV gave it to him; the other two turned him down because he refused to answer questions afterward. In the Faubus version of what had happened, Blake had been "a guest in a home." Troopers had run wild with "wholesale arrests." High school girls had been "taken by the FBI and held incommunicado for hours of questioning while their frantic parents knew nothing of their whereabouts." Young white southern womanhood was very much on the governor's mind; he held up a photograph for just a moment and said, "Evidence of the naked force of the federal government is here apparent in these unsheathed bayonets in the backs of schoolgirls." Again, he cried that he had returned from Georgia to find paratroopers "bludgeoning innocent bystanders, with bayonets in the backs of schoolgirls, and the warm, red blood of patriotic Americans staining the cold, naked, unsheathed knives." At the end he cried: "In the name of God, whom we all revere, in the name of liberty which we hold so dear, which we all cherish, what is happening in America?"

What was happening in Little Rock bore little relationship to his speech. Blake, of course, had been no one's guest. Only eight arrests had been made; four of the men had been fined for loitering, and the other four had been released at the police station. The FBI hadn't questioned anyone; J. Edgar Hoover said the governor was "disseminating falsehoods." As for the bayonets in girls' backs, the picture, which Faubus had quickly whipped out of sight, was of girls walking — and giggling — past a group of soldiers.

Those were the facts, and they testified to the good judgment of the troops from Fort Campbell. It continued to go unrecognized by Faubus. Two weeks later he descended to what the *Washington Post and Times Herald* called "the lavatory level," charging that troopers were entering the girls' locker room at Central High and staying to leer at their nudity. Reporters asked Faubus for eyewitness accounts or documentary proof. He replied, "I do not choose to release them at this time." Actually he never produced evidence to support any of his accusations. In November the Army withdrew all but a token force from the school, and the black children began attending Central High unescorted. By the following May the incident belonged to history. It had been a skillful if expensive use of force; keeping the nine Negro students in school had cost the federal government $4,051,000.

But the country paid another, far higher price for the events that autumn in Arkansas. The real significance of Little Rock lay in its impact on the white South. Deep in the southern consciousness lay tales of the Civil War and its aftermath, told to them in childhood by their grandparents, and the trouble at Central High evoked the martyred ghosts of that terrible era. On this subject they were beyond the reach of reason. Their reaction was compounded of the Stars and Bars, the strains of "Dixie," Jackson at Bull Run, Lee at Appomattox, and the dead on the field at Antietam. It rendered them blind to Faubus's clumsy lies. Northern soldiers on southern soil meant just one thing to them — an evil, loathsome presence to be attacked in righteous wrath, sounding a rebel yell that drowned out voices of sanity. Senator Richard Russell of Georgia accused Eisenhower of "applying tactics that must have been copied from the manual issued to the officers of Hitler's storm troopers."* Senator Olin Johnson of South Carolina said, "If I were Governor Faubus, I'd proclaim an insurrection down there, and I'd call out the National Guard, and I'd then find out who's going to run things in my state." Senator James O. Eastland of Mississippi charged, "Eisenhower has lit the fires of hate," and Senator Herman Talmadge of Georgia said, "We still mourn the destruction of Hungary. Now the South is threatened by the President of the United States using tanks [sic] and troops in the streets of Little Rock. I wish I could cast one vote for impeachment right now." Alabama's Governor James E. "Kissin' Jim" Folsom promised that he would disband his state's National Guard before he would let Eisenhower federalize it, and Governor James Bell Timmerman of South Carolina resigned his U.S. Navy reserve commission so he could not be called into service.

They were the leaders. In a thousand ways private southerners made it known that they regarded Faubus as their hero and the President as their enemy. Gallup found that while only 10 percent of the people in northern and western states thought Eisenhower had been wrong in sending the troopers to Central High, only a third of the southerners thought he had been right. In Jacksonville, Florida, an Air Corps veteran mailed his four Air Medals and six battle stars to the White House for distribution among the paratroopers. In Marshall, Texas, a speaker at a Kiwanian luncheon said, "This is the darkest day in Southern history since the reconstruction"; the Kiwanians then refused to pledge their allegiance to the flag. Near Dover, Delaware, two Negroes in business suits were ordered to leave a Howard Johnson restaurant by a waitress who said, "Colored people are not allowed to eat in here," thereby embarrassing the State Department;

---

*The President, indignant, wired Russell: "I must say I completely fail to understand your comparison of our troops to Hitler's storm troopers. In one case military power was used to further the ambitions of a ruthless dictator; in the other to preserve the institutions of free government."

one of the men was the finance minister of Ghana, who had entertained Richard Nixon in his home, and the other was his secretary. As always in the South, the raising of the racial issue was accompanied by intimations of terror. In Albany, Georgia, night riders put a college for Negroes to the torch, and at the height of the Little Rock crisis six Alabamans trapped a black named Judge Aaron on a lonely country road, took him to a deserted shack, castrated him with a razor blade, and poured turpentine into the wound. None of them had known Aaron; one of them said afterward, "We just wanted some nigger at random."

The subsequent career of Orval Faubus was a measure of southern feeling. The governor had played his role in full view of Arkansas voters. Elsewhere biased reporting may have clouded the judgment of readers, but not in Faubus's home state; one of the bravest chapters in American journalism was written by Harry Scott Ashmore of the *Arkansas Gazette,* who won a Pulitzer Prize for his superb coverage of the turmoil at Central High. Not all of his subscribers were appreciative. Ashmore's phone rang around the clock with threatening calls; Faubus denounced him as "an ardent integrationist"; Little Rock's racist Capital Citizens Council called him the state's "Public Enemy No. 1," and a statewide boycott cost the *Gazette* 3,000 subscriptions. He continued to print the truth, whereupon the people of Arkansas swept Faubus back into the statehouse in 1958 for a third term — he received 255,086 votes; the man who ran second got 56,966 — and continued to reelect him by massive majorities in subsequent elections. In 1967, after twelve years in the executive mansion, he retired.

Outside the South, and indeed beyond the United States, was another matter. The struggle to put the nine black children in Central High had global ramifications. Little Rock, an editor wrote at the time, had become "a name known wherever men could read newspapers and listen to radios, a symbol to be distorted in Moscow, misinterpreted in New Delhi," and "painfully explained in London." Americans solicitous of good opinion in foreign capitals were chagrined. They recognized the principles at stake in Arkansas, and saw them being flouted; and they felt shame.

And yet they had virtually nothing to say about the human dimensions of the episode. In perspective that silence is deafening. The voice of the American Negro was still unheard. The word southerner meant white southerner. There was no term for the South's blacks, and U.S. newspapers there and elsewhere seldom carried day-by-day news about them. The true meaning of the Howard Johnson episode was that a victim of racial discrimination had to be a cabinet member in a foreign country before the country's conscience was stirred, and even then it regretted not the wrong done, but the damage to America's image.

Black adults, bred to passivity, accepting the system because for so long there had been no alternative, turned inward as they always had, transmuting what should have been righteous anger into despair. For every American Negro who felt elation when the 101st Airborne triumphed in Arkansas there were dozens who feared — justifiably — the rage of aroused whites; who read of Judge Aaron and knew that there, but for the grace of God, went they. But their children reacted differently. Coming after the Montgomery bus boycott and the Supreme Court decisions outlawing discrimination, the confrontation at Central High confirmed the hope that the stereotypes of the past might be broken. It was in this sense, in the fall of 1957, that Little Rock left a profound impression on such young blacks as Stokely Carmichael, who was sixteen; Cassius Clay, fifteen; H. Rap Brown, thirteen; and Angela Davis, twelve.

In the first fortnight of November those who thought it their duty to cheer up America examined the bleak clouds that had been gathering, and in search of silver linings concentrated on repairing the havoc that had been wreaked upon U.S. morale by the sputniks. Von Braun told the press that the United States could launch a satellite with equipment already available. To the surprise of everyone, including those who had been working on it, Secretary McElroy announced that Vanguard was back on schedule. Emissaries from *Time,* dispatched to take soundings in 33 cities, found stout hearts in the president of the Kansas City Stock Yards Company, a Florida congressman, a group of bankers in Lincoln, Nebraska, and a Los Angeles sales engineer ("Six weeks ago I'd walk into an aircraft plant and it would look as if everybody from the chief engineer to the draftsmen was taking a coffee break at once. When I made my rounds this week, the recreation rooms were empty. Everybody was working.")

"Upward" was the inspirational title of a *Reader's Digest* article by Beirne Lay Jr., who suggested that "a Supreme Being" was America's silent ally in the space quest. By then the administration was responding to aroused public opinion. Rocket crews worked feverishly at Cape Canaveral, and at Nixon's urging the President reluctantly agreed that he must do something more to brighten the country's mood. After his appointment of Killian as special assistant for science and technology (to Ike's annoyance the press changed this to "missile czar") he named a Pentagon coordinator to crack down on interservice rivalries. Then he decided to deliver a series of five presidential TV talks. Much was expected of these, and the first went well. In it he displayed the four-foot nose cone of a retrieved Jupiter. He explained: "One difficult obstacle on the way to producing a long-range weapon is that of bringing a missile back from outer space without its burning up like a meteor . . . This one here in my office is the nose cone of an experimental missile. It has been hundreds of miles into outer space and back. Here it is, completely intact." It was his conviction, he said, that "as of today the overall military strength of the free world is distinctly greater than that of the Communist countries." ICBMs were on their way. Meantime SAC's B-52 jet bombers stood vigil.

The mail response was encouraging. His second chat was equally successful, and he set to work on a draft of the third, to be telecast from Cleveland.

It was slow going; he had a lot on his mind. The seasonal load of the Presidency is always at its heaviest between Labor Day and Christmas. On December 16 he was scheduled to preside over a NATO meeting in Paris. Before then he had to complete his legislative program for the coming year and explain it to the congressional leadership. The massive federal budget for the coming fiscal year demanded presidential attention, the new State of the Union address would be due in January, and it now appeared that the country was entering a major recession.

Still, restoring the nation's self-confidence was the most urgent issue before the President, and he was determined to complete the remaining TV talks. He didn't do it. On November 25, 1957, for the third time in twenty-six months the President of the United States was in bed, prostrate, unable to meet the simplest of his obligations. Dr. Snyder diagnosed his illness as a "vascular spasm." To the rest of the country it was a stroke.

That Monday before Thanksgiving, awaiting the arrival of Morocco's King Mohammed V on a state visit, the President had stood bareheaded in a raw autumn wind at Washington National Airport. Back in his White House office, Ike said he felt a chill coming on. He was afraid he might be catching the flu. It was graver than that. Dictating to Ann Whitman, his secretary, he was dismayed to find that the words wouldn't come. Near tears, she went to Sherman Adams. "The President has gone back to the house," she said. "He tried to tell me something but he couldn't express himself. Something seemed to have happened to him all of a sudden. And just now he gave up and went home. I can't imagine what's wrong with him."

In the presidential apartment upstairs, Adams found the President in pajamas. Snyder, on his way, had telephoned instructions for his patient to go to bed. Eisenhower smiled at his assistant. He said, "I suppose you are dis —" He couldn't finish it. Hesitating, he stammered: ". . . talking about the dinner tonight." Frustrated and angry over his inability to talk about plans for entertaining the African king, he struggled to say, "There's nothing the matter with me! I am perfectly all right!" But plainly he was having trouble forming words. As he continued to falter, he repeatedly came out with a word or syllable that had no relation to the word that was in his mind. In dismay Mrs. Eisenhower said to Adams, "We can't let him go down there in this condition." Adams agreed. He told the President that Nixon could take his place at the dinner. Ike shook his head violently. He managed to say, "If I cannot attend to my duties, I am simply going to give up this job. Now that is all there is to it."

Then the doctor arrived. On hearing a single word from Eisenhower — "international," which came out "internatt-nl" — Snyder reached his diagnosis. Ike's stroke had affected the speech center of the brain. He was suffering from aphasia, an impairment of the power to use words as symbols of ideas. It was impossible to say whether the lesion would heal, and if it did, how quickly. The doctor called Walter Reed and Adams called Nixon, who agreed to preside at the banquet. For the time being nothing was said to the press. Hagerty was in Paris advancing the NATO trip. When word of the President's illness reached him there, he wept.

But it was not an occasion for grief after all. Eisenhower's recovery was both speedy and miraculous. His improvement was noted in a matter of hours. Even as a Hagerty assistant briefed reporters on the findings of four neurological specialists ("an occlusion" accompanied by "slight difficulty in speaking"), the President was back in the White House watching Wyatt Earp on television. The next morning he awoke at 7:40 A.M., showered, and made his own breakfast. He painted awhile, picking up where he had left off on a portrait of Britain's Princess Anne. Feeling much better, he received his aides and the Moroccan king, worked on state papers for a half-hour, and signed or initialed a dozen of them. On Thursday, Thanksgiving, he went to church and shrugged off the helping hand of the pastor. In the Mansion he carved a forty-pound Thanksgiving turkey. Then, with Snyder as their house guest, the Eisenhowers drove to the Gettysburg farm. Saturday they watched the Army-Navy game. With Snyder's approval, Ike planned to return to a full schedule on Monday and preside over a cabinet meeting. The doctor told the press, "The President's progress continues to be excellent."

At Cape Canaveral, Vanguard scientists looked forward to giving the convalescing President's spirits a boost by putting an American sputnik in orbit on December 6. Everything seemed ready that Friday morning. The tall, three-stage, black-and-silver Navy Test Vehicle 3, or TV-3, stood in a spider-web gantry. Sunlight sparkled on a rime of frost crystals from its liquid oxygen fuel. TV-3 had been hurried along on orders from Washington; it was expected to throw into outer space a U.S. satellite the size of a small bowling ball — not much, to be sure, but a symbol of fine workmanship and American determination to enter and then win the space race. To reap a propaganda harvest the administration had made certain that the entire world knew what was coming. Although the Martin rocket had never been tested before, its performance was expected to be flawless. Pentagon PR men had kept 127 American and foreign journalists posted on latest developments, including details on the countdown, usually highly classified information. U.S. READY TO FIRE SATELLITE, said a *New York Times* head. The *Pittsburgh Sun-Telegram* predicted: MOON — MINUTES TO GO. The Associated Press distributed an advance story to member papers for release the moment the satellite went into orbit. In a thousand press rooms it was in type, ready to go:

> Cape Canaveral, December 6 (AP) — The radio-signalling baby moon circling the earth is the U.S.'s reply to Russia that it too can stake a claim to the space frontier.

After several postponements because of valve leaks, Cape Canaveral hoisted the red ball signifying that Vanguard blast-off was imminent. Observation planes — two old World War II B-17s and a new Cessna — took off and rose swiftly to gain altitude. They looked down on a multitude of spectators. None were allowed within three miles of the launching pad, but enormous crowds were watching from the barriers there. Children had been dismissed from schools throughout Florida's Canaveral peninsula; factories and offices had let their workers out; the streets, yards, and public beaches were dense with anticipative Americans awaiting the historic event.

At 10:42 A.M. the gantry was wheeled away; it was wheeled back fifty minutes later and then at last rolled away for good. The last cable connecting TV-3 to the disconnect pole dropped away at 1:44. Within seconds the first whiffs of white-hot vapor emerged from the rocket's base. In Washington the voice of Vanguard's deputy director, J. Paul Walsh, could be heard over an open phone. He called: "Zero! . . . *Fire!* . . . First ignition! . . ."

The massive rocket stirred and rose cumbersomely from the pad a foot, then two feet, then three. At that point, two seconds after launch time, it appeared to stand motionless, fixed in space. Suddenly Walsh cried, *"Explosion!"* A long orange flame spurted from beneath the doomed rocket, shot downward, and then surged upward in a billowing sheet of fire that enveloped TV-3's right side. Overhead one of the B-17 pilots was shouting: "There it goes! There is an explosion! Black smoke is now over the entire area — We do not see the rocket that is carrying our satellite — The rocket may not have gotten off — There is a very large black smoke cloud — a very large black area around the location that the explosion occurred."

The smoke was caused by streams of water and carbon dioxide from automatic extinguishers. As it drifted away the rocket's nose cone could be seen leaning against the disconnect pole. Here and there fires continued to burn. The charred and mutilated tail jutted into the pad. One part of the assembly was intact: the coconut-sized satellite had been thrown clear and lay on the ground, sending steady signals on its assigned frequency, 108 megacycles.

It was a public relations disaster. The scientists protested in vain that this had only been a test. Having summoned the world's attention in anticipation of its applause, the United States now had to endure its scorn and derision. Grinning Russians at the U.N. advised Americans to apply for Soviet technical assistance to backward nations. In London a calypso balladeer sang over the BBC, "Oh, from America comes the thought/ Their own little Sputnik won't go off," and the wits of five continents rechristened TV-3 the flopnik, sputternik, goofnik, dudnik, oopsnik, puffnik, stallnik, and kaputnik. Lyndon Johnson wailed in the Senate, "How long, how long, oh God, how long will it take us to catch up with Russia's two satellites?" Confronting a gloomy press conference in Washington, Vanguard's Dr. Hagen had a one-word comment: "Nuts." Editorial writers sought a new scapegoat — they settled on the public relations men, who joined the progressive educators in disgrace — and a professor in Pittsburgh said, "It's our worst humiliation since Custer's last stand."

In the age of instant communications the debacle seemed to be worse than it was. The fallen rocket wasn't the only one in the U.S. arsenal. Within a month, as soon as Cape Canaveral's launch pad could be repaired, the Navy would be ready for another satellite shot. The very week of the TV-3 fiasco the Air Force successfully retested Thor and Atlas missiles, and by March the Army would have eight Jupiter-Cs ready for the space program, each of them larger and more dependable than the Vanguard. The President had ordered the Jupiters withheld from civilian scientists because of military testing's absolute priority, but now he rescinded that order. Soon the people would forget the shame of December 6. The politicians would not forget, however. To them the risk of another such public roasting was unthinkable. From this point forward a succession of administrations would be committed to staying in the space race until it was won. No excuse for dropping out would be acceptable. Other calls upon the nation's resources, whatever their urgency — and by the late 1960s the need for some of them would be desperate — would have to wait until the Stars and Stripes had been firmly planted on the moon.

Portrait of an American

THE EDSEL

CONCEIVED IN 1948, the car was meant to solve a problem, not to become one. Satisfied Ford owners who grew more prosperous were ignoring the firm's Mercurys and trading up instead to Buicks, Pontiacs, and Oldsmobiles. "We have been growing customers for General Motors," said a Ford executive. Six years later company planners began investing a quarter-billion dollars on a new medium-price ($2,400 to $4,000) automobile. They knew they had to sell at least 200,000 in the first year to make money, but they were confident they could do it.

Lacking a name, they called it the E-Car, the E standing for "Experimental." Nothing was spared in its development. The mid-1950s were the salad days of motivational research, and among the advisers to the E-Car's stylists was the Columbia University Bureau of Applied Social Research, which appraised the "personalities" of other medium-priced cars, concluding, among other things, that the Buick was the wife of a professional man and the Mercury was sexy. After poring over this data, one of the Dearborn executives wrote: "The most advantageous personality for the E-Car might well be THE SMART CAR FOR THE YOUNGER EXECUTIVE OR PROFESSIONAL FAMILY ON ITS WAY UP," and added in explanation, "On Its Way Up: 'The E-Car has faith in you, son; we'll help you make it!' "

On August 15, 1955, the corporation's general staff, headed by Henry Ford II and Ernest R. Breech, witnessed the unveiling of a full-size clay model of the car, with tinfoil substituted for aluminum and chrome. They applauded. The stock market was booming that summer, and so was the medium-price market. Times seemed propitious for the E-Car. It already had the external features which were to become famous: the flaring gull-wing tail and the pinched-in oval radiator grille. Inside, it was to be what one designer called "the epitome of the push-button era."

After the motivational people had turned up 6,000 possible names, all of them alphabetized and cross-referenced, Breech christened it the Edsel, after Henry II's father, on a hunch. E-Day was set for September 4, 1957. On E minus 51 the first Edsels began rolling off assembly lines, but only a few people, all carefully screened, were allowed to see them. A tremendous aura of mystery was created by the car's promoters. Ads showed it as a blur, or as a shapeless hulk beneath canvas. Edsel buildings were fitted with special locks that could be changed in fifteen minutes should a key fall into the hands of Chrysler or General Motors spies. In July word was leaked that a model had been conveyed in a closed truck to Hollywood, where Cascade Pictures photographed it in a locked studio while armed guards patrolled outside. ("We took all the precautions we take for our AEC films," a Cascade spokesman said.) Ford's test track was encircled by barbed wire and camouflaged sentry boxes. In Dearborn telescopes kept watch on nearby roofs and hills for any competitors' agents who might be lurking there.

Business Week called the launching of the Edsel the most expensive such venture in the history of commerce. The stakes were enormous. Ford's Edsel division had its own plant, with 800 executives and 15,000 workers; 60 highly paid copywriters were turning out advertising copy, and nearly 1,200 auto dealers across the nation had surrendered profitable franchises for other makes to sell Edsels. They would become rich if it proved popular — and would lose their shirts if it failed.

In the last week of August Ford spent $90,000 on a three-day press conference at which 250 newsmen were shown the four main Edsel lines, which would be available in eighteen models. The affair was not an unqualified success. Daredevil drivers at the wheels of souped-up Edsels scared the daylights out of the reporters, and the music stands of a band hired for the occasion bore, in memory of Glenn Miller, the initials GM. These matters were slight but ominous. The new car appeared to be unlucky. Still, the public's curiosity was undoubtedly aroused. By the weekend that followed E-Day, almost three million people had entered dealers' showrooms to see what all the fuss was about. On E-Day itself, over 6,500 had bought Edsels. Dearborn was elated. If just one in fifteen of the remainder signed up, the car would finish its first year in the black.

It didn't happen. For one thing, the golden age of the medium-price car had begun to wane. In July the stock market had broken sharply, signaling the onset of the 1957–58 recession; *Automotive News* reported that dealers were experiencing the second worst season for sales in the history of the industry. More important, on E plus 30 — October 4, 1957, a date which will live in infamy at the Ford Motor Company — the Russians sent their first sputnik into orbit. Styles Bridges's thundering rhetoric in the Senate was typical of the American reaction: "The time has clearly come to be less concerned about the depth of pile on the new broadloom rug or the height of the tailfin on the new car and to be more prepared to shed blood, sweat, and tears." In this new climate of opinion *Business Week* called Dearborn's latest spawn "a nightmare." *Consumer Reports* said it represented "the many excesses" with which Detroit was "repulsing more and more potential car buyers," and *Time* wrote that it was "a classic case of the wrong car for the wrong market at the wrong time" and "a prime example of the limitations of market research, with its 'depth interviews' and 'motivational' mumbo-jumbo."

But there was more to it than that. The Edsel was a failure by other standards. The oval grille set vertically in the front end, with the aluminum letters EDSEL emblazoned in it, was not a success. Its designer had adopted the idea from contemporary European automobiles in the hope that it would give the car cachet. It didn't, partly because it was inconsistent with the rest of the front design, and the public's negative reaction to it was the first blow against the auto's success. One writer likened it to an egg. Others described it as a horse collar, Bugs Bunny, and — this may have been inspired by malicious counter public relations of General Motors or Chrysler — a toilet seat.

Even worse, fully half of the first Edsels to go on the market were lemons. Brakes failed, push buttons didn't work, oil pans fell out, trunks wouldn't open, hoods stuck, transmissions froze, paint peeled, hubcaps fell off, batteries died, doors wouldn't close — the list of defects seemed to have no end.

On E plus 3 the theft of an Edsel occurred in North Philadelphia. There were virtually no others. It was a sign of the car's diminishing glamour that it didn't even seem to be worth stealing. After the bloom wore off nationwide sales plummeted until the sales chart in Dearborn resembled a ski slope. Dealers were selling fewer than one-fifth of the number necessary if they were to break even. The promotion became defensive, frantic:

1959 Edsel. Looks right! Built right! Prices right! Makes history by making sense. Exciting new kind of car! A full-size practical beauty. Roomy without useless length. Soundly engineered. Powered to save. And priced with the most popular three!

On January 14, 1958, the Ford Motor Company merged its Edsel and Lincoln-Mercury departments. The new car had lost 400 million dollars. It was finished, and the entire country knew it. The time had come to throw in the towel. Unfortunately that was not yet possible. Just as new cars need a long lead time, so does a cessation of production. The Edsel's new models had been designed long ago; the steel dies had been cut, and the 1959s were plonking down at the end of their assembly lines. Finally, having sold fewer than 1 percent of the cars bought during their time on the market, the Edsel's manufacturers discontinued manufacture on November 19, 1959. Viewers of *Wagon Train,* a Western TV series sponsored by the car's advertising agency, were invited to participate in a contest. The purpose was promotional, but the prizes weren't Edsels. They were ponies.

TWENTY-FIVE

The Crusade Falters

I N 1958 Mike Todd's *Around the World in Eighty Days* entered its third year as the movie industry's greatest box office sensation since the arrival of the tube. Part of its appeal lay in the realization that in the late 1950s, as in Jules Verne's early 1870s, transportation was big news. The globe was growing noticeably smaller, and not only because of the satellites. British Overseas Airways Corporation introduced jet airliners for trans-Atlantic flights on October 4, 1958, and two months later, on December 10, U.S. jetliners made their first domestic appearance on the National Airlines New York to Miami run. The St. Lawrence Seaway was opened to traffic on April 25, 1959. U.S.S. *Wisconsin,* at that time the U.S. Navy's last battleship, was put in mothballs as Mamie Eisenhower christened N.S. *Savannah,* the first atom-powered merchant ship. Nuclear submarines surpassed Verne's wildest, 20,000-leagues-deep dream, circling the globe underwater and crossing the North Pole by passing beneath the Arctic ice cap. In June 1959 the 110-million-dollar sub *George Washington* slid stern first into the Thames River at Groton, Connecticut, carrying solid-fuel Polaris missiles, a guarantee that Russia could never level all U.S. nuclear bases in a sneak ICBM attack.

The American Telephone and Telegraph Company now had 100 million telephones in service, half the world total. Direct distance dialing (DDD), which had been introduced in Englewood, New Jersey, on November 10, 1951, was now being extended to overseas calls. Ocean telephone cables, radiophone, and over-the-horizon radio — soon to be joined by Telstar, the Bell System's first experimental communications satellite — linked Americans with 190 nations and territories overseas. Mark Cross, manufacturer of alligator handbags, provided some insight into the global character of modern American business when it announced a grant of financial aid to Zululand for the propagation of the crocodile species. At the same time, shrinking trade routes brought American auto dealers new competition from abroad. Foreign cars were accounting for 10 percent of all automobile sales in the United States. The leaders were West Germany's Volkswagen (1958 sales were 102,035), France's Renault (47,567), Italy's Fiat (23,000), and Britain's Hillman (18,663). Japan, Sweden, and Holland were about to enter the American market with other small cars, and Detroit, in a gesture toward reality, at last prepared to make little American autos. To distinguish them from automobiles made overseas they were to be called "compacts."

Asked what Americans might expect to find when they reached the moon, Edward Teller replied grimly, "Russians." In early January 1959 the Soviets launched Lunik I, a spectacular 3,245-pound satellite that came within 5,000 miles of the moon. Their head start in space exploration continued to be a tremendous advantage, though the United States had begun to take the first steps toward catching up. Cape Canaveral crews finally put a tiny American satellite in orbit with an Army Jupiter-C rocket. The National Defense Education Act of 1958 provided federal aid for improved teaching in science, mathematics, and foreign languages. In 1958 Congress also created the National Aeronautics and Space Administration (NASA). To test human endurance in space, Air Force Captain Joe Kittinger took the longest parachute jump in history, bailing out at 76,400 feet, falling twelve miles before a barometric device on his parachute blew it open, and landing safely in the New Mexican desert. Front pages on April 10, 1959, introduced the country to a new category of celebrities — the Project Mercury astronauts. All were veteran test pilots aged thirty-two to thirty-seven. Their names were Alan Shepard, Walter Schirra, Virgil Grissom, John H. Glenn Jr., Scott Carpenter, Gordon Cooper, and Donald Slayton. Each was white, a father, a native of small-town America, and a Protestant. Six of the seven had crew cuts.

The oceans on either side of the United States, which had been so comforting to isolationists in the 1930s, seemed at times to have shrunk to fordable streams. In August 1958 scientists debating the threat of fallout agreed that the bones of all Americans could be affected to some extent by any nuclear explosion anywhere on earth. Remote Indochina became less remote on July 10, 1959, when two American military advisers were killed and a third wounded at Bien Hoa, Vietnam, twenty miles north of Saigon. They had been watching a Jeanne Crain film, *The Tattered Dress*, on a home projector in a mess hall. Terrorists had surrounded the building, and when a sergeant switched on the lights to change reels, they had opened fire.

The first Eisenhower administration now belonged to the past, and some notable figures had vanished with it. Joe McCarthy died of drink on May 2, 1957. ("He was discouraged," George Sokolsky wrote. "He regarded himself as betrayed. He particularly felt that he was betrayed by Vice President Nixon, whom he had always trusted.") His widow, Jean Kerr McCarthy, continued to live in Washington; four years later she married a member of the Civil Aeronautics Board. Frank Lloyd Wright died at eighty-nine, leaving a time bomb of controversy over his last major work, New York City's three-million-dollar Solomon R. Guggenheim museum. Deaths in the entertainment world included Errol Flynn, Mario Lanza, Maxwell Anderson, and Lou Costello. John L. Lewis resigned as president of the United Mine Workers. Dave Beck of the Teamsters went to jail, leaving his successor, Jimmy Hoffa, locked in a desperate struggle with John F. Kennedy, a member of a Senate investigating committee, and Robert F. Kennedy, the committee's chief counsel. Maria Callas, thirty-five, left an Italian millionaire, Giovanni Meneghini, for the shipping czar Aristotle Socrates Onassis. Some gossips thought that at fifty-three Onassis was too old for her.

Increasingly the decade was being compared with the 1920s. Zany as they were, the 1950s had witnessed nothing comparable to the ukulele or flagpole sitting until 1958, when the deficiency was spectacularly remedied by two young toymen in San Gabriel, California. Richard Knerr and Arthur Melin, co-owners of an enterprise called the Wham-O Manufacturing Company, had started making slingshots after World War II with less than $1,000 capital. In 1957 they had racked up their first big score with Frisbees, light plastic saucers which could be skimmed slowly through the air from one thrower to another. At a New York toy fair in March 1958 an acquaintance told them that large wooden hoops had achieved swift and startling popularity in Australia; children rotated them on their hips. Back at Wham-O, Knerr and Melin went into production with wooden hoops. After twenty or so they stopped; they didn't like wood and wanted to experiment with plastics. In May they had what they wanted: three-foot hoops of gaudy polyethylene tubing which could be marketed at ninety-three cents each, representing a 16 percent gross profit. Wham-O's new toy was christened the hula hoop.

Patenting the hoops was impossible and by Labor Day a dozen other firms were turning out imitations under other trademarks. Even so, by early September Wham-O had sold two million hula hoops for a net profit of over $300,000. Then adults started using them for calisthenics. Wham-O's bookkeeper couldn't keep up with the production figures. Workers went into three shifts. Counting the copiers at home and abroad, hula hoop sales that autumn were reckoned in the tens of millions. So widespread was their use that European medical journals warned of injuries which might be sustained by enthusiasts. It was a long list. In Leiden, Holland, a Dutch woman was being wheeled into surgery for removal of her appendix when her physician found that what was really wrong with her was a torn abdominal muscle, the result of strenuous gyrations inside a hoop. In England, where a quarter-million hulas had been sold, the British Medical Association cautioned, "No one with a known heart disease should try it, and anyone who is out of training should not go hard at it right away." Japanese emergency wards were filling up with hoopers suffering from slipped discs and dislocated backbones. After a child was killed chasing a runaway hula the hoops were banned from Tokyo streets. Nevertheless sales there passed the three million mark. Lines of Japanese waiting to buy more stretched down the Ginza for blocks, and Premier Nobusuke Kishi received one as a gift on his sixty-second birthday.

Queen Mother Zaine of Jordan, returning from a visit to Europe, included a hula in her luggage. That should have been a guarantee of respectability, but some toymakers were nervous just the same. One of hooping's attractions for adult spectators was its suggestiveness on some hips. An unexpected pleasure at football games that autumn was a view of winsome drum majorettes pumping their loins in a frenzy of excitement as thousands cheered. A French manufacturer of hoops, Jacques de Saint-Phalle, was afraid the church might notice and object. Saint-Phalle had a reputation to safeguard; in hoopless times he made his living manufacturing plastic tubing for hospitals and laboratories. To protect himself he persuaded French celebrities to be photographed hooping. Finland solved the same problem by staging marathons in which participants had to keep three hulas going, at the neck, hips, and knees.

Elsewhere the American fad swept on, whatever watchers with coarse minds thought. In Germany it was popularized by the prizefighter Max Schmeling and his wife Anny Ondra. Germans who had no children, and therefore no easy explanation for buying toys, avoided embarrassment by having stores deliver them, wrapped, at night. A party of Belgian explorers leaving for the South Pole disclosed that twenty hoops were in their baggage; the expense was charged to morale. In some countries hoop shortages were serious. Correspondents in Johannesburg, where hulas were retailing at sixty-five cents, reported that only white customers could afford them; the natives were restless until charitable organizations started distributing free hoops. *Het Vrije Volk* of Amsterdam noted that Dutch industries requiring plastic tubing were at a standstill, and in Warsaw a weekly newspaper for young Poles observed, "If the Ministry of Light Industry and the Chamber of Artisans do not embark upon the production of hoops, we will be seriously delayed in hula hoop progress, especially on the international level." The ministry and the chamber continued to be dilatory, so hulas were smuggled in through East Germany.

The craze receded as quickly as it had spread. By the summer of 1959 discarded hoops had begun to pile up in city dumps, but the rage had been a singular illustration of how great a grasp even the trivia of American mass culture had on the rest of the world.

In Europe, Whitehall and the Quai d'Orsay had blamed Dulles for the Suez disaster; in Washington, a number of members of the Eisenhower administration were inclined to agree with them. Given the Mideast as it was after Suez, however, there were no two minds about what Washington's next move should be. It was an article of cold war faith that every desirable part of the world must belong to either the Communist world or the Free World. Sherman Adams wrote in 1961:

> The defeat of the attempt by Britain and France to settle the Suez Canal controversy by military force temporarily destroyed the prestige and political power of those two nations in the Middle East . . . Unless the United States undertook to fill the vacuum and made clear to the world the intention to do so, the President said, the Soviets could be counted upon to move into the Middle East and we would find ourselves in an intolerable situation.

The President told the congressional leadership, "I just do not believe that we can leave a vacuum in the Middle East," and to a joint session on the Hill he asked for authority to use U.S. troops there "to secure and protect the territorial integrity and political integrity and political independence of . . . nations requesting such aid against overt armed aggression from any nation controlled by International Communism." This was the Eisenhower Doctrine. Like FDR's undeclared war of 1940–41, Truman's decision to send American soldiers to Korea without consulting Congress, and the Formosa resolution of 1955, the doctrine was another long step toward presidential authority to use U.S. armed forces anywhere.

Adams put his finger on one weakness in the Eisenhower Doctrine. "The difficulty in any American attempt to stop the spread of Communism abroad," he wrote, "was in trying to prove that an internal upheaval which posed as a nationalist struggle was really under the direction of Moscow." The resolution supporting the doctrine passed the House easily but ran into trouble in the Senate. As in the Formosa resolution debate, critical senators were divided. Some believed the White House was trying to share responsibility for what should be an executive decision; others thought Eisenhower was asking for the right to make war. Richard Russell of Georgia and Fulbright of Arkansas were particularly apprehensive. Russell told Dulles, "We are being asked to buy a pig in a poke." Dulles replied that the issue was one of loyalty. He said to Russell, "If we are going to pinpoint everything, if Congress is not willing to trust the President . . . we can't win this battle."

But where was the battle? Britain and France having laid down their arms, the only Mideast danger spots were disputes between Arabs and Israel in the Gaza Strip and the Gulf of Aqaba. After two months of debate the Senate approved the resolution 72 to 19. "During the following year," Adams wrote, "there were a series of explosive developments in Jordan, Syria, and Lebanon, and all involved, directly or indirectly, the application of the Eisenhower Doctrine." In reality they mostly involved its inapplicability. Trouble in Jordan arose in a classic Mideastern form: anti-Israel Arabs rocked Amman, forcing the resignation of young King Hussein's premier. The king then appealed to Eisenhower, claiming that the crisis was "the responsibility of international Communism and its followers." Dulles endorsed this motion, and the President sent the Sixth Fleet to make a whiff-of-grape demonstration in the eastern Mediterranean. In the shadow of the guns Hussein selected a loyal government. The rioters having dispersed, the new premier survived. There is no evidence that the outcome would have been different without the warships.

The Syrian blowup came next, and it had an *opéra bouffe* air. Dulles was eager to show the flag in Damascus, but the Syrians weren't buying that. The government favored the Soviet Union; the opposition consisted of anti-American officers; each preferred to be left alone with the other. King Saud of Saudi Arabia assured Eisenhower that ideology had nothing to do with the feud, that no true Arab could be a Communist. The President replied that he had heard that one before; de Gaulle had told him that "no true Frenchman could be a Communist." "Obviously, the turmoil was Communist-inspired," Adams wrote, "but, in contrast to the situation in Jordan, the Syrian government wanted nothing to do with any assistance from the West, and there was therefore little that Eisenhower could do about it. This was an example of the weakness of the Eisenhower Doctrine."

On the morning of July 14, 1958, Washington awoke to learn that the Middle East was in the throes of one of its periodic convulsions. During the night pro-Nasser Arab nationalists in Iraq had seized the Baghdad radio station, post office, cable office, and the bridges over the Tigris River. Advancing on the royal palace, they put the king and the crown prince to the sword. Premier Nuri as-Said tried to escape disguised as a woman, but he, too, was captured and slain. This knocked out the central prop holding up Dulles's Baghdad Pact, which was only six months old.[*] It also panicked President Camille Chamoun of Lebanon. Earlier Chamoun had accused Arab Communists of a massive infiltration of his regime. Secretary General Dag Hammarskjöld had personally led a United Nations observation team investigating the charge. They had found no evidence supporting Chamoun's fears. Now, convinced that he was next on Nasser's list, he formally requested the dispatch of American troops to Beirut. Eisenhower consented.

This was 1930s isolationism turned on its head, the far swing of the interventionist pendulum. By no stretch of the imagination could American security be said to be in jeopardy. After 9,000 U.S. Marines had been put ashore under the watchful eye of 70 Sixth Fleet warships and 420 fighter planes, until then the greatest concentration of American armed might ever assembled in peacetime, the President issued a statement explaining that "The mission of these forces is to protect American lives — there are about 2,500 Americans in Lebanon," but there was not a shred of proof that any Americans (or Lebanese, for that matter) were in danger.

---

[*] Citing the Eisenhower Doctrine, Dulles had assured member countries that the United States would shield them from subversion with a "mobile power of great force." After the Baghdad coup the alliance was re-created, omitting Iraq, as the Central Treaty Organization (CENTO), with headquarters in Ankara, Turkey.

Moreover, by raising that issue the President in effect conceded that the Eisenhower Doctrine was irrelevant. Dulles tried to convince the congressional leadership that it was. If the United States did not act on Chamoun's request, the Secretary of State warned, "our prestige is gone; nobody will take our word again — ever. If we get there first, there might not be Communist intervention." Fail to act, he said, and the free world would lose not only the Mideast and nearly three-fourths of the free world's oil reserve with it, but also Africa and non-Communist Asia. This catechism was to be recited by cold-warriors as a justification for the use of force in every international crisis down to and including Vietnam. Eisenhower had resisted it in 1954. This time resistance came from the leaders on the Hill. They made it plain that they wanted no share in the responsibility for the Lebanese move.

To all intents and purposes, that was the end of the Eisenhower Doctrine. Four months later Chamoun was replaced by a neutralist president and premier, and at their request the marines were withdrawn. The episode had been "a frustrating and unhappy experience for Eisenhower," Adams concluded. Its implications were graver than they seemed at the time; the President had warned the senators and representatives that he might have to risk war in the Mideast without prior discussion in Congress — "In this case," he said, "if there has to be a public debate about the course of action, there would be no use in taking it at all" — thereby adding to the sanction of precedent under which presidential power to make war was expanding.

Gunboat diplomacy on the other side of the globe was something new for the United States. It suggested an imperial presence, and that is precisely what such Europeans as Reiner Hellman, author of *Amerika auf dem Europäischen Markt*, and J. J. Servan-Schreiber of *Le Défi Américain* (*The American Challenge*) believed they saw rising on the western rim of their horizon. To prewar Europeans the old America had appeared to be a land of affluence and ballyhoo, where everyone looked like Gary Cooper and Ginger Rogers and had children like Mickey Rooney and Ann Rutherford. That U.S.A. had been idealistic and innocent, the wonder and secret envy of the world. Except in time of natural disasters, when Americans were Good Samaritans, they had played virtually no role in world affairs.

Now they were all over the globe. Missionaries of Point Four, ECA, and technical assistance programs had fanned out across Africa and Asia. Congress had chartered the Development Loan Fund for underdeveloped countries, Fulbright scholarships, and Smith-Mundt exchanges for forty-two countries not covered by the Fulbright program. The number of American tourists abroad was increasing 12 percent annually; there were more than two million U.S. tourists in far lands in the late 1950s, and they were spending more than two billion dollars a year there.

It was not always spent wisely and gracefully. For every European who said with Churchill, "I love these Americans. They have behaved so generously," there was one or more who shared the contempt of Jean-Paul Sartre: *"Les Américains ne comprendront jamais rien à existentialisme."* Defenders of older cultures on the continent and in Asia felt threatened by the spread of Americanization. They were alarmed by the appeal of America's teen-age culture, especially its music, for the world's youth. Jazz could be heard almost everywhere. The young king of Thailand was writing songs for a Broadway musical called *Peep Show*, and the king of Cambodia taught himself to play a hot saxophone. And then there were the American soft drinks. In Bangkok the prime minister was the Coca-Cola concessionaire and the police chief had the Pepsi-Cola franchise; Adlai Stevenson called their rivalry "the ice cold war." Coke was ahead there and everywhere else. The sun never set on it. Every day people abroad consumed fifty billion bottles of it, enough Coke to float a light cruiser.

"What we are faced with," Servan-Schreiber wrote, "is not classic imperialism driven by a desire for conquest, but an overflow of power due to the difference in 'pressure' between America and the rest of the world." U.S. industry was in the process of investing 57.5 billion dollars in overseas plants, with a gross output of about 100 billion dollars a year. "One by one," Servan-Schreiber warned, "American firms are setting up headquarters to coordinate their activities throughout Western Europe."

As the American giants grew larger and stronger, Europeans, Asians and Africans became more curious about the quality of life in the United States. Not everything they heard was accurate and balanced. Admirers of the Soviet Union and the new China came down hard on racial discrimination, picturing the Montgomery bus boycott and Little Rock as race riots. Most accounts of American society emphasized the high standard of living; it was becoming a source of bitterness. The gap between the American standard and that of the rest of the world, particularly in the emerging countries, was steadily widening. In 1950 Premier Liaquat Ali Khan of Pakistan said on a visit to the United States: "As I let myself ponder over this, I suddenly see the United States of America as an island — a fabulously prosperous island. And all around this island I see the unhealthy sea of misery, poverty, and squalor in which millions of human beings are trying to keep their heads above water. At such moments I fear for this great nation as one fears for a dear friend."

U.S. embassies, USIS libraries, and cultural centers around the globe became targets in forty major riots. Spontaneous attacks on the American flag were now a common phenomenon, the reason in most cases being a long-smoldering anti-Americanism among the demonstrators which, for one reason or another, had reached the flash point. There were five such disturbances in Indonesia alone. They were by no means confined to nations whose leaders were critical of the United States. Demonstrations occurred in neutral capitals — Algiers, Cairo, and Khartoum among them — and even in those of U.S. allies, including Rio de Janeiro, Athens, Saigon, Taipeh, and Panama City.

Americans were puzzled. They had thought of themselves as being generous with foreign aid programs, unaware that, as Leon Keyserling wrote, the actual percentage of America's Gross National Product that flowed into international economic cooperation and assistance was "so imperceptible that one blushes to mention it." The American man in the street suspected that the rioters had been misled by agitators. If they understood the benefits of free enterprise, he thought, they would want it, too. In his naiveté he omitted the many other factors that made the U.S. mix so successfully, natural resources and the temperate climate being among them. He thought that if men in other lands only knew how prosperous the U.S. was, they would cheer the Stars and Stripes, not defile it. It never occurred to him that documenting that prosperity would be regarded as intolerable gloating.

It didn't occur to his leaders, either. In boning up for visits abroad, Vice President Nixon memorized charts and graphs showing how much better off Americans were than less fortunate people. After one of the visits he described how, in discussions with citizens in host countries, he had awaited an opening and then rammed his points home:

> I cited figures to show that the 44 million families in America own 56 million cars, 50 million television sets, 143 million radio sets, and that 31 million of those families own their own home. Then I made the point that so many people overlook. What these statistics dramatically demonstrate is this: that the United States, the world's largest capitalist country, has from the standpoint of the distribution of wealth come closest to the ideal of prosperity for all in a classless society.

By midpoint in the second Eisenhower administration, a considerable number of people overseas had heard this line of reasoning. President Eisenhower had taken to sending Mr. and Mrs. Nixon abroad a lot. In the interests of international good will the Vice President had endured diarrhea in Indonesia, Afghanistan, and Ethiopia, picketing in Burma, insults in Casablanca, and a sweaty hour trapped in a defective Mexico City elevator.

These efforts were to be capped, in the spring of 1958, by a strenuous eighteen-day tour of South America with stops in Uruguay, Colombia, Argentina, Paraguay, Bolivia, Ecuador, Peru, and Venezuela. It was to be a neighborly gesture, and Nixon expected it to be boring. Afterward he wrote: "Of all the trips I made abroad as Vice President the one I least wanted to take was my visit to South America in 1958 — not because I thought it would be difficult but because I thought it would be relatively unimportant and uninteresting compared with the assignments I had in Washington at that time." The CIA had assured him that the trip would be uneventful. To newspapermen who were hesitant about covering it he said that they would probably miss little if they stayed home.

There wasn't much in the beginning. South Americans of the ruling classes, who welcomed the Nixons to Montevideo, Buenos Aires, Asunción, and La Paz, were accustomed to North American policy makers taking them for granted. Under Assistant Secretary Henry Holland, who kept watch on Latin America for Dulles, the State Department fought all proposals for U.S. loans to countries there on the ground that if liberals came to power they might try to regulate businessmen, thus depressing business morale. The elite in the first countries Nixon visited knew that, appreciated it, and had no intention of rocking the boat.

Here and there on street corners intense young men held up signs calling the *yanqui* Vice President "Racist," "Imperialist," and "Son of a Dog." One placard advised him to "Go back to the U.S.A. where you enjoy the lynchings of Negroes and massacres of Indians." As a forthright politician, he paused wherever possible to explain that he wasn't a racist, an imperialist, or a son of a dog; that he didn't enjoy lynchings or massacres and had not, in fact, participated in any of them. But these incidents didn't amount to much. The number of pickets at his early stops were so few he didn't notice them. For every hostile placard there were greeters to welcome him with the Latin *abrazo*, a good-natured bear hug. He heard some students chanting "*Fuera Nixon*." His translator told him it meant "Go home, Nixon." He said smilingly that he didn't want to go; people were much friendlier here.

No one later could remember exactly when and where the chants changed to "*Muera Nixon*" — death to Nixon. He was jeered in Buenos Aires on the fifth day and booed in Asunción on the sixth, but on the whole the crowds remained cordial. Bolivians showered him with flying confetti; there were no visible signs of danger there. Actually he had been lucky. An attack on him had been narrowly averted in Bolivia by blowing up a railroad track to isolate a mining town where protesters wearing bandoliers of dynamite sticks had assembled. Elsewhere police vigilance had turned away men bent on violence. Such good fortune couldn't favor the Nixons all the way, and it didn't. Their first inkling that disaster might lie ahead came in Lima, Peru, on Wednesday, May 7, their eleventh day away from home.

The reception at Lima Airport was gracious, but as the motorcade entered the city Nixon observed that there were not many people on the streets and most of those who were there "did not seem to be aware" of who he was. The Peruvian official in his car explained that the motorcade route had not been published, to avoid "incidents." This, Nixon was to recall, was "somewhat disquieting since I had not anticipated any incidents in friendly Peru."

Little is known about the leaders of the mobs which were to confront Nixon there and later in Venezuela. They are shadowy figures, made more so by Nixon's later insistence that all his troubles could be traced to a centrally controlled Communist conspiracy. Upon his arrival at Lima's majestic Grand Hotel Bolívar, he wrote afterward, the extent of the plot was revealed to him: "It was apparent that the Communists, after the failure of their efforts to disrupt my tour in Uruguay, Argentina, or Bolivia, had decided to make an all-out effort to embarrass me and the United States at San Marcos University, an institution so well known throughout Latin America that whatever happened there would be front-page news everywhere." Watching the demonstrators, he thought, "How are they able to stir the people up to this pitch? Then I realized as this was going on that right here was the ruthlessness and the determination, the fanaticism of the enemy that we face. That was what I saw in the faces of the mob. This is really Communism as it is." Noting the youth of the crowds, he wrote, "My reaction was a feeling of absolute hatred for the tough Communist agitators who were driving children to this irrational state."

This is largely conjecture. Undoubtedly there were Communists in the forces which were forming against him in Peru and Venezuela, and clearly people were inflamed by the *Tribuna Popular*, the Communist weekly, which ran a front-page picture of him retouched so that his teeth looked like fangs and his expression was that of a madman. But to infer from this that all the Latin-American demonstrators protesting his trip were being manipulated and coordinated by agents of the Cominform is, to put it mildly, rich. The CIA was far from omniscient in these years — the agency had been caught napping by the Iraqi coup — but it is hard to believe that it would have missed something that big. A more reasonable interpretation is that poor people, regarding themselves as victims of injustice, saw an opportunity to express their hatred of the wealthy and — understandably — took it. Communists and extremists of other persuasions then added fuel to the flames of anti-American rage that had sprung up on their own.

The mobs in Lima were ugly, but there was a respite for the vice-presidential party afterward. Four days in Ecuador and Colombia provided an opportunity to regain the strength needed for the last and most risky stop: Caracas. The situation in Venezuela was volatile, the mood in the streets was ugly, and the ruling junta, which had been in power less than four months, had not taken the vigorous measures needed to suppress the troublemakers. Unwilling to acknowledge its helplessness, the new government responded to periodic inquiries from the American embassy with assurances that it foresaw no serious incidents for the Vice President and that it was prepared to deal with any which might arise.

Caracas was the one city in which Communist plotting against Nixon was probably a factor. South American Communists are proud of their ability to organize, and the Venezuelan mobs awaiting him had been well prepared. As the vice-presidential aircraft entered its glide pattern over Maiquetía Airport on the morning of Tuesday, May 13, five crowds took up strategic positions. One was at the air terminal. Three others lay in wait for the motorcade on the twelve-mile road between the airfield and the Panteón Plaza in the center of Caracas, where Nixon was scheduled to lay a wreath on the tomb of Simón Bolívar. The last and largest of the crowds, in the plaza itself, was armed with Molotov cocktails. At one place or another, the ringleaders expected Nixon to be torn to pieces and burned. In Venezuela that is regarded as the most degrading death possible. The previous January it had been the fate of policemen defending the outgoing regime, and the fresh memory of that doubtless accounts for the reluctance of surviving police officers to come to Nixon's aid.

Official laxity went beyond that, however, and some aspects of it are still puzzling. American correspondents covering the Vice President's tour landed before he did and found that five hundred anti-Nixon teen-agers had been bused to the airfield and deployed on the terminal's observation deck. Obviously they were there to make trouble. Already they were shaking fists and shouting insults at the plane overhead. Yet when Secret Service agents asked the Venezuelan security chief to make them move, he refused, saying, "They are harmless. They have a right to demonstrate." He then ordered the motorcade to form in the street beyond the terminal instead of at the customary place on the field. That meant the Nixons would have to walk another hundred yards, through demonstrators. His subsequent explanation — that the sleek motorcade limousines would have detracted from the splendor of the honor guard — was preposterous.

Other suspicious figures that day included the bandleader at the airport, who knew that whenever he struck up the American or Venezuelan national anthem the Vice President would have to stand at attention, and the authorities responsible for safeguarding the motorcade route. These last were the most derelict of all. They told Americans responsible for the Vice President's safety that all traffic on it had been halted an hour before his arrival. This was untrue; heavy traffic on it continued. In addition, men and material for the three ambushes had been assembled at points where even a casual inspection would have revealed them. Junta complicity in the plot is unthinkable, but hope for a newsworthy episode is not. Latin American editors had noted that the disorders in Lebanon and elsewhere had attracted American attention and aid. If shaking the Vice President up would end U.S. complacency about its southern neighbors, they implied, it would not be wholly deplorable. Nixon later found this explanation for the poor security persuasive. He noted, with commendable restraint, that those responsible cannot have known much about mobs.

In descending an airplane ramp he customarily sized up a crowd to see what kind of reception he might expect. One glance at these shrieking youths told him, as he put it afterward, that "here was one place where we would have an altogether different situation than we ever had in any country I visited." The interpreter said, "They aren't friendly, Mr. Vice President." Nixon didn't have to understand Spanish to know that; the din was so great that he could scarcely hear the national anthems and the 19-gun salute for him. Before the last 105 shells had been fired he decided to skip the other airport formalities, notably the greeting to him and his response. To the interpreter he said, "Look, we're not going to do the mike scene," and to Venezuela's foreign minister, Oscar García Lutín, "Let's dispense with the customary speeches here and go directly to our cars. No one could possibly hear what we said over the noise of this mob."

It was then that he missed the limousines. He turned to where they should have been and discovered instead that the red carpet ran all the way to the terminal building, through it, and out the other side. There in the distance the cars gleamed. In between angry teen-agers were forming ranks and brandishing gamy fruit and other refuse. The bayonets of the honor guard might have been useful, but their commander was nowhere to be found.

The situation was rapidly deteriorating when the Americans found unexpected allies: thirty aircraft mechanics at the field. They cheered him as the others booed, making themselves so conspicuous that they briefly distracted the crowd. That gave the Americans time to slip into the terminal building. Coming out of it, Nixon and his wife were just below the observation deck when the bandleader decided to replay the Venezuelan national anthem. The Nixons froze. The Vice President had what he afterward called "the sensation that rain was falling"; then he realized that it was spittle. The saliva was coming from the crowd overhead, and some of it, from tobacco chewers, fell on the new red suit Pat Nixon had bought for the trip, staining it with splotches of a dirty brown. A rubber noisemaker struck Nixon on the face. The music ended. He took Pat's arm and they waded into the throng, toward the cars, following a flying wedge of Secret Service agents and Americans from the embassy.

With a sudden lurch the wedge shoved the Vice President into the first car and Pat into the second. Secret Service agents and interpreters followed. As they rapidly rolled up windows and wiped the saliva from their faces and clothes, they were joined by their host and hostess, Foreign Minister García Lutín in Nixon's limousine and Señora García Lutín in Mrs. Nixon's. Both were mortified. García Lutín, a gentle, mild-mannered man, tried to clean the worst of the spittle from the Vice President's suit. "Don't bother," Nixon said sharply. "I am going to burn these clothes as soon as I can get out of them." The foreign minister then tried to explain. He said, "The Venezuelan people have been without freedom so long that they tend now to express themselves more vigorously perhaps than they should. In our new government we do not want to do anything which would be interpreted as a suppression of freedom." Nixon replied, "If your new government doesn't have the guts and good sense to control a mob like the one at the airport, there soon will be no freedom for anyone in Venezuela."

The ride into Caracas was hair-raising. Led by a police escort and a press truck, they were going 40 mph on the Autopista, a modern dual-lane highway, while demonstrators on motorcycles and motor scooters zigzagged in and out of the motorcade, shouting, spitting, and throwing rotten fruit at the lead car. The windows had to remain closed. The air inside —

there was no air-conditioning — became stifling. Approaching the city, Nixon noticed that the sidewalks were deserted and the shops locked and shuttered. He was about to remark that this was ominous when he heard a dull thud. Momentarily he thought the driver had hit a pothole. Then he heard another thud and then another; the car was being hit by flying rocks. Simultaneously the chauffeur slammed on his brakes and skidded to a halt. They had reached the city limits and the first ambush. A tattered mass of people of all ages and descriptions came boiling out of a dingy alley nearby and rushed into the street hurling heavy stones. The road-block here was unfinished, and the driver found a way around it, but a few minutes later he braked again. On a slope where the Autopista curves into the city and becomes the lower end of the Avenida Sucre, a six-lane roadway with a center divider, it bisects one of the poorest neighborhoods in Caracas, and the second trap was there. A huge dump truck and several buses and cars had been parked in the street and abandoned. Another ragged throng carrying placards and clubs came howling down on the stalled motorcade. There were more rocks here, and several wild-eyed demonstrators flung themselves at Nixon's limousine.

Here, too, a detour was found, and the motorcade raced on, tense and silent, until, in the very center of Caracas and almost at their destination, the way was blocked by the most elaborate barricade yet. Three banks of buses, trucks, and automobiles had been parked directly in the path of the motorcade. The chauffeur could not cross the center island because there the traffic was one-way, toward them, and it was hopelessly jammed anyhow. For a few seconds nothing happened. The silence was eerie. Then Agent Jack Sherwood said under his breath, "Here they come."

Later estimates of this mob put it between two and five hundred. Running full tilt and spitting as they came, the demonstrators brandished axes, poles, and sections of pipe. Watching from the motorcade's press car, Earl Mazo of the *New York Herald Tribune* thought the spectacle looked "like a scene from the French Revolution." This was the ultimate in mobs, a killer mob. The saliva streaming down the windshield was so thick that the driver turned on the windshield wiper. The leaders rode pickaback, shouting instructions and leading the chant: "Muera Nixon! Muera Nixon!" Their obvious aim was to get the Vice President and drag him out, by opening the doors if possible, by smashing the windows if not. A large stone hit one window and stuck in the special glass, spraying splinters from it into García Lutín's face. He cried, "It's in my eye! My eye!" Another window, the one by the interpreter, was hit by a length of iron pipe. It did not give way entirely, but pieces of it struck the interpreter's mouth. Sherwood, hit, began to bleed. Fragments struck Nixon in the face. Another piece of pipe, thrust through the opening, wobbled toward him.

The foreign minister, almost hysterical, sobbed, "This is terrible, terrible." Nixon looked out the back window. As he remembered afterward, he was relieved to see that Pat was chatting away with Señora García Lutín, "as though the trouble was no worse than an afternoon traffic jam on the Holly-wood Freeway." Her driver had showed presence of mind by pushing his front bumper against the front limousine, so that the mob couldn't get at the Vice President through the rear window. The demonstrators, Nixon saw, were not interested in Pat's car. Those were the only bright spots, how-ever. The violence had continued here for twelve minutes, and now it seemed that it could have but one outcome.

Inside the limousine they heard one of the pickaback commanders out-side shout an order. The car began to rock. To those who knew the ways of mobs — as all here did — this was the most frightening development yet. Rioters unable to get in an automobile rock it, trying to turn it over and set it afire, cremating the occupants. The window beside Nixon gave way. Sherwood and another agent, in the front seat, drew their guns.

At that moment, about 12:45 P.M. on May 13, 1958, Richard Nixon's chances of surviving the afternoon were even slighter than he knew. Four blocks away at the Bolívar Tomb an American scouting party, which in-cluded a Secret Service agent, the embassy's military attachés, and the Vice President's administrative assistant, had arrived early to appraise the situation for the wreath-laying ceremony. They were aghast. Between six and eight thousand angry people were milling around. Here, as at the airport, police protection had disappeared. In the place of law officers, surly demonstrators were waiting at strategic corners on the Avenida Sucre. Their hostility toward Americans was obvious. The attachés being in uni-form, they were kicked, spat upon, and manhandled, and a window in an embassy station wagon was broken. Thoroughly alarmed, the scouting party sent back three separate warning messages in code over a pre-arranged radio network centered at Caracas police headquarters.

At the third barricade the motorcade was disintegrating. Drivers behind the leading cars who could find a way clear were wheeling out of line and racing away down side streets, leaving the embattled American Vice President and his escorts to their fate. So chaotic had the situation become that to this day there is confusion over how Nixon escaped. According to his recollection, the driver of the truck carrying the correspondents who were covering the tour "somehow . . . edged his way into the oncoming lane of traffic, clearing a path for us like a football blocker leading a ball carrier. Our driver took us down the wrong side of the street with Mrs. Nixon's car following behind us." Mazo of the *Herald Tribune* was on that truck, however, and in his memory, just as the violence seemed to be reaching a murderous climax, "some Venezuelan soldiers showed up. They made a narrow opening in the traffic tie-up. Mrs. Nixon's car followed close behind."

The limousines at that time were still headed for the Panteón Plaza. In the last block before reaching it the Vice President told the chauffeur to swerve down an alley and take off in the opposite direction. The foreign minister cried, "We can't leave our protection!" Nixon said, "If that's the kind of protection we're going to get, we're better off going it alone." Once they were safe on another main boulevard he ordered a stop so that he could talk to Pat and take stock. The lead car was a wreck; all its windows were broken and its fenders smashed, and everyone in it had been scratched or cut. At the same time, no one had been seriously injured. The ladies were unhurt and the way ahead was clear. They drove directly to the U.S. embassy residence, located on the top of a steep, easily defensible hill in Caracas's exclusive Las Lomas neighborhood. Nixon took his first nap in twelve years of public life, sleeping the sleep of the exhausted; the rest of the men turned the hill into a fortress. The embassy's marine detachment and the Secret Service agents were reinforced by sixty American military men who were in the country as instructors of the Venezuelan armed forces. All messages, packages, and letters coming to the embassy were screened by security men. Plans were secretly drawn to leave Caracas at 3 P.M. the following day, nine hours ahead of schedule, and at Maiquetía Airport other guards prepared to defend the vice-presidential aircraft against possible attack.

Meanwhile, back in Washington, orders had been cut for a fantastic rescue mission. Lacking information about the Nixon party and warned to expect the worst, President Eisenhower had dispatched to Venezuela six destroyers, a guided-missile cruiser, and an aircraft carrier equipped to land marines by helicopter. A thousand marines and paratroopers were suiting up at Guantánamo Bay and on Puerto Rico, and Air Force fighters and bombers had been alerted to stand by. Nixon himself knew nothing of this. Dulles had cabled him the details, but this message, like the others that day, never reached its destination. The Nixons were dining alone in the privacy of their room at the embassy when the ambassador interrupted them. Word of the sensational new development had just reached him via a news report. The Pentagon had announced it at 6:05 P.M., explaining in a communiqué that "The movement is being undertaken so these troops will be in a position to cooperate with the Venezuelan government if assistance is requested."

This was an unexpected propaganda gift to the Venezuelan extremists responsible for the mobs. They had been in disgrace, but now they were almost forgotten as all Latin America protested the armada, which awakened in them the worst fears of North American imperialism. Nixon and the ambassador quickly issued a joint statement explaining that everyone was safe and there was no need for outside help. Next morning, when communications had been restored, the President was able to telephone the Vice President, who reassured him.

At Washington National Airport fifteen thousand people cheered Nixon as he came down the ramp. Eisenhower was there, accompanied by his entire cabinet. Nixon spoke briefly, saying that the best part of going away was coming home and that most of the people he had seen in his South American travels had been friendly.

Lima and Caracas had tested the Vice President and tempered him, but the effect of the incident on Nixon's popularity was as brief as it was immense. In June 1958, a month later, the Gallup poll showed him leading Adlai Stevenson for the first time and running a dead heat with Kennedy. It was the high point of his popularity in the 1950s. By the end of autumn it would be a memory. The Republicans were in trouble, and as their ranking politician he was, too.

Society knows few greater satisfactions than the discovery of a puritan caught practicing what he has preached against, and rarely does it happen so startlingly as in the month after Richard Nixon's return from Venezuela. The scandal was accompanied by a symbol as memorable as any in the influence-peddling 1940s. For 1958 not only produced the hula hoop, the big TV quiz shows, and Alec Guinness in neighborhood theaters showing the Japs how to build that bridge over the River Kwai; it was also the year of the vicuña coat. Before that summer possibly one American in ten thousand could have told you that the vicuña is a small fleet-footed hoofed mammal found in the Andes from Ecuador to Bolivia and much hunted for the wool of its fine lustrous undercoat, which is woven into fine cloth. By July 4 every taxpayer knew that a vicuña topcoat was to men what mink was to women — warm, handsome, stylish, and a status symbol. The taxpayer knew, if for no other reason, because every Democrat running for office was telling the vicuña story.

It is a curious fact that no one ever cleared up the question of how much vicuña wool there was in the vicuña coat, although that was one reason the government had brought the manufacturer, Bernard Goldfine, to book; he had been putting a "90% wool, 10% vicuña" label on cloth that actually contained some nylon. This and all other aspects of the story were eclipsed by testimony that the White House had intervened in Goldfine's behalf and that he, in appreciation, had seen to it that one of his top-quality, five-hundred-dollar coats hung in the closet of the assistant to the President of the United States, the former governor of New Hampshire, Sherman Adams. Other expressions of Goldfine's gratitude had included the gift to Adams of a $2,400 Oriental rug from Macy's and picking up the tab on twenty-one occasions between 1955 and May 1958 when members of the Adams family had stayed at Boston's elegant Sheraton Plaza Hotel, running up bills totaling $3,096.56. He had also paid for Adams's stays at the Waldorf Astoria in Manhattan. Goldfine had then claimed all of these expensive favors as business expenses on his tax returns.

They were deductible, under Internal Revenue regulations, provided some "ordinary and necessary" benefit or advantage had flowed to Goldfine businesses from the expenditure. It had, and he could prove it. The two men were very close. Subpoenaed telephone records were to reveal that over a six-month period Goldfine had placed 43 long distance calls to Adams, about one every four days. Adams had made countless others to the textile manufacturer and in his behalf. On December 30, 1953, the President's chief of staff had called Federal Trade Commission chairman Edward F. Howrey — who owed his appointment to Adams — to ask the source for the complaint against Goldfine for mislabeling textiles. On April 14, 1955, when the manufacturer was again under investigation for the same charge, Adams used his influence to get Goldfine an appointment with Howrey. During it, Goldfine wielded the name of his friend in a heavy-handed manner. "Please get me Sherman Adams on the line," he ordered a secretary in a voice loud enough to be heard in the next office. "Sherm, I'm over here at the FTC," he said on the phone. "I was well treated over here."

The following year Adams had asked Gerald Morgan, the White House special counsel, to ask Security and Exchange lawyers for confidential information about an SEC investigation of Goldfine's East Boston Company — a violation of the commission's rules. Later John Fox, publisher of the *Boston Post*, was an especially damaging witness. He testified that Goldfine regarded his friendship with the President's assistant as a license to make deals. "He told me," Fox said in one of his less plausible moments, "that as long as he had Sherman Adams in his pocket he could do it." Fox further testified, "I asked Mr. Goldfine just what his trouble . . . was and he told me they had accused him of mislabeling." Later, "as a matter of idle curiosity," Fox asked if Adams had taken care of the FTC matter, and Goldfine "told me that he had."

On that rare afternoon in June when the first choice Adams-Goldfine revelations were entered into the record of the House Special Subcommittee on Legislative Oversight, the presidential aide was delivering a baccalaureate address to the Holderness School for boys in New Hampshire on "the questions the Bible tells us shall be asked on Judgment Day." Adams had long been interested in what was going to happen to sinners on that Day. Democrats knew him as the stern moralist who had decried minks, freezers, and influence peddling during Truman's tenure, calling that administration an "Augean stables" in a memorable January 1952 speech and promising that Eisenhower would end such corruption. "Here is the man to do it," he had said. "The kind of people with whom he has surrounded himself is answer enough for that."

Conservative Republicans also resented Adams. They remembered his accusations that Taft was stealing GOP delegate votes in Texas. "Thou shalt not steal," he had cried, wagging a finger at them. To them he was the man who had delivered a ruthless judgment against Air Force Secretary Harold Talbott because he had solicited business for his efficiency-engineering firm on official Air Force stationery. One of the bitterest ironies of the Goldfine disclosures was that White House secretaries, one of whom worked within seventy-five feet of President Eisenhower's desk, had accepted cash gifts from the textile manufacturer ranging from $35 to $150. Until now that would have been enough to bring instant dismissal from Eisenhower's chief of staff, who had warned them to be on the lookout for improper requests for influence. Now they could not even be reprimanded. In the West Wing of the White House members of the President's staff moved on tiptoe and spoke in whispers, as though someone in the First Family were gravely ill.

How had it happened? All his life Adams had been, as his eighty-two-year-old father put it, "sound as a dollar and square as a brick." His wife Rachel fondly called him "the Great Stone Face." In the White House he scrupulously paid for office stamps he put on personal letters and insisted that he be billed for personal phone calls. Until recently he had still used stationery headed "Sherman Adams, Governor of New Hampshire," with "ex-" typed in. He was always at his desk by· 7:30 in the morning — that had been true in New Hampshire, too, where he had been known to wade through blizzards to get to work on time — and any member of the staff who came in after the office had opened would hear his sharp call: "You're late to work this morning!" In using the telephone he refused to waste valuable time saying "Hello" or "Good-bye." He began talking the instant the other person picked up the receiver, and when he had said his piece he promptly hung up, cutting off the other fellow in mid-sentence. No man had ever been more trusted by a President. He checked out every piece of paper, every visitor, and every decision headed for Eisenhower's desk, giving Ike clear options for choice, as in a short list of men eligible for a cabinet post. "Whatever I have to do," the President had told a press conference, "he has in some measure to do." Adams had never betrayed that enormous trust. How, then, had he wound up in the sticky embrace of a man like Bernard Goldfine?

Much of the answer lies in the fact that there were two Bernard Goldfines. One of them was a cheap, devious manipulator, always in and out of trouble with the government and capable of exploiting any relationship. That was the Goldfine who had attracted the interest of the House committee. But Adams had never met that man. The Goldfine he had known ever since the war was a self-made, humble, eager-to-please immigrant, a diamond in the rough eager to use his wealth in good causes. In Adams's words he was "an upright and honest citizen, trustworthy and reliable." The suggestion that he would stoop to underhanded practices was absurd. He didn't need to be underhanded; he was already rich. The Goldfine empire consisted of six textile mills in Maine, Vermont, New Hampshire, and Massachusetts and two real estate firms, East Boston Company and the Boston Port Development Company. Each year he gave $50,000 to charities. He, his wife, and his four children lived in a fashionable home in Boston's Chestnut Hill suburb.

Adams had been introduced to him by Norris Cotton, U.S. Senator from

New Hampshire, as a public-spirited millionaire who refused to follow other textile manufacturers in the exodus south to cheap southern labor and taxes. Adams made inquiries and found that Goldfine was known to be a sound businessman with a good reputation in his trade; he treated his employees well, paid good wages, and had never been in trouble with the textile union. Once he had held a good-will conference between representatives of labor and management. It had been attended by the governors of Maine, New Hampshire, Vermont, and Massachusetts. His friends and admirers included Cotton, Senator Frederick Payne of Maine, Speaker of the House John McCormack, Mayor John Hynes of Boston, and John Steelman and Maurice Tobin of the Truman administration.

The congressional investigation of Goldfine's manipulations revealed that some of these friendships had seamy sides. He owned the house in which Cotton lived, and he had made Payne's purchase of a home possible by lending him $3,500 for a down payment without interest, which had never been repaid. His relationship with Fox had begun when he had taken the extraordinary step of extending $400,000 credit to the *Post* in exchange for an editorial endorsement of Massachusetts Governor Paul A. Dever's campaign for reelection. Recently the Goldfine-Fox friendship had soured, which may account for the incriminating passages in Fox's testimony.

Goldfine and Adams had become and remained steadfast friends. Rachel Adams and Charlotte Goldfine were also close to one another. The four of them often spent weekends together — in his memoirs Adams describes Goldfine as "a man with a lot of good fun in him" — and when young Solomon Goldfine almost failed at Dartmouth, "Uncle Sherm" sternly lectured him and put him on the right track. In this context the gifts become more understandable. They went both ways; the Goldfines had an oil painting from Rachel, and Goldfine wore a gold Le Coultre wristwatch inscribed "To B.G. from S.A. Jan. 20, 1953." Adams was startled to learn that Goldfine had deducted the hotel bills on his tax returns. He had been under the impression that the suites were rented permanently by one of Goldfine's companies and would have been empty if Adams hadn't used them. As for the favors he had done for Goldfine, they weren't at all improper, he said. He hadn't guided him. Nor had he known that he had violated an FTC rule by making information available to his friend. In any event, that had been the extent of the accommodation. He would have done the same for any businessman bewildered by Washington bureaucracies.

White House correspondents hammered at Hagerty: "Does this indicate a departure from the administration's previous attitude toward freeloading by high officials?" He ducked: "I don't know what you mean by that. . . . This is a personal friend, if that's what you're talking about." They relentlessly pursued him: "It's all right for a personal friend?" He dodged again: "I stick with the letter that the governor issued. The facts are as they are."

The presidential assistant's failure to grasp the interpretation which others might put on his relationship with Goldfine stemmed in part from an inability to see himself as others might see him. Adams knew Adams to be honest; that was that. So was his friend; it couldn't be otherwise. Those close to the former governor believed that he had been flattered by the admiration of the Lithuanian immigrant who had followed the Horatio Alger course to the top. Adams's bedrock New England upbringing prevented him from being free with his own money, but he could not resist the lavish attentions of an openhanded big spender. Thus he had drifted thoughtlessly across a line.

Testifying before the subcommittee on June 7, a full week after the disclosure of his relationship with Goldfine, Adams acknowledged that he had been "imprudent." He said, "If . . . I have in any way so conducted myself as to cast any semblance of doubt upon such conduct, I can only say that the error was one of judgment and certainly not of intent." The question was whether that concession from him was adequate now. He had made it only after he had found that it was not enough to sit behind the White House gates and issue a statement attacking the "unwarranted and unfair insinuations" of his accusers. Newspaper editors, vigilant as always on the issue of morality in public servants, were reminding their readers that on May 4, 1956, President Eisenhower had said:

> If anyone ever comes to any part of this government . . . claiming some privilege . . . on the basis that he is part of my family or of my friends, that he has any connection with the White House, he is to be thrown out instantly . . . I can't believe that anybody on my staff would ever be guilty of an indiscretion. But if ever anything came to my attention of that kind, any part of this government, that individual would be gone.

Now, two years and fifty-five days later, Eisenhower faced 257 reporters in the Indian Treaty Room and doggedly declared that "Anyone who knows Sherman Adams has never had any doubt of his personal integrity and honesty. No one has believed that he could be bought." Adams had been accused of imprudence, and he had used that word himself. Ike said, "Now, the utmost prudence must necessarily be used by everyone attached to the White House . . . Carelessness must be avoided." But a valuable presidential aide should not be lost because he had skidded once, especially in these circumstances:

> I personally like Governor Adams. I admire his abilities. I respect him because of his personal and official integrity. I need him.
> Admitting the lack of that careful prudence in this incident . . . I believe with my whole heart that he is an invaluable public servant doing a difficult job efficiently, honestly, and tirelessly.

Ike had gone over the statement with Hagerty, who had approved it, believing that it would take the pressure off Adams. Only afterward did

THE CRUSADE FALTERS | 839

the presidential press secretary see the three damaging words leap from the pages: *I need him.* In a stroke the President had allowed his critics to depict him as a weak old man who could not govern without the help of an indispensable man and had permitted an exception to the White House rule that anyone on his staff involved in improper conduct should be fired.

The President, then, had gone bail for Adams's faith in his friend and benefactor Bernard Goldfine. Much would now depend upon the manner of the man with whom he had been imprudent. That came next and it destroyed Adams. The ensuing sessions on Capitol Hill turned into a burlesque. It began when Goldfine strode into the hearing room of the House subcommittee brandishing a twenty-five-page introductory statement. He had already angered the committee by releasing the text to the press at 7 A.M., three hours before he was scheduled to testify. Unperturbed and jaunty in a dark blue suit, wearing a blue silk tie initialed BG, he took the chair to read it. Then he removed his gold watch and passed it to the committeemen ("providing I get it back"), explaining, "The watch I am wearing now, on the back of it is written 'to B.G.' — that means Bernard Goldfine — 'from S.A.' — that's Governor Sherman Adams — dated 'Jan. 20, 1953,' and we all know that date. That is the inauguration date President Eisenhower was inaugurated." In the visitors' section Rachel Adams winced. She had just realized that that was how their friend had been introducing himself to strangers, including federal officials, all these years.

In the spectacle that followed, the star millionaire was assisted by a worshipful secretary named Mildred Paperman; an entourage of lawyers headed by Roger Robb, who had been the heavy-handed cross-examiner of J. Robert Oppenheimer; Tex McCrary, a Manhattan press agent; and a press headquarters in Washington's Sheraton-Carlton Hotel featuring caviar, free whiskey, and "Press Receptionist" Bea Duprey, a Boston Venus whose most conspicuous activity was urging reporters to get her measurements (35-22-35) right. There was also a New York flack named Jack Lotto, who identified himself as "a former ace reporter for INS" and who, in his press releases, spelled his client's name "Bernard Goldfein." Late one night Lotto caught two spies bugging the office from the next room. One of them was a private detective, Baron (name, not title) Ignatius Sacklette, who had been working for the subcommittee. He was instantly dismissed. The other was Drew Pearson's legman, Jack Anderson. Pearson refused to fire Anderson. He said, "I need him."

On the first page of Goldfine's opening statement McCrary had printed in block letters the message: YOU WILL BE GREAT! In reality Goldfine was awful. McCrary had also underlined words to be emphasized. Instead of stressing them, Goldfine yelled them. Periodically McCrary had written "Glass of water." Unfortunately he had neglected to check out the committee room. There were no glasses there, only floppy paper cups, with the result that from time to time his client peered around in confusion. But neither McCrary nor any of the others was responsible for the devastating impression Goldfine made. He appeared to be a sleazy, amoral, double-shuffle con man because he was, in fact, a sleazy, amoral, double-shuffle con man.

His voice rasping and his tone belligerent, he told how he had clawed his way upward in New England's savage textile and real estate world. It was a world of which Eisenhower and Adams knew little. Whenever they thought of a businessman they thought of George Humphrey. Goldfine was of a different breed. Waving the watch and calling Fox a character assassin, he backpedaled frantically when committee counsel questioned him about his troubles with federal regulatory agencies. No, he had no records; "Paperwork has been out of my line." Ask his secretary; "After all, I'm not a bookkeeper. She is." Loyal Miss Paperman, seated a few feet away, piped up at this point in an attempt to explain why there were no records, and Robb snarled, "Keep quiet, keep quiet, keep *quiet!*" Begging the congressmen for understanding, Goldfine explained that Adams had merely given him directions to "these giant federal agencies where a little man gets lost without some kind of guidance from a friend."

At this juncture the subcommittee trapped him in a lie. In his opening statement he had flatly said, "The first difficulty that any of my mills ever had with the Federal Trade Commission was in November . . . 1953. Neither I nor anyone else in our companies had had prior experience with the FTC in matters of this type." His point, essential to his case and Adams's plausibility, was that when the FTC charged him with mislabeling in November 1953 he was so mystified that he needed Sherman Adams to explain what it was all about. Now subcommittee investigators produced proof that Goldfine had been inundated in 1942 and every year thereafter with FTC complaints accusing him of using labels that made his products appear to be of a higher quality than they were. At the hearing he answered weakly that this was just more paperwork and, besides, that they were "minor matters" and therefore not likely to get to his level. The congressmen didn't challenge him. They knew what else was coming.

Among the topics that Goldfine and Paperman were keeping quiet about, on the ground that they had no files, was a sum of $776,879.16, all of it in treasurer's checks and cashier's checks dating back to 1941 and, as of May 8, 1958, still uncashed. People in shady enterprises like money that way because, among other things, such checks have no time limit. Also, the name of a bank official, not that of the person footing the bill, appears on them. Finally, public officials fearful of cashing them because of the possibility of scandal may put them up as prime collateral for loans.

Goldfine refused to answer questions about his treasurer's and cashier's checks, saying that they were irrelevant. The committee counsel countered that they could hardly be called that, inasmuch as thirty of those which had been cashed had been given to legislative aides on Capitol Hill. The names of men close to John McCormack and Styles Bridges entered the transcript. Goldfine replied: "At Christmas time these are all checks that we have sent at different times to some of the poor workers who work in different offices at Christmas time. If that is something that is bad, I would like to be told about it."

He was told that it was bad to ease in and out of firms through dummy organizations and straw men, bad to match loans, bad to disregard federal and state regulations designed to protect the public, bad to subsidize a pack of big and little politicians who thus became indebted to him, and bad to build an incredible record of litigation, including 89 lawsuits in the Boston area alone. It was bad, and it was also criminal, to plunder his own companies, thereby defrauding fellow shareholders, and there had been a lot of that.

As the hearings progressed, Goldfine played more and more to the gallery, blustering and shouting his answers. He tried to argue that his infractions of the law had been insignificant, that he was the victim of legalisms — neglecting to file an annual report with the Vermont secretary of state, in one instance, and failure to take up his legal responsibilities as a company officer in others. As in most cases of financial skulduggery, the path of guilt was sometimes hard to follow, but plenty of Goldfine swindles were easy to understand. Operating through his secretary, who held key posts as treasurer and director in his firms, he repeatedly helped himself to generous sums of stockholder money. The pretenses for taking it varied. It would be called a loan, a sales commission, or repayment for nonexistent expenses ($25,475 in the case of a local firm dealing in real estate). Sometimes there was no excuse at all. The cash just disappeared. Neither he nor Miss Paperman could account for some $89,000 taken out in the late 1940s. She blandly suggested that the bank had "made mistakes in the past, and these can be an error." It was hard to pin down exchanges because she and her employer were dealing every day with hundreds of thousands of dollars in liquid assets. In one respect ominous for Goldfine, however, the particulars didn't matter. Whatever had happened, he clearly owed the government far more than he had claimed on his tax returns.*

Afterward Adams wrote of his relationship with Goldfine that "I knew little or nothing about the details of his business dealings. I did not learn of his tax arrears until some of the facts began to unravel as a result of the hearings by the Legislative Oversight Committee; nor did I know about his troubles with his East Boston Company's financial operations." No one, of course, had suggested that he had. The question was one of judgment. The unavoidable conclusion was that Eisenhower's chief of staff had been gulled and the office of the Presidency demeaned. He would have to step down. It was both a public and a private tragedy. Adams had brought a rare talent to the White House, and one wonders how he could have fashioned an enduring social relationship with a cheat. Goldfine's indifference to the implications of his conduct is astonishing. Even after Adams had set up his

*Goldfine was sentenced to a year in jail and fined $1,000 for contempt of Congress following the 1958 hearings. The sentence was suspended and he was placed on probation.

appointment with the chairman of the FTC, he let matters drift until three of his firms had been slapped with "cease and desist" orders for label violations. His concept of friendship appears to have been a lopsided swap. In return for a rug, a coat, and payment of some $3,000 in hotel bills, he had compromised Adams's honor. A friend said of Goldfine, "He's a name dropper and a Scotch drinker, and he had a weakness of talking too much, dropping too many names and things." Now he had set in motion a chain of events which could only end in the dropping of Adams's name from the White House roster.

It didn't happen at once. Ike's executive officer was too valuable; he wouldn't give him up without a struggle. Another member of the White House staff explained, "Adams has been with the President since 1952, and he knows how he thinks better than any other man. He has talked with the President about policy more than any other man. The governor has got tucked away in his head all the policy decisions the President has ever made, all the policy questions that have been laid aside for the right time, all the questions that have been rejected. It would be impossible for any new man to operate like Adams operates. And the new man could never accumulate the knowledge that Adams has."

After the second week of the crisis — for that is what it amounted to — Ike and Adams persuaded themselves that the problem would go away. The President told Hagerty to announce meaningfully that "the Governor is back at his desk at White House business." In other words, Adams was staying.

Then came the Goldfine circus. When the House of Representatives voted August 13 to cite Adams's friend for contempt, the governor was through. A vast army of editorial writers and cartoonists, led by those who had supported Eisenhower in his two presidential campaigns, was waging an all-out war on him, and as the summer waned it grew more intense. That was the noisiest threat to Adams. It was secondary, however. The heart of the problem was political.

Democratic indignation was almost ritualistic — "I am tired of pious preaching from Sherman Adams," Adlai Stevenson said — but Republican censure came as a surprise to Eisenhower and Adams. It shouldn't have. This was an election year. Knowland, fighting a desperate battle for the California governorship, suggested that the President "should carefully weigh as to whether Adams has so hurt his usefulness that it might be harmful." Arthur Watkins of Utah was more blunt. "In the light of the record as measured by the high standards of ethics set by both the President and Mr. Adams," he said, "there seems to be no other possible conclusion than that Mr. Adams' usefulness is seriously impaired, if not completely destroyed."

The first test at the polls in 1958 came on September 8, when Maine voted. The Democratic slogan there was "Payne of Maine is mainly on the wane." If that was so, it was important; the results would be regarded as a measure of voter reaction to Goldfinian ethics. The Maine senator had never provided a convincing explanation of how he had acquired the $3,500 from Goldfine six years earlier, and his opponent, forty-four-year-old Governor Edmund S. Muskie, had made that the chief issue. The results made terrible reading in the White House. An incredible 20,000 registered Republicans had stayed home. Not only did Muskie become Maine's first popularly elected Democratic senator; his plurality was twice as large as he had predicted. The GOP slate had gone down with Payne. The Democrats had captured the statehouse, two of Maine's three congressional seats, and twelve seats in the state legislature. Senator Margaret Chase Smith said, "We took a shellacking." Hagerty said, "The President views it as I do. We took a beating," and Meade Alcorn, Republican national chairman, said that the results should "alert every Republican in the land to the urgency of an all-out effort on November 4."

Mainly it inspired them to redouble their insistence that Eisenhower dismiss Adams. "As Maine goes, so goes Adams," the Washington press corps prophesied. Alcorn's phone rang constantly. Goldwater said he was afraid that "the harm has already been done." Knowland, lagging now in the opinion polls, declared that Ike's assistant should resign "immediately," and New York's Congressman Kenneth Keating, running for the Senate, added that "the good of the country" required it.

Adams was a marked man, and he knew it. The pressure became intolerable, and he took a few days off for a fishing trip in southeast Canada with Rachel and Jerry and Alice Persons. They were up there in the stark beauty of the Miramichi valley when the boom was lowered upon him.

Nixon had called upon Ike with a painful message from virtually all Republicans running for Congress; Adams, they felt, was a sea anchor dragging them down. The President had promised to reconsider the subject. Then Alcorn reported that the party's big donors were keeping their checkbooks closed until "the Adams mess" had been cleaned up. The Republican National Committee was meeting in Chicago. Eisenhower asked Alcorn to make one more appraisal of party opinion. When the chairman returned shaken — Richard Simpson of Pennsylvania was threatening to lead a mutiny if Adams stayed another week — the President capitulated. He called it "the most hurtful, the hardest, the most heartbreaking decision" of his Presidency, and he refused to do the firing himself. He told Alcorn, "You've got to handle it. It's your job, the dirtiest I can give you."

Adams, meantime, was finding that not even the lonely Miramichi country was remote enough to hide him; Canadian reporters were asking him when he would resign. It seemed to be the only question people asked him any more. Then Gerry Morgan phoned from the White House and, according to Adams's recollection, said "he thought I ought to come back to

Washington because Nixon and Meade Alcorn . . . wanted to talk with me." He knew why: "So I went." At 8 A.M. the following day he was at his desk, ready for the blindfold and the last cigarette.

Nixon told him that most Republican candidates and political leaders would, as a matter of self-preservation, repudiate him, and that would make his position impossible. Alcorn spoke for an hour, mostly about GOP contributions drying up and the incipient revolt within the National Committee. Adams sat impassively in his great leather chair, his head thrown back, staring at the ceiling and nibbling a stem of his glasses. Then, with a weary nod, he agreed to go.

In *Six Crises* Nixon recalled how the 1958 election served "to virtually erase the public memory of my success in Caracas and put in its place an image of failure with which my name was associated." Friends urged him to avoid the campaign, since a Republican defeat was inevitable; Dewey said, "You have done enough for Republican candidates." But Eisenhower told him, "I would give a year of my salary if we could win either the House or the Senate." The President, "by personal and political inclination," did not want to become enmeshed in political battles which could destroy his ability to work constructively with Congress, Nixon wrote; therefore, "if anyone was to carry the major load for political cross-country campaigning, I was the one who had to do it."

> I could not stand aside and see my fellow Republicans go down to disastrous defeat. I had to risk my political prestige to avoid a disaster, if possible, knowing full well, as in 1954, we would probably lose, and I would be the big-name target for the defeat. . . . I ended up stumping more than 25,000 miles in twenty-five states.

What this account omits is the character of the Republican campaign and the zeal with which the President joined it in the last two weeks. Nixon's line of attack was narrow and highly partisan. The Democratic party, he warned, was a haven for "socialism" and "left-wing extremists." He accused the Democrats of "retreat and appeasement," scorned "the Acheson foreign policy" that "resulted in war," and rejoiced in the "military strength and diplomatic firmness" of the Republican administration. The President, appalled at first, told White House correspondents that he deplored "this kind of thing." That stirred up conservative protests, which turned him around so completely that he publicly praised his bellicose Vice President: "No one can do this more effectively than you." By the end of October Ike was sharing Nixon's mood. He vowed that "there will be no appeasing Communist aggression while I am President," declared that "the so-called missile gap is being rapidly filled," and called the Democrats "political radicals" and "self-styled liberals" with "the irresistible impulse . . . to squander money — your money."

On November 4 the roof fell in on the Republicans. They lost twelve seats in the Senate, forty-eight seats in the House, and thirteen of the twenty-one contests for governor. Knowland went down, and so, unexpectedly, did John Bricker in Ohio. Even rock-ribbed Republican Vermont was lost; for the first time in one hundred and six years a Democrat would represent it in Congress. Nixon summed up the nationwide results: "It was the worst defeat in history ever suffered by a party having control of the White House."

Three races were of national interest. In Massachusetts John F. Kennedy's margin was 874,608 — the largest ever for a candidate for any office in the state, and the largest in any senatorial race in 1958. Barry Goldwater ran against the Democratic tide in Arizona and was reelected decisively. And Rockefeller, even more impressively, rolled up a landslide plurality of a half-million votes. A TV commentator observed, "The big winner in this election is Nelson Rockefeller; the big loser, Richard Nixon." On November 9 New York's Governor-elect flew south to rest on his Venezuelan estate. At Maiquetía Airport, where the Nixons' baptism of Caracas spit had begun six months earlier, reporters asked him about Nixon. Rockefeller replied, *"No tengo nada que ver con Nixon"* — "I have nothing to do with Nixon."

Late Fifties Montage

Best actor of 1958: David Niven in *Separate Tables*

The Horse's Mouth   *The Inn of the Sixth Happiness*

The Long Hot Summer   *The Brothers Karamazov*

Come and click with Dick
The one that none can lick
He's the man to lead the U.S.A....
So let's all click with Dick

CRISIS IN FRANCE FADES AS DE GAULLE TAKES HELM

Best actor of 1959: Charlton Heston in **Ben-Hur**

Best actress of 1959: Simone Signoret in **Room at the Top**

Some Like It Hot

Just you wait, 'Enry 'Iggins, just you wait
You'll be sorry, but your tears will come too late
You'll be broke and I'll have money
Will I 'elp you? Don't be funny
Just you wait, 'Enry 'Iggins, just you wait

THE STATUS SEEKERS

An exploration of class behavior in America and the hidden barriers that affect you, your community, your future

VANCE PACKARD

Author of
The Hidden Persuaders

Now — Zenith brings you portable TV's biggest picture .... 21" Super Screen

Babies are FRAGILE — Handle with JOHNSON'S

Pillow Talk
North by Northwest

The Apartment   *Inherit the Wind*   *Sunrise at Campobello*
I'm All Right, Jack   *Hiroshima, Mon Amour*

The Nun's Story
On the Beach

GET RID OF TIRED BLOOD!

Take Geritol. It builds iron power in your blood fast.

MAXWELL HOUSE coffee: *TASTES* as good as it *SMELLS*

DURKEE'S Instant Minced Onion

"Funniest Musical in Years"
— *N.Y. News*

BEST SELLERS: Nonfiction
The Rise and Fall of the Third Reich by William L. Shirer
Only in America by Harry Golden
Born Free by Joy Adamson
How I Made $2,000,000 in the Stock Market by Nicholas Darvas
Aku, Aku by Thor Heyerdahl

BYE BYE BIRDIE

CHITA RIVERA   DICK VAN DYKE

Best actor of 1960: Burt Lancaster in *Elmer Gantry*

Best actress of 1960: Elizabeth Taylor in *BUtterfield 8*

54th Street Theater
150 West 54th Street

Anatomy of a Murder

K-E-Double-N-E-D-Y
Jack's the nation's favorite guy
Everyone wants to back Jack
Jack is on the right track

BEST SELLERS: Fiction
Doctor Zhivago by Boris Pasternak
Exodus by Leon Uris
Advise and Consent by Allen Drury
The Ugly American by William J. Lederer and Eugene Burdick
Lolita by Vladimir Nabokov

BAN *takes the worry out of being close*

noisiest potato chips in the world

1ST CLASS POSTAGE UP FROM 3c to 4c

little old wine-maker me

Hang down your head, Tom Dooley
Hang down your head and cry
Hang down your head, Tom Dooley
Poor boy, you're bound to die

MOSCOW, NEW YORK START JET PASSENGER SERVICE

POWER FAILURE HITS 500,000 NEW YORKERS: ANOTHER BIG BLACKOUT IS TERMED UNLIKELY

	1950	1960
U.S. homeowners	23,600,000	32,800,000
Powers mowers sold	1,000,000	2,600,000
Automatic washing machine sales	1,700,000	2,600,000
Children five to fourteen	24,300,000	35,500,000
Little Leagues	776	5,700
Girl Scouts, Brownies	1,800,000	4,000,000
Bowling lanes	52,500	108,000
Gallons of gin	6,000,000	19,000,000
Gallons of vodka	100,000	9,000,000
Pounds of aspirin	12,000,000	18,000,000

Things Go Better with **Coke**

Buy **Beech-Nut**, by Gum.

Any thirst you can get
7-UP can quench

REAL GUSTO
In a Great Light Beer
SCHLITZ

TWENTY-SIX

Tattoo for the General

H L. MENCKEN once observed that journalism is an inexact science. The last years of the Eisenhower era where rich in proof of it.

Six weeks after the Democrats' off-year sweep a special Arkansas legislative committee disclosed that it had "definitely proved that there was Communist influence" in the Little Rock integration dispute. The chairman, Representative Paul Van Dalsen, said that the committee's three-day public hearing had alerted Arkansas to the threat of Communism, and a colleague of Van Dalsen confidently predicted that American Negroes would reject invitations to join any new demonstrations instigated by the National Association for the Advancement of Colored People and "backed by the Communist Party." Racial peace, he said, lay dead ahead.

Clark Kerr, newly installed as the president of the University of California, took a close look at college students in 1959 and said, "The employers will love this generation. . . . They are going to be easy to handle. There aren't going to be any riots."

That November the Roman Catholic bishops of the United States, in opposing the use of federal money to promote artificial birth control at home and abroad, ridiculed the assertion that American Catholics would gradually come to accept contraception.

NBC, looking for a clean-cut young American to counterbalance Elvis Presley, chose Charles Van Doren, a $4,400-a-year Columbia University instructor who had just won $129,000 in fourteen spectacular weeks on the network's biggest quiz show, *Twenty-one.* Hired at $50,000 a year as an NBC consultant and *Today* show commentator, he edited an inspirational anthology, *Letters to Mothers.* In his own mail, three of every four letters were from parents or teachers grateful to him for the shining example he was setting for the country's youth. Late in 1958, when a New York County grand jury began looking into charges that quiz shows were rigged, reporters converged on his smart Greenwich Village home. He scorned the idea. "I never got any kind of hint or help," he said, "and as far as I know, nobody else ever did on the program." When they persisted he said sternly, "It is an insult to keep asking me these questions."

Whereupon Negroes, college students, Catholics, and Charles Van Doren proceeded to surprise those who thought they knew them.

The hope that black militancy would go away died a sudden death on February 1, 1960, when four black students at the North Carolina Agricultural and Technical College entered an F. W. Woolworth store on South Elm Street in nearby Greensboro, made several small purchases, took seats at the lunch counter, and ordered coffee. In conformity with the southern laws and tradition requiring segregation, the management ignored them. They stayed in silence until closing time, and the next morning they appeared at the counter again, this time with five black friends. They called it a sit-in. Each succeeding day there were more of them. Calm and well-behaved, ignoring catcalling white youths who dangled Confederate flags in front of them and flipped cigarette butts at them, the young blacks let it be known that they were going to stay until they got their coffee.

If it had been up to the store's Greensboro employees, they would never have been served. But Woolworth is a nationwide chain, and that was what they were counting on. In North Carolina the movement spread to Durham, Winston-Salem, Charlotte, Raleigh, and High Point, and outside the state lunch counters were occupied in Nashville, Chattanooga, Tallahassee, Richmond, and Rock Hill, South Carolina. Over the next fortnight blacks staged Woolworth sit-ins in fifteen cities, and in Boston four hundred students from Harvard, Brandeis, Boston University, and MIT picketed twelve Woolworth stores. That pleased the Greensboro blacks. What happened next astonished them and the country. Demonstrators appeared at Walgreen, S. H. Kress, W. T. Grant, and Liggett lunch counters. Englewood, New Jersey, sympathizers took up a collection to back the demonstrators. Yale Divinity School students marched through downtown New Haven in support. Exasperated dime store managers raised their coffee prices to a dollar a cup for Negroes, unscrewed the seats, and threatened to close the lunch counters. Nothing worked; the demonstrators met them at every turn with new forms of passive resistance. Then the movement leaped from the stools to every segregated facility in society. There were sleep-ins in motel lobbies, play-ins in parks, read-ins in public libraries, watch-ins in movie theaters, bet-ins in bingo halls, sweat-ins in Turkish baths, and, when spring approached, swim-ins on restricted beaches.

On May 10 the blacks scored their first victory when lunch counters were desegregated in six Nashville stores, the first such general action in any southern state except Texas. All spring battles of attrition were fought throughout the South, with the color bar moving a foot here, a yard there, and pressure on the diehards mounting. On June 5 the blacks' Southern

Regional Council reported desegregated counters in nine scattered border cities; there had been no violence in any of them, and none of the merchants had been hurt by the threat of retaliatory boycotts by angry whites. Virginia felt the opening wedge on June 23, when its Hot Shoppes were opened to Negroes. Knoxville stores ended lunch counter segregation July 18. July 25 was a day of black jubilation; the Woolworth and Kress stores in Greensboro, where it had all started six months earlier, were integrated. That same day four Virginia stores in the Norfolk-Portsmouth area also ended discrimination. After that the going was rougher. The never-say-die Deep South was digging in. On October 19 Atlanta policemen arrestĕd fifty-one sit-in demonstrators led by Martin Luther King. They refused to put up bail and were jailed. The great sit-in blitz of 1960 was over, and the blacks paused to consolidate their gains. But even the Arkansas legislature now knew that the respite would only be temporary. A Negro nation of 18,871,831 was stirring. American blacks were becoming visible at last.

The future was revealed to Clark Kerr on the cloudless afternoon of Friday, May 13, 1960. The House Committee on Un-American Activities, still tenaciously investigating California Communists after all these years, was holding hearings in San Francisco's rococo city hall. Among those subpoenaed were several public schoolteachers and a Berkeley sophomore, all of them rumored to be active leftists. Several busloads of Berkeley students arrived to give them moral support. No demonstrations had been contemplated; in that innocent day few undergraduates knew how to demonstrate. They merely wanted seats in the hearing room. But the building was already crowded. Policemen barred the door at the top of the steps. Somebody started to push. One cop lost his footing; afterward it was said that he was beaten. Nightsticks appeared, and then hoses. At the end of a wild half-hour twelve people were casualties and fifty-two were on their way to jail. Jessica Mitford of Oakland reported in the *Nation* that "the current crop of students has gone far to shake the label of apathy and conformity that had stuck through the Fifties." She predicted that in the coming decade they would be dedicated to "shaping the future of the world." One beaten undergraduate told a reporter, "I was a political virgin, but I was raped on the steps of city hall." To the country's 3,610,000 students the message from Berkeley was a challenge. Impatient faculty members had long been goading them to make a political commitment. Now they knew how to do it.

During those same tumultuous months, as black pride and collegiate political awareness grew, the curtain was rising on another instrument of social change. On May 9, 1960, the U.S. Food and Drug Administration announced that it had approved an oral contraceptive as safe.* The Pill was Enovid,

*The *New York Times* carried the story on page 75 of its May 10 issue.

made by G. D. Searle & Company, Chicago, which said it had proved to be 100 percent effective in a four-year test by 1,500 women. Twenty pills a month, obtainable by prescription, would provide assurance against pregnancy at a cost of $10 to $11 a month. This chemical form of birth control, combined with the new intrauterine devices and an increase in the acceptance of surgical birth control, offered women escape from the fear of pregnancy, the restraint that had inhibited their sexual activity since the beginning of time. Now, it seemed, they could go to bed as freely as men. Physicians and pharmaceutical houses were overwhelmed by the demand from millions of women for the Pill. Never had so many people taken a potent drug regularly for any purpose other than the control of a disease. And the Roman Catholic bishops were dismayed when Monsignor Irving A. LeBlanc, director of the National Catholic Family Life Bureau, reported that Catholic women were taking it as regularly as non-Catholics. As recently as November 1959 the bishops had reproved "some representatives of Christian bodies" — Protestant clergymen — for not practicing continence. Now even Catholic priests, and indeed some sisters in holy orders, were reappraising their vows in the light of the altered facts of life.

The clay figure of Charles Van Doren began to crumble in August 1958, when one Herbert M. Stempel, a CCNY student who had won $49,500 on *Twenty-one* before losing to Van Doren, took his troubled conscience to Manhattan District Attorney Frank Hogan and the *New York World-Telegram and Sun*. Stempel told them that the show was a fake. He said that contestants were given the answers in advance until their popularity began to wane; then they had to take a dive. He had been ordered to lose to Van Doren, who, like him, had been coached in facial expressions, lip-biting, brow-mopping, and stammering as he agonized over a question in the glass-walled isolation booth on camera. Rehearsed by the show's producer, Van Doren had then amazed 25 million televiewers by such feats as naming the only three baseball players to have collected more than 3,500 hits ("Ty Cobb, Cap Anson and . . . Tris Speaker!"), identifying the singer of the aria "Sempre libera" in *La Traviata* ("She sings it right at the end of the party given by . . . What's her name! Soprano. Her name is . . . Violetta!"), and spitting out the names of the Seven Dwarfs ("Sleepy, Sneezy, Dopey, Happy" — pause — "the grouchy one — ah, Grumpy — Doc — ah, the bashful one — Bashful!").

Stempel and other contestants on *Twenty-one* and CBS's *The $64,000 Challenge* told their story to a New York grand jury. Van Doren denied it under oath, and Judge Mitchell Schweitzer, deeply offended by the slandering of a contemporary American folk hero, impounded the record on the ground that it contained accusations which had not been proved. Outside the jury room, Van Doren told the press that he was "sad" and "shocked" by the lies about him. He repeated that he had played "honestly. . . . At no time was I coached or tutored."

The trouble with perjury is that those who commit it have no way of knowing whether there is someone who can prove they were lying. There is always the possibility that a Whittaker Chambers has the truth socked away in a pumpkin, and that is what happened to Van Doren. One James Snodgrass, an artist and a *Twenty-one* winner, produced registered letters that he had mailed to himself one to three days before the programs he was on, containing the questions and answers involved. These were then opened by the House Subcommittee on Legislative Oversight, the same stern tribunal which had been Bernard Goldfine's, and thus Sherman Adams's, downfall. The letters confirmed Snodgrass, and the committee, taking up where the Manhattan grand jury had left off, began building a trap of testimony and exhibits for that winning, handsome, loose-limbed, Ivy-clothed son of a distinguished literary family named Charles Van Doren.

They sprung it in October 1959. Van Doren, playing the outraged patrician like Hiss before him, wired the subcommittee a categorical denial of all the charges maligning him, declaring that he had not been "assisted in any form" and that he would be "available" to the subcommittee whenever it wished to question him. Back came a telegram inviting him to appear before the congressmen voluntarily, at which time he vanished. A formal subpoena was issued, but the process server could not find him. For six days the American people did not know whether he was alive or dead. On the seventh day, October 14, he materialized by prearrangement in New York's Roosevelt Hotel, accepted the subpoena, and confronted a packed press conference. He read a prepared statement. "Distressed" by the course of events, he said, he had taken a leave of absence from Columbia and gone with his wife to New England, "to gather my thoughts . . . in the October beauty of the region." He hadn't known he was wanted. The reporters boggled. How could he have been unaware of the subpoena when it was the lead story in every newspaper and news broadcast? Smiling wanly, he said out of respect for the U.S. Congress he would have no further comment until he appeared in the "appropriate forum," which was to say, its hearing room.

He surfaced there next on November 2, conservatively dressed and obviously tense as he confessed. "I would give almost anything I have to reverse the course of my life in the last three years. . . . I've learned a lot about good and evil. They are not always what they appear to be. I was involved, deeply involved, in a deception . . . I was almost able to convince myself that it did not matter what I was doing because it was having such a good effect on the national attitude toward teachers, education, and the intellectual life."

In time he became "terribly uncomfortable," he continued, and "very much afraid." He begged the producers "several times" to let him lose. They replied that it would have to be done in "a dramatic manner." At last a glamorous blonde lawyer became a contestant, and one of the producers "told me that . . . I would be defeated by her. I thanked him." When the public began to learn that the show had been a fraud, Van Doren said, he had been "horror-struck. . . . I simply ran away. . . . Most of all, I was running away from myself." There was "one way out which I had, of course, often considered, and that was simply to tell the truth." But "emotionally" this was not "possible." Then the subpoena was served upon him. ". . . it was a small thing that tipped the scales. A letter came to me from a woman, a complete stranger, who had seen me on the Garroway show and who said she admired my work there. She told me that the only way I could ever live with myself, and make up for what I had done — of course, she, too, did not know exactly what that was — was to admit it, clearly, openly, truly. Suddenly I knew she was right." Next morning, Van Doren went on, he summoned up the courage to phone his lawyer, who, when he had heard all, said, "God bless you." And that was the end of his statement. Putting it down, he turned to the attorney and smiled at him.

It was preposterous. It was the subpoena, not an unknown woman, which had forced him to own up. Furthermore, if he had really been "terribly uncomfortable" on the show there had been no need to plea for release from the producers; all he had to do was give a wrong answer to one question on the air. A Republican member of the subcommittee, Steven B. Derounian of New York, saw through Van Doren's fraudulence. He said to him, "I don't think an adult of your intelligence ought to be commended for telling the truth." But that was just what the other congressmen proceeded to do. Chairman Oren Harris said he wanted to "compliment" him on his candor. Representative William E. Springer of Illinois expressed the hope that Columbia would not "prematurely" dismiss him from its faculty, and Representative Peter F. Mack of Illinois said he trusted that NBC would forgive him. Others said they wanted to "commend" him for his "fortitude," and for the "forthrightness" of his "soul-searching" statement. Five hours later Columbia, seeing things differently, announced that it was dispensing with Van Doren's services; NBC discharged him the next day. But that was not a popular reaction. The crowd at the hearing had been with Van Doren, applauding him and his admirers on the subcommittee and greeting Congressman Derounian's comment with stony silence. Columbia students held a rally to protest his ouster. A poll showed that three of every four Americans felt that faced with the same situation "most people" would have done what he had done, and NBC's mail favored him, five to one.

No sooner had Van Doren and thirteen other celebrities been indicted in New York for perjury than the Harris subcommittee turned up new evidence of TV fraud. Dick Clark, the number one disc jockey in the teen-age subculture, admitted that he chose records in which he had a financial interest. This was called "payola." Chairman John C. Doerfer of the FCC in effect defended it. Nobody was harmed by it, he argued, and any attempt at regulation would "tamper with our cherished freedom of speech." At that point it was discovered that Doerfer himself had accepted payola from one of the big broadcasters he was supposed to be watching. Eisenhower accepted his resignation, but here, too, the public seemed to be indifferent. It is not surprising that viewers who showed no concern over any of this should have accepted the networks' tasteless programming in 1960. If 1959 had been the Year of the Quiz Show, *Variety* suggested, 1960 was the Year of the Western. There were eight such programs on CBS, nine on NBC, and eleven on ABC — a total of twenty-four and a half hours of prime viewing time every week.

After seven years of basking in Eisenhower sunshine, the nation's opinion makers, including those who had supported the President, were becoming restless. As early as 1958 the *Chicago Daily News* had asked, "Things are in an uproar. But what is Eisenhower doing? All you read about is that he's playing golf. Who's running the country?" Subscribers, however, remained apathetic. While the President was in Europe, the Vice President scored a personal triumph in negotiating the end of a 116-day steel strike. Opinion polls were virtually unaffected; the public hadn't been watching. The newly freed Congo was bleeding in a tragic civil war, and rebellious Laotian soldiers led by Captain Kong Le overturned the pro-Western government of Premier Tiao Samsonith; the average American couldn't have found either country on a map. At home a newspaper strike halted publication of all New York papers, there was a rash of prison riots, and another of bombs smuggled aboard airliners, including one planted by a greedy youth who thereby blew up his airbone mother, with everybody else on the flight, for her insurance. A survey reported that front pages were unread; readers preferred the comics and sports. When Caryl Chessman was executed in California after eight reprieves, opponents of capital punishment objected, but there were comparatively few of them, and the general lethargy seemed to be unaffected by a series of particularly brutal, senseless killings. One of them at this time was the murder of a Kansas farmer named Herbert Clutter with his wife, son, and daughter. *Time's* account of the crime appeared in the news magazine's November 30, 1959, issue. Its headline was "In Cold Blood," and its readers included a writer named Truman Capote.

The instant cliché that year was the use of the word "bit" as an all-purpose verbal punctuation mark. Greensboro's blacks were doing "the protest bit." Romance was "the love bit," Metrecal "the diet bit," and Alfred Hitchcock's *Psycho* "the thrill bit." The commonplace cropped up almost everywhere, but it was never applied to one department of the federal government. No one ever said John Foster Dulles was doing "the diplomacy bit." It would have been unseemly, and it would also have been inappropriate, for Dulles belonged to an earlier age, to a craft of statesmanship fashioned by foreign ministers in cutaways and striped pants. His haughty moralizing and simplistic "massive retaliation" had been outmoded by the statistics of Soviet rocket thrust, and in the early months of 1959, as he hobbled back and forth to Walter Reed Hospital in the agony of his last illness, he seemed to realize that the rigidity of the East-West posture which he had done so much to perpetuate was about to become obsolete. He defended it to the last. Grimacing with pain as he left Washington on his final journey to Europe, he told a friend, "If it isn't cancer, then I feel the trip is too important to be put off. If it is cancer, then any additional discomfort doesn't fundamentally matter anyway."

It was cancer. Blasted daily by million-volt X-rays in Walter Reed Hospital or resting in the Florida sun on Jupiter Island, the secretary became preoccupied with his desperate, losing battle with death, and as he struggled the reins of statecraft slipped at last from his hands. Outwardly the world's balance of power was unchanged. The United States was still committed by treaty to the defense of forty-two nations, and Dulles, to use another emerging cliché, was still a man with tremendous clout. American editorial writers paid tribute to the "wise counsel" and "single-minded strength" of this "indispensable man." Whitehall sent him word that it was "extraordinarily sorry," the Quai d'Orsay expressed concern over "the greatest possible loss for the West," and Bonn regretted that "a spoke" had been "torn from the wheels of Western policy making." But that was all diplomatic cant, and Dulles must have known it. Although he kept in close touch with the White House and his own office by telephone, alert for any sign of cold war heresy, to those who could read the signs — and he was one who could — it was clear that moves toward a detente between Washington and Moscow awaited only his departure from the scene. "The clenched fist of Dulles," Emmet John Hughes wrote, was about to be replaced by "the outstretched hand of Eisenhower."

In the aftermath of the GOP's off-year election defeat, Hagerty had put together a long memorandum looking toward the 1960 election, in which Eisenhower, campaigning for a Republican successor, would stand on his record as a man of peace. Based on conversations with the President, it set forth as goals everything Dulles had resisted in his six years at Foggy Bottom. Its frank assumption was that the time had arrived for diplomatic flexibility. The President must take the center of the international stage, the Eisenhower-Hagerty memo held, as a peacemaker. Continuing, it declared that he must play this role in appearances at the United Nations, in journeys to the far corners of the world, including neutral India, and in a hospitable attitude toward suggestions that he participate in summit conferences and conversations with Russia's Khrushchev.

The Soviet premier was ready for such overtures. In welcoming Premier Anastas Mikoyan home from a U.S. tour on January 26, 1959, Khrushchev had said that "the possibility of a thaw" in Russo-American relations was "not excluded." "Everything possible" must be done to improve relations between the two superpowers, he said, for thermonuclear war was unthinkable; those in the West who said that Khrushchev was "more frightened of war than anyone else" were absolutely correct. As always, Dulles had replied that any meeting would have to be preceded by Soviet demonstrations of good faith, and that he doubted that there would be any, for the USSR, in his opinion, was committed to winning the cold war, not ending it. But this time another administration spokesman had expressed a different view. Vice President Nixon said that the United States also wanted a thaw, "because we realize that if there is none we will all be eventually frozen in the ice so hard that only a nuclear bomb will break it."

On May 24 the death watch at Walter Reed ended with the bulletin: MR. JOHN FOSTER DULLES DIED QUIETLY IN HIS SLEEP AT 7:49 E.D.T. THIS MORNING. Already Undersecretary Christian A. Herter was running the State Department. His first priority was the most recent of the long, dreary series of crises over Berlin. Khrushchev had delivered an ultimatum to the western powers: if they weren't out of the city in six months, the Red Army would throw them out. The characteristic Dulles response would have been a counter ultimatum and a show of strength, forcing a showdown on the brink of war. Eisenhower had taken a different tack. The President read a careful statement to a press conference declaring that if there was any shooting in Berlin it would be "to stop us from doing our duty. We are not saying that we are going to shoot our way into Berlin. We say we are just going to go and continue carrying out our responsibilities to those people. So that if we are stopped, it will be somebody else using force." Herter treated the ultimatum as a maneuver in presummit bargaining, and that, it developed, was exactly what it was.

Once Dulles was in his grave, events moved with almost unseemly haste. Five weeks later, on June 28, Soviet Deputy Premier Frol R. Koslov led a delegation of Russian officials to New York to open a Soviet Exhibition of Science, Technology, and Culture. On July 11 Eisenhower personally drafted an invitation to Khrushchev to visit the United States. And on July 23, two months to the day after Dulles's death, the Vice President of the United States was in Moscow to open an American National Exhibition in Sokolniki Park, thus paying what Eisenhower called a "return courtesy" for the New York visit of the Soviet officials.

What followed can hardly be called a contribution to the slackening of East-West tensions, but it did provide some insight into the combative instincts of Nikita Khrushchev and Richard Nixon. The exhibition's most interesting display was a six-room model ranch house with a central viewing corridor, permitting visitors to see all its furnishings. The Soviet leader had worked himself into a rage over it. It touched a sensitive nerve; Russia's sputniks had been built at the expense of consumer products and services. The opening of the fair was being televised in the USSR, and Khrushchev felt that he had been somehow outmaneuvered. He was spoiling for a fight. Nixon was the man to give it to him. The ceremony was to appear on American television, too. He expected to be the Republican presidential nominee next year, and whatever Hagerty's views on campaign strategy, Nixon had plans of his own which did not include allowing himself to be bullied on TV by an angry Communist. The result was what the press called the "kitchen debate" or the "Sokolniki Summit."

It began when they paused at the model home's sleek, gadget-stocked kitchen. Nixon declared that this was a typical American house, and that almost any U.S. workman could afford it or one like it. The Soviet premier bridled.

KHRUSHCHEV: You think the Russians will be dumbfounded by this exhibit. But the fact is that all newly built Russian homes will have this equipment. You need dollars in the United States to get this house, but here all you need is to be born a citizen. If an American citizen does not have dollars he has the right to . . . sleep on the pavement. And you say we are slaves of Communism!

NIXON: . . . We don't think this fair will astound the Russian people, but it will interest them just as yours interested us. To us diversity, the right to choose, the fact that we have a thousand different builders, that's the spice of life. We don't want to have a decision made at the top by one government official saying that we will have one type of house. That's the difference —

KHRUSHCHEV (cutting in): On political differences, we will never agree. If I follow you, I will be led astray by Mikoyan. He likes spicy soups and I don't. But that doesn't mean we differ.

NIXON: Isn't it better to be talking about the relative merits of our washing machines than the relative strength of our rockets? Isn't this the kind of competition you want?

KHRUSHCHEV (pushing his thumb against Nixon's chest): Yes, that's the kind of competition we want, but your generals say they are so powerful they can destroy us. We can also show you something so you will know the Russian spirit. We are strong, we can beat you. But in this respect we can also show you something.

NIXON (wagging his finger at Khrushchev): To me, you are strong and we are strong. In some ways, you are stronger than we are. In others, we are stronger. . . .

Pausing at a table of California wines, they scored their final points. Khrushchev proposed a toast "To peace and the elimination of all military bases on foreign lands."

NIXON (without raising his glass): Let us just drink a toast to peace.

A RUSSIAN BYSTANDER: One hundred years to Premier Khrushchev!

NIXON: I will drink to that. We may disagree with your policy, but we want you to be of good health. May you live to be one hundred years old.

KHRUSHCHEV (after the toast): At ninety-nine years of age we shall discuss these questions further. Why should we be in haste?

NIXON (he has the last word): You mean that at ninety-nine, you will still be in power, with no free elections?

It was a curious exchange, less a debate than a quarrel between two aggressive men, each of them determined to impress the audience as more peaceful than the other. Both suffered from a self-imposed handicap. In a thousand speeches, the Soviet leader had created a crude stereotype of the typical capitalist politician as a Wall Street lackey, and Nixon didn't fit it. Nixon's handicap was a mirror image of Khrushchev's. His archetype of the evil Communist boss had as much substance as a man of straw, as much life as a Sunday supplement demon. The American Vice President had scored more forensic points, but the Russian premier had come across as warm, direct, and perhaps as better suited to his role. Nixon emerged as a man who liked ideas, Khrushchev as one who loved his people and would go to great lengths to champion them. As if to confirm that, he overlooked Nixon's insolence — plainly he regarded it as that — and accepted Eisenhower's invitation to visit America once Nixon had returned home. "I am prepared to turn out my pockets to show that I am harmless," he said in his disingenuous way. "In the old times people used to leave their weapons in the hall when they went in to talk peace. We should do that now, and there should be no saber rattling." With that, he quietly scuttled his Berlin ultimatum.

One reason Dulles had given for opposing such summitry had been his concern that U.S. allies might feel that they were being abandoned. To reassure them, the President flew to Europe at the end of August for two weeks of talks with Konrad Adenauer, Harold Macmillan, and Charles de Gaulle. It was an amazing trip. In Washington it was easy to forget the tremendous affection Europeans felt for Dwight D. Eisenhower. Their feeling for him was unclouded by partisanship or ideology. To them he was the kindly, straightforward, low-key American general who had led the victorious crusade to free them from Nazi rule. The Germans seemed as grateful as the British and French. As Eisenhower's Mercedes-Benz entered Bonn an estimated 315,000 people, twice the population of the city, lined the route, cheering him and holding up banners proclaiming, WE TRUST YOU and WE RELY ON YOU. In London his car was a dove-gray Rolls-Royce. There the shouts — from a crowd numbered in the hundreds of thousands — were "Glad to see you, Ike," and "Good for you, Ike," and as the motorcade entered Grosvenor Square, from which General Eisenhower had directed the coalition of armies that had routed Hitler, reporters saw tears in his eyes.

De Gaulle, now entering his difficult period, would have preferred that Parisians show more restraint, but it was impossible. At Le Bourget Airport the two generals-become-presidents exchanged tributes; then the throng's cry of "Ike!" which in French came out "Eek!" drowned out everything else. It never died out completely during Eek's two days in Paris, not even when he placed a wreath of pink lilies and red roses on the tomb of France's unknown soldier, beneath the Arc de Triomphe, or during his response to the continuing ovation at the Hôtel de Ville: "When the heart is full, the tongue is very likely to stumble. I have one small French phrase that, I think, expresses my feelings — *Je vous aime tous*." Obviously it was impractical to conduct serious talks against such a background. De Gaulle did press his plan for a NATO guided by a three-power directorate. Eisenhower warded him off with a promise to keep in closer touch over the transatlantic phone. ("I know he's a stubborn man," Ike told an aide, "but as long as he's stubborn on our side, everything's all right.") After a weekend at Scotland's Culzean Castle, where he occupied a nine-room apartment given to him by the Scottish people after V-E Day, the President flew home September 7. There he told a welcoming crowd: "I am quite certain that for the moment, at least, everything is going splendidly."

Nikita Khrushchev's barnstorming of the United States was to be the next stage in the slackening of world tensions. On September 15, at Andrews Field in Maryland, Soviet Ambassador Mikhail Menshikov called to a ramp, "Nikita Sergeyevich, I salute you on American soil," and as American spectators blinked in disbelief, down the steps he came, short, bald, and stocky, wearing three small medals on his black suit and accompanied by his shy wife, Nina Petrovna, his daughters Julia and Rada, his son Sergei, and a retinue of sixty-three Russian bureaucrats. President Eisenhower formally welcomed them, and then they were off on a two-week guided tour of the United States with U.N. Ambassador Henry Cabot Lodge as their host.

On the whole it was a successful journey. Americans are partial to curmudgeons, and this one was as salty as Thomas Edison and Henry Ford. In speeches before American businessmen, tours of rural Iowa, and luncheons with Mayor Robert Wagner of New York and Mayor Norris Poulson of Los Angeles, Khrushchev came on as shrewd, eccentric, and unscrupulous, but very human and determined to live in peace with his neighbors. Inevitably there were incidents. Khrushchev won an argument with Spyros P. Skouras, president of Twentieth Century–Fox, and lost one to Walter Reuther and his six union vice presidents. (He then denounced them as "agents for capitalists" and was puzzled when Reuther laughed.) After a Hollywood troupe had performed a cancan for him, the premier revealed a priggish streak, calling the dance "immoral" and adding, "A person's face is more beautiful than his backside."

At Camp David, the presidential retreat on Maryland's Catoctin Mountain, Khrushchev was on his best behavior. He said nothing offensive. In fact, he said almost nothing beyond vague generalities. His concept of discretion seemed to preclude getting down to brass tacks. Midway in the second day of their talks Eisenhower turned to him with a personal appeal: "You have the opportunity to make a great contribution to history by making it possible to ease tensions. It is within your hands." But the Russian leader refused to be pinned down. He praised American roast beef, enjoyed a western movie with Ike, and, after a helicopter hop to Gettysburg, admired the President's prize herd of Black Angus cattle. For the time being, that was going to be the extent of his contribution to a detente.

After their third day together the two leaders issued a joint statement. They had agreed that general disarmament was the most important question facing the world, that negotiations on the Berlin issue should be "reopened with a view to achieving a solution which would be in accordance with the views of all concerned and in the interest of the maintenance of peace," that "all outstanding international questions should be settled not by the application of force but by peaceful means through negotiation," and that President Eisenhower would visit the Soviet Union next year.

For a while the newspapers made much of "the spirit of Camp David." Briefly it seemed almost as substantive as the Roosevelt-Churchill Atlantic Charter. A turning point, men thought, had been reached in U.S. — USSR relations at last. It was all illusion. The President and the premier hadn't even touched upon the basic and critical problems arising from different views over the future of Germany and the world. The benign mood eventually turned out to be evanescent. In time it soured and was succeeded by disenchantment. Among the participants who resolved that a firmer groundwork should be prepared before any new conferences with the Russians was Richard Nixon.

Nixon did not, however, feel that the disappointing outcome vindicated Dulles's implacable opposition to meetings at the top. The world's statesmen had embarked on what *Time* called "the new global game of personal diplomacy," and none of them wanted a return to the arctic past. Their orchestrated journeys were now following a definite plot leading toward a desirable ending. The next step would be what was being called the "Western Summit," a kind of semifinal conference whose participants would be Eisenhower, Macmillan, Adenauer, and De Gaulle. These four would renew their vows to keep Berlin free and hammer out a joint approach for the final conference, which would be between them and Khrushchev.

The semifinal was held in Paris in December. Eisenhower was not going to limit the December trip to France, though. The ventures in personal diplomacy, made endurable by the new Boeing 707 jet airliners, were encouraging. The rousing welcome given him in the capitals of western Europe had given rise to a naive hope that the enthusiasm of the crowds that cheered motorcades could somehow be transformed into enduring good will and better international relations. With this in mind, and with Hagerty's memorandum before him, the President decided that as long as he was abroad he might as well call on the rulers of Italy, Turkey, Pakistan, Afghanistan, India, Iran, Greece, Tunisia, Spain, and Morocco. Before leaving on this 19-day, 19,500-mile trip to eleven nations on three continents, he delivered a televised report to the country. "During this mission of peace and good will," he said, "I hope to promote a better understanding of America and to learn more of our friends abroad."

Whether it led to a greater understanding is moot. It did provide staggering new evidence of the President's popularity, however. In Italy, where Romans stood in drenching rains for a glimpse of him — here "Ike" came out "Eekay" — a journalist worte in *Corriere Della Sera,* "We welcome this man who speaks to us with the accent of Kansas farmers who cultivate fields of wheat as vast as seas, of pioneers who went West not long before his birth. He speaks without rhetoric before the imminent peril as he calls for 'Peace, peace.' " Turkey was next. Eisenhower himself called his welcome to Ankara "the most stupendous I have ever seen." Over 750,000 Pakistanis welcomed him to Karachi, and in New Delhi he said he was "completely overwhelmed" by the crowds, as well he might have been: a million shouting Indians held aloft banners acclaiming him as, among other things, "Eisenhower, Prince of Peace," and they threw so many flowers at his open car that he stood a foot deep in blossoms. It was the same in every country. There were 750,000 cheering Iranians in Teheran, where he addressed a joint session of the Shah's parliament; 500,000 enthusiastic Athenians outside when he spoke to Greece's Chamber of Deputies; 500,000 Spaniards when Generalissimo Francisco Franco welcomed him to Madrid, and 500,000 to greet him in Casablanca.

It was numbing, and it was also rather baffling. Applause in western Europe could be traced back to World War II, but the only nation on this trip to have been in the war was Italy, and the Italians had been on the other side. Why should Indian untouchables walk forty miles to see the American President, or Afghan tribesmen spend days weaving floral tributes to lay before the wheels of his limousine? Part of the explanation seemed to lie in the recurring chants, in every tongue, of "Peace, peace." War was recognized everywhere as mankind's greatest scourge, even among peoples that had never heard gunfire. But that wasn't all that lay behind these awesome demonstrations. Clearly America was more beloved than Americans knew. Anti-Americans made more noise, but the vast majority in these countries seemed to admire and trust the United States.

Eisenhower returned home on December 22. That Christmas was a high point in his Presidency and in the history of U.S. diplomacy. In his annual Christmas message to the nation — beamed overseas this time in twenty-eight languages — he said of his journey: "My purpose was to improve the climate in which diplomacy might work more successfully; a diplomacy that seeks . . . peace with justice for all men." The test of his accomplishment lay less than five months away, when he and the three leaders of western Europe would confront Khrushchev in the summit of summits. It was scheduled to open on May 16, 1960, in Paris.

From time to time in the later 1950s subscribers to the *New York Times* read, under the byline of Herbert L. Matthews, captivating accounts of bearded young Cuban revolutionaries hiding out in the tangled jungles of that island's Sierra Maestra range. Their leader was a hulking, verbose lawyer in his early thirties, Fidel Castro Ruz. Castro had landed in Cuba on Christmas of 1956 with just twelve men. Taking to the hills before dictator Fulgencio Batista's soldiers could seize them, they unfurled the red and black flag of their 26th of July movement, so named for a desperate attack led by Castro on Santiago Batistianos on July 26, 1953, and called on Cuban lovers of freedom to join them.

In those early years Castro's movement was very popular in the United States. Batista's Cuba was a police state run by terrorists and corrupt bureaucrats who made fortunes in prostitution, gambling, and raids on the public till. Havana University was padlocked to suppress mutinous students; dissenters were murdered; their corpses were dismembered and sent to their parents, or dumped in gutters like garbage. Washington was elated at the prospect of a truly democratic Cuba. As early as March 1958 all deliveries of U.S. arms to Batista were halted. American correspondents like Matthews wrote sympathetic stories depicting Castro and his *barbudos*, or bearded rebels, as selfless Robin Hoods who wanted to give their countrymen liberty and justice. The reporters erred, but the error was common then, and it was shared by most members of the Cuban middle class and a great many influential Cuban army officers who were fed up with Batista. That was Batista's undoing. Castro had fewer than two thousand *barbudos* to put against forty thousand superbly equipped Batistianos, but businessmen and landowners were financing him, and the middle class was acclaiming the rebels, who were, for the most part, middle-class themselves — young professional men and intellectuals like Fidel, his brother Raul, and Major Ernesto "Che" Guevara, the Argentine physician who had become Castro's Trotsky.

In the last weeks of 1958 Guevera routed three thousand government troops in the province of Las Villas, one hundred and fifty miles from the capital, and captured the provincial capital, Santa Clara. A trainload of troops sent by Batista refused even to get out of the railroad cars. The old regime was through, and Batista knew it. On New Year's Day he flew off into exile. Castro then began a seven-day, six-hundred-mile march of triumph down Cuba's Central Highway. Fidel's men fired their pistols and tommy guns at the sky. In affection they called their leader "El Caballo," the horse. He was Gargantuan, a charismatic figure before the concept became popular. His personal life was ascetic. There were no women in it. Except for fifty-cent Montecristo cigars, he never indulged himself. Getting him to change his grimy green field jacket was next to impossible.

"Power does not interest me, and I will not take it," Castro said. "From now on the people are entirely free." He restored Cuba's lost pride, gave it a national identity, rooted out corruption, and launched vast programs to educate Cuba's children and inspire their parents. When whispering voices tried to spread reports that he was a Communist, the general reaction was scorn. Reactionaries always called reformers Reds; men like Matthews of the *Times* could remember their doing it in Spain twenty years earlier and they said so.

To demonstrate that he was a good neighbor to the United States, Fidel flew to Washington with a hundred cases of good-will rum. He lunched on steak and champagne with Acting Secretary of State Christian Herter — he wore his field jacket even there — and talked to eighteen congressmen in the Senate Foreign Relations Committee room. "The July 26 movement is not a Communist movement," he told them. "Its members are Roman Catholics, mostly." Asked about American investments in Cuba, he replied, "We have no intention of expropriating United States property, and any property we take we'll pay for." He was charming. To be sure, there was one sour note. After a three-hour conference with Castro, Vice President Nixon wrote a twelve-page confidential memorandum for distribution to the CIA, the State Department, and the White House, in which he said that he was convinced that Cuba's new leader was "either incredibly naive about Communism or under Communist discipline." But the CIA pigeon-holed it, State ignored it, and Eisenhower waved it away. The administration was getting a little tired of Nixon's seeing Communist bogeymen everywhere.

The rude awakening of the Americans, and the subsequent deterioration of U.S.-Cuban relations, came in that spring and summer of 1959. Castro's hatred of dictators vanished, it seemed, when the name of the dictator was Castro. His indifference to power also disappeared. With a ruthlessness that would have startled Batista, Fidel suspended habeas corpus, established military tribunals all over the island, and decreed an end to the right of convicted defendants to appeal their sentences. By September he was careening leftward. He recognized Red China, called the United States a "vulture . . . feeding on humanity," renounced Cuba's 1952 military pact with the U.S., and dared the *yanquis* to invade Cuba.

The idealists and visionaries of the 26th of July movement had been betrayed. When they realized it, all Cuba rocked with their thwarted rage. Over a hundred of them were jailed, and the others fled north to Florida. Manuel Ray, a radical young engineer who had commanded Castro's Havana underground, was one. Two were famous liberals: Mio Cardona, whom Castro had chosen to be the first premier of his new government, and Manuel Urrutia, also hand-picked, the regime's first president. Others who felt that they had been sold to the Reds included brave officers like José Peréz ("Pepe") San Román, Erneido Oliva, and Huber Matos, one of the 26th of July heroes of the Sierra Maestra. Some were incredulous when they first heard of Castro's treachery. They said they wouldn't believe until they saw it. Some literally witnessed it. Dr. Manuel Francisco Artime, the brilliant young manager of Oriente province, heard Castro himself outline his plan to communize Cuba within three years. "I realized," Artime later said, "that I was a democratic infiltrator in a Communist government."

Such men could not compromise with what they regarded as total evil. If they wanted to call their souls their own, they had to escape through what American reporters were calling "the cane curtain" in the hope that one day they could reclaim their homeland. Cubans have a certain style about them, and some of their escapes were dashing. Artime's was one. He wrote a personal note to Castro declaring that he was quitting the movement because he had "heard from your lips the complete plans to communize Cuba." Dressed as a priest and carrying a pistol inside a missal, he walked into the American embassy. There he was introduced to a certain man called "Williams," who saw to it that he sailed north in a secret compartment on a Honduran freighter. On the Tampa pier Artime was met by a tall American who identified himself as "Mr. Burnett, a friend of Williams." In Miami, which soon had so many refugees that it took on the air of a Cuban city, other friends of Williams and Burnett appeared and introduced themselves as "Jimmy," "Sonny," "Seabee," "Don," etc. All of them, Artime eventually discovered, were operatives of the United States Central Intelligence Agency.

They did not identify themselves as CIA agents, of course. Neither did they admit it if asked. Their cover story was that they were employed by a great American corporation which was determined to solve the Cuban problem. Their leader was particularly anxious to preserve this facade. He was tall and expensively dressed, and he was the only agent with a first and last name: "Frank Bender." "Remember, Manolo," Frank kept reminding Artime, "I am not a member of the United States government. I have nothing to do with the United States government. I am only working for a powerful company that wants to fight Communism." Later the Americans tried to give the impression that a Cuban millionaire was backing them. The Cubans winked at one another and joked that the "millionaire" was named "Uncle Sam." "At that time we were so stupid," one of them said long afterward. "We thought that Uncle Sam was behind us. He wanted to do this secretly. That was all right because he was Uncle Sam, and he is strong." The CIA agents solemnly told them that they all risked jail if the FBI found out what was going on. That, they explained, was why they could not disclose their real names. It was also given as the reason for a great deal of such hokey-pokey as blindfolds, passwords, and countersigns. The Americans were haunted by the fear that the operation might be penetrated by double agents. The Cubans were required to submit to lie detector tests, Rorschach tests, and lengthy interrogations by a genial, bespectacled psychiatrist with a heavy German accent. (He was "Max.") Those who passed were dispatched on mysterious errands — typically, one of them entailed flying to New York, registering at the Statler Hilton as "George L. Ringo," and following telephoned instructions from a series of callers — until their hosts' suspicions were allayed.

Those who had passed muster were divided into two groups. The younger men, who would do the actual fighting, were recruited for a brigade — La Brigada, as it was henceforth known. In Miami the older group formed a united political front, the Frente, which would eventually replace Castro's government. As an effective apparatus the Frente was a sieve, but it couldn't reveal much about its young soldiers because it wasn't told much. Not that that would have mattered. Had Fidel been told the strength of the tiny force to be sent against him, he wouldn't have believed it. He assumed it must have about 20,000 men. As late as November 1960 the actual figure was 450, and it never exceeded 1,200. To deceive the enemy if prisoners were taken, serial numbers began with 2500. When one recruit died in training, the brigade took its name from his number, 2506. Its emblem was the figure 2506 superimposed on a cross. They wore this on their uniforms and on a battle flag.

Later, after the agents' cover had been blown, it turned out that the operation had been guided by orders from the highest levels in Washington. Day-by-day supervision was the responsibility of the CIA's director, Allen Dulles; overall planning came from what was called "the special group" — a high command of officials from the White House, the Department of State, the Joint Chiefs of Staff, and the CIA. President Eisenhower did not attend their meetings, but he knew of them, and when Castro rejected the administration's last attempt to reach an understanding on March 17, 1960, the President approved a recommendation that the Cuban exiles be trained for possible use against Castro.

Many of La Brigada's operational details might have been lifted from one of Ian Fleming's bizarre spy novels about James Bond, which were then coming into vogue. The American officers who supervised the training of the exiles were borrowed from the Army and Marine Corps more or less on an old boy basis; frequently decorated in World War II and Korea, they tended to be high in personal courage and low in good judgment. Selecting sites for the training seems to have been almost haphazard. At first one of the Cubans used CIA money given to him by Frank Bender to lease the resort island of Useppa in the Gulf of Mexico; the Cubans were comfortably billeted at the Useppa country club, and the golfers among them improved their strokes. Next a C-54 transport plane flew them to the U.S. Army jungle warfare training camp at Fort Gulick in the Panama Canal Zone. They weren't supposed to know where they were, but one of their CIA instructors left a Panama City newspaper around, and the canal itself was clearly visible from a hill in the camp.

After eight weeks of lessons in guerrilla warfare — skills which, they were told, they would teach to a Cuban liberation army — they were transferred again, this time to Guatemala. Here, too, it was intended that they would be kept ignorant of their location. Leaving Panama, they were given only the code name of their destination, "little farm." But they knew what it meant soon after the two buses carrying them left Guatemala's San José Airport. The level of trainee sophistication was high. Many of them had traveled widely. The cobblestone streets and dirty adobe buildings in the Indian villages bespoke Central America, and the profusion of signs of American influence — Coca-Cola and Pepsi-Cola signs along the highway, and the number of filling stations selling Texaco, Shell, American or Esso gasoline — could only mean Guatemala. Soon the buses began climbing through the tropical foliage of the surrounding mountains, the Sierra Madre ridge on the Pacific coast of Guatamela. They were on their way to a vast coffee plantation, a *finca* belonging to Roberto Alejos, the brother of the Guatemalan ambassador to Washington. Alejos had given CIA operatives permission to use part of it for training after Miguel Ydígoras, the president of Guatemala, had agreed to look the other way. (In a sordid epilogue to the operation, Ydígoras would insist that the United States had agreed to press his claim for territory in British Honduras; Washington would vehemently deny it.) The camp there was christened Base Trax. It was characteristic of the operation that it was in the least desirable part of the *finca*. The volcano Santiaguito, still active, could be seen from base headquarters, and the camp's soil was volcanic ash. In some places the ash was six feet deep. Rainfall turned it into a thin porridge. The rains that year were the heaviest in memory. Much of the time the Cubans wallowed around in slime.

At this point some of them began to wonder aloud about the CIA's omniscience. They were hooted down by the others. The majority's trust in their *yanqui* advisers was complete. Surely, they reasoned, the mighty conquerors of Nazi Germany and Imperial Japan *must* know what they were doing. They agreed that La Brigada's strength was slight, but Castro, after all, had started his 26th of July movement with only a dozen guerrillas. At that time the parallel between them and him could be justified; their CIA advisers were planning to divide them into small guerrilla bands, each of which would be trained to infiltrate one of Cuba's six provinces. They were to be ready to go before the American presidential election; the deadline was September 19. It might have worked. Even if it hadn't, the consequences would have been bearable. Defeated bushfighters can usually fade away; small stigma is attached to their failure. Castro would be hard put to prove that the United States was behind them, and they might return to fight another time.

In August the special group in Washington began to doubt the wisdom of establishing guerrilla forces in the new Cuba. Castro's troops were far more formidable than Batista's had been. State Department figures put them at about 400,000 troops and militiamen, ten times his strength. A long bushwhacker campaign directed from the Sierra Maestra no longer seemed feasible. Moreover, Castro's men had been superbly equipped by his new friends in Moscow and Peking; the State Department study estimated that they had sent him 28,000 tons of military supplies. On top of all this, the vigilance and disposition of his coast watchers and aircraft spotters indicated that he had profited from Batista's mistakes in that regard, so that supplying guerrilla forces by airdrops now would be exceedingly difficult.

If these reasons were sound — and events the following year were to prove that they were, eminently so — then it would seem that they ought to have discouraged *any* military expedition. Not so; the men directing the operation from Washington began weighing the advantages of an amphibious landing by the Brigada with tactical air support provided by Cubans in American warplanes. Ship-to-shore invasions had been very effective in Europe and the Pacific in World War II, it was pointed out, and MacArthur had ravaged the North Korean supply lines by landing the 1st Marine Division at Inchon. No one appears to have pointed out to the group that La Brigada was the size of an American infantry battalion, and that no major amphibious operation had been attempted with fewer than nine battalions backed by artillery, air supremacy, and an armada of warships — 1,200 of them at Okinawa, World War II's last ship-to-shore attack.

Confident that the key to victory had been found, Washington abandoned plans for guerrilla activity, certain that once La Brigada had established a bridgehead all Cuba would flock to its standard. In a long cable to Base Trax, CIA headquarters in Langley, Virginia, ordered that the number of bushfighters be reduced to sixty; the agents in Guatemala were to "use conventional arms and training for everyone else." The Cubans took this to mean that once they were ashore an American army would land behind them, that being the only circumstance, they reasoned, which could justify the change. Their CIA advisers not only failed to correct them; "Frank Bender," the leader, told Pepe San Román and his fellow Cuban officers that they were "going to have protection by sea, by air, and even from under the sea." All the CIA operatives were enthusiastic about the new plan, and from that day forward they made it plain that they looked upon expression of doubt that it would succeed as a sign of weakness. Frank Bender came to believe that it superseded his loyalty to the President of the United States. He told Pepe San Román that powerful figures in Washington were trying to call off the invasion, and that it was conceivable that orders to that end might arrive from the White House. "If this happens," he said, "you come here and make some kind of show, as if you were putting us, the advisers, in prison, and you go ahead with the whole plan, even if we are your prisoners." To make sure that the amazed Cuban understood him, he became more specific. He explained that they would have to put an armed member of La Brigada at the door of each CIA adviser, cut communications with Washington, and go ahead with the invasion. He would tell them when and how to leave Base Trax for the staging area. He laughed and said, "In the end we will win."

Doubtless Frank's superiors in Washington knew nothing of this. Like everyone else who was involved, they couldn't piece together the whole picture until long afterward. To varying degrees it was a muddle to Dwight Eisenhower in the White House, Fidel Castro in Havana, Allen Dulles in Virginia, Frank Bender in Guatemala, the Joint Chiefs in the Pentagon, the Frente in Miami, and the brave men drilling on the coffee plantation beneath the Sierra Madre. Communication was faulty. The special group had neglected to tell Eisenhower of the switch from guerrilla tactics to plans for an amphibious landing. The Cubans in La Brigada continued to believe that they would constitute only the first wave of an invasion, and the Frente had understood the Americans to say that no attack would be mounted with fewer than five thousand men.

The CIA was trying to recruit as many fighters as possible. Wages were paid — $175 a month for a man, $50 for his wife, and $25 for each child. In this situation it was inevitable that security would be compromised. The word was out, and it was out everywhere. Castro was regularly predicting the imminent arrival of the "mercenaries," but his people didn't need him to tell them it was coming. The lowliest *guajiro* cutting sugar cane knew that counterrevolutionaries were on their way. Articles about La Brigada appeared in the city of Guatemala in *La Hora* and had been reprinted in most of the Spanish-language press, including some newspapers circulating in Cuba. Militiamen of the new Cuba slept with their rifles, and artillerymen beside their guns.

Americans could read accounts in English in the *Miami Herald* and the *New York Times*, though on the whole people in the United States were less interested than Cubans in the coming battle. They knew that something was going on down there, but they were distracted by other matters. It was not their country which was going to be invaded. They were likelier to be preoccupied by the dramatic struggle for the Democratic presidential nomination and the approaching climax to Eisenhower's White House years — the great Paris summit, to be followed by his tour of the Soviet Union. Advance parties of Secret Service men were already checking security arrangements in the Elysée Palace when, on May 1, sixteen days before the conference was to begin in France, a strange aircraft appeared high in the skies over Sverdlovsk, an industrial complex in the Ural Mountains some 1,200 miles inside Russia. Like the brigade in Guatemala, the flight was part of a CIA operation; the airplane had been built to CIA specifications by Lockheed. Its official designation was U-2. Presently the entire world would know it as "the spy plane."

Long and black, with a high tail, wide wings, and a single turbojet engine, the U-2 was piloted from a one-man cockpit. In the strict sense of the word, it was not a warplane. There were no guns. Instead it was equipped with sensitive infrared cameras aimed through seven portholes under the fuselage. They could photograph a strip of earth 125 miles wide and 3,000 miles long, producing prints in 4,000 paired frames. The detail was almost unbelievable. Photo interpreters studying huge enlargements could actually read a newspaper headline that had been nine or ten miles below the aircraft. Other instruments could test the air for evidence of secret nuclear tests and measure the efficiency of Russian radar. The U-2's protection was its height. Efficient cruising performance at very high altitudes had been achieved by careful aerodynamic and structural details; it was believed to be beyond the reach of Soviet radar. All in all it was the most sophisticated espionage device the world had ever seen. Its pilot that May Day was named Francis Gary Powers.

Powers was one of a new breed of soldiers of fortune. He flew, not for love of country, but for money. It was a job to him, and a good one; he was earning $30,000 a year as against an $8,400 combined income for him and his wife before he went to work for the CIA. That had been four years earlier, when he had been a twenty-seven-year-old Air Force first lieutenant. Beefy, thickset, and with a crew-cut, he looked like a professional football player — a defensive tackle, perhaps, with diligence and reliability, but little imagination.

He was not stupid, however. Earlier in the year he had asked an intelligence officer, "What if something happens and one of us goes down over Russia? That's an awfully big country and it could be a hell of a long walk to a border. Is there anyone there we can contact? Can you give us any names and addresses?" According to Powers this was the first time the question had been asked, despite the fact that Operation Overflight, as it was called, was about to enter its fifth year. The reply was "No, we can't." He persisted: "All right, say the worst happens. A plane goes down and the pilot is captured. What story does he use? Exactly how much should he tell?" It is Power's recollection — and no one has corrected him — that the intelligence officer's exact words were: "You may as well tell them everything because they're going to get it out of you anyway."

The lack of a well-rehearsed cover story is by no means the least credible aspect of the affair. Sherman Adams had been in the White House when Operation Overflight began in 1956, and he knew that none of the flights were made without the President's approval. Visiting Eisenhower after the Powers debacle, he asked him about it. "You're right," Ike said. "I made the decision, just as I have known about and personally approved every one of those flights. When they brought me the plan for this particular flight over Russia, I approved it as one among several within an intelligence policy already adopted. I had no thought of it having any possible bearing upon the summit meeting or on my forthcoming trip to Moscow. Except for unforeseen circumstances, it would not have had any."

Doubtless Eisenhower believed that, but it is untrue. The circumstances were foreseeable, or, at any rate, sufficiently within the range of possibilities to be weighed carefully. Powers's last trip was not routine. It was the first of two overflights after a long period without any, and it was the first attempt to cross the entire Soviet Union. From an American base in Peshawar, Pakistan, Powers was to fly 3,800 miles to Bodo, Norway. Taking off from one country and landing in another required two ground crews. That, too, was unprecedented. It was judged to be worth chancing because, by going deeper into Russia than ever before, the U-2 would pass over important targets never before photographed.

There was considerable speculation among the U-2 pilots over the timing of the mission. One theory was that the Russians were on the verge of a missile guidance breakthrough and that the CIA was trying to crowd in as many targets as possible beforehand. Another was that Eisenhower wanted the latest available data before sitting down with Khrushchev, and still another that an approaching detente with the Russians would make any covert operations unwise in the future. The fliers were well aware that they were part of a shady business. The suspicion had been growing among them that Soviet radar had been developed to the point where it was possible to track them. The possibilities of mechanical failure were also discussed. "One loose screw, in just the right place," as Powers put it, "could bring an aircraft down." In fact, this had happened. A U-2 had crash-landed near Tokyo the previous autumn. A Japanese journalist had inspected it, concluded that its mission was espionage, and reported that finding at length in the next issue of his magazine.

The designers of the plane had known it would run unusual risks, and they had equipped it with timed destruction mechanisms. Later the "granger," a device designed to throw off radar, had been installed as a further precaution. Despite the intelligence officer's rather casual answer to Powers's question about contingency planning, some thought had been given to forced landings. Colonel William M. Shelton, the Air Force officer commanding the Operation Overflight unit, told Powers that if he found he was running low on fuel over the Soviet city of Landalaksha, in the Murmansk region, he could take a shortcut to alternate landing fields in Finland and Sweden. He added, "Any place is preferable to going down in the Soviet Union."

The CIA had even considered the advantages of suicide for a downed pilot. Apparently the agency hadn't been able to make up its mind. The decision had been left with the fliers themselves. Cyanide tablets were available for those who wished them, and later they were shown a small device that looked like a good-luck charm. It was a silver dollar with a metal loop that permitted it to be fastened to a key chain or a chain around the neck. The loop unscrewed. Inside there was a straight pin, which in turn was a sheath that could be removed to expose a thin needle. Toward the end of the needle were tiny grooves. In the grooves was a sticky brown substance — curare, one prick of which brought instant death. Most of the pilots, including Powers, had decided against carrying either cyanide or curare, but when Colonel Shelton asked him during preparations for his last flight, "Do you want the silver dollar?" he changed his mind. He thought the deadly needle might make an effective weapon. "O.K.," he said, and slipped it into the pocket of his outer flight suit. He also carried a shaving kit, civilian clothes, a half-smoked packet of filter cigarettes, pictures of his wife, some German marks, Turkish liras, and Russian rubles; some gold coins, watches, and rings (to be used for bribery or barter if in need of help); about a hundred dollars in U.S. currency, some U.S. postage stamps, a Defense Department I.D. card, a NASA certificate, instrument rating cards, U.S. and international driver's licenses, a Selective Service card, a social security card, and an American flag poster that had "I am an American" printed on it in fourteen languages, including Russian. Long afterward Powers recalled that when he got into trouble he was asked whether he was an American. "It seemed," he said, "pointless to deny it."

The CIA facilities in Pakistan were surprisingly primitive; the airmen slept on folding cots and cooked their own food from rations. But they weren't there much. Most of the time they played poker and loafed at the U.S. Air Force base near Adana, Turkey. (A favorite topic in bull sessions was the coming summit meeting and how it could dispel world tension.) By March of 1960 they were champing at the bit. The number of flights had been drastically reduced now for nearly two years, and the fewer there were, the more apprehensive they became over the next one. Then, after a long pause, the two 1960 flights had been scheduled for April. Powers was the backup pilot for the first, April 9. It went smoothly. The second was to be his.

Things started to go wrong when, on arriving in Pakistan, he was told that the U-2 which had been reserved for this flight — it was the best they had — would be unavailable, having been grounded for a maintenance check. In its place he would fly a substitute, U-2 No. 360. This was bad news; No. 360 was a lemon; a "dog," they called it. There was always something going wrong with it. Its most recent malfunction was in the fuel tanks. Sometimes they wouldn't feed fuel to the engine. Colonel Shelton had them in mind when he authorized Powers to land in Finland or Sweden if necessary.

If the tanks behaved, and everything else went well, Powers's course would resemble a huge zigzag. Taking off from Peshawar, he would cross Afghanistan and the Hindu Kush, an extension of the Himalayas, and enter the Soviet Union near Stalinabad. Then he would pass over the Aral Sea, the Tyuratam Cosmodrome, Chelyabinsk, Sverdlovsk, Kirov, Archangel, Kandalaksha and Murmansk on the Kola peninsula; after Russia would come the Barents Sea and the northern coast of Norway to Bodo — some of the bleakest land in the world. The flight would take about nine hours. Three-fourths of it, 2,900 miles, would be inside the USSR. After the takeoff he would break radio contact with the Mobile Control Officer. The rest of the trip would be made in complete silence. It was, Powers said, "a lonely feeling."

For three agonizing days it seemed that the flight would never get off the ground. Washington was hemming and hawing over last-minute instructions. Thursday, April 28, was fixed as the departure date when Colonel Shelton, Powers, and eighteen other specialists and crew members flew down to Peshawar from Turkey. Powers went to bed at 4 P.M. Wednesday. At 2 A.M. Thursday he was awakened and told that the takeoff had been postponed twenty-four hours. The next night was the same. This time he was up and "on the house" — breathing oxygen — when word came of another twenty-four-hour wait. Saturday there was a third twenty-four-hour delay. Somebody at 1600 Pennsylvania Avenue couldn't make up his mind.

At last, at 5:30 A.M. Sunday, May 1, Powers climbed into the plane for the preflight check. There the delay continued. The scheduled departure time was 6 A.M. It came and went without the signal to go. The cockpit was fiercely hot; his long underwear was drenched with perspiration when Coloned Shelton came out to explain. They were awaiting final approval from the White House. This had never happened before. Presidential approval had always come through before the pilot was locked in his seat and ready to go. The wait lasted twenty excruciating minutes. Then Powers was given the green light. He roared off and, once up, completed his flight log entries: the aircraft number, 360; the sortie number, 4154; and the time. It was 6:26 A.M. local time, 1:26 Greenwich mean time, and 8:26 P.M. in Washington. In Moscow it was 3:26 A.M.

Crossing into Russia the cloud cover was solid. That didn't matter here; the CIA wasn't interested in this area. The sky cleared over the Aral Sea, and glancing down he glimpsed the condensation trail of another single-engine jet plane, moving parallel to his course but in the opposite direction. Shortly afterward he saw another contrail, this one moving in the opposite direction. Probably it was the same machine. He assumed that Soviet spotters had spotted him on their radar screens and were sending up scouts. He wasn't worried. The trails were so far below him that the Russian pilot couldn't possibly see him.

Some thirty miles to the east he passed over the Tyuratam Cosmodrome, Russia's Cape Canaveral, and looked down on the pads from which the Soviet sputniks and ICBM's had been launched. He flipped switches, turning on the cameras. The cloud cover thickened again; he switched them off. Fifty miles south of Chelyabinsk the skies cleared, giving him a good view of the snow-topped Ural mountain range, once considered the dividing line between Asia and Europe, and at that point the aircraft started giving him trouble. The autopilot had gone haywire; the U-2 was pitching nose-up. He turned the autopilot off, drove the plane manually for a while, and turned the autopilot on again. Again it pitched. He considered turning back to Pakistan — in an abort situation the decision was up to the pilot — but he had already crossed 1,300 miles of Russia and the visibility ahead was excellent. He decided to continue, flying manually. Passing over an enormous oil storage area and an industrial complex, he zigged toward Sverdlovsk, the Soviet Ruhr. There, at an altitude of 65,000 feet, he made a 90-degree turn for a zag northward. He was making log entries of the altitude, time, speed, exhaust-gas temperature and engine instrument readings when he felt a dull thud. The plane bucked forward, and a blinding flash of orange light flooded the cockpit.

It was about a half-hour after midnight in the White House. In the Kremlin it was 7:30 A.M. Powers thought: "My God, I've had it now!"

Out of control, the machine started to go down. He reached for the destruction switches and changed his mind; he wanted to get into position to use the ejection seat first. He couldn't quite make it. The metal canopy rail was pinning his legs. Ejecting in this position, he would lose both legs, each severed about three inches above the knee. He was down to 34,000 feet and losing altitude fast. Fleetingly he thought of the destruction switches again, but first he wanted to release his seat belt. He did, and the force of gravity pulled him halfway out of the plane. Now the oxygen hoses were holding him back. He had forgotten to unfasten them. Near panic, he kicked and squirmed away from them. He floated free and was thinking about pulling the parachute ripcord when he felt a tremendous jerk. At 15,000 feet it had opened automatically. Suddenly his plane passed him; it was intact, and hurling downward. He thought of the silver dollar. Unscrewing the loop of it, he slipped out the suicide needle and considered pricking himself. Then he dropped it into his pocket. He wanted to live.

That was on a Sunday. The following Thursday Nikita Khrushchev addressed the Supreme Soviet for three and a half hours. His remarks on the U-2, coming at the end, set off two weeks of pandemonium.

USSR	U.S. AND ALLIES
MAY 5 Khrushchev says: "I am duty bound to report to you on the aggressive acts . . . by the United States of America." Announces Russian gunners have shot down a U.S. aircraft over Soviet territory but does not say where. Charges that the mission of the operation was "one of aggressive provocation aimed at wrecking the summit conference." Is careful to exonerate Eisenhower of blame.	U.S. Aeronautics and Space Administration reports that a weather observation plane is missing over Turkey after pilot reported oxygen trouble. NASA says the pilot may have strayed over the Russo-Turkish border.
MAY 6	Lincoln White, State Department spokesman: "There was absolutely no — N-O — deliberate intention to violate the Soviet air space, and there has never been." NASA identifies the "weather" pilot as Francis G. Powers. This is what Khrushchev has been waiting for.

USSR	U.S. AND ALLIES
MAY 7 Khrushchev tells the Supreme Soviet that Powers has been captured "alive and kicking," that a Russian rocket brought the U-2 down from an altitude of 65,000 feet, and that at that time the plane was 1,300 miles from the Soviet-Afghan border. Powers, he says, has made a complete confession.	State Department admits it lied yesterday. Says these "surveillance" flights date from Soviet rejection of Ike's "open skies" proposal at Geneva in 1955.
MAY 8	Consternation among allies over timing of flights, the fact that U.S. has been caught in lie, and the implication that the President has been unaware of something so important.
MAY 9 Khrushchev warns that Soviet rockets will attack countries that allow U.S. spy planes to use their territory.	Secretary of State Herter says Ike approved the program but specific flights are not subject to presidential approval. U-2 flights will continue.
MAY 10 Soviet formally protests U-2 operation and states that Powers will be tried.	
MAY 11 Speaking at a display of the U-2 wreckage, Khrushchev says, "The Russian people would say I was mad to welcome a man who sends spy planes over here."	President Eisenhower assumes personal responsibility for the U-2 flights.
MAY 12	Eisenhower tells congressmen that he still plans to fly to Moscow unless the invitation is withdrawn.
MAY 14 Hopes that the summit can be retrieved rise when Khrushchev, arriving in Paris, pledges himself to work for its success.	

USSR	U.S. AND ALLIES
MAY 15 Khrushchev says he will not participate in the summit talks unless U.S. ends all U-2 flights, apologizes for past "aggressions," and punishes those responsible for the flights.	Eisenhower says the flights have been suspended and will not be resumed.

MAY 16

Khrushchev, Eisenhower, President de Gaulle, and Harold Macmillan meet in Elysée Palace in Paris for the opening session of the conference. The atmosphere is frigid.

Khrushchev takes the floor. He is curt and rude. He suggests that the summit be postponed for six months, accuses Ike of "treachery" and "bandit" acts, and cancels the invitation for the reciprocal Eisenhower visit to Russia.	Ike, grim, says that the overflights are over, but that Khrushchev's "ultimatum" is unacceptable to the U.S.
Khrushchev stalks from the palace, leaving behind the shambles of Ike's hopes for a detente and world conciliation.	Eisenhower returns to the U.S. embassy in Paris shaking with rage.
MAY 17 Khrushchev boycotts the meeting. One of his aides telephones the Elysée palace to ask whether Ike is ready to apologize for the U-2 and punish those responsible.	De Gaulle and Macmillan make last-ditch efforts to save the conference. At 3 P.M. Eisenhower, de Gaulle, and Macmillan meet for the conference's first business session.
	Eisenhower: no apologies, no punishment.

5 P.M.: *The summit ends.*

MAY 18 In a chaotic press conference attended by 3,000 people, Khrushchev denounces the U.S. as thief-like," "piratical," and "cowardly." The Soviet Union will now solve the Berlin problem by signing a separate treaty with Communist East Germany.	

MAY 25

General Thomas D. White, the U.S. Air Force chief of staff, says that the U-2 gamble was needless and that had he known about it he would have recommended suspension of the overflights before the summit.

On the way home Eisenhower landed in Lisbon; he had chosen this peculiar time to honor Antonio de Oliveira Salazar, Portugal's septuagenarian dictator. While strolling through the formal gardens of Queloz Palace he came upon an American reporter who was idly tossing French coins into a fountain. Wearily the President asked, "That how you're keeping busy?"

"No, sir," said the reporter. "This is just for luck."

Turning away, Eisenhower said, "Then you'd better throw some in for all of us."

But the President was not rid of the U-2 jinx. Japan, America's strongest Asian ally, was to be the last destination in his odyssey of personal diplomacy. Had the summit gone well, it would have been a triumphal tour. Now it became a desperate opportunity to patch up presidential prestige. Even that was denied him. Japan was known to be the Asian base for U-2 overflights. Three of the now notorious spy planes were there, and Japanese leftists, taking their cue from Khrushchev, made them an excuse for rioting. On June 11 Jim Hagerty landed at Tokyo's Haneda Airport to make arrangements for the visit. Like Nixon in Caracas, he was lucky to escape with his life. For over an hour a mob of twenty thousand kept him and Ambassador Douglas MacArthur II imprisoned in their automobile. They had to be rescued by a Marine helicopter.

Eisenhower was in Manila when the Japanese cabinet, meeting in emergency session, asked him to stay away for the sake of his own safety. Humiliated, he went to Formosa instead, convoyed by six warships and 100 aircraft of the Seventh Fleet. The ships raced through the water at speeds exceeding thirty knots, not because they didn't want to keep Chiang Kai-shek waiting but as a precaution against unfriendly submarines. On the Chinese mainland Radio Peking was denouncing the President as a "god of plague." To give him some idea of how they felt, they battered the offshore island of Quemoy with its heaviest shelling in years. It could be heard abroad his Seventh Fleet armada. Wry correspondents said that he was the only chief of staff ever to get an eighty-thousand-gun salute.

When Eisenhower landed back in Washington on June 27, his travels were over. In eighteen months he had covered 60,000 miles in pursuit of peace, and he had come home empty-handed. Surveying the wreckage and looking for the cause, he said wanly, "After all, Communists will act like Communists." Emmet John Hughes wrote sorrowfully:

All the gleam of political promise in his fantastic global journeys now was gone beyond recapturing. He had given unstintingly of his energy and his personality. He had been repaid in popular coin — the voices of millions yelling lusty ovations, the hands of millions waving gaudy banners. He had invested all this amassed political capital in the two great chances — one in Paris, one in Tokyo. Now it was spent — all of it.

The cold war was closing in again on all fronts. Travel to the Soviet Union became difficult. There were incidents at Checkpoint Charlie in Berlin. After the summit debris had been swept away, a ten-nation East-West disarmament conference, which had been going well all spring, resumed in Geneva; it, too, collapsed when Valerian A. Zorin, the chief Soviet delegate, denounced the West for ninety minutes and walked out. In July the Russians shot down an American RB-47 reconnaissance plane over international waters and vetoed a United States-sponsored U.N. resolution calling for an impartial investigation of it.

Then, in August, during the lull after the Democratic and Republican national conventions in the United States, Americans relived the mortification of the U-2 when Francis Gary Powers was convicted of espionage in Moscow. Powers had landed on a large state farm. Taking his pistol away from him, the farmers had held him at gunpoint until officers of the KGB — the Committee for State Security, the secret police — arrived to take him into custody. He told the Soviet court that he understood that the summit conference and Eisenhower's planned visit to the USSR had been called off because of his flight and that it had increased world tension. "I am sincerely sorry that I had anything to do with this," he said. He was sentenced to ten years in prison.*

During his last months in office the President became reflective. Government spending by his administration made Franklin Roosevelt's pump priming seem puny — the total cost of government, including state and local expenditures, was now 170 billion dollars, almost one-third of the Gross National Product — and he was chagrined by his party's failure to convert young independent voters who had supported him into Republicans. "What happened," he asked Sherman Adams when his former assistant returned to 1600 Pennsylvania Avenue for a visit, "to all those fine young people who sailed balloons and rang doorbells for us in 1952?"

He had one final word for his constituents, and he gave it the following January, three days before he left the White House. During the 1950s the Pentagon, and especially the Air Force, had fostered a growing band of corporations whose leaders were retired generals and admirals. Eisenhower warned of the dangers in this. In his farewell radio and television address to the American people he observed that "Disarmament, with mutual honor and confidence, is a continuing imperative. Because this need is sharp and

---

*After seventeen months the Russians exchanged him for Colonel Rudolf Abel, a Soviet spy who had been convicted in an American court. Lockheed gave Powers a job as a test pilot until 1970, when he was laid off.

apparent, I confess I lay down my official responsibilities in this field with a definite sense of disappointment." He continued, "I wish I could say tonight that a lasting peace is in sight. Happily, I can say that war has been avoided." He spoke of the prodigious growth of companies manufacturing munitions. Then:

"This conjunction of an immense military establishment and a large arms industry is new in the American experience. . . . We recognize the imperative need for this development. Yet we must not fail to comprehend its grave implications. . . . In the councils of government we must guard against the acquisition of unwarranted influence, whether sought or unsought, by the military-industrial complex. The potential for the disastrous rise of misplaced power exists and will persist."

It was a remarkable speech, but forces favoring an arms race between the United States and the Soviet Union were too strong. Despite their many differences they were, in essence, the world's two largest industrial nations. By 1966 the size of the American military-industrial complex, and its dependence on congressional appropriations, would become staggering. In that year Boeing and General Dynamics sold 65 percent of their output to the government; Raytheon sold 70 percent, Lockheed sold 81 percent, and Republic Aviation sold 100 percent. As Galbraith admonished readers of *The New Industrial State* six years later, a company developing a new generation of fighter aircraft, to cite but one example, was "in an admirable position to influence the design and equipment of the plane. It can have something to say on the mission for which it is adapted, the number of planes required, their deployment, and, by implication, on the choice of the enemy toward which it is directed."

The presidential election of 1960 shaped up as a classic duel. Both nominees were from the swing generation and had been young naval officers in World War II, each had entered public life in the months after World War II, and both were now vigorous men in their forties. Richard Nixon believed at the outset, in January 1960, that the coming race would be the closest presidential election in America up to that time. It was; but that was just about the only prediction about it which proved correct.

The United States was not the same country that Dwight D. Eisenhower and Adlai E. Stevenson had stumped in 1952, and it was even less like the country that had gone to war in Korea two years before that. By 1960 the wave of migrants to the new suburbia was at floodtide. The nation was richer. Washington, the new census revealed, had become the first American city with a black majority — 54 percent as against 35 percent in 1950. By 1960 40 million American families, or 88 percent of them, owned at least one television set. Fully aware of the hundred million viewers, the two candidates were pondering ways to beguile them. Afterward it was widely believed that the tube helped Kennedy most. Marshall McLuhan thought he knew why. Kennedy, he said, had projected the image of a "shy young sheriff" in a TV western, while Nixon resembled "the railway lawyer who signs leases that are not in the best interests of the folks in the little town." What McLuhan overlooked was that as Americans became more prosperous they were increasingly conservative; more of them were investing in the railway, and were therefore on the lawyer's, not the sheriff's, side.

Each candidate followed a strategic plan. Kennedy appealed to the young, to the blue-collar vote, and to the liberal constituency which Roosevelt had drawn into the Democratic party in the 1930s. The two great Kennedy bases were the Democratic South — holding it was to be the task of his running mate — and the industrial northeast. His campaign would be largely directed at nine big states: Massachusetts, California, New York, Texas, New Jersey, Illinois, Ohio, Michigan, and Pennsylvania. If they could be carried, they would give him 237 of the 269 electoral votes he needed to be elected. His techniques included the mass registration of seven million unregistered voters — seven of every ten new registrants now were Democrats — the articulation of ideas from an Ivy League brain trust — Schlesinger, Galbraith, et cetera — and the brilliant tactics of his young Irish-Americans from Massachusetts, led by Lawrence F. O'Brien and Kenneth O'Donnell.

Kennedy's built-in advantages were support from organized labor, his father's great wealth, his Pultizer Prize, a friendly press corps, his charisma — reporters were beginning to call it the Kennedy "style" — and his membership in the majority party.

His disadvantages were long memories of his father's support of appeasement twenty years earlier, his youth — forty-three to Nixon's forty-seven — his inexperience, and the widely held conviction, dating from Al Smith's candidacy in 1928, that a Roman Catholic could not be elected President.

Kennedy meant to run as hard as he could as far as he could as long as he could. Nixon took a different tack. He believed that a political campaign had high tides and low tides, and that to ignore them was to risk boring, and therefore alienating, the electorate. The object, in his view, was to "peak" a campaign — to bring it to a climax — on election day. Like Kennedy, Nixon planned to zero in on key states, seven of them in his case: New York, California, Michigan, Texas, Pennsylvania, Ohio, and Illinois. He also promised to campaign in each of the other forty-three states — a pledge he later regretted. He had no brain trust; now, as always, Nixon was a loner, a solitary, brooding introvert. While the theme of Kennedy's drive was that American prestige was slipping and that Americans must move ahead, the Republican nominee preached the virtues of free enterprise, individual responsibility, hard-nose anti-Communism, and Eisenhower peace with prosperity.

Nixon's built-in advantages were support from big businessmen, his greater experience (for example, in the steel strike settlement during the

President's illness, and in his kitchen debate with Khrushchev), his strong middle-class roots, and Eisenhower's occupancy of the White House.

His disadvantages were recollections of Hoover in the White House, still vivid in the minds of older voters; his reputation as a dirty fighter — the "old Nixon" — the bad luck which was to plague him throughout this campaign, and his membership in the minority party.

Each year there were fewer Republicans in the United States. GOP candidates had won 49 percent of the votes cast in the off-year elections of 1950. In 1954 the figure was 47 percent; in 1958, 43 percent. A Gallup poll published in 1960 traced the decline of Republican loyalties in various occupational groups over the past eight years. Asked which party "best served" their interests, 28 percent of the farmers had said the Republicans in 1950. In 1960 only 18 percent said so. Among white-collar workers the drop had been even sharper, from 44 to 29 percent. Everybody liked Ike in the White House, but that affection wasn't transferable to Republicans playing supporting roles, and the rate of attrition among the party's lesser figures was alarming.

Eisenhower's effect on the 1960 race was further blurred by his equivocal feelings about his Vice President. He clearly preferred him to Kennedy, whom he regarded as a young upstart ("that boy," he called him), but he had told too many people that "Dick just isn't presidential timber"; the word was out. Eisenhower's insensitivity in this regard was puzzling. He slighted Nixon again and again. Discussing possible successors in his second term, he came down hard in favor of his last Secretary of the Treasury, Robert Anderson — "Boy, I'd like to fight for him in 1960!" Making a mental list, he added "some good new other fellows," including Attorney General William Rogers. He loyally included Sherman Adams, "although he'll be sixty-one in 1960, and that's pretty old for this job." Only at the end did he say, ". . . and Dick Nixon." On August 24, 1960, Eisenhower dealt Nixon the worst blow in the campaign. He was asked in a press conference, "What major decisions of your administration has the Vice President participated in?" The President's almost unbelievable reply was, "If you give me a week, I might think of one." Nixon wrote in *Six Crises* that Eisenhower had telephoned to apologize, saying that he had merely meant to be "facetious." The justification is odd, and he never offered any public explanation.

In a trial heat taken by Gallup after the 1958 off-year election, the voters chose Kennedy over Nixon, 59 to 41 percent. Just before the Vice President's visit to Moscow in July 1959, it was Kennedy 61 to Nixon 39 — a greater margin than Eisenhower over Stevenson in 1956. After that trip the figures were Kennedy 52 to Nixon 48. In November 1959 Nixon moved ahead for the first time, 53 to 47. On the eve of the first presidential primary on March 8 that six-point margin held steady.

Between New Hampshire and the Democratic national convention in Los Angeles four months later, Kennedy captured the Democratic nomination by proving himself unbeatable. Other Democrats who had pursued it were

Hubert Humphrey, Lyndon Johnson, Stuart Symington and — his last hurrah — Adlai Stevenson. Humphrey had led the challengers in the primaries.
Kennedy bent Humphrey's lance in Wisconsin on April 5, taking 56 percent
of the vote, and then destroyed him in supposedly anti-Catholic West Virginia on May 10, outpolling him three to two. At that point Humphrey
quit; he had run out of money. Then the Kennedy bandwagon picked up
momentum, winning in Maryland, in Indiana, and Oregon. By June 27,
when Kennedy addressed the Montana legislature, in search of support, he
had 550 of the 761 delegate votes needed for the nomination.

On the eve of the Democratic convention, Gallup had him leading Nixon
52 percent to 48 percent.

When he moved into his Los Angeles command post, suite 8315 of the
Biltmore Hotel, the young Irish-American senator from Massachusetts had
600 delegate votes. Like all Democratic conventions, this one was boisterous, and rich in political talent. Chicago's retiring boss, Jake Arvey, was
there with his successor, Dick Daley, and the most eloquent speech was
that of Senator Eugene McCarthy, nominating Stevenson. Eleanor Roosevelt was for Stevenson; so was Marian Schlesinger. (Bob Kennedy scrawled
a note to her husband: "Can't you control your wife — or are you like
me?") The Stevenson people were well organized. They had packed the
galleries, and their placard carriers were numerous on the convention floor;
included among them was one whose sign delighted her candidate: an
enormously pregnant woman, she carried a placard reading, STEVENSON IS
THE MAN.

The Stevenson movement was exciting, at times it was even gallant, but
it altered nothing. John F. Kennedy was nominated on the first ballot with
806 votes; Wisconsin's 15 had put him over the top. He chose Lyndon
Johnson for the bottom of the ticket — no two men who were there can
agree exactly how it was done, but Kennedy knew he needed November
support in the South, and Johnson was the man likeliest to give it to him.
In his acceptance speech Kennedy spoke of "a New Frontier — the frontier
of the 1960s — a frontier of unknown opportunities and perils — a frontier
of unfulfilled hopes and threats." He warned, "the New Frontier of which I
speak is not a set of promises — it is a set of challenges. It sums up, not
what I intend to offer the American people, but what I intend to ask of
them." At the end he said, "Now begins another long journey, taking me
into your cities and homes all over America. Give me your help" — the
crowds cheered — "give me your hand" — they cheered again — "your
voice and your vote"; they gave him a standing ovation, cheering on and on.

Gallup figures after the Democratic convention showed Kennedy leading
55 to 45.

After Nixon's nomination at the Republican national convention the following week, he took the lead in Gallup's report, 51 to Kennedy's 49. The
week after that he lengthened the lead, 53 to 47. Late in August the two

were running neck and neck. In September the number of undecided voters pushed both candidates below the 50 percent mark, but Nixon remained in front, 49 to Kennedy's 46.

This was the low point in the Democratic campaign. Lyndon Johnson, convinced that he would be the party's nominee, had scheduled a special session of Congress in which he expected to shine. Kennedy was now trapped in it while Nixon jubilantly opened his first tour in Atlanta on August 26. Six days later the special session ended and Kennedy took off for Maine. Gallup's new figures were Nixon 50, Kennedy 50.

Luck now intervened. On the third day of his southern trip Nixon struck his right kneecap on an automobile door in Greensboro, North Carolina. The injury did not heal. At Walter Reed Hospital he was told that it had become infected with hemolytic *Staphylococcus aureus.* Unless he remained at Walter Reed for two weeks of intensive antibiotic treatment, he was told, the cartilage of the joint would be destroyed. Thus he lay on his back from August 29 to September 9 with his leg in traction, wretched at the thought of the lost time. Back in action, he caught cold in St. Louis. His voice grew hoarse. To compound his misery, the religious issue emerged at this time under the worst possible circumstances for him.

Nixon had repeatedly instructed his staff not to discuss Kennedy's religion with anyone, under any circumstances. Unfortunately he could not control Dr. Norman Vincent Peale, the best-known Protestant clergyman in the country and a Nixon friend. Dr. Peale led a group of ministers issuing a statement expressing doubt that a Roman Catholic President could free himself from the influence of the church hierarchy in Rome. Nixon couldn't attack Dr. Peale, though he came close to it on that Sunday's *Meet the Press* program. Kennedy, meanwhile, had seized the chance to deal with this most delicate of issues, one that he had known he must confront sooner or later. The Greater Houston Ministerial Association had just invited him to discuss his faith on September 12 in Houston's Rice Hotel. He accepted. With dignity and lucidity he told them that he firmly believed in the complete separation of church and state, and that if he could not solve a conflict between his conscience and his office, he would resign. They applauded.

Two weeks later Gallup announced that voter preferences were again narrowing. The figures were Nixon 47 and Kennedy 46, with 7 percent undecided.

The race was approaching the critical period. In two September weeks both candidates stumped the country from coast to coast. Nixon had now traveled fifteen thousand miles in twenty-five states, addressing crowds exceeding two million voters, but he realized, as he later put it, that "no matter how big the crowds or how extensive the local coverage, it was a drop in the bucket: the effect up to September 25 would be infinitesimal compared with the first joint debate for all-network coverage the next evening, Monday, September 26."

There were to be four debates — the others were on October 7, October 14 and October 21 — but the first one was the most important. It drew the largest audience, some seventy million Americans, twenty million more than the others, and it was a Kennedy triumph. That was dismaying for Nixon, and it came as a surprise. He was a skillful debater. Watching Kennedy's acceptance speech on television — unaware that Kennedy was exhausted — he had thought that his rival spoke too rapidly, that his voice was too high-pitched, and that his concepts were too complicated for the average American. That was why Nixon had accepted the challenge of the debates. Both men had crammed for the first debate as though they were boning up for a bar exam. In words and ideas it was a standoff. But that in itself was a victory for Kennedy. Until that evening Nixon had been the more famous of the two, holding as he did the higher office. But here they stood toe to toe with Howard K. Smith as referee, and Kennedy held his own. More important, he *looked* better. Those who heard them on radio thought both did well, but the larger television audience saw the senator as tanned and fit. Nixon, on the other hand, had lost five pounds in Walter Reed. He was haggard, and he wore a shirt collar a half size too large for him. He slouched, his expression was grim, and his complexion was pasty, a consequence of ill-advisedly coating his face with Lazy Shave, a pancake make-up meant to hide afternoon beard growth.

Gallup's new poll showed that Kennedy had moved ahead 49 to 46; 5 percent were undecided.

Drinking four chocolate milk shakes a day on his doctor's instructions, Nixon regained his lost weight. In subsequent debates he looked as fit as his rival. He scored more debating points, too. It was all to no avail; millions had seen all they wanted, and their minds were made up.

After the last debate, and before Nixon's last-minute surge, Gallup's findings were Kennedy 51, Nixon 45; 4 percent were undecided.

Two key incidents affected the Negro vote as the campaign approached the home stretch. Speaking in Harlem on October 12, Lodge, without consulting anyone, said: ". . . there ought to be a Negro in the Cabinet . . . It is part of our program and is offered as a pledge." Nixon angrily denied that it was part of any program of his — which unfairly but inevitably offended blacks. A week later, on October 19, a Martin Luther King sit-in once more collided with Georgia law. Arrested in an Atlanta department store for refusing to leave the store restaurant, King was sentenced to four months at hard labor. When reporters asked Nixon for an opinion, he answered that he had none. Privately he thought that King's constitutional rights had been violated, and he called Attorney General Rogers to ask for a Justice Department inquiry. Rogers agreed, but Eisenhower wanted no part of it and the matter was dropped. The Kennedys had reacted differently. The Democratic candidate put through a person-to-person call to Coretta King telling her of his sympathy and his desire to help in any way he could. Next he conferred with his brother. Bob phoned the Georgia judge who had sentenced King, and on the following day the black clergy-man was out on bail. At the time the press was unaware of all this, but Mrs. King told other black leaders about it. They spread the word, which undoubtedly contributed to the tremendous majorities Kennedy rolled up in northern cities on November 8. One of the voters who switched was Martin Luther King's father. He told reporters that he never thought he could cast his ballot for a Catholic, but a call from his daughter-in-law had won him over. Kennedy murmured, "Imagine Martin Luther King having a bigot for a father." Then he added, "Well, we all have fathers, don't we?"

In the last days of October Gallup concluded that the race was too close for prediction. The Elmo Roper, Lou Harris, and Claude Robinson polls agreed, and Lawrence O'Brien told Kennedy that it was "a toss-up." It wasn't a dead heat all the way, though. Political writers and politicians on both sides agree that two trends counterbalanced in October. A decided shift toward Kennedy two weeks before the election was followed by a last-minute surge to Nixon. Nixon subsequently took this to be confirmation that Kennedy had "peaked" too early, but there is another interpretation. The switch in momentum accompanied President Eisenhower's entry into the campaign. Neither the U-2 nor the Japanese humiliation had dimin-ished Ike's tremendous popularity in the country, but Nixon's relationship with him had continued to be difficult, which explains the Vice President's failure to ask for his help until Monday, October 21. The President plunged in then and turned the campaign around. Conceivably another week or even a few more days could have reversed the result.

Toward the end the election seemed to blur into a montage of sights and sounds: Kennedy reminding audiences in his cool clipped accents that Castro had put Communists "eight jet minutes from Florida," Nixon saying that America could not afford to use the White House "as a training ground for a man who wants to learn how to be President, at the expense of the United States of America," Kennedy repeating over and over, almost as an incantation, "This is a great country. But I think it can be greater. I think we can do better. I think we can make this country move again," Truman's profanity and Nixon's response, vowing never to sully the Presidency by using blasphemy while in the White House, Eisenhower reciting Republi-can accomplishments in the last eight years: a 48 percent increase in per-sonal income, a 45 percent growth in the Gross National Product, the ex-pansion of social security, the St. Lawrence Seaway, 41,000 miles of inter-state highways — "My friends, never have Americans achieved so much in so short a time" — the teen-age girl "jumpers" in motorcade crowds, bob-bing up for a glimpse of the candidate, the Vice President promising that a Nixon administration would never allow Red China into the U.N., thus giving "respectability to the Communist regime which would immensely increase its power and prestige in Asia, and probably irreparably weaken the non-Communist governments in that area," the enthusiasm on college campuses when Kennedy spoke of the years ahead, "the challenging, revolutionary Sixties," Nixon favoring a resumption of atom bomb tests, Kennedy's callused hand bursting with blood near the end when a Pennsylvania admirer squeezed it too hard, Nixon charging that Kennedy, by declaring that American prestige was at an all-time low, was "running America down and giving us an inferiority complex," the smiles of the women whenever Kennedy mentioned his pregnant wife, and Nixon urging audiences: "Vote for the man you think America and the world needs in this critical period. Whatever that decision is, it is the one that I know will be best for America..It is one that we will all abide by; one that we will all support."

Abruptly it was over. Bright weather and the closeness of the contest brought forth the largest turnout in history — 68,832,818 votes, 11 percent more than 1956. After voting, Nixon relaxed by driving three friends down the California coast and showing them Tijuana, the Mexican border town; Kennedy spent the day playing touch football in the family compound in Hyannisport. Elaborate electronic gear had been installed on the sun porch of Bob Kennedy's home there, and it was there that the Democratic candidate watched the results that night and Wednesday morning.

An IBM-CBS computer enlivened the early evening by predicting, on the basis of data available at 7:15 P.M., that Nixon would win — its incredible odds were 100 to 1 — with 459 electoral votes to Kennedy's 68. Then, as hard figures poured in, the country appeared to be going Democratic in a landslide. Kennedy took Connecticut, always the first state with complete returns, by 90,000. He was winning New York City by a huge margin and carrying Philadelphia by 331,000, 68.1 percent of the vote. Cook County, under the watchful eye of Dick Daley, was giving the Democratic ticket a lead that seemed to place it beyond the reach of downstate Republican Illinois. At 10:30 Kennedy's popular vote plurality was 1,500,-000. He was then being projected as the winner by 4,000,000 or 5,000,000. The IBM-CBS machine was giving him 311 electoral votes; NBC's RCA-501 computer was putting it at 401. Viewers in the eastern United States were switching off their sets and going to bed, believing that it was all over. Jacqueline Kennedy whispered to her husband, "Oh, Bunny, you're President now!" He replied quietly, "No . . . no . . . it's too early yet."

It was indeed. Kennedy's high-water mark came shortly after midnight. His margin then exceeded 2,000,000, and the first returns from Los Angeles County indicated that he might carry California by 8,000,000. It was at precisely that point that the ticket began to run into trouble. Something unexpected was happening on the far side of the Appalachians. In the swing county of Lexington, Kentucky, for example, Kennedy was running behind Stevenson in 1952 and far behind Truman in 1948. Early Kansas returns put Nixon ahead or abreast of Eisenhower in 1956. Over the next two hours the picture cleared. It was not reassuring to the watchers in Hyannisport. The GOP ticket was sweeping: Kansas by 60.4 percent, South Dakota by 58.3, North Dakota by 55.4, Nebraska by 62.1. Wisconsin, conceded to

Kennedy in all the polls, was going Republican by over 60,000 votes and the Democratic lead in California was disappearing as returns came in from the Los Angeles suburbs. Nationally, Kennedy's popular vote margin dwindled to 1,700,000 to 1,600,000 to 1,100,000. Plainly it was going to be less than a million. It might vanish altogether.

By 3 A.M. the country knew that Nixon was going to carry more states than Kennedy. That was small comfort to the Republicans, though; their ticket had virtually no chance of winning the 269 electoral votes needed for a Nixon triumph. The larger question was whether Kennedy would make it. Four big states hung in the balance: Illinois (27 electoral votes), Michigan (20), California (32), and Minnesota (11). Nixon could become President only if he carried all four, at that point a very remote possibility. Any two would cinch the election for Kennedy. But if he took only one of them, he would fall short. His triumph would be thwarted by 14 or 15 Dixiecrat electors, and the winner would be chosen by the House of Representatives.

By dawn everyone in Hyannisport had gone to bed except Bob Kennedy, who kept vigil over the teletypes, the television sets, and the telephone. (The Kennedy phone bill for that night was $10,000.) At 9:30 Michigan's Republicans threw in the towel, having concluded that Kennedy's 67,000 vote lead there would hold. The ticket was also carrying Minnesota and Illinois. That was good enough for U. E. Baugham, chief of the U.S. Secret Service. Baugham put through a call from Washington to a team of sixteen of his agents registered at Hyannis's Holiday Heath Inn, and they moved in on the Kennedy compound. The campaign belonged to history. Kennedy was now President-elect Kennedy.

Official returns in December gave him 34,226,925 to Nixon's 34,108,662 — a margin of 112,881, less than two-thirds of one percent of the popular vote. For Nixon it was a heartbreaker. A change of a half-vote per precinct would have given him the decision. He had run nearly five percentage points ahead of GOP congressional candidates, and of the country's eight geographic regions — New England, the mid-Atlantic states, the South, the farm states, the Rocky Mountain states, the industrial Midwest, the five Pacific states, and the border states — he had carried all but the first three. Some of his advisers wanted him to challenge the outcome. There was sufficient evidence of fraud in Illinois and Texas, among other states, to suggest the possibility of a turnaround. He was tempted, but decided against it. The barriers were too formidable. In Cook County, for example, a recount would have taken a year and a half, and there was no recount procedure at all in Texas. Meantime the country would have to be governed.

In January the U.S. Constitution played a cruel trick on this intense, driven man. Article II, Section 2, provides that after the presidential electors have cast their ballots, "the President of the Senate shall, in the presence of the Senate and House of Representatives, open all the certificates and the votes shall then be counted." The President of the Senate is the Vice President of the United States. Once before, in 1861, a Vice President, then John C. Breckinridge, had to attest thus to his defeat, then at the hands of Abraham Lincoln. Nixon solemnly announced the result, 303 to 219, with 15 Dixiecrats for Harry Byrd. He took the occasion to deliver a short, graceful speech congratulating Kennedy and Johnson and paying tribute to the stability of the American political process. In response the Congress gave him an ovation.

After he left an inaugural day luncheon at the F Street Club, his chauffeur gently reminded him that this was the last day that he, as Vice President, would have a limousine at his disposal. That evening Nixon rode to Capitol Hill. In the darkness the city seemed briefly deserted. He later wrote, "I got out of the car and looked once again down what I believe is the most magnificent vista in the world — the Mall, now completely snow-covered, with the Washington Monument and the Lincoln Memorial in the distance."

Here, as so often in his life, he found comfort in sententious reflections. "Defeat is a greater test of character than victory" was one. Another was in a handwritten letter from Robert O. Reynolds, the former Stanford All-American and Detroit Lions star who went on to become one of the owners of the Los Angeles Rams. "Sometimes one loses a battle to win the war," Reynolds wrote Nixon. Quoting one of his college professors, he explained:

> . . . defeats are poison to some men. Great men have become mediocre because of inability to accept and abide by a defeat. Many men have become great because they were able to accept and abide by a defeat. If you should achieve any kind of success and develop superior qualities as a man, chances are it will be because of the manner in which you meet the defeats that will come to you just as they come to all men.

Nixon liked that, and he remembered it while packing to go home to California and start all over again.

IV

REAPING
THE
WHIRLWIND
1961-1968

TWENTY-SEVEN

A New Generation of Americans

BITTER COLD had set in that week of Richard Nixon's farewell to Washington, and on Thursday, January 19, the day before Kennedy's inauguration, new snow began to fall. By late afternoon, when the government offices let out, streets and pavements were covered. Softly through the long blue winter twilight it sifted down in great powdery layers, and by 8 P.M., when the President-elect and his wife attended a concert in Constitution Hall, the District lay frozen under a thick coverlet which dismayed even hardy New Frontiersmen. Still it continued to fall, speckling the pink faces of soldiers using flamethrowers to melt the caked ice around the inauguration stand on the east side of the Capitol, deepening in the Capitol's many squares and circles, stitching the eaves of the Executive Office Building and the federal triangle complex with the same shimmering thread. Open fires were lit along the Mall in an attempt to keep it clear for traffic, but the flames had to be kept too low to help much, for the snow was accompanied by a wind that howled in from the Potomac and the Tidal Basin, sending the hard white silt scudding before its raw gusts. Shortly after 3:45 A.M., when the President-elect returned to his Georgetown home, the snow died away, but the cold continued to hold the city in its frigid grip. Drifts hung in the alleys of the Negro ghetto in northeast Washington, and there was an epidemic of broken oil burners in Cleveland Park.

At noon Friday the temperature was twenty degrees above zero; the winds were still punishing. Twenty minutes later the shivering crowd saw the new President appear on the stand and cheered, hoping to hear his speech soon. It didn't for a while. Instead it shivered some more while Richard Cardinal Cushing honked his way through an invocation that seemed endless. Like so many other chapters in John Kennedy's life, the inaugural was beginning in disarray. As the cardinal finished, smoke began to curl up from a short circuit in the wires under the lectern. Momentarily the horrified chief of the Secret Service envisaged the whole stand going up in flames. Three times he started to order it cleared and checked himself. Then the smoke stopped, only to be succeeded by another setback. Rising to read a poem, Robert Frost was blinded by the sun glaring on the snow; he had to put it away and recite a poem from memory. At last Chief Justice Warren administered the oath at 12:51. And with that, everything changed. Hatless and coatless, his voice frosting in the air, and his starchy vowels redolent of Boston, the vigorous young President set the tone of the new administration:

"Let the word go forth from this time and place, to friend and foe alike, that the torch has been passed to a new generation of Americans . . . tempered by war, disciplined by a hard and bitter peace, proud of our ancient heritage."

"That speech he made out there," Sam Rayburn said afterward, "was better than Lincoln." It was an occasion for extravagant remarks. After the tranquil, healing years under Eisenhower, the capital was witnessing the commencement of an innovative administration, the first since Franklin Roosevelt's. Now, as then, the accent was on youth. The new First Lady, who had been born the year of the Crash, was a young woman of stunning beauty. Joining her husband in the Capitol after his speech, she softly touched his face and said in her breathy way, "Oh, Jack, what a day!"

Subsequent days in those first weeks were equally radiant. Writing of Kennedy years afterward in a memoir on the swing generation, Joan Swallow Reiter said, "He was *our* President, the first born in our century, the youngest man ever elected to the office and, we were sure, certain to be one of the best." Among New Frontiersmen that faith was absolute: never had men picked up the symbols of command with greater confidence.

John Fitzgerald Kennedy had been chosen President by 34,221,463 Americans, or 49.7 percent of those who had voted. After his death in November 1963 a nationwide poll reported that 65 percent recalled casting their ballots for him, which meant that over ten million of his constituents had altered their memories of that election day. But they had been changing them even before he went to Dallas. In June 1963 another poll had found that 59 percent said they had voted Democratic three years earlier.

The phenomenon was not an accident. Kennedy had entered office determined to broaden his support in the country. During the interval between his election and his inauguration he had read Richard E. Neustadt's scholarly *Presidential Power,* in which Neustadt wrote that the public's impression of a chief executive "takes shape for most constituents no later than the time they first perceive him being President (a different thing from seeing him as a candidate)." Kennedy was determined that the first time Americans saw him as President he would be at the post and pulling away.

Noticing that there were no blacks among the Coast Guard cadets in the inaugural parade, he started an official inquiry on the spot. The next morning he was in his bare office early, witnessing the swearing in of his cabinet, pumping Harry Truman's hand — Truman was in the White House for the first time since his last day as tenant — and firing off Executive Order No. 1, to double the food rations of four million needy Americans. In the weeks which followed the new President continued to vibrate with energy. He would pace corridors while dictating rapidly, read on his feet, dart out for brisk constitutionals, and return in a fast walk that was almost a sprint, restlessly snapping his fingers. "He did everything today except shinny up the Washington Monument," James Reston wrote of one of those typical early days.

The rest of Washington was expected to keep pace with him. In the Kennedy administration, said Arthur J. Goldberg, the new Secretary of Labor, "the deadline for everything is day before yesterday." Charles E. Bohlen said, "I never heard of a President who wanted to know so much." Some members of the government were so hard-pressed by the new chief executive that routine work suffered. A committee chairman from the Hill complained, "*He* may have two hours to spend, but *I* don't," and Llewellyn Thompson, ambassador to Russia, who had seldom been alone with Eisenhower for more than ten minutes, had four two-hour sessions with Kennedy. The talk wasn't small talk. "When you see the President," a senator remarked, "you have to get in your car and drive like blazes back to the Capitol to beat his memo commenting on what you told him."

One day a hundred people were counted entering his West Wing office. One meeting there produced seventeen separate directives, and two months after taking the oath Kennedy had issued thirty-two official messages and legislative recommendations (Eisenhower had issued five in his first two months) while delivering twelve speeches, promulgating twenty-two executive orders and proclamations, sending twenty-eight communications to foreign chiefs of state, and holding seven press conferences. Reporters were fascinated: more of them came than for the press conferences of any other President before or since. A Washington wit observed that the new President seemed determined to be not only his own Secretary of State but his own Mrs. Roosevelt too. No detail seemed too small for him. At one early press conference he answered in a knowledgeable way a question about a proposal to ship $12,000,000 in Cuban molasses to the United States — information which had appeared four days earlier near the bottom of a departmental report. Noting that Army Special Forces troops had been deprived of their green berets, he ordered that they be returned. Conferring with generals about strategy in Southeast Asia, he tested the carbines being shipped to Vietnam, and as his first presidential spring approached he even detected crabgrass on the greening White House lawn and told the gardeners to get rid of it.

He was out to expand his all-important base. The people he needed were watching him, and he wanted to be sure they liked what they saw. The hatless, coatless vigor helped. Americans approve of self-starters. It was useful for reporters to report that the new President was very much in charge; useful, for example, to let the word get around that Dean Acheson had been given just four days to hammer out a detailed NATO report. The first televised sessions with the White House press corps were, of course, crucial. One of them — the third — was watched by some sixty-five million people in twenty-one and a half million homes. These performances were live. Kennedy had to be not only his own Mrs. Roosevelt but also his own Robert Montgomery. He did it; McLuhan acclaimed him as a virtuoso. And presently the wisdom of the Neustadt approach was reflected in studies by opinion samplers. Kennedy's racing start had converted an enormous segment of the electorate. These were Nixon voters who had changed their minds and would soon convince themselves that they had been for Kennedy all along. It was something of a political miracle: the new chief executive's base was as big as Ike's.

"Presidents, like great French restaurants, have an ambiance all their own," Douglass Cater observed. The Kennedy image was forming, an amalgam of, among other things, Jacqueline Kennedy's camellia beauty, three-year-old Caroline's Kate Greenaway charm, the elegant rhetoric of the President's speeches, the football on the attorney general's desk, and the new idealism. Gone were the former administration's flannel phrases — "bigger bang for a buck," "rolling readjustment," "agonizing reappraisal." Instead, the country learned, there was to be a dynamic policy of action, typified by the new Secretary of Labor, who settled a strike during his first twenty-four hours in office. Like the harassed senator, everyone in the new cabinet appeared to be driving like blazes, working twelve-hour days and displaying signs of Kennedy hypomania. It was mostly illusion, of course, and later there was bound to be some disillusion, but at the time it was undeniably impressive. One secretary was observed simultaneously signing his mail, carrying on a telephone conversation, and relaying instructions to an aide by crude semaphore; a second was said to be training himself to carry on with only six hours of sleep; and a third member of the cabinet, Robert McNamara, startled Pentagon guards by showing up at 7:30 each morning.

Restoration of green berets to the Special Forces reflected Kennedy's belief in excellence. Later David Halberstam would write of those first days that the members of the Kennedy team "carried with them an exciting sense of American elitism" — elitism was not yet a term of opprobrium — "a sense that the best men had been summoned forth from the country to harness this dream to a new American nationalism, bringing a new, strong, dynamic spirit to our historic role in world affairs." Examples abounded, particularly in the recruiting of distinguished scholars. An astonishing number of them came from Cambridge, Massachusetts; a mot of the time offered a new definition of a failure: a Yale man driving an Edsel with a Nixon sticker on it. Asked how he happened to be chosen Secretary of Agriculture, Orville Freeman said, "I'm not really sure, but I think it had something to do with the fact that Harvard does not have a school of agriculture." Freeman did indeed lack a Harvard degree, but what was more important in this administration was that at Minnesota he had been graduated magna cum laude and elected to Phi Beta Kappa. A Mauldin cartoon depicted a Phi Beta Kappa key as the new key to the capital. Disdain and even contempt for intellectuals, so conspicuous in Washington eight years earlier, had vanished. In cultivating this image, New Frontiersmen soft-pedaled certain inconvenient facts — their President loved golf, for example, and his two favorite songs, "Bill Bailey" and "Heart of My Heart," were anything but classical. Yet picturing him as a Brahmin was not inaccurate. As Truman had admired generals and Eisenhower tycoons, Kennedy turned to academics. Among his advisers were fifteen Rhodes scholars, led by the Secretary of State, and four professional historians. The Secretary of Defense, the Commissioner of Internal Revenue, the chairman of the Civil Service Commission, and the ambassadors to India, Japan, and Yugoslavia were former college teachers. The President's expert on gold was a professor. Even the President's military adviser, General Maxwell D. Taylor, came to him from the Lincoln Center for the Performing Arts, and for the first time in history the White House had a cultural coordinator.

The Best and the Brightest, Halberstam would later call them in a bitter reckoning of their foreign policy failures. His appraisal came eleven years later and was largely an indictment of their role in Vietnam. Unquestionably that was the worst of their handiworks, but it was not their only disaster, a fact to be weighed in putting the Kennedy years in perspective. The new administration had stumbled earlier. The responsibility for their first outstanding nonsuccess was far from theirs alone. They were executing a plan drawn up by the outgoing administration. Nevertheless, they should have been more skeptical of it. The fact that they were not is illustrative of how fallible the cleverest politicians can be. Their error lay in confusing image and reality. Looking back on those first weeks in power, Robert Kennedy would observe almost wistfully, "Those were the days when we thought we were succeeding because of the stories on how hard everybody was working." Their discovery of their mistake was a spin-off of one of American history's most farcical misadventures, which took its name from Cuba's Bahía de Cochinos, the Bay of Pigs.

Of that debacle Halberstam was to write: "How a President who seemed so contemporary could agree to a plan so obviously doomed to failure, a plan based on so little understanding of the situation, was astounding." Afterward Kennedy himself asked Ted Sorensen, "How could I have been so far off base? All my life I've known better than to depend on the experts. How could I have been so stupid, to let them go ahead?" Again and again, Arthur Schlesinger noted, the remorseful President would "recur incredulously to the Bay of Pigs, wondering how a rational and responsible government could ever have become involved in so ill-starred an adventure."

All that, of course, was after the fact. In the beginning the scheme had not seemed so harebrained. President-elect Kennedy had first learned of it from Allen Dulles on November 29, 1960. Two days after the inaugural, Dulles and General Lyman Lemnitzer, chairman of the Joint Chiefs, briefed the leading members of the new administration — Rusk, McNamara, Robert Kennedy. On January 28 the President called the first White House meeting to discuss the future of La Brigada. Schlesinger observed that Kennedy was "wary and reserved in his reaction." The CIA men told their new chief not to worry. There were no loose threads, they assured him; every base was covered.

Kennedy at that time had been President one week. He wanted time to mull the thing over, but the CIA said he couldn't have much of it. For La Brigada it was now or never. Castro was about to receive crated MIGs from Russia. By June 1 enough of them would be assembled and in service, piloted by Cuban fliers who were being trained in Czechoslovakia, to wipe out the brigade on the beaches. In addition, President Ydígoras said the trainees couldn't stay in Guatemala after April. By then the rainy season would turn the Sierra Madre into one vast bog. Further training there would be impossible. The CIA reported that La Brigada was fit and eager to fight. The liberation of Cuba awaited a word, a single word, from the President.

Still he hesitated. The pressure mounted. Allen Dulles bluntly put it to him: either he approved the plan or he would be refusing to allow freedom-loving exiles to deliver their homeland from a Communist dictatorship, encouraging Cuba to undermine democratic governments throughout Latin America, and creating an ugly '64 campaign issue as the disbanded, disillusioned brigade toured the United States under Republican auspices, revealing how Kennedy had betrayed them and the cause of anti-Communism. Dulles asked the President whether he was ready to tell this "group of fine young men" who asked "nothing other than the opportunity to try to restore a free government in their country" that they would "get no sympathy, no support, no aid from the United States?"

Kennedy asked what the chances of success were. Dulles reminded him that in June 1954 the CIA had overthrown Guatemala's Marxist government. He said, "I stood right here at Ike's desk, and I told him I was certain our Guatemalan operation would succeed, and, Mr. President, the prospects for this plan are even better than they were for that one." The Joint Chiefs unanimously endorsed it. Late in February Kennedy asked for a second opinion from the Chiefs. They sent an inspection team to the Guatemalan base. After reading the report and studying La Brigada's tactical plan, General Lemnitzer again predicted that it would succeed, and Admiral Arleigh Burke, chief of naval operations, seconded him. Looking for still another opinion, the President ordered to Guatemala a veteran Marine Corps colonel with a brilliant combat record. The result was this evaluation:

My observations have increased my confidence in the ability of this force to accomplish not only initial combat missions, but also the ultimate objective, the overthrow of Castro. The Brigade and battalion commanders now know all details of the plan and are enthusiastic.* These officers are young, vigorous, intelligent and motivated by a fanatical urge to begin battle. . . .

They say they know their own people and believe that after they have inflicted one serious defeat upon the opposition forces, the latter will melt away from Castro, whom they have no wish to support. They say it is a Cuban tradition to join a winner and they have supreme confidence they will win against whatever Castro has to offer.

I share their confidence.

At that, Kennedy yielded, conceding that there was some logic in the argument that an administration which was prepared to send U.S. troops to fight Communism in Laos, on the other side of the world, could not ignore an aggressive Communist regime ninety miles south of Florida. Yet even then he expressed misgivings. Schlesinger later believed that if one senior adviser had spoken out against the expedition, it would have been canceled. Only he and Senator William Fulbright protested. (Chester Bowles and Edward R. Murrow knew of it and were against it, but as their sources of information were unofficial, they couldn't appeal to the White House.) Schlesinger asked Kennedy, "What do you think about this damned invasion?" Kennedy replied dryly, "I think about it as little as possible."

On Monday, April 10, the brigade was moved by truck to its point of embarkation, Puerto Cabezas, in Nicaragua. Thursday the men boarded the boats. On Friday their CIA leaders told them their objectives: the capture of three beaches in the Bay of Pigs, with brigade paratroops seizing key points in the great marshy swamp — Cienaga de Zapata — that lay between the island proper and the sea. At noon Sunday the expedition passed the point of no return. The rebels, their armada, and their tiny air force were committed.

The real nature of that commitment and the plan Kennedy thought he had approved were not the same thing, however. The President had been assured that the brigade comprised 1,400 elite troops who had been trained as guerrillas. Their objective in the Bay of Pigs, he — and they — had been told, was a remote, abandoned beach whose only signs of habitation were deserted resort houses. Landing at night, the briefers explained, the rebels' presence would be unknown to Castro. CIA intelligence further assured the President that the Cuban dictator would be unable to act for at least seventy-two hours. Even then he would be bewildered; to divert him, 168 brigade commandos would make a diversionary landing on the coast of Oriente province over three hundred miles away.

Dulles, Richard Bissell — chief architect of the CIA plan — and their advisers, including E. Howard Hunt Jr., were confident that enough Cubans were disillusioned with Castro to guarantee the success of the main landing.

*The record shows that at that point the CIA had not shown any of them the plan.

They reported that 2,500 of them belonged to resistance organizations, that another 20,000 sympathized with the resistance, and that 25 percent of the population, at the very least, was prepared to give the insurgents active support. This was essential, for both in private and in public Kennedy had emphasized that the American military would play no part in an assault on Castro. He was locked in on this. At an April 12 press conference he said that "there will not be, under any conditions, any intervention in Cuba by United States forces, and this government will do everything it possibly can — and I think it can meet its responsibilities — to make sure that there are no Americans involved in any actions inside Cuba . . . The basic issue in Cuba is not one between the United States and Cuba; it is between the Cubans themselves."

Should the exiles fail to establish a beachhead in the Bay of Pigs and hold it, he was told, they would break off the action and "melt into the hills." With that, the President thought that all bets had been covered. Believing such a diversion would alter the plan from one for a spectacular amphibious assault to a low-key infiltration, he felt that any chance that U.S. credibility and prestige might be damaged had been eliminated.

He was mistaken. The CIA to the contrary, none of the exiles had received any instruction in guerrilla warfare since November 4, 1960, at which time their force had numbered just 300 men. Many of the more recent recruits were not fit for an arduous jungle campaign. Only 135 members of the brigade were really soldiers. The rest were clerks, lawyers, bankers, physicians, geologists, teachers, cattlemen, newspapermen, musicians, draftsmen, engineers, artists, and mechanics. Three were Catholic priests and one was a Protestant clergyman. Crack troops should be young, in their late teens or early twenties. The average age of these men was twenty-nine; some of them were in their sixties, and some of the late arrivals had not learned to fire a rifle.

That was only the beginning of Kennedy's misapprehensions. Actually the question of how the rebels would fare in the hills was never tested, because, incredibly, the nearest range was the Escambray Mountains, eighty miles inland and separated from the Bay of Pigs by a hopeless tangle of swamps. Being Cubans, the exiles might have pointed that out. The difficulty was that nothing had been said to them about the possibility of melting away there or anywhere else. On its own, without consulting either the President or the Joint Chiefs, the CIA had decided to withhold the alternative plan from the insurgents. Its reasoning was that if the exiles knew of it, their determination to fight might be weakened; they might be tempted to abandon their beachhead while they still had a good chance of winning.

Everything possible was done to build up the insurgents' morale, and that included making promises that could not be kept. Frank Bender said to them: "You will be so strong, you will be getting so many people to your side, that you won't want to wait for us. You will go straight ahead. You will put your hands out, turn left, and go straight into Havana." Furthermore, the CIA agents assured the exiles that if they foundered Americans would rescue them. Long afterward their leader, José Pérez San Román, learned of the option, the last resort of flight to the hills. He said bitterly, "We were never told about this. What we were told was, 'If you fail *we* will go in.'" In Miami, Manuel Ray of the Frente believed that U.S. troops would come in as a second wave. He said later, "We were told that the landings would be followed up by all necessary support. We were even told that ten to fifteen thousand men would be available."

The first setback came in the air, and it was crucial. CIA appraisals of the Cuban air force had been scornful. Its combat efficiency was rated "almost nonexistent," its planes "for the most part obsolete and inoperative," and its leadership "entirely disorganized." Castro had fifteen B-26 bombers, ten Sea Furies, and four fast T-33 jet trainers. To knock them out, the CIA scheduled a strike against Cuban airfields on Saturday, April 15, two days before the landing. Eight exiles were to fly World War II prop-driven B-26s; afterward two of them would identify themselves in Miami as defectors from the Cuban air force. It wasn't good enough. Castro, after all, knew who was deserting from him and who wasn't, and to assure confusion among the Americans a *real* defector chose this awkward time to land in Jacksonville. The lumbering B-26s were slow, unwieldy, and plagued by engine trouble. Saturday evening Frank Bender sent a message to Pepe San Román. The bombing mission had been a success, he said; nearly all Castro aircraft had been destroyed on the ground — twelve at his Santiago de Cuba airfield, six to eight at Ciudad Libertad, and eight to ten at San Antonio. This would have been marvelous if it were true, but it wasn't; the Cuban air force had been left with six B-26s, two Sea Furies, four fighters and, most important, two T-33 jets. Unaccountably, both the CIA and the Joint Chiefs had assigned no value to the T-33s because they were trainer planes. They were jets all the same, and as such could fly circles around the insurgents' B-26s. Armed with 50-caliber machine guns, they would hop on the tails of the B-26s. Moreover, the bombers were particularly vulnerable to attack from the rear. As flown in World War II, B-26s had been defended by tail gunners, but the CIA had eliminated tail guns in these planes to put in extra gas tanks, giving the fliers more time in the air over Cuba. Now the exiled fliers were doomed. Air mastery would belong to Castro. Always important in an amphibious operation, this was especially so for this one because of another CIA error. For reasons which have never been explained, the agents had ordered all the supplies for the first ten days of fighting — the ammunition, gasoline, food, hospital equipment — loaded on one ship.

The name of the vessel was the *Río Escondito*. It was one of five hulking old World War II troop transports and two escort ships bearing the cover name García Line for this operation, and in a way it was a symbol of the entire undertaking. Unpainted and covered with rust, its engines temperamental and its hold reeking of foul odors, the *Río* listed like *The African Queen*. The exiles were appalled by it. One of them, Enrique Ruiz-Williams, a mortarman with some knowledge of the sea, was shocked — it gave him what he later described as "a cold feeling" — and Erneido Oliva felt "a great deception when we got over to the ships. It was something we didn't expect. That was not what we were waiting for." The idea that such a boat had been chosen for a mission of stealth was ludicrous. Its hoists and winches shrieked when used. Its rust-caked loading machinery was even noisier. The *Río* was already in trouble. Moving down the Mississippi to the Gulf of Mexico, one of its propellers had struck a log. Brigade frogmen found it completely bent. Its maneuverability sharply limited, it limped onward on its way to a duel with enemy aircraft.

Kennedy's understanding that young Cuban patriots would be landed quietly on an isolated coast was first jarred by a Manhattan public relations firm. Without a word to the White House or anyone else, including the Cuban Frente, whose authority was being preempted, the CIA had hired Lem Jones Associates to issue press releases in the name of the "Cuban Revolutionary Council." The bulletins were being telephoned to Jones's Madison Avenue office by CIA agents and then distributed to the press. One, "for immediate release," reported: "The principal battle of the Cuban revolt against Castro will be fought in the next few hours. Action today was largely of a supply and support effort." At the end it called for "a coordinated wave of sabotage and rebellion."

In Washington administration insiders were beginning to wonder whether it wasn't the exiles who were being sabotaged. Everything was going wrong for them. The landing craft assigned to their assault waves turned out to be fourteen-foot open boats with no protection for those aboard. The 50-caliber machine guns on them were improperly sighted and aimed in the wrong direction. The boats were powered by outboard motors; at the peak of the coming action one of the invaders, jumping from his ship, struck a pilot and knocked him overboard, leaving the landing craft to drift in aimless circles. There were other mishaps; aboard the transport *Atlántico* three insurgents were practicing with a 50-caliber machine gun when it tore loose from its mounting and fired wildly in all directions, killing one of their comrades and wounding two others. More ominous for the outcome of the operation, the force of rebel commandos who were supposed to draw Castro's mission away from the Bay of Pigs by a feint in Oriente province never reached the shore. Twice they boarded their landing craft and twice returned to reembark on their ship, *La Playa*. The CIA agents accompanying them sent back word that the diversion had been "aborted primarily because of bad leadership." The leaders had been chosen by the CIA.

The Oriente landing was to have been part of a cunning design meant to throw Castro off balance. Even more important were plans for a general uprising in Cuba by the anti-Castro underground. President Kennedy had been told that the underground movement was vital to the success of the mission. The Joint Chiefs had agreed. The behavior of the CIA, however, had been curiously ambivalent. The underground was part of the over-all strategy. Agents had been in touch with Rogelio Gonzáles Corso, the almost legendary leader of the movement, known throughout Cuba under his code name, "Francisco." He and his men were on the alert. At the proper time they were to be told to create disorders and create a general air of insurgency which would then be capitalized upon by Radio Swan, the exiles' propaganda station; Radio Swan broadcasts would tell the populace how to help La Brigada, how to join its ranks, how to blow up power stations, and so on. This looked fine on paper, but in practice it raised a basic question of priorities. The difficulty was one of timing. The uprisings conflicted with the air strike meant to wipe out Castro's air force. Whichever one came first would alert him to the other. Command of the air was judged to be more important. It came first and it failed. The following night Radio Swan broadcast orders for the underground to rise. They were in code and lyrical in the most florid Howard Hunt prose:

Alert! Alert! Look well at the rainbow. The first will rise very soon. Chico is in the house. Visit him. The sky is blue. Place notice in the tree. The tree is green and brown. The letters arrived well. The letters are white. The fish will not take much time to rise. The fish is red.

The strangest thing about this message was that it seems to have beamed toward the wrong people. It was picked up by the Columbia and National broadcasting networks and by several Florida stations, none of which could fathom its meaning. But although it was repeated over and over, it reached none of the listeners for whom it was intended — the brigade, the commandos, the Frente, the infiltration teams, and the saboteurs in Cuba. In reality it didn't much matter, though. Castro, warned by the air attack the day before, had ordered a roundup of all Cubans whose loyalty to him was suspect. Instantly, in the words of nineteen-year-old Félix Rodríguez, one of those who was waiting to revolt, "The roads were closed, the houses were surrounded, and they were arresting thousands of people. I cried." In Havana alone more than two hundred thousand men and women were arrested and lodged in baseball parks, public buildings, theaters, and auditoriums. Thus the underground audience wasn't tuned in. It was being held at gunpoint. On the next day, D-day, Monday, April 17, 1961, Francisco himself was found guilty of treason and executed.

At 7:45 P.M. the previous evening the five rusty cargo ships and two escorts of the exiles' task force had arrived in the Bay of Pigs and cast anchor. One by one the subplots meant to support the insurgents on board had failed — the Oriente deception, the sabotage, Radio Swan's instructions, the rising of the underground — and now the amphibious landing would go in with as little subtlety as at Anzio. The men didn't know that. Like assault troops in all wars, they had been told as little as possible. They waited below deck dressed for combat, dozing fitfully. At 11 P.M. Pepe San

Román, their commander, came topside for a breath of air. What he saw stunned him. The shore, which he had been told would be forsaken, glittered with lights. His briefers had described the Bay of Pigs as it had been three years earlier, before Castro seized power. Since then the government had decided to turn this strip of coast into a public park. Modern roads now crossed the swamps, which the CIA thought were still impassable. Three tourist centers were in advanced stages of construction. One of them dominated the brigade's first objective, the town of Girón. Motels, snack bars, and bathhouses — nearly two hundred buildings altogether — were almost ready; they would accommodate a thousand Cubans at a time. The grand opening was scheduled for May 20, less than five weeks away. Every weekend since Three Kings' Day in January sightseers by the thousand had been driving down from Havana to inspect the progress. This being a Sunday, the last cars had left only a few hours before the brigade's transports sighted land. There were still people moving around on the beach; construction workers putting the finishing touches on the new buildings were living in Girón with their families. It was as though Russian conspirators had planned a hostile landing on Coney Island or Jones Beach. When Kennedy found out he was openmouthed. He remembered that Eisenhower had been in the White House when this venture was planned, and he said, "My God, the bunch of advisers we inherited. . . . Can you imagine being President and leaving someone like all these people there?"

That may have been the worst of it, but it wasn't all. If there was one kind of operation the American military had mastered in the past twenty years, it was the amphibious landing. From North Africa to Normandy, from Guadalcanal to Inchon, fighting men had been put ashore with practiced skill. Tide tables, underwater obstacles, undertow, surf, riptides — all obstacles had been overcome by brilliant seamanship, special landing craft, and ingenious amphibious techniques. Veterans of those operations were now CIA strategists. If they remembered anything, it should have been that no American commander in those battles had been foolhardy enough to increase the odds against him by scheduling a landing at night. Yet that was what they had laid out for the Cuban exiles. In addition, they had neglected to note a vital feature of the Bay of Pigs: every approach to it was guarded by sharp coral reefs just beneath the surface.

The first insurgents to go in were frogmen, former officers in the Cuban navy whose job was to place landing lights. (Despite Kennedy's order to the contrary, Americans were leading them.) Coming upon the reefs, they realized that they would have to chart a way through. At midnight their first flashing beacon, a guide to the troops who would be coming ashore, was placed beside a concrete pier. No sooner had it been switched on than the headlights of a jeep appeared on the beach. It was a militia patrol. The jeep swerved and stopped, its lights on the frogmen. They opened fire on it. Next a truck carrying armed Castro militia raced up to join the jeep. Gunners aboard one of the troopships, the *Blagar*, silenced that threat, but it was small comfort; the first wave of exiles hadn't even left the transports and already the element of surprise — the sole justification for a night landing — had been lost.

Now the frogmen set to work in earnest trying to find lanes through the coral for LCVPs and the wider, tank-bearing LCUs. In some cases it was impossible. Men halted as far as 150 yards from the shore waded through surf carrying weapons and radios which became inoperable in the salt water. The reefs knocked propellers off some boats. Impatient soldiers who leaped into deep water sank like stones because of heavy equipment lashed to them; comrades dragged them to safety. Some men yearned for dawn and even prayed for it, but daybreak, it became apparent, would only increase the odds against them. The officer who discovered that was Erneido Oliva. At 2:30 A.M., Oliva later testified, he reached the shore. The first building he saw was a shack with the antenna of a microwave station on top. He captured it at once, but as he said afterward, "You could see that they had transmitted from there recently." At 6 A.M. two more microwave stations had been discovered in Girón. In each the equipment was still warm. The failure of CIA intelligence to warn of them was one of the greatest oversights in the entire operation. Because of those sets, Castro knew they were here. Now he would be coming after them.

At 3:15 A.M. the bearded dictator had been roused in Havana and told that the enemy was landing troops at Girón and nearby Playa (beach) Larga. Wary of a trap, he asked for details. Operators at the microwave stations replied that they were under attack from naval gunfire, 50-caliber machine guns, bazookas, and recoilless cannons. Then they went off the air, obviously overrun. A beachhead had been established; at any moment a provisional government might be landed and recognized by the United States, creating a political problem. Castro was determined to throw the rebels into the sea.

It says much for the state of his defenses throughout Cuba that he had in that area, ready to march, a sufficient force to repel a landing much larger than this: a battalion commanded by Osmani Cienfuegos, his minister of public works; a battalion of militia armed with three mortar batteries; an infantry battalion; three battalions of reserves to guard the roads through the swamps, and several detachments of armed militia. Altogether 20,000 men barred the exiles' way out of the Zapata peninsula. In addition Castro still had his air force. At sunrise he ordered his six B-26s, each carrying a full bomb load, to take off from San Antonio de Los Baños airfield with a fighter escort and attack the ships at anchor in the Bay of Pigs.

There was a great deal of confusion on the beachhead that morning, part of it arising from the error of exiles on the ground who opened fire on their own planes. When Castro's pilots arrived over the beach the most vulnerable unit beneath them was La Brigada's heavy gun battalion. The frogmen had finished mapping a route through the coral at 6 A.M., and at 6:25 these big weapons began to come ashore. It was slow going, and it stopped altogether when the enemy swooped down from above. Briefly the action shifted to dogfights in the sky — the brigade's fliers were up there, too — but the T-33 jet trainers chased away the rebel aircraft. Then Castro's bombers zeroed in on the rusty cargo ships. The first to be lost was the *Houston,* loaded with ammunition and gasoline; twenty-six of her men drowned. Then came the *Río Escondido* and the ten days of supplies aboard her. A Sea Fury fighter put a rocket in the *Río,* which simply disintegrated in a blinding sheet of flame. That was enough for the task force commander. His crews, mostly Cubans with no strong political loyalties, were on the verge of mutiny. He notified Pepe San Román that although less than 10 percent of the brigade's ammunition had been unloaded, he and the surviving vessels were leaving now, immediately, at flank speed. He promised to come back that night.

In Washington the conflicting stories coming from Cuba at first seemed very far away. Cuba dominated the news that morning, however. In the United Nations Raúl Roa, Castro's foreign minister, had charged that in Saturday's air raid by rebel pilots in B-26s he detected the fine hand of the Central Intelligence Agency. Adlai Stevenson, disturbed, sent a query to Harlan Cleveland. Cleveland called the Bureau of Inter-American Affairs, which called the CIA, which solemnly denied the charge, thereby betraying America's most respected spokesman in foreign affairs. On the strength of that, Stevenson told the U.N. that the President had vowed "to make sure that no American participates in an action against Cuba." He then read from a bogus statement by a phony defector in Miami, which Stevenson believed to be true. He said, "These pilots and certain other crew members have apparently defected from Castro's tyranny." He added: "No United States personnel participated. No United States aircraft of any kind participated. These two planes, to the best of our knowledge, were Castro's own air force planes and, according to the pilots, they took off from Castro's own air force fields."

He held up a picture of one of the B-26s and said, "It has the marking of Castro's air force on the tail, which everyone can see for himself. The Cuban star and the initials F.A.R., *Fuerza Aerea Revolucionaria,* are clearly visible." Roa replied that anyone could have painted the insignia on, which of course was what had happened. The American ambassador assured him: "Steps have been taken to impound the Cuban planes and they will not be permitted to take off for Cuba."

There were to be no such steps. Already the CIA's cover story was becoming unstuck, leaving a humiliated Stevenson to extricate himself from the tangle of lies as best he could. As Robert F. Kennedy said afterward, "Things were beginning to surface." By Monday evening the worst was known. Kennedy's admirers abroad were dismayed. "In one day," said the *Cordiere della Sera* of Milan, "American prestige collapses lower than in eight years of Eisenhower timidity and lack of determination." The

Frankfurter Neue Presse declared that "Kennedy is to be regarded as politically and morally defeated." In the U.N. General Assembly diplomats from African and Asian countries, remembering John Foster Dulles's charges that neutralism was immoral, were having a field day. Stevenson said dryly that he wasn't sure who was attacking Cuba, but he knew who was attacking the United States.

The 6 P.M. edition of Monday's *Miami News* bore the headline: CUBAN NAVY IN REVOLT; INVASION FORCE MOVES IN. The story disclosed that the navy's mutiny bore the imaginative code name "Bounty," and that the exiles were slicing up Castro's disintegrating forces with gigantic pincer attacks. "Various accounts" were cited as sources for the claim that the invaders had "hit the beaches in four of Cuba's six provinces, sparing only Havana Province and Camaguey in Eastern Cuba." The accounts were all wrong. There was no operation called "Bounty"; the navy remained loyal to a man; and the only action was on the shores of the Bay of Pigs, where the 20,000 defenders of Castro's regime had the exiles trapped with their backs to the sea.

Deserted by their ships, the invaders were in a hopeless position. Yet they were fighting magnificently. The paratroopers, though they had been dropped in the wrong place, were beating back militia attacks. Outnumbered thirteen to one or more, facing an enemy with heavy artillery and tactical air support, the brigade had lost fewer than a hundred men that first day while holding every position. Oliva's command, just 370 rebels, had thrown back 2,100 Castro soldiers and twenty tanks. They had sustained fewer than a hundred casualties while inflicting on the government — the figures are from a Castro doctor — five hundred dead and over a thousand wounded.

They were exultant. Their overall plight was known only to their leaders, who clung to hope because they were being encouraged by radio messages from CIA agents on the dispersed troopships. ("Hello, Pepe. I want you to know that we will never abandon you, and if things are very rough there we will go in and evacuate you.") Afterward there was much controversy about these exchanges. There can be no doubt that by heartening the men on the beach the agents prolonged their resistance and thereby added to the bloodshed. It was generally believed by CIA critics that strategists in the agency had convinced one another that Kennedy wouldn't let the invasion fail, whatever his earlier position — that once he realized that American prestige was at stake he would intervene with U.S. might. Here, as in so many other ways, they were wrong. He meant what he had said. "What is prestige?" he asked those around him in the White House that day. "Is it the shadow of power or the substance of power? We are going to work on the substance of power. No doubt we will be kicked in the can for the next couple of weeks, but that won't affect the main business."

Most Americans seemed to understand, and to sympathize. The bitterness which was to divide them later in the 1960s lay ahead. The country had not yet split into hostile camps. As Robert F. Kennedy was to write afterward in *Thirteen Days,* "We had virtual unanimity at the time of the Bay of Pigs." Editor John Fischer expressed the general view when he observed in *Harper's* that "Every President needs about twelve months to get his executive team organized, to feel his way into the vast and dangerous machinery of the bureaucracy. . . . While [Kennedy] was still trying to move in the furniture, in effect, he found the roof falling in and the doors blowing off." The Gallup poll showed that 82 percent of his countrymen approved of the way he was handling his job. "It's just like Eisenhower," Kennedy said dourly. "The worse I do, the more popular I get."

To be sure, opinion wasn't unanimous. On the right were such hardliners as Richard Nixon, who was to reveal in the November 1964 *Reader's Digest* that he had advised Kennedy to "find a proper legal cover and . . . go in." But that was expected. What was surprising was the emergence at this time, and on this issue, of an abrasive New Left. Schlesinger noted that many "on the left, more than one would have thought, now saw full vindication of their pre-election doubts about Kennedy." Their placards demanded "Fair Play for Cuba." They filled Manhattan's Union Square with demonstrators. Norman Mailer joined them. Outside the White House a sandwich board worn by a tall woman poet reproached the First Lady: JACQUELINE, VOUS AVEZ PERDU VOS ARTISTES. The Fair Play movement found recruits on many campuses, especially in the humanities and the social sciences; H. Stuart Hughes, a member of the Harvard history department and an early New Left militant, led seventy college teachers who signed an open letter to the President demanding that the administration "reverse the present drift towards American military intervention in Cuba." Barrington Moore Jr., a sociologist, predicted "a militarist and reactionary government that covers its fundamental policies with liberal rhetoric," and from a hospital bed C. Wright Mills, author of *The Power Elite,* telegraphed a Fair Play rally in California:

> Kennedy and company have returned us to barbarism. Schlesinger and company have disgraced us intellectually and morally. I feel a desperate shame for my country. Sorry I cannot be with you. Were I physically able to do so I would at this moment be fighting alongside Fidel Castro.

Actually Castro wasn't fighting. It wasn't necessary. At the Bay of Pigs his subordinates had the situation well in hand, and he stood to one side, a spectator for once, while they relentlessly reduced the perimeter of the rebel beachhead. Latin America had never seen weapons like those of the government troops. Monday morning four batteries of their Soviet 122-mm howitzers started to rake the beach; the exiles who had been in the target area stumbled around in a daze. Rebel tank commanders fought gallantly, but the Russian T-34 tanks outgunned them. By Monday evening the exiles were desperately short of ammunition. "The night came and we were expecting the ships," Pepe San Román later told Haynes Johnson. "Everybody turned their faces to the sea waiting for the ships. We knew that without the ships we could not make it." Midnight came and there was nothing. In despair Pepe boarded an open boat with his radio operator and cruised six miles out, trying to reach the CIA boat. with his signal. Then he returned to his command post and sent another officer out to keep trying to reach the captains, whose mutinous crews had rendered them impotent. Hour after hour the message went out from the open boat: DOLORES. THIS IS BEACH. DOLORES. THIS IS BEACH. I AM TRYING TO FIND YOU. WE NEED YOU. WE NEED YOU.

At dawn Tuesday six of La Brigada's remaining B-26s tried to bomb the Cuban air force planes at San Antonio de Los Baños. Castro's luck held; cloud cover blanketed the field; there was no damage. On the ground at Girón, massed T-34s stood in a solid line, firing point-blank into the beach-head. Within the narrowing perimeter all omens were bad. The lack of air cover had been the exiles' undoing. Now they couldn't even be evacuated without it.

In the White House Tuesday evening the President was called away from the Mansion's annual congressional reception. Incongruously dressed in white tie and tails, he stood over a map in his office while Rusk, McNamara, two of the Joint Chiefs, and Richard Bissell of the CIA told him that only the U.S. air force could save the brigade from Castro's kangaroo courts. He compromised, authorizing a flight of six unmarked jets from the carrier *Essex*, on duty in the Caribbean off the Bay of Pigs. For one hour — from 6:30 A.M. to 7:30 A.M. Wednesday — the U.S. planes would keep the sky over the beachhead clear of Castro planes while the rebels' remaining B-26s attacked the government troops on the perimeter.*

The last act of the Bay of Pigs tragicomedy followed. The rebel fliers' base was at Puerto Cabezas in Nicaragua, a three-hour-and-twenty-minute flight from Cuba. They were exhausted by their previous missions; only two of them had the strength for another effort. Four American advisers, believing that jets from the *Essex* would protect them, volunteered to pilot the other B-26s. They then made the last and least plausible of all the CIA mistakes in the blunder-studded operation. Nicaragua and Cuba are in different time zones. The pilots forgot to reset their watches. They arrived over Girón an hour early, while the jets which were to shield them were still on the flight deck of the *Essex*. Castro's T-33s swarmed up and made short work of them; the four Americans were killed.

Only the final agony was left now. Pleas from Girón for reinforcements, tanks, and ammunition became fainter. Messages were terse: FIGHTING ON BEACH. SEND ALL AVAILABLE AIRCRAFT NOW. And: IN WATER. OUT OF AMMO. ENEMY CLOSING IN. HELP MUST ARRIVE IN NEXT HOUR. The last stand began Tuesday night. Encircled by Castro's artillery and tanks, the exiles' leader

*In *Give Us This Day* E. Howard Hunt Jr. has the effrontery to charge that Kennedy's failure to fill the sky with American warplanes was to blame for the failure of the Bay of Pigs expedition.

sent his last message at 4:32 P.M. Wednesday: AM DESTROYING ALL MY
EQUIPMENT AND COMMUNICATIONS. TANKS ARE IN SIGHT. I HAVE NOTHING TO
FIGHT WITH. AM TAKING TO THE WOODS. I CANNOT WAIT FOR YOU.

The woods could provide only temporary shelter. Lacking the fallback
plan, the rebels stumbled into enemy hands one by one. Castro's triumph
was complete. He had broken the invasion in less than seventy-two hours,
turning it into what Haynes Johnson in his excellent study of the battle
calls "perhaps the most heavily publicized of the many bungled, poorly
planned operations since the Light Brigade charged into oblivion at
Balaklava." Ahead for the survivors in the brigade lay the humiliation of a
public trial in Havana's Sports Palace and an imprisonment which was not
to end until Christmas 1962, when Robert F. Kennedy and James B.
Donovan led a successful movement to ransom them.

In the mid-1960s contemporary historians tended to believe that in the
long run the Bay of Pigs was really a blessing; that because of it Kennedy
became disillusioned with experts and was better equipped to face the
Cuban missile crisis eighteen months later. Seen from the 1970s, the
debacle at Girón, and his reaction to it, have a very different look. On
Thursday of that week, the day after the invasion collapsed, the President
spoke before the American Society of Newspaper Editors at the Statler-
Hilton Hotel in Washington. He took a fighting stance. He was letting
Castro go this time, he said, but he wanted the record to show that "our
restraint is not inexhaustible." The United States was ready to act, "alone, if
necessary," to "safeguard its security," and he warned Moscow that "should
that time ever come, we do not intend to be lectured on intervention by
those whose character was stamped for all time on the bloody streets of
Budapest."

This was cold war rhetoric at its most bleak. Implicit in it was the
assumption that the only danger to America lay outside the country's
borders. The country's one adversary was monolithic international Communism, whose forces were "not to be underestimated in Cuba or anywhere else in the world." The governments and peoples of the Western
Hemisphere were exhorted to "take an ever closer and more realistic look
at the menace of external Communist intervention and domination in
Cuba," for it was "clearer than ever before that we face a relentless struggle
in every corner of the globe that goes far beyond the clash of armies and
even nuclear armaments."

The great liberal turning of the 1960s still lay ahead then. Once it had
been taken, the threats to the nation would be viewed as internal — racism,
militarism, pollution, technology, bureaucracy, the population explosion,
"the establishment." But in the Kennedy years all that lay ahead. The
liberal hero of the hour, who in the 1930s had been the angry young workman, in the 1940s the GI, and in the 1950s the youth misunderstood by his
mother, had become, in the early 1960s, the dedicated Peace Corpsman

battling hunger, disease — and Communism — with tools of peace. As an American liberal of the time, Kennedy believed that the basic reasons for the revolutionary movements in underdeveloped countries were poverty and ignorance, which were being exploited by Communists for their own ends. He was sure that once those conditions had been changed by Point Four programs, the appeal of Communism would vanish. That was what the appeal of the Alianza was all about. A Latin America allied with the United States in pursuit of progress, it was held, would reject overtures from the Comintern.

These beliefs were deeply held. There was, perhaps for the last time, a liberal conviction that man would be able to solve his problems. The young idealist of the early 1960s was a pragmatist, to use a word much in vogue then. The hour of Ralph Nader, the liberal model of the next decade, had not yet struck. In the Kennedy years liberals believed, as they had believed since the years of Franklin Roosevelt, that the remedy for social wrongs lay in big government and stronger presidential powers. Later their disenchantment would shake the very foundations of the republic.

Kennedy's speech in the Statler-Hilton that Thursday might have been delivered in the Eisenhower years, perhaps even by John Foster Dulles. There were many differences in style, but not much in substance. Like all cold warriors Kennedy invoked the name of Munich toward the end, reminding his listeners of its meaning: that democracies which failed to stand up to totalitarian dictators were doomed; that "our security may be lost, piece by piece, country by country, without the firing of a single missile or the crossing of a single border." He intended "to profit by this lesson," he said, and he concluded: "History will record the fact that this bitter struggle reached its climax in the late 1950s and the early 1960s. Let me then make clear as the President of the United States that I am determined upon our system's survival and success, regardless of the cost and regardless of the peril."

Thus one of the worst guesses ever of what history would say. That address was Kennedy's public response to the Bay of Pigs. Back at the White House he took another, more symbolic step. McGeorge Bundy's status as national security adviser was sharply upgraded. He was moved from the relatively humble Executive Office Building, on the other side of West Executive Avenue, to the West Wing. There, much closer to the President's oval office, Bundy began presiding over regular morning meetings of his National Security Council staff. In addition he extended his sway over the White House war room, with its huge maps and brightly colored telephones. Next time the forces of world Communism plotted a blow at the free world, the United States would be on guard. If they dared subvert the anti-Communist government of another weak little country anywhere, they would meet a firmer will. The White House was ready. Bundy was ready. The war room was ready. The hot lines were plugged in. The aggressors would be taught a lesson they would never forget.

Among the thoughtful readers of reports from Cuba was Nikita Sergeyevich Khrushchev. The Chairman wasn't much impressed by cold war oratory, having delivered a lot of it himself. What interested him was that the new President, young and inexperienced, had stumbled badly. Kennedy seemed unsure of himself. This looked like a good time to pounce on him.

The White House knew that in the Kremlin this would be the interpretation of the debacle. It was the chief reason for Washington's dismay after taking stock of the wreckage of confidence left by the Bay of Pigs. In February a meeting between Kennedy and Khrushchev had been scheduled for early June, in Vienna. On May 12 the Chairman wrote that the invitation was still open. Kennedy thought of suggesting a postponement. But that, he decided, would be interpreted as a further sign of weakness. Better the summit, he said, than the brink. Instead of staying away he would redouble his preparations for the Vienna conference. He had been told that the Chairman had been disdainful of Eisenhower's failure to bone up on his homework before his two summits with Khrushchev; whenever a tough question came up, Ike had had to turn to aides for answers. Kennedy decided that the important talks there would be just the two of them and an interpreter.

Like him, Khrushchev was under pressure from hard-liners at home, Stalinists who believed that the only way to get what you wanted from the other side was to demand it, to grab it, to be coarse and abusive and intimidating. There was a lot of this in Khrushchev himself. Stalin had admired it in him. It was what gave him his aura of primitive power. The previous autumn he had provided the U.N. General Assembly with a memorable demonstration of it. The Congo in these years was a graveyard for the reputations of geopoliticians. Khrushchev, already frustrated by the U-2 incident, the aborting of the Geneva summit with Eisenhower, and the end of his hopes for a Soviet-American detente, had been maddened at fresh humiliations in Katanga. He had blamed Dag Hammarskjöld, calling him a tool of colonial powers. Demanding that the post of secretary general of the U.N. be abolished, he had proposed that it be replaced by an executive body of three men representing the three groups of nations, western, Communist, and neutral. He had called it a "troika," after the Russian wagon drawn by three horses abreast. For emphasis, he had removed his shoe and pounded his desk in rhythm. The General Assembly was in an uproar. Trying to restore order, the Irishman who was presiding at the time banged the gavel so hard that he broke it. The chaos delighted the Chairman. Returning to Moscow, he crowed, "How shaky the United Nations is! It's the beginning of the end."

On January 6, 1961, Khrushchev countered the American liberals' policy toward underdeveloped countries — a dual plan of economic aid, with military intervention if necessary — with what was to be Communism's great challenge of the 1960s: "unlimited support" to "peoples fighting for their liberation" in "just" wars. Six weeks later Patrice Lumumba, his Congolese ally, was murdered in Katanga. The infuriated Russian called the assassination "the crowning achievement of Hammarskjöld's criminal activities" and again demanded the secretary general's immediate removal.

The Russian right had other grievances for which Khrushchev was the spokesman. Laos, which had appeared to be about to drop into their lap, was veering toward a neutral course. Red Army hard-liners wanted a resumption of nuclear tests, suspended in the Soviet Union since the fall of 1958; they now had 20-, 30-, 50-, and 100-megaton weapons, and were eager to try them out. These were daily irritants, symptoms of the cold war which kept the diplomatic climate chilly without creating a world crisis. But for them one issue was vital, and transcended the others. Khrushchev had variously described it as a "bone stuck in the throat," "a sort of cancerous tumor requiring a surgical operation," and a "Sarajevo" likely to lead toward another world war. It was divided Berlin.

For fifteen years the Russians had regarded the presence of the West in the former German capital as unbearable. Stalin had tried to evict Allied troops in 1948 and had been thwarted by the great airlift. When the first sputnik raised Soviet stock, Khrushchev had seized the opportunity to demand that Berlin be made a demilitarized "free city." He had given the allies a six-month deadline then, and he had postponed it only when Eisenhower had made that a condition of Khrushchev's trip to the United States. Ike had made certain concessions. He had agreed that the Berlin situation was "abnormal." He had offered to negotiate the size of the western garrison there and the extent to which the city would serve as a base for West German propaganda and intelligence activities.

Now Khrushchev was stalking Kennedy with the same issue. In his wars-of-liberation speech the Chairman had come down hard on Berlin. He had openly threatened Kennedy. If "the imperialists" refused "to take into consideration the true situation," he had said, the Soviet Union would "take firm measures" and "sign a peace treaty with the German Democratic Republic." Thus Kennedy faced the demon Eisenhower had exorcised. Khrushchev made it clear that such an agreement would include guarantees that any "violation" of East Germany's frontiers would be considered "an act of aggression" against all members of the Warsaw Pact — meaning that the West would have to forsake Berlin or go to war. Did he mean it? Charles de Gaulle was doubtful. He urged the President to hold firm (*"tenir le coup"*). If Kennedy held fast and made plans for a new airlift, he said, the Chairman would back off. Looking to Vienna, Averell Harriman agreed, though he recommended different tactics. Khrushchev, he predicted, would be fierce. He would try to frighten the young President. The best response would be to turn him aside, but it should be done gently. And Kennedy mustn't overestimate his adversary. Khrushchev would be nervous too, Harriman said. The Chairman's only other trip to the West had failed. Furthermore, American Kremlinologists agreed that he had never forgotten his lowly origins. Inevitably there would be tension in Vienna. The Chairman would be offensive as only he knew how to be. The President, Harriman suggested, should rise above it and laugh it off.

This advice reached Kennedy in Paris, on the eve of his flight to Austria. The French leg of the trip had turned into a triumph for the young First Lady. Eleven years earlier, she had been a student here at the Sorbonne. Now she arrived with two truckloads of luggage, a blinding array of jewels, and a retinue that included Europe's leading hairdresser. De Gaulle could scarcely take his eyes off her. The French press cried *"Ravissante!"* *"Charmante!"* and *"Apothéose!"* Arriving at a press conference, the President said, "I do not think it altogether inappropriate for me to introduce myself. I am the man who accompanied Jacqueline Kennedy to Paris."

Vienna was different. Mrs. Kennedy teased Khrushchev — "Oh, Mr. Chairman, don't bore me with statistics" — but the gloomy pall was too heavy to be laughed away, even by her. Almost from the moment Khrushchev's black, Russian-built Chaika drove past the barbwire and up to the massive stone and stucco building that served as the U.S. embassy residence in the Austrian capital, the mood was as ugly as the weather. To an aide Kennedy described his adversary as a combination of external jocosity and "internal rage." During the two days of talks the rage was external, too. James Reston had asked to interview the President after the final encounter. Kennedy was wearing a hat that day, and as he entered the room where the reporter was waiting and sank down on a couch, he pushed the hat over his eyes and uttered a great sigh. Reston thought he seemed in a state of semi-shock. He asked the President, "Pretty rough?" Kennedy replied, "Roughest thing in my life."

Afterward Reston wrote:

> He [the President] came into a dim room in the American Embassy shaken and angry. He had tried, as always, to be calm and rational with Khrushchev, to get him to define what the Soviet Union would and would not do, and Khrushchev had bullied him and threatened him with war over Berlin. . . . Kennedy said just enough in that room to convince me of the following:
>
> Khrushchev had studied the events of the Bay of Pigs; he would have understood if Kennedy had left Castro alone or destroyed him; but when Kennedy was rash enough to strike at Cuba but not bold enough to finish the job, Khrushchev decided he was dealing with an inexperienced young leader who could be intimidated and blackmailed.

In their talks, Kennedy told Reston, the Chairman had been rude, savage; at times he had seemed to be about to lunge at Kennedy. On only one issue was he reasonable: Laos, which he regarded as unimportant. In discussing everything else his manner was vicious, sneering. Hammarskjöld had to go, he insisted; he must be replaced by the troika. Similarly, three executives from the world's three political camps would be needed to administer any disarmament agreement between the United States and the USSR. In vain Kennedy argued that an arrangement would be rendered impotent by a veto — "Even the Russian troika has but one driver." On the matter of Berlin Khrushchev delivered an ultimatum. The bone, he said, must be removed from the Soviet throat. With or without an American agreement, he would sign a treaty with East Germany before the end of the year. If the United States wanted to go to war on this question, there was nothing he could do about it. Madmen who sought war deserved only straitjackets.

During their last private meeting, held at Kennedy's request, the President desperately tried to dissuade him from so rash a step. Khrushchev bluntly refused. "I want peace," he said, "but if you want war that is your problem." His treaty decision was irreversible. He would sign it in December. As they parted Kennedy said, "It will be a cold winter."*

To Reston Kennedy said: "I've got two problems. First, to figure out why he did it, and in such a hostile way. And second, to figure out what we can do about it. I think the first part is pretty easy to explain. I think he did it because of the Bay of Pigs. I think he thought anyone who was so young and inexperienced as to get into a mess like that could be taken, and anyone who got into it, and didn't see it through, had no guts. So he just beat hell out of me. So I've got a terrible problem. If he thinks I'm inexperienced and have no guts, until we remove those ideas we won't get anywhere with him. So we have to act."

Khrushchev's credibility would be watched, too, and he knew it. Returning to Moscow, he ordered publication of the two aides-mémoire he had handed the President on nuclear testing and Berlin. Sharp eyes in the State Department saw that here there was no time limit attached to the Berlin demands, but it hardly mattered now. The whole world knew of the Russian ultimatum. Since then Khrushchev had increased the Soviet military budget by 3.144 billion rubles and had delivered a series of chauvinistic speeches.

Kennedy escalated with him. On June 25 he made a telecast report to the American people. "If war breaks out," he said, "it will have been started in Moscow and not in Berlin. . . . Only the Soviet government can use the Berlin frontier as a pretext for war." He asked Congress to approve authorization of $3,247,000,000 for the Pentagon, calling up reserves, tripling draft calls, raising the ceiling for combat troops, and reconditioning planes and ships which were in mothballs. Dean Acheson wanted him to declare a state of emergency, and Vice President Lyndon Johnson agreed. Kennedy preferred to leave the door open to negotiations. He hesitated to make an

---

*In *Khrushchev Remembers* the Chairman commented: ". . . I was genuinely pleased with our meeting in Vienna. Even though we came to no concrete agreement, I could tell that he was interested in finding a peaceful solution to world problems. . . . He was a reasonable man, and I think he knew that he wouldn't be justified in starting a new war over Berlin."

atomic bluff because it might be called. His chief fear, he told an editor of the *New York Post*, was that the Chairman "wants to rub my nose in the dirt," in which case "it's all over."

Pressure built up for both leaders. To reassure Germans in the old capital that they would not be abandoned, Kennedy sent his Vice President there with General Clay, the hero of the airlift. Khrushchev warned the world that the USSR could now create a bomb with an explosive power equal to 100 million tons of TNT and had rockets capable of delivering it. As though to prove his point, a Soviet astronaut had already been launched into orbit. Tension rose in the United States. Kennedy urged Americans to build bomb shelters. Meanwhile Berlin was in an uproar. During July, 30,444 refugees flowed into the western part of the city. In the first ten days of August another 16,500 crossed. On the twelfth alone 4,000 were counted, among them a high proportion of physicians, technicians, and skilled workers — the very people necessary for the Five-Year Program of the First Secretary of East Germany's Communist party, Walter Ulbricht.

At a half-hour past midnight on August 13, sirens screamed down the dark and deserted streets as squat tanks — T-34s and T-54s — led East German military convoys to the twenty-five-mile border that separated the western part of the city from the east. Trucks of steel-helmeted Vopos, East Berlin policemen, took up positions in the major intersections. Troops unloaded wooden horses, concertinas of barbed wire, concrete posts, stone blocks, and picks and shovels. Four hours later, at sunrise, the beginning of a wall was visible. Four days later it was complete, imprisoning the Germans who remained in East Berlin.

The western powers had been caught off balance. Kennedy was away from Washington. It took the State Department four days to deliver a formal protest in Moscow. Then, on September 1, Khrushchev gave the screw another turn. U.S. seismographs recorded unmistakable evidence that the Russians had resumed testing. Kennedy and Macmillan appealed to the Chairman to stop, citing the extent and toxicity of the new fallout. Khrushchev ignored them. Detection devices picked up a second test, and a third. Over the next month the Soviets detonated thirty major devices, nearly all of them in the atmosphere. At the end of the series the Russians had become responsible for more radioactive poison in the air than the Americans, the British, and the French combined. In a speech before the Communist Twenty-second Congress the Chairman announced the imminent explosion of a 50-megaton bomb — 2,500 times as large as the one which had been dropped on Hiroshima and five times the size of all high explosives used in all the wars in history. He drew laughter from the delegates at the next session when he told them that the resulting blast "proved somewhat bigger than the 50 megatons that the scientists had calculated," but that they would not be punished for the "mistake."

Kennedy decided that if this constituted Khrushchev's only answer to western proposals for an atmospheric test ban, he had to authorize a resumption of U.S. tests, though he approved only those underground, which had no fallout. In view of the acts of the Soviet government, he said, "we must now take those steps which prudent men find essential." It was now September 8, the peak of the crisis. The wall was complete, a corral of brick and jagged cement cutting through the heart of Berlin. Since August 22 all but one of the crossing points had been closed to the Allies, and there the Vopos insisted upon inspecting soldiers' papers. Any approach to the border closer than 100 meters (110 yards) was prohibited. Next notes to Paris, Bonn, and Washington formally demanded that West German leaders be forbidden to enter Berlin by plane. At that, the West stiffened. On September 8 Khrushchev's insistence that West German flights into Berlin should be controlled was curtly rejected. Ten days later, when Kennedy was about to leave Hyannisport to return to Washington, he was handed a grim note. Dag Hammarskjöld had been killed in a Congolese plane crash which has never been clearly explained. War had not seemed so close since V-J Day.

Two weeks later Khrushchev began to back away from the brink. To the Belgian diplomat Paul-Henri Spaak, who was visiting Moscow, he said, "I realize that contrary to what I had hoped the western powers will not sign the peace treaty. . . . I'm not trying to put you in an impossible situation; I know very well that you can't let yourself be stepped on." The bone in the throat wasn't intolerable, after all. "You know," he continued to the Belgian, "Berlin is not such a big problem for me. What are two million people among a billion Communists!" Nor was there any hurry now. He had given Kennedy an ultimatum — "by the end of the year" — but to Spaak he said, "I'm not bound by any deadline." Having built his wall, he now appeared to be trying to wring concessions from the West which would allow him to save face. He made several gestures intended to ease tensions, including generous comments about Kennedy's maturity and evident wisdom. When there was no response to them, he threw in his hand anyhow. Speaking once more to the Communist Party Congress, he declared on October 17, "The western powers are showing some understanding of the situation and are inclined to seek a solution to the German problem and the issue of West Berlin." He concluded, "If that is so, we shall not insist on signing a peace treaty absolutely before December 31, 1961."

With that, the confrontation ended. It seemed to be a victory for the Americans. Later the real price paid began to emerge. Given the attitude of Moscow, the Berlin question, and the resumption of nuclear testing, Schlesinger would write, "the President unquestionably felt that an American retreat in Asia might upset the whole world balance." Kennedy believed that there he must provide his adversaries with additional proof of fearlessness and backbone. To James Reston he observed that the only place where Communists were challenging the West in a shooting war was in Indochina, so "now we have a problem in trying to make our power credible, and Vietnam looks like the place."

This was a cheerless time for Lyndon Johnson. The year before, he had been the mighty majority leader of the U.S. Senate, and now, as Vice President, he occupied the emptiest, most exasperating position in the government. Every day Johnson's relative insignificance was driven home to him in countless ways. He was allowed only one parking place at the White House, and just one White House phone extension. (Attorney General Robert Kennedy had three.) His wife had never seen the inside of the presidential aircraft. He himself had been aboard, though not by invitation. Three times Kennedy aides had found him poking around its cabins alone. Inasmuch as they had been there because the President was about to use the plane, they had been obliged to ask him to leave. Each encounter should have been daunting, but he kept returning, fascinated, it seemed, by the symbols of real power.

Kennedy men treated Johnson people as outsiders. With the exception of Walter Jenkins, members of the vice-presidential staff were total strangers to the glamorous presidential advisers. Several lacked credentials to enter the White House and had seen it only as tourists. The obscurity even enveloped Secret Service agents assigned to the Johnson detail. Officially they were full equals of the men who guarded the President. In practice they were ostracized by the White House detail — excluded from their cars, their offices, their social functions. Most of them were philosophical about it. They knew there was nothing personal about the snubs. They had been banished by the elite because the man they were guarding was — there is no other word for it — unimpoitant.

Kennedy was largely unaware of this. Like most Presidents he kept the man next in line at arm's length. The occupants of America's first and second elective offices have never been congenial, for reasons rooted in historical precedent and, perhaps, in human nature. Some Vice Presidents who have been close to their chief executives in earlier years have been hurt to find friendship replaced by icy aloofness. They forget that to a President a Vice President is a daily reminder of his own mortality. He is more. Though individuals may contemplate the grave serenely, they are not constantly shadowed by understudies. Those who expect Presidents to provide Vice Presidents with detailed briefings rarely weigh the implications of it. To grasp it, one must understand the meaning of the Presidency, the legacy the second man stands to inherit. The head of a family may make out his will without flinching, but he would blanch if told that the man next door would, in the event of his death, become father to his children and husband to his wife.

Beyond this institutional difficulty lies another. It is a fact of political life that presidential campaign tickets are "balanced" by pairing two candidates from different parts of the country who appeal to different constituencies and whose make-ups may be antithetical. The husband, in short, must choose as his possible replacement a man who doesn't look like him, dress like him, talk like him, or share his values. Franklin Roosevelt and

Harry Truman bore only the faintest resemblance to one another. The same was true of Eisenhower and Nixon, and of Kennedy and Johnson. To Kennedy, Johnson was a marvelous and often comical prodigy. His self-aggrandizement was shameless and exuberant; on trips abroad he would telephone his Washington office daily for reports on how his activities were being played in the American press. He was always campaigning — "My God!" gasped an American doctor in Pakistan. "He's shaking hands with a leper!" — and his decision to transform a Karachi camel driver into an ambassador of good will delighted the country. "We have come to see you and your camel," he told the astonished Bashir Ahmed. "Our President wants to see your camel. He has plans to make things better for you." He had no such thing, and the stunt seemed certain to backfire. Yet in the end it didn't. Ahmed's trip to the United States was an enormous success. Kennedy was impressed. "If it had been me," he said, "I'd have wound up with camel shit on the White House lawn."

Knowing how unhappy the Vice President was, the President went out of his way to honor Johnson and invent missions abroad for him. Later some of them became important. It is ironic that the two which appealed to him the least in advance loom largest in retrospect. The first was to Berlin. He was glum before it, but he spoke well there and was on hand to greet the first U.S. reinforcements to enter the city. His hosts believed that his visit was a turning point for the beleaguered city, and he returned home deeply affected.

The other trip, that May, was to Saigon. In the end it was of even greater significance, although that wasn't apparent then. The journey was a tour of southern Asia. The Vice President was expected to bolster the confidence of non-Communist regimes. He was not, as he had been in Berlin, a symbol of America's resolve to fight alongside them. At that time U.S. commitments there had not gone that far. Nevertheless, his pledge to Saigon was very strong. Greatly taken with Ngo Dinh Diem, he publicly hailed him as "the Winston Churchill of south Asia." After the party had left Vietnam, Stan Karnow, a writer for the *Saturday Evening Post,* asked him whether he really believed that. "Shit, man," the Vice President replied, "he's the only boy we got out here."

The Winston Churchill of south Asia was a dark, stubby, chain-smoking bachelor whose most striking trait was his seeming inability to end a conversation. Survivors would emerge from his big yellow stucco Freedom Palace after nonstop Diem monologues that were said to last six, seven, even twelve hours. But he didn't have many other weaknesses. At sixty he was decisive, dedicated, and firm in purpose. Diem was an archetype of the strong man in power. His title was president, yet he didn't think much of democracy. He was more of an Oriental despot, or at any rate an aloof mandarin who firmly believed that it was the duty of his people to respect and to obey him. His rivals were sent to concentration camps. Under him there was no freedom of the press and no real reform. Army officers were political appointees, chosen for their loyalty, not their ability, and though Diem himself was honest, the halls of his palace swarmed with the corrupt and the ambitious. Rigid and inflexible, he seemed to feel that Roman Catholics should be privileged for no other reason than that he himself was a Catholic. To an astonishing degree, his responsibilities were undelegated — company commanders couldn't move their men without his permission, and until late in his regime, no passport was valid unless it bore the signature of Diem himself. With each passing month he held the reins of authority more tightly, consulting only a few trusted aides and the members of his family, particularly an aggressive brother, Ngo Dinh Nhu and Nhu's lovely, venomous wife, known to American foreign correspondents as "the Dragon Lady." "If we open the window," Madame Nhu once said, explaining the Ngo philosophy of government, "not only sunlight but many bad things will fly in."

Little went in and not much came out. This was especially true of information. The lack of hard facts explains one of the two great mysteries about the Vietnam War: why it became a graveyard for the reputations of experts from the West. Rarely in history have so many eminent men been so singularly wrong about such an important event. Right down to October 1972, when Henry Kissinger fell flat on his face by prematurely announcing a settlement of it, soldiers and statesmen misjudged the character of the war and its probable course. On April 6, 1954, a New England senator had diverted his colleagues by reciting some earlier appraisals of it: "the military situation appears to be developing favorably" (Dean Acheson, 1952), "In Indochina we believe the tide now is turning" (Assistant Secretary of State Walter Robertson, 1953), a French victory "is both possible and probable" (Secretary of Defense Charles E. Wilson, 1954), and "the French are going to win" (Admiral Radford, 1954). The French lost, having sacrificed 19,000 Frenchmen in seven years.* That would seem to have vindicated the skeptical New England senator, who was John F. Kennedy. Then Kennedy, too, became trapped. In the White House his policy toward Vietnam came to be based on such Lewis Carroll appraisals as a 1960 Senate committee report which predicted that "on the basis of the assurances of the head of the military aid mission in Vietnam . . . the U.S. military . . . can be phased out of Vietnam in the forseeable future," and early in 1961 President Kennedy approved an aid plan based on the assumption that the war would be won in eighteen months.

The second Vietnam mystery is why Americans of so many persuasions, including four Presidents, two Republican and two Democratic, felt obliged to rescue the Saigon government. The country was, after all, in Asia, over seven thousand miles away, a primitive land of rice paddies and dense jun-

---

*Compared with 45,882 Americans lost between 1961 and 1972. The usual figure given for French casualties is 92,000, but that includes Foreign Legionnaires, Africans, and Vietnamese who fought under the French flag. France, unlike the United States, sent no draftees to Vietnam.

gle curled around the remote Indochinese peninsula. Yet for over a decade administrations in Washington battled desperately to keep questionable men in power in there, even at the risk of domestic tranquillity at home. The American effort in Vietnam was ill-starred from the outset. Kennedy should have seen that. He was one of the few who had diagnosed the trouble in the beginning. As a congressman, he had toured Vietnam in 1951. "Without the support of the native population," he had said on *Meet the Press* on his return, "there is no hope of success in any of the countries of Southeast Asia." Later he, too, fell under the spell of cold war rhetoric. America had "lost" China, cold-warriors held; now it must not "lose" Indochina.

The original American commitment to Saigon had been made in 1954 and renewed in 1957. In a letter to Diem after the Geneva agreements had been signed, President Eisenhower pledged U.S. support "to assist the Government of Viet-Nam in developing and maintaining a strong, viable state, capable of resisting subversion or aggression through military means." Ike made this agreement with the understanding that it would be accompanied "by performance on the part of Viet-Nam in undertaking needed reforms." The purpose of his assurance was to "discourage any who might wish to impose a foreign ideology on your free people."

"Ike has made a promise," Lyndon Johnson would say of Vietnam during his years in the White House. "I have to keep it." But he didn't. This wasn't a pact. The Senate had nothing to do with it. It lacked even the legitimacy of an executive order. Yet both Johnson and Kennedy felt bound by it. To have withdrawn U.S. support, Theodore C. Sorensen wrote, would have caused "the world to wonder about the reliability of this nation's pledges." Arthur Schlesinger went further:

> Whether we had vital interests in South Vietnam before 1954, the Eisenhower letter created those interests. Whether we should have drawn the line where we did, once it was drawn we became every succeeding year more imprisoned by it. Whether the domino theory was valid in 1954, it had acquired validity seven years later, after neighboring governments had staked their own security on the ability of the United States to live up to its pledges to Saigon. Kennedy . . . had no choice but to work within the situation he had inherited.

"The cause in Vietnam," Theodore H. White wrote in *The Making of the President 1968*, was "the cause of America for half a century, a cause made clear to the world. . . . If there is any fragile form of world order today, 400,000 American battle deaths in four wars in this century have created that world order." President Johnson argued that to "cut and run," would have been to "say to the world in this case that we don't live up to our treaties and don't stand by our friends." *Time* explained to those who felt otherwise that:

. . . South Vietnam must be defended at all costs. . . . If the U.S. cannot or will not save South Viet Nam from the Communist assault, no Asian nation can ever again feel safe in putting its faith in the U.S. — and the fall of all of Southeast Asia would only be a matter of time.

The consequences of such a withdrawal were considered unthinkable. In support of sending American draftees to Vietnam, Robert McNamara and the Joint Chiefs of Staff flatly declared that the alternative was serious deterioration throughout that part of the world. General Lyman L. Lemnitzer, speaking for the Chiefs, predicted that in the event of a Viet Cong victory, "We would lose Asia all the way to Singapore," and General Maxwell Taylor, confident of success against the guerrilla enemy — North Vietnam was "extremely vulnerable to conventional bombing," he said — told President Kennedy that a "U.S. military task force" was "essential."

There was no sense in any of this. If the Kennedy administration hadn't felt bound to evacuate the Cuban brigade from its doomed beachhead, then it owed Diem nothing. Furthermore, the Eisenhower letter had no validity now because Diem had openly flouted the obligation of introducing "needed reforms." He had also refused to hold all-Vietnam elections in 1956. For him to have invoked the sanctity of treaties would have been absurd, even if the United States had been bound to him by a treaty, which of course it wasn't.

The real pressures binding Washington to Saigon were political. McCarthy was dead, but both Democrats and Republicans were haunted by the nightmarish possibility that Diem might become a second Chiang Kai-shek. It is all the more ironical, then, that they repeated the very mistake Americans counseling Chiang had made; though the problem was political there, too, the aid they gave was military. One reason for their error was the attitude of powerful figures on Capitol Hill who had great faith in the Joint Chiefs and little trust in the political officers on the State Department's Asian desk. Another explanation lay in the character of the two cabinet members advising the White House on Vietnam in the early 1960s. McNamara was decisive and forceful, Rusk was timid and vague; inevitably the more persuasive voice came from the Pentagon.

Vietnam had been comparatively placid in the latter Eisenhower years. Eight hundred U.S. military advisers and three hundred million dollars in military aid a year had sufficed to preserve the status quo. Then, in December 1960, the month before Kennedy's inaugural, Diem's adversaries announced the formation of a National Liberation Front. In Freedom Palace their rivals christened the NLF the Viet Cong (literally, "Vietnamese Communists"). Diem wasn't worried by it at first. The previous autumn he had easily turned back an attempted coup, and when Vice President Johnson asked him if he wanted some American soldiers, he said he didn't. But though ground troops weren't necessary then, he admitted needing some help. President Kennedy approved the dispatch of a 400-man Special

Forces group (the Green Berets) for training missions. For the first time the American commitment included troops.

Early in May 1961 a new U.S. ambassador, Frederick E. Nolting Jr., arrived in Saigon. His predecessor had tried to reason with Diem, and as a result had become, in effect, *persona non grata*. Nolting was resolved not to repeat that mistake. By now Viet Cong depredations were so obvious that even the mandarin president had to acknowledge them. The situation in the countryside was deteriorating. Guerrilla bands roamed at will, assassinating village chieftains. A U.S. intelligence estimate reported that an "extremely critical period" lay "immediately ahead" and warned that the Saigon regime's "reliance on virtually one-man rule" and "toleration of corruption" led many to "question Diem's ability to lead in this period."

In Washington the White House was being urged to step into the Vietnamese breach of its various bureaucratic constituencies. Deputy Undersecretary of State U. Alexis Johnson asked Kennedy to accept "defeat of the Vietcong" as a "real and ultimate" objective. The Joint Chiefs assured the President that 40,000 U.S. troops would "clean up the Vietcong threat," and that another 128,000 would be enough to turn back possible North Vietnam or Chinese Communist intervention. Roswell W. Gilpatric, McNamara's deputy at Defense, proposed talks with Diem on the "possibility of a defensive security alliance," and William P. Bundy, also in the Pentagon at that stage, urged "early and hard-hitting" American intervention in the war. Bundy gave it a 70 percent chance of success.

Kennedy authorized further studies, agreed to expand the 685-man U.S. military advisory group in Saigon, and approved plans to equip and pay 20,000 more Vietnamese troops for Diem (for a total of 150,000). Like Ike, he wanted aid contingent upon domestic reforms and mobilization of South Vietnamese resources against the Viet Cong, but he wasn't emphatic about it. He was preoccupied with Berlin and nuclear testing at the time. Schlesinger doubts that he ever gave Vietnam "his full attention." Observers attuned to the cold war continued to be baffled by Vietnam. "The situation gets worse almost week by week," Theodore H. White wrote in August 1961. White found that "guerrillas now control almost all the Southern delta — so much so that I could find no American who would drive me outside Saigon in his car even by day without military convoy." He reported a "political breakdown of formidable proportions." Then he wrote: ". . . what perplexes hell out of me is that the Commies, on their side, seem to be able to find people willing to die for their cause." The revolutionary spirit has often perplexed those not imbued with it.

The following month guerrillas captured a provincial capital and executed the governor. Diem's troops were in retreat everywhere. Reluctantly he summoned Nolting and asked for a bilateral defense treaty. Washington was in a responsive mood. All summer support had been coalescing around the Lyndon Johnson approach to Southeast Asia. The Vice President was voicing the classic liberal position: the real enemies in Vietnam, he had written on his return from there, were "hunger, ignorance, poverty, and disease." He believed that Americans "must — whatever strategies we evolve — keep those enemies the point of our attack, and make imaginative use of our scientific and technological capacity."

The President responded by sending to Saigon a high-level mission comprising two of his most trusted advisers, General Maxwell Taylor and Walt W. Rostow. Thus a general and a militant civilian — for Rostow, first to last, was the most uncompromising of the hawks — were to be the President's eyes and ears in Vietnam at this critical juncture. The absence of any American diplomat of stature was significant. It reflected, as Sorensen later wrote, "the State Department's inability to compete with the Pentagon." The result was further emphasis on military objectives at the expense of political considerations.

The Taylor-Rostow report marked one of the great turning points in the Vietnam War. To arrest the decline in Diem's fortunes, Kennedy was urged to send him a large contingent of American advisers, and — more important — American infantry: 8,000 at once and more as needed. Taylor, the dominant member of the team, wanted Vietnam to be the subject of a major presidential telecast. Some of his arguments for intervention were curious. In coming down hard on the side of an expeditionary force, for example, he compared Vietnam with Korea, "where U.S. troops learned to live and work without too much effort." Actually Korea and Vietnam were very different. The first was a conventional struggle, with enemy formations crossing a border and engaging Americans in fixed battles on terrain relatively familiar to U.S. soldiers. The second was irregular warfare in dense tropical jungle. Most important of all, the native population in South Korea wanted the Americans there. In Vietnam they didn't; Vietnamese villagers tended to regard U.S. Caucasian troops as successors to the French, and the Viet Cong as heroes.

Some members of the administration subcabinet — Chester Bowles, George Ball, and Averell Harriman among them — were appalled by this recommendation. The only senior man to question it, however, was Kennedy himself. He refused to go to the people on TV because that would confer upon Vietnam the status of Berlin. He also noted pointedly that Taylor and Rostow, unlike the Joint Chiefs, were optimistic about the effectiveness of U.S. intervention only if the North Vietnamese were prevented from infiltrating South Vietnam, and that they had no ideas for accomplishing that. What dismayed him most was the proposal to send soldiers. Sorensen wrote: "All his principal advisors on Vietnam favored it, calling it the 'touchstone' of our good faith, a symbol of our determination. But the President in effect voted 'no' — and only his vote counted." Kennedy told an aide: "They want a force of American troops. They say it's necessary in order to restore confidence and maintain morale. But it will be just like Berlin. The troops will march in; the bands will play; the crowds will cheer; and in four days everyone will have forgotten. Then we will be told we have to send more troops. It's like taking a drink. The effect wears off, and you have to take another."

Nevertheless, he was being manipulated. He vetoed U.S. troops but yielded on other points, and a buildup of U.S. strength in Vietnam began in December 1961. Like Eisenhower seven years earlier, the President affirmed the arrangement in a public exchange of letters with Diem. It wasn't all one-way; Diem conceded the need for reforms and acknowledged the need for more leadership and better morale in his army. But no limits were set for the amount of U.S. assistance or when it would end, other than when the Viet Cong had been pacified and the North Vietnamese driven out. Taylor saw no great peril in that. "The risks of backing into a major Asian war by way of South Vietnam," he cabled the President from the Philippines, "are present but not impressive." George Ball, on the other hand, was apprehensive. Diem wouldn't stop pressing until he got the administration to send infantrymen, he said. That was what Diem really wanted; it would allow him to stabilize his regime while the Americans did his fighting for him. Ball predicted that if that commitment was made it would not stay small. Within five years, he told the President, there would be 300,000 U.S. troops in Vietnam. Kennedy laughed and said, "George, you're crazier than hell."

One factor in the coming acceleration — which would vindicate Ball and then some — was the character of the Americans making decisions in Saigon. From early 1962 until the end of Kennedy's thousand days in power the two key figures were Ambassador Nolting and General Paul D. Harkins, the new head of the U.S. Military Assistance Advisory Group (MAAG), who reached Vietnam in February. The choice of both was tragic. Nolting, a member of an old Virginia family, was a traditionalist who knew nothing about Asia. His appointment had been recommended by the anti-Communist hard-liners in the State Department. In any crisis he would back Diem, and when Kennedy really needed him he would be found to be off cruising on the Aegean Sea on an extended vacation. Harkins was worse. He was the maverick son of a cultivated Boston family, a high school dropout who had risen in the Army solely because he was a good cavalryman, a spirited polo player, and a horsy companion for George S. Patton when Patton wanted to relax. In World War II Harkins had been Patton's deputy chief of staff; his nickname then had been "the ramrod" because of the way he drove Patton's orders home. Like Patton, he sometimes had trouble taking orders himself. This was to be particularly true when his instructions required him to send the President candid reports on how the war was going. Kennedy had made it plain that he wanted to know everything, the good news and the bad. But Harkins didn't like to relay bad news. He thought it might reflect on him. Instead he acted as though his mission were to make things look good on the surface. When he arrived in Saigon he told American correspondents that he was an optimist and liked to have optimists around him. Henceforth, he disclosed, the daily situation appraisal for Washington would be called "The Headway Report." He intended to leave no doubt that under him the fight against the Viet Cong would be making headway.

Nolting and Harkins agreed that Diem was the answer to all problems, that nothing could be done without him, and that since criticism of his regime would only anger him, there would be none of it. In the phrase of Homer Bigart of the *New York Times*, this became the policy of "Sink or Swim with Ngo Dinh Diem." Diem quickly realized that there was no limit to the ways he could take advantage of these two Americans.

The first drive against the Viet Cong after Harkins's arrival was called, appropriately, Operation Sunrise. Harkins told reporters that he was planning construction of a chain of fortified "strategic hamlets" which would be manned by home defense units; his co-planner was the Vietnamese president's brother Nhu. The next thing Washington knew, strategic hamlets were a thundering success, with over one-third of the total rural population living in them. The war seemed to be turning around. All the reports from Saigon were good. Skeptics could check Harkins's appreciations with those from Nolting, which also glowed.

In reality the experiments with the fortified hamlets were a failure. Nothing had changed except the men at the top. They were waging war through public relations releases. Reports from the field were being rewritten by Harkins, with pessimism and unwelcome information deleted and outright fiction substituted. Colonels and majors who objected — and some did, most memorably Lieutenant Colonel John Paul Vann — were transferred to unwelcome assignments with notations in their records that ended their military careers. When another general, junior to Harkins, toured the front and found a situation very different from that being depicted in the MAAG commander's self-serving dispatches, he gave Harkins an appraisal telling the truth about the war. Harkins scribbled in the margin — "Lies," "Lies," "More lies" — and stuck it in the back of a file cabinet. The real lies were his own, but the only sources to contradict him were the stories in American newspapers cabled back from correspondents in Vietnam. Harkins explained them away by calling the reporters sensation-mongers or, worse, traitors. When occasional reverses were acknowledged it was because Harkins had an ulterior motive. He wanted more men, more guns, more choppers. Failure to supply them, he warned, would mean that civilians were letting down the army, and anybody who remembered China knew what *that* would mean.

Had there been a Tet offensive or any other eruption in Viet Cong activity, this press-agentry might have been exposed in the beginning. As it happened, there was a drop in guerrilla activity. That was all the manipulators of news needed. Operation Sunrise, they declared, had brought blue skies over the battlefield. They were elated, and in Washington their elation was infectious. Maxwell Taylor said he sensed "a great national movement" in Vietnam to crush the Viet Cong. McNamara said, "Every quantitative measurement we have shows we're winning this war." President Kennedy, surprised and pleased, authorized an expansion of the Saigon command from 2,000 men to 16,000, and the U.S. Military Assistance Advisory Group (MAAG) was upgraded to the Military Assistance Command, Vietnam (MACV).

Montage: The Early Sixties

Michael row the boat ashore
Hal — le — lu —— jah
Michael row the boat ashore
Hal — le — lu —— jah

NEWBURGH MAYOR CUTS RELIEF TO MAKE UNEMPLOYED FIND JOBS

Are you smoking more and enjoying it less?

The Twist's origins are obscure, according to *Billboard*. It is said to have grown out of a dance called the Madison which originated in Philadelphia and was based on Rock 'n' Roll music. Nineteen-year-old Chubby Checker and twenty-two-year old Joe Dee are often considered the fathers of the Twist.

Margaret Mead, commenting on Mary Quant dresses which actually climb *above* the knee, observed, "We are going through a period of extreme exhibitionism."

bug out

Good night, David
Good night, Chet

VOTE HERE FOR MISS RHEINGOLD!

You gotta shake, rattle, 'n' roll

Maximilian Schell
in
JUDGMENT AT NUREMBERG

David Niven   Anthony Quinn
in
THE GUNS OF NAVARONE

FICTION

Advise and Consent, Drury
Hawaii, Michener
The Last of the Just, Schwarz-Bart
Decision at Delphi, MacInnes
The Agony and the Ecstasy, Stone
To Kill a Mockingbird, Lee
The Winter of Our Discontent, Steinbeck
Mila 18, Uris
The Carpetbagger, Robbins
A Burnt-Out Case, Greene.

HAL — LE — LU —— JAH

NONFICTION

The Rise and Fall of the Third Reich, Shirer
The Waste Makers, Packard
The New English Bible
A Nation of Sheep, Lederer
Born Free, Adamson
The Snake Has All the Lines, Kerr
Nobody Knows My Name, Baldwin
The Making of the President 1960, White
The Politics of Upheaval, Schlesinger
The Conscience of a Conservative, Goldwater

I like your thinkin'

You still using that greasy kid's stuff?

the *way* people get information, rather than the information itself, is the key fact in history; the *medium* is the message.

The river Jordan is deep and wide
Hal — le — lu —— jah

LORD'S PRAYER BANNED IN SCHOOLS

CUBA SI, YANQUI NO   ROCKY'S SON LOST IN NEW GUINEA

2,990,513 JOBS IN FEDERAL GOVT.

Hey, fun-ny

ASTRONAUT PROBES SPACE IN A B. F. GOODRICH SUIT

And today motoring is safer than ever before because the tubeless tire, originated by B.F. Goodrich, provides protection against bruise blowouts.

Just think how much you're going to be missing. You won't have Nixon to kick around any more, because, gentlemen, this is my last press conference.

Elizabeth Taylor and Richard Burton
WHO'S AFRAID OF VIRGINIA WOOLF?
from the play by Edward Albee
Directed by Mike Nichols

scrambles back to pass he's in trouble
always use Gillette. Closest, fastest, safest razor you can buy
doctor coming on the field
Gillette gives you your money's worth
bringing out a stretcher
So act sharp, feel sharp with Gillette blue blades
I mean he's really hurt

This land is my land
This land is your land

HAL — LU — LU —— JAH   *making out*

LA DOLCE VITA

Hey, getcha cold beah!
Hey, getcha Ballantine!

TWENTY-EIGHT

Now the Trumpet
Summoned Us Again

I N 1961 the troubled years of the decade lay in the future. The disorders at home would not begin until the summer of 1964, eight
months after President Kennedy's death. Later this would encourage the
myth that if only he had lived none of it would have happened. In fact, his
responsibility for the coming turmoil was substantial. The Vietnam buildup
was one of two major steps he took toward it. The second step was his decision to mount a program aimed at putting a man on the moon before the
end of the 1960s. Because Kennedy committed the country to the spending
of vast sums on space exploration — over 56 billion dollars before Apollo 11
reached the moon, and even that wasn't the end of it — successive administrations lacked the resources to provide imaginative, far-reaching responses to the ghetto upheavals which rocked the nation from Watts to
Harlem. Those riots, combined with anguished demonstrations against the
U.S. role in Vietnam, weakened the fabric of American society to an extent
unknown since the Civil War a hundred years earlier.

Kennedy agonized over both the Vietnam and space issues. In the
first of them he may even have been on the verge of withdrawing from
Indochina. Kenneth O'Donnell, his chief of staff, has said that he planned
to get out in his second term, and before flying to Texas on his last journey
the President had issued an order to bring back the first 1,000 U.S. military
advisers. (According to O'Donnell, Lyndon Johnson quietly rescinded the
order after the return from Dallas.) There are other signs that Kennedy
was moving toward disengagement. David Halberstam, who cannot be
called a friendly critic on this issue, believes that Kennedy had made up his
mind but "did not want to rush too quickly, to split his administration
unnecessarily. There was always time."

Space exploration is another matter. Here there are no extenuations.
Whatever the glory or lack of it attending that decision, all must go to

Kennedy, and with each passing year the scales tip farther against him. By 1961 the space race no longer had any bearing on national security. Paradoxically, the very fact that the Russians had larger rockets was evidence of their technological inferiority. Americans had found a way to design H-bomb warheads which were only a fraction of their former size and weight. Therefore they had no need of powerful rockets to send them toward their targets. Soviet scientists required enormous boosters — over 800,000 pounds of thrust — because their H-bombs remained crude and big. That meant that in this early phase of space exploration they had power to burn, charges which could hurl much heavier satellites into orbit, but that was all it meant, and it wasn't much. In later phases the superiority of American technology would pay off. Everyone in the White House knew it; so did everyone in the Kremlin.

The man on the street did not know it. As far as he could see, the Russians were showing America their heels, and somehow that was menacing to the free world. It was useless to explain to him that three out of every four satellites now in orbit were American, that in contrast to the clumsy Sputniks and Luniks the United States had launched whole families of Vanguards, Discoverers, Explorers, Pioneers, Samoses, Tiroses (weather), Transits (navigational), Midases (infrared detector of missiles), and Echos (communications). What counted in the public's eye was that the Russians were more spectacular. They had been first in orbit, the first to hit the moon and then to photograph it, the first to put a satellite in orbit around Venus with devices to radio back information about it. It was now clear that they were going to beat U.S. scientists to manned space flight. They had already put dogs into orbit, and now the first vehicle to put a man up was standing by on a launch pad near the Aral Sea, the site Francis Gary Powers had been trying to photograph on his ill-starred flight the year before.

This had nothing to do with either American security or the pursuit of knowledge. It was a matter of face or, as someone unkindly called it, of astropolitics. Given Kennedy elitism there was probably no question that the United States would have risen to the challenge anyhow, but the cold war had a lot to do with it. Like Acheson and Dulles — and Richard Nixon — Kennedy believed that the whole world was watching the rivalry between the two superpowers, and that destiny hung on the outcome of every contest between them. The thought that the Soviet Union might be more admired by the emerging nations in Africa and Asia was unbearable. In some vague way the freedom of mankind was at stake. This is clear from the memoirs of Theodore C. Sorensen. To Kennedy, Sorensen writes, the "space gap" which the new administration had inherited symbolized the country's lack of "initiative, ingenuity, and vitality."

He was convinced that Americans did not fully grasp the world-wide political and psychological impact of the space race. With East and West competing to convince the new and undecided nations which way to turn, which way was the future, the dramatic Soviet achievements, he feared, were helping to build a dangerous impression of unchallenged world leadership generally and scientific pre-eminence particularly.

In this view, the fact that the United States had superior weapons systems didn't count for much, because they didn't *seem* superior: "Other nations . . . assumed that a Soviet space lead meant a missile lead as well; and whether this assumption was true or false, it affected their attitudes in the cold war." Here, surely, was the triumph of image, the notion that in the huts and villages of the Third World peasants, weighing which way they would turn, were awaiting the latest word from outer space. The extraordinary implication was that Soviet rocketeering feats, if unchallenged, would be a greater blow to American prestige than anything else — greater, say, than oppressed American Negroes wrecking the centers of U.S. cities in riots of frustration.

This wasn't much of an improvement on the fantasies of John Foster Dulles, and Sorensen makes it clear that in this instance, unlike that of Vietnam, Kennedy was no reluctant convert: "The President was more convinced than any of his advisers that a second-rate, second-place space effort was inconsistent with this country's security and with the New Frontier spirit of discovery." Like Cuba, this had been one of his major themes in 1960. Campaigning in Manhattan, he had said: "These are entirely new times, and they require new solutions. The key decision which this [Eisenhower's] administration had to make in the field of international policy and prestige and power and influence was their recognition of the significance of outer space. . . . The Soviet Union is now first in outer space." In Pocatello, Idaho, he had charged: "They [other nations] have seen the Soviet Union first in space. They have seen it first around the moon, and first around the sun. . . . They come to the conclusion that the Soviet tide is rising and ours is ebbing. I think it is up to us to reverse that point." And in Oklahoma City five days before his election he had cried: "I will take my television black and white. I want to be ahead of them in rocket thrust."

On Monday of the second week in April, UPI began to move a story on the persistent Moscow rumor that Soviet rocketeers had sent a man into space and recovered him. Although that was premature, Tuesday evening the CIA reported that the flight was scheduled for that night. As Washington slept, Moscow's radios greeted the new day there with the slow, moving strains of the Russian patriotic anthem, "How Spacious Is My Country." It was followed by the momentous announcement: "The world's first spaceship, *Vostok*, with a man on board, has been launched on April 12 in the Soviet Union on a round-the-world orbit." To follow it, Russian children were released from classrooms, clerks from shops, workmen from factories. In the beginning they were silent, stunned. It seemed incredible that somewhere above them a fellow countryman could be soaring past the stars at 18,000 mph.

His name was Yuri Alekseyevich Gagarin, a twenty-seven-year-old Soviet major who had been chosen to be Russia's first "cosmonaut." Gagarin had been launched at 9:07 A.M. Moscow time — 1:07 A.M. in Washington — and at the time his niche in history appeared to be somewhat greater than it was. There are events whose chief significance lies in the popular response they evoke at the time. The reaction to the Orson Welles Martian broadcast of 1938 was one; so were the Wanna-Go-Home riots of 1946 and the support for the Bricker amendment in the early 1950s. Now people, and not just Russian people, were hungry for heroes. The Soviet Union gave them Gagarin. After 108 hours of flight, 89 of which were spent actually in orbit, he descended from his altitude of 188 miles to become a prized propaganda asset. Standing on the tomb of Lenin, he received a twenty-gun salute. A Moscow square was named after him, then a glacier. Soviet artists set to work designing a commemorative stamp bearing his picture. In Russian newspapers his name was printed in red. Adoring Soviet journalists christened him Gaga. One wrote breathlessly of him that "his eyes were shining as though still reflecting spatial starlight." In Red Square Khrushchev made a speech comparing him to Columbus. A nationwide Soviet radio broadcast carried a conversation between Khrushchev and the cosmonaut, whose most improbable revelations were "While in outer space I was thinking about our party and our homeland," and "When I was going down, I sang the song, 'The Motherland Hears, the Motherland Knows.'"

Americans gnashed their teeth. "Kennedy could lose the 1964 election over this," a space administrator said, and a NASA scientist said, "Wait until the Russians send up three men, then six, then a laboratory, start hooking them together and then send back a few pictures of New York for us to see." At Cape Canaveral a bitter astronaut told a reporter, "We could have got a man up there. We could have done it a month ago if somebody at the top two years ago had simply decided to push it." At four o'clock that afternoon Kennedy faced a tumultuous press conference in the New State Department auditorium. He was asked: "Mr. President, a member of Congress said today he was tired of seeing the United States second to Russia in the space field. I suppose he speaks for a lot of others. . . . What is the prospect that we will catch up with Russia and perhaps surpass Russia in this field?" The reply was defensive: "However tired anybody may be, and no one is more tired than I am, it is a fact that it is going to take some time [to catch up] . . . We are, I hope, going to go in other areas where we can be first, and which will bring perhaps more long-range benefits to mankind. But we are behind." Columnist Hugh Sidey commented that this "seemed hardly in the spirit of the New Frontier." One news magazine reported that the nation's mood was one of "frustration, shame, sometimes fury," and predicted: "Only a spectacular and extremely difficult bit of rocketeering, say a manned trip around the moon, will top Russian spacemen in the eyes of the world."

In fact, Kennedy learned that evening, it had to be the moon or nothing; on lesser objectives the Soviet lead was too great to overcome. The President had called a 7 P.M. meeting in the Cabinet Room to search for alternatives. One by one his advisers spoke up — Jerome Wiesner; James Webb, NASA head; Dr. Hugh Dryden, Webb's distinguished deputy; David Elliot Bell, director of the Bureau of the Budget; and Sorensen. The scientists had Kennedy at a disadvantage. Space was not his forte. He knew less about this issue than any other, hadn't been briefed on the projects at Cape Canaveral, and lacked the science background necessary to sort out scientific options and priorities. After Wiesner, Webb, and Dryden had spoken the President muttered gloomily, "We may never catch up." He said, "Now let's look at this. Is there any place we can catch them? What can we do?" He did know that three half-built U.S. rockets would produce over a million pounds of thrust each when finished. He asked of them: "What about Nova and Rover? When will Saturn be ready? Can we leapfrog?"

Dryden told him there was only one hope, and it would take a crash program similar to the Manhattan Project. That might put an American on the moon in ten years. It would be a gamble, though. And it would cost at least twenty billion dollars — perhaps twice that. The President was silent. Then he said, "The cost, that's what gets me." He looked hopefully at Bell, but there was no comfort there; Bell said that exploring space was a very expensive business. Kennedy asked, "Can't you fellows invent some other race here on earth that will do some good?" But nothing else had the fascination of a flight to the moon, and after drumming his fingernails on his teeth he asked Wiesner and the NASA men to take another look at the figures. Rising to go, he said, "When we know more, I can decide if it's worth it or not. If somebody can just tell me how to catch up. Let's find somebody — anybody. . . . There's nothing more important."

Three weeks later the American people showed that their judgment confirmed his. After twenty-eight months of delays and breakdowns, the first vehicle in NASA's Project Mercury rose from the gantries at Cape Canaveral. As a hundred million viewers held their breath, a tall, slender white Redstone rocket slowly climbed into the sky, emitting a widening vapor trail. Its passenger was naval Commander Alan B. Shepard Jr. The country was elated. On turnpikes and freeways drivers pulled over to the shoulder and turned up their car radios. An Indianapolis judge declared a recess so everyone in the courthouse could watch the picture on a television set which police had seized as part of a burglar's booty. The nation was eavesdropping on the exchanges between *Freedom 7*, as Shepard's space capsule was called, and his control in Florida. He was in outer space for fifteen minutes. His flight was nothing like Gagarin's complex trajectory, but for the moment Americans didn't care. As his capsule descended beside the carrier *Lake Champlain*, swinging widely beneath its parachute, the sailors cheered wildly. "It's a beautiful day," were his first words back on earth. "Boy, what a ride!" His ride to glory had only begun. New York gave him its biggest ticker tape welcome in history as of then. A new school in Deerfield, Illinois, was named for him. Greeting cards went on sale for admirers to send Shepard. Derry, New Hampshire, his home town, with a population of 6,987, staged a parade in his honor. People came from all over New England to march in it; Army, Navy, Marine Corps, Air Force, and National Guard troops passed in review while jet fighters roared overhead. Senator Styles Bridges in an eloquent speech described New Hampshire's pride in the new hero. Legislators debated renaming Derry "Spacetown, U.S.A."

None of this was lost on the White House, just then smarting from the Bay of Pigs defeat. On May 25 the President stood before Congress with a special message on "urgent national needs," his second State of the Union address in four months. He wanted "an estimated seven to nine billion dollars additional over the next five years" for the space program. He knew he was asking a lot, he said, but "These are extraordinary times. We face an extraordinary challenge." To him the issue was a matter of patriotism: "I am here to promote the freedom doctrine." He said: "I believe that this nation should commit itself to achieving the goal, before this decade is out, of landing a man on the moon and returning him safely to earth."

Congress approved by a thundering margin. Simultaneously ground was broken for expansion of facilities at Cape Canaveral and a mission control center in Houston. The aerospace industry was on its way.

In July, Air Force Captain Virgil I. Grissom completed a flight similar to Shepard's. The Russians sent Major Gherman S. Titov whirling around the earth seventeen times in August, and in November NASA orbited a male chimpanzee and recovered him after two trips around the earth; while up, the chimp responded to various lights by pulling levers which released sips of water or banana-flavored pellets. NASA then announced that the pilot of the first U.S. human orbital flight would be the oldest of the seven astronauts who had been chosen from 110 candidates, Marine Lieutenant Colonel John H. Glenn Jr. By then the tremendous popularity of the Mercury Project had been established. It was evident that if Glenn made it back he would be America's first aerospace superstar, a second Lindbergh. Teams of journalists explored his childhood in the tiny hamlet of New Concord, Ohio, and returned with reams of data which captivated the nation. As a boy he had been an avid reader of *Buck Rogers*. He had admired Glenn Miller and had played a loud trumpet himself in the New Concord band. As strict Presbyterians the Glenns had held that cigarettes were sinful, and New Concord was a Presbyterian stronghold; boys from surrounding towns called it "Saint's Rest." Glenn and his chums had taken a pledge never to use profanity. Once while singing "Hail, Hail, the Gang's

All Here," one besotted boy, throwing caution to the winds, had recklessly continued with the phrase, "What the hell do we care?" Now, a quarter-century later, the blasphemer told eager journalists how the future astronaut had rounded on him: "Johnny came up to me, white-faced and righteous, and told me to stop. I think he was ready to knock my block off." In 1962 Glenn's faith remained strong; he assured interviewers that he believed in "a power greater than I am that will certainly see that I am taken care of."

After ten frustrating postponements he lifted off the pad at 10 A.M., Tuesday, February 20, 1962. His departure was like Shepard's, but magnified many times. A great spurting gout of yellow-white flame licked out from the Atlas D rocket, casting weird shadows on the flat, sandy scrubland of Cape Canaveral. For four incredible seconds the rocket just hung there, balanced over its gantry. Then it ascended, gaining in momentum until it disappeared into the deep blue overarching sky. Glenn said, "Lift-off. The clock is operating. We're under way." From the Project Mercury Control Center the deep, calm voice of Lieutenant Colonel John "Shorty" Powers, NASA's public affairs officer, explained the next step to the country. It was the separation of the rocket and the capsule, *Friendship 7*, at the precise angle which would put Glenn in orbit. As it happened Glenn cried: "Capsule is turning around. Oh, that view is tremendous! I can see the booster doing turnarounds just a couple of hundred yards behind. Cape is go and I am go."

The temperature in the capsule had risen to 108 degrees, he noted, but the air-conditioning in his suit kept him cool. He had been instructed to explain his every sensation — the audience, after all, was paying for the trip — and he began by reporting that he had no feeling of speed. It was "about the same as flying in an airliner at, say, 30,000 feet, and looking down at clouds at 10,000 feet." Over the Atlantic he spotted the Gulf Stream, a river of blue in the gray sea. Over the West Coast he made out California's Salton Sea and the Imperial Valley, and he could pick out the irrigation canals near El Centro, where he had once lived. His first twilight was awesome: "As the sun goes down it's very white, brilliant light, and as it goes below the horizon you get a very bright orange color. Down close to the surface it pales out into a sort of blue, a darker blue, and then off into black." The stars were spectacular. "If you've been out on the desert on a very clear, brilliant night when there's no moon and the stars just seem to jump out at you, that's just about the way they look." Approaching Australia he radioed, "Just to my right I can see a big pattern of light, apparently right on the coast." From a tracking station below, Astronaut Gordon Cooper explained to him that this was the Australian city of Perth. Its 82,000 inhabitants had turned on all their light switches, to welcome him and test his night vision. Glenn replied, "Thank everybody for turning them on, will you?"

Glenn made other tests himself, exploring his weightless state. He swallowed some nutritious tablets and some applesauce which he squeezed out of a tube. No problems there, he reported: "It's all positive action. Your tongue forces it back in the throat and you swallow normally. It's all a positive displacement machine all the way through." He jiggled around as best he could to see if he could bring on giddiness or space sickness. There was none of it; "I have no ill effects at all from zero G. It's very pleasant, as a matter of fact. Visual acuity is still excellent. No astigmatic effects. No nausea or discomfort whatever." An amateur photographer, Glenn had brought a camera along. Instead of putting it on a shelf after he had taken some pictures through his window, he just stuck it out in the air, and there it stayed, suspended. Changing rolls, he let the film slip. He quickly reached for it, but as he explained to the enchanted millions, "instead of clamping onto it, I batted it and it went sailing around behind the instrument panel, and that was the last I saw of it."

Sometimes he ran out of words. "I don't know what you can say about a day in which you have seen four beautiful sunsets," he said. It was at that point that he forgot his travelogue commentary. So did his listeners. He was having trouble. As he passed over Mexico a small jet, meant to keep his capsule steady, developed a malfunction. He reported to the control center that the vehicle "drifts off in yaw to the right at about one degree per second. It will go to 20 degrees and hold at that." That was the end of the tests; the flight now commanded his entire attention; he had to take over the controls and fly it himself. That wasn't the end of his difficulties. During his second pass over the Pacific, his gyroscopes went out. The capsule began "rolling" — turning on its horizontal axis. Glenn eliminated that by skillful handling of the controls. Then, in his second orbit, he developed what looked like real trouble. An ominous light flashed on the control board at Cape Canaveral. It meant that *Friendship 7*'s fiberglas heat shield had come ajar. If the shield came off at any time before the capsule reentered the atmosphere, Glenn would be instantly incinerated. As it turned out, the fault was in the warning light, not the shield, but neither the astronaut nor his mentors on the ground knew that then. They made adjustments to change the reentry procedure, retaining the vehicle's retro-rockets — which were to be jettisoned — in the hope that their metal bands might help keep the shield in place. Then they prayed.

Glenn knew that this was the moment of maximum peril. His braking rockets were fired in sequence, and he braced himself. As the pressure on him mounted, *Friendship 7* shimmied. He gasped, "It feels like I'm going clear back to Hawaii." The G forces were mounting, squeezing him against his contour couch. He was coming down, and the heat shield was disintegrating, breaking up into growing fragments. Later he said, "You could see the fire and the glow from them — big flaming chunks." He couldn't explain it at the time because he had lost radio contact. That was to be expected; he was in the delicate process of reentering. The blackout lasted seven minutes and fifteen seconds. As it ended he could be heard shouting, "That was a real fireball!" At 2:43 P.M. the glowing capsule hit the waters of the Atlantic and was instantly enveloped in clouds of sizzling steam. At 3:01 the destroyer *Noa* rescued Glenn. A steward handed him a glass of iced tea. Glenn said, "It was hot in there."

Idolatry awaited him. His footprints on the carrier deck were traced in white paint for later exhibition in the Smithsonian Institution. Cameramen recorded the fact that his eyes were full at the moment of reunion with his wife and children, and after he had wiped his eyes the handkerchief was set aside so it, too, would be preserved. As he fielded questions from the press, reporters noted that in speaking of himself and *Friendship 7* he often said "We" — just like Lindy at Paris's Le Bourget Field thirty-five years earlier. Vice President Johnson was there to greet him. Johnson said, "In my country we'd say you're pretty tall cotton. Were you very tense at takeoff?" Glenn replied that he supposed so. LBJ said, "You were about as near the Lord's end as a person ever is."

At Cape Canaveral one banner read: WELCOME TO EARTH. There the Vice President was replaced by the President, who had just flown over from Palm Beach. There was a bit of byplay as Glenn tried to put a hard hat on Kennedy and failed — JFK had once seen a picture of Calvin Coolidge in an Indian headdress and had vowed never to pose in a funny hat — and then the country's first astronaut was off to address a joint session of Congress. "Usually the honor is reserved for heads of state," Johnson told him, "but in this case the whole country has elected you." A gala parade in New York was next, featuring Glenn, the other six of the original astronauts, and a star-studded cast of big-name scientists. After that Glenn flew abroad to tour other continents, telling America's allies and the uncommitted peoples that truly great achievements were possible in a free society. *Time* commented: "In terms of national prestige, Glenn's flight put the U.S. back in the space race with a vengeance, and gave the U.S. and the entire free world a huge and badly needed boost."

"This is a new ocean," said Kennedy, "and I believe the U.S. must sail on it." At Cape Canaveral American rocketeers, confident once more, talked enthusiastically of launching two-man capsules by 1964; of giant, solid-propellant boosters to lift great payloads off the earth; and of plans for Project Apollo, aimed at putting three men on the moon and bringing them back, perhaps as soon as 1968. A passionate interest in space travel took on the proportions of a national rage. It was the theme of that year's Century 21 Exposition, in Seattle. "Orbit" entered Madison Avenue's vocabulary as a noun and as a verb. Small boys launched water-propelled toy satellites that landed in trees, like kites before them. Wernher von Braun, whose skills had played a major part in the success of the Atlas, became a national celebrity. ("He aimed for the stars," Mort Sahl said of his earlier years, "and often hit London.") Europeans of all convictions were tremendously impressed. Even Pablo Picasso, no Americanophile, said of Glenn, "I am as proud of him as if he were my brother." Presently all sorts of people were launching satellites — American Tel & Tel, for example, put up Telstar, and even the Canadians sent a small vehicle into orbit.

It was in August that the Soviet Union's Major Gherman S. Titov circled the earth seventeen times. This was seized upon as a new evidence for the need to mobilize America's industrial and technological might in a great effort to surpass the Russians once and for all. By now there were some dissenters, particularly on the campuses and in the U.S. intellectual community. The President answered them in September. Speaking at Rice University in Houston he said:

"But why, some say, the moon? . . . And they may well ask, why climb the highest mountain? Why, thirty-five years ago, fly the Atlantic? Why does Rice play Texas? . . . Many years ago the great British explorer George Mallory, who was to die on Mount Everest, was asked why did he want to climb it, and he said, 'Because it is there.' Well, space is there, and . . . the moon and the planets are there, and new hopes for knowledge and peace are there."

The black problem was also there, however, and it was much closer. In retrospect Kennedy's underreckoning of it seems astonishing. He was, after all, a northern liberal and an admirer of Martin Luther King. But the liberals, and even King, were about to be pressed hard by militant young northern blacks. While America's eyes had been turned upward toward the stars, they had been searching for ways to distract the country. The first attempt, and it was memorable, came in the spring of 1961. On May 4, three weeks after Gagarin's flight, seven black and six white members of the Congress of Racial Equality (CORE) left Washington by bus for an expedition through the Deep South. Their purpose was to challenge segregation in interstate bus terminals in defiance of local custom — in waiting rooms, restaurants, and toilets. They called themselves freedom riders.

The course they had charted zigzagged across Dixie: south through Virginia, North Carolina, and South Carolina; southwestward to Atlanta; westward through Alabama, and then on across Mississippi and down to New Orleans. It was bound to be a memorable trip. Their flouting of the customs of the region was breathtaking. After four years Little Rock was all but forgotten, and Arkansas was a border state anyway. Here in the real southland the relationships between the races were still very precise and had scarcely changed in the ninety years since the departure of the last carpetbagger. In that respect there were almost no southern liberals as the term was understood above the Mason-Dixon line. The WPA guidebook to Alabama, written by native New Dealers in 1941, pictured the sort of welcome wayfarers might expect in Montgomery, one of the state's three largest cities:

The atmosphere of measured dignity tempered by cordiality is matched nowhere else in Alabama. A Negro boy — his face wreathed in smiles — usually accosts the traveler with, "You don't have to tote that grip, boss man; I'll do it cheap"; and a resident will willingly give directions and accompany the stranger a block or more to set him on the right road.

That was not an accurate description of the greeting awaiting the freedom riders, a fact so obvious that they can be fairly said to have been looking for trouble. The nature of their sponsorship was less clear. Under the leadership of James Farmer CORE was an independent, self-supporting organization and had been active since 1942. But in the seething days ahead many southern leaders and southern editorials would charge that the administration ("the Kennedys") was behind them or had at least encouraged them to come. The truth was that no one in the government had known of their journey until they had left on it. CORE had sent an advance copy of a press release about the trip to the Department of Justice, but it had wound up on the desk of Burke Marshall, chief of the Civil Rights Division, who was out with the mumps. Newspaper accounts of the departure had been buried on the inside pages. The White House first heard of it when the story erupted on front pages, and then its reaction was anger — directed at the riders.

From the administration's point of view, the timing was dreadful. Not only had the Russians just won the race for the first manned space flight to encircle the earth; the week after that the Cuban brigade had been overwhelmed on the beach. On June 3, less than a month away, Kennedy would meet Khrushchev in Vienna. The new President needed a victory or, if that was impossible, the absence of a fresh defeat. The last thing he wanted was an ugly racial incident. The Russians were still exploiting Little Rock for propaganda directed at the Third World, portraying America as racist. Any episode which could be interpreted as evidence of that would be a humiliation for the United States. That was how the White House first regarded the rides — as an embarrassment. Later John Kennedy, and particularly Robert Kennedy, would see the civil rights struggle as a moral imperative, but in their first months in office it was not yet that. An understanding of their position then is important, because it was shared by most liberal Democrats, including some who thought themselves to be very advanced.

Their commitment to end prejudice was total. It was a wrong, and they were determined to right it. It was intolerable to them that the Negro condition should be unchanged in the world's oldest and greatest democracy. Throughout that campaign John Kennedy had reminded audiences that "The Negro baby born in America today, regardless of the section of the nation in which he is born, has about one-half as much chance of completing high school as a white baby born in the same place on the same day, one-third as much chance of completing college, one-third as much chance of becoming a professional man, twice as much chance of becoming unemployed, about one-seventh as much chance of earning $10,000 a year, a life expectancy which is seven years shorter, and the prospects of earning only half as much." As President he had pledged himself to support programs aiming at correcting that injustice. What more could the blacks ask?

The first thing they asked was that liberals stop thinking of blacks as statistics. After that they expected an end to gradualism. They realized that the spring of 1961 was an awkward time for the government to deal with the freedom riders. Every season for the past century had been awkward, and so they had waited and waited and waited. What they expected their white sympathizers to understand was that to the new Negro, freedom for his people was more important than any issue in Vienna — or in Vietnam, or Cuba, or outer space.

In 1961 it was considered political bravery just to endorse equality before the law in front of an audience of southern whites. That was what Robert Kennedy did in his first major speech as attorney general, and he did it in Athens, Georgia, on May 6, two days after the departure from Washington of the freedom riders, of whose existence, however, he was still unaware. The occasion was Law Day at the University of Georgia. He went to explain to them that it was his sworn duty to uphold the law, a circumstance of which one might suppose law students would already be aware, but on this issue, in this part of the country, nothing could be assumed. "We are maintaining the orders of the courts," he told them. "We are doing nothing more nor less. And if any one of you were in my position, you would do likewise, for it would be required by your oath of office. You might not want to do it, you might not like to do it, but you would do it." This was hardly a passionate affirmation of the rights of an oppressed race, and there was even a hint in it that on this issue Robert Kennedy might be doing his duty against his better judgment, but there were no weasel words at the end: "Our position is clear. We are upholding the law. . . . In this case — in all cases — I say to you today that if the orders of the court are circumvented, the Department of Justice will act. We will not stand by or be aloof. We will move."

In civil rights, as in the Third World, liberals of the early 1960s believed in the eventual triumph of right. This perhaps more than anything else sets the Kennedy years apart from what lay ahead and makes them seem almost naive now. Send surplus wheat to an emerging nation, send Peace Corpsmen, send a Chester Bowles as the American ambassador, the catechism read, and you will have a bright new democracy, a credit to the free world and a potential ally in the eternal struggle against the powers of darkness in Moscow. So at home: strong leadership and the fundamental sense of decency in the American people would overcome the bigotry implanted by generations of ignorance. Integration was just good sense, and Americans were above all sensible; it was just a matter of showing them the light; if Eisenhower had taken a stand he could have accomplished it in the 1950s.

The notion that there were dark places in the American mind was illiberal and therefore rejected. The liberal vision had no explanation for the phenomenon of the McCarthyism, the most recent instance in which decency and good sense had been scorned by masses of Americans, but in 1961 nobody talked about McCarthy any more. Optimism was almost a requirement on the New Frontier. General Harkins had the right idea, his body counts were certainly encouraging, and why couldn't those American correspondents in Saigon join the team? On the domestic front good liberals would fight the good fight until the Negro baby born in America had just as much chance of completing his education as the white baby, no more chance of becoming unemployed, as much chance of earning $10,000 a year, and the same life expectancy. However, these things took *time*. They mustn't expect it all *now*.

But the freedom riders wanted it all now.

Richmond, Petersburg, Lynchburg — here they stopped, stretched their legs, had a bite together at lunch counters under signs reading "White" and ignored the toilets designated "Colored" with no more than a few ugly looks and muttered obscenities from bystanders. Then stories about the trip began appearing in the newspapers of cities farther along on their route. They weren't big news yet, not important enough to attract the attention of an attorney general or a governor; all they warranted was a couple of sticks, a squib or two, something to wrap around the ads. But that was enough to alert gas station attendants leafing through the inside pages in search of the comics, enough for ticket clerks in the bus terminals, for sheriff's deputies passing by and the kind of men who hang around stations and depots waiting for something to happen.

The first incident was in Charlotte, North Carolina: a black freedom rider strolled into the bus station barbershop and refused to leave. He was arrested for trespassing and the others proceeded without him. It wasn't much, but the word was sent ahead, passed on as such news is always passed, by a phone call, or another driver, or police radio. It doesn't matter. It was inevitable and they expected it; that was why they had come. Still, the tension on the bus grew. When they saw the crowd at the station in Rock Hill, South Carolina, they knew the violence had begun to escalate. Three of them were beaten; then the Rock Hill police intervened. Again in Winnsboro, thirty-seven miles to the south, police stepped in before anything could start and arrested two riders. Next came another quiet stretch: Sumter and Camden, South Carolina; Augusta and Atlanta, Georgia. Atlanta was an important stop. They divided there into two groups for the ride to Birmingham, one going on a Trailways bus and the other by Greyhound. There was no trouble here — Georgia troopers were everywhere — but after Rock Hill and Winnsboro they were on page one of every newspaper in the South. It was a Sunday, the day papers are read most. They assumed that the population of Alabama would know all about them. It did.

Today travelers between Atlanta and Birmingham cruise easily across eastern Alabama on Interstate Route 20, but in 1961 that was still under construction, and they had to follow the tortuous curves of U.S. 78 through a succession of remote crossroads communities virtually untouched by postwar change. This was "upcountry" Alabama, an untamed region clothed with scrub pine — mostly high, with elevations of nearly 1,800 feet in the Raccoon and Lookout ranges, the southernmost spurs of Appalachia. Coming down off their slopes to the Cumberland plateau, the road descended to fields soybean farmers had reclaimed after the devastations of the boll weevil, to the coal region, and, beyond, to the Black Belt. Cleburne County, Calhoun County — these were an old breeding ground of wool-hats and red-necks, the strongholds of the camp meeting and the revival, and it was here, six miles from Anniston on U.S. 78, that a gang of Ku Klux Klansmen armed with blackjacks, clubs, and tire chains ambushed the Greyhound bus. A rock sailed through one window, followed by an incendiary bomb. As it burst into flame the riders fled. Twelve of them were being methodically beaten when policemen arrived and fired pistols into the air. Ambulances carried away the injured. Then Birmingham blacks who had heard of the battle arrived in cars and rescued the others.

The riders on the Trailways bus escaped the Klan trap, but in Anniston eight young toughs boarded the bus, dragged them into the aisles, and began punching them. Anniston cops drove them off. Birmingham, the destination of the bus, was worse. A crowd of men carrying lengths of pipe had surrounded the Trailways terminal at Nineteenth Street and Sixth Avenue North. An informer had warned the FBI about them. Incredibly, the FBI had not relayed the information to Burke Marshall's Civil Rights Division or to the attorney general's office. Instead it passed the tip along to the Birmingham police, whose chief, Police Commissioner T. Eugene "Bull" Connor, pigeonholed it. Although Connor's headquarters were only two blocks from the terminal, he sent no one over. The hoodlums there dragged the riders into the station and clouted them for thirty minutes, injuring three seriously enough to require hospitalization. The next morning the *Birmingham News,* which had denounced the *New York Times* the year before for saying that fear and hatred stalked the streets of Birmingham, now admitted that "fear and hatred did stalk Birmingham's streets yesterday." But Alabama officials had no apologies. Governor John Patterson said, "I cannot guarantee protection for this bunch of rabble-rousers," and Bull Connor said, "Our people of Birmingham are a peaceful people, and we never have any trouble here unless some people come into our city looking for trouble." Asked why there had been no policemen at the terminal, Connor said he had been shorthanded because it was Mother's Day. It was a joke.

The Sunday beatings brought the freedom riders to the attention of the Justice Department for the first time, and Burke Marshall called Bob Kennedy at home to tell him of it. Bob thought he might be able to resolve the situation with a phone call. He knew Patterson, who had been the first southern governor to support John Kennedy for President and had stayed with him even after his delegation had gone over to Lyndon Johnson. He called the governor Monday morning and asked him to protect the buses. Passengers on them had a right to travel between the states, and local authorities had a clear responsibility to guarantee their safe passage. Patterson agreed. Then he called back and said he had changed his mind. He had been elected with Klan support, and now the Klansmen were cashing in their credit.

This was the first of several strange long distance exchanges the two Kennedy brothers were to have with southern governors on the race issue, and like the others it was exasperating. Bob tried to phone Patterson again. He was told that the governor couldn't come to the phone. He tried again on Tuesday, on Wednesday, and on Thursday. Each time aides expressed their regrets. The most they could do, they said, was take a message, and they couldn't guarantee that it would reach the governor. They couldn't be sure, but they thought he was "out on the Gulf" — unreachable in any case. Meanwhile the situation in Birmingham was deteriorating. The original group of freedom riders, battered and frightened, had flown on to New Orleans, but their places had been taken by volunteers from Fisk University in Nashville, from Martin Luther King's Southern Christian Leadership Conference, and from the younger civil rights organizations, one such newcomer being a cool nineteen-year-old immigrant from Trinidad named Stokely Carmichael. In Washington, Attorney General Kennedy issued a statement asking for restraint from both the freedom riders and their opposition. He said, "In order to insure that innocent people are not injured, maimed, or even killed, I would call upon all people who have paramount interest in the future of our country to exercise restraint and judgment over their activities in the next few weeks or the next few days." There was a sense of unreality in this. He seemed to be trying to play the role of an impartial arbiter between two equally responsible, equally strong adversaries. The riders solemnly promised not to attack Alabamans; the Alabamans said nothing. Then Kennedy issued another statement saying, "What is needed now is a cooling-off period." A CORE spokesman tartly commented that what was needed was an end to cooling off, that black Americans had been cooling off for a hundred years. By Friday, when the new freedom riders prepared to continue the journey that the others had started, it was clear that they would be heading into fresh trouble. At his brother's request, President Kennedy put in a call to

Governor Patterson. He was told that the governor was "out of town and still unreachable." He did get through to the lieutenant governor, who after several hours said he could arrange a meeting between the governor and a personal representative of the President.

The Kennedys chose John Seigenthaler, a handsome and brave young Tennessean and the attorney general's best friend. Seigenthaler was on a plane within an hour. At first his mission seemed successful. After he and Patterson had conferred for two hours they phoned Bob Kennedy. While Patterson listened and nodded Seigenthaler reported that he had been assured that Alabama had, as Patterson put it, "the means, ability, and the will to keep the peace without outside help." The governor said that he could protect everyone in the state, both Alabamans and visitors, in the cities and on the highways, and he said he would do it. Bobby then called Floyd Mann, the chief of Alabama's highway patrol, who backed up the governor's guarantee. With that, a biracial group of twenty-one students voted to board a Birmingham to New Orleans bus in the morning. An unexpected hitch developed when no driver could be found. Getting one required a long, abrasive phone conversation between the attorney general and George E. Cruit, the Greyhound representative in Birmingham, but in the end Cruit produced a man and the riders departed for Montgomery, which turned out to be even worse than Birmingham.

The trip there was uneventful. Mann's Highway Department did its part; both U.S. 65 and U.S. 31 were clear. The FBI had alerted the Montgomery police to the arrival of the bus, and when it was about fourteen miles from the city Mann radioed a second warning to Montgomery's police commissioner, Lester B. Sullivan. But Sullivan was no more ready than Connor to run interference for uppity blacks and renegade whites. He ignored the messages, and there were no policemen when the bus arrived at the Union Bus Terminal to confront a throng estimated at between a thousand and three thousand. The attorney general's office had a blow-by-blow account of what happened next because John Doar, second in command to Burke Marshall in the Civil Rights Division, was in the U.S. Attorney's office across the street from the terminal.* Doar had just put through a call to Kennedy when the bus drew up at the terminal. Kennedy and his deputy attorney general, Byron White, heard him say:

"The bus is in. The people are just standing there, watching. . . . Now the passengers are coming off. They're standing on a corner of the platform. Oh, there are fists, punching! A bunch of men led by a guy with a bleeding face are beating them. There are no cops. It's terrible. It's terrible. There's not a cop in sight. People are yelling, 'Get 'em, get 'em.' It's awful. . . . The cops are there now."

They were state troopers, not Montgomery policemen. ("We have no intention of standing police guard for a bunch of troublemakers coming

---

*On December 21, 1973, Doar became legal adviser to the House Judiciary Committee's inquiry into the possibility of impeachable offenses by President Nixon.

into our city," Sullivan told reporters.) And the troopers were too few to be effective. Mann saved one black by pulling his pistol, but the rest of the riders were beyond help. So were several bystanders who were unconnected with them, and who seem to have been attacked on general principle. One boy's leg was broken. A group of young whites poured inflammable liquid on another boy and set him on fire. One Montgomery woman held up her child so that he could reach out and beat on a black man with his fists. Other women swore at two white girls who had been among the riders and then slapped them with their purses. The girls begged a passing motorist for help. He said, "You deserve what you get. I hope they beat you up good." Another man in a rented car pulled over. "Come on, I'll help you," he called to the girls, "I'm a federal man." Before he could do anything, however, he was dragged to the pavement and slugged. He was John Seigenthaler, the President's personal envoy to the governor of Alabama, and he lay unconscious in his own blood on the sidewalk for twenty-five minutes before an ambulance arrived. Commissioner Sullivan later explained that no ambulance had been called for Seigenthaler because "every white ambulance in town reported their vehicles had broken down."

Bob Kennedy, livid, put Byron White on the next plane to Montgomery with Jim McShane, U.S. marshal for the District of Columbia. After Little Rock, Attorney General William P. Rogers had instituted riot training for U.S. marshals and their deputies to provide a federal law enforcement force other than the Army. At Maxwell Air Force Base outside Montgomery, Byron White now assembled four hundred men who had been so trained — revenue agents, border patrolmen, and guards from federal prisons — and who could be swiftly deputized for the occasion. Meanwhile Doar appeared in U.S. District Court and obtained an injunction enjoining the Ku Klux Klan and the National States' Rights Party, the two organizations most heavily represented in the mob, from interfering with interstate travel by bus. Governor Patterson then appeared at long last to protest that these moves were unconstitutional. Besides, he said, federal officers were unnecessary. On that he was simply proved wrong.

That Saturday afternoon the most famous civil rights activist, Martin Luther King, flew into Montgomery. At the home of the Reverend Ralph Abernathy he announced that he would speak that evening to a rally in the First Baptist Church. This presented the Ku Kluxers and their allies with a prize beyond their most vicious dreams. For a while King didn't seem to be an insurable risk. Byron White was supervising the preparations of the marshals when he received a startling phone call: Governor Patterson had called a meeting of Alabama law enforcement officers and was instructing them to arrest any federal men who broke state laws. White went to the meeting alone. It was open to the press, which took down the tense exchange between him and the governor. Patterson asked the deputy attorney general to share the government's information about

CORE. "No," said White. Then the governor asked for information about the freedom riders. "No," White said again. Then:

PATTERSON: You know where some of these freedom riders are, don't you?

WHITE: Yes, in the hospital.

PATTERSON: Do you know where the others are?

WHITE: No, I don't.

PATTERSON: If you knew where some of these people are, would you inform us?

WHITE: I will never know where these people are.

At that moment they were in the First Baptist Church with Martin Luther King. By nightfall some fifteen hundred Birmingham Negroes had arrived for the rally. It had scarcely begun when an ugly crowd began to gather in a park across the street. Learning that the local police were again absent, White dispatched his marshals by every conveyance he could find — postal delivery trucks, private automobiles, and a prison truck. They were wearing business suits and brassards and were armed with pistols, nightsticks, and tear gas guns. About a hundred of them had formed a skirmish line outside the church when the mob charged, hurling stones and broken bottles. With that, the governor declared marshal law. The marshals' skirmish line held until crucial reinforcements arrived: Floyd Mann at the head of his troopers, and Henry Graham, a National Guard major general, with a detachment of his men. Even so, before the attack of the mob was blunted the marshals had to fire several volleys of tear gas. The gas seeped into the hot, overcrowded church. At times the blacks there were close to panic. If the church had been put to the torch, which was the mob's intention, undoubtedly the loss of life would have been great. As it was, they were well shielded by the mixed force of state and federal law enforcement officers.

Governor Patterson phoned Attorney General Kennedy to protest that Alabama was being invaded.

"John, John," Bob said quietly. "What do you mean, you're being invaded? Who's invading you, John? You know better than that."

Patterson accused him of sending the freedom riders into the state and blamed him for the violence.

"Now John," Bob said. "You can say that on television. You can tell that to the people of Alabama, but don't tell me that. Don't tell me that, John."

Nevertheless Patterson did it again, repeating every word. Then he said that the National Guard would defend the church and the congregation inside, but could not guarantee the safety of King.

"I don't believe that," said Kennedy. "Have General Graham call me. I want to hear a general of the United States Army say he can't protect Martin Luther King."

By now the governor was yelling. He shouted shrilly that he was giving his opinion, not the general's. He cried that sending federal marshals had created "a very serious political situation" and shrilled, "You're destroying us politically!"

"John," Kennedy said in the same quiet tone. "It's more important that these people in the church survive physically than for us to survive politically."

That ended the threat of violence against the freedom riders. In the north, Patterson was regarded as the heavy loser in the episode. Southerners took a different view, however. Lost causes have had a special appeal to them since Appomattox. They rallied to his side, sent him money and encouragement, and promised to join the fight against integration. That was ominous; it committed them. Keeping the vow became a matter of honor, and by June it had been taken publicly by virtually every politician in Dixie, including George Corley Wallace, who the following year was elected to succeed Patterson.

Nevertheless, as such things go, the freedom riders were counted a success. No one had been killed, and Jim Crow had been routed. Enforced segregation in interstate travel, theoretically outlawed by the Supreme Court in 1950, now ended in fact. Bob Kennedy petitioned the Interstate Commerce Commission to issue regulations requiring desegregation in all interstate terminals, including airports and train depots, and four months later, on September 22, it did. A few cities cited local laws as an excuse for not complying; the Justice Department brought suit against them. By the end of 1961 Negroes could travel coast to coast without seeing "White" or "Colored" in waiting rooms.

Countless bastions of segregation remained, of course, and the most formidable of them were in Mississippi. In 1931 H. L. Mencken and Charles Angoff ran a two-part series in the *American Mercury* ranking the states from good to bad, "from civilized to barbaric." Their criteria included wealth, literacy, education, entries in *Who's Who in America,* symphony orchestras, crime, voter registration, infant mortality, transportation, and availability of medical attention. In the final standing Mississippi was last, behind the rest of the Deep South, and its situation hadn't changed in 1962; indeed, when John Bererdt repeated the Mencken-Angoff survey for the magazine *Lifestyle* ten years later, in November 1972, Mississippi was again on the bottom, just below Alabama.* The average Mississippian had less than nine years' schooling. Over a third of the people were poor, as the Department of Commerce *Statistical Abstract of the United States* defines poverty. One in four households lacked plumbing and 29 percent telephones; only 24 percent read a daily newspaper and only 3 percent a news magazine. "The Closed Society," Professor James W. Silver of the University of Mississippi called the state in 1964, and it became clear as the

---

*In 1931 Massachusetts was first. In 1972 Connecticut had replaced it.

1960s progressed that an astonishing number of its people, white and black, were actually unaware of the civil rights movement. There were no attacks on the freedom riders there because the state police didn't allow them the freedom of movement necessary to be mobbed. Their buses were met at the Alabama border and escorted to Jackson, and when they ignored the discriminatory signs in the terminal there, they were arrested and led to jail. Eventually federal courts overturned their convictions, but the rulings meant little to individual prisoners, who had served their time by then.

Burke Marshall, almost alone in the Justice Department, understood the inflexibility of Mississippi white supremacy. He knew that its prophets regarded the present period as a second Reconstruction. If they were just as single-minded in their resistance to it as their great-grandfathers had been, they thought, the federal challenge would fail and the problem would go away. But in 1961 most of the rest of the Justice Department (with the exception of Doar) wasn't on Marshall's wavelength. At the end of the year the attorney general submitted a report to his brother, the President, on civil rights progress. It almost sang with hope, and in a Voice of America broadcast a week after the confrontation at the First Baptist Church, Bob declared that racism was ebbing in the United States. He actually predicted that a black man could be elected President before the end of the century.

A brief conversation with one Mississippi black, James Meredith, would have tempered his optimism. Meredith was a nine-year veteran of the Air Force and one of ten children of a farmer in the mid-state town of Kosciusko. Inspired by President Kennedy's inaugural address, Meredith had written to the University of Mississippi the same evening he heard it, requesting an application for admission. He returned the completed form with an explanatory note: "I am an American-Mississippi-Negro citizen. With all of the occurring events regarding changes in our educational system taking place in our country in this new age, I feel certain that this application does not come as a surprise to you. I certainly hope that this matter will be handed in a manner that will be complimentary to the University and to the state of Mississippi."

Ole Miss, as the university at Oxford was known throughout the South, rejected him for complex academic reasons, but Meredith wasn't discouraged that easily, and he found a powerful ally in Medgar Evers, the state director of the NAACP. In June 1961 NAACP lawyers filed suit for Meredith in the federal district court, charging that he had been turned down solely because of his race. The litigation which followed is unique in the history of American jurisprudence. A district court judge ruled against Meredith twice. In June 1962 the court of appeals for the Fifth Circuit reversed the judge; then Judge Ben Cameron of the Fifth Circuit reversed the reversal. The appeals court vacated Cameron's order, but he promptly issued another. This went on until, after his fourth stay, he had made it clear that he intended to continue along this line indefinitely. The NAACP appealed for sanity to Supreme Court Justice Hugo Black. In September Black, a native Alabaman, upheld the court of appeals and ordered the university to admit Meredith at once. "Never!" cried Governor Ross Barnett, and two days later he went on statewide television to declare: "We will not surrender to the evil and illegal forces of tyranny."

Apart from his age — he was sixty-four in the autumn of 1962 — Ross Barnett was more like Meredith, whom he was about to engage in a duel by proxy, than he would have acknowledged. Like him he had been one of ten children, and had come to manhood in the hardscrabble clay wasteland of central Mississippi, the barren soil familiar to explorers of Yoknapataw-pha County, the creation of William Faulkner, whose nephew Murry Falkner would play a key role in the unfolding crisis just ahead. Like Meredith, Barnett was also a prisoner of the past, a fundamentalist who took the Old Testament to be the literal truth and believed it proscribed racial "mixing." In another time, under other stars, the two men might have become friends. Barnett would have liked that, for he was naturally warm and gentle, ready to do almost anything for someone in distress, including Negroes. But if the man was black he had to know his place. On the strength of his vow to keep the Merediths of Mississippi where they were, Barnett had been elected governor three years earlier with the endorsement of the state's White Citizens' Councils. As an elector in the last presidential election, he had bolted the Kennedy-Johnson ticket to vote for Harry Byrd. He was, in short, representative of his kind and his region: charming, ig-norant, friendly, suspicious, blindly loyal to the lost Confederacy, appalled by the present and frightened of the future. Martyrs are made of just such stuff, and only one trait kept Barnett from becoming one. He was a coward. Under great pressure he would look for a way out, a deal. His tragedy, which became Mississippi's, was that he just didn't know how to find or make one.

If Barnett resembled Meredith, his antithesis was Robert F. Kennedy, who completely misread him. On the strength of the fact that Mississippi's highway patrol had effectively convoyed the freedom riders to safety, Bob assumed that the authorities there believed in law and order. He mistook the patrol's commander, the felicitously but inaccurately named Colonel T. B. Birdsong, for another Floyd Mann. All the situation seemed to need was a plan, and Bob was very good at plans. On Saturday, September 15, he called Barnett and explained crisply how it would all be managed. He understood, of course, that as a southern governor Barnett would have to offer token resistance. Therefore Meredith would be escorted by several marshals brandishing court orders. The governor could throw up his hands and the university officials, bowing to the inevitable, would then enroll Meredith. Kennedy asked if Barnett understood, if there were any ques-tions. In what should have been recognized as a sign of how far apart they were, the governor said, "That will take about a year."

It took just five days. The following Thursday Meredith, accompanied by the marshals, appeared in Oxford to register. He was met by Barnett, who was attempting to shield the university administration by appearing himself in the role of a "special registrar." While two thousand white students chanted, "We want Ross, we want Ross," and "Glory, glory, segregation," the governor read a decree barring Meredith from the campus "now and forevermore." Then he handed it to him and said, "Take it and abide by it." One of the men from the Justice Department said, "Do you realize you are placing yourself in contempt of court?" Barnett said, "Are you telling me this or does it take a judge?"

His legal position, and he thought it unassailable, was what is called interposition — interposing himself, as a representative of the states' rights, between the administration in Washington and the people of Mississippi. He had asked his legislature to give him that authority, and it had complied. When American historians learned of that, they were incredulous. Interposition had been discredited as a doctrine before the Civil War. In fact, when John C. Calhoun had tried to invoke it in 1832, the Mississippi legislature of that time had rejected it as "a heresy, fatal to the existence of the Union . . . contrary to the letter and spirit of the Constitution and in direct conflict with the welfare, safety and independence of every state." Now, one hundred and thirty years later, the governor was trying to breathe life into the same dead dogma. The Fifth Circuit in New Orleans, undeceived and unwilling to recognize Barnett as a special registrar, ordered university officials to appear the following Monday and show cause why they should not be cited for contempt. Barnett protested bitterly to the press at the speed of the courts. Mississippi's Senator James Eastland phoned Bob Kennedy to say, "The governor thinks you can back down a little, and I think so, too." Bob replied, "You don't really believe that, Senator. You've been in the Senate too long to believe that."

In court the university officials promised to admit Meredith by 4 P.M. the next day. Barnett still refused to budge. Saying that he was "shocked" at the officials' "surrender," he announced that anyone from the Department of Justice who interfered with Mississippians doing their duty would be arrested and jailed. Kennedy phoned him to point out that the people of Mississippi, including their governor, were citizens of the United States of America and subject to its laws. Barnett said, "I consider the Mississippi courts as high as any other court and a lot more capable. . . . Our courts have acted too, and our legislature has acted too. I'm going to obey the laws of Mississippi!" His attorney general, Joe Patterson, then issued a statement saying that freedom had been dealt "a staggering blow. . . . The constitutional rights of over 5,000 students have been ignored to gratify the pretended constitutional rights of one."

Meredith made his second attempt to register the next day in Jackson, at the office of the university trustees. John Doar and Jim McShane were with him. They were met by Barnett, Colonel Birdsong, and a jeering crowd of onlookers. The university officials couldn't keep the commitment made yesterday in New Orleans, the governor said, because they had been sub-poenaed by a legislative committee investigating un-Mississippian activi-ties. Doar tried to serve court papers on the governor; Barnett put his hands in his pockets. Doar asked, "Do you refuse to let us through that door?" Courtly as always, the governor said, "Yes, sir, I do so politely." Doar said, "And we leave politely." The crowd was not polite. As Meredith and his escort departed there were cries of "Go home, nigger," and "Communists!"

Bob Kennedy had been trying to keep Barnett's name out of the court proceedings because he remembered how Faubus had made political capi-tal in Little Rock, but this was too much. The successive failures to admit Meredith were conveying the impression, in Mississippi at least, that the white supremacists were winning. Kennedy decided to ask for a Fifth Cir-cuit order showing the governor in contempt. He phoned Barnett to tell him he was going to do it. He said further that Meredith would appear in Oxford in the morning, ready to attend classes. Barnett was aggrieved. Didn't that boy know when he wasn't wanted? As governor he had other duties, he said; he couldn't keep "running all over the State of Mississippi" for one Mississippian, and a Negro at that. Kennedy thought Meredith's enrollment would work. He said, "Why don't you try it for six months and see how its goes?"

"It's best for him not to go to Ole Miss," Barnett said.

Bob replied softly, "But he likes Ole Miss."

On campus alarmed faculty members noted a growing swell of visitors from all over Dixie, hard-bitten men with brush-fire eyes who were often armed and who asked, "Where will the nigger come from?" Their leader was General Edwin A. Walker, now of Dallas. On Wednesday, September 26, the day before the confrontation in Jackson, the general had issued a somewhat incoherent radio appeal to those who shared his convictions: "It is time to move. We have talked, listened, and been pushed around far too much by the anti-Christ Supreme Court. Rise to a stand beside Governor Barnett at Jackson, Mississippi. Now is the time to be heard. Ten thousand strong from every state in the union. The battle cry of the republic. Barnett, yes; Castro, no. Bring your flags, your tents, and your skillets. . . . The last time in such a situation I was on the wrong side. . . . This time I am out of uniform and I am on the right side and I will be there."

That day Barnett went into temporary seclusion. When Meredith and his escorts approached the campus in Oxford they were turned back by Lieutenant Governor Paul Johnson, backed by detachments of state troopers and county sheriffs. This time there was some jostling as the federal men tried to walk around Johnson in the hope that, having resisted, he would bow to the inevitable. He didn't bow. It was clear that force would be required to get past him. The marshals had been told to stop short of that, and there weren't enough of them anyway. Meredith was turned back again.

By this point every civil rights leader in America and most of official

Washington thought that the Justice Department was being too patient, that the dignity of the federal government was in jeopardy. Robert Kennedy knew it, but he had sensed fear in Ross Barnett. The governor, he thought, would welcome an opportunity to save face; he seemed to be learning the peril of continuing to defy a federal court. On the phone the next morning, Thursday, Bob suggested that they explore the possibility of finding a way out. He had been right; the governor instantly agreed. If he had been as able a politician as George Wallace, the crisis might have been resolved then. But he wasn't able. His sense of timing (or Bob's timing in waiting this long to close with him) was wrong; too many hopes of total victory had been raised in diehard segregationists, emotions were running too high, too many Mississippians were calling for resistance "regardless of the cost in human life" — a phrase heard everywhere there. Most important, the governor didn't know how to strike a bargain. He knew he would have to sacrifice something to make peace, but he couldn't decide how much he would give up, how much resistance he could show for the sake of appearances and still remain below the flash point of violence.

Their first attempt to reach an understanding ended in ludicrous failure. They talked of Barnett and Lieutenant Governor Johnson at the campus gate, flanked by unarmed state troopers, facing McShane and thirty marshals. McShane would draw an unloaded pistol. The Mississippians would then step aside, and Meredith would pass through the gate and be registered. Barnett said one revolver wasn't enough. He wanted all thirty marshals to draw; that way, he could say he yielded to avoid bloodshed. Bobby proposed that the other marshals just slap their holsters. That wasn't sufficiently realistic for the governor, and so it was settled that all thirty guns would be drawn.

Earlier in the week this might have been enough, but now it would be dangerous. The fact that the troopers were unarmed was irrelevant; they would be counterbalanced by the guns carried by General Walker's followers in Oxford. In addition, Barnett was the only man on his side who knew of the deal. He might be the only one to step aside. The realization of this came to him while he was waiting for Meredith at the campus gate. The black Air Force veteran was then proceeding toward him in a thirteen-car convoy which was in radio contact with Washington. At 3:35 P.M. Mississippi time, 5:35 in Washington, Barnett called Kennedy to say that he couldn't control the crowd, it was too big and in too ugly a temper. That ended the showdown scenario. The convoy turned back. Meredith had been denied registration four times now, and that evening at the university white students held a wild demonstration.

But there would be no more failures. Bob Kennedy was conferring with General Maxwell Taylor, chairman of the Joint Chiefs, and his principal commanders, General Earle G. Wheeler and Major General Creighton W. Abrams. At the Justice Department an assistant attorney general was drafting documents for President Kennedy's signature putting Mississippi's National Guard in federal service, alerting U.S. infantry units at Fort Benning for action, and warning civilians in the streets of Oxford to go home and stay there. Another assistant attorney general was flying down to assume command of a growing force of marshals. From New Orleans came word that the Fifth Circuit had found Barnett guilty of contempt, ruling that if Meredith were not registered by Tuesday — it was now Friday — the governor would be fined $10,000 a day; for Lieutenant Governor Johnson, if Johnson took his place, it would be $5,000 a day.

The only card the government hadn't played was presidential prestige, and that was committed Saturday afternoon when the White House put through a call to the statehouse in Jackson. President Kennedy had already requested television time at 8 P.M. to lay the matter before the American people. He canceled it when Barnett proposed that Meredith be admitted secretly in Jackson on Monday while the governor was diverting the mob in Oxford. His manner didn't inspire confidence, however; hanging up, the President turned to the others and asked in wonder, "Do you know what that fellow said? He said, 'I want to thank you for your help on the poultry program.'"

At ten o'clock that evening the lack of confidence was justified. Barnett phoned the Justice Department to say that he had changed his mind. The agreement was off; he wouldn't go through with his part of it. Again the President requested television time, for 7:30 the following evening, Sunday, September 30. Sunday morning the governor called Robert Kennedy. It was another fruitless, frustrating conversation, and in the middle of it Bob lost his temper. He said his brother was going on TV to tell the country how Barnett had reached an agreement "with the President of the United States" and had then broken his word.

Alarmed, the governor said in a high-pitched voice, "That won't do at all."

"You broke your word to him."

"You don't mean the President is going to say that tonight?"

"He is."

Barnett, breathing hard, suggested flying Meredith in "this afternoon."

That seemed to be the end of it. Meredith, it appeared, would be enrolled that same day, and without bloodshed. He would be admitted quietly while state troopers kept the peace. Afterward Barnett would issue a furious statement saying that it had been done behind his back, that he was yielding to irresistible force but would fight it in the courts. Deputy Attorney General Nick Katzenbach flew down to supervise the details. At 5 P.M. Mississippi time, accompanied by Colonel Birdsong, he led four hundred marshals onto the Ole Miss campus, now almost deserted, through the little-used west gate. Meredith was taken quietly to Baxter Hall, at one end of the grounds, while Katzenbach and the marshals established a command post at the other end in the lovely old red brick Lyceum Building, the university's administration building. The President delayed his television address until 10 P.M. in the belief that the crisis would be all over by then. But this Sunday, like every other day in the Meredith case, seemed jinxed. Almost at once communications with Washington broke down, and they remained out until Monday morning. Even after Army units arrived on the scene, the Signal Corps was unable to establish a link to the White House. Throughout this, the height of the crisis, with the eyes of the nation and much of the world on Ole Miss, the President of the United States and the attorney general, his brother, received crucial reports from Katzenbach, who was dropping dimes into a pay phone in a campus booth.

As the sun sank over Mississippi it became evident that somehow word of what had happened was spreading in Oxford. A crowd of about a thousand quickly gathered outside the Lyceum. Meredith's whereabouts were unknown to them; throughout the coming nightmare he remained concealed a mile away, guarded by twenty-four marshals who had doffed their white helmets and orange vests so that they, too, would be inconspicuous. There can be little doubt about what would have happened to him, and possibly to them, if his presence in Baxter Hall had become known to the mob. Like Richard Nixon in Caracas, he was in very real danger of being torn apart. The marshals (all of whom were white southerners themselves) were being taunted with "Kill the nigger-loving bastards," "Go to Cuba, nigger lovers," and a chant: "Two-four-one-three, we hate Kennedy!" The evening deepened. The crowd doubled, and redoubled. Its shouts became obscene. The marshals were pelted with stones, then rocks, then lighted cigarettes. A Texas newsman and his wife were beaten by men swinging pieces of pipe. Many of the state troopers on the scene were unhelpful. Some stood aside with folded arms and did nothing.

It was 7:30 P.M. in Mississippi when the FBI monitored a radio signal ordering the state troopers to withdraw entirely and leave Meredith and the marshals to the mob. Later efforts to find out who had sent it were unsuccessful. Katzenbach phoned Bob Kennedy to tell him of it. In the background Bob could make out the ragged sounds of riot. Then — it was at 7:58 — he heard that thumping sound of gas grenades. Katzenbach said, "Bob, I'm very sorry to report we've had to fire tear gas. We had no choice."

In Washington the President went on television unaware of the latest developments. To the best of his knowledge then, Barnett was keeping his word to maintain order with the troopers. He explained to the national audience that Meredith was on the campus, explained the need to enforce court orders, spoke glowingly of the heroism of Mississippi men in the country's wars, and appealed to Ole Miss undergraduates: "The honor of your university and state are in the balance. I am certain that the great majority of the students will uphold that honor."

In Oxford the students watching him jeered. General Walker was moving among them purposefully. A fire engine and a bulldozer were seized by men who used them to try to crash through the line of marshals and into the Lyceum; well-lobbed grenades drove them off. The attackers hurled

Molotov cocktails fashioned from Coca-Cola bottles. Campus benches were demolished to make jagged concrete projectiles, iron bars and bricks from construction sites were thrown, and here and there the crack of rifles could be heard as invisible snipers zeroed in on the Lyceum. Two men were killed, a French foreign correspondent and an Oxford spectator. Over a third of the marshals — 166 — were injured, and 28 were wounded by snipers' bullets. The marshals carried sidearms; they were under fire; it seemed right to return it. They repeatedly asked for permission to do so, and Katzenbach relayed the requests to Washington. The Kennedy brothers rejected the appeals. There would be no federal use of live ammunition, they ruled, unless Meredith was in danger. The marshals, exhausted and bloodied, held out with only their black, stubby tear gas guns to protect them.* Edwin Guthman was in the Lyceum, on the phone with Bob Kennedy. Bob asked, "How's it going down there?" Ed answered, "Pretty rough. It's sort of like the Alamo." Bob said, "Well, you remember what happened to those fellows."

At ten o'clock in Oxford, Katzenbach reluctantly told Washington that troops were necessary. In three-quarters of an hour the first unit arrived, sixty National Guardsmen of Troop E, 108th Armored Cavalry, under the command of Captain Murry C. Falkner. Before daybreak sixteen of them would become casualties, among them Captain Falkner, two of whose bones were broken by a brickbat. To the exasperation and then the fury of the Kennedys, nearly five hours passed before regular Army contingents, who had been alerted, reached the scene. Three times the marshals almost ran out of tear gas. When the soldiers did arrive, they had to fight their way to the campus. Forty of them were hit by missiles or shotgun blasts. Most of the attackers vanished in the night. The 503rd Military Police Battalion, arriving with the main body of troops from Memphis, arrested over two hundred members of the mob, including General Walker. Only twenty-four of them were students; the others came from all over Dixie — Georgia, Alabama, Louisiana, Tennessee, and Texas, as well as Mississippi. At dawn the campus was seen to be littered with chunks of cement, tear gas canisters, wrecked vehicles, rocks, smashed window glass, and green chips from thousands of pulverized Coke bottles. Governor Barnett blamed the riot on "inexperienced, nervous, trigger-happy" marshals.

Shortly before eight o'clock Monday morning Jim McShane and two other marshals accompanied Meredith to the battered Lyceum. There, at last, he was admitted by Robert Byron Ellis, the stony-faced registrar. There was no resistance in the administration building, only resignation and studied courtesy. Meredith listed his academic goal as a degree in political science. With credits from extension courses already taken he would grad-

---

*"One would remember them," Ed Guthman wrote nine years later, "in the racial riots and wild campus demonstrations of the latter half of the 1960s and at Kent State and at Jackson State universities in 1970, when lawmen, with far, far less provocation and injury than the marshals endured, gunned people down."

uate in three semesters. As he left the Lyceum another student yelled, "Was it worth two lives, nigger?"

Booked and fingerprinted, Major General Edwin A. Walker was charged with assaulting an officer, resisting arrest, insurrection, and conspiracy. The charges were dropped three months later after he had been given a psychiatric examination at Parkland Memorial Hospital in Dallas, and on an April evening three months after *that* a sniper standing on his lawn and aiming a cheap mail order rifle tried to kill him. In December 1963 ballistics experts found that the owner of that rifle, and presumably the man who had fired it, was Lee Harvey Oswald, who, among other things, had become since then an active supporter of the Fair Play for Cuba Committee and the assassin of John F. Kennedy. The confusion of the radical left and radical right is puzzling unless one grasps that President Kennedy, supremely a man of the center, was hated by both. Their feelings for him had begun to harden at the time of the Bay of Pigs, when one extreme denounced him for backing the invasion of Castro Cuba while the other condemned him for not going all the way and wiping Castro out. By the end of his second year in office it was clear that among those at either end of the political spectrum Kennedy had become the most scorned President since Franklin Roosevelt.

The New Left had begun to organize for the long pull in June 1962, when forty-five quiet, neatly dressed young people met at an old UAW-CIO summer camp at Port Huron, Michigan, to found the Students for a Democratic Society. The SDS then was but a shadow of its future self. The principal activity at the meeting was discussion of a moderate, sixty-two-page manifesto drafted by a weedy, pock-marked twenty-two-year-old University of Michigan undergraduate named Tom Hayden. Hayden cited, as the two greatest challenges to society, racism and "the enclosing fact of the cold war, symbolized by the presence of the Bomb." He proposed "that we as individuals take the responsibility for encounter and resolution." There was nothing new in the diagnosis or the prescription for cure: "We would replace power rooted in possession, privilege, or circumstances by power and uniqueness rooted in love, reflectiveness, reason and creativity." Hayden specifically renounced what would later become an SDS trademark — violence as catalyst for change — on the ground that it "requires generally the transformation of the target, be it a human being or a community of people, into a depersonalized object of hate."

The right was much farther along. The John Birch Society, the SDS's mirror image, was four years old and flourishing. His membership in it had been the reason for General Walker's dismissal from the Army, and the Kennedy brothers had increased its fame by damning it, the attorney general calling it "ridiculous" and the President warning that it was an inept adversary of Communism. Robert Welch, "The Founder," as he called himself, continued to mastermind Birch activities from a two-story brick building in the Boston suburb of Belmont. He seemed to enjoy publicity and was doubtless aware that it helped recruit new Birchers. The basic unit in the society was the chapter, which was frankly based on the Communist cell. (Welch was fascinated by Communism and imitated it slavishly.) Each chapter numbered between ten and twenty members. By the early 1960s there were reported to be chapters in thirty-four states and the District of Columbia with a total membership of about one hundred thousand. Birch ranks were increased by what The Founder called "fronts," such as the Patrick Henry Society, the Sons of the American Revolution, and the Minute Women and Minutemen. In many communities the Birchers were treated as a joke, but it was no joke in places like Shreveport, Tampa, Houston, and Dallas, where, as the *New York Times* reported, "businessmen, management executives, physicians, lawyers, and other 'solid' people have joined chapters."

As the decade grew older the New Left would emerge as the greater threat to democratic institutions, but that was not apparent in the Kennedy years. The resources of the right overshadowed anything at the other extreme; during the Kennedy Presidency outlays by ultraconservative organizations rose from five million dollars a year to over fourteen million, while the national budget for a liberal enterprise like the Americans for Democratic Action ran to a mere $150,000. The worst the left could do then was an occasional ill-tempered remark — C. Wright Mills was reported to have said on his deathbed that he was "ashamed to be an American, ashamed to have John F. Kennedy as his President" — while Senator Fulbright uncovered a working political arrangement between ultraconservative organizations and career officers in the regular Army. When Fulbright held hearings to bring it to light, he was all but drowned out by charges that he was trying to "muzzle the military."

Among the more conspicuous activities of the ultras in those years were Dallas's National Indignation Convention, first convened in 1961 and again in 1963. In its first session the 1,800 delegates to the convention roared their approval of a speaker who protested that the chairman was becoming moderate — "All he wants to do is impeach Warren — I'm for hanging him." Two years later the convention counteracted United Nations Day by holding a "United States Day" — an event blessed by Governor John B. Connally Jr. with an official proclamation.

Under the ultra umbrella were gathered such groups as the Reverend Billy James Hargis's Christian Crusade and Dr. Fred Schwarz's Christian Anti-Communism Crusade. The farthest reaches of the right wing were dismissed as a refuge for impotent crackpots. It is true that George Lincoln Rockwell's American Nazi Party never threatened American liberties, but elsewhere ultras were both respectable and influential. C. D. Jackson, publisher of *Life*, bore reluctant witness to this. After an issue of his magazine had treated Schwarz with disdain the flak from powerful advertisers was so great that Jackson flew to a Schwarz rally in the Hollywood Bowl to eat crow: "I believe we were wrong, and I am profoundly sorry. It's a great privilege to be here tonight and align *Life* magazine with Senator Dodd, Representative Judd, Dr. Schwarz and the rest of these implacable fighters against Communism."

Extremists of both left and right were characterized by what Benjamin DeMott has called "the Spirit of Overkill." Susan Sontag wrote in the *Partisan Review* that "the white race is the cancer of history." The *Berkeley Barb* flatly declared, "The professors have nothing to teach. . . . We can learn more from any jail than we can from any university." An off-Broadway cast chanted, "The middle class/ Are just like pigs . . . The middle class/ Are just like pigs," and in 1961 Bertrand Russell said, "We used to call Hitler wicked for killing off the Jews, but Kennedy and Macmillan are much more wicked than Hitler. . . . They are the wickedest people who ever lived in the history of man and it is our duty to do what we can against them." On the opposite horizon The Founder of the Birchers said of the United States that "the whole country is one vast insane asylum and they're letting the worst patients run the place," while Dean Noebel, a Christian Crusade prophet, maintained that agents in the bowels of the Kremlin had formed a "Commie-Beatle Pact" — "the Communists have contrived an elaborate, calculating, and scientific technique directed at rendering a generation of American youth useless through nerve-jamming, mental deterioration, and retardation. . . . The destructive music of the Beatles . . . reinforces . . . mental breakdown."

John Kennedy was very much aware of both varieties of irreconcilables. At Seattle in November of 1961 he suggested that it was the very insolubility of the day's problems which engendered a yearning for simple answers. "There are two groups of these frustrated citizens," he said. "It is a curious fact that each . . . resembles the other. Each believes that we have only two choices: appeasement or war, suicide or surrender, humiliation or holocaust, to be either Red or dead." When possible he pricked them with wit. At a White House gathering, E. M. "Ted" Dealey of the morning *Dallas News* said, "We need a man on horseback to lead this nation, and many people in Texas and the southwest think that you are riding Caroline's tricycle." The editor of the evening paper in Dallas, the *Times Herald*, wrote Kennedy to say that Dealey did not speak for Texas. The President wrote back, "I'm sure the people of Dallas are glad when afternoon comes."

Ultra humor tended to be black humor. In milder versions it was innocuous. The sign on the marquee outside a Georgia theater showing *PT-109*, the story of the President's World War II heroism, read, "See How the Japs Almost Got Kennedy." A riddle ran, "If Jack, Bobby, and Teddy were on a sinking boat, who would be saved?" The answer: "The country." A mimeographed, widely circulated leaflet set forth plans for a Kennedy monument in Washington: "It was thought unwise to place it beside that of George Washington, who never told a lie, nor beside that of F. D. Roosevelt, who never told the truth, since John cannot tell the difference."* It continued:

> Five thousand years ago, Moses said to the children of Israel: "Pick up thy shovels, mount thy asses and camels, and I will lead you to the Promised Land." Nearly five thousand years later, Roosevelt said: "Lay down your shovels, sit on your asses, and light up a Camel; this *is* the Promised Land." Now Kennedy is stealing your shovels, kicking your asses, raising the price of Camels, and taking over the Promised Land.

From there to the outer limits of the lunatic fringe, however, ultra wit became increasingly unprintable. As in the Roosevelt years it was often* preoccupied with unusual sexual practices, and it involved not only the Kennedy men and women, but also their children and even their pets. The sons of men who had mimicked FDR's upper-class accent now mimicked JFK's while telling stories about hot lines running from the Pope's toilet and the sewers of Rome to the White House, about the strange ways he spent his father's money, about a woman who claimed to be his first wife — Joe Kennedy was supposed to have bought an annulment — and even about his illnesses. Arthur Schlesinger noted that virtually every aspect of Kennedy fed resentment: "His appearance, his religion, his wealth, his intelligence, his university, his section of the country, his wife, his brothers, his advisers, his support of the Negroes, his determination to de-emotionalize the cold war, his refusal to drop the bomb." The ultras simply hated everything they read about the President.

That was a lot. News of the First Family and its various affiliates at times seemed to have preempted the attention of the communications industry. Kennedy lore was featured in films, on television, on the Broadway stage, and in musical tributes. Every bookshop had its department of Kennedy books, of which by 1962 there were already over a hundred; book collectors were paying small ransoms for signed copies of *Profiles in Courage*. The fact that Lord David Cecil's biography of Melbourne was the President's favorite book was enough to turn what had been a book of limited appeal into a best seller; a report that Kennedy had enjoyed Ian Fleming's *From Russia With Love* made Fleming a millionaire. Caroline Kennedy's picture was on the cover of *Newsweek*, and three screen magazines adopted the rule that *every* cover, every issue, must feature a photograph of Caroline's mother.

Once it became known that the President had learned to read 1,200 words a minute at a speed-reading course, the number of such courses increased tenfold. Courses at hairdresser schools gave instruction in how to imitate the First Lady's bouffant coiffures. Because her husband usually appeared

---

*Many Roosevelt haters believe that there is an ostentatious FDR monument in the capital. In fact, Roosevelt had requested only that after his death a small plaque be placed on a rock outside the National Archives building on Pennsylvania Avenue, and that it bear simply his name and the dates of his birth and death. This was done in 1965. It is modest; few passersby notice it.

bareheaded, Danbury, Connecticut, the center of the hatting industry, entered a severe recession. The White House press revealed that his favorite cocktail was a daiquiri; suddenly bottled daiquiri mixes appeared on the shelves of package stores. Jackie believed it was smart to have small dinner parties at home. As a result, the names of the great party givers of the Eisenhower years — Pearl Mesta, Gwen Cafritz, etc. — went into eclipse. The word went out that busy as they were, such key figures in the administration as Robert McNamara and General Taylor were finding time to improve their minds at "Hickory Hill University," the evening and weekend seminars at Robert Kennedy's Virginia home. The idea spread to Alexandria and Arlington, to Georgetown and Cleveland Park, and presently such firms as Johnson & Johnson were offering self-improvement courses for their executives.

The Kennedys were very outdoorsy. Not since Theodore Roosevelt had so ardent an advocate of the strenuous life lived in the White House. There was touch football, and sailing off Hyannisport, and Jackie's waterskiing. One or another of them was enthusiastic about nearly every sport: tennis, swimming, horseback riding, badminton, golf, softball, isometrics, skiing at Aspen, and hiking before breakfast. The fact that Pierre Salinger, the White House press secretary, had a stocky build which was growing stockier made him an apostate, almost un-American, and the President tried to redeem him by challenging him to push-up matches. With Pierre in mind, Kennedy at one time asked everyone on his staff to lose five pounds each. The President himself faithfully went through special back exercises in the miniature White House gym, in hotel rooms on trips, and on the floor of *Air Force One*.

At times the preoccupation with keeping fit became obsessive. The Hyannisport version of touch football was a rough sport; catching a pass in the rose bushes could be dangerous; Jackie quit playing after she broke a leg. When Kennedy appointed Red Fay Undersecretary of the Navy, Red, a balding friend from PT days, toured Navy bases taking on gobs in push-up contests. Guests at Hickory Hill were expected to play at least one set of tennis before breakfast, and after the President saw his Green Beret guerrilla fighters master an almost unbelievable obstacle course at Fort Bragg, he told his three middle-aged military aides that he wanted them to do it, too.

The most memorable physical education exploit of those days became known as the Great Hike. It began with General David M. Shoup, commandant of the Marine Corps and a Kennedy favorite. Shoup unearthed a 1908 Theodore Roosevelt directive which had required Marine Corps company officers to march fifty miles in twenty hours, double-timing the last seven hundred yards. He sent a memo about it to the President, who after a little research wrote back: "President Roosevelt laid down such requirements not only for the officers of the Marine Corps but, when possible, for members of his own family, members of his staff and Cabinet, and even for unlucky foreign diplomats." Kennedy then challenged the Marine Corps. He asked Shoup whether today's marines could do as well as the marines of 1908. They could and did, but that was only the start of it. Robert Kennedy hiked the length of the C & O Canal path; assistant attorneys general and Justice Department secretaries followed him. The story reached the papers and engendered a craze. Walking long distances became the latest thing. People who seldom strolled farther than the distance from the armchair to the martini pitcher were on the road. Alarmed physicians pointed out that overenthusiasm in exercise was dangerous. At their behest the President warned against overdoing it, and Salinger, who had rashly agreed to lead the White House press corps fifty miles, gratefully backed down.

Salinger was pitched into the Hickory Hill swimming pool fully dressed at the end of an uproarious lawn party there, and on impulse Ted Kennedy dove in after him. When stories of the incident found their way into print the frowns on the faces of Kennedy haters deepened. For some reason the episode seemed particularly decadent to them. Private swimming pools were an affront to the Protestant ethic anyhow; entering them wearing anything except a bathing suit was almost a perversion. But those who felt that way received an even ruder shock. June 17, 1962, was the attorney general's twelfth wedding anniversary. He and Ethel gave a party to celebrate it. Tables were set around the pool; Ethel was at a table that teetered on an impromptu catwalk which actually crossed the pool. Arthur Schlesinger and a partner decided to dance between courses. That was a mistake. Their weight on the catwalk tilted it. The hostess's chair started to slide, and, splash, there was Ethel, in the drink. Schlesinger, mortified, plunged in after her. They put on dry clothes and the party continued, but that wasn't the way the Kennedy haters told it; in their accounts the cavorting around the pool had stopped just shy of Babylon. For the next year Ethel had to set new guests straight on what had really happened, and sometimes she had the uneasy feeling that they didn't believe her.

Like FDR, President Kennedy came to realize that the very intemperance of those who spread malicious stories about him and his family was a political asset. It offended decent Americans and thus redounded to his advantage. He expected Barry Goldwater to run against him in 1964, and he wanted to be sure that the country understood the difference between his centralism and Goldwater's extremism. In a speech he never lived to deliver — it was in his pocket when he died — he scorned those who confused "rhetoric with reality" and assumed "that vituperation is as good as victory." And earlier he had said of them:

> They look suspiciously at their neighbors and their leaders. They call for a "man on horseback" because they do not trust the people. They find treason in our churches, in our highest court, in our treatment of water. . . . Unwilling to face up to the danger from without [they] are convinced that the real danger is from within.

Despite C. Wright Mills and H. Stuart Hughes, Communism was then a threat to American security, and despite Robert Welch and the Christian Crusaders, the threat came from the Soviet Union and not fluoridated water. The tensions of the cold war were powerful enough to generate one more convulsion of terror. It would bring the country and the world to the very brink of nuclear oblivion, and it came, anomalously, in a month of unsurpassed autumnal glory, October 1962.

Ordinarily Senator Kenneth Keating of New York was not a suspicious man, but reports from Cuban refugees reaching Florida that summer had troubled him. Fidel Castro's brother Raúl, Cuba's war minister, was known to have been in Moscow on July 2. Late in that same month activity in Cuban harbors picked up sharply; large numbers of Soviet freighters from the Black Sea began arriving at Mariel, a deepwater port on the northern coast of Pinar del Río province. Their cargoes were unknown, and puzzling. The ships rode high in the water and were distinguished by very wide hatches. Equally odd, each vessel brought with it large teams of Soviet technicians.

By the end of August more than five thousand Russians were in Cuba, and refugees being questioned at the CIA interrogation center at Opa-Locka, Florida, reported seeing truck convoys hauling long tubular objects swathed in tarpaulins. A CIA agent reaching Opa-Locka from Cuba had seen the tailpiece of one object and had a sketch of it. That same week Castro's personal pilot boasted in a Havana bar that Cuba now had long-range missiles with atomic warheads. On October 3 word reached Opa-Locka of activity "probably connected with missiles" in Pinar del Río. How much of this information reached Senator Keating is unknown, but in a series of speeches that month he warned of a Soviet military buildup. On October 10 he said that according to his informants, who had been "100 percent reliable," six intermediate-range missile sites were being constructed on the island.

The administration was skeptical. The Soviets had never put missiles in other countries, not even in bordering eastern European satellites bound to them by the Warsaw Pact. On both sides of the Iron Curtain Castro was regarded as an unstable leader and an unreliable ally. It was inconceivable that Khrushchev would entrust such a man with weapons which could destroy the world. The Kremlin had not recognized Cuba as a member of the Soviet bloc, though Castro had so proclaimed it. Cuba was far from the Soviet Union; transportation and communication lines between them could be quickly cut by the United States. Finally, the Russians could be sure that any such move would trigger a violent reaction in Washington.

At 3 P.M. Sunday, October 14, McGeorge Bundy was interviewed on television by Edward P. Morgan and John Scali of the American Broadcasting Company. As the President's special assistant for national security, he was asked to comment on Keating's charges. He replied: "I know there is no present evidence, and I think there is no present likelihood, that the Cubans and the Cuban government and the Soviet government would, in combination, attempt to install a major offensive capability." That was the opinion of almost everyone in the CIA. Keating, they thought, was being had. Cuban informants were notoriously unreliable. The tubular objects were doubtless SAMs — surface-to-air missiles of the kind that shot down Francis Gary Powers's U-2 twelve hundred miles within the Soviet Union. The Russians had provided Egypt and Indonesia with them, and other SAMs were known to be on their way to Castro. They were defensive weapons, nothing to worry about.

One man disagreed with the majority: John A. McCone, the CIA director. Returning to the capital after a wedding trip, McCone learned that there had been no aerial reconnaissance of western Cuba for a month. The reason was that SAM installations had been discovered there. No one had been willing to risk the loss of another U-2 to SAMs. McCone said that the gamble would have to be taken. On October 4 he called for the immediate photographing of the entire island, with special vigilance over its western end. After various delays because of clouds over the target areas and instructions for new U-2 pilots, October 14 dawned cloudless, and two Air Force majors took off for western Cuba. They had been told to expect ground fire, but the SAM crews were either absent or dozing; their sweep was a milk run. On their return their film magazines were dispatched to Washington and developed at processing laboratories. At the interpretation center in the Pentagon skilled specialists began studying enlargements of each frame.

By Monday afternoon they had seen enough to vindicate Keating. A field near San Cristóbal had been laid out in a trapezoidal pattern which until now had been seen only in U-2 photographs of the Soviet Union. There were SAM sites at each corner of the field, guarding a launch pad. No ballistic missiles were in sight, but the analysts had identified missile transporters, erectors, and the launchers. The evidence was not conclusive, but it certainly required immediate attention on the highest levels of the American government. Secretary McNamara had left the Pentagon earlier than usual — he was attending a seminar at Hickory Hill University — so the commanding general at the Defense Intelligence Agency put through a hot-line call to the Washington apartment of Deputy Secretary of Defense Roswell Gilpatric. It was a few minutes after 7 P.M., Monday, October 15, 1962.

Gilpatric, dressing for dinner and overdue at General Taylor's Fort McNair quarters, decided that he would be even later than he had expected. He said he wanted to see the photographs. Two analysts brought them. After looking at them and issuing appropriate orders he continued on to the general's dinner, where the principal guests were already being called to the telephone, one by one, and given whispered information which, they were cautioned, could not be shared with their wives. Reports for the

President would be channeled through McGeorge Bundy, who was giving another dinner for Charles E. Bohlen, the newly appointed ambassador to France. Bundy received his call, from the deputy director of the CIA, at 8:30. He decided not to tell the President until the next day. There was nothing Kennedy could do that was not already being done except lose a night's sleep. "So," he explained to the President in a subsequent memo, "I decided that a quiet evening and a night of sleep was the best preparation you could have in the light of what you would face in the days ahead."

Dean Rusk, presiding at a third formal dinner on the eighth floor dining room at the State Department, was chatting with his guest of honor, Foreign Minister Gerhard Schroeder of West Germany, when he was called to a phone in the butler's pantry. The caller was Assistant Secretary of State Roger Hilsman. Rusk listened a moment, then said, "Do you, personally, think this is it?" Hilsman replied, "There has only been a preliminary analysis, but from what I can get over the phone there doesn't seem to be much doubt." Any unusual behavior by the Secretary of State would set loose a flood of rumors. Rusk, though wretched, saw no alternative to observing the amenities. He returned to his guest, and the thirteen-day crisis began the next morning.

Tuesday, October 16, 1962

Analysts have been up all night reexamining the photographs of San Cristóbal; McNamara sees them at 7:30 A.M., Bundy at eight. Bundy goes directly to the President's bedroom, where Kennedy is reading the morning papers, and breaks the news: "Mr. President, there is now hard photographic evidence, which you will see a little later, that the Russians have offensive missiles in Cuba." The President directs Bundy to summon key members of the administration to an 11:45 A.M. meeting in the Cabinet Room. Then he calls his brother.

In addition to the Kennedys, those present at the 11:45 meeting, or subsequent sessions of it, include Gilpatric, Bundy, McNamara, Rusk, O'Donnell, Lyndon Johnson, McCone, Maxwell Taylor, General Marshall Carter of the CIA, Sorensen, George Ball, Gilpatric's counterpart at the State Department; Secretary of the Treasury Dillon; Edward Martin, Assistant Secretary of State for Latin America; Ambassadors Bohlen, Llewellyn Thompson, and Adlai Stevenson; U. Alexis Johnson, Paul Nitze, and three men no longer in the government: Dean Acheson, John J. McCloy, and Robert A. Lovett. These men will enter history as the Executive Committee of the National Security Council, or simply the Ex Comm.

Reports from technicians indicate that the San Cristóbal site will be ready for firing in about ten days, and that completion will cut the warning time for an attack on the United States from fifteen minutes to between two and three minutes. Robert Kennedy makes a note of the dominant feeling: "shocked incredulity." There is a general awareness that any

American response might worsen the situation, but that not challenging Khrushchev would be the worst course of all.

The President orders a sharp increase in U-2 overflights. Other Ex Comm members will investigate possible choices — in Rusk's phrase, they will "box the compass." The State Department will explore the chances of support from Latin America and U.S. allies in Europe; the Defense Department will investigate the time factor, the kinds of units, and the number of men necessary for various military alternatives. At this point a majority feels that there is only one option: an air strike against the missile sites. Robert Kennedy passes a note to his brother: "I now know how Tojo felt when he was planning Pearl Harbor."

Wednesday, October 17

To maintain an appearance of calm, the President keeps a promise to campaign for Democratic candidates in Connecticut. He is away from the capital until midnight. The Ex Comm meets all day and most of the evening in George Ball's conference room on the seventh floor of the State Department. There is new U-2 evidence, and it is chilling. The Soviet technicians are working around the clock. Missiles are now visible in the photographs. Sixteen, and possibly thirty-two, sites may be ready for firing within a week. In addition to definite proof of medium-range missiles (1,000 miles) at San Cristóbal, there are intermediate-range sites (2,200 miles) in the Guanajay area, between San Cristóbal and Havana, and at Remedios in eastern Cuba. The intermediate-range weapons will be ready by December 1. They are what the military call "first-strike" weapons. With them, the U.S. Intelligence Board estimates, the USSR will be able to fire an initial salvo of forty nuclear warheads on targets in the United States as far west as Montana.

In the absence of his brother, Bob Kennedy emerges as the Ex Comm discussion leader. Majority opinion still favors an air attack — the euphemism for it is a "surgical operation." Bundy and Acheson are its chief advocates. McNamara proposes an alternative: a naval blockade of Cuba. Bombing and blockading are both acts of war, but the blockade has the advantage of avoiding bloodshed, at least in its first stages. An air strike would kill about 25,000 Cubans and an undetermined number of Soviet technicians. If Russians die, total war with the Soviet Union will be almost inevitable.

During the day six options, or "tracks," are pondered. Track A is to do nothing now. Track B would send an emissary to Khrushchev and try to settle matters quietly. Track C would hale the Russians before the U.N. Security Council. (Unfortunately Valerian Zorin of the USSR is chairman of the council this month.) Track D, known in the Ex Comm as "the slow track," is the blockade, Track E the air attack, and Track F an invasion of Cuba. Track F is put aside for restudy later; it cannot be weighed now because it must be preceded by elaborate preparations. However, these are under way.

Thursday, October 18

The U.S. intelligence community estimates that the weapons now in Cuba constitute about half the ICBM capacity of the entire Soviet Union. Photo analysis indicates that they are being aimed at specific American cities. If they are fired, eighty million Americans will be dead within a few minutes. According to the latest Intelligence Board reports, presented at the 11 A.M. session of the Ex Comm, the first missiles could be ready for launching in eighteen hours. The President says to Acheson, "This is the week I better earn my salary." While he is meeting with the Ex Comm, General Shoup says, "You are in a pretty bad fix, Mr. President." Kennedy replies swiftly, "You are in it with me."

The President has an appointment of long standing to receive Andrei Gromyko. He keeps it, talking with Gromyko for over two hours, giving him every opportunity to bring up the matter of missiles, but Gromyko misses all his cues. (Later there will be doubt that Gromyko knew what had been happening in Cuba.) Meanwhile, Rusk is suggesting to the Ex Comm that it regard Tuesday, October 23, as the deadline for action. If by then missile pads are still being built, he says, force should be used to remove them.

Air Force Chief of Staff Curtis LeMay joins the group and argues forcefully that a military attack is essential. The President asks LeMay what the Russian response might be. LeMay assures them that there would be none. Kennedy is skeptical: "They, no more than we, can let these things go by without doing something. They can't, after all their statements, permit us to take out their missiles, kill a lot of Russians, and then do nothing. If they don't take action in Cuba, they certainly will in Berlin." McNamara continues to build support for a blockade. A legal adviser from the State Department recalls Franklin Roosevelt's "quarantine-the-aggressor speech" and suggests it might be better if the blockade were called a quarantine. The weight of opinion is moving toward this option. Robert Kennedy is strongly in favor of it. With the memory of Pearl Harbor, he says, the United States cannot launch a surprise air attack in which thousands of innocent people would die. For a hundred and seventy-five years we have not been that kind of country, he says; surprise raids are not in the American tradition.

The evening session of the Ex Comm is held directly beneath a Rusk dinner for Gromyko on the eighth floor of the State Department Building. Reporters seeing the Secretary of Defense and the director of the CIA arriving sense something unusual. They are led to believe that McNamara and McCone are going to the dinner. To avoid another confrontation with the press, at the end of the meeting nine Ex Comm members — whose cars bear easily recognized license plates — pile into the attorney general's limousine. Their destination is the White House, where the President learns that the trend toward a blockade is continuing. Deputy Attorney General Katzenbach, a former professor of international law, is told to explore the legal basis for a blockade of Cuba.

Friday, October 19

Because the security lid is still on tight, the President leaves Washington again to honor an obligation, this time a commitment to campaign in Chicago. In the capital the Joint Chiefs put the Atlantic and Caribbean commands on alert at 1:20 P.M. The Pentagon announces that McNamara has asked the Chiefs to remain in Washington for six weeks to consult on "budget planning." Katzenbach reports that in his opinion a unilateral order for a blockade can be legally justified under the circumstances. The President decides to make a televised report to the American people Monday evening — the earliest time possible if all necessary steps are to be taken first.

The Ex Comm is in continuous session all day Friday and all Friday night. Now that there is a clear majority for the blockade, Acheson withdraws. The others split into groups to write out their recommendations and then exchange papers. Out of this the outline of a definite plan begins to emerge. The most important of Friday's developments is the decision to ask for an endorsement of the blockade by the Organization of American States (OAS). A two-thirds majority of twenty voting American republics will be necessary. If achievable it will be invaluable, the Kremlinologists believe, because the Russians are impressed by legalisms. As an adjunct to this, Ball gives the bare facts of the crisis to Don Wilson, deputy to ailing Edward R. Murrow at the United States Information Agency. Wilson asks a Bell Telephone executive to clear lines to Spanish-language radio stations without telling the stations why.

Saturday, October 20

Robert Kennedy phones his brother at the Sheraton Blackstone Hotel in Chicago: the Ex Comm is ready with a plan of action. The President summons Salinger to the presidential suite at the Sheraton Blackstone and hands him a slip of paper: "Slight upper respiratory [infection]. 1 degree temperature. Weather raw and rainy. Recommended return to Washington." At 9:35 Chicago time Salinger makes the announcement to the press. Aboard *Air Force One* he asks Kennedy, "There's nothing wrong with your health, is there, Mr. President?" Kennedy replies, "If you know nothing about it, you're lucky."

Robert Kennedy meets the presidential aircraft at Andrews Field. The afternoon session of the Ex Comm begins at 2:30 in the oval study on the second floor of the Executive Mansion. The President makes the final decision in favor of the blockade. The last small lingering doubt in his mind is removed when the commanding general of the U.S. Tactical Air Command tells him that even a major surprise air attack could not be certain to destroy all the missile sites and nuclear weapons in Cuba.

Adlai Stevenson, down for the day, suggests a deal. He proposes that the President tell the Russians that if they withdraw their missiles from Cuba, the United States will withdraw its missiles from Turkey and give up the American naval base at Guantánamo Bay. The general reaction is vehemently negative, a bitter aftertaste of which will stay with Stevenson until his death.

Elsewhere progress is smooth. Alexis Johnson has turned out a master scenario schedule of everything which must be done before the President's 7 P.M. speech Monday — instructions to U.S. embassies abroad, congressional briefings, etc. Acheson, recalled, agrees to tell Macmillan, de Gaulle, and Adenauer. Edward Martin prepares for the OAS meeting. As detailed arrangements are made and legal justifications marshaled, however, more and more government officials are brought into the discussions. As a consequence, word that something big is coming has begun to seep through to the press. Too many trips have been canceled, too many announcements made for odd reasons, too many lights have been burning late in unexpected places, too many high officers in the government have failed to appear at dinner parties or, having appeared, have left, murmuring excuses. James Reston of the *New York Times* and Alfred Friendly, managing editor of the *Washington Post*, have begun to stalk the truth, and Reston has most of the essential facts. At the President's personal request, both agree to publish less than they know until Tuesday.

The Navy has deployed 180 ships in the Caribbean. The B-52 bomber force has been ordered into the air fully loaded with atomic weapons; as one plane lands, another immediately takes its place in the air. Late Saturday night the 1st Armored Division begins to move out of Texas headed for embarkation ports in Georgia. Five other divisions are placed on alert.

Sunday, October 21

A golden fall day. In the State Department forty-three letters to heads of government and to Mayor Willy Brandt, mayor of West Berlin, are drafted for the President's signature. In addition, the President is writing a letter to Khrushchev; it will be delivered with a copy of his speech. American embassies and consulates abroad are warned to prepare for demonstrations and riots. U.S. ambassadors will receive explanatory telegrams at 6 P.M. tomorrow, an hour before Kennedy speaks. The U.S. Passport Office opens on a Sunday for one traveler — Dean Acheson's passport must be validated.

The secret won't keep much longer. An air of crisis hangs over Washington. The entire press corps now knows that something is afoot. The *New York Herald Tribune* spikes the story at McNamara's request, but other papers may be expected to divulge it at any time; the British embassy has found out what is coming, and the rest of the diplomatic corps have begun checking rumors. Sunday evening Dean Rusk advises his staff to get some sleep. "Gentlemen," he says, "by this time tomorrow we will be in a flaming crisis."

Monday, October 22

At noon Salinger announces that the President will speak on television at 7 P.M. The topic will be "of the greatest urgency."

Lawrence F. O'Brien phones twenty congressional leaders of both parties; the President wants to see them at 5 P.M. Those who can't make it by commercial airlines are picked up by Air Force planes — in some cases, jet fighters. The meeting turns out to be the most difficult of the crisis for Kennedy. The leaders condemn the quarantine-blockade as too weak. He leaves the room in a rage. Later, with his brother, he is more philosophical, recalling that though the congressional reaction is now more militant than his, it is close to what his was when he first learned of the missiles six days ago.

The diplomatic orchestration is flawless. Following the master scenario, separate briefings are given to forty-six allied diplomats, to Latin American ambassadors, and to envoys from the emerging nations. De Gaulle tells Acheson, "It is exactly what I would have done." At 6 P.M. Rusk sees Dobrynin, the Soviet ambassador; twenty-five minutes later Dobrynin emerges grim and shaken. (U.S. officials will come to believe afterward that Dobrynin had not known of the missiles in Cuba.) In France Acheson lays the matter before the NATO leadership. Adlai Stevenson delivers to Zorin of the USSR a request to convene a special meeting of the Security Council to deal with "the dangerous threat to the peace and security of the world by the secret establishment in Cuba" of missiles "capable of carrying thermonuclear warheads to most of North and South America."

The initial response to these moves is heartening, even among the governments of neutral nations. The Russians appear stunned. Only one allied leader is suspicious of the Americans: John Diefenbaker of Canada.

Kennedy's speech begins at 7 P.M. on all TV channels and on the Spanish language network:

"Good evening, my fellow citizens. The Government, as promised, has maintained the closest surveillance of the Soviet military buildup on the island of Cuba. Within the past week, unmistakable evidence has established the fact that a series of offensive missile sites is now in preparation on that imprisoned island. The purpose of these bases can be none other than to provide a nuclear strike capability against the Western Hemisphere."

He recites the Russian assurances, now revealed as "deliberate deception," and pledges that it will be his "unswerving objective" to remove the nuclear menace. The quarantine, he says, is only an initial step; it will be followed by stronger measures if that is necessary. The Organization of American States is meeting in emergency session to consider the threat, and U-2 flights over Cuba are being intensified. He warns Khrushchev: any missile launched from Cuba will be regarded as an attack by the Soviet Union on the United States, requiring full retaliatory response against the USSR. Any vessels attempting to run the blockade will be sunk by the U.S. Navy.

After his speech he is handed a confidential report from McNamara listing the resources being marshaled for further military action: warplanes capable of flying 2,000 sorties against targets in Cuba, 90,000 marines and paratroopers forming an invasion force, and 250,000 troops backing them up. An estimate of American casualties in the event of invasion puts the expected figure at over 25,000.

Unexpectedly, there is a light note in this. The Pentagon reports to the President that the Russians and Cubans have inexplicably lined up their planes wing tip to wing tip, ready to be destroyed, like the American planes at Pearl Harbor twenty-one years earlier. Kennedy asks General Taylor to put a U-2 photographic mission over the U.S. air bases in Florida. "It will be interesting if we have done the same thing," he says. We have. The Air Force hastily disperses them.

Tuesday, October 23

George Ball, who has spent the night in troubled sleep on his office couch, awakens to see Dean Rusk looking down on him, smiling for the first time in a week. "We have won a considerable victory," Rusk says. "You and I are still alive." The worst fears have not, in fact, materialized. The Russians have not bombed U.S. bases in the Middle East, blockaded Berlin, or moved to close the Dardanelles. Soviet strategy, whatever its intended thrust, has been checked by the President's challenge.

In Moscow there is no reaction for thirteen hours. Then the American ambassador there is handed a note accusing the United States of "piracy" and denying that the missiles in Cuba are intended for military purposes. The note is interpreted as betraying uncertainty; Khrushchev, caught off guard, appears to be playing for time to think things through. Even so, there is little time for maneuver. President Kennedy has signed the blockade proclamation; it will go into effect tomorrow morning. In it, contraband is defined as covering offensive missiles, their warheads and electronic equipment, and bomber aircraft. Already the Navy is tracking Russian submarines in the Caribbean. The twenty-five Soviet merchant ships on the way to Cuba have not changed course. They are receiving an extraordinary number of coded messages from Russia.

The Organization of American States meeting opens at 9 A.M., with Dean Rusk in the United States chair. The resolution supporting the quarantine must win fourteen Latin American votes, a two-thirds majority. Edward Martin believes that it will get exactly fourteen. The secretary hopes that his participation will widen the margin. It does — a few minutes after five o'clock the measure carries unanimously, 18-0, with only Uruguay abstaining. The Russians are reported to be astounded. At the same time, American ambassadors in Jamaica and Trinidad, Guinea, and Senegal report success in excluding the possibility that Soviet warheads might be flown to Cuba; their host governments have agreed to deny landing rights for Soviet bloc planes on their way there. Still another encouraging word comes from the U.N.: Stevenson has the support of seven of the eleven nations on the Security Council.

At the President's request, Robert Kennedy calls on Ambassador Dobrynin at the Russian embassy. Dobrynin spreads his hands; as far as he knows, there are no missiles in Cuba. Back at the White House, Bobby learns that the President has shortened the line of interception for the quarantine from eight hundred miles to five hundred miles, giving the Russians more time. McNamara phones from the Pentagon — the latest U-2 photographs show work continuing on the sites in Cuba.

President Kennedy has begun to show the tension. He talks rapidly, in staccato bursts, and his eyes are screwed up tight, as though he is squinting at the sun. A telegram arrives from Bertrand Russell: YOUR ACTION DESPERATE. . . . NO CONCEIVABLE JUSTIFICATION. WE WILL NOT HAVE MASS MURDER. . . . END THIS MADNESS. Kennedy replies, "I think your attention might well be directed to the burglars rather than to those who have caught the burglars."

Wednesday, October 24

Ten A.M.: the blockade line is drawn. Since Monday afternoon an American fleet, designated Task Force 136, has been racing at flank speed — 27 knots — to close off all five navigable channels through which ships from the mid-Atlantic can approach Cuba. Now they have reached their stations in a great arc five hundred miles out to sea from the eastern tip of Cuba. On the forward picket line there are thirteen destroyers; then two cruisers, each flanked by two more cruisers — nineteen ships altogether. Bearing down on them are the twenty-five Russian merchantmen, each of which has been spotted by Navy reconnaissance planes. Two of the vessels, the *Gagarin* and the *Komiles*, are within a few miles of the picket line. A Russian submarine has moved into position between them. In Washington the Ex Comm awaits the first interception, probably before noon.

Aerial photographs from special low-level reconnaissance missions of Cuba, supplementing the U-2s, show that feverish work continues on the ground there. Eight to ten bases are situated near the cities of San Cristóbal, Remedios, Guanajay, and Sagua la Grande. Each base has about four launchers. At least thirty missiles with nuclear warheads are in Cuba, and there are over twenty crated IL-28 (Ilyushin) jet light bombers capable of delivering nuclear bombs on American or Latin American cities. In the new photos the launching pads, the missiles, and the nuclear storage bunkers are clearly defined. Within a few days several of the launching pads will be ready for war.

At the U.N., Secretary General U Thant sends identical letters to Kennedy and Khrushchev urging suspension of the blockade and arms shipments for two to three weeks. Kennedy refuses to negotiate until the Russians agree to dismantle and remove the missile bases. In Moscow William Knox, an American industrialist, is invited to the Kremlin, where he finds Khrushchev in a state of near-exhaustion. The Soviet premier says he has a message for Washington. He looks like a man who has not slept all night; at times he is almost incoherent; the message is unimportant.

On his way to an Ex Comm session President Kennedy says to his brother, "It looks really mean, doesn't it? But then, really there was no other choice. If they get this mean on this one in our part of the world, what will they do on the next?" Bob tells him, "I just don't think there was any choice, and not only that, if you hadn't acted, you would have been impeached." The President says, "That's what I think — I would have been impeached."*

The first sign of hope comes at 10:32 A.M. Twenty Russian ships have stopped dead in the water. Six, then twelve, turn around. Rusk nudges Bundy and says softly, "We're eyeball to eyeball and I think the other fellow just blinked."

Thursday, October 25

At 8 A.M., twenty-two hours after the quarantine proclamation, the first interception of a Russian ship occurs at sea. She is the tanker *Bucharest*. Identifying herself by radio and declaring that her only cargo is petroleum, she is allowed to proceed through the line of American warships. At 8:35 A.M. the East German passenger ship *Völkerfreund*, carrying twenty students, also passes. The President has ordered that the captain of each vessel must be permitted sufficient time to consult Moscow.

The situation is still grave. In Cuba work on the missile sites continues at an extraordinarily rapid pace. The IL-28 bombers are also being uncrated and assembled. Kennedy keeps the pressure. To all offers of compromise he replies that the missiles and bombers must be removed; nothing else will do.

In the U.N. Security Council, Valerian Zorin makes the mistake of challenging Adlai Stevenson to produce evidence of the missiles. As millions of Americans watch — it is during the dinner hour — Stevenson turns on him

---

*In *Thirteen Days* Robert Kennedy wrote that this Wednesday and the following Saturday were the worst days of the crisis. Of that moment when they were awaiting the naval confrontation at sea on Wednesday, Bob wrote: "I think these few minutes were the time of gravest concern for the President. Was the world on the brink of a holocaust? Was it our error? A mistake? . . . His hand went up to his face and covered his mouth. His face seemed drawn, his eyes pained, almost gray. We stared at each other across the table. For a few fleeting seconds, it was almost as though no one else was there and he was no longer the President. Inexplicably, I thought of when he was ill and almost died; when he lost his child; when we learned that our oldest brother had been killed; of personal times of strain and hurt."

with superb scorn. He says he has proof, but first he asks Zorin to deny that the missiles are there. "*Yes* or *no*?" he snaps. "Don't wait for the translation, *yes* or *no*?" Zorin says he is not in an American courtroom. Stevenson says, "You are in the courtroom of world opinion right now and you can answer *yes* or *no*." Zorin, retreating, says, "You will have your answer in due course." Stevenson closes in: "I am prepared to wait for my answer until hell freezes over, if that's your decision. And I am also prepared to present the evidence in this room." With that, he unveils easels which have been shrouded, revealing blown-up photos of the sites.

Friday, October 26

At 7 A.M. the American destroyer *Joseph P. Kennedy Jr.* hails the freighter *Marucla* in the open sea about 180 miles northeast of Nassau. The *Kennedy* hoists the international signal "Oscar November," meaning "Heave to," and the *Marucla* does so. In less than an hour an armed boarding party of American sailors is searching her. There is no contraband; the ship is allowed to continue. The inference, which is encouraging, is that Moscow has instructed Soviet captains to submit to searches.

Nevertheless the Ex Comm is glum. In Cuba the Russians continue to work feverishly. The first missiles will be ready for firing in a matter of hours. At a White House press conference Salinger takes note of this and observes that the Soviet technicians are clearly trying to achieve "full operational capability as soon as possible." A State Department spokesman says ominously that if this continues, "further action" by the President "will be justified." Robert Kennedy tells Ambassador Dobrynin that the President cannot hold off more than forty-eight hours.

The first real break in the crisis comes at 1:30 P.M. It is highly unconventional. John Scali, a TV commentator who covers the State Department for the American Broadcasting Company, receives a telephone call from an acquaintance at the Soviet embassy. The caller is Alexander S. Fomin, a counselor at the embassy who is believed to be a colonel in the KGB, the Soviet secret police. Scali says he is busy. Fomin, highly agitated, says, "It's very important. Meet me at the Occidental in ten minutes." At the Occidental Restaurant on Pennsylvania Avenue, Fomin says he wants to know whether the State Department would discuss an agreement with three provisions: the removal of the missiles in Cuba under U.N. supervision, a promise from Castro to accept no offensive weapons in the future, and an American pledge not to invade Cuba. Scali says he will find out. At 7:35 the two men meet again in the coffee shop of the Statler Hilton. Scali, having talked to Rusk, informs the Russian that the United States government is definitely interested. Fomin rushes off.

At 6 P.M. (1 A.M. in Moscow) a long, emotional letter from Khrushchev starts coming through over the teletype linking the State Department with the American embassy in Moscow. The Soviet premier acknowledges for the first time that there are Russian missiles in Cuba. His proposal, he says, is this: no more weapons will go to Cuba, and those within Cuba will be either withdrawn or destroyed if Kennedy agrees not to attack Cuba. Essentially, these are Fomin's terms. At 10 P.M. the Ex Comm meets to consider the offer. The decision is to accept it as though it were a formal note and reply in the morning, pending a careful examination during the night by Kremlinologists at the State Department. The Fomin conditions will be studied at the same time. For the first time in ten days the President goes to bed believing that a peaceful solution may be found.

Saturday, October 27

The height of the crisis. Even as the reply to Khrushchev is being drafted, Radio Moscow broadcasts a second Khrushchev letter to Kennedy. This one is unacceptable. As a condition for withdrawal of the missiles he demands that NATO missile bases in Turkey be dismantled. The Ex Comm has already weighed the possibility of such a swap and rejected it. Though the bases in Turkey now have little military value (and will, in fact, be phased out soon), the Turks regard them as symbols of the American commitment. To bargain away the weapons of an ally in exchange for the security of the United States would, it is believed, shake, and perhaps shatter, the western alliance. This second letter is different in more than content; it lacks Khrushchev's style, and reads as though drafted by a committee. The FBI reports that Soviet diplomats in New York are preparing to destroy their documents. The bridges to sanity seem to be crumbling. On top of this there is another blow. An American U-2 pilot is shot down over Cuba, meaning that the SAM bases on the missile sites are operational; the missiles themselves will be next. The Joint Chiefs join the Ex Comm meeting. They recommend an air strike Monday, to be followed by an invasion of Cuba. With one exception the Ex Comm believes that there is no other course. The exception is the President. He says: "It isn't the first step that concerns me . . . but both sides escalating to the fourth and fifth step — and we don't go to the sixth because there is no one around to do so. We must remind ourselves we are embarking on a very hazardous course."

Robert Kennedy sees a way out. He proposes that they ignore the second letter and answer the first. Various drafts along these lines are submitted by Dean Rusk, George Ball, McGeorge Bundy, and Llewellyn Thompson. Bob doesn't like any of them. His brother tells him, "If you disagree so violently, go draft one yourself." Bob and Ted Sorensen leave the meeting to do just that. By choosing the terms they like best in each of the two letters and in the Fomin proposal, they agree to a proposal Khrushchev never made. The President approves it, sends it to Khrushchev at 8:05 P.M. — and tells the world he has accepted the Russian conditions. Bob then phones Dobrynin and asks him to come to the Justice Department. He tells the Soviet ambassador that they are running out of time. Only a few hours are left. The President must have a reply the next day. Dobrynin is pessimistic; the Kremlin, he says, is deeply committed to Castro.

At the White House the President remarks that the outcome seems to him to be touch and go, that it can now go "either way." McNamara, glancing at the sky on his way back to the Pentagon, wonders aloud how many more sunsets he will see. Thompson tells his wife that if he does not come home, he will let her know where she and the children will join him should the capital be evacuated.

Sunday, October 28

Another magnificent October day. A few minutes before 9 A.M. (4 P.M. in the Russian capital) Radio Moscow announces that an important announcement will be broadcast on the hour. This is the very last chance for peace. If Khrushchev rejects Kennedy's terms the American attack will go in. McNamara's estimate of U.S. casualties is now 40,000 to 50,000.

The Soviet announcer begins reading the Russian answer. The key to it is in the third paragraph:

> In order to eliminate as rapidly as possible the conflict which endangers the cause of peace . . . the Soviet government . . . has given a new order to dismantle the arms which you described as offensive, and to crate and return them to the Soviet Union.

Castro, who has not been consulted, declares that he has been betrayed, that he will ignore the settlement. But while he can delay the end of the crisis, he cannot stop it; though the missiles are on Cuban soil, they are in Russian hands, and there are no Cubans who know how to fire them anyhow. At 1:30 P.M. the Joint Chiefs signal Task Force 136: there will be no more boarding of ships, no show of force. The Ex Comm is jubilant, but the President speaks of how difficult it must have been for Khrushchev to back down; he warns them that there must be no claims of an American victory. He writes the Soviet premier a careful letter ending:

> I think we should give priority to questions relating to the proliferation of nuclear weapons, on earth and outer space, and to the great effort for a nuclear test ban.

That evening the Kennedy brothers review the thirteen days of crisis. At the end the President says, "Maybe this is the night I should go to the theater." Both of them laugh uproariously. Then Bob says, "If you go, I want to go with you."

Portrait of an American

———

PETER CARL GOLDMARK

BORN IN BUDAPEST on December 2, 1906, he was one of that generation of brilliant Hungarian scientists which included Edward Teller, John von Neumann, and Eugene Paul Wigner. But while they dedicated their talents to the technology of death, he became a leader in the communications revolution. They gave America the Bomb. He gave it the long-playing record, color television, and the promise of a whole new world of sight and sound.

His was a creative family. One great-uncle, Karl Goldmark, was one of the nineteenth century's most interesting composers of opera. Another great-uncle, Joseph Goldmark, discovered red phosphorus, essential to the manufacture of kitchen matches. Joseph defied the government of Austria-Hungary, fled to America, fought in the Civil War, and contributed to the defeat of Lee by inventing a new kind of percussion cap for the Union Army.

Peter was a precocious child. Showing the Joseph in him, he exasperated his parents by taking over the family bathroom for his experiments, and before the onset of adolescence he had assembled a huge motion-picture projector. Later in his youth he told his teachers that he had found a mistake in a paper by Britain's most celebrated physicist, Ernest Rutherford. They were amused — until he reconstructed the experiment for them and proved himself right.

In a magazine he read an article by an eccentric Scotch stocking salesman, John Logie Baird, who devised a primitive television system in the early 1920s, convinced the Royal Society that it would work, and talked the BBC into transmitting experimental broadcasts. The article told how to assemble a receiver and advertised a kit. Peter sent for one. Years afterward he described the result: "The picture came through in postage-stamp size. You could hardly make it out, it flickered so. It was also in color — all red. But it was the most exciting thing in my life."

It remained so. He took an engineering degree at the Berliner Technische Hochschule and a doctorate in physics at the University of Vienna, where he displayed the Karl Goldmark in him at a series of concerts in which he performed as a pianist and cellist. But Baird had captured his imagination; his dissertation, "A New Method for Determining the Velocity of Ions," which he read before the Academy of Science in Vienna, laid much of the groundwork for television projection. When his faculty advisers urged him to continue as a physicist, he politely declined, packed his cello, and sailed for England.

Hired by Pye Radio, Ltd., in Cambridge, he built a mechanical TV transmitter. Although it worked, the Pye studios seemed indifferent to its possibilities, and after two years he left Cambridge with savings of $250 and boarded a boat for New York. There he applied for American citizenship and a job at RCA. To the subsequent chagrin of David Sarnoff, Sarnoff's underlings at NBC turned the slight Hungarian scientist away. CBS then hired him.

The next thing Peter's new superiors knew, he was glimpsed atop the Chrysler Building putting up a television antenna. Four relatively fallow years followed. Then, while visiting Canada in the spring of 1940, he happened to drop in at a theater showing the Technicolor *Gone With the Wind*. Stunned by the beauty of the color, he said later, he came away with "an inferiority feeling about television in black and white." He developed color television in just three months.

His color system was built around a revolving disc with transparent color segments of green, blue, and red. The disc spun in front of the camera tube. When a picture representing, for example, the green in a scene was being sent out, the green transparency was in front of the camera; in the viewer's set another spinning disc, synchronized with the one in the camera, turned the picture into the right color, and the colors followed each other so rapidly that the viewer's eye mixed them together. In August 1940 Peter put on a demonstration for CBS executives. They saw an experimental set project, in succession, a lovely zinnia, black-eyed Susans, red sails in a sunset, a brunette with a red scarf, a blonde chasing a colorful beach ball into surf, and at the end — like a vaudeville show — an American flag waving in a spanking breeze.

Then war intervened. Peter led a team of engineers making devices to jam Nazi radar. In 1945 he turned again to color television. When the FCC held trials at the end of the decade, his pictures were beautiful, while RCA's, to the humiliation of David Sarnoff, showed green monkeys eating blue bananas. The FCC adopted the CBS system. Sarnoff hired a hundred expensive technicians, gave them a budget of 130 million dollars, and told them to develop better color. Meanwhile Peter came up with an improvement of his own called the shadow-mask tube. The FCC approved of RCA color, but RCA needed the shadow-mask tube for proper color projection — and had to pay CBS royalties for it. Later the Soviet Union and NASA's Apollo flights used Peter's original system.

One postwar evening he and several friends were listening to a record of Horowitz playing Brahms. "Suddenly," as he recalled afterward, "there was a click. The most horrible sound man ever invented, right in the middle of the music. Somebody rushed to change records. The mood was broken. I knew right there and then I had to stop that sort of thing."

After three years he had the 33⅓ rpm microgroove record as we know it, stamped from Vinylite to reduce surface noise. The old 78 rpm records had from 85 to 100 grooves to an inch; Peter increased this to from 224 to 300, which meant that 45 minutes of music could be played on the two sides of a 12-inch record — a whole concerto, or an entire symphony. Sarnoff announced that RCA had a 45-rpm record and ridiculed the notion that a slower speed was needed. But Columbia's first LP album was a tremendous success, offering everything from Bach to Harry James at prices ranging from $2.85 for a 10-inch popular disc to $4.85 for one of its 12-inch Masterworks, and RCA's challenge failed.

By Peter's fiftieth birthday CBS had assigned one executive to be his full-time factotum. (He was known as the "Vice President in Charge of Peter.") Then Peter was designated president of CBS laboratories, and the network built a workshop for him on a grassy knoll overlooking a Stamford thoroughfare not far from his home. Frank Stanton said, "The smartest thing we ever did was to build Peter a lab in the country to play with." From it CBS acquired patents on over a hundred of his inventions. One was the Reverbatron, which reproduces the vibrations of a large concert hall, adding depth to sound. Others included a record player for the blind and a miniature color television camera to transmit pictures for surgeons from inside the stomach, developed by Peter in one of his several roles — professor of medical electronics at the University of Pennsylvania. Perhaps his most extraordinary creation was EVR (Electronic Video Recording), a tiny device enabling the viewer to play programs on his home set without commercials — a seven-inch reel of tiny film covering a half-hour of color or an hour of black-and-white that would drop in place like a phonograph record and rewind automatically when finished.

In suburban Connecticut legends about him accumulated: stories of his musical evenings with Benny Goodman, a neighbor; his chess playing; his fantastic LP library; the speakers cunningly concealed about his house which could convert it into a church, with a choir singing in every corner. If a secretary came to work late and said her car was defective, Peter would repair it on the spot. Fastidious about his own Mercedes-Benz, he would clean up after the filling station attendants who serviced it. And he worked all hours, calling assistants at 3 A.M. or 5 A.M., saying, "Just thought of something, meet me at the lab," and hanging up.

There were tales about his temper, too. Yet he was one of the few scientists of his time with a social conscience, finding work for jobless blacks, heading the Stamford antipoverty office, and putting in long hours crusading for the use of educational television in public schools. He gave Stamford's Riverview Elementary School a complete television studio. Thanks in part to his efforts, by the time he retired in 1971 the teachers in nearly one-third of American schools were using film strips, projectors, or other visual teaching aids.

It was a measure of Peter's genius that CBS was very nervous about his retirement. The network offered him $75,000 a year for ten years to do nothing. He refused. Instead he threw his vast energies into a scheme for establishing as many as forty coast-to-coast TV channels by uniting domestic satellites and cable television. In his vision of the future there were nation-wide chains of movie theaters of the air, free TV access to the voters for campaigning politicians, home instruction for students, and national facsimile newspapers delivered through television sets.

Once in the late 1960s a radio interviewer asked him whether he thought mental telepathy would ever replace TV. Peter paused, adjusted his glasses, and said it was conceivable that undiscovered radiation from the brain might be used someday. He added: "But that's a long way off."

There was a protracted silence in the studio. With Peter you couldn't be sure.

TWENTY-NINE

Don't Let It Be Forgot

Now in the third year of the Kennedy Presidency a fundamental change loomed in the character of the civil rights movement. Beginning with the Montgomery bus boycott in 1955 and extending through Little Rock, the freedom rides, and Oxford, Mississippi, the struggle for racial equality had been in the form of a serial drama, with whites in the role of bullies and blacks as martyrs. The conscience of the nation's great white middle class had been aroused, and its indignation had become a solvent eroding barriers of law and custom which had endured for generations. But that era was about to end. Angrier, fiercer, more headstrong blacks were fighting their way to the center of the stage. The established black leadership was discovering that young Negroes were approaching the end of their patience. The emergence of the eye for an eye trend foreshadowed a new, darker period in the struggle for integration, but first there were a few more episodes in the serial to be played out. The bully who made black martyrs best was the police commissioner of Birmingham, T. Eugene "Bull" Connor, who had first come to the nation's attention during the freedom rides. Two years had passed; he was about to assume a star role.

Martin Luther King had called Birmingham "the most segregated city in the United States." Connor liked to quote him on that; he wore his bigotry like a badge of pride. For twenty-three years the commissioner had used terror and brutality to cow Negro leaders, always with success. Not only were Birmingham's schools completely segregated; so were its public toilets, drinking fountains, theaters, parks, playgrounds, restaurants, and even churches. Federal rulings prohibiting discrimination did not intimidate Bull Connor. To him they were just contrivances for disrupting law and order in Birmingham and, as such, opposition to be ruthlessly crushed. Until the spring of 1963 civil rights leaders tried to stay clear of him; he was running for mayor, and racial demonstrations would merely give him more white votes. In April the election was over. He had lost, which made him meaner, but they were ready for him.

King's campaign opened April 2 with sit-ins and marches. Connor retaliated swiftly, arresting over four hundred Negroes on charges of parading without a permit, loitering, or trespassing. King then sent groups to worship in white churches, defying the police to seize them there. Connor refused to be drawn. He counted on Birmingham's white Christians to draw the color line, and most of them did; four churches admitted the Negroes, seventeen turned them away. King called for a protest march on Good Friday, April 12. Connor obtained an injunction forbidding it. Burke Marshall urged the black leaders hold off until the inauguration of Albert Boutwell, the moderate mayor-elect. Little could be expected from Arthur Hanes, the outgoing mayor, who said of Robert Kennedy, "I hope that every drop of blood that's spilled he tastes in his throat, and I hope he chokes on it," and of King, "This nigger has got the blessing of the Attorney General and the White House." But the black leadership had no choice. Their people were ready to march without them. The demonstrations were held in defiance of the injunction, and the inevitable arrests, including King's, followed.

On May 2 about five hundred Negroes were locked up — high school students, most of them, carried to jail in school buses. Other students paraded in protest the next day. White spectators pelted them with brickbats and bottles. King held a mass meeting in the New Pilgrim Baptist Church to protest; a thousand blacks came, and Connor threw police lines around the church. There were no incidents then, but when twenty-five hundred Negroes surged into downtown Birmingham the following day in another demonstration, Connor met them with police dogs and fire hoses. The dogs were trained to rip clothing with their teeth, and the hoses, with 700 pounds of pressure, smashed the blacks against buildings or to the ground. On May 4 newspaper readers around the world were shocked by a brutal photograph showing a huge, snarling dog lunging at a frightened Negro woman. President Kennedy said the picture made him "sick," and he said, "I can well understand why the Negroes of Birmingham are tired of being asked to be patient." An ADA delegation asked him to intervene, but at this point there was little he could do under the Constitution. He did send Burke Marshall down to open the channels of communications. In quiet talks with Birmingham businessmen Marshall negotiated a fragile truce which lasted five days. On May 11 the home of a Negro leader and a desegregated hotel were bombed. The next day, Mother's Day, enraged blacks again erupted into the streets, and this time they were too much for the policemen, the dogs and the hoses. After a night of riots and fires Connor asked the new governor, George C. Wallace, for reinforcements.

This was the first the rest of the nation heard of Wallace. He had been expecting something of this sort, and he was ready with a motley force — seven hundred deputy sheriffs, game wardens, liquor agents, and highway patrolmen. Shouting threats, they stomped around the city shoving blacks into doorways and snapping the safety catches of their guns menacingly. The blacks weren't surprised. They distrusted Wallace, and with good reason; he had already told the press that he would use the power of his office to suppress King. Of Marshall's truce he said that he would not be party to any "compromise on the issues of segregation." It was his avowed purpose to sabotage Marshall, and the only thing that stopped him was the decision of President Kennedy to fly three thousand troops to an air base near Birmingham. "This government," the President said, "will do whatever must be done to preserve order, to protect the lives of its citizens, and to uphold the law of the land." Any misuse of force by the governor's officers now would bring in an overwhelming counterforce. Mayor Hanes denounced "bayonet brotherhood." Wallace, furious, filed suit with the Supreme Court, charging that the President's action was "unconstitutional and void." The governor said, "This military dictatorship must be nipped in the bud." The Justice Department quietly replied that as commander in chief of the nation's armed forces the President could move troops to any base he wished.

Marshall reconciled the black and white leaders once more, and this time a lasting peace returned to the littered but integrated streets of Birmingham. The outcome was clearly another triumph for Martin Luther King. Its implications were discernible far beyond the city; again the conscience of the country's white middle class had been stirred, and elsewhere protesting Negroes were marching in Selma, Alabama; Albany, Georgia; Cambridge, Maryland; Raleigh and Greensboro, North Carolina; Nashville and Clinton, Tennessee; Shreveport, Louisiana; Jackson and Philadelphia, Mississippi; and, in the north, in Chicago. "The fires of frustration and discord," the President said, "are burning in every city . . . where legal remedies are not at hand." In a phrase which would be remembered, Ken O'Donnell predicted "a long, hot summer." Before autumn ended fourteen thousand demonstrators would be in southern jails.

The next chapter in Wallace's burgeoning gubernatorial career put him in the path of Attorney General Kennedy. Robert Kennedy didn't want the conflict, and in the beginning he thought it might be avoidable. He had come to believe that the Mississippi crisis might have ended differently if he had cultivated Ross Barnett earlier. He hoped to do better with Wallace, though the prospects could hardly have been called auspicious. Not only had Wallace been elected as a racist; it had been, and still was, his only issue. In his campaign he had repeatedly vowed to stand in the doorway of any white Alabama school to drive away Negro children, and he had ended his florid inaugural address with the incendiary passage: "In the name of the greatest people that have ever trod on this earth, I draw the line in the dust and toss the gauntlet before the feet of tyranny. And I say: Segregation now! Segregation tomorrow! Segregation forever!" Still, Bob Kennedy thought a man-to-man exchange with him might prevent future grief. The fact that he thought that is curious. Demagogues have never been responsive to the voices of reason, and Bob's manner did not encourage moderation in those who differed with him. But he never saw himself as others saw him. He thought he might bring George Wallace around to his way of thinking.

His suit bogged down from the very beginning. Like his predecessor in Montgomery's executive mansion, Wallace was almost impossible to reach from Washington by telephone. Intermediaries arranged a meeting, and Bob did everything he could to make it seem casual, even scheduling other appointments in Alabama to make it seem one of many calls there. But Wallace had other ideas. He wanted his constituents fully informed about his battles for white supremacy, and to that end he did everything but greet the attorney general at the airport with a band playing "Dixie." The statehouse was ringed by state troopers. Pickets carried placards reading: CHRISTIANS AWAKE, "COME OUT FROM AMONGST THEM AND BE YE SEPARATE," and KOSHER TEAM: KENNEDY KASTRO KHRUSHCHEV. The place where Jefferson Davis was sworn in as President of the Confederacy was marked by a fresh wreath, and a Daughter of the Confederacy clad in spotless white stood guard there with folded arms, presumably to prevent Kennedy from defiling it. Inside, Wallace greeted him by turning on a tape recorder "as a precaution." It was a waste of electricity; nothing of substance was said. The most urgent racial problem in Alabama, which Bob hoped Wallace would share with him, arose from court orders ruling that the state university must admit black applicants. Over and over he told Wallace that the law must be enforced, that it was their sworn duty to do so; over and over Wallace said that this would mean violence and that the blood would be on Kennedy's hands. At the end of the conference the governor called in the press to announce that nothing which had been said altered his vow to stand in the schoolhouse door. Kennedy said he hoped local authorities would discourage mob violence. Ed Guthman, who was with him, thought that "Bob was dumbfounded by Wallace's attitude. It was the closest I ever saw him come to throwing up his hands in despair."

The Kennedys were determined to prevent another Oxford. They had the campus photographed with the same reconnaissance planes which had been used over Cuba, and troop commanders used the photos to map maneuvers. Flying down to Muscle Shoals, the President spoke from the same platform as Wallace and elliptically warned him not to defy the law. Again the governor told reporters that his mind was unchanged. They were moving rapidly toward confrontation. Under the terms of a court order three Negroes had been declared eligible for the university's summer term, beginning June 10, one of them to an extension course and two to the main campus at Tuscaloosa. These two, Vivian J. Malone and Jimmy A. Hood, were in the same situation as James Meredith twenty months earlier. Wallace, more audacious than Barnett, announced that he intended not only to bar Hood and Miss Malone from the Tuscaloosa campus; he also meant to force federal officers to arrest Alabama's governor. After a U.S. District Court enjoined him with interfering with their enrollment, he declared: "The action I am going to take involves even my personal freedom, but I intend to carry it out, regardless of what risk I take."

As Bob Kennedy's deputy, Nick Katzenbach was again cast in his difficult Oxford role, leading the federal officers at Tuscaloosa. In the name of states' rights Wallace had mobilized his seven hundred deputy sheriffs, game wardens, liquor agents, and state troopers, plus several National Guard companies. Unlike Barnett, Wallace wasn't taking university administrators into his confidence. They didn't know whether he planned to seal off the campus, issue guns, or what. The situation had comic aspects. The administrators reported to Katzenbach that Al Lingo, the state patrol chief, had painted a white line on the pavement in front of Foster Auditorium, where students would register. Wallace was occupying an office just inside the entrance. He had installed two air-conditioners, and there, as the sweating deputy attorney general tried to guess what he was up to, the bantam governor of Alabama sat coolly reading the *Montgomery Advertiser*. In the White House the President and his brother listened to Katzenbach's running analysis on an open telephone line and watched events develop on television.

They decided to let Wallace have his show. Katzenbach's plan, which was adopted, was to make the governor look ridiculous by robbing his doorway stand of meaning. Katzenbach would drive Miss Malone and Hood to the campus. Parking the car and leaving them in it, he would confront Wallace himself, telling the governor that going through the door was unimportant, that the government considered the two students enrolled, and that they would begin classes in the morning. The President would federalize the 31st National Guard division if Wallace continued to obstruct them.

That is more or less what happened. Katzenbach told the press that the two blacks would arrive at 10 A.M. Wallace appeared at 9:53 escorted by towering state policemen in combat gear — helmets, side arms, gas guns, and truncheons. When Katzenbach and the two Negroes drove up, accompanied by marshals in mufti, Wallace's public relations man darted out with a lectern and put it in front of the white line. The temperature was almost 100 degrees. The heat seemed to rise from the pavement in waves, and reporters and troopers tried to crowd in the building's shadow as Wallace took his stand. He raised his right arm like a traffic policeman. Katzenbach walked up with a marshal on either side and halted in front of him. He said, "I have a proclamation from the President of the United States ordering you to cease and desist from unlawful obstructions." Wallace replied by reading a proclamation of his own excoriating "the unwelcome, unwarranted and force-induced intrusion upon the campus of the University of Alabama of the might of the central government." He concluded: "Now, therefore I, George C. Wallace, as governor . . . do hereby denounce and forbid this illegal and unwarranted action by the central government."

Arms folded, Katzenbach answered mildly that all this was about two students who simply sought an education — "a simple problem scarcely worth this kind of attention." He asked the governor to reconsider, and, when Wallace refused to reply, he returned to the car and drove the two Negroes to dormitories which the administration had already assigned to them. Four hours later a brigadier general in the National Guard drove up. He saluted Wallace, who saluted back; he told him that the Guard had been federalized and asked him to "please stand aside so that the order of the court may be accomplished." After a last bitter volley at Yankee justice Wallace walked away.

The Kennedys thought he had been made to look ludicrous, and that the country would see his posturing for the absurdity it was. Millions of Americans agreed, and since more than three hundred blacks enrolled in the university after Hood and Malone without incident — indeed, without a word or even a glance from the statehouse — it appeared that the governor had been outwitted. George Wallace didn't see it that way, however, and neither did his admirers. He declared, "I stood eyeball to eyeball with them and they turned back." So they had, on television; all that viewers of the news had seen was the exchange of statements between him and Katzenbach and Katzenbach's departure. The registration of the two blacks had occurred off camera, and Wallace, then an underrated politician, had seen that in the eyes of the easily manipulated, his show in apparently staring down a federal official would carry more weight. In his book *Wallace* Marshall Frady wrote that the Alabama governor had "discovered a dark, silent, brooding mass of people whom no one — the newspapers, the political leaders, the intellectuals — no one but Wallace had suspected were there."

The race issue had emerged as one of the great themes of the 1960s. Already the civil rights movement was being described as revolutionary. In a televised speech on the evening of that June 10, the day of the Wallace-Katzenbach confrontation, President Kennedy called it "a moral issue" — "as old as the Scriptures and . . . as clear as the American Constitution." "A great change is at hand," he said, "and our task, our obligation, is to make that revolution, that change, peaceful and constructive for all." To that end he was asking Congress to enact a broad, sweeping civil rights bill committing it to the premise "that race has no place in American life or law."

Medgar Evers was returning that night to his home in Jackson, Mississippi, after attending a civil rights rally in a church. As the NAACP field secretary in that state, Evers had been James Meredith's friend and adviser, and that had marked him for Klansmen and the state's White Citizens' Councils. As he walked from his car he was murdered by a sniper lying in ambush. Discouraged and gloomy, the President said to Arthur Schlesinger, "I don't understand the South. I'm coming to believe that Thaddeus Stevens was right. I had always been taught to regard him as a man of vicious bias. But when I see this sort of thing I begin to wonder how else you can treat them."

When civil rights leaders told him that they were planning an enormous peaceful demonstration in Washington, he was appalled. "We want success in Congress," he said, "not just a big show." He was afraid it might get out of hand, or create "an atmosphere of intimidation." A. Philip Randolph, head of the Brotherhood of Sleeping Car Porters, answered him. The march was Randolph's idea. He had proposed it to Franklin Roosevelt twenty years earlier, and Roosevelt, equally apprehensive, had promised to establish a federal Committee on Fair Employment Practices if Randolph would call it off.* That had been the end of it then, but this time Randolph was determined to go ahead. "The Negroes are already in the streets," he said. "It is very likely impossible to get them off." He argued that it would be better that they be led by responsible leaders than by others who would exploit them and encourage violence.

The March on Washington, held on August 28, was a high point for those who believed that the grievances of the blacks could be redressed by working within the system. "We subpoenaed the conscience of the nation," Martin Luther King said. Nothing like it had ever been seen in the country — over two hundred thousand Americans, the largest crowd ever to gather in the capital, and all of them orderly. Most were Negroes, but thousands of whites came, too, led by Walter Reuther. They sang hymns and spirituals, and "We shall overcome," and they carried placards reading: EFFECTIVE CIVIL RIGHTS LAWS — NOW! INTEGRATED SCHOOLS — NOW! DECENT HOUSING — NOW!

Their self-discipline was a marvel. The District's fifty-nine hundred policemen had nothing to do but direct traffic; four thousand soldiers and marines who were standing by were never called. While the march was in progress the President received its leaders — among them King, Randolph, Reuther, Roy Wilkins, Whitney M. Young, Jr., Chairman John Lewis of the Student Nonviolent Coordinating Committee, and Floyd B. McKissick of CORE. Kennedy said he had been "impressed with the deep fervor and the quiet dignity" of the demonstration. They left and he watched the rest of it on television. The most memorable moment came when Martin Luther King spoke at the Lincoln Memorial:

"I have a dream that one day this nation will rise up, live out the true meaning of its creed: 'We hold these truths to be self-evident, that all men are created equal.' I have a dream that one day on the red hills of Georgia sons of former slaves and the sons of former slaveowners will be able to sit down together at the table of brotherhood. I have a dream that one day even the state of Mississippi, a state sweltering with the heat of injustice . . . will be transformed into an oasis of freedom and justice. I have a dream that my four little children will one day live in a nation where they will not be judged by the color of their skin but by the content of their character."

*See above, page 244.

"Dream some more!" cried his delighted listeners. Yet there were other Americans who were not delighted. Ward leaders in the great ethnic neighborhoods of the northern cities, keystones in the Democratic coalition Roosevelt had built, were stirring angrily. The Poles, the Irish, and the Italians, all of whom had given Kennedy wide margins in the election three years earlier, had struggled up from the bottom without the help of the government. Negroes, they argued, should do the same. They pointed out that congressmen who urged integration had withdrawn their own children from Washington classrooms and put them in private schools, and that a California study reportedly showed that outspoken liberals privately opposed Negroes in their schools and neighborhoods. A Lou Harris survey revealed that the administration's handling of the race issue had alienated over four million Democrats. In the South, naturally, the deterioration was greatest. "K.O. the Kennedys" was a political slogan in Mississippi. The governor of moderate North Carolina said that if an election were held then, Kennedy would lose it, and in Birmingham a Lubell poll found only one white voter who had supported Kennedy and didn't regret it.

The tragic fact is that this was a reaction to what had been, on the whole, exemplary black behavior. White Americans who were offended by the rhetoric of Martin Luther King and who thought James Meredith uppity were in for a shock. The same Negroes they regarded as upstarts were being called Uncle Toms by some black audiences. In Harlem young Negroes threw eggs at King, and in Chicago they booed Meredith. Their new heroes were Muslim leaders Jeremiah X, Malcolm X, and Elijah Mohammed, who preached the innate wickedness of the white race and dismissed nonviolence as folly. "The day of nonviolent resistance is over," Malcolm X told them. "If they have the Ku Klux Klan nonviolent, I'll be nonviolent. If they make the White Citizens' Councils nonviolent, I'll be nonviolent. But as long as you've got somebody else not being nonviolent, I don't want anybody coming to me talking any nonviolent talk."

The first administration figure to encounter the new blacks was Robert Kennedy. He was impressed by a James Baldwin article in the *New Yorker* in which Baldwin wrote of the Negro's past of:

> . . . rope, fire, torture, castration, infanticide, rape; death and humiliation; fear by day and night, fear as deep as the marrow of the bone; doubt that he was worthy of life, since everyone around him denied it; sorrow for his women, for his kinfolk, for his children, who needed his protection, and whom he could not protect; rage, hatred and murder, hatred for white men so deep that it often turned against him and his own and made all love, all trust, all joy impossible.

Baldwin believed that "the price of the liberation of the white people is the liberation of the blacks," and he quoted a Negro spiritual: *"God gave Noah the rainbow sign:/ No more water, the fire next time!"*

The comedian Dick Gregory suggested to Burke Marshall that the attorney general ought to meet Baldwin. Marshall passed the recommendation along, and the two men had breakfast together at Hickory Hill. Their talk was brief but amiable, and Kennedy proposed that they continue it in New York the next day in his father's Manhattan apartment. Burke Marshall would be with him. They wanted opinions about what the government should be doing, and they hoped that other blacks would join them. Baldwin said he would bring Kenneth B. Clark, the psychologist; Lorraine Hansberry, the writer; Lena Horne, Harry Belafonte, and Jerome Smith, a twenty-four-year-old CORE chairman who had been beaten and jailed during the freedom rides. Kennedy expected a serious discussion, the kind of talks he had had with Roy Wilkins and Martin Luther King. The first thing he got was a tirade from Smith, who said that being in the same room with Bob Kennedy made him feel like vomiting. From then on the meeting deteriorated.

Kennedy tried to explain what the government had done and was doing, and what its new bill would do. They didn't care. Baldwin didn't even know that a presidential civil rights message was before Congress. He said that the only reason the President had acted in Alabama was that a white man had been stabbed, and when Marshall protested that he had consulted Martin Luther King, they burst into laughter. This went on for three hours. Bob said afterward, "It was all emotion, hysteria. They stood up and orated. They cursed. Some of them wept and walked out of the room." Toward the end of it a young black said that he would not fight for the United States, and when Bob asked how he could say such a thing the youth repeated it.

The irony was that Bob's reason for coming to New York was to confer with several chain store executives over ways to end Jim Crow in their southern stores. That didn't impress the angry blacks either, and another attorney general might have become disenchanted with them. This one was different. He was resentful at the time; back in Washington, repeating the remark about refusing to defend the country, he added wonderingly, "Imagine anyone saying that." But later in the week he said thoughtfully, "I guess if I were in his shoes, if I'd gone through what he's gone through, I might feel differently about this country." It was the beginning of his real conversion to the movement, the realization that a rage that deep must have profound origins, and that if nothing was done about it the consequence would in fact be a fire next time.

On May 29 the President became forty-six years old. His staff had planned a surprise birthday party for him, getting him to it on the pretext that a call awaited him on the scramble phone in the situation room, but not much surprised this President, and he was grinning broadly when Mac Bundy led him into the White House mess. Pierre Salinger, the emcee, handed Kennedy a speech. "We know you usually write your speeches, Mr. President," he said, "but here is one written by a ghost writer, and we would like you to read it." It began, "Twoscore and six years ago there was brought forth at Brookline, Massachusetts . . ." Kennedy was handed a satellite model with a card reading, "Hope you have a good trip, Barry," and Jackie, teasing her husband over his pride in the new flower garden outside his office, gave him an enormous basket of dead grass. "From the White House Historical Society," the card read, "Genuine Antique Grass from the Antique Rose Garden." The evening was lovely. They spent it cruising down the Potomac in the presidential yacht, the *Honey Fitz*.

It was high tide for the Kennedy regime, but they didn't know that. They thought they had another five years in the White House, and when the President moved out he planned to start a new Washington newspaper. It would be a great one; the best newspapermen in the country would want to work for it. But that was a long way off, and they were not of an age to brood about the future. Youth continued to be a dominant theme in the administration. Their life-style in many ways was that of what were then called "the young marrieds." The three Kennedy wives, Jackie, Ethel, and Joan, were all pregnant that spring. Baby carriages and playpens had become familiar furniture in the homes of senior government officials who, in other years, would have been in their late fifties or sixties. That was part of the Kennedy era; like the Peace Corps it reminded young Americans that this was their President. To be sure, he had other constituencies, the intellectual community among them. Celebrating the end of his six-year term as a member of Harvard's board of overseers, he gave a stag dinner at the Executive Mansion for distinguished Harvard men. But even then he was conscious of his age. "It is difficult to welcome you to the White House," he said, "because at least two-thirds of you have attended more stag dinners here than I have."

His popularity, like that of any President, fluctuated. After the missile crisis in 1962 Gallup reported that 83 percent of the people approved of him; over the next ten months the figure fell to 61 percent and then 59. In September 1963, when the Senate ratified the nuclear test ban treaty with the Russians, the Gallup curve turned up. He had predicted that. The right-wingers, he believed, were misreading the country's mood. They made much of what they called a swing to conservatism on the campuses. They held that Admiral Lewis Strauss spoke for millions when he said, at the test ban hearings, "I am not sure that the reduction of tensions is necessarily a good thing," and that Edward Teller was reflecting the alarm of the entire middle class when he said at the same hearings, "If you ratify this treaty . . . you will have given away the future safety of this country." Kennedy didn't accept that. At Billings, Montana, and at Salt Lake City — in the very heart of what was thought to be Goldwater country — he was given standing ovations when, at midpoint in prepared speeches, he left his text to speak of his pride in the test ban. To friends he said that the treaty was the essence of his foreign policy; if he lost to Goldwater next year he would be willing to pay that price.

The signs of the coming detente were now unmistakable. The test ban, and the expressions of approval Kennedy heard across the country when it became an accomplished fact, had been possible because in Cuba the Russians had finally accepted the principle of verifying missile sites. The world had heard the last of the troika. In East Berlin Khrushchev said that the Wall had diminished the need for a separate German peace treaty. He had learned to live with the bone in his throat. Then Kennedy, speaking at American University on June 20, held out an olive branch to the Russians: "Our problems are man-made; therefore they can be solved by man . . . Some say that it is useless to speak of world peace . . . until the leaders of the Soviet Union adopt a more enlightened attitude. I hope they do. I believe we can help them do it. But I also believe that we must reexamine our own attitude."

The speech was largely ignored in the American press — his civil rights address, which came the following evening, preempted editorial attention — but the *Manchester Guardian* called it "one of the great state papers of American history," and Khrushchev, genuinely impressed, later told Harriman that it was "the greatest speech by an American President since Roosevelt."

On August 30 the Department of Defense announced that a hot line linking the White House and the Kremlin had gone into operation that same day. In October, when Russia's rift with China came into the open, Khrushchev said he did not share Mao's willingness to sacrifice millions of lives in a nuclear showdown with the West. Kennedy then authorized a sale of surplus wheat to the Soviet Union as "one more hopeful sign that a more peaceful world is both possible and beneficial to all."

The radical right was furious, but he relished its fury. He delighted in building a record as a liberal President. Kennedy chuckled when Ike, baffled by Keynesian economics, cried out in a magazine article: "What can those people in Washington be thinking about? Why would they deliberately do this to our country?" What Kennedy was doing to the country's economy, with the help of Douglas Dillon and Walter Heller, was producing the longest peacetime expansion in history, resulting in an annual increase in the Gross National Product of 5.6 percent a year. And if Congress would go along with his recommendation for a tax cut, he believed, there would be no recession in 1964, either.

That was by no means certain. The 88th Congress was mulish. The President was far ahead of its conservative instincts with his liberal program calling for Medicare, massive grants to encourage the rebuilding of decaying urban slums, a more sensible farm plan, the development and conservation of national resources, improved social security, his broad civil rights bill, and a growing commitment to the Alianza. At the time, critics gave him low marks in his struggle for legislation. Looking back, it is surprising that he did as well as he did. Of 107 recommendations he had sent to the 87th Congress, 73 had been enacted into law, and the early legislative victories of his successor were programs Kennedy had sent to the 88th.

Addressing the Irish Parliament in June, he recalled a line from George Bernard Shaw's *Back to Methuselah*: "You see things; and you say 'Why?' But I dream things that never were; and I say 'Why not?' "* That was the Kennedy outlook at its best, a blend of social prophecy and political vision. He was not always on that plane. At times he seemed to be looking toward wrong horizons. A decade later his pledges to support manned space flight and supersonic transport would be seen as dubious ventures. But even his errors of exuberance seemed preferable to the stagnation of the 1950s. Like Franklin Roosevelt he was using politics to expand the limits of the possible at home and abroad. In that context his triumphant ten-day tour of Europe five months before his death, of which the Irish visit was a part, is important to an understanding of him. More than anything else he resembled the statesmen of the European left, and they knew it. In him they saw their own idealized self-images. Willy Brandt in Germany, Gaston Defferre and Pierre Mendès-France in France, Harold Wilson in Britain, Pietro Nenni in Italy — all of them praised him, quoted him, and to some extent patterned their political styles after his. "Nenni, the old firebrand Socialist, cannot now contain his praise for Kennedy," Anthony Sampson wrote in the London *Observer*. ". . . There is hardly a word of anti-Americanism, except on the far right." As a liberal, Kennedy had, among other things, no patience with those who thought men should wear blinders to shield them from evil. Jailing students who wanted to see Castro's Cuba seemed to him absurd. "Why shouldn't they go?" he asked. "If I were twenty-one years old, that's what I would like to do this summer." And in Amherst on October 26, 1963, he spoke words which would be cherished by historians of his period: "It may be different elsewhere. But democratic society — in it, the highest duty of the writer, the composer, the artist is to remain true to himself and to let the chips fall where they may. In serving his vision of the truth, the artist best serves his nation."

At such times John Kennedy seemed inevitable. But there was another aspect of him. Astronomers are familiar with the phenomenon of the dark star, a star so feebly luminous as to be invisible, one which follows another star and eclipses it sporadically. Kennedy had a dark star, a shadow of imminent tragedy which was never far from him and those he loved and which would intervene unexpectedly to obscure their most splendid moments. It happened now. In early August Jacqueline Kennedy gave birth to a second son, who arrived five and a half weeks prematurely and with a lung ailment. Christened Patrick Bouvier Kennedy, the baby struggled for thirty-nine hours before expiring. The President, desolate, tried to lift the little coffin at the services to carry it to the grave; then Cardinal Cushing gently drew him away.

To lift his wife's spirits Kennedy suggested that she accept an invitation from Aristotle Onassis, the Greek shipping tycoon, for an Aegean cruise on his majestic yacht, the *Christina*. Later she would remember early October

*Later this was attributed to him, and then to Robert Kennedy. But it was Shavian.

as an unreal time, two dazzling weeks of sunshine between the loss of Patrick and the catastrophe that awaited in November. Dispatches from the Mediterranean traced her progress from Istanbul to Lesbos, Crete, Delphi, Marrakesh, and to an island in the Ionian Sea that Onassis owned. Royalty, beginning with the king and queen of Greece, entertained her and her sister Lee Radziwill; they toasted her, admired her, and gave her exotic gifts. When she returned to the White House on October 17, one member of the White House staff said, "Jackie has stars in her eyes — Greek stars." The President asked her if she would join him for a short campaign trip. She said fine, and she asked where, and he said Texas.

If there was any one place where things had seemed to be going exceptionally well for Kennedy earlier in the year, it was Saigon. Opening his State of the Union message on January 14, 1963, the President had reported: "The spearhead of aggression has been blunted in Vietnam." A Pentagon spokesman announced that "we have turned the corner in Vietnam," and General Harkins said that the war would be won "within a year." On April 22 Rusk said that the American effort in Saigon was "producing excellent results," and Ngo Dinh Diem and the Republic of Vietnam were "on their way to success." U. Alexis Johnson, Rusk's deputy undersecretary for political affairs, was particularly encouraged by "the intangible knitting together of government and people" in Vietnam and by the strategic hamlet program, which he called "the most important reason for guarded optimism."

Afterward this seemed puzzling. The fact that these prophets had been wildly wrong was bad enough; why had they been so eager to put themselves on the record? The answer was that they were trying to drown out other members of the government who were convinced that President Ngo Dinh Diem and everyone with him was doomed. The terms hawk and dove were not yet fashionable, but the administration was split along those lines. The chief hawks, or advocates of American involvement in the war, were the generals, including Maxwell Taylor, and McCone of the CIA, Rusk, Rostow, Ambassador Nolting in Saigon, and at this point McNamara, who was impressed by the force and precision of the reports from Saigon. Ranged against them were Robert Kennedy, George Ball, Averell Harriman, Roger Hilsman, Michael Forrestal, Richard Helms at the CIA, the American colonels in the field with Vietnamese troops, and American war correspondents, who sang to the tune of "Twinkle, Twinkle, Little Star":

> *We are winning, this we know.*
> *General Harkins tells us so.*
> *In the delta, things are rough.*
> *In the mountains, mighty tough.*
> *But we're winning, this we know.*
> *General Harkins tells us so.*

If you doubt this is true,
McNamara says so too.

As the third year of the Kennedy Presidency opened, no one could be said to be winning the war, because hardly anyone was fighting it. The Viet Cong was husbanding its strength, waiting to pounce, and the Republic of Vietnam's overcautious commanders had no intention of stirring them up. The calm was deceptive. The country was seething with resentment, and not all of Diem's critics were in the Viet Cong. Because he represented what might be called the Vietnamese establishment, the conservative, upper-class mandarins who spoke French and worshipped God as Roman Catholics, his natural adversaries in the non-Communist community were the young Buddhist priests and monks, who were poor, militant, middle- and lower-class, radical, and distrustful of everything western. Their religious faith was that of the majority, and they bitterly resented the privileges accorded the Catholics. Both sides were in a belligerent mood, needing only an incident to kindle a struggle between them.

It came in early May 1963. The Buddhists were celebrating Buddha's 2587th birthday in the ancient imperial city of Hue when officers commanding government troops ordered a group of them to disperse. They refused and the soldiers fired into the crowd, killing nine. Diem refused to express regrets — he said privately that he would lose face — and on June 11 a Buddhist monk, Quang Duc, protested with a spectacular demonstration of self-immolation. Sitting on the pavement, he waited patiently while his fellow monks drenched him with gasoline; then he struck a match and went up in flames. Other suicidal Buddhists followed his example, providing the press (which was notified in advance each time) with outstanding photographs. The newspaper-reading American public was appalled, but the government in Saigon was unmoved. President Diem at this point was almost entirely under the influence of his brother, Ngo Dinh Nhu, who was usually under the influence of opium. Madame Nhu demonstrated the ruling family's genius for public relations by telling reporters that she gaily clapped her hands each time one of these "so-called holy men" put on a "barbecue show."

Under great American pressure Diem tentatively agreed on June 15 to meet some of the Buddhist demands. Almost immediately it became clear that he had no intention of following through. On June 30 the Buddhist demonstrations were renewed. Students rioted in Vietnam schools, and American correspondents who were writing about the turmoil were attacked in the streets and beaten. This was too much for President Kennedy. The cold war thaw had provided him with a new incentive for wanting the shooting in Vietnam stopped. A truce was necessary before he could offer the world what he had called a "strategy of peace" at American University: "Not a *Pax Americana* enforced on the world by American weapons of war . . . not merely peace for Americans, but peace for all men; not merely peace in our time but peace for all time."

Apart from other considerations — such as corruption and ineffectuality — the rigid anti-Communism of Diem and the Nhus had no place in these plans for a new foreign policy. Kennedy wanted to take a strong hand with them, and when he discovered in early July that Nolting was absent on a two-month cruise in the remote Aegean, he decided that his first step should be to dispatch a new envoy to Saigon. Rusk picked the man, Henry Cabot Lodge. It was an excellent choice. Liberals in the administration were uneasy at first, fearing that as a patrician Lodge might favor South Vietnam's aristocracy. They didn't understand that as a Boston Brahmin Lodge expected the well-born to be gentlemen, which Diem and Nhu definitely were not. Among other things, gentlemen do not betray their friends. Whatever else may be said of Nolting's tenure, he had been a good friend to Diem, and they were about to repay him with an act of shocking treachery.

In a farewell speech at the airport Nolting spoke of bonds between the two countries: "humility and tolerance, respect for others and a deep sense of social justice." Correspondents thought these strange words in Vietnam, but Nolting believed them to be justified; the South Vietnamese president had just given him his word that there would be no more attacks on the Buddhists. Six days later Diem sent his secret police out on a midnight raid to seize the pagodas, arrest the priests and monks, and terrorize their followers. The raiders tried to camouflage their identity by wearing regular army uniforms, but the truth emerged forty-eight hours later after Madame Nhu, in a reference to a gang of cutthroats, which had been rooted out several years before, said that the sally had brought her "the happiest day in my life since we crushed the Binh Xuyen in 1955."

Lodge arrived in Saigon the following evening. He saw the raid as a studied act of scorn for the Americans. It was, in fact, a new low for Diem, and it marked the beginning of his isolation from other Vietnamese conservatives. His foreign minister quit in protest and shaved his head like a Buddhist monk. In Washington Madame Nhu's father, South Vietnam ambassador to the U.S., disowned his daughter. The Voice of America placed the blame for the storming of the pagodas squarely on the Nhus. Diem's generals, wanting no part of the atrocity, began plotting against him. Lodge cabled Washington that the plotters wanted to know what the American attitude would be if a coup was successful. What should he tell them?

The answer said much about the fissure in the Kennedy administration over the Vietnam question. It was August 24, a Saturday. The President was in Hyannisport. McNamara and McCone were on vacation, Rusk was out of town, and General Taylor could not be reached. Their key deputies were Gilpatric in the Pentagon, Helms at the CIA, and Ball at State, all critics of the regime in Saigon. The cable they approved was drafted by Ball, Harriman, Hilsman, and Forrestal, and it bluntly told the American ambassador that the Nhus must go. Afterward, when everyone was back in Washington, there were bitter recriminations, but when the President decided to put everyone on record no one was willing to take the responsibility for repudiating it.

The generals now had a green light from Lodge. On August 29 he cabled Rusk, "We are launched on a course from which there is no respectable turning back: the overthrow of the Diem government." Everything seemed set for it. Days passed, and then weeks, with no coup. The plotters appeared to have lost their nerve. The crackdown on the pagodas had cramped their style, sidelining several of their leaders, and Diem had tightened his control of the troops around Saigon. The State Department asked Lodge what was the matter with the generals. He said, "Perhaps they are like the rest of us, and afraid to die."

Encouraged by Diem's survival, the hawks in the administration took on new life. The need now, McNamara said at a council of war on August 31, was to reopen conversations with Diem. Rusk agreed, saying that this much was clear: the American presence must remain in Vietnam until the Viet Cong war was won, and the United States could not approve of a coup. General Taylor said they were both right. George Ball and Averell Harriman thought that this was absurd. Autumn was approaching, and each day the division between the two camps in Washington was wider. It became an abyss in September, when the National Security Council sent another fact-finding mission to Saigon. The investigators were Major General Victor H. "Brute" Krulak of the Marine Corps and, from the State Department, Joseph A. Mendenhall, a senior foreign service officer of comparable rank with experience in Vietnam. On their return President Kennedy reconvened the National Security Council, and each presented his report. General Krulak said that the war was being won and Diem's performance could hardly be improved upon. Mendenhall said that the Diem regime was at the point of collapse. There was a silence. Then the President said, "Were you two gentlemen in the same country?"

During all this the relationship between Lodge and General Harkins in Vietnam was deteriorating. Both were from Boston, and their families were old friends, but now they scarcely spoke to one another. Late in September McNamara and General Taylor arrived in Saigon on one more attempt to find out what was going on. At the airport Lodge, determined to reach McNamara first, detailed two of his men to obstruct Harkins's way. ("Please, gentlemen! Please let me through to the secretary!") Apart from that, Harkins was as cheerful as ever. His optimism was reflected in the opening paragraph of the subsequent McNamara-Taylor report, which declared that Diem's army "has made great progress and continues to progress." Because Diem's troops were victorious on all fronts, the appraisal continued, the first thousand American soldiers could be withdrawn before Christmas, and all of them would be home by the end of 1965. At the same time the report dealt a glancing blow to the heretical suggestion of

Robert Kennedy that the Americans pull out now. McNamara and Taylor took what would be the Pentagon line to the bitter end:

> The security of South Vietnam remains vital to United States security. For this reason, we adhere to the overriding objective of denying this country to Communism and of suppressing the Vietcong insurgency as promptly as possible.

But this view was now definitely losing support in the administration. The President himself was moving away from it. Interviewed on CBS-TV by Walter Cronkite on September 2, he had said pointedly that if the Republic of Vietnam was to be successful in its struggle against the Viet Cong it needed "changes in policy, and perhaps in personnel." He had then said: "I don't think the war can be won unless the people support the effort, and in my opinion, in the last two months the government has gotten out of touch with the people. . . . In the first analysis, it is their war. They are the ones who have to win it or lose it. We can help them, we can give them equipment, we can send our men there as advisers, but they have to win it, the people of Vietnam."

Early in October a ten-million-dollar-a-month program for Diem was quietly suspended. He and the Nhus angrily denounced Kennedy, and Madame Nhu arrived in California to open a lecture tour of the United States, condemning Kennedy with the support of right-wing groups. From the outset the trip was a fiasco. Official Washington boycotted her. When she attempted to call on her estranged father, Tran Van Chuong, she found the door locked and bolted; the ex-ambassador was in Manhattan speaking on what he called "the trail of stench" left by his daughter. She tried to follow him. At La Guardia Field she was met by a city official who curtly denied that he was greeting her; "I'm just here to see that the lady has sufficient police protection," he said. Madame Nhu snapped that she didn't need protection. "God is in my corner," she said. She never did find Tran. Speaking at Harvard, she was picketed by about five hundred students carrying such signs as NHU DEAL IS NHU DIEM GOOD. They pounded on the door of the lecture hall, spattered the side of the building with eggs, and rattled the windows as she spoke. After Cambridge, her crowds dwindled. Apart from ultraconservative claques, virtually the only people who turned out to see her were reporters.

Back in Saigon the government seemed to be losing its grip on reality. Nhu was threatening to form an alliance with Hanoi to drive the Americans out of the country. Diem's secret police, having purged the Buddhists, were attacking the country's schools. In a series of incomprehensible raids they jailed college students, then high school pupils, and finally children in the elementary schools. Even Catholics weren't safe from persecution. Vietnamese of all faiths and persuasions were appealing to General Duong Van Minh, "Big" Minh, the most prestigious officer in the army, begging him to oust Diem and Nhu. Minh approached John Richardson, the CIA station chief, and asked him for his advice. Bypassing General Harkins, Richardson arranged a meeting between Minh and Lodge. The ambassador told Minh that the Americans would do nothing to impede a coup, and that if it was successful U.S. aid would go to another anti-Communist government. This position was relayed to the White House, which approved it. Everyone in Washington and Saigon seemed to be aware of the coming revolt except Diem, Nhu, and General Harkins, who assured the President that there would be no coup, that it was all talk, that he had checked the rumors and found them to be groundless. Nothing could happen, Harkins said, without his knowing of it. It could, though. David Halberstam of the *New York Times* and another reporter had already received slips of paper with the message, "Please buy me one bottle of whisky at the PX" — the signal that the uprising was imminent.

Diem's hour struck at 1 P.M. Vietnamese time (1 A.M. in Washington) on Friday, November 1, All Saints' Day. In Saigon it was siesta time on a day of stupefying heat. The president and his brother had retired to their bedrooms in Gia Long palace, where they were presumably protected by the palace guard and seven-foot fences topped by barbed wire. But as they slept, truckloads of rebel marines wearing red kerchiefs had already launched an attack on their defenses while other soldiers threw up roadblocks at key intersections. The insurgents quickly seized the airport, the police station, navy headquarters on the banks of the Saigon River, and the government radio station, which broadcast a declaration in the name of fourteen generals and seven colonels: "Soldiers in the army, security service, civil defense force, and people's force! The Ngo Dinh Diem government, abusing power, has thought only of personal ambition and slighted the fatherland's interests. . . ."

That evening the siege of the palace began with a mortar and artillery barrage. In the early hours of the next morning a force of eighteen tanks began blowing holes in the fences. At 6:15 A.M. a rebel general ordered a five-minute cease-fire and called on Diem and Nhu to surrender. A white flag appeared in a first floor window, but Diem and Nhu were not there. They had fled through a secret tunnel to the Chinese suburb of Cholon, from which they sent word to the victorious junta that they were ready to open negotiations. Exactly what happened after that is unknown. Reportedly they accepted offers of safe conduct out of the country, but it was a ruse; they who had deceived so many were now betrayed themselves. Picked up by rebel soldiers, they were killed, on orders from the generals, in the back of an armored personnel carrier. Their bodies were found there, riddled with bullets and dressed in Roman Catholic priests' robes in which they had hoped to escape if nothing else worked. Diem had also been stabbed repeatedly.

Awakened with the news in the Beverly Wilshire Hotel in Beverly Hills, Madame Nhu sobbed that President Kennedy was to blame. The President was in fact shaken, depressed for the first time since the Bay of Pigs; whatever Diem's faults, he said, he had not deserved to be slain. Elsewhere in the administration the news was accepted with resignation, even relief. There was one significant exception. Vice President Johnson was bitter. The Vice President had given Diem his hand, had been his friend, and in Johnson's view the friendship had symbolized the American commitment to Diem. The same officials who had been Diem's critics in the administration were also critical of the Vice President. He knew it, and knew who they were, and he had long since come to despise them and everything about them, right down to their Cardin shirts and PT-109 tie clasps. On other issues Johnson admired Kennedy, but not here.

The people of Saigon did not share Johnson's view. They had turned the day into a holiday, dancing in the streets; statues of Diem, his brother, and his sister-in-law were smashed and posters of them were torn down, until the only likeness of the late President in the capital was on one-piaster coins. The triumphant generals were showered with confetti everywhere they went, and Lodge became the first American within recent memory to be cheered in public. Hope was running high in the U.S. embassy; the factions which had been united against the ruling family seemed popular enough to give the country a stable government.

A week passed, and then two weeks; the autumn days grew shorter, and President Kennedy's spirits rose. The McNamara-Taylor report, dated October 2, was still on his desk, but he felt no sense of urgency about the need to deal with it. As David Halberstam later wrote:

> He knew Vietnam was bad and getting worse, that he was on his way to a first-class foreign policy problem, but he had a sense of being able to handle it, of having time, that time was somehow on his side. He could afford to move his people slowly; too forceful a shove would bring a counter-shove. It was late 1963, and since 1964 was an election year, any delay on major decisions was healthy; if the Vietnamese could hold out a little longer, so could he.

On November 13 he summoned a conference of his chief strategists for the coming campaign. Meeting in the Cabinet Room late that Wednesday afternoon, they agreed that prospects for a landslide victory against Goldwater were encouraging. The economy was flourishing. The annual Gross National Product had grown 100 billion dollars since his inaugural; its rate of growth was greater than that of either Russia or Europe. The huge new Saturn rocket, which would be launched next month, would at last put the United States ahead of the Soviet Union in the manned spacecraft race. Except for Vietnam the world was calm, and to get more perspective on that the President cabled Ambassador Lodge suggesting that he come home for a long talk. Lodge replied that he was making arrangements to leave Saigon as soon as possible. That would be on Thursday, November 21.

Richard M. Nixon, then an attorney representing Pepsi-Cola, left Dallas,

Texas, aboard American Airlines Flight 82, bound for New York, at 9:05
A.M. on November 22, 1963, thus missing President Kennedy's arrival there
aboard *Air Force One* by about two and a half hours. Mr. Nixon had spent
the past two days at a Pepsi-Cola Bottlers Association meeting. He was just
beginning to learn the ropes as a corporation lawyer. He had filed a petition
for admission to the New York State bar only last Friday, and his name
was not yet on his office door, because he would not become a full partner
in the law firm of Mudge, Stern, Baldwin & Todd until January 1, 1964.

It was expected to remain there a long time. Earlier in the week during
a televised interview Dwight Eisenhower had spoken of Nixon's chances
in the next presidential election, but his remark is chiefly memorable as
vintage Eisenhowerese: "Now, if there should be one of those deadlocks,
I would think he would be one of the likely persons to be examined and
approached, because he is, after all, a very knowledgeable and a very
courageous type of fellow." Hardly anyone agreed with Ike. Certainly the
American Broadcasting Company didn't. Not only had the network called
a broadcast about him *The Political Obituary of Richard M. Nixon;* the
program, filmed the year before, had featured an interview with, of all
people, Alger Hiss. Two companies tried to cancel their advertising contracts with ABC because of it, but FCC Chairman Newton N. "Wasteland"
Minow turned them down with the cold observation that broadcasting must
be free from censorship by "those few, fearful advertisers who seek to influence the professional judgment of broadcast newsmen." President Kennedy said he agreed. Those were golden days for effete snobs.

Aboard Flight 82 a stewardess offered her distinguished passenger a
selection of current periodicals, and if one could return in time from the
mid-1970s to that fateful Friday, one of the differences to be noted in the
American scene would be the wider choice of magazines, *Look, Life,* and
the *Saturday Evening Post* then being alive, well, and on the stands. (The
long retreat from mass circulation was already well advanced among newspapers, however, and four weeks earlier, on October 16, the *New York
Mirror* had folded. Before the end of the decade 163 magazines and 160
daily newspapers, including the *Indianapolis Times,* the *San Francisco
News-Call-Bulletin,* the *Boston Traveler,* the *Portland Reporter,* and the
Houston Press would end publication.)

Nixon may well have picked *Time,* for he knew he would be in it. The
first news page carried an informal picture of him — he was fifty and looked
a young forty then — and in an accompanying interview he was quoted on
the political consequences of the Saigon coup: "If this Viet war goes sour,
Viet Nam could be a hot issue next year. If all goes well, it won't be. It's
strange to me, when we are fawning over Tito, catering to Kadar, accommodating Khrushchev, we don't even have the decency to express our sympathy to a family which was a real foe of Communism."

Barry Goldwater, who rarely fawned over Communists, was the front
runner for the 1964 Republican presidential nomination, Nelson Rocke-

feller having diminished his chances by marrying Happy Murphy the previous May. In that third week of November Goldwater had just scored a fresh triumph with one of his natural constituencies by telling a Better Business Bureau banquet in Chicago that the New Frontier had produced "1,026 days of wasted spending, wishful thinking, unwarranted intervention, wistful theories, and waning confidence."

Each time the Arizona senator tore into Kennedy reporters asked the President to reply. "Not yet," he would say, grinning; "not yet," but plainly he relished the prospect of running against him.

Among his valuable campaigners this time would be the First Lady. The Secret Service hoped Mrs. Kennedy could persuade her husband to be more careful in crowds. Eschewing SS advice the week before the Texas trip, he had ordered his driver to leave his car's motorcycle escort and detour through crowded downtown Manhattan. While the presidential limousine was halted at the traffic light an amateur photographer had darted up and fired a flash bulb at Kennedy's side of the car. A New York police official had told reporters, "She might well have been an assassin."

It was a year of technological innovations. Kodak introduced the Instamatic camera and Polaroid brought out color packs. Polyethylene appeared. Detroit's fall models featured sleekly sloping rear windows — "fastbacks," they were called; the one on the Sting Ray was particularly dramatic. On July 1, 1963, the Post Office Department, while announcing an increase in first-class postage from four cents to five, sprang the zip code system on a stunned and resentful public. The triumph of the digits moved one step closer with the conversion of the White House telephone number from NAtional 8-1414 to 456-1414. On the Bell systems' master map the hatched areas indicating switchovers to direct distance dialing were spreading like a vast cancer; DDD reached 44.2 million Bell subscribers in 1963. Students at liberal arts colleges displayed decals reading, "I Am a Human Being — Do Not Fold, Spindle, or Mutilate."

The sale of Barbie dolls reached its initial peak in 1963, and Barbie, who had acquired a boyfriend, Ken, two years earlier, was now joined by her "best friend," Midge. (Barbie's "black is beautiful" friend, Christie, would not appear in the Mattel sales line until 1968. In 1963 black beauty, like black power, was waiting to be discovered.) The question of how lifelike female dolls should be was still sparking lively debates among toymakers. A considerable number of parents objected to Barbie's firm little breasts. The public attitude in such matters remained comparatively conservative. In the matter of premarital intercourse it continued to hold that "Nice girls don't," although Gael Greene, researching *Sex and the College Girl* in 1963, was finding that more and more nice girls *did*. (A memorable passage in Miss Greene's book, startling at the time, described a sorority girl pretending to climb a wall in mock agony while crying out in frustration, "You don't know how long it's been since I got screwed.")

Few of collegiate America's mothers had any idea how casually some of their daughters were accustomed to being bedded. Parents would later rise up in righteous indignation to protest coed dorms, only to reel back when confronted by the new facts of campus life. One stunning fact was in a report of the infirmary at the University of California in Berkeley to the effect that venereal disease had become a serious health hazard among female undergraduates. Integrated dormitories was one answer to a problem which had other solutions. But in 1963 that belonged to the future. *Playboy* was then averaging fifty applications a week from young women whose aspiration was to appear on its gatefold in the altogether and who, in the judgment of the editors, were qualified to do so, yet even *Playboy* had to trim its sails somewhat to public opinion; for example, it did not yet dare show its Playmates' pubic hair. (It did, however, create an uproar in 1963 with a topless photo of a model who was an almost perfect double for the nation's First Lady.) Hard-core pornography was neither chic nor legal; in November 1963 a three-judge Manhattan court ruled that *Fanny Hill* was obscene and therefore forbidden. "While it is true that the book is well-written, such fact does not condone its indecency," the court found. "Filth, even if wrapped in the finest packaging, is still filth." It is startling to reflect that Linda Lovelace, who would rocket to fame ten years later as the superstar of *Deep Throat*, was then a twelve-year-old girl sucking lollipops in Bryan, Texas.

Among the names not in the news were Gloria Steinem, Kate Millet, Germaine Greer, and Bobby Riggs, then an executive for the American Photograph Corporation. Betty Friedan's *The Feminine Mystique* had just been published, but Women's Lib was, so to speak, still in the uterus. "Nobody," reported that November 22 issue of *Time,* "is more noisily dissatisfied these days than that symbol of stability — the fortyish housewife with teen-age children and a reasonably successful husband," but by the audiometers of the early 1970s the noise was almost imperceptible. The Seven College Conference, which had set up vocational workshops for college women "who are now ready for activity outside the home," had found just fifty such women. None described males as porcine. The vocations were largely limited to education, library science, social work, and — this was regarded as a breakthrough — public relations. Anne Cronin, director of the conference, fielded questions about what men might think with the defensiveness bluestockings had shown since the fall of the Claflin sisters. "In only one or two cases," she told a newspaperman, "have husbands gotten stuffy about their wives' going back into careers. For the most part, they're serious and understanding. We're not breaking up any homes that wouldn't break up anyway."

The fashions of the gentle sex were neither bold nor forward. There were no pantsuits, not even for toiling airline stewardesses. Styles were set by Jacqueline Kennedy — the pillbox hat, the shoes with very pointed toes and very slender heels, the hair length just below the ears and softly curled or bouffant. Skirts were a little below the knee, and the waistless sheath was popular. It was all very feminine. Male supremacy was riding high. No protests followed the showing, as a late movie, of Cary Grant and Myrna Loy in *Mr. Blandings Builds His Dream House* — nobody wondered what *Mrs.* Blandings might want in *her* dream house — and the author of a magazine profile of Dorothy Kilgallen, describing her race around the world as a journalistic stunt in 1936, was allowed to say: "Just like a woman, Dorothy came in late." In the summer of 1963 Ian Fleming's *The Spy Who Loved Me* appeared in paperback with this choice passage:

> All women love semi-rape. They love to be taken. It was his sweet bru-tality against my bruised body that had made his act of love so piercingly wonderful. That and the coinciding of nerves completely relaxed after the removal of tension and danger, the warmth of gratitude, and a woman's natural feelings for her hero. I had no regrets and no shame. . . . all my life I would be grateful to him, for everything. And I would remember him for-ever as my image of a man.

The *New York Times Magazine* carried a report on the campus mood that third week of November 1963. In it, undergraduate editors generally found their fellow students to be detached, determined to succeed, and concerned less with issues than with security and their personal lives. In their hours of relaxation Tarzan movies were the current thing. The University of Chicago was trying to revive football. Two Cornell fraternity teams had just played a thirty-hour touch football game; the final score was 664-538. LSU coeds had staged a "drawers raid" on a men's fraternity — all college residences were male or female, of course. Berkeley students, ever in the sexual vanguard, had asked the dispensary there to dispense contraceptives. They weren't militant about it, however; the demand was negotiable and was in fact ignored.

Camelot had ended its Broadway run in January 1963. *Tom Jones* was awarded the Academy Award as the best picture of the year. Sidney Poitier was voted the best actor for his performance in *Lilies of the Field*; Patricia Neal for hers in *Hud*. Films drawing big audiences in November 1963 were *Mary, Mary* and *It's a Mad, Mad, Mad, Mad World*. Popular television shows were *Dr. Kildare, Andy Griffith, My Three Sons, Perry Mason, Hazel, Lucy, The Beverly Hillbillies,* and *Twilight Zone*. NBC's Monday movie scheduled for November 25 — it would not be shown — was *Singing in the Rain*.

That year was the high point of the Ajax White Knight and White Tornado ("Cleans like a white tornado!") commercials, according to Harry McMahan of *Advertising Age*. Piel's Beer was presenting the Return of Bert and Harry. Maxwell House Instant Coffee offered a Cup and a Half. The Chevrolet commercial had a car riding on the water of a Venice canal, and Hertz commercials were dropping people into convertibles. Songs which were popular were "Go Away Little Girl," "Dominique," "If I Had a Hammer," "Puff the Magic Dragon," and "Blowing in the Wind."

Best-selling fiction included Mary McCarthy's *The Group*, Morris West's *The Shoes of the Fisherman*, James Michener's *Caravans*, and Helen MacInnes's *The Venetian Affair*. Best-selling nonfiction included James Baldwin's *The Fire Next Time*, Rachel Carson's *Silent Spring*, from which the ecology movement may be said to date, and two books which would be affected by the events of the coming weekend, Jessica Mitford's *The American Way of Death* and Victor Lasky's *J.F.K.: The Man and the Myth*. The first of these acquired historical significance because Robert Kennedy, who had read it, was guided by it in choosing a coffin for his brother's funeral. The Lasky book, which led the nonfiction best-seller lists, was a hatchet job and it would be withdrawn from the bookstores by its publisher.

In sports, Texas was ranked college football's number one. Darrell Royal's marvel that season was a shoeless field-goal kicker named Tony Crosby. The weekend before President Kennedy flew to Dallas, Crosby booted one 42 yards to beat TCU. Among the pros, Jimmy Brown of the Cleveland Browns was at the height of his remarkable powers. The New York Giants and the Chicago Bears were headed for a collision at the end of the National Football League season; Chicago would win the championship 14 to 10. In the American Football League finale, the San Diego Chargers would take the Boston Patriots 51 to 10. There was no superbowl. In hockey the big noise was Gordie Howe of the Detroit Red Wings. Having played 1,132 games in which he had lost twelve teeth and sustained wounds requiring 300 stitches, Gordie scored his 545th goal against the Montreal Canadiens in November 1963; it was a record. In basketball Bob Cousy of the Boston Celtics had hung up his jockstrap at the end of the 1962 season. As a consequence the Celts had been expected to be pushovers, but when Kennedy left the White House for the last time the 1963 season was two months old and the Celtics had lost only one game — by one point. Center Bill Russell was the big (six feet ten inches) reason.

Among the places not in the news that year were Woodstock, Watts, East Village, Grant Park, Wounded Knee, People's Park, My Lai, Khe Sanh, Kent State, Biafra, Lincoln Park, Bangladesh, Attica, the Ho Chi Minh Trail, Chappaquiddick, Bimini, Botswana, Qatar, and Watergate, though the Watergate office-and-apartment complex was under construction beside the State Department in Washington; President Kennedy's funeral procession would pass it. Haight-Ashbury was a drab working-class district in San Francisco. No one living in the Haight, as it would later be known, was then familiar with the hippy terms acid-zap, freak out, superstar, mindblowing, bummer, joints, munchies, turn on, tune in, rip off, drop out, commune, horse, crash pad, steam, zonked, love-in, be-in, share-in, flower power, trash, Panhandle Park, acid-American Dayglo art, role-playing, bunch-punching, past-blasting, guerrilla theater, psychedelic Satanism, and Christ vibes.

The *New York Times* carried a dispatch from its London bureau about "a group of four male pop singers now highly popular in Great Britain and the cause of numerous teen-age riots." They were the Beatles. In November 1963 they were on their way to the United States, preceded by recordings of their first three hits: "She Loves You," "Wanna Hold Your Hand," and "Standing There."

The Vietnamese generals who had staged the Saigon coup, David Halberstam reported, wanted to see General Harkins replaced, but the Pentagon expressed confidence that Harkins would fulfill his promises to beat the Viet Cong. Any suspicion that the United States might not be able to find a military solution in Vietnam was challenged by Deputy Secretary of Defense Roswell Gilpatric in an address to the Business Council in Hot Springs, Virginia. The U.S. had such lethal power, Gilpatric said, that defiance of it would be an act of self-destruction.

Nicole Alphand, the wife of the French ambassador, was on the cover of the November 22 *Time*. Jimmy Hoffa was being indicted. Charles de Gaulle was vetoing Britain's entrance into the Common Market. Governor Ross Barnett was endorsing the findings of a grand jury which blamed the federal government for the recent disorders that had accompanied the admission of James Meredith to the state university in Oxford. Richard Burton and Elizabeth Taylor, having fallen in love during the filming of *Cleopatra*, were divesting themselves of their spouses and planning an early wedding. The Mona Lisa was in the United States, heavily chaperoned.

In 1963 there were 189,242,000 Americans (in 1973 there would be 209,000,000), of whom 70,000,000 were employed (1973: 80,627,000). Five percent were unemployed. The population center of the United States lay four miles east of Salem, Illinois, having moved fifty-seven miles to the west in the 1950s, the greatest westward drift since the 1880s. World War II was no longer the paramount experience of most Americans. Because of the huge number of war babies, the median age was 29.5.

A startling figure came from organized labor: between 1960 and 1962 unions had lost about a half-million members. The percentage of workmen belonging to them had dropped from 24.4 percent in 1955 to 22.2 percent in 1962, and Murray Kempton, no enemy of unions, was talking about the "twilight" of the labor movement.

One reason for this was the passage of time. Fewer and fewer workers could remember the heroic strikes of the 1930s. At the same time, the character of the work force was changing. In the years since V-J Day the number of blue-collar workers had decreased by four million while the number of white-collar workers — managers, professionals, salesmen, office workers — had grown by nearly ten million.

Furthermore, the blue-collar of November 1963 would hardly have been recognized as a fellow worker by his oppressed father of the 1930s. In June 1963 the weekly pay of the average production worker for slightly more than forty hours' work passed $100 — four times the Depression wage for the same job. About 40 percent of all families now earned more than $7,000 a year. John Brooks pointed out that the word "proletarian" had virtually disappeared from the language. "People think that prices are going up," Caroline Bird wrote, "but it is their own standard of living that is rising."

The best place to measure the long-range impact of boom was in the classroom. In his comprehensive study of economic development, Edward F. Denison put education at the very top of factors contributing to economic expansion. Between the Crash in 1929 and the end of the Kennedy Presidency, America's investment in education increased tenfold, to 39 billion dollars a year.

The sociological implications of this can hardly be exaggerated. In 1900 only 4 percent of Americans of college age were enrolled in a college or university. In 1957 the figure was 32 percent; when Kennedy took office it was 40 percent, and when he died it was 50 percent. Andrew Hacker calculated that between 60 and 70 percent of all Americans now belonged to the middle class. It was, in fact, swiftly becoming the only class, the values of which were those which had once belonged to a small, highly educated upper middle class.

"The American economy has become so big," a European diplomat said, "that it is beyond the imagination to comprehend." U.S. editorial writers marveled at West Germany's *Wirtschaftswunder,* but a far greater economic miracle had been taking place at home. A few figures suggest its scope. Approximately 90,000 Americans were now millionaires — as against 27,000 in the early 1950s — and each year now the figure grew by 5,000. Since World War II American investments abroad had leaped from 12 billion dollars to 80 billion. The annual sales of a single corporation, General Motors, were 17 billion dollars, almost equal to a third of the Bundesrepublik's Gross National Product. The *increase* alone of the U.S. Gross National Product in the first four years of the 1960s would be greater than the *entire* GNP of Germany in one year, 1964 — 122 billion dollars to 100 billion. The value of New York Stock Exchange investments had grown from 46 billion dollars to 411 billion since the war; Wall Street's public relations men spoke glowingly of a "people's capitalism," and with considerable justification — the stocks listed on the Big Board were held by some twenty million Americans.

Social prophets of the time regarded this as an unmixed blessing. Some, like John Kenneth Galbraith, thought that profits should be distributed differently, but the assumption that affluence was benign was virtually unchallenged. Lenny Bruce was just an obscene comic one jump ahead of the law in 1963; Ralph Nader was an obscure lecturer in history and government at the University of Hartford. The New Left notion that the country was threatened not by international Communism but by technology and the sheer magnitude of American institutions — that the immensity of U.S. corporations and the Washington bureaucracy was mere obesity — lay quiet in the womb of time. The faith of liberals in big government was still strong.

"Change is the biggest story in the world today," James Reston said at Columbia University in 1963. Nowhere was this more evident than in the growing mobility of American society. The great internal migration of the early 1940s had continued in the postwar years, fueled by the conclusion of southern blacks that a better life awaited them in the northern cities and by technological innovation. American agriculture in 1963 produced 60 percent more food than in 1940, while the number of hours needed to do the nation's farming dropped from twenty million to nine million. As a consequence, by 1963 the number of Americans living in urban and suburban communities had reached 75 percent. The "farm bloc" no longer struck fear in the hearts of congressmen. The Grange had lost its political potency.

Even the vehicles of change were changing. The railroad depot was becoming one of the loneliest places in metropolitan America; for every passenger mile crossed on trains three were crossed on airplanes. (In 1973 the ratio would be one to thirteen.) Ninety percent of local transport was by auto; altogether, car traffic amounted to nearly 800 billion vehicle miles in 1963. The U.S. Department of Commerce reckoned that there were now 17,000 automobile graveyards in the United States, and with the completion of President Eisenhower's nonstop, limited-access, high-speed interstate highway system, the great American traffic jam was beginning to sprawl across state lines.

Across the street from the flyblown train depots the lights in the old mansard-roofed city hotels were darkening. Over 4,000 of them had shut down completely since V-J Day. The travelers who bypassed them were staying instead at motels, which had been evolving from shabby prewar "tourist cabins" into lush pavilions offering all the traditional services of hotels and a few new ones. Black-and-white television had become standard equipment in all but the grubbiest motels (color TV was still a novelty). There were now 56.4 million television sets in the United States. That fact, combined with the discovery of 1960 census takers that only 8.5 percent of the population lacked radios, meant that a communications system of unprecedented magnitude was ready to report any news flash of national importance. In the early afternoon of November 22 the source for all information would be two wire service reporters clutching commandeered telephones at Dallas's Parkland Memorial Hospital. An investigation conducted the following winter by the National Opinion Research Center of the University of Chicago found that by 1 P.M. Dallas time, a half-hour after the shooting, 68 percent of all adults in the United States — over 75 million people — knew about it. Before the end of the afternoon 99.8

percent knew. Even those without television or radio had ready access to those with it.

On September 2, 1963, the CBS *Evening News* increased its nightly news show to thirty minutes and NBC followed its example on September 9, developments which were to have the most profound implications for the Vietnam War; to fill the extra time, networks would run footage showing, among other things, American soldiers lopping off Viet Cong ears. In November 1963 it had not come to that. There weren't even any television commentators in Saigon then. That year just seventeen Americans were killed in Vietnam and 218 were wounded. The most interesting story from Saigon in the third week of November 1963 was a report on Colt's new M-16 rifle. It was smaller and lighter than the M-14. An Army spokesman explained it was one of the reasons anti-Communist forces were wiping out the Viet Cong so effortlessly in guerrilla warfare.

Polls in foreign countries, tabulated by the United States Information Agency, showed U.S. prestige to be very high in 1963. Other stories from abroad were a report from Katanga, which was ending its two-year secession from the Congo, and an appraisal of Sir Alec Douglas-Home's new Tory government in London. It was shaky; the country was still in a state of shock over Lord Denning's report on the Profumo scandal, starring Christine Keeler, that year's most eminent British prostitute.

At home the Dow Jones industrial average hovered around 732. A Roman Catholic prelate excommunicated New Orleans segregationists who refused to bow to the church's endorsement of integration. None of them had heard of the Fathers Berrigan. Other names not in the news included Daniel Ellsberg, Clifford Irving, William Calley, Jimi Hendrix, James Earl Ray, Jeb Stuart Magruder, Angela Davis, Andy Warhol, Arthur Bremer, Vida Blue, Archie Bunker, Myra Breckenridge, and Spiro T. Agnew, who was then in the second year of a four-year term as a local official in Baltimore County. No one had heard of Jesus freaks, the *Whole Earth Catalog, Crawdaddy, Screw, Money,* hotpants, waterbeds, *Sesame Street, Love Story,* the Black Liberation Army, or Gay Lib.

The November 1963 issue of the *Reader's Digest* anticipated the future with an article reprinted from *Good Housekeeping:* "Sleeping Pills and Pep Pills — Handle with Extreme Caution!" In the November 24, 1963, *New York Times Magazine,* which was fated to be one of its least read issues, Mary Anne Guitar analyzed some new expressions in subteen slang: "rat fink," "triple rat fink," a "real blast" (party), "fake out," "tough toenails," "the straight skinnies," "Jeez-o-man," "hung up," "hairy," "wuzza-wuzza," and "gasser." Of the preteens, who would become the college generation of 1973, Miss Guitar said that their coinages were no worse, and sometimes more imaginative, than their elders': "According to reliable reports, 'terrific' is the word on the New Frontier."

Among the living, in addition to President Kennedy, were Attorney General Robert F. Kennedy, Martin Luther King, Mary Jo Kopechne, Fred Hampton, Malcolm X, George Lincoln Rockwell, and 45,865 young American men who would die violently in Vietnam over the next nine years.

On November 12, 1963, Mrs. John F. Kennedy played hostess to two thousand underprivileged children on the White House lawn. It was her first official appearance since the death of Patrick the previous August, and while she supervised the distribution of two hundred gallons of cocoa and ten thousand sugar cookies among her guests, a detachment of Scotland's Black Watch Regiment strutted and skirled for them. Hearing the tunes and liking them, the President came out of his oval office to watch the performance. Ten days later she would remember his pleasure and ask them to play again, at his funeral.

Nearly every day now impressions were being imprinted on her memory, to be recalled, brooded over, relived, savored, or regretted after Dallas. The day before the Black Watch appearance for the children, the President took young John, not quite three, to Veterans Day ceremonies at Arlington National Cemetery. To the indignation of some, who thought the occasion should be solemn, the little boy was allowed to toddle into the procession and disrupt it. His father was delighted, and while he beamed down at the child, cameramen put the scene on celluloid. There were those who thought that Kennedy had brought the boy along with that in mind. *Look* was coming out with an exclusive spread of John Jr. pictures; it would have been like the President to stage something for photographers who would feel left out by it.

The admiring spectators at Arlington included Major General Philip C. Wehle, commanding officer of the military district in Washington. Twelve days later he would look down on Kennedy's body on the autopsy table at Bethesda Naval Hospital and recall A. E. Housman's lines "To an Athlete Dying Young":

> *Today, the road all runners come,*
> *Shoulder-high we bring you home*
> *And set you at your threshold down,*
> *Townsman of a stiller town. . . .*

Mrs. Kennedy had many recent recollections which would put the tragedy in context; General Wehle had one. Most Americans hadn't any. To them the blow that fell in Dallas came out of nowhere. They didn't even know that the President was in Texas. His visit was only of local interest there; he had come down to make peace between two feuding Democrats, Senator Ralph Yarborough, the liberal, and Governor John B. Connally Jr., the deviate. Non-Texans were unaware of the trip until the first incredible bulletin reached them with the news that the President had been gunned down by a sniper while riding in a downtown motorcade.

Afterward Americans, giving a shape to their grief, reconstructed the events there. They came to know the grid of downtown Dallas streets; the location of the Texas School Book Depository, from which the shots had come, and Parkland Memorial Hospital, to which the President and Governor Connally, who had also been wounded, had been rushed; and the identity of each figure in the tragedy and the part each had played. In time the country forgot its terrible ignorance in the first hours after the assassination, and how they had learned about it.

Merriman Smith of UPI had been riding in the press pool car, four cars behind the presidential limousine in the motorcade. Moments after the sound of the gunfire, at 1:30 P.M. Washington time, he dictated the first bulletin to his local bureau over the pool car's radiophone: "Three shots were fired at President Kennedy's motorcade in downtown Dallas." That went out on UPI printers at 1:34, two minutes before the presidential car reached the hospital. At 1:36 Don Gardiner of the ABC radio network cut into local programs with it. At 1:40 CBS-TV interrupted *As the World Turns*, a soap opera; viewers beheld a distraught Walter Cronkite relaying Smith's report of the three shots and adding, "The first reports say that the President was 'seriously wounded.'" At 1:45 NBC-TV scuttled another soap opera, *Bachelor Father*, to switch to Chet Huntley. That put the three networks on the air with the news, and they would remain there, with no interruptions for commercials, for three days and three nights, until the President had been buried in Arlington National Cemetery.

Some people first heard about the shooting from those early broadcasts and telecasts. One watcher in Fort Worth was Marguerite Oswald, the assassin's mother; she was tuned to WFAA-TV. In Irving, a Dallas suburb, her daughter-in-law Marina was another viewer. Elizabeth Pozen, the wife of a government official, was listening to WGMS over her car radio in Washington. One of her passengers was Caroline Kennedy, who was going to spend the night with a Pozen child, and when Mrs. Pozen heard the announcer say ". . . shot in the head and his wife Jackie . . ." she instantly switched it off. But most people did not learn what had happened that directly. The news reached them third or fourth hand, from a passing stranger, or a telephone call, or a public address system, or a waiter in a restaurant — often from sources which were so unlikely that a common reaction was utter disbelief. To make sure that it was false, they gathered around transistor radios, car radios, and television sets in bars — whatever was available — and there they learned that it was true after all.

(Some of the reports were inaccurate or misleading, however. At 2:18 Washington time the Associated Press circulated an unconfirmed report that Lyndon Johnson had been "wounded slightly," and at 3:14 Washington time AP teletypes chattered that "A Secret Service agent and a Dallas policeman were shot and killed today some distance from the area where President Kennedy was assassinated." This seemed to support theories of an elaborate plot. It wasn't corrected until 4:33 P.M.)

At 2 P.M. Washington time Kennedy was pronounced dead. The announcement was delayed until Lyndon Johnson could get away from the hospital. In that first hour it was widely assumed that the gunman had been part of a larger conspiracy. The new President left for the airport at 2:26 P.M. Six minutes later UPI quoted Father Oscar Huber, the Dallas priest who had performed the last rites, as saying, "He's dead, all right." Confirmation by the President's acting press secretary followed, and at 2:35 Washington time — an hour earlier in Dallas — UPI bells chimed on tele- type machines around the world:

> FLASH
>
> PRESIDENT KENNEDY DEAD
>
> JT135PCS

Meantime attention had shifted to another part of Dallas. Lee Harvey Oswald, having left his rifle in his sniper's nest on the sixth floor of the book depository, had caught a bus outside, ridden in it for seven blocks, and then switched to a taxi. He stopped at his rooming house for a pistol. At 2:15 he committed his second murder in less than a hour, gunning down J. D. Tippit, a Dallas policeman who tried to question him. Oswald was seized thirty-five minutes later in a nearby movie theater. The homicide squad then learned that its new prisoner worked as a stockman in the book depository and was, in fact, the only depository employee missing at the building. The net of circumstantial evidence began to build.

At 3:38 P.M. Lyndon Johnson took the presidential oath of office on *Air Force One* with a stunned and bloodstained Jacqueline Kennedy standing beside him. Nine minutes later the plane took off for Washington's An- drews Field. The flight took less than two and a half hours. Johnson made his first televised statement as President at Andrews Field and was then taken by helicopter to the White House. The Kennedy party followed the coffin to Bethesda and the autopsy, which continued through most of the night. It was 4:34 A.M. when the casket, now covered by an American flag, was carried into the White House and placed upon the catafalque in the East Room. Mrs. Kennedy knelt beside it and buried her face in the flag's field of stars.

The next three days passed in a blur. Saturday was accompanied by drenching rains and high winds in the capital. The groggy country would later remember it as a gap between days, between the shock of Friday's assassination and the murder of the assassin on Sunday. The University of Chicago study indicated that the average adult spent ten hours in front of his television set on Saturday, the weekend's peak, but the watchers didn't learn much. The body remained in the East Room; Kennedy's family, his friends, and senior members of the government called to pay their respects there. On Sunday the coffin was carried up Pennsylvania Avenue on a horse-drawn caisson led by a riderless horse with reversed boots in the stirrups, the symbol of a fallen chieftain. At the same time word of a new, unbelievable outrage came from Dallas. Lee Harvey Oswald, in the process of being transferred to another jail, was mortally wounded by a Dallas night club owner named Jack Ruby. The killing occurred in the presence of seventy uniformed Dallas policemen. Because NBC was televising the transfer, it was also television's first live murder. The President's widow was told about it when she returned to the White House. She called it "one more awful."

On Monday the coffin was taken on the caisson to St. Matthew's Cathedral for a funeral mass and thence to Arlington. Delegations from ninety-two nations, led by Charles de Gaulle, had come to participate in the funeral. Afterward they attended two receptions, one at the State Department and another, much smaller, at the White House; Mrs. Kennedy received them there. That was the end of it, though in a sense that weekend never ended; years later men would still be trying to fathom its meaning. It had been the greatest simultaneous experience in the history of this or any other people. Long afterward Americans would tell one another how they had first heard the news from Dallas, how they felt about the eternal flame Mrs. Kennedy had requested for the grave, and young John's saluting of his father's coffin, and the rest of it. David Brinkley concluded that the assassination was beyond understanding: "The events of those days don't fit, you can't place them anywhere, they don't go in the intellectual luggage of our time. It was too big, too sudden, too overwhelming, and it meant too much. It has to be separate and apart."

Nevertheless, people couldn't stop attempting to incorporate it into their lives. The most obvious approach was to name something after the President. Cape Canaveral was rechristened Cape Kennedy. Idlewild International Airport was renamed. The National Cultural Center was changed to the John F. Kennedy Center for the Performing Arts. The Treasury began minting fifty million Kennedy half-dollars — and couldn't keep them in circulation because they were being hoarded as souvenirs. In every part of the country committees and councils were voting to honor the President by altering local maps. Presently Jacqueline Kennedy was wondering whether she would be driving "down a Kennedy parkway to a Kennedy airport to visit a Kennedy school." The impulse reached abroad. Canada had its Mount Kennedy — the first man to climb it was Robert Kennedy — and the climax was reached when England set aside three acres of the historic meadow at Runnymede, where the Magna Carta was signed, as a Kennedy shrine. In May 1965 Queen Elizabeth presided at the ceremony, dedicating the tract to the President "whom in death my people still mourn and whom in life they loved." Mrs. Kennedy replied that it was "the deepest comfort to me to know that you share with me thoughts that lie too deep for tears."

The hundreds of thousands of letters which Americans sent to Mrs. Kennedy then were often touching precisely because they were emotive and unashamedly demonstrative. To David Bell the fallen President was "a warrior-king"; to Natalie Hemingway "a dear godfather"; and John Steinbeck wrote the widow of "this man who was the best of his people" and who "by his life, and his death, gave back the best of them for their own."

Buried in the bales of envelopes was another memorable letter which was found and answered long afterward:

Richard M. Nixon
810 Fifth Avenue
New York, N.Y. 10021

November 23

Dear Jackie,

In this tragic hour Pat and I want you to know that our thoughts and prayers are with you.

While the hand of fate made Jack and me political opponents I always cherished the fact that we were personal friends from the time we came to the Congress together in 1947. That friendship evidenced itself in many ways including the invitation we received to attend your wedding.

Nothing I could say now could add to the splendid tributes which have come from throughout the world to him.

But I want you to know that the nation will also be forever grateful for your service as First Lady. You brought to the White House charm, beauty and elegance as the official hostess for America, and the mistique [*sic*] of the young in heart which was uniquely yours made an indelible impression on the American consciousness.

If in the days ahead we could be helpful in any way we shall be honored to be at your command.

Sincerely,
DICK NIXON

Montage: JFK / LBJ

How many roads must a man walk down
Before they can call him a man
How many seas must a white dove sail
Before she sleeps in the sand
How many times must a cannonball fly
Before they're forever banned
The answer my friend is blowin' in the wind
The answer is blowin' in the wind

DISORDERS IN CANAL ZONE CAUSE U.S. - PANAMA DIPLOMATIC BREAK

There was only one catch and that was Catch-22, which specified that a concern for one's own safety in the face of dangers that were real and immediate was the process of a rational mind. . . . Orr would be crazy to fly more missions and sane if he didn't, but if he was sane he had to fly them. If he flew them he was crazy and didn't have to; but if he didn't want to he was sane and had to. Yossarian was moved very deeply by the absolute simplicity of this clause of Catch-22 and let out a respectful whistle.

"That's some catch, that Catch-22," he observed.

"It's the best there is," Doc Daneeka agreed.

TFX DEFENDED BY MCNAMARA

—— Pall Mall ——

WINSTON TASTES GOOD LIKE A CIGARETTE SHOULD

— What do you want: good grammar or good taste?

Best actor of 1963: Sidney Poitier in *Lilies of the Field*
Best actress of 1963: Patricia Neal in *Hud*

Tom Jones *The Great Escape* *How the West Was Won* *The Leopard*
Cleopatra *The L-Shaped Room*

Blacks have to fashion a world where they can live with dignity and restraint. I am not interested in being a murderer, but then I am not interested in being a dier, either. I am not going to kill you, but I am not going to let you kill me, said LeRoi Jones

BEST SELLERS: Nonfiction
The Warren Commission Report on the Assassination of President Kennedy
The Fire Next Time by James Baldwin
The American Way of Death by Jessica Mitford
Silent Spring by Rachel Carson
The Kennedy Wit edited by Dill Adler

MOURN POPE JOHN

the one beer to have when you're having more than one

SCHAEFER

SEVEN STEEL COMPANIES INDICTED FOR PRICE FIXING

LBJ: U.S. WILL DESTROY 480 B-47s IF RUSSIANS WILL GUT 480 TU-16s

HOOVER DEAD AT 90
— AJAX — ## MACARTHUR DEAD AT 84

fruiti-juici, fruiti-juici, say, pal, how 'bout a nice HAWAIIAN PUNCH!

HOOTENANNY!

SUB THRESHER LOST WITH 129 ABOARD

Gone was the glow of blue velvet
But in my heart there'll always be
Precious and warm a memory
through the years
And I still can see blue velvet through my tears

BEST SELLERS: Fiction
The Shoes of the Fisherman by Morris West
The Group by Mary McCarthy
The Venetian Affair by Helen MacInnes
The Spy Who Came In from the Cold by John le Carre
Herzog by Saul Bellow

Big John

GO-GO-GOODYEAR

Big Bad John

We demand that no more American youth be sent to fight in a war that is helping neither them nor the Vietnamese people. We have learned lessons from Nazi Germany, and will not go along with the aggressive war-making policies of any government even if it happens to be our own

EXILES BOMB CUBAN REFINERY

LINK PHILBY TO MACLEAN, BURGESS

Dr. Strangelove ## U.S. MOSCOW EMBASSY BUGGED

CASTRO'S DEFECTING SISTER AIDED CIA

THIRTY

The Long Arm

O N AN AUGUST AFTERNOON in 1964 Dwight Eisenhower described to this writer Lyndon Johnson as he saw him in the Executive Office Building that rainy Saturday, the day after the assassination:

"I'd known him for a long time. He was, as he always is, nervous — walking around and telephoning everyone. . . . I would mention someone in the conversation and he would snatch up the receiver and call the person. He asked my advice about many matters, including the tax cut. I told him that he had to show what he was going to do with his own budget. We also discussed foreign affairs. As far as I could see at that time, Lyndon Johnson's only intention was to find out what was going on and carry policy through. He suggested nothing new or different. He wanted to talk about Laos, Cuba, and so forth. He did seem to be less informed about foreign policy than about domestic policy."

"Lyndon," said the new President's wife, "acts as if there is never going to be a tomorrow." He himself defined his philosophy of leadership with his favorite Biblical quotation, from Isaiah 1:18: "Come now, and let us reason together, saith the Lord," but he confessed that he liked to "show a little garter" while doing it, and in practice he persuaded other men to join what he called his "consensus" less by reasoning with them than by imploring, bullying, and begging them, and he was not above outright extortion. As Senate majority leader he had become one of the greatest manipulators in the history of Capitol Hill; his arm-twisting had been highly regarded there. One of his problems as President was that he never understood that the same wheeler-dealer reputation was a handicap in the White House. Eric Goldman called him "a Machiavelli in a Stetson." The public might endorse his legislative goals, but his manner of reaching them was another matter. The pollster Samuel Lubell found that many Americans planning to vote for Johnson in 1964 were nevertheless suspicious of him. They had a feeling: he was a wheeler-dealer; you had to watch his hands; he was a master politician, useful at times, no doubt, but not entirely trustworthy. His admirers, and he had many of them, protested that this was unjust. While there was much to be said for this, the skepticism was not entirely unjustified. There is no blinking the fact that until early 1966 he deliberately misled the country about the extent of the American commitment in Vietnam, or that three of his closest associates — Bobby Baker, Walter Jenkins, and Abe Fortas — were involved in scandals during his administration.

Yet there was nothing dishonorable about Johnson himself, and nothing petty. At times in that first year he seemed to be everywhere at once, turning out the White House lights and cutting Kennedy's budget to display economy with garter; declaring war on poverty, lobbying personally for Medicare, conferring with the chiefs of state of six American allies ("my prime ministers," he explained to one journalist), settling the U.S.-Cambodian dispute (if only temporarily), offering to destroy 480 B-47 bombers if the Russians would demolish the same number of TU-16s, arranging a U.S.-USSR reduction in the supply of atomic materials, touring Appalachia, persuading the Republican presidential nominee to join him in a moratorium on the race issue during the 1964 campaign, intervening with armed force in the Dominican Republic, and, in a speech on October 31, 1964, envisioning "the Great Society." Everything about the man was gargantuan. As he stepped down from an address to a congressional joint session, a senator congratulated him. "Yes," said Johnson, "I got applause eighty times." The senator checked the record, which confirmed the President; he had been counting the house as he spoke.

In both the oval office and in his bedroom three television sets stood side by side, permitting him to watch commentators on CBS, NBC and ABC at the same time. His telephone console had forty-two buttons; he could put that many callers on hold and deal with them in turn or talk to all of them at once. To sign three bills he used 169 pens, a record. He liked to drive fast. In Texas he took four women reporters for a hair-raising ride, going ninety miles an hour while describing in graphic detail the sex life of a bull. One of his passengers looked at the speedometer and gasped; the President whipped off his five-gallon hat and covered the dashboard with it. His appeals to patriotism were shameless; asked what had happened during a jawbone session about a railroad strike, a labor leader said, "Lyndon has a flag in the corner of his office. He picked it up and ran around the room with it." He spoke of "my army," "my government," and "my taxes." To make certain that no one forgot who he was, he had the presidential seal emblazoned on his cuff links, his boots, his twill ranch jackets, even on plastic drinking cups. He ordered a 44-foot portrait of himself for the Democratic national convention in 1964, and he scheduled the convention for the week of his birthday, August 27, so that the party faithful could present him with the biggest cake of all time. He wanted to roll up the greatest landslide in the history of American politics that November, and he pulled out all the stops. Entering a new city at night, he would cruise through its neighborhoods shouting into a bullhorn, "Howdy, folks! Come to the meetin'! Come to the speakin'!" Jack Gould of the *New York Times* called him "the Y. A. Tittle of handshakers." Once in Los Angeles a pickpocket reaching into a pocket found his hand grasped by that of the President of the United States.

That year the White House press corps entertained themselves by drawing up a list of what could be the shortest books ever written. The top three were *Italian War Heroes,* the *Polish Who's Who,* and *Mistakes I Made,* by Lyndon Baines Johnson. Many of those who knew the President best believed that he never searched his own soul because he never felt secure enough to do it. His problem certainly wasn't a lack of intelligence. Eric Goldman, a Princeton professor who became a Johnson aide, wrote: "After years of meeting first-rate minds in and out of universities, I am sure I have never met a more intelligent person than Lyndon Johnson — intelligent in terms of sheer IQ's, a clear, swift, penetrating mind, with an abundance of its own type of imagination and subtleties." The difficulty appeared to be rooted in the realization that his youth had been culturally deprived. The high school he attended hadn't even been accredited by the easygoing standards of its region.

In a revealing outburst he once said to Hugh Sidey of *Time,* "I don't believe that I'll ever get credit for anything I do in foreign affairs, no matter how successful it is, because I didn't go to Harvard." That was absurd, though his suspicion of intellectuals was not. Their contempt for him — there is no other word for it — was a shocking phenomenon of the 1960s. They jeered at him for pulling the ears of his beagles, as though that mattered. Buttons worn on campuses read, "King Lyndon the First," "Sterilize LBJ: No More Ugly Children," "Hitler Is Alive — in the White House," and — most unforgivable of all — "Lee Harvey Oswald, Where Are You Now That We Need You?" They applauded *MacBird,* which in depicting him as an assassin was in far worse taste than any lapse of his, and they justified their conduct as an expression of mourning for Kennedy — unwilling or unable to realize that Kennedy had chosen Johnson as his Vice President precisely because he was so able. Theodore White noted that "Political jokes were resurrected from as far back as the days of Herbert Hoover and pinned on Johnson; bedroom jokes of the President's life with Lady Bird were of a pornography to match those about Franklin Roosevelt's life with Eleanor." The Secret Service reported that crank letters attacking the President jumped from a hundred a month to over a thousand.

Johnson's speaking manner did not help. He suppressed his natural warmth and earthiness and tried to appear solemn and humble instead. What came through on the TV tube was unction and sanctimony. Instinctively people realized that whatever the real Lyndon Johnson was like, this one was a fake. The feeling that he was a mountebank was heightened by his inability to cast aside the extravagant style of the southern politician, so alien to a nation which had become accustomed to Kennedy understatement. Johnson was derisively christened "Uncle Cornpone," and to some extent he deserved it. Addressing the nation over television after settling the railroad strike, he read a letter he had received from a seven-year-old child in Park Forest, Illinois, named Cathy May Baker. "My grandmother lives in New York," Cathy had written. "She is coming to see me make my first Holy Communion. Please keep the railroads running so that she can come to see me." The President said, "So Cathy's grandmother can now go to see her." As a senator he had been able to get away with this sort of thing, but no more; within twenty-four hours the country learned that the letter was ten days old. Cathy's grandmother had visited her, witnessed the Communion, and returned to New York. Johnson never learned to abandon such stratagems. Later, when the issue was Vietnam, his habitual stretching of the truth would be much more damaging.

Liz Carpenter, one of his devoted Texans, wrote: "When I think of Lyndon Johnson, I always seem to see a Long Arm — reaching out to pick up a telephone, to grab a sheaf of papers, to shake hands, to embrace, to comfort, to persuade, sometimes even to shove — but always to include, yes, always to include." But not everybody. Johnson excluded Robert F. Kennedy. They brought out the worst in each other. It was the strong, irrational dislike of two proud and sensitive men, and it had been evident long before the tragedy in Dallas. Robert Kennedy had opposed his brother's choice of Johnson in Los Angeles, and Johnson at times seemed to oppose the younger Kennedy's very existence. Johnsonians could be very bitter about their predecessors. Liz Carpenter wished her President had been given "some public words of encouragement from the bereaved family after the assassination . . . He never mentioned it, but being a woman and a partisan, I was conscious of the silence . . . the Kennedys looked at the living and wished for the dead and made no move to comfort the country."

Undoubtedly grief for the slain President made Johnson's task harder, but it was not confined to the Kennedy family. Shortly after the assassination Congressman Clarence Cannon of Missouri predicted that "Everything will be Kennedy for a while. Then people will forget." But they did not forget. Magazines issued JFK memorial editions which were quickly sold out. The demand for Kennedy books grew ever more insatiable. Collectors of Americana discovered that holographic Kennedy letters were as valuable as Lincoln letters. An autographed copy of *Profiles in Courage* brought $375. To point up the Kennedy-Johnson transition, the presidential staff took to distributing pictures of both Presidents during Johnsonian trips, but the practice was soon discontinued; for every Johnson picture the public took ten of Kennedy. The Secret Service raged when the new chief executive rebuked an agent for wearing a Kennedy PT boat tie clip, but Johnson's resentment was understandable. He was being shadowed by a ghost.

It must have sometimes seemed to him that he was encountering Kennedys whichever way he turned. He sent Bob and Ethel Kennedy off on a tour of the Far East and the tour was on every front page. Ted Kennedy was hurt in a plane crash and the accident obscured Johnson's announcement that U.S. military might was greater than the combined strength of all the armies and navies in the history of the world. Above all there was Jacqueline Kennedy, whose most trivial remark or appearance could eclipse a statement by the President. Gallup reported that the First Lady, in a break with tradition, was only the second most admired woman in the United States; her predecessor was still first. In July 1964 Mrs. Kennedy moved to New York, and there was hope in the White House that the country's idolatry of her might diminish. It didn't; the mere fact that she continued to prefer bouffant hairdos to hats was enough to do to the women's hat industry what her husband had done to the men's.

Francis B. Sayre, dean of the Episcopalian Washington Cathedral and a Kennedy friend, rose in the pulpit to call Johnson "a man whose public house is splendid in its every appearance but whose private lack of ethic most inevitably introduces termites at the very foundation." The *Washington Star* commented that Sayre's "harsh pronouncement, we suspect, sums up the real mood of a great part of the electorate." Even harder for the President to bear were the vicious rumors that he was implicated in his predecessor's death. A commission headed by Chief Justice Earl Warren found that Kennedy had been murdered by Lee Harvey Oswald, who had acted alone, and the Kennedy family did everything possible to encourage acceptance of the commission's findings, but irresponsible attacks on the Warren Report continued throughout Johnson's years in the White House, sometimes in respectable society. The *New York World Journal Tribune* commented that "Out of respect for the memory of a martyred President, we think it is time to ask the ghouls, the buck-chasers, the sensation-mongers and the character assassins to desist — to shut up until or unless they can put up, as so far they have so notoriously failed to do." It was wasted ink; assaults on the report continued, and reached a high-water mark when the British Broadcasting Company paid a discredited critic $40,000, a record price, for a two-hour film which proved nothing.

The "Bobby problem," as it was called in the White House, became a major headache for Johnson. The new President had been in office less than six months when Washington became aware that the previous President's brother was building a government-in-exile. Comprised of New Frontiersmen who had left the government, the Kennedy people met at Jacqueline Kennedy's Georgetown residence that spring and, after she left Washington, at the attorney general's home, Hickory Hill. They were united in hostility to Johnson. None of them believed that he had been responsible for the tragedy in Dallas, of course, but they did feel that the younger Kennedy had a right to become Johnson's Vice President. They had lost touch with reality. There was never any possibility that the two men might run on the same ticket. In one of his milder comments on Bob Kennedy, President Johnson said, "That upstart's come too far and too fast. He skipped the grades where you learn the rules of life. He never liked me, and that's nothing compared to what I think of him." Johnson people called Bob a former McCarthyite and a "liberal fascist"; they said he was "Rover Boy, without birth control," and that he supported "God and country — in that order, after the Kennedys."

At 1 P.M. on Wednesday, July 29, 1964, the President summoned Attorney General Kennedy to the oval office and told him that he would not be his running mate. Johnson said that he approved of the young Kennedy's ambition and thought it would be fine if Bob ran the country some day. But not yet. He offered him his choice of any other post in the government and asked him if he would run Johnson's coming presidential campaign, as he had his brother's. Bob declined. The manner of announcing the end of Kennedy's vice-presidential ambitions this year was left undecided. Kennedy left believing that the meeting had been confidential. Evidently Johnson didn't think so, for he invited three Washington correspondents to lunch the next day and told them about it. That was bad enough; what was worse was that he couldn't resist using his considerable talents as a mimic to show them how Kennedy had taken it. Bob hadn't said a word at first when he had been told, the President said. He had just gulped. Johnson showed how he had gulped. When the story reached Kennedy he was furious. He confronted the President and accused him of a breach of confidence. Johnson said he hadn't told anyone about the meeting, and when Bob bluntly called him a liar he said, well, maybe there was some conversation he had forgotten; he would have to check his records and his calendar.

The President wanted Kennedy to announce that he wouldn't be on the ticket. Bob wouldn't do it. That left Johnson with a dilemma. He didn't want to offend the national Kennedy following. On the other hand, he felt he couldn't risk leaving the question open; the delegates to the coming Democratic national convention in Atlantic City were Kennedy people, quite capable of choosing Bob themselves. His solution was bizarre and typically Johnsonian. On July 30 he announced: "With reference to the selection of the candidate for Vice President on the Democratic ticket I have reached the conclusion that it would be inadvisable for me to recommend to the convention any member of my Cabinet or any of those who meet regularly with the Cabinet." He gave no reason. It didn't make sense. In a stroke he had doomed the vice-presidential ambitions not only of Robert Kennedy but also of McNamara, Stevenson, Shriver, Rusk, and Orville Freeman. Johnson said, "Now that damn albatross is off my neck." Bob said, "I'm sorry I took so many nice fellows over the side with me."

In *The Making of the President 1964* Theodore H. White wrote of a historic encounter that summer: "The deft response of American planes to the jabbing of North Vietnam's torpedo boats in the Gulf of Tonkin had been carried off with the nicest balance between boldness and precision." So it seemed then. Later, when disenchantment with the Vietnam War was metastasizing through the country, the events in Tonkin Gulf turned out to be shadowy, imprecise, and, most disturbing, a consequence of deliberate American provocation.

The key to understanding what happened in those waters off North Vietnam during the first week of August 1964 is a U.S. plan for clandestine operations against the Communist forces there whose code designation was 34A. White had never heard of 34A; neither had the American people; neither had Congress, which on the strength of events for which it was responsible was asked to commit, and did commit, the country to a disastrous escalation of the Asian war. To some extent the Gulf of Tonkin incidents may have been misinterpreted and distorted by chance, but those errors would have been inconsequential if men in Washington had not been playing a deeper game. The chief intriguer was President Johnson. He in turn may have been deceived and manipulated by high officers in the Pentagon. All that can be said with certainty is that Congress was maneuvered into supporting hostilities.

Plan 34A was conceived in December 1963, the month after the assassination of President Kennedy. Secretary of Defense McNamara, in Saigon on one of his many inspection trips, liked what he heard of the scheme for stealthy actions against the North Vietnamese. He put General Krulak in charge of it. Back in Washington he described it to President Johnson, who was equally enthusiastic. In execution 34A proved disappointing, however. The attacks by South Vietnamese guerrillas, parachutists, and frogmen were well organized, but the population in North Vietnam liked the Hanoi regime; the saboteurs were betrayed every time. General Harkins and McGeorge Bundy, who were masterminding 34A, switched to commando raids on Communist shore installations by South Vietnamese torpedo boats. Hanoi regarded these as more an annoyance than a threat, but radio intercepts revealed a growing demand for retribution among Communist naval officers commanding the raided North Vietnamese bases.

On Thursday, July 30, 1964, the day that Johnson eliminated Attorney General Kennedy and the rest of his cabinet from the Vice Presidency, a flotilla of South Vietnamese PT boats sailed from Da Nang on a 34A errand. The U.S.S. *Maddox*, an American destroyer, was headed for the same waters; its task was to goad the shore installations into using their radar and then to plot the radar — the naval equivalent of spotting enemy artillery positions so that they can be destroyed by counterbattery fire. On August 1 the destroyer passed the PTs coming the other way; they had just completed their torpedo attack and were returning home. The destroyer entered the combat zone and began its task of provoking radar operators on the coast. North Vietnamese officers there assumed that the *Maddox* and the PT boats were part of the same mission. This assumption was clear to Americans who were monitoring radio messages from three North Vietnamese torpedo boats sent out to investigate the destroyer, and their report to that effect was sent back to the Pentagon. There it was filed in the back of a deep drawer without comment. In its report to the White House the Pentagon merely said that the three Communist PT boats had attacked the *Maddox*, which had responded by sinking one of them.

In the laundered version which was given to the public, the destroyer was said to have been thirty miles from the coast, peacefully sailing through international waters. There was no mention of its assignment, and nothing at all about the South Vietnamese boats. President Johnson ordered the *Maddox* to continue its activities, and a second destroyer, the *Turner Joy*, was told to join it. Thus the stage was set for a second Tonkin Gulf incident. The night of August 4, one sailor said later, was "darker than the hubs of hell." Captain John Herrick, the commander of the destroyer patrol, radioed back that it was clear from interceptions of the North Vietnamese radio that they continued to believe that the American vessels were part of a 34A attack. Like its predecessor, this message was suppressed in the Pentagon. The public was told that American vessels had been the target of a second act of unprovoked aggression, this time when they were sixty-five miles from the coast.

Considering the gravity of the actions based upon it, the evidence in this second episode was surprisingly thin. The Senate Foreign Relations Committee did not hear the full story until three and a half years later. To their astonishment, the senators then learned that there may have been no encounter at all. Blips had appeared on the *Turner Joy*'s radar screen; the destroyer had opened fire. The *Maddox* did, too, although its radar screen was clear. Both ships took evasive action. The captain of the *Maddox* noticed that his signalmen reported torpedoes each time the destroyer turned sharply. After three hours of this Herrick radioed back: "Review of action makes recorded contacts and torpedoes fired appear doubtful. Freak weather effects and overeager sonar man may have accounted for many reports. No actual visual sightings by *Maddox*. Suggest complete evaluation before further action." There were certainly North Vietnamese torpedo boats in the vicinity — destroyer gunfire and carrier-based aircraft sank two of them — but the American vessels were undamaged, and there was a very real doubt over which side had fired the first shot. Fourteen hours after the first reported contact the Pentagon was still asking the destroyers for the names of witnesses, their reliability, and the size, type, and number of attacking North Vietnamese forces.

Lyndon Johnson hadn't waited. On his orders American warplanes were already taking off from the carriers *Ticonderoga* and *Constellation*; their targets were four North Vietnamese torpedo boat bases and an oil depot. The next morning the country learned that thirty-five North Vietnamese boats and 90 percent of the depot had been damaged or destroyed. Johnson appeared on television to report that "aggression by terror against the peaceful villages of South Vietnam has now been joined by open aggression on the high seas against the United States of America." The response, he said, was "limited and fitting. We Americans know, although others appear to forget, the risks of spreading conflict. We seek no wider war."

Possibly his reaction to these brief clashes between small vessels would have been different if he had been facing another opponent in that election year. Three weeks earlier the Republicans had nominated Barry Goldwater in the San Francisco Cow Palace, and he was accusing the administration of "timidity before Communism." He brought his admirers to their feet, roaring, with the charge that "the Good Lord raised up this mighty republic to be a home for the brave . . . not to cringe before the bullying of Communism . . . Failures cement the wall of shame in Berlin. Failures blot the sands of shame at the Bay of Pigs. Failures mark the slow death of freedom in Laos. Failures infest the jungles of Vietnam."

By exploiting the events in Tonkin Gulf, Johnson could break the back of that Goldwater issue. All he needed to do was to wrap himself in the flag and ask Congress to give him a free hand to deal with the North Vietnamese pirates. To this end he called the congressional leaders to the White House and asked them for a resolution authorizing him to deal decisively with such challenges. What he wanted, he said, was a joint resolution similar to the ones Congress had given Eisenhower to oppose Communist threats in Formosa in 1955 and the Middle East in 1957. Bill Bundy had already drafted a version for him. The President asked Senator Fulbright, chairman of the Foreign Relations Committee and an old Johnson friend, to be the resolution's floor manager. To his subsequent sorrow, Fulbright agreed.

The cold war was still frigid in 1964; few men on the Hill were ready to urge a soft answer to Communist wrath. But there was one: Wayne Morse of Oregon. On the night after the second Tonkin Gulf incident Morse had a call from someone in the Pentagon. The caller had heard that the senator was going to fight the President's resolution. He suggested that the senator ask two questions. First, he should insist upon seeing the Maddox's log; it would show that the destroyer had been much closer to the shore than civilians realized. Second, he should demand to know the ship's mission; it had been far from innocent.

The next morning Morse studied the wording of the resolution and concluded that it was unconstitutional. Only Congress could declare war, he pointed out to Fulbright. This measure would give blanket approval to the waging of war by the chief executive with no war declaration. Fulbright reminded him of the Formosa and Middle East resolutions. Morse said they had been unconstitutional, too, but they had been more justifiable than this one. The crises which inspired them had been subject to quick solutions. Not so this one; the struggle in Vietnam seemed interminable, and this open-ended license would allow the President to intervene any time he saw fit. The wording was far too general, Morse said. He implored Fulbright to hold hearings. Impossible, said Fulbright; this was an emergency. Morse denied it, and he was right; but Fulbright had decided to ask for instant passage, making the issue one of senatorial patriotism. That isolated Morse and Ernest Gruening of Alaska, the only colleague to side with him. The measure passed the House 414 to 0, after just forty minutes of discussion. The Senate took longer — eight hours of debate — but that, as one observer later commented, was "less time than the Senate usually took to amend a fisheries bill."

There were few critical comments at the time. The move was seen as a logical extension of a line of thought reaching back to the decision, after Munich, never again to appease aggressors, relying instead on collective security. If we and SEATO's other signatories came to South Vietnam's rescue now, the reasoning went, they would help us if California found itself threatened by Ho Chi Minh, or by Ho and Mao. Dean Rusk flatly stated that to do less would put the United States in "mortal danger." Later there were hoots at this, but there was no derision at the time. The Rusk position was that of practically all public men in both parties; among the senators who voted for the resolution were Eugene McCarthy, George McGovern, Birch Bayh, Albert Gore, Jacob K. Javits, John Sherman Cooper, Frank Carlson, George D. Aiken, and Frank Church. The *New York Times* commented: "The nation's united confidence in the Chief Executive is vital." The *Washington Post* said: "President Johnson has earned the gratitude of the free world." Lou Harris reported that whereas 58 percent of the nation had been critical of Johnson's handling of the war in July, 72 percent now approved. Harris wrote: "In a single stroke Mr. Johnson has turned his greatest political vulnerability in foreign policy into one of his strongest assets." Even Walter Lippmann approved, believing that the President was telling the country that bombing would be the outer limit of American involvement in Vietnam, that he would never send troops. The friends of the administration, which in 1964 meant most of the nation, were jubilant. It was much later that Morse's prophetic words were recalled:

> I believe that history will record that we have made a great mistake in subverting and circumventing the Constitution of the United States . . . by means of this resolution. As I argued earlier today at great length, we are in effect giving the President . . . warmaking powers in the absence of a declaration of war. I believe that to be a historic mistake.

Johnson signed the document the day it was passed, August 7. Eight months later he told a group of visitors with a grin, "For all I know our Navy was shooting at whales out there."

In the summer of 1963 Eliot Janeway, the syndicated economic columnist, speculated about what might happen if black and white workmen found themselves competing for the same jobs. He suggested that the white workers might become resentful of the civil rights movement, and he gave the reaction a name: "backlash." During the winter after Dallas "backlash" acquired a political meaning. Specifically, it was applied to racist support for the presidential primary campaigns of Governor George C. Wallace of Alabama. After displays of strength in Indiana (where he won 30 percent of the vote on May 5) and in Maryland (43 percent on May 19), Wallace's national following dwindled. His popularity seemed to suffer from the dignified demeanor of most blacks, who were still turning their cheek to injustice. In July Wallace quit the race. Yet even as he with-drew, blacks in New York were making history by declining to turn a cheek. As a consequence, headlines began conveying news which was bound to stimulate backlash.

On July 16, the day the Republican presidential candidate accepted his party's nomination in San Francisco, a Manhattan janitor was hosing the sidewalk outside a building of luxury apartments at 215 East Seventy-sixth Street, near the edge of Harlem. Noticing three Negro youths lounging across the street, he impulsively turned the hose on them. That was unwise. To the boys the hose was reminiscent of Bull Connor and Birmingham. Infuriated, they attacked the janitor, holding trash can lids as shields and hurling missiles. A bottle hit him; he fled. One of the boys, James Powell, fifteen, went after him with a knife. At this point an off-duty police lieutenant, Thomas R. Gilligan, arrived on the scene. Gilligan drew his pistol and ordered Powell to drop the knife. Instead the boy lunged at the lieutenant, slashing his right forearm. Gilligan discharged one warning shot and then fired for keeps, killing him instantly.

Young Powell's death aroused all Harlem. For three days the Negroes' rage smoldered. On the third evening, a Saturday, CORE held a protest rally on West 123rd Street. Goaded by an impassioned speaker, a black mob marched to the nearby 29th Precinct station and demanded Gilligan's immediate suspension. When it wasn't forthcoming they rioted, throwing bottles and debris at the policemen. The riot spread and continued for five nights. Dying down there, it then broke out in the Bedford-Stuyvesant section of Brooklyn, and when the violence subsided in Brooklyn it erupted in Rochester, New York, three hundred miles away. On Sunday, August 2, Jersey City blew. Paterson and Elizabeth were next, then Dixmoor, a Chicago suburb, and finally Philadelphia. Hundreds had been injured, and nearly a thousand arrested. A thousand stores were damaged; losses were placed at several million dollars.

The FBI declared that there was no pattern to the riots, that they were "a senseless attack on all constituted authority, without purpose or objective." The report continued: "While in the cities racial tensions were a contributing factor, none of the . . . occurrences was a 'race riot' in the accepted meaning of the phrase." Essentially chaotic, the disorders were nevertheless far from lacking form and significance. Until 1964 whites had always been the aggressors in major American interracial disturbances, of which there had been thirty-three since the turn of the century. Now the situation was reversed; the initiative had passed to the blacks. The race riots of the 1960s shared other characteristics. They came in the summer, in ghettos marked by an absence of contact between the slum population and those who made the key decisions concerning it, and they were sparked by hostility between the Negroes and white policemen.

"Watch out," said Negro Congressman Adam Clayton Powell, often a shrewder man than his critics, black or white, knew. The "black revolution," as he called it, would, he said, have two phases. The first was southern and concerned with "middle-class matters": sitting on buses and at lunch counters, using public toilets, going to the same schools as whites — issues of status. The second phase was northern. It was just beginning, and it was going to be very different, he said. Powell called it "proletarian," and he predicted that it would be "rough." Northern Negroes had always had the rights their counterparts in the South sought. Their concern was what Powell called the "gut issue of who gets the money." They were in a mutinous mood, and they were not moved by Martin Luther King's appeals for nonviolence. Their war cry was: "Burn, baby, burn!"

Although no one knew it at the time, 1964 marked the beginning of a cycle which would devastate the northern cities within three years. In addition to the tumult in New York there were scattered disorders that summer in New Jersey, Philadelphia, Chicago, and St. Augustine, Florida. Race was becoming the country's overriding domestic issue. In northern schools it was the year of the boycott; black parents in New York and Cleveland, dissatisfied with the treatment of their children, kept them at home. Malcolm X formed the Black Nationalist Party in 1964. The consciences of the North had at last been aroused by the injustices in the South. That spring Mrs. Malcolm Peabody, the seventy-two-year-old mother of the governor of Massachusetts, was arrested for participating in the St. Augustine protests, and the declaration of a mistrial in the Medgar Evers murder case, which only a few years earlier would have been accepted passively by Negroes, stimulated recruitment for the most important civil rights program of the year, the Mississippi "Freedom Summer" of 1964.

The immediate importance of the events in Mississippi lay in their impact on the ghettoed blacks in the North. Until 1940, some 75 percent of American Negroes had lived in the South. The long emigration of southern Negroes northward and the coming of age of the children born in their new homes had created a new, militant generation of blacks. Washington, D.C., and Newark now had Negro majorities, and Cleveland, Baltimore, St. Louis, and Detroit were more than one-third Negro. The black birth rate — approximately 40 percent higher than that of whites — had replaced immigration as the U.S. population's expansional factor. The urban slums of the North were swarming with black youths. More than half the country's Negroes were now below the age of twenty-two, and great masses of them lacked parental supervision. Fully 30 percent of the black families in big cities were headed by women who lacked husbands; in New York City alone there were 100,000 illegitimate Negro children in 1964. The revolution in communications meant that TV news programs provided this volatile audience with vivid reports of civil rights developments in the South. "Amid all the sad statistics poured forth about the ghettoes," the *Economist* of London reminded its European readers, "it is worth remembering that . . . some 88 per cent of black American families have television sets."

The Freedom Summer was sponsored by the Council of Federated Organizations (CFO), principally SNCC and CORE. None of the participants expected a graceful reception from white Mississippians. Memories of James Meredith and Medgar Evers were still fresh, and the red-necks and wool-hats of the South were known to be resentful over the Civil Rights Act of 1964. Introduced by John Kennedy and shepherded through Congress by Lyndon Johnson, it extended the bans against discrimination into many new areas. CFO cast its recruiting nets on the campuses of northern colleges and universities, chiefly among white students whose consciences were troubled by injustices to Negroes. A thousand of them volunteered to participate in a drive to register as many voters as possible among Mississippi's 900,000 blacks. They were trained in Oxford, Ohio. On June 19 the first group of 200 left for the South, and on June 21 they reached Jackson.

Almost immediately — it was the following day — three of them were reported missing. They were Michael H. Schwerner, twenty-four, of Brooklyn; Andrew Goodman, twenty, of New York, and James E. Chaney, twenty-one, of Meridian, Mississippi. Schwerner and Goodman were white; Chaney was black. The three were traveling in a 1964 Ford station wagon, and they had been arrested for speeding in Neshoba County, in east central Mississippi. Sheriff Lawrence Rainey and his deputy, Cecil Price, said the youths had disappeared after paying a fine in Philadelphia, the county seat. The station wagon was found the next day fifteen miles northeast of Philadelphia. It had been burned.

The FBI, local law officers, and Navy men stationed in Mississippi conducted a massive search for the missing youths. Rivers and creeks were dragged; helicopters and a photoreconnaissance jet hovered overhead. At the request of the President, Allen Dulles flew down to confer with Governor Paul B. Johnson Jr. A considerable part of the state's white population believed that the three were in Cuba or, as one report had it, in a Chicago bar, drinking beer and laughing at the baffled lawmen looking for them. The prevailing opinion in white Mississippi was that the searchers had no expectation of finding the youths. They were there, the story went, to win Negro votes for President Johnson in the North.

Meanwhile the rest of the CFO volunteers were encountering other difficulties. In the Mississippi Delta their meetings with local blacks were bombed by the KAF — the Klan Air Force: private planes which soared overhead and dropped sachels of explosives. After several Negro homes had been demolished in McComb, in southwestern Mississippi, several white men were arrested; with them the arresting officers found four high-powered rifles, several carbines and pistols, fifteen dynamite bombs, a five-gallon can of explosive powder, a case of hand grenades, and several thousand rounds of ammunition.

CFO volunteers who distributed handbills in Belzoni, Mississippi, were arrested, charged with "criminal syndicalism," and held in the town jail. A dynamite charge tore out a wall in the home of the mayor of Natchez, who had promised blacks equal protection under the law. A circuit judge denounced men who burned churches, and a cross was burned on his lawn. As the summer waned the leaders of the Freedom Summer movement drew up a list of their casualties. Eighty of the volunteers had been beaten. Three had been wounded by gunfire in thirty-five shootings. Over a thousand had been arrested. Thirty-seven Negro churches and thirty-one homes had been burned or bombed. In addition there were several unsolved murders of blacks which were believed to be attributable to hostility toward the civil rights movement.

Robert Kennedy told the NAACP that the federal government could not undertake preventive police action in the state; it was impractical and probably unconstitutional. J. Edgar Hoover went further. Arriving in Jackson, he deplored what he called an "overemphasis" on civil rights and said his men "most certainly" would not provide the volunteers with protection. At the suggestion of Allen Dulles, however, the President sent more FBI agents to the state. Lights burned all night on the top two floors of a new office building in Jackson, the bureau's Mississippi headquarters. Governor Johnson appealed for public assistance in the search for the three missing civil rights workers. Predictably, that call was unheeded, but the FBI's offer of nearly $30,000 in reward money brought information from two informers. With it, agents rented excavation equipment and dug into a newly erected earthen dam on a farm some six miles southwest of Philadelphia. They found the bodies of the missing three near the base of the 25-foot-high red clay dam and at the center of its 250-foot length. They had been shot to death, and Chaney, the black, had been beaten savagely before being murdered.

On December 4 the FBI arrested twenty-one Neshoba County men, including Sheriff Rainey and Deputy Price. Price was accused of arresting the three youths and turning them over to a lynch mob, which he then joined. Most of the men were Klansmen, and one was the local Klan leader. Civil rights leaders doubted that any of them would be convicted, and for a while it certainly seemed unlikely. Governor Johnson and Mississippi Attorney General Joe Patterson announced that the state would not prefer charges; in their opinion the evidence was inadequate. A federal grand jury in Meridian, Mississippi, did hand down indictments against eighteen of the men, charging them with violating an obscure 1870 statute by conspiring to violate the constitutional rights of the slain men, but the U.S. District Judge was W. Harold Cox, who had helped delay due process in the James Meredith case. On one recent occasion Cox had compared black voter applicants to chimpanzees. He was not expected to give the defendants any trouble.

In the beginning he didn't. In February 1965 he dismissed the felony indictments against the accused, reducing the charges to misdemeanors. For a time it even appeared that the sheriff, his deputy, and a Philadelphia justice of the peace might be awarded damages against the government by a local jury. To reporters it seemed that the defendants were widely regarded as heroes. Confederate flags were displayed outside the federal building; one huge one was run up each morning at the barbershop directly across the street. Television and wire service cameramen were mauled by resentful bystanders. Although the U.S. Supreme Court reversed Judge Cox, ruling that the accused men must stand trial on the conspiracy charges brought by the Justice Department, most observers believed that the case was as good as dead. Certainly the accused thought so. Freed on bond during the trial, they were plainly enjoying their local fame. A battery of twelve defense lawyers called 114 witnesses, most of them to provide alibis or to attest to good character. One lawyer called the informers "traitors." The jury of seven women and five men was all white; eighteen Negro veniremen had been eliminated by defense challenges.

John Doar, prosecuting for the Justice Department, called forty-one witnesses. They revealed that the murders had been no crime of passion. Schwerner, who had preceded the main body of CFO volunteers, had been marked for death by the Klan nine days before he was killed for having eaten and slept in the homes of Negroes. He and his two companions had been seized after a wild chase and taken to a lonely dirt road. One of the Klansmen had spun Schwerner around and asked him, "Are you that nigger lover?" Schwerner had replied, "Sir, I know how you feel." Those had been his last words. Goodman, too, had been swiftly murdered. One Klansman had been disappointed because the two white volunteers had been put to death before he could fire. He had shot Chaney, saying, "At least I killed me a nigger."

One day after retiring to consider the evidence the jury reported that it was hopelessly deadlocked. Judge Cox refused to accept the stalemate. Instead he issued new instructions, among them the so-called "dynamite charge" which had been upheld by the Supreme Court in 1898 as a way to jolt a deadlocked jury into a decision. Under it jurors in the minority were urged to "carefully examine and reconsider" their opinions, weighing the feelings of the majority. The judge also told them that he would approve a mixed verdict. During a recess at this point Deputy Price and another defendant, Wayne Roberts, a salesman of automobile trailers, blundered. They told spectators in the federal building corridors that they were going to fix the judge. Roberts was heard to say, "Judge Cox gave the jury the dynamite charge. Well, we have some dynamite for him ourselves." Word of this reached the judge. Ordering them to the bench, he said, "If you think you can intimidate this court, you are sadly mistaken. I'm not going to let any wild man loose on any civilized society." With that, he ordered them locked up and denied them bail. On October 20 the jury found seven of the men, including Price and Roberts, guilty. Sheriff Rainey and seven others were acquitted. Over three years had passed since the crime, but the Justice Department was jubilant. The verdict had made history; for the first time, a federal jury of white Mississippians had convicted white defendants in a civil rights case. On December 29 Judge Cox sentenced the seven to jail terms ranging from three years to ten — the maximum.

It was the year of Goldwater. In seven consecutive national conventions of the past, beginning with the nomination of Landon in 1936, Republican conservatives had suppressed their yearning for a presidential candidate from their own ranks. This time they did not suppress it. This time they turned to $Au + H_2O = 1964$. They wanted A Choice, Not an Echo, as their placards proclaimed, and on July 15 they nominated Barry Morris Goldwater, Arizona's senior senator and a denizen of deep right field.

The fact is that the party felt desperate. George Gallup had discovered that during the past quarter-century the GOP had lost a third of its members; the number of Americans who regarded themselves as Republicans had diminished 13 percent, while the number of Democrats had increased 11 percent. Goldwater and his people had an explanation for this. The GOP, their argument went, had been choosing "me too" candidates — moderate Republicans who merely repeated Democratic promises. Their conclusion was that because the Democrats were originals and the Republican moderates mere carbon copies, the GOP had been repeatedly defeated, voters tending to prefer the real thing.

Here the skating reached thin ice. Polls indicated that a majority of the electorate favored the middle of the road. The Republican right-wingers denied it. They were convinced that out in the country there was a hidden conservative majority. It was, they insisted, the key fact in American politics. Lacking a home, these disgruntled conservatives had scorned both parties. On election days they went fishing or stayed home. To them the result was a matter of no consequence; either way they were going to be stuck with liberals, leftists, socialists, "collectivists," "bleeding hearts." Nominate a genuine conservative, said the Goldwater ideologues, and this hidden majority would come swarming into the streets and elect a real American.

Although President Kennedy had been convinced that Barry Goldwater would be the Republican nominee in 1964, Goldwater himself wasn't so sure, and other GOP leaders were slow in taking him seriously. The struggle over who would become the standard-bearer turned into an odd one. The Arizonan had announced his candidacy from his sun-drenched

Scottsdale, Arizona, patio on January 3. The next Republican to throw a hat in the ring had been a woman, Margaret Chase Smith. The first primary, in New Hampshire, was won with write-in votes by a man who hadn't announced at all, Henry Cabot Lodge. Nelson Rockefeller then divulged that he was available; next William Scranton of Pennsylvania said *he* was.

Until the last of the big primaries, in California on June 2, almost everyone seemed to believe that someone would take it away from Goldwater. The likeliest one was Rockefeller. Then, on May 30, a Saturday, the second Mrs. Rockefeller gave birth to Nelson A. Rockefeller Jr. — thereby reminding California Republicans of the New York governor's recent divorce. Overnight he lost seven percentage points in the Lou Harris poll. On Tuesday Goldwater received 51 percent of the primary vote and Rockefeller 49 percent. At the convention the Arizonan's well-organized legions then deflected all opposition and took the prize with an overwhelming 883 delegate votes on the first ballot. Thereupon the nominee deepened the division in the party by giving the moderates the rough side of his tongue in a memorable passage: "Extremism in the defense of liberty is no vice! And . . . moderation in the pursuit of justice is no virtue!"

Barry Goldwater was fifty-five years old, a man of absolute integrity, and one of the most charming politicians ever to run for the Presidency. Handsome, leonine, silver-haired, with the black horn-rimmed spectacles which were his trademark, he had become one of the most celebrated public men in the nation and certainly the best-known conservative. Goldwater represented a love for the best of the past and defiance toward the worst of the present. In his crisp, low southwestern drawl he reminded the country of American maxims and ethical certitudes which had lost their validity but not their fascination. It was his special talent that he could make them seem both plausible and relevant.

Away from the Senate he was a mishmash of anachronisms. For all his summoning of the legends of the past, he was a major general in the Air Force reserve, a hot jet pilot, and a tremendous admirer of sophisticated technology. (In San Francisco he buckled himself into the cockpit of his private jet and zoomed back and forth over the Cow Palace while his name was being placed in nomination.) He was an expert radio ham; he maintained expensive sending and receiving sets in his suburban Phoenix home and his Washington apartment, and he brought a third to the San Francisco convention. He was also a superb photographer; a volume of his desert studies had been issued. Perhaps his most significant acquisition was the twenty-five-foot flagpole at his Arizona home. It was equipped with a photoelectric device which automatically raised the colors when the dawn light reached it and lowered them as twilight deepened, thereby assuring a display of patriotism even when no one was home.

"*Viva olé! Viva olé!*" chanted his faithful followers. They were passionate, they were exuberant, and sometimes they were frightening. One unforgettable moment came in the Cow Palace when Nelson Rockefeller took the rostrum to urge the adoption of minority resolutions which had been drafted by the platform committee. The galleries, packed with Goldwaterites, booed him and shouted, "We want Barry!" Some men would be daunted by this, but Rockefeller relished it. "This is still a free country, ladies and gentlemen," he taunted, and as their fury mounted and they roared with rage, he described some of the tactics which had been used against him in the California primary: "These things have no place in America, but I can personally testify to their existence, and so can countless others who have also experienced midnight and early morning telephone calls, unsigned threatening letters, smear and hate literature, strong-arm and goon tactics, bomb threats and bombings, infiltration and take-over of established political organizations by Communist and Nazi methods."

By this time there were people in the galleries who were all but lying on the floor and drumming their heels. Chairman Thruston B. Morton vainly gaveled for order while the Goldwater delegates on the floor — aware that this demonstration of ferocity was hurting their man in the eyes of the television audience — pleaded for quiet. The storm of abuse continued unabated, and Rockefeller, grinning, delivered another thrust: "Some of you don't like to hear it, ladies and gentlemen, but it's the truth."

It was part of the truth. Goldwater and his managers permitted no little old ladies in tennis shoes in their organization. Indeed, one of the weaknesses of their campaign was that it was too disciplined, too lacking in spontaneity. After the convention the senator sent two of his very straight young men, Dean Burch and John Grenier, to take over the Republican National Committee, Burch as chairman and Grenier as executive director. They spent five full weeks putting it in order — five weeks when they should have been campaigning. The day after the election in November Goldwater's finance chairman elatedly announced that his books were in the black.

A shrewder politician would have used his acceptance speech to woo the losers. He might even have visited the vanquished, as Eisenhower had done with Taft in 1952. But Goldwater had been angered by dirty tricks, too, and for all his generosity of spirit he wasn't a healer. In August, too late, he sat down in Hershey, Pennsylvania, with the party's elders — Rockefeller, Eisenhower, Nixon, William Scranton, and George Romney — in an effort to bind up wounds and plan a master election strategy. It was a wasted day. They lacked a conciliatory spirit, and none had any useful campaign ideas. Mostly they complained. It was after this meeting, and in part as a consequence of it, that Republicans running for other offices began avoiding the presidential standard-bearer, even declining to share the same platform with him.

IN YOUR HEART YOU KNOW HE'S RIGHT, read the Goldwater billboards, pins, and bumper stickers. There was some truth to it. In his three books and eight hundred newspaper columns he had tackled many sacred cows which deserved it. Over the past half-century the federal bureaucracy had grown to something in the order of fifty or sixty times its original size. Its officials were often arrogant and overbearing, and some of the practices that the government either employed itself or encouraged in others had plainly outlived their usefulness — among them labor featherbedding, depletion allowances, farm price supports, and subsidies to peanut growers. Senator Goldwater was trenchant on the subject of these, and here millions of Americans knew in their hearts — or at any rate believed — that he was right.

The difficulty was that he had said, done, and written so many other things, some of them bizarre. He had offered to sell TVA for a dollar. He had said that he wished it were possible to saw off the eastern seaboard and let it float out to sea. He had depicted all of America's great cities as sin-steeped Babylons. At various times he had advocated the elimination of rural electrification, the replacement of the National Labor Relations Board, and a new U.S. Supreme Court. Here Americans knew in their hearts that he was wrong.

His opponent was one of the most masterful politicians in the history of the country; as a result, the flaws in Goldwater's armor were deftly exposed, over and over, so that he was put on the defensive and remained there. Atomic warfare was a particularly devastating issue. Speaking in Hartford on October 24, 1963, Goldwater had said that he believed the size of the American military presence could be reduced by as much as a third if NATO "commanders" were authorized to use tactical nuclear weapons in a crisis. That put the Bomb in the campaign, and it remained there to the end.

As exploited by Rockefeller in New Hampshire's January campaign, it was a legitimate campaign issue. The Democrats probably went too far in what became known as their "Daisy Girl" television spot, first shown on September 7. NBC's Monday Night at the Movies that evening, *David and Bathsheba,* starring Gregory Peck and Susan Hayward, was interrupted for an idyllic picture of a child pulling the petals off a daisy and counting them; as she did, the picture dissolved into a mushroom cloud. The Republicans were understandably incensed. Yet Goldwater had failed and continued to fail to clarify his Hartford remarks. At the very least his manner of referring to nuclear weapons was disturbing. A candidate for the Presidency of the United States ought not to speak of "lobbing one into the men's room at the Kremlin." On one occasion when Goldwater was supposed to be exorcising the shadow of the Bomb, Charles Mohr of the *New York Times* counted almost thirty such phrases as "push the button," "atomic holocaust," and "nuclear annihilation." That was not the way to reassure the people. IN YOUR HEART, the Democrats said in a wicked thrust, YOU KNOW HE MIGHT.

Another issue digging graves for Republican hopes was social security. Here the trouble had begun on January 6 in New Hampshire. In reply to a question, Goldwater said that he favored improving social security by making contributions voluntary. The next day's Concord, New Hampshire, *Monitor* carried the head, GOLDWATER SETS GOALS: END SOCIAL SECURITY. The senator protested, but plainly that would be the consequence of voluntary participation; payments to retired workers must come from young workers, who are no more eager than anyone else to pay taxes if they can get out of it. In the Democrats' TV spot on this, two hands tore up a social security card. Since social security affects a hundred million Americans, it would have been hard to find a theme of greater interest.

Goldwater had other problems; he had voted against the nuclear test ban treaty and — the previous June — the Kennedy-Johnson civil rights bill. The consequences of his record became clearer and clearer as one conservative newspaper after another endorsed Johnson, and ultimately even the Republican candidate could see it. Poll figures had never been so lopsided; Gallup had Johnson over Goldwater 65 to 29 percent. After the election the Arizonan remarked that he should have realized that it was all over in San Francisco, before the campaigning had even begun. As it was, he said, he knew in August that it was hopeless. That had the ring of hindsight. As late as October he was giving lip service, at least, to confidence in victory. Whatever his expectations, though, he never tried to improve his chances with low blows. He admonished audiences that hissed Johnson ("Don't boo the office of the Presidency"). When F. Clifton White, one of his advisers, produced a documentary film called *Choice*, exploiting the ghetto riots with shocking scenes of marauding Negroes, Goldwater called it racist and suppressed it. And he refused to capitalize on, or even to discuss, reports of an impending scandal in the Johnson campaign — the arrest of the President's chief aide on a charge of committing sodomy in a public toilet.

The aide was Walter Jenkins, who, exhausted by overwork, had yielded to temptations he might otherwise have suppressed. Jenkins had left the White House for a few hours on October 7 to attend a cocktail party celebrating the occupancy of new offices by *Newsweek*'s Washington bureau. After several drinks he left and walked two blocks to the Washington YMCA. The basement men's room was known to him as a trysting place for homosexuals. Unfortunately the Washington police knew it, too, and at about 7:30 P.M. Jenkins and an elderly army veteran were arrested by an officer who had been watching them through a peephole. They were taken to a police station, where it was discovered that five years earlier Jenkins had been arrested on the same charge. Newspapermen were reluctant to make this public, but they had no choice once Dean Burch called attention to "a report sweeping Washington that the White House is desperately trying to suppress a major news story affecting the national security" — an early instance of incautious use of this phrase by the Republican right. Once the report was public, Jenkins entered a hospital with a diagnosis of "extreme fatigue." Burch and many of Goldwater's other advisers begged him to avail himself of this opportunity to hammer away at what they called a shocking example of immorality on the highest level of the administration. He declined.

Johnson anxiously commissioned an Oliver Quayle survey to find out how many votes the disaster would cost. None to speak of, was Quayle's surprising conclusion, and the sad incident swiftly faded from public memory. Goldwater's compassion was only part of the explanation for this. Another part was that just as people had begun talking about Jenkins they were rocked by three startling developments in foreign affairs. Within forty-eight hours on October 15–16, Khrushchev was stripped of power and deposed, Communist China announced that it had exploded its first atomic bomb, and Sir Alec Douglas-Home's Conservative government fell. The White House press corps talked of Johnsonian luck. He was having a lot of it; when Lady Bird Johnson headed south with a group of southern administration wives on a sixteen-car train christened "The Lady Bird Special," they were met by hecklers — the one reception sure to win sympathy, and votes, elsewhere.

Johnson met the Lady Bird Special in New Orleans, where he then delivered his finest speech of the campaign. It was risky — a fiery appeal for civil rights, delivered against the advice of Senator Russell Long — and that alone would have made it memorable. The last line, however, made it unforgettable. After appealing for an end to bigotry he said that he was going to enforce and observe the Civil Rights Act of 1964 ("I'm not going to let them build up the hate and try to buy my people by appealing to their prejudice"), and then he told how, when Sam Rayburn first went to Congress, he had had a long talk with an ailing southern senator who said he wished he felt well enough to take one more trip home. "I would like to go back down there and make them one more Democratic speech," Johnson quoted the senator as saying. "I just feel I've got one more in me. Poor old state, they haven't heard a real Democratic speech in thirty years. All they ever hear at election time is *nigra, nigra, nigra.*" The audience gasped, recovered, and gave him a five-minute standing ovation.

The record of other LBJ campaign highlights does not always read so well. This is particularly true in regard to Vietnam. Accusing Goldwater of loose talk and loose thinking about nuclear weapons was powerful political medicine. The Democrats couldn't resist ever stronger doses of it. The "Daisy Girl" TV spot was followed by another on September 17 which was so outrageous that it was run but once; it showed a lovely child eating an ice cream cone while a voice told of strontium 90 poisoning the air and reminded viewers that Goldwater had voted against the test ban treaty. The senator's suggestion that atomic bombs might be used to "defoliate" the Ho Chi Minh Trail was cited as an example of his irresponsibility and militarism. But this was a dangerous topic for Johnson. It reminded voters that Americans were in a hot war in Vietnam and that Goldwater hadn't put them there. To keep the momentum of the peace issue, therefore, the President made certain pledges to the country which would not be forgotten.

In Eufaula, Oklahoma, on September 25 he said: "We don't want our American boys to do the fighting for Asian boys. We don't want to get involved . . . and get tied down in a land war in Asia."

Then in Manchester, New Hampshire, on September 28: "I have not thought we were ready for American boys to do the fighting for Asian boys. What I have been trying to do, with the situation that I found, was to get the boys in Vietnam to do their own fighting with our advice and with our equipment. . . . Now we have lost 190 American lives. . . . I often wake up in the night and think about how many I could lose if I made a misstep. . . . It is not any problem to start a war. . . . I know some folks who think I could start one mighty easy. But it is a pretty difficult problem for us to prevent one, and that is what we are trying to do."

In Akron, Ohio, on October 21: ". . . we are not about to send American boys nine or ten thousand miles away from home to do what Asian boys ought to be doing for themselves."

And in Pittsburgh on October 27: "There can be and will be, as long as I am President, peace for all Americans."

In a bitter joke a year later a girl said, "I was told if I voted for Goldwater we would be at war in six months. I did — and we were." Surely a voter whose sole motive was the preservation of peace, and who carefully followed accounts of speeches in the newspapers, would have voted for Johnson and against Goldwater in November 1964. Later he would feel betrayed, as many did. In El Paso during the campaign the President said, "I pledge you here today I will go to any remote corner of the world to meet anyone, any time, to promote freedom and peace," but the fact was that as long as he believed that American forces could impose a military solution on the Communists he rejected all gestures, including some promising ones, from the Viet Cong and the North Vietnamese. The issue during the campaign had seemed clear-cut. Goldwater recommended the dispatch of U.S. soldiers and aircraft to the support of South Vietnam, and Johnson accused him of reckless warmongering. The President appeared to be sincere. Yet it is difficult to think of any military proposal by Goldwater which Johnson had not taken, despite his vows to the contrary, by the following summer.

On November 3 Lyndon Johnson won election to a full term in the White House. He and Hubert Humphrey carried forty-four states and the District of Columbia, with an aggregate of 486 electoral votes. Goldwater and Congressman William E. Miller took Arizona, Mississippi, Alabama, South Carolina, Louisiana, and Georgia, with 52 electoral votes. The Democrats also swept the congressional races. They won 28 of the 35 senatorial seats, giving them 68 to the Republicans' 32, and picked up 41 House seats. They now dominated the House by better than a two-thirds majority, 295 to 140.

The Republicans did make a net gain of one statehouse, but they still had only 17 governors to 33 for the Democrats.

GOLDWATER FOR HALLOWEEN jeered one campaign bumper sticker that had been popular in Washington. Not all the cars displaying it had been owned by Democrats. On election day this writer lunched with Earl Warren in his chambers. The most vivid memory of that occasion was the vehemence with which the Chief Justice expressed the hope that Goldwater would be beaten soundly. Like many another GOP moderate, Warren wanted to see a total rout of the Goldwater conservatives. When disaster befell them the Republicans confirmed a theory of long standing, that their feuds are far more savage than those among Democrats. The conservatives had not only lost an election; in many cases they found themselves being cut dead by members of their own party.

Perhaps Richard Nixon best expressed the frustration and confusion among Republican regulars. Two days after the election he excoriated Nelson Rockefeller, charging that Rockefeller's refusal to help the Goldwater campaign had cost it votes. He called the New York governor a "divider." By the following Tuesday Nixon was having second thoughts. He urged his fellow Republicans to reject "right-wing extremism" while finding a place for all "responsible viewpoints," from liberal to conservative. Yet Nixon's observations were no longer compelling, even among his fellow Republicans. Unlike Rockefeller, he had campaigned tirelessly for the ticket, and apparently it had been a wasted effort. He had collected a lot of IOUs, but it was highly unlikely that they would ever prove valuable.

These were quiet years for Nixon, and in many ways they were good ones. He was making a lot of money. He had time to read and reflect. Except when he was speaking he saw as much of his family as fathers in private life. On the Sunday of that week that the campaign opened, Checkers, the little black and white cocker spaniel that he had turned into a political asset in 1952, died at the age of twelve, and he was there to comfort his daughters. (In October, while he was campaigning in Iowa, he was given another cocker and urged to call it Checkers II, but he gave it away; there was only one Checkers.) Eight weeks after the election his daughter Tricia led the parade at the International Debutante Ball in New York. He escorted her. Next day, the last day but one in 1964, he put a headstone over the grave of Checkers. To many it seemed symbolic.

Until November 1964 Lyndon Johnson had presided in the shadow of President Kennedy, but now he had been elected President in his own right. The hold of the Kennedy legend on the American imagination was still powerful — two of the most charismatic men on Capitol Hill were Robert Kennedy, the new senator from New York, as he now was, and Senator Edward M. Kennedy of Massachusetts, who had been swept back into office by over 900,000 votes — but Johnson was now number one, and the city began to reflect it. Among the songs heard most frequently in bars were "The Eyes of Texas" and "The Yellow Rose of Texas." Middle-aged men wearing cowboy boots and five-gallon hats with their business suits milled around in the lobby of the Washington Hotel on Fifteenth Street, beside the Treasury Building. Washington began to remind visitors of a frontier town, but then, so did the country; the wide-open, anything-goes 1960s were under way.

In 1964 Rudi Gernreich, the California designer, introduced the topless bathing suit, which led to all sorts of things. On a certain level of night club entertainment "topless" women employees became a feature attraction and then a commonplace; in the tawdry Washington cabarets down by the National Archives, as in other American metropolises, waitresses strode about with naked breasts swinging. Next Mary Quant created the miniskirt in London. Girls and many women wore skirts which shrank inch by tantalizing inch as the decade grew older, until, when the microskirt arrived, they had ceased to be tantalizing; all but the most handsome legs had lost their appeal.

Nudity was becoming fashionable in the theater, and as the mid-1960s wore on, seminudity became chic in society. Transparent, or "see-through" dresses were the new thing. Yves Saint Laurent brought out gauze shifts with coy sequins guarding the nipples and the crotch. In Italy the couturier Forquet created a South Seas skirt slung precariously on the hips; for a blouse he substituted a string of beads. Timid women wore either a flesh-colored something called a body stocking underneath, or "fun-derwear" — flashy, gay-colored undergarments to be glimpsed through gauze — but the more daring (and better-endowed) flaunted the works. Naked midriffs reached higher and lower. When the Smithsonian Institution acquired some of the more fantastic new gowns, Republican Congressman H. R. Gross of Iowa rose in the House to protest.

Both sexes in the rising generation insisted upon their right to say whatever they thought "relevant," relevance, like commitment, being one of the new things. Berkeley witnessed the rise of the Free Speech Movement, or the FSM, as it was known in California. That in turn led to the first great student-administration confrontation of the 1960s. The FSM, a coalition formed in the late summer of 1964 by undergraduates, graduate students, and junior faculty, ran the gamut ideologically from Goldwaterism to Maoism. All were united against a university prohibition of on-campus solicitation for political or civil rights demonstrations to be mounted off campus. Mobilizing under the leadership of Mario Savio, a twenty-two-year-old philosophy major from New York, the FSM reached the remarkable conclusion that the university's board of regents was trying to convert the campus into a concentration camp. The purpose of the conspiracy, as they saw it, was to make Berkeley a vast trade school turning out white-collar technicians useful to the establishment — industry, banks, publishing houses, the military, conservative labor unions. Savio cried, "The time has come to put our bodies on the machine and stop it!"

On September 14, 1964, a week before the opening of fall classes, the disorders began, and neither Berkeley nor any other American university would ever be the same. Those who called the FSM Communistic missed the point. It was anarchic, and it scorned all dialectic. A research fellow who approved of the movement explained, "All the old labels are out; if there were any orthodox Communists here, they would be a moderating influence." The movement's contempt for rationalism was at times ludicrous. When police dragged Savio and eight hundred of his followers out of Sproul Hall, the epicenter of the revolt, he cried, "This is wonderful! We'll bring the university to our terms!"

One lazy day the following March a barefoot, long-haired youth paraded through the main gate of the Berkeley campus holding aloft a placard emblazoned in blue with a single four-letter word. He wasn't a student. His name was John J. Thompson, and he was an unpublished poet, a member of Berkeley's so-called "hidden community" — unknown writers and political militants who would be blamed for much of the unrest there later in the decade. The following day a dozen other youths appeared carrying signs with similar messages; one shouted his cherished word into a campus microphone; another read a passage from *Lady Chatterley's Lover* aloud to an arresting officer. No one in the movement went bail for him and his friends. The campus newspaper deprecated this "filthy speech movement." To use another phrase which was entering the language, they suspected the odd crusaders of putting them on.

Yet both their demonstrations and the new uses of taboo words appear to have been aspects of a general revolt against constraints which characterized the 1960s. Thompson and his friends may have been pulling the FSM's leg, but many serious writers were in earnest about their right to use language which until now had been proscribed. They believed that the Supreme Court agreed with them (they were right), and in the long run their impact on society may prove to be more lasting than Savio's civil disobedience. Appearing in print, locker room language was next heard on the stage — for example, in *Who's Afraid of Virginia Woolf?*, which after 664 performances on Broadway became a film in 1966 — and then in mixed company, among the sophisticated at first, swiftly followed by the young. In what had once been called polite society one heard, frequently from the loveliest lips, short Anglo-Saxon words formerly limited to unmixed company. The effect on the inhibited older generation was often electrifying.

Like the Pill and the new nudity, this reflected an evolving life-style and a new morality. To many in the older generation it seemed to be no morality at all, and they came to identify it with excessive hair and communes. But the forbidden fruit was just as tasty on the palate of Goldwater's admirers in the Young Americans for Freedom. YAF members never marched in antiwar demonstrations or read *Ramparts,* but when the lights went out they were as active as the most erotic hippy. One survey of casual adulterers found that a majority were short-haired and politically conservative. A Los Angeles entrepreneur who dealt with a community of conservative hedonists told a reporter, "This is the America you don't hear about. It's clean-cut people who don't wear sandals and beards — guys and girls living very normal lives. It's almost blasphemous how American it is."

Colleges had long provided grounds suitable for pairing off, but until the mid-1960s finding a member of the opposite sex off campus who was attractive, agreeable, and prurient had been time-consuming and rather expensive. Now that, too, was changing. Two years before the Johnson-Goldwater race, Grossinger's Hotel in the Catskills held its first weekend for singles only. It was the beginning, though no one knew it then, of another movement. In 1964 a lonesome ensign named Michael G. O'Harro, stationed in Arlington, Virginia, established the beginning of a fortune and a way of life by throwing a party for other young unmarried people — officers, professional men, airline stewardesses, teachers, models, secretaries, and career girls. Three years later O'Harro was back in civilian life and president of an organization called the Junior Officers and Professional Association, with thirty thousand members, twelve local chapters, and a staff of fifty. By then it was possible to vacation at resorts for singles only, take Bahaman cruises or European tours in groups which accepted only bachelors and unmarried girls, and read such singles-only magazines as O'Harro's JOPA *Niteletter*. And O'Harro had competitors. In San Francisco the lonely could meet at Paoli's; Chicago had The Store, Dallas the TGIF (Thank God It's Friday), and Manhattan Mr. Laff's and Friday's.

The logical consequence of all this was the construction of apartment complexes in which the unmarried could rent apartments and visit one another at all hours, and that was what happened. In part it was a reflection of the balkanizing of generations — the tendency of people in one age group to go off by themselves, thus engendering misunderstandings and what would soon be known as "gaps." The first to do it were the elderly, not the young. The earliest "retirement town" was built by Del Webb in Arizona in 1960. Like O'Harro's enterprise it was a tremendous success, inspiring imitators and, in 1965, the first singles community, the South Bay Club in the Los Angeles suburb of Torrance. South Bay's 248 apartments were all rented while it was still going up. Ultimately the firm built thirteen such complexes, including one in Phoenix, with eight thousand tenants who could play bridge, engage in round-table discussions, attend barbecues, stage masked balls, participate in wine tastings, and cohabit without encountering anyone else's husband or wife.

Understandably, a popular topic in the singles-only round table discussions was birth control. Another was wedlock, often put as a proposition: "Marriage — Is It Defensible?" Matrimony was only one of many social institutions which were under attack in the mid-Sixties. Nothing was sacred any more; during Holy Week in 1966 *Time* asked on its cover, "Is God

Dead?" thereby generating an intense theological debate and one memorable bumper sticker: GOD IS ALIVE AND HIDING IN ARGENTINA. People who read *Time* — or anything else — were belittled as old-fashioned and "linear" in Marshall McLuhan's *The Gutenberg Galaxy: The Making of Typographic Man* (1962) and *Understanding Media: The Extensions of Man* (1964).

The iconoclasm of the mid-Sixties did not always pay. Ralph Ginzburg published *Eros* in 1962; the post office ruled that it was smut and he was sentenced to five years in prison. In 1964 he brought out *Fact;* it contained material about Barry Goldwater which was not factual, and when Goldwater sued he was awarded $75,000. In 1967 Ginzburg issued *Avant-Garde;* it flopped. Another loser, though no one would have guessed it in the beginning, was Cassius Clay. After winning the world's championship by knocking out Sonny Liston in one minute flat, the fastest kayo in heavyweight title history, Clay confused fight fans by becoming a Black Muslim, changing his name to Muhammad Ali, refusing induction into the Army on grounds of conscience, and then, like Ginzburg, going to jail.

But anyone could stumble in this hazardous time. The Strategic Air Command, which as the guardian of the U.S. nuclear striking capacity was supposed to be discreet, scared the country, not to mention Europe, when one of its B-52s collided with a jet tanker and dumped four hydrogen bombs in Spanish waters. Norman Mailer was reputed to know something about the writing of fiction, yet in 1965 *An American Dream,* his first novel in ten years, was mercilessly panned by critics. Lyndon Johnson was said to be determined to suppress vulgarian tendencies in order to achieve presidential dignity, but after undergoing an operation he yanked out his shirt so news cameramen could photograph the scar. James Pike, Episcopal bishop of California, resigned when accused of heresy, took up spiritualism, wrote a book about it called *The Other Side,* got lost in the Judean desert, and was found dead in a kneeling position. Betty Grable and Harry James, after twenty-two years of being regarded as the happiest couple in Beverly Hills, were divorced in Las Vegas.

Nothing, it appeared, was as it seemed. In a gubernatorial election Alabamans voted "for Lurleen" to "let George do it." Black militants blamed black lawlessness on tension between the races, but in 1964 the toughest enforcers of the law in the Crown Heights area of Brooklyn were the members of an organization of middle-class Negro vigilantes. The belief that Americans go to college to make more money took its lumps when the *Wall Street Journal* complained that few Ivy League graduates were going into business; instead they were taking jobs in churches, labor unions, the Peace Corps, and civil rights organizations. Even the cold war wasn't what it had been. In 1966 the United States and the Soviet Union introduced direct air service between Moscow and New York with one round trip each week by Pan American and Soviet Aeroflot.

In 1964 *Dr. Strangelove* faded from the marquees, to be supplanted, in 1965, by *Dr. Zhivago,* which inspired fashion fads for huge fur hats, thigh-high boots, and coat hems that swept the ground. The skateboard became the successor to the hula hoop in 1965, when its manufacturers grossed a hundred million dollars; a skateboard meet at Anaheim, California, was televised by the three networks, and the circulation of the *Skateboard Quarterly* reached fifty thousand. Then the dippy boards faded as the next toy sensation, the super ball, bounced into view. Bicycles returned to what would be a more lasting popularity that same year, when six million were sold and the Long Island Railroad installed bike racks for commuters.

An Associated Press writer observed of 1965 that "the more things were out, the more they were in." There were demands for, among other unlikely articles, tasseled lamps, and sailor suits. Bell-bottoms came on strong. Peter Max, a twenty-five-year-old commercial artist, had a vision of "a huge monumental wave of youth — the youth revolution coming," and in anticipation of it he created psychedelic art. Within five years his designs on decals, posters, scarves, etc., would provide him with an annual income of two million dollars. Pop art masterpieces included a woman's girdle with an enormous eye painted on the back. "Camp" entered the language and was applied to such artifacts as feather boas, antimacassars, bubble gum cards, Shirley Temple photographs, and souvenirs of Atlantic City. Humphrey Bogart and Jean Harlow films enjoyed revivals, and for a while girls again tried to look like Harlow. Big films included *Lord Jim, The Agony and the Ecstasy,* and two broad farces: *Cat Ballou* and *What's New, Pussycat?*

Lou Harris reported a "growing disenchantment with television on the part of the affluent, better-educated section of the adult American public." All three networks appeared to be searching for the lowest common denominator in popular taste, and they were virtually tied in the Nielsen ratings. ("It was inevitable," observed the *New Yorker.* "It shines with the clarity of a mathematical law.") The debasement of network programming was particularly painful at CBS, which in the great days of Edward R. Murrow had appealed to intelligent viewers. Now, under James T. Aubrey Jr., CBS offered mystery dramas, rural comedies, and peepshow sex.

Adlai Stevenson and Winston Churchill died in 1965. J. Edgar Hoover was still alive and running the FBI, but he was becoming senescent. FBI figures indicated that the national crime rate was rising 11 percent a year, and the President's Commission on Law Enforcement and Administration of Justice concluded that possibly three times as much crime was committed as was reported. Social protest was a growing category for law infractions. The anti-Vietnam teach-ins, which began with a twelve-hour all-night seminar at the University of Michigan on March 24, 1965, were perfectly legal, but that was not always true of the nude-ins, lie-ins, and love-ins which followed. Leaders of the Brooklyn chapter of CORE threatened to spoil the opening day of the New York World's Fair on April 22, 1964, with a stall-in — snarling traffic by allowing thousands of cars to run out of gas in the middle of it. They succeeded in cutting the opening day crowd from about 250,000 to 92,646. Nearly three hundred were arrested, including James Farmer, national director of CORE.

The level of violence in the country continued to appall. In the summer of 1966 an itinerant worker named Richard Speck murdered eight student nurses in Chicago. Two weeks later Charles Whitman, an honor student at the University of Texas, climbed to the top of the university's twenty-seven-story tower in Austin and opened fire on passersby below, killing fourteen and wounding thirty, and three months after that an eighteen-year-old student entered the Rose-Mar College of Beauty in Mesa, Arizona, with a pistol and killed four women and a child. He told police he had been inspired by the Chicago and Austin killings. Like Speck and Whitman, he said, he wanted "to get known."

Two legislators from opposite ends of the ideological spectrum were in trouble. Adam Clayton Powell had called a Harlem widow "a bag woman for the police department"; she had been awarded damages, but he ignored the verdict and avoided New York. Senator Tom Dodd of Connecticut was censured by his colleagues for misuse of campaign funds and selling influence to an agent for West German business interests. A New York undercover policeman infiltrated a conspiracy to blow up the Statue of Liberty, the Liberty Bell, and the Washington Monument; the causes of the various plotters ranged from Quebec independence and admiration for Fidel Castro to Negro rights and support of North Vietnam. In New York a Vacation Exchange served as a contact for homeowners who wanted to swap houses during holidays, and from a small city in eastern Massachusetts came the first word of young married couples who swapped spouses. A travel agency advertised a judo tour of Japan: two sweaty weeks for $1,396. President Sarah Gibson Blanding of Vassar told her 1,450 girls that she expected them either to abstain from sexual intercourse or leave the campus. Jack Valenti told an audience of advertising men that "I sleep each night a little better, a little more confidently because Lyndon Johnson is my President."

The Dallas trial of Jack Ruby opened on February 17, 1964, and ended March 14 with a guilty verdict. His lawyer, Melvin Belli, screamed: "This was a kangaroo court, a railroad court, and everyone knew it." Ruby would die of cancer in jail on January 3, 1967. Senator J. William Fulbright delivered a major speech on foreign policy, warning that unless the United States "cut loose from established myths" he would break with the administration. Pope Paul VI spent an October day in New York and addressed the United Nations. Hubert Humphrey, the new Vice President, seemed determined to demonstrate superloyalty to Johnson; echoing an Avis car rental ad, he said, "I'm number two and I have to try harder." Some observers wondered whether the winning Democratic ticket was developing a sadomasochistic relationship. The President almost seemed to enjoy humiliating his Vice President. "Boys, I just reminded Hubert I've got his balls in my pocket," he told reporters.

In 1966 *The Sound of Music* became one of the greatest hits in movie history. People went around saying, "You better believe it." Television was now almost 100 percent color during prime time. The two pro football leagues merged. *The Valley of the Dolls* and *How to Avoid Probate* were best-sellers. *Cabaret* and *Mame* were big on Broadway. David Merrick put $500,000 into *Breakfast at Tiffany's*; it failed. A clothing firm marketed disposable paper dresses which came in cans, cost a dollar or two, and were discarded when dirty. New male cosmetics included false eyelashes — called "Executive Eyelash" — and an after-shave powder puff — "Brass Knuckles." The summer of 1966 was spoiled for a lot of travelers by the longest and costliest airline strike ever; five major airlines were grounded for forty-three days. That fall the Dodgers lost four in a row — the World Series — to Baltimore. A wacky bumper sticker in California announced: MARY POPPINS IS A JUNKIE.

Labor troubles left New Yorkers without newspapers for 279 days in the mid-Sixties. The *World-Telegram, Journal-American,* and *Herald Tribune* merged into one paper, the *World Journal Tribune* — it was called the *Wijit* — which failed after nine months. After 190 years, superstition finally killed the two-dollar bill; the Treasury Department stopped printing the bills on August 10, 1966, citing "a lack of public demand."

The fall elections of 1966 marked a political turning point. Resentment against ghetto riots and civil rights demonstrations had finally coalesced, making white backlash a potent political force for the first time. Combined with inflation, high interest rates, a scarcity of mortgage money, and the rising cost of living, backlash provided Republican candidates with a powerful springboard. George Romney and Nelson Rockefeller were re-elected with huge majorities. Among the new Republican faces in the Senate were Howard Baker Jr. of Tennessee, Edward W. Brooke of Massachusetts, Mark Hatfield of Oregon, and Charles H. Percy of Illinois; new Republican governors included Ronald Reagan of California and Spiro T. Agnew of Maryland. Altogether the Republicans picked up three seats in the Senate, eight new governors, and 47 seats in the House of Representatives, more than they had lost in 1964.

But by then Johnson had lost interest in legislation. Increasingly, he had become preoccupied with the Vietnam War, believing that its outcome would determine his place in history. Nearly every night at 3 A.M., according to his brother, Sam Ealy Johnson Jr., he would "crawl out of bed, wearily slip on his robe and slippers, then go down to the Situation Room in the basement of the White House to get the latest reports coming in from Saigon."

He was increasingly isolated. Robert S. McNamara, Secretary of Defense in this administration as he had been in Kennedy's, was losing confidence in the ability of bombing to bring the enemy to his knees. McNamara was now engrossed in a fantastic scheme for building an electronic barrier across the waist of Vietnam to stop infiltration from the North. When he abandoned that, his faith in military technology would collapse. Soon the chief White House consultant on Vietnam would be Walt Rostow, whose relation to the embattled and lonely war President, said another aide, was "like Rasputin to a tsar under siege." The conservative 90th Congress would join Rostow in goading Johnson on, passing huge military appropriation bills, encouraging him to sink ever deeper in the Vietnamese mire.

By then it all seemed inevitable. Yet it hadn't been. After his rout of Goldwater, Johnson's consensus had been genuine. The nation had been behind him. His goals had been the country's goals. It had been a time of great hope for him and for the American people, and few gauged correctly the threat from "a raggedy-ass little fourth-rate country," as Johnson once called Vietnam. One member of the First Family was worried, though. "I just hope," Mrs. Johnson had said in the middle of 1965, "that foreign problems do not keep on mounting. They do not represent Lyndon's kind of Presidency."

THIRTY-ONE

A Dream of Greatness—
and Disenchantment

PRESIDENT KENNEDY had devoted his inaugural address to foreign affairs; President Johnson's four-thousand-word inaugural — which was delivered so slowly and deliberately that one observer said it sounded as though the President were dictating to a stonemason — almost ignored events abroad. The same was true of his second State of the Union message; Vietnam was covered in exactly 131 words. Considering what was to come, the emphasis on economy was odd. ("Last year we saved almost 35 hundred million dollars by eliminating waste in the national government. [Applause.] And I intend to do better this year. [Louder Applause.]") Johnson said that he wanted to be remembered as "the education President and the health President." He intended to complete the unfinished business of the New Deal and the Fair Deal.

He was also going to keep faith with Kennedy. From the New Frontier he had inherited four big bills: civil rights, a proposed tax cut, Medicare, and federal aid to education. Priority went to the first two, but he shepherded all of them through Congress. The battle for Medicare was a spectacular confrontation between a President who was a master parliamentarian and the mighty American Medical Association lobby. In 1945 President Truman had appeared personally before a joint session of Congress to ask for a comprehensive medical insurance program; the AMA had beaten him soundly, and he had taken it hard. This time, five presidential administrations and sixteen congressional sessions later, the AMA doctors came forward with something called Bettercare, which was to be voluntary, handled by the private insurance industry — and wholly inadequate, for the number of Americans over sixty-five had more than doubled since the Truman years.

To battle Johnson the AMA employed twenty-three full-time lobbyists and spent $5,000 a day. The President countered with personal telephone calls and invitations to the White House. He twisted arms and he twisted hearts. On July 30, 1965, just 204 days after Johnson had asked for Medicare, he signed the bill in Independence with eighty-one-year-old Harry Truman beaming alongside. On July 1, 1966, Medicare eligibility came to 160,000 elderly hospital patients in the United States. A New Jersey embroidery worker named Eugene Schneider, sixty-five, entered Polyclinic Hospital in New York at 12:01 that Friday, and treatment for his eye was paid for by the Social Security Administration, making him and Mrs. Robert Avery of Napierville, Illinois, the first Medicare patients. An Associated Press survey indicated that the program had increased hospital occupancy by 3 percent — about 100,000 new patients a week.

Five days after his call for Medicare Johnson had sent Congress another historic message, "Toward Full Education Opportunity," asking a billion dollars for public and parochial schools. Providing federal money for Catholic education was a profound break with the past and a guarantee of searing debate in the House. But Johnson knew that of the forty million American children in school, about six million were in overcrowded parochial schools — schools which would have to be replaced with public money if the church abandoned them. Moreover, excluding them had alienated Catholic legislators on the Hill, who had retaliated by voting against federal funds for public schools. Johnson had decided to include all, and he let it be known that he wanted no amendments, no changing of so much as a comma. All things were possible for him in the 89th Congress — the "Xerox Congress," Goldwater was beginning to call it — and the measure went through both houses of Congress in eighty-seven days. Designating it "the most important bill I will ever sign," the President staged this signing ceremony in the one-room Texas schoolhouse he had attended as a child, with his teacher, now seventy-two and retired, beside him.

A voting rights bill was next, a response to the ever more insistent civil rights movement. The measure was ready for his signature August 6. By now a blizzard of Great Society legislation was sweeping through Congress — over forty bills for education alone, including 2.4 billion dollars for college aid, more education legislation than in all American history until then. There were Johnsonian programs to fight heart disease, strokes, cancer, water pollution, air pollution, roadside billboards, and auto junkyards. Congress established a Department of Housing and Urban Development, a National Foundation for the Arts and the Humanities, and an Administration on Aging. A High-Speed Ground Transportation Act opened the way to a study of mass transit problems. The immigration service was reformed. A big excise tax cut — 4.7 billion dollars — was approved. Farm legislation and a Public Works and Economic Development Act gave the federal government a strong role in dealing with the changing face of the land for the first time since the 1930s.

Over 900 million dollars was set aside to deal with America's oldest rural slum, Appalachia. Under the ebullient leadership of Sargent Shriver, who had been the first director of the Peace Corps, the new Office of Economic Opportunity declared war on poverty. OEO programs included Job Opportunities in the Business Sector (JOBS), to provide special help in job placement for the hard-core unemployed; Head Start, for preschool children from poor families, which brightened the future for 1,300,000 of them in its first year; Volunteers in Service to America (VISTA), in effect a domestic peace corps; the Neighborhood Youth Corps, providing a half-million part-time jobs for teen-agers; Upward Bound, enrolling precollege youths in campus programs; the Community Action Program (CAP), coordinating local health, housing, and employment programs and offering the poor free legal advice; Foster Grandparents, to work with children without homes; and agencies to work with Indians, migrants, and seasonal workers.

Critics christened the Washington office building in which the OEO leased seven floors "The Poverty Palace." Republican Congressman Albert Quie of Minnesota said the OEO undertaking "could become not just a national disgrace but a national catastrophe." Richard Nixon said, "The war on poverty has been first in promises, first in politics, first in press releases — and last in performances." And even Shriver conceded that administration of the most successful of the OEO programs, Head Start, was marred in one state (Mississippi) by nepotism, conflict of interest, misuse of government automobiles, and payments to people who weren't even in the state.

But time would be kind to the OEO, as it was to Roosevelt's WPA. In five years the war on poverty programs would play a key role in lifting thirteen million people out of pauperism. Another part was played by Johnsonian prosperity. The Great Society appeared to be on its way, and Americans seemed appreciative; at the end of Johnson's second year in office the public opinion surveys reported that no other President in their thirty years of polling had received such strong, consistent support throughout the country.

His landslide triumph over Goldwater would have tempted another President to ride roughshod over Congress. Not Johnson; he remembered vividly how Roosevelt, after his great victory in 1936, had been humbled by the defeat of his plan to reorganize the Supreme Court. "I've watched the Congress from either the inside or the outside, man and boy, for more than forty years," he said in the aftermath of the 1964 election, "and I've never seen a Congress that didn't eventually take the measure of the President it was dealing with." Rather than aim for a spectacular Hundred Days, he said, he would send each bill to the Hill only when the legislators were ready for it. He explained: "It's like a bottle of bourbon. If you take a glass at a time, it's fine. But if you drink the whole bottle in one evening, you have troubles. I plan to take a sip at a time and enjoy myself."

The final result was stunning. When the first session of the 89th Congress rose on October 23, it had approved 89 major administration bills and rejected just two: home rule for the District of Columbia and repeal of Section 14(b) of the Taft-Hartley Act, permitting states to ban union shop contracts — and it had been by no means clear on the Hill that the President really wanted the Taft-Hartley change. He was entitled to rest on his laurels. He didn't do it. Ever dissatisfied, he kept casting about for new ways to dominate the news and convert his critics.

One of the oddest was a summit meeting with Soviet Premier Alexei N. Kosygin in Hollybush, the turreted stone home of the president of Glassboro State College in New Jersey. Glassboro was chosen because it was exactly halfway between Washington and U.N. headquarters in New York, where Kosygin was staying; neither leader would call on the other; the little campus was a compromise. The two leaders had no agenda — had, indeed, nothing specific to talk about. Afterward Johnson said, "It helps to try to reason together. That is why we went to Hollybush. Reasoning together was the spirit of Hollybush." There was little else to say, other than that "the exchange of views once more revealed profound differences between the United States and the Soviet Union." The President's popularity rating soared just the same. The very fact that the two men, with nuclear arsenals at their disposal, had talked together seemed to reassure people.

Yet there were many who were not reassured, who regarded Johnson with scorn and often with contempt. LBJ-haters continued to be found in large numbers among the creative communities in large cities and on university faculties. Visiting the United States in 1965, the British journalist Henry Fairlie wrote: "I have found nothing more strange or unattractive than the way in which American intellectuals take pleasure in reviling President Johnson." Fairlie noted that the strictures were "personal" and reflected a "fastidious disdain for the man. . . . He is a slob, one of them said to me. . . . Others say much of the same, if less briefly."

Dwight Macdonald, one of the most caustic of them, wrote of "tasteless, crude" Lyndon Johnson and minted a word, "midcult," to mock the President's middlebrow taste. Macdonald and others like him ridiculed Mrs. Johnson because her favorite television program was *Gunsmoke*. They despised LBJ for enjoying the New Christy Minstrels, telling photographers to "Use my left profile," disliking Peter Hurd's portrait of him, having a daughter who changed her name from Lucy to Luci, and calling the work of serious artists "artsy." Their discontent spread to the much larger number of Americans who were vaguely offended by Johnson's mountebank manner. Millions of others were susceptible because they had loved John Kennedy, grieved for him still, and irrationally felt that Johnson was a usurper. To all these, eventually, were added the vast mass of Americans who felt troubled or even threatened by the escalating violence in the Negro slums in large cities and the growing turmoil on campuses. Johnson's insistence that he was in charge made him an inviting target, and they let fly at him.

At the end of his unprecedented string of legislative successes on the

Hill in 1965 he entered Bethesda Naval Hospital for the removal of a stone-obstructed gallbladder. Convalescing, he brooded about the newspapers, which had been baiting him, and his taunters, "those people out there." In exasperation he blurted out, "What do they want — what *really* do they want? I'm giving them boom times and more good legislation than anybody else did, and what do they do — attack and sneer! Could FDR do better? Could anybody do better? What *do* they want?"

Senator Eugene McCarthy, whose role in the collapse of Johnson's consensus would become crucial, found half of the solution to the riddle when he suggested that Johnson was a kind of anachronistic President, providing New Deal remedies — social welfare legislation — for a nation whose dilemmas were very different. It was arguable, for example, that affluence, not poverty, was the great domestic challenge of the 1960s. McCarthy said that the President completely misjudged the temper of the liberal intellectuals: "he keeps going to them with the list of bills he's passed — the laundry list — and he doesn't know that they aren't interested any more."

Johnson raged, "Don't they know I'm the only President they've got?" Sometimes he would add, "Don't they know there's a war on?"

They knew. That was the other half of the answer to the riddle.

After the Gulf of Tonkin incidents there was a lull in American activity in Vietnam until November 1, 1964, when five U.S. military advisers were killed and 76 wounded in a Viet Cong mortar attack on an air base at Bienhoa, twenty miles north of Saigon. On Christmas Eve the guerrillas struck again, planting a bomb at the Brink's Hotel in Saigon. American casualties there were two dead and 58 wounded, and Lyndon Johnson's patriotic instincts were aroused. He strode around the White House saying that he wasn't going to let them kill our boys out there, that they were firing on the flag, that he'd show them he wasn't any "Chamberlain umbrella man." Plainly the North Vietnamese were guilty of aggression. ("Aggression is when one country won't let another one alone. Everybody knows when that is happening.") But depending on the United Nations to act would be a mistake. ("It couldn't pour piss out of a boot if the instructions were printed on the heel.") He wasn't going to go down in history as the President who lost Vietnam. The United States had the power to teach these little-biddy, raggedy-ass Communists a lesson. The Tonkin resolution gave him the authority to use it, and if the Viet Cong didn't back off he would do just that.

The difficulty was in deciding which approach to take. This new enemy, being unconventional, resisted conventional military solutions. The mighty American martial establishment wasn't equipped to deal with their hit-and-run tactics. President Kennedy had sent to Vietnam a 400-man Special Forces group, experts in antiguerrilla warfare, but the Joint Chiefs were unenthusiastic about these husky elitists. At one time, of over a hundred American generals in MACV, not one had gone through counter-insurgency training at Fort Bragg, North Carolina. And of all of them, none was more of a traditional soldier than MACV's new commander, William Childs Westmoreland.

What the Chiefs wanted was heavy bombing of North Vietnam. That would bring the enemy to his knees, they told the White House, and it would also bring him to the negotiating table. Clearly the bombing mystique had a powerful hold on the Johnson administration. Why this was so is less obvious. Two influential Democrats, George Ball and John Kenneth Galbraith, had participated in the U.S. Strategic Bombing Survey after World War II. That study had found that Allied bombing had not only failed to cripple German war production; it had strengthened the morale of the German people. And Germany was highly industrialized. If the Air Force had failed there, certainly its chances against the economy of a backward Asian country were at best doubtful.

Not all of Johnson's advisers had faith in the bombardiers. Ball and Galbraith didn't, and they were far from being alone. Early in 1964 the State Department's Policy Planning Council had conducted an exhaustive survey of the bombing question. The conclusion was that bombing North Vietnam would be ineffective, that it wasn't even likely to boost spirits in South Vietnam. Pier de Silva, John Richardson's successor as CIA station chief in Saigon, thought bombs would be useless; so did Westmoreland. As West Point graduates, both men knew that if you brought in planes you would need troops to protect the landing fields — that the decision to bomb would therefore bring the United States in all the way. Early in 1965, CIA analysts in Saigon completed two lengthy new reports on the same issue. The gist of them was that unleashing the bombers would be worse than futile; there was a strong probability that it would boomerang by touching off a massive infiltration of North Vietnamese troops down the Ho Chi Minh Trail.

That should have given the White House pause. At the very least the President ought to have listened intently to the counsels of caution. But something mysterious was happening to the doves, as opponents of escalation were beginning to be known. There were fewer and fewer of them in the halls of power. In October of 1964, when George Ball at State submitted his first memorandum protesting further American involvement in the war, he had plenty of company. Then, one by one, his allies were transferred or eased out of key positions. Roger Hilsman, Averell Harriman, Michael Forrestal, Paul Kattenburg, William Trueheart — all were gone by the time of Johnson's inaugural. Ball stood alone. Maxwell Taylor, who had agreed with Ball about bombing, was still an insider, but Taylor had changed his mind. He now wanted a green light for the Air Force. He thought the U.S. troop level in Vietnam could be controlled and need never rise above 100,000.

Now only one major White House special assistant was still uncommitted. He was McGeorge Bundy, the President's national security adviser.

On January 27, 1965, Bundy proposed that he visit Vietnam as the President's eyes and ears. McNamara concurred, and Johnson's security aide flew to Asia in the first week of February. It was a fateful trip. Bundy was brilliant and experienced, but he had never served in the field. All he knew of war was in memos and reports or on celluloid. The grime and the stench of combat were new to him, and when he encountered them he suffered a physical revulsion. Above all — and this would be decisive — he could not stand the sight of blood.

On the evening of February 5, while Bundy was being feted in Saigon, Spec. 5c Jesse A. Pyle of Marina, California, was taking up sentry duty in a foxhole outside a U.S. stronghold at Pleiku, a mountain town in Vietnam's central highlands. He was still there at 2 A.M. when he saw shadowy figures in black pajamas moving toward him through underbrush. Pyle opened fire; the Viet Cong guerrillas replied with a storm of grenades; Americans in their nearby barracks awoke and joined the fight. The Battle of Pleiku lasted fifteen furious minutes. At the end of it the guerrillas had demolished or damaged sixteen helicopters and six aircraft. Eight U.S. soldiers, Pyle among them, were dead. Another 126 were wounded.

At 2:38 P.M. in Washington, the first account of Pleiku reached the President. After a four-hour National Security Council meeting he ordered Navy jet fighter-bombers from three carriers to attack a Viet Cong staging area at Donghoi, forty miles north of the 17th Parallel. Whether or not the American combat role would grow, he announced, was a decision which "lies with the North Vietnamese aggressors." McNamara said, "I think it's quite clear that this was a test of will." But the most unexpected result of Pleiku was its impact on the President's national security adviser, who, being on the spot, visited the wounded and came away deeply moved. He flew home a hawk. "Well, they made a believer out of you, didn't they?" the President said to him. "A little fire will do that."

Ball was still opposed to the bombing. Vice President Hubert Humphrey was also against it, and he expressed himself so forcefully that Johnson, who now regarded such doubts as unmanly, excluded him from National Security Council meetings. The United States had entered the critical period of decision. McNamara later remarked that all the U.S. errors in Vietnam — and he conceded that there had been many — were committed by the late spring of 1965; after that, he said, there was no way out. In Washington it seemed that the Viet Cong was bent upon provoking the U.S. into massive intervention. Less than three days after Pleiku, black-pajamaed guerrillas blew up the Viet Cuong Hotel, a barracks for American soldiers in the Annamese port of Quinhon; 23 enlisted men were killed and 21 injured. Johnson, infuriated, gave orders for a three-hour bombing of Chanh Hoa and Chap Lee, military depots in North Vietnam.

On February 11 the Viet Cong hit Quinhon again. This time LBJ stayed his hand for forty-eight hours. When he did move, however, it was to take a long step down the road of escalation. Henceforth American reprisals from the air were not to be on a one-for-one, tit-for-tat basis. Instead Johnson ordered a sustained bombing campaign against the North, to be mounted without regard for provocation. Its code name was to be Operation Rolling Thunder. The justification for it was set forth in a sixty-four-page white paper, *Aggression from the North*, which, the State Department said, established "beyond question that North Viet Nam is carrying out a carefully conceived plan of aggression against the South." To defend Da Nang air base, fifty miles southeast of Hue, from which Rolling Thunder would be launched, General Westmoreland asked for two Marine Corps battalions. These 3,500 marines were the first U.S. ground troops to be committed to the war. On March 8 they splashed ashore under overcast skies at Nam O Beach, three miles from Da Nang. Awaiting them were ten smiling Vietnamese girls with flowers.

Elsewhere the landing was more controversial. In Moscow two thousand demonstrators hurled rocks and bricks at the American embassy; two western foreign correspondents were roughed up there. In the United States the teach-ins spread and reached a climax in Washington, where Bundy agreed to debate his critics on a program which would be broadcast to over a hundred campuses. (At the last minute he had to withdraw; the President needed him to deal with another foreign crisis in the Dominican Republic.) The administration sent a "truth team" to visit universities and reply to the charges of faculty doves. Dean Rusk caustically told the American Society of International Law, "I sometimes wonder at the gullibility of educated men and the stubborn disregard of plain facts by men who are supposed to be helping our young to learn — especially to learn how to think."

But the more the critics of the war learned about its South Vietnamese ally the stronger their reservations became. Half of U.S. aid, they learned, was going into the Saigon black market. Vietnamese youths from opulent families were buying their way out of the draft. The desertion rate in the South Vietnamese army was 15 percent. And the politicians in Saigon seemed to have a genius for bad timing. It seemed that at every critical moment in the conflict whatever government was in power would be overthrown by a new regime. Johnson, angered, told his staff that he wanted "no more of this coup shit," but he got it just the same. On February 21, 1965, Lieutenant General Nguyen Khanh was ousted and succeeded by Phan Huy Quat, a physician. (The secretary general of the junta behind Quat was Major General Nguyen Van Thieu, from this point forward a man to watch.) The Quat administration lasted exactly 111 days. When it toppled (the ninth change of government since Diem's assassination) the new prime minister was the colorful chief of the Vietnamese air force, Nguyen Cao Ky, and Thieu was deputy prime minister.

Each new sign of instability in Saigon increased the ranks of the doves, who were rapidly replacing the Republicans as Lyndon Johnson's most effective political opposition. Former Secretary of the Army Cyrus Vance said misgivings about the war were "threatening to tear the United States apart," and in the Senate Frank Church of Idaho, one of the first senatorial doves, warned: "There are limits to what we can do in helping any government surmount a Communist uprising. If the people themselves will not support the government in power, we cannot save it . . . The Saigon government is losing its war, not for lack of equipment, but for lack of any internal cohesion."

That was not yet a popular position, however. When Johnson asked for a 700-million-dollar supplemental appropriation to finance the escalation, the House approved, 408 to 7, in twenty-four hours, and the Senate followed suit, 88 to 3, in another twenty-four hours. In the popular press a certain stigma was attached to disapproval of American participation in the war. When Majority Leader Mike Mansfield gloomily told the Senate that it might go on "for four, five, or ten years," an Associated Press writer called this an "extreme view." (It was to be eight years.) In its annual review of that year's news the AP, ordinarily the most impartial of institutions, also reported that opponents of the war were giving aid and comfort to enemies of the United States. And when Senator Fulbright held Vietnam hearings in April, providing a forum for such distinguished critics of administration policy as George Kennan and General James Gavin, twenty-four NBC-TV stations refused to carry their network's coverage of them, while CBS-TV blacked them out entirely.

The war was becoming steadily hotter for the Americans in Vietnam. On March 30 a Vietnamese driver parked a black Citroën in front of the U.S. embassy in Saigon and roared off on a companion's motorcycle. In the car were 250 pounds of explosive, which went off at 10:55 A.M., tearing a hole in the side of the building and killing seventeen embassy employees. The next day U.S. planes bombed six North Vietnamese radar installations. It was their fifteenth raid across the border between the two Vietnams since Pleiku. The Viet Cong countered with more explosives. A bicycle loaded with nitroglycerin was parked one evening on the bank of the Saigon River beside My Canh, a floating restaurant popular with foreigners. When it went off forty-four people, twelve Americans among them, were killed. Still the U.S. troop buildup went on. At the beginning of the year there had been some 25,000 American servicemen in the country; by the end of spring the number had tripled.

On June 9 the White House announced that General Westmoreland had been authorized to send U.S. soldiers and marines into battle "when other effective reserves are not available and when in his judgment the general military situation urgently requires it." Four days later Westmoreland decided that circumstances at Dong Xoai, a district capital sixty miles north of Saigon, justified American intervention. After a clash in the night, 1,200 paratroopers of the U.S. 173rd Airborne joined 1,600 Vietnamese and Australians in aggressive pursuit of the guerrillas. Westmoreland called this a "search and destroy" mission, a phrase which would be used henceforth to describe the strategy, which evolved in these months, of seeking out and then wiping out Viet Cong bands. It was to be a costly and often frustrating process. The Dong Xoai melee was characteristic of the war; after the smoke had cleared it was impossible to say which side had come off best. All the commander of the 173rd could be sure of was that he had lost nineteen men. The casualty lists swiftly lengthened, for the Viet Cong were in the second month of their spring offensive. Long afterward Westmoreland would describe this as the time that the enemy won the war. No one knew it at the time, however. That same month Westmoreland asked Washington for forty-four fresh battalions and authority to use them as he saw fit, and he could not guarantee that even that would do the job.

It was in this period that Lyndon Johnson's deviousness and secretiveness began to shrivel public trust in him. Referring to it on May 23, a copyeditor on the *New York Herald Tribune* put the phrase "credibility gap" over a story by David Wise, the newspaper's White House correspondent. Then Murray Marder of the *Washington Post*, in an article analyzing the feeling, widespread in Washington, that the President was sometimes careless with the truth, wrote: "The problem could be called a credibility gap." Johnson's glittering peace promises in the 1964 campaign were being recalled and contrasted with his new martial stance. Marder noted a "growing doubt and cynicism concerning administration pronouncements in Washington." Reporters were particularly susceptible to it. Because the President had denounced Senator Goldwater for proposing the very policies he himself was now adopting, the press was becoming skeptical of new olive branches being extended by the White House.

Speaking at Johns Hopkins University on April 7, the President declared that the United States was ready for "unconditional discussions" leading toward a negotiated peace. The address was carried around the world by the U.S. Information Agency, and many of its details sounded new and exciting. He proposed that the nations of Southeast Asia, including North Vietnam, join in a crash Marshall Plan, and he said, "For our part, I will ask Congress to join in a billion-dollar American investment in this effort as soon as it is under way." U.S. farm surpluses would be sent to hungry Asians. He would "shortly name a special team of outstanding, patriotic, distinguished Americans" to guide the United States in all this. An end to the Vietnam War would, of course, be "necessary for final success. But we cannot and must not wait for peace to begin this job." It was all very sensible. It made Asia sound like central Texas.

David Wise's suspicious article was written in the aftermath of this speech, when many flaws in the President's proposition had become apparent. His proposal for truce discussions did have a condition, after all; he ruled out participation by the Viet Cong, which guaranteed Hanoi's rejection of it. Nothing more was heard about the billion-dollar commitment by the United States or the offer of U.S. surplus crops, and the panel of distinguished Americans was never chosen. Within a month what had appeared to be an imaginative approach to the problems of Southeast Asia had taken on the aspect of a publicity stunt. Not only had the President failed to follow through on any part of it; he was showing his real Asian policy in ever more vigorous prosecution of what was fast becoming a major American war.

The first six weeks of Rolling Thunder had been a total failure. Bombing hadn't brought the enemy to his knees, to the negotiating table, or even to what the Johnson administration conceived to be his senses. The Viet Cong were as disrespectful of the American flag as ever. The President decided to raise the ante again. In the third week of April he flew to Honolulu for a two-day conference with Ky and Thieu. Afterward McNamara announced that U.S. aid to Saigon in 1965 would jump from 207 million dollars to 330 million. Another 40,000 American soldiers — "grunts," as they had begun calling themselves — were ordered to Vietnam. Senator Gruening asked Johnson how long winning the war would take, and the President's answer was six months. Hanoi wouldn't be able to stand the bombing longer than that, he said; the Viet Cong would be begging MACV for terms before Christmas.

George Ball was deeply troubled. Intelligence, he knew, pointed toward a very different conclusion. John McCone reported that the CIA concluded the bombs were neither crippling Hanoi nor frightening it. Instead the raids were strengthening the hand of the hard-liners there. One North Vietnamese regiment had already been identified in South Vietnam, and a second was forming at the border. McCone told the National Security Council that a higher American troop level would be met by increased infiltration from the North; the U.S. troop transports on their way to Saigon would be neutralized before the grunts could even be landed. The Pentagon replied that the Air Force was preparing to commit its eight-engine B-52s, designed for nuclear weapons, and that nobody could stand up to B-52s, Phantoms, and F-111s.

But the air war was no longer the only event, nor even the main event, for the Americans in Vietnam. The U.S. military role there was subtly changing. The objective of the American troops was not limited to the protection of airfields now. The grunts were going to intimidate the guerrillas, persuading them that Uncle Sam meant business. Americans at home were unaware of the shift. Afterward James Reston would comment that the President had escalated the war by stealth. Under Johnson, David Halberstam would write years later, the decision makers in Washington "inched their way across the Rubicon without even admitting it" while the task of their press officers became "to misinform the public rather than inform it."

The next quantum jump in Washington's MACV commitment came in July. McNamara returned from his sixth fact-finding tour of Vietnam to report "deterioration" and recommend pledges of more men and more money. Johnson summoned his generals and advisers to Camp David for the weekend of July 17 to find a consensus, though the word, as he used it, had lost its original meaning; for him it had come to mean a ritual of agreement with a decision he had already made — to raise the number of U.S. troops in Vietnam by 50,000. The Joint Chiefs concurred reluctantly. They had hoped for much more; their greatest fear was involvement in partial war. Some of the men at Camp David refused to go along. "Whatever we do," Clark Clifford said prophetically of the Communists, "they will match it." Mike Mansfield also objected, telling the President that he, was opposed to sending any more troops, that he thought the war would divide the country. The others approved of the President's judgment; the domino theory, mutual security, containment, and the lesson of Munich still outweighed their misgivings.

After locking up the decision Johnson became furtive. He wanted no further debate. McNamara proposed a reserve call-up of 235,000 men. Instead the President doubled draft calls administratively, raising them from 17,000 to 35,000 a month, on the ground that it would attract less notice than a call-up. He also decided against asking Congress for more money. The new costs could be hidden in the Defense Department's huge budget. He said he didn't want to scare anyone, and for a time he considered making public only part of the increase in troops for Vietnam. Douglas Kiker of the *Herald Tribune* asked him about reports of the expansion. Rumors, Johnson assured him, nothing but rumors; he was just filling out a few units, and accounts predicting that U.S. troops in Vietnam would pursue the Viet Cong aggressively were also untrue. On July 28 he changed his mind and announced the full figure, together with the new, forceful nature of MACV's mission, thereby alienating Kiker and widening the credibility gap. "We did not choose to be the guardians at the gate," the President told an estimated 28 million Americans on noonday television, "but there is no one else."

Distrust was one evil crop he sowed that summer; another was eventual misunderstandings among those he was herding into consensus. The Joint Chiefs thought he was keeping the figures low until he could persuade the civilians that he must go higher; they were counting on an eventual force of a million men. Westmoreland, watching Hanoi reinforce at a faster rate than anyone dreamed possible and sending Washington reports of it, planned on between 640,000 and 648,000 Americans ultimately under his command, confident that when he needed them they would be there. His staff had a contingency plan under which the MACV force level could reach 750,000, a figure which it thought was both sensible and justifiable. But the assumption of the Secretary of Defense was the strangest of all. Years afterward it would still be comprehensible only to those who understood Robert McNamara's very orderly mind and his belief that disorderly events could be made to conform to it. McNamara arbitrarily decided in

1965 that the war would be over by June 30, 1967, the end of that fiscal year. It would be a perfect time for him, making his budget come out even, and he clung to it even after Westmoreland told him that it was impossible.

In one respect, however, McNamara and the Pentagon were more realistic than the White House. The Joint Chiefs urged the President to raise taxes. Their reasoning had nothing to do with economics. They wanted to see the country on a total war footing, and their textbook solution to civilian apathy was higher taxes. As it happened, the economists in the administration wholeheartedly agreed with them. Gardner Ackley, the Michigan professor who headed Johnson's Council of Economic Advisers, told the President that the administration could not have three things — prosecution of the war, continuance of his Great Society programs, and the absence of inflation — unless taxes were raised.

But this was the period in which Johnson was passing huge amounts of social legislation through Congress. If the true cost of the war were known, he feared, that process would come to a shuddering stop. "I don't know much about economics," he said to those around him, a confession that some of them later thought should be engraved on his tomb, "but I do know the Congress. And I can get the Great Society through right now — this is a golden time. We've got a good Congress and I'm the right President and I can do it. But if I talk about the cost of the war, the Great Society won't go through and the tax bill won't go through. Old Wilbur Mills will sit down there and he'll thank me kindly and send me back my Great Society, and then he'll tell me that they'll be glad to spend whatever we need for the war."

At this point he made the ultimate blunder. He fooled himself. Everything would come out all right, he reckoned, if victory could be bought cheap. Maybe that would happen; maybe Hanoi and the Viet Cong guerrillas would collapse. In that event, the estimates from the Pentagon would be overestimates. The wish became father to the thought, and when Ackley and his colleagues became insistent about the need for a 3 to 4 percent tax increase, the President responded by staging an extraordinary charade. Key Congressmen and leaders of the business community were invited to the White House and asked for their opinion about higher taxes. They in turn inquired about the cost of the war. He gave them phony figures. Thereupon they rejected the idea of a tax increase. Johnson then told the Council of Economic Advisers that a tax hike was impossible; he couldn't get it through Congress. Later Edwin Dale Jr., economic correspondent of the *New York Times*, called this the most single irresponsible presidential act in his fifteen years of covering Washington.

Johnson's decision against a tax raise, made in early 1966, was a stupendous blow to fiscal sanity. The federal deficit that year was 9.8 billion dollars. Even deeper vats of red ink lay ahead, for by then the war was costing between two and three billion dollars a month. The estimate the White House was putting out was 800 million dollars, and when Ralph

Lazarus of the Business Council said the government's figure was much too low, he received an indignant call from Abe Fortas, who told him that his calculations were wrong and were upsetting the President. Actually Lazarus was right on target. The war cost 27 billion dollars that year, and the deficit was a catastrophic 23 billion dollars. Johnson's legerdemain had brought the beginnings of runaway inflation.

Of all the war's aspects, perhaps the most incomprehensible was the lack of real planning. David Halberstam would later find that "the principals never defined either the mission or the number of troops. It seems incredible in retrospect, but it is true. There was never a clear figure and clear demonstration of what the strategy would be." All that was apparent in 1965 was that the numbers were going ever higher. U.S. soldiers were pouring into Vietnam in August, and by September it was obvious that the troop level was going to top 200,000.

Checking reports of a battle near Saigon, Peter Arnett of the Associated Press drove out of the capital to find clouds of smoke in three colors, South Vietnamese troops in action — and no enemy. He was told that the soldiers were making a color movie for the United States Information Service, "to show how things really are here." Arguments over how things really were there were going full blast on all fronts, including the home front. Lyndon Johnson talked at times as though he were responding to a personal challenge from Ho Chi Minh, the two of them striding toward one another in a *High Noon* confrontation. Terrorist bombings seemed closer to the truth in Saigon, where the list of atrocities lengthened; at dawn on December 4 another truck loaded with 250 pounds of explosives went off, this time outside the Metropole, a hotel for American servicemen; eight were killed and 137 wounded.

Westmoreland's spokesmen often sounded preoccupied with the daily "body count," a singularly insensate phrase which was used to describe Viet Cong casualties. To correspondent Neil Sheehan the war was typified by the enormous casualties among innocent civilians resulting from indiscriminate shelling and bombing. Sheehan asked Westmoreland if it didn't bother him, and the general replied, "Yes, but it does deprive the enemy of the population, doesn't it?"

In 1965 Americans demonstrating against the war were still a relative oddity in most of the country. Few people wished to be counted in favor of immediate, unconditional U.S. withdrawal from Indochina. Even college faculties, one of the most dovish groups in the country, were to be evenly divided as late as 1967 on the issue. Nevertheless, the vigor of the peace movement was already phenomenal. On the weekend of October 15–16 a crowd estimated at 14,000 paraded down Manhattan's Fifth Avenue. Simultaneously another 10,000 marched on the Oakland Army Base — they were turned back at the city line by police — and 2,000 demonstrated in Berkeley. Elsewhere during this "weekend of protest," as it was heralded, fifty students from the University of Wisconsin tried to arrest the commanding officer at Truax Air Force Base as a "war criminal," and protesters staged a "lie-in" at a draft board office in Ann Arbor.

The Fifth Avenue Vietnam Peace Parade Committee declared:

> We demand that no more American youth be sent to fight in a war that is helping neither them nor the Vietnamese people. We have learned lessons from Nazi Germany, and will not go along with the aggressive war-making policies of any government, even if it happens to be our own.

That was reasonable, but elsewhere the rhetoric of the demonstrators, like the war itself, was becoming hateful. It was in Washington the Saturday after Thanksgiving that 20,000 of them first chanted, "Hey! Hey! LBJ! How many kids did you kill today?" Members of the May 2nd Movement (M2M), named for May 2, 1964, when they first took to the streets to protest American involvement in the war, trooped around the White House carrying Viet Cong flags and advertised "bleed-ins" at which blood was collected for North Vietnamese soldiers. In Berkeley the Free Speech Movement had been succeeded by the Vietnam Day Committee, which twice tried to halt troop trains by occupying cars and sitting on the tracks.

On October 15, 1965, a new feature was introduced in demonstrations when David J. Miller, a twenty-two-year-old volunteer in a relief program, mounted a sound truck in New York, announced, "Instead of the speech I prepared I'll let this action speak for itself" — and held a match to his draft card. Miller was arrested a few weeks later, but burning Selective Service cards enjoyed a brief vogue, despite congressional action on August 31 making it a federal offense punishable by a $10,000 fine or five years in jail. Acts of self-immolation continued to be the ultimate protest; a Quaker outside the Pentagon and a Catholic relief worker outside the United Nations turned themselves into human torches.

Counterpickets from the American Nazi Party carried jerricans and placards reading, "Free Gas for Peace Creeps." As usual, nobody wanted any part of them. The tone of most antiprotest protests was relatively mild. A girl in New York carried a sign reading, "I Wish I Had a Draft Card." Earnest demonstrations were organized by the Young Americans for Freedom, the American Legion, and the Veterans of Foreign Wars. "Bomb Hanoi" was the most belligerent sentiment on signs of most of them. Placards at a typical march in Florida read, "We Love America," "Love Our Country," "My Country — Right or Wrong," "Will We Let Them Bury U.S.?" and "No Glory Like Old Glory." Bob Hope told one audience that "If we ever let the Communists win this war, we are in great danger of fighting for the rest of our lives and losing a million kids." That was an extravagant statement, but it was hardly in the same category with accusing the President of murdering children.

The gravest charges lodged by those favoring the war were suggestions that the other side was disloyal. "We won't creep around in the dark with candles like these traitors do," said the police chief of Charlestown, West

Virginia. "We'll march at high noon and let free people fall right in and march behind us." Some newspaper accounts of peace vigils in 1965 were inclined to hint broadly at Communist participation, and the FBI, which like Hope was shedding its nonpartisan reputation, virtually credited all such protests to the Kremlin. A government report said: "Control of the anti-Viet Nam movement has clearly passed from the hands of the moderate elements who may have controlled it at one time into the hands of the Communists and extremist elements who are openly sympathetic to the Viet Cong and openly hostile to the United States."

In fact the reverse was true. Despite the inflammatory language and provocative behavior of individual antiwar militants, each demonstration tended to be more respectable than the last. Middle-class conservative housewives and even servicemen in uniform were joining the movement. So, increasingly, were celebrities who felt a pull opposite to Bob Hope's. When stop-the-bombing marchers formed under cloudless skies in Washington on November 27, their number included, in addition to Norman Thomas and James Farmer, such strangers to political action as Dr. Benjamin Spock, cartoonist Jules Feiffer, novelist Saul Bellow, sculptor Alexander Calder, and author Michael Harrington.

That autumn dispatches from Vietnam reported that famous American military units were being mauled in Vietnam. It was the 101st Airborne Brigade at An Khe in September, the Green Berets at Plei Me in October, and, in November, the 1st Cavalry Division in the Ia Drang Valley. The encounter at Ia Drang, a week before the stop-the-bombing march in Washington, was of special significance; like the Viet Cong offensive the previous spring and the Tet offensive of early 1968, it was a turning point in the war. Troopers of the 1st Cav, pursuing enemy detachments in the aftermath of the Plei Me engagement, met stiff resistance in the valley, near Chupong Mountain, seven miles from the Cambodian border and two hundred miles north of Saigon in Vietnam's central highlands. This time the Americans faced not Viet Cong guerrillas, but the North Vietnamese 66th Regiment.

The 66th, an elite unit of the North Vietnamese army, faced a severe test. The 1st Cav was something new in military history, a heliborne division, equipped to take maximum advantage of superior American firepower. The tactics of the Communists, who knew all about the battlefield weapons designed by inventive Americans, called for grappling with the grunts at the closest range, hand to hand if possible, but at most within thirty-four yards, thus nullifying U.S. artillery and tactical air support.

The implications of the Ia Drang fighting were bound to be great. At the time of the Camp David conference in July there had been just two North Vietnamese regiments in the South. Now MACV had confirmed the presence of six regiments from the North, with two more probable and another possible. Others were on their way; General Vo Nguyen Giap,

Ho Chi Minh's commander, was continuing to break up his battalions into companies and platoons and send them down the trail faster than the Americans could bring in transports.

Both sides rushed reinforcements into the valley, and although a 1st Cav battalion, flown in, was ambushed and badly chewed up. when it was all over Westmoreland and his deputy, General William Depuy, claimed a victory. The figures seemed to support them; the enemy, attacking in waves like the World War II Japanese and yelling in English, "Kill GI!," had lost 1,200 to the Americans' 200. But other observers, among them John Paul Vann, who had returned to Vietnam as a civilian, had reached a very different conclusion. The Communists were prepared to accept such losses indefinitely. ("It is," one Viet Cong soldier wrote in his diary, "the duty of my generation to die for our country.") But the U.S. toll in Ia Drang, although much smaller, was a record for Westmoreland's troops; it put American casualties in the war at 1,335 dead and 6,131 wounded. While MACV believed that Westmoreland had found the strategic key to triumph and was eagerly planning more Ia Drangs, Giap took the Vann view. The North Vietnamese general was convinced, and events were to confirm him, that the American people would not accept such casualties in an open-ended commitment. Giap regarded the new phase of the war as a contest between his manpower and Westmoreland's technology, with U.S. public opinion as the referee.

In December McNamara urged a bombing pause on Johnson. Objections came from Rusk, now one of the toughest of the hawks, but the President grounded the B-52s and sent out diplomatic scouts to key world capitals, spreading the word that Washington was ready for peace. Two Italian professors arrived in Hanoi to sound out Ho. At first negotiations seemed possible, but just as word reached Rusk that the Communists were in a conciliatory mood, Hanoi denounced the whole thing as "sheer, groundless fabrication." The Americans were taken aback. After Ia Drang, they thought, it should be obvious to Ho that he faced defeat. The marines were reminded of the tagline of an old Corps joke: "There's always some son-of-a-bitch who doesn't get the word."

In appealing to a joint session of Congress for the voting Rights Act of 1965, Lyndon Johnson concluded his speech with a phrase which had become hallowed by the blood and tears of a new generation of black Americans marching for justice. He said that their cause "must be our cause too. Because it's not just Negroes, but really it's all of us who must overcome the crippling legacy of bigotry and injustice. *And we shall overcome.*"

That was fine liberal eloquence, but at times during the year it appeared to be a doubtful prediction. The eleventh anniversary of the Supreme Court's ruling in Brown v. Board of Education passed on May 17, and racism seemed stronger than ever. C. Vann Woodward, Sterling Professor of

History at Yale, said, "Negroes now have less contact with whites in schools than they did a generation ago." Between the middle of 1964 and the middle of 1965 the Ku Klux Klan made its greatest membership gains ever, including the Reconstruction era. In October of 1965 a Birmingham black reportedly bled to death because a white ambulance driver refused to take him to a hospital. An Alabama businessman, speaking of civil rights pickets, casually remarked to a *New York Times* correspondent, "The niggers are going to be in trouble around here when this is all over." The racial climate was not much better in the northern cities; speaking in Marquette Park, on Chicago's South Side, Martin Luther King Jr. said, "I have never seen such hate, not in Mississippi or Alabama, as I see here in Chicago." The attitude of millions of whites seemed symbolized in a lapel pin worn by Dallas County Sheriff James G. Clark Jr. in Selma. It simply read, "Never." Never, it appeared, would men like Clark, in the North as well as the South, accept Negroes as equals.

Confronted by this prejudice, the black mood continued to change. There was a splintering into various camps, many hostile to one another. The assassination of Malcolm X by fellow blacks in upper Manhattan's Audubon Ballroom on February 21, 1965, just as he had reached the threshold of leadership, reflected the depth of the division among the black militants. A sign of Negro despair was the upsurge in groups advocating "repatriation" — a "return to the African homeland." The Deacons for Defense were formed in some fifty Black Belt communities to combat the KKK. Others followed the preaching of Le Roi Jones, who told them that "The majority of American white men are evil"; and of James Forman, who issued a Black Manifesto demanding that white churches and synagogues (the very white institutions, ironically, which had been most ardent in support of the civil rights movement) pay Negroes 500 million dollars in "reparations."

The Muslims became the most famous of the groups advocating separatism, and in Oakland the first tiny pack of Black Panthers emerged in 1966. Daniel Patrick Moynihan came forward in November 1965 with the Moynihan Report, a closely reasoned document which argued that realistic approaches to internal problems in the Negro community must first deal with the worst legacies of slavery: Negro welfare dependency, a divorce rate 40 percent higher than that of whites, and the appalling rate of illegitimacy, one black birth in four being out of wedlock. Moynihan's facts were undisputed, but such was the Negro agony that year, and so shattering the impact of events on Negro pride, that blacks could not face them. Their leaders therefore branded the report racist propaganda and denounced its author as a "fascist."

C. Vann Woodward wrote in 1965 that "insofar as federal laws are capable of coping" with segregation and prejudice, "Congress has just about fulfilled its role." The capstone of such legislation was the voting act of that year. In January Martin Luther King called a press conference to point out that three million of the five million blacks in the South old enough to vote were not registered, and to announce that he was launching an all-out registration drive. It would open in Selma, Alabama, where 325 of 15,000 potential black voters were registered, as against 9,300 of 14,000 whites. Typically, Dr. King led the first group of Negroes ever to stay at Selma's Hotel Albert, previously all-white, and typically he was punched and kicked by a white segregationist while signing the hotel register. His assailant was fined one hundred dollars and sentenced to sixty days in jail, which King thought was a good start toward respect for the law, but then the drive stalled. The blunt truth was that most of Selma's Negroes were indifferent to the right to vote. Something dramatic was needed to arouse them. It was provided — again, this was characteristic — by rural whites who murdered a black would-be voter in nearby Perry County. Local civil rights leaders counted on that, on Sheriff Jim Clark's short temper, and on Governor Wallace's showboating to revive their campaign.

They declared that on March 7 they would stage a protest march. Negro and white sympathizers would hike from Selma to Montgomery, fifty-four miles away, moving straight down the middle of route 80, the Jefferson Davis Highway. Wallace promptly banned the demonstration as a menace to commerce and public safety and sent a hundred state troopers to reinforce Sheriff Clark, who gave a sign of his allegiance to the past by rounding up a mounted posse. On March 7 — which would enter Alabama history and folklore as "Black Sunday" — six hundred Negroes and a few white partisans of their cause defiantly marched from the Brown's Chapel African Methodist Episcopal Church to the Edmund Pettus Bridge, spanning the Alabama River. There they ran into Clark's horsemen and troopers wearing gas masks. When they ignored a two-minute warning to disperse, possemen waded into them swinging billy clubs and wet bullwhips. Yellow clouds of tear gas belched from the ranks of the troopers. Routed, the blacks stumbled and crawled back to the church. Accompanying them were television cameramen, whose footage guaranteed that Selma would become overnight a symbol of oppression.

Dr. King had been preaching in Atlanta on Black Sunday. Dropping everything, he flew to Selma, announced that he would lead a second march on Tuesday, and called on clergymen of both races to join him. Over three hundred white ministers, priests, and rabbis responded. Sympathy demonstrations were held in all the great cities of the North. Black activists staged sit-ins at the Department of Justice and the White House, and President Johnson issued a statement blaming Alabama officials for "the brutality with which a number of Negro citizens were treated." He sent John Doar and former Governor LeRoy Collins of Florida to Selma, and they succeeded in arranging a token march, back and forth across the bridge. Sheriff Clark and Dr. King agreed with many misgivings, which in King's case were justified. Militant black youths from SNCC accused him of Uncle Tomism. Coming off the bridge, they mocked him by singing the civil rights song "Ain't Gonna Let Nobody Turn Me Around."

King was turned around that same evening by the first of three murders arising from the Selma crisis, all of whites who sympathized with the civil rights movement. The Reverend James J. Reeb, a Boston Unitarian, was set upon by red-neck hoodlums as he left a Negro restaurant and beaten to death. James Forman of SNCC and five hundred of his followers then threatened to mutiny if Dr. King didn't take a bolder line. An angry crowd of fifteen hundred blacks held a rally in Montgomery's Beulah Baptist Church. King had encouraging news for them. A federal judge, Frank M. Johnson Jr. of Montgomery, had agreed to allow the march from Selma to Montgomery; although such a procession "reaches to the outer limits of what is constitutionally allowed," he had ruled, the mistreatment of the demonstrators had obviously surpassed "the outer limits of what is constitutionally permissible."

Governor Wallace, addressing a televised joint session of the Alabama legislature, condemned the imminent march as comparable to Communist "street warfare" that "ripped Cuba apart, that destroyed Diem in Vietnam, that raped China — that has torn civilization and established institutions of this world into bloody shreds." The state couldn't afford to protect all these outside agitators, he said, and he telegraphed the White House, calling upon the federal government to enforce the decision of the federal judge. That was exactly what Lyndon Johnson had been hoping he would do. The President now had an official request from Wallace to protect the demonstrators, and he complied by sending 1,863 federalized National Guardsmen, 250 U.S. marshals and FBI agents, two regular Army MP battalions, demolition experts to search the road and bridges ahead of those making the hike, and helicopters to hover overhead. In addition, the hikers were provided with huge tents for overnight stops, a 600-gallon water truck, latrine trucks, ambulances, trucks for rubbish, and scout cars to set up campsites in advance. Johnson was showing a little garter.

The march itself was a triumph. Veterans of the movement had become astute at providing TV cameramen with colorful material. Leading the procession were Dr. King, Ralph Bunche, a pretty coed, a sharecropper in overalls, a rabbi, a priest, a nun, and a one-legged marcher on crutches. (The white Alabamans along the way, hopelessly ignorant of how to cultivate a good image, made obscene gestures at the nun and guffawed while chanting, as a cadence for the man with one leg, "Left, left, left.") Although the Alabama legislature indignantly — and unanimously — fulminated against "the evidence of much fornication at the marchers' camps," behavior along the route was peaceful and orderly, a remarkable achievement in light of the number of people involved. Leaving Selma on March 21 there had been 3,200 in the procession; arriving in Montgomery four days later there were 25,000. Dr. King spoke to them on the grounds of the statehouse, which a century ago had been the capital of the Confederacy. He ended by crying four times, "Glory hallelujah!" They disbanded and heavy traffic carried them back on route 80 to Selma. A sullen clump of Ku Klux Klansmen watched them go. As the stream of cars thinned the Klansmen moved in for the second murder.

The victim was Viola Gregg Liuzzo, a red-haired Detroit housewife and the mother of five. Mrs. Liuzzo had told her husband, an agent for the Teamsters Union, "This is something I must do," and after the victorious rally on the statehouse lawn she volunteered to ferry Alabama marchers to their homes. On her last trip she was singing "We Shall Overcome" with her only passenger, a nineteen-year-old Negro barber, when a car full of Klansmen drew alongside on a lonely stretch of road. One of the white hoodlums, an auto mechanic, fired a 38-caliber pistol at her head. She collapsed with blood spurting from her temple; the car careened into a ditch; the terrified young barber hitchhiked into Selma for police help.

The third killing was of an Episcopalian seminarian from New Hampshire who was gunned down in a grocery. The killer, a part-time deputy sheriff, pleaded self-defense and was found innocent by a jury of twelve white Alabama men, though no weapon had been found on the seminarian and witnesses said there had been none. In the death of the Reverend Mr. Reeb, three men were charged a few hours after he had been battered to death. They, too, were acquitted; their jury deliberated just ninety-five minutes. The trial of Mrs. Liuzzo's murderers was the most interesting of the three. One of the Klansmen in the death car had in fact been an undercover man for the FBI; he identified each of his companions, their weapons, and what they had done and said. They were defended in their first trial by Matt H. Murphy Jr., a third-generation Klansman. Murphy's summation was one-hundred-proof racism: "When white people join up with them [blacks], they become white niggers. . . . God didn't intend for us to mix with the black race, I don't care what Lyndon Baines Johnson says." The FBI man, Murphy said, was a violator of his Klan oath, "as treacherous as a rattlesnake . . . purporting himself to be a white man and worse than a white nigger." That jury was hung (10 to 2 for conviction of manslaughter), but Murphy had made his last bow; he was killed in an auto accident during the interval before a second trial. A biased judge presided at those proceedings, which ended in an acquittal, but then the federal government stepped in and tried the Klansmen for violating Mrs. Liuzzo's civil rights. That curious law, which had been the downfall of the Klan killers in Mississippi's Freedom Summer and of the slayers of a Negro Army officer in Georgia, worked once more here with another jury of twelve southern men, and the judge sentenced the defendants to ten years, the maximum.

Selma inspired the voting rights act — Johnson said as much in asking Congress for it on March 15 — and the country credited it to Dr. King. It proved to be the peak of his reputation. The events of the previous year in Mississippi having created the first serious doubts about nonviolence, the Alabama murders confirmed the suspicions of the new generation of black activists. These skeptics left Selma convinced that King had nothing more to teach them. The vast majority of the Negro people disagreed; in a subsequent CBS public opinion poll where anonymity was preserved, only 4 percent said they would give active support to Stokely Carmichael, 2 percent to the more militant H. Rap Brown, and 1 percent to Ron Karenga, the most militant of the three, while 40 percent backed the ideals of Dr. King. Nevertheless, the activists had correctly gauged a change in mood. The majority yearned for peace — a majority has always wanted it — but the country was entering a new period, and one of its most striking qualities would be an affinity for violence. In retrospect the death of President Kennedy and the murder of his assassin now seemed to have been omens. Once more a gear had shifted somewhere in the universe. Search and destroy, emerging in Vietnam during the same months in 1965, was one expression of the emerging mood, the Selma murders were another; still others would crowd upon one another in the succeeding months and years as Negro rage and frustration which had been repressed for a century now erupted.

The new inner city temper emerged in Los Angeles on Wednesday, August 11, 1965, in a shabby Negro district of low, faded stucco houses, suggestive of certain poor areas in Puerto Rico, which lay under the approaches to Los Angeles International Airport. Trash never seemed to be properly collected there. There was litter everywhere — broken glass, rusty cans, rotting chicken bones, empty Tokay bottles — and the quality of life was further diminished by the typical white policeman, also known locally as The Man, who had a way of stopping black citizens and demanding, "Let's see your I.D."

That August evening Lee Minikus, an officer of the California Highway Patrol, wanted a look at the I.D. of a young Negro named Marquette Frye; he intended to take him in on suspicion of drunken driving. A knot of people, gathering around, kidded both Minikus and his suspect. It all seemed low-key and harmless, but beneath the surface tension was building. Los Angeles was in the fourth day of a brutal heat wave. People were outdoors, ready to assemble quickly at the promise of excitement. The arrest was taking place at the corner of Avalon Boulevard and Imperial Highway, a busy L.A. intersection through which passed a constant stream of white drivers, often behind the wheels of expensive cars. Most inauspicious of all was the neighborhood. It was 98 percent black, with a population density of 27.3 people per acre (the figure was 7.4 for Los Angeles County as a whole). Negro immigrants had been arriving here in massive numbers since the early 1940s, when an average of 2,000 each month came to work in war industries. Now 420,000 of the 2,731,000 inhabitants of the city were black. Yet in this ghetto there were just five blacks on the 205-man police force. And every month in 1965 another 1,000 Negroes poured into these swarming warrens, often looking for jobs that no longer existed. The temptations of drugs and alcohol awaited their children, and when the children went wrong The Man came after them. These snares, not the inhabitants, were the real transgressors in this district, a region known locally as Watts.

At 7:45 P.M. that Wednesday, California Highway Patrolman Minikus took the Frye youth into custody. Almost immediately he was in trouble. Among those attracted by the winking red light of his squad car was the prisoner's mother. At first she rebuked her son. Then she turned on the police officer. As her manner became distraught and the murmurs of the spectators less good-humored, Minikus nervously radioed for reinforcements. Then he made two mistakes. He attempted to force Frye into the squad car and he turned his back on Frye's mother. She jumped on it. As other officers arrived they pried her loose, and when the crowd began to mutter indignantly they held it at bay with shotguns. Minikus got away with his man, but the price had been exorbitant. Already the use of force was beginning to inspire distorted accounts of what had happened, and with each passing hour the stories grew taller. Two versions were widespread. One had it that a cop had struck a pregnant woman in the belly with his club. In the other, a cop had pushed a woman against the patrol car and tried to choke her. Aroused, the crowd pelted policemen with stones and bottles. By 10 P.M. the spectators had been transformed into a mob which set upon passersby, overturned cars, and smashed shop display windows. The familiar stages of riot escalation now appeared. Police sealed off eight blocks at 11 P.M. Two hours later the rioters burst free and roved Watts, two thousand strong, waylaying strangers, breaking everything fragile, and looting the stores.

At 3 A.M. the level of violence fell — rioters must sleep, too — and police patrols imposed a semblance of order in the ghetto. In the morning shop managers called their insurance companies, clerks cleaned up the mess, and those who knew nothing about riots assumed this one was over. Their disillusionment began at 7:45 P.M. that Thursday, just twenty-four hours after the arrest of young Frye. At first it was all a repetition of Wednesday evening: youths pouncing on passing autos, pelting cops with bricks, breaking windows. The change came at 4 A.M. At that hour the day before, a peace of exhaustion had fallen over the ghetto. This time a second shift of rioters spilled into the streets. These men were older and more vicious. They were also armed. Dick Gregory toured Watts with a bullhorn, begging for order, and was shot in the leg. The ghetto violence was approaching the force of an insurrection, but the authorities didn't realize it yet; a flying wedge of policemen cleared Watts's darkened streets and then announced that the situation was under control.

The truth was revealed to them at 10 A.M., when two white salesmen were attacked in the first incident of daytime violence. At 11 A.M. a policeman wounded a black looter. Governor Edmund Brown, on vacation in Greece, read reports of the growing disorders and hurried home; his lieutenant governor granted a request from the L.A. police chief for National Guard troops. The first contingent of Guardsmen reached Watts Friday afternoon. Even as they were being briefed in an elementary school the version they heard was being outdated by new developments in the ghetto. More than 5,000 rioters now roamed a 150-block area, firing buildings with Molotov cocktails and ambushing firemen who answered the alarms. Watts claimed its first fatality, a sheriff's deputy mortally wounded in the stomach, at 9:40 P.M. Three other deaths quickly followed. National Guard soldiers entering the district with fixed bayonets saw looters, their way illumined by a hundred major fires, carrying guns, appliances, liquor, jewelry — everything of value — from the shops of the ghetto. Crudely lettered signs outside some stores read "Black Brother," "Soul Brother," "Negro Owned," and "Owned by a Brother." Some had been robbed anyway. One gang was trying to burn Oak Park Community Hospital, which was crowded with Negroes hurt in the disorders. Robert Richardson, a black *Los Angeles Times* reporter, wrote: "The rioters were burning their city now, as the insane sometimes mutilate themselves."

On Saturday snipers on rooftops began picking off soldiers and policemen. Firemen were issued bulletproof vests. The Guard force grew to 10,000 men, then to 14,000; a curfew was imposed on 40 square miles Saturday and on 46 square miles Sunday. Intermittent shoot-outs continued until the early hours of Wednesday, August 18, when officers seized 35 blacks after a gunfight at a Black Muslim mosque. That was the end of it. During the six days of madness 34 had been killed, 898 hurt, and over 4,000 arrested. Losses were put at 45 million dollars.

The Watts devastation was called the worst race riot since Detroit in 1943, but it was really in a class by itself. While the death toll was the same, the damage in Detroit had been less than a million dollars. There was trouble elsewhere, too. Coincident with Watts, the West Side of Chicago ran amok when a fire truck, answering an alarm in West Garfield Park on August 12, struck and killed a black woman. Negroes fought cops and 2,000 Guardsmen for two nights, looting and hurling bottles at whites. Over 100 were arrested and 67 hurt. And in Springfield, Massachusetts, far from the ghettos of the great cities, the arrest of eighteen blacks outside a nightclub gave rise to accusations of brutality against seven cops; Molotov cocktail bombings of stores owned by whites then led to mass arrests and, once more, the calling of the National Guard. A protest march by 4,000 Springfield Negroes ended at City Hall, where George Wiley, assistant national director of CORE, told them that "the civil rights struggle in the North" would be "longer, bloodier, and more bitter" than it had been in the South.

It was characteristic of the 1960s that each outbreak of violence was followed by the appointment of a commission to study it. Governor Brown picked a panel of eminent citizens led by John A. McCone to look into Watts. Their findings were published under the title *Violence in the City:*

An End or a Beginning? By then everyone knew that Watts was only a beginning, but the searches for remedies followed various paths. The McCone Report came down hard on the need for law and order. Black militants protested that objection to laws oppressing Negroes was what Watts had been all about. Bayard Rustin called it "the first major rebellion of Negroes against their own masochism." Theodore H. White thought that television and radio reporting shared some of the responsibility. White charged that it had gone "beyond reporting and become a factor in itself," and he asked, "Can electronic reporting be curbed in the higher interest of domestic tranquillity?" Martin Luther King, touring the smoking ruins of Watts, received a mixed welcome. He was growing accustomed to this. The torch had been passed to the new generation of black leaders, and it had become a real torch.

If the summer of racial disorders had been hot in 1965, it had also been short. Until Watts burst into flame that second week in August there had been hope that the country might make it that year without a major riot. The next year was a different story. Again Los Angeles sounded the tocsin, but this time it was in March that a gang of Negro students stoned the auto of a white teacher there, attacked other whites, and turned to looting. Angeleno policemen had learned a lot the year before; this new threat was suppressed overnight with only two deaths. Yet if L.A. escaped with fewer scars, the rest of the nation did not. It almost seemed as though every large black community in the United States was in rebellion against society. In Washington, D.C., Negroes rose in April. By May three California cities were embattled. Cleveland erupted in late June, and Omaha, Des Moines, and Chicago two weeks after that. Next came Cleveland, and then in swift succession Brooklyn, Baltimore, Perth Amboy, Providence, Minneapolis, Milwaukee, Detroit, Dayton, Atlanta, San Francisco, and St. Louis; Pompano Beach, Florida; Cordele, Georgia; Cicero, Illinois; and Lansing, Muskegon, Benton Harbor, and Jackson, Michigan. By the end of the summer the toll was seven dead, over 400 hurt, some 3,000 arrested, and more than five million dollars lost to vandals, looters, and arsonists. By the end of 1966, America had been scarred by forty-three race riots that year.

In Cicero a Negro march for open housing ran into a counterdemonstration by hostile whites, who repeatedly tried to lunge past police to harm the blacks. Twelve were hurt; six officers were hit by missiles; 32 of the whites were arrested. Cicero was of special interest because it demonstrated that policemen, far from starting riots, often held together a fragile peace; when Negroes went after them it was often because the cops represented authority and were the only whites in sight. In working-class communities whites often matched, and more than matched, the black rage. The tension between the races was felt on both sides. It was in 1966 that backlash came into its own.

Originally the open housing demonstration had been in Cicero's Marquette Park and led by Martin Luther King. He called it off when a rock hit him and knocked him to his knees. Robert Lucas, Chicago chairman of CORE, defiantly sponsored the new march, explaining that "CORE wants to keep the pressure on." Lucas was one of the new militants, and 1966 was turning into their year, too. Floyd McKissick replaced the more moderate James Farmer as head of CORE and Stokely Carmichael succeeded John Lewis as chairman of SNCC. The development was not as auspicious for the movement as they thought. Carmichael had been in office just a month when an event that none of the civil rights leaders had taken seriously showed the extent of the divisions in their ranks.

On June 5 James H. Meredith announced that he was leaving Memphis to hike 225 miles to Mississippi's state capitol in Jackson. His motive was to prove that American Negroes were unafraid. The McKissicks and Carmichaels thought the idea impractical and visionary — "the silliest idea I ever heard of," one movement leader called it — and they decided to ignore him. Meredith was undaunted. Still guided by a feeling of "divine responsibility," as he had called it in *Three Years in Mississippi*, his account of his ordeal on the Ole Miss campus, he believed that destiny awaited him in his native state, and he was correct, destiny in this case being represented by a middle-aged, unemployed white Mississippian named Aubrey James Norvell. At 4:15 P.M. on the second day of the journey, Meredith and a convoy of FBI agents were striding along U.S. 51 just south of Hernando, Mississippi, when Norvell rose out of the bushes beside the road. "James Meredith!" he yelled. "James Meredith! I only want Meredith!" He fired three shotgun blasts. Doctors in a Memphis hospital found Meredith peppered with birdshot.

None of the wounds was serious. Norvell's real damage had been done to the notion that Meredith's walk needn't be taken seriously. The bursts of gunfire had turned it into a crusade, and everyone in the movement wanted to be part of it. Dick Gregory flew to Memphis to retrace Meredith's steps, and McKissick, Carmichael, and Martin Luther King headed south on foot from the stretch of pavement where Meredith had fallen. Dr. King, borrowing two thousand dollars to launch what he called the Meredith March for Freedom, ordered his Southern Christian Leadership Conference to mobilize resources for another Selma.

It wasn't possible. Selma had been an achievement of united Negro leadership advocating nonviolence. Now King's critics, and particularly those in SNCC, were out in the open. The day after Norvell's ambush Carmichael told a Memphis rally, "The Negro is going to take what he deserves from the white man." King deplored such demagoguery; Roy Wilkins of the NAACP and Whitney M. Young Jr. of the Urban League agreed. But the rhetoric of the young militants became more bellicose. In Philadelphia, Mississippi, where in the Freedom Summer of 1964 death had come to three members of the movement — two of them white — a white Mississippian was wounded by gunfire in the dark, and Ralph Featherstone of SNCC, far from regretting the incident, exulted that blacks were no longer meek, that "their reaction is shot for shot." Carmichael spoke up for the Black Panther political party. In Yazoo City young Negroes chanted, "Hey! Hey! Whattaya know! White folks must go — must go!" and that night in the Yazoo City fairgrounds Willie Ricks, a twenty-three-year-old member of SNCC known as "the Reverend" because of his evangelical style, mounted a flatbed truck and delivered a sermon of hate that made older Negro leaders shudder. He spoke of the blood of whites flowing and repeatedly described his goal in two explosive words: "Black power!"

In Greenwood, forty-five miles away, Carmichael was emerging from seven hours in jail. In a way his plight was a consequence of his militancy. White liberals, dismayed by it, were being far less generous with contributions than they had been at the time of Selma. Food and shelter were a problem, and Carmichael had been arrested while trying to erect tents on a Negro school playground. He heard about Ricks's speech just as he himself was climbing another flatbed truck to address a Greenwood rally. Using the repetition and question-and-response techniques which civil rights leaders had adopted so successfully from Negro preachers, he reminded his audience that he had been apprehended by police in a Negro schoolyard. "Everybody owns our neighborhoods except us. . . . Now we're going to get something and we're going to get some representing. We ain't going to worry about whether it's white — maybe black. Don't be ashamed. We . . . want . . . black . . . power!"

They shouted, "That's right!" and he took up the theme: "We . . . want . . . black power! We . . . want . . . black . . . power! We want black power! We want black power! That's right — that's what we want. . . . Now, from now on, when they ask you what you want, you know what to tell them. What do you want?"

"Black power!"

"What do you want?"

"Black power!"

"What do you want? Say it again!"

"Black power!"

What did it mean? Roy Wilkins had no doubts: "The term 'black power' means anti-white power . . . It has to mean going it alone. It has to mean separatism. We of the NAACP will have none of this." Wilkins called the phrase "the father of hatred and the mother of violence." Martin Luther King said much the same thing at first, though later, seeing that the coalition of civil rights groups was coming apart over the issue, he hedged, interpreting it as "an appeal to racial pride, an appeal to the Negro not to be ashamed of being black, and the transfer of the powerlessness of the Negro into positive, constructive power." McKissick saw it as an appeal to joint action: "Unless we can get around to unifying black power, we're going to be in bad shape." But Charles Evers, brother of the martyred Medgar Evers and the ranking NAACP worker in Mississippi, warned that

"If we are marching these roads for black supremacy, we are doomed," and A. Philip Randolph, deploring the war cry as "a menace to racial peace and prosperity" said that "No Negro who is fighting for civil rights can support black power, which is opposed to civil rights and integration."

A nationwide *New York Times* survey reported that the dissension among civil rights leaders in Mississippi was reducing public support for the movement. An opinion poll found that 77 percent of whites felt the black power creed was hurting the black cause. James Meredith agreed. "There seems to be a good bit of show going on down there," he said in New York, where he was convalescing. Fully recovered, he rejoined the march and was embraced by King and the others. Nevertheless his doubts remained. "I think something is wrong," he said, and he spoke of "some shenanigans going on that I don't like."

An open break between the old leaders and the new was inevitable. It came at Canton, near the end of the Meredith March, on June 23, after police had refused to let them pitch their tents on another school playground. Refusing to disperse, twenty-five hundred blacks stood their ground. Carmichael cried, "The time for running has come to an end." It hadn't really — when the police charged with nightsticks and tear gas the people scattered — but when King turned down a proposal that they try to put up the tents anyway, the SNCC leadership deserted him. One of them said, "What we do from now on we will do on our own." Then they proposed that the NAACP be excluded from the climactic rally in Jackson on the ground that its support of the march had been tepid. King and an organization of volunteer doctors and nurses, who had provided medical attention during the journey, opposed the resolution, but SNCC, CORE, and two other groups representing young blacks gave it a majority. Charles Evers said, "It's all right. I'll be here when they're all gone." He observed caustically that marches did nothing to register black voters. When the procession reached the statehouse grounds in Jackson, with a band playing "When the Saints Go Marching In," veterans of other civil rights demonstrations noted that the whites who had marched with King in other years were not there.

That did not end the liberal commitment to justice for blacks, of course. Nor did it block programs for Negro progress which were already under way. That same month a six-month boycott of white businesses in Fayette, Mississippi, ended with the hiring of black clerks in Fayette stores, the closing of filling station toilets for colored people, and the swearing in of black policemen and deputy sheriffs. Julian Bond, having been elected to the Georgia legislature three times in twelve months, was finally seated by order of the U.S. Supreme Court. In Selma Sheriff Jim Clark quietly removed his "Never" button as his job went on the ballot. It didn't save him; when Negro voters, registered under the voting act he had opposed, went to the polls, he lost.

Once it had been enough for all blacks that a few blacks made it. The entire race had been proud of the few. No more; typically, Carmichael quoted a Negro woman as saying that September, "The food that Ralph Bunche eats doesn't fill my stomach." The elevator operator and the three-dollar-a-day cotton picker wanted their share, too. It was human and it was natural, but the militants' way of going about it was hopelessly unrealistic. Negroes constituted only 11 percent of the U.S. population. The talk of black revolution — and there was a lot of it in 1966 — was senseless, and SNCC's demand that blacks reject integration was absurd.

Philip Randolph, appalled by the violent confrontations between slum blacks and policemen, suggested in September that "the time has come when the street marches and demonstrations have about run their course." He proposed a new approach, "a shift from the streets to the conference table." In October he, Wilkins, Young, Rustin, and three other veterans of the civil rights struggle signed a statement repudiating violence, rioting, and demagoguery, and concluding: "We not only welcome, we urge the full cooperation of white Americans." Martin Luther King, while approving in principle, declined to sign on the ground that he did not want to give the impression that he thought the spokesmen for black power were "conclusively and irrevocably committed to error."

For a time Carmichael took a conciliatory line, redefining black power as "black people coming together to form a political force and either electing representatives or forcing their representatives to speak their needs. . . . saying, 'Look, buddy, we're not laying a vote on you unless you lay so many schools, hospitals, playgrounds and jobs on us.' " It didn't last. Soon he was telling audiences that "If we don't get justice we're going to tear this country apart," and calling on Negroes to "fight for liberation by any means necessary." In Prattville, Alabama, he said, "We came here to tear this town up and we're going to tear it up." He called President Johnson a "hunky," a "buffoon," and a "liar." Increasingly he identified himself with the Panthers, whose "Power to the People" slogan meant power to black people and no one else. Then, like Danton being succeeded by Robespierre, Carmichael was replaced as SNCC's chairman by an even more violent racist, H. Rap Brown. When much of downtown Cincinnati went up in flames during five terrible days and nights of Molotov cocktails, Brown told reporters that there would be no peace "until the honky cops get out." Then he said: "SNCC has declared war."

The backlash vote in the 1966 elections was one response to the call for black power. Another was a shift in position by such sensitive politicians as Senator Everett Dirksen. Dirksen had supported civil rights legislation in 1964 and 1965 as "an idea whose time has come," but he scorned the 1966 bill, with Title IV, the "open housing" clause, as "a package of mischief," and that killed it. Curiously, it was a British periodical, the *Economist* of London, which took the most critical view of the new militants. "Many of these 'leaders' are of a lurid fascist type," said the *Economist*. It derided "liberal intellectuals" who "insultingly tell one another that the general anti-white mood among black Americans is similar to the anti-German mood among the French in 1943," observed that "robberies and assaults on white women" were being interpreted by some activists as "almost a noble act of black revolution," and predicted that "a temporary and rather extraordinary toleration by the American people of flamboyant violence is almost certainly about to turn to a harsh white intolerance of it."

Meantime the black racists were flourishing. The Panthers were acquiring what Tom Wolfe pungently called "radical chic" among some affluent urban liberals, and criminals whose notoriety would once have been limited to the police blotter were being seriously discussed as observers with fresh insight into the human dilemma. All were creatures of the ghettos, and the rise of some could be traced directly to the recent riots. Ron Karenga came from the depths of Watts; although he denied that members of US, his black nationalist organization, had engaged in riot activity, four of them had been so charged. Karenga's celebrity was a consequence of the Watts upheaval. The full bill for that convulsion, it was becoming clear, was incalculable. Some of the highest costs would be hidden for years. One item in the legacy of violence was a snub-nosed, eight-shot 22-caliber Iver-Johnson revolver, model 55SA, bought for protection by a frightened Angeleno for $31.95 late in August 1965 in the wake of the disorders. Later he gave it to his daughter, who passed it on to a Pasadena neighbor, who sold it to an employee in Nash's Department Store named Munir "Joe" Sirhan. Eventually Joe turned it over to his kid brother, Sirhan Bishara "Sol" Sirhan, who used it to assassinate Robert F. Kennedy in Los Angeles three years after Watts.

In the twelve-year cycle of the Vietnamese calender, the Year of the Snake, 1965, gave way to the Year of the Horse, 1966, which in turn was followed by the Year of the Goat, 1967. The Horse was supposed to be lucky, second only to the Year of the Dragon in auspiciousness, but almost half of America's total Vietnam dead by the end of the first ten weeks of 1966 — 2,559 men — had fallen to Communist guns and bombs in those ten weeks, and that, it turned out, was only the beginning. That year's toll was 4,800 U.S. soldiers killed in action. In May of the following year the total of U.S. dead passed 10,000, and as the war grew older, it grew bloodier. Average weekly losses in the Year of the Goat ran 33 percent higher than in the Year of the Horse. More men died in 1967 than in all the war's previous years. And during that same period there were 53,000 civilian deaths, a matter of increasing concern to the war critics at home.

The toll didn't deter the Pentagon from proposing an ever more vigorous, aggressive policy. The Joint Chiefs kept pressing McNamara to recommend to the President the bombing of petroleum, oil, and lubricant supplies (POL raids, they were called) in North Vietnam. Admiral U. S. Grant Sharp of CINCPAC predicted that this would "bring the enemy to the conference table or cause the insurgency to wither." McNamara finally agreed in March 1966, though the CIA prophesied that POL strikes would not halt infiltration of men and supplies. The CIA was right; despite heavy losses in combat, the number of North Vietnamese soldiers coming down the 1,000-mile Ho Chi Minh Trail grew from 1,500 a month to 3,500 and then to 4,000. By the end of the year Giap was sending an average of 8,800 men a month to the South. Soon the annual replacement rate would be 100,000 men.

Defense Department study groups advised McNamara that despite the bombing the flow of guerrillas southward was "undiminished" and that the raids "had no measurable direct effect" on Hanoi's capacity to make war below the 17th Parallel. The secretary flew over to see for himself; it was his eighth on-the-spot inspection. Returning, he told the President that "pacification has if anything gone backward," and that the air war had not "either significantly affected infiltration or cracked the morale of Hanoi." He recommended a reappraisal of the bombing campaign. The Joint Chiefs strenuously objected to any suggestion of a cutback in the raids. In a memorandum to the President they contended that the military situation had "improved substantially over the past year" and called bombing "a trump card." General Westmoreland, flying home to address a joint session of Congress, reported: "I have never been more encouraged in my four years in Vietnam. . . . We have reached an important point when the end begins to come in view."

McNamara was not encouraged. By now he had seen too many optimistic forecasts go glimmering. In Saigon he had spent a gloomy session with one of his men there who told him that the official cheerfulness was false, that there was no light at the end of the tunnel; the informant was Daniel Ellsberg. In fact Westmoreland was in Washington not to report victories but to ask for more troops. He had ended 1966 with 375,000. By April of 1967 he had 480,000, more than in the Korean War at its peak. He wanted 680,000 men by June 1968, or at the very least 565,000. With the higher figure, he told Johnson, he could end the war in two years; with the smaller figure it would take three years. The President noted unhappily that the Communist force in the South was at a record high. He asked the general, "When we add divisions, can't the enemy add divisions? If so, where does it all end?" Westmoreland said that if Giap's infiltration rate went much higher his supply problems would become difficult. Anyhow, the grunts were killing North Vietnamese quicker than they could be replaced. Johnson asked what would happen if Giap asked for Chinese volunteers. The general replied, "That's a good question."

Already American involvement in the Vietnam War had lasted longer than World War II or the Korean War. The conflict seemed more than ever a struggle between whites and Asians. MACV christened the battles with colorful names which became reminders of agony in the jungle and growing bitterness among an increasingly divided people at home. There was operation Attleboro, and Leatherneck Square, and operations Masher, Double Eagle, and White Wing. Then Dak To, Hill 881 North, Loc Ninh, and operations Crazy Horse, Hawthorne, and Hastings — Hastings, the costliest engagement since Ia Drang. And then Hill 881 South, Khe Sanh, the three red hills of Con Thien, and Ashu. The Iron Triangle, a three-cornered region of abandoned rubber plantations and rain forest between the Saigon River and Route 13 twenty miles north of Saigon, had been a Communist stronghold for twenty years. Operation Cedar Falls in January 1967, an attack on the Triangle by 30,000 grunts, was the largest American drive of the war till then. But operation Junction City, a month later, was even bigger: 45,000 American troops thrusting into Zone C near the Cambodian border to wipe out a Viet Cong base. They did it — and then had to let the enemy reclaim it, because ARVN (Army of the Republic of Vietnam) forces couldn't hold it, even as garrison troops.

Congress, meantime, was making dissent from Johnson's war policies respectable. By later standards the protests were muffled; addressing Hanoi, sixteen senators who opposed the administration's conduct of the war warned that there were limits to their dissent, that they were "steadfastly opposed to any unilateral withdrawal of American troops." Yet the Hill was growing restive. At the request of the President, five senators led by Mike Mansfield spent thirty-five days in Vietnam. When they issued their report Johnson was dismayed; they had found that a year of U.S. campaigning had not altered the progress of the war and that America was becoming trapped in an "open-ended" conflict: "how open is dependent upon the extent to which North Viet Nam and its supporters are willing and able to meet increased force by increased force." Senator Robert F. Kennedy charged that the administration had "switched" from the policy of his brother, so that now, "We're killing innocent people . . . because [the Communists] are 12,000 miles away and they might get 11,000 miles away."

That was the highest level of protest. Senatorial doves might object to Johnson's course in Indochina, but they voted him funds to continue on it, and their language was polite. Fulbright, the most outspoken of them, was never uncivil; when Westmoreland told a New York audience that he was "dismayed . . . by recent unpatriotic acts here at home" and accused the perpetrators of giving aid and comfort to the enemy, Fulbright merely replied that Westmoreland's visit had been planned by the administration "to pave the way for escalation," which was of course true. One step down was Martin Luther King, who called the United States "the greatest purveyor of violence in the world today," and compared American experiments with new weapons in Vietnam, where they were killing peasants, to Nazi tests of "new medicine and new tortures in the concentration camps of Europe." Eartha Kitt used much the same rhetoric in attacking the war at a White House luncheon given by Lady Bird. So did Dr. Spock in telling peace demonstrators that "Lyndon Johnson is the enemy"; so did folk singer Pete Seeger, censored by CBS for a number called "Waist Deep in the Big Muddy," which dealt contemptuously with the President's war policy ("And the old fool says, 'Push on'"), and Captain Howard Brett Levy, a Brooklyn physician who refused to train medical corpsmen assigned to the Army's Special Forces — Green Berets — on the ground that under the Nüremberg Doctrine he would thereby become an accessory to war crimes. One of the charges against Dr. Levy at his court-martial in June 1967 was that he had called the war a "diabolical evil." He was found guilty, sentenced to three years in prison, and led off in handcuffs.

Colleges and universities continued to be the centers of heavier protest. Job recruiters for the CIA, the Dow Chemical Company — manufacturers of napalm, the incendiary jelly — and the armed forces were treated roughly and sometimes ejected from campuses. The revelation on St. Valentine's Day 1967 that $200,000 a year in CIA funds had been subsidizing the National Student Association (NSA), which represented student governments on over three hundred campuses, was enough to cripple the NSA. Students provided the leadership for "Stop-the-Draft Week" in October 1967, including a march to the steps of the Pentagon by more than fifty thousand demonstrators, and they were responsible for imaginative and sometimes shocking protests against the draft — pasting eight draft cards on the door of the American embassy in London, battling Oakland police for five days while attempting to block buses carrying draftees from an induction center to military bases, and seizing and holding the administration building at the University of Chicago for three days to dramatize opposition to the war.

It was not all selfless idealism. College students were of the age most vulnerable to conscription, and as monthly draft calls in 1966 were boosted nearly tenfold over the 1965 average of five thousand, blanket deferments for students became rarer. Resistance to the draft was being expressed openly on posters, buttons, and bumper stickers. The theme of a 1967 hit tune, Arlo Guthrie's "Alice's Restaurant," was draft evasion, and virtually every undergraduate dormitory had a collection of leaflets providing tips on how to get rejected at Selective Service physical examinations. ("Arrive high. If you want to go about the addiction scene in a really big way, use a common pin on your arm for a few weeks in advance.") General Hershey struck back by sending a directive to the country's 4,088 draft boards instructing them to reclassify the protesters 1-A. Congressmen objected that Hershey was exceeding his authority, and the American Civil Liberties Union charged that using the draft to punish dissidents was "outrageous," but Hershey wouldn't back away. One consequence was that the flow of draft evaders to Canada grew until there were some ten thousand young American expatriates there, making new homes with the help of such groups as the Students Union for Peace Action in Toronto.

As the polarization of the country grew, the hawks became more hawkish. In response to back-to-back antiwar speeches by Morse of Oregon ("The United States is leading mankind into World War III out of which will come no victory") and Gruening of Alaska (who called a new war appropriation bill "a blank check for unlimited escalation"), Russell B. Long of Louisiana wrapped himself in the flag in attacking those who "encourage the Communists to prolong the war." Long said, "I swell with pride when I see Old Glory flying from the Capitol . . . My prayer is that there may never be a white flag of surrender up there." Everett Dirksen predicted that if Vietnam fell, "the whole Pacific coastline" of the United States would be "exposed." Manhattan hawks staged Operation Gratitude, a two-day vigil at Battery Park. At the same time, motorists who believed in the war were asked to drive with lights on — and suddenly every highway offered a vivid demonstration of how badly divided the people were.

Lyndon Johnson characteristically said one thing while believing the exact opposite. "No American, young or old, must ever be denied the right to dissent," he declared in June 1966, putting on his white hat. "No minority must be muzzled. Opinion and protest are the life breath of democracy — even when it blows heavy." His deeper feeling was that those who quarreled with his conduct of the war were un-American, and that it was his duty to battle them with any weapon that came to hand. Presidential publicity was effective, and at various times he conferred with Asian allies at Guam, Honolulu, Manila, and Melbourne, staging the trips to coincide with antiwar events he wanted to drive off the front page. It didn't always work. In Australia he discovered that American students weren't the only ones capable of mounting antiwar demonstrations; Melbourne hecklers tossed two plastic balloons filled with paint at his limousine, smearing it red and green, the Viet Cong colors.

His true feelings about opponents of the war boiled over on May 17, 1966, at a Democratic fund-raising dinner in Chicago, when he upbraided "Nervous Nellies" who "will turn on their leaders and on their country and on our own fighting men." By the end of that summer he was avoiding the phrase "Great Society." He had come to prefer the company of political conservatives to that of "knee-jerk liberals" who were such "trouble-makers that they force politicians to the right." In the privacy of the White House he would flatly state that Americans in the antiwar movement were disloyal, that "the Russians" were "behind the whole thing." The FBI and the CIA, he confided to his staff, were keeping him posted on what was "really going on." The doves in the Senate were in touch with Soviet agents, he said; they lunched with them, attended parties at the Russian embassy, and encouraged the children of their aides to date Soviet diplomats in Washington and at the U.N. He asserted, "The Russians think up things for the Senators to say. I often know before they do what their speeches are going to say." In June 1966 the parents of one of the winners of a Presidential Scholarship, a gifted seventeen-year-old girl, turned out to be critics of the war. Word went out to the staff that the girl was to be deprived of her medal. Eric Goldman protested and the order was rescinded, but Goldman was told that before Presidential Scholars were nominated in the future, they and their families would be subjected to FBI checks.

Hawks, following Johnson's example, saw the stain of disloyalty spreading. In 1966 CBS-TV showed marines in the "Zippo squads" — as they called themselves — setting fire to peasant huts, and the Pentagon virtually accused the commentators of treason. When McNamara opposed the bombing of Hanoi in a Montreal speech, noting that the weekly bomb tonnage dropped on North Vietnam already exceeded that of all the bombings of Germany in World War II, he too came under suspicion. He decided to resign in November 1967, joining Mac Bundy, George Ball, Jack Valenti, George Reedy, Richard Goodwin, and Horace Busby in the exodus of trusted Johnsonian advisers from Washington. The departure of Bill Moyers hurt the President most, but it was Johnson's equivocations which had made Moyers's role as press secretary untenable. Reston wrote of him that he had been wounded at Credibility Gap, and Moyers himself said that the gap had become so bad that "we can't even believe our own leaks." The President, stung by his resignation, accused Moyers of ingratiating himself with the Kennedys and exploiting the White House, using it to better himself at the expense of the administration. He read the clippings, LBJ stormed, and he wasn't stupid; he saw what had been happening; the press secretary had been getting a good press for himself while Johnson's grew worse and worse.

He was right about his public image. By 1967 it was terrible. The Secret Service disclosed that the number of people arrested for threatening the life of the chief executive had increased by over 500 percent since Dallas. The number of people holding Lyndon Johnson responsible for the death of John Kennedy was growing. By May 1967 there were, *Esquire* estimated, some sixty different versions of the Dallas tragedy on sale. Early that year District Attorney Jim Garrison of New Orleans told the press, "My staff and I solved the assassination weeks ago." Subsequent events made it plain that Garrison belonged in a padded cell, not a courtroom, but a Harris poll that May indicated that the number of Americans who doubted the Warren Report had jumped from 44 percent to 66. Many believed Garrison "had something"; others simply came to distrust everything about President Johnson, including the way he entered the White House.

His popularity dropped until in March 1968 Gallup's figures indicated that only 36 percent of the country approved of his conduct of the Presidency. Like Richard Nixon five years later, Johnson responded by withdrawing into a self-imposed isolation. During his campaign against Goldwater three years earlier he had alarmed the Secret Service by his way of wading joyously into seas of humanity. Now his public appearances were confined to reliable audiences — meetings of business executives or service families on military bases, where he could trust his listeners to be respectful. The White House became embattled. Getting past the gates became much more difficult; credentials had to be just so, and dispatch cases were rigorously searched. The President's staff urged him to get out among the people. Even if crowds were hostile the nation would sympathize and admire his courage. Anything would be an improvement on this seclusion. The Secret Service objected. Given the country's ugly mood, they felt that appearances before unscreened groups would be risky, and this time Johnson obeyed them.

More and more he kept watch on his staff and cabinet, alert for further defections. Those who wanted to stay, or who needed his approval for advancement now and his endorsement for future positions, felt they had to display excessive zeal and unquestioning devotion to him. Hubert Humphrey became a superhawk. Larry O'Brien drafted the dead in support of the war, telling an audience in Lexington, Virginia, that if General George C. Marshall were alive he would "no doubt" back Johnson's Vietnam policy in every particular. Nick Katzenbach, appointed attorney general, held in testimony before the Senate Foreign Relations Committee on August 17, 1967, that Congress had authorized the President "to use the armed forces of the United States in whatever way necessary" when it passed the Tonkin Gulf resolution three years earlier, and that this was indeed sufficient warrant for any military commitment the President might make in Indochina, including the bombing of targets close to the Chinese border. This exchange followed:

SENATOR FULBRIGHT: You think it is outmoded to declare war?

MR. KATZENBACH: In this kind of context I think the expression of declaring a war is one that has become outmoded in the international arena.

It was enough, Katzenbach said, that the Senate had approved of American participation in regional defense treaties, in this case SEATO. He intimated that a President could do whatever he liked with U.S. military power without consulting Congress. At that point a member of the committee rose and strode angrily out of the room muttering, "There is only one thing to do — take it to the country." The senator was Eugene McCarthy of Minnesota.

It was in May 1967, the third and ugliest year of black violence, that Stokely Carmichael resigned as chairman of the misnamed Student Nonviolent Coordinating Committee and flew off to tour Cuba and North Vietnam. "You'll be happy to have me back," he said, referring to his successor, H. Rap Brown, as "a bad man." The rise of Brown was a triumph for militants bent on the rejection of integration and the alienation of white liberals. "If you give me a gun I might just shoot Lady Bird," he said on July 26, and he told Detroit blacks, "The honky is your enemy."

Whites were barred from a national conference on black power in Newark the weekend of July 20–23. The delegates took their theme from Malcolm X: "The day of nonviolent resistance is over." Among the measures they endorsed were resolutions calling for the formation of a "black militia," for "a national dialogue on the desirability of partitioning the United States into two separate nations, one white and one black," and for recognition of "the right of black people to revolt when they deem it necessary and in their interests." Integration was dead, the nearly one thousand delegates declared; absolute segregation of the races was the new goal.

The August 14 issue of Brown's SNCC *Newsletter* denounced Zionism, attacked American Jews, and accused Israel of crushing Arabs "through terror, force, and massacre." That drove from SNCC membership such liberals as Harry Golden and Theodore Bikel and drew the fire of the Anti-Defamation League of B'nai B'rith. The militants were undaunted. To be sure white sympathizers got the message that they were unwelcome, CORE dropped "multiracial" from the constitutional description of its membership. Speaking for CORE, Floyd McKissick issued a Black Manifesto declaring that sit-ins, boycotts, and peaceful demonstrations belonged to the past. "The tactics and philosophy of the civil rights era can take us no further along the road to total equality," he said. "New methods must be found; a new era must begin." The long, hot summers of rioting, he suggested, might be remembered in the future as "the beginning of the black revolution."

Some honkies seemed to take an almost masochistic pleasure in their mortification. Perhaps the most vivid example was the National Conference for New Politics (NCNP), held in Chicago over Labor Day weekend in 1967. The conference was attended by three thousand delegates representing over two hundred groups with varied goals, among them an end to the Vietnam War, better treatment of the poor, and equity for black Americans. The number of votes represented by each delegate was determined by the number of active members in his organization back home. Women Strike for Peace, for example, had 1,000 votes; the Camden Citizens for Peace in Vietnam 31 votes. Negro groups had 5,000 votes. They wanted more. "Black people can't be a plank in someone else's platform," said McKissick. "They must be the platform itself." Forming a Black Caucus, the Negro delegates issued an ultimatum of thirteen points. Among them were a demand for 50 percent black representation on all committees, censure of the "imperial Zionist war," and approval of all measures passed by the Newark conference. They demanded that all this be accepted without change by 1 P.M. that Saturday. An editor of *Ramparts* suggested a modification of the language but withdrew it when a member of the Black Caucus shouted at him, "What right has a white man got amending the black man's resolution?"

After an elderly white woman explained that this was merely a test of the NCNP's "social barometer," the thirteen-point program was accepted by a three-to-one vote. The delegates then gave themselves a standing ovation. Then they received a jolt. The Black Caucus was still dissatisfied. The caucus groups wanted not the 5,000 votes they had been allocated but

28,498 votes — absolute control of the convention. Negro speakers explained from the podium that it was all a matter of trust; whites had to prove that they trusted blacks by adopting the proposal. "An extraordinary development took place," one of the white delegates said afterward. "The walls of the Palmer House began to drip with guilt." Adoption passed, two to one. Thereafter the fate of each resolution before the convention was determined by a young Negro in the front row of the Black Caucus holding a large pink card that represented 28,498 votes. In fact, not much was accomplished. A sizable number of whites had come hoping to nominate a presidential ticket, Martin Luther King for President and Dr. Spock for Vice President. It died stillborn: the Black Caucus regarded Dr. King as a black honky, and Dr. Spock, in his old-fashioned way, still used the word Negro.

Despite Brown-McKissick rhetoric, the flow of blacks into the middle class was increasing. Census figures would later show that the number of Negro families with annual incomes over $10,000 increased from 11 to 28 percent during the 1960s. The way was opening up spectacularly for talented blacks. In 1965 Benjamin O. Davis Jr. became a lieutenant general in the Air Force. Secretary of Housing and Urban Development Robert C. Weaver, U.S. Senator Edward W. Brooke, Bishop Robert Perry of the Catholic Church, and Judge Constance Baker Motley of the federal bench all reached their eminent offices in 1966. A survey by two private organizations revealed that 1,469 Negroes held public office. Thurgood Marshall was appointed to the Supreme Court in 1967; Air Force Major Robert H. Lawrence became the first Negro astronaut on June 30 (he was killed in December when his plane crashed on a training flight); Elizabeth D. Koontz was elected president of the National Education Association; Dean Rusk's daughter married a black, Guy Gibson Smith; Cleveland and Gary acquired Negro mayors, and Walter E. Washington was named commissioner of the District of Columbia. The very excesses of the black militants seemed to ease the way for some Negro moderates; James Meredith repeated his Mississippi march in 1967, and the only whites to interrupt him asked for his autograph or snapped his picture.

But backlash continued to deliver stinging blows elsewhere. In Boston Louise Day Hicks, a forty-four-year-old grandmother, became a popular figure, and later a congresswoman, on the strength of her stand against remedies for racial imbalance in schools. A black youth was murdered in Detroit's Algiers Motel while under police interrogation; the officer who shot him pleaded self-defense and was acquitted by an all-white jury, showing that such cases were not confined to the Deep South. Adam Clayton Powell was denied his seat in Congress. There was no doubt about his misconduct, but Thomas Dodd, it was noted, was merely censured by the Senate. Father James E. Groppi failed in his campaign for "open" (integrated) housing in Milwaukee. Lester Maddox was sworn in as governor of Georgia, and the winner of Mississippi's gubernatorial race was another racist, John Bell Williams.

But these developments were overshadowed by that summer's havoc in the metropolitan ghettos, bringing to a climax the Negro revolt which had begun two years earlier in Watts. In its fury and the desolation it left behind it was like a war, and indeed there were those who believed that it was a mirror image of the Vietnam violence which could be seen on the television screens in every living room now during the dinner hour. "The government is contradictory," said John Lewis, Carmichael's predecessor as chairman of SNCC, "telling oppressed black men not to be violent in the streets while it carries out the terrible slaughter in Vietnam and finances it with money it should be spending to get things right at home."

That year the first torches were lit on April 8. Nashville police ejected a Negro from a restaurant at Fisk University that evening. Two days of chaos followed, and during the next month Cleveland, Washington, Louisville, Montgomery, and Omaha exploded. May arrived, and June, and Molotov cocktails, looters' clubs, and snipers' rifles appeared with increasing frequency. Major cities hit were New York, Minneapolis, Tampa, Atlanta, Birmingham, Cincinnati, San Francisco, Buffalo, Dayton and Wichita. Then came the first weekend in July and the first real ghetto catastrophe of 1967.

It began according to the now established ritual, with policemen. Late that Friday afternoon squad cars were summoned to the Grove Hall welfare office in Roxbury, a black district in southeast Boston. An organization of women on relief was demonstrating against welfare policy. They wanted more money, and they wanted to be treated with greater civility. It was past closing time, but the women wouldn't leave, and they had locked arms at the doors to prevent the employees from leaving. The cops entered through the windows. A crowd of Negroes gathered. Bottles and stones were thrown. More police arrived with helmets and riot sticks. They charged the mob, as it now was, in a flying wedge. That broke it up, which turned out to be a mistake. Forming small bands, the Negroes roamed Roxbury smashing glass, looting, putting buildings to the torch, and clouting whites. Before dawn a thousand policemen were battling a thousand blacks, and by Sunday evening, when the riot was spent, seventy people had been injured and fifteen blocks of Blue Hill Avenue, a main artery between downtown Boston and the suburbs, were a vast junkyard.

The week after Roxbury was peaceful but tense; nothing in the past two summers encouraged complacency. Urbanists were watching Newark, New Jersey, with particular vigilance. Even in peaceful times Newark would have been considered volatile. In seeking Model Cities grants its administration had frankly described it as "a basic training camp for the poor." Crowded and slummy, its very air was polluted with offensive odors from its many factories. Newark had the country's highest rate of venereal

disease, the most crime, and the greatest percentage of condemned housing. Over the past century it had been successively inhabited by Protestants, Irish, Italians, and Jews, and by this time it was second only to
Washington as a major city with a black majority. In 1960 Newark's population had been 62 percent white. Now it was 52 percent black and 10
percent Puerto Rican. Most of the 208,000 blacks lived in the shabby
Central Ward. The unemployment figure there was twice the national
figure, and the black rate of joblessness was twice the city's. In Washington
the people at the new Department of Housing and Urban Development
whose job it was to watch such things had long been worried about
Newark. They thought the city awaited only a police incident to erupt. It
came on Wednesday, July 12.

At 9:45 P.M. a black cab driver, arrested for a traffic violation, was
brought into the 4th Precinct station in the Central Ward. He argued
heatedly with two police officers and exchanged blows with them. Word
spread outside that the cabby had been beaten to death. The customary
spectators gathered, but nothing much happened there; after they had left
officers reported downtown that they had been nothing more than "a bunch
of roving kids" anyway. At dusk the next day another crowd assembled,
carrying signs but apparently in good humor. Then the first bottle was
thrown, and the first brick. The policemen broke up the throng with
nightsticks. In twos and threes the Negroes disbanded — and began looting
stores. By 11 P.M. plundering was proceeding on a massive scale, snipers
were firing from roofs, and fires were blazing high. Newark's 1,400 police
couldn't handle it. By daybreak, when 2,600 National Guardsmen and 300
state police arrived, the sun shone down on what Governor Richard J.
Hughes called "a city in open rebellion." Almost half of Newark's twenty-
four square miles was in the hands of the rioters, and order was not
restored until Monday, July 17. By then twenty-seven were dead. The loss
was put at ten million dollars. It was the worst disorder since Watts.

Detroit blew the following Sunday after a police raid on a Twelfth Street
black nightclub which was selling liquor after 2 A.M., the legal closing time.
The crowd milled around, the rumors of brutality spread — this time it was
said that a boy wearing handcuffs had been kicked down a stairway — and
the crowd, scattered by police, wandered away in small groups and began
looting. In some ways this outburst was unusual. Unlike Newark, Detroit
had not been regarded as a potential trouble spot. The mayor, elected with
Negro support, had introduced measures which, together with the booming automobile business, had helped create a large black middle class. That,
in fact, was part of the trouble. The rioters, who had not made it, were as
resentful of middle-class Negroes as of whites. Another difference was that
looting was integrated in Detroit; blacks and whites ransacked stores side
by side. The extent of the arson was almost unbelievable — 1,600 fire
alarms in eleven days. But the most remarkable aspect of the Detroit riot
was its size. Henry Ford called it "the greatest internal violence since the

Civil War." The death toll was forty-three. Over seven thousand were arrested. Eighteen blocks of Twelfth Street and three miles of Grand River Avenue were burned to the ground. Aerial photographs of the city resembled Berlin in 1945. Five thousand people were without shelter. And many were insanely jubilant. "Those buildings going up was a pretty sight," said one of the Detroit rioters. "I sat right here and watched them go. And there wasn't nothing them honkies could do but sweat to put it out." He was speaking, of course, of Negro homes.

President Johnson appointed a commission headed by Governor Otto Kerner of Illinois to study outbreaks and find a way to prevent more of them. Hearings were scheduled by the Senate's Subcommittee on Investigations and the House Committee on Un-American Activities — which was under the impression that subversives were responsible for the disorders. And still that summer's rage in the ghettos was unspent. Altogether rioters struck 114 cities in 32 states. The complete toll would never be known, but there were at the very least 88 deaths, more than 4,000 other casualties, and 12,000 arrests. Among the grimmest upheavals were those in Wilmington, Toledo, South Bend, Grand Rapids, Pontiac, Milwaukee, New Haven, Providence, Saginaw, Flint, Portland (Oregon), and Cambridge (Maryland).

The Cambridge uprising was of particular interest. It was one of the few episodes which justified the Un-American Activities Committee's suspicions, and it had an unforeseen impact on national politics. Backlash had been a major factor in Maryland's 1966 gubernatorial campaign; when a racist candidate won the Democratic primary, black voters had backed the Republican nominee, Spiro T. Agnew, a moderate. Agnew's feelings about law and order were stronger than his views on race, however, and he was outraged when Rap Brown, an outside agitator if there ever was one, told a rally of Eastern Shore Negroes that "It's time for Cambridge to explode." Brown called a Negro school a firetrap which "should have burned down long ago." He urged them to "Get yourself some guns," said that the riots were a "dress rehearsal for revolution," and added that "Violence is as American as cherry pie."

Thereupon Cambridge exploded, the school was burned, and Agnew issued a warrant for Brown's arrest on charges of inciting to riot and arson. "Such a person," said the governor, "cannot be permitted to come into a state with the intention to destroy and then sneak away, leaving these poor people with the results of his evil scheme." Brown was arrested in Alexandria, Virginia, two days later. Afterward he faced other charges for carrying firearms across a state line while under indictment. Meanwhile Governor Agnew's resolute handling of the incident had attracted the attention of the Republican party's national leadership, winning him the admiration of, among others, Richard M. Nixon.

Montage: The Johnson Years

this button is just an attempt to communicate

GREAT SOCIETY ABOMINABLE SNOW JOB

REAGAN FIRES CLARK KERR AS BERKELEY CHANCELLOR: SCORES "PERMISSIVENESS"

Get your head together

APATHY

GOD IS DEAD

U.S. POPULATION SEEN SURPASSING 200 MILLION MARK

KEEP THE FAITH BABY

U.S., U.S.S.R. CATAPULT VENUS PROBES

"LSD is Western yoga," Dr. Leary explained. "The aim of all Eastern religion, like the aim of LSD, is basically to get high; that is, to expand your consciousness and find ecstasy and revelation within."

off the pigs

WE LOVE YOU AND ARE WORRIED,

PLEASE CALL COLLECT,

NO PUNISHMENT

Hare Krishna, Hare Krishna
Krishna Krishna, Hare Hare
Hare Rama, Hare Rama
Rama Rama, Hare Hare

COMPUTER, SET TO SELECT IDEAL MATES, PICKS BROTHER, SISTER

SPEED KILLS

Say it loud — I'm black and I'm proud

First you get a really strong sex urge. You get a fantastic rush — a feeling that you're speeded up, you think you can do anything. It opens up little doors to the channels in your mind so you actually believe you can do anything. After a while it induces acute paranoia.

Bangs manes bouffants beehives Beatle caps butter faces brush-on lashes decal eyes puffy sweaters French thrust bras flailing leather blue jeans stretch pants stretch jeans honeydew bottoms eclair shanks elf boots ballerinas Knight slippers, hundreds of them, these flaming little buds, bobbing and screaming, rocketing around inside the Academy of Music Theater underneath that vast old mouldering cherub dome up there — aren't they supermarvelous!

"There's no room for deathless prose in the novel," Miss Susann said.

3 ASTRONAUTS DIE; LAST PRAYERS TOLD

JACKIE VISITS CAMBODIA, LAUDS ORIENTAL CHARM

WARNING: YOUR LOCAL POLICE ARE ARMED AND DANGEROUS

IN COLD BLOOD: The show-place farm of Herbert Clutter, set in the peaceful, prosperous, picture-book country west of Garden City, Kans. (pop. 11,000), seemed the nation's least likely setting for cold-blooded, methodical murder.

LBJ, BIRD SET FOR LUCI VOWS

DE GAULLE: "VIVE LE QUEBEC LIBRE"

BOOKS MUST GO!

BAN THE BRA

power to the people

GREEK COLONELS SEIZE CONTROL IN ATHENS COUP

The new 100-mm. cigarette, six-tenths of an inch longer than the traditional king-sized ones, had jumped from 2 percent of the market at the beginning of 1967 to 15 percent at the year's close — about $1 billion worth

BLACK IS BEAUTIFUL

TURN ON TUNE IN DROP OUT

I'VE GONE TO POT

BLACK POWER

Good grief, Charlie Brown

THIRTY-TWO

Up Against the Wall

I N *The New Industrial State,* published in 1967, John Kenneth Galbraith noted "an interesting and widely remarked phenomenon of recent years," an "ill-defined discontent, especially among students and intellectuals, with the accepted and approved modalities of social thought." These, wrote Galbraith, "whether espoused by professed liberals or conservatives, are held to be the views of 'The Establishment.'"

Actually, by then, blacks, radicals, feminists, and just about everybody else who felt systematically cheated by organized society had taken to calling it and all its works the "establishment." Often the word was used so loosely as to render it meaningless — shoplifting was called a blow to the establishment; the establishment was blamed for poor television programming — but some applications of it indicated a profound instinct for the workings of the system. This was never truer than on the memorable night of Tuesday, November 9, 1965, when antiestablishmentarians felt vindicated, and others dismayed, by the extraordinary failure of one of society's essential services: electrical power.

The sun set over the eastern United States at 4:44 P.M. that afternoon, and the demand for electricity then began building toward its daily peak. Light switches were flipped on in homes and offices. Neon signs lit up. In places of business elevators came into maximum use as workers departed. Subways put on extra trains for commuters, farmers in the country beyond the skyline hitched cows to milking machines, and lighthouses commenced to flash. Children raced in from play and turned on TV sets, while their mothers started supper. The day being autumnal and the temperature 46, thermostats triggered millions of furnaces into operation. Greenhouse heating systems became more active, and reptile houses in zoos were provided with that extra margin of heat without which their vipers and crocodiles would perish. In bars, ice machines began hatching cubes for office workers pausing for that daily drink before setting out for home. On parkways and highways electrically powered gasoline pumps filled the tanks of homeward-bound cars.

All this was a matter of routine to Edward J. Nellis, a slender, balding man of sixty-two and a forty-one year veteran employee of the Consolidated Edison Company of New York. Nellis was seated in the controller's chair of Con Ed's Energy Control Center at 128 West End Avenue, Manhattan, near Sixty-fifth Street. The center, the hub of the company's electronic universe, is a high-ceilinged, antiseptic, rather Orwellian room whose dials and switches, bathed in brilliant fluorescent light, were all visible to Nellis. By vigilantly scanning them, he could be sure that Con Ed was fulfilling its role not only here in the metropolis, but also as chief member of the Ontario, New York, and New England electric power pool, an area of 80,000 square miles inhabited by 30 million people. At any rate, that was the theory. It entered the realm of intense controversy at about 5:16 P.M., when Nellis, starting from his chair, saw that the needles on all the dials had begun to oscillate wildly.

At the time neither he nor anyone else knew what was happening, though Con Ed's senior engineers had often discussed the possibility of a massive electric failure. They predicted — correctly — what they called a "cascade effect," in which an enormous, unexpected demand for power by one member of the pool would suck up the electricity of all the others. If that occurred, every generator in the pool, also known as the Northeast Power Grid, would automatically shut off to avoid damaging the equipment. All 80,000 square miles would be plunged into instant darkness.

The swinging needles at 128 West End Avenue were the consequence of such a cascade. The trouble lay 315 miles north of Manhattan and four miles west of Niagara Falls, in a Canadian hydrogenerating installation called the Sir Adam Beck Station No. 2. A relay — a device no larger than a breadbox — had been set for 1963 requirements and never readjusted, though power loads had been expanding steadily ever since. At 5 P.M. that afternoon electricity for Toronto was flowing north over six of the Adam Beck plant's lines. At 5:16:11, instruments showed later, the load increased slightly — just enough to trip the incorrectly set relay. That in turn set a circuit breaker in motion, putting one of the six lines out of action. Its load was instantly picked up by the other five, but they couldn't handle it. Overloaded, they were then cut off by their own relays. Two disasters followed almost simultaneously. About 1.6 million kilowatts of energy, destined for Toronto but unable to get through the invalided Adam Beck station, surged southward on the grid's great electric superhighway into upper New York State and New England, knocking out generating plants as it went. That created a power vacuum. The areas stricken by it demanded current from Manhattan — more than Manhattan had. The second calamity swiftly followed. Protective devices were activated all over the Northeast Power Grid. The cascade, or "falling domino" effect as some called it, was taking areas out of the pool automatically. It was complete at 5:38 P.M., when Vermont and southern New Hampshire joined the states to the south. Except for hospitals and other institutions, with their own generators, scarcely a light shone between Niagara and the Hudson. The great blackout had begun.

New York City went out at 5:27 P.M. Nellis had just decided to push the eight buttons which would have cut the metropolis free of the grid, but he was too late. It was a forgivable error: one of the few things unchanged about the consumption of electricity since Thomas Edison invented the first practical incandescent lamp in 1879 is that it still travels at the speed of light. But the consequences were stupefying. Except for Staten Island and one small Brooklyn neighborhood, the power was gone — all of it: illumination, appliances, subways; the works. In unaffected Montclair, New Jersey, a woman looking out her picture window had been admiring the fairylike spectacle of Manhattan alight. She called her teen-age son to share it with him, and when she turned back to the window the city had disappeared. Above Kennedy International Airport, Captain Ron George of Air Canada was entering his glide pattern. He looked down at the runway, glanced at his instruments, glanced back — and saw only Stygian blackness. The airport, too, had vanished.

Reactions in those first moments of the blackout varied, and to a certain extent they reflected individual fears. "The Chinese," thought a woman on Manhattan's East Side. "An attack from outer space!" cried a small boy in an apartment twenty stories above the East River. Two newspaper reporters were struck by the same thought — that the antiwar movement had scored a real coup. Others were too preoccupied with unexpected crises to wonder who was responsible. In hospitals awaiting the ninety-second shift to emergency power, surgeons were continuing to operate by flashlight. The management of Schrafft's was worrying about $200,000 worth of ice cream. (It all melted.) Governor Rockefeller was climbing fifteen stories of stairs to his apartment. Over 800,000 people were trapped underground in the subways. Sixty of them would spend a harrowing night in an Astoria line BMT train in the Sixtieth Street tunnel under the East River. Far above them, on the Williamsburg Bridge over the river, 1,700 commuters were stranded on four trains. After five hours they would be led to safety.

In department stores, floorwalkers either led their customers out by flashlight or put them to bed in the home furnishing departments. Farmers reacquired the skill of milking cows by hand. Children, deprived of television, were learning to play on their own. Zoo keepers kept mammals alive with blankets and warmed their reptile houses with portable propane gas heaters. Not much could be done for motorists in need of fuel from the electrically operated gas pumps or housewives with cold electric stoves, however. Many who were suddenly idle were calling friends or relatives.

The phones were working, and there was an 800 percent increase in local calls that evening. Others were doing other things. Nine months later to the day, all hospitals reported a sharp increase in births.

Thanks to transistors, radio broadcasts were getting through, but they cannot be said to have been much help to their bewildered audience. Breathless commentators spoke of "Canada in darkness . . . Cause unknown . . . worst power failure in the history of the world . . . President Johnson has summoned his emergency planning board . . . immediate investigation . . . sabotage feared." There were hints at war and nuclear holocaust until the Strategic Air Command in Colorado Springs reported "Condition Green," meaning normal. There were some local disturbances — looting in Springfield, Massachusetts, and a major riot at the Massachusetts state prison in Walpole — and a few tragic accidents. The body of one man was found at the bottom of a New York hotel elevator shaft, a burned-out candle in his hand.

In the early hours of that evening, virtually the only light in the grid was provided by candles, flashlights, automobile lights, and a full moon. Then the lights began returning, one area at a time. Vermont and southern New Hampshire came back after blackouts of thirty minutes to two hours. Connecticut had gone black at 5:30 and was slow to recover, but by 11:30 all but twelve of its towns were alight. Greater New York was the slowest of all. Brooklyn was back by 2 A.M. Wednesday, and thousands of sleepers there learned of it in a manner which would be repeated elsewhere; they had turned in leaving wall and lamp switches on, and were awakened when their bedrooms were suddenly flooded with light. Power returned to Queens at 4:20 A.M., to Manhattan and Westchester by 6:58 A.M., and to the Bronx at 7 A.M. Here and there stubborn pockets resisted the restoration of power. Pelham Manor in exclusive Westchester County didn't rejoin the grid until early Thursday. One Pelham Manor woman said afterward that she "burned a lot of candles," "kept the fireplace going," and "kept thinking about how people must have lived in Pelham Manor in the primitive days when there was no electricity."

The following Monday, November 15, 1965, six days after the power had failed, electrical engineers traced the blackout to the Beck plant. The Canadians were embarrassed; they had been insisting that the fault couldn't have been on their side of the border. American utilities spokesmen felt this proved that they had been blameless. But most of the public did not discriminate. They blamed the whole lot, Canadians and Americans alike. At the same time, the tales of their adventures during the blackout were improving in the telling. Eventually many forgot their anxieties at the time and were rejoicing in memories of the freedom from routine. Said a team of *New York Times* reporters:

> In every man there is a corner of rebellion against the machine. We were all delighted at the rediscovery of things that were not plugged into walls —

things that were almost forgotten by us — most of all, the wonderful, wonderful candle. What a moment of triumph to know that the huge computers we really did not like and that we suspected really did not like us were lying massively idle and useless, but the old pencil sharpener still worked.

It was all illusion, as the *Times* men conceded. In the end all were "recaptured and brought back submissively to the prison farm of modern technology." The candle and the pencil sharpener were all very well for a hiatus of a few hours, but they would not have seemed wonderful much longer. They could not have transported commuters, or warmed homes, or provided light for reading, or provided any one of the countless services and necessities for which men had come to rely upon technology. The way of life in Pelham Manor in the primitive days when there was no electricity would have come as a savage shock to them. Many would have been unable to survive it. Some thought of what the *Times* writers called "the plugged-in society" as a prison farm, and some had worse names for it, but not many were so vehement about the huge computers that they were prepared to scrap them. There were, however, a few.

Taking their name from a half-witted Leicestershire worker who had attacked a machine a generation earlier, British handcraftsmen thrown out of work by the industrial revolution declared war on shearing frames and power looms in 1811. From a mythical retreat in Sherwood Forest they issued a nonnegotiable demand:

We will never lay down Arms [till] The House of Commons passes an Act to put down all Machinery hurtful to Commonality, and repeal that to hang Frame Breakers. . . . We petition no more — that won't do — fighting must.
Signed by the General of the Army of Redressers
Ned Ludd Clerk

Soreheads standing in the way of laborsaving devices have been known as Luddites ever since, and critics of America's increasingly technocratic society during the Johnson years were frequently accused of Luddism. In instances of rioting students this was sometimes justified. Professors' notes were destroyed, equipment was damaged, and a sign plastered on one Cambridge computer accused it of drawing high wages and fringe benefits at the expense of American workmen. That was as absurd as Ned at his most futile, but the case against technocracy was not entirely preposterous. Intelligent men and women were tired of receiving punch-card mail, riding on push-button elevators, standing in check-out lines, reading about a war being judged by body counts, listening to recorded voices over telephones, and being treated during political campaigns as pollster percentages. As Nicholas von Hoffman pointed out, the demonstrating students were rebellious at being "admitted, tested, and flunked by computers." There was something chilling about Human Inventory, Inc., the Los Angeles matchmaking service which had 6,000 clients and was headed by a former executive in an aerospace company. Everyone had his computer horror stories, and some were choice. An Albany hospital sent a woman a bill for "ritual circumcision." And in 1966 Mayor John F. Collins of Boston was favored to win reelection until, three days before the primary, the city computer, all by itself, prepared, addressed, and mailed 30,000 delinquent sewer tax bills. The mayor was defeated.

Erich Fromm warned: "A specter is stalking in our midst. . . . It is a new specter: a completely mechanized society . . . directed by computers; and in this social process, man himself is being transformed into a part of the total machine." Millions of Americans by the late 1960s were carrying as many as twenty multiple numbers in their wallets, some indicating their various identities, some necessary for daily business, and all tending to reduce them to random particles — zip codes, area codes, blood types, drivers' licenses, automobile licenses, social security numbers, army serial numbers, and numbers of charge accounts, checking accounts, book club memberships, insurance policies, passports, birth and marriage certificates, mortgages, and Veterans Administration claims. The author of *The Beast of Business* recommended playing "computer-card roulette" by closing holes with tape, cutting new holes with a razor blade, and exposing the code number to an electromagnet. When a California janitor received a $5,000 check for two weeks' work, everyone cheered except the aeroelasticity investigators, inertial systems engineers, superconductivity research specialists, and digital circuit design specialists — those, in short, whose great age this was.

John Mauchly, the builder of the first U.S. commercial computers, had predicted that "only four or five giant firms will be able to employ these machines usefully." He underestimated his prodigies. There were 1,000 computers in the United States in 1955. In 1960 government engineers suggested that 15,000 might be in use within five years. The time arrived and 25,000 were in use. By 1967 there were 40,000 — some 2,000 for the federal government alone.

All this was disquieting to American humanists. Liberals in politics, they had become more and more traditional in their social attitudes. In the late 1940s they had been alarmed by *Nineteen Eighty-Four*. During the Eisenhower years a genteel shabbiness had acquired a certain cachet among them, for they were especially disturbed by the thing-oriented culture that had ridden in on the wave of technological advances. It appeared to them that the nation was becoming enslaved by manipulators of consumer appetites. Among the figures disgorged by the pullulating computers were analyses of what manipulation of the public was doing to consumer debt. Between 1956 and 1967 it increased 133 percent, to 99.1 billion dollars. Motor car paper alone was up 117 percent, to 31.2 billion dollars. It looked as though Will Rogers had been right; the country was going to the poorhouse in an automobile.

Autos would have been bad enough — thoughtful Americans were just beginning to learn what Detroit was doing to their environment — but the dismay of intellectuals over what was coming to be regarded as the blight of mass opulence went far beyond that. The voracity of the national vending machine seemed insatiable. Disposable personal income had almost doubled since the Eisenhower years, but the faith, so strong in the 1930s, that men would spend wisely if they just had the money, was in shreds. Then Edmund Wilson had written scornfully of "foods that do not nourish, disinfectants that do not disinfect," of "cosmetics that poison the face, lubricants that corrode your car," and "insecticides that kill your trees." But it was precisely these brands which were flourishing in the booming 1960s. At least in the Depression you hadn't been compelled to look at them in your own living room. Television commercials now spewed them forth in all their vulgarity — and in nauseous color to boot — until one wondered what the country was going to do with all the junk. An inspired Mobil commercial provided the answer during the 1969 American League baseball play-offs. With each $3 purchase it offered customers a plastic bag which would hold "22 pounds, four cubic feet" of trash. "You'll be glad you threw it away," said the commercial, and it was true.

Televised sport was a grievance in itself. It turned millions of men who ought to have been active outdoors — for their own health, if nothing else — into beer-drinking, flatulent spectators watching young athletes romp joyously in gilded playpens. The gaudiest pen of all was Houston's 32-million-dollar, air-conditioned Astrodome, with its 46,000 upholstered seats, 30,000-car parking lot, and a steel dome which eliminated the need to issue rain checks. So intent were the superstadium's designers upon making it playable in fog, rain, or darkness that they overlooked one possibility: the sun might shine. When that happened, they discovered to their horror, outfielders lost fly balls in the dazzling dome. Early games were played only on cloudy days, and even so the outfielders had to wear batting helmets. Then the skylights were painted gray — meaning that all games there would require lights, whatever the weather.

To skeptics of the new prosperity the Astrodome was a shrine of tastelessness and overconsumption. Its 53 private boxes, available for five-year leases, rented for $15,000 to $34,000 a season. Private clubrooms, for those bored with the game below, were outfitted with bars and TV and provided by decorators with such themes as "Tahitian Holiday," or "The French Hunt." Over fifty different uniforms were designed for Astrodome workers, depending on their tasks (ground crewmen wore space suits), and each was sent to school for three weeks to learn how to project the proper Astrodome image. The greatest spectacle in the stadium was a home run by the home team Astros. Fans never forgot it, and some visiting pitchers never recovered from it. The electric scoreboard went berserk. Rockets were launched and bombs exploded. Electric cattle wearing the American and Texas flags on their horns bucked wildly. Electric cowboys fired electronic bullets at them. An orchestra crashed through "The Eyes of Texas."

"When in doubt," went an advertising slogan that year, "buy the proven product." But the skeptics had no doubts. They recoiled from all mass merchandise. To them the marketplace was evil. The economic lessons they had learned in their youth had lost all relevance. "The essential mass problem had shifted," Eric Goldman wrote. It was "less food, housing and clothing than how to live with a weirdly uneasy affluence." Goldman described "a maldistribution no longer accepted by a significant section of the population." Certainly that section was highly articulate. Its polemics against maldistribution could be found in any bookstore. A common theme in them was that mass culture led to the garrison-prison state.

Some perceptive authors pointed out to intellectuals that they were not always logical. William H. Whyte Jr. remarked that it was "a retrograde point of view" which failed to recognize that a growth of Babbittry was "a consequence of making the benefits of our civilization available to more people." Caroline Bird noted that "People who are usually compassionate sometimes fail to see how the full employment of the 1960s is responsible for what they experience as a general decline in morals, competence, courtesy, energy, and discipline." John Kenneth Galbraith reminded liberal humanists that they could not pick and choose among technological advances. If they wanted some of them, they would have to put up with the rest. Nor could they accept the wonders of applied science and reject the special relationship between the state and industry which had made it possible: "It is open to every freeborn man to dislike this accommodation. But he must direct his attack to the cause. He must not ask that jet aircraft, nuclear power plants or even the modern automobile in its modern volume be produced by firms that are subject to unfixed prices and unmanaged demand. He must ask that they not be produced." Galbraith remained an eloquent advocate of a higher quality of life, but he told fellow critics that before dismissing the digital society entirely they should reflect that it has brought them much that they enjoy and take for granted; for example, "in the absence of automatic transmission of [telephone] calls, it would require approximately the entire female working force of the country to handle current traffic."

That was in 1967. Galbraith did not anticipate that within four years his assumption that all operators should be female would become fighting words. Yesterday's truism had become today's heresy. This, perhaps, was the overriding fact about the impact of science and technology on the United States. Its changes were convulsive, overwhelming. That was one reason for the jarring aspect of American life in the 1960s. Occupational skills became obsolete so rapidly that career planning was difficult and sometimes impossible for the young. In 1967, for example, the chemical industry calculated that half its business came from the sale of products which hadn't even existed ten years earlier. One of these, the contraceptive pill, played a crucial role in the dramatic revision of American female expectations. At the same time, life expectancy for white females was approaching

80 years (as against 75 years for white males). Science and technology was steadily altering the shape of the future. In 1968 Herman Kahn and the Hudson Institute issued a thousand-page study of what American life would be like in the year 2000. Their prediction was that by then the annual per capita income of Americans would be $7,500 a year. Seven-hour days and four-day weeks would be typical, the institute reported; so would thirteen-week annual vacations. With enjoyment replacing achievement as the goal of men and women, it appeared that the very reason for existence, and even existence itself, would be altered in ways which were now inconceivable.

But anticipating the future was not necessary to grasp what the technological revolution had already done to the United States. A glance backward could be breathtaking. In the early 1930s, when the now gray and balding swing generation was just approaching its teens, the largest category of Americans untouched by progress was the farm bloc — over 30 million people. In those days they lacked knowledge of even the fundamentals of conservation, which was one of the reasons for the devastating dust storms. Without rural electrification, farmers read by lamplight. Without electric power the typical farm wife had to carry as much as 28 tons of water each year from the pump or spring. Her butter churn was operated by hand. She did her laundry in a zinc tub and preserved meat in a brine barrel. Her husband's chores were even more backbreaking. After the morning milking he had two hours' work with the horses before he could set about whatever he had planned for the day. Horses and mules were his major source of locomotion — there were over 20 million of them in the country — and when he went to town he drove over dirt roads. Later his life would be sentimentalized by those who had no idea what it had really been like. Some of the most arrant nonsense would be written about the farm kitchen, when in fact, as Clyde Brion Davis pointed out in *The Age of Indiscretion*, "most of the cooking was frying — and not even in deep fat. The traditional American farmer . . . was scrawny-necked, flat-chested and potbellied from flatulent indigestion."

If the farmer's son was still living on the land a generation later, his world was entirely different. Trees planted by the CCC held the soil firm; strip-cropping and contour plowing made for greater yields and sturdier crops. Fifteen billion dollars in farm machinery had ended the tyranny of sweat and drudgery, and the 65 million acres once set aside for raising animal fodder were now used for produce. The development of hybrid corn had increased the nation's corn harvest 20 percent without boosting the acreage needed. Driven to abandon cotton by the boll weevil threat of the 1930s, southern farmers had learned to plant other crops — and had tripled their income. The new farmer in the new rural prosperity drove to market on macadam. And his wife, in a kitchen glittering with appliances, the brine barrel having been replaced by a commodious freezer, fed her family properly. Afternoons she had time to run into town herself. She went to the hairdresser regularly and wore the same synthetic fabrics as her city sisters instead of the gingham dresses and cotton stockings of her mother.

City toil had been transformed, too. The proletariat was disappearing. It was Norbert Wiener who had observed, in *Cybernetics; or, Control and Communication in the Animal and the Machine* (1948), that "There is no rate of pay which is low enough to compete with the work of a steam shovel and an excavator." Already in the first half of the twentieth century automation had cut the number of common laborers from 11 million to 6 million. Over the next thirteen years the country's work force grew by ten million — to 70.6 million — but the number of laborers continued to dwindle. Blue-collar workers were a shrinking minority. During the Eisenhower years the automobile industry's production force dropped by 172,000 while it turned out a half-million more cars each year. The stature of the once mighty trade unions diminished; machines can't strike. Labor leaders became conservative, suspicious of progress, and in some cases allies of their old foes, the corporations. Meanwhile, less need for male muscle was opening vast areas of employment to the women now entering the labor force, and the trend grew as the objectives of work changed. Instead of making goods, workers were joining the expanding service, amusement, and leisure industries. In the "new mass-consumption society," George E. Mowry wrote, "the old equation of man confronting materials and making something new of them had been changed to man confronting man and persuading him to act."

One masculine stronghold did not change. That was the executive suite. The Hudson Institute held out no hope that business executives might look forward to working less and loafing more in the year 2000. They could not be spared; too much depended upon them. This was a switch from the Roosevelt years. Executive illustriousness had been predicted in James Burnham's widely reviewed book of 1941, *The Managerial Revolution*, but Depression folklore had generally held bosses in contempt, and Depression novelists and dramatists had depicted them as knaves and fools. (Moviegoers may recall the character actor who portrayed this stock role most successfully. He was Edward Arnold.) Yet by the 1960s they were high in the saddle. To be sure, they had little in common with the piratical entrepreneurs of the past. "The Tycoon," said *Fortune*, "is dead." *Time* described the new businessmen as "the professional managers, the engineer-trained technicians" who "took over industrial societies so huge that the average owner" — stockholder — "seldom exercised more than theoretical control." Typically, they ruled not individually and by fiat but by committee, pooling information and expertise in what were variously called executive groups, task forces, assault groups, or, in the modish egalitarian spirit, "working parties." In *The New Industrial State* John Kenneth Galbraith called those who thus shared power the technostructure.

Bright, well-educated, and highly motivated, the men of the techno-structure suffered, ironically, in one area to which they gave great attention: public relations. The problem here was refractory and institutional. American industry had always deceived itself and others about its true nature. Professing faith in Herbert Spencer went with the job, like the key to the executive washroom and membership in the Republican party. Executives insisted upon the viability of the profit motive, even though their own careers frequently gave it the lie; they continued to drive themselves although taxes took huge bites of their salaries. The name of John Maynard Keynes was ritualistically hissed even as they defected from Barry Goldwater, who not only criticized Keynes but actually meant it. They encouraged stockholders to think possessively about their corporation, yet the influence of corporate investors, always minimal, had declined even further by the 1960s, and anyone attending their annual meetings could quickly perceive that the decisions made by individuals there depended upon the information which the technostructure chose to provide them.

This masquerade had been noted by economists. Usually the duplicity had been dismissed as harmless. After all, political ethics were honored more often in the breach. The technostructural deceit was graver than it seemed, however. As the Johnson administration grew older with no resolution of the Vietnam conflict, American businessmen were astonished to find that demonstrators were turning on them and accusing them of committing monstrous crimes with products like napalm. They couldn't understand it; didn't these angry people know that management and government were natural antagonists, not co-conspirators? They believed that and thought it should be obvious to everyone. But of course it was untrue. The truth was that by the late 1960s the military-industrial complex which had alarmed Eisenhower at the opening of the decade had continued to grow until the United States had — there is no other name for it — a planned economy.

In 1967 Jean-Jacques Servan-Schreiber startled U.S. readers with such blunt assertions as "Federal agencies have been collaborating with American corporations in developing advanced technology ever since the end of the war," and "In the United States nearly every major industry gets a substantial amount of federal assistance." It scarcely seemed credible. Roosevelt's heirs were still entrenched in Washington, scorning the economic royalists and the moneychangers; presidents of the National Association of Manufacturers condemned Washington paternalism; speakers at the U.S. Chamber of Commerce continued to explain that the government, since it never *made* anything, was essentially parasitic, and that the key to all economic progress was the businessman who was prepared to risk his capital in hope of gain.

This was perhaps true of the child's lemonade stand then being acclaimed in full-page ads extolling free enterprise — though where the child would be without paternal subsidies was unexplained — but it had lost all applicability for the five hundred giant corporations which, by the 1960s, accounted for two-thirds of the nation's industrial production. Where was the risk for the Rand Corporation, whose total budget was underwritten by the U.S. Air Force? What gamble did IBM run when it invested five billion dollars in the perfection of integrated circuits for its third generation of computers, knowing that the Pentagon stood behind every dollar? How could ITT's work on miniaturized electronic devices be called speculation when NASA knew that a manned flight to the moon would be impossible without them? As technology became more sophisticated and the lead time required for new developments lengthened, firms which were asked to break new ground demanded long-term contracts. Industrial executives and government bureaucrats, sharing the same goals, drew up budgets and reached decisions together. If the finished products were useful in marketable wares, there was nothing to stop the executives from cleaning up. Often they did. Integrated circuits — microcircuits which eliminate a chain of linked electronic parts: transistors, resistors, condensers, and tubes — are an example. Huge space rockets could not get off the pad without them. They made Polaris missiles and the swing-wing F-111 fighter possible. Boeing SSTs required them. So did the European Concorde prototype; governments in Europe had not been so cooperative, and when the manufacturers there needed the microcircuits, they had to deal with the only three firms making them, all American: Fairchild, Texas Instruments, and Motorola. The devices, they found, were expensive.

It would be wrong to suggest that the American taxpayer had been swindled in this process. The government was committed to space travel; the electronic computer had become indispensable to the machinery of national strategy; improved methods of transport were in the public interest; national prestige benefited. Indeed, Servan-Schreiber was lost in admiration for the ingenious Yankees: "Behind most of their recent innovations is a huge reservoir of federal funds that have financed the most profitable investment any people ever made for itself." The byproducts of space research alone included tremendous and invaluable gains in understanding refractory metals and equipment for working in vacuums. Through federal guarantees of large outlays of capital, the Pentagon, NASA, the AEC and the Federal Aviation Administration made possible the creation of marvels which would otherwise have waited a generation. Between the invention of photography and the manufacture of cameras, 112 years passed, from 1727 to 1839. The gap was 56 years for the telephone and 35 for radio. By paying for technical development and assuring a market for the end result, Washington had cut the lag to six years for the atomic bomb, five years for the transistor, and three years for the integrated circuit. There is a case to be made against the process, but it is a case against progress. That many Americans would find it persuasive is doubtful.

What was not possible, however, was to argue that industry had maintained its sovereignty — that it remained free to oppose decisions made in Washington. With the administration spending 15 billion dollars a year on research and development, as against 6 billion from business and private agencies, the presumption of domination by the government was inescapable. In 1929 federal, state, and municipal governments accounted for about 8 percent of all economic activity in the United States. By the 1960s the figure was between 20 and 25 percent, far exceeding that in India, a socialist country. The National Science Foundation reckoned that federal funds were paying for 90 percent of research in aviation and space travel, 65 percent in electrical and electronic devices, 42 percent in scientific instruments, 31 percent in machinery, 28 percent in metal alloys, 24 percent in automobiles, and 20 percent in chemicals. Washington was in a position to hold the very survival of great corporations as a hostage. It never came to that, no one was that crude, the matter was never discussed. Nevertheless, big industry had surrendered a large measure of autonomy.

In another time this circumstance would have concerned few Americans and aroused even fewer. Johnsonian prosperity was being enjoyed on all levels of society. Except in times of great distress the United States has rarely been troubled by protesters swarming in the streets and damning the government. Most people have a stake in the system; radical movements have been historically frustrated in their search for American recruits. But the Johnson years were witnessing another significant innovation. Since the war the nation had acquired an enormous student population. At the time of Pearl Harbor about 15 percent of Americans of college age were so enrolled. By the fall of 1965, 40 percent were — over five million youths between eighteen and twenty-one. Within four years the figure would be 6.7 million. Nearly a half-million bachelor degrees were now being awarded each year. More than 30 billion dollars was being spent annually on formal education. Going to class had, in fact, become the largest industry in the United States, making students the country's biggest single interest group.

In the rest of the population this was a source of pride — education had become almost a secular religion, the proposed cure for all social ills — but undergraduates were becoming discontented and restless. Their futures were clouded by the Vietnam War, which grew more hideous and frustrating every day. Their dissatisfaction with the prosecution of the conflict was encouraged by thousands of the nation's 150,000 tenure professors — men shielded from external discipline, who could be removed from their chairs only by death or personal scandal. Finally, many students were troubled by the realization that much of society's enthusiasm for higher education stemmed from its market value. Just as other federal programs enhanced technology by creating microcircuits, so the huge grants to education served to train future technicians, executives, and customers. Undergraduates found that after acquiring a healthy skepticism, a university's greatest gift to them, they were expected to stifle it and become cogs in industrial and governmental bureaucracies. Millions of parents saw nothing wrong with that. Many of the children were beginning to take another view, however. They said to one another: "They are snowing us. They are burying us. We cannot put up with it any more. We're going to overthrow it."

American technology has always been an American strength, a source of wonder and, sometimes, of anxiety. In 1853 a periodical called the *United States Review* had predicted that within fifty years "machinery will perform all work — automata will direct them," leaving people free "to make love, study and be happy." But as the campuses of the 1960s trembled on the verge of upheaval, John Kenneth Galbraith was less sanguine. He sensed a "danger that our educational system will be too strongly in the service of economic goals."

In some way the great student upheavals of the 1960s were even more significant than they seemed at the time. Like the revolutionary fever that swept western Europe in 1848, they may never be fully understood. They cut across national orders and cultural barriers that had long intimidated older generations. Neither oceans nor even the Iron Curtain checked them; as Columbia exploded and Berkeley seethed, campuses erupted in England, Italy, Germany, Holland, Sweden, Spain, Belgium, Japan, Formosa, Poland, Hungary, Yugoslavia, and Czechoslovakia. Americans were preoccupied with the disorders at home, but in at least two foreign capitals, Prague and Warsaw, the damage was more extensive than anything in the United States.

Doubtless part of the explanation for the chain reaction lies in the speed and sophistication of modern communications. The sense of world community was real and growing. Each of the emerging continents was to some degree aware of what was happening on other continents. "Establishment," in its new sense, had been translated into the language of every industrial nation. Student activists, as the riots would demonstrate, hadn't much use for it. This feeling was global. The antipathy was just as strong in Asia or eastern Europe as beneath the elms of Old Wabash.

Nevertheless, the American role was special. The turmoil began in the United States, the world's most affluent nation and the one with the most strongly defined youth subculture. Undergraduates abroad were very conscious of events on American campuses ("What is happening at Columbia?" Sorbonne demonstrators eagerly asked American foreign correspondents in 1968), while U.S. students were largely indifferent to the frenzies overseas. In America, moreover, it was possible to trace the powerful currents which were stirring youth. As Tocqueville noted, Americans have always taken a distinctive, almost Rousseauistic view of youth, and they have turned naturally to education as the solution to every problem, public and private.

But now youth itself had become a problem, and a major one at that. A great source of anxiety was the new political militance. A conservative educator declared that the campuses were harboring "a loose alliance of

Maoists, Trotskyites, Stalinists, Cheists, anarchists, utopians, and nihilists." Spiro Agnew made several memorable remarks on the subject. In St. Louis he called student demonstrators "malcontents, radicals, incendiaries, and civil and uncivil disobedients" and said, "I would swap the whole damn zoo for a single platoon of the kind of Americans I saw in Vietnam." On another occasion he described the universities as "circus tents or psychiatric centers for over-privileged, under-disciplined, irresponsible children of well-to-do blasé permissivists."

Parents denied that they were blasé or permissive, and those who disapproved of the demonstrations said they were the work of a minority. Gallup reported that 72 percent of all students had not participated in any of them; a *Fortune* poll concluded that just 12.5 percent of undergraduates held "revolutionary" or "radically dissident" views; SDS recruited just 7 percent. But Groucho Marx spoke for millions of older Americans when he remarked, "it's no good saying that the ones you read about are a minority. They're not a minority if they're all yours and you have to wait for the car to get home to know your daughter hasn't got pregnancy or leprosy."

The figures were deceptive anyhow. Extremists always attract a minority. A minority of northerners were abolitionists in 1861; probably a minority of colonists really wanted independence in 1776. Sympathies, not commitments, are the best indicator of a group's temper, and here the student pattern tells a different story. Gallup found that 81 percent of undergraduates were dissatisfied with college and university administrations. Another poll reported that more than 50 percent expressed major reservations about American foreign and domestic policies.

"The fear of being labeled radical, leftist, or subversive," Harvey Swados observed of academe in the early 1960s, "seems to have all but disappeared." Many, indeed, welcomed it. The undergraduates arriving on campus were often children of the middle-class liberals who had been most outraged — and in some instances had suffered most — during the McCarthy years. Their sons and daughters were determined not to be intimidated or repressed. They joined chapters of such organizations as SDS, Joan Baez's School for Nonviolence, the W. E. B. Du Bois Clubs, and the Young Socialist Alliance. They were in dead earnest but politically inept. Before the decade ended, the tactics of their New Left would offend virtually all potential allies, including their parents — which, some thought, might have been the point.

Yet in some areas they were highly skilled. Their demonstrations were often staged for TV news cameramen with a sense of what was good theater. The picketing in support of the Mississippi Freedom Party at the 1964 Democratic national convention was one example; the October 1967 march on the Pentagon was another. It is equally true that they frequently appeared to be shocking the country for the sake of shock. In 1965 SDS repealed its ban on admitting Communists and Birchers to membership.

The New Leftists proclaimed that their sacred trinity consisted of Marx, Mao, and Herbert Marcuse, and they enthusiastically embraced Marcuse's "discriminating tolerance"; *i.e.*, the suppression of points of view which the New Leftists regarded as unsound or dangerous. Their campaigns against ROTC, the draft, and napalm were logical, and walking out on commencement ceremonies was valid protest, but when they advocated dynamiting public buildings, even Marcuse demurred. Some SDS leaders all but salivated over violence. Of the Sharon Tate murders SDS's Bernardine Dohrn said: "Dig it, first they killed those pigs, then they ate dinner in the same room with them, then they even shoved a fork into a victim's stomach! Wild!"

The New Leftists' view of society was essentially conspirational. They saw it as dominated by an establishment which was itself manipulated by a "power elite" of industrialists, military leaders, and corporate giants. They talked darkly of revolution, yet a real revolution starts with strengthening the power of the state — which they were dead set against. Like all movements, theirs had a glossary of special terms: "dialogue," "creative tension," "nonnegotiable demands," and "nonviolent" among others. But their meanings were often obscure. Nonnegotiable demands could be negotiated, for example, and throwing rocks and bottles at policemen was deemed nonviolent.

The alienation of the young militants, expressing itself in disdain for conventional careers, clothing, and politics, had begun at Berkeley in 1964. The next spring, when that campus began to tremble again, President Kerr said, "The university and the Berkeley campus really couldn't face another such confrontation." In fact four more years of turmoil lay ahead. Berkeley was to be but one of many disturbed campuses. In 1965 Berkeley fallout first rocked the University of Kansas when 114 students were arrested there for staging a sit-in at the chancellor's office to protest fraternity and sorority discrimination. Then, within a few days, colleges and universities were embattled from coast to coast.

Yale undergraduates demonstrated after a popular philosophy instructor had been denied tenure. After an anti-ROTC rally at San Francisco State, five were hospitalized. At Fairfield University, a Jesuit school in Connecticut, students broke into a locked stack to put forbidden books on open shelves. Brooklyn College undergraduates booed their president off a platform. At St. John's in New York, the nation's biggest Catholic college, students demanded an end to censorship of their publications. Michigan students demonstrated against higher movie prices, and three deans resigned at Stanford over reading erotic poetry in the classroom. At Fairleigh Dickinson in New Jersey students picketed as "an expression of general student discontent." The uproar continued through 1966 and 1967, with major riots at San Jose State College, Wisconsin, Iowa, Cornell, Long Beach State College, and, once again, San Francisco State. And all this was merely a buildup for the cataclysmic year of 1968. "Yesterday's ivory tower," said the president of Hunter College, "has become today's foxhole."

For all their ardor, the militant undergraduates achieved little. Students are by definition transients; once they are graduated new students arrive, and there is no guarantee that the newcomers may not take a different line — as in fact those in this movement did. SDS, inherently unstable, split into two groups at the end of the decade: Revolutionary Youth Movement I, also known as the Weathermen, and Revolutionary Youth Movement II, which condemned the Weathermen as "adventuristic." The students had other difficulties. One of their basic premises was absurd. "The fantasy," wrote Benjamin DeMott, lay "in the notion that if you're upset about Vietnam, racism, poverty, or the general quality of life, the bridge to blow is college."

A second handicap was the students' exaggerated sense of their own power. In 1966 they confidently challenged the gubernatorial campaign of Ronald Reagan. To their amazement, he won by a margin of almost a million votes. That same day the Republicans gained fifty congressional seats. "One of the most obvious casualties of the 1966 elections," Hunter S. Thompson noted, "was the New Left's illusion of its own leverage. The radical-hippy alliance had been counting on the voters to repudiate the 'right-wing, warmonger' elements in Congress, but instead it was the 'liberal' Democrats who got stomped." Furthermore, analysts concluded that in California the New Left had actually boosted Reagan's vote by opposing him. Having found a popular issue, Reagan then capitalized on it, forcing Kerr's resignation on the ground that he had been too lenient with student dissidents and appointing Professor Samuel I. Hayakawa, a hard-liner, as president of San Francisco State.

Hostile reactions to politicized students were not confined to California. One Midwest legislature slashed over 38 million dollars from its state university's budget and raised tuition fees. Bills intended to stifle student dissent were introduced in most other legislatures, and eight of them were passed. "Americans," Oregon's Governor Tom McCall said of the demonstrators, were "fed up to their eardrums and eyeballs." Lou Harris reported that 62 percent of students' parents believed that it was more important for colleges to maintain discipline than to encourage intellectual curiosity. "Reduced to its simplest terms," *Life* commented, "the generations disagree on the most fundamental question of all: What is education for?"

Of course, they clashed over other issues, too. The demonstrations were one of the most visible manifestations of youth's subculture in the 1960s, but there was more to their subculture than that. Throughout the decade publicists wrote of "revolutions" in, among others, communications, sex, and drugs. Youth was active in all of them and was partly formed by them, if only because it had concluded that the election returns were what

Hunter Thompson called "brutal confirmation of the futility of fighting the Establishment on its own terms." The generation gap had arrived, and it was an abyss.

"Don't trust anyone over thirty!" said the banners and buttons displayed by the most arrogant, and it was cruel; so many Americans over thirty wanted to be young again, to share the fads and enthusiasms of youth. They slipped discs dancing the Watusi and the Swim and the Cottage Cheese, hopped about chasing Frisbees, endangered their lives riding motorcycles, laughed at *The Graduate* and even played with Super Balls. The Beatles having introduced long hair, the kids picked it up, and presently the middle-aged were imitating that, too. Both sexes wore wigs to make them look younger. Often the hippies set fashions for adults. "I watch what the kids are putting together for themselves," said Rudi Gernreich. "I formalize it, give it something of my own, perhaps, and that is fashion." Older Americans caught the discotheque bug and asked children where the action was; young wiseacres told them the Vincent Van Gogh-Gogh and the Long, Long Ago-go. Women went to plastic surgeons for eyelid lifts ($350), nose jobs ($500), rhytidectomies — face lifts — ($600), face peelings ($500), dermabrasions — removing acne scars — ($275), bosom implants ($165), belly lifts ($500) and thigh lifts ($650). "Being young was *right*," *Life* observed in a special issue on the 1960s; "as everybody once wanted to be rich, now everybody wanted to be, or seem to be, young. Fashion, films, books, music, even politics leaned toward youth."

Early in the decade half the U.S. population was under thirty. Then half was under twenty-seven, and then it was half under twenty-five, with 40 percent seventeen years old or younger and those under eighteen increasing four times as fast as the rest of the population. Even so, there were many who took a saturnine view of what one called youth's "vinyl-mini-inflatable Disneyland of pop culture." Defenders of the young reminded them that Socrates had written: "Our youth now loves luxury. They have bad manners, contempt for authority, disrespect for their elders. Children nowadays are tyrants." The implication was that since the Greeks were vexed by kids that long ago, today's worriers were making an issue over nothing. Grace and Fred M. Hechinger countered that real questions should be, "What happened to Greece? Or to Rome? Or to any civilization once it substituted self-indulgence for self-discipline?"

At times in the 1960s it almost seemed that America was becoming a filiarchy. Adolescence, wrote the Hechingers, had "evolved into a cult, to be prolonged, enjoyed, and commercially catered to as never before." In the new suburbs, especially, the young appeared to have been reared on a philosophy of instant gratification. Agnew, Billy Graham, and Al Capp distorted the issue, but it did exist and was debatable. "Self-expression" and "child-centered" were part of the permissive jargon; in the schools the trend frequently led to a system of "elective" subjects for pupils too young to know what they were electing. The teacher was to be regarded as a pal, not a superior being. Elementary school teachers were required to work with limited vocabularies, sometimes twenty words or less repeated endlessly. (The result was summed up in the deathless line attributed to a teacher who rammed a tree with her car: "Look look look, oh oh oh, damn damn damn.")

Children told that they were equal to their parents in every way believed that decisions in the home should be put to a vote. This was called "democratic living." Often it meant chaotic living. Writing in *Daedalus*, David Riesman noted the effect on a stranger: "As in the home of a poor peasant which is shared with goats, chickens, and other livestock, guests here may face the hazard of children who are treated as pets and who are not put away with a babysitter when company comes."

Henry A. Murray, another Harvard contributor to *Daedalus*, pointed to one unexpected consequence. Most teen-age aggregates, he observed, were "bound together by an anti-authoritarian, anti-father compact." It was a strong man who could command respect in his own house. Society seemed to be conspiring against him. One of the greatest offenders was television. TV fathers were pitiful weaklings. *Make Room for Daddy's* ineffectual daddy let his wife dominate him simply because she talked the loudest. Uncle Bentley in *Bachelor Father* was systematically humiliated by his niece and his servant, and Mr. Anderson, the antihero of a series sardonically called *Father Knows Best*, invariably responded to the strange antics of his children by saying, "Let's keep out of it and see what happens."

Advertisers were wary of offending youth; the nation's teen-agers were spending 25 billion dollars a year. It was ironic that student militants should take so vigorous a stand against materialism; their own generation was the most possession-conscious in history. In *The Lonely Crowd* Riesman wrote that in America "children begin their training as consumers at an increasingly young age," that "middle-class children have allowances of their own at four or five," and that the allowances "are expected to be spent, whereas in the earlier era they were often used as cudgels of thrift."

Advertisers courting them addressed teen-agers as "the Now Generation," the "New People," the "Pepsi Generation," and the "Go Anywhere, Do Anything Generation." John Brooks pointed out that they were the most conspicuous beneficiaries of Johnsonian prosperity: "American youth, like everybody else but more spectacularly, was getting rich. A combination of burgeoning national wealth and the settled national habit of indulging the young was putting unprecedented sums of cash in their hands." Keeping them solvent wasn't always easy. In 1964 the Harvard class of '39, hardly indigents, reported that providing their children with money was the chief paternal problem for 78 percent of them. Only 6 percent said that instilling moral values in them was as hard. And they weren't all that moral. For

$12.50 a boy could buy a girl a "Going Steady" ring which looked just like a wedding band; certainly no motel manager could tell the difference. If they felt guilty next day, in some places they could pray for forgiveness at teen-age churches. The Emmanuel Hospital in Portland, Oregon, even had a teen-age wing. It was described by Frank J. Taylor in a *Saturday Evening Post* article, "How to Have Fun in the Hospital." Patients enjoyed "unlimited snacks, jam sessions, and wheel-chair drag races." Priggish nutritionists kept their distance; the teen-agers were allowed to "eat hot dogs and hamburgers day after day for lunch and supper."

Literature for the young included *How to Be a Successful Teenager*, by one William C. Menninger. In a chapter on "How to Live with Parents" Menninger described techniques of handling mothers and fathers who tried to dictate to them: "One of the best ways to maintain family peace and insure cooperation is by holding family councils periodically about important matters." There were plenty of other sources of advice for youth. The *Chicago Daily News* carried a column of adolescent gossip called "Keen Teens"; the *Ladies' Home Journal* a department, "Profile of Youth." Pulps for adolescents included *Confidential Teen Romances, Teen Times, Hollywood Teenager, 16 Magazine, Teen World, Teen Parade, Modern Teen,* and *Teen Screen.* Among their magazines were *Ingenue, Calling All Girls,* and *Seventeen,* which observed its seventeenth year of publication in 1961 with a breathless editorial, "It's Our Birthday" — "*Seventeen* is 17 . . . Isn't Everybody?"

I Was a Teen-Age Frankenstein was one of the more memorable films produced for the adolescent trade. The editor of *Teen Magazine*, Charles Laufer, said that "the music market for the first time in history is completely dominated by the young set." They were the most musical generation ever, and their taste, at its best, was very good; the swing generation could hardly improve on the Beatles, Joan Baez, Bob Dylan, and forty-four-year-old B. B. King, whom the youth of the 1960s discovered after he had been ignored by his contemporaries for twenty-one years. Unfortunately the youngsters had other idols who belonged aesthetically with Andy Warhol's Brillo boxes and Campbell soup cans, among them the ruttish Presley. Presley's voice and appearance were at least his own. That wasn't true of most rock stars. To a striking degree they were all alike — short youths, running to fat, who were prepared for public consumption by strenuous dieting, nose surgery, contact lenses, and luxurious hair styles. And they couldn't sing. Most couldn't even have made themselves heard in the back of a theater. Their voices were amplified in echo chambers and then created on tape, a snippet here and a snippet there, destroying false notes. When they appeared in public, they would mouth the words while the records were being played over the loudspeakers. Wiggling their hips and snapping their fingers, their features always fixed in a sullen expression, they would desecrate good songs: "I loved, I loved, I loved yuh, once in si-ilence," or "The rain, yeah! stays mainly in the puh-lain."

"What I mean to kids," said Janis Joplin, shortly before she killed herself with whiskey and drugs, "is they can be themselves and win." John Lennon of the Beatles said, "We're more popular than Jesus now." Their listeners may have tuned such things out. They were, after all, accustomed to meaningless words — "Learn to forget," said a writer in *Crawdaddy;* it was one of the wiser apostrophes directed to that rock magazine's readers. Purdue polled two thousand teen-agers on the gravest problem facing American youth. A third of them said acne.

Policemen would have disagreed. Over the previous ten years arrests of the young had jumped 86 percent. "Teen-Agers on the Rampage," proclaimed a *Time* head after a single week which had seen violence "among high schools from California to Maine." Professor Ruth Shonle Cavan published the first sociology textbook to deal with upper- and middle-class delinquency, including what she called "alcohol-automobile-sex behavior." Felonies were almost commonplace in some neighborhoods which had once been serene. The FBI reported that Americans aged eighteen or younger accounted for almost half of all arrests for murder, rape, robbery, aggravated assault, burglary, and auto theft — and in the suburbs it was more than half. Beginning in 1960 suburbs began setting up teen-age codes of conduct, but they had no legal status, compliance was voluntary, and their chief value was evidence that parental authority was bankrupt. "Mit dose kids society is nix," said the cop of the Katzenjammer kids, and it often was. Gallup found a startling difference between the values of parents and those of their children. Three out of four youngsters said they knew that cheating on examinations was common. It didn't bother them, Gallup reported.

The first evidence of widespread teen-age drug parties in the paneled rumpus rooms of the affluent was turned up in 1960 by the Westchester County vice squad. After the shock had passed parents said that at least it wasn't liquor. Then police on Santa Catalina Island, the southern California resort, announced that drunkenness had become common among thirteen- and fourteen-year-old children in wealthy families, and in the future they would charge the parents $2.50 an hour to babysit teen-age drunks till parents came to take them home. Nationally the number of adolescents who drank regularly was put at between 50 and 66 percent. In Yonkers, New York, where it was 58 percent among high school juniors and seniors, 64 percent said they drove the family car while doing it. Parents in Rose Valley, a Philadelphia suburb, allowed children to bring their own bottles to parties. Their fathers did the bartending. One wondered what Clarence Day's father would have thought.

Among the recurring news stories of the 1960s — the ghetto disorders, the annual anniversary of Dallas, the war moratoriums — were accounts of rioting at the Newport Jazz Festival and at Fort Lauderdale, the watering places of the young. Yet the extent of teen-agers' drinking ought not to have been surprising. In a sense they were expressing their social role.

Opulence, the lack of genuine responsibility, and a position outside the unemployment pool gave them all the attributes of a leisure class.

In their ennui or their cups, youths of the 1960s frequently turned destructive. A brief item from Hannibal, Missouri, gave melancholy evidence of the revision of a cherished American myth. At the foot of Hannibal's Cardiff Hill stands a famous statue of Tom Sawyer and Huckleberry Finn, barefoot and carrying fishing poles; a plaque explains that this is the neighborhood where Tom and Huck "played and roamed at will." But any boys who attempted to emulate them after dark in the late 1960s would have risked arrest. Because of the rise in adolescent vandalism, loitering by the young on Cardiff Hill — and indeed anywhere in Hannibal — was forbidden after 10 P.M.

It was a harsh but necessary law; the vandalism was a real problem, in Missouri and elsewhere. During one week in February 1968 thirty New Haven high school students were arrested in the wake of china-smashing cafeteria riots, five hundred boys in the Chicago suburb of Maywood battled police at a rally protesting the selection of a homecoming queen, and nearly three thousand students at Chicago's Dunbar High left classes to pelt rocks at cars. In a typical suburban incident, an Alexandria, Virginia, gang, the children of government officials, did between $7,000 and $8,000 in damage by smashing automobile windshields with baseball bats. When arrested, they said they had done it "for fun." Another widespread expression of violence was party crashing. For a time there was a rash of such incidents each weekend in Westchester, Fairfield, Rockland, and Bucks counties — the exclusive suburbs ringing New York. Characteristically, six or eight uninvited youths would arrive at the height of a party, break open the parents' liquor cabinet, and destroy glassware and furniture.

Sometimes invited guests were worse. They would rival one another in seeing how much they could damage their host's home. One memorable debutante party celebrated the coming out of blonde Fernanda Wanamaker at her stepparent's thirty-room mansion in Southampton, Long Island. Over eight hundred children of what *Vogue* was then calling "the beautiful people" were invited. After the band had left, a hundred and twenty-seven of them wrecked the mansion, smashing windows, tearing down curtains, swinging on chandeliers, ripping out phones, breaking lamps, carting off appliances and throwing most of the furniture on the beach. The cost of the mischief was estimated to be somewhere between $3,000 and $10,000.

Affluent youths were often the worst offenders, but disorders could break anywhere. On one Independence Day five hundred drunken youths in Arnolds Park, Iowa, hurled rocks, beer bottles, and pieces of concrete at policemen; the tumult was set off when one of them yelled at the police chief, "Hey, punk, we're going to take over this place." In Chicago a free rock concert series — arranged by municipal officials to build camaraderie with youth — had to be canceled. At the first performance the audience rose up swinging tire chains and clubs; 135 were injured, including 65 policemen.

North Dakota University was one of the quietest, best-behaved campuses in the country until the *Student*, its undergraduate newspaper, proposed a weekend of fun in the nearby town of Zap. Zap's Mayor Norman Fuchs, delighted, wrote to all neighboring colleges promising "Zap-Burgers with special seasoning" and lots of "good, clean, beer-busting, food-munching, tear-jerking, rib-tickling fun." He acquired a sweatshirt with the legend "Zap, N.D. or Bust" and announced that the occasion would be called a "Zap-In." There was talk of Zap becoming the Fort Lauderdale of the North. The mayor could scarcely have understood the implications of all that. His town had a population of three hundred. By the evening of Friday, May 9, 1969, nearly a thousand students, 90 percent of them male, had arrived in Zap from five states. The town's three taverns were packed. When the thermometer dropped below freezing the students started a bonfire in the street, ripping out tables and booths from the taverns for firewood. Then they began breaking into stores and houses. Fistfights followed. A fire truck arrived; they seized it and dismantled it. Before five hundred National Guardsmen could arrive, the visitors had done $10,000 worth of damage.

The Fort Lauderdale of the South was never confronted with precisely that problem, freezing temperatures never having been recorded there in May. But Florida was afflicted with youthful firebugs that year just the same. Over a fifteen-month period an incredible number of unexplained fires (120) broke out on the University of Florida campus in Gainesville. Fire marshals thought it possible that the entire campus might be razed. The crisis was resolved when residents in Hume Hall confessed they had done it. Students in the east and west wings had been competing to see which could attract the most fire trucks. What made the incident particularly striking was a circumstance which would have been unthinkable in earlier generations. Hume Hall was a girls' dormitory.

Men's rooms in genteel establishments had long displayed a sign over urinals: PLEASE ARRANGE CLOTHING BEFORE LEAVING WASHROOM. Well-brought-up boys didn't need to be reminded; they had been taught never to fasten the flies of their trousers in public. They were therefore startled when Françoise Dorleac, in the 1966 film *Where the Spies Are*, emerged from a dressing room, reached for her crotch, and casually zipped up her slacks in the presence of her costar, David Niven. It was one of those moments which served as reminders that the delicate balance between the sexes had been altered, probably forever. Women were moving into jobs which had always been considered masculine: telephone linemen, mining engineers, ditch diggers, truck drivers, Secret Service agents. More of them were sharing men's vices, too: public drunkenness, juvenile delinquency, and assault and battery. Women's Liberation leader Ti-Grace Atkinson called marriage "slavery," "legalized rape," and "unpaid labor," and disapproved of love between the sexes as "tied up with a sense of dependency." The Women's Lib movement was not confined to the United States; in 1970 Bernadette Devlin was designated Ireland's Man of the Year by her admirers, and 1,162 pregnant Norwegian women sailors, who had conceived while on the high seas, claimed and were granted compensation from their government. But it was in America that women took to the streets at the end of the 1960s in massive rallies: 3,000 in Chicago, 2,000 in Indianapolis, 2,000 in Boston, and 50,000 in Manhattan, striding down Fifth Avenue with their breasts, unencumbered by brassieres, swaying visibly.

The disappearance of bras among members of the movement was but one of many changes in fashion. When Mia Farrow cropped her hair girls flocked to hairdressers so they, too, could look like boys. They crowded Army-Navy stores buying pea jackets, petty officer shirts, and bell-bottom trousers. Square-toed, low, heavy shoes became popular among them, and so many coeds were using after-shave lotion as perfume that the business journal *Forbes* protested that the sexes were beginning to smell alike. In 1966 Twiggy, the Cockney model, weighed in at ninety-one pounds, and women dieted to look like her, angularity being considered antifeminine. The idea was to look tough. Shiny plastic came into vogue, and hard, metallic fabrics. Pantsuits appeared — not cute slacks but mannish, tailored slacks. The zippers or buttons were no longer on the side; they went straight down the front, like Françoise Dorleac's, and some girls reportedly made them to go all the way through and up the back, so they could stand at urinals. Barbara Tuchman protested that too many women were beginning to look like Lolitas or liontamers. A Woman's Lib leader called her an Aunt Tom.

At the very top of the movement there was some female homosexuality and bisexuality; Kate Millett said she sometimes slept with women, and Joan Baez acknowledged that she had once had a lesbian affair. There was considerable resentment in the movement over being considered "sex objects"; girls objected to being whistled at and featured in fetching ads designed to appeal to males. Most girls in the movement preferred boys, however; Gloria Steinem, a heterosexual Lib leader, said, "Men think that once women become liberated, it will mean no more sex for men. But what men don't realize is that if women are liberated, there will be more sex and better." Betty Friedan attested to "the mounting sex-hunger of American women," and David Riesman noted that "millions of women" had become "knowing consumers of sex" and "pioneers, with men, on the frontier of sex." Elderly Americans, who had called aggressive women "bold" or "forward," couldn't grasp what was happening. Attending his granddaughter's commencement in 1967, General Eisenhower told miniskirted girls: "Ankles are nearly always neat and good-looking but knees are nearly always not." The girls, of course, knew that what interested boys was higher up.

Certainly more girls were on the prowl, often roaming the streets in pairs or appearing at weekends, available, on college campuses. Bachelors dropping in for a drink at Chicago's dating bars in the Rush Street district — The Jail, The Store, The Spirit of '76 — would be propositioned by girls who offered to "ball" them and tried to arouse them with a new gesture — the feminine hand, slipped between the man's thighs, squeezing him there. Over a third of the coeds at a New York university admitted to one-night affairs with total strangers. Nationally, during the 1960s, the number of girls reporting premarital intercourse in surveys more than doubled; in a five-year period it rose 65 percent. European surveyors found that twice as many boys as girls there volunteered to describe their sexual experiences; in the United States it was the other way around. The number of coeds reporting the petting of male genitals soared. High school girls tried to achieve a licentious air. To that end, *Seventeen* discovered, the number of its subscribers using mascara had jumped from one in five during the late 1940s to nine in ten. Rudi Gernreich said that twenty years earlier girls tried to look sweet and innocent; now, "before they are seventeen years old they cultivate a wild, consciously sexy look." Demure women all but vanished. Obscene language no longer shocked them; they used it themselves. If they wanted coitus they said so. In the film *All the Loving Couples,* a jaded wife waiting to be swapped said thickly, "When do we get laid?"

Presently she was in the throes of sexual intercourse, on camera, with another woman's husband. The movies, once straitlaced, were exploring all the visual possibilities of the sex act. Under the leadership of Jack Valenti, who left the White House to become president of the Motion Picture Association of America, Hollywood adopted a rating system for films in 1968. Those in the G category would be family movies; the others would be M (suggested for mature audiences), R (restricted to persons sixteen or older unless accompanied by a parent or guardian), or X (no one under sixteen admitted under any circumstances).

In the late 1960s each season's X movies went farther than the last. Even the movie ads in newspapers become something to put out of reach of children. *I Am Curious (Yellow)* was thought shocking when it appeared, showing nudity and coitus, but new productions rapidly made it obsolescent. Ads for *The Minx* said it "makes Curious Yellow look pale," and it did. Then *The Fox* depicted lesbians kissing passionately and a naked woman masturbating in front of a full-length mirror. A beast had intercourse with a woman in *Rosemary's Baby. Bob and Carol and Ted and Alice* was a comedy about wife swapping. *Blow-Up* provided a glimpse of a girl's pubic hair; it was thought daring at the time, but presently ingenious close-ups showed the genitals in intercourse from unusual angles — some from the bottom — and actresses masturbating actors to climax. The ultimate, or so it seemed at the time, was *Deep Throat,* a tremendous hit about cunnilingus and fellatio. At the conclusion of it the heroine took a man down to the hilt of his phallus, displaying a talent which the *New Yorker* compared to that of a sword swallower. The action was photographed at a range of a few feet, and when the man reached orgasm, so did the girl. Technicolor revealed her full body flush.

Dallas District Attorney Henry Wade said: "I wouldn't be too surprised to see a sex circus in the Cotton Bowl." On Manhattan's Forty-second Street, in the block between Seventh and Eighth avenues, a policeman said: "If a little old lady wants to buy the *Times,* she has to climb over three rows of *Screw* to get it." *Screw, Suck, Desire, Gay,* and *Coq* — all the smut magazines competed for circulation by trying to show more flesh of models in lewder poses than the others. In Miami, Bunny Dania, one of the more experienced models, said that when she began posing photographers would show nudes playing volleyball or swimming. "Now," she said, "you've got to have wife swapping and sadism and girls making out with girls. It's moved indoors."

On stage a performer named Jim Morrison described his latest sexual adventure; it had occurred five minutes before curtain time. *Oh Calcutta* was billed as "elegant erotica"; its sketches ranged in theme from wife swapping to rape. *Che!* provided a hundred minutes of faked sex acts. Those who preferred the real thing could find it in New York's "Mine-Cini Theater," or in San Francisco taverns where a boy and girl would strip, climb on the bar, and there engage in what was drolly called the act of love. Some spectacles shocked the most hardened observers. A reporter told of going backstage in one Manhattan show and seeing chorus girls, naked, shooting heroin into the backs of their knees while their illegitimate toddlers watched.

Sex became an issue in strange places. After searching his conscience for five years on contraception, Pope Paul rejected it in a 7,500-word encyclical entitled *Humanae Vitae (Of Human Life)* on July 29, 1969. Millions of American Catholics were furious. A study by the Urban Life Institute of the University of San Francisco, a Jesuit school, disclosed that 70 percent of them approved of birth control. The vast majority of young priests agreed (though over 90 percent of the older priests did not). In Washington several rebellious priests staged a sit-in, and a hundred and forty-two others sent a letter of protest to the head of their archdiocese, Patrick Cardinal O'Boyle. When the cardinal began a sermon on obedience in St. Matthew's Cathedral, two hundred members of the congregation rose from their pews and stalked out. Seven Buffalo priests were dismissed from a seminary for mutinous remarks. Still the revolt spread. The following year the former auxiliary bishop of the St. Paul–Minneapolis archdiocese married a New York divorcée. Soon stories about priests marrying — often to nuns who had leaped over the wall — lost their novelty.

A lot of carnal knowledge was being acquired in laboratories, observed by scientists in white coats holding stopwatches and other things. The most famous of them were Dr. William H. Masters and Virginia E. Johnson, who eventually married one another. Their findings at the Reproductive Biology Research Foundation in 'St. Louis were invaluable, but fastidious critics were appalled by the measuring and photographing of copulation; it smacked to them of charcoal filters and flip-top boxes. The most remarkable piece of Masters-Johnson equipment was an electrically powered plastic penis with a tiny camera inside and cold light illumination to allow observation and recording of what was happening inside the vagina. The size of this artificial phallus could be adjusted, and the woman using it could regulate the depth and speed of the thrust. Inevitably it inspired several novels. The best of them was Robert Kyle's *Venus Examined* (1968). At the end of it a disillusioned heroine returns to the sex laboratory, demolishes the plastic phallus, and is electrocuted.

All this was a great strain for the young. Previous generations had been protected from early sexual entanglements by social custom, the fear of disgrace, and the possibility of venereal disease or pregnancy — a catastrophe for the girl. Now mores had changed spectacularly; society took a tolerant view of premarital affairs. Venereal infection had vanished. (Late in the decade it would reappear as a nationwide epidemic, a consequence of the new promiscuity.) "If it feels good, I'll do it," read a pin popular among college students. Intercourse felt good, and they did it a lot, protected by the Pill, or diaphragms, and various intrauterine devices, loops and coils.

Late in the decade, when abortions became easier to obtain, girls felt even safer. But improved contraceptives were not responsible for the increase in pushovers. It preceded them. Illegitimate births doubled between 1940 and 1960, and 40 percent of the mothers were in their teens. The Hechingers found that in some sophisticated communities a girl was expected to begin sexual intercourse with her steady boyfriend on her sixteenth birthday; if she refrained, she lost status. Pregnancy was so common in an Oakland high school that girls were allowed to attend classes until their confinement. A New York hospital on the privileged East Side reported that the number of unwed mothers jumped 271 percent in six years, and the *New York Times* quoted Dr. Margaret L. McCormack as saying that pregnancy, "once a college problem, is now a high school and junior high school problem." One New York junior high, she said, had 240 pregnancies in one year. The Pill came into widespread use during the winter of 1961–62, and by 1967 the illegitimacy rate among schoolgirls was on the decline. But no one suggested that coitus had lost its popularity.

The sex-drenched state of American culture was undoubtedly responsible for much of the increase in premarital and extramarital intercourse. Sexiness was everywhere — on paperback book racks, television, in ads, magazines, popular songs, plays, musicals, and everyday conversation. Betty Friedan cited a psychological study which found that references to sex in mass media increased by over 250 percent in the 1960s. The *New York Times Book Review* noted the popularity of books about "love" affairs between animals and human beings. Complaints to the U.S. Post Office about smut doubled within six years, to 130,000 in 1965.

"Be Prepared!" proclaimed a poster showing an enormously pregnant girl, smiling broadly, in a Girl Scout uniform. The Scouts asked for damages; the court threw out the case. "Use Contraceptives: Take the Worry Out of Being Close," said a Planned Parenthood ad. The New York Hilton, Manhattan's largest hotel, was renting rooms by the hour. Frustrated persons (or couples) took out ads in the personal column of the *Saturday Review*, or in underground newspapers, soliciting new partners. Everybody knew about key parties for swapping couples; the men threw their house keys on a table and the wives picked them up at random, each then going to bed with the owner of whatever key she had.

Nicholas von Hoffman described a game, manufactured by the Diplomat Sales Company of Los Angeles, which provided "a safe, nicely structured way for two or three couples to end an evening naked, drunk, out of their minds, and lascivious as hell." Called Bumps and Grinds, it was played by the light of one candle (which was included). Players moved around a board like the one used in Monopoly, drawing "Tomcat" and "Pussycat" cards. These advised them to "Take one drink," or "Strip one article of clothing," and so on. The game was rigged for the girls to wind up nude and drunk first. Subsequent moves decided who was going to stagger to the bedroom with whom.

If wife swapping was permissible for the middle-aged, youths argued, what was wrong with wife testing for them? Some communities, troubled by the question and aware of the temptations which prompted it, tried to ward off the great landslide of sex with local regulations. For a while wearers of bikinis on some public beaches were required to have two inches of cloth on each hip. Then President Kennedy's widow was photographed in a three-ring bikini, and the regulations collapsed. Thus clad, or unclad, the young could caress 95 percent of each other's bodies with suntan lotion in public. And as they thus excited one another, transistor radios alongside broadcast suggestive lyrics:

> *If somebody loves you, it's no good unless she loves you*
> *All the way*

Or:

> *I'd like to teach you all,*
> *And get your love in return*

"There is," said a University of Michigan coed, "nobody saying 'No.'" So many were saying yes that it was a wonder one-third of female college undergraduates remained virgins. In some instances, parents actually regarded the absence of coital experience as troubling. All things being equal, they would have preferred that their daughters remained maidens. But in this generation everything else was unequal. A teen-age girl who lacked a normal interest in sex could be in the toils of another new snare for the young.

She was possibly — and in some communities probably — a user of heavy drugs.

Early developments in mid-century chemotherapy were benign. The sulfa drugs had arrived in the late 1930s. Then came penicillin (1943), streptomycin (1945), cortisone (1946), ACTH (1949), terramycin and aureomycin (1950), the Salk vaccine (1955), the Sabin vaccine (1960), and the tranquilizers, led by Miltown and Librium, which cut the length of the average mental hospital stay in half. All these were called "miracle drugs" when they first appeared. Because of them, diseases which had afflicted men since the dawn of history were tamed and, in some cases, eliminated. In 1959 over 579 *tons* of tranquilizers were prescribed, which gives some idea of the need they met. As recently as the early 1950s polio terrorized parents during the summer months; 57,000 cases were reported in 1952. Now that was merely a memory.

The first inkling that the drug revolution had a dark side came in 1962, when eight thousand European women who had been taking a new tranquilizer called Thalidomide gave birth to limbless babies. Thanks to Dr. Frances O. Kelsey of the Food and Drug Administration, Thalidomide had not been licensed for general use in the United States. Nevertheless, a few Thalidomide-deformed babies had been born to expectant mothers who had been taking the blue tablets on an investigative basis. If a drug could do that, anything was possible. And the amount of medication in American medicine cabinets was unprecedented. Doctors were now writing nearly two billion dollars' worth of prescriptions each year for pills which included new barbiturates and amphetamines, hypnotics, and antidepressants. In addition, an enormous black market was flourishing. Of the eight billion amphetamines, or pep pills, manufactured each year, about four billion were being sold illegally. Laymen might call the pep pills and barbiturates "soft" drugs and heroin, morphine, and cocaine "hard," but pharmacologists knew it should be the other way around; the older drugs calmed addicts, but the new ones created dangerous, unpredictable moods. Some became part of the culture, familiar enough to have popular nicknames. Among them were "bluejays" (sodium amytal), "redbirds" (seconal), "yellow jackets" (nembutal), and "goofballs" (barbiturates laced with benzedrine).

The most widely discussed of the new compounds was d-lysergic acid diethylamide — LSD. First isolated in 1938 by Dr. Albert Hofmann in the Sandoz Research Laboratories in Basle, Switzerland, it lay around his lab for five years, unappreciated, its properties awaiting discovery. That occurred on April 16, 1943. Absorbing some LSD through the skin of his fingers, Hofmann began hallucinating. His scientific curiosity aroused, he then deliberately took 250 micrograms of it — an amount about the size of a grain of salt. In his diary he explained the effect: "With closed eyes, multihued, metamorphizing, fantastic images overwhelmed me . . . Sounds were transposed into visual sensations so that from each tone or noise a comparable colored picture was evoked, changing in form and color kaleidoscopically." In short, he had taken a trip.

Dr. Humphrey Osmond of the New Jersey Neuropsychiatric Institute neologized a new name for LSD. He called it a psychedelic and said it meant mind-expanding. At the start of the 1960s, the colorless, odorless, tasteless drug was still unknown to the public. Then two Harvard psychologists, Timothy Leary and Richard Alpert, began experimenting with colleagues, writers, artists, clergymen, and volunteer prisoners. Leary and Alpert were dismissed from Harvard in 1963, but by then LSD had achieved its reputation. Taking a trip, or turning on, had come to convey status on campuses. Alarmed, the FDA warned college presidents that taking it was an "insidious and dangerous activity." Sandoz Laboratories stopped making it. Laws barring it in any form were passed in Michigan, New Jersey, Nevada, and California. None of that made any difference; the use of it continued to spread.

LSD became a household word in 1966. Even recluses knew what was meant by tripping, freaking out, and blowing one's mind. Priests and pastors held a conference on the religious aspects of LSD. In discotheques — and also in art galleries and museums — films, slides, and flashing colored lights suggested the impact of an LSD experience. Chilling stories, some of them apocryphal, were told to scare those who were tempted to take a trip. A youth high on LSD was said to have taken a swan dive into the front of a truck moving at 70 mph. Teen-agers under its influence reportedly lay in a field staring at the sun until they were permanently blinded. That was exposed as a lie, but the Associated Press verified the case of a young man who turned himself in to police saying he had been flying on LSD for three days and asking "Did I kill my wife? Did I rape anyone?" and was then charged with the murder of his mother-in-law.

Users described feeling depressed, even homicidal, and told how they had turned themselves into ravens, or Jesus Christ, or tiny people six inches tall. Distraught parents told what had happened to their children: "My boy is on drugs. He went to St. Louis because it's the astrological center of the universe. He has met Hitler and Lincoln." And "Our son came home for Christmas. He looked awful. He rode his little sister's bicycle barefoot through the snow. The neighbors took their children in. People are afraid of him."

But the users of LSD — they called it acid — described their trips as ecstatic. "Who needs jazz, or even beer," wrote a contributor to the *New York Times Magazine,* "when you can sit down on a public curbstone, drop a pill in your mouth, and hear fantastic music for hours at a time in your own head? A cap of good acid costs $5, and for that you can hear the Universal Symphony, with God singing solo and the Holy Ghost on drums."

The Beatles sang "Yellow Submarine," which was a euphemism for a freakout, and another song freighted with LSD meaning, "Strawberry

Field." Elementary school children dismayed their mothers by coming home chanting, to the tune of "Frère Jacques":

> Marijuana, marijuana,
> LSD, LSD,
> College kids are making it, high
>   school kids are taking it,
> Why can't we? Why can't we?

At times it seemed that an entire generation was turning on to drugs. In fact, the hippy movement, or counterculture, which sprang from the self-medication and narcotics, was at first smaller than it appeared to be. It was really an extension of the beat generation of the 1950s. In the early 1960s the beatniks moved into San Francisco's Haight-Ashbury district. A musical combo called the Jefferson Airplane was then playing the first acid rock in an obscure night spot called the Matrix. Their group and the Grateful Dead were being entertained by Ken Kesey and his band of Merry Pranksters at La Honda, Kesey's forest home fifty miles south of San Francisco. It was at La Honda that Kesey and the Pranksters served their guests Kool-Aid spiked with LSD, and there that he wrote *One Flew Over the Cuckoo's Nest* (1962) and *Sometimes a Great Notion* (1964).

Listening to the driving, drowning acid rock, the Pranksters experimented with light and color, wore spectacular clothes, and evolved a lifestyle which would later become familiar in virtually every American community and in many abroad. It wasn't popular then. The dances at which the Airplane and the Dead played were thinly attended. Most customers still preferred the Charlie Parker brand of jazz. The new musicians painted posters depicting the visual impact of an LSD trip. Few admired them. At first they gave away these early examples of psychedelic art, then they sold them for a dollar each. A *Ramparts* editor said the printing was "36-point illegible," but by 1967 some of the originals would be selling in the best San Francisco art galleries for $2,000.

By then a reporter for the *San Francisco Chronicle* had christened the new bohemians "hippies," and the movement had become first a national and then an international phenomenon. Hippy communes were flourishing in New York, Boston, Chicago, Los Angeles, and Atlanta, and hippy enclaves had been established in Mexico, Canada, London, Rome, Tokyo — even in Laos. By then many charter members of the movement had quit, disgusted by the exhibitionists who were giving colorful interviews to newspapermen and television commentators. "The best year to be a hippy was 1965," said Hunter S. Thompson, the Ernie Pyle of the movement, "but then there was not much to write about, because not much was happening in public and most of what was happening in private was illegal. The real year of the hippie was 1966, despite the lack of publicity, which in 1967 gave way to a nationwide avalanche."

Fortunes were made in the 1967 "Summer of Love" from the sale of

DMT, mescaline, methedrine, LSD, and the even more popular — and safer — marijuana to the disillusioned children of the middle and upper middle class who flocked to hippy communes, leaving what they regarded as a stifling straight life to Do Their Thing. Pot, boo, maryjane, grass, or Mary Warner — the various names under which marijuana was known to them — sold in Mexico for $35 a kilogram (2.2 pounds). Smuggled into the United States, a kilo brought $150 to $200. Meted out in 34-ounce bags, it went for as much as $25 an ounce, or $850 the kilo. Joints — marijuana cigarettes — sold on the street for a dollar each. The heroin racket was even more lucrative. Undercover chemists made $700 for every kilo of morphine converted to heroin in Marseilles. Manhattan entrepreneurs paid $10,000 for it and sold it on the street in plastic bags, each containing just 5 percent heroin cut with sugar or quinine powder. In that form the original 2.2 pounds earned $20,000. And the market was expanding rapidly. The Federal Bureau of Narcotics estimated that 68,000 Americans became addicted in a single year.

In literally scores of cities there were share-ins, be-ins, and love-ins. As in the case of the beatniks ten years earlier, San Francisco was the focal point of the movement. The San Francisco *Oracle,* the leading underground newspaper, was published there, and there the original band of Diggers — named for a seventeenth-century English brotherhood that raised food for the poor on land which had been uncultivated — became beggars in order to feed indigent hippies. The distribution was in what was called Panhandle Park; it was known as the Politics of Free.

The issue of how many youths participated in the counterculture depends entirely on definitions. If smokers of marijuana are counted, the number is enormous. Dr. Henry Brill, chairman of the American Medical Association's committee on drug dependence, estimated that the number of Americans who tried pot went from a few hundred thousand in the early 1960s to eight million at the end of the decade, most of them in their teens. That was by far the most conservative of the estimates; the U.S. Public Health Service put the figure at 20 million. A *Playboy* survey reported that 47 percent of the nation's college students admitted smoking marijuana, though only 13 percent said they used it frequently. Members of families with high incomes smoked it most often. Just 2 percent acknowledged injecting methedrine, or speed — liquid amphetamines — directly into their veins, and a mere 1 percent were addicted to other narcotics.

The great year of the hippy may be said to have begun on Easter Sunday, March 26, 1967, when ten thousand boys and girls assembled in New York Central Park's Sheep Meadow to honor love. They flew kites, tossed Frisbees, joined hands in "love circles," painted designs on each other's faces, and chanted: "Banana! Banana!" after a current hoax, that banana scrapings had psychedelic properties. On the other side of the country that Sunday fifteen thousand youths in San Francisco cheered Dr. Leary's Pied

Piper spiel: "Turn on to the scene; tune in to what's happening; and drop out — of high school, college, grade school . . . follow me, the hard way."

What came next was a nightmare for tens of thousands of mothers and fathers. With the memories of their Depression childhoods still vivid, the parents of the late 1960s could not grasp that the country had become so prosperous it could afford to support tramps, or that their own children would want to be among the tramps. "The kids looked like bums, often acted like bums," the Associated Press reported, "but they were no ordinary bums. Most had spent their lives in middle-class surroundings, finishing high school, often graduating from college — the American dream." Now their photographs, forwarded by their parents and accompanied by pathetic messages pleading for news of their whereabouts, were hung on bulletin boards in police stations. The pictures weren't much help. Taken when the youngsters were straight, they bore little relation to their new life-style.

The police did what they could. The Salvation Army opened a coffee house in East Village called The Answer, where flower children in their early teens were urged to return home. Runaways in Haight-Ashbury were sheltered at church-sponsored Huckleberry's while mothers and fathers were contacted. A physician opened a free clinic for hippies in San Francisco. Almost immediately he was overwhelmed by pregnancies, cases of venereal disease, and hepatitis caused by dirty syringes. Virtually every hippy in Hashbury had a cold or the flu. Many had tried sleeping in Golden Gate Park, unaware that a hidden sprinkling system automatically started up at dawn.

The greatest health hazard, of course, was the drugs. The hippies had no way of knowing what they were buying; Dr. Louis Lasagna found that many were getting veterinary anesthetics or even plain urine. In that summer many were experimenting with STP, a new compound named for a gasoline additive used in the Hell's Angels motorcycles. Between 5,000 and 10,000 STP capsules were given away. The flower children, liking it, christened it "the caviar of psychedelics." Doctors discovered that it was extremely dangerous; when taken in combination with chlorpromazine, an LSD antidote, STP could prove fatal. The "speed freaks" or "meth monsters," as other hippies called them, were taking methedrine; when high, they were capable of almost anything. Meantime, in Buffalo, Dr. Maimon M. Cohen announced that preliminary findings in an investigation of LSD and chlorpromazine indicated that mixed together the two could result in chromosome damage, spontaneous abortions, or deformed infants.

That summer tourist buses were routed through Haight-Ashbury to provide a glimpse of the strange scene there. (Sometimes a hippy would run alongside the bus, holding up a mirror.) There, and in East Village, part-time flower children, or "plastics," as they were known — straights who were in effect slumming — were spending their weekends as hippies, returning to their jobs on Monday morning conservatively dressed and well groomed. The attitude of the New Left toward the flower children was equally ambivalent. In the beginning, when Leary succeeded Mario Savio as youth's demigod, New Left writers praised the hippies for their candor and spontaneity. After the Reagan landslide the situation changed. Many disillusioned militants tossed in the sponge, abandoned hope, and chose instead to stay stoned for days at a time. Flower power, they said, was non-political. Stung, New Leftists retorted that the hippies lacked "stability" and "energy," that they were "intellectually flabby," and that they were really "nihilists" whose idea of love was "so generalized and impersonal as to be meaningless." Of course, the hippies replied; that was their thing, and they were going to do it, and up yours.

The immediate threat to the flower children was not from parents, policemen, tourists, or New Leftists. It came from lower-class ethnic groups into whose neighborhoods they had moved. Haight-Ashbury was a working-class district; New York's East Village was inhabited by Italians, Negroes, Poles, Jews, Puerto Ricans, and Ukrainians, all of them trying to climb into the lower middle class. The spectacle of idle youth scorning the class status to which the ghetto inhabitants aspired for their own children infuriated them. The AP quoted a twenty-year-old porter who had just been laid off: "These cats want to drop out. How do you think that makes a guy feel who is just trying to get in?"

"We hippies love people," a flute player protested; "we certainly aren't bigoted." The ethnics, he said wonderingly, thought of his neighborhood as "their turf." They did indeed. A black grumbled that the flower children had "taken over" Tompkins Square Park. The park had belonged to him and his; they didn't have much, but that, at least, had been theirs, and now these maddening, uninvited kids insisted on sharing it. The inevitable happened. Violence, always a menace in ghettos, erupted against the defenseless hippies. On Memorial Day of that year ethnic boys attacked a twenty-nine-year-old flower girl in Tompkins Square and stripped her naked. In Central Park a fifteen-year-old and her seventeen-year-old lover (characteristically she did not know his name; to her he was simply "The Poet") were attacked by blacks; she was raped and he was beaten insensible. In California a seller of drugs was murdered and his right forearm hacked off. A few days later another peddler was killed, stuffed into a sleeping bag, and left hanging from a cliff.

Clearly something ghastly was happening to that summer. Exploiters and predators were also stalking the young. In *The Family* Ed Sanders compared the flower movement to "a valley of plump rabbits surrounded by wounded coyotes." He wrote: "One almost had to live there to understand the frenzy that engulfed the Haight-Ashbury district of San Francisco in the spring and summer of 1967. The word was out all over America to come to San Francisco for love and flowers." But more awaited them in Hashbury than that. "The Haight attracted vicious criminals who grew long hair. Bikers tried to take over the LSD market with crude sadistic tactics. Bad dope was sold by acne-faced methedrine punks. Satanist and satanist-rapist death-freaks flooded the whirling crash pads. People began getting ripped off in the parks. There was racial trouble." In the midst of it, haunting Grateful Dead concerts in the Avalon Ballroom, was a bearded little psychotic who liked to curl up in a fetal position right on the dance floor, and whose secret ambitions were to persuade girls to perform fellatio with dogs and gouge out the eyes of a beautiful actress and smear them on walls. Later he would be well remembered in Hashbury. His name was Charles Manson.

Hippiedom would survive in one form or another, as beatism had — the bohemian strain runs wide and deep in America — but the movement as it had been known that year was doomed. All that was lacking was a final curtain. That came on the night of Saturday, October 8, 1967. A generation earlier, on June 8, 1931, the death of a New York girl bearing the singularly poetic name of Starr Faithfull had symbolized the magic and the depravity of an era then ending; John O'Hara had based *Butterfield 8* on it. Now the squalid Manhattan murder of another genteel girl ended the hippy summer of 1967. Her name was Linda Rae Fitzpatrick. She was eighteen, a blonde, the daughter of a wealthy spice and tea importer. Her home of record was her parents' mansion in Greenwich, Connecticut, but on Sunday, October 9, her naked corpse was found in a boiler room of a brownstone tenement at 169 Avenue B on the Lower East Side.

It was not a good address. Flanked by a flyblown junk shop and a dingy bar and grill, the boiler room reeked of dog excrement and rotting garbage. One naked light bulb shone down on peeling paint, decaying plaster, whitewashed bricks crawling with cockroaches, and a filthy mattress. Linda had come to this noisome trysting place with a tattooed drifter named James "Groovy" Hutchinson. As detectives and the police surgeon put the story together, she had stripped and sprawled on the mattress. At that point Linda and Groovy had discovered that they were not alone. This room was often used as an exchange point for the sale of drugs, and four speed-freaks, all of them flying, decided to share Groovy's girl with him. She refused. When Groovy tried to defend her, his face was bashed in with a brick. After Linda had been raped four times, her face was smashed, too. The bodies had been left face up; her black lace pants were found in a corner.

Three Negro men were swiftly arrested, but the public was more interested in the girl than in her victimizers. Linda had apparently led two lives. In Greenwich she had been the sheltered, well-bred child of an upper-class home. Like her parents she had been an Episcopalian; her favorite relaxation had been riding on the red-leafed bridle paths of the exclusive Round Hill Stables. The previous August, her father recalled, he had expressed his abhorrence of hippies, and her comments had been "much like mine." Her mother recalled that "Linda was never terribly boy crazy. She was very shy." Over Labor Day weekend she had told her mother that she didn't want to return to Oldfields, her expensive boarding school in Maryland. Instead she wanted to live in New York and paint.

"After all," her mother said afterward, "Linda's whole life was art. She had a burning desire to be something in the art world." Her parents agreed to her plan when she told them she had a room in a respectable Greenwich Village hotel. Her roommate, she said, was a twenty-two-year-old receptionist of a good family called Paula Bush.

"*Paula* Bush?" said the desk clerk. "Sure, I remember Linda, but there wasn't no Paula Bush. It was *Paul* Bush." In East Village she had consorted with many men, her family learned, and she had used money sent from Greenwich to buy drugs for them and herself. Late in September she thought she was pregnant, and she had confided to another girl that she was worried about the effect of LSD on the baby. Saturday evening, three hours before she died, she had told a friend that she had just shot some speed and was riding high. The cruelest part of the sequel for her parents was the discovery that her East Village acquaintances were indifferent to her death. One hippy girl said that though they mourned Groovy, "The chick wasn't anything to us."

In San Francisco's Golden Gate Park that same week hippies burned a gray coffin labeled "Summer of Love." In it were orange peels, peacock feathers, charms, flags, crucifixes, and a marijuana-flavored cookie. The ceremony was called "The Death of Hip." After the mourners had watched the fire while singing "God Bless America" and "Hare Krishna," they shouted, "Hippies are dead! Now the free men will come through!" Violence had crippled the movement, and so had commercialism. Tourists were crowding craft shops in both the Haight and East Village. Hippies hungering for money were acting in *Indian Givers,* a full-length psychedelic western, in which the sheriff was being played by, of all people, Dr. Timothy Leary. Ron Thelin, proprietor of San Francisco's Psychedelic Shop, said dolefully, "The spirit is gone"; then he went out of business, and Roger Ricco, a veteran member of The Group Image, said, "It isn't the same any more. Where have all the flowers gone?"

Portrait of an American

KARL HESS III

EITHER/OR.

As Karl Hess saw it, every serious man was obliged to take an unyielding stand at one extreme or the other.

Either he was a Minuteman or a Weatherman, a hard-core, better-dead-than-Red ultraconservative or a New Left militant, a Klansman or a Black

Panther, an anti-Semite or a gunman of the Symbionese Liberation Army. If you didn't want the SAC to lob one into the men's room at the Kremlin, you must advocate blowing up the Pan Am Building. There was no middle ground, just one faith and one enemy of the faith, one way to save the world and one way to destroy it. Society was not marvelously complex; it was magnificently simple. One must merely choose between absolutes, between the black and the white, the good and the evil.

In 1954, as a sleek, well-paid spokesman of the ultraconservative right, he wrote in *The American Mercury:*

> It would not be America really if it did not produce men who suddenly tire of palaver and reach for the rifle on the wall, to use themselves or to hand to the underdog who needs it.

In 1970, as a bearded, ragged oracle of the SDS and the Black Panthers, he proudly displayed an announcement of his appearance on the University of Texas campus:

> Union Speakers Comm. (the people who brought you Abbie Hoffman) present: Karl Hess, farout freak, militant, commie, anarchist, pervert!!! Currently assoc. editor of *Ramparts*.

He never saw that the two poles were really one. Superficially it seemed that he had swung from one to the other. In fact he had not budged an inch. He ended where he had begun — at the farthest possible distance from the political center.

Born on a great Philippines estate in 1923, he was molded not by his father, a flamboyant millionaire, but by his mother, a former Washington, D.C., working girl. When strong-minded Thelma Hess discovered that her husband was a philanderer, she left him, returned to Washington with young Karl, and went to work as a switchboard operator rather than accept alimony. She made a rule: before her little son could have a toy, he must read a book. Entering kindergarten, he had finished H. G. Wells's *Outline of History*.

By the time he reached adolescence the husky young Hess had read more than his teachers, and they bored him. To him education was an organized bureaucracy. Already, at fourteen, he had identified the system as his enemy. He fought it by enrolling in two high schools, filing the transfer papers of each at the other. Lying about his age — he looked older than his years — Hess got a job at the Mutual radio network. He was writing news programs when he borrowed his boss's car one day. A policemen gave him a ticket, his true age was discovered, and he was fired. The system had won. It always would, but he would never quit struggling.

Next, as a copyboy on the *Alexandria Gazette,* he became fascinated with politics; that, too, would be a lifelong obsession. The Democrats repelled him. He became a right-wing Republican because the ultraconservatives championed individual liberty. Whatever the merit of his views, there was no questioning his ability. By his twentieth birthday he was a rising star on the *Washington Daily News.* Then the editor phoned him at home to say that FDR had died and he was assigned to the story. Hess replied that Roosevelt's obituary wasn't worth getting out of bed; he was fired.

He became news editor of *Aviation Week,* author of a children's book on natural science, editor of *Fisherman Magazine,* and, between 1950 and 1955, press editor at *Newsweek.* Had he been able to shuck his ideological yoke, he might have had a distinguished journalistic career. As it was, he became increasingly preoccupied with right-wing doctrine, writing an anti-Communist column for the conservative weekly *Pathfinder,* editing *Counter-Attack* and H. L. Hunt's *Facts Forum,* and founding the *National Review* with, among others, William F. Buckley Jr. At the same time he was contributing regularly to the *American Mercury.* In its pages he denounced Robert Oppenheimer, the United Nations, and critics of the National Rifle Association, in which he held a lifetime membership. ("If everybody in Latin America had a pistol, they would have democracy.") The National Guard, he declared, was the country's greatest protection against federal dictatorship. He believed in order, deference to military rank, and the "discipline that comes from respect of an obedience to authority."

By 1960 Hess's lyrical praise of rugged individualism had brought him a sinecure as assistant to the president of Ohio's vast Champion Paper and Fibre Company. He lived in an expensive suburban home with a wife, two children, and seventeen custom-made suits. His job at Champion was to discourage aggressive union organizers and instill loyalty to the company in employees. From time to time the firm loaned him to right-wing think tanks. He compiled *The Conservative Papers* for Congressman Melvin Laird. In 1960 he wrote policy papers for Richard Nixon, and in 1964, as Barry Goldwater's chief adviser, he dashed off the speech in which the senator accepted his party's nomination. Goldwater, he said, offered "a choice, not an echo."

Then something snapped. Lyndon Johnson not only won the election; he won it with contributions from the very big businessmen who had been Hess's heroes. Hess discovered that the backer of one of his right-wing publications had been enriched by federal agricultural subsidies. Most traumatic of all, the magnitude of the Goldwater defeat had made Hess a pariah in GOP circles. By custom, men who have served ably in a losing campaign may expect a job in the service of other members of the party who are still in office. On Capitol Hill he went from door to door, hoping for a place on some Republican payroll. He found none. No one wanted him in any capacity. By the following spring he was broke and desperate, ready to settle for a place as a Capitol elevator operator. Even that was closed to him. He wound up welding bulldozers on the night shift in a Washington machine shop.

That was the year of Johnson's first big Vietnam build-up. Hess was appalled by it. This was the system run amok. He perceived his error, and concluded that "my enemy was not a particular state — not Cuba or North Vietnam, for example — but the state itself." As he saw it, the anti-Communist zeal of ultraconservatives had led them into a tragic error. They had trusted federal power, and had reaped the triumph of bureaucracy. His new heroes were the Panthers, who called for power to the people, and the Weathermen: "The SDS is raising essential political questions, and the police are beating them down for it." He began to read anarchist literature and to recommend resistance to authority — flouting of the law, draft resistance, hiding of political prisoners, refusing to move if the government condemns your house.

Slowly his life-style changed. He left his wife and grew a beard. The custom-made suits were left in the closet; he now wore a Castro cap, tennis shoes without socks, a tattered field jacket, and faded green denims. Because he refused to pay his taxes, he wasn't allowed to own property. He lived on the Anacostia River, in a houseboat belonging to a girlfriend. To a reporter he said, "I splice lines, paint the deck, and plot against the state." His plotting was limited to lecturing on campuses, exhorting Panther rallies, and writing for *Ramparts* and *Hard Times*, but the FBI was watching him carefully.

His old friends, who were now running the government under Nixon, were dumbfounded. In the corridors of power they whispered stories about him. He was poaching on federal property. He had competed in a motorcycle race and broken a leg. He was seen in the company of known felons, trotting around the District with a knapsack on his back. He had advocated the expropriation of all public and corporate wealth, was carrying an IWW membership card, had been arrested in an antiwar riot, had been gassed in a march on Fort Dix, had spoken at a radical rally from a stage dominated by an enormous black flag, had won a *Playboy* award for the best nonfiction article of the year — a paean to libertarianism.

Aboard the houseboat *Tranquil* the soft-voiced, beefily handsome Hess continued to scheme away. Mounted on the fore bulkhead was his beloved rifle, representing his everlasting belief in the right of a man to protect himself from the bureaucrats who would enslave him. Papers surrounded him: drafts of speeches, notes for an autobiography, pamphlets, the manuscript of a book on the wickedness of the capitalist state. He lamented as "tragic, very tragic" the fact "that Goldwater has now taken his stand on the side of established authority." He had heard that the senator refused to talk about him, but he understood that. "I wouldn't be surprised," he said reflectively, "if Barry thinks I'm crazy."

THIRTY-THREE

The Year Everything
Went Wrong

I T WAS THE YEAR of the Hong Kong flu and *Hair*. The hundred-and-twenty-one-year-old Pennsylvania Railroad and the hundred-and-fourteen-year-old New York Central merged, and service was twice as bad. First-class postage went from five cents an ounce to six. Helen Keller, Edna Ferber, and John Steinbeck died. Mia Farrow divorced Frank Sinatra. The American ambassador to Guatemala was assassinated.

In Washington the Willard Hotel, where at least seven Presidents, beginning with Franklin Pierce, had been guests at one time or another, went bankrupt. Red China, as it was still called then, exploded its seventh atom bomb, France its first hydrogen bomb. Hitler's bones turned up in Russia. A U.S. Strategic Air Command B-52 crashed in Greenland, near Thule, spilling wreckage contaminated with plutonium-235 over miles of ice, the thirteenth such accident. Biafra starved.

Some things went right. Barbra Streisand was marvelous in *Funny Girl*. Julie Nixon married David Eisenhower. Network censors cut Pete Seeger singing an antiwar song from a Smothers Brothers show, but six months later they changed their minds and let him do it. It was a big year for heart transplants, although only one patient in four lived more than six months. The *Washington Daily News* reported that one out of every eight Americans was getting social security benefits. Tiny Tim tiptoed into the limelight. The American Civil Liberties Union decided to support draft evaders. *Laugh-In* provided some lively graffiti: "Little Orphan Annie — call the eye bank," "This is your slum — keep it clean," "Forest fires prevent bears," and "George Wallace — your sheets are ready." Publishers issued John Updike's *Couples*, Charles Portis's *True Grit*, and Peter De Vries's *The Cat's Pajamas and Witch's Milk*. It was also the year of Allen Drury's *Preserve and Protect*. "When," asked *Time*, "will Drury cease and desist?"

The general thrust of events was suggested by the disclosure that the Defense Department budget this year would be 72 billion dollars, a record and a depressing one. (Roosevelt's *entire* annual budget, when he was accused of sending the country into the poorhouse, had been 8.8 billion dollars.) New Jersey Congressman Charles S. Joelson, told that the gun control bill had been watered down and that he would have to live with the new version, replied that "tens of thousands of Americans can die with it." The great American traffic jam became denser with the announcement, by the U.S. Bureau of the Census and Public Roads Administration, that 99.9 million automobiles were now registered in the United States, that 78.6 percent of all families owned at least one car, and that every fourth family owned two or more. If a man was younger than twenty-one the chances were that he had sideburns and wore bell-bottoms. The young expressed approval of something by calling it "tough" or saying it had "soul" or was "out of sight," and if you didn't agree you were either straight or sick.

That year Dancer's Image won the Kentucky Derby, was disqualified on charges that he had been drugged, and then, to confuse everyone, was designated the official winner — while losing the purse to the runner-up.

In West Virginia the Consolidated Coal Company's No. 9 mine blew, entombing seventy-eight men. The U.S. submarine *Scorpion* was lost with ninety-nine men, which would have been the greatest naval disaster of the year had it not been overshadowed by the spectacular fate of another U.S. ship in the waters off North Korea.

The U.S.S. *Pueblo* was labeled an "environmental research ship" by the Pentagon, but she was really an electronic snoop, bristling with antennas and complicated radar gear which enabled her to cruise slowly through the Sea of Japan, taking readings of what was happening to North Korean electronic devices on land. This was perfectly legal, provided she stayed twelve miles out. The North Koreans knew all about her. During the first two weeks of her first mission in 1968 they had tried to distract her with patrol boats and, overhead, low-flying MIGs. Her crew was therefore not surprised when, on January 23, a fleet of PTs sailed out and began circling her. Then one of the small boats signaled: "Heave to or I will open fire on you." That was new. Commander Lloyd M. Bucher, the *Pueblo*'s captain, replied, "I am in international waters." The PT said: "Follow in my wake." Bucher ignored that until another boat began backing toward him. Seeing that its fenders were rigged with rope mats and rubber tubes to cushion a collision, Bucher radioed his base in Japan: "These fellows are serious." Before the boarding party could arrive, he ordered his men to destroy as much of his intelligence ship's secret equipment as they could, shredding codes and wrecking the gear with sledgehammers, axes, and hand grenades.

The news that a U.S. Navy vessel had been captured — the first since the British seized the U.S.S. *Chesapeake* in 1807 — stunned the United States. Dean Rusk said it was "a matter of the utmost gravity" and an "act of war." Republican Senator Wallace F. Bennett of Utah demanded that American ships storm Wonsan harbor, recapture the *Pueblo,* and free her crew. Democratic Senator Thomas J. Dodd wanted the Navy to seize all ships flying the North Korean flag "wherever they may be found on the high seas." Most of Washington took the advice of Rusk to remain calm, however. North Dakota's Karl Mundt, no appeaser, pointed out that "We have enough war worries on our hands without looking for another one." Others on the Hill said that belligerence would merely doom the *Pueblo*'s crew. Two appeals to Russia, asking the Soviet Union to act as mediator, were rejected. Arthur Goldberg, the former Supreme Court justice who was now U.S. ambassador to the United Nations, tried to get the U.N. Security Council to review the incident. He failed.

In the end the case was taken up by American and North Korean negotiators in the tin-roofed Panmunjom shed where the armistice between their armies had been negotiated fifteen years ago. Meanwhile the North Korean Central News Agency was broadcasting what was called a confession by Commander Bucher, saying that he had committed a "criminal act" and "an act of sheer aggression" for which he had "no excuse whatever." An open letter from the commander and his crew said that they were being "provided with all the necessities of life," but the letter was stilted, almost in pidgin English, and therefore not reassuring. In the United States bumper stickers appeared reading, "Remember the *Pueblo*," as though it were possible to forget.

Exactly one week after the seizure of the *Pueblo*, the North Vietnamese launched their most spectacular offensive of the war three thousand miles to the south. General Westmoreland was expecting it, and he thought he knew where it would come: at the big U.S. Marine Corps base at Khe Sanh. Khe Sanh was in many ways like Dienbienphu, the bottom of a red clay, shell-pocked bowl of hills athwart the Communist enemy's chief infiltration route to the south. "This is the cork," an American major explained to reporters. "If they can get past us, they can tear up the countryside way over to the coast."

The bowl was in fact an enemy objective, and was invested by 20,000 North Vietnamese troops. It was to remain under siege for seventy-six days before Operation Pegasus, a force of 30,000 American troops, could break the siege. But Khe Sanh wasn't the chief target of General Vo Nguyen Giap. Giap planned instead to attack almost every population center of any size in South Vietnam.

Tet, the lunar New Year, was observed with a kind of fatalistic gaiety in South Vietnam's cities on the evening of Tuesday, January 30. The next day would be the first of the Year of the Monkey, the most inauspicious of them all. It was going to be worse than they dreamed. Evidence of that was around them, had they known how and where to look. One sign was the large number of husky young strangers arriving in the towns by sampan, scooter, and bicycle. Another was the incredible number of funerals, celebrated with the traditional gongs, flutes, firecrackers, and coffins — coffins packed, it would later be learned, with things other than corpses. Shortly after midnight, when those who had celebrated Tet were fast asleep, the strangers — all members of elite Viet Cong units — assembled and assaulted key points in the capital and a hundred other cities from one end of the country to another: police stations, military bases, government buildings, radio and power stations, and foreign embassies, including that of the United States, which had just been rebuilt after the last terrorist raid at a cost of two and a half million dollars.

Altogether some 60,000 Viet Cong were being committed to the Tet attack. After twenty-five days of the offensive they controlled large areas of the countryside, including most of the Mekong Delta. Inch by inch American and South Vietnamese troops drove them from the large population centers. The biggest battle was for the ancient imperial city of Hue, where 70 percent of the homes were in ruins. It was of Ben Tre, after air and artillery strikes there had routed the Communists, that an American officer made the memorable comment: "It became necessary to destroy the town to save it." After counting enemy bodies and finding that there were many more of them than of Americans and South Vietnamese, U.S. commanders triumphantly announced that they had won. President Johnson told a press conference that in military terms the Viet Cong drive had been "a complete failure." On television Secretary McNamara said, "It is quite clear that the military objective . . . has not been achieved."

"If this is failure," said Senator George D. Aiken of Vermont, "I hope the Viet Cong never have a major success." Robert F. Kennedy of New York warned against "the delusion" that the Tet campaign constituted "some sort of victory," and Eugene McCarthy of Minnesota said that "if capturing a section of the American embassy and several large cities constitutes complete failure, I suppose by this logic that if the Viet Cong captured the entire country, the administration would be claiming their total collapse." Another senator probably spoke for the largest number of Americans when he asked in bewilderment, "What happened? I thought we were supposed to be winning this war." Certainly that was what the country had been told. Only two months ago General Westmoreland had reported that he could see light at the end of the tunnel. And now this.

As David Halberstam later pointed out, the real casualties of the Tet offensive were "the credibility of the American strategy of attrition" and "the credibility of the man who was by now Johnson's most important political ally" — Westmoreland. If Westmoreland was no longer believable on the war, neither was Johnson. His administration began to come unstuck. John Gardner resigned as Secretary of Health, Education, and Welfare. Goldberg quit the U.N. McNamara left the Pentagon and was replaced by Clark Clifford.

By April 19, 1968, the American force level in Vietnam had risen to 549,000 troops. U.S. combat deaths reached 22,951, and on Sunday, June 23, the war became the longest in American history, surpassing the War of

Independence. Both of President Johnson's sons-in-law were there, which in another time would have elicited sympathy for him. But bitterness over the war was too intense now. Draft evaders and Army deserters were forming colonies in Canada and Sweden. Then, as summer and the national conventions of 1968 approached, two events swelled the ranks of the protesters: General Westmoreland asked for 206,000 more men and his headquarters announced that "the Khe Sanh base in Quang Tri province is being inactivated." So much for the cork. All those Marine Corps casualties, all that bravery, and now the general didn't even want it.

On April 10 the White House announced a change in command for U.S. troops in Vietnam. On June 30 the new chief would be a West Point classmate of Westmoreland's, General Creighton Abrams. ("A tough, plain-speaking New Englander," *Time* called him, ". . . who could inspire aggressiveness in a begonia.") What was needed was a man who could preside over an orderly withdrawal, for it was increasingly evident that it would come to that sooner or later. For a time there was hope that it might be soon. In May Hanoi proposed peace talks in Paris. They were scheduled to begin May 10 in the old Hotel Majestic, with Averell Harriman facing Xuan Thuy, who had retired as Ho Chi Minh's foreign minister three years earlier.

But nothing had changed. Six weeks of tortuous diplomacy were required before delegations could be brought into the same room, and then they quarreled about the shape of the table. Meantime enemy attacks had made May the bloodiest month of the war, with 2,000 Americans killed. President Johnson told American Legion and VFW conventions that there could be no truce until the Viet Cong showed some "restraint." Harriman advised him that that seemed unlikely. Clark Clifford toured Vietnam and reported that the Communists were "refitting, regrouping, and rearming" for another blitz. General Abrams studied Westmoreland's plans for a new campaign. They bore the code name Operation Complete Victory.

Angered by Nick Katzenbach's brusque claim that the Tonkin Gulf resolution was sufficient authority for waging war in Vietnam, Senator Eugene McCarthy was further aroused, in October 1967, by Dean Rusk's remark that the real threat to American security was "a billion Chinese." Afterward McCarthy said, "At this point, I thought I would call a halt." Urged by Allard K. Lowenstein, the leader of an antiwar campaign in search of a candidate, the Minnesota senator filed for the New Hampshire presidential primary. The polls predicted he would get at most 20 percent of the Democratic vote, but two factors increased his chances: the Tet offensive and the support of thousands of college student workers who shaved, scrubbed, and dressed to be "clean for Gene."

On March 12, the day of the primary, McCarthy electrified the country by polling 42 percent of the vote to Johnson's 48 percent. If Republican crossovers were counted, he almost defeated the President, with 28,791 to

Johnson's 29,201. Suddenly LBJ looked beatable. The most important immediate consequence of the vote was its impact on Robert F. Kennedy. Kennedy hadn't entered the primary, and as recently as January 20 he had said, "I would not oppose Lyndon Johnson under any foreseeable circumstances." He had explained then that he hesitated because his campaign would divide the party "in a very damaging way." Now he declared that he was "reassessing" his position, and on the Saturday after the New Hampshire primary he elated his admirers — and infuriated McCarthy's — by declaring: "I am announcing today my candidacy for the Presidency of the United States."

The next big primary was in Wisconsin, and the news from there was bad for Johnson. His organization was disintegrating; even the sons and daughters of loyal Democratic politicians there were stumping for McCarthy. Kennedy wasn't entered there, but each day's newspaper brought fresh evidence of his growing strength. Theodore Sorensen, Kenneth O'Donnell, and Arthur Schlesinger had joined his team, and Lawrence F. O'Brien had resigned as postmaster general to manage it. With that as background, President Johnson went on television March 31. He had ordered a reduction in the bombing of Vietnam, he said, and he spoke of the strife in the country, with "all of its ugly consequences." The nation needed unity, he said. Then:

"I have concluded that I should not permit the Presidency to become involved in the partisan divisions that are developing in this political year . . . I do not believe that I should devote an hour or a day of my time to any personal partisan causes . . . Accordingly, I shall not seek, and I will not accept, the nomination of my party for another term as your President."

Once the impact of Johnson's withdrawal had worn off, it became clear that the contest for the Democratic nomination was going to be a three-way race between McCarthy, Kennedy, and, once he was ready to declare, Vice President Humphrey. Of the three, only McCarthy was on the Wisconsin ballot; he had been running against Johnson there. It was too late to take the President's name off the ballot; McCarthy took 57.6 percent of the Democratic primary vote while Nixon, whose most serious opponents had been George Romney and Nelson Rockefeller, polled 81.3 percent of the Republican vote.

Humphrey announced his candidacy on April 27. Except for Oregon, in which McCarthy won narrowly, the rest of the primaries were all Kennedy. His strongest stands were against the war and for the poor and under-privileged. The leaders of the black movement were his natural allies. This was especially true of Martin Luther King, who had reached the conclusion that Vietnam was the largest serious obstacle to progress for his people; Negroes provided more than their share of combat troops, and money which should have been spent in the ghettos was going into the war. King said: "No one can pretend that the existence of the war is not profoundly affecting the destiny of civil rights progress."

In April 1968 King was in Memphis, supporting a two-month-old strike by 1,300 garbage men, most of them black. Newspapers had taunted him for staying at a plush Holiday Inn, paying $29 a night there, so he moved to a $13-a-night room in the Negro-owned Lorraine Motel. Before dinner on April 4 he was leaning on the second-floor iron railing outside room number 306 talking to fellow workers below. In a nondescript rooming house across the street a sniper crouched with a scope-sighted 30.06 Remington pump rifle. He fired one shot. It penetrated King's neck and exploded against his jaw, cutting his spinal column. He fell away from the rail and against the motel's wall, his hands rigid, reaching for his head.

Martin Luther King had been the greatest prophet of nonviolence since Gandhi, and it was the final irony of his life that the end of it should touch off the worst outburst of arson, looting, and criminal activity in the nation's history. In all, 168 cities and towns were stricken. Washington was the worst hit. An incredible 711 fires were set there. "Get your gun," Stokely Carmichael told blacks, and many did. There were ten deaths in the capital alone, one of them a white man who was dragged from his car and stabbed. President Johnson ordered the flag at half-mast on all federal buildings, the first time this had been done for a Negro, but the terror continued. Buildings within a few blocks of the White House were put to the torch. Nationwide, 2,600 fires were set, 2,600 people were arrested and 21,270 injured. To restore order 55,000 soldiers were required — ten times the number of marines defending Khe Sanh.

Accompanied by the music of spirituals and the tolling of church bells, Martin Luther King's coffin was transported to the grave on an old farm cart drawn by two mules. An estimated 120 million Americans watched the funeral march on television. There were between 50,000 and 100,000 marchers, including most of the nation's leaders, among them Robert Kennedy, Eugene McCarthy, Nelson Rockefeller, and Hubert Humphrey. Governor Lester Maddox of Georgia did not attend, although the funeral was in his state. Maddox refused to close the schools and protested lowering the flag to half-staff. But the man he refused to honor could never again be hurt by bigotry. The words of his epitaph, hewn in his tomb of Georgia marble, were from an old slave hymn; he had used them to close his oration at the Washington march five years before:

> *Free at last, free at last;*
> *Thank God Almighty, I'm free at last.*

John Willard, the name the sniper had used in renting the room from which he fired the shot, was an alias for Eric Starvo Galt, which also turned out to be an alias. Witnesses at the scene of the assassination had seen him race off in a white Mustang bearing Alabama license plates and Mexican tourist stickers. The car was found abandoned in Atlanta, Georgia. The FBI learned that he had bought it for $2,000 — cash — using the Galt name. A fugitive now, sought by police around the world, he fled to Toronto. There he adopted a new alias, Ramon George Sneyd, and acquired a Canadian passport by the only procedure necessary — swearing that was his name. Buying a $345 excursion ticket to Europe, he spent two days in Portugal before flying to London. There he vanished, no doubt he thought for good.

But he had made one irrevocable error. His fingerprints had been found in the Memphis rooming house. After a fifteen-day search in the 53,000 prints of wanted men in the Department of Justice, the FBI identified him as James Earl Ray. He had a long record of convictions for forgery, car theft, and armed robbery. In April 1967 Ray had escaped from the Missouri state penitentiary. Now Canadian Mounties picked up his trail from the FBI, and customs officials throughout Europe were alerted to be on the lookout for Ramon G. Sneyd. On June 8 he was picked up at London's Heathrow Airport. Extradited and handcuffed, he was flown back wearing a bulletproof vest, his legs encased in armored trousers; no one wanted another Oswald. He was transported to the Memphis jail in a six-and-a-half-ton truck. Heavy steel plates blocked his cell window. He pleaded guilty and was sentenced to ninety-nine years. The source of his money was never discovered.

Almost two months to the day after Martin Luther King was struck down, and the same week that Ray was arrested, another act of mindless violence cut down the front runner for the Democratic presidential nomination. "An assassin never changed the course of history," Robert Kennedy had said after his brother's death in Dallas, but it wasn't true; that one had, and now his did, too. He had beaten Eugene McCarthy in the Indiana primary, 42 percent to 27, and in Nebraska 51 to 31. On this day, Tuesday, June 4, 1968, he had defeated both Hubert Humphrey — in Humphrey's native state, South Dakota — and McCarthy in the biggest of all the primaries, California.

Kennedy had spent that morning on a beach near Los Angeles with six of his ten children and his wife Ethel, who was pregnant with their eleventh. He followed election reports in suite 512 of the city's Ambassador Hotel. At midnight he took the elevator down to his headquarters in the hotel's Embassy Room and spoke briefly to the elated volunteers there. At the end he said: "So my thanks to all of you and it's on to Chicago, and let's win there." Friends and members of his immediate entourage mimicked his accent, saying: "And it's on to The Factory," that being the name of the popular discotheque where they were going to celebrate with him. But first he had to say a few words in the press room. The crowd was so dense between the rostrum and the Embassy Room's entrance that one member of the party suggested that they leave by a back passageway. Bill Barry, the former FBI agent who was Kennedy's bodyguard, objected. He didn't like the idea. But the senator said, "It's all right," and they stepped into a hot, smelly corridor. Kennedy paused there to shake hands with a seventeen-year-old busboy, Jesus Perez, and answer a question about Humphrey: "It just goes back to the struggle for it —"

He never finished. A Pasadena reporter saw an arm and a gun come out of a knot of spectators. The assassin propped his right elbow on a serving counter and fired at Kennedy, just four feet away. He pumped off all eight shots in the snub-nosed Iver-Johnson revolver before Rafer Johnson, an Olympic champion and a Kennedy friend, could knock the pistol out of his hand. Six men lay bleeding on the floor of the hall, five with slight injuries. The sixth, Kennedy, was wounded mortally. One of the two bullets which had hit him was relatively harmless, but the other had pierced his skull and entered his brain. Ethel knelt beside him. Bobby asked for water. Then he asked, "Is everybody safe?" The busboy gave him a crucifix. Bobby's fingers held the beads, and Ethel prayed, and Roosevelt Grier, the three-hundred-pound Los Angeles Rams' lineman, held the slight, dark assassin in a bear hug.

"Why did you do it?" one member of the party yelled. The killer screamed, "I can explain! Let me explain!" Jesse Unruh, leader of California Democrats, shouted at him, "Why him? Why him?" The gunman answered: "I did it for my country." That seemed preposterous. Then the truth began to emerge. In his psychotic way he really believed he was being patriotic. To everyone else in Los Angeles this had been the day of the California primary, but to Kennedy's murderer it was the first anniversary of the Israeli-Arab six-day war. His name was Sirhan Bishara Sirhan, he was a native of Jordan, and he hated Israel, which Kennedy admired. On the surface that appeared to be the only motive the swarthy little Arab had.

The dying Kennedy was first taken to the Central Receiving Hospital and then to the larger Good Samaritan Hospital. Kept alive by adrenalin injections and by cardiac massage, he underwent surgery almost at once. But it was hopeless. At 1:44, after a few flutterings of life, he died. Lyndon Johnson denounced the country's "insane traffic" in guns. Then he sent a presidential jet to bring the body home, and once more the Kennedys and their friends flew eastward with a coffin in a Boeing 707. The United Nations lowered its flag to half-mast, an unprecedented tribute to one who had never been a chief of state. When the plane arrived in New York ten thousand people had already lined up outside St. Patrick's Cathedral to say goodbye. Candles were placed at each corner of the catafalque, and friends took turns standing vigil. Ted Kennedy, the surviving Kennedy brother, acted as paterfamilias, delivering the eulogy in a trembling voice.

Richard Cardinal Cushing presided. Andy Williams sang "The Battle Hymn of the Republic"; the choir, the Hallelujah Chorus. Then the motorcade proceeded to Pennsylvania Station, where a special train waited, drawn by two black engines. Its destination was Washington, but the crowds standing by the tracks along the way were so great that the trip took eight hours. By then it was night in the capital. With only streetlamps as illumination, the cavalcade wound past the city's huge dark government buildings and across the Potomac, to Arlington. There Bob's grave waited, a dark scar beneath a magnolia tree a few feet from his brother's tombstone. After a brief, simple service there the flag was folded in a triangle and presented to Ethel. The band played:

> *America! America!*
> *God shed his grace on thee!*
> *And crown thy good with brotherhood,*
> *From sea to shining sea!*

Between January 1 and June 15 of 1968 there were 221 major demonstrations, involving nearly 39,000 students, on 101 American campuses. Buildings were dynamited, college presidents and deans were roughed up, obscenities were painted on walls and shouted at policemen, sometimes by well-bred daughters of good families at the ivied Seven Sister colleges for women. Among the institutions of higher learning disrupted by student violence during those months were Temple in Philadelphia, the State University of New York in Buffalo, Oberlin, Princeton, Duke, Chicago's Roosevelt University, Southern Illinois University, Boston University, Marquette, Tufts, Stanford, Colgate, Howard, the University of Oregon, Northwestern, Ohio State, Barnard, Mills College, the University of Connecticut, Trinity, Tuskegee, the University of Chicago, Bowie State in Maryland, UCLA, the University of Miami —

And, of course, Columbia.

Until the third week after the assassination of Martin Luther King the newsiest event on the Morningside Heights campus was its reversal of a decision, made the year before, to accept a gift of royalties from the leasing of a new cigarette filter invented by Robert Strickman, an industrial chemist. That had brought much unwelcome publicity, but the Columbia uprising of April 1968 was much worse. It was the biggest campus confrontation since the Berkeley turmoil four years earlier, and in a way it was more significant, for it marked the emergence of the Students for a Democratic Society. Until then SDS was known to the public as merely one more campus political student organization. After eight years it had 5,500 members, chapters at 200 colleges, and a characteristic student distaste for centralization. In the mid-Sixties SDS had become committed to militancy, however. Its leaders were avowed enemies of oppression, racism, and imperialism, all three of them as defined by SDS. It held that American universities had become corrupted by them, and that Columbia was especially wicked.

A college marching song popular among undergraduates on Morningside Heights in merrier days went:

Who owns New York?

Who owns New York?
Why, we own New York!
Why, we own New York!
Who?
C-O-L-U-M-B-I-A!

The SDS reminded fellow students that in fact the university did own 230 million dollars' worth of real estate in Manhattan, including the land under Rockefeller Center, and that much of it was occupied by deteriorating Harlem tenements nearby, making Columbia, in effect, a big slumlord. Six years earlier the university had unwittingly provided the fuel for an eventual explosion by leasing from the city an additional 2.1 acres of nearby Morningside Heights Park's thirty acres. The idea was to build a magnificent 11.6-million-dollar gymnasium there. Negroes living in the adjacent, bottle-strewn Harlem slum would be welcome to enjoy a free gym and swimming pool on the ground floor; the university's department of physical education would use the upper floors. Since the neighborhood was at present infested with prostitutes and drug addicts, with one of the highest crime rates in the city, Columbia's trustees assumed that every resident with a spark of civic pride would embrace the project. They were wrong.

Protesting tenants called the plan "a land grab," and "a desecration of a public park." At that point the university's administration blundered. An architect's conception of the gym was published showing an elaborate, expensive entrance facing the campus and a small, plain door facing Harlem. Leaders of the community group denounced the "separate but unequal facilities," the chairman of the Harlem CORE angrily charged that "This community is being raped," and one hundred and fifty demonstrators shouting "Gym Crow must go!" marched to the gymnasium site and tore down a section of fence. White participants included Mark Rudd, the chairman of Columbia's SDS, and as many followers as he had been able to muster.

Rudd was the kind of New Leftist that J. Edgar Hoover dreamed about. Hoover had just described the SDS as "a militant youth group which receives support from the Communist Party, and which in turn supports Communist objectives and tactics." Columbia students said sarcastically, "The Communists can't take over SDS — they can't find it." It did in fact have few members there. However, their penchant for outrageous words and for outrages themselves gave them, in a phrase of the time, a high profile. Rudd was particularly noisy. On the day that the balloon went up over Morningside Heights he had just returned from a three-week visit to Castro's Cuba. As if to confirm Hoover, he praised it as an "extremely humanistic society."

His opposite number was Columbia's president, sixty-four-year-old Grayson Kirk, aloof, frosty, and a poor administrator. Later a commission headed by Archibald Cox would conclude that under Kirk the administration conveyed "an attitude of authoritarianism and invited mistrust." Kirk had been unresponsive earlier in April when SDS collected 1,500 signatures to a petition demanding that Columbia withdraw from the Institute for Defense Analysis (IDA), an organization of researchers working for the Pentagon on twelve campuses. SDS charged that IDA projects were "aimed at the oppression of the people in Vietnam" and included "riot equipment to commit mass genocide against black people" in the United States.

Leaving the downed fence at the putative gym site that Tuesday, Rudd and his band marched on ivy-covered Hamilton Hall, the headquarters of Columbia College. There, to their surprise, they were met by a conciliatory acting dean, who said that although he had "no intention of meeting any demands under a situation such as this," both the gym and IDA membership were negotiable issues. SDS wasn't interested in that now. Having tasted victory, the insurgents retained momentum by imprisoning the acting dean and two other officials for twenty-six hours. The siege of Columbia had begun.

During the first night the white students discovered something else: black power. The sixty Negro students among them demanded that the whites leave. SDS, they said, wasn't militant enough for them. One version had it that the blacks were carrying guns and planned a shoot-out with policemen. Their white soul brothers didn't think the gym was as bad as that. Some of them felt hurt. "Why should they run this thing?" one of them asked. "There's enough division and polarization in this country as it is." In any event, at 6 A.M. on the second day, Wednesday, April 24, Rudd announced that the whites weren't wanted in Hamilton Hall. Leaving it to the blacks, he and his honkies took over Low Library, where they put up a notice: "Liberated Area. Be Free to Join Us." President Kirk's office was in the library. They broke into it and ransacked it, photographing letters and documents, throwing others away, smoking his cigars, and drinking his sherry. And they had just begun. To reporters they said that they believed they were right in disrupting the university. They cited principles established at the Nuremberg trials of Nazi war criminals. Columbia's administration under Kirk, they said, was as bad as the Nazis.

There were seven hundred of them now. On Thursday a hundred seized Fayerweather Hall, the social science building. Another hundred took over Avery Hall, the architecture center, and on Friday a fifth hall was invaded. Over the balcony of that one they hung a banner: "Rudd Hall, Liberated Zone No. 5." They set up a command post and mimeographed proclamations. One demanded amnesty for all of them, but Kirk refused, saying that failure to take disciplinary action would "destroy the whole fabric of the university community." For a while it looked as though another group of students, the athletes, would evict the rebels. ("If this is a barbarian society," a wrestler said, "then it's survival of the fittest — and we're the fittest.") Kirk wanted no more violence, and he restrained them. He also made a concession: all work on the gymnasium was suspended. Not enough, the demonstrators shouted from the halls; they demanded secession from IDA and a lot of other things they had just thought up. Runners brought them food, blankets, and jars of vaseline. They wanted the vaseline because they had heard that it was protection from Mace. They expected Mace, fired by police.

They were right about the police coming. When the first detachment arrived on Morningside Heights, thirty members of Columbia's junior faculty barred the entrance to Low Hall. It was a deadlock. But then the university's trustees voted "to affirmatively direct" Kirk "to maintain the ultimate disciplinary power over the conduct of students." Thereupon he made what he later called "the most painful" decision of his life, to clear the buildings with force, if necessary — a thousand policemen in flying wedges. Hamilton Hall came first. The Negro students were docile. Black lawyers were there to represent them, and black police officers supervised the operation. After the Negroes left quietly, the building was found to be tidy.

The buildings occupied by whites were another matter. Whatever the provocation, the cops there clubbed, kicked, and punched the students, hurling them down concrete stairways. The police had assured spectators — there were several thousand of them — that they would be safe if they remained behind police barricades, but when it became clear that the spectators were prostudent, they, too were charged and beaten. All in all, 698 were arrested. Rudd and 72 other students were suspended for a year. Cox was asked to investigate the disorders. After twenty-one days of testimony from seventy-nine witnesses, he and four colleagues issued a 222-page report which was highly critical of both the university administration and the police. While holding no brief for the student ringleaders, the report found that their behavior "was in no way commensurate with the [police] brutality," which had "caused violence on a harrowing scale." Kirk and his staff had "regularly put the students at the bottom" of their priorities, the commission found, concluding that the gym and the IDA issue had in fact been mere surface manifestations of deep student dissatisfaction with the Vietnam War and racism in the United States.

According to a *New York Times* survey, the militant whites in campus riots at Columbia and elsewhere typically came from well-to-do homes in suburbia, had parents who were politically liberal, were students in the humanities rather than the sciences, were brilliant in class, and were predominantly Jewish. An example was Ted Gold, twenty-one, with Rudd a leader in the Columbia uprising and an SDS chairman. Gold said to reporters: "We are working, not just for a revolutionary Columbia, but for a revolutionary America."

At some point in the 1960s a man who had never run a stop sign did it. He was careful, nothing was coming; it was a silly statute, he reasoned; only robots obeyed it. He ran another; in a month he was doing it without qualms, and in another month he was running red lights if they turned red just as he was approaching an intersection. Though he overlooked the connection, he was annoyed because the attendant at his favorite filling station no longer checked his oil and cleaned his windshield unless asked. He switched filling stations; it was the same there. At about the same time a door in his new car developed a hideous rattle; he dismantled it and found that some anonymous worker on a Detroit assembly line had left a Coke bottle in it.

These were little things, but there were others. One morning you found a notice in your milk box. No more milk; the company had stopped deliveries; you had to go to the store. The postal system was a disgrace. Everybody had his horror story about the mails. Waitresses brought you somebody else's order. Cab drivers couldn't find your destination. Your evening paper wasn't delivered. The druggist filled the wrong prescription. The new washer-dryer was a lemon. Deliverymen double-parked and wouldn't move. By the end of the Johnson years it was a national joke. People displayed little signs:

PLAN AHEAD

The building industry was disgraceful; you were lucky if the job was done six months after the date promised. Airliners were late taking off; because they didn't reach your destination on time you had to wait, stacked over it, and when you did land you discovered that your baggage had gone on to another airport. This was so common that frequent travelers bought luggage expressly designed to fit under their seats. Bus and train timetables were fictive. Nearly everyone was dunned at one time or another for bills that were already paid. Nothing, it seemed, functioned any more. From the plumbing and the television to the F-111 swing-wing jet, all was snafu. A New York woman, billed for transatlantic telephone calls she hadn't made, picked up her phone to protest and heard violins playing; a Muzak line had crossed hers. Rex Reed, the writer, tried to use a credit card and was arrested on the ground that Rex Reed was dead. *Time* reported a man who had emptied a pistol firing at a vending machine.

Repairmen and salesclerks were as bad, or worse. The fault was difficult to pin down, but it was everywhere. People didn't seem to care whether things worked any more. The discipline that knits a society together was weakening and at some points giving way altogether. John Kenneth Galbraith attributed it to prosperity. Richard Nixon blamed it on permissiveness.

Jean-Jacques Servan-Schreiber likened the student demonstrators to General Giap in Vietnam, finding them different expressions of the same phenomenon. Clearly the war had something to do with it. Young men from the upper stratum of American society were evading the draft without guilt, encouraged by their parents and often with letters from physicians who lied about their health, also without guilt. Millions sympathized with the draft evaders and deserters making new lives in Toronto and Stockholm. Because the first four to arrive in Sweden had jumped ship from the aircraft carrier *Intrepid,* they were known as the "Intrepid Four." No one there thought the name ambiguous. One member of the colony, a nineteen-year-old South Carolinian, said: "We fall into two categories. There are those who are convinced the United States will blow up the world. There are others who think the United States can be saved before this catastrophe happens."

The war was only part of it. Not since Prohibition had so many people, concluding that some laws were senseless, proceeded to break them. Marijuana was an example. Unlike other drugs it was not habit-forming, unlike tobacco it was not harmful to the user, and unlike alcohol it was not dangerous to society. To the young it was often a matter of status; youths of the better families were known to be smoking it. For a time in 1969 police made a habit of "busting" — another new word — the sons and daughters of the famous.

Looters in the summer riots weren't arrested; you could see them helping themselves on the television news programs; policemen watched them and did nothing. "It seems to me," said Kenneth Clark, the Negro psychologist, "a high-policy decision was made to trade goods and appliances for human lives." Certainly it appeared that an arrest was determined by the identity of the person and place as much as by the act. In mid-May Ralph Abernathy, Martin Luther King's successor, set up a "Resurrection City," which King had planned, on the hallowed ground between the Lincoln Memorial and the Washington Monument. He led a thousand poor people on it, and the government not only failed to take any of them into custody; it gave them portable latrines, phone booths, power lines, showers, and even a zip number: 20013. Late in June, Alvin Johnson, the camp's chief security officer, resigned in anger, saying, "There are rapes, robberies, and cuttings every day, and there is nothing we can do about it." The National Capital Parks Police remained aloof.

In a previous generation Calvin Coolidge had won national recognition, and ultimately the Presidency, by breaking the Boston police strike of 1919. He said that there was "no right to strike against the public safety by anybody, anywhere, any time." In 1937 Franklin Roosevelt had called a strike by civil servants "unthinkable and intolerable." Since then the principle had been embodied in the Taft-Hartley Act and, in the states, by such laws as New York's Condon-Wadlin Act. Nevertheless, on January 1, 1966, Mike Quill led his Transport Workers Union in a strike that paralyzed downtown Manhattan by depriving the city, in effect, of 165 miles of subways and 530 miles of bus routes. When Quill was served with a court order to lead them back, he tore it up in front of television cameras. The city was forced to accept mediation and compromise with him.

Walkouts against the public interest in 1968 included that of the Memphis sanitation workers which Martin Luther King endorsed in his final hours. Another that same year left New York littered with a hundred thousands tons of reeking garbage on the streets before Governor Rocke-feller capitulated and granted the garbage workers a $425 pay raise which Mayor Lindsay had rejected earlier. Next, New York policemen picketed City Hall, shouting "Blue power!" They reported "sick" with imaginary ills or watched languidly while drivers left their cars parked at bus stops and in other no-parking zones. The head of the firemen's union bargained by telling his men to ignore such routine tasks as inspecting buildings and fire hydrants. On three separate occasions in the autumn of 1968 a majority of New York's 58,000 teachers walked out. Then air traffic controllers, alarmed at the dense stack-ups overhead, conspired in a deliberate slowdown.

The climax to defiance of public service came at the end of the decade, when over 200,000 of the country's 750,000 postmen decided to stop deliver-ing the mail for pay that started at $6,176 a year and reached $8,442 after twenty-one years. Despite the urging of their leaders, who reminded them that federal law threatened them with a $1,000 fine, a year in prison, the loss of pensions, and blacklisting from other government jobs, the 6,700 members of the Manhattan-Bronx local of the AFL-CIO National Associa-tion of Letter Carriers voted to walk out. Soon they were joined by the rest of greater New York's mailmen. The strike spread to Akron, Buffalo, Cleve-land, Chicago, Denver, St. Paul, and San Francisco.

It was the first walkout in the history of the U.S. Postal Service, and it was devastating. On an average day New York's post office moves about 25 million letters and packages; the national average is 270 million. Many firms had to suspend operations. New York banks couldn't receive their daily average of 300 million dollars in deposits, 400,000 welfare clients couldn't get their checks, and brokerage firms had to hire armored trucks to move securities on Wall Street. On the sixth day the National Guard began handling the New York mail, and on the eighth day the mailmen resumed their appointed rounds. Like other civil servants who had struck, they profited from their illegal walkout. Congress voted them an 8 percent raise, retroactive to the month before, and established an independent U.S. Postal Service which, among other things, was meant to be more attentive to their grievances.

Among the things that went wrong in 1968 was the choosing of a new Supreme Court Chief Justice. Earl Warren still felt vigorous, but he de-cided to retire because of his age; he had turned seventy-seven on March 19. On the morning of June 19 he telephoned President Johnson and told him. It was a historic moment. No Court had played a greater role in de-termining the direction of its time. Under Warren's leadership, the Court had led the way on school desegregation, school prayers, the rights of Communists, pornography, the arrest and conviction of defendants, and the "one man, one vote" ruling ordering legislative reapportionment. Warren had presided over fifteen Court terms. And now Lyndon Johnson, who wanted to do everything as President, could choose a new chief judge. He named Associate Justice Abe Fortas and picked Texas Congressman Homer Thornberry to take Fortas's place.

Both men were old friends of the President. Fortas was as close to the President as any man; the President had put him on the Court three years earlier. Johnson, being Johnson, had to make the new selections complicated. He would not accept Warren's resignation until the Senate had confirmed his choice of Fortas. Then, with Fortas securely in office, Thornberry could move into his old spot. But the Republicans, believing that they would capture the White House in November, were mulish. They called Fortas and Thornberry "lame duck" nominations and tarred Fortas as a "crony" of the President.

Senator Robert P. Griffin of Michigan emerged as the leader of seventeen hostile Republicans. In the beginning it seemed a lost cause. Everett Dirksen of Illinois, the minority leader in the Senate, called the "cronyism" and "lame duck" arguments "frivolous." "You do not go out looking for an enemy to put him on the Court," he said, and he remarked that Presidents Lincoln, Truman, and Kennedy had appointed friends. Rebuking Griffin, Dirksen said, "It's about time we be a little more circumspect about the kind of language we use." Even when the Senate Judiciary Committee decided to hold hearings — the first time for any nominee to the post of Chief Justice — Fortas seemed safe. The opening witness, Attorney General Ramsey Clark, pointed out that there was ample precedent for the President to keep Warren on the Court until Fortas's confirmation; many lesser federal judges were chosen while their predecessors remained in office.

The problem now was Fortas himself. He spent four terrible days being grilled. Under the Constitution he could not discuss his decisions while on the stand; that would be an outright violation of the principle of separation of powers. Nevertheless, opposition senators spent much of the time reading aloud liberal decisions in which he had participated. Then they questioned him about certain aspects of his conduct as an associate justice. That too was a matter of the separation of powers, but here it hurt him. As a member of the Court he was supposed to remain aloof from the executive department, and he hadn't been. He acknowledged that he had participated in White House meetings about the war and the ghetto riots, and that he had phoned Ralph Lazarus, the Columbus department store tycoon, to give him a tongue-lashing because of Lazarus's statement that Vietnam was affecting the economy.* Fortas protested that there was ample precedent for justices advising Presidents, but here, as always with Johnson, there was the

*See above, pages 1053–1054.

nagging feeling that something shady was going on. One straw was needed to break the camel's back now, and it came when the committee learned that Fortas had accepted $15,000 as the fee for teaching a series of summer groups, the money coming from businessmen who might figure in cases coming before the Court.

The judiciary committee approved the appointment 17 to 6, but the Republican and southern senators staged a filibuster. A two-thirds vote of the Senate was required to end it, and at that point Dirksen pulled the rug from under Fortas. He would not support the move to stop the filibuster, he said, and he wasn't even sure he would vote for the nomination; a Court ruling overturning the death penalty for the killing of a Chicago policeman angered him. The vote on cloture was 45 yes and 43 no, far short of the two-thirds needed. Fortas asked Johnson to withdraw the nomination. The President agreed "with deep regret" and said he would make no appointment at all. The following May *Life* revealed that Fortas had accepted another, $20,000 fee from the family foundation of Louis Wolfsen, whose conviction for stock manipulation had come before the Court. Although he had returned the money, Washington was shocked, and when still other revelations loomed, he resigned. With Fortas and Goldberg gone, and with a Republican in the White House, clearly the future Court would be less liberal.

Americans have a way of anointing and consecrating their heroes, putting them on pedestals that are impossibly high, and then knocking them off. In the autumn of 1968 it was the turn of a heroine: Jacqueline Bouvier Kennedy, who wanted neither the adoration of the past nor the calumny of the present, but merely privacy. She was a woman of beauty and charm. For one terrible weekend in its history the United States needed a presidential widow with those gifts and something else: a histrionic talent. Eleanor Roosevelt was a greater First Lady, but she could not have done that. Jackie Kennedy had given the country's grief dignity and nobility. No woman could have improved on it. But afterward she needed to be alone, and as long as she remained a widow that seemed to be impossible. In Washington tourist busses paused outside her home, and when she moved to New York cabbies recognized her and honked.

To avoid gossip she went out only with happily married public men. Arthur Schlesinger Jr., Robert S. McNamara, and Leonard Bernstein were familiar escorts. Lord Harlech, who as David Ormsby-Gore had been the British ambassador to the United States during the Kennedy years, was now a widower. The press suggested him as a new husband. Movie magazines proposed an elderly Greek shipping magnate, and the fans laughed.

They stopped laughing on October 17, 1968, when Jackie's mother announced: "My daughter, Mrs. John F. Kennedy, is planning to marry Mr. Aristotle Onassis" — the elderly shipping magnate. The son of a Smyrna tobacco merchant, Onassis had acquired a fortune which was estimated at 500 million dollars. Among other things he owned 100 ships, Olympic Airways, several corporations, a 325-foot yacht, the *Christina*, and the Greek island Skorpios. Those who believed the report — who weren't convinced that either the bride's mother was out of her mind or the announcement was a monstrous practical joke — speculated over what to give the couple. The New York Stock Exchange, the Taj Mahal, the *Queen Elizabeth 2*, and the De Beers diamond mines were among the suggestions.

JACKIE, HOW COULD YOU? asked the headline in the *Stockholm Expressen*. Onassis was two inches shorter and could have been her father — he was either twenty-three or twenty-nine years older, depending on which birth date you accepted. Onassis was divorced, which meant that Jackie could not hope for the church's blessing. Worst of all was the groom's total lack of a social conscience, the very heart of the Kennedy creed. He once said that his idea of the perfect home would be in a country without taxes. The taxes he did owe were outstanding in several different nations, including the United States. "She's gone from Prince Charming to Caliban," one former Kennedy appointee commented. Bob Hope said, "Nixon has a Greek running mate, and now everyone wants one." It was widely remarked that she wouldn't have done it if Bobby were alive.

The marriage was celebrated on October 20 in a tiny Chapel of the Little Virgin on Skorpios. Tulips had been airlifted from Holland by the tycoon's private jet fleet. The bride wore a lace Valentino original. Her two children were pages. The groom's children were witnesses. The Greek Orthodox ceremony took forty-five minutes; then the couple took communion from one chalice and were crowned with garlands of lemon blossoms, a sign of fertility and purity. After kissing the New Testament they circled the altar in a ritualistic dance. Afterward there was a reception on the white-hulled yacht. The Greek navy and Onassis's own patrol boats kept reporters off the island. His present to her was a ring with a huge ruby surrounded by big diamonds, with matching earrings — a gift worth 1.2 million dollars.

That was only the beginning. According to the veteran journalist Fred Sparks, the pair spent about twenty million dollars their first year together, and their expenditures then continued at the rate of about $384,000 a week. Onassis had given his new wife five million dollars in jewelry alone. And since he was making about fifty million dollars a year, he wasn't even dipping into capital. Keeping out of the newspapers was another matter. Mrs. Kennedy, as she still was, had agreed to hold one press conference on the eve of the wedding. She said then, "We wish our wedding to be a private moment in the little chapel among the cypresses of Skorpios, with only members of the family and their little children. Understand that even though people may be well known, they still hold in their hearts the emotion of a simple person for the moments that are the most important we know on earth — birth, marriage, and death."

Nevertheless, reporters stalked them. They were news and had to be covered. Photographers were worse. One, an Italian, managed, with telephoto lenses, to get a picture of her sunbathing in the nude. But the greatest blow to her new role came not from the secular press but from the Vatican's *L'Osservatore della Domenica.* Branding her "a public sinner," it reported that she would be denied church rites. In Boston Cardinal Cushing protested that "Only God knows" who sins and who doesn't; he pleaded for "love, mutual respect and esteem." Nevertheless, the canon lawyers in the Vatican held fast. In sharing Onassis's bed, they ruled, the wife of America's first Catholic President was profane in the eyes of God.

Richard Nixon's second presidential campaign had begun the previous February in Nashua, New Hampshire, when he registered at a Howard Johnson motel as Mr. Benjamin Chapman. Shortly thereafter pseudonyms became impossible, for his picture was back on front pages, and when he received 79 percent of the vote in the New Hampshire primary, he became the Republican front runner. Thereafter his campaign was one string of triumphs. George Romney was beaten early, after he had said he had been "brainwashed" into supporting the Vietnam War. Nelson Rockefeller dropped out, then came back after Johnson declared that he wouldn't run again, but the only effect of Rockefeller's in-out-in candidacy was to alienate an early supporter of his, Governor Spiro Agnew of Maryland.

Until Nixon chose him to share the ticket, Agnew was unknown outside his state. His name, as he conceded, was "not a household word." A few hours after his name went before the convention a reporter stopped pedestrians in downtown Atlanta and said, "I'm going to mention two words to you. You tell me what they mean. The words are Spiro Agnew." One Atlantan replied, "It's some kind of disease." Another said, "It's some kind of egg," and a third, a little closer to the mark, said, "He's a Greek that owns that shipbuilding firm."

Agnew's credentials, said *Time,* "are not convincing." But they had impressed Nixon. He wanted a running mate who would take the low road and thus serve the purpose he had served for Eisenhower. It was hard to assess Agnew's impact on the electorate, because his opposite number in the campaign turned out to be not the Democratic vice-presidential nominee, Senator Edmund Muskie of Maine, but a third-party candidate, Governor George Wallace of Alabama. Agnew denounced "phony intellectuals who don't understand what we mean by hard work and patriotism"; Wallace attacked "pointy-headed" newspapermen, "scummy anarchists" and "pseudo-intellectuals." Wallace said that if policemen "could run this country for about two years, they'd straighten it out." At the same time, Agnew was saying in Detroit, "If you've seen one ghetto area, you've seen them all." Agnew called a Nisei reporter a "fat Jap" and called Poles "Polacks." His manner was so graceless that a picket greeted him with a placard reading: APOLOGIZE NOW, SPIRO. IT WILL SAVE TIME LATER. Other pickets met Wallace with: IF YOU LIKED HITLER, YOU'LL LOVE WALLACE and WALLACE IS ROSEMARY'S BABY.

One reason the also-rans were so newsy in the early weeks of the campaign was the dreariness of the Republican convention, which came first. "Richard M. Nixon rode to victory," the Associated Press commented, "in a tedious ritual at Miami Beach." Theodore H. White wrote, "Boredom lay on the convention like a mattress." Glee clubs sang. Bands played. John Wayne gave an inspirational reading on "Why I am proud to be an American." Other celebrities supporting Nixon were equally dreary: Art Linkletter, Connie Francis, Pat Boone, Lawrence Welk. The arid speeches of the politicians seemed to go on forever. The only interesting moments came on the periphery of the convention. Senator Edward W. Brooke was reportedly barred from a reception because he was a Negro. Miami blacks rioted; the television commentators said that seventy policemen with shotguns entered the riot area, and the news later was that four Negroes had died. Nixon scribbled away a speech on the yellow legal-length pads which he soon would make famous. In it he called for a return to America's "lift of a driving dream."

The AP reported that the Republicans' security precautions were "the tightest in the memory of convention goers." The second Kennedy assassination had scared the Secret Service, which Johnson at that time had made responsible for the protection of all serious candidates. Agents in helicopters hovered over the convention city. Other agents with rifles and binoculars scanned the crowd from rooftops. A thirty-man riot squad was held in reserve, and the 1,333 delegates had to submit all packages and purses to inspection each time they entered the convention. Some Democrats said it was overdone. Two weeks later their own delegates assembled in Chicago.

The violence that lay ahead in Chicago was not inevitable, but all the ingredients were there. The Committee to End the War in Vietnam, an umbrella organization coordinating over eighty peace groups under David Dellinger, came to jeer at the Chicago police. Hippies, Yippies, peace pickets, McCarthy workers, disillusioned liberals — altogether, they predicted there would be 100,000 of them, and they would march on the convention in the International Amphitheater. Mayor Richard J. Daley took them seriously. He turned Chicago into an armed camp. Manholes around the amphitheater were sealed with tar. A chain link fence seven feet high, with barbed wire on top of it, was thrown around the hall. The city's 11,500 policemen were put on twelve-hour shifts, 5,500 National Guardsmen were alerted, and 7,500 troops of the U.S. Army, airlifted from Fort Hood in Texas on White House orders, were ordered to stand by. Despite the extravagant forecasts, only about 10,000 to 12,000 demonstrators came to confront them.

In the convention, the reason for all this, Humphrey was nominated on the first ballot; McCarthy and George McGovern of South Dakota lagged far behind him. The only real contest was over how the peace issue should be handled in the party platform. The administration plank, the more hawkish of the two, won with 1,567¾ to 1,041¼ for the dovish substitute plank. The figures reflected the depth of the division in the party on the war. Four years earlier Lyndon Johnson had been nominated by acclamation and had won in a landslide. The Chicago convention had been scheduled for the week of his sixtieth birthday, which came that Tuesday. Now he couldn't even come. The Secret Service advised him that it was too risky.

"Stop the war!" shouted the youths in the galleries. (The next day, in a ludicrous change, municipal employees took all the seats and waved banners reading WE LOVE DALEY.) But the most dramatic moment of the week was an outside echo of events inside the hall. Delegates were watching what was happening downtown on television screens, and Senator Abe Ribicoff, looking down from the rostrum on the Illinois delegation fifteen feet in front of him, condemned "Gestapo tactics in the streets of Chicago." Daley and his aides were on their feet, shaking fists and yelling obscenities at him — lip-readers watching television could identify the oaths — and Ribicoff said calmly, "How hard it is to accept the truth."

The full truth about what was happening was complicated. If the policemen had matched the courage and discipline of the U.S. marshals on the Ole Miss campus, their record would have been clean. At the same time, it is fair to point out that some of them were provoked. Afterward they displayed over a hundred weapons they had taken from those they arrested: switchblade knives, studded golf balls, clubs with nails embedded in them, bats with razor blades in the ends, chunks of concrete, and plain rocks.

The sequence of events which eventually erupted beneath the very hotel windows of the major candidates had begun on August 3, the Thursday before the convention, when the Youth International Party — the Yippies — arrived in Chicago with Pigasus, the 125-pound hog they announced they were going to nominate for President. Conspicuous in their beads, sandals, and beards, the Yippies and hippies settled down in Chicago's 1,185-acre Lincoln Park on the North Side. Over the weekend they played guitars, read poetry, and gave speeches. At 11 P.M. Saturday, curfew time, a dozen were arrested. None resisted. Sunday there were 2,000 of them. At 5 P.M. they asked police for permission to take a truck into the park and use it as a bandstand. The cops refused. They then arrested the Yippy leader Jerry Rubin. The crowd, incensed, chanted, "Hell, no, we won't go," "Oink, Oink!" and "Ho-Ho-Ho Chi Minh." Tom Hayden of the New Left explained to the officers that this last meant nothing; it was an international student chant which began in Germany. They ignored him. At curfew time they charged through the park swinging nightsticks. They did the same Monday night, except that this time they were tougher. The evicted demonstrators raced away through the North Side traffic.

On Tuesday seventy priests and ministers erected a ten-foot cross. The demonstrators sang, "We Shall Overcome" and "The Battle Hymn of the Republic." That evening three hundred policemen charged them with tear gas. Choking youths threw stones and bottles, shouting, "Shoot me, pig!"

and "Hit me, pig!" The climax came on Wednesday. Demonstration leaders had announced that the protesters would march from the Grant Park band shell to the amphitheater as a show of the solidarity of their opposition to the war. "This is a nonviolent march," Dellinger told an audience of eight thousand. "If you feel you can't respond nonviolently, please leave us." Many did. Nevertheless a Chicago official said, "There will be no march today."

And there wasn't. Instead there was what an investigatory commission later called a "police riot." Policemen with bullhorns shouted, "This is a final warning. Move out now." The crowd did, to a narrow strip of Grant Park across Michigan Avenue from the Conrad Hilton. As they moved they mocked the police with "Oink! Oink!" "Sieg Heil!" and other rude chants. At the intersection of Michigan and Balboa avenues a double line of cops awaited them. The scene was brightly illuminated by TV lights on trucks and the eaves of the Conrad Hilton Hotel, headquarters for the three candidates. As the crowd tensed and then surged back and forth taunting the officers, daring them to attack, the police swooped down on them in two flying wedges, nightsticks swinging, dragging individual demonstrators toward waiting wagons. Hundreds of girls in the throng screamed. The mayhem continued for eighteen mad minutes. What was happening, in a very real sense, was a battle between the upper middle and lower middle class. A journalist said, "Those are our children in the streets, and the policemen are attacking them." But of course the policemen had parents, too.

Apart from the major encounters there were skirmishes all week between patrolmen and demonstrators, and some between patrolmen and nondemonstrators. On Monday evening alone twenty-one newspapermen were hurt. At various times spectators, clergymen, and at least one cripple were clubbed. Hugh Hefner, the publisher of *Playboy,* was walloped, and Mrs. Anne Kerr, a British Labourite, was Maced outside the Conrad Hilton and thrown into a cell. Hotel guests in the lobby were also beaten and jailed. The hotel's air-conditioning shafts sucked up tear gas and wafted it into suite 2525A, where Hubert Humphrey was watching himself being nominated on television. On Friday policemen said they were being pelted by objects from windows above — sardines, herrings, beer cans, ashtrays, cocktail glasses, and ice cubes. They thought — they couldn't tell — that the missiles were coming from the fifteenth floor, corner suite 1505A and 1506A: McCarthy's command post. Without writ or warrant, they ran into the hotel, took elevators up, and clouted the occupants of the suite.

Bloodshed might have been averted in Chicago if Mayor Daley had consented when the demonstrators asked permission to sleep in the meadows and glens of Lincoln Park. Then the policemen could have guarded the fringes of the park until the protesters got bored and left. As it was, by enforcing the curfew the mayor made confrontation inevitable, and under the worst possible circumstances. "The whole world is watching," the youths had chanted at Michigan and Balboa. The world wasn't, but most of the country was — an estimated 89 million, including, at Key Biscayne, an elated Richard Nixon.

In Chicago, Theodore H. White had written in his notes at 8:05 P.M. Wednesday, "The Democrats are finished." Certainly it looked like it, and when Humphrey's campaign began with a sickening lurch his admirers despaired. Among his major handicaps were the alienation of Democrats whose hearts had been captured by McCarthy and who now wore blank campaign pins, lack of money, an inefficient organization, and his inability to free himself from the toils of Lyndon Johnson. Johnson wasn't helping. His attitude toward Humphrey was scornful. He seemed to regard him as contemptible. Asked to comment on him, Johnson said curtly, "He cries too much."

In those early autumn weeks he had something to cry over. Inadequately prepared, Humphrey swung through New Jersey, Delaware, Michigan, Louisiana, Texas, Pennsylvania, Colorado, and California, speaking as often as nine times a day, a sign of his energy — and the lack of judgment on the part of his staff. Advance men served him poorly; crowds were small and tepid. In Philadelphia, Joey Bishop, a local boy accompanying Humphrey, got more applause than Humphrey. There were hecklers at virtually every stop. In Boston an antiwar crowd booed Humphrey and Edward Kennedy off a platform. Humphrey, said one of his workers, "went to Chicago with one albatross," meaning Lyndon Johnson, "and came out with two," meaning Johnson and Daley.

His treasury was all but empty. His rhetoric, which could soar, was laced with bromides. At one point he actually said, "Government of the people, by the people, and for the people is as American as apple pie." Johnson seemed to be sabotaging him; when in September Humphrey said that the withdrawal of U.S. troops could begin at the end of the year, the President said that "no man can predict" when departure might start. Not counting Wallace votes, in August Gallup had Nixon leading by 16 points, and Harris put Nixon's margin at 40 to 31. Even Humphrey was discouraged. He said, "I have pursued impossible dreams before and maybe I am now."

Nixon's campaign was all the other way. He had plenty of money and exultant optimism. His schedule harmonized with deadlines of the network news programs, even allowing them plenty of time to develop their film. He dodged challenges to debate, and Republican senators filibustered a measure to allow public service TV debates without Wallace. He appealed to the "forgotten American" — the man who paid his taxes, didn't riot or break the law, went to church and raised his children to be "good Americans" who would wear the country's uniform with pride as "watchmen on the walls of freedom around the world."

Joe McGinniss described the advertising techniques used by the Nixon people in *The Selling of the President 1968*. One writer observed that to Nixon politics were "products . . . to be sold the public — this one today, that one tomorrow, depending on the discounts and the state of the market." Frank Shakespeare Jr., a Nixon aide, was tremendously excited by the Russian invasion of Czechoslovakia. "What a break!" McGinniss quoted him as saying. "This Czech thing is perfect! It puts the soft-liners in a hell of a box!"

Nixon said he had a plan to end the war; he couldn't divulge it now because it might disturb the peace talks going on in Paris. He promised to restore law and order by appointing a new attorney general, and he attacked the Supreme Court for being "patently guilty" of freeing defendants on technicalities. He favored approval of the nuclear nonproliferation treaty, but not now, because of Soviet treatment of the Czechs. Business would improve, he said, because he would give businessmen tax credits and other incentives which would create jobs and reduce the number of people on welfare. America, he said, became great, "not because of what government did for the people but because of what people did for themselves."

In October Humphrey began to gain.

He had put Chicago behind him, and as he forgot it, so did his audiences. He dismissed his mockers as "damned fools," introduced the clown, Emmett Kelly, as "Nixon's economic adviser," and accused Nixon of dodging issues. He backed the Supreme Court and the nonproliferation treaty. Union audiences were reminded of what Democratic administrations had done for them. Nixon was "Richard the chicken-hearted"; Wallace and General Curtis LeMay, his running mate, were the "bombsy twins." Humphrey developed a technique of naming the Democratic presidential champions — Roosevelt, Truman, Stevenson, Kennedy — and then, just as the applause started to build, slipping in the name of Lyndon Johnson. Meanwhile his running mate was savaging Agnew. Muskie would say, "Mr. Agnew tells us that we lack a sense of humor," and add dryly: "I think he is doing his best to restore it."

Salt Lake City was a pivot. When Humphrey declared there that he would stop the bombing in Vietnam as "an acceptable risk for peace," the tide started to turn. On October 21 Gallup reported that Humphrey had cut Nixon's lead in half. Fading memories of Chicago was part of it. The habit of voting Democratic for a generation was another part. That June Gallup had found that 46 percent of the people considered themselves Democratic, 27 percent said they were independents, and 27 percent Republicans. (In 1940 it had been 42, 20, and 38 percent, and in 1950 45, 22, and 33.) Liberals who had yearned for Robert Kennedy or McCarthy awoke to the fact that the choice was between Humphrey and Nixon, their bogey for the past twenty years. McCarthy himself, who had been pouting on the Riviera, announced his support of the Democratic ticket five days before the election. Finally there was the difference between the demeanor of the two candidates. Humphrey was at the top of his form; Nixon had begun to sound uncannily like Thomas E. Dewey.

On the afternoon before the election Gallup had 42 percent for Nixon,

40 for Humphrey, 14 percent for Wallace, with 4 percent undecided. Since September Humphrey had gained 12 percent to Nixon's 1 percent, both at the expense of the fading Wallace. That same Monday Harris had Humphrey in the lead with 43 percent over Nixon's 40 percent; Wallace had 14 percent and 4 percent were undecided.

Tuesday night was a spellbinder. Nixon had asked the electorate for a "mandate to govern." What he got was a surge of Humphrey votes which, in the opinion of many analysts, would have won the election if the campaign had lasted another day or two — as it would have, the Democrats reflected grimly, if they hadn't postponed their convention so that it would coincide with the week of Lyndon Johnson's birthday. The figures flashing on the networks' electric scoreboards showed the lead changing hands several times. It seemed at one point that the two leaders were, as the Associated Press put it, "trading state for state." Shortly after midnight Humphrey was leading by 33,000 votes. At dawn it appeared that although he couldn't win in the electoral college, he might win in the popular vote, and there was a distinct possibility that he could thwart a Nixon majority in electoral votes, throwing the election into the House of Representatives, where the Democrats had a majority.

The final electoral results were Nixon 301, Humphrey 191, and Wallace 45. The popular vote was 31,770,222 for Nixon (43.4 percent), 31,267,744 for Humphrey (42.7 percent), and 9,897,141 for Wallace (13.5 percent). The distance between the two leaders was less than .7 of one percentage point. Moreover, the Democrats had retained control of Congress. Nixon would be the first President in one hundred and twenty years to begin his administration with the opposition ruling both Houses on the Hill.

Campaigning in Ohio, Nixon had seen a thirteen-year-old schoolgirl holding a sign which read: "Bring Us Together." That, he said in his moment of triumph, had "touched me most." Did he mean it? With this complex man one could never be sure. "Watch what we do, not what we say," John Mitchell, his attorney-general designate, told a group of thirty southern black leaders. Later, during the Watergate scandals, James Reston would write of Nixon that "There is scarcely a noble principle in the American Constitution that he hasn't defended in theory or defied in practice." But in the pause after his election his credit was strong. Most Americans wanted to believe him, to persuade themselves that he knew how to leave the swamps of the 1960s for higher ground. He had promised to extricate the troops from Vietnam. Since 1961 there had been 24,291 American deaths in the war; it was an immense relief to know that soon the dying would end. The country needed a rest. Now partisan politics could be shelved.

From his windows on the thirty-ninth floor of Manhattan's Pierre Hotel, the President-elect could look out across the wooded sweep of Central Park and see America twinkling in the distance. Not since the pit of the

Depression had the country been so torn. Between those whose bumper stickers said LOVE IT OR LEAVE IT and those who said CHANGE IT OR LOSE IT yawned a chasm so broad that no reconciliation was possible now; finding common ground would have to wait until outstanding issues had been resolved, the war being the first of them. In the matter of social questions as liberal a commentator as Eric Sevareid found himself drifting to the right. He looked at the long list of crimes for which Black Panthers had been convicted and was appalled. He watched on television as a Baltimore girl, the mother of seven illegitimate children, furiously blamed society for her plight, and shook his head; he watched black women hurrying to reach home before sunset and said: "I just don't believe that 'law and order' are code words, except for a few. This issue is survival itself."

To those on the left side of the divide, the aroused young ideologues, nothing seemed to be sacred: not the American flag, God, motherhood, knowledge, honor, modesty, chastity, or simple honesty. In 1968 insurance actuaries reportedly discovered that the group in society which failed most often to repay its debts was the young collegians who owed tuition loans; a college president wrote to one defaulter who had just graduated, and back came a photograph of the new alumnus naked and in a cave. It was almost possible to believe that for some middle-class youths the Boy Scout pledge which their fathers had recited had become inverted: they strove to be untrustworthy, disloyal, unhelpful, hostile, discourteous, unkind, disobedient, cheerless, wasteful, craven, dirty, and irreverent.

The campuses of venerable institutions of learning had often become disagreeable and even dangerous places. The one at Wesleyan, a little ivy college in Connecticut, had to be floodlit at night; crossing it was unsafe; there had been an epidemic of muggings there. Universities were confronted with a new disciplinary problem: how to cope with the undergraduate who was putting himself through college by peddling dope to fellow students who had become drug addicts. Crime became commonplace in peculiar places. One respected physician in New England entertained dinner party guests by telling how he and his wife had started shoplifting as children, still did it, and in fact had stolen the centerpiece on the table only three days ago. An assistant dean explained in great detail the information he had given, to a recent undergraduate drafted into the tank corps, on the best way to sabotage a tank. And a July 1967 issue of the *New York Review of Books* carried on its front page a large drawing showing how to make a Molotov cocktail, with a rag soaked in gasoline as the stopper, a fuse of clothesline rope, and instructions to use as fuel a mixture two-thirds gas and one-third soap powder and dirt.

The election of Richard Nixon to the Presidency was a reaction against all this, and a healthy one. The nation wanted no more visionaries for the present. What was needed was a genuine conservative administration, another Eisenhower era. Such a government would resist temptations to cut taxes and try, insofar as possible, to balance the budget, assuring a sound dollar and no inflation. Hostilities in Indochina would be ended as soon as possible, and all foreign policies would be evaluated solely in terms of the national interest of the United States. At home the role of the federal government would be sharply limited and congressional preroga- tives restored, and ties would be strengthened between the generations, the races, the wealthy and the impoverished, the different regions in the country, and the religious faiths.

Nowhere was America's exhaustion in 1968 more evident than in the ghettos, which were calmer that year than anyone had prophesied. "We will have a bad summer," Lyndon Johnson had said in the spring. "We will have several bad summers before the deficiencies are erased." Nixon foresaw "war in the streets." The Justice Department had become so sophisticated on the subject of inner city disorders that it had established standards for a major riot. It had to be violent, had to have more than 300 participants, had to last at least twelve hours or more, and had to include gunfire, looting, arson, and vandalism. (A mere "serious disturbance" in- volved 150 people for three hours.) The Army had trained 15,000 men in seven task forces to cope with civil uprisings, and black leaders predicted that by spring they would be needed, that the biggest eruption ever lay ahead.

Certainly the leaders were setting an example. They taught courses in guerrilla warfare and house-to-house fighting. CORE joined SNCC and Martin Luther King's SCLC in a militant shift to the left, advocating com- pulsive separation of the races. Eldridge Cleaver's *Soul on Ice,* a best- seller of 1968, described Cleaver as a "full-time revolutionary in the struggle for black liberation in America." James Baldwin called the United States the "Fourth Reich," and the disciples of Malcolm X observed the third anniversary of his death with a lack of restraint beyond anything he had advocated. Even black celebrities were taking a hard line. Black sprinters Tommie Smith and John Carlos obscured the glory of American victories at the Olympic games in Mexico City by bowing their heads dur- ing the playing of "The Star-Spangled Banner" in honor of their victories and raising black-gloved clenched fists in a defiant gesture. When Cleveland blew in July, the general reaction was here-we-go-again. A tow truck, called to the scene of an accident, was fired upon by snipers. Policemen called to the scene became targets of the riflemen. Within thirty minutes three officers and four blacks were dead, and eight policemen were wounded. The National Guard was summoned, and losses from looting and burning were put at 1.5 million dollars. In the brick canyons of other ghettos police braced themselves for what seemed inevitable.

It didn't come. There were half as many riots as expected and none of the other big cities experienced the havoc of the past three years. "In terms of racial conflict," the AP reported, "it was the coolest summer in five years." There were just nineteen deaths, shocking by pre-Watts standards but nothing like the eighty-seven of the year before. One reason was that the most inflammatory of the inciters weren't in the streets any more. They were in jail, or fugitives. H. Rap Brown had been put away. Cleaver disappeared in late November when his parole was revoked. Huey P. Newton was tried in Oakland for killing a policeman; a jury with a black foreman found him guilty. "If Huey goes, the sky's the limit," said his black-jacketed followers, threatening to terrorize all whites, but when he was sent away for two to fifteen years for manslaughter, nothing happened.

Another reason for the comparative tranquillity was that blacks had realized they themselves were the chief victims of the riots. *Their* stores were looted, *their* cars were destroyed, *their* homes burned, and *their* children endangered. Dr. Hiawatha Harris, a Watts psychiatrist, said that "the rioting phase, where we burn down businesses in our own areas, is over. The whole movement is in another direction — toward implementing black power and finding our dignity as a people." Measured by education, wages, public service — "by every traditional index of progress," Theodore H. White wrote — American blacks were already moving forward. The change was evident in little ways. The television screen was one. Integration had become a reality there. Almost every serial had a black player now. The neurosurgeon in *Peyton Place* was a Negro — and one black, "Julia," was a heroine.

A new and more effective way to protest was put forward in Chicago by a Negro minister, Jesse Jackson, who forced white businessmen to hire blacks by telling his congregation to boycott their products. A & P made jobs for 970; Jewel Tea for 661. Operation Breadbasket, as Jackson called it, also persuaded businessmen to open accounts in two Negro banks, increasing their deposits from five million dollars to twenty-two million. Blacks had economic muscle to flex now. The Bureau of the Census later found that the number of Negro families making more than ten thousand dollars a year had risen in the 1960s from 11 percent to 28 percent. They were finally beginning to move into the middle class.

Montage: The Late Sixties

INTERSTATE HIGHWAY SURFACED
—— MILEAGE PASSES 42,500 MARK ——

HONOR U.S. HERO

Among the honors conferred upon General Westmoreland during his brief visit home were the USO Distinguished Service Award, a citation from the South Carolina Legislature, an honorary degree from the University of Buffalo, and the Boy Scout Silver Buffalo Award

Our battalion managed to retake the town by daybreak. When we moved in only one person was left alive in the place: a small boy who was badly wounded

This is the dawning of the Age of Aquarius,
The Age of Aquarius

Picture yourself in a boat on a river
With tangerine trees and marmalade skies
Somebody calls you, you answer quite slowly
A girl with kaleidoscopic eyes
Cellophane flowers of yellow and green

A boo-boo

SUPPORT OUR BOYS IN VIETNAM

No problem

GOD IS
LOVE IS
I AM

psychedelic, adj. Of, pertaining to, or generating hallucinations, distortions of perceptions, and, occasionally, states resembling psychosis.

COURT, 8-1, OKAYS STOP, FRISK

WOW! DIG ALL THE BEAUTIFUL FREAKS!

Put silver wings on my son's chest
Make him one of America's best
He'll be a man they'll test one day —
Have him win the green beret

GIVE A DAMN

I went up there, I said, "Shrink, I wanna kill. I wanna kill! I wanna see blood and gore and guts and veins in my teeth! Eat dead, burnt bodies! I mean kill, kill!" And I started jumpin' up and down yellin' "KILL! KILL!" ... and the sergeant came over, pinned a medal on me.

for **EXPERT** white collar girls ... get the Kelly Girl habit

The U.S. birth rate dropped to 17.9 births, the lowest on record, breaking a mark of 18.9 set in the Depression years of 1933 and 1938

Our motto comes from the novelist Hermann Hesse: "We are in a magic theatre, a world of pictures not reality/ Tonight at the magic theater for madmen only/the price of admission is your mind."

Take it off,
take it all off

NIXON'S THE ONE

U.S. TELSTAR RELAYS TV
PIX ACROSS ATLANTIC

"I'm for anything that gets you through the night — booze or religion," Mr. Sinatra said.

How does it feel, how does it feel
To be without a home
Like a complete unknown
Like a rolling stone?   No strain

frug

People try to put us down
Just because we get around
Things they do look awful cold
Hope I die before I get old

What the world needs now
Is love sweet love.

No sweat

DON'T TRUST ANYONE OVER 30

Had any lately?

MAKE LOVE NOT WAR

YOU FIGHT AND DIE BUT CAN'T DRINK AT 18

Poor People's Campaign 1968

WE SHALL OVER KILL

Student Power

POWs never have a nice day

STONED

No way

Have a nice day

HIPPY POWER

DROP IT

monkey

PEACE

GOD IS ON A TRIP

Would you believe fifty?

V

NIXON, AFTER ALL

1969-1972

THIRTY-FOUR

The Rise of the Silent Majority

RICHARD NIXON'S HEROES included a Democratic President, Woodrow Wilson, and upon learning that President-elect Wilson had announced all his cabinet choices at once in 1913, the President-elect of 1968 decided to do the same thing, on television. The ceremony was held in the Palladium Room of Washington's Shoreham Hotel on December 11, 1968. Nixon asked that each secretary-designate be accompanied by his wife; loyal helpmates, he explained, deserved to share in reflected glory — a condescension which was branded sexist by infuriated feminists. The wives of the new cabinet members seemed to enjoy the occasion, but the national audience was another matter. For viewers the thirty-minute production was flat — one critic rudely called it "a political *What's My Line?*" — and many noted that the star kept repeating himself. Each of the twelve secretaries-designate was identified by Nixon as a man who understood not only his specialty but psychology as well. This was called an "extra dimension," a phrase which the President-elect used no fewer than ten times.

In fact, the incoming cabinet was conspicuous for its lack of dimension. Its members were all affluent, white, male, middle-class, and Republican, and seven of them lived west of the Alleghenies, territory which had been the chief source of Republican votes. Nearly all were businessmen, with three — Walter Hickel (Interior), Winton Blount (postmaster general), and John Volpe (Transportation) — from the construction industry. The lack of breadth was not altogether Nixon's fault. He had tried for more diversity. Earlier he had pledged the formation of "a government made up of Republicans, Democrats, and independents," consisting of "the very best men and women I can find in the country, from government, from labor, from all the areas." But the principal areas of Democratic strength had not responded to his overtures. Three blacks, for example, had bluntly turned him down: Whitney Young Jr., Senator Edward Brooke, and Mrs. Ersa Poston, president of the New York Civil Service Commission. So he had wound up with homogeneity instead of a cross section. The Nixon cabinet, a magazine writer commented, "seems to be constructed more of gray fieldstone than glinting steel and glass." But so was its architect. "The men suggest cool competence rather than passion or brilliance," *Time* said. Whatever their shortcomings, no one doubted their integrity.

The presence in the cabinet of such Nixon intimates as William Rogers (State), John Mitchell (Justice), and Robert Finch (HEW) was interpreted as evidence that the new President intended to give it more power than Johnson had; the demise of the kitchen cabinet as a presidential institution was predicted by columnists who did not yet know H. R. Haldeman and John Ehrlichman. To be sure, the President watchers granted, there would be exceptions. As presidential assistant for national security Henry Kissinger was already emerging as a key adviser. Rogers was reported to be reading Kissinger's books. What no one then foresaw was that Nixon's first Secretary of State would be keeping in touch with American foreign policy developments by reading transcripts of Kissinger's press conferences.

Six months after entering the White House the new President received a tremendous psychological boost when NASA's long voyage to the moon, begun eight years earlier on orders from John F. Kennedy, reached its destination. The mission was Apollo 11. It was the capstone of an extraordinary effort — 20,000 contractors and 300,000 workers had contributed to it — and while men could argue endlessly over whether it had been worth the cost, its success was undeniably an American triumph. In a proclamation Richard Nixon noted that while exploration had been "a lonely enterprise" in the past, "today the miracles of space travel are matched by miracles of space communication; even across the vast lunar distance, television brings the moment of discovery into our homes and makes us all participants." By "all" he meant more than Americans. The lunar landing was witnessed by the largest television audience ever, some 528 million people.

The possibility of failure was small. U.S. space science had come a long way since its first failures twelve years earlier. Between 1961 and 1966 the sixteen manned flights of the Mercury and Gemini series had demonstrated that man could live and function in space, and the Ranger, Lunar Orbiter, and Surveyor programs had sent back proof that the surface of the moon was safe for astronauts. There had been one dreadful setback. In January 1967 a flash fire in the Apollo 1 capsule had killed the three-man crew. After twenty-one months of delays manned Apollo command modules had gone up, however, and in late 1968 and early 1969 NASA had followed a rigid schedule, sending up an Apollo every two and a half months in hopes of meeting the Kennedy deadline of May 1961: to land a man on the moon and return him safely to earth "before this decade is out."

Apollo 11, with its 36-story-high Saturn 5 rocket, was fired at Cape Kennedy's launch complex 39A at 9:32 on the morning of July 16, 1969.

Aboard were Neil A. Armstrong, the civilian commander, and two Air Force officers, Col. Edwin E. "Buzz" Aldrin Jr. and Lieutenant Colonel Michael Collins. The Saturn's third stage put them into an orbit at a height of 118 miles. After a two-and-a-half-hour check of all instruments systems, they refired the third stage. This gave them a velocity of 24,245 mph, sufficient to throw them beyond the earth's atmosphere and on their way to the moon, a quarter-million miles away.

At a distance of 50,000 miles from the earth Collins maneuvered the command vessel, which had been christened the *Columbia*, until it was nose to nose with the fragile lunar module, called the *Eagle* or simply the LM. Once the *Columbia* and the *Eagle* were hooked together, the Saturn's third stage was jettisoned. On Thursday, the second day of the trip, the men switched on *Columbia*'s engine just long enough to put them in a trajectory which would pass within 69 miles of the back side of the moon on Saturday. Friday afternoon, Cape Kennedy time, Armstrong and Aldrin crept through a tunnel connecting the two vessels and into the *Eagle*, and at the end of that day the astronauts entered the moon's field of gravity. They were now within 44,000 miles of it, and picking up speed.

Saturday afternoon they slowed to 3,736 mph and went into orbit around the moon. Mission Control, their radio link with NASA's Manned Spacecraft Center in Houston, awoke them at 7:02 A.M. on Sunday, July 20, which was to be the day of the landing. In the *Eagle* Armstrong and Aldrin extended the four landing legs of the ungainly lunar module. "You're 'go' for undocking," Mission Control told them. Now the LM and the *Columbia* separated, and Armstrong said, "The *Eagle* has wings!" At 3:08 P.M. he fired the spacecraft's engine, and down they went, toward the moon's Sea of Tranquillity.

At a distance of 9.8 miles from the surface of the moon they went into a low orbit, sailing over an awesome lunar scape of mountains and craters. At this point a Houston computer started flashing warning lights on their instruments. Rather than turn back this close to their goal, they went forward on instructions from a young guidance officer in Houston, with Armstrong at the controls and Buzz Aldrin calling out speed and altitude readings from the instruments. They had a bad moment during their final descent. The *Eagle* was less than 500 feet from the moon when Armstrong realized that they were about to land in the large, forbidding West Crater, so called because it was four miles west of their target. He flew beyond it, but this unexpected extension of the journey meant that he was rapidly running out of fuel; he had to decide immediately whether to turn about there or risk crashing. In that instant two lights on the panel in front of him glowed. They read LUNAR CONTACT. The *Eagle* had made it.

"Houston, Tranquillity Base here," he said. "The *Eagle* has landed." It was 4:17.42 P.M. Eastern Daylight Time, Sunday, July 20, 1969.

After three hours of checking instruments, the two astronauts asked Houston if they might omit a scheduled four-hour break and disembark now. "We will support it," Houston answered. They put on their $300,000 space suits and depressurized the LM cabin; then Armstrong, moving backward, began his slow descent of a nine-rung ladder. On the second step he pulled a cord, opening the lens of a TV camera and thus allowing half a billion people to watch him move cautiously down to the stark surface.

His 9½B boot touched it, and he said: "That's one small step for a man, one giant leap for mankind." It was 10:56.20 P.M. He shuffled around. "The surface is fine and powdery," he said. "It adheres in fine layers, like powdered charcoal, to the soles and sides of my boots. I only go in a fraction of an inch, maybe an eighth of an inch, but I can see the footprints of my boots and the treads in the fine, sandy particles."

Armstrong put some of the powder in a pocket on the leg of his space suit. Then, nineteen minutes after his debarkation, Aldrin joined him, saying, "Beautiful, beautiful; magnificent desolation." Armstrong drove a stake in the lunar soil and mounted the TV camera on it. The spidery *Eagle* was sixty feet away, and in the middle of the television picture; behind it was the eternal night of outer space. Gravity here was one-sixth G, 16.6 percent of that on earth. Viewers saw the two men bounding about like gazelles and heard Aldrin say, "When I'm about to lose my balance in one direction I find recovery is quite natural and very easy." They planted a three-by-five-foot U.S. flag, the cloth held out from the staff by wires; Aldrin saluted it. They also deposited a container bearing messages from the leaders of seventy-six countries and a stainless-steel plaque reading, "Here men from planet Earth first set foot upon the moon, July, 1969, A.D. We came in peace for all mankind."

Gathering some fifty pounds of rocks for scientific study, they measured the temperature outside their space suits: 234 degrees Fahrenheit in sunlight and 279 degrees below zero in the shade. A strip of foil was set out to collect solar particles, and two instruments were erected, a seismometer to mark lunar disturbances, and a reflector to send readings to telescopes on earth. At midnight they returned to the *Eagle,* and after 21 hours and 37 minutes on the moon they fired their engine and departed. ("You're cleared for takeoff," Mission Control said. "Roger, we're No. 1 on the runway," said Aldrin.) Back in orbit, they rendezvoused with Collins in the *Columbia.* He rehooked the two vessels together. They crawled back through the tunnel to join him, and the *Eagle* was cast loose to float through space and, eventually, to crash on the moon.

At 1:56 A.M. Collins pointed the *Columbia* earthward and fired its engine, freeing the command module from the moon's gravity. The trip home would take sixty hours. That evening, via television, the astronauts sent the world a picture of itself taken at a distance of 175,000 miles. "It's nice to sit here and watch the earth getting larger and larger and the moon smaller and smaller," said Aldrin. Armstrong said, "No matter where you travel, it's nice to get home." On Thursday, moving at a speed of

24,602 mph, they reentered the earth's atmosphere 757 miles over the Pacific. During the crucial part of this phase the spacecraft's shield was scorched by 4,000-degree heat. Clouds surrounded the command module, and radio contact was lost for three minutes.

Then radar aboard the waiting carrier *Hornet* picked up the descending *Columbia*, which was plunging down 13.8 miles away, beneath three 83-foot orange and white parachutes. The module splashed down in six-foot waves, capsized, and was righted when the three men inside inflated bags on the side. Helicopters from the *Hornet* hovered overhead, guiding the vessel to the spot. President Nixon was waving zoom binoculars on the bridge. The ship's band crashed into "Columbia, the Gem of the Ocean," and all over the United States, and in many foreign cities, church bells rang out, whistles blew, and motorists leaned on their horns.

Richard Nixon's greeting to the Apollo 11 astronauts came at the beginning of a nine-day presidential jet trip around the world. During it he visited six Asian nations: the Philippines, Indonesia, Thailand, South Vietnam, India, and Pakistan. His central purpose there was to drive home his determination to make sure there were no more Vietnams. Stopping overnight in Guam on his way to Manila, he spelled out the Nixon Doctrine for reporters: "Peace in Asia cannot come from the United States. It must come from Asia. The people of Asia, the governments of Asia — they are the ones who must lead the way." In Bangkok he said he wanted to speak plainly: "If domination by the aggressor can destroy the freedom of a nation, too much dependence on a protector can eventually erode its dignity."

That sounded unequivocal, but newspapermen were learning that often when the new President promised to make something perfectly clear, it was about to become opaque. So it was on this Asian swing. Even as he deplored America's overcommitment in Vietnam, he told U.S. troops there that he thought "history will record that this may have been one of America's finest hours," and he also pledged to the Thais: "The United States will stand proudly with Thailand against those who might threaten it from abroad or from within." Telling people what he thought they wanted to hear was an old Nixon weakness; if his hosts weren't elated by his assurances that he would send them some fragments of moon rock, it seemed, he was ready to hint that he might send a few divisions.

There was another explanation. This was a transitional period in his attitude toward Communism. Part of him was still the cold-warrior, ready to pick up any Red challenge, while another part believed that global stability depended on conciliation between Washington on the one hand and Moscow and Peking on the other. In this sense there was such a thing as a new Nixon. His flexibility emerged dramatically toward the end of this trip. He stopped in Bucharest to spend a day with Romanian President Nicolae Ceausescu, and as proof of his friendly feelings he rode through a downpour with the top of his car down. The crowd's response was amazing; people along the way not only cheered vigorously; they also vied with one another to pick up tiny paper American flags which fell to sidewalks, leaving flags of their own country where they lay.

In England Nixon paused for talks with Prime Minister Harold Wilson. This was his second European visit in five months; he had been in office only seventeen days when he had announced a trip to Belgium, Britain, West Germany, Italy, and France — "the blue-chip countries," as he called them. He had always believed that he had a special talent for foreign affairs, and he was certainly making friends among other chiefs of state, even though the most important of them, Wilson, Chancellor Kurt Kiesinger, and President Charles de Gaulle, were not to remain in office long. In that first year the new President was going out of his way to be cordial to a great many people at home and abroad, including some toward whom he had once been very chilly. He flew to Independence to give Harry Truman a grand piano which had once been in the White House and played "The Missouri Waltz" on it — Truman was too polite to tell him he had always hated the song — and he extolled retiring Chief Justice Earl Warren, as "a symbol of fairness, integrity, and dignity."

Even then Nixon kept his distance from the press, but most reporters were generous in their treatment of him. Hugh Sidey of *Life* wrote that the President had "devised a government in his own image — decent, thoughtful, competent, cautious." Although newsmen covering the White House felt that his public appearances were forced and contrived, they had a certain admiration for the pains he took for them, knowing how uncomfortable he was in such situations. They appreciated the diet he carefully followed to avoid appearing jowly, how he tried to stay tanned for television, and the time he spent choosing his wardrobe because he wanted his suits to give the public just the right impression of quiet good taste.

As his presidential image formed, he emerged as a thoughtful, rather lonely man who spent hours hunched over yellow legal tablets in various White House sanctuaries, notably a study off the Lincoln bedroom and a hideaway just across the street in the Executive Office Building. He liked paperwork more than Lyndon Johnson, and people less. The forty-two-button phone was removed from the oval office; Nixon needed only six buttons. He also appeared to be less interested in the news, even news about himself, than Johnson; the teletypes and the television sets of the previous administration were banished to an outer office. His favorite TV programs were Saturday afternoon football games in the autumn and winter, and he nearly always found time to watch them. "I know the job I have is supposed to be the most difficult job in the world," he said, "but it has not yet become for me that great, awesome burden that some have described it."

"Middle America" was a current journalistic phrase, and the new chief executive was its apotheosis. He liked the competitive spirit of Vince Lombardi, the music of Guy Lombardo, the novels of Allen Drury, the piety of Billy Graham, the wit of Bob Hope, and the sales techniques of J. Walter Thompson. Though most of his career had been spent in public service, he had the middle-class distrust of the federal bureaucracy; one of his first acts was to abolish the patronage system for selecting postmasters. (The following year Congress, at his request, established an independent U.S. Postal Service.) As a Middle American he believed in expert advice. The voices he listened to most were those of John Mitchell, Henry Kissinger, John D. Ehrlichman, and H. R. Haldeman. Sidey noted that although the President's programs were a little left of center on paper, "the men he named to high office leaned the other way — and in Washington experience suggested that in the end men would dominate blueprints." Doctrine seemed to mean little to Nixon himself anyway; he had Middle America's penchant for trying various approaches, zigging and zagging from the center, in hope of finding workable solutions. At various times in 1969 he proposed tax reform, tinkered with the ideological balance of the Supreme Court, reduced the troop level in Vietnam, returned Okinawa to Japan, tried to alter the welfare system, outlawed germ warfare, and made various attempts to restrain inflation. In that first year he also displayed Middle American modesty. When his advisers crowded around to congratulate him on his return from his first European journey, he called a halt. "Too soon, too soon," he said. "A year from now we'll know if it was a success."

He was not so modest as a spender. Like thousands of other American executives who had made it, the chief executive was overextending himself to support an elaborate new life-style. He was earning $290,000 a year in salary and expenses. He had a home near the office and a retreat at Camp David, but he mortgaged himself to the hilt just the same. First he bought a pair of brick-and-stucco bungalows on Florida's Biscayne Bay. The cost was put at over $250,000. There the President could spend his leisure hours with an old friend, C. G. "Bebe" Rebozo — a onetime chauffeur and filling station operator who had made a fortune in real estate — aboard Rebozo's elaborate houseboat, the *Cocolobo*. Yet even that wasn't enough for Nixon. While gardeners were still putting in a ten-foot hedge around the Key Biscayne home, the President was in San Clemente, California, buying a $340,000 fourteen-room adobe villa, ordering a $100,000 swimming pool for it, and planning a four-hole golf course on adjacent land, each tee to be marked with a tiny presidential seal.

Although the facts were unknown at the time, Rebozo and another Nixon intimate, aerosol spray valve inventor Robert H. Abplanalp, held mortgages of about $500,000 on the two properties. At the same time, the government was laying out a staggering 10.5 million dollars on the two presidential estates and on houses frequently visited by the Nixons, such as Abplanalp's island in the Bahamas. Much of the money went for such necessities as helipads and military communications, but sums of money running to six figures were spent on landscaping, furniture, and heating systems.

That wasn't the end of it. Indeed, in terms of sheer cost it was only a beginning. Four years later *Fortune* would quote a former official of the Bureau of the Budget as estimating that the expense of President Nixon's household, as of then, had been approximately 100 million dollars. Lyndon Johnson, who was not thrifty, had maintained three Boeing jetliners; when Lady Bird went shopping in New York, she had taken the Eastern Airlines shuttle. All Nixon's relatives, including his sons-in-law, traveled on government planes. At the President's exclusive disposal were five Boeing 707s, eleven Lockheed Jetstars, and sixteen helicopters. He installed an archery range, a swimming pool, and bowling alleys at Camp David; the annual operating costs of the camp went from $147,000 a year under Johnson to $640,000. In addition the chief executive was attended at his various homes by 75 butlers, maids, cooks, and caretakers, 21 gardeners and maintenance workers, 100 Secret Service agents, 300 guards, the crew of the presidential yacht, and the drivers of a fleet of official limousines. Under Richard Nixon the presidential style could only be called lordly.

In his first appearance as President he had appeared in the role of healer. "The greatest honor history can bestow is the title of peacemaker," he had said in his inaugural, and he had made it clear that he was not merely talking about Vietnam. "We find ourselves rich in goods, but ragged in spirit; reaching with magnificent precision for the moon, but falling into raucous discord on earth. . . . We are torn by division, wanting unity. We see around us empty lives, wanting fulfillment. We see tasks that need doing, waiting for hands to do them. To a crisis of the spirit, we need an answer of the spirit. And to find that answer, we need only look within ourselves. . . . We cannot learn from one another until we stop shouting at one another — until we speak quietly enough so that our words can be heard as well as our voices. For its part, government will listen."

It was a shrewd appraisal of the American dilemma, and during his first eight months in the White House Nixon's search for solutions was along those lines. He suppressed his own strong combative instincts, keeping his voice down, his profile low, and his ear to the ground. In seeking advice he cultivated an aura of responsible craftsmanship. He had promised a "small" White House staff in his campaign, and after he won had said that he would run an "open" administration with vigorous counsel from "independent thinkers." As Republicans, he and the members of his administration did not share the Johnsonian conviction that America's troubles could be traced to underprivilege and poverty, but they had their own guiding light. To them the national anguish arose from a loss of faith in religion, the family, the binding force of friendly neighborhood life, and *McGuffey's Reader* patriotism. These were the convictions of small-town America, the great keep of the Republican party. It was hardly their fault that most Americans no longer lived in small towns, or that the attack on the nation's most sacred institutions, from the flag to motherhood, had acquired an irresistible momentum. The furies of the 1960s were not yet spent. The period was still one of violent contention.

Yet some election results in 1969 suggested that backlash was turning the country rightward. Republicans won the Virginia statehouse for the first time in over eighty years and the New Jersey governorship after sixteen Democratic years. Barry Goldwater Jr. was elected to Congress by California's 27th District. Liberal Ralph Yarborough was in trouble in Texas; early the following year he would be toppled in the Democratic primary by a conservative challenger. In Minneapolis an astounding 62 percent of the voters swept Charles S. Stenvig, a previously unknown police detective, into the mayoralty on the strength of Stenvig's advocacy of tough law enforcement in black neighborhoods, and Los Angeles gave Sam Yorty, the closest thing to a racist mayor outside the South, a third term despite an appalling record of absenteeism, drift, strife, and the conviction, on charges of bribery, of three men Yorty had appointed city commissioners.

A trend toward the right did not explain some Nixon difficulties on the Hill. In a truly conservative climate the Pentagon would be sacrosanct, and in 1969 the Defense budget was in peril for the first time in twenty years. Ever since the North Koreans had crossed the 38th Parallel, astronomical annual sums had been appropriated for the military establishment, frequently without even a roll call. The Pentagon outlay had risen from eleven billion dollars to eighty-one billion, but now the generals were confronted by a balky Congress. Frustration over Vietnam was one reason; others included a scandal featuring senior Army noncoms who had been making fortunes through PX kickbacks, dissatisfaction with the excessive costs of Lockheed C-5A transport production, and the discovery that the Army's Chemical Warfare Service was transporting 7,000 tons of nerve and poison gas across the country and dumping it in the Atlantic Ocean. The immediate issue raising congressional hackles, however, was a matter of missilery. The Defense Department wanted to start work on an enormous antiballistic missile (ABM) system which could wind up costing the country as much as a hundred billion dollars.

The ABM was necessary, the Pentagon argued, to deprive the USSR of first-strike power — the ability to cripple U.S. ICBM installations with a single blow and therefore prevent American retaliation. Senate critics led by Edward M. Kennedy replied that the ABM would escalate the arms race, that it would waste money better spent on pollution and in slums, and that its radar and computers were too complicated to work. "History," one technical witness said dryly, "is littered with Maginot Lines." In the end an ABM appropriation passed the Senate by a single vote, but the victory was Pyrrhic. It laid the groundwork for future struggles over Defense programs and sowed seeds of bitterness between Congress and the new administration. Speaking at the Air Force Academy on June 4, President Nixon attacked the forty-nine anti-ABM senators as "new isolationists." Senator Fulbright replied: "The greatest threat to peace and domestic tranquillity is not in Hanoi, Moscow, or Peking but in our colleges and in the ghettos of cities throughout the land."

The split between the President and his adversaries on the Hill widened in two savage battles over Supreme Court nominees. Nixon's choice of Warren E. Burger to succeed Earl Warren as Chief Justice sailed through the Senate, but when he named federal Judge Clement F. Haynsworth Jr. of South Carolina to replace Abe Fortas he touched off a senatorial revolt. The AFL-CIO and the NAACP denounced Haynsworth as antilabor and racist. He might have survived that, but Birch Bayh of Indiana turned up evidence that the judge had ruled in favor of firms in which he held stock. The nomination was rejected 55 to 45, with seventeen Republicans, including Minority Leader Hugh Scott, in the majority. Nixon called the attacks on Haynsworth "brutal, vicious, and . . . unfair." Two months later he announced his second choice, federal Judge G. Harrold Carswell of Florida.

Carswell's chief qualification appeared to be that he wasn't rich and thus, unlike Haynsworth, couldn't be charged with conflict of interest in corporate verdicts. Unfortunately he had other liabilities. A reporter dug out a sentence from a 1948 Carswell speech: "Segregation of the races is proper and the only practical and correct way of life in our states." Confronted with the quotation, the nominee called it "obnoxious and abhorrent," but the NAACP came out against him anyway. Then it was revealed that Carswell had participated actively in a campaign to exclude blacks from a Tallahassee golf club, had insulted civil rights lawyers in his court, and had been often reversed on appeal. This last development inspired a well-meant comment by Senator Roman L. Hruska of Nebraska. He told a television interviewer that "even if he were mediocre, there are a lot of mediocre judges and people and lawyers. Aren't they entitled to a little representation and a little chance? We can't have all Brandeises and Cardozos and Frankfurters and stuff like that. I doubt we can. I doubt we want to."

Later Hruska was asked if he regretted saying it. "Indeed I do," he said, "indeed I do." A GOP floor leader remarked later, "Everywhere I go I hear that word — mediocre. If there was one single thing it was that. You could see the votes deserting in droves." Before Hruska said it, Senator Kennedy had forecast a maximum of 25 votes against Carswell, and Scott had predicted that the most the opposition could muster would be "in the 30s." In fact the ayes were 45 and the nays 51; "the nomination," said the presiding officer, Vice President Agnew, "is not agreed to." Two days later an angry President Nixon told newspapermen that as long as the Democrats controlled the Senate "I cannot successfully nominate to the Supreme

Court any federal appellate judge from the South who believes as I do in the strict construction of the Constitution."

This was a far cry from the bring-us-together theme of his inaugural, but it was deliberate. Nixon was abandoning nonpartisanship and was counter-attacking. The strategic shift had begun with a televised speech to the nation in response to the first in a series of new antiwar demonstrations which dramatized demands for peace in Vietnam. The President said they were unnecessary because he had "a plan . . . for the complete withdrawal of all United States ground combat forces and their replacement by South Vietnamese forces." He called this "Vietnamization." He said he believed it would succeed and asked for support from "the great silent majority of my fellow Americans." In a thrust at his critics he said: "Let us be united for peace. Let us also be united against defeat. Because let us understand: North Vietnam cannot defeat or humiliate the United States. Only Americans can do that."

Gallup reported that 77 percent of his audience approved of the speech — only 6 percent disapproved it — and Nixon, heartened, decided to send his Vice President into the breach with even more vivid rhetoric. This was to be what Agnew himself called the "politics of polarization," a deliberate effort to isolate the President's critics. He had won Nixon's warm congratulations for assailing the dissidents as "an effete corps of impudent snobs who characterize themselves as intellectuals" and their political supporters as "parasites of passion" and "ideological eunuchs." Because 70 million Americans watched television network news programs, and because the White House was unhappy with TV coverage of the President, Agnew made that his first target.

Speaking in Des Moines on November 13, he took out after "a small group of men; numbering perhaps no more than a dozen anchormen, commentators and executive producers," who "settle upon the twenty minutes or so of film and commentary that is to reach the public." This "unelected elite," he said, was "a tiny and closed fraternity of privileged men . . . enjoying a monopoly sanctioned and licensed by government." He accused it of distorting "our national search for internal peace and stability." A week later he zeroed in on the press, singling out the *New York Times* and the *Washington Post* and deploring "the monopolization of the great public information vehicles and the concentration of more and more power over public opinion in fewer and fewer hands." Both the networks and the newspapers reported a heavy run of mail supporting Agnew and condemning the "eastern liberal establishment." Washington wondered whether Agnew had been speaking for himself or for Nixon. Hubert Humphrey said "Anyone who thinks that the Vice President can take a position independent of the President or his administration simply has no knowledge of politics or government. You are his choice in a political marriage, and he expects your absolute loyalty."

His bombast identified Spiro Agnew as a man of the era, for it was a time of overstatement, of exaggerated gestures and posturing and hyperbole, when everything from eating grapes and lettuce to wearing (or not wearing) a brassiere carried political overtones, and CBS fired the Smothers Brothers, a comedy team, for encouraging guest stars to make flippant remarks about patriotism and the Vietnam War.

A number of courtrooms were preoccupied with political trials. James Earl Ray and Sirhan Sirhan, the assassins of Martin Luther King and Robert F. Kennedy, were being convicted, and in one of the most bizarre actions in American legal history, New Orleans District Attorney Jim Garrison was trying to convince a jury that Clay L. Shaw, a retired Louisiana businessman, had conspired to murder John Kennedy. The key witnesses were a former taxi driver who had vaguely incriminated Shaw while under hypnosis, a drug addict, a paranoid accountant, and a perjurer who ultimately confessed that he had invented his testimony. The trial lasted thirty-four days. The jury voted to acquit Shaw in less than an hour.

Norman Mailer ran for mayor of New York, Dr. Timothy Leary for governor of California. President Nixon appointed Shirley Temple Black, now forty-one, to the U.S. delegation to the United Nations ("because," someone said, "he wanted the world to have a happy ending"). Bernadette Devlin arrived from Ireland to ask New Yorkers for money that would be used for murdering British soldiers. At San Francisco State College, Timothy Peebles, black and nineteen, bungled while trying to set a crude time bomb and blinded himself. SDS Weathermen vowing to "Bring the War Home" rioted in Chicago; sixty were arrested and three shot. Over a five-month period in 1969 Manhattan terrorists bombed the Marine Midland Grace Trust Company, the Armed Forces Induction Center, the Federal Office Building, Macy's, a United Fruit Company pier, and the RCA, Chase Manhattan, and General Motors buildings. On the night of November 13 police arrested three young men and Jane Lauren Alpert, twenty-two, a brilliant Swarthmore student and the daughter of upper-middle-class parents, charging them with conspiring to bomb federal property. Miss Alpert's parents put up a $20,000 bond for her and forfeited it when she vanished.

Environmentalists were angry over the new jumbo jets, taxpayers over teacher strikes, cigarette manufacturers because they had been forbidden to advertise on television after the end of 1970. Honeymooners were irate because the water had been temporarily diverted from Niagara Falls. Believers in flying saucers were indignant at the Air Force, which concluded a two-year investigation of 11,000 reported sightings by declaring that the saucers did not exist. Squeamish theatergoers objected when the 1969 New York Drama Desk Award went to *Peace*, an antiwar play in which the God of War flushed nations down a huge toilet.

To millions of Americans the nation's abrasive new mood appeared to be symbolized when Mel Finkelstein, a *New York Daily News* photographer trying to photograph Jacqueline Kennedy Onassis as she left a Manhattan showing of *I Am Curious (Yellow)*, sprawled on the pavement outside the theater. He said she flipped him over her thigh in a judo maneuver; she said he slipped and fell. Whatever had happened, another cameraman snapped President Kennedy's widow striding away from Finkelstein and the Swedish blue movie. She was wearing a tight black leather miniskirt. In the background a sign advertised WINES AND LIQUORS. Camelot seemed very far away.

It was the roughest year yet on college campuses. Although Gallup found that 72 percent of the country's 6.7 million students had never joined a demonstration, and a *Fortune* poll reported that only 12.8 percent were "revolutionary" or "radically dissident," the minority disrupted or paralyzed institutions in every part of the country. San Francisco State was closed for three weeks. The home of San Mateo Junior College's dean was fire-bombed. A rally of a thousand students and two hundred faculty members forced the resignation of Rice's president, and desperate administrators summoned police to, among others, San Fernando State, Howard, Pennsylvania State, and the University of Massachusetts. At the University of Chicago Bruno Bettelheim said that "many of these kids are very sick — paranoid," and he compared them to German students who had backed Hitler. Their demands continued. Negroes sought more courses in black studies, whites called for an end to ROTC and Dow Chemical recruitment. And all wanted an end to the Vietnam War.

Campus clashes had a way of escalating rapidly, often reaching ugly proportions before authorities — or even some of the participants — clearly understood the issues at stake. At the University of Wisconsin an organization of Negro students, the Black People's Alliance, called a strike. Conservative students of the Young Americans for Freedom decided to cross the blacks' picket lines. Blows were exchanged, and in swift succession the governor called out 1,900 National Guardsmen, bayonets and tear gas were used on the Negroes, over five thousand whites marched on the state capitol to protest this use of force, faculty groups supported the black demands, and the Wisconsin legislature, lashing back, cut the university budget.

Puerto Rican students joined blacks at the City College of New York — CCNY, "the poor man's Harvard" — in locking themselves inside the South Campus and issuing a manifesto demanding that the college's enrollment reflect New York's racial balance, that a black studies program be introduced, and that they control it. Confronted by this threat to academic standards and consequently to the value of their diplomas, the white students mobilized. In the subsequent struggle an auditorium was burned. President Buell Gallagher closed the school twice and then resigned. The faculty senate then approved an almost unbelievable proposal under which 40 percent of the next freshman class would be blacks and Puerto Ricans who would not have to meet the academic requirements of CCNY, which as a consequence could no longer be called the poor man's Harvard.

Harvard itself blew on April 9, when undergraduates invaded University Hall, evicted the deans, and began rifling confidential files. President Nathan Pusey responded by calling on the state police, four hundred of whom fought their way into the building and arrested 197 students. Their classmates — six thousand of them — met in Harvard Stadium and voted to strike in protest. A faculty resolution asked that charges against the 197 be dropped. Pusey agreed, but the judge didn't; he fined them twenty dollars each for criminal trespass and sentenced a twenty-five-year-old graduate student to a year in prison for striking a dean. The university then formally endorsed a faculty resolution calling for agreement to the chief demand of the original group of demonstrators — an end to ROTC at Harvard.

Cornell was no more strife-torn than a dozen other campuses that spring, but a local aspect at Ithaca produced a sequence of photographs which shocked the world. Demanding an autonomous Afro-American college, two hundred and fifty Negro undergraduates took over Willard Straight Hall, the student union, on April 19. When rumors spread inside Willard Straight that a band of whites with guns was on its way, the Negroes acquired weapons themselves. That, said President James A. Perkins, made it "a whole new thing." He capitulated to every black demand, and the Negroes who had seized the building walked out — armed to the teeth, the newspaper pictures showed, with rifles in their hands and bandoliers of ammunition crisscrossed on their chests. The faculty rejected the president's settlement and then reversed itself. The university trustees announced an investigation and Perkins quit.

All this was being watched closely in Washington, where, as might be expected, the Nixon administration's sympathy was with everybody except the rebellious students. HEW Secretary Finch wrote to the head of every institution of higher learning in the country, pointing out that more than a million students were receiving aid which could be terminated if they abused their privileges. Nixon himself spoke out after Reverend Theodore M. Hesburgh, president of Notre Dame, warned his undergraduates that any who resorted to force would be expelled and charged with trespassing. In a "Dear Ted" letter, Nixon wrote Hesburgh, "I want to applaud the forthright stand you have taken," and asked him to forward his opinions on student unrest to Vice President Agnew, who was about to confer with the state governors. Hesburgh advised caution; "even the most far-out students," he observed, "are trying to tell society something that may be worth searching for today." His point was not lost on the governors, who rejected a proposal from Ronald Reagan for a federal inquiry into the student riots.

If Negro activists were busy on the campuses, they were lying low in most inner cities. For the second straight summer the ghettos were relatively quiet. The mood in the ghettos was changing. The turmoil of the mid-

1960s had opened new lines of communication with the city halls, and big cities could now field well-trained, well-equipped riot police. The new emphasis among blacks was on political action. With the upsurge in Negro registrations, the election of Negro candidates had become a realistic alternative in many areas to open revolt against society. Howard Lee became the first black mayor of Chapel Hill, North Carolina, in 1969, and Charles Evers won the mayoralty of Fayette, Mississippi, with the slogan: "Don't vote for a black man. Don't vote for a white man. Vote for a good man."

Nixon called the role of the new administration in race relations a "middle course." By any term it was a slowdown in desegregation. The Johnson policy had been to end federal subsidies to schools which failed to integrate. Nixon rejected it, saying, "I do not consider it a victory for integration when the federal government cuts off funds for a school and thereby, for both black and white students in that school, denies them the education they should have." In one of his first press conferences in the White House he conceded that Negroes distrusted him, believing him, despite his earlier record, to be indifferent now to their cause. In his campaign he had made much of promises of help for "black capitalism." Nothing more was heard about it. Instead, in August 1969 Finch proposed a delay in Mississippi school integration.

This was widely regarded as a stratagem to court the South's white voters. It was thwarted late in October when the Supreme Court, in its first major decision since Warren Burger's appointment as Chief Justice, unanimously ruled that "the obligation of every school district is to terminate dual school systems at once and to operate now and hereafter only unitary schools." Nixon responded that he would make every effort to enforce the decree with "full respect for the law."

Although student riots were the work of a minority, American youths in much larger numbers were continuing to assert their separate identity by dressing, speaking, and behaving in ways alien to adult society. Their extraordinarily high visibility was in large part a result of their life-style, which was, and was meant to be, conspicuous and even outrageous. But there were also more of them to be seen. This was the inevitable sequel to the postwar baby boom. In 1960 there had been 27 million Americans between the ages of fourteen and twenty-four. Now there were 40 million of them, accounting for a full 20 percent of the population. Their numbers and their affluence guaranteed that youth's counterculture would grow in magnitude, and that if a sizable proportion of them flocked to any one event, its popularity would be tremendous. Such an event occurred on the weekend of August 15–17, 1969. It was a rock music festival, and it was called Woodstock.

Actually that was a misnomer. Originally the two twenty-four-year-olds who conceived and promoted the festival planned to stage it in the Hudson

River village of Woodstock, New York, and it was so advertised. Zoning regulations and local opposition thwarted them there, however, and the event was moved to the six-hundred-acre dairy farm of one Max Yasgur in the Catskill town of Bethel, on White Lake, about seventy miles northwest of New York City. The promoters hoped the kids could find it. They were expecting to draw about 50,000 customers at seven dollars a ticket.

They grossly underestimated the festival's appeal. Max Yasgur's farm was stormed by a multitude of 400,000. Bethel briefly became the third largest city in the state. The surrounding road net was cluttered with abandoned cars, motorcycles, and microbuses decorated with psychedelic drawings. All adjacent exits from the Catskill highway were jammed. Collecting fees from so enormous a throng was impractical, and the promoters had to give up the idea, thereby losing two million dollars. That was one of two things which went wrong at Woodstock. The other was the weather. Two tremendous cloudbursts turned the farm into a swamp. The youths huddled in soggy sleeping bags and under plastic tents and lean-tos fashioned from blankets and pieces of clothing. The lack of normal supplies of food and water, or even of sanitation facilities, should have made Woodstock a disaster.

Instead it was a triumph. Looking out nervously over the huge crowd, one of the first performers said, "If we're going to make it, you had better remember that the guy next to you is your brother." They remembered. A police officer called the audience "the most courteous, considerate, and well-behaved group of kids that I have ever been in contact with in my twenty-four years of police work."

The most helpful hands came from their own ranks. A caravan of Ken Kesey's Merry Pranksters, who had driven all the way from Oregon, doled out a high-protein broth of raisins, oatmeal, and peanuts and set up a hospital tent; a hundred members of the Hog Farm, a Taos, New Mexico, commune, also provided essential services. What really made the event a success, however, was the magnet which had lured so many here: acid rock. The Jefferson Airplane, the Creedence Clearwater Revival, the Family Stone, Jimi Hendrix, Joan Baez, Janis Joplin — these were their folk heroes. They were here in person, and if they could not be seen, they could at least be heard from loudspeakers set atop eighty-foot scaffolds around the stage. And so, despite the rain and constant provocation, the youths in headbands, bell-bottoms, beads, and tie-dyed dungaree shirts made the festival so strong a symbol of generational unity that their future spokesmen would speak of them as the Woodstock Nation.

In an era of rapid change the strengthening of peer group bonds was inevitable. Woodstock was the most spectacular rock festival of 1969, but it was by no means unique. Others that year were held on a ranch near Tenino, Washington, after the state supreme court had overruled objections from the John Birch Society; at Lewisville, Texas ("This crowd is a lot better than Dallas football crowds," a security officer said, while the

Lewisville mayor told reporters that the only problem was created by older Texans who came to stare at naked young swimmers in the Garza–Little Elm Reservoir); and at Prairieville, Louisiana, where the attractions included the Grateful Dead, Canned Heat, Country Joe and the Fish, and the Iron Butterfly.

The festival phenomenon was not confined to the United States. It being an American phenomenon, and this being the age of American dominance, the sounds of rock were echoing in western Europe, and particularly in England. HELP BOb DYLAN SINK THE ISLE OF WIGHT, read banners over that English Channel island. Answering the appeal were 150,000 "oddly dressed people," as a local policeman put it, "of uncertain sex." Dylan himself arrived thirty-six hours after the music began; he wore a white suit, yellow shirt, and green boots. A young female admirer ripped off her clothes, danced nude, and screamed, "I just want to be free." Unlike Woodstock, the Isle of Wight concert wound up heavily in the black.

There was something anomalous here. Fortunes were being made by promoters and entertainers, yet the counterculture which supported them was aggressively antimaterialistic. Unlike swing music, rock was accompanied by an ideological strain. That was one reason many older Americans found it so objectionable. To them, the life-style and the social creed that went with it were unpatriotic, ungodly, immoral, and, if possible, worse. It was possible; their most hideous fears were realized when the ugliest murder of 1969 was committed by a band of hippies run amok. Those offended by the now generation saw it as a vindication of their direst predictions, and the failure of long-haired youth to accept responsibility for it merely deepened their rage.

The victims were actress Sharon Tate, honey blonde and pregnant, and four acquaintances. Their bodies, hideously mutilated and arranged in grotesque positions, were found one August morning in a Los Angeles mansion at 10050 Cielo Drive, overlooking Benedict Canyon. Four months later the killers — who had committed two other murders in the meantime — were found to be members of a commune on the fringe of Death Valley. Their leader was Charles Manson, a thirty-five-year-old ex-convict and, by all accounts, a sexual athlete. The slayers were his protégés: a demented Texas youth and three pretty girls who had been eager to do anything — literally anything — Manson required of them. Their days had been occupied with riding around on dune buggies fashioned from stolen Volkswagens and mounted with machine guns. (Manson had visions of war between the races.) At night they had explored unusual sexual activities — unless, of course, they had been busy stabbing strangers to death.

If Manson and his friends represented the dark side of hippy romanticism, the bright side was youth's social conscience. The best of young America was profoundly disturbed by man's abuse of his fellow man and his surroundings. The ecological issue was the least controversial; the need was obvious — pollution had become unconscionable. Gallup found that 70 percent of Americans put the environmental issue first among the country's domestic problems. Not only the younger generation but organizations on every level of society were awakening to the threat. The United Nations announced plans for a Conference on Human Environment. The President established an Environmental Quality Council. Governors and mayors appointed ecological committees. In Louisville, where a factory with ancient equipment was pouring eleven tons of dirt into the city's air each day, citizens wearing gas masks marched on City Hall bearing a protest petition with 13,000 signatures; the plant then installed new furnaces which cut the daily yield of soot to one hundred pounds.

That helped Louisville, but in the national view it hardly counted. There the dimensions of the problem were overwhelming. Combustion in the U.S. was disgorging 140 million tons of grime into the air every year. The automobiles in Los Angeles alone emitted each day 10,000 tons of carbon monoxide, 2,000 tons of hydrocarbons, and 530 tons of nitrogen oxides. Other pollutants rising into the great sewer in the sky over America were oxides of sulphur, sulphuric acid mists, fly ash, soot, and particles of arsenic, beryllium, cadmium, lead, chromium, and manganese. Annually they accounted for eleven billion dollars in property damage alone. Smog disintegrated nylon stockings, stripped paint from houses, turned other buildings a rusty orange, coated sidewalks with green slime, caused rubber to become brittle and crack, discolored clothing, etched windowpanes, attacked the enamel on teeth, induced pulmonary disease, and otherwise eroded, tarnished, soiled, corroded, and abraded man and his works.

All this had been going on for some time, but it was in 1969 that a combination of events forced the ecological issue into the forefront of the national consciousness. Nuclear power plants on the Hudson and Connecticut rivers on the East Coast, and the Columbia River in the West, were found to be killing fish by the ton with thermal pollution. DDT was also taking its toll of seafood and threatening the bald eagle, emblem of the nation, with extinction. Pedestrians in Manhattan were reported to be breathing air whose level of carbon monoxide was twice the danger level as determined by the federal government. And Everglades National Park in Florida and Sequoia National Park in California were threatened by plans for, respectively, a huge airport and an access road to a ski resort.

Construction of the airport was halted by nineteen groups of aroused conservationists who went to court. The Sierra Club also secured a court order stopping the building of the road by Walt Disney Productions, but the order was only temporary, and in other ways 1969 was a poor environmental year for the Golden State. Nature was partly to blame; three storms, dumping 52 inches of rain, hit the slopes of the San Gabriel Mountains in swift succession. Bridges were washed out and hundreds of homes literally slid down the hills — 291 houses in Carpenteria alone, with a population of just 7,200. Life was also edgy along the San Andreas fault, which cuts across one corner of San Francisco and runs twenty miles east of Los Angeles. Tension had been building along the fault since the calamity of 1906; another earthquake was overdue. Californians faced the possibility good-humoredly. Bumper stickers declared, "California Deserves a Fair Shake," and a local best seller in 1969 was *The Last Days of the Late, Great State of California,* a fictional account of a quake. In reality only one tremor of any substance was recorded, on April 28, and its center was in uninhabited desert country.

That, however, was not the full story of the state's experience with geological faults that year. The stresses along another of them, combined with man's folly, provided the nation's ecological horror story of 1969. Late in January an oil drill which had been boring into a high-pressure pool of petroleum and gas 3,486 feet beneath the bottom of the Pacific Ocean was withdrawn for the replacement of a worn bit. Suddenly the well erupted, sending up oil bubbles 200 feet in diameter around the drillers' platform. Meanwhile pressure from the runaway well was being relayed along unmapped fissures in the sand and shale of the sea floor. This was catastrophic; drillers capped the original hole in eleven days, but oil continued to boil forth over a wide area.

Six miles east of the platform lay the immaculate beaches of Santa Barbara, where shore-front property had been selling at as much as $2,000 a foot. In the first week of February the white sands cherished by Santa Barbarans — forty miles of superb waterfront — began turning black. Hundreds of thousands of gallons of gummy crude oil coated yachts and fishing craft with a thick scum which could only be removed by live steam. A *Sports Illustrated* writer reported that petroleum "lay so thick on the water that waves were unformed; they made a squishing sound. . . . The smell of oil followed me up the canyon to our house, a mile from the sea. . . . The tideline was a broad black band that looked from the air like something made on a map by a black crayon."

The most shocking aspect of the disaster was the destruction of marine life. Mussels and rock lobsters died instantly. Porpoises and sea lions disappeared. Pelicans dove straight into the oil and then sank, unable to raise their matted wings, and the beaches were studded with dead sandpipers, cormorants, gulls, grebes, and loons, their eyes horribly swollen and their viscera burned by petroleum. "A very sad-looking mess," said the Audubon Society; another spectator called it "a sickening sight." Residents held protest meetings, picketed government offices with placards demanding BAN THE BLOB, and joined a new ecological group called Get Oil Out (GOO). Damage suits totaling a billion dollars were filed; the cost of the cleanup was put at three million.

More than twelve thousand wires and letters went to Washington. At first the government seemed responsive. The Department of the Interior announced that in the future drills would have to be sheathed in pipe below the depth of 239 feet, which had been the previous requirement. Most important, drilling leases in the Santa Barbara Channel were suspended. Then the petroleum industry began applying pressure. Large sums of money were at stake; the leases, granting the right to drill in nearly one thousand square miles of the Pacific, had been signed a year earlier with a dozen firms which were paying 603 million dollars for the privilege. They wanted the privilege back, and in September the Nixon administration gave it to them — in spite of dire warnings from geologists as to other fissures, and in spite of continuing leaks from the original runaway well.

Youthful participants were conspicuous in all the environmental crusades, carrying petitions in Florida, marching on Louisville City Hall in large numbers, and setting up "laundries" to clean and save the California birds. How deep their convictions ran — to what degree they were merely caught up by the excitement of protest — was, however, another question. In some ways they seemed to be flagrantly inconsistent. Although vehemently opposed to pollution of the environment, for example, they enthusiastically supported by their patronage another form of pollution: the junk food industry.

Fast-food stands, peddling empty calories and little nourishment, had been a feature of the American roadside since the 1920s, but not until the 1960s did they impose a sameness on the landscape outside virtually all American cities by becoming the dominant force in the franchising business. Franchising itself — leasing the rights to a commercial name — was a sign of the times; among its creations were the Holiday Inns, Midas Muffler Shops, Citgo stations, and Howard Johnson's motels. These were conventional and sedate, however, when compared to the quick grill and ice cream shops. The going prices of top franchises in 1969 were $96,000 for a McDonald's ("Over 5 Billion Served") hamburger stand, $37,000 for an A & W stand, $24,500 for a Colonel Sanders ("Finger-Lickin' Good") Kentucky Fried Chicken stand, and from $7,500 to $30,000, depending on the location, for a Dairy Queen ice cream stand. Other emporia of the fatty snack, all of them drawing teen-agers by the millions, were doing business under the signs of Dunkin' Donuts, Bonanza, Hardee's, Burger King, Minnie Pearl's Chicken, Baskin-Robbins, Roy Rogers Roast Beef, and the International House of Pancakes.

If the young approved of these, they might have been expected to sanction another big financial phenomenon of the time, the conglomerates, of which the best known was ITT — the International Telephone and Telegraph Company — under whose banner hotels, car rental agencies, life insurance firms, bakeries, and manufacturers of communications equipment did business. But conglomerate was a dirty word among committed youths; it was associated with government contracts and therefore with the Vietnam War, which was an even greater enemy than pollution. Here passions ran highest, both for antiwar demonstrators and their critics, and here the rising generation was taking the stand for which it would be best remembered.

The word for protest that year was moratorium. The first M-day was scheduled for May 15. Richard Nixon said in advance, "Under no circumstances will I be affected whatever by it," thereby guaranteeing large turnouts to ring church bells, wear black armbands, carry signs and candles, and, above all, to march in thousands of American communities as proof of solidarity against the involvement in Indochina. That Wednesday there were 90,000 protesters on Boston Common, 20,000 in New York, and 22,000 in Washington. Some college campuses reported that half their students were gone. At Whittier College, whose most famous alumnus was in the White House, the wife of the acting president lit a flame which was to burn until the war was over.

November 15 fell on a weekend, and the New Mobe, as it was called, lasted for three days. This time the focus was Washington. Police put the crowd at 250,000; the New Mobe committee said 800,000 participated; there was really no way of reaching an accurate estimate, but certainly nothing like it had ever happened in America before. While the White House was announcing that President Nixon would stay inside, watching a football game on television, the first of 40,000 marchers passed by outside, each bearing a card with the name of an American who had died in Vietnam or the name of a Vietnamese community destroyed by the war. The marchers walked four miles, from Arlington to the Capitol, where the names were placed in huge, flag-draped coffins.

It was orderly. The Army had 9,000 troops in reserve to control unruly demonstrators, but they were not used, and praisers of the crowd's restraint included presidential aide Herbert G. Klein and Republican senators Hugh Scott and John Sherman Cooper. A minority view was expressed by Attorney General John N. Mitchell. Two minor episodes of violence had marred the weekend: an SDS band had attacked the South Vietnamese embassy, and a mob of Yippies had tried to rush the Justice Department building. Both had been turned back by tear gas. Taking note of them, Mitchell said that while "the great majority of participants" in the New Mobe had "obeyed the law," the march had been accompanied "by such extensive physical injury, property damage, and street confrontations that I do not believe that — overall — the gatherings here can be characterized as peaceful."

Spiro Agnew agreed. Washington was not surprised. By now it was clear that whatever other members of the administration might say, the attorney general and the Vice President would be pitiless with Americans who broke the law.

My Lai, which was to become the American Lidice, was a Vietnamese hamlet, too small to be known outside Quang Ngai province on the South China Sea until the hot, humid morning of Saturday, March 16, 1968, when it became an open grave for some 567 old men, women, and children. Even then the name was unfamiliar to most of its attackers, all members of Lieutenant William L. Calley Jr.'s Americal Division platoon. They called it Pinkville because the area was colored pink on the military maps issued the night before at the platoon leader's briefing.

Calley and his men were members of Task Force Barker, named for Lieutenant Colonel Frank A. Barker Jr., who would die in a helicopter crash three months later, leaving his role in the events of March 16 forever obscure. The question of provocation was also nebulous; it was to be raised at Calley's court-martial. Charlie Company of the division's 11th Infantry Brigade, to which his unit belonged, had been in Vietnam three and a half months. During that time the company had lost almost half of its 190 men to booby traps and sniper fire. At the briefing the lieutenant was told that My Lai was held by the 48th Battalion of the Viet Cong. Captain Ernest Medina, the company commander, later said that he did not know any women and children were there. He told Lieutenant Calley to clean the village out, and Calley passed the word among his men. At daybreak they were helicoptered in, their M-16 automatic rifles loaded and ready.

On landing they found no Viet Cong. Instead there were only defenseless civilians, who, according to Private Paul David Meadlo, were herded by the American soldiers into the center of the hamlet "like a little island." There, where two trails crossed, the lieutenant ordered his men to shoot the inhabitants. Meadlo was one who obeyed — "I poured about four clips" — 68 shots — "into them," he said afterward; "I might have killed ten or fifteen of them." Calley stood beside him, pumping automatic fire into the captives at point-blank range. Next the soldiers shoved seven or eight Vietnamese into one of the huts, or "hootches" as the grunts called them, and tossed a hand grenade in after them.

The third phase occurred in an L-shaped drainage ditch, which was to become infamous during the Fort Benning, Georgia, court-martial. There the mass murder took on aspects of an assembly line operation. "There was a variety of people there — men, women, and children," a rifleman testified at Fort Benning. ". . . There was being brought up small groups of people and they were being placed in the ditch and Lieutenant Calley was firing into it." Another witness told how the platoon leader had dealt with a Buddhist priest and a baby. The priest, who was wearing the flowing white robe of his office, held out supplicating hands as though in prayer. He kept repeating, "No Viet, no Viet." Calley, according to the testimony, smashed in the man's mouth with the butt of his M-16, reversed the rifle, "and pulled the trigger in the priest's face. Half his head was blown off." As for the infant, "Lieutenant Calley grabbed it by the arm and threw it into the ditch and fired."

Meanwhile, according to a Houston soldier named Herbert Carter, "We went through the village. We didn't see any VC. People began coming out of their hootches and the guys shot them down and then burned the hootches or burned the hootches and shot the people when they came out. Sometimes they would round up a bunch and shoot them together. It went on like this all day."

Sergeant Michael Bernhardt, whose comrades said he refused to participate, called it "point-blank murder." He said, "Only a few of us refused. I
told them the hell with this, I'm not doing it. I didn't think this was a law-
ful order." Most of the firing had died away before Private Richard Pendleton reached My Lai, "but," he later said, "some guys were still shooting
people. . . . There were big groups of bodies lying on the ground, in gullies
and in the paddies." Only one American was a casualty — a soldier who
had shot himself in the foot rather than take part in the killings.

Among the witnesses were two soldiers whose recollections would later
carry special weight. Ronald Haeberle, an Army photographer, recorded
the My Lai carnage on film with three cameras. One was official; he turned
that in. The other two were his personal property, and he kept them. The
second soldier was Warrant Officer Hugh C. Thompson Jr., a helicopter
pilot. Thompson saw the L-shaped gully from the air and alerted his commanding officer. "I thought something was wrong out there," he said later,
"because I couldn't foresee any way of how the bodies got in the ditch."
Thompson returned to the village and rescued sixteen children there. The
Army awarded him the Distinguished Flying Cross for "disregarding his
own safety."

That was the only sign of official awareness that anything unusual had
happened at My Lai. Twelve days later Colonel Barker filed a combat
action report describing the attack as "well-planned, well-executed, and
successful." In the words of a subsequent congressional report, "it can be
reasonably concluded that the My Lai matter was 'covered up' within the
Americal Division." Long afterward, when the cover-up had failed, the
divisional commander, Major General Samuel Koster — who had gone on
to become superintendent of West Point — was reduced in rank, and both
he and the assistant divisional commander were censured and deprived of
their Distinguished Service Medals. This could hardly have been foreseen
then or for some time afterward, however. The first man to do something
about My Lai hadn't been there that morning and didn't even hear about
it until a month later. He was Ronald Ridenhour, who had been with
Charlie Company earlier, in Hawaii; he learned about the massacre from
his former comrades. A year later, as a returned veteran, Ridenhour wrote
out an account of what had apparently happened and mailed twenty-three
copies of it to President Nixon, key congressmen, and officials in the Pentagon and the State Department. He charged that "something rather dark
and bloody did indeed occur sometime in March 1968 in a village called
'Pinkville' in the Republic of Vietnam."

That was on March 29, 1969. Within four weeks the Army opened a full-
scale inquiry into the slaughter. Evidence was turned over to the provost
marshal general on August 4; that same month the Pentagon received copies
of photographer Haeberle's slides. On September 5, the day before Calley
was scheduled to be discharged, he was accused of killing 109 Vietnamese
civilians. Others were charged, including Medina, but only Calley was later

found guilty, after a four-month trial which sent a shudder through the nation. Asked about the incident at a news conference when the story first broke, President Nixon said that it "was certainly a massacre," and that "under no circumstances was it justified." He continued: "One of the goals we are fighting for in Vietnam is to keep the people . . . from having imposed upon them a government which has atrocity against civilians as one of its policies."

When Calley was convicted in 1971 of murdering twenty-two Vietnamese and sentenced to life, however, an astonishing change swept the country, and the President's political antennae were quick to pick it up. A majority of Americans seemed to believe that the verdict was undeserved, either because the lieutenant was innocent or because he was being made a scapegoat. The mood, one observer said sardonically, was, "It didn't happen, and besides, they deserved it." Viking Press announced that it had paid $100,000 for Calley's memoirs, and in the first three days after his conviction a record on the Plantation label, "The Battle Hymn of Lieutenant Calley," sold 202,000 copies. After a saccharine voice-over about "a little boy who wanted to grow up and be a soldier and serve his country in whatever way he could," the song began:

> My name is William Calley, I'm a soldier of this land,
> I've vowed to do my duty and to gain the upper hand,
> But they've made me out a villain, they have stamped me with a brand,
> As we go marching on.

The White House reported that mail was running a hundred to one against the verdict and sentence. President Nixon ordered Calley released from the Benning stockade and moved to house arrest in his post apartment. Two days later the White House announced that "Yesterday the President made the decision that before any final sentence is carried out in the case of Lieutenant Calley the President will personally review the case and finally decide it." Later Nixon changed his mind, but at the time he seemed to be playing politics with a war crime. Indignant, the lieutenant's prosecutor, Captain Aubrey M. Daniel III, wrote the President that he was "shocked and dismayed at your decision to intervene in these proceedings in the midst of the public clamor."

Five weeks after Ronald Ridenhour put his My Lai statement in the mail, Secretary of the Navy John H. Chafee announced civilian intervention in the case of another embattled officer — Commander Lloyd M. Bucher of the *Pueblo*, back in the United States with his crew after the North Koreans had released them in exchange for an official American confession of espionage, an apology, and a promise that it would not happen again. Even as he handed it over at Panmunjom, Major General Gilbert H. Woodward said that the admission was false, that he had signed it "to free the crew, and only to free the crew." Still, the statement rankled in the Pentagon, and the Navy recommended a court-martial for Bucher. Chafee vetoed it. The commander and his men, he said, "have suffered enough."

The locust years continued for the military, despite the change in Presidents. Campaigning in 1968, Richard Nixon had said of Bucher's lost ship, "Unless the United States reacts to these slights, you are bound to encourage bigger slights and you are going to have more *Pueblos*. In a new administration I say we've got to stop that kind of action . . . before it gets started." Less than three months after he entered the White House he was confronted by a similar humiliation, and he was as helpless in responding to it as Lyndon Johnson had been. This time the vehicle of mortification was an airborne *Pueblo,* a converted Lockheed Super Constellation which the Navy called an EC121. Unarmed, the EC121 carried thirty-one crewmen and six tons of electronic gear designed to monitor the communications of a potential enemy. On April 15 the North Koreans shot it down, killing all hands. This time there could be no question about the location of the incident. Russian vessels agreed that it had occurred in international waters, between 100 and 120 miles off the coast.

Nixon's first impulse had been to retaliate, but the more he pondered his options, the fewer he had. Short of risking nuclear war, there was little he could do. In the end he could only say, "I have today ordered that these flights be continued. They will be protected. This is not a threat. It is simply a statement of fact."

It was also a statement of frustration, heightened by the year's events in Vietnam. In Paris American negotiators were telling the North Vietnamese that the United States had ruled out hopes for a military solution in Indochina; in Saigon President Thieu was being told that unilateral American withdrawal, or the acceptance of terms amounting to a disguised U.S. defeat, was also unacceptable. What lay between was impotence.

Human kamikazes — Viet Cong with dynamite lashed to their bodies to blow up barbed wire — led attackers on Fire Base Russell, a Marine position just south of the demilitarized zone, and savage fighting erupted around the big U.S. base at Bien Hoa, fifteen miles from Saigon. The most controversial action of the year was the American assault on Apbia Mountain, christened Hamburger Hill by the grunts. Continuing its strategy of the Johnson years, the Army was subjecting the Viet Cong to what the Pentagon called "maximum pressure." Hamburger Hill began as a typical search-and-destroy mission. Nine battalions were set down by helicopters in the A Shau Valley, a corridor for infiltration from Laos. During the subsequent sweep, the 3rd Battalion of the 187th Regiment, 101st Airborne Division, ran into what the divisional commander, Major General Melvin Zais, called "a hornets' nest" of opposition. Pulling back, the battalion dug in and sent a company up to storm the hill.

The attack failed. Two companies then assaulted the crest. They too were thrown back. The next day the whole battalion charged the defenders and was repulsed. Three more battalions were called in. Meanwhile U.S.

artillery and aircraft were battering the top of the hill; 2,000 shells and 155 air sorties defoliated the summit. Still the Viet Cong clung to it, sending the American attackers reeling backward each time in a tempest of rifle fire and exploding grenades. Ten successive U.S. charges were routed. On the eighth day 1,000 grunts and 400 South Vietnamese took the hill. General Zais called it "a great victory by a gutty bunch of guys." One week later an Army spokesman announced that Hamburger Hill was being abandoned. He said, "We feel we've gotten everything out of this mountain that we're going to get."

Senators reading the casualty lists — 46 Americans had been killed on the slopes of Apbia, and 308 wounded — reacted angrily. Edward M. Kennedy called such assaults "senseless and irresponsible." He asked, "How can we justify sending our boys up against a hill a dozen times or more, until soldiers themselves question the madness of the action?" Some Republicans were also aroused. Aiken of Vermont, the ranking minority member of the Senate Foreign Relations Committee, proposed that the White House "immediately" start "an orderly withdrawal," to turn the war over to "its rightful owners" — the Vietnamese. Scott of Pennsylvania, the GOP whip, urged the withdrawal of "a substantial number" of U.S. soldiers.

Nixon was listening. During his first term he was sensitive to the mood on Capitol Hill. In speeches he remained the irreconcilable cold-warrior, earnestly asserting his belief in a Free Asia, the domino theory, and the rest of it, but his actions were something else. "Vietnam might or might not make us," one of his aides acknowledged, "but there is no question it could break us." The Johnsonian strategy was clearly bankrupt. By March 1969 the number of dead Americans had exceeded the 33,639 killed in Korea. The cost of the war, which continued to top 25 billion dollars a year, continued to generate irresistible inflationary pressure; a 1958 dollar was now worth about seventy-five cents, and economist Milton Friedman was predicting what sounded like a politician's nightmare: an "inflationary recession."

It was now clear that Nixon's most influential foreign policy adviser was not Rogers but Kissinger. Writing in *Foreign Affairs* as a private citizen, Kissinger had proposed two parallel lines of negotiation. Washington and Hanoi, he suggested, might schedule mutual troop withdrawals while the Viet Cong and the South Vietnamese forged a political solution. Now Secretary of Defense Melvin Laird returned from a visit to Saigon with another component of the new President's war policy. Laird believed that the combat efficiency of Thieu's troops could be improved to the point where they might be left on their own. The White House seized on this as a way to implement Vietnamization. Breaking the news to Thieu on Midway, Nixon announced the first cut, of 25,000 men, on June 8.

That same month Clark Clifford proposed in *Foreign Affairs* that the administration "reduce the level of combat" by scheduling the pullout of

100,000 U.S. troops by the end of 1969 and the elimination of "all ground combat forces" by the end of 1970. Clifford wrote: "Nothing we might do could be so beneficial or could so add to the political maturity of South Vietnam as to begin to withdraw our combat troops. Moreover, in my opinion, we cannot realistically expect to achieve anything more through our military force, and the time has come to begin to disengage." Annoyed, Nixon told a national television audience, "I would hope that we could beat Mr. Clifford's timetable, just as I think we've done a little better than he did when he was in charge of our national defense." Aides hastily explained that this was not a commitment, but in September the President announced that he expected to bring home all fighting men "before the end of 1970 or the middle of 1971." A *Life* writer observed at the end of the year, "Politically there did not seem to be much choice. Nixon had to get the U.S. out of Vietnam or face almost certain defeat in the presidential election of 1972."

In Vietnam General Creighton Abrams introduced tactics meant to lower U.S. casualties. Instead of large-scale search-and-destroy missions, tactics on a typical day entailed sending out as many as a thousand patrols of from one hundred to two hundred men each; their orders were to destroy enemy troops and supplies if possible, but to avoid bloodlettings. "Maximum pressure" had been replaced by "protective reaction"; an offensive stance had become defensive. This sounded more impressive in Washington than it really was, however. Two great armies remained in the field, each capable of maiming the other and each led by aggressive commanders. Only forty-six skirmishes were announced in the seven days ending Saturday, July 5, a typical week, but 155 U.S. soldiers were killed. And Abrams's conservative posture did not eliminate the possibility of a big battle, which could flare up at any time.

It happened in late August amid the rolling hills southwest of Da Nang, an area known as the Rice Bowl. A U.S. helicopter crashed there, killing the eight men aboard, and two companies of the 196th Light Infantry Brigade were ordered to recover their bodies. Simultaneously, a thousand North Vietnamese were forming up there to assault the district capital of Hiep Duc. The two forces stumbled into one another and the Communist troops withdrew into a labyrinth of bunkers and trench lines. When the Americans went after them, it was Hamburger Hill all over again. Reinforcements were sucked in until about three thousand Americans and South Vietnamese were pitted against the North Vietnamese Second Division. Both sides battled for possession of a hummock called Hill 102. The struggle ended when grunts of the 196th reached the top — and found it deserted. "It's the old story," a U.S. officer said. "Five days of fighting like hell and on the sixth day they give it to you for nothing." But there was a new story from the Rice Bowl, too, and it was ominous. Company A of the 196th had refused to obey direct orders to descend into the labyrinth and bring back the dead from the wrecked helicopter. Eventually the men did move out, but the specter of mutiny remained, one more dissonant note in the Vietnamese din.

Speaking of crime at home, the President held his hand at neck level and told reporters that the people "have had it up to here." It was in fact a lawless time in the United States; the FBI reported an increase in felonies of 10.6 percent over the previous year. Larceny was up 19 percent, forcible rape 16.8 percent, robbery 12.5 percent, and one offense went right off the chart: skyjacking, the hijacking of airplanes. Between 1950 and 1967 the airlines had reported an average of 2.3 attempted skyjacks a year. In 1969 there were 71, of which 58 went to Cuba — three times as many as the year before. On NBC-TV's *Tonight Show* Johnny Carson said, "There are so many hijackings that one airline changed its slogan to 'Up, up, and olé.' "

The airlines did try a lot of things. Signs in terminals warned that sky-jacking was punishable by death, that passengers could be imprisoned just for carrying weapons aboard, and that they could be searched. The public was invited to offer some suggestions. Some memorable ones came in: stewardesses could be trained to seduce skyjackers, passengers should be required to travel naked, trapdoors could be built where the skyjackers would stand, the crew should play the Cuban national anthem over the public address system and then arrest everyone who stood up. Only one innovation worked. Although no U.S. airline scheduled regular flights to Cuba, every pilot flying over the South carried approach maps for Havana's José Martí Airport. With dismal regularity they were billed, through the Swiss government, for Cuban landing fees and incidental expenses.

That year's skyjacking climax came in November, when Captain Donald Cook of TWA's Los Angeles to San Francisco Flight 85 switched on the intercom and said, "There's a man here who wants to go some place, and he's just chartered himself an airplane. Drinks are on the house." The man was a twenty-year-old Marine Corps veteran of Vietnam, Raffaele Mini-chiello, and he was holding a pistol at the flight engineer's head. Minichiello was cagey about his destination. Cook said later, "Right away I suspected we would be heading south to pick up a few cigars, but that wasn't the way it was." The skyjacker ordered him to fly east.

After refueling at Bangor and Shannon, Ireland, they wound up over Leonardo da Vinci Airport in Rome. It seemed that Minichiello, a native Italian, was homesick. He ordered the control tower to park them in a far corner of the field; then he said he wanted an unarmed policeman as a hostage. Rome's police chief volunteered. The skyjacker made the chief drive him into the country and then released him. Several hours later Minichiello was arrested in a church. "Why did I do it?" he said. "I don't know." His sister said, "I think the war damaged my brother's mind." The Italian public appeared to regard him as a hero — he had, after all, estab-lished a skyjacking record: 17 hours in the air and 6,900 miles — but their government took another view. He was sentenced to six years and five months in prison.

Although the somewhat fey Minichiello was a comet in the world of crime, he was not the year's most famous miscreant. That distinction went to a motorist charged merely with leaving the scene of an accident without identifying himself. The misdeed became notorious because the culprit was a U.S. senator bearing a famous name — Edward M. Kennedy — and because the accident had tragic consequences. Until the night of July 18–19, 1969, Ted Kennedy had been the front runner for the next Democratic presidential nomination and a probable winner over Nixon and his minority party. Ted's eulogy at his brother Bob's funeral had moved the nation, and in January he had displayed his family's winning ways by blitzing Russell B. Long of Louisiana, beating him in a party caucus and thereby replacing him as the Senate's Democratic whip. The young Kennedy seemed to be on his way to greatness. Then came Chappaquiddick.

Among the many responsibilities Ted had inherited from his brothers was one for lifting the morale of the family's loyal campaigners. A cookout on July 18 was meant to do that. The hosts were Ted and several friends; their guests were six girls who had worked as volunteer drudges in the "boiler room" — back room — of Robert Kennedy's abortive presidential candidacy the year before. The place was Chappaquiddick Island, which lay just 250 yards off another island, Martha's Vineyard, on Cape Cod's Nantucket Sound.

According to Kennedy's testimony at the inquest six months later, he left the party in his Chrysler at about 11:15 P.M. with one of the girls, Mary Jo Kopechne. Mary Jo was attractive, twenty-eight, and known to her friends as "M.J." The senator said afterward that they were on their way to the two-car ferry which would have carried them back to Martha's Vineyard, where they were registered at different hotels, but the judge at the inquest didn't believe him, and neither did a lot of other people. Mary Jo left her pocketbook at the cookout. She told no one there she was departing, and she didn't ask her roommate for the key to their hotel room. When she and Ted drove off, they left behind ten people (including the Chrysler's chauffeur) who didn't intend to spend the night at the cookout and who, with the departure of the big car, were left with only one small rented auto, obviously inadequate for their return. Finally, and most compellingly, there was the question of the turn Kennedy took.

The blacktop road from the cookout to the ferry was the only surfaced road on Chappaquiddick. Ted left it for a bumpy gravel roadway that led to the beach. He said afterward that this was a mistake. But the turn was a hairpin curving back to the right, and the entrance to it was masked by bushes; you almost had to be looking for it to make it. The senator must have known the difference, the judge insisted; he had been driven over both more than once that day.

The bumpy way Ted and Mary Jo took was called the Dike Road, and a half-mile down it was the Dike Bridge, a narrow, humpbacked wooden structure. This span curved off the dirt road in a 25-degree angle to the left, rising to cross a slim channel in the dike which permitted sea water from the sound, on the right, to flow in and out of Poucha Pond. The bridge was their undoing. Ted didn't make the 25-degree turn. Instead the Chrysler plunged off the right side of the span, rolling as it fell, and hit the bottom of the ten-foot-deep channel wrong side up. At the inquest Kennedy testified that he didn't know he had turned on the wrong road until "the moment I went off the bridge."

> . . . the next thing I recall is the movement of Mary Jo next to me, the struggling, perhaps hitting or kicking me, and I at this time opened my eyes and realized I was upside down, that water was crashing in on me, that it was pitch black. . . . I can remember the last sensation of being completely out of air and inhaling what must have been a half a lung full of water and assuming that I was going to drown and the full realization that no one was going to be looking for us that night until the next morning and that I wasn't going to get out of the car alive, and then somehow I can remember coming up to the last energy of just pushing, pressing, and coming up to the surface.

Carried to the shore by the current, he waded back and dove into the ten feet of water for Mary Jo. He made seven or eight attempts to rescue her, he testified, but toward the end he was so out of breath that he could only hold his head under the water for a few seconds. For fifteen or twenty minutes he lay on the bank, coughing up water. Then, he said, he returned to the cookout, "walking, trotting, jogging, stumbling, as fast as I possibly could." There he told his story to two men, Joseph F. Gargan, a cousin, and Paul F. Markham, a Kennedy campaigner. Gargan and Markham returned to the scene with him and dove for Mary Jo without success. Like him, both men were lawyers, and they told him that this must be reported. He was deeply disturbed, they recalled afterward. He kept saying, "I just can't believe this happened."

At his request they drove him to the ferry slip. The lights of Edgartown, on Martha's Vineyard, lay just across the way. He told them to go back to the cookout but not to tell the girls what had happened. Then, he said, he "suddenly jumped into the water and impulsively swam across." As he crossed the narrow channel "the water got colder, the tide began to draw me out for the second time that evening, I knew I was going to drown." But he made it, rested on the far shore, and walked to the Shiretown Inn, where he was staying.

At the inn his behavior became increasingly incomprehensible. As he himself said later, "My conduct and conversations during the next several hours, to the extent that I can remember them, make no sense to me at all. I regard as indefensible the fact that I did not report the accident to the police immediately." He testified that he "just couldn't gain the strength within me, the moral strength to call Mrs. Kopechne at two o'clock in the morning and tell her that her daughter was dead."

What he did was to change into dry clothes and then complain to the hotel's co-owner that a party in the next room was keeping him awake. In the morning he discussed the weekend's yachting regatta with two couples. Then Gargan and Markham arrived and were aghast to learn that he hadn't reported the crash. He explained at the inquest: "I told them about my own thoughts and feelings as I swam across that channel and how I always willed that Mary Jo still lived." He also said that he wanted to make a telephone call, but apparently the phones in Edgartown wouldn't do; he passed two of them, both outdoors and both public. Taking the ferry back to Chappaquiddick, with Gargan and Markham accompanying him, he used a phone in the ferry-house on the other side. The ferryman asked them if they had heard about the accident. One replied, "We just heard about it." Only then, nearly eleven hours after the wreck, did Ted try to contact the Edgartown police.

Meanwhile the Chrysler had been discovered. At 7 A.M. two young men had crossed the bridge to fish in the surf; returning, they had noticed that the falling tide had exposed the wheel of a car. They had stopped to tell Mrs. Pierre Malm, who lived fifty yards away, and at 8:20 she had phoned Police Chief Dominick J. Arena. Borrowing trunks, the strapping Arena had come, dived down, radioed the automobile license number back for identification, and asked Fireman John Farrar to bring his scuba equipment. It was Farrar who found Mary Jo inside.

Arena's headquarters radioed back that the car was registered to Senator Edward M. Kennedy, and when the chief returned to Edgartown he found the senator waiting for him. Ted said: "I was driving. What do you want me to do? It has to be right." One thing he should do, Arena said, was make a proper report. Ted went into a back room with Markham and wrote one out; it was sketchy; he identified the victim as "one Miss Mary ——, a former secretary of my brother Robert Kennedy," omitting the rest of her name because, he said, he didn't know how to spell it. (Markham didn't, either.) Markham asked the chief to keep the news from the press until Ted could phone Burke Marshall for legal advice. Arena agreed. He waited three hours. Having heard nothing further from Kennedy by then, he gave the newspaper the story and charged Kennedy with leaving the scene of the accident. Of the senator's strange trip that morning to use the Chappaquiddick phone the chief said, "If he had time to take the ferry over and back, he had time to see me."

The medical examiner reported "a positive diagnosis of accidental drowning." Satisfied that there had been no foul play, he released the girl's body without an autopsy, and it was flown to her birthplace in Pennsylvania for burial — a move that brought criticism of the authorities later. In Hyannisport Ted went into seclusion. Seven days later he emerged to plead guilty in Edgartown's century-old courthouse. Judge James A. Boyle gave him the minimum sentence of two months in prison, suspended it, and took away his driver's license. That evening Kennedy went on nationwide television to explain the inexplicable. The speech was not a success. He answered questions which hadn't been asked, maintaining that he had not been "driving under the influence of liquor" and that there was "no truth, no truth whatever," to insinuations of "immoral conduct" by him and Mary Jo. He also seemed to imply that the damage to his career was more momentous than her death when he said that among his preoccupations the night after the accident had been "whether some awful curse actually did hang over all the Kennedys." The talk reminded some people of Nixon's Checkers performance in 1952. Like Nixon, Ted asked his constituents to help him decide whether he should continue in public life. Massachusetts being passionately pro-Kennedy, the response was favorable, and a week later he returned to his senatorial duties.

After the inquest reporters asked him about the judge's opinion that there was "probable cause to believe that Edward M. Kennedy operated his motor vehicle negligently," that "such operation appears to have contributed to the death of Mary Jo Kopechne," and that he found Ted's insistence that he and Mary Jo had been headed for the ferry incredible. Kennedy said: "In my personal view, the inference and the ultimate findings of the judge's report are not justified, and I reject them. . . . At the inquest I truthfully answered all the questions asked of me."

He also said: "I expect to be a candidate for the U.S. Senate in 1972, and I expect to serve out a full six-year term." The White House, taking no chances, was preparing to discredit him with the episode if he changed his mind and ran for President. Within six hours after the recovery of Mary Jo's body, presidential aides had sent a retired New York policeman to Chappaquiddick; according to John Dean, the man "posed as a newspaper reporter and always asked the most embarrassing questions at any press gathering." It was unnecessary. Temporarily, at least, Ted's national following had been diminished. He was no longer a charismatic figure on Capitol Hill. The following year he touched bottom there when Senator Robert C. Byrd of West Virginia challenged his right to continue as party whip. Kennedy had beaten Long 31 to 26. Now he lost to Byrd 31 to 24. Then, in the aftermath of a meeting at the White House, he was subjected to a new humiliation for a Kennedy: commiseration from Richard Nixon.

Portrait of an American

BENJAMIN McLANE SPOCK, M.D.

THE ELDEST OF SIX CHILDREN, born to a mother who wouldn't have a nurse, who wanted to do it all herself, he grew to love the idea of playing parent, feeding the others, even changing their diapers. He came naturally to think of children as very important, and — this from both his parents — was imbued with a New England hair-shirt conscience. Find a stern moral issue, they told him, and fight for it against all odds. He didn't want that. He decided to rebel. For a long time he thought he was going to succeed.

Hamden Hall Country Day School. Andover. Yale. Scroll and Key, and a flash of conventional glory as an oarsman in the 1924 Olympics. Aspiring briefly to becoming an architect, he fell into his parents' puritan mold while spending a summer as a counselor in a camp run by the Newington Crippled Children's Home near Hartford. He watched the orthopedic surgeon working with the children who had polio. Later he said: "I realized how much he was helping them and I decided that I wanted to be a doctor."

Columbia. An internship at New York's Presbyterian Hospital. A residency in pediatrics. Another in psychiatry. Six years of psychoanalytic training. His love for children grew and deepened, and they adored him. "The man with the gentle face and eyes," he was called. In his office toys were everywhere. He built a device for the shy ones — a small flight of steps led through a trap door to the examining table. He wanted them to *want* to be examined, and they did. Years afterward he said: "One of my faults as a pediatrician has always been that I whoop it up too much with the children." But he never really tried to change.

The standard handbook for baby care was Dr. John B. Watson's *Psychological Care of Infant and Child*, published the year after Spock, then a second-year medical student, married Jane Cheney. Watson said: "Never, never kiss your child. Never hold it on your lap. Never rock its carriage."

Young Dr. Spock set himself against all that. While in the Navy during World War II he wrote his *Common Sense Book of Baby and Child Care*. Its opening words set the tone: "You know more than you think you do." Jane typed it from his longhand, and he indexed it himself, from abscess to Zwieback, because, he explained, he knew he would have "a better notion of what words mothers would look for in an index."

Over the next twenty-three years the book sold 22 million copies and was translated into thirty languages. He wrote a column for the *Ladies' Home Journal,* then for *Redbook;* his half-hour television program was seen Sunday afternoons over fifty-two stations of NBC-TV. And all the time Dr. Spock was rising in that most exacting of professions, the teaching of medicine. He taught psychiatry at Minnesota, child psychiatry and development at Pitt, child development in the psychiatry department at Western Reserve in Cleveland. His stand against Watson had made him the champion of indulgence. Troubled by the far swing of the pendulum, he rewrote passages of *Baby and Child Care* in 1956, explaining, "I find that some uncertain parents are interpreting me as an advocate of extreme permissiveness, so in the revisions I'm making in the book, I'm having to emphasize the limits of permissiveness."

Then a deeper challenge stirred Spock's conscience. Raised a conservative Republican, he had been converted to Democratic liberalism by Franklin Roosevelt, and in 1960 he supported John F. Kennedy. But in March 1962, Kennedy resumed nuclear testing. Alarmed, Spock joined the National Committee for a Sane Nuclear Policy (SANE). He campaigned vigorously for Johnson against Goldwater and felt betrayed when, in February 1965, Johnson escalated the Vietnam War. Spock wrote the White House, protesting, and when that proved futile he took to the streets in demonstrations.

"Excruciatingly embarrassing," he said of this afterward, "like one of those bad dreams where suddenly you are downtown without any clothes on." Certainly he was unusually conspicuous — six foot four, with a strong craggy face, always wearing a suit with a vest and a watch chain — a grandfatherly figure articulating, with his taut Yankee twang, moral standards which other, younger demonstrators thought hopelessly old-fashioned. But he grew more militant, not less. His critics, and they were many and scathing in these years, ridiculed his concern as a new expression of permissiveness, which they were now presenting as a national bogey. To him the issue was simple decency and justice.

The National Mobilization Committee to End the War in Vietnam. The National Conference for a New Politics. Delivering 992 turned-in draft cards to a coldly furious functionary at the Department of Justice. Submitting to arrest for civil disobedience by crossing a police line at the armed forces induction center on Whitehall Street in Manhattan. Sitting on his long-legged stool at his drafting table, using a ballpoint pen to write — slowly and painfully, as always — "A Call to Resist Illegitimate Authority."

Authority finally struck back to salvage the pride of General Hershey, whose orders to draft antiwar demonstrators had been overruled by the Justice Department. Five antiwar leaders, virtual strangers to one another, were charged with conspiracy to subvert the draft law. They were not accused of committing a crime, just of plotting one. In a word, their offense was dissent. The most outstanding leader, literally towering over the other four, was Benjamin M. Spock, M.D.

The trial was held in Boston's District Court in May and June of 1968. The judge was eighty-five-year-old Francis Ford — rude, vain, and flagrantly partial. The verdict was guilty — "guilty," a juror explained afterward to a reporter, "as charged by the judge." The defendants were sentenced to two years in prison, and two of them, Spock and Chaplain William Sloane Coffin of Yale, were fined five thousand dollars each.

Spock said: "There is no shred of legality or constitutionality to this war; it violates the United Nations Charter, the Geneva Accords, and the United States' promise to obey the laws of international conduct. It is totally, abominably illegal. . . . I intend to go on working against the war."

And he did. The U.S. Court of Appeals for the First Circuit threw out the convictions, citing Judge Ford's prejudice. Spock went on, and on. They were still killing his children in the endless night of Vietnam, murdering the generation whose mothers he had counseled, and the sense of duty instilled in his own childhood gave him no rest. Sometimes it almost seemed to him that he could hear the dying crying out across half the world for mercy. Dr. Watson would have turned a deaf ear. ("Never, never kiss your child.") Dr. Spock could not. And slowly, as the nation in its agony turned from the shibboleths of mindless anti-Communism toward the peace of exhaustion, the wisdom of his compassion became clear.

Jesus said, Suffer little children, and forbid them not, to come unto me; for of such is the kingdom of heaven.

But President Nixon called Dr. Spock a bum.

THIRTY-FIVE

Nattering Nabobs

As AMERICA ENTERED the 1970s, the swing generation was in, or about to enter, its fifties, the age at which men begin to discover that the world they have loved is disintegrating. That year the impression carried special force, for there seemed to be an unusual number of reasons for feeling wronged, among them inflation, pollution, crime, the war, the stock market, the generation gap, immorality, riots, cyclamates, traffic, insulting bumper stickers and decals, strikes against the public, racism, and new skyjackings. Nothing worked as it once had. "Not only is there no God," said Woody Allen, "but try getting a plumber on weekends."

Hardly had three weeks of 1970 passed before a U.S. Navy ship set the tone for what was to come by tearing loose from its anchorage in a high wind and ripping a 375-foot hole in the Chesapeake Bay Bridge-Tunnel structure. To the superstitious it appeared that the new decade was off to an inauspicious start.

Nature appeared to be in a contrary mood elsewhere, too. After two hundred consecutive rainless days, Southern California was ravaged by the worst brush fires in its history, apparently caused by spontaneous combustion, denuding over 500,000 acres — an area nearly as large as Rhode Island. Eleven died in another fire of unexplained origin, in an eighty-five-year-old Minneapolis apartment building. All over the world natural disasters were besetting man; a Venice whirlwind left four dead, a cyclonic tidal wave in East Pakistan left 200,000 dead, and earthquakes in Peru, Turkey, and Iran left tens of thousands dead. Possibly God was angry with people like Woody Allen, who denied Him, or with the irreverent, like the flip college students who wore pins reading: "God Isn't Dead — He Just Doesn't Want to Get Involved."

Certainly religion wasn't the steady rock it had been. Christians who didn't regard God as a bigot were shaken by the new president of the Mormon Church, who said, "There is a reason why one man is born black and with other disadvantages, while another man is born white with great advantages. The Negro evidently is receiving the reward he merits." Episcopalians were agitated over the shelving, after three and a half centuries, of the King James Version of the Holy Bible for a New English Bible. Worst of all, from God's point of view, was the growing power of antichristianity — the worship of strange totems and even of Satan himself.

According to one reliable source, America was supporting 10,000 full-time and 175,000 part-time astrologers. Computers spewed forth ten-dollar horoscopes, a New York hairdresser employed a staff astrologer, a department store sold fifty-dollar annual subscriptions to a Dial-an-Astrologer service, and 300 newspapers with a combined circulation of 30 million carried a regular astrological column. Book clubs offered tarot cards as premiums. At the University of South Carolina 250 students were enrolled in a course on sorcery. Magazine advertisements inquired, "Tired of being on the outside of witchcraft looking in? Get in on the action yourself. Join our Diploma Course in Witchcraft and learn the age-old secrets, including raising power, meditation, prediction, fertility, and initiation rites." Mrs. Sybil Leek, a Houston sorceress who cast spells with a pet jackdaw named Hotfoot Jackson perched on her shoulder, calculated that there were "about eight million initiated witches in the world. I mean real witches, not Hollywood sex orgy, free-for-all types. I personally know of about four hundred regular covens in the United States. It is possible there are thousands of irregular ones."

If heaven was receiving insufficient respect, so were the authorities on earth. After one man had been killed and 105 wounded or injured during a People's Park riot in Berkeley, federal indictments were handed down accusing not the rioters, but ten deputies and two former deputies, who were charged with violating the civil rights of the demonstrators. ("This is the sickest operation any level of government was ever involved in," the sheriff raged.) Black Panthers seemed to be literally getting away with murder; juries or appeals courts threw out homicide charges against them in San Francisco, New Haven, and New York, and in Chicago a special federal grand jury criticized police conduct during the raid in which Panthers Fred Hampton and Mark Clark had been killed. Even the American Indians, who had been at the bottom of the status pyramid since the country was founded, were feeling feisty. The Senate didn't give the country back to them, but a bill did return New Mexico's Blue Lake and 48,000 surrounding acres to the Pueblo tribe.

It was a hard time for U.S. generals, and not just in Vietnam. The Russians arrested two of them on charges of violating Soviet air space. The commanding general of the European Exchange System was stripped of his rank for irregularities by subordinates, and Benjamin O. Davis Jr., who had retired from the Air Force as a lieutenant general, the highest rank ever held by a black, resigned as director of public safety in Cleveland because, he said, the city's black mayor was providing "support and comfort to the enemies of law enforcement." Anyone wearing a uniform was liable to be subjected to abuse by the tormentors of authority, though it did seem that President Nixon gave the White House police a special handicap. Impressed by the fancy uniforms of Romanian police, the President commissioned Jimmie Muscatello, a Washington tailor, to design new regalia for guards at the Executive Mansion. The result was a $16,000 joke — double-breasted white tunics with gold braid, brass buttons bearing the presidential seal, and black plastic Ruritanian hats. One guard muttered that if he had to wear such livery he wanted a bass drum to go with it. A designer said, "This is not the time for Gilbert and Sullivan at the White House." "You can't please everybody," said Muscatello, who hadn't pleased anybody, not even the President; the tunics stayed in service, but the hats were quietly shelved.

New York gravediggers struck in January. The air traffic controllers went out in April. Grounded passengers were bitter, but they may have been lucky; heavier-than-air transport wasn't at its most reliable in 1970. Air piracy continued, and an Arizonan named A. G. Barkley added a new wrinkle when he entered a TWA cabin with a gun, a razor, and a can of gasoline and announced that he wanted 100 million dollars. He was seized after a gun battle during which the pilot was wounded in the stomach. Boeing's 21-million-dollar jumbo jet, the 747, was off to a slow start, running as much as six hours behind schedule. Even a lunar flight, Apollo 13, broke down some 200,000 miles from home. The three astronauts aboard had to turn back.

Ironically, one of the most successful journeys of 1970 was a 3,200-mile ocean voyage by a papyrus boat, the Ra II, built and sailed by Norwegian explorer Thor Heyerdahl to prove that the ancient Egyptians could have crossed the Atlantic. At least the Ra II reached its destination, Barbados, and while it didn't make money, neither did many commercial carriers, including, most conspicuously, the biggest railroad in the United States. In bankruptcy court with 2.6 billion dollars in debts, the Penn Central was one of many American institutions which were having trouble balancing their books. Another was the motion picture industry; five major Hollywood studios were in the red, with total debts of over 100 million dollars. The great boom of the 1960s seemed to have ended with the decade, and the best evidence was in Wall Street, where the Dow Jones industrial average, which had been within striking distance of 1,000 in December 1968, sank to 631 on May 27.

The gallery at the New York Stock Exchange had been crowded with eager spectators in the years of the Johnson bull market. After the long slide of May 1970 it became a lonelier place. Indeed, the entire city of New York — which its mordant inhabitants now called Fun City — was less popular with tourists. There was the street crime, and there were other perils. On June 1 the city increased its towing fee for illegally parked cars from twenty-five to fifty dollars. That day a Springfield, Massachusetts, mother came to New York and took her children to a film. When she emerged her auto was gone and she owed the city fifty dollars plus a fine. The movie was *The Out-of-Towners,* dealing with the hazards of visiting Manhattan.

While 1970 was a year of doldrums on most California motion picture lots, a director named Russ Meyer finished his twenty-first successful movie that year. He had known from the outset that it would be big box office. None of its predecessors had lost money or grossed less than six figures, and one of them, *Vixen,* filmed for $72,000, had earned over six million. Meyer said: "I don't play games with an audience. In my films you know where you're at in fifteen seconds — the first fifteen seconds." Where you were at was in the middle of what the trade described as "erotica" and others called pornography. Peddling sex had become a big business in the United States, netting over 500 million dollars a year, and the market seemed insatiable.

The merchandise came in various packages. Main Street theaters showed X-rated films; 1970 hits included *Sexual Freedom in Denmark, The Minx* ("Makes *Curious Yellow* look pale" — *New York Daily News*), and Allen Funt's *What Do You Say to a Naked Lady?* ("What *can* you say?" asked its ads. "We say wow"), which was grossing one San Francisco movie house $7,000 a week for round-the-clock showings. Manhattan was supporting two hundred "adult bookstores," and those in the twenty-four-hour-a-day block between Seventh and Eighth avenues displayed their goods like supermarkets, with overhead signs advertising the various departments — heterosexual, homosexual (male), bestiality, flagellation, lesbian, incest, fellatio and cunnilingus. Arcade machines offered skin flicks in color at a quarter a showing. Picture packets contained "Eight revealing poses! $2." Onstage in New York were *Grin and Bare It* with nine nudes in the cast, *The Boys in the Band,* which AP dramatic critic William Glover called "the most unabashed and forthright account of homosexuality yet seen in this era of growing artistic permissiveness," and *Futz,* which dealt with the problems of a yokel who enjoyed coupling with a sow. But the market was much bigger than Broadway. The Arcadian bachelor could resolve his frustrations by sending for obscene LP records; a lonely bachelor girl could purchase a vibrator in a hometown store or a plastic dildo through the mails, and as Professor Morse Peckham of the University of South Carolina observed, in the corner drugstore the public could now "buy for very little money pornographic works which a short time ago were unobtainable for any amount of money."

To Americans over the age of thirty the change was mind-boggling. In their childhoods the word "ass" had been forbidden in mixed company, and the swing generation could remember the uproar over the Hays Office decision to let Clark Gable say "Frankly, my dear, I don't give a damn" in *Gone With the Wind.* Now Jack Valenti approved "horseshit" and "Piss on you" in movies rated for the whole family. Part of the latitude studios now took could be traced to the Supreme Court's 1957 decision, in the case of Roth v. U.S., that to be obscene material must be prurient, offensive to community standards, and "utterly without redeeming social value." Another part of the new license was a byproduct of the new contraceptives, liberalized abortion legislation, and the consequent emancipation of women from the fear of unwanted pregnancy. And much of it, as William Glover had noted, was rooted in the era, in the sexual revolution and the mini-micro-bikini-topless-bottomless mood of the times. Curiosity about sex appeared to be insatiable; Nicholas von Hoffman wrote about a female reporter who, while collecting material for an article about prostitution, went to bed with a strange man for money and reported that the climax was "a moment of stunning pleasure." A mother in Braintree, Massachusetts, came home one afternoon to find her teen-age daughter and a girlfriend in bed naked, experimenting with Sapphic techniques. The word "indiscretion" in its sexual sense all but dropped out of the language, because hardly anybody was discreet any more. A Pennsylvania legislator opposing abortion legislation was unmasked as a hypocrite when a young woman came forward to tell the press that he had been her lover and had paid for her abortion. There had been a time when she would have kept that to herself.

All this was hard on children, who were exposed to it, were more precocious in their dating customs than their parents, and attained puberty at an earlier age. The remedy most often proposed was sex education in the schools. Gallup found that 71 percent of the people approved it, with 55 percent in favor of courses explaining birth control. Among the groups endorsing the teaching of sex were the AMA, the National Education Association, the Sex Education Association, and the Sex Information and Education Council in the United States (SIECUS). Dr. Mary Calderone, executive director of SIECUS, said sex should be taught "not as something you do but as something you are."

SIECUS issued no material; it merely offered professional advice to school systems. That point was obscured by the articulate minority, which was outraged by the very suggestion that reproduction might be discussed in the classroom. "Is the Schoolhouse the Proper Place to Teach Raw Sex?" asked Billy James Hargis's Christian Crusade, firing the opening gun in the ultraright's attack on sex education. The Reverend Billy called SIECUS the "pornographic arm of liberal education," and state boards of education in Oklahoma, California, and Utah rejected sound film strips because they had been approved by SIECUS.

Other organizations in the antisex coalition were the Movement to Restore Decency (MOTOREDE), a Birch front; Parents United for a Responsible Education (PURE), the Mothers Organization for Moral Stability (MOMS), Sanity on Sex (SOS), Parents Opposed to Sex Education (POSE), and Parents Against Unconstitutional Sex Education (PAUSE). "I doubt that one parent in a thousand had heard about sex education a year ago," said a Birch coordinator. "Now they've heard about it, and they don't like what they hear." One group accused the schools of planning to "reveal all the details of intercourse and masturbation to small children"; a school in Parsippany, New Jersey, was called an "academic whorehouse"; a PAUSE leader accused the schools of "undermining what should be taught in the home." An eighth-grade mathematics teacher was jailed for disseminating lewd materials, and a California school superintendent was fired. Ultrarightists also won in Racine, Wisconsin, after charging that sex education was a Communist plot to undermine the morals of the pupils. One of the wilder battles was in San Francisco over an innocuous book titled *A Doctor Talks to Five-to-Eight-Year-Olds.* The ultras there printed a leaflet reproducing an illustration from the book of one toad on another's back. The book explained that it was a mother carrying her baby. The leaflet lost sex education a lot of supporters by changing the caption to "Mating Toads."

At the peak of the controversy sex education was an issue in twenty-seven states. Toward the end of 1970 sanity triumphed and the courses were introduced, to the bewilderment of the children, who wondered what all the fuss had been about. Then, just as superintendents and school boards thought they could divert their professional attention to other matters, their presentation of sex came under attack from an entirely different movement: Women's Lib. Liberated women took it as an article of faith that all except physical differences between males and females were taught, not inherent. They believed that girls were trained to want motherhood and cultivate domestic science, and they regarded the public schools as a major training ground. Demanding that textbooks be revised and teachers reoriented, they joined battle with their adversaries in a struggle which was certain to endure as a major issue of the 1970s.

Millions of Americans had first become aware of the new feminism when Robin Morgan, until then best known as a TV actress in *I Remember Mama,* marched into the 1968 Miss America Pageant pulling a train of blazing brassieres. She was there, she told startled reporters, in her role as founder of the Women's International Terrorist Conspiracy from Hell (WITCH). Feminists paraded through metropolitan shopping districts on August 26, 1970, the fiftieth anniversary of ratification of the Nineteenth Amendment. All that year liberated women were demonstrating that they, like the members of other protest movements, understood the uses of publicity. "Take it off!" one of them yelled at a construction worker, and when she was asked if she meant his hard hat she said, "No, his jockstrap." One June Conlan won a ten-year court fight to become a day laborer digging ditches. Marlene Dixon wrote that "in all classes and groups, the institution functions to a greater or lesser degree to oppress women; the unity of women of different classes hinges upon our understanding of that common oppression." Abby Aldrich Rockefeller, a great-granddaughter of John D., denounced romantic love between men and women as "counter-revolutionary."

"I've had Women's Lib up to here," said Dr. Edgar F. Berman, a physician active in Democratic politics. Democratic Congresswoman Patsy Mink of Hawaii promptly accused Berman of being a sexist with the "basest sort of prejudice against women." As the year wore on, the rhetoric grew more heated. Margaret Mead said, "Women's liberation has to be terribly conscious of the danger of provoking men to kill women. You have quite literally driven them mad." One male spectator at the women's march in New York screamed at them, "All you pigs can't get a man!" while another stood silently by wearing a brassiere. "These chicks," said Hugh Hefner in a memo to his staff, "are our natural enemy. It's time to do battle with them. They are inalterably opposed to the romantic boy-girl society *Playboy* promotes."

Some of the women sounded as frivolous as Hefner. They devoted a great deal of energy to debates over whether they should be known as Mrs., Miss, or Ms.; to attempts to have chairmen called chairpersons, and to attacks on National Airlines for running ads of pretty stewardesses saying, "I'm Doris. Fly me." But the deeper questions they raised were anything but trivial. Over 23 million American women now held full-time jobs; another eight million had part-time jobs. Four of every ten married women were employed, 12 million of them with children at home under eighteen. Superficially this indicated a challenge to male supremacy in the job market, but the nature of the employment and the pay for it still reflected a society in which men, not women, were expected to support families. Men still dominated the most lucrative professions and brought home the bigger slices of bacon. Just 7.6 percent of America's 300,000 doctors, and only 1 percent of the surgeons, were women, while 90 percent of the phone operators and stenographers were female. The average woman was making $3 for every $5 made by a man with the same job. *Life* calculated that a woman needed a B.A. degree to earn as much as a man who left school after the eighth grade. The typical salesman made $8,549; the typical saleswoman $3,461.

By 1970 Women's Lib arguments for equality in employment and education were supported by many men. Demands for free abortions and free day-care centers for children were more controversial, and the masculine population seemed evenly divided on the proposed Twenty-seventh Amendment to the Constitution — the Equal Rights Amendment (ERA), ensuring women complete equality before the law. Yet within two years the Senate would approve ERA and send it to the state legislatures. Under it, women would no longer be required to change their names when they married; they would be given an equal voice in where the family would live; if the husband's job obliged him to move elsewhere, and his wife stayed behind, she would not be liable to a charge of desertion. On the other hand, should a marriage break up, the wife might have to pay alimony. Laws shielding women from danger and physical strain on the job and protecting them from certain sexual outrages would be void. (Rape was an exception.) In addition, women might be drafted and even sent into battle. A pro-ERA contributor to the *Yale Law Journal* argued:

> . . . the effectiveness of the modern soldier is due more to equipment and training than to individual strength. Women are physically as able as men to perform many jobs classified as combat duty, such as piloting an airplane or engaging in naval operations. . . . There is no reason to assume that in a dangerous situation women will not be as serious and well-disciplined as men.

It is doubtful that many housewives wanted to become machine gunners or BAR men, or identified with Elizabeth P. Hoisington, director of the Women's Army Corps, who became America's first female general in June 1970. Nevertheless, millions of American women — especially younger women — had been changed by the movement. There was a new spunkiness about them, a plucky defiance toward those who would manipulate them for selfish ends, and this was illustrated by the disaster which befell the new fashion known to readers of *Women's Wear Daily* as the longuette and to the rest of the country as the midi. Nearly a quarter-century earlier independent women had tried to lead a revolt against the long-skirted New Look, signing manifestos, forming LBK (Little Below the Knee) clubs, and demonstrating against the couturiers.* They had been routed then. Now the modistes were again turning out longer skirts. James Galanos said, "Long is where the direction is," Adele Simpson said, "It's good-bye thigh," and Leo Narducci said, "Women are definitely ready for a fashion change." All were confident that the female herd would grovel and buy their wares.

The first mutinous mutters came from Los Angeles, where one Juli Hutner, president of something called POOFF (Preservation of Our Femininity and Finances), told a reporter: "We're not going to let them pull the wool over our legs as well as our eyes. I know women who'd wear a tin box if Galanos said it was in. I think that's sick. All we ask is a choice." KEEP THE MINI ON THE MARKET and LEGS! LEGS! LEGS! said the placards carried by demonstrating members of Girls Against More Skirt (GAMS). Some of them suggested that the midi was a plot against Women's Lib, that the designers were trying to isolate the feminists by bringing femininity back; others blamed older matrons whose legs weren't sexy any more and who wanted to make nubile girls hide theirs. Gilman Ostrander, a social historian, said the falling stock market was responsible for the midi, and that it was bound to prevail: "The middle-aged, who like long skirts, determine social standards in times of depression or recession. And young people, who like short skirts, determine standards in times of prosperity."

By winter the stock market had gone up, however, and the fashion industry's enthusiasm for the midi had plunged. A *New York Times* survey

*See above, pages 422–424.

found that while a few shop owners gallantly professed faith in the longer look ("It's here! Everybody's accepting and loving and buying it!"), most conceded that it had failed wretchedly: "Stores that last fall said they bought lots of midis are now saying they didn't really. What they did buy didn't sell very well. And women's knees are not yet obsolete." To be sure, more skirts covered the knee. But the dress designers had insisted that the midi was a specific length, measuring 44 to 45 inches from shoulder to hem, which put it at mid-calf for most women. The *Times* found that only 20 percent of dresses sold at that length, and at the end of the year just 5 percent of the women were wearing them. The other frocks had been returned for shortening or left in the closet.

Bitter retailers said the style had "bombed," or "laid an egg"; one said it "certainly did fashion a disservice and didn't take as a look," and another told a newswoman, "Our customers didn't want it. . . . We were never really able to sell it." The massive attempt to push the calf-length hem did trigger an unintended sartorial shift, however. "The midi," said the *Times,* "virtually killed the dress . . . suddenly there were kickers, gauchos, and pants, pants, pants." Older women bought pantsuits, and their daughters kept their bare knees by donning very short shorts. Bergdorf Goodman called the shorts "cool pants." *Women's Wear Daily,* closer to the mood of the new women, gave them the name that stuck: hotpants.

The streak of violence which had blighted Johnson's administration continued under Nixon, growing, if anything, more lurid. The great metropolitan ghettos continued to be relatively quiet, but the assassin and the pyromaniac now moved with murderous stealth in the black neighborhoods of smaller cities. Six Negroes were shot to death in Augusta, Georgia. A boy was stabbed in an Oklahoma City racial incident. A church which had been used for civil rights meetings in Carthage, Mississippi, was bombed. And there were riots in East Los Angeles, Miami, Houston, Highland Park, Michigan; Michigan City, Indiana; New Bedford, Massachusetts; Asbury Park, New Jersey; South Melbourne, Florida; Aliquippa, Pennsylvania; Oxford, North Carolina; Hot Springs, Arkansas; River Rouge, Michigan; Cairo, Illinois; and three Georgia communities: Perry, Macon, and Athens.

In New York bomb threats were running at a thousand a month. Over a fifteen-month period 368 of the devices had actually exploded in the city, one of them in a second-floor men's room at police headquarters, and Commissioner Howard Leary told a U.S. Senate subcommittee that he could not guarantee the safety of visitors to precinct stations. At times it seemed as though an open season had been declared on American policemen. In 1970 the FBI reported 35,202 assaults on them, almost quadruple the number in 1960, and fifteen officers were killed, most of them by ambushers, in nine months of the year.

The Little Rock police chief said attacks on cops had become "practically a daily occurrence . . . It seemed everyone from school age on up is assaulting police officers." Commissioner Frank L. Rizzo of Philadelphia said, "We are dealing with a group of fanatics — psychopaths," and the director of public safety in Omaha suggested that "the problem being experienced by police departments throughout the nation gives all indications that there is a conspiracy. The timing gives another indication. We are piecing together all the information available and we hope to prove a conspiracy." He didn't do it, and most law enforcement officials thought it wasn't possible — "We look upon the assaults as separate and independent incidents," Leary said — but there was general agreement that at a time when authority was under widespread attack, cops were inevitable targets. As Quinn Tamm of the International Association of Chiefs of Police put it: "Attacks on police are becoming more and more violent as radical groups exhort their members to 'kill the pigs' . . . That blue uniform makes the wearer a highly visible representative of the establishment."

Hostility to the established order was responsible for the bombings. In some instances the bombers boasted about it. After blasts tore into the Manhattan offices of International Business Machines, the General Telephone and Electronics Corporation, and Mobil Oil, a group called Revolutionary Force 9 took credit for them, declaring that the firms were profiteering in Vietnam. In other cases the terrorists, not being skilled in the use of explosives, blew themselves up. Within a month of the IBM, General Telephone, and Mobil eruptions one revolutionist was killed and another gravely injured when their bomb factory fulminated in a tenement on New York's Lower East Side. In Baltimore two black militants, protégés of H. Rap Brown, died after one of their bombs detonated prematurely in their automobile. And on March 6 Greenwich Village was rocked by the most sensational bomb disaster of 1970, killing three young nihilists and involving the names of several wealthy families.

Cathlyn Platt Wilkerson was a recent graduate of Swarthmore; Diana Oughton and Kathy Boudin were Bryn Mawr alumnae; all three were Weatherwomen. Diana was the daughter of an ultraconservative, highly respectable Illinois multimillionaire whose extraordinary family estate had been visited by King Edward VII, then Prince of Wales, a century earlier. Kathy was the niece of I. F. Stone. Her father, Leonard B. Boudin, was a famous lawyer whose clients included Paul Robeson, Judith Coplon, and Julian Bond; later he would defend Daniel Ellsberg. Cathlyn's father owned a chain of radio stations. He and his second wife were on holiday in the Caribbean that month. In his absence Cathlyn was entertaining Diana and Kathy, Ted Gold, who had been active in Columbia's SDS chapter, and another young man — whose identity was to remain a mystery — in the elegant $100,000 Wilkerson town house at 18 West Eleventh Street in Manhattan.

At noon on the day of the catastrophe the sky was clear and sunny over New York, with just a suggestion of approaching spring in the air. No one was in the house next door, which belonged to Dustin Hoffman, the actor, and number 18 appeared to be quiet. Inside, however, the young revolutionaries were busy. Two current Weatherman slogans were "If you don't believe in guns and violence, then you aren't a revolutionary" and "Bring the war home." On Monday one of the boys, dressed as a priest, had driven to New Hampshire to buy two cases of dynamite. Now fifty-seven sticks of TNT were strewn about in a makeshift basement workshop, together with friction tape, roofing nails, clockwork timing mechanisms, doorbell wire, thirty blasting tapes, and lengths of plumbing pipe meant to contain the charges.

Probably no one will ever know exactly what went wrong, but somebody bungled and set the lot off. It may have been Diana; her body was the most mutilated — the head, both hands and a foot were blown off, and the torso was riddled with roofing nails. Gold and the unidentified youth were also dead. The first explosion ripped through the living room wall of Hoffman's house, shattered windows across the street, and rocked a kitchen sixteen doors away. Then the gas mains ignited, touching off two more blasts, and the floors started to collapse.

Inside, stunned and bleeding, were Cathlyn and Kathy, one of them naked and the other partially dressed. Two policemen and a retired fireman — "the girls," John Neary wryly noted in *Life*, "would have called them 'pigs'" — came to their rescue, and a neighbor gave them the use of her shower and loaned them clothing. Then they disappeared. At first firemen thought leaking gas was responsible for the disaster. Then they found the dynamite, the blasting caps, and stacks of SDS pamphlets. Suddenly they wanted to question the survivors. New York authorities learned that Kathy and Cathlyn were out on bail after indictment in Chicago for participating in the Weathermen's Days of Rage the previous October. When they failed to appear there for trial March 16 the FBI joined the hunt. Their families said the girls had sent word that they were alive but gave no details.

On the other side of the country a weird blend of radical politics and witchcraft was blamed for the worst mass murder in California since the Manson killings. Sheriff's deputies on a routine patrol saw flames in the $250,000 home of Dr. Victor Ohta, an eye surgeon, overlooking Monterey Bay. They called firemen, who went to the Ohta swimming pool in search of water and there found the bodies of the surgeon, his wife, their two sons, and the doctor's secretary. All had been tied up with gaudy scarves and shot in the back of the head. Police found a scribbled message under the windshield wiper of the surgeon's car: "From this day forward anyone . . . who misuses the natural environment or destroys same will suffer the penalty of death. . . . I and my comrades from this day forth will fight until death or freedom against anything or anyone who does not support natural life on this planet. Materialism must die or mankind will stop." The signature was taken from tarot cards: "Knight of Wands, Knight of Cups, Knight of Pentacles, Knight of Swords." The signer, found living in a ramshackle hut a half-mile away, was a bearded youth named John F. Frazier. Frazier's lawyer said that his client had hurt his head in a car accident and had then "changed radically."

That year's most famous black advocate of revolutionary action in California was a dusky twenty-six-year-old beauty, Angela Davis. A daughter of the black middle class, she had been a Birmingham Girl Scout, apparently contented with society until four of her Negro girlfriends were killed in the September 1963 bombing of a church there. At Brandeis University, where she was elected to Phi Beta Kappa, she became an enthusiastic reader of Marx and Herbert Marcuse, and after graduate work at the Sorbonne and in Germany she became Marcuse's student on the San Diego campus of the University of California. There she joined the Black Panthers and the Communist Party. In one speech she told undergraduates that "the government has to be overthrown"; in another she said that "revolution must be tied to dealing with specific problems now, not a lot of rhetoric about revolution, but real, fundamental problems." She participated in the storming of a campus building in San Diego and was arrested for refusing to leave a police station.

As an assistant professor on the university's Los Angeles campus she was teaching philosophy when, in April 1970, Governor Reagan's Board of Regents voted to fire her, citing a board resolution barring Communists from the faculty. Since both the California and U.S. Supreme Courts had held that Communist membership was insufficient reason to disqualify a professor from teaching in a state university, the board changed the grounds for dismissal to incompetence. A majority of students and UCLA faculty members took Angela's side. Her fellow professors adopted a resolution expressing "our shock, our dismay, our rage" at her removal. They voted to defy the regents by keeping her on the faculty, and the issue was unresolved when a new development put her case in an entirely different light.

As a black militant, Angela had been among those who were agitating for the release of the "Soledad Brothers" — three Negro prisoners, not actually related to one another, who had been charged with killing a white guard at Soledad Prison on January 16. The most interesting of the three was George Jackson, twenty-seven, who was serving five years to life for a 1961 filling station robbery. As the author of *Soledad Brother,* a collection of his prison letters, Jackson would become one of the most famous convicts in the country that fall. Some of the most moving notes in the book were written to Angela, who had first seen him during a hearing in a Salinas courtroom that May. In her own letters to him, and in a diary, she declared that she had "spontaneously" fallen in love with him. She called herself his "lifelong wife" and said she would dedicate her life to freeing him. She added that she didn't care what means she used, a passage which aroused much subsequent interest.

In the first week of August Angela was seen frequently in the company of Jonathan Jackson, George's seventeen-year-old brother. Three guns she owned found their way into Jonathan's possession; so did a twelve-gauge sawed-off shotgun she bought on August 5. That was a Wednesday. On Thursday she and Jonathan were driving around in a small, bright yellow enclosed Ford panel truck he had rented the day before. On Friday the van was parked in a lot outside the San Rafael courthouse, thirteen miles north-west of San Francisco. Minutes later Jonathan, slim and intense, entered a courtroom wearing a raincoat and carrying a small bag.

On the stand at the time was Ruchell Magee, a San Quentin convict who was testifying in the case of James McLain, a fellow prisoner accused of stabbing a guard. Another black inmate, William Christmas, was waiting to be called. Magee, McLain, and Christmas were powerfully built young men, and McLain, who was sitting at the counsel's table, was known at San Quentin as a firebrand, an agitator, and a Panther. Superior Court Judge Harold J. Haley was on the bench. The deputy district attorney was Gary W. Thomas, who was married to the judge's niece. There was a jury, but young Jackson was the only spectator. It was a boring case.

It became much livelier when Jonathan unzipped his bag, drew out one of Angela's revolvers, and slipped a 30-caliber carbine from under his raincoat. "This is it!" he yelled. "I've got an automatic weapon. Everybody freeze!" He ordered the unarmed bailiffs to unlock the handcuffs on McLain, Magee, and Christmas, and handed each of the three unshackled convicts a weapon. He gave the shotgun to McLain, who taped it around the judge's neck so that the muzzle hung a few inches from Haley's chin. The other prisoners tied Thomas and three women jurors together with piano wire. McLain commanded the judge to call the sheriff's office and direct him to give the inmates safe passage out. "I am in the courtroom," Haley said into the telephone on the bench. "There are a number of armed convicts here." McLain grabbed the phone and shouted into it, "You're going to call off your pig dogs. We're going to get out of here. Call them off!"

Herding the hostages before them, the blacks paused before the press room, fifty feet down the hall, but the door was locked. As they continued down the corridor McLain called, "We want the Soledad Brothers released by twelve-thirty today!" In the parking lot they shoved the five hostages into the Ford van. McLain slid behind the wheel; Jonathan gave him the keys; Magee took over the guarding of the judge, and they headed for U.S. 101, about two hundred yards away. Watching them were some hundred law enforcement officers, crouched behind other vehicles and the building. Suddenly a San Quentin guard darted in front of the panel truck and yelled, "Halt!"

The next minute was madness, with gunfire pouring into the panel truck and out from it. At one point the shotgun roared in the back of the van. That was the end for the judge; his jaw and part of his face were blown off. Thomas had a bullet in his spine; he would be paralyzed from the waist down for the rest of his life. One of the jurors was wounded in the arm. Magee had been shot in the chest but was still alive. McLain, Christmas, and Jonathan Jackson were dead.

Three hours later Angela Davis bought an airplane ticket at the San Francisco terminal. Then she vanished.

Under California law, anyone abetting a killer before the act is equally guilty of murder, and a warrant was issued for her arrest. Panther leader Huey P. Newton said he believed that she had been responsible for the courthouse shootings, was proud of her, and hoped others would follow her "courageous example." Charles Garry, a white attorney for the Panthers, cried, "More power to Angela Davis! May she live long in liberty." In fact she remained at large for over two months. On October 13 FBI agents arrested her in Manhattan after she had checked into a Howard Johnson's motel with David Rudolph Poindexter Jr., a wealthy Negro. Poindexter was charged with harboring a fugitive; Angela was extradited and lodged in a San Rafael prison less than five miles from George Jackson's cell in San Quentin.

Nearly a year later, on a hot August day in 1971, Jackson received a visit from his lawyer, Stephen Mitchell Bingham. Bingham was white, a Yale alumnus, and the grandson of Hiram Bingham, who had served Connecticut as governor and U.S. senator. Prison officials later became convinced that the younger Bingham, who had been active in the cause of minority groups, was on a smuggling mission that day. He was carrying two parcels which guards did not search: an expanding brown envelope and a small portable tape recorder. After he completed an hour-long session with Jackson and left, a guard noticed something different about the convict's Afro hairdo. Asked about it, the Negro yanked off a wig and pulled a small automatic pistol from it.

Terror and death followed. On Jackson's orders, twenty-seven prisoners, including the convalescing Ruchell Magee, were released. Then three white guards and two white trusties were murdered; two were shot in the back of the head, and the throats of the others were cut with a dull razor blade. The corpses were piled in a corner of Jackson's cell like bloody rugs. By now San Quentin's sirens were screaming. Still holding the pistol, Jackson bolted out a door and sprinted some seventy-five feet across an open courtyard before sharpshooters in the towers overhead cut him down.

Stephen Bingham was indicted for the murder of the guards and the trusties — the county district attorney said, "There is no way Jackson could have gotten the death gun except during his visit with Bingham" — but he disappeared without a trace, and by the following year authorities were suggesting that he might be dead: that black militants, having used him, may have then killed him. Law enforcement officers were embittered by the deaths of August 21. Negro activists were also outraged. Jackson became a martyr to them. His body was dressed in the Panther uniform — black leather jacket, black beret, and black shirt — and buried beside that of Jonathan. Julian Bond spoke of his "assassination" and of "the expected outcome of his constant attacks on a vicious system which was unable to crush his spirit or his body." California Assemblyman Willie Brown said, "The people in the street are saying this is an execution, that it's ridiculous Jackson could hide a gun in his hair," and Angela Davis wrote of "the loss of an irretrievable love."

Angela's trial in the late spring of 1972 was an international event. Her elegant profile, with the high cheekbones and vast Afro coiffure — she had cut it off while a fugitive, but it had grown back — adorned posters around the world. Militant slogans called her a "political prisoner" and demanded "Free Angela!" The prosecution, protesting that the proceedings had nothing to do with politics or race, that this was a criminal trial, submitted 201 exhibits and testimony from ninety-five witnesses. Three people identified her as Jonathan's companion at a gas station across the street from the courthouse the day before the escape attempt, and others put her with him on each of the three days beforehand.

The defense presented testimony from twelve witnesses (Angela chose not to take the stand) and ridiculed the idea that "a brilliant college professor" could have been implicated in such a harebrained scheme. She and Jonathan hadn't been together as often as some people claimed, her lawyers said. Admittedly she had given him the shotgun, but it had been with the understanding that he would use it only to guard the headquarters of the Soledad Brothers Defense Committee. She had kept the other weapons on a rack in her home for target practice by members of the Che-Lumumba Club. Jonathan had visited her there six days before the courthouse tragedy; probably he had stolen them then.

The attorney presenting the defense summation said that the only evidence against her was "that Angela was closely related to Jonathan Jackson, that her guns were used, that she expressed a desire to free the Soledad Brothers, that Angela expressed love for George Jackson, and that on August 7 Angela made herself unavailable to the authorities." The jury would have fled, too, the lawyer declared, if they had been Negro and had discovered that four guns they owned had been used in the escape attempt at the courthouse: "I say to you, when you look at the situation through the eyes of a black person, you would not wonder why she fled. You would only wonder why she allowed herself to be caught."

After thirteen hours of deliberation the panel found her not guilty. Turning her back on the jurors, Angela left the courtroom to address her admirers outside. A reporter asked her if she thought she had received a fair trial. She said she didn't. "The very fact of an acquittal," she said, "means that there was no fair trial, because a fair trial would have been no trial at all." Setting out on a triumphant tour of the country, she told her supporters: "Starting from this day forward, we must work to free every political prisoner and every oppressed person in this country and the whole world."

Four weeks after the Soledad murder, which had started the chain of events that culminated in Angela's fame, Chicago had witnessed the end of another remarkable trial. It had opened with eight defendants: Yippies Jerry Rubin and Abbie Hoffman; Rennie Davis, David Dellinger, and SDS's Tom Hayden, the three leaders of the National Mobilization Committee which had brought the antiwar demonstrators to Chicago; Bobby Seale of the Panthers; and Lee Weiner and John R. Froines. Before their arrests some of the defendants had scarcely known one another, and in fact the key complaint against them was not the conspiracy count, but the accusation that they had entered Illinois individually to incite a riot — "crossing state lines with a state of mind," said chief counsel William M. Kunstler, while Leonard I. Weinglass, their other attorney, called the statute — which had been passed as a rider to the 1968 Civil Rights Act — "the only federal law where the government can punish someone without the commission of an overt act." They were the first defendants to be indicted under it, though that fact and a great many others were forgotten during the circus into which the proceedings deteriorated.

Kunstler set the tone on the first day of the trial, when he moved for a mistrial because of the way Judge Julius J. Hoffman read the charges to the jury. "Your Honor sounded like Orson Welles reciting the Declaration of Independence," said the lawyer.

"I've never been compared to that great actor, Orson Welles," said the judge, "but I deny the motion."

Altogether, the defense would make more than a score of mistrial motions, and to a great degree the tempestuous character of the proceedings arose from the chasm between Kunstler, Weinglass, and their clients on the one hand, and Judge Hoffman and the state's attorneys on the other. "The trial," wrote Richard Ciccone of the AP Chicago Bureau, "was a collision of generations, ideologies, and life-styles." Judge Hoffman wore a vest; Abbie Hoffman wore love beads and buckskin, and during one uproarious session he and Rubin appeared in judicial robes. Rubin and Hoffman had beards. The defendants and their lawyers grew their hair long, a fact caustically noted by the well-barbered prosecutors, Thomas A. Foran and Richard G. Schultz.

At one point, when Allen Ginsberg was testifying for the defense, the witness showed how he had quieted antiwar Chicago demonstrators in 1968 — with a ten-second grunt: "Ah-ooom!" Kunstler protested that the judge was laughing. His Honor denied it. "I just don't understand the language," he said. Ginsberg explained, "It's Sanskrit." The judge said, "That's one I don't know." The transcript shows that there was a great deal the court did not know, but Hoffman did have a clear concept of the decorum which should be observed in his courtroom. During the seventy-four years since his birth in a humble Chicago neighborhood he had come to expect respect from the people who came before him, and neither the Chicago Eight nor their defense staff gave it to him. The first signs of what lay ahead came during a pretrial hearing. Kunstler and Weinglass wanted to ask veniremen how they felt about protest demonstrations, American slums, and the Vietnam War. Judge Hoffman turned them down; he said they couldn't even ask prospective jurors their opinion of hippies and Yippies. The next defense request was for a postponement of the trial until Seale's attorney, Charles Garry, could recover from an operation. Hoffman rejected that, too, and when he followed it by denying Seale's appeal for the right to address the court, telling him that he would have to allow Kunstler to speak for him, he touched off judicial chaos.

"I can only see the judge as a blatant racist," Seale said. The dwarfish judge bounded to his feet. "Did you hear that?" he asked a clerk in disbelief. The Panther leader was cautioned, then and repeatedly afterward, that interruptions would be "dealt with appropriately at some time in the future." Seale retorted, "What can you do to me that hasn't been done to black people for three hundred years?" In the eighth week of the trial the judge started to respond to a series of Seale outbursts: "Look, young man, if you keep this up —" Seale replied: "Look, old man, if you keep denying me my constitutional rights you are being exposed to the world —" Hoffman said: "Mr. Seale, do you want to stop or do you want me to direct the marshal —" Seale said: "I want to argue about this so you can get an understanding of the facts."

His patience exhausted, the judge told the marshal, "Take that defendant into the room there and deal with him as he should be dealt with." After a recess the Panther was carried in gagged and handcuffed to a metal folding chair. Even that didn't silence him. He rattled his fetters against the chair and cried in a muffled voice, "That means I object!" He was moved to a wooden chair and the gag was tightened. At the next session he managed to work free of the gag and shout at the bench: "You fascist dog, you rotten low-life son-of-a-bitch!" Abbie Hoffman and Rubin jumped up, screaming, and Kunstler asked the court: "Your Honor, when are we going to stop this medieval torture? This is an unholy disgrace to the law ... I feel so utterly ashamed at this time to be an American lawyer." Judge Hoffman, who had frequently said that he blamed Kunstler and Weinglass for the misconduct of his clients, snapped: "You should be." The following week he ordered the gag removed, and when Seale persisted in his interruptions he sentenced him to four years in prison for contempt. Now those left were christened the Chicago Seven.

They weren't chastened. While Davis was on the stand he accused the judge of being asleep — His Honor warned him that his insolence would be "dealt with appropriately at some time in the future" — and Abbie Hoffman created pandemonium by coming into the courtroom walking on his hands and calling Judge Hoffman a "tyrant," a "Nazi," and "a disgrace to the Jews."

The sharpest exchanges were between the court and the chief defense counsel. The judge explicitly directed Kunstler not to ask in the presence of the jury that Mayor Daley — who had insisted the trial be held despite Justice Department doubts — be declared a hostile witness. The attorney did it anyway, and he almost gave the judge apoplexy by asking Daley pointblank whether he had shouted an obscenity at Senator Abraham Ribicoff during the convention. At one point Abbie Hoffman raised his shirt. "Let the record show," the judge said, "that man bared his body in open court." Kunstler said, "Your Honor, I remember when President Johnson showed his stomach scar to a whole nation on television." "Maybe that's why he isn't President any more," His Honor replied. When the lawyer chuckled and was rebuked he said, "Come on, Your Honor, what's the harm in laughter? Sometimes we can't help ourselves." The judge said, "Oh yes, I can see that you can't help yourself."

Toward the end of the trial the court's hostility toward the defendants became flagrant. For two days Hoffman refused to let them use the toilet in the hall; the latrine in the jail, he said, was good enough for them. One day he said they would start a half-hour earlier the following morning. When Kunstler asked the reason he was told, "Because it will be at nine-thirty." The lawyer commented, "That's like a child saying, 'Because, because.'" The judge said, "Let the record show that, in the presence of the jury, Mr. Kunstler compared me to a child." The lawyer was effusive in court, often hilarious or in tears. Sometimes he hugged men, and he kissed Weinglass and one of the witnesses, the Reverend Ralph D. Abernathy. "Let the record show," Judge Hoffman said acidly each time, "that Mr. Kunstler kissed that man." As the end of the trial was to prove, his reasons for these insertions in the transcript were not frivolous.

Defense witnesses included Pete Seeger, William Styron, Judy Collins, Norman Mailer, Julian Bond, Reverend Jesse Jackson, Terry Southern, and Ginsberg, who at Prosecutor Foran's insistence read aloud some of his poems on homosexuality and masturbation, apparently because Foran thought they would offend the ten women jurors. Kunstler and Weinglass argued that Daley and the Chicago police had provoked the violence at the Democratic convention.

Most of the evidence against the Seven came from informers who had mingled with the antiwar demonstrators in Lincoln and Grant parks and had taken everything they heard literally. An undercover policewoman testified that Abbie Hoffman had yelled: "We need a lot of weapons. Get rocks, bricks, stones. Break the bricks in half — they're easier to conceal that way and the girls can carry them." An undercover policeman said the defendants had been determined to create violence as "the first step of the revolution." A Chicago official told the court that Abbie had said to him: "If the city was smart, it would give $100,000 to sponsor our festival.

Better yet, give me $100,000 and I'll leave town." The official had construed this as attempted extortion.

After nearly five months of testimony and argument the jury retired and the judge, with obvious relish, began meting out sentences for contempt. It took him two days, with time out for the defendants' screams. As Kunstler heard his clients and his co-counsel being sent away — Weinglass was given two months — he staggered all over the courtroom and collapsed, sobbing, "My life has come to naught at your hands, Judge. Come to mine. Come to mine. Take me next, I don't want to be here any more." The judge took him last. Saying, "No lawyer has ever said the things to me that you said during this trial," he gave him four years and thirteen days in prison.

The jury acquitted all the defendants of conspiracy but convicted Davis, Dellinger, Hayden, Hoffman, and Rubin of crossing state lines to incite a riot. The judge sentenced each of them to five years in prison, fined each $5,000, and assessed them the costs of the prosecution — another $50,000. But the sentences didn't stand. Nearly three years later a U.S. Court of Appeals reversed the convictions. The appellate court found the controversial antiriot statute — the so-called Rap Brown Act — constitutional by a two to one vote but threw out the verdict, citing Judge Hoffman's "antagonistic" behavior and finding that his "deprecatory" attitude toward the defense was "evident in the record from the very beginning."

Indeed, far from vindicating the prosecution, the case of the Chicago Seven became the first of an unparalleled series of judicial disasters for the government. It was followed by the trials of the Harrisburg Seven, the Camden Seventeen, the Seattle Seven, the Kansas City Four, the Evanston Four, the Pentagon Papers case, and the Gainesville Eight. In each of them the defendants were heretics in the eyes of the established order, and in every case the accused were vindicated by a jury, a judge, or an appeals court. Hostility to informers and judicial bias were common threads in the findings. In addition, as Martin Arnold pointed out in the *New York Times*, "despite all evidence to the contrary, people generally believe that the government is competent, and it angers them when the government goes into court with a weak case, often incompetently presented."

The Vietnam War, the real fuel for the riots which had been blamed on the Seven, continued to divide and abrade the country in 1970. At the beginning of the year there had been hope for something better. During the first four months the news from Saigon had been mildly encouraging. U.S. troops under General Abrams were avoiding big battles with the Viet Cong and the North Vietnamese. Nixon was reducing American troops from 543,000 to 340,000, and he assured the country that another 60,000 grunts would be withdrawn by May 1. But an end to the war seemed as remote as ever. In Paris the Communists scorned a five-point Nixon peace proposal, saying, "Our rejection is firm, total, and categorical." David K. E.

Bruce, the chief American negotiator, turned down a Communist plan, calling it "old wine in new bottles."

U.S. combat deaths, which had stood at 25,000 during the Chicago protests two years earlier, now passed the 44,000 mark. Barring a breakthrough, Washington let it be known, some 200,000 American soldiers would stay in Vietnam for years. War weariness was becoming increasingly evident in the United States, among the South Vietnamese, and in fighting units. Grunts in the 4th U.S. Division refused to go into battle until they had been persuaded by desperate officers; troops in another division reviled Nixon, shouting obscenities about him when they spotted a war correspondent; soldiers wore peace medals with their dog tags; estimates of marijuana use among U.S. servicemen ran as high as 80 percent, while deaths from overdoses of hard drugs almost tripled. Augmenting all this was an appearance of incompetence at the highest levels of the American military effort. U.S. paratroopers executed a daring raid on a POW camp at Son Tay, twenty-three miles from Hanoi; seventy to a hundred American fliers were believed to be imprisoned there. The raid would have been a success, but intelligence had blundered — all the POWs had been moved. That same week U.S. warplanes pounded North Vietnam for twenty-four hours. The Pentagon first said the sorties were part of a "protective reaction" operation, protecting unarmed American aircraft, then changed its story to acknowledge that supply bases were being attacked. In fact, the shocked nation later learned, the targets of the bombardiers had included hospitals.

Abandonment of the Saigon government was out of the question, the White House declared, because the Communists were said to have a list of three million Vietnamese who would be "dealt with" in a "blood bath." The existence of the list was a matter of some skepticism, and Americans in increasing numbers were ready to desert the regime of General Nguyen Van Thieu anyway. The South Vietnamese seemed unappreciative of their American ally, even hostile toward it. Saigon rioters burned Nixon in effigy, shouting "Down with the Americans" and accusing the United States of prolonging the war. Ominously, Buddhists with kerosene and matches were immolating themselves, as other bonzes had just before the overthrow of Ngo Dinh Diem. David Truong, the son of a South Vietnamese politician, toured the U.S. telling audiences that the grunts and the ARVN troops fighting beside them shared only a mutual hatred of each other.

Meantime the notion that Americans were fighting to defend an Asian democracy was becoming difficult to sustain. David's father ran against Thieu and was clapped in jail, becoming one of over 80,000 political prisoners of the Saigon government. Americans in the field reported the torture of the regime's critics and their convictions by kangaroo courts; the courts continued to sit even after Saigon's supreme court ruled that they were unconstitutional. And Thieu's demands for U.S. wealth appeared to be insatiable. After nearly a decade of unstinting support of Saigon by

Washington, he continued to say that he needed more equipment from the United States, more time to train his troops, and a lot more money. Unless he got them, he said, he couldn't take responsibility for the consequences.

The last thing Americans wanted that year was a war in another Southeast Asian country, but that was what the administration gave them. Actually their Air Force had been hammering Communist bases in eastern Cambodia for over a year, though few of them knew it. On orders from the White House, B-52s had conducted 3,630 secret raids on jungle sanctuaries there. The Joint Chiefs had long wanted to send in the infantry. Nixon had demurred at that; he knew that Cambodia's ruler, Prince Norodom Sihanouk, would protest the violation of his country's neutrality. With double bookkeeping and tight security it was possible to suppress information about the B-52 sorties. Once U.S. troops lunged across the frontier that would be impracticable.

On March 18, however, the Cambodian situation was changed dramatically by a coup. Sihanouk, aware that his administration was threatened, was in Russia asking for Soviet help in his effort to get 40,000 Viet Cong and North Vietnamese troops out of his country, when Cambodian General Lon Nol took over the government. Lon Nol was a rightist; he wouldn't denounce a U.S.–ARVN expedition to drive out the Communist intruders. Six weeks after the coup Nixon went on television to tell Americans that an operation to do just that was under way. Its goal was to be the destruction of the Vietnam nerve center, base camps, and underground arsenals above the "Parrot's Beak" northwest of Saigon. "For five years," the President said, "neither the United States nor South Vietnam has moved against these sanctuaries because we did not want to violate the territory of a neutral nation." He did not mention the clandestine bombing of Cambodia, which at that time had been in process for fourteen months.

The military value of the invasion of Cambodia was disputed. While it was still being mounted Nixon described it as "an enormous success — far exceeding expectations." Asked about Pentagon claims that the Viet Cong would need six to nine months to recover from it, Thieu said, "I say they will never recover. Cambodia from 1964 to 1969 was a second North Vietnam, a whole rear area." In Saigon, MACV claimed the seizure of 15 million rounds of ammunition, 7,250 tons of food, and 25,000 guns; the death of 11,285 enemy soldiers; and the capture of 2,156. Allied casualties were 1,138 killed and 4,911 wounded.

But now Cambodia had been drawn into the war. The Communist troops which had been squatting in the Parrot's Beak responded to the offensive by driving westward against Lon Nol's army, conquering half the country, threatening its capital, Phnom Penh, and establishing a new, secure supply route in the Mekong valley. Washington was now committed to a new regime which was even less defensible than Thieu's. And some of the expedition's Cambodian goals were unachieved because they had been wholly unrealistic. "American officials," Frances FitzGerald noted in *Fire in the Lake*, "spoke of plans to capture the enemy's command headquarters for the south as if there existed a reverse Pentagon in the jungle complete with Marine guards, generals, and green baize tables." No such command post was found because, of course, there had never been any.

The greatest damage wrought by the Cambodian adventure was its impact on the home front. So great was the public outcry against this new involvement that the Senate, stirring at last to invoke the congressional right to declare war, passed a measure demanding an evacuation of American troops from Cambodia and an end to air support there by July. On campuses the reaction eclipsed all previous protests. By the end of May 415 colleges and universities had been disrupted. It was the first general student strike in the country's history, and it was entirely spontaneous. At the end of the semester 286 schools were still paralyzed, and while 129 others in forty-three states had officially reopened, many classrooms were empty.

On the weekend of May 9–10, more than 100,000 students stormed Washington. The White House was transformed into an armed camp behind a bumper-to-bumper wall of transit buses. The President's first response was contemptuous; talking informally with some Pentagon secretaries, he called the protesters "bums." Then he decided to make a conciliatory gesture. On Friday night of that week he went to the Lincoln Memorial with his valet and Secret Service agents and tried to talk to students sleeping there. "I feel just as deeply as you do about this," he said to them. Trying to find common ground, he launched into a discussion of football and asked one of the students, a Californian, if he enjoyed surfing. "The two Americas," wrote a team of reporters for the London *Sunday Times*, "met and drifted apart in a state of mutual incomprehension."

Equally bewildering for the President was a letter to him from Secretary of the Interior Walter J. Hickel. Hickel had been a conversative businessman, but he was also the father of six sons. He protested that the administration was alienating youth. He was particularly incensed over attacks on the young by Vice President Agnew. Nixon's public response was propitiatory; he assured the secretary that members of the administration would cool their rhetoric. But Hickel had committed a cardinal sin. His letter had appeared in the newspapers before it reached the oval office. On Thanksgiving eve Nixon summoned him to the White House and fired him for lack of "mutual confidence." Within a few hours one of H. R. Haldeman's assistants arrived at the Department of the Interior with a list of men to be purged. Six senior officials were told: "We want your resignation, and we want you out of the building by five o'clock."

If that was tough, the actions on some campuses were rougher. A revolutionist's bomb tore out the sides of the University of Wisconsin's Army

Mathematics Research Center, killing a physicist, wounding four, and doing six million dollars' worth of damage.* At predominantly black Jackson State, in Mississippi, an encounter between students and police in front of a dormitory ended tragically when officers opened fire with buckshot, machine gun, rifle and armor-piercing shells, killing two students and wounding nine. A presidential commission headed by former Pennsylvania Governor William W. Scranton called the 28-second fusillade "an unreasonable, unjustified overreaction," but a local grand jury blamed the students, declaring that "when people . . . engage in civil disorders and riots, they must expect to be injured or killed when law enforcement officers are required to reestablish order."

Mississippians weren't the only Americans in that troubled year to feel that students were fair game, and Negroes weren't the only victims. Flag-carrying hardhat Manhattan construction workers who marched into a crowd of antiwar demonstrators that May were enormously popular; when the White House commended them it was interpreted as smart politics. Hostility toward youth cut deep. Older Americans were offended by almost every facet of the youthful subculture: the long hair, the tie-dyed jeans, the loud music, the language, the gestures, the very names of the rock groups — the Cream, the Stones, the Grand Funk Railroad. Most objectionable of all were the heavy drugs. The college students, whom younger teen-agers slavishly aped, put up outrageous psychedelic posters of bleeding colors and distorted images; they spoke casually of getting spaced out, turned on, tuned in, getting it on, getting into it, getting funky or freaky or heavy from narcotics, and they lured adolescents away from parents with rock jamborees which appeared to be, and sometimes were, steeped in sin.

Woodstock had been the high-water mark for the rock bacchanals. According to John Morthland, assistant editor of the weekly *Rolling Stone,* of the forty-eight major festivals slated the following year, only eighteen were held. "The major reason," said Morthland, "is political. The day after a festival is announced, the city council and police come up with some emergency ordinance that makes it impossible to hold it." Authorities taking such steps were acting with the approval — often the entreaties — of residents who had seen and heard enough of the subculture to know that they didn't want it celebrated in their backyards. They felt vindicated and then some by stories about 1970's most notorious rock gala: the Powder Ridge festival in Middlefield, Connecticut.

Actually Powder Ridge was a nongala; it never went on as scheduled. Promoters had signed up twenty-five bands to play at the three-hundred-acre ski area, but four days before the affair was to begin a citizens' committee convinced a judge that the tiny community didn't have to endure

---

*In November 1973 Karleton Lewis Armstrong, twenty-seven, was convicted of the bombing and sentenced to twenty-three years in prison. His counsel was William Kunstler.

the noise, the pot, the kids in the buff, and the Viet Cong flags. He issued an injunction. That turned the musicians away, but it was too late to stop the audience from gathering; the occasion had been advertised in underground newspapers as far away as Los Angeles, the throng was already on its way, and it arrived, 35,000 strong, on the Friday of that first weekend in August. No entertainment awaited it, no food, no adequate plumbing facilities. Powder Ridge was a disaster waiting to happen, and it happened.

The heat was sweltering, and after pitching their colorful tents the youths divested themselves of clothes. On the first day they swam nude in a small pond beside the ski lodge, but so many of them voided and defecated in it that on Saturday the pond was declared a health hazard. Sanitation was a concern of Dr. William Abruzzi, a bearded, bald physician who was there as a volunteer, but it wasn't his chief worry; that was narcotics. Peddlers roamed through the crowd hawking marijuana, cocaine, heroin ("only a dollar-five-oh for magic magic"), barbiturates, speed, and LSD ("Acid here, the quality goes in before the name goes on"). State police arrested seventy pushers leaving the crowd, one of them with $13,000 in his pocket, but most of them got away. Kids who couldn't afford the hucksters' prices could drink free from vast buckets of "electric water," into which passers-by were asked to drop any drugs they could spare. This ugly stew was blamed by Abruzzi for many of the thousand bad trips he treated, more than the number at Woodstock, where the multitude had been over ten times as large. Every Middlefield resident had tales of what the doped youngsters did. One of the more sensational scenes, attested to by several witnesses, occurred in a small wood near some homes. A boy and a girl, both naked and approaching from different directions, met under the trees. On impulse they suddenly embraced. She dropped to her knees, he mounted her from behind, and after he had achieved his climax they parted — apparently without exchanging a word.

Obviously Powder Ridge had nothing to do with antiwar protest, but to its critics the subculture of the young was all of a piece; any one aspect of it reminded them of the others. The most memorable symbol of college backlash in the days after Nixon's announcement of the Cambodian invasion, the Kent State tragedy, didn't start as a protest. By all accounts the first phases of the disorders there would have occurred anyhow. Unlike Columbia and Berkeley, the university in Kent, Ohio, had no tradition of activism. Football was still big in Kent; after a triumph students would ring the Victory Bell on the Commons. There were proms and bull-and-beer joints in the town. Indeed, the trouble started with a beer bust that muggy Friday night.

Spilling out from a bar, students decided to dance in the street. An angry motorist gunned his engine as if to drive into them. Several young drunks climbed on the car, broke its windows, set fires in trash barrels, and smashed store windows. On orders from Mayor LeRoy Satrom, Kent policemen turned the roisterers out of the taverns. Driving them back toward the campus, they broke up the diehards with tear gas. The next day Kent State's few political militants secured administration approval for a rally that evening. Out of an enrollment of nearly twenty thousand, about eight hundred students came. Shouting "One two three four, we don't want your fucking war!" at faculty members and student marshals, the crowd turned the rally into a demonstration. It got out of hand and disrupted a dance; lighted railroad flares were thrown through the windows of a one-story ROTC building facing the Commons. When firemen appeared, the demonstrators pelted them with rocks and chopped up their hoses with machetes. The building burned to the ground.

Without notifying the university administration, Mayor Satrom appealed for help from the National Guard. Governor James Rhodes responded by sending a five-hundred-man contingent equipped with M-1 rifles, Colt revolvers, and tear gas. Students greeted them by spraying trees with gasoline and setting them afire, but by midnight on Sunday the fires were out and everything seemed to be under control. Meantime Governor Rhodes had arrived on campus. On Tuesday Ohio Republicans were going to vote in a senatorial primary, and Rhodes was one of the candidates. He was trailing badly — in the event he would lose — but he was making a last effort to turn the tide. The situation in Kent seemed exploitable. Calling a press conference, he declared an emergency and said of the students, "We're going to use every weapon of law enforcement to drive them out of Kent . . . They're worse than the Brownshirts, and the Communist element and also the night riders and the vigilantes. They're the worst type of people that we harbor in America."

In fairness to Governor Rhodes, it should be pointed out that he was not the only student-baiter whose words reached the National Guardsmen. Attorney General Mitchell had attacked campus militants as rowdies; so had President Nixon and Vice President Agnew, who had been widely quoted as saying that "The troublemakers among the younger generation are only a bunch of hoodlums who don't deserve to bear the title of American youth." In Kent, Mayor Satrom was making inflammatory remarks, while Brigadier General Robert H. Canterbury of the Guard was virtually inciting to riot. Having sowed the wind, they reaped the whirlwind at noon Monday. Classes were resumed that day and the campus at first appeared to be quiet. Several students rang the Victory Bell at midday and about a thousand gathered for a peaceful demonstration on the Commons while another two thousand watched. Two jeeps appeared. Guardsmen in them shouted through bullhorns: "Evacuate the Commons area. You have no right to assemble." Students raised their middle fingers, flung some stones and yelled: "Pigs off campus! We don't want your war." Brigadier General Canterbury told reporters, "These students are going to have to find out what law and order is all about." Major General Sylvester Del Corso of the Guard, in full view of his troops, picked up several rocks and threw them back at students.

It was now about a quarter past twelve. Two skirmish lines of Guardsmen fired tear gas canisters into the crowd; a few students tossed them back, but they fell short. Other students fled, and a unit of about a hundred troopers chased some of them between two buildings. There the Guardsmen found themselves hemmed in, with a fence in front of them and rock-throwing students on either side. Their plight was not really serious; the rocks didn't come close enough to hit them, and many of the onlookers were laughing. At this point the troopers ran out of tear gas and began retreating up a hill, looking apprehensively over their shoulders. It was a dangerous situation. The Guardsmen were capable of savagery — over the weekend they had bayoneted three students — and their M-1 rifles were loaded with live ammunition. As a presidential commission headed by former Pennsylvania Governor William W. Scranton later put it, "all that stood between the Guardsmen and firing was a flick of a thumb on a safety mechanism and the pull of an index finger on a trigger."

There were suggestions afterward that a group of troopers decided to fire on their tormentors. Photographs show eight or ten of them gathered in what witnesses described as a "huddle." Another curious piece of evidence is a tape of the incident. On it, the fatal thirteen-second salvo is preceded by a single shot. This could have been fired, either as a signal or from fear, by Terence F. Norman, a spurious "freelance photographer" who was really an informer on the FBI payroll. (In addition he may have been in the employ of the university, which also had undercover men.) Norman had a gun, and some spectators say he drew it and fired it, either just before or just after the crucial moment. What is certain is that on reaching the top of the slope at 12:24 P.M. the troopers knelt, aimed at the students, who were hundreds of feet away, too far to harm them, and fired as though on command. (Brigadier General Canterbury, in their midst, managed to be looking the other way.) The fusillade was followed by an awful silence. Into it a girl screamed, "My God, they're killing us!"

Thirteen students had been shot, and four — none of them a militant and one an ROTC cadet — were dead. A stream of blood was gushing from the head of one youth, drenching the textbooks he had been carrying; another boy was holding a cloth against a friend's stomach, trying vainly to stem the bleeding. The troopers made no attempt to help their victims.

In the immediate aftermath none of them were prosecuted for the killings. Although Attorney General Mitchell declared that American education was experiencing the "saddest semester" in its history — "There can be no greater evidence of disorder in society than the sound of gunfire on a college campus," he said — and though an investigation by three hundred FBI agents concluded that the Guardsmen had been in no physical danger, and that they conspired afterward to blame the incident on a threatening mob which never existed, the Justice Department declined even to convene a federal grand jury. Long afterward this was done, but not until March of 1974 were eight indictments handed down.

At the time, an Ohio grand jury exonerated the troopers — and indicted instead twenty-five others, including the president of the student body. Although none of them were convicted, there was a widespread feeling that the victims had got what was coming to them. It was strengthened when President Nixon implied that violent protest had brought violence in return; the incident, he said, "should remind us once again that when dissent turns to violence it invites tragedy." The Scranton Commission said that "61 shots by Guardsmen certainly cannot be justified." Vice President Agnew called their report "pablum for permissiveness," and added that responsibility for what had happened lay with the students, "on the steps of the university administration, and at the door of the faculty lounge." Any other interpretation, he said, would be "scapegoating of the most irresponsible sort."

The campus disorders which greeted Nixon's announcement of the Cambodian adventure formed a key link in the chain of events which led, ultimately, to the burglarizing of the Democratic National Committee's offices in the Watergate complex in Washington two years later. The first link had been a story in the *New York Times* of May 19, 1969, under the byline of William Beecher, who covered the Defense Department for the paper. It began: "American B-52 bombers in recent weeks have raided several Vietcong and North Vietnamese supply dumps in Cambodia for the first time, according to Nixon administration sources, but Cambodia has not made any protest."

Nixon was dismayed. He felt that his worst fears about the irresponsibility of the eastern establishment press had been confirmed, and believed them reconfirmed when the *Times* published technical details of American preparation for the Strategic Arms Limitation Talks (SALT) talks with Russia. Under the Constitution there was little he could do about Beecher and his paper, but he could at least hunt the unknown informants in his administration who were leaking classified information to newspapermen. He consulted Henry Kissinger, who drew up a list of thirteen officials, including five of his own National Security Council aides, who knew about the secret Cambodian bombing. On orders from the President, their telephones were tapped by the FBI; so were the phones of four journalists who had published leaked material: Beecher; Hedrick Smith, the *Times* man at the State Department; Marvin Kalb of CBS; and Henry Brandon of the London *Sunday Times*. It was the White House's first incursion into the twilight zone of questionable activity, and it was fruitless; Beecher's source was never found.

The President began to entertain misgivings about the efficiency of both Hoover's FBI and Richard Helms's CIA. His doubts deepened after the events of May 1970. Nixon was convinced that the campus outbreaks were the work of foreign instigators, probably Cubans, Egyptians, and eastern Europeans. He asked the CIA to identify them. After an extensive investi-

NATTERING NABOBS | 1217

gation the agency reported that all the agitators were native Americans. The President gave the FBI the same assignment; the bureau brought back the same explanation. Still dissatisfied, the oval office ordered more wire-taps and — something new — house break-ins to search suspected offices and homes. The programs were to be directed by a new domestic security panel consisting of the country's top intelligence men: Hoover, Helms, and the directors of the Defense Intelligence Agency and the National Security Agency. Their marching orders were to be drawn up by a twenty-nine-year-old Hoosier lawyer and presidential speech writer named Tom Charles Huston.

On June 5, 1970, the four intelligence chiefs met in the President's office, were photographed with him, and were told that he wanted them to form a committee supervising national security, with Hoover as chairman. They were to go into action on August 1. Meantime Huston would draft operational plans with the FBI director. During one of their early meetings Hoover tried to dampen the young lawyer's enthusiasm for illegal schemes by explaining the historical development of objective intelligence. Huston replied impatiently, "We're not talking about the dead past; we're talking about the living present." In addition to electronic surveillance and surreptitious entry, his plan envisaged opening mail, recruiting more FBI informers on campuses, and CIA spying on students and other Americans living abroad.

As an attorney, the Indianan was aware that second-story jobs and what he called "mail coverage" were felonies, but he wanted to go ahead anyway. He wrote: "Use of this technique is clearly illegal; it amounts to burglary. It is also highly risky and could result in great embarrassment if exposed. However, it is also the most fruitful tool and can produce the type of intelligence which cannot be obtained in any other fashion." He argued that the advantages "outweigh the risks." Hoover disagreed. In a footnote to the Huston report the director said he didn't want to be chairman of the panel and didn't even want to be a member of it. Huston felt wounded. He sent Haldeman a memorandum in early July commenting on the FBI director's comment: "His objections are generally inconsistent and frivolous — most express concern about possible embarrassment to the intelligence community (i.e., Hoover) from public exposure." On July 23 Nixon signed a "decision memo," drafted by the young lawyer, approving the plan, but when Hoover saw it he protested to Mitchell, who discussed it with the President, who dropped the whole thing. Embittered, Huston resigned that fall and went home to practice law in Indianapolis. His intelligence duties were assigned to a White House newcomer, presidential counsel John Wesley Dean III.

The following spring the *Times* began publishing fresh Pentagon leaks, and Nixon concluded that his administration had become a sieve, that something must be done, that he would have to bypass Hoover. Accordingly, the President established a Special Investigations Unit whose job, as he himself later explained, was to "stop security leaks and to investigate other sensitive security matters."

Unknown to one another then, the men who would make presidential burglary the prelude to the American scandal of the century had been emerging from governmental careers, thus becoming available for new employment. E. Howard Hunt, whose CIA career had been going downhill since the American ambassador in Madrid refused to approve his assignment as deputy station chief there, on the ground that he was an intriguer, had retired at the time of the Kent State tragedy. Four months later James W. McCord Jr. resigned from the CIA, and eight months after that G. Gordon Liddy was fired by the Treasury Department because of an unauthorized speech praising gun ownership at a National Rifle Association rally.

David Young, a thirty-two-year-old lawyer from Kissinger's staff, opened the Special Investigations Unit's headquarters in room 16 in the basement of the Executive Office Building. The *New York Times* carried a brief item reporting that Young and a colleague, Egil Krogh Jr., were doing something about leaks. One of Young's relatives read it and said to him, "Your grandfather would be proud of you, working on leaks at the White House. He was a plumber." David put a sign on the door of his new office: "Mr. Young — Plumber."

The off-year elections of 1970 were waged by the GOP leadership on the basis of a principle laid down by Murray Chotiner, Richard Nixon's first campaign mentor. It was, quite simply, that Americans vote against candidates, not for them. An aspirant for office following Chotiner's precept gave only nominal attention to his own program. Instead he blazed away at the least attractive aspects of his opponent's record, ideas, mannerisms, and private life. If the aspirant couldn't find anything, he invented something. These tactics were what the President's critics had in mind when they spoke of the Old Nixon. The GOP strategy that autumn was to convert all the party's nominees into Old Nixons. It was to be the first hundred-million-dollar congressional election, and the chief Republican firehorse would be the Vice President, or, as presidential adviser Bryce Harlow called him, "Power-pack Agnew."

Certainly the party needed a boost of some sort. The previous November Nixon's approval rating in the Gallup poll had touched 68 percent, but since then it had been eroded by worsening inflation, Cambodia, the Calley case, and rising unemployment. Early in the year Nixon told GOP leaders that they would lose in November if the jobless rate touched 5.5 percent. It went to 5.8 and hit 6 percent before the end of the year. The SALT talks were going well, and in March the nuclear nonproliferation pact was signed, yet neither these nor the administration's plan for revenue sharing generated much interest in the electorate. Its welfare reform plans also lacked appeal. Nixon's vow to preserve "neighborhood schools" without busing was well received in the South, but it angered Negroes in the

North, and with the emergence of the black middle class the Negro vote was becoming formidable. By November the country would have thirteen black congressmen, 81 black mayors, 198 black state legislators, and 1,567 local black officeholders.

In the White House the Vice President was regarded as admirably suited to campaign under Chotiner's colors. During his first year in Washington he had been remarkably active at the lectern, delivering seventy-seven major speeches, and his audiences had been large and appreciative. A Gallup poll in 1970 placed him third among America's most respected men, just behind the President and Billy Graham. To be sure, eleven faculty members at the University of Minnesota had appealed to him to stop "driving moderates into the hands of the extremists." Senator George Mc-Govern had called him "a divisive, damaging influence," and Republican Governor Francis Sargent had announced that he was unwelcome in Massachusetts. But college professors and McGovern were already recognized as the administration's natural enemies, while Sargent's state, with 300,000 students among its inhabitants, had become identified as the most liberal in the union. In any event, Agnew had been among the first members of the administration to spurn the President's inaugural plea to Americans to "stop shouting at one another" ("I intend to be heard over the din," the Vice President had said, "even if it means raising my voice"), and Middle Americans delighted in the choicer passages of Agnewian bombast:

> Some newspapers dispose of their garbage by printing it.
>
> Asking Senator Fulbright's advice on foreign policy is like asking the Boston Strangler to massage your neck.
>
> If, in challenging, we polarize the American people, I say it is time for a positive polarization.
>
> Violence rewarded breeds further violence and perpetual violence ultimately produces a brutal counterreaction.
>
> The disease of our times is an artificial and masochistic sophistication — the vague uneasiness that our values are false, that there is something wrong with being patriotic, honest, moral, and hardworking.

Agnew covered 32,000 miles while stumping thirty-two states in the fall of 1970. He set the tone for his campaign in a Palm Springs, California, press conference on September 13, when he called on the electorate to reject the Democrats as "radical liberals." Subsequently he capsulized this as "radic-libs," explaining that the politicians he had in mind could be "depended upon to vote against the interests of law and order and against the interests of a representative society and against the foreign policy of the United States virtually every time." While not endorsing all aspirants in his own party — "I would have to put one Republican senator who seeks election in that group. That's Senator Goodell of New York" — he condemned all opposition nominees: "The Democratic candidates are a team of permissive candidates who have a penchant for indulging the disorderly and fawning upon lawbreakers." His sesquipedalian prose was enlivened by two presidential speech writers, William Safire and Pat Buchanan. With them as phrasemakers, he denounced senatorial doves as "solons of sellout" and "pampered prodigies." All Democratic nominees were lumped together as "nattering nabobs of negativism," "pusillanimous pussyfooters," "vicars of vacillation," "troglodytic leftists," and "hopeless, hysterical hypochondriacs of history" catering to "foolish fads of phony intellectualism." Of his fustian rhetoric he said he liked metaphors and alliteration, "but I don't need gimmicks to get my message across. I am simply stating what America is all about."

Agreeing with him, the President sounded much the same theme while campaigning 17,240 miles in twenty-two states over twenty-three days. In all of them he was on the attack. Like Agnew, he defended no record, described no goals, acclaimed no ideals; that would have violated Chotiner's rule. Instead he stumped against students, narcotics, the SDS, rioters, draft dodgers, flag burners, homosexuals, criminals, promiscuity, and pornography, identifying all of them with the Democrats. The climax came the night before the election, when the Republicans rebroadcast on television one of the President's most strident speeches. The previous Thursday evening in San Jose, California, demonstrators had pelted his limousine with eggs and rocks, tried to smash the windows, and hammered on the doors. "You had to see their faces," an aide who was with him said later; "the hate in those faces — it got to him." *Time* noted that the episode had been "condemned in all responsible and even quasi-responsible quarters." Nevertheless, speaking after it in Phoenix, the President had seemed to blame all his critics for what had happened. He pledged that "No band of violent thugs is going to keep me from going out and speaking with the American people" — the implication was that Democrats were out to stop him — and said of the dissenters, "They're not romantic revolutionaries. They're the same thugs and hoodlums that have always plagued the good people." He concluded: "Our approach, the new approach, demands new and strong laws that will give the peace forces new muscle to deal with the criminal forces in the United States."

The quality of the election eve rebroadcast, like the message it bore, was scratchy, and at times all but incoherent. It lasted fifteen minutes. The next quarter-hour was given over to a paid reply from Senator Edmund Muskie of Maine, speaking for the other party. Muskie was calm, measured — and devastating. Noting that Nixon and Agnew had maligned Democrats and accused them of disloyalty, he said: "That is a lie, and the American people know it is a lie. . . . There are only two kinds of politics . . . the politics of fear and the politics of trust. One says: you are encircled by monstrous dangers. . . . The other says: the world is a baffling and hazardous place, but it can be shaped to the will of men. . . . Thus in voting for the Democratic Party tomorrow you cast your vote for trust . . . for trusting your fellow citizens . . . and most of all for trust in yourself."

Everyone, Muskie pointed out, believes in law and order; the Democrats had voted for the administration's bills to control crime. But what about racial tension, the environment, the economy? And what about national unity? He said: "There are those who seek to turn our common distress to partisan advantages, not by offering better solutions but with empty threat and malicious slander." He called on the voters to repudiate them.

They did. The Democrats gained twelve House seats, widening their margin to 255–180. The Republicans lost eleven governorships. They had led, with 32 statehouses to 18; now they trailed 29–21. The average Democratic candidate ran three percentage points ahead of 1968. Early in the campaign the GOP had entertained hopes of winning eight Senate seats and regaining control there. It had seemed possible, for the Democrats had twice as many Senate seats at stake. After the smoke had cleared, the Republicans had picked up just two of them, and one was of doubtful value; in Connecticut a conservative Democrat, Thomas J. Dodd, had been replaced by a liberal Republican, Lowell P. Weicker Jr.

Trying to put the best possible face on the results, Nixon claimed an "ideological victory," pointing to the defeat of Albert Gore in Tennessee, Joseph Tydings in Maryland, and Charles Goodell in New York, where Conservative party candidate James Buckley had won a three-way race with only 39 percent of the vote. But these gains were offset by the successes of Adlai Stevenson III in Illinois and John V. Tunney in California, and the Texas defeat of George Bush, whom the administration had strongly backed. Most discouraging for the White House were omens for the 1972 election. Apart from Tennessee, the celebrated GOP southern strategy had achieved nothing. Elsewhere Republicans had lost several key legislatures. Special Nixon-Agnew efforts had failed in New Jersey, Wisconsin, North Dakota, Florida, Nevada, and New Mexico, and they had done badly in big states — California, Pennsylvania, Ohio, and Michigan — where the next presidential race would probably be decided.

The president of the liberal Republican Ripon Society summed up the outcome as the GOP's "worst showing since 1964," and said of Nixon's interpretation that "to the degree he claims he has a working ideological majority now, he cannot use Congress as a scapegoat in 1972." The standing joke among Republican governors assembling after the election in Sun Valley, Idaho, was that they should have met in Death Valley. The governor of Indiana, which had given the President his biggest plurality two years earlier, said he was in trouble even there; the governor of New Mexico warned his fellow Republicans that the GOP had "lost the election because the strategy was completely negative." "In November 1970," wrote columnists Rowland Evans and Robert Novak, "the Presidency of Richard Nixon . . . hit bottom." In fact it sank lower. That winter Gallup showed the percentage of Americans who approved of the President dropping from 56 percent to 51 to 50 to 49. In the Harris poll Muskie surged ahead of Nixon by three points, and in subsequent months his margin widened to five points and then to eight points — 47 to 39. *Newsweek* raised the possibility that Nixon might be a one-term President.

It was against this background that Nixon and his chief political advisers gathered in Key Biscayne for a postmortem — one of them, reflecting their host's fondness for sports cant, called it "going over the game plan." Mitchell, who was particularly gloomy, said the President had acted as though he had been "running for sheriff." All agreed that they could not afford a repeat performance two years hence. Starting now, Nixon must appear to be aloof from partisan politics, doing his job as President. The new chairman of the Republican National Committee would be Senator Robert Dole of Kansas, a GOP stalwart and a hard-liner.

But that wasn't the most important decision at the meeting. As one who was there put it afterward, "We knew we were in a damn tough fight, and we weren't going to entrust it to a bunch of cautious old hacks down at the committee." Another said later, "The decision was to get politics the hell out of the White House and across the street" — across the street being the steel and glass tower at 1701 Pennsylvania Avenue, a hundred and fifty yards from the White House. There the independent Citizens Committee for the Reelection of the President opened its second-floor offices in March 1971 amid new furniture, fashionable interior decoration, and deep orange pile carpeting. Until John Mitchell resigned from the Justice Department and took it over, it would be run by a protégé of Haldeman's, Jeb Stuart Magruder. Magruder's director of security was to be James W. McCord Jr. His counsel was G. Gordon Liddy. The committee itself was to become known to all, Republicans and Democrats alike, as CREEP.

Early Seventies Montage

IS MOTHER'S MILK FIT FOR HUMAN CONSUMPTION?

AT&T UP 1000% SINCE 1932

Hello darkness, my old friend
I've come to talk with you again
Because a vision softly creeping
Left its seeds while I was sleeping
And the vision that was planted in my brain
Still remains,
Echoing the sound of silence.

You don't need to be a weatherman
To know which way the wind blows

Masters and Johnson estimate that one-half of the marriages in the United States are threatend by sexual dysfunction

Virginia Slims

INSTAMATIC SALES HIT 50,000,000

NIXON PLEDGES SMALL STAFF, OPEN ADMINISTRATION

SILENT MAJORITY

They Ran Out of Tear Gas

Kent State 1970

Allison Krause, 19
Sandra Lee Scheuer, 20
Jeffrey Glenn Miller, 20
William K. Schroeder, 19

Best Sellers   FICTION
Love Story Segal
Islands in the Stream Hemingway
Crystal Cave Stewart
God Is an Englishman Delderfield
The French Lieutenant's Woman Fowles

AMERICAN GIs SPREAD CHRISTMAS JOY TO CHILDREN AROUND WORLD

That's what it's all about
This has to be the richest country ever

1 IN 8 AMERICANS GET SOCIAL SECURITY CHECKS

— It can't be all that bad —

IKE DEAD

moratorium

THE WHITE HOUSE
WASHINGTON   August 17, 1971
TO: The Staff
From: John Dean
     This memorandum addresses the matter of how we can maximize the fact of our incumbency in dealing with persons known to be active in their opposition to our Administration. Stated a bit more bluntly -- how we can use the available federal machinery to screw our political enemies. **HOMOSEXUALS MARCH IN NEW YORK**

Is that all there is?
Is that all there is?
If that's not all there is, my friend,
Then let's keep dancing

Letting it all hang out

OUR AMERICAN MADNESS: WHY WE WORK SO HARD AT HAVING FUN

Portnoy's Complaint (port'-noiz kəm-plānt') *n.* (after Alexander Portnoy 1933-   ) A disorder in which strongly felt ethical and altruistic impulses are perpetually warring with extreme sexual longings, often of a preverse nature . . . It is believed by Spielvogel that many of the symptoms can be traced to the bonds obtaining in the mother-child relationship.

SELL 3,000 TOPLESS SWIM SUITS Effete Snobs for Peace

Q: (to witness Atkins) Did there come a time when you killed Miss Tate?
— You better believe it —
A: Yes. I killed her
Q: Describe to the court what happened.
A: Well, I stabbed her, and she fell. And I stabbed her again. I don't know how many times I stabbed her and I don't know why I stabbed her . . .
Q: But how can it be right to kill somebody?
A: How can it not be right when it's done with love?

Raindrops keep falling on my head
But I'm not complaining
That my eyes will soon be red
Crying's not for me

Sorry about that

How's that for starters?

Ninety percent of all scientists who ever lived are alive now.

BLACK NATIONALISTS PICK CITY AS TARGET

Best Sellers NONFICTION
The Sensuous Woman "j"
Everything You Always Wanted to Know About Sex Reuben
Inside the Third Reich Speer
Future Shock Toffler
Zelda Milford

Go Naked

THIRTY-SIX

The Divided States of America

T HAT WINTER NOSTALGIA became big business. Wooden cigar store Indians were bringing as much as $4,000 each; *Superman* comic books issued in 1938, $400. An Italian designer reintroduced the Rita Hayworth look, and his models, showing the shirt dresses and the flaring skirts, strolled to the piped rhythms of swing music. Coeds, reaching even farther back into the past, wore ankle-length turn-of-the-century frocks and steel-rimmed granny glasses. Arrow Shirts were displayed in 1906 layouts; Hertz advertisements featured sepia-toned prints and obsolete Victorian type faces. Hippies wore Mickey Mouse watches. Over three hundred radio stations observed Halloween by rebroadcasting Orson Welles's *War of the Worlds.* One of the most remarkable — and profitable — shows on Broadway was a revival of the 1920s *No, No, Nanette.* In its first week it earned $35,000; tickets went for $25 apiece; "I Want to Be Happy" became a hit again. The choreography was by Busby Berkeley. The star was sixty-year-old Ruby Keeler. When she skipped into her first tap dance to the tune of "Tea for Two," the opening night audience leaped to its feet to give her a roaring ovation.

Among the extraordinary examples of yesterday's appeal was the 1971 reissue of Sears, Roebuck's Catalogue No. 104, for 1897, with new introductions by S. J. Perelman and Richard Rovere. The publishers expected it to be bought only by libraries for reference shelves. Instead it sold 200,000 copies at $14.95. Presently a Nostalgia Book Club opened offices, offering books of old movie ads, collections of pulp magazine stories, and the adventures of Dick Tracy, Little Orphan Annie, and Buck Rogers. Nancy Drew and Hardy Boys mysteries were selling briskly. The Longines Symphonette Recording Society was reaching millions with albums of 1930s songs and radio broadcasts under such titles as *Remember the Golden Days of Radio, The Great Vocalists of the Big Band Era, Thanks for the Memory, The Years to Remember, Those Memory Years,* and

Theme Songs of the Big Band Era. The most ambitious project along these lines was a series of Time-Life albums which re-recorded, in stereo sound, the great swing hits of Glenn Miller, Harry James, Artie Shaw, Tommy Dorsey, Les Brown, Woody Herman, Charlie Barnet, Jimmie Lunceford, Claude Thornhill, Lionel Hampton, and, of course, Benny Goodman.

The message was clear: Americans were yearning for the past because they were fed up with the present. Though 1971 was an eventful year, the character of the events was no improvement over 1970. Later inflation would make that of 1971 seem mild, but at the time it seemed outrageous. In February wholesale prices took their sharpest jump in seventeen years. Overall, the cost of living had risen 25 percent in five years. At the same time, FBI figures indicated that serious crimes had increased 176 percent in the 1960s. During the previous year there had been 5.5 million of them in the United States, and whereas one crime in three had been solved in 1960, the rate now was only one in five. Venereal disease had spread dismayingly. The incidence of gonorrhea had attained the proportions of a nationwide epidemic — with no vaccine to prevent infection.

Change continued to alter the country at a startling pace. The figures from the new census, now becoming available, showed among other things that the flight from U.S. farms in the 1960s had reduced the population living on the land by another 40 percent. Rootlessness was up again; six million Americans now lived in trailers. One useful measure of the shifting patterns in urban life was the growth of shopping centers. The first one had been built outside Portland, Maine, in 1959, and over the next decade retail business in the central city there plunged 71 percent. By the second year of the Nixon administration the nation had more than thirteen thousand shopping centers, with more devastating consequences for the stores of downtown America. Another set of figures with ominous implications — which were unappreciated by the Nixon administration — foretold the energy crisis. Since 1945 the consumption of gasoline in the United States had increased fourfold, and the use of electricity sixfold.

It was a rough year for tradition. Rolls-Royce went into receivership. The Army declared that henceforth married WACs and nurses could have babies and remain in uniform. Capitol Hill was rocked when a Weatherman bomb exploded in a men's lavatory just below the Senate chamber. The Roman Catholic Church announced that 1,400 parochial schools had closed their doors in the past five years. *Look* observed National Magazine Week by folding. The Bon Vivant Company, makers of fine soups, collapsed when New Jersey health authorities discovered that what they were selling was botulism; over 1.2 million cans of its vichyssoise had to be destroyed. Radicals won three of four available seats on the Berkeley City Council. The judgment "Thirty dollars or thirty days" was heard for the last time when the Supreme Court ruled that a defendant could not be imprisoned because he was unable to pay a fine.

Campuses were quiet in 1971. The impact of Kent State was obvious. A

Playboy survey of student opinion found that only 36 percent said, "I would protest now," and even they added, "but not violently." A contributor to the *Daily Californian* wrote: "The level of life in Berkeley has degenerated. The despair of the junkie pervades much of the community. We sit around smoking dope or drinking or thinking of new stereos . . . all too many people are just waiting for life rather than living." John L. Erlich, professor of social work at the University of Michigan, said that "large numbers of students have become discouraged and alienated." Erlich also noted that "larger numbers are still committed to change," however. The chief difference was that activists had stopped demonstrating on campus. The zealots, and there were still a lot of them, were now concentrating on Washington. The cause of their loudest clamor — the war — was drearily the same. If 1970 had been the year of Cambodia in Indochina, 1971 was the year of Laos. In addition it marked an end to any lingering illusions that South Vietnam, under President Nguyen Van Thieu, was on its way to becoming a democracy.

The Gilbert and Sullivan character of South Vietnam's 1971 presidential campaign could be traced to the 1967 election. The Thieu-Ky ticket had won then, but because eleven candidates had been running, the winners had carried only 35 percent of the vote. Thieu hadn't liked that. It still rankled; he felt he had lost face. This time would be different. At his direction the Vietnamese assembly required future nominees who wanted a place on the ballot to secure the signatures of either forty assemblymen or a hundred provincial and municipal councilors. (Under the second option, each councilor's endorsement must be countersigned by his province chief.)

Thieu had two serious challengers: Ky and the popular General Duong Van Minh. Ky and Minh reached a gentleman's agreement: they would stay out of each other's way. Minh also said that he would withdraw if he suspected electoral fraud. Fraud followed; Thieu's supreme court threw out Ky's candidacy on a technicality. Angered, Minh called at the U.S. embassy with proof of other Thieu measures showing that the president was rigging the election, among them written instructions to province chiefs to buy votes, to shift "unfriendly civil servants to other jobs," and to stuff ballot boxes. Minh then quit the race, explaining that he could not "put up with a disgusting farce that strips away all the people's hope of a democratic regime and bars reconciliation of the Vietnamese people."

That left Thieu without opposition, a situation which delighted him but alarmed Washington. After U.S. Ambassador Ellsworth Bunker had protested, the Vietnamese supreme court obligingly reversed itself, ruling that Ky was a valid nominee and that his name could be printed on the ballot. But Ky had pride, too. In addition he suspected that Thieu's orders to the province chiefs had effectively fixed the race. Thereupon *he* withdrew, naming the president as "the principal actor in the farce." The election was held as scheduled, and the principal actor in the farce received 94.3 percent of the vote, the balance representing mutilated ballots. Thieu announced that he was gratified by this "astounding" display of confidence in his leadership, but this was no time for him to be winning Pyrrhic victories. By the end of the year the American troop level there would be down to 158,000, and the ability of his army to stand on its own was in grave doubt.

A South Vietnamese campaign in Laos multiplied the doubts, which was ironic, because it was supposed to do the opposite. To prove the effectiveness of Vietnamization, 16,000 ARVN troops were ordered to cross the demilitarized zone (DMZ), penetrate Laos along route 9, and cut the Ho Chi Minh Trail, that legendary spiderweb of supply paths which by now was fifty miles wide at some points. Few planners in military history had been so careless of secrecy. For weeks in advance confident U.S. officers in Saigon briefed the press on the Hobson's choice which lay ahead for the enemy: the North Vietnamese would either have to abandon their Laotian bases or stand and fight, and if they fought they would be annihilated. To advertise the native character of the drive, a billboard was erected on route 9 two hundred yards from the border of Laos, reading NO U.S. PERSONNEL BEYOND THIS POINT. When reporters pointed out that the operation bore an American code name — Dewey Canyon II — the name was hastily changed to Lam Son 719.

Lam Son 719 was launched on February 8, 1971, to the accompaniment of the continuing drumbeat of publicity. The first reports claimed success. War correspondents knew only that the troops were moving slowly against no apparent opposition. An armored column took two weeks to move eleven miles. Then disaster struck. The enemy attacked with tanks, heavy rockets, massed artillery, and four of North Vietnam's best divisions. In Saigon the deputy U.S. commander, Major General Frederick Weyland, acknowledged that South Vietnam's losses were "worse than Tet." Stalled, the battalion commanders of Thieu's supposedly elite 1st Division asked permission to fall back. They were turned down because, Frances FitzGerald wrote in *Fire in the Lake*, "The American command and the White House had claimed that the ARVN would stay in Laos and occupy the trail until the end of the dry season in May, and the ranking ARVN officers did not dare contradict the Americans."

Infantrymen of the 1st Division panicked, abandoned their positions, blew up their artillery, and desperately hacked their way through jungle to clearings where U.S. helicopters could rescue them. Americans watching televised evening newscasts that week saw terrified ARVN soldiers clinging to the helicopters' skids. Only the intervention of American air power averted total catastrophe. At the end of the forty-five-day campaign the South Vietnamese units had suffered over 50 percent casualties — 3,800 killed and 5,200 wounded. Eight battalions were unable to take the field. Traffic on the trail actually increased. When Nixon told the nation in early April, "Tonight I can report that Vietnamization has succeeded," his critics accused him of insulting the country's intelligence.

A response from America's antiwar movement was inevitable. On April 18 the Vietnam Veterans Against the War encamped below Capitol Hill and picketed the Supreme Court. Presidential counsel Charles W. Colson hurriedly organized the Veterans for a Just Peace, and the Reverend Carl McIntire formed another countergroup, the Patriots for Victory, which called on Nixon to jettison his timid Vietnam policy and "use the sword as God intended." Administration officials accused commentators of exposing their leftist sympathies by failing to give the VJP and the PFV sufficient publicity, but events were moving too fast for both the government and the press. On April 24 a peaceful Washington march was held by some 200,000 protesters. The next week a "People's Lobby" swarmed over the Hill and into draft headquarters, buttonholing congressmen and Selective Service authorities, and the end of the month brought the climax of the capital demonstrations — the arrival of the "Mayday Tribe," which invoked the international distress call on behalf of its avowed objective: "stopping the government."

Just how violent the Tribe's intentions were later became a matter of some controversy. The leaders pointed out that their symbol had been the image of Mohandas Gandhi. It adorned their pamphlets, posters, buttons, and the cover of their tactical manual, which explained the principle of organized civil disobedience. Yet some of their methods were rougher than Gandhi's. Techniques included throwing junk in the street, abandoning autos at key intersections, and lying in front of cars. The Washington police force, which was known as one of the most relaxed in the nation, decided to adopt a strategy of killing the protesters with kindness. It was never given a chance to work. The President sent new instructions from San Clemente. He wanted the government to react more aggressively.

As coordinator of law enforcement tactics he chose Attorney General Mitchell. At the time of the November 1969 demonstrations, Mitchell had told his wife Martha that the peace marchers reminded him of Russian revolutionaries. More recently he had argued before a group of attorneys that the government's right to protect itself must override the right of individuals to privacy. The example he had chosen then was the need, as he saw it, for wiretaps without court orders. The Mayday disorders provided another illustration of the Mitchell approach to law enforcement in a time of political dissent. Under normal procedures, a policeman making an arrest must complete a form, filling in the name of the person charged, the offense, the arresting officer, and the time and place of the alleged infraction. Confronted by an invasion of 12,000 to 15,000 youths, many of them bent upon disrupting Washington traffic, Mitchell decided to cut through what he regarded as red tape.

On the evening of May 1 the vanguard of the Tribe was listening to a rock concert in West Potomac Park, near the Lincoln Memorial, when 750 helmeted officers swinging riot sticks drove them into the streets. Two days later the main battle was joined. Law enforcement officials had been given an overriding mission: keep the traffic flowing. Policemen, National Guardsmen, and regular Army troops broke up large concentrations of demonstrators with tear gas and truncheons. Assault units hovered overhead in military helicopters, ready to pounce. On that first day of the dragnet 7,200 were arrested, many of them peaceful pickets and spectators. It was a record. Altogether 12,614 were taken into custody over a four-day period. The jails wouldn't hold them; the overflow was penned in an open-air stockade at Robert F. Kennedy Memorial Stadium.

There they sang "God Bless America" — derisively — and "We all live in a con-cen-tra-tion camp," to the tune of the Beatles' "Yellow Submarine." Among them was Dr. Spock, shivering in a light raincoat. Abbie Hoffman was arrested in New York and accused of being a Mayday conspirator. He said, "I had about as much to do with the demonstrations in Washington as the Capitol bombing or the earthquake in Los Angeles, which I also expect to be indicted for." He had been picked up after a scuffle, and his nose was injured and taped. He said, "Like, man, that's defacing a national monument."

Congressional doves were appalled by the demonstrations. Tunney of California told reporters that the "foolish and useless" disorders "might well have ruined several months of hard work by the real advocates of peace." As it turned out, the courts rejected the arrests as clear violations of the prisoners' civil rights. The American Civil Liberties Union had anticipated that outcome, but it had been by no means certain at the time. The administration thought the law enforcement officers had performed admirably. Returning from California, Nixon told Republican leaders that he thought the Washington police chief had done "a magnificent job." He said, "John Mitchell and the Department of Justice did a fine job, too. I hope you will all agree to make that point when you leave here." Mitchell said, "I am proud of the Washington city police. I am proud that they stopped a repressive mob from robbing the rights of others." Then he compared the peace demonstrators to Hitler's Nazi brownshirts.

Six weeks after the great Mayday bust the *New York Times* of Sunday, June 13, carried on its first page the dull head: "VIETNAM ARCHIVE: PENTAGON STUDY TRACES 3 DECADES OF GROWING U.S. INVOLVEMENT." The story jumped to six inside pages, where column after column of dense type reprinted U.S. communiqués, recommendations, position papers, cables, and presidential orders, all concerning American activity in Indochina. It was perhaps the most extraordinary leak of classified documents in the history of governments, and it was only a beginning. Subsequent installments, the editors promised, would reveal more.

What the *Times* had acquired was a copy of a massive study commissioned by Robert S. McNamara shortly before his resignation as Secretary of Defense. The Pentagon Papers, as the newspaper called the archive, had been assembled by thirty-five scholars, including analysts from the Rand

Corporation think tank, in an office adjoining McNamara's. Altogether there were forty-seven volumes of typescript — 4,000 pages of records and 3,000 pages of explication, a total of 2.5 million words. It was all secret, but the secrets were not military. None of it compromised American troops still in Vietnam, and there was nothing from the Nixon years. McNamara had wanted to know how the United States had become entangled in Vietnam's swamps. The papers told how. Some of the documents went back to the Truman administration. They made a lot of officials look inept, foolish, or worse. Among other things the documents revealed that Lyndon Johnson had ordered the drafting of the Tonkin Gulf resolution months before the alleged incident there. Worse, on the very day in 1965 that he had decided to commit American infantry in Vietnam he had told a press conference that he was aware of "no far-reaching strategy that is being suggested or promulgated."

Clark Clifford, McNamara's successor as Secretary of Defense, had never found time to read the study. Henry Kissinger had been one of its researchers, but he hadn't seen the completed project. President Nixon didn't even know of its existence until that fateful Sunday morning that the *Times* began publishing it. Although it affected neither him nor his conduct of the war, he was infuriated. He felt that the ability of a government to keep secrets was vital. The fact that none of his own confidences were involved here was, he thought, beside the point; next time could be different. Furthermore, at a time when he and Kissinger were carefully defining their own Vietnam policy, these documents opened old wounds and raised again the ugly issue of the government's credibility.

On Monday, June 14, the *Times* published its second installment of the papers. Mitchell called the White House and suggested that the administration tackle the newspaper in the courts. Nixon agreed. Mitchell telegraphed the paper, "respectfully" suggesting that it print no more. If the editors went ahead, he warned, they could be convicted under the espionage statute, fined $10,000, and sentenced to ten years in prison. And the government would prosecute; the leak was causing "irreparable injury to the defense interests of the United States." The *Times* ran a front-page account of the attorney general's threat, and published the third installment of the papers alongside it.

That was a wild fortnight in city rooms and courtrooms. A team of government lawyers under Assistant Attorney General Robert Mardian went into federal court in New York on Tuesday, asking for an injunction against the editors. The judge, who had been on the bench exactly five days, scheduled a hearing for Friday and issued a temporary restraining order. The *Times* obediently stopped publication, but on Friday the *Washington Post* began running its own account of the papers. Clearly the *Post's* editors had access to the same source. Four days later the *Boston Globe* began printing the documents. Meantime the Associated Press had begun sending the *Post* version around the world. Among the papers printing it was the *New York Times*.

Mardian took the *Post* to court, but the federal judge in Washington refused to hand down even a temporary order. The government, he found, could not "impose a prior restraint on publication of essentially historical data." The U.S. Appellate Court voted 2 to 1 to restrain the *Post*. The New York judge refused a permanent injunction against the *Times* but extended his temporary order until appeals courts could rule. Finally, on the following Friday, the two cases — numbers 1873 and 1875 — came before the U.S. Supreme Court, which found for the press 6 to 3. Then nine justices handed down no fewer than six opinions. Along with John Harlan, Nixon appointees Burger and Harry A. Blackmun were in the minority.

Mardian had taken the position that the Justice Department was merely attempting to recover stolen papers necessary for national security. The identity of the putative thief was unmentioned then, but the FBI knew. He was Daniel Ellsberg, a summa cum laude graduate of Harvard who had written his doctoral dissertation on the decision making process, worked for Rand, become a McNamara protégé, and helped put the Pentagon Papers together. A hawk at first, he had, like so many others, been transformed by events into a dove. Resigning from Rand because he had become an embarrassment to it, he had become a fellow at the Massachusetts Institute of Technology. He had brooded long over whether to make the papers public. The invasion of Cambodia had finally decided him.

On June 23 Ellsberg, still in hiding, appeared on television at an undisclosed location and identified himself as the source of the documents. The United States, he declared, was to blame for the Vietnam tragedy: "There has never been a year when there would have been a war in Indochina without American money." He said, "I felt as an American citizen, a responsible citizen, I could no longer cooperate in concealing this information from the American people. I took this action on my own initiative, and I am prepared for all the consequences." On June 28 he surrendered to authorities in Boston and was released on $50,000 bail. That same day he was indicted in Los Angeles for stealing government property and violating the Espionage Act. Six months later twelve more criminal charges, including conspiracy, were leveled against him. A former Rand colleague, Anthony J. Russo Jr., was also indicted, together with a Los Angeles advertising woman and a former South Vietnamese ambassador to the United States. Ellsberg said: "I stole nothing and I did not commit espionage. I violated no laws and I have not intended to harm my country."

Surveying the Watergate wreckage in 1973, a team of London *Sunday Times* reporters concluded that "The Pentagon Papers tipped the Nixon administration over the edge." The White House Special Investigations Unit — the Plumbers — acquired the services of two former New York cops, a Runyonesque pair named Jack Caulfield and Tony Ulasewicz.

They had been hired by John Ehrlichman two years earlier for political investigations; their assignments, first from Ehrlichman and then from John Dean, had included inquiries into Chappaquiddick, My Lai critics, the drinking habits of anti-Nixon senators, the private life of a Washington columnist, and reports that the brother of an eminent Democrat was a homosexual. In the aftermath of the Pentagon Papers case they received their first assignment as Plumbers.

Anyone who had worked with Ellsberg had a lot of explaining to do in those days, and a man high on everyone's list of possible co-conspirators was Morton B. Halperin, who had directed the assembly of the Pentagon Papers. Halperin had been an Ellsberg friend and later a Kissinger aide. Leaving the government, he had moved to the Brookings Institution, a liberal think tank in Washington. Charles Colson believed that Halperin had been a source of leaks and probably still had classified material. If so, it might be in his Brookings office. Colson sent Ulasewicz on a reconnoitering mission; the ex-cop returned to report that there was no way to burglarize the institution. According to a subsequent account by John Dean, Colson, a hard man to discourage, told Caulfield that "if necessary he should plant a fire-bomb in the building and retrieve the documents during the commotion that would ensue."

That was too much for the New Yorkers. Someone, they felt, should restrain the impulsive Colson. They took the story to Dean, who caught the next plane to San Clemente. He laid the tale before Ehrlichman; Ehrlichman phoned Washington, and no more was said about fire-bombs. It was a costly triumph for Caulfield and Ulasewicz, however. The White House suddenly lost interest in their talents. Jobs which would have come their way in the past now went to the two rising stars in the Plumbers unit: E. Howard Hunt and G. Gordon Liddy. After three months in the cold, Caulfield decided to devise a master plan for political espionage. He hoped to sell it to the Committee for the Reelection of the President. Its code name was Operation Sand Wedge. On November 24 Dean secured an appointment for him with Mitchell. The presentation was not a success. Caulfield had a hunch that someone else was going to get the work, and as he left he knew he was right; sitting in the attorney general's outer office was Gordon Liddy.

During the spring and summer of 1971, when Richard Nixon was secretly having his White House offices wired for sound, his popularity rating in public opinion polls continued to sag. Presidential aides were agonizing over the refractory nature of the Vietnam War, still the most important issue before the country, and debating among themselves how best to reverse the electorate's political mood, so discouragingly expressed in the previous autumn's off-year election. This much was clear to them: they were going to need a lot of money. Fortunately, they were in much better shape than the debt-ridden Democrats. Herbert Kalmbach, the President's personal attorney, had custody of nearly two million dollars in unspent campaign funds from 1968. In January 1971 Kalmbach deposited the first $500,000 of the 1972 war chest in the Newport Beach, California, branch of the Bank of America. It is a matter of some interest that the money was in the form of cashier's checks which he had bought, with cash, in the Security Pacific National Bank branch just across the street. Even then he was taking steps to see that contributions could not be easily traced, because even then he knew that much of the means for the coming campaign would be coming from dubious sources.

Some of those sources emerged during the next few months. The first, in March, was the dairy industry. Early in the month Secretary of Agriculture Clifford Hardin announced that price supports for "manufacturing milk" — used to make cheese and butter — would be $4.66 per hundredweight, unchanged from the year before. The milk manufacturers took steps to reverse the decision. On March 22 they formed a GOP slush fund called the Trust for Agricultural Political Development and put $10,000 in it. The next day sixteen leaders of dairy cooperatives were invited to meet Nixon and Hardin in the oval office. They told the President and the secretary that they wanted a higher federal subsidy. The following day they gave the Nixon war chest another $25,000. The day after that Hardin changed his mind and pegged milk supports at $4.93. The dairy leaders then poured a total of $527,500 into Republican bank accounts.

Another lode was opened a few weeks later. Since the early days of the Nixon administration Harold S. Geneen, president of the International Telephone and Telegraph Corporation (ITT), had been trying to block a Justice Department task force which was working to prevent a merger of ITT and the Hartford Fire Insurance Corporation. Department career lawyers were determined to establish the principle that business competition is illegally crippled by huge sprawling conglomerates like ITT. The government's campaign was being directed by Richard W. McLaren, head of Justice's antitrust division. McLaren was reporting to Deputy Attorney General Kleindienst; Mitchell had supposedly withdrawn from the case because his New York law firm had represented ITT. On April 19, 1971, McLaren and Kleindienst conferred and agreed to carry an appeal to the Supreme Court. Kleindienst telephoned ITT's lawyer to tell him of the decision.

Later that same day Kleindienst received a call from John Ehrlichman, who told him that President Nixon was "directing" Kleindienst to drop the ITT case entirely. The deputy attorney general said that was impossible; he, McLaren, and Solicitor General Erwin Griswold were committed. "Oh?" Ehrlichman said curtly. "We'll see about that." A few minutes later Kleindienst's phone rang again. It was Nixon, who began by saying, "You son of a bitch, don't you understand the English language?" He ordered Kleindienst not to appeal. Disturbed, the deputy attorney general told Mitchell that he would resign rather than capitulate, and he thought

McLaren and Griswold would go with him. Shortly thereafter Mitchell told his deputy that he had talked to Nixon and "He says do anything you want on antitrust cases."

The President and the attorney general were being less than candid with Kleindienst. In a subsequent memo to Haldeman, Colson said he was trying to suppress all White House – ITT correspondence because it "would lay this case on the President's doorstep." And Mitchell, for all his talk of having turned the whole thing over to his deputy, had been holding regular meetings with Geneen for the past year. As early as September 1970 Ehrlichman had written to Mitchell criticizing McLaren's attitude and mentioning an "understanding" with Geneen.

Bargaining between the administration and the conglomerate was apparently concluded at a lunch given by the governor of Kentucky at the Kentucky Derby the month after Kleindienst and McLaren thought they had committed the government to a Supreme Court trial. The mediators were Mitchell and Dita Beard, ITT's salty Washington lobbyist. ITT agreed to pay $400,000 and the administration agreed to forget about the antitrust action. In a highly incriminating memorandum dated June 25, 1971, Mrs. Beard told her immediate superior that the only Republicans to know "from whom the 400 thousand commitment had come" were Nixon, Mitchell, Haldeman, and the lieutenant governor of California. She said: "I am convinced that our noble commitment has gone a long way toward our negotiations on the mergers eventually coming out as Hal [Geneen] wants them. Certainly the President has told Mitchell to see that things are worked out fairly. It is still only McLaren's mickeymouse we are suffering. . . . Mitchell is definitely helping us, but it cannot be known."

She ended the memo, "Please destroy this, huh?" It wasn't destroyed, and when it surfaced in a Jack Anderson column the following February 29, ITT's response was to shred all other documents relating to the case and claim that this one had been a forgery. But the Dita Beard note does not stand alone. It is braced by the Ehrlichman correspondence, including a May 5 letter to Mitchell referring to a talk between the President and the attorney general in which they had settled the "agreed-upon ends" in the ITT case. Certain events of that time are also supportive. On May 15 Geneen pledged the $400,000 to the GOP, and at the end of July the Justice Department and the government settled their differences without an appeal to the Supreme Court. ITT was allowed to keep Hartford Fire. "Quite clearly," *Fortune* commented, "Harold S. Geneen has achieved something of a victory."

The key figure in a third deal between the administration and people trying to solve legal problems was Robert L. Vesco, a controversial financier with several ties to the Nixon family. Vesco had given $50,000 to the 1968 Republican campaign through the President's brother, F. Donald Nixon. He was close to the President's other brother, Edward, and beginning in the summer of 1971 he employed the President's nephew Donald as his personal assistant. "He is the one person who has never lied to me, ever," Donald once said of Vesco, a strange statement from a young man with such an eminent relative, and one not many people would make; within two years Vesco would be a fugitive from American justice, living in Costa Rica rather than face Securities and Exchange Commission charges that he had looted Investors Overseas Services, a mutual fund, of 224 million dollars.

Vesco was already in trouble in the early summer of 1971, when, according to the indictment against him, he involved Mitchell and Nixon's Secretary of Commerce, Maurice Stans, in an attempt to buy his way out of the SEC accusations. The understanding was that Vesco would give Stans $250,000 in cash and Mitchell, according to the charges, would "exert his influence on the SEC on behalf of Robert L. Vesco." Edward Nixon later acted as bagman, delivering to Stans $200,000 in a brown attaché case. (The remaining $50,000 came in a second installment.) Mitchell set up meetings between Vesco, the SEC chairman, and the commission's general counsel. The SEC continued to prosecute anyway.

While cash began to accumulate in the GOP war chest, the White House was engaging in various parapolitical activities in 1971, most of them with a view toward the next year's presidential election. One was the compilation of a list of political enemies, which under Colson's guidance expanded to fill a file four inches thick. It included the names of Jack Anderson, James Reston, Jane Fonda, Barbra Streisand, Paul Newman, Gregory Peck, and Carol Channing. The president of the Otis Elevator Company was there — apparently because the Otis elevator in Nixon's San Clemente house didn't work properly — and so was Detroit's black Congressman John Conyers. A notation after Conyers's name read, "Has known weakness for white females." On September 9, 1971, Colson designated twenty names for "go status," but no one on the presidential staff could think of an effective method of attack. Daniel Schorr of CBS ("a real media enemy," Colson called him) was subjected to an FBI check that summer, but the sole consequence was frustration for the White House. Ronald Ziegler put out the explanation that Schorr had been investigated because he was being considered for a government job.

Various Nixon aides — Huston, Dean, Caulfield — tried to talk the Internal Revenue Service into harassing selected taxpayers. All failed, and Commissioner Randolph Thrower resigned for reasons which, he said at the time, were "between me and the President." The White House was driven to the absurd lengths of writing anonymous letters to the IRS hinting at tax evasions by people on Colson's list. It was perhaps an inevitable outgrowth of this malicious foolishness that at some point the conspirators should conclude that someone was conspiring against *them*. The someone, they thought, was J. Edgar Hoover, who kept in his office safe logs of wiretaps he had carried out on White House orders. Robert Mardian persuaded one of Hoover's assistants to steal the logs, and they were locked up in Ehrlichman's safe. Hoover missed them in July 1971. He was enraged.

Men who did not shrink from doing a bag job on the director of the FBI had no qualms about playing rough with Democratic presidential candidates, and it was in these months that what later became famous as Republican "dirty tricks" made their appearance. Mailings critical of Ted Kennedy went out in fake Muskie envelopes; a spurious Muskie aide phoned the Associated Press bureau in Boston with charges that Kennedy was a "divisive influence"; Rowland Evans and Robert Novak were gulled into printing counterfeit Muskie memos which seemed to suggest that he was engaging in questionable activities. On December 1, 1972, Donald H. Segretti gave fifty dollars to the president of the Tampa Young Republicans Club with the understanding that it would be used to discredit the primary campaigns of Senators Muskie and Jackson in Florida. It was the first installment on a project which would eventually lead to Segretti's disbarment, conviction, and imprisonment.

Some tricks were intricate. On the assumption that a third-party Wallace candidacy would hurt Nixon more than any Democratic candidate, various projects were undertaken to sabotage Wallace's American Independent Party. One of the more fantastic of them, masterminded by Mitchell and Jeb Magruder, involved paying the American Nazi Party $10,000 to persuade AIP voters in California to change their registration. The rationale behind this was that if enough voters switched, Wallace's party would have too few registrants to qualify for the ballot. It failed; the AIP actually gained 6,500 members during the period.

Another plot was directed at Ted Kennedy, the most formidable vote getter among President Nixon's possible challengers. Here the reasoning was that since young Kennedy's popularity was a reflection of John Kennedy's charisma, reducing the late President's appeal would hurt Ted. At a press conference on September 16, 1971, Nixon was asked about a recent statement by Senator Henry Jackson to the effect that the Saigon regime would be stronger if it were more democratic. Nixon replied, "If what the senator is suggesting is that the United States should use its leverage now to overthrow Thieu, I would remind all concerned that the way we got into Vietnam was through overthrowing Diem, and the complicity in the murder of Diem, and the way to get out of Vietnam, in my opinion, is not to overthrow Thieu." This was the first time anyone in the government had accused the Kennedy administration of connivance in Diem's death, and it gave Howard Hunt an idea.

Hunt had been poring over the Pentagon Papers. He told Colson that a Kennedy role in the Diem assassination might be assumed "inferentially" from State Department cables of the time. According to Hunt, Colson suggested that he "improve on them" — doctor them. Using a razor blade and a photocopier, Hunt forged two cables. One, dated three days before the

Diem assassination, began: AT HIGHEST-LEVEL MEETING TODAY, DECISION RELUCTANTLY MADE THAT NEITHER YOU NOR HARKINS SHOULD INTERVENE IN BEHALF OF DIEM OR NHU IN EVENT THEY SEEK ASYLUM. Colson referred a *Life* reporter to Hunt, saying of Nixon's accusation, "There's a big story there," but the reporter suspected duplicity and didn't bite.

The failure of this intrigue was Hunt's second disappointment that month. The other, the more bitter of the two, dated back to the previous April. On the tenth anniversary of the Bay of Pigs Hunt had flown to Miami for lunch with a Cuban-American named Bernard L. Barker who had been his principal subordinate then and was now a successful Florida real estate man. It was the opening link in a historic chain of events. The second was Ellsberg's massive leak of the Pentagon Papers. The third began with four men — Nixon, Kissinger, Haldeman, and Ehrlichman — on a helicopter ride between Los Angeles and San Clemente. The four leaders raged over the leak, which the President equated with the Alger Hiss case, and discussed bypassing the FBI with an undercover operation to learn more about it. The decision was made to detach David Young from Kissinger's National Security staff to work full-time with the Plumbers. Young then put the Ellsberg ball in Hunt's court; Hunt put it in Barker's.

But not right away. In the beginning the Plumbers explored what appeared at the time to be an innocent area. Toward the end of July they discovered, from an FBI report which was routinely routed through their office, that for two years Ellsberg had been psychoanalyzed by a Dr. Lewis B. Fielding of Beverly Hills. Two of Hoover's agents had attempted to grill the psychiatrist, but he had demurred, invoking the sanctity of the doctor-patient relationship. Hunt remembered that the CIA had a psychiatric section which drew up analytic profiles of men whose personalities were of special interest to the government. Under the CIA's congressional mandate the subjects were supposed to be foreigners — the most successful had been an analysis of Nikita Khrushchev, prepared just before President Kennedy's Vienna summit with him — but there had been one exception: Captain Lloyd Bucher of the *Pueblo*. Young asked CIA Director Richard Helms to make Ellsberg a second exception. Helms agreed. Early in August the finished profile was forwarded to the CIA.

Nobody there liked it. It wasn't at all what the Plumbers had in mind. The CIA psychiatrists seemed to admire Ellsberg. ("There is no suggestion that the subject [saw] anything treasonous in his act. Rather he seemed to be responding to what he deemed a higher order of patriotism.") On August 11 Young and Egil Krogh sent a minute on the study to Ehrlichman, rejecting it as "very superficial" and underscoring their belief that the CIA could do a better job. They wrote: "We will meet tomorrow with the head psychiatrist, Dr. Bernard Malloy, to impress upon him the detail and depth we expect." They then crossed the line into contemplation of criminal activity. "In this connection," they continued, "*we would recommend* that a covert operation be undertaken to examine all the medical files still held by

Ellsberg's psychiatrist covering the two-year period in which he was undergoing analysis." At the bottom of the memorandum were the words "Approve _____ Disapprove _____." After "Approve" Ehrlichman scrawled his initial. He added: "If done under your assurance that it is not traceable."

It was this condition, stipulating that the Plumbers must use undercover operatives with no White House ties, which prompted Hunt to recruit Barker and, through him, two fellow Cubans, Felipe DeDiego and Eugenio R. Martinez. All Hunt told Barker was that he needed him to explore a "national security matter" on authorization from officials "above both the CIA and the FBI." The job, he said, concerned a traitor who was passing information to the Soviet embassy. Except for the fact that the Russians subscribe to the *New York Times*, this was untrue. Later, in prison, Barker found the deception unforgivable. Morality apart (and none of the principals seemed to see any moral issue at the time), Hunt was guilty of incredible carelessness. He failed to tell Barker not to carry in his pocket a telephone number and abbreviated address ("W.H." and "W. House") linking him with Hunt. He didn't even check to be certain that Barker's men were free of government connections. In fact one of them, Martinez, was on the CIA payroll as a Cuban informant.

Meanwhile Hunt and Liddy, his partner in this strange venture, were being outfitted by the CIA — another violation of the provision in the agency's charter forbidding domestic activity. Ehrlichman phoned Marine General Robert E. Cushman Jr., Helms's deputy, asking him to do all in his power to help Hunt, whom he identified as "a bona fide employee, a consultant on security matters." Ehrlichman didn't specify the nature of the mission. During their subsequent meeting Hunt told Cushman that he had been "charged with quite a highly sensitive mission by the White House to visit and elicit information from an individual whose ideology we aren't entirely sure of" and that he needed "flash alias documentation," "pocket litter of some sort," and "some degree of physical disguise, for a one-time op — in and out."

With the approval of Helms, the CIA's technical services division provided Hunt with a social security card and a driving license, both made out to "Edward Joseph Warren." Liddy was given identification in the name of "George Leonard." Hunt was issued a reddish-brown wig and a device, resembling false teeth, to alter the sound of his voice when telephoning. In addition Liddy received a tiny camera hidden in a tobacco pouch. On August 25, 1971, the two Plumbers flew to California on a preliminary reconnaissance mission. They didn't achieve much. After taking a picture of Liddy standing outside Dr. Fielding's office at 450 North Bedford Drive in Beverly Hills, Hunt entered the office, told a cleaning woman that he was a physician, and photographed the room. Both men timed a drive from there to the doctor's home. Then they flew back to Washington, where the plane was met by a CIA messenger who took the films from Hunt and had them developed. At the White House the two Plumbers persuaded their superiors that burglarizing the psychiatrist's office was justifiable. Young brought Ehrlichman up to date and proposed in a new minute that a committee on Capitol Hill be persuaded to look into the leak of the Pentagon Papers: "We have already started on a negative press image of Ellsberg. If the present Liddy/Hunt project is successful, it will be absolutely essential to have an overall game plan developed foı its use in conjunction with the congressional investigation."

D-day for the Beverly Hills break-in was September 3, 1971; H-hour was 9 P.M. The operation was staged with all the meticulous attention to detail which had marked Hunt's participation in the Bay of Pigs, and it was just about as successful. Shortly before zero the Cubans checked in at the Beverly Hilton Hotel under assumed names. Two of them donned delivery men's uniforms and took a huge suitcase plastered with labels reading "Rush to Dr. Fielding" to North Bedford Drive. The cleaning woman admitted them and they left the bag with her, unlocking the door as they departed. Liddy was driving around outside, watching for suspicious policemen. Hunt was outside the Fielding home with a walkie-talkie to flash the alarm if the psychiatrist emerged and headed for his office.

At about midnight the Cubans returned to the office, only to discover — an omen of what was to come at the Watergate offices of the Democratic National Committee — that the cleaning woman had relocked the door. Forcing it, they removed a camera and a spotlight from the suitcase. The plan was to photograph Ellsberg's medical history. Unfortunately they couldn't find it. They dumped Dr. Fielding's files on the floor, but there was nothing for them there. All they turned up was an address book with Ellsberg's name in it. They took pictures of that and of the strewn files, to show that they had done their best. After four frustrating hours the team returned to the hotel, where Liddy phoned Washington to tell Krogh that it had been a "clean job" — Dr. Fielding would have disagreed, but Liddy meant only that they hadn't been caught. That was putting the best possible face on it. Back in the capital Hunt had to tell the White House that the mission had been a failure. Ehrlichman, according to his subsequent testimony, said he didn't want them to try again. Ehrlichman had another piece of bad news for Hunt. On instructions from Helms, General Cushman had called to say that while the CIA had been glad to help out, a repetition would be out of the question. The Plumbers were on their own now, and the pressure to produce something to justify their jobs was mounting.

The week after the first second-story job masterminded from the White House a tragic episode pointed up one of the issues deeply dividing Americans during the Nixon years. It lay between the holders of one set of values, who regarded their critics as illiberal and ınhumane, and the critics, who scorned the liberals as "permissivists." The incident was the bloodiest prison revolt in the country's history. It occurred in an unlikely setting, amid the white clapboard homes, red barns, and tall silvery silos of western New

York's Wyoming County. There, surrounded by dense fields of sweet corn and goldenrod, stood a fifty-five-acre penitentiary compound enclosed by thirty-foot turreted gray concrete walls. Christened after the nearby town, it bore the classical name of the ancient Athenian plain: Attica.

The state called Attica a "correctional facility," but not much correcting was done there. Under the stern administration of Superintendent Vincent Mancusi there was little vocational training and less compassion. Solitary confinement — "the box" — was the penalty for the slightest infraction of the rules, and inmates were systematically beaten in the elevator on the way there. They were allowed one bar of soap and one roll of toilet paper a month. If they worked in the hundred-degree heat of the metal shop, known to them as "the Black Hole of Calcutta," they were paid as little as 25 cents a day. Ugliest of all was the regime's naked racism. Of the 2,254 convicts, 75 percent were black or Puerto Rican, while all 383 guards were white. The keepers openly favored white prisoners, taunted the Negroes, and called their clubs "nigger sticks."

Warden Mancusi's reply to civil libertarians was that he was running a maximum security institution and that Attica's inmates included some of the country's most hardened criminals. It was true. It was also true, and an ill omen, that among them were many of a new convict breed, black militants who regarded themselves as victims of an imperialist society. Attica was, in fact, where other wardens shipped self-styled revolutionists who gave them trouble. Arriving, they smuggled in books by George Jackson and Eldridge Cleaver, held secret rallies when they were supposed to be at sports or in chapel, and circulated inflammatory pamphlets which they wrote in their cells. "If we cannot live as people, we will at least try to die like men," wrote a convict named Charles "Brother Flip" Crowley, and a poem being passed around began:

> *If we must die — let it not be like hogs,*
> *Hunted and penned in an inglorious spot,*
> *While round us bark the mad and hungry dogs,*
> *Making their mock at our accursed lot.*

In July 1971 an organization of militant inmates calling themselves the Attica Liberation Faction sent a proclamation demanding reforms to State Corrections Commissioner Russell G. Oswald. It was a clever move. Oswald had been appointed by Governor Rockefeller because his sweeping improvements in Wisconsin's prison system had been widely acclaimed by penologists, and though he had been in office only six months, he and Mancusi were already at odds on almost every administrative question. After Labor Day Oswald taped a message to the convicts asking for time to make profound changes. Among other things he pledged "meaningful rehabilitative methods, evening vocational programs, better law libraries."

He may have been too late. After the revolt guards found enormous circles drawn around the date September 9 on cell calendars. In July the militants had told Oswald that they felt there was "no need to dramatize our demands," but they changed their minds the following month. The decisive event seems to have been the death of George Jackson in San Quentin on August 21. At breakfast next morning Attica's Negroes protested by fasting. "It was the weirdest thing," a turnkey said afterward. "Nobody picked up a tray or a spoon, and nobody took any food. They just walked through the line and went to their seats and they sat down. They looked straight ahead and nobody made a sound . . . Then we noticed that almost all had some black on them. . . . It scared us because a thing like that takes a lot of organization, a lot of solidarity, and we had no idea they were so well organized."

The evangelical rhetoric of two revolutionists who were later identified as the key leaders, Herbert X. Blyden and "Brother Richard" Clarke, became more strident. Both were New Yorkers and Black Muslims; both had been convicted of armed robbery. Like George Jackson, Blyden was self-taught, a reader of history and philosophy who had been sent to Attica after leading a prison riot in the Tombs, Manhattan's House of Detention. Clarke had been transferred to Attica from a medium security prison whose warden said he had been advocating "the violent overthrow of the institution." His family had noticed that in Attica he was becoming increasingly bitter. Once when his wife was visiting him he said, "Feed the animals, feed the animals. That's what they treat us like here — animals."

On Wednesday, September 8, eighteen days after Jackson had been killed on the other side of the country, an Attica guard was punched by a convict while breaking up a fight in one of the prison exercise yards. That night the two who had been fighting were put in "the box." Other inmates said they were abused as they were dragged away, and a Puerto Rican prisoner threw a tumbler at one of the guards, cutting his face. The riot exploded the following morning. Precisely what touched it off is unclear. According to one account, a work party refused to line up at the rap of keepers' clubs. Another story put the responsibility on guards who, as a reprisal for the previous day's events, arbitrarily canceled the prisoners' exercise period. In a third version, Brother Richard led five convicts who were on their way to breakfast on a rampage, freeing Blyden, who was working in the metal shop, along the way.

However it started, the results were spectacular. Fewer than one hundred guards were on duty. They were overwhelmed, and many were captured. The prison school, the chapel, and the machine shop were put to the torch. While they were being reduced to smoldering debris, raiding parties of inmates raced through the galleries, gates, and catwalks of three of the four rectangular cellblocks — B, C and D. According to a Wyoming County deputy sheriff, they were armed with pipes which they had hidden under loaves of bread on trays in the mess halls. That may be apocryphal; the credibility of Attica's authorities was to be severely damaged before the uprising was over. But even if the inmates lacked weapons at the outset, they soon equipped themselves with them. Using grinding wheels acquired while looting the shops, some of them fashioned spears from scissor blades and broom handles. Others turned out clubs and knives which, when the keepers tried to extinguish the fires, were used to shred the hoses. With tear gas, guards managed to regain control of cellblock C and part of B, but the prisoners retained the rest, locking gates and even welding some of them shut with shop equipment.

Four hours after the revolt had begun, the battlefront hardened along lines which would remain substantially unchanged over the next four days. Cellblock D, the farthest from the administration building and the nearest to the shop, was the rebel stronghold, commanded by Blyden and Clarke. Wearing football helmets or turbans, the rebels — there were 1,280 of them — sprawled under makeshift tents in D yard, and a crude bench at one end of the yard was the epicenter of the revolt. There a rebel secretariat, the People's Central Committee, sat in continuous session, assigning work details, dictating defense measures, and even confining unruly prisoners in a "people's jail." Contacts between the convicts and state authorities were made in negotiating sessions at the table and in an A block corridor, a kind of no-man's-land dubbed the DMZ. A point of special interest was the geographical center of the prison, "Times Square," where catwalks leading to all four cellblocks met. It was held by the rebels. They had wrested it from a twenty-eight-year-old guard, William Quinn, who had battled them with a nightstick and had been overcome only after his skull had been fractured in two places. Some guards swore that they had seen him being brutally thrown from a high catwalk. There was no question that he had been gravely injured. When Clarke saw blood dripping from the unconscious guard's ear he ordered him passed through the DMZ to the authorities. Quinn's condition was a matter of great interest to both sides; if he died, every inmate participating in the uprising could be tried for murder.

Around noon Captain Henry F. Williams of the state police mustered two hundred and fifty troopers with riot equipment and told them: "If somebody on the other side gets killed, well, that's the way it's got to be. You're to take no crap from anybody. Don't lose your weapon and don't lose your buddy." That was tough talk, but it was deprived of much of its force by the fact that precipitate action was likely to lose them thirty-nine buddies — guards being held by the rebels as hostages. The captive keepers had been dressed in convict uniforms, blindfolded, and tied up in D yard. An inmate shouting through a megaphone warned that the hostages would be the first to suffer if the troopers charged, and no one in a position of responsibility, not even Superintendent Mancusi, was eager to call their bluff.

The man with the legal responsibility of dealing with the situation was Commissioner Oswald, who flew in at 2 P.M. Against Mancusi's advice, Oswald decided to enter D yard with Herman Schwartz, a Buffalo law professor trusted by the leaders of the revolt, and confront the rebels in person. He intended to tell them that he could not discuss their complaints until the hostages had been released, an unbreakable rule in penal administration. He did demand their release, but he also listened while Blyden dictated a list of fifteen demands to him. The rebels wanted, among other things, permission to hold political meetings "without intimidation," "religious freedom" for Muslims, an end to mail censorship, the right to communicate with anyone they wished, regular grievance procedures, more recreation and less time in cells, more exercise yards, a full-time physician, a better school, more fruit and less pork, the removal of Warden Mancusi, a committee of outsiders to "oversee" the behavior of the authorities during the revolt, and a federal court injunction against any "physical and mental reprisals" for the inmates' acts during the revolt. To the end of the list Blyden added that some of the convicts, at least, insisted upon "Speedy and safe transportation out of confinement to a nonimperialist country." He said: "We are men. We are not beasts, and do not intend to be beaten or driven. What has happened here is but the sound before the fury of those oppressed."

Oswald's personal courage in entering D yard was considerable. Even as he sat before the secretariat of rebel leaders, some of them were suggesting that he be added to the group of hostages, and though state police sharpshooters atop the prison walls were lining up the inmates around him in their sights, his chances of surviving a real row were negligible. His wisdom in going was another matter. Once he had heard them out and concluded that many of their points were reasonable, the pressure on him to open negotiations was almost irresistible. He yielded to it. As proof of his good faith he agreed to appoint a committee of overseers and to dispatch Schwartz to Federal Judge John T. Curtin, who was at a Vermont judicial conference, in pursuit of the injunction. Oswald did something else which was deeply resented by Mancusi and his staff. He signed a pledge of "No administrative reprisals against prisoners for activities of Sept. 9, 1971." The rebels interpreted this as a guarantee of clemency. The governor's office quickly pointed out that exoneration for criminal acts was out of the question; the commissioner didn't have the power to grant that. But the seeds of misunderstanding had been sown and were bound to bear bitter fruit.

That night Oswald returned to the floodlit prison yard, now further illumined by convicts' campfires. With him he brought a contingent of reporters — a concession to another rebel demand. Much of the time was spent putting together the panel of overseers. The inmates' choices included William Kunstler, Huey P. Newton, Bobby Seale, State Senator John R. Dunne, Tom Wicker of the *New York Times,* who had written sympathetically of George Jackson; Herman Badillo, the first Puerto Rican elected to Congress; and Clarence Jones, Negro publisher of Manhattan's *Amsterdam News.* Later Rockefeller added a number of selections of his own: his secretary, a school superintendent, a retired general, and various legislators and penologists. At one point there were thirty overseers. That was too many to be effective, and the ideological splits among them further weakened the committee.

Schwartz brought back the injunction signed by Judge Curtin. It had been drafted by one of the white prisoners, Jerome S. Rosenberg from Brooklyn, murderer of a policeman, but now the rebels rejected it as inadequate. The overseers were off to a lumbering start. Wicker, Jones, and Julian Tepper of the National Legal Aid and Defenders Association breakfasted with Wyoming County District Attorney Louis James; the best they could wangle from him was a written promise of no "indiscriminate mass prosecutions" — an assurance hardly likely to diminish the fears of the edgy convict secretariat. Another shaky agreement was broken at 4 A.M. Saturday, as the revolt approached the end of its second twenty-four-hour period, when the press pool was barred from the prison. Police hostility toward the reporters had been growing, a grim sign which usually foreshadows actions that policemen do not want outsiders to watch.

Yet Oswald was optimistic that morning. The inmates' demands had grown to thirty, but he had agreed to twenty-eight of them, drawing the line only at complete amnesty, which he now called "nonnegotiable," and the firing of Mancusi. Just as he was expressing confidence that these could be resolved, however, new developments shriveled hopes for a peaceful end to the riot. Quinn died, ending any possibility of leniency for the rebel leaders. Then Bobby Seale arrived. Before entering the prison he told fifty cheering radical demonstrators outside the walls that "If anything happens to those guards, the state and the governor should be charged with murder." Then his entourage passed out copies of a statement from the Panther Central Committee: "The prison guards, called 'hostages,' have actually in reality been placed under arrest by the 1,280 prisoners who are rightly redressing their grievances concerning the harassing, brutal, and inhuman treatment to which they are constantly subjected. . . . A promise of amnesty is the first thing that must be done to start negotiations of the prisoners' . . . demands. This is the only bail the arrested guards can have, from the analysis of the Black Panther party."

Obviously Seale had no interest in a resolution of the crisis. Inside, he told the inmates that they must make their own decisions in dealing with Oswald. In a pathetic display of trust, they begged him for advice. He replied that he could offer them no counsel without the approval of Huey P. Newton. After participating briefly in the overseers' deliberations he left, telling newspapermen that their questions and the armed state troopers were upsetting him. To cap this, Kunstler, in an act of extraordinary irresponsibility, told the rebel secretariat that representatives of "Third World nations are waiting for you across the street." Presumably he meant the fifty demonstrators, but he didn't explain, and the prisoners, now hoping for total victory, lost interest in bargaining with Oswald.

Sunday was a day of mobilization for both sides. Throughout the afternoon trucks arrived to disgorge National Guardsmen, powerful fire hoses, and crates of gas cylinders and gas masks. The overseers issued a statement warning that they were "now convinced that a massacre of prisoners and guards may ·take place at this institution." Wicker, Jones, Badillo, and Dunne spent over a half an hour on the telephone pleading with Rockefeller to come to Attica, but the governor issued a statement of his own saying that "In view of the fact that the key issue is total amnesty . . . I do not feel that my physical presence on the site can contribute to a peaceful settlement." He and Oswald had already agreed that if the convict leadership did not respond to a final ultimatum, they would have to resort to force. They were not sanguine. Plainly the mood of the prisoners was turning uglier. Gates were being wired to make them electrically hot, trenches were filled with gasoline. Booby traps of peat moss and oil were wired with time charges. Crude rocket catapults were fixed in position; the spears were resharpened. Barricades of metal tables were built along the main catwalk leading from A block to Times Square — a route invading troopers would have to follow. That afternoon rebels paying off old scores stabbed two white convicts to death.

The point of no return was reached early Monday. At 7 A.M. teams of policemen were assigned to specific functions: marksmanship, rescue, barricade demolition, and reserve strength. Two helicopters hovered overhead reporting on the disposition of convict forces and the situation of the hostages. At 8:35 Oswald met Richard Clarke in the DMZ. Brother Richard insisted that the rebels must be assured of "complete, total, unadulterated amnesty" and the dismissal of "that guy Mancusi." He said he wanted another half-hour to confer with other members of the secretariat. Oswald gave it to him. At 9:05 an inmate shouted through a megaphone that all the hostages would be killed by inmate "executioners" if rebel positions were attacked. An Oswald aide called back, "Release the prisoners now. Then the commissioner will meet with you." The convict yelled, "Negative." That was, literally, the last word in the negotiations. Only savagery was left.

Minutes later one of the helicopters radioed that four hostages were "at each corner of Times Square with knives at their throats." It was a chilling sight: each captive's head was yanked back by the hair, arching his neck; the blades, held by cocked hands, were biting into the flesh. Actually this looked more desperate than it really was. What officials could not know was that they were witnessing a prime example of militant overstatement. The hostages weren't going to die at the rebels' hands. Like the demand for resettlement in "a nonimperialist country" (which had been withdrawn the first time Oswald had raised an eyebrow), the grisly gestures with the homemade daggers were a kind of rhetoric, designed to impress the world and, perhaps, the convicts themselves. There have always been men prepared to die for acts of bravado. Some were about to fall here now, and they were going to take helpless victims with them.

Convinced that the hostages were in grave peril, that they might be massacred anyway — that the danger was imminent and time was of the essence — Oswald said to his aides, "There's no question now — we've got to go in." More than five hundred local law enforcement officers and yellow-clad state troopers were coiled at the doors leading to the catwalks as *Jackpot Two,* a CH-34 helicopter, swooped down on Times Square with a load of tear gas, pepper gas, and mustard gas. The radio dispatcher's voice crackled: "Move in! Move in! The drop has been made! Base to all posts — move in. Launch the offensive!"

Troopers burst through the doors and blasted away at the barricades; marksmen on the gray walls began picking off inmates. Clearing the cat-walks of obstacles took ninety minutes. Then the main attack went in. With clouds of turbid gas drifting across Times Square and D yard, it was difficult to see what was going on, and the fact that the hostages were wearing convict uniforms didn't help. Troopers insisted afterward that strong resistance persisted for about two and a half minutes. One said, "They came at us like a banzai charge, waving knives and spears. Those we had to shoot." Another said, "The ones that resisted — throwing spears and Molotov cocktails — were cut down. We caught some men with arms extended to throw weapons. Anybody that resisted was killed."

But some who didn't resist were killed, too. Sporadic firing continued for almost an hour. The New York State Special Commission on Attica (the McKay Commission) later found that the police assault had been "marred by excesses," which included "much unnecessary shooting." Some of the needless violence was attributable to carelessness, possibly even to a contempt for human life. Rockefeller had specifically forbidden prison guards to participate in the assault, but they went in anyhow and were responsible for at least two homicides. Some of the policemen fired shotguns loaded with "oo" buckshot which spread at distances exceeding thirty yards, hitting "unintended targets," the McKay investigators found, and creating "a high risk of injury and death to unresisting inmates and hostages." An attending physician, Dr. Lionel Sifontes of Buffalo, reported afterward that "Many of the ringleaders were approached by guards and shot systematically. Some had their hands in the air surrendering. Some were lying on the ground."

More than 120 men lay wounded or dying. Counting Quinn and the convicts who had been murdered by other prisoners during the uprising, Attica's death toll was 32 inmates and 11 guards or administrative officers — a total of 43. Compounding the confusion in the hours after the recapture of the prison were highly inaccurate reports about how the hostages had died. One Oswald aide said that a guard had been found emasculated, his testicles stuffed in his mouth. Another aide told reporters that "Several of the hostages had their throats slashed." Stories that the guards had been butchered by their captors gained credence from the fact that their blood-stained blindfolds had fallen around their necks. In fact, three surviving guards had suffered throat wounds, but when the medical examiner issued his report the following morning, he found no castrations and no mutilations among the dead. All had been killed from gunfire. And only policemen had carried guns.

Governor Rockefeller said the hostages had "died in the crossfire." Oswald lamely suggested that they "could very well have been used as shields." The rescued hostages vigorously endorsed the police assault, and in Washington President Nixon said that the "painful, excruciating" decision to storm Attica had been the only thing the authorities "could possibly do." The conflict of opinion over what had happened was rapidly becoming ideological. Those who distrusted liberals, penal reforms, "bleeding hearts" and "do-gooders" rejected all criticism of the troopers. They blamed the convicts — in a fierce editorial the *Atlanta Constitution* denounced "the animals of Attica" for trying to impose "kangaroo justice" on the hostages — and many also blamed the overseers. As an exhausted Wicker left Attica a guard at the door hissed at him, "You people will never again be allowed inside this facility under any circumstances."

The other side was also vehement. Newark Mayor Kenneth Gibson called the crushing of the prison revolt "one of the most callous and blatantly repressive acts ever carried out by a supposedly civilized society." Wicker later noted that although sixty inmates had been indicted on some 1,300 counts, not a single law enforcement officer had been charged with anything, despite "evidence of official negligence, official brutality, official indiscipline, official excess — possibly even official murder." After the rebellion had been suppressed, the McKay Commission found there had been "widespread beatings, proddings, kickings." Prisoners had been stripped and forced to run a gauntlet of guards with hickory billy clubs. Wounded guards had been swiftly treated, their families quickly notified. Wounded inmates had been left without medical attention for four hours, their bodies tagged "P1, P2, P3." Four days later the families of some prisoners were still frantically trying to learn whether their sons or husbands were alive or dead. Often Attica wouldn't tell them even that. Those who did hear received curt wires: REGRET TO INFORM YOU THAT YOUR HUSBAND RAYMOND RIVERA NUMBER 29533 HAS DECEASED. THE BODY REPOSES AT THIS INSTITUTION.

"All right we are two nations," John Dos Passos had written bitterly of the chasm between the rich and the starving in an earlier America. The rupture was along different lines now, but it cut equally deep. Three years earlier a new occupant of the White House had vowed to "bring us together." He hadn't done it. The people were as far apart as ever, unable to agree on the most elementary issues — justice and mercy, war and peace, right and wrong — and with a new presidential election a year away Americans were beginning to eye anew Richard Nixon's standings in the polls. Here, however, there was a change. As late as early August pollster Albert Sindlinger found that only 27 percent of the voters wanted to see

Nixon reelected, but before the month was out his popularity curve paused, leveled out, and slowly rose. The decisive factor was resolute executive action at home and abroad.

The thirty-first world table tennis championships were held in Nagoya, Japan, that April, and the composition of the U.S. team was a tribute to the sport's widespread appeal: a Chrysler personnel supervisor, a Du Pont chemist, an editor of *Sports Illustrated,* a college professor, a black federal employee, an IBM programmer, an immigrant from the Dominican Republic, an employee of a Wall Street bank, two teen-age girls, two housewives, and two college undergraduates. One of the students, Glenn Cowan of Santa Monica, was the most flamboyant member of the party; he wore tie-dyed purple bell-bottoms and a shirt with a peace symbol, and he kept his shoulder-length hair under control during play with a headband. Possibly because the headband was red, possibly because he was alert and extroverted, Cowan was singled out by players from the People's Republic of China for a historic proposal. How, he was asked, would he and his teammates like to make an all-expenses-paid tour of Red China?

They were delighted — "To quote Chairman Mao," Cowan said after consulting his teammates, "I seem to have struck the spark that started a prairie fire" — and a formal invitation to them from Secretary General Sung Chung of the Chinese table tennis delegation quickly followed. Washington had no objection; just a few weeks earlier the State Department had lifted all restrictions on Americans who wanted to travel in the People's Republic. Everyone concerned, including the ping-pong players, knew that the relationship between the two events was not coincidental. It was generally interpreted as an opening move toward detente, a reflection of the new confidence in Peking since the violent three-year power struggle there, known as the Great Proletarian Cultural Revolution, had ended in the final triumph of Mao and Premier Chou En-lai two years earlier. When seven western newspapermen were granted permission to enter China and cover the tour, it was clear that the world had reached a historic turning point. Obviously the Chinese, like the Russians before them, were using sport for diplomatic purposes. Table tennis acquired a new status overnight. Even President Nixon told his staff that "I was quite a Ping Pong player in my days at law school. I might say I was fairly good at it." Moscow sulked. The Kremlin called Peking's overture to the Americans "unprincipled."

On April 10 the U.S. team crossed from Hong Kong to the border station of Lo Wu via a short, steel-trussed bridge and continued on over another, tin-roofed bridge to the Chinese city of Shumchun. There smiling Communist officials led them to an immaculate cream and blue train. Their first destination was Canton, which since the rupture between Washington and Peking twenty-one years earlier had been rechristened Kwangchow. Along the twenty-three-mile journey there they saw banana groves, lichee trees, rice paddies, and, at strategic intervals, gigantic billboards bearing pictures of Mao. At Canton's new airport they boarded a Soviet-built Ilyushin-18 airliner while loudspeakers blared military marches and quotations from *The Thoughts of Chairman Mao*. An exhortatory sign in the terminal read PEOPLE OF THE WORLD UNITE AND DEFEAT THE U.S. AGGRESSORS AND THEIR RUNNING DOGS. It wasn't meant as an insult to the visitors. Mao's government at that point was drawing a fine line between the American people, whose friendship it wanted, and its government, which Peking Radio continued to excoriate as a conspiracy of "bloodthirsty gangsters."

Even in April Peking's climate retains the bite of winter, but apart from that the capital's reception for the U.S. ping-pong group was all hospitality. Quartered in the elegant Hsinchiao Hotel, they were entertained at banquets and taken on a tour of the nineteenth-century summer palace of the Manchu emperors and the Great Hall of the People. They saw a "revolutionary ballet," *The Red Detachment of Women*, and heard an opera celebrating the victory of Communism over capitalism, *Taking Tiger Mountain by Strategy*. Arriving at Peking's Indoor Stadium for an exhibition match with members of the Chinese team, they were greeted by 18,000 cheering fans and a huge banner reading WELCOME TO THE TABLE TENNIS TEAM FROM THE UNITED STATES. A band struck up the stirring strains of "Sailing the Seas Depends on the Helmsman, Making Revolution Depends on the Thought of Mao Tse-tung." Cowan did the frug.

Chinese tact continued in the table tennis competition. Holding back their first team, which could have crushed the Americans, they sent in second-string players who only won the men's matches 5-3 and the women's 5-4. The hosts called the contests "friendly games." They were not the most striking act of friendship. The following day Chou En-lai met China's ping-pong guests in the red-carpeted reception room of the Great Hall. The members of the United States delegation weren't the only table tennis visitors that week, and since Chinese protocol is rigidly alphabetical, they were preceded by players from Canada, Colombia, England, and Nigeria. But Chou spent most of his time — one and three-quarter hours — with them. He told them, "We have opened a new page in the relations of the Chinese and the American people." To the U.S. newsmen he said that now American correspondents could "come in batches."

That same day, as the Americans left for Hong Kong, President Nixon eased the twenty-year U.S. embargo on trade with China and Peking resumed telephone contact with Washington and London. There was a lot to talk about; less than two weeks later a presidential commission headed by Henry Cabot Lodge recommended that the People's Republic be admitted to the United Nations provided a way could be found for Nationalist China to retain its seat. Already plans were being laid for a secret visit to Peking by National Security Adviser Henry Kissinger at which the chief topic of conversation would be a state visit by the President himself.

Early in July Kissinger flew to Asia, officially for conferences in Saigon, Thailand, India, and Pakistan. After a ninety-minute talk with Pakistani

President Agha Muhommad Yahya Khan, Kissinger announced a change in his schedule; he would spend a brief working holiday in the mountain resort of Nathia Gali, thirty-eight miles north of Rawalpindi. The trip wasn't turning out to be particularly newsworthy, and the curiosity of newsmen covering it was unstirred when the Yahya Khan government announced that Kissinger would have to spend an additional day in the resort because of a slight indisposition. He was thought to be suffering from Asian dysentery — "Delhi belly" — and the U.S. embassy encouraged the assumption by putting out word that a doctor had been dispatched to examine him. A correspondent suggested that the presidential adviser would be more comfortable in an air-conditioned Rawalpindi hotel. The embassy spokesman replied that the visitor did not want to embarrass anyone in the capital by his illness.

Actually Kissinger had driven to the Rawalpindi airport with three aides and boarded a Pakistan International Airlines plane for Peking. At noon on July 9 they landed on a deserted field outside the Chinese capital. Driven to a villa on a nearby lake, they lunched and were then joined, at mid-afternoon, by Chou En-lai. Chou and Kissinger conferred late that Friday night, Saturday evening, and Sunday morning. Five pounds heavier because of Chinese hospitality, the presidential adviser — who was still believed to be laid low by a stomach ailment — flew back to Pakistan and rejoined his party after a two-and-a-half day absence. Nothing more was heard from Peking Radio about American officials being gangsters or running dogs. Five days after the Kissinger mission President Nixon flew by helicopter from San Clemente to a Burbank television studio and delivered a four-minute address which astounded the world. He had been invited to visit Red China, he announced, and he was accepting with pleasure. He said: "I have taken this action because of my profound conviction that all nations will gain from a reduction of tensions and a better relationship between the United States and the People's Republic of China." In a reference to Nationalist China the President added that "seeking a new relationship" with Peking would not be "at the expense of our old friends."

It was a promise he could not keep. His plan to seat both Chinas in the United Nations was doomed. Each year the U.N. had come closer to expelling the Taiwan delegation, and this was enough to put it over the top. On October 25 the General Assembly voted Peking in and Chiang Kai-shek's representatives out. American conservatives watching television that day beheld a spectacle of humiliation which would have been unbelievable in the days when Dean Acheson and John Foster Dulles ran U.S. foreign policy; the Algerians and the Albanians embraced, and the Tanzanians danced a jig in the aisles. The reaction in Washington was sharp and angry. Barry Goldwater demanded that the United States quit the U.N. and consign the General Assembly to "some place like Moscow or Peking." Hugh Scott of Pennsylvania spoke contemptuously of "hot-pants principalities" like Tanzania, and presidential press secretary Ronald Ziegler condemned "the shocking demonstration and undisguised glee among some of the delegates following the vote." But these were mere political rituals. The fact was that Chiang's continuing pretensions to great-power status had been doomed from the moment of the first conciliatory gesture toward Glenn Cowan in Nagoya.

One month to the day after his telecast announcing that he would be flying to Peking, Nixon went on the air again with news of another momentous step, this one to rescue the American economy. It badly needed help. The country was sliding into its worst money crisis since the Depression. Then the nation's crippled finances had been further hobbled by Hoover's rigid faith in the economic gospels of Adam Smith and John Stuart Mill. Nixon paid them lip service, but in practice he was anything but inflexible. Hugh Sidey of *Time* observed that the President "clings to what is familiar until the last moment. Then, when the evidence overwhelms him or something happens in his gut, he decides to act, and nothing stands very long in his way. He abandons his philosophy, his promises, his speeches, his friends, his counselors. He marches out of one life into a new world without any apologies or glancing back." At times this could be disconcerting, but in that August of 1971, with the dollar tottering on the brink of disaster, it was heartening.

At the close of World War II the United States had been the wealthiest country in the history of civilization, holding 35 billion of the world's 40-odd billions of monetary gold. The structure of postwar finance had been established the year before at Bretton Woods, New Hampshire, where gold and dollars had been established as the reserves behind the money of every major nation outside the Communist bloc. There wasn't enough gold to support the anticipated flow of foreign trade, so the dollar, the world's strongest money, was made equal to gold. Debts between countries could be paid with either one. America pledged to redeem all available dollars with an ounce of gold for every $35, and other countries expressed the value of their currency in dollars. It worked. Trade prospered. Whenever a country managed to tip the balance of its U.S. trade in its favor — exporting more goods to America than it imported from there — its surplus dollars were used to back new issues of its own money.

Since the United States was rich and the rest of the world was comparatively poor, large sums went overseas to help the needy. It didn't matter; there was so much. Then came the Korean War and the revival of European commerce. By 1961, the end of the Common Market's first year, U.S. gold reserves were down to 17 billion dollars. In 1962 they dropped to 16 billion, in 1963 to 15 billion. At the beginning of the 1970s the reserves stood at 11 billion — almost the bare minimum, since American law required a dollar's worth of gold in Fort Knox for each four dollars in circulation, and the nation's business needed 40 billion in paper and silver. Meantime the balance of trade had become less and less favorable to the

United States. In 1960 the country had imported 15 billion dollars' worth of goods and sold 20 billion abroad, leaving a surplus of five billion. By 1970 this margin was down to two billion. In May 1971 it vanished. The nation was trading in the red, and with the Pentagon still hemorrhaging wealth in Vietnam there was no hope of a quick turnaround. Secretary of Commerce Maurice Stans warned that the U.S. faced its first trade deficit since 1893.

That month economists received anxious signals from Germany. The *Wirtschaftswunder* had transformed the Federal Republic into a heavy exporter. Twice during the previous decade the deutsche mark had been revalued upward, altering its value vis-à-vis the dollar and enriching speculators who accumulated reserves of it. Now the pressure was mounting for another revaluation. As a member of the International Monetary Fund established at Bretton Woods, Bonn was obliged to maintain the relationship between the dollar and the mark, buying dollars and selling marks as the mark became more valuable. Because of the unfavorable balance in American trade, speculators had a lot of dollars — or "Eurodollars," as dollars owned abroad were called — to invest. In the first four months of 1971 the stocks of Eurodollars on the continent had taken a frightening jump, from five billion to between 50 and 60 billion, and the German central bank was being flooded with them.

Die Zentralbank bought and bought until Bonn, recognizing early signs of inflation, notified the International Monetary Fund on May 9 that it wouldn't buy any more, Bretton Woods or no Bretton Woods. Instead the Germans proposed to let their currency find its own level under the law of supply and demand. In the idiom of economists they would "float" the mark. It floated up from 25 cents to 27 cents and hung there, relieving the pressure on their central bank and, incidentally, improving the U.S. balance of trade with the Federal Republic, since American goods were now cheaper there. But the respite was brief. Because of what Larry Stuntz of the Associated Press called "that huge pool of Eurodollars sloshing around Europe" — it amounted to the equivalent of all the money circulating in America — speculators were bound to turn elsewhere. They built a fire under the French franc, but Paris, which had been watching the German agony, quickly cut loose from the International Monetary Fund and limited dollar trades. The wildcatters went after the Swiss franc next. Bern followed the example of Paris. It was becoming increasingly hard to unload dollars. Bretton Woods was coming unstuck; *Barron's* was predicting a worldwide panic by fall. Then, early in August, came an authoritative forecast that the U.S. trade deficit for the second quarter would exceed seven billion dollars. This was swiftly followed by a report of the Joint Congressional Economic Committee which declared that the dollar was overvalued, that other currencies should be revalued upward, and that if this wasn't done the United States should stop buying gold. The stock market dove; the Dow Jones industrial average dropped 100 points from its April high. There was virtually no market for Eurodollars now. American tourists in Europe found that the once mighty dollar had become unacceptable currency. World trade was at a standstill; merchants could no longer be sure what their money would buy next week, or even tomorrow.

Americans were getting bad economic news at home, too. Nixon, predicting that 1971 would be a good year and 1972 a bad year, had based his budget on an anticipated Gross National Product of 1,065 billion dollars. It came in at 1,050 billion, and half the gain was inflation. Production was down; unemployment, at 6 percent, was nearing the recession level. At the end of June the administration ended the fiscal year with an appalling 23.2-billion-dollar deficit, just two billion less than Johnson's record-breaking 1968 shortfall and an incredible 24.5 billion below Nixon's expectations. The President had alarmed his conservative supporters by talking in terms of a "full employment balance," a Keynesian concept which holds that a budget is "balanced" if the amount of spending does not exceed the amount which would be collected in taxes if everyone had a job. But even with that yardstick the administration was eight billion in the red. And the future was glum. New labor contracts promised rail workers a hike of 42 percent in 42 months; steelworkers would get 30 percent in three years. Inflation would jump accordingly.

Congress had given the President the Economic Stabilization Act of 1970, authorizing him to "issue such orders as he may deem appropriate to stabilize prices, rents, wages, and salaries." Nixon had opposed the bill. He had been forced to sign it because it set aside basic resources needed for national defense, but he had vowed he would never use it. His plans excluded controls. He didn't even believe in voluntary guidelines or jawboning — using presidential prestige to persuade labor and management to forego wage or price increases.

All this changed in one short weekend at Camp David with his economic advisers. Summoned on twenty-four hours' notice, they drafted an economic message invoking the very powers he rejected, and on Sunday, August 15, he was on television with it. He called the program his New Economic Policy. Among the measures he ordered, or asked Congress for, was a closing of the "gold window" — the United States would no longer exchange dollars for gold. Most imports would be subjected to a 10 percent surtax, designed to make American goods more competitive at home with those from abroad, and in some cases Americans would receive tax breaks if they bought U.S. merchandise. Industry would get tax credit for new investment. The 7 percent excise tax on automobiles would be repealed, an average saving of $200 per car. With few exceptions, all U.S. prices, wages, rents, and dividends would be frozen for ninety days at their present levels. A Cost of Living Council headed by Treasury Secretary John Connally would preside over the freeze.

Nixon had floated the dollar, and the effect was the same as devaluation. In money markets it amounted to 2 percent in the first two weeks. Foreign bankers were understanding; they indicated that they were prepared to revalue their currencies if the U.S. would drop the surcharge. Meanwhile there was little retaliation abroad. The Danes did introduce a surcharge of their own, and the French muttered about imposing one, but there were few threats to build tariff walls against American goods which had suddenly become cheaper. Connally was not a popular man in foreign chancelleries; his insistence that the United States must quickly achieve a 13-billion-dollar swing in its balance of payments provoked protests that so rapid a reversal would destroy the Common Market. But at a September meeting of the International Monetary Fund, financiers from the "Group of Ten" wealthiest nations continued to be sympathetic to the U.S. position. Connally, in turn, hinted that America might reopen the gold window and raise its price — direct devaluation. Subsequent talks in Rome led to an agreement, announced at the Smithsonian Institution in Washington, under which the U.S. surcharge was canceled, the value of other currencies was raised, and the price of gold was provisionally boosted to $38.

On Wall Street the day after Nixon's announcement of the freeze — or Phase One, as it was already being called — the Dow Jones industrial average jumped 32.93 to 888.95 on what was then the busiest day in its history; 31,720,000 shares were traded. In September, the first full month of Phase One, the nation's rise in living costs was held to 2.4 percent and the wholesale price index posted its biggest decline in five years. A few holes were poked in the wage and price ceilings, and inevitably there was a great deal of confusion in some industries, but for the most part the thing worked. Unfortunately it was, by definition, only the first step. On November 13 it would expire. Before then the administration had to find guidelines which provided hope of preserving relative stability while rectifying the injustices which had been frozen into the system.

On October 8 Nixon spoke to the nation again, this time setting up the machinery for Phase Two. The challenge was greater now. Economist Herbert Stein, the chief planner of the new stage, had anticipated the difficulties at the time of the first message. He said, "I knew immediately the problem would not be the freeze, but the unfreeze, the thaw." The goal of this second program was to hold inflation to between 2 and 3 percent a year. Controls would be administered by a seven-man Price Commission and a fifteen-member pay board. There would be no ceiling on profits, the President said, and the success or failure of the plan would depend upon "the voluntary cooperation of the American people."

Fear that both labor and capital might withdraw their representatives from the supervisory panels doomed hopes of keeping inflation below 3 percent. "If the President doesn't want our membership on the Pay Board on our terms, he knows what he can do," Meany told delegates to an AFL-CIO convention in Miami Beach. Nixon boldly flew to the convention hall to reply: "I know exactly what I can do. And I am going to do it."

Nevertheless, the board capitulated to Meany in the last week of Phase One, announcing full recognition of deferred wage increases and establishment of 5.5 percent as the annual norm for new raises. Even that line wasn't held; in its first decision under Phase Two the board granted a 15 percent pay boost for coal miners. The price commission was no more effective. It began by approving 7 percent increases in the cost of tinplate manufactured by two steel companies. Within three weeks one-third of the country's 1,500 largest corporations had applied for endorsement of price hikes, and acceptances surpassed rejections by a ratio of 20 to 1.

In December the stock market plunged again. The board continued its conciliatory treatment of labor, but three months later Meany and two other top union leaders pulled out anyway, accusing the majority of bias. The next day Leonard Woodcock of the UAW also quit. That left only one labor member: Frank E. Fitzsimmons, the Teamsters president. Since Nixon's Christmas Week pardon of Jimmy Hoffa, the Teamsters had been in the President's pocket. That clemency had been universally attributed to politics, but few blamed Nixon. Though his standing in the polls had improved somewhat since the lows of summer, it was generally believed that if he was going to be reelected he would need all the help he could get.

Portrait of an American

RALPH NADER

In the Connecticut manufacturing city of Winsted his Lebanese immigrant father was the local populist, a familiar American type. Customers at Nadra Nader's Highland Sweet Shop, a restaurant and bakery, complained that the proprietor never let them eat in peace. Nadra was always lecturing them about the wrongs, the inequities, the injustices of the system. Like many immigrants, he was a more ardent Democrat than the natives. He went on about the crimes of the Interests and was forever threatening to sue them. In time nearly everyone there tuned him out, with one exception: his youngest son Ralph.

In 1938, at the age of four, Ralph Nader was a tiny spectator when lawyers harangued juries in the local courthouse. At fourteen he became a daily reader of the *Congressional Record.* He won a scholarship to Princeton, where he refused to wear white bucks or other symbols of sartorial conformity and staged a protest against the spraying of campus trees with DDT. He was locked so often in the university library after hours that he was given a key. Characteristically he responded by denouncing the administration for callous disregard of other students' legal rights. In 1955 he was elected to Phi Beta Kappa, graduated magna cum laude, and admitted to Harvard Law School, which he described as a "high-priced tool factory" turning out servants of power.

His reputation as a puritan grew. He foreswore the reading of novels; they were a waste of time. So were movies; he would limit himself to two a year. He scorned plays, tobacco, alcohol, girls, and parties. At Harvard he also quit driving automobiles, but here his motive was different. He had become interested in auto injury cases, and after some research in car technology at nearby MIT he wrote an article for the *Harvard Law Record* entitled "American Cars: Designed for Death."

The problem continued to bother him. Throughout his career he was to be concerned with the protection of the human body — from unsafe natural gas pipelines, food additives, tainted meat, pollution, mining health hazards, herbicides, unwholesome poultry, inadequate nursing homes, and radiation emission from color TVs — but the auto threat was basic. He opened a private law practice in Hartford (which rapidly became a source of free legal advice for the poor) and continued to urge stronger car safety regulations on local governments. Early in 1964 he took his campaign to Washington, where Assistant Secretary of Labor Daniel Patrick Moynihan hired him as a fifty-dollar-a-day consultant to the Labor Department.

Working with Connecticut's Senator Abraham Ribicoff, Nader turned out a two-hundred-page brief calling for auto safety legislation with teeth. A General Motors engineer became the first of his many secret contacts in industry by pointing out the Chevrolet Corvair's tendency to flip over. In November 1965 Nader's first book, *Unsafe at Any Speed: The Designed-in Dangers of the American Automobile,* called the Corvair "one of the nastiest-handling cars ever built" and charged that the industry had taken "four years of the model and 1,124,076 Corvairs before they decided to do something."

Unsafe at Any Speed, which sold 450,000 copies in cloth and paper, brought its author before a Ribicoff committee on February 10, 1966, as an expert witness on hazardous autos. Three weeks later Nader became a national figure when he accused General Motors of harassing him with private detectives, abusive telephone calls, and women who tried to entice him into compromising situations. A GM operative admitted under oath that he had been instructed by his superiors "to get something somewhere on this guy . . . get him out of their hair . . . shut him up." Nader filed suit for 26 million dollars and collected $280,000. Like his book royalties, the money went to the cause; when the National Traffic and Motor Vehicle Safety Act was passed that summer the *Washington Post* declared that "Most of the credit for making possible this important legislation belongs to one man — Ralph Nader . . . a one-man lobby for the public prevailed over the nation's most powerful industry."

Nader set himself up as a watchdog of the National Traffic Safety Agency and then went after the meat packers; the result was the Wholesome Meat Act of 1967. He broadened his attack on exploiters of the consumer to include the Food and Drug Administration, Union Carbide smokestacks, think tanks, unsafe trucks, pulp and paper mills, property taxes, bureaucrats, consumer credit, banks, and supermarkets. One observer said, "Ralph is not a consumer champion. He is just plain against consumption."

Unlike the muckrakers of the Lincoln Steffens era, Nader acquired a conservative constituency. At a time of anarchy and disorder he believed in working within the system. He was a linear thinker, an advocate of law and industrial order. Stockbrokers contributed to his causes. Miss Porter's School sent him volunteer workers. He was acquiring lieutenants now — "Nader's Raiders," a reporter dubbed them — and they were mostly white upper-middle-class graduates of the best schools, with names like Pullman cars: Lowell Dodge, William Harrison Wellford, Reuben B. Robertson III, and William Howard Taft IV. One of them, Edward F. Cox, became a son-in-law of President Nixon.

He installed them in cubbyhole offices in the National Press Building furnished with secondhand desks, chairs bought at rummage sales, apple crate files, and shelves made from planks and bricks. He worked them a hundred hours a week and paid them poverty-level salaries. Royalties from the books they turned out went into his campaigns. They didn't complain; he himself was earning $200,000 a year and spending $5,000.

He lived in an $80-a-month furnished room near Dupont Circle, paid $97 a month office rent, and had no secretary. People gave him briefcases; he turned them into files and traveled instead with his papers in a sheaf of manila envelopes. His black shoes were scuffed, the laces broken and knotted. He wore a gray rumpled suit, frayed white shirts, and narrow ties which had been out of style for years. Standing six feet four inches, with wavy black hair and a youthful face, he was compared by *Newsweek* to a "Jimmy Stewart hero in a Frank Capra movie." His only unusual expense was his telephone bill. It was enormous. He was paying for calls from all his volunteer spies in industry.

Most of his income came from lecture fees. Each week he received fifty invitations to speak; he accepted 150 a year, charging as much as $2,000. He became known as the most long-winded speaker since Walter Reuther, rarely relinquishing the lectern before an hour and forty-five minutes. There was never any flourish at the end. He would simply stop talking and pivot away. College audiences gave him wild ovations, but he never turned back to acknowledge them. If asked to autograph a book he would curtly reply, "No." A friend said, "Ralph is so afraid of being turned into a movie star, of having his private life romanticized, that he has renounced his own private life."

He was an impossible customer. To a waitress he would say when ordering, "Is the ham sliced for each sandwich? Is that genuine or processed cheese? Do *you* eat sugar? You do? Let me tell you something — it's absolutely useless, no food value." To an airline stewardess he said, "The only thing you should be proud to serve on this whole plane is the little bag of nuts. And you should take the salt off the nuts." When Allegheny Airlines had the temerity to bump him from a flight on which he had a confirmed reservation, he filed suit and was awarded $50,000 in punitive damages, half for him and half for the consumer group he had been unable to address because of the missed flight.

Asked by Robert F. Kennedy why he was "doing all this," he answered, "If I were engaged in activities for the prevention of cruelty to animals, nobody would ask me that question." His ultimate goal, he said, was "nothing less than the qualitative reform of the industrial revolution," and he refused to be lured from it by any bait. Nicholas von Hoffman and Gore Vidal proposed him for the Presidency. He said, "I'm not interested in public office. The biggest job in this country is citizen action. Politics follows that."

Yet for all his evangelism, his devotion to the public good, and his monastic life, Nader's impact on society was questionable. At times he seemed to know it. "We always fail," he said once. "The whole thing is limiting the degree of failure." His audiences appeared to regard him as a performer. They applauded him, but it was as though they were applauding an act. Few of them felt compelled to get involved, to follow his example or even his advice. They went right on driving big Detroit cars, eating processed foods, coating themselves with expensive cosmetics and smoking poisonous cigarettes.

In a pensive moment he reflected that "A couple of thousand years ago in Athens, a man could get up in the morning, wander around the city, and inquire into matters affecting his well-being and that of his fellow citizens. No one asked him 'Who are you with?' " Americans of the 1970s did not inquire about him; they knew. Yet they themselves remained uncommitted. The painful fact — excruciating for him — was that however loud their cheers for Ralph Nader, however often they said that they were for him, in this Augustan age of materialism they were not really with him.

THIRTY-SEVEN

Pride Goeth

THE AGE OF PUBLICITY, as Louis Kronenberger called it, may be said to have begun in the 1920s with flagpole sitting and the ordeal of Floyd Collins, an unlucky youth whose entrapment and eventual death in a Kentucky cave-in was page one news for two weeks in 1925. Ballyhoo became increasingly conspicuous after World War II with the emergence of such exhibitionists as those who took their marriage vows on carnival carrousels, spent their honeymoons in department store windows, bore children under floodlights, and hired halls to celebrate their divorces. "The trouble with us in America," Kronenberger wrote in 1954, "isn't that the poetry of life has turned to prose, but that it has turned to advertising copy." He suggested that next to Marx and Freud, the ideologue with the greatest impact on U.S. lives was Phineas Taylor Barnum.

As American influence spread abroad, so did the Barnum spirit. Among the bizarre stunts overseas which put their perpetrators on front pages in 1972 was a telephoned threat to blow up the luxury liner *Queen Elizabeth 2* and the defacing of Michelangelo's *Pietà* in St. Peter's Basilica by an Australian geologist with a twelve-pound hammer, a perverted sense of theater, and the conviction that he was the son of God. They were outrageous, but at least they weren't homicidal, which was more than could be said for many foreign self-promoters. That year was memorable for what might be called the hoopla of death. Murders committed abroad for their publicity value included those of three NATO electronics experts executed by Turkish leftists, twenty-six travelers in Tel Aviv's Lod Airport by a squad of Japanese terrorists, eleven Israeli athletes at the Munich Olympics by Palestinian Arabs of the Black September ring, and 469 Ulster Catholics and Protestants by Ulster Protestants and Catholics. In addition, Japan's Yasunari Kawabata, the 1968 Nobel Prize winner in literature, took his own life. He thereby followed the example of Yukio Mishima, a young colleague who had protested western influence in his homeland by committing ritualistic hara-kiri in the good old way, eviscerating himself and submitting to decapitation by his best friend.

Americans had no reason to feel smug about this lengthening roll of dishonor overseas. It was Lee Harvey Oswald of Dallas who had first demonstrated to his countrymen in the 1960s that attention must be paid to a daring murderer, and his example had been followed in the United States by, among others, Sirhan Sirhan, of Los Angeles, Charles Whitman of the Austin bell tower, and Robert Benjamin Smith, who had committed mayhem in the Mesa, Arizona, beauty school. In 1972 they were joined by others with similar motivation. Mobster "Crazy Joe" Gallo was gunned down in New York's Little Italy. His sister told reporters, "He changed his image, that's why this happened." When George Jackson's two Soledad colleagues were acquitted in the death of a prison guard, Angela Davis managed to transform it into a public relations triumph; "It's beautiful," she said. The end of *Life* magazine on December 29, closing a big publicity artery, was treated by some politicians as a death in the family. The name of four-star Air Force General John D. Lavelle began appearing on reference books after he had been reprimanded and reduced in rank for unauthorized bombing raids in North Vietnam; his name had been in the papers. Most memorable was Arthur Herman Bremer, who gunned down George Wallace in a Laurel, Maryland, shopping center on the eve of the presidential primary there. On the way to jail Bremer asked officers, "How much do you think I'll get for my memoirs?"

While these malefactions were drearily familiar, some Americans did break new publicity ground that year. Two police cases deserve special recognition because, unlike the Soledad, Gallo, and Wallace incidents, they displayed remarkable imaginative powers on the part of criminals or accusers. The first was the skyjacking of a Southern Airways DC9 jet by pirates who lifted extortion from the realm of the ordinary by threatening to crash the plane into the nuclear research plant at Oak Ridge unless their demands were met. Though the airliner's tires were shot out by FBI agents, the skyjackers collected two million dollars at the Chattanooga airport and landed in Havana, where, like so many of their predecessors, they were dismayed to find themselves under Cuban arrest and their loot confiscated. The other episode followed a charge by J. Edgar Hoover that peace workers were plotting to kidnap Henry Kissinger and blow up steam pipes beneath Washington, D.C., which carried heat to all federal buildings in the capital. Indicted for conspiracy, six Catholics and a Moslem were tried. The government lost the case, and nine months afterward two of the defendants, Father Philip Berrigan and Sister Elizabeth McAlister, startled their associates at, respectively, the Society of St. Joseph and the Sacred Heart of Mary community, by getting married.

That was thought strange by practitioners of traditional religion, but an even zanier approach to piety was that of the "Jesus people," also known as the "Jesus freaks" or the "street Christians." In reality they represented the latest stage in the youth movement, which had evolved from the beats to the hippies and was searching for a new kick. "Jesus, am I ever high on Jesus!" was one of their rallying cries. Three years earlier Theodore Roszak had declared in *The Making of a Counter Culture* that the movement had clearly defined spiritual aspects. He meant Zen and even odder sects; Christianity was then considered hopelessly square and establishmentarian. Now, however, the cats were wearing crucifixes and Christ T-shirts — "You Have a Lot to Live," read one, echoing a Pepsi-Cola jingle, "And Jesus Has a Lot to Give." They established communes called God's Love, Zion's Inn, and Soul Inn, attended Jesus rock concerts and Christian nightclubs, and made some parents yearn for the days when kids got stoned on old-fashioned marijuana.

As the colleges continued to be almost serene in 1972, peace militants talked about a public relations failure, but administrators of state universities were relieved; taxpayers had been rejecting school bond issues by lopsided votes. President Nixon's press office claimed that he had "scored points" with his constituents by a colorful turn of phrase; he had said he planned to spend more time at Camp David because "I find that up here on top of a mountain, it is easier for me to get on top of the job." On November 14 the New York Stock Exchange achieved a breakthrough in good publicity when the Dow Jones industrial average closed at 1006.16, above 1,000 for the first time in history. (It was, though no one knew it then, a good time to sell.) The public image of Jacqueline Kennedy Onassis shone more brightly, and that of one of her tormentors more dully, after a federal judge in New York ruled that a freelance photographer named Ronald E. Galella had "relentlessly invaded" Mrs. Onassis's privacy. In the future, the court ruled, Galella would be required to stay 50 yards from her, 75 yards from her children, and 100 yards from the family's homes and schools.

These varied events in the Age of Publicity, while noteworthy, were, however, rendered pallid by the accomplishments of two giants of the age. Both were American, both were passionately devoted to advertisements of themselves, and both achieved international recognition in 1972. One was an outlaw, the other merely ill-tempered.

Robert James Fischer, the irascible one, played chess. It is not recorded that he ever did anything else except insult his opponents, fail to make scheduled appearances, alienate his supporters, display greed, break his word, deliver ultimatums, throw temper tantrums, disappear at crucial moments, and become, after a classic tournament with Russia's Boris Spassky in Reykjavik, Iceland, the winner of the world chess championship. His countrymen agreed that it couldn't happen to a worse competitor. He stalked off angrily counting a record $156,000 in prize money.

The desperado was named Clifford Irving.

Shortly before Christmas 1971 the publishing firm of McGraw-Hill dispatched a 550-word publicity release of special interest to the New York offices of major editors, newscasters, and wire services. After nearly four-teen years of refusing to be interviewed, photographed, or even seen by members of the press, Howard Hughes, America's reclusive billionaire, had apparently completed, with the help of a collaborator, a 230,000-word account of his life. The clothbound edition of the work would be issued on March 27, 1972, and *Life* would publish three 10,000-word installments from it. "Call this autobiography," the announcement quoted Hughes as saying. "Call it my memoirs. Call it what you please. It is the story of my life in my own words." Also attributed to Hughes in the release were phrases singing the praises of his assistant in the project, Clifford Irving. In the billionaire's putative words, Irving had been picked "because of his sympathy, discernment, discretion and, as I learned, his integrity as a human being."

Hughes's recollections, it seemed, had been taped: "The words in this book — other than some of the questions which provoked them — are my own spoken words." At first editors assumed that the taping sessions had been held in the Bahamas hotel where he had been hiding out for the past year, but the truth seemed to be more dramatic than that; the two men had held over a hundred meetings "in various motel rooms and parked cars throughout the Western Hemisphere."

That was the claim advanced in the publisher's announcement. It would be accepted by the public for a month, and another month would pass before it was withdrawn. In the meantime the story was to become one of the most sensational in the history of the book trade. At one point it drove news of the President's inspection of the Great Wall of China off tabloid front pages. More newspapermen were covering Hughes and Irving than the Vietnam War — nine reporters from the *Los Angeles Times* alone. Thirty postal inspectors were tracking clues in the mails. Paramount re-issued *The Carpetbaggers*, a thinly disguised fictional account of Hughes's life. An X-rated film entitled *Helga and Howard* was being shown in Man-hattan, Hughes T-shirts were selling well at two dollars apiece, and people were wearing pins which said, "This is a genuine Howard Hughes button."

The genuineness of the autobiography was first questioned in the wake of the December announcement. A spokesman for the Hughes Tool Com-pany denied "the existence of a Hughes autobiography." But the recluse was celebrated for his furtiveness with his closest associates; those who knew him best thought the disclaimer was completely in character, and in fact the editors of the book had expected it. When managing Editor Ralph Graves of *Life* showed his staff a handwritten letter from Hughes approv-ing serialization of the text, one of them asked, "How do we know the let-ter's not a forgery?" Graves replied, "It's authentic, all right. We've had it checked by an expert." Albert Leventhal, a McGraw-Hill vice president, told the *New York Times*, "We have gone to considerable efforts to ascer-tain that this is indeed the Hughes autobiography," and Donald M. Wilson, a *Life* vice president, told another newsman, "Oh, we're absolutely positive. Look, we're dealing with people like McGraw-Hill, and, you know, we're not exactly a movie magazine! This is Time, Inc. and McGraw-Hill talking. We've checked this thing out. We have proof."

To another questioner Wilson said, "We never dealt with the Hughes Tool Company. It doesn't surprise us that they know nothing of this, since Mr. Hughes was totally secretive about the project." The person they had dealt with was Irving, who had been a McGraw-Hill author for twelve years. He had written four unsuccessful novels and, more recently, *Fake!*, an account of Elmyr de Hory, an art forger and Irving's neighbor on the Spanish island of Ibiza. In retrospect it seems that his publishers should have taken a closer look at the author's preoccupation with fraudulence and his story that Hughes insisted upon discussing the matter with no one but him. The truth was that the book was a complete fabrication. Irving had never met Hughes, let alone taped him, and Hughes had never heard of the man who claimed to be his ghost. At first glance McGraw-Hill and *Life* seem to have been inexcusably gullible. But in fact the hoaxer had shown remarkable cunning, and he had also been lucky.

The plot had begun a year earlier with the reproduction in *Newsweek* of an eleven-line handwritten note by Hughes. A month later *Life* published the letter in color. Irving was the son of a cartoonist; he had inherited his father's clever fingers, and he found that with a little practice he could produce whole pages of writing which looked like that of Hughes. The tycoon was in the news that season, and much was being made of his secrecy. Some writers suggested that he might even be dead; no one in the outside world would know. It struck Irving that a book of reminiscences purporting to bear Hughes's imprimatur might go unchallenged by him, especially since he might already be in his grave. He persuaded Richard Suskind, a fellow hack living on the neighboring island of Majorca, to collaborate with him. Later, when the names of both men had become household words, their photographs would be familiar on front pages around the world — Irving, tall and ruggedly handsome, and Suskind, "built," as a friend put it, "like an avalanche with a gargoyle on top." Ultimately their likenesses would represent the ultimate in literary chicanery. In the beginning, however, they appeared to the editors at McGraw-Hill as a writer known for reliability if not talent and his diligent researcher. The editors had no way of knowing that Irving proposed to share the swag with his crony, 75 percent for himself and 25 percent for Suskind. A third member of the conspiracy was Irving's wife Edith, an attractive Swiss painter and the mother of his two children.

Irving played McGraw-Hill with consummate skill, forwarding them apparently genuine letters from Howard Hughes in which the billionaire expressed growing interest in the collaboration. At the appropriate time Hughes's signature appeared on a contract, clause 22 of which specified that "The Publisher agrees that it shall undertake no advertising or promotion or sale of the Work prior to 30 days after acceptance by the Publisher of a complete and satisfactory manuscript for the Work." *Life,* which bought first serial rights for $250,000, also agreed to stay mum. Taking what seemed to be reasonable precautions, the publisher submitted specimens of Hughes's supposed handwriting to an expert, who compared it with samples of the real thing and reported: "The chances that another person could copy this handwriting even in a similar way are less than one in a million." Later another firm of analysts concurred, declaring that it was "impossible, based on our years of experience in the field of questioned handwriting and signatures," that anyone except Howard Hughes could have written the material which had come from Irving.

Most ingenious of all, Irving told his publisher that the eccentric tycoon insisted that checks made out to him bear only his initials: "H. R. Hughes." When the author got them, he turned them over to his wife. Edith, wearing a wig and carrying an altered passport and a stolen identity card, flew to Zurich and opened a Swiss Credit Bank account in the name of "Helga R. Hughes." Into this account, number 320496, she ultimately deposited nearly a million dollars of McGraw-Hill money, which she then withdrew and put in the Swiss Banking Corporation across the street. Meanwhile her husband and Suskind had also been traveling, researching Hughes's life in the New York Public Library, the Library of Congress, Palm Springs, California, the morgues of the *Houston Chronicle* and the *Houston Post,* and — the unkindest cut of all — the files of Time-Life. Their most valuable acquisition was the unpublished manuscript of the memoirs of Hughes's retired chief lieutenant. Irving borrowed it from one of the man's associates and photocopied it. Pooling their information, he and Suskind took turns being "Hughes" and interviewing one another on tape. The tapes were then transcribed, and Irving wrote marginal comments on the resulting thousand-page manuscript in the billionaire's hand. The result seemed so authentic that it fooled men who had known Hughes intimately years earlier.

The conspiracy began to come apart on the afternoon of January 7, 1972, when Hughes, speaking from the Bahamas, held a two-and-a-half-hour press conference over the telephone with seven journalists who had covered him before his withdrawal into seclusion. He branded Irving's book a humbug and, while he was at it, denied reports that his fingernails were six inches long, that he was emaciated, and that his hair hung to his waist. All seven of his listeners agreed that the voice was his. Irving called it a fake, but time was beginning to run out for him. Edith's end of the plot had begun to come to light. A Hughes lawyer had asked his client to fill out a questionnaire, establishing its authenticity with his fingerprints. One of the questions was: "When is the last time you personally endorsed a check for any reason?" Hughes answered in his own hand: "More than ten years ago." The conspirators had assumed that numbered accounts in Swiss banks were inviolate under all circumstances. Not so: in cases of suspected crime details could be revealed, and when the Swiss learned that checks meant for

Howard R. Hughes had been cashed by a German-speaking woman calling herself Helga R. Hughes, they knew something was rotten in Zurich. A worldwide search for the mysterious Helga began.

On Thursday, January 20, the day word of this sensational new development reached New York, Irving attended a conference of McGraw-Hill and *Life* executives. Coolly he advanced three possible explanations for it: that he had taped a charlatan pretending to be Hughes, that Hughes had used a "loyal servant" to deposit the checks, and that he, Irving, was a mountebank. Searching the eyes of everyone there, he said in his most sincere voice, "The last of these possibilities I intend to discard, and I hope that you do, too." His presence was superb; they all nodded. Flying back to Ibiza — to the indignation of *Life*, whose editors thought he should stay in New York until the crisis had been resolved — he replied to reporters pointing out the resemblance between Edith and the Swiss descriptions of Helga: "Do you really think I'd involve my family in an enterprise like this?" Back in Manhattan his lawyer, whose suspicions had not yet been aroused, confided to reporters that he thought his client had been duped by a gang of impostors, two of them gifted forgers and the third a six-foot-three beanpole who looked like Howard Hughes.

This was a crucial moment in the conspiracy, and a grasp of it is essential to an understanding of what was happening to Clifford Irving. He had a large part of the money in cash, he had his freedom, and he could have kept both. Other fugitives from justice were living comfortably on Ibiza and Majorca. He, Edith, and Suskind might have remained where they were or flown to any one of several South American countries where their crimes were not extraditable. Expense was no problem; they could have afforded almost anything. The alternative was grim; exposure was now inevitable. Why, then, did Irving fly back to New York and into the trap? The answer, in the opinion of those who were close to him, was that he couldn't resist the publicity. All his life he had craved attention. His books hadn't brought it, but this caper had, and the knowledge that an eager press corps awaited him at Kennedy Airport drew him as though he were helpless. The moth simply could not resist the flame. It is one of the sad little ironies of his story that when he landed there he couldn't answer their questions. He had laryngitis. "Gentlemen, this is a horrible experience," he whispered to them. For once one believes him.

Another irony followed swiftly. Two reporters believed that Irving had been in touch with a former Hughes aide named John Meier. Calling to see him at his lawyer's house, they sent in word: "Just tell Cliff we know all about Meier." Irving had never heard of Meier, but when the message reached him he was stunned. He thought they meant *Meyer*, which sounded the same. The man who had slipped him the unpublished memoirs of Hughes's retired assistant was named Stanley Meyer. If the newsmen had been tipped off to Meyer's role, the plotters were finished, and Irving might as well own up to it. He went out to the district attorney's office, made a partial confession there, and then returned to confront the two waiting newspapermen. "There's something I have to tell you guys," he said, "but it's got to be off the record, O.K.?" Under the circumstances an off-the-record confidence was impossible, but they nodded. He took a deep breath and said, "Well, you may have guessed it and you may not. Helga Hughes is Edith. Edith is Helga."

That should have been the end of it, but it wasn't. Improvising, he said that his wife had been acting at Hughes's direction, and so convincing was the manuscript — and the opinions of the handwriting experts — that the hoax limped along for a few more days. Then two blows demolished it. The manuscript of the retired Hughes assistant's unpublished memoirs surfaced, and the story of Irving's taping sessions with Hughes in various exotic settings was unmasked. He had in fact traveled to those places, sending back picture postcards to McGraw-Hill, but he had made the mistake of mixing pleasure with business. One of his companions had been a willowy blonde scuba diving instructor who had accompanied him to St. Croix in the Virgin Islands; she told the *Chicago Tribune* that she had grown very fond of Irving, whom she had thought was separated from his wife, but that neither of them had encountered Howard Hughes. The second and more damaging of the hoaxer's playmates was a beautiful Danish baroness and entertainer named Nina Van Pallandt. Irving had been indiscreet enough to brag about Nina to a McGraw-Hill editor and reveal her name. Located by postal inspectors, Nina admitted that she had traveled with Irving and said they had, in fact, copulated their way across Mexico. Since Cliff had been constantly at her side, she said, he couldn't possibly have kept any rendezvous with Hughes.

That was the end for Irving. But not for Nina. It is a provocative comment on the value of publicity — *any* publicity — that it was only a beginning for her. For years she had been limping along as an obscure folksinger. Now, suddenly, she was in demand everywhere. She appeared twice on the *David Frost Show*, twice on the *Mike Douglas Show*, twice on the *Dick Cavett Show,* once on the *Today Show*, once on the *Johnny Carson Show,* and on a television special. Manhattan's St. Regis Hotel booked her for three weeks, and she was signed up for appearances in Miami, Dallas, San Juan, and San Francisco. Her manager said the Irving happening was "worth five hit records and an Academy Award." Without doubt she was the most distinguished fornicatrix of 1972.

Howard Hughes was not so fortunate. The uproar had become so great that the Bahaman government began to investigate the fact that his staff lacked work permits and immigration clearance, whereupon he fled to Nicaragua accompanied by six television sets, several crates of Poland water, a document shredder, blood plasma, a refrigerator, a hospital bed, mattresses, office furniture, pots and pans, various boxes of film, several hundred yards of cable, an old electric stove, a heater, and a cheap vinyl couch.

Life was reimbursed by McGraw-Hill, which got most of its money back from the Irvings and Suskind, all three of whom briefly went to prison. But that wasn't the extent of McGraw-Hill's disasters that year. The publisher suffered a long streak of bad luck. After Irving had been led away the publishers had just begun to patch up their image with the success of a book about Indians, *The Memoirs of Chief Red Fox,* when an awkward truth emerged: *Red Fox* was plagiarized from a work published in 1940. Next the editor of the Irving book was accused of an unethical practice: borrowing money from two other authors, the sum amounting to 10 percent of their advances from the publisher. Then a final touch assured the firm's wretched situation as the laughingstock of the New York communications industry that year. Before the hoax the first floor of the new McGraw-Hill Building on the Avenue of the Americas had been leased to a branch bank. Now the tenant was moving in. Horrified publishing executives saw the gilt lettering going up on the plate-glass windows and realized that there was absolutely nothing they could do about it, because the contracts had long been executed and filed. The signs read: THE IRVING TRUST COMPANY.

On the frosty morning of February 21, 1972, the silver, blue and white fuselage of the *Spirit of '76*, as Nixon called the presidential aircraft, flitted across the muddy ribbon of the Yangtze, headed northward, and entered its glide pattern over Peking. American reporters who had covered China a quarter-century earlier were amazed by the changes in the landscape below: paved roads, irrigation canals, huge collective farms, and trees ("Trees in China!" wrote Theodore H. White) lining the highways. On this historic day the masters of Red China would once more grasp the hands of American leaders in friendship. Anti-Communism would cease to be the dominant note in U.S. foreign policy. It was an occasion for good omens, the eve of George Washington's birthday in the United States and, in Peking, the seventh day of the Year of the Rat, an auspicious time on the Chinese calendar.

The presidential jet touched down at 11:30. A moment of consternation followed. Except for U.S. correspondents and TV technicians, the airport was almost deserted. There were placards, but they had nothing to do with Nixon — LONG LIVE THE CHINESE COMMUNIST PARTY and LONG LIVE THE GREAT SOLIDARITY OF ALL THE WORLD'S PEOPLE. Fewer than four hundred troops were on hand; they were singing a Red Army ballad of the 1930s, "The Three Rules of Discipline and the Eight Points of Attention." America's peripatetic thirty-seventh President had greeted the rulers of Romania, Pakistan, Yugoslavia, Spain, Canada, Brazil, Australia, Japan, India, Ireland, Italy, Germany, Belgium, France, Britain, Austria, and the Vatican. Always there had been crowds. Here there were none. Dismayed aides wondered what to do if he were left in the lurch. Could they fly home and say it had all been a mistake? At the last moment the inscrutable

Chinese became scrutable. Premier Chou En-lai appeared with a handful of officials. Nixon extended his hand, and as millions of Americans watched on television, Chou took it.

The Chinese people were not watching. News of the visitors had been kept from them. The presidential motorcade entered the city on silent streets. All the inhabitants seemed to be elsewhere. But five hours later, when Nixon was still settling down in a two-story buff brick guesthouse, he was unexpectedly summoned to the private study of seventy-eight-year-old Mao, the living legend of the new China. The President and the Chairman chatted for a full hour, accompanied only by Chou and Henry Kissinger. The substance of the conversation remained secret, but obviously there was rapport; at one point the No. 1 International Bandit reached across the tea table and softly held the hand of the No. 1 Imperialist Dog, and next morning a picture of the meeting, with the principals smiling, appeared on the front page of the *People's Daily*. The message was clear: the visit had the Chairman's blessing. Now there was excitement in the streets. When Nixon appeared there, people clapped hands — in unison, to be sure, but that was how things were done here — and Mao designated his fourth wife, the revolutionary firebrand Chiang Ching, to be the President's official hostess.

Each day for five days Nixon and Chou conferred for four hours at a long green table. There was less there than met the eye, as the vague communiqué at the end made clear; it mostly dealt with the need for more friendship among the Chinese and American peoples, and the only real concession came from the President, a promise to withdraw U.S. military forces from Taiwan. But the real significance of the talks is that they were held at all. The President and the First Lady were determined to be amicable. It showed, and was appreciated. Every evening they sat through a three-hour ceremonial banquet in the Great Hall of the People, pluckily grappling their way through eight courses with ivory chopsticks and drinking toasts with *mao tai* while a Chinese orchestra played such tunes as "Billy Boy" and "She'll Be Coming 'Round the Mountain." They watched exhibitions of ping-pong, badminton, and gymnastics, and one evening Chiang Ching took them to a ballet, *The Red Detachment of Women*, which was all about cruel landlords. Nixon, who was trying to reduce the taxes landlords paid in the United States, nevertheless applauded heartily, and next morning his wife gamely continued her inspections of nursing homes, kitchens, agriculture communes and acupuncture clinics, though she was squeamish about the needles.

After a visit to Peking's Forbidden City and a walk along the ramparts of the twenty-two-hundred-year-old Great Wall of China, the Nixons left the *Spirit of '76* behind and flew to Hangchow with Chou on a white Ilyushin airliner. There, in the city which Marco Polo had proclaimed as the greatest in the world seven centuries earlier, the President roamed through parks and cruised on historic West Lake with the premier. From

Hangchow the presidential party flew on to Shanghai, their last stop, where the communiqué was issued, and then home for a report to the American people.

On the whole his countrymen gave Nixon high marks for his performance, though some thought that at times he had been obsequious. In his Peking speeches he had proposed that the two nations "start a Long March together," and he repeatedly quoted Chairman Mao, saying that "so many deeds cry out to be done, and always urgently," and recommending that his audience "Seize the day, seize the hour." He had also been banal. Shown the elaborately carved sedan chair on which each Ming emperor was carried from the Hall of Supreme Harmony to the red gates of the Forbidden City, the President remarked, "He didn't get much exercise if he was always carried on the chair." Of the Great Wall he said, "A people that can build a wall like this certainly have a great past to be proud of, and a people who have this kind of a past must also have a great future." Then: "As we look at this wall, we do not want walls of any kind between people."

Among the people on the far side of this particular wall were the Russians, and they were uneasy about possible implications of the visit. Tension between Moscow and Peking had been growing since Stalin's death nineteen years earlier. It had reached a peak the previous autumn when Lin Piao, vice chairman of the Chinese Communist Party and Mao's designated successor, had tried to fly to the USSR in a military plane. On orders from Mao and Chou, the craft had been shot down. The Soviets had regarded that as a slur on their hospitality, and now they suspected that the Chinese and the Americans were up to no good. In a Mandarin language broadcast beamed to Mao's subjects, Radio Moscow declared that nothing was "more shameless and hypocritical" than the Shanghai communiqué. China, said the Muscovite commentator, was entering into a "dangerous plot with the ruling circles of the U.S.A."

This was less a sign of anti-Americanism than of the growing friction within the Communist world. The Russians were jealous — unreasonably so, since the Nixons were going to visit them three months later. The prospect of that summit, in turn, had aroused Radio Hanoi, which called it "dark and despicable." Here there was a difference, however. Unlike Peking and Moscow, Hanoi was not interested in detente. On the contrary, the North Vietnamese were prepared to sabotage friendly relations between Washington and the two Communist capitals to the north. They didn't succeed, but they tried hard, and for a time it seemed that they were going to prevail.

News of the Peking talks reached troops of South Vietnam's 3rd Division, just south of the DMZ, over the small Japanese transistor radios then popular among ARVN forces. Not much was happening in that sector, and with the Americans and the Communists sitting down together, Thieu's men had let their guard down. There was another reason for their complacency. Since Nixon's submission of a new eight-point peace plan to the North Vietnamese there seemed to be a real movement toward peace. Thus the 3rd Division didn't feel threatened by the reports of a fresh buildup of Democratic Republic of (North) Vietnam (DRVN) forces across the 17th Parallel. As the sullen gray clouds of the northeast winter monsoon began to clear in March there was a noticeable increase in artillery fire from the north, but the South Vietnamese were unalarmed. They remained in their bunkers and sent out few patrols. Better troops would have been warier, but the 3rd Division was not a crack unit, which was precisely why the DRVN's General Vo Nguyen Giap had marked them as the first target of a new offensive, his biggest drive since Tet four years earlier.

Led by tanks, infantrymen of Giap's 304th Division bounded across the DMZ on March 30 in a savage attack which was the exact opposite of Tet — a power play, a blitz meant to overwhelm Saigon's forces with sophisticated Soviet weapons and the sheer weight of numbers. The assault units quickly captured fifteen border outposts. Over the next five weeks they advanced twenty-two miles in heavy fighting, taking ground which had been successfully and bloodily defended by U.S. Marines. The 3rd Division was virtually destroyed and the provincial capital of Quang Tri was lost. It was, as Defense Secretary Laird called it, a "massive invasion," and it was to be only one of four major North Vietnamese thrusts into South Vietnamese territory.

On April 6, four days after Easter, a DRVN tank column struck from Cambodia, driving ARVN forces from Loc Ninh. In less than a week the attackers had surrounded the provincial capital of An Loc, sixty miles north of Saigon, penning up the entire South Vietnamese 5th Division, which was one of the key units assigned to the defense of Thieu's capital. On April 18 another Red drive routed defenders in the coastal province of Binh Dinh, threatening to cut South Vietnam in half across its narrow waist. Finally, on April 22, four DRVN divisions burst into the Central Highlands, seizing Dak To and virtually encircling the provincial capital of Kontum.

Nixon responded by sending the B-52s north, pounding Hanoi and Haiphong in the first raids there in over three years. Antiwar senators reacted swiftly; Muskie of Maine introduced a resolution calling for an immediate end to all American military activity in North Vietnam. Laird, unmoved, warned Hanoi that the B-52 sorties would continue until all DRVN forces were withdrawn from South Vietnam. He said that the administration regarded the offensive as a "flagrant" violation of the 1954 Geneva accords and that Washington would spare nothing in its determination to turn the invaders back. In reality the White House mood was compounded of as much embarrassment as outrage. For three years the President had been proclaiming the success of Vietnamization, and the dispatches from Saigon strongly suggested that that policy was a failure.

The prospect of humiliation made Nixon a dangerous adversary. On May 8 he took a breathtaking step which he called Operation Linebacker. To cripple the DRVN's war-making capacity he ordered a massive air-sea blockade; the U.S. Navy would mine the waters of Haiphong and other North Vietnamese ports, and U.S. aerial sorties would smash rail lines leading out of southern China. This took him to the brink of confrontation with the very men in Peking and Moscow that he and Kissinger were wooing. He acknowledged the conflict with the Russians. In his televised address he said: "I particularly direct my comments tonight to the Soviet Union. We respect the Soviet Union as a great power. We recognize the right of the Soviet Union to defend its interests when they are threatened. The Soviet Union in turn must recognize our right to defend our interests. . . . Let us and let all great powers help our allies for the purpose of their defense — not for the purpose of launching invasions against their neighbors."

The President's aggressive response to Giap's drive gave new life to the antiwar movement, and the Committee for the Reelection of the President spent thousands of dollars to fake support for it which did not, in fact, exist. So many bogus telegrams were sent that the White House could announce with complete honesty a five-to-one ratio in favor of the move. In addition, a *New York Times* editorial critical of it was answered by a spurious ad headed "The People vs. the *New York Times*," the "People" being Charles Colson and a few aides. That was illegal, and, as it turned out, unnecessary. By the end of that month the North Vietnamese offensive had begun to falter. After laying waste 75 percent of Binh Dinh the DRVN forces there melted away. An Loc and Kontum held out, and a widely heralded Giap attempt to capture Hue never materialized. Abruptly the Hanoi menace seemed diminished. The Communists had committed all but two training divisions to the push, had lost one hundred thousand men, and had won little of strategic value. Their all-or-nothing gamble had failed. Le Duc Tho, a member of North Vietnam's politburo and Hanoi's chief negotiator, sent word to Kissinger that he was ready to reopen the talks in Paris. He still insisted that a cease-fire would be conditional upon Thieu's dismissal, but a genuine suit for peace appeared to be very near.

Moscow had something to do with that. In early May the blockade had made the likelihood of a Nixon-Brezhnev summit seem remote, but the Russians were determined to make the detente work. This became clear when Nikolai S. Patolichev, the Soviet foreign trade minister, called at the White House to exchange a few ideas about world trade. Reporters summoned to the oval office were astonished to find Nixon, Patolichev, and Ambassador Anatoly Dobrynin grinning, laughing, and bantering over how to say "friendship" in the two languages. A correspondent asked the minister whether the President's May 22 visit to Moscow was still on. "We never had any doubts about it," Patolichev replied. "I don't know why you asked." The Russians were simultaneously urging Hanoi to break off hostilities and readying a Kremlin apartment which had once belonged to the czars for occupancy by the President. The North Vietnamese were outraged by the prospect of Soviet and American leaders feasting on caviar and champagne with Giap's dead still warm in their graves, but nothing could stop deals between the world's two dominant powers — which was one of the points the Soviets wanted to make.

Improbable as it seemed to anyone aware of the history of the past two decades, American flags were waving beside the hammer and sickle when the *Spirit of '76*, arriving from Austria, descended over the glittering domes of the Kremlin churches and taxied to a stop beside the waiting figures of the Soviet president, premier, and foreign minister. Brezhnev was not there; like Mao he postponed his reception of Nixon until after the President had unpacked. That evening the Americans were guests of honor at a welcoming banquet in the Grand Kremlin Palace. In the morning the First Lady was off on tours of Soviet schools, Red Square, the famous Moscow subway, and the state-run GUM department store. Her husband's picture was on the front page of *Pravda;* it would be there every day throughout the week of talks. Appearing on the "blue screen," as Russians call their television, Nixon greeted viewers with *"Dobry vecher"* (Good evening), and parted at the end with *"Spasibo i do svidaniya"* (Thank you and goodbye). In between, another voice translated his cordial message, which was rich in the earthy Russian maxims that they cherish.

Unlike the Peking trip, this summit was more than symbolic. The banquets, the toasts, and the ballet performances were lavish, but the real meaning of the visit emerged in conferences beneath the huge gilt chandelier of the Kremlin's St. Vladimir Hall. The White House described the sessions as "frank and businesslike"; Brezhnev, bluff and hearty all week, called them "businesslike and realistic." A routine developed. The two national leaders would reach an agreement, or endorse a Russo-American understanding which might have been negotiated over a period of months or even years. Kissinger and Foreign Minister Andrei Gromyko would settle the details. Then protocol aides would appear with blue and red leather folders, and Nixon and Brezhnev would sign the documents. The two agreed to collaborate in space exploration, achieving a joint docking of a manned spacecraft in 1975. Joint research projects would examine problems of public health, cancer, heart disease, and pollution. Each consented to stop molesting the other's ships on the high seas. Both acknowledged the need to reduce troop strength in central Europe and the necessity for a conference on European security. Most important, they concurred on missile control. The two nations would limit their deployment of ABMs and freeze offensive missiles at current levels for five years.

There were some disappointments. There was no meeting of minds on the Middle East. Nixon wanted the Russians to talk Hanoi into a cease-fire; they wouldn't do it. Brezhnev was eager for a trade pact; the issue had to be referred to a commission for further discussion. The Soviet World War II lend-lease debt of 10.8 billion dollars was unresolved; they offered 300 million, Nixon wanted 800 million, all attempts at a compromise failed. On the other hand, the talks had yielded a dividend, a twelve-point statement of principles to establish rules of diplomacy for great powers, a breakthrough in international law. "We have laid out a road map," said Kissinger. "Will we follow this road? I don't know. It isn't automatic." But unless all signs failed, the implications for the future were vast. The difference between the two great systems of government were now likely to be expressed in treaties, not ideological jehads. Russia, through the coming European security conference, would draw closer to the continent and away from Asia. Trade and technology would continue to draw the two superpowers together, and understandings between them, not the fissioning of a multipolar world, which had been widely predicted, would be the paramount fact of world politics for a long time to come. The cold war was over, ended in large part through the efforts of an American President who had been one of the most resolute of the cold-warriors.

Not the least of its attractions for Nixon was the fact that it had occurred in an election year. In Peking, and then in the Kremlin, he had taken two giant steps toward four more years in the White House. Each passing day now seemed to bring him closer to victory in November. Unfortunately for his place in history, some of those around him weren't satisfied with that. They wanted to be absolutely sure. It was to be his tragedy that they were prepared to go to any lengths to guarantee a second Nixon term. Their attitude was summed up by one of them, Charles Colson, when he posted over his bar the slogan, "If you've got 'em by the balls, their hearts and minds will follow," and said, "For the President I would walk over my grandmother, if necessary." There was a word for the more extreme measures they were taking in pursuit of their goal: criminal. It was about to acquire a synonym: Watergate.

The 1972 campaign had begun to simmer in January, when a Harris poll showed Edmund Muskie running neck and neck with the President in public favor — 42 percent for him, 42 percent for Nixon, and 11 percent for George Wallace. The Maine senator was clearly the strongest Democratic candidate; that same month Gallup reported that in a trial free-for-all Muskie emerged with 32 percent, Edward Kennedy with 27, Humphrey with 17, and McGovern with 3. Whoever their opponent, Republicans were preparing to come on strong. Appearing on the *Today Show*, H. R. Haldeman said that critics of the war were "consciously aiding and abetting the enemy," and the White House moved swiftly to exploit suburban indignation over the January decision of Federal Judge Robert R. Merhige Jr., who ordered busing of white schoolchildren in the two counties surrounding Richmond, Virginia, to achieve racial balance in the city's 70-percent-black schools. Judge Merhige would be reversed in June, but by then Muskie's potential adversaries would have rung all the changes on his support of busing.

In Florida Republican zealots were putting the finishing touches on a bogus letter to the Manchester, New Hampshire, *Union Leader* charging that while campaigning in the South Muskie had referred to French Canadians as "Canucks"; this would cripple him in the New Hampshire primary. Other Nixon operatives were taking similar steps to torpedo the senator's campaign, or — in the case of Howard Hunt — planning to burglarize the safe of a Las Vegas editor which was supposed to contain anti-Muskie dirt. At 1701 Pennsylvania Avenue in Washington CREEP was fleshing out its staff. Within a month John Mitchell would resign as attorney general to become in title what he already was in fact: CREEP's director.

Meanwhile the Republican war chest was rapidly being filled while that of the Democrats remained six million dollars in debt. There had always been some truth in the Democratic charge that the GOP was the party of big business. This year there would be no doubt of it. A bill requiring the naming of big donors would become law on April 10. The two chief GOP fund raisers, Secretary of Commerce Maurice Stans and Herbert Kalmbach, the President's personal attorney, were crisscrossing the country in a successful pursuit of contributions from the wealthy before the deadline. As the Nixon men warmed to their task they began to skirt the borders of indiscretion, and sometimes to cross them. Gifts totaling $114,000 were deposited in the Miami bank account of Bernard L. Barker, Hunt's chief burglar. And although political donations from corporations were illegal even under the old law, the fund raisers solicited them and got them — $100,000 from Ashland Oil, $100,000 from Gulf, $100,000 from Phillips Petroleum, $55,000 from American Airlines, $40,000 from Goodyear, $30,000 from Minnesota Mining and Manufacturing. Ultimately they refused sums of less than $100,000; smaller donations were not worth the trouble. A list of two thousand secret donors was kept in the desk of Rose Mary Woods, the President's secretary, at the White House, where it was known as "Rose Mary's baby."

As the amounts collected mounted into the tens of millions, fertile minds brooded over ways to use them. By far the boldest ideas were the brainchildren of Gordon Liddy, and he outlined them at 4 P.M. on January 27, 1972, in the office of the attorney general at the Department of Justice. His audience consisted of Mitchell, Magruder, and John Dean, special counsel to the President. Displaying colored diagrams with such code names as Target and Gemstone, Liddy lectured for a half-hour on a million-dollar operation which included the tapping of Democrats' phones, bludgeoning anti-Nixon demonstrators, and kidnapping antiwar leaders, who would be held in Mexican camps during the Republican national convention, then scheduled to be held in San Diego. One of the more imaginative aspects of the plan called for leasing a yacht and hiring prostitutes during the Democratic convention in Miami Beach. The girls (who would be "the best in the business," Liddy promised) would elicit important information from lusty Democrats and lure them into lewd positions. They would then be photographed by hidden cameras.

It is impossible to say what effect all this had on Liddy's eminent listeners. He himself never talked to federal prosecutors afterward, preferring to remain in jail. Mitchell later told congressional investigators that the submission had been "beyond the pale," Magruder said he was "appalled," and Dean called it "mind-boggling." All that can be said with certainty is that Liddy was invited back the following week for another try, and on the afternoon of February 4 he presented a cheaper, $500,000 version, featuring the clandestine cameras and wiretaps. He passed around eight-by-ten-inch charts describing proposed breaking-and-entering operations at the Fontainebleau Hotel in Miami Beach, McGovern's campaign offices on First Street in southwest Washington, and the Washington headquarters of the Democratic National Committee in the Watergate complex. According to Magruder, the attorney general "didn't feel comfortable" with this rendition either, and Liddy was told to try once again.

The winter wore on, the President flew to China and back, and Liddy still hadn't received a green light for the project. Early in March he and Hunt approached Colson, asking him to intercede with the Republican high command. Phoning Magruder, Colson said, "Gordon Liddy's upset. He's trying to get started on an intelligence operation, and he can't seem to see anybody." He urged Magruder to "get off the stick and get the budget approved for Liddy's plans." The undertaking was now budgeted at $250,000. There were no provisions for assault, abductions, or prostitution, but the proposal to burglarize and bug Democratic and McGovern headquarters remained. On March 30 Magruder flew down to Key Biscayne, where Mitchell was taking a brief holiday in the sun, and laid this final presentation before him. Three men were present — Magruder, Mitchell, and Fred LaRue, a southern Republican strategist — and later each had a different recollection of what transpired. Whatever the precise words used, the plan was accepted, and only Mitchell had the power to do that. Liddy had his green light.

The following week Magruder authorized CREEP's treasurer, Hugh Sloan Jr., to pay out $83,000 to Liddy. Of this, $65,000 was turned over to McCord on April 12; he spent most of it in New York on electronic surveillance equipment. McCord added another man to the assembling Watergate cast on May 1 when he contacted Alfred C. Baldwin III, whose name he had found in the register of the Society of Former Agents of the FBI. All the recruit was told then was that he was wanted as a temporary bodyguard for Martha Mitchell — no plum, as Baldwin realized, but he was assured that if he did a good job it might be "a stepping-stone to a permanent position." Martha didn't think much of her new escort. She later said that he deliberately led her into a hostile demonstration, told all her friends that he was a Democrat, and "walked around in front of everybody in New York barefoot." He was, she said, "the most gauche character I have ever met." But McCord liked Baldwin. He promoted him, moved him into room 419 of Washington's Howard Johnson motel, just across Virginia Avenue from the Watergate, and told him he would be doing some undercover surveillance of radicals in the capital. Returning to the room on the afternoon of Friday, May 26, the former FBI man was surprised to find McCord there, twirling the dials of an elaborate radio receiver. "We're going to put some units over there tonight," McCord said, gesturing across the street, "and you'll be monitoring them." To show how bugs worked, he dismantled the phone in the motel room, inserted a device, and tested it by dialing a local number for a recorded message. If Baldwin handled this job well, he was told, he would be given a similar assignment at the Democratic national convention.

Four days earlier a team of Cuban exiles led by Barker had flown to Washington from Miami and registered at another hotel under assumed names. Now they were moved into the Watergate Hotel. Baldwin's motel room had the advantage of providing a view of Democratic headquarters on the sixth floor of the Watergate complex, but the Cubans' new rooms were closer to the objective. Closer still was the Continental Room of the Watergate Hotel, and it was there, that evening, that Hunt, Liddy, and the Cubans opened the first act of what would turn out to be a classic comedy of errors. With wealthy Republican campaign contributors paying the bill, they ordered $236 in food and wine — almost $30 per man. After the meal everyone left the Continental Room except Hunt and Virgilio Gonzales, Barker's locksmith. These two hid in an adjoining room until waiters had locked up; then Gonzales tried to open a door at the end of the hall which would have let them into a stairwell leading to the sixth floor and the offices of the Democratic National Committee, or, as those familiar with it called it, the DNC. But the latch there was too difficult for Gonzales. So, to their dismay, was the other lock, leading to their escape route through the dining room. Left with no alternative, they settled down for a long and uncomfortable night while their gastric juices gently broke down their share of the banquet.

The others hadn't been idle, but they had been just as ineffectual. Led by Liddy, they had left Virginia Avenue for First Street and McGovern headquarters. The entrance was bathed in light from a nearby street lamp. Opening a dispatch case, Liddy produced a high-powered pellet pistol wrapped in a towel. "Shall I take that out?" he asked, gesturing at the bright light. He was capable of it; a few days earlier he had fired it in a toilet at the staid Hay-Adams Hotel, just across Lafayette Square from the White House. This time McCord discouraged him. The mission had to be aborted anyway. A drunk was loitering in the entrance of the building. He wouldn't leave, and at 5 A.M. they gave up and returned to their beds on Virginia Avenue.

The next evening Hunt took an elevator to the DNC headquarters and walked down through the building, taping door locks open as he went so that McCord and the Cubans could reach their goal from the garage in the Watergate basement. Wearing rubber gloves and carrying walkie-talkies, cameras, and flashlights, the raiding party reached the target area at 1:30 A.M. Two hours later McCord had planted taps in the telephones of Lawrence F. O'Brien's secretary and of R. Spencer Oliver, a party official. Barker, who was under the impression that they were looking for proof that Castro was financing the Democrats, found no evidence of it. In fact, this night was as unproductive as the one before. They were again unable to penetrate McGovern's offices. And the bugs were a disappointment. One didn't work at all, and the other phone, Baldwin discovered, was largely used by secretaries to arrange assignations with married politicians. According to Magruder, Mitchell, after reviewing some two hundred conversations that Baldwin had monitored, said that the information was "worthless," that the money had been wasted, and that he wanted them to try again.

The second and final act of the farce was played out on the night of Saturday, June 17. It began when the Cubans checked into rooms 214 and 314 in the Watergate Hotel and sat down to another banquet. McCord taped the garage door and then crossed to Baldwin's room at Howard Johnson's, where he checked new equipment — soldering irons, batteries, wires, and screwdrivers — which he had purchased earlier in the day. At 12:45 A.M. an important new actor appeared onstage. His name was Frank Wills, and he was a Negro watchman at the Watergate. Discovering the tape, he concluded that it had been left by a maintenance man; removing it, he crossed to Howard Johnson's for a cup of coffee. At about the same time McCord, looking out of Baldwin's window, saw the lights go off in the DNC offices. He phoned Hunt, who was in Watergate room 214 with Liddy, to say that the coast was clear. Patting the radio receiver, McCord said to Baldwin, "Any activity you see across the street, you just get on this unit and let us know." Then he joined the Cubans — Barker, Gonzales, Frank Sturgis, and Eugenio R. Martinez — in the garage. Aghast at finding the door again fastened, they appealed to Gonzales, and this time the locksmith was able to pick the lock open. There was some discussion over whether continuing with the job was an unacceptable risk. They decided to go ahead and mounted steps to the sixth floor, taping latches on the way. At 1:50 A.M. watchman Wills, finishing his coffee, returned to find the garage door taped for the second time. He telephoned the police, and at 1:52 A.M. his call was relayed to Metropolitan Police Car 727, an unmarked cruiser. Inside were three members of the District's "Bum Squad" — plainclothes men wearing T-shirts, windbreakers, and cheap slacks.

It is now 2 A.M., a historic hour. The Bum Squad parks and enters the Watergate, observed by Baldwin, who is standing on the little balcony outside his Howard Johnson's room, enjoying, in his later words, the "beautiful night." Since the three policemen are in informal clothes, he is unalarmed, but when lights begin appearing across the way he quickly radios: "Base headquarters, base one, do you read me?" In room 214 of the Watergate Hotel Hunt replies: "I read you; go on; what have you got?" Baldwin: "The lights went on on the entire eighth floor." Hunt: "We know about that. That is the two o'clock guard check. Let us know if anything else happens." At this point the thrifty Barker, who has been listening to the exchange, turns off his walkie-talkie to save the batteries. Minutes later lights start flickering on and off on the sixth floor, and Baldwin sees two of the plainclothesmen there. One of them is holding a pistol. Baldwin: "Base one, unit one, are our people in suits or are they dressed casually?" Hunt: "Our people are dressed in suits. Why?" Baldwin: "You have some trouble, because there are some individuals out there who are dressed casually and have got their guns out." Hunt — sounding, according to Baldwin, "a bit frantic" — tries to rouse the raiding party, yelling: "Are you reading this? Are you reading this?" Because of the economy-minded Barker, there is no response. It is probably too late anyway. McCord is in the process of dismantling O'Brien's phone when one of the officers sees an arm. He shouts: "Hold it! Stop! Come out!" Baldwin and Hunt hear a walkie-talkie switched on; a hoarse voice whispers into it: "They got us." Then the officers see ten rubber-gloved hands go up. McCord asks: "Are you gentlemen the Metropolitan Police?" The plainclothesmen affirm it, and the Watergate Five are placed under arrest.

Hunt called Howard Johnson's: "Are you still across the street?" Baldwin replied, "Yes I am," and Hunt told him, "Well, we'll be right over." Looking down from his balcony, Baldwin saw Hunt and Liddy emerge. Shortly thereafter Hunt burst into his room. Distraught, he asked, "What is going on, what is going on?" Baldwin said, "Come and see." The street below was swarming with uniformed patrolmen, motorcycles, and police cruisers; McCord, Barker, Gonzales, Sturgis, and Martinez were being led off in handcuffs. Hunt moaned, "I have got to use the bathroom," ran into the toilet, used it, ran out, called a lawyer, and asked Baldwin for McCord's address. They looked about at the electronic litter. Logs of previously intercepted conversations lay around; McCord's wallet and keys were on the bed. "Get all the stuff out of here and get yourself out of here!" Hunt said. "We will be in touch. You will get further instructions." As he dashed for the door Baldwin called after him, "Does this mean I won't be going to Miami?"

The *Washington Post*'s account of the break-in appeared on the front page of its Sunday edition, but few papers gave it that much prominence. The *New York Times* carried thirteen inches inside under the head FIVE

CHARGED WITH BURGLARY AT DEMOCRATIC QUARTERS, and most other editors played it down even more. Nevertheless, it was the most interesting story in the papers for certain high officers of the U.S. government and the Republican party, among them H. R. Haldeman, John Ehrlichman, John Mitchell, Maurice Stans, Charles Colson, Gordon Strachan, John Dean, Jeb Magruder, Fred LaRue, and, probably, the President of the United States.

A year later, during the hearings of the Senate Select Committee on Presidential Campaign Activities, chaired by Sam J. Ervin Jr. of North Carolina, Magruder was asked when this glittering array of outlaws decided to cover its tracks, and he answered in a puzzled tone, "I don't think there was ever any discussion that there would not be a cover-up." It was an involuntary reaction, and it began that morning of June 18 in Los Angeles, where several of them were holding meetings on campaign strategy. They were at breakfast in the Beverly Hills Hotel when, at about 8:30 A.M., Magruder took a call in the dining room from Liddy. "Can you get to a secure phone?" Liddy asked. Magruder said he couldn't and asked what was wrong. Liddy said, "There has been a problem." Magruder asked, "What kind of problem?" Liddy told him: "Our security chief has been arrested at the Watergate." "Do you mean Jim McCord?" "Yes." Hanging up, Magruder muttered to LaRue, "You know, I think last night was the night they were going into the DNC." LaRue told Mitchell, who said, "This is incredible."

Their first response was to protect McCord, then the only one of the five captives known to them. According to Magruder, Mitchell proposed that Liddy approach Richard Kleindienst, the new attorney general, and ask him to spring McCord. Mitchell denied it, but someone at the Beverly Hills Hotel phoned Liddy at 9 A.M. California time — noon in Washington — and told him to do just that. Liddy found Kleindienst at the Burning Tree Country Club and put it to him in the locker room. Kleindienst not only refused to go along; he ordered his visitor to leave the club at once and then called Henry Petersen, who headed the Justice Department's criminal division, and instructed him that under no circumstances would he tolerate special treatment for the Watergate Five.

The FBI had already entered the case, which was beginning to develop unusual aspects. The papers implicating Hunt had been found in Barker's pocket. The prisoners had been carrying $1,300 in $100 bills, and another $3,200 in $100 bills had been discovered in the Cubans' rooms at the Watergate Hotel. Liddy, trying to destroy all evidence of his involvement, had used the shredder at CREEP headquarters to get rid of all documents in his possession, including his $100 bills. Strachan was searching Haldeman's White House files on his instructions and removing everything linking him to the burglars. Magruder phoned an assistant and directed him to take home a Gemstone file because, he said, he was afraid Democrats might raid his office in retaliation. And Howard Hunt was on the lam.

Dean, Colson, and Ehrlichman had held a hurried council of war over what advice they should give to Hunt. According to Dean, Ehrlichman proposed that he be told to leave the country. Dean made the call and then began to worry. Is it, he asked the others, really wise for the White House to give orders of that sort? "Why not?" Ehrlichman replied. "He's not a fugitive from justice." But Colson agreed with Dean, who made a second call canceling the instruction. Hunt decided to flee anyway. He cleaned out his desk, leaving only an empty whiskey bottle and a few Librium tablets. Then he flew to California, where he holed up in the home of a friend until he could no longer resist the pressure to turn himself in. The FBI was on his trail. They had already found Liddy, who had aroused suspicion by refusing to talk to them. Mitchell fired him for that, which seems hypocritical of him, but Liddy understood; he had told Magruder and Dean that he had "goofed," that "I am a good soldier and will never talk," and that "if anyone wants to shoot me on the street I am ready."

Meantime the presidential staff had been agonizing over the fact that disowning Hunt was almost impossible, since he was still on the White House payroll. Dean ordered Hunt's safe in room 552 of the Executive Office Building cleaned out. An aide brought him the contents: a black briefcase or dispatch case and a cardboard box containing, among other things, four walkie-talkies, a tear gas canister, four shoulder harnesses, the forged State Department Vietnam cables from 1963, evidence of his attempt to persuade *Life* that the forgeries were genuine, a folder of the Pentagon Papers, the CIA's Ellsberg profile, and Hunt's reports on Chappaquiddick. Dean looked over this extraordinary accumulation and gasped, "Holy shit!"

In California, meantime, Mitchell had issued a hurried statement trying to explain away McCord, who, he said:

> . . . is the proprietor of a private security agency who was employed by our committee months ago to assist with the installation of our security system. He has, as we understand it, a number of business clients and interests, and we have no knowledge of those relationships. We want to emphasize that this man and the other people involved were not operating either on our behalf or with our consent. I am surprised and dismayed at these reports. There is no place in our campaign or in the electoral process for this type of activity, and we will not permit or condone it.

Among the people who knew that this was a lie was Mitchell's wife. When he returned to Washington on Monday he persuaded her to stay in Los Angeles, where, she said afterward, she was held as a "political prisoner" by Baldwin's successor as her bodyguard. According to her, the guard yanked the phone wires out of the wall when she was telling a UPI reporter that "they don't want me to talk"; then he held her down while another man injected a sedative into her buttocks. There was no way to keep Martha Mitchell quiet, though. Three days later she was calling the reporter again, saying, "I'm not going to stand for all those dirty things that go on." It made a good story, but Martha's credibility was low, and most Americans accepted the official line, which was that the administration had not known anything about those dirty things. Tuesday morning Ronald Ziegler, the former adman who served as Richard Nixon's press secretary, spelled it out. In a scornful mood, he declined even to add to Mitchell's statement. "I am not going to comment from the White House on a third-rate burglary attempt," Ziegler said. "This is something that should not fall into the political process." However, when a handful of *Post* men continued to pursue the story, Ziegler did comment from the White House. He said, "I don't respect the type of journalism, the shabby journalism, that is being practiced by the *Washington Post*." And Mitchell, referring to the paper's publisher, told one of its reporters, "Katie Graham is going to get her teat caught in a big fat wringer."

In a sense the campaign which followed was the story of Richard Nixon's growing invincibility. Early trial heats had suggested a standoff. Then, as the summer progressed, the President moved ahead until all the polls conceded him about 60 percent of the vote. From then on he was beyond reach. CREEP's tremendous financial advantage — 60 million dollars compared to 25 million for the Democrats — had little to do with the outcome. Watergate had even less. He had been elected four years earlier on a tide of protest against the Vietnam War. Ending the hostilities seemed to take him forever, and some 17,000 Americans had been killed there while he was doing it, but by the beginning of 1972 he had reduced the U.S. troop commitment in Vietnam from 549,500 to 139,000, and the Pentagon's weekly casualty list, which had been running at about 300 when he entered the White House, would on September 21, 1972, reach zero and remain near there. Being a political animal, he was quick to exploit this and other opportunities as they arose. In the Florida Democratic primary, for example, George Wallace campaigned on the slogan, "Send them a message," promising that if Floridians voted for him, "President Nixon will do something to halt this busing within thirty days." Wallace knew his Nixon. The President didn't wait thirty days. He demanded a busing moratorium just two days after the returns from there.

The sum of Nixon's skills was a united party led by a nominee who, his past notwithstanding, was now identified as the candidate of peace and detente. His only two rivals for the Republican nomination were Congressmen Paul N. McCloskey Jr. of California on the left and John M. Ashbrook of Ohio on the right. They merely served to point up the President's preemption of the GOP center. McCloskey arrived at the Republican convention — switched to Miami Beach after Dita Beard and ITT had made San Diego too embarrassing — with a single vote, pledged to him by New Mexico's primary law. He expected to have his name placed before the convention, thereby giving critics of Nixon's racial and military policies a chance to be heard, but the Rules Committee limited nominations to candidates controlling the delegations of at least three states. The final vote on the first ballot was: Nixon 1,347, McCloskey 1. The lone New Mexican apologized to the hall.

As a piece of stage management it was awesome. The President had eliminated any possibility of suspense by announcing his intention to keep Agnew on the ticket. Everyone in the party seemed eager to do his bidding. Ronald Reagan chaired the convention, Nelson Rockefeller put Nixon's name in nomination. Knowing the President's passion for order, floor managers limited the demonstration in his behalf to exactly twenty minutes, and to refute claims that the Democrats represented young America, 3,000 conservatively dressed youths were brought to Miami Beach on chartered buses. The boys wore their hair so short that they appeared to belong to another era — which was, of course, the idea.

To be sure, they were not the only young Americans there. Over 5,000 scruffy antiwar militants had camped in the city's Flamingo Park. During the Democratic week they were relatively quiescent, but when the GOP arrived they erupted, and 1,200 were arrested for slashing tires, blocking traffic, smashing store windows, setting bonfires in the streets, and trying to prevent delegates from attending the convention. The Republicans were elated. This, they seemed to be saying to those who objected to their tidy sessions, is what happens when you allow untidiness in politics. During the campaign which followed (in which Nixon hardly participated; he left most of the politicking to surrogates and never mentioned his opponent's name) GOP speakers spoke proudly of their unity and hammered away at the disarray on the other side.

They had a point. Riven in Chicago four years earlier, the Democrats were still absorbed in savage internecine feuds. The new presidential sweepstakes opened all their old wounds and inflicted new ones. At one time or another during the primary months the party's nomination was being sought by Muskie, McGovern, Humphrey, George Wallace, Eugene McCarthy, Fred Harris of Oklahoma, Vance Hartke of Indiana, Henry Jackson of Washington, John Lindsay of New York, Sam Yorty of Los Angeles, Wilbur Mills of Arkansas, Shirley Chisholm of New York, and Edward T. Coll, a young poverty worker from Connecticut who scared the pants off a Democratic National Committeewoman by dangling a rubber rat in front of her during a televised debate. The battle to head the ticket was a melee. Harry Truman, who had called the primaries "just so much eyewash," was vindicated. Like the Republican struggle in 1964, this one routed promising candidates and left the field in the possession of a nominee who would prove hopelessly weak in the general election and whose vulnerability had, in fact, been demonstrated in the very process which had brought him the prize.

Speaking in New Hampshire early in the year of his ill-starred race,

Barry Goldwater had sunk a nail in his own coffin by calling, in effect, for the end of social security. On January 13, 1972, eight years later almost to the day, George McGovern told a college audience in Ames, Iowa, that he favored giving every American $1,000 from the federal treasury and limiting inheritances to $500,000 each. The speech didn't attract much attention at the time because McGovern was still a minor figure; in one recognition poll a few months earlier he had scored exactly 2 percent. But later it would return to haunt him, alienating millions who thought the government was too generous already and vast numbers of others who dreamed that one day they would hit the lottery, or something, big.

Part of McGovern's strength lay in the skill with which his organization exploited his obscurity. In New Hampshire, the first test, they successfully established the line that since Muskie was the front runner and from a neighboring state, any showing below 50 percent would be a defeat for him and a McGovern victory. That put the pressure on the Maine senator, who was hurt by the spurious "Canuck" letter and by the *Manchester Union Leader*'s tasteless charge that Mrs. Muskie told dirty jokes. In a televised speech outside the newspaper's office Muskie called its publisher William Loeb a "gutless coward," said "It's fortunate for him he's not on this platform beside me," and wept — perhaps the most expensive tears ever shed by a public man. Even so, Muskie won 46.4 percent of the vote on March 7 as against McGovern's 37 percent. The margin was a sweep, if not a landslide, yet so adroitly had the South Dakotan's aides depicted him as a dark horse that the spotlight was on him.

Florida, the next joust in the primary tournament, had eleven entries. McGovern sensibly said that it was not a state where he "expected to do well," and in fact he did poorly, receiving 6.1 percent of the vote. Wallace was the big winner, surprising everyone, including himself — "We beat the face cards of the Democratic deck," he crowed — and he was trailed by Humphrey, Jackson, and Muskie. The following week Muskie won in Illinois, taking 63 percent to McCarthy's 37 percent. Wisconsin came next. McGovern's troops were superbly organized there, and he led the pack of twelve candidates with 30 percent, followed by Wallace, Humphrey, and Muskie. McGovern won in liberal Massachusetts; Humphrey took Ohio and Indiana; in Nebraska McGovern beat Humphrey by six percentage points; Humphrey walloped Wallace in West Virginia 67 to 33 percent, and North Carolina went to Wallace.

By the middle of May Muskie was out of it and the marathon was settling down to a three-way contest between Wallace, Humphrey, and McGovern. Support for the Alabaman was generally interpreted as a protest vote; he said he would use it to win concessions at the national convention. Then came May 15 in Maryland. Wallace was successively hit by a rock in Frederick, eggs in Hagerstown, popsicles in Salisbury — and six bullets in Laurel. Next day he won both the Maryland and Michigan primaries, but for him, wounded and paralyzed, it was all over. It was, in fact, the end for all the Democratic candidates; without the third-party threat of Wallace siphoning off votes on the right, a Nixon victory was assured. But few realized that at the time, and the winner-take-all California primary on June 6 loomed as a titanic battle between the two survivors. The results were 1,527,392 votes, or 47.1 percent, for McGovern; 1,352,379, or 41.7 percent, for Humphrey. After that plums began toppling into the South Dakotan's lap, and he went to Miami Beach with 1,492.75 delegates — for all practical purposes, the nomination.

What was unappreciated at the time was the impact of the California campaign on McGovern's popularity. Until then no one had cast a harsh light on his program. He was seen as a handsome, decent, plainspoken man who was outraged by the Vietnam War. In three bruising televised debates, Humphrey had destroyed that image, pointing to McGovern's sometimes inconsistent and often quixotic stands on Israel, defense spending, welfare, labor law, unemployment compensation, taxation, and even, in the beginning, on Vietnam. "It was Hubert Humphrey who put McGovern away; no other Democrat could have done it to him like Hubert," pollster Robert M. Teeter said afterward. "Not only did Hubert give it to him, but it was the first time McGovern got adversary treatment."

The second time was at Miami Beach, when the watching nation saw what had happened to the Democratic party. Four years earlier, on the humid night of August 27, 1968, the Chicago convention had approved by voice vote a Credentials Committee resolution calling for a reform of the process by which convention delegates were chosen. Under the chairmanship of George McGovern, a reform commission had approved by a 10–9 vote a resolution which established a quota for blacks, and then — on a motion from a member who said, "There is no reason why our national convention shouldn't have 50 percent women, 10 to 15 percent young people" — quotas for women and youth. A majority of the commission thought that made sense, but it didn't. The quotas were a denial of the whole principle of representation. Worse, they had the effect of legitimatizing discrimination against all classifications who had no quotas — for example, the elderly, ethnic groups, and organized labor, three traditional sources of the party's strength.

In his keynote address Governor Reubin Askew of Florida declared, "It is impossible to look upon this group without feeling that one has seen the face of America." Certainly he was looking at newcomers to politics. Eight of every ten delegates were attending their first convention; 15 percent were black, 36 percent were women, and 22 percent were under thirty years of age. "Don't pass up any hitchhikers, they might be delegates," said one candidate. There were some hitchhikers — and some others. In their anxiety to assure representation to the underprivileged, the California delegation had included eighty-nine people who were on welfare. McGovern was so determined to offend no minority that he ordered kid-glove treatment of Gay Liberationists, who chanted — on television — "Two-four-six-eight, we don't overpopulate" and "Three-five-seven-nine, lesbians are mighty fine." At the same time an extraordinary number of elected Democrats were being excluded from the floor: 225 of the party's 255 congressmen and the Democratic mayors of Philadelphia, Detroit, Boston, San Francisco, Los Angeles, and Chicago.

Inevitably, the amateurs committed blunders which professionals would have avoided. The few politicians left in the hall were painfully aware of them. "I think we may have lost Illinois tonight," Frank Mankiewicz said glumly when that state's elected delegation was expelled from the convention by McGovern enthusiasts, and on the platform committee Ben Wattenberg sighed, "They just lost Michigan to the Republicans today with their busing plank. No one seemed impressed by the fact that in Macomb County they voted against busing in a referendum last fall by fourteen to one." Hugh Scott chided McGovern as a "triple A" champion who advocated "Acid, amnesty, and abortion." That was unfair, but at one time or another various McGovern supporters did speak well of all three, despite the anguished remonstrations of observers like David Riesman, who pointed out that the floor of a national political convention is not the best place to discuss so sensitive an issue as abortion. The impact of all this on the national television audience cannot be determined with precision, but subsequent events suggest that the number of blacks, women, and youths won over by the requirement that delegations "reasonably" reflect their constituencies by race, sex, and age was overwhelmed by the swarms of voters who were offended by the spectacle in Miami Beach. Of the three groups, only the Negroes went for McGovern in November, and they had been for him long before.

By the time McGovern won the nomination it was probably not worth much. He further devalued it by delivering his acceptance speech at 3 A.M., when most voters were asleep. The first in a series of disasters came less than twelve hours later at a meeting of the Democratic National Committee in the Fontaine Room of the Fontainebleau. McGovern began by announcing that Larry O'Brien had "reached a judgment that he will not stay on as the chairman of the party." That was false — O'Brien was willing to remain — and a number of people there knew it. Mrs. Jean Westwood was chosen as the new chairman. McGovern nominated Pierre Salinger as vice chairman. Charles Evers rose to say that "inasmuch as we are going to try to stay in line with the McGovern rules, I would . . . strongly urge that if we are going to have a female chairman . . . I would like to place in nomination a black man to be co-chairman or vice chairman." He then nominated an unknown Negro — whereupon McGovern said that was fine with him, thus publicly scuttling Salinger.

Unlucky Pierre was betrayed a second time. Later that same day, McGovern asked him to serve as his representative in talks with the North Vietnamese in Paris. Salinger flew to France, the story leaked to UPI, and McGovern issued a statement to the press saying, "Pierre Salinger had no instructions whatsoever from me. He told me he was going to Paris, and he said while he was there he might try to make some determinations of what was going on in the negotiations. But there wasn't the slightest instruction on my part to him." Once again there were people who knew better, among them David Dellinger, who had acted as liaison between McGovern and Hanoi. The nominee challenging Nixon's integrity was himself losing credibility fast.

Then the Eagleton affair exploded. McGovern had just begun a pre-campaign holiday in the Black Hills when reporters learned that Senator Thomas Eagleton of Missouri, his running mate, had twice been hospital-ized for psychiatric care, including electroshock therapy. Up to that point the nominee could scarcely be held responsible for that calamity. He hadn't known about Eagleton's medical history at the time he picked him, and when Mankiewicz had asked Eagleton if there were any skeletons in his closet, the reply had been that there were none. The Missourian was at fault there. American ignorance of mental health being what it is, even a mild history of depression disqualifies a politician from running for national office, and the problems of a patient subjected to electroshock treatments are not mild. The obvious solution was to let Eagleton resign gracefully. McGovern didn't do it.

Instead he issued a statement saying that he was "1,000 percent for Tom Eagleton" and had "no intention of dropping him from the ticket." The mimeograph machine in the Black Hills was still warm when the *New York Post*, the *Washington Post*, and the *New York Times* — the most liberal papers in the country — said Eagleton had to go. Matthew Troy, a prominent New York Democrat whose support for McGovern had been unwavering, was quoted as saying, "I have nine kids. I don't want to see them destroyed because some unstable person might become President." Democratic headquarters were deluged with mail, wires, and calls de-manding that the vice-presidential nominee quit, and the head of the ticket decided that his support of him wasn't 1,000 percent after all. He agreed to let Mrs. Westwood say on *Meet the Press* that it would be "a noble thing" for the Missourian to withdraw. Then, greeting Eagleton, he told him, "Tom, believe me I had no idea what she was going to say." His running mate replied, "Don't shit me, George." According to Eagleton, "George smirked. Not a smile of faint amusement. Not a frown of slight irritation. A smirk, that's what it was." Eagleton retired from the ticket on July 31, and after five Democrats, including Muskie, had declined to replace him, Sargent Shriver consented. The episode had been one of the most disastrous in the history of presidential politics. McGovern would never recover from it.

From that moment on the Democratic campaign was on the skids. The nominee belatedly courted LBJ, Mayor Daley, organized labor, and the Jewish vote; all were cool. His Washington headquarters disintegrated. Important letters were unanswered. Speaking schedules disappeared. Distinguished Democrats who called with offers to help were insulted by shaggy young volunteers and turned away. At one time — in May — McGovern had been within five percentage points of Nixon. By July, the month of the Democratic convention, he was twenty points behind. After the Eagleton debacle he slipped farther behind. In October, as he furiously rushed back and forth across the country, logging 65,000 miles in the air, he gained slightly. It didn't last. Both Gallup and Harris predicted on election eve that the vote would split 61 percent for Nixon and 39 percent for McGovern. Actually it was 60.7 to 37.5, with splinter candidates getting 1.8.

Nixon had carried forty-nine states; Massachusetts and the District of Columbia went to McGovern. But that was not the full story. The voter turnout was the lowest in twenty-four years. Only 55 percent of the country's registered voters went to the polls; the rest, presumably, rejected *both* candidates. And while the President had forged a historic electoral triumph, his party hadn't done at all well. Democratic congressional candidates had held the GOP to a 12-seat gain in the House — rather than the 41 they needed for control — while gaining two Senate seats, making their margin there 57 to 43, and picking up one statehouse.

McGovern said he was not disheartened. His central issue had been the Vietnam War, and he believed he had done much to end it. In conceding defeat he told his workers, "I want every one of you to remember that if we pushed the day of peace just one day closer, then every minute and every hour and every bone-crushing effort in this campaign was worth the entire effort." That was putting the best possible face on it. Not everyone agreed. Marquis Childs said it had been "one of the most unhappy campaigns in American history." Understandably, Richard Nixon took a different view. Greeting his supporters in Washington's Shoreham Hotel, he said, "I've never known a national election when I could go to bed earlier." As he turned away to retire there, they set up a terrific din, chanting, "*Four more years!*" It was a top-drawer Republican crowd, well-barbered and expensively dressed. The television audience had no way of knowing that some of the most eminent chanters were felons.

In a reference to Watergate, McGovern had described the Nixon administration as "the most corrupt in history," but Gallup had reported in October that barely half the voters had heard of the break-in. Of those, four out of every five did not see it as a reason to vote Democratic. Teeter had found that only 6 percent thought the President was involved. The others tended to blame CREEP — a tribute to the party leadership's wisdom in establishing a reelection headquarters outside the White House. It was an illusion. The big campaign decisions were made at 1600 Pennsylvania Avenue. The men around Nixon continued to be deeply involved in the Watergate cover-up, which, according to subsequent testimony before the Ervin committee, took the following course.

John Dean's immediate problem, once he had seen the contents of Hunt's safe, was how to get rid of it. He took the matter up with Ehrlichman, who suggested he "shred the documents and deep-six the briefcase." Ehrlichman said, "You drive across the river on your way home at night, don't you? Well, when you cross over the bridge, just toss the briefcase in the river." Dean pointed out that it wasn't that simple; too many White House employees, including his own assistant, had seen at least part of what had been in the safe. Ehrlichman's solution was to summon to his office L. Patrick Gray, who had been acting director of the FBI since J. Edgar Hoover's death in May. On June 28, eleven days after the Watergate burglary, Dean gave him the sensitive material there, calling it "political dynamite" which "should never see the light of day." Gray kept it until the end of the year — possibly to blackmail the White House should the President fail to recommend him as permanent director — and then burned it with the Christmas trash, thereby assuring his eventual resignation in disgrace.

That same week the White House made an effort to cloak at least part of the Watergate incident with the mantle of "national security." The President himself was involved in this; later he justified his intervention by saying, "I was advised that there was a possibility of CIA involvement in some way." His concern included the possibility that Hunt's role in the Plumbers might be revealed, exposing other sensitive "national security matters," including, presumably, the burgling of Ellsberg's psychiatrist's office. CIA director Richard Helms and his new deputy, General Vernon Walters, were called to the White House, where Haldeman told him that the DNC break-in was embarrassing Nixon. He said it was "the President's wish" that Walters suggest to Gray that the arrest of five housebreakers "should be sufficient," and that it was not useful to press the investigation any farther, "especially in Mexico" — a reference to the route political contributions had followed in finding their way into Barker's bank account.

At meetings on June 26 and June 28 Dean proposed to Walters that the CIA furnish bail and pay the salaries of the five prisoners. The general said he didn't think that was a good idea, that it might hurt the "apolitical" reputation of the agency. Walters did approach Gray, but not to carry out White House suggestions; instead he warned him that presidential aides were trying to exploit both the agency and the bureau for questionable purposes. Gray already knew this. In addition to his own personal experience he was beginning to feel heat from below; FBI subordinates were telling him that a cover-up had begun and urging him to alert the President. On July 6 he did it with a phone call, cautioning Nixon that "people on your staff are trying to mortally wound you by using the CIA and the FBI and by confusing the question of CIA interest in, or not in, people the FBI wishes to interview." After a pause the President said, "Pat, you just continue to conduct your aggressive and thorough investigation," and hung up.

It was now nearly three weeks since the Watergate arrests, and efforts to conceal the trail of those behind the break-in were in full swing. Gray, having sent up his rocket and seen it sputter into nothing, allowed himself to be duped by Dean. The presidential counsel was permitted to kibitz at FBI interviews with eight White House aides and was given copies of some eighty FBI reports on Watergate. In addition he persuaded Petersen not to call five members of the staff — Colson, Young, Krogh, Strachan, and Dwight Chapin — before the federal grand jury that was looking into Watergate. Instead they testified in a separate room, where jurors could not question them. It was at this time that Kleindienst, Petersen's superior, assured the public that the Justice Department's pursuit of the truth about the break-in was "the most extensive, thorough, and comprehensive investigation since the assassination of President Kennedy."

On August 29 Nixon did some reassuring of his own. He told the country that besides giving all assistance required by the FBI, he had launched his own inquiry: "Within our own staff, under my direction, Counsel to the President, Mr. Dean, has conducted a complete investigation of all leads which might involve any present members of the White House or anybody in the government. I can say categorically that his investigation indicates that no one in the White House staff, no one in this administration, presently employed, was involved in this very bizarre incident." Dean heard this on a newscast and was astonished. He had only been following orders from Haldeman and Ehrlichman. He had conducted no investigation, had written no report, and had not even seen the President. (A year later the White House acknowledged this, saying that Nixon's confidence had been inspired by "assurances" from Ehrlichman.)

In that same statement the President said: "What really hurts in matters of this sort is not the fact that they occur, because over-zealous people in campaigns do things that are wrong. What hurts is if you try to cover it up." This, of course, is precisely what was happening. John Mitchell was presiding over cover-up strategy sessions in his office, and, after July 1, when he resigned from CREEP at the importuning of Martha, in his apartment in the Watergate complex. Among those who attended were LaRue, Assistant Attorney General Mardian and Jeb Magruder. At one point Magruder volunteered to take the rap for all of them. This received serious consideration, but in the end it was decided that since he had lacked authority to approve the vast sums Liddy had spent, a guilty plea from him would merely lead to Mitchell and jeopardize Nixon's reelection.

Instead it was decided to make Liddy the cutoff point. Though an eccentric, he was reliable; he wouldn't talk, and they could build a plausible story around him, exaggerating the sums of money given to him for legitimate purposes and saying he had decided on his own to spend it on the burglary. Bart Porter, a Magruder aide, agreed to perjure himself. He would testify that he had given Liddy $100,000 to infiltrate organizations of antiwar radicals. There was one difficulty. Hugh Sloan Jr., CREEP's treasurer, was an honest man. In April he had asked Stans about Liddy's huge budget. ("I don't want to know," Stans answered, "and you don't want to know.") Now, when Magruder told him they were going to alter the figures, saying that Liddy had received only $75,000 or $80,000, Sloan replied, "I have no intention of perjuring myself." Magruder said, "You may have to."

Sloan, under the mistaken impression that he was not the only scrupulous man in the leadership of the reelection campaign, tried to warn several presidential aides that something was terribly wrong at 1701 Pennsylvania Avenue. He went to Chapin first and was advised to take a vacation. Chapin said that "the important thing is that the President must be protected." Then Sloan went to Ehrlichman, recommending that an outsider investigate the committee. "Don't tell me any details," Ehrlichman said, and, like Stans, "I do not want to know." Finally, with FBI agents waiting in his office to question him, Sloan appealed to Mitchell for guidance. The former attorney general said, "When the going gets tough, the tough get going." Sloan got going. He had no choice; Stans told the FBI that he had already resigned.

On September 15 the grand jury indicted Hunt, Liddy, the five men who had been captured in the DNC — and no others. The trail had stopped with them, and the President was greatly relieved. Late that afternoon Dean was summoned to the oval office, where Nixon and Haldeman greeted him warmly. As Dean later testified before the Ervin committee, Nixon said he hoped there would be no trial before the election and that he wanted Dean to keep a list of people giving the administration trouble, because he meant to make life difficult for them after the election. The principal thorn here continued to be the *Washington Post*, which on October 10 reported that the Watergate burglary was part of "a massive campaign of political spying and sabotage . . . directed by officials of the White House and the Committee for the Reelection of the President." The reelection high command reacted swiftly and angrily. Clark MacGregor, Mitchell's successor at CREEP, called the story "vicious and contemptible." Another committee spokesman described it as "a collection of absurdities." To Stans it was "a senseless pack of lies"; to Ron Ziegler, "the shoddiest type of journalism." Their indignation was widely accepted as righteous. The Fourth Estate had fallen sharply in public esteem during the Nixon Presidency. Symbolically, that summer the Supreme Court had ruled 5 to 4 — with the administration's four appointees in the majority — that newspapermen could be required to reveal confidences by judges and grand juries. The American Civil Liberties Union declared that "in a relatively short time the press in the United States has moved from what many considered a position of extreme security to one of extreme vulnerability." The men responsible for that were now threatened by vigorous reporting. They responded by stirring the suspicion of "the media" which they themselves had planted in the public mind. Their reward was a short-term success — at the expense of ultimate disgrace.

One plank of the scaffold which awaited them fell into place at 2:27 P.M. on the foggy afternoon of December 8, when United Airlines Flight 553, approaching Chicago's Midway Airport, crashed a mile and a half short of the runway, killing thirty of its forty-five passengers. Among the dead was Mrs. E. Howard Hunt, in whose purse investigators of the accident found $10,000 in cash. A relative said she had been on her way to make a down payment on a Holiday Inn franchise. But where, the authorities wondered, did she get the money? The Hunts had always been strapped. He had wanted badly to buy a partnership in a Washington public relations firm but had been unable to round up the $2,000 required for a down payment. Now his wife's body had been found with a small fortune in $100 notes — just like the Watergate Five.

The money was hush money, and there was a lot more of it. Eleven days after the Watergate arrests the council of war over which Mitchell was presiding had decided, in Dean's words, to raise funds "in exchange for the silence of the men in jail." Herbert Kalmbach was the first to be given the assignment, though apparently he wasn't told the full story. He had arrived the next morning on a night flight from Los Angeles, and after being sketchily briefed by Dean at a rendezvous in Lafayette Park he phoned Stans, who produced $75,100 in campaign funds, all of it in the ubiquitous $100 bills. Over the next two months Kalmbach rounded up between $210,000 and $230,000, of which $154,000 went to Dorothy Hunt. The Californian had qualms over the propriety of this, and on July 26 he went to Ehrlichman with them. "John," he began, "I am looking right into your eyes." He said he wanted to know whether Dean had the authority to give him these instructions, and whether it was right. According to him, Ehrlichman answered, "Herb, John Dean does have the authority, it is proper, and you are to go forward."

At the end of August Kalmbach quit anyway and LaRue became the new paymaster. Altogether between $423,000 and $548,000 was paid to the Watergate defendants, most of it channeled through Mrs. Hunt. Tony Ulasewicz, who actually delivered the cash, or "the laundry," as he called it, said he came to the conclusion that "something here is not kosher." Not to put too fine a point on it, CREEP was being blackmailed. Shortly after the arrests Hunt had sent Dean a dark message: "The writer has a manuscript of a play to sell." Later, according to McCord, Hunt said that unless his wife's demands were met he would "blow the White House out of the water" and produce "information which could impeach the President." Not only did he want money; he insisted on pledges of presidential clemency. Colson sent him a "general assurance" of this through Hunt's lawyer. In exchange, Hunt agreed to plead guilty and tell the press he knew of no involvement of "higher-ups."

The cover-up strategy seemed to be working. Actually it was about to unravel. The key to the imminent exposure was McCord, who felt a continuing loyalty to his old organization, the CIA, or, as he and other insiders called it, "the company." On June 30, the week presidential aides began trying to involve the agency in the toils of the cover-up, McCord sent Helms an unsigned letter promising to keep him informed and ending: "From time to time I will send along things you may be interested in." It was the first of seven anonymous letters he mailed to the director, and was followed, on December 22, by a warning to an old friend in the agency's security office: "There is tremendous pressure to put the operation off on the company." That same week he wrote John J. Caulfield:

Dear Jack,
I am sorry to have to tell you this but the White House is bent on having the CIA take the blame for the Watergate. If they continue to pursue this course, every tree in the forest will fall and it will be scorched earth. The whole matter is at the precipice right now. Pass the message that if they want it to blow, they are on exactly the right course. I am sorry that you will get hurt in the fallout.

There was no signature, but none was necessary. Caulfield spread the word that McCord was planning to confess everything, and frantic efforts were made to change his mind — pledges of financial support for his family, executive clemency, rehabilitation and a job when he got out; even what McCord construed as a threat on his life from Caulfield: "You know that if the administration gets its back to the wall, it will have to take steps to defend itself." McCord answered, "I have already thought through the risks and will take them when I'm ready. I have had a good life and my will is made out." Caulfield said, "Everybody is on track but you. You are not following the game plan. Keep silent." But the old spy didn't want any part of this game plan. His mind was made up. In a letter to Judge John J. Sirica, which was read from the bench at the end of the court proceedings, he said that "Others involved in the Watergate operation were not identified during the trial," that "perjury occurred during the trial," and that "there was political pressure applied to the defendants to plead guilty and remain silent." It was a sensational moment, and one of the most fateful in the history of American jurisprudence. With it, the collapse of the Nixon Presidency began.

The President's reelection campaign had been enormously enhanced in its last days by electrifying news from Henry Kissinger: he and Le Duc Tho, Hanoi's chief negotiator, had achieved a breakthrough in their Paris talks. On October 8 the North Vietnamese had dropped their insistence that Thieu be ejected and a coalition government installed in Saigon. Eighteen days later Kissinger told a televised press conference that a final accord could be reached in one more meeting. "Peace," he said, "is at hand."

But it wasn't. On October 23 the White House announced that the signing of the cease-fire agreement was being postponed pending new sessions needed to "clarify" some matters. At least part of the difficulty seemed to lie in Saigon. South Vietnamese Foreign Minister Tran Van Lam attacked the imminent agreement as "unacceptable," and Thieu said it would amount to "a surrender of the South Vietnamese people to the Communists." If necessary, Thieu vowed, his nation would continue the war alone.

When Kissinger tried to reopen certain sensitive topics, Hanoi accused Washington of bad faith and demanded that the settlement be signed as negotiated. The Americans refused, and Le Duc Tho, furious, began advancing counterproposals on such matters as the size of the international truce supervision team and — the most vital subject for the United States — the return of U.S. prisoners of war. Kissinger announced that the other side was raising "one frivolous issue after another," that the team from Hanoi was trying to make substantive alterations "in the guise of linguistic changes."

The President was reported to be angry with both Vietnams; with Saigon for being mulish and with Hanoi for, as he saw it, going back on its word. On December 14 Kissinger left Paris in despair and Nixon cabled North Vietnam's Premier Pham Van Dong, warning him that unless serious negotiations were resumed within seventy-two hours he would reseed Haiphong harbor with mines and unleash America's aerial might: B-52s, F-4 Phantoms, and Navy fighter-bombers. General Curtis LeMay had once proposed bombing the North back into the Stone Age, and clearly the President had something like that in mind. It was no light threat; his Air Force generals assured him that in two weeks they could saturate the enemy homeland with more tonnage than in virtually all the great raids of World War II. Furthermore, this would be terror bombing on a scale never known before. The B-52 guaranteed that. Pinpoint attacks by them were impossible. Each carried forty tons of bombs in its belly. Flying in "cells" of three, each cell laid its missiles in "boxes" a mile and a half long by a half-mile wide. Until now they had never assailed a city. If they unloaded over Hanoi, massive civilian casualties would be unavoidable.

The seventy-two hours passed, Pham Van Dong did not reply, and Nixon sent the word to U.S. air bases on Guam and in Thailand and carriers in the Gulf of Tonkin: start the blitz. The result was the most savage chapter in the long history of American involvement in Vietnam. Hanoi was pounded around the clock by every type of American aircraft in every kind of weather. Using 100 of the huge green and brown B-52s, U.S. airmen flew over 1,400 sorties in the first week alone. Americans were stunned. Only a few days earlier — until mid-December, in fact — they had been expecting total U.S. disengagement in Indochina, with the prospect that American POWs, some of whom had been in captivity for nearly ten years, might be home for Christmas. Now they were confronted by this bewildering volte-face. And they were offered no presidential explanation. In the past, Nixon, like Johnson before him, had appeared on television to announce new developments in Vietnam. Now he made no attempt at justification. The only White House official to comment was Ziegler, who told reporters that the bombing "will continue until such time as a settlement is arrived at."

The Pentagon briskly ticked off the military targets: truck parks, communications towers, power plants, warehouses, bridges, railways, shipyards, factories, roads, barracks, supply points, landing fields, and antiaircraft and surface-to-air missile (SAM) installations. But most of the objectives were in heavily populated parts of North Vietnam's cities. The Hanoi thermal power plant, for example, was only a thousand yards from the center of the capital. Diplomats and foreign newsmen stationed there sent out descriptions of a stricken city, lacking electricity and often water. Vast neighborhoods were cratered and pocked by explosives. Schools were reduced to smoking sockets in the ground. Torn copybooks lay in the rubble. Parents frantically searched for their children among jagged chunks of shattered concrete.

In the Hanoi suburb of Thai Nguyen almost a thousand civilians were dead or wounded. Coffins were stacked on street corners. The Bach Thai hospital for tuberculars was razed. So was Bach Mai general hospital; doctors carried patients piggyback from the debris. A dispensary was destroyed. One bomb hit a POW camp — incensing Nixon, who reportedly blamed the North Vietnamese for putting prisoners where missiles might fall. The Polish freighter *Josef Conrad* was sunk in Hanoi harbor, killing three of her crew; a Russian and a Chinese ship were mangled. Men in the State Department, which was charged with apologizing for these outrages, were bitter. "The way things are going," one American diplomat said gloomily, "we'll hit the cathedral in Hanoi on Christmas Eve."

In fact Nixon declared a thirty-six-hour truce over Christmas, but the moment it was over the deluge of death resumed. On walls still standing North Vietnamese chalked, "We will avenge our compatriots massacred by the Americans," and "Nixon, you will pay this blood debt." These were gestures of helplessness; the White House was over seven thousand miles away, and soon the last American ground troops would have left Indochina. North Vietnam's only real hostages against the terror were captured U.S. fliers. In the seven years before this blitz B-52s had flown 100,000 sorties and only one had been lost to enemy gunners. Now Hanoi had the strongest antiaircraft defenses in the world, and in these last two weeks of 1972 their fuming muzzles brought down sixteen of the aerial dreadnoughts, each representing fifteen million dollars. More important, ninety-eight crewmen had been captured. The American onslaught over Tonkin had increased the stakes in Paris. There was more pressure on Kissinger as well as on Le Duc Tho.

Other incentives for peace had appeared. Nixon had, not for the last time, misjudged the public's capacity for moral indignation. James Reston called the massive raids "war by tantrum," and Republican Senator William Saxbe of Ohio, who had supported the President's Vietnam policy, now came out against it, saying he was troubled "as an American" and thought most of his countrymen felt "the same way." In Europe the reaction was sharper. London's *Daily Mirror* said, "The American resumption of the bombing of North Vietnam has made the world recoil in revulsion." In Paris *Le Monde* compared the air offensive to the Nazi leveling of Guernica in the Spanish Civil War. Premier Olof Palme of Sweden went farther, equating it with the German extermination of the Jews. That angered the administration, which called the Swedish ambassador to protest, but the feeling in all western chancelleries was almost as strong.

If Washington had underestimated the depth of allied resentment, Hanoi had overestimated the wrath of the Communist world. Comment in Moscow and Peking was perfunctory. Speaking on the fiftieth anniversary of the Soviet Union, Leonid Brezhnev made the mildest of references to the B-52 strikes, and he pointedly sent his children to meet Tricia Nixon Cox and her husband at a U.S. embassy reception there. Both the Russians and the Chinese were urging the North Vietnamese to settle with the Americans. The United States had lost its enthusiasm for opposing "wars of liberation," but the eagerness of the USSR and the People's Republic of China to support them had also diminished. This, perhaps more than the bombing, led Hanoi to send out urgent signals calling for new talks. On December 30 the White House announced a bombing halt and the rescheduling of talks between Kissinger and Le Duc Tho for January 8. It was a sign of the American determination to find a solution that when Thieu sent two South Vietnamese diplomats to Washington with a threat to fight any treaty that did not meet his requirements, Nixon responded by dispatching General Alexander Haig to Saigon with a letter to Thieu telling him, in effect, to shut up.

Soon Kissinger was commuting between Paris and Key Biscayne with a briefcase containing fresh proposals. The break came in late January when the two bargainers met for their twenty-fourth round of talks in forty-two months. Two more days of dickering had been anticipated, but a final understanding was reached in just four hours. The formal end of the war came in the silk-walled conference room of Paris's old Majestic Hotel; simultaneous announcements were broadcast in Washington, Hanoi, and Saigon. (Just working out that process, said Kissinger, had "aged us all by several years.") President Nixon led the nation in prayer, praising the 2.5 million Americans who had served in Vietnam "in one of the most selfless enterprises in the history of nations." He declared that he had achieved "Peace with honor."

But honor had little to do with it. Kissinger appreciated that. In his thoughtful press briefing he observed that "it should be clear by now that no one in the war has had a monopoly of anguish and that no one has had a monopoly of insight." He made no reference to honor, or valor, or glory, or any of the other martial concepts which had become irrelevant to this conflict. "Together with healing the wounds in Indochina," he said, "we can begin to heal the wounds in America." That was the right note to strike, because that was the issue for Americans. After some 46,000 U.S. battle deaths, 300,000 wounded, and the expenditure of 110 billion dollars, they were left, as a direct result of the war, with a grave domestic problem, a spiritual malaise. In the McLuhanesque global village it was not possible to lay waste a distant land without inflicting hideous scars on the United States. Among the casualties had been public esteem for the Presidency, which had led the country into the war; for Congress, which had continued to appropriate vast sums for it; for the courts, which had failed to find it unconstitutional; and for the institution of democracy itself, which, having proved ineffectual in attempting to influence the makers of policy, had degenerated into chaos in the streets. "There has been a sharp decline in respect for authority in the United States as a result of the war," Reston wrote on the occasion of the cease-fire, "a decline in respect not only for the civil authority of government but also for the moral authority of the schools, the universities, the press, the church, and even the family . . . something has happened to American life — something not yet understood or agreed upon, something that is different, important, and probably enduring."

The week of the truce there was an ugly row at Madison Square Garden over whether "The Star-Spangled Banner" should be played before athletic events. At the same time a fresh epidemic of teacher strikes was disrupting classrooms across the country. Neither would have been conceivable during the Depression, the last great trial of the American spirit. The flag had flown over a poorer land then; there had been a great deal of physical suffering in the United States. Teachers had been among the greatest victims of the economic crisis. Often they had been paid in worthless scrip or not all, and some had shared the little food they had with starving children. But in that tightly disciplined society strikes by them, like disrespect for the national anthem, would have been inconceivable. That does not mean that America was a better country then; plainly it was not. It does mean that it was a different country, inhabited by other people facing challenges wholly unrelated to those of the 1970s.

Perhaps this was what Henry Adams meant when he wrote, in the early years of this century, that the test of twentieth-century Americans would be their capacity for adjustment. Change is a constant theme in the American past. The United States is the only nation in the world to worship it for its own sake, and to regard change and progress as indistinguishable. "We want change. We want progress," Lyndon Johnson said in 1965, "and we aim to get it."

But if that is one aspect of the American national character, there is another, the reverse of the same coin, which reemerged with the end of the Vietnam War. It is the yearning to renounce the present and find restoration in the unconsummated past. "America," John Brooks observed, "has an old habit of regretting a dream just lost, and resolving to capture it next time." The theme is a familiar one in American literature. One thinks of Willa Cather's lost lady and Robert Frost's "The Road Not Taken." Thomas Wolfe wrote: "Remembering speechlessly we seek the great forgotten language, the lost lane-end into heaven, a stone, a leaf, an unfound door. Where? When? O lost, and by the wind grieved, ghost, come back again." So it was that after intervening in foreign conflicts for a third of a century, the people of the United States turned inward once more, seeking comfort in insularity and renewal in isolation. "So we beat on, boats against the current," F. Scott Fitzgerald wrote at the end of his finest novel, "borne back ceaselessly into the past."

EPILOGUE

Echoes

Surrounded by happy perjurers, Richard Nixon celebrated his second inauguration in a three-day, four-million-dollar extravaganza directed by up-and-coming young Jeb Stuart Magruder. The rhetoric of the January 20 inaugural address, in keeping with the retreat from far-flung world commitments, was less a promise of what the government would do than what it wouldn't. Twelve years earlier another President of the same generation had vowed that "we shall pay any price, bear any burden, meet any hardship, support any friend, oppose any foe, in order to assure the survival and the success of liberty." Now Nixon declared that "the time has passed when America will make every other nation's conflicts our own, or presume to tell the people of other nations how to manage their own affairs." At the same time he prepared to liquidate the domestic programs of liberal administrations with a paraphrase of President Kennedy's most memorable line. Nixon said, "Let each of us ask, not just what will government do for me, but what I can do for myself."

As he paused for effect, a faint sound could be heard from several blocks away. A group of youths was chanting: "Murderer!" "Out now!" "End racism!"

"It's disgusting," a woman from Iowa told a *New York Times* reporter. "Just disgusting. I don't see why we can't do something about these kids." Certainly it was indecorous. Yet counterdemonstrations, like the counter-culture, were an expression of the continuing divisions in America, and they had to be endured. There is really no effective way to stifle dissent in an open society; if there were one, Magruder and his employer would have been the first to use it. The chanters — five hundred to a thousand Yippies, SDS militants, and members of the Maoist Progressive Labor Party — were the smallest and rudest band of protesters in the multitude of demonstrators roaming Washington that weekend. With them they carried a loathsome effigy — a ten-foot-long papier-mâché rat with Nixon's face, bearing in its teeth a bloodstained baby doll. That was too much even for the indulgent District police, and they confiscated it. But apart from that group the only really ugly gesture at the inaugural was the lowering of American flags around the Washington Monument and the hoisting of Viet Cong banners in their stead.

The stateliest protest had been held in the Washington Cathedral on Wisconsin Avenue at 9 P.M. the previous evening. After brief remarks by Dean Francis B. Sayre Jr. and former Senator Eugene McCarthy, Leonard Bernstein led a pickup orchestra of local musicians in the gentle, contemplative strains of Haydn's *Mass in Time of War,* with its urgent kettledrums and its final plea, *"Dona nobis pacem"* (Give us peace). In counterpoint, across the city Eugene Ormandy and the Philadelphia Orchestra were saluting the President with Tchaikovsky's bombastic *1812 Overture.* Sixteen of Ormandy's musicians had been excused because they felt it would be demeaning to play before such an audience. Presumably their absence removed any threat to Nixon's life. Even so, the firing of blanks in a cannon, usually the climax of the overture, was omitted at the request of the Secret Service. It was one of the service's less expensive suggestions under that President.

That same evening, critics of Nixon's record in Vietnam delivered to a White House guard a petition setting forth their views. On the sidewalk outside, Father Philip Berrigan performed in a crude skit meant to show how the authorities had mistreated those who had dared to speak out against them. Berrigan pretended to manhandle a woman carrying a peace placard. Lest anyone miss the point of the drama, the priest wore a large sign around his neck reading POLICE. The next day Daniel Ellsberg, who at that time faced possible conviction and sentences totaling 115 years for publishing the Pentagon Papers, addressed a testimonial dinner held by the National Peace Action Coalition. Ellsberg ridiculed the President's inaugural promise of a generation of peace, saying, "He's winding down the war like he's winding down my indictment," and comparing the manufacturers of Vietnam war matériel to the designers of the Nazi death camp at Auschwitz.

Berrigan and Ellsberg were seen by few, but most of the counter-inauguration events were well attended. The Bernstein concert was heard by 3,000 people in the cathedral and another 12,000 to 15,000 who stood in the dank night outside and listened to it over loudspeakers. The petition had been signed by 50,000. And the largest demonstration of all, timed, like the SDS march, to coincide with the President's address on Capitol Hill, drew between 75,000 and 100,000. It began when 2,500 members of the Vietnam Veterans Against the War marched from Arlington National Cemetery to the Washington Monument, continued with the signing of a mock peace treaty there, and ended with an address by New York Congresswoman Bella Abzug, who had been listening to Nixon's speech over a transistor radio and bellowed out her opinion of it.

Some youths in the audience carried obsolete signs reading STOP THE BOMBING. That was ludicrous. The blitz had been stopped three weeks earlier. Other gestures of protest also bordered on the ridiculous. Some of them were wholly unrelated to Vietnam; as Nixon spoke, a tiny biplane, rented by a disgruntled millionaire and closely shepherded by police and Air Force helicopters, trailed a banner which read LEGALIZE GOLD. But there was nothing absurd about the concept of protest. It was far truer to the American spirit than the inaugural address, the cannonless Tchaikovsky overture, and the 1,976 saucily dressed Virginia high school musicians who paraded past the White House, a tribute to Jeb Magruder's vision of what the nation's second centennial would be all about.

In the darkest year of Joe McCarthy a West Virginia college president, testifying in behalf of an embattled liberal, was asked by counsel what America represented to him. He replied that it was "the right to be different." He did not mean merely the eccentric and the whimsically wrong, though there will always be room in the United States for, say, the astrologists, the believers in flying saucers, and the Republican statesmen who bought big Washington houses in 1948 for occupancy during the first Dewey administration. But if liberty is to signify anything substantive, it must also be extended to the last limits of the endurable, shielding under its broad tent the genuinely unpopular champions of causes which the majority regards as reprehensible. Any people can cheer an Eisenhower, a MacArthur, a John Glenn, a Neil Armstrong; it takes generosity of spirit to suffer the Weathermen who hated LBJ, the Birchers who baited JFK, the Liberty Leaguers who heckled FDR.

In the lengthening memories of Americans who were entering their fifties in the Nixon years, the strains on the nation's tolerance had been great. Sometimes it had been too much, and the names of the places where patience was exhausted stain the pages of U.S. history with shame: Attica, Kent State, My Lai, Birmingham, Oxford, the Republic Steel plant in Chicago, the California camps where Americans of Japanese descent were penned up during World War II; and the Bonus Army camp on Anacostia Flats whose destruction was described in the first pages of this book.

Yet they were exceptions. A list of examples of forbearance would be many times longer, and might be regarded as a national roll of libertarian honor. It would include the names of Angela Davis, the Berrigans, Stokely Carmichael, Dr. Spock, the Chicago Seven, Woodstock, Ti-Grace Atkinson, the American Nazis who carried "Free Gas for Peace Creeps" signs, the captain of the *Pueblo*, the Fair Play for Cuba Committee, Edwin Walker, SANE's Linus Pauling, Rosa Parks, the America Firsters, Earl Browder, the Shrine of the Little Flower, William Dudley Pelley, Huey Long, Gerald L. K. Smith, and the emaciated wraiths who greeted the 72nd

Congress, on its return to Washington in December 1932, by singing "The International."

Defiers of the popular will, like those who give it voice, deserve remembrance; but so do the silent witnesses who kept the key figures alert and honest and strengthened the country's democratic institutions simply by their presence. In time of crisis they gathered quietly in Lafayette Park, just across Pennsylvania Avenue from the White House; a President had but to look out a window and there they were, reminding him that his employers were watching. They were conspicuously in attendance at the great congressional hearings in which the country's temper was being tested, and often its policy forged, through the past forty years, weighing the Vietnam War, Sherman Adams and Bernard Goldfine, the Bricker Amendment, the Army-McCarthy controversy, the hoodlums exposed by Estes Kefauver, Hiss and Chambers, the five-percenters, Pearl Harbor, Roosevelt's plan for Supreme Court reform, and the part played by Wall Street in the Great Depression. They were the spectators when the Taft bell tower was dedicated, they mourned when Roosevelt and Eisenhower lay in state, and they stood in stricken silence on November 25, 1963, as a caisson bearing the body of John Kennedy clattered across Memorial Bridge toward Arlington and the eternal flame.

There is a school of historians which holds that great events may tell us less about the past than the trivia accumulated by ordinary people — the letters, pressed flowers, prom programs, cherished toys and the like saved by those who loved them and could not bear to throw them away. From time to time construction workers will stumble across such caches, sometimes entombed in old mansions. Occasionally they may find something almost as elaborate as the Westinghouse time capsule which was buried at the New York World's Fair of 1939. Such discoveries always excite curiosity, and the older ones stir speculation over what this or that article meant to people at the time it was put away. With the growing mobility of Americans the accumulation of such troves is rarer, but if members of the swing generation had one — put away, perhaps, in a storeroom the size of Fibber McGee's fabled closet — it might provide insight into what they had been like, what they had endured, what their dreams had been, and which had been realized and which dashed.

Envisaging such a cupboard, we see in front on the top shelf a steel tennis racket, several dieting books, a wide necktie, and a pantsuit broad in the beam. Just behind them are a "Welcome Home POWs" bumper sticker, one for MIAs ("Only Hanoi Knows"), and a peace decal; then a brass-colored PT boat tie clip, and cassette recordings of *Camelot*, Arlo Guthrie's *Alice's Restaurant*, and Carol Channing's *Hello, Dolly*. Behind them, well hidden in a corner beneath a pile of tie-dyed jeans, are well-thumbed copies of *Fanny Hill* and *The Autobiography of a Flea*.

Various items of clothing occupy much of the space on the second shelf:

a sheath dress, a gray flannel suit, a man's narrow-brimmed felt hat, several incredibly narrow neckties, a child's coonskin cap, and a straw boater with the legend I LIKE IKE on the hatband. Concealed beneath them is an obsolete item of female apparel: a diaphragm in a white plastic case. Beyond is a curious little silver lapel pin. It resembles the bottom of a man's shoe with a hole in the sole. Nearby are a *My Fair Lady* album, a record of Edith Piaf singing "*Il Pleut*," a Winky Dink kit, a Mouseketeer cap, and a collapsed Bayby-Tenda. Copies of *Fireman Small* and *Peyton Place* lie on top of miscellaneous papers: a pamphlet on how to stop smoking, a Fish House Punch recipe, an *Around the World in Eighty Days* program, a batch of bills from a diaper service, and an envelope containing plans for a home bomb shelter (never opened).

Near the front of the third shelf is a Dior New Look skirt, an Eisenhower jacket which appears to have been worn by a slender man, early nylons, a freshman beanie, a copy of *Tropic of Cancer*, and under it a packet of three Trojans. (They sold for a dollar.) Various certificates: military discharge, marriage license, college diplomas. A ruptured duck pin. An Army divisional patch. Rationing stamps. Navy dog tags, long tarnished. A packet of V-letters. A Nazi helmet; a samurai sword. A Kate Smith Columbia record: "God Bless America." A rhinestone V-for-Victory pin.

The bottom shelf is rather junky. A pair of Thom McAn saddle shoes, very dirty, stand on top of an equally soiled reversible raincoat, beneath which is a sport coat with a belted back. A dead corsage is pressed between two 78 rpm records — "Deep Purple" and "Stardust." Beside them lie campaign pins reading "We Want Willkie" and "FDR." A third pin is shaped like a sunflower. Then: a shabby Philco radio in the form of an arch, a tattered copy of *Gone With the Wind*, a copy of *Ulysses* in which only the last forty pages seem to have been read, Boy and Girl Scout handbooks, and several square Big Little Books. There is a dusty Lionel train transformer, a jump rope, several marbles and one steelie, a splintered hockey stick, a well-oiled first baseman's mitt, a Shirley Temple doll, a sheaf of bubble gum cards, a G-man cap gun. Two Post Toasties box tops. A box of cherry bombs. A Bolo ball attached by elastic to a paddle. A pair of brown corduroy knickers. A hair ribbon. An old stand-up telephone.

Lastly, on the floor of the closet, are a batch of snapshots taken with a box Brownie. There are automobiles in them: a Model A Ford with the windshield down in some, a Chevy sporting a sassy rumble seat in others, and in the older ones, brown with age, a Model T. People are posing by the running boards. It is summer, yet the adults look very formal. The men are wearing stiff collars, the women vast hats and shapeless cotton dresses. But it is the children who seem oddest. Like their parents they are quaintly dressed. There is something else, though. It takes a moment to realize why they look so peculiar. Then you see it. There is an intensity in their expressions. They are leaning slightly forward, as though trying to see into the future. And they are smiling.

ACKNOWLEDGMENTS
CHAPTER NOTES
BIBLIOGRAPHY
COPYRIGHT ACKNOWLEDGMENTS
INDEX

Acknowledgments

HARRY SIONS, the editor of this book, died in Philadelphia on March 26, 1974, when the manuscript was in the final stages of preparation for the press. He had completed his final review of the text just a few days earlier. For over seventeen years he was a colleague and a cherished friend; his skill and high intelligence left their mark on every page of this volume, as well as on much of my earlier work.

Don Congdon, my literary agent for a quarter-century, planted the seed for the book by suggesting a study of the American national character. Together with Harry and J. Randall Williams of Little, Brown, he was an unfailing source of encouragement and sound advice. The support of Don and Randy Williams was immense, and is most gratefully acknowledged.

Several other associates and acquaintances were generous with suggestions and insight. I am particularly indebted to Henry Anatole Grunwald, Herman Kahn, Louis Lasagna M.D., Daniel Patrick Moynihan, Arthur M. Schlesinger Jr., and Eric Sevareid. In addition, Harry McMahan of *Advertising Age* was a treasure of information in his special field.

My invaluable assistant, Margaret Kennedy Rider, was loyal, resourceful, and tireless during the long years of research and writing. Epsey Farrell was of great help in her role as researcher, and I am appreciative of the assistance of Ellen G. D'Oench in annotating the manuscript.

No expression of thanks to Wyman Parker, Librarian of Wesleyan University, and the staff of the university's Olin Library, can really be adequate. For fifteen years they have sheltered me, cheered me, guarded my privacy, and given unstintingly of their considerable technical skills. At a time when their stacks are crammed, all I can give them in return is another book, and an outsize one at that. Moreover, it is imperfect, as all books are. It is true, insofar as diligence and research can establish truth, but it is not the whole truth. No volume, nor even a whole library, can provide that. All an author can offer is a fragment of reality — that, and the hope that it will endure.

Chapter Notes

In these Notes, works are generally cited by the author's name only; for full listings see the Bibliography. If the note is citing an author with more than one work in the Bibliography, a brief title for the work cited is also given in the note. Other forms of citation are:

Fab   Time-Life series *This Fabulous Century* (see entries at Maitland A. Edey and Jerry Korn in the Bibliography)

NYT   *New York Times*

TA   Time Annual *1969: The Year in Review*

T   *Time* magazine

TC   Time-Life series *Time Capsule* (see entry at Maitland A. Edey in the Bibliography)

W   Associated Press series *The World in——* (see listing at Keith Fuller in the bibliography)

WA   *World Almanac* (cited with the year)

WM   Author's interviews

The words identifying each note are the *end* of the paragraph which the note covers.

PROLOGUE: ROCK BOTTOM
(pages 3–28)

3 "Bonus Expeditionary Force": NYT 1/31/32; T 8/15/32; Schlesinger *Crisis* 256; *Baltimore Sun* 7/17/32. off to jail: Fab IV 25. 4 and multiplying misery: *Baltimore Sun* 7/17/32. to the country: *Baltimore Sun* 7/27/32; WM/Herman Kahn 6/5/70; *Washington* 29; Acheson 16–17, 91. 5 on ruling them: Mullett 3–8; "Who's in the Army Now?". elaborate buzzer system: Daniels 181; Gene Smith 12, 48; *Washington* 11. Ike came scurrying: *Saturday Evening Post* 12/20/30; Gene Smith 48; *Washington* 11; NYT 12/25/29, 7/27/41; WM/Herman Kahn; *Foreign Service Journal* February 1955; Eisenhower *Ease* 210; WM/Eisenhower 8/27/64. 6 was rich: *Ease* 219–20; "Who's in the Army Now?" Rovere *Years* 13; NYT 10/2/43; Mellor 129–30; Farago 105; *Washington* 601. colonies in 1776: T 2/8/32; "Who's in the Army Now?". "an ungraceful angle": "Who's in the Army Now?" 7 trolley car: NYT 9/1/43; WM/Eisenhower; Adams 155. a cottage industry: WM/Herman Kahn; *Washington* xix; Phillips *Blitz* 294–95. "Dat's de propolition": *Washington* xxi, 3, 83, 87; Schlesinger *Upheaval* 428. 8 great god macadam: NYT 5/15/48; Van Camp. D.C. was like: Sylvia Porter "The Vanishing Trains" *Middletown Press* 12/9/69. 9 to American business: NYT 4/29/32, 5/11/32, 4/24/32, 1/17/32; *Washington* 945; "Washington Through the Years"; NYT 2/4/32, 11/9/32; *Washington* 117, 918. 10 scheduled for razing: "Washington Through the Years"; NYT 2/4/32, 11/9/32; *Washington* 117,

918; Shuster 64, 105. exactly what he did: Galbraith *State* 359; *Baltimore Sun* 7/27/32; NYT 7/29/32; Daniels 193. "anywhere in the world": NYT 7/21/32; *Baltimore Sun* 6/5/32, 6/8/32, 6/9/32, 6/10/32, 6/19/32, 6/27/32; T 6/13/32; Gene Smith 136. *11* "their individual cases": NYT 6/19/32; *Ease* 209; Gene Smith 135. about patriotism: NYT 7/29/32; Daniels 192; Gene Smith 152. *12* Chicago's southwest side: NYT 8/17/32, 8/2/32, 7/29/32; T 8/8/32. chief of staff: NYT 7/29/32; *Baltimore Sun* 7/29/32; *Boston Herald* 7/29/32; T 8/8/32; Gene Smith 156. *13* bitterly resented it: Congdon 117; Rovere and Schlesinger 31–33; *Ease* 159, 212. solicitude toward civilians: Gene Smith 159. *14* suit, and all: *Baltimore Sun* 7/29/32; Walter Johnson 3–5; Gene Smith 161. "his mouth again": T 8/8/32. drove him out: Gene Smith 161. *15* his next move: *Ease* 213. disobey a President: Walter Johnson 3–5; *Ease* 213; Fab IV 25–26; *Ease* 213. *16* "feel for them": Fab IV 25–26; T 8/8/32; *Ease* 213; Gene Smith 162. George S. Patton Jr.: Daniels 194; *Crisis* 263; NYT 7/30/32; T 8/8/32; Mellor 103–28. "heroes just now": T 8/8/32. *17* "would surprise me": NYT 7/29/32, 8/4/32; T 8/8/32; Gene Smith 164, 166. "law and order": NYT 7/30/32; Congdon 119; *New Republic* 11/2/32; *Crisis* 263–64. *18* a difficult task: *Baltimore Sun* 7/29/32; "Who's in the Army Now?". "the Bonus marchers?" *Crisis* 261; Daniels 193. "in terrible shape": Gene Smith 169. *19* land in 1932: NYT 7/30/32; Bird 56; *Nation* 8/17/32. "the next station": *Blitz* 40–41; Congdon 102; *Crisis* 251; T 2/6/33; *Blitz* 285; Mowry 75; Walter Johnson 16; WM/Eric Sevareid; Congdon 102, 110. far from home: Sevareid *Dream* 49; *Nation* 8/24/32; Walter Johnson 23; NYT 12/11/32. *20* his old menus: NYT 5/4/32. "real estate company": NYT 9/19/31. *21* "with very pity": *Esquire* June 1960; Bird 24; Wolfe 413–14. "Yes, sir": Goldman *Tragedy* 377; *Time* editors 24; *Tragedy* 274; *Relief for Unemployed Transients* 35–38. venereal infection: Minehan 67–71. *22* and, later, militancy: NYT 3/26/31, 1/20/32; *Upheaval* 428–29; Congdon 171; Bird 130; T 4/10/33, 4/17/33, 12/11/33. day was inevitable: Minehan 18–83. for a quarter: NYT 8/2/41; T 5/12/41. "them at night": Congdon 152; Gene Smith 80; NYT 3/5/29; Gene Smith 206. *23* return of prosperity: Gene Smith 66. such incredible speed: Wolff 198; Gene Smith 97. *24* "both of them": NYT 3/2/32. might be softened: *Years* 78; Walter Johnson 27. people be tabled: Galbraith *Affluent* 15; NYT 1/5/32; Isabel Leighton 277. *25* legislatures, not Congress: Fab IV 25; Leary; Bird 208–209. the building trades: *Crisis* 57; Childs "Main Street"; Sulzberger 27. "make things worse": NYT 1/20/32; *Crisis* 164; *Affluent* 16; Gene Smith 76. would win: Schwartz xiii, xiv; *Affluent* 45; Gene Smith 68. *26* "political log-rolling!": T 5/30/32. "grandiloquent egotists": Mowry 57; *Crisis* 80. "Depression is over": Bird 13. *27* "spare a dime": NYT 12/3/30; Bird 58; *Crisis* 241; T 4/4/32. Business Confidence Week: *Crisis* 177. "worn-out private belongings": Fab IV 76; NYT 1/4/32; Isabel Leighton 222. *28* on American newsstands: *Middletown Press* 7/27/32; headlines T 8/8/32.

I THE CRUELEST YEAR
(pages 31–69)

31 could not understand: Gene Smith 103. "protect my children?": NYT 9/6/29; Mowry 68; Gene Smith 81. *32* "to the community": *Commonweal* 9/3/54; Bird 41. overextension of credit: Allen *Change* 144. "got too little": Mowry 64. *33* without historical precedent: Bird 115. jobs was $16.21: Shannon 73; Phillips *Blitz* 32, 34. *34* Howard Johnson, survived: Allen *Since* 132; *Time* editors 63; NYT 3/2/33, 2/6/32; *Theatre Arts* April 1931. "off my pants" *Time* editors 65; Bird 12; T 12/19/32; *Since* 108. *35* a peculiar gait: Bird 226; Schlesinger *Crisis* 167. she could imagine: Bird 227. and an undertaker: Fab IV 46; Bird 40, 116; Shannon 12, 26. *36* dunes of garbage: Shannon 10; Bird 21. an entire family: *Crisis* 167; Bird 36. of their own: *Fortune* September 1932. of two hundred: Gene Smith 174; NYT 1/19/33; Shannon 23. *37* "the Depression, huh?": *Blitz* 34; Fab IV 54; Shannon 23. called starvation wages: Bird 68; Shannon 26. *38* until after sunset: Congdon 36, 45, 47. began to disintegrate: *Crisis* 248; T 3/13/33. and the indigent: Bird 63. *39* game called Eviction: ibid 27. population of 600,000: *American Academy* January 1933. "bill before delivery": Bird 134. excluded from churches: ibid 26. *40* filthy old sheepskin: Schlesinger *Coming* 268; *Blitz* 257. began to disappear: Shannon 93–103 passim. twenty million dollars: ibid 94. *41* thin pocketbooks: ibid 99. "poor people were": NYT 3/8/32. "to our children?": *Crisis* 3; Shannon 53; Fab IV 53. *42* dying of hunger: *Fortune* September 1932; Bird 32. "days of 1932": *Crisis* 250; Wolfe 412. might be misunderstood: Bird 19. *43* "mighty vaults": Wolfe 414 "went to hell": *Newsweek* 2/17/33; NYT 2/6/32; Gene Smith 24. *44* "of the lowest": NYT 3/30/32; Congdon 612. couldn't help them: *Crisis* 190; NYT 3/11/32; Daniels 189. "policeman searches you": NYT 6/29/32, 4/14/32; T 10/17/32; *Crisis* 118. *45* taxes in full: *Blitz* 134; Bird 10; NYT 4/26/33; Daniels 183. "ammunition for radicals": NYT 5/12/33, 2/11/32; *New Republic* 5/29/35; T 1/25/32. from trusting investors: T 3/21/32; NYT 3/13/32. *46* "completely shattered": NYT 5/21/33; T 6/19/33; *Time* editors 31. it had become: NYT 6/7/32, 7/29/32; *Crisis* 109;

John Brooks *Golconda* 137. he liked it: Mowry 55; NYT 11/8/28; *Crisis* 280. "economic pyramid": NYT 4/8/32. 47 "rich against poor!": NYT 4/14/32; T 4/25/32. "have another Hoover": *Crisis* 175, 280, 288; NYT 7/10/32, 6/11/32; T 7/4/32. "still a Hoover": Rovere *Years* 18; *Crisis* 290. 48 were very direct: NYT 4/27/32, 5/5/32; Gene Smith 116. "here again!" Gene Smith 114. 49 campaign had begun: *Crisis* 309; T 8/8/32. to "brain trust": NYT 7/3/32, 5/23/32; *Since* 78. 50 danger of accidents: T 7/31/33; Fab IV 141. endorse any candidate: *Crisis* 428; *Mowry* 86. General MacArthur: Gene Smith 178; NYT 11/11/32, 10/16/32. 51 "this extraordinary hour": *Crisis* 434; *Nation* 7/13/32. four years later: T 11/21/32; NYT 9/24/32, 6/17/33; *Crisis* 413, 416. 52 "of lost children": *Crisis* 428. Johnson of California: NYT 9/13/32; Walter Johnson 37. 53 phoned Calvin Coolidge: *Crisis* 194, 199, 204; NYT 11/6/32. would be dead: *Crisis* 201; NYT 10/12/32; T 10/24/32. words had become: Walter Johnson 37; T 11/7/32; NYT 11/8/32; *Crisis* 437. 54 Franklin Delano Ragin: NYT 11/9/32; *Crisis* 218, 437; *Blitz* 73. "do this job": Gene Smith 214. was right: Walter Johnson 45; NYT 11/13/32; Bird 78. 55 "world's in birth": NYT 12/6/32; *Crisis* 448; Shannon 120. "and farmers' republic": NYT 11/8/32; Congdon 148. 56 smashed her face: NYT 1/15/33; *Blitz* 5; *Crisis* 166. "the American system": NYT 3/23/32; Shannon 114; *Coming* 22. 57 "left-wing state": *Crisis* 208; NYT 8/30/32; Bird 116. of Columbia University: *Crisis* 204, 460; NYT 1/26/32, 1/6/32; Schlesinger *Upheaval* 82. 58 "one now": NYT 11/11/32; *Crisis* 266. in Sioux City: Bird 131; *Crisis* 266. "was illegal too": NYT 8/14/32; Daniels 195; Shannon 123, 125. 59 "of other days": NYT 8/22/32; Shannon 121. "eat their gold": *Crisis* 174; *Time* editors 32. about mortgage foreclosures: NYT 8/26/32. press prosecution afterward: *Crisis* 459; T 5/8/33. 60 "than twelve months": T 1/16/33, 2/6/33; NYT 2/12/33; *Crisis* 459. 61 thirty-four years: Bird 4. these. O Pioneers!: ibid 2. before a bath: Gold *1940–41* 7. 62 aluminum juice extractor: T 4/27/42. about hair "coloring": Gold *1940–41* 9, 12. 63 59 million dollars: *Science* 5/12/33; WM/Louis Lasagna; Bird 133. "Uncle Don": *Blitz* 433. 64 best friend's thoughts: Sevareid *Dream* 4. Lindbergh's *We*: NYT 8/7/27. "destined to encounter": Gold *1940–41* 11. 65 "coal beds" . . . "in a monarchy": Theodore White *1968* 99, 97. 66 clearly visible: T 10/10/32. palms of his hands: NYT 6/16/32; *Since* 16. and cherry bombs: Gold *1940–41* 10. 67 R.N. stewardesses: Bird 2. service improves: Bird 264. 68 "ten years ago": NYT 5/4/37, 11/10/32; T 4/4/32. "my band, son": Bird 30; Gold *1940–41* 48. 69 paper victory: NYT 8/20/32, 9/23/32; Fab V 66. death or even illness: NYT 2/28/32, 8/24/32; T 4/11/32.

II ROOSEVELT!
(pages 71–93)

71 the outgoing President: Schlesinger *Crisis* 440; NYT 2/5/53, 7/31/32; Gene Smith 222. 72 "in the future": NYT 11/23/32, 1/8/33; *Crisis* 441. it a holiday: NYT 2/14/33. was "a madman": NYT 2/16/33; *Crisis* 474. 73 had gone under: *Crisis* 466. song for children: Bird 92; NYT 3/2/33, 2/5/33. 74 "could not be greater": *Holiday* February 1960. fog, toward Washington: NYT 3/6/33, 3/2/33. barometer was falling: NYT 3/3/33, 3/2/33. 75 two financial strongholds: NYT 3/3/33. "don't want to": NYT 3/4/33. "must go now": Gene Smith 225. 76 "we can do": NYT 3/3/33, 3/4/33; Fab IV 116. with a cameraman: Schlesinger *Coming* 424; NYT 3/1/33, 3/5/33. 77 "a foreign foe": NYT 3/5/33. tell him so: Walter Johnson 49; Isabel Leighton 275; *Coming* 1. 78 without moneychangers: NYT 3/5/33, 3/6/33; Bird 96. "going any lower": *Holiday* February 1960. 79 they had done: ibid. going into action: NYT 3/10/33. 80 "Are Here Again": NYT 3/9/33; Phillips *Blitz* 120; John Brooks *Golconda* 155. "bit shell-shocked": NYT 3/10/33, 6/17/33; Gunther 139. "Hitler much more": *Blitz* 106. 81 one vast classroom: *Coming* 555. President's own wife: NYT 3/9/33; *Blitz* 473. "wheels turning around": NYT 3/13/33; *Coming* 557. 82 had won it: *Coming* 530, 574. "is the President": ibid 511; NYT 3/5/33; T 7/31/33. 83 one note ran: Gunther 147; NYT 1/22/61. "President like you": Fab IV 136. "and in itself": ibid; *Coming* 424; T 3/13/33; NYT 3/19/33. "why they left": WM/Herman Kahn. 84 Kleberg's constituents: NYT 5/9/33; Bird 111; *Blitz* 234. "Lord, God Almighty": Acheson 151. them, especially Hiss: WM/Herman Kahn. those of congressmen: NYT 3/7/33, 2/27/33; T 8/21/33. 85 Texas to Canada: NYT 3/25/33; *Coming* 338; Fab IV 130. "the deflationary forces": *Golconda* 154, 155. control for hogs: Isabel Leighton 284; NYT 5/13/33; T 8/21/33. 86 "the United States!": NYT 5/21/33; TC 1930 145. and Ickes achieved: *Coming* 264; NYT 11/8/33. the Florida mainland: NYT 11/9/33; Bird 108. 87 first Nixon administration: NYT 7/12/36, 9/12/36, 5/7/46. anything was possible: NYT 1/22/33. "ax won't work": NYT 6/17/33; Isabel Leighton 291. 88 "authority of government": NYT 6/17/33, 5/8/33; *Coming* 98. "restraint of competition": *Blitz* 218; NYT 11/2/33. it looked real: NYT 8/14/33; T 7/31/33. 89 "on the nose": Walter Johnson 68; T 8/7/33; *Blitz* 48. "back good times": NYT 7/25/33; *Blitz* 220. 90 "American economic life": *Coming* 119, 123; T 11/13/33. had saved capitalism: Fab IV 116; *Blitz*

128. *91* to ask him: T 8/14/33; Schlesinger *Upheaval* 451. *91–93* Eleanor Roosevelt portrait: *Current Biography 1949*, 1963; NYT 11/8/62.

III STIRRINGS
(pages 94–122)

94 "am for Johnny": NYT 10/26/34; Fab IV 100, 109. *95* in her purse: NYT 7/23/34, 2/8/34; Daniels 240. and Clyde Barrow: NYT 7/26/34. he had left: NYT 6/5/34, 6/10/34; Schlesinger *Coming* 294. *96* nascent Liberty League: NYT 9/26/34, 7/3/34; *Coming* 153, 463; John Brooks *Golconda* 198. "virtually terminated": T 4/3/33. *97* concern was espionage: *Coming* 53; NYT 4/6/34. left he could get: Kendrick 136. do the job: NYT 11/7/34. *98* New Year's Day: NYT 5/20/34, 8/30/34, 1/11/34, 8/8/34, 2/23/33. get some rain: NYT 5/29/34. was blowing away: NYT 1/27/37, 9/22/38; *Coming* 70; Brogan 82. *99* threatened with famine: Brogan 81; Walter Johnson 67; Shannon 131. on their floors: NYT 6/21/34; *Coming* 69; Fab IV 60. at 108 degrees: Fab IV 61; NYT 8/13/34; Congdon 289. *100* "off the earth": Phillips *Blitz* 240. of Upton Sinclair: Daniels 247; Sevareid *Dream* 11; NYT 4/14/39; Fab IV 64. a generation later: Schlesinger *Upheaval* 117. *101* the regular Democratic organization: *Upheaval* 111; Daniels 248. "going on before": NYT 9/2/34; *Upheaval* 34. *I Got Licked:* NYT 2/24/35; Daniels 248; *Upheaval* 118. *102* New York City: NYT 9/10/36, 11/6/36, 11/8/33. or his effectiveness: NYT 9/17/33; Congdon 195. "support for reaction": NYT 11/18/34; *Upheaval* 176, 182. *103* "be USSA then": NYT 10/29/50; Schulberg 20; Allen *Since* 251. *104* "TAKE IT CLUB": NYT 8/23/34. his own good: NYT 10/25/34. *105* Days of 1935: NYT 10/16/34, 4/1/36, 6/5/35. "perturbed at developments": NYT 1/5/35; *Upheaval* 391, 226. *106* response was a fraud: NYT 4/2/35; *Upheaval* 311. "hand, Mr. Chairman": NYT 8/9/35; Burns *Soldier* 362; *Blitz* 289. cents an hour: NYT 6/20/35. *107* bosses, and Negroes: NYT 5/30/34. "other crime bills": NYT 6/14/34, 7/5/34. *108* the early 1970s: NYT 1/23/35, 1/10/35, 2/5/35, 4/1/35. claim was undisputed: NYT 12/1/35; *Upheaval* 4; Isabel Leighton 242. "let me know": Spivak 6. *109* "toes against eternity": *Upheaval* 20; NYT 12/26/35; T 4/10/33. ground between them: Carlson 58. *110* the political center: NYT 6/9/36, 4/29/34. "the labor problem": Isabel Leighton 241. "we will win": NYT 7/20/35; T 4/10/33; Carlson 57; Isabel Leighton 243. *111* "a holy war": Carlson 58. "unbalanced college professors": Daniels 253. *112* William Howard Taft: NYT 8/18/46. in American politics: NYT 2/1/35. "still weep here": Daniels 204. *113* "of my path": NYT 1/26/32. Avenue in Washington: *Upheaval* 56. "lead the mob": NYT 9/22/35; Daniels 240–43; *Upheaval* 66. *114* his own constituents: Walter Johnson 83–86; Congdon 315. "you want it": *Upheaval* 243–44. "honestly conducted election": Isabel Leighton 357. *115* "has an intellect": NYT 6/26/35; *Upheaval* 249. over the country: NYT 3/8/35. "man a king": *Upheaval* 65. *116* "in knee breeches": NYT 9/29/35. "kill Huey Long": NYT 9/9/35; *Blitz* 302; NYT 9/10/35, 9/15/35; *Upheaval* 340. *117* been dramatically different: *Upheaval* 341. resembling a sermon: NYT 6/17/36. "in the scale": Schlesinger *Thousand* 720. *118* a chain reaction: *Blitz* 296; NYT 7/5/36. a familiar form: *Blitz* 420. King of Swing: Gold *1936–37* 4. in the future: Gold *1940–41* 21. *120* "censorship as possible": Fab IV 180; Mowry 25; *Time* editors 151; T 2/20/33. United States in 1935: Mowry 5. *121* "their Bewildering Offspring": ibid 3. introduced to him: *Blitz* 442. *122* the New Deal: *Time* editors 63; Mowry 112.

IV THE ROOSEVELT REFERENDUM
(pages 124–148)

124 to threats overseas: NYT 12/31/33. *125* America was chickenhearted: NYT 7/4/37. aggression in Manchuria: NYT 9/1/35. "is fairly certain": NYT 6/5/34; Gunther 300. *126* was forty-three: NYT 7/27/34; "Who's in the Army Now?" *127* Swarthmore '32; NYT 4/13/35; Schlesinger *Upheaval* 199; Simon 157, 168–69. abolished it: Sevareid *Dream* 59. "right-minded students here": Phillips *Blitz* 477; T 10/3/32. desperately needed cash: NYT 11/9/35. *128* "starving by degrees": Simon 155; *Fortune* June 1936; Simon 155. the university library: Bird 242; Congdon 400. of juvenile distinction: *New Republic* 10/9/35. *129* and roller skates: Gold *1940–41* 21; Fab V 48. suits and white bucks: Gold *1940–41* 4. all Duke dances: Fab IV 241; Gold *1940–41* 21. *130* yet to come: Bird 238. progressive union policies: Fab IV 164; NYT 1/28/32. "return their blows": Schlesinger *Coming* 138, 413. *131* "of his youth": NYT 12/8/35; *Coming* 143. "a quieting influence": Fab IV 164; *Coming* 394. "mines without them": *Coming* 385; NYT 7/17/34; Fab IV 162. *132* "dinkey parlez vous": Bird 149; NYT 2/16/36; *Blitz* 516. "just join up!": NYT 12/8/35. over 400,000: NYT 9/28/34, 11/5/34. *133* time for persuasion: NYT 12/1/34, 3/13/35, 5/17/35. "their goddam heads": Daniels 255; Graham and Gurr 332; *Coming* 396; Bird 152. *134* "of the race": Graham and Gurr 336 ff, 387; NYT 5/22/34;

Coming 388. underpaid, and sweated: NYT 7/1/34, 2/15/35; *Coming* 406. *135* of Industrial Organizations: Simon 107; NYT 10/20/35, 11/24/35, 12/8/35. "makes us strong": *Coming* 415. *136* it was illegal: *Upheaval* 448, 451; Mowry 116, 118; NYT 10/30/35. regulate interstate commerce: NYT 5/28/35. *137* issuing a warning: NYT 5/30/35. problems was forbidden: NYT 1/7/36, 5/19/36, 5/26/36; *Upheaval* 488. *138* ceiling over hours: NYT 6/2/36. "of the Court": NYT 10/31/36. one-term President: NYT 12/15/36. *139* from the President; *Upheaval* 633. than half that: Gunther 300; NYT 3/24/35; Daniels 305. OF COUNTRY LEADS: *Upheaval* 571. political assets, luck: ibid 502, 590. *140* the American temper: NYT 1/26/36. died before November: NYT 6/12/36, 6/14/36. paused for breath: NYT 6/11/36. "for to free!": *Blitz* 484. *141* Bell was cracked: Spivak 32; NYT 8/16/36; *Upheaval* 629. for a prayer: NYT 10/16/36. "within the gates": NYT 6/24/36. *142* "you ever saw": Congdon 435; NYT 6/28/36; *Upheaval* 584. in New Orleans: NYT 6/1/36, 11/3/36. was a Communist: NYT 10/16/36. *143* Landon didn't win: *Upheaval* 616. social security number: NYT 10/24/36; *Upheaval* 635. bonfire in him: Congdon 439, 442; NYT 1/1/36. *144* after his departure: NYT 11/1/36; *Upheaval* 639. "campaign manager's prophecies?": WM/DPMoynihan; *Blitz* 488; Bird 181; *Upheaval* 608. out to *Time:* NYT 12/15/36, 11/4/36, 2/19/37; Wish 471; Daniels 275. *145* "known conservative tendencies": *Upheaval* 656. *145–147* Whitney portrait: John Brooks *Once in Golconda* 210–29; T 11/23/36, 3/21/38, 5/9/38, 5/16/38.

V THE CONSERVATIVE PHOENIX
(pages 149–171)

149 Dutch East Indies: NYT 6/23/37, 6/8/37. oxygen bomb calorimeter: Congdon 615 and passim. (were Gap-Free): NYT 5/24/37. *150* awaited television: Jack Goodman 279; NYT 3/19/37. kind of year: NYT 1/21/37. "with muffled oars": Schlesinger *Upheaval* 494; Gunther 61; Schlesinger *Thousand* 869. *151* "Chief Justice understood": NYT 1/7/37; *Time* editors 36. the "Court Pack": NYT 2/4/37. the same decision: NYT 3/11/37; Phillips *Blitz* 501. *152* "rendezvous with death": *Blitz* 501; NYT 3/10/37, 3/5/37. "the caucus room": *Blitz* 503; Simon 205. in his hand: NYT 3/30/37, 7/7/37, 7/15/37; Congdon 468. *153* was now acceptable: NYT 7/22/37; WA 1937; Congdon 475. including Johnson himself: Goldman *Tragedy* 258. be kept moving: Daniels 285; NYT 3/21/34. *154* "that's the trouble": NYT 3/6/37; Fab IV 164. burst into tears: NYT 12/19/36, 12/29/36; Daniels 266. *155* past the police: NYT 3/25/37. major GM stockholder: NYT 1/1/37; Gunther 147. issuing a statement: Spivak 110; NYT 8/1/37; Gunther 147. SHALL NOT PASS: NYT 2/3/37. "the right thing?": Fab IV 167; Bird 155. outside the plants: *Time* editors 70; Allen *Since* 82; NYT 2/7/37. he was underpaid: Fab IV 170; NYT 4/7/37. *157* "is nothing there": T 5/15/39, 12/2/40. meant to change: NYT 5/16/37; Fab IV 172; Daniels 267. *158* another conversation: NYT 10/27/37; *Since* 292. "Yes, Mr. Fairless": NYT 3/8/37. meet workers' demands: *Blitz* 522–23; Bird 147; NYT 5/28/37. *159* Court, was unmentioned: NYT 5/27/37; Fab IV 172, 175. "Solidarity Forever": NYT 5/31/37; Isabel Leighton 383 ff. *160* "women doing there?": NYT 6/20/37; Isabel Leighton 386ff; Fab IV 176. much for them: Isabel Leighton 398; NYT 7/28/37. "intimidate the strikers": NYT 6/16/37; Fab IV 176. *161* except Bethlehem Steel: Isabel Leighton 396. "in our history": NYT 5/27/37. expanding middle class: Walter Johnson 159; NYT 10/29/37. *162* ideals to work: NYT 9/23/37, 2/28/37, 9/25/37. "fifty times more": Bird 183; NYT 9/29/37. of 1929–30: *Since* 305ff; NYT 10/20/37. *163* was on relief: Mowry 295. days, lay ahead: Galbraith *Affluent* 16; *Thousand* 626; NYT 5/1/38, 4/15/38; *Since* 311. "you would wish": Bird 184. *164* not party lines: *Saturday Evening Post* 9/22/34; Schlesinger *Coming* 483. "Grand!" across it: Daniels 301; *Coming* 569. *165* businessmen, was battening: NYT 12/5/38. "that man's skin": Gunther 56. (Colonel van Rosenfeld): Daniels 300; John Brooks *Golconda* 215. *166* businessmen to Washington: Gunther 50. had syphilis: Simon 111; *Golconda* 216. *167* breathe freely again: NYT 8/15/39. in the fall: *Since* 232. "the New Deal": NYT 7/13/38 could sense it: Mowry 120, 122; *Fortune* January 1939. *168* for Roosevelt's signature: *Time* editors 37. ugly overture: *Blitz* 507–508. "my own name": NYT 6/25/38. *169* "a commanding position": Burns *Lion* 363, 365. had been committed: NYT 7/9/38, 7/14/38, 7/17/38. *170* New Deal legislation: NYT 7/8/38; *Lion* 363. "a working majority": NYT 9/18/40; *Thousand* 708. "to the forest": *Lion* 366. *171* "President's foreign policy": Childs "They Hate" and "They Still Hate." Empire of Japan: NYT 12/13/37.

VI A SHADOW OF PRIMITIVE TERROR
(pages 173–209)

173 convoying anybody: NYT 12/13/37. *174* to declare war: NYT 2/16/32. "remembered the *Maine*": NYT 4/20/38; Fehrenbach 294; Phillips *Blitz* 532. Depression become comprehensible: T 5/29/39; NYT 2/2/37, 7/15/38; *Blitz* 532. *175* doted on Europe: Rovere and Schlesinger 229. "find no one there": NYT 10/6/37; Daniels 295; *Time* editors 292. *176* "less given up": NYT 2/9/37; Daniels 295. Canada were attacked: NYT 12/22/37; *Blitz* 548; Cooke 2; Fehrenbach 294. eight thousand casualties: NYT 7/22/37; Spivak 137; T 3/6/39. *177* United States with impunity: NYT 4/30/37, 1/11/38; Congdon 606. Americans in 1914–18: Daniels 295; NYT 10/9/38. *178* "two-ocean" Navy: NYT 1/29/38. for June 6: NYT 3/22/38, 10/16/38. to the dictators: NYT 10/7/38. a ringside seat: NYT 9/13/37. *179* "you do it?" NYT 5/13/37; *Time* editors 173; *Atlantic* September 1940. said they would try: Kendrick 157ff. American public opinion: ibid. *180* "'Heils' ('Hail Victory')": NYT 9/13/38. The Siegfried Line: Congdon 574. *181* the United States: ibid 575. *182* were still preferred: ibid 578. *183* "basely betrayed": NYT 9/21/38. "on its way": ibid. *184* say about it: McCarthy *Hurricane* 3. anything after all: NYT 9/20/38. *185* out to sea: NYT 9/21/38, 9/20/38, 9/22/38. that same night: NYT 9/22/38. *186* house blew away: *Hurricane* 14. only that morning: ibid 3. *187* twenty-nine corpses: NYT 9/23/38. in a nightmare: ibid. was carried away: *Hurricane* 63. *188* "in smoking ruins": ibid 57. U.S. Weather Bureau: ibid 141. of American history: NYT 9/22/38, 9/23/38. "a social power": NYT 9/30/38. *189* "will bring peace": Daniels 303; Fab IV 39. Halloween in 1938: NYT 10/31/38. *190* Sunday prime time: *Blitz* 383; T 11/20/44. *191* everyone agreed: NYT 9/26/38, 10/31/38. *192–195* Quotations from the script are from Cantril. *194* "lot to do": Congdon 589. *195* "Jersey and fire": Cantril 67, 112. *197* time would come: T 4/10/39; NYT 6/29/39. had in mind: Fab IV 112. voice was changing: T 3/13/39; Gold *1940–41* 54. *198* him "Mr. Christian": NYT 7/30/39. had ever known: *Time* editors 124. no Grover Whalen: NYT 2/19/39. *198n Harper's* March 1933. American society: NYT 2/5/39; Fab IV 268. own food: NYT 5/17/39. fourteen-lane turnpikes: Fab IV 280. *200* "of Hell": NYT 5/15/39. to Hyde Park: NYT 6/11/39. was "half-caste": NYT 6/12/39. tried to retire: T 7/24/39. *201* of bad weather: NYT 9/16/39, 7/6/39; Rovere and Schlesinger 130. *202* "in my belt": NYT 7/19/39. the experimental stage: NYT 5/24/39. *203* "Bullitt, Mr. President" (and next three paragraphs): T 9/11/39; NYT 9/1/39. "Deutschland über Alles": T 9/18/39, 9/25/39. *203* "about salt water": Fehrenbach 29. *204* meant by neutrality: NYT 9/4/39, 9/14/39; T 9/18/39. "willing to answer": NYT 11/3/40. *205* epithet stuck: Fehrenbach 45. *206* however, sleep long: NYT 4/21/39, 5/14/39.

VII THROUGH THE NIGHT WITH A LIGHT FROM ABOVE
(pages 210–236)

210 was Viennese: *Saturday Evening Post* 9/7/40. life in ruins: Laurence 32. *211* "that so long?" NYT 11/11/38, 1/29/39. destroy the world: Jungk 71, 75. powerful as TNT: NYT 1/3/39; Laurence 34. on the blackboard: Laurence 35, 44. *213* spread the news: NYT 4/30/39; Laurence 37. ahead of them: Laurence 48. *215* "surrounding territory": Burns *Soldier* 249; Laurence 85. and two glasses: Laurence 83. "requires action": ibid 86. *216* on another ship: ibid 88. across the Atlantic: NYT 1/20/40; *Scholastic* 10/14/40. by Reynaud himself: NYT 5/15/40, 6/1/40. *217* "liberation of the Old": NYT 6/23/40, 8/23/40. "shall never surrender": NYT 11/16/40. hundred feet below: Fehrenbach 210. "to fight alone": NYT 6/14/40. *218* "wish to live": NYT 12/18/40. "them all dead": NYT 9/8/40. "talk about that": NYT 6/19/40. *219* movements ever since: NYT 7/14/40, 6/5/42, 11/27/42. diamonds, for $5,000: T 7/28/41. United States intervened: ibid. *220* Air Corps colonel: NYT 4/26/41, 4/29/41. the speech "inexcusable": NYT 5/13/42; Fehrenbach 272. *221* "name in Indochina": T 7/8/40; Fehrenbach 84. on their hands: Fehrenbach 59, 101. *222* the American people: NYT 3/1/40. freighters to England: NYT 2/24/42. planes a year: Fab V 22. "the two deals": NYT 6/11/40. *223* board of directors: Fehrenbach 175; NYT 1/21/41. booed Churchill's name: NYT 4/24/41. *Washington Times-Herald:* NYT 9/4/40. Training and Service Bill: NYT 9/17/40, 9/2/40. *224* as U.S. citizens: *American Mercury* April 1940. was Lewis B. Hershey: *Life* 9/30/40; NYT 9/30/40. "have been selected": *Vital Speeches* 9/1/40. *225* Roosevelt was skating: *Life* 8/18/41. "rendered in this": Fehrenbach 267. them Wendell L. Willkie: John Brooks *Leap* 307; T 7/8/40. after the election: T 9/23/40. *226* "the White House!": Daniels 309, 319. the Nazis' choice: Fehrenbach 109; Daniels 317. Superintendent of Sewers: Fab V 23. "any foreign wars": NYT 10/31/40. the White House: Walter Johnson 137. *227 Wall Street Journal:* NYT 11/7/40. the same boat: T 8/26/40. *228* "are at war": T 6/24/40. *229* "to the bone?" NYT 12/4/40. as lend-lease: Burns *Soldier* 25. *230* it "in kind": NYT 12/18/40; *Soldier* 26. "the United States": *Soldier* 45. to start now: NYT 12/30/40. "devoutly hope not": Fab V 25; *Christian Century* 2/19/41. *231* Duce any more?: T 3/3/41, 3/24/41. the western hemisphere: NYT 12/13/41, 4/11/41. *232* "North Atlantic war": Fehrenbach 227. policy, was inevitable: NYT 6/29/41. "OK FDR": *Soldier* 91. *233* "probably the time": NYT 7/8/41. dangerous Murmansk run: NYT 6/22/41, 6/24/41. he said wryly: NYT 2/19/41. *234* the Atlantic Charter: T 4/28/41. "no formal document": NYT 8/22/41. *235* that they approved: NYT 9/5/41. "of our nation": NYT 10/18/41; *Soldier* 147. "good *Reuben James?*" NYT 11/1/41. *236* on Japan, too: *Life* 10/7/40. the American Navy: *Soldier* 142. in the theater: *Soldier* 149. December 10, 1941: NYT 12/7/41.

VIII AMERICA ON THE BRINK

(pages 238–260)

238 for sheer survival: NYT 7/14/40; *Newsweek* 4/28/41. $832 a year: Burns *Soldier* 53; T 5/12/41, 9/22/41. *239* rheumatic heart disease: T 5/12/41. times a week: *American Journal of Sociology* November 1942; Lifton 199. friend five cents: NYT 1/13/42, 4/15/42, 6/30/42, 9/22/42, 12/11/42. condoms than haircuts: Bird 213; *Fortune* December 1937. *240* on a battlefield: John Brooks *Leap* 30; NYT 5/21/40. cost a quarter: *Leap* 29; NYT 6/13/34. *241* in "illicit relations": Gold *1940–41* 31; *American Magazine* August 1941; *Leap* 28. no longer used: Chapman 28. *242* separate fraternities: NYT 2/23/41. *243* fighting this war: T 10/28/40; *Soldier* 266. "straight to hell": *Fortune* June 1942; *Soldier* 463; Bird 46; T 6/16/41; *Current Biography* 1943. in the North: *Leap* 276; Bird 45; *Time* editors 153; *Soldier* 463. 1960s were born: *Leap* 279. *244* "next Brown Bomber": T 9/29/41; Gold *1940–41* 10. "NAACP-type production": Gold *1941–42* 25, 27. her own people: ibid 27. *245* American Presidents: *Survey* November 1942; *Soldier* 123. in Constitution Hall: *Leap* 275; NYT 2/23/29. outdoor concert possible: NYT 3/31/39. "I can, too": NYT 2/28/39; Congdon 622. *246* the assembly line: NYT 6/26/40; T 1/6/41. and Virginia Woolf: T 1/27/41, 2/10/41, 4/7/41, 4/14/41. "unmolested by authority": *Time* editors 155; *Life* 5/12/41; NYT 5/4/48, 5/9/41; Eisinger 235, 240. *247* December 7, 1941; NYT 7/21/41, 5/3/41. from behind: Allen *Since* 138. *248* sharp hostesses: T 1/31/44; Gold *1940–41* 21 and passim. substitute "outlets": *Leap* 238. "on beaches": ibid 10; NYT 9/11/41. demanding private showers: T 4/1/40. *249* "he is mad": T 3/4/40. "and moral views": NYT 3/11/40; T 3/11/40. won round two: T 3/25/40. and "narrow-minded": T 4/8/40. *250* happier about it: WA 1940. the United States: T 4/8/40. *251* urgent, inexplicable request: WA 1941; NYT 10/6/41, 8/12/41, 8/17/41; Daniels 336. cruises to Hawaii: Daniels 336. kill 2,403 Americans: NYT 12/9/41. armed forces — oil: Fehrenbach 297. vehemently anti-Japanese: NYT 12/7/41. *252* Germany and Italy: *Life* 10/7/40; *Soldier* 20. "are no taxicab": T 8/4/41, 9/22/41. neighboring countries: *Soldier* 135–36; Fehrenbach 304. in the Orient: NYT 10/17/41; *Soldier* 146. *253* "at Pearl Harbor": T 11/26/45. *254* know about war: *Soldier* 78; T 12/10/45. "on Pearl Harbor": T 12/31/45. *255* NOT A DRILL: Daniels 341. *255–56* bow them out . . . toward the door: *Soldier* 162–63. *256* ATTACK PEARL HARBOR: Sulzberger 144. THE STATE DEPARTMENT: ibid. *257* would be back: NYT 12/18/41; Fab V 71. "fishy to me": Fab V 71. treacherous Orientals: NYT 12/8/41. *258* a Pacific fleet: Gunther 330. "in Valdosta, Georgia": Daniels 343. "Come anyway" . . . "of peace": Kendrick 239. *259* "On the *ground!*": Fab V 71. "fog of battle": ibid. *260* would dive: ibid. "national interest required" Acheson 37.

IX COUNTERATTACK

(pages 263–287)

General source for WWII in the Pacific: William Manchester "Our War in the Pacific" *Holiday* November 1960 pp 110–11, 152–67. *263* lost a war: NYT 11/29/45. the sky then: T 1/12/42. *264* offensive at once: NYT 1/2/42. coastal waters: NYT 1/2/42, 1/17/42, 1/15/42, 1/20/42, 3/4/42. *265* and San Francisco: NYT 2/3/43, 4/29/42; *Life* 8/10/42; *Time* editors 43; Burns *Soldier* 212. Malaya: NYT 12/15/41. couldn't be turned: NYT 12/8/41, 1/28/42, 1/3/42. "gives a damn": NYT 12/11/41, 3/18/42; T 3/30/42; Rovere and Schlesinger 56. *266* to their fate: NYT 9/27/42, 2/22/42. Abandon Ship: NYT 3/14/42, 3/15/42. the New Hebrides: NYT 9/30/42. *267* lovely flame trees: NYT 11/2/43. *268* unearthly splendor: *Life* 3/22/43; NYT 1/30/43. *269* "come, the better": T 7/9/45. "time to die": NYT 5/7/42. planes and killed him: *Newsweek* 2/1/43; NYT 5/21/43. *270* after he was dead: *Current Biography* 1942; NYT 5/21/43. sealing off China: NYT 2/16/42. "States Marines hiding?": NYT 2/16/42, 2/2/41. and troop movements: NYT 5/6/42, 12/18/42. *271* "men, still unafraid": NYT 1/15/42, 5/6/42. time for Midway: NYT 5/8/42, 6/13/42, 7/15/42, 9/17/42. "Seattle by air": NYT 7/18/42, 9/17/43, 6/5/42; T 6/15/42. *272* patched-up *Yorktowns* NYT 6/5/42; *Life* 11/16/42. sipping rice broth: NYT 6/5/42; T 6/22/42, 6/7/43. *273* hospitalized by October: NYT 8/9/42, 11/22/42; WM/Dr. Louis Lasagna 8/4/70. hundred one night: *Soldier* 284. could win all: Fab V 75; NYT 10/31/42. *274* U-boat challenge: *Soldier* 183. off to combat: NYT 8/11/42, 11/5/43, 8/11/42. *275* "work to do": Fab V 198; T 6/22/42, 2/22/43. as Los Alamos: Jungk 133. *276* "of

October 3": T 5/4/42, 6/22/42; NYT 10/4/42. couldn't remember it: Mazo 36. *277* "him to bed": NYT 11/22/42. ready to move: NYT 7/10/42, 9/27/42; T 11/9/42. operation was Torch: Walter Johnson 173. "a cruel initiative": *Scholastic Magazine* 1/11/43; T 11/16/42; NYT 11/9/42; T 11/16/42; *Soldier* 291. *278* "are striking back": *Soldier* 291. through Kasserine Pass: *Saturday Evening Post* 5/29/43; NYT 2/22/43. just 18,500 casualties: *Collier's* 11/9/43. *279* Italians and Sicilians: NYT 5/9/43, 6/12/43. of Axis troops: NYT 8/18/43; *Soldier* 394; NYT 7/26/43; T 9/20/43. "another Dunkerque": NYT 9/16/43, 7/18/43, 7/21/46. toward Naples: NYT 9/11/43. *280* pitiless as ever: NYT 10/2/43, 2/16/44. winters in memory: NYT 2/18/44, 1/19/44. *281* water, and time: NYT 1/3/43. *282* warmth of socks: Mauldin *Front* 36. gasoline called napalm: ibid 93; *Soldier* 344. *283* "deadpan face" NYT 11/21/48; Walter Johnson 156. "a little superfluous": *Front* 32. over to Hitler: NYT 10/2/43. and David Niven: T 6/7/43; NYT 2/21/42. *284* Hopkins's youngest boy: NYT 1/10/42, 11/17/43, 12/25/44, 11/13/44, 4/12/44, 8/19/44, 8/15/44, 2/13/44; John Brooks *Leap* 286. *285* "killed same": *Soldier* 271. *286* to GI prurience: NYT 12/31/43. "einst Lilli Marlene": NYT 10/17/43.

X THE HOME FRONT
(pages 289–327)

289 "boy on Bataan": T 3/23/42. the same again: Sevareid *Dream* 215. *290* those of 1929: Burns *Soldier* 460; Jack Goodman 19. "so do comforts": NYT 5/3/45, 4/28/65; Walter Johnson 157; Fab V 148. "in the black": T 3/15/43; Brogan 164. *291* "a hothouse growth": NYT 12/14/60; Allen *Change* 188–90. dismissed as "eggheads": NYT 4/13/38; *Soldier* 461. *292* an overstatement: NYT 3/23/44. "Win-the-War": NYT 12/29/43, 12/8/41. permitted to vote: NYT 12/29/43, 12/8/41. *One World*: NYT 11/4/42; *Soldier* 280; Walter Johnson 165; *Soldier* 337; T 2/7/44, 3/6/44; NYT 2/25/44, 6/16/43, 4/8/43. *293* to the Army: NYT 2/28/43; T 6/26/44. knew, but still: T 4/13/42. "sergeant over there": NYT 2/6/44. *294* (brands as Fleetwoods): T 7/3/44. by 22 percent: T 7/17/44; NYT 2/7/42. *295* on the West Coast: NYT 4/28/44; T 12/21/42; Jack Goodman 50. admirals wanted them: Liddell Hart 384. loss of quality: NYT 2/20/41; *Soldier* 244; *Time* editors 45. *296* of the profits: NYT 8/1/42, 8/24/42; T 8/31/42. and overwhelming them: Sulzberger 418. 44,000,000,000: Fab V 150. *297* country was fighting: NYT 6/20/43; *Soldier* 213 and passim. "the alien Japanese": Walter Johnson 156; NYT 2/1/42, 10/6/53. *298* next three weeks: Fab V 201. "welcome in Kansas": ibid 204. "American or not": ibid 201, 206. *299* it to Washington: NYT 4/23/41. "elder statesman": NYT 11/3/43. "or all persons": NYT 6/19/42, 3/19/42, 2/21/42; Fab V 201. *300* in horse stalls: T 4/6/42; Fab V 204. 1,862 funerals: NYT 11/4/42; Fab V 206. *301* could go hang: *Soldier* 216. were "disloyal": NYT 12/19/44, 12/20/44. more than sing: Fab V 205. *302* "rates were appalling": NYT 10/14/43; Fab V 206. overt outrages subsided: Mauldin *Home* 168. said a word: ibid 170. *303* victory gardens: NYT 1/23/42. *304* asylum and tranquillity: NYT 1/2/42, 2/6/42, 5/1/42, 5/10/42, 5/3/42, 9/7/44, 9/6/42, 10/18/42, 11/22/45, 12/3/45, 11/27/42, 11/1/42; Jack Goodman 467. in Broadway alleys: NYT 7/1/42, 5/2/44, 1/28/45; T 1/15/45. they sold well: NYT 7/23/42, 3/21/42, 9/13/42, 1/21/43, 4/8/43, 10/28/43, 11/21/44, 2/29/44. *305* "frustrated women": Jack Goodman 418. pajamas at night: Rovere *Years* 8; Fab V 256. Walter Annenberg's *Seventeen*: Jack Goodman 594. *306* called bobby-soxers: Fab V 27. quietly died: NYT 11/12/44. *307* were at peace: T 8/21/44; Fab V 46–49. "they're nice kids": T 7/5/43. her feet, shrieking: NYT 12/10/43. *308* twenty squad cars: NYT 10/13/44. later, Mia Farrow: NYT 10/31/51, 11/8/51. "*My* lifetime?": Jack Goodman 379. *309* "Sinatra is baffling": *Reader's Digest* January 1945. bobby-soxer rite: NYT 3/6/45; Fab V 47. "like the Paramount": NYT 6/22/45, 6/11/45; Fab V 48. *310* Allies with nothing: Jungk 131; *Soldier* 249. the three tons: Laurence 68–69. 311 might reach 1.07: ibid 70. liquid at it: ibid 76–77. technological problem: ibid 74; NYT 8/7/45. *312* "realistic traditions": *Soldier* 550. "to the project": NYT 11/4/44. *313* whole-souled Communist: NYT 6/16/50, 5/24/50, 6/17/50, 2/4/50. *314* just been formed: NYT 7/18/50; West 217–21. in fact killed: NYT 8/19/50. history greatly altered: NYT 5/25/46. *315* was Klaus Fuchs: Jungk 193; NYT 6/29/46. desert remains obscure: NYT 8/7/45. criminal investigation: NYT 12/7/45. *316* and Winston Churchill: NYT 1/8/43; *Soldier* 316. great battles ahead: *Soldier* 389. "triumphant success": ibid 17, 298, 300, 546. *317* their prewar dreams: ibid 302, 489. "was once white!": ibid 498; NYT 7/27/43. *318* three heart attacks: NYT 10/2/43, 10/8/44; T 4/17/44; *Soldier* 274, 511. "the United States": *Soldier* 453; NYT 7/12/44; Walter Johnson 166. *319* "to the convention": Gunther 360; NYT 7/19/44. would be Truman: NYT 7/19/44, 7/20/44; Phillips *Truman* 37–40. "Senator from Missouri": NYT 7/22/44; T 7/31/44. *320* "about my dog": NYT 11/8/44; *Soldier* 168. value was doubtful: *Soldier* 525. *321* " 'the *Chicago Tribune* ' ": NYT 10/29/44. "an old man": T 10/23/44, 5/22/44. "they are not true": NYT 10/13/44; T 10/24/44. *322* utterly wretched: NYT 10/22/44. image of vitality: *Soldier* 525. been forever laid:

NYT 11/8/44, 11/10/44, 11/12/44; T 11/13/44; Gunther 92. with no scars: *Soldier* 530. *323* seemed so robust: NYT 11/20/44. battery of specialists: T 10/23/44; NYT 4/5/44. *324* a frequent visitor: *Soldier* 448; NYT 4/11/44. "killed himself trying": NYT 4/27/44, 2/25/44; Gunther 340. *325* deliver a speech: *Soldier* 507. "goddamned ghouls": ibid 509. *326* "close to nonsense": ibid 508–509; Acheson 102; Gunther 38. been "a sellout": NYT 2/8/44. his first inaugural: *Soldier* 594.

XI LILACS IN THE DOORYARD
(pages 329–362)

329 "was beyond us": NYT 1/23/44, 1/31/44. *330* act of war: NYT 4/17/45, 2/14/44. "the Fifth Army": NYT 5/13/44, 6/5/44. D-Day in Normandy: NYT 6/6/44, 6/7/44. "is mine alone": NYT 6/6/44. *331* "up and consolidated": NYT 7/10/44. stubborn defenders: Burns *Soldier* 475. *332* "O.K. We'll go": NYT 7/11/43; *Soldier* 475. "our united crusade": *Soldier* 475; NYT 6/6/44. sunk off Arromanches: NYT 6/27/44. *333* "men at arms": NYT 7/10/44, 7/19/44, 8/8/44; T 7/3/44. "working for Vichy": NYT 8/26/44, 8/24/44; T 10/16/44. *334* "Fatherland and Führer!": NYT 9/7/44, 9/12/44, 10/21/44; T 10/25/44. "American soldier myself": NYT 12/28/44; T 1/15/45. to celebrate it: NYT 3/9/45, 4/2/45, 4/12/45. U.S.-RUSS JUNCTURE: NYT 4/12/45; *Soldier* 599. *335* Lucy's daughter: *Soldier* 599. "cause for alarm": ibid 595. *336* atom armaments race; Jungk 179. this was done: NYT 8/13/45, 9/28/45, 10/1/66. *337* sharply changed: Speer 227. with the enemy. Jungk 163. uranium research: ibid. "an atom bomb": ibid 164, 166. *338* a textile mill: NYT 9/28/45; Jungk 167. "going to use it": NYT 8/13/45, 9/28/45; Jungk 171. *339* "politics or physics?": Jungk 174. or be annihilated: NYT 11/28/45. *340* "agreed to that": NYT 4/9/46; Jungk 175. began a counteroffensive: NYT 7/23/42. *341* no military significance: NYT 1/3/43, 1/10/43, 1/20/43. range of Rabaul: NYT 7/2/43, 8/29/43. unloaded overhead: NYT 12/28/43. *342* anticipated a Tarawa: NYT 12/4/44. 75 percent casualties: NYT 11/25/43, 2/22/44. *343* approaching Tarawa's: NYT 4/25/44, 5/28/44. were cut off: NYT 6/21/44, 8/11/44. *344* "God protect you": NYT 7/26/44; *Soldier* 489. was to come: NYT 10/20/44. of all time: NYT 10/21/44. *345 Banzai:* NYT 10/26/44. moments of daylight: NYT 10/28/44. power was finished: NYT 10/26/44. early March, Manila: NYT 12/16/44. *346* Japs on Iwo: NYT 12/25/44. bee in the face: NYT 3/10/45. GIs at leisure: NYT 3/30/45, 4/2/45, 4/13/45. *347* absolutely secure: *Soldier* 599. "laundry to dry": ibid 600; NYT 4/16/45. state documents: Asbell 33. *348* "expert in explosives": NYT 2/13/45. Outer Mongolia: T 2/26/45. *349* "fifteen minutes more": NYT 4/16/45. filling in colors: T 6/4/45. "beautiful woman": Asbell 36. 1:15 P.M.: NYT 4/13/45; *Soldier* 600. *350* on the couch: NYT 4/13/45. anguished snores: Asbell 41. "3:35 o'clock": ibid 44. *351* reach Eleanor Roosevelt: ibid 46. "concert is finished": NYT 4/13/45; *Soldier* 602. Truman at once: NYT 4/13/45; Asbell 53. "was talking about": Truman I 6. *352* "when you can" ibid. "in trouble now": T 4/23/45; Asbell 63. "WARM SPRINGS, GA.": Asbell 78. *353* "man at Warm Springs": ibid 81. with her hands: ibid 84, 91, 99. "So long — out": ibid 93, 150. *354* "most clearly": ibid xi. "lost a friend": ibid 94, 117. "the great man" ibid 94. *355* "the White House": T 4/23/45. "for us all!": NYT 4/13/45; Asbell 87. the man's cheek: Asbell 91. *356* "the next curve": Gunther 144. "Hi, Dad" . . . to be vacated: Asbell 105–106. *357* Early drew up: ibid 124. chief improviser: ibid 113. to view it: ibid 128, 134; NYT 4/14/45. *358* clasped hands: Asbell 156. "Lincoln home again": ibid 158, 160. passed overhead: NYT 4/15/45. *359* "be any man's": Asbell 170. President's widow: NYT 4/14/45. Executive Mansion: Asbell 178. *360* sealed forever: NYT 4/15/45; Asbell 183. *360–61* said his son . . . "remember it": *New Yorker* 4/21/45. *362* "Thy servant sleeping": Margaret Truman 90; Asbell 194. "is over": T 4/30/45.

XII A NEW WORLD, UNDER A NEW SUN
(pages 364–391)

364 "single moment": Phillips *Truman* 62; Asbell 136. return to obscurity: T 4/23/45; *Truman* 62–63. in history: NYT 11/7/34, 9/15/40. *365* "the President": Asbell 136–37. "for me now": ibid 137. "have ever done": NYT 4/14/45; Asbell 111. *366* "son and bro": NYT 4/13/45; *Truman* 65. *367* "through her teeth": NYT 4/21/45; Margaret Truman 91, 95, 96; *Truman* 62, 144; Asbell 166. "supporter below": T 12/18/50. with greater dignity: ibid. *368* "be game, too": *Truman* 140; T 9/24/45, 9/18/50. "what they meant": *Truman* 63, 71, 169, 79; T 6/4/45; NYT 4/19/45. "the new President": *Truman* 80. *369* "not Henry Wallace": Acheson 104; NYT 7/1/45. "he died?" . . . "it just now": NYT 4/18/45; Asbell 168. *370* of the question: NYT 5/2/45, 5/3/45, 5/5/45, 5/8/45, 5/9/45, 5/10/45; T 5/14/45. larger than Newark: NYT 8/9/45, 7/27/45, 12/16/45. *371* a hand grenade?: Manchester "Our War in the Pacific"; NYT 5/4/45. on Allied losses: NYT 1/28/47; Stimson "The Decision to Use the Atomic Bomb." *372* been even greater: NYT 6/2/45, 6/8/44; Truman I 332; NYT 6/6/45, 7/23/45. "the gadget": NYT 6/6/45; Burns *Soldier* 459, 251; Jungk 175. "do something different": Jungk 178. *373* "have come in": NYT 12/7/45. "winning the war": Laurence 201. *374* stadium in Chicago: Jungk 192. *375* of a second: Laurence 168–70. as yet undetermined: NYT 8/1/45; *Soldier* 558. same conclusions: NYT 4/26/45; *Truman* 53. *376* "The Fat Man": Jungk 180. greatest war criminals: *Reader's Digest* March 1947; NYT 1/28/47; *Harper's* February 1947; Compton "If the Atomic Bomb Had Not Been Used." *377* no one said much: Jungk 198 and passim. perfecting the mesh: *Current Biography* 1947. *377–78* right microsecond . . . "there be light": NYT 8/7/45; Laurence 10. *378* their windowpanes: Laurence 12. blown away: ibid 195. instant peace: Jungk 197, 202. *379* "the Japanese": Truman I 416. "Japanese home islands": ibid 417. "utter destruction": NYT 7/28/45; *Truman* 58. *380* had been passed: *Truman* 59; T 8/13/45. intelligence officer: NYT 8/8/45; Laurence 196, 202–206. *380–81* "of TNT" . . . any of them: Laurence 208–11. "from the Empire": NYT 8/18/45; Laurence 220. "long now, folks": Laurence 221; NYT 11/22/45. *382* "do with it": T 8/13/45, 8/20/45. *383* "I don't": T 10/22/45; NYT 8/9/45; Laurence 225, 228. "devised by man": NYT 7/28/45; *Truman* 68; Laurence 242. *384* turning somersaults: Jungk 211. "such devastation": ibid 213; NYT 11/24/45. of his doing: NYT 8/9/45. *386* countermanded the order: *Harper's* February 1947. formalities of capitulation: NYT 8/15/45; T 8/20/45. followed his example: NYT 8/15/45. *387* "very fragile arch": Morison *Two-Ocean* 572. the United States: NYT 9/2/45. *388* war against Japan: T 7/30/45. *General Henry Taylor:* NYT 8/19/45; T 8/27/45. *388–91* Reuther portrait: *Holiday* November and December 1959; NYT 3/28/46, 5/10/70; *Hartford Courant* 5/16/70.

XIII THE FRAYING FLAGS OF TRIUMPH
(pages 392–416)

392 in trusting them: NYT 5/13/45; Phillips *Truman* 132, 156. *393* "his own death": NYT 4/23/61, 4/4/61. U.N. General Assembly: NYT 2/20/45. *394* the other leg: NYT 3/17/46; Rovere *McCarthy* 95–98. their way there: NYT 11/6/46; Fab V 221. *395* "Richard M. Nixon": NYT 11/7/46; Mazo 41. "police the world": NYT 7/18/46. *and Child Care:* NYT 9/22/46. from the hills: T 9/9/46. political war chests: NYT 8/15/45. *396* "little fellow there": T 9/3/45; Goldman *Decade* 16. *397* rapid extinction: *Decade* 7; NYT 2/9/40, 9/26/45, 8/14/46; Bird 255; Jungk 341. the black market: *Truman* 101; NYT 8/22/45; *Decade* 251; NYT 1/7/46. "about inflation?" . . . Truman called back: T 9/24/45. *398* postwar inflation *Decade* 14. in his refrigerator: T 5/6/46; *Decade* 27. *399* "campaign of 1946": NYT 9/6/45; *Truman* 103–104. had ruined them: NYT 1/15/46. "below the belt": NYT 3/11/46. *400* dipped in the polls: NYT 7/26/46; Truman I 487ff; NYT 1/22/46, 11/10/46. collars than blue: NYT 7/22/44. was intolerable: NYT 9/2/46. *401* of his Presidency: *Commonweal* 2/8/46; T 10/8/45. their heads stubbornly: NYT 1/12/46, 4/26/46; WA 1946. "of the government": T 6/3/46. was deplorable: NYT 5/18/46, 5/24/46. *402* "sons of bitches": *Decade* 23. "do the job!": *Truman* 114ff. to General Hershey: *U.S. News and World Report* 5/3/46. *403* "has been settled": NYT 5/26/46. "coal with bayonets": *Decade* 25. burned coal: T 6/28/43. *404* and Wagner Acts: NYT 5/22/46; *U.S. News and World Report* 10/11/46. was 3,510,000: NYT 11/22/46, 12/4/46. *405* work at once: NYT 12/6/46. "his balls clank": NYT 12/8/46; *Truman* 124. a heavy blow: NYT 1/8/46. *406* out of uniform: T 6/18/45. stars could, too: NYT 9/18/45, 4/11/51; Acheson 127. *407* point freeze: NYT 7/4/46. TO SPEED SAILINGS: NYT 1/7/46. *408* "wanna go home": NYT 1/12/46. "the nation accepted": NYT 1/10/46. *409* and other instigators: NYT 1/9/46, 1/8/46. "Manila and Le Havre": NYT 9/13/45. departments to himself: NYT 6/16/46. "out of Army": NYT 6/6/46; T 10/22/45; *Newsweek* 1/28/46. *410* "some other country": NYT 11/2/46. in the Ruhr: Acheson 86; Mowry 163. *411* "my way home": NYT 7/10/45; Truman I 334, 337, 411, 412. "not be I": NYT 7/27/45; *Truman* 92, 98. "a great pity": NYT 7/25/46, 11/15/45; Acheson 130, 634. *412* would warn them: Walter Johnson 163. and his President: ibid 226; NYT 9/21/46, 2/14/46. to his speech: NYT 3/6/46, 9/11/46; *Truman* 150. *413* "of his administration": ibid 151; NYT 9/13/46. "my resignation immediately": T 9/23/46. *414* "exactly in line": ibid; Acheson 192. "this subject again": Acheson 191; NYT 9/22/46. "I'm right": Truman I 560. *415* sometime in 1946: *Life* 11/26/45. "Had enough?": NYT 1/11/47; Mazo 47; *Truman* 128; *Decade* 45. "a Republican country": NYT 11/4/48. *416* returned to them: Walter Johnson 228.

XIV LIFE WITH HARRY
(pages 418–432)

418 "come to responsibility": Schlesinger *Thousand* 287. *419* bowed your head: NYT 6/11/50; *Business Week* 1/22/49, 2/21/49. *420* as a Red: NYT 12/31/49. teachers looked on: NYT 5/20/56. bipartisan support: NYT 12/23/41; Burns *Soldier* 184, 515; T 2/28/44, 6/28/43, 7/23/45; NYT 5/26/44, 1/22/44, 8/7/45, 12/11/46. *421* "requires it": T 12/10/45; NYT 1/11/45; Eisinger 487. serious uprising: *NYT* 10/2/45. *422* started to go: NYT 1/3/42. (expensive) New Look: Gold *1940–41* 31; Fab V 248. *423* on the roads: Fab V 251, 253. he didn't know: *Life* 3/1/48. *424* Stalin had become: NYT 1/27/45, 4/24/45, 12/22/45. the absolute limit: Allen *Change* 263; Fab V 221, 260. *426* presidential campaign: NYT 6/23/46, 9/30/47; Kendrick 40. ran one headline: Fab V 210. *426–27* "after the war?" . . . "most astonishing": O'Neill 3–4. *427* all-time high: O'Neill 4; NYT 10/18/45, 6/17/43, 6/16/45, 4/22/45, 1/1/48, 11/10/46; Fab V 212; WA 1946. *428* game was security: T 6/18/45. *429* was blushing: Friedan 174; Bird 259; Kinsey 194. their enthusiasm: O'Neill 13. Spock had begun: NYT 7/14/46; Gold *1940–41* 31. *430* finding a home: NYT 11/2/47, 6/15/45; Mauldin *Home* 48. "understand our problems": Mauldin *Home* 65; T 12/24/45. *431* "pla-ace to stay": T 1/15/45. well under $10,000: *Newsweek* 10/6/69; O'Neill 38ff. *432* standard specifications: O'Neill 41; T 7/3/60. "think big" . . . much choice: Kimball "Dream Town."

XV A LITTLE TOUCH OF HARRY IN THE NIGHT
(pages 433–471)

433 wait until Monday?: NYT 2/23/47; Acheson 217. *434* own silk hat: NYT 2/28/47, 3/2/47, 3/18/47. after September 1945: Acheson 217; Walter Johnson 203, 207; T 12/31/45. no viable alternative: NYT 5/13/45; T 10/1/45. *435* not much else: NYT 7/14/46; T 9/25/44. unprecedented scale: NYT 2/8/47, 3/18/46; Acheson 212; Phillips *Truman* 174. "give the conquered": Goldman *Decade* 33, 34. *436* "it back again": NYT 4/2/47; Rovere and Schlesinger 241. "it at all": NYT 4/17/47; *Decade* 60; T 5/29/50. only as "X": Walter Johnson 208; NYT 7/8/47. *437* under its spell: *Truman* 258, 262. "do the same": ibid 305; Acheson 219. Muehlebach Hotel: NYT 3/13/47, 5/23/47; Mowry 922; *Truman* 171, 176. Kennan's reasoning: NYT 3/14/47; Rovere and Schlesinger 238. *438* "strategic monstrosity": NYT 11/30/47; Lippmann 16–23. strategic nightmare: NYT 10/17/49. few sparks there: Acheson 226. "human beings": NYT 5/9/47; Acheson 227, 229. "in his hand": NYT 6/6/47; George Marshall *European Initiative* 494. *440* could take hold: Walter Johnson 209; *Truman* 184. or foreign bases: NYT 4/14/48, 4/4/48; WA 1952; Mowry 76; *Truman* 192. *441* blockade on Berlin: NYT 2/24/48, 6/25/48. complete rupture: Acheson 260. on either side: ibid 262. *442* be done — yet: NYT 9/11/48; T 9/27/48. French fliers: *Newsweek* 7/12/48; NYT 7/1/48; Clay 381–86. blew it up: ibid; NYT 12/17/48. *443* they were beaten: NYT 4/17/49. grace and generosity: NYT 5/12/49; Walter Johnson 217. their own money: Clay 381–86; NYT 1/25/48. *444* "who owned it": Sevareid *Dream* 392. across the water: Walter Johnson 221. *445* "colonial empire": NYT 7/16/45, 3/1/50; T 3/12/50. "elsewhere rejected?": Kronenberger 216. *446* "in the night": Acheson 730, 731. could hardly wait: NYT 11/4/48. MacArthur or Vandenberg: Ross 95. *447* he would lose: *Washington Post* 7/7/48. in the ring: NYT 3/2/48, 3/9/48; Ross 72. *448* General Eisenhower!: Ross 11, 64, 66, 75; *Truman* 946; NYT 11/7/46; *Nation* 3/13/48; T 3/13/48. Draft Eisenhower Committee: *N.Y. Herald-Tribune* 7/10/48. to lead them then: ibid. NYT 7/10/48. issues in November: Ross 33. *449* trial run: NYT 4/18/48; Ross 77. problems with Congress?: NYT 9/7/48. like a debacle: *Washington Post* 6/4/48. *450* presidential politics: NYT 6/4/48. "growing entertainment value": Ross 84. "and Czechoslovakia?": ibid 85ff. *451* "the biggest whistle-stop!": NYT 6/12/48. "what I'm doing!": NYT 6/19/48; T 6/28/48; *Truman* 215. that was something: NYT 7/11/48; Ross 92. *452* this convention year: NYT 9/27/48; John Brooks *Leap* 288. "Federal payrolls": Ross 54. "to dislike him": NYT 1/17/48; Ross 38, 53. *453* their little jokes: NYT 3/29/48; Rovere and Schlesinger 231. "within ourselves": NYT 5/23/48, 6/25/48; *N.Y. World-Telegram* 6/14/48. bargain prices: NYT 9/20/48. *454* run the race: NYT 7/13/48, 7/15/48; Ross 109. to the door: NYT 7/15/48; Ross 116. alone, and waiting: T 7/26/48; NYT 7/15/48. "for real": NYT 7/15/48. *455* fouler than that: ibid; T 7/26/48. "in the world": T 7/26/48; NYT 7/15/48; Ross 125. *456* "run for office": T 7/26/48. "what they say!": T 7/26/48. "in the stocks!": *Truman* 222; T 7/26/48. "political courage": T 7/26/48. the Democratic South: NYT 7/18/48. *457* to be flourishing: NYT 12/30/47, 9/11/48, 12/31/47; *Truman* 204. "announce his candidacy": NYT 6/13/48; Ross 136. He refused: NYT 8/9/50, 9/11/48; Ross 145, 149. *458* "Christian martyrs": NYT 7/26/48; T 8/2/48, 7/26/48. independent center: NYT 8/30/48, 8/21/48; *Washington Post* 10/22/48. hastened their victories: NYT 11/3/48, 9/11/48. *459* "end of it": NYT 7/27/48; Ross 132. judgment of it: NYT 7/28/48. Congress in history: NYT 8/13/48. espionage hearings?: NYT 8/1/48, 8/4/48. *460* always quotable: NYT 9/6/48. "do exactly that": *Truman* 230ff. "the farmer's back": NYT 9/17/48. *461* have written it: *Truman* 243. wished to say: Ross 180ff; *Truman* 242. *461–462* "Democratic incumbent" . . . and irrigation": Ross 182–85. *462* "of the world": NYT 9/21/48. over the country: Ross 206; *Truman* 242. *463* water, and faith: NYT 6/27/48; Ross 203. have a chance: Ross 167;

NYT 10/30/48. "that they cherish": Ross 12. *464* would win, handily: ibid 196; *Life* 11/1/48, 11/15/48; NYT 10/31/48. "the poorhouse": *Detroit Free Press* 11/3/48. *465* Dewey's inaugural: *Life* 11/15/48. one instance, arrogant: ibid. *466* hedge his bet: NYT 9/10/48. almost hourly: NYT 11/25/48; *N.Y. World-Telegram* 9/24/48; Ross 226. *467* drama outside: Ross 227ff; Rovere *Years* 48; *Truman* 245ff. almost instantly: *Life* 11/15/48. *468* DEWEY DEFEATS TRUMAN: NYT 11/15/48. *469* back to sleep: Truman II 220ff. stared at him: NYT 11/4/48. had some sleep: T 11/8/48. "claims," he said: Ross 227. *470* governor of Illinois: NYT 11/4/48; *Truman* 247. "in American politics": *Truman* 251; Walter Johnson 233. *471* "out of this": NYT 11/6/48, 11/4/48; Ross 230; T 11/15/48. him he shouldn't; NYT 11/23/48; Ross 235.

XVI THE AGE OF SUSPICION
(pages 473–516)

473 1648 Pennsylvania Avenue: NYT 4/14/45. *474* Great Society: Phillips *Truman* 163, 164. "of underdeveloped areas": NYT 11/4/64, 1/6/49, 1/21/49; *Truman* 272. *475* was coming from: *Truman* 273. "first proposed it": NYT 6/6/50. on the Hill: NYT 12/1/48, 3/4/49. Secretaries of State: Acheson 249; NYT 1/22/49. *476* suburbia themselves: Whyte 312. *477* amaze the country: NYT 3/14/48. *478* "took up sex": T 9/3/56. *480* "lack of opportunity": Fab V 217; Gold *1940–41* 15. *481* even to society: Eisinger 153; Kronenberger 197. *482* into Bloomington's computers: Guiles 90. solvent of custom: Goldman *Decade* 119. *483* bottle of Hadacol: NYT 1/23/48. "loved in return": Gold *1940–41* 32. "double-breasted suits": ibid. *484* professional athlete: Fab V 221. kill a President: NYT 7/4/46, 11/2/50. lordly spaniel: Fab IV 240. *485* "who like it": Fab V 342. *486* (at the Sorbonne): NYT 9/16/50; Fab V 218. the new decade: NYT 2/5/50. *487* died with it: NYT 4/4/49, 4/25/49, 12/9/49. *488* "but could not": NYT 8/6/49; Acheson 303. *489* "nations having it": Jungk 260; NYT 9/24/49, 3/29/49; *Decade* 100. *490* be heard again: Ross 134. *491* "frittered away": NYT 3/3/48. *492* "down the river": Walter Johnson 214. "I deeply believe": NYT 11/2/46. *493* its Canadian allies: NYT 3/5/46, 2/11/50. *494* for International Peace: NYT 7/30/48, 8/4/48, 8/1/48, 2/11/49, 8/4/48. "bad security risks": NYT 12/5/47. rulings were final: NYT 11/18/49; *Truman* 360. *496* nine years old: NYT 8/19/49. with orthodoxy: NYT 11/9/47. *497* "was sacked anyway": Truman 351; NYT 11/18/48. "their reliability": *Truman* 352. *498* the vigilantes: ibid. "question of espionage": ibid 364. plain paper wrappers: NYT 12/10/49. *499* "smoke, there's fire": *Truman* 373. *500* "be all right": NYT 5/20/50, 5/24/50, 7/18/50; West 224. both of them: NYT 6/17/50, 7/18/50, 8/12/50. *502* "Russian code": NYT 8/3/48, 8/1/48. "of the hearings": *New Yorker* 9/4/48. *503* was Alger Hiss: NYT 8/18/48, 11/25/54. *504* him a liar: Acheson 250. heavily lidded eyes: NYT 6/7/49. could prove it: NYT 12/12/48. *505* face to face: NYT 8/4/48. than he knew: Cooke 71. *506* McDowell, and Russell: NYT 8/18/48. "until I return": Cooke 80. *507* anyone named Crosley: NYT 8/26/48. to the Russians: NYT 9/28/48, 11/4/48. *508* he was trapped: NYT 12/7/48, 6/7/49. had the story: NYT 12/11/48, 12/5/48. "expense of Austria": Cooke 92. *509* "the United States": NYT 12/19/48. were chagrined: NYT 12/10/48, 12/16/48. *510* "looks like faltering": Mazo 65–66. on both counts: NYT 11/18/49, 1/22/50, 3/6/49. was a mystery: NYT 12/15/49. *511* it to him: *Truman* 369. had Priscilla Hiss: Cooke 298. he had been: NYT 1/22/50. *512* "with verse 34": NYT 5/13/47, 1/26/50; Acheson 360. "was not easy": ibid 359. "America can do?": NYT 2/13/50, 2/4/50. *513* "do it again": Griffin 28. Murrow portrait: *Current Biography* 1953; NYT 4/8/65; *Cue* 2/21/53; Kendrick passim.

XVII INTO THE ABYSS
(pages 517–550)

517 "sensible course": Acheson 354. from Hoover: Rovere and Schlesinger 213. *518* "for that purpose": NYT 12/17/49, 2/4/50, 5/24/50; Acheson 355. "chain to Alaska": NYT 3/2/49. January 12, 1950: NYT 1/13/50. *519* the United Nations: Acheson 354; NYT 1/13/50. fend for themselves: NYT 1/13/50. " 'back in there' ": NYT 12/30/49; Acheson 293. *520* "long road back": NYT 1/21/50; Acheson 358. seven years left: NYT 11/6/46, 5/3/57. *521* "recognizes me": *Harper's* August 1950. "shape our policy": NYT 5/4/50. *New Yorker*: *Harper's* August 1950; Rovere *McCarthy* 128. *522* speak of *traitors*: NYT 2/23/50. "the State Department": *McCarthy* 126. the fugitive list: ibid 127. *523* "curtain of secrecy": NYT 2/20/50; *McCarthy* 130. "not a Communist?": *McCarthy* 132. *524* "in the Department": ibid. "reckless performance": NYT 2/21/50. *525* except McCarthy himself: NYT 2/23/50, 2/26/50. see him discredited: NYT 5/21/50. Levine's *Plain Talk*: NYT 1/27/50, 4/7/50, 5/11/50. *526* "contact you later": *McCarthy* 144, mud-bespattered buckets: ibid 12. "its sleeves rolled": ibid 11. *527* to be had: NYT 4/26/50; Griffith 72. "the State Department": NYT 3/22/50, 3/27/50; *McCarthy* 151, 152. *528* with laughter: NYT 3/27/50, 4/2/50; *McCarthy* 153. "as a Communist": NYT 4/7/50, 4/12/50. *529* all the headlines: NYT 4/2/50, 4/21/50, 4/26/50, 5/2/50. general election: NYT 6/2/50, 6/25/50, 5/3/50, 11/8/50. "the United States": Griffith 73, 100; NYT 4/19/50. *530* "half months ago": *McCarthy* 55. "but Russia's": NYT 6/25/50. *531* "the United States": NYT 1/20/50, 7/6/50. "shine their boots": NYT 3/24/50. *532* around the clock: NYT 8/16/50; Acheson 402. before Monday: NYT 6/25/50; Phillips *Truman* 289. Forest Hills: NYT 1/11/50. "like a cobra": NYT 6/25/50. *533* of their lives: ibid. "Republic of Korea": Acheson 402. White House switchboard: NYT 6/26/50. *534* Success, New York: Acheson 404; NYT 6/26/50. passed 9 to 0: NYT 9/7/50. neutrality impossible: NYT 6/26/50; *Truman* 291. *535* in Indochina: NYT 6/27/50. an earlier Vietnam: NYT 6/29/50, 6/26/50. *536* was unanimous: NYT 6/28/50. "with the subject": NYT 6/29/50. "the Armed Forces": NYT 7/1/50; Acheson 410. *537* in June 1950: NYT 7/6/50. "it amounts to": NYT 6/27/50; *Truman* 302. negative aim: NYT 6/30/50. *538* "battle area": ibid.; *Truman* 302. at once: NYT 7/1/50. for an opinion: ibid; *Truman* 311. *539* the high command: NYT 7/21/50. "want from me?": NYT 7/21/50, 9/1/50. the country's pride: NYT 7/12/50. other U.N. members: NYT 8/1/50. *540* NKPA rear: NYT 9/16/50. a little talk: NYT 10/1/50. "fight communism": NYT 7/31/50. *541* Wake Island: *Truman* 318; NYT 8/29/50. "greatest slaughter": NYT 10/15/50; *Truman* 321. *542* to move north: NYT 10/15/50. "Kim Buck Too?": NYT 10/21/50. history of warfare: NYT 11/10/50. *543* other was doing: NYT 11/24/50, 10/25/50; *Truman* 323. it in Korea: NYT 11/1/50. "Little Big Horn": NYT 11/3/50. *544* had found five: NYT 11/5/50. "of my command": NYT 11/6/50. and power installations: *Truman* 325. *545* Monroe Doctrine: Rovere and Schlesinger 149. "intervention in Korea": *Truman* 322; NYT 10/12/50. *546* "extraordinarily light": NYT 11/10/50, 11/24/50. *547* outcome was different: NYT 12/1/50. help, at Hungnam: NYT 12/7/50. was evacuated: NYT 12/11/50, 12/25/50. *548* "military matters": *Truman* 327. "publicly announced": Acheson 47; NYT 11/29/50. win the war: Acheson 474. *549* "is concurred in": NYT 12/13/50; Rovere and Schlesinger 156; *Truman* 329. *550* along the Yalu: NYT 12/28/50. the U.N. lines: NYT 1/1/50.

XVIII A HOUSE DIVIDED
(pages 555–598)

555 "spiritless defeat": NYT 1/4/51; Acheson 489. of the war: NYT 1/24/51, 3/2/51, 3/15/51, 3/31/51. short of treason: Rovere and Schlesinger 245; Walter Johnson 239. *556* balancing the budget: NYT 12/13/50, 12/21/50. the Great Debate: NYT 1/8/51; Mowry 177. Roosevelt's Hundred Days: NYT 1/6/51, 1/9/51, 2/10/51, 1/16/51; WA 1951. *557* "rebuilding of Europe": Truman II 380. to future increases: NYT 12/20/50, 2/2/51; Acheson 494. *558* his doing it: NYT 4/5/51; Walter Johnson 243. "tolls for thee": NYT 11/8/50; Griffith 126. some time ago: NYT 3/3/51; Mazo 141. twelve years later: NYT 4/11/51. *559* STILL SEEN POSSIBLE: NYT 4/11/51; Phillips *Truman* 346; Rovere and Schlesinger 172. "commander in chief": NYT 10/15/50; *U.S. News* 9/1/50; *Truman* 330, 334; Acheson 518; Truman II 435. *560* Joe Martin: Truman II 442; NYT 4/24/51, 4/6/51. "discussion would be": NYT 4/10/51, 4/6/51; *Truman* 340; Acheson 520. "foregoing message": NYT 4/11/51, 4/9/51; Truman II 448; Acheson 523. Magnuson of Washington: Rovere and Schlesinger 174. daylight in Tokyo: NYT 4/12/51; *Truman* 345. *562* THE PRESIDENTIAL CHAIR: Rovere and Schlesinger 8. might be tried: ibid 8, 12; NYT 4/22/51; *Truman* 345. "God Bless America!": *Truman* 347; NYT 4/14/51, 4/18/51, 4/19/51. *563* "Douglas MacArthur": NYT 4/19/51, 4/20/51. "could not answer": NYT 4/20/51. "duty. Good-bye": NYT 4/20/51. *564* "in my heart": NYT 4/13/51; Rovere and Schlesinger 15; NYT 4/20/51. "just fade away": NYT 4/21/51, 4/20/51; Rovere and Schlesinger 9. Republican national convention: NYT 4/22/51, 6/11/52. *565* village of Panmunjom: NYT 5/19/51, 5/24/51. "one big boom": Goldman *Decade* 181. New 49. "lot of money": Michener 49. the United States: NYT 12/25/52. "irreducible minimum": NYT 7/10/51, 10/10/51; Acheson 532, 538. *567* most persuasive: NYT 4/7/49, 2/4/52. "just as stupid": NYT 8/3/47, 2/12/50, 11/5/50, 5/13/51, 8/5/51. *569* increasingly resentful: WA 1952. other people's wars: NYT 1/6/51; Acheson 281. *570* growing much bigger: NYT 8/7/45; Rovere *Years* 244. "Atomic Bombers": Jungk 242. "the hydrogen bomb": *Life* 9/6/54. *571* Super, the better: Jungk 265. leave it to him: ibid 270. "saner than Hitler?": ibid 270ff. *572* fissionable materials: ibid 274; NYT 9/25/49; Mowry 192. "or super bomb": NYT 1/22/50, 2/4/50, 2/1/50. *573* of a button: NYT 2/5/50, 1/26/64; Jungk 265, 288. it was MANIAC: Jungk 300ff; NYT 2/28/52. *574* two, and sank: NYT 11/17/52; WA 1952. reporters, "beckons": Fab VI 30; Jungk 305; NYT 8/9/53; *Decade* 137. *575* "militarily acceptable": Jungk 307. came of it: Fab VI 30. *576* "play in, too": Fab VI 25. five days underground: ibid 30, 72. of this one: ibid 1; NYT 8/12/51. *577* themselves in it: John Brooks *Leap* 232; T 3/30/59. "they could picket!": Bird 259; Kluckhohn "Mid-Century"; Schlesinger *Thousand* 740. and stayed there: Fab V 44; O'Neill 19. *578* part of him: NYT 12/9/56; Whyte 147. "on company time": Whyte 74, 81; Riesman 273. *579* largest undergraduate group: Whyte 93.

"spot for you": NYT 11/12/52, 7/17/55. *580* what to do: Kronenberger 184. economic security: quoted in Kluckhohn "Evolution." "than he knows": *Decade* 291. *581* on American campuses: Rovere *McCarthy* 9; NYT 12/17/52, 12/21/52, 10/8/54, 6/29/55. torn asunder: Stanley Walker "Book Branding." *582* free enterprise: NYT 10/8/51. "(group-forming) society": *NYT Magazine* 5/25/58; O'Neill 83; Kluckhohn "Evolution." *583* in Dwight, Illinois: T 3/23/70, 3/30/70. *584* his own blood: NYT 3/27/49; Wertham 369. he could get: ibid 365, 377; Fab V 215. *585* larger than radio's: Fab V 215; *Leap* 161; T 5/15/50. "barefoot voice": *Time* editors 176; T 2/27/50. *586* television began: NYT 9/5/51; T 1/16/50. Milton Berle: T 11/20/50. working for pay: Theodore White *1960* 279. toilets in unison: NYT 2/3/54; *Leap* 163; *Decade* 266; Wertham 369. *587* "program or that": Kronenberger 81. Murrow retired: NYT 11/19/51, 7/2/52, 5/12/55. "the . . . the paper": NYT 7/4/41. *588* or documentary film: T 7/23/56. *Break the Bank:* NYT 12/19/52, 6/19/56, 6/29/62. *589* of peeping Toms: T 2/27/56; Kronenberger 24; Tate "The Man of Letters." and Louis Kronenberger: Allen *Change* 272; Kluckhohn "Evolution." went into eclipse: *Time* editors 127; T 1/2/56; *Leap* 168. *590* and used contraceptives: Bird 51. prewar constellations: NYT 10/18/56, 6/28/56, 12/16/55, 10/6/55, 5/21/56, 12/19/57. *591* in the millions: *Leap* 168. a ghost town: NYT 1/10/54. would come later: T 12/24/56; Hechinger and Hechinger 142; NYT 9/5/56. *592* American experience: NYT 12/31/46. *Without a Cause:* NYT 12/27/55; Howe "Notes on Popular Culture." *593* regional speech; Goldman *Tragedy* 528; Steinbeck 106. political campaigns: *Leap* 57. crucial shopping moment: T 8/14/44. *594* "off at Westport": NYT 5/26/46. consumer dollar: Fab V 219. motivational research: *Leap* 86; Kendrick 480. among your creditors: *Decade* 302. *595* credit card living: ibid 303. American Gas Association: T 4/27/59. in the USSR also: NYT 4/13/55. *596* Pets in Chicago: NYT 3/10/50, 8/15/51, WA 1950. "name of style": Kronenberger 106. "the money is": WA 1952; Acheson 658; WM/Louis Lasagna; NYT 3/18/55; WA 1952. "get seasick": NYT 11/21/48; WA 1952. *597* a free press: NYT 3/11/52. U.S. had tripled: NYT 11/15/55; T 6/5/50. *598* Hammarskjöld of Sweden: NYT 10/4/51, 12/4/52, 4/8/53.

XIX RIGHT TURN
(pages 599–641)

599 nationwide crime: Walter Johnson 247–48. *600* Mayor William O'Dwyer: NYT 3/18/51, 3/13/51. already been developed: NYT 5/8/50. mean treatment: Fab VI 96; NYT 3/15/51. *601* "to walk out": Fab VI 100–101. autumn's World Series: NYT 8/16/52. "do about it?": NYT 3/22/51; Goldman *Decade* 198–99. University of Kentucky: NYT 12/1/51. cheating on examinations: NYT 3/17/53, 1/4/52; Walter Johnson 247–48. *603* five hundred dollars: NYT 4/17/51. a $520 Deepfreeze: NYT 2/6/51; Phillips *Truman* 406. *604* a $9,540 mink coat: NYT 2/3/51, 7/26/51, 2/28/51. "discriminating taste": *Decade* 188. literally wicked: NYT 2/3/51. had hung on: NYT 12/5/51; *Truman* 408–11; NYT 12/5/51, 12/6/51, 12/16/51. *605* appointments secretary: NYT 10/24/51, 7/28/51; *Truman* 409. McGrath and Justice: NYT 7/7/51, 12/23/51, 1/11/52. *606* dismissed McGrath: NYT 2/2/52, 4/4/52, 4/6/52. trying to avert: NYT 4/9/52, 6/3/52. honorable objectives: NYT 12/20/50; Acheson 400. *607* "living American": NYT 9/24/50; Rovere *McCarthy* 172; Griffith 115–16. "history of man": NYT 6/15/51; *McCarthy* 178–79. between the parties: Acheson 435. *608* " 'done his damnedest' ": Neustadt 96; NYT 4/18/52. Adlai Stevenson: NYT 1/24/52; Truman II 490; *Truman* 417. *609* "has any politics": NYT 7/23/52; Adams 13. Eisenhower jacket: Rovere *Years* 13–20. "respect to me": NYT 1/7/52; Kenneth Davis 258. *610* "from Dwight Eisenhower": NYT 1/24/52; *Truman* 415. "was flabbergasted": Truman II 491–92. *611* Democratic nominee: *Years* 342. of that inconceivable: T 1/28/52. "seek the nomination": Kenneth Davis 236; Truman II 492. *612* "seemed thin": NYT 3/30/52; Acheson 632. "Good": NYT 3/31/52; Kenneth Davis 240. "No": Kenneth Davis 240. "beside Alger Hiss": ibid. *612n* misspelled "Stephenson": Mazo 86. *613* "ultimate timidity": NYT 3/31/52. "doesn't inhale": Kenneth Davis 263. he was packing: NYT 3/13/52, 3/20/52. for the nomination: NYT 3/20/52, 4/3/52, 4/2/52, 4/9/52, 4/16/52, 4/23/52; Pusey 16–17. *614* had to say: NYT 6/20/52; *Years* 22. to stamp out: Fab VI 108; *Years* 33. *615* to its hangar: NYT 7/8/52. cattle prod: NYT 7/10/52. a nice point: Mazo 84–86; *Years* 61–62; *Life* 7/19/52. *616* "of another man": NYT 7/11/52; *Years* 27. be turned back: *Years* 27. the national convention: Pusey 15. *617* demanded "fair play": NYT 7/2/52; Walter Johnson 249–50. "that road again!": NYT 7/11/52; Adams 35. *618* Ike had it: NYT 7/7/52, 7/8/52, 7/12/52. "in his administration": NYT 7/12/52. *619* "of the party": Mazo 66–68. on television, too: Adams 34; Mazo 97. *620* chosen their nominee: NYT 11/1/50. friends and admirers: Mazo 100. the White House: *Years* 105. was badly divided: ibid; *Chicago Tribune* 7/13/52. *621* "to his nomination": NYT 4/17/52; Kenneth Davis 264. "should be nominated": NYT 7/21/52; Kenneth Davis 268. "and fair contest": NYT 7/22/52. *622* "for the carnage": Kenneth Davis 269. "be too late": *Years* 342; NYT 7/22/52. "Stevenson of Illinois": NYT 7/23/52. "it embarrass me?" Truman II 496. choice of 1952: NYT 7/26/52. *623* "Thy will be done": Walter Johnson 260; NYT 7/26/52. "rest of them": Hughes 196. "consequences of each": Kenneth Davis 273–75. "misgovern the people": ibid. and Stevenson friend: NYT 7/27/52, 7/29/52; Kenneth Davis 276–77. "I do not know": Acheson 699–700. *624* proud of it: Kenneth Davis 314; *Decade* 234. "often rather thin": *Years* 36–37. "about his backbone": NYT 9/13/52; Donovan 103. *625* "well concede defeat": *Decade* 222; Walter Johnson 257. next five years: Kronenberger 157. "eggheads are there?": WM/John Alsop 3/23/74. *626* "psychopathic instability": *Decade* 224. of Governor Stevenson: *Truman* 427–28; Walter Johnson 225. his dander up: NYT 9/4/52; *Years* 38; Hughes 493. *627* "his family life": Walter Johnson 259. "discussed them": Hughes 41–43; Pusey 29–32. "few weeks ago": NYT 10/4/52; Pusey 31; Hughes 41–43; Donovan 244; Adams 31–32. *628* state ticket: Griffith 195; *McCarthy* 184. "apply to method": NYT 10/28/52; *McCarthy* 182–83; Pusey 29; NYT 10/4/52. "Stevenson's part": Mazo 66–67; NYT 10/14/52. *629* "was revealed today": *N.Y. Post* 9/18/52. "the beneficiaries": Mazo 118. *630* "to smear me": NYT 9/21/52, 9/19/52; Mazo 117. out of the question: Mazo 116; Nixon 85–87. *631* "hound's tooth?": *Decade* 227. "out all right": Mazo 119–20. seat of power: ibid 120–21. the Ambassador Hotel: Nixon 100. *632* "common people" . . . "to be said": Mazo 124; Nixon 108. "television and listen": Mazo 124–25. *633* against the wall: Adams 37; Mazo 126. up the receiver . . . "about politics, too!": Nixon 110; Adams 40–41; Nixon 110–11. "has been questioned": NYT 9/24/52. "everything I own" . . . "is honestly ours": Nixon 115. *635* "to keep it": NYT 9/24/52. "Irish never quit": Nixon 117. *636* "your $75,000 worth": Mazo 132. burst into tears: ibid 131. "beyond expectations": Nixon 118. "dog world, anyhow": Hughes 40. from Dwight Eisenhower: Adams 38–39; Nixon 119. *637* "any time thereafter": NYT 9/25/52. *637n* "genre of weepers": Mazo 136. *638* "Nixon rejoices us": ibid. "ended that night": NYT 10/17/52; Hughes 32–33; NYT 10/25/52; Adams 44. *639* "not much": Adams 44. would be defeated: Kenneth Davis 289–90. went Republican: NYT 11/3/52; 11/5/52. 69.4 percent: Whyte 332. *640* Senate, merely one: *Years* 112–15. said Stevenson: Kenneth Davis 290. "much to laugh": ibid 291. *641* the Secret Service: NYT 11/6/52; Donovan 200–201.

XX WHAT WAS GOOD FOR GENERAL MOTORS
(pages 643–691)

643 audience laughed: Fab VI 136. *644* "fallow period": ibid 152; Donovan 202, 203; Davis 320; Acheson 694. sold at $5.95 . . . from her mother: Fab VI 70–71; NYT 4/9/56, 4/23/56; *Life* 6/25/56; T 3/19/56, 6/18/56. *645* as Vitaphone: Fab VI 222, 58; NYT 11/28/52. great as ever: Fab VI 68. frame was plastic: ibid 182–83. sharp, chill wind: NYT 12/6/52; Donovan 17–18. *646* fateful one: NYT 12/6/52; Donovan 17; NYT 11/21/52. "massive retaliation": Donovan 19; NYT 5/13/53; Goldman *Decade* 248–49. *647* "since my return": NYT 12/6/52, 12/10/52; Donovan 19–20. outgoing administrations: Donovan 20; NYT 12/11/52. *648* January 12 and 13: NYT 11/25/52; Adams 5; Hughes 52. Labor Department: NYT 1/17/53; Donovan 105; NYT 9/11/53. do the same; NYT 4/8/53, 4/3/53; Donovan 77; Hughes 77; NYT 2/11/53. "grocery store": Rovere *Years* 111; Donovan 25; NYT 1/24/53; Fab VI 43; Hughes 75–76. *649* "free economy": Hughes 76; NYT 8/28/52; *Decade* 280, 243. times as large: Hughes 67; *Years* 74. "illustrious ruler": Hughes 134; NYT 1/22/53; Mazo 150; NYT 10/1/53; Mazo 251. *650* "East issues settled": Hughes 134–35; Donovan 9; Hughes 76; Adams 99. "except to kids": Donovan 20–21; NYT 1/19/53, 1/25/53, 1/21/53; Donovan 23. *651* senator's fire: Acheson 707; NYT 3/5/53. into history: Phillips *Truman* 431–32; NYT 1/21/53. it every morning: NYT 1/22/53, 1/25/53; Adams 71; Donovan 206. *652* is his reward: NYT 1/22/53. in "deportment": Donovan 69–70; T 1/9/56; Donovan 61. his famous grin: Donovan 3; Hughes 103. *653* "rock the boat": Donovan 200; NYT 2/12/53; Donovan 204–205; Adams 73; *New Republic* 2/18/57. "not to interfere": Donovan 69, 207, 208. "every other individual": Adams 74; NYT 1/22/53; Walter Johnson 321, 319. *654* "Sincerely, DE": Donovan 207, 195; Adams 426. Bernard Baruch: *Years* 315. *655* with Sherman Adams: Donovan 196; Adams 427. "do any harm": NYT 1/3/53; Mowry 329; *Years* 103; Rovere *McCarthy* 188. be reckoned with: NYT 2/8/53, 1/11/53. had to lose: NYT 3/19/53; Griffith 101–102. *656* only seem worse: NYT 3/21/ 53; Adams 94; Hughes 93; Griffith 202; Donovan 89. "of Mr. Bohlen": Adams 95; NYT 3/26/53. votes to 13: NYT 3/28/53. Joseph R. McCarthy: Adams 95; *McCarthy* 33; Donovan 89; Griffith 204; NYT 3/31/53; *McCarthy* 33–34. *657* half of 1954: NYT 4/26/53, 2/7/53; Walter Johnson 280. "this is done": NYT 6/28/50. applauded vigorously: Hughes 109. IS RESCINDED: *Donovan* 28. *658* "releashing Chiang": NYT 2/3/53; *Years* 266; Walter Johnson 301. extremely awkward: *Years* 91; Donovan 86–87. *659* and the Russians: Adams 91–92. was deadlocked: Donovan 87. "horse of containment": *McCarthy* 240–41; Donovan 70–71. *660* stricken in Moscow: Schlesinger *Thousand* 187; *Years* 106; NYT 3/6/63. "his death makes": Donovan 41; NYT 3/6/53; Hughes 99–101. "their own toil": Hughes 103–104. *661* "speech about it": ibid. at the end: Hughes 112; NYT 4/17/53; Hughes

110, 105, 112; Adams 97–98. *662* "out to be": Adams 117–18. of the talks: NYT 5/8/52. "with the Communists": Adams 98. *663* a major offensive: Fontaine 66–67; Adams 96; Donovan 122–23. Rhee gave in: Fontaine 67; Adams 101–102; NYT 7/12/53; Donovan 124. "present agreement": *Years* 149. "has been implemented": T 8/10/53. *664* "against Communism": *Years* 145. "Eisenhower's appeasement": Donovan 119, 126. "noticed no change": ibid 125–26. Robert A. Taft: T 10/3/53. *665* further reductions: NYT 1/10/53. strategy followed: Adams 21–22; Donovan 110. counsel despair: NYT 6/5/53. in ill health: T 6/22/53, 8/10/53. *666* "Howard Roberts": NYT 6/14/53. "back in January!": NYT 6/11/53; Adams 25. postponed indefinitely: NYT 7/5/53. *667* "futile battle": NYT 7/27/53. he was dead: NYT 8/1/53. "beyond calculation": NYT 8/1/53. "man, go on": NYT 1/4/53, 8/4/53. "now under discussion": NYT 1/25/54; Donovan 239. *668* "into their business": NYT 8/5/53; Hughes 28–29. "to the ministry": Donovan 85; NYT 3/31/53; Donovan 87. *669* for the demagogue: Hughes 132. "nearly impotent": Walter Johnson 279; *Washington Post* 7/20/53; Donovan 143–44. *670* the House 265–2: Hughes 119–20; NYT 6/2/53; Donovan 133; *Years* 216. late Joseph Stalin: NYT 10/21/53, 10/25/53; Kendrick 36–37; NYT 9/24/53. *671* other Radulovichs: NYT 11/25/53. and the press: NYT 4/16/54; Donovan 287–88. Communists in Asia: NYT 12/19/54; Donovan 285–86, 297–98. "national security": NYT 4/29/53. *672* from the payroll: Donovan 289; NYT 10/24/53; Adams 150, 152; NYT 1/8/54; Mazo 155–56. side down: Donovan 298; NYT 4/29/53. Bricker amendment: Donovan 105, 239; NYT 8/19/53. *673* half-million Americans?: Donovan 238–39; Hughes 144. "for this amendment": NYT 2/18/54, 4/7/53; Hughes 144. "of Almighty God": *Years* 206. *674* listening to him yet: NYT 1/31/54. executive agreements: Donovan 240–41. individual states: Hughes 142–44. *675* "treated that way!": Adams 410. "forty-eight governments": NYT 7/15/53; Donovan 237. *676* and 42 opposed: NYT 2/26/54, 2/27/54. to resist it: NYT 2/4/54; Donovan 241; Adams 108–109. *677* rejected as unconstitutional: NYT 2/27/54. lost India's friendship: Donovan 309; Hughes 205; Kenneth Davis 343–44; NYT 5/12/53. "embrace this principle": Hughes 147; NYT 7/18/53. *678* "their captivity": Hughes 147–48; Adams 88–89; NYT 7/2/53, 12/1/53. "of this country": Walter Johnson 298; Hughes 285; *Parade* 9/28/69; *N.Y. Herald Tribune* 8/12/58. "enemy attack": Adams 399–400. *679* it would be: ibid. "and then some": NYT 7/7/57; Walter Johnson 309; *Years* 199. *680* "does not happen": NYT 2/11/54. "war may go?" . . . "with large units": Donovan 263. "not look back": NYT 12/31/49, 2/8/50; Acheson 672, 674. *681* Roy 194–95, 172. *682* declare war: Donovan 263. force in Korea: Burns *Soldier* 379. "totalitarian sea": Rostow "The American National Style." *683* and he did: Acheson 677–78. ask for it: NYT 5/16/54; Roy 225, 240; NYT 3/23/54. "resolute today": Jungk 310; NYT 3/30/54. *684* "power in Indochina": *Years* 193. London and Paris: Donovan 259; Adams 122–23. "profound influences": NYT 4/8/54; Adams 120. *685* Congress could act: Roy 271. "such a decision": NYT 4/17/54; Mazo 255–56. was "unlikely": NYT 4/20/54. *686* fire upon himself: NYT 4/17/54. honor of France: T 5/8/72; Roy 340. "may prove inescapable": Kendrick 359. *687* "with a crash": Donovan 267. Cambodia, and Laos: ibid 268. "relations as now": Adams 126–27. "blessing in disguise": Hughes 208. Norma Jean Baker portrait: Guiles passim; *Current Biography* 1962; NYT 8/6/62; T 8/17/62.

XXI MR. CHAIRMAN, MR. CHAIRMAN
(*pages 692–729*)

692 "rolling readjustment": NYT 1/3/54, 2/7/54, 3/2/54, 3/18/54. St. Lawrence Seaway: NYT 5/7/54, 5/8/54. *693* in September: NYT 6/20/53; Donovan 247; NYT 9/1/54. heart disease: NYT 10/8/54, 12/22/54, 7/3/54. called a *hippy:* Fab VI 80. *694* staying in Hollywood; NYT 5/21/54, 4/16/54. telecast March 7, 1955: NYT 10/21/54, 2/26/54; Kendrick 374–75; NYT 7/8/55, 12/26/51, 9/13/54, 11/30/55. morning sickness: NYT 1/16/53; Goldman *Decade* 266. *695* any previous year: Mazo 155. "H-bomb program": NYT 2/7/54; *Decade* 260; NYT 4/13/54; Donovan 294. "except Communists": NYT 6/17/54; Kendrick 41. *696* Hall of Fame: NYT 6/11/54. behind Borden: NYT 6/16/54; Schlesinger *Thousand* 457. he knew it: NYT 7/1/54, 11/11/54; Jungk 317. *697* Joseph R. McCarthy: Donovan 295. refused to take it: Jungk 318. "for the occasion": NYT 4/13/54; Jungk 322, 324. *697–698* interrogation of Oppenheimer: Jungk 325–26. *698* "the devil's work": ibid 324. "interests of security": Donovan 296; Jungk 330. not be overlooked: NYT 7/2/54, 6/30/54. *699* had already formed: Jungk 229–38; NYT 12/3/63, 2/19/67, 6/16/54. flying over India: NYT 2/16/55; Jungk 310; NYT 3/16/54, 4/26/55. *700* everyone on earth: NYT 10/16/55. named Irving Peress: NYT 1/8/55. investigative powers: NYT 2/20/54; Adams 145; NYT 1/31/54. *701* "from him, too": T 3/22/54. Permanent Investigations Subcommittee: ibid; NYT 9/5/52; 1/3/53. *702* "directions please": *Harvard Crimson* 5/7/54. he met McCarthy: T 3/22/54; Rovere *Years* 130. they might go: Rovere *McCarthy* 191. *703* "Cohn Schines best": T 3/22/54; *McCarthy* 200. "issue in 1954": NYT 11/17/53, 11/25/53. "of American money": NYT 11/25/53.

704 "friendly countries": Donovan 247; NYT 12/2/53. the President: NYT 12/5/53, 12/4/53. *705* Joseph R. McCarthy: *McCarthy* 23; NYT 2/3/54; *Years* 97. McCarthy support: *McCarthy* 22. needed Schine: ibid; NYT 11/5/53. *706* Reber about that: Griffith 245; NYT 3/12/54. Reber-Welch exchange: *McCarthy* 208–209. of the Navy: Straight 30–31. "routine step": ibid 27. *707* "unreasonable about": *McCarthy* 206. "of the Army": Adams 143–45. "to regret it": Donovan 250; Walter Johnson 292; NYT 2/21/54; Straight 200. *708* "will be available": NYT 2/25/54; Straight 61; NYT 2/24/54, 2/25/54. "on his knees": *McCarthy* 31; Griffith 247–48. *709* "known Communists": NYT 3/4/54; Griffith 248–49; NYT 3/5/54. "wreck the Army": NYT 3/5/54, 3/10/54; Griffith 273; NYT 3/11/54, 2/28/54. in the chair: Walter Johnson 292–93; NYT 3/13/54, 3/17/54. *710* "point of order": NYT 4/23/54, 7/11/53. "be so named": Straight 9. "of the Army": Straight 12. *711* "the Communist Party": NYT 4/23/54; Straight 235–36. "any place, anywhere": *McCarthy* 221. *712* "to the end": NYT 11/14/54; Straight 84–85. "not get the information": ibid. 125; NYT 5/5/54; *McCarthy* 216–17. *712–16* Welch-Cohn-Mundt-McCarthy: NYT 6/10/54; Straight 249–53; Transcript of the Hearings 2428–30. *713* "from a pixie": NYT 4/28/54. *716* and the CIA: NYT 6/18/54; Transcript 2973–77; NYT 6/19/54. *717* with disfavor: Griffith 264; NYT 11/4/54, 7/20/54. they had won: *Congressional Record* 83rd Congress 2nd Session 6/11/54 8032–33; NYT 7/1/54, 8/1/54. *718* the previous January: *McCarthy* 227; NYT 12/3/54; *McCarthy* 229. "is McCarthy-wasm": *McCarthy* 231. with a sling: NYT 7/20/54, 11/30/54; *McCarthy* 235–36; NYT 11/18/54. "in the United States": Donovan 280. *719* "of the United States": ibid 277; Adams 164–66; Mazo 152; NYT 9/16/54; Donovan 280–81; Kenneth Davis 300. cheered him accordingly: Walter Johnson 285. exposed as myth: Donovan 274–75. *720* the jitters: NYT 10/12/54; Hughes 75–76. "through with politics": Mazo 138, 152–57; NYT 6/13/54; Mazo 157. "at the polls": NYT 11/5/54; *Years* 230; *Washington Post* 11/4/54. *721* "that goddamned drum": Donovan 282–84. *722* withering "Hardeeharhar": Fab VI 81. bombing or spooking: Hechinger and Hechinger 82; Fab VI 80. *723* "highly emotionalized child": Hechinger and Hechinger 144, 147. *724* "women of means": ibid 148, 154. "her life": ibid 125, 126. "by their families": John Brooks *Leap* 233; Hechinger and Hechinger 126. a billion dollars: *Leap* 233. *725* "the wild frontier": *Newsweek* 12/27/54; Fab VI 58–59; NYT 6/1/55. *726* carried too far: Hechinger and Hechinger 142–43. of the 1950s: Fab VI 86. "beautiful to feel!": quoted in Fab VI 89. *727* "just your glassy flesh": NYT 3/2/50; quoted in Fab VI 88. "to the wheel": NYT 9/5/57; quoted in Fab VI 89. *728* SMOKE POT: Fab VI 90; *Leap* 237. *729* "everybody goes 'Awww!'": quoted in Fab VI 84.

XXII WITH ALL DELIBERATE SPEED
(pages 731–771)

731–734 American Institute of Public Opinion *The 1954 Pocket Almanac.* *734* "to see me?": Schlesinger *Thousand* 924. *735* in states' rights: NYT 9/9/53, 5/17/54; T 10/12/53, 5/24/54. are inherently unequal: NYT 5/18/54. *737* "just plain nuts": Hughes 241–47, 201. expected of others: Walter Johnson 273; Donovan 159, 154–55. the White South: Walter Johnson 273–74. *738* expanding rapidly: Lerner 78; Donovan 390; Graham and Gurr 389. permanent expulsion: T 2/20/56; John Brooks *Leap* 289; T 3/12/56. closed its file: NYT 9/2/55. *739* "and us white": T 9/10/56. *740* nearly three to one: T 12/10/56, 12/17/56. "machinery had shifted": NYT 12/6/55; T 1/16/56. *741* "to their demands": T 2/6/56. *742* "to hate them": NYT 3/20/56; T 3/5/56. "boycotting the buses": T 2/6/56. "black ape": NYT 3/23/56; T 3/5/56. *743* roared "No!": T 4/2/56. for civil rights: T 11/26/56. "humility and meekness": T 11/26/56. "That's right": T 12/31/56. *744* "interest demands it": Phillips *Truman* 399. *745* "Chinese civil war": Kenneth Davis 303; Donovan 301. and for all: Adams 131; Donovan 303. "seven-thousand-mile frontier": Donovan 302. *746* Eisenhower's message: NYT 1/25/55. "or anything else": Rovere *Years* 264. offshore islands: Adams 130; Donovan 305; Hughes 166. *747* "of this resolution": Donovan 306. had been removed: NYT 1/30/55; Donovan 307; Kenneth Davis 303. as the Soviets: Walter Johnson 303; *Years* 269–75. *748* in the past: Donovan 75. he said grimly: NYT 6/23/55. "What they're doing": Adams 114, 91. in his briefcase: ibid 177. *749* Parc des Eaux-Vives: *Years* 280; NYT 7/18/55. in helicopters overhead: NYT 7/19/55; *Years* 287. democratic Germany: NYT 7/19/55; Donovan 350. *750* "all our peoples": Donovan 349; NYT 7/22/55; Donovan 344; NYT 7/22/55. just stared: Donovan 344. *751* have proposed it: ibid 345. with MIGSs: *Years* 290–91. it didn't melt: Adams 179; Donovan 350. *752* vacation in Denver: NYT 7/25/55; Donovan 352. to Open Skies: NYT 9/25/55; Donovan 359–60. across the hall: NYT 9/25/55; Donovan 360–61; Adams 183. "better come over": Donovan 362–63. *753* President's chances: NYT 9/25/55; Donovan 363; Adams 183. oxygen tent: Adams 154; Donovan 363–65. "to the car": Donovan 366. "My God!": Mazo 189; NYT 9/25/55. *754* into the car: Mazo 190. for some time: Adams 181–82. since the crash: NYT 9/26/55. *755* chief's absence: Donovan 369; NYT 9/26/55. due until January: *Years* 319–28; *Donovan* 370–71; Adams 186. "some other guy": Adams 187–88; Donovan

378. accompanied recovery: NYT 10/15/55; Donovan 376; NYT 10/23/55; Donovan 376. *756* "agreeably surprised": NYT 11/12/55, 11/15/55; Donovan 385; Adams 191. to think about: Hughes 174–76; Donovan 397. of this term: NYT 1/9/56; T 1/16/56. *757* "his own appointees": Donovan 393–95; Adams 226. vote for him: Adams 224–26; NYT 2/15/56. "that is, affirmative": T 1/2/56; NYT 3/1/56. hearing aid: T 3/26/56. *758* "in this matter": NYT 3/1/56. "an egghead": T 3/12/56. "Secretary of Agriculture": T 3/19/56. future President: T 1/2/56 (Man of the Year). ribbons of concrete: Chapman 38. six cents to seven: NYT 5/6/56, 7/7/56. *759* year for humor: T 2/27/56. "Aw rutti!": NYT 12/10/56, 8/12/56, 10/18/56, 4/22/56. a million copies: NYT 11/16/56. "through the fence?": T 5/14/56. *760* "the same response": NYT 5/14/56. of American culture: NYT 10/2/58. implications then: NYT 4/21/56, 7/20/56. criminal irresponsibility: NYT 5/5/56, 3/19/56, 4/10/56, 1/13/56, 7/27/56; T 11/12/56. things personally: T 7/2/56. *761* "just plain loaf": *Ladies' Home Journal* October 1960. "came back with": *Redbook* September 1960; NYT 4/22/56, 4/20/56, 8/5/55; T 1/16/56. *762* a million francs: T 1/16/56, 1/23/56. "like the Kellys": NYT 4/5/56, 4/16/56, 4/19/56, 4/20/56; T 4/23/56. *763* IN FEBRUARY: NYT 4/19/56, 4/20/56; T 4/30/56; NYT 8/3/56; T 8/13/56. campaign for reelection: NYT 6/25/56. "Egyptians!": NYT 7/20/56, 7/27/56; T 8/6/56. Eden in 1956: NYT 8/1/56. *764* "quite a combination": TC 1956 106; Hughes 212. "may be necessary": NYT 10/30/56. "honor our pledge": Hughes 214. *765* "the Hungarian people": NYT 11/1/56, 11/4/56; Adams 258–59; NYT 11/6/56; Hughes 220. without outside help: NYT 11/2/56, 11/4/56, 11/3/56. "how *are* you?": NYT 11/7/56. "involved answer": Adams 259. *766* a major issue: NYT 7/18/56. "known and respected": *Years* 368. operating table: NYT 9/25/55, 6/9/56. *767* Walter Reed Hospital: NYT 6/9/56; T 6/18/56. SAY DOCTORS: NYT 6/10/56. him gingerly: Kenneth Davis 327–28. be a catastrophe: NYT 10/12/56; T 11/5/56, 10/29/56; Kenneth Davis 256–57; Mazo 179, 169, 180; NYT 8/14/56. "presidential timber": NYT 7/24/56; Hughes 173. "the Vice President": Mazo 165; NYT 4/27/56, 6/27/56. a major issue: *Thousand* 596; NYT 8/23/56; Kenneth Davis 335. *769* of his "image": McGinniss 27; Kenneth Davis 323. "need to win": NYT 8/12/56; Kenneth Davis 332–35; Hughes 190; NYT 4/22/56; Davis 343. *770* for the challenger: Kenneth Davis 340; NYT 9/6/56. against odds: NYT 10/24/56, 11/6/56. Hoover's in 1928: NYT 11/7/56; Walter Johnson 285–86. "the way I feel": Hughes 224–28. *771* "across the nation": NYT 8/18/56; *Thousand* 8–9; Adams 253; McCarthy *Kennedys* 119; Burns *Kennedy* 190. "for President": McCarthy *Kennedys* 119.

XXIII THE PURSUIT OF HAPPINESS
(pages 772–785)

772 as cloudless: NYT 10/5/57. Auto Buy Now: Steinbeck 95; Goldman *Decade* 305; NYT 10/1/58. *773* *it's gone:* NYT 1/2/58; Steinbeck 47. size of Poland's: John Brooks *Leap* 53. "in Detroit": Walter Johnson 263; *Fortune* May 1954. *774* handling their credit: NYT 9/4/57; Galbraith *Affluent* 171–72; Whyte 360. "apparatus of it": Whyte 354–55, 362, 363. *775* "importance of thrift": Bird 259; Whyte 353; Riesman 18; Whyte 19–20. *776* sense of identity: Galbraith *State* 49; Whyte 78, 338. week to spend: Spectorsky 7–8; Whyte 401. *777* "lead the bland": *Affluent* 135, 193–94; Mowry 222; *Affluent* 4–5. community playgrounds: Whyte 350. "policemen, and rats": *Leap* 104–105, 108, 114–15. *778* "well-adjusted": Riesman 16, 26. "and weakness": ibid xviii; Whyte 5. *779* they liked it: *Leap* 138; Whyte 3–4. only natural: Eisinger xiv–xvi; *Leap* 53–54. "fundamental decency": Steinbeck 183; Whyte 321, 319; NYT 12/2/56. *780* her own party: Whyte 316, 368, 389, 315–16. "Man-Trap Set": Spectorsky 191; NYT 11/16/56; Whyte 337; NYT 9/16/55; Friedan 12. *781* "feminist ideology": Friedan 13, 17; Lifton 203. luck elsewhere: Friedan 12; Lifton 202; Friedan 154. *782* considered worse: Packard *Wilderness* 22–23; Walter Johnson 266. coalition faltered: Whyte 332. "his problem?": ibid 389. *783* and resented: Kronenberger 120, 122–23, 223–24. the next generation: Spectorsky 197, 248; Murray "Individuality." *784* "less than ninety": Whyte 428. polled one another: ibid 429. *785* "dreams into reality": *Decade* 307; T 10/21/57; NYT 10/6/57.

XXIV BEEP BEEP
(pages 787–817)

787 "their achievement": NYT 10/1/57; T 10/14/57. "if they did": NYT 10/5/57. *788* ("of the de-emphasis"): Hughes 246; Adams 415. "too late": Adams 416–18; T 11/18/57. "windshield wipers": T 10/21/57; Walter Johnson 313; Hughes 247. *789* "book was home": Goldman *Decade* 313; T 10/21/57; Galbraith *Affluent* xxviii. "be successful": T 10/21/57. *790* source of power: T 11/4/57. coup in itself: T 10/21/57. from outer space: T 10/14/57. *791* the reason why: T 10/14/57. tail-twitching cheerleaders: Rovere *Years* 124. *792* the national income: T 10/14/57; NYT 10/3/57; T 11/18/57. "as we are": T 10/21/57, 11/18/57. of the language: T 10/21/57. *793* or entertain, pupils: ibid; Lynd and Lynd 23. "it the better": T 12/2/57; NYT 11/23/57; T 12/2/57. "or *with* information?": T 11/4/57. *794* survive in space: NYT 10/27/57; T 10/28/57; NYT 11/3/57, 11/14/57. to Columbus: NYT 11/2/57. MOON, IKE: T 11/11/57. *795* would vanish: NYT 10/10/57. a U.S. ICBM: NYT 6/6/57, 8/27/57, 11/29/58. *796* "to the good": Adams 415; Hughes 429. of a solution: Adams 414–15; NYT 12/21/57. "on the moon": Adams 416–18; NYT 11/8/57. *797* "into its interior": T 10/28/57. U.S. IGY committee: T 3/17/58. *798* starcrossed Edsel: 9/30/54. across the skies: T 10/21/57, 11/18/57. would tell him: NYT 10/10/57. *799* "at this moment": ibid. "err, bollix": T 10/7/57. promises of glory: T 9/26/57. *800* by local police: T 9/16/57. possible demonstrators: NYT 8/31/57. *801* "become a deluge!": T 9/16/57. delay of integration: NYT 9/5/57, 9/16/57, 9/8/57. "at my command": NYT 9/21/57; Adams 345–46. *802* a federal court: NYT 9/15/57; Adams 349–53; T 9/23/57, 9/30/57; NYT 9/25/57. "and judgment": NYT 9/21/57. "got up and bowed": T 9/30/57. *803* phone booth: NYT 9/25/57; T 10/7/57. "do my job": T 10/7/57. to be hostile: ibid. *804* "good judgment": NYT 9/24/57; T 10/7/57. "the Federal Court": Adams 332, 351; NYT 9/24/57; Adams 354. *805* "read it": Adams 354–55; T 10/7/57. "anarchy would result": Adams 355; NYT 9/25/57. Army rule: NYT 9/25/57. *806–807* "Roadblock Alpha" . . . "base of the neck": T 10/7/57. *807* "in America?": NYT 9/27/57; T 10/7/57. *808* government $4,051,000: T 5/19/58. called into service: Adams 356; T 10/7/57. *808n* "of free government": Adams 356. *809* "at random": T 10/14/57, 11/11/57. he retired: T 10/14/57, 5/19/58; NYT 7/31/58. felt shame: NYT 8/2/62, T 10/7/57. *810* ("was working"): NYT 11/10/57; T 11/18/57; *Saturday Review* 11/2/57; T 11/4/57. stood vigil: T 10/4/57; NYT 11/8/57. *811* a major recession: T 11/14/57. was a stroke T 11/27/57. "wrong with him": Adams 195; T 12/9/57; NYT 11/26/57. "is to it": Adams 196–97. *812* there, he wept: T 12/9/57; NYT 11/27/57; Adams 198. "to be excellent": NYT 11/29/57, 11/30/57. *813* "First ignition!" . . . "explosion occurred": NYT 12/7/57; T 12/16/57. *814* "Custer's last stand": T 12/16/57. *814–17* Edsel portrait: John Brooks *Edsel*; Cone; Galbraith *Affluent*; Goldman *Decade; Consumer Reports* January and April 1958; *Life* 7/22/57, 8/5/57, 8/21/57; NYT 11/20/56, 8/27/57, 8/29/57, 10/5/57, 10/6/57, 11/28/57, 11/20/59; T 10/21/57, 11/30/59.

XXV THE CRUSADE FALTERS
(pages 818–845)

818 ICBM attack: NYT 7/22/59; T 12/7/59; NYT 6/10/59. *819* called "compacts": T 4/6/59. crew cuts: NYT 1/3/59; TC 1959; NYT 3/3/59; Adams 311; NYT 7/16/58, 11/22/59, 4/10/59. opened fire: NYT 7/10/59; T 7/20/59. *820* old for her: NYT 5/3/57, 9/6/61, 4/10/59, 10/15/59, 10/8/59, 5/7/59, 3/1/59, 1/15/60, 7/25/61. the hula hoop: T 9/15/58; NYT 8/11/57. *821* sixty-second birthday: T 12/1/58; NYT 12/7/58. through East Germany: T 12/1/58. *822* "intolerable situation": Adams 271. armed forces anywhere: NYT 1/6/57. "this battle": Adams 274. *823* the warships: ibid 289; NYT 4/26/57. "Eisenhower Doctrine": Adams 289. Eisenhower consented: NYT 7/15/58, 7/4/58. *824* Lebanese move: T 7/28/58; Adams 291. was expanding: NYT 9/24/58; Adams 293. in world affairs: NYT 7/16/58; *Time* editors 75. *825* a light cruiser: DeMott 172. western Europe: Servan-Schreiber 59, 36. "a dear friend": Walter Johnson 266. and Panama City: John Brooks *Leap* 339. *826* intolerable gloating: *New Republic* 10/27/58. "classless society": Nixon 259. stayed home: NYT 4/28/58. *827–33* Nixon trip: Mazo 206–46; Nixon 183–228. *827* rocking the boat: Schlesinger *Thousand* 189. *828* "irrational state": NYT 5/9/58; Mazo 233; Nixon 219. *829* to Nixon's aid: NYT 5/14/58. was preposterous: Mazo 222. *830* "of this mob": Mazo 225. *831* Nixon's limousine: NYT 5/14/58. wobbled toward him: ibid. *833* against possible attack: ibid. "assistance is requested": ibid. *834* had been friendly: NYT 5/16/58. he was, too: Nixon 231; T 6/23/58. vicuña story: NYT 1/12/58. tax returns T 7/14/58; NYT 6/11/58. *835* "that he had": T 7/7/58. *836* like Bernard Goldfine?: T 6/30/58. *837* Washington bureaucracies: Adams 440; T 7/14/58. "as they are": T 6/23/58. *838* "would be gone": T 6/30/58. "and tirelessly": NYT 6/19/58; Hughes 266–67; Adams 445–46. *839* should be fired: T 6/30/58. all these years (and following paragraphs): T 7/14/58. *840* collateral for loans: NYT 7/4/58. *841* "told about it": T 7/14/58. a lot of that: NYT 6/19/58. *842* White House roster: NYT 6/23/58. was political: NYT 8/14/58. *843* "on November 4": NYT 9/10/58; WA 1959 120. lowered upon him: Adams 446–47. "I can give you": NYT 9/28/58. *844* last cigarette: Adams 447. agreed to go: Hughes 269; Adams 451. "twenty-five states": Nixon 232–33. "your money": NYT 10/14/58, 10/16/58, 10/17/58, 10/21/58, 10/22/58, 10/23/58. *845* "the White House": NYT 11/6/58, 11/5/58; Nixon 233. "do with Nixon": NYT 11/5/58; Nixon 234; NYT 11/5/58, 11/10/58.

XXVI TATTOO FOR THE GENERAL
(pages 847–886)

847 proof of it: Mencken 264. dead ahead: NYT 12/19/58. "be any riots": Fab VII 28. accept contraception: NYT 11/26/59. 848 "these questions": Kendrick 410; Goldman Decade 319; NYT 8/28/58. got their coffee: NYT 10/1/58, 1/3/60. on restricted beaches: NYT 2/24/60. 849 visible at last: NYT 5/11/60, 6/16/60, 7/19/60, 6/6/60, 7/19/60, 7/26/60, 10/20/60; WA 1962 251. to do it: NYT 5/14/60; Fab VII 28–29. 850 facts of life: NYT 5/10/60; WA 1961 168; W 1966 163; NYT 11/26/59. ("Bashful!"): Kendrick 429–30; Decade 318; Fab VI 44; NYT 8/29/58; T 10/19/59. "coached or tutored": NYT 11/3/59. 851 its hearing room: Decade 319; NYT 10/15/59. "intellectual life": Fab VI 44; Decade 321–22; NYT 11/3/59. 852 smiled at him: Decade 322. five to one: NYT 11/5/59, 11/6/59. 853 every week: Kendrick 440. named Truman Capote: NYT 3/11/60; Kendrick 437; Chicago Daily News 9/20/58; Nixon 304; NYT 1/5/60, 5/3/60, 11/16/59; T 11/30/59. 854 "matter anyway": T 2/23/59. "hand of Eisenhower": NYT 4/16/59; Hughes 342. 855 "will break it": NYT 1/27/59. what it was: T 6/1/59; NYT 5/25/59; T 3/2/59. Soviet officials: WA 1960 108; T 8/3/59; NYT 7/24/59; Hughes 287; NYT 7/24/59. the "Sokolniki Summit": NYT 7/25/59; Nixon 255–58; T 8/3/59. 856 "we are stronger" . . . "no free elections": WA 1960 111; Nixon 255–58; T 8/3/59. 857 Berlin ultimatum: NYT 8/6/59. in his eyes: NYT 8/26/59, 8/27/59; WA 1960 117; T 9/7/59; NYT 8/8/59. 858 "going splendidly": NYT 9/3/59; T 9/14/59; NYT 9/5/59, 9/8/59. as their host: NYT 9/16/59. "than his backside": NYT 9/20/59. to a detente: NYT 9/26/59; T 10/5/59. 859 Soviet Union next year: NYT 9/28/59. them and Khrushchev: T 10/5/59. "our friends abroad": NYT 11/5/59, 12/4/59. 860 in Casablanca: T 12/14/59, 12/15/59. 1960, in Paris: T 12/23/59, 12/24/59. 861 to join them: T 1/12/59; NYT 8/2/53. Castro's Trotsky: Schlesinger Thousand 220. next to impossible: T 1/12/59, 1/25/59. and they said so: T 1/12/59. 862 bogeymen everywhere: T 4/27/59; Nixon 351–52; Haynes Johnson 25. to invade Cuba: T 11/9/59, 3/16/59; NYT 2/21/59, 1/22/59; Haynes Johnson 49. "a Communist government": NYT 1/6/59. 863 suspicions were allayed: Haynes Johnson 30–31, 37. 864 battle flag: ibid 76. in the camp: ibid 38. 865 around in slime: ibid 44. 866 "we will win": ibid 81, 75–76. 867–72 general sources: see under Powers in the Bibliography. 868 Francis Gary Powers: NYT 5/6/60. "have had any": Adams 455. 869 of his magazine: Hughes 303. 872 weeks of pandemonium: NYT 5/8/60. 872–75 general sources: WA 1961 171; Hughes 300–302; Decade 335–38. 873 complete confession: NYT 5/8/60. flights will continue: NYT 5/10/60. "planes over here": NYT 5/12/60. 874 is frigid: NYT 5/17/60. world conciliation: T 5/30/60. no punishment: NYT 5/18/60. 875 before the summit: NYT 5/26/60. "keeping busy?": NYT 5/20/60. "all of us": Hughes 306. Marine helicopter: NYT 6/11/60. eighty-thousand-gun salute: NYT 6/17/60. 876 "all of it": Theodore White 1960 117; Hughes 310–11. years in prison: NYT 8/20/60. "us in 1952?": Adams 453. 876n was laid off: NYT 2/10/62. 877 munitions. Then . . . "and will persist": Galbraith State 399–400; Adams 325–30; WA 1962 90; NYT 1/18/61. "it is directed": State 317–19. 878 sheriff's, side: NYT 9/27/60; McGinniss 32. 879 public explanation: Hughes 319, 250; NYT 8/25/60; Nixon 339. margin held steady: NYT 3/10/60. 880 on and on: NYT 7/14/60. 881 to Kennedy's 46: NYT 7/27/60. Kennedy 50: NYT 8/27/60. circumstances for him: Nixon 326; NYT 8/30/60. They applauded: NYT 9/8/60, 9/13/60; Sorensen 190–91. percent undecided: Theodore White 1960 320. "September 26": Nixon 336; NYT 9/27/60. 882 beard growth: NYT 10/8/60, 10/14/60, 10/22/60. 883 "fathers, don't we?": NYT 10/13/60, 10/20/60; Nixon 363; Thousand 73–74. reversed the result: Sorensen 209. 884 "will all support": Nixon 409; Theodore White 1960 304; Nixon 376–79. Wednesday morning: NYT 12/16/60. "early yet": White 1960 18. 885 to be governed: NYT 12/16/60. 886 "in the distance": Nixon 417. "to all men": Nixon 402.

XXVII A NEW GENERATION OF AMERICANS
(pages 889–923)

889 in Cleveland Park: NYT 1/20/61; Schlesinger Thousand 1–2. 890 new administration . . . "our ancient heritage": NYT 1/21/61. "what a day!": Fab VII 37; Thousand 5. with greater confidence: Gold 1940–41 27. three years earlier: NYT 12/16/60; Manchester Death 505. and pulling away: Manchester Portrait 11–12; NYT 12/18/60; Neustadt 94. 891 typical early days: NYT 1/22/61. "what you told him": Agronsky 9; NYT 1/22/61; Portrait 12–13. rid of it: NYT 2/19/61; WM/Ronald L. Ziegler; Agronsky 9; NYT 12/16/61. 892 as big as Ike's: NYT 2/26/61; Portrait 15. each morning: NYT 2/26/51; Portrait 15–16. 893 cultural coordinator: Halberstam 41; U.S. News and World Report 5/1/61; Thousand 144; NYT 1/22/61, 6/27/61. Bay of Pigs: NYT 4/21/61; Haynes John-

son 67. "ill-starred an adventure": Halberstam 66, 69; *Thousand* 292. *894* base was covered: *Thousand* 238; WM/John F. Kennedy October 1961. from the President: Sorensen 296; *Thousand* 239–40. "the United States?": Sorensen 295–96; NYT 4/21/61. *895* "share their confidence": Sorensen 296; NYT 4/21/61; Haynes Johnson 65; *Thousand* 239, 267. "little as possible": *Thousand* 249, 259, 246. force were committed: Haynes Johnson 82, 70; NYT 4/17/61. miles away: Haynes Johnson 69, 84. *896* "the Cubans themselves": *Thousand* 247; NYT 4/13/61; Sorensen 298. fire a rifle: *Thousand* 250; Haynes Johnson 69. chance of winning: NYT 4/21/61. *897* "would be available": *Thousand* 269, 250; *U.S. News and World Report* 1/7/63; *Thousand* 281; NYT 5/28/61. on one ship: *Thousand* 270; NYT 4/16/61; Haynes Johnson 94; *U.S. News and World Report* 1/14/63; Haynes Johnson 113. *898* enemy aircraft: Haynes Johnson 77–79; *U.S. News and World Report* 1/14/63. "and rebellion": Haynes Johnson 128–29; *Thousand* 274–75. by the CIA: Haynes Johnson 95. *899* "fish is red": NYT 4/26/61; *U.S. News and World Report* 1/14/63; Haynes Johnson 100. and executed: Haynes Johnson 60, 120–22. *900* "these people there?": ibid 100, 83, 105, 295; *Thousand* 295. *901* had been lost: Haynes Johnson 103. *902* back that night: ibid 111, 113. "air force fields": NYT 4/18/61; *Thousand* 271; Haynes Johnson 92; NYT 4/18/61. "off for Cuba": Haynes Johnson 93. *903* the United States: *Thousand* 291; Haynes Johnson 152. a thousand wounded: Johnson 136–38. "the main business": ibid 143; *Thousand* 276. *904* "popular I get": John Kennedy 112; Sorensen 291; *Thousand* 292. "alongside Fidel Castro": *Reader's Digest* November 1964; *Thousand* 285; NYT 4/23/61; *Militant* 5/1/61. *905* WE NEED YOU: Haynes Johnson 129–30. Americans were killed: ibid 154–56; *Thousand* 278. *906* WAIT FOR YOU: Haynes Johnson 161, 167. to ransom them: ibid 349; NYT 4/22/61, 12/24/62. "streets of Budapest": Haynes Johnson 174; NYT 4/21/61, 4/19/61. "nuclear armaments": NYT 4/21/61; *Thousand* 287–88. *907* from the Comintern: NYT 3/2/61. "of the peril": NYT 4/21/61; Haynes Johnson 175. never forget: *Thousand* 297. *908* and an interpreter: Halberstam 72; NYT 5/20/61; Fontaine 413. "beginning of the end": NYT 5/8/60, 9/24/60, 9/30/60, 10/13/60. *909* immediate removal: Fontaine 390; NYT 2/14/61. divided Berlin: NYT 8/31/61; Fontaine 315, 423. intelligence activities: NYT 6/27/48, 5/15/60, 10/23/60. *910* laugh it off: Fontaine 412–13, 314–15; T 6/9/61; Halberstam 74–75. "Jacqueline Kennedy to Paris": T 6/9/61; NYT 6/3/61. "in my life": *Thousand* 367; Halberstam 76; NYT 6/4/61. "and blackmailed": NYT 11/15/64. *911* only straitjackets: NYT 6/6/61, 6/11/61; Fontaine 416. "cold winter": Fontaine 416. "have to act": Halberstam 76. chauvinistic speeches WA 1962 113. *911n* "war over Berlin": Khrushchev 458. *912* "it's all over": WA 1962 113; Fontaine 418. Walter Ulbricht: WA 1962 115; NYT 8/6/61. in East Berlin: T 8/25/61; NYT 8/13/61, 8/16/61; *Thousand* 395. for the "mistake": WA 1962 121; NYT 9/8/61, 9/28/61, 9/2/61; *Thousand* 460–61; Fontaine 425; NYT 10/18/61. *913* since V-J Day: Fontaine 421–22; NYT 9/19/61. "December 31, 1961": Fontaine 423–25; *Thousand* 400; NYT 10/18/61. "like the place": *Thousand* 548; Halberstam 76. *914* of real power: NYT 3/19/61. for it — unimportant: NYT 3/1/61. *915* "White House lawn": NYT 2/24/61; Carpenter 50; Goldman *Tragedy* 388–90; NYT 10/23/61. deeply affected: *Thousand* 396; NYT 8/21/61. "got out here": NYT 5/10/61; Halberstam 135. *916* "will fly in": NYT 5/13/61; *Life* 10/26/62. eighteen months: NYT 10/27/72; *Thousand* 322, 539, 541; NYT 5/5/61. *916n* draftees to Vietnam: WA 1972 88. *917* not "lose" Indochina: *Thousand* 321; NYT 1/13/51. "your free people": Sorensen 651; *Thousand* 536. "he had inherited": T 1/29/73; Sorensen 652; *Thousand* 537–38. *918* "matter of time": Theodore White *1968* 16; *Thousand* 542; T 8/4/61. was "essential": Halberstam 173; Sheehan 81. *919* included troops: Sorensen 650; NYT 5/13/61, 11/10/61; Halberstam 129. "in this period": NYT 3/15/61, 3/16/61, 5/5/61, 5/9/61; Sheehan 80. chance of success: Sheehan 81, 97. imbued with it: Langer 1271; NYT 10/17/61; *Tragedy* 399; *Thousand* 544. *920* "technological capacity": NYT 1/10/62; *Thousand* 542. political considerations: Sorensen 655. Viet Cong as heroes: NYT 10/16/61; Sorensen 655; Sheehan 142–43. *921* "to take another": Sorensen 653; *Thousand* 547. "crazier than hell": Halberstam 177; NYT 11/10/61; Sorensen 655; Halberstam 174. *922* making headway: NYT 2/9/62, 2/14/62; Halberstam 186. also glowed: NYT 3/27/62; *Current Biography* 1969; Langer 1271; Sheehan 111; NYT 7/25/62. *922* that would mean: *Thousand* 548–49; Halberstam 203. *923* (MACV): *Thousand* 549–50; NYT 7/24/62; FitzGerald 165.

XXVIII NOW THE TRUMPET SUMMONED US AGAIN
(pages 925–971)

925 hundred years earlier: NYT 5/26/61. "was always time": O'Donnell and Powers 16–17; Halberstam 286. *926* in the Kremlin: T 4/21/61, 4/28/61. the year before: Sidey 112; NYT 4/12/61. *927* preeminence particularly: Sorensen 524ff. "rocket thrust": Sidey 114–15. *928* at 18,000 mph: NYT 4/11/61; Sidey 111–12; NYT 4/12/61. " 'the Motherland Knows' ": NYT 4/12/61, 4/15/61; T 4/21/61. *929* "of the world": NYT 4/13/61; T 4/21/61. "Can we leapfrog?": Sidey 129–32; NYT 4/14/61. "nothing more important":

NYT 4/14/61; *Newsweek* 7/7/69; Sidey 131. *930* "Spacetown, U.S.A.": NYT 5/6/61. "safely to earth": NYT 5/26/61; T 6/2/61; Armstrong et al 18. on its way: Sorensen 526. *931* "taken care of": WA 1963 150; NYT 7/22/61, 8/6/61; WA 1962 128; NYT 2/21/62, 3/4/62; T 3/2/62. "I am go": NYT 2/21/62. "will you?": T 3/2/62, 2/22/62, 2/21/62. *932* "saw of it": NYT 2/21/62, 2/24/62. they prayed: NYT 2/22/62. *933* "hot in there": NYT 2/24/62, 2/21/62. "person ever is": NYT 2/24/62. "needed boost": NYT 2/23/62, 2/27/62, 3/2/62. *934* into orbit: T 5/12/61; Armstrong et al 17; T 3/12/62. Houston he said: NYT 8/6/61. peace are there: Sorensen 527–28. freedom riders: NYT 5/5/61. *935* "the right road": ibid; *Alabama* 221. at the riders: NYT 5/5/61, 5/15/61. very advanced: NYT 3/6/61. *936* the blacks ask? Guthman 157; NYT 6/25/60. "We will move": NYT 5/7/61; Guthman 162. *938* It did: NYT 5/9/61; Guthman 166–67; NYT 5/14/61; T 5/26/61. rescued the others: NYT 5/15/61. *939* was a joke: NYT 5/20/61; Guthman 167; WM/David E. Swift; T 5/26/61. in their credit: NYT 5/16/61. *940* of the President: NYT 5/20/61, 5/16/61. than Birmingham: NYT 5/21/61, 6/1/61. heard him say: NYT 5/21/61. "are there now": Guthman 171. *941* "had broken down": NYT 5/21/61; T 6/2/61. simply proved wrong: NYT 5/21/61. *942* again. Then: NYT 5/22/61. "these people are": Guthman 172–73. law enforcement officers: NYT 5/22/61. *943* "survive politically": Schlesinger *Thousand* 936; Guthman 178. succeed Patterson: NYT 11/7/62. in waiting rooms: NYT 5/30/61; *Thousand* 936; NYT 9/23/61; Sorensen 478. *944* time by then: Angoff and Mencken; NYT 6/25/61. of the century: Guthman 180–81. of Mississippi: *Thousand* 940; NYT 9/28/62. *945* "of tyranny": NYT 6/26/62, 9/13/62, 9/11/62, 9/14/62. or make one: NYT 11/4/59. "about a year": Guthman 185. *946* "take a judge?": *Thousand* 941; NYT 9/26/62. "to believe that": NYT 9/14/62, 9/21/62; Guthman 189. "rights of one": NYT 9/25/62. *947* "Communists!": NYT 9/26/62. "how it goes?": NYT 10/1/62. "will be there": NYT 9/30/62; *Thousand* 943. turned back again: NYT 9/28/62; Lord 165–66. *948* point of violence: Guthman 93. *949* $5,000 a day: NYT 11/16/62. "poultry program": *Thousand* 944. broken his word: NYT 10/1/62. in "this afternooon?" Lord 196. *950* a campus booth: NYT 10/1/62; Sorensen 287. "had no choice": NYT 10/1/62, 10/5/62; Lord 209. "uphold that honor": NYT 10/1/62. *951* "to those fellows": NYT 10/1/62; T 10/12/62; NYT 10/5/62. "trigger-happy" marshals: NYT 10/2/62; T 10/12/62; NYT 10/2/62. *952* "lives, nigger?": Guthman 203; T 10/12/62; *Thousand* 948. Franklin Roosevelt: NYT 10/2/62, 10/7/62, 1/21/63, 4/12/63, 12/7/62. "of hate": NYT 6/14/69. *951n* Guthman 204. *953* "joined chapters": NYT 5/14/61; T 2/16/61. "muzzle the military": *Thousand* 743; NYT 7/21/61; *Thousand* 1020; *Life* 2/9/62. official proclamation: *Thousand* 1020. *954* "against Communism": *Life* 2/9/62; NYT 10/29/61. "mental breakdown": DeMott 72, 77. "afternoon comes": *Thousand* 752, 753; NYT 11/17/61, 10/28/61. *955* "the Promised Land": *Thousand* 755. about the President: NYT 9/18/62; *Thousand* 755. *955n* "never notice it": NYT 4/4/65. *956* Air Force One: Sidey 272–73. do it, too: NYT 1/23/61. *957* "backed down": Sidey 289–90. didn't believe her: ibid 272; *Thousand* 643; NYT 6/21/62. "is from within": Sorensen 335. *958* Soviet technicians: Abel 6, 29–30. on the island: NYT 10/11/62. *959* to worry about: Abel 1. *960* "days ahead": ibid 17. the next morning: ibid 21. calls his brother: ibid 32. *961* "planning Pearl Harbor": Robert Kennedy 31; Abel 31–42 passim. *962* are under way: NYT 10/18/62; Abel 43–53 passim. American tradition: Robert Kennedy 36; *Thousand* 806–807. *963* blockade of Cuba: NYT 11/3/62; Abel 54–68 passim. taken first: NYT 10/20/62. the stations why: Abel 69–75 passim. *964* weapons in Cuba: Robert Kennedy 48–49. until Tuesday: NYT 10/23/62. on alert: Abel 76–83 passim. *965* "flaming crisis": Abel 84–94 passim. "greatest urgency": NYT 10/23/62. six days ago: Robert Kennedy 55. "Western Hemisphere": NYT 10/23/62. *966* hastily disperses them: Abel 95–109 passim. *967* the Security Council: NYT 10/24/62. "caught the burglars": *Thousand* 817; Abel 123–38 passim. before noon: NYT 10/24/62. *968* ready for war: NYT 10/27/62. is unimportant: NYT 10/25/62, 10/27/62. "have been impeached": Robert Kennedy 17. "just blinked": ibid 71; Abel 123–38 passim. *968n* "strain and hurt": Robert Kennedy 69–70. *969* "of the sites": NYT 10/26/62; Abel 139–51 passim. submit to searches: NYT 10/27/62. *970* be found: NYT 10/28/62; Abel 152–64 passim. "very hazardous course": NYT 10/28/62; Robert Kennedy 96–97. committed to Castro: Robert Kennedy 109; NYT 11/3/62. *971* capital be evacuated: Abel 165–79 passim. 40,000 to 50,000: *Thousand* 831. "the Soviet Union": NYT 10/29/62. "nuclear test ban": Abel 180–86 passim. "go with you": Abel 186; Robert Kennedy 110. Goldmark portrait: *Current Biography* 1940, 1950; *Newsweek* 1/28/48; T 12/4/50; NYT 12/17/67, 11/27/70, 7/26/71, 8/2/71, 8/3/71.

XXIX DON'T LET IT BE FORGOT
(pages 976–1008)

976 star role: Fab VII 138; Sorenson 489–90. *977* ready for him: WA 1963 102; NYT 4/3/63. King's, followed: NYT 4/13/63, 4/14/63, 5/10/63, 4/13/63. for reinforcements:

NYT 5/3/63, 5/8/63, 5/4/63, 5/8/63. *978* base he wished: T 5/24/63; NYT 5/13/63, 5/24/63, 5/19/63. southern jails: NYT 5/16/63; Sidey 396; NYT 5/16/63, 5/1/63, 5/13/63; Sorensen 489; Schlesinger *Thousand* 964. *979* way of thinking: Guthman 207–208; NYT 1/5/63. "hands in despair": Guthman 207–10. *980* "risk I take": NYT 5/19/63, 5/22/63, 6/6/63. on television: NYT 6/10/63. obstruct them: Guthman 215; WA 1963 106, 109–10; Sidey 399–403; *Thousand* 964; Sorensen 493. "central government": NYT 6/12/63. *981* Wallace walked away: Sidey 401; NYT 6/12/63. "suspected were there": NYT 6/13/63; Guthman 217–18. "life or law": *Thousand* 965; NYT 6/12/63. *982* "can treat them": NYT 6/12/63; *Thousand* 966. encourage violence: Fab VII 144; Sidey 405; Sorensen 504–505; *Thousand* 969. HOUSING—NOW!: NYT 8/29/63. Lincoln Memorial . . . "of their character": ibid. *983* didn't regret it: Sorensen 505. "nonviolent talk": NYT 5/10/63; Fab VII 154; NYT 5/15/63. *"fire next time!":* Guthman 219–20. *984* meeting deteriorated: NYT 9/19/63. youth repeated it: Guthman 220–21; *Thousand* 962–63. fire next time: Guthman 221. *985* the *Honey Fitz*: Sidey 405; NYT 5/30/63. "than I have"; NYT 5/14/63. pay that price: Sidey 416; *Thousand* 978; Halberstam 295. *986* "our own attitude": *Thousand* 891; NYT 6/11/63; Sorensen 733. "since Roosevelt": Sorensen 733. "beneficial to all": *Thousand* 920. in 1964, either: Sidey 388. to the 88th: *Thousand* 713. *987* "serves his nation": NYT 6/29/63, 6/6/63; *Thousand* 881; NYT 10/27/63; John Kennedy 817. *988* he said Texas: NYT 9/4/63, 9/9/63, 10/4–11/63, 10/13/63. "guarded optimism": John Kennedy 11; NYT 1/15/63; *Thousand* 982–86; NYT 4/23/63. *989* "McNamara says so too": *Thousand* 983. struggle between them: Halberstam 250. a "barbecue show": NYT 5/10/63, 6/11/63; Sorensen 657. *990* "for all time": NYT 6/16/63, 7/8/63; John Kennedy 459–64. shocking treachery: NYT 6/28/63. "Binh Xuyen in 1955": Halberstam 261; *Thousand* 989–90; NYT 8/16/63. he tell them?: NYT 8/23/63. *991* "afraid to die": Halberstam 264–65. "same country?": ibid 266–67; *Thousand* 993. *992* "promptly as possible": Halberstam 283–84; NYT 10/3/63; Goldman *Tragedy* 399. "people of Vietnam": T 11/8/63; Sorensen 658–59; NYT 9/3/63; Halberstam 272. were reporters: NYT 10/8/63; *Thousand* 966; Halberstam 283; T 11/8/63; NYT 11/1/63; T 10/25/63. *993* was imminent: NYT 11/3/63, 11/2/63, 11/13/63; T 11/8/63. "fatherland's interests": NYT 11/2/63, 11/3/63. stabbed repeatedly: NYT 11/2/63; T 12/6/63. *994* but not here: NYT 11/14/63; *Thousand* 997; T 12/6/63; Halberstam 291–93. stable government: NYT 11/3/63. "so could he": NYT 12/3/63; Halberstam 286. Thursday, November 21: NYT 11/25/63. *995* January 1, 1964: Rose Mary Woods to the author 8/4/64. effete snobs: NYT 11/20/62; T 11/22/63. (would end publication): NYT 10/16/63; Fab VII 130. "foe of Communism": T 11/22/63. *996* "waning confidence": NYT 5/5/63, 11/16/63. "been an assassin": NYT 11/16/63. "Spindle, or Mutilate": NYT 9/4/63, 9/4/64; Customer Relations Office, U.S. Post Office, New York City; NYT 7/1/63; Sally Morgan to the author 4/10/63. ("I got screwed"): *Life* 8/23/63; NYT 4/21/63; Greene 115. *997* in Bryan, Texas: T 6/21/63, 12/6/63, 11/22/63, 1/21/73. "break up anyway": T 11/22/63, 10/20/63. *998* "of a man": T 10/5/63. in fact ignored: NYT 11/17/63; T 11/22/63. *in the Rain:* NYT 4/14/64. *999* by its publisher: NYT 8/25/63, 5/27/63, 8/9/63, 1/31/63, 8/25/63, 1/31/63, 9/8/63. (ten inches) reason: NYT 11/18/63, 12/30/63, 11/11/63, 4/25/63; T 11/22/63. *1000* and "Standing There": NYT 12/1/63; T 11/15/63; DeMott 78. of self-destruction: NYT 11/3/63. heavily chaperoned: NYT 11/22/63, 12/7/63, 2/2/63. the labor movement: John Brooks *Leap* 157–58. nearly ten million: Bird 257. *1001* "that is rising": ibid 267. dollars a year: Servan-Schreiber 83–90. upper middle class: *Leap* 138. million Americans: Theodore White *1964* 365. *1002* political potency: *Leap* 11; NYT 4/16/63; *Leap* 104. across state lines: *Leap* 120–21. *1003* those with it: Manchester *Death* 189–91. in guerrilla warfare: T 9/10/73, 11/22/63. British prostitute: Sidey 390–91; NYT 11/13/63, 6/7/63. "the New Frontier": *Reader's Digest* November 1963; NYT 11/24/63. *1004* at his funeral: NYT 11/14/63; T 11/22/63. "a stiller town": *Death* 462. *1005* Arlington National Cemetery: ibid. 190. *1006* DEAD JT135PCS: NYT 11/23/63; *Death* 221, began to build: NYT 11/23/63. field of stars: *Death* 442. *1007* "one more awful": NYT 11/25/63. "separate and apart": NYT 11/26/63; *Death* 572, 627. "deep for tears": NYT 11/29/63, 12/25/63, 12/4/63, 12/11/63, 5/5/65. *1008* "for their own": NYT 11/30/63; *Death* 642.

XXX THE LONG ARM
(pages 1010–1040)

1010 "domestic policy": WM/Dwight D. Eisenhower 8/27/64. *1011* "his administration": Goldman *Tragedy* 20–21, 523; NYT 1/30/67, 10/15/64, 10/3/68. as he spoke: NYT 1/5/65, 11/1/64, 8/20/64. *1012* the United States: NYT 1/21/64; T 1/5/68; NYT 8/28/64; Theodore White *1964* 413. of its region: NYT 2/4/64; *Tragedy* 525. over a thousand: NYT 1/19/66, 4/28/64; Theodore White *1968* 103–104. *1013* much more damaging: NYT 11/18/67, 4/23/64. "comfort the country": Carpenter 31, 331. *1014* to the men's: NYT 6/20/64, 7/7/64. proved nothing: NYT 9/15/64; *Tragedy* 228–29;

NYT 9/25/64. *1015* "after the Kennedys": *Tragedy* 78–79. his calendar: NYT 7/31/64; Theodore White *1964* 315–16, 317. "side with me": NYT 7/31/64; *Tragedy* 199. *1016* American provocation: White *1964* 328; W 1964 152–56. supporting hostilities: NYT 8/8/64, 8/5/64. *1017* one of them: W 1968 46; NYT 8/3/64. from the coast: NYT 8/2/64, 8/4/64, 8/3/64. North Vietnamese forces: NYT 2/21/68; W 1964 152–56, 1968 46. *1018* "no wider war": Halberstam 413–14; *Tragedy* 175; NYT 3/6/64. "jungles of Vietnam": NYT 7/16/64; WA 1965 41. Fulbright agreed: NYT 8/6/64. *1019* "a fisheries bill": NYT 8/6/64, 8/8/64. "historic mistake": Fab VII 204; *Tragedy* 181–83; Halberstam 442; NYT 8/7/64; Halberstam 419. *1020* stimulate backlash: Theodore White *1964* 281; NYT 5/6/64, 5/20/64, 7/20/64; WA 1965 166. killing him instantly: White *1964* 266–68; NYT 7/17/64. million dollars: NYT 7/21/64. *1021* and white policemen: White *1964* 278; Graham and Gurr 51; *Collier's* 86. "Burn, baby, burn!": *Tragedy* 172–73. "Freedom Summer" of 1964: NYT 8/3/64, 8/29/64, 8/17/64, 4/3/64. *1022* "television sets": White *1964* 269; John Brooks *Leap* 291–92; *Economist* 5/10/69; White *1964* 277. reached Jackson: NYT 11/8/64; White *1964* 220–22; NYT 6/21/64. had been burned: NYT 6/23/64; W 1964 233–35. in the North: NYT 11/8/64. *1023* rounds of ammunition: NYT 7/9/64. being murdered: NYT 7/11/64; W 1964 233–35. *1024* any trouble: W 1967 210–11; T 10/27/67; NYT 12/5/67, 1/17/65, 2/26/65, 10/29/66, 10/21/67. defense challenges: NYT 2/26/65, 12/14/64; W 1967 220–21. "me a nigger": W 1967 211. *1025* the maximum: NYT 10/21/67; T 10/27/67; NYT 12/30/67. deep right field: NYT 7/16/64. the real thing: *Leap* 319; White *1964* 458. *1026* said *he* was: NYT 1/4/64, 1/28/64, 3/11/64, 1/3/64, 6/7/64. "is no virtue!": White *1964* 151, 153; NYT 5/31/64, 6/3/64, 7/17/64. no one was home: White *1964* 252. *1027* "Nazi methods": NYT 7/15/64. "it's the truth": ibid. in the black: NYT 7/18/64; White *1964* 377–79. platform with him: NYT 8/13/64. *1028* he was right: *Daedalus* Spring 1958; White *1964* 359. he was wrong: NYT 11/1/63. to the end. T 11/1/63. KNOW HE MIGHT: White *1964* 384; NYT 9/7/64; White *1964* 387. *1029* of greater interest: NYT 10/23/64; White *1964* 361. public toilet: NYT 6/19/64; White *1964* 385, 375. *1030* He declined: T 10/23/64; NYT 10/15/64; WA 1964 175–76. votes, elsewhere: NYT 10/14/64, 10/16–17/64, 8/15/64; *Tragedy* 359–61. standing ovation: *Tragedy* 245–48. *1031* "war in Asia": NYT 9/26/64. "trying to do": NYT 9/29/64; *Tragedy* 235–37, 412; NYT 10/22/64, 10/28/64. "for themselves": NYT 10/22/64. "all Americans": NYT 10/28/64. the following summer: *Tragedy* 224, 412–13. *1032* for the Democrats: NYT 11/4/64; WA 1964 40; NYT 12/15/64; W 1964 206–10. prove valuable: NYT 11/6/64, 11/11/64. seemed symbolic: NYT 9/9/64, 10/4/64, 12/30/64, 12/31/64. *1033* were under way; NYT 11/4/64, 11/5/64. lost their appeal: W 1966 38; NYT 6/16/64. House to protest: W 1966 38. "and stop it!": NYT 1/3/65, 2/14/65, 11/21/64; Raskin "Berkeley." *1034* "to our terms!": NYT 12/4/64. putting them on: W 1965 54; NYT 3/11/64. was often electrifying: Fab VII 181. *1035* "American it is": ibid 246. Laff's and Friday's: Ruffner 939; Fab VII 238. husband or wife: Fab VII 248. *1036 of Man* (1964): T 4/8/66. going to jail: NYT 12/20/63; W 1965 96–97. in Las Vegas: WA 1967 93; W 1965 186; Fab VII 172; W 1965 206. Soviet Aeroflot: W 1966 98; Graham and Gurr 187–89; NYT 2/4/65; Bird 235; W 1965 114, 254, 1966 234. *1037* for commuters: NYT 1/26/64; Fab VII 109; NYT 12/23/65, 3/3/65; *Life* 5/14/65. *New, Pussycat?*: W 1965 252, 254; Fab VII 177. peepshow sex: Kendrick 509. *1038* director of CORE: NYT 7/15/65, 1/24/65; W 1965 24, 1967 47, 120; NYT 4/23/64. "to get known": NYT 7/17/66; WA 1967 78, 85; NYT 8/2/66; W 1966 232. "is my President": NYT 4/15/63; W 1966 208; NYT 4/28/67; W 1965 107, 264; Fab VII 178. *1039* told reporters: NYT 2/18/64, 3/15/64, 1/4/67, 3/26/64, 10/5/65; Carpenter 48; Halberstam 533. IS A JUNKIE: NYT 11/20/66, 2/4/66; W 1966 239–41; T 3/18/66, 10/10/66. "of public demand": Fab VII 132; NYT 3/22/66; W 1966 164. lost in 1964: W 1966 228–29; NYT 11/9/66; WA 1967 42; NYT 11/10/66; *Tragedy* 334. "from Saigon": *Tragedy* 498; Fab VII 204–205. *1040* the Vietnamese mire: Halberstam 630; NYT 11/28/67, 2/28/66, 4/26/66; *Tragedy* 509; NYT 4/24/66, 9/16/65, 12/15/66, 4/1/66; Halberstam 628. "kind of Presidency": *Tragedy* 378.

XXXI A DREAM OF GREATNESS — AND DISENCHANTMENT
(*pages 1041–1081*)

1041 the Fair Deal: NYT 1/21/61; W 1965 9; Goldman *Tragedy* 281–82; NYT 1/13/66. Truman years: NYT 9/7/45; Truman II 29. *1042* patients a week: *Tragedy* 285ff; W 1966 136; NYT 7/31/65, 1/2/66. retired, beside him: NYT 1/13/65; *Tragedy* 307; NYT 4/12/65. since the 1930s; NYT 5/26/65, 7/3/64, 8/11/65, 4/1/65, 12/2/65; W 1965 187; *Tragedy* 332–33. *1043* seasonal workers: NYT 3/5/61; *Economist* 5/10/69; W 1966 204–205; NYT 5/19/65. in the state: W 1966 204–206, 1965 172. throughout the country: Carpenter 15; *Tragedy* 335. "and enjoy myself": NYT 11/5/64; *Tragedy* 259–60. *1044* convert his critics: NYT 10/23/65; *Tragedy* 333; W 1965 187; NYT

5/19/65. to reassure people: NYT 6/26/67; W 1967 118–21; *Life* 6/30/67; T 6/30/67. "if less briefly": *Tragedy* 439. fly at him: ibid. 446. *1045* "*do* they want?": W 1965 168; NYT 10/6/65; *Tragedy* 337. "interested any more": NYT 12/1/67; Halberstam 429. "a war on?": *Tragedy* 451. do just that: NYT 11/1/64, 12/25/64. *1046* William Childs Westmoreland: Halberstam 129; NYT 11/17/61, 11/15/64. Ho Chi Minh trail: Halberstam 355–57, 503, 507–508. rise above 100,000: NYT 2/26/64, 2/15/65; Halberstam 369–70; NYT 1/8/65. *1047* sight of blood: NYT 2/3/65. were wounded: NYT 2/6/65; W 1965 28–30. "will do that": W 1965 30; Halberstam 521. in North Vietnam: Halberstam 534; Theodore White *1968* 23; NYT 2/11/65. *1048* girls with flowers: Halberstam 237; NYT 7/4/65, 2/28/65, 3/9/65. "how to think": NYT 2/10/65, 5/16/65, 4/24/65. deputy prime minister: Fab VII 205; Halberstam 351; NYT 2/22/65; W 1965 32; NYT 6/31/65. *1049* "internal cohesion": Fab VII 205; W 1965 32; NYT 6/25/65. blacked them out entirely: NYT 5/10–12/65; W 1965 119, 223; Kendrick 16–17. number had tripled: NYT 3/31/65, 4/1/65, 6/26/65, 5/8/65, 6/17/65. *1050* do the job: NYT 6/10/65, 6/14/65; Halberstam 582–83. the White House: *Tragedy* 409; *N.Y. Herald Tribune* 5/23/65; *Washington Post* 12/5/65. like central Texas: W 1965 119; NYT 4/8/65; *Tragedy* 407–409. *1051* terms before Christmas: NYT 4/20–21/65; Halberstam 576–78. and F-111s: Halberstam 575–79; W 1965 123. "than inform it": Halberstam 584. *1052* outweighed their misgivings: NYT 7/21/65; W 1965 123; NYT 7/22/65, 7/29/65; Halberstam 597, 600. "no one else": Theodore White *1968* 23; NYT 7/24/65; Halberstam 599; NYT 7/29/65; W 1965 118. *1053* it was impossible: Halberstam 594, 595, 606, 614. "for the war": ibid 604–10. *1054* runaway inflation: NYT 5/13/68. to top 200,000: Halberstam 594, 602; NYT 8/4/65; W 1965 26. and 137 wounded: W 1965 240; NYT 12/4/65. "doesn't it?": NYT 10/9/66; Halberstam 550. *1055* in Ann Arbor: *Tragedy* 432, 433; NYT 10/17/65, 10/16/65; WA 1966 87; W 1965 222–23. "be our own": Fab VII 206. on the tracks: W 1965 222–23. into human torches: NYT 10/16/65, 9/1/65, 11/3/65. murdering children: Fab VII 218–19. *1056* "the United States": W 1965 223. author Michael Harrington: NYT 11/28/65. 66th Regiment: NYT 11/21/65; WA 1966 90–91. *1057* bring in transports: Halberstam 612–14. as the referee: NYT 8/27/66; W 1965 240; NYT 12/4/66; Halberstam 167; WA 1966 91; Halberstam 621; W 1965 238–39. "get the word": NYT 12/3/66; *Tragedy* 322; NYT 3/16/65. "*we shall overcome*": NYT 3/16/65. *1058* Negroes as equals: NYT 8/29/65, 4/20/65; W 1966 168. in "reparations": NYT 2/22/65; W 1965 35–37, 153; *Collier's* 90; W 1969 194. as a "fascist": Theodore White *1968* 102; NYT 11/25/65. *1059* revive their campaign: *Tragedy* 308–11; WA 1966 48, 52; NYT 1/2/65, 3/12/65. symbol of oppression: NYT 3/7/65, 3/8/65. *1060* "Turn Me Around": NYT 3/8/65, 3/9/65. "constitutionally permissible": NYT 3/10/65. a little garter: *Tragedy* 315; NYT 3/19/65, 3/21/65; W 1965 52–53. *1061* the second murder: NYT 3/22/65; *Tragedy* 324; NYT 3/26/65. police help: NYT 3/26/65. the maximum: NYT 8/21/65, 10/1/65, 3/11/65, 11/30/65; W 1965 196–99; NYT 8/21/65, 12/4/65. *1062* now erupted: WA 1966 57–58; NYT 3/16/65; *Economist* 5/10/69; NYT 5/27/66. "see your I.D.": NYT 6/12/66. *1063* locally as Watts: NYT 8/12/65; W 1965 138. looting the stores: NYT 8/12/65. under control: NYT 8/11/65, 8/14/65. *1064* "mutilate themselves": NYT 8/14/65; W 1965 142. 45 million dollars: NYT 8/19/65. in the South: *Collier's* 88; W 1965 154–55; NYT 7/20/65. *1065* a real torch: NYT 8/20/65, 12/7/65; *Collier's* 89; Theodore White *1968* 26–27. riots that year: *Collier's* 88–89; Theodore White *1968* 201; NYT 3/16/66; W 1966 166–71. into its own: NYT 10/17/66. *1066* in their ranks: NYT 8/27/66, 8/31/66, 1/4/66. peppered with birdshot: NYT 6/6/66; W 1966 112; NYT 6/7/66. another Selma: NYT 6/7/66, 6/8/66. *1067* "Black power!": W 1964 233–35; NYT 12/5/64. "black . . . power!": NYT 9/10/66. "Black power!": W 1966 166–67. *1068* "rights and integration": NYT 7/3/66. "I don't like": W 1966 116. were not there: NYT 6/24/66, 6/27/66. polls, he lost: W 1966 124; NYT 12/6/66, 6/1/66. *1069* was absurd: Fab VII 155; Graham and Gurr 671. "committed to error": NYT 9/22/66; W 1966 171; NYT 10/14/66, 10/15/66. "declared war": *Life: The 1960s;* W 1967 106; Theodore White *1968* 201; T 1/5/68; NYT 6/16/67. *1070* "intolerance of it": W 1966 226–29; NYT 10/15/66; *Economist* 5/10/69. years after Watts: NYT 5/27/66; T 6/14/68, 6/21/68; W 1968 119. critics at home: *Collier's* vi; W 1967 34; Sheehan 513. *1071* be 100,000 men: NYT 6/30/66; W 1966 126, 251, 249. "come in view": Sheehan 512; W 1967 248–49; NYT 4/29/67. "a good question": W 1966 249, 1967 92–94; Halberstam 641; W 1967 91; Halberstam 642. *1072* garrison troops: W 1967 90. "11,000 miles away"; W 1967 94, 1966 32, 1967 251. *1073* off in handcuffs: WA 1968 75–76 W 1967 95; Rovere *Muddy* 8, 9; *Collier's* 158; W 1967 132; NYT 6/4/67. to the war: NYT 12/11/67; W 1967 41–43; Graham and Gurr 515–16; NYT 10/22/67; W 1967 252; Fab VII 212. in Toronto: NYT 11/11/67; W 1967 252. *1074* the people were: W 1966 36; NYT 12/1/66. Viet Cong colors: *Life: The 1960s;* NYT 3/19/67, 10/18/66, 10/23/66, 10/22/66; W 1966 189; *U.S. News and World Report* 10/31/66. *1075* FBI checks: WA 1967 69; NYT 5/18/66; *Tragedy* 499–502. worse and worse: Kendrick 24; NYT 11/28/67, 1/25/67; Halberstam 640; Fab VII 30. the White House: Fab VII 97–98. *1076* obeyed them: NYT 11/7/67; *Tragedy* 511; Halberstam 640. of Minnesota: *Tragedy* 265; NYT 8/18/67; WA 1968 85. "is your enemy": *Collier's* 196, 422; NYT 5/13/67. *1077* the new goal: W 1967 143–44; NYT 7/21/67. "black revolution": NYT 8/16–21/67. "black man's resolution?": Walter Goodman "Black Power." *1078* the word Negro: ibid. snapped his picture: NYT 6/23/73, 4/17/65, 1/14/66, 1/7/66, 8/25/66, 6/14/67, 7/1/67, 12/9/67, 7/8/67, 9/22/67, 11/8/67, 9/7/67, 6/25/67; W 1966 24, 1970 137. *1079* John Bell Williams: NYT 9/27/67, 8/8/67, 1/11/67, 6/24/67, 11/8/67. "right at home": Good "Odyssey." catastrophe of 1967: WA 1968 77; NYT 4/9/67. vast junkyard: NYT 1/3/67. *1080* Wednesday, July 12: W 1967 137–39; Theodore White *1968* 201. since Watts: NYT 7/13/67, 7/14/67, 7/18/67. *1081* of Negro homes: NYT 7/24/67, 8/7/67; Fab VII 148. Cambridge (Maryland): NYT 7/28/67. "as cherry pie": W 1967 142–43. Richard M. Nixon: NYT 5/23/68.

XXXII UP AGAINST THE WALL
(pages 1083–1121)

1083 "of 'the Establishment' ": Galbraith *State* 330–31. electrical power: NYT 11/10/65. *1084* oscillate wildly: Rosenthal and Gelb 17; W 1965 206–13. *1085* blackout had begun: Rosenthal and Gelb 85; W 1965 208–13; NYT 11/16/65. too, had vanished: NYT 11/13/65. led to safety: *Life* 11/19/65. *1086* increase in births: NYT 8/10–12/66. candle in his hand: Rosenthal and Gelb 37. "no electricity": ibid 66. *1087* "sharpener still worked": NYT 11/16/65; Rosenthal and Gelb 12. NED LUDD Clerk: Graham and Gurr 19. *1088* mayor was defeated: Theodore White *1968* 426–27; *Middletown Press* 10/7/70; NYT 6/11/66, 6/7/67; Fab VII 267. federal government alone: Servan-Schreiber 103, 134. in an automobile: Galbraith *Affluent* 171–72; Schlesinger *Crisis* 264. *1089* it was true: *Affluent* 171–72; Bird 150. whatever the weather: NYT 7/21/68. "Eyes of Texas": W 1965 78–81. *1090* garrison prison state: Goldman *Tragedy* 257; Arendt 451–59. "handle current traffic": Whyte 441; Bird 262; *State* 45. *1091* now inconceivable: Servan-Schreiber 55–61. "flatulent indigestion": *Statistical Abstract of the United States 1969* table 891 p 590; *Time* editors 73. *1092* of her mother: *Time* editors 72–73. "him to act": *State* 243, 247; Mowry 206, 207. the technostructure: *Time* editors 66; *State* 82. *1093* planned economy: NYT 1/21/68. hope of gain: Servan-Schreiber 81, 141. *1094* were expensive: Mowry 200; Servan-Schreiber 134–35. is doubtful: Servan-Schreiber 163. *1095* of autonomy: John Brooks *Leap* 250; *State* 13, 14; Servan-Schreiber 81–82, 141. interest group: W 1965 55, 1969 122; Servan-Schreiber 69. *1096* "overthrow it": Theodore White *1968* 424; "Democracy Has/Hasn't a Future." "economic goals": *Leap* 269; *State* 20; *Affluent* 249. the United States: NYT 4/24/68, 7/1/68, 3/9/68. Old Wabash: NYT 6/10/68. *1097* "blasé permissivists": *New Republic* 9/12/70; NYT 10/26/69; W 1970 202. "or leprosy": W 1969 122; Fab VII 59. domestic policies: *New Republic* 9/12/70; NYT 7/24/70; *U.S. News and World Report* 8/3/70. been the point: *Leap* 327. *1098* "stomach! Wild!": NYT 8/25/64, 10/22/67, 3/15/70. deemed nonviolent: Theodore White *1968* 214. coast to coast: NYT 12/4/64, 3/11/65; W 1965 44–45; NYT 3/9/65. *1099* "today's foxhole": NYT 9/2/65, 4/15/65, 3/9/65, 2/21/65, 3/24/65, 2/23/67; Graham and Gurr 516–17; NYT 1/21/67; *Leap* 241. "blow is college": NYT 10/9/69. San Francisco State: NYT 11/10/66; *Collier's* 79; NYT 1/21/67; W 1967 128; NYT 11/27/68. "education for?": W 1969 125; NYT 3/12/67; W 1969 128. *1100* an abyss: *Collier's* 79. "toward youth": *Life: The 1960s; Hartford Courant* 11/8/69. "for self-discipline?": Hechinger and Hechinger 177. *1101* ("damn damn"): Fab V 28. "company comes": Lifton 80. "see what happens": Murray "Individuality": *Leap* 145–46. "cudgels of thrift": *Leap* 233; Riesman 100; Packard *Wilderness* 25. *1102* "lunch and supper": *Leap* 233, 145; *Saturday Evening Post* 10/28/61. "Isn't Everybody?": Hechinger and Hechinger 121; Fab V 128; Hechinger and Hechinger 116–17; *Seventeen* September 1961. "the puh-lain": Hechinger and Hechinger 94, 89–90; *Life: The 1960s*; W 1966 149. *1103* said acne: NYT 10/5/70; W 1966 150; NYT 8/5/66, 8/12/66; W 1966 163; Fab VI 148–49, V 28. Gallup reported: Lifton 111–12; T 2/23/68; Loth 15; Hechinger and Hechinger 165. would have thought: Hechinger and Hechinger 16. *1104* leisure class: W 1969 185; NYT 7/7/69. after 10 P.M.: W 1970 128. and furniture: T 2/23/68; Loth 101–102, 106–107. $3,000 and $10,000: NYT 9/5/63; T 9/13/63. *1105* 65 policemen: *Leap* 234; *Hartford Courant* 7/29/70. worth of damage: W 1969 119. girls' dormitory: *Hartford Courant* 3/13/70. *1106* swaying visibly: NYT 1/27/66; W 1970 192–94; *Wilderness* 353; W 1970 193; *Hartford Courant* 1/27/70; W 1970 190. Aunt Tom: W 1967 258; *Wilderness* 85; NYT 3/29/67; *Life* 2/3/67; *Wilderness* 81; NYT 2/10/66. higher up: W 1970 193; Friedan 249; Riesman 156; W 1967 134; NYT 6/16/67. *1107* "do we get laid?": *Wilderness* 144–45, 60–61. (under any circumstances): NYT 10/8/68. *1108* full body flush: NYT 1/19/68, 11/22/69, 1/14/69, 10/9/69. toddlers watched: DeMott 53; *Collier's* 131. lost their novelty: W 1968 186–90: NYT 7/30/68, 10/1/68, 9/23/68. *1109* is electrocuted: NYT 4/20/69, 2/12/71; DeMott 112; NYT

2/11/68. loops and coils: *Wilderness* 68; NYT 6/1/70. in 1965: *Wilderness* 250–51; W 1966 62; NYT 3/18/62, 12/20/63; Fab VII 176. *1110* key she had: W 1967 258; T 8/9/68. bedroom with whom: *Middletown Press* 3/6/70. "love in return": *Wilderness* 60. *1111* heavy drugs: ibid 149. merely a memory: NYT 9/26/43; T 6/11/45; NYT 4/13/55, 8/25/60; Phillips *Blitz* 358. (with benzedrine): NYT 4/12/62; T 8/10/62; NYT 12/13/62; *Newsweek* 8/17/70. *1112* taken a trip: W 1966 91. continued to spread: NYT 5/29/63. his mother-in-law: W 1966 91. "afraid of him": ibid; W 1967 197; NYT 5/14/67. *1113 Great Notion* (1964): *Collier's* 76; NYT 2/4/62, 7/27/64. "nationwide avalanche": *Collier's* 73. *1114* a single year: W 1967 196, 1970 254. Politics of Free: Sanders 39; W 1967 197. other narcotics: Fab VII 84; *Hartford Courant* 8/10/70; W 1967 200. *1115* "the hard way": W 1967 196. up at dawn: ibid 198; NYT 5/5/67. deformed infants: NYT 6/28/67, 5/5/68. *1116* and up yours: NYT 6/8/66; *Collier's* 79. "to get in": W 1967 201. from a cliff: NYT 5/31/67. *1117* Charles Manson: Sanders 39–40; NYT 8/19/67; Sanders 37–38. Lower East Side: NYT 10/9/69, 10/10/69. *1117–1118* in a corner . . . "anything to us": W 1967 202; T 10/20/67, 10/13/67; NYT 10/16/67. *1118* "the flowers gone?": T 10/13/67; NYT 10/5/67. *1118–21* Hess portrait: NYT 9/28/69; Theodore White *1968* 32; Stan Lehr and Louis Rossetto Jr. "The New Right Credo — Libertarianism" *New York Times Magazine* 1/10/71; *Newsweek* 9/29/69; Murray Kempton "Karl Hess: Goldwater Finds His Sorensen" *New Republic* 8/8/64; James Boyd "From Far Right to Far Left — and Farther" *New York Times Magazine* 12/6/70.

XXXIII THE YEAR EVERYTHING WENT WRONG
(pages 1122–1150)

1122 was assassinated: T 12/13/68; NYT 12/31/68, 1/10/68, 6/2/68, 4/17/68, 12/21/68, 8/17/68, 1/17/68. Biafra starved: NYT 7/16/68, 8/2/68, 1/23/68, 12/13/68. "cease and desist?": NYT 9/19/68; Fab VII 176; NYT 9/13/67, 2/15/68, 7/16/68, 7/19/68; T 5/17/68. *1123* straight or sick: NYT 9/13/68. the runner-up: NYT 5/5/68, 5/8/68, 12/24/68. off North Korea: NYT 11/21/68, 5/28/68. and hand grenades: W 1969 110; NYT 1/24/68. *1124* He failed: W 1968 22; NYT 1/25/68. possible to forget: NYT 1/25/68, 1/27/68. "to the coast": W 1968 84. in South Vietnam: NYT 2/5/68; W 1968 84. *1125* million dollars: NYT 1/30/68. "not been achieved": T 3/1/68; NYT 1/25/68; W 1968 28–35. now this: *Life: The 1960s.* by Clark Clifford: Halberstam 647–48; NYT 4/26/68, 1/19/68. *1126* even want it: W 1968 35, 88; T 4/12/68. three years earlier: T 4/19/68; NYT 4/11/68; T 5/10/68. Complete Victory: W 1968 247–48. "clean for Gene": Theodore White *1968* 79. *1127* "the United States": NYT 3/16/68, 3/17/68. said. Then . . . "as your President": NYT 4/4/68, 4/1/68; T 3/22/68, 4/5/68. Republican vote: NYT 4/3/68. "civil rights progress": NYT 4/28/68, 5/29/68; W 1967 97. *1128* for his head: NYT 4/5/68. defending Khe Sanh: NYT 4/6/68. "free at last": W 1969 74; NYT 4/10/68. *1129* never discovered: NYT 4/20/68; T 7/26/68, 7/9/68, 3/11/69; WA 1970 913. primaries, California: TC 1968 34; NYT 5/8/68; W 1968 119; NYT 5/15/68, 6/5/68. *1130* "struggle for it —": NYT 6/6/68. a bear hug: TC 1968 34. little Arab had: ibid; W 1968 118, 115; NYT 6/6/68. trembling voice: NYT 6/5/68, 6/7/68; T 6/14/68; NYT 6/9/68. *1131* "to shining sea!": NYT 6/9/68. University of Miami —: W 1968 100. especially wicked: TC 1968 227–33; NYT 4/24/68; T 5/24/68. *1132* They were wrong: W 1968 101–103; TC 1968 227–33. able to muster: NYT 5/18/68, 5/12/68. "humanistic society": W 1968 101. *1133* as the Nazis: NYT 4/25/68, 4/30/68. *1134* to be tidy: NYT 4/27/68, 4/28/68. the United States: NYT 10/6/68. "revolutionary America": W 1968 101, 1970 58; NYT 3/8/68. *1135* vending machine: T 3/23/70. *1136* "catastrophe happens": Servan-Schreiber xvi; W 1968 53. remained aloof: T 4/19/68; NYT 5/26/68. *1137* compromise with him: NYT 1/4/66; T 2/4/66; W 1966 15–19. deliberate slowdown: T 2/16/68; NYT 2/3/68, 11/2/68; T 11/1/68; NYT 10/20/68, 10/24/68, 9/10/68, 10/15/68, 7/4/68. and San Francisco: NYT 3/20/70, 3/18/70, 3/20/70. their grievances: NYT 3/27/70, 4/3/70. *1138* take Fortas's place: NYT 6/22/68, 6/27/68. remained in office: NYT 7/17/68. *1139* before the court: NYT 7/20/68, 9/14/68. be less liberal: NYT 10/3/68; *Life* 5/9/69; W 1968 210–12, 1969 77–79. the fans laughed: NYT 2/22/68. *1140* among the suggestions: NYT 10/18/68. 1.2 million dollars: NYT 10/21/68; W 1968 201. "marriage, and death": W 1968 201. *1141* eyes of God: NYT 11/25/68, 11/7/68, 10/24/68. Agnew of Maryland: NYT 3/14/68, 2/29/68, 3/22/68, 5/1/68. "shipbuilding firm": NYT 8/9/68; T 8/16/68. IS ROSEMARY'S BABY: T 10/25/68. *1142* "driving dream": W 1968 151; Theodore White *1968* 243; NYT 8/6/68; McGinniss 77; NYT 8/12/68. in Chicago: W 1968 151. confront them: NYT 8/21/68, 8/26/68. *1143* too risky: NYT 8/29/68. "accept the truth": ibid. North Side traffic: W 1968 161–66. *1144* "no march today": NYT 8/24/68. had parents too: NYT 8/26/68; *New Republic* 9/7/68. of the suite: Theodore White *1968* 308–309; NYT 8/31/68. *1145* elated Richard Nixon: Theodore White *1968* 320. "cries too much": T 9/20/68; *Columbia Journalism*

Review Winter 1969. Johnson and Daley: T 9/20/68. "the world": NYT 9/10/68. *1146* "of a box!": McGinniss 31. Thomas E. Dewey: NYT 10/1/68; WA 1972 19. *1147* Houses on the Hill: NYT 11/6/68, 11/7/68. could be shelved: T 7/25/69; NYT 8/17/73. *1148* "survival itself": *Middletown Press* 1/28/70; WM/Eric Sevareid 6/24/70. powder and dirt: Theodore White *1968* 196. *1149* ever lay ahead: W 1968 181. seemed inevitable: T 6/21/68; NYT 1/19/68, 10/17/68, 7/24/68. *1150* nothing happened: W 1968 181; NYT 5/23/68; T 10/4/68, 9/20/68; NYT 9/28/68. was a heroine: T 9/13/68; Theodore White *1968* 200; T 5/24/68. into the middle class: T 3/1/68; NYT 6/24/73.

XXXIV THE RISE OF THE SILENT MAJORITY
(*pages 1155–1189*)

1155 ten times: NYT 12/12/68; T 12/20/68. *1156* doubted their integrity: T 12/20/68. 528 million people: NYT 7/21/69. "decade is out": TA 180–81; NYT 1/28/67. *1157–1159* general sources: W 1969 141–52; TA 180–89. *1157* miles away: NYT 7/17/69. picking up speed: W 1969 141–46. had made it: NYT 7/25/69. July 20, 1969: NYT 7/21/69. *1158* "fine, sandy particles": NYT 7/21/69. "for all mankind": ibid. on the moon: NYT 7/22/69. *1159* on their horns: W 1969 147; NYT 7/25/69. "erode its dignity": NYT 7/23/69, 7/26/69; W 1969 188; TA 11. *1160* where they lay: NYT 8/3/69. "and dignity": NYT 8/4/69, 2/7/69, 3/22/69, 6/24/69. quiet good taste: TA 10. "have described it": W 1969 189. *1161* "was a success": NYT 2/6/69, 8/7/70; TA 10–11; NYT 11/22/69, 5/15/72. presidential seal: TA 18; NYT 1/19/69, 4/28/69, 6/15/69. *1162* heating systems: T 8/20/73, 9/10/73; *Middletown Press* 10/18/73. "government will listen": NYT 1/21/69. *1163* violent contention: TA 11; NYT 6/17/70; *Economist* 5/10/69. city commissioners: NYT 11/5/69; *Hartford Courant* 5/4/70; NYT 5/28/69. hundred billion dollars. TA 22. *1164* "throughout the land": NYT 2/5/69; W 1969 246–48; Chayes and Wiesner 2; NYT 6/5/69. Carswell of Florida: NYT 6/4/69, 11/22/69, 12/5/69; W 1969 237. "we want to": NYT 1/22/70, 3/17/70; W 1970 96–99. *1165* "the Constitution": NYT 4/9/70. "can do that": NYT 11/4/69; Pater and Pater 244. his first target: WA 1970 40; NYT 11/14/69. "absolute loyalty": NYT 11/14/69, 11/21/69. *1166* Vietnam War: NYT 4/5/69. than an hour: NYT 3/11/69, 4/18/69, 3/1/69. she vanished: NYT 6/18/69, 8/30/69, 8/23/69, 8/22/69, 8/23/69, 11/11/69, 11/13/69, 12/1/69, 5/15/69. a huge toilet: NYT 3/22/69; TA 134. *1167* very far away: *Middletown Press* 10/6/69; NYT 10/6/69. Vietnam War: WA 1970 907; W 1969 122–28; NYT 3/23/69. university budget: NYT 2/14/25. *1168* poor man's Harvard: NYT 4/23/69, 5/10/69, 6/3/69. ROTC at Harvard: NYT 4/10/69, 4/11/69, 5/12/69. Perkins quit: NYT 6/1/69. student riots: NYT 2/18/69, 2/28/69. *1169* "a good man": NYT 5/7/69; TA 32; NYT 6/5/69. school integration: NYT 8/27/69. "for the law": TA 12; NYT 10/30/69. called Woodstock: Theodore White *1972* 149. *1170* dollars a ticket: *Life: The 1960s;* W 1969 180–85; TA 112–23; NYT 7/17/69. a disaster: NYT 8/16/69, 8/17/69. "police work": *Life: The 1960s;* NYT 8/18/69. Woodstock Nation: NYT 8/17/69. *1171* Iron Butterfly: NYT 8/31/69, 9/1/69. in the black: W 1969 181. to death: NYT 8/10/69, 12/3/69; Sanders 356. *1172* one hundred pounds: T 1/27/67; W 1969 31–35; TA 112–23; Galbraith *State* 354. a ski resort: TA 113; NYT 4/28/69, 1/28/69. *1173* desert country: NYT 1/16/70; W 1969 125–26, 35; NYT 1/18/70, 4/29/69. a wide area: W 1969 33–34; TA 113–15; NYT 1/31/69. "black crayon": NYT 2/5/69. at three million: NYT 2/9/69. *1174* runaway well: NYT 2/8/69. House of Pancakes: TA 176. *1175* huge, flag-draped coffins: NYT 11/16/69; W 1969 220–22. "as peaceful": NYT 11/15/69; W 1969 222. *1176* leader's briefing: "The Massacre at Mylai" *Life* 12/5/69; TA 62; W 1969 257, 1971 68–72; NYT 9/7/69. loaded and ready: NYT 1/29/69. in after them . . . "ditch and fired": W 1971 69–70. "this all day": W 1969 257. *1177* the killings: NYT 11/21/70. "his own safety": NYT 11/19/70, 11/24/70. "Republic of Vietnam": NYT 5/20/71; T 5/31/71; NYT 9/28/70. *1178* "of its policies": NYT 9/7/69. "go marching on": T 4/12/71; NYT 3/30/71, 4/9/71. "public clamor": NYT 4/4/71. *1179* "suffered enough": NYT 12/22/68. off the coast: NYT 5/7/69. "statement of fact": NYT 5/5/69. storm the hill: W 1969 94–95; TA 220; W 1969 95. *1180* "going to get": W 1969 95. of U.S. soldiers: NYT 5/22/69. "inflationary recession": TA 58. on June 8: NYT 2/19/70; TA 54. *1181* "election of 1972": NYT 6/20/69; W 1969 96; TA 59. at any time: NYT 10/5/69. *1182* Vietnamese din: NYT 8/26/69. "up, and olé": TA 13; WA 1971 78; TA 36, 37; W 1969 85–87, 240. to fly east: NYT 11/1/69. *1183* in prison: W 1970 231; NYT 11/12/70. Nantucket Sound: NYT 7/20/69; TA 212; W 1969 26; TA 29; W 1969 249–53; W 1970 74–78. turn Kennedy took: NYT 1/6/70, 4/30/70. *1184* "to the surface": NYT 1/6/70; W 1970 76. "this happened" . . . "see me": TA 28–29; W 1969 249–53, 1970 75–78. *1186* senatorial duties: NYT 7/26/69. "asked of me": NYT 4/30/70. from Richard Nixon: NYT 7/22/70. *1187–89* Spock portrait: *Current Biography* 1956, 1969; *Newsweek* 9/15/69; *Time* 5/31/68; Jessica Mitford *The Trial of Dr. Spock* New York 1969.

XXXV NATTERING NABOBS
(pages 1190–1222)

1190 inauspicious start: NYT 1/22/70, 2/23/70; W 1970 13–15. "Get Involved": NYT 3/8/70, 9/20/70, 11/15/70, 6/1/70, 3/29/70, 3/15/70. *1191* Satan himself: NYT 1/19/70, 1/25/70, 3/15/70. "irregular ones": NYT 10/31/69; W 1970 173–75. the Pueblo tribe: NYT 12/5/69, 12/3/70. *1192* quietly shelved: NYT 7/28/70, 1/28/70; W 1970 23. to turn back: NYT 1/13/70, 3/18/70, 6/5/70, 4/14/70; W 1970 61–68. on May 27: *U.S. News and World Report* 7/27/70; NYT 6/22/70, 5/28/70. *1193* visiting Manhattan: NYT 5/19/70; W 1970 122. seemed insatiable: W 1970 110–13; *Middletown Press* 7/3/70. "amount of money": NYT 2/19/70; W 1970 113; NYT 3/18/70. *1194* that to herself: *Newsweek* 11/12/73; WA 1958 47. "something you are": *Hartford Courant* 6/23/69; W 1970 38. by SIECUS: T 7/25/69. *1195* "Mating Toads": W 1970 39. as "counterrevolutionary": NYT 8/27/70; W 1970 193; Hargreaves 559; NYT 3/17/70. *1196* "*Playmate* promotes": W 1970 191. saleswoman $3,461: Hargreaves 561–63. *1197* "as men": ibid 564–65; NYT 3/23/72. buy their wares: W 1970 53–54; NYT 6/12/60, 2/26/70. "of prosperity": W 1970 54. *1198* in the closet: NYT 10/25/70, 1/1/71. Macon, and Athens: NYT 5/13/70. of the year: NYT 6/10/70, 6/17/70; W 1970 122. *1199* "of the establishment": W 1970 179. wealthy families: NYT 3/13/70; *Hartford Courant* 3/13/70; NYT 3/12/70; W 1970 58; NYT 3/7/70. in Manhattan: NYT 3/9/70; *Hartford Times* 3/14/70; NYT 7/12/72; W 1970 58. *1200* contain the charges: NYT 3/7/70; *Life* 3/27/70. to collapse: NYT 3/18/70. no details: *Life* 3/27/70. *1201* "changed radically": NYT 10/21/70, 10/23/70. police station: T 10/17/69, 6/29/70, 8/31/70, 10/26/70, 1/4/71; W 1970 153–57, 1972 66–67, 118–21. subsequent interest: NYT 9/14/70. *1202* a boring case: NYT 8/8/70. "them off!": T 8/17/70. yelled "Halt!": ibid. *1203* were dead: *Life* 8/21/70. in San Quentin: NYT 10/14/70. pistol from it: W 1971 168–71; NYT 8/22/71, 8/18/71, 1/6/72; W 1971 168–71. cut him down: NYT 8/22/71. *1204* "irretrievable love": NYT 9/4/71, 8/29/71; W 1971 168–71. "to be caught": NYT 6/5/72; W 1972 119. *1205* "the whole world": NYT 6/5/72. *1205–1208* general source (Chicago Seven): W 1970 34–37. *1205* said the lawyer: NYT 3/21/69. Richard G. Schultz: W 1970 34; NYT 2/7/70. *1206* judicial chaos: NYT 12/13/69. Chicago Seven: NYT 10/30/69, 10/31/69, 11/4/69, 11/6/69. *1207* "can't help yourself": NYT 9/9/73; W 1970 36. *1208* days in prison: NYT 2/16/70; W 1970 34–37. "the very beginning": NYT 2/19/70, 2/21/70; W 1972 225. "incompetently presented": NYT 9/9/73. *1209* "in new bottles": NYT 4/2/70, 7/2/70. included hospitals: W 1970 239; NYT 10/24/70. of each other: W 1970 239; FitzGerald 448–49. *1210* fourteen months: NYT 5/1/70; Chester et al 24–25. and 4,911 wounded: W 1970 236. *1211* never been any: FitzGerald 186. "mutual incomprehension": NYT 5/10/70, 5/9/70; Chester et al 29. "by five o'clock": NYT 5/7/70, 11/26/70. *1212* "reestablish order": T 11/12/73; NYT 5/16/70, 10/2/70, 7/30/70. Middlefield, Connecticut: W 1970 161. *1213* and it happened: NYT 7/17/70, 7/31/70. exchanging a word: NYT 8/2/70, 8/3/70. muggy Friday night: T 5/18/70. *1214* to the ground: NYT 5/4/70, 5/3/70. "harbor in America": NYT 5/4/70, 5/7/70. back at students: NYT 9/2/73. "on a trigger": W 1970 187. "killing us!": NYT 5/15/70. their victims: W 1970 187; NYT 5/5/70. handed down: NYT 5/19/70, 3/30/74. *1216* "irresponsible sort": NYT 10/17/70, 5/5/70; W 1970 190. "any protest": NYT 5/15/69. *1217* Tom Charles Huston: Chester et al 39–40. living abroad: ibid 41. John Wesley Dean III: W 1973 150. *1218* "security matters": NYT 6/29/71, 7/22/73. "Mr. Young — Plumber": Lukas "The Story So Far." "Power-pack Agnew": Theodore White 1972. 49. *1219* black officeholders: ibid. 62; NYT 3/6/70. "and hardworking": W 1970, 24, 202. *1220* "all about": NYT 12/14/70. "the United States": T 11/16/70; NYT 10/30/70; Theodore White 1972 295. "in yourself": NYT 11/3/70; Theodore White 1972 76. *1221* repudiate them: T 11/16/70. Lowell P. Weicker Jr.: T 11/16/70; NYT 11/5/70, 11/4/70. be decided: Chester et al 11–13; NYT 11/4/70. *1222* one-term President: Theodore White 1972 59; Chester et al 12–13, a hard-liner: NYT 7/22/73, 1/6/61. alike, as CREEP: NYT 1/6/71; Chester et al 1; Theodore White 1972 49; Lukas "The Story So Far."

XXXVI THE DIVIDED STATES OF AMERICA
(pages 1224–1258)

1224 roaring ovation: NYT 1/21/71, *1225* to prevent infection: NYT 4/4/71, 4/11/71. electricity sixfold: Theodore White 1972 155–56, xv. pay a fine: NYT 2/5/71, 3/2/71, 9/18/71, 7/24/71, 3/3/71. *1226* becoming a democracy: W 1971 174. (his province chief): NYT 9/4/67, 6/3/71. "Vietnamese people": NYT 8/20/71, 8/6/71, 8/21/71. *1227* in grave doubt: NYT 9/2/71, 8/21/71, 8/23/71, 10/4/71. "Lam Son 719": Theodore White 1972 58; W 1971 239–41; FitzGerald 553–55. "the Americans": NYT 2/9/71; FitzGerald

554. country's intelligence: NYT 4/8/71. *1228* "the government": NYT 4/24/71, 4/25/71, 4/27/61; Chester et al 31–34. more aggressively: NYT 4/27/71. as red tape: NYT 1/15/69; Chester et al 8. *1229* Memorial Stadium: W 1971 84–87; NYT 5/3/71, 5/4/71. "national monument": NYT 5/6/71. Nazi Brownshirts: Chester et al 34; NYT 5/11/71. reveal more: W 1971 182–85; NYT 6/13/71. *1230* "or promulgated": NYT 4/28/65. government's credibility: NYT 6/13/71. alongside it: NYT 6/15/71. *1231 New York Times:* NYT 6/16/71. in the minority: NYT 6/27/71. finally decided him: ibid. "harm my country": NYT 6/24/71, 6/29/71, 12/31/71. *1232* as Plumbers: Chester et al 52. "that would ensue": NYT 7/5/71; Chester et al 54–55. *1233* dubious sources: NYT 7/11/71. bank accounts: *Nation* 12/20/71; NYT 9/28/71; T 12/17/73. of the decision: NYT 6/11/69, 3/2/72. *1234* "antitrust cases": T 11/12/73. "understanding" with Geneen: Chester et al 147. "cannot be known": NYT 3/1/72. "of a victory": ibid. *1235* 224 million dollars: T 5/21/73, 6/11/73, NYT 11/28/72. prosecute anyway: NYT 5/23/73. a government job: NYT 2/1/72; Chester et al 85. *1236* and imprisonment: Theodore White *1972* 89. Hunt an idea: NYT 9/17/71; Lukas "The Story So Far." *1237* it in Barker's: NYT 12/16/73. to the CIA: Lukas "The Story So Far." *1238* "not traceable": Chester et al 68. Cuban informant: ibid 70. *1239* "congressional investigation": ibid 69. for his office: Lukas "The Story So Far." was mounting: ibid. *1240:* plain: Attica: T 9/27/71; W 1971 160–67; WA 1972 964; NYT 11/18/73, 9/10/71. clubs "nigger sticks": T 9/27/71. "our accursed lot": ibid. *1241* "so well organized": NYT 9/27/71, 8/22/71; W 1971 161. "like here — animals": NYT 9/17/71; T 9/27/71. along the way: T 9/20/71. *1242* tried for murder: T 9/27/71. call their bluff: NYT 9/14/71. *1243* "those oppressed": NYT 9/10/71. bitter fruit: T 9/27/71; NYT 9/11/71. *1244* the committee: NYT 9/11/71. "Black Panther Party": NYT 7/13/71. with Oswald: NYT 9/12/71. *1245* to death: NYT 9/13/71, 9/14/71. victims with them: W 1971 165. *1246* "the offensive!" NYT 9/14/71; W 1971 160. "was killed": NYT 9/14/71. "on the ground": NYT 11/18/73. *1247* carried guns: NYT 9/14/71. "any circumstances": NYT 9/17/71; W 1971 167. AT THIS INSTITUTION: NYT 9/17/71; T 9/27/71. *1248* home and abroad: T 8/30/71. of Red China?: NYT 4/1/71; T 4/26/71; W 1971 62–66; WA 1972 950; NYT 4/7/71. Americans "unprincipled": NYT 4/8/71. *1249* "bloodthirsty gangsters": NYT 4/10/71. "come in batches": NYT 4/14/71, 4/15/71. President himself: NYT 4/14/71. *1250* by his illness: T 7/26/71; NYT 7/16/71. "our old friends": NYT 7/17/71; T 3/6/72; NYT 7/16/71; WA 1972 957. *1251* Cowan in Nagoya: NYT 10/27/71; W 1971 204–205; NYT 10/28/71. was heartening: NYT 8/5/71; T 8/30/71. its own money: W 1971 193. *1252* deficit since 1893: T 8/30/71. flooded with them: W 1971 194. *1253* jump accordingly: ibid 216; NYT 7/29/71. price increases: T 8/30/71. over the freeze: W 1971 217; NYT 8/15/71. *1254* into the system: NYT 8/17/73. "American people": NYT 10/8/71; WA 1972 964. *1255* he could get: NYT 3/23/72, 12/24/71. *1255–58* Nader portrait: *Current Biography* 1966; T 4/26/71, 7/31/72, 3/14/71, 3/21/71, 10/29/73; *Life* 1/21/72; Charles McCarry *Citizen Nader* New York 1972.

XXXVII PRIDE GOETH
(pages 1259–1297)

1259 Phineas Taylor Barnum: Kronenberger 25. *1260* his best friend: T 5/29/72; NYT 5/22/72, 5/31/72, 9/6/72, 4/18/72, 11/36/70, 4/17/72. "my memoirs?": W 1972 71; NYT 4/8/72, 3/28/72, 12/9/72, 5/16/72. getting married: NYT 11/13/72, 11/14/72; T 6/4/73. *1261* old-fashioned marijuana: NYT 3/7/69. homes and schools: NYT 11/15/72, 7/6/72. *1262* "human being": W 1972 102–106; NYT 12/8/71, 1/10/72; Fay et al 3–4. "Western Hemisphere": Fay et al 2–3. *1263* "We have proof": Fay et al 5; NYT 12/9/72, 1/11/72. also been lucky: NYT 2/12/72. his two children: Fay et al 28. *1264* come from Irving: ibid 72. years earlier: NYT 1/29/72. *1265* Helga began: NYT 1/10/72, 1/22/72. like Howard Hughes: Fay et al 179, 181. one believes him: NYT 1/27/72. *1266* "is Helga": Fay et al 189–90; NYT 1/29/72. fornicatrix of 1972: *Life* 12/29/72; Fay et al 303. vinyl couch: Fay et al 228; NYT 6/17/72. *1267* TRUST COMPANY: Fay et al 204. Chinese calendar: NYT 2/21/72; Theodore White *1972* viii. *1268* Chou took it: W 1972 76–82; T 3/6/72; NYT 2/22/72. official hostess: NYT 2/22/72. about needles: ibid. *1269* the American people: NYT 2/24/72. "kind between people": ibid. "of the U.S.A.": W 1972 81–82. *1270* four years earlier: W 1972 230–35, 1973 1003; NYT 1/26/72. of Kontum: NYT 4/7/72, 4/20/72. was a failure: NYT 4/22/72. *1271* "their neighbors": NYT 5/9/72. *1272* wanted to make: NYT 5/12/72, 5/13/72, 5/24/72; T 5/22/72. that they cherish: NYT 5/23/72; T 6/5/72; WA 1972 1010; W 1972 82–83; NYT 5/27/72. for five years: NYT 5/27/72. *1273* of the cold-warriors: W 1972 83. synonym: Watergate: NYT 7/22/73. *1274* support of busing: Theodore White *1972* 75; NYT 1/23/72, 2/8/72, 1/11/72, 6/7/72. CREEP's director: NYT 3/5/72, 7/2/72. "Rose Mary's baby": NYT 6/11/72. *1275* by hidden cameras: NYT 6/15/72; Lukas "The Story So Far." try once again: Chester et al 136. his green light: NYT 10/23/72. *1276* national convention: Lukas "The Story So Far"; Chester et al 152; NYT 9/17/72. of the banquet: NYT 6/19/72; Lukas "The Story So Far." *1277* on Virginia Avenue: Chester et al 156. to try again: Lukas "The Story So Far." cheap slacks: NYT 6/18/72. *1278* under arrest: ibid; Lukas "The Story So Far." "going to Miami?": Lukas. *1279* of the United States: NYT 6/18/72. "is incredible": Chester et al 165. on the lam: NYT 7/2/72. *1280* "I am ready": Lukas "The Story So Far." "Holy shit!": Chester et al 176. "or condone it": ibid 168. *1281* "big fat wringer": NYT 9/13/72; Chester et al 202. returns from there: NYT 3/15/72, 3/17/72. *1282* to the hall: NYT 8/7/72, 8/23/72. course, the idea: NYT 8/23/72. the other side: NYT 8/25/72. him the prize: NYT 1/5/72, 1/11/72, 1/19/72, 2/12/72, 1/26/72, 2/12/72. *1283* something, big: Theodore White *1964* 129, *1972* 118–19; NYT 1/14/72. was on him: NYT 3/8/72, 3/14/72. went to Wallace: NYT 3/15/72, 3/22/72, 4/5/72, 4/26/72, 5/5/72, 5/11/72. *1284* the nomination: NYT 5/15/72, 5/16/72, 5/17/72, 6/7/72. "adversary treatment": NYT 5/29/72, 5/31/72, 6/5/72. party's strength: NYT 8/28/68; Theodore White *1972* 29–30. *1285* and Chicago: NYT 7/11/72, 6/3/72; Theodore White *1972* 172. him long before: Theodore White *1972* 166, 161. scuttling Salinger: NYT 7/13/72, 7/14/72, 7/15/72. *1286* credibility fast: NYT 8/17/72; Theodore White *1972* 214. didn't do it: NYT 7/26/72; W *1972* 144; NYT 7/26/72. recover from it: Theodore White *1972* 203; NYT 7/31/72; White *1972* 205–206; NYT 8/6/72. *1287* getting 1.8: NYT 11/8/72. one statehouse: NYT 11/9/72. were felons: W *1972* 203–204. the following course: Chester et al 207; NYT 10/5/72; Theodore White *1972* 327. *1288* in disgrace: Chester et al 183–84. and hung up: ibid. 191. *1289* "of President Kennedy": NYT 8/29/72. (from Ehrlichman): NYT 8/30/72. Nixon's reelection: NYT 7/2/72; Lukas "The Story So Far." *1290* "may have to": Chester et al 196. already resigned: ibid 198. *1291* ultimate disgrace: NYT 9/16/72; Lukas "The Story So Far": NYT 10/11/72, 6/30/72. Watergate Five: NYT 12/10/72; Szulc "The Spy Compulsion." "are to go forward": Chester et al 219. of "higher-ups": ibid. 220. *1292* "in the fallout": ibid 225–26. Presidency began: ibid 229. "is at hand": W *1972* 233–35; T 12/25/72, 1/1/73, 1/8/73, 1/15/73, 1/22/73, 2/5/73. *1293* the war alone: NYT 10/24/72. would be unavoidable: NYT 12/14/72. *1294* "is arrived at": NYT 12/19/72. "on Christmas Eve": NYT 12/23/72. Le Duc Tho: NYT 12/25/72; T 8/4/52. *1295* to shut up: NYT 12/31/72. "Peace with honor": NYT 1/24/72; W 1973 9/13. *1296* "probably enduring": NYT 1/24/73. "to get it": John Brooks *Leap* 13. *1297* "into the past": *Leap* 359; Thomas Wolfe *Look Homeward Angel* (foreword); F. Scott Fitzgerald *The Great Gatsby* (conclusion).

EPILOGUE: ECHOES
(pages 1298–1302)

1298 "do for myself": NYT 1/21/73. "End racism!": ibid. *1299* in their stead: NYT 1/20/73, 1/21/73. under that President: NYT 1/20/73. camp at Auschwitz: NYT 1/21/73. *1300* opinion of it: ibid. heckled FDR: *Baltimore Sun* 12/20/51.

Bibliography

Aaron, Daniel *Writers on the Left* Harcourt, Brace and World, New York 1961

Abel, Elie, *The Missile Crisis* Lippincott, New York and Philadelphia 1966 (Bantam, New York 1966)

Acheson, Dean *Present at the Creation: My Years at the State Department* Norton, New York 1969

Adamic, Louis *My America* Harper, New York 1938

Adams, Sherman *Firsthand Report: The Story of the Eisenhower Administration* Harper, New York 1961

Agronsky, Martin, and others, commentary by *Let Us Begin: The First Hundred Days of the Kennedy Administration* Simon and Schuster, New York 1961

Alabama: A Guide to the Deep South, compiled by workers of the Writers Program of the Works Progress Administration in Alabama; Richard R. Smith, New York 1941

Aldridge, John W. "In the Country of the Young" *Harper's Magazine* October–November 1969

Allen, Frederick Lewis *The Big Change: America Transforms Itself 1900–1950* Harper and Row, New York 1952

———— *Only Yesterday: An Informal History of the Nineteen-Twenties* Harper, New York 1931

———— *Since Yesterday: The Nineteen-Thirties in America, September 3, 1929–September 3, 1939* Harper, New York 1940

Alsop, Stewart "The Lessons of the Cuban Disaster" *Saturday Evening Post* June 24, 1961

American Institute of Public Opinion, ed. *The 1954 Pocket Almanac* Pocket Books, New York 1953

"America's Military Decline: Where We'd Stand in a Fight" *U.S. News and World Report* March 22, 1946

Angoff, Charles, and H. L. Mencken "The Worst American State" *American Mercury* September–November 1931

Appleman, Roy E. *The United States Army in the Korean War: South to the Naktong, North to the Yalu (June–November 1950)* U.S. Government Printing Office, Washington 1961

Arendt, Hannah *The Origins of Totalitarianism* Meridian, New York 1958

Armstrong, Neil, Michael Collins, and Edwin E. Aldrin Jr. *First on the Moon* (written with Gene Farmer and Dora Jane Hamblin) Little, Brown, Boston 1970

Arnold, Thurman "How *Not* to Get Investigated: Ten Commandments for Government Employees" *Harper's Magazine* November 1948

Asbell, Bernard *When F.D.R. Died* Holt, Rinehart and Winston, New York 1961

Asch, Berta, and A. R. Magnus *Farmers on Relief and Rehabilitation* (WPA Research Monograph VIII) U. S. Government Printing Office, Washington 1937

Asch, Nathan *The Road* Norton, New York 1937

Bakal, Carl *The Right to Bear Arms* McGraw-Hill, New York 1966

Barnouw, Erik *A Tower in Babel: A History of Broadcasting in the United States* (Volume I, to 1933) Oxford, New York 1966

———— *The Golden Web: A History of Broadcasting in the United States* (Volume II, 1933–1953) Oxford, New York 1968

Barrett, George "Close-up of the Birchers' 'Founder'" *New York Times Magazine* May 14, 1961

——— "Jim Crow, He's Real Tired" *New York Times Magazine* March 3, 1957

Barrett, William "Dialogue on Anxiety" *Partisan Review* March–April 1947

Barth, Alan *The Loyalty of Free Men* Viking, New York 1951

Bell, Daniel, ed. *The Radical Right: The New American Right* Doubleday, New York 1963 (Anchor, New York 1964)

Bell, Jack *The Johnson Treatment: How Lyndon B. Johnson Took Over the Presidency and Made It His Own* Harper, New York 1965

Bendiner, Robert "Great Expectations, a Quarter of a Century Later" *New York Times Magazine* April 26, 1970

Berger, Peter L. and Brigitte "The Blueing of America" *New Republic* April 3, 1971

Bernstein, Irving *The Lean Years* Houghton Mifflin, Boston 1960

Bird, Caroline *The Invisible Scar* McKay, New York 1966 (Pocket Books, New York 1967)

Bishop, Joseph W. Jr. "The Warren Court Is Not Likely to Be Overruled" *New York Times Magazine* September 7, 1969

Bliven, Bruce, "Boulder Dam" *New Republic* December 11, 1935

——— "Sitting Down in Flint" *New Republic* January 27, 1937

Bohr, Niels "On Atoms and Human Knowledge" *Daedalus* Spring 1958

Brecher, Edward M., and Consumer Report Editors *Licit and Illicit Drugs: The Consumers Union Report on Narcotics, Stimulants, Depressants, Inhalants, Hallucinogens, and Marijuana — Including Caffeine, Nicotine, and Alcohol* Little, Brown, Boston 1972

Brogan, D. W. *The American Character* Knopf, New York 1944

Brooks, John *The Fate of the Edsel and Other Business Ventures* Harper and Row, New York 1963

——— *The Great Leap: The Past Twenty-five Years in America* Harper and Row, New York 1966

——— *Once in Golconda: A True Drama of Wall Street 1920–1938* Harper and Row, New York 1969

Brooks, Thomas R. "The New Left Is Showing Its Age" *New York Times Magazine* June 14, 1969

——— "Voice of the New Campus 'Underclass'" *New York Times Magazine* November 7, 1965

Brzezinski, Zbigniew "America in the Technocratic Age" *Encounter* January 1968

Burns, James MacGregor *John Kennedy: A Political Profile* Harcourt, Brace, New York 1960

——— *Roosevelt: The Lion and the Fox* Harcourt, Brace, New York 1956

——— *Roosevelt: The Soldier of Freedom* Harcourt Brace Jovanovich, New York 1970

Butz, Otto "Defense of the Class of '58" *New York Times Magazine* May 25, 1958

Buxton, Frank, and Bill Owen *The Big Broadcast 1920–1950* (A new, revised, and greatly expanded edition of *Radio's Golden Age*) Viking, New York 1972

Byrnes, James F. *Speaking Frankly* Harper, New York 1947

Cantril, Hadley *The Invasion from Mars: A Study in the Psychology of Panic, With the Complete Script of the Famous Orson Welles Broadcast* Princeton University, Princeton 1940

Carlson, Avis D. "Deflating the Schools" *Harper's Magazine* November 1933

Carlson, John Roy *Under Cover: My Four Years in the Nazi Underworld of America* Blakiston, Philadelphia 1943

Carpenter, Liz *Ruffles and Flourishes* Doubleday, New York 1970

Chalmers, Allan K. *They Shall Be Free* Doubleday, New York 1951

Chambers, Whittaker *Witness* Random House, New York 1952

Chapman, C. C., and others *Crisis — Transportation* Caterpillar Tractor Company n.d.

Chayefsky, Paddy *Television Plays* Simon and Schuster, New York 1955

Chayes, Abram, and Jerome B. Wiesner, eds. *ABM: An Evaluation of the Decision to Deploy an Antiballistic Missile System* Signet, New York 1969

Chester, Lewis, Cal McCrystal, Stephen Aris, and William Shawcross *Watergate: The Full Inside Story* Ballantine, New York 1973

Childs, Marquis "Main Street Twenty Years After" *New Republic* January 18, 1933

——— "They Hate Roosevelt" *Harper's Magazine* May 1936

——— "They Still Hate Roosevelt" *New Republic* September 14, 1938

Clark, George R. "Beckerstown, 1932: An American Town Faces the Depression" *Harper's Magazine* October 1932

Clay, Lucius D. *Decision in Germany* Doubleday, New York 1950

Cohen, Morris R. "The Future of American Liberalism" in his *The Faith of a Liberal: Selected Essays* Holt, New York 1946

Cohn, David L. *The Good Old Days: A History of American Morals and Manners As Seen Through the Sears, Roebuck Catalog 1905 to the Present* Simon and Schuster, New York 1950

Collier's 1968 Year Book: Covering the Year 1967 Crowell-Collier, New York 1968

Colton, F. Barrows "The Geography of a Hurricane" *National Geographic Magazine* April 1939

Compton, Karl T. "If the Atomic Bomb Had Not Been Used" *Atlantic Monthly* December 1946

Cone, Fairfax M. *With All Its Faults: A Candid Account of Forty Years in Advertising* Little, Brown, Boston 1969

Congdon, Don, ed. *The Thirties: A Time to Remember* Simon and Schuster, New York 1962

Cooke, Alistair *A Generation on Trial: U.S.A. v. Alger Hiss* Knopf, New York 1950

Cowley, Malcolm "The Flight of the Bonus Army" *New Republic* August 17, 1932

Crane, Burton *A Century of Financial Advertising in the New York Times* New York Times, New York 1957

Daniels, Jonathan *The Time Between the Wars: Armistice to Pearl Harbor* Doubleday, New York 1966

Davis, Forrest *Huey Long: A Biography* Dodge, New York 1935

Davis, Kenneth S. *The Politics of Honor: A Biography of Adlai E. Stevenson* Putnam, New York 1967

"Democracy Has/Hasn't a Future . . . a Present" *New York Times Magazine* May 26, 1968

DeMott, Benjamin *Supergrow: Essays and Reports on Imagination in America* Dutton, New York 1969

Didion, Joan "Just Folks at a School for Nonviolence" *New York Times Magazine* February 27, 1966

Donovan, Robert J. *Eisenhower: The Inside Story* Harper, New York 1956

Dorman, Michael *We Shall Overcome: A Reporter's Eyewitness Account of the Year in Racial Strife and Triumph* Dell, New York 1964

Edey, Maitland A., ed. *This Fabulous Century: Sixty Years of American Life* (Volumes IV, 1930–1940, and V, 1940–1950) Time-Life Books, New York 1969

——— *TIME Capsule: A History of the Year Condensed from the Pages of TIME* (Volumes for 1933, 1941 and 1950, published 1967; for 1932, 1939, 1940, 1942, 1943, 1944, 1945, 1956 and 1959, published 1968; and for 1968, published 1969) Time-Life Books, New York

——— *1969: The Year in Review* Time-Life Books, New York 1970

"The Edsel" *Consumer Reports* January 1958

"The Edsel Story" *Consumer Reports* April 1958

Ehrlich, Paul R. *The Population Bomb* Ballantine, New York 1968

"Eight Scientists Protest Thomas Committee's Methods" *Bulletin of the Atomic Scientists* October 1948

Einstein, Albert, as told to Raymond Swing "Einstein on the Atomic Bomb" *Atlantic Monthly* November 1945

Eisenhower, Dwight D. *At Ease: Stories I Tell to Friends* Doubleday, New York 1967 (Avon, New York 1968)

——— *Crusade in Europe* Doubleday, New York 1948

Eisinger, Chester E., ed. *The 1940s: Profile of a Nation in Crisis* Doubleday Anchor Books, New York 1969

Evans, Rowland Jr., and Robert D. Novak "Nixonomics: How the Game Plan Went Wrong" *Saturday Review* July 1971

Farago, Ladislas *Patton: Ordeal and Triumph* Ivan Obolensky, New York 1963

Faulk, John Henry *Fear on Trial* Simon and Schuster, New York 1964

Fay, Stephen, Lewis Chester, and Magnus Linklater *Hoax: The Inside Story of the Howard Hughes – Clifford Irving Affair* Bantam, New York 1972

Federal Aid for Unemployment Relief: Hearings Before a Subcommittee of the Committee on Manufactures, U.S. Senate, 72nd Congress, 1st Session, on S.174 and S.262 U.S. Government Printing Office, Washington 1932

Federal Aid for Unemployment Relief: Hearings Before a Subcommittee of the Committee on Manufactures, U.S. Senate, 72nd Congress, 2nd Session, on S.5125 U.S. Government Printing Office, Washington 1932

Federal Cooperation in Unemployment Relief: Hearings Before a Subcommittee of the Committee on Manufactures, U.S. Senate, 72nd Congress, 1st Session, on S.4592 U.S. Government Printing Office, Washington 1932

Fehrenbach, T. R. *F.D.R.'s Undeclared War* McKay, New York 1967

Ferguson, Otis "The Spirit of Jazz" *New Republic* December 30, 1936

Fischer, John "Black Panthers and Their White Hero-Worshippers" *Harper's Magazine* August 1970

FitzGerald, Frances *Fire in the Lake: The Vietnamese and the Americans in Vietnam* Little, Brown, Boston 1972 (Vintage, New York 1973)

Fontaine, André *History of the Cold War: From the Korean War to the Present* Pantheon, New York 1969

Frady, Marshall "Gary, Indiana" *Harper's Magazine* August 1969

Friedan, Betty, *The Feminine Mystique* Norton, New York 1963

Fuller, Keith, project supervisor *The World in 1964: History As We Lived It* Associated Press, New York 1965, and similar volumes for 1965 (published 1966), 1966 (1967), 1967 (1968), 1968 (1968), 1969 (1970), 1970 (1971), 1971 (1972), 1972 (1973), and 1973 (1974)

Galbraith, John Kenneth *The Affluent Society* 2nd ed. Houghton Mifflin, Boston 1969

———— *The New Industrial State* Houghton Mifflin, Boston 1967 (Signet, New York 1968)

Garson, Barbara *MacBird!* Grove, New York 1966

Gellhorn, Walter *Security, Loyalty, and Science* Cornell University, Ithaca 1950

Glass, Remley J. "Gentlemen, the Corn Belt!" *Harper's Magazine* July 1933

Gold, Jay, ed. *The Swing Era (1936–1937: The Movies, Between Vitaphone and Video. 1940–1941: How It Was to Be Young Then. 1941–1942: Swing As a Way of Life)* Time-Life Records, New York 1970

Goldman, Eric F. *The Crucial Decade — and After: America, 1945–1960* Vintage, New York 1960

———— *The Tragedy of Lyndon Johnson,* Knopf, New York 1969

Good, Paul "Odyssey of a Man — and a Movement" *New York Times Magazine* June 25, 1967

Goodman, Jack, ed. *While You Were Gone: A Report on Wartime Life in the United States* Simon and Schuster, New York 1946

Goodman, Paul "The Chance for Popular Culture" *Poetry* June 1949

———— *Growing Up Absurd: Problems of Youth in the Organized Society* Knopf, New York 1956 (Vintage, New York 1960)

Goodman, Walter "The Question of Repression" *Commentary* August 1970

———— "When Black Power Runs the New Left" *New York Times Magazine* September 24, 1967

Goodstone, Tony, ed. *1929 Johnson Smith & Co. Catalogue* Chelsea House, New York 1970

Graham, Hugh Davis, and Ted Robert Gurr *Violence in America: Historical and Comparative Perspectives. A Report to the National Commission on the Causes and Prevention of Violence, June 1969* Signet, New York 1969

"The Great American Roadside" *Fortune* September 1934

"The Great Hurricane and Tidal Wave — Rhode Island: September 21, 1938" Providence Journal Company 1938

Greeley, Andrew N. "Turning Off the People" *New Republic* June 27, 1970

Greene, Gael *Sex and the College Girl* Dial, New York 1964

Greenfield, Jeff "A Member of the First TV Generation Looks Back" *New York Times Magazine* July 4, 1971

Griffith, Robert *The Politics of Fear: Joseph R. McCarthy and the Senate* University Press of Kentucky, Lexington 1970

Grosvenor, Gilbert "Washington Through the Years" *National Geographic Magazine* November 1931

Guiles, Fred Lawrence *Norma Jean: The Life of Marilyn Monroe* McGraw-Hill, New York 1969

Gunther, John *Roosevelt in Retrospect: A Profile in History* Harper, New York 1950 (Pyramid 1962)

Guthman, Edwin *We Band of Brothers* Harper and Row, New York 1971

Halberstam, David *The Best and the Brightest* Random House, New York 1972

Hargreaves, Robert *Superpower: A Portrait of America in the 1970s* St. Martin, New York 1973

Harris, Herbert *American Labor* Yale University, New Haven 1939

Hart, *see* Liddell Hart

Hayek, Friedrich A. *The Road to Serfdom* University of Chicago, Chicago 1944

Hechinger, Grace and Fred M. *Teen-Age Tyranny* Morrow, New York 1962 (Fawcett, New York 1963)

Heffernan, Joseph L. "The Hungry City: A Mayor's Experience with Unemployment" *Atlantic Monthly* May 1932

Heinl, Robert Debs Jr. *Victory at High Tide: The Inchon-Seoul Campaign* Lippincott, Philadelphia and New York 1968

Herbers, John "Communiqué from the Mississippi Front" *New York Times Magazine* November 8, 1964

Hersey, John *Hiroshima* Knopf, New York 1946

Hersh, Seymour M. "My Lai: The First Detailed Account of the Vietnam Massacre" *Harper's Magazine* May 1970

Hicks, Granville "On Leaving the Communist Party" *New Republic* October 4, 1939

Hillman, William *Mr. President: The First Publication from the Personal Diaries, Private Letters, Papers and Revealing Interviews of Harry S. Truman* Farrar, Straus and Young, New York 1952

Hiss, Alger *In the Court of Public Opinion* Knopf, New York 1957

Holmes, Clellon "This Is the Beat Generation" *New York Times Magazine* November 16, 1952

Hook, Sidney "The New Failure of Nerve" *Partisan Review* January–February 1943

Howe, Irving "Notes on Popular Culture" *Politics* Spring 1948

Hughes, Emmet John *The Ordeal of Power: A Political Memoir of the Eisenhower Years* Atheneum, New York 1963

"Hurricane Sweeps Across Northeast, Kills Hundreds" *Life* October 3, 1938

Irving, Clifford, with Richard Suskind *What Really Happened: His Untold Story of the Hughes Affair* Grove, New York 1972

Jackson, George *Soledad Brother: The Prison Letters of George Jackson* Coward-McCann, New York 1970

Jeffries, Ona Griffin *In and Out of the White House: From Washington to the Eisenhowers* Wilfred Funk, New York 1960

Johnson, Haynes, and others *The Bay of Pigs: The Leaders' Story of Brigade 2506* Norton, New York 1964

Johnson, Walter *1600 Pennsylvania Avenue: Presidents and the People Since 1929* Little, Brown, Boston 1963

Jungk, Robert *Brighter Than a Thousand Suns: A Personal History of the Atomic Scientists* Harcourt, Brace and World, New York 1958

Kaplan, Abraham "American Ethics and Public Policy" *Daedalus* Spring 1958

Kateb, George "The Political Thought of Herbert Marcuse" *Commentary* January 1970

Kendrick, Alexander *Prime Time: The Life of Edward R. Murrow* Little, Brown, Boston 1969

Kennan, George F. *American Diplomacy 1900–1950* Mentor, Chicago 1951

———— "America's Administrative Response to Its World Problems" *Daedalus* Spring 1958

———— [X] "The Sources of Soviet Conduct" *Foreign Affairs* July 1947

Kennedy, John F. *Public Messages, Speeches, and Statements of the President, January 1 to November 22, 1963* (in *Public Papers of the Presidents of the United States*) U.S. Government Printing Office, Washington 1964

Kennedy, Robert F. *Thirteen Days: A Memoir of the Cuban Missile Crisis* Norton, New York 1969 (Signet, New York 1969)

Khrushchev, Nikita S. *Khrushchev Remembers* Little, Brown, Boston 1970

Kimball, Penn " 'Dream Town' — Large Economy Size" *New York Times Magazine* December 14, 1952

Kinsey, Alfred C. and others *Sexual Behavior in the Human Male* Saunders, Philadelphia and London 1948

———— *Sexual Behavior in the Human Female* Saunders, Philadelphia and London 1953

Kirk, Russell *The Conservative Mind* Henry Regnery, Chicago 1953

Kluckhohn, Clyde "The Evolution of Contemporary American Values" *Daedalus* Spring 1958

———— "Mid-Century Manners and Morals" in *Twentieth Century Unlimited* (ed. Bruce Bliven) Lippincott, Philadelphia 1950

Korn, Jerry, ed. *This Fabulous Century* Volumes VI (1950–1960) and VII (1960–1970) Time-Life Books, New York 1970

Kronenberger, Louis *Company Manners: A Cultural Inquiry into American Life* Bobbs-Merrill, New York 1954

Langer, William L., ed. *An Encyclopedia of World History* Houghton Mifflin, Boston 1968

Lasagna, Louis, M.D. *The Doctors' Dilemmas* Gollancz, London 1962

Lash, Joseph P. *Eleanor and Franklin: The Story of Their Relationship, Based on Eleanor Roosevelt's Private Papers* Norton, New York 1971

Lasswell, Harold D. "The Universal Peril: Perpetual Crisis and the Garrison-Prison State" in *Perspectives on a Troubled Decade: Science, Philosophy, and Religion 1939–1949* (ed. Lyman Bryson, Louis Finkelstein, and R. M. MacIver) Harper, New York 1950

Lattimore, Owen *Ordeal by Slander* Little, Brown, Boston 1950

Laurence, William L. *Dawn Over Zero: The Story of the Atomic Bomb* Knopf, New York 1946

Lear, Martha "The Second Feminist Wave" *New York Times Magazine* March 10, 1968

Leary, John L. Jr. "If We Had the Dole" *American Magazine* December 1931

Leighton, George R. "And If the Revolution Comes . . . ?" *Harper's Magazine* March 1932

Leighton, Isabel, ed. *The Aspirin Age 1919–1941* Simon and Schuster, New York 1949

Lerner, Max *Tocqueville and American Civilization* Harper and Row, New York 1966

Lescohier, Don Divance *Working Conditions* (Volume III of *The History of Labor in the U.S. 1896–1932*) Macmillan, New York 1935

Leuchtenburg, William E., ed. *Franklin D. Roosevelt: A Profile* Hill and Wang, New York 1967

Levine, Mark L., George C. McNamee, and Daniel Greenberg eds. *The Tales of Hoffman, Edited from the Official Transcript,* Bantam, New York 1970

Levinson, Leonard Louis *Wall Street: A Pictorial History* Ziff-Davis, New York 1961

Lewin, Nathan "Kent State Revisited" *New Republic* August 8 and 25, 1973

Liddell Hart, B. H. *History of the Second World War* Putnam, New York 1970

Liebling, A. J. *The Press* Ballantine, New York 1961

———— "The Red Blonde Spy Queen" *New Yorker* August 28, 1948

Life, special double issue, *The 1960s: Decade of Tumult and Change*, vol. 47, no. 13

Lifton, Robert Jay, ed. *The Woman in America* Beacon, Boston 1965

Lilienthal, David E. *This I Do Believe* Harper, New York 1949

Lilly, Doris "Jackie's Fabulous Greek" *Look* June 30, 1970

Lindley, Betty and Ernest K. *A New Deal for Youth: The Story of the National Youth Administration* Viking, New York 1938

Lippmann, Walter *The Cold War: A Study in U.S. Foreign Policy* Harper, New York 1947

Lipset, Seymour Martin, and Earl Raab "The Non-Generation Gap" *Commentary* August 1970

Long-Term Economic Growth 1860–1965 (U.S. Department of Commerce, Bureau of the Census) U.S. Government Printing Office, Washington 1966

Lord, Walter *The Past That Would Not Die* Harper and Row, New York 1965

Loth, David *Crime in the Suburbs* Morrow, New York 1967

Love, Gilbert "College Students Are Beating the Depression" *School and Society* June 10, 1933

Lukas, J. Anthony "The Story So Far" *New York Times Magazine* July 22, 1973

———— "The Story Continued" *New York Times Magazine* January 13, 1974

Lynd, Albert *Quackery in the Public Schools* Little, Brown, Boston 1950

Lynd, Robert S. and Helen Merrell *Middletown in Transition: A Study in Cultural Conflicts* Harcourt, Brace and World, New York 1937

MacLeish, Archibald "The Irresponsibles" *Nation* May 18, 1940

Mailer, Norman *Miami and the Siege of Chicago: An Informal History of the Republican and Democratic Conventions of 1968* Signet, New York 1968

———— "The Steps of the Pentagon" *Harper's Magazine* March 1968

Manchester, William "The Great Bank Holiday" *Holiday* February 1960

———— *The Death of a President, November 20 – November 25, 1963* Harper and Row, New York 1967

———— "Our War in the Pacific" *Holiday* November 1960

———— *Portrait of a President: John F. Kennedy in Profile* Little, Brown, Boston 1962

Marcuse, Herbert *One-Dimensional Man: Studies in the Ideology of Advanced Industrial Society* Beacon, Boston 1964

Markel, Lester *World in Review* Rand McNally, New York 1972

Marshall, E. Kennerly Jr. "Historical Perspectives in Chemotherapy" in *Advances in Chemotherapy* (Volume I ed. Abraham Goldin and Frank Hawking) Academic Press, New York 1964

———— "The Revolution in Drug Therapy" *Johns Hopkins Magazine* June 1955

Marshall, George C. *European Initiative Essential to Economic Recovery* (Department of State Publication 2882, European Series 25) U.S. Government Printing Office, Washington 1947

Mauldin, Bill *Back Home* William Sloane, New York 1947

———— *Up Front* Holt, New York 1945

Mazo, Earl *Richard Nixon: A Political and Personal Portrait* Harper, New York 1959

McCarry, Charles *Citizen Nader* Saturday Review Press, New York 1972

McCarthy, Joe *Hurricane!* American Heritage Press, New York 1969

———— *The Remarkable Kennedys* Dial, New York 1960

McGinniss, Joe *The Selling of the President 1968* Trident, New York 1969

McLuhan, Marshall *The Gutenberg Galaxy: The Making of Typographic Man* Signet, New York 1962

———— *Understanding Media: The Extensions of Man* McGraw-Hill, New York 1964

McMahan, Harry W. " 'Best of the Year' TV Commercials" *Advertising Age* December 16, 1963

Mellor, William Bancroft *Patton: Fighting Man* Putnam, New York 1946

Mencken, H. L. *Newspaper Days 1899–1906* Knopf, New York 1945

Meryman, Richard "George McGovern Talks" *Life* July 7, 1972

Michael, Paul, ed. *The American Movies Reference Book: The Sound Era* Prentice-Hall, Englewood Cliffs, N.J. 1970

Michener, James A. *America vs. America: The Revolution in Middle-Class Values* Signet, New York 1968

Millis, Walter, ed. *The Forrestal Diaries* Viking, New York 1951

Mills, C. Wright *White Collar: The American Middle Classes* Oxford, New York 1951

Milstein, Tom "A Perspective on the Panthers" *Commentary* September 1970

Minehan, Thomas *Boy and Girl Tramps of America* Farrar and Rinehart, New York 1934

Mitchell, Broadus *Depression Decade: From New Era Through New Deal, 1929–1941* Rinehart, New York 1947

Mitford, Jessica *The Trial of Dr. Spock* Knopf, New York 1969

Modell, John "American Concentration Camps" *Pennsylvania Gazette* February 1974

Moley, Raymond *The First New Deal* Harcourt, Brace and World, New York 1966

Mooney, Booth *The Lyndon Johnson Story* Farrar, Straus, New York 1956

Moorehead, Alan *The Traitors* Scribner, New York 1952

Morison, Samuel Eliot *History of United States Naval Operations in World War II* (15 volumes) Little, Brown, Boston 1947–1962

———— *The Two-Ocean War: A Short History of the United States Navy in the Second World War* Little, Brown, Boston 1963

Morris, Richard B. *Encyclopedia of American History* Harper and Row, New York 1965

Mowry, George E. *The Urban Nation 1920–1960* Hill and Wang, New York 1965

Mullett, Charles F. *The British Empire* Holt, New York 1938

Murray, Henry A. "Individuality: The Meaning and Content of Individuality in Contemporary America" *Daedalus* Spring 1958

Murrow, Edward R. *This Is London* (ed. Elmer Davis) Simon and Schuster, New York 1941

Navasky, Victor S. "Notes on Cult; or, How to Join the Intellectual Establishment" *New York Times Magazine* March 27, 1966

Neary, John "Bombs Blast a Message of Hate" *Life* March 27, 1970

Nelson, Walter Henry *Small Wonder: The Amazing Story of the Volkswagen* Little, Brown, Boston 1965

"The Neurotic Trillionaire" *Economist* May 10, 1969

Neustadt, Richard E. *Presidential Power: The Politics of Leadership* Wiley, New York 1960

Niebuhr, Reinhold *The Children of Light and the Children of Darkness: A Vindication of Democracy and a Critique of Its Traditional Defense* Scribner, New York 1944

———— "Is There a Revival of Religion?" *New York Times Magazine* November 19, 1950

Nixon, Richard M. *Six Crises* Doubleday, New York 1962

"No One Has Starved" *Fortune* September 1932

Northeast Power Failure November 9 and 10, 1965: A Report to the President by the Federal Power Commission U.S. Government Printing Office, Washington 1965

O'Donnell, Kenneth P. "LBJ and the Kennedys" *Life* August 7, 1970

———— and David F. Powers, with Joseph McCarthy *"Johnny, We Hardly Knew Ye": Memories of John Fitzgerald Kennedy* Little, Brown, Boston 1972

One Hundred Years of Famous Pages from the New York Times, 1851–1951 Simon and Schuster, New York 1951

O'Neill, William L., ed. *American Society Since 1945* Quadrangle, Chicago 1969

Packard, Vance "Resurvey of 'Hidden Persuaders' " *New York Times Magazine* May 11, 1958

———— *The Sexual Wilderness* David McKay, New York 1968

Pater, Alan F. and Jason R. *What They Said in 1969: The Yearbook of Spoken Opinion* Monitor, Beverly Hills, California 1970

Pauling, Linus, and Edward Teller "Fallout and Disarmament" *Daedalus* Spring 1958

Phillips, Cabell *From the Crash to the Blitz* Macmillan, New York 1969

———— *The Truman Presidency: The History of a Triumphant Succession* Macmillan, New York 1966

Pound, Arthur "Bankruptcy Mill" *Atlantic Monthly* February 1932

Powers, Francis Gary "Francis Gary Powers Tells His Story" *New York Times Magazine* April 19, 1970

———— with Curt Gentry *Operation Overflight: The U-2 Spy Pilot Tells His Story for the First Time* Holt, Rinehart, and Winston, New York 1970

Pusey, Merlo J. *Eisenhower, The President* Macmillan, New York 1956

Pyle, Ernie *This Is Your War* Holt, New York 1943

Pynchon, Thomas "A Journey into the Mind of Watts" *New York Times Magazine* June 12, 1966 (Pyramid 1966)

Raskin, A. H. "The Berkeley Affair: Mr. Kerr vs. Mr. Savio & Co." *New York Times Magazine* February 14, 1965

———— "Report on the Communist Party (U.S.A.)" *New York Times Magazine* March 30, 1947

Relief for Unemployed Transients: Hearings Before a Subcommittee of the Committee on Manufactures, U.S. Senate, 72nd Congress, 2nd Session, on S.5121 U.S. Government Printing Office, Washington 1933

Report of the President's Commission on the Assassination of President John F. Kennedy U.S. Government Printing Office, Washington 1964

Report on the International Control of Atomic Energy, A (Prepared for the Secretary of State's Committee on Atomic Energy by a board of consultants) Doubleday, New York 1946

Ridgeway, James "The Cops and the Kids" *New Republic* September 7, 1968

Ridgway, Matthew B. (as told to Harold H. Martin) *Soldier* Harper, New York 1956

Riesman, David, in collaboration with Reuel Denney and Nathan Glazer *The Lonely Crowd: A Study of the Changing American Character* Yale, New Haven 1950

Roosevelt, James, and Sidney Shalett *Affectionately, F.D.R.: A Son's Story of a Lonely Man* Harcourt, Brace, New York 1959

"Roosevelt Wins" *Nation* July 13, 1932

Rosenthal, A. M., and Arthur Gelb, eds. *The Night the Lights Went Out* Signet, New York 1965

Ross, Irwin *The Loneliest Campaign: The Truman Victory of 1948* Signet, New York 1968

Rossiter, Clinton *The American Presidency* Harcourt, Brace, New York 1956 (Mentor, New York 1960)

Rostow, W. W. "The American National Style" *Daedalus* Spring 1958

Rovere, Richard H. *Affairs of State: The Eisenhower Years* Farrar, Straus, and Cudahy, New York 1956

———— *Senator Joe McCarthy* Harcourt, Brace, New York 1959

———— *Waist Deep in the Big Muddy* Little, Brown, Boston 1968

———— and Arthur M. Schlesinger Jr. *The General and the President: And the Future of American Foreign Policy* Farrar, Straus and Young, New York 1951

Roy, Jules *The Battle of Dienbienphu* Harper, New York 1965

Ruffner, Frederick G. Jr., ed. *National Organizations of the United States* (Volume I of *Encyclopedia of Organizations*) Gale Research, Detroit 1968

Salisbury, Harrison E. *The Shook-Up Generation* Harper, New York 1958

Sanders, Ed *The Family: The Story of Charles Manson's Dune Buggy Attack Battalion* Avon, New York 1972

Scheinfeld, Amram "Kinsey's Study of Female Sexual Behavior" *Cosmopolitan* September 1953

Schlesinger, Arthur M. Jr. *The Coming of the New Deal* Houghton Mifflin, Boston 1958

———— *The Crisis of the Old Order* Houghton Mifflin, Boston 1957

———— *The Politics of Upheaval* Houghton Mifflin, Boston 1960

———— *A Thousand Days: John F. Kennedy in the White House* Houghton Mifflin, Boston 1965

Schrag, Peter "The Forgotten American" *Harper's Magazine* August 1969

———— "Is Main Street Still There?" *Saturday Review* January 17, 1970

Schulberg, Budd *The Disenchanted* Random House, New York 1950

Schwarz, Jordan *1933: Roosevelt's Decision. The United States Leaves the Gold Standard* Chelsea House, New York 1969

Servan-Schreiber, J. J. *The American Challenge* Avon, New York 1969

Sevareid, Eric "The American Dream" *Look* July 9, 1968

———— *Not So Wild a Dream* Knopf, New York 1946

Shannon, David A., ed. *The Great Depression* Prentice-Hall, Englewood Cliffs, N.J. 1960

Shapiro, Nat, ed. *Popular Music: An Annotated Index of American Popular Songs* (Volume I, 1950–1959) Adrian Press, New York 1964

Sheehan, Neil, Hedrick Smith, E. W. Kenworthy, and Fox Butterfield *The Pentagon Papers* Bantam, New York 1971

Sherrill, Robert *Gothic Politics in the Deep South: Stars of the New Confederacy* Ballantine, New York 1968

Shirer, William L. *The Rise and Fall of the Third Reich: A History of Nazi Germany* Simon and Schuster, New York 1960

Shuster, Alvin, ed. *Washington: The New York Times Guide to the Nation's Capital* Robert B. Luce, Washington 1967

Sidey, Hugh *John F. Kennedy, President* Atheneum, New York 1963

Silber, Irwin, ed. *Songs America Voted By* Stackpole, Harrisburg, Pennsylvania 1971

Simon, Rita James, ed. *As We Saw the Thirties* University of Illinois, Urbana 1967

Smith, A. Robert, and Eric Sevareid *Washington: Magnificent Capital* Doubleday, New York 1965

Smith, Gene *The Shattered Dream: Herbert Hoover and the Great Depression* Morrow, New York 1970

Smith, John M., and Tim Cankwell, eds. *The World Encyclopedia of the Film* World, New York 1972

Sorensen, Theodore C. *Kennedy* Harper and Row, New York 1965

Soule, George "Are We Going to Have a Revolution?" *Harper's Magazine* August 1932

Sparks, Fred *The $20,000,000 Honeymoon: Jackie and Ari's First Year* Dell, New York 1970

Sparrow, John *After the Assassination: A Positive Appraisal of the Warren Report* Chilmark Press, New York 1967

Spectorsky, A. C. *The Exurbanites* Lippincott, Philadelphia and New York 1955

Speer, Albert *Inside the Third Reich* Macmillan, New York 1970

Spivak, John L. *Shrine of the Silver Dollar* Modern Age, New York 1940

Spock, Benjamin, M.D. *The Common Sense Book of Baby and Child Care* Duell, Sloan and Pearce, New York 1945

Stearns, Marshall *The Story of Jazz* Oxford, New York 1956

Steinbeck, John *Travels with Charley: In Search of America* Viking, New York 1962 (Bantam, New York 1963)

Steiner, Paul *The Stevenson Wit and Wisdom* Pyramid, New York 1965

Stevenson, Adlai *Speeches of Adlai Stevenson* Random House, New York 1952

Stimson, Henry L. "The Decision to Use the Atomic Bomb" *Harper's Magazine* February 1947

Storr, Anthony *Human Aggression* Atheneum, New York 1968

Straight, Michael *Trial by Television* Beacon, Boston 1954

Streit, Peggy "Why They Fight for the P.A.T." *New York Times Magazine* September 20, 1964

Sullivan, Frank *A Pearl in Every Oyster* Little, Brown, Boston 1938

Sulzberger, C. L., ed. *The American Heritage Picture History of World War II* Simon and Schuster, New York 1966

"A Survey of Unemployed Alumni" *School and Society* March 10, 1934

Symes, Lillian "Blunder on the Left: The Revolution and the American Scene" *Harper's Magazine* December 1933

Szulc, Tad "The Spy Compulsion" *New York Times Magazine* June 3, 1973

Tate, Allen "The Man of Letters in the Modern World" *Hudson Review* Autumn 1952

Terkel, Studs *Hard Times: An Oral History of the Great Depression* Pantheon, New York 1970

Tessler, Mark A., and Ronald D. Hedlund "Students Aren't Crazies" *New Republic* September 12, 1970

Thayer, George *The War Business: The International Trade in Armaments* Simon and Schuster, New York 1969

Thompson, Hunter S. "The 'Hashbury' Is the Capital of the Hippies" *New York Times Magazine* May 14, 1967

Time, Editors of *Live Them Again: The Three Decades from Flappers to Flying Saucers, 1923–1953* Simon and Schuster, New York 1953

Tocqueville, Alexis de *Democracy in America* ed. Phillips Bradley (Vol. I) Vintage, New York 1945

Toland, John *But Not in Shame: The Six Months After Pearl Harbor* Random House, New York 1961

Truman, Harry S. *Memoirs,* volumes I (*Year of Decisions,* 1955) and II (*Years of Trial and Hope,* 1956) Doubleday, New York

Truman, Margaret, with Margaret Cousins *Souvenir: Margaret Truman's Own Story* McGraw-Hill, New York 1956

"200,000 Trailers" *Fortune* March 1937

Unemployment in the United States: Hearings Before a Subcommittee of the Committee on Labor, House of Representatives, 72nd Congress, 1st Session, on H.R.206, H.R.6011, H.R.6066 U.S. Government Printing Office, Washington 1932

Van Camp, Sarah "Growing Up in D.C. in Song and Story" (unpublished manuscript)

Vandenberg, Arthur H. *The Private Papers of Senator Vandenberg,* ed. Arthur H. Vandenberg Jr. Houghton Mifflin, Boston 1952

Vanderlip, Frank A. "What About the Banks?" *Saturday Evening Post* November 5, 1932

Villard, Oswald Garrison "An Open Letter to Governor Roosevelt" *Nation* May 11, 1932

———— "Roosevelt and Hoover Militarists Both" *Nation* October 26, 1932

Vorse, Mary Heaton "Rebellion in the Cornbelt: American Farmers Beat Their Plowshares into Swords" *Harper's Magazine* December 1932

Walker, Daniel *Rights in Conflict* Signet, New York 1968

Walker, John and Katherine *The Washington Guidebook* Metro Publishers, Washington 1969

Walker, Stanley " 'Book Branding' — A Case History" *New York Times Magazine* July 12, 1953

Warner, W. Lloyd, and others *Yankee City* Yale University, New Haven 1963

———— and others *Social Class in America: A Manual of Procedure for the Measurement of Social Status* Harper Torchbooks, New York 1960

Washington, City and Capital (Federal Writers' Project, Works Progress Administration, American Guide Series) U.S. Government Printing Office, Washington 1937

"Washington and Its Approaches" *Saturday Evening Post* December 20, 1930

Weaver, Richard M. *Ideas Have Consequences* University of Chicago, Chicago 1948

Webb, John N. *The Migratory-Casual Worker* (WPA Research Monograph VII) U.S. Government Printing Office, Washington 1937

Webbink, Paul "Unemployment in the United States, 1930–1940" *Papers and Proceedings of the American Economic Association* February 1941

Weber, Max *The Protestant Ethic and the Spirit of Capitalism* Scribner, New York 1958

Wecter, Dixon *The Age of the Great Depression* Macmillan, New York 1948

Wertham, Frederic *Seduction of the Innocent* Rinehart, New York 1954

West, Rebecca *The New Meaning of Treason* Viking, New York 1964 (Time-Life Books 1966)

White, Theodore H. *The Making of the President 1960* Atheneum, New York 1961
——— *The Making of the President 1964* Atheneum, New York 1965
——— *The Making of the President 1968* Atheneum, New York 1969
——— *The Making of the President 1972* Atheneum, New York 1973

White, William S. *The Professional: Lyndon B. Johnson* Houghton Mifflin, Boston 1964 (Crest, New York 1964)

Whitehead, Donald F. *The FBI Story: A Report to the People* Random House, New York 1956

White House Historical Association *The White House: An Historic Guide* Washington 1962

Whiteside, Thomas "Corridor of Mirrors: The Television Editorial Process, Chicago" *Columbia Journalism Review* Winter 1968/1969

"Who's in the Army Now?" *Fortune* September 1935

Whyte, William H. Jr. *The Organization Man* Simon and Schuster, New York 1956 (Anchor, New York)

Wiener, Norbert "A Scientist Rebels" *Atlantic Monthly* January 1947

Willkie, Wendell *One World* Simon and Schuster, New York 1943

Wills, Garry *Nixon Agonistes: The Crisis of the Self-Made Man* Houghton Mifflin, Boston 1970 (Signet, New York 1971)

Wilson, Sloan *The Man in the Gray Flannel Suit* Simon and Schuster, New York 1955

Wish, Harvey *Contemporary America* 4th ed. Harper and Row, New York 1966

Wolfe, Thomas *You Can't Go Home Again* Harper, New York 1934

Wolfert, Ira *American Guerrilla in the Philippines* Simon and Schuster, New York 1945

Wolff, Perry Sidney *A Tour of the White House with Mrs. John F. Kennedy* (television program) Doubleday, New York 1962

"Women in Business" *Fortune* September 1935

X [See George F. Kennan]

Yank, Editors of, selected by *The Best from Yank* World, Cleveland 1945

"Youth in College" *Fortune* June 1936

Zeiger, Henry A. *Inquest! Ted Kennedy – Mary Jo Kopechne: Prosecution or Persecution?* Tower, New York 1970

Copyright
Acknowledgments

Index

AAA (Agricultural Adjustment Administration). *See* agriculture
Abel, Rudolf, 876n
Abernathy, Ralph, 941, 1136, 1207
ABM (anti-ballistic missile), 1163–64
Abplanalp, Robert H., 1161
Abrams, Gen. Creighton, 334, 948, 1126, 1181, 1208
Abruzzi, Dr. William, 1213
Abt, John, 84, 503
Abzug, Bella, 1300
Acheson, Alice (Mrs. Dean), 611–12
Acheson, Dean, 202, 228, 250, 260, 437, 475, 532, 596, 612, 644, 651, 748; and New Deal, 83, 96, 105, 138; on FDR, 325, 354; on Truman, 369, 413, 446; and MacArthur, 406, 548, 559, 560, 561; and Soviet-American friendship, 411; accusations against, 411n, 491–92; and aid to Europe, 433, 437, 438–39; and collapse of Kuomintang, 487–88; and Hiss case, 501, 511–12; Far East policy, 517–20, 657, 916, 1250; and Korean War, 531, 533–34, 536, 549, 555; hostility of, toward Communism, 536–37; and Vietnam, 537, 647, 680; and nuclear weapons, 572, 679; Republican attacks on, 606; and Formosa, 744; JFK and, 892, 911; and Cuban missile crisis, 960–65
Acheson, Mary. *See* Bundy, Mary Acheson
Ackley, Gardner, 1053
Adamic, Louis, 38
Adams, Henry, 1296
Adams, John G., 707
Adams, Phelps, 203
Adams, Rachel (Mrs. Sherman), 639, 836, 837, 839, 843
Adams, Sherman, 679, 769, 801, 868, 876, 879; and 1952 presidential campaign, 608–609, 632–33, 639; as chief of Eisenhower's staff, 647, 651–52, 653, 656, 672, 764, 765, 768; on Dulles,

661–62; on Korea, 662; and Eisenhower's illnesses, 754–57, 811; on Sputnik, 788; Eisenhower Doctrine, 822, 823; and Goldfine scandal, 834–44
Adenauer, Konrad, 597, 857, 859, 964
Adjusted Compensation Act of 1924, 3
Adkins, Homer M., 298
adolescents. *See* teen-agers
Adonis, Joe, 597
advertising: in Depression, 25, 27, 149; and radio polls, 190, 191; in World War II, 284–87, 304–305, 593; postwar, 424–25; (1950s) 593–95, 775–76; Nixon on campaign use of, 720–21; and the young, 723–25, 1101–1102; commercials (1963), 998. *See also* exploitation; public relations
AFL. *See* American Federation of Labor
Aga Khan III, 762
Aging, Administration on, 1042
Agnew, Spiro T., 108, 246–47, 476, 1039, 1081, 1100; and youth, 1097, 1175, 1211, 1214, 1216; in campaigns, 1141, 1146, 1218–21, 1282; attacks mass media, 1165
agriculture, 1042; (1930s) 5, 32–33, 36–37, 137, 1091; and farmers' revolt, 58–60; and AAA (Agricultural Adjustment Administration), 80, 84, 85, 90, 98, 100, 107, 137, 141; and dust storms, 98–100; and REA, 106, 238; (1940) 238–39; "breadbasket of the world," 290; World War II, 302–303; (1950s) 732, 766, 777; (1960s) 1002, 1091–92; and technology, 1091–92; (1970s) 1225; dairy industry, 1233
Ahbez, Eden, 483
Aiken, George D., 1019, 1125, 1180
Aiken, Howard, 431
AIP (American Independent Party), 1236
aircraft and air power, 4, 178, 202, 222, 342, 345, 596; German, 217, 218, 278, 285; and U.S. production, 246, 274,

293, 296; Japanese, 263, 272, 343; Soviet, 530, 531, 967, 968; and Bay of Pigs, 897, 901–902, 905. *See also* Air Force, U.S.; air transportation
Air Force, U.S., 231, 645, 678, 1094; expansion, 178, 202; in battles in Pacific, 270–72, 342, 345–46; and delivery of atom bomb, 372–74, 376, 380, 381; Strategic Air Command, 383, 574–75, 810, 1036, 1122; and Berlin airlift, 441–443; reconnaissance flights, 488, 876, 1179 (*see also* U–2 affair *below*); in Vietnam, 680, 1049, 1051, 1056–57, 1209, 1270–71, 1293–95; in space race, 814; and U–2 affair, 867–76; in Cuban missile crisis, 959, 961, 964–66; at Gulf of Tonkin, 1017; in Cambodia, 1210–1211. *See also* aircraft and air power; air transportation
Air Force Academy, 692
air transportation: (1930s) 8, 34, 49, 67, 174; helicopters, 240, 293; (1940s) 241; (1950s) 596, 818; (1960s) 1002, 1036, 1039; and hijacking, 1182, 1192, 1260
Alcorn, Meade, 843, 844
Aldrin, Col. Edwin E. "Buzz" Jr., 1157–1159
Alejos, Roberto, 865
Ali, Muhammad (Cassius Clay), 810, 1036
Allen, Fred, 191, 585
Allen, Frederick Lewis, 102, 144, 167, 247, 291, 396
Allen, Hervey: *Anthony Adverse,* 97
Allen, Oscar A., 74
Allen, Robert S., 135
Allen, Steve, 588
Allen, Woody, 1190
Allies, World War II, 204, 216, 266, 271; in Europe, 273, 277–80, 329–34, 909; summit meetings of, 316, 327, 348, 674
Alpert, Jane Lauren, 1166
Alpert, Richard, 1112
Alphand, Nicole, 1000
Alsop, John, 625, 627
Alsop, Joseph, 446, 464–65, 470, 525–26, 532, 766
Alsop, Stewart, 60, 446, 464–65, 470, 525–526, 625
Alsos (intelligence unit). *See* atomic weapons
Alvarez, Luis W., 213, 374, 571
Ameche, Don, 190
Amerasia (journal), 489–90, 494, 521
America First movement, 220, 221, 223, 228, 569, 1300. *See also* isolationism
American Bankers Association, 103. *See also* banks
American Bar Association, 676
American Civil Liberties Union (ACLU), 111, 206, 250, 403, 490, 582, 1229, 1290; and the Japanese, 300–301; and the draft, 1073, 1122
American Communist party. *See* Communist party
American Federation of Labor (AFL), 56, 110, 130, 1164; (1930s) 37, 131, 134–

135, 158; and CIO, 135, 153–56, 157; and auto workers, 153, 155, 156
American Friends Service Committee, 41, 92
American Girl magazine, 723
American Independent Party (AIP), 1236
American Legion, 17, 57, 219, 582, 718, 1055
American Liberty League. *See* Liberty League, American
American Magazine, 25, 241
American Medical Association (AMA), 63, 239, 474, 1041, 1194
American Mercury, 56, 1119, 1120
American Nazi Party, 953, 1055, 1236
American Red Cross, 188
Americans for Democratic Action (ADA), 389, 448, 457, 605, 953, 977
American Society of Newspaper Editors, 661, 685, 906
American Student Union, 127
American Youth Congress, 224
Ameringer, Oscar, 58–59
Amtorg (Russian trading agency), 35
Anami, Gen. S., 384–86
Anastasia, Albert, 694
Anderson, Jack, 839, 1234, 1235
Anderson, Marian, 245
Anderson, Maxwell, 820
Anderson, Robert, 879
Anderson, Sherwood, 12, 57, 246
Andrews, Bert, 637; *Washington Witch Hunt,* 496
Andrews, Dana, 427
Andrews, Julie, 217, 218, 333, 369
Angelino, Joseph T., 16
Angoff, Charles, 943
Annenberg, Walter, 305
anti-Americanism. *See* image of U.S. abroad
anti-ballistic missile (ABM), 1163–64
Anti-Defamation League of B'nai B'rith, 1077
anti-Semitism: in U.S., 8, 107, 110–11, 115, 176, 242, 243, 318, 483, 1077; in Germany, 336. *See also* Jews
Anzio, battle for, 329–30
Apollo 11 (moon landing),1156–59
Appalachia, 1042
Arab Republic of Egypt. *See* Egypt
Arden, Eve, 586
Arena, Dominick J., 1185
Arizona Republic, 257
Arkansas Gazette, 809
Arliss, George, 198
armed forces, U.S.: and military spending, 274 (*see also* budget, federal); unification of, 392, 409, 531; strength, 409, 531; in Korea, 535, 537–50, 555; and NATO, 569. *See also* Air Force, U.S.; Army, U.S.; Navy, U.S.; Marine Corps, U.S.; Vietnam and Vietnam War
arms race, 572, 1011; Einstein and, 335–336, 512, 571, 574; and "massive retaliation," 646–47, 679, 696, 1179; Eisenhower and, 660–61, 876–77
Armstrong, Karleton Lewis, 1212n
Armstrong, Neil A., 1157–59

Army, U.S., 284, 953; (1930s) 6, 57, 125–127, 177–78, 202; and demonstrations, 11–18, 1060, 1142, 1149, 1229; and ROTC, 126, 127, 388, 1098; blacks in, 242, 737; troop brutalities, 269 (see also war crimes and atrocities); and military spending, 274 (see also budget, federal); and draft evasion, 283 (see also draft); demobilization, 320, 387–88, 405–10, 430, 531; new look, 597, 679; Eisenhower reduces, 678–79; -McCarthy hearings, 700–16; and Cuban missile crisis, 964; and demonstrators, 1060, 1142, 1149, 1229; civilian intervention with, 1178–79. See also Air Force, U.S.; Green Berets; Korea and Korean War; National Guard; Pentagon; Vietnam and Vietnam War; World War II

Army and Navy Register, 87

Army Special Forces troops. See Green Berets

Arnaz, Desi, 694

Arnett, Peter, 1054

Arno, Peter, 164, 477

Arnold, Edward, 1092

Arnold, Gen. Henry H. "Hap," 178

Arnold, Martin, 1208

Arnold, Thurmond, 84

arson. See crime

art(s): future of, 246; painting by numbers, 645; and the White House, 893; Mona Lisa in U.S., 1000; psychedelic and pop, 1037; National Foundation for, 1042. See also books; music and musicians; theater

Artime, Dr. Manuel Francisco, 862–63

Arvey, Jacob M., 448, 880

Asbell, Bernard, 359

Asch, Nathan, 99

Ashbrook, John M., 1281

Ashmore, Harry Scott, 809

Askew, Reubin, 1284

Associated Press, 81, 118, 522

Astaire, Fred, 68, 98

Astor, Vincent, 71

astrology, 1191

astronauts. See space travel and satellite programs

Athenia, sinking of, 204

Atkinson, Ti-Grace, 1106, 1300

Atlanta Constitution, 334–35, 1247

Atlantic Charter, 234, 297

Atlantic Monthly, 41, 56

Atomic Energy, Joint Congressional Committee on, 572

Atomic Energy Commission (AEC), 314, 571–72, 693, 695–700, 1094

atomic weapons: early development, 87, 211, 213–16, 792; moral implications, 208, 338–40, 375, 376, 570–73, 576; Germany and, 210–13, 275, 309, 313, 336–39; and secrecy, 275, 312, 372, 373, 376; Manhattan Project, 309–15, 337, 338, 339, 348, 365, 375, 792; and espionage, 309, 313–14, 372–75, 379, 493, 499–502; Alsos and, 315, 336, 337–338; Einstein warns against, 335–36, 512; means of delivery, 372–74, 376,

380, 381; bomb described, 374, 383; decision to use bomb, 375, 376, 379–380; bomb tests, 375–78, 699–700 (see also test ban below); at Hiroshima and Nagasaki, 381, 382, 384; and armament control, 411, 412, 1218; USSR and, 488–89, 510, 512, 517, 571, 574, 597, 912–13; and international politics, 569–570, 854–55; H-bomb, 570–76, 699–700, 769, 792, 797; and troop maneuvers, 597; and "massive retaliation," 646–47, 679, 696, 1179; and Oppenheimer case, 695–700; and strontium 90, 699; "Open Skies" proposal, 748, 750–751; test ban, 769–70, 909, 913, 971, 985–86; and nationwide shelter program, 796, 912; and Cuban missile crisis, 958–971; as campaign issue, 1028; bombs submerged off Spain, 1036. See also fallout; nuclear power

Attica prison revolt, 1239–47

Attlee, Clement, 549

Aubrey, James T. Jr., 1037

Auden, W. H., 246

Augusta (warship), 233, 234, 411

Austen, Jane, paperback edition, 589

Austin, Warren, 231, 532, 533

Australia, defense of, 266–74, 340–43

automation. See technology

automobile(s), 199; industry and unions, 7, 34, 119, 153–56, 246, 758, 816, 818–819, 1092, 1253; travel, 7, 67, 100, 118–19, 241, 294, 1002, 1123; and highways, 169, 241, 758, 766, 883, 1002; VWs, 198, 483, 819; models, 240, 595; teen-agers and, 722; compacts, 758, 819; Ralph Nader and, 1256

Autry, Gene, 197

Avery, Sewell, 96, 294

Axis powers, 222, 230, 231, 264, 278. See also Germany; Japan

Baber, Eric, 784

Bacall, Lauren, 366

Bacher, Robert F., 377

backlash: against black militance, 1020–1021, 1039, 1065, 1069–70, 1078, 1081; against youth, 1098–1100

Badillo, Herman, 1243, 1245

Badoglio, Marshal Pietro, 279

Baer, Buddy, 283

Baer, Max, 98

Baez, Joan, 1097, 1102, 1106

Baghdad Pact, 823. See also CENTO

Bailey, Dorothy, 496–98, 499

Bailey, Jim, 758

Bailey, John, 448

Bailey, Pearl, 244

Baker, Bonnie, 205

Baker, Charles P., 383

Baker, Howard Jr., 1039

Baker, Newton D., 19–20, 22, 138

Baker, Norma Jean. See Monroe, Marilyn

Baker, Robert G., 1011

Baldwin, Alfred C. III, 1275–78

Baldwin, Hanson W., 406, 664, 709

Baldwin, James, 60, 983–84, 999, 1149

Baldwin, Roger N., 206
Ball, George, 1075; and Vietnam, 920, 921, 988, 990, 991, 1046, 1047, 1051; and Cuban missile crisis, 960, 961, 963, 966, 970
Ball, Lucille, 694
Baltimore Sun, 73, 164, 243, 334, 526, 707
bands and bandleaders. *See* music and musicians
Bankhead, William B., 177
banks: and RFC, 24 (*see also* Reconstruction Finance Corporation); manipulations, 44, 45, 46; failures and closings, 53, 72–76; holiday (1933), 78–81; FDR and American Bankers Association, 104; Swiss, in Hughes hoax, 1264
Bao Dai, Prince, 680
Bardot, Brigitte, 590, 644, 689
Barker, Bernard L., 1237, 1238, 1274, 1276–78, 1279, 1288
Barker, Col. Frank A. Jr., 1176, 1177
Barker, "Ma," 95
Barkley, Alben W., 352, 608; FDR and, 141, 152, 168, 324; as candidate and Vice President, 319, 454–55, 621
Barnett, Ross, 945–50, 978, 979, 1000
Barnum, Phineas Taylor, 1259
Barrett, William, 246
Barrie, James M., 68
Barrington, Lowell, 236
Barrow, Clyde, 95
Barry, Bill, 1129
Barrymore, John Jr., 597
Barrymore, Lionel, 121
Barton, Bruce, 176, 320; *The Man Nobody Knows*, 25
Baruch, Bernard, 47, 51, 171, 324, 436, 654, 748
Basie, Count, 248
Bataan. *See* Philippine Islands
Batista, Gen. Fulgencio, 597, 860–61, 862, 865
Batten, Barton, Durstine, and Osborn, 631, 695
Baugham, U. E., 885
Baxter, Anne, 486
Bayh, Birch, 1019
Bay of Pigs. *See* Cuba
Beard, Charles A., 73, 81, 125, 139
Beard, Dita, 1234, 1281
"beat" generation, 726–29
Beatles, The, 954, 1000, 1100, 1102, 1112
Beauvoir, Simone de, 761
Beaverbrook, Lord, 333
Beck, David, 390, 391, 820
Beebe, Dr. William, 68
Beecher, William, 1216
Beedy, Carroll L., 86
BEF. *See* Bonus Expeditionary Force
Behrens, Earl, 619
Belafonte, Harry, 643, 984
Bel Geddes, Norman, 199
Belgium, 216, 251
Bell, David Elliot, 929, 1007
Bell, Elliott, 462
Belli, Melvin, 1038
Bellow, Saul, 60, 1056

"Bender, Frank" (CIA agent). *See* CIA
Bender, George, 717
Bendetsen, Maj. Karl R., 299
Bendiner, M. Robert, 791
Benedict, Ruth, 589
Benes, Eduard, 183
Benét, Stephen Vincent, 51
Ben-Gurion, David, 763–64, 765
Bennett, Harry, 154
Bennett, Rear Adm. Rawson, 788
Bennett, Wallace F., 1123
Benny, Jack, 98, 198n, 586
Benson, Ezra Taft, 648, 649, 650, 671, 758
Bentley, Elizabeth, 459, 462, 493, 502
Bererdt, John, 943
Bergen, Edgar, 121, 190, 191
Berger, Meyer, 199
Bergman, Ingrid, 303, 486
Bergoff, Pearl, 131
Beria, Lavrenti P., 595
Berigan, Bunny, 248
Berkeley, Busby, 66, 68, 88, 120, 1224
Berkeley, California, 1225, 1226; demonstrations at, 849, 1054, 1098, 1191; Free Speech Movement, 1033–34
Berkeley Barb, 954
Berkner, Lloyd, 787
Berle, Adolf, 84, 105, 197, 773
Berle, Milton, 66, 585, 586, 759
Berlin: fall of, 369; blockade and airlift, 441–43, 464, 909; crises, (1959) 855, 857, 874, (1961) 909–13; Wall built, 912–13
Berman, Dr. Edgar F., 1196
Bernhardt, Michael, 1177
Bernstein, Leonard, 102, 304, 1139, 1299
Bernstein, Morey: *The Search for Bridey Murphy*, 644
Berrigan, Philip, 1260, 1299, 1300
best sellers. *See* books
Bethe, Hans, 572, 573
Bettelheim, Bruno, 1167
Bevin, Ernest, 439
Biafra, 1122
Bidault, Georges, 440, 677, 684, 685
Biddle, Anthony D. Jr., 203
Biddle, Francis, 133, 297, 299, 318
Bigart, Homer, 511, 548, 922
Bikel, Theodore, 1077
Bilbo, Theodore G., 57, 114, 116, 243
Billboard magazine, 759
Bingham, Barry, 611
Bingham, Hiram, 14, 1203
Bingham, J. A., 12
Bingham, Stephen Mitchell, 1203
Birch, Capt. John, and Birch Society, 393, 782, 952–53, 954, 1194
Bird, Caroline, 41, 67, 239, 428, 1001, 1090
Birdsong, T. B., 945, 946
Birmingham, Alabama, civil rights campaign (1963), 976–978
Birmingham News, 938
birth control, 998, 1035; the church and, 847, 850, 1108; and the pill, 849–50, 1090, 1109; and abortion legislation, 1194. *See also* population explosion

birth rate, 781, 1021
Bishop, John Peale, 246
Bissell, Richard, 895, 905
Black, Hugo, 17, 106, 152, 297, 301, 945
Black, Shirley Temple. *See* Temple, Shirley
black(s), 65, 167, 199, 238, 245; (1930s)
  7, 21–22, 112, 119, 207; education, 7,
  107, 735–36, 936, 944–52, 979–81,
  1021; in music, 119, 244; vote, 141,
  142, 457, 882–83, 1219; in armed
  forces, 242–43, 283, 447; in sports, 243,
  283, 1036; economic status, 243, 936,
  937, 1021–22, 1078, 1150; as political
  issue, 304, 452, 458; "invisible," 734;
  and 1954 Supreme Court decision, 734–
  738; in Montgomery bus boycott, 740–
  743; and Republican party, 770, 1147;
  and Little Rock, 800–10; population,
  849, 877, 1021–22, 1062, 1069, 1078,
  1080, 1150; and "Uncle Tomism," 983,
  1059; in North, 1020–22; "revolution,"
  1021, 1069, 1077 (*see also* riots and demonstrations); Freedom Summer, 1021–
  1023, 1066; and Moynihan report, 1058;
  in government, 1078, 1169, 1219; and
  Chicago boycotts, 1150; and 1969 student riots, 1158–69; Mormon Church
  and, 1190–91; and "Soledad" case,
  1201–1205, 1260. *See also* black groups
  and societies; black militants and militancy; civil rights; nonviolence; racism;
  segregation
Black Caucus, NCNP, 1077–78
"black market" (1930s), 21
black market, wartime and postwar, 293,
  397–98
black militants and militancy, 243; and sit-
  ins, 848–49, 882–83; growth of, 976–78,
  1036, 1066–69, 1076–78; and separatism, 983–84, 1133; division among,
  1058; denounced by conservative leadership, 1067; Black Power, 1067–68,
  1133; and "Soledad" murders, 1201–
  1204; at Attica, 1239–47. *See also*
  black(s); crime; racism; riots and demonstrations
"Black Monday," 136
Blackmun, Harry A., 1231
Black Muslims, 738, 1036, 1058, 1241
Black Nationalist Party, 1021
blackout of 1965, 1083–86
Black Panthers, 1058, 1067, 1069, 1070,
  1119, 1148, 1191, 1201, 1203, 1244.
  See also Newton, Huey P.; Seale, Bobby
Black People's Alliance, 1167
Black Power. *See* black militants and mili-
  tancy
"Black Sunday," 1059
Blagonravov, Gen. Anatoly Arkadievich,
  790–91, 793
Blair, William McCormick Jr., 611, 640
Blake, C. E., 807
Blanchard, Doc, 306
Blanding, Sarah Gibson, 1038
Bleyer, Archie, 694
blitzkrieg, 203, 216
Bliven, Bruce, 483

Block, Herbert ("Herblock"), 526, 673,
  708
Blondell, Joan, 88
Blossom, Virgil, 804
blue eagle. *See* National Recovery Adminis-
  tration
Blyden, Herbert X., 1241, 1242, 1243
B'nai B'rith, Anti-Defamation League of,
  1077
bobby-soxers. *See* teen-agers
Boddy, Manchester, 529
Bogart, Humphrey, 1037
Bohlen, Charles E. "Chip," 535, 655–56,
  891, 960
Bohr, Niels, 210–11, 212, 213, 315, 339
Bolte, Charles G. "Chuck," 221
Bond, Julian, 1068, 1199, 1204, 1207
Bone, Homer, 230–31
Bonus Expeditionary Force (BEF), 23, 26,
  54; Washington encampment (1932) and
  attack on, 3–4, 10–18; MacArthur and,
  11, 13–18; aftermath, 18–19
books: text, 40; (1930s) 64, 68; World
  War II, 304; (1950) 532; (1968) 1122;
  best sellers, 97–98, 251, 420, 424, 644,
  999, 1039, 1122, 1187–88; paperbacks,
  240, 589; anti-Communist violence and,
  567–69; as "Communist propaganda,"
  581; presidential favorites, 653, 955;
  and Hughes hoax, 1262–66
booms, economic. *See* economy, U.S.
"boondoggling," 86
Boone, Pat, 1142
Borah, William, 17, 52, 108, 111, 152,
  176, 177, 216; and neutrality, 202, 204,
  205
Borden, William L., 695–96
Borge, Victor, 587
Boston Evening Transcript, 80, 246
Boston Globe, 188, 1230
Boston Herald, 17
Boston Post, 835, 837
Boudin, Kathy, 583, 1199–1200
Boudin, Leonard B., 1199
Boutwell, Albert, 977
Bow, Clara, 689
Bowes, "Major" Edward, 121, 148
Bowles, Chester, 390, 399, 448, 895, 920
Boyd, William, 584
Boyle, James A., 1185
Boyle, William M. Jr., 603, 604
Braddock, James, 148
Bradley, Charles C., 59
Bradley, Gen. Omar, 280, 332, 353, 438;
  as chairman of Joint Chiefs, 532, 542,
  546, 560, 572, 606, 646
"brain trust," 49, 51
Brandeis, Louis D., 136, 152, 250
Brando, Marlon, 725
Brandon, Henry, 1216
Brandt, Willy, 964, 987
Braun, Wernher von, 332, 333, 797–98,
  810, 933
breadlines. *See* food
Breckinridge, John C., 886
Breech, Ernest R., 815
Breen, Bobby, 197

Breen Office, 120, 592
Bremer, Arthur Herman, 1260
Brennan, Bernard, 620
Brewster, Owen, 527, 529
Brezhnev, Leonid, 1271–72, 1295
Bricker, John, 170, 319, 618, 667, 675–76, 845
Bricker amendment, 672–77
Bridges, Styles, 415, 447, 564, 655, 657, 669, 816, 840, 930
Bright, J. Fulmer, 56
Brill, Dr. Henry, 1114
Brinkley, David, 353, 587, 1007
Brinkley, Dr. John "Goat Glands," 50
Brink's robbery, 482, 760
British Broadcasting Company, 1014
Broadway. See theater
Brodsky, A. I., 212
Brogan, D. W., 290, 589
Bromfield, Louis, 625–26, 705
Brooke, Edward W., 60, 1039, 1078, 1142, 1155
Brookhouser, Frank, 196
Brooklyn Eagle, 42
Brooklyn Tablet, 109, 275
Brooks, John, 199–200, 777, 1101, 1297
Brotherhood of Sleeping Car Porters, 244, 982
Broun, Heywood, 47, 49, 89, 133
Browder, Earl, 97, 111, 201, 320, 475, 526n, 1300
Brown, Clarence J., 618
Brown, Edmund, 1063, 1064
Brown, H. Rap, 396, 810, 1062, 1069, 1076–78, 1081, 1150; and "Rap Brown Act," 1208
Brown, Jimmy, 999
Brown, John Mason, 623
Brown, Les, 128
Brown, Phyllis, 760
Brown, Walter F., 76
Brown, Willie, 1204
Brown v. Board of Education of Topeka, 735, 804, 1057
Brownell, Herbert: Dewey and, 458–59, 462–63, 468, 469; and Eisenhower campaign, 618–19, 630; as attorney general, 648, 651, 668, 697, 740, 754, 757, 804–805
Bruce, David K. E., 1209–10
Bruce, Lenny, 1001
Bruenn, Lt. Cdr. Howard G., 323–24, 325, 326, 327, 335, 349–50
Brundage, Percival, 788
Brussels Defense Pact, 441
Buchanan, Pat, 1220
Bucher, Cdr. Lloyd M., 1123–24, 1178–79, 1237
Buckley, James, 1221
Buckley, William F. Jr., 705, 1120
Buddhists, 989, 990, 992, 1176, 1209
Budenz, Louis, 55, 528
budget, federal, 1095; Hoover and, 24–25; FDR and, 51, 138, 162–63, 274, 324, 1123; and military spending, 274, 289–290, 388, 519, 531, 569, 646–47, 657, 678–79, 877, 911, 1047, 1052, 1053–

1054, 1122, 1163, 1180, 1296; Eisenhower and, 649, 664–65, 678–79, 760, 811, 876; and space race, 792, 799, 930; JFK and, 911, 930; LBJ and, 1011, 1049, 1052, 1053–54; Nixon and, 1163, 1253. See also economy, U.S.
Bulganin, Nikolai, 748–51, 765
Bulge, Battle of the, 334
Bullitt, William C., 203, 491
Bunche, Ralph, 483, 1060, 1069
Bundy, Mary Acheson (Mrs. William P.), 512, 517, 520
Bundy, McGeorge, 60, 907, 984, 1075; and Cuban missile crisis, 958, 960, 961, 968, 970; and Vietnam, 1016, 1046–47, 1048
Bundy, William P., 512n, 919, 1018
Bunker, Ellsworth, 1226
Burch, Dean, 1027, 1029, 1030
Burd, Laurence H., 755
bureaucracy, growth of, 1028
Bureau of Internal Revenue. See Internal Revenue Service
Burger, Warren E., 1164, 1231
Burke, Adm. Arleigh, 894
Burke, Edward R., 152, 162
Burnham, James, 705; The Managerial Revolution, 1092
Burns, James MacGregor, 169, 229, 233, 291, 312, 326, 771
Burton, Richard, 1000
bus boycott, Montgomery, Alabama, 740–743
Busby, Horace, 1075
Bush, George, 1221
Bush, Vannevar, 375
business and industry: Coolidge and Hoover and, 25–28, 42, 106; and conglomerates, 44, 1002, 1174; and NRA, 88–90; and FDR, 103, 105, 106, 141, 143–44, 163–164, 166, 239; Republican party and, 106, 766, 1274; and aid to Britain, 228; and World War II, 244, 246, 290–91, 603; and Truman, 399; college students and, 578–79; merchandising changes, 721, 1174, 1225; investments abroad, 773, 825; and social conformity, 778–779, 781, 784; and personnel relocation, 781; and military-industrial complex, 877, 1093–95; management, 1092–94; power of Washington over, 1095; and education, 1095; and environment, 1173, 1174; tax credits for, 1253. See also advertising; economy, U.S.; Reconstruction Finance Corporation
Business Week, 35, 669, 815, 816
busing issue (school integration), 1273–1274, 1281, 1285
Butler, Hugh, 655
Butler, John Marshall, 558
Butler, Nicholas Murray, 27, 57
Butler, Pierce, 136, 137
Butler, Samuel, 775
Butler, Gen. Smedley D., 10, 57
Butz, Otto, 577, 582
Byoir, Carl, 118
Byrd, Harry, 48, 456, 886, 945
Byrd, Robert C., 1186

Byrnes, James F., 274, 293, 319, 326, 360, 365, 400, 736; as Secretary of State, 369, 375, 380, 385, 392, 412–14, 433, 521

Caesar, Sid, 586, 694
Cafritz, Gwen, 956
Cagney, James, 95, 101
Cain, Harry P., 672
Calder, Alexander, 1056
Calderone, Dr. Mary, 1194
Caldwell, Erskine, 57, 66; God's Little Acre, 120
Calhoun, John C., 946
California: loyalty oath in, 597; hippies in, 1113–14; environmental problems in, 1172–74.
Callas, Maria, 820
Calley, Lt. William, 341n, 1175–78
Cambodia, 680, 825, 1011, 1216; U.S. invasion of, 1210–11
Cambridge, Maryland, riots, 1081
Cameron, Ben, 944
Campbell, Sir Malcolm, 98
Cannon, Clarence, 1013
Canterbury, Brig. Gen. Robert H., 1214, 1215
Capehart, Homer, 512
Capote, Truman, 757, 853
Capp, Al, 1101
Capra, Frank, 197, 283
Caraway, Mrs. Hattie W., 115
Cardona, Mio, 862
Cardozo, Benjamin N., 136
Carlos, John, 1149
Carlson, Eric, 12
Carlson, Frank, 655, 1019
Carmichael, Stokely, 810, 939, 1062, 1066–1069, 1076, 1128, 1300
Carney, Adm. Robert B., 692, 745
Carpenter, Liz, 1013
Carpenter, Scott, 819
Carroll, Earl, 66
Carson, Johnny, 1182
Carson, Rachel, 999
Carswell, G. Harrold, 1164
Carter, Herbert, 1176
Carter, Hodding, 113, 114
Carter, Gen. Marshall, 960
Cary, Joyce, 532
Casablanca, 316
Castro Ruz, Fidel, 1277; takeover of Cuba, 860–63; Nixon on, 862; and counterrevolution (Bay of Pigs), 863–64, 866–867, 894–906; and missile crisis, 958, 970, 971
Castro Ruz, Raul, 861, 958
casualties: in riots and demonstrations, 10, 12–16, 849, 951, 1023, 1060–61, 1064, 1065, 1080, 1081, 1128, 1142, 1149–1150, 1191, 1198, 1212, 1215; in strikes, 131, 133–34, 156, 159–61; World War II, 235, 264, 266, 268–69, 271–73, 278–80, 316, 332, 340–43, 346, 347, 371, 376, 381, 383; Vietnam, 283, 819, 916n, 1003, 1004, 1045, 1047, 1049, 1050, 1054, 1057, 1070,

1125–26, 1147, 1180, 1181, 1209, 1210, 1281, 1293, 1294, 1296; Hiroshima and Nagasaki, 382; Korea, 537, 539, 547, 566, 663, 1180; Bay of Pigs, 902, 903, 905; potential, in Cuban missile crisis, 961, 962, 966, 971; space program, 1156; police, 1198; terrorist bombings, 1199–1200, 1201; in Laos, 1227; at Attica prison, 1246–47. See also crime
Cater, Douglass, 892
Cather, Willa, 1297
Catholicism: as political handicap, 771, 878, 881; and birth control, 847, 850, 1108; and segregation, 1003; and education, 1042, 1225
Catholic League of Decency, 120
Catledge, Turner, 115
Catton, Bruce, Civil War trilogy, 653
Caudle, T. Lamar, 605
Caulfield, John J., 1231, 1232, 1235, 1292
Cavan, Ruth Shonle, 1103
Cavendish, Henry, 792
Ceausescu, Nicolae, 1159
Cecil, Lord David, 955
censorship: movie, 120, 591–92 (see also Breen Office; Hays Office); radio, 121, 995; in Europe, 182, 387; German, and atomic development, 213–14; TV, 588
CENTO (Central Treaty Organization), 678, 823n
Central Intelligence Agency. See CIA
Cerf, Bennett, 165
Cermak, Anton, 55, 72
CFO (Council of Federated Organizations), 1022–23
Chadwick, Sir James, 69, 210
Chafee, John H., 1178–79
Chai Ung Jun, Gen., 533
Chamberlain, John, 50, 415, 705
Chamberlain, Neville, 178, 182, 189, 201, 216
Chamber of Commerce, U.S., 88, 151, 399, 400, 1093
Chambers, Whittaker, 96, 148, 197, 247, 459, 462, 493–94; testimony of, 501–511; "George Crosley," 505–507
Chamoun, Camille, 823, 824
Chandler, A. B. "Happy," 168, 169, 448
Chandler, Douglas, 317
Chaney, James E., 1022–24
Chang, Dr. John Myun, 535
Channing, Carol, 1235
Chapin, Dwight, 1289, 1290
Chaplin, Charles, 427; Modern Times, 157
Chaplin, Oona O'Neill (Mrs. Charles), 305, 427
Chappaquiddick, 1183–86, 1232, 1280
Chasanow, Abraham, 671
Chase, Ilka, 304
Chase, Stuart, 51, 100; A New Deal, 49, 57
Chayefsky, Paddy, 587
Cherne, Leo, 396
Cherwell, Lord, 339
Chessman, Caryl, 853
Chevalier, Maurice, 68

Chiang Ching (wife of Mao Tse-tung), 1268

Chiang Kai-shek, 111, 173, 252, 316, 379, 434, 491, 528; Stalin and, 348; defeat of, and flight to Taiwan, 487–89, 510, 534; and Korean War, 536, 540, 541, 545; Eisenhower and, 657–58, 875; and Formosa crisis, 744; and U.N., 1250–1251

Chiang Kai-shek, Madame (Soong Mei-ling), 491, 528

Chicago, 40–41, 55, 76; riots in, 159–60, 1064; Metallurgical Project (atomic research), 310–12; and Democratic national convention (1968), 1142–44; and "Operation Breadbasket," 1150

Chicago American, 644

Chicago Daily News, 853, 1102

Chicago Seven trial, 1205–1208, 1300

Chicago Tribune, 24, 160, 223, 318, 517, 521, 522, 525, 536, 762; and FDR, 54, 138, 196, 250, 321; and elections, 467–468, 639; and Stevenson, 613; and Republican party, 620

child labor. *See* labor and labor unions

Childs, Marquis, 141, 143, 165, 166, 171, 627, 1287

Chiles, Henry P., 367

China, 178, 597, 657–58, 1295; Japan and, 68, 74, 124, 125, 174, 176, 252; during World War II, 270, 383; Nationalist flight to Taiwan, 487–88, 512, 517; U.S. aid to, 488; -Soviet relations, 488, 986; rise of People's Republic, 517; and U.N., 535, 549, 564, 669–70, 883, 1249–50; and Korean War, 540–50, 555–56, 560, 566; anti-U.S. propaganda, 661, 662; offshore islands (Quemoy, Matsu), 692, 744–47, 875; and Cuba, 862, 865; and atomic weapons, 1030, 1122; U.S. ping-pong group in, 1248–49; -U.S. relations, 1249–51, 1267–69; Nixon visits, 1262, 1267–69. *See also* Chiang Kai-shek; Mao Tse-tung

China Lobby, 491, 525, 555

Chisholm, Shirley, 1282

Chmedelin, M., 222

Choate, Robert, 143

Chotiner, Murray, 619, 620, 631–33, 636, 637, 720, 1218–20

Chou En-lai, 545, 1248, 1249, 1250, 1268, 1269

Christian Science Monitor, 475

Christmas, William, 1202–1203

Church, Frank, 60, 1019, 1049

church, the. *See* religion

Churchill, Randolph, 762

Churchill, Winston, 68, 92, 121, 144–45, 223, 315, 339, 354, 367, 369, 379, 488; on Munich Pact, 189; and Battle of Britain, 216, 217; and U.S. aid, 229, 232, 434, 440, 443, 824; meets FDR at sea, 234; and Pacific war, 258, 259, 265, 273; visits U.S., 274, 420; and summit meetings, 316, 327, 348, 674, 693, 703, 747; loses election, 370; and Iron Curtain speech, 410, 412; and Vietnam, 684; death, 1037

Chu Teh, Gen., 487

CIA (Central Intelligence Agency), 790, 826, 828, 927, 1073; on Korea, 531, 546; and Cuban counterrevolution (Bay of Pigs), 862, 863–67, 894–903, 905; "Frank Bender" and, 863, 864, 866, 896, 897; and U–2, 867–71; and Cuban missile crisis, 958–60, 962; and Vietnam bombing, 1046, 1051, 1071; Nixon and, 1216–17; and Ellsberg case, 1237–39, 1280; and Watergate, 1288. *See also* intelligence, military

Ciccone, Richard, 1205

Cienfuegos, Osmani, 901

Cierva, Juan de la, 9

CIO (Congress of Industrial Organizations), 158, 320, 389, 403, 447, 630; and AFL, 135, 153–56; and steel and auto industries, 153, 155–61; and Communists, 159, 161

Citizens Committee for the Reelection of the President (CREEP). *See* CREEP

City College of New York, 127

City Lights Bookshop, 726

civil defense, 258, 259, 265, 303, 575–76

Civilian Conservation Corps (CCC), 80, 84–85, 98, 107

civil rights, 111, 976; and labor, 131–33; World War II, 244–45, 297–302, (1948) 452, 454; Fair Deal and, 474; and segregation, 735–37, 743 (*see also* segregation); and Little Rock incident, 800–10; Kennedys and, 939–43, 981–84 (*see also* Kennedy, John F.; Kennedy, Robert F.); in Mississippi, 943–51; and backlash, 1020; Acts, 1022, 1030, 1205; J. Edgar Hoover and, 1023; (1960s) 1057–1059, 1064; in North, 1064; black power and, 1068; of rioters, 1191. *See also* American Civil Liberties Union; black groups and societies

Civil Service Commission, 740

Civil Works Administration (CWA), 86, 103

Clark, Bennett Champ, 219, 230

Clark, Chase, 298

Clark, Dick, 852

Clark, James G. Jr., 1058, 1059, 1068

Clark, Kenneth B., 735, 984, 1136

Clark, Mark, 1191

Clark, Gen. Mark, 278, 279, 329–30, 646

Clark, Ramsay, 1138

Clark, Tom C., 494, 496

Clarke, "Brother Richard," 1241, 1242, 1245

Clay, Cassius (Muhammad Ali), 810, 1036

Clay, Gen. Lucius, 442, 912

Clayton, Will, 413, 439

Cleaver, Eldridge, 740, 1150, 1240; *Soul on Ice*, 1149

Cleveland, Harlan, 902

Cleveland *Plain Dealer*, 17

Clevenger, Cliff, 450

Clifford, Clark, 413; and Truman, 402–403, 405, 447–66 passim, 474; on Vietnam, 1052, 1180–81; at Pentagon, 1125, 1126, 1230

Clifton, Maj. Gen. Chester V., 559
Clutter, Herbert, 853
Coca, Imogene, 694
Coca-Cola, 444–45, 825
Coffin, Henry Sloane, 283
Coffin, William Sloane, 1189
Cohan, George M., 68
Cohen, Ben, 105
Cohen, Dr. Maimon M., 1115
Cohn, Harry, 486
Cohn, Roy, 701–18
Colbert, Claudette, 68, 198
cold war, 436, 501, 1036; Lippmann's study of, 437–38; deepens, 510, 566, 598, 692; Eisenhower and, 646, 665; Dulles and, 854–55; and U–2 affair, 876; JFK and, 906–13, 917, 927, 958; LBJ and, 1018; Nixon and, 1159, 1180, 1273
Cole, Nat King, 483
Coleman, Tom, 493
Coll, Edward T., 1282
Collier's magazine, 90, 528
Collins, Floyd, 1259
Collins, Gen. J. Lawton, 538, 559
Collins, John F., 1088
Collins, Judy, 1207
Collins, LeRoy, 1059
Collins, Lt. Michael, 1157–59
Collyer, Clayton "Bud," 588
Colman, Ronald, 198
Colson, Charles W., 1228, 1234, 1235, 1271, 1272; and Pentagon Papers, 1232, 1236–37; and Watergate, 1275, 1279–1280, 1289, 1291
Columbia University riots, 1131–34
Combined Chiefs. See Joint Chiefs of Staff
comic strips and books. See mass media
commercialism. See exploitation
Committee to Defend America by Aiding the Allies, 204, 223
Committee to Defend America First. See America First movement
Committee to End War in Vietnam, 1142
Committee to Reelect the President. See CREEP
Commodity Credit Corporation, 347
Common Market (European Economic Community), 440, 1000, 1251, 1254
Commonweal magazine, 275
communications, 426; revolution in, 118, 589, 757, 1022; telephones and Telstar, 818, 934; (1960s) 996, 1002–1003; and spread of youth counterculture, 1096. See also radio and radio programs; television
Communists and Communism, 22, 56, 71, 97, 176, 207–208, 243, 411; and BEF, 13, 17; and intellectuals, 50, 56–57, 103, 1201; FDR and, 84, 142, 143; American Communist Party, 96, 494, 670; and fascism, 110, 111; in CIO, 159, 161; and atomic research, 312–14; and U.S. presidential campaigns, 320, 457–58; and loyalty issue, 372, 489–98; and postwar Europe, 433, 435–36, 437; legislation regarding, 452, 670; and Ko-

rea, 519, 530 (see also Korea and Korean War); McCarthy and, 520–21 (see also McCarthy, Joseph, and McCarthyism); as monolithic, 557, 906–907; and anti-Communism, 566–67, 580–82, 588, 597, 630, 650, 671–72, 718, 953–954, 1267; global struggle against, 682, 822–24; conspiracy trials, 692; influence "proved" in integration disputes, 847; and Cuba, 862–63, 894–95 (see also Cuba); and Vietnam, 918, 919, 995, 1056 (see also Vietnam and Vietnam War); and missile crisis, 958; students and faculty, 1132, 1201. See also China; espionage; subversion; House Un-American Activities Committee; Soviet Union
Como, Perry, 483, 643, 693
Compton, Arthur H., 310, 311, 313, 375
Compton, Karl T., 375, 376
computers and computerization. See technology
Comstock, William A., 72
Conant, James Bryant, 375, 571, 574, 655
Condon, Eddie, 34
Condon, Edward U., 490
Condon-Wadlin Act, 1136
Confidential magazine, 693
conformity, social. See society
Congo, Republic of (Zaire), 853, 908, 909, 1003
Congress, U.S.: and Hoover, 10, 26, 35, 44, 54–55; and presidential power, 58 (see also presidential power); and FDR, 78, 90, 104, 105, 144, 150, 152–53, 168–169, 170, 231, 243, 274, 292; and neutrality, 125, 176, 177, 200, 204, 235; and the draft, 224–25; declares war, 260; and Truman, 398–99, 415, 447, 448, 449, 451, 455–56, 458–59, 470, 490, 530–31, 538, 557; and Korea, 530–31; and Eisenhower, 655, 668, 720, 745–47; and amendments to Constitution, 673–77; and civil rights, 740; and JFK, 965, 986; and Vietnam War, 1016, 1018–19, 1040, 1072; and LBJ, 1040, 1042, 1043; and Nixon, 1147
Congressional Record, 521
Congress of Industrial Organizations. See CIO
Congress of Racial Equality. See CORE
Conlan, June, 1195
Connally, John B. Jr., 60, 106, 953, 1003–1004, 1253, 1254
Connally, Tom, 169, 408–409, 524
Connelly, Matthew H., 605
Connery, William P. Jr., 134, 144
Connor, T. Eugene "Bull," 243, 938–40, 976–77
Connors, W. Bradley, 532, 533
conscription. See draft
conservation. See ecology
Constitution, U.S.: and presidential powers, 58, 556 (see also presidential powers); FDR and, 81, 150–51; Charles Evans Hughes and, 135, 151; amendments to, 673–77; Warren Court and, 740; and

presidential electors, 885–86; and Equal Rights Amendment, 1196–97
consumer(s): credit, 32, 240, 594, 595, 724, 774–75, 1088; "crusade" for OPA, 399; stereotyped, 773; exploitation, 775–777, 784–85; Ralph Nader and, 1256–1258. *See also* advertising
Consumer Reports, 816
containment policy. *See* foreign policy, U.S.
Continentalism. *See* Fortress America concept
Conyers, John, 1235
Coogan, Jackie, 283
Cook, Donald, 1182
Cooke, Alistair, 587
Coolidge, Calvin, 5, 24, 25, 32, 43, 48, 53, 106, 1136
Coons, Hannibal, 484
Cooper, Gary, 303, 643
Cooper, Gordon, 819, 931
Cooper, Jackie, 11
Cooper, John Sherman, 709, 1019, 1175
Coplon, Judith, 510, 1199
Corcoran, Tom, 105, 170
CORE (Congress of Racial Equality), 934–935, 939, 942, 982, 1020, 1022, 1037–1038, 1066, 1068, 1077, 1132, 1149
Corregidor. *See* Philippine Islands
corruption. *See* crime
Corso, Gregory, 726
Corso, Rogelio Gonzáles "Francisco," 899
cost: of World War II, 289–90; of Korean War, 519; of NATO, 569; of interstate highway system, 758; to USSR of Sputnik, 789, 855; of space race, 796, 797, 799, 929, 930; of Little Rock incident, 808; of riots, 949, 1021, 1058, 1064, 1070, 1149; of Vietnam War, 1049, 1052–54, 1180, 1296; of teen-age vandalism, 1104–1105; of Nixon life-style, 1161–62; of living, 1225; (*see also* economy, U.S.); of Watergate, 1275–1276. *See also* budget, federal; casualties; property damage
Costello, Frank, 599–601
Costello, Lou, 820
Costigan, Edward P., 21, 22
Cotten, Joseph, 486
Cotton, Norris, 836, 837
Coughlin, Charles E., 100, 107–11, 114, 115, 117, 141, 142, 144, 155, 176
Coulter, Maj. Gen. John B., 546
Council of Federated Organizations (CFO), 1022–23. *See also* Freedom Summer
Counter-Attack (blacklist), 498–499, 1120
Cousins, Norman, 586, 589
Cousy, Robert J., 999
Cowan, Glenn, 1248, 1249, 1251
Coward, Noel, 588
Cowley, Malcolm, 57
Cox, Archibald, 1132, 1134
Cox, Edward F., 1257
Cox, Mrs. Edward F. *See* Nixon, Tricia
Cox, Eugene, 491n
Cox, W. Harold, 1024–25
Cozzens, James Gould, 242
Crawford, Broderick, 486

Crawford, Joan, 68
Crawford, Kenneth, 203
"credibility gap": under Hoover, 24; under FDR, 222, 226, 232; under LBJ, 1011, 1013, 1050, 1052, 1053, 1075, 1138–1139, 1230; under Nixon, 1230
CREEP (Citizens Committee for Reelection of the President), 1222, 1271; and Watergate, 1274, 1275, 1279, 1281, 1287, 1289–91
Crew Cuts, The, 693
crime, 27, 597; vagrancy and, 19, 21, 37; Lindbergh case, 23; stock manipulation, 44–46, 145–47; mortgage foreclosures and, 59; assassinations, 72, 116–17, 1004–1006, 1068, 1128–30; J. Edgar Hoover and public enemies, 94–95; strikes and, 133–35, 159–61, 389 (*see also* strikes); wiretapping, 197, 1216, 1217, 1235–36, 1274–76, 1278; Brink's robbery, 482, 760; TV and, 584, 852–53; and corruption in Truman years, 599–606, 694; bribery and blackmail, 603–604, 834–42, 1289–91; shoplifting, 721, 776, 1148; and juvenile delinquency, 734, 1103–1104; perjury, 852, 1289–1290, 1292; rise of, 1037, 1182, 1225, 1259–60; Selma murders, 1060–61; arson, 1080, 1081, 1105, 1128; Sharon Tate murders, 1098, 1171; vandalism, 1103–1105; hippies and, 1116–18; blacks and, 1078, 1148, 1150, 1191; terrorist threats and bombings, 1166, 1198–1200, 1211–12; skyjacking, 1182, 1192, 1260; mass murder, 1200; Soledad murders, 1202–1203; illegal entry, 1217, 1232, 1238–39, 1276–78; political forgery, 1236–37, 1274–75, 1280, 1283; and Attica prison riot, 1239–47; exhibitionism and, 1259. *See also* espionage; police; war crimes and atrocities
Crockett, Davy, 725
Cronin, Anne, 997
Cronin, John, 505
Cronkite, Walter, 992, 1005
Crosby, Bing, 303, 308, 444, 585
Crosby, John, 624
Crosby, Tony, 999
Cross, Mark, 818
Crossley radio survey, 190, 304, 466
Crowley, Charles "Brother Flip," 1240
Crowther, Bosley, 303
Cruit, George E., 940
Cuba, 537, 597; Castro takes over, 860–63; counterrevolution (Bay of Pigs), 863–67, 893–908; missile crisis in, 958–71
Cummings, Homer, 96, 137, 151, 454
Cunningham, Glenn, 98
Curie, Irène, 498
Curley, James Michael, 89
currency. *See* money
Currie, Lauchlin, 459, 493–94, 502
Curtice, Harlow H., 758
Curtin, John T., 1243, 1244
Curtis, Charles, 10
Curtis, Tony, 198n, 690

Cushing, Richard Cardinal, 889, 987, 1130, 1141
Cushman, Gen. Robert E. Jr., 1238, 1239
Custer, Gen. George A., 341
Cutler, Robert, 697
Czechoslovakia, 441, 597, 894, 1146; 1938 crisis, 177–83, 188–89, 200

Daedalus (journal), 580, 682, 1101
Dagnian, Harry, 314
Daily Californian, 1226
Daily Oklahoman, 561
Daily Pacifican, 407–408
Daily Worker, 457, 528
Daladier, Edouard, 216
Dale, Edwin Jr., 1053
D'Alesandro, Thomas Jr., 476
Daley, Richard J., 880, 884, 1142–44, 1145, 1207, 1287
Dallas Times Herald, 954
Daly, John Charles, 587
Damrosch, Walter, 89
dance bands and bandleaders. See music and musicians
dancing, 127, 129, 248, 1100
Dania, Bunny, 1108
Daniel, Capt. Aubrey M. III, 1178
Daniels, Jonathan, 107, 317
Darby, Harry, 463
D'Argenlieu, Adm. Thierry, 395
Darrow, Clarence, 100
Daughters of the American Revolution (DAR), 151, 245, 563–64, 718
Davidson, C. Girard, 474n
Davies, John Paton, 655
Davies, Ronald, 800, 801–802
Davis, Angela, 810, 1201–1205, 1260, 1300
Davis, Lt. Gen. Benjamin O. Jr., 1078, 1191
Davis, Bette, 197, 206, 486, 688
Davis, Clyde Brion, 1091
Davis, Elmer, 47, 50, 57
Davis, Forrest: Huey Long, 115
Davis, John W., 138, 503
Davis, Junior, 306
Davis, Kenneth S., 767
Davis, Miles, 693
Davis, Rennie, 1205, 1206, 1208
Dawes, Charles G., 25, 46, 85
Dawes, Chester L., 240
Dawson, Donald, 603, 604, 672
Deacons for Defense, 1058
Dealey, E. M. "Ted," 954
Dean, James, 592
Dean, John Wesley III, 1186, 1217, 1232, 1235, 1274, 1275, 1279–80, 1288–91
Dean, Gen. William F., 531
Debs, Eugene, 206, 207, 388, 404
de Castries, Gen. Christian, 685–86
DeDiego, Felipe, 1238–39
Defender (newspaper), 240
Defense, Department of, 409, 986, 1122, 1163
defense industries, 244, 246, 603
Defferre, Gaston, 987
deficit spending. See economy, U.S.

de Galard-Terraube, Geneviève, "Angel of Dienbienphu," 686
de Gaulle, Gen. Charles, 216, 278, 333, 434, 823, 857, 859, 1007, 1160; at summit meetings, 874, 909, 910; and Cuban missile crisis, 964, 965; and Common Market, 1000
Degler, Carl N., 781
de Hory, Elmyr, 1263
Delaney, Dennis, 605
Delano, Laura, 347, 351
de Laveleye, Victor, 219
Del Corso, Maj. Gen. Sylvester, 1214
Dellinger, David, 1142, 1144, 1205, 1208, 1286
Delmar, Kenneth, 191
Del Rio, Dolores, 98
De Mille, Cecil B., 614
Democratic National Committee, 115, 139, 317, 319, 466–67, 603, 1285; and Watergate, 1216, 1275–80 (see also Watergate)
Democratic national conventions: (1932) 48–49; (1936) 141–42, 145, 164; (1940) 226; (1944) 318–19, 344; (1948) 448, 451, 453–56, 457; (1952) 620–23; (1960) 880; (1964) 1011, 1015, 1097; (1968) 1142–44, 1207; (1972) 1284–85
Democratic party: (1932) 48, 51, (1934) 104, (1940) 225, (1952) 599, 640, (1958) 845, (1964) 1028–32, (1968) 1142–43, 1145, (1970) 1219–21, (1971) 1232, (1972) 1274, 1282–87; "destruction" of, 50; and coalition, 107, 139, 141, 153, 167–71, 400, 475, 640; campaign contributions, 139; in South, 153, 170, 454, 456, 458, 878, 880; and Truman, 415–16, 453–54, 470; and loyalty issue, 490–94, 504, 508–509, 524
Democrats for Eisenhower, 448, 450, 453
demonstrations. See riots and demonstrations
DeMott, Benjamin, 954, 1099
Denison, Edward F., 1001
Denney, Reuel, 592
Dennis, Eugene, 457
Dennis, Lawrence, 111, 318
Denver Post, 522, 644
Depression, Great, 8, 31, 42, 56; and BEF, 3–4; and transient population, 18–22; "Hoovervilles," 23–24; Hoover's view of, 24–27; business and production, 27–28, 32–33; prices, income and wages, 32, 36–38, 67, 134, 137–38, 148; relief structure, 38–40; public schools and police, 40–41, 54–56, 65, 1296; and public behavior, 55–60; and foreign policy, 125, 174–75; and students, 127–28
Depuy, Gen. William, 1057
Derounian, Stephen B., 852
De Sapio, Carmine, 600
desegregation. See segregation
de Silva, Pierre, 1046
Detroit: in Depression, 34, 40n, 52, 55, 72; race riots in, 1064, 1080–81
Detroit Free Press, 10, 464

Detroit News, 73
Dever, Paul A., 837
Devereux, Maj. James, 266
Devlin, Bernadette, 1106, 1166
De Voto, Bernard, 396
De Vries, Peter, 1122
Dewey, John, 50, 793
Dewey, Thomas E., 147, 170, 197, 220, 225, 535–36, 613, 659, 844; in 1944 presidential campaign, 318–23; in 1948 presidential campaign, 446, 452–53, 458–59, 461–71; and NATO, 557; and 1952 presidential campaign, 616–17, 619, 631, 632–33
De Witt, Lt. Gen. John L., 298, 302
Diebner, Karl, 338
Diefenbaker, John, 965
Diem, Ngo Dinh. *See* Ngo Dinh Diem
Dienbienphu, siege and battle of, 681–86, 687
Dies, Martin, 167; and Dies Committee, 176. *See also* House Un-American Activities Committee
Dietrich, Marlene, 309
Dilling, Elizabeth, 107, 111, 318
Dillinger, John, 94–95
Dillon, C. Douglas, 684, 960, 986
DiMaggio, Joe, 247, 283, 689, 690, 691, 759
Dionne quintuplets, 98, 596
Dior, Christian, 422, 423. *See also* New Look
Dirksen, Everett M., 612–13, 617, 669, 674, 708, 709, 1069, 1074, 1138–39
disarmament: Dulles and, 677; and "Open Skies" proposal, 748, 750–51, 873; and test ban, 769, 770, 909, 913, 971, 985–986; Soviet Union and, 876, 911, 1272; Eisenhower on, 876–77. *See also* arms race
disasters: (1968) 1123; (1969) 1172, 1173; (1970) 1190. *See also* storms and weather
discount houses, growth of, 721
Disney, Walt, 532, 725
Displaced Persons Plan, 440, 459
Dix, Dorothy, 64, 305
Dixiecrats, 451, 454, 456, 470, 885, 886
Dixon, Edgar H., 693
Dixon, Marlene, 1195
Doar, John, 940, 941, 944, 946–47, 1024, 1059
Dobrynin, Anatoly F., 965, 967, 969, 970, 1271
Dodd, Bella, 528
Dodd, Thomas J., 954, 1038, 1078, 1124, 1221
Dodge, Joseph M., 664
Dodge, Lowell, 1257
Doerfer, John C., 852
Dohrn, Bernardine, 1098
Dole, Robert, 1222
"dole," the, 24–25, 86. *See also* welfare, public
Dominick, Peter, 60
"domino" theory, 684, 686, 917, 1052, 1180

Donat, Robert, 198
Dönitz, Adm. Karl, 295
Donnell, Forrest, 569
Donovan, James B., 906
Donovan, Robert J., 687
Dorleac, Françoise, 1105
Dorsey, Tommy, 68, 119, 129, 248, 307
Dos Passos, John, 12, 56–57, 68, 120, 1247; *Number One,* 111
Douglas, Helen Gahagan, 322, 529, 620
Douglas, Kirk, 198n, 590
Douglas, Paul, 283
Douglas, Paul H., 50, 105, 454, 463, 470, 557, 611, 663, 705
Douglas, William O., 147, 319, 453–54
Douglas-Home, Sir Alec, 1003, 1030
Dow Chemical Company, 78, 1073, 1167
Dow Jones averages: (1933) 80; (1936) 139; (1937) 163; (1940) 239; (1949) 485; (1950s) 597; (1955) 754; (1963) 1003; (1970) 1192; (1971) 1252, 1254; (1972) 1261. *See also* stock market; Wall Street
Downey, Morton, 121
draft, 226, 407, 539, 549, 1098; Selective Service Bill, 223–25; rejections, 238; evasion of, 283, 1073, 1122, 1126, 1136; extended, 597; Vietnam and, 1052; card burning, 1055
Dreiser, Theodore, 12, 100
Dressler, Marie, 68
drinking, teen-age, 1103–1104
drugs: (1930s) 63, 1111, (1950s) 776, (1960s) 1111–16, 1148; and malaria, 272–73; LSD, 596, 1111–13, 1115, 1116, 1118; tranquilizers, 759, 776, 1111; amphetamines, 763, 1111; and teen-agers, 1103, 1114, 1212–13; "miracle," 1111; Thalidomide, 1111; psychedelic, and hippies, 1112–15; marijuana, 1114, 1136; and U.S. troops in Vietnam, 1209; at youth festivals, 1212–13
Drum, Lt. Gen. Hugh, 202
Drummond, Roscoe, 669
Drury, Allen, 326, 1122, 1161
Dryden, Hugh, 929
Dubinsky, David, 132
Du Bois, W. E. B., 1097
Duff, James H., 564, 655
Duggan, Laurence, 503
Dulles, Allen, 309, 764, 1022, 1023; and Bay of Pigs, 864, 866, 894, 895. *See also* CIA
Dulles, John Foster; 464, 503, 540, 755, 757, 766, 833, 903, 1250; and America First, 221, 222, 615; and NATO, 557; at 1952 Republican convention, 615; as Secretary of State, 646, 649, 650, 651, 670; and "massive retaliation," 646, 853; background and character of, 650, 677–678; and Bohlen appointment, 656; on "secret agreements," 658–59; policy and "brinksmanship," 661–63, 677–79, 853–54, 857, 859; and loyalty issue, 672; and Bricker amendment, 673, 675; and Vietnam, 682–84, 685, 687; and Joseph McCarthy, 703–704; and For-

Dulles, John Foster (*continued*)
  mosa crisis, 745; and Geneva conference, 747–49; and Middle East, 763–64, 821–824; illness and death, 764, 853–55
Dumbarton Oaks conference, 292
Dun, Bishop Angus, 359
Dunham, Walter, 604
Dunne, Irene, 68
Dunne, John R., 1243, 1245
Duong Van Minh, Gen., 992–93, 1226
Du Pont, Pierre S., 83, 140, 141, 156
Du Pont family, 43
Durante, Jimmy, 587
Durkheim, Emile, 32
Durkin, Martin P., 648
dust storms, 98–100
Dutch East Indies. *See* Indonesia
Dylan, Bob, 1102, 1171

Eagleton, Thomas, 1286, 1287
Earhart, Amelia, 124, 126
Earle, George, 170
Early, Stephen, 351, 352, 353, 357
Earp, Wyatt, 812
East Germany (German Democratic Republic). *See* Germany
Eastland, James O., 808, 946
Eastman, Max, 705
Eccles, Marriner S., 105
ecology: dust storms, 98–100; movement starts, 999; and pollution, 1089, 1163, 1172–74
Economic Stabilization Act of 1970, 1253
economy, U.S.: Hoover and, 23–28, 32, 1251; and gold standard, 24, 72–74, 79–80, 85, 124, 1251–53; Gross National Product, 33, 239, 290, 594, 758, 773, 826, 876, 883, 986, 1001, 1253; FDR and, 85–90; deficit spending, 95, 162; laissez-faire, 136–37; inflation, 139, 397–398, 399, 452, 474, 758, 1054, 1180, 1225, 1253, 1254; and war boom, 238, 289–91; pre–World War II, 238–39; blacks and, 243, 936, 1021–22, 1078, 1150; civilian spending, 290, 291; and profits, 290, 1094, 1095, 1096; black market, 293, 397–98; postwar, 396–400, 403, 430, 1251; affluence and public values, 592, 594–95, 722–25, 1045, 1089, 1090; and tariff, 597, 1254; recessions, 657, 692, 720, 816; boom, 695, 766, 773–79; (1960s) 986, 1001, 1054, 1094, 1252; (1970s) 1180, 1252; Nixon's New Economic Policy, 1251–55. *See also* budget, federal; business and industry; cost; Depression, Great; income; prices; stock market; wages and hours
Eddy, Nelson, 68, 149, 304
Eden, Anthony, 326, 327, 658, 748, 763–765
Edgerton, John E., 31, 38
Edison, Thomas A., 792, 1085
Edsel, the, 791, 798, 814–17
education, 60, 67, 1001; blacks and, 7, 107, 735–36, 936, 944–52, 979–81, 1021; for veterans, 292, 324, 397; pro-
gressive, 784; (1950s) 784–85, 791–93; U.S. compared with Russian, 791–93; federal aid to, 819, 1042; (1960s) 1036, 1095–96; parochial, 1042, 1255; and permissiveness, 1097; and busing issue, 1273–74, 1281. *See also* schools and teachers; sex education; student(s)
Edward VIII of England, 68
Edwards, Willard, 521, 525
Egan, Leo, 461
"eggheads." *See* intellectuals
Egypt, 231, 959; Suez crisis, 763–65, 821–824
Ehrlichman, John, 1156, 1161, 1232, 1236; and ITT, 1233–34; and Pentagon Papers, 1237–39; and Watergate, 1279–1280, 1288–91
Eichelberger, Gen. Robert L., 269, 340
Einstein, Albert, 69, 211, 382, 792; letters to FDR, 214–15, 335–36; opposes use of atomic weapons, 335–36, 512, 571, 574
Eisenhower, David, 1122
Eisenhower, Gen. Dwight D., 11, 125, 250, 532, 580, 613, 718, 763, 833, 1106; early career, 5–7, 13, 15–16, 84, 233, 256, 296; and blacks, 242–43; as ETO commander, 276–78, 280, 316, 317, 324, 330–32, 353, 368; *Crusade in Europe*, 282, 596; and D-Day, 330–33; and Russia, 348–49, 372, 854–55; and eastern Europe, 348–49; and demobilization, 408–10; Truman and, 411, 446–47, 450, 647; Democrats for, 448, 450, 453; and NATO, 557, 609; presidential campaigns: (1952) 558, 593, 608–609, 613–14, 616–19, 622–28, 630–33, 636–41, (1956) 769–70, (1960) 883, (1964) 1027; and Stevenson, 610, 623–27; and Joseph McCarthy, 627–29, 656, 703–704, 718; and Korea, 638, 645–47, 661–663, 666; cabinet members and meetings, 647–50, 667–68, 756; and budget, 649, 664–65, 678–79, 760, 876; and Nixon, 649, 719–20, 768, 826, 879, 883, 915, 995; first inauguration, 650–651; routines and diversions of, 651–55; accomplishments of, 652–53, 766, 891; domestic policy, 657, 719, 766; foreign policy, 657–63, 666–67, 678, 747–51, 854–55; "Chance for Peace" speech, 661; and Dulles, 661, 854; and divisions within party, 664–65, 667–69; powers of, 667–68, 675–76, 684, 744–47; and Bricker/George amendments, 667, 674–677; and security program, 670–72; and Vietnam, 680, 682–85, 687, 744, 745–747, 917, 918, 919; and Chinese offshore islands, 692; and Bermuda conference, 693, 704; political philosophy, 693, 695; and Oppenheimer case, 695, 696–697; and integration issue, 737, 882; and Geneva conference, 747–51, 908; illnesses, 752–53, 766–67, 811–12; decision for second term, 756–58; and Suez crisis, 764, 765; popularity of, 766, 767, 794, 883; and space race, 794–99,

810–11; and Little Rock school integration crisis, 801, 804–805, 808; Doctrine and Middle East, 822–24; and Adams scandal, 838–44; Khrushchev's visit to, 855, 857, 858–59, 909; visits Europe and Middle East, 857–58, 859–60; and Paris conference, 860, 866, 873–74, 908; and Cuba, 862, 864, 866; and U–2 affair, 868, 872–76; on disarmament, 876–877; and Bay of Pigs, 900; on JFK, 986; on LBJ, 1010

Eisenhower, Julie (Mrs. David), 1122

Eisenhower, Mamie (Mrs. Dwight D.), 616, 618, 633, 752, 753, 755, 756, 767, 811, 818

Eisenhower, Milton, 297, 299, 300, 757

elections. See presidential campaigns and elections

Elijah Mohammed, 983

Eliot, Maj. George Fielding, 222, 316

Eliot, T. S., 486

Elizabeth, wife of George VI of England, 177, 200

Elizabeth II of England, 762, 1007

Ellington, Duke, 244

Ellis, Handy, 454

Ellis, Havelock, 479

Ellis, Robert Byron, 951

Ellison, Ralph, 734

Ellsberg, Daniel, 1071, 1199; and Pentagon Papers, 1231–32, 1237–39, 1280, 1299

Elsey, George M., 449, 461

Ely, Joseph B., 138

Ely, Gen. Paul, 683

Emerson, Faye, 586, 588

energy crisis, 1225. See also blackout of 1965

Engels, Friedrich, 411, 498

England. See Great Britain

Enterprise (aircraft carrier), 271, 272

environment, pollution of, 1089, 1163, 1172–74. See also ecology

Equal Rights Amendment, 1196–97

Erlich, John L., 1226

Ernst, Morris, 51, 100

ERP (European Recovery Program). See Marshall Plan

Ervin, Sam J., and Ervin committee, 1279, 1287, 1290

espionage, 97; German, 274, 309; and atomic research, 309, 313–14, 372–75, 379, 493, 499–502; Bentley testimony, 459, 462, 493–94; and Chambers-Hiss case, 459, 462, 493–94, 502–11; and loyalty issue, 489, 491, 498; McCarthyism and, 527–28; U–2 affair, 867–76; political, 1232 (see also Watergate). See also security, national; subversives and subversion

Esquire magazine, 286, 715n, 1075

Essary, J. F., 13

Essex (aircraft carrier), 341

establishment, the, 1098; student revolt against, 1033–34, 1096; defined, 1083. See also society

Ethiopian War, 108

Etting, Ruth, 121

Europe, 175; aid to, 434–38 (see also Marshall Plan); eastern, Dulles incitement of, 677–78; and "Eurodollars," 1252–1253

European Coal and Steel Community, 440

European Defense Community, 597

European Economic Community. See Common Market

European Exchange System, 1191

European Recovery Program (ERP). See Marshall Plan

European Theater of Operations (ETO). See World War II

Evans, Dale, 427

Evans, Linda Sue, 583

Evans, Rowland, 1221, 1236

Evans, Ward V., 697, 698

Evers, Charles, 1067, 1068, 1285

Evers, Medgar, 944, 981, 1021

Ewing, Oscar, 474

executive branch. See presidency; presidential power

exhibitionism. See publicity, age of

exploitation: and commercialism, 649–95; of consumer, 775–77, 784–85; of hippies, 1116; of youth's counterculture, 1171

Fadiman, Clifton, 57

fads. See fashions and fads

Fairbanks, Douglas Jr., 283

Fair Deal (Truman), 473–75

Fair Employment Practices Committee, 244, 982

Fair Labor Standards Act, 167–68

Fairless, Benjamin, 158

Fairlie, Henry, 1044

Faithful, Starr, 1117

Falkenberg, Jinx, 596

Falkner, Capt. Murry C., 945, 951

fallout, 512, 575, 699–700, 819, 912. See also atomic weapons

family: relations and "togetherness," 692, 694; marriage, 780, 1035; generation gap, 1100; parents, 1101, 1103; teenagers and, 1101–1103; background of hippies, 1115. See also birth control

Fanny Hill, 997

Faraday, Michael, 792

Farley, James, 48, 74, 114, 115, 144, 145, 168–69, 226, 465–66

Farmer, James, 60, 935, 1038, 1056, 1066

farms and farming. See agriculture

Farouk I of Egypt, 596, 762, 763

Farrar, John, 1185

Farrell, Charles, 11, 68

Farrell, Gen. T. F., 380

Farrow, Mia, 308, 1122

fascist movements, prewar U.S., 57–58, 102, 107, 110–111, 142, 176

fashions and fads: (1930s) 62, 128; (1940s) 247, 248; World War II, 305, 306, 333; postwar, 422–24, 1197; teenage, 722–24; (1950s) 722–24, 779–780; Davy Crockett craze, 725; hula hoop fad, 820–21; Kennedy family and,

fashions and fads (*continued*)
955–57, 997; (1960s) 997–98, 1033, 1037, 1039; (1970s) 1197–98
Faubus, Orval, 799–805, 807–809, 947
Faulk, John Henry, 588
Faulkner, William, 58, 945; *Intruder in the Dust*, 452
Faure, Edgar, 748, 751
Fay, Paul B. Jr., "Red," 956
FBI (Federal Bureau of Investigation), 760, 950, 970, 1182, 1200, 1260; and gangsters, 94–95; Nixon and, 148, 1216–17, 1235; and loyalty issue, 498; and espionage, 500; and race issue, 738, 1020, 1022, 1023; at Little Rock, 801, 807; and freedom riders, 938; and Vietnam protests, 1056; at Selma, 1060, 1061; and James Meredith, 1066; and teen-age crime, 1103; and Kent State, 1215; and Pentagon Papers, 1237, 1238; and Watergate, 1275, 1279, 1280, 1288–89. *See also* crime; Hoover, J. Edgar
FDR. *See* Roosevelt, Franklin D.
Featherstone, Ralph, 1066
Federal Communications Commission, 196, 588, 973
Federal Emergency Relief Act, 85
Federal Employee Loyalty Program, 490. *See also* loyalty issue
Federal Housing Administration, 107
federal relief. *See* welfare, public
Federal Republic of Germany. *See* Germany
Federal Reserve Board, 24, 79, 90, 106
Federal Trade Commission (FTC), 835, 840
Fehrenbach, T. R., 227, 232
Feiffer, Jules, 1056
Feller, Bob, 247
Ferber, Edna, 1122
Ferebee, Capt. Tom, 381
Ferguson, Homer, 527, 560, 655
Ferlinghetti, Lawrence, 726
Fermi, Enrico, 117, 210, 212, 213, 214, 311, 313, 375, 378, 699
Fermi, Laura (Mrs. Enrico), 117
Ferrer, José, 236
Field, Marshall, 238
Fielding, Dr. Lewis B., 1237–39
Fields, Howard, 18
Fields, W. C., 179
Finch, Robert, 1156, 1168
Finkelstein, Mel, 1167
Finnegan, James P., 604
Fischer, John, 425, 904
Fischer, Robert James, 1261
Fish, Hamilton Jr., 58, 177, 219, 230, 250, 318, 320, 322
Fisher, Dorothy Canfield, 100
Fisher, Frederick G., 714–16
Fitzgerald, Barry, 303
FitzGerald, Frances: *Fire in the Lake*, 1211, 1227
Fitzgerald, F. Scott, 57, 102, 246, 1297
Fitz-Gibbon, Bernice, 723–24
Fitzpatrick, Linda Rae, 1117–18
Fitzsimmons, Frank E., 1255

Flair magazine, 483, 693
Flanders, Ralph E., 88, 709, 717, 747
Fleming, Ian, 955, 998
Flesch, Rudolph: *Why Johnny Can't Read*, 793
Fletcher, Henry P., 140
floods. *See* storms and weather
"flower people." *See* hippies
Floyd, "Pretty Boy," 95
Flügge, S., 213–14
Flynn, Edward J., 82, 170, 447
Flynn, Errol, 820
Flynn, John T., 83
Folsom, James E. "Kissin' Jim," 808
Fomin, Alexander S., 969–70
Fonda, Henry, 283
Fonda, Jane, 1235
Fontaine, Joan, 303
food: garbage as, 20, 42–43; and breadlines, 22, 35; and malnutrition, 22, 41–42, 238; in White House, 23, 81–82; prices, 36–37, 64; shortages and hoarding, 205; and victory gardens, 302–303; and eating habits, 732
Food and Drug Administration, 1111, 1112
Foran, Thomas A., 1205, 1207
Forbes magazine, 1106
Ford, Francis, 1189
Ford, Gerald, 60
Ford, Henry, 22, 25, 55, 89, 125, 140, 155, 204, 223, 246. *See also* Ford Motor Company
Ford, Henry II, 815, 1080
Ford, John, 283
Ford Motor Company, 34, 52, 400; demonstration at Dearborn plant, 10, 26, 41n; and Willow Run, 274; and Walter Reuther, 388, 389. *See also* Edsel
Foreign Affairs, 436, 437, 1180
foreign policy, U.S.: (1930s) 68, 69, 80, 108, 124–27, 171, 174–77, 201–206; postwar, 318; Henry Wallace and, 411–414, 510; and aid to Europe, 436–41 (*see also* Marshall Plan); and cold war, 436–38 (*see also* cold war); containment policy, 437, 438, 532, 555, 659, 696; Acheson and, 519 (*see also* Acheson, Dean); MacArthur and, 540–41, 548; Korean War, 548, 667 (*see also* Korea and Korean War); coexistence, 555; and "massive retaliation," 646–47, 679, 696, 1179; Dulles and, 661–63 (*see also* Dulles, John Foster); and Bricker/George amendments, 673–77; and Vietnam, 680–87 (*see also* Vietnam and Vietnam War); and Formosa, 744–747; and Cuban counterrevolution, 863–867, 893–908; and U–2 affair, 867–76; and missile crisis, 958–71; and China, 1267 (*see also* China). *See also* interventionism; isolationism; neutrality; *and names of individual presidents*
Foreign Relations Committee. *See* Senate Foreign Relations Committee
forgeries, political, 1236–37, 1274, 1280
"forgotten man," 49, 51, 164, 634
Forman, James, 1058, 1060

Formosa (Taiwan). *See* Chiang Kai-shek; China
Formosa resolution (1955), 744–47
Forquet (couturier), 1033
Forrestal, James, 385, 475
Forrestal, Michael, 988, 990, 1046
Forstmeyer, Kurt von, 180
Fortas, Abe, 84, 297, 299, 300, 528, 1011, 1054, 1138–39
Fortress America concept, 178, 222, 556. *See also* isolationism
Fortune magazine, 196, 239; on arms and Army, 5, 6, 125; on General MacArthur, 6, 17–18; on Depression, 19, 25, 36, 38, 41; on FDR administration, 105, 167; polls of, 128, 167, 189, 191, 228, 420; on labor, 161; on H-bomb, 575; on consumer, 773; on women, 781; on "Tycoon," 1092; on Nixon, 1162; on ITT, 1234
Fosdick, Harry Emerson, 223
Foster, William C., 530
Foster, William Z., 10, 50
Four Aces, The, 694
Fowler, Henry, 84
Fox, John, 835, 837, 840
Frady, Marshall, 981
France, 177, 180, 181, 205, 221, 443, 445, 682, 740, 1122, 1252; nuclear physicists of, 215–16; fall of, 216, 217, 222, 251; Vichyites, 270, 333; FDR's message to, 277; liberation of Paris, 333; and Indochina, 395, 421, 535, 647, 680–87, 916; U.S. occupation troops in, 406; and Marshall Plan, 440; and Suez, 763–65, 822. *See also* de Gaulle, Charles
Francis, Connie, 1142
Francis, Kay, 11
Franco, Gen. Francisco, 176, 860
Frank, Anne, 300
Frank, Jerome N., 84
Frankfurter, Felix, 95, 105
Franklin, Benjamin, 227, 775
Frazier, John F., 1200–1201
freedom riders, 934–43, 944
Freedom Summer, 1021–23, 1066
Freeman, Bud, 248
Freeman, Orville, 60, 892–93, 1015
Freeman (publication), 525
Free Speech Movement (FSM), 1033–34
"free world," 556–57, 682
French, Samuel, 582
Freyberg, Gen. Bernard, 329
Friedan, Betty, 286, 393, 428, 777, 1106, 1109; *The Feminine Mystique*, 997
Friedman, Milton, 1180
Friendly, Alfred, 521n, 964
Friendly, Fred W., 514
Frisch, O. R., 211, 212, 314, 315
Froines, John R., 1205
Fromm, Erich, 1088
Frost, Robert, 577, 890, 1297
Fry, Christopher, 486
Frye, Marquette, 1062–63
FTC. *See* Federal Trade Commission
Fuchs, Klaus Emil, 213, 313–14, 315, 493, 500, 502n, 512, 572

Fuchs, Norman, 1105
Fulbright, J. William, 83, 322, 444, 788, 822, 953; and peace organization, 292, 420; and Truman, 415, 447; investigates RFC, 603–604; and Joseph McCarthy, 704, 718; and Fulbright program, 824; and Bay of Pigs, 895; and Vietnam War, 1018–19, 1049, 1072; foreign policy, 1038, 1219; on ABM, 1164
Fuller, Alfred C., 33–34
funds, campaign: FDR and, 139; Nixon "Secret Fund," 620, 629–38; questionable contributions, 1232–35, 1274, 1288
Funk, Wilfred J., 471
Furness, Betty, 614, 621

Gable, Clark, 68, 198, 283, 1193
Gabrielson, Guy, 529
Gagarin, Yuri A., 928, 929
Gaither, H. Rowan Jr., 796
Gaitskell, Hugh, 440
Galanos, James, 1197
Galbraith, John Kenneth, 24, 67, 878, 1001, 1046, 1090, 1096; on life-style, 775, 776, 777, 1135; *The Affluent Society*, 789; *The New Industrial State*, 877, 1083, 1092
Galella, Ronald E., 1261
Galento, Tony, 197
Galíndez, Dr. Jesús de, 760
Gallagher, Buell, 1167
Gallagher, Bishop Michael, 110
Gallo, "Crazy Joe," 1260
Gallup, George, and Gallup polls, 118, 126; and FDR, 139, 415; and war issues, 174, 201, 224, 228, 231; and Truman, 415, 446, 562, 607; and elections: (1948) 446, 453, 458, 465–66, 468, 470, 471, (1960) 879, 880–83, (1964) 1029, (1968) 1145, 1146–47, (1972) 1273, 1287; on loyalty issue, 489; on Joseph McCarthy, 526, 704; on Nixon, 619, 834, 1165, 1218, 1221, 1287; 1954 study of American life, 731–34; on Eisenhower administration, 751–52, 766, 794, 808; on Republican party, 879, 1025; on Kennedys, 904, 985, 1014; on LBJ, 1075; on students and education, 1097, 1103, 1167, 1194; on environment, 1171–72; on Agnew, 1219; on Watergate, 1287
Galsworthy, John, 68
Gamelin, Gen. Maurice, 216
"game plan," 1222, 1239, 1292
Gandhi, Mohandas K. (Mahatma), 111, 1228
Ganeval, Gen. Jean, 442
gangsters. *See* crime
Gannett, Frank, 151
Gannon, Joseph W., 481
Garbo, Greta, 68
Gardiner, Don, 1005
Gardner, Ava, 308, 427
Gardner, John, 1125
Gardner, O. Max, 55
Gardner, Trevor, 788
Gargan, Joseph F., 1184–85

Garland, Judy, 197, 198n, 427
Garner, John Nance, 48, 51, 76, 114, 140, 151, 152, 155, 157, 200, 202, 226
Garrison, Jim, 1075, 1166
Garry, Charles, 1203, 1206
Gathings, Ezekiel, 596
Gavin, Gen. James, 1049
Gay, Charles R., 147
Gayle, W. A., 741, 742, 743
Gaynor, Janet, 68
Gehrig, Lou, 197, 247
Geneen, Harold S., 1233–34
General Motors, 33, 119, 485, 648, 773, 814, 1001; strikes against, 153–56, 400–401; and Ralph Nader, 1256
"generation gap," 1100. See also family
Geneva conference (1955), 747–51, 760, 873
George, Ron, 1085
George, Walter, 170, 200, 456, 557, 747; and George amendment, 676
George VI of England, 177, 179, 200
Germany, 68, 229n, 231, 235, 1046; rise of Hitler, 74, 171, 175, 178, 180 (see also Hitler, Adolf); Jews in, 96, 124, 370; prelude to World War II, 178–183, 202–203, 205; atomic research, 210–16, 275, 309, 313, 336–39, 374, 574; offenses and atrocities, 217; and U.S. 1940 election, 225; and USSR, 233, 236, 260, 264, 273, 279, 334, 874, 909 (see also East Germany below); and Allied invasion, 273, 278–79, 329, 331–334; espionage of, 274, 309; defeated, 347, 369; U.S. occupation of, 408, 441–443; West German sovereignty, 487; and European Defense Community Pact, 597; East Germany (German Democratic Republic) and USSR, 909, 911; and currency revaluation, 1252. See also Berlin
Gernreich, Rudi, 1033, 1107
Gervasi, Frank, 179
Gesell, Arnold, 424
Getty, J. Paul, 34
Giap, Vo Nguyen. See Vo Nguyen Giap
Gibbons, Floyd, 179
Gibbs, Wolcott, 304
Gibson, Kenneth, 1247
Gilbert, Eugene, 723, 724
Gillette, Guy, 200
Gilpatrick, Roswell W., 919, 959, 960, 990, 1000
Ginsberg, Allen, 393, 483, 727, 728, 1205, 1207
Ginzburg, Ralph, 1036
Girdler, Tom M., 96, 158–59, 160, 161
GIs, 280–87, 289, 333, 334, 409; and GI Bill, 292, 324, 397. See also Army, U.S.; veterans, war; World War II
Glass, Carter, 48, 78–79, 164, 230
Glassford, Gen. Pelham D., 10, 11, 12, 15, 17
Glenn, Lt. Col. John H. Jr., 60, 819, 930–934
Glover, William, 1193, 1194

GNP (Gross National Product). See economy, U.S.
Godfrey, Arthur, 359, 585, 588
Goebbels, Joseph Paul, 178, 213, 219, 290, 354
gold, hoarding, 72–73
Gold, Harry, 312–13, 375, 500, 501, 502n
Gold, Ted, 1134, 1199–1200
Goldberg, Arthur, 209, 891, 1124, 1125, 1139
Golden, Harry, 1077
Goldfine, Bernard, 834–43
Goldfine, Charlotte (Mrs. Bernard), 836, 837
Goldman, Eric F., 565, 594, 1010, 1012, 1075, 1090
Goldmark, Peter Carl, 972–75
Goldsborough, T. Alan, 404
gold standard. See economy, U.S.
Gold Star mothers, 7
Goldstein, Joseph, 249
Goldwater, Barry, 845, 957, 985, 994, 1036, 1042, 1050, 1093, 1120, 1121, 1250; campaigns: (1964) 995–96, 1018, 1025–29, 1030, 1031–32, (1972) 1283
Goldwater, Barry Jr., 1163
Goldwyn, Samuel, 382
Golos, Jacob, 502n
Gompers, Samuel, 404
Gonzales, Donald, 533
Gonzales, Virgilio, 1276–78
Goodell, Charles, 1219, 1221
Good Housekeeping magazine, 1003
Goodman, Al, 179
Goodman, Andrew, 1022–24
Goodman, Benny, 68, 119, 244, 248, 430, 975
Goodpaster, Col. Andrew J., 754
Goodwin, Richard, 1075
GOP. See Republican party
Gore, Albert, 770, 1019, 1221
"Gorgeous George," 484
Göring, Hermann, 222, 336, 382
Gorki, Maxim, 23
Goudsmit, Samuel A., 315, 336, 337, 338, 374
Gould, Chester, 94–95
Gould, Jack, 584, 1012
Gouzenko, Igor, 493, 500, 501
Grable, Betty, 286, 1036
Grace, Eugene, 166
Grafton, Samuel, 355–56, 415
Graham, Frank P., 529
Graham, Maj. Gen. Henry, 942
Graham, William Franklin "Billy," 60, 484, 594, 749, 1100, 1161, 1219
Grant, Cary, 120, 998
Graves, Ralph, 1262
Gray, Gordon, 573, 697, 698
Gray, Harold, 166–67
Gray, L. Patrick, 1288–89
Great Britain, 24, 25, 68, 125, 174, 371, 484, 574, 590, 591; as world leader, 4–5, 201, 316, 433; king and queen visit America, 177, 200; and developments toward war in Europe, 177, 178, 180, 182–83; and "cash-and-carry," 204–

205; Battle of Britain, 217–19; -U.S. destroyer swap, 222, 226, 228; aid and lend-lease, 227–31; and war in Pacific, 265–66, 270; U.S. troops in, 277; and rocket attacks, 332, 333; postwar conditions in, 433–35, 440; and Korea, 536, 539, 555; and Suez, 763–65, 822
Great Debate, 556–58
Great Society (LBJ), 474, 1011, 1042, 1043, 1053, 1074
Greece, 217, 433–37, 438, 464
Green, Edward, 645
Green, Theodore Francis, 524
Green, William, 84, 130, 132–35, 155, 157, 223–24
Green Berets (Special Forces group), 891, 892, 918–19, 956, 1045, 1056, 1073
Greenberg, Hank, 283
Greene, Gael: *Sex and the College Girl*, 996
Greenglass, David and Ruth, 313–14, 374, 500
Greenland–U.S. treaty, 231
Gregory, Dick, 983, 1063, 1066
Grenier, John, 1027
Grew, Joseph C., 173–74, 251–52, 254
Grey, Zane, 532
Grier, Roosevelt, 1130
Griffin, Robert P., 1138
Griffith, Robert, 491n
Grissom, Capt. Virgil I., 819, 930
Griswold, Erwin, 1233–34
Gromyko, Andrei A., 368, 411, 962, 1272
Groppi, James E., 1078
Gross, Ernest, 532, 533, 535
Gross, H. R., 1033
Gross National Product (GNP). *See* economy, U.S.
Groves, Gen. Leslie R., 212, 312, 315, 375, 378, 379
Gruening, Ernest, 1019, 1051, 1074
Gruenther, Gen. Alfred M., 654, 754
Guadalcanal, 267, 268, 270, 272–73, 274, 340, 342, 343
Guam, 176, 265, 343
Guatemala, 677, 864–65, 894, 1122
Guevara, Ernesto "Che," 861
Guffey, Joseph, 157
Guffey-Snyder Coal Act, 106, 137
Guinness, Alec, 420, 590, 834
Guitar, Mary Anne, 1003
Gunther, John: on FDR, 49, 80, 150, 165, 226, 325–26, 355; *Inside Russia Today*, 791
Guthman, Edwin, 951, 979
Guthrie, Arlo, 1073
Guthrie, Woody, 235

Hacker, Andrew, 1001
Haeberle, Ronald, 1177
Hagen, John P., 798, 799, 813
Hagerty, James A., 319, 788; and Dewey, 452, 463, 466, 468, 469; and Eisenhower, 633, 646, 647, 652, 703, 753, 756, 757, 767, 768, 812, 859, 875; and Adams scandal, 837, 838, 842, 843; and 1960 campaign strategy, 854, 855

Hague, Frank, 47, 207, 448, 482, 627
Hahn, Otto, 210–11
Haig, Gen. Alexander, 1295
Halberstam, David, 892, 893, 925, 993, 1000; on Vietnam, 994, 1051, 1054, 1125
Haldeman, H. R., 1156, 1161, 1211, 1217, 1234, 1237, 1273; and Watergate, 1279, 1288–90
Haley, Bill, 725
Haley, Harold J., 1202
Hall, James Norman, 68
Hall, Leonard, 708, 757
Hallanan, Walter, 615
Halleck, Charles, 447, 450, 452
Halley, Rudolph, 600
Halperin, Morton B., 1232
Halsey, Adm. William F. Jr., 263, 269, 344, 345, 346
Halverson, Carl S., 443
Hamilton, John D. M., 143, 144
Hammarskjöld, Dag, 598, 823, 908, 909, 910, 913
Hammerstein, Oscar, 304
Hampton, Fred, 1004, 1191
Hampton, Lionel, 244
Hanes, Arthur, 977, 978
Hannegan, Robert, 317, 318, 319
Hansberry, Lorraine, 984
Hara, Admiral, 271
hardhats, demonstration by, 1212
Hardin, Clifford, 1233
Harding, Warren G., 206, 357
Hargis, Billy James, 953, 1194
Hargrove, Marion, 304
Harkins, Gen. Paul D., 921–22, 937, 988, 991, 993, 1000, 1016
Harlan, John, 1231
Harlech, Lord (David Ormsby-Gore), 1139
Harlow, Bryce, 703, 1218
Harlow, Jean, 101, 148, 592n, 689, 1037
Harper's Magazine, 56, 90
Harriman, Averell, 45, 105, 233, 326, 348, 368, 369, 540, 608, 769, 986; on Berlin crisis, 909–10; and Vietnam, 920, 988, 990, 991, 1046, 1126
Harriman, Joseph Wright, 45
Harrington, Michael, 1056
Harris, Fred, 1282
Harris, Dr. Hiawatha, 1150
Harris, Louis, and Harris polls, 883, 983, 1019, 1026, 1037, 1075, 1099, 1145, 1147, 1221, 1273, 1287
Harris, Oren, 852
Harrison, Gen. William K., 666
Harrison, Pat, 113, 152
Hart, Adm. Tom, 266
Hartford Courant, 187
Hartke, Vance, 1282
Harvard *Crimson*, 702
Harvard University, 1168
Hassett, William D., 316, 322, 335, 347, 350, 356–57
Hatch Act, 168, 495
Hatfield, Mark, 60, 1039
Hawaii, Japanese attack on. *See* Pearl Harbor

Haw-Haw, Lord, 279
Hawkins, Jack, 590
Hayakawa, Samuel I., 1099
Hayden, Tom, 952, 1143, 1205, 1208
Haynsworth, Clement F. Jr., 1164
Hays, Brooks, 801
Hays, Will H., and Hays Office, 66, 120, 592, 1193
Hayter, Sir William, 410
Hayward, Louis, 283
Hayward, Susan, 1028
Haywood, Bill, 388
Hayworth, Rita, 198n, 286, 689
health, 1225; conditions in 1930s, 20–22, 39, 66, 69; and medical insurance, 63, 239; cancer research, 240; cigarettes and, 693; physical fitness and, 956–57; and promiscuity, 997, 1109, 1225; of hippies, 1111, 1115; poliomyelitis, 1111; heart transplants, 1122. See also drugs; food
Health, Education and Welfare, Department of, 648
Hearst, William Randolph, and Hearst press, 48, 111, 301, 302, 525, 564, 596; and FDR, 83, 90, 106, 107, 108, 137, 138, 143
Hebert, F. Edward, 757
Hechinger, Fred M., 725, 1100, 1109
Hechinger, Grace, 1100, 1109
Hecht, Ben, 727
Heeton, Dr. Leonard D., 767
Hefner, Hugh, 1144, 1196
Heiman, Kurt, 180
Heinl, Col. Robert D. Jr., 530
Heisenberg, Werner, 336, 337
helicopters, 240, 293. See also air transportation
Heller, Walter, 60, 986
Hellman, Reiner, 824
Helms, Richard, 988, 990, 1216, 1217, 1237–39, 1288, 1292
Hemingway, Ernest, 98; Across the River and Into the Trees, 486; The Old Man and the Sea, 649
Hemingway, Natalie, 1007
Henderson, Fletcher, 119
Henderson, Leon, 162, 163, 448
Henderson, Loy, 433
Hepburn, Katharine, 187, 303
"Herblock" (Herbert Block), 526, 673, 708
Herman, Woody, 483
Herrick, Capt. John, 1017
Hersey, John, 304
Hershey, Gen. Lewis B., 224, 320, 402, 407, 1073, 1188
Herter, Christian A., 855, 862, 873
Hess, Karl III, 1118–21
Heyerdahl, Thor, 1192
Hickel, Walter J., 1155, 1211
Hickenlooper, Bourke B., 524, 527
Hickerson, John, 533
Hickok, Lorena, 99
Hicks, Granville, 57, 205
Hicks, Louise Day, 1078
Hien, Captain, 681

highways. See automobile(s)
Hildegarde, 197, 247
Hill, George Washington, 121–22, 148, 149
Hill, Joe, 135; ballad of, 391
Hill, John, 118
Hill, Lister, 448
Hillary, Sir Edmund, 693
Hillman, Sidney, 132, 153–54, 320
Hilsman, Roger, 960, 988, 990, 1046
Hilton, Conrad, 762
Hilton, James: Lost Horizon, 240
Himmler, Heinrich, 198, 203
Hindenburg, Paul von, 68, 296
hippies, 483, 693, 999–1000, 1100, 1113–1118, 1143–44. See also "beat" generation
Hirohito, Emperor, 124, 251, 273, 383, 384–87
Hiroshima. See Japan
Hiss, Alger, 84, 96, 126, 148, 247, 393, 572, 674, 995; Hiss case, 459, 494, 503–512; Acheson and, 501, 511–12; Adlai Stevenson and, 503, 611–12, 628, 629; Eisenhower and, 613
Hiss, Priscilla (Mrs. Alger), 148, 503, 505, 507, 511
Hitchcock, Alfred, 120, 197, 303
Hitler, Adolf, 68, 80, 110, 115, 126, 166, 175, 198, 204, 229, 231, 296, 354, 519; and Munich Pact, 124, 182; and Czechoslovakia, 177, 178–83, 200; speeches of, 180, 181; FDR and, 190, 200, 201, 206, 225, 233, 236, 260, 331; and Poland, 201–203; and western campaign, 205, 216–18, 219; and physicists, 210–16, 336–37; and Soviet Union, 233, 260; declares war on U.S., 260; and European invasion, 278, 333–34; and U-boat campaign, 295; and "secret weapons," 315; death of, 369, 1122. See also Germany; World War II
Hobby, Oveta Culp, 648, 649
hoboes. See population
Ho Chi Minh, 395, 421, 680, 681, 684, 1057
Hoffa, James, 389, 390, 391, 820, 1000, 1255
Hoffman, Abbie, 1205–1208, 1229
Hoffman, Dustin, 1200
Hoffman, Julius J., 1205–1208
Hoffman, Nicholas von, 1087, 1110, 1194, 1258
Hoffman, Paul G., 436, 582, 618, 630, 703
Hofmann, Dr. Albert, 1111
Hogan, Frank, 850
Hoisington, Gen. Elizabeth P., 1197
Holden, William, 590
Holding Company Act, 105, 116
Holiday, Billie, 244
Holland, 216, 222, 251, 266. See also Indonesia
Holland, Henry, 827
Hollenbeck, Don, 515
Holliday, Judy, 198n, 486, 590
Hollywood. See moving pictures and performers

Holman, Frank E., 676
home front, World War II, 289–309; shortages and rationing, 205, 293–94, 303, 333; dimouts, 274; government agencies, 275; black markets, 293; women on, 305
Homma, Gen. Masaharu, 265, 268
Hood, Jimmy A., 979–81
Hooper polls, 190, 304, 584, 585
Hoover, Herbert Clark, 5, 7, 9, 22, 31, 54, 88, 89, 106, 112, 125, 140, 239, 366, 518, 603, 652, 654, 793; and BEF, 3–4, 10, 12–13, 15–18; and economy, 23–28, 32, 37, 38, 138, 1251; on starvation, 41–42; and FDR, 47, 49–53 passim, 72, 75, 77, 141, 320; and interregnum, 71–74, 76; and blacks, 107; on postwar Europe, 435; on Hiss case, 511; and isolationism, 556; and MacArthur, 563, 564; on Nixon, 630
Hoover, J. Edgar, 94–95, 241, 243, 297, 529, 738, 1037, 1261, 1288; and Communism, 97, 197, 493; and Oppenheimer, 695, 696–97; and civil rights demonstrations, 807, 1023, 1132; and Nixon aides, 1216–17, 1235–36
Hoover, Lou (Mrs. Herbert), 23
Hope, Bob, 1055, 1056, 1140, 1161
Hopkins, Eric, 305
Hopkins, Harry, 89, 97, 103, 105, 163, 170, 226, 227, 232, 284, 674; and federal relief, 85–86, 106–107, 188; and survey of air power, 178; on FDR and lend-lease, 229; as second in command, 233–34, 276–77, 278, 316, 324, 360
Hopkins, Miriam, 118
Hopkins, Stephen P., 284
Hopper, Hedda, 246
Hopson, Howard, 45
Horii, General, 268
Horne, Lena, 244, 984
Horner, Henry, 75
Hornet (aircraft carrier), 272, 1159
hot line, U.S./USSR, 907, 986
House Labor Committee, 59
Houseman, John, 190, 195–96
House Subcommittee on Legislative Oversight, 835, 851
House Un-American Activities Committee, 97, 167, 176, 459, 489, 495, 498n, 502, 525, 668; and Hiss case, 504–11; and riots, 849, 1081
housing, 447, 474; wartime shortages, 293; postwar developments, 430–32, 476, 777–778, 779–80; "singles," 1035; blacks and, 1065, 1069, 1080
Housing and Urban Development, Department of, 1042, 1080
Housman, A. E., 1004
Houston (cruiser), 266
Howard, Trevor, 486
Howard University, 7
Howe, Gordon, 999
Howe, Irving, 592
Howe, Louis McHenry, 47, 48, 54, 77, 107
Howrey, Edward F., 835
Hoyt, Palmer, 708, 717

Hrushka, William, 12
Hruska, Roman L., 1164
Huber, Oscar, 1006
Hughes, Charles Evans, 5, 76, 90, 135, 136, 318; Hughes Court and FDR, 137, 140, 151–53
Hughes, Emmet John, 607, 626, 627, 648, 649, 659–61, 676, 769, 770, 796, 854, 876
Hughes, Howard, 174n, 274, 296, 1262–1266
Hughes, H. Stuart, 904, 958
Hughes, J. J., 173
Hughes, Richard J., 1080
Hu Hsiu-chuan, Gen., 549
hula hoops, 820–21
Hull, Cordell, 96, 114, 124, 222; and war developments in Europe, 177, 201–202, 222; and Pearl Harbor, 251–52, 255–56, 258, 259
Hume, Paul, 367
Hummer, Ed, 505
Humphrey, George M., 96, 647–49, 657, 664, 678, 755, 756, 840
Humphrey, Hubert H., 83, 128, 209, 448, 454, 470, 670, 704, 746, 1128, 1165; in presidential campaigns: (1956) 770, (1960) 880, (1968) 1127, 1129, 1142, 1145–47, (1972) 1273, 1282–84, 1286; as Vice President, 1031, 1038–39, 1047; and Vietnam, 1047, 1076
Hungary, 597, 764, 765
Hunt, Dorothy (Mrs. E. Howard Jr.), 1291
Hunt, E. Howard Jr., 895, 899, 905n, 1218; and "Plumbers," 1232, 1236–39, 1274, 1288; and Watergate, 1275–80, 1288, 1290–91
Hunt, James V., 603
Hunter, Ken, 525
Huntley, Chet, 587, 1005
Hurd, Peter, 1044
Hurley, Gen. Patrick J., 348, 488; as Secretary of War, 12, 14, 16–18, 42, 57, 58, 130–31
hurricane of 1938, 183–88
Hurst, Fannie, 286
Hussein, king of Jordan, 822–23
Huston, John, 283, 690
Huston, Tom Charles, 1217, 1235
Hutcheson, Bill, 135
Hutchinson, James "Groovy," 1117
Hutner, Juli, 1197
Hutton, Barbara, 132
Hutton, Betty, 486, 694
Hutton, Marion, 248
Huxley, Aldous, 68
Hynek, Joseph A., 790
Hynes, John, 837

ICBMs (intercontinental ballistic missiles). See missiles and rocket programs
Iceland, U.S. troops in, 232–33
Ickes, Harold, 84, 86, 115, 138, 151, 204, 231, 245, 250, 360, 412, 415
IDA (Institute for Defense Analysis), 1133–1134
IGY. See International Geophysical Year

image, 118, 425, 448; of GIs, 280–81, 283, 284–86; of management, 1093; of press, 1290
image of U.S. abroad: (1930s) 124–25; and Hitler, 296; and demobilization riots, 405–10; anti-Americanism, 435, 492, 824–33, 875; postwar, 443–46; in Third World, 548, 824–25; and arms race, 572; and integration issue, 737; and space race, 789, 794, 926–29, 933, 934; Little Rock crisis and, 809; (1960s) 860, 873, 875, 1003; U–2 affair and, 873, 875; Bay of Pigs and, 902–903
immigration, 581, 670
impeachment, 45, 177, 561–62, 940n, 953, 968
income: (1929) 32, (1932) 36, 67, (1937) 148, 165–66, (1940) 238, 773; black, 243, 1078, 1150; World War II, 290; (1950s) 773, 775, 776, 784, 883; national, 792; (1960s) 1001, 1089, 1091. See also prices; wages and hours
income taxes, 25, 73, 106, 165–66, 240; avoidance of, 45, 148, 604–605. See also Internal Revenue Service; taxes
independent voters. See third party
India, 484, 566, 860
Indians, American, 224, 1191
Indochina: Japan and, 177, 251, 252, 265; U.S. aid and intervention, 535, 680–87, 819, 1229; Eisenhower and war in, 680, 682–85, 687. See also Cambodia; Laos; Vietnam and Vietnam War
Indonesia, 266, 484, 825, 959
inflation. See economy, U.S.
Ingalls, David S., 615–16
Inge, William, 486
Insull, Samuel, 44, 67
integration, 447, 936; in Truman years, 482–83; Brown v. Board of Education, Topeka, 734–38; Little Rock crisis, 799–810; TV and, 1150. See also black(s); busing; segregation
intellectuals, 102–103, 126, 228, 1090; and Communism, 50, 56–57, 103; and FDR, 77; "eggheads," 291, 625–26, 695, 758, 792; defined by Eisenhower, 580; and Stevenson, 610, 625–26; and LBJ, 1012, 1044–45
intelligence, military, 264, 343, 787, 909, 919, 961, 962, 1051, 1123, 1209. See also CIA (Central Intelligence Agency)
intercontinental ballistic missiles (ICBMs). See missile and rocket programs
Internal Revenue Service, 73, 604–606, 1235. See also income taxes
"International, The," 55, 102, 1301
International Apple Shippers Association, 26
International Geophysical Year (IGY), 787, 797–98
internationalism, 420–21. See also isolationism; United Nations
International Ladies Garment Workers Union, 132
International Monetary and Economic Conference, 124

International Monetary Fund, 1252, 1254
International Telephone and Telegraph Corporation (ITT), 1174, 1233–34, 1281
Interstate Commerce Commission (ICC), 740, 943
interventionism, 219–22, 228, 230–31; and Vietnam, 682–87, 760, 919–23; in Middle East, 823–24; JFK and, 906, 919–23. See also isolationism; neutrality
Inverchapel, Lord, 433–34
Iraq, 823
Iron Curtain speech (Churchill), 410, 412
IRS. See Internal Revenue Service
Irving, Clifford, 1261–67
Irving, Edith (Mrs. Clifford), 1263–66
isolationism, (1930s) 108, 125–27, 174–75, 177–78; FDR and, 175, 176, 177, 202–203, 204, 226, 321; in World War II, 219–22, 235, 292, 318; America First movement, 223; as 1940 campaign issue, 225–26; and lend-lease, 230–31; and Japan, 251; vs internationalism, 420–21; return to, 445, 555–58, 569–570. See also neutrality
Israel, 8, 763–64, 822. See also Jews
Italy, 175, 180, 217, 222, 590; U.S. and, 231, 235; and Tripartite Pact, 235, 252, 260; invasion of, 279–80
Ives, Irving M., 655
Iwo Jima, 266, 267, 345–46, 347, 371, 385
Izvestia, 749

Jackson, C. D., 703, 953
Jackson, George, 1201–1204, 1240, 1241, 1260
Jackson, Graham, 357
Jackson, Henry, 788, 1236, 1282, 1283
Jackson, Jesse, 1150, 1207
Jackson, Jonathan, 1202–1204
Jackson, Robert H., 301, 734–35
Jackson State affair, 951n, 1212
Jacob, Philip E., 582–83
Jacob Jones (destroyer), 264
Jacobson, Eddie, 397
James, Harry Haig, 68, 197, 307, 308, 1036
James, Louis, 1244
Janeway, Eliot, 1019
Japan, 177, 221, 229, 235–36, 339, 1248; and China, 68, 74, 124, 125, 174, 176, 252; Pearl Harbor, 69, 251–60; and the Panay, 171, 173–76; and Tripartite Pact, 230, 235, 251–52, 260; and Vietnam, 251–52; Pacific campaigns, 263–74, 340–346; armed strength of, 263–64, 265–266, 271, 346; morale, 263, 346, 370, 371, 376, 383; army brutalities of, 268–269; on defensive, 340–46, 347, 371; and Soviet declaration of war, 348, 384, 411; kamikaze pilots, 370, 371, 385, 386–87; prospect of long war with, 371, 386–87, 388; and Potsdam Declaration, 379–80, 384, 385; Hiroshima and Nagasaki bombed, 379–84; surrender of, 384–387; U.S. occupation troops in, 406–407, 409–10, 531; and Korean War, 539, 544; Peace Treaty, 541, 586; anti-

American riots in, 875; and terrorists, 1259

Japanese-Americans, in World War II, 208, 297–302

Jaudon, Capt. Leonard B., 388

Javits, Jacob K., 1019

Jeffers, Robinson, 68

Jenkins, Ray, 709–13

Jenkins, Walter W., 914, 1011, 1029–30

Jenner, William E., 475, 491, 527, 562, 627, 664, 668, 674

Jeremiah X, 983

Jervis, Richard, 90

Jessup, Philip, 541

Jews, 68, 142, 165, 176, 220, 242, 447; in Germany, 96, 124, 370; SNCC and, 1077. *See also* anti-Semitism; Israel

JFK. *See* Kennedy, John F.

Jodl, Gen. Alfred, 369

Joelson, Charles S., 1123

John Birch Society. *See* Birch

Johnson, Alvin, 1136

Johnson, Frank M. Jr., 1060

Johnson, Haynes, 905, 906

Johnson, Hiram, 17, 52, 108, 152, 176, 292, 395

Johnson, Howard, 34

Johnson, Gen. Hugh S. "Ironpants," 51, 84, 104, 115, 221, 230; and NRA, 87–90, 95–96, 105, 132

Johnson, Lady Bird (Mrs. Lyndon B.), 21, 106, 914, 1010, 1030, 1040, 1044, 1072

Johnson, Louis, 316, 475, 489, 531, 532, 534, 572

Johnson, Lyndon B., 8, 21, 65, 170, 209, 470, 593n, 771, 1038, 1081, 1160, 1286, 1296; as newcomer to Washington, 84, 106, 153, 395; FDR and, 169, 355; in Senate, 659, 666, 1010; and Joseph McCarthy, 704, 709, 717; on satellites, 788, 813; in 1960 campaign, 880, 881; as Vice President, 911–12, 914, 915, 933, 960; and Vietnam, 917–20, 925, 994, 1016–19, 1039–40, 1045–57, 1074, 1125, 1145, 1230; sworn in as president, 1006; character and image, 1010–14, 1036, 1075–76; calumny against, 1012, 1044–45, 1068, 1073; relations with Kennedys, 1013–15, 1075; powers of, 1018–19, 1076; and civil rights, 1022, 1030, 1042, 1057, 1060, 1149; 1964 campaign and election, 1029–32, 1120, 1143; peace promises, 1031, 1050; foreign relations, 1040, 1044; social and economic legislation, 1041–44, 1053; meets Kosygin, 1044; announces withdrawal, 1127, 1141; and Supreme Court, 1137–39. *See also* credibility gap; Great Society

Johnson, Mary, 245

Johnson, Nunnally, 689

Johnson, Olin, 447, 808

Johnson, Paul B., 947–49, 1022, 1023

Johnson, Rafer, 1130

Johnson, Sam Ealy Jr., 1039

Johnson, U. Alexis, 919, 960, 964, 988

Johnson, Van, 149

Johnson, Virginia E., 1108–1109

Johnson, Walter, 282

Johnson Debt Default Act, 125

Johnston, Eric, 589

Joint Chiefs of Staff, 227, 372, 572, 646; and war in Pacific, 344, 370–71, 388; and Korea, 409, 518, 531, 540; MacArthur and, 542, 544, 545–46, 548, 550, 559–60, 562, 606; and Formosa crisis, 745; and Bay of Pigs, 866, 894, 899; and Vietnam, 919, 920, 1045, 1046, 1052, 1053, 1070–71; and Cuban missile crisis, 963, 970, 971; and Cambodia, 1210

Joliot-Curie, Frédéric, 210, 211, 216

Jolson, Al, 89, 734

Jones, Clarence, 1243, 1244, 1245

Jones, Jennifer, 303

Jones, Jesse, 104, 369

Jones, Le Roi, 1058

Jones, Spike, 119

Joplin, Janis, 1103

Jordan, 822, 823

Joslin, Theodore, 27

Joyce, James, 246; *Ulysses*, 98

Judd, Walter, 512, 954

Jung, Dr. Carl Gustav, 82

Justice Department, 1149; J. Edgar Hoover and, 94; and Little Rock crisis, 800, 802, 804; and civil rights in South, 935, 939, 944, 946, 948–49, 978, 1024; and Kent State, 1215; and ITT, 1233; and Watergate, 1279, 1289

Kaiser, Henry J., 274, 295–96

Kalb, Marvin, 1216

Kallen, Kitty, 693

Kalmbach, Herbert, 1232–33, 1274, 1291

Kaltenborn, H. V., 180, 181, 182, 189, 469

Kansas City, 18, 21

Kansas City Star, 364

Kaplan, Joseph, 787, 792

Karam, James "Jimmy the Flash," 803, 804, 805

Karam, Mrs. James, 803

Karenga, Ron, 1062, 1070

Karnow, Stan, 915

Kasper, John, 739

Katcher, Leo, 629

Kattenburg, Paul, 1046

Katzenbach, Nicholas, 60, 949–51, 963, 980–81, 1076, 1126

Kawabata, Yasunari, 1259

Kawabe, Lt. Gen. T., 383–84

Kaye, Sammy, 256

Keating, Kenneth, 843, 958–59

Keeler, Christine, 1003

Keeler, Ruby, 88, 1224

Kefauver, Estes, 470, 705; Costello hearings, 600–601; as candidate: (1952) 601, 608, 613, 622, (1956) 770

Keitel, Field Marshal Wilhelm, 369

Keller, Helen, 1122

Kelly, Colin, 270

Kelly, Edward J., 159, 226, 448

Kelly, Gene, 149

Kelly, Grace, 22; marriage to Prince Rainier, 761–62
Kelly, John B., 22, 761–62
Kelly, Patsy, 120
Kelsey, Frances O., 1111
Kemp, Hal, 128
Kempton, Murray, 390, 1000
Kennan, George F., 348, 436–38, 518, 519, 535, 566, 677, 1049
Kennedy, Caroline, 892, 955, 1005
Kennedy, Edward, 957, 1014, 1032, 1130, 1145, 1163, 1180, 1236; and Chappaquiddick, 1183–86; in 1972 campaign, 1273
Kennedy, Ethel (Mrs. Robert F.), 957, 985, 1014, 1129–31
Kennedy, Jacqueline Bouvier (Mrs. John F.), 356n, 486, 884, 890, 892, 985, 987–988, 996; popularity of, 910, 955–56, 1014, 1139; and death and funeral of JFK, 1004, 1005–1008; remarriage, 1139–41. See also Onassis, Jacqueline (Mrs. Aristotle)
Kennedy, Joan (Mrs. Edward), 985
Kennedy, John F., 8, 60, 170, 204, 247, 276, 356n, 394, 466, 516, 933, 995, 1003, 1025, 1166; as Senator, 486, 674, 820; statement on Yalta, 491; and Joseph McCarthy, 704; in elections: (1956) 770–71, (1958) 845, (1960) 877–86; inauguration and early days as President, 889–93; powers of, 890, 907; and blacks, 890, 935–36, 977–78, 982; image and popularity of, 892–93, 985; and Bay of Pigs, 893–98, 900, 903–908, 930, 935; and cold war, 906–13; and Vienna conference, 908–11, 935; and Berlin crisis, 911–13; and Vietnam War, 913, 916–23, 925, 988–94, 1045, 1236–37; and space program, 925–30, 934, 1156; and civil rights, 935, 939–40, 949–50, 981–83, 1022; hatred of, 952, 954, 957; Profiles in Courage, 955, 1013; and physical fitness, 956–57; and Cuban missile crisis, 960–71; foreign policy, 985–86, 994; liberal programs, 986–87; death and funeral of, 1004–1008; posthumous honors and popularity, 1007–1008, 1013. See also New Frontier
Kennedy, John F. Jr., 1004, 1007
Kennedy, Joseph P., 46, 92, 96, 146, 204, 221, 242, 284; and Father Coughlin, 109, 117; and isolationism, 223, 556, 557
Kennedy, Joseph P. Jr., 284
Kennedy, Patrick Bouvier, 987
Kennedy, Renwick C., 435
Kennedy, Robert F., 60, 820, 880, 885, 914, 957, 999, 1004, 1007, 1127, 1128, 1258; and Army-McCarthy hearings, 710; and Bay of Pigs, 894, 902, 904, 906; Thirteen Days, 904, 968; and civil rights, 935, 936, 939–43, 944–48, 950–51, 978–81, 1023; and Cuban missile crisis, 960–63, 965, 967–71; extremists and, 977, 979; and new blacks, 983–84; and Vietnam, 988, 992, 1072, 1125; LBJ and, 1013–15; as New York Senator, 1032; assassination, 1070, 1129–31
Kent, Atwater, 166
Kent, Frank R., 164
Kenton, Stan, 483
Kent State tragedy, 951n, 1213–16, 1225–1226
Kentucky Derby, 1123
Kenyon Review, 246
Kerley, Lawrence, 525
Kerner, Otto, 1081
Kerouac, Jack (Jean-Louis), 726–29; On the Road, 729
Kerr, Clark, 127, 847, 849, 1098, 1099
Kesey, Ken, 1113
Kesselring, Field Marshal Albert, 329
Keyes, Robert M., 664
Keynes, John Maynard, 31, 95, 99, 124, 163, 1093
Keyserling, Leon, 474n, 826
Khanh, Nguyen. See Nguyen Khanh
Khrushchev, Nikita, 514, 928, 1237; and Geneva conference, 748–51; on Sputnik, 785, 795–96; "kitchen debate" with Nixon, 855–57; visit to U.S., 855, 857, 858–59, 909; and U–2 affair, 869, 872–874; and Paris conference, 873–74; and Vienna conference, 908–11, 935; at U.N., 908; and Berlin, 909–13, 986; and Cuban missile crisis, 958, 961, 964, 966, 968, 969–71; on JFK speech, 986; deposed, 1030
Kieran, James, 49
Kiesinger, Kurt, 1160
Kiker, Douglas, 1052
Kilgallen, Dorothy, 998
Killian, James R., 796, 798, 810
Kilpatrick, William H., 248, 793
Kim Il Sung, 531, 663
Kimmel, Adm. Husband E., 253, 254, 257
King, B. B., 1102
King, Coretta (Mrs. Martin Luther), 882–883
King, Dennis, 120
King, Adm. Ernest J., 270, 343–44, 345
King, Martin Luther, 934, 984, 1004, 1021, 1058, 1065, 1067, 1069, 1078, 1137, 1166; and Montgomery bus boycott, 741–743; and sit-ins, 849, 882–83; and freedom riders, 939, 941–42; and Birmingham civil rights campaign, 976–78; and March on Washington, 982–83; and Selma voting march, 1058–62; and James Meredith, 1066, 1068; on Vietnam, 1072, 1127; assassinated, 1128
King, Wayne, 119
Kinkaid, Adm. Thomas, 344, 345
Kinsey, Dr. Alfred C., 248, 429; Kinsey Report, 477–81, 482
Kipling, Rudyard, 68
Kiplinger, Willard M., 82, 164, 464
Kirk, Grayson, 1132–34
Kishi, Nobusuke, 821
Kissinger, Henry, 1156, 1161, 1260, 1271,

1272, 1273; *Nuclear Weapons and Foreign Policy,* 679; on Vietnam War, 916, 1180; and Vietnam peace, 1180, 1292–1296; and Cambodian bombing leaks, 1216; and Pentagon Papers, 1230, 1232, 1237; and visits to China, 1249–50, 1268
Kitt, Eartha, 1072
Kittinger, Capt. Joe, 819
Kleberg, Richard, 84
Klein, Herbert G., 1175
Kleindienst, Richard G., 1233–34, 1279, 1289
Klimpton, Lawrence A., 793
Kluckhohn, Clyde, 481
KMT. *See* Kuomintang
Knight, Frances G., 670
K-9 Corps, 275, 284
Knowland, Joseph Russell, 395
Knowland, William Fife, 283, 395, 536, 618, 630, 655, 842, 843, 845; and foreign policy, 557, 657, 659, 664; as majority leader, 666–69, 674–76, 717, 745; and Joseph McCarthy, 669, 717; and space race, 788, 796
Knox, Frank, 139, 225, 232, 254, 257, 259
Knox, William, 968
Knudsen, William S., 154, 156
Koch, Howard, 190
Koestler, Arthur, 597
Kohlberg, Alfred, 525, 527
Kohler, Walter J. Jr., 627
Konoye, Fumimaro, 252
Koontz, Elizabeth D., 1078
Kopechne, Mary Jo, 1004, 1183–86
Korea and Korean War, 348, 409, 920; prelude to, 517–20, 530, 531; Republic of, invaded, 530–35; NKPA (North Korea People's Army), 530–43 passim; ROK (Army of the Republic of Korea), 530–543 passim, 565; as "police action," 537; expansion of, 538–47; stalemate in, 539, 549, 555; Chinese troops in, 540–50; defeat of MacArthur in, 547–50, 555–556; and "Great Debate," 556–58; U.S. apathy toward, 565–67; armistice in, 661–64, 666–67; and *Pueblo* affair, 1123–24
Koslov, Frol R., 855
Koster, Maj. Gen. Samuel, 1177
Kosygin, Alexei N., 1044
Kovacs, Ernie, 589
Kramer, Stanley, 725, 726
Krause, Maj. Gustav, 393
Kreuger, Ivar, 45
Krishna Menon, V. K., 566
Krock, Arthur, 74, 76, 77, 82, 144, 528, 626
Krogh, Egil Jr., 1218, 1237, 1239, 1289
Kronenberger, Louis, 445, 481, 586–87, 588–89, 625, 776, 1259
Krueger, Gen. Walter, 344
Krulak, Gen. Victor H. "Brute," 991, 1016
Kuchel, Thomas H., 705
Kuhn, Fritz, 142, 201
Ku Klux Klan, 108, 112, 597, 737, 938–941, 981, 983, 1022–24, 1056, 1058, 1061
Kunstler, William M., 1205–1208, 1212n, 1243, 1244
Kuomintang (KMT), 487–88, 491. *See also* Chiang Kai-shek; China
Kurita, Adm. Takeo, 345
Kurusu, Saburo, 252–53, 255, 256
Kuzume, Col. Naoyuki, 342–43, 344
Ky, Nguyen Cao. *See* Nguyen Cao Ky
Kyle, Robert, 1109
Kyser, Kay, 119

labor and labor unions, 161, 170n, 295, 766, 778; NRA and, 88–89, 132–33; John L. Lewis and, 130–35, 153–58; violence against, 130–35, 154–61; child labor, 132, 140, 164, 168; and blacks, 244; public attitude toward, 306, 400; Truman and, 400–405; (1950s) 782, 1092; (1960s) 1000–1001, 1092; (1971) 1253, 1254–55. *See also* American Federation of Labor (AFL); CIO (Congress of Industrial Organizations); strikes; *and individual unions*
Ladejinsky, Wolf I., 671
Ladies' Home Journal, 761, 1102, 1188
La Follette, Philip, 170
La Follette, Robert M., 97, 101, 458
La Follette, Robert M. Jr., and Civil Liberties Committee, 131, 160
La Guardia, Fiorello, 17, 46, 86, 101–102, 110, 170, 258, 322, 370
Lahr, Bert, 197
Laine, Frankie, 483
Laird, Melvin, 1120, 1180, 1270
Lamont, Thomas W., 27, 74, 147
Lamour, Dorothy, 190, 246, 267
Lampell, Millard, 358
Landis, James M., 105
Landon, Alfred M., 50, 58, 76, 138–44, 320
Langer, William, 655
Langlis, Arthur B., 618
language, 1034, 1037, 1193. *See also* slang
Lanza, Mario, 820
Laos, 681, 853, 895, 909, 910, 1226–27
Lapp, Ralph, 700
Lardner, John, 485
LaRue, Fred, 1275, 1279, 1289, 1291
Lasagna, Dr. Louis, 596, 1115
Laski, Harold, 50
Lasky, Victor, 999
Latin America, 56, 125, 203, 474, 597, 677, 894, 907; anti-American riots (1958), 826–33. *See also* Organization of American States (OAS)
Lattimore, Owen, 491, 527–28, 580–81, 674, 701
Laue, Max von, 336
Laufer, Charles, 1102
Laughton, Charles, 198
Laurence, William L., 211, 310, 311, 377–378, 382–83
Laval, Pierre, 216
Lavelle, Gen. John D., 1260

Lawrence, David, 164
Lawrence, Ernest O., 375, 571
Lawrence, Maj. Robert H., 1078
Lawyers Guild, 714–15
Lay, Beirne Jr., 810
Lazarus, Ralph, 1053–54, 1138
LBJ. See Johnson, Lyndon B.
Le, Capt. Kong, 853
Leach, Margaret: Reveille in Washington, 251
League of Nations, 48, 124, 175, 317
Leahy, Adm. William D., 326, 347, 365, 368, 369, 385
Leary, Howard, 1198, 1199
Leary, Dr. Timothy, 1112, 1114–15, 1116, 1118, 1166
Lebanon, 823–24
LeBlanc, Irving A., 850
Leclerc, Gen. Jacques, 333
Ledbetter, Huddie, 486
Le Duc Tho, 1271, 1292–95
Lee, Howard, 1169
Lee, J. Bracken, 718
Lee, Gen. Robert E., 341
Lee, Robert E., 490, 521, 523, 525
Lee, Higginson & Company, 45
Leek, Sybil, 1191
Leffingwell, Russell, 85
Lehman, Herbert, 75–76, 170, 284, 705
Lehman, Peter G., 284
leisure class, 43–44
LeMay, Gen. Curtis, 962, 1146
Lemke, William, 141, 144
Lemmon, Jack, 690
Lemnitzer, Gen. Lyman L., 894, 918
lend-lease, 227–32, 233, 434
Lennon, John, 1102
Lerner, Max, 102, 586, 589
Lester, Jerry, 588
Leventhal, Albert, 1262
Leviero, Anthony, 626
Levine, Isaac Don, 525
Levine, Nathan, 508
Levitt, I. M., 798
Levitt, William J., and Levittowns, 431–432
Levy, Capt. Howard Brett, 1073
Lewis, Anthony, 671
Lewis, Fulton Jr., 525, 526
Lewis, John, 982, 1066, 1079
Lewis, John Llewellyn, 165, 168, 223, 322, 389, 820; rise of, 130–35; and auto and steel workers, 153–58, 160; in disfavor, 161, 227; Truman and, 402–405, 447
Lewis, Capt. Robert A., 381
Lewis, Sinclair, 284
Lewis, Wells, 284
Lexington (aircraft carrier), 271
Leyte Gulf, Battle of, 344–45
Liaquat Ali Khan, 825
Liberace, 759
Liberty League, American, 96, 134, 136, 156; vs FDR, 103, 105, 107, 139, 141, 151
Liberty ships, 295
Liddell Hart, B. H., 331
Liddy, G. Gordon, 1218, 1222; and

"Plumbers," 1232, 1238–39; and Watergate, 1274–76, 1278–80, 1289–90
Lie, Trygve, 532–35, 598
Liebling, A. J., 502, 508, 510
Life magazine, 118, 120, 304, 308, 415, 463, 491, 555, 577, 615, 626, 689, 724, 780, 804, 953–54, 995, 1099, 1100, 1139, 1181, 1237, 1260, 1280; and Hughes hoax, 1262–65, 1267
Lifestyle magazine, 943
life-styles and attitudes: (1930s) 7–8, 31–32, 33–44, 56, 60–69, 117–22, 129–130; teen-agers, 63, 305–309, 480, 1169, 1171; (1937) 148–49; (1939–40) 196–200, 204–206; (1941) 238–50; war years, 274, 289–94, 303–309; and GIs, 280–87, 289; Truman years, 418–420, 422–32, 476–87, 556–69, 576–98; "Organization Men," 476, 578; comparison of Truman-Nixon eras, 481; Eisenhower years, 643–45, 692–95, 720–29, 731–34, 758–62, 772–85, 818–21; (1960s) 877, 996–1004, 1090–92, 1134–1137, 1162–63; in Mississippi, 943–44; (1970s) 1190–98, 1224–26, 1259–61. See also family
Lilienthal, David E., 317, 492, 570, 572
Lindbergh, Anne Morrow (Mrs. Charles): The Wave of the Future, 204
Lindbergh, Charles, 23, 124; We, 64; and isolationism, 200, 204, 220, 223
Lindley, Ernest K., 50
Lindsay, John, 60, 209, 1137, 1282
Linkletter, Art, 1142
Lin Piao, 1269
Lippman, Lois, 737
Lippmann, Walter, 776, 792; on aspects of Depression, 18, 25, 31, 44; on FDR and administration, 47, 50, 58, 83, 90, 139, 232; and Japanese, 251, 297, 299; The Cold War, 437–38; on Truman era, 470, 526, 560; on foreign policy, 664, 678, 745, 1019; on Nixon, 637n, 719
Lipset, Seymour Martin, 778
Literary Digest, 42, 52, 64, 90; predicts 1936 Republican victory, 144, 167, 465
literature. See books; poetry
Little Rock crisis, 799–810, 934, 935
Liuzzo, Viola Gregg, 1061
Lloyd, David, 608
Lloyd's of London, 5, 409, 689
lobbyists, 105–106, 1041, 1234
Locke, Richard Adams, 189
Lodge, Henry Cabot, Jr., 283, 524, 557, 609, 617, 659, 757, 882, 1026, 1249; at U.N., 765, 858; as ambassador to Vietnam, 990–91, 993, 994
Loeb, William, 1283
Lollobrigida, Gina, 590
Lombardi, Vince, 1161
Lombardo, Guy, 119, 1161
London Economist, 440, 789, 1022, 1069
Long, Huey Pierce Jr., 57, 108, 142, 144, 1300; and FDR, 50, 71, 107; rise of, 111–15; My First Days in the White House, 113; assassination of, 116–17, 175

Long, Russell, 60, 705, 1030, 1074, 1183, 1186
Longworth, Alice, 223
Lon Nol, Gen., 1210
Look magazine, 118, 995, .004, 1225
Lopez, Vincent, 119
Los Alamos, atomic project site, 309, 376
Los Angeles Daily News, 632
Los Angeles Herald-Examiner, 561
Los Angeles Times, 415, 1262
Lothian, Lord, 221
Lotto, Jack, 839
Louis, Joe, 148, 197, 243, 283, 759
Lovelace, Linda, 997
Lovett, Robert A., 548, 960
Lowell, Robert, 283
Lowenstein, Allard K., 1126
Loy, Myrna, 998
loyalty issue, 127, 597; and Truman administration, 489–98; and loyalty oaths in business and professions, 498–99, 515, 582; and Eisenhower administration, 668–73. *See also* McCarthy, Joseph R.
LSD (lysergic acid diethylamide). *See* drugs
Lubell, Samuel, and Lubell polls, 983, 1010
Lucas, Robert, 1066
Lucas, Scott, 524, 529
Luce, Clare Boothe Brokaw (Mrs. Henry), 58, 227, 446, 450, 793
Luce, Henry, 198, 246, 348, 411, 491, 564, 626, 793
Luce, Robert, 85
Luciano, Charles "Lucky," 101, 600
Lucy, Autherine, 738
Luddites, 1087
Ludlow, Louis, 177
Lukas, Paul, 595
Lumumba, Patrice, 909
Lundeen, Ernest, 97, 221
Lutín, Oscar García, 830, 831
Lynd, Robert and Helen, 133, 248
Lynes, Russell, 485–86, 780

MAAG (U.S. Military Assistance Advisory Group), 921–22. *See also* MACV (Military Assistance Command, Vietnam)
Mabley, Jack, 799
McAlister, Elizabeth, 1260
MacArthur, Arthur II, 562
MacArthur, Gen. Douglas, 51, 76, 127, 257, 263, 316, 348, 438, 443, 532; (1930s) 5–7, 46, 84; and BEF, 11, 13–18; FDR on, 18, 50; and Philippines, 265, 271, 342–44, 370; and Japanese, 269–74, 371, 385, 387; and presidential campaigns: (1944) 318, 344, (1948) 446, 452–53, (1952) 564, 614–15, 616, 618; Truman and, 392, 541, 545, 546, 549, 558–62; and demobilization, 406; and Korean War, 518, 534, 535, 537–550, 555–56, 558–61, 647, 662; and foreign policy, 540–42; insubordination and dismissal, 541, 545–46, 558–65, 606; during Eisenhower presidency, 646, 647, 654, 662
MacArthur, Douglas II, 875

MacArthur, Jean (Mrs. Douglas), 561, 562
McAuliffe, Brig. Gen. Anthony C., 334
McCall, Tom, 1099
McCall's magazine, 692, 761
McCarran, Patrick A., 169, 627, 655
McCarran-Walter Immigration Act, 581, 670
"McCarthy, Charlie," 121, 190, 191, 192
McCarthy, Eugene, 60, 880, 1019, 1125, 1128, 1299; on LBJ, 1045, 1076; and campaigns: (1964) 1126–27, 1129, (1968) 1142, 1144–46, (1972) 1282, 1283
McCarthy, Jean Kerr (Mrs. Joseph R.), 819
McCarthy, Joseph R., and McCarthyism, 107–108, 246, 390, 394, 415, 440, 452, 562, 572, 612, 651, 668, 673, 720, 937; search for campaign issue, 512–13; character and image, 513, 520; Edward R. Murrow and, 514, 515; use of spurious data, 521, 523–25, 527–30, 557, 615; vs State Department, 522–30; public and political support of, 525–27, 529, 530, 705, 716–17; and Drew Pearson, 558; students and, 578, 580–81; attacks General Marshall, 607; at 1952 Republican convention, 615; Eisenhower and, 627–628, 669, 670; and Stevenson, 628; and Republican appointees, 655–56, 672; and China, 657; and Oppenheimer case, 697; –Army hearings, 700–16; Senate censure of, 717–18; death, 819
McCarthy, Mary, 483, 999
McClellan, John, 710
McCloskey, Paul N. Jr., 1281–82
McCloy, John J., 223, 297, 299, 309, 960
McCluskey, Lt. Cdr. Clarence, 272
MacColl, René, 439
McCone, John A., 959, 960, 962, 988, 990, 1051; and McCone report, 1064–65
McCord, James W. Jr., 1218, 1222; and Watergate, 1275–80, 1291–92
McCormack, John W., 97, 837, 840
McCormack, Dr. Margaret L., 1109
McCormick, Anne O'Hare, 83, 354, 622
McCormick, Col. Robert R., 24, 45, 196, 197, 251, 517, 525, 564, 620, 669
McCrary, Tex, 596, 839
McCullers, Carson, 486
McCulloch, Spencer, 390
Macdonald, Dwight, 1044
MacDonald, Jeannette, 149
McDowell, John, 505–506
McDuffie, Irvin, 82
McDuffie, Lizzie, 349
McElroy, Neil, 794, 796, 810
McGeehan, John E., 249–50
McGinniss, Joe: *The Selling of the President 1968,* 1145–46
McGovern, George, 1019, 1142, 1219; and 1972 campaign, 1273, 1275–77, 1282–1287
McGranery, James, 701
McGrath, J. Howard, 447, 453, 605–606
McGraw-Hill, Inc., 1261–67
MacGregor, Clark, 1290
McGuire, Dorothy, 694

MacInnes, Helen, 999
McIntire, Carl, 1228
McIntire, Adm. Ross T., 316, 321, 322, 324, 349, 350, 351, 353, 357
Mack, Connie, 596
Mack, John E., 48
Mack, Peter F., 852
McKay, Douglas, 648, 672
McKay Commission, 1246–47
McKellar, Kenneth D., 492, 524
McKinney, Frank, 623
McKissick, Floyd, 60, 982, 1066, 1067, 1077, 1078
McLain, James, 1202–1203
MacLaine, Shirley, 590
McLaren, Richard W., 1233–34
MacLeish, Archibald, 100, 250
McLemore, Henry, 298
McLeod, R. W. Scott, 656, 670, 671
McLuhan, Marshall, 118, 189, 592, 877–878, 892, 1036
McMahan, Harry, 998
McMahon, Brien, 322, 524, 695
Macmillan, Harold, 857, 859, 874, 912, 954, 964
MacMurray, Fred, 303
McNair, Gen. Lesley J., 269
McNamara, Robert S., 60, 82n, 291, 892, 956, 1015, 1139; and Bay of Pigs, 894, 905; and Vietnam War, 918, 923, 988–992, 994, 1016, 1039–40, 1047, 1051–1053, 1057, 1070–71, 1075, 1125; and Cuban missile crisis, 959–64, 966, 967, 971; and Pentagon Papers, 1229–30, 1231
McNarney, Gen. Joseph G., 408
McNutt, Paul, 295, 454
McPhail, Larry, 424
McPherson, Aimee Semple, 101
McReynolds, James C., 136, 151
McShane, James, 941, 946, 948, 951
MACV (Military Assistance Command, Vietnam), 923, 1045–46, 1051, 1052, 1056–1057, 1071, 1210
McWilliams, Joseph E., 111, 318
Maddox, Lester, 1078, 1128
Maddox (destroyer), 1016–17
Madison Avenue. See advertising
Mad magazine, 693
magazines. See newspapers and magazines
Magee, Ruchell, 1202–1203
Magnani, Anna, 590
Magnuson, Warren, 101, 561, 705
Magruder, Jeb Stuart, 1222, 1236, 1298, 1300; and Watergate, 1274–75, 1277, 1279–80, 1289–90
Mailer, Norman, 60, 251, 904, 1166, 1207; The Naked and the Dead, 481, 589; An American Dream, 1036
Maine, in 1932 election, 52
Malan, Daniel F., 597
Malaya, Japanese invasion of, 265
Malcolm X, 244, 983, 1004, 1021, 1058, 1076, 1149
Malenkov, Georgi, 574
Malik, Jacob, 532, 535, 566
Malloy, Dr. Bernard, 1237

Malm, Mrs. Pierre, 1185
malnutrition. See food
Malone, George W., 664
Malone, Vivian J., 979–81
Malraux, André, 698
Manchester Guardian, 440, 986
Manchester (N.H.) Union Leader, 1274, 1283
Manchuria, 74, 125, 383, 541, 542, 544, 549, 555
Mancusi, Vincent, 1240, 1242–45
Manhattan Project. See atomic weapons
MANIAC (Mathematical Analyzer, Numerical Integrator and Computer), 573
Manion, Clarence E., 672, 674
Mankiewicz, Frank, 1285, 1286
Mankiewicz, Joseph L., 486
Mann, Floyd, 940, 942
Mann, Woodrow W., 800, 801, 804–805
Manning, Bishop William T., 249–50
Mansfield, Mike, 408, 705, 1049, 1052, 1072
Manson, Charles, 1117, 1171
Mao Tse-tung, 487–89, 491, 519, 534, 541, 657, 662, 986, 1098, 1248–49; Stalin and, 348, 517; Nixon and, 1268–1269. See also China
Marcelle, Joseph, 605
March on Washington (1963), 982–83
Marconi, Guglielmo, 118
Marcuse, Herbert, 102, 1098, 1201
Marder, Murray, 1050
Mardian, Robert, 1230–31, 1236, 1289
Marine Corps, U.S., 10, 367, 387, 406, 956–57; World War II battles in Pacific, 176, 267, 270, 272–73, 340–44; in Iceland, 232–33; casualties, 346, 760 (see also casualties); in Korea, 540, 544, 547; in Middle East, 823–24; in Vietnam, 1048, 1126, 1270
Markel, Lester, 305
Markham, Paul F., 1184–85
Markos, General, 436, 438
Marquand, John P., 242
marriage, 780, 1035. See also family
Marshall, Burke, 935, 938–40, 944, 977, 978, 983–84, 1185
Marshall, Gen. George C., 84, 296, 368, 369, 488, 557, 625, 1076; as chief of staff, 202, 223, 258, 259, 276, 324, 372, 375, 491; as Secretary of State, 421, 433, 437, 439, 475, 560; attacks on, 464, 491–92, 606–607, 627. See also Marshall Plan
Marshall, Robert, 86
Marshall, Thomas: American History, 65
Marshall, Thurgood, 735–36, 738, 1078
Marshall Plan (European Recovery Program), 208, 422, 438–40, 464, 474, 488
Martin, Edward, 960, 964, 966
Martin, Lt. Gen. H. G., 560
Martin, Joseph, 320, 447, 452, 475, 560, 562, 607
Martin, Mary, 148, 419, 694
Martin, Peter D., 726
Martinez, Eugenio R., 1238–39, 1277–78
Marx, Groucho, 588, 689, 694, 1097

Marx, Karl, and Marxism, 57, 102, 411, 498, 1098
Masaryk, Thomas, 178
Massing, Hede, 102
massive retaliation. *See* arms race
mass media, 220, 304, 592, 1049, 1065; comic strips and books, 27, 94, 166–67, 568–69; manipulation of, 100, 143, 160, 176, 769; and pornography, 1107–1109. *See also* moving pictures and performers; press; radio and radio programs; television
Masters, Dr. William H., 1108–1109
Masters and Johnson laboratories, 478, 1109
Mathews, William R., 518n
Matos, Huber, 862
Matsu. *See* China
Matthews, Herbert L., 860, 861
Matthews, J. B., 525
Mature, Victor, 303
Mauchly, John, 1088
Maugham, Somerset, 762
Mauldin, William H., 280, 283, 286, 429, 430, 893
Maulnier, Thierry, 789
Maverick, Maury, 169, 170; and Maverick family, 581
Max, Peter, 1037
Maxwell, Elsa, 309
May, Alan Nunn, 314, 493, 500
Mayday Tribe, 1228–29
Mayer, Louis B., 100, 101, 121, 148
Mazey, Emil, 405, 407, 409
Mazo, Earl, 631, 831, 832
Mead, Margaret, 1196
Meadlo, Paul David, 1176
Mechanics Illustrated, 119
mechanization of society, 1086–92. *See also* technology
media. *See* mass media
Medicare, 474, 986, 1011; birth of, 1041–1042. *See also* health
medicine. *See* drugs; health
Meany, George, 1254–55
Medina, Capt. Ernest, 1176, 1177
Meet the Press (radio, TV program), 507, 612, 613, 881, 917, 1286
Meier, John, 1265
Meitner, Lise, 210, 211, 212, 314
Mellon, Andrew, 24, 25, 42, 45
Mellon, Richard B., 131
Memorial Day Massacre, 160
Mencken, H. L., 49, 111, 189, 485, 593, 847, 943
Mendenhall, Joseph A., 991
Mendès-France, Pierre, 987
Meneghini, Giovanni, 820
Menninger, Dr. William C., 1102
Menotti, Gian-Carlo, 486, 694
Menshikov, Mikhail, 858
Mercer, Lucy. *See* Rutherfurd, Lucy Mercer
Meredith, James H., 944–52, 979, 981, 983, 1000; Meredith March, 1066–68, 1078
Merhige, Robert R. Jr., 1273
Merman, Ethel, 198n, 486

Merriam, Frank, 101
Mesta, Pearl, 956
Metro-Goldwyn-Mayer, 101
Meyer, Eugene, 74
Meyer, Russ, 1193
Meyer, Stanley, 1265
Miall, Leonard, 439
Miami News, 903
Michelson, Charles, 80
Michener, James A., 565–66, 999
Michigan, bank failures in, 72–73
Midway, Battle of, 271–72, 342
Mifune, Toshiro, 590
Mikoyan, Anastas, 854, 856
military-industrial complex. *See* business and industry
military spending. *See* budget, federal
Milland, Ray, 303
Millay, Edna St. Vincent, 217
Miller, Alice Duer: *The White Cliffs,* 218
Miller, Arthur, 60, 128, 689
Miller, David J., 1055
Miller, Glenn, 119, 284, 815
Miller, Mitch, 643
Miller, Mordecai, 605
Miller, William E., 1031
Millet, Kate, 1106
Millikin, Eugene, 447, 655, 669
Mills, C. Wright, 904, 953, 958
Mills, Ogden, 74, 75
Mills, Wilbur, 1053, 1282
Mindszenty, Joseph Cardinal, 765
Minehan, Thomas, 22
Minh, Duong Van. *See* Duong Van Minh
Minichiello, Raffaele, 1182, 1183
Minikus, Lee, 1062–63
Mink, Patsy, 1196
Minnelli, Vincente, 427
Minow, Newton N. "Wasteland," 995
Mishima, Yukio, 1259–60
missile and rocket programs: "buzz bombs," 332, 333, 370; H-bomb, 575; IRBMs, 792, 795, 797, 798, 814; U.S. and Soviet, 795–98, 814, 926–27, 1272; ICBMs, 795–97, 810, 926–27; Eisenhower and, 796–97; separated from satellite program, 797–99; Soviet, in Cuba, 958–71; ABMs, 1163–64. *See also* space travel and satellites
Mississippi: life-style in, 943–44; University of, integration, 944–951
Mississippi Freedom Party, 1097
Missouri (battleship), 386–87
Mitchell, Charles E., 44–45
Mitchell, Hugh, 448
Mitchell, John N., 1156, 1161; and blacks, 1147; and students, 1175, 1214, 1215; and FBI, 1217; and CREEP, 1222, 1274; and Mayday Tribe, 1228–29; and Pentagon Papers, 1230; and Watergate, 1232, 1274–75, 1279–81, 1289, 1291–1292; and ITT, 1233–34; and SEC, 1234–35; and AIP, 1236
Mitchell, Martha (Mrs. John N.), 1228, 1275–76, 1280–81
Mitchell, Jonathan, 128
Mitchell, R. S., 21, 22

Mitchell, Stephen A., 623, 630, 632
Mitchell, Gen. William "Billy," 4, 10
Mitchell, William D., 10, 12
Mitford, Jessica, 849, 999
Mohammed V of Morocco, 811, 812
Mohawk Indians, 224
Mohr, Charles, 1028
Moley, Raymond, 78, 84, 90, 96, 105, 138, 166
Mollet, Guy, 763–65
Molotov, V. M., 277, 368, 410
Monde, Le (Paris), 749, 1295
money: pound sterling, 4, 229; currency, 72, 78–80, 1039, 1252; "Eurodollars," 1252–53. *See also* economy, U.S.; income; prices; wages and hours
Monk, Thelonious, 693
Monnet, Jean, 440
Monroe, Marilyn (Norma Jean Baker), 250, 394, 482, 590, 592n, 688–91
Montand, Yves, 590, 689
Montgomery, Field Marshal Sir Bernard, 278, 279, 280, 331, 334
Montgomery, Robert, 283, 593, 758
Montgomery, Alabama: bus boycott, 740–743; WPA *Guide* description, 934–35
Montgomery Advertiser, 638
Montgomery Ward, 294, 324
Moody, Mrs. Blair, 604
moon, exploration of, 929, 934, 1156–59. *See also* space travel and satellites
Moore, Barrington Jr., 904
Moore, C. F., 608–609
morale, 290; in Depression, 23; Japanese attacks and, 259–60, 270; of Japanese, 263, 346, 370, 371, 376, 383; of armed forces, 281–83, 284–87, 405–10, 539, 1181–82; loyalty issue and, 496; postwar deterioration of, 531; Korea and, 539, 542, 544, 565–66, 646; and space race, 787–90, 810–11, 812–14, 816, 926–30, 933; German, in World War II, 1046
morality, 1101; and use of atomic and H-bombs, 208, 338–40, 375, 376, 570–73, 576; of students, 582, 601, 996–97, 1148; TV, 588; government corruption in Truman era, 599–601, 602–606; shoplifting, 721, 776, 1148; Elvis Presley and, 759; "new," 1034–36; of teen-agers, 1101–1105; "Plumbers" and, 1238; Vietnam War and, 1296. *See also* crime; permissiveness; sex and attitude toward
Moran, Lord, 326
More, Paul Elmer, 64
Morehead v. Tipaldo, 137
Morgan, Edward P., 958
Morgan, Frank, 197
Morgan, Gerald "Gerry," 835, 843
Morgan, Henry, 594
Morgan, J. P., 43–45, 74, 85, 145, 147, 186, 202
Morgan, Robin, 1195
Morgan, Thomas A., 697, 698
Morgenthau, Henry, 82, 110, 162, 259, 360
Mori, Admiral, 268
Morison, Samuel Eliot, 174, 177, 387

Morley, Christopher, 27, 68
Morris, Newbold, 605–606
Morrison, Jim, 1108
Morrison, Dr. Philip, 373
Morrow, E. Frederic, 737
Morrow, Elizabeth Cutter, 204, 223
Morse, David A., 474n
Morse, Wayne, 651, 657, 1018–19, 1074
mortgage foreclosures, 37, 59–60
Morthland, John, 1212
Morton, Sterling, 223
Morton, Thruston B., 659, 1027
Moseley, Gen. George, 11, 15
Motley, Constance Baker, 1078
moving pictures and performers, 246, 998; (early 1930s) 11, 33, 68, 74, 88, 95, 98, 120–21; (1937–40) 148–49, 197–98, 206; World War II, 216n, 218–19, 283, 303–304; Truman years, 419, 420, 425, 427, 486, 532; (1953–58) 643, 644, 694, 818; (1963–69) 998, 1028, 1037, 1039, 1107–1108; (1970s) 1192, 1193, 1262; political use and suppression, 100–101, 160, 176; Technicolor, 118; name changes of stars, 198n; decline of, 589–92; European, 590–91; and free speech, 597
Mowrer, Edgar Ansel, 179
Mowry, George E., 122, 1092
Moyers, Bill D., 1075
Moynihan, Daniel Patrick, 55, 144, 1256; and Moynihan Report, 1058
Muccio, John J., 533, 534
Muggeridge, Malcolm, 439
Muir, Jean, 499
Mumford, Lewis, 50
Mundelein, George William Cardinal, 175
Mundt, Karl, 491, 502, 505, 627, 1124; and Joseph McCarthy, 527, 708, 709–710, 714, 716
Munich Pact, 188–89, 200
Municipal Bankruptcy Act, 137
Murphy, Charles S., 449, 474n
Murphy, Frank, 155–56, 170, 301
Murphy, Matt H. Jr., 1061
Murphy, Thomas F., 605
Murray, Gerry, 485
Murray, Henry A., 783, 1101
Murray, Philip, 158, 402
Murrow, Edward R., 97, 220, 251, 258–259, 290, 332, 333, 451, 585, 601, 963, 1037; and 1938 crisis in Europe, 179, 181, 182, 189, 514; portrait of, 513–16; loyalty investigations, 514, 515, 670–71; and *See It Now*, 515, 516, 587, 670; on Indochina, 686; on Bay of Pigs, 895
Murrow, Janet (Mrs. Edward R.), 258–59
Muscatello, Jimmie, 1192
music and musicians, 1299; jazz, 34, 483, 693, 825; recording industry, 34, 119, 248, 419, 444, 724, 759, 972, 973–74, 1224–25; dance bands and bandleaders, 68, 119, 121, 128, 244; swing, 119, 129, 248; black, 119, 244; unions and, 306; rock, 1102, 1170. *See also* dancing; song(s)

Muskie, Edmund S., 843, 1141, 1146, 1270; and 1970 elections, 1220–21; and fake charges, 1236; in 1972 campaign, 1273–74, 1282, 1283
Muskie, Jane (Mrs. Edmund S.), 1283
Mussolini, Benito, 124, 177, 231, 260, 278, 279, 296, 329
Mutual Security Act, 672, 765, 788
My Lai killings. See Calley, Lt. William
Myrdal, Gunnar, 735

NAACP. See National Association for the Advancement of Colored People
Nader, Ralph, 1001, 1255–58
Nagasaki. See Japan
Naguib, Gen. Mohammed, 596, 677
Nagy, Imre, 765
Nam Il, Gen., 666
Narducci, Leo, 1197
NASA (National Aeronautics and Space Administration), 819, 872, 930, 1094, 1156–57
Nasser, Gamal Abdel, 596, 763
Nast, Condé, 305
Nation, 47, 51, 457
National Association for the Advancement of Colored People (NAACP), 107, 245, 389, 735, 738, 847, 944, 1067–68, 1164
National Association of Manufacturers (NAM), 27, 31, 38, 88, 134, 136, 151, 155, 399–400, 415, 1093
National Bureau of Standards, 310, 672
National Conference for New Politics (NCNP), 1077–78
National Council for the Prevention of War, 176
National Defense Education Act, 819
National Emergency Council, 114
National Farmers Union, 60
National Football League. See sports and games
National Guard, 1142; and strikes, 37, 131, 133, 134, 155, 1137; and Korea, 539; and racism, 739; and Little Rock, 800–802, 805, 808; in Mississippi, 942, 948–951; in Alabama, 980, 981, 1060; and riots, 1064, 1080, 1105, 1149, 1167; at Kent State, 1214–16; and Mayday Tribe, 1229; at Attica prison, 1245
National Industrial Recovery Act (NIRA). See National Recovery Administration
National Labor Relations Board, 106, 134, 160
National Liberation Front (Viet Cong). See Vietnam and Vietnam War
National Loyalty Review Board, 494, 496. See also loyalty issue
National Nutrition Conference, 238
National Peace Action Coalition, 1299
National Recovery Administration (NRA), 80, 87–90, 95–96, 105, 132–34, 136–137, 144
National Resources Planning Board, 99, 106, 292
National Review, 1120
National Science Foundation, 792, 1095

National Security Council, 437, 519, 651, 797, 798, 907; "Ex Comm" of, in Cuban missile crisis, 960–64, 967–71; and Vietnam, 991, 1047, 1051; and Cambodian bombing leaks, 1216
National States' Rights Party, 941
National Student Association (NSA), 1073
National Youth Administration (NYA), 106, 128
Nation's Business, 42
NATO (North Atlantic Treaty Organization), 487, 488, 510, 748, 811, 812, 890, 1028, 1259; and Fortress America concept, 556–57; U.S. forces in, 569; and Bricker amendment, 675; Dulles and, 677; USSR and, 749; de Gaulle and, 857; and Cuban missile crisis, 965, 970
Navarre Plan, 682
Navy, U.S., 236, 290, 818, 1190; maneuvers at Pearl Harbor, 69, 253–54; and Panay incident, 171–76; Vinson Naval Act, 178; in Battle of the Atlantic, 232–233, 235–36, 260, 264, 295; blacks in, 242, 737; in Pacific (World War II), 251, 253–58, 266–73, 295, 316, 340, 343–45, 346; Nixon and JFK in, 276; and invasion of Europe, 278; and unification of armed forces, 324, 392; and demobilization, 387, 406, 409, 430; and Korea, 534, 536, 540; Seventh Fleet, (Formosa) 534, 657, 658, 692, 747, 875, (Vietnam) 684, 1271; and missile program, 790, 798, 812–14; in Cuban missile crisis, 964, 966, 967; at Gulf of Tonkin, 1016–18; and Pueblo affair, 1123–24. See also submarines.
NCNP (National Conference for New Politics), 1077
Neal, Patricia, 998
Neary, John, 1200
Negroes. See black(s)
Nehru, Jawaharlal, 390, 661, 677
Nellis, Edward J., 1084, 1085
Nelson, "Baby Face," 95
Nelson, Donald, 250
Nenni, Pietro, 987
Nesbitt, Henrietta, 259
Netherlands. See Holland; Indonesia
Neumann, John von, 573, 972
Neustadt, Richard E., 892; Presidential Power, 890
neutrality and the Neutrality Act (1935), 108, 126, 177, 200, 201–202, 204, 235; FDR and, 125, 175, 203–204, 222. See also isolationism
Newark, New Jersey, riots, 1079–80
New Deal, 49, 87–90, 95, 102, 103, 107, 114, 125, 167, 170, 176, 208, 292; litigation concerning, 96, 136, 137, 152
New Economic Policy (Nixon), 1251–55
"New Era" prosperity, 32, 36, 106, 594
New Frontier (Kennedy), 474, 880, 996, 1003, 1041
New Guinea campaign, World War II, 270, 340–41. See also Australia, defense of
New Left, 489n, 904, 952, 953, 1001, 1097, 1098, 1099, 1115–16

New Look (fashions), 422–24, 1197
Newman, Lewis I., 580
Newman, Paul, 1235
New Masses, 102
New Outlook, 103
New Republic, 47, 51, 102, 457, 648, 652
New Russia's Primer, 57
Newsom, Earl, 118
newspapers and magazines, 189; and Czech crisis, 180–81; decline of, 246, 995, 1039, 1225, 1260; World War II, 304–305; postwar, 425, (1950s) 589, 693; newspaper strike, 1039; and pornography, 1108. *See also* mass media; press
Newsweek, 309, 461, 1120, 1222, 1257, 1263
Newton, Huey P., 583, 1150, 1203, 1243, 1244
Newton, Robert, 532
New York City: during Depression, 5, 23, 35–36, 41; World's Fairs in, 198–200, 240, 1037–38, 1301; and tourism, 1192–1193; bombings in, 1198–1200
New York Daily Mirror, 762
New York Daily News, 3, 78, 289, 318, 321, 397, 1167
New Yorker, 58, 92, 284, 360, 521, 702, 1037
New York Herald Tribune, 17, 164, 308, 334, 548, 637, 653, 696, 771, 964, 1050
New York Journal-American, 525
New York Magazine, 102
New York Post, 33n, 355, 457, 629–30, 661, 707, 912, 1286
New York Sun, 157, 321, 470
New York Times, 177, 213, 334, 387, 481, 522, 526, 650, 658, 812, 953, 1000, 1068, 1109, 1165, 1286; on aspects of Depression, 11, 17, 27; on FDR, 90, 143, 354; on Truman era, 319, 399, 409, 449, 456; on elections: (1948) 453, 464, 465, (1952) 621, 638, 639; on Eisenhower, 638, 661; on LBJ, 1019; on mechanization, 1086–87; on student riots, 1134; on fashions, 1197–98; and Pentagon leaks and Papers, 1216–17, 1229–32; and Watergate, 1278
New York Times Magazine, 998, 1003, 1112
New York World Journal Tribune, 1014, 1039
New York World Telegram and Sun, 502, 850
Ngo Dinh Diem, 915–22, 988–94, 1209, 1236
Ngo Dinh Nhu, 916, 922, 989–90, 992–93
Ngo Dinh Nhu, Mme., 916, 989–90, 992–993
Nguyen Cao Ky, 1048, 1051, 1226
Nguyen Khanh, Lt. Gen., 1048
Nguyen Van Thieu, Gen., 1048, 1051, 1179, 1209, 1210, 1226, 1269, 1271, 1292–1293, 1295
Nhu, Ngo Dinh. *See* Ngo Dinh Nhu
Nhu, Mme. Ngo Dinh. *See* Ngo Dinh Nhu, Mme.
Nichlos, John B., 42

Nichols, Maj. Gen. Kenneth D., 697
Nicholson, Henry, 467
Niebuhr, Reinhold, 51
Nielsen, A. C., and Nielsen polls, 149, 584, 636
Nielsen, Aksel, 752
Niemöller, Martin, 749
Nimitz, Adm. Chester W., 257, 270, 271, 316, 341, 342–43, 387, 409, 596
Nishina, Yoshio, 384
Niteletter magazine, 1035
Nitze, Paul, 572, 669, 960
Niven, David, 197, 283, 1105
Nixon, Donald, 1235
Nixon, Edward, 1234, 1235
Nixon, F. Donald, 1234
Nixon, Julie (Mrs. David Eisenhower), 1122
Nixon, Pat (Mrs. Richard M.), 250, 276, 633–37 passim, 830–33, 1268–69, 1272
Nixon, Richard M., 8, 25, 36, 101n, 276, 294, 367, 452, 529, 994–95, 1008, 1075, 1120, 1135, 1172, 1247, 1248; during Depression, 60, 106, 148, 250; and Hiss case, 247, 504–506, 508–12, 521, 612, 619, 620, 628, 629; as Congressional candidate, 394–95, 415; and loyalty issue, 491, 504–506, 508–11, 520, 529, 672; and Joseph McCarthy, 515, 558, 703, 718; and Stevenson, 612, 628, 629, 634; in presidential campaigns: (1952) 615, 619–20, 628–38, (1956) 766–69, (1960) 855, 877–86, (1964) 995, 1027, 1032, (1968) 1127, 1141, 1145–47, (1972) 1273–82, 1287, 1292; character and image, 619–20, 629–30, 634–36, 638, 719, 720, 879, 1159–62, 1209, 1218, 1219, 1221, 1232, 1248; and campaign funds, 620, 629–38, 1232–36, 1274; *Six Crises,* 636, 844, 879; as Vice President, 649, 670, 672, 673, 685, 757, 853, 916; and Vietnam, 685, 996, 1165, 1180–81; 1208–1209, 1220, 1270–72, 1281, 1293–95; as chief Republican spokesman, 718–21, 843–45; and civil rights, 737, 1149; and presidential powers, 744, 1161–62 (*see also* Watergate); and Eisenhower's illnesses, 753–54, 811; and the press, 768, 1160, 1216, 1290; and space race, 796, 798; visits Latin America, 826–33; -Khrushchev "kitchen debate," 855–57; and Russia, 859, 1271–1273; and Castro, 862, 904; on war on poverty, 1043; political vacillation, 1155–1156, 1159–65, 1168–69, 1178; cabinet, 1155–56; 1969 trip to Asia and Europe, 1159–60; extravagance of, 1161–1162; and student riots, 1168, 1169, 1175, 1214, 1216; and Calley case, 1178; and international incidents, 1179; on crime, 1182; and Cambodia, 1210–1211, 1216; and CIA, 1216–17; and 1970 elections, 1218–22; and Negro vote, 1218–19; and Pentagon Papers, 1230–31, 1237; and ITT, 1233–34; political enemies of, 1235–37; and China, 1249, 1250, 1262, 1267–69; and New Economic Policy, 1251–55; -Brezhnev

meeting, 1271–73; and Watergate, 1287–1289, 1292 (*see also* Watergate); second inauguration, 1298
Nixon, Tricia (Mrs. Edward Cox), 754, 1032, 1295
NKPA (North Korea Peoples Army), 530–543 passim
Nobel Prize winners, 57, 118, 210, 211, 214, 483, 1259
Noble, Ray, 121
Noebel, Dean, 954
Nolting, Frederick E. Jr., 919, 921–22, 988, 990
Nomura, Kichisaburo, 252, 255–56
nonviolence, 208, 982, 983, 1021, 1098, 1128. *See also* black militants and militancy; violence
Nordhoff, Charles, 68
Norman, Terence F., 1215
Normandie (French liner), 231
Normandy, invasion of, 331–33
Norris, George, 87
Norris, Kathleen, 223
Norris – La Guardia Act, 404
North Africa, in World War II, 264, 273, 277–78
Norvell, Aubrey James, 1066
nostalgia (1970s), 1224–26
Novak, Robert, 1221, 1236
NRA. *See* National Recovery Administration (NRA)
nuclear power, 199; development of, 69, 117–18, 210–16; and submarines, 692, 818; and environment, 1172. *See also* atomic weapons
Nuremberg trials, 336. *See also* war crimes and atrocities
Nuri as-Said, 823
Nye, Gerald P., 126, 200, 220, 230, 250, 257, 321, 322
Nylon, 149

Oberon, Merle, 197
O'Boyle, Patrick Cardinal, 1108
O'Brian, John Lord, 496
O'Brien, John P., 56
O'Brien, Lawrence F., 60, 878, 883, 965, 1076, 1128, 1277, 1278, 1285
occultism, 1191
O'Connell, Helen, 248
O'Connell, William Cardinal, 110
O'Connor, John J., 170
O'Donnell, P. Kenneth, 878, 925, 960, 978, 1127
O'Dwyer, William, 600
Office of Economic Opportunity (OEO), 1043
Office of Price Administration (OPA), 276, 294, 398–400
Office of Strategic Services (OSS), 490
Office of War Mobilization, 293
O'Hara, John, 242, 1117
O'Harro, Michael G., 1035
Ohly, John, 680, 687
Ohta, Dr. Victor, 1200
Okinawa, battle for, 346, 347, 371, 385
Oldendorf, Adm. Jesse, 345

Oliva, Erneido, 862, 898, 901, 903
Oliver, R. Spencer, 1277
Olivier, Laurence, 197
Olson, Culbert L., 297
Olson, Floyd B., 57, 101
Olson, John, 12
Olympic games, 247, 1149, 1187, 1259
O'Mahoney, Joseph C., 162
Onassis, Aristotle Socrates, 596, 762, 820, 987–88, 1139–41
Onassis, Jacqueline (Mrs. Aristotle Socrates), 1167, 1261. *See also* Kennedy, Jacqueline Bouvier (Mrs. John F.)
O'Neal, Edward A. III, 60
O'Neill, Eugene: *Strange Interlude,* 34
O'Neill, Oona. *See* Chaplin, Oona O'Neill
O'Neill, William L., 427, 577
OPA. *See* Office of Price Administration
Open Door policy, 174
"Open Skies." *See* disarmament
Oppenheimer, J. Robert, 213, 309, 312, 374, 375, 515; at atomic bomb test, 377–378; and arms control, 411, 571, 572–573, 574; security proceedings against, 695–700
Organization of American States (OAS), 678; in Cuban missile crisis, 963–64, 966–67
Ormandy, Eugene, 1299
Ormsby-Gore, David (Lord Harlech), 1139
Orwell, George, 486, 589
Osmond, Dr. Humphrey, 1112
Ostrander, Gilman, 1197
Oswald, Lee Harvey, 396, 584, 952, 1006–1007, 1014, 1260
Oswald, Marguerite, 396, 1005
Oswald, Russell G., 1240–41, 1242–47
Oughton, Diana, 583, 1199–1200
Owens, Hamilton, 463
Owens, Jesse, 243
Ozawa, Adm. Jisaburo, 343, 345

Pace, Frank C. Jr., 534, 538, 560–61
Pacific islands, World War II in. *See* World War II
pacifism, 126–27, 174–75, 283. *See also* draft; nonviolence
Paine, Tom, 496
Pakistan, 860, 868, 870
Palestine, 68
Palme, Olof, 1295
Panay (gunboat), sinking of, 171, 173–76
Panikkar, Sirdar K. M., 545
Paperman, Mildred, 839–41
Paris conference (1960), 859–60, 873–74
Paris-Soir, 145
Parker, Bonnie, 95
Parker, Dorothy, 246
Parker, Fess, 725
Parker, Suzy, 595
Parks, Rosa, 740–41, 743, 1300
Parsons, Louella, 246
Parsons, Capt. William S., 380, 381
Pash, Boris, 312
Patman, Wright, 45
Patolichev, Nikolai S., 1271

patriotism. See loyalty issue
Patterson, Eleanor "Cissy," 318
Patterson, Floyd, 759
Patterson, Joe, 946, 1023
Patterson, John, 938–943
Patterson, Joseph Medill, 103
Patterson, Robert P., 339, 406, 407
Patton, Gen. George S. Jr., 6, 13, 16, 51, 353, 371, 921; and European invasion, 278, 280, 333, 334, 337, 349
Paul VI, Pope, 1038, 1108
Paul, Elliot, 304
Paul, Randolph, 291
Pauling, Linus, 1300
Paullin, Dr. James D., 350
Payne, Frederick, 837
Peabody, Endicott, 49
Peabody, Mrs. Malcolm, 1021
Peace Corps, 906, 1043
Peale, Norman Vincent, 76, 881
Pearl Harbor: 1932 maneuvers at, 69, 253–254; investigation, 227, 254; attack on, 251–60, 297, 466
Pearson, Drew, 4, 10, 135, 407, 464, 527, 558, 707, 839
Peck, Gregory, 486, 1028, 1235
Peckham, Morse, 1193
Peebles, Timothy, 1166
Pegler, Westbrook, 92, 97, 111, 298
Pelley, William Dudley, 107, 1300
Pendleton, Richard, 1177
Pentagon, 87, 223, 304, 324, 1094; and military spending, 270, 530, 531 (see also budget, federal); and Army-McCarthy hearings, 706, 707; and Vietnam, 918, 920, 1000, 1051, 1070; and IDA, 1133–34. See also Army, U.S.
Pentagon Papers, 1229–32, 1236–39, 1280, 1299
People's Daily (China), 1268
Pepper, Claude, 448, 529
Pepsi-Cola, 825, 994
Percival, Lt. Gen. A. E., 270
Percy, Charles H., 60, 1039
Perelman, S. J., 1224
Peress, Irving, 515, 700, 707, 708
Perkins, Frances, 82, 85, 106, 107, 133, 155, 161, 325
Perkins, James A., 1168
permissiveness, 694, 782, 1097, 1100, 1135, 1193
Perry, Herman, 394–95
Perry, Bishop Robert, 1078
Pershing, Gen. John J., 222, 367
Persons, Gen. Wilton B. "Jerry," 627, 648, 652, 656, 754, 757, 764, 768, 770, 843
Pétain, Marshal Henri Philippe, 216, 277
Peters, J., 96
Peters, Jean, 694
Petersen, Henry, 1279, 1289
Petrillo, James C., 306
Pham Van Dong, 1293
Phan Huy Quat, 1048
Philbrick, Herbert: I Led Three Lives, 566
Philippine Islands, 252, 253; taken by Japanese, 257, 265; Corregidor, 266, 269–271, 345; U.S. drive on, 342–43, 345,

370; demobilization riots in, 405–10; independence of, 407, 484
Phillips, Cabell, 20, 354, 405, 454, 467, 468, 473, 475
Phillips, Adm. Sir Tom, 265
physicists. See science and scientists
Piaf, Edith, 419
Picasso, Pablo, 934
Piccard, Auguste, 68
Pidgeon, Walter, 218
Piel Brothers, 594
Pike, Bishop James, 1036
pill, the. See birth control
Pinchot, Gifford, 74
ping-pong tournaments in Japan and China, 1248–49
Pinkerton National Detective Agency, 131
Pittman, Key, 176, 220–21
Pittman Neutrality Resolution, 125
Pittsburgh Sun-Times, 812
Pius XI, Pope, 110
Pius XII, Pope, 197, 248, 250
Plain Dealer (Cleveland), 17
Plain Talk (publication), 525
Playboy magazine, 592, 690, 693, 997, 1114, 1121, 1226
plays and playwrights. See theater
Plumbers, the, 1217–18; and Pentagon Papers, 1231–32, 1237–39; at Watergate, 1274–79, 1288
PM, 238, 457, 477
Poe, Edgar Allan, 189
poetry, 218, 246
Poindexter, David Rudolph Jr., 1203
Point Four program, 474–75
Poitier, Sidney, 998
Poland, 773; Hitler and, 201–203; Stalin and, 327, 348, 368, 597
police: and BEF, 3–4, 10, 18; in strikes, 10, 133, 155–56, 159–60; during Depression, 40, 41, 54–56; and riots, 1062–1064, 1065, 1069, 1078, 1136, 1149, 1169, 1191, 1213–14, 1299; at Columbia University, 1134; strike of, 1136, 1137; and 1968 Democratic national convention, 1142–44, 1207; White House, 1192; attacks on, 1198–99; and Mayday Tribe, 1228–29; at Attica prison, 1242–47; and Watergate, 1277–78
Pollard, John Garland, 18
Pollock, Jackson, 759
polls and surveys: Literary Digest, 52, 144, 167; Democratic, 115; first Gallup, 118 (see also Gallup, George, and Gallup polls); and students, 128, 1097, 1099, 1134, 1226; advertising and radio, 149, 190, 191, 194, 195, 304; on FDR, 167; on war and war issues, 189, 205, 227–228, 230–32, 235, 424; Truman and, 400, 449, 461; on U.N., 420; on elections: (1948) 449, 461, 462, 464–66, 468, 471, (1960) 879–83, 890, (1964) 1025–26, 1029, 1030, (1968) 1126, (1972) 1273, 1287; on TV programs, 584, 588, 601, 1037; on Nixon, 636, 853, 1247–48, 1287; on Eisenhower, 654, 853; Republican, 695; on JFK,

983; on LBJ, 1010, 1019, 1043, 1075; on black leadership, 1062, 1068; on birth control, 1108; on Watergate, 1287. *See also individual polls and pollsters*

pollution, 1089, 1163, 1172–74

Pomerene, Atlee, 46

Pons, Lily, 333

Popular Front, 97

population: transient (vagrant), 18–22, 100; farm, 36, 238, 732, 777, 1002, 1225; student, 40, 849, 1001, 1095; of U.S., 239, 596, 1000; of Japan, 371n; and vote: (1956) 765, (1960) 884–85, 890, (1968) 1146–47, (1972) 1287; cities vs suburbs, 777–78, 1225; blue collar and white collar, 778, 1000, 1001; and birth rate, 781, 1021; black, 849, 877, 1021–22, 1062, 1069, 1078, 1080, 1150; by age groups, 1100, 1169

population explosion, 429, 724, 781, 1000. *See also* birth control.

pornography, 129, 596, 997, 1036, 1107–1109, 1193–94

Porter, Bart, 1289

Porter, Paul, 497, 528

Porter, Sylvia Field, 33, 239

Portis, Charles, 1122

Portland *Oregonian*, 789

Post, Emily, 305

postal rates, 758, 996, 1122

Postal Service, U.S., strike of, 1137

Poston, Mrs. Ersa, 1155

Potsdam Conference and Declaration, 371, 372, 379, 380, 384, 385, 410–11, 534, 658, 674

Poulson, Norris, 858

poverty: during Depression, 33–36, 41; in Mississippi, 943; LBJ and war on, 1011, 1043

Powder Ridge festival, 1212–13

Powell, Adam Clayton, 322, 1021, 1038, 1078

Powell, Dick, 88

Powell, James, 1020

Powell, Thomas Reed, 90

Powell, William, 11

Power, Tyrone, 197, 205, 283, 303

Powers, Francis Gary, 868–73, 876, 959

Powers, Lt. Col. John "Shorty," 931

POWs. *See* prisoners of war

Pozen, Elizabeth, 1005

Pravda, 689, 749, 789

Prensa, La (Buenos Aires), 597

presidency, and relationship to vice-presidency, 914–15, 1165

presidential campaigns and elections, 640; (1932) 47–54, 640; (1936) 122, 138–145, 164; (1940) 221–27; (1944) 317–327, 400; (1948) 446–71, 608; (1952) 608–41; (1956) 754, 756–58, 765–71; (1960) 877–86; (1964) 429, 1025–32; (1968) 1126–27; (1972) 1281–87

presidential powers: 58, 437, 684; FDR and, 77, 80, 125, 167, 177–78, 292, 294, 556, 744, 822; and war, 125, 177–178, 536–37, 538, 556–57, 569, 744–747, 822, 824, 1018–19, 1076; Truman and, 398, 399–400, 459, 536, 538, 556–557, 606, 744, 822; Eisenhower and, 667–68, 675–76, 684, 744–47, 822, 824; and Bricker/George amendments, 674–77; JFK and, 890, 907; LBJ and, 1018–19, 1076; Nixon and, 1161–62 (*see also* Watergate)

President's commissions: on Intergovernmental Relations, 672; on Law Enforcement, 1037; on Violence, 131

Presley, Elvis Aaron, 588, 759–60, 1102

press, the, 28, 118, 138, 179, 195; and FDR, 90, 107, 137, 138–39, 143, 145, 325; and Yalta agreement, 348; and Patton, 371; and Republican party, 465; Eisenhower berates, 768; Nixon and, 768, 1160, 1216, 1290; on Sputnik, 789; and Vietnam, 922; and Pentagon Papers, 1229–32; Watergate and, 1278, 1290; and Supreme Court decision, 1290. *See also* mass media; newspapers and magazines

press conferences: FDR and, 81, 90, 136, 150, 166, 170, 203, 229; and Mrs. FDR, 92; Truman and, 413–14; JFK and, 891; Nixon and, 1160

Pressman, Lee, 84, 161, 457, 458, 503

Price, Cecil, 1022, 1023–25

Price, G. Ward, 518n

price controls, 1253–55

prices: (1930s) 32, 36–37, 64–65, 67, 162; (1940) 239, 240; postwar, 397–400; (1948) 451–52; (1954) 693; (1960s) 1001; (1970s) 1253–55. *See also* inflation

prisoners of war: German, 278, 334, 369; Korean, 662–63; Russian, 662; U.S., in Vietnam, 1209, 1293, 1294

prison riots, 1086; Attica, 1239–47

productivity and production: 32–33, 246, 274, 290–93, 295–96, 397, 400, 1253

profits. *See* economy, U.S.

Progressive Labor Party, 1298

Progressive Party, 97

Progressive Party of America, 389, 456–58

Prohibition, 27, 124, 146; repeal, 48, 73

propaganda, 126, 516, 909; moving pictures, 218–19; "V for Victory," 219; Japanese, and Tokyo Rose, 268, 270, 272; German, 279; Chinese, 661, 662; for TV-3 satellite, 812; anti-American, 833, 935; and Bay of Pigs, 899

property damage, 596; dust storms, 98–100; at Hiroshima, 382; in North Vietnam, 1017; in riots and terrorist demonstrations, 1020, 1023, 1064–65, 1069, 1212; vandalism, 1103–1105; to Chesapeake Bay Bridge, 1190. *See also* cost; storms and weather

protests, 1037. *See also* riots and demonstrations

publicity, age of, 1259–61

public relations, 118, 425, 593; Nixon and, 720–21; and satellite failure, 812–14; CIA and, 898; and Vietnam, 922; of executives, 1093. *See also* advertising

Public Relations Society of America, 593

Public Works Administration (PWA), 86
Pueblo incident, 1123–24, 1178–79
Puerto Rico, 596
Pulitzer Prize, 671, 809, 878
Puller, Col. Lewis B. "Chesty," 547
"pumpkin papers," 508–509
Purvis, Melvin, 94, 95
Pusey, Nathan, 1168
Pyle, Ernie, 286, 304
Pyle, Howard, 649, 757

Quant, Mary, 1033
Quat, Phan Huy, 1048
Quayle, Oliver, 1030
Quemoy. *See* China
Quie, Albert, 1043
Quill, Michael, 457, 1136
Quinn, William, 1242, 1244, 1246
Quislings, 219

Rabaul campaign, 270, 341
racism, 8; (1940s) 243–44; and Japanese, 297–302; in Truman years, 482–83; and U.S. image abroad, 737; increase of, after Supreme Court decision, 738–39, 799; Little Rock and, 799–810; and southern politicians, 808–809, 943, 945; and freedom riders, 937–43; in Mississippi, 944–51; of blacks, 983–84, 1020–1021, 1070, 1133 (*see also* black militants and militancy); (1960s) 1058–70; at Attica prison, 1240–47. *See also* black(s); riots and demonstrations; segregation
Radford, Adm. Arthur W., 392, 646, 683, 684, 685, 745, 764, 916
radio and radio programs, 24, 149, 425, 507, 1002; *Amos 'n' Andy,* 7, 243; (1930s–40s) 63, 76, 98, 118, 121–22, 197, 584; FDR and, 81, 92, 117, 353, 359; Father Coughlin, 108–109, 111, 117; and presidential campaigns, 142–143, 451, 467, 468–69; and Czech crisis, 178–83, 188–89; Orson Welles (Martian invasion panic), 189–96, 1224; World War II, 216, 217, 256–57, 304; soap operas and singing commercials, 239, 721, 774; Truman years, 484; (1960s) 995; (1970s) 1224; and loyalty issue, 498–99, 515; and TV, 585–86; transistor, 757, 772–73, 1086; and Bay of Pigs, 899
Radio Daily, 586
Radio Free Europe, 597, 760
radium poisoning, 69
Radulovich, Lt. Milo, 670
Radziwill, Lee, 988
Raeder, Adm. Erich, 233, 235, 264
Raft, George, 66
railroads: (1930s) 8, 11, 18–21, 34; Railway Brotherhoods, 88, 244, 982; (1940s) 240–41; World War II, 294; strikes, 401–403; (1960s) 1002, 1122; (1970s) 1192
Rainey, Lawrence, 1022, 1023–25
Rainier III of Monaco, 761–62

Rains, Claude, 595
Ramparts magazine, 1077, 1113, 1121
Rand, Sally, 34, 40, 481–82
Randall, Clarence, 788
Randolph, A. Philip, 244, 982, 1068, 1069
Randolph, John, 150
Rank, J. Arthur, 590
Rankin, John, 243, 408, 505
Ransom, John Crowe, 589
Raskob, John J., 138
rationing. *See* home front; Office of Price Administration; World War II
Ratner, Payne, 298
Rauschenbusch, Walter, 206
Ray, James Earl, 1128–29, 1166
Ray, Manuel, 862, 897
Rayburn, Sam, 48, 352, 364, 367, 455, 491, 890, 1030
Raymond, Gene, 98
Reader's Digest, 1003
Reagan, Ronald, 729, 1039, 1099, 1116, 1168, 1201, 1282
Reber, Brig. Gen. Miles, 706
Rebozo, C. G. "Bebe," 1161
reconnaissance flights, 488; and "Open Skies" proposal, 750 (*see also* disarmament); U–2 affair, 867–76; and Cuban missile crisis, 959, 961, 966, 967; EC121 shot down, 1179
Reconstruction Finance Corporation (RFC), 24, 25, 46, 104; Fulbright's investigation of, 603–604, 605
recordings, phonograph. *See* music and musicians
Redbook magazine, 761, 1188
Red Channels (blacklist), 499
Redgrave, Michael, 590
Reeb, James J., 1060, 1061
Reece, Carroll, 449
Reed, Carroll, 486
Reed, David A., 58, 72
Reed, Harold W., 604
Reed, Rex, 1135
Reedy, George, 1075
Reeves, George, 584
Reilly, Mike, 325
Reinecke, Jean Otis, 424
relief. *See* welfare, public
religion, 595, 1035–36; and Protestant ethic, 65, 774, 957; Father Coughlin, 108–11; and pacifism, 126; Billy Graham, 484, 594; "subversion" in, 668–69; as campaign issue, 771, 878, 881; (1950s) 733, 772, 776, 783; and color line, 977; and contraception, 1108; (1970s) 1190–1191; New English Bible, 1191; "Jesus people," 1260–61. *See also* Catholicism.
Remington, William T., 459, 494, 503
Reno, Milo, 58–59
Republican National Committee, 72, 142, 225, 520, 695, 843, 844, 1027, 1222
Republican national conventions: (1936) 140; (1940) 225; (1948) 448, 451, 457, 585–86; (1952) 614–20; (1956) 768; (1960) 880; (1964) 1018, 1020, 1026–1027; (1968) 1142; (1972) 1274, 1281–1282

Republican party, 23, 52; (1934) 101, 104; (1936) 143, 144, 170; (1940s) 170, 225–27; (1944) 318–20; (1945–48) 398–400, 415–16, 446, 453, 470; (1950s) 558, 695, 842–45, 879; (1952) 656–58; (1956) 770; (1964) 1025–28, 1031–32; (1966) 1039, 1099; (1969) 1163; (1970) 1221; (1972) 1273–76, 1279, 1281–82, 1287; and big business, 106, 766, 1274; and blacks, 107, 770; and federal judges, 136, 150, 153; campaign contributions to, 139, 629–38, 1232–35, 1274, 1288; and coalition, 139 (see also Democratic party); and loyalty issue, 489–93, 501, 504, 507; and Korea, 537, 664–65; and search for government corruption, 599, 604–607; in South, 616–18, 770; division in, 620, 667–77, 766, 1032; and Nixon, 634, 1287; and Joseph McCarthy, 716–17; Old Guard opposition to Soviet meeting, 747–48; and U.N., 766; and Supreme Court, 1138; "dirty tricks," 1236–39

Reston, James, 439, 964, 1002, 1075; on Truman, 414, 470, 475; on Eisenhower, 557, 627, 719; and Oppenheimer case, 695, 697; and Khrushchev interview, 794; and JFK, 891, 910, 911, 913; on Vietnam, 1051, 1294–95, 1296; and Nixon, 1147, 1235

Reuben James (destroyer), 235

Reuther, Victor, 388–89

Reuther, Walter, 388–391, 448, 457, 458, 858, 982

revolution, social. See society

Rexroth, Kenneth, 728

Rey, Alvino, 128

Reynaud, Paul, 216

Reynolds, Jackson E., 104

Reynolds, Robert O., 886

Rhee, Syngman, 530, 534, 537, 662–63, 666

Rhinelander, Alice, 243

Rhodes, James, 1214

Ribbentrop, Joachim von, 260

Ribicoff, Abraham, 1143, 1256

Ricco, Roger, 1118

Rich, Buddy, 307

Rich, Robert F., 408, 491

Richards, Ray, 525

Richardson, John, 992–93, 1046

Richardson, Robert, 1064

Richardson, Seth, 496, 497–98

Richberg, Donald R., 87, 105

Rickover, Adm. Hyman G., 793

Ricks, Willie "the Reverend," 1067

Ridenhour, Ronald, 1177

Ridgway, Gen. Matthew B., 555, 560–61, 565, 566, 613, 683, 745

Riesel, Victor, 761

Riesman, David, 64, 577, 592, 723, 777, 1101, 1106; The Lonely Crowd, 31–32

riots and demonstrations, 847, 925, 1070, 1093; Bonus Expeditionary Force, 3–4, 10–19, 23, 26, 54; pacifist, 126–27; demobilization ("Wanna-Go-Home"), 405–410, 531; and Korea, 539; French, 684–

685; bus boycott, 740–43; anti-American, abroad, 825–33, 875, 964; black sit-ins, 848–49, 1059; Berkeley, 849, 1033–34, 1054, 1191; racist, in Mississippi, 945–952; Birmingham, 976–78; March on Washington, 982–83; in Vietnam, 989; black, in North, 1020–22, 1037, 1079–1081, 1149; against the U.S. war in Vietnam, 1037, 1048, 1054–56, 1207; draft card burning, 1055; Selma voting march, 1058–62, 1068; Watts, 1062–1066, 1070; countrywide, 1064–66, 1069, 1079–81, 1131; Meredith March for Freedom, 1066–68; Roxbury, Newark, Detroit, Cambridge, 1079–81; in blackout, 1086; at foreign universities, 1096; student, 1096, 1098, 1099, 1167, 1168; teen-age, 1103–1105; after death of Martin Luther King, 1128; at Columbia University, 1131–34; at Democratic national convention, 1142–44; "standards" established, 1149; Cleveland, 1149; M-day, 1174–75; Nixon years, 1175, 1198, 1298–1300; Jackson State, 1212; Kent State, 1213–16, 1225–26; Mayday Tribe, 1228–29; Attica prison, 1239–47; at 1972 Republican convention and inaugural, 1282, 1298–1300. See also casualties; freedom riders

Ripley, William Z., 42

Ripon Society, 1221

Ritchie, Albert C., 18, 73, 138

Ritchie, William, 450

Rizzo, Frank L., 1199

Roa, Raúl, 902

Robb, Robert, 697–98, 699, 839, 840

Robbins, Harold, 589

Roberts, Clifford, 654

Roberts, Owen J., 136, 137, 301

Roberts, Roy, 364

Roberts, Wayne, 1024–25

Roberts, William L., 531

Robertson, Reuben B. III, 1257

Robertson, Walter S., 663, 916

Robeson, Paul, 419, 1199

Robin Hood, as anti-Communist issue, 581

Robinson, Claude, and Robinson polls, 883

Robinson, Edward G., 218, 303

Robinson, Joseph, 71, 113, 152

Robinson, William, 633

Robinson, William E., 654

Rockefeller, Abby Aldrich, 1195

Rockefeller, David, 60

Rockefeller, Happy (Mrs. Nelson), 996, 1026

Rockefeller, John D., 149

Rockefeller, Nelson, 209, 748, 1085, 1128, 1240; as governor of N.Y., 845, 1039, 1137; and campaigns: (1964) 995–96, 1026–27, 1028, 1032, (1968) 1127, 1141, (1972) 1282; and Attica prison, 1240, 1243, 1245, 1246, 1247

Rockefeller, Winthrop, 800

Rockefeller Foundation, 478

rockets. See missile and rocket programs

Rockne (automobile), 34

Rockwell, George Lincoln, 953, 1004

Rodgers, Richard, 304
Rodin, Odile, 761
Rodríguez, Gen. Nicholas, 155
Roffo, A. H., 240
Rogers, Ginger, 68, 98, 149
Rogers, Roy, 427
Rogers, Will, 10, 44, 49, 50, 57, 59, 77, 81, 108, 1088
Rogers, William P., 631, 633, 754, 800, 879, 882, 941, 1156
ROK (Army of the Republic of Korea), 530–43 passim
Roland, Arthur, 275
Roller Derby, 485
Roman Catholicism. See Catholicism
Rommel, Field Marshal Gen. Erwin, 264, 278, 331
Romney, George, 758, 1027, 1039, 1127, 1141
Rooney, Mickey, 197
Roosevelt, Anna, 323, 326, 360
Roosevelt, (Anna) Eleanor (Mrs. Franklin D.), 18, 71, 75, 77, 79, 83, 111, 224, 258, 366, 407–408, 880, 1139; portrait of, 91–93; threats to, 95; and blacks, 107, 245; on neutrality, 204, 228; and FDR's health, 322, 323, 326; and death of FDR, 350–54, 356–62; on Walter Reuther, 390
Roosevelt, Elliott, 448
Roosevelt, Franklin D., 181, 188, 196, 250, 282, 315, 487, 488, 652, 682; on Hoover administration, 18, 46; and public welfare, 25, 84, 85–87, 95; campaigns, 47–54, 138–44, 221–27, 317–21; public reaction to, 49–51, 53–54; and budget, 51, 138, 162–63, 274, 324, 1123; and interregnum, 71–74; inaugurations, 74–77, 92, 124, 150; takes office and declares bank holiday, 78–80, 81; and presidential powers, 77, 80, 125, 167, 177–78, 292, 294, 556, 744, 822; fireside chats, 81, 88, 89, 104, 105, 152, 163, 168, 230, 264; routine of, 82–83; Communism and, 84, 142, 143; and government agencies, 84–87; and Keynesian theory, 95, 124; business and, 103–106, 141, 143–44, 163–64, 166, 239; plans and accomplishments, 105–108, 150–153, 162–71, 222, 226–36, 324, 327; and Democratic coalition, 107, 139, 141, 153, 167–71, 400; foreign policy, 108, 171, 177–78, 190, 221, 223; Father Coughlin and, 109–11, 117; and Huey Long, 111, 113–15, 117; neutrality and isolationism, 125, 175–77, 189, 200–202, 203–204, 226, 235–36; and organized labor, 132–33, 400; and Supreme Court, 136–38, 150–53, 162, 167–169; campaign contributions to, 139, 156; and strikes, 153, 155, 156, 159, 160, 1136; calumny against, 164–67, 954–55; "warmongering" of, 175–76, 250; visited by king and queen of England, 177, 200; and Hitler, 190, 200, 201, 206, 225, 236, 251, 260, 331; Einstein and commitment to atomic bomb,
215, 309, 311–12, 339–40; deviousness of, 222, 226, 232, 339, 396; and lend-lease, 227–32, 233; meets Churchill at sea, 234; and blacks, 245; and Japanese, 251, 299; and declaration of war, 258–259; and battles in Pacific, 270, 271, 273; and second front, 273–74, 277–78; pronounces New Deal dead, 292; as commander in chief, 315–17, 318; and fourth term, 317–21; and Truman, 319–320, 364, 365, 915; health, 321–27; and D-Day, 331–32; illness and death, 334, 335, 347–62, 466; and Manhattan Project, 339; and Philippine issue, 344; and Yalta agreement, 348, 410, 489, 491, 674 (see also Yalta agreement)
Roosevelt, Franklin D. Jr., 283–84, 353
Roosevelt, James (FDR's father), 361
Roosevelt, James, 54, 74, 163, 324–25, 448, 458
Roosevelt, John, 353
Roosevelt, Sara Delano, 91
Roosevelt, Theodore, 49, 81, 91, 167, 956
Root, Elihu, 5
Roper, Elmo, and Roper polls, 205, 465–466, 883
Rose, David, 427
Rosenberg, Jerome S., 1244
Rosenberg, Julius and Ethel, 313, 500, 692
Rosenman, Sam, 84, 226, 317–18, 325, 326, 454
Rosenwald, Lessing, 223
Ross, Charles G., 401, 402, 413, 414
Ross, Irwin, 455
Ross, Lillian, 486
Ross, Murray, 577
Rossellini, Roberto, 486
Rostow, Elspeth, 418
Rostow, Walt W., 682, 920, 988, 1040
Roszak, Theodore: The Making of a Counter Culture, 1261
ROTC (Reserve Officers' Training Corps) See Army, U.S.
Rovere, Richard H., 126, 174, 521, 523, 679, 1224; on Truman, 460, 469; on Eisenhower, 624, 661, 766; on Korea, 663–64
Rowley, Jim, 467, 469
Roxbury, Massachusetts, riots, 1079
Roy, Jules, 684n
Royall, Kenneth C., 408, 446–47
Royce City, Texas, doctors in, 39
Rubin, Jerry, 1143, 1205, 1206, 1208
Rubirosa, Porfirio, 761
Ruby, Charles P., 12
Ruby, Jack, 1007, 1038
Rudd, Mark, 583, 701, 1132–34
Rundstedt, Field Marshal Gerd von, 334
Runyon, Damon, 298
Rural Electrification Act, 106
Rushmore, Howard, 525
Rusk, Dean, 532, 533, 894, 905, 918, 1015, 1078; and Cuban missile crisis, 960–62, 965, 966, 968–70; and Vietnam, 988, 990, 991, 1019, 1048, 1057, 1126; and Pueblo affair, 1123–24

Russell, Bertrand, 249–50, 954, 967
Russell, Bill, 999
Russell, Jane, 303
Russell, Louis, 506
Russell, Richard, 448, 454, 456, 608, 705, 736, 808, 822
Russia. *See* Soviet Union
Russo, Anthony J. Jr., 1231
Rustin, Bayard, 1065, 1069
Rutherford, Lord Ernest, 69, 972
Rutherford, Lucy Mercer, 92, 93, 324, 335, 347, 349, 353, 357, 360
Ryerson, Edward Jr., 223

Sabath, Adolph J., 521
Sachs, Alexander, 215, 339
Sacklette, Baron Ignatius, 839
Safire, William, 1220
Sahl, Mort, 933
St. Clair, James D., 715n
Saint Laurent, Yves, 1033
St. Louis Post-Dispatch, 160, 526
Saipan, battle for, 343, 371
Salazar, Antonio de Oliveira, 875
Sale, Chic, 11
Salinger, Pierre, 956–57, 963, 965, 969, 984, 1285–86
Salisbury, Marquess of, 677
Salk, Dr. Jonas, 60
SALT. *See* Strategic Arms Limitation Talks
Saltonstall, Leverett, 170, 284, 303, 669, 709
Saltonstall, Peter B., 284
Sampson, Anthony, 987
Samsonith, Tiao, 853
Sander, Dr. Herman N., 595
Sanders, Ed, 1116
Sanders, George, 486
San Francisco Chronicle, 41, 49, 1113
San Francisco Examiner, 302
San Francisco Golden Gate Exposition, 198
San Román, José Peréz "Pepe," 862, 866, 897, 899–900, 902, 904–905
Sargent, Francis, 1219
Sarnoff, David, 973, 974
Sartre, Jean-Paul, 825
satellites. *See* space travel and satellites
Satrom, LeRoy, 1213–14
Saturday Evening Post, 5, 31, 164, 995, 1102
Saturday Review, 1110
Saud, Ibn, king of Saudi Arabia, 823
Savio, Mario, 583, 701, 1033–34, 1116
Savo, Jimmy, 304
Sawyer, Charles, 606
Saxbe, William, 1295
Sayre, Francis B., 510, 1014, 1299
Scali, John, 958, 969
Schary, Dore, 596
Schechter, Joseph, 144
Schell, Maria and Maximilian, 590
Schenectady Star, 25
Schine, G. David, 700–703, 705–708, 709, 713
Schirra, Walter, 819
Schlesinger, Arthur M. Jr., 42, 60, 82, 83, 100, 174, 878, 957; and Bay of Pigs,

893, 895, 904; on Vietnam War, 913, 917, 919; on JFK, 955, 981–82; and RFK, 1127
Schlesinger, Marian (Mrs. Arthur M. Jr.), 880
Schmeling, Max, 98, 821
Schoenman, George J., 605
schools and teachers, 266; (1930s) 40–41, 65, 1296; (1940) 238; (1950s) 784–85, 793; (1960s) 1137; (1970s) 1296; federal aid to, 474; and loyalty issue, 498; and segregation, 735–36 (*see also* segregation); and Little Rock incident, 799–810; black boycotts of, 1021; parochial, 1042, 1225. *See also* busing issue; education
Schorr, Daniel, 1235
Schramm, Jim, 716
Schricker, Henry F., 622
Schroeder, Gerhard, 960
Schulberg, Budd: *The Disenchanted,* 102
Schultz, Benjamin, 702
Schultz, Richard G., 1205
Schumach, Murray, 561
Schumann Heink, Mme., 121
Schwab, Charles M., 56
Schwartz, Herman, 1242, 1243, 1244
Schwarz, Fred, 953, 954
Schweitzer, Dr. Albert, 595
Schweitzer, Mitchell, 850
Schwellenbach, Lewis B., 179
Schwerner, Michael H., 1022–24
Schwinn, Hermann, 155
science and scientists: German, 210–16, 275, 309, 313, 336–39, 374, 574; U.S. nuclear, 212–14, 309–15, 336–40, 373–378, 411, 498, 572–73, 696, 792, 794, 797; French, 215–16; Japanese, 339, 384; and scientific politics in U.S., 696; Soviet, 791–93; and space race, 814. *See also* technology
Science magazine, 699
SCLC. *See* Southern Christian Leadership Conference
Scott, Hugh D. Jr., 456, 459, 461, 1175, 1180, 1250, 1285
Scottsboro Boys, 21–22
Scranton, William W., 1027, 1212, 1215
Scribner's magazine, 56
Scripps-Howard newspapers, 47, 168, 625
SDS. *See* Students for a Democratic Society
Seabees, 284
Seale, Bobby, 1205, 1206, 1243, 1244
SEATO (Southeast Asia Treaty Organization), 678, 687, 1076
Secret Service, U.S., 325, 1142; and presidential protection, 27, 113, 365, 1076, 1143, 1299
"secret war" .(S-1), 215–16, 372
Securities and Exchange Commission (SEC), 96, 103, 137, 162, 1235. *See also* Wall Street
security, national, 489, 581; and atomic research, 212–13, 215, 315, 372; NKVD and, 493–94; and "pumpkin papers," 508–509; Eisenhower administration and, 670–72; and space race, 926; and Re-

security, national (*continued*)
  publican right, 1029; Nixon and, 1216–1217. *See also* espionage
Sedov, Leonid I., 789
Seeger, Pete, 458, 1073, 1122, 1207
segregation: Supreme Court and schools, 735–37; of transportation, 735, 740–43, 934–44; and sit-ins, 848–49, 882–83; freedom riders, 934–43, 944; Birmingham and, 976–78; black militants and, 1077 (*see also* black militants and militancy); and busing issue, 1273–74. *See also* civil rights; integration
Segretti, Donald H., 1236
Seigenthaler, John, 940, 941
Seldes, Gilbert, 61
Selective Service. *See* draft; Hershey, Gen. Lewis B.
Selective Training and Service Bill. *See* draft
Selma registration march, 1058–62, 1068
Senate Foreign Relations Committee, 200, 220, 524, 655, 659, 676, 862, 1017, 1076
Senate Judiciary Committee, 1138
Senate Military Affairs Committee, 222
Senate Munitions Investigating Subcommittee, 126
Senate Select Committee on Presidential Campaign Activities (Ervin committee), 1279, 1287, 1290
separatism. *See* black militants and militancy
Servan-Schreiber, Jean-Jacques, 824, 825, 1093, 1095, 1135
Sevareid, Eric, 127, 181, 233, 290, 330, 1148; as vagrant, 19, 22, 100; on strike-breaking, 133–34; on GIs in Europe, 443–44
Seventh Fleet. *See* Navy, U.S.
Seversky, Maj. Alexander de, 304
sex and attitudes toward, 286, 1171; (1930s) 21, 33, 66, 129; (1940s) 248–250; (1950s) 601–602, 694, 722–23; (1960s) 996–97, 1103, 1106–11; (1970s) 1193–95; of troops, 426–27; Kinsey report, 477–82; teen-agers and, 480, 722–23, 1102–1103, 1109, 1194; prostitution, 601–602; contraception and abortion, 847, 849–50, 1090, 1108, 1109, 1194; at colleges and universities, 996–97, 998, 1038, 1107; and "singles only," 1035; "literature," stage and screen, 1107–1109, 1193–94; and drugs, 1213; Gay Liberation, 1284–85. *See also* morality; pornography
sex education, 1194–95
Shakespeare, Frank Jr., 1146
Shalett, Sidney M., 199
Sharp, Adm. U. S. Grant, 1070
Shaw, Artie, 119, 244, 427
Shaw, Clay L., 1166
Shaw, George Bernard, 68, 987
Shea, Catherine, 75
Shearer, Norma, 198, 688
Sheehan, Neil, 1054
Sheen, Bishop Fulton J., 587

Shelton, Col. William M., 869, 870–71
Shepard, Cdr. Alan B. Jr., 819, 929–30
Sheppard, Dr. Samuel H., 693
Sheridan, Ann, 148
Sherman, Arthur G., 34, 118, 119
Sherman, Adm. Forrest, 436
Sherrod, Robert, 233
Sherwood, Jack, 831, 832
Sherwood, Robert, 56, 73, 223, 226, 236
shipping: and World War II, 231–33, 234–236, 264, 295, 341; in blockade of Cuba, 968–69
Shirer, William L., 179, 181, 182, 189, 200, 514
Shivers, Allan, 736
Shore, Dinah, 695
Short, Dewey, 563, 607
Short, Luke, 653
Short, Gen. Walter, 253, 254, 257
Shoumatoff, Mme. Elizabeth, 347, 349, 353
Shoup, Gen. David M., 956–57, 962
show business. *See* moving pictures and performers; radio and radio programs; television; theater
Shriver, Sargent, 1015, 1042–43, 1286
Sichell, H. M., 433
Sicily, invasion of, 278–79
Sidey, Hugh, 928, 1012, 1251
Sifontes, Dr. Lionel, 1246
Signal Corps, U.S., 269, 271–72
Sihanouk, Norodom, 1210
Sikorsky, Igor, 240, 293
Silver, James W., 943
Simpson, Adele, 1197
Simpson, John A., 60
Simpson, Richard, 843
Simpson, Mrs. Wallis (Duchess of Windsor), 68
Sinatra, Frank, 128–29, 197, 307–309, 483, 693, 1122
Sinclair, Upton, 57, 97, 100–101, 394
Sindlinger, Albert, and Sindlinger polls, 1247–48
Singapore, capture of, 265, 270
Singer, Saul, 45
Sirhan, Sirhan Bishara "Sol," 1070, 1130, 1166, 1260
Sirica, John J., 1292
sit-ins. *See* segregation
Skelton, Red, 283
Skouras, Spyros, P., 858
slang and jargon, 150, 241, 693, 722–23, 853, 999–1000, 1003
Slansky, Rudolf, 597
Slayton, Donald, 819
Slessor, Sir John, 570
Sloan, Alfred P. Jr., 119
Sloan, Hugh Jr., 1275, 1289–90
Slotin, Louis, 314–15
slum clearance. *See* housing
Smathers, George A., 529
Smith, Adam, 136
Smith, Alfred E., 46–48, 51, 58, 85, 103, 138, 140
Smith, "Cotton Ed," 141, 170, 303
Smith, Dana C., 627
Smith, Gene, 22

Smith, Gerald L. K., 107, 116–17, 141, 142, 321, 1300
Smith, Guy Gibson, 1078
Smith, Hedrick, 1216
Smith, Lt. Gen. Holland M. "Howlin' Mad," 343
Smith, Howard K., 882
Smith, James H. Jr., 671
Smith, Jerome, 984
Smith, Kate, 121, 200, 218, 238
Smith, Lillian, 304
Smith, Margaret Chase, 529, 607, 705, 709, 843, 1026
Smith, Merriman, 358, 755, 1005
Smith, Paul, 632
Smith, Red, 485
Smith, Robert Benjamin, 1260
Smith, Tommie, 1149
Smith, Gen. Walter Bedell, 655
Smith, Willis, 529
Smith Act, 494, 510, 672
Smith-Mundt program, 444, 824
Smyth, Henry D., 698
Smyth, James G., 604
SNCC. See Student Nonviolent Coordinating Committee
Snodgrass, James, 851
Snyder, Dr. Howard McC., 752–53, 767, 811–12
Snyder, John W., 369, 392, 604
Sobell, Morton, 314
Socialism, 56, 206–208
Social Justice magazine, 109, 110
social security, 116, 240, 447, 766, 883, 1122; FDR and, 103, 106, 107, 122, 137, 143; Republican party and, 143, 415, 1028–29; Supreme Court and, 152. See also Medicare
society: youth and, 63, 420, 1033–34, 1096 (see also teen-agers; youth counterculture); revolt against, 289, 291, 406–410 (see also riots and demonstrations); conformity to, 476–77, 576–82, 592, 777–79, 781, 784; nonconformity and "beat" generation, 725–29; double standard of, 776–77; growing mobility of, 1002; and the establishment, 1083, 1098. See also backlash; black(s); life-styles and attitudes
Soil Conservation Act, 106
Sokolsky, George, 46, 525, 669, 701, 702, 819
Soledad case, 1201–1205, 1260
Sollazo, Salvatore T., 601
Somervell, Gen. Brehon, 306
song(s), 73; "Brother, Can You Spare a Dime?", 27; chants and, 43, 128, 131, 218, 583; political themes and ditties, 48, 84, 101, 115, 140; "Happy Days Are Here Again," 48, 89; "The International," 55, 102, 103; Iowa farmers', 59; ballad for Huey Long, 116; popular: (1930–41) 121, 150, 197, 205, 247–48, (World War II) 218, 235, 247–48, 265, 275, 277, 286–87, 304–307 passim, (1947–49) 420, 483, 486, (1950s) 539, 549, 564, 643, 693–94, 725, 759,

(1960s) 998–1000, 1110, 1113; ballad of Joe Hill, 135, 391; singing commercials, 239, 721, 774; "Lili Marlene," 286; "Nature Boy," 483; "Tennessee Waltz," 549; "Davy Crockett," 725; "We Shall Overcome," 742; in Vietnam War, 988–89, 1178; Columbia song, 1131–32. See also music and musicians
Sontag, Susan, 954
Sorensen, Theodore C., 893, 917, 920, 926–27, 929, 960, 970, 1127
South: Democratic party in, 153, 170, 454, 456, 458, 878, 880; war fever in, 228; Republican party in, 616–18, 770; and segregation decision, 736–37, 799, 943; Eisenhower's popularity in, 794; -North antipathy, 808–809
South Africa, 597
Southern, Terry, 1207
Southern Christian Leadership Conference (SCLC), 939, 1066, 1149
Southern Regional Council, 848–49
"South Sea bubble," 33
Soviet Union, 35, 57, 65, 597; diplomatic recognition of, 84, 97; and atomic developments, 87, 212, 313–15, 379, 488, 499–501, 510, 512, 517, 571, 574, 597, 912–13; Hitler and, 233, 236, 260; as U.S. ally, 233, 320, 347, 348, 371–72, 436; and Atlantic Charter, 234; siege of Stalingrad, 264; and Yalta agreement, 326, 327, 348–49, 371, 410; troops in Europe, 334, 410; and Potsdam Conference, 372, 410–11, 534; invades Manchuria, 383; declares war on Japan, 384, 411; postwar foreign policy, 410–13, 440, 441, 443; as world leader, 434, 435–36, 441; and China, 488, 986, 1248; espionage, 489, 493–94, 499–502, 507–10; NKVD, 493, 597, 751; in eastern Europe, 510, 677–78, 909; and Korea, 519, 530, 541, 543, 549, 566, 1124; and Vietnam, 680, 1295; and Geneva conference, 747–51; and Hungarian uprising, 764, 765; Sputnik and satellites, 785, 791–94, 797, 798, 816, 818, 819, 855, 926, 930, 935; ICBMs, 795–98, 962, 1163; –U.S. relations, 854–55, 858–59, 869, 874, 908–13, 986–87, 1271–73; and Bay of Pigs, 865, 894, 904; and U-2 affair, 868–69, 871–74, 876; and Berlin, 874, 909–13; and test ban, 909, 913, 971; military budget increased, 911; manned space flights, 926–28, 930, 935, 994; and Cuban missile crisis, 958–71; arrest of U.S. generals, 1191; and Cambodia, 1210; SALT and, 1216; and China–U.S. relations, 1269; Nixon-Brezhnev meeting, 1271–73. See also United Nations
Spaak, Paul-Henri, 913
Spaatz, Lt. Gen. Carl, 383
space travel and satellites: U.S. and USSR, 785, 788–90, 794, 813, 819, 926–28, 935, 994, 1272; development, 788, 790, 794, 796–99, 812–14, 818, 819, 925–

space travel and satellites (*continued*) 930, 934; manned flights, 929–34, 994, 1156–59, 1192; byproducts of, 1094; moon landing, 1156–59. *See also* Soviet Union

Spain, 176, 178, 198, 1036

Sparkman, John, 448, 623, 656

Sparks, Fred, 1141

Spassky, Boris, 1261

Special Forces. *See* Green Berets

Special Investigations Unit. *See* Plumbers

Speck, Richard, 1038

Spectorsky, A. C., 776

Spedding, Frank H., 311

Speer, Albert, 296, 336–37

Spellman, Francis Cardinal, 197, 564, 654

Spencer, Herbert, 1093

Spillane, Mickey, 567, 568–69

Spina, Frank, 368

Spivak, Lawrence, 613

Spock, Dr. Benjamin M., 395, 780, 1078, 1300; "Age of," 429; and peace demonstrations, 1056, 1072, 1229; portrait of, 1187–89

sports and games, 98, 118, 148, 197, 247, 256, 257, 1296; World Series, 98; football and National Football League, 149, 205, 256, 257, 483, 998, 999, 1039; blacks in, 243, 283, 1036; during World War II, 306; TV, 484–85, 594, 1089; (1950s) 732; (1960s) 998, 999, 1036, 1039, 1089; Astrodome, 1089; ping-pong, 1248–49; chess, 1261. *See also* toys

Sports Illustrated, 1173

Sprague, Russell, 462

Springer, William E., 852

Springfield, Mass., riots, 1064

Sputnik, 785, 787–91, 797, 816, 855. *See also* Soviet Union

Stalin, Joseph V., 201, 277, 296, 315, 316, 349, 369, 488, 519, 594, 908; Truman and, 233, 365, 368, 372, 379, 450; and Yalta agreement, 327, 348, 410, 674; and Eisenhower, 372; and Potsdam Conference, 410–11; and coexistence, 436; and Berlin blockade, 441, 909; and Mao, 517; death, 660, 661

Stalingrad, siege of, 264, 273, 279, 340, 530

standard of living. *See* income; wages and hours

Stanley, Thomas, 736

Stans, Maurice, 1235, 1252, 1274, 1279, 1290, 1291

Stanton, Frank, 974

Stanwyck, Barbara, 303

Stars and Stripes, 284, 309

starvation. *See* food

Stassen, Harold, 276, 318, 415, 446, 452, 557, 613, 618, 671, 677, 749, 768

State Department, U.S., 125, 222, 314, 344, 357, 808, 827; *Panay* incident, 174, 176; Vietnam, 177, 1046, 1048, 1294; fall of Kuomintang, 487–88; and loyalty investigations, 490, 491, 518–30, 668; and Korean War, 566; and travel in Communist countries, 581, 1248; and "secret" agreements, 658; and Cuba, 862, 865; and U-2 affair, 872–73; and Berlin Wall, 912; and Pentagon, 920; cables forged, 1236–37, 1280. *See also* names of *Secretaries of State*

states' rights, 735, 946; and National States' Rights Party, 941

Status of Forces treaties, 675

Steelman, John, 837

steelworkers. *See* United Steel Workers

Steen, Marguerite: *The Sun Is My Undoing,* 251

Steffens, Lincoln, 57, 102

Stein, Herbert, 1254

Steinbeck, John, 20, 286, 779, 1007–1008, 1122; *The Grapes of Wrath,* 100; *The Moon Is Down,* 304

Steinem, Gloria, 1106

Stemple, Herbert M., 850

Stennis, John, 682

Stenvig, Charles S., 1163

Stephens, Tom, 757

Sterling, Len, 256, 257

Stern, Curt, 699–700

Stettinius, Edward R., 326

Stevens, Robert T., 706–708, 711

Stevenson, Adlai E., 84, 93, 233, 454, 463, 470, 644, 648, 672, 825, 834, 842, 880, 1015; and Alger Hiss, 503, 612–13, 628, as presidential candidate: (1952) 608, 610–11, 621–26, 627–30, 634, 638–40, (1956) 766–70; character and image, 610–11, 613, 623; Nixon and, 612, 628, 629, 634, 718, 719, 767–68; Joseph McCarthy and, 628–29; on Formosa crisis, 745; on presidential powers, 747; on Eisenhower, 758; and Bay of Pigs, 902, 903; and Cuban missile crisis, 960, 964, 965, 967–69; death, 1037

Stevenson, Adlai E. III, 1221

Stewart, James, 206, 283

Stilwell, Gen. Joseph, 264, 488

Stimson, Henry L., 5, 72, 175, 387; on FDR, 77, 316, 324, 339–40; as Secretary of War, 224, 225, 232, 254, 259, 278, 320, 324, 339–40, 365, 371, 372, 375, 379; and Japanese, 263–64, 297, 299, 376, 379, 385

Stock Exchange, New York, 76, 96, 145, 146, 162, 594, 1001, 1192, 1261. *See also* Dow Jones; Wall Street

stock market, 46, 96, 594; 1929 crash, 26, 31, 32–33, 36, 145; (1937) 162, 163; (1957) 816; (1971) 1252, 1255; (1972) 1261; and Eisenhower's illnesses, 754–755; and fashions, 1197. *See also* Dow Jones; Wall Street

Stokowski, Leopold Antoni, 427

Stolper, Gustav, 215

Stone, Harlan Fiske, 136

Stone, I. F., 102, 1199

storms and weather: 98–100, 596–97, 692–693, 1190; 1938 hurricane, 183–88

Strachan, Gordon, 1279, 1289

Straight, Michael: *Trial by Television,* 712

Strang, Ruth, 793

Strassmann, Fritz, 210
Strategic Air Command (SAC). *See* Air Force, U.S.
Strategic Arms Limitation Talks (SALT), 1216, 1218
Straus, Roger, 466
Strauss, Adm. Lewis A., 572, 696, 697, 699, 985
Strawn, Silas, 25
Streisand, Barbra, 1122, 1235
Stribling, T. S., 68
Strickman, Robert, 1131
strikes, 55, 133, 853, 892; violence in, 131, 133–35, 159–61; in auto industry, 133, 153–56, 389–90, 400–401; sit-down, 154–55, 156, 161; and stock market, 162–63; Truman and, 400–405, 606; wartime, 400, 403; (1960s) 1136–37; (1970s) 1192, 1296. *See also* labor and labor unions
strontium, 90, 699
Stuart, R. Douglas Jr., 223
student(s), 951; unrest in Kentucky, 26; pacifism, 126–27, 221; employment, 127–28; and draft, 224, 283, 1073, 1136; apathy, 576–81; Berkeley, 849, 1098; and CFO, 1022; Free Speech Movement, 1033–34; riots and demonstrations, 1033–34, 1096, 1098, 1131–1134; attitudes and heroes, 1098, 1135–1136, 1225–26; and politics, 1099, 1219; strike to protest Cambodia invasion, 1211; Kent State tragedy, 1213–16. *See also* riots and demonstrations
Student League for Industrial Democracy (SLID). *See* Students for a Democratic Society (SDS)
Student Nonviolent Coordinating Committee (SNCC), 982, at Selma march, 1059; growth of militancy in, 1066–69, 1076–1077, 1149; anti-Semitism of, 1077
Students for a Democratic Society (SDS), 126–27, 952, 1097, 1098, 1119, 1175, 1205, 1298, 1299; split in, 1099, 1131–1133
Students Union for Peace Action, 1073
Stuntz, Larry, 1252
Sturgis, Frank, 1277, 1278
Sturtevant, A. H., 699
Styer, Lt. Gen. W. D., 407
Styron, William, 1207
submarines: loss of *Squalus*, 202; German, 204, 231–33, 235–36, 264, 274, 295; Japanese, 265; U.S., (World War II) 269, 341, 345, (atomic) 692, 818; Soviet, 631, 967; loss of *Scorpion*, 1123
suburbs: life-style, 242, 775, 777–84; postwar growth of, 431–32, 476; returns from, in 1952 election, 639; blacks in, 779; and teen-agers, 1103; shopping centers, 1225
subversives and subversion, 491n, 597, 668, 672, 1081; World War II and postwar, 270, 275, 410; and loyalty issue, 495–96, 510, 521. *See also* Communists and Communism; espionage
Suckley, Margaret "Daisy," 347, 349

Suez crisis, 763–65, 821–24
suicide: "altruistic," 32; rate, 55, 759; kamikaze, 370, 371, 385–87, 1179; U-2 pilots and, 869, 872; self-immolation, 989, 1055, 1209; hara-kiri, 1259–1260
Sukarno, Dr. Achmed, 596
Sullivan, Ed, 588, 694
Sullivan, Lester B., 940–41
Sullivan, Mark, 28, 139, 164, 482
Sullivan, Walter, 787
Summerfield, Arthur E., 630, 633, 635, 637, 648, 757
summit meeting(s), 316, 327; 348, 674; Geneva (1955), 747–51; Paris (1960), 859–60, 873–74; Vienna (1961), 908–911, 935; Nixon-Mao, 1268–69; Nixon-Brezhnev, 1271–73
Sumner, William Graham, 49
Sumners, Hatton, 151
Sung Chung, 1248
Sun Yat-sen, 487
Supreme Court, U.S., 159, 170n, 597, 1024; Scottsboro case, 22; FDR and, 96, 135–38, 150–53, 162, 167–69; and NRA, 105, 136, 144; on sit-down strikes, 161; and Japanese-Americans, 301; and Communism, 597, 1201; and integration, 734–38, 743, 799, 804, 1057, 1068; George Wallace and, 978; LBJ and, 1137–39; Nixon and, 1146, 1164–65; on unitary schools, 1169; on obscenity, 1194; on ability to pay, 1225; and Pentagon Papers, 1231; and press confidences, 1290. *See also names of chief justices*
Suskind, Richard, 1263, 1264, 1265, 1267
Sutherland, George, 136, 137
Sutton, Willie, 596
Suzuki, Adm. Kantaro, 354, 380, 384–86
Swados, Harvey, 1097
Swanson, Claude A., 48
Swanson, Gloria, 486
Swayze, John Cameron, 587
sweatshops, 38, 86
Swing, Raymond Gram, 110
Swope, Herbert Bayard, 436
Symington, Stuart, 711, 788, 880
synthetics, 149
Syria, 823
Szilard, Leo, 211, 214–15, 335–36

Taft, Robert A., 97, 170, 197, 225, 231, 297, 440, 445, 475, 518, 524, 564, 648; on Vietnam, 221, 665; and FDR, 354, 664; and Truman, 400, 403, 447, 448, 450–51, 459, 470, 664; on presidential powers, 437, 459, 536; as presidential candidate, 452, 493, 613–14, 616–18, 619, 620, 624, 626, 630, 835; and loyalty issue, 493, 518, 527; and Korean War, 536; and isolationism, 556, 557, 569; as majority leader, 655–56, 659, 664–65; on Charles Bohlen, 656; illness and death, 665–68
Taft, Robert A. Jr., 60
Taft, William Howard, 112

Taft, William Howard IV, 1257
Taft-Hartley bills, 403, 462, 474, 1044, 1136
Taiwan (Formosa). *See* Chiang Kai-shek; China; Formosa resolution
Takamatsu, Prince, 387
Takijishi, Admiral, 386
Talbott, Harold E., 670, 835
Talmadge, Eugene D., 131, 138
Talmadge, Herman, 736, 808
Talmadge, Norma, 688
Tamm, Quinn, 1199
Tarawa campaign, 270, 342–43
tariff, 597, 1254
Tass, 785
Tate, Allen, 588, 589
Tate, Sharon, 1098, 1171
Tatlock, Dr. Jean, 312
taxes, 106, 165, 474; income, 25, 45, 73, 106, 148, 165–66, 240; real estate, 38–39; and social security, 103, 106, 107, 240; payroll, 103, 106, 240; LBJ and, 1042, 1053–54; Nixon and, 1253
Taylor, Davidson, 193–94
Taylor, Elizabeth, 486, 1000
Taylor, Frank J., 1102
Taylor, Glen, 430, 457
Taylor, Gen. Maxwell D., 805, 893, 918, 949, 956; and Vietnam, 920, 922, 988, 990, 991, 992, 994, 1046; and Cuban missile crisis, 959, 960, 966
Taylor, Myron Charles, 157–58, 250
Taylor, Brig. Gen. Telford, 485
Teamsters Union, 320, 820, 1255
technology: automation, 118, 1092, 1096; and 1939 World's Fair, 199–200; World War II, 291; computers and computerization, 573, 884, 1087–88; and life-style, 772–73, 785, 996, 1002, 1087, 1091; and space race, 772, 926; revolution in, 1091–92, 1094; and agriculture, 1091–1092. *See also* science and scientists
teen-agers: (1930s) 63; (1940s) 420; (1950s) 592, 720–25; (1960s) 1003, 1100–1104; bobby-soxers, 305–306, 483; and Sinatra craze, 307–309; and sex clubs, 480; purchasing power, 722–25, 1101; delinquency and crime, 734, 1103–1105; culture abroad, 825, 1107; drugs and drunkenness, 1103–1104, 1114; "literature," music and movies, 1102–1103. *See also* youth counterculture
Teen Times magazine, 724
Teeter, Robert M., 1284, 1287
Teheran conference, 316, 658
television, 118, 121, 133, 1166; (1930s) 61, 240; (1940s) 425, 451, 484–85; (1948–50, "Age of") 583–89; (1950s) 694; (1960s) 877–78, 995, 998, 1002, 1037, 1089; Edward R. Murrow and, 514–15, 516; U.N. and, 535; and children, 583–84, 723; advertising, 593, 595, 723; and Kefauver hearings, 599–601; and 1952 conventions, 614, 618, 624; Nixon and, 631–37, 720, 855, 882, 1268, 1272; and Army-McCarthy hearings, 709–16, 717; and Little Rock, 805,

807; rigged quiz shows, 847–48; and "payola," 852–53; and "kitchen debate," 855; development of color, 972–74, 1039; and civil rights movement, 981, 1022, 1065, 1097; Vietnam War and, 1003; and teen-agers, 1101; and integration, 1150
Teller, Edward, 211, 214, 215, 314, 338, 972; and H-bomb, 570–73; and Oppenheimer case, 696, 698–99; on U.S. and USSR, 792, 819; on test ban, 985
Temple, Shirley, 68, 197, 1166
Tennessee Valley Authority (TVA), 80, 87, 107
Tepper, Julian, 1244
test ban. *See* atomic weapons
Texas, Republican caucuses in, 616
Thailand, 265, 825, 1159
Thant, U, 968
theater, 236; (1930s) 83; (1960s) 998, 1039; (1970s) 1167, 1224; *Oklahoma!*, 304; *South Pacific*, 486; and loyalty issue, 498–99, 582, 668. *See also* moving pictures and performers
Thelin, Ron, 1118
Thieu, Nguyen Van. *See* Nguyen Van Thieu, Gen.
third party: LaFollette's Progressive Party, 97; Coughlin's Union Party, 117, 141; Progressive Party (1948), 389, 456–58; "Dixiecrats," 451, 454, 456, 470, 885, 886; Independents, 640; American Independent Party, 1236. *See also* Communists and Communism; Socialism
Third World, 548, 824–25, 908, 926–27, 935, 936. *See also* Point Four
Thomas, Gary W., 1202–1203
Thomas, J. Parnell, 498
Thomas, Lowell, 179
Thomas, Norman, 50, 54, 56, 101, 166, 206–209, 223, 388, 1056
Thompson, Dorothy, 139, 194, 303
Thompson, Hugh C. Jr., 1177
Thompson, Hunter S., 1099, 1100, 1113
Thompson, John J., 1034
Thompson, J. Walter, 1161
Thompson, Llewellyn, 891, 960, 970, 971
Thomsen, Hans, 225
Thornberry, Homer, 1138
Thrower, Randolph, 1235
Thurmond, Strom, 447, 456, 458, 461, 464, 466, 468, 482
Thye, Edward J., 618
Tibbetts, Col. Paul W. Jr., 380, 382
Till, Emmett, 738
Tillstrom, Burr, 584
Tilton, Martha, 248
Time magazine, 68, 88, 101, 144, 247, 284, 308, 420, 458, 477, 531, 702, 758, 759, 853, 1000; on Hoover, 17, 54; on business and economy, 38, 162, 290, 1092; and FDR, 51, 164, 222, 323; censoriousness of, 66, 120, 588, 591, 644; and Father Coughlin, 109; isolationism of, 176; and Germany, 198, 203, 233; on Army and Navy, 202, 254, 531; on Truman, 319, 364, 413, 450, 456,

470; on aid to Europe, 434, 445; on Joseph McCarthy, 526; on Korea, 547–548; on TV, 585; on Stevenson, 611; on women, 761, 781, 997; on Sputnik and space race, 789, 793, 794, 797, 810, 933; on Edsel, 816; on global diplomacy, 859; on Vietnam, 917–18; on Nixon, 995; on religion, 1036; on juvenile delinquency, 1103; on Agnew, 1141

Timmerman, James Bell, 808

Tinkham, George Holden, 177

Tin Pan Alley. *See* song(s)

Tiny Tim, 1122

Tippit, J. D., 1006

Tito, Josip Broz, 438

Titov, Maj. Gherman S., 930, 934

Tobey, Charles, 600

Tobin, Maurice, 837

Tocqueville, Alexis de, 230, 737, 778, 1096

Todd, Mike: *Around the World in 80 Days*, 590, 818

Todd, Thelma, 120

"togetherness," 692, 694. *See also* family

Togo, Shigenori, 380, 384–85

Tojo, Gen. Hideki, 252, 264, 265, 270, 343

Tokyo Rose, 270, 272, 346, 373

Tonkin, Gulf of, and Tonkin Resolution. *See* Vietnam and Vietnam War

Tower, John, 60

Townsend, Francis Everett, 42, 111, 117, 142; Townsend Plan, 101, 107, 116, 140

Toyoda, Adm. S., 384–386

toys, 820–21, 996, 1037. *See also* sports and games

"Tracy, Dick," 94–95

Tracy, Spencer, 197, 303, 486

Trading with the Enemy Act, 78

tranquilizers. *See* drugs

transportation and travel: (1930s) 7, 8, 34, 67, 118, 174; (1940s) 240–41, 294, 401; (1950s) 732–33, 818; (1960s) 1002, 1037, 1042; (1970s) 1225; and transient population, 18–22, 100; and merchandising changes, 721; and segregation, 735, 740–43, 934–43, 944; and tourism abroad, 824; busing issue, 1273–1274, 1281. *See also* air transportation; automobile(s); railroads; shipping

Transport Workers Union, 457, 1136

Tran Van Chuong, 990, 992

Tran Van Lam, 1293

Tregaskis, Richard, 304

Trendex polls, 588

trial(s): political, 1166; Calley court-martial, 1177–78; Chappaquiddick, 1185–1186; Dr. Spock, 1188–89; Angela Davis, 1204; Chicago Seven, 1205–1208, 1300; Harrisburg Seven and others, 1208; and Watergate, 1290, 1292

Tripartite Pact, 230, 235, 252, 260

Trohan, Walter, 525

Trotsky, Leon, 208

Trout, Robert, 141, 181, 182

Troy, Matthew, 1286

True, James, 111

Truehart, William, 1046

Trujillo Molina, Rafael, 649, 760

Truman, Bess (Mrs. Harry S.), 356, 366, 367, 392, 450, 460, 461

Truman, Harry S., 106, 114, 250, 275, 515, 597, 651, 652, 891, 915, 1041–42, 1160, 1230; in 1934 election, 97, 99, 104; and Stalin, 233, 410, 450; campaign for Vice President, 319, 320, 323, 400; letters and memoirs quoted, 351–352, 366, 367, 414, 610; and death of FDR, 351–52, 354, 355, 358–60; character and image of, 364–69, 392, 396, 405, 412–15, 446, 448, 465, 607; and Molotov, 368, 411; powers of, 398, 399–400, 459, 536, 538, 556–57, 606, 744, 822; and Potsdam Conference/Declaration, 371, 379, 380, 410–11; decision on atomic bomb, 375, 379–80, 382, 572; and Hirohito, 385–86; and MacArthur, 392, 541, 545, 546, 549, 558–62, 647; and postwar economy, 396–400, 430; and strikes, 400–405, 606; and demobilization, 406–407, 409–10; and Eisenhower, 411, 446–47, 450, 647, 650; foreign policy and Point Four, 413–14, 441, 446, 474–75, 519; Truman Doctrine, 434–37, 438–40, 464, 488; campaign and reelection, 446–51, 453–56, 458–71, 489; Fair Deal, 473–75; assassination attempt on, 484; loyalty issue, 489–98, 509, 519, 671; and Korea, 518, 530, 532–38, 541, 545, 546, 549, 662, 663; and Joseph McCarthy, 525, 703; and NATO, 556–58; at Japanese Peace Treaty Conference, 586; and "mess in Washington," 605; and later campaigns, 610–12, 622, 623, 626, 769, 883, 1282

Truman, Margaret (Mrs. E. Clifton Daniel Jr.), 356, 361, 366, 367, 392, 450, 460, 461, 651, 761; *Souvenir*, 420

Truman, Vivian, 532

Truong, David, 1209

Tugwell, Rexford G., 18, 84, 95, 99, 100, 102, 105, 457–58

Tully, Grace, 278, 323, 350, 357

Tunney, John V., 1221, 1229

Turkey, 547, 860; 1947 crisis, 433–34, 435, 437, 438; U.S. bases in, 870, 964, 970

Turner, Richmond Kelly, 254

TVA. *See* Tennessee Valley Authority

TV Guide magazine, 584, 693

Twiggy, 1106

Twining, Gen. Nathan F., 745

Tydings, Joseph, 1221

Tydings, Millard E., 170, 226, 524, 527–529; Joseph McCarthy and, 557, 628

Tyner, Evalyn, 351

U-boats. *See* submarines

Udall, Stewart, 60

UFOs, 645, 1166

Ulasewicz, Tony, 1231, 1232, 1291

Ulbricht, Walter, 912

Umezu, Gen. Y., 384–86

underdeveloped countries. *See* Point Four; Third World
unemployment and employment: (1930s) 19–22, 28, 33–36, 44, 54–56, 128, 139; (1940–41) 238, 290; World War II and postwar, 290, 397; (1960s) 1000, 1062, 1080; (1970s) 1218, 1253. *See also* welfare, public
unemployment insurance, 25, 131, 397, 474
Union League Club, 139, 157
Union Party, 117, 141, 142
unions. *See* labor and labor unions; *names of individual unions*
United Automobile Workers, 133, 134, 154–156, 389–91
United Electrical Workers, 458
United Mine Workers, 37, 130–32, 306, 403–405, 820
United Nations, 292, 488, 674, 1124; FDR and, 317, 322; Soviet Union and, 348, 368, 532, 598; Charter signed, 370; origin and naming of, 420–22; and Point Four, 474–75; and Korean conflict, 519, 533–35, 539, 540, 542–46, 548–50, 555, 566, 662, 663, 682; China and, 535, 549, 564, 669–70, 883, 1249, 1250–51; and "security risks," 581; and Vietnam, 682; and Hungary, 765; and Bay of Pigs, 902, 903; Khrushchev at, 908; and Cuban missile crisis, 961, 965, 967, 968; and environment, 1172
United Nations Relief and Rehabilitation Administration (UNRRA), 434, 439
United States: and world leadership, 4–5, 144–45, 316, 433–41; emigration from, 35; destroyer swap (Great Britain), 222, 226, 228; prepares for war, 231–36; –Greenland treaty, 231; World War II convoys, 231–33, 234–36; ultimatum to Japan, 251–52; declares war, 258–59, 260; and possibility of invasion, 271; war agencies, 275; as "incorporation," 290; occupation troops, 406–10, 435, 531; anti-Americanism, 435, 825–34; diplomatic defeat in China, 487–88 (*see also* China); defense of non-Communist nations, 678–79, 854 (*see also* Korea and Korean War; Vietnam and Vietnam War); aid to Hungary, 765; investments abroad, 773, 825, 1001. *See also* economy, U.S.; image of U.S. abroad; World War II
U.S. Army. *See* Army, U.S.
United States Information Agency (USIA), 516, 1003, 1050, 1054
U.S. News and World Report, 164, 654
United States Steel, 33, 34, 37, 157–61
United Steel Workers, 606
Unruh, Jesse, 1130
Updike, John, 1122
uranium, 69, 275, 596; development of fission, 210–15, 309–10, 337–38, 374. *See also* atomic weapons
Urey, Harold C., 489
Urrutia, Manuel, 862
US, 1070. *See also* Karenga, Ron
Ushijima, Gen. Mitsuri, 346

USSR. *See* Soviet Union
U Thant, 968
Utley, Freda, 528
U-2 reconnaissance: U-2 (Powers) affair, 867–876, 959; in Cuban missile crisis, 959, 961, 967–968, 970; in Alabama, 979

vagrants. *See* population
Valenti, Jack, 1038, 1075, 1107, 1193
Vallee, Rudy, 27, 121
Van Buren, Martin, 150
Vance, Cyrus, 1048
vandalism, 1103–1105
Van Dalsen, Paul, 847
Vandenberg, Arthur H., 200, 204, 205, 221, 251, 292, 409, 413, 437, 569; on internationalism, 420–21; and 1948 election, 446, 452, 456, 459
Vandenberg, Gen. Hoyt S., 559, 678
Vanderbilt, Gloria, 427
Van Devanter, Willis, 136, 152
Van Doren, Charles, 847–48, 850–52
Van Druten, John, 486
Van Fleet, Gen. James A., 565, 646, 664
Vanity Fair magazine, 58
van Loon, Hendrik Willem, 68
Vann, Lt. Col. John Paul, 922, 1057
Van Pallandt, Nina, 1266
Variety magazine, 180, 181, 191, 637n, 694, 853
Vaughan, Gen. Harry H., 392, 562, 602–604, 672
Velde, Harold R., 491, 668
Vesco, Robert L., 1234–35
veterans, war: and BEF, 3–4, 28 (*see also* Bonus Expeditionary Force); and Veterans Administration, 17; and FDR, 84, 141; World War II, 406, Vietnam, 1228, 1299. *See also* GIs
Veterans of Foreign Wars, 4, 126, 1055
"V for Victory," 219
Victor Emmanuel III of Italy, 279
Vidal, Gore, 121, 1258
Videodex surveys, 601
Vienna conference (1961), 908–11, 935
Vietnam and Vietnam War, 177, 208, 221, 438; Japan and, 251–52; atrocities in, 269, 1175–78, 1209; France and, 395, 647, 680; Viet Minh, 395, 680, 681, 684, 686; country declared independent, 421; and U.S. presidential powers, 676–677, 744–47, 1018–19; U.S. commitment and aid to, 680–87, 913, 916–19, 920–23, 925, 994, 1000, 1048, 1051, 1209, 1227, 1294; and siege of Dienbienphu, 681–86, 687; and elections, 687, 760, 918; Viet Cong, 918–23, 989, 1000, 1031, 1045–57 passim, 1125–26, 1179; false reports on, 921–22, 988, 993; U.S. optimism, 988, 991, 993, 994; hawk-dove split, 988–89, 991, 1046, 1047, 1054, 1071–75, 1143, 1208, 1231; Buddhists in, 989, 990, 992, 1209; TV and, 1003; Gulf of Tonkin and Tonkin Resolution, 1016–19, 1045, 1076, 1128, 1230; escalation under LBJ, 1031,

1045–57; bombing question, 1046–48, 1051, 1057, 1070–72, 1075, 1293–95; U.S. "victory," 1056–57; compared to World War II and Korea, 1071; ARVN forces, 1072, 1209, 1210, 1227, 1270; Tet offensive, 1124–26; length of war, 1125–26; "Vietnamization" and troop withdrawal, 1165, 1180–81, 1208–1209, 1227, 1236, 1271, 1281; U.S. military incompetence, 1179–81, 1209; and Cambodia, 1210–11; and Laos, 1226–27; DRVN attack, 1270–71; peace talks, 1292–93, 1295; U.S. volte-face, 1293–1294. *See also* casualties; cost; Green Berets

Vietnam Veterans against the War, 1228, 1299

Villard, Oswald Garrison, 47, 51, 223

Vincent, John Carter, 651

Vinson, Fred M., 392, 398, 608, 649

Vinson Naval Act, 178

violence: labor unions and, 56, 131, 133–135, 159–61; President's Commission on, 131; accomplishments of, 161; in mass media, 566–69, 584, 725–26; racism and, 739, 801–804, 983, 1128 (*see also* racism); and freedom riders, 937–943; and students, 952, 1098; backlash and, 1020–21; (1960s and 1970s) 1038, 1076, 1079–81, 1098, 1198–1203; police and, 1065, 1069, 1134. *See also* black militants and militancy; crime; nonviolence; riots and demonstrations

Volkswagen, 198, 483, 819

Volpe, John, 1155

Vo Nguyen Giap, Gen., 681, 683, 686, 1056–57, 1071, 1124, 1135, 1270–72

Voorhis, Jerry, 101n, 394

Vorse, Mary Heaton, 58

Voting Rights Act of 1965, 1057

Wade, Henry, 1108

Wadleigh, Henry Julian, 508

wages and hours: (1930s) 33, 37–38, 134, 137–38, 152, 157; postwar, 397, 606; (1960s) 1001, 1091; (1970s) 1196, 1253–55; legislation, 37, 137, 150, 153, 167–68, 399, 400; for women, 137–38, 152, 1196; and 40-hour week, 149, 156, 397; of physicists, 212; Walter Reuther and, 389, 391; for Cuban counterrevolutionaries, 876; of postmen, 1137. *See also* economy, U.S.; income

Wagner, Robert, 133, 134, 239, 322, 770, 858

Wagner (Connery) Act, 106, 134, 136, 137, 152, 159, 404, 415

Wakeman, Frederic: *The Hucksters*, 424, 594

Wald, Lillian, 41

Walker, Maj. Gen. Edwin A., 806n, 947, 948, 950–51, 952, 1300

Walker, Frank, 286

Walker, Lt. Gen. Walton H., 543, 547

Wallace, George Corley, 60, 107, 943, 977, 1036; and Meredith case, 978–81; presidential campaigns of, 1020, 1141, 1145,

1146, 1147, 1273, 1281–83; and Selma voting march, 1059–60; and AIP, 1236; shooting of, 1260

Wallace, Henry A., 88, 360, 389, 392, 400, 440, 674; as Secretary of Agriculture, 84, 85, 98, 139; Communist Party and, 208, 457–58; as candidate and Vice President, 226, 319, 323; and Progressive Party, 389, 456–58; and foreign policy, 411–14, 510; in 1948 election, 447, 454, 456–58, 466, 468, 469

Wallace, Lurleen (Mrs. George C.), 1036

Wall Street, 126, 137, 139, 1001, 1192; FDR and, 85, 96, 104, 141; Richard Whitney and, 145–47; Eisenhower's illnesses and, 754–55. *See also* Dow Jones; stock market

Wall Street Journal, 227, 595, 781, 1036

Walsh, J. Paul, 813

Walters, Gen. Vernon, 1288

Wanamaker, Fernanda, 1104

"Wanna-Go-Home" riots. *See* riots and demonstrations

war crimes and atrocities, 126, 1072, 1073; German, 217, 700; Japanese, 268–69; American, 297, 1175–78; and Nuremberg trials, 336; Korean, 538, 1178, 1179; Vietnamese, 1054, 1209

war debts (World War I), 125, 177

Ware, Harold, 96, 503

Warhol, Andy, 1102

War Labor Board, 294

War of the Worlds broadcast, 190–96; Princeton study, 191, 194, 195

War Production Board, 294

Warren, Earl, 50, 140, 395, 452, 453, 557, 649, 890, 953, 1032, 1160, 1164; and Japanese in California, 297, 298; and 1952 Republican convention, 613, 618; and integration decision, 735–37, 804; "Warren Court" and Constitution, 740, 1137–38; and Warren Report, 1014, 1075

Warren, Robert Penn: *All the King's Men*, 111

Warsaw Pact, 765, 909, 958

Washington, Walter E., 1078

Washington, D.C., 4–5, 7–9, 81, 233, 877; Bonus Expeditionary Force in, 3–4, 10–18; detention camp in, 54–55; wartime, 274; society in, 485–86; March on, 982–983; "Resurrection City," 1136; M-days in, 1174–75; Mayday Tribe in, 1228–1229; demonstrations at Nixon's second inauguration, 1298–1300

Washington Daily News, 1120

Washington Evening Star, 11, 753, 1014

Washington Post, 334, 365, 367, 470, 526, 559, 669, 1019, 1165, 1256, 1286; and Pentagon Papers, 1230–31; and Watergate, 1278–81, 1290

Washington Post and Times-Herald, 720, 807

Washington Times-Herald, 223, 558, 669

Watergate, 1147, 1231, 1274–79, 1287–1292

Waters, George, 525

Watkins, Arthur V., 717, 842
Watson, Gen. Edwin "Pa," 215, 332
Watson, James E., 225
Watson, Dr. John B., 1187, 1188, 1189
Watson, Thomas J., 148
Wattenberg, Ben, 1285
Watts riots, 1062–66, 1070
Wavell, Gen. Sir Archibald, 266
Wayne, John, 1142
weather. See storms and weather
Weather Bureau, U.S., 183–88
Weathermen, 1099, 1166, 1199–1200, 1225
Weaver, Robert C., 107, 1078
Webb, Clifton, 694
Webb, Del, 1035
Webb, James, 929
Weber, Max, 774
Wechsler, James, 102, 127
Weckler, Herman L., 131
Wedemeyer, Gen. Albert C., 348, 408, 437, 531
Weeks, Sinclair, 639, 648, 649, 672
Wehle, Maj. Gen. Philip C., 1004
Weicker, Lowell P. Jr., 1221
Weiner, Lee, 1205
Weinglass, Leonard I., 1205–1208
Weiss, Dr. Carl Austin, 116
Weisskopf, Victor F., 211
Weizsäcker, Carl von, 336, 337
Welch, Joseph N., 706, 711–16
Welch, Robert, 952–53, 958
welfare, public, 128, 163; Hoover and, 24–26, 38, 52; FDR and, 25, 84–87, 95; stigma and inadequacy of, 32, 39–40, 55; RFC and, 46; Republican party and, 415
Welk, Lawrence, 68, 476, 595, 1142
Welles, Orson, 118, 486, 1205; Martian broadcast, 189–196
Welles, Sumner, 204, 258, 509; The Time for Decision, 420
Wellford, William Harrison, 1257
Wells, H. G., 397; War of the Worlds, 190
West, Mae, 66, 120
West Berlin. See Berlin
Westmoreland, Gen. William C., 60, 1046, 1048–50, 1052–54, 1071, 1072, 1124–1126
West Germany (Federal Republic of Germany). See Germany
West Point, 306, 601
Westwood, Mrs. Jean, 1285, 1286
Weygand, Gen. Maxime, 216
Weyl, Nathaniel, 84
Weyland, Maj. Gen. Frederick, 1227
Whalen, Grover Aloysius, 198–99, 200, 240
Wheeler, Burton K., 80, 152, 162, 176, 204, 221, 224, 251, 257
Wheeler, Gen. Earle G., 948
Wheeling Intelligencer, 521, 522
Wherry, Kenneth S., 447, 475, 524, 527, 529, 556, 557
Whitaker, John T., 181
White, Byron "Whizzer," 148, 205, 940, 941

White, F. Clifton, 1029
White, Harry Dexter, 494, 501, 503, 515, 674
White, Lincoln, 872
White, Paul, 179
White, Dr. Paul Dudley, 754–56, 757, 767
White, Theodore H., 60, 415, 917, 919, 1012, 1015–16, 1267; on racism, 1065, 1150; on 1968 conventions, 1142, 1145
White, Gen. Thomas D., 875
White, Walter, 107, 245
White, William Allen, 22, 37, 53, 57, 204, 223
White, William L., 304
White, William S., 528, 667
White Citizens' Councils, 737, 739, 741, 945, 981, 983
White House: "oval rooms" in, 5, 654n; food at, 23, 81–82; renovation of, 473; and the arts, 893; police uniforms, 1192
Whiteleather, Melvin, 181
Whitman, Ann, 653, 753, 811
Whitman, Charles, 1038, 1260
Whitney, Maj. Gen. Courtney, 562
Whitney, George, 145, 147
Whitney, Richard, 96, 145–47, 250, 291
Whyte, William H. Jr., 476, 774, 779, 1090; The Organization Man, 578
Wickard, Claude R., 302
Wicker, Tom, 1243, 1244, 1245, 1247
Wiegand, Karl von, 179
Wiener, Norbert, 792, 1092
Wiesner, Jerome, 929
Wiggin, Albert H., 44
Wigner, Eugene Paul, 214, 972
Wilder, Billy, 689
Wiley, Alexander, 352
Wiley, George, 1064
Wilhelmina, queen of Holland, 372
Wilk, Ruth, 236
Wilkerson, Cathlyn Platt, 583, 1199–1200
Wilkins, Roy, 982, 984, 1066, 1067, 1069
Williams, Andrew, 163
Williams, Andy, 1130
Williams, G. Mennen, 470
Williams, Capt. Henry F., 1242
Williams, John Bell, 1079
Williams, John J., 705
Williams, Tennessee, 60, 589
Willkie, Wendell L., 105, 231, 610; presidential campaign, 225–26, 318, 320; One World, 292, 304; FDR and, 317–318
Willoughby, Maj. Gen. Charles A., 543, 544–45
Wills, Frank, 1277
Wilson, Charles Edward, 648
Wilson, Charles Erwin "Engine Charlie," 645, 646, 648–51, 669, 674, 692, 709, 805, 916; and Oppenheimer case, 696–697; and Sputnik, 787, 788, 792
Wilson, Don, 963
Wilson, Donald M., 1262–63
Wilson, Edmund, 57, 77, 776, 1089
Wilson, Harold, 987, 1160

Wilson, Sloan: *The Man in the Gray Flannel Suit*, 579
Wilson, Teddy, 244
Wilson, Woodrow, 49, 317, 1155
Winchell, Walter, 283, 407, 701
Winninger, Charles, 89
Wise, David, 1050
Wise, Stephen S., 175
witchcraft, 1191
Witt, Nathan, 84
Wolfe, Thomas, 20–21, 42, 43, 1297
Wolfe, Tom, 102, 1070
Wolfsen, Louis, 1139
women, 481, 1155; (1930s) 62–63; World War II, 305; postwar, 397, 426–30; (1950s) 731, 760–61, 777, 780–81, 1092; (1960s) 996–98, 1090–92, 1105–1107; (1970s) 1194–98; and ILGWU, 132; minimum wage for, 137–38; employment of, 239, 1105, 1195–97; "Women's Lib," 997, 1106, 1195–98; life expectancy of, 1090
Women's Army Corps (WACs), 274–75, 387, 1197, 1225
Women's Trade Union League, 91
Women's Wear Daily, 274, 1197, 1198
Wood, Gen. Robert A., 223
Woodcock, Leonard, 1255
Woodin, William H., 73–80 passim, 110
Woods, Rose Mary, 637, 1274
Woodstock festival, 1169–71, 1300
Woodward, C. Vann, 1057, 1058
Woodward, Maj. Gen. Gilbert H., 1178
Woolf, Virginia, 246
Woolley, Monty, 303
Works Progress Administration (WPA), 86, 87, 107, 114, 115, 168, 190, 238, 934
World Court, 108, 125
World Series, 98
World's Fair: Chicago, 40; New York, (1939) 198–200, 240, 1301, (1964) 1037–38; San Francisco, 198
World War II: Hitler's western campaign, 205, 216–18, 219; Battle of Britain, 217–19; and "V for Victory," 219; U.S. first involved in, 232, 234–35; war boom, 238, 289–91; Pearl Harbor attack, 251–260; U.S. enters, 258–60; in Pacific, 263–74, 340–46, 371; first U.S. offensive (Guadalcanal), 272–73; second front, 273–74, 277–78, 348 (*see also* in Europe *below*); home front, 274, 275, 289–309, 333; in Europe, 276–87, 316, 324, 329–34, 370; in North Africa, 277–78; "GIs" of, 280–87 (*see also* GIs); cost of, 289–90; military secrets, 318 (*see also* espionage); D-Day, 330–33; V-E Day, 369–70; post V-E Day, 370–71, 379–380; atom bomb and surrender of Japan, 378–87; Potsdam Declaration, 379–80; V-J Day, 386. *See also* casualties; productivity and production

Wouk, Herman, 60
Wright, Col. Clement B., 15
Wright, Fielding L., 456
Wright, Frank Lloyd, 820
Wright, Richard, 304
Wyatt, Wilson, 448
Wylie, Philip, 275, 776

Xuan Thay, 1126

YAF. *See* Young Americans for Freedom
Yahya Khan, Agha Muhammad, 1250
Yakovlev, Anatoli A., 313–14, 499–500
Yale Law Journal, 1197
Yale Review, 56
Yalta agreement, 371, 655; FDR and, 326, 327, 348, 410, 489; JFK on, 491; and "secret agreements," 658, 659, 674
Yamamoto, Adm. Isoroku, 252–53, 269–272, 273, 342, 344
Yamashita, Gen. Tomoyuki, 265, 270, 344, 345
Yank (GI weekly), 282, 284, 286, 355, 688
Yarborough, Ralph, 1006, 1163
Yates, Eugene A., 693
Yazgur, Max, 1170
Ydígoras, Miguel, 865, 894
York Gazette and Daily, 457, 495
Yorktown (aircraft carrier), 271, 272
Yorty, Sam, 1163, 1282
Young, David, 1218, 1237, 1239, 1289
Young, E. Merle, 603–604
Young, Owen D., 27
Young, Robert, 303
Young, Robert R., 223
Young, Whitney M. Jr., 60, 982, 1066, 1069, 1155
Young Americans for Freedom (YAF), 1034, 1055, 1167
Young & Rubicam, 601
youth counterculture, 1103–1107; backlash against, 1098–1100; Woodstock, 1169–1171, 1300; Powder Ridge, 1212–13; "Jesus people," 1260–61. *See also* student(s); teen-agers
Youth International Party (Yippies), 1142, 1143, 1175, 1205, 1298
Yugoslavia, 6

Zaine, queen mother of Jordan, 821
Zaire. *See* Congo
Zais, Maj. Gen. Melvin, 1179, 1180
Zanuck, Darryl, 283, 636
Zhukov, Marshal Georgi, 369, 749, 751
Ziegler, Ronald, 1230, 1235, 1281, 1294
Zinn, W. H., 311
Zionism, 1077. *See also* Jews
Zorin, Valerian A., 876, 961, 965, 968–69
Zweifel, Henry, 616
Zwicker, Brig. Gen. Ralph W., 707–708

ABOUT THE AUTHOR

In 1932, when the narrative of *The Glory and the Dream* opens, WILLIAM MANCHESTER was ten years old and already an avid reader of newspapers. The son of a Massachusetts social worker, he saw the sufferings of the Great Depression firsthand. Fourteen years old when Franklin Roosevelt ran for reelection in 1936, he was a volunteer at Democratic headquarters in Springfield, Massachusetts. After Pearl Harbor he joined the Marine Corps and was gravely wounded on Okinawa. Discharged as totally disabled, Manchester recovered in graduate school, where he wrote his dissertation on the literary criticism of H. L. Mencken. His first book, a biography of Mencken entitled *Disturber of the Peace*, was written when he was twenty-seven and was an instant critical success. As a correspondent for the *Baltimore Sun*, and later as a magazine writer, he has had a front-row seat for the key events of our time since the late 1940s. For many years he has also been a member of the Wesleyan University community, as a teacher and a Fellow of the University. Mr. Manchester's books have been translated into seventeen languages and braille. His many bestselling books include *The Arms of Krupp*, *The Death of a President*, *American Caesar*, and the first two volumes of his heralded biography of Winston Churchill, *The Last Lion: Visions of Glory* and *The Last Lion: Alone*.